KING JAMES BIBLE

1611 EDITION with Apocrypha

NOTE FOR THE READER

Welcome to this faithful reproduction of the 1611 King James Bible with Apocryoha. This edition preserves the original spellings and typographical practices of the early 17th century, offering you an authentic glimpse into the linguistic and printing conventions of the time.

You will notice that English spelling had not yet been standardized, resulting in varied spellings of the same words. The letter 'v' is used for both initial 'u' and 'v' sounds, while 'u' appears for 'u' and 'v' in other contexts. The long 's' (ſ) is used for non-final 's', and the letter 'j' only appears after 'i'. These unique features may seem unusual, but they provide a true representation of the original 1611 printing.

We hope this edition enriches your understanding and appreciation of this historic text.

TIMELESS SCRIPTURES

OLD TESTAMENT

APOCRYPHA

NEW TESTAMENT

EPISTLE DEDICATORIE

TO THE MOſT HIGH AND MIGHTIE Prince, IAMEſ by the grace of God King of Great Britaine, France and Ireland, Defender of the Faith, &c.

THE TRANSLATORS OF *THE BIBLE,* *with Grace, Mercie, and Peace, through* IEſVſ CHRIſT *our* LORD.

Great and manifold were the bleſſings (moſt dread Soueraigne) which Almighty GOD, the Father of all Mercies, beſtowed vpon vs the people of ENGLAND, when firſt he ſent your Maieſties Royall perſon to rule and raigne ouer vs. For whereas it was the expectation of many, who wiſhed not well vnto our SION, that vpon the ſetting of that bright *Occidentall Starre* Queene ELIZABETH of moſt happy memory, ſome thicke and palpable cloudes of darkeneſſe would ſo haue ouerſhadowed this land, that men ſhould haue bene in doubt which way they were to walke, and that it ſhould hardly be knowen, who was to direct the vnſetled State: the appearance of your MAIEſTIE, as of the *Sunne* in his ſtrength, inſtantly diſpelled thoſe ſuppoſed and ſurmiſed miſts, and gaue vnto all that were well affected, exceeding cauſe of comfort; eſpecially when we beheld the gouernment eſtabliſhed in your HIGHNEſSE, and your hopefull Seed, by an vndoubted Title, and this alſo accompanied with Peace and tranquillitie, at home and abroad.

But amongſt all our Ioyes, there was no one that more filled our hearts, then the bleſſed continuance of the Preaching of GODſ ſacred word amongſt vs, which is that ineſtimable treaſure, which excelleth all the riches of the earth, becauſe the fruit thereof extendeth it ſelfe, not onely to the time ſpent in this tranſitory world, but directeth and diſpoſeth men vnto that Eternall happineſſe which is aboue in Heauen.

Then, not to ſuffer this to fall to the ground, but rather to take it vp, and to continue it in that ſtate, wherein the famous predeceſſour of your HIGHNEſSE did leaue it; Nay, to goe forward with the confidence and reſolution of a man in maintaining the trueth of CHRIſT, and propagating it farre and neere, is that which hath ſo bound and firmely knit the hearts of all your MAIEſTIEſ loyall and Religious people vnto you, that your very Name is precious among them, their eye doeth behold you with comfort, and they bleſſe you in their hearts, as that ſanctified perſon, who vnder GOD, is the immediate authour of their true happineſſe. And this their contentment doeth not diminiſh or decay, but euery day increaſeth and taketh ſtrength, when they obſerue that the zeale of your Maieſtie towards the houſe of GOD, doth not ſlacke or goe backward, but is more and more kindled, manifeſting it ſelfe abroad in the furtheſt parts of *Chriſtendome*, by writing in defence of the Trueth, (which hath giuen ſuch a blow vnto that man of Sinne, as will not be healed) and euery day at home, by Religious and learned diſcourſe, by frequenting the houſe of GOD, by hearing the word preached, by cheriſhing the teachers therof, by caring for the Church as a moſt tender and louing nourcing Father.

There are infinite arguments of this right Chriſtian and Religious affection in your MAIEſTIE: but none is more forcible to declare it to others, then the vehement and perpetuated deſire of the accompliſhing and publiſhing of this Worke, which now with all humilitie we preſent vnto your MAIEſTIE. For when your Highneſſe had once out of deepe iudgment apprehended, how conuenient it was, That out of the Originall ſacred tongues, together with comparing of the labours, both in our owne and other forreigne Languages, of many worthy men who went before vs, there ſhould be one more exact Tranſlation of the holy Scriptures into the *Engliſh tongue*; your MAIEſTIE did neuer deſiſt, to vrge and to excite thoſe to whom it was commended, that the worke might be haſtened, and that the buſineſſe might be expedited in ſo decent a maner, as a matter of ſuch importance might iuſtly require.

And now at laſt, by the Mercy of GOD, and the continuance of our Labours, it being brought vnto ſuch a concluſion, as that we haue great hope that the Church of *England* ſhall reape good fruit thereby; we hold it our duety to offer it to your MAIEſTIE, not onely as to our King and Soueraigne, but as to the principall moouer and Author of the Worke. Humbly crauing of your moſt Sacred Maieſtie, that ſince things of this quality haue euer bene ſubiect to the cenſures of ill meaning and diſcontented perſons, it may receiue approbation and Patronage from ſo learned and iudicious a Prince as your Highneſſe is, whoſe allowance and acceptance of our Labours, ſhall more honour and incourage vs, then all the calumniations and hard interpretations of other men ſhall diſmay vs. So that, if on the one ſide we ſhall be traduced by Popiſh perſons at home or abroad, who therefore will maligne vs, becauſe we are poore Inſtruments to make GODſ holy Trueth to be yet more and more knowen vnto the people, whom they deſire ſtill to keepe in ignorance and darkneſſe: or if on the other ſide, we ſhall be maligned by ſelfe-conceited brethren, who runne their owne wayes, and giue liking vnto nothing but what is framed by themſelues, and hammered on their Anuile; we may reſt ſecure, ſupported within by the trueth and innocencie of a good conſcience, hauing walked the wayes of ſimplicitie and integritie, as before the Lord; And ſuſtained without, by the powerfull Protection of your Maieſties grace and fauour, which will euer giue countenance to honeſt and Chriſtian endeuours, againſt bitter cenſures, and vncharitable imputations.

The LORD of Heauen and earth bleſſe your Maieſtie with many and happy dayes, that as his Heauenly hand hath enriched your Highneſſe with many ſingular, and extraordinary Graces; ſo you may be the wonder of the world in this later age, for happineſſe and true felicitie, to the honour of that Great GOD, and the good of his Church, through IESVS CHRIST our Lord and onely Sauiour.

THE TRANSLATORS
TO THE READER

Zeale to promote the common good, whether it be by deuiſing any thing our ſelues, or reuiſing that which hath bene laboured by others, deſerueth certainly much reſpect and eſteeme, but yet findeth but cold intertainment in the world. It is welcommed with ſuſpicion in ſtead of loue, and with emulation in ſtead of thankes: and if there be any hole left for cauill to enter, (and cauill, if it doe not finde a hole, will make one) it is ſure to bee miſconſtrued, and in danger to be condemned. This will eaſily be granted by as many as know ſtory, or haue any experience. For, was there euer any thing proiected, that ſauoured any way of newneſſe or renewing, but the ſame endured many a ſtorme of gaine-ſaying, or oppoſition? A man would thinke that Ciuilitie, holeſome Lawes, learning and eloquence, Synods, and Church-maintenance, (that we ſpeake of no more things of this kinde) ſhould be as ſafe as a Sanctuary, and I of ſhot, as they ſay, that no man would lift vp the heele, no, nor dogge mooue his tongue againſt the motioners of them. For by the firſt, we are diſtinguiſhed from bruit-beaſts led with ſenſualitie: By the ſecond, we are bridled and reſtrained from outragious behauiour, and from doing of iniuries, whether by fraud or by violence: By the third, we are enabled to informe and reforme others, by the light and feeling that we haue attained vnto our ſelues: Briefly, by the fourth being brought together to a parle face to face, we ſooner compoſe our differences then by writings, which are endleſſe: And laſtly, that the Church be ſufficiently prouided for, is ſo agreeable to good reaſon and conſcience, that thoſe mothers are holden to be leſſe cruell, that kill their children aſſoone as they are borne, then thoſe nourſing fathers and mothers (whereſoeuer they be) that withdraw from them who hang vpon their breaſts (and vpon whoſe breaſts againe themſelues doe hang to receiue the Spirituall and ſincere milke of the word) liuelyhood and ſupport fit for their eſtates. Thus it is apparent, that theſe things which we ſpeake of, are of moſt neceſſary vſe, and therefore, that none, either without abſurditie can ſpeake againſt them, or without note of wickedneſſe can ſpurne againſt them.

Yet for all that, the learned know that certaine worthy men haue bene brought to vntimely death for none other fault, but for ſeeking to reduce their Countrey-men to good order and diſcipline: and that in ſome Common-weales. it was made a capitall crime, once to motion the making of a new Law for the abrogating of an old, though the ſame were moſt pernicious: And that certaine, which would be counted pillars of the State, and paternes of Vertue and Prudence, could not be brought for a long time to giue way to good Letters and refined ſpeech, but bare themſelues as auerſe from them, as from rocks or boxes of poiſon: And fourthly, that hee was no babe, but a great clearke, that gaue foorth (and in writing to remaine to poſteritie) in paſſion peraduenture, but yet he gaue foorth, that hee had not ſeene any profit to come by any Synode, or meeting of the Clergie, but rather the contrary: And laſtly, againſt Church-maintenance and allowance, in ſuch ſort, as the Embaſſadors and meſſengers of the great King of Kings ſhould be furniſhed, it is not vnknowen what a fiction or fable (ſo it is eſteemed, and for no better by the reporter himſelfe, though ſuperſtitiouſ) was deuiſed; Namely, that at ſuch time as the profeſſours and teachers of Chriſtianitie in the Church of Rome, then a true Church, were liberally endowed, a voyce forſooth was heard from heauen, ſaying; Now is poiſon powred down into the Church, &c. Thus not only as oft as we ſpeake, as one ſaith, but alſo as oft as we do anything of note or conſequence, we ſubiect our ſelues to euery ones cenſure, and happy is he that leaſt toſſed vpon tongues; for vtterly to eſcape the ſnatch of them it is impoſſible. If any man conceit, that this is the lot and portion of the meaner ſort onely, and that Princes are priuiledged by their high eſtate, he is deceiued. Aſ *the ſword deuoureth aſwell one as the other*, as it is in *Samuel*; nay as the great Commander charged his ſouldiers in a certaine battell, to ſtrike at no part of the enemie, but at the face; And as the King of *Syria* commanded his chiefe Captaineſ *to fight neither with ſmall nor great, ſaue onely againſt the King of Iſrael*: ſo it is too true, that Enuie ſtriketh moſt ſpitefully at the faireſt, and at the chiefeſt. *Dauid* was a worthy Prince, and no man to be compared to him for his firſt deedes, and yet for as worthy an acte as euer he did (euen for bringing backe the Arke of God in ſolemnitie) he was ſcorned and ſcoffed at by his owne wife. *Solomon* was greater then *Dauid*, though not in vertue, yet in power: and by his power and wiſdome he built a Temple to the LORD, ſuch a one as was the glory of the land of Iſrael, and the wonder of the whole world. But was that his magnificence liked of by all? We doubt of it. Otherwiſe, why doe they lay it in his ſonnes diſh, and call vnto him for ‖ eaſing of the burden, *Make*, ſay they, *the grieuous ſeruitude of thy father, and his ſore yoke, lighter*. Belike he had charged them with ſome leuies, and troubled them with ſome cariages; Hereupon they raiſe vp a tragedie, and wiſh in their heart the Temple had neuer bene built. So hard a thing it is to pleaſe all, euen when we pleaſe God beſt, and doe ſeeke to approue our ſelues to euery ones conſcience.

If wee will deſcend to later times, wee ſhall finde many the like examples of ſuch kind, or rather vnkind acceptance. The firſt Romane Emperour did neuer doe a more pleaſing deed to the learned, nor more profitable to poſteritie, for conſeruing the record of times in true ſupputation; then when he corrected the Calender, and ordered the yeere according to the courſe of the Sunne: and yet this was imputed to him for noueltie, and arrogancie, and procured to him great obloquie. So the firſt Chriſtened Emperour (at the leaſtwiſe that openly profeſſed the faith himſelfe, and allowed others to doe the like) for ſtrengthening the Empire at his great charges, and prouiding for the Church, as he did, got for his labour the name *Pupillus,* as who would ſay, a waſtefull prince, that had neede of a Guardian, or ouerſeer. So the beſt Chriſtened Emperour, for the loue that he bare vnto peace, thereby to enrich both himſelfe and his ſubiects, and becauſe he did not ſeeke warre but find it, was iudged to be no man at armes, (though in deed he excelled in feates of chiualrie, and ſhewed ſo much when he was prouked) and condemned for giuing himſelfe to his eaſe, and to his pleaſure. To be ſhort, the moſt learned Emperour of former times, (at the leaſt, the greateſt politician) what thanks had he for cutting off the ſuperfluities of the lawes, and digeſting them into ſome order and method? This, that he hath been blotted by ſome to bee an Epitomiſt, that is, one that extinguiſhed worthy whole volumes, to bring his abridgements into requeſt. This is the meaſure that hath been rendred to excellent Princes in former times, euen, *Cum benè facerent, malè audire*, For their good deedes to be euill ſpoken of. Neither is there any likelihood, that enuie and malignitie died, and were buried with the ancient. No, no, the reproofe of *Mosef* taketh hold of moſt ages; *You are riſen vp in your fathers ſtead, an increaſe of ſinfull men.What is that that hath been done? that which ſhall be done: and there is no new thing vnder the Sunne,* ſaith the wiſeman: and S. *Steuen*, *As your fathers did, ſo doe you.* This, and more to this purpoſe, His maieſtie that now reigneth (and long, and long may he reigne, and his offpring for euer, *Himſelfe and children and childrens children alwayeſ*) knew full well, according to the ſingular wiſedome giuen vnto him by God, and the rare learning and experience that he hath attained vnto; namely that whoſoeuer attempteth any thing for the publike (ſpecially if it pertaine to Religion, and to the opening and clearing of the word of God) the ſame ſetteth himſelfe vpon a ſtage to be glouted vpn by euery euil eye, yea, he caſteth himſelfe headlong vpon pikes, to be gored by euery ſharpe tongue. For he that medleth with mens Religion in any part, medleth with their cuſtome, nay, with their freehold; and though they finde no content in that which they haue, yet they cannot abibe to heare of altering. Notwithſtanding his Royall heart was not daunted or diſcouraged for this or that colour, but ſtood reſolute, *as a ſtatue immoueable, and an anuile not eaſie to be beaten into plates,* as one ſayth; he knew who had choſen him to be a Souldier, or rather a Captaine, and being aſſured that the courſe which he intended made much for the glory of God, & the building vp of his Church, he would not ſuffer it to be broken off for whatſoeuer ſpeaches or practiſes. It doth certainely belong vnto Kings, yea, it doth ſpecially belong vnto them, to haue care of Religion, yea, to know it aright, yea, to profeſſe it zealouſly, yea to promote it to the vttermoſt of their power. This is their glory before all nations which meane well, and this will bring vnto them a farre moſt excellent weight of glory in the day of the Lord Ieſus. For the Scripture ſaith not in vaine, *Them that honor me, I will honor*, neither was it a vaine word that *Euſebiuſ* deliuered long agoe, that pietie towards God was the weapon, and the onely weapon that both preſerued *Conſtantineſ* perſon, and auenged him of his enemies.

But now what pietie without trueth? what trueth (what ſauing trueth) without the word of God? what word of God (whereof we may be ſure) without the Scripture? The Scriptures we are commanded to ſearch. Ioh.5.39
. Eſa.8.20 . They are commended that ſearched & ſtudied them. Act.17.11. and 8.28,29
. They are reproued that were vnſkilful in them, or ſlow to beleeue them. *Mat.*22.29
. *Luk.*24.25. They can make vs wiſe vnto ſaluation. 2.*Tim.*3.15. If we be ignorant, they will inſtruct vs; if out of the way, they will bring vs home; if out of order, they will reforme vs, if in heauines, comfort vs, if dull, quicken vs, if colde, inflame vs. *Tolle, lege, Tolle, Lege,* Take vp and read, take vp and read the Scriptures, (for vnto them was the direction) it was ſaid vnto *S. Auguſtine* by a ſupernaturall voyce. *Whatſoeuar is in the Scriptures, beleeue me,* ſaith the ſame S.*Auguſtine, is high and diuine; there is verily trueth, and a doctrine moſt fit for the refreſhing and renewing of mens mindes, and truely ſo tempered, that euery one may draw from thence that which is ſufficient for him, if hee come to draw with a deuout and pious minde, as true Religion requireth.* Thus S. *Auguſtine*. And. S. *Hierome*: *Ama ſcipturas, & amabit te ſapientia &c.* Loue the Scriptures, and wiſedome will loue thee. And S.*Cyrill* againſt *Iulian*; *Euen boyes that are bred vp in the Scriptures, become moſt religious, &c.* But what mention wee three or foure vſes of the Scriptrue, whereas whatſoeuer is to be beleeued or practiſed, or hoped for, is contained in them? or three or foure ſentences of the Fathers, ſince whoſoeuer is worthy the name of a Father, from Chriſts time downeward, hath likewiſe written not onely of the riches, but alſo of the perfection of the Scripture? *I adore the fulneſſe of the Scripture,* ſaith *Terullian* againſt *Hermogenes.* And againe, to *Apelleſ* an Heretike of the like ſtampe, he ſaith; *I doe not admit that which thou bringeſt in* (or concludeſt) *of thine owne* (head or ſtore, *de tuo*) without Scripture. So Saint *Iuſtin Martyr* before him; *Wee muſt know by all meanes,* ſaith hee, *that it is not lawfull* (or poſſible οἷόν τε) *to learne* (anything) *of God or of right pietie, ſaue onely out of the Prophets, who teach vs by diuine inſpiration.* So Saint *Baſill* after *Tertullian, It is a manifeſt falling away from the Faith, and a fault of preſumption, either to reiect any of thoſe things that are written, or to bring in* (vpon the head of them, ἐπεισαγεῖν) *any of thoſe things that* are not written. Wee omit to cite to the ſame effect, S.*Cyrill* B. of *Hieruſalem* in his 4.*Cataches.* Saint *Hierome* againſt *Heluidius,* Saint *Auguſtine* in his 3. booke againſt the letters of *Petilian*, and in very many other places of his workes. Alſo we forbeare to deſcend to latter Fathers, becauſe wee will not wearie the reader. The Scriptures then being acknowledged to bee ſo full and ſo perfect, how can wee excuſe our ſelues of negligence, if we doe not ſtudie them, of curioſitie, if we be not content with them? Men talke much of how many ſweete and goodly things it had hanging on it; of the Philoſophers ſtone, that it turneth copper into gold; of *Cornu-copia*, that it had all things neceſſary for foode in it, of *Panaceſ* the herbe, that it was good for all diſeaſes; of *Catholicon* the drugge, that it is in ſtead of all purges; of *Vulcanſ* armour, that is was an armour of proofe againſt all thruſts, and all blowes, &c. Well, that which they falſly or vainely attributed to theſe things for bodily good, wee may iuſtly and with full meaſure aſcribe vnto the Scripture, for ſpitituall. It is not onely an armour, but alſo a whole armorie of weapons, both offenſiue, and defenſiue; whereby we may ſaue our ſelues and put the enemie to flight. It is not an herbe, but a tree, or rather a whole paradiſe of trees of life, which bring foorth fruit euery moneth, and the fruit thereof is for meate, and the leaues for medicine. It is not a pot of *Manna*, or a cruſe of oyle, which were for memorie only, or for a meales meate or two, but as it were a ſhowre of heauenly bread ſufficient for a whole hoſt, be it neuer ſo great; and as it were a whole cellar full of oyle veſſels; whereby all our neceſſities may be prouided for, and our debts diſcharged. In a word, it is a Panary of holeſome foode, againſt fenowed traditions; a Phyſionſ-ſhop Saint *Baſill* calleth it) of preſeruatiues againſt poiſſoned hereſies; a Pandect of profitable laws, againſt rebellious ſpirits; a treaſurie of moſt coſtly iewels, againſt beggarly rudiments; Finally a fountiane of moſt pure water ſpringing vp vnto euerlaſting life. And what maruaile? The originall thereof being from heauen, not from earth; the authour being God, not man; the enditer, the holy ſpirit, not the wit of the Apoſtles or Prophets; the Pen-men ſuch as were ſanctified from the wombe, and endewed with a principall portion of Gods ſpirit; the matter, veritie, pietie, puritie, vprightneſſe; the forme, Gods word, Gods teſtimonie, Gods oracles, the word of trueth, the word of ſaluation, &c. the effects, light of vnderſtanding, ſtableneſſe of perſwaſion, repentance from dead workes, newneſſe of life, holineſſe, peace, ioy in the holy Ghoſt; laſtly, the end and reward of the ſtudie thereof, fellowſhip with the Saints, participation of the heauenly nature, fruition of an inheritance immortall, vndefiled, and that neuer ſhall fade away: Happie is the man that delighteth in the Scripture, and thriſe happie that meditateth in it day and night.

But how ſhall men meditate in that, which they cannot vnderſtand? How ſhall they vnderſtand that which is kept cloſe in an vnknowen tongue? as it is written, *Except I know the power of the voyce, I ſhall be to him that ſpeaketh, a Barbarian, and he that ſpeaketh, ſhalbe a Barbarian to me.* The Apoſtle excepteth no tongue; not Hebrewe the ancienteſt, not Greeke the moſt copious, not Latine the fineſt.

Nature taught a naturall man to confeſſe, that all of vs in thoſe tongues which wee doe not vnderſtand, are plainely deafe; wee may turne the deafe eare vnto them. The *Scythian* counted the *Athenian*, whom he did not vnderſtand, barbarous: ſo the *Romane* did the *Syrian*, and the *Iew*, (euen *S. Hieronym. Damaſo.*S. *Hierome* himſelfe calleth the Hebrew tongue barbarous, belike becauſe it was ſtrange to ſo many) ſo the Emperour of *Conſtantinople* calleth the *Latine* tongue, barbarous, though Pope *Nicolaſ* do ſtorme at it: ſo the *Ieweſ* long before *Chriſt*, called all other nations, *Lognazim*, which is little better than barbarous. Therefore as one complaineth, that alwayes in the Senate of *Rome*, there was one or other that called for an interpreter: ſo leſt the Church be driuen to the like exigent, it is neceſſary to haue tranſlations in a readineſſe. Tranſlation it is that openeth the window, to let in the light; that breaketh the ſhell, that we may eat the kernel; that putteth aſide the curtaine, that we may looke into the moſt Holy place; that remooueth the couer of the well, that wee may come by the water, euen aſ *Iacob* rolled away the ſtone from the mouth of the well, by which meanes the flockes of *Laban* were watered. Indeede without tranſlation into the vulgar tongue, the vnlearned are but like children at *Iacobſ* well (which was deepe) without a bucket or ſome thing to draw with: or as that perſon mentioned by *Eſau*, to whom when a ſealed booke was deliuered, with this motion, *Reade this, I pray thee,* hee was ſaine to make this anſwere, *I cannot, for it is ſealed.*

While God would be knowen onely in *Iacob*, and haue his Name great in *Iſrael*, and in none other place, while the dew lay on *Gideonſ* fleece onely, and all the earth beſides was drie; then for one and the ſame people, which ſpake all of them the language of *Canaan*, that is, *Hebrewe*, one and the ſame originall in *Hebrew* was ſufficient. But when the fulneſſe of time drew neere, that the Sunne of righteouſneſſe, the Sonne of God ſhould come into the world, whom God ordeined to be a reconciliation through faith in his blood, not of the *Iew* onely, but alſo of the *Greeke*, yea, of all them that were ſcattered abroad; then loe, it pleaſed the Lord to ſtirre vp the ſpirit of a *Greeke* Prince (*Greeke* for deſcent and language) euen of *Ptolome Philadelph* King of *Egypt*, to procure the tranſlating of the Booke of God out of *Hebrew* into *Greeke*. This is the tranſlation of the *Seuentie* Interpreters, commonly ſo called, which prepared the way for our Sauiour among the Gentiles by written preaching, as Saint *Iohn* Baptiſt did among the *Ieweſ* by vocall. For the *Grecianſ* being deſirous of learning, were not wont to ſuffer bookes of worth to lye moulding in Kings Libraries, but had many of their ſeruants, ready ſcribes, to copie them out, and ſo they were diſperſed and made common. Againe, the *Greeke* tongue was well knowen and made familiar to moſt inhabitants in *Aſia*, by reaſon of the conqueſt that there the *Grecianſ* had made, as alſo by the Colonies, which thither they had ſent. For the ſame cauſes alſo it was well vnderſtood in many places of *Europe*, yea, and of *Affrike* too. Therefore the word of God being ſet foorth in *Greeke*, becommeth hereby like a candle ſet vpon a candleſticke, which giueth light to all that are in the houſe, or like a proclamation ſounded foorth in the market place, which moſt men preſently take knowledge of; and therefore that language was fitteſt to containe the Scriptures, both for the firſt Preachers of the Goſpel to appeale vnto for witneſſe, and for the learners alſo of thoſe times to make ſearch and triall by. It is certaine, that the Tranſlation was not ſo ſound and ſo perfect, but that it needed in many places correction; and who had bene ſo ſufficient for this worke as the Apoſtles or Apoſtolike men? Yet it ſeemed good to the holy Ghoſt and to them, to take that which they found, (the ſame being for the greateſt part true and ſufficient) rather then by making a new, in that new world and greene age of the Church, to expoſe themſelues to many exceptions and cauillations, as though they made a Tranſlation to ſerue their owne turne, and therefore bearing witneſſe to themſelues, their witneſſe not to be regarded. This may be ſuppoſed to bee ſome cauſe, why the Tranſlation of the *Seuentie* was allowed to paſſe for currant. Notwithſtanding, though it was commended generally, yet it did not fully content the learned, no not of the *Iewes*. For not long after *Chriſt*, *Aquila* fell in hand with a new Tranſlation, and after him *Theodotion*, and after him *Symmachus:* yea, there was a fift and a ſixt edition, the Authours wherof were not knowen. Theſe with the *Seuentie* made vp the *Hexapla*, and were worthily and to great purpoſe compiled together by *Origen*. Howbeit the Edition of the *Seuentie* went away with the credit, and therefore not onely was placed in the midſt by *Origen* (for the worth and excellencie thereof aboue the reſt, aſ *Epiphaniuſ* gathereth) but alſo was vſed by the *Greeke* fathers for the ground and foundation of their Commentaries. Yea, *Epiphaniuſ* aboue named doeth attribute ſo much vnto it, that he holdeth the Authours thereof not onely for Interpreters, but alſo for Prophets in ſome reſpect: and *Iuſtinian* the Emperour enioyning the *Ieweſ* his ſubiects to vſe ſpecially the Tranſlation of the *Seuentie*, rendreth this reaſon thereof, becauſe they were as it were enlighted with propheticall grace. Yet for all that, as the *Egyptianſ* are ſaid of the Prophet to bee men and not God, and their horſes fleſh and not ſpirit: ſo it is euident, (and Saint *Hieromes* affirmeth as much) that the *Seuentie* were Interpreters, they were not Prophets; they did many things well, as learned men; but yet as men they ſtumbled and fell, one while through ouerſight, another while through ignorance, yea, ſometimes they may be noted to adde to the Originall, and ſometimes to take from it; which made the Apoſtles to leaue them many times, when they left the *Hebrew*, and to deliuer the ſence thereof according to the trueth of the word, as the ſpirit gaue them vtterance. This may ſuffice touching the Greeke Tranſlations of the old Teſtament.

.There were alſo within a few hundreth yeeres after CHRIſT, tranſlations many into the Latine tongue: for this tongue alſo was very fit to conuey the Law and the Goſpel by, becauſe in thoſe times very many Countreys of the Weſt, yea of the South, Eaſt and North, ſpake or vnderſtood Latine, being made Prouinces to the *Romanes*. But now the Latine Tranſlations were too many to be all good, for they were infinite (*Latini Interpretes nullo modo numerari poſſunt*, ſaith *S. Auguſtine*) Againe they were not out of the *Hebrew* fountaine (wee ſpeake of the *Latine* Tranſlations of the Old Teſtament) but out of the *Greeke* ſtreame, therefore the *Greeke* being not altogether cleare, the *Latine* from it muſt needs be muddie. This moved S. Jerome a moſt learned father, and the beſt linguiſt without controverſie, of his age, or of any that went before him, to undertake the tranſlating of the Old Teſtament, out of the very fountaines themſelves; which hee performed with that evidence of great learning, judgement, induſtrie and faithfulnes, that he hath for ever bound the Church unto him, in a debt of ſpeciall remembrance and thankefulneſse.

Now though the Church were thus furniſhed with Greeke and Latine Tranſlations, even before the faith of CHRIST was generally embraced in the Empire: (for the learned know that even in S. Jeroms time, the Conſul of Rome and his wife were both Ethnicks, and about the ſame time the greateſt part of the Senate alſo) yet for all that the godly-learned were not content to have the Scriptures in the Language which themſelves underſtood, Greeke and Latine, (as the good Lepers were not content to fare well themſelves, but acquainted their neighbours with the ſtore that God had ſent, that they alſo might provide for themſelveſ) but alſo for the behoofe and edifying of the unlearned which hungred and thirſted after Righteouſneſſe, and had ſoules to be ſaved as well as they, they provided Tranſlations into the vulgar for their Countreymen, inſomuch that moſt nations under heaven did ſhortly after their converſion, heare CHRIST ſpeaking unto them in their mother tongue, not by the voyce of their Miniſter onely, but alſo by the written word tranſlated. If any doubt hereof, he may be ſatiſfied by examples enough, if enough will ſerve the turne. Firſt S. Jerome ſaith, Multarum gentiu linguis Scriptura antè tranſlata, docet falſa eſse quæ addita ſunt, &c.i. The Scripture being tranſlated before in the languages of many Nations, doth ſhew that thoſe things that were added (by Lucian or Heſychiuſ) are falſe. So S. Jerome in that place. The ſame Jerome elſewhere affirmeth that he, the time was, had ſet forth the tranſlation of the Seventy, ſuæ linguæ hominibus.i. for his countreymen of Dalmatia. Which words not only Eraſmus doth underſtand to purport, that S. Jerome tranſlated the Scripture into the Dalmatian tongue, but alſo Sixtus Senenſis, and Alphonſus à Caſtro (that we ſpeake of no more) men not to be excepted againſt by them of Rome, doe ingenuouſly confeſse as much. So, S. Chryſoſtome that lived in S. Hieromes time, giveth evidence with him: The doctrine of S. John (ſaith he) did not in ſuch ſort (as the Philoſophers did) vaniſh away: but the Syrians, Egyptians, Indians, Perſians. Ethiopians, and infinite other nations being barbarous people, tranſlated it into their (mother) tongue, and have learned to be (true) Philoſophers, he meaneth Chriſtians. To this may be added Theodorit, as next unto him, both for antiquitie, and for learning. His words be theſe, Every Countrey that is under the Sunne, is full of theſe wordes (of the Apoſtles and Prophetſ) and the Hebrew tongue (he meaneth the Scriptures in the Hebrew tongue) is turned not onely into the Language of the Grecians, but alſo of the Romanes, and Egyptians, and Perſians, and Indians, and Armenians, and Scythians, and Sauromatians, and briefly into all the Languages that any Nation uſeth. So he. In like maner, Ulpilas is reported by Paulus Diaconus and Iſidor (and before them by Sozomen) to have tranſlated the Scriptures into the Gothicke tongue: John Biſhop of Sivil by Vaſſeus, to have turned them into Arabicke, about the yeere of our Lord 717: Beda by Ciſtertienſis, to have turned a great part of them into Saxon: Efnard by Trithemius, to have abridged the French Pſalter, as Beda had done the Hebrew, about the yeere 800: King Alured by the ſaid Ciſtertienſis, to have turned the Pſalter into Saxon: Methodius by Aventinus (printed at Ingolſtad) to have turned the Scriptures into ll Sclavonian: Valdo, Biſhop of Friſing by Beatus Rhenanus, to have cauſed about that time, the Goſpels to be tranſlated into Dutch-rithme, yet extant in the Library of Corbinian: Valdus, by divers to have turned them himſelfe, or to have gotten them turned into French, about the yeere 1160: Charles the 5. of that name, ſurnamed The wiſe, to have cauſed them to be turned into French, about 20

0. yeeres after Valdus his time, of which tranſlation there be many copies yet extant, as witneſſeth Beroaldus. Much about that time, even in our King Richard the ſeconds dayes, John Treviſa tranſlated them into Engliſh, and many Engliſh Bibles in written hand are yet to be ſeene with divers, tranſlated as it is very probable, in that age. So the Syrian tranſlation of the New Teſtament is in moſt learned mens Libraries, of Widminſtadius his ſetting forth, and the Pſalter in Arabicke is with many, of Auguſtinus Nebienſis ſetting foorth. So Poſtel affirmeth, that in his travaile he ſaw the Goſpels in the Ethiopian tongue; And Ambroſe Theſius alleageth the Pſalter of the Indians, which he teſtifieth to have bene ſet forth by Potken in Syrian characters. So that, to have the Scriptures in the mother-tongue is not a quaint conceit lately taken up, either by the Lord Cromwell in England, or by the Lord Radevil in Polonie, or by the Lord Ungnadius in the Emperours dominion, but hath bene thought upon, and put in practiſe of old, even from the firſt times of the converſion of any Nation; no doubt, becauſe it was eſteemed moſt profitable, to cauſe faith to grown in mens hearts the ſooner, and to make them to be able to ſay with the words of the Pſalme, As we have heard, ſo we have ſeene.

Now the Church of Rome would ſeeme at the length to beare a motherly affection towards her children, and to allow them the Scriptures in their mother tongue: but indeed it is a gift, not deſerving to be called a gift, an unprofitable gift: they muſt firſt get a Licence in writing before they may uſe them, and to get that, they muſt approve themſelves to their Confeſsor, that is, to be ſuch as are, if not frozen in the dregs, yet ſoured with the leaven of their ſuperſtition. Howbeit, it ſeemed too much to Clement the 8. that there ſhould be any Licence granted to have them in the vulgar tongue, and therefore he overruleth and fruſtrateth the grant of Pius the fourth. So much are they afraid of the light of the Scripture, (Lucifugæ Scripturarum, as Tertullian ſpeaketh) that they will not truſt the people with it, no not as it is ſet foorth by their owne ſworne men, no not with the Licence of their owne Biſhops and Inquiſitors. Yea, ſo unwilling they are to communicate the Scriptures to the peoples underſtanding in any ſort, that they are not aſhamed to confeſse, that wee forced them to tranſlate it into Engliſh againſt their wills. This ſeemeth to argue a bad cauſe, or a bad conſcience, or both. Sure we are, that it is not he that hath good gold, that is afraid to bring it to the touch-ſtone, but he that hath the counterfeit; neither is it the true man that ſhunneth the light, but the malefactour, leſt his deedes ſhould be reproved: neither is it the plaine dealing Merchant that is unwilling to have the waights, or the meteyard brought in place, but he that uſeth deceit. But we will let them alone for this fault, and returne to tranſlation.

Many mens mouths have bene open a good while (and yet are not ſtopped) with ſpeeches about the Tranſlation ſo long in hand, or rather peruſals of Tranſlations made before: and aſke what may be the reaſon, what the neceſsitie of the employment: Hath the Church bene deceived, ſay they, all this while? Hath her ſweet bread bene mingled with leaven, her ſilver with droſse, her wine with water, her milke with lime? (Lacte gypſum malè miſcetur, ſaith S. Ireney,) We hoped that we had bene in the right way, that we had had the Oracles of God delivered unto us, and that though all the world had cauſe to be offended and to complaine, yet that we had none. Hath the nurſe holden out the breaſt, and nothing but winde in it? Hath the bread bene delivered by the fathers of the Church, and the ſame proved to be lapidoſus, as Seneca ſpeaketh? What is it to handle the word of God deceitfully, if this be not? Thus certaine brethren. Alſo the adverſaries of Judah and Jeruſalem, like Sanballat in Nehemiah, mocke, as we heare, both at the worke and workemen, ſaying; What doe theſe weake Jewes, &c. will they make the ſtones whole againe out of the heapes of duſt which are burnt? although they build, yet if a foxe goe up, he ſhall even breake downe their ſtony wall. Was their Tranſlation good before? Why doe they now mend it? Was it not good? Why then was it obtruded to the people? Yea, why did the Catholicks (meaning Popiſh Romaniſtſ) alwayes goe in jeopardie, for refuſing to goe to heare it? Nay, if it muſt be tranſlated into Engliſh, Catholicks are fitteſt to doe it. They have learning, and they know when a thing is well, they can manum de tabulá. Wee will anſwere them both briefly: and the former, being brethren, thus, with S. Jerome, Damnamus veteres? Minimè, ſed poſt priorum ſtudia in domo Domini quod poſsumus laboramus. That is, Doe we condemne the ancient? In no caſe: but after the endevours of them that were before us, wee take the beſt paines we can in the houſe of God. As if hee ſaid, Being provoked by the example of the learned that lived before my time, I have thought it my duetie, to aſſay whether my talent in the knowledge of the tongues, may be profitable in any meaſure to Gods Church, leſt I ſhould ſeeme to have laboured in them in vaine, and leſt I ſhould be thought to glory in men, (although ancient,) above that which was in them. Thus S. Jerome may be thought to ſpeake.

And to the ſame effect ſay wee, that we are ſo farre off from condemning any of their labours that traveiled before us in this kinde, either in this land or beyond ſea, either in King Henries time, or King Edwards (if there were any tranſlation, or correction of a tranſlation in his time) or Queene Elizabeths of ever-renoumed memorie, that we acknowledge them to have beene raiſed up of God, for the building and furniſhing of his Church, and that they deſerve to be had of us and of poſteritie in everlaſting remembrance. The Judgement of Ariſtotle is worthy and well knowen: If Timotheus had not bene, we had not had much ſweet muſicke; but if Phrynis (Timotheus his maſter) had not beene, wee had not had Timotheus. Therefore bleſſed be they, and moſt honoured be their name, that breake the ice, and glueth onſet upon that which helpeth forward to the ſaving of ſoules. Now what can bee more availeable thereto, then to deliever Gods booke unto Gods people in a tongue which they underſtand? Since of an hidden treaſure, and of a fountaine that is ſealed, there is no profit, as Ptolomee Philadelph wrote to the Rabbins or maſters of the Jewes, as witneſſeth Epiphanius: and as S. Auguſtine ſaith; A man had rather be with his dog then with a ſtranger (whoſe tongue is ſtrange unto him.) Yet for all that, as nothing is begun and perfited at the ſame time, and the later thoughts are thought to be the wiſer: ſo, if we building upon their foundation that went before us, and being holpen by their labours, doe endevour to make that better which they left ſo good; no man, we are ſure, hath cauſe to miſlike us; they, we perſuade our ſelves, if they were alive, would thanke us. The vintage of Abiezer, that ſtrake the ſtroake: yet the gleaning of grapes of Ephraim was not to be deſpiſed. ſee Judges 8. verſe 2. Joaſh the king of Iſrael did not ſatiſfie himſelfe, till he had ſmitten the ground three times; and yet hee offended the Prophet, for giving over then. Aquila, of whom wee ſpake before, tranſlated the Bible as carefully, and as ſkilfully as he could; and yet he thought good to goe over it againe, and then it got the credit with the Jewes, to be called , that is accuratly done, as Saint Jerome witneſſeth. How many bookes of profane learning have bene gone over againe and againe, by the ſame tranſlators, by others? Of one and the ſame booke of Ariſtotles Ethikes, there are extant not ſo few as ſixe or ſeven ſeverall tranſlations. Now if this coſt may bee beſtowed upon the goord, which affordeth us a little ſhade, and which to day flouriſheth, but to morrow is cut downe; what may we beſtow, nay what ought we not to beſtow upon the Vine, the fruite whereof maketh glad the conſcience of man, and the ſtemme whereof abideth for ever? And this is the word of God, which we tranſlate. What is the chaffe to the wheat, ſaith the Lord? Tanti vitreum, quanti verum margaritum (ſaith Tertullian,) if a toy of glaſſe be of that rekoning with us, how ought wee to value the true pearle? Therefore let no mans eye be evill, becauſe his Majeſties is good; neither let any be grieved, that wee have a Prince that ſeeketh the increaſe of the ſpirituall wealth of Iſrael (let Sanballats and Tobiahs doe ſo, which therefore doe beare their juſt reproofe) but let us rather bleſſe God from the ground of our heart, for working this religious care in him, to have the tranſlations of the Bible maturely conſidered of and examined. For by this meanes it commeth to paſſe, that whatſoever is found alreadie (and all is found for ſubſtance, in one or other of our editions, and the worſt of ours farre better then their autentike vulgar) the ſame will ſhine as gold more brightly, being rubbed and poliſhed; alſo if any thing be halting, or ſuperfluous, or not ſo agreeable to the originall, the ſame may bee corrected, and the trueth ſet in place. And what can the King command to bee done, that will bring him more true honour then this? and wherein could they that have beene ſet a worke, approve their duetie to the King, yea their obedience to God, and love to his Saints more, then by yeelding their ſervice, and all that is within them, for the furniſhing of the worke? But beſides all this, they were the principall motives of it, and therefore ought leaſt to quarrell it: for the very Hiſtoricall trueth is, that upon the importunate petitions of the Puritanes, at this Majeſties comming to this Crowne, the Conference at Hampton Court having bene appointed for hearing their complaints: when by force of reaſon they were put from all other grounds, they had recourſe at the laſt, to this ſhift, that they could not with good conſcience ſubſcribe to the Communion booke, ſince it maintained the Bible as it was there tranſlated, which was as they ſaid, a moſt corrupted tranſlation. And although this was judged to be but a very poore and emptie ſhift; yet even hereupon did his Majeſtie beginne to bethinke himſelfe of the good that might enſue by a new tranſlation, and preſently after gave order for this Tranſlation which is now preſented unto thee. Thus much to ſatiſfie our ſcrupulous Brethren.

Now to the later we anſwere; that wee doe not deny, nay wee affirme and avow, that the very meaneſt tranſlation of the Bible in Engliſh, ſet foorth by men of our profeſsion (for wee have ſeene none of theirs of the whole Bible as yet) containeth the word of God, nay, is the word of God. As the Kings Speech which hee uttered in Parliament, being tranſlated into French, Dutch, Italian and Latine, is ſtill the Kings Speech, though it be not interpreted by every Tranſlator with the like grace, nor peradventure ſo fitly for phraſe, nor ſo expreſly for ſence, every where. For it is confeſsed, that things are to take their denomination of the greater part; and a naturall man could ſay, Verùm ubi multa nitent in carmine, non ego paucis offendor maculis, &c. A man may be counted a vertuous man, though hee have made many ſlips in his life, (els, there were none vertuous, for in many things we offend all) alſo a comely man and lovely, though hee have ſome warts upon his hand, yea, not onely freakles upon his face, but all ſkarres. No cauſe therefore why the word tranſlated ſhould bee denied to be the word, or forbidden to be currant, notwithſtanding that ſome imperfections and blemiſhes may be noted in the ſetting foorth of it. For what ever was perfect under the Sunne, where Apoſtles or Apoſtolike men, that is, men indued with an extraordinary meaſure of Gods ſpirit, and priviledged with the priviledge of infallibilitie, had not their hand? The Romaniſtes therefore in refuſing to heare, and daring to burne the Word tranſlated, did no leſſe then deſpite the ſpirit of grace, from whom originally it proceeded, and whoſe ſenſe and meaning, as well as mans weaknefse would enable, it did expreſse. Judge by an example or two. Plutarch writeth, that after that Rome had beene burnt by the Galles, they fell ſoone to builde it againe: but doing it in hafte, they did not caft the ftreets, nor proportion the houfes in fuch comely fafhion, as had bene moft fightly and convenient; was Catiline therefore an honeft man, or a good Patriot, that fought to bring it to a combuftion? or Nero a good Prince, that did indeed fet it on fire? So, by the ftory of Ezrah, and the prophefie of Haggai it may be gathered, that the Temple build by Zerubbabel after the returne from Babylon, was by no meanes to bee compared to the former built by Solomon (for they that remembred the former, wept when they confidered the latter) notwithftanding, might this later either have bene abhorred and forfaken by the Jewes, or prophaned by the Greekes? The like wee are to thinke of Tranflations. The tranflation of the Seventie difsenteth from the Originall in many places, neither doeth it come neere it, for perfpicuitie, gratvitie, majeftie; yet which of the Apoftles did condemne it? it? Condemne it? Nay, they ufed it, (as it is apparent, and as Saint Jerome and moft learned men doe confefse) which they would not have done, nor by their example of ufing it, fo grace and commend it to the Church, if it had bene unworthy the appellation and name of the word of God. And whereas they urge for their fecond defence of their vilifying and abufing of the Englifh Bibles, or fome pieces thereof, which they meete with, for that heretikes (forfooth) were the Authours of the tranflations, (heretikes they call us by the fame right that they call themfelves Catholikes, both being wrong) wee marveile what divinitie taught them fo. Wee are fure Tertullian was of another minde: Ex perfonis probamus fidem, an ex fide perfonas? Doe we trie mens faith by their perfons? we fhould trie their perfons by their faith. Alfo S. Auguftine was of an other minde: for he lighting upon certaine rules made by Tychonius a Donatift, for the better underftanding of the word, was not afhamed to make ufe of them, yea, to infert them into his owne booke, with giving commendation to them fo farre foorth as they were worthy to be commended, as is to be feene in S. Auguftines third booke De doctrinâ Chriftianâ. To be fhort, Origen, and the whole Church of God for certain hundred yeeres, were of an other minde: for they were fo farre from treading under foote, (much more from burning) the Tranflation of Aquila a Profelite, that is, one that had turned Jew; of Symmachus, and Theodotion, both Ebionites, that is, moft vile heretikes, that they joyned them together with the Hebrew Originall, and the Tranflation of the Seventie (as hath bene before fignified out of Epiphaniuf) and fet them forth openly to be confidered of and perufed by all. But we weary the unlearned, who need not know fo much, and trouble the learned, who know it already.

Yet before we end, we muft anfwere a third cavill and objection of theirs againft us, for altering and amending our Taanflations [fic] fo oft; wherein truely they deale hardly, and ftrangely with us. For to whom ever was it imputed for a fault (by fuch as were wife) to goe over that which hee had done, and to amend it where he faw caufe? Saint Auguftine was not afraide to exhort S. Jerome to a Palinodia or recantation; the fame S. Auguftine was not afhamed to retractate, we might fay revoke, many things that had paffed him, and doth even glory that he feeth his infirmities. If we will be fonnes of the Trueth, we muft confider what it fpeaketh, and trample upon our owne credit, yea, and upon other mens too, if either be any way an hinderance to it. This to the caufe: then to the perfons we fay, that of all men they ought to bee moft filent in this cafe. For what varieties have they, and what alterations have they made, not onely of their Service bookes, Portefses and Breviaries, but alfo of their Latine Tranflation? The Service booke fuppofed to be made by S. Ambrofe (Officium Ambrofianum) was a great while in fpeciall ufe and requeft: but Pope Hadrian calling a Councill with the ayde of Charles the Emperour, abolifhed it, yea, burnt it, and commanded the Service-booke of Saint Gregorie univerfally to be ufed. Well, Officium Gregorianum gets by this meanes to be in credit, but doeth it continue without change or altering? No, the very Romane Service was of two fafhions, the New fafhion, and the Old, (the one ufed in one Church, the other in another) as is to bee feene in Pamelius a Romanift, his Preface, before Micrologus. The fame Pamelius reporteth out of Radulphus de Rivo, that about the yeere of our Lord, 127

7. Pope Nicolas the third removed out of the Churches of Rome, the more ancient bookes (of Service) and brought into ufe the Mifsals of the Friers Minorites, and commaunded them to bee obferved there; infomuch that about an hundred yeeres after, when the above named Radulphus happened to be at Rome, he found all the bookes to be new, (of the new ftampe.) Neither was there this chopping and changing in the more ancient times onely, but alfo of late: Pius Quintus himfelfe confefseth, that every Bifhopricke almoft had a peculiar kind of fervice, moft unlike to that which others had: which moved him to abolifh all other Breviaries, though never fo ancient, and priviledged and publifhed by Bifhops in their Diocefes, and to eftablifh and ratifie that onely which was of his owne fetting foorth, in the yeere 1568. Now, when the father of their Church, who gladly would heale the foare of the daughter of his people foftly and fleightly, and make the beft of it, findeth fo great fault with them for their oddes and jarring; we hope the children have no great caufe to vaunt of their uniformitie. But the difference that appeareth betweene our Tranflations, and our often correcting of them, is the thing that wee are fpecially charged with; let us fee therefore whether they themfelves bee without fault this way, (if it be to be counted a fault, to correct) and whether they bee fit men to throw ftones at us: O tandem major parcas infane minori: they that are leffe found themfelves, ought not to object infirmities to others. If we fhould tell them that Valla, Stapulenfis, Erafmus, and Vives found fault with their vulgar Tranflation, and confequently wifhed the fame to be mended, or a new one to be made, they would anfwere peradventure, that we produced their enemies for witneffes againft them; albeit, they were in no other fort enemies, then as S. Paul was to the Galatians, for telling them the trueth: and it were to be wifhed, that they had dared to tell it them plainlier and oftner. But what will they fay to this, that Pope Leo the tenth allowed Erafmus Tranflation of the New Teftament, fo much different from the vulgar, by his Apoftolike Letter & Bull; that the fame Leo exhorted Pagnin to tranflate the whole Bible, and bare whatfoever charges was necefsary for the worke? Surely, as the Apoftle reafoneth to the Hebrewes, that if the former Law and Teftament had bene fufficient, there had beene no need of the latter: fo we may fay, that if the olde vulgar had bene at all points allowable, to fmall purpofe had labour and charges bene undergone, about framing of a new. If they fay, it was one Popes private opinion, and that he confulted onely himfelfe; then wee are able to goe further with them, and to averre, that more of their chiefe men of all forts, even their owne Trent-champions Paiva & Vega, and their owne Inquifitors, Hieronymus ab Oleaftro, and their own Bifhop Ifidorus Clarius, and their owne Cardinall Thomas à Vio Caietan, doe either make new Tranflations themfelves, or follow new ones of other mens making, or note the vulgar Interpretor for halting; none of them feare to diffent from him, nor

yet to except againſt him. And call they this an uniforme tenour of text and judgement about the text, ſo many of their Worthies diſclaiming the now received conceit? Nay, we wil yet come neerer the quicke: doth not their Pariſ-edition differ from the Louaine, and Hentenius his from them both, and yet all of them allowed by authoritie? Nay, doth not Sixtus Quintus confeſse, that certaine Catholikes (he meaneth certainte of his owne ſide) were in ſuch an humor of tranſlating the Scriptures into Latine, that Satan taking occaſion by them, though they thought of no ſuch matter, did ſtrive what he could, out of ſo uncertaine and manifold a varietie of Tranſlations, ſo to mingle all things, that nothing might ſeeme to be left certaine and firme in them, &c? Nay, further, did not the ſame Sixtus ordaine by an inviolable decree, and that with the counſell and conſent of his Cardinals, that the Latine edition of the olde and new Teſtament, which the Councill of Trent would have to be authenticke, is the ſame without controverſie which he then ſet forth, being diligently corrected and printed in the Printing-houſe of Vatican? Thus Sixtus in his Preface before his Bible. And yet Clement the eight his immediate ſucceſsour, publiſheth another edition of the Bible, containing in it infinite differences from that of Sixtus, (and many of them waightie and materiall) and yet this muſt be authenticke by all meanes. What is to have the faith of our glorious Lord JESUS CHRIST with Yea and Nay, if this be not? Againe, what is ſweet harmonie and conſent, if this be? Therfore, as Demaratus of Corinth adviſed a great King, before he talked of the diſsentions among the Grecians, to compoſe his domeſticke broiles (for at that time his Queene and his ſonne and heire were at deadly fuide with him) ſo all the while that our adverſaries doe make ſo many and ſo various editions themſelves, and doe jarre ſo much about the worth and authoritie of them, they can with no ſhow of equitie challenge us for changing and correcting.

But it is high time to leave them, and to ſhew in briefe what wee propoſed to our ſelves, and what courſe we held in this our peruſall and ſurvay of the Bible. Truly (good Chriſtian Reader) wee never thought from the beginning, that we ſhould neede to make a new Tranſlation, nor yet to make of a bad one a good one, (for then the imputation of Sixtus had bene true in ſome ſort, that our people had bene fed with gall of Dragons in ſtead of wine, with whey in ſtead of milke:) but to make a good one better, or out of many good ones, one principall good one, not juſtly to be excepted againſt; that hath bene our indeavour, that our marke. To that purpoſe there were many choſen, that were greater in other mens eyes then in their owne, and that ſought the truth rather then their own praiſe. Againe, they came or were thought to come to the worke, not exercendi cauſâ (as one ſaith) but exercitati, that is, learned, not to learne: For the chiefe overſeer and under his Majeſtie, to whom not onely we, but alſo our whole Church was much bound, knew by his wiſedome, which thing alſo Nazianzen taught ſo long agoe, that it is a prepoſterous order to teach firſt and to learne after, yea that to learne and practiſe together, is neither commendable for the workeman, nor ſafe for the worke. Therefore ſuch were thought upon, as could ſay modeſtly with Saint Jerome, Et Hebrææum Sermonem ex parte didicimus, & in Latino penè ab ipſis incunabulis &c. detriti ſumus. Both we have learned the Hebrew tongue in part, and in the Latine wee have beene exerciſed almoſt from our verie cradle. S. Jerome maketh no mention of the Greeke tongue, wherein yet hee did excell, becauſe hee tranſlated not the old Teſtament out of Greeke, but out of Hebrewe. And in what ſort did theſe aſſemble? In the truſt of their owne knowledge, or of their ſharpeneſse of wit, or deepeneſse of judgement, as it were in an arme of fleſh? At no hand. They truſted in him that hath the key of David, opening and no man ſhutting: they prayed to the Lord the Father of our Lord, to the effect that S. Auguſtine did; O let thy Scriptures be my pure delight, let me not be deceived in them, neither let me deceive by them. In this confidence, and with this devotion did they aſſemble together; not too many, leſt one ſhould trouble another; and yet many, leſt many things haply might eſcape them. If you aſke what they had before them, truely it was the Hebrew text of the Olde Teſtament, the Greeke of the New. Theſe are the two golden pipes, or rather conduits, where-through the olive branches emptie themſelves into the golde. Saint Auguſtine calleth them precedent, or originall tongues; Saint Jerome, fountaines. The ſame Saint Jerome affirmeth, and Gratian hath not ſpared to put it into his Decree, That as the credit of the olde Bookes (he meaneth of the Old Teſtament) is to bee tryed by the Hebrewe Volumes, ſo of the New by the Greeke tongue, he meaneth by the originall Greeke. If trueth be to be tried by theſe tongues, then whence ſhould a Tranſlation be made, but out of them? Theſe tongues, therefore, the Scriptures wee ſay in thoſe tongues, wee ſet before us to tranſlate, being the tongues wherein God was pleaſed to ſpeake to his Church by his Prophets and Apoſtles. Neither did we run over the worke with that poſting haſte that the Septuagint did, if that be true which is reported of them, that they finiſhed it in 72. dayes; neither were we barred or hindered from going over it againe, having once done it, like S. Jerome, if that be true which himſelfe reporteth, that he could no ſooner write any thing, but preſently it was caught from him, and publiſhed, and he could not have leave to mend it: neither, to be ſhort, were we the firſt that fell in hand with tranſlating the Scripture into Engliſh, and conſequently deſtitute of former helpes, as it is written of Origen, that hee was the firſt in a maner, that put his hand to write Commentaries upon the Scriptures, and therefore no marveile, if he overſhot himſelfe many times. None of theſe things: the worke hath not bene hudled up in 72. dayes, but hath coſt the workemen, as light as it ſeemeth, the paines of twiſe ſeven times ſeventie two dayes and more: matters of ſuch weight and conſequence are to bee ſpeeded with maturitie: for in a buſineſse of moment a man feareth not the blame of convenient ſlackneſse. Neither did wee thinke much to conſult the Tranſlators or Commentators, Chaldee, Hebrewe, Syrian, Greeke, or Latine, no nor the Spaniſh, French, Italian, or Dutch; neither did we diſdaine to reviſe that which we had done, and to bring backe to the anvill that which we had hammered: but having and uſing as great helpes as were needfull, and fearing no reproch for ſlowneſse, nor coveting praiſe for expedition, wee have at the length, through the good hand of the Lord upon us, brought the worke to that paſſe that you ſee.

Some peradventure would have no varietie of ſences to be ſet in the margine, leſt the authoritie of the Scriptures for deciding of controverſies by that ſhew of uncertaintie, ſhould ſomewhat be ſhaken. But we hold their judgmet not to be ſo be ſo ſound in this point. For though, whatſoever things are neceſsary are manifeſt, as S. Chryſoſtome ſaith, and as S. Auguſtine, In thoſe things that are plainely ſet downe in the Scriptures, all ſuch matters are found that concerne Faith, hope, and Charitie. Yet for all that it cannot be diſsembled, that partly to exerciſe and whet our wits, partly to weane the curious from loathing of them for their every-where-plaineneſse, partly alſo to ſtirre up our devotion to crave the aſsiſtance of Gods ſpirit by prayer, and laſtly, that we might be forward to ſeeke ayd of our brethren by conference, and never ſcorne thoſe that be not in all reſpects ſo complete as they ſhould bee, being to ſeeke in many things our ſelves, it hath pleaſed God in his divine providence, heere and there to ſcatter wordes and ſentences of that difficultie and doubtfulneſse, not in doctrinall points that concerne ſalvation, (for in ſuch it hath beene vouched that the Scriptures are plaine) but in matters of leſſe moment, that fearefulneſse would better beſeeme us then confidence, and if we will reſolve, to reſolve upon modeſtie with S. Auguſtine, (though not in this ſame caſe altogether, yet upon the ſame ground) Melius eſt dubitare de occultis, quàm litigare de incertis, it is better to make doubt of thoſe things which are ſecret, then to ſtrive about thoſe things that are uncertaine. There be many words in the Scriptures, which be never found there but once, (having neither brother nor neighbour, as the Hebrewes ſpeake) ſo that we cannot be holpen by conference of places. Againe, there be many rare names of certaine birds, beaſtes and precious ſtones, &c. concerning which the Hebrewes themſelves are ſo divided among themſelves for judgement, that they may ſeeme to have defined this or that, rather becauſe they would ſay ſomething, the becauſe they were ſure of that which they ſaid, as S. Jerome ſomewhere ſaith of the Septuagint. Now in ſuch a caſe, doth not a margine do well to admoniſh the Reader to ſeeke further, and not to conclude or dogmatize upon this or that peremptorily? For as it is a fault of incredulitie, to doubt of thoſe things that are evident: ſo to determine of ſuch things as the Spirit of God hath left (even in the judgment of the judiciouſ) queſtionable, can beno leſſe then preſumption. Therfore as S. Auguſtine ſaith, that varietie of Tranſlations is profitable for the finding out of the ſenſe of the Scriptures: ſo diverſitie of ſignification and ſenſe in the margine, where the text is not ſo cleare, muſt needes doe good, yea is neceſsary, as we are perſwaded. We know that Sixtus Quintus expreſly forbiddeth, that any varietie of readings of their vulgar edition, ſhould be put in the margine, (which though it be not altogether the ſame thing to that we have in hand, yet it looketh that way) but we thinke he hath not all of his owne ſide his favourers, for this conceit. They that are wiſe, had rather have their judgements at libertie in differences of readings, then to be captivated to one, when it may be the other. If they were ſure that their hie Prieſt had all lawes ſhut up in his breſt, as Paul the ſecond bragged, and that he were as free from errour by ſpeciall priviledge, as the Dictators of Rome were made by law inviolable, it were an other matter; then his word were an Oracle, his opinion a deciſion. But the eyes of the world are now open, God be thanked, and have bene a great while, they find that he is ſubject to the ſame affections and infirmities that others be, that his ſkin is penetrable, and therefore ſo much as he prooveth, not as much as he claimeth, they grant and embrace. An other thing we thinke good to admoniſh thee of (gentle Reader) that wee have not tyed our ſelves to an uniformitie of phraſing, or to an identitie of words, as ſome peradventure would wiſh that we had done, becauſe they obſerve, that ſome learned men ſome where, have beene as exact as they could that way. Truly, that we might not varie from the ſenſe of that which we had tranſlated before, if the word ſignified the ſame thing in both places (for there bee ſome wordes that bee not of the ſame ſenſe every where) we were eſpecially carefull, and made a conſcience, according to our duetie. But, that we ſhould expreſse the ſame notion in the ſame particular word; as for example, if we tranſlate the Hebrew or Greeke word once by Purpoſe, never to call it Intent; if one where Journeying, never Traveiling; if one where Thinke, never Suppoſe; if one where Paine, never Ache; if one where Joy, never Gladneſse, &c. Thus to minſe the matter, wee thought to ſavour more of curioſitie then wiſedome, and that rather it would breed ſcorne in the Atheiſt, then bring profite to the godly Reader. For is the kingdome of God become words or ſyllables? why ſhould wee be in bondage to them if we may be free, uſe one preciſely when wee may uſe another no leſſe fit, as commodiouſly? A godly Father in the Primitive time ſhewed himſelfe greatly moved, that one of the newfanglenes called , though the difference be little or none; and another reporteth, that he was much abuſed for turning Cucurbita (to which reading the people had beene uſed) into Hedera. Now if this happen in better times, and upon ſo ſmall occaſions, wee might juſtly feare hard cenſure, if generally wee ſhould make verball and unneceſsary changings. We might alſo be charged (by ſcofferſ) with ſome unequall dealing towards a great number of good Engliſh wordes. For as it is written of a certaine great Philoſopher, that he ſhould ſay, that thoſe logs were happie that were made images to be worſhipped; for their fellowes, as good as they, lay for blockes behinde the fire: ſo if wee ſhould ſay, as it were, unto certaine words, ſtand up higher, have a place in the Bible alwayes, and to others of like qualitie, Get ye hence, be baniſhed for ever, wee might be taxed peradventure with S. James his words, namely, To be partiall in our ſelves and judges of evill thoughts. Adde hereunto, that niceneſse in wordes was alwayes counted the next ſtep to trifling, and ſo was to bee curious about names too: alſo that we cannot follow a better patterne for elocution then God himſelfe; therefore hee uſing divers words, in his holy writ, and indifferently for one thing in nature: we, if wee will not be ſuperſtitious, may uſe the ſame libertie in our Engliſh verſions out of Hebrew & Greeke, for that copie or ſtore that he hath given us. Laſtly, wee have on the one ſide avoided the ſcrupuloſitie of the Puritanes, who leave the olde Eccleſticall words, and betake them to other, as when they put waſhing for Baptiſme, and Congregation in ſtead of Church: as alſo on the other ſide we have ſhunned the obſcuritie of the Papiſts, in their Azimes, Tunike, Rational, Holocauſts, Præpuce, Paſche, and a number of ſuch like, whereof their late Tranſlation is full, and that of purpoſe to darken the ſence, that ſince they muſt needs tranſlate the Bible, yet by the language thereof, it may bee kept from being underſtood. But we deſire that the Scripture may ſpeake like it ſelfe, as in the language of Canaan, that it may bee underſtood even of the very vulgar.

Many other things we might give thee warning of (gentle Reader) if wee had not exceeded the meaſure of a Preface alreadie. It remaineth, that we commend thee to God, and to the Spirit of his grace, which is able to build further then we can aſke or thinke. Hee removeth the ſcales from our eyes, the vaile from our hearts, opening our wits that wee may underſtand his word, enlarging our hearts, yea correcting our affections, that we may love it above gold and ſilver, yea that we may love it to the end. Ye are brought unto fountaines of living water which yee digged not; doe not caſt earth into them with the Philiſtines, neither preferre broken pits before them with the wicked Jewes. Others have laboured, and you may enter into their labours; O receive not ſo great things in vaine, O deſpiſe not ſo great ſalvation! Be not like ſwine to treade under foote ſo precious things, neither yet like dogs to teare and abuſe holy things. ſay not to our Saviour with the Gergeſites, Depart out of our coaſts; neither yet with Eſau ſell your birthright for a meſse of potage. If light be come into the world, love not darkneſſe more then light; if foode, if clothing be offered, goe not naked, ſtarve not your ſelves. Remember the adviſe of Nazianzene, It is a grievous thing (or dangerouſ) to neglect a great faire, and to ſeeke to make markets afterwards: alſo the encouragement of S. Chryſoſtome, It is altogether impoſsible, that he that is ſober (and watchfull) ſhould at any time be neglected: Laſtly, the admonition and menacing of S. Auguſtine, They that deſpiſe Gods will inviting them, ſhal feele Gods will taking vengeance of them. It is a fearefull thing to fall into the hands of the living God; but a bleſſed thing it is, and will bring us to everlaſting bleſſednes in the end, when God ſpeaketh unto us, to hearken; when he ſetteth his word before us, to reade it; when hee ſtretcheth out his hand and calleth, to anſwere, Here am I; here wee are to doe thy will, O God. The Lord worke a care and conſcience in us to know him and ſerve him, that we may be acknowledged of him at the appearing of our Lord Jeſus Chriſt, to whom with the holy Ghoſt, be all prayſe and thankeſgiving. Amen.

GENEſIS (GENESIS)

CHAPTER 1 1In the beginning God created the Heauen, and the Earth.2And the earth was without forme, and voyd, and darkeneſſe was vpon the face of the deepe: and the Spirit of God mooued vpon the face of the waters.3And God ſaid, Let there be light: and there was light.4And God ſaw the light, that it was good: and God diuided the light from the darkeneſſe.5And God called the light, Day, and the darkneſſe he called Night: and the euening and the morning were the firſt day.6And God ſaid, Let there be a firmament in the midſt of the waters: and let it diuide the waters from the waters.7And God made the firmament; and diuided the waters, which were vnder the firmament, from the waters, which were aboue the firmament: and it was ſo.8And God called the firmament, Heauen: and the euening and the morning were the ſecond day.9And God ſaid, Let the waters vnder the heauen be gathered together vnto one place, and let the dry land appeare: and it was ſo.10And God called the drie land, Earth, and the gathering together of the waters called hee, ſeas: and God ſaw that it was good.11And God ſaid, Let the Earth bring foorth graſſe, the herbe yeelding ſeed, and the fruit tree, yeelding fruit after his kinde, whoſe ſeed is in it ſelfe, vpon the earth: and it was ſo.12And the earth brought foorth graſſe, and herbe yeelding ſeed after his kinde, and the tree yeelding fruit, whoſe ſeed was in it ſelfe, after his kinde: and God ſaw that it was good.13And the euening and the morning were the third day.14And God ſaid, Let there bee lights in the firmament of the heauen, to diuide the day from the night: and let them be for ſignes and for ſeaſons, and for dayes and yeeres.15And let them be for lights in the firmament of the heauen, to giue light vpon the earth: and it was ſo.16And God made two great lights: the greater light to rule the day, and the leſſer light to rule the night: he made the ſtarres alſo.17And God ſet them in the firmament of the heauen, to giue light vpon the earth:18And to rule ouer the day, and ouer the night, and to diuide the light from the darkeneſſe: and God ſaw that it was good.19And the euening and the morning were the fourth day.20And God ſaid, Let the waters bring foorth aboundantly the mouing creature that hath life, and foule that may flie aboue the earth in the open firmament of heauen.21And God created great whales, and euery liuing creature that moueth, which the waters brought forth aboundantly after their kinde, and euery winged foule after his kinde: and God ſaw that it was good.22And God bleſſed them, ſaying, Be fruitfull, and multiply, and fill the waters in the ſeas, and let foule multiply in the earth.23And the euening and the morning were the fift day.24And God ſaid, Let the earth bring forth the liuing creature after his kinde, cattell, and creeping thing, and beaſt of the earth after his kinde: and it was ſo.25And God made the beaſt of the earth after his kinde, and cattell after their kinde, and euery thing that creepeth vpon the earth, after his kinde: and God ſaw that it was good.26And God ſaid, Let vs make man in our Image, after our likeneſſe: and let them haue dominion ouer the fiſh of the ſea, and ouer the foule of the aire, and ouer the cattell, and ouer all the earth, and ouer euery creeping thing that creepeth vpon the earth.27So God created man in his owne Image, in the Image of God created hee him; male and female created hee them.28And God bleſſed them, and God ſaid vnto them, Be fruitfull, and multiply, and repleniſh the earth, and ſubdue it, and haue dominion ouer the fiſh of the ſea, and ouer the foule of the aire, and ouer euery liuing thing that mooueth vpon the earth.29And God ſaid, Behold, I haue giuen you euery herbe bearing ſeede, which is vpon the face of all the earth, and euery tree, in the which is the fruit of a tree yeelding ſeed, to you it ſhall be for meat:30And to euery beaſt of the earth, and to euery foule of the aire, and to euery thing that creepeth vpon the earth, wherein there is life, I haue giuen euery greene herbe for meat: and it was ſo.31And God ſaw euery thing that hee had made: and behold, it was very good. And the euening and the morning were the ſixth day.

CHAPTER 2 1Thus the heauens and the earth were finiſhed, and all the hoſte of them.2And on the ſeuenth day God ended his worke, which hee had made: And he reſted on the ſeuenth day from all his worke, which he had made.3And God bleſſed the ſeuenth day, and ſanctified it: becauſe that in it he had reſted from all his worke, which God created and made.4Theſe are the generations of the heauens, & of the earth, when they were created; in the day that the LORD God made the earth, and the heauens,5And euery plant of the field, before it was in the earth, and euery herbe of the field, before it grew: for the LORD God had not cauſed it to raine vpon the earth, and there was not a man to till the ground.6But there went vp a miſt from the earth, and watered the whole face of the ground.7And the LORD God formed man of the duſt of the ground, & breathed into his noſtrils the breath of life; and man became a liuing ſoule.8And the LORD God planted a garden Eaſtward in Eden; and there he put the man whom he had formed.9And out of the ground made the LORD God to grow euery tree that is pleaſant to the ſight, and good for food: the tree of life alſo in the midſt of the garden, and the tree of knowledge of good and euill.10And a riuer went out of Eden to water the garden, and from thence it was parted, and became into foure heads.11The name of the firſt is Piſon: that is it which compaſſeth the whole land of Hauilah, where there is gold.12And the gold of that land is good: There is Bdellium and the Onix ſtone.13And the name of the ſecond riuer is Gihon: the ſame is it that compaſſeth the whole land of Ethiopia.14And the name of the third riuer is Hiddekel: that is it which goeth toward the Eaſt of Aſſyria: and the fourth riuer is Euphrates.15And the LORD God tooke the man, and put him into the garden of Eden, to dreſſe it, and to keepe it.16And the LORD God commanded the man, ſaying, Of euery tree of the garden thou mayeſt freely eate.17But of the tree of the knowledge of good and euill, thou ſhalt not eate of it: for in the day that thou eateſt thereof, thou ſhalt ſurely die.18And the LORD God ſaid, It is not good that the man ſhould be alone: I will make him an helpe meet for him.19And out of yͤ ground the LORD God formed euery beaſt of the field, and euery foule of the aire, and brought them vnto Adam, to ſee what he would call them: and whatſoeuer Adam called euery liuing creature, that was the name thereof.20And Adam gaue names to all cattell, and to the foule of the aire, and to euery beaſt of the fielde: but for Adam there was not found an helpe meete for him.21And the LORD God cauſed a deepe ſleepe to fall vpon Adam, and hee ſlept; and he tooke one of his ribs, and cloſed vp the fleſh in ſtead thereof.22And the rib which the LORD God had taken from man, made hee a woman, & brought her vnto the man.23And Adam ſaid, This is now bone of my bones, and fleſh of my fleſh: ſhe ſhalbe called woman, becauſe ſhee was taken out of man.24Therefore ſhall a man leaue his father and his mother, and ſhall cleaue vnto his wife: and they ſhalbe one fleſh.25And they were both naked, the man & his wife, and were not aſhamed.

CHAPTER 3 1Now the ſerpent was more ſubtill then any beaſt of the field, which the LORD God had made, and he ſaid vnto the woman, Yea, hath God ſaid, Ye ſhall not eat of euery tree of the garden?2And the woman ſaid vnto the ſerpent, Wee may eate of the fruite of the trees of the garden:3But of the fruit of the tree, which is in the midſt of the garden, God hath ſaid, Ye ſhal not eate of it, neither ſhall ye touch it, leſt ye die.4And the Serpent ſaid vnto the woman, Ye ſhall not ſurely die.5For God doeth know, that in the day ye eate thereof, then your eyes ſhalbee opened: and yee ſhall bee as Gods, knowing good and euill.6And when the woman ſaw, that the tree was good for food, and that it was pleaſant to the eyes, and a tree to be deſired to make one wiſe, ſhe tooke of the fruit thereof, and did eate, and gaue alſo vnto her huſband with her, and hee did eate.7And the eyes of them both were opened, & they knew that they were naked, and they ſewed figge leaues together, and made themſelues aprons.8And they heard the voyce of the LORD God, walking in the garden in the coole of the day: and Adam and his wife hid themſelues from the preſence of the LORD God, amongſt the trees of the garden.9And the LORD God called vnto Adam, and ſaid vnto him, Where art thou?10And he ſaid, I heard thy voice in the garden: and I was afraid, becauſe I was naked, and I hid my ſelfe.11And he ſaid, Who told thee, that thou waſt naked? Haſt thou eaten of the tree, whereof I commanded thee, that thou ſhouldeſt not eate?12And the man ſaid, The woman whom thou gaueſt to be with mee, ſhee gaue me of the tree, and I did eate.13And the LORD God ſaid vnto the woman, What is this that thou haſt done? And the woman ſaid, The Serpent beguiled me, and I did eate.14And the LORD God ſaid vnto the Serpent, Becauſe thou haſt done this, thou art curſed aboue all cattel, and aboue euery beaſt of the

field: vpon thy belly ſhalt thou goe, and duſt ſhalt thou eate, all the dayes
of thy life.[15]And I will put enmitie betweene thee and the woman, and
betweene thy ſeed and her ſeed: it ſhal bruiſe thy head, and thou ſhalt
bruiſe his heele.[16]Unto the woman he ſaid, I will greatly multiply thy
ſorowe and thy conception. In ſorow thou ſhalt bring forth children:
and thy deſire ſhall be to thy huſband, and hee ſhall rule ouer thee.[17]And
vnto Adam he ſaid, Becauſe thou haſt hearkened vnto the voyce of thy
wife, and haſt eaten of the tree, of which I commaunded thee, ſaying,
Thou ſhalt not eate of it: curſed is the ground for thy ſake: in ſorow ſhalt
thou eate of it all the dayes of thy life.[18]Thornes alſo and thiſtles ſhall it
bring forth to thee: and thou ſhalt eate the herbe of the field.[19]In the
ſweate of thy face ſhalt thou eate bread, till thou returne vnto the
ground: for out of it waſt thou taken, for duſt thou art, and vnto duſt
ſhalt thou returne.[20]And Adam called his wiues name Eue, becauſe ſhe
was the mother of all liuing.[21]Unto Adam alſo, and to his wife, did the
LORD God make coates of ſkinnes, and cloathed them.[22]And the
LORD God ſaid, Behold, the man is become as one of vs, to know good
& euill. And now leſt hee put foorth his hand, and take alſo of the tree
of life, and eate and liue for euer:[23]Therefore the LORD God ſent him
foorth from the garden of Eden, to till the ground, from whence he was
taken.[24]So he droue out the man: and he placed at the Eaſt of the garden
of Eden, Cherubims, and a flaming ſword, which turned euery way, to
keepe the way of the tree of life.

CHAPTER 4[1]And Adam knew Eue his wife, and ſhee conceiued, and
bare Cain, and ſaid, I haue gotten a man from the LORD.[2]And ſhe
againe bare his brother Abel, and Abel was a keeper of ſheep, but Cain
was a tiller of the ground.[3]And in proceſſe of time it came to paſſe, that
Cain brought of the fruite of the ground, an offering vnto the
LORD.[4]And Abel, he alſo brought of the firſtlings of his flocke, and of
the fat thereof: and the LORD had reſpect vnto Abel, and to his
offering.[5]But vnto Cain, and to his offring he had not reſpect: and Cain
was very wroth, and his countenance fell.[6]And the LORD ſaid vnto
Cain, Why art thou wroth? And why is thy countenance fallen?[7]If thou
doe well, ſhalt thou not be accepted? and if thou doeſt not well, ſinne
lieth at the doore: And vnto thee ſhall be his deſire, and thou ſhalt rule
ouer him.[8]And Cain talked with Abel his brother: and it came to paſſe
when they were in the field, that Cain roſe vp againſt Abel his brother,
and ſlew him.[9]And the LORD ſaid vnto Cain, Where is Abel thy
brother? And hee ſaid, I know not: Am I my brothers keeper?[10]And he
ſaid, What haſt thou done? the voyce of thy brothers blood cryeth vnto
me, from the ground.[11]And now art thou curſed from the earth, which
hath opened her mouth to receiue thy brothers blood from thy
hand.[12]When thou tilleſt the ground, it ſhall not henceforth yeeld vnto
thee her ſtrength: A fugitiue and a vagabond ſhalt thou be in the
earth.[13]And Cain ſaid vnto the LORD, My puniſhment is greater, then
I can beare.[14]Behold, thou haſt driuen me out this day from the face of
the earth, and from thy face ſhall I be hid, and I ſhall be a fugitiue, and
a vagabond in the earth: and it ſhall come to paſſe, that euery one that
findeth me, ſhall ſlay me.[15]And the LORD ſaid vnto him, Therefore
whoſoeuer ſlayeth Cain, vengeance ſhalbe taken on him ſeuen fold. And
the LORD ſet a marke vpon Cain, leſt any finding him, ſhould kill
him.[16]And Cain went out from the preſence of the LORD, and dwelt in
the land of Nod, on the Eaſt of Eden.[17]And Cain knew his wife, and
ſhe conceiued and bare Enoch, and hee builded a City, and called the
name of the City, after the name of his ſonne, Enoch.[18]And vnto Enoch
was borne Irad: and Irad begate Mehuiael, and Mehuiael begate
Methuſael, and Methuſael begate Lamech.[19]And Lamech tooke vnto
him two wiues: the name of the one was Adah, and the name of the
other Zillah.[20]And Adah bare Iabal: he was the father of ſuch as dwell
in tents, and of ſuch as haue cattell.[21]And his brothers name was Iubal:
hee was the father of all ſuch as handle the harpe and organ.[22]And Zillah,
ſhe alſo bare Tubal-Cain, an inſtructer of euery artificer in braſſe and
iron: and the ſiſter of Tubal-Cain was Naamah.[23]And Lamech ſayd vnto
his wiues, Adah and Zillah, Heare my voyce, yee wiues of Lamech,
hearken vnto my ſpeech: for I haue ſlaine a man to my wounding, and
a yong man to my hurt.[24]If Cain ſhall bee auenged ſeuen fold, truely
Lamech ſeuenty and ſeuen folde.[25]And Adam knew his wife againe, and
ſhe bare a ſonne, & called his name Seth: For God, ſaid ſhe, hath
appointed mee another ſeed in ſtead of Abel, whom Cain ſlew.[26]And to
Seth, to him alſo there was borne a ſonne, and he called his name Enos:
then began men to call vpon the Name of the LORD.

CHAPTER 5[1]This is the booke of the generations of Adam: In the day
that God created man, in the likenes of God made he him.[2]Male and
female created hee them, and bleſſed them, and called their name Adam,
in the day when they were created.[3]And Adam liued an hundred and
thirtie yeeres, and begate a ſonne in his owne likeneſſe, after his image;
and called his name Seth.[4]And the dayes of Adam, after he had begotten
Seth, were eight hundred yeeres: and he begate ſonnes and
daughters.[5]And all the dayes that Adam liued, were nine hundred and
thirtie yeeres: and he died.[6]And Seth liued an hundred and fiue yeeres:
and begate Enos.[7]And Seth liued, after he begate Enos, eight hundred
and ſeuen yeeres, and begate ſonnes and daughters.[8]And all the dayes
of Seth, were nine hundred and twelue yeeres, and he died.[9]And Enos
liued ninetie yeeres, and begate Cainan.[10]And Enos liued after hee
begate Cainan, eight hundred and fifteene yeeres, and begate ſonnes &
daughters.[11]And all the dayes of Enos were nine hundred & fiue yeres;
and he died.[12]And Cainan liued ſeuentie yeeres, and begate
Mahalaleel.[13]And Cainan liued after he begate Mahalaleel, eight hundred
and fourtie yeeres, & begate ſonnes and daughters.[14]And al the dayes of
Cainan were nine hundred & ten yeres; and he died.[15]And Mahalaleel
liued ſixtie and fiue yeeres, and begat Iared.[16]And Mahalaleel liued after
he begate Iared, eight hundred and thirtie yeeres, and begate ſonnes &
daughters.[17]And all the dayes of Mahalaleel, were eight hundred ninetie
and fiue yeeres, and he died.[18]And Iared liued an hundred ſixtie and two
yeeres, & he begat Enoch.[19]And Iared liued after he begate Enoch, eight
hundred yeres, and begate ſonnes and daughters.[20]And all the dayes of
Iared were nine hundred ſixtie and two yeeres, and he died.[21]And Enoch
liued ſixtie and fiue yeeres, and begate Methuſelah.[22]And Enoch walked
with God, after he begate Methuſelah, three hundred yeeres, and begate
ſonnes and daughters.[23]And all the dayes of Enoch, were three hundred
ſixtie and fiue yeeres.[24]And Enoch walked with God: and he was not;
for God tooke him.[25]And Methuſelah liued an hundred eightie and
ſeuen yeeres, and begat Lamech.[26]And Methuſelah liued, after hee
begate Lamech, ſeuen hundred, eightie and two yeeres, and begate
ſonnes and daughters.[27]And all the dayes of Methuſelah were nine
hundred, ſixtie and nine yeeres, and he died.[28]And Lamech liued an
hundred eightie and two yeeres: and begate a ſonne.[29]And he called his
name Noah, ſaying; This ſame ſhall comfort vs, concerning our woorke
and toyle of our hands, becauſe of the ground, which the LORD hath
curſed.[30]And Lamech liued, after hee begate Noah, fiue hundred ninetie
and fiue yeeres, and begate ſonnes and daughters.[31]And all the dayes of
Lamech were ſeuen hundred ſeuentie and ſeuen yeeres, and he
died.[32]And Noah was fiue hundred yeeres olde: and Noah begate Sem,
Ham, and Iapheth.

CHAPTER 6[1]And it came to paſſe, when men began to multiply on
the face of the earth, and daughters were borne vnto them:[2]That the
ſonnes of God ſaw the daughters of men, that they were faire, and they
took them wiues, of all which they choſe.[3]And the LORD ſaid, My Spirit
ſhall not alwayes ſtriue with man; for that hee alſo is fleſh: yet his dayes
ſhalbe an hundred and twenty yeeres.[4]There were Giants in the earth in
thoſe daies: and alſo after that, when the ſonnes of God came in vnto
the daughters of men, & they bare children to them; the ſame became
mightie men, which were of old, men of renowme.[5]And God ſaw, that
the wickednes of man was great in the earth, and that euery imagination
of the thoughts of his heart was onely euill continually.[6]And it repented
the LORD that he had made man on the earth, and it grieued him at his
heart.[7]And the LORD ſaid, I will deſtroy man, whom I haue created,
from the face of the earth: both man and beaſt, and the creeping thing,
and the foules of the aire: for it repenteth me that I haue made
them.[8]But Noah found grace in the eyes of the LORD.[9]Theſe are the
generations of Noah: Noah was a iuſt man, and perfect in his
generations, and Noah walked with God.[10]And Noah begate three
ſonnes: Sem, Ham, and Iapheth.[11]The earth alſo was corrupt before
God; and the earth was filled with violence.[12]And God looked vpon the
earth, and behold, it was corrupt: for all fleſh had corrupted his way
vpon the earth.[13]And God ſaid vnto Noah, The end of all fleſh is come
before mee; for the earth is filled with violence through them; and
behold, I will deſtroy them with the earth.[14]Make thee an Arke of

Gopher-wood: roomes ſhalt thou make in the arke, and ſhalt pitch it within and without with pitch.15And this is the faſhion, which thou ſhalt make it of: the length of the arke ſhalbe three hundred cubits, the breadth of it fifty cubits, and the height of it thirtie cubits.16A window ſhalt thou make to the arke, and in a cubite ſhalt thou finiſh it aboue; and the doore of the arke ſhalt thou ſet in the ſide thereof: With lower, ſecond, and third ſtories ſhalt thou make it.17And behold, I, euen I doe bring a flood of waters vpon the earth, to deſtroy all fleſh, wherein is the breath of life from vnder heauen, and euery thing that is in the earth ſhall die.18But with thee wil I eſtabliſh my Couenant: and thou ſhalt come into the Arke, thou, and thy ſonnes, and thy wife, and thy ſonnes wiues with thee.19And of euery liuing thing of all fleſh, two of euery ſort ſhalt thou bring into the Arke, to keepe them aliue with thee: they ſhall be male and female.20Of fowles after their kinde, and of cattel after their kinde: of euery creeping thing of the earth after his kinde, two of euery ſort ſhall come vnto thee, to keepe them aliue.21And take thou vnto thee of all food that is eaten, and thou ſhalt gather it to thee; and it ſhall be for food, for thee, and for them.22Thus did Noah; according to all that God commanded him, ſo did he.

CHAPTER 71And the LORD ſaide vnto Noah, Come thou and all thy houſe into the Arke: for thee haue I ſeene righteous before me, in this generation.2Of euery cleane beaſt thou ſhalt take to thee by ſeuens, the male and his female: and of beaſtes that are not cleane, by two, the male and his female.3Of fowles alſo of the aire, by ſeuens, the male & the female; to keepe ſeed aliue vpon the face of all the earth.4For yet ſeuen dayes, and I will cauſe it to raine vpon the earth, fortie dayes, and forty nights: and euery liuing ſubſtance that I haue made, will I deſtroy, frō off the face of the earth.5And Noah did according vnto all that the LORD commanded him.6And Noah was ſixe hundred yeeres old, when the flood of waters was vpon the earth.7And Noah went in, and his ſonnes, and his wife, and his ſonnes wiues with him, into the Arke, becauſe of the waters of the Flood.8Of cleane beaſts, & of beaſts that are not cleane, & of fowles, and of euery thing that creepeth vpon the earth,9There went in two and two vnto Noah into the Arke, the male & the female, as God had commanded Noah.10And it came to paſſe after ſeuen dayes, that the waters of the Flood were vpon the earth.11In the ſixe hundredth yeere of Noahs life, in the ſecond moneth, the ſeuenteenth day of the moneth, the ſame day, were al the fountaines of the great deepe broken vp, and the windowes of heauen were opened.12And the raine was vpon the earth, fortie dayes, and fortie nights.13In the ſelfe ſame day entred Noah, and Sem, and Ham, and Iapheth, the ſonnes of Noah, and Noahs wife, and the three wiues of his ſonnes with them, into the Arke,14They, and euery beaſt after his kinde, & all the cattell after their kinde: and euery creeping thing that creepeth vpon the earth after his kinde, and euery foule after his kinde, euery birde of euery ſort.15And they went in vnto Noah into the Arke, two and two of all fleſh, wherein is the breath of life.16And they that went in, went in male and female of all fleſh, as God had commaunded him: and the LORD ſhut him in.17And the Flood was fortie dayes vpon the earth, and the waters increaſed, and bare vp the Arke, and it was lift vp aboue the earth.18And the waters preuailed, and were encreaſed greatly vpon the earth: and the Arke went vpon the face of the waters.19And the waters preuailed exceedingly vpon the earth, and all the high hils, that were vnder the whole heauen, were couered.20Fifteene cubits vpward, did the waters preuaile; and the mountaines were couered.21And all fleſh died, that mooued vpon the earth, both of fowle, & of cattell, and of beaſt, and of euery creeping thing that creepeth vpon the earth, and euery man.22All in whoſe noſethrils was the breath of life, of all that was in the dry land, died.23And euery liuing ſubſtance was deſtroyed, which was vpon the face of the ground, both man and cattell, and the creeping things, and the foule of the heauen; and they were deſtroyed from the earth: and Noah onely remained aliue, and they that were with him in the Arke.24And the waters preuailed vpon the earth, an hundred and fifty dayes.

CHAPTER 81And God remembred Noah, and euery liuing thing, and all the cattell that was with him in the Arke: and God made a winde to paſſe ouer the earth, and the waters aſſwaged.2The fountaines alſo of the deepe, and the windowes of heauen were ſtopped, and the raine from heauen was reſtrained.3And the waters returned from off the earth, continually: and after the end of the hundred and fiftie dayes, the waters were abated.4And the Arke reſted in the ſeuenth moneth, on the ſeuenteenth day of the moneth, vpon the mountaines of Ararat.5And the waters decreaſed continually vntill the tenth moneth: in the tenth moneth, on the firſt day of the moneth, were the tops of the mountaines ſeene.6And it came to paſſe at the end of forty dayes, that Noah opened the window of the Arke which he had made.7And he ſent forth a Rauen, which went foorth to and fro, vntill the waters were dried vp from off the earth.8Alſo hee ſent foorth a doue from him, to ſee if the waters were abated from off the face of the ground.9But the doue found no reſt for the ſole of her foote, and ſhe returned vnto him into the Arke: for the waters were on the face of the whole earth. Then he put foorth his hand, and tooke her, and pulled her in vnto him, into the Arke.10And hee ſtayed yet other ſeuen dayes; and againe hee ſent foorth the doue out of the Arke.11And the doue came in to him in the euening, and loe, in her mouth was an Oliue leafe pluckt off: So Noah knew that the waters were abated from off the earth.12And hee ſtayed yet other ſeuen dayes, and ſent forth the doue, which returned not againe vnto him any more.13And it came to paſſe in the ſixe hundredth and one yeere, in the firſt moneth, the firſt day of the moneth, the waters were dryed vp from off the earth: and Noah remooued the couering of the Arke, and looked, and behold, the face of the ground was drie.14And in the ſecond moneth, on the ſeuen and twentieth day of the moneth, was the earth dried.15And God ſpake vnto Noah, ſaying,16Goe foorth of the Arke, thou, and thy wife, and thy ſonnes, and thy ſonnes wiues with thee:17Bring foorth with thee euery liuing thing that is with thee, of all fleſh, both of fowle, and of cattell, and of euery creeping thing that creepeth vpon the earth, that they may breed abundantly in the earth, and be fruitfull, and multiply vpon the earth.18And Noah went foorth, and his ſonnes, and his wife, and his ſonnes wiues with him:19Euery beaſt, euery creeping thing, and euery fowle, and whatſoeuer creepeth vpon the earth, after their kinds, went foorth out of the Arke.20And Noah builded an Altar vnto the LORD, and tooke of euery cleane beaſt, and of euery cleane fowle, and offred burnt offrings on the Altar.21And the LORD ſmelled a ſweete ſauour, and the LORD ſaid in his heart, I will not againe curſe the ground any more for mans ſake; for the imagination of mans heart is euil from his youth: neither will I againe ſmite any more euery thing liuing, as I haue done.22While the earth remaineth, ſeed-time and harueſt, and cold, and heat, and Summer, and Winter, and day and night, ſhall not ceaſe.

CHAPTER 91And God bleſſed Noah, and his ſonnes, and ſaid vnto them, Bee fruitfull and multiply, and repleniſh the earth.2And the feare of you, & the dread of you ſhall be vpon euery beaſt of the earth, and vpon euery fowle of the aire, vpon all that mooueth vpon the earth, and vpon all the fiſhes of the ſea; into your hand are they deliuered.3Euery mouing thing that liueth, ſhalbe meat for you; euen as the greene herbe haue I giuen you all things.4But fleſh with the life thereof, which is the blood thereof, ſhall you not eate.5And ſurely your blood of your liues will I require: at the hand of euery beaſt will I require it, & at the hand of man, at the hand of euery mans brother will I require the life of man.6Who ſo ſheddeth mans blood, by man ſhall his blood be ſhed: for in the image of God made he man.7And you, be ye fruitfull, and multiply, bring foorth aboundantly in the earth, and multiply therein.8And God ſpake vnto Noah, and to his ſonnes with him, ſaying;9And I, behold, I eſtabliſh my couenant with you, and with your ſeede after you:10And with euery liuing creature that is with you, of the fowle, of the cattell, and of euery beaſt of the earth with you, from all that goe out of the Arke, to euery beaſt of the earth.11And I wil eſtabliſh my couenant with you, neither ſhal all fleſh be cut off any more, by the waters of a flood, neither ſhall there any more be a flood to deſtroy the earth.12And God ſaid, This is the token of the Couenant which I make betweene mee and you, and euery liuing creature that is with you, for perpetuall generations.13I doe ſet my bow in the cloud, and it ſhall be for a token of a couenant, betweene me and the earth.14And it ſhall come to paſſe, when I bring a cloud ouer the earth, that the bow ſhall be ſeene in the cloud.15And I will remember my couenant, which is betweene mee and you, and euery liuing creature of all fleſh: and the waters ſhall no more become a flood to deſtroy all fleſh.16And the bow ſhalbe in the cloud; and I will looke vpon it, that I may remember the euerlaſting couenant betweene God and euery liuing creature, of all fleſh that is vpon the earth.17And God ſaid vnto Noah, This is the token of the couenant, which I haue eſtabliſhed betweene mee and all fleſh, that is vpon the earth.18And the ſonnes of Noah that went forth of the Arke, were Shem, and Ham, and Iaphet: and Ham is the father of Canaan.19Theſe are the three ſonnes of Noah: and of them was the whole earth ouerſpread.20And Noah began to bee an huſbandman, and he planted a vineyard.21And he dranke of the wine, and was drunken, and hee was vncouered within his tent.22And Ham, the father of Canaan, ſaw the nakedneſſe of his father, and told his two brethren without.23And Shem and Iaphet tooke a garment, and layed it vpon both their ſhoulders , and went backward, and couered the nakedneſſe of their father, and their faces were backward, and they ſaw not their fathers nakedneſse.24And Noah awoke from his wine, and knew what his yonger ſonne had done vnto him.25And he ſaid, Curſed bee Canaan: a ſeruant of ſeruants ſhall hee be vnto his brethren.26And hee ſaide, Bleſſed bee the LORD God of Shem, and Canaan ſhalbe his ſeruant.27God ſhall enlarge Iaphet, and he ſhal dwel in the tents of Shem, and Canaan ſhalbe his ſeruant.28And Noah liued after the flood, three hundred and fifty yeeres.29And all the dayes of Noah were nine hundred & fifty yeeres, and he died.

CHAPTER 101Now theſe are the generations of the ſonnes of Noah; Shem, Ham, and Iaphet: and vnto them were ſonnes borne after the Flood.2The ſonnes of Iaphet: Gomer, and Magog, and Madai, and Iauan, & Tubal, and Meſhech, & Tiras.3And the ſonnes of Gomer: Aſhkenaz, and Riphath, and Togarmah.4And the ſons of Iauan: Eliſhah, and Tarſhiſh, Kittim, and Dodanim.5By theſe were the Iles of the Gentiles diuided in their lands, euery one after his tongue: after their families, in their nations.6And the ſonnes of Ham: Cuſh, and Mizraim, and Phut, and Canaan.7And the ſonnes of Cuſh, Seba, and Hauilah, and Sabtah, and Raamah, and Sabtecha: and the ſonnes of Raamah: Sheba, and Dedan.8And Cuſh begat Nimrod: he began to be a mighty one in the earth.9He was a mighty hunter before the LORD: wherefore it is ſaide, Euen as Nimrod the mightie hunter before the LORD.10And the beginning of his kingdome was Babel, and Erech, and Accad, and Calneh, in the land of Shinar.11Out of that land went forth Aſshur, and builded Nineueh, and the citie Rehoboth, and Calah,12And Reſen betweene Nineueh and Calah: the ſame is a great citie.13And Mizraim begat Ludim, and Anamim, and Lehabim, and Naphtuhim,14And Pathruſim, and Caſluhim (out of whome came Philiſtiim) and Caphtorim.15And Canaan begate Sidon his firſt borne, and Heth,16And the Iebuſite, and the Emorite, and the Girgaſite,17And the Hiuite, and the Arkite, and the Sinite,18And the Aruadite, and the Zemarite, and the Hamathite: and afterward were the families of the Canaanites ſpread abroad.19And the border of the Canaanites, was from Sidon, as thou commeſt to Gerar, vnto Gaza, as thou goeſt vnto Sodoma and Gomorah, and Admah, & Zeboim, euen vnto Laſha.20Theſe are the ſonnes of Ham, after their families, after their tongues, in their countries, and in their nations.21Unto Shem alſo the father of all the children of Eber, the brother of Iaphet the elder, euen to him were children borne.22The children of Shem: Elam, and Aſshur, and Arphaxad, and Lud, and Aram.23And the children of Aram: Uz, and Hul, and Gether, and Maſh.24And Arphaxad begate Salah, and Salah begate Eber.25And vnto Eber were borne two ſonnes: the name of one was Peleg, for in his dayes was the earth diuided, and his brothers name was Ioktan.26And Ioktan begate Almodad, and Sheleph, and Hazarmaueth, and Ierah,27And Hadoram, and Uzal, and Diklah,28And Obal, and Abimael, and Sheba,29And Ophir, and Hauilah, & Iobab: all theſe were the ſonnes of Ioktan.30And their dwelling was from Meſha, as thou goeſt vnto Sephar, a mount of the Eaſt.31Theſe are the ſonnes of Shem, after their families, after their tongues, in their lands after their nations.32Theſe are the families of the ſonnes of Noah after their generations, in their nations: and by theſe were the nations diuided in the earth after the Flood.

CHAPTER 111And the whole earth was of one language, and of one ſpeach.2And it came to paſſe as they iourneyed from the Eaſt, that they found a plaine in the land of Shinar, and they dwelt there.3And they ſayd one to another; Goe to, let vs make bricke, and burne them thorowly. And they had bricke for ſtone, and ſlime had they for morter.4And they ſaid; Goe to, let vs build vs a city and a tower, whoſe top may reach vnto heauen, and let vs make vs a name, leſt we be ſcattered abroad vpon the face of the whole earth.5And the LORD came downe to ſee the city and the tower, which the children of men builded.6And the LORD ſaid; Behold, the people is one, and they haue all one language: and this they begin to doe: and now nothing will be reſtrained from them, which they haue imagined to doe.7Goe to, let vs go downe, and there cōfound their language, that they may not vnderſtand one anothers ſpeech.8So the LORD ſcattered them abroad from thence, vpon the face of all the earth: and they left off to build the Citie.9Therefore is the name of it called Babel, becauſe the LORD did there confound the language of all the earth: and from thence did the LORD ſcatter them abroad vpon the face of all the earth.10Theſe are the generations of Shem. Shem was an hundred yeres old, and begate Arphaxad two yeeres after the Flood.11And Shem liued, after he begate Arphaxad, fiue hundred yeeres, and begate ſonnes and daughters.12And Arphaxad liued fiue and thirtie yeeres, and begate Salah.13And Arphaxad liued, after he begate Salah, foure hundred and three yeeres, and begate ſonnes and daughters.14And Salah liued thirtie yeeres, and begate Eber.15And Salah liued, after hee begate Eber, foure hundred and three yeeres, and begate ſonnes and daughters.16And Eber liued foure and thirty yeeres, and begate Peleg.17And Eber liued, after hee begate Peleg, foure hundred and thirtie yeres, and begate ſonnes and daughters.18And Peleg liued thirtie yeeres, and begate Reu.19And Peleg liued, after hee begate Reu, two hundred and nine yeeres, and begate ſonnes and daughters.20And Reu liued two and thirtie yeeres, and begate Serug.21And Reu liued, after hee begate Serug, two hundreth and ſeuen yeres, and begate ſonnes and daughters.22And Serug liued thirtie yeeres, and begate Nahor.23And Serug liued, after he begate Nahor, two hundred yeeres, and begat ſonnes and daughters.24And Nahor liued nine and twentie yeeres, and begate Terah.25And Nahor liued, after he begate Terah, an hundred & nineteene yeeres, and begate ſonnes and daughters.26And Terah liued ſeuenty yeeres, and begate Abram, Nahor, & Haran.27Now theſe are the generations of Terah: Terah begate Abram, Nahor, and Haran: And Haran begate Lot.28And Haran died, before his father Terah in the land of his natiuity, in Ur of the Chaldees.29And Abram and Nahor tooke them wiues: the name of Abrams wife was Sarai, and the name of Nahors wife, Milcah, the daughter of Haran, the father of Milcah, and the father of Iſcah.30But Sarai was barren; ſhe had no childe.31And Terah tooke Abram his ſonne, and Lot the ſonne of Haran his ſonnes ſonne, and Sarai his daughter in lawe, his ſonne Abrams wife, and they went foorth with them from Ur of the Chaldees, to goe into the land of Canaan: and they came vnto Haran, and dwelt there.32And the dayes of Terah, were two hundred and fiue yeres: and Terah died in Haran.

CHAPTER 121And the whole earth was of one language, and of one ſpeach.2And it came to paſſe as they iourneyed from the Eaſt, that they found a plaine in the land of Shinar, and they dwelt there.3And they ſayd one to another; Goe to, let vs make bricke, and burne them thorowly. And they had bricke for ſtone, and ſlime had they for morter.4And they ſaid; Goe to, let vs build vs a city and a tower, whoſe top may reach vnto heauen, and let vs make vs a name, leſt we be ſcattered abroad vpon the face of the whole earth.5And the LORD came downe to ſee the city and the tower, which the children of men builded.6And the LORD ſaid; Behold, the people is one, and they haue all one language: and this they begin to doe: and now nothing will be reſtrained from them, which they haue imagined to doe.7Goe to, let vs go downe, and there cōfound their language, that they may not vnderſtand one anothers ſpeech.8So the LORD ſcattered them abroad from thence, vpon the face of all the earth: and they left off to build the Citie.9Therefore is the name of it called Babel, becauſe the LORD did there confound the language of all the earth: and from thence did the LORD ſcatter them abroad vpon the face of all the earth.10Theſe are the generations of Shem. Shem was an hundred yeres old, and begate Arphaxad two yeeres after the Flood.11And Shem liued, after he begate Arphaxad, fiue hundred yeeres, and begate ſonnes and daughters.12And Arphaxad liued fiue and thirtie yeeres, and begate Salah.13And Arphaxad liued, after he begate Salah, foure hundred and three yeeres, and begate ſonnes and daughters.14And Salah liued thirtie yeeres, and begate Eber.15And Salah liued, after hee begate Eber, foure hundred and three yeeres, and begate ſonnes and daughters.16And Eber liued foure and thirty yeeres, and begate Peleg.17And Eber liued, after hee begate Peleg, foure hundred and thirtie yeres, and begate ſonnes and daughters.[18]And Peleg liued thirtie yeeres, and begate Reu.[19]And Peleg liued, after hee begate Reu, two hundred and nine yeeres, and begate ſonnes and daughters.[20]And Reu liued two and thirtie yeeres, and begate Serug.[21]And Reu liued, after hee begate Serug, two hundreth and ſeuen yeres, and begate ſonnes and daughters.[22]And Serug liued thirtie yeeres, and begate Nahor.[23]And Serug liued, after he begate Nahor, two hundred yeeres, and begat ſonnes and daughters.[24]And Nahor liued nine and twentie yeeres, and begate Terah.[25]And Nahor liued, after he begate Terah, an hundred & nineteene yeeres, and begate ſonnes and daughters.[26]And Terah liued ſeuenty yeeres, and begate Abram, Nahor, & Haran.[27]Now theſe are the generations of Terah: Terah begate Abram, Nahor, and Haran: And Haran begate Lot.[28]And Haran died, before his father Terah in the land of his natiuity, in Ur of the Chaldees.[29]And Abram and Nahor tooke them wiues: the name of Abrams wife was Sarai, and the name of Nahors wife, Milcah, the daughter of Haran, the father of Milcah, and the father of Iſcah.[30]But Sarai was barren; ſhe had no childe.[31]And Terah tooke Abram his ſonne, and Lot the ſonne of Haran his ſonnes ſonne, and Sarai his daughter in lawe, his ſonne Abrams wife, and they went foorth with them from Ur of the Chaldees, to goe into the land of Canaan: and they came vnto Haran, and dwelt there.[32]And the dayes of Terah, were two hundred and fiue yeres: and Terah died in Haran.

CHAPTER 13[1]And Abram went vp out of Egypt, he and his wife, and all that he had, and Lot with him, into the South.[2]And Abram was very rich in cattell, in ſiluer, and in gold.[3]And hee went on his iourneyes from the South, euen to Beth-el, vnto the place where his tent had bene at the beginning, betweene Beth-el and Hai:[4]Unto the place of the altar, which he had made there at the firſt: and there Abram called on the Name of the LORD.[5]And Lot alſo which went with Abram, had flocks and heards, & tents.[6]And the land was not able to beare them, that they might dwell together: for their ſubſtance was great, ſo that they could not dwell together.[7]And there was a ſtrife betweene the heardmen of Abrams cattell, and the heardmen of Lots cattell: And the Canaanite, and the Perizzite dwelled then in the land.[8]And Abram ſaid vnto Lot, Let there be no ſtrife, I pray thee, betweene mee and thee, and betweene my heardmen and thy heardmen: for wee bee brethren.[9]Is not the whole land before thee? Separate thy ſelfe, I pray thee, from mee: if thou wilt take the left hand, then I will goe to the right: or if thou depart to the right hand, then I will goe to the left.[10]And Lot lifted vp his eyes, and beheld all the plaine of Iordane, that it was well watered euery where before the Lord deſtroyed Sodome and Gomorah, euen as the garden of the LORD, like the land of Egypt, as thou commeſt vnto Zoar.[11]Then Lot choſe him all the plaine of Iordane: and Lot iourneyed Eaſt; and they ſeparated themſelues the one from the other.[12]Abram dwelled in the land of Canaan, and Lot dwelled in the cities of the plaine, and pitched his tent toward Sodome.[13]But the men of Sodome were wicked, and ſinners before the LORD exceedingly.[14]And the LORD ſaid vnto Abram, after that Lot was ſeparated from him, Lift vp now thine eyes, and looke from the place where thou art, Northward, and Southward, and Eaſtward, and Weſtward.[15]For all the land which thou ſeeſt, to thee will I giue it, and to thy ſeede for euer.[16]And I will make thy ſeede as the duſt of the earth: ſo that if a man can number the duſt of the earth, then ſhall thy ſeed alſo be numbred.[17]Ariſe, walke through the land, in the length of it, and in the breadth of it: for I will giue it vnto thee.[18]Then Abram remoued his tent, and came and dwelt in the plaine of Mamre, which is in Hebron, and built there an altar vnto the LORD.

CHAPTER 14[1]And it came to paſſe in the dayes of Amraphel King of Shinar, Arioch King of Ellaſar, Chedorlaomer King of Elam, and Tidal King of nations:[2]That theſe made warre with Bera King of Sodome, and with Birſha King of Gomorrah, Shinab King of Admah, and Shemeber King of Zeboiim, and the King of Bela, which is Zoar.[3]All theſe were ioyned together in the vale of Siddim; which is the ſalt ſea.[4]Twelue yeeres they ſerued Chedorlaomer, and in the thirteenth yeere they rebelled.[5]And in the fourteenth yeere came Chedorlaomer, and the Kings that were with him, and ſmote the Rephaims, in Aſhteroth Karnaim, & the Zuzims in Ham, and the Emims in Shaueh Kiriathaim;[6]And the Horites in their mount Seir, vnto El-Paran, which is by the wilderneſſe.[7]And they returned, and came to En-miſhpat, which is Kadeſh, & ſmote all the countrey of the Amalekites, and alſo the Amorites, that dwelt in Hazezon-tamar.[8]And there went out the King of Sodome, and the King of Gomorrah, and the King of Admah, and the King of Zeboiim, and the King of Bela, (the ſame is Zoar) and they ioyned battell with them, in the vale of Siddim,[9]With Chedorlaomer the King of Elam, and with Tidal King of nations, and Amraphel King of Shinar, and Arioch King of Ellaſar; foure Kings with fiue.[10]And the vale of Siddim was full of ſlime-pits: and the Kings of Sodome & Gomorrah fled, and fell there: and they that remained, fled to the mountaine.[11]And they tooke all the goods of Sodome and Gomorrah, and all their victuals, and went their way.[12]And they tooke Lot, Abrams brothers ſonne, (who dwelt in Sodome) and his goods, and departed.[13]And there came one that had eſcaped, and told Abram the Hebrew, for hee dwelt in the plaine of Mamre the Amorite, brother of Eſhcol, and brother of Aner: and theſe were confederate with Abram.[14]And when Abram heard that his brother was taken captiue, he armed his trained ſeruants borne in his owne houſe, three hundred and eighteene, and purſued them vnto Dan.[15]And hee diuided himſelfe againſt them, he and his ſeruants by night, and ſmote them, and purſued them vnto Hoba, which is on the left hand of Damaſcus:[16]And hee brought backe all the goods, and alſo brought againe his brother Lot, and his goods, and the women alſo, and the people.[17]And the king of Sodome went out to meete him, (after his returne from the ſlaughter of Chedorlaomer, and of the Kings that were with him) at the valley of Saueh, which is the Kings dale.[18]And Melchizedek King of Salem brought foorth bread and wine: and he was the Prieſt of the moſt high God.[19]And hee bleſſed him, and ſaide; Bleſſed bee Abram of the moſt high God, poſſeſſour of heauen and earth,[20]And bleſſed bee the moſt high God, which hath deliuered thine enemies into thy hand: and hee gaue him tithes of all.[21]And the King of Sodome ſaid vnto Abram, giue me the perſons, and take the goods to thy ſelfe.[22]And Abram ſaid to the King of Sodome, I haue lift vp my hand vnto the LORD, the moſt high God, the poſſeſſour of heauen and earth,[23]That I wil not take from a threed euen to a ſhoe latchet, and that I will not take any thing that is thine, leſt thou ſhouldeſt ſay, I haue made Abram rich:[24]Saue onely that which the yong men haue eaten, and the portion of the men which went with mee, Aner, Eſchol, and Mamre; let them take their portion.

CHAPTER 15[1]After theſe things, the word of the LORD came vnto Abram in a viſion, ſaying; Feare not, Abram: I am thy ſhield, and thy exceeding great reward.[2]And Abram ſaid, Lord GOD, what wilt thou giue me, ſeeing I goe childleſſe? and the ſteward of my houſe is this Eliezer of Damaſcus.[3]And Abram ſaid; Behold, to mee thou haſt giuen no ſeed: and loe, one borne in my houſe is mine heire.[4]And behold, the word of the LORD came vnto him, ſaying; This ſhall not be thine heire: but he that ſhall come foorth out of thy owne bowels, ſhalbe thine heire.[5]And he brought him forth abroad, and ſaid, Looke now towards heauen, and tell the ſtarres, if thou be able to number them. And hee ſaid vnto him, So ſhall thy ſeed be.[6]And he beleeued in the LORD; and hee counted it to him for righteouſneſſe.[7]And he ſaid vnto him; I am the LORD that brought thee out of Ur of the Caldees, to giue thee this land, to inherit it.[8]And he ſaid, Lord GOD, whereby ſhal I know that I ſhall inherit it?[9]And he ſaid vnto him, Take me an heifer of three yeeres old, and a ſhee goat of three yeeres old, and a ramme of three yeeres old, and a turtle doue, and a yong pigeon.[10]And he tooke vnto him all theſe, and diuided them in the midſt, and layd each peece one againſt another: but the birds diuided he not.[11]And when the fowles came downe vpon the carcaſes, Abram droue them away.[12]And when the Sunne was going downe, a deepe ſleepe fell vpon Abram: and loe, an horrour of great darkeneſſe fell vpon him.[13]And he ſaid vnto Abram, Know of a ſurety, that thy ſeed ſhalbe a ſtranger, in a land that is not theirs, and ſhal ſerue them, and they ſhall afflict them foure hundred yeeres.[14]And alſo that nation whom they ſhall ſerue, wil I iudge: and afterward ſhall they come out with great ſubſtance.[15]And thou ſhalt goe to thy fathers in peace; thou ſhalt be buried in a good old age.[16]But in the fourth generation they ſhall come hither againe: for the iniquitie of the Amorites is not yet full.[17]And it came to paſſe that when the Sunne went downe, and it was darke, behold, a ſmoking furnace, and a burning lampe that paſſed betweene thoſe pieces.[18]In that ſame day the LORD made a couenant with Abram, ſaying; Unto thy ſeed haue I giuen this land from the riuer of Egypt vnto the great riuer, the riuer Euphrates:[19]The Kenites, and the Kenizites, and the Kadmonites:[20]And the Hittites, and the

Perizzites, and the Rephaims,[21]And the Amorites, and the Canaanites, and the Girgaſhites, and the Iebuſites.

CHAPTER 16[1]Now Sarai Abrams wife bare him no children: and ſhe had an handmaide, an Egyptian, whoſe name was Hagar.[2]And Sarai ſaid vnto Abram, Behold now, the LORD hath reſtrained me from bearing: I pray thee go in vnto my maid: it may bee that I may obtaine children by her: and Abram hearkened to the voice of Sarai.[3]And Sarai Abrams wife, tooke Hagar her maid, the Egyptian, after Abram had dwelt ten yeeres in the land of Canaan, and gaue her to her huſband Abram, to be his wife.[4]And he went in vnto Hagar, and ſhe conceiued: And when ſhee ſaw that ſhee had conceiued, her miſtreſſe was deſpiſed in her eyes.[5]And Sarai ſaid vnto Abram, My wrong be vpon thee: I haue giuen my maid into thy boſome, and when ſhee ſaw that ſhe had conceiued, I was deſpiſed in her eyes: the LORD iudge betweene me and thee.[6]But Abram ſaid vnto Sarai, Behold, thy maid is in thy hand; doe to her as it pleaſeth thee. And when Sarai dealt hardly with her, ſhee fled from her face.[7]And the Angel of the LORD found her by a fountaine of water, in the wilderneſſe, by the fountaine, in the way to Shur:[8]And he ſaid, Hagar Sarais maid, whence cameſt thou? and whither wilt thou goe? And ſhe ſaid, I flee from the face of my miſtreſſe Sarai.[9]And the Angel of the LORD ſaid vnto her, Returne to thy miſtreſſe, and ſubmit thy ſelfe vnder her hands.[10]And the Angel of the LORD ſaid vnto her, I will multiply thy ſeede exceedingly, that it ſhall not be numbred for multitude.[11]And the Angel of the LORD ſaid vnto her, Behold, thou art with child, and ſhalt beare a ſonne, and ſhalt call his name Iſhmael; becauſe the LORD hath heard thy affliction.[12]And he will be a wilde man; his hand will be againſt euery man, and euery mans hand againſt him: & he ſhal dwell in the preſence of all his brethren.[13]And ſhee called the name of the LORD that ſpake vnto her, Thou God ſeeſt me: for ſhe ſaid, Haue I alſo here looked after him that ſeeth me?[14]Wherefore the well was called, Beer-lahai-roi: Behold, It is betweene Cadeſh and Bered.[15]And Hagar bare Abram a ſonne: and Abram called his ſonnes name, which Hagar bare, Iſhmael.[16]And Abram was foureſcore and ſixe yeeres old, when Hagar bare Iſhmael to Abram.

CHAPTER 17[1]And when Abram was ninetie yeres old and nine, the LORD appeared to Abram, and ſaid vnto him, I am the almightie God, walke before me, and be thou perfect.[2]And I wil make my couenant betweene me and thee, and will multiply thee exceedingly.[3]And Abram fell on his face, and God talked with him, ſaying,[4]As for me, behold, my couenant is with thee, and thou ſhalt be a father of many nations.[5]Neither ſhall thy name any more be called Abram, but thy name ſhall bee Abraham: for a father of many nations haue I made thee.[6]And I will make thee exceeding fruitfull, and I will make nations of thee, and Kings ſhall come out of thee.[7]And I will eſtabliſh my couenant betweene me and thee, and thy ſeede after thee, in their generations for an euerlaſting couenant, to bee a God vnto thee, and to thy ſeed after thee.[8]And I will giue vnto thee, and to thy ſeed after thee, the land wherein thou art a ſtranger, all the land of Canaan, for an euerlaſting poſſeſſion, and I will be their God.[9]And God ſaid vnto Abraham, Thou ſhalt keepe my couenant therefore, thou, and thy ſeede after thee, in their generations.[10]This is my couenant, which yee ſhall keepe betweene me and you, and thy ſeed after thee: euery man child among you ſhall be circumciſed.[11]And ye ſhall circumciſe the fleſh of your foreſkinne; and it ſhal be a token of the couenant betwixt me and you.[12]And he that is eight dayes olde, ſhalbe circumciſed among you, euery man child in your generations, he that is borne in the houſe, or bought with money of any ſtranger, which is not of thy ſeed.[13]He that is borne in thy houſe, and he that is bought with thy money, muſt needs be circumciſed: and my couenant ſhall be in your fleſh, for an euerlaſting couenant.[14]And the vncircumciſed man-child, whoſe fleſh of his foreſkinne is not circumciſed, that ſoule ſhall be cut off from his people: hee hath broken my couenant.[15]And God ſaid vnto Abraham, As for Sarai thy wife, thou ſhalt not call her name Sarai, but Sarah ſhall her name be.[16]And I will bleſſe her, and giue thee a ſonne alſo of her: yea I wil bleſſe her, and ſhe ſhalbe a mother of nations; Kings of people ſhall be of her.[17]Then Abraham fell vpon his face, and laughed, and ſaid in his heart, Shall a child be borne vnto him that is an hundred yeeres old? and ſhal Sarah that is ninetie yeeres old, beare?[18]And Abraham ſaid vnto God, O that Iſhmael might liue before thee.[19]And God ſaid, Sarah thy wife ſhall beare thee a ſonne in deede, and thou ſhalt call his name Iſaac: and I will eſtabliſh my couenant with him, for an euerlaſting couenant, and with his ſeed after him.[20]And as for Iſhmael, I haue heard thee: behold, I haue bleſſed him, and will make him fruitfull, and will multiplie him exceedingly: Twelue princes ſhall he beget, and I will make him a great nation.[21]But my couenant wil I eſtabliſh with Iſaac, which Sarah ſhall beare vnto thee, at this ſet time, in the next yeere.[22]And he left off talking with him, and God went vp from Abraham.[23]And Abraham tooke Iſhmael his ſonne, and all that were borne in his houſe, and all that were bought with his money, euery male, among the men of Abrahams houſe, and circumciſed the fleſh of their foreſkinne, in the ſelfeſame day, as God had ſaid vnto him.[24]And Abraham was ninety yeeres old and nine, when he was circumciſed in the fleſh of his foreſkinne.[25]And Iſhmael his ſonne was thirteene yeeres old, when he was circumciſed in the fleſh of his foreſkinne.[26]In the ſelfe ſame day was Abraham circumciſed, and Iſhmael his ſonne.[27]And all the men of his houſe, borne in the houſe, and bought with money of the ſtranger, were circumciſed with him.

CHAPTER 18[1]And the LORD appeared vnto him, in the plaines of Mamre: and he ſate in the tent doore, in the heat of the day.[2]And he lift vp his eyes and looked, and loe, three men ſtood by him: and when he ſaw them, hee ranne to meete them from the tent doore, and bowed himſelfe toward the ground,[3]And ſaid, My Lord, If now I haue found fauour in thy ſight, paſſe not away, I pray thee, frō thy ſeruant:[4]Let a little water, I pray you, be fetched, and waſh your feete, and reſt your ſelues vnder the tree:[5]And I will fetch a morſell of bread; and comfort ye your hearts, after that you ſhall paſſe on: for therefore are you come to your ſeruant. And they ſaid; So doe, as thou haſt ſaid.[6]And Abraham haſtened into the tent, vnto Sarah, & ſaid; Make ready quickly three meaſures of fine meale, knead it, and make cakes vpon the hearth.[7]And Abraham ranne vnto the heard, and fetcht a calfe, tender and good, and gaue it vnto a yong man: and he haſted to dreſſe it.[8]And he tooke butter, and milke, and the calfe which he had dreſſed, and ſet it before them; and he ſtood by them vnder the tree: and they did eate.[9]And they ſaid vnto him, Where is Sarah thy wife? And he ſaid, Behold, in the tent.[10]And he ſaid, I will certainly returne vnto thee according to the time of life; and loe, Sarah thy wife ſhall haue a ſonne. And Sarah heard it in the tent doore, which was behind him.[11]Now Abraham and Sarah were old, and well ſtricken in age: and it ceaſed to be with Sarah after the maner of women.[12]Therefore Sarah laughed within her ſelfe, ſaying, After I am waxed old, ſhall I haue pleaſure, my lord being old alſo?[13]And the LORD ſaid vnto Abraham, Wherefore did Sarah laugh, ſaying; Shall I of a ſurety beare a childe, which am old?[14]Is any thing too hard for the LORD? At the time appointed will I returne vnto thee, according to the time of life, and Sarah ſhall haue a ſonne.[15]Then Sarah denied, ſaying, I laughed not: for ſhe was afraid. And he ſaid, Nay, but thou diddeſt laugh.[16]And the men roſe vp from thence, and looked toward Sodome: and Abraham went with them, to bring them on the way.[17]And the LORD ſaid, Shall I hide from Abraham that thing which I doe;[18]Seeing that Abraham ſhall ſurely become a great and mighty nation, and all the nations of the earth ſhall be bleſſed in him?[19]For I know him, that hee will command his children, and his houſehold after him, and they ſhall keepe the way of the LORD, to doe iuſtice and iudgement, that the LORD may bring vpon Abraham, that which hee hath ſpoken of him.[20]And the LORD ſaid, Becauſe the cry of Sodome and Gomorrah is great, and becauſe their ſinne is very grieuous:[21]I will goe downe now, and ſee whether they haue done altogether according to the cry of it, which is come vnto me: and if not, I will know.

CHAPTER 19[1]And there came two Angels to Sodome at euen, and Lot ſate in the gate of Sodome: and Lot ſeeing them, roſe vp to meet them, and he bowed himſelfe with his face toward the ground.[2]And he ſaid, Beholde now my Lords, turne in, I pray you, into your ſeruants houſe, and tarie all night, and waſh your feete, and ye ſhall riſe vp early and goe on your wayes. And they ſaid, Nay: but we wil abide in the ſtreet all night.[3]And he preſſed vpon them greatly, and they turned in vnto him, and entred into his houſe: and he made them a feaſt, and did bake vnleauened bread, and they did eate.[4]But before they lay downe, the men of the citie, euen the men of Sodom, compaſſed the houſe round, both old and yong, all the people from euery quarter.[5]And they called vnto Lot, and ſaid vnto him, Where are the men which came in to thee this night? bring them out vnto vs, that we may know them.[6]And Lot went out at the doore vnto them, & ſhut the doore after him,[7]And ſaid,

I pray you, brethren, doe not ſo wickedly.8Behold now, I haue two
daughters, which haue not knowen man; let mee, I pray you, bring them
out vnto you, and doe ye to them, as is good in your eyes: onely vnto
theſe men do nothing: for therefore came they vnder the ſhadow of my
roofe.9And they ſaid, ſtand backe. And they ſaid againe, This one fellow
came in to ſoiourne, and he will needs bee a Iudge: Now wil we deale
worſe with thee, then with them. And they preſſed ſore vpon the man,
euen Lot, and came neere to breake the doore.10But the men put forth
their hand, and pulled Lot into the houſe to them, and ſhut to the
doore.11And they ſmote the men that were at the doore of the houſe,
with blindnes, both ſmall and great: ſo that they wearied themſelues to
finde the doore.12And the men ſaid vnto Lot, Haſt thou here any
beſides? ſonne in law, and thy ſonnes, and thy daughters, and
whatſoeuer thou haſt in the citie, bring them out of this place.13For we
will deſtroy this place, becauſe the crie of them is waxen great before
the face of the LORD: and the LORD hath ſent vs to deſtroy it.14And
Lot went out, and ſpake vnto his ſonnes in law, which married his
daughters, and ſaid, Up, get yee out of this place: for the LORD wil
deſtroy this citie: but hee ſeemed as one that mocked, vnto his ſonnes
in law.15And when the morning aroſe, then the Angels haſtened Lot,
ſaying, Ariſe, take thy wife, & thy two daughters, which are here, leſt
thou be conſumed in the iniquitie of the citie.16And while he lingred,
the men laid hold vpon his hand, and vpon the hand of his wife, and
vpon the hand of his two daughters, the LORD being mercifull vnto
him: and they brought him forth, and ſet him without the citie.17And it
came to paſſe, when they had brought them forth abroad, that he ſaid,
Eſcape for thy life, looke not behind thee, neither ſtay thou in all the
plaine: eſcape to the mountaine, leſt thou bee conſumed.18And Lot ſaid
vnto them, Oh not ſo, my Lord.19Beholde now, thy ſeruant hath found
grace in thy ſight, and thou haſt magnified thy mercy, which thou haſt
ſhewed vnto me, in ſauing my life, and I cannot eſcape to the mountaine,
leſt ſome euill take me, and I die.20Behold now, this citie is neere to flee
vnto, and it is a litle one: Oh let me eſcape thither, (is it not a litle one?)
and my ſoule ſhall liue.21And he ſaid vnto him, See, I haue accepted thee
concerning this thing, that I will not ouerthrow this citie, for the which
thou haſt ſpoken.22Haſte thee, eſcape thither: for I cannot doe any thing
till thou bee come thither: therefore the name of the citie was called
Zoar.23The ſunne was riſen vpon the earth, when Lot entred into
Zoar.24Then the LORD rained vpon Sodome & vpon Gomorrah,
brimſtone and fire, from the LORD out of heauen.25And he ouerthrew
thoſe cities, and all the plaine, and all the inhabitants of the cities, and
that which grew vpon the ground.26But his wife looked backe from
behind him, and ſhe became a pillar of ſalt.27And Abraham gate vp
earely in the morning, to the place, where hee ſtood before the
LORD.28And he looked toward Sodome and Gomorrah, & toward all
the land of the plaine, and beheld, and loe, the ſmoke of the countrey
went vp as the ſmoke of a furnace.29And it came to paſſe, when God
deſtroyed the cities of the plaine, that God remembred Abraham, and
ſent Lot out of the midſt of the ouerthrow, when he ouerthrew the cities,
in the which Lot dwelt.30And Lot went vp out of Zoar, and dwelt in the
mountaine, and his two daughters with him: for hee feared to dwell in
Zoar, and he dwelt in a caue, he and his two daughters.31And the firſt
borne ſaide vnto the yonger, Our father is old, and there is not a man in
the earth, to come in vnto vs, after the maner of all the earth.32Come,
let vs make our father drinke wine, and we will lye with him, that we
may preſerueſeed of our father.33And they made their father drinke wine
that night, & the firſt borne went in, and lay with her father: and he
perceiued not, when ſhee lay downe, nor when ſhe aroſe.34And it came
to paſſe on the morrow, that the firſt borne ſaid vnto the yonger,
Behold, I lay yeſternight with my father: let vs make him drinke wine
this night alſo, and goe thou in, and lye with him, that we may
preſerueſeed of our father.35And they made their father drinke wine that
night alſo, and the yonger aroſe, and lay with him: and he perceiued not,
when ſhe lay downe, nor when ſhe aroſe.36Thus were both the daughters
of Lot with childe by their father.37And the firſt borne bare a ſonne, and
called his name Moab: the ſame is the father of the Moabites vnto this
day.38And the yonger, ſhe alſo bare a ſonne, and called his name, Ben-
ammi: the ſame is the father of the children of Ammon, vnto this day.
CHAPTER 201And Abraham iourneyed from thence, toward the
South-Countrey, and dwelled betweene Cadeſh and Shur, and ſoiourned
in Gerar.2And Abraham ſaid of Sarah his wife, She is my ſiſter: And
Abimelech King of Gerar ſent, and tooke Sarah.3But God came to
Abimelech in a dreame by night, and ſaid to him, Behold, thou art but a
dead man, for the woman which thou haſt taken: for ſhee is a mans
wife.4But Abimelech had not come neere her: and he ſaid, LORD, wilt
thou ſlay alſo a righteous nation?5Said he not vnto me, She is my ſiſter?
and ſhe, euen ſhe herſelfe ſaid, Hee is my brother: in the integritie of my
heart, and innocencie of my hands haue I done this.6And God ſaide
vnto him in a dreame, Yea, I know that thou didſt this in the integritie
of thy heart: for I alſo withheld thee from ſinning againſt mee, therefore
ſuffered I thee not to touch her.7Now therefore reſtore the man his
wife: for he is a Prophet, and he ſhal pray for thee, and thou ſhalt liue:
and if thou reſtore her not, know thou that thou ſhalt ſurely die, thou,
and all that are thine.8Therefore Abimelech roſe earely in the morning,
and called all his ſeruants, and told all theſe things in their eares: and the
men were ſore afraid.9Then Abimelech called Abraham, and ſaid vnto
him, What haſt thou done vnto vs? and what haue I offended thee, that
thou haſt brought on me, and on my kingdome a great ſinne? thou haſt
done deeds vnto mee that ought not to be done.10And Abimelech ſaid
vnto Abraham, What ſaweſt thou, that thou haſt done this thing?11And
Abraham ſaid, Becauſe I thought, Surely the feare of God is not in this
place: and they will ſlay mee for my wiues ſake.12And yet indeed ſhee is
my ſiſter: ſhe is the daughter of my father, but not the daughter of my
mother; and ſhee became my wife.13And it came to paſſe when God
cauſed me to wander from my fathers houſe, that I ſaid vnto her, This
is thy kindneſſe which thou ſhalt ſhew vnto me; at euery place whither
wee ſhall come, ſay of me, He is my brother.14And Abimelech tooke
ſheepe and oxen, and men-ſeruants, and women ſeruants, and gaue
them vnto Abraham, and reſtored him Sarah his wife.15And Abimelech
ſaid, Behold, my land is before thee; dwel where it pleaſeth thee.16And
vnto Sarah hee ſaid, Behold, I haue giuen thy brother a thouſand pieces
of ſiluer: behold, he is to thee a couering of the eyes, vnto all that are
with thee, and with all other: thus ſhee was reproued.17So Abraham
prayed vnto God: and God healed Abimelech, and his wife, and his
maid-ſeruants, and they bare children.18For the LORD had faſt cloſed
vp all the wombes of the houſe of Abimelech, becauſe of Sarah
Abrahams wife.
CHAPTER 211And the LORD viſited Sarah as he had ſaid, and the
LORD did vnto Sarah as he had ſpoken.2For Sarah conceiued, and bare
Abraham a ſonne in his old age, at the ſet time, of which God had
ſpoken to him.3And Abraham called the name of his ſonne, that was
borne vnto him, whom Sarah bare to him, Iſaac.4And Abraham
circumciſed his ſonne Iſaac, being eight dayes old, as God had
commanded him.5And Abraham was an hundred yeeres old, when his
ſonne Iſaac was borne vnto him.6And Sarah ſaid, God hath made me to
laugh, ſo that all that heare, will laugh with me.7And ſhe ſaid, Who
would haue ſaid vnto Abraham, that Sarah ſhould haue giuen children
ſucke? for I haue borne him a ſonne in his old age.8And the child grew,
and was weaned: and Abraham made a great feaſt, the ſame day that
Iſaac was weaned.9And Sarah ſaw the ſonne of Hagar the Egyptian,
which ſhee had borne vnto Abraham, mocking.10Wherfore ſhe ſaid vnto
Abraham, Caſt out this bond woman, and her ſonne: for the ſonne of
this bond woman ſhall not be heire with my ſonne, euen with
Iſaac.11And the thing was very grieuous in Abrahams ſight, becauſe of
his ſonne.12And God ſaid vnto Abraham, Let it not be grieuous in thy
ſight, becauſe of the lad, and becauſe of thy bond woman. In all that
Sarah hath ſaid vnto thee, hearken vnto her voice: for in Iſaac ſhall thy
ſeed be called.13And alſo, of the ſonne of the bond woman will I make
a nation, becauſe he is thy ſeed.14And Abraham roſe vp earely in the
morning, and tooke bread, and a bottle of water, and gaue it vnto Hagar,
(putting it on her ſhoulder,) and the child, and ſent her away: and ſhee
departed, and wandered in the wilderneſſe of Beer-ſheba.15And the
water was ſpent in the bottle, and ſhee caſt the child vnder one of the
ſhrubs.16And ſhe went, and ſate her downe ouer againſt him, a good
way off, as it were a bow ſhoot: for ſhe ſaid, Let me not ſee the death of
the child. And ſhee ſate ouer againſt him, and lift vp her voice, and
wept.17And God heard the voice of the lad, and the Angel of God called
to Hagar out of heauen, and ſaid vnto her, What aileth thee, Hagar? feare
not: for God hath heard the voice of the ladde, where he is.18Ariſe, lift
vp the lad, and hold him in thine hand: for I will make him a great

nation.19And God opened her eyes, and ſhe ſaw a well of water, and
ſhee went, and filled the bottle with water, and gaue the lad drinke.20And
God was with the lad, and he grew, and dwelt in the wilderneſſe, and
became an archer.21And hee dwelt in the wilderneſſe of Paran: and his
mother tooke him a wife out of the land of Egypt.22And it came to paſſe
at that time, that Abimelech and Phichol the chiefe captaine of his hoſte
ſpake vnto Abraham, ſaying, God is with thee in all that thou
doeſt.23Now therefore ſweare vnto mee here by God, that thou wilt not
deale falſly with me, nor with my ſonne, nor with my ſonnes ſonne: but
according to the kindneſſe that I haue done vnto thee, thou ſhalt doe
vnto me, and to the land wherein thou haſt ſoiourned.24And Abraham
ſaide, I will ſweare.25And Abraham reproued Abimelech, becauſe of a
well of water, which Abimelechs ſeruants had violently taken
away.26And Abimelech ſaide, I wote not who hath done this thing:
neither didſt thou tell me, neither yet heard I of it, but to day.27And
Abraham tooke ſheepe and oxen, and gaue them vnto Abimelech: and
both of them made a couenant.28And Abraham ſet ſeuen ewe lambes of
the flocke by themſelues.29And Abimelech ſaid vnto Abraham, What
meane theſe ſeuen ewe lambes, which thou haſt ſet by themſelues?30And
he ſaid, For theſe ſeuen ewe lambs ſhalt thou take of my hand, that they
may be a witneſſe vnto me, that I haue digged this well.31Wherefore he
called that place, Beer-ſheba: becauſe there they ſware both of
them.32Thus they made a couenant at Beeer-ſheba: then Abimelech roſe
vp, and Phichol the chiefe captaine of his hoſte, and they returned into
the land of the Philiſtines.33And Abraham planted a groue in Beer-ſheba,
and called there on the Name of the LORD, the euerlaſting God.34And
Abraham ſoiourned in the Philiſtines land, many dayes.
CHAPTER 221And it came to paſſe after theſe things, that God did
tempt Abraham, and ſaid vnto him, Abraham. And hee ſaid, Beholde,
heere I am.2And he ſaid, Take now thy ſonne, thine onely ſonne Iſaac,
whom thou loueſt, and get thee into the land of Moriah: and offer him
there for a burnt offering vpon one of the Mountaines which I will tell
thee of.3And Abraham roſe vp earely in the morning, and ſadled his aſſe,
and tooke two of his yong men with him, and Iſaac his ſonne, and claue
the wood for the burnt offering, and roſe vp, and went vnto the place
of which God had told him.4Then on the third day Abraham lift vp his
eyes, and ſaw the place afarre off.5And Abraham ſaid vnto his yong
men, Abide you here with the aſſe, and I and the lad will goe yonder and
worſhip, and come againe to you.6And Abraham tooke the wood of the
burnt offering, and layd it vpon Iſaac his ſonne: and he tooke the fire in
his hand, and a knife: and they went both of them together.7And Iſaac
ſpake vnto Abraham his father, and ſaid, My father: and he ſaid, Here
am I, my ſonne. And hee ſaid, Behold the fire and wood: but where is
the lambe for a burnt offring?8And Abraham ſaid, My ſonne, God will
prouide himſelfe a lambe for a burnt offering: ſo they went both of them
together.9And they came to the place which God had tolde him of, and
Abraham built an Altar there, and layd the wood in order, and bound
Iſaac his ſonne, and layde him on the Altar vpon the wood.10And
Abraham ſtretched foorth his hand, and tooke the knife to ſlay his
ſonne.11And the Angel of the LORD called vnto him out of heauen, and
ſaid, Abraham, Abraham. And he ſaid, Here am I.12And he ſaid, Lay not
thine hand vpon the lad, neither do thou any thing vnto him: for now I
know that thou feareſt God, ſeeing thou haſt not withhelde thy ſonne,
thine onely ſonne from mee.13And Abraham lifted vp his eyes, and
looked, and beholde, behinde him a Ramme caught in a thicket by his
hornes: And Abraham went and tooke the Ramme, and offered him vp
for a burnt offering, in the ſtead of his ſonne.14And Abraham called the
name of that place Iehouah-ijreh, as it is ſaid to this day, In the Mount
of the LORD it ſhalbe ſeene.15And the Angel of the LORD called vnto
Abraham out of heauen the ſecond time,16And ſaid, By my ſelfe haue I
ſworne, ſaith the LORD, for becauſe thou haſt done this thing, and haſt
not withheld thy ſonne, thine onely ſonne,17That in bleſſing I will bleſſe
thee, and in multiplying, I will multiply thy ſeed as the ſtarres of the
heauen, and as the ſand which is vpon the ſea ſhore, and thy ſeed ſhall
poſſeſſe the gate of his enemies.18And in thy ſeed ſhall all the nations of
the earth be bleſſed, becauſe thou haſt obeyed my voice.19So Abraham
returned vnto his yong men, and they roſe vp, and went together to
Beer-ſheba, and Abraham dwelt at Beer-ſheba.20And it came to paſſe
after theſe things, that it was told Abraham, ſaying, Behold Milcah, ſhee
hath alſo borne children vnto thy brother Nahor,21Huz his firſt borne,
and Buz his brother, and Kemuel the father of Aram,22And Cheſed, and
Hazo, and Pildaſh, and Iidlaph, and Bethuel.23And Bethuel begate
Rebekah: theſe eight Milcah did beare to Nahor, Abrahams
brother.24And his concubine whoſe name was Reumah, ſhe bare alſo
Tebah, and Gaham, and Thahaſh, and Maachah.
CHAPTER 231And Sarah was an hundred and ſeuen and twenty yeeres
olde: theſe were the yeeres of the life of Sarah.2And Sarah died in Kiriath
arba, the ſame is Hebron in the land of Canaan: And Abraham came to
mourne for Sarah, and to weepe for her.3And Abraham ſtood vp from
before his dead, & ſpake vnto the ſonnes of Heth, ſaying,4I am a
ſtranger and a ſoiourner with you: giue me a poſſeſſion of a burying
place with you, that I may bury my dead out of my ſight.5And the
children of Heth anſwered Abraham, ſaying vnto him,6Heare vs, my
Lord, thou art a mightie Prince amongſt vs: in the choiſe of our
ſepulchres bury thy dead: none of vs ſhall withhold from thee his
ſepulchre, but that thou mayeſt bury thy dead.7And Abraham ſtood vp
and bowed himſelfe to the people of the land, euen to the children of
Heth.8And hee communed with them, ſaying, if it be your mind that I
ſhould bury my dead out of my ſight, heare me, and entreat for me to
Ephron the ſonne of Zohar:9That he may giue me the caue of
Machpelah, which he hath, which is in the end of his field: for as much
money as it is worth he ſhall giue it mee, for a poſſeſſion of a burying
place amongſt you.10And Ephron dwelt amongſt the children of Heth.
And Ephron the Hittite anſwered Abraham in the audience of the
children of Heth, euen of all that went in at the gates of his citie,
ſaying,11Nay, my lord, heare mee: the field giue I thee, and the caue that
is therein, I giue it thee, in the preſence of the ſonnes of my people giue
I it thee: bury thy dead.12And Abraham bowed downe himſelfe before
the people of the land.13And he ſpake vnto Ephron in the audience of
the people of the land, ſaying, But if thou wilt giue it, I pray thee, heare
mee: I will giue thee money for the field: take it of me, and I will bury
my dead there.14And Ephron anſwered Abraham, ſaying vnto him,15My
lord, hearken vnto mee: the land is worth foure hundred ſhekels of
ſiluer: what is that betwixt mee and thee? bury therefore thy dead.16And
Abraham hearkened vnto Ephron, and Abraham weighed to Ephron
the ſiluer, which he had named, in the audience of the ſonnes of Heth,
foure hundred ſhekels of ſiluer, currant money with the merchant.17And
the field of Ephron which was in Machpelah, which was before Mamre,
the fielde and the caue which was therein, and all the trees that were in
the field, that were in all the borders round about, were made ſure18Unto
Abraham for a poſſeſſion in the preſence of the children of Heth, before
all that went in at the gates of his Citie.19And after this Abraham buried
Sarah his wife in the caue of the field of Machpelah, before Mamre: the
ſame is Hebron in the land of Canaan.20And the field, and the caue that
is therein, were made ſure vnto Abraham, for a poſſeſſion of a burying
place, by the ſonnes of Heth.
CHAPTER 241And Abraham was olde and well ſtricken in age: And
the LORD had bleſſed Abraham in all things.2And Abraham ſaid vnto
his eldeſt ſeruant of his houſe, that ruled ouer all that he had, Put, I pray
thee, thy hand vnder my thigh:3And I will make thee ſweare by the
LORD the God of heauen, and the God of the earth, that thou ſhalt not
take a wife vnto my ſonne of the daughters of the Canaanites amongſt
whom I dwell.4But thou ſhalt go vnto my countrey, and to my kinred,
and take a wife vnto my ſonne Iſaac.5And the ſeruant ſaid vnto him,
Peraduenture the woman will not bee willing to follow mee vnto this
land: muſt I needes bring thy ſonne againe, vnto the land from whence
thou cameſt?6And Abraham ſaid vnto him, Beware thou, that thou
bring not my ſonne thither againe.7The LORD God of heauen which
tooke mee from my fathers houſe, and from the land of my kindred,
and which ſpake vnto mee, and that ſware vnto me, ſaying, Unto thy
ſeed will I giue this land, he ſhall ſend his Angel before thee, and thou
ſhalt take a wife vnto my ſonne from thence.8And if the woman wil not
be willing to follow thee, then thou ſhalt bee cleare from this my othe:
onely bring not my ſonne thither againe.9And the ſeruant put his hand
vnder the thigh of Abraham his maſter, and ſware to him concerning
that matter.10And the ſeruant tooke ten camels, of the camels of his
maſter, and departed, (for all the goods of his maſter were in his hand)
and he aroſe, and went to Meſopotamia, vnto the citie of Nahor.11And
he made his camels to kneele downe without the citie, by a well of water,
at the time of the euening, euen the time that women goe out to draw

water.12And he ſaid, O LORD, God of my maſter Abraham, I pray thee ſend me good ſpeed this day, and ſhew kindneſſe vnto my maſter Abraham.13Behold, I ſtand here by the well of water; and the daughters of the men of the Citie come out to draw water:14And let it come to paſſe, that the damſell to whom I ſhall ſay, Let downe thy pitcher, I pray thee, that I may drinke, and ſhe ſhall ſay, Drinke, and I will giue thy camels drinke alſo; let the ſame be ſhee that thou haſt appointed for thy ſeruant Iſaac: and thereby ſhall I know that thou haſt ſhewed kindneſſe vnto my maſter.15And it came to paſſe before hee had done ſpeaking, that behold, Rebekah came out, who was borne to Bethuel, ſonne of Milcah, the wife of Nahor Abrahams brother, with her pitcher vpon her ſhoulder.16And the damſell was very faire to looke vpon, a virgine, neither had any man knowen her; and ſhee went downe to the wel, and filled her pitcher, and came vp.17And the ſeruant ranne to meete her, and ſaid, Let mee (I pray thee) drinke a little water of thy pitcher.18And ſhe ſaid, Drinke, my lord: and ſhe haſted, and let downe her pitcher vpon her hand, and gaue him drinke.19And when ſhee had done giuing him drinke, ſhe ſaid, I will draw water for thy camels alſo, vntill they haue done drinking.20And ſhe haſted and emptied her pitcher into the trough, and ranne againe vnto the well to draw water, and drew for all his camels.21And the man wondering at her, helde his peace, to wit, whether the LORD had made his iourney proſperous, or not.22And it came to paſſe as the camels had done drinking, that the man tooke a golden eare-ring, of halfe a ſhekel weight, & two bracelets for her handes, of ten ſhekels weight of gold,23And ſaid, whoſe daughter art thou? tell mee, I pray thee: is there roome in thy fathers houſe for vs to lodge in?24And ſhe ſaid vnto him, I am the daughter of Bethuel the ſonne of Milcah, which ſhe bare vnto Nahor:25She ſaid moreouer vnto him, We haue both ſtraw & prouender ynough, and roome to lodge in.26And the man bowed downe his head, and worſhipped the LORD.27And hee ſaide, Bleſſed bee the LORD God of my maſter Abraham, who hath not left deſtitute my maſter of his mercy, and his trueth: I being in the way, the LORD led me to the houſe of my maſters brethren.28And the damſell ranne, and told them of her mothers houſe, theſe things.29And Rebekah had a brother, and his name was Laban: and Laban ranne out vnto the man, vnto the well.30And it came to paſſe when he ſaw the eare-ring, and bracelets vpon his ſiſters hands, and when hee heard the wordes of Rebekah his ſiſter, ſaying, Thus ſpake the man vnto me, that he came vnto the man; and behold, hee ſtood by the camels, at the well.31And he ſaid, Come in, thou bleſſed of the LORD, wherefore ſtandeſt thou without? for I haue prepared the houſe, and roome for the camels.32And the man came into the houſe: and he vngirded his camels, and gaue ſtraw and prouender for the camels, and water to waſh his feet, and the mens feet that were with him.33And there was ſet meat before him to eate: but he ſaid, I will not eate, vntill I haue tolde mine errand. And hee ſaid, Speake on.34And he ſaid, I am Abrahams ſeruant.35And the LORD hath bleſſed my maſter greatly, and hee is become great: and hee hath giuen him flocks, and heards, and ſiluer, and gold, and men ſeruants, and mayd ſeruants, and camels, and aſſes.36And Sarah my maſters wife bare a ſonne to my maſter when ſhee was old: and vnto him hath hee giuen all that he hath.37And my maſter made me ſweare, ſaying, Thou ſhalt not take a wife to my ſonne, of the daughters of the Canaanites, in whoſe land I dwell:38But thou ſhalt goe vnto my fathers houſe, and to my kinred, and take a wife vnto my ſonne.39And I ſaid vnto my maſter, Peraduenture the woman will not followe me.40And hee ſaide vnto me, The LORD, before whom I walke, will ſend his Angel with thee, and proſper thy way: and thou ſhalt take a wife for my ſonne, of my kinred, and of my fathers houſe.41Then ſhalt thou bee cleare from this my oath, when thou commeſt to my kinred, and if they giue not thee one, thou ſhalt be cleare from my oath.42And I came this day vnto the well, and ſaid, O LORD God of my maſter Abraham, if now thou doe proſper my way, which I goe:43Behold, I ſtand by the well of water; and it ſhall come to paſſe, that when the virgine commeth foorth to draw water, and I ſay to her, Giue me, I pray thee, a litle water of thy pitcher to drinke;44And ſhe ſay to me, Both drinke thou, and I will alſo draw for thy camels: let the ſame be the woman, whō the LORD hath appointed out for my maſters ſonne.45And before I had done ſpeaking in mine heart, behold, Rebekah came forth, with her pitcher on her ſhoulder; and ſhe went downe vnto the well, and drew water: and I ſaid vnto her, Let me drinke, I pray thee.46And ſhe made haſte, & let downe her pitcher from her ſhoulder, and ſaide, Drinke, and I will giue thy camels drinke alſo: ſo I dranke, and ſhe made the camels drinke alſo.47And I aſked her, and ſaid, whoſe daughter art thou? and ſhe ſaid, The daughter of Bethuel, Nahors ſonne, whom Milcah bare vnto him: and I put the earering vpon her face, and the bracelets vpon her hands.48And I bowed downe my head, and worſhipped the LORD, and bleſſed the LORD God of my maſter Abraham, which had led mee in the right way to take my maſters brothers daughter vnto his ſonne.49And now if you wil deale kindly and truely with my maſter, tell me: and if not, tell me, that I may turne to the right hand, or to the left.50Then Laban and Bethuel anſwered and ſaid, The thing proceedeth from the LORD: we cannot ſpeake vnto thee bad or good.51Behold, Rebekah is before thee, take her, and goe, and let her be thy maſters ſonnes wife, as the LORD hath ſpoken.52And it came to paſſe, that when Abrahams ſeruant heard their words, he worſhipped the LORD, bowing himſelfe to the earth.53And the ſeruant brought foorth iewels of ſiluer, and iewels of gold, and raiment, and gaue them to Rebekah: He gaue alſo to her brother, and to her mother precious things.54And they did eate and drinke, he and the men that were with him, and taried all night, and they roſe vp in the morning, and he ſaid, Send me away vnto my maſter.55And her brother and her mother ſaid, Let the damſell abide with vs a few dayes, at the leaſt ten; after that, ſhe ſhall goe.56And he ſaid vnto them, Hinder me not, ſeeing the LORD hath proſpered my way: ſend me away, that I may goe to my maſter.57And they ſaid, wee will call the Damſell, and enquire at her mouth.58And they called Rebekah, and ſaid vnto her, Wilt thou go with this man? and ſhe ſaid, I will goe.59And they ſent away Rebekah their ſiſter, and her nurſe, and Abrahams ſeruant, and his men.60And they bleſſed Rebekah, and ſaid vnto her, Thou art our ſiſter, bee thou the mother of thouſands of millions, and let thy ſeed poſſeſſe the gate of thoſe which hate them.61And Rebekah aroſe, and her damſels, & they rode vpon the camels, and followed the man: and the ſeruant tooke Rebekah, and went his way.62And Iſaac came from the way of the well Lahai-roi, for he dwelt in the South countrey.63And Iſaac went out, to meditate in the field, at the euentide: and hee lift vp his eyes, and ſaw, and behold, the camels were comming.64And Rebekah lift vp her eyes, and when ſhe ſaw Iſaac, ſhe lighted off the camel.65For ſhe had ſaid vnto the ſeruant, What man is this that walketh in the field to meet vs? and the ſeruant had ſaid, It is my maſter: therefore ſhee tooke a vaile and couered her ſelfe.66And the ſeruant tolde Iſaac all things that he had done.67And Iſaac brought her into his mother Sarahs tent, and tooke Rebekah, and ſhe became his wife, and he loued her: and Iſaac was comforted after his mothers death.

CHAPTER 251Then againe Abraham tooke a wife, & her name was Keturah.2And ſhee bare him Zimran, and Iokſhan, and Medan, and Midian, and Iſhbak, and Shuah.3And Iokſhan begat Sheba, and Dedan. And the ſonnes of Dedan were Aſſhurim, and Letuſhim, and Leummim.4And the ſonnes of Midian, Ephah, and Epher, and Hanoch, and Abida, and Eldaah: all theſe were the children of Keturah.5And Abraham gaue all that he had, vnto Iſaac.6But vnto the ſonnes of the concubines which Abraham had, Abraham gaue gifts, and ſent them away from Iſaac his ſonne (while he yet liued) Eaſtward, vnto the Eaſt country.7And theſe are the dayes of the yeres of Abrahams life which he liued; an hundred, threeſcore & fifteene yeeres.8Then Abraham gaue vp the ghoſt, and died in a good old age, an old man, and full of yeeres, and was gathered to his people.9And his ſonnes Iſaac and Iſhmael buried him in the caue of Machpelah, in the field of Ephron the ſonne of Zohar the Hittite, which is before Mamre;10The field which Abraham purchaſed of the ſonnes of Heth: there was Abraham buried, and Sarah his wife.11And it came to paſſe after the death of Abraham, that God bleſſed his ſonne Iſaac, and Iſaac dwelt by the well Lahai-roi.12Now theſe are the generations of Iſhmael Abrahams ſonne, whom Hagar the Egyptian Sarahs handmayd, bare vnto Abraham:13And theſe are the names of the ſonnes of Iſhmael, by their names, according to their generations; The firſt borne of Iſhmael, Nebaioth, and Kedar, and Adbeel, and Mibſam,14And Miſhma, and Dumah, and Maſſa,15Hadar, and Tema, Ietur, Naphiſh, and Kedemah.16Theſe are the ſonnes of Iſhmael, and theſe are their names, by their townes and by their caſtels; twelue princes according to their nations.17And theſe are the yeeres of the life of Iſhmael; an hundred and thirty and ſeuen yeeres: and he gaue vp the ghoſt and died, and was gathered vnto his people.[18]And they dwelt from Hauilah vnto Shur, that is before Egypt, as thou goeſt towards Aſſyria: and hee died in the preſence of all his brethren.[19]And theſe are the generations of Iſaac, Abrahams ſonne: Abraham begate Iſaac.[20]And Iſaac was fortie yeeres old when hee tooke Rebekah to wife, the daughter of Bethuel the Syrian of Padan Aram, the ſiſter to Laban the Syrian.[21]And Iſaac intreated the LORD for his wife, becauſe ſhe was barren: and the LORD was intreated of him, and Rebekah his wife conceiued.[22]And the children ſtruggled together within her; and ſhe ſaid, If it be ſo, why am I thus? and ſhee went to enquire of the LORD.[23]And the LORD ſaid vnto her, Two nations are in thy wombe, and two maner of people ſhall be ſeparated from thy bowels: and the one people ſhalbe ſtronger then the other people: and the elder ſhall ſerue the yonger.[24]And when her dayes to be deliuered were fulfilled, behold, there were twinnes in her wombe.[25]And the firſt came out red, all ouer like an hairy garment: and they called his name, Eſau.[26]And after that came his brother out, and his hand tooke holde on Eſaus heele; and his name was called Iacob: and Iſaac was threeſcore yeres old, when ſhee bare them.[27]And the boyes grew; and Eſau was a cunning hunter, a man of the fielde: and Iacob was a plaine man, dwelling in tents.[28]And Iſaac loued Eſau, becauſe he did eate of his veniſon: but Rebekah loued Iacob.[29]And Iacob ſod pottage: and Eſau came from the field, and hee was faint.[30]And Eſau ſaid to Iacob, Feed me, I pray thee, with that ſame red pottage: for I am faint; therefore was his name called Edom.[31]And Iacob ſaid, Sell me this day thy birthright.[32]And Eſau ſaid, Behold, I am at the point to die: and what profit ſhall this birthright doe to me?[33]And Iacob ſaid, Sweare to mee this day: and he ſware to him: and he ſold his birthright vnto Iacob.[34]Then Iacob gaue Eſau bread and pottage of lentiles; and he did eate and drinke, and roſe up, and went his way: thus Eſau deſpiſed his birthright.

CHAPTER 26[1]And there was a famine in the land, beſides the firſt famine that was in the dayes of Abraham. And Iſaac went vnto Abimelech King of the Philiſtims, vnto Gerar.[2]And the LORD appeared vnto him and ſaid, Goe not downe into Egypt; dwell in the land which I ſhall tell thee of.[3]Soiourne in this land, and I wil be with thee, and will bleſſe thee: for vnto thee, and vnto thy ſeed I will giue all theſe countreys, and I wil performe the othe, which I ſware vnto Abraham thy father.[4]And I wil make thy ſeed to multiply as the ſtarres of heauen, and will giue vnto thy ſeed all theſe countreys: and in thy Seed ſhall all the nations of the earth be bleſſed:[5]Becauſe that Abraham obeyed my voyce, and kept my charge, my Commandements, my Statutes and my Lawes.[6]And Iſaac dwelt in Gerar.[7]And the men of the place aſked him of his wife: and he ſaid, She is my ſiſter: for he feared to ſay, She is my wife; leſt, ſaid he, the men of the place ſhould kill me for Rebekah, becauſe ſhee was faire to looke vpon.[8]And it came to paſſe when he had bene there a long time, that Abimelech king of the Philiſtims looked out at a window, and ſaw, and behold, Iſaac was ſporting with Rebekah his wife.[9]And Abimelech called Iſaac and ſaid, Behold, of a ſuretie ſhe is thy wife: and how ſaidſt thou, She is my ſiſter? And Iſaac ſaid vnto him, Becauſe I ſaid, Leſt I die for her.[10]And Abimelech ſaid, What is this thou haſt done vnto vs? one of the people might lightly haue lien with thy wife, and thou ſhouldeſt haue brought guiltineſſe vpon vs.[11]And Abimelech charged all his people, ſaying, Hee that toucheth this man or his wife, ſhall ſurely bee put to death.[12]Then Iſaac ſowed in that land, and receiued in the ſame yeere an hundred fold: & the LORD bleſſed him.[13]And the man waxed great, and went forward, and grew vntill he became very great.[14]For he had poſſeſſion of flocks, and poſſeſſion of heards, and great ſtore of ſeruants, and the Philiſtims enuied him.[15]For all the wels which his fathers ſeruants had digged in the dayes of Abraham his father, the Philiſtims had ſtopped them, & filled them with earth.[16]And Abimelech ſaid vnto Iſaac, Goe from vs: for thou art much mightier then we.[17]And Iſaac departed thence, and pitched his tent in the valley of Gerar, and dwelt there.[18]And Iſaac digged againe the wels of water, which they had digged in the dayes of Abraham his father: for the Philiſtims had ſtopped them after the death of Abraham, and he called their names after the names by which his father had called them.[19]And Iſaacs ſeruants digged in the valley, and found there a well of ſpringing water.[20]And the heardmen of Gerar did ſtriue with Iſaacs heardmen, ſaying, The water is ours; and hee called the name of the well, Eſek, becauſe they ſtroue with him.[21]And they digged another well, and ſtroue for that alſo: and hee called the name of it, Sitnah.[22]And he remoued from thence, and digged another well, and for that they ſtroue not: and he called the name of it Rehoboth: and he ſaid, For now the LORD hath made roome for vs, and we ſhall be fruitfull in the land.[23]And he went vp from thence to Beer-ſheba.[24]And the LORD appeared vnto him the ſame night, and ſaide, I am the God of Abraham thy father: feare not, for I am with thee, and will bleſſe thee, and multiply thy ſeede, for my ſeruant Abrahams ſake.[25]And he builded an altar there, and called vpon the name of the LORD, and pitched his tent there: and there Iſaacs ſeruants digged a well.[26]Then Abimelech went to him from Gerar, and Ahuzzath one of his friends, and Phichol the chiefe captaine of his armie.[27]And Iſaac ſaide vnto them, Wherefore come ye to me, ſeeing ye hate me, and haue ſent me away from you?[28]And they ſaid, we ſaw certainly that the LORD was with thee: and wee ſaid, Let there be now an othe betwixt vs, euen betwixt vs and thee, and let vs make a couenant with thee,[29]That thou wilt doe vs no hurt, as we haue not touched thee, and as we haue done vnto thee nothing but good, and haue ſent thee away in peace: thou art now the bleſſed of the LORD.[30]And he made them a feaſt, and they did eate and drinke.[31]And they roſe vp betimes in the morning, and ſware one to another: and Iſaac ſent them away, and they departed from him in peace.[32]And it came to paſſe the ſame day, that Iſaacs ſeruants came, and tolde him concerning the well which they had digged, and ſaid vnto him, we haue found water.[33]And he called it Shebah: therefore the name of the citie is Beer-ſheba vnto this day.[34]And Eſau was forty yeeres old, when he tooke to wife Iudith, the daughter of Beeri the Hittite, and Baſhemath the daughter of Elon the Hittite:[35]Which were a griefe of minde vnto Iſaac and to Rebekah.

CHAPTER 27[1]And it came to paſſe that when Iſaac was old, and his eyes were dimme, ſo that he could not ſee, hee called Eſau his eldeſt ſon, and ſaid vnto him, My ſonne. And hee ſaid vnto him, Behold, here am I.[2]And he ſaid, Behold now, I am old, I know not the day of my death.[3]Now therefore take, I pray thee, thy weapons, thy quiuer, and thy bow, and goe out to the field, and take mee ſome veniſon.[4]And make me ſauoury meat, ſuch as I loue, and bring it to mee, that I may eate, that my ſoule may bleſſe thee before I die.[5]And Rebekah heard when Iſaac ſpake to Eſau his ſonne: and Eſau went to the fielde to hunt for veniſon, and to bring it.[6]And Rebekah ſpake vnto Iacob her ſonne, ſaying, Behold, I heard thy father ſpeake vnto Eſau thy brother, ſaying,[7]Bring me veniſon, and make mee ſauoury meat, that I may eate, and bleſſe thee before the LORD, before my death.[8]Now therefore, my ſonne, obey my voyce, according to that which I command thee.[9]Goe now to the flocke, and fetch me from thence two good kids of the goates, and I will make them ſauoury meat for thy father, ſuch as he loueth.[10]And thou ſhalt bring it to thy father, that he may eate, and that he may bleſſe thee, before his death.[11]And Iacob ſaid to Rebekah his mother, Behold, Eſau my brother is a hairy man, and I am a ſmooth man.[12]My father peraduenture will feele me, and I ſhall ſeeme to him as a deceiuer, and I ſhall bring a curſe vpon me, and not a bleſſing.[13]And his mother ſaid vnto him, Upon me be thy curſe, my ſonne: onely obey my voice, and go fetch me them.[14]And hee went, and fetched, and brought them to his mother, and his mother made ſauoury meat, ſuch as his father loued.[15]And Rebekah tooke goodly raiment of her eldeſt ſonne Eſau, which were with her in the houſe, and put them vpon Iacob her yonger ſonne:[16]And ſhee put the ſkinnes of the kids of the goats vpon his hands, and vpon the ſmooth of his necke.[17]And ſhe gaue the ſauoury meate, and the bread, which ſhe had prepared, into the hand of her ſonne Iacob.[18]And he came vnto his father, and ſaid, My father: And he ſaid, Here am I: who art thou, my ſonne?[19]And Iacob ſaid vnto his father, I am Eſau, thy firſt borne; I haue done according as thou badeſt mee: Ariſe, I pray thee, ſit, and eate of my veniſon, that thy ſoule may bleſſe me.[20]And Iſaac ſaid vnto his ſonne, How is it that thou haſt found it ſo quickly, my ſonne? And he ſaid, Becauſe the LORD thy God brought it to me.[21]And Iſaac ſaide vnto Iacob, Come neere, I pray thee, that I may feele thee, my ſonne, whether thou bee my very ſonne Eſau, or not.[22]And Iacob went neere vnto Iſaac his father: and hee felt him, and ſaid, The voyce is Iacobs voyce, but the hands are the hands of Eſau.[23]And he diſcernedhim not, becauſe his hands were hairie, as his brother Eſaus hands: So he bleſſed him.[24]And he ſaid, Art thou my very

ſonne Eſau? and he ſaid, I am.25And he ſaid, Bring it neere to me, and I
will eate of my ſonnes veniſon, that my ſoule may bleſſe thee: and hee
brought it neere to him, and he did eate: and he brought him wine, &
he dranke.26And his father Iſaac ſaide vnto him, Come neere now, and
kiſſe me, my ſonne.27And hee came neere, and kiſſed him: and he
ſmelled the ſmell of his raiment, and bleſſed him, and ſaid, See, the ſmell
of my ſonne is as the ſmell of a field, which the LORD hath
bleſſed.28Therefore God giue thee of the dew of heauen, and the
fatneſſe of the earth, and plenty of corne and wine.29Let people ſerue
thee, and nations bow downe to thee: bee lord ouer thy brethren, & let
thy mothers ſonnes bow downe to thee: Curſed bee euery one that
curſeth thee, and bleſſed be hee that bleſſeth thee.30And it came to
paſſe, as ſoone as Iſaac had made an ende of bleſſing Iacob, and Iacob
was yet ſcarce gone out from the preſence of Iſaac his father, that Eſau
his brother came in from his hunting.31And hee alſo had made ſauoury
meate, and brought it vnto his father, and ſaid vnto his father, Let my
father Ariſe, and eat of his ſonnes veniſon, that thy ſoule may bleſſe
me.32And Iſaac his father ſaid vnto him, Who art thou? and he ſaid, I
am thy ſonne, thy firſt borne Eſau.33And Iſaac trembled very
exceedingly, and ſaid, Who? Where is he that hath taken veniſon, and
brought it me, and I haue eaten of all before thou cameſt, and haue
bleſſed him? yea and he ſhalbe bleſſed.34And when Eſau heard the
words of his father, he cried with a great and exceeding bitter cry, and
ſaid vnto his father, Bleſſe mee, euen me alſo, O my father.35And hee
ſaid, Thy brother came with ſubtilty, and hath taken away thy
bleſſing.36And he ſaid, Is not he rightly naned Iacob? for he hath
ſupplanted me theſe two times: hee tooke away my birthright, and
behold, now he hath taken away my bleſſing: and hee ſaid, Haſt thou
not reſerueda bleſſing for mee?37And Iſaac anſwered and ſaide vnto
Eſau, Behold, I haue made him thy lord, and all his brethren haue I
giuen to him for ſeruants: and with corne and wine haue I ſuſteined him:
and what ſhall I doe now vnto thee, my ſonne?38And Eſau ſaid vnto his
father, Haſt thou but one bleſſing, my father? bleſſe mee, euen mee alſo,
O my father. And Eſau lift vp his voyce, and wept.39And Iſaac his father
anſwered, and ſaid vnto him, Behold, thy dwelling ſhall be the fatneſſe
of the earth, and of the dew of heauen from aboue.40And by thy ſword
ſhalt thou liue, and ſhalt ſerue thy brother: and it ſhall come to paſſe
when thou ſhalt haue the dominion, that thou ſhalt breake his yoke from
off thy necke.41And Eſau hated Iacob, becauſe of the bleſſing,
wherewith his father bleſſed him: and Eſau ſaid in his heart, The dayes
of mourning for my father are at hand; then will I ſlay my brother
Iacob.42And theſe words of Eſau her elder ſonne were told to Rebekah:
And ſhee ſent and called Iacob her yonger ſonne, and ſaid vnto him,
Behold, thy brother Eſau, as touching thee, doeth comfort himſelfe,
purpoſing to kill thee.43Now therefore my ſonne, obey my voice: and
Ariſe, flee thou to Laban my brother, to Haran.44And tary with him a
few dayes, vntill thy brothers furie turne away;45Untill thy brothers
anger turne away from thee, and hee forget that, which thou haſt done
to him: then I will ſend, and fetch thee from thence: why ſhould I be
depriued alſo of you both in one day?46And Rebekah ſaid to Iſaac, I am
weary of my life, becauſe of the daughters of Heth: If Iacob take a wife
of the daughters of Heth, ſuch as theſe which are of the daughters of
the land, what good ſhall my life doe me?

CHAPTER 281And Iſaac called Iacob, and bleſſed him, and charged
him, and ſaide vnto him, Thou ſhalt not take a wife, of the daughters of
Canaan.2Ariſe, goe to Padan Aram, to the houſe of Bethuel thy mothers
father, and take thee a wife from thence, of the daughters of Laban thy
mothers brother.3And God Almighty bleſſe thee, and make thee
fruitfull, and multiply thee, that thou mayeſt be a multitude of
people:4And giue thee the bleſſing of Abraham, to thee and to thy ſeede
with thee, that thou mayeſt inherit the lande wherein thou art a ſtranger,
which God gaue vnto Abraham.5And Iſaac ſent away Iacob, and hee
went to Padan-Aram vnto Laban, ſonne of Bethuel the Syrian, the
brother of Rebekah, Iacobs and Eſaus mother.6When Eſau ſawe that
Iſaac had bleſſed Iacob, and ſent him away to Padan-Aram, to take him
a wife from thence; and that as he bleſſed him, he gaue him a charge,
ſaying, Thou ſhalt not take a wife of the daughters of Canaan;7And that
Iacob obeyed his father, and his mother, and was gone to Padan-
Aram;8And Eſau ſeeing that the daughters of Canaan pleaſed not Iſaac
his father.9Then went Eſau vnto Iſhmael, and tooke vnto the wiues
which hee had, Mahalath the daughter of Iſhmael Abrahams ſonne, the
ſiſter of Nebaioth, to be his wife.10And Iacob went out from Beer-
ſheba, and went toward Haran.11And hee lighted vpon a certaine place,
and taried there all night, becauſe the ſunne was ſet: and hee tooke of
the ſtones of that place, and put them for his pillowes, and lay downe in
that place to ſleepe.12And he dreamed, and beholde, a ladder ſet vp on
the earth, and the top of it reached to heauen: and beholde the Angels
of God aſcending and deſcending on it.13And behold, the LORD ſtood
aboue it, and ſaid, I am the LORD God of Abraham thy father, and the
God of Iſaac: the land whereon thou lieſt, to thee will I giue it, and to
thy ſeede.14And thy ſeed ſhall be as the duſt of the earth, and thou ſhalt
ſpread abroad to the Weſt, and to the Eaſt, and to the North, and to the
South: and in thee, and in thy ſeed, ſhall all the families of the earth be
bleſſed.15And behold, I am with thee, and will keepe thee in all places
whither thou goeſt, and will bring thee againe into this land: for I will
not leaue thee, vntill I haue done that which I haue ſpoken to thee
of.16And Iacob awaked out of his ſleepe, and he ſaid, Surely the LORD
is in this place, and I knew it not.17And he was afraid, and ſaid, How
dreadful is this place? this is none other, but the houſe of God, and this
is the gate of heauen.18And Iacob roſe vp earely in the morning, and
tooke the ſtone that hee had put for his pillowes, and ſet it vp for a pillar,
and powred oile vpon the top of it.19And hee called the name of that
place Beth-el: but the name of that citie was called Luz, at the firſt.20And
Iacob vowed a vow, ſaying, If God will be with me, and will keepe me
in this way that I goe, and will giue me bread to eate, and raiment to put
on,21So that I come againe to my fathers houſe in peace: then ſhall the
LORD be my God.22And this ſtone which I haue ſet for a pillar, ſhall
be Gods houſe: and of all that thou ſhalt giue me, I will ſurely giue the
tenth vnto thee.

CHAPTER 291Then Iacob went on his iourney, and came into the land
of the people of the Eaſt.2And he looked, and behold, a well in the field,
and loe, there were three flocks of ſheepe lying by it: for out of that wel
they watered the flocks: and a great ſtone was vpon the welles
mouth.3And thither were all the flockes gathered, and they rolled the
ſtone from the wels mouth, & watered the ſheepe, and put the ſtone
againe vpon the wels mouth in his place.4And Iacob ſaid vnto them, My
brethren, whence be ye? and they ſaide, Of Haran are we.5And he ſaid
vnto them, Know ye Laban the ſonne of Nahor? And they ſayde, We
knowe him.6And he ſaid vnto them, Is hee well? and they ſaid, He is
well: and behold, Rachel his daughter commeth with the ſheepe.7And
hee ſaid, Loe, it is yet high day, neither is it time that the cattell ſhould
be gathered together: water yee the ſheepe, and goe and feed them.8And
they ſaid, We cannot, vntill all the flockes bee gathered together, and till
they rolle the ſtone from the welles mouth: then wee water the
ſheepe.9And while hee yet ſpake with them, Rachel came with her
fathers ſheepe: for ſhe kept them.10And it came to paſſe, when Iacob
ſaw Rachel the daughter of Laban his mothers brother, and the ſheepe
of Laban his mothers brother; that Iacob went neere, and rolled the
ſtone from the wels mouth, and watered the flocke of Laban his mothers
brother.11And Iacob kiſſed Rachel, and lifted vp his voyce, and
wept.12And Iacob told Rachel, that hee was her fathers brother, and that
hee was Rebekahs ſonne: and ſhe ranne, and told her father.13And it
came to paſſe, when Laban heard the tidings of Iacob his ſiſters ſonne,
that he ranne to meete him, and imbraced him, and kiſſed him, &
brought him to his houſe: and hee tolde Laban all theſe things.14And
Laban ſaid to him, Surely thou art my bone and my fleſh: and he abode
with him the ſpace of a moneth.15And Laban ſaid vnto Iacob, Becauſe
thou art my brother, ſhouldeſt thou therefore ſerue me for nought? tell
me, what ſhall thy wages be?16And Laban had two daughters: the name
of the elder was Leah, and the name of the yonger was Rachel.17Leah
was tender eyed: but Rachel was beautiful and well fauoured.18And
Iacob loued Rachel, and ſaid, I will ſerue thee ſeuen yeeres for Rachel
thy yonger daughter.19And Laban ſaid, It is better that I giue her to thee,
then that I ſhould giue her to another man: abide with mee.20And Iacob
ſerued ſeuen yeeres for Rachel: and they ſeemed vnto him but a few
dayes, for the loue hee had to her.21And Iacob ſaid vnto Laban, Giue
me my wife (for my dayes are fulfilled) that I may goe in vnto her.22And
Laban gathered together all the men of the place, and made a feaſt.23And
it came to paſſe in the euening, that he tooke Leah his daughter, and
brought her to him, and he went in vnto her.24And Laban gaue vnto his

daughter Leah, Zilpah his mayde, for a handmayd.[25]And it came to paſſe, that in the morning, behold it was Leah: and he ſaid to Laban, What is this thou haſt done vnto mee? did not I ſerue with thee for Rachel? wherefore then haſt thou beguiled me?[26]And Laban ſaid, It muſt not be ſo done in our countrey, to giue the yonger, before the firſt borne.[27]Fulfill her weeke, and wee will giue thee this alſo, for the ſeruice which thou ſhalt ſerue with mee, yet ſeuen other yeeres.[28]And Iacob did ſo, and fulfilled her weeke: and he gaue him Rachel his daughter to wife alſo.[29]And Laban gaue to Rachel his daughter, Bilhah his handmayd, to be her mayd.[30]And hee went in alſo vnto Rachel, and he loued alſo Rachel more then Leah, and ſerued with him yet ſeuen other yeeres.[31]And when the LORD ſaw that Leah was hated, hee opened her wombe: but Rachel was barren.[32]And Leah conceiued and bare a ſonne, and ſhee called his name Reuben: for ſhe ſaid, Surely, the LORD hath looked vpon my affliction; now therefore my huſband will loue me.[33]And ſhee conceiued againe, and bare a ſonne, and ſaide, Becauſe the LORD hath heard that I was hated, hee hath therefore giuen mee this ſonne alſo, and ſhe called his name Simeon.[34]And ſhee conceiued againe, and bare a ſonne, and ſaid, Now this time will my huſband be ioyned vnto me, becauſe I haue borne him three ſonnes: therefore was his name called Leui.[35]And ſhee conceiued againe, and bare a ſonne: and ſhe ſaid, Now wil I praiſe the LORD: therefore ſhe called his name Iudah, and left bearing.

CHAPTER 30[1]And when Rachel ſaw that ſhee bare Iacob no children, Rachel enuied her ſiſter, and ſaid vnto Iacob, Giue mee children, or els I die.[2]And Iacobs anger was kindled againſt Rachel, and he ſaid, Am I in Gods ſtead, who hath withheld from thee the fruit of the wombe?[3]And ſhe ſaid, Behold my mayde Bilhah: goe in vnto her, and ſhe ſhall beare vpon my knees, that I may alſo have children by her.[4]And ſhee gaue him Bilhah her handmayd to wife: and Iacob went in vnto her.[5]And Bilhah conceiued and bare Iacob a ſonne.[6]And Rachel ſaid, God hath iudged me, and hath alſo heard my voyce, and hath giuen me a ſonne; therefore called ſhe his name Dan.[7]And Bilhah Rachels mayd conceiued againe, and bare Iacob a ſecond ſonne.[8]And Rachel ſaide, With great wraſtlings haue I wraſtled with my ſiſter, and I haue preuailed: and ſhe called his name Naphtali.[9]When Leah ſaw that ſhe had left bearing, ſhee tooke Zilpah her mayde, and gaue her Iacob to wife.[10]And Zilpah Leahs mayde bare Iacob a ſonne.[11]And Leah ſaid, A troupe commeth: and ſhe called his name Gad.[12]And Zilpah Leahs mayde bare Iacob a ſecond ſonne.[13]And Leah ſaid, Happy am I, for the daughters will call me bleſſed: and ſhe called his name Aſher.[14]And Reuben went in the dayes of wheat harueſt, & found Mandrakes in the field, and brought them vnto his mother Leah. Then Rachel ſaide to Leah, Giue me, I pray thee, of thy ſonnes Mandrakes.[15]And ſhee ſaid vnto her, Is it a ſmall matter, that thou haſt taken my huſband? and wouldſt thou take away my ſonnes Mandrakes alſo? and Rachel ſaid, Therefore hee ſhall lye with thee to night, for thy ſonnes Mandrakes.[16]And Iacob came out of the field in the euening, and Leah went out to meet him, and ſaid, Thou muſt come in vnto mee: for ſurely I haue hired thee with my ſonnes Mandrakes. And hee lay with her that night.[17]And God hearkened vnto Leah, and ſhe conceiued, and bare Iacob the fift ſonne.[18]And Leah ſaid, God hath giuen mee my hire, becauſe I haue giuen my mayden to my huſband: and ſhe called his name Iſſachar.[19]And Leah conceiued againe, and bare Iacob the ſixth ſonne.[20]And Leah ſaid, God hath endued me with a good dowry: Now will my huſband dwel with me, becauſe I haue borne him ſixe ſonnes: and ſhee called his name Zebulun.[21]And afterwardes ſhee bare a daughter, and called her name Dinah.[22]And God remembred Rachel, and God hearkened to her, and opened her wombe.[23]And ſhee conceiued and bare a ſonne, and ſaid; God hath taken away my reproch:[24]And ſhee called his name Ioſeph, and ſaide, The LORD ſhall adde to me another ſonne.[25]And it came to paſſe when Rachel had borne Ioſeph, that Iacob ſaid vnto Laban, Send me away, that I may goe vnto mine owne place, and to my countrey.[26]Giue mee my wiues and my children, for whom I haue ſerued thee, and let me goe: for thou knoweſt my ſeruice which I haue done thee.[27]And Laban ſaid vnto him, I pray thee, if I haue found fauour in thine eyes, tary: for I haue learned by experience, that the LORD hath bleſſed me for thy ſake.[28]And he ſaid, Appoint me thy wages, and I will giue it.[29]And hee ſaid vnto him, Thou knoweſt how I haue ſerued thee, and how thy cattell was with me.[30]For it was little which thou hadſt before I came; and it is now increaſed vnto a multitude; and the LORD hath bleſſed thee ſince my comming: and now when ſhall I prouide for mine owne houſe alſo?[31]And hee ſaid, what ſhall I giue thee? and Iacob ſaid, Thou ſhalt not giue me any thing; if thou wilt doe this thing for mee, I will againe feed and keepe thy flocke.[32]I will paſſe through all thy flocke to day, remoouing from thence all the ſpeckled and ſpotted cattell: and all the browne cattell among the ſheepe, and the ſpotted and ſpeckled among the goates, and of ſuch ſhalbe my hire.[33]So ſhall my righteouſneſſe anſwere for mee in time to come, when it ſhall come for my hire, before thy face: euery one that is not ſpeckled and ſpotted amongſt the goates, and browne amongſt the ſheepe, that ſhalbe counted ſtollen with me.[34]And Laban ſaide, Beholde, I would it might bee according to thy word.[35]And he remoued that day the hee goates that were ring-ſtraked, and ſpotted, and all the ſhee goats that were ſpeckled and ſpotted, and euery one that had ſome white in it, and all the browne amongſt the ſheepe, and gaue them into the hand of his ſonnes.[36]And hee ſet three dayes iourney betwixt himſelfe and Iacob: and Iacob fed the reſt of Labans flocks.[37]And Iacob tooke him rods of greene poplar, and of the haſel and cheſnut tree, and pilled white ſtrakes in them, and made the white appeare which was in the rods.[38]And he ſet the rods which he had pilled, before the flockes in the gutters in the watering troughes when the flocks came to drinke, that they ſhould conceiue when they came to drinke.[39]And the flockes conceiued before the rods, and brought forth cattell ringſtraked, ſpeckled and ſpotted.[40]And Iacob did ſeparate the lambes, and ſet the faces of the flockes toward the ring-ſtraked, and all the browne in the flocke of Laban: and he put his owne flocks by themſelues, and put them not vnto Labans cattell.[41]And it came to paſſe whenſoeuer the ſtronger cattell did conceiue, that Iacob layd the rods before the eyes of the cattell in the gutters, that they might conceiue among the rods.[42]But when the cattel were feeble, hee put them not in: ſo the feebler were Labans, and the ſtronger Iacobs.[43]And the man increaſed exceedingly, and had much cattell, and maydſeruants, and men ſeruants, and camels, and aſſes.

CHAPTER 31[1]And he heard the words of Labans ſonnes, ſaying, Iacob hath taken away all that was our fathers; and of that which was of our fathers, hath hee gotten all this glory.[2]And Iacob behelde the countenance of Laban, and behold, it was not toward him as before.[3]And the LORD ſaid vnto Iacob, Returne vnto the land of thy fathers, and to thy kindred; and I wil be with thee.[4]And Iacob ſent and called Rachel and Leah, to the field vnto his flocke,[5]And ſaid vnto them, I ſee your fathers countenance, that it is not toward mee as before: but the God of my father hath bene with me.[6]And yee know, that with all my power I haue ſerued your father.[7]And your father hath deceiued mee, and changed my wages ten times: but God ſuffered him not to hurt me.[8]If hee ſaid thus, The ſpeckled ſhall be thy wages, then all the cattell bare ſpeckled: and if he ſaid thus, The ring-ſtraked ſhalbe thy hire, then bare all the cattell ring-ſtraked.[9]Thus God hath taken away the cattell of your father, and giuen them to mee.[10]And it came to paſſe at the time that the cattell conceiued, that I lifted vp mine eyes and ſaw in a dreame, and behold, the rammes which leaped vpon the cattell were ring-ſtraked, ſpeckled and griſled.[11]And the Angel of God ſpake vnto me in a dreame, ſaying, Iacob; And I ſaid, Here am I.[12]And hee ſaid, Lift vp now thine eyes, and ſee, all the rammes which leape vpon the cattell are ring-ſtraked, ſpeckled and griſled: for I haue ſeene all that Laban doeth vnto thee.[13]I am the God of Bethel, where thou annoyntedſt the pillar, and where thou vowedſt a vow vnto mee: now Ariſe, get thee out from this land, and returne vnto the land of thy kindred.[14]And Rachel and Leah anſwered, and ſaid vnto him; Is there yet any portion or inheritance for vs in our fathers houſe?[15]Are we not counted of him ſtrangers? for he hath ſold vs, and hath quite deuoured alſo our money.[16]For all the riches which God hath taken from our father, that is ours, and our childrens: now then whatſoeuer God hath ſaid vnto thee, doe.[17]Then Iacob roſe vp, and ſet his ſonnes and his wiues vpon camels.[18]And he caried away all his cattell, and all his goods which he had gotten, the cattell of his getting, which hee had gotten in Padan Aram, for to goe to Iſaac his father in the land of Canaan.[19]And Laban went to ſheare his ſheepe: and Rachel had ſtollen the Images that were her fathers.[20]And Iacob ſtale away vnawares to Laban the Syrian, in that he told him not that he fled.21So hee fled with all that hee had, and he roſe vp and paſſed ouer the Riuer, and ſet his face toward the mount Gilead.22And it was tolde Laban on the third day, that Iacob was fled.23And hee tooke his brethren with him, and purſued after him ſeuen dayes iourney, and they ouertooke him in the mount Gilead.24And God came to Laban the Syrian in a dreame by night, and ſaide vnto him, Take heed that thou ſpeake not to Iacob either good or bad.25Then Laban ouertooke Iacob. Now Iacob had pitched his tent in the mount: and Laban with his brethren pitched in the mount of Gilead.26And Laban ſaid to Iacob, What haſt thou done, that thou haſt ſtollen away vnawares to me, and caried away my daughters, as captiues taken with the ſword?27Wherefore didſt thou flie away ſecretly, and ſteale away from me, and didſt not tell mee? that I might haue ſent thee away with mirth, and with ſongs, with tabret, and with harpe,28And haſt not ſuffered me to kiſſe my ſonnes and my daughters? thou haſt now done fooliſhly in ſo doing.29It is in the power of my hand to doe you hurt: but the God of your father ſpake vnto mee yeſternight, ſaying, Take thou heed, that thou ſpeake not to Iacob either good or bad.30And now though thou wouldeſt needes bee gone, becauſe thou ſore longedſt after thy fathers houſe; yet wherefore haſt thou ſtollen my gods?31And Iacob anſwered and ſaid to Laban, Becauſe I was afraid: for I ſaid, Peraduenture thou wouldeſt take by force thy daughters from me.32With whomſoeuer thou findeſt thy gods, let him not liue: before our brethren diſcerne thou what is thine with me, and take it to thee: for Iacob knew not that Rachel had ſtollen them.33And Laban went into Iacobs tent, and into Leahs tent, and into the two maid ſeruants tents: but he found them not. Then went he out of Leahs tent, and entred into Rachels tent.34Now Rachel had taken the images, and put them in the camels furniture, and ſate vpon them: and Laban ſearched all the tent, but found them not.35And ſhee ſaid to her father, Let it not diſpleaſe my lord, that I cannot riſe vp before thee; for the cuſtome of women is vpon mee: and he ſearched, but found not the images.36And Iacob was wroth, and chode with Laban: and Iacob anſwered and ſaid to Laban, what is my treſpaſſe? what is my ſinne, that thou haſt ſo hotly purſued after me?37Whereas thou haſt ſearched all my ſtuffe, what haſt thou found of all thy houſhold ſtuffe? ſet it here before my brethren, and thy brethren, that they may iudge betwixt vs both.38This twentie yeeres haue I bene with thee: thy ewes and thy ſhee goates haue not caſt their yong, and the rammes of thy flocke haue I not eaten.39That which was torne of beaſts, I brought not vnto thee: I bare the loſſe of it; of my hand didſt thou require it, whether ſtollen by day, or ſtollen by night.40Thus I was in þe day, the drought conſumed mee, and the froſt by night, aud my ſleep departed from mine eyes.41Thus have I bene twentie yeres in thy houſe: I ſerued thee fourteene yeeres for thy two daughters, and ſixe yeres for thy cattel; and thou haſt changed my wages ten times.42Except the God of my father, the God of Abraham, and the feare of Iſaac had bin with me, ſurely thou hadſt ſent me away now emptie: God hath ſeene mine affliction, and the labour of my hands, & rebuked thee yeſternight.43And Laban anſwered and ſaid vnto Iacob, Theſe daughters are my daughters, and theſe children are my children, and theſe cattell are my cattell, and all that thou ſeeſt, is mine: and what can I doe this day vnto theſe my daughters, or vnto their children which they haue borne?44Now therefore come thou, let vs make a couenant, I and thou: and let it be for a witneſſe betweene me and thee.45And Iacob tooke a ſtone, and ſet it vp for a pillar.46And Iacob ſaide vnto his brethren, Gather ſtones: and they tooke ſtones, and made an heape, and they did eate there vpon the heape.47And Laban called it Iegar-Sahadutha: but Iacob called it Galeed.48And Laban ſaid, This heape is a witneſſe betweene mee and thee this day. Therefore was the name of it called Galeed,49And Mizpah: for he ſaid, The LORD watch betweene me and thee when we are abſent one from another.50If thou ſhalt afflict my daughters, or if thou ſhalt take other wiues beſide my daughters, no man is with vs; See, God is witneſſe betwixt mee and thee.51And Laban ſaid to Iacob, Behold this heape, and behold this pillar, which I haue caſt betwixt me and thee.52This heape be witneſſe, and this pillar be witneſſe, that I will not paſſe ouer this heape to thee, and that thou ſhalt not paſſe ouer this heape, and this pillar vnto me, for harme.53The God of Abraham, and the God of Nahor, the God of their father, iudge betwixt vs. And Iacob ſware by the feare of his father Iſaac.54Then Iacob offred ſacrifice vpon the mount, and called his brethren to eate bread, and they did eate bread, and taried all night in the mount.55And earely in the morning, Laban roſe vp and kiſſed his ſonnes, and his daughters, and bleſſed them: and Laban departed, and returned vnto his place.

CHAPTER 321And Iacob went on his way, and the Angels of God met him.2And when Iacob ſaw them, he ſaid, This is Gods hoſte: and hee called the name of that place Mahanaim.3And Iacob ſent meſſengers before him, to Eſau his brother, vnto the land of Seir, the countrey of Edom.4And he commaunded them, ſaying, Thus ſhall ye ſpeake vnto my lord Eſau, Thy ſeruant Iacob ſaith thus, I haue ſoiourned with Laban, and ſtayed there vntill now.5And I haue oxen, and aſſes, flockes, and men ſeruants and women ſeruants: and I haue ſent to tell my lord, that I may find grace in thy ſight.6And the meſſengers returned to Iacob, ſaying, Wee came to thy brother Eſau, and alſo he commeth to meet thee, and foure hundred men with him.7Then Iacob was greatly afraid, and diſtreſſed, and he diuided the people that was with him, and the flockes, and herdes, and the camels into two bands,8And ſaid, If Eſau come to the one company, and ſmite it, then the other company which is left, ſhall eſcape.9And Iacob ſaid, O God of my father Abraham, and God of my father Iſaac, the LORD which ſaidſt vnto me, Returne vnto thy countrey, and to thy kinred, and I will deale well with thee:10I am not worthy of the leaſt of all the mercies, and of all the trueth, which thou haſt ſhewed vnto thy ſeruant: for with my ſtaffe I paſſed ouer this Iordan, and now I am become two bands.11Deliuer me, I pray thee, from the hand of my brother, from the hand of Eſau: for I feare him, leſt he will come, and ſmite me, and the mother with the children.12And thou ſaidſt, I will ſurely doe thee good, and make thy ſeed as the ſand of the ſea, which cannot be numbred for multitude.13And he lodged there that ſame night, and tooke of that which came to his hand, a preſent for Eſau his brother:14Two hundred ſhee goats, and twentie hee goats, two hundred ewes, and twentie rammes,15Thirtie milch camels with their colts, fortie kine, and ten bulles, twenty ſhee aſhes, and ten foales.16And hee deliuered them into the hand of his ſeruants, euery droue by themſelues, and ſaid vnto his ſeruants, Paſſe ouer before me, and put a ſpace betwixt droue and droue.17And he commanded the formoſt, ſaying, When Eſau my brother meeteth thee, and aſketh thee, ſaying, whoſe art thou? and whither goeſt thou? and whoſe are theſe before thee?18Then thou ſhalt ſay, They be thy ſeruant Iacobs: it is a preſent ſent vnto my lord Eſau: and behold alſo, he is behind vs.19And ſo commanded he the ſecond, and the third, and all that followed the droues, ſaying, On this maner ſhal you ſpeake vnto Eſau, when you find him.20And ſay ye moreouer, Beholde, thy ſeruant Iacob is behind vs: for he ſaid, I will appeaſe him with the preſent that goeth before me, and afterward I will ſee his face; peraduenture he will accept of me.21So went the preſent ouer before him: and himſelfe lodged that night in the company.22And hee roſe vp that night, and tooke his two wiues, and his two women ſeruants, and his eleuen ſonnes, and paſſed ouer the foord Iabbok.23And he tooke them, and ſent them ouer the brooke, and ſent ouer that hee had.24And Iacob was left alone: and there wreſtled a man with him, vntill the breaking of the day.25And when he ſaw, that he preuailed not againſt him, he touched the hollow of his thigh: and the hollow of Iacobs thigh was out of ioynt, as hee wreſtled with him.26And he ſaid, Let me goe, for the day breaketh: and he ſaid, I will not let thee goe, except thou bleſſe me.27And he ſaid vnto him, what is thy name? and he ſaid, Iacob.28And he ſaid, Thy name ſhall be called no more Iacob, but Iſrael: for as a prince haſt thou power with God, and with men, and haſt preuailed.29And Iacob aſked him, and ſaide, Tell me, I pray thee, thy name: and he ſaid, wherefore is it, that thou doeſt aſke after my name? and he bleſſed him there.30And Iacob called the name of the place Peniel: for I haue ſeene God face to face, and my life is preſerued.31And as he paſſed ouer Penuel, the ſunne roſe vpon him, and he halted vpon his thigh.32Therefore the children of Iſrael eate not of the ſinewe which ſhranke, which is vpon the hollow of the thigh, vnto this day: becauſe hee touched the hollow of Iacobs thigh, in the ſinewe that ſhranke.

CHAPTER 331And Iacob lifted vp his eyes, and looked, and behold, Eſau came, and with him foure hundreth men: and hee diuided the children vnto Leah, and vnto Rachel, and vnto the two handmaids.2And he put the handmaides, and their chidren foremoſt, and Leah and her children after, and Rachel and Ioſeph hindermoſt.3And hee paſſed ouer before them, and bowed himſelfe to the ground ſeuen times, vntill hee came neere to his brother.4And Eſau ran to meete him, and imbraced him, and fell on his necke, and kiſſed him, and they wept.5And he lift vp his eyes, and ſawe the women, and the children, and ſaid, who are thoſe with thee? And he ſaid, The children which God hath graciouſly giuen thy ſeruant.6Then the handmaidens came neere; they and their children, and they bowed themſelues.7And Leah alſo with her children came neere, and bowed themſelues: and after came Ioſeph neere and Rachel, and they bowed themſelues.8And he ſaid, What meaneſt thou by all this droue, which I met? And he ſaid, Theſe are to find grace in the ſight of my lord.9And Eſau ſaid, I haue enough: my brother, keepe that thou haſt vnto thy ſelfe.10And Iacob ſaide, Nay, I pray thee: if now I haue found grace in thy ſight, then receiue my preſent at my hand: for therefore I haue ſeene thy face, as though I had ſeene the face of God; and thou waſt pleaſed with me.11Take, I pray thee, my bleſſing that is brought to thee; becauſe God hath dealt graciouſly with mee, and becauſe I haue enough: and hee vrged him, and he tooke it.12And he ſaid, Let vs take our iourney, and let vs goe, and I will goe before thee.13And hee ſaid vnto him, My lord knoweth, that the children are tender, and the flockes and heards with yong are with mee: and if men ſhould ouer-driue them one day, all the flocke will die.14Let my lord, I pray thee, paſſe ouer before his ſeruant, and I will leade on ſoftly, according as the cattell that goeth before me, and the children be able to endure, vntill I come vnto my lord vnto Seir.15And Eſau ſaid, Let me now leaue with thee ſome of the folke that are with me: And hee ſaid, What needeth it? let me finde grace in the ſight of my lord.16So Eſau returned that day, on his way vnto Seir.17And Iacob iourneyed to Succoth, and built him an houſe, and made boothes for his cattell: therefore the name of the place is called Succoth.18And Iacob came to Shalem, a citie of Shechem, which is the land of Canaan, when he came from Padan Aram, and pitched his tent before the Citie.19And he bought a parcell of a field where hee had ſpread his tent, at the hand of the children of Hamor Shechems father, for an hundred pieces of money.20And hee erected there an Altar, and called it El-Elohe-Iſrael.

CHAPTER 341And Dinah the daughter of Leah, which ſhee bare vnto Iacob, went out to ſee the daughters of the land.2And when Shechem the ſonne of Hamor the Hiuite, prince of the countrey ſaw her, he tooke her, and lay with her, and defiled her.3And his ſoule claue vnto Dinah the daughter of Iacob, and hee loued the damſell, and ſpake kindly vnto the damſell.4And Shechem ſpake vnto his father Hamor, ſaying, Get mee this damſell to wife.5And Iacob heard that he had defiled Dinah his daughter (now his ſonnes were with his cattel in the field) and Iacob helde his peace vntill they were come.6And Hamor the father of Shechem went out vnto Iacob to commune with him.7And the ſonnes of Iacob came out of the field when they heard it, and the men were grieued: and they were very wroth, becauſe hee had wrought folly in Iſrael, in lying with Iacobs daughter; which thing ought not to be done.8And Hamor communed with them, ſaying, The ſoule of my ſonne Shechem longeth for your daughter: I pray you giue her him to wife.9And make ye mariages with vs, and giue your daughters vnto vs, and take our daughters vnto you.10And ye ſhall dwell with vs, and the land ſhall be before you: dwell and trade you therein, and get you poſſeſſions therein.11And Shechem ſaid vnto her father, and vnto her brethren, Let mee finde grace in your eyes, and what yee ſhall ſay vnto me, I will giue.12Aſke mee neuer ſo much dowrie and gift, and I will giue according as yee ſhall ſay vnto mee: but giue me the damſell to wife.13And the ſonnes of Iacob anſwered Shechem, and Hamor his father deceitfully, and ſaid, becauſe he had defiled Dinah their ſiſter.14And they ſaide vnto them, wee cannot doe this thing, to giue our ſiſter to one that is vncircumciſed: for that were a reproch vnto vs.15But in this will we conſent vnto you: If ye will be as we be, that euery male of you be circumciſed:16Then wil we giue our daughters vnto you, and we wil take your daughters to vs, and we will dwell with you, and we will become one people.17But if ye will not hearken vnto vs, to be circumciſed, then will we take our daughter, and we will be gone.18And their words pleaſed Hamor, and Shechem Hamors ſonne.19And the yong man deferred not to doe the thing, becauſe he had delight in Iacobs daughter: and he was more honourable then all the houſe of his father.20And Hamor and Shechem his ſonne came vnto the gate of their citie, and communed with the men of their citie, ſaying:21Theſe men are peaceable with vs, therefore let them dwel in the land, and trade therein: for the land, behold, it is large enough for them: let vs take their daughters to vs for wiues, and let vs giue them our daughters.22Onely herein will the men conſent vnto vs, for to dwell with vs to be one people, if euery male among vs bee circumciſed, as they are circumciſed.23Shall not their cattell, and their ſubſtance, and euery beaſt of theirs bee ours? onely let vs conſent vnto them, and they will dwell with vs.24And vnto Hamor and vnto Shechem his ſonne, hearkened all that went out of the gate of his citie; and euery male was circumciſed, all that went out of the gate of his citie.25And it came to paſſe on the thirde day when they were ſore, that two of the ſonnes of Iacob, Simeon and Leui, Dinahs brethren, tooke each man his ſword and came vpon the citie boldly, and ſlew all the males.26And they ſlew Hamor and Shechem his ſonne, with the edge of the ſword, and tooke Dinah out of Shechems houſe, and went out.27The ſonnes of Iacob came vpon the ſlaine, and ſpoiled the citie, becauſe they had defiled their ſiſter.28They tooke their ſheepe, and their oxen, and their aſſes, and that which was in the citie, and that which was in the field.29And all their wealth, and all their little ones, and their wiues tooke they captiue, and ſpoiled euen all that was in the houſe.30And Iacob ſaid to Simeon and Leui, Ye haue troubled me to make me to ſtinke among the inhabitants of the land, amongſt the Canaanites, and the Perizzites: and I being few in number, they ſhall gather themſelues together againſt me, and ſlay me, and I ſhal be deſtroyed, I and my houſe.31And they ſaid, Should hee deale with our ſiſter, as with an harlot?

CHAPTER 351And God ſaid vnto Iacob, Ariſe, goe vp to Bethel, and dwel there: and make there an Altar vnto God, that appeared vnto thee, when thou fleddeſt from the face of Eſau thy brother.2Then Iacob ſaid vnto his houſehold, and to all that were with him, Put away the ſtrange gods that are among you, and bee cleane, and change your garments,3And let vs Ariſe, and goe vp to Bethel, and I will make there an Altar vnto God, who anſwered me in the day of my diſtreſſe, and was with me in the way which I went.4And they gaue vnto Iacob all the ſtrange gods which were in their hand, and all their eare-rings which were in their eares, and Iacob hid them vnder the oke which was by Shechem.5And they iourneyed: and the terrour of God was vpon the cities that were round about them, and they did not purſue after the ſonnes of Iacob.6So Iacob came to Luz, which is in the land of Canaan (that is Bethel) hee and all the people that were with him.7And hee built there an Altar, and called the place El-Bethel, becauſe there God appeared vnto him, when he fled from the face of his brother.8But Deborah Rebekahs nurſe died, and ſhe was buried beneath Bethel vnder an oke: and the name of it was called Allon Bachuth.9And God appeared vnto Iacob againe, when he came out of Padan Aram, and bleſſed him.10And God ſaid vnto him, Thy name is Iacob: thy name ſhall not bee called any more Iacob, but Iſrael ſhall bee thy name; and hee called his name Iſrael.11And God ſaide vnto him, I am God Almightie: be fruitfull and multiply: a nation and a company of nations ſhall be of thee, and Kings ſhall come out of thy loynes.12And the land which I gaue Abraham, and Iſaac, to thee I will giue it, and to thy ſeed after thee will I giue the land.13And God went vp from him, in the place where he talked with him.14And Iacob ſet vp a pillar in the place where he talked with him, euen a pillar of ſtone: and hee powred a drinke offering thereon, and he powred oile thereon.15And Iacob called the name of the place where God ſpake with him, Bethel.16And they iourneyed from Bethel: and there was but a litle way to come to Ephrath; and Rachel traueiled, and ſhe had hard labour.17And it came to paſſe when ſhee was in hard labour, that the midwife ſaid vnto her, Feare not: thou ſhalt haue this ſonne alſo.18And it came to paſſe as her ſoule was in departing, (for ſhe died) that ſhe called his name Ben-oni: but his father called him Beniamin.19And Rachel died, and was buried in the way to Ephrath, which is Bethlehem.20And Iacob ſet a pillar vpon her graue: that is the pillar of Rachels graue vnto this day.21And Iſrael iourneyed and ſpread his tent beyond the towre of Edar.22And it came to paſſe when Iſrael dwelt in that land, that Reuben went & lay with Bilhah his fathers concubine: and Iſrael heard it. Now the ſonnes of Iacob were twelue.23The ſonnes of Leah: Reuben Iacobs firſt borne, and Simeon, and Leui, and Iudah, and Iſſachar, and Zebulun.24The ſonnes of Rachel: Ioſeph, and Beniamin.25And the ſonnes of Bilhah, Rachels handmaid:

Dan and Naphtali.[26]And the ſonnes of Zilpah, Leahs handmaid: Gad, and Aſher. Theſe are the ſonnes of Iacob, which were borne to him in Padan Aram.[27]And Iacob came vnto Iſaac his father vnto Mamre, vnto the citie of Arbah (which is Hebron) where Abraham and Iſaac ſoiourned.[28]And the dayes of Iſaac were an hundred and foureſcore yeeres.[29]And Iſaac gaue vp the ghoſt and died, and was gathered vnto his people, being old and full of dayes: and his ſonnes Eſau and Iacob buried him.

CHAPTER 36[1]Now theſe are the generations of Eſau, who is Edom.[2]Eſau tooke his wiues of the daughters of Canaan: Adah the daughter of Elon the Hittite, and Aholibamah the daughter of Anah the daughter of Zibeon the Hiuite:[3]And Baſhemath Iſhmaels daughter, ſiſter of Nebaioth.[4]And Adah bare to Eſau, Eliphaz: and Baſhemath bare Reuel.[5]And Aholibamah bare Ieuſh, and Iaalam, and Korah: theſe are the ſonnes of Eſau, which were borne vnto him in the land of Canaan.[6]And Eſau tooke his wiues, and his ſonnes, and his daughters, and all the perſons of his houſe, and his cattell, and all his beaſts, and all his ſubſtance, which he had got in the lande of Canaan: and went into the countrey from the face of his brother Iacob.[7]For their riches were more then that they might dwell together: and the land wherein they were ſtrangers, could not beare them, becauſe of their cattell.[8]Thus dwelt Eſau in mount Seir: Eſau is Edom.[9]And theſe are the generations of Eſau, the father of the Edomites in mount Seir.[10]Theſe are the names of Eſaus ſonnes: Eliphaz the ſonne of Adah the wife of Eſau, Reuel the ſonne of Baſhemath, the wife of Eſau.[11]And the ſonnes of Eliphaz were, Teman, Omar, Zepho, and Gatam, and Kenaz.[12]And Timna was concubine to Eliphaz Eſaus ſonne, and ſhee bare to Eliphaz Amalek: theſe were the ſonnes of Adah Eſaus wife.[13]And theſe are the ſonnes of Reuel: Nahath and Zerah, Shammah, and Mizzah: theſe were the ſonnes of Baſhemath, Eſaus wife.[14]And theſe were the ſonnes of Aholibamah, the daughter of Anah, daughter of Zibeon Eſaus wife: and ſhe bare to Eſau, Ieuſh and Iaalam, and Korah.[15]Theſe were dukes of the ſonnes of Eſau: the ſonnes of Eliphaz the firſt borne ſonne of Eſau, duke Teman, duke Omar, duke Zepho, duke Kenaz,[16]Duke Korah, duke Gatam, and duke Amalek: Theſe are the dukes that came of Eliphaz, in the land of Edom: Theſe were the ſonnes of Adah.[17]And theſe are the ſonnes of Reuel Eſaus ſonne: duke Nahath, duke Zerah, duke Shammah, duke Mizzah. Theſe are the dukes that came of Reuel, in the land of Edom: theſe are the ſonnes of Baſhemath, Eſaus wife.[18]And theſe are the ſonnes of Aholibamah Eſaus wife: duke Ieuſh, duke Iaalam, duke Korah: theſe were the dukes that came of Aholibamah the daughter of Anah Eſaus wife.[19]Theſe are the ſonnes of Eſau, (who is Edom) and theſe are their dukes.[20]Theſe are the ſonnes of Seir the Horite, who inhabited the land, Lotan, and Shobal, and Zibeon, and Anah.[21]And Diſhon, and Ezer, and Diſhan: theſe are the dukes of the Horites the children of Seir in the lande of Edom.[22]And the children of Lotan, were Hori, and Hemam: and Lotans ſiſter was Timna.[23]And the children of Shobal were theſe: Aluan, and Manahath, and Ebal, Shepho, and Onam.[24]And theſe are the children of Zibeon, both Aiah, and Anah: this was that Anah that found the mules in the wilderneſſe, as he fed the aſſes of Zibeon his father.[25]And the children of Anah were theſe: Diſhon, and Aholibamah the daughter of Anah.[26]And theſe are the children of Diſhon: Hemdan and Eſhban, & Ithran, and Cheran.[27]The children of Ezer are theſe: Bilhan and Zaauan, and Akan.[28]The children of Diſhan are theſe: Uz, and Aran.[29]Theſe are the dukes that came of the Horites: duke Lotan, duke Shobal, duke Zibeon, duke Anah,[30]Duke Diſhon, duke Ezer, duke Diſhan: theſe are the dukes that came of Hori, among their dukes in the land of Seir.[31]And theſe are the kings that reigned in the land of Edom, before there reigned any king ouer the children of Iſrael.[32]And Bela the ſonne of Beor reigned in Edom: and the name of his citie was Dinhabah.[33]And Bela died, and Iobab the ſonne of Zerah of Bozra reigned in his ſtead.[34]And Iobab died, and Huſham of the land of Temani reigned in his ſtead.[35]And Huſham died, and Hadad the ſonne of Bedad, (who ſmote Midian in the field of Moab,) reigned in his ſtead: & the name of his citie was Auith.[36]And Hadad died, and Samlah of Maſrekah, reigned in his ſtead.[37]And Samlah died, and Saul of Rehoboth, by the riuer, reigned in his ſtead.[38]And Saul died, and Baal-hanan the ſonne of Achbor reigned in his ſtead.[39]And Baal-hanan the ſonne of Achbor died, and Hadar reigned in his ſtead: and the name of his citie was Pau, and his wiues name was Mehetabel, the daughter of Matred, the daughter of Mezahab.[40]And theſe are the names of the dukes that came of Eſau, according to their families, after their places, by their names: duke Timnah, duke Aluah, duke Ietheth,[41]Duke Aholibamah, duke Elah, duke Pinon,[42]Duke Kenaz, duke Teman, duke Mibzar,[43]Duke Magdiel, duke Iram. Theſe be the dukes of Edom, according to their habitations, in the land of their poſſeſſion: he is Eſau the father of the Edomites.

CHAPTER 37[1]And Iacob dwelt in the land wherein his father was a ſtranger, in the land of Canaan.[2]Theſe are the generations of Iacob: Ioſeph being ſeuenteene yeeres old, was feeding the flocke with his brethren, and the lad was with the ſonnes of Bilhah, and with the ſonnes of Zilpah, his fathers wiues: and Ioſeph brought vnto his father their euill report.[3]Now Iſrael loued Ioſeph more then all his children, becauſe he was the ſonne of his old age: and he made him a coat of many colours.[4]And when his brethren ſaw that their father loued him more then all his brethren, they hated him, and could not ſpeake peaceably vnto him.[5]And Ioſeph dreamed a dreame, and he told it his brethren, and they hated him yet the more.[6]And he ſaid vnto them, Heare, I pray you, this dreame which I haue dreamed.[7]For beholde, wee were binding ſheaues in the field, and loe, my ſheafe aroſe, and alſo ſtood vpright; and behold, your ſheaues ſtood round about, and made obeiſance to my ſheafe.[8]And his brethren ſaide to him, Shalt thou indeed reigne ouer vs? or ſhalt thou indeed haue dominion ouer vs? and they hated him yet the more, for his dreames, and for his words.[9]And hee dreamed yet another dreame, and told it his brethren, and ſaid, Behold, I haue dreamed a dreame more: and behold, the ſunne and the moone, and the eleuen ſtarres made obeiſance to me.[10]And he told it to his father, and to his brethren: and his father rebuked him, and ſaid vnto him, What is this dreame that thou haſt dreamed? ſhal I, and thy mother, and thy brethren indeed come to bow downe our ſelues to thee, to the earth?[11]And his brethren enuied him: but his father obſerued the ſaying.[12]And his brethren went to feed their fathers flocke in Shechem.[13]And Iſrael ſaide vnto Ioſeph, Doe not thy brethren feed the flocke in Shechem? Come, and I will ſend thee vnto them: & he ſaid to him, Here am I.[14]And he ſaid to him, Goe, I pray thee, ſee whether it bee well with thy brethren, and well with the flockes, and bring me word againe: ſo hee ſent him out of the vale of Hebron, and he came to Shechem.[15]And a certaine man found him, and behold, hee was wandring in the field, and the man aſked him, ſaying, What ſeekeſt thou?[16]And he ſaid, I ſeeke my brethren: tell me, I pray thee, where they feede their flockes.[17]And the man ſaid, They are departed hence: for I heard them ſay, Let vs goe to Dothan. And Ioſeph went after his brethren, and found them in Dothan.[18]And when they ſaw him a farre off, euen before he came neere vnto them, they conſpired againſt him, to ſlay him.[19]And they ſaid one to another, Behold, this dreamer commeth.[20]Come now therefore, and let vs ſlay him, and caſt him into ſome pit, and we will ſay, Some euill beaſt hath deuoured him: and we ſhall ſee what will become of his dreames.[21]And Reuben heard it, and he deliuered him out of their hands, and ſaid; Let vs not kill him.[22]And Reuben ſaide vnto them, Shed no blood, but caſt him into this pit that is in the wilderneſſe, and lay no hand vpon him; that he might rid him out of their hands, to deliuer him to his father againe.[23]And it came to paſſe when Ioſeph was come vnto his brethren, that they ſtript Ioſeph out of his coate, his coat of many colours that was on him.[24]And they tooke him and caſt him into a pit: and the pit was emptie, there was no water in it.[25]And they ſate downe to eat bread: and they lift vp their eyes and looked, and behold, a company of Iſhmeelites came from Gilead, with their camels, bearing ſpicery, & baulme, and myrrhe, going to cary it downe to Egypt.[26]And Iudah ſaide vnto his brethren, What profit is it if we ſlay our brother, and conceale his blood?[27]Come, and let vs ſell him to the Iſhmeelites, and let not our hand bee vpon him: for he is our brother, and our fleſh; and his brethren were content.[28]Then there paſſed by Midianites merchant men, and they drew and lift vp Ioſeph out of the pit, and ſold Ioſeph to the Iſhmeelites for twentie pieces of ſiluer: and they brought Ioſeph into Egypt.[29]And Reuben returned vnto the pit, and behold, Ioſeph was not in the pit: and he rent his clothes.[30]And hee returned vnto his brethren and ſaid, The childe is not, and I, whither ſhall I goe?[31]And they tooke Ioſephs coat, and killed a kid of the goats, and dipped the coat in the blood.[32]And they ſent the coat of many colours, and they brought it to their father, and ſaid, This haue we found: know now whether it bee thy ſonnes coat or no.33And he knew it, and ſaid, It is my ſonnes coat: an euil beaſt hath deuoured him; Ioſeph is without doubt rent in pieces.34And Iacob rent his clothes, and put ſackcloth vpon his loines, & mourned for his ſonne many dayes.35And all his ſonnes, and all his daughters roſe vp to comfort him: but he refuſed to be comforted: and he ſaid, For I will goe downe into the graue vnto my ſonne, mourning; thus his father wept for him.36And the Medanites ſold him into Egypt vnto Potiphar, an officer of Pharaohs, and captaine of the guard.

CHAPTER 381And it came to paſſe at that time, that Iudah went downe from his brethren, and turned in to a certaine Adullamite, whoſe name was Hirah:2And Iudah ſaw there a daughter of a certaine Canaanite, whoſe name was Shuah: and he tooke her, and went in vnto her.3And ſhe conceiued & bare a ſonne, and he called his name Er.4And ſhee conceiued againe, and bare a ſonne, and ſhee called his name, Onan.5And ſhe yet againe conceiued and bare a ſonne, and called his name Shelah: and hee was at Chezib, when ſhee bare him.6And Iudah tooke a wife for Er his firſt borne, whoſe name was Tamar.7And Er, Iudahs firſt borne was wicked in the ſight of the LORD, and the LORD ſlew him.8And Iudah ſaid vnto Onan, Goe in vnto thy brothers wife, and marrie her, and raiſe vp ſeed to thy brother.9And Onan knew that the ſeed ſhould not be his; and it came to paſſe when hee went in vnto his brothers wife, that hee ſpilled it on the ground, leaſt that hee ſhould giue ſeed to his brother.10And the thing which he did, diſpleaſed the LORD: wherefore hee ſlew him alſo.11Then ſaid Iudah to Tamar his daughter in law, Remaine a widow at thy fathers houſe, til Shelah my ſonne be growen: (for he ſaid, Leſt peraduenture he die alſo as his brethren did) and Tamar went and dwelt in her fathers houſe.12And in proceſſe of time, the daughter of Shuah Iudahs wife died: and Iudah was comforted, and went vp vnto his ſheepe-ſhearers to Timnath, he and his friend Hirah the Adullamite.13And it was told Lamar, ſaying, Behold, thy father in law goeth vp to Timnath to ſheare his ſheepe.14And ſhee put her widowes garments off from her, and couered her with a vaile, and wrapped her ſelfe, and ſate in an open place, which is by the way to Timnath: for ſhee ſawe that Shelah was growen, and ſhe was not giuen vnto him to wife.15When Iudah ſaw her, he thought her to be an harlot: becauſe ſhe had couered her face.16And hee turned vnto her by the way, and ſaid, Goe to, I pray thee, let me come in vnto thee: (for he knew not that ſhe was his daughter in law) and ſhe ſaid, what wilt thou giue mee, that thou mayeſt come in vnto me?17And hee ſaid, I will ſend thee a kid from the flocke: and ſhee ſaide, Wilt thou giue mee a pledge, till thou ſend it?18And he ſaid, What pledge ſhall I giue thee? And ſhe ſaid, Thy ſignet, and thy bracelets, and thy ſtaffe, that is in thine hand: and he gaue it her, & came in vnto her, and ſhe conceived by him.19And ſhee aroſe and went away, and laid by her vaile from her, and put on the garments of her widowhood.20And Iudah ſent the kidde by the hand of his friend the Adullamite, to receive his pledge from the womans hand: but he found her not.21Then hee aſked the men of that place, ſaying, where is the harlot, that was openly by the way ſide? And they ſaid, There was no harlot in this place.22And he returned to Iudah, and ſaid, I cannot finde her: and alſo the men of the place ſaid, That there was no harlot in this place.23And Iudah ſaid, Let her take it to her, leſt we bee ſhamed: behold, I ſent this kidde, and thou haſt not found her.24And it came to paſſe about three moneths after, that it was tolde Iudah, ſaying, Tamar thy daughter in law hath played the harlot, and alſo behold, ſhe is with child by whoredom: and Iudah ſaid, Bring her foorth, and let her be burnt.25When ſhe was brought forth, ſhe ſent to her father in law, ſaying, By the man whoſe theſe are, am I with child: and ſhee ſaid, Diſcerne, I pray thee, whoſe are theſe, the ſignet, and bracelets, and ſtaffe.26And Iudah acknowledged them, and ſaid, She hath bin more righteous then I: becauſe that I gaue her not to Shelah my ſonne: and he knew her againe no more.27And it came to paſſe in the time of her trauaile, that beholde, twinnes were in her wombe.28And it came to paſſe when ſhee trauailed, that the one put out his hand, and the midwife tooke and bound vpon his hand a ſkarlet threed, ſaying, This came out firſt.29And it came to paſſe as he drewe backe his hand, that behold, his brother came out: and ſhe ſaid, how haſt thou broken foorth? this breach bee vpon thee: Therefore his name was called Pharez.30And afterward came out his brother that had the ſkarlet threed vpon his hand, and his name was called Zarah.

CHAPTER 391And Ioſeph was brought downe to Egypt, and Potiphar an Officer of Pharaoh, captaine of þe guard, an Egyptian, bought him of the hand of the Iſhmeelites, which had brought him downe thither.2And the LORD was with Ioſeph, and hee was a proſperous man, and hee was in the houſe of his maſter the Egyptian.3And his maſter ſawe that the LORD was with him, and that the LORD made all that he did, to proſper in his hand.4And Ioſeph found grace in his ſight, and he ſerued him; and hee made him ouerſeer ouer his houſe, and all that he had he put into his hand.5And it came to paſſe from the time that hee had made him overſeer in his houſe, and ouer all that he had, that the LORD bleſſed the Egyptians houſe for Ioſephs ſake: and the bleſſing of the LORD was vpon all that he had in the houſe, and in the field.6And he left all that he had, in Ioſephs hand: and he knew not ought he had, ſaue the bread which he did eate: and Ioſeph was a goodly perſon, and well fauoured.7And it came to paſſe after theſe things, that his maſters wife caſt her eyes vpon Ioſeph, and ſhee ſaid, Lie with me.8But he refuſed, and ſaid vnto his maſters wife, Behold, my maſter wotteth not what is with mee in the houſe, and he hath committed all that he hath, to my hand.9There is none greater in this houſe then I: neither hath hee kept backe any thing from me, but thee, becauſe thou art his wife: how then can I doe this great wickedneſſe, and ſinne againſt God?10And it came to paſſe as ſhe ſpake to Ioſeph day by day, that hee hearkened not vnto her, to lie by her, or to bee with her.11And it came to paſſe about this time, that Ioſeph went in to the houſe, to doe his buſines, and there was none of the men of the houſe there within.12And ſhee caught him by his garment, ſaying, Lie with me: and he left his garment in her hand, and fled, and got him out.13And it came to paſſe, when ſhe ſaw that hee had left his garment in her hand, and was fled forth;14That ſhe called vnto the men of her houſe, and ſpake vnto them, ſaying, See, he hath brought in an Hebrew vnto vs, to mocke vs: he came in vnto me to lie with me, and I cried with a loud voice.15And it came to paſſe, when hee heard that I lifted vp my voice, and cried, that he left his garment with mee, and fled, and got him out.16And ſhe laid vp his garment by her, vntill her lord came home.17And ſhe ſpake vnto him, according to theſe words, ſaying, The Hebrew ſeruant which thou haſt brought vnto vs, came in vnto me to mocke me.18And it came to paſſe as I lift vp my voice, and cried, that he left his garment with me, and fled out.19And it came to paſſe when his maſter heard the words of his wife, which ſhe ſpake vnto him, ſaying, After this maner did thy ſeruant to me, that his wrath was kindled.20And Ioſephs maſter tooke him, and put him into the priſon, a place, where þe kings priſoners were bound: and he was there in the priſon.21But the LORD was with Ioſeph, and ſhewed him mercie, and gaue him fauour in the ſight of the keeper of the priſon.22And the keeper of the priſon committed to Ioſephs hand all the priſoners that were in the priſon, and whatſoeuer they did there, he was the doer of it:23The keeper of the priſon looked not to any thing, that was vnder his hand, becauſe the LORD was with him: & that which he did, the LORD made it to proſper.

CHAPTER 401And it came to paſſe after theſe things, that the Butler of the King of Egypt, and his Baker, had offended their lord the King of Egypt.2And Pharaoh was wroth againſt two of his officers, againſt the chiefe of the Butlers, and againſt the chiefe of the Bakers.3And he put them in ward in the houſe of the captaine of the guard, into the priſon, the place where Ioſeph was bound.4And the captaine of the guard charged Ioſeph with them, and he ſerued them, and they continued a ſeaſon in warde.5And they dreamed a dreame both of them, each man his dreame in one night, each man according to the interpretation of his dreame, the Butler and the Baker of the king of Egypt, which were bound in the priſon.6And Ioſeph came in vnto them in the morning, and looked vpon them, and behold, they were ſad.7And he aſked Pharaohs officers that were with him in the warde of his lords houſe, ſaying, wherefore looke ye ſo ſadly to day?8And they ſaid vnto him, we haue dreamed a dreame, and there is no interpreter of it. And Ioſeph ſaid vnto them, Doe not interpretations belong to God? tell me them, I pray you.9And the chiefe Butler tolde his dreame to Ioſeph, and ſaid to him; In my dreame, beholde, a vine was before mee:10And in the vine were three branches, and it was as though it budded, and her bloſsoms ſhot foorth; and the cluſters thereof brought forth ripe grapes.11And Pharaohs cup was in my hand, and I tooke the grapes and preſſed them into Pharaohs cup: and I gaue the cup into Pharaohs hand.[12]And Ioſeph ſaid vnto him, This is the interpretation of it: the three branches are three dayes,[13]Yet within three dayes ſhall Pharaoh lift vp thine head, and reſtore thee vnto thy place, and thou ſhalt deliuer Pharaohs cup into his hand, after the former manner when thou waſt his Butler.[14]But thinke on me, when it ſhall be well with thee, and ſhew kindeneſse, I pray thee, vnto mee, and make mention of me vnto Pharaoh, and bring me out of this houſe.[15]For indeed I was ſtollen away out of the land of the Hebrewes: and here alſo haue I done nothing, that they ſhould put me into the dungeon.[16]When the chiefe Baker ſaw, that the interpretation was good, he ſaid vnto Ioſeph, I alſo was in my dreame, and behold, I had three white baſkets on my head.[17]And in the vppermoſt baſket there was of all maner of bake-meats for Pharaoh, and the birds did eat them out of the baſket vpon my head.[18]And Ioſeph anſwered, and ſaid, This is the interpretation thereof: the three baſkets are three dayes:[19]Yet within three dayes ſhall Pharaoh lift vp thy head from off thee, and ſhall hang thee on a tree, and the birds ſhall eate thy fleſh from off thee.[20]And it came to paſſe the third day, which was Pharaohs birth day, that hee made a feaſt vnto all his ſeruaunts: and he lifted vp by the head of the chiefe Butler, and of the chiefe Baker among his ſeruants.[21]And he reſtored the chiefe Butler vnto his Butlerſhip againe, and hee gaue the cup into Pharaohs hand.[22]But he hanged the chiefe Baker, as Ioſeph had interpreted to them.[23]Yet did not the chiefe Butler remember Ioſeph, but forgate him.

CHAPTER 41[1]And it came to paſſe at the end of two ful yeeres, that Pharaoh dreamed: and beholde, hee ſtood by the riuer.[2]And behold, there came vp out of the riuer ſeuen well fauoured kine, and fat fleſhed, and they fed in a medow.[3]And behold, ſeuen other kine came vp after them out of the riuer, ill fauoured and leane fleſhed, and ſtood by the other kine, vpon the brinke of the riuer.[4]And the ill fauoured and leane fleſhed kine, did eate vp the ſeuen well fauoured and fat kine: So Pharaoh awoke.[5]And hee ſlept and dreamed the ſecond time: and beholde, ſeuen eares of corne came vp vpon one ſtalke, ranke and good.[6]And beholde, ſeuen thinne eares and blaſted with the Eaſtwind, ſprang vp after them.[7]And the ſeuen thinne eares deuoured the ſeuen ranke and full eares: and Pharaoh awoke, and behold, it was a dreame.[8]And it came to paſſe in the morning, that his ſpirit was troubled, and he ſent and called for all the Magicians of Egypt, and all the wiſe men thereof: and Pharaoh tolde them his dreame; but there was none that could interprete them vnto Pharaoh.[9]Then ſpake the chiefe Butler vnto Pharaoh, ſaying, I doe remember my faults this day.[10]Pharaoh was wroth with his ſeruants, and put mee in warde, in the captaine of the guards houſe, both mee, and the chiefe Baker.[11]And we dreamed a dreame in one night, I and he: we dreamed each man according to the interpretation of his dreame.[12]And there was there with vs a yong man an Hebrew, ſeruant to the captaine of the guard: and wee told him, and he interpreted to vs our dreames, to each man according to his dreame, he did interpret.[13]And it came to paſſe, as he interpreted to vs, ſo it was; mee he reſtored vnto mine office, and him he hanged.[14]Then Pharaoh ſent and called Ioſeph, and they brought him haſtily out of the dungeon: And he ſhaued himſelfe, and changed his raiment, and came in vnto Pharaoh.[15]And Pharaoh ſaid vnto Ioſeph, I haue dreamed a dreame, and there is none that can interpret it: and I haue heard ſay of thee, that thou canſt vnderſtand a dreame, to interpret it.[16]And Ioſeph anſwered Pharaoh, ſaying; It is not in me: God ſhall giue Pharaoh an anſwere of peace.[17]And Pharaoh ſaid vnto Ioſeph; In my dreame, behold, I ſtood vpon the banke of the riuer.[18]And behold, there came vp out of the riuer ſeuen kine, fat fleſhed and well fauoured, and they fed in a medow.[19]And behold, ſeuen other kine came vp after them, poore and very ill fauoured, and leane fleſhed, ſuch as I neuer ſaw in all the land of Egypt for badnes.[20]And the leane, & the ill fauoured kine, did eate vp the firſt ſeuen fat kine.[21]And when they had eaten them vp, it could not bee knowen that they had eaten them, but they were ſtill ill fauoured, as at the beginning: So I awoke.[22]And I ſaw in my dreame, and behold, ſeuen eares came vp in one ſtalke, full and good.[23]And behold, ſeuen eares withered, thin & blaſted with the Eaſt wind, ſprung vp after them.[24]And the thin eares deuoured the ſeuen good eares: and I told this vnto the magicians, but there was none that could declare it to me.[25]And Ioſeph ſaid vnto Pharaoh, the dreame of Pharaoh is one; God hath ſhewed Pharaoh what he is about to doe.[26]The ſeuen good kine are ſeuen yeeres: and the ſeuen good eares are ſeuen yeeres: the dreame is one.[27]And the ſeuen thin and ill fauoured kine that came vp after them, are ſeuen yeeres: and the ſeuen emptie eares blaſted with the Eaſt wind, ſhall bee ſeuen yeeres of famine.[28]This is the thing which I haue ſpoken vnto Pharaoh: what God is about to doe, he ſheweth vnto Pharaoh.[29]Behold, there come ſeuen yeeres of great plentie, throughout all the land of Egypt.[30]And there ſhall Ariſe after them, ſeuen yeeres of famine, and all the plentie ſhall be forgotten in the land of Egypt: and the famine ſhall conſume the land.[31]And the plentie ſhal not be knowen in the land, by reaſon of that famine following: for it ſhalbe very grieuous.[32]And for that the dreame was doubled vnto Pharaoh twice, it is becauſe the thing is eſtabliſhed by God: and God will ſhortly bring it to paſſe.[33]Now therfore let Pharaoh looke out a man diſcreet and wiſe, and ſet him ouer the land of Egypt.[34]Let Pharaoh doe this, and let him appoint officers ouer the land, & take vp the fift part of the land of Egypt, in the ſeuen plenteous yeeres.[35]And let them gather all the food of thoſe good yeeres that come, and lay vp corne vnder the hand of Pharaoh, and let them keepe food in the cities.[36]And that food ſhall be for ſtore to the land, againſt the ſeuen yeeres of famine, which ſhall bee in the land of Egypt, that the land periſh not through the famine.[37]And the thing was good in the eyes of Pharaoh, and in the eyes of all his ſeruants.[38]And Pharaoh ſaid vnto his ſeruants, Can we find ſuch a one, as this is, a man in whom the ſpirit of God is?[39]And Pharaoh ſaid vnto Ioſeph, Foraſmuch as God hath ſhewed thee all this, there is none ſo diſcreete and wiſe, as thou art:[40]Thou ſhalt be ouer my houſe, and according vnto thy word ſhall all my people be ruled: only in the throne will I be greater then thou.[41]And Pharaoh ſaid vnto Ioſeph, See, I haue ſet thee ouer all the land of Egypt.[42]And Pharaoh tooke off his ring from his hand, & put it vpon Ioſephs hand, and arayed him in veſtures of fine linnen, and put a gold chaine about his necke.[43]And he made him to ride in the ſecond charet which he had: and they cried before him, Bow the knee: and he made him ruler ouer all the land of Egypt.[44]And Pharaoh ſaid vnto Ioſeph, I am Pharaoh, and without thee ſhall no man lift vp his hand or foote, in all the land of Egypt.[45]And Pharaoh called Ioſephs name, Zaphnath-Paaneah, and he gaue him to wife Aſenath the daughter of Poti-pherah, prieſt of On: and Ioſeph went out ouer all the lande of Egypt.[46](And Ioſeph was thirtie yeeres old when he ſtood before Pharaoh king of Egypt) and Ioſeph went out from the preſence of Pharaoh, and went thorowout all the land of Egypt.[47]And in the ſeuen plenteous yeres the earth brought forth by handfuls.[48]And he gathered vp all the foode of the ſeuen yeeres, which were in the land of Egypt, and laid vp the foode in the cities: the foode of the field which was round about euery citie, laid he vp in the ſame.[49]And Ioſeph gathered corne as the ſand of the ſea, very much, vntill he left numbring: for it was without number.[50]And vnto Ioſeph were borne two ſonnes, before the yeeres of famine came: which Aſenath the daughter of Poti-pherah, Prieſt of On bare vnto him.[51]And Ioſeph called the name of the firſt borne Manaſſeh: for God, ſaid hee, hath made me forget all my toile, and all my fathers houſe.[52]And the name of the ſecond called he Ephraim: for God hath cauſed mee to be fruitfull in the land of my affliction.[53]And the ſeuen yeeres of plenteouſneſse, that was in the land of Egypt, were ended.[54]And the ſeuen yeeres of dearth beganne to come according as Ioſeph had ſaide, and the dearth was in all lands: but in all the land of Egypt there was bread.[55]And when all the land of Egypt was famiſhed, the people cried to Pharaoh for bread: and Pharaoh ſaid vnto all the Egyptians, Goe vnto Ioſeph: what he ſaith to you, doe.[56]And the famine was ouer all the face of the earth; and Ioſeph opened all the ſtorehouſes, and ſolde vnto the Egyptians: and the famine waxed ſore in the land of Egypt.[57]And all countreys came into Egypt to Ioſeph, for to buy corne, becauſe that the famine was ſo ſore in all lands.

CHAPTER 42[1]Now when Iacob ſaw that there was corne in Egypt, Iacob ſaid vnto his ſonnes, Why doe ye looke one vpon an other?[2]And hee ſaid, Beholde, I haue heard that there is corne in Egypt: get you downe thither and buy for vs from thence, that we may liue, and not die.[3]And Ioſephs ten brethren went downe to buy corne in Egypt.[4]But Beniamin Ioſephs brother, Iacob ſent not with his brethren: for he ſaid, Leſt peraduenture miſchiefe befall him.[5]And the ſonnes of Iſrael came to buy corne among thoſe that came: for the famine was in the land of Canaan.[6]And Ioſeph was the gouernour ouer the land, and hee it was

that ſold to all the people of the land: and Ioſephs brethren came, &
bowed downe themſelues before him, with their faces to the earth.7And
Ioſeph ſaw his brethren, and he knew them, but made himſelfe ſtrange
vnto them, and ſpake roughly vnto them; and hee ſaide vnto them,
Whence come ye? And they ſaid, From the land of Canaan, to buy
food.8And Ioſeph knew his brethren, but they knew not him.9And
Ioſeph remembred the dreames which hee dreamed of them, and ſaid
vnto them, Ye are ſpies: to ſee the nakednes of the land you are
come.10And they ſaid vnto him, Nay, my lord, but to buy food are thy
ſeruants come.11We are all one mans ſonnes, we are true men: thy
ſeruants are no ſpies.12And he ſaid vnto them, Nay: but to ſee the
nakedneſſe of the land, you are come.13And they ſaid, Thy ſeruants are
twelue brethren, the ſonnes of one man in the land of Canaan: and
behold, the yongeſt is this day with our father, and one is not.14And
Ioſeph ſaid vnto them, That is it that I ſpake vnto you, ſaying, Ye are
ſpies.15Hereby ye ſhall be proued: by the life of Pharaoh ye ſhall not goe
foorth hence, except your yongeſt brother come hither.16Send one of
you, and let him fetch your brother, and ye ſhalbe kept in priſon, that
your wordes may be proued, whether there be any trueth in you: or els
by the life of Pharaoh ſurely ye are ſpies.17And he put them all together
into warde, three dayes.18And Ioſeph ſaid vnto them the third day, This
doe, and liue: for I feare God.19If ye be true men, let one of your
brethren be bound in the houſe of your priſon: goe ye, carry corne for
the famine of your houſes.20But bring your yongeſt brother vnto mee,
ſo ſhall your wordes be verified, and yee ſhall not die: and they did
ſo.21And they ſaid one to another, We are verily guiltie concerning our
brother, in that we ſaw the anguiſh of his ſoule, when he beſought vs,
and we would not heare: therefore is this diſtreſſe come vpon vs.22And
Reuben anſwered them, ſaying, ſpake I not vnto you, ſaying, Doe not
ſinne againſt the childe, and ye would not heare? therefore behold alſo,
his blood is required.23And they knew not that Ioſeph vnderſtood them:
for hee ſpake vnto them by an interpreter.24And hee turned himſelfe
about from them and wept, and returned to them againe, and
communed with them, and tooke from them Simeon, and bound him
before their eyes.25Then Ioſeph commanded to fill their ſackes with
corne, and to reſtore euery mans money into his ſacke, and to giue them
prouiſion for the way: and thus did he vnto them.26And they laded their
aſſes with the corne, and departed thence.27And as one of them opened
his ſacke, to giue his aſſe prouender in the Inne, he eſpied his money:
for behold, it was in his ſackes mouth.28And he ſaid vnto his brethren,
My money is reſtored, and loe, it is euen in my ſacke: and their heart
failed them, and they were afraid, ſaying one to an other, What is this
that God hath done vnto vs?29And they came vnto Iacob their father,
vnto the land of Canaan, and told him all that befell vnto them,
ſaying;30The man who is the lord of the land, ſpake roughly to vs, and
tooke vs for ſpies of the countrey.31And we ſaid vnto him, We are true
men; we are no ſpies.32We be twelue brethren, ſonnes of our father: one
is not, and the yongeſt is this day with our father, in the land of
Canaan.33And the man the lord of the countrey ſaid vnto vs, Hereby
ſhall I know that ye are true men: leaue one of your brethren here with
me, and take foode for the famine of your houſholds, and be
gone.34And bring your yongeſt brother vnto me: then ſhall I know that
you are no ſpies, but that you are true men: ſo will I deliuer you your
brother, and ye ſhall traffique in the land.35And it came to paſſe as they
emptied their ſacks, that behold, euery mans bundle of money was in
his ſacke: and when both they and their father ſaw the bundels of
money, they were afraid.36And Iacob their father ſaid vnto them, We
haue ye bereaued of my children: Ioſeph is not, and Simeon is not, and
ye wil take Beniamin away: all theſe things are againſt me.37And Reuben
ſpake vnto his father, ſaying; Slay my two ſonnes, if I bring him not to
thee: deliuer him into my hand, and I will bring him to thee againe.38And
he ſaid, My ſonne ſhall not goe downe with you, for his brother is dead,
and he is left alone: if miſchiefe befall him by the way in the which yee
goe, then ſhall ye bring downe my gray haires with ſorrow to the graue.
CHAPTER 43 1And the famine was ſore in the land.2And it came to
paſſe when they had eaten vp the corne, which they had brought out of
Egypt, their father ſaid vnto them, Goe againe, buy vs a little foode.3And
Iudah ſpake vnto him, ſaying, The man did ſolemnly proteſt vnto vs,
ſaying, Ye ſhall not ſee my face, except your brother be with you.4If
thou wilt ſend our brother with vs, we will goe downe and buy thee
food.5But if thou wilt not ſend him, we will not goe downe: for the man
ſaide vnto vs, Ye ſhall not ſee my face, except your brother be with
you.6And Iſrael ſaid, Wherefore dealt ye ſo ill with me, as to tell the man
whether ye had yet a brother?7And they ſaid, The man aſked vs ſtraitly
of our ſtate, and of our kindred, ſaying, Is your father yet aliue? haue yee
another brother? and we tolde him according to the tenour of theſe
words: Could we certainely knowe that he would ſay, Bring your brother
downe?8And Iudah ſaid vnto Iſrael his father, Send the lad with me, and
wee will Ariſe and go, that we may liue, and not die, both we, and thou,
and alſo our little ones.9I will be ſurety for him; of my hand ſhalt thou
require him: if I bring him not vnto thee, and ſet him before thee, then
let me beare the blame for euer.10For except we had lingred, ſurely now
wee had returned this ſecond time.11And their father Iſrael ſaid vnto
them, If it muſt bee ſo now, doe this: take of the beſt fruits in the land
in your veſſels, and carie downe the man a Preſent, a litle balme, and a
litle honie, ſpices, and myrrhe, nuts, and almonds.12And take double
money in your hand, and the money that was brought againe in the
mouth of your ſackes: carie it againe in your hand, peraduenture it was
an ouerſight.13Take alſo your brother, and Ariſe, goe againe vnto the
man.14And God Almightie giue you mercie before the man, that he may
ſend away your other brother, and Beniamin: If I be bereaued of my
children, I am bereaued.15And the men tooke that Preſent, and they
tooke double money in their hand, and Beniamin, and roſe vp, and went
downe to Egypt, and ſtood before Ioſeph.16And when Ioſeph ſawe
Beniamin with them, hee ſaid to the ruler of his houſe, Bring theſe men
home, and ſlay, and make ready: for theſe men ſhall dine with me at
noone.17And the man did as Ioſeph hade: and the man brought the men
into Ioſephs houſe.18And the men were afraid, becauſe they were
brought into Ioſephs houſe, and they ſaid, Becauſe of the money that
was returned in our ſackes at the firſt time are we brought in, that hee
may ſeeke occaſion againſt vs, and fall vpon vs, and take vs for
bondmen, and our aſſes.19And they came neere to the ſteward of
Ioſephs houſe, and they communed with him at the doore of the
houſe,20And ſaid, O Sir, we came indeed downe at the firſt time to buy
food.21And it came to paſſe when wee came to the Inne, that wee
opened our ſackes, and behold, euery mans money was in the mouth of
his ſacke, our money in ful weight: and we haue brought it againe in our
hand.22And other money haue wee brought downe in our handes to buy
food: we cannot tell who put our money in our ſackes.23And he ſaid,
Peace be to you, feare not: your God, and the God of your father, hath
giuen you treaſure in your ſackes: I had your money. And hee brought
Simeon out vnto them.24And the man brought the men into Ioſephs
houſe, and gaue them water, and they waſhed their feete, and he gaue
their aſſes prouender.25And they made ready the Preſent againſt Ioſeph
came at noone: for they heard that they ſhould eate bread there.26And
when Ioſeph came home, they brought him the Preſent which was in
their hand, into the houſe, and bowed themſelues to him to the
earth.27And he aſked them of their welfare, and ſaid, Is your father well,
the old man of whom ye ſpake? Is he yet aliue?28And they anſwered,
Thy ſeruant our father is in good health, hee is yet aliue: & they bowed
downe their heads, and made obeiſance.29And he lift vp his eyes, and
ſawe his brother Beniamin, his mothers ſonne, and ſaid, Is this your
yonger brother, of whom yee ſpake vnto mee? and he ſaid, God be
gracious vnto thee, my ſonne.30And Ioſeph made haſte: for his bowels
did yerne vpon his brother: and he ſought where to weepe, and hee
entred into his chamber, & wept there.31And he waſhed his face, and
went out, and refrained himſelfe, and ſaide, Set on bread.32And they ſet
on for him by himſelfe, and for them by themſelues, and for the
Egyptians which did eate with him, by themſelues: becauſe the
Egyptians might not eate bread with the Hebrewes: for that is an
abomination vnto the Egyptians.33And they ſate before him, the firſt
borne according to his birthright, and the yongeſt according to his
youth: and the men marueiled one at another.34And hee tooke and ſent
meaſſes vnto them from before him: but Beniamins meaſſe was fiue
times ſo much as any of theirs: and they drunke, and were merry with
him.
CHAPTER 44 1And hee commaunded the ſteward of his houſe, ſaying,
Fill the mens ſackes with food, as much as they can carie, and put euery
mans money in his ſacks mouth.2And put my cup, the ſiluer cup, in the
ſackes mouth of the youngeſt, and his corne money: and he did

according to the word that Ioſeph had ſpoken.3Aſsoone as the morning was light, the men were ſent away, they, and their aſſes.4And when they were gone out of the citie, and not yet farre off, Ioſeph ſaid vnto his ſteward, Up, follow after the men; and when thou doeſt ouertake them, ſay vnto them, Wherefore haue ye rewarded euill for good?5Is not this it, in which my lord drinketh? and whereby indeed he diuineth? ye haue done euill in ſo doing.6And he ouertooke them, and he ſpake vnto them theſe ſame words.7And they ſaid vnto him, Wherefore ſaith my lord theſe words? God forbid that thy ſeruants ſhould doe according to this thing.8Behold, the money which wee found in our ſackes mouthes, wee brought againe vnto thee, out of the land of Canaan: how then ſhould wee ſteale out of thy lords houſe, ſiluer or golde?9With whom ſoeuer of thy ſeruants it be found, both let him die, and we alſo will be my lords bondmen.10And he ſaid, Now alſo let it be according vnto your wordes: hee with whom it is found, ſhall be my ſeruant: and ye ſhall be blameleſſe.11Then they ſpeedily tooke downe euery man his ſacke to the ground, and opened euery man his ſacke.12And he ſearched, and began at the eldeſt, and left at the yongeſt: and the cup was found in Beniamins ſacke.13Then they rent their clothes, and laded euery man his aſſe, and returned to the citie.14And Iudah and his brethren came to Ioſephs houſe: (for he was yet there) and they fell before him on the ground.15And Ioſeph ſaid vnto them, What deed is this that ye haue done? wote ye not, that ſuch a man as I can certainely diuine?16And Iudah ſaid, What ſhall wee ſay vnto my lord? what ſhal we ſpeake? or how ſhall we cleare our ſelues? God hath found out the iniquitie of thy ſeruants: beholde, wee are my lords ſeruants, both we, and he alſo with whom the cup is found.17And he ſaid, God forbid that I ſhould doe ſo: but the man in whoſe hand the cup is found, he ſhal be my ſeruant; and as for you, get you vp in peace vnto your father.18Then Iudah came neere vnto him, and ſaid, Oh my lord, let thy ſeruant, I pray thee, ſpeake a word in my lords eares, & let not thine anger burne againſt thy ſeruant: for thou art euen as Pharaoh.19My lord aſked his ſeruants, ſaying; Haue ye a father, or a brother?20And we ſaid vnto my lord, Wee haue a father, an olde man, and a childe of his old age, a little one: and his brother is dead, and he alone is left of his mother, and his father loueth him.21And thou ſaidſt vnto thy ſeruants, Bring him downe vnto mee, that I may ſet mine eyes vpon him.22And we ſaid vnto my lord, The lad cannot leaue his father: for if hee ſhould leaue his father, his father would die.23And thou ſaidſt vnto thy ſeruants, Except your yongeſt brother come downe with you, you ſhall ſee my face no more.24And it came to paſſe when wee came vp vnto thy ſeruant my father, we told him the words of my lord.25And our father ſaid, Goe againe, and buy vs a little food.26And we ſaide, Wee cannot goe downe: if our yongeſt brother be with vs, then will we goe downe: for wee may not ſee the mans face, except our yongeſt brother be with vs.27And thy ſeruant my father ſaid vnto vs, Ye know that my wife bare me two ſonnes.28And the one went out from me, and I ſaid, Surely he is torne in pieces: and I ſaw him not ſince.29And if ye take this alſo from me, and miſchiefe befall him, ye ſhall bring downe my gray haires with ſorrow to the graue.30Now therefore when I come to thy ſeruant my father, and the lad bee not with vs; (ſeeing that his life is bound vp in the lads life.)31It ſhall come to paſſe, when he ſeeth that the lad is not with vs, that he will die, and thy ſeruants ſhall bring downe the gray haires of thy ſeruant our father with ſorrow to the graue.32For thy ſeruant became ſurety for the lad vnto my father, ſaying, If I bring him not vnto thee, then I ſhall beare the blame to my father, for euer.33Now therefore, I pray thee, let thy ſeruant abide in ſtead of the lad, a bondman to my lord, and let the lad goe vp with his brethren.34For how ſhall I goe vp to my father, and the lad be not with mee, leſt peraduenture I ſee the euill that ſhall come on my father?

CHAPTER 451Then Ioſeph could not refraine himſelfe before all them that ſtood by him: and he cried, Cauſe euery man to goe out from me; and there ſtood no man with him, while Ioſeph made himſelfe knowen vnto his brethren.2And he wept aloud: and the Egyptians, and the houſe of Pharaoh heard.3And Ioſeph ſaid vnto his brethren, I am Ioſeph; Doeth my father yet liue? and his brethren could not anſwere him: for they were troubled at his preſence.4And Ioſeph ſaid vnto his brethren, Come neere to me, I pray you: and they came neere; and he ſaid, I am Ioſeph your brother, whom ye ſold into Egypt.5Now therefore bee not grieued, nor angry with your ſelues, that yee ſold me hither: for God did ſend me before you, to preſeruelife.6For theſe two yeeres hath the famine bene in the land: and yet there are fiue yeeres, in the which there ſhall neither be earing nor harueſt.7And God ſent me before you, to preſerueyou a poſteritie in the earth, and to ſaue your liues by a great deliuerance.8So now it was not you that ſent me hither, but God: and he hath made me a father to Pharaoh, and lord of all his houſe, and a ruler throughout all the land of Egypt.9Haſte you, and goe vp to my father, and ſay vnto him, Thus ſaith thy ſonne Ioſeph; God hath made me lord of all Egypt; come downe vnto me, tary not.10And thou ſhalt dwell in the land of Goſhen, and thou ſhalt be neere vnto me, thou, and thy children, and thy childrens children, and thy flockes, and thy heards, and all that thou haſt.11And there wil I nouriſh thee, (for yet there are fiue yeeres of famine) leſt thou and thy houſhold, and all that thou haſt, come to pouertie.12And behold, your eyes ſee, and the eyes of my brother Beniamin, that it is my mouth that ſpeaketh vnto you.13And you ſhall tell my father of all my glory in Egypt, and of all that you haue ſeene, and ye ſhall haſte, and bring downe my father hither.14And he fel vpon his brother Beniamins necke, and wept: and Beniamin wept vpon his necke.15Moreouer hee kiſſed all his brethren, and wept vpon them: and after that, his brethren talked with him.16And the fame thereof was heard in Pharaohs houſe, ſaying, Ioſephs brethren are come: and it pleaſed Pharaoh well, and his ſeruants.17And Pharaoh ſaid vnto Ioſeph, ſay vnto thy brethren, This doe yee, lade your beaſts and goe, get you vnto the land of Canaan.18And take your father, and your houſholds, and come vnto mee: and I wil giue you the good of the land of Egypt, and ye ſhall eat the fat of the land.19Now thou art commanded, this doe yee; Take you wagons out of the land of Egypt for your little ones, and for your wiues, and bring your father, and come.20Alſo regard not your ſtuffe: for the good of all the land of Egypt is yours.21And the children of Iſrael did ſo: and Ioſeph gaue them wagons, according to the commandement of Pharaoh, and gaue them prouiſion for the way.22To all of them he gaue each man changes of raiment: but to Beniamin hee gaue three hundred pieces of ſiluer, and fiue changes of raiment.23And to his father hee ſent after this maner: ten aſſes laden with the good things of Egypt, and ten ſhee aſſes laden with corne, and bread and meat for his father by the way.24So he ſent his brethren away, and they departed: and hee ſaid vnto them, ſee that yee fall not out by the way.25And they went vp out of Egypt, and came into the land of Canaan vnto Iacob their father,26And told him, ſaying, Ioſeph is yet aliue, and he is gouernour ouer all the land of Egypt. And Iacobs heart fainted, for he beleeued them not.27And they told him all the words of Ioſeph, which hee had ſaide vnto them: and when hee ſaw the wagons which Ioſeph had ſent to carie him, the ſpirit of Iacob their father reuiued.28And Iſrael ſaid, It is enough; Ioſeph my ſonne is yet aliue: I will goe and ſee him before I die.

CHAPTER 461And Iſrael tooke his iourney with all that hee had, and came to Beerſheba, and offered ſacrifices vnto the God of his father Iſaac.2And God ſpake vnto Iſrael in the viſions of the night, and ſaid, Iacob, Iacob. And he ſaid, Here am I.3And he ſaid, I am God, the God of thy father, feare not to goe downe into Egypt: for I will there make of thee a great nation.4I will goe downe with thee into Egypt; and I will alſo ſurely bring thee vp againe: and Ioſeph ſhall put his hand vpon thine eyes.5And Iacob roſe vp from Beerſheba: and the ſonnes of Iſrael caried Iacob their father, and their litle ones, and their wiues, in the wagons which Pharaoh had ſent to cary him.6And they tooke their cattell, and their goods which they had gotten in the land of Canaan, and came into Egypt, Iacob, and all his ſeed with him:7His ſonnes, and his ſonnes ſonnes with him, his daughters, and his ſonnes daughters, and all his ſeed brought he with him into Egypt.8And theſe are the names of the children of Iſrael, which came into Egypt, Iacob and his ſonnes: Reuben Iacobs firſt borne;9And the ſonnes of Reuben, Hanoch, and Phallu, and Hezron, and Carmi.10And the ſonnes of Simeon: Iemuel, and Iamin, and Ohad, and Iachin, and Zohar, and Shaul the ſonne of a Canaanitiſh woman.11And the ſonnes of Leui: Gerſhon, Kohath, and Merari.12And the ſonnes of Iudah: Er, and Onan, and Shelah, and Pharez, and Zerah: But Er & Onan died in the land of Canaan. And the ſonnes of Pharez, were Hezron, and Hamul.13And the ſonnes of Iſſachar: Tola, and Phuuah, and Iob, and Shimron.14And the ſonnes of Zebulun: Sered, and Elon, and Iahleel.15Theſe bee the ſonnes of Leah, which ſhe bare vnto Iacob in Padan-Aram, with his daughter Dinah: all the ſoules of his ſonnes and his daughters, were thirtie and three.16And the ſonnes of

Gad: Ziphion, and Haggi, Shuni, and Ezbon, Eri, and Arodi, and
Areli.[17]And the ſonnes of Aſher: Iimnah, and Iſhuah, and Iſui, and
Beriah, and Serah their ſiſter: And the ſonnes of Beriah: Heber, and
Malchiel.[18]Theſe are the ſonnes of Zilpah, whome Laban gaue to Leah
his daughter: and theſe ſhe bare vnto Iacob, euen ſixteene ſoules.[19]The
ſonnes of Rachel Iacobs wife: Ioſeph, and Beniamin.[20]And vnto Ioſeph
in the lande of Egypt, were borne Manaſſeh and Ephraim, which
Aſenath the daughter of Poti-pherah Prieſt of On bare vnto him.[21]And
the ſonnes of Beniamin were Belah, and Becher, and Aſhbel, Gera, and
Naaman, Ehi and Roſh, Muppim, and Huppim, and Ard.[22]Theſe are the
ſonnes of Rachel which were borne to Iacob: all the ſoules were
fourteene.[23]And the ſonnes of Dan: Huſhim.[24]And the ſonnes of
Naphtali: Iahzeel, and Guni, and Iezer, and Shillem.[25]Theſe are the
ſonnes of Bilhah, which Laban gaue vnto Rachel his daughter, and ſhe
bare theſe vnto Iacob: all the ſoules were ſeuen.[26]All the ſoules that
came with Iacob into Egypt, which came out of his loines, beſides
Iacobs ſonnes wiues, all the ſoules were threeſcore and ſixe.[27]And the
ſonnes of Ioſeph, which were borne him in Egypt, were two ſoules: all
the ſoules of the houſe of Iacob, which came into Egypt, were
threeſcore and ten.[28]And he ſent Iudah before him vnto Ioſeph, to
direct his face vnto Goſhen, and they came into the lande of
Goſhen.[29]And Ioſeph made ready his charet, and went vp to meet Iſrael
his father, to Goſhen, and preſented himſelfe vnto him: and he fell on
his necke, and wept on his necke a good while.[30]And Iſrael ſaide vnto
Ioſeph, Now let me die, ſince I haue ſeene thy face, becauſe thou art yet
aliue.[31]And Ioſeph ſaid vnto his brethren, and vnto his fathers houſe, I
will goe vp, and ſhew Pharaoh, and ſay vnto him, My brethren, & my
fathers houſe, which were in the land of Canaan, are come vnto
me.[32]And the men are ſheapheards, for their trade hath bene to feed
cattell: and they haue brought their flocks, and their heards, and all that
they haue.[33]And it ſhall come to paſſe when Pharaoh ſhall call you, and
ſhall ſay, What is your occupation?[34]That ye ſhall ſay, Thy ſeruants trade
hath bene about cattell, from our youth euen vntill now, both we, and
alſo our fathers: that ye may dwell in the land of Goſhen; for euery
ſhepheard is an abomination vnto the Egyptians.
CHAPTER 47[1]Then Ioſeph came and tolde Pharaoh, and ſaide, My
father and my brethren, and their flockes, and their heards, and all that
they haue, are come out of the land of Canaan: and behold, they are in
the land of Goſhen.[2]And hee tooke ſome of his brethren, euen fiue men,
& preſented them vnto Pharaoh.[3]And Pharaoh ſaid vnto his brethren,
What is your occupation? And they ſaid vnto Pharaoh, Thy ſeruants are
ſhepheards, both wee and alſo our fathers.[4]They ſaid moreouer vnto
Pharaoh, For to ſoiourne in the land are we come: for thy ſeruants haue
no paſture for their flockes, for the famine is ſore in the land of Canaan:
now therefore we pray thee, let thy ſeruants dwel in the land of
Goſhen.[5]And Pharaoh ſpake vnto Ioſeph, ſaying, Thy father and thy
brethren are come vnto thee.[6]The land of Egypt is before thee: in the
beſt of the land make thy father and brethren to dwell, in the lande of
Goſhen let them dwell: and if thou knoweſt any man of actiuitie amongſt
them, then make them rulers ouer my cattell.[7]And Ioſeph brought in
Iacob his father, and ſet him before Pharaoh: and Iacob bleſſed
Pharaoh.[8]And Pharaoh ſaid vnto Iacob, How old art thou?[9]And Iacob
ſaid vnto Pharaoh, The dayes of the yeeres of my pilgrimage are an
hundred & thirtie yeres: few and euill haue the dayes of the yeeres of my
life bene, and haue not attained vnto the dayes of the yeeres of the life
of my fathers, in the dayes of their pilgrimage.[10]And Iacob bleſſed
Pharaoh, and went out from before Pharaoh.[11]And Ioſeph placed his
father, and his brethren, and gaue them a poſſeſſion in the land of Egypt,
in the beſt of the land, in the land of Rameſes, as Pharaoh had
commanded.[12]And Ioſeph nouriſhed his father and his brethren, and all
his fathers houſhold with bread, according to their families.[13]And there
was no bread in all the land: for the famine was very ſore, ſo that the
land of Egypt and all the land of Canaan fainted by reaſon of the
famine.[14]And Ioſeph gathered vp all the money that was found in the
land of Egypt, and in the land of Canaan, for the corne which they
bought: and Ioſeph brought the money into Pharaohs houſe.[15]And
when money failed in the land of Egypt, and in the land of Canaan, all
the Egyptians came vnto Ioſeph, and ſaid, Giue vs bread: for why ſhould
we die in thy preſence? for the money faileth.[16]And Ioſeph ſaid, Giue
your cattell: and I will giue you for your catell, if money faile.[17]And they
brought their cattel vnto Ioſeph: and Ioſeph gaue them bread in
exchange for horſes, and for the flockes, and for the cattell of the heards,
and for the aſſes, and he fed them with bread, for all their cattel, for that
yeere.[18]When that yeere was ended, they came vnto him the ſecond
yeere, and ſaid vnto him, We will not hide it from my lord, how that our
money is ſpent, my lord alſo had our heards of cattell: there is not ought
left in the ſight of my lord, but our bodies, and our lands.[19]Wherfore
ſhall we die before thine eyes, both we, and our land? buy vs and our
land for bread, and we and our land will be ſeruants vnto Pharaoh: and
giue vs ſeede that we may liue and not die, that the land be not
deſolate.[20]And Ioſeph bought all the land of Egypt for Pharaoh: for the
Egyptians ſold euery man his field, becauſe the famine preuailed ouer
them: ſo the land became Pharaohs.[21]And as for the people, he remoued
them to cities from one end of the borders of Egypt, euen to the other
ende thereof.[22]Onely the land of the Prieſts bought he not: for the
prieſts had a portion aſsigned them of Pharaoh, and did eate their
portion which Pharaoh gaue them: wherefore they ſolde not their
lands.[23]Then Ioſeph ſaid vnto the people, Behold, I haue bought you
this day, and your land for Pharaoh: Loe, here is ſeed for you, and ye
ſhall ſow the land.[24]And it ſhall come to paſſe in the increaſe, that you
ſhall giue the fift part vnto Pharaoh, and foure parts ſhall be your owne,
for ſeed of the field, and for your food, and for them of your
houſeholds, and for food for your litle ones.[25]And they ſaid, Thou haſt
ſaued our liues: let vs find grace in the ſight of my lord, and we will be
Pharaohs ſeruants.[26]And Ioſeph made it a law ouer the land of Egypt
vnto this day, that Pharaoh ſhould haue the fift part: except the land of
the prieſts onely, which became not Pharaohs.[27]And Iſrael dwelt in the
land of Egypt in the countrey of Goſhen, and they had poſſeſſions
therein, and grew, and multiplied exceedingly.[28]And Iacob liued in the
land of Egypt ſeuenteene yeres: ſo the whole age of Iacob was an
hundred fourtie and ſeuen yeeres.[29]And the time drew nigh that Iſrael
muſt die, and he called his ſonne Ioſeph, and ſaid vnto him, If now I
haue found grace in thy ſight, put, I pray thee, thy hand vnder my thigh,
and deale kindly and truely with mee, bury me not, I pray thee, in
Egypt.[30]But I will lie with my fathers, and thou ſhalt carie mee out of
Egypt, and bury me in their burying place: and he ſaid, I will doe as thou
haſt ſaid.[31]And he ſaid, Sweare vnto mee: and he ſware vnto him. And
Iſrael bowed himſelfe vpon the beds head.
CHAPTER 48[1]And it came to paſſe after theſe things, that one told
Ioſeph, Behold, thy father is ſicke: and he tooke with him his two
ſonnes, Manaſſeh and Ephraim.[2]And one told Iacob, and ſaid, Behold,
thy ſonne Ioſeph commeth vnto thee: and Iſrael ſtrengthened himſelfe,
and ſate vpon the bed.[3]And Iacob ſaide vnto Ioſeph, God Almightie
appeared vnto mee at Luz in the land of Canaan, and bleſſed mee,[4]And
ſaid vnto me, Behold, I wil make thee fruitfull, and multiplie thee, and I
will make of thee a multitude of people, and will giue this land to thy
ſeede after thee, for an euerlaſting poſſeſſion.[5]And now thy two ſonnes,
Ephraim and Manaſſeh, which were borne vnto thee in the land of
Egypt, before I came vnto thee into Egypt, are mine: as Reuben and
Simeon, they ſhalbe mine.[6]And thy iſſue which thou begetteſt after
them, ſhall be thine, and ſhall be called after the name of their brethren
in their inheritance.[7]And as for me, when I came from Padan, Rachel
died by me in the land of Canaan, in the way, when yet there was but a
little way to come vnto Ephrath: and I buried her there in the way of
Ephrath, the ſame is Bethlehem.[8]And Iſrael behelde Ioſephs ſonnes,
and ſaid, Who are theſe?[9]And Ioſeph ſaid vnto his father, They are my
ſonnes, whom God hath giuen me in this place: and he ſaid, Bring them,
I pray thee, vnto me, and I will bleſſe them.[10](Now the eyes of Iſrael
were dimme for age, ſo that he could not ſee,) and hee brought them
neere vnto him, and he kiſſed them, and imbraced them.[11]And Iſrael
ſaid vnto Ioſeph, I had not thought to ſee thy face: and loe, God hath
ſhewed me alſo thy ſeed.[12]And Ioſeph brought them out from betweene
his knees, and hee bowed himſelfe with his face to the earth.[13]And
Ioſeph tooke them both, Ephraim in his right hand, toward Iſraels left
hand, and Manaſſeh in his left hand towards Iſraels right hand, and
brought them neere vnto him.[14]And Iſrael ſtretched out his right hand,
and layd it vpon Ephraims head who was the yonger; and his left hand
vpon Manaſſehs head, guiding his hands wittingly: for Manaſſeh was the
firſt borne.[15]And he bleſſed Ioſeph and ſaid, God before whom my
fathers Abraham and Iſaac did walke, the God which fedde mee all my

life long vnto this day,[16]The Angel which redeemed mee from all euill, bleſſe the laddes, and let my name be named on them, and the name of my fathers Abraham and Iſaac, and let them grow into a multitude in the midſt of the earth.[17]And when Ioſeph ſaw that his father laide his right hand vpon the head of Ephraim, it diſpleaſed him: and he held vp his fathers hand, to remoue it from Ephraims head, vnto Manaſſehs head.[18]And Ioſeph ſaide vnto his father, Not ſo my father: for this is the firſt borne; put thy right hand vpon his head.[19]And his father refuſed, and ſaid, I know it, my ſonne, I know it: he alſo ſhall become a people, and he alſo ſhall be great: but truely his yonger brother ſhall be greater then he; and his ſeede ſhall become a multitude of nations.[20]And he bleſſed them that day, ſaying, In thee ſhall Iſrael bleſſe, ſaying, God make thee as Ephraim, and as Manaſſeh: and he ſet Ephraim before Manaſſeh.[21]And Iſrael ſaide vnto Ioſeph, Behold, I die: but God ſhall be with you, and bring you againe vnto the land of your fathers.[22]Moreouer I haue giuen to thee one portion aboue thy brethren, which I tooke out of the hand of the Amorite with my ſword, and with my bow.

CHAPTER 49[1]And Iacob called vnto his ſonnes, and ſaid, Gather your ſelues together, that I may tell you that which ſhall befall you in the laſt dayes.[2]Gather your ſelues together, and heare ye ſonnes of Iacob, and hearken vnto Iſrael your father.[3]Reuben, thou art my firſt borne, my might, and the beginning of my ſtrength, the excellencie of dignitie, and the excellencie of power:[4]Unſtable as water, thou ſhalt not excell, becauſe thou wenteſt vp to thy fathers bed: then defiledſt thou it. He went vp to my couche.[5]Simeon and Leui are brethren, inſtruments of crueltie are in their habitations.[6]O my ſoule, come not thou into their ſecret: vnto their aſſembly mine honour be not thou vnited: for in their anger they ſlew a man, and in their ſelfe will they digged downe a wall.[7]Curſed be their anger, for it was fierce; and their wrath, for it was cruell: I will diuide them in Iacob, and ſcatter them in Iſrael.[8]Iudah, thou art he whom thy brethren ſhall praiſe: thy hand ſhall be in the necke of thine enemies, thy fathers children ſhall bow downe before thee.[9]Iudah is a Lyons whelpe: from the pray my ſonne thou art gone vp: he ſtouped downe, hee couched as a Lyon, and as an old Lyon: who ſhall rouſe him vp?[10]The ſcepter ſhall not depart from Iudah, nor a Law-giuer from betweene his feete, vntill Shiloh come: and vnto him ſhall the gathering of the people be:[11]Binding his foale vnto the vine, and his aſſes colt vnto the choice vine; he waſhed his garments in wine, and his clothes in the blood of grapes.[12]His eyes ſhall be red with wine, and his teeth white with milke.[13]Zebulun ſhall dwell at the hauen of the ſea, and hee ſhall be for an Hauen of ſhips: and his border ſhall be vnto Zidon.[14]Iſſachar is a ſtrong aſſe, couching downe betweene two burdens.[15]And he ſaw that reſt was good, and the land that it was pleaſant: and bowed his ſhoulder to beare, and became a ſeruant vnto tribute.[16]Dan ſhall iudge his people, as one of the tribes of Iſrael.[17]Dan ſhalbe a ſerpent by the way, an adder in the path, that biteth the horſe heeles, ſo that his rider ſhall fall backward.[18]I haue waited for thy ſaluation, O LORD.[19]Gad, a troupe ſhall ouercome him: but he ſhall ouercome at the laſt.[20]Out of Aſher his bread ſhall be fat, and he ſhall yeeld royall dainties.[21]Naphtali is a hinde let looſe: He giueth goodly words.[22]Ioſeph is a fruitfull bough, euen a fruitfull bough by a well, whoſe branches runne ouer the wall.[23]The archers haue ſorely grieued him, and ſhot at him, and hated him.[24]But his bow abode in ſtrength, and the armes of his hands were made ſtrong, by the hands of the mighty God of Iacob: from thence is the Sheapheard, the ſtone of Iſrael,[25]Euen by the God of thy father who ſhall helpe thee, and by the Almightie, who ſhall bleſſe thee with bleſſings of heauen aboue, bleſſings of the deepe that lyeth vnder, bleſſings of the breaſts and of the wombe.[26]The bleſſings of thy father haue preuailed aboue the bleſſings of my progenitors: vnto the vtmoſt bound of the euerlaſting hils, they ſhall bee on the head of Ioſeph, and on the crowne of the head of him that was ſeparate from his brethren.[27]Beniamin ſhall rauine as a wolfe: In the morning hee ſhall deuoure the pray, and at night he ſhall diuide the ſpoile.[28]All theſe are the twelue tribes of Iſrael, and this is it that their father ſpake vnto them, and bleſſed them: euery one according to his bleſſing he bleſſed them.[29]And hee charged them and ſaid vnto them, I am to bee gathered vnto my people: burie me with my fathers, in the caue that is in the field of Ephron the Hittite,[30]In the caue that is in the field of Machpelah, which is before Mamre, in the land of Canaan, which Abraham bought with the field of Ephron the Hittite, for a poſſeſſion of a burying place.[31](There they buried Abraham and Sarah his wife, there they buried Iſaac and Rebekah his wife, and there I buried Leah.)[32]The purchaſe of the field and of the caue that is therein, was from the children of Heth.[33]And when Iacob had made an end of commanding his ſonnes, he gathered vp his feete into the bed, and yeelded vp the ghoſt, and was gathered vnto his people.

CHAPTER 50[1]And Ioſeph fell vpon his fathers face, and wept vpon him, and kiſſed him.[2]And Ioſeph commanded his ſeruants the phyſicians to imbalme his father: and the phyſicians imbalmed Iſrael.[3]And fortie dayes were fulfilled for him, (for ſo are fulfilled the dayes of thoſe which are imbalmed) and the Egyptians mourned for him threeſcore and ten dayes.[4]And when the dayes of his mourning were paſt, Ioſeph ſpake vnto the houſe of Pharaoh, ſaying, If now I haue found grace in your eyes, ſpeake, I pray you, in the eares of Pharaoh, ſaying,[5]My father made me ſweare, ſaying, Loe, I die: in my graue which I haue digged for me, in the land of Canaan, there ſhalt thou bury me. Now therfore let me goe vp, I pray thee, and bury my father, and I will come againe.[6]And Pharaoh ſaid, Goe vp, and bury thy father, according as he made thee ſweare.[7]And Ioſeph went vp to bury his father: and with him went vp all the ſeruants of Pharaoh, the elders of his houſe, and all the elders of the land of Egypt,[8]And all the houſe of Ioſeph, and his brethren, and his fathers houſe: onely their litle ones, and their flockes, and their heards, they left in the land of Goſhen.[9]And there went vp with him both charets and horſemen: and it was a very great company.[10]And they came to the threſhing floore of Atad, which is beyond Iordan, and there they mourned with a great and very ſore lamentation: and he made a mourning for his father ſeuen dayes.[11]And when the inhabitants of the land, the Canaanites ſawe the mourning in the floore of Atad, they ſaide, This is a grieuous mourning to the Egyptians: wherfore the name of it was called, Abel Mizraim, which is beyond Iordan.[12]And his ſonnes did vnto him according as he commanded them.[13]For his ſonnes caried him into the land of Canaan, and buried him in the caue of the field of Machpelah, which Abraham bought with the field for a poſſeſſion of a burying place, of Ephron the Hittite, before Mamre.[14]And Ioſeph returned into Egypt, he and his brethren, and all that went vp with him, to bury his father, after he had buried his father.[15]And when Ioſephs brethren ſaw that their father was dead, they ſaid, Ioſeph will peraduenture hate vs, and will certainely requite vs all the euill which we did vnto him.[16]And they ſent a meſſenger vnto Ioſeph, ſaying, Thy father did command before he died, ſaying,[17]So ſhall ye ſay vnto Ioſeph, Forgiue, I pray thee now, the treſpaſſe of thy brethren, and their ſinne: for they did vnto thee euill: And now wee pray thee, forgiue the treſpaſſe of the ſeruants of the God of thy father. And Ioſeph wept, when they ſpake vnto him.[18]And his brethren alſo went and fell downe before his face, and they ſaid, Behold, we be thy ſeruants.[19]And Ioſeph ſaide vnto them, Feare not: for am I in the place of God?[20]But as for you, yee thought euill againſt me, but God meant it vnto good, to bring to paſſe, as it is this day, to ſaue much people aliue.[21]Now therefore feare yee not: I will nouriſh you, and your litle ones. And hee comforted them, and ſpake kindly vnto them.[22]And Ioſeph dwelt in Egypt, he, and his fathers houſe: and Ioſeph liued an hundred and ten yeeres.[23]And Ioſeph ſawe Ephraims children, of the third generation: the children alſo of Machir, the ſonne of Manaſſeh were brought vp vpon Ioſephs knees.[24]And Ioſeph ſaide vnto his brethren, I die: and God will ſurely viſit you, and bring you out of this land, vnto the land which hee ſware to Abraham, to Iſaac, and to Iacob.[25]And Ioſeph tooke an othe of the children of Iſrael, ſaying, God will ſurely viſite you, and ye ſhal carie vp my bones from hence.[26]So Ioſeph died, being an hundred and ten yeeres old: and they imbalmed him, and he was put in a coffin, in Egypt.

EXODUS

CHAPTER 1[1]Nowe theſe are the names of the children of Iſrael, which came into Egypt, euery man & his houſehold, came with Iacob.[2]Reuben, Simeon, Leui, and Iudah,[3]Iſſachar, Zebulun and Beniamin,[4]Dan, and Naphtali, Gad, and Aſher.[5]And all the ſoules that came out of the loynes of Iacob, were ſeuentie ſoules: for Ioſeph was in Egypt already.[6]And

Ioſeph died, and all his brethren, and all that generation.7And the children of Iſrael were fruitfull, and increaſed aboundantly, and multiplied, and waxed exceeding mighty, and the land was filled with them.8Now there aroſe vp a new King ouer Egypt, which knew not Ioſeph.9And he ſaid vnto his people, Behold, the people of the children of Iſrael are moe and mightier then we.10Come on, let vs deale wiſely with them, leſt they multiply, and it come to paſſe that when there falleth out any warre, they ioyne alſo vnto our enemies, and fight againſt vs, and ſo get them vp out of the land.11Therefore they did ſet ouer them taſk-maſters, to afflict them with their burdens: And they built for Pharaoh treaſure-cities, Pithom and Raamſes.12But the more they afflicted them, the more they multiplied and grew: and they were grieued becauſe of the children of Iſrael.13And the Egyptians made the children of Iſrael to ſerue with rigour.14And they made their liues bitter, with hard bondage, in morter and in bricke, and in all maner of ſeruice in the fielde: all their ſeruice wherein they made them ſerue, was with rigour.15And the King of Egypt ſpake to the Hebrew midwiues, (of which the name of one was Shiphrah, and the name of the other Puah.)16And he ſaid, When ye do the office of a midwife to the Hebrew-women, and ſee them vpon the ſtooles, if it be a ſonne, then ye ſhall kill him: but if it be a daughter, then ſhee ſhall liue.17But the midwiues feared God, and did not as the King of Egypt commanded them, but ſaued the men children aliue.18And the King of Egypt called for the midwiues, & ſaid vnto them, Why haue ye done this thing, and haue ſaued the men children aliue?19And the midwiues ſaid vnto Pharaoh, Becauſe the Hebrew women are not as the Egyptian women: for they are liuely, and are deliuered ere the midwiues come in vnto them.20Therefore God dealt well with the midwiues: and the people multiplied and waxed very mighty.21And it came to paſſe, becauſe the midwiues feared God, that hee made them houſes.22And Pharaoh charged all his people, ſaying, Euery ſonne that is borne, yee ſhall caſt into the riuer, and euery daughter ye ſhall ſaue aliue.

CHAPTER 21And there went a man of the houſe of Leui, & tooke to wife a daughter of Leui.2And the woman conceiued, and bare a ſonne: and when ſhee ſaw him that hee was a goodly childe, ſhee hid him three moneths.3And when ſhee could not longer hide him, ſhe tooke for him an arke of bul-ruſhes, and daubed it with ſlime, and with pitch, and put the childe therein, and ſhee layd it in the flags by the riuers brinke.4And his ſiſter ſtood afarre off, to wit what would be done to him.5And the daughter of Pharaoh came downe to waſh her ſelfe at the riuer, and her maydens walked along by the riuer ſide: and when ſhee ſaw the arke among the flags, ſhe ſent her maid to fetch it.6And when ſhe had opened it, ſhe ſaw the childe: and beholde, the babe wept. And ſhe had compaſſion on him, and ſaid, This is one of the Hebrewes children.7Then ſaid his ſiſter to Pharaohs daughter, Shall I goe, and call to thee a nurſe of the Hebrew-women, that ſhe may nurſe the childe for thee?8And Pharaohs daughter ſaid to her, Goe: And the mayd went and called the childs mother.9And Pharaohs daughter ſaid vnto her, Take this child away, and nurſe it for me, and I will giue thee thy wages. And the woman tooke the childe, and nurſed it.10And the childe grew, and ſhee brought him vnto Pharaohs daughter, and he became her ſonne. And ſhe called his name Moſes: And ſhe ſaid, Becauſe I drew him out of the water.11And it came to paſſe in thoſe dayes, when Moſes was growen, that he went out vnto his brethren, and looked on their burdens, and he ſpied an Egyptian ſmiting an Hebrew, one of his brethren.12And he looked this way and that way, and when he ſaw that there was no man, he ſlew the Egyptian, and hid him in the ſand.13And when he went out the ſecond day, behold, two men of the Hebrewes ſtroue together: And hee ſaid to him that did the wrong, Wherefore ſmiteſt thou thy fellow?14And he ſaid, Who made thee a Prince and a iudge ouer vs? intendeſt thou to kill me, as thou killedſt the Egyptian? And Moſes feared, and ſaid, Surely this thing is knowen.15Now when Pharaoh heard this thing, he ſought to ſlay Moſes. But Moſes fled from the face of Pharaoh, and dwelt in the land of Midian: and he ſate downe by a well.16Now the Prieſt of Midian had ſeuen daughters, and they came and drew water, and filled the troughes to water their fathers flocke.17And the ſhepheards came and droue them away: but Moſes ſtood vp and helped them, & watred their flocke.18And when they came to Reuel their father, he ſaid, How is it that you are come ſo ſoone to day?19And they ſaid, An Egyptian deliuered vs out of the hand of the ſhepheards, and alſo drew water enough for vs, and watered the flocke.20And he ſaid vnto his daughters, And where is he? why is it that yee haue left the man? Call him, that hee may eate bread.21And Moſes was content to dwel with the man, and he gaue Moſes Zipporah his daughter.22And ſhe bare him a ſonne, and he called his name Gerſhom: for he ſaid, I haue bene a ſtranger in a ſtrange land.23And it came to paſſe in proceſſe of time, that the king of Egypt died, and the children of Iſrael ſighed by reaſon of the bondage, and they cried, and their cry came vp vnto God, by reaſon of the bondage.24And God heard their groning, and God remembred his Couenant with Abraham, with Iſaac, and with Iacob.25And God looked vpon the children of Iſrael, and God had reſpect vnto them.

CHAPTER 31Nowe Moſes kept the flocke of Iethro his father in law, the Prieſt of Midian: and hee led the flocke to the backeſide of the deſert, and came to the mountaine of God, euen to Horeb.2And the Angel of the Lord appeared vnto him, in a flame of fire out of the midſt of a buſh, and he looked, and behold, the buſh burned with fire, and the buſh was not conſumed.3And Moſes ſaide, I will nowe turne aſide, and ſee this great ſight, why the buſh is not burnt.4And when the Lord ſawe that he turned aſide to ſee, God called vnto him out of the midſt of the buſh, and ſaid, Moſes, Moſes. And he ſaide, Here am I.5And he ſaid, Drawe not nigh hither: put off thy ſhooes from off thy feete, for the place whereon thou ſtandeſt, is holy ground.6Moreouer hee ſaid, I am the God of thy father, the God of Abraham, the God of Iſaac, and the God of Iacob. And Moſes hid his face: for he was afraid to looke vpon God.7And the Lord ſaid, I haue ſurely ſeene the affliction of my people which are in Egypt, and haue heard their crie, by reaſon of their taſke-maſters: for I know their ſorrowes,8And I am come downe to deliuer them out of the hand of the Egyptians, and to bring them vp out of that land, vnto a good land and a large, vnto a lande flowing with milke and hony, vnto the place of the Canaanites, and the Hittites, and the Amorites, and the Perizzites, and the Hiuites, and the Iebuſites.9Now therefore behold, the crie of the children of Iſrael is come vnto me: and I haue alſo ſeene the oppreſſion wherewith the Egyptians oppreſſe them.10Come now therefore, and I will ſend thee vnto Pharaoh, that thou mayeſt bring forth my people the children of Iſrael out of Egypt.11And Moſes ſaide vnto God, Who am I, that I ſhould goe vnto Pharaoh, and that I ſhould bring forth the children of Iſrael out of Egypt?12And he ſaid, Certainely I will be with thee, and this ſhall be a token vnto thee, that I haue ſent thee: When thou haſt brought foorth the people out of Egypt, ye ſhall ſerue God vpon this mountaine.13And Moſes ſaide vnto God, Behold, when I come vnto the children of Iſrael, and ſhall ſay vnto them, The God of your fathers hath ſent me vnto you; and they ſhall ſay to me, What is his name? what ſhall I ſay vnto them?14And God ſaide vnto Moſes, I AM THAT I AM: And he ſaid, Thus ſhalt thou ſay vnto the children of Iſrael, I AM hath ſent me vnto you.15And God ſaid moreouer vnto Moſes, Thus ſhalt thou ſay vnto the children of Iſrael; The Lord God of your fathers, the God of Abraham, the God of Iſaac, and the God of Iacob hath ſent me vnto you: this is my name for euer, and this is my memoriall vnto all generations.16Goe and gather the Elders of Iſrael together, and ſay vnto them, The Lord God of your fathers, the God of Abraham, of Iſaac, and of Iacob appeared vnto me, ſaying, I haue ſurely viſited you, and ſeene that which is done to you in Egypt.17And I haue ſaid, I will bring you vp out of the affliction of Egypt, vnto the land of the Canaanites, and the Hittites, and the Amorites, and the Perizzites, and the Hiuites, and the Iebuſites, vnto a land flowing with milke and hony.18And they ſhall hearken to thy voyce: and thou ſhalt come, thou and the Elders of Iſrael vnto the King of Egypt, and you ſhall ſay vnto him, The Lord God of the Hebrewes hath met with vs: and now let vs goe, (wee beſeech thee) three dayes iourney into the wildernes, that we may ſacrifice to the Lord our God.19And I am ſure that the King of Egypt will not let you goe, no not by a mightie hand.20And I will ſtretch out my hand, and ſmite Egypt with all my wonders which I will doe in the midſt thereof: and after that he will let you goe.21And I will giue this people fauour in the ſight of the Egyptians, and it ſhall come to paſſe that when ye goe, ye ſhall not goe empty:22But euery woman ſhal borrow of her neighbour, and of her that ſoiourneth in her houſe, iewels of ſiluer, and iewels of gold, and rayment: and ye ſhall put them vpon your ſonnes and vpon your daughters, and yee ſhall ſpoile the Egyptians.

CHAPTER 41And Moſes anſwered, and ſaid, But behold, they will not beleeue mee, nor hearken vnto my voice: for they will ſay, The Lord hath not appeared vnto thee.2And the Lord ſaid vnto him, What is that in thine hand? and hee ſaid, A rod.3And he ſaid, Caſt it on the ground: And he caſt it on the ground, and it became a ſerpent: and Moſes fled from before it.4And the Lord ſaid vnto Moſes, Put forth thine hand, and take it by the taile: And he put foorth his hand, and caught it, and it became a rod in his hand:5That they may beleeue that the Lord God of their fathers, the God of Abraham, the God of Iſaac, and the God of Iacob hath appeared vnto thee.6And the Lord ſaid furthermore vnto him, Put now thine hand into thy boſome. And he put his hand into his boſome: and when hee tooke it out, behold, his hand was leprous as ſnowe.7And he ſaid, Put thine hand into thy boſome againe. And hee put his hand into his boſome againe, and plucked it out of his boſome, and behold, it was turned againe as his other fleſh.8And it ſhall come to paſſe, if they wil not beleeue thee, neither hearken to the voice of the firſt ſigne, that they will beleeue the voice of the latter ſigne.9And it ſhall come to paſſe, if they will not beleeue alſo theſe two ſignes, neither hearken vnto thy voice, that thou ſhalt take of the water of the riuer, and powre it vpon the drie land: and the water which thou takeſt out of the riuer, ſhall become blood vpon the drie land.10And Moſes ſaide vnto the Lord, O my lord, I am not eloquent, neither heretofore, nor ſince thou haſt ſpoken vnto thy ſeruant: but I am ſlow of ſpeach, and of a ſlow tongue.11And the Lord ſaid vnto him, Who hath made mans mouth? or who maketh the dumbe or deafe, or the ſeeing, or þe blind? haue not I the Lord?12Now therefore goe, and I will be with thy mouth, and teach thee what thou ſhalt ſay.13And he ſaid, O my Lord, ſend, I pray thee, by the hand of him whom thou wilt ſend.14And the anger of the Lord was kindled againſt Moſes, and hee ſaid, Is not Aaron the Leuite thy brother? I know that he can ſpeake well. And alſo behold, he commeth foorth to meet thee: and when he ſeeth thee, hee will be glad in his heart.15And thou ſhalt ſpeake vnto him, and put words in his mouth, and I wil be with thy mouth, & with his mouth, and will teach you what ye ſhall doe.16And he ſhal be thy ſpokeſman vnto the people: and he ſhall be, euen hee ſhall be to thee in ſtead of a mouth, and thou ſhalt be to him in ſtead of God.17And thou ſhalt take this rod in thine hand, wherewith thou ſhalt doe ſignes.18And Moſes went and returned to Iethro his father in law, and ſaid vnto him, Let me goe, I pray thee, and returne vnto my brethren, which are in Egypt, and ſee whether they bee yet aliue. And Iethro ſaid to Moſes, Goe in peace.19And the Lord ſaid vnto Moſes in Midian, Goe, returne into Egypt: for all the men are dead which ſought thy life.20And Moſes tooke his wife, and his ſonnes, and ſet them vpon an aſſe, and he returned to the land of Egypt. And Moſes tooke the rod of God in his hand.21And the Lord ſaid vnto Moſes, When thou goeſt to returne into Egypt, ſee that thou doe all thoſe wonders before Pharaoh, which I haue put in thine hand: but I wil harden his heart, that hee ſhall not let the people goe.22And thou ſhalt ſay vnto Pharaoh, Thus ſaith the Lord, Iſrael is my ſonne, euen my firſt borne.23And I ſay vnto thee, let my ſonne goe, that he may ſerue mee: and if thou refuſe to let him goe, behold, I will ſlay thy ſonne, euen thy firſt borne.24And it came to paſſe by the way in the Inne, that the Lord met him, and ſought to kill him.25Then Zipporah tooke a ſharpe ſtone, and cut off the foreſkinne of her ſonne, and caſt it at his feete, and ſaid, Surely a bloody huſband art thou to mee.26So he let him goe: then ſhe ſaid, A bloody huſband thou art, becauſe of the Circumciſion.27And the Lord ſaid to Aaron, Goe into the wilderneſſe to meete Moſes. And hee went and met him in the mount of God, and kiſſed him.28And Moſes tolde Aaron all the wordes of the Lord, who had ſent him, and all the ſignes which hee had commanded him.29And Moſes and Aaron went, and gathered together all the elders of the children of Iſrael.30And Aaron ſpake all the wordes which the Lord had ſpoken vnto Moſes, and did the ſignes in the ſight of the people.31And the people beleeued: And when they heard that the Lord had viſited the children of Iſrael, and that he had looked vpon their affliction, then they bowed their heads and worſhipped.

CHAPTER 51And afterward Moſes and Aaron went in, and tolde Pharaoh, Thus ſaith the Lord God of Iſrael, Let my people goe, that they may holde a feaſt vnto mee in the wilderneſſe.2And Pharaoh ſaid, Who is the Lord, that I ſhould obey his voyce to let Iſrael goe? I know not the Lord, neither will I let Iſrael goe.3And they ſaid, The God of the Hebrewes hath met with vs: let vs goe, we pray thee, three dayes iourney into the deſert, and ſacrifice vnto the Lord our God, leſt hee fall vpon vs with peſtilence, or with the ſword.4And the King of Egypt ſaid vnto them, Wherfore doe ye, Moſes and Aaron, let the people from their workes? get you vnto your burdens.5And Pharaoh ſaid, Behold, the people of the land now are many, & you make them reſt from their burdens.6And Pharaoh commanded the ſame day the taſke-maſters of the people, and their officers, ſaying;7Yee ſhall no more giue the people ſtraw to make bricke, as heretofore: let them goe and gather ſtraw for themſelues.8And the tale of the brickes which they did make heretofore, you ſhall lay vpon them: you ſhall not diminiſh ought thereof: for they be idle; therefore they cry, ſaying, Let us goe and ſacrifice to our God.9Let there more worke be layde vpon the men, that they may labour therein, and let them not regard vaine wordes.10And the taſke-maſters of the people went out, and their officers, and they ſpake to the people, ſaying, Thus ſaith Pharaoh, I will not giue you ſtraw.11Goe ye, get you ſtraw where you can find it: yet not ought of your worke ſhall be diminiſhed.12So the people were ſcattered abroad throughout al the land of Egypt, to gather ſtubble in ſtead of ſtraw.13And the taſke-maſters haſted them, ſaying; Fulfill your workes, your dayly taſkes, as when there was ſtraw.14And the officers of the children of Iſrael, which Pharaohs taſk-maſters had ſet ouer them, were beaten, and demanded, Wherefore haue ye not fulfilled your taſke, in making bricke, both yeſterday and to day, as heretofore?15Then the officers of the children of Iſrael came and cryed vnto Pharaoh, ſaying, Wherefore dealeſt thou thus with thy ſeruants?16There is no ſtraw giuen vnto thy ſeruants, and they ſay to vs, Make bricke: and beholde, thy ſeruants are beaten; but the fault is in thine owne people.17But he ſaid, Ye are idle, ye are idle: therefore ye ſay, Let vs goe and doe ſacrifice to the Lord.18Goe therefore now and worke: for there ſhall no ſtraw bee giuen you, yet ſhall ye deliuer the tale of brickes.19And the officers of the children of Iſrael did ſee that they were in euill caſe, after it was ſaid, Yee ſhall not miniſh ought from your brickes of your dayly taſke.20And they met Moſes and Aaron, who ſtood in the way, as they came foorth from Pharaoh.21And they ſaid vnto them; The Lord looke vpon you, and iudge, becauſe you haue made our ſauour to be abhorred in the eyes of Pharaoh, and in the eyes of his ſeruants, to put a ſword in their hand to ſlay vs.22And Moſes returned vnto the Lord, and ſaid, Lord, Wherefore haſt thou ſo euill intreated this people? Why is it that thou haſt ſent me?23For ſince I came to Pharaoh to ſpeake in thy Name, he hath done euill to this people, neither haſt thou deliuered thy people at all.

CHAPTER 61Then the Lord ſaid vnto Moſes, Now ſhalt thou ſee what I will doe to Pharaoh: for with a ſtrong hand ſhall hee let them goe, and with a ſtrong hand ſhall he driue them out of his land.2And God ſpake vnto Moſes, and ſaid vnto him, I am the Lord.3And I appeared vnto Abraham, vnto Iſaac, and vnto Iacob, by the Name of God Almighty, but by my name IEHOVAH was I not knowen to them.4And I haue alſo eſtabliſhed my Couenant with them, to giue them the land of Canaan, the land of their pilgrimage, wherein they were ſtrangers.5And I haue alſo heard the groning of the children of Iſrael, whom the Egyptians keepe in bondage: and I haue remembred my Couenant.6Wherefore ſay vnto the children of Iſrael, I am the Lord, and I will bring you out from vnder the burdens of the Egyptians, and I will rid you out of their bondage: and I will redeeme you with a ſtretched out arme, and with great iudgements.7And I will take you to mee for a people, and I will be to you a God: and ye ſhall know that I am the Lord your God, which bringeth you out from vnder the burdens of the Egyptians.8And I will bring you in vnto the lande concerning the which I did ſweare to giue it, to Abraham, to Iſaac, and to Iacob, and I will giue it you for an heritage, I am the Lord.9And Moſes ſpake ſo vnto the children of Iſrael: but they hearkened not vnto Moſes, for anguiſh of ſpirit, and for cruell bondage.10And the Lord ſpake vnto Moſes, ſaying,11Goe in, ſpeake vnto Pharaoh King of Egypt, that he let the children of Iſrael goe out of his land.12And Moſes ſpake before the Lord, ſaying, Behold, the children of Iſrael haue not hearkened vnto me: how then ſhal Pharaoh heare me, who am of vncircumciſed lips?13And the Lord ſpake vnto Moſes and vnto Aaron, & gaue them a charge vnto the children of Iſrael, and vnto Pharaoh King of Egypt, to bring the children of Iſrael out of the land of Egypt.14Theſe be the heads of their fathers houſes: The ſonnes of Reuben the firſt borne of Iſrael, Hanoch, and

Pallu, Hezron, and Carmi: theſe be the families of Reuben. 15 And the
ſonnes of Simeon: Iemuel, and Iamin, and Ohad and Iachin, and Zohar,
and Shaul the ſonne of a Canaanitiſh woman: theſe are the families of
Simeon. 16 And theſe are the names of the ſonnes of Leui, according to
their generations: Gerſhon and Kohath and Merari: and the yeeres of
the life of Leui, were an hundred, thirtie and ſeuen yeeres. 17 The ſonnes
of Gerſhon: Libni and Shimi, according to their families. 18 And the
ſonnes of Kohath: Amram, and Izhar, and Hebron, and Uzziel. And the
yeeres of the life of Kohath, were an hundred thirtie and three
yeeres. 19 And the ſonnes of Merari: Mahali and Muſhi: theſe are the
families of Leui, according to their generations. 20 And Amram tooke him
Iochebed his fathers ſiſter to wife, and ſhee bare him Aaron and Moſes:
and the yeeres of the life of Amram were an hundred, and thirtie and
ſeuen yeeres. 21 And the ſonnes of Izhar: Korah and Nepheg, and
Zichri. 22 And the ſonnes of Uzziel: Miſhael, and Elzaphan, and
Zithri. 23 And Aaron tooke him Eliſheba daughter of Amminadab ſiſter
of Naaſhon to wife, and ſhe bare him Nadab and Abihu, Eleazar and
Ithamar. 24 And the ſonnes of Korah, Aſsir, and Elkanah, and Abiaſaph:
theſe are the families of the Korhites. 25 And Eleazar Aarons ſonne tooke
him one of the daughters of Putiel to wife, and ſhe bare him Phinehas:
theſe are the heads of the fathers of the Leuites, according to their
families. 26 Theſe are that Aaron and Moſes, to whom the Lord ſaid,
Bring out the children of Iſrael from the land of Egypt, according to
their armies. 27 Theſe are they which ſpake to Pharaoh king of Egypt, to
bring out the children of Iſrael from Egypt: Theſe are that Moſes and
Aaron. 28 And it came to paſſe on the day when the Lord ſpake vnto
Moſes in the land of Egypt, 29 That the Lord ſpake vnto Moſes, ſaying, I
am the Lord: ſpeake thou vnto Pharaoh king of Egypt, all that I ſay vnto
thee. 30 And Moſes ſaid before the Lord, Behold, I am of vncircumciſed
lips, and how ſhall Pharaoh hearken vnto mee?
CHAPTER 7 1 And the Lord ſaid vnto Moſes, See, I haue made thee a
god to Pharaoh, and Aaron thy brother ſhalbe thy prophet. 2 Thou ſhalt
ſpeake all that I command thee, and Aaron thy brother ſhall ſpeake vnto
Pharaoh, that he ſend the children of Iſrael out of his land. 3 And I will
harden Pharaohs heart, and multiplie my ſignes and my wonders in the
land of Egypt. 4 But Pharaoh ſhall not hearken vnto you, that I may lay
my hand vpon Egypt, and bring forth mine armies, and my people the
children of Iſrael, out of the land of Egypt, by great iudgments. 5 And the
Egyptians ſhall knowe that I am the Lord, when I ſtretch forth mine
hand vpon Egypt, and bring out the children of Iſrael from among
them. 6 And Moſes and Aaron did as the Lord commanded them, ſo did
they. 7 And Moſes was foureſcore yeres olde, and Aaron foureſcore and
three yeeres old, when they ſpake vnto Pharaoh. 8 And the Lord ſpake
vnto Moſes, and vnto Aaron, ſaying: 9 When Pharaoh ſhall ſpeake vnto
you, ſaying, ſhew a miracle for you: then thou ſhalt ſay vnto Aaron, Take
thy rod and caſt it before Pharaoh, and it ſhall become a ſerpent. 10 And
Moſes and Aaron went in vnto Pharaoh, and they did ſo as the Lord had
commanded: and Aaron caſt downe his rod before Pharaoh, and before
his ſeruants, and it became a ſerpent. 11 Then Pharaoh alſo called the wiſe
men and the ſorcerers; now the Magicians of Egypt, they alſo did in like
maner with their enchantments. 12 For they caſt downe euery man his
rod, and they became ſerpents: but Aarons rod ſwallowed vp their
rods. 13 And hee hardened Pharaohs heart, that hee hearkened not vnto
them, as the Lord had ſaid. 14 And the Lord ſaide vnto Moſes, Pharaohs
heart is hardened: he refuſeth to let the people goe. 15 Get thee vnto
Pharaoh in the morning, loe, he goeth out vnto the water, and thou ſhalt
ſtand by the riuers brinke, againſt hee come: and the rod which was
turned to a ſerpent, ſhalt thou take in thine hand. 16 And thou ſhalt ſay
vnto him, The Lord God of the Hebrewes hath ſent me vnto thee,
ſaying; Let my people goe, that they may ſerue mee in the wilderneſſe:
and beholde, hitherto thou wouldeſt not heare. 17 Thus ſaith the Lord, In
this thou ſhalt know that I am the Lord: behold, I will ſmite with the
rod that is in my hand, vpon the waters which are in the riuer, and they
ſhalbe turned to blood. 18 And the fiſh that is in the riuer ſhall die, and
the riuer ſhall ſtincke, and the Egyptians ſhall loathe to drinke of the
water of the riuer. 19 And the Lord ſpake vnto Moſes, ſay vnto Aaron,
Take thy rod, & ſtretch out thine hand vpon the waters of Egypt, vpon
their ſtreames, vpon their riuers, and vpon their ponds, and vpon all
their pooles of water, that they may become blood, and that there may
be blood throughout all the land of Egypt, both in veſſels of wood, and
in veſſels of ſtone. 20 And Moſes and Aaron did ſo, as the Lord
commanded: and he lift vp the rod and ſmote the waters that were in
the riuer, in the ſight of Pharaoh, and in the ſight of his ſeruants: and all
the waters that were in the riuer, were turned to blood. 21 And the fiſh
that was in the riuer died: and the riuer ſtunke, and the Egyptians could
not drinke of the water of the riuer: and there was blood throughout all
the land Egypt. 22 And the Magicians of Egypt did ſo, with their
enchantments: and Pharaohs heart was hardened, neither did he hearken
vnto them, as the Lord had ſaid. 23 And Pharaoh turned and went into
his houſe, neither did hee ſet his heart to this alſo. 24 And all the
Egyptians digged round about the riuer for water to drinke: for they
could not drinke of the water of the riuer. 25 And ſeuen dayes were
fulfilled after that the Lord had ſmitten the riuer.
CHAPTER 8 1 And the Lord ſpake vnto Moſes, Goe vnto Pharaoh, and
ſay vnto him; Thus ſayeth the Lord, Let my people goe, that they may
ſerue me. 2 And if thou refuſe to let them goe, beholde, I will ſmite all thy
borders with frogges. 3 And the riuer ſhall bring foorth frogges
abundantly, which ſhall goe vp and come into thine houſe, and into thy
bed-chamber, and vpon thy bed, and into the houſe of thy ſeruants, and
vpon thy people, and into thine ouens, and into thy kneading
troughes. 4 And the frogges ſhall come vp both on thee, and vpon thy
people, and vpon all thy ſeruants. 5 And the Lord ſpake vnto Moſes; ſay
vnto Aaron, Stretch foorth thine hand with thy rodde ouer the ſtreames,
ouer the riuers, and ouer the ponds, and cauſe frogges to come vp vpon
the land of Egypt. 6 And Aaron ſtretched out his hand ouer the waters of
Egypt, and the frogges came vp, and couered the land of Egypt. 7 And
the Magicians did ſo with their inchantments, and brought vp frogges
vpon the land of Egypt. 8 Then Pharaoh called for Moſes, and Aaron,
and ſaid, Intreat the Lord, that hee may take away the frogges from me,
and from my people: and I will let the people goe, that they may doe
ſacrifice vnto the Lord. 9 And Moſes ſaide vnto Pharaoh, Glory ouer
mee: when ſhall I entreat for thee, and for thy ſeruants, and for thy
people, to deſtroy the frogges from thee, and thy houſes, that they may
remaine in the riuer onely? 10 And he ſaid, To morrow. And hee ſaid, Bee
it according to thy word: That thou mayeſt know that there is none like
vnto the Lord our God. 11 And the frogs ſhall depart from thee, and from
thy houſes, and from thy ſeruants, and from thy people; they ſhall
remaine in the riuer onely. 12 And Moſes and Aaron went out from
Pharaoh, and Moſes cried vnto the Lord becauſe of the frogs which he
had brought againſt Pharaoh. 13 And the Lord did according to the word
of Moſes: and the frogges died out of the houſes, out of the villages, and
out of the fields. 14 And they gathered them together vpon heapes, and
the land ſtanke. 15 But when Pharaoh ſaw that there was reſpit, he
hardned his heart, and hearkened not vnto them, as the Lord had
ſaid. 16 And the Lord ſaide vnto Moſes, ſay vnto Aaron, Stretch out thy
rod, and ſmite the duſt of the land, that it may become lice, thorowout
all the land of Egypt. 17 And they did ſo: for Aaron ſtretched out his hand
with his rod, and ſmote the duſt of the earth, and it became lice, in man
and in beaſt: all the duſt of the land became lice throughout all the land
of Egypt. 18 And the Magicians did ſo with their enchantments to bring
foorth lice, but they could not: ſo there were lice vpon man and vpon
beaſt. 19 Then the Magicians ſaid vnto Pharaoh; This is the finger of God.
And Pharaohs heart was hardned, and he hearkened not vnto them, as
the Lord had ſaid. 20 And the Lord ſaide vnto Moſes, Riſe vp early in the
morning, and ſtand before Pharaoh: loe, he commeth foorth to the
water, and ſay vnto him; Thus ſaith the Lord, Let my people goe, that
they may ſerue me. 21 Els, if thou wilt not let my people goe, beholde, I
will ſend ſwarmes of flies vpon thee, and vpon thy ſeruants, and vpon
thy people, and into thy houſes: and the houſes of the Egyptians ſhall
bee full of ſwarmes of flies, and alſo the ground whereon they are. 22 And
I will ſeuer in that day the lande of Goſhen in which my people dwell,
that no ſwarmes of flies ſhall be there, to the end thou maieſt know that
I am the Lord in the midſt of the earth. 23 And I will put a diuiſion
betweene my people and thy people: to morrow ſhall this ſigne be. 24 And
the Lord did ſo: and there came a grieuous ſwarme of flies into the houſe
of Pharaoh, and into his ſeruants houſes, and into all the lande of Egypt:
the land was corrupted by reaſon of the ſwarme of flies. 25 And Pharaoh
called for Moſes and for Aaron, and ſaid, Goe yee, ſacrifice to your God
in the land. 26 And Moſes ſaid, It is not meete ſo to doe; for we ſhal
ſacrifice the abomination of the Egyptians, to the Lord our God: Loe,

ſhall we ſacrifice the abomination of the Egyptians before their eyes,
and will they not ſtone vs?27We will goe three dayes iourney into the
wilderneſſe, and ſacrifice to the Lord our God, as he ſhall command
vs.28And Pharaoh ſaid, I wil let you goe that ye may ſacrifice to the Lord
your God, in the wildernes: onely you ſhall not goe very farre away:
intreate for me.29And Moſes ſaid, Behold, I goe out from thee, and I
will intreate the Lord that the ſwarmes of flies may depart from Pharaoh,
from his ſeruants, and from his people to morrow: but let not Pharaoh
deale deceitfully any more, in not letting the people goe to ſacrifice to
the Lord.30And Moſes went out from Pharaoh, and intreated the
Lord:31And the Lord did according to the word of Moſes: and he
remooued the ſwarmes of flies from Pharaoh, from his ſeruants, and
from his people: there remained not one.32And Pharaoh hardened his
heart at this time alſo, neither would hee let the people goe.
CHAPTER 91Then the Lord ſaid vnto Moſes, Goe in vnto Pharaoh,
and tell him, Thus ſaith the Lord God of the Hebrewes, Let my people
goe, that they may ſerue me.2For if thou refuſe to let them goe, and wilt
hold them ſtill,3Behold, the hand of the Lord is vpon thy cattell which
is in the field, vpon the horſes, vpon the aſſes, vpon the camels, vpon
the oxen, and vpon the ſheepe: there ſhall be a very grieuous
murraine.4And the Lord ſhall ſeuer betweene the cattell of Iſrael, and
the cattell of Egypt, and there ſhall nothing die of all that is the childrens
of Iſrael.5And the Lord appointed a ſet time, ſaying, To morrow the
Lord ſhall doe this thing in the land.6And the Lord did that thing on the
morrow; and all the cattell of Egypt died, but of the cattell of the
children of Iſrael died not one.7And Pharaoh ſent, and beholde, there
was not one of the cattell of the Iſraelites dead. And the heart of
Pharaoh was hardened, and he did not let the people goe.8And the Lord
ſaide vnto Moſes, and vnto Aaron, Take to you handfuls of aſhes of the
fornace, and let Moſes ſprinkle it towards the heauen, in the ſight of
Pharaoh:9And it ſhall become ſmall duſt in all the land of Egypt, and
ſhall bee a boyle breaking forth with blaines, vpon man and vpon beaſt,
throughout all the land of Egypt.10And they tooke aſhes of the fornace,
and ſtood before Pharaoh, and Moſes ſprinkled it vp toward heauen:
and it became a boile breaking forth with blaines, vpon man and vpon
beaſt.11And the Magicians could not ſtand before Moſes, becauſe of the
boiles: for the boile was vpon the magicians, and vpon all the
Egyptians.12And the Lord hardened the heart of Pharaoh, and hee
hearkened not vnto them, as the Lord had ſpoken vnto Moſes.13And
the Lord ſaide vnto Moſes, Riſe vp earely in the morning, and ſtand
before Pharaoh, and ſay vnto him, Thus ſaith the Lord God of the
Hebrewes, Let my people goe, that they may ſerue me.14For I will at this
time ſend all my plagues vpon thine heart, and vpon thy ſeruants, and
vpon thy people: that thou mayeſt knowe that there is none like me in
all the earth.15For now I will ſtretch out my hand, that I may ſmite thee
and thy people, with peſtilence, and thou ſhalt be cut off from the
earth.16And in very deede, for this cauſe haue I raiſed thee vp, for to
ſhewe in thee my power, and that my name may be declared throughout
all the earth.17As yet exalteſt thou thy ſelfe againſt my people, that thou
wilt not let them goe?18Behold, to morrow about this time, I wil cauſe
it to raine a very grieuous haile, ſuch as hath not bene in Egypt, ſince
the foundation thereof euen vntill now.19Send therefore now, and
gather thy cattell, and all that thou haſt in the field: for vpon euery man
and beaſt which ſhal be found in the field, and ſhal not bee brought
home, the haile ſhall come downe vpon them, and they ſhall die.20Hee
that feared the word of the Lord amongſt the ſeruants of Pharaoh, made
his ſeruants and his cattell flee into the houſes.21And he that regarded
not the word of the Lord, left his ſeruants and his cattell in the
field.22And the Lord ſaide vnto Moſes, Stretch forth thine hand toward
heauen, that there may be haile in all the land of Egypt, vpon man and
vpon beaſt, and vpon euery herbe of the field, thorowout the land of
Egypt.23And Moſes ſtretched foorth his rod toward heauen, and the
Lord ſent thunder and haile, and the fire ranne along vpon the ground,
and the Lord rained haile vpon the land of Egypt.24So there was haile,
and fire mingled with the haile, very grieuous, ſuch as there was none
like it in all the land of Egypt, ſince it became a nation.25And the haile
ſmote throughout all the land of Egypt, all that was in the field, both
man and beaſt: and the haile ſmote euery herbe of the fielde, and brake
euery tree of the field.26Onely in the land of Goſhen where the children
of Iſrael were, was there no haile.27And Pharaoh ſent, and called for
Moſes and Aaron, and ſaid vnto them, I haue ſinned this time: the Lord
is righteous, and I and my people are wicked.28Entreat the Lord, (for it
is enough) that there be no more mighty thunderings and haile, and I
will let you goe, and ye ſhall ſtay no longer.29And Moſes ſaide vnto him,
Aſsoone as I am gone out of the citie, I will ſpread abroad my hands
vnto the Lord, and the thunder ſhall ceaſe, neither ſhall there be any
more haile: that thou mayeſt know how that the earth is the Lords.30But
as for thee and thy ſeruants, I know that ye will not yet feare the Lord
God.31And the flaxe, and the barley was ſmitten: for the barley was in
the eare, and the flaxe was bolled:32But the wheat and the rye were not
ſmitten: for they were not growen vp.33And Moſes went out of the city
from Pharaoh, and ſpread abroad his hands vnto the Lord: and the
thunders and haile ceaſed, and the raine was not powred vpon the
earth.34And when Pharaoh ſaw that the raine, and the haile and the
thunders were ceaſed, hee ſinned yet more, and hardened his heart, he
and his ſeruants.35And the heart of Pharaoh was hardened, neither
would he let the children of Iſrael goe, as the Lord had ſpoken by Moſes.
CHAPTER 101And the Lord ſaid vnto Moſes, Goe in vnto Pharaoh:
for I haue hardned his heart, and the heart of his ſeruants, that I might
ſhew theſe my ſignes before him:2And that thou mayeſt tell in the eares
of thy ſonne, and of thy ſonnes ſonne, what things I haue wrought in
Egypt, and my ſignes which I haue done amongſt them, that ye may
know how that I am the Lord.3And Moſes and Aaron came in vnto
Pharaoh, and ſaide vnto him, Thus ſaith the Lord God of the Hebrewes,
How long wilt thou refuſe to humble thy ſelfe before mee? Let my
people goe, that they may ſerue me.4Els, if thou refuſe to let my people
goe, behold, to morrow will I bring the locuſts into thy coaſt.5And they
ſhall couer the face of the earth, that one cannot be able to ſee the earth,
and they ſhall eate the reſidue of that which is eſcaped, which remaineth
vnto you from the haile, and ſhall eate euery tree, which groweth for you
out of the field.6And they ſhall fill thy houſes, and the houſes of all thy
ſeruants, and the houſes of all the Egyptians, which neither thy fathers,
nor thy fathers fathers haue ſeene, ſince the day that they were vpon the
earth, vnto this day. And he turned himſelfe, and went out from
Pharaoh.7And Pharaohs ſeruants ſaid vnto him, How long ſhall this
man be a ſnare vnto vs? Let the men goe, that they may ſerue the Lord
their God: Knoweſt thou not yet, that Egypt is deſtroyed?8And Moſes
and Aaron were brought againe vnto Pharaoh: and he ſaid vnto them,
Goe, ſerue the Lord your God: but who are they that ſhall goe?9And
Moſes ſaid, We wil goe with our yong, and with our old, with our ſonnes
and with our daughters, with our flockes and with our heards will we
goe: for we muſt hold a feaſt vnto the Lord.10And he ſaid vnto them;
Let the Lord bee ſo with you, as I will let you goe, and your litle ones.
Looke to it, for euill is before you.11Not ſo: goe now yee that are men,
and ſerue the Lord, for that you did deſire: and they were driuen out
from Pharaohs preſence.12And the Lord ſaid vnto Moſes, Stretch out
thine hand ouer the land of Egypt for the locuſts, that they may come
vp vpon the land of Egypt, and eate euery herbe of the land, euen all
that the haile hath left.13And Moſes ſtretched forth his rod ouer the land
of Egypt, and the Lord brought an Eaſt wind vpon the land all that day,
and all that night: and when it was morning, the Eaſt wind brought the
locuſts.14And the locuſts went vp ouer all the land of Egypt, and reſted
in all the coaſts of Egypt: very grieuous were they: before them there
were no ſuch locuſts as they, neither after them ſhall be ſuch.15For they
couered the face of the whole earth, ſo that the land was darkned, and
they did eate euery herbe of the land, and all the fruit of the trees, which
the haile had left, and there remained not any greene thing in the trees,
or in the herbes of the field, through all the land of Egypt.16Then
Pharaoh called for Moſes and Aaron in haſte: and he ſaid, I haue ſinned
againſt the Lord your God, and againſt you.17Now therefore forgiue, I
pray thee, my ſinne onely this once, and intreat the Lord your God, that
hee may take away from mee this death onely.18And he went out from
Pharaoh, and intreated the Lord.19And the Lord turned a mighty ſtrong
Weſt wind, which tooke away the locuſts, and caſt them into the red ſea:
there remained not one locuſt in all the coaſts of Egypt.20But the Lord
hardened Pharaohs heart, ſo that hee would not let the children of Iſrael
goe.21And the Lord ſaid vnto Moſes, Stretch out thine hand toward
heauen, that there may be darkeneſſe ouer the land of Egypt, euen
darkenes which may be felt.22And Moſes ſtretched foorth his hand
toward heauen: and there was a thicke darkeneſſe in all the land of Egypt

three dayes.23They ſaw not one another, neither roſe any from his place for three dayes: but all the children of Iſrael had light in their dwellings.24And Pharaoh called vnto Moſes, and ſaid, Goe ye, ſerue the Lord: onely let your flockes and your herds be ſtayed: let your litle ones alſo goe with you.25And Moſes ſaide, Thou muſt giue vs alſo ſacrifices, and burnt offerings, that we may ſacrifice vnto the Lord our God.26Our cattell alſo ſhall goe with vs: there ſhall not an hoofe bee left behind: for thereof muſt we take to ſerue the Lord our God: and we knowe not with what wee muſt ſerue the Lord, vntill we come thither.27But the Lord hardened Pharaohs heart, and he would not let them goe.28And Pharaoh ſaid vnto him, Get thee from me, take heed to thy ſelfe: ſee my face no more: for in that day thou ſeeſt my face, thou ſhalt die.29And Moſes ſaid, Thou haſt ſpoken well, I will ſee thy face againe no more.

CHAPTER 111And the Lord ſaid vnto Moſes, Yet will I bring one plague more vpon Pharaoh, and vpon Egypt, afterwards hee will let you goe heuce: when hee ſhall let you goe, he ſhall ſurely thruſt you out hence altogether.2Speake now in the eares of the people, and let euery man borrowe of his neighbour, and euery woman of her neighbour, iewels of ſiluer, and iewels of gold.3And the Lord gaue the people fauour in the ſight of the Egyptians. Moreouer the man Moſes was very great in the land of Egypt, in the ſight of Pharaohs ſeruants, and in the ſight of the people.4And Moſes ſaid, Thus ſaith the Lord, about midnight will I goe out into the midſt of Egypt.5And all the firſt borne in the lande of Egypt ſhall die, from the firſt borne of Pharaoh, that ſitteth vpon his throne, euen vnto the firſt borne of the maid ſeruant that is behind the mill, and all the firſt borne of beaſts.6And there ſhall bee a great crie throughout all the land of Egypt, ſuch as there was none like it, nor ſhall bee like it any more.7But againſt any of the children of Iſrael, ſhal not a dog moue his tongue, againſt man or beaſt: that ye may know how that the Lord doth put a difference betweene the Egyptians and Iſrael.8And all theſe thy ſeruants ſhall come downe vnto me, and bow downe themſelues vnto me, ſaying, Get thee out, and all the people that follow thee; and after that I wil goe out: and he went out from Pharaoh in a great anger.9And the Lord ſaid vnto Moſes, Pharaoh ſhall not hearken vnto you, that my wonders may be multiplied in the land of Egypt.10And Moſes and Aaron did all theſe wonders before Pharaoh: and the Lord hardened Pharaohs heart, ſo that he would not let the children of Iſrael goe out of his land.

CHAPTER 121And the Lord ſpake vnto Moſes and Aaron in the land of Egypt, ſaying,2This moneth ſhalbe vnto you the beginning of moneths: it ſhall be the firſt moneth of the yeere to you.3Speake ye vnto all the Congregation of Iſrael, ſaying, In the tenth day of this moneth they ſhall take to them euery man a lambe, according to the houſe of their fathers, a lambe for an houſe.4And if the houſhold be too little for the lambe, let him and his neighbour next vnto his houſe, take it according to the number of the ſoules: euery man according to his eating ſhall make your count for the lambe.5Your lambe ſhall be without blemiſh, a male of the firſt yeere: yee ſhall take it out from the ſheepe or from the goates.6And ye ſhall keepe it vp vntill the fourteenth day of the ſame moneth: and the whole aſſembly of the congregation of Iſrael ſhall kill it in the euening.7And they ſhall take of the blood and ſtrike it on the two ſide poſtes, and on the vpper doore poſte, of the houſes wherin they ſhall eate it.8And they ſhall eat the fleſh in that night roſte with fire, and vnleauened bread, and with bitter herbes they ſhall eate it.9Eate not of it raw, nor ſodden at all with water, but roſte with fire: his head, with his legs, and with the purtenance thereof.10And ye ſhall let nothing of it remaine vntill the morning: and that which remaineth of it vntill the morning, ye ſhall burne with fire.11And thus ſhall ye eate it: with your loines girded, your ſhooes on your feet, and your ſtaffe in your hand: and ye ſhall eate it in haſte: it is the Lords Paſſeouer.12For I will paſſe through the land of Egypt this night, and will ſmite all the firſt borne in the land of Egypt, both man & beaſt, and againſt all the gods of Egypt I will execute iudgement: I am the Lord.13And the blood ſhall be to you for a token vpon the houſes where you are: and when I ſee the blood, I will paſſe ouer you, and the plague ſhall not bee vpon you to deſtroy you, when I ſmite the land of Egypt.14And this day ſhall be vnto you for a memoriall: and you ſhall keepe in a feaſt to the Lord, throughout your generations: you ſhall keepe it a feaſt by an ordinance for euer.15Seuen dayes ſhall ye eate vnleauened bread, euen the firſt day yee ſhall put away leauen out of your houſes: For whoſoeuer eateth leauened bread, from the firſt day vntil the ſeuenth day, that ſoule ſhall be cut off from Iſrael.16And in the firſt day there ſhalbe an holy conuocation, and in the ſeuenth day there ſhall be an holy conuocation to you: no maner of worke ſhalbe done in them, ſaue that which euery man muſt eate, that onely may bee done of you.17And yee ſhall obſerue the feaſt of vnleauened bread: for in this ſelfe ſame day haue I brought your armies out of the land of Egypt; therefore ſhall ye obſerue this day in your generations, by an ordinance for euer.18In the firſt moneth, on the fourteenth day of the moneth at euen, ye ſhall eate vnleauened bread vntill the one and twentieth day of the moneth at euen.19Seuen dayes ſhall there bee no leauen found in your houſes: for whoſoeuer eateth that which is leauened, euen that ſoule ſhall be cut off from the congregation of Iſrael, whether he be a ſtranger, or borne in the land.20Yee ſhall eate nothing leauened: in all your habitations ſhall ye eate vnleauened bread.21Then Moſes called for all the Elders of Iſrael, and ſaid vnto them; Draw out and take you a lambe, according to your families, and kill the Paſſeouer.22And ye ſhall take a bunch of hyſope, and dip it in the blood that is in the baſon, and ſtrike the lintel and the two ſide poſtes with the blood that is in the baſon: and none of you ſhall goe out at the doore of his houſe, vntill the morning.23For the Lord wil paſſe through to ſmite the Egyptians: and when hee ſeeth the blood vpon the lintel, and on the two ſide-poſtes, the Lord will paſſe ouer the doore, and will not ſuffer the deſtroyer to come in vnto your houſes to ſmite you.24And ye ſhall obſerue this thing for an ordinance to thee, and to thy ſonnes for euer.25And it ſhall come to paſſe when yee bee come to the land, which the Lord will giue you, according as he hath promiſed, that ye ſhall keepe this ſeruice.26And it ſhall come to paſſe, when your children ſhall ſay vnto you, What meane you by this ſeruice?27That ye ſhall ſay, It is the ſacrifice of the Lords Paſſeouer, who paſſed ouer the houſes of the children of Iſrael in Egypt, when he ſmote the Egyptians, and deliuered our houſes. And the people bowed the head, and worſhipped.28And the children of Iſrael went away, and did as the Lord had commanded Moſes and Aaron, ſo did they.29And it came to paſſe that at midnight the Lord ſmote all the firſt borne in the land of Egypt, from the firſt borne of Pharaoh that ſate on his throne, vnto the firſt borne of the captiue that was in the dungeon, and all the firſt borne of cattell.30And Pharaoh roſe vp in the night, hee and all his ſeruants, and all the Egyptians; and there was a great cry in Egypt: for there was not a houſe, where there was not one dead.31And hee called for Moſes and Aaron by night, and ſaid, Riſe vp, and get you forth from amongſt my people, both you and the children of Iſrael: and goe, ſerue the Lord, as ye haue ſaid.32Alſo take your flockes and your heards, as ye haue ſaid: and bee gone, and bleſſe me alſo.33And the Egyptians were vrgent vpon the people that they might ſend them out of the land in haſte: for they ſaid, We be all dead men.34And the people tooke their dough before it was leauened, their kneading troughes beeing bound vp in their clothes vpon their ſhoulders .35And the children of Iſrael did according to the word of Moſes: and they borrowed of the Egyptians iewels of ſiluer, and iewels of gold, and raiment.36And the Lord gaue the people fauour in the ſight of the Egyptians, ſo that they lent vnto them ſuch things as they required: and they ſpoiled the Egyptians.37And the children of Iſrael iourneyed from Rameſes to Succoth, about ſixe hundred thouſand on foote that were men, beſide children.38And a mixed multitude went vp alſo with them, and flocks and heards, euen very much cattell.39And they baked vnleauened cakes of the dough, which they brought forth out of Egypt; for it was not leauened: becauſe they were thruſt out of Egypt, and could not tarry, neither had they prepared for themſelues any victuall.40Now the ſoiourning of the children of Iſrael, who dwelt in Egypt, was foure hundred and thirtie yeeres.41And it came to paſſe at the end of the foure hundred and thirtie yeeres, euen the ſelfe ſame day it came to paſſe, that all the hoſts of the Lord went out from the land of Egypt.42It is a night to be much obſerued vnto the Lord, for bringing them out from the land of Egypt: This is that night of the Lord to be obſerued of all the children of Iſrael, in their generations.43And the Lord ſaide vnto Moſes and Aaron, This is the ordinance of the Paſſeouer: there ſhall no ſtranger eate thereof.44But euery mans ſeruant that is bought for money, when thou haſt circumciſed him, then ſhall he eate thereof.45A forreiner, and an hired ſeruant ſhall not eate thereof.46In one houſe ſhall it be eaten, thou ſhalt not carie foorth ought of the fleſh abroad out of the houſe, neither ſhall ye breake a bone thereof.47All the

Congregation of Iſrael ſhall keepe it.48And when a ſtranger ſhall
ſoiourne with thee, and will keepe the Paſſeouer to the Lord, let all his
males be circumciſed, and then let him come neere, and keepe it: and he
ſhall be as one that is borne in the land: for no vncircumciſed perſon
ſhall eate thereof.49One law ſhall be to him that is home-borne, and
vnto the ſtranger that ſoiourneth among you.50Thus did all the children
of Iſrael: as the Lord commanded Moſes and Aaron, ſo did they.51And
it came to paſſe the ſelfe ſame day, that the Lord did bring the children
of Iſrael out of the land of Egypt, by their armies.
CHAPTER 131And the Lord ſpake vnto Moſes, ſaying,2ſanctifie vnto
me all the firſt borne, whatſoeuer openeth the wombe, among the
children of Iſrael, both of man and of beaſt: it is mine.3And Moſes ſaid
vnto the people, Remember this day, in which yee came out from Egypt,
out of the houſe of bondage: for by ſtrength of hand the Lord brought
you out from this place: there ſhall no leauened bread be eaten.4This
day came yee out, in the moneth Abib.5And it ſhalbe when the Lord
ſhall bring thee into the land of the Canaanites, and the Hittites, and the
Amorites, and the Hiuites, and the Iebuſites, which he ſware vnto thy
fathers to giue thee, a land flowing with milke and hony, that thou ſhalt
keepe this ſeruice in this moneth.6Seuen dayes thou ſhalt eate
vnleauened bread, and in the ſeuenth day ſhall be a feaſt to the
Lord.7Unleauened bread ſhall be eaten ſeuen dayes: and there ſhall no
leauened bread bee ſeene with thee: neither ſhall there be leauen ſeene
with thee in all thy quarters.8And thou ſhalt ſhew thy ſonne in that day,
ſaying, This is done becauſe of that which the Lord did vnto mee, when
I came forth out of Egypt.9And it ſhall bee for a ſigne vnto thee, vpon
thine hand, and for a memoriall betweene thine eyes, that the Lords law
may be in thy mouth: for with a ſtrong hande hath the Lord brought
thee out of Egypt.10Thou ſhalt therfore keepe this ordinance in his
ſeaſon from yeere to yere.11And it ſhalbe when the Lord ſhall bring thee
into the land of the Canaanites as he ſware vnto thee, and to thy fathers,
and ſhall giue it thee:12That thou ſhalt ſet apart vnto the Lord all that
openeth the matrix, and euery firſtling that commeth of a beaſt, which
thou haſt, the males ſhall be the Lords.13And euery firſtling of an aſſe
thou ſhalt redeeme with a lambe: and if thou wilt not redeeme it, then
thou ſhalt breake his necke, and all the firſt borne of man amongſt thy
children ſhalt thou redeeme.14And it ſhalbe when thy ſonne aſketh thee
in time to come, ſaying, What is this? That thou ſhalt ſay vnto him; By
ſtrength of hand the Lord brought vs out from Egypt, from the houſe
of bondage.15And it came to paſſe when Pharaoh would hardly let vs
goe, that the Lord ſlew all the firſt borne in the land of Egypt, both the
firſt borne of man, and the firſt borne of beaſt: Therefore I ſacrifice to
the Lord all that openeth the matrix, being males: but all the firſt borne
of my children I redeeme.16And it ſhall be for a token vpon thine hand,
and for frontlets betweene thine eyes. For by ſtrength of hand the Lord
brought vs foorth out of Egypt.17And it came to paſſe when Pharaoh
had let the people goe, that God led them not through the way of the
land of the Philiſtines, although that was neere: For God ſaide, Leſt
peraduenture the people repent when they ſee warre, and they returne
to Egypt:18But God ledde the people about through the way of the
wilderneſſe of the Red ſea: and the children of Iſrael went vp harneſſed
out of the land of Egypt.19And Moſes tooke the bones of Ioſeph with
him: for hee had ſtraitly ſworne the children of Iſrael, ſaying; God will
ſurely viſite you, and ye ſhall cary vp my bones away hence with
you.20And they tooke their iourney from Succoth, and encamped in
Etham, in the edge of the wilderneſſe.21And the Lord went before them
by day in a pillar of a cloud, to lead them the way, and by night in a pillar
of fire, to giue them light to goe by day and night.22He tooke not away
the pillar of the cloud by day, nor the pillar of fire by night, from before
the people.
CHAPTER 141And the Lord ſpake vnto Moſes, ſaying,2Speake vnto
the children of Iſrael, that they turne and encampe before Pi-hahiroth,
betweene Migdol and the ſea, ouer againſt Baal-Zephon: before it ſhall
ye encampe by the ſea.3For Pharaoh will ſay of the children of Iſrael,
They are intangled in the land, the wilderneſſe hath ſhut them in.4And
I will harden Pharaohs heart, that he ſhall follow after them, and I will
be honoured vpon Pharaoh, and vpon all his hoſte, That the Egyptians
may know that I am the Lord. And they did ſo.5And it was told the King
of Egypt, that the people fled: And the heart of Pharaoh and of his
ſeruants was turned againſt the people, and they ſaid, Why haue wee
done this, that we haue let Iſrael goe from ſeruing vs?6And hee made
ready his charet, and tooke his people with him.7And hee tooke ſixe
hundred choſen charets, and all the charets of Egypt, and captaines ouer
euery one of them.8And the Lord hardened the heart of Pharaoh King
of Egypt, and he purſued after the children of Iſrael: and the children of
Iſrael went out with an high hand.9But the Egyptians purſued after them
(all the horſes and charets of Pharaoh, and his horſemen, and his army)
and ouertooke them encamping by the ſea, beſide Pi-hahiroth before
Baal-Zephon.10And when Pharaoh drew nigh, the children of Iſrael lift
vp their eyes, and behold, the Egyptians marched after them, and they
were ſore afraid: and the children of Iſrael lift vp their eyes, and beholde,
the Egyptians marched after them, and they were ſore afraid: and the
children of Iſrael cried out vnto the Lord.11And they ſaid vnto Moſes,
Becauſe there were no graues in Egypt, haſt thou taken vs away to die
in the wilderneſſe? Wherefore haſt thou dealt thus with vs, to cary vs
foorth out of Egypt?12Is not this the word that wee did tell thee in Egypt,
ſaying, Let vs alone, that we may ſerue the Egyptians? For it had bene
better for vs to ſerue the Egyptians, then that wee ſhould die in the
wilderneſſe.13And Moſes ſaide vnto the people, Feare ye not, ſtand ſtill,
and ſee the ſaluation of the Lord, which he will ſhew to you to day: for
the Egyptians whom ye haue ſeene to day, ye ſhall ſee them againe no
more for euer.14The Lord ſhall fight for you, and ye ſhall hold your
peace.15And the Lord ſaide vnto Moſes, Wherefore crieſt thou vnto me?
Speake vnto the children of Iſrael, that they goe forward.16But lift thou
vp thy rodde, and ſtretch out thine hand ouer the ſea, and diuide it: and
the children of Iſrael ſhall goe on dry ground thorow the mids of the
ſea.17And I, beholde, I will harden the hearts of the Egyptians, and they
ſhall follow them: and I will get mee honour vpon Pharaoh, and vpon
all his hoſte, vpon his charets, and vpon his horſemen.18And the
Egyptians ſhall know that I am the Lord, when I haue gotten me honour
vpon Pharaoh, vpon his charets, and vpon his horſemen.19And the
Angel of God which went before the campe of Iſrael, remoued and went
behind them, and the pillar of the cloud went from before their face,
and ſtood behinde them.20And it came betweene the campe of the
Egyptians, and the campe of Iſrael, and it was a cloud and darkeneſſe to
them, but it gaue light by night to theſe: ſo that the one came not neere
the other all the night.21And Moſes ſtretched out his hand ouer the ſea,
and the Lord cauſed the ſea to goe backe by a ſtrong Eaſt winde all that
night, and made the ſea dry land, and the waters were diuided.22And the
children of Iſrael went into the midſt of the ſea vpon the dry ground,
and the waters were a wall vnto them on their right hand, and on their
left.23And the Egyptians purſued, and went in after them, to the midſt
of the ſea, euen all Pharaohs horſes, his charets and his horſemen.24And
it came to paſſe, that in the morning watch the Lord looked vnto the
hoſte of the Egyptians, through the pillar of fire, and of the cloude, and
troubled the hoſte of the Egyptians,25And tooke off their charet
wheeles, that they draue them heauily: So that the Egyptians ſaid, Let vs
flee from the face of Iſrael: for the Lord fighteth for them, againſt the
Egyptians.26And the Lord ſaide vnto Moſes, Stretch out thine hand ouer
the ſea, that the waters may come againe vpon the Egyptians, vpon their
charets, and vpon their horſemen.27And Moſes ſtretched foorth his
hand ouer the ſea, and the ſea returned to his ſtrength when the morning
appeared: and the Egyptians fled againſt it: and the Lord ouerthrew the
Egyptians in the midſt of the ſea.28And the waters returned, and couered
the charets, and the horſemen, and all the hoſte of Pharaoh that came
into the ſea after them: there remained not ſo much as one of
them.29But the children of Iſrael walked vpon drie land, in the midſt of
the ſea, and the waters were a wall vnto them on their right hand, and
on their left.30Thus the Lord ſaued Iſrael that day out of the hand of the
Egyptians: and Iſrael ſawe the Egyptians dead vpon the ſea ſhore.31And
Iſrael ſaw that great worke which the Lord did vpon the Egyptians: &
the people feared the Lord, and beleeued the Lord, and his ſeruant
Moſes.
CHAPTER 151Then ſang Moſes and the children of Iſrael this ſong
vnto the Lord, and ſpake, ſaying, I will ſing vnto the Lord: for he hath
triumphed glorioufly, the horſe and his rider hath he throwen into the
ſea.2The Lord is my ſtrength and ſong, and he is become my ſaluation:
he is my God, and I will prepare him an habitation, my fathers God, and
I wil exalt him.3The Lord is a man of warre: the Lord is his
Name.4Pharaohs charets and his hoſte hath he caſt into the ſea: his

choſen captaines alſo are drowned in the red ſea.5The depths haue couered them: they ſanke into the bottome as a ſtone.6Thy right hand, O Lord, is become glorious in power, thy right hand, O Lord, hath daſhed in pieces the enemie.7And in the greatneſſe of thine excellencie thou haſt ouerthrowen them, that roſe vp againſt thee: thou ſenteſt forth thy wrath, which conſumed them as ſtubble.8And with the blaſt of thy noſtrils the waters were gathered together: the floods ſtood vpright as an heape, and the depths were congealed in the heart of the ſea.9The enemie ſaid, I will purſue, I wil ouertake, I wil diuide the ſpoile: my luſt ſhall be ſatiſfied vpon them: I will draw my ſword, mine hand ſhall deſtroy them.10Thou didſt blow with thy wind, the ſea couered them, they ſanke as lead in the mighty waters.11Who is like vnto thee, O Lord, amongſt the gods? who is like thee, glorious in holineſſe, fearefull in praiſes, doing wonders!12Thou ſtretchedſt out thy right hand, the earth ſwallowed them.13Thou in thy mercie haſt led forth the people which thou haſt redeemed: thou haſt guided them in thy ſtrength vnto thy holy habitation.14The people ſhall heare, and be afraid: ſorrow ſhall take hold on the inhabitants of Paleſtina.15Then the dukes of Edom ſhal be amaſed: the mighty men of Moab trembling ſhall take hold vpon them: all the inhabitants of Canaan ſhal melt away.16Feare and dread ſhall fall vpon them, by the greatneſſe of thine arme they ſhall be as ſtill as a ſtone, till thy people paſſe ouer, O Lord, till the people paſſe ouer which thou haſt purchaſed.17Thou ſhalt bring them in, and plant them in the mountaine of thine inheritance, in the place, O Lord, which thou haſt made for thee to dwell in, in the Sanctuary, O Lord, which thy hands haue eſtabliſhed.18The Lord ſhal reigne for euer and euer.19For the horſe of Pharaoh went in with his charets and with his horſemen into the ſea, and the Lord brought againe the waters of the ſea vpon them: But the children of Iſrael went on drie land in the mids of the ſea.20And Miriam the prophetefse the ſiſter of Aaron, tooke a timbrell in her hand, and all the women went out after her, with timbrels & with dances.21And Miriam anſwered them, Sing ye to the Lord, for he hath triumphed glorioufly: the horſe and his rider hath he throwen into the ſea.22So Moſes brought Iſrael from the red ſea, and they went out into the wilderneſſe of Shur: and they went three dayes in the wilderneſſe, and found no water.23And when they came to Marah, they could not drinke of the waters of Marah, for they were bitter: therefore the name of it was called Marah.24And the people murmured againſt Moſes, ſaying, What ſhall wee drinke?25And he cried vnto the Lord: and the Lord ſhewed him a tree, which when hee had caſt into the waters, the waters were made ſweete: there he made a ſtatute & an ordinance, and there he proued them,26And ſaid, If thou wilt diligently hearken to the voice of the Lord thy God, and wilt doe that which is right in his ſight, and wilt giue eare to his Commandements, and keepe all his Statutes, I will put none of theſe diſeaſes vpon thee, which I haue brought vpon the Egyptians: for I am the Lord that healeth thee.27And they came to Elim: where were twelue wels of water, and threeſcore and ten palme trees, and they encamped there by the waters.

CHAPTER 161And they tooke their iourney from Elim, and all the Congregation of the children of Iſrael came vnto the wilderneſſe of Sin, which is betweene Elim and Sinai, on the fifteenth day of the ſecond moneth after their departing out of the land of Egypt.2And the whole Congregation of the children of Iſrael murmured againſt Moſes and Aaron in the wilderneſſe.3And the children of Iſrael ſaide vnto them, Would to God wee had died by the hand of the Lord in the land of Egypt, when wee ſate by the fleſh pots, and when we did eate bread to the full: for ye haue brought vs forth into this wilderneſſe, to kill this whole aſſembly with hunger.4Then ſaid the Lord vnto Moſes, Behold, I will raine bread from heauen for you: and the people ſhall goe out, and gather a certaine rate euery day, that I may proue them, whether they will walke in my Law, or no.5And it ſhall come to paſſe, that on the ſixt day, they ſhall prepare that which they bring in, and it ſhall be twice as much as they gather dayly.6And Moſes and Aaron ſaid vnto all the children of Iſrael, At euen, then ye ſhall know that the Lord hath brought you out from the land of Egypt.7And in the morning, then ye ſhall ſee the glory of the Lord, for that he heareth your murmurings againſt the Lord: And what are wee, that yee murmure againſt vs?8And Moſes ſaid, This ſhalbe when the Lord ſhal giue you in the euening fleſh to eate, and in the morning bread to the full: for that the Lord heareth your murmurings which ye murmure againſt him; and what are wee? your murmurings are not againſt vs, but againſt the Lord.9And Moſes ſpake vnto Aaron, ſay vnto all the Congregation of the children of Iſrael, Come neere before the Lord: for hee hath heard your murmurings.10And it came to paſſe as Aaron ſpake vnto the whole Congregation of the children of Iſrael, that they looked toward the wilderneſſe, and behold, the glory of the Lord appeared in the cloude.11And the Lord ſpake vnto Moſes, ſaying,12I haue heard the murmurings of the children of Iſrael: Speake vnto them, ſaying, At euen ye ſhall eat fleſh, and in the morning ye ſhalbe filled with bread: and ye ſhal know that I am the Lord your God.13And it came to paſſe, that at euen the Quailes came vp, and couered the campe: and in the morning the dew lay round about the hoſte.14And when the dewe that lay was gone vp, behold, vpon the face of the wilderneſſe there lay a ſmall round thing, as ſmall as the hoare froſt on the ground.15And when the children of Iſrael ſaw it, they ſaid one to another, It is Manna: for they wiſt not what it was. And Moſes ſaid vnto them, This is the bread which the Lord hath giuen you to eate.16This is the thing which the Lord hath commanded: gather of it euery man according to his eating: an Omer for euery man, according to the number of your perſons, take yee euery man for them which are in his tents.17And the children of Iſrael did ſo, and gathered ſome more, ſome leſſe.18And when they did mete it with an Omer, he that gathered much, had nothing ouer, and he that gathered litle, had no lacke: they gathered euery man according to his eating.19And Moſes ſaide, Let no man leaue of it till the morning.20Notwithſtanding they hearkened not vnto Moſes, but ſome of them left of it vntill the morning, and it bred wormes, and ſtanke: and Moſes was wroth with them.21And they gathered it euery morning, euery man according to his eating: and when the Sunne waxed hot, it melted.22And it came to paſſe that on the ſixt day they gathered twice as much bread, two Omers for one man: and all the rulers of the Congregation came and told Moſes.23And he ſaid vnto them, This is that which the Lord hath ſaid, To morrow is the reſt of the holy Sabbath vnto the Lord: bake that which you will bake, to day, and ſeethe that ye will ſeethe, and that which remaineth ouer, lay vp for you to be kept vntill the morning.24And they laid it vp till the morning, as Moſes bade: and it did not ſtinke, neither was there any worme therein.25And Moſes ſaide, Eate that to day, for to day is a Sabbath vnto the Lord: to day yee ſhall not finde it in the field.26Sixe dayes ye ſhall gather it, but on the ſeuenth day which is the Sabbath, in it there ſhall be none.27And it came to paſſe, that there went out ſome of the people on the ſeuenth day for to gather, and they found none.28And the Lord ſaid vnto Moſes, How long refuſe yee to keepe my Commandements, and my Lawes?29See, for that the Lord hath giuen you the Sabbath, therefore hee giueth you on the ſixt day the bread of two dayes: abide yee euery man in his place: let no man goe out of his place on the ſeuenth day.30So the people reſted on the ſeuenth day.31And the houſe of Iſrael called the name thereof Manna: and it was like Coriander ſeed, white: and the taſte of it was like wafers made with hony.32And Moſes ſaid, This is the thing which the Lord commandeth: Fill an Omer of it to bee kept for your generations, that they may ſee the bread wherewith I haue fed you in the wilderneſſe, when I brought you forth from the land of Egypt.33And Moſes ſayd vnto Aaron, Take a pot, and put an Omer full of Manna therein, and lay it vp before the Lord, to be kept for your generations.34As the Lord commaunded Moſes, ſo Aaron layd it vp before the Teſtimonie, to be kept.35And the children of Iſrael did eat Manna fortie yeeres, vntill they came to a land inhabited: they did eate Manna, vntill they came vnto the borders of the land of Canaan.36Now an Omer is the tenth part of an Ephah.

CHAPTER 171And all the Congregation of the children of Iſrael iourneyed from the wilderneſſe of Sin after their iourneys, according to the commandement of the Lord, and pitched in Rephidim: and there was no water for the people to drinke.2Wherefore the people did chide with Moſes and ſaid, Giue vs water that wee may drinke. And Moſes ſaid vnto them, Why chide you with mee? Wherefore doe ye tempt the Lord ?3And the people thirſted there for water, and the people murmured againſt Moſes, and ſaid, Wherefore is this that thou haſt brought vs vp out of Egypt, to kill vs and our children, and our cattell with thirſt?4And Moſes cried vnto the Lord, ſaying, What ſhall I doe vnto this people? They be almoſt ready to ſtone me.5And the Lord ſaid vnto Moſes, Goe on before the people, and take with thee of the Elders

of Iſrael: and thy rod wherewith thou ſmoteſt the riuer, take in thine
hand, and goe.6Behold, I will ſtand before thee there, vpon the rocke in
Horeb, and thou ſhalt ſmite the rocke, and there ſhall come water out
of it, that the people may drinke. And Moſes did ſo, in the ſight of the
Elders of Iſrael.7And hee called the name of the place Maſſah, and
Meribah, becauſe of the chiding of the children of Iſrael, and becauſe
they tempted the Lord, ſaying, Is the Lord amongſt vs, or not?8Then
came Amalek, & fought with Iſrael in Rephidim.9And Moſes ſaid vnto
Ioſhua, Chooſe vs out men, and goe out, fight with Amalek: to morrow
I will ſtand on the top of the hill, with the rodde of God in mine
hand.10So Ioſhua did as Moſes had ſaid to him, and fought with Amalek:
and Moſes, Aaron, and Hur went vp to the top of the hill.11And it came
to paſſe when Moſes held vp his hand, that Iſrael preuailed: and when
he let downe his hand, Amalek preuailed.12But Moſes hands were
heauie, and they tooke a ſtone, and put it vnder him, and he ſate thereon:
and Aaron and Hur ſtayed vp his hands, the one on the one ſide, and
the other on the other ſide, and his handes were ſteady vntill the going
downe of the Sunne.13And Ioſhua diſcomfited Amalek, and his people,
with the edge of the ſword.14And the Lord ſaid vnto Moſes, Write this
for a memoriall in a booke, and rehearſe it in the eares of Ioſhua: for I
will vtterly put out the remembrance of Amalek from vnder
heauen.15And Moſes built an Altar, and called the name of it
IEHOUAH Niſsi.16For he ſaid, Becauſe the Lord hath ſworne that the
Lord will haue warre with Amalek from generation to generation.
CHAPTER 181When Iethro the Prieſt of Midian, Moſes father in law,
heard of all that God had done for Moſes, and for Iſrael his people, and
that the Lord had brought Iſrael out of Egypt:2Then Iethro Moſes father
in law tooke Zipporah Moſes wife, after he had ſent her backe,3And her
two ſonnes, of which the name of the one was Gerſhom: for he ſaid, I
haue bene an alien in a ſtrange land.4And the name of the other was
Eliezer: for the God of my father, ſaid he, was mine helpe, and deliuered
me from the ſword of Pharaoh.5And Iethro Moſes father in law came
with his ſonnes and his wife vnto Moſes into the wildernes, where he
encamped at the mount of God.6And he ſaid vnto Moſes, I thy father
in law Iethro am come vnto thee, and thy wife, and her two ſonnes with
her.7And Moſes went out to meete his father in law, and did obeyſance,
and kiſſed him: and they aſked each other of their welfare, and they came
into the tent.8And Moſes told his father in law, all that the Lord had
done vnto Pharaoh, and to the Egyptians for Iſraels ſake, and all the
trauaile that had come vpon them by the way, and how the Lord
deliuered them.9And Iethro reioyced for all the goodneſſe which the
Lord had done to Iſrael: whom he had deliuered out of the hand of the
Egyptians.10And Iethro ſaid, Bleſſed be the Lord, who hath deliuered
you out of the hand of the Egyptians, and out of the hand of Pharaoh,
who hath deliuered the people from vnder the hand of the
Egyptians.11Now I know that the Lord is greater then all gods: for in the
thing wherein they dealt proudly, hee was aboue them.12And Iethro,
Moſes father in law, tooke a burnt offering and ſacrifices for God: and
Aaron came, and all the Elders of Iſrael, to eat bread with Moſes father
in law before God.13And it came to paſſe on the morrow, that Moſes
ſate to iudge the people: and the people ſtood by Moſes, from the
morning vnto the euening.14And when Moſes father in law ſaw all that
he did to the people, he ſaid, What is this thing that thou doeſt to the
people? Why ſitteſt thou thy ſelfe alone, and all the people ſtand by thee
from morning vnto euen?15And Moſes ſaid vnto his father in law,
Becauſe the people come vnto me to enquire of God.16When they haue
a matter, they come vnto mee, and I iudge betweene one and another,
and I doe make them know the ſtatutes of God and his Lawes.17And
Moſes father in law ſaide vnto him, The thing that thou doeſt, is not
good.18Thou wilt ſurely weare away, both thou, and this people that is
with thee: for this thing is too heauy for thee; thou art not able to
performe it thy ſelfe alone.19Hearken now vnto my voyce, I will giue
thee counſell, and God ſhall be with thee: Be thou for the people to
Godward, that thou mayeſt bring the cauſes vnto God:20And thou ſhalt
teach them ordinances and lawes, and ſhalt ſhew them the way wherein
they muſt walke, and the worke that they muſt doe.21Moreouer thou
ſhalt prouide out of all the people able men, ſuch as feare God, men of
trueth, hating couetouſneſſe, and place ſuch ouer them, to bee rulers of
thouſands, and rulers of hundreds, rulers of fifties, and rulers of
tennes.22And let them iudge the people at all ſeaſons: and it ſhall bee
that euery great matter they ſhall bring vnto thee, but euery ſmall matter
they ſhal iudge: ſo ſhall it be eaſier for thy ſelfe, and they ſhall beare the
burden with thee.23If thou ſhalt doe this thing, and God command thee
ſo, then thou ſhalt bee able to endure, and all this people ſhall alſo goe
to their place in peace.24So Moſes hearkened to the voice of his father
in law, and did all that he had ſaid.25And Moſes choſe able men out of
all Iſrael, and made them heads ouer the people, rulers of thouſands,
rulers of hundreds, rulers of fifties, and rulers of tennes.26And they
iudged the people at all ſeaſons: the hard cauſes they brought vnto
Moſes, but euery ſmall matter they iudged themſelues.27And Moſes let
his father in law depart, and he went his way into his owne land.
CHAPTER 191In the third moneth when the children of Iſrael were
gone forth out of the land of Egypt, the ſame day came they into the
wilderneſſe of Sinai.2For they were departed from Rephidim, and were
come to the deſert of Sinai, and had pitched in the wilderneſſe, and there
Iſrael camped before the mount.3And Moſes went vp vnto God: and
the Lord called vnto him out of the mountaine, ſaying, Thus ſhalt thou
ſay to the houſe of Iacob, and tell the children of Iſrael:4Ye haue ſeene
what I did vnto the Egyptians, and how I bare you on Eagles wings, and
brought you vnto my ſelfe.5Now therfore if ye will obey my voice
indeed, and keepe my couenant, then ye ſhall be a peculiar treaſure vnto
me aboue all people: for all the earth is mine.6And ye ſhall be vnto me
a kingdome of Prieſtes, and an holy nation. Theſe are the wordes which
thou ſhalt ſpeake vnto the children of Iſrael.7And Moſes came and
called for the Elders of the people, and layd before their faces all theſe
wordes which the Lord commanded him.8And all the people anſwered
together, and ſaid, All that the Lord hath ſpoken, we will doe. And
Moſes returned the wordes of the people vnto the Lord.9And the Lord
ſaid vnto Moſes, Loe, I come vnto thee in a thicke cloud, that the people
may heare when I ſpeake with thee, and beleeue thee for euer: And
Moſes told the wordes of the people vnto the Lord.10And the Lord ſaide
vnto Moſes, Goe vnto the people, and ſanctifie them to day and to
morrow, and let them waſh their clothes.11And be ready againſt the
thirde day: for the third day the Lord will come downe in the ſight of all
the people, vpon mount Sinai.12And thou ſhalt ſet bounds vnto the
people round about, ſaying, Take heed to your ſelues, that ye goe not vp
into the mount, or touch the border of it: whoſoeuer toucheth the
mount, ſhall be ſurely put to death.13There ſhall not a hand touch it, but
he ſhall ſurely be ſtoned or ſhot thorow, whether it be beaſt, or man, it
ſhall not liue: when the trumpet ſoundeth long, they ſhall come vp to
the mount.14And Moſes went downe from the mount vnto the people,
and ſanctified the people; and they waſhed their clothes.15And hee ſaid
vnto the people, Be ready againſt the third day: come not at your
wiues.16And it came to paſſe on the third day in the morning, that there
were thunders and lightnings, and a thicke cloud vpon the mount, and
the voyce of the trumpet exceeding lowd, ſo that all the people that was
in the campe, trembled.17And Moſes brought foorth the people out of
the campe to meete with God, and they ſtood at the nether part of the
mount.18And mount Sinai was altogether on a ſmoke, becauſe the Lord
deſcended vpon it in fire: and the ſmoke thereof aſcended as the ſmoke
of a furnace, and the whole mount quaked greatly.19And when the voyce
of the trumpet ſounded long, and waxed lowder and lowder, Moſes
ſpake, and God anſwered him by a voyce.20And the Lord came downe
vpon mount Sinai, on the top of the mount: and the Lord called Moſes
vp to the top of the mount, and Moſes went vp.21And the Lord ſaid
vnto Moſes, Goe downe, charge the people, leſt they breake thorow
vnto the Lord to gaze, and many of them periſh.22And let the Prieſtes
alſo which come neere to the Lord, ſanctifie themſelues, leſt the Lord
breake foorth vpon them.23And Moſes ſaid vnto the Lord, The people
cannot come vp to mount Sinai: for thou chargedſt vs, ſaying, Set
bounds about the mount, and ſanctifie it.24And the Lord ſaid vnto him,
Away, get thee downe, and thou ſhalt come vp, thou, and Aaron with
thee: but let not the Prieſtes and the people breake through, to come vp
vnto the Lord, leſt hee breake foorth vpon them.25So Moſes went
downe vnto the people, and ſpake vnto them.
CHAPTER 201And God ſpake all theſe words, ſaying,2I am the Lord
thy God, which haue brought thee out of the land of Egypt, out of the
houſe of bondage:3Thou ſhalt haue no other Gods before me.4Thou
ſhalt not make vnto thee any grauen Image, or any likeneſſe of any thing
that is in heauen aboue, or that is in the earth beneath, or that is in the

water vnder the earth.5Thou ſhalt not bow downe thy ſelfe to them, nor
ſerue them: For I the Lord thy God am a iealous God, viſiting the
iniquitie of the fathers vpon the children, vnto the thirde and fourth
generation of them that hate me:6And ſhewing mercy vnto thouſands
of them that loue mee, and keepe my Commandements.7Thou ſhalt not
take the Name of the Lord thy God in vaine: for the Lord will not holde
him guiltleſſe, that taketh his Name in vaine.8Remember the Sabbath
day, to keepe it holy.9Sixe dayes ſhalt thou labour, and doe all thy
worke:10But the ſeuenth day is the Sabbath of the Lord thy God: in it
thou ſhalt not doe any worke, thou, nor thy ſonne, nor thy daughter, thy
man ſeruant, nor thy mayd ſeruant, nor thy cattell, nor thy ſtranger that
is within thy gates:11For in ſixe dayes the Lord made heauen and earth,
the ſea, and all that in them is, and reſted the ſeuenth day: wherefore the
Lord bleſſed the Sabbath day, and halowed it.12Honour thy father and
thy mother: that thy dayes may bee long vpon the land, which the Lord
thy God giueth thee.13Thou ſhalt not kill.14Thou ſhalt not commit
adultery.15Thou ſhalt not ſteale.16Thou ſhalt not beare falſe witnes
againſt thy neighbour.17Thou ſhalt not couet thy neighbours houſe, thou
ſhalt not couet thy neighbours wife, nor his man ſeruant, nor his maid
ſeruant, nor his oxe, nor his aſſe, nor any thing that is thy
neighbours.18And all the people ſaw the thundrings, and the lightnings,
and the noiſe of the trumpet, and the mountaine ſmoking: and when the
people ſaw it, they remooued, and ſtood a farre off.19And they ſaide
vnto Moſes, Speake thou with vs, and wee will heare: But let not God
ſpeake with vs, leſt we die.20And Moſes ſaid vnto the people, Feare not:
for God is come to prooue you, and that his feare may bee before your
faces, that ye ſinne not.21And the people ſtood afarre off, and Moſes
drew neere vnto the thicke darkenes, where God was.22And the Lord
ſaid vnto Moſes, Thus thou ſhalt ſay vnto the children of Iſrael, Yee
haue ſeene that I haue talked with you from heauen.23Ye ſhall not make
with me gods of ſiluer, neither ſhall ye make vnto you gods of gold.24An
Altar of earth thou ſhalt make vnto me, and ſhalt ſacrifice thereon thy
burnt offerings, and thy peace offerings, thy ſheepe, and thine oxen: In
all places where I record my Name, I will come vnto thee, and I will
bleſſe thee.25And if thou wilt make mee an Altar of ſtone, thou ſhalt not
build it of hewen ſtone: for if thou lift vp thy toole vpon it, thou haſt
polluted it.26Neither ſhalt thou goe vp by ſteps vnto mine Altar, that thy
nakedneſſe be not diſcouered thereon.
CHAPTER 211Now theſe are the Iudgements which thou ſhalt ſet
before them.2If thou buy an Hebrew ſeruant, ſixe yeeres he ſhall ſerue,
and in the ſeuenth he ſhall goe out free for nothing.3If he came in by
himſelfe, he ſhal goe out by himſelfe: if he were married, then his wife
ſhall goe out with him.4If his maſter haue giuen him a wife, and ſhe haue
borne him ſonnes or daughters; the wife and her children ſhall be her
maſters, and he ſhall go out by himſelfe.5And if the ſeruant ſhall plainely
ſay, I loue my maſter, my wife, and my children, I will not goe out
free:6Then his maſter ſhall bring him vnto the Iudges, hee ſhall alſo
bring him to the doore, or vnto the doore poſt, and his maſter ſhall
boare his eare through with an aule, and he ſhall ſerue him for euer.7And
if a man ſell his daughter to be a mayd ſeruant, ſhee ſhall not goe out as
the men ſeruants doe.8If ſhe pleaſe not her maſter, who hath betrothed
her to himſelfe, then ſhall he let her be redeemed: To ſell her vnto a
ſtrange nation hee ſhall haue no power, ſeeing he hath dealt deceitfully
with her.9And if he haue betrothed her vnto his ſonne, he ſhall deale
with her after the maner of daughters.10If he take him another wife, her
food, her rayment, and her duety of mariage ſhall he not diminiſh.11And
if he doe not theſe three vnto her, then ſhall ſhe goe out free without
money.12He that ſmiteth a man, ſo that he die, ſhalbe ſurely put to
death.13And if a man lye not in wait, but God deliuer him into his hand,
then I will appoint thee a place whither hee ſhall flee:14But if a man
come preſumptuouſly vpon his neighbour to ſlay him with guile, thou
ſhalt take him from mine Altar, that he may die.15And he that ſmiteth
his father, or his mother, ſhall bee ſurely put to death.16And he that
ſtealeth a man, and ſelleth him, or if he be found in his hand, he ſhall
ſurely be put to death.17And hee that curſeth his father or his mother,
ſhall ſurely bee put to death.18And if men ſtriue together, and one ſmite
another with a ſtone, or with his fiſt, and he die not, but keepeth his
bed:19If hee riſe againe, and walke abroad vpon his ſtaffe, then ſhall hee
that ſmote him, be quit: onely he ſhall pay for the loſſe of his time, and
ſhall cauſe him to be throughly healed.20And if a man ſmite his ſeruant,
or his mayd, with a rod, and hee die vnder his hand, hee ſhall bee ſurely
puniſhed:21Notwithſtanding, if he continue a day or two, hee ſhall not
be puniſhed, for he is his money.22If men ſtriue, and hurt a woman with
child, ſo that her fruit depart from her, and yet no miſchiefe follow, he
ſhalbe ſurely puniſhed, according as the womans huſband will lay vpon
him, and hee ſhall pay as the Iudges determine.23And if any miſchiefe
follow, then thou ſhalt giue life for life,24Eye for eye, tooth for tooth,
hand for hand, foote for foote,25Burning for burning, wound for
wound, ſtripe for ſtripe.26And if a man ſmite the eye of his ſeruant, or
the eye of his mayd, that it periſh, hee ſhall let him goe free for his eyes
ſake.27And if he ſmite out his man ſeruants tooth, or his mayde ſeruants
tooth, hee ſhal let him goe free for his tooths ſake.28If an oxe gore a
man, or a woman, that they die, then the oxe ſhal be ſurely ſtoned, and
his fleſh ſhall not be eaten: but the owner of the oxe ſhall be quitte.29But
if the oxe were wont to puſh with his horne in time paſt, and it hath
bene teſtified to his owner, and he hath not kept him in, but that he hath
killed a man or a woman; the oxe ſhall be ſtoned, and his owner alſo
ſhall bee put to death.30If there be layed on him a ſumme of money,
then he ſhall giue for the ranſome of his life, whatſoeuer is layd vpon
him.31Whether hee haue gored a ſonne, or haue gored a daughter,
according to this iudgement ſhall it bee done vnto him.32If the oxe ſhall
puſh a man ſeruant, or a mayd ſeruant, hee ſhall giue vnto their maſter
thirty ſhekels, and the oxe ſhalbe ſtoned.33And if a man ſhall open a pit,
or if a man ſhall digge a pit, and not couer it, and an oxe or an aſſe fall
therein:34The owner of the pit ſhall make it good, and giue money vnto
the owner of them, and the dead beaſt ſhalbe his.35And if one mans oxe
hurt anothers, that he die, then they ſhall ſell the liue oxe, and diuide the
money of it, and the dead oxe alſo they ſhall diuide.36Or if it bee knowen
that the oxe hath vſed to puſh in time paſt, and his owner hath not kept
him in, hee ſhall ſurely pay oxe for oxe, and the dead ſhall be his owne.
CHAPTER 221If a man ſhal ſteale an oxe, or a ſheepe, and kill it, or
ſell it; he ſhall reſtore fiue oxen for an oxe, and foure ſheepe for a
ſheepe.2If a thiefe bee found breaking vp, and be ſmitten that he die,
there ſhal no blood be ſhed for him.3If the Sunne be riſen vpon him,
there ſhall be blood ſhed for him: for hee ſhould make full reſtitution: if
he haue nothing, then he ſhall bee ſold for his theft.4If the theft be
certainely found in his hand aliue, whether it bee oxe or aſſe, or ſheepe,
he ſhall reſtore double.5If a man ſhall cauſe a field or vineyard to be
eaten, and ſhall put in his beaſt, and ſhall feede in another mans field: of
the beſt of his owne field, and of the beſt of his owne vineyard ſhall he
make reſtitution.6If fire breake out, and catch in thornes, ſo that the
ſtackes of corne, or the ſtanding corne, or the field be conſumed
therewith; hee that kindled the fire, ſhall ſurely make reſtitution.7If a
man ſhal deliuer vnto his neighbour money or ſtuffe to keepe, and it be
ſtollen out of the mans houſe; if the thiefe be found, let him pay
double.8If the thiefe be not found, then the maſter of the houſe ſhall be
brought vnto the Iudges, to ſee whether he haue put his hande vnto his
neighbours goods.9For all maner of treſpaſſe, whether it be for oxe, for
aſſe, for ſheepe, for raiment, or for any maner of loſt thing, which
another challengeth to be his: the cauſe of both parties ſhall come before
the Iudges, and whome the Iudges ſhall condemne, he ſhall pay double
vnto his neighbour.10If a man deliuer vnto his neighbour an aſſe, or an
oxe, or a ſheepe, or any beaſt to keepe, and it die, or be hurt, or driuen
away, no man ſeeing it,11Then ſhall an othe of the Lord be betweene
them both, that hee hath not put his hand vnto his neighbours goods:
and the owner of it ſhall accept thereof, and he ſhall not make it
good.12And if it be ſtollen from him, he ſhall make reſtitution vnto the
owner thereof.13If it be torne in pieces, then let him bring it for witneſſe,
and hee ſhall not make good that which was torne.14And if a man
borrowe ought of his neighbour, and it be hurt, or die, the owner thereof
being not with it, he ſhall ſurely make it good.15But if the owner thereof
be with it, he ſhall not make it good: If it bee an hired thing, it came for
his hire.16And if a man entice a maide that is not betrothed, and lie with
her, he ſhall ſurely endow her to be his wife.17If her father vtterly refuſe
to giue her vnto him, he ſhall pay money according to the dowrie of
virgins.18Thou ſhalt not ſuffer a witch to liue.19Whoſoeuer lieth with a
beaſt, ſhall ſurely be put to death.20Hee that ſacrificeth vnto any god
ſaue vnto the Lord onely, hee ſhall be vtterly deſtroyed.21Thou ſhalt
neither vexe a ſtranger, nor oppreſſe him: for ye were ſtrangers in the

land of Egypt.22Yee ſhall not afflict any widow, or fatherleſſe child.23If thou afflict them in any wiſe, and they crie at all vnto mee, I will ſurely heare their crie.24And my wrath ſhall waxe hote, and I will kill you with the ſword: and your wiues ſhall be widowes, and your children fatherleſſe.25If thou lend money to any of my people that is poore by thee, thou ſhalt not be to him as an vſurer, neither ſhalt thou lay vpon him vſurie.26If thou at all take thy neighbors raiment to pledge, thou ſhalt deliuer it vnto him by that the ſun goeth downe.27For that is his couering onely, it is his raiment for his ſkinne: wherein ſhal he ſleepe? and it ſhal come to paſſe, when he crieth vnto mee, that I will heare: for I am gracious.28Thou ſhalt not reuile the Gods, nor curſe the ruler of thy people.29Thou ſhalt not delay to offer the firſt of thy ripe fruits, and of thy liquors: the firſt borne of thy ſonnes ſhalt thou giue vnto me.30Likewiſe ſhalt thou do with thine oxen, and with thy ſheepe: ſeuen dayes it ſhall be with his damme, on the eight day thou ſhalt giue it me.31And ye ſhall be holy men vnto me: neither ſhall ye eate any fleſh that is torne of beaſts in the field: yee ſhall caſt it to the dogs.

CHAPTER 23 Thou ſhalt not raiſe a falſe report: put not thine hand with the wicked to bee an vnrighteous witneſſe.2Thou ſhalt not follow a multitude to doe euill: neither ſhalt thou ſpeake in a cauſe, to decline after many, to wreſt iudgement:3Neither ſhalt thou countenance a poore man in his cauſe.4If thou meete thine enemies oxe or his aſſe going aſtray, thou ſhalt ſurely bring it backe to him againe.5If thou ſee the aſſe of him that hateth thee, lying vnder his burden, and wouldeſt forbeare to helpe him, thou ſhalt ſurely helpe with him.6Thou ſhalt not wreſt the iudgement of thy poore in his cauſe.7Keepe thee farre from a falſe matter: and the innocent and righteous ſlay thou not: for I will not iuſtifie the wicked.8And thou ſhalt take no gift: for the gift blindeth the wiſe, and peruerteth the words of the righteous.9Alſo thou ſhalt not oppreſſe a ſtranger: for yee know the heart of a ſtranger, ſeeing yee were ſtrangers in the land of Egypt.10And ſixe yeres thou ſhalt ſow thy land, and ſhalt gather in the fruites thereof:11But the ſeuenth yeere thou ſhalt let it reſt, and lie ſtill, that the poore of thy people may eate, and what they leaue, the beaſts of the field ſhall eate. In like maner thou ſhalt deale with thy vineyard, and with thy oliue yard.12Sixe dayes thou ſhalt doe thy worke, and on the ſeuenth day thou ſhalt reſt: that thine oxe and thine aſſe may reſt, and the ſonne of thy handmayd, & the ſtranger may be refreſhed.13And in all things that I haue ſaid vnto you, be circumſpect: and make no mention of the names of other gods, neither let it be heard out of thy mouth.14Three times thou ſhalt keepe a feaſt vnto me in the yeere.15Thou ſhalt keepe the feaſt of vnleauened bread: thou ſhalt eate vnleauened bread ſeuen daies, as I commanded thee in the time appointed of the moneth Abib: for in it thou cameſt out from Egypt: and none ſhall appeare before me emptie:16And the feaſt of harueſt, the firſt fruits of thy labours, which thou haſt ſowen in the field: and the feaſt of ingathering which is in the end of the yeere, when thou haſt gathered in thy labours out of the field.17Three times in the yeere all thy males ſhall appeare before the Lord God.18Thou ſhalt not offer the blood of my ſacrifice with leauened bread, neither ſhall the fat of my ſacrifice remaine vntill the morning.19The firſt of the firſt fruits of thy land thou ſhalt bring into the houſe of the Lord thy God: thou ſhalt not ſeethe a kid in his mothers milke.20Behold, I ſend an Angel before thee to keepe thee in the way, and to bring thee into the place which I haue prepared.21Beware of him, and obey his voice, prouoke him not: for he will not pardon your tranſgreſſions: for my name is in him.22But if thou ſhalt indeed obey his voice, and doe all that I ſpeake, then I wil be an enemie vnto thine enemies, and an aduerſarie vnto thine aduerſaries.23For mine Angel ſhall goe before thee, and bring thee in vnto the Amorites, and the Hittites, and the Perizzites, and the Canaanites, the Hiuites, and the Iebuſites: and I will cut them off.24Thou ſhalt not bow downe to their gods, nor ſerue them, nor doe after their workes: but thou ſhalt vtterly ouerthrowe them, and quite breake downe their images.25And yee ſhall ſerue the Lord your God, and he ſhall bleſſe thy bread, and thy water: and I will take ſicknes away from the midſt of thee.26There ſhall nothing caſt their yong, nor bee barren in thy land: the number of thy dayes I will fulfill.27I will ſend my feare before thee, and will deſtroy all the people to whom thou ſhalt come, and I will make all thine enemies turne their backes vnto thee.28And I will ſend hornets before thee, which ſhall driue out the Hiuite, the Canaanite, and the Hittite from before thee.29I will not driue them out from before thee in one yeere, leſt the land become deſolate, and the beaſt of the field multiply againſt thee.30By little and little I will driue them out from before thee, vntill thou be increaſed and inherit the land.31And I will ſet thy bounds from the Red ſea, euen vnto the ſea of the Philiſtines, and from the deſert vnto the riuer: for I will deliuer the inhabitants of the land into your hand: and thou ſhalt driue them out before thee.32Thou ſhalt make no couenant with them, nor with their gods.33They ſhall not dwell in thy land, leſt they make thee ſinne againſt me: for if thou ſerue their gods, it will ſurely be a ſnare vnto thee.

CHAPTER 241And hee ſaid vnto Moſes, Come vp vnto þe Lord,thou, and Aaron, Nadab and Abihu, and ſeuentie of the Elders of Iſrael: and worſhip ye a farre off.2And Moſes alone ſhall come neere the Lord: but they ſhall not come nigh, neither ſhall the people goe vp with him.3And Moſes came and told the people all the words of the Lord, and all the iudgements: and all the people anſwered with one voyce, and ſaid, All the words which the Lord hath ſaid, will we doe.4And Moſes wrote all the words of the Lord, and roſe vp early in the morning, and builded an Altar vnder the hill, and twelue pillars, according to the twelue tribes of Iſrael.5And he ſent yong men of the children of Iſrael, which offered burnt offerings, and ſacrificed peace offerings of oxen, vnto the Lord.6And Moſes tooke halfe of the blood, and put it in baſons, and halfe of the blood he ſprinkled on the Altar.7And he tooke the booke of the couenant, and read in the audience of the people: and they ſaide, All that the Lord hath ſaid, will we doe, and be obedient.8And Moſes tooke the blood and ſprinkled it on the people, and ſaid, Behold the blood of the Couenant which the Lord hath made with you, concerning all theſe words.9Then went vp Moſes and Aaron, Nadab and Abihu, and ſeuenty of the Elders of Iſrael:10And they ſaw the God of Iſrael: and there was vnder his feet, as it were a paued worke of a Saphire ſtone, and as it were the body of heauen in his cleareneſſe.11And vpon the Nobles of the children of Iſrael he layd not his hand: alſo they ſaw God, and did eate and drinke.12And the Lord ſayd vnto Moſes, Come vp to me into the mount, and be there, and I will giue thee Tables of ſtone, and a Law, and Commandements which I haue written, that thou mayeſt teach them.13And Moſes roſe vp, and his miniſter Ioſhua: and Moſes went vp into the mount of God.14And hee ſaide vnto the Elders, Tary ye here for vs, vntill wee come againe vnto you: and behold, Aaron and Hur are with you: If any man haue any matters to doe, let him come vnto them.15And Moſes went vp into the Mount, and a cloud couered the Mount.16And the glory of the Lord abode vpon mount Sinai, and the cloud couered it ſixe dayes: and the ſeuenth day hee called vnto Moſes out of the midſt of the cloud.17And the ſight of the glory of the Lord was like deuouring fire, on the top of the mount, in the eyes of the children of Iſrael.18And Moſes went into the midſt of the cloud, and gate him vp into the mount: and Moſes was in the mount forty dayes, and forty nights.

CHAPTER 251And the Lord ſpake vnto Moſes, ſaying,2Speake vnto the children of Iſrael, that they bring me an offering: of euery man that giueth it willingly with his heart, ye ſhall take my offering.3And this is the offering which ye ſhall take of them; Gold, and ſiluer, and braſſe,4And blew, and purple, and ſcarlet, and fine linnen, and goats haire:5And rammes ſkinnes died red, and badgers ſkinnes, and Shittim wood:6Oile for the light, ſpices for anointing oile, and for ſweet incenſe:7Onix ſtones, and ſtones to be ſet in the Ephod, and in the breſt plate.8And let them make mee a Sanctuary, that I may dwell amongſt them:9According to all that I ſhew thee, after the patterne of the Tabernacle, and the patterne of all the inſtruments thereof, euen ſo ſhall ye make it.10And they ſhall make an Arke of Shittim wood: two cubites and a halfe ſhalbe the length thereof, and a cubite and an halfe the breadth thereof, and a cubite & a halfe the height thereof.11And thou ſhalt ouerlay it with pure gold, within and without ſhalt thou ouerlay it: and ſhalt make vpon it a crowne of gold round about.12And thou ſhalt caſt foure rings of gold for it, and put them in the foure corners thereof, and two rings ſhal be in the one ſide of it, and two rings in the other ſide of it.13And thou ſhalt make ſtaues of Shittim wood, and ouerlay them with gold.14And thou ſhalt put the ſtaues into the rings, by the ſides of the Arke, that the Arke may be borne with them.15The ſtaues ſhall be in the rings of the Arke: they ſhal not be taken from it.16And thou ſhalt put into the Arke the Teſtimonie which I ſhall giue thee.17And thou

ſhalt make a Mercieſeat of pure gold: two cubites and a halfe ſhalbe the
length thereof, and a cubite and a halfe the breadth thereof.18And thou
ſhalt make two Cherubims of gold: of beaten worke ſhalt thou make
them, in the two endes of the Mercie-ſeat.19And make one Cherub on
the one end, and the other Cherub on the other end: euen of the Mercie-
ſeat ſhall yee make the Cherubims, on the two ends thereof.20And the
Cherubims ſhall ſtretch forth their wings on high, couering the Mercie-
ſeat with their wings, and their faces ſhall looke one to another: toward
the Mercie-ſeat ſhall the faces of the Cherubims be.21And thou ſhalt put
the Mercie-ſeat aboue vpon the Arke, and in the Arke thou ſhalt put the
Teſtimonie that I ſhall giue thee.22And there I wil meet with thee, and I
will commune with thee, from aboue the Mercie-ſeat, from betweene
the two Cherubims which are vpon the Arke of the Teſtimonie, of all
things which I will giue thee in commaundement vnto the children of
Iſrael.23Thou ſhalt alſo make a table of Shittim wood: two cubites ſhall
bee the length thereof, and a cubite the bredth thereof, and a cubite and
a halfe the height thereof.24And thou ſhalt ouerlay it with pure gold, and
make thereto a crowne of gold round about.25And thou ſhalt make vnto
it a border of an hand bredth round about, and thou ſhalt make a golden
crowne to the border thereof round about.26And thou ſhalt make for it
foure rings of gold, and put the rings in the foure corners that are on
the foure feete thereof.27Ouer againſt the border ſhall the rings be for
places of the ſtaues to beare the table.28And thou ſhalt make the ſtaues
of Shittim wood, and ouerlay them with gold, that the table may be
borne with them.29And thou ſhalt make the diſhes thereof, and ſpoones
therof, and couers thereof, and bowles thereof, to couer withall: of pure
gold ſhalt thou make them.30And thou ſhalt ſet vpon the Table Shew-
bread before me alway.31And thou ſhalt make a Candleſticke of pure
gold: of beaten worke ſhall the candleſticke bee made; his ſhaft and his
branches, his bowles, his knops, and his flowers ſhall be of the
ſame.32And ſixe branches ſhall come out of the ſides of it: three
branches of the candleſticke out of the one ſide, and three branches of
the candleſticke out of the other ſide:33Three bowles made like vnto
almonds, with a knop and a flower in one branch: and three bowles
made like almonds in the other branch, with a knop and a flower: ſo in
the ſixe branches that come out of the candleſticke.34And in the
candleſticke ſhall bee foure bowles made like vnto almonds, with their
knops and their flowers.35And there ſhal be a knop vnder two branches
of the ſame, and a knop vnder two branches of the ſame, and a knop
vnder two branches of the ſame, according to the ſixe branches that
proceede out of the candleſticke.36Their knops and their branches ſhall
be of the ſame: all it ſhall bee one beaten worke of pure gold.37And thou
ſhalt make the ſeuen lamps thereof: and they ſhall light the lampes
thereof, that they may giue light ouer againſt it.38And the tongs thereof,
and the ſnuffe diſhes therof ſhalbe of pure gold.39Of a talent of pure
gold ſhall hee make it, with all theſe veſſels.40And looke that thou make
them after their patterne, which was ſhewed thee in the mount.
CHAPTER 261Moreouer thou ſhalt make the Tabernacle with ten
curtaines of fine twined linnen, and blew, and purple, and ſcarlet: with
Cherubims of cunning worke ſhalt thou make them.2The length of one
curtaine ſhalbe eight and twenty cubits, and the bredth of one curtaine,
foure cubits: and euery one of the curtaines ſhall haue one meaſure.3The
fiue curtaines ſhalbe coupled together one to another: and other fiue
curtaines ſhalbe coupled one to another.4And thou ſhalt make loopes
of blew vpon the edge of the one curtaine, from the ſeluedge in the
coupling, and likewiſe ſhalt thou make in the vttermoſt edge of another
curtaine, in the coupling of the ſecond.5Fiftie loopes ſhalt thou make in
the one curtaine, and fiftie loopes ſhalt thou make in the edge of the
curtaine, that is in the coupling of the ſecond, that the loopes may take
hold one of another.6And thou ſhalt make fiftie taches of gold, and
couple the curtaines together with the taches: and it ſhall be one
tabernacle.7And thou ſhalt make curtaines of goats haire, to be a
couering vpon the tabernacle: eleuen curtaines ſhalt thou make.8The
length of one curtaine ſhalbe thirtie cubites, and the bredth of one
curtaine foure cubites: and the eleuen ſhalbe all of one meaſure.9And
thou ſhalt couple fiue curtaines by themſelues, and ſixe curtaines by
themſelues, and ſhalt double the ſixt curtaine in the forefront of the
tabernacle.10And thou ſhalt make fiftie loopes on the edge of the one
curtaine, that is outmoſt in the coupling, and fiftie loopes in the edge of
the curtaine which coupleth the ſecond.11And thou ſhalt make fiftie
taches of braſſe, and put the taches into the loopes, and couple the tent
together, that it may be one.12And the remnant that remaineth of the
curtaines of the tent, the halfe curtaine that remaineth ſhall hang ouer
the backe ſide of the tabernacle.13And a cubite on the one ſide, and a
cubite on the other ſide of that which remaineth in the length of the
curtaines of the tent, it ſhall hang ouer the ſides of the tabernacle, on
this ſide, and on that ſide to couer it.14And thou ſhalt make a couering
for the tent of rammes ſkinnes died red, and a couering aboue of badgers
ſkinnes.15And thou ſhalt make boards for the Tabernacle of Shittim
wood ſtanding vp.16Ten cubits ſhall be the length of a board, and a
cubite and an halfe ſhall be the breadth of one board.17Two tenons ſhall
there be in one board ſet in order one againſt another: thus ſhalt thou
make for all the boards of the Tabernacle.18And thou ſhalt make the
boards for the Tabernacle, twentie boards on the Southſide
Southward.19And thou ſhalt make fourtie ſockets of ſiluer, vnder the
twenty boards: two ſockets vnder one board for his two tenons, and two
ſockets vnder another board for his two tenons.20And for the ſecond
ſide of the Tabernacle on the Northſide there ſhall bee twentie
boards,21And their fourtie ſockets of ſiluer: two ſockets vnder one
board, and two ſockets vnder another board.22And for the ſides of the
Tabernacle Weſtward thou ſhalt make ſixe boards.23And two boards
ſhalt thou make for the corners of the tabernacle in the two ſides.24And
they ſhall be coupled together beneath, and they ſhall be coupled
together aboue the head of it vnto one ring: thus ſhall it bee for them
both; they ſhall be for the two corners.25And they ſhall be eight boards,
and their ſockets of ſiluer ſixteene ſockets: two ſockets vnder one board,
and two ſockets vnder another board.26And thou ſhalt make barres of
Shittim wood: fiue for the boards of the one ſide of the
Tabernacle,27And fiue barres for the boards of the other ſide of the
Tabernacle, and fiue barres for the boards of the ſide of the Tabernacle
for the two ſides Weſtward.28And the middle barre in the mids of the
boards, ſhall reach from ende to ende.29And thou ſhalt ouerlay the
boards with gold, and make their rings of gold for places for the barres:
and thou ſhalt ouerlay the barres with gold.30And thou ſhalt reare vp the
Tabernacle according to the faſhion therof, which was ſhewed thee in
the mount.31And thou ſhalt make a Uaile of blew, and purple, and
ſcarlet, and fine twined linnen of cunning worke: with Cherubims ſhall
it be made.32And thou ſhalt hang it vpon foure pillars of Shittim wood,
ouerlayd with gold: their hookes ſhalbe of gold, vpon the foure ſockets
of ſiluer.33And thou ſhalt hang vp the Uaile vnder the taches, that thou
maiſt bring in thither within the Uaile, the Arke of the Teſtimony: and
the Uaile ſhall diuide vnto you, betweene the holy place and the moſt
holy.34And thou ſhalt put the Mercie-ſeat vpon the Arke of the
Teſtimony, in the moſt holy place.35And thou ſhalt ſet the table without
the Uaile, and the candleſticke ouer againſt the table, on the ſide of the
Tabernacle toward the South: and thou ſhalt put the table on the North
ſide.36And thou ſhalt make an Hanging for the doore of the Tent, of
blew, and purple and ſcarlet, and fine twined linnen, wrought with
needle worke.37And thou ſhalt make for the Hanging fiue pillars of
Shittim wood, and ouerlay them with gold, and their hookes ſhalbe of
gold: and thou ſhalt caſt fiue ſockets of braſſe for them.
CHAPTER 271And thou ſhalt make an Altar of Shittim wood, fiue
cubits long, and fiue cubites broad: the Altar ſhall be foure ſquare, and
the height thereof ſhalbe three cubits.2And thou ſhalt make the hornes
of it vpon the foure corners thereof: his hornes ſhall be of the ſame: and
thou ſhalt ouerlay it with braſſe.3And thou ſhalt make his pannes to
receiue his aſhes, and his ſhouels, and his baſons, and his fleſhhooks,
and his firepannes: all the veſſels thereof thou ſhalt make of braſſe.4And
thou ſhalt make for it a grate of networke of braſſe; and vpon the net
ſhalt thou make foure braſen rings in the foure corners thereof.5And
thou ſhalt put it vnder the compaſſe of the Altar beneath, that the net
may bee euen to the midſt of the Altar.6And thou ſhalt make ſtaues for
the Altar, ſtaues of Shittim wood, and ouerlay them with braſſe.7And
the ſtaues ſhalbe put into the rings, and the ſtaues ſhall be vpon the two
ſides of the Altar, to beare it.8Hollow with boards ſhalt thou make it: as
it was ſhewed thee in the mount, ſo ſhall they make it.9And thou ſhalt
make the Court of the Tabernacle for the Southſide, Southward: there
ſhall be hangings for the Court, of fine twined linnen of an hundred
cubits long, for one ſide.10And the twenty pillars thereof, and their
twenty ſockets, ſhall be of braſſe: the hookes of the pillars, and their

fillets ſhalbe of ſiluer.11And likewiſe for the Northſide in length, there ſhall be hangings of an hundred cubits long, and his twenty pillars, and their twenty ſockets of braſſe: the hookes of the pillars, and their fillets of ſiluer.12And for the breadth of the Court, on the Weſtſide ſhalbe hangings of fifty cubits: their pillars tenne, and their ſockets ten.13And the breadth of the Court on the Eaſtſide Eaſtward, ſhall bee fiftie cubits.14The hangings of one ſide of the gate ſhalbe fifteene cubits: their pillars three, and their ſockets three.15And on the other ſide ſhalbe hangings, fifteene cubits: their pillars three, and their ſockets three.16And for the gate of the Court ſhall be an hanging of twenty cubits of blew, and purple, and ſcarlet, and fine twined linnen, wrought with needle worke: and their pillars ſhall be foure, and their ſockets foure.17All the pillars round about the Court ſhalbe filletted with ſiluer: their hookes ſhalbe of ſiluer, and their ſockets of braſſe.18The length of the Court ſhalbe an hundred cubits, and the breadth fiftie euery where, and the height fiue cubits of fine twined linnen, and their ſockets of braſſe.19All the veſſels of the Tabernacle in all the ſeruice thereof, and all the pinnes thereof, and all the pinnes of the Court, ſhalbe of braſſe.20And thou ſhalt command the children of Iſrael, that they bring thee pure oyle Oliue beaten, for the light, to cauſe the lampe to burne alwayes.21In the Tabernacle of the Congregation without the Uaile, which is before the Teſtimony, Aaron and his ſonnes ſhall order it from euening to morning before the Lord: It ſhall be a ſtatute for euer, vnto their generations, on the behalfe of the children of Iſrael.

CHAPTER 281And take thou vnto thee Aaron thy brother, and his ſonnes with him, from among the children of Iſrael, that he may miniſter vnto me in the Prieſts office, euen Aaron, Nadab, and Abihu, Eleazar, and Ithamar, Aarons ſonnes.2And thou ſhalt make holy garments for Aaron thy brother, for glory and for beauty.3And thou ſhalt ſpeake vnto all that are wiſe hearted, whom I haue filled with the ſpirit of wiſedome, that they may make Aarons garments to conſecrate him, that hee may miniſter vnto me in the Prieſts office.4And theſe are the garments which they ſhall make; a breaſtplate, and an Ephod, and a robe, and a broidered coat, a Miter, and a girdle: and they ſhall make holy garments for Aaron thy brother, and his ſonnes, that hee may miniſter vnto mee in the Prieſtes office.5And they ſhall take gold, and blew, and purple, and ſcarlet, and fine linnen.6And they ſhall make the Ephod of gold, of blew and of purple, of ſcarlet, and fine twined linnen, with cunning worke.7It ſhall haue the two ſhoulder pieces thereof, ioyned at the two edges thereof; and ſo it ſhall bee ioyned together.8And the curious girdle of the Ephod which is vpon it, ſhall bee of the ſame, according to the worke thereof, euen of gold, of blew, and purple, and ſcarlet, and fine twined linnen.9And thou ſhalt take two Onix ſtones, and graue on them the names of the children of Iſrael:10Sixe of their names on one ſtone, and the other ſixe names of the reſt on the other ſtone, according to their birth:11With the worke of an engrauer in ſtone; like the engrauings of a ſignet ſhalt thou engraue the two ſtones, with the names of the children of Iſrael; thou ſhalt make them to be ſet in ouches of gold.12And thou ſhalt put the two ſtones vpon the ſhoulders of the Ephod, for ſtones of memoriall vnto the children of Iſrael. And Aaron ſhall beare their names before the Lord, vpon his two ſhoulders for a memoriall.13And thou ſhalt make ouches of gold;14And two chaines of pure gold at the ends; of wreathen worke ſhalt thou make them, and faſten the wreathen chaines to the ouches.15And thou ſhalt make the breſtplate of Iudgement, with cunning worke, after the worke of the Ephod thou ſhalt make it: of gold, of blew, and of purple, and of ſcarlet, and of fine twined linnen ſhalt thou make it.16Foure ſquare it ſhall be being doubled; a ſpanne ſhalbe the length thereof, and a ſpan ſhalbe the breadth thereof.17And thou ſhalt ſet in it ſettings of ſtones; euen foure rowes of ſtones: the firſt row ſhalbe a Sardius, a Topaz, and a Carbuncle: this ſhall be the firſt row.18And the ſecond row ſhall be an Emeraude, a Saphir, and a Diamond.19And the third row a Lygure, an Agate, and an Amethiſt.20And the fourth row, a Berill, and an Onix, and a Iaſper: they ſhalbe ſet in gold in their incloſings.21And the ſtones ſhall bee with the names of the children of Iſrael, twelue, according to their names, like the engrauings of a ſignet: euery one with his name ſhall they bee according to the twelue tribes.22And thou ſhalt make vpon the breſtplate chaines at the ends, of wreathen worke, of pure gold.23And thou ſhalt make vpon the breſtplate two rings of gold, and ſhalt put the two rings on the two endes of the breſtplate.24And thou ſhalt put the two wreathen chaines of gold in the two rings, which are on the ends of the breſtplate.25And the other two endes of the two wreathen chaines, thou ſhalt faſten in the two ouches, and put them on the ſhoulder pieces of the Ephod before it.26And thou ſhalt make two rings of gold, and thou ſhalt put them vpon the two ends of the breaſtplate, in the border thereof, which is in the ſide of the Ephod inward.27And two other rings of gold thou ſhalt make, and ſhalt put them on the two ſides of the Ephod vnderneath towards the forepart thereof, ouer againſt the other coupling thereof, aboue the curious girdle of the Ephod.28And they ſhall bind the breſtplate by the rings thereof, vnto the rings of the Ephod with a lace of blewe, that it may be aboue the curious girdle of the Ephod, and that the breaſtplate be not looſed from the Ephod.29And Aaron ſhal beare the names of the children of Iſrael in the breaſtplate of iudgement, vpon his heart, when hee goeth in vnto the holy place, for a memoriall before the Lord continually.30And thou ſhalt put in the breaſtplate of iudgement, the Urim and the Thummim, and they ſhall bee vpon Aarons heart, when he goeth in before the Lord: and Aaron ſhall beare the iudgement of the children of Iſrael vpon his heart, before the Lord continually.31And thou ſhalt make the robe of the Ephod all of blew.32And there ſhall bee an hole in the top of it, in the mids thereof: it ſhall haue a binding of wouen worke, round about the hole of it, as it were the hole of an habergeon, that it be not rent.33And beneath vpon the hemme of it thou ſhalt make pomegranates of blew, and of purple, and of ſcarlet, round about the hemme thereof, and belles of gold betweene them round about.34A golden bell and a pomegranate, a golden bell and a pomegranate, vpon the hemme of the robe round about.35And it ſhall be vpon Aaron, to miniſter: and his ſound ſhall be heard when he goeth in vnto the holy place before the Lord, and when he commeth out, that he die not.36And thou ſhalt make a plate of pure gold, and graue vpon it, like the engrauings of a ſignet, HOLINES TO THE LORD.37And thou ſhalt put it on a blewe lace, that it may be vpon the miter; vpon the forefront of the miter it ſhall be.38And it ſhall be vpon Aarons forehead, that Aaron may beare the iniquitie of the holy things, which the children of Iſrael ſhall hallow, in all their holy gifts: and it ſhall be alwayes vpon his forehead, that they may be accepted before the Lord.39And thou ſhalt embroider the coat of fine linnen, and thou ſhalt make the miter of fine linnen, and thou ſhalt make the girdle of needle worke.40And for Aarons ſonnes thou ſhalt make coats, and thou ſhalt make for them girdles, and bonnets ſhalt thou make for them, for glory and for beautie.41And thou ſhalt put them vpon Aaron thy brother, and his ſonnes with him: and ſhalt annoint them, and conſecrate them, and ſanctifie them, that they may miniſter vnto mee in the Prieſts office.42And thou ſhalt make them linnen breeches, to couer their nakednes, from the loines euen vnto the thighes they ſhall reach.43And they ſhall be vpon Aaron, & vpon his ſonnes, when they come in vnto the Tabernacle of the Congregation, or when they come neere vnto the Altar to miniſter in the holy place, that they beare not iniquitie, and die. It ſhall be a ſtatute for euer vnto him and his ſeede after him.

CHAPTER 291And this is the thing that thou ſhalt doe vnto them, to hallow them, to miniſter vnto me in the Prieſts office: Take one yong bullocke, and two rammes without blemiſh,2And vnleauened bread, and cakes unleauened, tempered with oyle, and wafers vnleauened, annointed with oile: of wheaten flowre ſhalt thou make them.3And thou ſhalt put them into one baſket, and bring them in the baſket, with the bullocke and the two rammes.4And Aaron and his ſonnes thou ſhalt bring vnto the doore of the Tabernacle of the Congregation, and ſhalt waſh them with water.5And thou ſhalt take the garments, and put vpon Aaron the coat, and the robe of the Ephod, and the Ephod, and the breſtplate, and gird him with the curious girdle of the Ephod.6And thou ſhalt put the Miter vpon his head, and put the holy Crowne vpon the Miter.7Then ſhalt thou take the annointing oyle, and powre it vpon his head, and annoint him.8And thou ſhalt bring his ſonnes, and put coats vpon them.9And thou ſhalt gird them with girdles, (Aaron and his ſonneſ) and put the bonnets on them: and the prieſts office ſhall be theirs for a perpetuall ſtatute: and thou ſhalt conſecrate Aaron and his ſonnes.10And thou ſhalt cauſe a bullocke to bee brought before the Tabernacle of the Congregation: and Aaron and his ſonnes ſhall put their hands vpon the head of the bullocke.11And thou ſhalt kill the bullocke before the Lord, by the doore of the Tabernacle of the

Congregation.[12]And thou ſhalt take of the blood of the bullocke, and put it vpon the hornes of the altar with thy finger, and powre all the blood beſide the bottome of the Altar.[13]And thou ſhalt take all the fat that couereth the inwards, and the caule that is aboue the liuer, and the two kidneis, and the fat that is vpon them, and burne them vpon the altar.[14]But the fleſh of the bullocke, and his ſkinne, and his doung ſhalt thou burne with fire without the campe, it is a ſinne offering.[15]Thou ſhalt alſo take one ram, and Aaron and his ſonnes ſhall put their hands vpon the head of the ram.[16]And thou ſhalt ſlay the ramme, and thou ſhalt take his blood, and ſprinkle it round about vpon the altar.[17]And thou ſhalt cut the ramme in pieces, and waſh the inwards of him, and his legs, and put them vnto his pieces, and vnto his head.[18]And thou ſhalt burne the whole ramme vpon the Altar: it is a burnt offering vnto the Lord: It is a ſweet ſauour, an offering made by fire vnto the Lord.[19]And thou ſhalt take the other ramme: and Aaron and his ſonnes ſhall put their hands vpon the head of the ramme.[20]Then ſhalt thou kill the ramme, and take of his blood, and put it vpon the tip of the right eare of Aaron, and vpon the tip of the right eare of his ſonnes, and vpon the thumbe of their right hand, and vpon the great toe of their right foot, and ſprinckle the blood vpon the Altar round about.[21]And thou ſhalt take of the blood that is vpon the Altar, and of the anointing oyle, and ſprinkle it vpon Aaron, and vpon his garments, and vpon his ſonnes, and vpon the garments of his ſonnes with him: and hee ſhall be hallowed, and his garments, and his ſonnes, and his ſonnes garments with him.[22]Alſo thou ſhalt take of the ram the fat and the rumpe, and the fat that couereth the inwards, & the caule aboue the liuer, and the two kidneis, and the fat that is vpon them, and the right ſhoulder, for it is a ram of conſecration:[23]And one loafe of bread, and one cake of oyled bread, and one wafer out of the baſket of the vnleauened bread, that is before the Lord.[24]And thou ſhalt put all in the hands of Aaron, and in the hands of his ſonnes, and ſhalt waue them for a waue-offering before the Lord.[25]And thou ſhalt receiue them of their hands, and burne them vpon the Altar for a burnt offering, for a ſweet ſauour before the Lord: it is an offering made by fire vnto the Lord.[26]And thou ſhalt take the breſt of the ramme of Aarons conſecrations, and waue it for a waue-offering before the Lord, and it ſhalbe thy part.[27]And thou ſhalt ſanctifie the breſt of the waue-offering, and the ſhoulder of the heaue offering, which is waued, and which is heaued vp of the ramme of the conſecration, euen of that which is for Aaron, and of that which is for his ſonnes.[28]And it ſhalbe Aarons, and his ſonnes by a ſtatute for euer, from the children of Iſrael: for it is an heaue offering: and it ſhall be an heaue offering from the children of Iſrael, of the ſacrifice of their peace offrings, euen their heaue offering vnto the Lord.[29]And the holy garments of Aaron ſhall be his ſonnes after him, to bee anoynted therein, and to be conſecrated in them.[30]And that ſonne that is Prieſt in his ſtead, ſhal put them on ſeuen dayes, when he commeth into the Tabernacle of the Congregation to miniſter in the holy place.[31]And thou ſhalt take the ramme of the conſecration, and ſeethe his fleſh in the holy place.[32]And Aaron and his ſonnes ſhall eate the fleſh of the ramme, and the bread that is in the baſket, by the doore of the Tabernacle of the Cōgregation.[33]And they ſhall eate thoſe things, wherewith the atonement was made, to conſecrate and to ſanctifie them: but a ſtranger ſhall not eate thereof, becauſe they are holy.[34]And if ought of the fleſh of the conſecrations, or of the bread remaine vnto the morning, then thou ſhalt burne the remainder with fire: it ſhall not be eaten, becauſe it is holy.[35]And thus ſhalt thou doe vnto Aaron, and to his ſonnes, according to all things which I haue commaunded thee: ſeuen dayes ſhalt thou conſecrate them.[36]And thou ſhalt offer euery day a bullocke for a ſinne offering, for atonement: and thou ſhalt clenſe the Altar, when thou haſt made an atonement for it, and thou ſhalt anoynt it, to ſanctifie it.[37]Seuen dayes thou ſhalt make an atonement for the Altar, and ſanctifie it: and it ſhalbe an Altar moſt holy: whatſoeuer toucheth the Altar, ſhalbe holy.[38]Now this is that which thou ſhalt offer vpon the Altar; two lambs of the firſt yere, day by day continually.[39]The one lambe thou ſhalt offer in the morning: and the other lambe thou ſhalt offer at euen:[40]And with the one lambe a tenth deale of flowre mingled with the fourth part of an Hin of beaten oyle: and the fourth part of an Hin of wine for a drinke offering.[41]And the other lambe thou ſhalt offer at Euen, and ſhalt doe thereto, according to the meat offering of the morning, and according to the drinke offering thereof, for a ſweet ſauour, an offering made by fire vnto the Lord.[42]This ſhalbe a continuall burnt offering throughout your generations, at the doore of the Tabernacle of the Congregation, before the Lord,where I wil meete you, to ſpeake there vnto thee.[43]And there I will meet with the children of Iſrael: and the Tabernacle ſhalbe ſanctified by my glory.[44]And I will ſanctifie the Tabernacle of the Congregation, and the Altar: I will ſanctifie alſo both Aaron and his ſonnes, to miniſter to me in the Prieſts office.[45]And I will dwell amongſt the children of Iſrael, and will be their God.[46]And they ſhall know that I am the Lord their God, that brought them foorth out of the land of Egypt, that I may dwell amongſt them: I am the Lord their God.

CHAPTER 30[1]Andthou ſhalt make an Altar to burne incenſe vpon: of Shittim wood ſhalt thou make it.[2]A cubite ſhall bee the length thereof, and a cubite the breadth thereof, (foure ſquare ſhall it bee) and two cubits ſhalbe the height thereof: the hornes thereof ſhalbe of the ſame.[3]And thou ſhalt ouerlay it with pure gold, the top therof, and the ſides thereof round about, and the hornes thereof: and thou ſhalt make vnto it a crowne of gold round about.[4]And two golden rings ſhalt thou make to it vnder the crowne of it, by the two corners thereof, vpon the two ſides of it ſhalt thou make it: and they ſhalbe for places for the ſtaues to beare it withall.[5]And thou ſhalt make the ſtaues of Shittim wood, and ouerlay them with gold.[6]And thou ſhalt put it before the Uaile, that is by the Arke of the Teſtimonie before the Mercie-ſeat, that is, ouer the Teſtimonie where I will meet with thee.[7]And Aaron ſhall burne thereon ſweet incenſe euery morning: when he dreſſeth the lamps he ſhal burne incenſe vpon it.[8]And when Aaron lighteth the lampes at euen, he ſhall burne incenſe vpon it, a perpetuall incenſe before the Lord,throughout your generations.[9]Ye ſhall offer no ſtrange incenſe thereon, nor burnt ſacrifice, nor meate offering, neither ſhall ye powre drinke offering thereon.[10]And Aaron ſhall make an atonement vpon the hornes of it once in a yeere, with the blood of the ſinne offering of atonements: once in the yeere ſhall hee make atonement vpon it, throughout your generations: it is moſt holy vnto the Lord.[11]And the Lord ſpake vnto Moſes, ſaying,[12]When thou takeſt the ſumme of the children of Iſrael, after their number, then ſhall they giue euery man a ranſome for his ſoule vnto the Lord, when thou numbreſt them, that there be no plague amongſt them, when thou numbreſt them.[13]This they ſhall giue, euery one that paſſeth among them that are numbred: halfe a ſhekel after the ſhekel of the Sanctuary: A ſhekel is twenty gerahs: an halfe ſhekel ſhall be the offering of the Lord.[14]Euery one that paſſeth among them that are numbred from twentie yeeres old and aboue, ſhall giue an offering vnto the Lord.[15]The rich ſhal not giue more, and the poore ſhall not giue leſſe then halfe a ſhekel, when they giue an offering vnto the Lord, to make an atonement for your ſoules.[16]And thou ſhalt take the atonement money of the children of Iſrael, and ſhalt appoint it for the ſeruice of the Tabernacle of the Congregation, that it may be a memoriall vnto the children of Iſrael before the Lord, to make an atonement for your ſoules.[17]And the Lord ſpake vnto Moſes, ſaying,[18]Thou ſhalt alſo make a Lauer of braſſe, and his foote alſo of braſſe, to waſh withall, and thou ſhalt put it betweene the Tabernacle of the Congregation, and the altar, and thou ſhalt put water therein.[19]For Aaron and his ſonnes ſhall waſh their hands and their feet thereat.[20]When they goe into the Tabernacle of the Congregation, they ſhall waſh with water, that they die not: or when they come neere to the altar to miniſter, to burne offering made by fire vnto the Lord.[21]So they ſhall waſh their handes and their feet, that they die not: and it ſhall be a ſtatute for euer to them, euen to him and to his ſeed throughout their generations.[22]Moreouer the Lord ſpake vnto Moſes, ſaying,[23]Take thou alſo vnto thee principall ſpices, of pure myrrhe fiue hundred ſhekels, and of ſweet cinamon halfe ſo much, euen two hundred and fifty ſhekels, and of ſweet calamus two hundred and fiftie ſhekels,[24]And of Caſſia fiue hundred ſhekels, after the ſhekel of the Sanctuary, and of oyle oliue an Hin.[25]And thou ſhalt make it an oyle of holy oyntment, an oyntment compound after the arte of the Apothecarie: it ſhalbe an holy anointing oyle.[26]And thou ſhalt anoint the Tabernacle of the Congregation therewith, and the Arke of the Teſtimonie:[27]And the Table and all his veſſels, and the Candleſticke, and his veſſels, and the Altar of incenſe:[28]And the Altar of burnt offering with all his veſſels, and the Lauer and his foot.[29]And thou ſhalt ſanctifie them, that they may bee moſt holy: whatſoeuer toucheth them, ſhall be holy.[30]And thou

ſhalt annoint Aaron and his ſonnes, and conſecrate them, that they may
miniſter vnto mee in the prieſts office.31And thou ſhalt ſpeake vnto the
children of Iſrael, ſaying, This ſhall bee an holy anointing oile vnto mee,
throughout your generations.32Upon mans fleſh ſhall it not bee powred,
neither ſhall ye make any other like it, after the compoſition of it: it is
holy, and it ſhall be holy vnto you.33Whoſoeuer compoundeth any like
it, or whoſoeuer putteth any of it vpon a ſtranger, ſhall euen be cut off
from his people.34And the Lord ſaid vnto Moſes, Take vnto thee ſweete
ſpices, Stacte, and Onicha, and Galbanum: theſe ſweete ſpices with pure
frankincenſe, of each ſhall there be a like weight.35And thou ſhalt make
it a perfume, a confection after the arte of the Apothecarie, tempered
together, pure and holy.36And thou ſhalt beat ſome of it very ſmall, and
put of it before the teſtimony in the tabernacle of the Congregation,
where I will meet with thee: it ſhalbe vnto you moſt holy.37And as for
the perfume which thou ſhalt make, you ſhall not make to your ſelues,
according to the compoſition thereof: it ſhall be vnto thee holy for the
Lord.38Whoſoeuer ſhall make like vnto that, to ſmell thereto, ſhall euen
bee cut off from his people.
CHAPTER 311And the Lord ſpake vnto Moſes, ſaying,2See, I haue
called by name, Bezaleel the ſonne of Uri, the ſonne of Hur, of the tribe
of Iudah:3And I haue filled him with the Spirit of God, in wiſedome,
and in vnderſtanding, and in knowledge, and in all maner of
workemanſhip,4To deuiſe cunning workes, to worke in golde, and in
ſiluer, and in braſſe,5And in cutting of ſtones, to ſet them, and in caruing
of timber, to worke in all maner of workemanſhip.6And I, behold, I
haue giuen with him, Aholiab the ſonne of Ahiſamach, of the tribe of
Dan, and in the hearts of all that are wiſe hearted I haue put wiſedome,
that they may make all that I haue commanded thee:7The Tabernacle of
the Congregation, and the Arke of the Teſtimony, and the Mercie-ſeat
that is thereupon, & all the furniture of the Tabernacle:8And the Table,
and his furniture, and the pure Candleſticke, with all his furniture, and
the Altar of incenſe:9And the Altar of burnt offering, with all his
furniture, and the Lauer and his foote:10And the clothes of ſeruice, and
the holy garments for Aaron the Prieſt, and the garments of his ſonnes,
to miniſter in the Prieſts office:11And the anointing oyle, and ſweet
incenſe for the Holy place: according to all that I haue commanded thee,
ſhall they doe.12And the Lord ſpake vnto Moſes, ſaying,13Speake thou
alſo vnto the children of Iſrael, ſaying, Uerely my Sabbaths ye ſhall
keepe: for it is a ſigne betweene me and you, throughout your
generations, that ye may know that I am the Lord, that doth ſanctifie
you.14Yee ſhall keepe the Sabbath therefore: for it is holy vnto you:
Euery one that defileth it, ſhall ſurely be put to death: for whoſoeuer
doth any worke therein, that ſoule ſhall be cut off from amongſt his
people.15Sixe dayes may worke bee done, but in the ſeuenth is the
Sabbath of reſt, holy to the Lord: whoſoeuer doth any worke in the
Sabbath day, he ſhall ſurely be put to death.16Wherefore the children of
Iſrael ſhall keepe the Sabbath, to obſerue the Sabbath throughout their
generations, for a perpetuall couenant.17It is a ſigne betweene me and
the children of Iſrael for euer: for in ſixe dayes the Lord made heauen
and earth, and on the ſeuenth day he reſted, and was refreſhed.18And he
gaue vnto Moſes, when hee had made an end of communing with him
vpon mount Sinai, two tables of Teſtimonie, tables of ſtone, written with
the finger of God.
CHAPTER 321And when the people ſaw that Moſes delayed to come
downe out of the mount, the people gathered themſelues together vnto
Aaron, and ſaid vnto him, Up, make vs gods which ſhall goe before vs:
for as for this Moſes, the man that brought vs vp out of the land of
Egypt, we wot not what is become of him.2And Aaron ſaide vnto them,
Breake off the golden earerings which are in the eares of your wiues, of
your ſonnes, and of your daughters, and bring them vnto me.3And all
the people brake off the golden earerings, which were in their eares, and
brought them vnto Aaron.4And hee receiued them at their hand, and
faſhioned it with a grauing toole, after hee had made it a molten calfe:
and they ſaid, Theſe be thy gods, O Iſrael, which brought thee vp out of
the land of Egypt.5And when Aaron ſaw it, he built an altar before it,
and Aaron made proclamation, and ſaid, To morrow is a feaſt to the
Lord.6And they roſe vp early on the morrow, and offered burnt
offerings, and brought peace offerings: and the people ſate downe to
eate and to drinke, and roſe vp to play.7And the Lord ſaid vnto Moſes,
Goe, get thee downe: for thy people which thou broughteſt out of the
land of Egypt, haue corrupted themſelues.8They haue turned aſide
quickly out of the way which I commaunded them: they haue made
them a molten Calfe, and haue worſhipped it, and haue ſacrificed
thereunto, and ſaide, Theſe bee thy gods, O Iſrael, which haue brought
thee vp out of the land of Egypt.9And the Lord ſaid vnto Moſes, I haue
ſeene this people, and behold, it is a ſtiffenecked people.10Now
therefore let me alone, that my wrath may waxe hot againſt them, and
that I may conſume them: and I will make of thee a great nation.11And
Moſes beſought the Lord his God, and ſaid, Lord, why doeth thy wrath
waxe hot againſt thy people, which thou haſt brought foorth out of the
land of Egypt, with great power, and with a mighty hand?12Wherefore
ſhould the Egyptians ſpeake and ſay, For miſchiefe did he bring them
out, to ſlay them in the mountaines, & to conſume them from the face
of the earth? Turne from thy fierce wrath, and repent of this euill againſt
thy people.13Remember Abraham, Iſaac, and Iſrael thy ſeruants, to
whom thou ſwareſt by thine owne ſelfe, and ſaideſt vnto them, I will
multiply your ſeed as the ſtarres of heauen: and all this land that I haue
ſpoken of, will I giue vnto your ſeed, and they ſhall inherit it for
euer.14And the Lord repented of the euill which he thought to doe vnto
his people.15And Moſes turned, and went downe from the Mount, and
the two Tables of the Teſtimony were in his hand: the Tables were
written on both their ſides; on the one ſide, and on the other were they
written.16And the Tables were the worke of God; and the writing was
the writing of God, grauen vpon the Tables.17And when Ioſhua heard
the noiſe of the people as they ſhouted, hee ſaid vnto Moſes, There is a
noiſe of warre in the campe.18And he ſaid, It is not the voyce of them
that ſhout for maſtery, neither is it the voyce of them that cry for being
ouercome: but the noyſe of them that ſing doe I heare.19And it came to
paſſe, aſſoone as he came nigh vnto the campe, that he ſaw the Calfe,
and the dancing: and Moſes anger waxed hot, and he caſt the Tables out
of his hands, and brake them beneath the mount.20And he tooke the
Calfe which they had made, and burnt it in the fire, and ground it to
powder, and ſtrawed it vpon the water, and made the children of Iſrael
drinke of it.21And Moſes ſaid vnto Aaron, What did this people vnto
thee, that thou haſt brought ſo great a ſinne vpon them?22And Aaron
ſaid, Let not the anger of my lord waxe hot: thou knoweſt the people,
that they are ſet on miſchiefe.23For they ſaid vnto me, Make vs gods
which ſhall goe before vs: for as for this Moſes, the man that brought
vs vp out of the land of Egypt, we wot not what is become of him.24And
I ſaid vnto them, Whoſoeuer hath any gold, let them breake it off: So
they gaue it mee: then I caſt it into the fire, & there came out this
Calfe.25And when Moſes ſaw that the people were naked, (for Aaron
had made them naked vnto their ſhame, amongſt their enemieſ)26Then
Moſes ſtood in the gate of the campe, and ſaide, Who is on the Lords
ſide? let him come vnto mee. And all the ſonnes of Leui gathered
themſelues together vnto him.27And hee ſaid vnto them, Thus ſaith the
Lord God of Iſrael, Put euery man his ſword by his ſide, and go in and
out from gate to gate throughout the campe, and ſlay euery man his
brother, and euery man his companion, and euery man his
neighbour.28And the children of Leui did according to the word of
Moſes; and there fell of the people that day about three thouſand
men.29For Moſes had ſaid, Conſecrate your ſelues to day to the Lord,
euen euery man vpon his ſonne, and vpon his brother, that he may
beſtow vpon you a bleſſing this day.30And it came to paſſe on the
morrow, that Moſes ſaid vnto the people, Ye haue ſinned a great ſinne:
And now I will goe vp vnto the Lord; peraduenture I ſhall make an
atonement for your ſinne.31And Moſes returned vnto the Lord, and ſaid,
Oh, this people haue ſinned a great ſinne, and haue made them gods of
gold.32Yet now, if thou wilt forgiue their ſinne; and if not, blot me, I
pray thee, out of thy Booke, which thou haſt written.33And the Lord ſaid
vnto Moſes, Whoſoeuer hath ſinned againſt me, him will I blot out of
my Booke.34Therefore now goe, leade the people vnto the place of
which I haue ſpoken vnto thee: Behold, mine Angel ſhall goe before
thee; Neuertheleſſe in the day when I viſit, I will viſit their ſinne vpon
them.35And the Lord plagued the people, becauſe they made the Calfe,
which Aaron made.
CHAPTER 331And the Lord ſaid vnto Moſes, Depart, and goe vp
hence, thou and the people which thou haſt brought vp out of the land
of Egypt, vnto the land which I ſware vnto Abraham, to Iſaac, & to
Iacob, ſaying, Unto thy ſeed will I giue it.2And I will ſend an Angel

before thee, and I will driue out the Canaanite, the Amorite, and the
Hittite, and the Perizzite, the Hiuite, and the Iebufite:3Unto a land
flowing with milke and hony: For I will not goe vp in the midft of thee:
for thou art a ftiffenecked people, left I confume thee in the way.4And
when the people heard thefe euill tidings, they mourned: and no man
did put on him his ornaments.5For the Lord had faide vnto Mofes, fay
vnto the children of Ifrael, Ye are a ftiffenecked people: I wil come vp
into the midft of thee in a moment, & confume thee: Therefore now
put off thy ornaments from thee, that I may know what to doe vnto
thee.6And the children of Ifrael ftript themfelues of their ornaments, by
the mount Horeb.7And Mofes tooke the Tabernacle, & pitched it
without the campe, a farre off from the campe, and called it the
Tabernacle of the Congregation: And it came to paffe, that euery one
which fought the Lord, went out vnto the Tabernacle of the
Congregation, which was without the campe.8And it came to paffe
when Mofes went out vnto the Tabernacle, that all the people rofe vp,
and ftood euery man at his tent doore, and looked after Mofes, vntill he
was gone into the Tabernacle.9And it came to paffe as Mofes entred
into the Tabernacle, the cloudy pillar defcended, and ftood at the doore
of the Tabernacle, and the Lord talked with Mofes.10And all the people
faw the cloudy pillar ftand at the Tabernacle doore: and all the people
rofe vp, and worfhipped euery man in his tent doore.11And the Lord
fpake vnto Mofes face to face, as a man fpeaketh vnto his friend. And
he turned againe into the campe, but his feruant Iofhua the fonne of
Nun, a yong man, departed not out of the Tabernacle.12And Mofes faide
vnto the Lord, See, thou fayeft vnto mee, Bring vp this people, and thou
haft not let mee know whome thou wilt fend with me. Yet thou haft
faid, I knowe thee by name, and thou haft alfo found grace in my
fight.13Now therefore, I pray thee, If I haue found grace in thy fight,
fhewe mee now thy way that I may know thee, that I may find grace in
thy fight: and confider that this nation is thy people.14And he faid, My
prefence fhall go with thee, and I will giue thee reft.15And he faid vnto
him, If thy prefence goe not with mee, carie vs not vp hence.16For
wherein fhall it bee knowen here, that I and thy people haue found grace
in thy fight? is it not in that thou goeft with vs? So fhall we be feparated,
I and thy people, from all the people that are vpon the face of the
earth.17And the Lord faid vnto Mofes, I will doe this thing alfo that thou
haft fpoken: for thou haft found grace in my fight, and I know thee by
name.18And he faid, I befeech thee, fhew me thy glory.19And he faid, I
will make all my goodneffe paffe before thee, and I will proclaime the
name of the Lord before thee: and will bee gracious to whom I wil be
gracious, and wil fhew mercie on whom I will fhew mercie.20And he
faid, Thou canft not fee my face: for there fhall no man fee mee, and
liue.21And the Lord faid, Beholde, there is a place by mee, and thou fhalt
ftand vpon a rocke.22And it fhall come to paffe, while my glory paffeth
by, that I will put thee in a clift of the rocke, and will couer thee with
my hand, while I paffe by.23And I wil take away mine hand, and thou
fhalt fee my backe parts: but my face fhall not be feene.
CHAPTER 341And the Lord faid vnto Mofes, Hew thee two Tables
of ftone, like vnto the firft: and I will write vpon thefe Tables, the words
that were in the firft Tables which thou brakeft.2And be ready in the
morning, and come vp in the morning vnto mount Sinai, and prefent
thy felfe there to me, in the top of the mount.3And no man fhall come
vp with thee, neither let any man bee feene throughout all the mount,
neither let the flockes nor herds feede before that mount.4And he
hewed two Tables of ftone, like vnto the firft, and Mofes rofe vp earely
in the morning, and went vp vnto mount Sinai, as the Lord had
commanded him, and tooke in his hand the two tables of ftone.5And
the Lord defcended in the cloud, and ftood with him there, and
proclaimed the Name of the Lord.6And the Lord paffed by before him,
and proclaimed, The Lord, The Lord God, mercifull and gracious, long
fuffering, and abundant in goodneffe and trueth,7Keeping mercie for
thoufands, forgiuing iniquitie and tranfgreffion and finne, and that will
by no meanes cleere the guiltie, vifiting the iniquitie of the fathers vpon
the children, and vpon the childrens children, vnto the third and to the
fourth generation.8And Mofes made hafte, and bowed his head toward
the earth, and worfhipped.9And he faid, If now I haue found grace in
thy fight, O Lord, let my Lord, I pray thee, goe amongft vs, (for it is a
ftiffenecked people,) and pardon our iniquitie, and our finne, and take
vs for thine inheritance.10And he faid, Behold, I make a couenant:
before all thy people, I wil doe marueiles, fuch as haue not beene done
in all the earth, nor in any nation: and all the people amongft which thou
art, fhall fee the worke of the Lord: for it is a terrible thing that I will
doe with thee.11Obferue thou that which I command thee this day:
Behold, I driue out before thee the Amorite, and the Canaanite, and the
Hittite, and the Perizzite, and the Hiuite, and the Iebufite.12Take heed
to thy felfe, left thou make a couenant with the inhabitants of the land
whither thou goeft, left it be for a fnare in the midft of thee.13But ye
fhall deftroy their altars, breake their images, and cut downe their
groues.14For thou fhalt worfhip no other god: for the Lord, whofe name
is Ielous, is a Ielous God:15Left thou make a couenant with the
inhabitants of the land, and they goe a whoring after their gods, and doe
facrifice vnto their gods, and one call thee, and thou eate of his
facrifice,16And thou take of their daughters vnto thy fonnes, and their
daughters goe a whoring after their gods, and make thy fonnes goe a
whoring after their gods.17Thou fhalt make thee no molten gods.18The
feaft of vnleauened bread fhalt thou keepe: Seuen dayes thou fhalt eate
vnleauened bread, as I commanded thee in the time of the moneth Abib:
for in the moneth Abib thou cameft out from Egypt.19All that openeth
the matrixe is mine: and euery firftling amongft thy cattell, whether oxe
or fheepe, that is male.20But the firftling of an Afse thou fhalt redeeme
with a lambe: and if thou redeeme him not, then fhalt thou breake his
necke. All the firft borne of thy fonnes thou fhalt redeeme: and none
fhall appeare before me empty.21Sixe dayes thou fhalt worke, but on the
feuenth day thou fhalt reft: in earing time and in harueft thou fhalt
reft.22And thou fhalt obferue the feaft of weekes, of the firft fruits of
wheat harueft, and the feaft of ingathering at the yeeres end.23Thrice in
the yeere fhall all your men children appeare before the Lord God, the
God of Ifrael.24For I will caft out the nations before thee, and enlarge
thy borders: neither fhall any man defire thy land, when thou fhalt goe
vp to appeare before the Lord thy God, thrice in the yeere.25Thou fhalt
not offer the blood of my facrifice with leauen, neither fhall the facrifice
of the feaft of Paffeouer be left vnto the morning.26The firft of the firft
fruits of thy land thou fhalt bring vnto the houfe of the Lord thy God.
Thou fhalt not feeth a kid in his mothers milke.27And the Lord faid vnto
Mofes, Write thou thefe words: for after the tenour of thefe wordes, I
haue made a couenant with thee, and with Ifrael.28And hee was there
with the Lord forty dayes and forty nights: he did neither eat bread, nor
drinke water; and he wrote vpon the Tables the words of the couenant,
the ten Commandements.29And it came to paffe when Mofes came
downe from mount Sinai (with the two Tables of Teftimony in Mofes
hand, when hee came downe from the mount) that Mofes wift not that
the fkin of his face fhone, while he talked with him.30And when Aaron
and all the children of Ifrael faw Mofes, behold, the fkinne of his face
fhone, and they were afraid to come nigh him.31And Mofes called vnto
them, and Aaron and all the rulers of the Congregation returned vnto
him, and Mofes talked with them.32And afterward all the children of
Ifrael came nigh: and he gaue them in commandement all that the Lord
had fpoken with him in mount Sinai.33And till Mofes had done fpeaking
with them, he put a vaile on his face.34But when Mofes went in before
the Lord to fpeake with him, hee tooke the vaile off, vntill he came out:
And hee came out and fpake vnto the children of Ifrael, that which he
was commanded.35And the children of Ifrael faw the face of Mofes, that
the fkinne of Mofes face fhone: and Mofes put the vaile vpon his face
againe, vntill hee went in to fpeake with him.
CHAPTER 351And Mofes gathered all the Congregation of the
children of Ifrael together, and faid vnto them; Thefe are the wordes
which the Lord hath commanded, that yee fhould doe them.2Sixe dayes
fhall worke be done, but on the feuenth day there fhall be to you an holy
day, a Sabbath of reft to the Lord: whofoeuer doeth worke therein, fhall
be put to death.3Ye fhall kindle no fire throughout your habitations
vpon the Sabbath day.4And Mofes fpake vnto all the Congregation of
the children of Ifrael, faying, This is the thing which the Lord
commanded, faying,5Take ye from amongft you an offring vnto the
Lord: Whofoeuer is of a willing heart, let him bring it, an offering of the
Lord, gold, and filuer, and braffe,6And blew, and purple, and fcarlet, and
fine linnen, and goats haire,7And rammes fkinnes died red, & badgers
fkinnes, and Shittim wood,8And oyle for the light, and fpices for
anoynting oyle, and for the fweet incenfe:9And Onix ftones, and ftones
to be fet for the Ephod, and for the breftplate.10And euery wife hearted

among you, ſhall come and make all that the Lord hath commanded:11The Tabernacle, his tent, and his couering, his taches, & his barres, his pillars, and his ſockets:12The Arke and the ſtaues thereof, with the Mercy ſeat, and the Uaile of the couering:13The Table and his ſtaues, and all his veſſels, and the Shewbread,14The Candleſticke alſo for the light, and his furniture, and his lamps, with the oyle for the light,15And the incenſe Altar, and his ſtaues, and the anoynting oyle, and the ſweet incenſe, and the hanging for the doore, at the entring in of the Tabernacle:16The Altar of burnt offering with his braſen grate, his ſtaues, and all his veſſels, the Lauer and his foot:17The hangings of the Court, his pillars, and their ſockets, and the hanging for the doore of the Court:18The pinnes of the Tabernacle, and the pinnes of the Court, and their coards:19The cloathes of ſeruice, to doe ſeruice in the holy place, the holy garments for Aaron the Prieſt, and the garments of his ſonnes to miniſter in the Prieſts office.20And all the Congregation of the children of Iſrael departed from the preſence of Moſes.21And they came euery one whoſe heart ſtirred him vp, and euery one whom his ſpirit made willing, and they brought the Lords offering to the worke of the Tabernacle of the Congregation, and for all his ſeruice, and for the holy garments.22And they came both men and women, as many as were willing hearted, and brought bracelets, and earerings, and rings, & tablets, all iewels of gold: and euery man that offered, offered an offering of gold vnto the Lord.23And euery man with whom was found blew, and purple, and ſcarlet, and fine linnen, and goates haire, and red ſkinnes of rammes, and badgers ſkinnes, brought them.24Euery one that did offer an offering of ſiluer and braſſe, brought the Lords offering: and euery man with whom was found Shittim wood for any worke of the ſeruice, brought it.25And all the women that were wiſe hearted, did ſpin with their hands, and brought that which they had ſpun, both of blew, and of purple, and of ſcarlet, and of fine linnen.26And all the women whoſe heart ſtirred them vp in wiſedome, ſpunne goats haire.27And the rulers brought Onix ſtones, and ſtones to be ſet for the Ephod, and for the breſtplate:28And ſpice, and oyle for the light, and for the anoynting oyle, and for the ſweet incenſe.29The children of Iſrael brought a willing offering vnto the Lord, euery man and woman, whoſe heart made them willing to bring for all maner of worke, which the Lord had commanded to be made by the hands of Moſes.30And Moſes ſaid vnto the children of Iſrael, See, the Lord hath called by name Bezaleel the ſonne of Uri, the ſonne of Hur, of the tribe of Iudah.31And he hath filled him with the Spirit of God, in wiſedome, in vnderſtanding, and in knowledge, and in all maner of workemanſhip:32And to deuiſe curious workes, to worke in gold, & in ſiluer, and in braſſe,33And in the cutting of ſtones, to ſet them, and in caruing of wood, to make any maner of cunning worke.34And he hath put in his heart that he may teach, both he and Aholiab the ſonne of Ahiſamach of the tribe of Dan.35Them hath hee filled with wiſedome of heart, to worke all manner of worke, of the ingrauer, and of the cunning workeman, and of the embroiderer, in blew, and in purple, in ſcarlet, and in fine linnen, and of the weauer, euen of them that doe any worke, and of thoſe that deuiſe cunning worke.

CHAPTER 36 Then wrought Bezaleel and Aholiab, and euery wiſe hearted man, in whome the Lord put wiſedome and vnderſtanding, to know how to worke all maner of worke for the ſeruice of the Sanctuary, according to all that the Lord had commanded.2And Moſes called Bezaleel and Aholiab, and euery wiſe hearted man, in whoſe heart the Lord had put wiſedome, euen euery one whoſe heart ſtirred him vp to come vnto the worke to doe it.3And they receiued of Moſes all the offering which the children of Iſrael had brought, for the worke of the ſeruice of the Sanctuarie, to make it withall. And they brought yet vnto him free offerings euery morning.4And al the wiſemen that wrought all the worke of the Sanctuary, came euery man from his worke which they made.5And they ſpake vnto Moſes, ſaying, The people bring much more then enough for the ſeruice of the worke which the Lord commaunded to make.6And Moſes gaue commandement, and they cauſed it to bee proclaimed throughout the campe, ſaying, Let neither man nor woman make any more worke for the offering of the Sanctuarie: ſo the people were reſtrained from bringing.7For the ſtuffe they had was ſufficient for all the worke to make it, and too much.8And euery wiſe hearted man, among them that wrought the worke of the Tabernacle, made ten curtaines, of fine twined linnen, and blew, and purple, and ſcarlet: with Cherubims of cunning worke made he them.9The length of one curtaine was twentie & eight cubites, and the breadth of one curtaine foure cubites: the curtaines were all of one ciſe.10And he coupled the fiue curtaines one vnto another: and the other fiue curtaines he coupled one vnto another.11And he made loopes of blew, on the edge of one curtaine, from the ſeluedge in the coupling: likewiſe hee made in the vttermoſt ſide of another curtaine, in the coupling of the ſecond.12Fiftie loopes made he in one curtaine, and fiftie loopes made hee in the edge of the curtaine which was in the coupling of the ſecond: the loopes held one curtaine to another.13And he made fiftie taches of gold, and coupled the curtaines one vnto another with the taches. So it became one tabernacle.14And he made curtaines of goats haire, for the tent ouer the Tabernacle: eleuen curtaines he made them.15The length of one curtaine was thirtie cubites, and foure cubites was the breadth of one curtaine: the eleuen curtaines were of one ciſe.16And he coupled fiue curtaines by themſelues, and ſixe curtaines by themſelues.17And he made fiftie loopes vpon the vttermoſt edge of the curtaine in the coupling, and fiftie loopes made he vpon the edge of the curtaine, which coupleth the ſecond.18And he made fiftie taches of braſſe to couple the tent together that it might be one.19And he made a couering for the tent of rammes ſkinnes died red, and a couering of badgers ſkinnes aboue that.20And hee made boards for the Tabernacle of Shittim wood, ſtanding up.21The length of a board was ten cubites, and the breadth of a board one cubite and a halfe.22One board had two tenons, equally diſtant one from another: thus did he make for all the boards of the tabernacle.23And he made boards for the Tabernacle: twentie boards for the South ſide, Southward.24And fourtie ſockets of ſiluer hee made vnder the twentie boards: two ſockets vnder one board for his two tenons, and two ſockets vnder another board, for his two tenons.25And for the other ſide of the Tabernacle which is toward the North corner, he made twentie boards.26And their fourtie ſockets of ſiluer: two ſockets vnder one board, and two ſockets vnder another board.27And for the ſides of the Tabernacle Weſtward, he made ſixe boards.28And two boards made he for the corners of the Tabernacle, in the two ſides.29And they were coupled beneath and coupled together at the head thereof, to one ring: thus hee did to both of them in both the corners.30And there were eight boards, and their ſockets were ſixteene ſockets of ſiluer: vnder euery board two ſockets.31And he made barres of Shittim wood: five for the boards of the one ſide of the Tabernacle,32And fiue barres for the boards of the other ſide of the Tabernacle, and fiue barres for the boards of the Tabernacle for the ſides Weſtward.33And he made the middle barre to ſhoot thorow the boards from the one end to the other.34And he ouerlaid the boards with gold, and made their rings of golde to be places for the barres, and ouerlaide the barres with gold.35And he made a Uaile of blew, and purple, and ſcarlet, and fine twined linnen: with Cherubims made he it of cunning worke.36And he made thereunto foure pillars of Shittim wood, and ouerlaide them with golde: their hookes were of gold: and he caſt for them foure ſockets of ſiluer.37And hee made an hanging for the Tabernacle doore of blew and purple, and ſcarlet, and fine twined linnen, of needle worke,38And the fiue pillars of it with their hooks: and he ouerlaid their chapiters and their fillets with gold: but their fiue ſockets were of braſſe.

CHAPTER 371And Bezaleel made the Arke of Shittim wood: two cubites and a halfe was the length of it, and a cubite and a halfe the breadth of it, and a cubite and a halfe the height of it.2And he ouerlaid it with pure gold within & without, and made a crowne of gold to it round about.3And hee caſt for it foure rings of gold, to be ſet by the foure corners of it: euen two rings vpon the one ſide of it, and two rings vpon the other ſide of it.4And he made ſtaues of Shittim wood, and ouerlaid them with gold.5And hee put the ſtaues into the rings, by the ſides of the Arke, to beare the Arke.6And he made the Mercie ſeat of pure gold: two cubites and an halfe was the length thereof, and one cubite and an halfe the breadth thereof.7And he made two Cherubims of gold, beaten out of one piece made hee them, on the two endes of the Mercie ſeate:8One Cherub on the end on this ſide, and another Cherub on the other end, on that ſide: out of the Mercie ſeat made hee the Cherubims on the two ends thereof.9And the Cherubims ſpread out their wings on high, and coucred with their wings ouer the Mercie ſeat with their faces one to another: euen to the Mercie ſeat ward were the faces of the Cherubims. 10 And hee made the Table of Shittim wood: two cubites was the length thereof, and a cubite the breadth thereof, and a cubite and a halfe the height thereof. 11 And he ouerlaid it with pure gold, and made thereunto a crowne of gold round about. 12 Alſo he made thereunto a border of an handbreadth, round about: and made a crowne of gold for the border thereof round about. 13 And hee caſt for it foure rings of gold, and put the rings vpon the foure corners that were in the foure feete thereof. 14 Ouer againſt the border were the rings, the places for the ſtaues, to beare the Table. 15 And he made the ſtaues of Shittim wood, and ouerlayed them with gold, to beare the Table. 16 And hee made the veſſels which were vpon the Table, his diſhes, and his ſpoones, and his bowles, and his couers to couer withall, of pure gold. 17 And he made the Candleſticke of pure gold, of beaten worke made he the Candleſticke, his ſhaft & his branch, his bowles, his knops, and his flowers were of the ſame. 18 And ſixe branches going out of the ſides thereof: three branches of the candleſticke out of the one ſide thereof, and three branches of the candleſticke out of the other ſide thereof. 19 Three bowles made he after the faſhion of almonds, in one branch, a knop and a flower: and three bowles made like almonds, in another branch, a knop and a flower: ſo throughout the ſixe branches, going out of the Candleſticke. 20 And in the candleſticke were foure bowles made like almonds, his knops, and his flowers: 21 And a knop vnder two branches of the ſame, & a knop vnder two branches of the ſame, and a knop vnder two branches of the ſame, according to the ſixe branches going out of it. 22 Their knops and their branches were of the ſame: all of it was one beaten worke of pure gold. 23 And he made his ſeuen lampes, and his ſnuffers, and his ſnuffe-diſhes of pure gold. 24 Of a talent of pure gold made he it, and all the veſſels thereof. 25 And he made the incenſe Altar of Shittim wood: the length of it was a cubit, and the breadth of it a cubit: it was foure ſquare, and two cubites was the height of it; the hornes thereof were of the ſame. 26 And he ouerlayed it with pure gold, both the top of it and the ſides thereof round about, and the hornes of it: alſo he made vnto it a crowne of gold round about. 27 And he made two rings of gold for it vnder the crowne thereof, by the two corners of it, vpon the two ſides thereof, to bee places for the ſtaues to beare it withall. 28 And he made the ſtaues of Shittim wood, and ouerlayed them with gold. 29 And he made the holy anoynting oyle, and the pure incenſe of ſweet ſpices, according to the worke of the Apothecary.

CHAPTER 38 1 And he made the Altar of burnt offring of Shittim wood: fiue cubits was the length thereof, and fiue cubits the breadth thereof: it was foure ſquare, and three cubits the height thereof. 2 And hee made the hornes thereof on the foure corners of it: the hornes thereof were of the ſame, and he ouerlayed it with braſſe. 3 And he made all the veſſels of the Altar, the pots and the ſhouels, and the baſons, and the fleſhhookes, and the firepannes: all the veſſels thereof made he of braſſe. 4 And he made for the Altar a braſen grate of networke, vnder the compaſſe thereof, beneath vnto the midſt of it. 5 And hee caſt foure rings for the foure ends of the grate of braſſe, to bee places for the ſtaues. 6 And he made the ſtaues of Shittim wood, and ouerlayed them with braſſe. 7 And hee put the ſtaues into the rings on the ſides of the Altar, to beare it withall; hee made the Altar hollow with boards. 8 And hee made the Lauer of braſſe, and the foot of it of braſſe, of the looking glaſſes of the women aſſembling, which aſſembled at the doore of the Tabernacle of the Congregation. 9 And he made the Court: on the Southſide Southward, the hangings of the Court were of fine twined linnen, a hundred cubits. 10 Their pillars were twenty, and their braſen ſockets twentie: the hooks of the pillars, and their fillets were of ſiluer. 11 And for the North ſide, the hangings were an hundred cubites, their pillars were twentie, and their ſockets of braſſe twentie: the hoopes of the pillars, and their fillets of ſiluer. 12 And for the Weſt ſide were hangings of fiftie cubites, their pillars ten, and their ſockets ten: the hookes of the pillars, and their fillets of ſiluer. 13 And for the Eaſt ſide Eaſtward fiftie cubites. 14 The hangings of the one ſide of the gate were fifteene cubites, their pillars three, and their ſockets three. 15 And for the other ſide of the court gate on this hand and that hand were hangings of fifteene cubites, their pillars three, and their ſockets three. 16 All the hangings of the court round about, were of fine twined linnen. 17 And the ſockets for the pillars were of braſſe, the hookes of the pillars, and their fillets of ſiluer, and the ouerlaying of their chapiters of ſiluer, and all the pillars of the court were filleted with ſiluer. 18 And the hanging for the gate of the Court was needle worke, of blew, and purple, and ſcarlet, and fine twined linnen: and twentie cubites was the length, and the height in the breadth was fiue cubites, anſwerable to the hangings of the Court. 19 And their pillars were foure, and their ſockets of braſſe foure, their hookes of ſiluer, and the ouerlaying of their chapiters, & their fillets of ſiluer. 20 And all the pinnes of the Tabernacle, and of the court round about, were of braſſe. 21 This is the ſumme of the Tabernacle, euen of the Tabernacle of Teſtimonie, as it was counted, according to the commaundement of Moſes, for the ſeruice of the Leuites, by the hand of Ithamar, ſon to Aaron the Prieſt. 22 And Bezaleel the ſonne of Uri, the ſonne of Hur, of the tribe of Iudah, made all that the Lord commanded Moſes. 23 And with him was Aholiab, ſonne of Ahiſamach, of the tribe of Dan, an engrauer, and a cunning workeman, and an embroiderer in blew, and in purple, and in ſcarlet, and fine linnen. 24 All the gold that was occupied for the worke in all the worke of the holy place, euen the gold of the offring, was twentie and nine talents, and ſeuen hundred and thirtie ſhekels, after the ſhekel of the Sanctuary. 25 And the ſiluer of them that were numbred of the Congregation, was an hundred talents, and a thouſand, ſeuen hundred and threeſcore and fifteene ſhekels, after the ſhekel of the Sanctuary. 26 A Bekah for euery man, that is, halfe a ſhekel, after the ſhekel of the Sanctuary, for euery one that went to be numbred, from twentie yeeres olde and vpward, for ſixe hundred thouſand, and three thouſand, and fiue hundred, and fiftie men. 27 And of the hundred talents of ſiluer, were caſt the ſockets of the Sanctuary, and the ſockets of the vaile: an hundred ſockets of the hundred talents, a talent for a ſocket. 28 And of the thouſand, ſeuen hundred, ſeuentie and fiue ſhekels, he made hookes for the pillars, and ouerlaide their chapiters, and filleted them. 29 And the braſſe of the offring was ſeuentie talents, and two thouſand and foure hundred ſhekels. 30 And therewith he made the ſockets to the doore of the Tabernacle of the Congregation, and the braſen Altar, and the braſen grate for it, and all the veſſels of the Altar, 31 And the ſockets of the court round about, and the ſockets of the court gate, and all the pinnes of the Tabernacle, and all the pinnes of the court round about.

CHAPTER 39 1 And of the blew, and purple, and ſcarlet, they made clothes of ſeruice, to doe ſeruice in the holy place, and made the holy garments for Aaron, as the Lord commanded Moſes. 2 And he made the Ephod of gold, blew, and purple, and ſcarlet, and fine twined linnen. 3 And they did beate the golde into thinne plates, and cut it into wiers, to worke it in the blew, and in the purple, and in the ſcarlet, and in the fine linnen, with cunning worke. 4 They made ſhoulder pieces for it, to couple it together; by the two edges was it coupled together. 5 And the curious girdle of his Ephod that was vpon it, was of the ſame, according to the worke thereof: of gold, blew, and purple, and ſcarlet, and fine twined linnen, as the Lord commanded Moſes. 6 And they wrought Onix ſtones encloſed in ouches of gold, grauen as ſignets are grauen, with the names of the children of Iſrael. 7 And hee put them on the ſhoulderſof the Ephod, that they ſhould be ſtones for a memoriall to the children of Iſrael, as the Lord commanded Moſes. 8 And he made the breſtplate of cunning worke, like the worke of the Ephod, of gold, blew, and purple, and ſcarlet, and fine twined linnen. 9 It was foure ſquare, they made the breſtplate double: a ſpanne was the length therof, and a ſpanne the breadth thereof being doubled. 10 And they ſet in it foure rowes of ſtones: the firſt row was a Sardius, a Topaz, and a Carbuncle: this was the firſt row. 11 And the ſecond row an Emeraude, a Saphire and a Diamond. 12 And the third row a Lygure, an Agate, and an Amethiſt. 13 And the fourth row, a Berill, an Onix and a Iaſper: they were encloſed in ouches of gold in their incloſings. 14 And the ſtones were according to the names of the children of Iſrael, twelue according to their names, like the ingrauings of a ſignet, euery one with his name, according to the twelue tribes. 15 And they made vpon the breſtplate chaines, at the ends, of wrethen worke of pure gold. 16 And they made two ouches of gold, and two gold rings: and put the two rings in the two ends of the breſtplate. 17 And they put the two wreathen chaines of golde in the two rings on the ends of the breſtplate. 18 And the two endes of the two wreathen chaines they faſtened in the two ouches, and put them on the ſhoulder pieces of the Ephod, before it. 19 And they made two rings of gold, and put them on the two endes of the breſt plate vpon the border of it, which was on the ſide of the Ephod inward. 20 And they made two other golden rings, and put them on the two ſides of the Ephod vnderneath, toward the forepart of it, ouer againſt the other coupling thereof, aboue the curious girdle of the Ephod.21And they did bind the breſt plate by his rings vnto the rings of the Ephod, with a lace of blew, that it might be aboue the curious girdle of the Ephod, and that the breſt plate might not bee looſed from the Ephod, as the Lord commanded Moſes.22And he made the robe of the Ephod of wouen worke, all of blew.23And there was a hole in the midſt of the robe as the hole of an habergeon, with a band round about the hole, that it ſhould not rent.24And they made vpon the hemmes of the robe pomegranates, of blew, and purple, and ſcarlet, and twined linnen.25And they made belles of pure gold, and put the belles betweene the pomegranates, vpon the hemme of the robe, round about betweene the pomegranates.26A bell and a pomegranate, a bell and a pomegranate round about the hemme of the robe to miniſter in, as the Lord commanded Moſes.27And they made coats of fine linnen, of wouen worke, for Aaron and for his ſonnes.28And a miter of fine linnen, and goodly bonnets of fine linnen, and linnen breeches of fine twined linnen,29And a girdle of fine twined linnen and blew, and purple, and ſcarlet of needle worke, as the Lord commanded Moſes.30And they made the plate of the holy Crowne of pure gold, and wrote vpon it a writing, like to the engrauings of a ſignet, HOLINES TO THE LORD.31And they tied vnto it a lace of blew to faſten it on high vpon the mitre, as the Lord commanded Moſes.32Thus was all the worke of the Tabernacle of the tent of the Congregation finiſhed: and the children of Iſrael did according to al that the Lord commanded Moſes, ſo did they.33And they brought the Tabernacle vnto Moſes, the tent, and all his furniture, his taches, his boards, his barres, and his pillars, and his ſockets.34And the couering of rammes ſkinnes died red, and the couering of badgers ſkinnes, and the vaile of the couering:35The Arke of the Teſtimony, and the ſtaues thereof, and the Mercie ſeat,36The Table, and all the veſſels thereof, and the ſhew bread:37The pure Candleſticke, with the lampes thereof, euen with the lampes to be ſet in order, and all the veſſels thereof, and the oyle for light:38And the golden altar, and the anointing oyle, and the ſweet incenſe, and the hanging for the Tabernacle doore:39The braſen altar, and his grate of braſſe, his ſtaues, and all his veſſels, the lauer and his foote:40The hangings of the Court, his pillars, and his ſockets, and the hanging for the court gate, his coards, and his pinnes, and all the veſſels of the ſeruice of the Tabernacle, for the tent of the Congregation:41The clothes of ſeruice to doe ſeruice in the holy place, and the holy garments for Aaron the Prieſt, and his ſonnes garments to miniſter in the Prieſts office.42According to all that the Lord commanded Moſes, ſo the children of Iſrael made all the worke.43And Moſes did looke vpon all the worke, and behold, they had done it as the Lord had commanded, euen ſo had they done it: and Moſes bleſſed them.

CHAPTER 401And the Lord ſpake vnto Moſes, ſaying,2On the firſt day of the firſt moneth ſhalt thou ſet vp the Tabernacle of the Tent of the Congregation.3And thou ſhalt put therein the Arke of the Teſtimonie, and couer the Arke with the Uaile:4And thou ſhalt bring in the Table, and ſet in order the things that are to be ſet in order vpon it, and thou ſhalt bring in the Candleſticke, and light the lampes thereof.5And thou ſhalt ſet the Altar of gold for the incenſe before the Arke of the Teſtimonie, and put the hanging of the doore to the Tabernacle.6And thou ſhalt ſet the Altar of the burnt offering, before the doore of the Tabernacle of the Tent of the Congregation.7And thou ſhalt ſet the Lauer betweene the Tent of the Congregation and the Altar, and ſhalt put water therein.8And thou ſhalt ſet vp the Court round about, and hang vp the hanging at the Court gate.9And thou ſhalt take the annoynting oyle, and annoynt the Tabernacle and all that is therein, and ſhalt hallow it, and all the veſſels thereof: and it ſhalbe holy.10Aud thou ſhalt annoynt the Altar of the burnt offering, and all his veſſels, and ſanctifie the Altar: and it ſhalbe an Altar moſt Holy.11And thou ſhalt annoynt the Lauer and his foot, and ſanctifie it.12And thou ſhalt bring Aaron and his ſonnes vnto the doore of the Tabernacle of the Congregation, and waſh them with water.13And thou ſhalt put vpon Aaron the holy garments, and anoynt him, and ſanctifie him, that he may miniſter vnto me in the Prieſts office.14And thou ſhalt bring his ſonnes, and clothe them with coats.15And thou ſhalt anoynt them, as thou didſt anoynt their father, that they may miniſter vnto mee in the Prieſts office: For their anoynting ſhall ſurely be an euerlaſting Prieſthood, throughout their generations.16Thus did Moſes: according to all that the Lord commanded him, ſo did he.17And it came to paſſe in the firſt moneth, in the ſecond yeere, on the firſt day of the moneth, that the Tabernacle was reared vp.18And Moſes reared vp the Tabernacle, and faſtened his ſockets, and ſet vp the boards thereof, and put in the barres thereof, and reared vp his pillars.19And he ſpread abroad the tent ouer the Tabernacle, and put the couering of the Tent aboue vpon it, as the Lord commanded Moſes.20And he tooke and put the teſtimony into the Arke, and ſet the ſtaues on the Arke, and put the Mercie-ſeat aboue vpon the Arke.21And he brought the Arke into the Tabernacle, and ſet vp the Uaile of the couering, and couered the Arke of the Teſtimony, as the Lord commanded Moſes.22And hee put the Table in the Tent of the Congregation, vpon the ſide of the Tabernacle Northwaed, without the Uaile.23And he ſet the bread in order vpon it, before the Lord, as the Lord had commanded Moſes.24And he put the candleſticke in the Tent of the Congregation, ouer againſt the Table, on the ſide of the Tabernacle Southward.25And he lighted the lampes before the Lord, as the Lord commanded Moſes.26And he put the golden Altar in the Tent of the Congregation, before the Uaile.27And he burnt ſweet incenſe thereon, as the Lord commanded Moſes.28And hee ſet vp the hanging, at the doore of the Tabernacle.29And he put the Altar of burnt offering by the doore of the Tabernacle of the Tent of the Congregation, and offered vpon it the burnt offering, and the meat offring, as the Lord commanded Moſes.30And he ſet the Lauer betweene the Tent of the Congregation and the Altar, & put water there, to waſh withall.31And Moſes, and Aaron and his ſonnes, waſhed their hands, and their feet thereat.32When they went into the Tent of the Congregation, and when they came neere vnto the Altar, they waſhed, as the Lord commanded Moſes.33And hee reared vp the Court round about the Tabernacle, and the Altar, & ſet vp the hanging of the Court gate: ſo Moſes finiſhed the worke.34Then a cloud couered the Tent of the Congregation, and the glory of the Lord filled the Tabernacle.35And Moſes was not able to enter into the Tent of the Congregation, becauſe the cloud abode thereon, and the glory of the Lord filled the Tabernacle.36And when the cloud was taken vp from ouer the Tabernacle, the children of Iſrael went onward in all their iourneys:37But if the cloud were not taken vp, then they iourneyed not, till the day that it was taken vp.38For the cloud of the Lord was vpon the Tabernacle by day, and fire was on it by night, in the ſight of all the houſe of Iſrael, throughout all their iourneys.

LEUITICUS (LEVITICUS)

CHAPTER 11And the Lord called vnto Moſes, and ſpake vnto him out of the Tabernacle of the Congregation, ſaying,2Speake vnto the children of Iſrael, and ſay vnto them, If any man of you bring an offering vnto the Lord, ye ſhall bring your offering of the cattell, euen of the herd, and of the flocke.3If his offering be a burnt ſacrifice of the herd, let him offer a male without blemiſh: he ſhall offer it of his owne voluntary will, at the doore of the Tabernacle of the Congregation before the Lord.4And he ſhall put his hand vpon the head of the burnt offering: and it ſhall be accepted for him to make atonement for him.5And he ſhall kill the bullocke before the Lord: and the Prieſts Aarons ſonnes ſhall bring the blood, and ſprinkle the blood round about vpon the altar, that is by the doore of the Tabernacle of the Congregation.6And hee ſhall ſlay the burnt offering, and cut it into his pieces.7And the ſonnes of Aaron the Prieſt ſhall put fire vpon the Altar, and lay the wood in order vpon the fire.8And the Prieſts Aarons ſonnes ſhall lay the parts, the head and the fat in order vpon the wood that is in the fire which is vpon the altar.9But the inwards and his legges ſhall he waſh in water, and the Prieſt ſhall burne all on the altar, to be a burnt ſacrifice, an offering made by fire, of a ſweet ſauour vnto the Lord.10And if his offring be of the flocks, namely of the ſheepe, or of the goates for a burnt ſacrifice, he ſhall bring it a male without blemiſh.11And hee ſhall kill it on the ſide of the Altar Northward, before the Lord: and the Prieſtes Aarons ſonnes ſhall ſprinkle his blood round about vpon the altar.12And he ſhall cut it into his pieces, with his head and his fat: and the Prieſt ſhall lay them in order on the wood that is on the fire, which is vpon the altar:[13]But hee ſhall waſh the inwards and the legs with water, and the Prieſt ſhall bring it all, and burne it vpon the altar: it is a burnt ſacrifice, an offering made by fire, of a ſweet ſauour vnto the Lord.[14]And if the burnt ſacrifice for his offring to the Lord be of foules, then he ſhall bring his offering of turtle doues, or of yong pigeons.[15]And the Prieſt ſhall bring it vnto the altar, and wring off his head, and burne it on the altar: and the blood thereof ſhall be wrung out at the ſide of the altar.[16]And he ſhall plucke away his crop with his feathers, and caſt it beſide the altar on the Eaſt part, by the place of the aſhes.[17]And hee ſhall cleane it with the wings thereof, but ſhall not diuide it aſunder: And the Prieſt ſhall burne it vpon the altar, vpon the wood that is vpon the fire: it is a burnt ſacrifice, an offering made by fire of a ſweet ſauour vnto the Lord.

CHAPTER 2[1]And when any will offer a meate offering vnto the Lord, his offring ſhall be of fine flowre: and hee ſhall powre oyle vpon it, and put frankincenſe thereon.[2]And he ſhall bring it to Aarons ſonnes the Prieſts: and hee ſhall take thereout his handfull of the flowre thereof, and of the oile thereof, with all the frankincenſe thereof, and the Prieſt ſhall burne the memoriall of it vpon the altar, to be an offering made by fire of a ſweet ſauour vnto the Lord.[3]And the remnant of the meat offering ſhall be Aarons and his ſonnes: it is a thing moſt holy of the offerings of the Lord made by fire.[4]And if thou bring an oblation of a meate offering baken in the ouen, it ſhall bee an vnleauened cake of fine flowre mingled with oyle, or vnleauened wafers anointed with oyle.[5]And if thy oblation be a meate offering baken in a panne, it ſhall bee of fine flowre vnleauened, mingled with oyle.[6]Thou ſhalt part it in pieces, and powre oyle thereon: it is a meate offering.[7]And if thy oblation be a meate offering baken in the frying pan, it ſhalbe made of fine flowre with oyle.[8]And thou ſhalt bring the meat offering that is made of theſe things vnto the Lord, and when it is preſented vnto the Prieſt, he ſhall bring it vnto the Altar.[9]And the Prieſt ſhall take from the meat offering a memoriall thereof, and ſhall burne it vpon the Altar, it is an offering made by fire of a ſweet ſauour vnto the Lord.[10]And that which is left of the meat offering, ſhalbe Aarons and his ſonnes: It is a thing moſt holy, of the offerings of the Lord made by fire.[11]No meat offering, which ye ſhall bring vnto the Lord, ſhall be made with leauen: For ye ſhall burne no leauen, nor any hony, in any offering of the Lord made by fire.[12]As for the oblation of the firſt fruits, yee ſhall offer them vnto the Lord, but they ſhall not be burnt on the Altar for a ſweet ſauour.[13]And euery oblation of thy meat offering ſhalt thou ſeaſon with ſalt; neither ſhalt thou ſuffer the ſalt of the Couenant of thy God to bee lacking from thy meat offering: with all thine offerings thou ſhalt offer ſalt.[14]And if thou offer a meat offering of thy firſt fruits vnto the Lord, thou ſhalt offer for the meat offering of thy firſt fruits, greene eares of corne dried by the fire, euen corne beaten out of full eares.[15]And thou ſhalt put oyle vpon it, and lay frankincenſe theron; it is a meat offering.[16]And the Prieſt ſhall burne the memoriall of it, part of the beaten corne thereof, and part of the oyle thereof, with all the frankincenſe thereof: it is an offering made by fire vnto the Lord.

CHAPTER 3[1]And if his oblation be a ſacrifice of peace offering, if hee offer it of the herd, whether it be a male or female, he ſhal offer it without blemiſh before the Lord.[2]And he ſhall lay his hand vpon the head of his offering, and kil it at the doore of the Tabernacle of the Congregation: and Aarons ſonnes the Prieſts ſhall ſprinckle the blood vpon the Altar round about.[3]And he ſhall offer of the ſacrifice of the peace offering, an offering made by fire vnto the Lord; the fat that couereth the inwards, and all the fat that is vpon the inwards.[4]And the two kidneys, and the fat that is on them, which is by the flanks: and the caule aboue the liuer with the kidneys, it ſhall he take away.[5]And Aarons ſonnes ſhall burne it on the Altar vpon the burnt ſacrifice, which is vpon the wood that is on the fire: it is an offering made by fire of a ſweet ſauour vnto the Lord.[6]And if his offering for a ſacrifice of peace offering vnto the Lord, be of the flocke, male or female, he ſhall offer it without blemiſh.[7]If hee offer a lambe for his offering, then ſhall he offer it before the Lord.[8]And he ſhall lay his hand vpon the head of his offering, and kill it before the Tabernacle of the Congregation: And Aarons ſonnes ſhall ſprinkle the blood thereof, round about vpon the Altar.[9]And he ſhall offer of the ſacrifice of the peace offering, an offering made by fire vnto the Lord: the fat thereof and the whole rumpe, it ſhall he take off hard by the backe bone: and the fat that couereth the inwards, and all the fat that is vpon the inwards.[10]And the two kidneys, and the fat that is vpon them, which is by the flankes, and the caule aboue the liuer, with the kidneys, it ſhall he take away.[11]And the Prieſt ſhall burne it vpon the Altar: it is the food of the offering made by fire vnto the Lord.[12]And if his offering be a goat, then he ſhall offer it before the Lord.[13]And he ſhall lay his hand vpon the head of it, and kill it before the Tabernacle of the Congregation: and the ſonnes of Aaron ſhall ſprinckle the blood thereof vpon the Altar, round about.[14]And he ſhall offer thereof his offering, euen an offering made by fire vnto the Lord; the fat that couereth the inwards, and al the fat that is vpon the inwards.[15]And the two kidneys, and the fat that is vpon them, which is by the flancks, and the caule aboue the liuer with the kidneys, it ſhall he take away.[16]And the Prieſt ſhall burne them vpon the Altar: it is the food of the offering made by fire, for a ſweet ſauour: All the fat is the Lords.[17]It ſhall be a perpetuall ſtatute for your generations, throughout all your dwellings, that ye eat neither fat, nor blood.

CHAPTER 4[1]And the Lord ſpake vnto Moſes, ſaying,[2]Speake vnto the children of Iſrael, ſaying, If a ſoule ſhall ſinne through ignorance againſt any of the commandements of the Lord (concerning things which ought not to bee done) and ſhall do againſt any of them:[3]If the Prieſt that is anointed, doe ſinne according to the ſinne of the people, then let him bring for his ſinne which he hath ſinned, a yong bullocke without blemiſh, vnto the Lord for a ſinne offering.[4]And hee ſhall bring the bullocke vnto the doore of the Tabernacle of the Congregation before the Lord, and ſhall lay his hand vpon the bullockes head, and kill the bullocke before the Lord.[5]And the Prieſt that is anointed, ſhall take of the bullocks blood, and bring it to the Tabernacle of the Congregation.[6]And the Prieſt ſhall dip his finger in the blood, and ſprinkle of the blood ſeuen times before the Lord, before the Uaile of the Sanctuary.[7]And the Prieſt ſhall put ſome of the blood vpon the hornes of the Altar of ſweet incenſe before the Lord, which is in the Tabernacle of the Congregation, and ſhal powre all the blood of the bullocke at the bottome of the altar of the burnt offering, which is at the doore of the Tabernacle of the Congregation.[8]And he ſhall take off from it all the fat of the bullocke for the ſinne offering: the fat that couereth the inwards, and all the fat that is vpon the inwards.[9]And the two kidneis, and the fat that is vpon them, which is by the flankes, and the caule aboue the liuer with the kidneis, it ſhall he take away,[10]As it was taken off from the bullocke of the ſacrifice of peace offerings: and the Prieſt ſhall burne them vpon the altar of the burnt offering.[11]And the ſkinne of the bullocke, and all his fleſh, with his head, and with his legs, and his inwards, and his doung,[12]Euen the whole bullocke ſhall he carie foorth without the campe, vnto a cleane place, where the aſhes are powred out, and burne him on the wood with fire: where the aſhes are powred out, ſhall he be burnt.[13]And if the whole Congregation of Iſrael ſinne through ignorance, and the thing be hid from the eyes of the aſſembly, and they haue done ſomewhat againſt any of the Commandements of the Lord, concerning things which ſhould not be done, and are guiltie:[14]When the ſinne which they haue ſinned againſt it, is knowen, then the Congregation ſhall offer a yong bullocke for the ſinne, and bring him before the Tabernacle of the Congregation.[15]And the Elders of the Congregation ſhall lay their hands vpon the head of the bullocke, before the Lord: and the bullocke ſhall be killed before the Lord.[16]And the Prieſt that is anointed, ſhall bring of the bullockes blood to the Tabernacle of the Congregation.[17]And the Prieſt ſhall dip his finger in ſome of the blood, and ſprinkle it ſeuen times before the Lord, euen before the vaile.[18]And he ſhal put ſome of the blood vpon the hornes of the altar, which is before the Lord, that is in the Tabernacle of the Congregation, and ſhall powre out all the blood at the bottome of the altar of the burnt offring, which is at the doore of the Tabernacle of the Congregation.[19]And he ſhall take all his fat from him, and burne it vpon the altar.[20]And he ſhall do with the bullocke as he did with the bullocke for a ſinne offring, ſo ſhall he do with this: And the Prieſt ſhall make an atonement for them, and it ſhall be forgiuen them.[21]And he ſhall carie foorth the bullocke without the campe, and burne him as he burned the firſt bullocke: it is a ſinne offering for the Congregation.[22]When a ruler hath ſinned and done ſomewhat through ignorance againſt any of the Commandements of the Lord his God, concerning things which ſhould not be done, and is guilty:[23]Or if his ſinne wherein hee hath ſinned, come to his knowledge: he ſhall bring his offering, a kid of the goates, a male without blemiſh.24And hee ſhall lay his hand vpon the head of the goate, and kill it in the place where they kill the burnt offering before the Lord: it is a ſinne offring.25And the Prieſt ſhall take of the blood of the ſinne offering with his finger, and put it vpon the hornes of the Altar of burnt offring, and ſhall powre out his blood at the bottome of the Altar of burnt offering.26And he ſhall burne all his fat vpon the Altar, as the fat of the ſacrifice of peace offerings: and the Prieſt ſhall make an atonement for him, as concerning his ſinne, and it ſhall be forgiuen him.27And if any one of the common people ſinne through ignorance, while he doeth ſomewhat againſt any of the commandements of the Lord, concerning things which ought not to be done, and be guiltie:28Or if his ſinne which he hath ſinned come to his knowledge, then hee ſhall bring his offering, a kidde of the goats, a female without blemiſh, for his ſinne which he hath ſinned.29And he ſhall lay his hand vpon the head of the ſinne offering, and ſlay the ſin offering in the place of the burnt offering.30And the Prieſt ſhall take of the blood thereof with his finger, and put it vpon the hornes of the Altar of burnt offering, and ſhall powre out all the blood thereof at the bottome of the Altar.31And he ſhall take away all the fat thereof, as the fat is taken away from off the ſacrifice of peace offerings: and the Prieſt ſhall burne it vpon the Altar, for a ſweet ſauour vnto the Lord, and the Prieſt ſhall make an atonement for him, and it ſhall be forgiuen him.32And if he bring a lambe for a ſinne offering, he ſhall bring it a female without blemiſh.33And he ſhall lay his hand vpon the head of the ſinne offering, and ſlay it for a ſinne offering, in the place where they kill the burnt offering.34And the Prieſt ſhall take of the blood of the ſinne offering with his finger, and put it vpon the hornes of the Altar of burnt offring, and ſhall powre out all the blood thereof at the bottome of the Altar.35And he ſhall take away all the fat thereof, as the fat of the lambe is taken away from the ſacrifice of the peace offerings: and the Prieſt ſhall burnt them vpon the Altar, according to the offerings made by fire vnto the Lord, and the Prieſt ſhall make an atonement for his ſinne that he hath committed, and it ſhalbe forgiuen him.

CHAPTER 51And if a ſoule ſinne, and heare the voyce of ſwearing, and is a witneſſe, whether he hath ſeene or knowen of it, if he doe not vtter it, then he ſhall beare his iniquity.2Or if a ſoule touch any vncleane thing, whether it be a carcaſe of an vncleane beaſt, or a carcaſe of vncleane cattell, or the carcaſe of vncleane creeping things, and if it be hidden from him, he alſo ſhall be vncleane, and guilty:3Or if he touch the vncleanneſſe of man, whatſoeuer vncleanneſſe it be that a man ſhalbe defiled withall, and it be hid from him, when he knoweth of it, then he ſhalbe guilty.4Or if a ſoule ſweare, pronouncing with his lips to do euill, or to do good, whatſoeuer it be that a man ſhall pronounce with an oath, and it be hid from him, when he knoweth of it, then he ſhalbe guilty in one of theſe.5And it ſhalbe when he ſhalbe guiltie in one of theſe things, that he ſhall confeſse that hee hath ſinned in that thing.6And he ſhall bring his treſpaſſe offering vnto the Lord for his ſinne which he hath ſinned, a female from the flocke, a lambe, or a kidde of the goates, for a ſinne offering: And the Prieſt ſhal make an atonement for him concerning his ſinne.7And if hee be not able to bring a lambe, then he ſhall bring for his treſpaſſe which hee hath committed, two turtle doues, or two yong pigeons vnto the Lord: one for a ſinne offring, and the other for a burnt offering.8And he ſhall bring them vnto the Prieſt, who ſhall offer that which is for the ſinne offering firſt, and wring off his head from his necke, but ſhall not diuide it aſunder.9And he ſhall ſprinckle of the blood of the ſinne offering vpon the ſide of the Altar, and the reſt of the blood ſhall be wrung out at the bottome of the altar: it is a ſinne offering.10And hee ſhall offer the ſecond for a burnt offering, according to the maner: and the Prieſt ſhal make an atonement for him for his ſinne, which he had ſinned, and it ſhall be forgiuen him.11But if hee be not able to bring two turtle doues, or two yong pigeons; then he that ſinned, ſhall bring for his offring the tenth part of an Ephah of fine flowre for a ſinne offering: hee ſhall put no oyle vpon it, neither ſhall he put any frankincenſe thereon: for it is a ſinne offering.12Then ſhall hee bring it to the Prieſt, and the Prieſt ſhall take his handfull of it, euen a memoriall thereof, and burne it on the altar, according to the offerings made by fire vnto the Lord: it is a ſinne offering.13And the Prieſt ſhall make an atonement for him as touching his ſinne that he hath ſinned in one of theſe, and it ſhall be forgiuen him: and the remnant ſhall be the Prieſts, as a meat offering.14And the Lord ſpake vnto Moſes, ſaying,15If a ſoule commit a treſpaſſe, and ſinne through ignorance, in the holy things of the Lord; then hee ſhall bring for his treſpaſſe vnto the Lord, a ramme without blemiſh, out of the flockes, with thy eſtimation by ſhekels of ſiluer, after the ſhekel of the Sanctuarie, for a treſpaſſe offering.16And hee ſhall make amends for the harme that he hath done in the holy thing, and ſhall adde the fift part thereto, and giue it vnto the Prieſt: and the Prieſt ſhall make an atonement for him with the ramme of the treſpaſſe offering, and it ſhall be forgiuen him.17And if a ſoule ſinne, and commit any of theſe things which are forbidden to be done by the commaundements of the Lord, though he wiſt it not, yet is hee guiltie, and ſhall beare his iniquitie.18And he ſhall bring a ramme without blemiſh out of the flocke, with thy eſtimation, for a treſpaſſe offering vnto the Prieſt: and the Prieſt ſhall make an atonement for him concerning his ignorance wherein he erred, and wiſt it not: and it ſhall be forgiuen him.19It is a treſpaſſe offring: he hath certainly treſpaſſed againſt the Lord.

CHAPTER 61And the Lord ſpake vnto Moſes, ſaying,2If a ſoule ſinne, and commit a treſpaſſe againſt the Lord, and lie vnto his neighbour in that which was deliuered him to keepe, or in fellowſhip, or in a thing taken away by violence, or hath deceiued his neighbour:3Or haue found that which was loſt, and lieth concerning it, and ſweareth falſly: in any of all theſe that a man doth, ſinning therein:4Then it ſhall be, becauſe he hath ſinned, and is guiltie, that hee ſhall reſtore that which he tooke violently away, or the thing which he hath deceitfully gotten, or that which was deliuered him to keepe, or the loſt thing which he found:5Or all that about which hee hath ſworne falſly: hee ſhall euen reſtore it in the principall, and ſhall adde the fift part more thereto, and giue it vnto him to whom it apperteineth, in the day of his treſpaſſe offering.6And hee ſhall bring his treſpaſſe offering vnto the Lord, a ramme without blemiſh out of the flocke, with thy eſtimation, for a treſpaſſe offering vnto the Prieſt.7And the Prieſt ſhall make an atonement for him, before the Lord: and it ſhall bee forgiuen him, for any thing of all that he hath done, in treſpaſsing therein.8And the Lord ſpake vnto Moſes, ſaying,9Command Aaron and his ſonnes, ſaying, This is the law of the burnt offring: (It is the burnt offring, becauſe of the burning vpon the Altar all night vnto the morning, and the fire of the altar ſhall be burning in it.)10And the Prieſt ſhal put on his linnen garment, & his linnen breeches ſhal he put vpon his fleſh, and take vp the aſhes which the fire hath conſumed with the burnt offering on the Altar, and he ſhall put them beſides the Altar.11And he ſhal put off his garments, and put on other garments, and carry foorth the aſhes without the Campe, vnto a cleane place.12And the fire vpon the Altar ſhall be burning in it: it ſhall not be put out; And the Prieſt ſhall burne wood on it euery morning, and lay the burnt offering in order vpon it, and he ſhall burne thereon the fatte of the peace offerings.13The fire ſhall euer be burning vpon the Altar: it ſhall neuer goe out.14And this is the law of the meat offering: the ſonnes of Aaron ſhall offer it before the Lord, before the Altar.15And he ſhall take of it his handfull, of the flowre of the meat offering, and of the oyle therof, and all the frankincenſe which is vpon the meat offring, and ſhall burne it vpon the Altar, for a ſweet ſauour, euen the memoriall of it vnto the Lord.16And the remainder thereof ſhall Aaron and his ſonnes eat: with vnleauened bread ſhall it be eaten in the holy place: in the court of the Tabernacle of the Congregation they ſhall eat it.17It ſhall not be baken with leauen: I haue giuen it vnto them for their portion of my offerings made by fire: it is moſt holy, as is the ſin offering, and as the treſpaſſe offering.18All the males among the children of Aaron ſhall eat of it: It ſhalbe a ſtatute for euer in your generations concerning the offerings of the Lord made by fire: euery one that toucheth them ſhalbe holy.19And the Lord ſpake vnto Moſes, ſaying,20This is the offering of Aaron, and of his ſonnes which they ſhall offer vnto the Lord, in the day when he is anoynted: The tenth part of an Ephah of fine flowre for a meat offering perpetuall, halfe of it in the morning, and halfe thereof at night.21In a panne it ſhalbe made with oyle, and when it is baken, thou ſhalt bring it in: and the baken pieces of the meat offering ſhalt thou offer for a ſweet ſauour vnto the Lord.22And the Prieſt of his ſonnes that is anoynted in his ſtead, ſhal offer it: It is a ſtatute for euer vnto the Lord, it ſhalbe wholly burnt.23For euery meat offering for the Prieſt ſhal be wholly burnt: it ſhall not be eaten.24And the Lord ſpake vnto Moſes, ſaying,25Speake vnto Aaron and to his ſonnes, ſaying, This is the law of the ſinne offering: In the

place where the burnt offering is killed, ſhall the ſinne offering be killed
before the Lord: it is moſt holy.26The Prieſt that offereth it for ſinne,
ſhall eat it: In the holy place ſhal it be eaten, in the court of the
Tabernacle of the Congregation.27Whatſoeuer ſhall touch the fleſh
thereof, ſhalbe holy: and when there is ſprinckled of the blood thereof
vpon any garment, thou ſhalt waſh that whereon it was ſprinckled, in
the holy place.28But the earthen veſſell wherein it is ſodden, ſhall be
broken: And if it be ſodden in a braſen pot, it ſhall be both ſcowred, and
rinſed in water.29All the males among the Prieſts ſhall eate thereof: it is
moſt holy.30And no ſinne offering whereof any of the blood is brought
into the Tabernacle of the Congregation to reconcile withall in the holy
place, ſhall be eaten: it ſhall be burnt in the fire.
CHAPTER 7 1Likewiſe this is the lawe of the treſpaſſe offering: it is
moſt holy.2In the place where they kil the burnt offring, ſhall they kil the
treſpaſſe offering; and the blood thereof ſhall hee ſprinckle round about
vpon the Altar.3And he ſhall offer of it, all the fat thereof; the rumpe,
and the fat that couereth the inwards,4And the two kidneys, and the fat
that is on them, which is by the flankes, and the caule that is aboue the
liuer, with the kidneys, it ſhall he take away.5And the Prieſt ſhall burne
them vpon the Altar, for an offering made by fire vnto the Lord: it is a
treſpaſſe offering.6Euery male among the Prieſtes ſhall eate thereof: it
ſhall be eaten in the holy place: it is moſt holy.7As the ſinne offering is,
ſo is the treſpaſſe offering: there is one law for them: the Prieſt that
maketh atonement therewith, ſhall haue it.8And the Prieſt that offereth
any mans burnt offering, euen the Prieſt ſhall haue to himſelfe the ſkinne
of the burnt offering which he hath offered.9And all the meate offering
that is baken in the ouen, and all that is dreſſed in the frying panne, and
in the panne, ſhall be the Prieſts that offereth it.10And euery meate
offering mingled with oyle, and drie, ſhall all the ſonnes of Aaron haue,
one as much as another.11And this is the law of the ſacrifice of peace
offerings, which he ſhall offer vnto the Lord.12If hee offer it for a
thankeſgiuing, then he ſhall offer with the ſacrifice of thankeſgiuing
vnleauened cakes mingled with oyle, and vnleauened wafers anointed
with oile, and cakes mingled with oyle of fine flowre fried.13Beſides the
cakes, hee ſhall offer for his offring leauened bread, with the ſacrifice of
thankeſgiuing of his peace offerings.14And of it he ſhall offer one out of
the whole oblation, for an heaue offering vnto the Lord, and it ſhall bee
the Prieſts that ſprinkleth the blood of the peace offerings.15And the
fleſh of the ſacrifice of his peace offerings for thankeſgiuing, ſhall be
eaten the ſame day that it is offered: he ſhall not leaue any of it vntill the
morning.16But if the ſacrifice of his offering be a vow, or a voluntary
offering, it ſhall be eaten the ſame day that he offereth his ſacrifice: and
on the morrowe alſo the remainder of it ſhall be eaten.17But the
remainder of the fleſh of the ſacrifice on the third day ſhall bee burnt
with fire.18And if any of the fleſh of the ſacrifice of his peace offerings
be eaten at all on the third day, it ſhall not be accepted, neither ſhal it be
imputed vnto him that offereth it: it ſhall be an abomination, and the
ſoule that eateth of it, ſhall beare his iniquitie.19And the fleſh that
toucheth any vncleane thing, ſhal not be eaten: it ſhal be burnt with fire,
and as for the fleſh, all that be cleane ſhall eate thereof.20But the ſoule
that eateth of the fleſh of the ſacrifice of peace offerings, that pertaine
vnto the Lord, hauing his vncleaneſse vpon him, euen that ſoule ſhall be
cut off from his people.21Moreouer, the ſoule that ſhall touch any
vncleane thing, as the vncleanneſſe of man, or any vncleane beaſt, or
any abominable vncleane thing, and eate of the fleſh of the ſacrifice of
peace offerings which pertaine vnto the Lord, euen that ſoule ſhall be
cut off from his people.22And the Lord ſpake vnto Moſes,
ſaying,23Speake vnto the children of Iſrael, ſaying, Ye ſhall eat no maner
fat of oxe, or of ſheepe, or of goat.24And the fat of the beaſt that dieth
of it ſelfe, and the fat of that which is torne with beaſts, may be vſed in
any other vſe: but yee ſhall in no wiſe eate of it.25For whoſoeuer eateth
the fat of the beaſt, of which men offer an offring made by fire vnto the
Lord, euen the ſoule that eateth it, ſhall be cut off from his
people.26Moreouer ye ſhall eat no maner of blood, whether it bee of
foule or of beaſt in any of your dwellings.27Whatſoeuer ſoule it be that
eateth any maner of blood, euen that ſoule ſhalbe cut off from his
people.28And the Lord ſpake vnto Moſes, ſaying,29Speake vnto the
children of Iſrael, ſaying, Hee that offereth the ſacrifice of his peace
offerings vnto the Lord, ſhall bring his oblation vnto the Lord, of the
ſacrifice of his peaceofferings.30His owne hands ſhall bring the offerings
of the Lord made by fire, the fat with the breſt, it ſhall hee bring, that
the breſt may be waued for a waue offering before the Lord.31And the
Prieſt ſhall burne the fat vpon the Altar: but the breſt ſhalbe Aarons and
his ſonnes.32And the right ſhoulder ſhall ye giue vnto the Prieſt for an
heaue offering of the ſacrifices of your peace offerings.33Hee among the
ſonnes of Aaron that offereth the blood of the peace offerings, and the
fat, ſhall haue the right ſhoulder for his part.34For the waue breſt and
the heaue ſhoulder haue I taken of the children of Iſrael, from off the
ſacrifices of their peace offerings, and haue giuen them vnto Aaron the
Prieſt, and vnto his ſonnes, by a ſtatute for euer, from among the
children of Iſrael.35This is the portion of the anointing of Aaron, and of
the anointing of his ſonnes, out of the offerings of the Lord made by
fire, in the day when he preſented them, to miniſter vnto the Lord in the
Prieſts office:36Which the Lord commanded to be giuen them of the
children of Iſrael, in the day that hee anointed them, by a ſtatute for
euer, throughout their generations.37This is the law of the burnt
offering, of the meate offering, and of the ſinne offering, and of the
treſpaſſe offering, and of the conſecrations, and of the ſacrifice of the
peace offerings:38Which the Lord commanded Moſes in mount Sinai, in
the day that he commanded the children of Iſrael to offer their oblations
vnto the Lord, in the wilderneſſe of Sinai.
CHAPTER 8 1And the Lord ſpake vnto Moſes, ſaying,2Take Aaron and
his ſonnes with him, and the garments, and the anointing oyle, and a
bullocke for the ſinne offering, and two rammes, and a baſket of
vnleauened bread.3And gather thou all the Congregation together vnto
the doore of the Tabernacle of the Congregation.4And Moſes did as the
Lord commanded him, & the aſſembly was gathered together vnto the
doore of the Tabernacle of the Congregation.5And Moſes ſaide vnto the
Congregation, This is the thing which the Lord commanded to be
done.6And Moſes brought Aaron and his ſonnes, and waſhed them with
water.7And he put vpon him the coate, and girded him with the girdle,
and clothed him with the robe, and put the Ephod vpon him, and he
girded him with the curious girdle of the Ephod, and bound it vnto him
therewith.8And hee put the breſt plate vpon him: alſo he put in the breſt
plate the Urim and the Thummim.9And he put the miter vpon his head;
alſo vpon the miter, euen vpon his forefront did hee put the golden
plate, the holy crowne, as the Lord commanded Moſes.10And Moſes
tooke the anointing oile, and anointed the tabernacle and all that was
therein, and ſanctified them.11And he ſprinkled thereof vpon the altar
ſeuen times, and anointed the altar and all his veſſels, both the lauer and
his foot, to ſanctifie them.12And he powred of the anointing oile vpon
Aarons head, and anointed him, to ſanctifie him.13And Moſes brought
Aarons ſonnes, and put coats vpon them, and girded them with girdles,
and put bonnets vpon them, as the Lord commanded Moſes.14And he
brought the bullocke for the ſinne offering, and Aaron and his ſonnes
laid their hands vpon the head of the bullocke for the ſinne
offering.15And he ſlew it, and Moſes tooke the blood, and put it vpon
the hornes of the altar round about with his finger, and purified the altar,
and powred the blood at the bottome of the altar, and ſanctified it, to
make reconciliation vpon it.16And he tooke all the fat that was vpon the
inwards, and the kall aboue the liuer, and the two kidneis, and their fat,
and Moſes burned it vpon the Altar.17But the bullocke, and his hide, his
fleſh and his doung, he burnt with fire without the campe, as the Lord
commanded Moſes.18And he brought the ramme for the burnt offring:
and Aaron and his ſonnes laid their hands vpon the head of the
ramme.19And he killed it, and Moſes ſprinkled the blood vpon the Altar
round about.20And he cut the ramme into pieces, and Moſes burnt the
head, and the pieces, and the fat.21And he waſhed the inwards and the
legges in water, and Moſes burnt the whole ramme vpon the Altar: It
was a burnt ſacrifice for a ſweet ſauour, and an offering made by fire
vnto the Lord, as the Lord commanded Moſes.22And hee brought the
other ramme, the ramme of conſecration: and Aaron and his ſonnes layd
their hands vpon the head of the ramme.23And he ſlew it, and Moſes
tooke of the blood of it, and put it vpon the tip of Aarons right eare,
and vpon the thumbe of his right hand, and vpon the great toe of his
right foot.24And he brought Aarons ſonnes, and Moſes put of the blood
vpon the tippe of their right eare, and vpon the thumbs of their right
hands, and vpon the great toes of their right feete: and Moſes ſprinkled
the blood vpon the Altar round about.25And hee tooke the fat, and the
rumpe, and all the fat that was vpon the inwards, and the caule aboue

the liuer, and the two kidneys and their fat, and the right ſhoulder.26And out of the baſket of vnleauened bread, that was before the Lord, he tooke one vnleauened cake, and a cake of oyled bread, and one wafer, and put them on the fat, and vpon the right ſhoulder.27And hee put all vpon Aarons hands, and vpon his ſonnes hands, and waued them for a waue offering before the Lord.28And Moſes tooke them from off their hands, and burnt them on the Altar, vpon the burnt offering: They were conſecrations for a ſweet ſauour: It is an offering made by fire vnto the Lord.29And Moſes tooke the breſt, and waued it for a waue offering before the Lord: For of the ramme of conſecration it was Moſes part, as the Lord commanded Moſes.30And Moſes tooke of the anoynting oyle, and of the blood which was vpon the Altar, and ſprinckled it vpon Aaron, and vpon his garments, and vpon his ſonnes, and vpon his ſunnes garments with him: and ſanctified Aaron, and his garments, and his ſonnes, and his ſonnes garments with him.31And Moſes ſaid vnto Aaron and to his ſonnes, Boile the fleſh at the doore of the Tabernacle of the Congregation: and there eat it with the bread that is in the baſket of conſecrations, as I commanded, ſaying, Aaron and his ſonnes ſhall eat it.32And that which remaineth of the fleſh, and of the bread, ſhall yee burne with fire.33And ye ſhall not goe out of the doore of the Tabernacle of the Congregation in ſeuen dayes, vntill the dayes of your conſecration be at an end: for ſeuen dayes ſhall he conſecrate you.34As he hath done this day, ſo the Lord hath commanded to doe, to make an atonement for you.35Therefore ſhall ye abide at the doore of the Tabernacle of the Congregation day and night, ſeuen dayes, and keepe the charge of the Lord, that ye die not: for ſo I am commanded.36So Aaron and his ſonnes did all things which the Lord commanded by the hand of Moſes.

CHAPTER 91And it came to paſſe on the eight day, that Moſes called Aaron and his ſonnes, and the elders of Iſrael.2And hee ſaide vnto Aaron, Take thee a yong calfe for a ſinne offering, and a ramme for a burnt offering, without blemiſh, and offer them before the Lord.3And vnto the children of Iſrael thou ſhalt ſpeake, ſaying, Take ye a kid of the goats, for a ſinne offering, and a calfe, and a lambe, both of the firſt yeere without blemiſh, for a burnt offering.4Alſo a bullocke and a ramme, for peace offerings, to ſacrifice before the Lord, and a meat offring mingled with oyle: for to day the Lord will appeare vnto you.5And they brought that which Moſes commanded, before the Tabernacle of the Congregation: and all the Congregation drew neere and ſtood before the Lord.6And Moſes ſaid, This is the thing which the Lord commanded that ye ſhould doe: and the glory of the Lord ſhall appeare vnto you.7And Moſes ſaid vnto Aaron, Goe vnto the Altar, and offer thy ſinne offering, and thy burnt offering, and make an atonement for thy ſelfe, and for the people: and offer the offering of the people, and make an atonement for them, as the Lord commanded.8Aaron therefore went vnto the Altar, and ſlew the calfe of the ſinne offering, which was for himſelfe.9And the ſonnes of Aaron brought the blood vnto him, and he dipt his finger in the blood, and put it vpon the hornes of the Altar, and powred out the blood at the bottome of the Altar.10But the fat and the kidneys, and the caule aboue the liuer of the ſinne offering he burnt vpon the Altar, as the Lord commanded Moſes.11And the fleſh and the hide he burnt with fire, without the campe.12And hee ſlew the burnt offering, and Aarons ſonnes preſented vnto him the blood, which he ſprinckled round about vpon the Altar.13And they preſented the burnt offering vnto him, with the pieces thereof, and the head: and he burnt them vpon the Altar.14And he did waſh the inwards, and the legs, and burnt them vpon the burnt offering on the Altar.15And he brought the peoples offering, and tooke the goat, which was the ſinne offering for the people, and ſlew it, and offered it for ſinne, as the firſt.16And he brought the burnt offring, and offered it according to the maner.17And he brought the meat offring, and tooke an handfull thereof, and burnt it vpon the Altar, beſide the burnt ſacrifice of the morning.18He ſlew alſo the bullocke and the ramme, for a ſacrifice of peace offerings, which was for the people: And Aarons ſonnes preſented vnto him the blood, (which hee ſprinckled vpon the Altar round about)19And the fat of the bullocke and of the ramme, the rumpe, and that which couereth the inwards, and the kidneys, and the caule aboue the liuer,20And they put the fat vpon the breſts, & he burnt the fat vpon the altar:21And the breaſts and the right ſhoulder, Aaron waued for a waue offering before the Lord, as Moſes commanded.22And Aaron lift up his hand towards the people, and bleſſed them, and came downe from offering of the ſinne offering, and the burnt offering, and peace offerings.23And Moſes and Aaron went into the Tabernacle of the Congregation, and came out, and bleſſed the people: and the glory of the Lord appeared vnto all the people.24And there came a fire out from before the Lord, and conſumed vpon the Altar the burnt offering, and the fat: which when all the people ſaw, they ſhouted, and fell on their faces.

CHAPTER 101And Nadab and Abihu, the ſonnes of Aaron, tooke either of them his cenſer, and put fire therein, and put incenſe thereon, and offered ſtrange fire before the Lord, which hee commaunded them not.2And there went out fire from the Lord and deuoured them, and they died before the Lord.3Then Moſes ſaid vnto Aaron, This is it that the Lord ſpake, ſaying, I will bee ſanctified in them that come nigh me, and before all the people I will be glorified: And Aaron held his peace.4And Moſes called Miſhael and Elzaphan the ſonnes of Uzziel, the vncle of Aaron, and ſaid vnto them, Come neere, cary your brethren from before the Sanctuary, out of the campe.5So they went neere, and caried them in their coats out of the campe, as Moſes had ſaid.6And Moſes ſaid vnto Aaron, and vnto Eleazar and vnto Ithamar his ſonnes, Uncouer not your heads, neither rend your clothes, leſt you die, and leſt wrath come vpon all the people: But let your brethren, the whole houſe of Iſrael, bewaile the burning which the Lord hath kindled.7And ye ſhal not goe out from the doore of the Tabernacle of the Congregation, leſt you die: for the anointing oyle of the Lord is vpon you: and they did according to the word of Moſes.8And the Lord ſpake vnto Aaron, ſaying,9Doe not drinke wine nor ſtrong drinke, thou, nor thy ſonnes with thee, when ye goe into the Tabernacle of the Congregation, leſt yee die: It ſhall bee a ſtatute for euer, throughout your generations:10And that ye may put difference betweene holy and vnholy, and betweene vncleane and cleane:11And that ye may teach the children of Iſrael all the ſtatutes which the Lord hath ſpoken vnto them by the hand of Moſes.12And Moſes ſpake vnto Aaron, and vnto Eleazar and vnto Ithamar his ſonnes that were left, Take the meate offering that remaineth of the offerings of the Lord made by fire, and eate it without leauen, beſide the altar: for it is moſt holy.13And ye ſhal eat it in the holy place, becauſe it is thy due, and thy ſonnes due of the ſacrifices of the Lord, made by fire: for ſo I am commanded.14And the waue breaſt and heaue ſhoulder ſhall ye eate in a cleane place, thou, and thy ſonnes, and thy daughters with thee: For they be thy due and thy ſonnes due, which are giuen out of the ſacrifice of peace offerings, of the children of Iſrael.15The heaue ſhoulder, and the waue breaſt ſhal they bring, with the offrings made by fire of the fat, to waue it for a waue offering before the Lord: and it ſhall bee thine, and thy ſonnes with thee, by a ſtatute for euer, as the Lord hath commanded.16And Moſes diligently ſought the goate of the ſinne offering, and behold, it was burnt: and he was angry with Eleazar and Ithamar, the ſonnes of Aaron, which were left aliue, ſaying,17Wherefore haue ye not eaten the ſinne offering in the holy place, ſeeing it is moſt holy, and God hath giuen it you to beare the iniquitie of the Congregation, to make atonement for them, before the Lord?18Behold, the blood of it was not brought in, within the holy place: yee ſhould indeed haue eaten it in the holy place, as I commanded.19And Aaron ſaid vnto Moſes, Behold, this day haue they offered their ſinne offering, and their burnt offering before the Lord: and ſuch things haue befallen me: and if I had eaten the ſinne offering to day, ſhould it haue bin accepted in the ſight of the Lord?20And when Moſes heard that, he was content.

CHAPTER 111And the Lord ſpake vnto Moſes, and to Aaron, ſaying vnto them,2Speake vnto the children of Iſrael, ſaying, Theſe are the beaſts which ye ſhal eat among all the beaſts that are on the earth:3Whatſoever parteth the hoofe, and is clouen footed, & cheweth cud among the beaſts, that ſhall ye eate.4Neuertheleſſe, theſe ſhall ye not eate, of them that chewe the cud, or of them that diuide the hoofe: as the camel, becauſe hee cheweth the cud, but diuideth not the hoofe, he is vncleane vnto you.5And the conie, becauſe he cheweth the cud, but diuideth not the hoofe, he is vncleane vnto you.6And the hare, becauſe he cheweth the cud, but diuideth not the hoofe, he is vncleane vnto you.7And the ſwine, though he diuide the hoofe, and be clouen footed, yet hee cheweth not the cud: he is vncleane to you.8Of their fleſh ſhall ye not eat, and their carcaſe ſhall ye not touch: they are vncleane to you.9Theſe ſhal ye eat, of all that are in the waters: whatſoeuer hath

finnes and ſcales in the waters, in the ſeas, and in the riuers, them ſhall
ye eate.[10]And all that haue not finnes nor ſcales in the ſeas, and in the
riuers, of all that moue in the waters, and of any liuing thing which is in
the waters, they ſhalbe an abomination vnto you:[11]They ſhalbe euen an
abomination vnto you: ye ſhall not eat of their fleſh, but you ſhall haue
their carcaſes in abomination.[12]Whatſoeuer hath no finnes nor ſcales in
the waters, that ſhalbe an abomination vnto you.[13]And theſe are they
which ye ſhall haue in abomination among the foules, they ſhall not be
eaten, they are an abomination: The Eagle, and the Oſsifrage, and the
Oſpray,[14]And the Uulture, and the Kite, after his kinde:[15]Euery Rauen
after his kinde:[16]And the Owle, and the nighthauke, & the Cuckow, and
the Hawke after his kinde,[17]And the little Owle, and the Cormorant, and
the great Owle,[18]And the Swanne, and the Pellicane, and the Gier-
eagle,[19]And the Storke, the Heron after her kinde, and the Lapwing, and
the Batte.[20]All foules that creepe, going vpon all foure, ſhalbe an
abomination vnto you.[21]Yet theſe may ye eat, of euery flying creeping
thing that goeth vpon all foure, which haue legges aboue their feet, to
leape withall vpon the earth.[22]Euen theſe of them ye may eate: the
Locuſt, after his kinde, and the Bald-locuſt after his kinde, and the Beetle
after his kinde, and the Graſſehopper after his kinde.[23]But al other flying
creeping things which haue foure feet, ſhall be an abomination vnto
you.[24]And for theſe ye ſhalbe vncleane: whoſoeuer toucheth the
carkaſſe of them, ſhall be vncleane vntill the euen.[25]And whoſoeuer
beareth ought of the carkaſſe of them, ſhall waſh his clothes, & be
vncleane vntill the euen.[26]The carkaſſes of euery beaſt which diuideth
the hoofe, and is not clouen footed, nor cheweth the cud, are vncleane
vnto you: euery one that toucheth them, ſhalbe vncleane.[27]And
whatſoeuer goeth vpon his pawes, among all maner of beaſts, that goe
on all foure, thoſe are vncleane vnto you: who ſo toucheth their carkaſſe,
ſhall be vncleane vntill the Euen.[28]And he that beareth the carkaſſe of
them, ſhall waſh his clothes, and be vncleane vntill the Euen: they are
vncleane vnto you.[29]Theſe alſo ſhalbe vncleane vnto you, among the
creeping things that creepe vpon the earth: the Weaſell, and the Mouſe,
and the Tortois, after his kinde,[30]And the Ferret, and the Cameleon, and
the Lyzard, and the Snaile, and the Molle.[31]Theſe are vncleane to you
among all that creepe: whoſoeuer doth touch them when they bee dead,
ſhall be vncleane vntill the Euen.[32]And vpon whatſoeuer any of them,
when they are dead, doeth fall, it ſhalbe vncleane, whether it be any
veſsel of wood, or raiment, or ſkinne, or ſacke, whatſoeuer veſſell it be,
wherein any worke is done, it muſt be put into water, and it ſhall be
vncleane vntill the Euen; ſo it ſhalbe cleanſed.[33]And euery earthen
veſsel, whereinto any of them falleth, whatſoeuer is in it ſhall bee
vncleane; and yee ſhall breake it.[34]Of all meat which may be eaten, that
on which ſuch water commeth, ſhall be vncleane: And all drinke that
may be drunkein euery ſuch veſſell, ſhalbe vncleane.[35]And euery thing,
whereupon any part of their carkaſſe falleth, ſhall be vncleane, whether
it be ouen, or ranges for pots, they ſhalbe broken downe: for they are
vncleane, and ſhall be vncleane vnto you.[36]Neuertheleſſe, a fountaine or
pit, wherein there is plenty of water, ſhalbe cleane: but that which
toucheth their carkaſſe ſhalbe vncleane.[37]And if any part of their
carkaſſe fall vpon any ſowing ſeed which is to be ſowen, it ſhalbe
cleane:[38]But if any water be put vpon the ſeed, and any part of their
carkaſſe fall thereon, it ſhalbe vncleane vnto you.[39]And if any beaſt of
which ye may eat, die, he that toucheth the carkaſſe thereof, ſhall be
vncleane vntill the Euen.[40]And hee that eateth of the carkaſſe of it, ſhall
waſh his clothes, and be vncleane vntil the Euen: he alſo that beareth
the carkaſſe of it, ſhal waſh his clothes, and bee vncleane vntill the
Euen.[41]And euery creeping thing that creepeth vpon the earth, ſhalbe
an abomination: it ſhall not be eaten.[42]Whatſoeuer goeth vpon the
bellie, and whatſoeuer goeth vpon all foure, or whatſoeuer hath more
feet among all creeping things that creepe vpon the earth, them ye ſhall
not eate, for they are an abomination.[43]Yee ſhall not make your ſelues
abominable with any creeping thing that creepeth, neither ſhall ye make
your ſelues vncleane with them, that ye ſhould be defiled thereby.[44]For
I am the Lord your God: yee ſhall therefore ſanctifie your ſelues, and ye
ſhall be holy, for I am holy: neither ſhall ye defile your ſelues with any
maner of creeping thing that creepeth vpon the earth.[45]For I am the
Lord that bringeth you vp out of the land of Egypt to be your God: ye
ſhal therefore be holy, for I am holy.[46]This is the law of the beaſts, and
of the foule, and of euery liuing creature that moueth in the waters, and
of euerie creature that creepeth vpon the earth:[47]To make a difference
betweene the vncleane and the cleane, & betweene the beaſt that may
be eaten, and the beaſt that may not be eaten.

CHAPTER 12[1]And the Lord ſpake vnto Moſes, ſaying,[2]Speake vnto
the children of Iſrael, ſaying, If a woman haue conceiued ſeed, and borne
a man child, then ſhe ſhal be vncleane ſeuen dayes: according to the
dayes of the ſeparation for her infirmitie ſhall ſhe be vncleane.[3]And in
the eight day, the fleſh of his foreſkinne ſhall be circumciſed.[4]And ſhe
ſhal then continue in the blood of her purifying three and thirtie dayes:
Shee ſhall touch no hallowed thing, nor come into the Sanctuary, vntill
the dayes of her purifying be fulfilled.[5]But if ſhe beare a maid child, then
ſhe ſhalbe vncleane two weekes, as in her ſeparation: and ſhe ſhall
continue in the blood of her purifying threeſcore and ſixe dayes.[6]And
when the dayes of her purifying are fulfilled, for a ſonne, or for a
daughter, ſhe ſhall bring a lambe of the firſt yeere for a burnt offring, &
a yong pigeon, or a turtle doue for a ſinne offering, vnto the doore of
the Tabernacle of the Congregation, vnto the Prieſt:[7]Who ſhall offer it
before the Lord, and make an atonement for her, and ſhe ſhall be
cleanſed from the iſſue of her blood. This is the law for her that hath
borne a male or a female.[8]And if ſhe be not able to bring a lambe, then
ſhe ſhall bring two turtles, or two yong pigeons, the one for the burnt
offering, and the other for a ſinne offering: and the Prieſt ſhall make an
atonement for her, and ſhee ſhall bee cleane.

CHAPTER 13[1]And the Lord ſpake vnto Moſes and Aaron,
ſaying,[2]When a man ſhall haue in the ſkinne of his fleſh, a riſing, a
ſcabbe, or bright ſpot, and it bee in the ſkinne of his fleſh like the plague
of leproſie, then he ſhall bee brought vnto Aaron the Prieſt, or vnto one
of his ſonnes the Prieſts.[3]And the Prieſt ſhall looke on the plague in the
ſkinne of the fleſh: and when the haire in the plague is turned white, and
the plague in ſight be deeper then the ſkin of his fleſh, it is a plague of
leproſie: and the Prieſt ſhall looke on him, and pronounce him
vncleane.[4]If the bright ſpot be white in the ſkinne of his fleſh, and in
ſight bee not deeper then the ſkinne, and the haire thereof be not turned
white, then the Prieſt ſhall ſhut vp him that hath the plague, ſeuen
dayes.[5]And the Prieſt ſhall looke on him the ſeuenth day: and beholde,
if the plague in his ſight be at a ſtay, and the plague ſpread not in the
ſkinne, then the Prieſt ſhall ſhut him vp ſeuen dayes more.[6]And the
Prieſt ſhall looke on him againe the ſeuenth day: and beholde, if the
plague be ſomewhat darke, and the plague ſpread not in the ſkin; the
Prieſt ſhall pronounce him cleane: it is but a ſcab: and he ſhall waſh his
clothes, and be cleane.[7]But if the ſcab ſpread much abroad in the ſkinne
after that hee hath beene ſeene of the Prieſt, for his cleanſing hee ſhall
be ſeene of the Prieſt againe.[8]And if the Prieſt ſee, that behold, the ſcab
ſpreadeth in the ſkin, then the Prieſt ſhall pronounce him vncleane: it is
a leproſie.[9]When the plague of leproſie is in a man, then he ſhall be
brought vnto the Prieſt;[10]And the Prieſt ſhall ſee him: and behold, if the
riſing be white in the ſkin, and it haue turned the haire white, and there
be quicke raw fleſh in the riſing:[11]It is an old leproſie in the ſkinne of his
fleſh, and the Prieſt ſhall pronounce him vncleane, and ſhal not ſhut him
vp: for he is vncleane.[12]And if a leproſie breake out abroad in the ſkin,
and the leproſie couer all the ſkin of him that hath the plague, from his
head euen to his foot, whereſoeuer the Prieſt looketh:[13]Then the Prieſt
ſhall conſider: and behold, if the leproſie haue couered al his fleſh, he
ſhal pronounce him cleane that hath the plague, it is all turned white; he
is cleane.[14]But when raw fleſh appeareth in him, he ſhall be
vncleane.[15]And the Prieſt ſhall ſee the raw fleſh, and pronounce him to
bee vncleane: for the raw fleſh is vncleane: it is a leproſie.[16]Or if the raw
fleſh turne againe, and bee changed vnto white, hee ſhall come vnto the
Prieſt:[17]And the Prieſt ſhall ſee him: and beholde, if the plague bee
turned into white, then the Prieſt ſhall pronounce him cleane that hath
the plague; hee is cleane.[18]The fleſh alſo, in which, euen in the ſkinne
thereof was a bile, and is healed,[19]And in the place of the bile there be
a white riſing, or a bright ſpot white, and ſomewhat reddiſh, and it be
ſhewed to the Prieſt:[20]And if when the Prieſt ſeeth it, behold, it be in
ſight lower then the ſkinne, and the haire thereof be turned white, the
Prieſt ſhall pronounce him vncleane: it is a plague of leproſie broken out
of the bile.[21]But if the Prieſt looke on it, and behold, there be no white
haires therein, and if it be not lower then the ſkin, but be ſomewhat
darke; then the Prieſt ſhall ſhut him vp ſeuen dayes.[22]And if it ſpread

much abroad in the ſkinne, then the Prieſt ſhall pronounce him vncleane; it is a plague.[23]But if the bright ſpot ſtay in his place, and ſpread not, it is a burning bile; and the Prieſt ſhall pronounce him cleane.[24]Or if there be any fleſh in the ſkin whereof there is a hot burning, and the quicke fleſh that burneth haue a white bright ſpot, ſomewhat reddiſh, or white;[25]Then the Prieſt ſhall looke vpon it: and behold, if the haire in the bright ſpot be turned white, and it bee in ſight deeper then the ſkinne, it is a leproſie broken out of the burning: wherefore the Prieſt ſhal pronounce him vncleane: it is the plague of leproſie.[26]But if the Prieſt looke on it, and behold, there be no white haire in the bright ſpot, and it be no lower then the other ſkin, but be ſomewhat darke, then the Prieſt ſhal ſhut him vp ſeuen dayes.[27]And the Prieſt ſhall looke vpon him the ſeuenth day: and if it be ſpread much abroad in the ſkin, then the Prieſt ſhall pronounce him vncleane; it is the plague of leproſie.[28]And if the bright ſpot ſtay in his place, and ſpread not in the ſkin, but it be ſomewhat darke; it is a riſing of the burning, and the Prieſt ſhall pronounce him cleane: for it is an inflammation of the burning.[29]If a man or woman hath a plague vpon the head or the beard,[30]Then the Prieſt ſhall ſee the plague: and behold, if it be in ſight deeper then the ſkin, and there be in it a yellow thin haire, then the Prieſt ſhall pronounce him vncleane, it is a dry ſkall, euen a leproſie vpon the head or beard.[31]And if the Prieſt looke on the plague of the ſkall, and behold, it be not in ſight deeper then the ſkin, and that there is no blacke haire in it; then the Prieſt ſhall ſhut vp him that hath the plague of the ſkall, ſeuen dayes.[32]And in the ſeuenth day the Prieſt ſhall looke on the plague: and behold, if the ſkall ſpread not, and there be in it no yellow haire, and the ſkall be not in ſight deeper then the ſkin;[33]He ſhall be ſhauen, but the ſkall ſhall he not ſhaue: and the Prieſt ſhall ſhut vp him that hath the ſkall, ſeuen dayes more.[34]And in the ſeuenth day the Prieſt ſhall looke on the ſkall: and behold, if the ſkall be not ſpread in the ſkin, nor be in ſight deeper then the ſkin, then the Prieſt ſhall pronounce him cleane: and he ſhall waſh his clothes, and be cleane.[35]But if the ſkall ſpread much in the ſkinne after his cleanſing,[36]Then the Prieſt ſhall looke on him, and behold, if the ſkall be ſpread in the ſkinne, the Prieſt ſhall not ſeeke for yellow haire: he is vncleane.[37]But if the ſkall be in his ſight at a ſtay, and that there is blacke haire growen vp therein: the ſkall is healed, he is cleane, and the Prieſt ſhall pronounce him cleane.[38]If a man alſo or a woman haue in the ſkinne of their fleſh bright ſpots, euen white bright ſpots,[39]Then the Prieſt ſhall looke: and behold, if the bright ſpots in the ſkinne of their fleſh bee darkiſh white, it is a freckled ſpot that groweth in the ſkin: he is cleane.[40]And the man whoſe haire is fallen off his head, he is bald: yet is hee cleane.[41]And he that hath his haire fallen off from the part of his head toward his face, he is forehead-bald: yet is hee cleane.[42]And if there be in the bald head, or bald forehead a white reddiſh ſore, it is a leproſie ſprung vp in his bald-head, or his bald forehead.[43]Then the Prieſt ſhall looke vpon it: and beholde, if the riſing of the ſore bee white reddiſh in his balde head, or in his bald forehead, as the leproſie appeareth in the ſkinne of the fleſh,[44]Hee is a leprous man, he is vncleane: the Prieſt ſhall pronounce him vtterly vncleane, his plague is in his head.[45]And the leper in whom the plague is, his clothes ſhall be rent, and his head bare, and he ſhall put a couering vpon his vpper lip, and ſhall cry, Uncleane, vncleane.[46]All the dayes wherein the plague ſhall bee in him, he ſhall bee defiled, hee is vncleane: he ſhall dwell alone, without the campe ſhall his habitation be.[47]The garment alſo, that the plague of leproſie is in, whether it bee a woollen garment, or a linnen garment,[48]Whether it bee in the warpe, or woofe of linnen or of woollen, whether in a ſkin, or in any thing made of ſkinne:[49]And if the plague be greeniſh or reddiſh in the garment, or in the ſkin, either in the warpe, or in the woofe, or in any thing of ſkinne, it is a plague of leproſie, and ſhall be ſhewed vnto the Prieſt.[50]And the Prieſt ſhall looke vpon the plague, and ſhut vp it that hath the plague, ſeuen dayes.[51]And he ſhall looke on the plague on the ſeuenth day: if the plague be ſpread in the garment, either in the warpe, or in the woofe, or in a ſkin, or in any worke that is made of ſkinne, the plague is a fretting leproſie; it is vncleane.[52]Hee ſhall therefore burne that garment, whether warpe or woofe, in wollen or in linnen, or any thing of ſkinne, wherein the plague is: for it is a fretting leproſie; it ſhall bee burnt in the fire.[53]And if the Prieſt ſhall looke, and behold the plague be not ſpread in the garment, either in the warpe, or in the woofe, or in any thing of ſkinne;[54]Then the Prieſt ſhall command that they waſh the thing wherein the plague is, and he ſhall ſhut it vp ſeuen dayes more.[55]And the Prieſt ſhall looke on the plague after that it is waſhed: and behold, if the plague haue not changed his colour, and the plague be not ſpread, it is vncleane, thou ſhalt burne it in the fire, it is fret inward, whether it be bare within or without.[56]And if the Prieſt looke, and behold, the plaine be ſomewhat darke after the waſhing of it, then he ſhall rend it out of the garment, or out of the ſkin, or out of the warpe, or out of the woofe.[57]And if it appeare ſtill in the garment, either in the warpe, or in the woofe, or in any thing of ſkinne, it is a ſpreading plague, thou ſhalt burne that wherein the plague is, with fire.[58]And the garment, either warpe, or woofe, or whatſoeuer thing of ſkin it bee, which thou ſhalt waſh, if the plague be departed from them, then it ſhall be waſhed the ſecond time, and ſhalbe cleane.[59]This is the law of the plague of leproſie in a garment of woollen or linnen, either in the warpe, or woofe, or any thing of ſkinnes, to pronounce it cleane, or to pronounce it vncleane.

CHAPTER 14[1]And the Lord ſpake vnto Moſes, ſaying,[2]This ſhalbe the law of the leper, in the day of his cleanſing: he ſhall be brought vnto the Prieſt.[3]And the Prieſt ſhall goe forth out of the campe, and the Prieſt ſhall looke: and beholde, if the plague of leproſie be healed in the leper,[4]Then ſhall the Prieſt command to take for him that is to bee cleanſed, two birds aliue, and cleane, and Cedar wood, and ſcarlet, and hyſope.[5]And the Prieſt ſhall command that one of the birds bee killed in an earthen veſſell, ouer running water.[6]As for the liuing bird, he ſhal take it, and the Cedar wood, and the ſcarlet, and the hyſope, and ſhall dip them and the liuing bird in the blood of the bird that was killed ouer the running water.[7]And he ſhall ſprinckle vpon him that is to be cleanſed from the leproſie, ſeuen times, and ſhall pronounce him cleane, and ſhall let the liuing bird looſe into the open field.[8]And he that is to be cleanſed ſhall waſh his clothes, and ſhaue off all his haire, and waſh himſelfe in water, that he may be cleane: And after that hee ſhall come into the Campe, and ſhall tary abroad out of his tent ſeuen dayes.[9]But it ſhall be on the ſeuenth day, that he ſhall ſhaue all his haire off his head and his beard, and his eyebrowes, euen all his haire he ſhal ſhaue off: And he ſhall waſh his clothes, alſo he ſhall waſh his fleſh in water, and he ſhall be cleane.[10]And on the eight day he ſhall take two hee lambes without blemiſh, and one ewe-lambe of the firſt yeere, without blemiſh, and three tenth deales of fine flowre for a meat offering, mingled with oyle, and one log of oyle.[11]And the Prieſt that maketh him cleane, ſhall preſent the man that is to be made cleane, and thoſe things before the Lord, at the doore of the Tabernacle of the Congregation:[12]And the Prieſt ſhall take one hee lambe, and offer him for a treſpaſſe offering, and the log of oile, and waue them for a waue offering before the Lord.[13]And he ſhall ſlay the lambe in the place where he ſhall kil the ſin-offering, and the burnt offring in the holy place: for as the ſinne offering is the Prieſts, ſo is the treſpaſſe offering: it is moſt Holy.[14]And the Prieſt ſhall take ſome of the blood of the treſpaſſe offering, and the Prieſt ſhall put it vpon the tip of the right eare of him that is to be cleanſed, and vpon the thumbe of his right hand, and vpon the great toe of his right foot.[15]And the Prieſt ſhall take ſome of the log of oile, and powre it into the palme of his owne left hand:[16]And the Prieſt ſhall dip his right finger in the oile that is in his left hand, and ſhall ſprinckle of the oile with his finger, ſeuen times before the Lord.[17]And of the reſt of the oile that is in his hand, ſhall the Prieſt put vpon the tip of the right eare of him that is to be cleanſed, and vpon the thumbe of his right hande, and vpon the great toe of his right foot, vpon the blood of the treſpaſſe offering.[18]And the remnant of the oile that is in the Prieſts hand, he ſhall powre vpon the head of him that is to be cleanſed: and the Prieſt ſhall make an atonement for him before the Lord.[19]And the Prieſt ſhal offer the ſinne offering, and make an atonement for him that is to be cleanſed from his vncleanneſſe, and afterward he ſhall kill the burnt offering.[20]And the Prieſt ſhall offer the burnt offering, and the meat offering vpon the Altar: and the Prieſt ſhall make an atonement for him, and he ſhalbe cleane.[21]And if he be poore, and cannot get ſo much, then hee ſhall take one lambe for a treſpaſſe offring to be waued, to make an atonement for him, and one tenth deale of fine flowre mingled with oile, for a meat offering, and a log of oile,[22]And two turtle doues, or two yong pigeons, ſuch as he is able to get: and the one ſhalbe a ſinne offering, and the other a burnt offering.[23]And hee ſhall bring them on the eight day, for his cleanſing vnto the Prieſt, vnto the doore of the Tabernacle of the Congregation, before the Lord.[24]And the Prieſt ſhall take the lambe of the treſpaſſe offering, and the log of oile, and the Prieſt ſhall waue them for a waue offering before the Lord.[25]And he ſhall kill the lambe of the treſpaſſe offering, and the Prieſt ſhall take ſome of the blood of the treſpaſſe offering, and put it vpon the tip of the right eare of him that is to be cleanſed, and vpon the thumbe of his right hand, and vpon the great toe of his right foote.[26]And the Prieſt ſhall powre of the oyle into the palme of his owne left hand.[27]And the Prieſt ſhal ſprinkle with his right finger, ſome of the oile that is in his left hand, ſeuen times before the Lord.[28]And the Prieſt ſhall put of the oile that is in his hand, vpon the tip of the right eare of him that is to be cleanſed, and vpon the thumbe of his right hand, and vpon the great toe of his right foot; vpon the place of the blood of the treſpaſſe offering.[29]And the reſt of the oile that is in the Prieſts hand, he ſhall put vpon the head of him that is to bee cleanſed, to make an atonement for him before the Lord.[30]And he ſhall offer the one of the turtle doues, or of the yong pigeons, ſuch as he can get:[31]Euen ſuch as he is able to get, the one for a ſinne offering, and the other for a burnt offering, with the meat offering. And the Prieſt ſhall make an atonement for him that is to be cleanſed, before the Lord.[32]This is the law of him in whom is the plague of leproſie, whoſe hand is not able to get that which pertaineth to his cleanſing.[33]And the Lord ſpake vnto Moſes, and vnto Aaron, ſaying,[34]When ye be come into the land of Canaan, which I giue to you for a poſſeſſion, and I put the plague of leproſie in a houſe of the land of your poſſeſſion;[35]And hee that oweth the houſe ſhall come, and tell the Prieſt, ſaying, It ſeemeth to me there is as it were a plague in the houſe:[36]Then the Prieſt ſhall command that they emptie the houſe, before the Prieſt goe into it to ſee the plague, that all that is in the houſe be not made vncleane: and afterward the Prieſt ſhall goe in, to ſee the houſe.[37]And he ſhal looke on the plague: and behold, if the plague be in the walls of the houſe, with hollow ſtrakes, greeniſh or reddiſh, which in ſight are lower then the wall;[38]Then the Prieſt ſhall goe out of the houſe, to the doore of the houſe, and ſhut vp the houſe ſeuen dayes.[39]And the Prieſt ſhall come againe the ſeuenth day, and ſhall looke: and behold, if the plague bee ſpread in the walls of the houſe;[40]Then the Prieſt ſhall command that they take away the ſtones in which the plague is, and they ſhall caſt them into an vncleane place without the Citie.[41]And hee ſhall cauſe the houſe to be ſcraped within round about, and they ſhall powre out the duſt that they ſcrape off, without the citie into an vncleane place.[42]And they ſhall take other ſtones, and put them in the place of thoſe ſtones; and hee ſhall take other morter, and ſhall plaiſter the houſe.[43]And if the plague come againe, and breake out in the houſe, after that he hath taken away the ſtones, and after he hath ſcraped the houſe, and after it is plaſtered;[44]Then the Prieſt ſhall come and looke, and behold, if the plague bee ſpread in the houſe, it is a fretting leproſie in the houſe: it is vncleane.[45]And he ſhall breake downe the houſe, the ſtones of it, and the timber thereof, and all the morter of the houſe: and he ſhall cary them foorth out of the city into an vncleane place.[46]Moreouer, he that goeth into the houſe all the while that it is ſhut vp, ſhalbe vncleane vntill the Euen.[47]And hee that lieth in the houſe, ſhall waſh his clothes: and hee that eateth in the houſe, ſhall waſh his clothes.[48]And if the Prieſt ſhall come in, and looke vpon it, and behold, the plague hath not ſpread in the houſe, after the houſe was plaſtered: then the Prieſt ſhall pronounce the houſe cleane, becauſe the plague is healed.[49]And he ſhall take to cleanſe the houſe, two birds, and Cedar wood, and ſcarlet, and hyſope.[50]And he ſhall kill the one of the birds in an earthen veſſell, ouer running water.[51]And he ſhall take the Cedar-wood and the hyſope, and the ſcarlet, and the liuing bird, and dip them in the blood of the ſlaine bird, and in the running water, and ſprinkle the houſe ſeuen times.[52]And he ſhall clenſe the houſe with the blood of the bird, and with the running water, and with the liuing bird, and with the Cedar wood, and with the hyſope, and with the ſcarlet.[53]But hee ſhall let goe the liuing bird out of the citie into the open fields, and make an atonement for the houſe: and it ſhall be cleane.[54]This is the law for all manner plague of leproſie and ſkall,[55]And for the leproſie of a garment, and of an houſe,[56]And for a riſing, and for a ſcabbe, and for a bright ſpot:[57]To teach when it is vncleane, and when it is cleane: this is the lawe of leproſie.

CHAPTER 15[1]And the Lord ſpake vnto Moſes, and to Aaron, ſaying,[2]Speake vnto the children of Iſrael, and ſay vnto them, when any man hath a running iſſue out of his fleſh, becauſe of his iſſue he is vncleane.[3]And this ſhall be his vncleanneſſe in his iſsue: whether his fleſh run with his iſsue, or his fleſh be ſtopped from his iſsue, it is his vncleanneſſe.[4]Euery bed whereon he lieth, that hath the iſsue, is vncleane: and euery thing whereon he ſitteth, ſhall bee vncleane.[5]And whoſoeuer toucheth his bed, ſhall waſh his clothes, and bath himſelfe in water, and bee vncleane vntill the Euen.[6]And hee that ſitteth on any thing whereon hee ſate that hath the iſsue, ſhall waſh his clothes, and bath himſelfe in water, and bee vncleane vntill the Euen.[7]And he that toucheth the fleſh of him that hath the iſsue, ſhall waſh his clothes, and bathe himſelfe in water, and be vncleane vntill the Euen.[8]And if he that hath the iſsue, ſpit vpon him that is cleane, then hee ſhall waſh his clothes, and bathe himſelfe in water, and bee vncleane vntill the Euen.[9]And what ſaddle ſoeuer he rideth vpon, that hath the iſsue, ſhall bee vncleane.[10]And whoſoeuer toucheth any thing that was vnder him, ſhall be vncleane vntil the Euen: And he that beareth any of thoſe things, ſhall waſh his clothes, and bathe himſelfe in water, and be vncleane vntill the Euen.[11]And whomſoeuer hee toucheth that hath the iſſue (and hath not rinſed his hands in water) he ſhall waſh his clothes, and bathe himſelfe in water, and be vncleane vntill the Euen.[12]And the veſſell of earth that hee toucheth which hath the iſsue, ſhall bee broken: and euery veſſell of wood ſhall be rinſed in water.[13]And when hee that hath an iſsue, is cleanſed of his iſsue, then hee ſhall number to himſelfe ſeuen dayes for his cleanſing, and waſh his clothes, and bathe his fleſh in running water, and ſhall be cleane.[14]And on the eight day hee ſhall take to him two turtle doues, or two yong pigeons, and come before the Lord, vnto the doore of the Tabernacle of the Congregation, and giue them vnto the Prieſt.[15]And the Prieſt ſhall offer them, the one for a ſinne offering, and the other for a burnt offering, and the Prieſt ſhall make an atonement for him before the Lord for his iſsue.[16]And if any mans ſeede of copulation goe out from him, then hee ſhall waſh all his fleſh in water, and bee vncleane vntill the Euen.[17]And euery garment and euery ſkinne whereon is the ſeede of copulation, ſhall be waſhed with water, and be vncleane vntill the Euen.[18]The woman alſo with whom man ſhall lie with feed of copulation, they ſhall both bath themſelues in water, and be vncleane vntill the Euen.[19]And if a woman haue an iſsue, and her iſſue in her fleſh be blood, ſhee ſhall bee put apart ſeuen dayes: and whoſoeuer toucheth her, ſhall bee vncleane vntil the Euen.[20]And euery thing that ſhe lieth vpon in her ſeparation, ſhall be vncleane: euery thing alſo that ſhe ſitteth vpon, ſhalbe vncleane.[21]And whoſoeuer toucheth her bed, ſhall waſh his clothes, and bathe himſelfe in water, and be vncleane vntill the Euen.[22]And whoſoeuer toucheth any thing that ſhe ſate vpon, ſhall waſh his clothes, and bathe himſelfe in water, and be vncleane vntill the Euen.[23]And if it be on her bed, or on any thing whereon ſhe ſitteth, when hee toucheth it, he ſhall be vncleane vntill the Euen.[24]And if any man lye with her at all, and her flowers be vpon him, hee ſhall be vncleane ſeuen dayes: and all the bed whereon he lyeth, ſhall be vncleane.[25]And if a woman haue an iſſue of her blood many dayes out of the time of her ſeparation, or if it runne beyond the time of her ſeparation, all the dayes of the iſſue of her vncleanneſſe, ſhall be as the dayes of her ſeparation: ſhe ſhalbe vncleane.[26]Euery bed whereon ſhe lyeth all the dayes of her iſsue, ſhall be vnto her as the bed of her ſeparation: and whatſoeuer ſhee ſitteth vpon, ſhall bee vncleane, as the vncleanneſſe of her ſeparation.[27]And whoſoeuer toucheth thoſe things, ſhalbe vncleane, and ſhall waſh his clothes, and bathe himſelfe in water, and be vncleane vntill the Euen.[28]But if ſhe be cleanſed of her iſsue, then ſhe ſhall number to her ſelfe ſeuen dayes: and after that, ſhe ſhalbe cleane.[29]And on the eight day ſhe ſhall take vnto her two turtles or two yong pigeons, & bring them vnto the Prieſt, to the doore of the Tabernacle of the Congregation.[30]And the Prieſt ſhall offer the one for a ſinne offering, and the other for a burnt offering, and the Prieſt ſhall make an atonement for her before the Lord, for the iſſue of her vncleanneſſe.[31]Thus ſhall yee ſeparate the children of Iſrael from their vncleanneſſe, that they die not in their vncleanneſſe, when they defile my Tabernacle that is among them.[32]This is the law of him that hath an iſsue, and of him whoſe ſeed goeth from him, and is defiled therewith;33And of her that is ſicke of her flowers, and of him that hath an iſsue, of the man, and of the woman, & of him that lyeth with her which is vncleane.

CHAPTER 161And the Lord ſpake vnto Moſes, after the death of the two ſonnes of Aaron, when they offered before the Lord, and died.2And the Lord ſayd vnto Moſes, Speake vnto Aaron thy brother, that hee come not at all times in to the Holy place within the Uaile, before the Mercy ſeat, which is vpon the Arke, that hee die not: for I will appeare in the cloud vpon the Mercy ſeat.3Thus ſhall Aaron come into the Holy place: with a yong bullocke for a ſinne offering, and a ramme for a burnt offering.4Hee ſhall put on the holy linnen coate, and he ſhall haue the linnen breeches vpon his fleſh, and ſhall be girded with a linnen girdle, and with the linnen Miter ſhall hee be attired. Theſe are holy garments: therefore ſhall he waſh his fleſh in water, and ſo put them on.5And he ſhall take of the Congregation of the children of Iſrael, two kiddes of the Goates for a ſinne offering, and one ramme for a burnt offering.6And Aaron ſhall offer his bullocke of the ſinne offering, which is for himſelfe, and make an atonement for himſelfe, and for his houſe.7And he ſhall take the two goats, and preſent them before the Lord at the doore of the Tabernacle of the Congregation.8And Aaron ſhall caſt lottes vpon the two Goates: one lot for the Lord, and the other lot for the Scape goat.9And Aaron ſhall bring the goate vpon which the Lords lot fell, and offer him for a ſinne offering.10But the goat on which the lot fell to be the Scape goate, ſhalbe preſented aliue before the Lord, to make an atonement with him, and to let him goe for a Scape goate into the wilderneſſe.11And Aaron ſhal bring the bullocke of the ſinne offering, which is for himſelfe, and ſhall make an atonement for himſelfe, and for his houſe, and ſhal kill the bullocke of the ſinne offering which is for himſelfe.12And he ſhall take a cenſer full of burning coales of fire from off the Altar before the Lord, and his handes full of ſweet incenſe beaten ſmall, and bring it within the vaile.13And he ſhall put the incenſe vpon the fire before the Lord, that the cloud of the incenſe may couer the mercie ſeate that is vpon the teſtimonie, that he die not.14And he ſhall take of the blood of the bullocke, and ſprinkle it with his finger vpon the Mercie ſeat Eaſtward: and before the Mercie ſeate ſhall hee ſprinkle of the blood with his finger ſeuen times.15Then ſhall he kill the goate of the ſinne offering that is for the people, and bring his blood within the Uaile, and doe with that blood as he did with the blood of the bullocke, and ſprinkle it vpon the Mercie ſeat, and before the Mercie ſeat.16And he ſhall make an atonement for the holy place, becauſe of the vncleanneſſe of the children of Iſrael, and becauſe of their tranſgreſſions in all their ſinnes: and ſo ſhall hee doe for the Tabernacle of the Congregation that remaineth among them, in the middeſt of their vncleanneſſe.17And there ſhall bee no man in the Tabernacle of the Congregation, when hee goeth in to make an atonement in the holy place, vntill hee come out, and haue made an atonement for himſelfe, and for his houſhold, and for all the Congregation of Iſrael.18And he ſhall goe out vnto the Altar that is before the Lord, and make an atonement for it, & ſhall take of the blood of the bullocke, and of the blood of the goate, and put it vpon the hornes of the Altar round about.19And he ſhall ſprinkle of the blood vpon it with his finger ſeuen times, and clenſe it, and hallow it from the vncleanneſſe of the children of Iſrael.20And when hee hath made an end of reconciling the holy place, and the Tabernacle of the Congregation, and the Altar, hee ſhall bring the liue goate.21And Aaron ſhall lay both his hands vpon the head of the liue goate, and confeſse ouer him all the iniquities of the children of Iſrael, and all their tranſgreſſions in all their ſinnes, putting them vpon the head of the goate, and ſhall ſend him away by the hand of a fit man into the wilderneſſe.22And the goate ſhall beare vpon him all their iniquities, vnto a land not inhabited; and he ſhall let goe the goat in the wilderneſſe.23And Aaron ſhall come into the Tabernacle of the Congregation, and ſhal put off the linnen garments which he put on, when he went in to the holy place, and ſhall leaue them there.24And he ſhall waſh his fleſh with water in the holy place, and put on his garments, and come foorth, and offer his burnt offering, and the burnt offering of the people, and make an atonement for himſelfe, and for the people.25And the fat of the ſinne offering ſhall he burne vpon the Altar.26And he that let goe the goat for the Scape-goat, ſhal waſh his clothes, and bathe his fleſh in water, and afterward come into the Campe.27And the bullocke for the ſinne offering, and the goat for the ſin offering, whoſe blood was brought in, to make atonement in the holy place, ſhall one cary foorth without the Campe, and they ſhal burne in the fire their ſkinnes and their fleſh, and their doung.28And he that burneth them, ſhall waſh his clothes, and bathe his fleſh in water, and afterward he ſhall come into the Campe.29And this ſhall be a ſtatute for euer vnto you: that in the ſeuenth moneth, on the tenth day of the moneth, ye ſhall afflict your ſoules, & doe no worke at all, whether it bee one of your owne countrey, or a ſtranger that ſoiourneth among you.30For on that day ſhal the Prieſt make an atonement for you, to cleanſe you, that yee may bee cleane from all your ſinnes before the Lord.31It ſhall be a Sabbath of reſt vnto you, and ye ſhall afflict your ſoules by a ſtatute for euer.32And the Prieſt whom he ſhall anoynt, and whom he ſhall conſecrate to miniſter in the Prieſts office in his fathers ſtead, ſhall make the atonement, and ſhal put on the linnen clothes, euen the holy garments.33And he ſhall make an atonement for the holy Sanctuary, and hee ſhall make an atonement for the Tabernacle of the Congregation, and for the Altar: and he ſhall make an atonement for the Prieſts, and for all the people of the Congregation.34And this ſhall be an euerlaſting ſtatute vnto you, to make an atonement for the children of Iſrael, for all their ſinnes once a yeere. And he did as the Lord commanded Moſes.

CHAPTER 171And the Lord ſpake vnto Moſes, ſaying,2Speake vnto Aaron and vnto his ſonnes, and vnto all the children of Iſrael, and ſay vnto them; This is the thing which the Lord hath commanded, ſaying;3What man ſoeuer there bee of the houſe of Iſrael, that killeth an oxe, or lambe, or goat in the Campe, or that killeth it out of the Campe,4And bringeth it not vnto the doore of the Tabernacle of the Congregation, to offer an offering vnto the Lord before the Tabernacle of the Lord, blood ſhall be imputed vnto that man; he hath ſhed blood, and that man ſhall be cut off from among his people:5To the end that the children of Iſrael may bring their ſacrifices, which they offer in the open field, euen that they may bring them vnto the Lord, vnto the doore of the Tabernacle of the Congregation vnto the Prieſt, and offer them for peace offerings vnto the Lord.6And the Prieſt ſhall ſprinckle the blood vpon the Altar of the Lord, at the doore of the Tabernacle of the Congregation, and burne the fat for a ſweet ſauour vnto the Lord.7And they ſhall no more offer their ſacrifices vnto deuils, after whom they haue gone a whoring: This ſhall be a ſtatute for euer vnto them throughout their generations.8And thou ſhalt ſay vnto them, whatſoeuer man there be of the houſe of Iſrael, or of the ſtrangers which ſoiourne among you, that offreth a burnt offering or ſacrifice,9And bringeth it not vnto the doore of the Tabernacle of the Congregation, to offer it vnto the Lord, euen that man ſhall be cut off from among his people.10And whatſoeuer man there be of the houſe of Iſrael, or of the ſtrangers that ſoiourne among you, that eateth any maner of blood, I will euen ſet my face againſt that ſoule that eateth blood, and will cut him off from among his people.11For the life of the fleſh is in the blood, and I haue giuen it to you vpon the Altar, to make an atonement for your ſoules: for it is the blood, that maketh an atonement for the ſoule.12Therefore I ſaid vnto the children of Iſrael, No ſoule of you ſhall eat blood, neither ſhall any ſtranger that ſoiourneth among you, eat blood.13And whatſoeuer man there be of the children of Iſrael, or of the ſtrangers that ſoiourne among you, which hunteth and catcheth any beaſt or foule that may be eaten, he ſhall euen powre out the blood thereof, and couer it with duſt.14For it is the life of all fleſh, the blood of it is for the life thereof: therefore I ſaid vnto the children of Iſrael, Ye ſhall not eat the blood of no maner of fleſh: for the life of all fleſh is the blood thereof: whoſoeuer eateth it, ſhalbe cut off.15And euery ſoule that eateth that which died of it ſelfe, or that which was torne with beaſts, whether it bee one of your owne countrey, or a ſtranger, he ſhall both waſh his clothes, and bathe himſelfe in water, and be vncleane vntill the Euen: then ſhall he be cleane.16But if he waſh them not, nor bathe his fleſh, then he ſhal beare his iniquity.

CHAPTER 181And the Lord ſpake vnto Moſes, ſaying,2Speake vnto the children of Iſrael, and ſay vnto them, I am the Lord your God.3After the doings of the land of Egypt wherein ye dwelt, ſhal ye not doe: and after the doings of land of Canaan whither I bring you, ſhall ye not doe: neither ſhall yee walke in their ordinances.4Ye ſhall doe my iudgements, and keepe mine ordinances, to walke therein: I am the Lord your God.5Yee ſhall therefore keepe my ſtatutes, and my iudgements: which if a man doe, hee ſhall liue in them: I am the Lord.6None of you ſhall approche to any that is neere of kinne to him, to vncouer their nakedneſse: I am the Lord.7The nakedneſſe of thy father, or the nakedneſſe of thy mother, ſhalt thou not vncouer: ſhe is thy mother, thou ſhalt not vncouer her nakedneſse.8The nakedneſſe of thy fathers wife ſhalt thou not vncouer: it is thy fathers nakedneſse.9The nakedneſſe of thy ſiſter, the daughter of thy father, or daughter of thy mother, whether ſhee be borne at home, or borne abroad, euen their nakedneſſe thou ſhalt not vncouer.10The nakedneſſe of thy ſonnes daughter, or of thy daughters daughter, euen their nakedneſſe thou ſhalt not vncouer: for theirs is thine owne nakedneſse.11The nakedneſſe of thy fathers wiues daughter, begotten of thy father, (ſhe is thy ſiſter,) thou ſhalt not vncouer her nakedneſse.12Thou ſhalt not vncouer the nakedneſſe of thy fathers ſiſter: ſhe is thy fathers neere kinſwoman.13Thou ſhalt not vncouer the nakedneſſe of thy mothers ſiſter: for ſhe is thy mothers neere kinſwoman.14Thou ſhalt not vncouer the nakedneſſe of thy fathers brother, thou ſhalt not approche to his wife: ſhee is thine aunt.15Thou ſhalt not vncouer the nakedneſſe of thy daughter in law: ſhee is thy ſonnes wife, thou ſhalt not vncouer her nakedneſse.16Thou ſhalt not vncouer the nakedneſſe of thy brothers wife: it is thy brothers nakedneſse.17Thou ſhalt not vncouer the nakedneſſe of a woman and her daughter, neither ſhalt thou take her ſonnes daughter, or her daughters daughter, to vncouer her nakedneſse: For they are her neere kinſewomen: it is wickedneſſe.18Neither ſhalt thou take a wife to her ſiſter, to vexe her, to vncouer her nakednes beſides the other, in her life time.19Alſo thou ſhalt not approche vnto a woman to vncouer her nakednes, as long as ſhee is put apart for her vncleanneſſe.20Moreouer, thou ſhalt not lie carnally with thy neighbours wife, to defile thy ſelfe with her.21And thou ſhalt not let any of thy ſeed paſſe through the fire to Molech, neither ſhalt thou prophane the Name of thy God: I am the Lord.22Thou ſhalt not lie with mankinde, as with womankinde: it is abomination.23Neither ſhalt thou lie with any beaſt, to defile thy ſelfe therewith: neither ſhall any woman ſtand before a beaſt to lie downe thereto: It is confuſion.24Defile not you your ſelues in any of theſe things: for in all theſe, the nations are defiled which I caſt out before you.25And the land is defiled: Therefore I doe viſit the iniquitie thereof vpon it, and the land it ſelfe vomiteth out her inhabitants.26Ye ſhall therefore keepe my Statutes and my Iudgements, and ſhall not commit any of theſe abominations; neither any of your owne nation, nor any ſtranger that ſoiourneth among you:27(For all theſe abominations haue the men of the land done, which were before you, and the land is defiled.)28That the land ſpew not you out alſo, when ye defile it, as it ſpewed out the nations that were before you.29For whoſoeuer ſhall commit any of theſe abominations, euen the ſoules that commit them, ſhall be cut off from among their people.30Therefore ſhal ye keepe mine Ordinance, that ye commit not any one of theſe abominable cuſtomes, which were committed before you, and that ye defile not your ſelues therein: I am the Lord your God.

CHAPTER 191And the Lord ſpake vnto Moſes, ſaying,2Speake vnto all the Congregation of the children of Iſrael, and ſay vnto them, Ye ſhalbe holy: for I the Lord your God am holy.3Yee ſhall feare euery man his mother, and his father, and keepe my Sabbaths: I am the Lord your God.4Turne ye not vnto idoles, nor make to your ſelues molten gods: I am the Lord your God.5And if ye offer a ſacrifice of peace offerings vnto the Lord, ye ſhall offer it, at your owne will.6It ſhall be eaten the ſame day ye offer it, and on the morrow: and if ought remaine vntill the third day, it ſhalbe burnt in the fire.7And if it be eaten at all on the third day, it is abominable; it ſhall not be accepted.8Therefore euery one that eateth it, ſhal beare his iniquitie, becauſe he hath prophaned the halowed thing of the Lord; and that ſoule ſhalbe cut off from among his people.9And when ye reape the harueſt of your land, thou ſhalt not wholly reape the corners of thy field, neither ſhalt thou gather the gleanings of thy harueſt.10And thou ſhalt not gleane thy vineyard, neither ſhalt thou gather euery grape of thy vineyard; thou ſhalt leaue them for the poore and ſtranger: I am the Lord your God.11Ye ſhall not ſteale, neither deale falſly, neither lie one to another.12And ye ſhall not ſweare by my Name falſly, neither ſhalt thou prophane the Name of thy God: I am the Lord.13Thou ſhalt not defraud thy neighbour, neither rob him: the wages of him that is hired, ſhal not abide with thee all night, vntill the morning.14Thou ſhalt not curſe the deafe, nor put a ſtumbling blocke before the blind, but ſhalt feare thy God: I am the Lord.15Ye ſhall doe no vnrighteouſnes in iudgement; thou ſhalt not reſpect the perſon of the poore, nor honour the perſon of the mightie: but in righteouſneſſe ſhalt thou iudge thy neighbour.16Thou ſhalt not goe vp and downe as a tale-bearer among thy people: neither ſhalt thou ſtand againſt the blood of thy neighbour: I am the Lord.17Thou ſhalt not hate thy brother in thine heart: thou ſhalt in any wiſe rebuke thy neighbour, and not ſuffer ſinne vpon him.18Thou ſhalt not auenge nor beare any grudge againſt the children of thy people, but thou ſhalt loue thy neighbor as thy ſelfe: I am the Lord.19Yee ſhall keepe my Statutes: Thou ſhalt not let thy cattell gender with a diuerſe kinde: Thou ſhalt not ſowe thy field with mingled ſeed: Neither ſhall a garment mingled of linnen and woollen come vpon thee.20And whoſoeuer lieth carnally with a woman that is a bondmaid, ſhe ſhall be ſcourged: they ſhall not be put to death, becauſe ſhe was not free:21And he ſhall bring his treſpaſſe offering vnto the Lord, vnto the doore of the Tabernacle of the Congregation, euen a ramme for a treſpaſſe offering.22And the Prieſt ſhall make an atonement for him with the ramme of the treſpaſſe offering before the Lord for his ſinne which hee hath done: and the ſinne which he hath done ſhall bee forgiuen him.23And when yee ſhall come in to the land, and ſhall haue planted all maner of trees for food, then ye ſhall count the fruit therof as vncircumciſed: three yeeres ſhall it be as vncircumciſed vnto you: it ſhall not be eaten of.24But in the fourth yeere all the fruit thereof ſhall be holy to praiſe the Lord withall.25And in the fift yeere ſhall ye eate of the fruit thereof, that it may yeelde vnto you the increaſe thereof: I am the Lord your God.26Ye ſhall not eate any thing with the blood, neither ſhall ye vſe inchantment, nor obſerue times.27Ye ſhall not round the corners of your heads, neither ſhalt thou marre the corners of thy beard.28Ye ſhall not make any cuttings in your fleſh for the dead, nor print any markes vpon you: I am the Lord.29Doe not proſtitute thy daughter, to cauſe her to be a whore, leſt the land fall to whoredome, and the land become full of wickedneſſe.30Ye ſhall keepe my Sabbaths, and reuerence my Sanctuary: I am the Lord.31Regard not them that haue familiar ſpirits, neither ſeeke after Wizards, to be defiled by them: I am the Lord your God.32Thou ſhalt riſe vp before the hoary head, and honour the face of the old man, and feare thy God: I am the Lord.33And if a ſtranger ſoiourne with thee in your land, yee ſhall not vexe him.34But the ſtranger that dwelleth with you, ſhalbe as one borne amongſt you, and thou ſhalt loue him as thy ſelfe, for ye were ſtrangers in the land of Egypt: I am the Lord your God.35Ye ſhall doe no vnrighteouſnes in iudgment, in meteyard, in weight, or in meaſure.36Iuſt ballances, iuſt weights, a iuſt Ephah, and a iuſt Hin ſhall ye haue: I am the Lord your God, which brought you out of the land of Egypt.37Therefore ſhall ye obſerue all my Statutes, and all my Iudgements, and doe them: I am the Lord.

CHAPTER 201And the Lord ſpake vnto Moſes, ſaying,2Againe, thou ſhalt ſay to the children of Iſrael; whoſoeuer he be of the children of Iſrael, or of the ſtrangers that ſoiourne in Iſrael, that giueth any of his ſeed vnto Molech, he ſhall ſurely be put to death: the people of the land ſhall ſtone him with ſtones.3And I wil ſet my face againſt that man, and will cut him off from among his people: becauſe he hath giuen of his ſeed vnto Molech, to defile my Sanctuary, and to prophane my holy Name.4And if the people of the land doe any wayes hide their eyes from the man, when he giueth of his ſeed vnto Molech, and kill him not:5Then I will ſet my face againſt that man, and againſt his family, and will cut him off, and all that goe a whoring after him, to commit whoredome with Molech, from among their people.6And the ſoule that turneth after ſuch as haue familiar ſpirits, and after wizards, to goe a whoring after them, I will euen ſet my face againſt that ſoule, and will cut him off from among his people.7ſanctifie your ſelues therefore, and bee yee holy: for I am the Lord your God.8And ye ſhall keepe my Statutes, and do them: I am the Lord which ſanctifie you.9For euery one that curſeth his father or his mother, ſhalbe ſurely put to death: hee hath curſed his father or his mother; his blood ſhalbe vpon him.10And the man that committeth adulterie with another mans wife, euen he that committeth adulterie with his neighbours wife, the adulterer, and the adultereſse ſhall ſurely bee put to death.11And the man that lieth with his fathers wife, hath vncouered his fathers nakedneſse: both of them ſhalbe put to death; their blood ſhalbe vpon them.12And if a man lie with his daughter in law, both of them ſhall ſurely be put to death: they haue wrought confuſion; their blood ſhall be vpon them.13If a man alſo lie with mankind, as hee lyeth with a woman, both of them haue committed an abomination: they ſhall ſurely be put to death; their blood ſhalbe vpon them.14And if a man take a wife, and her mother, it is wickedneſſe: They ſhalbe burnt with fire, both he and they, that there be no wickedneſſe among you.15And if a man lie with a beaſt, he ſhall ſurely be put to death: and ye ſhall ſlay the beaſt.16And if a woman approch vnto any beaſt, and lie downe thereto, thou ſhalt kill the woman and the beaſt: they ſhall ſurely be put to death, their blood ſhalbe vpon them.17And if a man ſhall take his ſiſter, his fathers daughter, or his mothers daughter, and ſee her nakedneſse, and ſhe ſee his nakedneſse, it is a wicked thing, and they ſhall bee cut off in the ſight of their people: he hath vncouered his ſiſters nakedneſse, he ſhall beare his iniquitie.18And if a man ſhall lie with a woman hauing her ſickeneſse, and ſhal vncouer her nakedneſse: he hath diſcouered her fountaine, and ſhe hath vncouered the fountaine of her blood: and both of them ſhall bee cut off from among their people.19And thou ſhalt not vncouer the nakedneſſe of thy mothers ſiſter, nor of thy fathers ſiſter: for hee vncouereth his neere kinne: they ſhall beare their iniquitie.20And if a man ſhall lie with his vncles wife, he hath vncouered his vncles nakedneſse: they ſhall beare their ſinne, they ſhall die childleſſe.21And if a man ſhall take his brothers wife, it is an vncleane thing: hee hath vncouered his brothers nakedneſse, they ſhall be childleſſe.22Ye ſhall therefore keepe all my Statutes, and all my Iudgements, and doe them: that the lande whither I bring you to dwell therein, ſpue you not out.23And ye ſhall not walke in the maners of the nation, which I caſt out before you: for they committed all theſe things, & therefore I abhorred them.24But I haue ſaid vnto you, Yee ſhall inherit their land, and I will giue it vnto you, to poſſeſſe it, a land that floweth with milke and hony: I am the Lord your God, which haue ſeparated you from other people.25Ye ſhall therefore put difference betweene cleane beaſts, and vncleane, and betweene vncleane foules, and cleane: & ye ſhall not make your ſoules abominable by beaſt or by foule, or by any maner of liuing thing, that creepeth on the ground, which I haue ſeparated from you as vncleane.26And ye ſhal be holy vnto me: for I the Lord am holy, & haue ſeuered you from other people, that ye ſhould be mine.27A man alſo or woman that hath a familiar ſpirit, or that is a wizzard, ſhall ſurely be put to death: they ſhall ſtone them with ſtones: their blood ſhalbe vpon them.

CHAPTER 211And the Lord ſaid vnto Moſes; Speake vnto the Prieſts the ſonnes of Aaron, and ſay vnto them, There ſhall none be defiled for the dead among his people:2But for his kinne, that is neere vnto him, that is, for his mother, and for his father, and for his ſonne, and for his daughter, and for his brother,3And for his ſiſter a virgin, that is nigh vnto him, which hath had no huſband: for her may he be defiled.4But hee ſhall not defile himſelfe being a chiefe man among his people, to prophane himſelfe.5They ſhall not make baldneſse vpon their head, neither ſhall they ſhaue off the corner of their beard, nor make any cuttings in their fleſh:6They ſhalbe holy vnto their God, and not profane the name of their God: for the offrings of the Lord made by fire, and the bread of their God they doe offer: therefore they ſhall be holy.7They ſhall not take a wife that is a whore, or profane, neither ſhall they take a woman put away from her huſband: for he is holy vnto his God.8Thou ſhalt ſanctifie him therfore, for he offereth the bread of thy God: he ſhalbe holy vnto thee: for I the Lord which ſanctifie you, am holy.9And the daughter of any Prieſt, if ſhe profane her ſelfe, by playing the whore, ſhe profaneth her father: ſhee ſhall be burnt with fire.10And he that is the high Prieſt among his brethren, vpon whoſe head the anointing oyle was powred, and that is conſecrated to put on the garments, ſhall not vncouer his head, nor rent his clothes:11Neither ſhall he goe in to any dead body, nor defile himſelfe for his father, or for his mother:12Neither ſhall hee goe out of the Sanctuary, nor prophane the Sanctuary of his God; for the crowne of the anointing oile of his God is vpon him: I am the Lord.13And he ſhall take a wife in her virginitie.14A widow, or a diuorced woman, or prophane, or an harlot, theſe ſhall he not take: but he ſhall take a virgine of his owne people to wife.15Neither ſhal he prophane his ſeed among his people: for I the Lord doe ſanctifie him.16And the Lord ſpake vnto Moſes, ſaying,17Speake vnto Aaron, ſaying, Whoſoeuer he be of thy ſeed in their generations, that hath any blemiſh, let him not approche to offer the bread of his God:18For whatſoeuer man hee be that hath a blemiſh, he ſhall not approche: a blind man, or a lame, or he that hath a flat noſe, or any thing ſuperfluous,19Or a man that is broken footed, or broken handed,20Or crooke backt, or a dwarfe, or that hath a blemiſh in his eye, or be ſcuruy, or ſcabbed, or hath his ſtones broken:21No man that hath a blemiſh, of the ſeed of Aaron the Prieſt, ſhall come nigh to offer the offrings of the Lord made by fire: he hath a blemiſh; he ſhall not come nigh to offer the bread of his God.22He ſhall eat the bread of his God, both of the moſt Holy, and of the holy:23Onely he ſhall not goe in vnto the Uaile, nor come nigh vnto the Altar, becauſe he hath a blemiſh, that he prophane not my Sanctuaries: for I the Lord doe ſanctifie them.24And Moſes told it vnto Aaron, and to his ſonnes, and vnto all the children of Iſrael.

CHAPTER 221And the Lord ſpake vnto Moſes, ſaying,2Speake vnto Aaron, and to his ſonnes, that they ſeparate themſelues from the holy things of the children of Iſrael, and that they prophane not my holy Name, in thoſe things which they halow vnto me: I am the Lord.3ſay vnto them, Whoſoeuer he be of all your ſeed, among your generations, that goeth vnto the holy things, which the children of Iſrael hallow vnto the Lord, hauing his vncleanneſſe vpon him, that ſoule ſhalbe cut off from my preſence: I am the Lord.4What man ſoeuer of the ſeed of Aaron is a leper, or hath a running iſsue, he ſhall not eat of the holy things, vntill he be cleane. And who ſo toucheth any thing that is vncleane by the dead, or a man whoſe ſeed goeth from him:5Or whoſoeuer toucheth any creeping thing, whereby he may be made vncleane, or a man of whom hee may take vncleanneſſe, whatſoeuer vncleanneſſe he hath:6The ſoule which hath touched any ſuch, ſhalbe vncleane vntill Euen, and ſhall not eate of the holy things, vnleſſe he waſh his fleſh with water.7And when the Sunne is downe, he ſhall be cleane, and ſhall afterward eate of the holy things, becauſe it is his food.8That which dieth of it ſelfe, or is torne with beaſts, hee ſhall not eate to defile himſelfe therewith: I am the Lord.9They ſhall therefore keepe mine Ordinance, leſt they beare ſinne for it, and die therefore, if they prophane it: I the Lord doe ſanctifie them.10There ſhall no ſtranger eat of the holy thing; a ſoiourner of the Prieſts, or an hired ſeruant ſhall not eate of the holy thing.11But if the Prieſt buy any ſoule with his money, he ſhall eat of it, and he that is borne in his houſe: they ſhall eat of his meat.12If the Prieſts daughter alſo bee married vnto a ſtranger, ſhe may not eate of an offering of the holy things.13But if the Prieſts daughter be a widow, or diuorced, and haue no childe, and is returned vnto her fathers houſe, as in her youth, ſhe ſhall eat of her fathers meat, but there ſhall no ſtranger eate thereof.14And if a man eate of the holy thing vnwittingly, then he ſhall put the fift part thereof vnto it; and ſhall giue it vnto the Prieſt, with the holy thing.15And they ſhall not profane the holy things of the children of Iſrael, which they offer vnto the Lord:16Or ſuffer them to beare the iniquitie of treſpaſſe, when they eate their holy things: for I the Lord do ſanctifie them.17And the Lord ſpake vnto Moſes, ſaying,18Speake vnto Aaron and to his ſonnes, and vnto all the children of Iſrael, and ſay vnto them, Whatſoeuer he be of the houſe of Iſrael, or of the ſtrangers in Iſrael, that will offer his oblation for all his vowes, and for all his free will offerings, which they will offer vnto the Lord for a burnt offering:19Ye ſhal offer at your owne wil a male without blemiſh, of the beeues, of the ſheepe, or of the goats.20But whatſoeuer hath a blemiſh, that ſhall ye not offer: for it ſhall not be acceptable for you.21And whoſoeuer offereth a ſacrifice of peace offerings vnto the Lord, to accompliſh his vow, or a free will offring in beeues or ſheepe, it ſhalbe perfect, to be accepted: there ſhall be no blemiſh therein.22Blind, or broken, or maimed, or hauing a wenne, or ſcuruie, or ſcabbed, ye ſhal not offer theſe vnto the Lord, nor make an offring by fire of them vpon the Altar vnto the Lord.23Either a bullocke, or a lambe that hath any thing ſuperfluous or lacking in his parts, that mayeſt thou offer for a free will offring: but for a vow it ſhal not be accepted.24Ye ſhal not offer vnto the Lord that which is bruiſed, or cruſhed, or broken, or cut, neither ſhall you make any offering thereof in your land.25Neither from a ſtrangers hand ſhall ye offer the bread of your God of any of theſe; becauſe their corruption is in them, and blemiſhes bee in them: they ſhall not be accepted for you.26And the Lord ſpake vnto Moſes, ſaying,27When a bullocke, or a ſheepe, or a goat is brought forth, then it ſhall bee ſeuen dayes vnder the damme, and from the eight day and thencefoorth, it ſhal be accepted for an offering made by fire vnto the Lord.28And whether it be cowe or ewe, ye ſhall not kill it, and her yong, both in one day.29And when yee will offer a ſacrifice of thankeſgiuing vnto the Lord, offer it at your owne will.30On the ſame day it ſhall be eaten vp, ye ſhall leaue none of it vntill the morrow: I am the Lord.31Therefore ſhall ye keepe my Commandements, and doe them: I am the Lord.32Neither ſhal ye profane my holy Name, but I will be hallowed among the children of Iſrael: I am the Lord which hallow you,33That brought you out of the land of Egypt, to be your God: I am the Lord.

CHAPTER 231And the Lord ſpake vnto Moſes, ſaying,2Speake vnto the children of Iſrael, and ſay vnto them, Concerning the feaſts of the Lord, which yee ſhall proclaime to be holy conuocations, euen theſe are my feaſts.3Sixe dayes ſhall worke be done, but the ſeuenth day is the Sabbath of reſt, an holy conuocation; ye ſhall doe no worke therein: it is the Sabbath of the Lord in all your dwellings.4Theſe are the feaſtes of the Lord, euen holy conuocations, which ye ſhall proclaime in their ſeaſons.5In the fourteenth day of the firſt moneth at euen, is the Lords Paſſeouer.6And on the fifteenth day of the ſame moneth, is the feaſt of vnleauened bread vnto the Lord: ſeuen dayes ye muſt eate vnleauened bread.7In the firſt day ye ſhall haue an holy conuocation: ye ſhall do no ſeruile worke therein.8But ye ſhal offer an offring made by fire vnto the Lord ſeuen dayes: in the ſeuenth day is an holy conuocation, Ye ſhall doe no ſeruile worke therein.9And the Lord ſpake vnto Moſes, ſaying,10Speake vnto the children of Iſrael, and ſay vnto them, When yee be come into the land which I giue vnto you, and ſhal reape the harueſt thereof, then ye ſhall bring a ſheafe of the firſt fruits of your harueſt vnto the Prieſt:11And hee ſhall waue the ſheafe before the Lord to be accepted for you: on the morrow after the Sabbath the Prieſt ſhall waue it.12And ye ſhall offer that day, when ye waue the ſheafe, an hee lambe without blemiſh of the firſt yeere, for a burnt offering vnto the Lord.13And the meat offring thereof ſhall be two tenth deales of fine flowre, mingled with oile, an offering made by fire vnto the Lord, for a ſweet ſauour: and the drinke offering thereof ſhalbe of wine, the fourth part of an Hin.14And ye ſhall eate neither bread, nor parched corne, nor greene eares, vntill the ſelfe ſame day that yee haue brought an offering vnto your God: It ſhalbe a ſtatute for euer, throughout your generations, in all your dwellings.15And ye ſhall count vnto you from the morrow after the Sabbath, from the day that ye brought the ſheafe of the waue offering; ſeuen Sabbaths ſhalbe complete.16Euen vnto the morrow after the ſeuenth Sabbath, ſhall ye number fifty dayes, and ye ſhall offer a new meat offering vnto the Lord.17Ye ſhall bring out of your habitations two waue-loaues, of two tenth deales: they ſhalbe of fine flowre, they ſhall be baken with leauen, they are the firſt fruits vnto the Lord.18And ye ſhall offer with the bread ſeuen lambes without blemiſh, of the firſt yeere, and one yong bullocke and two rammes: they ſhall be for a burnt offering vnto the Lord, with their meat offring and their drinke offrings, euen an offering made by fire of ſweet ſauour vnto the Lord.19Then ye ſhall ſacrifice one kid of the goates, for a ſinne offering, and two lambes of the firſt yeere, for a ſacrifice of peace offerings.20And the Prieſt ſhall waue them with the bread of the firſt fruits, for a waue-offring before the Lord, with the two lambs: they ſhalbe holy to the Lord for the Prieſts.21And ye ſhal proclaime on the ſelfe ſame day, that it may be an holy conuocation vnto you: ye ſhall doe no ſeruile worke therein: it ſhall be a ſtatute for euer in all your dwellings throughout your generations.22And when ye reape the harueſt of your land, thou ſhalt not make cleane riddance of the corners of the field, when thou reapeſt, neither ſhalt thou gather any gleaning of thy harueſt: thou ſhalt leaue them vnto the poore, and to the ſtranger: I am the Lord your God.23And the Lord ſpake vnto Moſes, ſaying,24Speake vnto the children of Iſrael, ſaying, In the ſeuenth moneth, in the firſt day of the moneth ſhall yee haue a Sabbath, a memoriall of blowing of trumpets, an holy conuocation.25Ye ſhall do no ſeruile worke therein; but ye ſhall offer an offering made by fire vnto the Lord.26And the Lord ſpake vnto Moſes, ſaying,27Alſo on the tenth day of this ſeuenth moneth, there ſhalbe a day of atonement, it ſhalbe an holy conuocation vnto you, & ye ſhall afflict your ſoules, and offer an offering made by fire vnto the Lord.28And ye ſhall doe no worke in that ſame day: for it is a day of atonement, to make an atonement for you, before the Lord your God.29For whatſoeuer ſoule it bee that ſhall not bee afflicted in that ſame day, hee ſhall bee cut off from among his people.30And whatſoeuer ſoule it bee that doeth any worke in that ſame day, the ſame ſoule will I deſtroy from among his people.31Ye ſhall doe no maner of worke: it ſhall be a ſtatute for euer throughout your generations, in all your dwellings.32It ſhalbe vnto you a Sabbath of reſt, and yee ſhall afflict your ſoules in the ninth day of the moneth at Euen, from Euen vnto Euen ſhall ye celebrate your Sabbath.33And the Lord ſpake vnto Moſes, ſaying,34Speake vnto the children of Iſrael, ſaying, The fifteenth day of this ſeuenth moneth, ſhall be the feaſt of Tabernacles for ſeuen dayes vnto the Lord.35On the firſt day ſhalbe an holy conuocation: ye ſhall doe no ſeruile worke therein.36Seuen dayes ye ſhall offer an offring made by fire vnto the Lord, on the eight day ſhall be an holy conuocation vnto you, and ye ſhall offer an offering made by fire vnto the Lord: It is a ſolemne aſſembly, and ye ſhall doe no ſeruile worke therein.37Theſe are the feaſts of the Lord which ye ſhall proclaime to be holy conuocations, to offer an offering made by fire vnto the Lord, a burnt offering, and a meat offering, a ſacrifice, & drinke offerings, euery thing vpon his day;38Beſide the Sabbaths of the Lord, and beſide your gifts, and beſide all your vowes, and beſide all your free will offerings, which ye giue vnto the Lord.39Alſo in the fifteenth day of the ſeuenth moneth when yee haue gathered in the fruit of the land, ye ſhall keepe a feaſt vnto the Lord ſeuen dayes. On the firſt day ſhall bee a Sabbath, and on the eight day ſhall bee a Sabbath.40And ye ſhall take you on the firſt day the boughes of goodly trees, branches of Palme trees, and the boughes of thicke trees, and willowes of the brooke, and yee ſhall reioyce before the Lord your God ſeuen dayes.41And yee ſhall keepe it a feaſt vnto the Lord ſeuen dayes in the yeere: It ſhalbe a ſtatute for euer in your generations, ye ſhall celebrate it in the ſeuenth moneth.42Ye ſhall dwell in boothes ſeuen dayes: all that are Iſraelites borne, ſhall dwell in boothes;43That your generations may know that I made the children of Iſrael to dwell in boothes, when I brought them out of the land of Egypt: I am the Lord your God.44And Moſes declared vnto the children of Iſrael the feaſtes of the Lord.

CHAPTER 241And the Lord ſpake vnto Moſes, ſaying,2Command the children of Iſrael, that they bring vnto thee pure oyle Oliue, beaten, for the light, to cauſe the lampes to burne continually.3Without the Uaile of the Teſtimonie, in the Tabernacle of the Congregation, ſhal Aaron order it from the euening vnto the morning, before the Lord continually: It ſhall be a ſtatute for euer in your generations.4He ſhall order the lampes vpon the pure Candleſticke before the Lord continually.5And thou ſhalt take fine flowre, and bake twelue cakes thereof: two tenth deales ſhall be in one cake.6And thou ſhalt ſet them in two rowes, ſixe on a row vpon the pure Table, before the Lord.7And thou ſhalt put pure frankincenſe vpon ech row, that it may bee on the bread for a memorial, euen an offering made by fire vnto the Lord.8Euery Sabbath he ſhall ſet it in order before the Lord continually, being taken from the children of Iſrael by an euerlaſting couenant.9And it ſhall be Aarons and his ſonnes, and they ſhall eate it in the holy place: for it is moſt holy vnto him, of the offerings of the Lord made by fire, by a perpetuall ſtatute.10And the ſonne of an Iſraelitiſh woman, whoſe father was an Egyptian, went out among the children of Iſrael: and this ſonne of the Iſraelitiſh woman, and a man of Iſrael ſtroue together in the campe.11And the Iſraelitiſh womans ſonne blaſphemed the name of the Lord, and curſed, and they brought him vnto Moſes: and his mothers name was Shelomith, the daughter of Dibri, of the tribe of Dan.12And they put him in ward, that the minde of the Lord might bee ſhewed them.13And the Lord ſpake vnto Moſes, ſaying,14Bring forth him that hath curſed, without the Campe, and let all that heard him, lay their hands vpon his head, and let all the Congregation ſtone him.15And thou ſhalt ſpeake vnto the children of Iſrael, ſaying, Whoſoeuer curſeth his God, ſhall beare his ſinne.16And hee that blaſphemeth the Name of the Lord, he ſhall ſurely be put to death, and all the Congregation ſhall certainely ſtone him: Aſwell the ſtranger, as he that is borne in the land, when he blaſphemeth the Name of the Lord, ſhall be put to death.17And he that killeth any man, ſhall ſurely be put to death.18And he that killeth a beaſt, ſhall make it good; beaſt for beaſt.19And if a man cauſe a blemiſh in his neighbour; as he hath done, ſo ſhal it be done to him:20Breach, for breach, eye for eye, tooth for tooth: as he hath cauſed a blemiſh in a man, ſo ſhall it be done to him againe.21And hee that killeth a beaſt, hee ſhall reſtore it: and hee that killeth a man, he ſhall be put to death.22Ye ſhall haue one maner of law, aſwell for the ſtranger, as for one of your owne countrey: for I am the Lord your God.23And Moſes ſpake to the children of Iſrael, that they ſhould bring foorth him that had curſed, out of the Campe, and ſtone him with ſtones: and the children of Iſrael did as the Lord commanded Moſes.

CHAPTER 251And the Lord ſpake vnto Moſes in Mount Sinai, ſaying,2Speake vnto the children of Iſrael, and ſay vnto them: when yee come into the land which I giue you, then ſhall the land keepe a Sabbath vnto the Lord.3Sixe yeeres thou ſhalt ſow thy field, and ſixe yeeres thou ſhalt prune thy Uineyard, and gather in the fruit thereof.4But in the ſeuenth yeere ſhalbe a Sabbath of reſt vnto the land, a Sabbath for the Lord: thou ſhalt neither ſow thy field, nor prune thy Uineyard.5That which groweth of it owne accord of thy harueſt, thou ſhalt not reape, neither gather the grapes of thy Uine vndreſſed: for it is a yeere of reſt vnto the land.6And the Sabbath of the land ſhall be meat for you; for thee, and for thy ſeruant, and for thy mayd, and for thy hired ſeruant, and for the ſtranger that ſoiourneth with thee,7And for thy cattel, and for the beaſt that are in thy land, ſhall all the encreaſe thereof be meat.8And thou ſhalt number ſeuen Sabbaths of yeeres vnto thee, ſeuen times ſeuen yeeres, and the ſpace of the ſeuen Sabbaths of yeeres, ſhall be vnto thee fourtie and nine yeeres.9Then ſhalt thou cauſe the trumpet of the Iubile to ſound, on the tenth day of the ſeuenth moneth; in the day of atonement ſhall ye make the trumpet ſound throughout all your land.10And ye ſhall hallow the fiftieth yeere, and proclaime libertie throughout all the land, vnto al the inhabitants thereof: It ſhalbe a Iubile vnto you, and ye ſhall returne euery man vnto his poſſeſſion, and ye ſhall returne euery man vnto his family.11A Iubile ſhall that fiftieth yeere be vnto you: Ye ſhall not ſow, neither reape that which groweth of it ſelfe in it, nor gather the grapes in it of thy Uine vndreſſed.12For it is the Iubile, it ſhall be holy vnto you: ye ſhall eate the encreaſe thereof out of the field.13In the yeere of this Iubile yee ſhall returne euery man vnto his poſſeſſion.14And if thou ſell ought vnto thy neighbour, or buyeſt ought of thy neighbours hand, ye ſhall not oppreſſe one another.15According to the number of yeres after the Iubile, thou ſhalt buy of thy neighbour, and according vnto the number of yeeres of the fruits, he ſhall ſell vnto thee.16According to the multitude of yeeres, thou ſhalt encreaſe the price thereof, and according to the fewneſse of yeeres, thou ſhalt diminiſh the price of it: for according to the number of the yeeres of the fruites doeth hee ſell vnto thee.17Yee ſhall not therefore oppreſſe one another; but thou ſhalt feare thy God: For I am the Lord your God.18Wherefore ye ſhall do my Statutes, and keepe my Iudgements, and doe them, and ye ſhall dwell in the land in ſafetie.19And the land ſhall yeeld her fruit, and ye ſhal eat your fill, and dwell therin in ſafetie.20And if ye ſhall ſay, What ſhall we eate the ſeuenth yeere? Behold, we ſhall not ſow, nor gather in our increaſe:21Then I will command my bleſſing vpon you in the ſixt yeere, and it ſhall bring forth fruit for three yeeres.22And ye ſhall ſow the eight yeere, and eat yet of old fruit, vntill the ninth yeere: vntill her fruits come in, ye ſhall eate of the old ſtore.23The land ſhall not be ſold for euer: for the land is mine, for ye were ſtrangers and ſoiourners with me.24And in all the land of your poſſeſſion, ye ſhall grant a redemption for the land.25If thy brother be waxen poore, and hath ſold away ſome of his poſſeſſion, and if any of his kinne come to redeeme it, then ſhall hee redeeme that which his brother ſold.26And if the man haue none to redeeme it, and himſelfe bee able to redeeme it:27Then let him count the yeeres of the ſale therof, and reſtore the ouerplus vnto the man, to whom he ſold it, that he may returne vnto his poſſeſſion.28But if he be not able to reſtore it to him, then that which is ſold, ſhall remaine in the hand of him that hath bought it, vntill the yeere of Iubile: and in the Iubile it ſhall goe out, and he ſhall returne vnto his poſſeſſion.29And if a man ſell a dwelling houſe in a walled citie, then he may redeeme it within a whole yeere after it is ſolde: within a full yeere may he redeeme it.30And if it be not redeemed within the ſpace of a full yeere, then the houſe that is in the walled citie, ſhall be ſtabliſhed for euer to him that bought it, throughout his generations: it ſhall not goe out in the Iubile.31But the houſes of the villages which haue no walles round about them, ſhall bee counted as the fields of the countrey: they may ee redeemed, and they ſhall goe out in the Iubile.32Notwithſtanding, the cities of the Leuites, and the houſes of the cities of their poſſeſſion, may the Leuites redeeme at any time.33And if a man purchaſe of the Leuites, then the houſe that was ſold, and the citie of his poſſeſſion ſhall goe out in the yeere of Iubile: for the houſes of the cities of the Leuites are their poſſeſſion among the children of Iſrael.34But the field of the ſuburbs of their cities may not be ſold, for it is their perpetuall poſſeſſion.35And if thy brother bee waxen poore, and fallen in decay with thee, then thou ſhalt relieue him, yea though he be a ſtranger, or a ſoiourner, that hee may liue with thee.36Take thou no vſurie of him, or increaſe: but feare thy God, that thy brother may liue with thee.37Thou ſhalt not giue him thy money vpon vſurie, nor lend him thy victuals for increaſe.38I am the Lord your God, which brought you foorth out of the land of Egypt, to giue you the land of Canaan, and to be your God.39And if thy brother that dwelleth by thee be waxen poore, and be ſold vnto thee, thou ſhalt not compell him to ſerue as a bond ſeruant.40But as an hired ſeruant, and as a ſoiourner he ſhall be with thee, and ſhall ſerue thee vnto the yere of Iubile.41And then ſhall hee depart from thee, both he and his children with him, and ſhall returne vnto his owne familie, and vnto the poſſeſſion of his fathers ſhall he returne.42For they are my ſeruants, which I brought forth out of the land of Egypt: they ſhall not be ſold as bond men.43Thou ſhalt not rule ouer him with rigour, but ſhalt feare thy God.44Both thy bondmen, and thy bondmaids, which thou ſhalt haue, ſhall be of the Heathen, that are round about you: of them ſhall ye buy bondmen and bondmaids.45Moreouer, of the children of the ſtrangers that do ſoiourne among you, of them ſhall ye buy, and of their families that are with you, which they begat in your land: and they ſhalbe your poſſeſſion.46And ye ſhall take them as an inheritance for your children after you, to inherite them for a poſſeſſion, they ſhal bee your bondmen for euer: but ouer your brethren the children of Iſrael, ye ſhall not rule one ouer another with rigour.47And if a ſoiourner or ſtranger waxe rich by thee, and thy brother that dwelleth by him waxe poore, and ſell himſelfe vnto the ſtranger or ſoiourner by thee, or to the ſtocke of the ſtrangers family:48After that he is ſold, hee may be redeemed againe: one of his brethren may redeeme him.49Either his vncle, or his vncles ſonne may redeeme him, or any that is nigh of kinne vnto him, of his family, may redeeme him: or if he be able, hee may redeeme himſelfe.50And he ſhall reckon with him that bought him, from the yeere that he was ſold to him, vnto the yeere of Iubile, and the price of his ſale ſhalbe according vnto the number of yeeres, according to the time of an hired ſeruant ſhall it be with him.51If there be yet many yeeres behinde, according vnto them hee ſhall giue againe the price of his redemption, out of the money that hee was bought for.52And if there remaine but few yeeres vnto the yeere of Iubile, then he ſhall count with him, and according vnto his yeeres ſhall he giue him againe the price of his redemption.53And as a yeerely hired ſeruant ſhall he be with him: and the other ſhall not rule with rigour ouer him in thy ſight.54And if hee be not redeemed in theſe yeeres, then he ſhall goe out in the yeere of Iubile, both he, and his children with him.55For vnto me the children of Iſrael are ſeruants, they are my ſeruants whom I brought forth out of the land of Egypt: I am the Lord your God.

CHAPTER 261Yee ſhall make you no Idoles nor grauen Image, neither reare you vp a ſtanding image, neither ſhall yee ſet vp any Image of ſtone in your land, to bow downe vnto it: For I am the Lord your God.2Ye ſhal keepe my Sabbaths, and reuerence my Sanctuary: I am the Lord.3If ye walke in my Statutes, and keepe my Commandements, and doe them;4Then I will giue you raine in due ſeaſon, and the land ſhall yeeld her increaſe, and the trees of the field ſhall yeeld their fruit.5And your threſhing ſhall reach vnto the vintage, and the vintage ſhall reach vnto the ſowing time: and yee ſhal eat your bread to the full, and dwel in your land ſafely.6And I wil giue peace in the land, and ye ſhall lye downe, and none ſhall make you afraid: and I will rid euill beaſts out of the land, neither ſhall the ſword goe through your land.7And ye ſhall chaſe your enemies, and they ſhall fall before you by the ſword.8And fiue of you ſhal chaſe an hundred, and an hundred of you ſhall put ten thouſand to flight: and your enemies ſhall fall before you by the ſword.9For I wil haue reſpect vnto you, and make you fruitfull, and multiply you, & eſtabliſh my couenant with you.10And yee ſhall eate old ſtore, and bring forth the old, becauſe of the new.11And I will ſet my Tabernacle amongſt you: and my ſoule ſhall not abhorre you.12And I will walke among you, and will be your God, and ye ſhall be my people.13I am the Lord your God, which brought you forth out of the land of Egypt, that yee ſhould

not be their bondmen, & I haue broken the bandes of your yoke, and
made you go vpright.14But if ye will not hearken vnto me, and will not
doe all theſe Commandements:15And if ye ſhall deſpiſe my Statutes, or
if your ſoule abhorre my Iudgements, ſo that ye wil not doe all my
Commandements, but that yee breake my Couenant:16I alſo will doe this
vnto you, I will euen appoint ouer you terrour, conſumption, and the
burning ague, that ſhall conſume the eyes, and cauſe ſorrow of heart:
and ye ſhall ſow your ſeede in vaine, for your enemies ſhall eate it.17And
I will ſet my face againſt you, and ye ſhall be ſlaine before your enemies:
they that hate you ſhall reigne ouer you, and ye ſhall flee when none
purſueth you.18And if ye will not yet for all this hearken vnto me, then
I will puniſh you ſeuen times more for your ſinnes.19And I will breake
the pride of your power, and I will make your heauen as yron, and your
earth as braſſe:20And your ſtrength ſhall be ſpent in vaine: for your land
ſhall not yeeld her increaſe, neither ſhall the trees of the land yeeld their
fruits.21And if ye walke contrary vnto me, and will not hearken vnto
mee, I will bring ſeuen times moe plagues vpon you, according to your
ſinnes.22I will alſo ſend wilde beaſts among you, which ſhall rob you of
your children, and deſtroy your cattell, and make you few in number,
and your high wayes ſhall be deſolate.23And if ye will not be reformed
by theſe things, but will walke contrary vnto me:24Then will I alſo walke
contrary vnto you, and will puniſh you yet ſeuen times for your
ſinnes.25And I will bring a ſword vpon you, that ſhall auenge the quarell
of my couenant: and when yee are gathered together within your cities,
I wil ſend the peſtilence among you, and ye ſhalbe deliuered into the
hand of the enemie.26And when I haue broken the ſtaffe of your bread,
ten women ſhall bake your bread in one ouen, and they ſhall deliuer you
your bread againe by weight: and ye ſhall eate, and not bee
ſatiſfied.27And if ye wil not for all this hearken vnto me, but walke
contrary vnto mee,28Then I wil walke contrary vnto you alſo in fury, and
I, euen I will chaſtiſe you ſeuen times for your ſinnes.29And ye ſhal eate
the fleſh of your ſonnes, and the fleſh of your daughters ſhall ye
eate.30And I will deſtroy your high places, and cut downe your images,
and caſt your carkeiſes vpon the carkeiſes of your idoles, and my ſoule
ſhall abhorre you.31And I wil make your cities waſte, and bring your
ſanctuaries vnto deſolation, and I will not ſmell the ſauour of your ſweet
odours.32And I will bring the land into deſolation: and your enemies
which dwel therein, ſhall be aſtoniſhed at it.33And I will ſcatter you
among the heathen, and will draw out a ſword after you: and your land
ſhall be deſolate, and your cities waſte.34Then ſhall the lande enioy her
Sabbaths, as long as it lieth deſolate, and yee be in your enemies land,
euen then ſhall the land reſt, and enioy her Sabbaths.35As long as it lieth
deſolate, it ſhall reſt: becauſe it did not reſt in your Sabbaths, when ye
dwelt vpon it.36And vpon them that are left aliue of you, I will ſend a
faintneſse into their hearts in the lands of their enemies, and the ſound
of a ſhaken leafe ſhall chaſe them, and they ſhall flee, as fleeing from a
ſword: and they ſhall fall, when none purſueth.37And they ſhall fall one
vpon another, as it were before a ſword, when none purſueth: and yee
ſhall haue no power to ſtand before your enemies.38And yee ſhall periſh
among the Heathen, and the land of your enemies ſhall eate you
vp.39And they that are left of you ſhall pine away in their iniquitie in
your enemies lands, and alſo in the iniquities of their fathers ſhall they
pine away with them.40If they ſhall confeſse the iniquitie of their fathers,
with their treſpaſſe which they treſpaſſed againſt me, and that alſo they
haue walked contrary vnto me:41And that I alſo haue walked contrary
vnto them, and haue brought them into the land of their enemies: if then
their vncircumciſed hearts bee humbled, and they then accept of the
puniſhment of their iniquitie:42Then will I remember my couenant with
Iacob, and alſo my couenant with Iſaac, and alſo my couenant with
Abraham will I remember, and I will remember the land.43The land alſo
ſhalbe left of them, and ſhall enioy her Sabbaths, while ſhe lieth deſolate
without them: and they ſhall accept of the puniſhment of their iniquitie:
becauſe, euen becauſe they deſpiſed my Iudgements, and becauſe their
ſoule abhorred my Statuteſ44And yet for all that, when they be in the
land of their enemies, I will not caſt them away, neither will I abhorre
them, to deſtroy them vtterly, and to breake my couenant with them:
for I am the Lord their God.45But I wil for their ſakes remember the
couenant of their Anceſtours, whom I brought forth out of the land of
Egypt, in the ſight of the Heathen, that I might be their God: I am the
Lord.46Theſe are the Statutes, and Iudgements, and Lawes which the
Lord made betweene him and the children of Iſrael, in mount Sinai, by
the hand of Moſes.
CHAPTER 271And the Lord ſpake vnto Moſes, ſaying,2Speake vnto
the children of Iſrael, and ſay vnto them, When a man ſhal make a
ſingular vow, the perſons ſhall be for the Lord, by thy eſtimation.3And
thy eſtimation ſhall be: Of the male from twentie yeeres old, euen vnto
ſixtie yeeres old: euen thy eſtimation ſhall be fiftie ſhekels of ſiluer, after
the ſhekel of the Sanctuary.4And if it be a female, then thy eſtimation
ſhall be thirtie ſhekels.5And if it be from fiue yeeres olde, euen vnto
twentie yeeres old, then thy eſtimation ſhall be of the male twentie
ſhekels, and for the female ten ſhekels.6And if it be from a moneth old,
euen vnto fiue yeeres old, then thy eſtimation ſhall be of the male, fiue
ſhekels of ſiluer, and for the female, thy eſtimation ſhall be three ſhekels
of ſiluer.7And if it be from ſixtie yeeres old, and aboue, if it be a male,
then thy eſtimation ſhall be fifteene ſhekels, and for the female ten
ſhekels.8But if he bee poorer then thy eſtimation, then he ſhall preſent
himſelfe before the Prieſt, and the Prieſt ſhall value him: according to
his abilitie that vowed, ſhall the Prieſt value him.9And if it be a beaſt
whereof men bring an offering vnto the Lord, all that any man giueth
of ſuch vnto the Lord, ſhall be holy.10He ſhall not alter it, nor change it,
a good for a bad, or a bad for a good: And if hee ſhall at all change beaſt
for beaſt, then it, and the exchange thereof ſhall be holy.11And if it be
any vncleane beaſt, of which they doe not offer a ſacrifice vnto the Lord,
then he ſhall preſent the beaſt before the Prieſt:12And the Prieſt ſhall
value it, whether it be good or bad: as thou valueſt it who art the Prieſt:
ſo ſhall it be.13But if hee will at all redeeme it, then he ſhall adde a fift
part thereof vnto thy eſtimation.14And when a man ſhall ſanctifie his
houſe to be holy vnto the Lord, then the Prieſt ſhal eſtimate it, whether
it be good or bad: as the Prieſt ſhall eſtimate it, ſo ſhall it ſtand.15And if
he that ſanctified it, will redeeme his houſe, then he ſhall adde the fift
part of the money of thy eſtimation vnto it, and it ſhall be his.16And if a
man ſhall ſanctifie vnto the Lord ſome part of a field of his poſſeſſion,
then thy eſtimation ſhall be according to the ſeed thereof: An Homer of
barley ſeed ſhall be valued at fiftie ſhekels of ſiluer.17If hee ſanctifie his
field from the yeere of Iubile, according to thy eſtimation it ſhall
ſtand.18But if hee ſanctifie his field after the Iubile, then the Prieſt ſhall
reckon vnto him the money, according to the yeeres that remaine, euen
vnto the yeere of the Iubile, and it ſhall be abated from thy
eſtimation.19And if he that ſanctified the field, will in any wiſe redeeme
it, then he ſhal adde the fift part of the money of thy eſtimation vnto it,
and it ſhall be aſsured to him.20And if hee will not redeeme the field, or
if he haue ſold the field to another man, it ſhall not be redeemed any
more.21But the field, when it goeth out in the Iubile, ſhall be holy vnto
the Lord, as a field deuoted: the poſſeſſion thereof ſhalbe the
Prieſts.22And if a man ſanctifie vnto the Lord a field which he hath
bought, which is not of the fieldes of his poſſeſſion:23Then the Prieſt
ſhall reckon vnto him the worth of thy eſtimation, euen vnto the yeere
of the Iubile, and hee ſhall giue thine eſtimation in that day, as a holy
thing vnto the Lord.24In the yeere of the Iubile, the field ſhall returne
vnto him of whom it was bought, euen to him to whom the poſſeſſion
of the land did belong.25And all thy eſtimations ſhall be according to the
ſhekel of the Sanctuarie: twentie Gerahs ſhall bee the ſhekel.26Onely the
firſtling of the beaſts which ſhould be the Lords firſtling, no man ſhall
ſanctifie it, whether it bee oxe, or ſheepe: It is the Lords.27And if it be
of an vncleane beaſt, then hee ſhall redeeme it according to thine
eſtimation, and ſhall adde a fifth part of it thereto: Or if it be not
redeemed, then it ſhalbe ſold according to thy
eſtimation.28Notwithſtanding, no deuoted thing that a man ſhall deuote
vnto the Lord, of all that he hath, both of man and beaſt, and of the
field of his poſſeſſion, ſhall be ſold or redeemed: euery deuoted thing is
moſt holy vnto the Lord.29None deuoted, which ſhalbe deuoted of men,
ſhall be redeemed: but ſhall ſurely be put to death.30And all the tithe of
the land, whether of the ſeed of the land, or of the fruit of the tree, is
the Lords: it is holy vnto the Lord.31And if a man will at all redeeme
ought of his tithes, he ſhall adde thereto the fifth part thereof.32And
concerning the tithe of the herde, or of the flocke, euen of whatſoeuer
paſſeth vnder the rod, the tenth ſhalbe holy vnto the Lord.33He ſhall not
ſearch whether it be good or bad, neither ſhall he change it: and if he
change it at all, then both it, and the change thereof, ſhall be holy; it ſhall

not be redeemed.[34]Theſe are the Commandements which the Lord commanded Moſes, for the children of Iſrael in mount Sinai.

NUMBERS

CHAPTER 1[1]And the Lord ſpake vnto Moſes in the wilderneſſe of Sinai, in the Tabernacle of the Congregation, on the firſt day of the ſecond moneth, in the ſecond yeere, after they were come out of the land of Egypt, ſaying,[2]Take yee the ſumme of all the Congregation of the children of Iſrael, after their families, by the houſe of their fathers, with the number of their names, euery male by their polle:[3]From twentie yeeres old and vpward, all that are able to goe foorth to warre in Iſrael: thou and Aaron ſhall number them by their armies.[4]And with you there ſhalbe a man of euery Tribe: euery one head of the houſe of his fathers.[5]And theſe are the names of the men that ſhall ſtand with you: of the tribe of Reuben, Elizur the ſonne of Shedeur.[6]Of Simeon: Shelumiel the ſon of Zuriſhaddai.[7]Of Iudah: Nahſhon, the ſonne of Amminadab.[8]Of Iſſachar: Nethaneel, the ſonne of Zuar.[9]Of Zebulun: Eliab the ſonne of Helon.[10]Of the children of Ioſeph: of Ephraim, Eliſhama the ſonne of Ammihud: of Manaſſeh, Gamaliel the ſonne of Pedahzur.[11]Of Beniamin: Abidan, the ſonne of Gideoni.[12]Of Dan: Ahiezer, the ſonne of Ammiſhaddai.[13]Of Aſher: Pagiel the ſonne of Ocran.[14]Of Gad: Eliaſaph, the ſonne of Deuel.[15]Of Naphthali: Ahira the ſonne of Enan.[16]Theſe were the renowned of the Congregation, Princes of the tribes of their fathers, heads of thouſands in Iſrael.[17]And Moſes and Aaron tooke theſe men, which are expreſſed by their names.[18]And they aſſembled all the Congregation together on the firſt day of the ſecond moneth, and they declared their pedegrees after their families, by the houſe of their fathers, according to the number of the names, from twenty yeres old and vpward by their polle.[19]As the Lord commaunded Moſes, ſo he numbred them in the wilderneſſe of Sinai.[20]And the children of Reuben Iſraels eldeſt ſonne, by their generations after their families, by the houſe of their fathers, according to the number of the names, by their polle, euery male from twenty yeeres old and vpward, all that were able to go forth to warre:[21]Thoſe that were numbred of them, euen of the tribe of Reuben, were fourty and ſixe thouſand and fiue hundred.[22]Of the children of Simeon by their generations, after their families, by the houſe of their fathers, thoſe that were numbred of them, according to the number of the names, by their polles, euery male from twenty yeeres old and vpward, all that were able to goe foorth to warre:[23]Thoſe that were numbred of them, euen of the tribe of Simeon, were fiftie and nine thouſand, and three hundred.[24]Of the children of Gad by their generations, after their families by the houſe of their fathers, according to the number of the names, from twenty yeeres old and vpward, all that were able to goe foorth to warre:[25]Thoſe that were numbred of them, euen of the tribe of Gad, were fourty and fiue thouſand, ſixe hundred and fiftie.[26]Of the children of Iudah by their generations, after their families by the houſe of their fathers, according to the number of the names, from twenty yeeres old and vpward, all that were able to goe foorth to warre:[27]Thoſe that were numbred of them, euen of the tribe of Iudah, were threeſcore and fourteene thouſand, and ſixe hundred.[28]Of the children of Iſſachar, by their generations, after their families by the houſe of their fathers, according to the number of the names, from twenty yeres old and vpward, all that were able to goe foorth to warre:[29]Thoſe that were numbred of them, euen of the tribe of Iſſachar, were fiftie and foure thouſand, and foure hundred.[30]Of the children of Zebulun, by their generations, after their families, by the houſe of their fathers, according to the number of the names, from twenty yeres old and vpward, all that were able to goe foorth to warre:[31]Thoſe that were numbred of them, euen of the tribe of Zebulun, were fiftie and ſeuen thouſand and foure hundred.[32]Of the children of Ioſeph; namely of the children of Ephraim, by their generations, after their families, by the houſe of their fathers, according to the number of the names, from twenty yeres old and vpward, all that were able to goe foorth to warre:[33]Thoſe that were numbred of them, euen of the tribe of Ephraim, were fourty thouſand and fiue hundred.[34]Of the children of Manaſſeh by their generations, after their families, by the houſe of their fathers according to the number of the names, from twenty yeeres old and vpward, all that were able to go forth to warre:[35]Thoſe that were numbred of them, euen of the tribe of Manaſſeh, were thirty and two thouſand, and two hundred.[36]Of the children of Beniamin, by their generations, after their families, by the houſe of their fathers, according to the number of the names from twenty yeeres old and vpward, all that were able to goe foorth to warre:[37]Thoſe that were numbred of them, euen of the tribe of Beniamin, were thirtie and fiue thouſand, and foure hundred.[38]Of the children of Dan, by their generations, after their families, by the houſe of their fathers, according to the number of the names, from twentie yeeres old and vpward, all that were able to goe forth to warre:[39]Thoſe that were numbred of them, euen of the tribe of Dan, were threeſcore and two thouſand, and ſeuen hundred.[40]Of the children of Aſher, by their generations, after their families, by the houſe of their fathers, according to the number of the names, from twentie yeres old and vpward, all that were able to goe forth to warre:[41]Thoſe that were numbred of them, euen of the tribe of Aſher, were fourtie and one thouſand, and fiue hundred.[42]Of the children of Naphtali, throughout their generations, after their families by the houſe of their fathers, according to the number of the names, from twentie yeeres olde and vpward, all that were able to goe forth to warre:[43]Thoſe that were numbred of them, euen of the tribe of Naphtali, were fiftie and three thouſand, and foure hundred.[44]Theſe are thoſe that were numbred, which Moſes and Aaron numbred, and the Princes of Iſrael, being twelue men: each one was for the houſe of his fathers.[45]So were all thoſe that were numbred of the children of Iſrael, by the houſe of their fathers, from twenty yeeres old and vpward, all that were able to goe forth to warre in Iſrael:[46]Euen all they, that were numbred, were ſixe hundred thouſand, and three thouſand, and fiue hundred and fiftie.[47]But the Leuites after the tribe of their fathers, were not numbred among them.[48]For the Lord had ſpoken vnto Moſes, ſaying,[49]Onely thou ſhalt not number the tribe of Leui, neither take the ſumme of them among the children of Iſrael.[50]But thou ſhalt appoint the Leuites ouer the Tabernacle of Teſtimonie, and ouer all the veſſels thereof, and ouer all things that belong to it: they ſhall beare the Tabernacle, and all the veſſels thereof, and they ſhall miniſter vnto it, and ſhall encampe round about the Tabernacle.[51]And when the Tabernacle ſetteth forward, the Leuites ſhall take it downe: and when the Tabernacle is to be pitched, the Leuites ſhall ſet it vp: and the ſtranger that commeth nigh, ſhall be put to death.[52]And the children of Iſrael ſhall pitch their tents euery man by his own campe, and euery man by his owne ſtanderd, throughout their hoſtes.[53]But the Leuites ſhall pitch round about the Tabernacle of Teſtimonie, that there be no wrath vpon the Congregation of the children of Iſrael: and the Leuites ſhall keepe the charge of the Tabernacle of Teſtimonie.[54]And the children of Iſrael did according to all that the Lord commanded Moſes, ſo did they.

CHAPTER 2[1]And the Lord ſpake vnto Moſes, and vnto Aaron, ſaying,[2]Euery man of the children of Iſrael ſhall pitch by his owne ſtanderd, with the enſigne of their fathers houſe: farre off about the Tabernacle of the Congregation ſhall they pitch.[3]And on the Eaſt ſide toward the riſing of the Sunne, ſhall they of the ſtanderd of the campe of Iudah pitch, throughout their armies: and Nahſhon the ſonne of Amminadab, ſhall bee captaine of the children of Iudah.[4]And his hoſte, and thoſe that were numbred of them, were threeſcore and fourteene thouſand, and ſixe hundred.[5]And thoſe that doe pitch next vnto him, ſhall be the tribe of Iſſachar: and Nethaneel the ſonne of Zuar, ſhall bee captaine of the children of Iſſachar.[6]And his hoſte, and thoſe that were numbred thereof, were fiftie and foure thouſand, and foure hundred.[7]Then the tribe of Zebulun: and Eliab the ſonne of Helon, ſhalbe captaine of the children of Zebulun.[8]And his hoſte and thoſe that were numbred thereof, were fiftie and ſeuen thouſand, and foure hundred.[9]All that were numbred in the Campe of Iudah, were an hundred thouſand, and foureſcore thouſand, and ſixe thouſand, and foure hundred, throughout their armies: theſe ſhall firſt ſet foorth.[10]On the Southſide ſhall be the ſtanderd of the Campe of Reuben, according to their armies: and the captaine of the children of Reuben ſhall be Elizur the ſonne of Shedeur.[11]And his hoſte, and thoſe that were numbred thereof, were fourtie and ſixe thouſand, and fiue hundred.[12]And thoſe which pitch by him, ſhall bee the tribe of Simeon, and the captaine of the children of Simeon ſhall be Shelumiel the ſonne of Zuriſhaddai.[13]And his hoſte, and thoſe that were numbred of them, were fiftie and nine thouſand, and three hundred.14Then the tribe of Gad: and the captaine of the ſonnes of Gad ſhall be Eliaſaph the ſonne of Reuel.15And his hoſte, and thoſe that were numbred of them, were fourtie and fiue thouſand, and ſixe hundred and fiftie.16All that were numbred in the Campe of Reuben were an hundred thouſand, and fiftie and one thouſand, and foure hundred and fiftie throughout their armies: and they ſhall ſet foorth in the ſecond ranke.17Then the Tabernacle of the Congregation ſhall ſet forward with the Campe of the Leuites, in the midſt of the Campe: as they encampe, ſo ſhall they ſet forward, euery man in his place by their ſtanderds.18On the Weſt ſide ſhall bee the ſtanderd of the Campe of Ephraim, according to their armies: and the captaine of the ſonnes of Ephraim, ſhall be Eliſhama the ſonne of Ammihud.19And his hoſte, and thoſe that were numbred of them, were fourtie thouſand and fiue hundred.20And by him ſhall be the tribe of Manaſſeh: and the captaine of the children of Manaſſeh, ſhalbe Gamaliel the ſonne of Pedahzur.21And his hoſte, and thoſe that were numbred of them, were thirtie and two thouſand, and two hundred.22Then the tribe of Beniamin: and the captaine of the ſonnes of Beniamin, ſhall bee Abidan the ſonne of Gideoni.23And his hoſte, and thoſe that were numbred of them, were thirtie and fiue thouſand, and foure hundred.24All that were numbred of the Campe of Ephraim, were an hundred thouſand, and eight thouſand, and an hundred, throughout their armies: and they ſhall goe forward in the third ranke.25The ſtanderd of the Campe of Dan ſhall be on the Northſide by their armies: and the captaine of the children of Dan ſhall be Ahiezer, the ſonne of Ammiſhaddai.26And his hoſte, and thoſe that were numbred of them, were threeſcore and two thouſand, and ſeuen hundred.27And thoſe that encampe by him, ſhalbe the tribe of Aſher: and the captaine of the children of Aſher, ſhalbe Pagiel the ſonne of Ocran.28And his hoſte, and thoſe that were numbred of them, were fourtie and one thouſand, and fiue hundred.29Then the tribe of Naphtali: and the captaine of the children of Naphtali, ſhall bee Ahira the ſonne of Enan.30And his hoſte, and thoſe that were numbred of them, were fiftie and three thouſand, and foure hundred.31All they that were numbred in the Campe of Dan, were an hundred thouſand, and fifty and ſeuen thouſand, and ſixe hundred: they ſhall goe hindmoſt with their ſtanderds.32Theſe are thoſe which were numbred of the children of Iſrael, by the houſe of their fathers; all thoſe that were numbred of the Campes throughout their hoſtes, were ſixe hundred thouſand, and three thouſand, and fiue hundred and fiftie.33But the Leuites were not numbred among the children of Iſrael, as the Lord commanded Moſes.34And the children of Iſrael did according to all that the Lord commanded Moſes: ſo they pitched by their ſtanderds, and ſo they ſet forward euery one after their families, according to the houſe of their fathers.

CHAPTER 31Theſe alſo are the generations of Aaron and Moſes, in the day that the Lord ſpake with Moſes in Mount Sinai.2And theſe are the names of the ſonnes of Aaron: Nadab the firſt borne, and Abihu, Eleazar and Ithamar.3Theſe are the names of the ſonnes of Aaron the Prieſts, which were anointed, whom he conſecrated to miniſter in the Prieſts office.4And Nadab and Abihu died before the Lord, when they offered ſtrange fire before the Lord in the wilderneſſe of Sinai, and they had no children: and Eleazar and Ithamar miniſtred in the Prieſts office in the ſight of Aaron their father.5And the Lord ſpake vnto Moſes, ſaying,6Bring the tribe of Leui neere, and preſent them before Aaron the Prieſt, that they may miniſter vnto him.7And they ſhall keepe his charge, and the charge of the whole Congregation before the Tabernacle of the Congregation, to doe the ſeruice of the Tabernacle.8And they ſhall keepe all the inſtruments of the Tabernacle of the Congregation, and the charge of the children of Iſrael, to doe the ſeruice of the Tabernacle.9And thou ſhalt giue the Leuites vnto Aaron and to his ſonnes: they are wholly giuen vnto him out of the children of Iſrael.10And thou ſhalt appoint Aaron and his ſonnes, and they ſhall waite on their prieſts office: and the ſtranger that commeth nigh, ſhall bee put to death.11And the Lord ſpake vnto Moſes, ſaying,12And I, behold, I haue taken the Leuites from among the children of Iſrael, in ſtead of all the firſt borne that openeth the matrice among the children of Iſrael: therefore the Leuites ſhall be mine,13Becauſe all the firſt borne are mine: for on the day that I ſmote all the firſt borne in the land of Egypt, I halowed vnto mee all the firſt borne in Iſrael, both man, and beaſt, mine they ſhall be: I am the Lord.14And the Lord ſpake vnto Moſes, in the wilderneſſe of Sinai, ſaying,15Number the children of Leui, after the houſe of their fathers, by their families: euery male from a moneth old and vpward ſhalt thou number them.16And Moſes numbred them according to the word of the Lord, as he was commanded.17And theſe were the ſonnes of Leui, by their names: Gerſhon, and Kohath, and Merari.18And theſe are the names of the ſonnes of Gerſhon, by their families: Libni, and Shimei.19And the ſonnes of Kohath by their families: Amram, and Izehar, Hebron and Uzziel.20And the ſonnes of Merari by their families: Mahli, and Muſhi: theſe are the families of the Leuites, according to the houſe of their fathers.21Of Gerſhon was the familie of the Libnites, and the familie of the Shimites: theſe are the families of the Gerſhonites.22Thoſe that were numbred of them, according to the number of all the males, from a moneth old and vpward, euen thoſe that were numbred of them, were ſeuen thouſand and fiue hundred.23The families of the Gerſhonites ſhal pitch behind the Tabernacle Weſtward.24And the chiefe of the houſe of the father of the Gerſhonites, ſhall be Eliaſaph the ſonne of Lael.25And the charge of the ſonnes of Gerſhon, in the Tabernacle of the Congregation, ſhall be the Tabernacle, and the tent, the couering thereof, and the hanging for the doore of the Tabernacle of the Congregation:26And the hangings of the Court, and the curtaine for the doore of the court, which is by the Tabernacle, and by the Altar round about, and the cords of it, for all the ſeruice therof.27And of Kohath was the familie of the Amramites, and the familie of the Izeharites, and the familie of the Hebronites, and the familie of the Uzzielites: theſe are the families of the Kohathites.28In the number of all the males, from a moneth olde and vpward, were eight thouſand, and ſixe hundred, keeping the charge of the Sanctuary.29The families of the ſonnes of Kohath, ſhall pitch on the ſide of the Tabernacle Southward.30And the chiefe of the houſe of the father of the families of the Kohathites ſhalbe Elizaphan the ſonne of Uzziel.31And their charge ſhall be the Arke, and the Table, and the Candleſticke, and the altars, and the veſſels of the Sanctuarie, wherewith they miniſter, and the hanging, and all the ſeruice thereof.32And Eleazar the ſonne of Aaron the Prieſt, ſhall be chiefe ouer the chiefe of the Leuites, and haue the ouerſight of them that keepe the charge of the Sanctuary.33Of Merari was the family of the Mahlites, and the family of the Muſhites: theſe are the families of Merari.34And thoſe that were numbred of them, according to the number of all the males from a moneth old & vpward, were ſixe thouſand and two hundred.35And the chiefe of the houſe of the father of the families of Merari, was Zuriel the ſonne of Abihail: theſe ſhall pitch on the ſide of the Tabernacle Northwards.36And vnder the cuſtody and charge of the ſonnes of Merari, ſhall bee the boards of the Tabernacle, and the barres thereof, and the pillars thereof, and the ſockets thereof, & all the veſſels thereof, and all that ſerueth thereto:37And the pillars of the Court round about, and their ſockets, and their pinnes, and their cords.38But thoſe that encampe before the Tabernacle toward the Eaſt, euen before the Tabernacle of the Congregation Eaſtward, ſhall be Moſes and Aaron, and his ſonnes, keeping the charge of the Sanctuary, for the charge of the children of Iſrael: and the ſtranger that commeth nigh, ſhall be put to death.39All that were numbred of the Leuites, which Moſes and Aaron numbred at the commaundement of the Lord, throughout their families, all the males from a moneth old and vpward, were twenty and two thouſand.40And the Lord ſaid vnto Moſes, Number all the firſt borne of the males of the children of Iſrael, from a moneth old and vpward, and take the number of their names.41And thou ſhalt take the Leuites for me, (I am the Lord) in ſtead of all the firſt borne among the children of Iſrael, and the cattell of the Leuites, in ſtead of all the firſtlings among the cattell of the children of Iſrael.42And Moſes numbred as the Lord commanded him, all the firſt borne among the children of Iſrael.43And all the firſt borne males, by the number of names, from a moneth old & vpward, of thoſe that were numbred of them, were twenty and two thouſand, two hundred, and threeſcore and thirteene.44And the Lord ſpake vnto Moſes, ſaying,45Take the Leuites in ſtead of all the firſt borne among the children of Iſrael, and the cattell of the Leuites in ſtead of their cattell, and the Leuites ſhalbe mine: I am the Lord.46And for thoſe that are to be redeemed of the two hundred and threeſcore and thirteene, of the firſt borne of the children of Iſrael, which are more then the Leuites;47Thou ſhalt euen take fiue ſhekels a piece, by the polle, after the ſhekel of the Sanctuary ſhalt thou take them; the ſhekel is twenty gerahs.48And thou ſhalt giue the money, wherewith the odde number of them is to be redeemed, vnto Aaron and to his ſonnes.49And Moſes tooke the redemption money, of them that were ouer and aboue them that were redeemed by the Leuites.50Of the firſt borne of the children of Iſrael tooke he the money; a thouſand, three hundred, and threeſcore and fiue ſhekels, after the ſhekel of the Sanctuary.51And Moſes gaue the money of them that were redeemed, vnto Aaron and to his ſonnes, according to the word of the Lord, as the Lord commanded Moſes.

CHAPTER 41And the Lord ſpake vnto Moſes, and vnto Aaron, ſaying,2Take the ſumme of the ſonnes of Kohath, from among the ſonnes of Leui, after their families, by the houſe of their fathers.3From thirty yeeres old and vpward, euen vntil fifty yeres old, all that enter into the hoſte, to doe the worke in the Tabernacle of the Congregation.4This ſhall bee the ſeruice of the ſonnes of Kohath, in the Tabernacle of the Congregation, about the moſt Holy things.5And when the Campe ſetteth forward, Aaron ſhall come, and his ſonnes, and they ſhall take downe the couering Uaile, and couer the Arke of Teſtimony with it:6And ſhall put thereon the couering of badgers ſkinnes, & ſhall ſpread ouer it a cloth wholly of blew, and ſhall put in the ſtaues thereof.7And vpon the table of Shewbread they ſhall ſpread a cloth of blew, and put thereon the diſhes, and the ſpoones, and the bowles, and couers to couer withall: and the continual bread ſhalbe thereon.8And they ſhall ſpread vpon them a clothe of ſcarlet, and couer the ſame with a couering of badgers ſkinnes, and ſhall put in the ſtaues thereof.9And they ſhall take a cloth of blew, and couer the candleſticke of the light, and his lampes, and his tongs, and his ſnuffe diſhes, and all the oyle veſſels thereof, wherewith they miniſter vnto it.10And they ſhall put it, and all the veſſels thereof, within a couering of badgers ſkinnes, and ſhall put it vpon a barre.11And vpon the golden Altar they ſhall ſpread a cloth of blew, and couer it with a couering of badgers ſkinnes, and ſhall put to the ſtaues thereof.12And they ſhall take all the inſtruments of miniſtery, wherewith they miniſter in the Sanctuary, and put them in a cloth of blew, and couer them with a couering of badgers ſkinnes, and ſhall put them on a barre.13And they ſhall take away the aſhes from the Altar, and ſpread a purple cloth thereon:14And they ſhall put vpon it all the veſſels thereof, wherewith they miniſter about it, euen the cenſers, the fleſhhookes, and the ſhouels, and the baſons, all the veſſels of the Altar: and they ſhall ſpread vpon it a couering of badgers ſkinnes, and put to the ſtaues of it.15And when Aaron and his ſonnes haue made an end of couering the Sanctuary, and all the veſſels of the Sanctuary, as the campe is to ſet forward; after that, the ſonnes of Kohath ſhall come to beare it: but they ſhal not touch any holy thing, leſt they die. Theſe things are the burden of the ſonnes of Kohath in the Tabernacle of the Congregation.16And to the office of Eleazar the ſonne of Aaron the Prieſt, perteineth the oile for the light, and the ſweet incenſe, and the dayly meat offering, and the anoynting oyle, and the ouerſight of all the Tabernacle, and of all that therein is, in the Sanctuary, and in the veſſels thereof.17And the Lord ſpake vnto Moſes, and vnto Aaron, ſaying,18Cut ye not off the tribe of the families of the Kohathites, from among the Leuites.19But thus doe vnto them, that they may liue, and not die: when they approche vnto the moſt Holy things, Aaron and his ſonnes ſhall goe in, and appoint them euery one to his ſeruice, and to his burden.20But they ſhall not goe in to ſee when the holy things are couered, leſt they die.21And the Lord ſpake vnto Moſes, ſaying,22Take alſo the ſumme of the ſonnes of Gerſhon, throughout the houſes of their fathers, by their families:23From thirtie yeeres old and vpward, vntill fiftie yeeres old ſhalt thou number them: all that enter in to performe the ſeruice, to doe the worke in the Tabernacle of the Congregation.24This is the ſeruice of the families of the Gerſhonites, to ſerue, and for burdens.25And they ſhall beare the curtaines of the Tabernacle, and the Tabernacle of the Congregation; his couering, and the couering of the badgers ſkinnes that is aboue vpon it, and the hanging for the doore of the Tabernacle of the Congregation:26And the hangings of the Court, and the hanging for the doore of the gate of the Court which is by the Tabernacle, and by the Altar round about, and their cords, and all the inſtruments of their ſeruice, and all that is made for them: ſo ſhall they ſerue.27At the appointment of Aaron and his ſonnes, ſhall be all the ſeruice of the ſonnes of the Gerſhonites, in all their burdens, and in all their ſeruice: and yee ſhall appoint vnto them in charge all their burdens.28This is the ſeruice of the families of the ſonnes of Gerſhon, in the Tabernacle of the Congregation: and their charge ſhalbe vnder the hande of Ithamar the ſonne of Aaron the Prieſt.29As for the ſonnes of Merari, thou ſhalt number them after their families, by the houſe of their fathers:30From thirty yeeres old and vpward, euen vnto fiftie yeeres old ſhalt thou number them, euery one that entreth in to the ſeruice, to doe the worke of the Tabernacle of the Congregation.31And this is the charge of their burden, according to all their ſeruice, in the Tabernacle of the Congregation, the boards of the Tabernacle, and the barres thereof, and the pillars thereof, and ſockets thereof:32And the pillars of the Court round about, and their ſockets, and their pinnes, and their coards, with all their inſtruments, and with all their ſeruice: and by name yee ſhall reckon the inſtruments of the charge of their burden.33This is the ſeruice of the families of the ſonnes of Merari, according to all their ſeruice in the Tabernacle of the Congregation, vnder the hand of Ithamar the ſonne of Aaron the Prieſt.34And Moſes and Aaron, and the chiefe of the Congregation, numbred the ſonnes of the Kohathites, after their families, and after the houſe of their fathers;35From thirtie yeeres old and vpward, euen vnto fiftie yeeres old, euery one that entreth in to the ſeruice, for the worke in the Tabernacle of the Congregation.36And thoſe that were numbred of them by their families, were two thouſand, ſeuen hundred and fiftie.37Theſe were they that were numbred of the families of the Kohathites; all that might doe ſeruice in the Tabernacle of the Congregation, which Moſes and Aaron did number, according to the commandement of the Lord, by the hand of Moſes.38And thoſe that were numbred of the ſonnes of Gerſhon, throughout their families, and by the houſe of their fathers;39From thirtie yeeres old and vpward, euen vnto fiftie yeeres old, euery one that entreth in to the ſeruice, for the worke in the Tabernacle of the Congregation:40Euen thoſe that were numbred of them, throughout their families, by the houſes of their fathers, were two thouſand, and ſixe hundred and thirtie.41Theſe are they that were numbred of the families of the ſonnes of Gerſhon, of all that might doe ſeruice in the Tabernacle of the Congregation, whom Moſes and Aaron did number, according to the commandement of the Lord.42And thoſe that were numbred of the families of the ſonnes of Merari, throughout their families, by the houſe of their fathers:43From thirtie yeeres old and vpward, euen vnto fiftie yeeres old, euery one that entreth in to the ſeruice, for the worke in the Tabernacle of the Congregation:44Euen thoſe that were numbred of them after their families, were three thouſand and two hundred.45Theſe be thoſe that were numbred of the families of the ſonnes of Merari, whom Moſes & Aaron numbred according to the word of the Lord by the hand of Moſes.46All thoſe that were numbred of the Leuites, whom Moſes and Aaron, and the chiefe of Iſrael numbred, after their families, and after the houſe of their fathers:47From thirty yeeres old and vpward, euen vnto fifty yeeres old, euery one that came to doe the ſeruice of the miniſtery, and the ſeruice of the burden in the Tabernacle of the Congregation:48Euen thoſe that were numbred of them, were eight thouſand, and fiue hundred, and foureſcore.49According to the commandement of the Lord, they were numbred by the hand of Moſes, euery one according to his ſeruice, and according to his burden: Thus were they numbred of him, as the Lord commanded Moſes.

CHAPTER 51And the Lord ſpake vnto Moſes, ſaying,2Commaund the children of Iſrael, that they put out of the campe euery leper, and euery one that hath an iſsue, and whoſoeuer is defiled by the dead:3Both male and female ſhal ye put out, without the campe ſhall yee put them, that they defile not their campes in the middeſt whereof I dwell.4And the children of Iſrael did ſo, and put them out, without the campe: as the Lord ſpake vnto Moſes, ſo did the children of Iſrael.5And the Lord ſpake vnto Moſes, ſaying,6Speake vnto the children of Iſrael, When a man or woman ſhall commit any ſinne that men commit, to doe a treſpaſſe againſt the Lord, and that perſon be guiltie;7Then they ſhall confeſse their ſinne, which they haue done: and hee ſhall recompenſe his treſpaſſe, with the principall thereof, and adde vnto it the fifth part thereof, and giue it vnto him againſt whom he hath treſpaſſed.8But if the man haue no kinſman to recompenſe the treſpaſſe vnto, let the treſpaſſe be recompenſed vnto the Lord, euen to the Prieſt: beſide the ramme of the atonement, whereby an atonement ſhall be made for him.9And euery offering of all the holy things of the children of Iſrael, which they bring vnto the Prieſt, ſhall be his.[10]And euery mans halowed things ſhall be his: whatſoeuer any man giueth the Prieſt, it ſhall be his.[11]And the Lord ſpake vnto Moſes, ſaying,[12]Speake vnto the children of Iſrael, and ſay vnto them, If any mans wife goe aſide, and commit a treſpaſſe againſt him;[13]And a man lye with her carnally, and it be hid from the eyes of her huſband, and be kept cloſe, and ſhe be defiled, and there be no witneſſe againſt her, neither ſhe be taken with the maner;[14]And the ſpirit of ielouſie come vpon him, and he be ielous of his wife, and ſhee be defiled: or if the ſpirit of ielouſie come vpon him, and hee be ielous of his wife, and ſhe be not defiled:[15]Then ſhall the man bring his wife vnto the Prieſt, and he ſhall bring her offering for her, the tenth part of an Ephah of barley meale: hee ſhall powre no oyle vpon it, nor put frankincenſe thereon; for it is an offering of ielouſie, an offering of memoriall, bringing iniquitie to remembrance:[16]And the Prieſt ſhall bring her neere, and ſet her before the Lord.[17]And the Prieſt ſhall take holy water in an earthen veſſell, and of the duſt that is in the floore of the Tabernacle the Prieſt ſhall take, and put it into the water:[18]And the Prieſt ſhall ſet the woman before the Lord, and vncouer the womans head, and put the offering of memoriall in her hands, which is the Ielouſie offering: and the Prieſt ſhall haue in his hand the bitter water that cauſeth the curſe.[19]And the Prieſt ſhall charge her by an othe, and ſay vnto the woman, If no man haue lyen with thee, and if thou haſt not gone aſide to vncleanneſſe with another in ſtead of thy huſband, be thou free from this bitter water that cauſeth the curſe.[20]But if thou haſt gone aſide to another in ſtead of thy huſband, and if thou be defiled, and ſome man hath lien with thee beſide thine huſband:[21]Then the Prieſt ſhall charge the woman with an othe of curſing, and the Prieſt ſhall ſay vnto the woman, The Lord make thee a curſe, and an othe among thy people, when the Lord doth make thy thigh to rot, and thy belly to ſwell.[22]And this water that cauſeth the curſe, ſhall go into thy bowels, to make thy belly to ſwell, and thy thigh to rot: and the woman ſhall ſay, Amen, Amen.[23]And the Prieſt ſhall write theſe curſes in a booke, and hee ſhall blot them out with the bitter water:[24]And he ſhall cauſe the woman to drinke the bitter water, that cauſeth the curſe: and the water that cauſeth the curſe ſhall enter into her, and become bitter.[25]Then the Prieſt ſhall take the ielouſie offering out of the womans hand, and ſhall waue the offering before the Lord, and offer it vpon the Altar.[26]And the Prieſt ſhal take an handfull of the offering, euen the memoriall thereof, and burne it vpon the Altar, and afterward ſhall cauſe the woman to drinke the water.[27]And when he hath made her to drinke the water, then it ſhall come to paſſe, that if ſhee be defiled, and haue done treſpaſſe againſt her huſband, that the water that cauſeth the curſe, ſhall enter into her, and become bitter, and her belly ſhall ſwell, and her thigh ſhal rot: and the woman ſhalbe a curſe among her people.[28]And if the woman be not defiled, but be cleane, then ſhe ſhall be free, and ſhall conceiue ſeed.[29]This is the law of ielouſies, when a wife goeth aſide to another in ſtead of her huſband, and is defiled:[30]Or when the ſpirit of ielouſie commeth vpon him, and hee be ielous ouer his wife, and ſhall ſet the woman before the Lord, and the Prieſt ſhal execute vpon her all this law.[31]Then ſhall the man bee guiltleſſe from iniquitie, and this woman ſhall beare her iniquitie.

CHAPTER 6[1]And the Lord ſpake vnto Moſes, ſaying,[2]Speake vnto the children of Iſrael, and ſay vnto them, When either man or woman ſhall ſeparate themſelues to vow a vow of a Nazarite, to ſeparate themſelues vnto the Lord:[3]Hee ſhall ſeparate himſelfe from wine, and ſtrong drinke, and ſhal drinke no vineger of wine, or vineger of ſtrong drinke, neither ſhal he drinke any liquor of grapes, nor eate moiſt grapes, or dried.[4]All the dayes of his ſeparation ſhall he eat nothing that is made of the vine tree, from the kernels euen to the huſke.[5]All the dayes of the vow of his ſeparation, there ſhall no raſour come vpon his head: vntill the dayes bee fulfilled in the which hee ſeparateth himſelfe vnto the Lord, he ſhall be holy, and ſhall let the lockes of the haire of his head grow.[6]All the dayes that he ſeparateth himſelfe vnto the Lord, hee ſhall come at no dead body.[7]Hee ſhall not make himſelfe vncleane for his father, or for his mother, for his brother, or for his ſiſter, when they die: becauſe the conſecration of his God is vpon his head.[8]All the dayes of his ſeparation he is holy vnto the Lord.[9]And if any man die very ſuddenly by him, and he hath defiled the head of his conſecration, then he ſhall ſhaue his head in the day of his cleanſing, on the ſeuenth day ſhall he ſhaue it.[10]And on the eight day he ſhal bring two turtles or two yong pigeons to the Prieſt, to the doore of the Tabernacle of the Congregation.[11]And the Prieſt ſhall offer the one for a ſinne offering, and the other for a burnt offering, and make an atonement for him, for that hee ſinned by the dead, and ſhall hallow his head that ſame day.[12]And hee ſhall conſecrate vnto the Lord the dayes of his ſeparation, and ſhall bring a lambe of the firſt yeere for a treſpaſſe offering: but the dayes that were before ſhall be loſt, becauſe his ſeparation was defiled.[13]And this is the Lawe of the Nazarite: when the dayes of his ſeparation are fulfilled, he ſhall be brought vnto the doore of the Tabernacle of the Congregation.[14]And he ſhall offer his offring vnto the Lord, one hee lambe of the firſt yeere without blemiſh, for a burnt offering, and one ewe lambe of the firſt yeere without blemiſh, for a ſinne offering, and one lambe without blemiſh for peace offerings,[15]And a baſket of vnleauened bread, cakes of fine flowre mingled with oyle, and wafers of vnleauened bread anointed with oyle, and their meate offering, and their drinke offerings.[16]And the Prieſt ſhall bring them before the Lord, and ſhall offer his ſinne offering, and his burnt offering.[17]And he ſhall offer the ramme for a ſacrifice of peace offerings vnto the Lord, with the baſket of vnleauened bread: the Prieſt ſhall offer alſo his meate offering, and his drinke offering.[18]And the Nazarite ſhal ſhaue the head of his ſeparation, at the doore of the Tabernacle of the Congregation, and ſhall take the haire of the head of his ſeparation, and put it in the fire which is vnder the ſacrifice of the peace offerings.[19]And the Prieſt ſhall take the ſodden ſhoulder of the ramme, and one vnleauened cake out of the baſket, and one vnleauened wafer, and ſhall put them vpon the hands of the Nazarite, after the haire of his ſeparation is ſhauen.[20]And the Prieſt ſhall waue them for a waue offring before the Lord: this is holy for the Prieſt, with the waue breaſt, and heaue ſhoulder: and after that, the Nazarite may drinke wine.[21]This is the Law of the Nazarite, who hath vowed, and of his offering vnto the Lord for his ſeparation, beſides that, that his hand ſhall get: according to the vow which he vowed, ſo he muſt do after the law of his ſeparation.[22]And the Lord ſpake vnto Moſes, ſaying,[23]Speake vnto Aaron, and vnto his ſonnes, ſaying, On this wiſe ye ſhall bleſſe the children of Iſrael, ſaying vnto them:[24]The Lord bleſſe thee, and keepe thee:[25]The Lord make his face ſhine vpon thee, and be gracious vnto thee:[26]The Lord lift vp his countenance vpon thee, and giue thee peace.[27]And they ſhall put my Name vpon the children of Iſrael, and I will bleſſe them.

CHAPTER 7[1]And it came to paſſe on the day that Moſes had fully ſet vp the Tabernacle, and had anointed it, and ſanctified it, and all the inſtruments thereof, both the Altar, and all the veſſels thereof, and had anointed them, and ſanctified them:[2]That the Princes of Iſrael, heads of the houſe of their fathers, (who were the Princes of the tribes, and were ouer them that were numbred) offered:[3]And they brought their offering before the Lord, ſixe couered wagons, and twelue oxen: a wagon for two of the Princes, and for each one an oxe, and they brought them before the Tabernacle.[4]And the Lord ſpake vnto Moſes, ſaying,[5]Take it of them, that they may be to doe the ſeruice of the Tabernacle of the Congregation, and thou ſhalt giue them vnto the Leuites, to euery man according to his ſeruice.[6]And Moſes tooke the wagons, and the oxen, and gaue them vnto the Leuites.[7]Two wagons and foure oxen he gaue vnto the ſonnes of Gerſhon, according to their ſeruice.[8]And foure wagons and eight oxen he gaue vnto the ſonnes of Merari, according vnto their ſeruice, vnder the hand of Ithamar the ſonne of Aaron the Prieſt.[9]But vnto the ſonnes of Kohath he gaue none: becauſe the ſeruice of the Sanctuary belonging vnto them, was that they ſhould beare vpon their ſhoulders .[10]And the Princes offered for dedicating of the Altar, in the day that it was anointed, euen the Princes offered their offering before the Altar.[11]And the Lord ſaid vnto Moſes, They ſhall offer their offering eche Prince on his day, for the dedicating of the Altar.[12]And he that offered his offring the firſt day, was Nahſhon the ſonne of Amminadab, of the tribe of Iudah.[13]And his offering was one ſiluer charger, the weight thereof was an hundred and thirty ſhekels, one ſiluer bowle of ſeuentie ſhekels, after the ſhekel of the Sanctuary; both of them were full of fine flowre mingled with oile for a meat offering:[14]One ſpoone of ten ſhekels of gold, full of incenſe:[15]One yong bullocke, one ramme, one lambe of the firſt yeere, for a burnt offering,[16]One kid of the goats for a ſinne offering:[17]And for a ſacrifice of peace offerings, two oxen, fiue rammes, fiue hee goats, fiue lambes of the firſt yeere: this was the offering of Nahſhon the ſonne of Amminadab.[18]On the ſecond day Nethaneel the ſonne of Zuar, Prince of Iſſachar did offer.19He offered for his offering one ſiluer charger, the weight whereof was an hundred and thirtie ſhekels, one ſiluer bowle of ſeuenty ſhekels, after the ſhekel of the Sanctuary, both of them full of fine flowre mingled with oile, for a meat offering:20One ſpoone of gold of ten ſhekels, full of incenſe:21One yong bullocke, one ramme, one lambe of the firſt yeere for a burnt offering:22One kid of the goats for a ſinne offering:23And for a ſacrifice of peace offerings, two oxen, fiue rammes, fiue hee goats, fiue lambes of the firſt yeere: this was the offering of Nethaneel the ſonne of Zuar.24On the third day Eliab the ſonne of Helon, Prince of the children of Zebulun did offer.25His offering was one ſiluer charger, the weight whereof was an hundred and thirtie ſhekels, one ſiluer bowle of ſeuentie ſhekels, after the ſhekel of the Sanctuary, both of them full of fine flowre mingled with oile, for a meat offering:26One golden ſpoone of ten ſhekels, full of incenſe:27One yong bullocke, one ramme, one lambe of the firſt yeere for a burnt offering:28One kid of the goats for a ſinne offering:29And for a ſacrifice of peace offerings, two oxen, fiue rammes, fiue hee goats, fiue lambes of the firſt yeere: This was the offring of Eliab the ſonne of Helon.30On the fourth day Elizur the ſonne of Shedeur, Prince of the children of Reuben did offer.31His offering was one ſiluer charger of an hundred and thirty ſhekels, one ſiluer bowle of ſeuentie ſhekels, after the ſhekel of the Sanctuary, both of them full of fine flowre mingled with oyle, for a meat offering:32One golden ſpoone of tenne ſhekels, full of incenſe:33One yong bullocke, one ramme, one lambe of the firſt yeere for a burnt offering:34One kid of the goats for a ſinne offering:35And for a ſacrifice of peace offerings, two oxen, fiue rammes, fiue hee goats, fiue lambs of the firſt yere: This was the offering of Elizur the ſonne of Shedeur.36On the fifth day Shelumiel the ſonne of Zuriſhaddai Prince of the children of Simeon, did offer.37His offring was one ſiluer charger, the weight whereof was an hundred and thirtie ſhekels, one ſiluer bowle of ſeuentie ſhekels, after the ſhekel of the Sanctuary, both of them full of fine flowre, mingled with oyle, for a meate offering:38One golden ſpoone of ten ſhekels, full of incenſe:39One yong bullocke, one ramme, one lambe of the firſt yeere for a burnt offering:40One kidde of the goates for a ſinne offering:41And for a ſacrifice of peace offerings, two oxen, fiue rammes, fiue hee goates, fiue lambes of the firſt yeere: This was the offering of Shelumiel the ſonne of Zuriſhaddai.42On the ſixt day, Eliaſaph the ſonne of Deuel, Prince of the children of Gad, offered:43His offering was one ſiluer charger of the weight of an hundred and thirtie ſhekels, a ſiluer bowle of ſeuentie ſhekels, after the ſhekel of the Sanctuarie, both of them ful of fine flowre mingled with oyle, for a meate offering:44One golden ſpoone of ten ſhekels, full of incenſe:45One yong bullocke, one ramme, one lambe of the firſt yeere, for a burnt offering:46One kid of the goates for a ſinne offering:47And for a ſacrifice of peace offerings, two oxen, fiue rammes, fiue hee goates, fiue lambes of the firſt yeere. This was the offering of Eliaſaph the ſonne of Deuel.48On the ſeuenth day, Eliſhama the ſonne of Ammiud, Prince of the children of Ephraim offered.49His offering was one ſiluer charger, the weight whereof was an hundred and thirtie ſhekels, one ſiluer bowle of ſeuentie ſhekels, after the ſhekel of the Sanctuarie, both of them full of fine flowre mingled with oile for a meat offering:50One golden ſpoone of ten ſhekels, full of incenſe:51One yong bullocke, one ramme, one lambe of the firſt yeere, for a burnt offering:52One kid of the goates for a ſinne offering:53And for a ſacrifice of peace offrings, two oxen, fiue rammes, fiue hee goats, fiue lambes of the firſt yeere. This was the offering of Eliſhama the ſonne of Ammiud.54On the eight day offered Gamaliel the ſonne of Pedazur, Prince of the children of Manaſſeh.55His offering was one ſiluer charger of an hundred and thirtie ſhekels, one ſiluer bowle of ſeuentie ſhekels, after the ſhekel of the Sanctuary, both of them full of fine flowre mingled with oile, for a meate offering:56One golden ſpoone of ten ſhekels, full of incenſe:57One yong bullocke, one ramme, one lambe of the firſt yeere, for a burnt offering:58One kid of the goates for a ſinne offering:59And for a ſacrifice of peace offerings, two oxen, fiue rammes, fiue hee goats, fiue lambes of the firſt yeere. This was the offering of Gamaliel the ſonne of Pedazur.60On the ninth day, Abidan the ſonne of Gideoni, prince of the children of Beniamin offered.61His offering was one ſiluer charger, the weight whereof was an hundred and thirtie ſhekels, a ſiluer bowle of ſeuentie ſhekels, after the ſhekel of the Sanctuary, both of them full of fine flowre mingled with oyle, for a meate offering:62One golden ſpoone of ten ſhekels, full of incenſe:63One yong bullocke, one ramme, one lambe of the firſt yeere for a burnt offering:64One kid of the goats for a ſinne offering:65And for a ſacrifice of peace offerings, two oxen, fiue rammes, fiue hee goates, fiue lambes of the firſt yeere. This was the offering of Abidan, the ſonne of Gideoni.66On the tenth day Ahiezer the ſonne of Ammiſhaddai, Prince of the children of Dan offered.67His offring was one ſiluer charger, the weight whereof was an hundred and thirtie ſhekels, one ſiluer bowle of ſeuentie ſhekels, after the ſhekel of the Sanctuarie, both of them full of fine flowre mingled with oyle, for a meate offering:68One golden ſpoone of ten ſhekels, full of incenſe:69One yong bullocke, one ramme, one lambe of the firſt yeere, for a burnt offering:70One kid of the goates for a ſinne offering:71And for a ſacrifice of peace offerings, two oxen, fiue rammes, fiue hee goats, fiue lambes of the firſt yeere. This was the offering of Ahiezer the ſonne of Ammiſhaddai.72On the eleuenth day, Pagiel the ſonne of Ocran, Prince of the children of Aſher offered.73His offering was one ſiluer charger, the weight whereof was an hundred and thirtie ſhekels, one ſiluer bowle of ſeuentie ſhekels, after the ſhekel of the Sanctuarie, both of them full of fine flowre mingled with oyle, for a meat offering:74One golden ſpoone of ten ſhekels, full of incenſe:75One yong bullocke, one ramme, one lambe of the firſt yeere for a burnt offering:76One kid of the goates for a ſinne offering:77And for a ſacrifice of peace offrings, two oxen, fiue rammes, fiue hee goats, fiue lambs of the firſt yeere. This was the offering of Pagiel the ſonne of Ocran.78On the twelfth day, Ahira the ſonne of Enan, Prince of the children of Naphtali, offered.79His offering was one ſiluer charger, the weight whereof was an hundred and thirtie ſhekels, one ſiluer bowle of ſeuentie ſhekels, after the ſhekel of the Sanctuary, both of them full of fine flowre mingled with oyle, for a meate offering:80One golden ſpoone of ten ſhekels, full of incenſe:81One yong bullocke, one ramme, one lambe of the firſt yeere for a burnt offering:82One kidde of the goats for a ſinne offering:83And for a ſacrifice of peace offrings, two oxen, fiue rammes, fiue hee goats, fiue lambs of the firſt yeere. This was the offering of Ahira the ſonne of Enan.84This was the dedication of the Altar (in the day when it was annointed) by the Princes of Iſrael: twelue chargers of ſiluer, twelue ſiluer bowles, twelue ſpoones of gold:85Each charger of ſiluer weighing an hundred and thirtie ſhekels, each bowle ſeuentie: all the ſiluer veſſels weighed two thouſand and foure hundred ſhekels, after the ſhekel of the Sanctuary.86The golden ſpoones were twelue, full of incenſe, weighing ten ſhekels a piece, after the ſhekel of the Sanctuary: all the gold of the ſpoones, was an hundred and twentie ſhekels.87All the oxen for the burnt offering, were twelue bullocks, the rams twelue, the lambes of the firſt yeere twelue, with their meat offering: and the kids of the goats for ſinne offering, twelue.88And all the oxen for the ſacrifice of the peace offerings, were twenty and foure bullocks, the rammes ſixtie, the hee goates ſixtie, the lambes of the firſt yeere ſixtie. This was the dedication of the Altar, after that it was anoynted.89And when Moſes was gone into the Tabernacle of the Congregation, to ſpeake with him, then he heard the voyce of one ſpeaking vnto him, from off the Mercie ſeat, that was vpon the Arke of Teſtimony from betweene the two Cherubims: and he ſpake vnto him.

CHAPTER 81And the Lord ſpake vnto Moſes, ſaying,2Speake vnto Aaron, and ſay vnto him, When thou lighteſt the lampes, the ſeuen lampes ſhall giue light, ouer againſt the candleſticke.3And Aaron did ſo; he lighted the lampes therof, ouer againſt the candleſtick, as the Lord comanded Moſes.4And this worke of the candleſtick was of beaten gold, vnto the ſhaft thereof, vnto the flowres thereof was beaten worke: according vnto the paterne which the Lord had ſhewed Moſes, ſo he made the candleſticke.5And the Lord ſpake vnto Moſes, ſaying,6Take the Leuites from among the children of Iſrael, and cleanſe them.7And thus ſhalt thou doe vnto them, to cleanſe them: ſprinkle water of purifying vpon them, and let them ſhaue all their fleſh, and let them waſh their clothes, and ſo make themſelues cleane.8Then let them take a yong bullocke with his meat offering, euen fine flowre mingled with oyle, and an other yong bullock ſhalt thou take for a ſinne offering.9And thou ſhalt bring the Leuites before the Tabernacle of the Congregation; and thou ſhalt gather the whole aſſembly of the children of Iſrael together.10And thou ſhalt bring the Leuites before the Lord, and the children of Iſrael ſhall put their hands vpon the Leuites.11And Aaron ſhall offer the Leuites before the Lord for an offring of the children of Iſrael, that they may execute the ſeruice of the Lord.12And the Leuites ſhall lay their hands vpon the heads of the bullocks: and thou ſhalt offer the one for a ſinne offering, and the other for a burnt offering vnto the Lord, to make an atonement for the Leuites.13And thou ſhalt ſet the Leuites before Aaron, and before his ſonnes, and offer them for an offering vnto the Lord.14Thus ſhalt thou ſeparate the Leuites from among the children of Iſrael: and the Leuites ſhalbe mine.15And after that, ſhall the Leuites goe in; to doe the ſeruice of the Tabernacle of the Congregation: and thou ſhalt clenſe them, and offer them for an offering.16For they are wholly giuen vnto me, from among the children of Iſrael: in ſtead of ſuch as open euery wombe, euen in ſtead of the firſt borne of all the children of Iſrael, haue I taken them vnto me.17For all the firſt borne of the children of Iſrael, are mine, both man and beaſt: on the day that I ſmote euery firſt borne in the land of Egypt, I ſanctified them for my ſelfe.18And I haue taken the Leuites for all the firſt borne of the children of Iſrael.19And I haue giuen the Leuites as a gift to Aaron, and to his ſonnes, from among the children of Iſrael, to do the ſeruice of the children of Iſrael, in the Tabernacle of the Congregation, and to make an atonement for the children of Iſrael: that there bee no plague among the children of Iſrael, when the children of Iſrael come nigh vnto the Sanctuarie.20And Moſes and Aaron, and all the Congregation of the children of Iſrael did to the Leuites according vnto all that the Lord commanded Moſes, concerning the Leuites, ſo did the children of Iſrael vnto them.21And the Leuites were purified, and they waſhed their clothes: and Aaron offered them as an offering before the Lord, and Aaron made an atonement for them to cleanſe them.22And after that, went the Leuites in, to do their ſeruice in the Tabernacle of the Congregation before Aaron and and before his ſonnes: as the Lord had commanded Moſes concerning the Leuites, ſo did they vnto them.23And the Lord ſpake vnto Moſes, ſaying,24This is it that belongeth vnto the Leuites: from twentie and fiue yeeres old, and vpward, they ſhall goe in to waite vpon the ſeruice of the Tabernacle of the Congregation.25And from the age of fiftie yeeres they ſhall ceaſe waiting vpon the ſeruice thereof, and ſhall ſerue no more:26But ſhall miniſter with their brethren in the Tabernacle of the Congregation, to keepe the charge, and ſhall doe no ſeruice: thus ſhalt thou doe vnto the Leuites, touching their charge.

CHAPTER 91And the Lord ſpake vnto Moſes in the wilderneſſe of Sinai, in the firſt moneth of the ſecond yeere; after they were come out of the land of Egypt, ſaying,2Let the children of Iſrael alſo keepe the Paſſeouer, at his appointed ſeaſon.3In the fourteenth day of this moneth at euen, ye ſhall keepe it in his appointed ſeaſon: according to all the rites of it, and according to all the ceremonies thereof ſhall ye keepe it.4And Moſes ſpake vnto the children of Iſrael that they ſhould keepe the Paſſeouer.5And they kept the Paſſeouer on the fourteenth day of the firſt moneth at Euen, in the wilderneſſe of Sinai: according to all that the Lord commanded Moſes, ſo did the children of Iſrael.6And there were certaine men who were defiled by the dead body of a man, that they could not keepe the Paſſeouer on that day: and they came before Moſes, and before Aaron on that day.7And thoſe men ſaid vnto him, We are defiled by the dead body of a man: wherefore are we kept backe, that wee may not offer an offring of the Lord in his appointed ſeaſon among the children of Iſrael?8And Moſes ſaide vnto them, ſtand ſtill, and I will heare what the Lord wil command concerning you.9And the Lord ſpake vnto Moſes, ſaying,10Speake vnto the children of Iſrael, ſaying, If any man of you, or of your poſteritie ſhall be vncleane by reaſon of a dead body, or bee in a iourney afarre off, yet he ſhall keepe the Paſſeouer vnto the Lord.11The fourteenth day of the ſecond moneth at Euen they ſhall keepe it, and eat it with vnleauened bread and bitter herbes.12They ſhall leaue none of it vnto the morning, nor breake any bone of it: according to all the ordinances of the Paſſeouer they ſhall keepe it.13But the man that is cleane, and is not in a iourney, and forbeareth to keep the Paſſeouer, euen the ſame ſoule ſhall be cut off from his people, becauſe hee brought not the offering of the Lord in his appointed ſeaſon: that man ſhall beare his ſinne.14And if a ſtranger ſhall ſoiourne among you, and will keepe the Paſſeouer vnto the Lord; according to the ordinance of the Paſſeouer, and according to the maner thereof, ſo ſhall he doe: ye ſhall haue one ordinance, both for the ſtranger, and for him that was borne in the land.15And on the day that the Tabernacle was reared vp, the cloud couered the Tabernacle, namely the Tent of the Teſtimony: and at Euen there was vpon the Tabernacle, as it were the appearance of fire, vntill the morning.16So it was always: the cloud couered it by day, and the appearance of fire by night.17And when the cloud was taken vp from the Tabernacle, then after that, the children of Iſrael iourneyed, and in the place where the cloud abode, there the children of Iſrael pitched their tents.18At the commandement of the Lord the children of Iſrael iourneied, and at the commandement of the Lord they pitched: as long as the cloud abode vpon the Tabernacle, they reſted in the tents.19And when the cloud taried long vpon the Tabernacle many daies, then the children of Iſrael kept the charge of the Lord, and iourneyed not.20And ſo it was when the cloude was a few daies vpon the Tabernacle, according to the commandement of the Lord, they abode in their tents, and according to the commandement of the Lord, they iourneyed.21And ſo it was when the cloude abode from Euen vnto the morning, and that the cloude was taken vp in the morning, then they iourneyed: whether it was by day or by night that the cloude was taken vp, they iourneyed.22Or whether it were two dayes, or a moneth, or a yeere that the cloude taried vpon the Tabernacle, remayning thereon, the children of Iſrael abode in their tents, and iourneyed not: but when it was taken vp, they iourneyed.23At the commandement of the Lord they reſted in the tents, and at the commaundement of the Lord they iourneyed: they kept the charge of the Lord, at the commandement of the Lord by the hand of Moſes.

CHAPTER 101And the Lord ſpake vnto Moſes, ſaying,2Make thee two trumpets of ſiluer: of an whole piece ſhalt thou make them, that thou mayeſt vſe them for the calling of the aſſembly, and for the iourneying of the campes.3And when they ſhall blow with them, all the aſſembly ſhall aſſemble themſelues to thee, at the doore of the Tabernacle of the Congregation.4And if they blow but with one trumpet, then the Princes, which are heads of the thouſands of Iſrael, ſhall gather themſelues vnto thee.5When ye blow an alarme, then the campes that lie on the Eaſt parts, ſhall goe forward.6When you blow an alarme the ſecond time, then the campes that lye on the Southſide, ſhall take their iourney: they ſhall blow an alarme for their iourneys.7But when the Congregation is to be gathered together, you ſhal blow: but you ſhall not ſound an alarme.8And the ſonnes of Aaron the Prieſts ſhall blow with the trumpets; and they ſhalbe to you for an ordinance for euer throughout your generations.9And if ye goe to warre in your land, againſt the enemie that oppreſseth you, then ye ſhall blow an alarme with the trumpets, and ye ſhalbe remembred before the Lord your God, and yee ſhalbe ſaued from your enemies.10Alſo in the day of your gladneſſe, and in your ſolemne dayes, and in the beginnings of your monethes, ye ſhall blow with the trumpets ouer your burnt offerings, and ouer the ſacrifices of your peace offerings, that they may bee to you for a memoriall before your God: I am the Lord your God.11And it came to paſſe on the twentieth day of the ſecond moneth, in the ſecond yeere, that the cloude was taken vp from off the Tabernacle of the Teſtimony.12And the children of Iſrael tooke their iourneys out of the wilderneſſe of Sinai; and the cloud reſted in the wilderneſſe of Paran.13And they firſt tooke their iourney, according to the commandement of the Lord, by the hand of Moſes.14In the firſt place went the ſtanderd of the campe of the children of Iudah, according to their armies, and ouer his hoſte was Nahſhon the ſonne of Amminadab.15And ouer the hoſte of the tribe of the children of Iſſachar, was Nethaneel the ſonne of Zuar.16And ouer the hoſte of the tribe of the children of Zebulun, was Eliab the ſonne of Helon.17And the Tabernacle was taken downe, and the ſonnes of Gerſhon, and the ſonnes of Merari ſet forward, bearing the Tabernacle.18And the ſtanderd of the campe of Reuben ſet forward according to their armies: and ouer his hoſte was Elizur the ſonne of Shedeur.19And ouer the hoſte of the tribe of the children of Simeon, was Shelumiel the ſonne of Zuriſhaddai.20And ouer the hoſte of the tribe of the children of Gad, was Eliaſaph the ſonne of Deuel.21And the Kohathites ſet forward, bearing the Sanctuary, and the other did ſet vp the Tabernacle againſt they came.22And the ſtanderd of the campe of the children of Ephraim ſet forward, according to their armies, and ouer his hoſte was Eliſhama the ſonne of Ammiud.23And ouer the hoſte of the tribe of the children of Manaſſeh was Gamaliel the ſonne of Pedazur.24And ouer the hoſte of the tribe of the children of Beniamin, was Abidan the ſoune of Gideoni.[25]And the ſtanderd of the campe of the children of Dan ſet forward, which was the rere-ward of all the campes throughout their hoſtes: and ouer his hoſte was Ahiezer the ſonne of Ammiſhaddai.[26]And ouer the hoſte of the tribe of the children of Aſher, was Pagiel the ſonne of Ocran.[27]And ouer the hoſte of the tribe of the children of Naphtali was Ahira the ſonne of Enan.[28]Thus were the iourneyings of the children of Iſrael, according to their armies, when they ſet forward.[29]And Moſes ſaid vnto Hobab the ſonne of Raguel the Midianite Moſes father in law, Wee are iourneying vnto the place of which the Lord ſaid, I wil giue it you: come thou with vs, and we will doe thee good: for the Lord hath ſpoken good concerning Iſrael.[30]And he ſaid vnto him, I will not goe, but I will depart to mine owne land, and to my kinred.[31]And he ſaid, Leaue vs not, I pray thee, foraſmuch as thou knoweſt how we are to encampe in the wilderueſse, and thou mayeſt bee to vs in ſtead of eyes.[32]And it ſhall bee if thou goe with vs, yea it ſhall be, that what goodneſſe the Lord ſhall doe vnto vs, the ſame will we doe vnto thee.[33]And they departed from the Mount of the Lord three dayes iourney: and the Arke of the Couenant of the Lord went before them in the three dayes iourney, to ſearch out a reſting place for them.[34]And the cloude of the Lord was vpon them by day, when they went out of the campe.[35]And it came to paſſe when the Arke ſet forward, that Moſes ſaid, Riſe vp Lord, and let thine enemies be ſcattered, and let them that hate thee, flee before thee.[36]And when it reſted, he ſaid, Returne, O Lord, vnto the many thouſands of Iſrael.

CHAPTER 11[1]And when the people complained, it diſpleaſed the Lord: and the Lord heard it: and his anger was kindled, and the fire of the Lord burnt among them, and conſumed them that were in the vttermoſt parts of the campe.[2]And the people cried vnto Moſes, and when Moſes prayed vnto the Lord, the fire was quenched.[3]And hee called the name of the place Taberah: becauſe the fire of the Lord burnt among them.[4]And the mixt multitude that was among them, fell a luſting, and the children of Iſrael alſo wept againe, and ſaid, Who ſhal giue vs fleſh to eate?[5]We remember the fiſh which wee did eate in Egypt freely: the cucumbers and the melons, and the leekes, and the onions, and the garlicke.[6]But now our ſoule is dried away, there is nothing at all, beſides this Manna, before our eyes.[7]And the Manna was as Coriander ſeed, and the colour thereof as the colour of Bdelium:[8]And the people went about, and gathered it, and ground it in milles, or beat it in a morter, and baked it in pans, and made cakes of it: and the taſte of it was as the taſte of freſh oyle.[9]And when the dew fell vpon the campe in the night, the Manna fell vpon it.[10]Then Moſes heard the people weepe throughout their families, euery man in the doore of his tent, and the anger of the Lord was kindled greatly, Moſes alſo was diſpleaſed.[11]And Moſes ſaid vnto the Lord, Wherefore haſt thou afflicted thy ſeruant? and wherefore haue I not found fauour in thy ſight, that thou layeſt the burden of all this people vpon me?[12]Haue I conceiued all this people? haue I begotten them, that thou ſhouldeſt ſay vnto me, Cary them in thy boſome (as a nurſing father beareth the ſucking child) vnto the land which thou ſwareſt vnto their fathers?[13]Whence ſhould I haue fleſh to giue vnto all this people? for they weep vnto me, ſaying, Giue vs fleſh, that we may eate.[14]I am not able to beare all this people alone, becauſe it is too heauie for mee.[15]And if thou deale thus with mee, kill me, I pray thee out of hand, if I haue found fauour in thy ſight, and let me not ſee my wretchedneſse.[16]And the Lord ſaid vnto Moſes, Gather vnto me ſeuentie men, of the Elders of Iſrael, whome thou knoweſt to be the elders of the people, and officers ouer them: and bring them vnto the Tabernacle of the Congregation, that they may ſtand there with thee.[17]And I will come downe and talke with thee there, and I will take of the ſpirit which is vpon thee, and wil put it vpon them, and they ſhall beare the burden of the people with thee, that thou beare it not thy ſelfe alone.[18]And ſay thou vnto the people, ſanctifie your ſelues againſt to morrow, and yee ſhall eate fleſh: (for you haue wept in the eares of the Lord, ſaying, Who ſhall giue vs fleſh to eate? for it was well with vs in Egypt:) therfore the Lord wil giue you fleſh, and ye ſhall eate.[19]Ye ſhall not eate one day, nor two dayes, nor fiue dayes, neither ten dayes, nor twentie dayes:[20]But euen a whole moneth, vntill it come out at your noſtrels, and it bee loathſome vnto you, becauſe that yee haue deſpiſed the Lord which is among you, and haue wept before him, ſaying, Why came we foorth out of Egypt?[21]And Moſes ſaid, The people amongſt whome I am, are ſixe hundred thouſand footmen, and thou haſt ſaid, I will giue them fleſh, that they may eate a whole moneth.[22]Shall the flockes and the herds be ſlaine for them to ſuffice them? or ſhal all the fiſh of the ſea bee gathered together for them, to ſuffice them?[23]And the Lord ſaid vnto Moſes, Is the Lords hand waxed ſhort? thou ſhalt ſee now whether my word ſhall come to paſſe vnto thee, or not.[24]And Moſes went out, and tolde the people the wordes of the Lord, and gathered the ſeuenty men of the Elders of the people, and ſet them round about the Tabernacle.[25]And the Lord came downe in a cloude, and ſpake vnto him, and tooke of the ſpirit that was vpon him, and gaue it vnto the ſeuentie Elders: and it came to paſſe that when the ſpirit reſted vpon them, they propheſied, and did not ceaſe.[26]But there remained two of the men in the campe, the name of the one was Eldad, & the name of the other Medad: and the Spirit reſted vpon them, (and they were of them that were written, but went not out vnto the Tabernacle) and they propheſied in the campe.[27]And there ranne a yong man, and tolde Moſes, and ſaid, Eldad and Medad doe propheſie in the campe.[28]And Ioſhua the ſonne of Nun the ſeruant of Moſes, one of his yong men, anſwered and ſaid, My lord Moſes, Forbid them.[29]And Moſes ſaid vnto him, Enuieſt thou for my ſake? Would God that all the Lords people were Prophets, and that the Lord would put his Spirit vpon them.[30]And Moſes gate him into the campe, he, and the Elders of Iſrael.[31]And there went forth a winde from the Lord, and brought quailes from the ſea, and let them fall by the campe, as it were a dayes iourney on this ſide, and as it were a dayes iourney on the other ſide round about the campe, and as it were two cubits high vpon the face of the earth.[32]And the people ſtood vp all that day, and all that night, and all the next day, and they gathered the quailes: he that gathered leaſt, gathered ten homers: and they ſpread them all abroad for themſelues round about the campe.[33]And while the fleſh was yet betweene their teeth, yer it was chewed, the wrath of the Lord was kindled againſt the people, and the Lord ſmote the people with a very great plague.[34]And he called the name of that place, Kibroth-Hattaauah: becauſe there they buried the people that luſted.[35]And the people iourneyed from Kibroth-Hattaauah, vnto Hazeroth: and abode at Hazeroth.

CHAPTER 12[1]And Miriam and Aaron ſpake againſt Moſes, becauſe of the Ethiophian woman, whom hee had married: for he had married an Ethiopian woman.[2]And they ſaid, Hath the Lord indeed ſpoken onely by Moſes? Hath hee not ſpoken alſo by vs? And the Lord heard it.[3](Now the man Moſes was very meeke, aboue all the men which were vpon the face of the earth.)[4]And the Lord ſpake ſuddenly vnto Moſes, and vnto Aaron, and vnto Miriam, Come out ye three vnto the Tabernacle of the Congregation: and they three came out.[5]And the Lord came downe in the pillar of the cloude, and ſtood in the doore of the Tabernacle, and called Aaron and Miriam: and they both came foorth.[6]And hee ſaide, Heare now my words: If there be a Prophet among you, I the Lord will make my ſelfe knowen vnto him in a viſion, and will ſpeake vnto him in a dreame:[7]My ſeruant Moſes is not ſo, who is faithfull in all mine houſe.[8]With him will I ſpeake mouth to mouth euen apparantly, and not in darke ſpeeches, and the ſimilitude of the Lord ſhall hee behold: wherefore then were yee not afraid to ſpeake againſt my ſeruant Moſes?[9]And the anger of the Lord was kindled againſt them, and he departed.[10]And the cloud departed from off the Tabernacle, and behold, Miriam became leprous, white as ſnow: and Aaron looked vpon Miriam, and behold, ſhe was leprous.[11]And Aaron ſaid vnto Moſes, Alas my lord, I beſeech thee, lay not the ſinne vpon vs, wherein we haue done fooliſhly, and wherein we haue ſinned:[12]Let her not bee as one dead, of whom the fleſh is halfe conſumed, when he commeth out of his mothers wombe.[13]And Moſes cryed vnto the Lord, ſaying, Heale her now, O God, I beſeech thee.[14]And the Lord ſaid vnto Moſes, If her father had but ſpit in her face, ſhould ſhe not bee aſhamed ſeuen dayes? let her be ſhut out from the campe ſeuen dayes, and after that let her be receiued in againe.[15]And Miriam was ſhut out from the campe ſeuen dayes: and the people iourneied not, til Miriam was brought in againe.[16]And afterward the people remoued from Hazeroth, and pitched in the wilderneſſe of Paran.

CHAPTER 13[1]And the Lord ſpake vnto Moſes, ſaying,[2]Send thou men, that they may ſearch the lande of Canaan, which I giue vnto the children of Iſrael: of euery tribe of their fathers ſhal ye ſend a man, euery one a ruler among them.[3]And Moſes by the commaundement of the Lord, ſent them from the wildernes of Paran: all thoſe men were heads of the children of Iſrael.4And theſe were their names. Of the tribe of Reuben, Shammua the ſonne of Zaccur.5Of the tribe of Simeon, Shaphat the ſonne of Hori.6Of the tribe of Iudah, Caleb the ſonne of Iephunneh.7Of the tribe of Iſſachar, Igal the ſonne of Ioſeph.8Of the tribe of Ephraim, Oſhea the ſonne of Nun.9Of the tribe of Beniamin, Palti the ſonne of Raphu.10Of the tribe of Zebulun, Gaddiel the ſonne of Sodi.11Of the tribe of Ioſeph, namely of the tribe of Manaſſeh, Gaddi the ſonne of Suſi.12Of the tribe of Dan, Ammiel the ſonne of Gemalli.13Of the tribe of Aſher, Sethur the ſonne of Michael.14Of the tribe of Naphtali, Nahbi the ſonne of Uophſi.15Of the tribe of Gad, Geuel the ſonne of Machi.16Theſe are the names of the men which Moſes ſent to ſpie out the land: and Moſes called Oſhea the ſonne of Nun, Iehoſhua.17And Moſes ſent them to ſpie out the land of Canaan, and ſaid vnto them, Get you by this way Southward, and goe vp into the mountaine:18And ſee the lande what it is, and the people that dwelleth therein, whether they bee ſtrong or weake, fewe or many:19And what the lande is that they dwell in, whether it be good or bad, and what cities they bee that they dwell in, whether in tents, or in ſtrong holds:20And what the land is, whether it be fat or leane, whether there be wood therein, or not. And be ye of good courage, and bring of the fruit of the land: (Now the time was the time of the firſt ripe grapeſ)21So they went vp, and ſearched the land, from the wilderneſſe of Zin, vnto Rehob, as men come to Hamath.22And they aſcended by the South, and came vnto Hebron: where Ahiman, Sheſhai, and Talmai, the children of Anak were: Now Hebron was built ſeuen yeeres before Zoan in Egypt.23And they came vnto the brooke of Eſhcol, and cut downe from thence a branch with one cluſter of grapes, and they bare it betweene two vpon a ſtaffe, and they brought of the pomegranates and of the figs.24The place was called the brooke Eſhcol, becauſe of the cluſter of grapes which the children of Iſrael cut downe from thence.25And they returned from ſearching of the land after fourty dayes.26And they went and came to Moſes, and to Aaron, and to all the Congregation of the children of Iſrael vnto the wilderneſſe of Paran, to Kadeſh, and brought backe word vnto them, and vnto all the Congregation, and ſhewed them the fruit of the land.27And they told him, and ſaid, We came vnto the land whither thou ſenteſt vs, & ſurely it floweth with milke and honie; and this is the fruit of it.28Neuertheleſſe, the people bee ſtrong that dwell in the land, and the cities are walled and very great: and moreouer, we ſaw the children of Anak there.29The Amalekites dwell in the land of the South: and the Hittites, and the Iebuſites, and the Amorites dwell in the mountaines: and the Canaanites dwell by the ſea, and by the coaſt of Iordane.30And Caleb ſtilled the people before Moſes, and ſaid, Let vs goe vp at once, and poſſeſſe it, for we are well able to ouercome it.31But the men that went vp with him, ſaid, Wee be not able to goe vp againſt the people, for they are ſtronger then we.32And they brought vp an euill report of the land which they had ſearched, vnto the children of Iſrael, ſaying, The land through which we haue gone, to ſearch it, is a land that eateth vp the inhabitants thereof, and all the people that we ſaw in it, are men of a great ſtature.33And there we ſaw the giants, the ſonnes of Anak, which come of the giants: and wee were in our owne ſight as graſhoppers, and ſo wee were in their ſight.

CHAPTER 141And all the Congregation lifted vp their voyce and cried; and the people wept that night.2And all the children of Iſrael murmured againſt Moſes, and againſt Aaron: and the whole Congregation ſaid vnto them, Would God that we had died in the land of Egypt, or would God we had died in this wilderneſſe.3And wherefore hath the Lord brought vs vnto this land, to fall by the ſword, that our wiues, and our children ſhould be a pray? Were it not better for vs to returne into Egypt?4And they ſaide one to another, Let vs make a captaine, and let vs returne into Egypt.5Then Moſes and Aaron fell on their faces before all the aſſembly of the Congregation of the children of Iſrael.6And Ioſhua the ſonne of Nun, and Caleb the ſonne of Iephunneh, which were of them that ſearched the land, rent their clothes.7And they ſpake vnto all the company of the children of Iſrael, ſaying. The land which wee paſſed thorow to ſearch it, is an exceeding good land.8If the Lord delight in vs, then he will bring vs into this land, and giue it vs, a land which floweth with milke and hony.9Onely rebell not yee againſt the Lord, neither feare yee the people of the land, for they are bread for vs: their defence is departed from them, and the Lord is with vs: feare them not.10But all the Congregation bade ſtone them with ſtones: and the glory of the Lord appeared in the Tabernacle of the Congregation, before all the children of Iſrael.11And the Lord ſaid vnto Moſes, How long will this people prouoke me? and how long will it bee, yer they beleeue me, for all the ſignes which I haue ſhewed among them?12I will ſmite them with the peſtilence, and diſinherite them, and will make of thee a greater nation, and mightier then they.13And Moſes ſaid vnto the Lord, Then the Egyptians ſhall heare it, (for thou broughteſt vp this people in thy might from among them:)14And they will tell it to the inhabitants of this land: for they haue heard that thou Lord art among this people, that thou Lord art ſeene face to face, and that thy cloud ſtandeth ouer them, and that thou goeſt before them, by day time in a pillar of a cloud, and in a pillar of fire by night.15Now if thou ſhalt kill all this people, as one man, then the nations which haue heard the fame of thee, will ſpeake, ſaying,16Becauſe the Lord was not able to bring this people into the lande which he ſware vnto them, therefore he hath ſlaine them in the wilderneſſe.17And now, I beſeech thee, let the power of my Lord be great, according as thou haſt ſpoken, ſaying,18The Lord is long ſuffering, and of great mercie, forgiuing iniquitie and tranſgreſsion, and by no meanes clearing the guiltie, viſiting the iniquity of the fathers vpon the chldren, vnto the third and fourth generation.19Pardon, I beſeech thee, the iniquitie of this people, according vnto the greatneſſe of thy mercie, and as thou haſt forgiuen this people, from Egypt, euen vntill now.20And the Lord ſaid, I haue pardoned, according to thy word.21But as truly as I liue, all the earth ſhalbe filled with the glory of the Lord.22Becauſe all thoſe men which haue ſeene my glory, and my miracles which I did in Egypt, and in the wilderneſſe, and haue tempted mee now theſe ten times, and haue not hearkened to my voice,23Surely they ſhall not ſee the land which I ſware vnto their fathers, neither ſhall any of them that prouoked me, ſee it.24But my ſeruant Caleb, becauſe hee had another ſpirit with him, (and hath followed mee fully) him will I bring into the land, whereinto he went, and his ſeed ſhall poſſeſſe it.25(Now the Amalekites, and the Canaanites dwelt in the valley) to morrow turne you and get you into the wilderneſſe, by the way of the Red ſea.26And the Lord ſpake vnto Moſes, and vnto Aaron, ſaying,27How long ſhall I beare with this euil congregation which murmure againſt mee? I haue heard the murmurings of the children of Iſrael, which they murmure againſt mee.28ſay vnto them, As truly as I liue, ſaith the Lord, as ye haue ſpoken in mine eares, ſo will I doe to you:29Your carcaſes ſhall fall in this wilderneſſe, and all that were numbred of you, according to your whole number from twentie yeeres old and vpward, which haue murmured againſt mee,30Doubtleſſe ye ſhall not come into the land concerning which I ſware to make you dwell therein, ſaue Caleb the ſonne of Iephunneh, and Ioſhua the ſonne of Nun.31But your little ones, which yee ſaid ſhould be a pray, them will I bring in, and they ſhall know the land which ye haue deſpiſed.32But as for you, your carkaſes, they ſhall fall in this wilderneſſe.33And your children ſhall wander in the wildernes forty yeres, and beare your whoredomes, vntill your carkaſes be waſted in the wilderneſſe.34After the number of the dayes in which ye ſearched the land, euen fortie dayes (each day for a yeere) ſhall yee beare your iniquities, euen forty yeeres, and yee ſhall know my breach of promiſe.35I the Lord haue ſaid, I will ſurely doe it vnto all this euill Congregation, that are gathered together againſt mee: in this wilderneſſe they ſhalbe conſumed, & there they ſhall die.36And the men which Moſes ſent to ſearch the land, who returned, and made all the Congregation to murmure againſt him, by bringing vp a ſlander vpon the land,37Euen thoſe men that did bring vp the euill report vpon the land, died by the plague, before the Lord.38But Ioſhua the ſonne of Nun, and Caleb the ſonne of Iephunneh, which were of the men that went to ſearch the land, liued ſtill.39And Moſes told theſe ſayings vnto all the children of Iſrael, and the people mourned greatly.40And they roſe vp early in the morning, and gate them vp into the top of the mountaine, ſaying, Loe, we be here, and will goe vp vnto the place which the Lord hath promiſed: for we haue ſinned.41And Moſes ſaid, Wherefore now doe you tranſgreſse the commaundement of the Lord ? but it ſhall not proſper.42Goe not vp, for the Lord is not among you, that ye be not ſmitten before your enemies.43For the Amalekites, and the Canaanites are there before you, and yee ſhall fall by the ſword, becauſe yee are turned away from the Lord; therefore the Lord will not bee with you.44But they preſumed to go vp vnto the hill top: neuertheles the Arke of the Couenant of the Lord, and Moſes departed not out of the campe.[45]Then the Amalekites came downe, and the Canaanites which dwelt in that hill, and ſmote them, and diſcomfited them, euen vnto Hormah.

CHAPTER 15[1]And the Lord ſpake vnto Moſes, ſaying,[2]Speake vnto the children of Iſrael, and ſay vnto them, When ye be come into the land of your habitations, which I giue vnto you,[3]And will make an offering by fire vnto the Lord, a burnt offering or a ſacrifice in performing a vow, or in a free will offering, or in your ſolemne feaſts, to make a ſweet ſauour vnto the Lord, of the herd or of the flocke:[4]Then ſhall he that offereth his offering vnto the Lord, bring a meat offring of a tenth deale of flowre, mingled with the fourth part of an Hyn of oyle.[5]And the fourth part of an Hyn of wine for a drinke offring ſhalt thou prepare, with the burnt offering or ſacrifice for one lambe.[6]Or for a ramme, thou ſhalt prepare for a meate offering two tenth deales of flowre mingled with the third part of an Hyn of oyle.[7]And for a drinke offering, thou ſhalt offer the third part of an Hyn of wine, for a ſweete ſauour vnto the Lord.[8]And when thou prepareſt a bullocke for a burnt offering, or for a ſacrifice in performing a vow, or peace offerings vnto the Lord:[9]Then ſhall hee bring with a bullocke a meate offering of three tenth deales of flowre, mingled with halfe an Hyn of oyle.[10]And thou ſhalt bring for a drinke offering halfe an Hyn of wine, for an offering made by fire of a ſweet ſauour vnto the Lord.[11]Thus ſhall it be done for one bullocke, or for one ramme, or for a lambe, or a kidde.[12]According to the number that yee ſhall prepare, ſo ſhall yee doe to euery one, according to their number.[13]All that are borne of the countrey ſhall doe theſe things after this maner, in offering an offering made by fire of a ſweet ſauour, vnto the Lord.[14]And if a ſtranger ſoiourne with you, or whoſoeuer bee among you in your generations, and will offer an offering made by fire of a ſweete ſauour vnto the Lord: as ye doe, ſo hee ſhall doe.[15]One ordinance ſhall be both for you of the Congregation, and alſo for the ſtranger that ſoiourneth with you, an ordinance for euer in your generations: as ye are, ſo ſhall the ſtranger bee, before the Lord.[16]One law, and one maner ſhall be for you, and for the ſtranger that ſoiourneth with you.[17]And the Lord ſpake vnto Moſes, ſaying,[18]Speake vnto the children of Iſrael, and ſay vnto them, When ye come into the land whither I bring you,[19]Then it ſhall be that when ye eate of the bread of the land, yee ſhall offer vp an heaue offring vnto the Lord.[20]Ye ſhall offer vp a cake of the firſt of your dough, for an heaue offring: as ye doe the heaue offering of the threſhing floore, ſo ſhall ye heaue it.[21]Of the firſt of your dough ye ſhal giue vnto the Lord, an heaue offering in your generations.[22]And if yee haue erred, and not obſerued all theſe Commaundements which the Lord hath ſpoken vnto Moſes,[23]Euen all that the Lord hath commanded you, by the hand of Moſes from the day that the Lord commanded Moſes, and henceforward among your generations:[24]Then it ſhalbe, if ought be committed by ignorance without the knowledge of the Congregation, that all the Congregation ſhall offer one yong bullocke for a burnt offering, for a ſweet ſauour vnto the Lord, with his meate offering, and his drinke offering, according to the manner, and one kid of the goats for a ſinne offering.[25]And the Prieſt ſhall make an atonement for all the Congregation of the children of Iſrael, and it ſhal be forgiuen them, for it is ignorance: and they ſhall bring their offring, a ſacrifice made by fire vnto the Lord, and their ſinne offering before the Lord, for their ignorance.[26]And it ſhall bee forgiuen all the Congregation of the children of Iſrael, and the ſtranger that ſoiourneth among them, ſeeing all the people were in ignorance.[27]And if any ſoule ſinne through ignorance, then hee ſhall bring a ſhee goat of the firſt yeere for a ſinne offring.[28]And the Prieſt ſhall make an atonement for the ſoule that ſinneth ignorantly, when he ſinneth by ignorance before the Lord, to make an atonement for him, & it ſhalbe forgiuen him.[29]You ſhall haue one law for him that ſinneth through ignorance, both for him that is borne amongſt the children of Iſrael, and for the ſtranger that ſoiourneth among them.[30]But the ſoule that doeth ought preſumptuouſly, whether he be borne in the land, or a ſtranger, the ſame reprocheth the Lord: and that ſoule ſhall be cut off from among his people.[31]Becauſe he hath deſpiſed the word of the Lord, and hath broken his commandement, that ſoule ſhall vtterly be cut off: his iniquitie ſhall be vpon him.[32]And while the children of Iſrael were in the wildernes, they found a man that gathered ſtickes vpon the Sabbath day.[33]And they that found him gathering ſticks, brought him vnto Moſes and Aaron, and vnto all the Congregation.[34]And they put him in ward, becauſe it was not declared what ſhould be done to him.[35]And the Lord ſaid vnto Moſes, The man ſhall bee ſurely put to death: all the Congregation ſhall ſtone him with ſtones without the campe.[36]And all the Cogregation brought him without the campe, and ſtoned him with ſtones, and he died, as the Lord commanded Moſes.[37]And the Lord ſpake vnto Moſes, ſaying,[38]Speake vnto the children of Iſrael, and bidde them that they make them fringes in the borders of their garments, throughout their generations, and that they put vpon the fringe of the borders a ribband of blew.[39]And it ſhall bee vnto you for a fringe, that ye may looke vpon it, and remember all the commandements of the Lord, and doe them: and that ye ſeeke not after your owne heart, and your owne eyes, after which ye vſe to goe a whoring:[40]That ye may remember, and doe all my commandements, and be holy vnto your God.[41]I am the Lord your God, which brought you out of the land of Egypt, to bee your God: I am the Lord your God.

CHAPTER 16[1]Now Korah the ſonne of Izhar, the ſonne of Kohath, the ſonne of Leui, and Dathan, and Abiram the ſonnes of Eliab, and On the ſonne of Peleth, ſonnes of Reuben, tooke men.[2]And they roſe vp before Moſes, with certaine of the children of Iſrael, two hundred and fiftie Princes of the aſſembly, famous in the Congregation, men of renowne.[3]And they gathered themſelues together againſt Moſes, and againſt Aaron, and ſaid vnto them, Ye take too much vpon you, ſeeing all the Congregation are holy euery one of them, and the Lord is among them: wherfore then lift you vp your ſelues aboue the Congregation of the Lord ?[4]And when Moſes heard it, he fell vpon his face.[5]And hee ſpake vnto Korah, and vnto all his company, ſaying, Euen to morrow the Lord will ſhew who are his, and who is holy, and will cauſe him to come neere vnto him: euen him whom he hath choſen, will he cauſe to come neere vnto him.[6]This doe: take you cenſers, Korah, and all his company:[7]And put fire therein, and put incenſe in them, before the Lord to morrow; And it ſhall be, that the man whom the Lord doeth chooſe, hee ſhall be holy: yee take too much vpon you, ye ſonnes of Leui.[8]And Moſes ſaide vnto Korah, Heare, I pray you, ye ſonnes of Leui.[9]Seemeth it but a ſmall thing vnto you, that the God of Iſrael hath ſeparated you from the Congregation of Iſrael, to bring you neere to himſelfe, to doe the ſeruice of the Tabernacle of the Lord, and to ſtand before the Congregation to miniſter vnto them?[10]And he hath brought thee neere to him, and all thy brethren the ſonnes of Leui with thee: and ſeeke ye the Prieſthood alſo?[11]For which cauſe both thou, and all thy company are gathered together againſt the Lord: and what is Aaron, that ye murmure againſt him?[12]And Moſes ſent to call Dathan and Abiram the ſonnes of Eliab: which ſaid, We will not come vp.[13]Is it a ſmall thing that thou haſt brought vs vp out of a land that floweth with milke and hony, to kill vs in the wilderneſſe, except thou make thy ſelfe altogether a prince ouer vs?[14]Moreouer, thou haſt not brought vs into a land that floweth with milke and hony, or giuen vs inheritance of fields and vineyards: wilt thou put out the eyes of theſe men? we will not come vp.[15]And Moſes was very wroth, and ſaid vnto the Lord, Reſpect not thou their offering: I haue not taken one aſſe from them, neither haue I hurt one of them.[16]And Moſes ſaid vnto Korah, Be thou and all thy company before the Lord, thou, and they, and Aaron to morrow.[17]And take euery man his cenſer, and put incenſe in them, and bring yee before the Lord euery man his cenſer, two hundred and fiftie cenſers, thou alſo and Aaron, each of you his cenſer.[18]And they tooke euery man his cenſer, and put fire in them, and laide incenſe thereon, and ſtood in the doore of the Tabernacle of the Congregation with Moſes and Aaron.[19]And Korah gathered all the Congregation againſt them, vnto the doore of the Tabernacle of the Congregation: and the glory of the Lord appeared vnto all the Congregation.[20]And the Lord ſpake vnto Moſes, and vnto Aaron, ſaying,[21]Separate your ſelues from among this Congregation, that I may conſume them in a moment.[22]And they fell vpon their faces, and ſaid, O God, the God of the ſpirits of all fleſh, ſhal one man ſinne, and wilt thou be wroth with all the Congregation?[23]And the Lord ſpake vnto Moſes, ſaying,[24]Speake vnto the Congregation, ſaying, Get you vp from about the tabernacle of Korah, Dathan, and Abiram.[25]And Moſes roſe vp, and went vnto Dathan and Abiram: and the Elders of Iſrael followed him.[26]And hee ſpake vnto the Congregation, ſaying, Depart, I pray you, from the tents of theſe wicked men, and touch nothing of theirs, leſt ye be conſumed in all their ſinnes.[27]So they gate vp from the tabernacle of Korah, Dathan, and Abiram, on euery ſide: and Dathan and Abiram came out, and ſtood in the doore of their tents, and their wiues, & their ſonnes, and their little children.[28]And Moſes ſaid, Hereby ye ſhall know that the Lord hath ſent me to doe all theſe workes: for I haue not done them of mine owne mind.[29]If theſe men die the common death of all men, or if they be viſited after the viſitation of all men, then the Lord hath not ſent me:[30]But if the Lord make a new thing, and the earth open her mouth, and ſwallow them vp, with all that appertaine vnto them, and they go downe quicke into the pit: then ye ſhall vnderſtand that theſe men haue prouoked the Lord.[31]And it came to paſſe as he had made an ende of ſpeaking all theſe words, that the ground claue aſunder that was vnder them:[32]And the earth opened her mouth, and ſwallowed them vp, and their houſes, and all the men that appertained vnto Korah, and all their goods.[33]They, and all that appertained to them, went downe aliue into the pit, and the earth cloſed vpon them: and they periſhed from among the Congregation.[34]And all Iſrael that were round about them, fled at the crie of them: for they ſaid, Leſt the earth ſwallow vs vp alſo.[35]And there came out a fire from the Lord, and conſumed the two hundred and fiftie men that offered incenſe.[36]And the Lord ſpake vnto Moſes, ſaying,[37]Speake vnto Eleazar the ſonne of Aaron the Prieſt, that he take vp the cenſers out of the burning, and ſcatter thou the fire yonder, for they are hallowed.[38]The cenſers of theſe ſinners againſt their owne ſoules, let them make them broad plates for a couering of the Altar: for they offered them before the Lord, therefore they are hallowed, and they ſhall be a ſigne vnto the children of Iſrael.[39]And Eleazar the Prieſt tooke the braſen cenſers, wherewith they that were burnt had offered, and they were made broad plates for a couering of the Altar:[40]To bee a memoriall vnto the children of Iſrael, that no ſtranger, which is not of the ſeed of Aaron, come neere to offer incenſe before the Lord, that he be not as Korah, and as his company, as the Lord ſaid to him by the hand of Moſes.[41]But on the morrow, all the Congregation of the children of Iſrael murmured againſt Moſes and againſt Aaron, ſaying, Ye haue killed the people of the Lord.[42]And it came to paſſe when the Congregation was gathered againſt Moſes and againſt Aaron, that they looked toward the Tabernacle of the Congregation: and behold, the cloud couered it, and the glory of the Lord appeared.[43]And Moſes and Aaron came before the Tabernacle of the Congregation.[44]And the Lord ſpake vnto Moſes, ſaying,[45]Get you vp from among this Congregation, that I may conſume them, as in a moment: and they fell vpon their faces.[46]And Moſes ſaid vnto Aaron, Take a cenſer, and put fire therein from off the Altar, and put on incenſe, and goe quickly vnto the Congregation, and make an atonement for them: for there is wrath gone out from the Lord; the plague is begun.[47]And Aaron tooke as Moſes commanded, and ranne into the midſt of the Congregation: and behold, the plague was begun among the people, and he put on incenſe, and made an atonement for the people.[48]And he ſtood betweene the dead and the liuing, and the plague was ſtayed.[49]Now they that died in the plague, were foureteene thouſand and ſeuen hundred, beſide them that died about the matter of Korah.[50]And Aaron returned vnto Moſes, vnto the doore of the Tabernacle of the Congregation; and the plague was ſtayed.

CHAPTER 17[1]And the Lord ſpake vnto Moſes, ſaying,[2]Speake vnto the children of Iſrael, and take of euery one of them a rod, according to the houſe of their fathers, of all their princes, according to the houſe of their fathers, twelue rods: write thou euery mans name vpon his rodde.[3]And thou ſhalt write Aarons name vpon the rod of Leui: for one rod ſhall be for the head of the houſe of their fathers.[4]And thou ſhalt lay them vp in the Tabernacle of the Congregation, before the Teſtimony, where I will meet with you.[5]And it ſhall come to paſſe, that the mans rod whom I ſhall chooſe, ſhall bloſsome: and I will make to ceaſe from mee the murmurings of the children of Iſrael, whereby they murmure againſt you.[6]And Moſes ſpake vnto the children of Iſrael, and euery one of their Princes gaue him a rod a piece, for each Prince one, according to their fathers houſes, euen twelue rods: and the rod of Aaron was among their rods.[7]And Moſes layd vp the rods before the Lord, in the Tabernacle of Witneſse.[8]And it came to paſſe that on the morrow Moſes went into the Tabernacle of Witneſse, and behold, the rod of Aaron for the houſe of Leui was budded, and brought forth buds, and bloomed bloſsomes, and yeelded almonds.[9]And Moſes brought out all the rods from before the Lord, vnto all the children of Iſrael: and they looked, and tooke euery man his rod.[10]And the Lord ſaid vnto Moſes, Bring Aarons rod againe before the Teſtimony, to be kept for a token againſt the rebels, and thou ſhalt quite take away their murmurings from me, that they die not.[11]And Moſes did ſo: as the Lord commanded him, ſo did he.[12]And the children of Iſrael ſpake vnto Moſes, ſaying, Behold, wee die, we periſh, we all periſh.[13]Whoſoeuer commeth any thing neere vnto the Tabernacle of the Lord, ſhall die: Shall wee be conſumed with dying?

CHAPTER 18[1]And the Lord ſayd vnto Aaron, Thou and thy ſonnes, and thy fathers houſe with thee, ſhall beare the iniquitie of the Sanctuary: and thou and thy ſonnes with thee, ſhall beare the iniquitie of your Prieſthood.[2]And thy brethren alſo of the tribe of Leui, the tribe of thy father, bring thou with thee, that they may be ioyned vnto thee, and miniſter vnto thee: but thou and thy ſonnes with thee ſhall miniſter before the Tabernacle of Witneſse.[3]And they ſhall keepe thy charge, and the charge of all the Tabernacle: onely they ſhall not come nigh the veſſels of the Sanctuarie, and the Altar, that neither they, nor you alſo die.[4]And they ſhall bee ioyned vnto thee, and keepe the charge of the Tabernacle of the Congregation, for all the ſeruice of the Tabernacle: and a ſtranger ſhall not come nigh vnto you.[5]And yee ſhall keepe the charge of the Sanctuary, and the charge of the Altar, that there be no wrath any more vpon the children of Iſrael.[6]And I, beholde, I haue taken your brethren the Leuites from among the children of Iſrael: to you they are giuen as a gift for the Lord, to doe the ſeruice of the Tabernacle of the Congregation.[7]Therefore thou and thy ſonnes with thee, ſhall keepe your Prieſts office for euery thing of the Altar, and within the Uaile, and yee ſhall ſerue: I haue giuen your Prieſts office vnto you, as a ſeruice of gift: and the ſtranger that commeth nigh, ſhall bee put to death.[8]And the Lord ſpake vnto Aaron, Behold, I alſo haue giuen thee the charge of mine heaue offerings, of all the hallowed things of the children of Iſrael, vnto thee haue I giuen them by reaſon of the anointing, and to thy ſonnes by an ordinance for euer.[9]This ſhall bee thine of the moſt holy things, reſeruedfrom the fire: euery oblation of theirs, euery meat offering of theirs, and euery ſinne offering of theirs, and euery treſpaſſe offering of theirs, which they ſhal render vnto me, ſhall be moſt holy for thee, and for thy ſonnes.[10]In the moſt holy place ſhalt thou eate it, euery male ſhall eate it: it ſhall be holy vnto thee.[11]And this is thine: the heaue offering of their gift, with all the waue offrings of the children of Iſrael: I haue giuen them vnto thee, & to thy ſonnes, and to thy daughters with thee, by a ſtatute for euer: euery one that is cleane in thy houſe, ſhall eate of it.[12]All the beſt of the oyle, and all the beſt of the wine, and of the wheat, the firſt fruits of them which they ſhall offer vnto the Lord, them haue I giuen thee.[13]And whatſoeuer is firſt ripe in the land, which they ſhall bring vnto the Lord, ſhall be thine, euery one that is cleane in thine houſe, ſhall eat of it.[14]Euery thing deuoted in Iſrael, ſhall be thine.[15]Euery thing that openeth the matrice in all fleſh, which they bring vnto the Lord, whether it bee of men or beaſts, ſhall be thine: Neuertheles the firſt borne of man ſhalt thou ſurely redeeme, and the firſtling of vncleane beaſts ſhalt thou redeeme.[16]And thoſe that are to be redeemed, from a moneth old ſhalt thou redeeme according to thine eſtimation, for the money of fiue ſhekels, after the ſhekel of the Sanctuary, which is twentie gerahs.[17]But the firſtling of a cowe, or the firſtling of a ſheepe, or the firſtling of a goat thou ſhalt not redeeme, they are holy: thou ſhalt ſprinckle their blood vpon the Altar, and ſhalt burne their fat for an offering made by fire, for a ſweet ſauour vnto the Lord.[18]And the fleſh of them ſhall bee thine: as the waue breaſt, and as the right ſhoulder are thine.[19]All the heaue offerings of the holy things, which the children of Iſrael offer vnto the Lord, haue I giuen thee and thy ſonnes, and thy daughters with thee, by a ſtatute for euer: it is a couenant of ſalt for euer, before the Lord vnto thee, and to thy ſeed with thee.[20]And the Lord ſpake vnto Aaron, Thou ſhalt haue no inheritance in their land, neither ſhalt thou haue any part among them: I am thy part, and thine inheritance among the children of Iſrael.[21]And behold, I haue giuen the children of Leui all the tenth in Iſrael, for an inheritance, for their ſeruice which they ſerue, euen the ſeruice of the Tabernacle of the Congregation.[22]Neither muſt the children of Iſrael hencefoorth come nigh the Tabernacle of the Congregation, leſt they beare ſinne, and die.[23]But the Leuites ſhall doe the ſeruice of the Tabernacle of the Congregation, and they ſhal beare their iniquitie: it ſhall be a ſtatute for euer throughout your generations, that among the children of Iſrael they haue no inheritance.[24]But the tithes of the children of Iſrael which they offer as an heaue offering vnto the Lord, I haue giuen to the Leuites to inherite: therefore I haue ſaid vnto them, Among the children of Iſrael they ſhall haue no inheritance.[25]And the Lord ſpake vnto Moſes, ſaying,[26]Thus ſpeake vnto the Leuites, and ſay vnto them, When ye take of the children of Iſrael the tithes, which I haue giuen you from them for your inheritance, then ye ſhal offer vp an heaue offering of it for the Lord, euen a tenth part of the tithe.[27]And this your heaue offering ſhall be reckoned vnto you, as though it were the corne of the threſhing floore, and as the fulneſse of the wine preſse.[28]Thus you alſo ſhal offer an heaue offering vnto the Lord of all your tithes which ye receiue of the children of Iſrael, and ye ſhall giue thereof the Lords heaue offering to Aaron the Prieſt.[29]Out of all your gifts ye ſhall offer euery heaue offering of the Lord, of all the beſt thereof, euen the hallowed part thereof, out of it.[30]Therefore thou ſhalt ſay vnto them, When yee haue heaued the beſt thereof from it, then it ſhall be counted vnto the Leuites, as the encreaſe of the threſhing floore, and as the encreaſe of the wine preſse.[31]And ye ſhall eate it in euery place, ye and your houſholds: for it is your reward for your ſeruice, in the Tabernacle of the Congregation.[32]And yee ſhall beare no ſinne by reaſon of it, when ye haue heaued from it the beſt of it: neither ſhall ye pollute the holy things of the children of Iſrael, leſt ye die.

CHAPTER 19[1]And the Lord ſpake vnto Moſes, and vnto Aaron, ſaying,[2]This is the ordinance of the Law, which the Lord hath commaunded, ſaying, Speake vnto the children of Iſrael, that they bring thee a red heifer without ſpot, wherein is no blemiſh, and vpon which neuer came yoke.[3]And ye ſhall giue her vnto Eleazar the Prieſt, that hee may bring her forth without the campe, and one ſhall ſlay her before his face.[4]And Eleazar the Prieſt ſhall take of her blood with his finger, and ſprinckle of her blood directly before the Tabernacle of the Congregation ſeuen times.[5]And one ſhall burne the heifer in his ſight: her ſkinne, and her fleſh, and her blood, with her doung, ſhall he burne.[6]And the Prieſt ſhall take Cedarwood, and hyſope, and ſcarlet, and caſt it into the midſt of the burning of the heifer.[7]Then the Prieſt ſhall waſh his clothes, and hee ſhall bathe his fleſh in water, and afterward he ſhall come into the campe, and the Prieſt ſhalbe vncleane vntill the euen.[8]And he that burneth her, ſhall waſh his clothes in water, and bathe his fleſh in water, and ſhall be vncleane vntill the Euen.[9]And a man that is cleane, ſhall gather vp the aſhes of the heifer, and lay them vp without the campe in a cleane place, and it ſhall bee kept for the Congregation of the children of Iſrael, for a water of ſeparation: it is a purification for ſinne.[10]And he that gathereth the aſhes of the heifer, ſhall waſh his clothes, and be vncleane vntil the Euen: and it ſhall be vnto the children of Iſrael, and vnto the ſtranger that ſoiourneth among them, for a ſtatute for euer.[11]He that toucheth the dead body of any man, ſhall bee vncleane ſeuen dayes.[12]He ſhall purifie himſelfe with it on the third day, and on the ſeuenth day he ſhall be cleane: but if he purifie not himſelfe the third day, then the ſeuenth day he ſhall not be cleane.[13]Whoſoeuer toucheth the dead bodie of any man that is dead, and purifieth not himſelfe, defileth the Tabernacle of the Lord, and that ſoule ſhall be cut off from Iſrael, becauſe the water of ſeparation was not ſprinckled vpon him: he ſhall be vncleane, his vncleanneſſe is yet vpon him.[14]This is the law, when a man dieth in a tent; all that come into the tent, and all that is in the tent, ſhalbe vnclean ſeuen dayes.[15]And euery open veſsel which hath no couering bound vpon it, is vncleane.[16]And whoſoeuer toucheth one that is ſlaine with a ſword in the open fields, or a dead body, or a bone of a man, or a graue, ſhall be vncleane ſeuen dayes.[17]And for an vncleane perſon they ſhall take of the aſhes of the burnt heifer of purification for ſinne, and running water ſhall bee put thereto in a veſſell:[18]And a cleane perſon ſhall take hyſope, and dippe it in the water, and ſprinckle it vpon the tent, and vpon all the veſſels, and vpon the perſons that were there, and vpon him that touched a bone, or one ſlaine, or one dead, or a graue.[19]And the cleane perſon ſhal ſprinkle vpon the vncleane on the third day, and on the ſeuenth day: and on the ſeuenth day he ſhall purifie himſelfe, and waſh his clothes, and bathe himſelfe in water, and ſhall be cleane at Euen.[20]But the man that ſhall bee vncleane, and ſhall not purifie himſelfe, that ſoule ſhall bee cut off from among the Congregation: becauſe he hath defiled the Sanctuary of the Lord, the water of ſeparation hath not beene ſprinkled vpon him, he is vncleane.[21]And it ſhall be a perpetuall ſtatute vnto them, that he that ſprinkleth the water of ſeparation, ſhall waſh his clothes: and he that toucheth the water of ſeparation, ſhall be vncleane vntill Euen.[22]And whatſoeuer the vncleane perſon toucheth, ſhall be vncleane: and the ſoule that toucheth it, ſhall bee vncleane vntill Euen.

CHAPTER 20[1]Then came the children of Iſrael, euen the whole Congregation, into the deſert of Zin, in the firſt moneth: and the people abode in Kadeſh, and Miriam died there, and was buried there.[2]And there was no water for the Congregation: and they gathered themſelues together againſt Moſes and againſt Aaron.[3]And the people chode with Moſes, and ſpake, ſaying, Would God that we had died when our brethren died before the Lord.[4]And why haue yee brought vp the Congregation of the Lord into this wilderneſſe, that we and our cattell ſhould die there?[5]And wherefore haue ye made vs to come vp out of Egypt, to bring vs in vnto this euil place? it is no place of ſeed, or of figges, or vines, or of pomegranates, neither is there any water to drinke.[6]And Moſes and Aaron went from the preſence of the aſſembly, vnto the doore of the Tabernacle of the congregation, and they fell vpon their faces: and the glory of the Lord appeared vnto them.[7]And the Lord ſpake vnto Moſes, ſaying,[8]Take the rodde, and gather thou the aſſembly together, thou and Aaron thy brother, and ſpeake yee vnto the rocke before their eyes, and it ſhall giue foorth his water, and thou ſhalt bring foorth to them, water out of the rocke: ſo thou ſhalt giue the Congregation, and their beaſts drinke.[9]And Moſes tooke the rod from before the Lord, as he commanded him.[10]And Moſes and Aaron gathered the Congregation together before the rocke, and hee ſaid vnto them, Heare now, ye rebels; muſt we fetch you water out of this rocke?[11]And Moſes lift vp his hand, and with his rod he ſmote the rocke twice: and the water came out abundantly, and the Congregation dranke, and their beaſts alſo.[12]And the Lord ſpake vnto Moſes and Aaron, Becauſe ye beleeue me not, to ſanctifie me in the eyes of the children of Iſrael, therefore ye ſhall not bring this Congregation into the land which I haue giuen them.[13]This is the water of Meribah, becauſe the children of Iſrael ſtroue with the Lord; and he was ſanctified in them.[14]And Moſes ſent meſſengers from Kadeſh, vnto the King of Edom; Thus ſaith thy brother Iſrael, Thou knoweſt all the trauaile that hath befallen vs:[15]How our fathers went downe into Egypt, and we haue dwelt in Egypt a long time: and the Egyptians vexed vs, and our fathers.[16]And when wee cryed vnto the Lord, he heard our voyce, and ſent an Angel, and hath brought vs foorth out of Egypt: and behold, wee are in Kadeſh, a citie in the vttermoſt of thy border.[17]Let vs paſſe, I pray thee, thorow thy countrey: we will not paſſe thorow the fields, or thorow the Uineyards, neither will we drinke of the water of the wells: wee will goe by the Kings high-way, we wil not turne to the right hand nor to the left, vntill wee haue paſſed thy borders.[18]And Edom ſaid vnto him, Thou ſhalt not paſſe by me, leſt I come out againſt thee with the ſword.[19]And the children of Iſrael ſaid vnto him, We will goe by the high-way: and if I and my cattell drinke of thy water, then I will pay for it: I will onely (without doing any thing elſe) go thorow on my feet.[20]And he ſaid, Thou ſhalt not goe thorow. And Edom came out againſt him with much people, and with a ſtrong hand.[21]Thus Edom refuſed to giue Iſrael paſsage thorow his border: wherefore Iſrael turned away from him.[22]And the children of Iſrael, euen the whole Congregation, iourneyed from Kadeſh, and came vnto mount Hor.[23]And the Lord ſpake vnto Moſes and Aaron in mount Hor, by the coaſt of the land of Edom, ſaying;[24]Aaron ſhall bee gathered vnto his people: for hee ſhall not enter into the land which I haue giuen vnto the children of Iſrael, becauſe yee rebelled againſt my word at the water of Meribah.[25]Take Aaron, and Eleazar his ſonne, and bring them vp vnto mount Hor.[26]And ſtrippe Aaron of his garments, and put them vpon Eleazar his ſonne, and Aaron ſhall be gathered vnto his people, and ſhall die there.[27]And Moſes did as the Lord commaunded: and they went vp into mount Hor, in the ſight of all the Congregation.[28]And Moſes ſtripped Aaron of his garments, and put them vpon Eleazar his ſonne, and Aaron died there in the top of the mount: and Moſes and Eleazar came downe from the mount.[29]And when all the Congregation ſaw that Aaron was dead, they mourned for Aaron thirty dayes, euen all the houſe of Iſrael.

CHAPTER 21[1]And when king Arad the Canaanite, which dwelt in the South, heard tell that Iſrael came by the way of the ſpies, then hee fought againſt Iſrael, and tooke ſome of them priſoners.2And Iſrael vowed a vow vnto the Lord, and ſaid, If thou wilt in deed deliuer this people into my hand, then I wil vtterly deſtroy their cities.3And the Lord hearkened to the voyce of Iſrael, and deliuered vp the Canaanites: and they vtterly deſtroyed them, and their cities, and hee called the name of the place Hormah.4And they iourneyed from mount Hor, by the way of the red ſea, to compaſſe the land of Edom: and the ſoule of the people was much diſcouraged becauſe of the way.5And the people ſpake againſt God and againſt Moſes, Wherefore haue ye brought vs vp out of Egypt, to die in the wilderneſſe? for there is no bread, neither is there any water, and our ſoule loatheth this light bread.6And the Lord ſent fierie ſerpents among the people, and they bit the people, and much people of Iſrael died.7Therefore the people came to Moſes, and ſaid, We haue ſinned: for wee haue ſpoken againſt the Lord, and againſt thee: pray vnto the Lord that hee take away the ſerpents from vs: and Moſes prayed for the people.8And the Lord ſaid vnto Moſes, Make thee a fierie ſerpent, and ſet it vpon a pole: and it ſhall come to paſſe, that euery one that is bitten, when hee looketh vpon it, ſhall liue.9And Moſes made a ſerpent of braſſe, and put it vpon a pole, and it came to paſſe, that if a ſerpent had bitten any man, when hee beheld the ſerpent of braſſe, he liued.10And the children of Iſrael ſet forward, and pitched in Oboth.11And they iourneyed from Oboth, and pitched at Iie-Abarim, in the wildernes which is before Moab, toward the Sunne riſing.12From thence they remooued, and pitched in the valley of Zared.13From thence they remooued, and pitched on the other ſide of Arnon, which is in the wilderneſſe that commeth out of the coaſts of the Amorites: for Arnon is the border of Moab, betweene Moab and the Amorites.14Wherefore it is ſaid in the booke of the warres of the Lord, what he did in the Red ſea, and in the brookes of Arnon,15And at the ſtreame of the brookes that goeth downe to the dwelling of Ar, & lieth vpon the border of Moab.16And from thence they went to Beer: that is the well whereof the Lord ſpake vnto Moſes, Gather the people together, and I will giue them water.17Then Iſrael ſang this ſong, Spring vp O well, Sing ye vnto it:18The Princes digged the well, the nobles of the people digged it, by the direction of the Law-giuer, with their ſtaues. And from the wilderneſſe they went to Mattanah:19And from Mattanah, to Nahaliel, and from Nahaliel to Bamoth:20And from Bamoth in the valley, that is in the countrey of Moab, to the toppe of Piſgah, which looketh toward Ieſhimon.21And Iſrael ſent meſſengers vnto Sihon king of the Amorites, ſaying,22Let me paſſe thorow thy land, we will not turne into the fields, or into the vineyards, we will not drinke of the waters of the well: but we will goe along by the kings high way, vntill wee be paſt thy borders.23And Sihon would not ſuffer Iſrael to paſſe thorow his border: but Sihon gathered all his people together, and went out againſt Iſrael into the wildernes: and he came to Iahaz, and fought againſt Iſrael.24And Iſrael ſmote him with the edge of the ſword, and poſſeſſed his land from Arnon vnto Iabok, euen vnto the children of Ammon: for the border of the children of Ammon was ſtrong.25And Iſrael tooke all theſe cities: and Iſrael dwelt in all the cities of the Amorites, in Heſhbon, and in all the villages thereof.26For Heſhbon was the citie of Sihon the King of the Amorites, who had fought againſt the former King of Moab, and taken all his land out of his hand, euen vnto Arnon.27Wherefore they that ſpeake in prouerbes, ſay, Come into Heſhbon: let the citie of Sihon bee built and prepared.28For there is a fire gone out of Heſhbon, a flame from the citie of Sihon: it hath conſumed Ar of Moab, and the lordes of the high places of Arnon.29Woe to thee, Moab, thou art vndone, O people of Chemoſh: he hath giuen his ſonnes that eſcaped, and his daughters, into captiuitie vnto Sihon King of the Amorites.30We haue ſhot at them; Heſhbon is periſhed euen vnto Dibon, and we haue layde them waſte euen vnto Nophah, which reacheth vnto Medeba.31Thus Iſrael dwelt in the land of the Amorites.32And Moſes ſent to ſpy out Iaazer, and they tooke the villages thereof, and droue out the Amorites that were there.33And they turned and went vp by the way of Baſhan: and Og the King of Baſhan went out againſt them, he, and all his people, to the battell at Edrei.34And the Lord ſaid vnto Moſes, Feare him not: for I haue deliuered him into thy hand, and all his people, and his land, and thou ſhalt doe to him as thou didſt vnto Sihon King of the Amorites, which dwelt at Heſhbon.35So they ſmote him & his ſonnes, and all his people, vntill there was none left him aliue, and they poſſeſſed his land.

CHAPTER 221And the children of Iſrael ſet forward, and pitched in the plaines of Moab, on this ſide Iordane by Iericho.2And Balak the ſonne of Zippor, ſaw all that Iſrael had done to the Amorites.3And Moab was ſore afraid of the people, becauſe they were many, and Moab was diſtreſſed, becauſe of the children of Iſrael.4And Moab ſaid vnto the elders of Midian; Now ſhall this company licke vp all that are round about vs, as the oxe licketh vp the graſſe of the field. And Balak the ſonne of Zippor, was King of the Moabites at that time.5He ſent meſſengers therefore vnto Balaam the ſonne of Beor, to Pethor, which is by the riuer of the land of the children of his people, to call him, ſaying, Behold, there is a people come out from Egypt: beholde, they couer the face of the earth, and they abide ouer againſt me.6Come now therefore, I pray thee, curſe mee this people, for they are too mightie for me: peraduenture I ſhall preuaile, that we may ſmite them, and that I may driue them out of the land: for I wot that he whom thou bleſſeſt, is bleſſed, and hee whom thou curſeſt, is curſed.7And the elders of Moab, and the elders of Midian departed, with the rewards of diuination in their hand; and they came vnto Balaam, and ſpake vnto him the words of Balak.8And hee ſaid vnto them, Lodge here this night, and I will bring you word againe as the Lord ſhal ſpeake vnto mee: and the Princes of Moab abode with Balaam.9And God came vnto Balaam, and ſaid, What men are theſe with thee?10And Balaam ſaid vnto God, Balak the ſonne of Zippor, King of Moab, hath ſent vnto me, ſaying;11Behold, there is a people come out of Egypt, which couereth the face of the earth: Come now, curſe me them; peraduenture I ſhalbe able to ouercome them, and driue them out.12And God ſaide vnto Balaam; Thou ſhalt not goe with them, thou ſhalt not curſe the people: for they are bleſſed.13And Balaam roſe vp in the morning, and ſaid vnto the Princes of Balak, Get you into your land: for the Lord refuſeth to giue mee leaue to goe with you.14And the Princes of Moab roſe vp, and they went vnto Balak, and ſaid, Balaam refuſeth to come with vs.15And Balak ſent yet againe Princes, moe, and more honourable then they.16And they came to Balaam, and ſaid to him, Thus ſaith Balak the ſon of Zippor; Let nothing, I pray thee, hinder thee from comming vnto me:17For I wil promote thee vnto very great honour, and I will do whatſoeuer thou ſaieſt vnto me: Come therefore, I pray thee, curſe me this people.18And Balaam anſwered and ſaid vnto the ſeruants of Balak, If Balak would giue me his houſe full of ſiluer and gold, I cannot goe beyond the word of the Lord my God, to doe leſſe or more.19Now therefore, I pray you, tarie yee alſo here this night, that I may know what the Lord will ſay vnto me more.20And God came vnto Balaam at night, and ſaid vnto him, If the men come to call thee, riſe vp, and goe with them: but yet the word which I ſhall ſay vnto thee, that ſhalt thou doe.21And Balaam roſe vp in the morning, and ſadled his aſſe, and went with the princes of Moab.22And Gods anger was kindled, becauſe he went: and the Angel of the Lord ſtood in the way for an aduerſarie againſt him: Now he was riding vpon his aſſe, and his two ſeruants were with him.23And the Aſse ſawe the Angel of the Lord ſtanding in the way, and his ſword drawen in his hand: and the aſſe turned aſide out of the way, and went into the field: and Balaam ſmote the aſſe, to turne her into the way.24But the Angel of the Lord ſtood in a path of the vineyards, a wall being on this ſide, & a wall on that ſide.25And when the aſſe ſaw the Angel of the Lord, ſhe thruſt her ſelfe vnto the wall, and cruſht Balaams foote againſt the wall: and hee ſmote her againe.26And the Angel of the Lord went further, and ſtood in a narrowe place, where was no way to turne, either to the right hand, or to the left.27And when the aſſe ſawe the Angel of the Lord, ſhee fell downe vnder Balaam, and Balaams anger was kindled, and hee ſmote the aſſe with a ſtaffe.28And the Lord opened the mouth of the aſſe, and ſhee ſaide vnto Balaam, What haue I done vnto thee, that thou haſt ſmitten mee theſe three times?29And Balaam ſaid vnto the aſſe, Becauſe thou haſt mocked mee: I would there were a ſword in mine hand, for now would I kill thee.30And the aſſe ſaid vnto Balaam, Am not I thine aſſe, vpon which thou haſt ridden euer ſince I was thine, vnto this day? was I euer wont to do ſo vnto thee? And he ſaid, Nay.31Then the Lord opened the eyes of Balaam, and hee ſaw the Angel of the Lord ſtanding in the way, and his ſword drawen in his hand: and hee bowed downe his head, and fell flat on his face.32And the Angel of the Lord ſaid vnto him, Wherefore haſt thou ſmitten thine aſſe theſe three times? Behold, I went out to withſtand thee, becauſe thy way is peruerſe before me.33And the aſſe ſaw me, and turned from me theſe three times: vnleſſe ſhee had

turned from me, ſurely now alſo I had ſlaine thee, and ſaued her
aliue.34And Balaam ſaid vnto the Angel of the Lord, I haue ſinned: for
I knew not that thou ſtoodeſt in the way againſt mee: Now therefore if
it diſpleaſe thee, I will get mee backe againe.35And the Angel of the Lord
ſaid vnto Balaam, Goe with the men: but onely the word that I ſhall
ſpeake vnto thee, that thou ſhalt ſpeake: So Balaam went with the
princes of Balak.36And when Balak heard that Balaam was come, hee
went out to meete him, vnto a citie of Moab, which is in the border of
Arnon, which is in the vtmoſt coaſt.37And Balak ſaid vnto Balaam, Did
I not earneſtly ſend vnto thee to call thee? wherefore cameſt thou not
vnto me? Am I not able indeed to promote thee to honour?38And
Balaam ſaide vnto Balak, Loe, I am come vnto thee: haue I now any
power at all to ſay any thing? the worde that God putteth in my mouth,
that ſhall I ſpeake.39And Balaam went with Balak, and they came vnto
Kiriath-Huzoth.40And Balak offered oxen, and ſheepe, and ſent to
Balaam, and to the princes that were with him.41And it came to paſſe
on the morrow, that Balak tooke Balaam, and brought him vp into the
high places of Baal, that thence hee might ſee the vtmoſt part of the
people.
CHAPTER 231And Balaam ſaide vnto Balak, Build me here ſeuen
Altars, and prepare mee here ſeuen oxen, and ſeuen rammes.2And Balak
did as Balaam had ſpoken, and Balak & Balaam offered on euery altar a
bullocke and a ramme.3And Balaam ſaid vnto Balak, ſtand by thy burnt
offring, and I wil goe: peraduenture the Lord will come to meete mee;
and whatſoeuer he ſheweth me, I will tell thee. And he went to an high
place.4And God met Balaam, and he ſaid vnto him, I haue prepared
ſeuen altars, and I haue offered vpon euery altar a bullocke and a
ramme.5And the Lord put a word in Balaams mouth, and ſaid, Returne
vnto Balak, & thus thou ſhalt ſpeake.6And he returned vnto him, and
loe, he ſtood by his burnt ſacrifice, hee, and all the Princes of
Moab.7And he tooke vp his parable, and ſaid, Balak the King of Moab
hath brought mee from Aram, out of the mountaines of the Eaſt, ſaying,
Come, curſe me Iacob, and come, defie Iſrael.8How ſhall I curſe, whom
God hath not curſed? or how ſhall I defie, whom the Lord hath not
defied?9For from the top of the rockes I ſee him, and from the hilles I
behold him: loe, the people ſhall dwell alone, and ſhall not bee reckoned
among the nations.10Who can count the duſt of Iacob, and the number
of the fourth part of Iſrael? Let mee die the death of the righteous, &
let my laſt end be like his.11And Balak ſaide vnto Balaam, What haſt thou
done vnto me? I tooke thee to curſe mine enemies, and behold, thou
haſt bleſſed them altogether.12And he anſwered, and ſaid, Muſt I not
take heede to ſpeake that which the Lord hath put in my mouth?13And
Balak ſaid vnto him, Come, I pray thee, with me, vnto another place,
from whence thou mayeſt ſee them: thou ſhalt ſee but the vtmoſt part
of them, and ſhalt not ſee them all: and curſe me them from
thence.14And hee brought him into the fielde of Zophim, to the toppe
of Piſgah, and built ſeuen altars, and offered a bullocke and a ramme on
euery altar.15And he ſaid vnto Balak, ſtand here by thy burnt offering,
while I meete the Lord yonder.16And the Lord met Balaam, and put a
word in his mouth, and ſaide, Goe againe vnto Balak, and ſay thus.17And
when hee came to him, behold, he ſtood by his burnt offring, and the
Princes of Moab with him. And Balak ſaid vnto him, What hath the
Lord ſpoken?18And he tooke vp his parable, and ſaid, Riſe vp Balak, &
heare; hearken vnto me, thou ſonne of Zippor:19God is not a man that
he ſhould lie, neither the ſonne of man, that hee ſhould repent: hath he
ſaid, and ſhall he not doe it? or, hath hee ſpoken, and ſhall he not make
it good?20Behold, I haue receiued commandement to bleſſe: and hee
hath bleſſed, and I cannot reuerſe it.21Hee hath not beheld iniquitie in
Iacob, neither hath he ſeene peruerſeneſse in Iſrael: the Lord his God is
with him, and the ſhoute of a King is among them.22God brought them
out of Egypt; he hath as it were the ſtrength of an Unicorne.23Surely
there is no inchantment againſt Iacob, neither is there any diuination
againſt Iſrael: according to this time it ſhalbe ſaid of Iacob, and of Iſrael,
What hath God wrought!24Beholde, the people ſhall riſe vp as a great
Lion, and lift vp himſelfe as a yong Lion: hee ſhall not lie downe vntill
he eate of the pray, and drinke the blood of the ſlaine.25And Balak ſaid
vnto Balaam, Neither curſe them at all, nor bleſſe them at all.26But
Balaam anſwered, and ſaid vnto Balak, Told not I thee, ſaying, All that
the Lord ſpeaketh, that I muſt doe?27And Balak ſaide vnto Balaam,
Come, I pray thee, I will bring thee vnto another place, peraduenture it
will pleaſe God, that thou mayeſt curſe me them from thence.28And
Balak brought Balaam vnto the top of Peor, that looketh toward
Ieſhimon.29And Balaam ſaide vnto Balak, Build mee here ſeuen altars,
and prepare me here ſeuen bullocks, and ſeuen rammes.30And Balak did
as Balaam had ſaid, and offred a bullocke and a ramme on euery altar.
CHAPTER 241And when Balaam ſawe that it pleaſed the Lord to
bleſſe Iſrael, hee went not, as at other times to ſeeke for inchantments,
but hee ſet his face toward the wilderneſſe.2And Balaam lift vp his eyes,
and he ſaw Iſrael abiding in his tents, according to their Tribes: and the
Spirit of God came vpon him.3And he tooke vp his parable, and ſaid,
Balaam the ſonne of Beor hath ſaid, and the man whoſe eyes are open
hath ſaid:4Hee hath ſaid, which heard the words of God, which ſaw the
viſion of the Almightie, falling into a trance, but hauing his eyes
open:5How goodly are thy tents, O Iacob, and thy Tabernacles, O
Iſrael!6As the valleyes are they ſpread forth, as gardens by the riuer ſide,
as the trees of Lign-Aloes which the Lord hath planted, and as Cedar
trees beſide the waters.7He ſhall powre the water out of his buckets, and
his ſeed ſhall be in many waters, and his King ſhall be higher then Agag,
and his Kingdome ſhall be exalted.8God brought him forth out of
Egypt, he hath as it were the ſtrength of an Unicorne: he ſhall eate vp
the nations his enemies, and ſhall breake their bones, and pierce them
thorow with his arrowes.9Hee couched, he lay downe as a Lyon, and as
a great Lyon: who ſhal ſtirre him vp? Bleſſed is hee that bleſſeth thee,
and curſed is hee that curſeth thee.10And Balaks anger was kindled
againſt Balaam, and hee ſmote his hands together: and Balak ſaid vnto
Balaam, I called thee to curſe mine enemies, and behold, thou haſt
altogether bleſſed them theſe three times.11Therefore now, flee thou to
thy place: I thought to promote thee vnto great honour, but loe, the
Lord hath kept thee backe from honour.12And Balaam ſaid vnto Balak,
ſpake I not alſo to thy meſſengers which thou ſenteſt vnto me,
ſaying,13If Balak would giue mee his houſe full of ſiluer and gold, I
cannot goe beyond the commandement of the Lord, to doe either good
or bad of mine owne mind? But what the Lord ſaith, that will I
ſpeake.14And now beholde, I goe vnto my people: come therefore, and
I will aduertiſe thee, what this people ſhall doe to thy people in the latter
dayes.15And hee tooke vp his parable, and ſaid, Balaam the ſonne of
Beor hath ſaid, and the man whoſe eyes are open, hath ſaid:16He hath
ſaid which heard the words of God, and knewe the knowledge of the
moſt High, which ſawe the viſion of the Almightie, falling into a trance,
but hauing his eyes open.17I ſhall ſee him, but not now: I ſhall behold
him, but not nigh: There ſhall come a ſtarre out of Iacob, and a Scepter
ſhall riſe out of Iſrael, and ſhall ſmite the corners of Moab, and deſtroy
all the children of Sheth.18And Edom ſhall bee a poſſeſſion, Seir alſo
ſhall be a poſſeſſion for his enemies, and Iſrael ſhall doe valiantly.19Out
of Iacob ſhall come he that ſhall haue dominion, and ſhall deſtroy him
that remaineth of the citie.20And when he looked on Amalek, he tooke
vp his parable, and ſayd, Amalek was the firſt of the nations, but his
latter end ſhall bee, that hee periſh for euer.21And hee looked on the
Kenites, and tooke vp his parable, and ſaide, Strong is thy dwelling place,
and thou putteſt thy neſt in a rocke:22Neuertheleſſe, the Kenite ſhall be
waſted, vntil Aſhur ſhal carie thee away captiue.23And he tooke vp his
parable, and ſaid, Alas! who ſhall liue when God doeth this?24And
ſhippes ſhall come from the coaſt of Chittim, and ſhal afflict Aſhur,
and ſhall afflict Eber, and hee alſo ſhall periſh for euer.25And Balaam
roſe vp, and went and returned to his place: and Balak alſo went his way.
CHAPTER 251And Iſrael abode in Shittim, and the people begun to
commit whoredome with the daughters of Moab.2And they called the
people vnto the ſacrifices of their gods: and the people did eate, and
bowed downe to their gods.3And Iſrael ioyned himſelfe vnto Baal-Peor:
and the anger of the Lord was kindled againſt Iſrael.4And the Lord ſaid
vnto Moſes, Take all the heads of the people, and hang them vp before
the Lord againſt the Sunne, that the fierce anger of the Lord may be
turned away from Iſrael.5And Moſes ſaid vnto the Iudges of Iſrael, Slay
ye euery one his men, that were ioyned vnto Baal-Peor.6And behold,
one of the children of Iſrael came and brought vnto his brethren a
Midianitiſh woman, in the ſight of Moſes, and in the ſight of all the
Congregation of the children of Iſrael, who were weeping before the
doore of the Tabernacle of the Congregation.7And when Phinehas the
ſonne of Eleazar, the ſonne of Aaron the Prieſt ſaw it, hee roſe vp from
amongſt the Congregation, and tooke a iauelin in his hand.8And he went

after the man of Iſrael into the tent, and thruſt both of them thorow, the man of Iſrael, and the woman, thorow her belly: So the plague was ſtayed from the children of Iſrael.9And thoſe that died in the plague, were twentie and foure thouſand.10And the Lord ſpake vnto Moſes, ſaying,11Phinehas the ſonne of Eleazar, the ſonne of Aaron the Prieſt, hath turned my wrath away from the children of Iſrael, (while hee was zealous for my ſake among them) that I conſumed not the children of Iſrael in my ieloufie.12Wherefore ſay, Behold, I giue vnto him my Couenant of peace.13And he ſhall haue it, and his ſeed after him, euen the Couenant of an euerlaſting Prieſthood, becauſe he was zealous for his God, and made an atonement for the children of Iſrael.14Now the name of the Iſraelite that was ſlaine, euen that was ſlaine with the Midianitiſh woman, was Zimri the ſonne of Salu, a Prince of a chiefe houſe among the Simeonites.15And the name of the Midianitiſh woman that was ſlaine, was Cozbi, the daughter of Zur, hee was head ouer a people, and of a chiefe houſe in Midian.16And the Lord ſpake vnto Moſes, ſaying,17Uexe the Midianites, and ſmite them:18For they vexe you with their wiles, wherewith they haue beguiled you, in the matter of Peor, and in the matter of Cozbi, the daughter of a Prince of Midian their ſiſter, which was ſlaine in the day of the plague, for Peors ſake.

CHAPTER 261And it came to paſſe after the plague, that the Lord ſpake vnto Moſes, and vnto Eleazar the ſonne of Aaron the Prieſt, ſaying,2Take the ſumme of all the Congregation of the children of Iſrael, from twenty yeeres old and vpward, throughout their fathers houſe, all that are able to goe to warre in Iſrael.3And Moſes & Eleazar the Prieſt ſpake with them in the plaines of Moab by Iordane neere Iericho, ſaying,4Take the ſumme of the people from twenty yeeres old and vpward, as the Lord commanded Moſes, and the children of Iſrael which went foorth out of the land of Egypt.5Reuben the eldeſt ſonne of Iſrael: the children of Reuben, Hanoch, of whom commeth the family of the Hanochites: of Pallu the family of the Palluites:6Of Heſron the family of the Heſronites: of Carmi the family of the Carmites.7Theſe are the families of the Reubenites: and they that were numbred of them, were fourtie and three thouſand, and ſeuen hundred and thirtie.8And the ſonnes of Pallu, Eliab.9And the ſonnes of Eliab, Nemuel, and Dathan, and Abiram: this is that Dathan & Abiram, which were famous in the Congregation, who ſtroue againſt Moſes and againſt Aaron in the companie of Korah, when they ſtroue againſt the Lord:10And the earth opened her mouth, and ſwallowed them vp together with Korah when that companie died, what time the fire deuoured two hundred and fiftie men: and they became a ſigne.11Notwithſtanding, the children of Korah died not.12The ſonnes of Simeon, after their families: Of Nemuel, the family of the Nemuelites: Of Iamin, the familie of the Iaminites: Of Iachin, the familie of the Iachinites:13Of Zerah, the familie of the Zarhites: Of Shaul, the familie of the Shaulites.14Theſe are the families of the Simeonites, twentie and two thouſand, and two hundred.15The children of Gad after their families: Of Zephon, the familie of the Zephonites: of Haggi the familie of the Haggites: of Shuni the familie of the Shunites.16Of Ozni, the familie of the Oznites: Of Eri the familie of the Erites.17Of Arod the familie of the Arodites: of Areli the familie of the Arelites.18Theſe are the families of the children of Gad, according to thoſe that were numbred of them, fourtie thouſand and fiue hundred.19The ſonnes of Iudah, were Er and Onan: and Er and Onan died in the land of Canaan.20And the ſonnes of Iudah after their families were: Of Shelah the familie of the Shelanites: Of Pharez the familie of the Pharzites: Of Zerah the familie of the Zarhites.21And the ſonnes of Pharez were: Of Heſron the familie of the Heſronites: Of Hamul the familie of the Hamulites.22Theſe are the families of Iudah according to thoſe that were numbred of them, threeſcore and ſixteene thouſand and fiue hundred.23Of the ſonnes of Iſſachar after their families: Of Tola the familie of the Tolaites: of Pua the familie of the Punites.24Of Iaſhub the familie of the Iaſhubites: of Shimron the familie of the Shimronites.25Theſe are the families of Iſſachar according to thoſe that were numbred of them, threeſcore and foure thouſand, and three hundred.26Of the ſonnes of Zebulun after their families, of Sered the familie of the Sardites: Of Elon the familie of the Elonites: of Iahleel the familie of the Iahleelites.27Theſe are the families of the Zebulunites, according to thoſe that were numbred of them, threeſcore thouſand and fiue hundred.28The ſonnes of Ioſeph after their families, were Manaſſeh and Ephraim.29Of the ſonnes of Manaſſeh: Of Machir the familie of the Machirites: and Machir begate Gilead: Of Gilead come the familie of the Gileadites.30Theſe are the ſonnes of Gilead: Of Ieezer the family of the Ieezerites: Of Helek the familie of the Helekites.31And of Aſriel the family of the Aſrielites: and of Shechem the familie of the Shechemites.32And of Shemida the familie of the Shemidaites: and of Hepher the familie of the Hepherites.33And Zelophehad the ſonne of Hepher had no ſonnes, but daughters: and the names of the daughters of Zelophehad, were Mahlah, and Noah, Hoglah, Milcah, and Tirzah.34Theſe are the families of Manaſſeh, and thoſe that were numbred of them, fiftie and two thouſand and ſeuen hundred.35Theſe are the ſonnes of Ephraim, after their families: Of Shuthelah the familie of the Shuthalhites: Of Becher the familie of the Bachrites: Of Tahan the familie of the Tahanites.36And theſe are the ſonnes of Shuthelah: Of Eran the familie of the Eranites.37Theſe are the families of the ſonnes of Ephraim, according to thoſe that were numbred of them, thirtie and two thouſand, and fiue hundred. Theſe are the ſonnes of Ioſeph after their families.38The ſonnes of Beniamin after their families: Of Bela the familie of the Belaites: Of Aſhbel the familie of the Aſhbelites: Of Ahiram the family of the Ahiramites:39Of Shupham the family of the Shuphamites: Of Hupham the family of the Huphamites.40And the ſonnes of Bela were Ard and Naaman: of Ard, the family of the Ardites: and of Naaman the family of the Naamites.41Theſe are the ſonnes of Beniamin after their families; and they that were numbred of them, were fourty and fiue thouſand, and ſixe hundred.42Theſe are the ſonnes of Dan after their families: Of Shuham the family of the Shuhamites. Theſe are the families of Dan, after their families.43All the families of the Shuhamites, according to thoſe that were numbred of them, were three ſcore and foure thouſand, and foure hundred.44Of the children of Aſher after their families: Of Iimna the family of the Iimnites: Of Ieſui the family of the Ieſuites: Of Beriah the family of the Beriites.45Of the ſonnes of Beriah; of Heber the family of the Heberites: of Malchiel, the family of the Malchielites.46And the name of the daughter of Aſher, was Sarah.47Theſe are the families of the ſonnes of Aſher, according to thoſe that were numbred of them; who were fiftie and three thouſand, and foure hundred.48Of the ſonnes of Naphtali, after their families, of Iahzeel the family of the Iahzeelites: Of Guni, the family of the Gunites:49Of Iezer, the family of the Iezerites: Of Shillem the family of the Shillemites.50Theſe are the families of Naphtali, according to their families: and they that were numbred of them, were fourty and fiue thouſand, and foure hundred.51Theſe were the numbred of the children of Iſrael, ſixe hundred thouſand, and a thouſand, ſeuen hundred and thirtie.52And the Lord ſpake vnto Moſes, ſaying,53Unto theſe the land ſhall be diuided for an inheritance, according to the number of names.54To many thou ſhalt giue the more inheritance, and to few thou ſhalt giue the leſſe inheritance: to euery one ſhall his inheritance be giuen, according to thoſe that were numbred of him.55Notwithſtanding the land ſhall bee diuided by lot: according to the names of the tribes of their fathers, they ſhall inherite.56According to the lot ſhall the poſſeſſion thereof be diuided betweene many and few.57And theſe are they that were numbred of the Leuites, after their families: Of Gerſhon, the family of the Gerſhonites: Of Kohath the family of the Kohathites: Of Merari the family of the Merarites.58Theſe are the families of the Leuites: the family of the Libnites, the family of the Hebronites, the family of the Mahlites, the family of the Muſhites, the family of the Korathites: and Kohath begate Amram.59And the name of Amrams wife was Iochebed the daughter of Leui, whom her mother bare to Leui in Egypt: And ſhee bare vnto Amram, Aaron and Moſes, and Miriam their ſiſter.60And vnto Aaron was borne Nadab and Abihu, Eleazar and Ithamar.61And Nadab and Abihu died, when they offered ſtrange fire before the Lord.62And thoſe that were numbred of them, were twenty and three thouſand, all males from a moneth old and vpward: for they were not numbred among the children of Iſrael, becauſe there was no inheritance giuen them among the children of Iſrael.63Theſe are they that were numbred by Moſes and Eleazar the Prieſt, who numbred the children of Iſrael in the plaines of Moab, by Iordane neere Iericho.64But among theſe there was not a man of them, whom Moſes and Aaron the Prieſt numbred, when they numbred the children of Iſrael in the wilderneſſe of Sinai.65For the Lord had ſaid of them, They ſhall ſurely die in the wilderneſſe: and there was not left a man of them, ſaue Caleb the ſonne of Iephunneh, and Ioſhua the ſonne of Nun.

CHAPTER 27 1Then came the daughters of Zelophehad, the ſonne of Hepher, the ſonne of Gilead, the ſonne of Machir, the ſonne of Manaſſeh, of the families of Manaſſeh, the ſonne of Ioſeph; and theſe are the names of his daughters: Mahlah, Noah, and Hoglah, and Milcah, and Tirzah. 2And they ſtood before Moſes, and before Eleazar the Prieſt, and before the Princes, and all the Congregation, by the doore of the Tabernacle of the Congregation, ſaying, 3Our father died in the wilderneſſe, and he was not in the company of them that gathered themſelues together againſt the Lord in the company of Korah: but died in his owne ſinne, and had no ſonnes. 4Why ſhould the name of our father be done away from among his family, becauſe he hath no ſonne? Giue vnto vs therefore a poſſeſſion among the brethren of our father. 5And Moſes brought their cauſe before the Lord. 6And the Lord ſpake vnto Moſes, ſaying, 7The daughters of Zelophehad ſpeake right: thou ſhalt ſurely giue them a poſſeſſion of an inheritance among their fathers brethren, and thou ſhalt cauſe the inheritance of their father to paſſe vnto them. 8And thou ſhalt ſpeake vnto the children of Iſrael, ſaying, If a man die, and haue no ſonne, then yee ſhall cauſe his inheritance to paſſe vnto his daughter. 9And if he haue no daughter, then yee ſhall giue his inheritance vnto his brethren. 10And if he haue no brethren, then yee ſhall giue his inheritance vnto his fathers brethren. 11And if his father haue no brethren, then ye ſhall giue his inheritance vnto his kinſeman that is next to him of his family, and hee ſhall poſſeſſe it: And it ſhall be vnto the children of Iſrael a ſtatute of iudgement, as the Lord commanded Moſes. 12And the Lord ſaide vnto Moſes, Get thee vp into this mount Abarim, and ſee the land which I haue giuen vnto the children of Iſrael. 13And when thou haſt ſeene it, thou alſo ſhalt be gathered vnto thy people, as Aaron thy brother was gathered. 14For ye rebelled againſt my Commandement (in the deſart of Zin, in the ſtrife of the Congregation) to ſanctifie me at the water, before their eyes: that is the water of Meribah in Kadeſh in the wilderneſſe of Zin. 15And Moſes ſpake vnto the Lord, ſaying, 16Let the Lord, the God of the ſpirits of all fleſh, ſet a man ouer the Congregation, 17Which may goe out before them, and which may goe in before them, and which may lead them out, and which may bring them in, that the Congregation of the Lord bee not as ſheepe which haue no ſhepheard. 18And the Lord ſaide vnto Moſes, Take thee Ioſhua the ſonne of Nun, a man in whom is the ſpirit, and lay thine hand vpon him. 19And ſet him before Eleazar the Prieſt, and before all the Congregation: and giue him a charge in their ſight. 20And thou ſhalt put ſome of thine honour vpon him, that all the Congregation of the children of Iſrael may be obedient. 21And he ſhall ſtand before Eleazar the Prieſt, who ſhall aſke counſell for him, after the iudgement of Urim before the Lord: at his word ſhal they goe out, and at his word they ſhal come in, both he, and al the children of Iſrael with him, euen all the Congregation. 22And Moſes did as the Lord commanded him: and he tooke Ioſhua and ſet him before Eleazar the Prieſt, and before all the Congregation. 23And hee layd his handes vpon him, and gaue him a charge, as the Lord commaunded by the hand of Moſes.

CHAPTER 28 1And the Lord ſpake vnto Moſes, ſaying, 2Command the children of Iſrael, and ſay vnto them, My offering, and my bread for my ſacrifices, made by fire for a ſweet ſauour vnto mee, ſhall yee obſerue, to offer vnto me, in their due ſeaſon. 3And thou ſhalt ſay vnto them, This is the offering made by fire, which ye ſhall offer vnto the Lord: Two lambes of the firſt yeere without ſpot day by day, for a continuall burnt offering. 4The one lambe ſhalt thou offer in the morning, and the other lambe ſhalt thou offer at Euen. 5And a tenth part of an Ephah of flowre for a meate offering, mingled with the fourth part of an Hyn of beaten oyle. 6It is a continuall burnt offering which was ordeined in mount Sinai for a ſweete ſauour, a ſacrifice made by fire vnto the Lord. 7And the drinke offering thereof ſhall be the fourth part of an Hyn for the one lambe: in the holy place ſhalt thou cauſe the ſtrong wine to bee powred vnto the Lord for a drinke offring. 8And the other lambe ſhalt thou offer at Euen: as the meate offring of the morning, and as the drinke offering thereof, thou ſhalt offer it, a ſacrifice made by fire of a ſweet ſauour vnto the Lord. 9And on the Sabbath day, two lambes of the firſt yeere without ſpot, and two tenth deales of flowre for a meate offering mingled with oyle, and the drinke offering thereof. 10This is the burnt offring of euery Sabbath, beſide the continuall burnt offering, and his drinke offering. 11And in the beginnings of your moneths, ye ſhall offer a burnt offering vnto the Lord: Two yong bullocks and one ramme, ſeuen lambs of the firſt yeere, without ſpot, 12And three tenth deales of flowre for a meate offering, mingled with oyle, for one bullocke, and two tenth deales of flowre for a meat offering, mingled with oyle, for one ramme: 13And a ſeueral tenth deale of flowre mingled with oyle for a meate offering, vnto one lambe, for a burnt offering of a ſweet ſauour, a ſacrifice made by fire vnto the Lord. 14And their drinke offerings ſhal be halfe an Hin of wine vnto a bullocke, and the third part of an Hin vnto a ramme, and a fourth part of an Hin vnto a lambe: This is the burnt offring of euery moneth, throughout the moneths of the yeere. 15And one kidde of the goates for a ſinne offering vnto the Lord ſhalbe offered, beſides the continuall burnt offring and his drinke offering. 16And in the fourteenth day of the firſt moneth, is the Paſſeouer of the Lord. 17And in the fifteenth day of this moneth is the feaſt: ſeuen dayes ſhall vnleauened bread be eaten. 18In the firſt day ſhall bee an holy conuocation, yee ſhall doe no maner of ſeruile worke therein. 19But ye ſhall offer a ſacrifice made by fire for a burnt offering vnto the Lord, two yong bullockes, and one ramme, and ſeuen lambes of the firſt yeere: they ſhall be vnto you without blemiſh. 20And their meate offering ſhall be of flowre mingled with oyle: three tenth deales ſhall ye offer for a bullocke, and two tenth deales for a ramme. 21A ſeuerall tenth deale ſhalt thou offer for euery lambe, throughout the ſeuen lambes: 22And one goat for a ſinne offering, to make an atonement for you. 23Ye ſhal offer theſe beſide the burnt offering in the morning, which is for a continuall burnt offering. 24After this maner yee ſhall offer dayly throughout the ſeuen dayes, the meat of the ſacrifice made by fire, of a ſweet ſauour vnto the Lord: it ſhal be offred beſide the continuall burnt offring, and his drinke offering. 25And on the ſeuenth day yee ſhall haue an holy conuocation: yee ſhall doe no ſeruile worke. 26Alſo in the day of the firſt fruits when ye bring a new meat offering vnto the Lord, after your weekes bee out: ye ſhall haue an holy conuocation, ye ſhall doe no ſeruile worke. 27But yee ſhall offer the burnt offering for a ſweete ſauour vnto the Lord, two yong bullockes, one ramme, ſeuen lambes of the firſt yeere. 28And their meat offering of flowre mingled with oyle, three tenth deales vnto one bullocke, two tenth deales vnto one ramme, 29A ſeuerall tenth deale vnto one lambe, thorowout the ſeuen lambes, 30And one kidde of the goates, to make an atonement for you. 31Ye ſhall offer them beſides the continuall burnt offering, and his meat offering, (they ſhall be vnto you without blemiſh) and their drinke offerings.

CHAPTER 29 1And in the ſeuenth moneth, on the firſt day of the moneth, ye ſhall haue an holy conuocation, yee ſhall doe no ſeruile worke: it is a day of blowing the trumpets vnto you. 2And ye ſhall offer a burnt offering for a ſweet ſauour vnto the Lord, one yong bullocke, one ramme, and ſeuen lambes of the firſt yeere without blemiſh. 3And their meat offering ſhall be of floure mingled with oyle, three tenth deales for a bullocke, and two tenth deales for a ramme: 4And one tenth deale for one lambe thorowout the ſeuen lambes: 5And one kidde of the goats for a ſinne offering to make an atonement for you: 6Beſide the burnt offering of the moneth, and his meat offering, and the dayly burnt offering, and his meat offering, and their drinke offerings, according vnto their maner, for a ſweet ſauour, a ſacrifice made by fire vnto the Lord. 7And ye ſhall haue on the tenth day of this ſeuenth moneth an holy conuocation; and yee ſhall afflict your ſoules: yee ſhall not doe any worke therein. 8But ye ſhall offer a burnt offering vnto the Lord for a ſweet ſauour, one yong bullock, one ramme, and ſeuen lambes of the firſt yeere, they ſhall bee vnto you without blemiſh. 9And their meate offering ſhall be of floure mingled with oyle, three tenth deales to a bullocke, and two tenth deales to one ramme: 10A ſeuerall tenth deale for one lambe, thorowout the ſeuen lambes; 11One kidde of the goats for a ſinne offering, beſide the ſinne offering of atonement, and the continuall burnt offering, and the meat offering of it, and their drinke offerings. 12And on the fifteenth day of the ſeuenth moneth, yee ſhall haue an holy conuocation, yee ſhall doe no ſeruile worke, and ye ſhall keepe a feaſt vnto the Lord ſeuen dayes. 13And ye ſhall offer a burnt offring, a ſacrifice made by fire, of a ſweet ſauour vnto the Lord, thirteene yong bullocks, two rammes, and fourteene lambes of the firſt yeere: They ſhall be without blemiſh. 14And their meat offering ſhall be of floure mingled with oyle, three tenth deales vnto euery bullocke of the thirteene bullocks, two tenth deales to each ramme of the two rammes:15And a ſeuerall tenth deale to each lambe of the foureteene lambes:16And one kidde of the goats for a ſinne offring, beſide the continual burnt offering, his meate offering, and his drinke offering.17And on the ſecond day ye ſhal offer twelue yong bullocks, two rammes, foureteene lambes of the firſt yeere without ſpot.18And their meat offring, and their drinke offerings for the bullockes, for the rammes, and for the lambes, ſhall be according to their number, after the maner:19And one kidde of the goats for a ſinne offering, beſide the continuall burnt offering, and the meate offering thereof, and their drinke offerings.20And on the third day eleuen bullocks, two rammes, foureteene lambs of the firſt yere without blemiſh.21And their meate offering, and their drinke offerings for the bullocks, for the rammes, and for the lambes, ſhall be according to their number after the maner:22And one goat for a ſinne offering, beſide the continuall burnt offering, and his meate offering, and his drinke offering.23And on the fourth day ten bullocks, two rammes, and foureteene lambs of the firſt yere without blemiſh.24Their meat offering, and their drinke offerings, for the bullocks, for the rammes, and for the lambes, ſhall be according to their number after the maner:25And one kidde of the goats for a ſin offering, beſide the continuall burnt offering, his meate offering, and his drinke offering.26And on the fift day, nine bullockes, two rammes, and fourteene lambes of the firſt yeere, without ſpot:27And their meat offring and their drinke offerings, for the bullockes, for the rammes, and for the lambes, ſhall be according to their number after the maner:28And one goate for a ſinne offring, beſide the continuall burnt offring, and his meate offering and his drinke offering.29And on the ſixt day eight bullockes, two rammes, and fourteene lambes of the firſt yeere without blemiſh:30And their meat offring, and their drinke offerings, for the bullockes, for the rammes, and for the lambes, ſhall be according to their number, after the maner:31And one goat for a ſinne offering, beſide the continuall burnt offering, his meate offering and his drinke offering.32And on the ſeuenth day, ſeuen bullockes, two rammes, and fourteene lambes of the firſt yeere without blemiſh.33And their meate offring, and their drinke offerings, for the bullockes, for the rammes, and for the lambes, ſhall be according to their number, after the maner:34And one goat for a ſinne offring, beſide the continuall burnt offering, his meate offering, and his drinke offring.35On the eight day, ye ſhall haue a ſolemne aſſembly: ye ſhall do no ſeruile worke therein:36But ye ſhal offer a burnt offring, a ſacrifice made by fire, of a ſweet ſauour vnto the Lord, one bullocke, one ramme, ſeuen lambes of the firſt yeere without blemiſh:37Their meate offering, and their drinke offrings, for the bullocke, for the ramme, and for the lambes ſhall be according to their number, after the maner:38And one goat for a ſinne offering, beſide the continuall burnt offring, and his meate offering, and his drinke offering.39Theſe things ye ſhall doe vnto the Lord in your ſet feaſts, beſides your vowes, and your free will offerings, for your burnt offerings, and for your meate offerings, and for your drinke offerings, and for your peace offerings.40And Moſes tolde the children of Iſrael, according to all that the Lord commanded Moſes.

CHAPTER 301And Moſes ſpake vnto the heads of the tribes, concerning the children of Iſrael, ſaying, This is the thing which the Lord hath commanded.2If a man vowe a vow vnto the Lord, or ſweare an othe to bind his ſoule with a bond: he ſhall not breake his word, hee ſhall doe according to all that proceedeth out of his mouth.3If a woman alſo vow a vow vnto the Lord, and binde her ſelfe by a bond, being in her fathers houſe in her youth;4And her father heare her vow, and her bond wherewith ſhee hath bound her ſoule, and her father ſhall holde his peace at her: then all her vowes ſhall ſtand, and euery bond wherewith ſhee hath bound her ſoule, ſhall ſtand.5But if her father diſallow her in the day that he heareth; not any of her vowes or of her bonds, wherewith ſhe hath bound her ſoule, ſhall ſtand: and the Lord ſhall forgiue her, becauſe her father diſallowed her.6And if ſhe had at all an huſband when ſhe vowed, or vttered ought out of her lips, wherewith ſhee bound her ſoule,7And her huſband heard it, and held his peace at her in the day that hee heard it: then her vowes ſhall ſtand, and her bonds wherewith ſhee bound her ſoule, ſhall ſtand.8But if her huſband diſallowe her on the day that he heard it, then he ſhall make her vowe which ſhe vowed, and that which ſhe vttered with her lippes wherewith ſhee bound her ſoule, of none effect, and the Lord ſhall forgiue her.9But euery vow of a widow, and of her that is diuorced, wherewith they haue bound their ſoules, ſhall ſtand againſt her.10And if ſhe vowed in her huſbands houſe, or bound her ſoule by a bond with an oath;11And her huſband heard it, and held his peace at her, and diſallowed her not: then all her vowes ſhall ſtand, and euery bond wherewith ſhee bound her ſoule, ſhall ſtand.12But if her huſband hath vtterly made them voyd on the day hee heard them: then whatſoeuer proceeded out of her lips concerning her vowes, or concerning the bond of her ſoule, ſhall not ſtand: her huſband hath made them voyd, and the Lord ſhal forgiue her.13Euery vow, and euery binding othe to afflict the ſoule, her huſband may eſtabliſh it, or her huſband may make it voyd.14But if her huſband altogether hold his peace at her, from day to day, then he eſtabliſheth all her vowes, or all her bonds which are vpon her: hee confirmeth them, becauſe hee held his peace at her, in the day that hee heard them.15But if hee ſhall any wayes make them voyd after that he hath heard them, then he ſhall beare her iniquitie.16Theſe are the ſtatutes which the Lord commanded Moſes betweene a man and his wife, betweene the father and his daughter, being yet in her youth, in her fathers houſe.

CHAPTER 311And the Lord ſpake vnto Moſes, ſaying,2Auenge the children of Iſrael of the Midianites: afterward ſhalt thou be gathered vnto thy people.3And Moſes ſpake vnto the people, ſaying, Arme ſome of your ſelues vnto the warre, and let them goe againſt the Midianites, and auenge the Lord of Midian.4Of euery tribe a thouſand, throughout all the tribes of Iſrael, ſhall ye ſend to the warre.5So there were deliuered out of the thouſands of Iſrael, a thouſand of euery tribe, twelue thouſand armed for warre.6And Moſes ſent them to the warre, a thouſand of euery tribe, them and Phinehas the ſonne of Eleazar the Prieſt, to the warre, with the holy inſtruments, and the trumpets to blow, in his hand.7And they warred againſt the Midianites, as the Lord commanded Moſes, and they ſlew all the males.8And they ſlew the Kings of Midian, beſide the reſt of them that were ſlaine; namely Eui, and Rekem, and Zur, and Hur, and Reba, fiue Kings of Midian; Balaam alſo the ſonne of Beor they ſlew with the ſword.9And the children of Iſrael tooke all the women of Midian captiues, and their little ones, and tooke the ſpoile of all their cattell, and all their flocks, and all their goods.10And they burnt all their cities wherein they dwelt, and all their goodly caſtles with fire:11And they tooke all the ſpoile, and all the pray, both of men and of beaſts.12And they brought the captiues, and the pray, and the ſpoile vnto Moſes and Eleazar the Prieſt, and vnto the Congregation of the children of Iſrael, vnto the campe at the plaines of Moab, which are by Iordan neere Iericho.13And Moſes and Eleazar the Prieſt, and all the Princes of the Congregation went foorth to meete them without the campe.14And Moſes was wroth with the officers of the hoſte, with the captaines ouer thouſands, and captaines ouer hundreds, which came from the battel.15And Moſes ſaid vnto them, Haue ye ſaued all the women aliue?16Behold, theſe cauſed the children of Iſrael, through the counſell of Balaam, to commit treſpaſſe againſt the Lord in the matter of Peor, and there was a plague among the Congregation of the Lord.17Now therefore kill euery male among the little ones, and kill euery woman that hath knowen man, by lying with him.18But all the women children that haue not knowen a man by lying with him, keepe aliue for your ſelues.19And doe yee abide without the campe ſeuen dayes: whoſoeuer hath killed any perſon, and whoſoeuer hath touched any ſlaine, purifie both your ſelues, and your captiues, on the third day, and on the ſeuenth day.20And purifie all your raiment, and all that is made of ſkinnes, and all worke of goates haire, and all things made of wood.21And Eleazar the Prieſt ſaid vnto the men of warre which went to the battell, This is the ordinance of the law which the Lord commaunded Moſes.22Onely the gold, and the ſiluer, the braſſe, the yron, the tinne, and the lead,23Euery thing that may abide the fire, yee ſhall make it goe through the fire, and it ſhall be cleane: neuertheleſſe, it ſhall be purified with the water of ſeparation: and all that abideth not the fire, yee ſhall make goe through the water.24And ye ſhall waſh your clothes on the ſeuenth day, and ye ſhalbe cleane, and afterward yee ſhall come into the campe.25And the Lord ſpake vnto Moſes, ſaying,26Take the ſumme of the pray, that was taken, both of man and of beaſt, thou and Eleazar the Prieſt, and the chiefe fathers of the Congregation:27And diuide the pray into two parts, betweene them that tooke the warre vpon them, who went out to battell, and betweene all the Congregation.28And leuie a tribute vnto the Lord of the men of warre which went out to battell: one ſoule of fiue hundred, both of the perſons, and of the beeues, and of the aſſes, and of the ſheepe. 29 Take it of their halfe, and giue it vnto Eleazar the Prieſt, for an heaue offering of the Lord. 30 And of the children of Iſraels halfe, thou ſhalt take one portion of fiftie, of the perſons, of the beeues, of the aſſes, and of the flockes, of all maner of beaſts, and giue them vnto the Leuites, which keepe the charge of the Tabernacle of the Lord. 31 And Moſes and Eleazar the Prieſt did as the Lord commanded Moſes. 32 And the bootie being the reſt of the pray which the men of war had caught, was ſix hundred thouſand, and ſeuenty thouſand, and fiue thouſand ſheepe, 33 And threeſcore and twelue thouſand beeues, 34 And threeſcore and one thouſand aſſes: 35 And thirtie and two thouſand perſons in all, of women that had not knowen man by lying with him. 36 And the halfe which was the portion of them that went out to warre, was in number three hundred thouſand, and ſeuen and thirtie thouſand, and fiue hundred ſheepe. 37 And the Lords tribute of the ſheepe was ſixe hundred and threeſcore and fifteene. 38 And the beeues were thirtie and ſixe thouſand, of which the Lords tribute was threeſcore and twelue. 39 And the aſſes were thirtie thouſand and fiue hundred, of which the Lords tribute was threeſcore and one. 40 And the perſons were ſixteene thouſand, of which the Lords tribute was thirtie and two perſons. 41 And Moſes gaue the tribute which was the Lords heaue offering, vnto Eleazar the Prieſt, as the Lord commanded Moſes. 42 And of the children of Iſraels halfe, which Moſes diuided from the men that warred: 43 (Now the halfe that perteined vnto the Congregation, was three hundred thouſand, and thirtie thouſand, and ſeuen thouſand, and fiue hundred ſheepe: 44 And thirtie and ſixe thouſand beeues: 45 And thirtie thouſand aſſes, and fiue hundred: 46 And ſixteene thouſand perſonſ) 47 Euen of the children of Iſraels halfe, Moſes tooke one portion of fiftie, both of man and of beaſt, and gaue them vnto the Leuites, which kept the charge of the Tabernacle of the Lord, as the Lord commanded Moſes. 48 And the officers which were ouer thouſands of the hoſte, the captaines of thouſands, and captaines of hundreds came neere vnto Moſes. 49 And they ſaid vnto Moſes, Thy ſeruants haue taken the ſumme of the men of warre which are vnder our charge, and there lacketh not one man of vs. 50 Wee haue therefore brought an oblation for the Lord, what euerie man hath gotten, of iewels of golde chaines, and bracelets, rings, earerings, and tablets, to make an atonement for our ſoules before the Lord. 51 And Moſes and Eleazar the Prieſt tooke the gold of them: euen all wrought iewels. 52 And all the gold of the offring that they offered vp to the Lord, of the captaines of thouſands, and of the captaines of hundreds, was ſixteene thouſand, ſeuen hundred and fiftie ſhekels. 53 (For the men of warre had taken ſpoile, euery man for himſelfe.) 54 And Moſes and Eleazar the Prieſt tooke the gold of the captaines, of thouſands, and of hundreds, and brought it into the Tabernacle of the Congregation, for a memoriall for the children of Iſrael before the Lord.

CHAPTER 32 1 Now the children of Reuben, and the children of Gad, had a very great multitude of cattell: and when they ſaw the land of Iazer, and the land of Gilead, that behold, the place was a place for cattell; 2 The children of Gad, and the children of Reuben, came and ſpake vnto Moſes, and to Eleazar the Prieſt, and vnto the Princes of the Congregation, ſaying, 3 Ataroth, and Dibon, and Iazer, and Nimrah, and Heſhbon, and Elealeh, and Shebam, and Nebo, and Beon, 4 Euen the countrey which the Lord ſmote before the Congregation of Iſrael, is a land for cattell, and thy ſeruants haue cattell. 5 Wherefore, ſaid they, if wee haue found grace in thy ſight, let this lande be giuen vnto thy ſeruants for a poſſeſſion, and bring vs not ouer Iordane. 6 And Moſes ſaid vnto the children of Gad, and to the children of Reuben, Shall your brethren goe to warre, and ſhall ye ſit here? 7 And wherefore diſcourage yee the heart of the children of Iſrael from going ouer into the lande, which the Lord hath giuen them? 8 Thus did your fathers, when I ſent them from Kadeſh Barnea to ſee the land. 9 For when they went vp vnto the valley of Eſhcol, and ſaw the land, they diſcouraged the heart of the children of Iſrael, that they ſhould not goe into the land which the Lord had giuen them. 10 And the Lords anger was kindled the ſame time, and hee ſware, ſaying, 11 Surely none of the men that came vp out of Egypt, from twentie yeeres old and vpward, ſhall ſee the lande which I ſware vnto Abraham, vnto Iſaac, and vnto Iacob, becauſe they haue not wholly followed me: 12 Saue Caleb the ſonne of Iephunneh the Kenezite, and Ioſhua the ſonne of Nun: for they haue wholly followed the Lord. 13 And the Lords anger was kindled againſt Iſrael, and hee made them wander in the wilderneſſe fourty yeeres, vntill all the generation that had done euill in the ſight of the Lord was conſumed. 14 And beholde, ye are riſen vp in your fathers ſtead, an increaſe of ſinfull men, to augment yet the fierce anger of the Lord toward Iſrael. 15 For if yee turne away from after him, hee will yet againe leaue them in the wilderneſſe, and ye ſhall deſtroy all this people. 16 And they came neere vnto him, and ſaid, Wee will build ſheepfoldes here for our cattell, and cities for our litle ones. 17 But we ourſelues will goe ready armed before the children of Iſrael, vntill wee haue brought them vnto their place: and our litle ones ſhall dwell in the fenced cities, becauſe of the inhabitants of the land. 18 Wee will not returne vnto our houſes, vntill the children of Iſrael haue inherited euery man his inheritance: 19 For wee will not inherite with them on yonder ſide Iordane, or forward, becauſe our inheritance is fallen to vs on this ſide Iordane Eaſtward. 20 And Moſes ſaid vnto them, If ye will doe this thing, if ye will goe armed before the Lord to warre, 21 And will goe all of you armed ouer Iordane before the Lord, vntill he hath driuen out his enemies from before him, 22 And the land bee ſubdued before the Lord: then afterward ye ſhall returne, and bee guiltleſſe before the Lord, and before Iſrael; and this land ſhall be your poſſeſſion before the Lord. 23 But if ye will not doe ſo, behold, yee haue ſinned againſt the Lord: and bee ſure your ſinne will finde you out. 24 Build ye cities for your litle ones, and folds for your ſheepe, and doe that which hath proceeded out of your mouth. 25 And the children of Gad, and the children of Reuben ſpake vnto Moſes, ſaying, Thy ſeruants will doe as my lord commandeth. 26 Our little ones, our wiues, our flocks, and all our cattell ſhall be there in the cities of Gilead. 27 But thy ſeruants will paſſe ouer, euery man armed for warre, before the Lord to battell, as my lord ſaith. 28 So concerning them Moſes commaunded Eleazar the Prieſt, and Ioſhua the ſonne of Nun, and the chiefe fathers of the tribes of the children of Iſrael: 29 And Moſes ſaid vnto them, If the children of Gad, and the children of Reuben will paſſe with you ouer Iordane, euery man armed to battell before the Lord, and the land ſhall be ſubdued before you, then ye ſhall giue them the land of Gilead for a poſſeſſion: 30 But if they will not paſſe ouer with you armed, they ſhall haue poſſeſſions among you in the land of Canaan. 31 And the children of Gad, and the children of Reuben anſwered, ſaying, As the Lord hath ſaid vnto thy ſeruants, ſo will we doe. 32 Wee will paſſe ouer armed before the Lord into the land of Canaan, that the poſſeſſion of our inheritance on this ſide Iordane may be ours. 33 And Moſes gaue vnto them, euen to the children of Gad, and to the children of Reuben; and vnto halfe the tribe of Manaſſeh the ſonne of Ioſeph, the kingdome of Sihon King of the Amorites, and the kingdome of Og King of Baſhan, the land with the cities thereof, in the coaſtes, euen the cities of the countrey round about. 34 And the children of Gad built Dibon, and Ataroth, and Aroer, 35 And Atroth, Shophan, and Iaazer, and Iogbehah, 36 And Bethnimrah, and Bethharan, fenced cities: and foldes for ſheepe. 37 And the children of Reuben built Heſhbon, and Elealeh, and Kiriathaim, 38 And Nebo, and Baalmeon (their names being changed) and Shibmah: and gaue other names vnto the cities which they builded. 39 And the children of Machir, the ſonne of Manaſſeh, went to Gilead, and tooke it, and diſpoſſeſſed the Amorite which was in it. 40 And Moſes gaue Gilead vnto Machir the ſonne of Manaſſeh, and he dwelt therein. 41 And Iair the ſonne of Manaſſeh went and tooke the ſmall townes thereof, and called them Hauoth-Iair. 42 And Nobah went and tooke Kenath, and the villages thereof, and called it Nobah, after his owne name.

CHAPTER 33 1 Theſe are the iourneyes of the children of Iſrael, which went foorth out of the land of Egypt, with their armies, vnder the hand of Moſes and Aaron. 2 And Moſes wrote their goings out according to their iourneyes, by the commandement of the Lord: and theſe are their iourneyes according to their goings out. 3 And they departed from Rameſes in the firſt moneth, on the fifteenth day of the firſt moneth: on the morrow after the Paſſeouer, the children of Iſrael went out with an high hand in the ſight of all the Egyptians. 4 (For the Egyptians buried all their firſt borne, which the Lord had ſmitten among them: vpon their gods alſo the Lord executed iudgements.) 5 And the children of Iſrael remoued from Rameſes, and pitched in Succoth. 6 And they departed from Succoth, and pitched in Etham, which is in the edge of the wilderneſſe.7And they remoued from Etham, and turned againe vnto Pihahiroth, which is before Baal-zephon: and they pitched before Migdol.8And they departed from before Pihahiroth, and paſſed thorow the midſt of the ſea, into the wildernes, and went three dayes iourney in the wilderneſſe of Etham, and pitched in Marah.9And they remoued from Marah, and came vnto Elim, and in Elim were twelue fountaines of water, and three ſcore and ten palme trees, and they pitched there.10And they remooued from Elim, and encamped by the red ſea.11And they remooued from the red ſea, and encamped in the wilderneſſe of Sin.12And they tooke their iourney out of the wilderneſſe of Sin, and encamped in Dophkah.13And they departed from Dophkah, and encamped in Aluſh.14And they remoued from Aluſh, and encamped at Rephidim, where was no water for the people to drinke.15And they departed from Rephidim, and pitched in the wilderneſſe of Sinai.16And they remoued from the deſert of Sinai, and pitched at Kibroth Hattaauah.17And they departed from Kibroth Hattaauah, and encamped at Hazeroth.18And they departed from Hazeroth, and pitched in Rithmah.19And they departed from Rithmah, and pitched at Rimmon Parez.20And they departed from Rimmon Parez, and pitched in Libnah.21And they remoued from Libnah, and pitched at Riſſah.22And they iourneyed from Riſſah, and pitched in Kehelathah.23And they went from Kehelathah, and pitched in mount Shapher.24And they remoued from mount Shapher, and encamped in Haradah.25And they remooued from Haradah, and pitched in Makheloth.26And they remooued from Makheloth, and encamped at Tahath.27And they departed from Tahath, and pitched at Tarah.28And they remoued from Tarah, and pitched in Mithcah.29And they went from Mithcah, and pitched in Haſhmonah.30And they departed from Haſhmonah, and encamped at Moſeroth.31And they departed from Moſeroth, and pitched in Bene-Iaakan.32And they remooued from Bene-Iaakan, & encamped at Horhagidgad.33And they went from Horhagidgad, and pitched in Iotbathah.34And they remooued from Iotbathah, and encamped at Ebronah.35And they departed from Ebronah, and encamped at Ezion-gaber.36And they remoued from Ezion-gaber, and pitched in the wildernes of Zin, which is Kadeſh.37And they remooued from Kadeſh, and pitched in mount Hor, in the edge of the land of Edom.38And Aaron the Prieſt went vp into mount Hor, at the commandement of the Lord, and died there in the fourtieth yeere, after the children of Iſrael were come out of the lande of Egypt, in the firſt day of the fift moneth.39And Aaron was an hundred and twentie and three yeeres old, when hee died in mount Hor.40And King Arad the Canaanite (which dwelt in the South, in the land of Canaan) heard of the comming of the children of Iſrael.41And they departed from mount Hor, and pitched in Zalmonah.42And they departed from Zalmonah, and pitched in Punon.43And they departed from Punon, and pitched in Oboth.44And they departed from Oboth, and pitched in Iie-Abarim, in the border of Moab.45And they departed from Iim, and pitched in Dibon Gad.46And they remoued from Dibon Gad, and encamped in Almon-Diblathaim.47And they remooued from Almon-Diblathaim, and pitched in the mountaines of Abarim, before Nebo.48And they departed from the mountaines of Abarim, and pitched in the plaines of Moab, by Iordan neere Iericho.49And they pitched by Iordane from Beth-Ieſimoth, euen vnto Abel Shittim, in the plaines of Moab.50And the Lord ſpake vnto Moſes, in the plaines of Moab by Iordane, neere Iericho, ſaying,51Speake vnto the children of Iſrael, and ſay vnto them, When ye are paſſed ouer Iordane into the land of Canaan;52Then ye ſhall driue out all the inhabitants of the land from before you, and deſtroy all their pictures, and deſtroy all their molten images, and quite plucke downe all their high places.53And ye ſhall diſpoſſeſſe the inhabitants of the land, and dwell therein: for I haue giuen you the land to poſſeſſe it.54And ye ſhall diuide the land by lot, for an inheritance among your families, and to the moe ye ſhall giue the more inheritance, and to the fewer yee ſhall giue the leſſe inheritance: euery mans inheritance ſhall bee in the place where his lot falleth, according to the tribes of your fathers, ye ſhall inherite.55But if ye will not driue out the inhabitants of the land from before you, then it ſhall come to paſſe that thoſe which ye let remaine of them, ſhall be prickes in your eyes, and thornes in your ſides, and ſhal vexe you in the land wherein ye dwell.56Moreouer, it ſhall come to paſſe, that I ſhall do vnto you, as I thought to doe vnto them.

CHAPTER 341And the Lord ſpake vnto Moſes, ſaying,2Command the children of Iſrael, and ſay vnto them, When ye come into the land of Canaan, (this is the land that ſhall fall vnto you for an inheritance, euen the land of Canaan, with the coaſts thereof.)3Then your South quarter ſhall be from the wilderneſſe of Zin, along by the coaſt of Edom, and your South border ſhall be the outmoſt coaſt of the ſalt ſea Eaſtward.4And your border ſhal turne from the South to the aſcent of Akrabbim, and paſſe on to Zin: and the going foorth thereof ſhall be from the South to Kadeſh-Barnea, and ſhall goe on to Hazar-Addar, and paſſe on to Azmon.5And the border ſhall fetch a comcompaſſe from Azmon vnto the riuer of Egypt, and the goings out of it ſhall be at the ſea.6And as for the Weſterne border, you ſhall euen haue the great ſea for a border: this ſhall be your Weſt border.7And this ſhall be your North border: from the great ſea, you ſhall point out for you, mount Hor.8From mount Hor, ye ſhall point out your border vnto the entrance of Hamath: and the goings foorth of the border ſhall be to Zedad.9And the border ſhall goe on to Ziphron, and the goings out of it ſhall bee at Hazar Enan: this ſhall be your North border.10And ye ſhall point out your Eaſt border, from Hazar Enan to Shepham.11And the coaſt ſhall goe downe from Shepham to Riblah, on the Eaſt ſide of Ain: and the border ſhall deſcend and ſhall reach vnto the ſide of the ſea of Chinnereth Eaſtward.12And the border ſhall goe downe to Iordane, and the goings out of it ſhall be at the ſalt ſea: this ſhall be your land with the coaſtes thereof round about.13And Moſes commanded the children of Iſrael, ſaying, This is the land which ye ſhall inherite by lot, which the Lord commanded to giue vnto the nine tribes, and to the halfe tribe.14For the tribe of the children of Reuben, according to the houſe of their fathers, and the tribe of the children of Gad, according to the houſe of their fathers, haue receiued their inheritance, and halfe the tribe of Manaſſeh haue receiued their inheritance.15The two tribes, and the halfe tribe haue receiued their inheritance on this ſide Iordane neere Iericho, Eaſtward, toward the Sunne riſing.16And the Lord ſpake vnto Moſes, ſaying,17Theſe are the names of the men which ſhall diuide the land vnto you: Eleazar the Prieſt, and Ioſhua the ſonne of Nun.18And yee ſhall take one Prince of euery tribe, to diuide the land by inheritance.19And the names of the men are theſe: Of the tribe of Iudah, Caleb the ſonne of Iephunneh.20And of the tribe of the children of Simeon, Shemuel the ſonne of Ammihud.21Of the tribe of Beniamin, Elidad the ſonne of Chiſlon.22And the Prince of the tribe of the children of Dan, Bukki the ſonne of Iogli.23The Prince of the children of Ioſeph: for the tribe of the children of Manaſſeh, Hanniel the ſonne of Ephod.24And the Prince of the tribe of the children of Ephraim, Kemuel the ſonne of Shiphtan.25And the Prince of the tribe of the children of Zebulun, Elizaphan the ſonne of Parnach.26And the Prince of the tribe of the children of Iſſachar, Paltiel the ſonne of Azzan.27And the Prince of the tribe of the children of Aſher, Ahihud the ſonne of Shelomi.28And the Prince of the tribe of the children of Naphtali, Pedahel the ſonne of Ammihud.29Theſe are they whom the Lord commaunded to diuide the inheritance vnto the children of Iſrael in the land of Canaan.

CHAPTER 351And the Lord ſpake vnto Moſes in the plaines of Moab by Iordane, neere Iericho, ſaying,2Command the children of Iſrael, that they giue vnto the Leuites of the inheritance of their poſſeſſion, cities to dwell in: and yee ſhall giue alſo vnto the Leuites ſuburbs for the cities round about them.3And the cities ſhall they haue to dwell in, and the ſuburbs of them ſhall be for their cattell, and for their goods, and for all their beaſts.4And the ſuburbs of the cities, which yee ſhall giue vnto the Leuites, ſhall reach from the wall of the citie, and outward, a thouſand cubites round about.5And ye ſhall meaſure from without the city on the Eaſtſide two thouſand cubites, and on the Southſide two thouſand cubites, and on the Weſtſide two thouſand cubites, & on the Northſide two thouſand cubites: and the citie ſhall be in the midſt; this ſhalbe to them the ſuburbs of the cities.6And among the cities which yee ſhal giue vnto the Leuites, there ſhalbe ſixe cities for refuge, which ye ſhall appoint for the manſlayer, that hee may flee thither: And to them ye ſhall adde fourty and two cities.7So all the cities which ye ſhall giue to the Leuites, ſhall be fourty and eight cities: them ſhall yee giue with their ſuburbs.8And the cities which ye ſhal giue, ſhalbe of the poſſeſſion of

the children of Iſrael: from them that haue many ye ſhall giue many; but
from them that haue few, ye ſhall giue few. Euery one ſhal giue of his
cities vnto the Leuites, according to his inheritance which he
inheriteth.9And the Lord ſpake vnto Moſes, ſaying,10Speake vnto the
children of Iſrael, and ſay vnto them, When ye bee come ouer Iordane,
into the land of Canaan:11Then ye ſhall appoint you cities, to be cities of
refuge for you; that the ſlayer may flee thither which killeth any perſon
at vnawares.12And they ſhall be vnto you cities for refuge from the
auenger, that the man-ſlayer die not, vntill he ſtand before the
Congregation in iudgement.13And of theſe cities which ye ſhall giue, ſixe
cities ſhall ye haue for refuge.14Yee ſhall giue three cities on this ſide
Iordane, and three cities ſhall yee giue in the land of Canaan, which ſhall
be cities of refuge.15Theſe ſixe cities ſhall be a refuge, both for the
children of Iſrael, and for the ſtranger, and for the ſoiourner among
them: that euery one that killeth any perſon vnawares, may flee
thither.16And if he ſmite him with an inſtrument of Iron, (ſo that he
die,) hee is a murderer: the murderer ſhall ſurely be put to death.17And
if he ſmite him with throwing a ſtone, (wherewith hee may die) and he
die, he is a murderer: the murderer ſhall ſurely be put to death.18Or if
he ſmite him with an handweapon of wood, (wherewith he may die) and
he die, hee is a murderer: the murderer ſhall ſurely be put to death.19The
reuenger of blood himſelfe ſhall ſlay the murtherer: when he meeteth
him, he ſhall ſlay him.20But if he thruſt him of hatred, or hurle at him
by laying of waite that he die,21Or in enmitie ſmite him with his hand,
that he die: hee that ſmote him ſhall ſurely be put to death, for hee is a
murderer: the reuenger of blood ſhall ſlay the murderer, when hee
meeteth him.22But if hee thruſt him ſuddenly without enmitie, or haue
caſt vpon him any thing without laying of wait,23Or with any ſtone
wherewith a man may die, ſeeing him not, and caſt it vpon him, that he
die, and was not his enemie, neither ſought his harme:24Then the
Congregation ſhall iudge betweene the ſlayer, and the reuenger of blood,
according to theſe iudgements.25And the Congregation ſhall deliuer the
ſlayer out of the hand of the reuenger of blood, and the Congregation
ſhal reſtore him to the city of his refuge, whither he was fled: and he
ſhall abide in it vnto the death of the high Prieſt, which was annoynted
with the holy oyle.26But if the ſlayer ſhall at any time come without the
border of the citie of his refuge, whither he was fled:27And the reuenger
of blood finde him without the borders of the citie of his refuge, and
the reuenger of blood kill the ſlayer, he ſhall not be guiltie of
blood:28Becauſe he ſhould haue remained in the citie of his refuge, vntill
the death of the high Prieſt: but after the death of the hie Prieſt, the
ſlayer ſhal returne into the land of his poſſeſſion.29So theſe things ſhall
be for a ſtatute of iudgment vnto you, thorowout your generations in al
your dwellings.30Who ſo killeth any perſon, the murderer ſhall be put to
death, by the mouth of witneſſes: but one witneſſe ſhall not teſtifie
againſt any perſon, to cauſe him to die.31Moreouer, yee ſhall take no
ſatiſfaction for the life of a murderer, which is guiltie of death, but he
ſhalbe ſurely put to death.32And yee ſhall take no ſatiſfaction for him
that is fled to the citie of his refuge, that hee ſhould come againe to dwell
in the land, vntil the death of the Prieſt.33So ye ſhall not pollute the lande
wherein ye are: for blood, it defileth the land: and the land cannot bee
cleanſed of the blood that is ſhed therein, but by the blood of him that
ſhed it.34Defile not therefore the lande which yee ſhall inhabite, wherein
I dwell: for I the Lord dwell among the children of Iſrael.
CHAPTER 361And the chiefe fathers of the families of the children of
Gilead, the ſonne of Machir, the ſonne of Manaſſeh, of the families of
the ſonnes of Ioſeph, came neere, and ſpake before Moſes, and before
the Princes the chiefe fathers of the children of Iſrael.2And they ſaid,
The Lord commanded my lord to giue the lande for an inheritance by
lot to the children of Iſrael: and my lord was commanded by the Lord,
to giue the inheritance of Zelophehad our brother, vnto his
daughters.3And if they bee married to any of the ſonnes of the other
tribes of the children of Iſrael, then ſhall their inheritance be taken from
the inheritance of our fathers, and ſhall bee put to the inheritance of the
tribe, whereinto they are receiued: ſo ſhal it be taken from the lot of our
inheritance.4And when the Iubile of the children of Iſrael ſhall be, then
ſhall their inheritance be put vnto the inheritance of the tribe, whereunto
they are receiued: So ſhal their inheritance be taken away from the
inheritance of the tribe of our fathers.5And Moſes commanded the
children of Iſrael, according to the worde of the Lord, ſaying, The tribe
of the ſonnes of Ioſeph hath ſaid well.6This is the thing which the Lord
doeth command concerning the daughters of Zelophehad, ſaying, Let
them marry to whom they thinke beſt: onely to the family of the tribe
of their father ſhall they marry.7So ſhall not the inheritance of the
children of Iſrael remooue from tribe to tribe: for euery one of the
children of Iſrael ſhall keepe himſelfe to the inheritance of the tribe of
his fathers.8And euery daughter that poſſeſſeth an inheritance, in any
tribe of the children of Iſrael, ſhall be wife vnto one of the family of the
tribe of her father, that the children of Iſrael may enioy euery man the
inheritance of his fathers.9Neither ſhall the inheritance remoue from
one tribe to another tribe: but euery one of the tribes of the children of
Iſrael, ſhall keepe himſelfe to his owne inheritance.10Euen as the Lord
commanded Moſes, ſo did the daughters of Zelophehad.11For Mahlah,
Tirzah, and Hoglah, and Milcah, and Noah the daughters of
Zelophehad, were married vnto their fathers brothers ſonnes.12And they
were married into the families of the ſonnes of Manaſſeh, the ſonne of
Ioſeph, and their inheritance remained in the tribe of the family of their
father.13Theſe are the commandements and the iudgements which the
Lord commanded by the hand of Moſes, vnto the children of Iſrael in
the plaines of Moab, by Iordane, neere Iericho.

DEUTERONOMIE (DEUTERONOMY)

CHAPTER 11Theſe bee the woordes which Moſes ſpake vnto all Iſrael,
on this ſide Iordane in the wildernes, in the plaine ouer againſt the Red
ſea, betweene Paran, and Tophel, and Laban, and Hazeroth, and
Dizahab.2(There are eleuen daies iourney from Horeb, by the way of
mount Seir, vnto Kadeſh Barnea.)3And it came to paſſe in the fourtieth
yeere, in the eleuenth moneth, on the firſt day of the moneth, that Moſes
ſpake vnto the children of Iſrael, according vnto all that the Lord had
giuen him in commandement vnto them:4After hee had ſlaine Sihon the
King of the Amorites, which dwelt in Heſhbon, and Og the King of
Baſhan, which dwelt at Aſtaroth, in Edrei.5On this ſide Iordane, in the
land of Moab, began Moſes to declare this law, ſaying,6The Lord our
God ſpake vnto vs in Horeb, ſaying, Ye haue dwelt long ynough in this
mount:7Turne you, and take your iourney, and goe to the mount of the
Amorites, and vnto all the places nigh thereunto, in the plaine, in the
hills, and in the vale, and in the South, and by the ſea ſide, to the land of
the Canaanites, and vnto Lebanon, vnto the great riuer, the riuer
Euphrates.8Behold, I haue ſet the land before you: Goe in, and poſſeſſe
the land, which the Lord ſware vnto your fathers, Abraham, Iſaac, and
Iacob, to giue vnto them, and to their ſeed after them.9And I ſpake vnto
you at that time, ſaying, I am not able to beare you my ſelfe alone:10The
Lord your God hath multiplied you, and beholde, you are this day as the
ſtarres of heauen for multitude.11(The Lord God of your fathers make
you a thouſand times ſo many moe as ye are, and bleſſe you as he hath
promiſed you.)12How can I my ſelfe alone beare your cumbrance, and
your burden, and your ſtrife?13Take ye wiſe men, and vnderſtanding, and
knowen among your tribes, and I will make them rulers ouer you.14And
ye anſwered me, and ſaide, The thing which thou haſt ſpoken, is good
for vs to doe.15So I tooke the chiefe of your tribes, wiſe men, and
knowen, and made them heads ouer you, captaines ouer thouſands, and
captaines ouer hundreds, and captaines ouer fifties, and captaines ouer
tennes, and officers among your tribes.16And I charged your Iudges at
that time, ſaying, Heare the cauſes betweene your brethren, and iudge
righteouſly betweene euery man and his brother, & the ſtranger that is
with him.17Ye ſhall not reſpect perſons in iudgement, but you ſhall heare
the ſmall aſwell as the great: you ſhall not bee afraid of the face of man,
for the iudgment is Gods: and the cauſe that is too hard for you, bring
it vnto me, and I will heare it.18And I commanded you at that time all
the things which ye ſhould doe.19And when wee departed from Horeb,
we went through all that great and terrible wildernes, which you ſaw by
the way of the mountaine of the Amorites, as the Lord our God
commanded vs: and wee came to Kadeſh Barnea.20And I ſaid vnto you,
Ye are come vnto the mountaine of the Amorites, which the Lord our
God doth giue vnto vs.21Behold, the Lord thy God hath ſet the land
before thee: Goe vp, and poſſeſſe it, as the Lord God of thy fathers hath
ſaid vnto thee: Feare not, neither be diſcouraged.22And ye came neere

vnto mee euery one of you, and ſaid, We will ſend men before vs, and
they ſhall ſearch vs out the land, and bring vs word againe, by what way
we muſt goe vp, and into what cities we ſhall come.23And the ſaying
pleaſed mee well: and I tooke twelue men of you, one of a tribe.24And
they turned and went vp into the mountaine, and came vnto the valley
of Eſhcol, and ſearched it out.25And they tooke of the fruit of the land
in their handes, and brought it downe vnto vs, and brought vs worde
againe, and ſaid, It is a good lande which the Lord our God doeth giue
vs.26Notwithſtanding, ye would not goe vp, but rebelled againſt the
commandement of the Lord your God.27And ye murmured in your
tents and ſaid, Becauſe the Lord hated vs, he hath brought vs forth out
of the land of Egypt, to deliuer vs into the hand of the Amorites, to
deſtroy vs:28Whither ſhall wee goe vp? our brethren haue diſcouraged
our heart, ſaying, The people is greater and taller then we, the cities are
great, and walled vp to heauen, and moreouer we haue ſeene the ſonnes
of the Anakims there.29Then I ſaid vnto you, Dread not, neither be
afraid of them.30The Lord your God which goeth before you, he ſhall
fight for you, according to all that hee did for you in Egypt before your
eyes:31And in the wildernes, where thou haſt ſeene how that the Lord
thy God bare thee, as a man doth beare his ſonne, in all the way that ye
went, vntil ye came into this place.32Yet in this thing ye did not beleeue
the Lord your God,33Who went in the way before you to ſearch you out
a place to pitch your tents in, in fire by night, to ſhew you by what way
ye ſhould goe, and in a cloud by day.34And the Lord heard the voice of
your words, and was wroth, and ſware, ſaying,35Surely there ſhall not
one of theſe men of this euill generation ſee that good land, which I
ſware to giue vnto your fathers:36Saue Caleb the ſonne of Iephunneh,
he ſhall ſee it, and to him will I giue the land that he hath troden vpon,
and to his children, becauſe hee hath wholly followed the Lord.37Alſo
the Lord was angry with me for your ſakes, ſaying, Thou alſo ſhalt not
goe in thither.38But Ioſhua the ſonne of Nun, which ſtandeth before
thee, he ſhall goe in thither. Encourage him: for he ſhall cauſe Iſrael to
inherite it.39Moreouer, your litle ones, which ye ſaid ſhould be a pray,
and your children, which in that day had no knowledge betweene good
and euil, they ſhall goe in thither; and vnto them will I giue it, and they
ſhall poſſeſſe it.40But as for you, turne ye, and take your iourney into
the wilderneſſe, by the way of the Red ſea.41Then ye anſwered, and ſaid
vnto mee, Wee haue ſinned againſt the Lord, we will goe vp and fight,
according to all that the Lord our God commanded vs. And when ye
had girded on euery man his weapons of warre, yee were ready to goe
vp into the hill.42And the Lord ſaid vnto me, ſay vnto them, Goe not
vp, neither fight, for I am not among you: leaſt ye be ſmitten before your
enemies.43So I ſpake vnto you, and you would not heare, but rebelled
againſt the commandement of the Lord, and went preſumptuouſly vp
into the hill.44And the Amorites which dwelt in that mountaine, came
out againſt you, and chaſed you, as Bees doe, and deſtroyed you in Seir,
euen vnto Hormah.45And ye returned and wept before the Lord; but
the Lord would not hearken to your voyce, nor giue eare vnto you.46So
yee abode in Kadeſh many dayes, according vnto the dayes that ye abode
there.
CHAPTER 21Then we turned, and tooke our iourney into the
wilderneſſe, by the way of the Red ſea, as the Lord ſpake vnto mee: and
wee compaſſed mount Seir many dayes.2And the Lord ſpake vnto me,
ſaying,3Yee haue compaſſed this mountaine long enough: turne you
Northward.4And commaund thou the people, ſaying, Ye are to paſſe
through the coaſt of your brethren the children of Eſau, which dwell in
Seir, and they ſhall be afraid of you: take ye good heed vnto your ſelues
therefore.5Meddle not with them, for I will not giue you of their land,
no not ſo much as a foote breadth, becauſe I haue giuen mount Seir
vnto Eſau for a poſſeſſion.6Ye ſhall buy meat of them for money, that
ye may eat, and yee ſhall alſo buy water of them for money, that yee may
drinke.7For the Lord thy God hath bleſſed thee, in all the workes of thy
hand: hee knoweth thy walking thorow this great wilderneſſe: theſe
fourtie yeres the Lord thy God hath bene with thee, thou haſt lacked
nothing.8And when we paſſed by from our brethren the children of
Eſau, which dwelt in Seir, thorow the way of the plaine from Elath, and
from Ezion-Gaber, wee turned and paſſed by the way of the wilderneſſe
of Moab.9And the Lord ſaid vnto mee, Diſtreſſe not the Moabites,
neither contend with them in battell: for I wil not giue thee of their land
for a poſſeſſion, becauſe I haue giuen Ar vnto the children of Lot for a
poſſeſſion.10The Emims dwelt therein in times paſt, a people great, and
many, and tall, as the Anakims:11Which alſo were accounted giants, as
the Anakims, but the Moabites call them Emims.12The Horims alſo
dwelt in Seir beforetime, but the children of Eſau ſucceeded them when
they had deſtroyed them from before them, & dwelt in their ſtead, as
Iſrael did vnto the land of his poſſeſſion, which the Lord gaue vnto
them.13Now riſe vp, ſaid I, and get you ouer the brooke Zered: and we
went ouer the brooke Zered.14And the ſpace in which we came from
Kadeſh Barnea, vntill we were come ouer the brooke Zered, was thirtie
and eight yeeres; vntill all the generation of the men of warre were
waſted out from among the hoſte, as the Lord ſware vnto them.15For
indeed the hand of the Lord was againſt them, to deſtroy them from
among the hoſte, vntill they were conſumed.16So it came to paſſe, when
all the men of warre were conſumed and dead from among the
people,17That the Lord ſpake vnto me, ſaying,18Thou art to paſſe ouer
thorow Ar, the coaſt of Moab, this day.19And when thou commeſt nigh
ouer againſt the children of Ammon, diſtreſſe them not, nor meddle
with them: for I will not giue thee of the lande of the children of Ammon
any poſſeſſion, becauſe I haue giuen it vnto the children of Lot for a
poſſeſſion:20(That alſo was accounted a land of Giants: giants dwelt
therein in old time, and the Ammonites call them Zamzummims.21A
people great, and many, and tall, as the Anakims: but the Lord deſtroyed
them before them, and they ſucceeded them & dwelt in their ſtead:)22As
he did to the children of Eſau which dwelt in Seir, when he deſtroyed
the Horims from before them, and they ſucceeded them, and dwelt in
their ſtead euen vnto this day.23And the Auims which dwelt in Hazerim,
euen vnto Azzah, the Caphtorims which came foorth out of Caphtor,
deſtroyed them, and dwelt in their ſtead.24Riſe ye vp, take your iourney,
and paſſe ouer the riuer Arnon: Behold, I haue giuen into thy hand
Sihon the Amorite king of Heſhbon, and his land: begin to poſſeſſe it,
and contend with him in battell.25This day will I begin to put the dread
of thee, and the feare of thee vpon the nations, that are vnder the whole
heauen, who ſhall heare report of thee, and ſhall tremble, and be in
anguiſh becauſe of thee.26And I ſent meſſengers out of the wilderneſſe
of Kedemoth, vnto Sihon king of Heſhbon, with wordes of peace,
ſaying,27Let me paſſe through thy land: I will goe along by the high way,
I will neither turne vnto the right hand, nor to the left.28Thou ſhalt ſell
me meat for money, that I may eate, and giue me water for money that
I may drinke: Only I will paſſe through on my feet:29As the children of
Eſau which dwell in Seir, and the Moabites which dwell in Ar, did vnto
me, vntill I ſhall paſſe ouer Iordan, into the land which the Lord our
God giueth vs.30But Sihon King of Heſhbon would not let vs paſſe by
him: for the Lord thy God hardened his ſpirit, and made his heart
obſtinate, that hee might deliuer him into thy hand, as appeareth this
day.31And the Lord ſaid vnto mee, Behold, I haue begun to giue Sihon
and his land before thee: begin to poſſeſſe, that thou mayeſt inherit his
land.32Then Sihon came out againſt vs, he & all his people to fight at
Iahaz.33And the Lord our God deliuered him before vs, and wee ſmote
him, and his ſonnes, and all his people.34And we tooke all his cities at
that time, and vtterly deſtroyed the men, and the women, and the litle
ones of euery citie, we left none to remaine:35Onely the cattell wee tooke
for a pray vnto our ſelues, and the ſpoyle of the cities, which we
tooke:36From Aroer, which is by the brinke of the riuer of Arnon, and
from the citie that is by the riuer euen vnto Gilead, there was not one
citie too ſtrong for vs: the Lord our God deliuered all vnto vs.37Onely
vnto the land of the children of Ammon thou cameſt not, nor vnto any
place of the riuer Iabbok, nor vnto the cities in the mountaines, nor vnto
whatſoeuer the Lord our God forbade vs.
CHAPTER 31Then we turned, and went vp the way to Baſhan: and Og
the King of Baſhan came out againſt vs, hee, and all his people to battell
at Edrei.2And the Lord ſaid vnto mee, Feare him not: for I will deliuer
him, and all his people, and his land into thy hand, and thou ſhalt doe
vnto him as thou didſt vnto Sihon king of the Amorites, which dwelt at
Heſhbon.3So the Lord our God deliuered into our hands Og alſo the
King of Baſhan, and all his people: and wee ſmote him vntill none was
left to him remayning.4And we tooke all his cities at that time, there was
not a citie which wee tooke not from them; threeſcore cities, all the
region of Argob, the kingdome of Og in Baſhan.5All theſe cities were
fenced with high walles, gates and barres, beſide vnwalled townes a great
many.6And we vtterly deſtroyed them, as we did vnto Sihon King of

Heſhbon, vtterly deſtroying the men, women, and children of euery citie.7But all the cattell, and the ſpoile of the cities, we tooke for a pray to our ſelues.8And we tooke at that time out of the hand of the two Kings of the Amorites, the land that was on this ſide Iordan, from the riuer of Arnon, vnto mount Hermon:9(Which Hermon the Sidonians call Syrion: and the Amorites call it Shenir.)10All the cities of the plaine, and all Gilead, and all Baſhan, vnto Salchah, and Edrei, cities of the kingdome of Og in Baſhan.11For onely Og King of Baſhan remained of the remnant of giants; behold, his bedſted was a bedſted of yron: is it not in Rabbath of the children of Ammon? Nine cubites was the length thereof, and foure cubites the breadth of it, after the cubite of a man.12And this land which we poſſeſſed at that time, from Aroer which is by the riuer Arnon, and halfe mount Gilead, and the cities thereof, gaue I vnto the Reubenites, and to the Gadites.13And the reſt of Gilead, and all Baſhan, being the kingdome of Og, gaue I vnto the halfe tribe of Manaſſeh: All the region of Argob with all Baſhan, which was called the land of Giants.14Iair the ſonne of Manaſſeh tooke all the countrey of Argob, vnto the coaſtes of Geſhuri, and Maachathi; and called them after his owne name, Baſhan Hauoth Iair, vnto this day.15And I gaue Gilead vnto Machir.16And vnto the Reubenites, and vnto the Gadites, I gaue from Gilead, euen vnto the riuer Arnon, halfe the valley, and the border, euen vnto the riuer Iabbok, which is the border of the children of Ammon:17The plaine alſo, and Iordan, and the coaſt thereof, from Chinnereth, euen vnto the ſea of the plaine, euen the ſalt ſea, vnder Aſhdoth Piſgah Eaſtward.18And I commanded you at that time, ſaying, The Lord your God hath giuen you this land to poſſeſſe it: ye ſhall paſſe ouer armed before your brethren the children of Iſrael, all that are meet for the warre.19But your wiues, and your little ones, and your cattell (for I know that ye haue much cattel) ſhall abide in your cities, which I haue giuen you:20Untill the Lord haue giuen reſt vnto your brethren, as well as vnto you, and vntill they alſo poſſeſſe the land which the Lord your God hath giuen them beyond Iordan: and then ſhall ye returne euery man vnto his poſſeſſion, which I haue giuen you.21And I commanded Ioſhua at that time, ſaying, Thine eyes haue ſeene all that the Lord your God hath done vnto theſe two Kings: ſo ſhal the Lord doe vnto all the kingdomes whither thou paſſeſt.22Ye ſhall not feare them: for the Lord your God, he ſhal fight for you.23And I beſought the Lord at that time, ſaying,24O Lord God, thou haſt begun to ſhew thy ſeruant thy greatneſse, and thy mighty hand: for what God is there in heauen, or in earth, that can do according to thy workes, and according to thy might?25I pray thee let me goe ouer, and ſee the good land that is beyond Iordan, that goodly mountaine and Lebanon.26But the Lord was wroth with me for your ſakes, and would not heare mee: and the Lord ſaid vnto me, Let it ſuffice thee, ſpeake no more vnto me of this matter.27Get thee vp into the top of Piſgah, and lift vp thine eyes Weſtward, and Northward, and Southward, and Eaſtward, and beholde it with thine eyes: for thou ſhalt not goe ouer this Iordan.28But charge Ioſhua, and encourage him, and ſtrengthen him: for hee ſhall goe ouer before this people, and he ſhall cauſe them to inherite the land which thou ſhalt ſee.29So we abode in the valley, ouer againſt Beth-Peor.

CHAPTER 41Nowe therefore hearken, O Iſrael, vnto the Statutes, and vnto the Iudgments which I teach you, for to do them, that ye may liue, and goe in and poſſeſſe the lande, which the Lord God of your fathers giueth you.2Ye ſhall not adde vnto the word which I command you, neither ſhall you diminiſh ought from it, that ye may keepe the Commaundements of the Lord your God, which I command you.3Your eyes haue ſeene what the Lord did becauſe of Baal Peor: for all the men that followed Baal Peor, the Lord thy God hath deſtroyed them from among you.4But yee that did cleaue vnto the Lord your God, are aliue euery one of you this day.5Behold, I haue taught you Statutes, and Iudgements, euen as the Lord my God commanded me, that ye ſhould do ſo, in the land whither ye goe to poſſeſſe it.6Keepe therefore, and doe them; for this is your wiſedome and your vnderſtanding in the ſight of the nations, which ſhall heare all theſe ſtatutes, and ſay, Surely this great nation is a wiſe and vnderſtanding people.7For what nation is there ſo great, who hath God ſo nigh vnto them, as the Lord our God is in all things, that we call vpon him for?8And what nation is there ſo great, that hath Statutes and Iudgements ſo righteous, as all this Law which I ſet before you this day?9Onely take heed to thy ſelfe, and keepe thy ſoule diligently, leſt thou forget the things which thine eyes haue ſeene, and leſt they depart from thy heart all the dayes of thy life: but teach them thy ſonnes, & thy ſonnes ſonnes:10Specially, the day that thou ſtoodſt before the Lord thy God in Horeb, when the Lord ſaid vnto mee, Gather me the people together, and I will make them heare my wordes, that they may learne to feare mee all the dayes that they ſhall liue vpon the earth, and that they may teach their children.11And ye came neere and ſtood vnder the mountaine, and the mountaine burnt with fire vnto the midſt of heauen, with darkenes, cloudes, and thicke darkeneſſe.12And the Lord ſpake vnto you out of the midſt of the fire: ye heard the voyce of the words, but ſaw no ſimilitude, onely ye heard a voyce.13And he declared vnto you his couenant, which he commanded you to performe, euen ten cōmandements, and he wrote them vpon two tables of ſtone.14And the Lord commanded me at that time, to teach you Statutes, and Iudgements, that yee might doe them in the land whither ye goe ouer to poſſeſſe it.15Take ye therfore good heed vnto your ſelues, (for ye ſaw no maner of ſimilitude on the day that the Lord ſpake vnto you in Horeb, out of the midſt of the fire)16Leſt yee corrupt your ſelues, and make you a grauen image, the ſimilitude of any figure, the likenes of male, or female,17The likeneſſe of any beaſt that is on the earth, the likenes of any winged foule that flieth in the aire,18The likeneſſe of any thing that creepeth on the ground, the likeneſſe of any fiſh that is in the waters beneath the earth:19And leſt thou lift vp thine eyes vnto heauen, and when thou ſeeſt the ſun, and the moone, and the ſtarres, euen all the hoſte of heauen, ſhouldeſt be driuen to worſhip them, and ſerue them, which the Lord thy God hath diuided vnto all nations vnder the whole heauen.20But the Lord hath taken you, and brought you foorth out of the yron fornace, euen out of Egypt, to bee vnto him a people of inheritance, as ye are this day.21Furthermore, the Lord was angry with mee for your ſakes, and ſware that I ſhould not goe ouer Iordan, and that I ſhould not goe in vnto that good land which the Lord thy God giueth thee for an inheritance.22But I muſt die in this lande, I muſt not goe ouer Iordan: but ye ſhall goe ouer and poſſeſſe that good land.23Take heed vnto your ſelues, leſt ye forget the couenant of the Lord your God, which hee made with you, and make you a grauen image, or the likenes of any thing which the Lord thy God hath forbidden thee.24For the Lord thy God is a conſuming fire, euen a iealous God.25When thou ſhalt beget children, and childrens children, and ſhalt haue remained long in the land, and ſhal corrupt your ſelues, & make a grauen image, or the likenes of any thing, and ſhall doe euil in the ſight of the Lord thy God, to prouoke him to anger:26I call heauen and earth to witneſſe againſt you this day, that ye ſhall ſoone vtterly periſh from off the land whereunto you goe ouer Iordan, to poſſeſſe it: yee ſhall not prolong your dayes vpon it, but ſhall vtterly bee deſtroyed.27And the Lord ſhall ſcatter you among the nations, and ye ſhall be left few in number among the heathen, whither the Lord ſhall lead you.28And there ye ſhall ſerue gods, the worke of mens hands, wood and ſtone, which neither ſee, nor heare, nor eate, nor ſmell.29But if from thence thou ſhalt ſeeke the Lord thy God, thou ſhalt finde him, if thou ſeeke him with all thy heart, and with all thy ſoule.30When thou art in tribulation, and all theſe things are come vpon thee, euen in the latter dayes, if thou turne to the Lord thy God, and ſhalt be obedient vnto his voice:31(For the Lord thy God is a mercifull God) he will not forſake thee, neither deſtroy thee, nor forget the couenant of thy fathers, which he ſware vnto them.32For aſke now of the dayes that are paſt, which were before thee, ſince the day that God created man vpon earth, and aſke from the one ſide of heauen vnto the other, whether there hath bene any ſuch thing as this great thing is, or hath bene heard like it?33Did euer people heare the voyce of God ſpeaking out of the midſt of the fire, as thou haſt heard, and liue?34Or hath God aſsayed to goe and take him a nation from the midſt of another nation, by temptations, by ſignes, and by wonders, and by warre, and by a mighty hand, and by a ſtretched out arme, and by great terrors, according to all that the Lord your God did for you in Egypt before your eyes?35Unto thee it was ſhewed, that thou mighteſt know, that the Lord hee is God; there is none elſe beſides him.36Out of heauen hee made thee to heare his voice, that he might inſtruct thee: and vpon earth hee ſhewed thee his great fire, and thou heardeſt his words out of the midſt of the fire.37And becauſe he loued thy fathers, therefore he choſe their ſeed after them, and brought thee out in his ſight with his mightie power out of Egypt:38To driue out nations from before thee, greater and mightier then thou art, to bring thee in, to giue thee their land for an inheritance, as it is this day.39Know therefore this day, & conſider it in thine heart, that the Lord hee is God in heauen aboue, and vpon the earth beneath: there is none elſe.40Thou ſhalt keepe therefore his Statutes, and his Commandements, which I command thee this day; that it may goe well with thee, and with thy children after thee, and that thou mayeſt prolong thy dayes vpon the earth, which the Lord thy God giueth thee, for euer.41Then Moſes ſeuered three cities on this ſide Iordan, toward the Sunne riſing:42That the ſlayer might flee thither, which ſhould kill his neighbour vnawares, and hated him not in times paſt, and that fleeing vnto one of theſe cities he might liue:43Namely, Bezer in the wilderneſſe, in the plaine countrey of the Reubenites; and Ramoth in Gilead of the Gadites; and Golan in Baſhan, of the Manaſsites.44And this is the Law which Moſes ſet before the children of Iſrael:45Theſe are the Teſtimonies, and the Statutes, and the Iudgements, which Moſes ſpake vnto the children of Iſrael, after they came foorth out of Egypt;46On this ſide Iordan in the valley ouer againſt Beth-Peor, in the land of Sihon King of the Amorites, who dwelt at Heſhbon, whom Moſes and the children of Iſrael ſmote, after they were come foorth out of Egypt.47And they poſſeſſed his land, and the land of Og king of Baſhan, two kings of the Amorites, which were on this ſide Iordan toward the ſun riſing,48From Aroer, which is by the banke of the riuer Arnon, euen vnto mount Sion, which is Hermon,49And all the plaine of this ſide Iordan Eaſtward, euen vnto the ſea, of the plaine vnder the ſprings of Piſgah.

CHAPTER 51And Moſes called all Iſrael, and ſayd vnto them, Heare, O Iſrael, the Statutes and Iudgements which I ſpeake in your eares this day, that ye may learne them, and keepe and doe them.2The Lord our God made a couenant with vs in Horeb.3The Lord made not this couenant with our fathers, but with vs: euen vs, who are all of vs here aliue this day.4The Lord talked with you, face to face, in the mount, out of the midſt of the fire,5(I ſtood betweene the Lord and you, at that time, to ſhew you the word of the Lord: for ye were afraid by reaſon of the fire, and went not vp into the mount,) ſaying,6I am the Lord thy God, which brought thee out of the lande of Egypt, from the houſe of bondage.7Thou ſhalt haue none other gods before me.8Thou ſhalt not make thee any grauen image, or any likeneſſe of any thing that is in heauen aboue, or that is in the earth beneath, or that is in the waters beneath the earth.9Thou ſhalt not bow downe thy ſelfe vnto them, nor ſerue them: for I the Lord thy God am a ielous God, viſiting the iniquity of the fathers vpon the children, vnto the third and fourth generation of them that hate me,10And ſhewing mercy vnto thouſands, of them that loue me, and keepe my commandements.11Thou ſhalt not take the name of the Lord thy God in vaine: for the Lord will not holde him guiltleſſe that taketh his name in vaine.12Keepe the Sabbath day to ſanctifie it, as the Lord thy God hath commanded thee.13Sixe dayes thou ſhalt labour, and doe all thy worke.14But the ſeuenth day is the Sabbath of the Lord thy God: in it thou ſhalt not doe any worke, thou, nor thy ſonne, nor thy daughter, nor thy man ſeruant, nor thy maid ſeruant, nor thine oxe, nor thine aſſe, nor any of thy cattel, nor thy ſtranger that is within thy gates, that thy man ſeruant and thy maid ſeruant may reſt as well as thou.15And remember that thou waſt a ſeruant in the land of Egypt, and that the Lord thy God brought thee out thence, through a mightie hand, and by a ſtretched out arme: Therefore the Lord thy God commaunded thee to keepe the Sabbath day.16Honour thy father and thy mother, as the Lord thy God hath commanded thee, that thy daies may be prolonged, and that it may goe well with thee, in the land which the Lord thy God giueth thee.17Thou ſhalt not kill.18Neither ſhalt thou commit adulterie.19Neither ſhalt thou ſteale.20Neither ſhalt thou beare falſe witneſſe againſt thy neighbour.21Neither ſhalt thou deſire thy neighbours wife, neither ſhalt thou couet thy neighbours houſe, his field, or his man ſeruant, or his maide ſeruant, his oxe, or his aſſe, or any thing that is thy neighbours.22Theſe wordes the Lord ſpake vnto all your aſſembly in the mount out of the midſt of the fire, of the cloud, and of the thicke darkeneſſe, with a great voice, and he added no more, and he wrote them in two Tables of ſtone, and deliuered them vnto me.23And it came to paſſe when yee heard the voice out of the midſt of the darkenes (for the mountaine did burne with fire) that ye came neere vnto mee, euen all the heads of your tribes, and your elders.24And ye ſaid, Behold, the Lord our God hath ſhewed vs his glory, and his greatneſse, and we haue heard his voice out of the midſt of the fire: wee haue ſeene this day that God doth talke with man, and he liueth.25Now therefore why ſhould wee die? for this great fire will conſume vs. If we heare the voyce of the Lord our God any more, then we ſhall die.26For who is there of all fleſh that hath heard the voice of the liuing God, ſpeaking out of the midſt of the fire (as we haue) and liued?27Goe thou neere, and heare all that the Lord our God ſhall ſay; and ſpeake thou vnto vs all that the Lord our God ſhall ſpeake vnto thee, and we will heare it, and doe it.28And the Lord heard the voice of your words, when ye ſpake vnto me, and the Lord ſaid vnto me, I haue heard the voice of the wordes of this people, which they haue ſpoken vnto thee: they haue well ſaid, all that they haue ſpoken.29O that there were ſuch an heart in them, that they would feare me, and keepe my commandements alwayes, that it might bee well with them, and with their children for euer.30Goe, ſay to them, Get you into your tents againe.31But as for thee, ſtand thou here by me, and I will ſpeake vnto thee all the Commandements, and the Statutes, and the Iudgements, which thou ſhalt teach them, that they may doe them in the land which I giue them to poſſeſſe it.32Ye ſhall obſerue to doe therefore, as the Lord your God hath commanded you: you ſhall not turne aſide to the right hand, or to the left.33You ſhall walke in all the wayes which the Lord your God hath commanded you, that ye may liue, and that it may be well with you, and that ye may prolong your dayes in the land which ye ſhall poſſeſſe.

CHAPTER 61Now theſe are the Commaundements, the Statutes, & the Iudgements, which the Lord your God commanded to teach you, that ye might doe them in the land whither ye goe to poſſeſſe it:2That thou mighteſt feare the Lord thy God, to keepe all his Statutes, and his Commandements which I command thee; thou, and thy ſonne, and thy ſonnes ſonne, all the dayes of thy life: and that thy dayes may be prolonged.3Heare therefore, O Iſrael, and obſerue to do it, that it may be wel with thee, and that ye may increaſe mightily, as the Lord God of thy fathers hath promiſed thee, in the land that floweth with milke and hony.4Heare, O Iſrael, the Lord our God is one Lord.5And thou ſhalt loue the Lord thy God with all thine heart, and with all thy ſoule, and with all thy might.6And theſe words which I command thee this day, ſhall bee in thine heart.7And thou ſhalt teach them diligently vnto thy children, and ſhalt talke of them when thou ſitteſt in thine houſe, and when thou walkeſt by the way, and when thou lieſt downe, and when thou riſeſt vp.8And thou ſhalt binde them for a ſigne vpon thine hand, and they ſhalbe as frontlets betweene thine eyes.9And thou ſhalt write them vpon the poſts of thy houſe, and on thy gates.10And it ſhall be when the Lord thy God ſhall haue brought thee into the land which hee ſware vnto thy fathers, to Abraham, to Iſaac, and to Iacob to giue thee, great and goodly cities, which thou buildedſt not,11And houſes full of all good things which thou filledſt not, and welles digged which thou diggedſt not, vineyards and oliue trees which thou plantedſt not, when thou ſhalt haue eaten and be full,12Then beware leſt thou forget the Lord which brought thee forth out of the land of Egypt, from the houſe of bondage.13Thou ſhalt feare the Lord thy God, and ſerue him, & ſhalt ſweare by his Name.14Yee ſhall not goe after other gods, of the gods of the people which are round about you:15(For the Lord thy God is a ielous God among you) leſt the anger of the Lord thy God bee kindled againſt thee, and deſtroy thee from off the face of the earth.16Ye ſhall not tempt the Lord your God, as yee tempted him in Maſſah.17You ſhall diligently keepe the Commandements of the Lord your God, and his Teſtimonies, and his Statutes, which he hath commanded thee.18And thou ſhalt doe that which is right and good in the ſight of the Lord: that it may be well with thee, and that thou mayeſt goe in, and poſſeſſe the good land which the Lord ſware vnto thy fathers:19To caſt out all thine enemies from before thee, as the Lord hath ſpoken.20And when thy ſonne aſketh thee in time to come, ſaying, What meane the Teſtimonies, & the Statutes, and the Iudgements, which the Lord our God hath commanded you?21Then thou ſhalt ſay vnto thy ſonne, We were Pharaohs bondmen in Egypt, and the Lord brought vs out of Egypt with a mighty hand.22And the Lord ſhewed ſignes and wonders, great and ſore vpon Egypt, vpon Pharaoh, and vpon all his houſhold, before our eyes:23And hee brought vs out from thence, that hee might bring vs in, to giue vs the land which hee ſware vnto our fathers.24And the Lord commanded vs to doe all theſe Statutes, to feare the Lord our God, for our good alwayes, that he might preſeruevs aliue, as it is at this

day.25And it ſhall be our righteouſnes, if we obſerue to doe all theſe
Commandements, before the Lord our God, as he hath commanded vs.
CHAPTER 71When the Lord thy God ſhall bring thee into the land
whither thou goeſt to poſſeſſe it, and hath caſt out many nations before
thee, the Hittites, and the Girgaſhites, and the Amorites, and the
Canaanites, and the Perizzites, and the Hiuites, and the Iebuſites, ſeuen
nations greater and mightier then thou:2And when the Lord thy God
ſhall deliuer them before thee, thou ſhalt ſmite them, and vtterly deſtroy
them, thou ſhalt make no couenant with them, nor ſhew mercy vnto
them.3Neither ſhalt thou make marriages with them: thy daughter thou
ſhalt not giue vnto his ſonne, nor his daughter ſhalt thou take vnto thy
ſonne.4For they will turne away thy ſonne from following mee, that they
may ſerue other gods: ſo will the anger of the Lord be kindled againſt
you, and deſtroy thee ſuddenly.5But thus ſhal ye deale with them; ye
ſhall deſtroy their altars, and breake downe their images, and cut downe
their groues, and burne their grauen images with fire.6For thou art an
holy people vnto the Lord thy God: the Lord thy God hath choſen thee
to be a ſpecial people vnto himſelfe, aboue all people that are vpon the
face of the earth.7The Lord did not ſet his loue vpon you, nor chooſe
you, becauſe yee were moe in number then any people: (for ye were the
feweſt of all people,)8But becauſe the Lord loued you, and becauſe hee
would keepe the othe which hee had ſworne vnto your fathers, hath the
Lord brought you out with a mighty hand, and redeemed you out of the
houſe of bondmen, from the hand of Pharaoh king of Egypt.9Know
therefore that the Lord thy God, he is God, the faithfull God, which
keepeth Couenant and Mercy with them that loue him, and keepe his
Commandements, to a thouſand generations;10And repaieth them that
hate him to their face, to deſtroy them: he wil not be ſlacke to him that
hateth him, he will repay him to his face.11Thou ſhalt therefore keepe
the Commandements, and the Statutes, and the Iudgements, which I
command thee this day, to doe them.12Wherefore it ſhal come to paſſe,
if ye hearken to theſe iudgements, and keepe and do them: That the
Lord thy God ſhall keepe vnto thee the Couenant and the Mercy which
he ſware vnto thy fathers.13And hee will loue thee, and bleſſe thee, and
multiply thee: Hee will alſo bleſſe the fruit of thy wombe, and the fruit
of thy land, thy corne, and thy wine, and thine oile, the encreaſe of thy
kine, and the flockes of thy ſheepe, in the land which hee ſware vnto thy
fathers to giue thee.14Thou ſhalt bee bleſſed aboue all people: there ſhall
not bee male or female barren among you or among your cattell.15And
the Lord will take away from thee all ſickeneſse, and will put none of
the euill diſeaſes of Egypt (which thou knoweſt) vpon thee: but will lay
them vpon all them that hate thee.16And thou ſhalt conſume all the
people which the Lord thy God ſhall deliuer thee: thine eye ſhall haue
no pitie vpon them, neither ſhalt thou ſerue their gods, for that will be
a ſnare vnto thee.17If thou ſhalt ſay in thine heart, Theſe nations are moe
then I, howe can I diſpoſſeſſe them?18Thou ſhalt not be afraid of them:
but ſhalt well remember, what the Lord thy God did vnto Pharaoh, and
vnto all Egypt,19The great temptations which thine eyes ſawe, and the
ſignes and the wonders, and the mightie hand, and the ſtretched out
arme, whereby the Lord thy God brought thee out: ſo ſhall the Lord thy
God doe vnto all the people of whom thou art afraid.20Moreouer, the
Lord thy God will ſend the hornet among them, vntill they that are left
and hide themſelues from thee, be deſtroyed.21Thou ſhalt not bee
affrighted at them: for the Lord thy God is among you, a mightie God,
and terrible.22And the Lord thy God will put out thoſe nations before
thee by litle and litle: thou mayeſt not conſume them at once, leſt the
beaſtes of the field increaſe vpon thee.23But the Lord thy God ſhall
deliuer them vnto thee, and ſhall deſtroy them with a mightie
deſtruction, vntill they be deſtroyed.24And he ſhall deliuer their kings
into thine hand, and thou ſhalt deſtroy their name from vnder heauen:
There ſhal no man be able to ſtand before thee, vntil thou haue
deſtroyed them.25The grauen images of their gods ſhall yee burne with
fire: thou ſhalt not deſire the ſiluer or golde that is on them, nor take it
vnto thee, leſt thou bee ſnared therein: for it is an abomination to the
Lord thy God.26Neither ſhalt thou bring an abomination into thine
houſe, leſt thou bee a curſed thing like it: but thou ſhalt vtterly deteſt it,
and thou ſhalt vtterly abhorre it, for it is a curſed thing.
CHAPTER 81All the commaundements which I commaund thee this
day, ſhall yee obſerue to doe, that yee may liue, and multiply, and goe in,
and poſſeſſe the land which the Lord ſware vnto your fathers.2And thou
ſhalt remember all the way which the Lord thy God led thee theſe fourtie
yeeres in the wilderneſſe, to humble thee, and to proue thee, to know
what was in thine heart, whether thou wouldeſt keepe his
commandements, or no.3And he humbled thee, and ſuffred thee to
hunger, and fed thee with Manna, which thou kneweſt not, neither did
thy fathers know: that he might make thee know, that man doth not liue
by bread onely, but by euery word that proceedeth out of the mouth of
the Lord doth man liue.4Thy raiment waxed not old vpon thee, neither
did thy foote ſwell theſe fourtie yeeres.5Thou ſhalt alſo conſider in thine
heart, that as a man chaſteneth his ſon, ſo the Lord thy God chaſteneth
thee.6Therefore thou ſhalt keepe the Commandements of the Lord thy
God, to walke in his wayes, and to feare him.7For the Lord thy God
bringeth thee into a good land, a lande of brookes of water, of
fountaines, and depths that ſpring out of valleys and hilles,8A land of
wheate, and barley, and vines, and fig trees, and pomegranats, a land of
oyle oliue, and hony,9A lande wherein thou ſhalt eate bread without
ſcarcenes, thou ſhalt not lacke any thing in it: a lande whoſe ſtones are
yron, and out of whoſe hils thou mayeſt digge braſſe.10When thou haſt
eaten and art full, then thou ſhalt bleſſe the Lord thy God, for the good
lande which hee hath giuen thee.11Beware that thou forget not the Lord
thy God, in not keeping his Commandements, and his Iudgements, and
his Statutes which I command thee this day:12Leſt when thou haſt eaten
and art full, and haſt built goodly houſes, and dwelt therein;13And when
thy heards and thy flocks multiply, and thy ſiluer and thy gold is
multiplied, and all that thou haſt is multiplied:14Then thine heart bee
lifted vp, and thou forget the Lord thy God (which brought thee foorth
out of the land of Egypt, from the houſe of bondage,15Who led thee
through that great and terrible wilderneſſe, wherein were fierie ſerpents,
and ſcorpions, & drought, where there was no water, who brought thee
foorth water out of the rocke of flint,16Who fed thee in the wilderneſſe
with Manna, which thy fathers knew not, that hee might humble thee,
and that hee might prooue thee, to doe thee good at thy latter
end:)17And thou ſay in thine heart, My power, and the might of mine
hand hath gotten me this wealth.18But thou ſhalt remember the Lord
thy God: for it is he that giueth thee power to get wealth, that he may
eſtabliſh his Couenant, which he ſware vnto thy fathers, as it is this
day.19And it ſhalbe, if thou doe at all forget the Lord thy God, and walke
after other gods, and ſerue them, and worſhip them; I teſtifie againſt you
this day, that ye ſhall ſurely periſh.20As the nations which the Lord
deſtroyeth before your face, ſo ſhall yee periſh; becauſe ye would not be
obedient vnto the voice of the Lord your God.
CHAPTER 91Heare, O Iſrael, thou art to paſſe ouer Iordan this day,
to goe in, to poſſeſſe nations greater & mightier then thy ſelfe, Cities
great, and fenced vp to heauen,2A people great and tall, the children of
the Anakims, whom thou knoweſt, and of whom thou haſt heard ſay,
Who can ſtand before the children of Anak?3Underſtand therefore this
day, that the Lord thy God is he, which goeth ouer before thee, as a
conſuming fire: he ſhall deſtroy them, and he ſhall bring them downe
before thy face: So ſhalt thou driue them out, and deſtroy them quickly,
as the Lord hath ſaid vnto thee.4Speake not thou in thine heart, after
that the Lord thy God hath caſt them out from before thee, ſaying, For
my righteouſneſſe the Lord hath brought mee in to poſſeſſe this land:
but for the wickedneſſe of theſe nations, the Lord doeth driue them out
from before thee.5Not for thy righteouſneſſe, or for the vprightneſse of
thine heart, doeſt thou goe to poſſeſſe their land: But for the
wickedneſſe of theſe nations the Lord thy God doeth driue them out
from before thee, and that he may performe the word which the Lord
ſware vnto thy fathers, Abraham, Iſaac and Iacob.6Underſtand
therefore, that the Lord thy God giueth thee not this good land to
poſſeſſe it, for thy righteouſneſſe; for thou art a ſtiffe-necked
people.7Remember and forget not, how thou prouokedſt the Lord thy
God to wrath in the wilderneſſe: from the day that thou didſt depart out
of the land of Egypt, vntill ye came vnto this place, yee haue bene
rebellious againſt the Lord.8Alſo in Horeb yee prouoked the Lord to
wrath, ſo that the Lord was angry with you, to haue deſtroyed
you.9When I was gone vp into the mount, to receiue the Tables of ſtone,
euen the Tables of the Couenant which the Lord made with you, then I
abode in the mount fortie dayes, and fortie nights, I neither did eate
bread, nor drinke water:10And the Lord deliuered vnto me two Tables
of ſtone, written with the finger of God, and on them was written

according to all the words which the Lord ſpake with you in the mount, out of the midſt of fire, in the day of the aſſembly.[11]And it came to paſſe at the end of fortie dayes, and fortie nights, that the Lord gaue mee the two Tables of ſtone, euen the Tables of the Couenant.[12]And the Lord ſaid vnto mee, Ariſe, get thee downe quickly from hence; for thy people which thou haſt brought foorth out of Egypt, haue corrupted themſelues: they are quickly turned aſide out of the way which I commanded them; they haue made them a molten image.[13]Furthermore, the Lord ſpake vnto me, ſaying, I haue ſeene this people, and behold, it is a ſtifnecked people.[14]Let me alone, that I may deſtroy them, and blot out their name from vnder heauen: and I will make of thee a nation mightier and greater then they.[15]So I turned and came downe from the mount, and the mount burned with fire: and the two Tables of the Couenant were in my two hands.[16]And I looked, and behold, ye had ſinned againſt the Lord your God, and had made you a molten calfe: ye had turned aſide quickly out of the way which the Lord had commanded you.[17]And I tooke the two Tables, and caſt them out of my two hands, and brake them before your eyes.[18]And I fell downe before the Lord, as at the firſt, fortie dayes and fortie nights, I did neither eate bread nor drinke water, becauſe of all your ſinnes which ye ſinned, in doing wickedly in the ſight of the Lord, to prouoke him to anger.[19](For I was afraid of the anger, and whot diſpleaſure wherewith the Lord was wroth againſt you, to deſtroy you.) But the Lord hearkned vnto me at that time alſo.[20]And the Lord was very angry with Aaron, to haue deſtroyed him: And I prayed for Aaron alſo the ſame time.[21]And I tooke your ſinne, the calfe which ye had made, and burnt it with fire, and ſtamped it, and ground it very ſmall, euen vntill it was as ſmall as duſt: and I caſt the duſt therof into the brooke that deſcended out of the mount.[22]And at Taberah, and at Maſſah, and at Kibroth-Hattaauah, ye prouoked the Lord to wrath.[23]Likewiſe when the Lord ſent you from Kadeſh Barnea, ſaying, Goe vp and poſſeſſe the land which I haue giuen you, then you rebelled againſt the commandement of the Lord your God, and ye beleeued him not, nor hearkened to his voyce.[24]You haue bin rebellious againſt the Lord, from the day that I knew you.[25]Thus I fell downe before the Lord fourtie dayes, and fourtie nights, as I fel downe at the firſt, becauſe the Lord had ſaid, he would deſtroy you.[26]I prayed therefore vnto the Lord, and ſaid, O Lord God, deſtroy not thy people, and thine inheritance, which thou haſt redeemed through thy greatnes, which thou haſt brought foorth out of Egypt, with a mightie hand.[27]Remember thy ſeruants, Abraham, Iſaac, and Iacob, looke not vnto the ſtubburnneſse of this people, nor to their wickednes, nor to their ſinne:[28]Leſt the land whence thou broughteſt vs out, ſay, Becauſe the Lord was not able to bring them into the land which hee promiſed them, and becauſe hee hated them, hee hath brought them out, to ſlay them in the wilderneſſe.[29]Yet they are thy people, and thine inheritance which thou broughteſt out by thy mightie power, and by thy ſtretched out arme.

CHAPTER 10[1]At that time the Lord ſaid vnto me, Hew thee two Tables of ſtone, like vnto the firſt, and come vp vnto mee into the mount, and make thee an Arke of wood.[2]And I will write on the Tables the words that were in the firſt Tables which thou brakeſt, and thou ſhalt put them in the Arke.[3]And I made an Arke of Shittim wood, and hewed two Tables of ſtone like vnto the firſt, and went vp into the mount, hauing the two Tables in mine hand.[4]And he wrote on the Tables, according to the firſt writing, the tenne Commandements, which the Lord ſpake vnto you in the mount, out of the midſt of the fire, in the day of the aſſembly: and the Lord gaue them vnto me.[5]And I turned my ſelfe and came downe from the mount, and put the Tables in the Arke which I had made, and there they be, as the Lord commanded me.[6]And the children of Iſrael tooke their iourney from Beeroth, of the children of Iaakan, to Moſera; there Aaron died, and there he was buried, and Eleazar his ſonne miniſtred in the Prieſts office in his ſtead.[7]From thence they iourneyed vnto Gudgodah, and from Gudgodah to Iotbath, a land of riuers of waters.[8]At that time the Lord ſeparated the tribe of Leui, to beare the Arke of the Couenant of the Lord, to ſtand before the Lord, to miniſter vnto him, and to bleſſe in his Name, vnto this day.[9]Wherefore Leui hath no part nor inheritance with his brethren: the Lord is his inheritance, according as the Lord thy God promiſed him.[10]And I ſtayed in the mount, according to the firſt time, fortie dayes, and fortie nights: and the Lord hearkened vnto mee at that time alſo, and the Lord would not deſtroy thee.[11]And the Lord ſaid vnto me, Ariſe, take thy iourney before the people, that they may goe in, and poſſeſſe the land which I ſware vnto their fathers to giue vnto them.[12]And now Iſrael, what doeth the Lord thy God require of thee, but to feare the Lord thy God, to walke in all his waies, and to loue him, and to ſerue the Lord thy God, with all thy heart, and with all thy ſoule,[13]To keepe the Commandements of the Lord, and his Statutes, which I commaund thee this day for thy good?[14]Behold, the heauen, & the heauen of heauens is the Lords thy God, the earth alſo, with all that therein is.[15]Onely the Lord had a delight in thy fathers, to loue them, and hee choſe their ſeed after them, euen you, aboue all people, as it is this day.[16]Circumciſe therefore the foreſkin of your heart, and bee no more ſtiffenecked.[17]For the Lord your God is God of gods, and Lord of lords, a great God, a mighty, and a terrible, which regardeth not perſons, nor taketh reward.[18]He doeth execute the iudgement of the fatherleſſe, and widow, and loueth the ſtranger, in giuing him food and raiment.[19]Loue yee therefore the ſtranger: for yee were ſtrangers in the land of Egypt.[20]Thou ſhalt feare the Lord thy God; him ſhalt thou ſerue, and to him ſhalt thou cleaue, and ſweare by his Name.[21]He is thy praiſe, and he is thy God that hath done for thee theſe great and terrible things, which thine eyes haue ſeene.[22]Thy fathers went downe into Egypt with threeſcore and ten perſons: and now the Lord thy God hath made thee as the ſtarres of heauen, for multitude.

CHAPTER 11[1]Therefore thou ſhalt loue the Lord thy God, and keepe his charge, and his Statutes, and his Iudgements, and his Commandements alway.[2]And know you this day: for I ſpeake not with your children which haue not knowen, and which haue not ſeene the chaſtiſement of the Lord your God, his greatneſse, his mighty hand, and his ſtretched out arme,[3]And his miracles, and his actes, which he did in the midſt of Egypt, vnto Pharaoh the King of Egypt, and vnto all his land,[4]And what hee did vnto the army of Egypt, vnto their horſes, and to their charets, how he made the water of the Red ſea to ouerflow them as they purſued after you, and how the Lord hath deſtroyed them vnto this day,[5]And what hee did vnto you in the wilderneſſe, vntill yee came into this place,[6]And what he did vnto Dathan, and Abiram, the ſonnes of Eliab the ſonne of Reuben: how the earth opened her mouth and ſwallowed them vp, and their houſholds, and their tents, and all the ſubſtance that was in their poſſeſſion in the middeſt of all Iſrael.[7]But your eyes haue ſeene all the great acts of the Lord, which he did.[8]Therefore ſhall yee keepe all the Commandements which I command you this day, that ye may be ſtrong and goe in, and poſſeſſe the land whither ye goe to poſſeſſe it:[9]And that yee may prolong your dayes in the lande which the Lord ſware vnto your fathers to giue vnto them, and to their ſeed, a land that floweth with milke and hony.[10]For the land whither thou goeſt in to poſſeſſe it, is not as the lande of Egypt from whence ye came out, where thou ſowedſt thy ſeed, and wateredſt it with thy foot, as a garden of herbes:[11]But the lande whither ye goe to poſſeſſe it, is a lande of hilles and valleys, and drinketh water of the raine of heauen:[12]A lande, which the Lord thy God careth for: the eyes of the Lord thy God are alwayes vpon it, from the beginning of the yeere, euen vnto the end of the yeere.[13]And it ſhall come to paſſe, if you ſhall hearken diligently vnto my Commandements which I command you this day, to loue the Lord your God, and to ſerue him with all your heart, and with all your ſoule;[14]That I will giue you the raine of your land in his due ſeaſon, the firſt raine and the latter raine, that thou mayeſt gather in thy corne, and thy wine, and thine oyle.[15]And I will ſend graſſe in thy fields for thy cattell, that thou mayeſt eate and be full.[16]Take heede to your ſelues, that your heart be not deceiued, and ye turne aſide, and ſerue other gods, and worſhip them:[17]And then the Lords wrath be kindled againſt you, and hee ſhut vp the heauen, that there be no raine, and that the land yeeld not her fruit, and leſt ye periſh quickly from off the good land which the Lord giueth you.[18]Therefore ſhall ye lay vp theſe my words in your heart, and in your ſoule, and bind them for a ſigne vpon your hand, that they may bee as frontlets betweene your eyes.[19]And ye ſhal teach them your children, ſpeaking of them, when thou ſitteſt in thine houſe, and when thou walkeſt by the way, when thou lieſt downe, and when thou riſeſt vp.[20]And thou ſhalt write them vpon the doore poſts of thine houſe, and vpon thy gates:[21]That your dayes may bee multiplied, and the dayes of your children, in the land which the Lord ſware vnto your fathers to giue them, as the dayes of heauen vpon the

earth.22For if ye ſhall diligently keepe all theſe Commaundements which
I command you, to doe them, to loue the Lord your God, to walke in
all his wayes, and to cleaue vnto him:23Then will the Lord driue out all
theſe nations from before you, and ye ſhall poſſeſſe greater nations, and
mightier then your ſelues.24Euery place whereon the ſoles of your feet
ſhall tread, ſhall be yours: from the wilderneſſe, and Lebanon, from the
riuer, the riuer Euphrates, euen vnto the vttermoſt ſea, ſhall your coaſt
be.25There ſhall no man bee able to ſtand before you: for the Lord your
God ſhall lay the feare of you, and the dread of you vpon all the land
that yee ſhall tread vpon, as hee hath ſaid vnto you.26Behold, I ſet before
you this day, a bleſſing and a curſe:27A bleſſing, if ye obey the
Commandements of the Lord your God which I command you this
day:28And a curſe, if ye will not obey the Commandements of the Lord
your God, but turne aſide out of the way, which I command you this
day, to goe after other gods which yee haue not knowen.29And it ſhall
come to paſſe when the Lord thy God hath brought thee in, vnto the
land whither thou goeſt to poſſeſſe it, that thou ſhalt put the bleſſing
vpon mount Gerizim, and the curſe vpon mount Ebal.30Are they not
on the other ſide Iordan, by the way where the Sunne goeth downe, in
the land of the Canaanites, which dwell in the champion ouer againſt
Gilgal, beſide the plaines of Moreh?31For ye ſhall paſſe ouer Iordan, to
goe in to poſſeſſe the land which the Lord your God giueth you, and ye
ſhall poſſeſſe it, and dwell therein.32And yee ſhall obſerue to doe all the
Statutes, and Iudgements, which I ſet before you this day.
CHAPTER 121Theſe are the Statutes, and Iudgements, which ye ſhal
obſerue to do, in the land which the Lord God of thy fathers giueth thee
to poſſeſſe it, all the dayes that yee liue vpon the earth.2Yee ſhall vtterly
deſtroy all the places, wherein the nations which yee ſhall poſſeſſe,
ſerued their gods, vpon the high mountaines, and vpon the hils, and
vnder euery greene tree.3And you ſhall ouerthrow their altars, and
breake their pillars, and burne their groues with fire, and you ſhall hew
downe the grauen images of their gods, and deſtroy the names of them
out of that place.4Yee ſhall not doe ſo vnto the Lord your God.5But
vnto the place which the Lord your God ſhall chuſe out of all your
tribes, to put his name there, euen vnto his habitation ſhall yee ſeeke,
and thither thou ſhalt come:6And thither yee ſhall bring your burnt
offrings, and your ſacrifices, and your tithes, and heaue offrings of your
hand, and your vowes, and your free wil offerings, and the firſtlings of
your heards, and of your flocks.7And there ye ſhall eate before the Lord
your God, and yee ſhall reioyce in all that you put your hand vnto, ye
and your houſholds, wherein the Lord thy God hath bleſſed thee.8Ye
ſhall not do after all the things that we doe here this day, euery man
whatſoeuer is right in his owne eyes.9For yee are not as yet come to the
reſt, and to the inheritance which the Lord your God giueth you.10But
when yee goe ouer Iordan, and dwel in the land which the Lord your
God giueth you to inherite, and when he giueth you reſt from all your
enemies round about, ſo that ye dwell in ſafety:11Then there ſhall be a
place which the Lord your God ſhall chooſe to cauſe his name to dwell
there, thither ſhall ye bring all that I command you; your burnt offerings,
and your ſacrifices, your tithes, and the heaue offring of your hand, &
all your choice vowes, which ye vow vnto the Lord.12And yee ſhall
reioyce before the Lord your God, ye and your ſonnes and your
daughters, and your men ſeruants, and your maid ſeruants, and the
Leuite that is within your gates, foraſmuch as hee hath no part nor
inheritance with you.13Take heed to thy ſelfe, that thou offer not thy
burnt offerings in euery place that thou ſeeſt:14But in the place which
the Lord ſhal chooſe in one of thy tribes, there thou ſhalt offer thy burnt
offerings, and there thou ſhalt do all that I command
thee.15Notwithſtanding, thou mayeſt kill and eate fleſh in all thy gates,
whatſoeuer thy ſoule luſteth after, according to the bleſſing of the Lord
thy God which he hath giuen thee: the vncleane and the cleane may eate
thereof, as of the Roe bucke, and as of the Hart.16Onely ye ſhall not eat
the blood: yee ſhall powre it vpon the earth as water.17Thou mayeſt not
eate within thy gates the tithe of thy corne, or of thy wine, or of thy oyle,
or the firſtlings of thy heards, or of thy flocke, nor any of thy vowes
which thou voweſt, nor thy free will offerings, or heaue offering of thine
hand:18But thou muſt eate them before the Lord thy God, in the place
which the Lord thy God ſhall chooſe, thou and thy ſonne, and thy
daughter, and thy man ſeruant, and thy maid ſeruant, and the Leuite that
is within thy gates: and thou ſhalt reioyce before the Lord thy God, in
all that thou putteſt thine hands vnto.19Take heed to thy ſelfe, that thou
forſake not the Leuite, as long as thou liueſt vpon the earth.20When the
Lord thy God ſhall enlarge thy border, as hee hath promiſed thee, and
thou ſhalt ſay, I will eate fleſh (becauſe thy ſoule longeth to eat fleſh)
thou mayeſt eat fleſh whatſoeuer thy ſoule luſteth after.21If the place
which the Lord thy God hath choſen to put his Name there, be too farre
from thee, then thou ſhalt kill of thy herd and of thy flocke, which the
Lord hath giuen thee, as I haue commaunded thee, and thou ſhalt eate
in thy gates, whatſoeuer thy ſoule luſteth after.22Euen as the Roe bucke
and the Hart is eaten, ſo thou ſhalt eate them: the vncleane and the
cleane ſhall eate of them alike.23Onely be ſure that thou eate not the
blood: for the blood is the life, and thou mayeſt not eate the life with
the fleſh.24Thou ſhalt not eate it; thou ſhalt powre it vpon the earth as
water.25Thou ſhalt not eate it, that it may goe well with thee, and with
thy children after thee, when thou ſhalt doe that which is right in the
ſight of the Lord.26Onely thy holy things which thou haſt, and thy
vowes, thou ſhalt take, and goe vnto the place which the Lord ſhall
chuſe.27And thou ſhalt offer thy burnt offerings, the fleſh and the blood,
vpon the altar of the Lord thy God: and the blood of thy ſacrifices ſhall
be powred out vpon the altar of the Lord thy God, and thou ſhalt eat
the fleſh.28Obſerue & heare all theſe words which I command thee, that
it may go well with thee, and with thy children after thee for euer, when
thou doeſt that which is good and right in the ſight of the Lord thy
God.29When the Lord thy God ſhall cut off the nations from before
thee, whither thou goeſt to poſſeſſe them, and thou ſucceedeſt them,
and dwelleſt in their land:30Take heede to thy ſelfe that thou be not
ſnared by following them, after that they be deſtroyed from before thee,
and that thou enquire not after their gods, ſaying, How did theſe nations
ſerue their gods? euen ſo will I doe likewiſe.31Thou ſhalt not doe ſo vnto
the Lord thy God: for euery abomination to the Lord which hee hateth,
haue they done vnto their gods: for euen their ſonnes and their
daughters they haue burnt in the fire to their gods.32What thing ſoeuer
I command you, obſerue to doe it: thou ſhalt not adde thereto, nor
diminiſh from it.
CHAPTER 131If there Ariſe among you a prophet, or a dreamer of
dreames, and giueth thee a ſigne, or a wonder:2And the ſigne or the
wonder come to paſſe, wherof he ſpake vnto thee, ſaying, Let vs go after
other gods (which thou haſt not knowen) and let vs ſerue them:3Thou
ſhalt not hearken vnto the words of that prophet, or that dreamer of
dreames: for the Lord your God prooueth you, to know whether you
loue the Lord your God with all your heart, and with all your ſoule.4Ye
ſhall walke after the Lord your God, and feare him, and keepe his
commandements, and obey his voyce, and you ſhall ſerue him, and
cleaue vnto him.5And that prophet or that dreamer of dreames ſhalbe
put to death (becauſe hee hath ſpoken to turne you away from the Lord
your God, which brought you out of the land of Egypt, and redeemed
you out of the houſe of bondage, to thruſt thee out of the way which
the Lord thy God commanded thee to walke in) So ſhalt thou put the
euill away from the midſt of thee.6If thy brother, the ſonne of thy
mother, or thy ſonne, or thy daughter, or the wife of thy boſome, or thy
friend, which is as thine owne ſoule, entiſe thee ſecretly, ſaying, Let vs
goe and ſerue other gods which thou haſt not knowen, thou, nor thy
fathers:7Namely of the gods of the people which are round about you,
nigh vnto thee, or farre off from thee, from the one end of the earth,
euen vnto the other end of the earth:8Thou ſhalt not conſent vnto him
nor hearken vnto him, neither ſhall thine eye pitie him, neither ſhalt thou
ſpare, neither ſhalt thou conceale him.9But thou ſhalt ſurely kill him:
Thine hand ſhall be firſt vpon him, to put him to death, and afterwards
the hand of all the people.10And thou ſhalt ſtone him with ſtones, that
hee die: becauſe hee hath ſought to thruſt thee away from the Lord thy
God, which brought thee out of the land of Egypt, from the houſe of
bondage.11And all Iſrael ſhall heare, and feare, and ſhall doe no more
any ſuch wickedneſſe as this is, among you.12If thou ſhalt heare ſay in
one of thy cities, which the Lord thy God hath giuen thee to dwell there,
ſaying,13Certaine men, the children of Belial, are gone out from among
you, and haue withdrawen the inhabitants of their citie, ſaying, Let vs
goe & ſerue other gods, which ye haue not knowen:14Then ſhalt thou
enquire and make ſearch, and aſke diligently: and behold, if it be trueth,
and the thing certaine, that ſuch abomination is wrought among
you:15Thou ſhalt ſurely ſmite the inhabitants of that citie with the edge

of the ſword, deſtroying it vtterly, and all that is therein, and the cattell thereof, with the edge of the ſword.[16]And thou ſhalt gather all the ſpoile of it, into the midſt of the ſtreet thereof, and ſhalt burne with fire the citie, and all the ſpoile thereof euery whit, for the Lord thy God: and it ſhall be an heape for euer, it ſhall not bee built againe.[17]And there ſhall cleaue nought of the curſed thing to thine hand, that the Lord may turne from the fiercenefse of his anger, and ſhew thee mercy, and haue compaſſion vpon thee, and multiply thee, as he hath ſworne vnto thy fathers;[18]When thou ſhalt hearken to the voyce of the Lord thy God, to keepe all his Commaundements which I command thee this day, to doe that which is right in the eyes of the Lord thy God.

CHAPTER 14[1]Yee are the children of the Lord your God: yee ſhall not cutte your ſelues, nor make any baldneſse betweene your eyes for the dead.[2]For thou art an holy people vnto the Lord thy God, and the Lord hath choſen thee to be a peculiar people vnto himſelfe, aboue all the nations that are vpon the earth.[3]Thou ſhalt not eate any abominable thing.[4]Theſe are the beaſts which yee ſhall eate: the oxe, the ſheepe, and the goat,[5]The Hart, and the Roe bucke, and the fallow deere, and the wilde goat, and the Pygarg, and the wilde oxe, and the chamois.[6]And euery beaſt that parteth the hoofe, and cleaueth the clift into two clawes, and cheweth the cud amongſt the beaſts: that ye ſhall eate.[7]Neuertheleſſe theſe yee ſhall not eate, of them that chew the cud, or of them that diuide the clouen hoofe, as the camel, and the hare, and the cony: for they chew the cudde, but diuide not the hoofe, therefore they are vncleane vnto you.[8]And the ſwine, becauſe it diuideth the hoofe, yet cheweth not the cud, it is vncleane vnto you: ye ſhall not eate of their fleſh, nor touch their dead carkeiſe.[9]Theſe yee ſhall eate of all that are in the waters: all that haue finnes and ſcales ſhall ye eate:[10]And whatſoeuer hath not finnes and ſcales, ye may not eat: it is vncleane vnto you.[11]Of all cleane birds ye ſhall eate.[12]But theſe are they of which ye ſhall not eat: the Eagle, and the oſsifrage, and the oſpray,[13]And the glede, and the kite, and the vulture after his kinde,[14]And euery rauen after his kinde,[15]And the owle, & the night hawke, and the cuckow, and the hawke after his kinde,[16]The little owle, and the great owle, and the ſwanne,[17]And the pellicane, and the Geer-eagle, and the cormorant,[18]And the Storke, and the Heron after her kind, and the lapwing, and the batte.[19]And euery creeping thing that flyeth, is vncleane vnto you: they ſhall not be eaten.[20]But of all cleane foules ye may eat.[21]Ye ſhall not eate of any thing that dieth of it ſelfe: thou ſhalt giue it vnto the ſtranger that is in thy gates, that he may eate it, or thou mayeſt ſell it vnto an alien: for thou art an holy people vnto the Lord thy God. Thou ſhalt not ſeethe a kidde in his mothers milke.[22]Thou ſhalt truely tithe all the increaſe of thy ſeede, that the field bringeth forth yeere by yeere.[23]And thou ſhalt eate before the Lord thy God, in the place which he ſhall chuſe to place his Name there, the tithe of thy corne, of thy wine, and of thine oyle, and the firſtlings of thy herdes, and of thy flockes: that thou mayeſt learne to feare the Lord thy God alwayes.[24]And if the way bee too long for thee, ſo that thou art not able to carie it, or if the place be too farre from thee, which the Lord thy God ſhall chuſe to ſet his name there, when the Lord thy God hath bleſſed thee:[25]Then ſhalt thou turne it into money, and binde vp the money in thine hand, and ſhalt goe vnto the place which the Lord thy God ſhal chuſe.[26]And thou ſhalt beſtow that money for whatſoeuer thy ſoule luſteth after, for oxen, or for ſheepe, or for wine, or for ſtrong drinke, or for whatſoeuer thy ſoule deſireth: and thou ſhalt eat there before the Lord thy God, and thou ſhalt reioyce, thou and thine houſhold.[27]And the Leuite that is within thy gates, thou ſhalt not forſake him: for he hath no part nor inheritance with thee.[28]At the end of three yeres thou ſhalt bring forth all the tithe of thine increaſe the ſame yeere, and ſhalt lay it vp within thy gates.[29]And the Leuite, becauſe he hath no part nor inheritance with thee, and the ſtranger, and the fatherleſſe, and the widowe which are within thy gates, ſhall come and ſhal eate, and be ſatiſfied, that the Lord thy God may bleſſe thee, in all the worke of thine hande which thou doeſt.

CHAPTER 15[1]At the end of euery ſeuen yeeres thou ſhalt make a releaſe.[2]And this is the maner of the releaſe: Euery creditour that lendeth ought vnto his neighbour, ſhall releaſe it: hee ſhall not exact it of his neighbour, or of his brother, becauſe it is called the Lords releaſe.[3]Of a forreiner thou mayeſt exact it againe: but that which is thine with thy brother, thine hand ſhall releaſe.[4]Saue when there ſhall bee no poore among you: for the Lord ſhal greatly bleſſe thee in the land which the Lord thy God giueth thee for an inheritance to poſſeſſe it:[5]Onely if thou carefully hearken vnto the voice of the Lord thy God, to obſerue to doe all theſe commandedements, which I commaund thee this day.[6]For the Lord thy God bleſſeth thee, as he promiſed thee, and thou ſhalt lend vnto many nations, but thou ſhalt not borrow, and thou ſhalt reigne ouer many nations, but they ſhall not reigne ouer thee.[7]If there be among you a poore man of one of thy brethren within any of thy gates, in thy lande which the Lord thy God giueth thee, thou ſhalt not harden thy heart, nor ſhut thine hand from thy poore brother:[8]But thou ſhalt open thine hand wide vnto him, and ſhalt ſurely lend him ſufficient for his neede, in that which he wanteth.[9]Beware that there bee not a thought in thy wicked heart, ſaying, The ſeuenth yeere, the yeere of releaſe is at hand, and thine eye be euill againſt thy poore brother, and thou giueſt him nought, and hee crie vnto the Lord againſt thee, and it be ſinne vnto thee.[10]Thou ſhalt ſurely giue him, and thine heart ſhall not bee grieued when thou giueſt vnto him: becauſe that for this thing the Lord thy God ſhall bleſſe thee in all thy workes, and in all that thou putteſt thine hand vnto.[11]For the poore ſhall neuer ceaſe out of the land: therefore I command thee, ſaying, Thou ſhalt open thine hand wide vnto thy brother, to thy poore, and to thy needy in the land.[12]And if thy brother, an Hebrew man, or an Hebrew woman, be ſold vnto thee, and ſerue thee ſixe yeres, then in the ſeuenth yeere thou ſhalt let him goe free from thee.[13]And when thou ſendeſt him out free from thee, thou ſhalt not let him go away emptie:[14]Thou ſhalt furniſh him liberally out of thy flocke, and out of thy floore, and out of thy wine preſse, of that wherewith the Lord thy God hath bleſſed thee thou ſhalt giue vnto him.[15]And thou ſhalt remember that thou waſt a bondman in the land of Egypt, and the Lord thy God redeemed thee: therefore I command thee this thing to day.[16]And it ſhall be if he ſay vnto thee, I will not goe away from thee, becauſe he loueth thee, and thine houſe, becauſe he is well with thee:[17]Then thou ſhalt take an aule, and thruſt it through his eare vnto the doore, and hee ſhall be thy ſeruant for euer: and alſo vnto thy mayd ſeruant thou ſhalt doe likewiſe.[18]It ſhall not ſeeme hard vnto thee when thou ſendeſt him away free from thee: for hee hath bene worth a double hired ſeruant to thee, in ſeruing thee ſixe yeeres: and the Lord thy God ſhall bleſſe thee in all that thou doeſt.[19]All the firſtling males that come of thy heard, and of thy flock, thou ſhalt ſanctifie vnto the Lord thy God: thou ſhalt doe no worke with the firſtling of thy bullocke, nor ſheare the firſtling of thy ſheepe.[20]Thou ſhalt eate it before the Lord thy God yeere by yeere, in the place which the Lord ſhall chooſe, thou and thy houſhold.[21]And if there be any blemiſh therein; as if it be lame, or blinde, or haue any ill blemiſh, thou ſhalt not ſacrifice it vnto the Lord thy God.[22]Thou ſhalt eate it within thy gates: the vncleane and the cleane perſon ſhall eat it alike, as the Roe bucke, and as the Hart.[23]Onely thou ſhalt not eate the blood thereof: thou ſhalt powre it vpon the ground as water.

CHAPTER 16[1]Obſerue the moneth of Abib, and keepe the Paſſeouer vuto the Lord thy God: for in the moneth of Abib the Lord thy God brought thee foorth out of Egypt by night.[2]Thou ſhalt therefore ſacrifice the Paſſeouer vnto the Lord thy God, of the flocke and the heard, in the place which the Lord ſhall chooſe to place his name there.[3]Thou ſhalt eat no leauened bread with it: ſeuen dayes ſhalt thou eat vnleauened bread therewith, euen the bread of affliction, (for thou cameſt forth out of the land of Egypt in haſte) that thou mayeſt remember the day when thou cameſt foorth out of the land of Egypt, all the dayes of thy life.[4]And there ſhall bee no leauened bread ſeene with thee in all thy coaſts ſeuen dayes, neither ſhall there any thing of the fleſh, which thou ſacrificedſt the firſt day at Euen, remaine all night, vntill the morning.[5]Thou mayeſt not ſacrifice the Paſſeouer within any of the gates, which the Lord thy God giueth thee.[6]But at the place which the Lord thy God ſhall chooſe to place his Name in, there thou ſhalt ſacrifice the Paſſeouer at Euen, at the going downe of the Sunne, at the ſeaſon that thou cameſt foorth out of Egypt.[7]And thou ſhalt roſte and eate it in the place which the Lord thy God ſhall chooſe, and thou ſhalt turne in the morning, and goe vnto thy tents.[8]Sixe dayes thou ſhalt eate vnleauened bread, and on the ſeuenth day ſhall be a ſolemne aſſembly to the Lord thy God: thou ſhalt doe no worke therein.[9]Seuen weekes ſhalt thou number vnto thee: beginne to number the ſeuen weekes, from ſuch time as thou beginneſt to put the ſickle to the corne.[10]And thou ſhalt keepe the feaſt of weekes vnto the Lord thy God with a tribute of a free will offering of thine hand, which thou ſhalt giue vnto the Lord thy God, according as the Lord thy God hath bleſſed thee.11And thou ſhalt reioyce before the Lord thy God, thou, and thy ſonne, and thy daughter, and thy man ſeruant and thy maid ſeruant, and the Leuite that is within thy gates, and the ſtranger, and the fatherleſſe, and the widow, that are among you, in the place which the Lord thy God hath choſen to place his Name there.12And thou ſhalt remember that thou waſt a bondman in Egypt: and thou ſhalt obſerue & do theſe Statutes.13Thou ſhalt obſerue the feaſt of Tabernacles ſeuen dayes, after that thou haſt gathered in thy corne, and thy wine.14And thou ſhalt reioice in thy feaſt, thou, and thy ſonne, and thy daughter, and thy man ſeruant, and thy maid ſeruant, and the Leuite, the ſtranger, and the fatherleſſe, and the widow, that are within thy gates.15Seuen dayes ſhalt thou keepe a ſolemne feaſt vnto the Lord thy God, in the place which the Lord ſhall chuſe: becauſe the Lord thy God ſhall bleſſe thee in all thy increaſe, and in all the workes of thine handes, therefore thou ſhalt ſurely reioyce.16Three times in a yeere ſhal all thy males appeare before the Lord thy God, in the place which hee ſhall chuſe: in the feaſt of Unleauened bread, and in the feaſt of Weekes, and in the feaſt of Tabernacles: and they ſhal not appeare before the Lord emptie.17Euery man ſhall giue as hee is able, according to the bleſſing of the Lord thy God, which he hath giuen thee.18Iudges and officers ſhalt thou make thee in all thy gates which the Lord thy God giueth thee throughout thy tribes: and they ſhall iudge the people with iuſt iudgement.19Thou ſhalt not wreſt iudgement, thou ſhalt not reſpect perſons, neither take a gift: for a gift doth blind the eyes of the wiſe, and peruert the wordes of the righteous.20That which is altogether iuſt ſhalt thou followe, that thou mayeſt liue, and inherite the land which the Lord thy God giueth thee.21Thou ſhalt not plant thee a groue of any trees neere vnto the Altar of the Lord thy God, which thou ſhalt make thee:22Neither ſhalt thou ſet thee vp any image, which the Lord thy God hateth.

CHAPTER 171Thou ſhalt not ſacrifice vnto the Lord thy God any bullocke, or ſheepe wherein is blemiſh, or any euilfauourednes: for that is an abomination vnto the Lord thy God.2If there bee found among you within any of thy gates which the Lord thy God giueth thee, man or woman that hath wrought wickednes in the ſight of the Lord thy God, in tranſgreſsing his couenant,3And hath gone and ſerued other gods, and worſhipped them, either the Sunne, or Moone, or any of the hoſte of heauen, which I haue not commanded,4And it be told thee, and thou haſt heard of it, and inquired diligently, and behold, it be true, and the thing certaine, that ſuch abomination is wrought in Iſrael:5Then ſhalt thou bring forth that man, or that woman (which haue committed that wicked thing) vnto thy gates, euen that man, or that woman, and ſhalt ſtone them with ſtones till they die.6At the mouth of two witneſſes, or three witneſſes, ſhall he that is worthy of death, be put to death: but at the mouth of one witneſſe he ſhall not bee put to death.7The hands of the witneſſes ſhall be firſt vpon him, to put him to death, and afterward the hands of all the people: ſo thou ſhalt put the euil away from among you.8If there Ariſe a matter too hard for thee in iudgement, betweene blood and blood, betweene plea and plea, and betweene ſtroke and ſtroke, being matters of controuerſie within thy gates: then ſhalt thou Ariſe, and get thee vp into the place, which the Lord thy God ſhall chooſe;9And thou ſhalt come vnto the Prieſts the Leuites, & vnto the Iudge that ſhal be in thoſe dayes, and enquire; and they ſhall ſhew thee the ſentence of Iudgement.10And thou ſhalt doe according to the ſentence which they of that place (which the Lord ſhall chooſe) ſhall ſhew thee, and thou ſhalt obſerue to do according to all that they enforme thee:11According to the ſentence of the Law which they ſhall teach thee, and according to the Iudgement which they ſhall tell thee thou ſhalt doe: thou ſhalt not decline from the Sentence which they ſhall ſhew thee, to the right hand, nor to the left.12And the man that will doe preſumptuouſly, and will not hearken vnto the Prieſt (that ſtandeth to miniſter there before the Lord thy God) or vnto the Iudge, euen that man ſhall die, and thou ſhalt put away the euill from Iſrael.13And all the people ſhal heare, and feare, and doe no more preſumptuouſly.14When thou art come vnto the land which the Lord thy God giueth thee, and ſhalt poſſeſſe it, and ſhalt dwell therein, and ſhalt ſay, I will ſet a King ouer mee, like as all the nations that are about me:15Thou ſhalt in any wiſe ſet him King ouer thee, whom the Lord thy God ſhall chooſe. One from among thy brethren ſhalt thou ſet King ouer thee: thou mayeſt not ſet a ſtranger ouer thee, which is not thy brother.16But he ſhall not multiply horſes to himſelfe, nor cauſe the people to returne to Egypt, to the ende that hee ſhould multiply horſes: for as much as the Lord hath ſaid vnto you, Yee ſhall hencefoorth returne no more that way.17Neither ſhall he multiply wiues to himſelfe, that his heart turne not away: neither ſhall hee greatly multiply to himſelfe ſiluer and gold.18And it ſhall be when he ſitteth vpon the Throne of his kingdome, that he ſhall write him a copy of this Law in a booke, out of that which is before the Prieſts the Leuites.19And it ſhall be with him, and hee ſhall reade therein all the dayes of his life, that hee may learne to feare the Lord his God, to keep all the words of this Law, and theſe Statutes, to do them:20That his heart bee not lifted vp aboue his brethren, and that hee turne not aſide from the Commandement, to the right hand, or to the left: to the end that hee may prolong his dayes in his kingdome, hee, and his children in the midſt of Iſrael.

CHAPTER 181The Prieſts, the Leuites, and all the tribe of Leui, ſhall haue no part nor inheritance with Iſrael: they ſhall eate the offerings of the Lord made by fire, and his inheritance.2Therefore ſhall they haue no inheritance among their brethren: the Lord is their inheritance, as he hath ſaid vnto them.3And this ſhalbe the Prieſts due from the people, from them that offer a ſacrifice, whether it bee oxe or ſheepe: and they ſhall giue vnto the Prieſt the ſhoulder, and the two cheekes, and the maw.4The firſt fruit alſo of thy corne, of thy wine, and of thy oyle, and the firſt of the fleece of thy ſheepe, ſhalt thou giue him.5For the Lord thy God hath choſen him out of all thy tribes, to ſtand to miniſter in the Name of the Lord, him, and his ſonnes for euer.6And if a Leuite come from any of thy gates out of all Iſrael, where he ſoiourned, and come with all the deſire of his minde, vnto the place which the Lord ſhall chooſe;7Then hee ſhall miniſter in the Name of the Lord his God, as all his brethren the Leuites doe, which ſtand there before the Lord.8They ſhall haue like portions to eate, beſide that which commeth of the ſale of his patrimonie.9When thou art come into the land which the Lord thy God giueth thee, thou ſhalt not learne to doe after the abominations of thoſe nations.10There ſhall not be found among you any one that maketh his ſonne, or his daughter to paſſe thorow the fire, or that vſeth diuination, or an obſeruer of times, or an inchanter, or a witch,11Or a charmer, or a conſulter with familiar ſpirits, or a wyzard, or a Necromancer.12For all that do theſe things, are an abomination vnto the Lord: and becauſe of theſe abominations, the Lord thy God doth driue them out from before thee.13Thou ſhalt bee perfite with the Lord thy God.14For theſe nations which thou ſhalt poſſeſſe, hearkened vnto obſeruers of times, and vnto diuiners: but as for thee, the Lord thy God hath not ſuffered thee ſo to doe.15The Lord thy God will raiſe vp vnto thee a Prophet from the midſt of thee, of thy brethren, like vnto me, vnto him ye ſhall hearken,16According to all that thou deſiredſt of the Lord thy God in Horeb, in the day of the aſſembly, ſaying, Let mee not heare again the voice of the Lord my God, neither let mee ſee this great fire any more, that I die not.17And the Lord ſaid vnto mee, They haue well ſpoken that which they haue ſpoken.18I will raiſe them vp a Prophet from among their brethren, like vnto thee, and will put my wordes in his mouth, and hee ſhall ſpeake vnto them all that I ſhall command him.19And it ſhall come to paſſe, that whoſoeuer will not hearken vnto my words, which hee ſhall ſpeake in my name, I will require it of him.20But the prophet which ſhall preſume to ſpeake a word in my name, which I haue not commanded him to ſpeake, or that ſhall ſpeake in the name of other gods, euen that prophet ſhall die.21And if thou ſay in thine heart, How ſhall wee know the word which the Lord hath not ſpoken?22When a prophet ſpeaketh in the name of the Lord, if the thing follow not, nor come to paſſe, that is the thing which the Lord hath not ſpoken, but the prophet hath ſpoken it preſumptuouſly: thou ſhalt not bee afraid of him.

CHAPTER 191When the Lord thy God hath cut off the nations, whoſe lande the Lord thy God giueth thee, and thou ſucceedeſt them, and dwelleſt in their cities, and in their houſes:2Thou ſhalt ſeparate three cities for thee in the midſt of thy land, which the Lord thy God giueth thee to poſſeſſe it.3Thou ſhalt prepare thee a way, and diuide the coaſts of thy land (which the Lord thy God giueth thee to inherit) into three parts, that euery ſlayer may flee thither.4And this is the caſe of the ſlayer which ſhall flee thither, that hee may liue: who ſo killeth his neighbour ignorantly, whom he hated not in time paſt,5As when a man goeth into the wood with his neighbor, to hew wood, and his hand fetcheth a ſtroke with the axe to cut downe the tree, and the head ſlippeth from the helue, and lighteth vpon his neighbour that he die, he ſhall flee vnto one of thoſe cities, and liue:6Leſt the auenger of the blood purſue the ſlaier, while his heart is hot, and ouertake him, becauſe the way is long, and ſlay him, whereas he was not worthy of death, in as much as hee hated him not in time paſt.7Wherefore I command thee, ſaying, Thou ſhalt ſeparate three cities for thee.8And if the Lord thy God enlarge thy coaſt (as he hath ſworne vnto thy fatherſ) and giue thee all the lande which hee promiſed to giue vnto thy fathers:9(If thou ſhalt keepe all theſe commandements to doe them, which I command thee this day, to loue the Lord thy God, and to walke euer in his wayeſ) then ſhalt thou adde three cities moe for thee, beſide theſe three:10That innocent blood be not ſhed in thy land which the Lord thy God giueth thee for an inheritance, and ſo blood be vpon thee.11But if any man hate his neighbour and lie in wait for him, and riſe vp againſt him, and ſmite him mortally that hee die, and fleeth into one of theſe Cities:12Then the Elders of his citie ſhall ſend and fetch him thence, and deliuer him into the hand of the auenger of blood, that he may die.13Thine eye ſhall not pittie him, but thou ſhalt put away the guilt of innocent blood from Iſrael, that it may goe wel with thee.14Thou ſhalt not remooue thy neighbours land-marke, which they of old time haue ſet in thine inheritance, which thou ſhalt inherite, in the land that the Lord thy God giueth thee to poſſeſſe it.15One witneſſe ſhall not riſe vp againſt a man for any iniquitie, or for any ſinne, in any ſinne that he ſinneth: at the mouth of two witneſſes, or at the mouth of three witneſſes, ſhall the matter be ſtabliſhed.16If a falſe witnes riſe vp againſt any man to teſtifie againſt him that which is wrong:17Then both the men betweene whom the controuerſie is, ſhall ſtand before the Lord, before the Prieſts, and the Iudges, which ſhall be in thoſe dayes.18And the Iudges ſhall make diligent inquiſition: and behold, if the witneſſe be a falſe witneſſe, and hath teſtified falſly againſt his brother:19Then ſhall ye doe vnto him, as he had thought to haue done vnto his brother: ſo ſhalt thou put the euil away from among you.20And thoſe which remaine ſhall heare, and feare, and ſhall hencefoorth commit no more any ſuch euill among you.21And thine eye ſhall not pitie, but life ſhall goe for life, eye for eye, tooth for tooth, hand for hand, foot for foot.

CHAPTER 201When thou goeſt out to battell againſt thine enemies, and ſeeſt horſes and charets, and a people more then thou, be not afraid of them: for the Lord thy God is with thee, which brought thee vp out of the land of Egypt.2And it ſhall bee when ye are come nigh vnto the battell, that the Prieſt ſhall approach and ſpeake vnto the people,3And ſhall ſay vnto them, Heare O Iſrael, you approach this day vnto battell againſt your enemies: let not your hearts faint, feare not, and doe not tremble, neither be ye terrified becauſe of them.4For the Lord your God is hee that goeth with you, to fight for you againſt your enemies, to ſaue you.5And the Officers ſhall ſpeake vnto the people, ſaying, What man is there that hath built a new houſe, and hath not dedicated it? let him goe and returne to his houſe, leſt hee die in the battell, and an other man dedicate it.6And what man is hee that hath planted a Uineyard, and hath not yet eaten of it? let him alſo go and returne vnto his houſe, leſt he die in the battell, and an other man eate of it.7And what man is there that hath betrothed a wife, and hath not taken her? let him goe and returne vnto his houſe, leſt he die in battell, and another man take her.8And the Officers ſhall ſpeake further vnto the people: and they ſhall ſay, What man is there that is fearefull and faint hearted? let him goe and returne vnto his houſe, leſt his brethrens heart faint as well as his heart.9And it ſhall be when the Officers haue made an end of ſpeaking vnto the people, that they ſhall make Captaines of the armies to leade the people.10When thou commeſt nigh vnto a City to fight againſt it, then proclaime peace vnto it.11And it ſhall be, if it make thee anſwere of peace, and open vnto thee, then it ſhalbe that all the people that is found therein, ſhall be tributaries vnto thee, and they ſhall ſerue thee.12And if it will make no peace with thee, but will make warre againſt thee, then thou ſhalt beſiege it.13And when the Lord thy God hath deliuered it into thine hands, thou ſhalt ſmite euery male thereof with the edge of the ſword.14But the women, and the litle ones, and the cattell, and all that is in the citie, euen all the ſpoile thereof, ſhalt thou take vnto thy ſelfe, and thou ſhalt eate the ſpoile of thine enemies, which the Lord thy God hath giuen thee.15Thus ſhalt thou doe vnto all the cities which are very far off from thee, which are not of the cities of theſe nations.16But of the cities of theſe people which the Lord thy God doth giue thee for an inheritance, thou ſhalt ſaue aliue nothing that breatheth:17But thou ſhalt vtterly deſtroy them, namely, the Hittites, and the Amorites, the Canaanites, and the Perizzites, the Hiuites, and the Iebuſites, as the Lord thy God hath commanded thee:18That they teach you not to do after all their abominations, which they haue done vnto their gods, ſo ſhould ye ſinne againſt the Lord your God.19When thou ſhalt beſiege a citie a long time, in making warre againſt it to take it, thou ſhalt not deſtroy the trees thereof, by forcing an axe againſt them: for thou mayeſt eate of them, and thou ſhalt not cut them downe (for the tree of the field is mans life) to employ them in the ſiege.20Only the trees which thou knoweſt that they be not trees for meate, thou ſhalt deſtroy, and cut them downe, and thou ſhalt build bulwarkes againſt the city that maketh warre with thee, vntil it be ſubdued.

CHAPTER 211If one bee found ſlaine in the lande, which the Lord thy God giueth thee to poſſeſſe it, lying in the fielde, and it bee not knowen who hath ſlaine him:2Then thy Elders and thy Iudges ſhall come forth, and they ſhall meaſure vnto the cities which are round about him that is ſlaine.3And it ſhall be that the citie which is next vnto the ſlaine man, euen the Elders of that citie ſhall take an heifer which hath not bene wrought with, and which hath not drawen in the yoke.4And the Elders of that citie ſhall bring downe the heifer vnto a rough valley, which is neither eared nor ſowen, and ſhall ſtrike off the heifers necke there in the valley.5And the Prieſts the ſonnes of Leui ſhall come neere (for them the Lord thy God hath choſen to miniſter vnto him, and to bleſſe in the Name of the Lord:) and by their worde ſhall euery controuerſie and euery ſtroke bee tried.6And all the Elders of that city that are next vnto the ſlaine man, ſhal waſh their hands ouer the heifer that is beheaded in the valley.7And they ſhall anſwere, and ſay, Our hands haue not ſhedde this blood, neither haue our eyes ſeene it.8Be merciful, O Lord, vnto thy people Iſrael, whom thou haſt redeemed, and lay not innocent blood vnto thy people of Iſraels charge, and the blood ſhall be forgiuen them.9So ſhalt thou put away the guilt of innocent blood from among you, when thou ſhalt do that which is right in the ſight of the Lord.10When thou goeſt forth to warre againſt thine enemies, and the Lord thy God hath deliuered them into thine hands, & thou haſt taken them captiue,11And ſeeſt among the captiues a beautifull woman, and haſt a deſire vnto her, that thou wouldeſt haue her to thy wife:12Then thou ſhalt bring her home to thine houſe, and ſhee ſhall ſhaue her head, and pare her nailes.13And ſhee ſhall put the raiment of her captiuitie from off her, and ſhall remaine in thine houſe, and bewaile her father and her mother a full moneth: and after that, thou ſhalt go in vnto her and be her huſband, and ſhe ſhall be thy wife.14And it ſhall be if thou haue no delight in her, then thou ſhalt let her goe whither ſhe will, but thou ſhalt not ſell her at al for money, thou ſhalt not make merchandize of her, becauſe thou haſt humbled her.15If a man haue two wiues, one beloued and another hated, and they haue borne him children, both the beloned, and the hated: and if the firſt borne ſonne be hers that was hated:16Then it ſhall be, when he maketh his ſonnes to inherite that which hee hath, that he may not make the ſonne of the beloued, firſt borne, before the ſonne of the hated, which is indeed the firſt borne:17But hee ſhall acknowledge the ſonne of the hated for the firſt borne, by giuing him a double portion of all that hee hath: for hee is the beginning of his ſtrength; the right of the firſt borne is his.18If a man haue a ſtubborne and rebellious ſonne, which will not obey the voice of his father, or the voice of his mother, and that when they haue chaſtened him, wil not hearken vnto them:19Then ſhall his father and his mother lay hold on him, and bring him out vnto the Elders of his citie, and vnto the gate of his place:20And they ſhall ſay vnto the Elders of his citie, This our ſonne is ſtubborne, and rebellious, hee will not obey our voice: he is a glutton, & a drunkard.21And all the men of his city ſhall ſtone him with ſtones, that hee die: ſo ſhalt thou put euill away from among you, and all Iſrael ſhall heare, & feare.22And if a man haue committed a ſinne worthy of death, and he be to be put to death, and thou hang him on a tree:23His body ſhall not remaine all night vpon the tree, but thou ſhalt in any wiſe bury him that day: for he that is hanged, is accurſed of God: that thy land be not defiled, which the Lord thy God giueth thee for an inheritance.

CHAPTER 221Thou ſhalt not ſee thy brothers oxe, or his ſheepe go
aſtray, and hide thy ſelfe from them: thou ſhalt in any caſe bring them
againe vnto thy brother.2And if thy brother be not nigh vnto thee, or if
thou know him not, then thou ſhalt bring it vnto thine owne houſe, and
it ſhall be with thee, vntil thy brother ſeeke after it, and thou ſhalt reſtore
it to him againe.3In like maner ſhalt thou do with his aſſe, and ſo ſhalt
thou doe with his raiment: and with all loſt thing of thy brothers which
he hath loſt, and thou haſt found, ſhalt thou do likewiſe: thou mayeſt
not hide thy ſelfe.4Thou ſhalt not ſee thy brothers aſſe or his oxe fall
downe by the way, and hide thy ſelfe from them: thou ſhalt ſurely helpe
him to lift them vp againe.5The woman ſhall not weare that which
pertaineth vnto a man, neither ſhall a man put on a womans garment:
for all that doe ſo, are abomination vnto the Lord thy God.6If a birds
neſt chance to be before thee in the way in any tree, or on the ground,
whether they be yong ones, or egges, and the damme ſitting vpon the
yong, or vpon the egges, thou ſhalt not take the damme with the
yong.7But thou ſhalt in any wiſe let the damme goe, and take the yong
to thee, that it may be well with thee, and that thou mayeſt prolong thy
dayes.8When thou buildeſt a new houſe, then thou ſhalt make a
battlement for thy roofe, that thou bring not blood vpon thine houſe, if
any man fall from thence.9Thou ſhalt not ſow thy vineyard with diuers
ſeeds: leſt the fruit of thy ſeed which thou haſt ſowen, and the fruit of
thy Uineyard be defiled.10Thou ſhalt not plow with an oxe and an aſſe
together.11Thou ſhalt not weare a garment of diuers ſorts, as of woollen,
and linnen together.12Thou ſhalt make thee fringes vpon the foure
quarters of thy veſture, wherewith thou coureſt thy ſelfe.13If any man
take a wife, and go in vnto her, and hate her,14And giue occaſions of
ſpeach againſt her, and bring vp an euill name vpon her, and ſay, I tooke
this woman, and when I came to her, I found her not a mayd:15Then
ſhal the father of the damoſell, and her mother take, and bring forth the
tokens of the damoſels virginitie, vnto the Elders of the citie in the
gate.16And the damoſels father ſhall ſay vnto the Elders, I gaue my
daughter vnto this man to wife, & he hateth her:17And loe, he hath giuen
occaſions of ſpeech againſt her, ſaying, I found not thy daughter a maid:
and yet theſe are the tokens of my daughters virginity; and they ſhall
ſpread the cloth before the Elders of the citie.18And the Elders of that
citie ſhall take that man, and chaſtiſe him.19And they ſhall amearſe him
in an hundred ſhekels of ſiluer, and giue them vnto the father of the
damoſell, becauſe he hath brought vp an euill name vpon a virgine of
Iſrael: and ſhe ſhall be his wife, hee may not put her away all his
dayes.20But if this thing be true, and the tokens of virginitie be not found
for the damoſel:21Then they ſhall bring out the damoſell to the doore of
her fathers houſe, and the men of her city ſhal ſtone her with ſtones that
ſhe die, becauſe ſhe hath wrought folly in Iſrael, to play the whore in her
fathers houſe: ſo ſhalt thou put euill away from among you.22If a man
be found lying with a woman married to an huſband, then they ſhall
both of them die, both the man that lay with the woman, and the
woman: ſo ſhalt thou put away euill from Iſrael.23If a damoſell that is a
virgin be betrothed vnto an huſband, and a man find her in the citie, and
lie with her:24Then yee ſhall bring them both out vnto the gate of that
citie, and yee ſhall ſtone them with ſtones that they die; the damoſel,
becauſe ſhee cried not, being in the citie; and the man, becauſe he hath
humbled his neighbours wife: ſo thou ſhalt put away euill from among
you.25But if a man find a betrothed damoſel in the field, and the man
force her, and lie with her: then the man only that lay with her, ſhall
die.26But vnto the damoſel thou ſhalt doe nothing, there is in the
damoſel no ſinne worthy of death: for as when a man riſeth againſt his
neighbour, and ſlayeth him, euen ſo is this matter.27For he found her in
the field, and the betrothed damoſel cried, and there was none to ſaue
her.28If a man finde a damoſel that is a virgin, which is not betrothed,
and lay hold on her, and lie with her, and they be found:29Then the man
that lay with her, ſhall giue vnto the damoſels father fifty ſhekels of
ſiluer, and ſhe ſhalbe his wife, becauſe he hath humbled her: he may not
put her away all his dayes.30A man ſhall not take his fathers wife, nor
diſcouer his fathers ſkirt.

CHAPTER 231Hee that is wounded in the ſtones, or hath his priuie
member cut off, ſhall not enter into the Congregation of the Lord.2A
baſtard ſhall not enter into the Congregation of the Lord: euen to his
tenth generation ſhall he not enter into the Congregation of the
Lord.3An Ammonite, or Moabite ſhall not enter into the Congregation
of the Lord, euen to their tenth generation ſhall they not enter into the
Congregation of the Lord for euer,4Becauſe they met you not with bread
and with water in the way when ye came forth out of Egypt, and becauſe
they hired againſt thee Balaam the ſon of Beor of Pethor of
Meſopotamia, to curſe thee.5Neuertheleſſe, the Lord thy God would
not hearken vnto Balaam: but the Lord thy God turned the curſe into a
bleſſing vnto thee, becauſe the Lord thy God loued thee.6Thou ſhalt not
ſeek their peace, nor their proſperity all thy dayes for euer.7Thou ſhalt
not abhorre an Edomite, for he is thy brother: thou ſhalt not abhorre an
Egyptian, becauſe thou waſt a ſtranger in his land.8The children that are
begotten of them, ſhal enter into the cõgregation of the Lord, in their
third generation.9When the hoſte goeth foorth againſt thine enemies,
then keepe thee from euery wicked thing.10If there bee among you any
man that is not cleane, by reaſon of vncleanneſſe that chanceth him by
night, then ſhall hee goe abroad out of the campe, hee ſhall not come
within the campe.11But it ſhalbe when euening commeth on, he ſhall
waſh himſelfe with water: and when the Sunne is downe, he ſhall come
into the campe againe.12Thou ſhalt haue a place alſo without the campe,
whither thou ſhalt goe foorth abroad.13And thou ſhalt haue a paddle
vpon thy weapon: and it ſhall be when thou wilt eaſe thy ſelfe abroad,
thou ſhalt digge therewith, and ſhalt turne backe and couer that which
commeth from thee.14For the Lord thy God walketh in the midſt of thy
campe, to deliuer thee, and to giue vp thine enemies before thee:
therefore ſhall thy campe be holy, that he ſee no vncleane thing in thee,
and turne away from thee.15Thou ſhalt not deliuer vnto his maſter, the
ſeruant which is eſcaped from his maſter vnto thee.16He ſhall dwell with
thee, euen among you, in that place which he ſhall chooſe, in one of thy
gates where it liketh him beſt: thou ſhalt not oppreſſe him.17There
ſhalbe no whore of the daughters of Iſrael, nor a Sodomite of the ſonnes
of Iſrael.18Thou ſhalt not bring the hire of a whore, or the price of a
dogge into the houſe of the Lord thy God for any vow: for euen both
theſe are abomination vnto the Lord thy God.19Thou ſhalt not lend
vpon vſury to thy brother; vſury of money, vſury of victuals, vſury of
any thing that is lent vpon vſury.20Unto a ſtranger thou maieſt lend vpon
vſury, but vnto thy brother thou ſhalt not lend vpon vſury: that the Lord
thy God may bleſſe thee, in all that thou ſetteſt thine hand to, in the land
whither thou goeſt to poſſeſſe it.21When thou ſhalt vow a vow vnto the
Lord thy God, thou ſhalt not ſlacke to pay it: for the Lord thy God will
ſurely require it of thee; and it would be ſinne in thee.22But if thou ſhalt
forbeare to vow, it ſhall be no ſinne in thee.23That which is gone out of
thy lippes, thou ſhalt keepe and performe; euen a freewill offering
according as thou haſt vowed vnto the Lord thy God, which thou haſt
promiſed with thy mouth.24When thou commeſt into thy neighbors
Uineyard, then thou mayeſt eate grapes thy fill, at thine owne pleaſure,
but thou ſhalt not put any in thy veſſell.25When thou commeſt into the
ſtanding corne of thy neighbours, then thou maieſt plucke the eares with
thine hand: but thou ſhalt not mooue a ſickle vnto thy neighbours
ſtanding corne.

CHAPTER 241When a man hath taken a wife and married her, and it
come to paſſe that ſhee find no fauour in his eyes, becauſe hee hath
found ſome vncleanneſſe in her: then let him write her a bill of
diuorcement, and giue it in her hand, and ſend her out of his houſe.2And
when ſhee is departed out of his houſe, ſhe may goe and be another
mans wife.3And if the latter huſband hate her, and write her a bill of
diuorcement, and giueth it in her hand, and ſendeth her out of his houſe:
Or if the latter huſband die, which tooke her to be his wife,4Her former
huſband which ſent her away, may not take her againe to be his wife,
after that ſhe is defiled: for that is abomination before the Lord, and
thou ſhalt not cauſe the land to ſinne, which the Lord thy God giueth
thee for an inheritance.5When a man hath taken a new wife, he ſhal not
goe out to warre, neither ſhall hee be charged with any buſineſse: but
hee ſhall be free at home one yeere, and ſhall cheere vp his wife which
he hath taken.6No man ſhall take the nether or the vpper milſtone to
pledge: for hee taketh a mans life to pledge.7If a man bee found ſtealing
any of his brethren of the children of Iſrael, and maketh merchandize
of him, or ſelleth him: then that thiefe ſhall die, and thou ſhalt put euill
away from among you.8Take heede, in the plague of leproſie, that thou
obſerue diligently, and doe according to all that the Prieſts the Leuites
ſhall teach you: as I commanded them, ſo ye ſhall obſerue to
doe.9Remember what the Lord thy God did vnto Miriam by the way,

after that yee were come forth out of Egypt. 10 When thou doeſt lend thy brother any thing, thou ſhalt not goe into his houſe to fetch his pledge. 11 Thou ſhalt ſtand abroad, and the man to whome thou doeſt lend, ſhall bring out the pledge abroad vnto thee. 12 And if the man be poore, thou ſhalt not ſleepe with his pledge: 13 In any caſe thou ſhalt deliuer him the pledge againe when the Sun goeth downe, that he may ſleepe in his owne raiment, and bleſſe thee: and it ſhall be righteouſneſſe vnto thee before the Lord thy God. 14 Thou ſhalt not oppreſſe an hired ſeruant that is poore and needy, whether he be of thy brethren, or of thy ſtrangers that are in thy lande within thy gates. 15 At his day thou ſhalt giue him his hire, neither ſhall the Sun goe downe vpon it, for he is poore, and ſetteth his heart vpon it, leſt hee crie againſt thee vnto the Lord, and it bee ſinne vnto thee. 16 The fathers ſhall not bee put to death for the children, neither ſhall the children be put to death for the fathers: euery man ſhall be put to death for his owne ſinne. 17 Thou ſhalt not peruert the iudgement of the ſtranger, nor of the fatherles, nor take a widowes raiment to pledge. 18 But thou ſhalt remember that thou waſt a bondman in Egypt, and the Lord thy God redeemed thee thence: therefore I command thee to doe this thing. 19 When thou cutteſt downe thine harueſt in thy field, and haſt forgot a ſheafe in the field, thou ſhalt not go againe to fetch it: it ſhalbe for the ſtranger, for the fatherleſſe, and for the widow: that the Lord thy God may bleſſe thee in all the worke of thine hands. 20 When thou beateſt thine oliue tree thou ſhalt not goe ouer the boughes againe: it ſhall be for the ſtranger, for the fatherleſſe, and for the widow. 21 When thou gathereſt the grapes of thy vineyard, thou ſhalt not gleane it afterward, it ſhalbe for the ſtranger, for the fatherleſſe, and for the widow. 22 And thou ſhalt remember that thou waſt a bondman in the land of Egypt: therfore I command thee to doe this thing.

CHAPTER 25 1 If there bee a controuerſie betweene men, and they come vnto iudgment, that the Iudges may iudge them, then they ſhall iuſtifie the righteous, and condemne the wicked. 2 And it ſhall be, if the wicked man be worthy to be beaten, that the Iudge ſhall cauſe him to lie downe, and to bee beaten before his face, according to his fault, by a certaine number. 3 Fourtie ſtripes he may giue him, and not exceed: leſt if he ſhould exceede, and beate him aboue theſe, with many ſtripes, then thy brother ſhould ſeeme vile vnto thee. 4 Thou ſhalt not muſſell the oxe when he treadeth out the corne. 5 If brethren dwell together, and one of them die, and haue no child, the wife of the dead ſhall not marrie without, vnto a ſtranger: her huſbands brother ſhall go in vnto her, and take her to him to wife, and performe the duetie of an huſbands brother vnto her. 6 And it ſhall be, that the firſt borne which ſhe beareth, ſhall ſucceede in the name of his brother which is dead, that his name be not put out of Iſrael. 7 And if the man like not to take his brothers wife, then let his brothers wife go vp to the gate, vnto the Elders, and ſay, My huſbands brother refuſeth to raiſe vp vnto his brother a name in Iſrael: he will not performe the dutie of my huſbands brother. 8 Then the Elders of his citie ſhall call him and ſpeake vnto him: and if he ſtand to it, and ſay, I like not to take her: 9 Then ſhal his brothers wife come vnto him in the preſence of the Elders, and looſe his ſhooe from off his foote, and ſpit in his face, and ſhall anſwere, and ſay, So ſhall it bee done vnto that man that will not build vp his brothers houſe. 10 And his name ſhall bee called in Iſrael, the houſe of him that hath his ſhooe looſed. 11 When men ſtriue together one with another, and the wife of the one draweth neere, for to deliuer her huſband out of the hand of him that ſmiteth him, and putteth foorth her hand and taketh him by the ſecrets: 12 Then thou ſhalt cut off her hand, thine eye ſhall not pitie her. 13 Thou ſhalt not haue in thy bagge diuers weights, a great, and a ſmall. 14 Thou ſhalt not haue in thine houſe diuers meaſures, a great, and a ſmall. 15 But thou ſhalt haue a perfect and iuſt weight, a perfect and iuſt meaſure ſhalt thou haue: that thy dayes may bee lengthened in the land which the Lord thy God giueth thee. 16 For all that doe ſuch things, and all that doe vnrighteouſly, are an abomination vnto the Lord thy God. 17 Remember what Amalek did vnto thee by the way, when ye were come foorth out of Egypt: 18 How he met thee by the way, and ſmote the hindmoſt of thee, euen all that were feeble behinde thee, when thou waſt faint and weary; and he feared not God. 19 Therefore it ſhall bee when the Lord thy God hath giuen thee reſt from all thine enemies round about, in the land which the Lord thy God giueth thee for an inheritance to poſſeſſe it; that thou ſhalt blot out the remembrance of Amalek from vnder heauen: thou ſhalt not forget it.

CHAPTER 26 1 And it ſhall be when thou art come in vnto the land which the Lord giueth thee for an inheritance, and poſſeſſeſt it, and dwelleſt therein: 2 That thou ſhalt take of the firſt of all the fruit of the earth, which thou ſhalt bring of thy land that the Lord thy God giueth thee, and ſhalt put it in a baſket, and ſhalt goe vnto the place which the Lord thy God ſhal chooſe to place his Name there: 3 And thou ſhalt goe vnto the Prieſt that ſhall be in thoſe dayes, and ſay vnto him, I profeſse this day vnto the Lord thy God, that I am come vnto the countrey which the Lord ſware vnto our fathers for to giue vs. 4 And the Prieſt ſhall take the baſket out of thine hand, and ſet it downe before the Altar of the Lord thy God. 5 And thou ſhalt ſpeake and ſay before the Lord thy God, A Syrian ready to periſh was my father, and hee went downe into Egypt, and ſoiourned there with a few, and became there a nation, great, mighty, and populous. 6 And the Egyptians euil intreated vs, and afflicted vs, and layd vpon vs hard bondage. 7 And when wee cryed vnto the Lord God of our fathers, the Lord heard our voyce, and looked on our affliction, and our labour, and our oppreſſion. 8 And the Lord brought vs foorth out of Egypt with a mightie hand, and with an out-ſtretched arme, and with great terribleneſſe, and with ſignes, and with wonders. 9 And he hath brought vs into this place, and hath giuen vs this land, euen a land that floweth with milke and honie. 10 And now behold, I haue brought the Firſt fruits of the land, which thou, O Lord, haſt giuen mee: and thou ſhalt ſet it before the Lord thy God, and worſhip before the Lord thy God. 11 And thou ſhalt reioyce in euery good thing, which the Lord thy God hath giuen vnto thee, and vnto thine houſe, thou, and the Leuite, and the ſtranger that is among you. 12 When thou haſt made an end of tithing all the tithes of thine increaſe, the third yeere, which is the yeere of tything, and haſt giuen it vnto the Leuite, the ſtranger, the fatherleſſe, and the widow, that they may eate within thy gates, and be filled: 13 Then thou ſhalt ſay before the Lord thy God, I haue brought away the hallowed things out of mine houſe, and alſo haue giuen them vnto the Leuite, and vnto the ſtranger, to the fatherleſſe, and to the widow, according to all thy commandements, which thou haſt commanded me: I haue not tranſgreſſed thy commandements, neither haue I forgotten them. 14 I haue not eaten thereof in my mourning, neither haue I taken away ought thereof for any vncleane vſe, nor giuen ought thereof for the dead: but I haue hearkened to the voyce of the Lord my God, and haue done according to all that thou haſt commaunded me. 15 Looke downe from thy holy habitation, from heauen, and bleſſe thy people Iſrael, and the land which thou haſt giuen vs, as thou ſwareſt vnto our fathers, a land that floweth with milke and hony. 16 This day the Lord thy God hath commanded thee to doe theſe Statutes and Iudgements: thou ſhalt therefore keepe and doe them with all thine heart, and with all thy ſoule. 17 Thou haſt auouched the Lord this day to be thy God, and to walke in his wayes, and to keepe his Statutes, and his Commaundements, and his Iudgements, and to hearken vnto his voice. 18 And the Lord hath auouched thee this day to be his peculiar people, as he hath promiſed thee, and that thou ſhouldeſt keepe all his Commaundements: 19 And to make thee high aboue all nations which he hath made, in praiſe and in name, and in honour, and that thou mayeſt be an holy people vnto the Lord thy God, as he hath ſpoken.

CHAPTER 27 1 And Moſes with the Elders of Iſrael commaunded the people, ſaying, Keepe all the Commandements which I command you this day. 2 And it ſhall be on the day when you ſhall paſſe ouer Iordan, vnto the land which the Lord thy God giueth thee, that thou ſhalt ſet thee vp great ſtones, and plaiſter them with plaiſter. 3 And thou ſhalt write vpon them all the words of this Law when thou art paſſed ouer, that thou mayeſt goe in vnto the land which the Lord thy God giueth thee, a land that floweth with milke and hony, as the Lord God of thy fathers hath promiſed thee. 4 Therefore it ſhall be when ye bee gone ouer Iordan, that yee ſhall ſet vp theſe ſtones, which I command you this day, in mount Ebal, and thou ſhalt plaiſter them with plaiſter. 5 And there ſhalt thou build an Altar vnto the Lord thy God, an altar of ſtones: thou ſhalt not lift vp any yron toole vpon them. 6 Thou ſhalt build the Altar of the Lord thy God of whole ſtones: and thou ſhalt offer burnt offerings theron vnto the Lord thy God. 7 And thou ſhalt offer peace offerings, and ſhalt eate there, and reioyce before the Lord thy God. 8 And thou ſhalt write vpon the ſtones all the words of this Law very plainely. 9 And

Moſes, and the Prieſtes the Leuites, ſpake vnto all Iſrael, ſaying, Take heed, and hearken O Iſrael, this day thou art become the people of the Lord thy God.10Thou ſhalt therefore obey the voyce of the Lord thy God, and doe his Commandements, and his Statutes which I command thee this day.11And Moſes charged the people the ſame day, ſaying,12Theſe ſhall ſtand vpon mount Gerizzim to bleſſe the people, when yee are come ouer Iordan: Simeon, and Leui, and Iudah, and Iſſachar, and Ioſeph, and Beniamin.13And theſe ſhall ſtand vpon mount Ebal to curſe: Reuben, Gad, and Aſher, and Zebulun, Dan, & Naphtali.14And the Leuites ſhal ſpeake, and ſay vnto all the men of Iſrael with a loud voyce:15Curſed be the man that maketh any grauen or molten image, an abomination vnto the Lord, the worke of the handes of the craftesman, and putteth it in a ſecret place: and all the people ſhall anſwere and ſay, Amen.16Curſed be he that ſetteth light by his father or his mother: and all the people ſhall ſay, Amen.17Curſed be he that remooueth his neighbours land-marke: and all the people ſhall ſay, Amen.18Curſed be hee that maketh the blinde to wander out of the way: and all the people ſhall ſay, Amen.19Curſed be hee that peruerteth the iudgement of the ſtranger, fatherleſſe, and widow: and all the people ſhall ſay, Amen.20Curſed be hee that lieth with his fathers wife, becauſe he vncouereth his fathers ſkirt: and all the people ſhall ſay, Amen.21Curſed be hee that lieth with any maner of beaſt: and all the people ſhall ſay, Amen.22Curſed be hee that lieth with his ſiſter, the daughter of his father, or the daughter of his mother: and all the people ſhall ſay, Amen.23Curſed be hee that lieth with his mother in law: and all the people ſhall ſay, Amen.24Curſed be hee that ſmiteth his neighbour ſecretly: and all the people ſhall ſay, Amen.25Curſed be he that taketh reward to ſlay an innocent perſon: and all the people ſhall ſay, Amen.26Curſed be hee that confirmeth not all the words of this Law to doe them: and al the people ſhal ſay, Amen.

CHAPTER 281And it ſhall come to paſſe, if thou ſhalt hearken diligently vnto the voyce of the Lord thy God, to obſerue and to doe all his Commandements which I command thee this day; that the Lord thy God will ſet thee on high aboue all nations of the earth.2And all theſe bleſſings ſhall come on thee, and ouertake thee, if thou ſhalt hearken vnto the voice of the Lord thy God.3Bleſſed ſhalt thou bee in the citie, and bleſſed ſhalt thou be in the field.4Bleſſed ſhall be the fruit of thy body, and the fruit of thy ground, and the fruit of thy cattell, the increaſe of thy kine, and the flocks of thy ſheepe.5Bleſſed ſhall be thy baſket and thy ſtore.6Bleſſed ſhalt thou bee when thou commeſt in, and bleſſed ſhalt thou bee when thou goeſt out.7The Lord ſhall cauſe thine enemies that riſe vp againſt thee, to bee ſmitten before thy face: they ſhall come out againſt thee one way, and flee before thee ſeuen wayes.8The Lord ſhall command the bleſſing vpon thee in thy ſtore-houſes, and in all that thou ſetteſt thine hand vnto, and he ſhall bleſſe thee in the land which the Lord thy God giueth thee.9The Lord ſhall eſtabliſh thee an holy people vnto himſelfe, as hee hath ſworne vnto thee, if thou ſhalt keepe the Commaundements of the Lord thy God, and walke in his wayes.10And all people of the earth ſhall ſee, that thou art called by the Name of the Lord, and they ſhall bee afraid of thee.11And the Lord ſhal make thee plenteous in goods, in the fruit of thy body, and in the fruit of thy cattell, and in the fruit of thy ground, in the land which the Lord ſware vnto thy fathers to giue thee.12The Lord ſhal open vnto thee his good treaſure, the heauen to giue the raine vnto thy land in his ſeaſon, and to bleſſe all the worke of thine hand: and thou ſhalt lend vnto many nations, and thou ſhalt not borrow.13And the Lord ſhall make thee the head, and not the taile, and thou ſhalt be aboue onely, and thou ſhalt not be beneath: if that thou hearken vnto the Commandements of the Lord thy God, which I command thee this day, to obſerue, and to doe them:14And thou ſhalt not go aſide from any of the wordes which I command thee this day, to the right hand, or to the left, to goe after other gods, to ſerue them.15But it ſhal come to paſſe, if thou wilt not hearken vnto the voyce of the Lord thy God, to obſerue to doe all his Commandements and his Statutes, which I command thee this day, that all theſe curſes ſhall come vpon thee, and ouertake thee.16Curſed ſhalt thou be in the city, and curſed ſhalt thou be in the field.17Curſed ſhall be thy baſket and thy ſtore.18Curſed ſhalbe the fruit of thy body, and the fruit of thy land, the increaſe of thy kine, and the flocks of thy ſheepe.19Curſed ſhalt thou bee when thou commeſt in, and curſed ſhalt thou bee when thou goeſt out.20The Lord ſhall ſend vpon thee curſing, vexation, and rebuke, in all that thou ſetteſt thine hand vnto, for to doe, vntill thou be deſtroyed, and vntill thou periſh quickely, becauſe of the wickedneſſe of thy doings, whereby thou haſt forſaken me.21The Lord ſhall make the peſtilence cleaue vnto thee, vntill he haue conſumed thee from off the land, whither thou goeſt to poſſeſſe it.22The Lord ſhall ſmite thee with a conſumption, and with a feuer, and with an inflammation, & with an extreme burning, and with the ſword, and with blaſting, and with mildewe: and they ſhall purſue thee vntill thou periſh.23And the heauen that is ouer thy head ſhall be braſſe, and the earth that is vnder thee ſhall be yron.24The Lord ſhall make the raine of thy land powder & duſt: from heauen ſhall it come downe vpon thee, vntill thou be deſtroyed.25The Lord ſhall cauſe thee to be ſmitten before thine enemies: thou ſhalt go out one way againſt them, and flee ſeuen wayes before them, and ſhalt be remoued into all the kingdomes of the earth.26And thy carkeiſeſhalbe meat vnto all foules of the aire, and vnto the beaſts of the earth, and no man ſhall fray them away.27The Lord wil ſmite thee with the botch of Egypt, and with the emerods, and with the ſcabbe, and with the itch, whereof thou canſt not bee healed.28The Lord ſhall ſmite thee with madneſse, and blindneſse, and aſtoniſhment of heart.29And thou ſhalt grope at noone dayes, as the blind gropeth in darknes, and thou ſhalt not proſper in thy waies: and thou ſhalt be onely oppreſſed, and ſpoiled euermore, and no man ſhal ſaue thee.30Thou ſhalt betrothe a wife, and another man ſhall lie with her: thou ſhalt build an houſe, and thou ſhalt not dwell therein: thou ſhalt plant a vineyard, and ſhalt not gather the grapes thereof.31Thine oxe ſhall be ſlaine before thine eyes, and thou ſhalt not eat thereof: thine aſſe ſhall be violently taken away from before thy face, and ſhal not be reſtored to thee: thy ſheepe ſhall bee giuen vnto thine enemies, and thou ſhalt haue none to reſcue them.32Thy ſonnes, and thy daughters ſhall be giuen vnto another people, and thine eyes ſhal looke, and faile with longing for them al the day long: and there ſhall be no might in thine hand.33The fruit of thy land, and all thy labours, ſhall a nation which thou knoweſt not, eate vp: and thou ſhalt be onely oppreſſed and cruſhed alway:34So that thou ſhalt bee mad, for the ſight of thine eyes which thou ſhalt ſee.35The Lord ſhall ſmite thee in the knees, and in the legges with a ſore botch that cannot bee healed, from the ſole of thy foot, vnto the top of thy head.36The Lord ſhal bring thee, and thy king which thou ſhalt ſet ouer thee, vnto a nation which neither thou, nor thy fathers haue knowen, and there ſhalt thou ſerue other gods, wood and ſtone.37And thou ſhalt become an aſtoniſhment, a prouerbe, and a by-worde, among all nations whither the Lord ſhall leade thee.38Thou ſhalt carie much ſeede out into the field, and ſhalt gather but litle in: for the locuſt ſhall conſume it.39Thou ſhalt plant vineyards and dreſſe them, but ſhalt neither drinke of the wine, nor gather the grapes: for the wormes ſhall eate them.40Thou ſhalt haue Oliue trees throughout al thy coaſts, but thou ſhalt not anoint thy ſelfe with the oyle: for thine Oliue ſhall caſt his fruit.41Thou ſhalt beget ſonnes and daughters, but thou ſhalt not enioy them: for they ſhall goe into captiuitie.42All thy trees and fruit of thy land ſhall the locuſts conſume.43The ſtranger that is within thee ſhall get vp aboue thee very high: and thou ſhalt come downe very low.44He ſhall lend to thee, and thou ſhalt not lend to him: he ſhall bee the head, and thou ſhalt be the taile.45Moreouer, all theſe curſes ſhall come vpon thee, and ſhall purſue thee, and ouertake thee, til thou be deſtroied: becauſe thou hearkenedſt not vnto the voice of the Lord thy God, to keepe his Commandements, and his Statutes which he commanded thee.46And they ſhall be vpon thee for a ſigne, and for a wonder, and vpon thy ſeed for euer:47Becauſe thou ſeruedſt not the Lord thy God with ioyfulneſse, and with gladneſſe of heart, for the aboundance of all things.48Therefore ſhalt thou ſerue thine enemies, which the Lord ſhall ſend againſt thee, in hunger, and in thirſt, and in nakedneſse, and in want of all things: and he ſhall put a yoke of iron vpon thy necke, vntill he haue deſtroyed thee.49The Lord ſhall bring a nation againſt thee from farre, from the end of the earth, as ſwift as the Eagle fleeth, a nation whoſe tongue thou ſhalt not vnderſtand:50A nation of fierce countenance, which ſhal not regard the perſon of the old, nor ſhew fauour to the yong:51And hee ſhall eat the fruit of thy cattell, and the fruit of thy land, vntill thou be deſtroyed: which alſo ſhall not leaue thee either corne, wine, or oyle, or the increaſe of thy kine, or flockes of thy ſheepe, vntill he haue deſtroyed thee.52And he ſhall beſiege thee in all thy gates, vntill thy high and fenced walles come downe wherein thou truſtedſt throughout all thy land: and hee ſhall beſiege thee in all thy gates, throughout all thy land which the Lord thy God hath giuen thee.53And thou ſhalt eate the fruit of thine owne body, the fleſh of thy ſonnes, and of thy daughters (which the Lord thy God hath giuen thee) in the ſiege, and in the ſtraitneſse wherewith thine enemies ſhall diſtreſſe thee.54So that the man that is tender among you, and very delicate, his eye ſhalbe euill toward his brother, and toward the wife of his boſome, and towards the remnant of his children which he ſhall leaue:55So that he wil not giue to any of them of the fleſh of his children whom he ſhall eate: becauſe hee hath nothing left him in the ſiege, and in the ſtraitneſse wherewith thine enemies ſhal diſtreſſe thee, in all thy gates.56The tender and delicate woman among you, which would not aduenture to ſet the ſole of her foote vpon the ground, for delicateneſse and tenderneſse, her eye ſhall be euill towards the huſband of her boſome, and towards her ſonne, and towards her daughter,57And towards her yong one that commeth out from betweene her feete, and towards her children which ſhee ſhall beare: for ſhee ſhall eate them for want of all things ſecretly in the ſiege and ſtraitnes, wherewith thine enemie ſhall diſtreſſe thee in thy gates.58If thou wilt not obſerue to doe all the wordes of this Law that are written in this booke, that thou mayeſt feare this glorious and fearefull Name, The Lord thy God:59Then the Lord wil make thy plagues wonderfull, and the plagues of thy ſeed, euen great plagues, and of long continuance, and ſore ſickneſses, and of long continuance.60Moreouer, hee will bring vpon thee all the diſeaſes of Egypt, which thou waſt afraid of, and they ſhal cleaue vnto thee.61Alſo euery ſickeneſse, and euery plague which is not written in the booke of this Law, them will the Lord bring vpon thee, vntill thou be deſtroyed.62And ye ſhall be left few in number, whereas ye were as the ſtarres of heauen for multitude: becauſe thou wouldeſt not obey the voyce of the Lord thy God.63And it ſhall come to paſſe, that as the Lord reioyced ouer you to doe you good, and to multiply you; ſo the Lord will reioyce ouer you to deſtroy you, and to bring you to nought; and ye ſhalbe plucked from off the land whither thou goeſt to poſſeſſe it.64And the Lord ſhall ſcatter thee among all people, from the one end of the earth, euen vnto the other: and there thou ſhalt ſerue other gods, which neither thou nor thy fathers haue knowen, euen wood and ſtone.65And among theſe nations ſhalt thou finde no eaſe, neither ſhall the ſole of thy foote haue reſt: but the Lord ſhall giue thee there a trembling heart, and failing of eyes, & ſorrow of minde.66And thy life ſhall hang in doubt before thee, and thou ſhalt feare day and night, and ſhalt haue none aſsurance of thy life.67In the morning thou ſhalt ſay, Would God it were Euen: and at Euen thou ſhalt ſay, Would God it were morning, for the feare of thine heart wherewith thou ſhalt feare, and for the ſight of thine eyes which thou ſhalt ſee.68And the Lord ſhall bring thee into Egypt againe, with ſhips, by the way whereof I ſpake vnto thee, Thou ſhalt ſee it no more againe: and there ye ſhall bee ſold vnto your enemies for bondmen, and bondwomen, and no man ſhall buy you.

CHAPTER 291Theſe are the woordes of the Couenant which the Lord commanded Moſes to make with the children of Iſrael in the land of Moab, beſide the Couenant which he made with them in Horeb.2And Moſes called vnto all Iſrael, and ſaid vnto them, Yee haue ſeene all that the Lord did before your eyes in the land of Egypt vnto Pharaoh, and vnto all his ſeruants, and vnto all his land;3The great temptations which thine eyes haue ſeene, the ſignes and thoſe great miracles:4Yet the Lord hath not giuen you an heart to perceiue, and eyes to ſee, and eares to heare, vnto this day.5And I haue led you fourtie yeres in the wildernes: your clothes are not waxen old vpon you, and thy ſhooe is not waxen old vpon thy foot.6Ye haue not eaten bread, neither haue you drunke wine, or ſtrong drink: that yee might knowe that I am the Lord your God.7And when yee came vnto this place, Sihon the king of Heſhbon, and Og the King of Baſhan, came out againſt vs vnto battell, and wee ſmote them.8And wee tooke their lande, and gaue it for an inheritance vnto the Reubenites, and to the Gadites, and to the halfe tribe of Manaſſeh.9Keepe therefore the wordes of this Couenant and doe them, that yee may proſper in all that ye doe.10Ye ſtand this day all of you before the Lord your God: your captaines of your tribes, your Elders, and your officers, with all the men of Iſrael,11Your litle ones, your wiues, and thy ſtranger that is in thy campe, from the hewer of thy wood, vnto the drawer of thy water:12That thou ſhouldeſt enter into Couenant with the Lord thy God, and into his othe which the Lord thy God maketh with thee this day:13That he may eſtabliſh thee to day for a people vnto himſelfe, and that hee may be vnto thee a God, as he hath ſaid vnto thee, and as he hath ſworne vnto thy fathers, to Abraham, to Iſaac, and to Iacob.14Neither with you onely doe I make this couenant and this othe:15But with him that ſtandeth here with vs this day before the Lord our God, and alſo with him that is not here with vs this day:16(For ye know how we haue dwelt in the land of Egypt, and how we came thorow the nations which ye paſſed by.17And ye haue ſeene their abominations, and their idoles, wood, and ſtone, ſiluer, and gold, which were among them.)18Leſt there ſhould be among you man or woman, or familie, or tribe, whoſe heart turneth away this day frō the Lord our God, to goe and ſerue the gods of theſe nations: leſt there ſhould bee among you a root that beareth gall and wormewood,19And it come to paſſe when he heareth the wordes of this curſe, that hee bleſſe himſelfe in his heart, ſaying, I ſhall haue peace, though I walke in the imagination of mine heart, to adde drunkenneſse to thirſt:20The Lord wil not ſpare him, but then the anger of the Lord, and his ielouſie ſhall ſmoke againſt that man, and all the curſes that are written in this booke ſhall lie vpon him, and the Lord ſhall blot out his name from vnder heauen.21And the Lord ſhall ſeparate him vnto euill, out of all the tribes of Iſrael, according to all the curſes of the Couenant, that are written in this booke of the Law:22So that the generation to come of your children, that ſhall riſe vp after you, and the ſtranger that ſhall come from a farre land, ſhall ſay, when they ſee the plagues of that land, and the ſickneſses which the Lord hath layd vpon it;23And that the whole land thereof is brimſtone and ſalt, and burning, that it is not ſowen, nor beareth, nor any graſſe groweth therein, like the ouerthrow of Sodome, and Gomorah, Admah, and Zeboim, which the Lord ouerthrew in his anger, and in his wrath:24Euen al nations ſhal ſay, Wherefore hath the Lord done thus vnto this land? what meaneth the heat of this great anger?25Then men ſhall ſay, Becauſe they haue forſaken the Couenant of the Lord God of their fathers, which he made with them when he brought them foorth out of the land of Egypt.26For they went and ſerued other gods, & worſhipped them, gods whom they knew not, and whom he had not giuen vnto them.27And the anger of the Lord was kindled againſt this land, to bring vpon it all the curſes, that are written in this booke.28And the Lord rooted them out of their land, in anger and in wrath, and in great indignation, and caſt them into another land, as it is this day.29The ſecret things belong vnto the Lord our God: but thoſe things which are reuealed belong vnto vs, and to our children for euer, that wee may doe all the words of this Law.

CHAPTER 301And it ſhall come to paſſe when all theſe things are come vpon thee, the bleſſing, and the curſe, which I haue ſet before thee, and thou ſhalt call them to minde among all the nations whither the Lord thy God hath driuen thee,2And ſhalt returne vnto the Lord thy God, and ſhalt obey his voyce according to all that I command thee this day, thou and thy children with al thine heart, and with all thy ſoule:3That then the Lord thy God will turne thy captiuitie, and haue compaſſion vpon thee, and wil returne and gather thee from all the nations whither the Lord thy God hath ſcattered thee.4If any of thine be driuen out vnto the outmoſt parts of heauen, from thence will the Lord thy God gather thee, and from thence will he fetch thee.5And the Lord thy God will bring thee into the land which thy fathers poſſeſſed, and thou ſhalt poſſeſſe it: and he will doe thee good, and multiply thee aboue thy fathers.6And the Lord thy God will circumciſe thine heart, and the heart of thy ſeed, to loue the Lord thy God with all thine heart, and with all thy ſoule, that thou mayeſt liue.7And the Lord thy God will put all theſe curſes vpon thine enemies, and on them that hate thee, which perſecuted thee.8And thou ſhalt returne and obey the voice of the Lord, and doe all his Commandements which I command thee this day.9And the Lord thy God will make thee plenteous in euery worke of thine hand, in the fruit of thy body, and in the fruit of thy cattell, and in the fruit of thy land, for good: for the Lord will againe reioyce ouer thee for good, as he reioyced ouer thy fathers:10If thou ſhalt hearken vnto the voyce of the Lord thy God to keepe his Commandements, and his Statutes which are written in this booke of the Law, and if thou turne vnto the Lord thy God with all thine heart, and with all thy ſoule.11For this Commaundement which I command thee this day, it is not hidden from thee, neither is it farre off.12It is not in heauen, that thou ſhouldeſt ſay, Who ſhal goe vp for vs to heauen, and bring it vnto vs, that wee may heare it, and doe it?13Neither is it beyond the ſea, that thou

ſhouldeſt ſay, Who ſhall goe ouer the ſea for vs, and bring it vnto vs,
that we may heare it, and doe it? 14 But the word is very nigh vnto thee,
in thy mouth, and in thy heart, that thou mayeſt doe it. 15 See, I haue ſet
before thee this day, life and good, and death, and euill: 16 In that I
command thee this day to loue the Lord thy God, to walke in his wayes,
and to keepe his Commandements, and his Statutes, and his
Iudgements, that thou maieſt liue and multiply: and the Lord thy God
ſhall bleſſe thee in the land, whither thou goeſt to poſſeſſe it. 17 But if
thine heart turne away, ſo that thou wilt not heare, but ſhalt bee drawen
away, and worſhip other gods and ſerue them: 18 I denounce vnto you
this day, that ye ſhall ſurely periſh, and that yee ſhall not prolong your
dayes vpon the land, whither thou paſſeſt ouer Iordan, to goe to poſſeſſe
it. 19 I call heauen and earth to record this day againſt you, that I haue ſet
before you life and death, bleſſing and curſing: therefore chooſe life, that
both thou and thy ſeed may liue: 20 That thou maieſt loue the Lord thy
God, and that thou mayeſt obey his voyce, and that thou mayeſt cleaue
vnto him: for he is thy life, and the length of thy dayes, that thou mayeſt
dwell in the land, which the Lord ſware vnto thy fathers, to Abraham,
to Iſaac, and to Iacob, to giue them.

CHAPTER 31 1 And Moſes went & ſpake theſe wordes vnto all
Iſrael. 2 And hee ſaide vnto them, I am an hundred and twentie yeeres old
this day; I can no more goe out and come in: alſo the Lord hath ſaid
vnto mee, Thou ſhalt not goe ouer this Iordan. 3 The Lord thy God, hee
will goe ouer before thee, and he will deſtroy theſe nations from before
thee, and thou ſhalt poſſeſſe them: and Ioſhua, hee ſhall goe ouer before
thee, as the Lord hath ſaid. 4 And the Lord ſhall doe vnto them, as hee
did to Sihon, and to Og Kings of the Amorites, and vnto the land of
them, whom he deſtroyed. 5 And the Lord ſhall giue them vp before your
face, that ye may doe vnto them according vnto all the Commandements
which I haue commanded you. 6 Be ſtrong, and of a good courage, feare
not, nor be afraid of them: for the Lord thy God, he it is that doeth goe
with thee, he will not faile thee, nor forſake thee. 7 And Moſes called vnto
Ioſhua, and ſaid vnto him in the ſight of all Iſrael, Bee ſtrong, and of a
good courage: for thou muſt goe with this people vnto the land, which
the Lord hath ſworne vnto their fathers to giue them; and thou ſhalt
cauſe them to inherite it. 8 And the Lord, he it is that doth goe before
thee, he will be with thee, hee will not faile thee, neither forſake thee:
feare not, neither be diſmayed. 9 And Moſes wrote this Law, and
deliuered it vnto the Prieſts the ſonnes of Leui, which bare the Arke of
the Couenant of the Lord, and vnto all the Elders of Iſrael. 10 And Moſes
commanded them, ſaying, At the end of euery ſeuen yeeres, in the
ſolemnitie of the yeere of releaſe, in the feaſt of Tabernacles, 11 When all
Iſrael is come to appeare before the Lord thy God, in the place which
hee ſhall chooſe; thou ſhalt reade this Law before all Iſrael, in their
hearing. 12 Gather the people together, men, and women and children,
and thy ſtranger that is within thy gates, that they may heare, and that
they may learne, and feare the Lord your God, and obſerue to doe all
the wordes of this Law: 13 And that their children which haue not knowen
any thing, may heare, and learne to feare the Lord your God, as long as
yee liue in the land, whither ye goe ouer Iordan to poſſeſſe it. 14 And the
Lord ſaide vnto Moſes, Beholde, thy dayes approach that thou muſt die:
call Ioſhua, and preſent your ſelues in the Tabernacle of the
Congregation, that I may giue him a charge. And Moſes and Ioſhua went
and preſented themſelues in the Tabernacle of the Congregation. 15 And
the Lord appeared in the Tabernacle in a pillar of a cloud: and the pillar
of the cloude ſtood ouer the doore of the Tabernacle. 16 And the Lord
ſaide vnto Moſes, Behold, thou ſhalt ſleepe with thy fathers, and this
people wil riſe vp, and goe a whoring after the gods of the ſtrangers of
the land whither they goe to be amongſt them, and wil forſake me, and
breake my couenant which I haue made with them. 17 Then my anger
ſhall be kindled againſt them in that day, and I will forſake them, and I
will hide my face from them, and they ſhall be deuoured, and many euils
and troubles ſhall befall them, ſo that they will ſay in that day, Are not
theſe euils come vpon vs, becauſe our God is not amongſt vs? 18 And I
will ſurely hide my face in that day, for all the euils which they ſhal haue
wrought, in that they are turned vnto other gods. 19 Now therefore, write
ye this ſong for you, and teach it the children of Iſrael: put it in their
mouthes, that this ſong may be a witneſſe for mee, againſt the children
of Iſrael. 20 For when I ſhall haue brought them into the land which I
ſware vnto their fathers, that floweth with milke and hony; and they ſhall
haue eaten and filled themſelues, and waxen fat; then will they turne
vnto other gods, and ſerue them, and prouoke me, and breake my
couenant. 21 And it ſhall come to paſſe, when many euils and troubles are
befallen them, that this ſong ſhall teſtifie againſt them as a witneſſe: for
it ſhall not bee forgotten out of the mouthes of their ſeed: for I know
their imagination which they goe about euen now, before I haue brought
them into the land, which I ſware. 22 Moſes therefore wrote this ſong the
ſame day, and taught it the children of Iſrael. 23 And he gaue Ioſhua the
ſonne of Nun a charge, and ſaid, Bee ſtrong, and of a good courage: for
thou ſhalt bring the children of Iſrael into the land which I ſware vnto
them: and I will be with thee. 24 And it came to paſſe when Moſes had
made an ende of writing the wordes of this Law in a booke, vntill they
were finiſhed, 25 That Moſes commaunded the Leuites which bare the
Arke of the Couenant of the Lord, ſaying, 26 Take this booke of the Law,
and put it in the ſide of the Arke of the Couenant of the Lord your God,
that it may bee there for a witneſſe againſt thee. 27 For I know thy
rebellion, and thy ſtiffe necke: Beholde, while I am yet aliue with you
this day, yee haue bene rebellious againſt the Lord; and how much more
after my death? 28 Gather vnto mee all the Elders of your tribes, and your
Officers, that I may ſpeake theſe words in their eares, and call heauen
and earth to record againſt them. 29 For I know, that after my death yee
will vtterly corrupt your ſelues, and turne aſide from the way, which I
haue commauded you: and euil wil befall you in the latter dayes, becauſe
yee wil doe euil in the ſight of the Lord, to prouoke him to anger through
the worke of your hands. 30 And Moſes ſpake in the eares of al the
Cōgregation of Iſrael the words of this ſong, vntill they were ended.

CHAPTER 32 1 Giue eare, O yee heauens, and I will ſpeake; And heare,
O earth, the words of my mouth. 2 My doctrine ſhall drop as the raine:
my ſpeech ſhall diſtill as the deaw, as the ſmal raine vpon the tender
herbe, and as the ſhowres vpon the graſſe. 3 Becauſe I wil publiſh the
Name of the Lord: aſcribe yee greatneſſe vnto our God. 4 He is the rocke,
his worke is perfect: for all his wayes are Iudgement: A God of trueth,
and without iniquity, iuſt and right is he. 5 They haue corrupted
themſelues, their ſpot is not the ſpot of his children: they are a peruerſe
and crooked generation. 6 Doe ye thus requite the Lord, O fooliſh
people, & vnwiſe? Is not he thy Father that hath bought thee? Hath he
not made thee, and eſtabliſhed thee? 7 Remember the dayes of olde,
conſider the yeeres of many generations: aſke thy father, and he will
ſhewe thee, thy Elders, and they wil tell thee. 8 When the moſt High
diuided to the nations their inheritance, when he ſeparated the ſonnes
of Adam, hee ſet the bounds of the people according to the number of
the children of Iſrael. 9 For the Lords portion is his people: Iacob is the
lot of his inheritance. 10 He found him in a deſert land, and in the waſte
howling wilderneſſe: Hee ledde him about, he inſtructed him, hee kept
him as the apple of his eye. 11 As an Eagle ſtirreth vp her neſt, fluttereth
ouer her yong, ſpreadeth abroad her wings, taketh them, beareth them
on her wings: 12 So the Lord alone did leade him, and there was no ſtrange
God with him. 13 He made him ride on the high places of the earth, that
he might eate the increaſe of the fields, and he made him to ſucke hony
out of the rocke, and oyle out of the flintie rocke, 14 Butter of kine, &
milke of ſheepe, with fat of lambes, and rammes of the breed of Baſhan,
& goats, with the fat of kidneis of wheat, and thou diddeſt drinke the
pure blood of the grape. 15 But Ieſurun waxed fat, and kicked: Thou art
waxen fat, thou art growen thicke, thou art couered with fatnes: then he
forſooke God which made him, and lightly eſteemed the Rocke of his
ſaluation. 16 They prouoked him to ielouſie with ſtrange gods, with
abominations prouoked they him to anger. 17 They ſacrificed vnto deuils,
not to God: to gods whom they knew not, to new gods, that came newly
vp, whom your fathers feared not. 18 Of the Rocke that begate thee thou
art vnmindfull, and haſt forgotten God that formed thee. 19 And when
the Lord ſaw it, he abhorred them, becauſe of the prouoking of his
ſonnes, & of his daughters. 20 And he ſaid, I will hide my face from them,
I will ſee what their ende ſhall be: for they are a very froward generation,
children in whom is no faith. 21 They haue mooued me to ielouſie with
that which is not god, they haue prouoked me to anger with their
vanities: And I will moue them to ielouſie with thoſe which are not a
people, I will prouoke them to anger with a fooliſh nation. 22 For a fire is
kindled in my anger, and ſhall burne vnto the loweſt hell, and ſhall
conſume the earth with her increaſe, and ſet on fire the foundations of
the mountaines. 23 I will heape miſchiefes vpon them, I will ſpend mine

arrowes vpon them.24They ſhall bee burnt with hunger and deuoured
with burning heat, and with bitter deſtruction: I will alſo ſend the teeth
of beaſts vpon them, with the poiſon of ſerpents of the duſt.25The
ſword without, and terrour within ſhall deſtroy both the yong man, and
the virgin, the ſuckling alſo with the man of gray haires.26I ſaid, I would
ſcatter them into corners, I would make the remembrance of them to
ceaſe frō among men:27Were it not that I feared the wrath of the enemie,
leſt their aduerſaries ſhould behaue themſelues ſtrangely, and leſt they
ſhould ſay, Our hande is high, and the Lord hath not done all this.28For
they are a nation voide of counſel, neither is there any vnderſtanding in
them.29O that they were wiſe, that they vnderſtood this, that they would
conſider their latter end.30How ſhould one chaſe a thouſand, and two
put ten thouſand to flight, except their Rocke had ſold them, and the
Lord had ſhut them vp?31For their rocke is not as our Rocke, euen our
enemies themſelues being iudges.32For their vine is of the vine of
Sodome, and of the fields of Gomorah: their grapes are grapes of gall,
their cluſters are bitter.33Their wine is the poiſon of dragons, and the
cruell venime of Aſpes.34Is not this laide vp in ſtore with me, and ſealed
vp among my treaſures?35To me belongeth vengeance, and recompence,
their foot ſhall ſlide in due time: for the day of their calamitie is at hand,
and the things that ſhal come vpon them, make haſte.36For the Lord
ſhall iudge his people, and repent himſelfe for his ſeruants, when he
ſeeth that their power is gone; and there is none ſhut vp, or left.37And
he ſhall ſay, where are their gods? their Rocke in whom they
truſted;38Which did eat the fat of their ſacrifices, & dranke the wine of
their drinke offerings? let them riſe vp and helpe you, and be your
protection.39ſee now, that I, euen I am he, and there is no god with mee;
I kill, and I make aliue: I wound, and I heale: neither is there any that
can deliuer out of my hand.40For I lift vp my hand to heauen, and ſay,
I liue for euer.41If I whet my glittering ſword, and mine hand take holde
on Iudgement, I will render vengeance to mine enemies, and will reward
them that hate me.42I will make mine arrowes drunke with blood, (and
my ſword ſhal deuoure fleſh) and that with the blood of the ſlaine, and
of the captiues, from the beginning of reuenges vpon the
enemie.43Reioyce, O ye nations with his people, for he will auenge the
blood of his ſeruants, and will render vengeance to his aduerſaries, and
wil be mercifull vnto his land, and to his people.44And Moſes came and
ſpake all the wordes of this ſong in the eares of the people, he and
Hoſhea the ſonne of Nun.45And Moſes made an end of ſpeaking all
theſe words to all Iſrael.46And hee ſaid vnto them, Set your hearts vnto
all the wordes which I teſtifie among you this day, which yee ſhall
commaund your children to obſerue to doe all the wordes of this
Law.47For it is not a vaine thing for you: becauſe it is your life, and
through this thing yee ſhall prolong your dayes, in the land whither yee
goe ouer Iordan to poſſeſſe it.48And the Lord ſpake vnto Moſes that
ſelfe ſame day, ſaying,49Get thee vp into this mountaine Abarim, vnto
mount Nebo, which is in the land of Moab, that is ouer againſt Iericho,
and behold the land of Canaan which I giue vnto the children of Iſrael
for a poſſeſſion:50And die in the mount whither thou goeſt vp, and bee
gathered vnto thy people, as Aaron thy brother died in mount Hor, and
was gathered vnto his people:51Becauſe ye treſpaſſed againſt me among
the children of Iſrael, at the waters of Meribah Kadeſh, in the
wilderneſſe of Zin: becauſe yee ſanctified mee not in the midſt of the
children of Iſrael.52Yet thou ſhalt ſee the land before thee, but thou ſhalt
not goe thither vnto the land which I giue the children of Iſrael.
CHAPTER 331And this is the bleſſing, wherewith Moſes the man of
God bleſſed the children of Iſrael before his death.2And he ſaid, The
Lord came from Sinai, and roſe vp from Seir vnto them, hee ſhined
foorth from mount Paran, and hee came with ten thouſands of Saints:
from his Right hand went a fierie Law for them.3Yea hee loued the
people; all his Saints are in thy hand: and they ſate downe at thy feete;
euery one ſhall receiue of thy wordes.4Moſes commaunded vs a Law,
euen the inheritance of the Congregation of Iacob.5And hee was King
in Ieſurun, when the heads of the people, and the Tribes of Iſrael were
gathered together.6Let Reuben liue, and not die, and let not his men be
few.7And this is the bleſſing of Iudah: and he ſaid, Heare, Lord, the
voice of Iudah, and bring him vnto his people: let his hands bee
ſufficient for him, and bee thou an helpe to him from his enemies.8And
of Leui hee ſaid, Let thy Thummim and thy Urim be with thy holy one,
whom thou diddeſt prooue at Maſſah, & with whom thou didſt ſtriue at
the waters of Meribah:9Who ſaid vnto his father & to his mother, I haue
not ſeene him, neither did hee acknowledge his brethren; nor knew his
owne children: for they haue obſerued thy word, and kept thy
Couenant.10They ſhal teach Iacob thy iudgments, and Iſrael thy Lawe:
they ſhall put incenſe before thee, and whole burnt ſacrifice vpon thine
Altar.11Bleſſe, Lord, his ſubſtance, and accept the worke of his handes,
ſmite thorow the loines of them that riſe againſt him, and of them that
hate him, that they riſe not againe.12And of Beniamin he ſaid, The
beloued of the Lord ſhall dwell in ſafetie by him, and the Lord ſhall
couer him all the day long, and he ſhall dwell betweene his ſhoulders
.13And of Ioſeph he ſaid, Bleſſed of the Lord be his land, for the precious
things of heauen, for the dew, and for the deep that coucheth
beneath;14And for the precious fruits brought forth by the ſunne, and
for the precious things put forth by the moone,15And for the chiefe
things of the ancient mountaines, and for the precious things of the
laſting hils,16And for the precious things of the earth, and fulneſse
thereof, and for the good will of him that dwelt in the buſh: let the
bleſſing come vpon the head of Ioſeph, and vpon the top of the head
of him that was ſeparated frō his brethren.17His glory is like the firſtling
of his bullocke, & his hornes are like the hornes of Unicornes: with them
he ſhall puſh the people together, to the ends of the earth: and they are
the ten thouſands of Ephraim, and they are the thouſands of
Manaſſeh.18And of Zebulun he ſaid, Reioyce, Zebulun, in thy going out;
and Iſſachar, in thy tents.19They ſhall call the people vnto the
mountaine, there they ſhal offer ſacrifices of righteouſneſſe: for they
ſhall ſucke of the abundance of the ſeas, and of treaſures hid in the
ſand.20And of Gad he ſaid, Bleſſed be he that enlargeth Gad: he dwelleth
as a lyon, and teareth the arme with the crowne of the head.21And he
prouided the firſt part for himſelfe, becauſe there, in a portion of the
lawgiuer was he ſeated, and hee came with the heads of the people, he
executed the iuſtice of the Lord, and his iudgments with Iſrael.22And of
Dan he ſaid, Dan is a Lyons whelpe: hee ſhall leape from Baſhan.23And
of Naphtali he ſaid, O Naphtali, ſatiſfied with fauour, and full with the
bleſſing of the Lord: poſſeſſe thou the Weſt and the South.24And of
Aſher hee ſaid, let Aſher be bleſſed with children, Let him be acceptable
to his brethren, and let him dip his foot in oile.25Thy ſhooes ſhall bee
yron and braſſe, and as thy dayes, ſo ſhall thy ſtrength bee.26There is
none like vnto the God of Ieſurun, who rideth vpon the heauen in thy
helpe, and in his excellencie on the ſkie.27The eternall God is thy refuge,
and vnderneath are the euerlaſting armes: and he ſhall thruſt out the
enemie from before thee, and ſhall ſay, Deſtroy them.28Iſrael then ſhall
dwell in ſafetie alone: the fountaine of Iacob ſhalbe vpon a land of corne
and wine, alſo his heauens ſhall drop downe deaw.29Happy art thou, O
Iſrael: Who is like vnto thee, O people! ſaued by the Lord, the ſhield of
thy helpe, and who is the ſword of thy excellencie: and thine enemies
ſhal be found liars vnto thee, and thou ſhalt tread vpon their high places.
CHAPTER 341And Moſes went vp from the plaines of Moab, vnto the
mountaine of Nebo, to the top of Piſgah, that is ouer againſt Iericho:
and the Lord ſhewed him all the land of Gilead, vnto Dan,2And all
Naphtali, and the lande of Ephraim, and Manaſſeh, and all the land of
Iudah, vnto the vtmoſt ſea.3And the South, and the plaine of the valley
of Iericho, the citie of palme trees vnto Zoar.4And the Lord ſaid vnto
him, This is the land which I ſware vnto Abraham, vnto Iſaac, and vnto
Iacob, ſaying, I will giue it vnto thy ſeed: I haue cauſed thee to ſee it with
thine eyes, but thou ſhalt not go ouer thither.5So Moſes the ſeruant of
the Lord died there in the land of Moab, according to the word of the
Lord.6And hee buried him in a valley in the land of Moab, ouer againſt
Beth-Peor: but no man knoweth of his Sepulchre vnto this day.7And
Moſes was an hundred and twentie yeeres olde when he died: his eye
was not dimme, nor his naturall force abated.8And the children of Iſrael
wept for Moſes in the plaines of Moab thirty dayes: So the dayes of
weeping and mourning for Moſes were ended.9And Ioſhua the ſonne of
Nun was full of the Spirit of wiſedome: for Moſes had layd his handes
vpon him, and the children of Iſrael hearkened vnto him, and did as the
Lord commanded Moſes.10And there aroſe not a Prophet ſince in Iſrael
like vnto Moſes, whom the Lord knew face to face:11In al the ſignes and
the wonders which the Lord ſent him to doe in the land of Egypt, to
Pharaoh, and to all his ſeruants, and to all his land,12And in all that

mighty hand, and in all the great terrour, which Moſes ſhewed in the ſight of all Iſrael.

IOſHUA (JOSHUA)

CHAPTER 11Nowe after the death of Moſes the ſeruant of the Lord, it came to paſſe, that the Lord ſpake vnto Ioſhua the ſonne of Nun, Moſes miniſter, ſaying,2Moſes my ſeruant is dead: now therefore Ariſe, goe ouer this Iordan, thou, and all this people, vnto the land which I doe giue to them, euen to the children of Iſrael.3Euery place that the ſole of your foote ſhall tread vpon, that haue I giuen vnto you, as I ſaid vnto Moſes.4From the wilderneſſe and this Lebanon, euen vnto the great Riuer, the riuer Euphrates, all the land of the Hittites, and vnto the great ſea, toward the going downe of the Sunne, ſhalbe your coaſt.5There ſhall not any man be able to ſtand before thee all the dayes of thy life: as I was with Moſes, ſo I will be with thee: I will not faile thee, nor forſake thee.6Bee ſtrong, and of a good courage: for vnto this people ſhalt thou diuide for an inheritance the land which I ſware vnto their fathers to giue them.7Onely bee thou ſtrong, and very courageous, that thou mayeſt obſerue to doe according to all the Law, which Moſes my ſeruant commaunded thee: turne not from it to the right hand, or to the left, that thou mayeſt proſper whither ſoeuer thou goeſt.8This booke of the Law ſhal not depart out of thy mouth, but thou ſhalt meditate therein day and night, that thou mayeſt obſerue to doe according to all that is written therein: for then thou ſhalt make thy way proſperous, and then thou ſhalt haue good ſuccefse.9Haue not I commanded thee? be ſtrong, and of a good courage, bee not afraid, neither be thou diſmayed: for the Lord thy God is with thee, whither ſoeuer thou goeſt.10Then Ioſhua commanded the Officers of the people, ſaying,11Paſſe through the hoſte, and command the people, ſaying, Prepare you victuals: for within three dayes ye ſhal paſſe ouer this Iordan, to goe in to poſſeſſe the land which the Lord your God giueth you, to poſſeſſe it.12And to the Reubenites, and to the Gadites, and to halfe the tribe of Manaſſeh, ſpake Ioſhua, ſaying,13Remember the word which Moſes the ſeruant of the Lord commanded you, ſaying, The Lord your God hath giuen you reſt, and hath giuen you this land:14Your wiues, your litle ones, and your cattell ſhall remaine in the lande which Moſes gaue you on this ſide Iordan; but ye ſhall paſſe before your brethren armed, all the mightie men of valour, and helpe them:15Untill the Lord haue giuen your brethren reſt, as he hath giuen you, and they alſo haue poſſeſſed the lande which the Lord your God giueth them: then yee ſhall returne vnto the land of your poſſeſſion, and enioy it, which Moſes the Lords ſeruant gaue you on this ſide Iordan toward the Sunne riſing.16And they anſwered Ioſhua, ſaying, All that thou commandeſt vs, we will doe, and whither ſoeuer thou ſendeſt vs, we will goe.17According as we hearkened vnto Moſes in all things, ſo will we hearken vnto thee: onely the Lord thy God be with thee, as he was with Moſes.18Whoſoeuer he be that doth rebell againſt thy commandement, and will not hearken vnto thy words, in all that thou commandeſt him, he ſhall bee put to death: onely be ſtrong, and of a good courage.

CHAPTER 21And Ioſhua the ſonne of Nun ſent out of Shittim two men, to ſpie ſecretly, ſaying, Go, view the land, euen Iericho: and they went, and came into an harlots houſe, named Rahab, and lodged there.2And it was told the king of Iericho, ſaying, Behold, there came men in hither to night, of the children of Iſrael, to ſearch out the countrey.3And the king of Iericho ſent vnto Rahab, ſaying, Bring forth the men that are come to thee, which are entred into thine houſe: for they bee come to ſearch out all the countrey.4And the woman tooke the two men, and hid them, & ſaid thus: There came men vnto mee, but I wiſt not whence they were:5And it came to paſſe about the time of ſhutting of the gate, when it was darke, that the men went out: whither the men went, I wote not: purſue after them quickely, for ye ſhall ouertake them.6But ſhee had brought them vp to the roofe of the houſe, and hid them with the ſtalkes of flaxe, which ſhe had laid in order vpon the roofe.7And the men purſued after them the way to Iordan, vnto the foords: and aſſoone as they which purſued after them were gone out, they ſhut the gate.8And before they were laide downe, ſhee came vp vnto them vpon the roofe.9And ſhe ſaid vnto the men, I know that the Lord hath giuen you the land, and that your terrour is fallen vpon vs, and that all the inhabitants of the land faint becauſe of you:10For wee haue heard how the Lord dried vp the water of the red ſea for you; when you came out of Egypt, and what you did vnto the two kings of the Amorites that were on the other ſide Iordan, Sihon and Og; whom ye vtterly deſtroyed.11And aſſoone as we had heard theſe things, our hearts did melt, neither did there remaine any more courage in any man, becauſe of you: for the Lord your God, he is God in heauen aboue, and in earth beneath.12Now therfore, I pray you, ſweare vnto me by the Lord, ſince I haue ſhewed you kindneſse, that ye will alſo ſhew kindneſſe vnto my fathers houſe, and giue me a true token:13And that ye will ſaue aliue my father, and my mother, and my brethren, and my ſiſters, and all that they haue, and deliuer our liues from death.14And the men anſwered her, Our life for yours, if yee vtter not this our buſineſse. And it ſhall bee when the Lord hath giuen vs the land, that wee will deale kindely and truely with thee.15Then ſhee let them downe by a coard thorow the window: for her houſe was vpon the towne wall, and ſhe dwelt vpon the wall.16And ſhe ſaid vnto them, Get you to the mountaine, leſt the purſuers meete you; and hide your ſelues there three dayes, vntill the purſuers bee returned, and afterward may ye goe your way.17And the men ſaid vnto her, Wee will bee blameleſſe of this thine oath which thou haſt made vs ſweare:18Behold, when we come into the land, thou ſhalt binde this line of ſcarlet threed in the window which thou didſt let vs downe by: and thou ſhalt bring thy father and thy mother, and thy brethren, and all thy fathers houſhold home vnto thee.19And it ſhall bee, that whoſoeuer ſhall goe out of the doores of thy houſe into the ſtreet, his blood ſhalbe vpon his head, and wee will bee guiltleſſe: and whoſoeuer ſhall bee with thee in the houſe, his blood ſhalbe on our head, if any hand be vpon him.20And if thou vtter this our buſineſse, then we wilbe quit of thine oath which thou haſt made vs to ſweare.21And ſhee ſaide, According vnto your words, ſo be it. And ſhe ſent them away, & they departed: and ſhe bound the ſcarlet line in the window.22And they went, and came vnto the mountaine, and abode there three dayes, vntill the purſuers were returned. And the purſuers ſought them thorowout all the way, but found them not.23So the two men returned, and deſcended from the mountaine, and paſſed ouer, and came to Ioſhua the ſonne of Nun, and told him all things that befell them.24And they ſaide vnto Ioſhua, Truely the Lord hath deliuered into our hands all the land; for euen all the inhabitants of the countrey doe faint becauſe of vs.

CHAPTER 31And Ioſhua roſe early in the morning, and they remooued from Shittim, and came to Iordan, hee and all the children of Iſrael, and lodged there before they paſſed ouer.2And it came to paſſe after three dayes, that the Officers went thorow the hoſte;3And they commanded the people, ſaying, When ye ſee the Arke of the Couenant of the Lord your God, and the Prieſts the Leuites bearing it, then yee ſhall remoone from your place, and goe after it.4Yet there ſhalbe a ſpace betweene you and it, about two thouſand cubites by meaſure: come not neere vnto it, that ye may know the way by which ye muſt goe: for yee haue not paſſed this way heretofore.5And Ioſhua ſaid vnto the people, ſanctifie your ſelues: for to morrow the Lord wil do wōders among you.6And Ioſhua ſpake vnto the Prieſts, ſaying, Take vp the Arke of the Couenant, and paſſe ouer before the people. And they tooke vp the Arke of the Couenant, and went before the people.7And the Lord ſaide vnto Ioſhua, This day wil I begin to magnifie thee in the ſight of all Iſrael, that they may know that as I was with Moſes, ſo I will be with thee.8And thou ſhalt commaund the Prieſts that beare the Arke of the Couenant, ſaying; When ye are come to the brinke of the water of Iordan, yee ſhall ſtand ſtill in Iordan.9And Ioſhua ſaid vnto the children of Iſrael, Come hither, and heare the words of the Lord your God.10And Ioſhua ſaid, Hereby ye ſhall know that the liuing God is among you, and that he will without faile driue out from before you the Canaanites, and the Hittites, and the Hiuites, and the Perizzites, and Girgaſhites, and the Amorites, and the Iebuſites.11Behold, the Arke of the Couenant, euen the Lord of all the earth, paſſeth ouer before you, into Iordan.12Now therefore take yee twelue men out of the Tribes of Iſrael, out of euery Tribe a man.13And it ſhall come to paſſe, aſſoone as the ſoles of the feete of the Prieſtes that beare the Arke of the Lord, the Lord of all the earth, ſhall reſt in the waters of Iordan, that the waters of Iordan ſhall be cut off, from the waters that come downe from aboue: and they ſhall ſtand vpon

an heape.[14]And it came to paſſe when the people remooued from their
tents, to paſſe ouer Iordan, and the Prieſts bearing the Arke of the
Couenant before the people;[15]And as they that bare the Arke were come
vnto Iordan, and the feet of the Prieſtes that bare the Arke, were dipped
in the brimme of the water, (for Iordan ouerfloweth all his banks at the
time of harueſt)[16]That the waters which came downe from aboue, ſtood
and roſe vp vpon an heape very farre, from the city Adam, that is beſide
Zaretan: and thoſe that came downe toward the ſea of the plaine, euen
the ſalt ſea, failed, and were cut off: and the people paſſed ouer right
againſt Iericho.[17]And the Prieſtes that bare the Arke of the Couenant of
the Lord, ſtood firme on drie ground, in the midſt of Iordan, and all the
Iſraelites paſſed ouer on drie ground, vntill all the people were paſſed
cleane ouer Iordan.
CHAPTER 4[1]And it came to paſſe when all the people were cleane
paſſed ouer Iordan, that the Lord ſpake vnto Ioſhua, ſaying,[2]Take you
twelue men out of the people, out of euery tribe a man,[3]And command
you them, ſaying, Take you hence out of the mids of Iordan, out of the
place where the Prieſts feet ſtood firme, twelue ſtones, and yee ſhal cary
them ouer with you, and leaue them in the lodging place where you ſhall
lodge this night.[4]Then Ioſhua called the twelue men, whom he had
prepared of the children of Iſrael, out of euery tribe a man:[5]And Ioſhua
ſaid vnto them, Paſſe ouer before the Arke of the Lord your God into
the mids of Iordan, and take ye vp euery man of you a ſtone vpon his
ſhoulder, according vnto the number of the tribes of the children of
Iſrael:[6]That this may be a ſigne among you, that when your children aſke
their fathers in time to come, ſaying, What meane you by theſe
ſtones?[7]Then yee ſhall anſwere them, That the waters of Iordan were
cut off before the Arke of the Couenant of the Lord, when it paſſed
ouer Iordan, the waters of Iordan were cut off: and theſe ſtones ſhall
bee for a memoriall vnto the children of Iſrael for euer.[8]And the
children of Iſrael did ſo as Ioſhua commanded, and tooke vp twelue
ſtones out of the midſt of Iordan, as the Lord ſpake vnto Ioſhua,
according to the number of the tribes of the children of Iſrael, and caried
them ouer with them, vnto the place where they lodged, and laid them
downe there.[9]And Ioſhua ſet vp twelue ſtones in the midſt of Iordan, in
the place where the feet of the Prieſts which bare the Arke of the
Couenant, ſtood: and they are there vnto this day.[10]For the Prieſts which
bare the Arke, ſtood in the midſt of Iordan, vntill euery thing was
finiſhed that the Lord commanded Ioſhua to ſpeake vnto the people,
according to all that Moſes commanded Ioſhua: and the people haſted
and paſſed ouer.[11]And it came to paſſe when all the people were cleane
paſſed ouer, that the Arke of the Lord paſſed ouer, and the Prieſts in
the preſence of the people.[12]And the children of Reuben, and the
children of Gad, and halfe the tribe of Manaſſeh, paſſed ouer armed
before the children of Iſrael, as Moſes ſpake vnto them:[13]About fourty
thouſand prepared for war, paſſed ouer before the Lord vnto battell, to
the plaines of Iericho.[14]On that day the Lord magnified Ioſhua in the
ſight of all Iſrael, and they feared him, as they feared Moſes all the dayes
of his life.[15]And the Lord ſpake vnto Ioſhua, ſaying,[16]Command the
Prieſts that beare the Arke of the Teſtimony, that they come vp out of
Iordan.[17]Ioſhua therefore commaunded the Prieſts, ſaying, Come yee
vp out of Iordan.[18]And it came to paſſe when the Prieſts that bare the
Arke of the Couenant of the Lord, were come vp out of the mids of
Iordan, and the ſoles of the Prieſts feete were lift vp vnto the dry land,
that the waters of Iordan returned vnto their place, and flowed ouer all
his banks, as they did before.[19]And the people came vp out of Iordan
on the tenth day of the firſt moneth, and encamped in Gilgal, in the Eaſt
border of Iericho.[20]And thoſe twelue ſtones which they tooke out of
Iordan, did Ioſhua pitch in Gilgal.[21]And he ſpake vnto the children of
Iſrael, ſaying, When your children ſhal aſke their fathers in time to come,
ſaying, What meane theſe ſtones?[22]Then yee ſhall let your children
know, ſaying, Iſrael came ouer this Iordan on dry land.[23]For the Lord
your God dried vp the waters of Iordan from before you, vntill yee were
paſſed ouer, as the Lord your God did to the Red ſea, which hee dried
vp from before vs, vntill we were gone ouer:[24]That all the people of the
earth might know the hand of the Lord, that it is mighty, that ye might
feare the Lord your God for euer.
CHAPTER 5[1]And it came to paſſe when all the Kings of the Amorites
which were on the ſide of Iordan Weſtward, and all the Kings of the
Canaanites, which were by the ſea, heard that the Lord had dried vp the
waters of Iordan from before the children of Iſrael, vntill we were paſſed
ouer, that their heart melted; neither was there ſpirit in them any more,
becauſe of the children of Iſrael.[2]At that time the Lord ſaid vnto Ioſhua,
Make thee ſharpe kniues, and circumciſe againe the children of Iſrael the
ſecond time.[3]And Ioſhua made him ſharpe kniues, and circumciſed the
children of Iſrael at the hill of the foreſkinnes.[4]And this is the cauſe why
Ioſhua did circumciſe: all the people that came out of Egypt, that were
males, euen all the men of warre, died in the wildernes by the way after
they came out of Egypt.[5]Now all the people that came out, were
circumciſed, but all the people that were borne in the wilderneſſe by the
way, as they came foorth out of Egypt, them they had not
circumciſed.[6]For the children of Iſrael walked fourtie yeeres in the
wilderneſſe, till all the people that were men of warre which came out
of Egypt were conſumed, becauſe they obeyed not the voyce of the
Lord, vnto whome the Lord ſware that hee would not ſhew them the
land which the Lord ſware vnto their fathers, that he would giue vs, a
land that floweth with milke & honie.[7]And their children, whom hee
raiſed vp in their ſtead, them Ioſhua circumciſed, for they were
vncircumciſed: becauſe they had not circumciſed them by the way.[8]And
it came to paſſe when they had done circumciſing all the people, that
they abode in their places in the campe, till they were whole.[9]And the
Lord ſaide vnto Ioſhua, This day haue I rolled away the reproch of
Egypt from off you: Wherefore the name of the place is called Gilgal
vnto this day.[10]And the children of Iſrael incamped in Gilgal, and kept
the Paſſeouer, on the fourteenth day of the moneth at euen, in the
plaines of Iericho.[11]And they did eate of the olde corne of the land, on
the morrow after the Paſſeouer, vnleauened cakes, and parched corne
in the ſelfe ſame day.[12]And the Manna ceaſed on the morrow after they
had eaten of the old corne of the land, neither had the children of Iſrael
Manna any more, but they did eate of the fruit of the land of Canaan
that yeere.[13]And it came to paſſe when Ioſhua was by Iericho, that he
lift vp his eyes, and looked, and beholde, there ſtood a man ouer againſt
him, with his ſword dawen in his hand: and Ioſhua went vnto him, and
ſaid vnto him, Art thou for vs, or for our aduerſaries?[14]And he ſaid,
Nay, but as captaine of the hoſte of the Lord am I now come. And
Ioſhua fell on his face to the earth, and did worſhip, and ſaid vnto him,
What ſaith my Lord vnto his ſeruant?[15]And the captaine of the Lords
hoſte ſaid vnto Ioſhua, Looſe thy ſhooe from off thy foote, for the place
whereon thou ſtandeſt, is holy: And Ioſhua did ſo.
CHAPTER 6[1]Now Iericho was ſtraitly ſhut vp, becauſe of the children
of Iſrael: none went out, & none came in.[2]And the Lord ſaid vnto
Ioſhua, See, I haue giuen into thine hand Iericho, and the King thereof,
and the mighty men of valour.[3]And ye ſhall compaſſe the city, all yee
men of warre, and goe round about the city once: thus ſhalt thou doe
ſixe dayes.[4]And ſeuen Prieſts ſhall beare before the Arke ſeuen trumpets
of rams hornes: and the ſeuenth day yee ſhall compaſſe the city ſeuen
times, and the Prieſts ſhall blow with the trumpets.[5]And it ſhall come to
paſſe that when they make a long blaſt with the rammeſ-horne, and
when ye heare the ſound of the trumpet, all the people ſhall ſhout with
a great ſhout: and the wall of the citie ſhall fall downe flat, and the people
ſhall aſcend vp euery man ſtraight before him.[6]And Ioſhua the ſonne of
Nun called the Prieſts, and ſaid vnto them, Take vp the Arke of the
Couenant, and let ſeuen Prieſts beare ſeuen trumpets of rammeſ-hornes,
before the Arke of the Lord.[7]And he ſaid vnto the people, Paſſe on, and
compaſſe the city, and let him that is armed paſſe on before the Arke of
the Lord.[8]And it came to paſſe when Ioſhua had ſpoken vnto the
people, that the ſeuen Prieſtes bearing the ſeuen trumpets of rammes
hornes, paſſed on before the Lord, and blew with the trumpets: and the
Arke of the Couenant of the Lord followed them.[9]And the armed men
went before the Prieſts that blew with the trumpets: and the rereward
came after the Arke, the Prieſts going on, and blowing with the
trumpets.[10]And Ioſhua had commanded the people, ſaying, Ye ſhall not
ſhout, nor make any noiſe with your voice, neither ſhall any word
proceed out of your mouth, vntill the day I bid you ſhoute, then ſhall ye
ſhoute.[11]So the Arke of the Lord compaſſed the citie, going about it
once: and they came into the campe, and lodged in the campe.[12]And
Ioſhua roſe earely in the morning, and the Prieſts tooke vp the Arke of
the Lord.[13]And ſeuen Prieſts bearing ſeuen trumpets of rammes hornes
before the Arke of the Lord, went on continually, and blew with the
trumpets: and the armed men went before them, but the rereward came

after the Arke of the Lord, the Prieſts going on and blowing with the trumpets.14And the ſecond day they compaſſed the citie once, and returned into the campe: ſo they did ſixe dayes.15And it came to paſſe on the ſeuenth day, that they roſe early about the dawning of the day, and compaſſed the citie after the ſame maner, ſeuen times: only on that day they compaſſed the citie ſeuen times.16And it came to paſſe at the ſeuenth time, when the Prieſts blewe with the trumpets, Ioſhua ſaid vnto the people, Shout, for the Lord hath giuen you the citie.17And the citie ſhalbe accurſed, euen it, and all that are therein, to the Lord: onely Rahab the harlot ſhal liue, ſhe, and all that are with her in the houſe, becauſe ſhe hid the meſſengers that we ſent.18And you, in any wiſe keepe your ſelues from the accurſed thing, leſt yee make your ſelues accurſed, when yee take of the accurſed thing, and make the campe of Iſrael a curſe, and trouble it.19But all the ſiluer, and gold, and veſſels of braſſe and yron, are conſecrated vnto the Lord: they ſhall come into the treaſurie of the Lord.20So the people ſhouted when the Prieſts blew with the trumpets: and it came to paſſe when the people heard the ſound of the trumpet, and the people ſhouted with a great ſhout, that the wall fell downe flat, ſo that the people went vp into the citie, euery man ſtraight before him, and they tooke the citie.21And they vtterly deſtroyed all that was in the city, both man and woman, yong and old, and oxe, and ſheepe, and aſſe, with the edge of the ſword.22But Ioſhua had ſaid vnto the two men that had ſpied out the countrey; Goe into the harlots houſe, and bring out thence the woman and all that ſhe hath, as ye ſware vnto her.23And the yong men that were ſpies, went in, and brought out Rahab, and her father, and her mother, and her brethren, and all that ſhe had: and they brought out all her kinred, and left them without the campe of Iſrael.24And they burnt the city with fire, and all that was therein: onely the ſiluer & the gold, and the veſſels of braſſe and of yron, they put into the Treaſury of the houſe of the Lord.25And Ioſhua ſaued Rahab the harlot aliue, and her fathers houſhold, and all that ſhe had: and ſhe dwelleth in Iſrael euen vnto this day, becauſe ſhe hid the meſſengers which Ioſhua ſent to ſpy out Iericho.26And Ioſhua adiured them at that time, ſaying, Curſed be the man before the Lord, that riſeth vp and buildeth this city Iericho: he ſhall lay the foundation therof in his firſt borne, and in his yongeſt ſonne ſhall hee ſet vp the gates of it.27So the Lord was with Ioſhua, and his fame was noiſed throughout all the countrey.

CHAPTER 71But the children of Iſrael committed a treſpaſſe in the accurſed thing: for Achan the ſonne of Carmi, the ſonne of Zabdi, the ſonne of Zerah, of the tribe of Iudah, tooke of the accurſed thing: and the anger of the Lord was kindled againſt the children of Iſrael.2And Ioſhua ſent men from Iericho to Ai, which is beſide Beth-auen, on the Eaſt ſide of Bethel, and ſpake vnto them, ſaying, Goe vp and view the countrey. And the men went vp, and viewed Ai.3And they returned to Ioſhua, and ſaid vnto him, Let not all the people goe vp: but let about two or three thouſand men goe vp, and ſmite Ai, and make not all the people to labour thither, for they are but few.4So there went vp thither of the people about three thouſand men, and they fled before the men of Ai.5And the men of Ai ſmote of them about thirty and ſixe men: for they chaſed them from before the gate euen vnto Shebarim, and ſmote them in the going downe: Wherefore the hearts of the people melted, & became as water.6And Ioſhua rent his clothes, and fell to the earth vpon his face, before the Arke of the Lord, vntill the euentide, he and the Elders of Iſrael, and put duſt vpon their heads.7And Ioſhua ſaid, Alas, O Lord God, wherefore haſt thou at all brought this people ouer Iordan, to deliuer vs into the hand of the Amorites, to deſtroy vs? Would to God we had bene content, and dwelt on the other ſide Iordan.8Oh Lord! what ſhall I ſay, when Iſrael turneth their backes before their enemies?9For the Canaanites, and all the inhabitants of the land ſhall heare of it, and ſhall enuiron vs round, and cut off our name from the earth: and what wilt thou doe vnto thy great Name?10And the Lord ſaide vnto Ioſhua, Get thee vp; wherefore lieſt thou thus vpon thy face?11Iſrael hath ſinned, and they haue alſo tranſgreſſed my Couenant which I commaunded them: for they haue euen taken of the accurſed thing, and haue alſo ſtollen, and diſsembled alſo, and they haue put it euen amongſt their owne ſtuffe.12Therefore the children of Iſrael could not ſtand before their enemies, but turned their backs before their enemies, becauſe they were accurſed: neither will I bee with you any more, except yee deſtroy the accurſed from amongſt you.13Up, ſanctifie the people, and ſay, ſanctifie your ſelues againſt to morrow: for thus ſaith the Lord God of Iſrael, There is an accurſed thing in the midſt of thee, O Iſrael: thou canſt not ſtand before thine enemies, vntill ye take away the accurſed thing from among you.14In the morning therefore ye ſhal be brought, according to your tribes: and it ſhall be that the tribe which the Lord taketh, ſhall come according to the families thereof, and the familie which the Lord ſhall take, ſhal come by houſholdes: and the houſholdes which the Lord ſhall take, ſhal come man by man.15And it ſhalbe that he that is taken with the accurſed thing, ſhall bee burnt with fire, he, and all that hee hath: becauſe he hath tranſgreſſed the couenant of the Lord, and becauſe hee hath wrought folly in Iſrael.16So Ioſhua roſe vp earely in the morning, and brought Iſrael by their tribes, and the tribe of Iudah was taken.17And hee brought the familie of Iudah, and he tooke the familie of the Zarhites: and he brought the familie of the Zarhites, man by man, and Zabdi was taken.18And hee brought his houſhold, man by man, and Achan the ſonne of Carmi, the ſonne of Zabdi, the ſonne of Zerah, of the tribe of Iudah, was taken.19And Ioſhua ſaid vnto Achan, My ſonne, giue, I pray thee, glory to the Lord God of Iſrael, and make confeſsion vnto him, and tel me now, what thou haſt done, hide it not from me.20And Achan anſwered Ioſhua, and ſaid, Indeed I haue ſinned againſt the Lord God of Iſrael, and thus and thus haue I done.21When I ſaw among the ſpoiles a goodly Babyloniſh garment, and two hundred ſhekels of ſiluer, and a wedge of gold of fiftie ſhekels weight, then I coueted them, and tooke them, and behold, they are hid in the earth in the midſt of my tent, and the ſiluer vnder it.22So Ioſhua ſent meſſengers, and they ran vnto the tent, and behold, it was hid in his tent, and the ſiluer vnder it.23And they tooke them out of the midſt of the tent, and brought them vnto Ioſhua, and vnto all the children of Iſrael, and laid them out before the Lord.24And Ioſhua and all Iſrael with him tooke Achan the ſonne of Zerah, and the ſiluer, and the garment, and the wedge of golde, and his ſonnes, and his daughters, and his oxen, and his aſſes, and his ſheepe, and his tent, and all that he had: and they brought them vnto the valley of Achor.25And Ioſhua ſaid, Why haſt thou troubled vs? the Lord ſhall trouble thee this day. And all Iſrael ſtoned him with ſtones, and burned them with fire, after they had ſtoned them with ſtones.26And they raiſed ouer him a great heape of ſtones vnto this day: ſo the Lord turned from the fierceneſse of his anger: Wherefore the name of the place was called, The valley of Achor, vnto this day.

CHAPTER 81And the Lord ſaid vnto Ioſhua, Feare not, neither be thou diſmaid: take all the people of warre with thee, and Ariſe, goe vp to Ai: See, I haue giuen into thy hand the king of Ai, and his people, and his citie, and his land.2And thou ſhalt doe to Ai and her king, as thou diddeſt vnto Iericho and her king: Onely the ſpoile thereof and the cattell thereof ſhall ye take for a pray vnto your ſelues: lay thee an ambuſh for the citie, behind it.3So Ioſhua aroſe, and all the people of warre, to goe vp againſt Ai: and Ioſhua choſe out thirtie thouſand mighty men of valour, and ſent them away by night:4And he commanded them, ſaying, Behold, ye ſhall lie in wait againſt the citie, euen behind the citie: goe not very farre from the citie, but be ye all ready:5And I, and all the people that are with mee, will approch vnto the citie: and it ſhall come to paſſe when they come out againſt vs, as at the firſt, that we will flee before them,6(For they will come out after vſ) till we haue drawen them from the citie; for they will ſay, They flee before vs, as at the firſt: therefore we will flee before them.7Then yee ſhall riſe vp from the ambuſh, and ſeiſe vpon the citie: for the Lord your God will deliuer it into your hand.8And it ſhall be when yee haue taken the citie, that ye ſhall ſet the citie on fire: according to the commandement of the Lord ſhall ye do. See, I haue commanded you.9Ioſhua therefore ſent them foorth, and they went to lie in ambuſh, and abode betweene Bethel and Ai, on the Weſt ſide of Ai: but Ioſhua lodged that night among the people.10And Ioſhua roſe vp early in the morning, and numbred the people, and went vp; he, and the Elders of Iſrael, before the people to Ai.11And all the people, euen the people of warre that were with him, went vp, and drew nigh, and came before the city, and pitched on the North ſide of Ai: now there was a valley betweene them and Ai.12And he tooke about fiue thouſand men, and ſet them to lye in ambuſh betweene Bethel and Ai, on the Weſt ſide of the citie.13And when they had ſet the people, euen all the hoſte that was on the North of the city, and their liers in wait on the Weſt of the citie: Ioſhua went that night

into the midſt of the valley.14And it came to paſſe when the King of Ai
ſaw it, that they haſted, and roſe vp early, and the men of the citie went
out againſt Iſrael to battell, hee, and all his people, at a time appointed,
before the plaine, but hee wiſt not that there were liers in ambuſh againſt
him behind the city.15And Ioſhua and all Iſrael made as if they were
beaten before them, and fled by the way of the wilderneſſe.16And all the
people that were in Ai, were called together to purſue after them: and
they purſued after Ioſhua, and were drawen away from the city.17And
there was not a man left in Ai or Bethel, that went not out after Iſrael:
and they left the citie open, and purſued after Iſrael.18And the Lord ſaid
vnto Ioſhua, Stretch out the ſpeare that is in thy hand, toward Ai; for I
will giue it into thine hand. And Ioſhua ſtretched out the ſpeare that hee
had in his hand, toward the city.19And the ambuſh aroſe quickly out of
their place, and they ranne as ſoone as he had ſtretched out his hand:
and they entred into the city, and tooke it, and haſted, and ſet the citie
on fire.20And when the men of Ai looked behind them, they ſaw, and
behold, the ſmoke of the city aſcended vp to heauen, and they had no
power to flee this way or that way: and the people that fled to the
wilderneſſe, turned backe vpon the purſuers.21And when Ioſhua and all
Iſrael ſaw that the ambuſh had taken the city, and that the ſmoke of the
city aſcended, then they turned againe and ſlew the men of Ai.22And the
other iſſued out of the citie againſt them, ſo they were in the midſt of
Iſrael; ſome on this ſide, and ſome on that ſide, and they ſmote them; ſo
that they let none of them remaine or eſcape.23And the King of Ai they
tooke aliue, and brought him to Ioſhua.24And it came to paſſe when
Iſrael had made an end of ſlaying all the inhabitants of Ai, in the field,
in the wilderneſſe wherein they chaſed them, and when they were all
fallen on the edge of the ſword, vntill they were conſumed, that all the
Iſraelites returned vnto Ai, and ſmote it with the edge of the
ſword.25And ſo it was that all that fell that day, both of men and women,
were twelue thouſand, euen all the men of Ai.26For Ioſhua drew not his
hand backe wherewith hee ſtretched out the ſpeare, vntill he had vtterly
deſtroyed all the inhabitants of Ai.27Onely the cattell, and the ſpoile of
that city Iſrael tooke for a pray vnto themſelues, according vnto the
word of the Lord, which he commaunded Ioſhua.28And Ioſhua burnt
Ai, and made it an heape for euer, euen a deſolation vnto this day.29And
the king of Ai he hanged on a tree vntil euentide: and aſſoone as the
ſunne was downe, Ioſhua commaunded that they ſhould take his
carkeiſedowne from the tree, and caſt it at the entring of the gate of the
citie, and raiſe thereon a great heape of ſtones that remaineth vnto this
day.30Then Ioſhua built an Altar vnto the Lord God of Iſrael in mount
Ebal,31As Moſes the ſeruant of the Lord commaunded the children of
Iſrael, as it is written in the booke of the Law of Moſes, an Altar of
whole ſtones, ouer which no man hath lift vp any yron: and they offred
theron burnt offerings vnto the Lord, and ſacrificed peace
offerings.32And he wrote there vpon the ſtones a copie of the Lawe of
Moſes, which hee wrote in the preſence of the children of Iſrael.33And
all Iſrael, and their Elders, and Officers, and their Iudges, ſtood on this
ſide the Arke, and on that ſide, before the Prieſts the Leuites, which bare
the Arke of the Couenant of the Lord, aſwell the ſtranger, as he that was
borne among them: halfe of them ouer againſt mount Gerizim, and
halfe of them ouer againſt mount Ebal, as Moſes the ſeruant of the Lord
had commanded before, that they ſhould bleſſe the people of
Iſrael.34And afterward hee read all the words of the Law, the bleſſings
and curſings, according to all that is written in the booke of the
Law.35There was not a word of all that Moſes commanded, which
Ioſhua read not before all the Congregation of Iſrael, with the women
and the litle ones, and the ſtrangers that were conuerſant among them.
CHAPTER 9 1And it came to paſſe when all the kings which were on
this ſide Iordan in the hilles, and in the valleys, and in all the coaſts of
the great ſea, ouer againſt Lebanon, the Hittite, and the Amorite, the
Canaanite, the Perizzite, the Hiuite, and the Iebuſite heard thereof:2That
they gathered themſelues together to fight with Ioſhua, and with Iſrael,
with one accord.3And when the inhabitants of Gibeon heard what
Ioſhua had done vnto Iericho, and to Ai,4They did worke wilily, and
went and made as if they had beene embaſſadours, and tooke old ſackes
vpon their aſſes, and wine-bottels, old, and rent, and bound vp,5And
old ſhooes and clowted vpon their feet, & olde garments vpon them,
and all the bread of their prouiſion was drie and mouldie.6And they went
to Ioſhua vnto the campe at Gilgal, and ſaid vnto him, and to the men
of Iſrael, Wee be come from a farre countrey: Now therefore make ye a
league with vs.7And the men of Iſrael ſaid vnto the Hiuites,
Peraduenture yee dwell among vs, and how ſhall wee make a league with
you?8And they ſaid vnto Ioſhua, Wee are thy ſeruants. And Ioſhua ſaid
vnto them, Who are ye? And from whence come ye?9And they ſaid vnto
him, From a very farre countrey thy ſeruants are come, becauſe of the
Name of the Lord thy God: for wee haue heard the fame of him, and
all that hee did in Egypt,10And all that hee did to the two kings of the
Amorites, that were beyond Iordan, to Sihon king of Heſhbon, and to
Og king of Baſhan, which was at Aſhtaroth.11Wherefore our Elders and
all the inhabitants of our countrey, ſpake to vs, ſaying, Take victuals with
you for the iourney, and goe to meete them, and ſay vnto them, Wee are
your ſeruants: therefore now make ye a league with vs.12This our bread,
wee tooke hote for our prouiſion out of our houſes, on the day we came
forth to goe vnto you: but now behold, it is dry, & it is mouldy.13And
theſe bottels of wine which we filled, were new, and behold, they be
rent: and theſe our garments, and our ſhooes are become old, by reaſon
of the very long iourney.14And the men tooke of their victuals, and
aſked not counſell at the mouth of the Lord.15And Ioſhua made peace
with them, and made a league with them, to let them liue: and the princes
of the Congregation ſware vnto them.16And it came to paſſe at the end
of three dayes, after they had made a league with them, that they heard
that they were their neighbours, and that they dwelt among them.17And
the children of Iſrael iourneyed, and came vnto their cities on the third
day: now their cities were Gibeon, and Chephirah, and Beeroth, and
Kiriath iearim.18And the children of Iſrael ſmote them not, becauſe the
Princes of the Congregation had ſworne vnto them by the Lord God of
Iſrael: And all the Congregation murmured againſt the Princes.19But all
the Princes ſaid vnto all the Congregation, We haue ſworne vnto them
by the Lord God of Iſrael: now therefore we may not touch them.20This
we will doe to them; wee will euen let them liue, leſt wrath be vpon vs,
becauſe of the oath which wee ſware vnto them.21And the Princes ſaid
vnto them, Let them liue, (but let them bee hewers of wood, and drawers
of water, vnto all the Congregation,) as the Princes had promiſed
them.22And Ioſhua called for them, and he ſpake vnto them, ſaying,
Wherefore haue ye beguiled vs, ſaying, We are very farre from you?
when ye dwell among vs.23Now therefore ye are curſed, and there ſhall
none of you bee freed from being bondmen, and hewers of wood, and
drawers of water, for the houſe of my God.24And they anſwered Ioſhua,
and ſaid, Becauſe it was certainely told thy ſeruants, how that the Lord
thy God commanded his ſeruant Moſes to giue you all the land, and to
deſtroy all the inhabitants of the land from before you, therefore we
were ſore afraid of our liues becauſe of you, and haue done this
thing.25And now behold, we are in thine hand: as it ſeemeth good and
right vnto thee to doe vnto vs, doe.26And ſo did he vnto them, and
deliuered them out of the hand of the children of Iſrael, that they ſlew
them not.27And Ioſhua made them that day, hewers of wood, and
drawers of water for the Congregation, and for the Altar of the Lord,
euen vnto this day, in the place which he ſhould chooſe.
CHAPTER 10 1Now it came to paſſe when Adoni-zedek King of
Ieruſalem, had heard how Ioſhua had taken Ai, and had vtterly deſtroyed
it, (as he had done to Iericho, and her King, ſo hee had done to Ai, and
her King) and how the inhabitants of Gibeon had made peace with
Iſrael, and were among them,2That they feared greatly becauſe Gibeon
was a great citie, as one of the royall cities, and becauſe it was greater
then Ai, and all the men thereof were mighty.3Wherefore Adoni-zedek
King of Ieruſalem, ſent vnto Hoham King of Hebron, and vnto Piram,
king of Iarmuth, and vnto Iaphia king of Lachiſh, and vnto Debir king
of Eglon, ſaying,4Come vp vnto me, and helpe me, that we may ſmite
Gibeon: for it hath made peace with Ioſhua, and with the children of
Iſrael.5Therefore the fiue Kings of the Amorites, the king of Ieruſalem,
the king of Hebron, the king of Iarmuth, the king of Lachiſh, the king
of Eglon, gathered themſelues together, and went vp, they, and all their
hoſtes, and encamped before Gibeon, and made warre againſt it.6And
the men of Gibeon ſent vnto Ioſhua to the campe to Gilgal, ſaying,
Slacke not thy hand from thy ſeruants, come vp to vs quickly, and ſaue
vs, and helpe vs: for all the kings of the Amorites that dwell in the
mountaines, are gathered together againſt vs.7So Ioſhua aſcended from
Gilgal, he, and all the people of warre with him, and all the mighty men
of valour.8And the Lord ſaid vnto Ioſhua, Feare them not: for I haue

deliuered them into thine hand; there ſhall not a man of them ſtand
before thee.9Ioſhua therefore came vnto them ſuddenly, and went vp
from Gilgal all night.10And the Lord diſcomfited them before Iſrael, and
ſlewe them with a great ſlaughter at Gibeon, and chaſed them along the
way that goeth vp to Bethoron, and ſmote them to Azekah and vnto
Makkedah.11And it came to paſſe as they fled from before Iſrael, and
were in the going downe to Bethoron, that the Lord caſt downe great
ſtones from heauen vpon them, vnto Azekah, and they died: they were
moe which died with haileſtones, then they whome the children of Iſrael
ſlew with the ſword.12Then ſpake Ioſhua to the Lord in the day when
the Lord deliuered vp the Amorites before the children of Iſrael, and
hee ſaid in the ſight of Iſrael, Sunne, ſtand thou ſtill vpon Gibeon, and
thou Moone in the valley of Aialon.13And the Sunne ſtood ſtill, and the
Moone ſtayed, vntill the people had auenged themſelues vpō their
enemies. Is not this written in the booke of Iaſher? So the Sunne ſtood
ſtill in the midſt of heauen, and haſted not to goe downe, about a whole
day.14And there was no day like that, before it, or after it, that the Lord
hearkened vnto the voyce of a man: for the Lord fought for Iſrael.15And
Ioſhua returned, and all Iſrael with him, vnto the campe to Gilgal.16But
theſe fiue kings fled, and hid themſelues in a caue at Makkedah.17And it
was told Ioſhua, ſaying, The fiue kings are found hid in a caue at
Makkedah.18And Ioſhua ſaid, Roule great ſtones vpon the mouth of the
caue, and ſet men by it, for to keepe them.19And ſtay you not, but purſue
after your enemies, and ſmite the hindmoſt of them, ſuffer them not to
enter into their cities: for the Lord your God hath deliuered them into
your hand.20And it came to paſſe when Ioſhua and the children of Iſrael
had made an end of ſlaying them with a very great ſlaughter, till they
were conſumed, that the reſt which remained of them, entred into
fenced cities.21And all the people returned to the campe to Ioſhua at
Makkedah in peace: none mooued his tongue againſt any of the children
of Iſrael.22Then ſaid Ioſhua, Open the mouth of the caue, and bring out
thoſe fiue kings vnto me out of the caue.23And they did ſo, and brought
forth thoſe fiue kings vnto him out of the caue, the king of Ieruſalem,
the king of Hebron, the king of Iarmuth, the king of Lachiſh, and the
king of Eglon.24And it came to paſſe when they brought out thoſe kings
vnto Ioſhua, that Ioſhua called for all the men of Iſrael, and ſaide vnto
the captaines of the men of war which went with him, Come neere, put
your feete vpon the neckes of theſe kings. And they came neere, and put
their feet vpon the necks of them.25And Ioſhua ſaid vnto them, Feare
not, nor be diſmaid, bee ſtrong, and of good courage: for thus ſhall the
Lord doe to all your enemies againſt whom ye fight.26And afterward
Ioſhua ſmote them, and ſlew them, and hanged them on fiue trees: and
they were hanging vpon the trees vntill the euening.27And it came to
paſſe at the time of the going downe of the Sunne, that Ioſhua
commanded, and they tooke them downe off the trees, and caſt them
into the caue, wherein they had beene hid, and laid great ſtones in the
caues mouth, which remain vntil this very day.28And that day Ioſhua
tooke Makkedah, and ſmote it with the edge of the ſword, and the king
thereof hee vtterly deſtroyed, them, and all the ſoules that were therein,
he let none remaine: and he did to the king of Makkedah, as hee did
vnto the king of Iericho.29Then Ioſhua paſſed from Makkedah, and all
Iſrael with him, vnto Libnah, and fought againſt Libnah.30And the Lord
deliuered it alſo and the king thereof, into the hand of Iſrael, and he
ſmote it with the edge of the ſword, and all the ſoules that were therein:
He let none remaine in it, but did vnto the king therof, as he did vnto
the king of Iericho.31And Ioſhua paſſed from Libnah and all Iſrael with
him, vnto Lachiſh, and encamped againſt it, and fought againſt it.32And
the Lord deliuered Lachiſh into the hande of Iſrael, which tooke it on
the ſecond day, and ſmote it with the edge of the ſword, and all the
ſoules that were therein, according to all that he had done to
Libnah.33Then Horam king of Gezer, came vp to helpe Lachiſh, and
Ioſhua ſmote him and his people, vntill he had left him none
remayning.34And from Lachiſh, Ioſhua paſſed vnto Eglon, and all Iſrael
with him, and they encamped againſt it, and fought againſt it.35And they
tooke it on that day, and ſmote it with the edge of the ſword, and all the
ſoules that were therein he vtterly deſtroyed that day, according to all
that he had done to Lachiſh.36And Ioſhua went vp from Eglon, and all
Iſrael with him, vnto Hebron, and they fought againſt it.37And they
tooke it, and ſmote it with the edge of the ſword, and the king thereof,
and all the cities thereof, and all the ſoules that were therein, he left none
remaining, according to all that he had done to Eglon: but deſtroyed it
vtterly, and all the ſoules that were therein.38And Ioſhua returned, and
all Iſrael with him to Debir, and fought againſt it.39And hee tooke it, and
the King thereof, and all the cities thereof, and they ſmote them with
the edge of the ſword, and vtterly deſtroyed all the ſoules that were
therein, he left none remayning: as he had done to Hebron, ſo he did to
Debir, and to the king thereof, as he had done alſo to Libnah, and to
her king.40So Ioſhua ſmote all the countrey of the hils, and of the South,
and of the vale, and of the ſprings, and all their kings, hee left none
remayning, but vtterly deſtroyed all that breathed, as the Lord God of
Iſrael commanded.41And Ioſhua ſmote them from Kadeſh-Barnea,
euen vnto Gaza, and all the countrey of Goſhen, euen vnto
Gibeon.42And all theſe Kings and their land did Ioſhua take at one time:
becauſe the Lord God of Iſrael fought for Iſrael.43And Ioſhua returned
& al Iſrael with him, vnto the campe to Gilgal.
CHAPTER 111And it came to paſſe, when Iabin king of Hazor had
heard thoſe things, that hee ſent to Iobab king of Madon, and to the
king of Shimron, & to the king of Achſhaph,2And to the kings that were
on the North of the mountaines, and of the plaines South of Cinneroth,
and in the valley, and in the borders of Dor, on the Weſt;3And to the
Canaanite on the Eaſt and on the Weſt, and to the Amorite, and the
Hittite, and the Perizzite, and the Iebuſite in the mountaines, and to the
Hiuite vnder Hermon in the land of Mizpeh.4And they went out, they
and all their hoſtes with them, much people, euen as the ſand that is
vpon the ſeaſhore in multitude, with horſes and charets very many.5And
when all theſe Kings were met together, they came and pitched together
at the waters of Merom, to fight againſt Iſrael.6And the Lord ſaide vnto
Ioſhua, Be not afraid becauſe of them: for to morrow about this time
will I deliuer them vp al ſlaine before Iſrael: thou ſhalt hough their
horſes, and burne their charets with fire.7So Ioſhua came, and all the
people of warre with him, againſt them by the waters of Merom
ſuddenly, and they fell vpon them.8And the Lord deliuered them into
the hand of Iſrael, who ſmote them, and chaſed them vnto great Zidon,
and vnto Miſrephothmaim, and vnto the valley of Mizpeh Eaſtward, and
they ſmote them, vntill they left them none remayning.9And Ioſhua did
vnto them as the Lord bade him: hee houghed their horſes, and burnt
their charets with fire.10And Ioſhua at that time turned backe, and tooke
Hazor, and ſmote the king thereof with the ſword: for Hazor beforetime
was the head of all thoſe kingdomes.11And they ſmote all the ſoules that
were therein with the edge of the ſword, vtterly deſtroying them: there
was not any left to breathe; and he burnt Hazor with fire.12And all the
cities of thoſe kings, and all the kings of them, did Ioſhua take, and
ſmote them with the edge of the ſword, and he vtterly deſtroied them,
as Moſes the ſeruant of the Lord commanded.13But as for the cities that
ſtood ſtill in their ſtrength, Iſrael burned none of them, ſaue Hazor
onely; that did Ioſhua burne.14And all the ſpoile of theſe cities, and the
cattell, the children of Iſrael tooke for a pray vnto themſelues: but euery
man they ſmote with the edge of the ſword, vntill they had deſtroyed
them, neither left they any to breathe.15As the Lord commanded Moſes
his ſeruant, ſo did Moſes command Ioſhua, and ſo did Ioſhua: hee left
nothing vndone of all that the Lord commanded Moſes.16So Ioſhua
tooke all that land, the hilles, and all the South countrey, and all the land
of Goſhen, and the valley, and the plaine, and the mountaine of Iſrael,
and the valley of the ſame:17Euen from the mount Halak, that goeth vp
to Seir, vnto Baal-Gad, in the valley of Lebanon, vnder mount Hermon:
and all their kings he tooke, and ſmote them, and ſlew them.18Ioſhua
made warre a long time, with all thoſe kings.19There was not a citie that
made peace with the children of Iſrael, ſaue the Hiuites the inhabitants
of Gibeon; all other they tooke in battell.20For it was of the Lord to
harden their hearts, that they ſhould come againſt Iſrael in battell, that
he might deſtroy them vtterly, & that they might haue no fauour: but
that hee might deſtroy them, as the Lord commanded Moſes.21And at
that time came Ioſhua and cut off the Anakims from the mountaines,
from Hebron, from Debir, from Anab, and from all the mountaines of
Iudah, and from all the mountaines of Iſrael: Ioſhua deſtroyed them
vtterly with their cities.22There was none of the Anakims left in the land
of the children of Iſrael: onely in Gaza, in Gath, and in Aſhdod, there
remained.23So Ioſhua tooke the whole land according to all that the
Lord ſaide vnto Moſes, and Ioſhua gaue it for an inheritance vnto Iſrael,

according to their diuiſions by their tribes: and the land reſted from warre.

CHAPTER 121Now theſe are the kings of the land, which the children of Iſrael ſmote, and poſſeſſed their land on the other ſide Iordan, toward the riſing of the Sunne: from the riuer Arnon, vnto mount Hermon, and all the plaine on the Eaſt.2Sihon king of the Amorites who dwelt in Heſhbon, and ruled from Aroer, which is vpon the banke of the riuer of Arnon, and from the middle of the riuer, and from halfe Gilead vnto the riuer Iabbok; which is the border of the children of Ammon:3And from the plaine, to the ſea of Cinneroth on the Eaſt, and vnto the ſea of the plaine, euen the ſalt ſea on the Eaſt, the way to Beth-Ieſhimoth: and from the South, vnder Aſhdoth-Piſgah.4And the coaſt of Og king of Baſhan, which was of the remnant of the Giants, that dwelt at Aſhtaroth, and at Edrei,5And reigned in mount Hermon, and in Salcah, and in all Baſhan, vnto the border of the Geſhurites, and the Maachathites, and halfe Gilead, the border of Sihon king of Heſhbon.6Them did Moſes the ſeruant of the Lord, and the children of Iſrael ſmite, and Moſes the ſeruant of the Lord gaue it for a poſſeſſion vnto the Reubenites, and Gadites, and the halfe tribe of Manaſſeh.7And theſe are the kings of the countrey which Ioſhua and the children of Iſrael ſmote on this ſide Iordan on the Weſt, from Baal Gad in the valley of Lebanon, euen vnto the mount Halak, that goeth vp to Seir, which Ioſhua gaue vnto the tribes of Iſrael for a poſſeſſion, according to their diuiſions:8In the mountaines and in the valleys, and in the plaines, and in the ſprings, and in the wilderneſſe, and in the South countrey: the Hittites, the Amorites, and the Canaanites, the Perizzites, the Hiuites, and the Iebuſites.9The king of Iericho, one: the king of Ai, which is beſide Bethel, one:10The king of Ieruſalem, one: the king of Hebron, one:11The king of Iarmuth, one: the king of Lachis, one:12The king of Eglon, one: the king of Gezer, one:13The king of Debir, one: the king of Geder, one:14The king of Hormah one: the king of Arad, one:15The king of Libnah, one: the king of Adullam, one:16The king of Makkedah, one: the king of Bethel, one:17The king of Tappuah, one: the king of Hepher, one:18The king of Aphek, one: the king of Laſharon, one:19The king of Madon, one: the king of Hazor, one:20The king of Shimron-Meron, one: the king of Achſhaph, one:21The king of Taanach, one: the king of Megiddo, one:22The king of Kedeſh, one: the king of Iokneam of Carmel, one:23The king of Dor, in the coaſt of Dor, one: the king of the nations of Gilgal, one:24The king of Tirzah, one: all the kings thirtie and one.

CHAPTER 131Now Ioſhua was old and ſtricken in yeeres, and the Lord ſaide vnto him; Thou art old, and ſtricken in yeres, and there remaineth yet very much land to bee poſſeſſed.2This is the land that yet remaineth: all the borders of the Philiſtines, and all Geſhuri,3From Sihor, which is before Egypt, euen vnto the borders of Ekron Northward, which is counted to the Canaanite: fiue lords of the Philiſtines; the Gazathites, and the Aſhdothites, the Eſhkalonites, the Gittites, and the Ekronites; Alſo the Auites.4From the South, all the land of the Canaanites, and Mearah that is beſide the Sidonians, vnto Aphek, to the borders of the Amorites:5And the land of the Giblites, and al Lebanon toward the Sunne riſing, from Baal-Gad vnder mount Hermon, vnto the entring into Hamath.6All the inhabitants of the hill countrey, from Lebanon vnto Miſrephothmaim, and all the Sidonians, them will I driue out from before the children of Iſrael: onely diuide thou it by lot vnto the Iſraelites, for an inheritance, as I haue commanded thee.7Now therefore, diuide this land for an inheritance vnto the nine tribes, and the halfe tribe of Manaſſeh,8With whom the Reubenites, and the Gadites haue receiued their inheritance, which Moſes gaue them, beyond Iordan Eaſtward, euen as Moſes the ſeruant of the Lord gaue them:9From Aroer that is vpon the banke of the riuer Arnon, and the citie that is in the middeſt of the riuer, and all the plaine of Medeba vnto Dibon:10And all the cities of Sihon king of the Amorites, which reigned in Heſhbon, vnto the border of the children of Ammon:11And Gilead, and the border of the Geſhurites, and Maachathites, and all mount Hermon, and all Baſhan vnto Salcah:12All the kingdome of Og in Baſhan, which reigned in Aſhtaroth and in Edrei, who remained of the remnant of the giants: for theſe did Moſes ſmite, and caſt them out.13Neuertheleſſe, the children of Iſrael expelled not the Geſhurites, nor the Maachathites: but the Geſhurites and the Maachathites dwel among the Iſraelites vntill this day.14Onely vnto the tribe of Leui hee gaue none inheritance: the ſacrifices of the Lord God of Iſrael made by fire, are their inheritance, as he ſaid vnto them.15And Moſes gaue vnto the tribe of the children of Reuben inheritance according to their families:16And their coaſt was from Aroer that is on the banke of the riuer Arnon, and the city that is in the midſt of the riuer, and all the plaine by Medeba.17Heſhbon and all her cities that are in the plaine: Dibon, and Bamoth-Baal, and Beth-Baalmeon,18And Iahazah, and Kedemoth, and Mephaath,19And Kiriathaim, and Sibmah, and Zareth-ſhahar, in the mount of the valley,20And Bethpeor, and Aſhdoth-Piſgah, and Beth-ieſhimoth:21And all the cities of the plaine, and all the kingdome of Sihon king of the Amorites, which reigned in Heſhbon, whom Moſes ſmote with the princes of Midian, Eui, and Rekem, and Zur, and Hur, and Reba, which were dukes of Sihon, dwelling in the countrey.22Balaam alſo the ſonne of Beor the Sooth-ſayer did the children of Iſrael ſlay with the ſword, among them that were ſlaine by them.23And the border of the children of Reuben, was Iordan and the border therof: This was the inheritance of the children of Reuben after their families, the cities, and villages thereof.24And Moſes gaue inheritance vnto the tribe of Gad, euen vnto the children of Gad, according to their families:25And their coaſt was Iazer, and all the cities of Gilead, and halfe the land of the children of Ammon, vnto Aroer that is before Rabbah:26And from Heſhbon vnto Ramath-Mizpeh, and Betonim: and from Mahanaim vnto the border of Debir.27And in the valley, Beth-aram, and Beth-nimrah, and Succoth, and Zaphon the reſt of the kingdome of Sihon king of Heſhbon, Iordan, and his border, euen vnto the edge of the ſea of Cinneroth, on the other ſide Iordan Eaſtward.28This is the inheritance of the children of Gad after their families: the cities and their villages.29And Moſes gaue inheritance vnto the halfe tribe of Manaſſeh: and this was the poſſeſſion of the halfe tribe of Manaſſeh, by their families.30And their coaſt was frō Mahanaim all Baſhan, all the kingdome of Og king of Baſhan, and all the townes of Iair, which are in Baſhan, threeſcore cities:31And halfe Gilead, and Aſhtaroth, and Edrei, cities of the kingdom of Og in Baſhan, were perteining vnto the children of Machir the ſonne of Manaſſeh, euen to the one halfe of the children of Machir by their families.32Theſe are the countreyes which Moſes did diſtribute for inheritance in the plaines of Moab, on the other ſide Iordan by Iericho Eaſtward.33But vnto the tribe of Leui Moſes gaue not any inheritance: the Lord God of Iſrael was their inheritance, as he ſaid vnto them.

CHAPTER 141And theſe are the countreys which the children of Iſrael inherited in the lande of Canaan, which Eleazar the Prieſt, & Ioſhua the ſonne of Nun, and the heads of the fathers of the tribes of the children of Iſrael diſtributed for inheritance to them:2By lot was their inheritance, as the Lord commanded by the hande of Moſes, for the nine tribes, and for the halfe tribe.3For Moſes had giuen the inheritance of two tribes and an halfe tribe, on the other ſide Iordan: but vnto the Leuites hee gaue none inheritance among them.4For the children of Ioſeph were two tribes, Manaſſeh and Ephraim: therefore they gaue no part vnto the Leuites in the land, ſaue cities to dwell in, with their ſuburbs for their cattell, and for their ſubſtance.5As the Lord commaunded Moſes, ſo the children of Iſrael did, and they diuided the land.6Then the children of Iudah came vnto Ioſhua in Gilgal: and Caleb the ſonne of Iephunneh the Kenezite, ſaid vnto him, Thou knoweſt the thing that the Lord ſaid vnto Moſes the man of God concerning me and thee, in Kadeſh Barnea.7Fourtie yeeres olde was I when Moſes the ſeruant of the Lord ſent me from Kadeſh Barnea, to eſpie out the land, and I brought him worde againe, as it was in mine heart.8Neuertheleſſe, my brethren that went vp with me, made the heart of the people melt: but I wholly followed the Lord my God.9And Moſes ſware on that day, ſaying, Surely the land whereon thy feet haue troden, ſhall be thine inheritance, and thy childrens for euer, becauſe thou haſt wholly followed the Lord my God.10And now beholde, the Lord hath kept me aliue, as he ſaid, theſe forty and fiue yeres, euen ſince the Lord ſpake this word vnto Moſes, while the children of Iſrael wandered in the wilderneſſe: and now loe, I am this day foureſcore and fiue yeeres old.11As yet I am as ſtrong this day, as I was in the day that Moſes ſent mee: as my ſtrength was then, euen ſo is my ſtrength now, for warre, both to goe out and to come in.12Now therefore giue mee this mountaine, whereof the Lord ſpake in that day, (for thou heardeſt in that day how the Anakims were there, and that the cities were great and fenced) if ſo be the Lord will be with me, then I ſhall bee able to driue them out, as the Lord ſaid.13And Ioſhua

bleſſed him, and gaue vnto Caleb the ſonne of Iephunneh, Hebron for
an inheritance.14Hebron therefore became the inheritance of Caleb the
ſonne of Iephunneh the Kenezite vnto this day: becauſe that hee wholly
followed the Lord God of Iſrael.15And the name of Hebron before, was
Kiriath-Arba, which Arba was a great man among the Anakims: and the
land had reſt from warre.

CHAPTER 15 1This then was the lot of the tribe of the children of
Iudah by their families, euen to the border of Edom; the wilderneſſe of
Zin Southward, was the vttermoſt part of the South coaſt:2And their
South border was from the ſhore of the ſalt ſea, from the bay that
looketh Southward.3And it went out to the Southſide to
Maalehacrabbim, and paſſed along to Zin, and aſcended vp on the
Southſide vnto Kadeſh-Barnea: and paſſed along to Hezron, and went
vp to Adar, and fetched a compaſſe to Karkaa.4From thence it paſſed
toward Azmon, and went out vnto the riuer of Egypt, and the goings
out of that coaſt were at the ſea: this ſhalbe your South coaſt.5And the
Eaſt border was the ſalt ſea, euen vnto the end of Iordan: and their
border in the North quarter, was from the bay of the ſea, at the vttermoſt
part of Iordan.6And the border went vp to Bethhogla, and paſſed along
by the North of Beth-arabah, and the border went vp to the ſtone of
Bohan the ſonne of Reuben.7And the border went vp toward Debir
from the valley of Achor, and ſo Northward, looking toward Gilgal, that
is before the going vp to Adummim, which is on the Southſide of the
riuer: and the border paſſed towards the waters of Enſhemeſh, and the
goings out thereof were at En-Rogel.8And the border went vp by the
valley of the ſonne of Hinnom, vnto the South ſide of the Iebuſite, the
ſame is Ieruſalem: and the border went vp to the top of the mountaine,
that lieth before the valley of Hinnom, Weſtward, which is at the end of
the valley of the giants, Northward.9And the border was drawen from
the top of the hill vnto the fountaine of the water of Nephtoah, and
went out to the cities of mount Ephron, and the border was drawen to
Baalah, which is Kiriath-iearim.10And the border compaſſed from
Baalah Weſtward vnto mount Seir, and paſſed along vnto the ſide of
mount Iearim, (which is Cheſalon) on the North ſide, and went downe
to Bethſhemeſh, and paſſed on to Timnah.11And the border went out
vnto the ſide of Ekron Northward: and the border was drawen to
Shicron, and paſſed along to mount Baalah, and went out vnto Iabneel;
and the goings out of the border were at the ſea.12And the Weſt border
was to the great ſea, and the coaſt therof: this is the coaſt of the children
of Iudah round about, according to their families.13And vnto Caleb the
ſonne of Iephunneh, he gaue a part among the children of Iudah,
according to the cōmandement of the Lord to Ioſhua, euen the citie of
Arba the father of Anak, which citie is Hebron.14And Caleb droue
thence the three ſonnes of Anak, Sheſhai, and Ahiman, and Talmai, the
children of Anak.15And he went vp thence to the inhabitants of Debir:
and the name of Debir before was Kiriath-Sepher.16And Caleb ſaid, He
that ſmiteth Kiriath-Sepher, and taketh it, to him will I giue Achſah my
daughter to wife.17And Othniel the ſonne of Kenaz, the brother of
Caleb, tooke it: and hee gaue him Achſah his daughter to wife.18And it
came to paſſe as ſhee came vnto him, that ſhe moued him to aſke of her
father a field, and ſhe lighted off her aſſe; and Caleb ſaid vnto her, What
wouldeſt thou?19Who anſwered, Giue mee a bleſſing; for thou haſt
giuen mee a Southland, giue me alſo ſprings of water; and he gaue her
the vpper ſprings, and the nether ſprings.20This is the inheritance of the
tribe of the children of Iudah according to their families.21And the
vttermoſt cities of the tribe of the children of Iudah toward the coaſt of
Edom Southward, were Kabzeel, and Eder, and Iagur,22And Kinah, and
Dimonah, and Adadah,23And Kedeſh, and Hazor, and Ithnan,24Ziph,
and Telem, and Bealoth,25And Hazor, Hadattah, and Kerioth: and
Hezron, which is Hazor,26Amam, and Shema, and Moladah,27And
Hazar-Gaddah, and Heſhmon, and Beth-palet,28And Hazarſhual, and
Beerſheba, and Biziothiah,29Baalah, and Iim, and Azem,30And Eltolad,
and Cheſil, and Hormah,31And Ziklag, and Madmannah, and
Sanſannah,32And Lebaoth, and Shilhim, and Ain, and Rimmon: all the
cities are twentie and nine, with their villages.33And in the valley,
Eſthaol, and Zoreah, and Aſhnah,34And Zanoah, and Engannim,
Tappuah, and Enam,35Iarmuth, and Adullam, Socoh, and
Azekah,36And Sharaim, and Adithaim, and Gederah, and Gederothaim:
fourteene cities with their villages.37Zenam, and Hadaſhah, &
Migdalgad,38And Dileam, and Mizpeh, and Ioktheel,39Lachiſh, and
Bozkath, & Eglon,40And Cabbon, and Lahmam, and Kithliſh,41And
Gederoth, Beth-dagon, and Naamah, and Makkedah: ſixteene cities with
their villages.42Lebnah, and Ether, and Aſhan,43And Iiphta, and
Aſhnah, and Nezib,44And Keilah, and Achzib, and Mareſhah: nine cities
with their villages.45Ekron with her townes, and her villages.46From
Ekron euen vnto the ſea, all that lay neere Aſhdod, with their
villages.47Aſhdod with her townes and her villages, Gaza with her
townes and her villages, vnto the riuer of Egypt, and the great ſea and
the border thereof.48And in the mountaines, Shamir, and Iattir, and
Socoh,49And Dannah, & Kiriath-Sannath, which is Debir,50And Anab,
and Aſhtemoh, and Anim,51And Goſhen, and Holon, and Giloh: eleuen
cities with their villages.52Arab, and Dumah, and Eſhean,53And Ianum,
and Beth-tappuah, and Aphekah,54And Humtah, and Kiriatharba
(which is Hebron) and Zior, nine cities with their villages.55Maon,
Carmel, and Ziph, and Iuttah,56Ind Iezreel, and Iokdeam, and
Zanoah,57Cain, Gibbeah, and Timnah: ten cities with their
villages.58Halhul, Beth-zur, and Gedor,59And Maarah, and Bethanoth,
& Eltekon: ſix cities with their villages.60Kiriath-baal, which is
Kiriathiearim, and Rabbah: two cities with their villages.61In the
wilderneſſe, Beth-arabah, Middin, and Secacah,62And Nibſhan, and the
city of Salt, and Engedi: ſixe cities with their villages.63As for the
Iebuſites the inhabitants of Ieruſalem, the children of Iudah could not
driue them out: but the Iebuſites dwell with the children of Iudah at
Ieruſalem vnto this day.

CHAPTER 16 1And the lot of the children of Ioſeph fell from Iordan
by Iericho, vnto the water of Iericho on the Eaſt, to the wilderneſſe that
goeth vp from Iericho throughout mount Bethel;2And goeth out from
Bethel to Luz, and paſſeth along vnto the borders of Archi, to
Ataroth,3And goeth downe Weſtward, to the coaſt of Iaphleti, vnto the
coaſt of Bethoron the nether, and to Gezer: and the goings out thereof
are at the ſea.4So the children of Ioſeph, Manaſſeh, and Ephraim, tooke
their inheritance.5And the border of the children of Ephraim according
to their families, was thus: euen the border of their inheritance on the
Eaſt ſide was Ataroth-Addar, vnto Bethoron the vpper.6And the border
went out toward the ſea, to Michmethah on the Northſide, and the
border went about Eaſtward vnto Taanath Shiloh, and paſſed by it on
the Eaſt to Ianohah:7And it went downe from Ianohah to Ataroth and
to Naarath, and came to Iericho, and went out at Iordane.8The border
went out from Tappuah Weſtward vnto the riuer Kanah: and the goings
out thereof were at the ſea. This is the inheritance of the tribe of the
children of Ephraim by their families.9And the ſeparate cities for the
children of Ephraim were among the inheritance of the children of
Manaſſeh, all the cities with their villages.10And they draue not out the
Canaanites that dwelt in Gezer: but the Canaanites dwell among the
Ephramites vnto this day, and ſerue vnder tribute.

CHAPTER 17 1There was alſo a lot for the tribe of Manaſſeh; (for hee
was the firſt borne of Ioſeph) to wit, for Machir the firſt borne of
Manaſſeh the father of Gilead: becauſe he was a man of warre, therefore
hee had Gilead and Baſhan.2There was alſo a lot for the reſt of the
children of Manaſſeh by their families; for the children of Abiezer, and
for the children of Helek, and for the children of Aſriel, and for the
children of Shechem, and for the children of Hepher, and for the
children of Shemida: theſe were the male children of Manaſſeh, the
ſonne of Ioſeph by their families.3But Zelophehad the ſonne of Hepher,
the ſonne of Gilead, the ſonne of Machir, the ſonne of Manaſſeh, had
no ſonnes but daughters: And theſe are the names of his daughters,
Mahlah, and Noah, Hoglah, Milcah, and Tirzah.4And they came neere
before Eleazar the Prieſt, and before Ioſhua the ſonne of Nun, and
before the Princes, ſaying, The Lord commanded Moſes to giue vs an
inheritance among our brethren: therefore according to the
commaundement of the Lord, hee gaue them an inheritance among the
brethren of their father.5And there fel ten portions to Manaſſeh, beſide
the land of Gilead and Baſhan, which were on the other ſide
Iordan;6Becauſe the daughters of Manaſſeh had an inheritance among
his ſonnes: and the reſt of Manaſſehs ſonnes had the land of
Gilead.7And the coaſt of Manaſſeh was from Aſher to Michmethah, that
lieth before Shechem, and the border went along on the right hand, vnto
the inhabitants of Entappuah.8Now Manaſſeh had the land of Tappuah:
but Tappuah on the border of Manaſſeh belonged to the children of

Ephraim. 9 And the coaſt deſcended vnto the riuer Kanah, Southward of the riuer: theſe cities of Ephraim are among the cities of Manaſſeh: the coaſt of Manaſſeh alſo was on the North ſide of the riuer, and the outgoings of it were at the ſea. 10 Southward it was Ephraims, and Northward it was Manaſſehs, and the ſea is his border, and they met together in Aſher on the North, and in Iſſachar on the Eaſt. 11 And Manaſſeh had in Iſſachar and in Aſher, Bethſhean & her townes, and Ibleam and her townes, and the inhabitants of Dor and her townes, and the inhabitants of Endor and her townes, and the inhabitants of Taanach and her townes, and the inhabitants of Megiddo and her townes, euen three countreyes. 12 Yet the children of Manaſſeh could not driue out the inhabitants of thoſe cities, but the Canaanites would dwell in that land. 13 Yet it came to paſſe when the children of Iſrael were waxen ſtrong, that they put the Canaanites to tribute: but did not vtterly driue them out. 14 And the children of Ioſeph ſpake vnto Ioſhua, ſaying, Why haſt thou giuen me but one lot and one portion to inherit, ſeeing I am a great people, foraſmuch as the Lord hath bleſſed me hitherto? 15 And Ioſhua anſwered them, If thou be a great people, then get thee vp to the wood countrey, and cut downe for thy ſelfe there in the land of the Perizzites, and of the giants, if mount Ephraim be too narrow for thee. 16 And the children of Ioſeph ſaide, The hill is not enough for vs: and all the Canaanites that dwell in the lande of the valley, haue charets of yron, both they who are of Bethſhean and her townes, and they who are of the valley of Iezreel. 17 And Ioſhua ſpake vnto the houſe of Ioſeph, euen to Ephraim, and to Manaſſeh, ſaying, Thou art a great people, and haſt great power: Thou ſhalt not haue one lot onely. 18 But the mountaine ſhalbe thine, for it is a wood, and thou ſhalt cut it downe: and the outgoings of it ſhalbe thine: for thou ſhalt driue out the Canaanites, though they haue yron charets, and though they be ſtrong.

CHAPTER 18 1 And the whole Congregation of the children of Iſrael aſſembled together at Shiloh, & ſet vp the Tabernacle of the Congregation there, and the land was ſubdued before them. 2 And there remained among the children of Iſrael ſeuen tribes, which had not yet receiued their inheritance. 3 And Ioſhua ſaid vnto the children of Iſrael, how long are you ſlacke to goe to poſſeſſe the lande which the Lord God of your fathers hath giuen you? 4 Giue out from among you three men, for each tribe: and I will ſend them, and they ſhall riſe, & goe through the land, and deſcribe it according to the inheritance of them, and they ſhal come againe to me. 5 And they ſhall diuide it into ſeuen parts: Iudah ſhall abide in their coaſt on the South, and the houſe of Ioſeph ſhall abide in their coaſts on the North. 6 Ye ſhall therfore deſcribe the land into ſeuen parts, and bring the deſcription hither to me: that I may caſt lots for you here before the Lord our God. 7 But the Leuites haue no part among you, for the Prieſthood of the Lord is their inheritance: and Gad and Reuben, and halfe the tribe of Manaſſeh, haue receiued their inheritance beyond Iordan on the Eaſt, which Moſes the ſeruant of the Lord gaue them. 8 And the men aroſe, and went away: and Ioſhua charged them that went to deſcribe the land, ſaying, Goe, and walke through the land, & deſcribe it, and come againe to me, that I may here caſt lots for you, before the Lord in Shiloh. 9 And the men went, and paſſed thorow the land, and deſcribed it by cities, into ſeuen parts in a booke, and came againe to Ioſhua to the hoſte at Shiloh. 10 And Ioſhua caſt lots for them in Shiloh, before the Lord: and there Ioſhua diuided the land vnto the children of Iſrael according to their diuiſions. 11 And the lot of the tribe of the children of Beniamin came vp according to their families: and the coaſt of their lot came foorth betweene the children of Iudah, and the children of Ioſeph. 12 And their border on the Northſide was from Iordan, and the border went vp to the ſide of Iericho, on the North ſide, and went vp through the mountaines Weſtward, and the goings out thereof were at the wilderneſſe of Beth-auen. 13 And the border went ouer from thence toward Luz, to the ſide of Luz, (which is Bethel) Southward, and the border deſcended to Ataroth-Adar, neere the hill that lieth on the South ſide of the nether Beth-horon. 14 And the border was drawen thence, and compaſſed the corner of the ſea Southward, from the hill that lieth before Beth-horon Southward: and the goings out thereof were at Kiriath-baal (which is Kiriath-iearim) a city of the children of Iudah: This was the Weſt quarter. 15 And the South quarter was from the end of Kiriath-iearim, & the border went out on the Weſt, and went out to the well of waters of Nephtoah. 16 And the border came downe to the end of the mountaine, that lieth before the valley of the ſonne of Hinnom, and which is in the valley of the Giants on the North, and deſcended to the valley of Hinnom to the ſide of Iebuſi on the South, and deſcended to En-Rogel, 17 And was drawen frō the North, and went foorth to Enſhemeſh, and went foorth toward Geliloth, which is ouer againſt the going vp of Adummim, and deſcended to the ſtone of Bohan the ſonne of Reuben, 18 And paſſed along toward the ſide ouer againſt Arabah Northward, and went downe vnto Arabah. 19 And the border paſſed along to the ſide of Beth-hoglah Northward: and the outgoings of the border were at the North bay of the ſalt ſea at the South end of Iordane: This was the South coaſt. 20 And Iordane was the border of it on the Eaſt ſide: this was the inheritance of the children of Beniamin, by the coaſts thereof round about, according to their families. 21 Now the cities of the tribe of the children of Beniamin according to their families, were Iericho, and Bethhoglah, and the valley of Keziz, 22 And Betharabah, and Zemaraim, and Bethel, 23 And Auim, and Parah, and Ophrah, 24 And Chephar-Haammonai, and Ophni, and Gaba, twelue cities with their villages. 25 Gibeon, and Ramah, and Beeroth, 26 And Mizpeh, and Chephirah, and Mozah, 27 And Rekem, and Irpeel, and Taralah, 28 And Zela, Eleph, and Iebuſi, (which is Ieruſalem) Gibeath, and Kiriath, foureteene cities with their villages. This is the inheritance of the children of Beniamin according to their families.

CHAPTER 19 1 And the ſecond lot came foorth to Simeon, euen for the tribe of the children of Simeon according to their families: and their inheritance was within the inheritance of the children of Iudah. 2 And they had in their inheritance Beer-ſheba, or Sheba, and Moladah, 3 And Hazarſhual, and Balah, and Azem, 4 And Eltolad, and Bethul, and Hormah, 5 And Ziklag, and Beth-marcaboth, and Hazar-ſuſah, 6 And Beth-lebaoth, and Sharuhen: thirteene cities and their villages. 7 Ain, Remmon, and Ether, and Aſhan: foure cities and their villages, 8 And all the villages that were round about theſe cities, to Baalath-Beer, Ramath of the South: This is the inheritance of the tribe of the children of Simeon according to their families. 9 Out of the portion of the children of Iudah was the inheritance of the children of Simeon: for the part of the children of Iudah was too much for them: therefore the children of Simeon had their inheritance within the inheritance of them. 10 And the third lot came vp for the children of Zebulun, according to their families: and the border of their inheritance was vnto Sarid. 11 And their border went vp toward the ſea, and Maralah, and reached to Dabbaſheth, and reached to the riuer that is before Iokneam, 12 And turned from Sarid Eaſtward, toward the Sunne riſing, vnto the border of Chiſloth Tabor, and then goeth out to Daberath, and goeth vp to Iaphia, 13 And from thence paſſeth on along on the Eaſt to Gittah-Hepher, to Ittah-Kazin, and goeth out to Remmon Methoar to Neah. 14 And the border compaſſeth it on the North ſide to Hannathon: and the outgoings thereof are in the valley of Iiphthah-el. 15 And Kattath, and Nahallal, and Shimron, and Idalah, and Bethlehem: twelue cities with their villages. 16 This is the inheritance of the children of Zebulun according to their families, theſe cities with their villages. 17 And the fourth lot came out to Iſſachar for the children of Iſſachar according to their families. 18 And their border was toward Izreel, and Cheſulloth, and Shunem, 19 And Hapharaim, and Shion, and Anaharath, 20 And Rabbith, and Kiſhion, and Abez, 21 And Remeth, and Engannim, and Enhaddah, and Bethpazzez. 22 And the coaſt reacheth to Tabor, and Shahazimath, and Bethſhemeſh, and the outgoings of their border were at Iordan, ſixteene cities with their villages. 23 This is the inheritance of the tribe of the children of Iſſachar according to their families, the cities, and their villages. 24 And the fift lot came out for the tribe of the children of Aſher according to their families. 25 And their border was Helkath, and Hali, and Beten, and Achſhaph, 26 And Alammelech, and Amad, and Miſheal, and reacheth to Carmel Weſtward, and to Shihor-Libnath, 27 And turneth toward the Sunne riſing to Beth-dagon, and reacheth to Zebulun, and to the valley of of Iiphthahel toward the Northſide of Bethemek, and Neiel, and goeth out to Cabul on the left hand, 28 And Hebron, and Rehob, and Hammon, and Kanah, euen vnto great Zidon: 29 And then the coaſt turneth to Ramah, and to the ſtrong citie Tyre, and the coaſt turneth to Hoſah: and the outgoings thereof are at the ſea from the coaſt to Achzib. 30 Ummah alſo, and Aphek, and Rehob: twentie and two cities with their villages. 31 This is the inheritance of the tribe of the children of Aſher according to their families, theſe cities with their villages. 32 The ſixt lot came out to the children of Naphtali: euen for the children of Naphtali according to their families.33And their coaſt was from Heleph, from Allon to Zaanannim, and Adami, Nekeb, and Iabneel vnto Lakum: and the outgoings thereof were at Iordan.34And then the coaſt turneth Weſtward to Aznoth-Tabor, and goeth out from thence to Hukkok, and reacheth to Zebulun on the Southſide, and reacheth to Aſher on the Weſtſide, and to Iudah vpon Iordan toward the Sun riſing.35And the fenced cities are Ziddim, Zer, and Hammath, Rakkath, and Cinnereth,36And Adamah, and Ramah, and Hazor,37And Kedeſh, and Edrei, and Enhazor,38And Iron, and Migdal-el, Horem, and Bethanah, and Bethſhemeſh, nineteene cities with their villages.39This is the inheritance of the tribe of the children of Naphtali according to their families, the cities and their villages.40And the ſeuenth lot came out for the tribe of the children of Dan according to their families:41And the coaſt of their inheritance was Zorah, and Eſhtaol, and Irſhemeſh,42And Shaalabbin, and Aiialon, and Iethlah,43And Elon, and Thimnathah, and Ekron,44And Eltekeh, and Gibbethon, and Baalah,45And Iehud, and Bene-berak, and Gath-rimmon,46And Meiarkon, and Rakkon, with the border before Iapho.47And the coaſt of the children of Dan went out too little for them: therefore the children of Dan went vp to fight againſt Leſhem, and tooke it, and ſmote it with the edge of the ſword, and poſſeſſed it, and dwelt therein, and called Leſhem, Dan, after the name of Dan their father.48This is the inheritance of the tribe of the children of Dan according to their families, theſe cities with their villages.49When they had made an end of diuiding the land for inheritance by their coaſts, the children of Iſrael gaue an inheritance to Ioſhua the ſonne of Nun among them:50According to the word of the Lord, they gaue him the citie which he aſked, euen Timnath-Serah in mount Ephraim: and he built the citie, and dwelt therein.51Theſe are the inheritances which Eleazar the Prieſt, and Ioſhua the ſonne of Nun, and the heads of the fathers of the tribes of the children of Iſrael, diuided for an inheritance by lot, in Shiloh before the Lord, at the doore of the Tabernacle of the Congregation: ſo they made an end of diuiding the countrey.

CHAPTER 201The Lord alſo ſpake vnto Ioſhua, ſaying,2Speake to the children of Iſrael, ſaying, Appoint out for you cities of refuge, whereof I ſpake vnto you by the hand of Moſes:3That the ſlayer that killeth any perſon vnawares and vnwittingly, may flee thither: and they ſhall be your refuge from the auenger of blood.4And when he that doeth flee vnto one of thoſe cities, ſhall ſtand at the entring of the gate of the city, and ſhall declare his cauſe in the eares of the Elders of that citie; they ſhall take him into the citie vnto them, and giue him a place, that he may dwell among them.5And if the auenger of blood purſue after him, then they ſhal not deliuer the ſlayer vp into his hand: becauſe hee ſmote his neighbour vnwittingly, and hated him not beforetime.6And hee ſhall dwell in that citie, vntill he ſtand before the Congregation for iudgement, and vntill the death of the high Prieſt that ſhall bee in thoſe dayes: then ſhall the ſlayer returne, and come vnto his owne city, and vnto his owne houſe, vnto the citie from whence he fled.7And they appointed Kedeſh in Galilee, in mount Naphtali, and Shechem in mount Ephraim, and Kiriath-arba (which is Hebron) in the mountaine of Iudah.8And on the other ſide Iordan by Iericho Eaſtward, they aſsigned Bezer in the wilderneſſe vpon the plaine, out of the tribe of Reuben, and Ramoth in Gilead out of the tribe of Gad, and Golan in Baſhan out of the tribe of Manaſſeh.9Theſe were the cities appointed for all the children of Iſrael, and for the ſtranger that ſoiourneth among them, that whoſoeuer killeth any perſon at vnawares might flee thither, & not die by the hand of the auenger of blood, vntill he ſtood before the Congregation.

CHAPTER 211Then came neere the heads of the fathers of the Leuites vnto Eleazar the Prieſt, and vnto Ioſhua the ſonne of Nun, and vnto the heads of the fathers of the tribes of the children of Iſrael.2And they ſpake vnto them at Shiloh in the land of Canaan, ſaying, The Lord commaunded by the hand of Moſes, to giue vs Cities to dwell in, with the ſuburbs thereof for our cattell.3And the children of Iſrael gaue vnto the Leuites out of their inheritance at the commandement of the Lord, theſe cities and their ſuburbs.4And the lot came out for the families of the Kohathites: and the children of Aaron the Prieſt, which were of the Leuites, had by lot out of the tribe of Iudah, and out of the tribe of Simeon, and out of the tribe of Beniamin, thirteene cities.5And the reſt of the children of Kohath had by lot, out of the families of the tribe of Ephraim, and out of the tribe of Dan, and out of the halfe tribe of Manaſſeh, ten cities.6And the children of Gerſhon had by lot out of the families of the tribe of Iſſachar, and out of the tribe of Aſher, and out of the tribe of Naphtali, and out of the halfe tribe of Manaſſeh in Baſhan, thirteene cities.7The children of Merari by their families, had out of the tribe of Reuben, and out of the tribe of Gad, and out of the tribe of Zebulun, twelue cities.8And the children of Iſrael gaue by lot vnto the Leuites theſe cities with their ſuburbs, as the Lord commanded by the hand of Moſes.9And they gaue out of the tribe of the children of Iudah, and out of the tribe of the children of Simeon, theſe cities which are here mentioned by name,10Which the children of Aaron being of the families of the Kohathites, who were of the children of Leui, had: (for theirs was the firſt lot.)11And they gaue them the citie of Arbah the father of Anak (which citie is Hebron) in the hill countrey of Iudah, with þe ſuburbs thereof round about it.12But the fields of the citie, and the villages thereof, gaue they to Caleb the ſonne of Iephunneh, for his poſſeſſion.13Thus they gaue to the children of Aaron the Prieſt Hebron with her ſuburbs to bee a citie of refuge for the ſlayer, and Libnah with her ſuburbs,14And Iattir with her ſuburbs, and Eſhtemoa with her ſuburbs:15And Holon with her ſuburbs, and Debir with her ſuburbs:16And Ain with her ſuburbs, and Iuttah with her ſuburbs, and Bethſhemeſh with her ſuburbs, nine cities out of thoſe two tribes.17And out of the tribe of Beniamin, Gibeon with her ſuburbs, Geba with her ſuburbs,18Anathoth with her ſuburbs, and Almon with her ſuburbs, foure cities.19All the cities of the children of Aaron the Prieſts, were thirteene cities with their ſuburbs.20And the families of the children of Kohath the Leuites, which remained of the children of Kohath, euen they had the cities of their lot out of the tribe of Ephraim.21For they gaue them Shechem with her ſuburbs in mount Ephraim, to be a citie of refuge for the ſlayer: and Gezer with her ſuburbs,22And Kibzaim with her ſuburbs, and Beth-horon with her ſuburbs, foure cities.23And out of the tribe of Dan, Eltekeh with her ſuburbs, Gibethon with her ſuburbs,24Aijalon with her ſuburbs, Gathrimmon, with her ſuburbs: foure cities.25And out of the halfe tribe of Manaſſeh, Tanach with her ſuburbs, and Gathrimmon with her ſuburbs, two cities.26All the cities were ten with their ſuburbs, for the families of the children of Kohath that remained.27And vnto the children of Gerſhon of the families of the Leuites, out of the other halfe tribe of Manaſſeh, they gaue Golan in Baſhan, with her ſuburbs, to be a citie of refuge for the ſlayer: and Beeſhterah with her ſuburbs, two cities.28And out of the tribe of Iſſachar, Kiſhon with her ſuburbs, Dabareh with her ſuburbs,29Iarmuth with her ſuburbs, Engannim with her ſuburbs, foure cities.30And out of the tribe of Aſher Miſhal with her ſuburbs, Abdon with her ſuburbs,31Helkah with her ſuburbs, and Rehob with her ſuburbs, foure cities.32And out of the tribe of Naphtali, Kedeſh in Galilee with her ſuburbs, to be a citie of refuge for the ſlayer, and Hammoth-dor with her ſuburbs, and Kartan with her ſuburbs, three cities.33All the cities of the Gerſhonites according to their families were thirteen cities with their ſuburbs.34And vnto the families of the children of Merari the reſt of the Leuites, out of the tribe of Zebulun, Iokneam, with her ſuburbs, and Kartah with her ſuburbs,35Dimnah with her ſuburbs, Nahalal with her ſuburbs, foure cities.36And out of the tribe of Reuben, Bezer with her ſuburbs, and Iahazah with her ſuburbs,37Kedemoth with her ſuburbs, and Mephaath with her ſuburbs, foure cities.38And out of the tribe of Gad, Ramoth in Gilead with her ſuburbs, to be a city of refuge for the ſlayer; and Mahanaim with her ſuburbs,39Heſhbon with her ſuburbs, Iazer with her ſuburbs, foure cities in all.40So all the cities for the children of Merari by their families, which were remayning of the families of the Leuites, were by their lot, twelue cities.41All the cities of the Leuites within the poſſeſſion of the children of Iſrael, were fourty and eight cities, with their ſuburbs.42Theſe cities were euery one with their ſuburbs round about them: thus were all theſe cities.43And the Lord gaue vnto Iſrael all the land which hee ſware to giue vnto their fathers: and they poſſeſſed it, and dwelt therein.44And the Lord gaue them reſt round about, according to all that he ſware vnto their fathers, and there ſtood not a man of all their enemies before them: the Lord deliuered all their enemies into their hand.45There failed not ought of any good thing which the Lord had ſpoken vnto the houſe of Iſrael: all came to paſſe.

CHAPTER 22 1 Then Ioſhua called the Reubenites, and the Gadites, and the halfe tribe of Manaſſeh, 2 And ſaid vnto them, Yee haue kept all that Moſes the ſeruant of the Lord commanded you, and haue obeyed my voyce in all that I commanded you. 3 Yee haue not left your brethren theſe many dayes vnto this day, but haue kept the charge of the commandement of the Lord your God. 4 And now the Lord your God hath giuen reſt vnto your brethren, as hee promiſed them: therefore now returne yee, and get yee vnto your tents, and vnto the land of your poſſeſſion, which Moſes the ſeruant of the Lord gaue you on the other ſide Iordane. 5 But take diligent heed, to doe the Commandement and the Law, which Moſes the ſeruant of the Lord charged you, to loue the Lord your God, and to walke in all his wayes, and to keepe his Commaundements, and to cleaue vnto him, and to ſerue him with all your heart, and with all your ſoule. 6 So Ioſhua bleſſed them, and ſent them away: and they went vnto their tents. 7 Now to the one halfe of the tribe of Manaſſeh Moſes had giuen poſſeſſion in Baſhan: but vnto the other halfe therof gaue Ioſhua among their brethren on this ſide Iordane Weſtward. And when Ioſhua ſent them away alſo vnto their tents, then hee bleſſed them, 8 And he ſpake vnto them, ſaying; Returne with much riches vnto your tents, and with very much cattell, with ſiluer and with gold, and with braſſe, and with iron, and with very much raiment: Diuide the ſpoile of your enemies with your brethren. 9 And the children of Reuben, and the children of Gad, and the halfe tribe of Manaſſeh returned, and departed from the children of Iſrael out of Shiloh which is in the land of Canaan, to goe vnto the countrey of Gilead, to the land of their poſſeſſion, whereof they were poſſeſſed, according to the word of the Lord by the hand of Moſes. 10 And when they came vnto the borders of Iordan, that are in the land of Canaan, the children of Reuben, and the children of Gad, and the halfe tribe of Manaſſeh built there an altar by Iordan, a great altar to ſee to. 11 And the children of Iſrael heard ſay, Behold, the children of Reuben, and the children of Gad, and the halfe tribe of Manaſſeh, haue built an altar ouer againſt the land of Canaan, in the borders of Iordan, at the paſsage of the children of Iſrael. 12 And when the children of Iſrael heard of it, the whole Congregation of the children of Iſrael gathered themſelues together at Shiloh, to goe vp to warre againſt them. 13 And the children of Iſrael ſent vnto the children of Reuben, and to the children of Gad, and to the halfe tribe of Manaſſeh into the lande of Gilead, Phinehas ſon of Eleazar the Prieſt, 14 And with him ten princes, of ech chiefe houſe a prince, throughout all the tribes of Iſrael, and each one was an head of the houſe of their fathers, among the thouſands of Iſrael. 15 And they came vnto the children of Reuben, and to the children of Gad, and to the halfe tribe of Manaſſeh vnto the land of Gilead, and they ſpake with them, ſaying, 16 Thus ſaith the whole Congregation of the Lord, What treſpaſſe is this that ye haue committed againſt the God of Iſrael, to turne away this day from following the Lord, in that ye haue builded you an altar, that yee might rebell this day againſt the Lord ? 17 Is the iniquitie of Peor too litle for vs, from which we are not cleanſed vntil this day, (although there was a plague in the Congregation of the Lord) 18 But that ye muſt turne away this day from following the Lord ? And it will be, ſeeing yee rebell to day againſt the Lord, that to morrow he will be wroth with the whole Congregation of Iſrael. 19 Notwithſtanding, if the lande of your poſſeſſion be vncleane, then paſſe yee ouer vnto the land of the poſſeſſion of the Lord, wherein the Lords Tabernacle dwelleth, and take poſſeſſion among vs: but rebell not againſt the Lord, nor rebell againſt vs, in building you an altar, beſide the Altar of the Lord our God. 20 Did not Achan the ſonne of Zerah commit a treſpaſſe in the accurſed thing, and wrath fell on all the Congregation of Iſrael? and that man periſhed not alone in his iniquitie. 21 Then the children of Reuben, and the children of Gad, and the halfe tribe of Manaſſeh, anſwered and ſaide vnto the heads of the thouſands of Iſrael, 22 The Lord God of gods, the Lord God of gods, hee knoweth, and Iſrael he ſhall know; if it bee in rebellion, or if in tranſgreſſion againſt the Lord, (ſaue vs not this day,) 23 That wee haue built vs an altar to turne from following the Lord, or if to offer thereon burnt offering, or meat offering, or if to offer peace offerings thereon, let the Lord himſelfe require it; 24 And if we haue not rather done it for feare of this thing, ſaying, In time to come your children might ſpeake vnto our children, ſaying, What haue you to doe with the Lord God of Iſrael? 25 For the Lord hath made Iordan a border betweene vs and you, yee children of Reuben, and children of Gad, yee haue no part in the Lord: ſo ſhal your children make our children ceaſe from fearing the Lord: 26 Therefore we ſaid, Let vs now prepare to build vs an altar, not for burnt offering, nor for ſacrifice, 27 But that it may bee a witneſſe betweene vs and you, and our generations after vs, that we might do the ſeruice of the Lord before him with our burnt offrings, and with our ſacrifices, and with our peace offerings, that your children may not ſay to our children in time to come, Ye haue no part in the Lord. 28 Therefore ſaid we, that it ſhalbe, when they ſhould ſo ſay to vs, or to our generations in time to come, that wee may ſay againe, Beholde the paterne of the altar of the Lord, which our fathers made, not for burnt offrings, nor for ſacrifices, but it is a witnes betweene vs and you. 29 God forbid that we ſhould rebell againſt the Lord, and turne this day from following the Lord, to build an altar for burnt offerings, for meate offerings, or for ſacrifices, beſides the Altar of the Lord our God that is before his Tabernacle. 30 And when Phinehas the Prieſt and the Princes of the Congregation, and Heads of the thouſands of Iſrael which were with him, heard the words that the children of Reuben and the children of Gad, and the children of Manaſſeh ſpake, it pleaſed them. 31 And Phinehas the ſonne of Eleazar the Prieſt ſaid vnto the children of Reuben, and to the children of Gad, and to the children of Manaſſeh, This day we perceiue that the Lord is among vs, becauſe ye haue not committed this treſpaſſe againſt the Lord: now ye haue deliuered the children of Iſrael out of the hand of the Lord. 32 And Phinehas the ſonne of Eleazar the Prieſt, and the Princes, returned from the children of Reuben, and from the children of Gad, out of the land of Gilead, vnto the land of Canaan, to the children of Iſrael, & brought them word againe. 33 And the thing pleaſed the children of Iſrael, and the children of Iſrael bleſſed God, and did not intend to goe vp againſt them in battel, to deſtroy the land wherein the children of Reuben and Gad dwelt. 34 And the children of Reuben, and the children of Gad called the altar Ed: for it ſhall bee a witneſſe betweene vs, that the Lord is God.

CHAPTER 23 1 And it came to paſſe, a long time after that the Lord had giuen reſt vnto Iſrael from all their enemies round about, that Ioſhua waxed old, and ſtricken in age. 2 And Ioſhua called for all Iſrael, and for their Elders, & for their Heads, and for their Iudges, and for their Officers, and ſaid vnto them; I am old, and ſtricken in age. 3 And yee haue ſeene all that the Lord your God hath done vnto all theſe nations, becauſe of you; for the Lord your God is hee that hath fought for you. 4 Behold, I haue diuided vnto you by lot theſe nations that remaine, to bee an inheritance for your tribes, from Iordan, with all the nations that I haue cut off, euen vnto the great ſea Weſtward. 5 And the Lord your God, hee ſhall expell them from before you, and driue them from out of your ſight, & ye ſhall poſſeſſe their land, as the Lord your God hath promiſed vnto you. 6 Be ye therefore very courageous to keepe and to doe all that is written in the booke of the Law of Moſes, that yee turne not aſide therefrom, to the right hand, or to the left, 7 That yee come not among theſe nations, theſe that remaine amongſt you, neither make mention of the name of their gods, nor cauſe to ſweare by them, neither ſerue them, nor bow your ſelues vnto them. 8 But cleaue vnto the Lord your God, as yee haue done vnto this day. 9 For the Lord hath driuen out from before you, great nations, and ſtrong: But as for you, no man hath beene able to ſtand before you vnto this day. 10 One man of you ſhall chaſe a thouſand: for the Lord your God, he it is that fighteth for you, as hee hath promiſed you. 11 Take good heed therefore vnto your ſelues, that ye loue the Lord your God. 12 Elſe, if ye do in any wiſe go backe, and cleaue vnto the remnant of theſe nations, euen theſe that remaine among you, and ſhall make marriages with them, and goe in vnto them, and they to you: 13 Know for a certainety, that the Lord your God will no more driue out any of theſe nations from before you: but they ſhalbe ſnares and traps vnto you, and ſcourges in your ſides, and thornes in your eyes, vntill yee periſh from off this good land which the Lord your God hath giuen you. 14 And behold, this day I am going the way of all the earth, and ye know in all your hearts, and in all your ſoules, that not one thing hath failed of all the good things which the Lord your God ſpake concerning you; all are come to paſſe vnto you, and not one thing hath failed thereof. 15 Therefore it ſhall come to paſſe, that as all good things are come vpon you, which the Lord your God promiſed you: ſo ſhall the Lord bring vpon you all euill things, vntill he haue deſtroyed you from off this good land which the Lord your God hath giuen you. 16 When yee haue tranſgreſſed the Couenant of the Lord your God, which hee commaunded you, and haue gone and ſerued other gods, and bowed your ſelues to them: then ſhall the anger of the Lord bee kindled againſt you, and yee ſhall periſh quickly from off the good land which hee hath giuen vnto you.

CHAPTER 241And Ioſhua gathered all the Tribes of Iſrael to Shechem, and called for the Elders of Iſrael, and for their Heads, and for their Iudges, and for their Officers, and they preſented themſelues before God.2And Ioſhua ſaid vnto all the people, Thus ſaith the Lord God of Iſrael, Your fathers dwelt on the other ſide of the flood in old time, euen Terah the father of Abraham, and the father of Nachor: and they ſerued other gods.3And I tooke your father Abraham frō the other ſide of the flood, and led him throughout all the land of Canaan, and multiplied his ſeed, and gaue him Iſaac.4And I gaue vnto Iſaac, Iacob and Eſau: & I gaue vnto Eſau mount Seir, to poſſeſſe it: but Iacob and his children went downe into Egypt.5I ſent Moſes alſo and Aaron, and I plagued Egypt, according to that which I did amongſt them: and afterward, I brought you out.6And I brought your fathers out of Egypt: and you came vnto the ſea, and the Egyptians purſued after your fathers with charets and horſemen vnto the red ſea.7And when they cried vnto the Lord, hee put darkeneſſe betweene you and the Egyptians, and brought the ſea vpon them, and couered them, and your eyes haue ſeene what I haue done in Egypt, and ye dwelt in the wildernes a long ſeaſon.8And I brought you into the land of the Amorites, which dwelt on the other ſide Iordan: and they fought with you, and I gaue them into your hand, that ye might poſſeſſe their land, and I deſtroyed them from before you.9Then Balak the ſonne of Zippor king of Moab, aroſe and warred againſt Iſrael, and ſent and called Balaam the ſonne of Beor to curſe you:10But I would not hearken vnto Balaam, therefore he bleſſed you ſtill: ſo I deliuered you out of his hand.11And ye went ouer Iordan, and came vnto Iericho: and the men of Iericho fought againſt you, the Amorites, and the Perizzites, & the Canaanites, and the Hittites, and the Girgaſhites, the Hiuites, and the Iebuſites, and I deliuered them into your hand.12And I ſent the hornet before you, which draue them out from before you, euen the two kings of the Amorites: but not with thy ſword, nor with thy bow.13And I haue giuen you a land for which ye did not labour, & cities which ye built not, and yee dwell in them: of the vineyards and Oliue-yards which ye planted not, doe ye eate.14Now therefore, feare the Lord, and ſerue him in ſinceritie, and in trueth, and put away the gods which your fathers ſerued on the other ſide of the flood, and in Egypt: and ſerue yee the Lord.15And if it ſeeme euill vnto you to ſerue the Lord, chooſe you this day whome you will ſerue, whether the gods which your fathers ſerued that were on the other ſide of the flood, or the gods of the Amorites, in whoſe lande ye dwell: but as for mee and my houſe, we will ſerue the Lord.16And the people anſwered and ſaid, God forbid that wee ſhould forſake the Lord, to ſerue other gods.17For the Lord our God, he it is that brought vs vp and our fathers out of the land of Egypt, from the houſe of bondage, & which did thoſe great ſignes in our ſight, and preſerued vs in all the way wherein we went, and among all the people through whom we paſſed.18And the Lord draue out from before vs all the people, euen the Amorites which dwelt in the land: therefore will we alſo ſerue the Lord, for he is our God.19And Ioſhua ſaid vnto the people, Ye cannot ſerue the Lord: for hee is an holy God: he is a ielous God, he will not forgiue your tranſgreſſions nor your ſinnes.20If yee forſake the Lord, and ſerue ſtrange gods, then he will turne, and doe you hurt, and conſume you, after that he hath done you good.21And the people ſaid vnto Ioſhua, Nay, but we will ſerue the Lord.22And Ioſhua ſaid vnto the people, Yee are witneſſes againſt your ſelues, that yee haue choſen you the Lord, to ſerue him. And they ſaid, We are witneſſes.23Now therefore put away, ſaid he, the ſtrange gods which are among you, and encline your heart vnto the Lord God of Iſrael.24And the people ſaide vnto Ioſhua; The Lord our God will we ſerue, and his voice will we obey.25So Ioſhua made a couenant with the people that day, and ſet them a Statute, & an Ordinance in Shechem.26And Ioſhua wrote theſe words in the booke of the Law of God, and tooke a great ſtone, and ſet it vp there, vnder an oake, that was by the Sanctuary of the Lord.27And Ioſhua ſaide vnto all the people, Behold, this ſtone ſhalbe a witneſſe vnto vs; for it hath heard all the words of the Lord which hee ſpake vnto vs; it ſhall be there for a witneſſe vnto you, leſt ye deny your God.28So Ioſhua let the people depart, euery man vnto his inheritance.29And it came to paſſe after theſe things, that Ioſhua the ſonne of Nun the ſeruant of the Lord died, being an hundred and ten yeeres old.30And they buried him in the border of his inheritance in Timnath-Serah, which is in mount Ephraim, on the North ſide of the hill of Gaaſh.31And Iſrael ſerued the Lord all the dayes of Ioſhua, & all the dayes of the Elders that ouerliued Ioſhua, and which had knowen al the works of the Lord, that he had done for Iſrael.32And the bones of Ioſeph, which the children of Iſrael brought vp out of Egypt, buried they in Shechem, in a parcell of ground which Iacob bought of the ſonnes of Hamor the father of Shechem, for an hundred pieces of ſiluer; and it became the inheritance of the children of Ioſeph.33And Eleazar the ſonne of Aaron died, and they buried him in a hill that pertained to Phinehas his ſon, which was giuen him in mount Ephraim.

IUDGES (JUDGES)

CHAPTER 11Now after the death of Ioſhua, it came to paſſe, that the children of Iſrael aſked the Lord, ſaying, Who ſhal goe vp for vs againſt the Canaanites firſt, to fight againſt them?2And the Lord ſayd, Iudah ſhall goe vp: Behold, I haue deliuered the land into his hand.3And Iudah ſaide vnto Simeon his brother, Come vp with me into my lot, that wee may fight againſt the Canaanites, and I likewiſe will goe with thee into thy lot. So Simeon went with him.4And Iudah went vp, and the Lord deliuered the Canaanites and the Perizzites into their hand: and they ſlew of them in Bezek ten thouſand men.5And they found Adoni-bezek in Bezek: and they fought againſt him, and they ſlew the Canaanites, and the Perizzites.6But Adoni-bezek fled, and they purſued after him, and caught him, and cut off his thumbes, and his great toes.7And Adoni-bezek ſaid, Threeſcore & ten kings, hauing their thumbs and their great toes cut off, gathered their meate vnder my table: as I haue done, ſo God hath requited mee, and they brought him to Ieruſalem, and there he died.8(Now the children of Iudah had fought againſt Ieruſalem, and had taken it, and ſmitten it with the edge of the ſword, and ſet the citie on fire)9And afterward the children of Iudah went downe to fight againſt the Canaanites that dwelt in the moūtaine, & in the South, and in the valley.10And Iudah went againſt the Canaanites that dwelt in Hebron (nowe the name of Hebron before was Kiriath-arba) and they ſlew Sheſhai, and Ahiman, and Talmai.11And from thence he went againſt the inhabitants of Debir, (& the name of Debir before was Kiriath-ſepher)12And Caleb ſaid, Hee that ſmiteth Kiriath-ſepher, and taketh it, to him will I giue Achſah my daughter to wife.13And Othniel the ſonne of Kenaz Calebs yonger brother tooke it: and he gaue him Achſah his daughter to wife.14And it came to paſſe when ſhee came to him, that ſhe moued him to aſke of her father a field: and ſhee lighted from off her aſſe, and Caleb ſaid vnto her, What wilt thou?15And ſhe ſaid vnto him, Giue me a bleſſing: for thou haſt giuen mee a South land, giue me alſo ſprings of water. And Caleb gaue her the vpper ſprings, and the nether ſprings.16And the children of the Kenite, Moſes father in law, went vp out of the citie of palme trees, with the children of Iudah into the wilderneſſe of Iudah, which lieth in the South of Arad, and they went and dwelt among the people.17And Iudah went with Simeon his brother, and they ſlew the Canaanites that inhabited Zephath, and vtterly deſtroyed it, (and the name of the citie was called Hormah.)18Alſo Iudah tooke Gaza with the coaſt thereof, and Aſkelon with the coaſt thereof, and Ekron with the coaſt thereof.19And the Lord was with Iudah, and hee draue out the inhabitants of the mountaine, but could not driue out the inhabitants of the valley, becauſe they had charets of yron.20And they gaue Hebron vnto Caleb, as Moſes ſaide: and hee expelled thence the three ſonnes of Anak.21And the children of Beniamin did not driue out the Iebuſites that inhabited Ieruſalem: but the Iebuſites dwel with the children of Beniamin in Ieruſalem, vnto this day.22And the houſe of Ioſeph, they alſo went vp againſt Bethel: and the Lord was with them.23And the houſe of Ioſeph ſent to deſcrie Bethel (now the name of the citie before was Luz)24And the ſpies ſawe a man come forth out of the citie, and they ſaid vnto him, ſhew vs, wee pray thee, the entrance into the citie, and we will ſhew thee mercie.25And when hee ſhewed them the entrance into the citie, they ſmote the citie with the edge of the ſword: but they let goe the man and all his familie.[26]And the man went into the lande of the Hittites, and built a citie, and called the name thereof Luz: which is the name thereof vnto this day.[27]Neither did Manaſſeh driue out the inhabitants of Bethſhean, and her townes, nor Taanach and her townes, nor the inhabitants of Dor, and her townes, nor the inhabitants of Ibleam, and her townes, nor the inhabitants of Megiddo, and her townes: but the Canaanites would dwel in that land.[28]And it came to paſſe when Iſrael was ſtrong, that they put the Canaanites to tribute, and did not vtterly driue them out.[29]Neither did Ephraim driue out the Canaanites that dwelt in Gezer: but the Canaanites dwelt in Gezer among them.[30]Neither did Zebulun driue out the inhabitants of Kitron, nor the inhabitants of Nahalol: but the Canaanites dwelt among them, and became tributaries.[31]Neither did Aſher driue out the inhabitants of Accho, nor the inhabitants of Zidon, nor of Ahlab, nor Achzib, nor Helbath, nor Aphik, nor of Rehob:[32]But the Aſherites dwelt among the Canaanites, the inhabitants of the land: for they did not driue them out.[33]Neither did Naphtali driue out the inhabitants of Bethſhemeſh, nor the inhabitants of Bethanath, but hee dwelt among the Canaanites, the inhabitants of the land: neuertheleſſe, the inhabitants of Bethſhemeſh, and of Bethanath, became tributaries vnto them.[34]And the Amorites forced the children of Dan into the mountaine: for they would not ſuffer them to come downe to the valley.[35]But the Amorites would dwell in mount Heres in Aiialon, & in Shaalbim: yet the hand of the houſe of Ioſeph preuailed, ſo that they became tributaries.[36]And the coaſt of the Amorites was from the going vp to Akrabbim, from the rocke, and vpward.

CHAPTER 2[1]And an Angel of the Lord came vp from Gilgal to Bochim, and ſaid, I made you to goe vp out of Egypt, and haue brought you vnto the land which I ſware vnto your fathers, and I ſaid, I will neuer breake my Couenant with you.[2]And yee ſhall make no league with the inhabitants of this land, you ſhal throw downe their altars: But ye haue not obeyed my voyce; Why haue ye done this?[3]Wherefore I alſo ſaid, I will not driue them out from before you: but they ſhalbe as thornes in your ſides, and their gods ſhalbe a ſnare vnto you.[4]And it came to paſſe when the Angel of the Lord ſpake theſe words vnto all the children of Iſrael, that the people lift vp their voice, and wept.[5]And they called the name of that place Bochim: and they ſacrificed there vnto the Lord.[6]And when Ioſhua had let the people goe, the children of Iſrael went euery man vnto his inheritance, to poſſeſſe the land.[7]And the people ſerued the Lord all the dayes of Ioſhua, and all the dayes of the Elders that outliued Ioſhua, who had ſeene all the great workes of the Lord, that hee did for Iſrael.[8]And Ioſhua the ſonne of Nun, the ſeruant of the Lord died, being an hundred and ten yeeres old.[9]And they buried him in the border of his inheritance in Timnath-Heres, in the mount of Ephraim, on the North ſide of the hill Gaaſh.[10]And alſo all that generation were gathered vnto their fathers: and there aroſe another generation after them, which knew not the Lord, nor yet the woorkes which hee had done for Iſrael.[11]And the children of Iſrael did euil in the ſight of the Lord, and ſerued Baalim:[12]And they forſooke the Lord God of their fathers, which brought them out of the land of Egypt, and followed other gods, of the gods of the people that were round about them, and bowed themſelues vnto them, and prouoked the Lord to anger.[13]And they forſooke the Lord, and ſerued Baal and Aſhtaroth.[14]And the anger of the Lord was hote againſt Iſrael, and he deliuered them into the hands of ſpoilers that ſpoiled them, and he ſold them into the hands of their enemies round about, ſo that they could not any longer ſtand before their enemies.[15]Whither ſoeuer they went out, the hand of the Lord was againſt them for euill, as the Lord had ſaid, and as the Lord had ſworne vnto them: and they were greatly diſtreſſed.[16]Neuertheleſſe, the Lord rayſed vp Iudges, which deliuered them out of the hand of thoſe that ſpoyled them.[17]And yet they would not hearken vnto their Iudges, but they went a whoring after other gods, and bowed themſelues vnto them: they turned quickly out of the way, which their fathers walked in, obeying the Commandements of the Lord; but they did not ſo.[18]And when the Lord raiſed them vp Iudges, then the Lord was with the Iudge, and deliuered them out of the hand of their enemies, all the dayes of the Iudge (for it repented the Lord, becauſe of their gronings by reaſon of them that oppreſſed them, and vexed them:)[19]And it came to paſſe when the Iudge was dead, that they returned, and corrupted themſelues more then their fathers, in following other gods, to ſerue them, and to bow downe vnto them: they ceaſed not from their owne doings, nor from their ſtubborne way.[20]And the anger of the Lord was hote againſt Iſrael, and he ſaid, Becauſe that this people hath tranſgreſſed my Couenant which I commanded their fathers, and haue not hearkened vnto my voice:[21]I alſo will not henceforth driue out any from before them of the nations which Ioſhua left when he died:[22]That through them I may proue Iſrael, whether they will keepe the way of the Lord, to walke therein, as their fathers did keepe it, or not.[23]Therefore the Lord left thoſe nations, without driuing them out haſtily, neither deliuered he them into the hand of Ioſhua.

CHAPTER 3[1]Now theſe are the nations which the Lord left, to prooue Iſrael by them, (euen as many of Iſrael as had not knowen all the warres of Canaan;[2]Onely that the generations of the children of Iſrael might know to teach them warre, at the leaſt ſuch as before knew nothing thereof:)[3]Namely fiue lords of the Philiſtines, and all the Canaanites, and the Sidonians, and the Hiuites that dwelt in mount Lebanon, from mount Baal-Hermon, vnto the entring in of Hamath.[4]And they were to prooue Iſrael by them, to know whether they would hearken vnto the Commandements of the Lord, which hee commaunded their fathers by the hand of Moſes.[5]And the children of Iſrael dwelt among the Canaanites, Hittites, and Amorites, and Perizzites, and Hiuites, and Iebuſites,[6]And they tooke their daughters to be their wiues, and gaue their daughters to their ſonnes, and ſerued their gods.[7]And the children of Iſrael did euill in the ſight of the Lord, and forgate the Lord their God, and ſerued Baalim, and the groues.[8]Therefore the anger of the Lord was hote againſt Iſrael, and he ſold them into the hand of Chuſhan-Riſhathaim king of Meſopotamia: and the children of Iſrael ſerued Chuſhan-Riſhathaim eight yeeres.[9]And when the children of Iſrael cryed vnto the Lord, the Lord raiſed vp a deliuerer to the children of Iſrael, who deliuered them, euen Othniel the ſonne of Kenaz, Calebs yonger brother.[10]And the Spirit of the Lord came vpon him, and he iudged Iſrael, and went out to warre, & the Lord deliuered Chuſhan-Riſhathaim king of Meſopotamia into his hand; and his hand preuailed againſt Chuſhan-Riſhathaim.[11]And the land had reſt forty yeres: and Othniel the ſonne of Kenaz died.[12]And the children of Iſrael did euill againe in the ſight of the Lord: and the Lord ſtrengthened Eglon the king of Moab againſt Iſrael, becauſe they had done euill in the ſight of the Lord.[13]And hee gathered vnto him the children of Ammon, and Amalek, and went and ſmote Iſrael, and poſſeſſed the city of Palme-trees.[14]So the children of Iſrael ſerued Eglon the King of Moab eighteene yeeres.[15]But when the children of Iſrael cried vnto the Lord, the Lord raiſed them vp a deliuerer, Ehud the ſonne of Gera, a Beniamite, a man left handed: and by him the children of Iſrael ſent a Preſent vnto Eglon the king of Moab.[16]But Ehud made him a dagger (which had two edgeſ) of a cubite length, and he did gird it vnder his raiment, vpon his right thigh,[17]And he brought the preſent vnto Eglon king of Moab: and Eglon was a very fat man.[18]And when he had made an end to offer the Preſent, he ſent away the people that bare the Preſent.[19]But hee himſelfe turned againe from the quarries that were by Gilgal, and ſaid, I haue a ſecret errand vnto thee, O king: who ſaid, Keepe ſilence. And all that ſtood by him, went out from him.[20]And Ehud came vnto him, and he was ſitting in a Summer parlour, which hee had for himſelfe alone: And Ehud ſaid, I haue a meſsage from God vnto thee. And he aroſe out of his ſeat.[21]And Ehud put forth his left hand, and tooke the dagger from his right thigh, and thruſt it into his belly.[22]And the haft alſo went in after the blade: and the fatte cloſed vpon the blade, ſo that hee could not drawe the dagger out of his belly, and the dirt came out.[23]Then Ehud went forth through the porche, and ſhut the doores of the parlour vpon him, and locked them.[24]When he was gone out, his ſeruants came, and when they ſaw, that behold, the doores of the parlour were locked, they ſaid, Surely he couereth his feet in his Summer chamber.[25]And they taried till they were aſhamed: and behold, he opened not the doores of the parlour, therefore they tooke a key, and opened them: and behold, their lord was fallen downe dead on the earth.[26]And Ehud eſcaped while they taried: and paſſed beyond the quarries, and eſcaped vnto Seirath.[27]And it came to paſſe when hee was come, that hee blew a trumpet in the mountaine of Ephraim, and the children of Iſrael went downe with him from the mount, & he before them.[28]And hee ſaid vnto them, Follow after me: for the Lord hath deliuered your enemies the Moabites into your hand. And they went downe after him, and tooke the foords of Iordan toward Moab, and ſuffered not a man to paſſe ouer.[29]And they ſlewe of Moab at that time about ten thouſand men, all luſty, and all men of valour, and there eſcaped not a man.30So Moab was ſubdued that day vnder the hand of Iſrael: and the land had reſt foureſcore yeeres.31And after him was Shamgar the ſonne of Anath, which ſlew of the Philiſtines ſixe hundred men with an oxe goad, and he alſo deliuered Iſrael.

CHAPTER 41And the children of Iſrael againe did euil in the ſight of the Lord, when Ehud was dead.2And the Lord ſold them into the hande of Iabin king of Canaan: that reigned in Hazor, the captaine of whoſe hoſt was Siſera, which dwelt in Haroſheth of the Gentiles.3And the children of Iſrael cried vnto the Lord: for he had nine hundred charets of yron: and twentie yeres hee mightily oppreſſed the children of Iſrael.4And Deborah a prophetefſe, the wife of Lapidoth, ſhee iudged Iſrael at that time.5And ſhee dwelt vnder the palme tree of Deborah, betweene Ramah and Bethel in mount Ephraim: and the children of Iſrael came vp to her for iudgement.6And ſhee ſent and called Barak the ſonne of Abinoam, out of Kedeſh-Naphtali, and ſaid vnto him, Hath not the Lord God of Iſrael commaunded, ſaying, Goe, and drawe toward mount Tabor, and take with thee ten thouſand men of the children of Naphtali, and of the children of Zebulun?7And I wil draw vnto thee to the riuer Kiſhon, Siſera the captaine of Iabins army, with his charets, and his multitude, and I will deliuer him into thine hand.8And Barak ſaid vnto her, If thou wilt goe with me, then I wil goe: but if thou wilt not goe with mee, then I will not goe.9And ſhe ſaid, I wil ſurely go with thee, notwithſtanding the iourney that thou takeſt, ſhal not be for thine honor: for the Lord ſhall ſell Siſera into the hand of a woman. And Deborah aroſe, & went with Barak to Kedeſh.10And Barak called Zebulun, and Naphtali to Kedeſh, and he went vp with ten thouſand men at his feete: and Deborah went vp with him.11Now Heber the Kenite, which was of the children of Hobab the father in law of Moſes, had ſeuered himſelfe from the Kenites, and pitched his tent vnto the plaine of Zaanaim, which is by Kedeſh.12And they ſhewed Siſera, that Barak the ſonne of Abinoam was gone vp to mount Tabor.13And Siſera gathered together all his charets, euen nine hundred charets of iron, and al the people that were with him, from Haroſheth of the Gentiles, vnto the riuer of Kiſhon.14And Deborah ſaid vnto Barak, Up, for this is the day in which the Lord hath deliuered Siſera into thine hand: Is not the Lord gone out before thee? ſo Barak went downe from mount Tabor, and ten thouſand men after him.15And the Lord diſcomfited Siſera, and all his charets, and all his hoſte with the edge of the ſword, before Barak: ſo that Siſera lighted downe off his charet, and fled away on his feet.16But Barak purſued after the charets, and after the hoſte vnto Haroſheth of the Gentiles, and all the hoſt of Siſera fell vpon the edge of the ſword; and there was not a man left.17Howbeit Siſera fled away on his feet, to the tent of Iael the wife of Heber the Kenite: for there was peace betweene Iabin the king of Hazor, and the houſe of Heber the Kenite.18And Iael went out to meete Siſera, and ſaid vnto him, Turne in, my lord, turne in to me, feare not. And when hee had turned in vnto her, into the tent, ſhee couered him with a mantle.19And he ſaid vnto her, Giue me, I pray thee, a litle water to drinke, for I am thirſtie. And ſhe opened a bottle of milke, and gaue him drinke, and couered him.20Againe he ſaid vnto her, ſtand in the doore of the tent, and it ſhall bee when any man doeth come and enquire of thee and ſay, Is there any man here? that thou ſhalt ſay, No.21Then Iael Hebers wife, tooke a naile of the tent, and tooke an hammer in her hand, and went ſoftly vnto him, and ſmote the naile into his temples, and faſtened it into the ground: (for he was faſt aſleepe, and weary;) ſo he died.22And behold, as Barak purſued Siſera, Iael came out to meet him, and ſaid vnto him, Come, and I will ſhew thee the man whom thou ſeekeſt. And when he came into her tent, behold, Siſera lay dead, and the naile was in his temples.23So God ſubdued on that day, Iabin the king of Canaan, before the children of Iſrael.24And the hand of the children of Iſrael proſpered, & preuailed againſt Iabin the king of Canaan, vntill they had deſtroyed Iabin king of Canaan.

CHAPTER 51Then ſang Deborah, and Barak the ſon of Abinoam, on that day, ſaying,2Praiſe ye the Lord, for the auenging of Iſrael, when the people willingly offered themſelues.3Heare, O ye kings, giue eare, O ye Princes: I, euen I will ſing vnto the Lord, I wil ſing praiſe to the Lord God of Iſrael.4Lord, when thou wenteſt out of Seir, when thou marchedſt out of the field of Edom, the earth trembled, and the heauens dropped, the clouds alſo dropped water.5The mountaines melted from before the Lord, euen that Sinai, from before the Lord God of Iſrael.6In the dayes of Shamgar the ſon of Anath, in the dayes of Iael, the high wayes were vnoccupied, and the traueilers walked thorow by-wayes.7The inhabitants of the villages ceaſed, they ceaſed in Iſrael, vntill that I Deborah aroſe, that I aroſe a mother in Iſrael.8They choſe new gods; then was warre in the gates: was there a ſhield or ſpeare ſeene among fourtie thouſand in Iſrael?9My heart is toward the gouernours of Iſrael, that offered themſelues willingly among the people: Bleſſe ye the Lord.10Speake yee that ride on white aſſes, yee that ſit in Iudgement, and walke by the way.11They that are deliuered from the noiſe of Archers in the places of drawing water; there ſhall they rehearſe the righteous acts of the Lord, euen the righteous acts towards the inhabitants of his villages in Iſrael: then ſhall the people of the Lord goe downe to the gates.12Awake, awake Deborah: awake, awake, vtter a ſong: Ariſe Barak, and leade thy captiuitie captiue, thou ſonne of Abinoam.13Then hee made him that remaineth, haue dominion ouer the Nobles among the people: the Lord made me haue dominion ouer the mightie.14Out of Ephraim was there a roote of them againſt Amalek, after thee Beniamin, among thy people: Out of Machir came downe gouernours, and out of Zebulun they that handle the pen of the writer.15And the princes of Iſſachar were with Deborah: euen Iſſachar, and alſo Barak, he was ſent on foot into the valley: for the diuiſions of Reuben, there were great thoughts of heart.16Why abodeſt thou among the ſheepefolds, to heare the bleatings of the flocks? for the diuiſions of Reuben there were great ſearchings of heart.17Gilead abode beyond Iordan: and why did Dan remaine in ſhips? Aſher continued on the ſea ſhore, and abode in his breaches.18Zebulun and Naphtali were a people that ieoparded their liues vnto the death, in the high places of the field.19The kings came and fought, then fought the kings of Canaan in Taanach by the waters of Megiddo, they tooke no gaine of money.20They fought from heauen, the ſtarres in their courſes fought againſt Siſera.21The riuer of Kiſhon ſwept them away, that ancient riuer, the riuer Kiſhon: O my ſoule, thou haſt troden downe ſtrength.22Then were the horſe hoofes broken, by the meanes of the pranſings, the pranſings of their mightie ones.23Curſe ye Meroz (ſaid the Angel of the Lord) curſe ye bitterly the inhabitants thereof: becauſe they came not to the helpe of the Lord, to the helpe of the Lord againſt the mighty.24Bleſſed aboue women ſhal Iael the wife of Heber the Kenite be, bleſſed ſhall ſhe be aboue women in the tent.25He aſked water, and ſhe gaue him milke, ſhee brought foorth butter in a lordly diſh.26Shee put her hand to the naile, and her right hand to the workemens hammer: and with the hammer ſhee ſmote Siſera, ſhee ſmote off his head, when ſhe had pearſed & ſtriken through his temples.27At her feete he bowed, he fell, he lay downe: at her feet he bowed, he fell; where he bowed, there he fel down dead.28The mother of Siſera looked out at a window, and cried through the lattefſe, Why is his charet ſo long in comming? Why tarie the wheeles of his charets?29Her wiſe ladies anſwered her, yea ſhe returned anſwere to her ſelfe,30Haue they not ſped? haue they not diuided the pray to euery man a damoſell or two? To Siſera a pray of diuers colours, a pray of diuers colours, of needle worke, of diuers colours of needle worke on both ſides, meet for the necks of them that take the ſpoile?31So let all thine enemies periſh, O Lord: but let them that loue him, be as the Sunne when he goeth foorth in his might. And the land had reſt fourtie yeeres.

CHAPTER 61And the children of Iſrael did euill in the ſight of the Lord: and the Lord deliuered them into the hande of Midian ſeuen yeeres.2And the hand of Midian preuailed againſt Iſrael: and becauſe of the Midianites, the children of Iſrael made them the dennes which are in the mountaines, and caues, & ſtrong holds.3And ſo it was when Iſrael had ſowen, that the Midianites came vp, & the Amalekites, & the children of the Eaſt, euen they came vp againſt them,4And they encamped againſt them, and deſtroyed the encreaſe of the earth, till thou come vnto Gaza, and left no ſuſtenance for Iſrael, neither ſheepe, nor oxe, nor aſſe.5For they came vp with their cattell and their tents, and they came as Graſhoppers for multitude, for both they and their camels were without number: and they entred into the land to deſtroy it.6And Iſrael was greatly impoueriſhed, becauſe of the Midianites, and the children of Iſrael cryed vnto the Lord.7And it came to paſſe when the children of Iſrael cryed vnto the Lord, becauſe of the Midianites,8That the Lord ſent a Prophet vnto the children of Iſrael, which ſaid vnto them; Thus ſaith the Lord God of Iſrael, I brought you vp from Egypt,

and brought you forth out of the houſe of bondage,9And I deliuered
you out of the hand of the Egyptians, and out of the hand of al that
oppreſſed you, and draue them out from before you, and gaue you their
land:10And I ſaid vnto you, I am the Lord your God, feare not the gods
of the Amorites in whoſe land ye dwel: But ye haue not obeyed my
voice.11And there came an Angel of the Lord, and ſate vnder an Oake
which was in Ophrah, that pertained vnto Ioaſh the Abi-Ezrite: and his
ſonne Gideon threſhed wheat by the winepreſſe , to hide it from the
Midianites.12And the Angel of the Lord appeared vnto him, and ſaid
vnto him, The Lord is with thee, thou mightie man of valour.13And
Gideon ſaid vnto him, Oh my Lord, if the Lord bee with vs, why then
is all this befallen vs? and where be all his miracles which our fathers
tolde vs of, ſaying, Did not the Lord bring vs vp from Egypt? But now
the Lord hath forſaken vs, and deliuered vs into the hands of the
Midianites.14And the Lord looked vpon him, and ſaid, Goe in this thy
might, and thou ſhalt ſaue Iſrael from the hand of the Midianites: haue
not I ſent thee?15And hee ſaid vnto him, Oh my lord, wherewith ſhall I
ſaue Iſrael? behold, my family is poore in Manaſſeh, and I am the leaſt
in my fathers houſe.16And the Lord ſaid vnto him, Surely I will be with
thee, and thou ſhalt ſmite the Midianites, as one man.17And he ſaid vnto
him, If now I haue found grace in thy ſight, then ſhew me a ſigne, that
thou talkeſt with me.18Depart not hence, I pray thee, vntil I come vnto
thee, and bring forth my Preſent, and ſet it before thee. And hee ſaide,
I will tary vntill thou come againe.19And Gideon went in, and made
ready a kid, and vnleauened cakes of an Ephah of floure: the fleſh he
put in a baſket, and he put the broth in a pot, and brought it out vnto
him vnder the oake, and preſented it.20And the Angel of God ſayd vnto
him, Take the fleſh, and the vnleauened cakes, and lay them vpon this
rocke, and powre out the broth. And he did ſo.21Then the Angel of the
Lord put foorth the end of the ſtaffe that was in his hand, and touched
the fleſh, and the vnleauened cakes, and there roſe vp fire out of the
rocke, and conſumed the fleſh and the vnleauened cakes: then the Angel
of the Lord departed out of his ſight.22And when Gideon perceiued that
hee was an Angel of the Lord, Gideon ſaid, Alas, O Lord God: for
becauſe I haue ſeene an Angel of the Lord face to face.23And the Lord
ſaid vnto him, Peace be vnto thee, feare not, thou ſhalt not die.24Then
Gideon built an Altar there vnto the Lord, and called it Iehouah ſhalom:
vnto this day it is yet in Ophrah, of the Abi-Ezrites.25And it came to
paſſe the ſame night, that the Lord ſaid vnto him, Take thy fathers yong
bullocke, euen the ſecond bullocke of ſeuen yeeres old, and throw
downe the altar of Baal that thy father hath, and cut downe the groue
that is by it:26And builde an Altar vnto the Lord thy God vpon the top
of this rocke, in the ordered place, and take the ſecond bullocke, and
offer a burnt ſacrifice with the wood of the groue, which thou ſhalt cut
downe.27Then Gideon tooke ten men of his ſeruants, and did as the
Lord had ſaid vnto him: And ſo it was becauſe hee feared his fathers
houſhold, and the men of the city, that he could not doe it by day, that
hee did it by night.28And when the men of the citie aroſe earely in the
morning, behold, the altar of Baal was caſt downe, and the groue was
cut downe that was by it, and the ſecond bullocke was offered vpon the
altar that was built.29And they ſaid one to another, Who hath done this
thing? And when they enquired and aſked, they ſaid, Gideon the ſonne
of Ioaſh hath done this thing.30Then the men of the citie ſaid vnto Ioaſh,
Bring out thy ſonne, that he may die: becauſe he hath caſt downe the
altar of Baal, and becauſe hee hath cut downe the groue that was by
it.31And Ioaſh ſaid vnto all that ſtood againſt him, Will ye pleade for
Baal? will ye ſaue him? He that will plead for him, let him be put to death
whileſt it is yet morning: if he be a god, let him plead for himſelfe,
becauſe one hath caſt down his altar.32Therefore on that day hee called
him Ierubbaal, ſaying, Let Baal plead againſt him, becauſe hee hath
throwen downe his altar.33Then all the Midianites, and the Amalekites,
and the children of the Eaſt were gathered together, and went ouer, and
pitched in the valley of Iezreel.34But the Spirit of the Lord came vpon
Gideon, and hee blewe a trumpet, and Abiezer was gathered after
him.35And he ſent meſſengers throughout all Manaſſeh, who alſo was
gathered after him, and hee ſent meſſengers vnto Aſher, and vnto
Zebulun, and vnto Naphtali, and they came vp to meete them.36And
Gideon ſaid vnto God, If thou wilt ſaue Iſrael by mine hand, as thou
haſt ſaid,37Beholde, I will put a fleece of wooll in the floore: and if the
deaw be on the fleece onely, and it bee drie vpon all the earth beſide,
then ſhall I know that thou wilt ſaue Iſrael by my hande, as thou haſt
ſaid.38And it was ſo: for he roſe vp early on the morrow, and thruſt the
fleece together, and wringed the deaw out of the fleece, a bowle full of
water.39And Gideon ſaid vnto God, Let not thine anger be hote againſt
me, and I will ſpeake but this once: Let mee prooue, I pray thee, but this
once with the fleece. Let it now be drie onely vpon the fleece, and vpon
all the ground let there be deaw.40And God did ſo that night: for it was
drie vpon the fleece onely, and there was deaw on all the ground.
CHAPTER 71Then Ierubbaal (who is Gideon) and all the people that
were with him, roſe vp earely, and pitched beſide the well of Harod: ſo
that the hoſte of the Midianites were on the North ſide of them by the
hill of Moreh, in the valley.2And the Lord ſaid vnto Gideon, The people
that are with thee, are too many for me to giue the Midianites into their
handes, leſt Iſrael vaunt themſelues againſt mee, ſaying, Mine owne hand
hath ſaued me.3Now therefore go to, proclaime in the eares of the
people, ſaying, Whoſoeuer is fearefull and afraid, let him returne and
depart earely from mount Gilead: and there returned of the people
twentie and two thouſand, & there remained ten thouſand.4And the
Lord ſaid vnto Gideon, The people are yet too many: bring them downe
vnto the water, and I wil trie them for thee there: and it ſhall bee that of
whome I ſay vnto thee, This ſhall goe with thee, the ſame ſhall goe with
thee: and of whomſoeuer I ſay vnto thee, This ſhal not goe with thee,
the ſame ſhall not goe.5So he brought downe the people vnto the water:
and the Lord ſayd vnto Gideon, Euery one that lappeth of the water
with his tongue as a dog lappeth, him ſhalt thou ſet by himſelfe, likewiſe
euery one that boweth downe vpon his knees to drinke.6And the
number of them that lapped putting their hand to their mouth, were
three hundred men: but all the reſt of the people bowed downe vpon
their knees to drinke water.7And the Lord ſaid vnto Gideon, By the
three hundred men that lapped, will I ſaue you, and deliuer the
Midianites into thine hand: and let all the other people goe euery man
vnto his place.8So the people tooke victuals in their hand, and their
trumpets: and he ſent all the reſt of Iſrael, euery man vnto his tent, and
reteined thoſe three hundred men: and the hoſte of Midian was beneath
him in the valley.9And it came to paſſe the ſame night, that the Lord
ſayd vnto him, Ariſe, get thee downe vnto the hoſte, for I haue deliuered
it into thine hand.10But if thou feare to goe downe, goe thou with
Phurah thy ſeruant downe to the hoſte.11And thou ſhalt heare what they
ſay, and afterward ſhall thine handes be ſtrengthened to goe downe vnto
the hoſte. Then went hee downe, with Phurah his ſeruant, vnto the
outſide of the armed men, that were in the hoſte.12And the Midianites,
and the Amalekites, and all the children of the Eaſt, lay along in the
valley like graſhoppers for multitude, and their camels were without
number, as the ſand by the ſea ſide for multitude.13And when Gideon
was come, beholde, there was a man that tolde a dreame vnto his fellow,
and ſayd, Behold, I dreamed a dreame, and loe, a cake of Barley bread
tumbled into the hoſte of Midian, and came vnto a tent, and ſmote it
that it fell, and ouerturned it, that the tent lay along.14And his fellow
anſwered, and ſaid, This is nothing els ſaue the ſword of Gideon the
ſonne of Ioaſh, a man of Iſrael: for into his hand hath God deliuered
Midian, and all the hoſte.15And it was ſo, when Gideon heard the telling
of the dreame, and the interpretation thereof, that hee worſhipped, and
returned into the hoſt of Iſrael, and ſayd, Ariſe, for the Lord hath
deliuered into your hand the hoſt of Midian.16And he diuided the three
hundred men into three companies, and hee put a trumpet in euery mans
hand, with empty pitchers, and lampes within the pitchers,17And hee
ſaid vnto them, Looke on mee, and doe likewiſe; and beholde, when I
come to the outſide of the campe, it ſhall be that as I doe, ſo ſhall ye
doe.18When I blow with a trumpet, I and all that are with mee, then
blow ye the trumpets alſo on euery ſide of all the campe, and ſay, The
ſword of the Lord, and of Gideon.19So Gideon and the hundred men
that were with him, came vnto the outſide of the campe, in the beginning
of the middle watch, and they had but newly ſet the watch, and they
blew the trumpets, and brake the pitchers that were in their hands.20And
the three companies blew the trumpets, and brake the pitchers, and held
the lampes in their left hands, and the trumpets in their right hands to
blow withall: and they cryed, The ſword of the Lord, and of
Gideon.21And they ſtood euery man in his place, round about the
campe: and all the hoſt ranne, and cried, and fled.22And the three
hundred blew the trumpets, and the Lord ſet euery mans ſword againſt

his fellow, euen throughout all the hoſt: and the hoſt fled to Beth-
ſhittah, in Zererath, and to the border of Abel Meholah, vnto
Tabbath.23And the men of Iſrael gathered themſelues together out of
Naphtali, and out of Aſher, and out of all Manaſſeh, and purſued after
the Midianites.24And Gideon ſent meſſengers throughout all mount
Ephraim, ſaying; Come downe againſt the Midianites, and take before
them the waters vnto Beth-barah, and Iordan. Then all the men of
Ephraim gathered themſelues together, and tooke the waters vnto Beth-
barah, and Iordane.25And they tooke two Princes of the Midianites,
Oreb, and Zeeb; and they ſlew Oreb vpon the rocke Oreb, and Zeeb
they ſlew at the winepreſſe of Zeeb, and purſued Midian, and brought
the heads of Oreb and Zeeb, to Gideon on the other ſide Iordan.
CHAPTER 81And the men of Ephraim ſaid vnto him, Why haſt thou
ſerued vs thus, that thou calledſt vs not when thou wenteſt to fight with
the Midianites? And they did chide with him ſharpely.2And he ſaid vnto
them, What haue I done now in compariſon of you? Is not the gleaning
of the grapes of Ephraim better then the vintage of Abiezer?3God hath
deliuered into your hands the princes of Midian, Oreb and Zeeb: and
what was I able to doe in compariſon of you? then their anger was
abated toward him, when he had ſaid that.4And Gideon came to Iordan,
and paſſed ouer, hee, and the three hundred men that were with him,
faint, yet purſuingthem.5And he ſaid vnto the men of Succoth, Giue, I
pray you, loaues of bread vnto the people that follow me, for they bee
faint, and I am purſuingafter Zebah and Zalmunna, kings of
Midian.6And the princes of Succoth ſaid, Are the hands of Zebah and
Zalmunna now in thine hands, that wee ſhould giue bread vnto thine
armie?7And Gideon ſaid, Therfore when the Lord hath deliuered Zebah
and Zalmunna into mine hand, then I wil teare your fleſh with the
thornes of the wilderneſſe, and with briers.8And he went vp thence to
Penuel, and ſpake vnto them likewiſe: and the men of Penuel anſwered
him, as the men of Succoth had anſwered him.9And he ſpake alſo vnto
the men of Penuel, ſaying, When I come againe in peace, I will breake
downe this towre.10Now Zebah and Zalmunna were in Karkor, and
their hoſtes with them, about fifteene thouſand men, all that were left
of all the hoſts of the children of the Eaſt: for there fell an hundred and
twentie thouſand men that drew ſword.11And Gideon went vp by the
way of them that dwelt in tents, on the Eaſt of Nobah, and Iogbehah,
and ſmote the hoſt: for the hoſt was ſecure.12And when Zebah and
Zalmunna fled, he purſued after them, and took the two kings of
Midian, Zebah, and Zalmunna, & diſcomfited all the hoſt.13And Gideon
the ſonne of Ioaſh returned from battel before the Sunne was vp,14And
caught a yong man of the men of Succoth, and enquired of him: and he
deſcribed vnto him the princes of Succoth and the elders thereof, euen
threeſcore and ſeuenteene men.15And he came vnto the men of
Succoth, and ſaid, Behold Zebah and Zalmunna, with whom ye did
vpbraid me, ſaying, Are the handes of Zebah and Zalmunna now in
thine hand, that we ſhould giue bread vnto thy men that are
wearie?16And hee tooke the Elders of the citie, and thornes of the
wildernes, and briers, and with them hee taught the men of
Succoth.17And he beat downe the towre of Penuel, and ſlew the men of
the citie.18Then ſaid he vnto Zebah and Zalmunna, What maner of men
were they whom ye ſlew at Tabor? And they anſwered, As thou art, ſo
were they, ech one reſembled the children of a king.19And hee ſaid, They
were my brethren, euen the ſonnes of my mother: as the Lord liueth, if
yee had ſaued them aliue, I would not ſlay you.20And he ſaid vnto Iether
his firſt borne, Up, and ſlay them: but the youth drew not his ſword: for
he feared, becauſe he was yet a youth.21Then Zebah and Zalmunna ſaid,
Riſe thou, and fall vpon vs: for as the man is, ſo is his ſtrength. And
Gideon aroſe, and ſlewe Zebah and Zalmunna, & tooke away the
ornaments that were on their camels neckes.22Then the men of Iſrael
ſaide vnto Gideon, Rule thou ouer vs, both thou, and thy ſonne, & thy
ſonnes ſonne alſo: for thou haſt deliuered vs from the hand of
Midian.23And Gideon ſaid vnto them, I will not rule ouer you, neither
ſhall my ſonne rule ouer you: the Lord ſhall rule ouer you.24And Gideon
ſaid vnto them, I would deſire a requeſt of you, that you would giue me
euery man the earerings of his pray. For they had golden eare-rings,
becauſe they were Iſhmaelites.25And they anſwered, We will willingly
giue them. And they ſpread a garment, and did caſt therein, euery man
the earerings of his pray.26And the weight of the golden eare-rings that
hee requeſted, was a thouſand and ſeuen hundred ſhekels of gold, beſide
ornaments, and collars, & purple raiment that was on the kings of
Midian, and beſide the chaines that were about their camels necks.27And
Gideon made an Ephod thereof, and put it in his citie, euen in Ophrah:
and all Iſrael went thither a whoring after it; which thing became a ſnare
vnto Gideon, and to his houſe.28Thus was Midian ſubdued before the
children of Iſrael; ſo that they lifted vp their heads no more: and the
countrey was in quietneſse fourtie yeeres, in the dayes of Gideon.29And
Ierubbaal the ſonne of Ioaſh went & dwelt in his owne houſe.30And
Gideon had threeſcore and ten ſonnes of his body begotten: for he had
many wiues.31And his concubine that was in Shechem, ſhee alſo bare
him a ſonne, whoſe name he called Abimelech.32And Gideon the ſonne
of Ioaſh died, in a good olde age, and was buried in the ſepulchre of
Ioaſh his father, in Ophrah of the Abi-Ezrites.33And it came to paſſe as
ſoone as Gideon was dead, that the children of Iſrael turned againe, and
went a whoring after Baalim, and made Baal-Berith their god.34And the
children of Iſrael remembred not the Lord their God, who had deliuered
them out of the hands of all their enemies, on euery ſide:35Neither
ſhewed they kindneſſe to the houſe of Ierubbaal, namely Gideon,
according to all the goodneſſe which he had ſhewed vnto Iſrael.
CHAPTER 91And Abimelech the ſonne of Ierubbaal went to
Shechem, vnto his mothers brethren, and communed with them, and
with all the family of the houſe of his mothers father, ſaying;2Speake, I
pray you, in the eares of all the men of Shechem; Whether is better for
you, either that all the ſonnes of Ierubbaal (which are threeſcore and ten
perſonſ) reigne ouer you, or that one reigne ouer you? Remember alſo,
that I am your bone, and your fleſh.3And his mothers brethren ſpake of
him in the eares of all the men of Shechem, all theſe wordes, and their
hearts inclined to follow Abimelech: for they ſaid, He is our
brother.4And they gaue him threeſcore and ten pieces of ſiluer, out of
the houſe of Baal-Berith, wherewith Abimelech hired vaine & light
perſons, which followed him.5And hee went vnto his fathers houſe at
Ophrah, and ſlewe his brethren the ſonnes of Ierubbaal, being
threeſcore and tenne perſons, vpon one ſtone: notwithſtanding, yet
Iotham the youngeſt ſonne of Ierubbaal was left; for he hid
himſelfe.6And all the men of Shechem gathered together, and all the
houſe of Millo, and went, and made Abimelech King, by the plaine of
the pillar that was in Shechem.7And when they told it to Iotham, he
went and ſtood in the top of mount Gerizim, and lift vp his voice, and
cried, and ſaid vnto them, Hearken vnto mee, you men of Shechem, that
God may hearken vnto you.8The trees went foorth on a time to annoint
a King ouer them, and they ſaid vnto the Oliue tree, Reigne thou ouer
vs.9But the Oliue tree ſaide vnto them, Should I leaue my fatneſſe,
wherewith by mee they honour God and man, and goe to bee promoted
ouer the trees?10And the trees ſaid to the Figge tree, Come thou, and
reigne ouer vs.11But the Figge tree ſaide vnto them, Should I forſake my
ſweeteneſse, and my good fruit, and goe to be promoted ouer the
trees?12Then ſaide the trees vnto the Uine, Come thou, and reigne ouer
vs.13And the Uine ſaid vnto them, Should I leaue my wine, which
cheareth God and man, and goe to bee promoted ouer the trees?14Then
ſaid all the trees vnto the Bramble, Come thou, and reigne ouer vs.15And
the Bramble ſaid vnto the trees, If in trueth ye anoint me King ouer you,
then come, and put your truſt in my ſhadow: and if not, let fire come
out of the Bramble, and deuoure the Cedars of Lebanon.16Now
therefore, if yee haue done truely and ſincerely, in that yee haue made
Abimelech King, and if yee haue dealt well with Ierubbaal, and his
houſe, and haue done vnto him according to the deſeruing of his
hands:17(For my father fought for you, and aduentured his life farre, and
deliuered you out of the hand of Midian:18And yee are riſen vp againſt
my fathers houſe this day, and haue ſlaine his ſonnes, threeſcore aud ten
perſons, vpon one ſtone, and haue made Abimelech the ſonne of his
maidſeruant, king ouer the men of Shechem, becauſe he is your
brother.)19If yee then haue dealt truely and ſincerely with Ierubbaal, and
with his houſe this day, then reioyce yee in Abimelech, aud let him alſo
reioyce in you.20But if not, let fire come out from Abimelech, and
deuoure the men of Shechem and the houſe of Millo: and let fire come
out from the men of Shechem, and from the houſe of Millo, and
deuoure Abimeleeh.21And Iotham ran away, and fled, and went to Beer,
and dwelt there for feare of Abimeleeh his brother.22When Abimelech
had reigned three yeeres ouer Iſrael,23Then God ſent an euill ſpirit
betweene Abimelech & the men of Shechem: and the men of Shechem

dealt treacherouſly with Abimelech:24That the crueltie done to the threeſcore and ten ſonnes of Ierubbaal might come, and their blood be laid vpon Abimelech their brother which ſlew them, and vpon the men of Shechem which aided him in the killing of his brethren.25And the men of Shechem ſet lyers in wait for him in the toppe of the mountaines, and they robbed all that came along that way by them: and it was told Abimelech.26And Gaal the ſonne of Ebed came with his brethren, and went ouer to Shechem: and the men of Shechem put their confidence in him.27And they went out into the fields, and gathered their vineyards, and trode the grapes, and made merry, and went into the houſe of their god, and did eate and drinke, and curſed Abimelech.28And Gaal the ſonne of Ebed ſaid, Who is Abimelech, and who is Shechem, that we ſhould ſerue him? Is not he the ſonne of Ierubbaal? and Zebul his officer? ſerue the men of Hamor the father of Shechem: for why ſhould we ſerue him?29And would to God this people were vnder my hand; then would I remoue Abimelech. And he ſaid to Abimelech, Increaſe thine armie and come out.30And when Zebul the ruler of the citie heard the wordes of Gaal the ſonne of Ebed, his anger was kindled.31And he ſent meſſengers vnto Abimelech priuily, ſaying, Behold, Gaal the ſonne of Ebed, and his brethren, be come to Shechem, and behold, they fortifie the citie againſt thee.32Now therefore vp by night, thou and the people that is with thee, and lie in wait in the field.33And it ſhalbe, that in the morning aſsoone as the Sunne is vp, thou ſhalt riſe earely, and ſet vpon the citie: and behold, when he and the people that is with him, come out againſt thee, then mayeſt thou doe to them as thou ſhalt finde occaſion.34And Abimelech roſe vp, and all the people that were with him, by night, and they laid wait againſt Shechem in foure companies.35And Gaal the ſonne of Ebed went out, and ſtood in the entring of the gate of the citie: and Abimelech roſe vp, and the people that were with him, from lying in waite.36And when Gaal ſaw the people, he ſaid to Zebul, Behold, there come people downe frō the top of the mountaines. And Zebul ſaide vnto him, Thou ſeeſt the ſhadow of the mountaines, as if they were men.37And Gaal ſpake againe, and ſaid, See, there come people downe by the middle of the land, and another companie come along by the plaine of Meonenim.38Then ſaid Zebul vnto him, Where is now thy mouth, wherwith thou ſaidſt, Who is Abimelech, that wee ſhould ſerue him? Is not this the people that thou haſt deſpiſed? Goe out, I pray now, and fight with them.39And Gaal went out before the men of Shechem, and fought with Abimelech.40And Abimelech chaſed him, and hee fledde before him, and many were ouerthrowen and wounded, euen vnto the entring of the gate.41And Abimelech dwelt at Arumah: and Zebul thruſt out Gaal and his brethren, that they ſhould not dwell in Shechem.42And it came to paſſe on the morrow, that the people went out into the field, and they tolde Abimelech.43And he tooke the people, and diuided them into three companies, and laide waite in the field, and looked, and behold, the people were come forth out of the citie, and he roſe vp againſt them, and ſmote them.44And Abimelech, and the companie that was with him, ruſhed forward, and ſtood in the entring of the gate of the citie: and the two other companies ranne vpon all the people that were in the fields, and ſlew them.45And Abimelech fought againſt the citie all that day, and he tooke the citie, and ſlewe the people that was therein, and beat downe the citie, and ſowed it with ſalt.46And when all the men of the tower of Shechem heard that, they entred into an holde of the houſe of the god Berith.47And it was told Abimelech, that all the men of the towre of Shechem were gathered together.48And Abimelech gate him vp to mount Zalmon, hee and all the people that were with him, & Abimelech tooke an axe in his hand, and cut downe a bough from the trees, and tooke it, and laide it on his ſhoulder, and ſaid vnto the people that were with him, What ye haue ſeene me doe, make haſte, and doe as I haue done.49And all the people likewiſe cut downe euery man his bough, and followed Abimelech, and put them to the holde, and ſet the holde on fire vpon them: ſo that all the men of the towre of Shechem died alſo, about a thouſand men and women.50Then went Abimelech to Thebez, and encamped againſt Thebez, and tooke it.51But there was a ſtrong towre within the city, and thither fled all the men and women, and all they of the citie, and ſhut it to them, and gate them vp to the top of the towre.52And Abimelech came vnto the towre, and fought againſt it, and went hard vnto the doore of the towre, to burne it with fire.53And a certaine woman caſt a piece of a milſtone vpon Abimelechs head, and all to brake his ſcull.54Then hee called haſtily vnto the young man his armour-bearer, and ſaid vnto him, Draw thy ſword, and ſlay me, that men ſay not of me, A woman ſlewe him: and his young man thruſt him through, and he died.55And when the men of Iſrael ſaw that Abimelech was dead, they departed euery man vnto his place.56Thus God rendred the wickedneſſe of Abimelech which hee did vnto his father, in ſlaying his ſeuentie brethren.57And all the euill of the men of Shechem, did God render vpon their heads: and vpon them came the curſe of Iotham the ſonne of Ierubbaal.

CHAPTER 101And after Abimelech, there aroſe to defend Iſrael, Tola the ſonne of Puah, the ſonne of Dodo, a man of Iſſachar, and he dwelt in Shamir in mount Ephraim.2And he iudged Iſrael twenty and three yeeres, and died, and was buried in Shamir.3And after him aroſe Iair a Gileadite, and iudged Iſrael twentie and two yeeres.4And hee had thirtie ſonnes that rode on thirtie aſſe-colts, and they had thirtie cities, which are called Hauoth-Iair vnto this day, which are in the land of Gilead.5And Iair died, and was buried in Camon.6And the children of Iſrael did euill againe in the ſight of the Lord, and ſerued Baalim and Aſhtaroth, and the gods of Syria, and the gods of Zidon, and the gods of Moab, and the gods of the children of Ammon, and the gods of the Philiſtines, and forſooke the Lord, and ſerued not him.7And the anger of the Lord was hot agaiuſt Iſrael, and hee ſolde them into the hands of the Philiſtines, and into the hands of the children of Ammon.8And that yere they vexed and oppreſſed the children of Iſrael: eighteene yeeres, all the children of Iſrael that were on the other ſide Iordan, in the land of the Amorites, which is in Gilead.9Moreouer, the children of Ammon paſſed ouer Iordan, to fight alſo againſt Iudah, and againſt Beniamin, and againſt the houſe of Ephraim; ſo that Iſrael was ſore diſtreſſed.10And the children of Iſrael cried vnto the Lord, ſaying, Wee haue ſinned againſt thee, both becauſe wee haue forſaken our God, and alſo ſerued Baalim.11And the Lord ſaid vnto the children of Iſrael, Did not I deliuer you from the Egyptians, and from the Amorites, from the children of Ammon, and from the Philiſtines?12The Zidonians alſo and the Amalekites, and the Maonites did oppreſſe you, and ye cried to me, and I deliuered you out of their hand.13Yet ye haue forſaken me, and ſerued other gods: wherefore I will deliuer you no more.14Go, and cry vnto the gods which ye haue choſen, let them deliuer you in the time of your tribulation.15And the children of Iſrael ſaid vnto the Lord, We haue ſinned, doe thou vnto vs whatſoeuer ſeemeth good vnto thee, deliuer vs onely, wee pray thee, this day.16And they put away the ſtrange gods from among them, and ſerued the Lord: and his ſoule was grieued for the miſery of Iſrael.17Then the children of Ammon were gathered together, and encamped in Gilead: and the children of Iſrael aſſembled themſelues together, and encamped in Mizpeh.18And the people and Princes of Gilead, ſaid one to another, What man is hee that will begin to fight againſt the children of Ammon? he ſhall be Head ouer all the inhabitants of Gilead.

CHAPTER 111Now Iephthah the Gileadite was a mightie man of valour, and he was the ſonne of an harlot: and Gilead begate Iephthah.2And Gileads wife bare him ſonnes, and his wiues ſonnes grew vp, and they thruſt out Iephthah, and ſaid vnto him, Thou ſhalt not inherite in our fathers houſe, for thou art the ſon of a ſtrange woman.3Then Iephthah fled from his brethren, and dwelt in the land of Tob: and there were gathered vaine men to Iephthah, and went out with him.4And it came to paſſe, in proceſſe of time, that the children of Ammon made warre againſt Iſrael.5And it was ſo, that when the children of Ammon made war againſt Iſrael, the Elders of Gilead went to fetch Iephthah out of the land of Tob,6And they ſaid vnto Iephthah, Come and bee our Captaine, that wee may fight with the children of Ammon.7And Iephthah ſaid vnto the Elders of Gilead, Did not ye hate me, and expell me out of my fathers houſe? And why are ye come vnto mee now when ye are in diſtreſſe?8And the Elders of Gilead ſaid vnto Iephthah, Therefore we turne againe to thee now, that thou mayeſt go with vs, and fight againſt the children of Ammon, and bee our head ouer all the inhabitants of Gilead.9And Iephthah ſaid vnto the Elders of Gilead, If ye bring me home againe to fight againſt the children of Ammon, and the Lord deliuer them before me; ſhall I be your Head?10And the Elders of Gilead ſaid vnto Iephthah, The Lord be witnes betweene vs, if we doe not ſo according to thy words.11Then

Iephthah went with the Elders of Gilead, and the people made him head
and captaine ouer them: and Iephthah vttered all his words before the
Lord in Mizpeh. 12 And Iephthah ſent meſſengers vnto the king of the
children of Ammon, ſaying, What haſt thou to do with me, that thou art
come againſt mee to fight in my land? 13 And the king of the children of
Ammon anſwered vnto the meſſengers of Iephthah; Becauſe Iſrael
tooke away my land when they came vp out of Egypt, from Arnon euen
vnto Iabbok, and vnto Iordan: now therfore reſtore thoſe lands againe
peaceably. 14 And Iephthah ſent meſſengers againe vnto the king of the
children of Ammon: 15 And ſaid vnto him, Thus ſaith Iephthah; Iſrael
tooke not away the land of Moab, nor the land of the children of
Ammon: 16 But when Iſrael came vp from Egypt, and walked through
the wilderneſſe, vnto the red ſea, and came to Kadeſh; 17 Then Iſrael ſent
meſſengers vnto the king of Edom ſaying, Let me, I pray thee, paſſe
through thy land. But the king of Edom would not hearken thereto: And
in like maner they ſent vnto the king of Moab: but hee would not
conſent: & Iſrael abode in Kadeſh. 18 Then they went along through the
wildernes, and compaſſed the land of Edom, and the land of Moab, and
came by the Eaſtſide of the land of Moab, and pitched on the other ſide
of Arnon, but came not within the border of Moab: for Arnon was the
border of Moab. 19 And Iſrael ſent meſſengers vnto Sihon king of the
Amorites, the king of Heſhbon, and Iſrael ſaid vnto him, Let vs paſſe,
we pray thee, thorow thy land, vnto my place. 20 But Sihon truſted not
Iſrael, to paſſe through his coaſt: but Sihon gathered all his people
together, and pitched in Iahaz, and fought againſt Iſrael. 21 And the Lord
God of Iſrael deliuered Sihon and all his people into the hand of Iſrael,
and they ſmote them: ſo Iſrael poſſeſſed all the land of the Amorites,
the inhabitants of that countrey. 22 And they poſſeſſed all the coaſts of
the Amorites, from Arnon euen vnto Iabbok, and from the wilderneſſe
euen vnto Iordan. 23 So nowe the Lord God of Iſrael hath diſpoſſeſſed
the Amorites from before his people Iſrael, and ſhouldeſt thou poſſeſſe
it? 24 Wilt not thou poſſeſſe that which Chemoſh thy god giueth thee to
poſſeſſe? ſo whomſoeuer the Lord our God ſhal driue out from before
vs, them will we poſſeſſe. 25 And now, art thou any thing better then
Balak the ſonne of Zippor king of Moab? Did hee euer ſtriue againſt
Iſrael, or did hee euer fight againſt them, 26 While Iſrael dwelt in
Heſhbon, and her townes, and in Aroer, and her townes, and in all the
cities that bee along by the coaſts of Arnon, three hundred yeeres? Why
therefore did yee not recouer them within that time? 27 Wherefore, I haue
not ſinned againſt thee, but thou doeſt me wrong to warre againſt mee:
the Lord the Iudge, bee Iudge this day betweene the children of Iſrael,
and the children of Ammon. 28 Howbeit, the king of the children of
Ammon hearkened not vnto the words of Iephthah which hee ſent
him. 29 Then the Spirit of the Lord came vpon Iephthah, and he paſſed
ouer Gilead and Manaſſeh, and paſſed ouer Mizpeh of Gilead, and from
Mizpeh of Gilead hee paſſed ouer vnto the children of Ammon. 30 And
Iephthah vowed a vowe vnto the Lord, and ſaid, If thou ſhalt without
faile deliuer the children of Ammon into mine hands, 31 Then it ſhall be,
that whatſoeuer commeth forth of the doores of my houſe to meete me,
when I returne in peace from the children of Ammon, ſhall ſurely be the
Lords, and I will offer it vp for a burnt offering. 32 So Iephthah paſſed
ouer vnto the children of Ammon to fight againſt them, and the Lord
deliuered them into his hands. 33 And he ſmote them from Aroer, euen
till thou come to Minnith, euen twentie cities, and vnto the plaine of the
vineyards, with a very great ſlaughter: thus the children of Ammon were
ſubdued before the children of Iſrael. 34 And Iephthah came to Mizpeh
vnto his houſe, and beholde, his daughter came out to meete him with
timbrels and with dances, and ſhe was his onely childe: beſide her he
had neither ſonne nor daughter. 35 And it came to paſſe when he ſaw her,
that he rent his clothes, and ſaid, Alas, my daughter, thou haſt brought
me very low, and thou art one of them that trouble me: for I haue
opened my mouth vnto the Lord, and I cannot goe backe. 36 And ſhe ſaid
vnto him, My father, if thou haſt opened thy mouth vnto the Lord, doe
to me according to that which hath proceeded out of thy mouth;
foraſmuch as the Lord hath taken vengeance for thee of thine enemies,
euen of the children of Ammon. 37 And ſhe ſaid vnto her father, Let this
thing be done for me: Let me alone two moneths, that I may goe vp and
downe vpon the mountaines, and bewaile my virginitie, I, and my
fellowes. 38 And he ſaid, Goe. And he ſent her away for two moneths,
and ſhee went with her companions, and bewailed her virginitie vpon
the mountaines. 39 And it came to paſſe at the ende of two moneths that
ſhee returned vnto her father, who did with her according to his vow
which he had vowed: and ſhe knew no man: & it was a cuſtome in
Iſrael, 40 That the daughters of Iſrael went yeerely to lament the daughter
of Iephthah the Gileadite foure dayes in a yeere.

CHAPTER 12 1 And the men of Ephraim gathered themſelues together,
and went Northward, & ſaid vnto Iephthah, Wherefore paſſedſt thou
ouer to fight againſt the children of Ammon, and didſt not call vs to goe
with thee? Wee will burne thine houſe vpon thee with fire. 2 And
Iephthah ſaide vnto them, I and my people were at great ſtrife with the
children of Ammon: and when I called you, ye deliuered me not out of
their hands. 3 And when I ſawe that ye deliuered me not, I put my life in
my handes, and paſſed ouer againſt the children of Ammon, and the
Lord deliuered them into my hand: Wherfore then are ye come vp vnto
me this day, to fight againſt me? 4 Then Iephthah gathered together all
the men of Gilead, and fought with Ephraim: and the men of Gilead
ſmote Ephraim, becauſe they ſaid, Yee Gileadites are fugitiues of
Ephraim, among the Ephraimites and among the Manaſsites. 5 And the
Gileadites tooke the paſsages of Iordan before the Ephraimites: and it
was ſo that when thoſe Ephraimites which were eſcaped ſaide, Let me
go ouer, that the men of Gilead ſaid vnto him, Art thou an Ephraimite?
If he ſaid, Nay: 6 Then ſaid they vnto him, ſay now, Shibboleth: and he
ſaid, Sibboleth: for hee could not frame to pronounce it right. Then they
tooke him, and ſlewe him at the paſsages of Iordan: and there fell at that
time of the Ephraimites, fourtie & two thouſand. 7 And Iephthah iudged
Iſrael ſixe yeeres: then died Iephthah the Gileadite, and was buried in
one of the cities of Gilead. 8 And after him Ibzan of Bethlehem iudged
Iſrael. 9 And hee had thirtie ſonnes, and thirtie daughters, whome hee
ſent abroad, and tooke in thirtie daughters from abroad for his ſonnes.
And hee iudged Iſrael ſeuen yeeres. 10 Then died Ibzan, and was buried
at Bethlehem. 11 And after him, Elon, a Zebulonite iudged Iſrael, and he
iudged Iſrael ten yeeres. 12 And Elon the Zebulonite died, and was buried
in Aiialon in the countrey of Zebulun. 13 And after him, Abdon, the ſonne
of Hillel a Pirathonite iudged Iſrael. 14 And he had fourty ſonnes, and
thirtie nephewes, that rode on threeſcore and ten aſſe-colts: and he
iudged Iſrael eight yeeres, 15 And Abdon the ſonne of Hillel the
Pirathonite died, and was buried in Pirathon in the land of Ephraim, in
the mount of the Amalekites.

CHAPTER 13 1 And the children of Iſrael did euill againe in the ſight of
the Lord, and the Lord deliuered them into the hand of the Philiſtines
forty yeeres. 2 And there was a certaine man of Zorah, of the family of
the Danites, whoſe name was Manoah, and his wife was barren, and bare
not. 3 And the Angel of the Lord appeared vnto the woman, and ſaid vnto
her, Behold now, thou art barren, and beareſt not: but thou ſhalt
conceiue and beare a ſonne. 4 Now therefore beware I pray thee, and
drinke not wine, nor ſtrong drinke, and eat not any vncleane thing. 5 For
loe, thou ſhalt conceiue, and beare a ſonne, and no raſor ſhall come on
his head: for the child ſhall be a Nazarite vnto God from the wombe:
and he ſhall begin to deliuer Iſrael out of the hand of the
Philiſtines. 6 Then the woman came, and told her huſband, ſaying; A man
of God came vnto mee, and his countenance was like the countenance
of an Angel of God, very terrible: but I aſked him not whence he was,
neither told he me his name: 7 But he ſaid vnto mee, Behold, thou ſhalt
conceiue and beare a ſonne; and now, drinke no wine nor ſtrong drinke,
neither eate any vncleane thing: for the childe ſhal be a Nazarite to God,
from the wombe, to the day of his death. 8 Then Manoah entreated the
Lord, and ſaid, O my Lord, let the man of God which thou didſt ſend,
come againe vnto vs, & teach vs what we ſhall do vnto the childe that
ſhall be borne. 9 And God hearkened to the voyce of Manoah; and the
Angel of God came againe vnto the woman as ſhee ſate in the field: But
Manoah her huſband was not with her. 10 And the woman made haſte,
and ranne, and ſhewed her huſband, and ſaid vnto him; Behold, the man
hath appeared vnto me, that came vnto me the other day. 11 And Manoah
aroſe, and went after his wife, and came to the man, and ſaid vnto him,
Art thou the man that ſpakeſt vnto the woman? And he ſaid, I am. 12 And
Manoah ſaid, Now let thy words come to paſſe: How ſhall wee order
the childe, and how ſhall we doe vnto him? 13 And the Angel of the Lord
ſaid vnto Manoah, Of all that I ſaid vnto the woman, let her
beware. 14 She may not eate of any thing that commeth of the Uine,
neither let her drinke wine or ſtrong drinke, nor eat any vncleane thing:

all that I commanded her, let her obſerue. 15 And Manoah ſaide vnto the Angel of the Lord, I pray thee let vs deteine thee, vntill wee ſhall haue made ready a kid for thee. 16 And the Angel of the Lord ſaid vnto Manoah, Though thou deteine mee, I will not eat of thy bread: and if thou wilt offer a burnt offering, thou muſt offer it vnto the Lord: for Manoah knew not that he was an Angel of the Lord. 17 And Manoah ſaid vnto the Angel of the Lord, What is thy name, that when thy ſayings come to paſſe, we may doe thee honour? 18 And the Angel of the Lord ſaid vnto him, Why aſkeſt thou thus after my name, ſeeing it is ſecret? 19 So Manoah tooke a kid, with a meat offering, and offered it vpon a rocke vnto the Lord: and the Angel did wonderouſly, and Manoah and his wife looked on. 20 For it came to paſſe, when the flame went vp toward heauen from off the altar, that the Angel of the Lord aſcended in the flame of the altar: and Manoah and his wife looked on it, and fell on their faces to the ground. 21 (But the Angel of the Lord did no more appeare to Manoah and to his wife:) then Manoah knewe that he was an Angel of the Lord. 22 And Manoah ſaid vnto his wife, Wee ſhall ſurely die, becauſe wee haue ſeene God. 23 But his wife ſaid vnto him, If the Lord were pleaſed to kill vs, he would not haue receiued a burnt offering and a meat offering at our hands, neither would hee haue ſhewed vs all theſe things, nor would as at this time haue told vs ſuch things as theſe. 24 And the woman bare a ſonne, and called his name Samſon: and the child grew, & the Lord bleſſed him. 25 And the Spirit of the Lord beganne to mooue him at times in the campe of Dan, betweene Zorah and Eſhtaol.

CHAPTER 14 1 And Samſon went down to Timnath, and ſawe a woman in Timnath, of the daughters of the Philiſtines. 2 And hee came vp, and told his father and his mother, and ſaid, I haue ſeene a woman in Timnath, of the daughters of the Philiſtines: nowe therefore get her for me to wife. 3 Then his father and his mother ſaid vnto him, Is there neuer a woman among the daughters of thy brethren, or among all my people, that thou goeſt to take a wife of the vncircumciſed Philiſtines? And Samſon ſaid vnto his father, Get her for me, for ſhee pleaſeth me well. 4 But his father and his mother knew not that it was of the Lord, that hee ſought an occaſion againſt the Philiſtines: for at that time the Philiſtines had dominion ouer Iſrael. 5 Then went Samſon downe, and his father & his mother, to Timnath, and came, to the vineyards of Timnath: and behold, a young Lion roared againſt him. 6 And the Spirit of the Lord came mightily vpon him, and hee rent him as he would haue rent a kid, and he had nothing in his hand: but hee told not his father or his mother what hee had done. 7 And hee went downe and talked with the woman, and ſhe pleaſed Samſon well. 8 And after a time hee returned to take her, and he turned aſide to ſee the carkeis of the Lion: and beholde, there was a ſwarme of Bees, and honie in the carkeis of the Lion. 9 And hee tooke thereof in his handes, and went on eating, and came to his father and mother, and hee gaue them, and they did eate: but he told not them that he had taken the hony out of the carkeis of the Lion. 10 So his father went downe vnto the woman, and Samſon made there a feaſt: for ſo vſed the young men to doe. 11 And it came to paſſe when they ſaw him, that they brought thirtie companions to be with him. 12 And Samſon ſaid vnto them, I will now put foorth a riddle vnto you: if you can certeinly declare it me, within the ſeuen dayes of the feaſt, and finde it out, then I will giue you thirtie ſheetes, and thirtie change of garments: 13 But if ye cannot declare it me, then ſhall yee giue me thirtie ſheetes, and thirtie change of garments. And they ſaid vnto him, Put foorth thy riddle, that we may heare it. 14 And hee ſaid vnto them, Out of the eater came foorth meate, aud out of the ſtrong came foorth ſweetneſse. And they could not in three dayes expound the riddle. 15 And it came to paſſe on the ſeuenth day, that they ſaid vnto Samſons wife, Entice thy huſband, that hee may declare vnto vs the riddle, leſt we burne thee and thy fathers houſe with fire: Haue yee called vs, to take that wee haue? is it not ſo? 16 And Samſons wife wept before him, and ſaid, Thou doeſt but hate me, and loueſt me not: thou haſt put foorth a riddle vnto the children of my people, and haſt not tolde it me. And hee ſaid vnto her, Behold, I haue not tolde it my father nor my mother, and ſhall I tell it thee? 17 And ſhee wept before him the ſeuen dayes, while the feaſt laſted: and it came to paſſe on the ſeuenth day, that he tolde her, becauſe ſhee lay ſore vpon him: and ſhe tolde the riddle to the children of her people. 18 And the men of the city ſaid vnto him on the ſeuenth day before the ſunne went downe, What is ſweeter then honie? and what is ſtronger then a Lion? And he ſaid vnto them, If ye had not plowed with my heifer, yee had not found out my riddle. 19 And the Spirit of the Lord came vpon him, and hee went downe to Aſhkelon, and ſlewe thirtie men of them, and tooke their ſpoile, and gaue change of garments vnto them which expounded the riddle, and his anger was kindled; and hee went vp to his fathers houſe. 20 But Samſons wife was giuen to his companion, whom hee had vſed as his friend.

CHAPTER 15 1 But it came to paſſe within a while after, in the time of wheat harueſt, that Samſon viſited his wife with a kid, and he ſaid, I will goe in to my wife into the chamber. But her father would not ſuffer him to goe in. 2 And her father ſaide, I verily thought that thou haddeſt vtterly hated her, therfore I gaue her to thy companion: is not her younger ſiſter fairer then ſhe? take her, I pray thee, in ſtead of her. 3 And Samſon ſaid concerning them, Now ſhal I be more blameleſſe then the Philiſtines, though I do them a diſpleaſure. 4 And Samſon went and caught three hundred foxes, and tooke firebrands, and turned taile to taile, and put a firebrand in the midſt betweene two tailes. 5 And when hee had ſet the brands on fire, he let them goe into the ſtanding corne of the Philiſtines, and burnt vp both the ſhockes, and alſo the ſtanding corne, with the vineyards and oliues. 6 Then the Philiſtines ſaide, Who hath done this? and they anſwered, Samſon the ſonne in law of the Timnite, becauſe hee had taken his wife, and giuen her to his companion. And the Philiſtines came vp, and burnt her and her father with fire. 7 And Samſon ſaid vnto them, Though ye haue done this, yet will I be auenged of you, and after that, I wil ceaſe. 8 And he ſmote them hip and thigh, with a great ſlaughter; and hee went down and dwelt in the top of the rocke Etam. 9 Then the Philiſtines went vp, and pitched in Iudah, and ſpread themſelues in Lehi. 10 And the men of Iudah ſaid, Why are ye come vp againſt vs? and they anſwered, To bind Samſon are we come vp, to doe to him, as he hath done to vs. 11 Then three thouſand men of Iudah went to the top of the rocke Etam, and ſayd to Samſon; Knoweſt thou not that the Philiſtines are rulers ouer vs? What is this that thou haſt done vnto vs? And he ſaid vnto them, As they did vnto me, ſo haue I done vnto them. 12 And they ſaid vnto him, Wee are come downe to binde thee, that we may deliuer thee into the hand of the Philiſtines. And Samſon ſaid vnto them, Sweare vnto me, that yee will not fall vpon me your ſelues. 13 And they ſpake vnto him, ſaying; No: but wee will binde thee faſt, and deliuer thee into their hand: but ſurely we will not kill thee. And they bound him with two new cordes, and brought him vp from the rocke. 14 And when he came vnto Lehi, the Philiſtines ſhouted againſt him: and the Spirit of the Lord came mightily vpon him, and the cordes that were vpon his armes became as flaxe that was burnt with fire, & his bands looſed from off his hands. 15 And he found a new iawbone of an aſſe, and put foorth his hand, and tooke it, and ſlewe a thouſand men therewith. 16 And Samſon ſaid, With the iawbone of an aſſe, heapes vpon heapes, with the iaw of an aſſe haue I ſlaine a thouſand men. 17 And it came to paſſe when he had made an end of ſpeaking, that hee caſt away the iaw bone out of his hand, and called that place Ramath-Lehi. 18 And hee was ſore athirſt, and called on the Lord, and ſaid, Thou haſt giuen this great deliuerance into the hand of thy ſeruant: and now ſhall I die for thirſt, and fall into the hand of the vncircumciſed? 19 But God claue an hollow place that was in the iawe, and there came water thereout, & when he had drunke, his ſpirit came againe, and he reuiued: wherefore hee called the name thereof En-hakkore, which is in Lehi, vnto this day: 20 And he iudged Iſrael in the dayes of the Philiſtines twentie yeeres.

CHAPTER 16 1 Then went Samſon to Gaza, and ſaw there an harlot, and went in vnto her. 2 And it was told the Gazites, ſaying, Samſon is come hither. And they compaſſed him in, and layd wait for him all night in the gate of the citie, and were quiet all the night, ſaying, In the morning when it is day, we ſhall kill him. 3 And Samſon lay till midnight, and aroſe at midnight, and tooke the doores of the gate of the city, and the two poſts, and went away with them, barre and all, and put them vpon his ſhoulders , and caried them vp to the toppe of an hill that is before Hebron. 4 And it came to paſſe afterward, that he loued a woman in the valley of Sorek, whoſe name was Delilah. 5 And the lords of the Philiſtines came vp vnto her, and ſaid vnto her, Entice him, and ſee wherein his great ſtrength lieth, and by what meanes we may preuaile againſt him, that we may bind him, to afflict him: and we will giue thee euery one of vs, eleuen hundreth pieces of ſiluer. 6 And Delilah ſaid to Samſon, Tel me, I pray thee, wherein thy great ſtrength lyeth, and wherewith thou mighteſt be bound, to afflict thee.7And Samſon ſaid vnto her, If they binde mee with ſeuen greene withs, that were neuer dried, then ſhall I be weake, and be as another man.8Then the lords of the Philiſtines brought vp to her ſeuen greene withs, which had not bene dried, & ſhe bound him with them.9Now there were men lying in wait, abiding with her in the chamber: and ſhe ſaid vnto him, The Philiſtines be vpon thee, Samſon. And he brake the withs, as a threed of tow is broken, when it toucheth the fire: ſo his ſtrength was not knowen.10And Delilah ſaid vnto Samſon, Behold, thou haſt mocked me, and told mee lies: now tell mee, I pray thee, wherewith thou mighteſt be bound.11And he ſaid vnto her, If they bind me faſt with newe ropes that neuer were occupied, then ſhall I bee weake, and be as another man.12Delilah therfore tooke new ropes, and bound him therewith, and ſaid vnto him, The Philiſtines be vpon thee, Samſon. (And there were liers in wait abiding in the chamber.) and hee brake them from off his armes, like a threed.13And Delilah ſaid vnto Samſon, Hitherto thou haſt mocked me, and told me lies: tell me wherewith thou mighteſt be bound. And he ſaid vnto her, If thou weaueſt the ſeuen lockes of my head with the web.14And ſhe faſtened it with the pinne, and ſaid vnto him, The Philiſtines be vpon thee, Samſon. And hee awaked out of his ſleepe, and went away with the pinne of the beame, & with the web.15And ſhee ſaid vnto him, How canſt thou ſay, I loue thee, when thine heart is not with mee? Thou haſt mocked mee theſe three times, and haſt not told me wherin thy great ſtrength lieth.16And it came to paſſe, when ſhe preſſed him daily with her wordes, and vrged him ſo that his ſoule was vexed vnto death,17That he told her all his heart, and ſaid vnto her, There hath not come a raſor vpon mine head: for I haue bene a Nazarite vnto God from my mothers wombe: If I bee ſhauen, then my ſtrength will goe from me, and I ſhall become weake, and bee like any other man.18And when Delilah ſaw that he had told her all his heart, ſhe ſent and called for the Lords of the Philiſtines, ſaying, Come vp this once, for hee hath ſhewed me all his heart. Then the lords of the Philiſtines came vp vnto her, & brought money in their hand.19And ſhe made him ſleepe vpon her knees, and ſhe called for a man, and ſhe cauſed him to ſhaue off the ſeuen lockes of his head, and ſhe began to afflict him, and his ſtrength went from him.20And ſhe ſaid, The Philiſtines be vpon thee, Samſon. And hee awoke out of his ſleepe, and ſaid, I will go out as at other times before, and ſhake my ſelfe. And he wiſt not that the Lord was departed from him.21But the Philiſtines tooke him and put out his eyes, and brought him downe to Gaza, and bound him with fetters of braſſe, and he did grind in the priſon houſe.22Howbeit, the haire of his head began to grow againe, after he was ſhauen.23Then the lords of the Philiſtines gathered them together, for to offer a great ſacrifice vnto Dagon their god, and to reioyce: for they ſaid, Our god hath deliuered Samſon our enemy into our hand.24And when the people ſaw him, they praiſed their god: for they ſaid, Our god hath deliuered into our hands our enemy, and the deſtroyer of our countrey, which ſlew many of vs.25And it came to paſſe when their hearts were merry, that they ſaid, Call for Samſon, that hee may make vs ſport. And they called for Samſon out of the priſon houſe, and he made them ſport, and they ſet him betweene the pillars.26And Samſon ſaid vnto the lad that held him by the hand, Suffer mee, that I may feele the pillars whereupon the houſe ſtandeth, that I may leane vpon them.27Now the houſe was full of men and women, and all the lords of the Philiſtines were there: and there were vpon the roofe about three thouſand men and women, that behelde while Samſon made ſport.28And Samſon called vnto the Lord, and ſaid, O Lord God, remember me, I pray thee, & ſtrengthen mee, I pray thee, onely this once, O God, that I may be at once auenged of the Philiſtines, for my two eyes.29And Samſon tooke hold of the two middle pillars, vpon which the houſe ſtood, and on which it was borne vp, of the one with his right hand, and of the other with his left.30And Samſon ſaid, Let me die with the Philiſtines: & he bowed himſelfe with all his might: and the houſe fel vpon the lords, and vpon all the people that were therein: ſo the dead which he ſlew at his death, were moe, then they which he ſlew in his life.31Then his brethren, and all the houſe of his father, came downe, and tooke him, and brought him vp, and buried him betweene Zorah and Eſhtaol, in the burying place of Manoah his father: and hee iudged Iſrael twentie yeeres.

CHAPTER 171And there was a man of mount Ephraim, whoſe name was Micah.2And he ſaid vnto his mother, The eleuen hundred ſhekels of ſiluer, that were taken from thee, about which thou curſedſt, and ſpakeſt of alſo in mine eares, behold, the ſiluer is with mee, I tooke it. And his mother ſaid, Bleſſed be thou of the Lord, my ſonne.3And when hee had reſtored the eleuen hundred ſhekels of ſiluer to his mother, his mother ſaid, I had wholly dedicated the ſiluer vnto the Lord, from my hand, for my ſonne, to make a grauen image and a molten image: now therefore I will reſtore it vnto thee.4Yet hee reſtored the money vnto his mother, and his mother tooke two hundred ſhekels of ſiluer, and gaue them to the founder, who made thereof a grauen image and a molten image, and they were in the houſe of Micah.5And the man Micah had an houſe of gods, and made an Ephod, and Teraphim, and conſecrated one of his ſonnes, who became his Prieſt.6In thoſe dayes there was no king in Iſrael, but euery man did that which was right in his owne eyes.7And there was a young man out of Bethlehem Iudah, of the family of Iudah, who was a Leuite, and he ſoiourned there.8And the man departed out of the citie from Bethlehem Iudah, to ſoiourne where he could finde a place: and he came to mount Ephraim to the houſe of Micah, as he iourneyed.9And Micah ſaid vnto him, Whence commeſt thou? And he ſaid vnto him, I am a Leuite, of Bethlehem Iudah, and I goe to ſoiourne where I may finde a place.10And Micah ſaid vnto him, Dwell with me, and be vnto me a father and a Prieſt, and I will giue thee ten ſhekels of ſiluer by the yeere, and a ſuite of apparell, and thy victuals. So the Leuite went in.11And the Leuite was content to dwell with the man, and the yong man was vnto him as one of his ſonnes.12And Micah conſecrated the Leuite, and the young man became his Prieſt, and was in the houſe of Micah.13Then ſaid Micah, Now know I that the Lord will doe me good, ſeeing I haue a Leuite to my Prieſt.

CHAPTER 181In thoſe dayes there was no king in Iſrael: and in thoſe daies the tribe of the Danites ſought them an inheritance to dwel in: for vnto that day, all their inheritance had not fallen vnto them, among the tribes of Iſrael.2And the children of Dan ſent of their family, fiue men from their coaſts, men of valour, from Zorah, and from Eſhtaol, to ſpy out the land, and to ſearch it, and they ſaid vnto them, Goe, ſearch the land: Who when they came to mount Ephraim, to the houſe of Micah, they lodged there.3When they were by the houſe of Micah, they knew the voice of the yong man the Leuite: and they turned in thither, & ſaid vnto him, Who brought thee hither? And what makeſt thou in this place? and what haſt thou here?4And hee ſaid vnto them, Thus and thus dealeth Micah with me, and hath hired me, and I am his Prieſt.5And they ſayd vnto him, Aſke counſell, we pray thee, of God, that we may know, whether our way which we goe, ſhall be proſperous.6And the Prieſt ſaid vnto them, Goe in peace: before the Lord is your way wherein ye goe.7Then the fiue men departed, and came to Laiſh, and ſaw the people that were therein, how they dwelt careleſſe, after the maner of the Zidonians, quiet and ſecure, and there was no magiſtrate in the land that might put them to ſhame in any thing, and they were farre from the Zidonians, and had no buſineſse with any man.8And they came vnto their brethren to Zorah, and Eſhtaol: and their brethren ſaid vnto them, What ſay yee?9And they ſaid, Ariſe, that we may goe vp againſt them: for we haue ſeene the land, and behold, it is very good: and are ye ſtill? Bee not ſlothfull to goe, and to enter to poſſeſſe the land.10When ye goe, ye ſhall come vnto a people ſecure, and to a large land: for God hath giuen it into your handes: a place where there is no want of any thing, that is in the earth.11And there went from thence of the family of the Danites out of Zorah, and out of Eſhtaol, ſixe hundred men, appoynted with weapons of warre.12And they went vp, and pitched in Kiriath-iearim, in Iudah: Wherefore they called that place Mahaneh-Dan, vnto this day: behold, it is behinde Kiriath-iearim.13And they paſſed thence vnto mount Ephraim, and came vnto the houſe of Micah.14Then anſwered the fiue men that went to ſpie out the countrey of Laiſh, and ſaide vnto their brethren, Doe ye know that there is in theſe houſes an Ephod, and Teraphim, and a grauen image, and a molten image? Now therefore conſider what ye haue to doe.15And they turned thitherward, and came to the houſe of the yong man the Leuite, euen vnto the houſe of Micah, and ſaluted him.16And the ſix hundred men appointed with their weapons of war, which were of the children of Dan, ſtood by the entring of the gate.17And the fiue men that went to ſpie out the land, went vp and came in thither, and tooke the grauen image, and the Ephod, and the Teraphim, and the molten image: and the Prieſt ſtood in the entring of the gate, with the ſixe hundreth men that were appointed with weapons of warre. 18 And theſe went into Micahs houſe, and fetched the carued image, the Ephod, and the Teraphim, and the molten image: then ſaid the Prieſt vnto them, What doe ye? 19 And they ſaid vnto him, Hold thy peace, lay thine hand vpon thy mouth, and goe with vs, and bee to vs a father and a Prieſt: Is it better for thee to bee a Prieſt vnto the houſe of one man, or that thou be a Prieſt vnto a tribe and a family in Iſrael? 20 And the Prieſts heart was glad, and he tooke the Ephod, and the Teraphim, and the grauen image, and went in the middeſt of the people. 21 So they turned, and departed, and put the little ones, and the cattell, and the cariage before them. 22 And when they were a good way from the houſe of Micah, the men that were in the houſes neere to Micahs houſe, were gathered together, and ouertooke the children of Dan. 23 And they cried vnto the children of Dan: and they turned their faces, and ſaid vnto Micah, What aileth thee, that thou commeſt with ſuch a company? 24 And he ſaid, Yee haue taken away my gods which I made, and the Prieſt, and ye are gone away: and what haue I more? and what is this that yee ſay vnto me, What aileth thee? 25 And the children of Dan ſaid vnto him, Let not thy voyce bee heard among vs, leſt angry fellowes run vpon thee, and thou loſe thy life, with the liues of thy houſhold. 26 And the children of Dan went their way: and when Micah ſawe that they were too ſtrong for him, he turned and went backe vnto his houſe. 27 And they tooke the things which Micah had made, and the Prieſt which hee had, and came vnto Laiſh, vnto a people that were at quiet, and ſecure, and they ſmote them with the edge of the ſword, and burnt the citie with fire. 28 And there was no deliuerer, becauſe it was farre from Zidon, and they had no buſineſse with any man: and it was in the valley that lieth by Beth-rehob, and they built a citie, and dwelt therein. 29 And they called the name of the city, Dan, after the name of Dan their father, who was borne vnto Iſrael: howbeit the name of the citie was Laiſh at the firſt. 30 And the children of Dan ſet vp the grauen image: and Ionathan the ſonne of Gerſhom, the ſonne of Manaſſeh, hee and his ſonnes, were Prieſts to the tribe of Dan, vntill the day of the captiuitie of the land. 31 And they ſet them vp Micahs grauen image, which hee made, all the time that the houſe of God was in Shiloh.

CHAPTER 19 1 And it came to paſſe in thoſe dayes, when there was no King in Iſrael, that there was a certaine Leuite ſoiourning on the ſide of mount Ephraim, who tooke to him a concubine out of Bethlehem Iudah. 2 And his concubine played the whore againſt him, and went away from him vnto her fathers houſe to Bethlehem Iudah, and was there foure whole moneths. 3 And her huſband aroſe, and went after her to ſpeake friendly vnto her, and to bring her againe, hauing his ſeruant with him, and a couple of aſſes: and ſhee brought him into her fathers houſe, and when the father of the damſell ſaw him, he reioyced to meet him. 4 And his father in law, the damoſels father, reteined him, and hee abode with him three dayes: ſo they did eate and drinke, and lodged there. 5 And it came to paſſe on the fourth day, when they aroſe earely in the morning, that he roſe vp to depart: and the damoſels father ſaide vnto his ſonne in lawe, Comfort thine heart with a morſell of bread, and afterward goe your way. 6 And they ſate downe, and did eat and drinke both of them together: for the damoſels father had ſaide vnto the man, Be content, I pray thee, and tary all night, and let thine heart be merrie. 7 And when the man roſe vp to depart, his father in law vrged him: therfore he lodged there againe. 8 And hee aroſe early in the morning on the fift day to depart, and the damoſels father ſayd, Comfort thine heart, I pray thee. And they taried vntill after noone, and they did eate both of them. 9 And when the man roſe vp to depart, hee and his concubine, and his ſeruant; his father in law, the damſels father, ſaid vnto him, Behold, now the day draweth towardes euening, I pray you tarie all night: behold, the day groweth to an ende, lodge heere, that thine heart may be merrie; and to morrow get you early on your way, that thou mayeſt goe home. 10 But the man would not tary that night, but he roſe vp and departed, and came ouer againſt Iebus (which is Ieruſalem:) and there were with him two aſſes ſadled, his concubine alſo was with him. 11 And when they were by Iebus, the day was farre ſpent, and the ſeruant ſaid vnto his maſter, Come, I pray thee, and let vs turne in into this citie of the Iebuſites, and lodge in it. 12 And his maſter ſaid vnto him, We will not turne aſide hither into the citie of a ſtranger, that is not of the children of Iſrael, we will paſſe ouer to Gibeah. 13 And hee ſayde vnto his ſeruant, Come, and let vs draw neere to one of theſe places to lodge all night, in Gibeah, or in Ramah. 14 And they paſſed on and went their way, and the ſunne went downe vpon them when they were by Gibeah, which belongeth to Beniamin. 15 And they turned aſide thither, to go in and to lodge in Gibeah: and when he went in, he ſate him downe in a ſtreet of the citie: for there was no man that tooke them into his houſe to lodging. 16 And behold, there came an olde man from his worke out of the field at euen, which was alſo of mount Ephraim; and hee ſoiourned in Gibeah, but the men of the place were Beniamites. 17 And when he had lift vp his eyes, he ſaw a wayfaring man in the ſtreete of the citie: and the old man ſaid, Whither goeſt thou? and whence commeſt thou? 18 And he ſaid vnto him, We are paſsing from Bethlehem Iudah, toward the ſide of mount Ephraim, from thence am I: and I went to Bethlehem Iudah, but I am now going to the houſe of the Lord, and there is no man that receiueth me to houſe. 19 Yet there is both ſtraw and prouender for our aſſes, and there is bread and wine alſo for me and for thy handmaid, and for the young man which is with thy ſeruants: there is no want of any thing. 20 And the olde man ſaid, Peace be with thee; howſoeuer, let all thy wants lie vpon me; only lodge not in the ſtreet. 21 So he brought him into his houſe, and gaue prouender vnto the aſſes: and they waſhed their feet, and did eate and drinke. 22 Now as they were making their hearts merrie, behold, the men of the citie, certaine ſonnes of Belial, beſet the houſe round about, and beat at the doore, and ſpake to the maſter of the houſe, the olde man, ſaying; Bring foorth the man that came into thine houſe, that we may know him. 23 And the man, the maſter of the houſe, went out vnto them, and ſaid vnto them, Nay my brethren, nay, I pray you doe not ſo wickedly; ſeeing that this man is come into mine houſe, doe not this folly. 24 Behold, here is my daughter, a maiden, and his concubine, them I wil bring out now, and humble yee them, and doe with them what ſeemeth good vnto you: but vnto this man doe not ſo vile a thing. 25 But the men would not hearken to him: ſo the man tooke his concubine, and brought her foorth vnto them, and they knew her, and abuſed her all the night vntil the morning: and when the day began to ſpring, they let her goe. 26 Then came the woman in the dawning of the day, and fell downe at the doore of the mans houſe, where her lord was, till it was light. 27 And her lord roſe vp in the morning, & opened the doores of the houſe, and went out to goe his way: and behold, the woman his concubine was fallen downe at the doore of the houſe, and her hands were vpon the threſhold. 28 And he ſaid vnto her, Up, and let vs be going. But none anſwered: then the man tooke her vp vpon an aſſe, and the man roſe vp, and gate him vnto his place. 29 And when he was come into his houſe, hee tooke a knife, and layd hold on his concubine, and diuided her, together with her bones, into twelue pieces, and ſent her into all the coaſts of Iſrael. 30 And it was ſo that all that ſaw it, ſaid, There was no ſuch deed done nor ſeene, from the day that the children of Iſrael came vp out of the land of Egypt, vnto this day: conſider of it, take aduiſe, and ſpeake your mindes.

CHAPTER 20 1 Then all the children of Iſrael went out, and the Congregation was gathered together as one man, from Dan euen to Beer-ſheba, with the land of Gilead, vnto the Lord in Mizpeh. 2 And the chiefe of al the people, euen of all the tribes of Iſrael, preſented themſelues in the aſſembly of the people of God, foure hundred thouſand footmen that drew ſword. 3 (Now the children of Beniamin heard that the children of Iſrael were gone vp to Mizpeh.) Then ſaid the children of Iſrael, Tell vs, how was this wickedneſſe? 4 And the Leuite the huſband of the woman that was ſlaine, anſwered and ſaid, I came into Gibeah that belongeth to Beniamin, I and my concubine, to lodge. 5 And the men of Gibeah roſe againſt me, and beſet the houſe round about vpon me by night, and thought to haue ſlaine mee, and my concubine haue they forced that ſhe is dead. 6 And I tooke my concubine, and cut her in pieces, and ſent her throughout all the countrey of the inheritance of Iſrael: for they haue committed lewdneſse and folly in Iſrael. 7 Behold, ye are all children of Iſrael, giue here your aduiſe and counſell. 8 And all the people aroſe as one man, ſaying, We will not any of vs goe to his tent, neither will wee any of vs turne into his houſe: 9 But now, this ſhall bee the thing which we will doe to Gibeah, we will goe vp by lot againſt it: 10 And we wil take ten men of a hundred throughout all the tribes of Iſrael, and an hundred of a thouſand, and a thouſand out of ten thouſand, to fetch victuall for the people, that they may doe, when they come to Gibeah of Beniamin, according to all the folly that they haue wrought in Iſrael. 11 So all the men of Iſrael were gathered againſt the citie, knit together as one man. 12 And the tribes of Iſrael ſent men thorow

all the tribe of Beniamin, ſaying, What wickedneſſe is this that is done
among you?13Now therfore deliuer vs the men, the children of Belial
which are in Gibeah, that wee may put them to death, and put away euill
from Iſrael: but the children of Beniamin would not hearken to the voice
of their brethren the children of Iſrael.14But the children of Beniamin
gathered themſelues together out of the cities, vnto Gibeah, to goe out
to battell againſt the children of Iſrael.15And the children of Beniamin
were numbred at that time out of the cities, twentie and ſixe thouſand
men that drew ſword, beſide the inhabitants of Gibeah, which were
numbred ſeuen hundred choſen men.16Among all this people there were
ſeuen hundred choſen men left handed, euery one could ſling ſtones at
an haire breadth, and not miſse.17And the men of Iſrael, beſide
Beniamin, were numbred foure hundred thouſand men that drewe
ſword; all theſe were men of warre.18And the children of Iſrael aroſe,
and went vp to the houſe of God, and aſked counſell of God, and ſaide,
Which of vs ſhall goe vp firſt to the battell againſt the children of
Beniamin? And the Lord ſaid, Iudah ſhall goe vp firſt.19And the children
of Iſrael roſe vp in the morning, and encamped againſt Gibeah.20And
the men of Iſrael went out to battell againſt Beniamin, and the men of
Iſrael put themſelues in aray to fight againſt them at Gibeah.21And the
children of Beniamin came forth out of Gibeah, and deſtroied downe
to the ground of the Iſraelites that day, twenty & two thouſand
men.22And the people the men of Iſrael incouraged themſelues, & ſet
their battel againe in aray, in the place where they put themſelues in aray
the firſt day.23(And the children of Iſrael went vp and wept before the
Lord vntill Euen, and aſked counſel of the Lord, ſaying, Shall I goe vp
againe to battell againſt the children of Beniamin my brother? And the
Lord ſaide, Goe vp againſt him.)24And the children of Iſrael came neere
againſt the children of Beniamin, the ſecond day.25And Beniamin went
foorth againſt them out of Gibeah the ſecond day, & deſtroyed down to
the ground of the children of Iſrael againe, eighteene thouſand men, all
theſe drew the ſword.26Then all the children of Iſrael, and all the people
went vp, and came vnto the houſe of God, and wept, and ſate there
before the Lord, and faſted that day vntill Euen, and offered burnt
offerings, and peace offerings before the Lord.27And the children of
Iſrael enquired of the Lord, (for the Arke of þe couenant of God was
there in thoſe daies,28And Phinehas the ſonne of Eleazar the ſonne of
Aaron ſtood before it in thoſe dayes.) ſaying; Shall I yet againe goe out
to battel againſt the children of Beniamin my brother, or ſhall I ceaſe?
And the Lord ſaid, Goe vp; for to morrow I will deliuer them into thine
hand.29And Iſrael ſet lyers in waite round about Gibeah.30And the
children of Iſrael went vp againſt the children of Beniamin on the third
day, and put themſelues in aray againſt Gibeah, as at other times.31And
the children of Beniamin went out againſt the people, and were drawen
away from the citie, and they began to ſmite of the people and kill as at
other times, in the high wayes, of which one goeth vp to the houſe of
God, and the other to Gibeah in the field, about thirtie men of
Iſrael.32And the children of Beniamin ſaid, They are ſmitten downe
before vs, as at the firſt: But the children of Iſrael ſaid, Let vs flee, and
draw them from the citie, vnto the high wayes.33And all the men of Iſrael
roſe vp out of their place, and put themſelues in aray at Baal Tamar: and
the lyers in waite of Iſrael came foorth out of their places, euen out of
the medowes of Gibeah.34And there came againſt Gibeah ten thouſand
choſen men, out of all Iſrael, and the battell was ſore: but they knew not
that euill was neere them.35And the Lord ſmote Beniamin before Iſrael,
and the children of Iſrael deſtroyed of the Beniamites that day, twentie
and fiue thouſand, and an hundred men; all theſe drew the ſword.36So
the children of Beniamin ſaw that they were ſmitten: for the men of
Iſrael gaue place to the Beniamites, becauſe they truſted vnto the lyers
in wait, which they had ſet beſide Gibeah.37And the liers in wait haſted,
and ruſhed vpon Gibeah, and the liers in wait drew themſelues along,
and ſmote all the citie with the edge of the ſword.38Nowe there was an
appointed ſigne between the men of Iſrael and the liers in wait, that they
ſhould make a great flame with ſmoke riſe vp out of the citie.39And
when the men of Iſrael retired in the battell, Beniamin began to ſmite
and kill of the men of Iſrael about thirtie perſons; for they ſaide, Surely
they are ſmitten downe before vs, as in the firſt battell.40But when the
flame began to Ariſe vp out of the citie, with a pillar of ſmoke, the
Beniamites looked behind them, and behold, the flame of the citie
aſcended vp to heauen.41And when the men of Iſrael turned againe, the
men of Beniamin were amaſed; for they ſaw that euill was come vpon
them.42Therefore they turned their backs before the men of Iſrael, vnto
þe way of the wildernes, but the battel ouertooke them: & them which
came out of the cities, they deſtroyed in the midſt of them.43Thus they
incloſed the Beniamites round about, and chaſed them, and trode them
downe with eaſe ouer againſt Gibeah toward the ſunne riſing.44And
there fell of Beniamin eighteene thouſand men; all theſe were men of
valour.45And they turned and fled toward the wilderneſſe vnto the rocke
of Rimmon: and they gleaned of them in the high wayes fiue thouſand
men: and purſued hard after them vnto Gidom, and ſlew two thouſand
men of them.46So that all which fell that day of Beniamin, were twentie
and fiue thouſand men that drew the ſword; all theſe were men of
valour.47But ſixe hundred men turned and fledde to the wilderneſſe
vnto the rocke Rimmon, and abode in the rocke Rimmon foure
moneths.48And the men of Iſrael turned againe vpon the children of
Beniamin, and ſmote them with the edge of the ſword, as well the men
of euery citie, as the beaſt, and all that came to hand: alſo they ſet on fire
all the cities that they came to.

CHAPTER 211Nowe the men of Iſrael had ſworne in Mizpeh, ſaying,
There ſhall not any of vs giue his daughter vnto Beniamin to wife.2And
the people came to the houſe of God, and abode there till euen before
God, and lift vp their voices, and wept ſore:3And ſaid, O Lord God of
Iſrael, why is this come to paſſe in Iſrael, that there ſhould bee to day
one tribe lacking in Iſrael?4And it came to paſſe on the morrow, that the
people roſe early, and built there an Altar, and offered burnt offerings,
and peace offerings.5And the children of Iſrael ſayd, Who is there
among all the tribes of Iſrael, that came not vp with the congregation
vnto the Lord ? for they had made a great oath concerning him that
came not vp to the Lord to Mizpeh, ſaying, He ſhall ſurely be put to
death.6And the children of Iſrael repented them for Beniamin their
brother, and ſaid, There is one tribe cut off from Iſrael this day:7How
ſhall wee doe for wiues for them that remaine, ſeeing wee haue ſworne
by the Lord, that wee will not giue them of our daughters to wiues?8And
they ſaid, What one is there of the tribes of Iſrael, that came not vp to
Mizpeh to the Lord ? And beholde, there came none to the campe from
Iabeſh Gilead to the aſſembly.9For the people were numbred, and
behold, there were none of the inhabitants of Iabeſh Gilead there.10And
the congregation ſent thither twelue thouſand men of the valianteſt, and
commaunded them, ſaying, Goe, and ſmite the inhabitants of Iabeſh
Gilead with the edge of the ſword, with the women and the
children.11And this is the thing that yee ſhall doe, Yee ſhall vtterly
deſtroy euery male, and euery woman that hath lien by man.12And they
found among the inhabitants of Iabeſh Gilead, foure hundred yong
virgins that had knowen no man, by lying with any male: and they
brought them vnto the campe to Shiloh, which is in the land of
Canaan.13And the whole Congregation ſent ſome to ſpeake to the
children of Beniamin that were in the rocke Rimmon, and to call
peaceably vnto them.14And Beniamin came againe at that time, and they
gaue them wiues which they had ſaued aliue of the women of Iabeſh
Gilead: and yet ſo they ſufficed them not.15And the people repented
them for Beniamin, becauſe that the Lord had made a breach in the
tribes of Iſrael.16Then the Elders of the Congregation ſaid, How ſhall
we doe for wiues for them that remaine? ſeeing the women are deſtroyed
out of Beniamin.17And they ſaid, There muſt be an inheritance for them
that bee eſcaped of Beniamin, that a tribe be not deſtroyed out of
Iſrael.18Howbeit wee may not giue them wiues of our daughters. For
the children of Iſrael haue ſworne, ſaying, Curſed be he that giueth a
wife to Beniamin.19Then they ſaid, Behold, there is a feaſt of the Lord
in Shiloh yerely, in a place which is on the Northſide of Bethel on the
Eaſt ſide of the hie way that goeth vp from Bethel to Shechem, and on
the South of Lebanon.20Therefore they commanded the children of
Beniamin, ſaying, Goe and lie in wait in the vineyards.21And ſee, and
behold, if the daughters of Shiloh come out to daunce in daunces, then
come yee out of the vineyards, and catch you euery man his wife of the
daughters of Shiloh, and goe to the land of Beniamin.22And it ſhall bee
when their fathers or their brethren come vnto vs to complaine, that we
will ſay vnto them, Bee fauourable vnto them for our ſakes: becauſe we
reſeruednot to each man his wife in the warre: for yee did not giue vnto
them at this time, that you ſhould be guiltie.23And the children of
Beniamin did ſo, and tooke them wiues according to their number, of

them that daunced, whome they caught: and they went and returned vnto their inheritance, and repaired the cities, and dwelt in them.24And the children of Iſrael departed thence at that time, euery man to his tribe, and to his family, and they went out from thence euery man to his inheritance.25In thoſe dayes there was no King in Iſrael: euery man did that which was right in his owne eyes.

RUTH

CHAPTER 11Nowe it came to paſſe in the dayes when þe Iudges ruled, that there was a famine in the land: and a certaine man of Bethlehem Iudah, went to ſoiourne in the countrey of Moab, he, and his wife, and his two ſonnes.2And the name of the man was Elimelech, and the name of his wife, Naomi, and the name of his two ſonnes, Mahlon, and Chilion, Ephrathites of Bethlehem Iudah: and they came into the countrey of Moab, and continued there.3And Elimelech Naomies huſband died, and ſhee was left, and her two ſonnes;4And they tooke them wiues of the women of Moab: the name of the one was Orpah, and the name of the other Ruth: and they dwelled there about ten yeeres.5And Mahlon and Chilion died alſo both of them, and the woman was left of her two ſonnes, and her huſband.6Then ſhee aroſe with her daughters in law, that ſhee might returne from the countrey of Moab: for ſhee had heard in the countrey of Moab, how that the Lord had viſited his people, in giuing them bread.7Wherefore ſhe went foorth out of the place where ſhe was, and her two daughters in law with her: and they went on the way to returne vnto the land of Iudah.8Aud Naomi ſaid vnto her two daughters in law, Goe, returne each to her mothers houſe: the Lord deale kindly with you, as ye haue dealt with the dead, and with me.9The Lord graunt you, that you may finde reſt each of you in the houſe of her huſband. Then ſhe kiſſed them, and they lift vp their voyce and wept.10And they ſaid vnto her, Surely wee will returne with thee, vnto thy people.11And Naomi ſaid, Turne againe, my daughters: why will you goe with mee? Are there yet any moe ſonnes in my wombe, that they may be your huſbands?12Turne againe, my daughters, go your way, for I am too old to haue an huſband: if I ſhould ſay, I haue hope, if I ſhould haue a huſband alſo to night, and ſhould alſo beare ſonnes:13Would ye tary for them till they were growen? would ye ſtay for them from hauing huſbands? nay my daughters: for it grieueth me much for your ſakes, that the hand of the Lord is gone out againſt me.14And they lift vp their voyce, and wept againe: and Orpah kiſſed her mother in law, but Ruth claue vnto her.15And ſhe ſaid, Behold, thy ſiſter in law is gone backe vnto her people, and vnto her gods: returne thou after thy ſiſter in law.16And Ruth ſaid, Intreate mee not to leaue thee, or to returne from following after thee: for whither thou goeſt, I will goe; and where thou lodgeſt, I will lodge: thy people ſhall be my people, and thy God my God:17Where thou dieſt, wil I die, and there will I bee buried: the Lord doe ſo to me, and more alſo, if ought but death part thee and me.18When ſhee ſawe that ſhee was ſtedfaſtly minded to goe with her, then ſhee left ſpeaking vnto her.19So they two went vntill they came to Bethlehem: And it came to paſſe when they were come to Bethlehem, that all the citie was mooued about them, and they ſaid, Is this Naomi?20And ſhe ſaid vnto them, Call me not Naomi; call mee Mara: for the Almightie hath dealt very bitterly with me.21I went out full, and the Lord hath bought me home againe emptie: Why then call ye me Naomi, ſeeing the Lord hath teſtified againſt me, and the Almighty hath afflicted me?22So Naomi returned, and Ruth the Moabiteſſe her daughter in law with her, which returned out of the countrey of Moab: and they came to Bethlehem, in the beginning of barley harueſt.

CHAPTER 21And Naomi had a kinſeman of her huſbands, a mighty man of wealth, of the familie of Elimelech, and his name was Boaz.2And Ruth the Moabiteſſe ſaide vnto Naomi, Let me now goe to the field, and gleane eares of corne after him, in whoſe ſight I ſhall finde grace. And ſhee ſaide vnto her, Goe, my daughter.3And ſhe went, and came, and gleaned in the field after the reapers: and her happe was to light on a part of the fielde belonging vnto Boaz, who was of the kinred of Elimelech.4And behold, Boaz came from Bethlehem, and ſaid vnto the reapers, The Lord bee with you; and they anſwered him, The Lord bleſſe thee.5Then ſaid Boaz vnto his ſeruant, that was ſet ouer the reapers, Whoſe damoſell is this?6And the ſeruaunt that was ſet ouer the reapers, anſwered and ſaid, It is the Moabitiſh damoſell that came backe with Naomi out of the countrey of Moab:7And ſhe ſaid, I pray you, let mee gleane and gather after the reapers amongſt the ſheaues: ſo ſhee came, and hath continued euen from the morning vntill now, that ſhe taried a little in the houſe.8Then ſaid Boaz vnto Ruth, Heareſt thou not, my daughter? Goe not to gleane in another field, neither goe from hence, but abide here faſt by my maidens.9Let thine eyes be on the field that they doe reape, and go thou after them: Haue I not charged the young men, that they ſhall not touch thee? and when thou art athirſt, goe vnto the veſſels, and drinke of that which the yong men haue drawen.10Then ſhe fel on her face, and bowed her ſelfe to the ground, and ſaid vnto him, Why haue I found grace in thine eyes, that thou ſhouldeſt take knowledge of me, ſeeing I am a ſtranger?11And Boaz anſwered and ſaid vnto her, It hath fully bene ſhewed me, all that thou haſt done vnto thy mother in law ſince the death of thine huſband: and how thou haſt left thy father and thy mother, and the land of thy natiuitie, and art come vnto a people, which thou kneweſt not heretofore.12The Lord recompenſe thy worke, and a full reward be giuen thee of the Lord God of Iſrael, vnder whoſe wings thou art come to truſt.13Then ſhe ſaid, Let me finde fauour in thy ſight, my lord, for that thou haſt comforted mee, and for that thou haſt ſpoken friendly vnto thine handmaid, though I be not like vnto one of thy hand-maidens.14And Boaz ſayde vnto her, At meale time come thou hither, and eate of the bread, and dip thy morſell in the vineger. And ſhee ſate beſide the reapers: and he reached her parched corne, and ſhe did eate, and was ſufficed, and left.15And when ſhee was riſen vp to gleane, Boaz commanded his young men, ſaying, Let her gleane euen among the ſheaues, & reproch her not.16And let fall alſo ſome of the handfuls of purpoſe for her, and leaue them that ſhe may gleane them, and rebuke her not.17So ſhe gleaned in the field vntill euen, and beat out that ſhe had gleaned: and it was about an Ephah of barley.18And ſhee tooke it vp, and went into the citie: and her mother in lawe ſaw what ſhee had gleaned; and ſhee brought foorth, and gaue to her that ſhe had referued, after ſhe was ſufficed.19And her mother in law ſaid vnto her, Where haſt thou gleaned to day? and where wroughteſt thou? bleſſed be hee that did take knowledge of thee. And ſhee ſhewed her mother in lawe with whom ſhee had wrought, and ſaid, The mans name with whom I wrought to day, is Boaz.20And Naomi ſaid vnto her daughter in law, Bleſſed be he of the Lord, who hath not left off his kindneſſe to the liuing and to the dead. And Naomi ſaid vnto her, The man is neere of kin vnto vs, one of our next kinſemen.21And Ruth the Moabiteſſe ſaid, He ſaid vnto me alſo, Thou ſhalt keepe faſt by my yong men, vntill they haue ended all my harueſt.22And Naomi ſaid vnto Ruth her daughter in law, It is good, my daughter, that thou goe out with his maidens, that they meete thee not in any other field.23So ſhee kept faſt by the maidens of Boaz to gleane, vnto the end of barley harueſt, and of wheat harueſt, and dwelt with her mother in law.

CHAPTER 31Then Naomi her mother in law ſaid vnto her, My daughter, ſhal I not ſeeke reſt for thee, that it may be well with thee?2And now is not Boaz of our kinred, with whoſe maidens thou waſt? Behold, he winnoweth barley to night in the threſhing floore.3Waſh thy ſelfe therefore, and annoint thee, and put thy raiment vpon thee, and get thee downe to the floore: but make not thy ſelfe knowen vnto the man, vntill hee ſhall haue done eating and drinking.4And it ſhall be when hee lieth downe, that thou ſhalt marke the place where hee ſhall lie, and thou ſhalt goe in, and vncouer his feete, and lay thee downe, and he will tell thee what thou ſhalt doe.5And ſhee ſaid vnto her, All that thou ſayeſt vnto me, I will doe.6And ſhe went downe vnto the floore, and did according to all that her mother in law bade her.7And when Boaz had eaten and drunke, and his heart was merrie, hee went to lie downe at the ende of the heape of corne: and ſhe came ſoftly, and vncouered his feet, and laid her downe.8And it came to paſſe at midnight, that the man was afraid, and turned himſelfe: and behold, a woman lay at his feete.9And hee ſaid, Who art thou? And ſhe anſwered, I am Ruth thine handmaid: ſpread therefore thy ſkirt ouer thine handmaid, for thou art a neare kinſeman.10And hee ſaid, Bleſſed be thou of the Lord, my daughter: for thou haſt ſhewed more kindneſſe in the latter ende, then at the beginning, in as much as thou followedſt not yong men, whether poore, or rich.11And now my daughter, feare not, I will doe to thee all that thou requireſt: for all the citie of my people doeth know, that thou art a vertuous woman.[12]And now it is true, that I am thy neare kinſeman: howbeit there is a kinſeman nearer then I.[13]Tary this night, and it ſhall be in the morning, that if hee will performe vnto thee the part of a kinſeman, well, let him doe the kinſemans part; but if hee will not doe the part of a kinſeman to thee, then will I doe the part of a kinſeman to thee, as the Lord liueth: lie downe vntill the morning.[14]And ſhee lay at his feete vntill the morning: and ſhe roſe vp before one could know another. And he ſaid, Let it not be knowen, that a woman came into the floore.[15]Alſo he ſaid, Bring the vaile that thou haſt vpon thee, and holde it. And when ſhe helde it, he meaſured ſixe meaſures of barley, and laide it on her: and he went into the citie.[16]And when ſhee came to her mother in law, ſhe ſaid, Who art thou, my daughter? and ſhe tolde her all that the man had done to her.[17]And ſhe ſaid, Theſe ſixe meaſures of barley gaue he me, for he ſaid to me, Go not emptie vnto thy mother in law.[18]Then ſaid ſhe, Sit ſtill, my daughter, vntill thou know how the matter will fall: for the man will not be in reſt, vntil he haue finiſhed the thing this day.

CHAPTER 4[1]Then went Boaz vp to the gate, and ſate him downe there: and beholde, the kinſeman of whome Boaz ſpake, came by, vnto whom he ſaid, Ho, ſuch a one: turne aſide, ſit downe here. And hee turned aſide, and ſate downe.[2]And hee tooke ten men of the Elders of the citie, and ſaid, Sit ye downe here. And they ſate downe.[3]And he ſaid vnto the kinſeman: Naomi that is come againe out of the countrey of Moab, ſelleth a parcell of land, which was our brother Elimelechs.[4]And I thought to aduertiſe thee, ſaying, Buy it before the inhabitants, and before the Elders of my people. If thou wilt redeeme it, redeeme it, but if thou wilt not redeeme it, then tell mee, that I may know: for there is none to redeeme it, beſides thee, and I am after thee. And he ſaid, I will redeeme it.[5]Then ſaid Boaz, What day thou buyeſt the field of the hand of Naomi, thou muſt buy it alſo of Ruth the Moabiteſse, the wife of the dead, to raiſe vp the name of the dead vpon his inheritance.[6]And the kinſeman ſaid, I cannot redeeme it for my ſelfe, leſt I marre mine owne inheritance: redeeme thou my right to thy ſelfe, for I cannot redeeme it.[7]Now this was the maner in former time in Iſrael, concerning redeeming and concerning changing, for to confirme all things: a man plucked off his ſhooe, and gaue it to his neighbour: and this was a teſtimonie in Iſrael.[8]Therfore the kinſeman ſaid vnto Boaz, Buy it for thee: ſo he drew off his ſhooe.[9]And Boaz ſaide vnto the Elders, and vnto all the people, Ye are witneſſes this day, that I haue bought all that was Elimelechs, and all that was Chilions, and Mahlons, of the hande of Naomi.[10]Moreouer, Ruth the Moabiteſse, the wife of Mahlon, haue I purchaſed to be my wife, to raiſe vp the name of the dead vpon his inheritance, that the name of the dead be not cut off from among his brethren, and from the gate of his place: ye are witneſſes this day.[11]And all the people that were in the gate, and the Elders ſaid, Wee are witneſſes: The Lord make the woman that is come into thine houſe, like Rachel and like Leah, which two did build the houſe of Iſrael: and do thou worthily in Ephratah, and bee famous in Bethlehem.[12]And let thy houſe be like the houſe of Pharez, (whom Tamar bare vnto to Iudah) of the ſeed which the Lord ſhall giue thee of this yong woman.[13]So Boaz tooke Ruth, and ſhe was his wife: and when he went in vnto her, the Lord gaue her conception, and ſhe bare a ſonne.[14]And the women ſaid vnto Naomi, Bleſſed be the Lord which hath not left thee this day without a kinſeman, that his name may bee famous in Iſrael:[15]And he ſhalbe vnto thee a reſtorer of thy life, and a nouriſher of thine old age: for thy daughter in law which loueth thee, which is better to thee then ſeuen ſonnes, hath borne him.[16]And Naomi tooke the childe, and laid it in her boſome, and became nurſe vnto it.[17]And the women her neighbours gaue it a name, ſaying, There is a ſonne borne to Naomi, and they called his name Obed: hee is the father of Ieſſe the father of Dauid.[18]Now theſe are the generations of Pharez: Pharez begate Hezron,[19]And Hezron begate Ram, and Ram begate Amminadab,[20]And Amminadab begate Nahſhon, and Nahſhon begate Salmon,[21]And Salmon begate Boaz, and Boaz begate Obed,[22]And Obed begat Ieſſe, and Ieſſe begate Dauid.

1 SAMUEL

CHAPTER 1[1]Now there was a certaine man of Ramathaim Zophim, of mount Ephraim, & his name was Elkanah, the ſonne of Ieroham, the ſonne of Elihu, the ſonne of Tohu, the ſonne of Zuph, an Ephrathite;[2]And he had two wiues, the name of the one was Hannah, and the name of the other Peninnah: and Peninnah had children, but Hannah had no children.[3]And this man went vp out of his citie yeerely, to worſhip and to ſacrifice vnto the Lord of hoſtes in Shiloh; and the two ſonnes of Eli, Hophni, and Phinehas, the Prieſts of the Lord, were there.[4]And when the time was, that Elkanah offered, he gaue to Peninnah his wife, and to all her ſonnes, and her daughters, portions.[5]But vnto Hannah he gaue a worthy portion: (for he loued Hannah, but the Lord had ſhut vp her wombe.[6]And her aduerſary alſo prouoked her ſore, for to make her fret, becauſe the Lord had ſhut vp her wombe.)[7]And as he did ſo yeere by yeere, when ſhe went vp to the houſe of the Lord, ſo ſhe prouoked her; therefore ſhe wept, and did not eat.[8]Then ſaid Elkanah her huſband to her, Hannah, why weepeſt thou? and why eateſt thou not? and why is thy heart grieued? Am not I better to thee, then ten ſonnes?[9]So Hannah roſe vp after they had eaten in Shiloh, and after they had drunke; (now Eli the Prieſt ſate vpon a ſeat by a poſte of the Temple of the Lord.)[10]And ſhee was in bitterneſse of ſoule, and prayed vnto the Lord, and wept ſore.[11]And ſhe vowed a vow, and ſaid, O Lord of hoſtes, if thou wilt indeed looke on the affliction of thine handmayd, and remember me, and not forget thine handmayd, but wilt giue vnto thine handmayd a man childe, then I will giue him vnto the Lord all the dayes of his life, and there ſhall no raſor come vpon his head.[12]And it came to paſſe as ſhe continued praying before the Lord, that Eli marked her mouth.[13]Now Hannah, ſhee ſpake in her heart; onely her lippes mooued, but her voice was not heard: therefore Eli thought ſhe had beene drunken.[14]And Eli ſaid vnto her, How long wilt thou be drunken? put away thy wine from thee.[15]And Hannah anſwered, and ſaid, No, my lord, I am a woman of a ſorrowfull ſpirit: I haue drunke neither wine nor ſtrong drinke, but haue powred out my ſoule before the Lord.[16]Count not thine handmaid for a daughter of Belial: for out of the abundance of my complaint and griefe, haue I ſpoken hitherto.[17]Then Eli anſwered, and ſaid, Goe in peace: and the God of Iſrael grant thee thy petition, that thou haſt aſked of him.[18]And ſhe ſaid, Let thine handmaid finde grace in thy ſight. So the woman went her way, and did eate, and her countenance was no more ſad.[19]And they roſe vp in the morning early, and worſhipped before the Lord, and returned, and came to their houſe to Ramah: and Elkanah knewe Hannah his wife, and the Lord remembred her.[20]Wherefore it came to paſſe when the time was come about, after Hannah had conceiued, that ſhee bare a ſonne, and called his name Samuel, ſaying; Becauſe I haue aſked him of the Lord.[21]And the man Elkanah, and all his houſe, went vp to offer vnto the Lord the yeerely ſacrifice, and his vowe.[22]But Hannah went not vp; for ſhee ſaid vnto her huſband, I will not goe vp vntill the childe be weaned, and then I will bring him, that he may appeare before the Lord, and there abide for euer.[23]And Elkanah her huſband ſaid vnto her, Do what ſeemeth thee good, tary vntill thou haue weaned him, only the Lord eſtabliſh his word: ſo the woman abode, and gaue her ſonne ſucke vntill ſhe weaned him.[24]And when ſhee had weaned him, ſhee tooke him vp with her, with three bullocks, and one Ephah of floure, and a bottle of wine, and brought him vnto the houſe of the Lord in Shiloh: and the childe was young.[25]And they ſlew a bullocke, and brought the childe to Eli.[26]And ſhe ſaid, Oh my lord, as thy ſoule liueth, my lord, I am the woman, that ſtood by thee heere, praying vnto the Lord.[27]For this childe I prayed, and the Lord hath giuen me my petition, which I aſked of him:[28]Therefore alſo I haue lent him to the Lord as long as hee liueth, he ſhall be lent to the Lord. And he worſhipped the Lord there.

CHAPTER 2[1]And Hannah prayed, and ſaid, My heart reioyceth in the Lord, mine horne is exalted in the Lord: my mouth is inlarged ouer mine enemies: becauſe I reioyce in thy ſaluation.[2]There is none holy as the Lord: for there is none beſide thee: neither is there any Rocke like our God.[3]Talke no more ſo exceeding proudly, let not arrogancie come out of your mouth: for the Lord is a God of knowledge, and by him actions are weighed.[4]The vowes of the mightie men are broken, and they that ſtumbled are girt with ſtrength.[5]They that were full, haue hired out themſelues for bread: and they that were hungry, ceaſed: ſo that the barren hath borne ſeuen, and ſhe that hath many children, is waxed feeble.6The Lord killeth and maketh aliue, he bringeth downe to the graue, and bringeth vp.7The Lord maketh poore, and maketh rich: he bringeth low, and lifteth vp.8He raiſeth vp the poore out of the duſt, and lifteth vp the begger from the dunghill, to ſet them among princes, and to make them inherit the throne of glory: for the pillars of the earth are the Lords, and hee hath ſet the world vpon them.9He will keepe the feet of his ſaints, and the wicked ſhall bee ſilent in darkeneſſe; for by ſtrength ſhall no man preuaile.10The aduerſaries of the Lord ſhalbe broken to pieces: out of heauen ſhal he thunder vpon them: the Lord ſhall iudge the ends of the earth, and he ſhal giue ſtrength vnto his king, and exalt the horne of his Anointed.11And Elkanah went to Ramah to his houſe, and the child did miniſter vnto the Lord before Eli the Prieſt.12Now the ſonnes of Eli were ſonnes of Belial, they knewe not the Lord.13And the prieſts cuſtome with the people was, that when any man offred ſacrifice, the prieſtes ſeruant came, while the fleſh was in ſeething, with a fleſhhooke of three teeth in his hand,14And he ſtrooke it into the panne, or kettle, or caldron, or pot: all that the fleſh-hooke brought vp, the prieſt tooke for himſelfe: ſo they did in Shiloh vnto all the Iſraelites that came thither.15Alſo before they burnt the fat, the prieſts ſeruant came, & ſaid to the man that ſacrificed, Giue fleſh to roſte for the prieſt, for he wil not haue ſodden fleſh of thee, but raw.16And if any man ſaid vnto him, Let them not faile to burne the fat preſently, and then take as much as thy ſoule deſireth: then hee would anſwere him, Nay, but thou ſhalt giue it mee now: and if not, I will take it by force.17Wherefore the ſinne of the yong men was very great before the Lord: for men abhorred the offering of the Lord.18But Samuel miniſtred before the Lord, being a child, girded with a linnen Ephod.19Moreouer, his mother made him a litle coate, and brought it to him from yeere to yeere, when ſhe came vp with her huſband, to offer the yeerely ſacrifice.20And Eli bleſſed Elkanah, and his wife, and ſaid, The Lord giue thee ſeed of this woman, for the loane which is lent to the Lord. And they went vnto their owne home.21And the Lord viſited Hannah, ſo that ſhee conceiued, and bare three ſonnes, and two daughters: and the child Samuel grew before the Lord.22Now Eli was very olde, and heard all that his ſonnes did vnto all Iſrael, and how they lay with the women that aſſembled at the doore of the Tabernacle of the Congregation23And he ſaid vnto them, Why doe ye ſuch things? for I heare of your euil dealings, by all this people.24Nay my ſonnes: for it is no good report that I heare; yee make the Lords people to tranſgreſſe.25If one man ſinne againſt another, the Iudge ſhall iudge him: but if a man ſinne againſt the Lord, who ſhall intreat for him? Notwithſtanding they hearkened not vnto the voice of their father, becauſe the Lord would ſlay them.26(And the child Samuel grew on, and was in fauour, both with the Lord, and alſo with men.)27And there came a man of God vnto Eli, and ſaide vnto him, Thus ſaith the Lord, Did I plainely appeare vnto the houſe of thy father, when they were in Egypt in Pharaohs houſe?28And did I chuſe him out of all the tribes of Iſrael, to be my Prieſt, to offer vpon mine altar, to burne incenſe, to weare an Ephod before me? and did I giue vnto the houſe of thy father, all the offerings made by fire of the children of Iſrael?29Wherefore kicke ye at my ſacrifice, and at mine offering, which I haue commaunded in my habitation, and honoureſt thy ſonnes aboue mee, to make your ſelues fat with the chiefeſt of all the offrings of Iſrael my people?30Wherefore the Lord God of Iſrael ſaith, I ſayd indeede that thy houſe, & the houſe of thy father ſhould walke before me for euer: but now the Lord ſaith, Be it farre from mee; for them that honour me, I will honour, and they that deſpiſe me, ſhall be lightly eſteemed.31Behold, the dayes come, that I will cut off thine arme, and the arme of thy fathers houſe, that there ſhall not be an old man in thine houſe.32And thou ſhalt ſee an enemie in my habitation, in all the wealth which God ſhall giue Iſrael, and there ſhall not bee an olde man in thine houſe for euer.33And the man of thine, whom I ſhall not cut off from mine Altar, ſhall be to conſume thine eyes, and to grieue thine heart: and all the increaſe of thine houſe ſhall die in the floure of their age.34And this ſhall bee a ſigne vnto thee, that ſhall come vpon thy two ſonnes, on Hophni and Phinehas: in one day they ſhall die both of them.35And I will raiſe me vp a faithfull Prieſt, that ſhall doe according to that which is in my heart and in my mind, and I will build him a ſure houſe, and hee ſhall walke before mine Anointed for euer.36And it ſhall come to paſſe, that euery one that is left in thine houſe, ſhal come and crouch to him for a piece of ſiluer, and a morſel of bread, and ſhall ſay, Put me (I pray thee) into one of the Prieſts offices, that I may eat a piece of bread.

CHAPTER 31And the child Samuel miniſtred vnto the Lord before Eli: and the word of the Lord was precious in thoſe daies; there was no open viſion.2And it came to paſſe at that time, when Eli was layd downe in his place, and his eyes beganne to waxe dimme, that he could not ſee;3And yer the lampe of God went out in the Temple of the Lord, where the Arke of God was, and Samuel was layd downe to ſleepe;4That the Lord called Samuel, and he anſwered, Here am I.5And he ranne vnto Eli, and ſayd, Here am I, for thou calledſt me. And he ſaid, I called not; lie downe againe. And he went and lay downe.6And the Lord called yet againe, Samuel. And Samuel aroſe, and went to Eli, and ſaid, Here am I, for thou diddeſt call me. And he anſwered, I called not, my ſonne; lie downe againe.7Now Samuel did not yet know the Lord, neither was the word of the Lord yet reuealed vnto him.8And the Lord called Samuel againe the third time. And hee aroſe, and went to Eli, and ſaid, Here am I, for thou diddeſt call me. And Eli perceiued that the Lord had called the childe.9Therefore Eli ſaid vnto Samuel, Go, lie downe, & it ſhal be, if he call thee, that thou ſhalt ſay, Speake Lord, for thy ſeruant heareth. So Samuel went, and lay downe in his place.10And the Lord came, and ſtood and called as at other times, Samuel, Samuel. Then Samuel anſwered, Speake, for thy ſeruant heareth.11And the Lord ſayd to Samuel, Behold, I will doe a thing in Iſrael, at which, both the eares of euery one that heareth it, ſhall tingle.12In that day, I will performe againſt Eli, all things which I haue ſpoken concerning his houſe: when I begin, I will alſo make an end.13For I haue tolde him, that I will iudge his houſe for euer, for the iniquitie which hee knoweth: becauſe his ſonnes made themſelues vile, and he reſtrained them not.14And therefore I haue ſworne vnto the houſe of Eli, that the iniquitie of Elies houſe ſhall not be purged with ſacrifice, nor offering for euer.15And Samuel lay vntill the morning, and opened the doores of the houſe of the Lord: and Samuel feared to ſhew Eli the viſion.16Then Eli called Samuel, and ſaid, Samuel my ſonne. And he anſwered, Here am I.17And he ſaid, What is the thing that the Lord hath ſaid vnto thee? I pray thee hide it not from mee: God doe ſo to thee, and more alſo, if thou hide any thing from me, of all the things that hee ſaid vnto thee.18And Samuel tolde him euery whit, and hid nothing from him. And he ſaid, It is the Lord: Let him doe what ſeemeth him good.19And Samuel grew, and the Lord was with him, and did let none of his words fall to the ground.20And all Iſrael from Dan euen to Beer-ſheba, knew that Samuel was eſtabliſhed to bee a Prophet of the Lord.21And the Lord appeared againe in Shiloh: for the Lord reueiled himſelfe to Samuel in Shiloh, by the word of the Lord.

CHAPTER 41And the word of Samuel came to all Iſrael. Now Iſrael went out againſt the Philiſtines to battell, and pitched beſide Eben-ezer: and the Philiſtines pitched in Aphek.2And the Philiſtines put themſelues in aray againſt Iſrael: and when they ioyned battell, Iſrael was ſmitten before the Philiſtines: and they ſlew of the armie in the field, about foure thouſand men.3And when the people were come into the campe, the Elders of Iſrael ſaid, Wherefore hath the Lord ſmitten vs to day before the Philiſtines? Let vs fetch the Arke of the Couenant of the Lord out of Shiloh vnto vs, that when it commeth among vs, it may ſaue vs out of the hand of our enemies.4So the people ſent to Shiloh, that they might bring from thence the Arke of the Couenant of the Lord of hoſtes, which dwelleth betweene the Cherubims: and the two ſonnes of Eli, Hophni, and Phinehas were there, with the Arke of the Couenant of God.5And when the Arke of the Couenant of the Lord came into the campe, all Iſrael ſhouted with a great ſhout, ſo that the earth rang againe.6And when the Philiſtines heard the noiſe of the ſhout, they ſaid, What meaneth the noiſe of this great ſhout in the campe of the Hebrewes? And they vnderſtood, that the Arke of the Lord was come into the campe.7And the Philiſtines were afraid, for they ſaide, God is come into the campe. And they ſaid, Woe vnto vs: for there hath not bene ſuch a thing heretofore.8Woe vnto vs: who ſhall deliuer vs out of the hand of theſe mightie Gods? theſe are the Gods that ſmote the Egyptians with all the plagues in the wilderneſſe.9Bee ſtrong, and quit your ſelues like men, O ye Philiſtines, that yee be not ſeruants vnto the Hebrewes, as they haue bene to you: quit your ſelues like men, and fight.10And the Philiſtines fought, and Iſrael was ſmitten, and they fled euery man into his tent: and there was a very great ſlaughter, for there fell of Iſrael thirtie thouſand footmen.11And the Arke of God was taken, and the two ſonnes of Eli, Hophni, and Phinehas were ſlaine.[12]And there ran a man of Beniamin out of the army, and came to Shiloh the ſame day with his clothes rent, and with earth vpon his head.[13]And when hee came, loe, Eli ſate vpon a ſeat by the way ſide, watching: for his heart trembled for the Arke of God. And when the man came into the citie, and told it, all the city cried out.[14]And when Eli heard the noiſe of the crying, hee ſaid; What meaneth the noiſe of this tumult? And the man came in haſtily, and told Eli.[15]Now Eli was ninetie and eight yeeres old, and his eyes were dimme, that he could not ſee.[16]And the man ſaid vnto Eli, I am he, that came out of the army, and I fled to day out of the army. And he ſaid, What is there done, my ſonne?[17]And the meſſenger anſwered, and ſaid, Iſrael is fled before the Philiſtines, and there hath bene alſo a great ſlaughter among the people, and thy two ſonnes alſo, Hophni & Phinehas, are dead, and the Arke of God is taken.[18]And it came to paſſe when hee made mention of the Arke of God, that he fell from off the ſeat backward by the ſide of the gate, and his necke brake, and hee died: for hee was an old man, and heauie, and hee had iudged Iſrael fortie yeeres.[19]And his daughter in law Phinehas wife was with childe neere to be deliuered: and when ſhee heard the tidings that the Arke of God was taken, and that her father in law, and her huſband were dead, ſhee bowed her ſelfe and traueyled; for her paines came vpon her.[20]And about the time of her death, the women that ſtood by her, ſaid vnto her: Feare not, for thou haſt borne a ſonne. But ſhe anſwered not, neither did ſhe regard it.[21]And ſhe named the childe Ichabod, ſaying, The glory is departed from Iſrael, (becauſe the Arke of God was taken, and becauſe of her father in law and her huſband.)[22]And ſhe ſaid, The glory is departed from Iſrael: for the Arke of God is taken.

CHAPTER 5[1]And the Philiſtines tooke the Arke of God, and brought it from Ebenezer vnto Aſhdod.[2]When the Philiſtines tooke the Arke of God, they brought it into the houſe of Dagon, and ſet it by Dagon.[3]And when they of Aſhdod aroſe earely on the morrow, behold, Dagon was fallen vpon his face to the earth, before the Arke of the Lord: and they tooke Dagon, and ſet him in his place againe.[4]And when they aroſe earely on the morrow morning, behold, Dagon was fallen vpon his face to the ground, before the Arke of the Lord: and the head of Dagon, and both the palmes of his hands were cut off vpon the threſhold, only the ſtumpe of Dagon was left to him.[5]Therefore neither the prieſts of Dagon, nor any that come into Dagons houſe, tread on the threſhold of Dagon in Aſhdod vnto this day.[6]But the hand of the Lord was heauy vpon them of Aſhdod, and he deſtroyed them, and ſmote them with Emerods, euen Aſhdod, and the coaſtes thereof.[7]And when the men of Aſhdod ſaw that it was ſo, they ſaid, The Arke of the God of Iſrael ſhall not abide with vs: for his hand is ſore vpon vs, and vpon Dagon our god.[8]They ſent therefore, and gathered all the lords of the Philiſtines vnto them, and ſaid, What ſhall we doe with the Arke of the God of Iſrael? And they anſwered, Let the Arke of the God of Iſrael bee caried about vnto Gath. And they caried the Arke of the God of Iſrael about thither.[9]And it was ſo, that after they had caried it about, the hand of the Lord was againſt the citie with a very great deſtruction: and hee ſmote the men of the citie both ſmall and great, and they had Emerods in their ſecret parts.[10]Therfore they ſent the Arke of God to Ekron: and it came to paſſe as the Arke of God came to Ekron, that the Ekronites cried out, ſaying, They haue brought about the Arke of the God of Iſrael to vs, to ſlay vs, and our people.[11]So they ſent and gathered together all the lords of the Philiſtines, and ſaid, Send away the Arke of the God of Iſrael, and let it goe againe to his owne place, that it ſlay vs not, and our people: for there was a deadly deſtruction throughout all the citie: The hand of God was very heauy there.[12]And the men that died not, were ſmitten with the Emerods: and the cry of the citie went vp to heauen.

CHAPTER 6[1]And the Arke of the Lord was in the countrey of the Philiſtines ſeuen moneths.[2]And the Philiſtines called for the prieſts and the diuiners, ſaying, What ſhall we doe to the Arke of the Lord ? Tell vs wherewith we ſhall ſend it to his place?[3]And they ſaid, If yee ſend away the Arke of the God of Iſrael, ſend it not empty: but in any wiſe returne him a treſpaſſe offring: then ye ſhall be healed, and it ſhall be knowen to you, why his hand is not remooued from you.[4]Then ſaid they, What ſhall be the treſpaſſe offering, which wee ſhall returne to him? They anſwered, Fiue golden Emerods, and fiue golden mice, according to the number of the lordes of the Philiſtines: for one plague was on you all, and on your lords.[5]Wherefore ye ſhall make images of your Emerodes, and images of your Mice, that marre the land, and ye ſhall giue glory vnto the God of Iſrael: peraduenture hee will lighten his hand from off you, and from off your gods, and from off your land.[6]Wherefore then doe yee harden your hearts, as the Egyptians and Pharaoh hardened their hearts? when he had wrought wonderfully among them, did they not let the people goe, and they departed?[7]Now therefore make a new cart, and take two milch-kine, on which there hath come no yoke, and tie the kine to the cart, and bring the calues home from them.[8]And take the Arke of the Lord, and lay it vpon the cart, and put the iewels of golde, which ye returne him for a treſpaſſe offering, in a coffer by the ſide thereof, and ſend it away, that it may goe.[9]And ſee, if it goeth vp by the way of his owne coaſt to Bethſhemeſh, then he hath done vs this great euill: but if not, then wee ſhall know that it is not his hand that ſmote vs; it was a chance that happened to vs.[10]And the men did ſo: and tooke two milch-kine, and tied them to the cart, and ſhut vp their calues at home.[11]And they layde the Arke of the Lord vpon the cart, and the coffer, with the mice of golde, and the images of their Emerods.[12]And the kine tooke the ſtraight way to the way of Bethſhemeſh, and went along the high way, lowing as they went, and turned not aſide to the right hand, or to the left: and the lords of the Philiſtines went after them, vnto the border of Bethſhemeſh.[13]And they of Bethſhemeſh were reaping their wheat harueſt in the valley: and they lifted vp their eyes, and ſaw the Arke, and reioyced to ſee it.[14]And the cart came into the field of Ioſhua a Bethſhemite, & ſtood there, where there was a great ſtone: and they claue the wood of the cart, and offered the kine, a burnt offering vnto the Lord.[15]And the Leuites tooke downe the Arke of the Lord, and the coffer that was with it, wherein the iewels of golde were, and put them on the great ſtone: And the men of Bethſhemeſh offered burnt offrings, and ſacrificed ſacrifices the ſame day vnto the Lord.[16]And when the fiue lordes of the Philiſtines had ſeene it, they returned to Ekron the ſame day.[17]And theſe are the golden Emerods which the Philiſtines returned for a treſpaſſe offering vnto the Lord; for Aſhdod one, for Gaza one, for Aſkelon one, for Gath one, for Ekron one.[18]And the golden Mice according to the number of all the cities of the Philiſtines, belonging to the fiue lordes, both of fenced cities, and of countrey villages, euen vnto the great ſtone of Abel, whereon they ſet downe the Arke of the Lord; which ſtone remaineth vnto this day, in the field of Ioſhua the Bethſhemite.[19]And he ſmote the men of Bethſhemeſh, becauſe they had looked into the Arke of the Lord, euen he ſmote of the people fiftie thouſand, and threeſcore and tenne men: and the people lamented, becauſe the Lord had ſmitten many of the people with a great ſlaughter.[20]And the men of Bethſhemeſh ſaid, Who is able to ſtand before this holy Lord God? and to whom ſhal he goe vp from vs?[21]And they ſent meſſengers to the inhabitants of Kiriath-iearim, ſaying, The Philiſtines haue brought againe the Arke of the Lord; come ye downe, and fetch it vp to you.

CHAPTER 7[1]And the men of Kiriath-iearim came, and fetcht vp the Arke of the Lord, and brought it into the houſe of Abinadab in the hill, and ſanctified Eleazar his ſonne, to keepe the Arke of the Lord.[2]And it came to paſſe while the Arke abode in Kiriath-iearim, that the time was long: for it was twentie yeeres: and all the houſe of Iſrael lamented after the Lord.[3]And Samuel ſpake vnto all the houſe of Iſrael, ſaying, If ye doe returne vnto the Lord with all your hearts, then put away the ſtrange gods, and Aſhtaroth from among you, and prepare your hearts vnto the Lord, and ſerue him onely: & he will deliuer you out of the hand of the Philiſtines.[4]Then the children of Iſrael did put away Baalim, and Aſhtaroth, and ſerued the Lord onely.[5]And Samuel ſaid, Gather all Iſrael to Mizpeh, and I will pray for you vnto the Lord.[6]And they gathered together to Mizpeh, and drew water, and powred it out before the Lord, and faſted on that day, and ſaid there, We haue ſinned againſt the Lord. And Samuel iudged the children of Iſrael in Mizpeh.[7]And when the Philiſtines heard that the children of Iſrael were gathered together to Mizpeh, the lords of the Philiſtines went vp againſt Iſrael: and when the children of Iſrael heard it, they were afraid of the Philiſtines.[8]And the children of Iſrael ſaid to Samuel, Ceaſe not to crie vnto the Lord our God for vs, that he will ſaue vs out of the hand of the Philiſtines.[9]And Samuel tooke a ſucking lambe, and offered it for a burnt offering wholly vnto the Lord; and Samuel cried vnto the Lord for Iſrael, and the Lord heard him.[10]And as Samuel was offering vp the burnt offering, the Philiſtines drewe neere to battell againſt Iſrael: but the Lord thundred

with a great thunder on that day vpon the Philiſtines, and diſcomfited
them, and they were ſmitten before Iſrael. 11And the men of Iſrael went
out of Mizpeh, and purſued the Philiſtines, and ſmote them, vntill they
came vnder Bethcar. 12Then Samuel tooke a ſtone, and ſet it betweene
Mizpeh and Shen, and called the name of it Eben-Ezer, ſaying, Hitherto
hath the Lord helped vs. 13So the Philiſtines were ſubdued, and they
came no more into the coaſt of Iſrael: and the hand of the Lord was
againſt the Philiſtines, all the dayes of Samuel. 14And the cities which the
Philiſtines had taken from Iſrael, were reſtored to Iſrael, from Ekron
euen vnto Gath, and the coaſts thereof did Iſrael deliuer out of the hands
of the Philiſtines: and there was peace betweene Iſrael and the
Amorites. 15And Samuel iudged Iſrael all the dayes of his life. 16And he
went from yeere to yeere in circuit to Bethel, and Gilgal, and Mizpeh,
and iudged Iſrael in all thoſe places. 17And his returne was to Ramah: for
there was his houſe: and there hee iudged Iſrael, and there hee built an
altar vnto the Lord.
CHAPTER 8 1And it came to paſſe, when Samuel was old, that he made
his ſonnes Iudges ouer Iſrael. 2Now the name of his firſt borne was Ioel,
and the name of his ſecond, Abiah: they were Iudges in Beer-ſheba. 3And
his ſonnes walked not in his wayes, but turned aſide after lucre, and
tooke bribes, & peruerted iudgement. 4Then all the Elders of Iſrael
gathered themſelues together, and came to Samuel vnto Ramah, 5And
ſaid vnto him, Behold, thou art olde, and thy ſonnes walke not in thy
wayes: now make vs a King to iudge vs, like all the nations. 6But the
thing diſpleaſed Samuel, when they ſaid, Giue vs a King to iudge vs: and
Samuel prayed vnto the Lord. 7And the Lord ſaid vnto Samuel, Hearken
vnto the voyce of the people in all that they ſay vnto thee: for they haue
not reiected thee, but they haue reiected mee, that I ſhould not reigne
ouer them. 8According to all the works which they haue done ſince the
day that I brought them vp out of Egypt euen vnto this day, wherewith
they haue forſaken me, and ſerued other gods: ſo doe they alſo vnto
thee. 9Nowe therefore hearken vnto their voyce: howbeit, yet proteſt
ſolemnly vnto them, and ſhew them the maner of the King that ſhall
reigne ouer them. 10And Samuel told all the words of the Lord vnto the
people, that aſked of him a King. 11And hee ſayd, This will be the maner
of the king that ſhall reigne ouer you: Hee will take your ſonnes, and
appoint them for himſelfe for his charets, and to bee his horſemen, and
ſome ſhall runne before his charets. 12And hee will appoint him
Captaines ouer thouſands, and captaines ouer fifties, and will ſet them
to eare his ground, and to reape his harueſt, and to make his inſtruments
of warre, and inſtruments of his charets. 13And he will take your
daughters to be confectionaries, and to be cookes, and to be
bakers. 14And he will take your fields, and your vineyards, and your oliue-
yards, euen the beſt of them, and giue them to his ſeruants. 15And he will
take the tenth of your ſeed, and of your vineyards, and giue to his
officers, and to his ſeruants. 16And hee will take your men ſeruants, and
your mayd ſeruants, and your goodlieſt young men, and your aſſes, and
put them to his worke. 17Hee will take the tenth of your ſheepe, and ye
ſhall be his ſeruants. 18And ye ſhall cry out in that day, becauſe of your
king which ye ſhall haue choſen you; and the Lord will not heare you in
that day. 19Neuertheleſſe, the people refuſed to obey the voyce of
Samuel; and they ſaid, Nay, but we will haue a King ouer vs: 20That we
alſo may be like all the nations, and that our King may iudge vs, and goe
out before vs, and fight our battels. 21And Samuel heard all the words of
the people, and he rehearſed them in the eares of the Lord. 22And the
Lord ſaid to Samuel, Hearken vnto their voyce, and make them a King.
And Samuel ſaid vnto the men of Iſrael, Goe yee euery man vnto his
citie.
CHAPTER 9 1Now there was a man of Beniamin, whoſe name was
Kiſh, the ſonne of Abiel, the ſonne of Zeror, the ſonne of Bechorath,
the ſonne of Aphiah, a Beniamite, a mighty man of power. 2And he had
a ſonne, whoſe name was Saul, a choice young man, and a goodly: and
there was not among the children of Iſrael a goodlier perſon then hee:
from his ſhoulderſand vpward, hee was higher then any of the
people. 3And the aſſes of Kiſh, Sauls father, were loſt; and Kiſh ſaid to
Saul his ſonne, Take nowe one of the ſeruants with thee, and Ariſe, goe
ſeeke the aſſes. 4And he paſſed thorow mount Ephraim, and paſſed
thorow the land of Shaliſha, but they found them not: then they paſſed
thorow the land of Shalim, and there they were not: and hee paſſed
thorow the land of the Beniamites, but they found them not. 5And when
they were come to the land of Zuph, Saul ſaid to his ſeruant that was
with him, Come, and let vs returne, leſt my father leaue caring for the
aſſes, and take thought for vs. 6And hee ſaid vnto him, Behold now,
there is in this citie a man of God, and he is an honourable man; all that
he ſaith, commeth ſurely to paſſe: Now let vs goe thither; peraduenture
he can ſhew vs our way that we ſhould goe. 7Then ſaid Saul to his
ſeruaunt, But behold, if we goe, what ſhall wee bring the man? for the
bread is ſpent in our veſſels, and there is not a preſent to bring to the
man of God: What haue wee? 8And the ſeruant anſwered Saul againe,
and ſaid, Behold, I haue here at hand the fourth part of a ſhekel of ſiluer;
that wil I giue to the man of God, to tell vs our way. 9(Beforetime in
Iſrael, when a man went to enquire of God, thus he ſpake; Come, and
let vs go to the Seer: for he that is now called a Prophet, was beforetime
called a Seer.) 10Then ſaid Saul to his ſeruant, Wel ſaid, come, let vs go:
ſo they went vnto the city where the man of God was. 11And as they
went vp the hill to the city, they found yong maydens going out to draw
water, and ſaid vnto them, Is the Seer here? 12And they anſwered them,
and ſaid, He is: behold, he is before you, make haſte now: for he came
to day to the citie; for there is a ſacrifice of the people to day in the hie
place. 13Aſſoone as ye be come into the citie, ye ſhall ſtraightway finde
him, before he goe vp to the high place to eate: for the people will not
eate vntill hee come, becauſe he doth bleſſe the ſacrifice, and afterwards
they eat that be bidden: Now therefore get you vp, for about this time
ye ſhall finde him. 14And they went vp into the citie: and when they were
come into the citie, behold, Samuel came out againſt them, for to goe
vp to the hie place. 15Now the Lord had told Samuel in his eare a day
before Saul came, ſaying, 16To morrow about this time I will ſend thee a
man out of the land of Beniamin, and thou ſhalt anoynt him to be
Captaine ouer my people Iſrael, that he may ſaue my people out of the
hand of the Philiſtines: for I haue looked vpon my people, becauſe their
cry is come vnto me. 17And when Samuel ſaw Saul, the Lord ſaid vnto
him, Behold the man whom I ſpake to thee of: this ſame ſhall reigne
ouer my people. 18Then Saul drew neere to Samuel in the gate, and ſaid,
Tell me, I pray thee, where the Seers houſe is. 19And Samuel anſwered
Saul, and ſaid, I am the Seer: Goe vp before me vnto the high place, for
ye ſhall eate with me to day, and to morrow I will let thee goe, and will
tell thee all that is in thine heart. 20And as for thine aſſes that were loſt
three dayes agoe, ſet not thy minde on them, for they are found: And
on whom is all the deſire of Iſrael? is it not on thee, & on all thy fathers
houſe? 21And Saul anſwered, and ſaid, Am not I a Beniamite, of the
ſmalleſt of the tribes of Iſrael? and my family the leaſt of all the families
of the tribe of Beniamin? Wherefore then ſpeakeſt thou ſo to me? 22And
Samuel tooke Saul, and his ſeruant, and brought them into the parlour,
& made them ſit in the chiefeſt place among them that were bidden,
which were about thirtie perſons. 23And Samuel ſaid vnto the cooke,
Bring the portion which I gaue thee, of which I ſaid vnto thee, Set it by
thee. 24And the cooke took vp the ſhoulder, and that which was vpon it,
and ſet it before Saul, and Samuel ſaid, Behold, that which is left, ſet it
before thee, and eate: for vnto this time hath it bene kept for thee, ſince
I ſaid I haue inuited the people: So Saul did eat with Samuel that
day. 25And when they were come downe from the high place into the
citie, Samuel communed with Saul vpon the top of the houſe. 26And they
aroſe early: and it came to paſſe about the ſpring of the day, that Samuel
called Saul to the top of the houſe, ſaying, Up, that I may ſend thee away:
And Saul aroſe, and they went out both of them, hee and Samuel,
abroad. 27And as they were going downe to the end of the city, Samuel
ſaid to Saul, Bid the ſeruant paſſe on before vs, (and he paſſed on) but
ſtand thou ſtill a while, that I may ſhew thee the word of God.
CHAPTER 10 1Then Samuel tooke a viall of oile, and powred it vpon
his head, & kiſſed him, and ſaid, Is it not becauſe the Lord hath anoynted
thee to be captain ouer his inheritance? 2When thou art departed from
me to day, then thou ſhalt find two men by Rachels ſepulchre in the
border of Beniamin, at Zelzah: and they will ſay vnto thee, The aſſes
which thou wenteſt to ſeeke, are found: and loe, thy father hath left the
care of the aſſes, and ſorroweth for you, ſaying, What ſhall I doe for my
ſonne? 3Then ſhalt thou goe on forward from thence, and thou ſhalt
come to the plaine of Tabor, and there ſhall meete thee three men, going
vp to God to Bethel, one carying three kids, and another carying three
loaues of bread, and another carying a bottle of wine. 4And they will
ſalute thee, and giue thee two loaues of bread, which thou ſhalt receiue

of their hands.5After that thou ſhalt come to the hill of God, where is the gariſon of the Philiſtines: and it ſhall come to paſſe when thou art come thither to the citie, that thou ſhalt meet a company of prophets comming downe from the high place, with a pſalterie, and a tabret, and a pipe, and a harpe before them, and they ſhall prophecie.6And the Spirit of the Lord will come vpon thee, and thou ſhalt prophecie with them, and ſhalt be turned into another man.7And let it be when theſe ſignes are come vnto thee, that thou doe as occaſion ſerue thee, for God is with thee.0And thou ſhalt goe downe before me to Gilgal, and behold, I will come downe vnto thee, to offer burnt offerings, and to ſacrifice ſacrifices of peace offerings: ſeuen dayes ſhalt thou tarie, till I come to thee, and ſhew thee what thou ſhalt doe.9And it was ſo that when he had turned his backe to go from Samuel, God gaue him another heart: and all thoſe ſignes came to paſſe that day.10And when they came thither to the hill, behold, a company of the prophets met him, and the ſpirit of God came vpon him, and hee propheſied among them.11And it came to paſſe when all that knew him beforetime, ſaw, that behold, hee propheſied among the prophets, then the people ſaid one to another, What is this that is come vnto the ſonne of Kiſh? Is Saul alſo among the prophets?12And one of the ſame place anſwered, and ſayd, But who is their father? Therefore it became a prouerbe, Is Saul alſo among the Prophets?13And when he had made an end of propheſying, he came to the high place.14And Sauls vncle ſaide vnto him, and to his ſeruant, Whither went ye? And he ſaid, To ſeeke the aſſes: and when we ſaw that they were no where, we came to Samuel.15And Sauls vncle ſaid, Tell me, I pray thee, what Samuel ſaid vnto you.16And Saul ſayd vnto his vncle; He told vs plainely that the aſſes were found. But of the matter of the kingdome, whereof Samuel ſpake, he told him not.17And Samuel called the people together vnto the Lord to Mizpeh;18And ſaid vnto the children of Iſrael, Thus ſaith the Lord God of Iſrael, I brought vp Iſrael out of Egypt, and deliuered you out of the hand of the Egyptians, and out of the hand of all kingdomes, and of them that oppreſſed you.19And ye haue this day reiected your God, who himſelfe ſaued you out of all your aduerſities & your tribulations: and ye haue ſaid vnto him, Nay, but ſet a king ouer vs. Now therefore preſent your ſelues before the Lord by your tribes, and by your thouſands.20And when Samuel had cauſed all the tribes of Iſrael to come neere, the tribe of Beniamin was taken.21When he had cauſed the tribe of Beniamin to come neere by their families, the familie of Matri was taken, and Saul the ſonne of Kiſh was taken: and when they ſought him, he could not be found.22Therefore they enquired of the Lord further, if the man ſhould yet come thither: and the Lord anſwered, Behold, hee hath hid himſelfe among the ſtuffe.23And they ranne, and fetched him thence, and when he ſtood among the people, he was higher then any of the people, from the ſhoulderſ& vpward.24And Samuel ſaid to all the people, ſee ye him whome the Lord hath choſen, that there is none like him among all the people? And all the people ſhouted, and ſaide, God ſaue the King.25Then Samuel tolde the people the maner of the kingdome, and wrote it in a booke, and layd it vp before the Lord, and Samuel ſent all the people away, euery man to his houſe.26And Saul alſo went home to Gibeah, and there went with him a band of men, whoſe hearts God had touched.27But the children of Belial ſayd, Howe ſhall this man ſaue vs? and they deſpiſed him, and brought him no preſents: but he held his peace.

CHAPTER 111Then Nahaſh the Ammonite came vp, and encamped againſt Iabeſh Gilead: and all the men of Iabeſh ſayde vnto Nahaſh, Make a couenant with vs, and we will ſerue thee.2And Nahaſh the Ammonite anſwered them, On this condition will I make a couenant with you, that I may thruſt out all your right eyes, and lay it for a reproch vpon all Iſrael.3And the Elders of Iabeſh ſayd vnto him, Giue vs ſeuen daies reſpite, that we may ſend meſſengers vnto all the coaſts of Iſrael: and then, if there be no man to ſaue vs, we will come out to thee.4Then came the meſſengers to Gibeah of Saul, and told the tidings in the eares of the people: and all the people lift vp their voyces, and wept.5And behold, Saul came after the herd out of the field, and Saul ſayd, What aileth the people that they weep? and they told him the tidings of the men of Iabeſh.6And the Spirit of God came vpon Saul, when he heard thoſe tydings, and his anger was kindled greatly.7And he tooke a yoke of oxen, and hewed them in pieces, and ſent them throughout all the coaſts of Iſrael by the hands of meſſengers, ſaying, Whoſoeuer commeth not foorth after Saul and after Samuel, ſo ſhall it bee done vnto his oxen: and the feare of the Lord fell on the people, and they came out with one conſent.8And when he numbred them in Bezek, the children of Iſrael were three hundred thouſand, and the men of Iudah thirty thouſand.9And they ſaid vnto the meſſengers that came, Thus ſhall yee ſay vnto the men of Iabeſh Gilead, To morrow by that time the ſunne be hote, ye ſhal haue helpe. And the meſſengers came, and ſhewed it to the men of Iabeſh, and they were glad.10Therfore the men of Iabeſh ſaid, To morrow wee will come out vnto you, and ye ſhall doe with vs all that ſeemeth good vnto you.11And it was ſo on the morrow, that Saul put the people in three cōpanies, and they came into the midſt of the hoſt in the morning watch, and ſlewe the Ammonites, vntill the heat of the day: and it came to paſſe, that they which remained were ſcattered, ſo that two of them were not left together.12And the people ſaid vnto Samuel, Who is he that ſaid, Shall Saul reigne ouer vs? bring the men, that we may put them to death.13And Saul ſaid, There ſhall not a man be put to death this day: for to day the Lord hath wrought ſaluation in Iſrael.14Then ſaid Samuel to the people, Come, and let vs goe to Gilgal, and renew the kingdome there.15And all the people went to Gilgal, and there they made Saul King before the Lord in Gilgal: and there they ſacrificed ſacrifices of peace offerings before the Lord: and there Saul and all the men of Iſrael reioyced greatly.

CHAPTER 121And Samuel ſaide vnto all Iſrael, Beholde, I haue hearkned vnto your voice in all that ye ſaid vnto mee, and haue made a King ouer you.2And now behold, the King walketh before you: and I am olde, and gray headed, and behold, my ſonnes are with you: and I haue walked before you from my childhood vnto this day.3Behold, here I am, witneſſe againſt me before the Lord, and before his Anoynted: Whoſe oxe haue I taken? or whoſe aſſe haue I taken? or whom haue I defrauded? whom haue I oppreſſed? or of whoſe hand haue I receiued any bribe to blinde mine eyes therewith? and I will reſtore it you.4And they ſaid, Thou haſt not defrauded vs, nor oppreſſed vs, neither haſt thou taken ought of any mans hand.5And hee ſaid vnto them, The Lord is witneſſe againſt you, and his Anointed is witneſſe this day, that ye haue not found ought in my hand: And they anſwered, He is witneſſe.6And Samuel ſaid vnto the people, It is the Lord that aduanced Moſes and Aaron, and that brought your fathers vp out of the land of Egypt.7Now therefore ſtand ſtill, that I may reaſon with you before the Lord, of all the righteous acts of the Lord, which he did to you and your fathers.8When Iacob was come into Egypt, and your fathers cried vnto the Lord, then the Lord ſent Moſes and Aaron, which brought foorth your fathers out of Egypt, and made them dwell in this place.9And when they forgat the Lord their God, he ſold them into the hand of Siſera captaine of the hoſte of Hazor, and into the hand of the Philiſtines, and into the hand of the king of Moab, and they fought againſt them.10And they cried vnto the Lord, and ſaid, Wee haue ſinned, becauſe we haue forſaken the Lord, and haue ſerued Baalim and Aſhtaroth: but now deliuer vs out of the hand of our enemies, and we will ſerue thee.11And the Lord ſent Ierubbaal, and Bedan, and Iephthah, and Samuel, and deliuered you out of the hand of your enemies on euery ſide, and yee dwelled ſafe.12And when ye ſaw that Nahaſh the king of the children of Ammon came againſt you, ye ſaid vnto me, Nay, but a King ſhall reigne ouer vs, when the Lord your God was your King.13Now therefore, behold the King whom yee haue choſen, and whom yee haue deſired: and behold, the Lord hath ſet a King ouer you.14If ye will feare the Lord, and ſerue him, and obey his voice, and not rebell againſt the Commandement of the Lord, then ſhall both ye and alſo the King that reigneth ouer you, continue following the Lord your God.15But if ye wil not obey the voice of the Lord, but rebel againſt the Commandement of the Lord, then ſhall the hand of the Lord be againſt you, as it was againſt your fathers.16Now therefore ſtand and ſee this great thing which the Lord will doe before your eyes.17Is it not wheat harueſt to day? I will call vnto the Lord, and hee ſhall ſend thunder and raine, that ye may perceiue and ſee that your wickedneſſe is great, which ye haue done in the ſight of the Lord, in aſking you a King.18So Samuel called vnto the Lord, and the Lord ſent thunder and raine that day: and all the people greatly feared the Lord and Samuel.19And all the people ſaid vnto Samuel, Pray for thy ſeruants vnto the Lord thy God, that we die not: for we haue added vnto all our ſinnes, this euil, to aſke vs a King.20And Samuel ſaide vnto the people, Feare not: (ye haue done al this wickedneſſe, yet turne not aſide from following the Lord, but ſerue the Lord with all your heart:21And turne ye not aſide, for then ſhould ye goe after vaine things, which cannot profit, nor deliuer, for they are vaine.)22For the Lord wil not forſake his people, for his great Names ſake: becauſe it hath pleaſed the Lord to make you his people.23Moreouer, as for me, God forbid that I ſhould ſin againſt the Lord, in ceaſing to pray for you: but I will teach you the good and the right way.24Onely feare the Lord, and ſerue him in trueth with all your heart: for conſider how great things he hath done for you.25But if yee ſhall ſtill doe wickedly, yee ſhall be conſumed, both yee and your King.

CHAPTER 131Saul reigned one yeere, and when he had reigned two yeeres ouer Iſrael,2Saul choſe him three thouſand men of Iſrael: whereof two thouſand were with Saul in Michmaſh, and in mount Bethel, and a thouſand were with Ionathan in Gibeah of Beniamin: and the reſt of the people he ſent euery man to his tent.3And Ionathan ſmote the gariſon of the Philiſtines that was in Geba, and the Philiſtines heard of it: and Saul blew the trumpet thorowout all the land, ſaying, Let the Hebrewes heare.4And all Iſrael heard ſay, that Saul had ſmitten a gariſon of the Philiſtines, and that Iſrael alſo was had in abomination with the Philiſtines: and the people were called together after Saul to Gilgal.5And the Philiſtines gathered themſelues together, to fight with Iſrael, thirtie thouſand charets, and ſixe thouſand horſemen, and people as the ſand which is on the ſea ſhore in multitude, and they came vp, and pitched in Michmaſh, Eaſtward from Bethauen.6When the men of Iſrael ſaw that they were in a ſtrait: (for the people were diſtreſſed:) then the people did hide themſelues in caues, and in thickets, and in rocks, and in high places, and in pits.7And ſome of the Hebrewes went ouer Iordane, to the land of Gad and Gilead; as for Saul, he was yet in Gilgal, and all the people followed him trembling.8And he taried ſeuen dayes, according to the ſet time that Samuel had appointed: but Samuel came not to Gilgal, and the people were ſcattered from him.9And Saul ſaid, Bring hither a burnt offring to me, and peace offrings. And he offered the burnt offering.10And it came to paſſe that aſſoone as he had made an end of offering the burnt offering, behold, Samuel came, and Saul went out to meete him, that he might ſalute him.11And Samuel ſaid, What haſt thou done? And Saul ſaid, Becauſe I ſawe that the people were ſcattered from me, and that thou cameſt not within the dayes appointed, and that the Philiſtines gathered themſelues together to Michmaſh:12Therfore ſaid I, The Philiſtines will come downe now vpon me to Gilgal, and I haue not made ſupplication vnto the Lord: I forced my ſelfe therefore, and offered a burnt offering.13And Samuel ſaid to Saul, Thou haſt done fooliſhly: thou haſt not kept the commandement of the Lord thy God, which hee commanded thee: for now would the Lord haue eſtabliſhed thy kingdome vpon Iſrael for euer.14But now thy kingdome ſhall not continue: the Lord hath ſought him a man after his owne heart, and the Lord hath commanded him to bee captaine ouer his people, becauſe thou haſt not kept that which the Lord commanded thee.15And Samuel aroſe, and gate him vp from Gilgal, vnto Gibeah of Beniamin, and Saul numbred the people that were preſent with him, about ſixe hundred men.16And Saul and Ionathan his ſonne, and the people that were preſent with them, abode in Gibeah of Beniamin: but the Philiſtines encamped in Michmaſh.17And the ſpoilers came out of the campe of the Philiſtines, in three companies: one company turned vnto the way that leadeth to Ophrah, vnto the land of Shual.18And another company turned the way to Bethoron: and another companie turned to the way of the border, that looketh to the valley of Zeboim toward the wilderneſſe.19Now there was no ſmith found thorowout all the land of Iſrael: for the Philiſtines ſaid, Leſt the Hebrewes make them ſwords or ſpeares.20But all the Iſraelites went downe to the Philiſtines, to ſharpen euery man his ſhare and his coulter, and his axe, and his mattocke.21Yet they had a file for the mattocks, and for the coulters, and for the forkes, and for the axes, and to ſharpen the goads.22So it came to paſſe in the day of battell, that there was neither ſword nor ſpeare found in the hand of any of the people that were with Saul and Ionathan: but with Saul & with Ionathan his ſonne was there found.23And the gariſon of the Philiſtines went out to the paſſage of Michmaſh.

CHAPTER 141Now it came to paſſe vpon a day, that Ionathan the ſonne of Saul ſaid vnto the yong man that bare his armour, Come, and let vs goe ouer to the Philiſtines gariſon, that is on the other ſide: but hee told not his father.2And Saul taried in the vttermoſt part of Gibeah, vnder a Pomegranate tree, which is in Migron: and the people that were with him, were about ſixe hundred men:3And Ahiah the ſonne of Ahitub, Ichabods brother, the ſonne of Phinehas, the ſonne of Eli, the Lords Prieſt in Shiloh, wearing an Ephod: and the people knew not that Ionathan was gone.4And betweene the paſſages, by which Ionathan ſought to go ouer vnto the Philiſtines gariſon, there was a ſharpe rocke on the one ſide, and a ſharp rocke on the other ſide: and the name of the one was Bozez, and the name of the other Seneh.5The forefront of the one was ſituate Northward ouer againſt Michmaſh, and the other Southward ouer againſt Gibeah.6And Ionathan ſaid to the young man that bare his armour, Come, and let vs goe ouer vnto the gariſon of theſe vncircumciſed; it may be that the Lord will worke for vs: for there is no reſtraint to the Lord, to ſaue by many, or by few.7And his armour bearer ſayd vnto him, Doe all that is in thine heart: turne thee, behold, I am with thee, according to thy heart.8Then ſaid Ionathan, Behold, we will paſſe ouer vnto theſe men, and we will diſcouer our ſelues vnto them.9If they ſay thus vnto vs, Tary vntill we come to you: then wee will ſtand ſtill in our place, and will not goe vp vnto them.10But if they ſay thus, Come vp vnto vs: then we will goe vp; for the Lord hath deliuered them into our hand: and this ſhall be a ſigne vnto vs.11And both of them diſcouered themſelues vnto the gariſon of the Philiſtines: and the Philiſtines ſayd, Behold, the Hebrewes come foorth out of the holes, where they had hid themſelues.12And the men of the gariſon anſwered Ionathan and his armour bearer, and ſaid, Come vp to vs, and wee will ſhew you a thing. And Ionathan ſaid vnto his armour bearer, Come vp after me; for the Lord hath deliuered them into the hand of Iſrael.13And Ionathan climed vp vpon his hands, and vpon his feete, and his armour bearer after him: and they fell before Ionathan; and his armour bearer ſlew after him.14And that firſt ſlaughter which Ionathan and his armour-bearer made, was about twentie men, within as it were an halfe acre of land, which a yoke of oxen might plow.15And there was trembling in the hoſte, in the field, and among all the people: the gariſon and the ſpoilers, they alſo trembled, and the earth quaked: ſo it was a very great trembling.16And the watchmen of Saul in Gibeah of Beniamin looked: and behold, the multitude melted away, and they went on beating downe one another.17Then ſaid Saul vnto the people that were with him, Number now, and ſee who is gone from vs. And when they had numbred, behold, Ionathan and his armour bearer were not there.18And Saul ſaid vnto Ahiah, Bring hither the Arke of God: (for the Arke of God was at that time with the children of Iſrael.)19And it came to paſſe while Saul talked vnto the Prieſt, that the noiſe that was in the hoſte of the Philiſtines went on, and increaſed: And Saul ſaid vnto the Prieſt, Withdraw thine hand.20And Saul and all the people that were with him aſſembled themſelues, and they came to the battel, and behold, euery mans ſword was againſt his fellow, and there was a very great diſcomfiture.21Moreouer, the Hebrewes that were with the Philiſtines before that time, which went vp with them into the campe from the countrey round about; euen they alſo turned to be with the Iſraelites, that were with Saul and Ionathan.22Likewiſe all the men of Iſrael, which had hid themſelues in mount Ephraim, when they heard that the Philiſtines fled, euen they alſo followed hard after them in the battell.23So the Lord ſaued Iſrael that day: and the battell paſſed ouer vnto Beth-auen.24And the men of Iſrael were diſtreſſed that day; for Saul had adiured the people, ſaying, Curſed bee the man that eateth any foode vntill euening, that I may be auenged on mine enemies: ſo none of the people taſted any food.25And all they of the land came to a wood, and there was honie vpon the ground.26And when the people were come into the wood, behold, the honie dropped, but no man put his hand to his mouth: for the people feared the oath.27But Ionathan heard not when his father charged the people with the oath; wherefore he put foorth the ende of the rodde that was in his hand, and dipt it in an hony combe, and put his hand to his mouth, and his eyes were enlightened.28Then anſwered one of the people, and ſaid, Thy father ſtraitly charged the people with an oath, ſaying, Curſed be the man that eateth any food this day. And the people were faint.29Then ſaid Ionathan, My father hath troubled the land: ſee, I pray you, how mine eyes haue beene enlightened, becauſe I taſted a little of this honie:30How much more, if haply the people had eaten freely to day of the ſpoile of their enemies which they found? for had there not beene now a much greater ſlaughter among the Philiſtines?31And they ſmote the Philiſtines

that day from Michmaſh to Aiialon: and the people were very
faint.32And the people flewe vpon the ſpoile, and tooke ſheepe, and
oxen, and calues, and ſlew them on the ground, and the people did eate
them with the blood.33Then they tolde Saul, ſaying, Behold, the people
ſinne againſt the Lord, in that they eate with the blood. And he ſaid, Yee
haue tranſgreſſed: roule a great ſtone vnto mee this day.34And Saul ſaid,
Diſperſe your ſelues among the people, and ſay vnto them, Bring me
hither euery man his oxe, and euery man his ſheepe, and ſlay them here,
and eat, and ſinne not againſt the Lord in eating with the blood. And all
the people brought euery man his oxe with him that night, and ſlew
them there.35And Saul built an altar vnto the Lord: the ſame was the
firſt altar that he built vnto the Lord.36And Saul ſaide, Let vs goe downe
after the Philiſtines by night, and ſpoile them vntil the morning light,
and let vs not leaue a man of them. And they ſaid, Do whatſoeuer
ſeemeth good vnto thee. Then ſaid the prieſt, Let vs draw neere hither
vnto God.37And Saul aſked counſell of God, Shall I goe downe after the
Philiſtines? Wilt thou deliuer them into the hand of Iſrael? But he
anſwered him not that day.38And Saul ſaid, Draw yee neere hither all the
chiefe of the people: and know and ſee, wherein this ſinne hath beene
this day.39For as the Lord liueth, which ſaueth Iſrael, though it bee in
Ionathan my ſonne, he ſhall ſurely die: But there was not a man among
all the people that anſwered him.40Then ſaid he vnto all Iſrael, Be ye on
one ſide, and I, and Ionathan my ſonne will be on the other ſide. And
the people ſaid vnto Saul, Doe what ſeemeth good vnto
thee.41Therefore Saul ſaide vnto the Lord God of Iſrael, Giue a perfect
lot. And Saul and Ionathan were taken: but the people eſcaped.42And
Saul ſaid, Caſt lots betweene me and Ionathan my ſonne. And Ionathan
was taken.43Then Saul ſaid to Ionathan, Tell me what thou haſt done.
And Ionathan tolde him, and ſaid, I did but taſte a litle hony with the
end of the rodde that was in mine hand, and loe, I muſt die.44And Saul
anſwered, God do ſo, and more alſo: for thou ſhalt ſurely die,
Ionathan.45And the people ſaid vnto Saul, Shall Ionathan die, who hath
wrought this great ſaluation in Iſrael? God forbid: as the Lord liueth,
there ſhal not one haire of his head fall to the ground: for hee hath
wrought with God this day. So the people reſcued Ionathan, that hee
died not.46Then Saul went vp from following the Philiſtines: and the
Philiſtines went to their owne place.47So Saul tooke the kingdom ouer
Iſrael, and fought againſt all his enemies on euery ſide, againſt Moab,
and againſt the children of Ammon, and againſt Edom, and againſt the
kings of Zobah, and againſt the Philiſtines: and whitherſoeuer hee
turned himſelfe, he vexed them.48And he gathered an hoſte, and ſmote
the Amalekites, and deliuered Iſrael out of the handes of them that
ſpoiled them.49Now the ſonnes of Saul, were Ionathan, and Iſhui, and
Melchiſhua: and the names of his two daughters were theſe: the name
of the firſt borne Merab, and the name of the yonger Michal:50And the
name of Sauls wife was Ahinoam, the daughter of Ahimaaz, and the
name of the captaine of his hoſt was Abner, the ſonne of Ner, Sauls
vncle.51And Kiſh was the father of Saul, and Ner the father of Abner
was the ſonne of Abiel.52And there was ſore warre againſt the
Philiſtines, all the dayes of Saul: and when Saul ſaw any ſtrong man, or
any valiant man, he tooke him vnto him.
CHAPTER 151Samuel alſo ſaide vnto Saul, The Lord ſent me to
annoint thee to bee king ouer his people, ouer Iſrael: nowe therefore
hearken thou vnto the voyce of the words of the Lord.2Thus ſaith the
Lord of hoſts, I remember that which Amalek did to Iſrael, how he laid
wait for him in the way when he came vp from Egypt.3Now goe, and
ſmite Amalek, and vtterly deſtroy all that they haue, and ſpare them not;
but ſlay both man and woman, infant and ſuckling, oxe and ſheepe,
camell and aſſe.4And Saul gathered the people together, and numbred
them in Telaim, two hundred thouſand footmen, and ten thouſand men
of Iudah.5And Saul came to a citie of Amalek, and laid waite in the
valley.6And Saul ſaide vnto the Kenites, Goe, depart, get you downe
from among the Amalekites, leſt I deſtroy you with them: for yee ſhewed
kindneſſe to all the children of Iſrael when they came vp out of Egypt.
So the Kenites departed from among the Amalekites.7And Saul ſmote
the Amalekites from Hauilah, vntill thou commeſt to Shur, that is ouer
againſt Egypt.8And hee tooke Agag the king of the Amalekites aliue,
and vtterly deſtroyed all the people with the edge of the ſword.9But Saul
and the people ſpared Agag, and the beſt of the ſheepe, and of the oxen,
and of the fatlings, and the lambes, and all that was good, and would
not vtterly deſtroy them: but euery thing that was vile, and refuſe, that
they deſtroyed vtterly.10Then came the word of the Lord vnto Samuel,
ſaying;11It repenteth me that I haue ſet vp Saul to be king: for hee is
turned backe from following me, and hath not performed my
commandements. And it grieued Samuel; and he cried vnto the Lord all
night.12And when Samuel roſe early to meet Saul in the morning, it was
tolde Samuel, ſaying, Saul came to Carmel, and behold, he ſet him vp a
place, and is gone about, and paſſed on, and gone downe to Gilgal.13And
Samuel came to Saul, and Saul ſaid vnto him, Bleſſed be thou of the
Lord: I haue performed the commandement of the Lord.14And Samuel
ſaid, What meaneth then this bleating of the ſheepe in mine eares, and
the lowing of the oxen which I heare?15And Saul ſayde, They haue
brought them from the Amalekites: for the people ſpared the beſt of the
ſheepe, and of the oxen, to ſacrifice vnto the Lord thy God, and the reſt
we haue vtterly deſtroyed.16Then Samuel ſayd vnto Saul, Stay, and I will
tell thee what the Lord hath ſaid to mee this night. And he ſaid vnto
him, ſay on.17And Samuel ſaid, When thou waſt litle in thine owne ſight,
waſt thou not made the Head of the tribes of Iſrael, and the Lord
anointed thee King ouer Iſrael?18And the Lord ſent thee on a iourney,
and ſaid, Goe, and vtterly deſtroy the ſinners the Amalekites, and fight
againſt them, vntill they be conſumed.19Wherefore then didſt thou not
obey the voice of the Lord, but didſt flie vpon the ſpoile, and didſt euill
in the ſight of the Lord ?20And Saul ſaid vnto Samuel; Yea, I haue
obeyed the voice of the Lord, and haue gone the way which the Lord
ſent me, and haue brought Agag the king of Amalek, and haue vtterly
deſtroyed the Amalekites.21But the people tooke of the ſpoile, ſheepe
and oxen, the chiefe of the things which ſhould haue bene vtterly
deſtroyed, to ſacrifice vnto the Lord thy God in Gilgal.22And Samuel
ſaide, Hath the Lord as great delight in burnt offerings and ſacrifices, as
in obeying the voice of the Lord ? Behold, to obey, is better then
ſacrifice: and to hearken, then the fat of rammes.23For rebellion is as the
ſin of witchcraft, and ſtubburnneſe is as iniquitie and idolatrie: becauſe
thou haſt reiected the word of the Lord, he hath alſo reiected thee from
being king.24And Saul ſaid vnto Samuel, I haue ſinned: for I haue
tranſgreſſed the Commandement of the Lord, and thy wordes; becauſe
I feared the people, and obeyed their voice.25Now therefore, I pray thee,
pardon my ſinne, and turne againe with me, that I may worſhip the
Lord.26And Samuel ſaid vnto Saul, I will not returne with thee: for thou
haſt reiected the word of the Lord, and the Lord hath reiected thee from
being king ouer Iſrael.27And as Samuel turned about to goe away, he
laid hold vpon the ſkirt of his mantle, and it rent.28And Samuel ſaid vnto
him, The Lord hath rent the kingdome of Iſrael from thee this day, and
hath giuen it to a neighbour of thine, that is better then thou.29And alſo
the ſtrength of Iſrael will not lie, nor repent: for he is not a man that he
ſhould repent.30Then he ſaid, I haue ſinned; yet honour me now, I pray
thee, before the Elders of my people, and before Iſrael, and turne againe
with me, that I may worſhip the Lord thy God.31So Samuel turned
againe after Saul, and Saul worſhipped the Lord.32Then ſaid Samuel,
Bring you hither to me Agag the king of the Amalekites: and Agag came
vnto him delicately. And Agag ſaid, Surely the bitterneſſe of death is
paſt.33And Samuel ſaid, As thy ſword hath made women childleſſe, ſo
ſhall thy mother bee childleſſe among women. And Samuel hewed Agag
in pieces before the Lord in Gilgal.34Then Samuel went to Ramah, and
Saul went vp to his houſe to Gibeah of Saul.35And Samuel came no
more to ſee Saul vntill the day of his death: neuertheleſſe, Samuel
mourned for Saul: and the Lord repented that he had made Saul king
ouer Iſrael.
CHAPTER 161And the Lord ſaid vnto Samuel, How long wilt thou
mourne for Saul, ſeeing I haue reiected him from reigning ouer Iſrael?
Fill thine horne with oile, and goe, I will ſend thee to Ieſſe the
Bethlehemite: for I haue prouided mee a King among his ſonnes.2And
Samuel ſaid, How can I goe? if Saul heare it, he will kill mee. And the
Lord ſaid, Take an heifer with thee, and ſay, I am come to ſacrifice to
the Lord.3And call Ieſſe to the ſacrifice, and I will ſhew thee what thou
ſhalt doe: and thou ſhalt anoynt vnto mee him whom I name vnto
thee.4And Samuel did that which the Lord ſpake, and came to
Bethlehem: and the elders of the towne trembled at his comming, and
ſaid, Commeſt thou peaceably?5And hee ſaid, Peaceably: I am come to
ſacrifice vnto the Lord: ſanctifie your ſelues, and come with me to the
ſacrifice: and he ſanctified Ieſſe, and his ſonnes, and called them to the

ſacrifice.6And it came to paſſe when they were come, that he looked on
Eliab, and ſaid, Surely the Lords anointed is before him.7But the Lord
ſaid vnto Samuel, Looke not on his countenance, or on the height of his
ſtature, becauſe I haue refuſed him: for the Lord ſeeth not, as man ſeeth;
For man looketh on the outward appearance, but the Lord looketh on
the heart.8Then Ieſſe called Abinadab, and made him paſſe before
Samuel: and he ſaid, Neither hath the Lord choſen this.9Then Ieſſe
made Shammah to paſſe by: and he ſaid, Neither hath the Lord choſen
this.10Againe Ieſſe made ſeuen of his ſonnes to paſſe before Samuel; and
Samuel ſaid vnto Ieſſe, The Lord hath not choſen theſe.11And Samuel
ſaide vnto Ieſſe, Are here all thy children? And he ſaid, There remaineth
yet the yongeſt, and behold, he keepeth the ſheepe. And Samuel ſaid
vnto Ieſſe, Send, and fetch him: for we will not ſit downe, till hee come
hither.12And he ſent, and brought him in: now he was ruddy, and withal
of a beautifull countenance, and goodly to looke to: And the Lord ſaid,
Ariſe, anoint him: for this is he.13Then Samuel tooke the horne of oile,
and annointed him in the midſt of his brethren: and the Spirit of the
Lord came vpon Dauid, from that day forward: So Samuel roſe vp and
went to Ramah.14But the ſpirit of the Lord departed from Saul, and an
euil ſpirit from the Lord troubled him.15And Sauls ſeruants ſaid vnto
him, Behold now, an euill ſpirit from God troubleth thee.16Let our lord
now command thy ſeruants which are before thee, to ſeeke out a man,
who is a cunning player on an harpe: and it ſhall come to paſſe when the
euill ſpirit from God is vpon thee, that hee ſhall play with his hand, and
thou ſhalt be well.17And Saul ſaid vnto his ſeruants, Prouide mee now a
man, that can play well, and bring him to me.18Then anſwered one of
the ſeruants, and ſaid, Behold, I haue ſeene a ſonne of Ieſſe the
Bethlehemite, that is cunning in playing, and a mighty valiant man, and
a man of warre, and prudent in matters, and a comely perſon, and the
Lord is with him.19Wherefore Saul ſent meſſengers vnto Ieſſe, and ſaid,
Send me Dauid thy ſonne, which is with the ſheepe.20And Ieſſe tooke
an aſſe laden with bread, and a bottle of wine, and a kid, and ſent them
by Dauid his ſonne vnto Saul.21And Dauid came to Saul, and ſtood
before him: and hee loued him greatly, and hee became his armour
bearer.22And Saul ſent to Ieſſe, ſaying, Let Dauid, I pray thee, ſtand
before me: for hee hath found fauour in my ſight.23And it came to paſſe,
when the euill ſpirit from God was vpon Saul, that Dauid tooke an
harpe, and played with his hand: So Saul was refreſhed, and was well,
and the euill ſpirit departed from him.
CHAPTER 171Now the Philiſtines gathered together their armies to
battell, and were gathered together at Shochoh, which belongeth to
Iudah, and pitched betweene Shochoh and Azekah, in Epheſ-
Dammim.2And Saul and the men of Iſrael were gathered together, and
pitched by the valley of Elah, and ſet the battell in aray againſt the
Philiſtines.3And the Philiſtines ſtood on a mountaine on the one ſide,
and Iſrael ſtood on a mountaine on the other ſide: and there was a valley
betweene them.4And there went out a champion out of the campe of
the Philiſtines, named Goliath of Gath: whoſe height was ſixe cubites
and a ſpan.5And he had an helmet of braſſe vpon his head, and he was
armed with a coate of male: and the weight of the coat was fiue thouſand
ſhekels of braſſe.6And he had greaues of braſſe vpon his legs, and a
target of braſſe betweene his ſhoulders .7And the ſtaffe of his ſpeare was
like a weauers beame, and his ſpeares head weighed ſixe hundred ſhekels
of yron: and one bearing a ſhield, went before him.8And hee ſtood and
cried vnto the armies of Iſrael, and ſaid vnto them, Why are yee come
out to ſet your battell in aray? am not I a Philiſtine, and you ſeruants to
Saul? chuſe you a man for you, and let him come downe to me.9If he be
able to fight with mee, and to kill me, then will we be your ſeruants: but
if I preuaile againſt him, and kill him, then ſhall yee be our ſeruants, and
ſerue vs.10And the Philiſtine ſaid, I defie the armies of Iſrael this day;
giue me a man, that we may fight together.11When Saul and all Iſrael
heard thoſe words of the Philiſtine, they were diſmayed, and greatly
afraid.12Now Dauid was the ſonne of that Ephrathite of Bethlehem
Iudah, whoſe name was Ieſſe, and hee had eight ſonnes: and the man
went among men for an old man in the dayes of Saul.13And the three
eldeſt ſonnes of Ieſſe went, and followed Saul to the battell: and the
names of his three ſonnes that went to the battell, were, Eliab the firſt
borne, and next vnto him, Abinadab, and the third, Shammah.14And
Dauid was the yongeſt: and the three eldeſt followed Saul.15But Dauid
went, and returned from Saul, to feed his fathers ſheepe at
Bethlehem.16And the Philiſtine drewe neere, morning and euening, and
preſented himſelfe forty dayes.17And Ieſſe ſaid vnto Dauid his ſonne,
Take now for thy brethren an ephah of this parched corne, and theſe
ten loaues, and run to the campe to thy brethren.18And carie theſe ten
cheeſes vnto the Captaine of their thouſand, and looke how thy brethren
fare, and take their pledge.19Now Saul, and they, and all the men of Iſrael
were in the valley of Elah, fighting with the Philiſtines.20And Dauid roſe
vp earely in the morning, and left the ſheepe with a keeper, and tooke,
and went, as Ieſſe had commanded him; and he came to the trench, as
the hoſt was going forth to the fight, and ſhouted for the battell.21For
Iſrael and the Philiſtines had put the battel in aray, army againſt
armie.22And Dauid left his cariage in the hand of the keeper of the
cariage, and ranne into the armie, and came and ſaluted his
brethren.23And as he talked with them, behold, there came vp the
champion (the Philiſtine of Gath, Goliath by name) out of the armies of
the Philiſtines, and ſpake according to the ſame words: and Dauid heard
them.24And all the men of Iſrael, when they ſaw the man, fled from him,
and were ſore afraid.25And the men of Iſrael ſaid, Haue yee ſeene this
man that is come vp? Surely to defie Iſrael is he come vp: and it ſhall be
that the man who killeth him, the king wil enrich him with great riches,
and will giue him his daughter, and make his fathers houſe free in
Iſrael.26And Dauid ſpake to the men that ſtood by him, ſaying; What
ſhall bee done to the man that killeth this Philiſtine; and taketh away the
reproch from Iſrael? for who is this vncircumciſed Philiſtine, that he
ſhould defie the armies of the liuing God?27And the people anſwered
him after this maner, ſaying, So ſhall it be done to the man that killeth
him.28And Eliab his eldeſt brother heard when he ſpake vnto the men,
and Eliabs anger was kindled againſt Dauid, and he ſaid, Why cameſt
thou down hither? and with whom haſt thou left thoſe few ſheepe in
the wilderneſſe? I know thy pride, and the naughtineſse of thine heart;
for thou art come downe, that thou mighteſt ſee the battell.29And Dauid
ſaide, What haue I now done? Is there not a cauſe?30And hee turned
from him towards another, and ſpake after the ſame maner: and the
people anſwered him againe after the former maner.31And when the
words were heard which Dauid ſpake, they rehearſed them before Saul:
and he ſent for him.32And Dauid ſaid to Saul, Let no mans heart faile,
becauſe of him: thy ſeruant will goe and fight with this Philiſtine.33And
Saul ſaid to Dauid, Thou art not able to goe againſt this Philiſtine, to
fight with him: for thou art but a youth, and he a man of warre from his
youth.34And Dauid ſaid vnto Saul, Thy ſeruant kept his fathers ſheepe,
and there came a Lyon, and a Beare, and tooke a lambe out of the
flocke:35And I went out after him, and ſmote him, and deliuered it out
of his mouth: and when he aroſe againſt me, I caught him by his beard,
and ſmote him, and ſlew him.36Thy ſeruant ſlew both the Lyon and the
Beare: and this vncircumciſed Philiſtine ſhall be as one of them, ſeeing
he hath defied the armies of the liuing God.37Dauid ſaide moreouer,
The Lord that deliuered me out of the paw of the Lyon, and out of the
pawe of the Beare, he will deliuer me out of the hand of this Philiſtine.
And Saul ſaid vnto Dauid, Goe, and the Lord be with thee.38And Saul
armed Dauid with his armour, and hee put an helmet of braſſe vpon his
head, alſo he armed him with a coat of male.39And Dauid girded his
ſword vpon his armour, and he aſsayed to goe, for he had not proued
it: and Dauid ſaid vnto Saul, I cannot goe with theſe: for I haue not
proued them. And Dauid put them off him.40And hee tooke his ſtaffe
in his hand, and choſe him fiue ſmoothe ſtones out of the brooke, and
put them in a ſhepheards bag which he had, euen in a ſcrip, and his ſling
was in his hande, and he drew neere to the Philiſtine.41And the Philiſtine
came on and drew neere vnto Dauid, and the man that bare the ſhield,
went before him.42And when the Philiſtine looked about, and ſaw
Dauid, hee diſdained him: for he was but a youth, and ruddy, and of a
faire countenance.43And the Philiſtine ſaid vnto Dauid, Am I a dog, that
thou commeſt to me with ſtaues? and the Philiſtine curſed Dauid by his
gods.44And the Philiſtine ſaid to Dauid, Come to me, and I will giue thy
fleſh vnto the foules of the aire, and to the beaſts of the field.45Then
ſaid Dauid to the Philiſtine, Thou commeſt to mee with a ſword, and
with a ſpeare, and with a ſhield: but I come to thee in the Name of the
Lord of hoſtes, the God of the armies of Iſrael, whom thou haſt
defied.46This day wil the Lord deliuer thee into mine hand, and I will
ſmite thee, and take thine head from thee, and I wil giue the carkeiſes of
the hoſt of the Philiſtines this day vnto the foules of the aire, and to the

wild beaſts of the earth, that all the earth may know that there is a God
in Iſrael. 47 And all this aſſembly ſhal know that the Lord ſaueth not with
ſword & ſpeare (for the battell is the Lords) and he will giue you into
our hands. 48 And it came to paſſe when the Philiſtine aroſe, and came,
and drewe nigh to meet Dauid, that Dauid haſted, and ran toward the
armie to meete the Philiſtine. 49 And Dauid put his hande in his bag, and
tooke thence a ſtone, and ſlang it, & ſmote the Philiſtine in his forehead,
that the ſtone ſunke into his forehead, and he fell vpon his face to the
earth. 50 So Dauid preuailed ouer the Philiſtine with a ſling and with a
ſtone, and ſmote the Philiſtine, and ſlew him, but there was no ſword in
the hande of Dauid. 51 Therefore Dauid ran and ſtood vpon the
Philiſtine, and tooke his ſword, and drewe it out of the ſheath thereof,
and ſlew him, and cut off his head therewith. And when the Philiſtines
ſawe their champion was dead, they fled. 52 And the men of Iſrael, and
of Iudah aroſe, and ſhouted, and purſued the Philiſtines, vntill thou
come to the valley, and to the gates of Ekron: and the wounded of the
Philiſtines fell downe by the way to Shaaraim, euen vnto Gath, and vnto
Ekron. 53 And the children of Iſrael returned from chaſing after the
Philiſtines, and they ſpoiled their tents. 54 And Dauid tooke the head of
the Philiſtine, and brought it to Ieruſalem, but he put his armour in his
tent. 55 And when Saul ſawe Dauid goe forth againſt the Philiſtine, he
ſayd vnto Abner the captaine of the hoſte, Abner, whoſe ſonne is this
youth? And Abner ſaid, As thy ſoule liueth, O king, I cannot tell. 56 And
the king ſaid, Enquire thou whoſe ſonne the ſtripling is. 57 And as Dauid
returned from the ſlaughter of the Philiſtine, Abner tooke him, &
brought him before Saul, with the head of the Philiſtine in his
hand. 58 And Saul ſaide to him, Whoſe ſonne art thou, thou yong man?
And Dauid anſwered, I am the ſonne of thy ſeruant Ieſſe, the
Bethlehemite.
CHAPTER 18 1 And it came to paſſe when hee made an ende of
ſpeaking vnto Saul, that the ſoule of Ionathan was knit with the ſoule of
Dauid, and Ionathan loued him as his owne ſoule. 2 And Saul tooke him
that day, and would let him go no more home to his fathers houſe. 3 Then
Ionathan and Dauid made a couenant, becauſe he loued him as his owne
ſoule. 4 And Ionathan ſtript himſelfe of the robe that was vpon him, and
gaue it to Dauid, and his garments, euen to his ſword, and to his bow,
and to his girdle. 5 And Dauid went out, whither ſoeuer Saul ſent him,
and behaued himſelfe wiſely: and Saul ſet him ouer the men of warre,
and he was accepted in the ſight of all the people, and alſo in the ſight
of Sauls ſeruants. 6 And it came to paſſe as they came when Dauid was
returned from the ſlaughter of the Philiſtine, that the women came out
of all cities of Iſrael, ſinging and dancing, to meete king Saul, with
tabrets, with ioy, and with inſtruments of muſicke. 7 And the women
anſwered one another as they played, and ſaid, Saul hath ſlaine his
thouſands, and Dauid his ten thouſands. 8 And Saul was very wroth, and
the ſaying diſpleaſed him, and he ſayd, They haue aſcribed vnto Dauid
tenne thouſands, and to me they haue aſcribed but thouſands: and what
can he haue more, but the kingdome? 9 And Saul eyed Dauid from that
day, and forward. 10 And it came to paſſe on the morrow, that the euill
ſpirit from God came vpon Saul, and he prophecied in the midſt of the
houſe: and Dauid played with his hand, as at other times: and there was
a iauelin in Sauls hand. 11 And Saul caſt the iauelin; for hee ſaid, I will
ſmite Dauid euen to the wall with it: and Dauid auoided out of his
preſence twice. 12 And Saul was afraid of Dauid, becauſe the Lord was
with him, and was departed from Saul. 13 Therefore Saul remooued him
from him, and made him his captaine ouer a thouſand, and hee went
out and came in before the people. 14 And Dauid behaued himſelfe wiſely
in all his wayes; & the Lord was with him. 15 Wherefore when Saul ſaw
that hee behaued himſelfe very wiſely, hee was afraid of him. 16 But all
Iſrael and Iudah loued Dauid, becauſe hee went out and came in before
them. 17 And Saul ſaid to Dauid, Behold, my elder daughter Merab, her
will I giue thee to wife: onely be thou valiant for me, and fight the Lords
battels: for Saul ſaid, Let not mine hand be vpon him, but let the hand
of the Philiſtines be vpon him. 18 And Dauid ſaid vnto Saul, Who am I?
and what is my life, or my fathers family in Iſrael, that I ſhould be ſonne
in law to the king? 19 But it came to paſſe at the time when Merab Sauls
daughter ſhould haue beene giuen to Dauid, that ſhee was giuen vnto
Adriel the Meholathite to wife. 20 And Michal Sauls daughter loued
Dauid: and they tolde Saul, and the thing pleaſed him. 21 And Saul ſaid, I
will giue him her, that ſhe may be a ſnare to him, and that the hand of
the Philiſtines may be againſt him. Wherefore Saul ſaid to Dauid, Thou
ſhalt this day be my ſonne in law, in the one of the twaine. 22 And Saul
commanded his ſeruants, ſaying, Commune with Dauid ſecretly, and ſay,
Behold, the king hath delight in thee, and all his ſeruants loue thee: now
therefore be the kings ſonne in law. 23 And Sauls ſeruants ſpake thoſe
wordes in the eares of Dauid: And Dauid ſaid, Seemeth it to you a light
thing to be a kings ſonne in law, ſeeing that I am a poore man, and lightly
eſteemed? 24 And the ſeruants of Saul tolde him, ſaying; On this manner
ſpake Dauid. 25 And Saul ſaid, Thus ſhall yee ſay to Dauid, The King
deſireth not any dowrie, but an hundred foreſkinnes of the Philiſtines,
to be auenged of the kings enemies. But Saul thought to make Dauid fal
by the hand of the Philiſtines. 26 And when his ſeruants told Dauid theſe
wordes, it pleaſed Dauid well to be the kings ſonne in lawe: and the
dayes were not expired. 27 Wherefore Dauid aroſe, hee and his men, and
ſlew of the Philiſtines two hundred men, and Dauid brought their
foreſkinnes, and they gaue them in full tale to the king, that hee might
be the kings ſonne in law: and Saul gaue him Michal his daughter to
wife. 28 And Saul ſaw and knew that the Lord was with Dauid, and that
Michal Sauls daughter loued him. 29 And Saul was yet the more afraid of
Dauid; and Saul became Dauids enemie continually. 30 Then the Princes
of the Philiſtines went foorth: and it came to paſſe after they went
foorth, that Dauid behaued himſelfe more wiſely then all the ſeruants of
Saul, ſo that his name was much ſet by.
CHAPTER 19 1 And Saul ſpake to Ionathan his ſonne, and to all his
ſeruants, that they ſhould kill Dauid. 2 But Ionathan Sauls ſonne delighted
much in Dauid, and Ionathan told Dauid, ſaying, Saul my father ſeeketh
to kill thee: Now therefore, I pray thee, take heed to thy ſelfe vntill the
morning, and abide in a ſecret place, and hide thy ſelfe: 3 And I will goe
out and ſtand beſide my father in the field where thou art, and I will
commune with my father of thee, and what I ſee, that I will tell
thee. 4 And Ionathan ſpake good of Dauid vnto Saul his father, and ſaid
vnto him, Let not the King ſinne againſt his ſeruant, againſt Dauid:
becauſe hee hath not ſinned againſt thee, and becauſe his workes haue
bene to thee ward very good. 5 For he did put his life in his hand, and
ſlew the Philiſtine, & the Lord wrought a great ſaluation for all Iſrael:
thou ſaweſt it, and didſt reioyce: Wherefore then wilt thou ſinne againſt
innocent blood, to ſlay Dauid without a cauſe? 6 And Saul hearkened
vnto the voyce of Ionathan; and Saul ſware, As the Lord liueth, he ſhall
not be ſlaine. 7 And Ionathan called Dauid, and Ionathan ſhewed him all
thoſe things: and Ionathan brought Dauid to Saul, and he was in his
preſence, as in times paſt. 8 And there was warre againe, and Dauid went
out, and fought with the Philiſtines, and ſlew them with a great ſlaughter,
& they fled from him. 9 And the euill ſpirit from the Lord was vpon Saul,
as he ſate in his houſe with his iauelin in his hand: and Dauid played
with his hand. 10 And Saul ſought to ſmite Dauid euen to the wall with
the iauelin: but hee ſlipt away out of Sauls preſence, and he ſmote the
iauelin into the wall: and Dauid fled, and eſcaped that night. 11 Saul alſo
ſent meſſengers vnto Dauids houſe, to watch him, and to ſlay him in the
morning: and Michal Dauids wife tolde him, ſaying, If thou ſaue not thy
life to night, to morrow thou ſhalt be ſlaine. 12 So Michal let Dauid downe
thorow a window: and hee went and fled, and eſcaped. 13 And Michal
tooke an image, and laid it in the bedde, and put a pillow of goats haire
for his bolſter, and couered it with a cloth. 14 And when Saul ſent
meſſengers to take Dauid, ſhe ſaid, He is ſicke. 15 And Saul ſent the
meſſengers againe to ſee Dauid, ſaying, Bring him vp to me in the bedde,
that I may ſlay him. 16 And when the meſſengers were come in, behold,
there was an image in the bed, with a pillow of goates haire for his
bolſter. 17 And Saul ſaid vnto Michal, Why haſt thou deceiued me ſo, and
ſent away mine enemie, that he is eſcaped? And Michal anſwered Saul,
Hee ſaid vnto me, Let mee goe; Why ſhould I kill thee? 18 So Dauid
fledde, and eſcaped, and came to Samuel to Ramah, and told him all that
Saul had done to him: and hee and Samuel went, and dwelt in
Naioth. 19 And it was told Saul, ſaying, Behold, Dauid is at Naioth in
Ramah. 20 And Saul ſent meſſengers to take Dauid: and when they ſawe
the company of the Prophets prophecying, and Samuel ſtanding as
appointed ouer them, the Spirit of God was vpon the meſſengers of
Saul, and they alſo prophecied. 21 And when it was tolde Saul, he ſent
other meſſengers, and they prophecied likewiſe: and Saul ſent
meſſengers againe the third time, and they prophecied alſo. 22 Then went
hee alſo to Ramah, and came to a great well that is in Sechu: and he

aſked, and ſaid, Where are Samuel and Dauid? And one ſaid, Behold, they be at Naioth in Ramah.23And hee went thither to Naioth in Ramah: and the Spirit of God was vpon him alſo, and he went on and prophecied vntill hee came to Naioth in Ramah:24And he ſtript off his clothes alſo, and prophecied before Samuel in like manner, and lay downe naked all that day, and all that night: wherefore they ſay, Is Saul alſo among the Prophets?

CHAPTER 201And Dauid fled from Naioth in Ramah, and came and ſaid before Ionathan, What haue I done? what is mine iniquity? and what is my ſinne before thy father, that he ſeeketh my life?2And he ſaid vnto him, God forbid, thou ſhalt not die; beholde, my father will doe nothing, either great or ſmall, but that he will ſhew it me: and why ſhould my father hide this thing from me? it is not ſo.3And Dauid ſware moreouer, and ſaid, Thy father certeinly knoweth that I haue found grace in thine eyes, and he ſayth, Let not Ionathan know this, leſt he be grieued: but truely, as the Lord liueth, and as thy ſoule liueth, there is but a ſtep betweene me & death.4Then ſaid Ionathan vnto Dauid, Whatſoeuer thy ſoule deſireth, I will euen doe it for thee.5And Dauid ſaid vnto Ionathan, Behold, to morrow is the new moone, and I ſhould not faile to ſit with the king at meate: but let me goe, that I may hide my ſelfe in the fields vnto the third day at euen.6If thy father at all miſse me, then ſay, Dauid earneſtly aſked leaue of me that he might runne to Bethlehem his citie: for there is a yeerely ſacrifice there for all the family.7If he ſay thus, It is well, thy ſeruant ſhall haue peace: but if he be very wroth, then be ſure that euill is determined by him.8Therefore thou ſhalt deale kindly with thy ſeruant, for thou haſt brought thy ſeruant into a couenant of the Lord with thee: notwithſtanding, if there be in me iniquitie, ſlay me thy ſelfe: for why ſhouldeſt thou bring me to thy father?9And Ionathan ſaid, Farre be it from thee: for if I knew certainely that euill were determined by my father to come vpon thee, then would not I tell it thee?10Then ſaid Dauid to Ionathan, Who ſhall tell me? or what if thy father anſwere thee roughly?11And Ionathan ſaid vnto Dauid, Come, and let vs goe out into the field. And they went out both of them into the field.12And Ionathan ſaid vnto Dauid, O Lord God of Iſrael, when I haue ſounded my father, about to morrow any time, or the third day, and behold, if there be good toward Dauid, and I then ſend not vnto thee, and ſhew it thee;13The Lord doe ſo and much more to Ionathan: but if it pleaſe my father to doe thee euill, then I wil ſhew it thee, and ſend thee away, that thou mayeſt goe in peace, and the Lord be with thee, as hee hath beene with my father.14And thou ſhalt not onely while yet I liue, ſhew me the kindneſſe of the Lord, that I die not:15But alſo thou ſhalt not cut off thy kindneſſe from my houſe for euer: no not when the Lord hath cut off the enemies of Dauid, euery one from the face of the earth.16So Ionathan made a couenant with the houſe of Dauid, ſaying, Let the Lord euen require it at the hande of Dauids enemies.17And Ionathan cauſed Dauid to ſweare againe, becauſe he loued him: for he loued him as he loued his owne ſoule.18Then Ionathan ſaid to Dauid, To morrow is the newe moone: and thou ſhalt be miſsed, becauſe thy ſeat wil be emptie.19And when thou haſt ſtayed three dayes, then thou ſhalt goe downe quickly, and come to the place where thou diddeſt hide thy ſelfe, when the buſineſse was in hand, and ſhalt remaine by the ſtone Ezel.20And I will ſhoot three arrowes on the ſide thereof, as though I ſhot at a marke.21And behold, I will ſend a ladde, ſaying, Goe, find out the arrowes. If I expreſly ſay vnto the lad, Behold, the arrowes are on this ſide of thee, take them: then come thou, for there is peace to thee, and no hurt, as the Lord liueth.22But if I ſay thus vnto the yong man, Behold, the arrowes are beyond thee: goe thy way, for the Lord hath ſent thee away.23And as touching the matter which thou and I haue ſpoken of, behold, the Lord be betweene thee and mee for euer.24So Dauid hid himſelfe in the field: and when the newe moone was come, the king ſate him downe to eate meate.25And the king ſate vpon his ſeate, as at other times, euen vpon a ſeate by the wall: and Ionathan aroſe, and Abner ſate by Sauls ſide, and Dauids place was emptie.26Neuertheleſſe, Saul ſpake not any thing that day: for hee thought, Some thing hath befallen him, hee is not cleane; ſurely he is not cleane.27And it came to paſſe on the morrow which was the ſecond day of the moneth, that Dauids place was emptie: and Saul ſaid vnto Ionathan his ſonne, Wherefore commeth not the ſonne of Ieſſe to meat, neither yeſterday nor to day?28And Ionathan anſwered Saul, Dauid earneſtly aſked leaue of me, to goe to Bethlehem.29And he ſaid, Let me goe, I pray thee, for our familie hath a ſacrifice in the citie, and my brother, hee hath commanded mee to be there: and now if I haue found fauour in thine eyes, let me get away, I pray thee, and ſee my brethren: Therefore he commeth not vnto the kings table.30Then Sauls anger was kindled againſt Ionathan, and hee ſaid vnto him, Thou ſonne of the peruerſe rebellious woman, doe not I know that thou haſt choſen the ſonne of Ieſſe to thine owne confuſion, and vnto the confuſion of thy mothers nakedneſse?31For as long as the ſonne of Ieſſe liueth vpon the ground, thou ſhalt not be ſtabliſhed, nor thy kingdome: wherefore now ſend and fetch him vnto mee, for he ſhall ſurely die.32And Ionathan anſwered Saul his father, and ſaid vnto him, Wherefore ſhall hee be ſlaine? what hath hee done?33And Saul caſt a iauelin at him to ſmite him, whereby Ionathan knewe that it was determined of his father to ſlay Dauid.34So Ionathan aroſe from the table in fierce anger, and did eate no meat the ſecond day of the moneth: for hee was grieued for Dauid, becauſe his father had done him ſhame.35And it came to paſſe in the morning, that Ionathan went out into the field, at the time appointed with Dauid, and a little ladde with him.36And he ſaid vnto his lad, Runne, finde out now the arrowes which I ſhoote. And as the ladde ranne, he ſhot an arrow beyond him.37And when the ladde was come to the place of the arrow, which Ionathan had ſhot, Ionathan cryed after the ladde, and ſaid, Is not the arrow beyond thee?38And Ionathan cryed after the ladde, Make ſpeed, haſte, ſtay not. And Ionathans ladde gathered vp the arrowes, and came to his maſter.39But the lad knew not any thing: onely Ionathan and Dauid knew the matter.40And Ionathan gaue his artillery vnto his ladde, and ſaid vnto him, Goe, cary them to the citie.41And aſsoone as the ladde was gone, Dauid aroſe out of a place toward the South, and fell on his face to the ground, and bowed himſelfe three times: and they kiſſed one another, and wept one with another, vntill Dauid exceeded.42And Ionathan ſaid to Dauid, Goe in peace, foraſmuch as wee haue ſworne both of vs in the Name of the Lord, ſaying; The Lord be betweene me and thee, and betweene my ſeede and thy ſeede for euer. And hee aroſe, and departed: and Ionathan went into the citie.

CHAPTER 211Then came Dauid to Nob, to Ahimelech the Prieſt, and Ahimelech was afraide at the meeting of Dauid, and ſaid vnto him, Why art thou alone, and no man with thee?2And Dauid ſaid vnto Ahimelech the Prieſt, The king hath commanded me a buſineſse, and hath ſaid vnto me, Let no man know any thing of the buſineſse whereabout I ſend thee, and what I haue commanded thee: and I haue appointed my ſeruants to ſuch and ſuch a place.3Now therefore what is vnder thine hand? giue me fiue loaues of bread in mine hand, or what there is preſent.4And the Prieſt anſwered Dauid, and ſaid, There is no common bread vnder mine hand, but there is hallowed bread: if the young men haue kept themſelues at leaſt from women.5And Dauid anſwered the Prieſt, and ſaid vnto him, Of a trueth women haue beene kept from vs about theſe three dayes, ſince I came out, and the veſſels of the young men are holy, and the bread is in a manner common, yea, though it were ſanctified this day in the veſſell.6So the Prieſt gaue him hallowed bread; for there was no bread there, but the Shewbread that was taken from before the Lord, to put hote bread in the day when it was taken away.7Now a certaine man of the ſeruants of Saul was there that day, detained before the Lord, and his name was Doeg an Edomite, the chiefeſt of the heardmen that belonged to Saul.8And Dauid ſaid vnto Ahimelech, And is there not here vnder thine hand ſpeare or ſword? for I haue neither brought my ſword nor my weapons with mee, becauſe the kings buſineſse required haſte.9And the Prieſt ſaid, The ſword of Goliath the Philiſtine, whome thou ſleweſt in the valley of Elah, behold, it is heere wrapt in a cloth behinde the Ephod: if thou wilt take that, take it; for there is no other ſaue that, here. And Dauid ſaide, There is none like that, giue it me.10And Dauid aroſe, and fled that day, for feare of Saul, and went to Achiſh, the king of Gath.11And the ſeruants of Achiſh ſayd vnto him, Is not this Dauid the king of the land? Did they not ſing one to another of him in daunces, ſaying, Saul hath ſlaine his thouſands, and Dauid his ten thouſands?12And Dauid layd vp theſe wordes in his heart, and was ſore afraid of Achiſh the king of Gath.13And he changed his behauiour before them, and fained himſelfe mad in their hands, and ſcrabled on the doores of the gate, and let his ſpittle fall downe vpon his beard.14Then ſaide Achiſh vnto his ſeruants, Loe, you ſee the man is mad: wherefore then haue yee brought him to mee?15Haue I need of

mad-men, that ye haue brought this fellow to play the mad-man in my
preſence? Shall this fellow come into my houſe?
CHAPTER 22 1Dauid therefore departed thence, and eſcaped to the
caue Adullam: and when his brethren, and all his fathers houſe heard it,
they went downe thither to him. 2And euery one that was in diſtreſſe,
and euery one that was in debt, and euery one that was diſcontented,
gathered themſelues vnto him, and he became a captaine ouer them: and
there were with him about foure hundred men. 3And Dauid went thence
to Mizpeh of Moab; and he ſaid vnto the king of Moab, Let my father,
and my mother, I pray thee, come foorth, and be with you, till I know
what God will doe for me. 4And he brought them before the king of
Moab: and they dwelt with him all the while that Dauid was in the
hold. 5And the Prophet Gad ſaid vnto Dauid, Abide not in the hold;
depart, and get thee into the land of Iudah. Then Dauid departed, and
came into the forreſt of Hareth. 6When Saul heard that Dauid was
diſcouered, and the men that were with him: (now Saul abode in Gibeah
vnder a tree in Ramah, hauing his ſpeare in his hand, and all his ſeruants
were ſtanding about him.) 7Then Saul ſaide vnto his ſeruants that ſtood
about him, Heare now, ye Beniamites: Will the ſonne of Ieſſe giue euery
one of you fields, and Uineyards, and make you all captaines of
thouſands, and captaines of hundreds: 8That all of you haue conſpired
againſt me, and there is none that ſheweth mee, that my ſonne hath
made a league with the ſonne of Ieſſe, and there is none of you that is
ſory for me, or ſheweth vnto me that my ſonne hath ſtirred vp my
ſeruant againſt me, to lye in wait, as at this day? 9Then anſwered Doeg
the Edomite, (which was ſet ouer the ſeruants of Saul) and ſaide, I ſaw
the ſonne of Ieſſe comming to Nob, to Ahimelech the ſonne of
Ahitub. 10And hee enquired of the Lord for him, and gaue him victuals,
and gaue him the ſword of Goliath the Philiſtine. 11Then the king ſent to
call Ahimelech the Prieſt, the ſonne of Ahitub, and all his fathers houſe,
the Prieſts that were in Nob: and they came all of them to the king. 12And
Saul ſaid, Heare now thou ſonne of Ahitub: and hee anſwered, Here I
am, my lord. 13And Saul ſaide vnto him, Why haue ye conſpired againſt
me, thou and the ſonne of Ieſſe, in that thou haſt giuen him bread, and
a ſword, and haſt enquired of God for him, that he ſhould riſe againſt
mee, to lye in waite, as at this day? 14Then Ahimelech anſwered the king,
and ſaid, And who is ſo faithfull among all thy ſeruants, as Dauid, which
is the kings ſonne in law, and goeth at thy bidding, and is honourable in
thine houſe? 15Did I then beginne to enquire of God for him? be it farre
from mee: let not the king impute any thing vnto his ſeruant, nor to all
the houſe of my father: for thy ſeruant knew nothing of all this, leſſe or
more. 16And the king ſaide, Thou ſhalt ſurely die, Ahimelech, thou, and
all thy fathers houſe. 17And the king ſaid vnto the footmen that ſtood
about him, Turne and ſlay the Prieſts of the Lord, becauſe their hand
alſo is with Dauid, and becauſe they knew when he fled, and did not
ſhew it to mee. But the ſeruants of the king would not put foorth their
hand to fall vpon the Prieſtes of the Lord. 18And the king ſaid to Doeg,
Turne thou and fall vpon the Prieſts. And Doeg the Edomite turned,
and hee fell vpon the Prieſts, and ſlew on that day foure ſcore and fiue
perſons that did weare a linnen Ephod. 19And Nob the citie of the Prieſts
ſmote he with the edge of the ſword, both men and women, children
and ſucklings, and oxen and aſſes, and ſheepe, with the edge of the
ſword. 20And one of the ſonnes of Ahimelech, the ſonne of Ahitub,
named Abiathar, eſcaped and fled after Dauid: 21And Abiathar ſhewed
Dauid that Saul had ſlaine the Lords Prieſts. 22And Dauid ſaid vnto
Abiathar, I knew it that day, when Doeg the Edomite was there, that he
would ſurely tell Saul: I haue occaſioned the death of all the perſons of
thy fathers houſe. 23Abide thou with me, feare not: for he that ſeeketh
my life, ſeeketh thy life: but with me thou ſhalt bee in ſafegard.
CHAPTER 23 1Then they told Dauid, ſaying, Beholde, the Philiſtines
fight againſt Keilah, and they rob the threſhing floores. 2Therefore Dauid
enquired of the Lord, ſaying, Shall I go and ſmite theſe Philiſtines? And
the Lord ſaid vnto Dauid, Goe, and ſmite the Philiſtines, and ſaue
Keilah. 3And Dauids men ſaid vnto him, Behold, we be afraid here in
Iudah: how much more then if wee come to Keilah againſt the armies
of the Philiſtines? 4Then Dauid enquired of the Lord yet againe: And the
Lord anſwered him, and ſaid, Ariſe, go down to Keilah: for I will deliuer
the Philiſtines into thine hand. 5So Dauid and his men went to Keilah,
and fought with the Philiſtins, and brought away their cattell, and ſmote
them with a great ſlaughter: ſo Dauid ſaued the inhabitants of
Keilah. 6And it came to paſſe when Abiathar the ſonne of Ahimelech
fled to Dauid to Keilah, that hee came downe with an Ephod in his
hand. 7And it was told Saul that Dauid was come to Keilah: and Saul
ſaid, God hath deliuered him into mine hand: for he is ſhut in, by entring
into a towne that hath gates and barres. 8And Saul called all the people
together to warre, to goe downe to Keilah, to beſiege Dauid, and his
men. 9And Dauid knewe that Saul ſecretly practiſed miſchiefe againſt
him, and hee ſaid to Abiathar the Prieſt, Bring hither the Ephod. 10Then
ſaide Dauid, O Lord God of Iſrael, thy ſeruant hath certainly heard that
Saul ſeeketh to come to Keilah, to deſtroy the citie for my ſake. 11Will
the men of Keilah deliuer me vp into his hande? will Saul come downe,
as thy ſeruant hath heard, O Lord God of Iſrael? I beſeech thee tell thy
ſeruant. And the Lord ſaid, He will come downe. 12Then ſaid Dauid, Will
the men of Keilah deliuer me, and my men, into the hand of Saul? And
the Lord ſaid, They will deliuer thee vp. 13Then Dauid and his men,
which were about ſixe hundred, aroſe, and departed out of Keilah, and
went whitherſoeuer they could goe: and it was told Saul that Dauid was
eſcaped from Keilah, and hee forbare to goe foorth. 14And Dauid abode
in the wilderneſſe in ſtrong holds, and remained in a mountaine in the
wildernes of Ziph: and Saul ſought him euery day, but God deliuered
him not into his hand. 15And Dauid ſaw that Saul was come out to ſeeke
his life: and Dauid was in the wildernes of Ziph in a wood. 16And
Ionathan Sauls ſonne aroſe, & went to Dauid into the wood, and
ſtrengthened his hand in God. 17And he ſaid vnto him, Feare not; for
the hand of Saul my father ſhall not finde thee, and thou ſhalt be king
ouer Iſrael, and I ſhall be next vnto thee: and that alſo Saul my father
knoweth. 18And they two made a couenant before the Lord: and Dauid
abode in the wood, and Ionathan went to his houſe. 19Then came vp the
Ziphites to Saul to Gibeah, ſaying, Doth not Dauid hide himſelfe with
vs in ſtrong holds in the wood, in the hill of Hachilah, which is on the
South of Ieſhimon? 20Now therefore, O king, come downe according to
all the deſire of thy ſoule to come downe, and our part ſhall be to deliuer
him into the kings hand. 21And Saul ſaid, Bleſſed be yee of the Lord, for
yee haue compaſſion on me. 22Goe, I pray you, prepare yet, and know,
and ſee his place where his haunt is, and who hath ſeene him there: for
it is told mee that he dealeth very ſubtilly. 23ſee therefore, and take
knowledge of all the lurking places where he hideth himſelfe, and come
ye againe to me with the certainty, and I will goe with you: and it ſhall
come to paſſe, if he be in the land, that I will ſearch him out throughout
all the thouſands of Iudah. 24And they aroſe, & went to Ziph before Saul:
but Dauid and his men were in the wilderneſſe of Maon, in the plaine
on the South of Ieſhimon. 25Saul alſo and his men went to ſeeke him,
and they told Dauid: wherefore he came downe into a rocke, and abode
in the wilderneſſe of Maon: and when Saul heard that, he purſued after
Dauid in the wildernes of Maon. 26And Saul went on this ſide of the
mountaine, and Dauid and his men on that ſide of the mountaine: and
Dauid made haſte to get away for feare of Saul: for Saul and his men
compaſſed Dauid and his men round about to take them. 27But there
came a meſſenger vnto Saul, ſaying, Haſte thee, and come: for the
Philiſtines haue inuaded the land. 28Wherefore Saul returned from
purſuingafter Dauid, & went againſt the Philiſtines; therefore they called
that place Sela-Hammahlekoth. 29And Dauid went vp from thence, and
dwelt in ſtrong holds at En-gedi.
CHAPTER 24 1And it came to paſſe when Saul was returned from
folowing the Philiſtines, that it was told him, ſaying, Behold, Dauid is in
the wilderneſſe En-gedi. 2Then Saul tooke three thouſand choſen men
out of all Iſrael, and went to ſeeke Dauid and his men vpon the rockes
of the wilde goates. 3And hee came to the ſheepe coates by the way,
where was a caue, and Saul went in to couer his feete: and Dauid and
his men remained in the ſides of the caue. 4And the men of Dauid ſayd
vnto him, Beholde the day of which the Lord ſayd vnto thee, Behold, I
wil deliuer thine enemy into thine hand, that thou mayeſt doe to him as
it ſhall ſeeme good vnto thee. Then Dauid aroſe, and cut off the ſkirt of
Sauls robe priuily. 5And it came to paſſe afterward, that Dauids heart
ſmote him, becauſe he had cut off Sauls ſkirt. 6And hee ſayd vnto his
men, The Lord forbid that I ſhould doe this thing vnto my maſter the
Lords Anoynted, to ſtretch forth mine hand againſt him, ſeeing he is the
Anoynted of the Lord. 7So Dauid ſtayed his ſeruants with theſe wordes,
and ſuffered them not to riſe againſt Saul: but Saul roſe vp out of the
caue, and went on his way. 8Dauid alſo roſe afterward, and went out of

the caue, and cryed after Saul, ſaying, My lord the king. And when Saul looked behinde him, Dauid ſtouped with his face to the earth, and bowed himſelfe.9And Dauid ſaid to Saul, Wherfore heareſt thou mens words, ſaying, Behold, Dauid ſeeketh thy hurt?10Behold, this day thine eyes haue ſeene, how that the Lord had deliuered thee to day into mine hand in the caue: and ſome bade me kill thee, but mine eye ſpared thee, and I ſaid, I will not put foorth mine hand againſt my lord, for hee is the Lords Anointed.11Moreouer my father, See, yea ſee the ſkirt of thy robe in my hand: for in that I cut off the ſkirt of thy robe, and killed thee not, know thou and ſee, that there is neither euill nor tranſgreſſion in mine hand, and I haue not ſinned againſt thee; yet thou hunteſt my ſoule, to take it.12The Lord iudge betweene me and thee, and the Lord auenge me of thee: but mine hand ſhall not be vpon thee.13As ſaith the prouerbe of the ancients, Wickedneſſe proceedeth from the wicked: but mine hand ſhall not be vpon thee.14After whom is the king of Iſrael come out? after whom doeſt thou purſue? After a dead dogge, after a flea.15The Lord therfore be Iudge, and iudge betweene me and thee, and ſee, and plead my cauſe, and deliuer me out of thine hand.16And it came to paſſe when Dauid had made an ende of ſpeaking theſe words vnto Saul, that Saul ſaid, Is this thy voice, my ſonne Dauid? And Saul lift vp his voice, and wept.17And he ſaid to Dauid, Thou art more righteous then I: for thou haſt rewarded mee good, whereas I haue rewarded thee euill.18And thou haſt ſhewed this day how that thou haſt dealt well with me: foraſmuch as when the Lord had deliuered me into thine hand, thou killedſt me not.19For if a man finde his enemie, will hee let him goe well away? wherefore the Lord reward thee good, for that thou haſt done vnto me this day.20And now behold, I know well that thou ſhalt ſurely be King, and that the kingdome of Iſrael ſhall be eſtabliſhed in thine hand.21Sweare now therefore vnto me by the Lord, that thou wilt not cut off my ſeede after mee, and that thou wilt not deſtroy my name out of my fathers houſe.22And Dauid ſware vnto Saul, and Saul went home: but Dauid and his men gate them vp vnto the holde.

CHAPTER 251And Samuel died, and all the Iſraelites were gathered together, and lamented him, and buried him in his houſe at Ramah. And Dauid aroſe, & went downe to the wilderneſſe of Paran.2And there was a man in Maon, whoſe poſſeſſions were in Carmel, and the man was very great, and hee had three thouſand ſheepe, and a thouſand goates: and he was ſhearing his ſheepe in Carmel.3Now the name of the man was Nabal, and the name of his wife, Abigail: and ſhee was a woman of good vnderſtanding, and of a beautifull countenance: but the man was churliſh and euill in his doings, and hee was of the houſe of Caleb.4And Dauid heard in the wilderneſſe, that Nabal did ſheare his ſheepe.5And Dauid ſent out ten yong men, and Dauid ſaid vnto the young men, Get you vp to Carmel, and goe to Nabal, and greete him in my name;6And thus ſhall ye ſay to him that liueth in proſperitie, Peace be both to thee, and peace be to thine houſe, and peace be vnto all that thou haſt.7And now, I haue heard that thou haſt ſhearers: now thy ſhepheards which were with vs, wee hurt them not, neither was there ought miſsing vnto them, all the while they were in Carmel.8Aſke thy yong men, and they will ſhew thee: wherefore let the yong men finde fauour in thine eyes: (for we come in a good day) giue, I pray thee, whatſoeuer commeth to thine hand, vnto thy ſeruants, and to thy ſonne Dauid.9And when Dauids yong men came, they ſpake to Nabal according to all thoſe words in the name of Dauid, and ceaſed.10And Nabal anſwered Dauids ſeruants, and ſaid, Who is Dauid? and who is the ſonne of Ieſſe? There bee many ſeruants now a daies that breake away euery man from his maſter.11Shall I then take my bread and my water, and my fleſh that I haue killed for my ſhearers, and giue it vnto men, whom I know not whence they bee?12So Dauids yong men turned their way, and went againe, and came and told him all thoſe ſayings.13And Dauid ſaid vnto his men, Gird you on euery man his ſword. And they girded on euery man his ſword, and Dauid alſo girded on his ſword: and there went vp after Dauid about foure hundred men, and two hundred abode by the ſtuffe.14But one of the yong men told Abigail Nabals wife, ſaying, Behold, Dauid ſent meſſengers out of the wilderneſſe to ſalute our maſter: and he railed on them.15But the men were very good vnto vs, and we were not hurt, neither miſsed we any thing as long as wee were conuerſant with them, when we were in the fields.16They were a wall vnto vs both by night and day, all the while we were with them keeping ſheepe.17Now therefore know and conſider what thou wilt doe: for euill is determined againſt our maſter, and againſt all his houſhold: for he is ſuch a ſonne of Belial, that a man cannot ſpeake to him.18Then Abigail made haſte, and tooke two hundred loaues, and two bottles of wine, and fiue ſheepe readie dreſſed, and fiue meaſures of parched corne, and an hundred cluſters of raiſins, and two hundred cakes of figges, and laid them on aſſes.19And ſhe ſaid vnto her ſeruants, Goe on before me, behold, I come after you: but ſhe told not her huſband Nabal.20And it was ſo as ſhe rode on the aſſe, that ſhe came downe by the couert of the hill, and behold, Dauid and his men came downe againſt her, and ſhe met them.21(Now Dauid had ſaid, Surely in vaine haue I kept all that this fellow hath in the wilderneſſe, ſo that nothing was miſsed of all that pertained vnto him: and he hath requited me euil for good.22So and more alſo doe God vnto the enemies of Dauid, if I leaue of all that pertaine to him by the morning light, any that piſseth againſt the wall.)23And when Abigail ſaw Dauid, ſhe haſted, and lighted off the aſſe, and fell before Dauid on her face, and bowed her ſelfe to the ground,24And fell at his feet, and ſaid, Upon me, my lord, vpon me let this iniquitie be, and let thine handmaid, I pray thee, ſpeake in thine audience, and heare the words of thine handmaid.25Let not my lord, I pray thee, regard this man of Belial, euen Nabal: for as his name is, ſo is he: Nabal is his name, and folly is with him: But I thine handmaid ſaw not the yong men of my lord, whom thou didſt ſend.26Now therefore, my lord, as the Lord liueth, and as thy ſoule liueth, ſeeing the Lord hath withholden thee from comming to ſhed blood, and from auenging thy ſelfe with thine owne hand: now let thine enemies and they that ſeeke euill to my lord, bee as Nabal.27And now this bleſſing which thine handmaid hath brought vnto my lord, let it euen be giuen vnto the yong men that follow my lord.28I pray thee, forgiue the treſpaſſe of thine handmaide: for the Lord will certainely make my lord a ſure houſe, becauſe my lord fighteth the battels of the Lord, and euill hath not bene found in thee all thy dayes.29Yet a man is riſen to purſue thee, and to ſeeke thy ſoule: but the ſoule of my lord ſhall be bound in the bundle of life with the Lord thy God, and the ſoules of thine enemies, them ſhall he ſling out, as out of the middle of a ſling.30And it ſhall come to paſſe when the Lord ſhal haue done to my lord, according to all the good that hee hath ſpoken concerning thee, and ſhall haue appointed thee ruler ouer Iſrael;31That this ſhall bee no griefe vnto thee, nor offence of heart vnto my lord, either that thou haſt ſhed blood cauſeleſſe, or that my lord hath auenged himſelfe: But when the Lord ſhall haue dealt well with my lord, then remember thine handmayd.32And Dauid ſayd to Abigail, Bleſſed be the Lord God of Iſrael, which ſent thee this day to meet me.33And bleſſed bee thy aduice, and bleſſed be thou, which haſt kept me this day from comming to ſhed blood, and from auenging my ſelfe with mine owne hand.34For in very deed, as the Lord God of Iſrael liueth, which hath kept mee backe from hurting thee, except thou hadſt haſted and come to meet me, ſurely there had not bene left vnto Nabal, by the morning light, any that piſseth againſt the wall.35So Dauid receiued of her hand that which ſhee had brought him, and ſayd vnto her, Goe vp in peace to thine houſe; See, I haue hearkened to thy voyce, and haue accepted thy perſon.36And Abigail came to Nabal, and behold, he held a feaſt in his houſe like the feaſt of a king; & Nabals heart was merry within him, for hee was very drunken: wherefore ſhee tolde him nothing, leſſe or more, vntill the morning light.37But it came to paſſe in the morning, when the wine was gone out of Nabal, and his wife had told him theſe things, that his heart died within him, and he became as a ſtone.38And it came to paſſe about ten dayes after, that the Lord ſmote Nabal, that he died.39And when Dauid heard that Nabal was dead, he ſaid, Bleſſed be the Lord, that hath pleaded the cauſe of my reproch from the hand of Nabal, and hath kept his ſeruant from euil: for the Lord hath returned the wickedneſſe of Nabal vpon his owne head. And Dauid ſent, and communed with Abigail, to take her to him to wife.40And when the ſeruants of Dauid were come to Abigail to Carmel, they ſpake vnto her, ſaying, Dauid ſent vs vnto thee, to take thee to him to wife.41And ſhee aroſe, and bowed her ſelfe on her face to the earth, and ſayd, Beholde, let thine handmayd bee a ſeruant to waſh the feet of the ſeruants of my lord.42And Abigail haſted, and roſe, and rode vpon an aſſe, with fiue damoſels of hers that went after her; and ſhe went after the meſſengers of Dauid, and became his wife.43Dauid alſo tooke Ahinoam of Iezreel, and they were alſo both of them his wiues.44But

Saul had giuen Michal his daughter, Dauids wife, to Phalti the ſonne of Laiſh, which was of Gallim.

CHAPTER 26 1And the Ziphites came vnto Saul to Gibeah, ſaying, Doeth not Dauid hide himſelfe in the hill of Hachilah, which is before Ieſhimon? 2Then Saul aroſe, and went downe to the wilderneſſe of Ziph, hauing three thouſand choſen men of Iſrael with him, to ſeeke Dauid in the wilderneſſe of Ziph. 3And Saul pitched in the hill of Hachilah, which is before Ieſhimon by the way: but Dauid abode in the wilderneſſe, and he ſaw that Saul came after him into the wilderneſſe. 4Dauid therefore ſent out ſpies, and vnderſtood that Saul was come in very deed. 5And Dauid aroſe, and came to the place where Saul had pitched: and Dauid beheld the place where Saul lay, and Abner the ſonne of Ner the captaine of his hoſte: and Saul lay in the trench, and the people pitched round about him. 6Then anſwered Dauid, and ſayd to Ahimelech the Hittite, and to Abiſhai the ſonne of Zeruiah brother to Ioab, ſaying, Who will goe downe with me to Saul to the campe? And Abiſhai ſayd, I will goe downe with thee. 7So Dauid and Abiſhai came to the people by night, and behold, Saul lay ſleeping within the trench, and his ſpeare ſtucke in the ground at his bolſter: but Abner and the people lay round about him. 8Then ſaid Abiſhai to Dauid, God hath deliuered thine enemie into thine hand this day: now therefore let mee ſmite him, I pray thee, with the ſpeare, euen to the earth at once, and I will not ſmite him the ſecond time. 9And Dauid ſayd to Abiſhai, Deſtroy him not: for who can ſtretch forth his hand againſt the Lords Anointed, and be guiltleſſe? 10Dauid ſaid furthermore, As the Lord liueth, the Lord ſhal ſmite him, or his day ſhall come to die, or hee ſhall deſcend into battell, and periſh. 11The Lord forbid that I ſhould ſtretch foorth mine hand againſt the Lords Anointed: but I pray thee, take thou now the ſpeare that is at his bolſter, and the cruſe of water, and let vs goe. 12So Dauid tooke the ſpeare and the cruſe of water from Sauls bolſter, and they gate them away, and no man ſaw it, nor knew it, neither awaked: for they were all aſleepe, becauſe a deepe ſleepe from the Lord was fallen vpon them. 13Then Dauid went ouer to the other ſide, and ſtood on the toppe of an hill afarre off (a great ſpace being betweene them:) 14And Dauid cryed to the people, and to Abner the ſonne of Ner, ſaying, Anſwereſt thou not, Abner? Then Abner anſwered, and ſayd, Who art thou that cryeſt to the King? 15And Dauid ſaid to Abner, Art not thou a valiant man? and who is like to thee in Iſrael? Wherefore then haſt thou not kept thy lord the king? for there came one of the people in, to deſtroy the king thy lord. 16This thing is not good that thou haſt done: as the Lord liueth, ye are worthy to die, becauſe yee haue not kept your maſter the Lords Anointed: and now ſee where the Kings ſpeare is, and the cruſe of water that was at his bolſter. 17And Saul knew Dauids voyce, and ſaid, Is this thy voice, my ſonne Dauid? And Dauid ſaide, It is my voice, my lord, O king. 18And he ſaid, Wherefore doeth my lord thus purſue after his ſeruant? for what haue I done? or what euill is in mine hand? 19Now therefore, I pray thee, let my lord the king heare the words of his ſeruant: If the Lord haue ſtirred thee vp againſt mee, let him accept an offering: but if they be the children of men, curſed be they before the Lord: for they haue driuen me out this day from abiding in the inheritance of the Lord, ſaying, Goe ſerue other gods. 20Now therefore, let not my blood fall to the earth before the face of the Lord: for the king of Iſrael is come out to ſeeke a flea, as when one doeth hunt a partridge in the mountaines. 21Then ſaid Saul, I haue ſinned: Returne, my ſonne Dauid, for I will no more doe thee harme, becauſe my ſoule was precious in thine eyes this day: behold, I haue played the foole, and haue erred exceedingly. 22And Dauid anſwered, and ſayd, Behold the kings ſpeare, and let one of the yong men come ouer and fetch it. 23The Lord render to euery man his righteouſneſſe, and his faithfulneſse: for the Lord deliuered thee into my hand to day, but I would not ſtretch foorth mine hand againſt the Lords Anointed. 24And behold, as thy life was much ſet by this day in mine eyes: ſo let my life bee much ſet by in the eyes of the Lord, and let him deliuer me out of all tribulation. 25Then Saul ſaid to Dauid, Bleſſed be thou, my ſonne Dauid: thou ſhalt both doe great things, and alſo ſhalt ſtill preuaile. So Dauid went on his way, and Saul returned to his place.

CHAPTER 27 1And Dauid ſayd in his heart, I ſhall now periſh one day by the hand of Saul: there is nothing better for me, then that I ſhould ſpeedily eſcape into the land of the Philiſtines; and Saul ſhal deſpaire of me, to ſeeke me any more in any coaſt of Iſrael: ſo ſhall I eſcape out of his hand. 2And Dauid aroſe, and hee paſſed ouer with the ſixe hundred men that were with him, vnto Achiſh the ſonne of Maoch king of Gath. 3And Dauid dwelt with Achiſh at Gath, he, and his men, euery man with his houſhold, euen Dauid with his two wiues, Ahinoam the Iezreelitefſe, and Abigail the Carmelitefse Nabals wife. 4And it was told Saul, that Dauid was fled to Gath, and he ſought no more againe for him. 5And Dauid ſaid vnto Achiſh, If I haue now found grace in thine eyes, let them giue mee a place in ſome towne in the countrey, that I may dwel there: for why ſhould thy ſeruant dwell in the royall citie with thee? 6Then Achiſh gaue him Ziklag that day: wherfore Ziklag pertaineth vnto the kings of Iudah vnto this day. 7And the time that Dauid dwelt in the countrey of the Philiſtines, was a full yeere, and foure moneths. 8And Dauid and his men went vp and inuaded the Geſhurites, and the Gezrites, and the Amalekites: for thoſe nations were of old the inhabitants of the land, as thou goeſt to Shur, euen vnto the land of Egypt. 9And Dauid ſmote the land, and left neither man nor woman aliue, and tooke away the ſheepe, and the oxen, and the aſſes, and the camels, and the apparell, and returned, and came to Achiſh. 10And Achiſh ſaid, Whither haue ye made a rode to day? And Dauid ſaid, Againſt the South of Iudah, and againſt the South of the Ierahmeelites, and againſt the South of the Kenites. 11And Dauid ſaued neither man nor woman aliue, to bring tidings to Gath, ſaying, Leſt they ſhould tell on vs, ſaying, So did Dauid, and ſo will be his maner, all the while he dwelleth in the countrey of the Philiſtines. 12And Achiſh beleeued Dauid, ſaying, Hee hath made his people Iſrael vtterly to abhorre him, therefore hee ſhall be my ſeruant for euer.

CHAPTER 28 1And it came to paſſe in thoſe dayes, that the Philiſtines gathered their armies together for warfare, to fight with Iſrael: And Achiſh ſaid vnto Dauid, Knowe thou aſsuredly, that thou ſhalt goe out with me to battell, thou, and thy men. 2And Dauid ſaid to Achiſh, Surely thou ſhalt know what thy ſeruant can doe. And Achiſh ſaid to Dauid, Therfore will I make thee keeper of mine head for euer. 3Now Samuel was dead, and all Iſrael had lamented him, and buried him in Ramah, euen in his owne citie: and Saul had put away thoſe that had familiar ſpirits, and the wyzards, out of the land. 4And the Philiſtines gathered themſelues together, and came and pitched in Shunem: and Saul gathered all Iſrael together, and they pitched in Gilboa. 5And when Saul ſaw the hoſte of the Philiſtines, he was afraid, and his heart greatly trembled. 6And when Saul enquired of the Lord, the Lord anſwered him not, neither by dreames, nor by Urim, nor by Prophets. 7Then ſaid Saul vnto his ſeruants, Seeke me a woman that hath a familiar ſpirit, that I may goe to her, and enquire of her. And his ſeruant ſaid to him, Beholde, there is a woman that hath a familiar ſpirit at Endor. 8And Saul diſguiſed himſelfe, and put on other raiment, and hee went, and two men with him, and they came to the woman by night, and he ſaid, I pray thee diuine vnto me by the familiar ſpirit, and bring me him vp whom I ſhall name vnto thee. 9And the woman ſaide vnto him, Beholde, thou knoweſt what Saul hath done, how hee hath cut off thoſe that haue familiar ſpirits, and the wyzards out of the land: wherefore then layeſt thou a ſnare for my life, to cauſe me to die? 10And Saul ſware to her by the Lord, ſaying, As the Lord liueth, there ſhall no puniſhment happen to thee for this thing. 11Then ſaid the woman, Whome ſhall I bring vp vnto thee? and he ſaid, Bring me vp Samuel. 12And when the woman ſaw Samuel, ſhe cried with a lowd voyce; and the woman ſpake to Saul, ſaying, Why haſt thou deceiued me? for thou art Saul. 13And the king ſayd vnto her, Be not afraid: for what ſaweſt thou? And the woman ſaid vnto Saul, I ſaw gods aſcending out of the earth. 14And he ſaid vnto her, What forme is he of? And ſhe ſaid, An old man commeth vp, and he is couered with a mantle. And Saul perceiued that it was Samuel, and hee ſtouped with his face to the ground, and bowed himſelfe. 15And Samuel ſaid to Saul, Why haſt thou diſquieted me, to bring me vp? And Saul anſwered, I am ſore diſtreſſed; for the Philiſtins make war againſt me, and God is departed from me, and anſwereth me no more, neither by Prophets, nor by dreames: therefore I haue called thee, that thou mayſt make knowen vnto me, what I ſhall doe. 16Then ſaid Samuel, Wherefore then doeſt thou aſke of mee, ſeeing the Lord is departed from thee, and is become thine enemy? 17And the Lord hath done to him, as hee ſpake by mee: for the Lord hath rent the kingdome out of thine hand, and giuen it to thy neighbour, euen to Dauid: 18Becauſe thou obeiedſt not the voice of the Lord, nor executedſt his fierce wrath vpon Amalek, therefore hath the Lord done this thing vnto thee this day.19Moreouer, the Lord will alſo deliuer Iſrael with thee, into the hand of the Philiſtines: and to morrow ſhalt thou and thy ſonnes bee with mee: the Lord alſo ſhall deliuer the hoſte of Iſrael into the hand of the Philiſtines.20Then Saul fell ſtraightway all along on the earth, and was ſore afraid, becauſe of the words of Samuel, & there was no ſtrength in him: for he had eaten no bread all the day, nor al the night.21And the woman came vnto Saul, and ſaw that he was ſore troubled, and ſayd vnto him, Behold, thine handmayd hath obeyed thy voice, and I haue put my life in my hand, and haue hearkened vnto thy words which thou ſpakeſt vnto me:22Now therefore, I pray thee, hearken thou alſo vnto the voyce of thine handmaid, & let me ſet a morſel of bread before thee; & eat, that thou mayeſt haue ſtrength, when thou goeſt on thy way.23But hee refuſed, and ſaid, I will not eate. But his ſeruants together with the woman compelled him, and he hearkened vnto their voyce: ſo he aroſe from the earth, & ſate vpon the bed.24And the woman had a fat calfe in the houſe, and ſhe haſted, and killed it, and tooke flower and kneaded it, and did bake vnleauened bread thereof.25And ſhe brought it before Saul, and before his ſeruants, and they did eate: then they aroſe vp, and went away that night.

CHAPTER 291Now the Philiſtines gathered together all their armies to Aphek: and the Iſraelites pitched by a fountaine which is in Iezreel.2And the lords of the Philiſtines paſſed on by hundreds, and by thouſands: but Dauid and his men paſſed on in the rere-ward with Achiſh.3Then ſaid the princes of the Philiſtines, What doe theſe Hebrewes here? And Achiſh ſaid vnto the princes of the Philiſtines, Is not this Dauid the ſeruant of Saul the king of Iſrael, which hath bene with me theſe dayes, or theſe yeeres, and I haue found no fault in him ſince he fell vnto me, vnto this day?4And the princes of the Philiſtines were wroth with him, and the princes of the Philiſtines ſaid vnto him, Make this fellow returne, that he may goe againe to his place which thou haſt appointed him, and let him not go downe with vs to battel, leſt in the battell he be an aduerſary to vs: for wherewith ſhould hee reconcile himſelfe vnto his maſter? ſhould it not be with the heads of theſe men?5Is not this Dauid, of whom they ſang one to another in daunces, ſaying, Saul ſlew his thouſands, and Dauid his ten thouſands?6Then Achiſh called Dauid, and ſaid vnto him, Surely, as the Lord liueth, thou haſt bene vpright, and thy going out and thy comming in with me in the hoſte is good in my ſight: for I haue not found euil in thee, ſince the day of thy comming vnto me vnto this day: neuertheles, the lords fauour thee not.7Wherefore now returne and goe in peace, that thou diſpleaſe not the lords of the Philiſtines.8And Dauid ſaid vnto Achiſh, But what haue I done? and what haſt thou found in thy ſeruant ſo long as I haue bene with thee vnto this day, that I may not goe fight againſt the enemies of my lord the king?9And Achiſh anſwered, and ſaid to Dauid, I know that thou art good in my ſight, as an Angel of God: notwithſtanding the Princes of the Philiſtines haue ſaid, Hee ſhall not goe vp with vs to the battell.10Wherfore now riſe vp early in the morning, with thy maſters ſeruants that are come with thee: and aſsoone as yee be vp early in the morning, and haue light, depart.11So Dauid and his men roſe vp early to depart in the morning, to returne into the land of the Philiſtines; and the Philiſtines went vp to Iezreel.

CHAPTER 301And it came to paſſe when Dauid and his men were come to Ziklag on the third day, that the Amalekites had inuaded the South and Ziklag, and ſmitten Ziklag, and burnt it with fire:2And had taken the women captiues, that were therein; they ſlewe not any either great or ſmal, but caried them away, and went on their way.3So Dauid and his men came to the citie, and beholde, it was burnt with fire, and their wiues, and their ſonnes, and their daughters were taken captiues.4Then Dauid and the people that were with him, lift vp their voice, and wept, vntill they had no more power to weepe.5And Dauids two wiues were taken captiues, Ahinoam the Iezreelitefse, and Abigail the wife of Nabal the Carmelite.6And Dauid was greatly diſtreſſed: for the people ſpake of ſtoning him, becauſe the ſoule of all the people was grieued, euery man for his ſonnes, and for his daughters: but Dauid encouraged himſelfe in the Lord his God.7And Dauid ſaid to Abiathar the Prieſt Ahimelechs ſonne, I pray thee, bring mee hither the Ephod: and Abiathar brought thither the Ephod to Dauid.8And Dauid enquired at the Lord, ſaying; Shall I purſue after this troupe? ſhall I ouertake them? And he anſwered him, Purſue, for thou ſhalt ſurely ouertake them, and without faile recouer all.9So Dauid went, hee, and the ſixe hundred men that were with him, and came to the brooke Beſor, where thoſe that were left behinde, ſtayed.10But Dauid purſued, he and foure hundred men: (for two hundred abode behinde, which were ſo faint that they could not goe ouer the brooke Beſor.)11And they found an Egyptian in the field, and brought him to Dauid, and gaue him bread, and he did eate, and they made him drinke water.12And they gaue him a piece of a cake of figges, and two cluſters of raiſins: and when hee had eaten, his ſpirit came againe to him: for hee had eaten no bread, nor drunke any water, three dayes and three nights.13And Dauid ſayde vnto him, To whome belongeſt thou? and whence art thou? And he ſaid, I am a yong man of Egypt, ſeruant to an Amalekite, and my maſter left me, becauſe three dayes agone I fell ſicke.14Wee made an inuaſion vpon the South of the Cherethites, and vpon the coaſt which belongeth to Iudah, and vpon the South of Caleb, and wee burnt Ziklag with fire.15And Dauid ſayde to him, Canſt thou bring me downe to this company? And he ſaid, Sweare vnto me by God, that thou wilt neither kill me, nor deliuer mee into the handes of my maſter, and I will bring thee downe to this company.16And when he had brought him downe, behold, they were ſpread abroad vpon all the earth, eating and drinking, and dauncing, becauſe of all the great ſpoile that they had taken out of the land of the Philiſtines, and out of the land of Iudah.17And Dauid ſmote them from the twilight, euen vnto the euening of the next day: and there eſcaped not a man of them, ſaue foure hundred yong men which rode vpon camels, and fled.18And Dauid recouered all that the Amalekites had caried away: and Dauid reſcued his two wiues.19And there was nothing lacking to them, neither ſmall nor great, neither ſonnes nor daughters, neither ſpoile, nor any thing that they had taken to them: Dauid recouered all.20And Dauid tooke all the flockes, and the herds, which they draue before thoſe other cattell, and ſaid, This is Dauids ſpoile.21And Dauid came to the two hundred men which were ſo faint that they could not follow Dauid, whome they had made alſo to abide at the brook Beſor: and they went forth to meet Dauid, and to meete the people, that were with him; and when Dauid came neere to the people, he ſaluted them.22Then anſwered all the wicked men, and men of Belial, of thoſe that went with Dauid, and ſaid, Becauſe they went not with vs, we wil not giue them ought of the ſpoile, that wee haue recouered, ſaue to euery man his wife and his children, that they may leade them away, and depart.23Then ſaid Dauid, Ye ſhall not do ſo, my brethren, with that which the Lord hath giuen vs, who hath preſerued vs, and deliuered the companie that came againſt vs, into our hand.24For who will hearken vnto you in this matter? But as his part is that goeth downe to the battell, ſo ſhall his part bee that tarieth by the ſtuffe: they ſhall part alike.25And it was ſo from that day forward, that he made it a ſtatute, and an ordinance for Iſrael, vnto this day.26And when Dauid came to Ziklag, hee ſent of the ſpoile vnto the Elders of Iudah, euen to his friends, (ſaying, Behold a Preſent for you, of the ſpoile of the enemies of the Lord)27To them which were in Bethel, and to them which were in South Ramoth, and to them which were in Iattir,28And to them which were in Aroer, and to them which were in Siphmoth, and to them which were in Eſhtemoa,29And to them which were in Rachal, and them which were in the cities of the Ierahmeelites, and to them which were in the cities of the Kenites,30And to them which were in Hormah, and to them which were in Choraſhan, and to them which were in Athach,31And to them which were in Hebron, and to all the places where Dauid himſelfe and his men were wont to haunt.

CHAPTER 311Nowe the Philiſtines fought againſt Iſrael: and the men of Iſrael fled from before the Philiſtines, and fell downe ſlaine in mount Gilboa.2And the Philiſtines followed hard vpon Saul, and vpon his ſonnes, and the Philiſtines ſlewe Ionathan, and Abinadab, and Malchiſhua, Sauls ſonnes.3And the battell went ſore againſt Saul, and the archers hit him, and he was ſore wounded of the archers.4Then ſaid Saul vnto his armour bearer, Draw thy ſword, and thruſt me through therewith, leſt theſe vncircumciſed come and thruſt me through, and abuſe mee. But his armour bearer would not, for he was ſore afraid: therfore Saul tooke a ſword, & fell vpon it.5And when his armour bearer ſaw that Saul was dead, he fell likewiſe vpon his ſword, and died with him.6So Saul died, and his three ſons, and his armour bearer, and all his men that ſame day together.7And when the men of Iſrael that were on the other ſide of the valley, and they that were on the other ſide Iordane, ſaw that the men of Iſrael fled, and that Saul and his ſonnes were dead, they forſooke the cities and fled, and the Philiſtines came and dwelt in them.8And it came to paſſe on the morrow when the Philiſtines came to ſtrip the ſlaine, that they found Saul, and his three ſons fallen in mount Gilboa.9And they cut off his head, and ſtripped off his armour, and ſent into the land of the Philiſtines round about to publiſh it in the houſe of their idoles, and among the people.10And they put his armour in the houſe of Aſhtaroth: and they faſtened his body to the wall of Bethſhan.11And when the inhabitants of Iabeſh Gilead heard of that which the Philiſtines had done to Saul:12All the valiant men aroſe, and went all night, and tooke the body of Saul, and the bodies of his ſonnes from the wall of Bethſhan, and came to Iabeſh, and burnt them there.13And they tooke their bones, and buried them vnder a tree at Iabeſh, and faſted ſeuen dayes.

2 SAMUEL

CHAPTER 11Now it came to paſſe after þe death of Saul, when Dauid was returned from the ſlaughter of the Amalekites, and Dauid had abode two daies in Ziklag,2It came euen to paſſe on the third day, that behold, a man came out of the campe from Saul, with his clothes rent, and earth vpon his head: and ſo it was when he came to Dauid, that hee fell to the earth, and did obeyſance.3And Dauid ſaid vnto him, From whence commeſt thou? And he ſaid vnto him, Out of the campe of Iſrael am I eſcaped.4And Dauid ſaid vnto him, How went the matter? I pray thee, tell mee. And he anſwered, That the people are fled from the battell, and many of the people alſo are fallen and dead, and Saul and Ionathan his ſonne are dead alſo.5And Dauid ſaid vnto the yong man that told him, How knoweſt thou that Saul and Ionathan his ſonne be dead?6And the yong man that told him, ſaid, As I happened by chance vpon mount Gilboa, behold, Saul leaned vpon his ſpeare: and loe, the charets and horſemen followed hard after him.7And when he looked behind him, he ſaw me, and called vnto mee: and I anſwered, Here am I.8And hee ſaid vnto mee, Who art thou? and I anſwered him, I am an Amalekite.9He ſaid vnto me againe, Stand, I pray thee, vpon me, and ſlay me: for anguiſh is come vpon mee, becauſe my life is yet whole in me.10So I ſtood vpon him, and ſlew him, becauſe I was ſure that hee could not liue after that hee was fallen: And I tooke the crowne that was vpon his head, and the bracelet that was on his arme, and haue brought them hither vnto my lord.11Then Dauid tooke hold on his clothes, and rent them, and likewiſe all the men that were with him.12And they mourned and wept, and faſted vntill Euen, for Saul and for Ionathan his ſonne, and for the people of the Lord, and for the houſe of Iſrael, becauſe they were fallen by the ſword.13And Dauid ſaid vnto the yong man that told him, Whence art thou? And he anſwered, I am the ſonne of a ſtranger, an Amalekite.14And Dauid ſaid vnto him, How waſt thou not afraid to ſtretch foorth thine hand, to deſtroy the Lords Anointed?15And Dauid called one of the yong men, and ſayd, Goe neere, and fall vpon him. And hee ſmote him, that hee dyed.16And Dauid ſaid vnto him, Thy blood be vpon thy head: for thy mouth hath teſtified againſt thee, ſaying, I haue ſlaine the Lords Annoynted.17And Dauid lamented with this lamentation ouer Saul, and ouer Ionathan his ſonne:18(Alſo hee bade them teach the children of Iudah the vſe of the bow: behold, it is written in the booke of Iaſher.)19The beauty of Iſrael is ſlaine vpon thy high places: how are the mightie fallen!20Tell it not in Gath, publiſh it not in the ſtreetes of Aſkelon: leſt the daughters of the Philiſtines reioyce, leſt the daughters of the vncircumciſed triumph.21Yee mountaines of Gilboa, let there bee no dewe, neither let there be raine vpon you, nor fields of offerings: for there the ſhield of the mightie is vilely caſt away, the ſhield of Saul, as though hee had not beene annointed with oile.22From the blood of the ſlaine, from the fat of the mightie, the bow of Ionathan turned not backe, and the ſword of Saul returned not emptie.23Saul and Ionathan were louely and pleaſant in their liues, and in their death they were not diuided: they were ſwifter then Eagles, they were ſtronger then Lions.24Yee daughters of Iſrael, weepe ouer Saul, who clothed you in ſcarlet, with other delights, who put on ornaments of golde vpon your apparell.25How are the mightie fallen in the midſt of the battell! O Ionathan, thou waſt ſlaine in thine high places.26I am diſtreſſed for thee, my brother Ionathan, very pleaſant haſt thou beene vnto mee: thy loue to mee was wonderfull, paſsing the loue of women.27How are the mightie fallen, and the weapons of warre periſhed!

CHAPTER 21And it came to paſſe after this, that Dauid enquired of the Lord, ſaying, Shall I goe vp into any of the Cities of Iudah? And the Lord ſaid vnto him, Goe vp. And Dauid ſaid, Whither ſhall I goe vp? And he ſaid, Unto Hebron.2So Dauid went vp thither, and his two wiues alſo, Ahinoam the Iezreeliteſse, and Abigail Nabals wife the Carmelite.3And his men that were with him, did Dauid bring vp, euery man with his houſhold: and they dwelt in the cities of Hebron.4And the men of Iudah came, and there they anointed Dauid king ouer the houſe of Iudah: and they tolde Dauid, ſaying; That the men of Iabeſh Gilead were they that buried Saul.5And Dauid ſent meſſengers vnto the men of Iabeſh Gilead, and ſaid vnto them, Bleſſed be ye of the Lord, that ye haue ſhewed this kindneſſe vnto your lord, euen vnto Saul, and haue buried him.6And now the Lord ſhewe kindneſſe and trueth vnto you: and I alſo will requite you this kindneſse, becauſe ye haue done this thing.7Therefore now let your handes be ſtrengthened, and be ye valiant: for your maſter Saul is dead, and alſo the houſe of Iudah haue anointed me king ouer them.8But Abner the ſonne of Ner, captaine of Sauls hoſte, tooke Iſhboſheth the ſonne of Saul, and brought him ouer to Mahanaim.9And hee made him king ouer Gilead, and ouer the Aſhurites, and ouer Iezreel, and ouer Ephraim, and ouer Beniamin, and ouer all Iſrael.10Iſhboſheth Sauls ſonne was fortie yeeres olde when he began to reigne ouer Iſrael, and reigned two yeres: but the houſe of Iudah followed Dauid.11(And the time that Dauid was King in Hebron ouer the houſe of Iudah, was ſeuen yeeres, and ſixe moneths)12And Abner the ſonne of Ner, and the ſeruants of Iſhboſheth the ſonne of Saul, went out from Mahanaim, to Gibeon.13And Ioab the ſonne of Zeruiah, and the ſeruants of Dauid went out, and met together by the poole of Gibeon: and they ſate downe, the one on the one ſide of the poole, and the other on the other ſide of the poole.14And Abner ſaid to Ioab, Let the yong men now Ariſe, and play before vs: and Ioab ſaide, Let them Ariſe.15Then there aroſe and went ouer by number twelue of Beniamin, which pertained to Iſhboſheth the ſonne of Saul, and twelue of the ſeruants of Dauid.16And they caught euery one his fellow by the head, and thruſt his ſword in his fellowes ſide, ſo they fell downe together: Wherfore that place was called Helkath-hazzurim, which is in Gibeon.17And there was a very ſore battell that day: and Abner was beaten, and the men of Iſrael, before the ſeruants of Dauid.18And there were three ſonnes of Zeruiah there, Ioab, and Abiſhai, and Aſahel: and Aſahel was as light of foot as a wilde Roe.19And Aſahel purſued after Abner, and in going he turned not to the right hand nor to the left from following Abner.20Then Abner looked behind him, and ſaid, Art thou Aſahel? And he anſwered, I am.21And Abner ſaid to him, Turne thee aſide to thy right hand, or to thy left, and lay thee holde on one of the yong men, and take thee his armour. But Aſahel would not turne aſide from following of him.22And Abner ſaid againe to Aſahel, Turne thee aſide from following me: Wherefore ſhould I ſmite thee to the ground? how then ſhould I holde vp my face to Ioab thy brother?23Howbeit he refuſed to turne aſide: wherefore Abner with the hinder ende of the ſpeare ſmote him vnder the fift ribbe, that the ſpeare came out behinde him, and hee fell downe there, and died in the ſame place: and it came to paſſe, that as many as came to the place where Aſahel fell downe and died, ſtood ſtill.24Ioab alſo and Abiſhai purſued after Abner: and the Sunne went downe when they were come to the hill of Ammah, that lieth before Giah by the way of the wilderneſſe of Gibeon.25And the children of Beniamin gathered themſelues together after Abner, and became one troupe, and ſtood on the top of an hill.26Then Abner called to Ioab, and ſaid, Shall the ſword deuoure for euer? Knoweſt thou not that it wil be bitterneſse in the latter end? How long ſhall it bee then, yer thou bid the people returne from following their brethren?27And Ioab ſaid, As God liueth, vnleſſe thou hadſt ſpoken, ſurely then in the morning the people had gone vp euery one from following his brother.28So Ioab blew a trumpet, and all the people ſtood ſtill, and purſued after Iſrael no more, neither fought they any more.29And Abner and his men walked all that night thorow the plaine, and paſſed ouer Iordane, and went thorow all Bithron, and they came to

Mahanaim.30And Ioab returned from folowing Abner; and when he had gathered all the people together, there lacked of Dauids ſeruants nineteene men, and Aſahel.31But the ſeruants of Dauid had ſmitten of Beniamin and of Abners men, ſo that three hundred and threeſcore men died.32And they tooke vp Aſahel, and buried him in the ſepulchre of his father which was in Bethlehem: and Ioab and his men went all night, and they came to Hebron at breake of day.

CHAPTER 31Now there was long war betweene the houſe of Saul, and the houſe of Dauid: but Dauid waxed ſtronger and ſtronger, and the houſe of Saul waxed weaker and weaker.2And vnto Dauid were ſonnes borne in Hebron: and his firſt borne was Ammon, of Ahinoam the Iezreelitesſe.3And his ſecond, Chileab, of Abigail the wife of Nabal the Carmelite: and the third, Abſalom the ſonne of Maacah, the daughter of Talmai king of Geſhur;4And the fourth, Adoniiah the ſon of Haggith: and the fifth, Shephatiah the ſonne of Abital;5And the ſixth, Ithream by Eglah Dauids wife: theſe were borne to Dauid in Hebron.6And it came to paſſe while there was warre between the houſe of Saul and the houſe of Dauid, that Abner made himſelfe ſtrong for the houſe of Saul.7And Saul had a concubine, whoſe name was Rizpah, the daughter of Aiah: and Iſhboſheth ſaide to Abner, Wherefore haſt thou gone in vnto my fathers concubine?8Then was Abner very wroth for the words of Iſhboſheth, and ſaid, Am I a dogs head, which againſt Iudah doe ſhew kindneſſe this day vnto the houſe of Saul thy father, to his brethren, and to his friends, and haue not deliuered thee into the hand of Dauid, that thou chargeſt mee to day with a fault concerning this woman?9So doe God to Abner, and more alſo, except, as the Lord hath ſworne to Dauid, euen ſo I doe to him:10To tranſlate the kingdome from the houſe of Saul, and to ſet vp the throne of Dauid ouer Iſrael, and ouer Iudah, from Dan euen to Beer-ſheba.11And he could not anſwere Abner a word againe, becauſe he feared him.12And Abner ſent meſſengers to Dauid on his behalfe, ſaying, Whoſe is the land? ſaying alſo, Make thy league with me, and behold, my hand ſhall bee with thee, to bring about all Iſrael vnto thee.13And he ſaid, Well, I will make a league with thee: but one thing I require of thee, that is, Thou ſhalt not ſee my face, except thou firſt bring Michal Sauls daughter, when thou commeſt to ſee my face.14And Dauid ſent meſſengers to Iſhboſheth Sauls ſonne, ſaying, Deliuer mee my wife Michal, which I eſpouſed to mee for an hundred foreſkinnes of the Philiſtines.15And Iſhboſheth ſent, and tooke her from her huſband, euen from Phaltiel the ſonne of Laiſh.16And her huſband went with her along weeping behinde her to Bahurim: then ſaid Abner vnto him, Goe, returne. And he returned.17And Abner had communication with the Elders of Iſrael, ſaying, Yee ſought for Dauid in times paſt, to be king ouer you.18Now then doe it, for the Lord hath ſpoken of Dauid, ſaying; By the hand of my ſeruant Dauid I will ſaue my people Iſrael out of the hand of the Philiſtines, and out of the hand of all their enemies.19And Abner alſo ſpake in the eares of Beniamin: and Abner went alſo to ſpeake in the eares of Dauid in Hebron, all that ſeemed good to Iſrael, and that ſeemed good to the whole houſe of Beniamin.20So Abner came to Dauid to Hebron, and twenty men with him: and Dauid made Abner, and the men that were with him, a feaſt.21And Abner ſaid vnto Dauid, I will Ariſe, and goe, and will gather all Iſrael vnto my lord the king, that they may make a league with thee, and that thou mayeſt raigne ouer all that thine heart deſireth. And Dauid ſent Abner away, and he went in peace.22And behold, the ſeruants of Dauid, and Ioab came from purſuinga troupe, and brought in a great ſpoile with them: (but Abner was not with Dauid in Hebron, for he had ſent him away, and he was gone in peace.)23When Ioab and all the hoſt that was with him, were come, they told Ioab, ſaying, Abner the ſonne of Ner came to the king, and he hath ſent him away, and he is gone in peace.24Then Ioab came to the king, and ſaid, What haſt thou done? behold, Abner came vnto thee, why is it that thou haſt ſent him away, & he is quite gone?25Thou knoweſt Abner the ſonne of Ner, that he came to deceiue thee, and to know thy going out, and thy comming in, & to know all that thou doeſt.26And when Ioab was come out from Dauid, hee ſent meſſengers after Abner, which brought him againe from the well of Siriah; but Dauid knew it not.27And when Abner was returned to Hebron, Ioab tooke him aſide in the gate to ſpeake with him quietly: and ſmote him there vnder the fift ribbe, that he died, for the blood of Aſahel his brother.28And afterward when Dauid heard it, hee ſaid, I and my kingdome are guiltleſſe before the Lord for euer, from the blood of Abner the ſonne of Ner:29Let it reſt on the head of Ioab, and on all his fathers houſe, & let there not faile from the houſe of Ioab one that hath an iſsue, or that is a leper, or that leaneth on a ſtaffe, or that falleth on the ſword, or that lacketh bread.30So Ioab and Abiſhai his brother ſlew Abner, becauſe he had ſlaine their brother Aſahel at Gibeon in the battell.31And Dauid ſaid to Ioab, and to all the people that were with him, Rent your clothes, and girde you with ſackecloth, and mourne before Abner. And king Dauid himſelfe followed the biere.32And they buried Abner in Hebron, and the king lift vp his voice, and wept at the graue of Abner; and all the people wept.33And the king lamented ouer Abner, and ſaid, Died Abner as a foole dieth?34Thy hands were not bound, nor thy feete put into fetters: as a man falleth before wicked men, ſo felleſt thou. And all the people wept againe ouer him.35And when all the people came to cauſe Dauid to eate meate while it was yet day, Dauid ſware, ſaying, So doe God to mee, and more alſo, if I taſte bread or ought elſe, till the Sunne be downe.36And all the people tooke notice of it, and it pleaſed them: as whatſoeuer the King did, pleaſed all the people.37For all the people, and all Iſrael vnderſtood that day, that it was not of the King to ſlay Abner the ſonne of Ner.38And the King ſaid vnto his ſeruants, Knowe yee not that there is a prince and a great man fallen this day in Iſrael?39And I am this day weake, though anointed King, and theſe men the ſonnes of Zeruiah be too hard for me: the Lord ſhall reward the doer of euill, according to his wickedneſſe.

CHAPTER 41And when Sauls ſonne heard that Abner was dead in Hebron, his hands were feeble, and all the Iſraelites were troubled.2And Sauls ſonne had two men that were captaines of bands: the name of the one was Baanah, and the name of the other Rechab, the ſonnes of Rimmon a Beerothite, of the children of Beniamin: (for Beeroth alſo was reckoned to Beniamin:3And the Beerothites fled to Gittaim, and were ſoiourners there vntill this day.)4And Ionathan, Sauls ſonne, had a ſonne that was lame of his feete, and was fiue yeeres olde when the tidings came of Saul and Ionathan out of Iezreel, and his nource tooke him vp, and fled: and it came to paſſe as ſhe made haſte to flee, that hee fell, and became lame, and his name was Mephiboſheth.5And the ſonnes of Rimmon the Beerothite, Rechab and Baanah, went, and came about the heat of the day to the houſe of Iſhboſheth, who lay on a bed at noone.6And they came thither into the midſt of the houſe, as though they would haue fetched wheat, and they ſmote him vnder the fift rib, and Rechab and Baanah his brother eſcaped.7For when they came into the houſe, hee lay on his bedde in his bedchamber, and they ſmote him, and ſlew him, and beheaded him, and tooke his head, and gate them away thorow the plaine all night.8And they brought the head of Iſhboſheth vnto Dauid to Hebron, and ſaid to the King, Behold the head of Iſhboſheth the ſonne of Saul, thine enemie, which ſought thy life, and the Lord hath auenged my lord the king this day of Saul and of his ſeed.9And Dauid anſwered Rechab and Baanah his brother, the ſonnes of Rimmon the Beerothite, and ſaid vnto them, As the Lord liueth, who hath redeemed my ſoule out of all aduerſitie,10When one told me, ſaying, Behold, Saul is dead, (thinking to haue brought good tidingſ) I tooke hold of him, and ſlew him in Ziklag, who thought that I would haue giuen him a reward for his tidings:11How much more, when wicked men haue ſlaine a righteous perſon, in his owne houſe, vpon his bed? Shall I not therefore now require his blood of your hand, and take you away from the earth?12And Dauid commanded his yong men, and they ſlew them, and cut off their hands and their feete, and hanged them vp ouer the poole in Hebron: but they tooke the head of Iſhboſheth, and buried it in the ſepulchre of Abner, in Hebron.

CHAPTER 51Then came all the tribes of Iſrael to Dauid vnto Hebron, and ſpake, ſaying, Behold, we are thy bone, and thy fleſh.2Alſo in time paſt when Saul was king ouer vs, thou waſt hee that leddeſt out and broughteſt in Iſrael: and the Lord ſaid to thee, Thou ſhalt feed my people Iſrael, and thou ſhalt bee a captaine ouer Iſrael.3So all the Elders of Iſrael came to the King to Hebron, and King Dauid made a league with them in Hebron before the Lord: and they anointed Dauid King ouer Iſrael.4Dauid was thirtie yeeres old when he began to reigne, and he reigned fourtie yeeres.5In Hebron he reigned ouer Iudah ſeuen yeeres, and ſixe moneths: and in Ieruſalem he reigned thirty and three yeres ouer all Iſrael and Iudah.6And the king and his men went to Ieruſalem, vnto the Iebuſites, the inhabitants of the land: which ſpake

vnto Dauid, ſaying, Except thou take away the blind and the lame, thou
ſhalt not come in hither: Thinking, Dauid cannot come in
hither.7Neuertheleſſe, Dauid tooke the ſtrong hold of Zion: the ſame is
the citie of Dauid.8And Dauid ſaid on that day, Whoſoeuer getteth vp
to the gutter, and ſmiteth the Iebuſites, and the lame, and the blind, that
are hated of Dauids ſoule, he ſhall be chiefe and captaine: Wherefore
they ſaid, The blind and the lame ſhall not come into the houſe.9So
Dauid dwelt in the fort, and called it the citie of Dauid, and Dauid built
round about, from Millo and inward.10And Dauid went on, and grew
great, and the Lord God of hoſts was with him.11And Hiram king of
Tyre ſent meſſengers to Dauid, and Cedar trees, and carpenters, and
Maſons: and they built Dauid an houſe.12And Dauid perceiued that the
Lord had eſtabliſhed him King ouer Iſrael, and that he had exalted his
kingdome for his people Iſraels ſake.13And Dauid tooke him mo
concubines and wiues out of Ieruſalem, after he was come from
Hebron, and there were yet ſonnes and daughters borne to Dauid.14And
theſe be the names of thoſe that were borne vnto him in Ieruſalem,
Shammua, & Shobab, and Nathan, and Solomon:15Ibhar alſo, and
Eliſhua, and Nepheg, and Iaphia,16And Eliſhama, and Eliada, and
Eliphalet.17But when the Philiſtines heard that they had anointed Dauid
King ouer Iſrael, all the Philiſtines came vp to ſeeke Dauid, and Dauid
heard of it, and went downe to the hold.18The Philiſtines alſo came, and
ſpred themſelues in the valley of Rephaim.19And Dauid enquired of the
Lord, ſaying, Shall I goe vp to the Philiſtines? wilt thou deliuer them into
mine hand? And the Lord ſaid vnto Dauid, Goe vp: for I will doubtleſſe
deliuer the Philiſtines into thine hand.20And Dauid came to Baal-
Perazim, and Dauid ſmote them there, and ſaid, The Lord hath broken
foorth vpon mine enemies before me, as the breach of waters. Therefore
he called the name of that place, Baal-Perazim.21And there they left their
images, and Dauid and his men burnt them.22And the Philiſtines came
vp yet againe, and ſpread themſelues in the valley of Rephaim.23And
when Dauid enquired of the Lord, he ſaid, Thou ſhalt not goe vp: but
fetch a compaſſe behinde them, and come vpon them ouer againſt the
Mulbery trees.24And let it be when thou heareſt the ſound of a going in
the tops of the mulbery trees, that then thou ſhalt beſtirre thy ſelfe: for
then ſhal the Lord goe out before thee, to ſmite the hoſt of the
Philiſtines.25And Dauid did ſo, as the Lord had commaunded him; and
ſmote the Philiſtines from Geba, vntil thou come to Gazer.
CHAPTER 61Againe, Dauid gathered together all the choſen men of
Iſrael, thirtie thouſand:2And Dauid aroſe and went with all the people
that were with him, from Baale of Iudah, to bring vp from thence the
Arke of God, whoſe Name is called by the Name of the Lord of hoſtes,
that dwelleth betweene the Cherubims.3And they ſet the Arke of God
vpon a new cart, and brought it out of the houſe of Abinadab that was
in Gibeah: and Uzzah and Ahio the ſonnes of Abinadab, draue the new
cart.4And they brought it out of the houſe of Abinadab which was at
Gibeah, accompanying the Arke of God; and Ahio went before the
Arke.5And Dauid and all the houſe of Iſrael played before the Lord on
all manner of inſtruments made of Firrewood, euen on harpes, and on
Pſalteries, and on timbrels, and on cornets, and on cimbals.6And when
they came to Nachons threſhing floore, Uzzah put forth his hand to the
Arke of God, and tooke hold of it, for the oxen ſhooke it.7And the anger
of the Lord was kindled againſt Uzzah, and God ſmote him there for
his errour, and there he died by the Arke of God.8And Dauid was
diſpleaſed, becauſe the Lord had made a breach vpon Uzzah: And hee
called the name of the place, Perez-Uzzah to this day.9And Dauid was
afraide of the Lord that day, and ſaid, How ſhall the Arke of the Lord
come to me?10So Dauid would not remoue the Arke of the Lord vnto
him into the citie of Dauid: but Dauid caried it aſide into the houſe of
Obed Edom, the Gittite.11And the Arke of the Lord continued in the
houſe of Obed Edom the Gittite, three moneths: and the Lord bleſſed
Obed Edom, and all his houſehold.12And it was told king Dauid, ſaying,
The Lord hath bleſſed the houſe of Obed Edom, and all that pertained
vnto him, becauſe of the Arke of God. So Dauid went, and brought vp
the Arke of God, from the houſe of Obed Edom, into the citie of Dauid,
with gladneſſe.13And it was ſo, that when they that bare the Arke of the
Lord, had gone ſixe paces, hee ſacrificed oxen and fatlings.14And Dauid
daunced before the Lord with all his might, and Dauid was girded with
a linnen Ephod.15So Dauid and all the houſe of Iſrael brought vp the
Arke of the Lord with ſhouting, and with the ſound of the
trumpet.16And as the Arke of the Lord came into the citie of Dauid,
Michal Sauls daughter looked through a window, and ſaw king Dauid
leaping and dauncing before the Lord, and ſhe deſpiſed him in her
heart.17And they brought in the Arke of the Lord, and ſet it in his place,
in the midſt of the Tabernacle that Dauid had pitched for it: and Dauid
offered burnt offerings, and peace offrings before the Lord.18And
aſſoone as Dauid had made an end of offering burnt offerings and peace
offerings, hee bleſſed the people in the Name of the Lord of
hoſtes.19And hee dealt among all the people, euen among the whole
multitude of Iſrael, as well to the women as men, to euery one a cake of
bread, and a good piece of fleſh, and a flagon of wine: ſo all the people
departed euery one to his houſe.20Then Dauid returned to bleſſe his
houſhold: and Michal the daughter of Saul came out to meete Dauid,
and ſaid, How glorious was the King of Iſrael to day, who vncouered
himſelfe to day in the eyes of the handmaids of his ſeruants, as one of
the vaine fellowes ſhameleſſely vncouereth himſelfe!21And Dauid ſaid
vnto Michal, It was before the Lord, which choſe me before thy father,
& before all his houſe, to appoint me ruler ouer the people of the Lord,
ouer Iſrael: therefore will I play before the Lord.22And I will yet be more
vile then thus, and will be baſe in mine owne ſight: and of the maid
ſeruants which thou haſt ſpoken of, of them ſhall I be had in
honour.23Therefore Michal the daughter of Saul had no childe vnto the
day of her death.
CHAPTER 71And it came to paſſe, when the King ſate in his houſe,
and the Lord had giuen him reſt round about frō all his enemies;2That
the king ſaid vnto Nathan the Prophet, ſee now, I dwell in an houſe of
Cedar, but the Arke of God dwelleth within curtaines.3And Nathan
ſayde to the King, Go, doe all that is in thine heart: for the Lord is with
thee.4And it came to paſſe that night, that the word of the Lord came
vnto Nathan, ſaying;5Goe and tell my ſeruant Dauid, Thus ſayth the
Lord, Shalt thou build me an houſe for me to dwell in?6Whereas I haue
not dwelt in any houſe, ſince the time that I brought vp the children of
Iſrael out of Egypt, euen to this day, but haue walked in a tent and in a
tabernacle.7In all the places wherein I haue walked with all the children
of Iſrael, ſpake I a word with any of the tribes of Iſrael, whome I
commanded to feede my people Iſrael, ſaying, Why build ye not me an
houſe of Cedar?8Now therefore ſo ſhalt thou ſay vnto my ſeruant
Dauid; Thus ſayth the Lord of hoſtes, I tooke thee from the ſheepe-
cote, from following the ſheepe, to be ruler ouer my people, ouer
Iſrael.9And I was with thee witherſoeuer thou wenteſt, and haue cut off
all thine enemies out of thy ſight, and haue made thee a great name, like
vnto the name of the great men that are in the earth.10(Moreouer I will
appoint a place for my people Iſrael, and will plant them, that they may
dwell in a place of their owne, and mooue no more: neither ſhall the
children of wickedneſſe afflict them any more, as beforetime,11And as
ſince the time that I commanded Iudges to bee ouer my people Iſrael,
and haue cauſed thee to reſt from all thine enemies:) Alſo the Lord
telleth thee, that he will make thee an houſe.12And when thy dayes be
fulfilled, and thou ſhalt ſleepe with thy fathers, I will ſet vp thy ſeede
after thee, which ſhall proceede out of thy bowels, and I will eſtabliſh
his kingdome.13Hee ſhall build an houſe for my Name, and I will ſtabliſh
the throne of his kingdome for euer.14I will be his father, and he ſhall
be my ſonne: if hee commit iniquitie, I will chaſten him with the rodde
of men, and with the ſtripes of the children of men.15But my mercie
ſhall not depart away from him, as I tooke it from Saul, whom I put
away before thee.16And thine houſe, and thy kingdome ſhall be
ſtabliſhed for euer before thee: thy throne ſhall be ſtabliſhed for
euer.17According to all theſe words, and according to all this viſion, ſo
did Nathan ſpeake vnto Dauid.18Then went king Dauid in, and ſate
before the Lord, and hee ſaid, Who am I, O Lord God? and what is my
houſe, that thou haſt brought me hitherto?19And this was yet a ſmall
thing in thy ſight, O Lord God: but thou haſt ſpoken alſo of thy ſeruants
houſe for a great while to come, and is this the maner of man, O Lord
God?20And what can Dauid ſay more vnto thee? for thou, Lord God,
knoweſt thy ſeruant.21For thy words ſake, and according to thine own
heart haſt thou done all theſe great things, to make thy ſeruant know
them.22Wherefore thou art great, O Lord God: for there is none like
thee, neither is there any God beſide thee, according to all that we haue
heard with our eares.23And what one nation in the earth is like thy
people, euen like Iſrael, whom God went to redeeme for a people to

himſelfe, & to make him a name, and to doe for you great things, and terrible, for thy lande, before thy people which thou redeemedſt to thee from Egypt, from the nations, and their gods? 24 For thou haſt confirmed to thy ſelfe thy people Iſrael to be a people vnto thee for euer: and thou, Lord art become their God. 25 And now, O Lord God, the word that thou haſt ſpoken, concerning thy ſeruant, and concerning his houſe, eſtabliſh it for euer, and doe as thou haſt ſaid. 26 And let thy name bee magnified for euer, ſaying, The Lord of hoſts is the God ouer Iſrael: and let the houſe of thy ſeruant Dauid bee eſtabliſhed before thee. 27 For thou, O Lord of hoſtes, God of Iſrael, haſt reuealed to thy ſeruant, ſaying, I will build thee an houſe: therfore hath thy ſeruant found in his heart to pray this prayer vnto thee. 28 And now, O Lord GOD, (thou art that God, and thy words be true, and thou haſt promiſed this goodneſſe vnto thy ſeruant.) 29 Therefore now let it pleaſe thee to bleſſe the houſe of thy ſeruant, that it may continue for euer before thee: for thou, O Lord God, haſt ſpoken it, and with thy bleſſing let the houſe of thy ſeruant be bleſſed for euer.

CHAPTER 8 1 And after this it came to paſſe, that Dauid ſmote the Philiſtines, and ſubdued them: and Dauid tooke Metheg-Ammah out of the hand of the Philiſtines. 2 And he ſmote Moab, and meaſured them with a line, caſting them downe to the ground: euen with two lines meaſured he, to put to death, and with one full line to keepe aliue: and ſo the Moabites became Dauids ſeruants, and brought gifts. 3 Dauid ſmote alſo Hadadezer the ſonne of Rehob, king of Zobah, as he went to recouer his border at the riuer Euphrates. 4 And Dauid tooke from him a thouſand charets, and ſeuen hundred horſemen, and twentie thouſand footemen: and Dauid houghed all the charet horſes, but referuedof them for an hundred charets. 5 And when the Syrians of Damaſcus came to ſuccour Hadadezer king of Zobah, Dauid ſlew of the Syrians two and twentie thouſand men. 6 Then Dauid put gariſons in Syria of Damaſcus: And the Syrians became ſeruants to Dauid, and brought gifts: and the Lord preſerued Dauid whitherſoeuer he went. 7 And Dauid tooke the ſhields of gold that were on the ſeruants of Hadadezer, and brought them to Ieruſalem. 8 And from Betah and from Berothai, cities of Hadadezer, King Dauid tooke exceeding much braſſe. 9 When Toi king of Hamath heard that Dauid had ſmitten all the hoſte of Hadadezer, 10 Then Toi ſent Ioram his ſonne vnto king Dauid to ſalute him, and to bleſſe him, becauſe hee had fought againſt Hadadezer, and ſmitten him: (for Hadadezer had warres with Toi) and Ioram brought with him veſſels of ſiluer, and veſſels of gold, and veſſels of braſſe; 11 Which alſo king Dauid did dedicate vnto the Lord, with the ſiluer and gold that he had dedicate of all nations which he ſubdued: 12 Of Syria, and of Moab, and of the children of Ammon, and of the Philiſtines, & of Amalek, and of the ſpoile of Hadadezer ſonne of Rehob king of Zobah. 13 And Dauid gate him a name when he returned from ſmiting of the Syrians in the valley of ſalt, being eighteene thouſand men. 14 And he put garriſons in Edom; thorowout all Edom put he garriſons, and all they of Edom became Dauids ſeruants: and the Lord preſerued Dauid whitherſoeuer he went. 15 And Dauid reigned ouer all Iſrael, and Dauid executed iudgement and iuſtice vnto all his people. 16 And Ioab the ſonne of Zeruiah was ouer the hoſt, and Iehoſhaphat the ſonne of Ahilud was Recorder. 17 And Zadok the ſonne of Ahitub, and Ahimelech the ſonne of Abiathar, were the Prieſts, and Seraiah was the ſcribe. 18 And Benaiah the ſonne of Iehoiada was ouer both the Cherethites, and the Pelethites, and Dauids ſonnes were chiefe rulers.

CHAPTER 9 1 And Dauid ſaid, Is there yet any that is left of the houſe of Saul, that I may ſhew him kindneſſe for Ionathans ſake? 2 And there was of the houſe of Saul, a ſeruant whoſe name was Ziba: and when they had called him vnto Dauid, the king ſaid vnto him, Art thou Ziba? And he ſaid, Thy ſeruant is he. 3 And the king ſaid, Is there not yet any of the houſe of Saul, that I may ſhew the kindneſſe of God vnto him? and Ziba ſaid vnto the king, Ionathan hath yet a ſonne, which is lame on his feete. 4 And the king ſaide vnto him, Where is hee? and Ziba ſaid vnto the king, Behold, he is in the houſe of Machir the ſonne of Ammiel, in Lodebar. 5 Then king Dauid ſent, and fet him out of the houſe of Machir the ſon of Ammiel, from Lodebar. 6 Now when Mephiboſheth the ſonne of Ionathan the ſonne of Saul, was come vnto Dauid, hee fell on his face, and did reuerence: and Dauid ſaid, Mephiboſheth! And he anſwered, Behold thy ſeruant. 7 And Dauid ſaide vnto him, Feare not; for I will ſurely ſhew thee kindneſse, for Ionathan thy fathers ſake, and will reſtore thee all the land of Saul thy father, and thou ſhalt eate bread at my table continually. 8 And hee bowed himſelfe, and ſaide, What is thy ſeruant, that thou ſhouldeſt looke vpon ſuch a dead dogge as I am? 9 Then the king called to Ziba Sauls ſeruant, and ſaid vnto him, I haue giuen vnto thy maſters ſonne all that pertained to Saul, and to all his houſe. 10 Thou therefore and thy ſonnes, and thy ſeruants, ſhall till the land for him, and thou ſhalt bring in the fruits, that thy maſters ſonne may haue food to eate: but Mephiboſheth thy maſters ſonne ſhall eat bread alway at my table. Now Ziba had fifteene ſonnes, and twenty ſeruants. 11 Then ſaide Ziba vnto the king, According to all that my lord the king hath commanded his ſeruant, ſo ſhall thy ſeruant doe: as for Mephiboſheth, ſaid the King, he ſhall eate at my table, as one of the kings ſonnes. 12 And Mephiboſheth had a yong ſonne whoſe name was Micha: and all that dwelt in the houſe of Ziba, were ſeruants vnto Mephiboſheth. 13 So Mephiboſheth dwelt in Ieruſalem: for hee did eate continually at the kings table, and was lame on both his feete.

CHAPTER 10 1 And it came to paſſe, after this, that the king of the children of Ammon died, and Hanun his ſonne reigned in his ſtead. 2 Then ſaid Dauid, I will ſhewe kindnes vnto Hanun the ſonne of Nahaſh, as his father ſhewed kindnes vnto me. And Dauid ſent to comfort him by the hand of his ſeruants, for his father: and Dauids ſeruants came into the land of the children of Ammon. 3 And the princes of the children of Ammon ſaide vnto Hanun their lord, Thinkeſt thou that Dauid doeth honour thy father, that he hath ſent comforters vnto thee? Hath not Dauid rather ſent his ſeruants vnto thee, to ſearch the citie, and to ſpie it out, and to ouerthrow it? 4 Wherefore Hanun tooke Dauids ſeruants, and ſhaued off the one halfe of their beards, and cut off their garments in the middle, euen to their buttocks, and ſent them away. 5 When they told it vnto Dauid, he ſent to meet them, becauſe the men were greatly aſhamed: and the King ſaide, Tarie at Iericho vntill your beards be growen, and then returne. 6 And when the children of Ammon ſaw that they ſtanke before Dauid, the children of Ammon ſent, and hired the Syrians of Beth-Rehob, and the Syrians of Zoba, twentie thouſand footmen, and of king Maacah, a thouſand men, and of Iſhtob twelue thouſand men. 7 And when Dauid heard of it, he ſent Ioab, and all the hoſte of the mightie men. 8 And the children of Ammon came out, and put the battell in aray at the entring in of the gate: and the Syrians of Zoba and of Rehob, and Iſhtob, and Maacah, were by themſelues in the field. 9 When Ioab ſaw that the front of the battell was againſt him, before and behind, he choſe of all the choiſe men of Iſrael, and put them in aray againſt the Syrians. 10 And the reſt of the people he deliuered into the hand of Abiſhai his brother, that he might put them in aray againſt the children of Ammon. 11 And he ſaid, If the Syrians bee too ſtrong for me, then thou ſhalt helpe me: but if the children of Ammon bee too ſtrong for thee, then I will come and helpe thee. 12 Be of good courage, and let vs play the men, for our people, and for the cities of our God: and the Lord doe that which ſeemeth him good. 13 And Ioab drew nigh, and the people that were with him, vnto the battell againſt the Syrians: and they fled before him. 14 And when the children of Ammon ſaw that the Syrians were fledde, then fled they alſo before Abiſhai, and entred into the citie: ſo Ioab returned from the children of Ammon, and came to Ieruſalem. 15 And when the Syrians ſawe that they were ſmitten before Iſrael, they gathered themſelues together. 16 And Hadarezer ſent, and brought out the Syrians that were beyond the riuer, and they came to Helam, and Shobach the captaine of the hoſte of Hadarezer went before them. 17 And when it was told Dauid, he gathered all Iſrael together, and paſſed ouer Iordane, and came to Helam: and the Syrians ſet themſelues in aray againſt Dauid, and fought with him. 18 And the Syrians fled before Iſrael, and Dauid ſlew the men of ſeuen hundred charets of the Syrians, and fourtie thouſand horſemen, and ſmote Shobach the captaine of their hoſte, who died there. 19 And when all the kings that were ſeruants to Hadarezer ſawe, that they were ſmitten before Iſrael, they made peace with Iſrael, and ſerued them: ſo the Syrians feared to helpe the children of Ammon any more.

CHAPTER 11 1 And it came to paſſe, that after the yeere was expired, at the time when kings goe foorth to battell, that Dauid ſent Ioab and his ſeruants with him, and all Iſrael; and they deſtroyed the children of Ammon, and beſieged Rabbah: but Dauid taried ſtill at Ieruſalem. 2 And it came to paſſe in an euening tide, that Dauid aroſe from off his bed, and walked vpon the roofe of the kings houſe: and from the roofe he ſaw a woman waſhing her ſelfe; and the woman was very beautifull to looke vpon.3And Dauid ſent and enquired after the woman: and one ſaid, Is not this Bath-ſheba the daughter of Eliam, the wife of Uriah the Hittite?4And Dauid ſent meſſengers, and tooke her, and ſhee came in vnto him, and he lay with her, (for ſhe was purified from her vncleanneſſe) and ſhee returned vnto her houſe.5And the woman conceiued, and ſent and tolde Dauid, and ſaid, I am with childe.6And Dauid ſent to Ioab, ſaying, Send me Uriah the Hittite. And Ioab ſent Uriah to Dauid.7And when Uriah was come vnto him, Dauid demanded of him how Ioab did, and how the people did, and how the warre proſpered.8And Dauid ſaid to Uriah, Goe downe to thy houſe, and waſh thy feete. And Uriah departed out of the Kings houſe, and there followed him a meſse of meat from the king.9But Uriah ſlept at the doore of the kings houſe, with all the ſeruants of his lord, and went not downe to his houſe.10And when they had tolde Dauid, ſaying, Uriah went not downe vnto his houſe, Dauid ſaid vnto Uriah, Cameſt thou not from thy iourney? why then diddeſt thou not goe downe vnto thine houſe?11And Uriah ſaid vnto Dauid, The Arke, and Iſrael, and Iudah abide in tents, and my lord Ioab, and the ſeruants of my lord are encamped in the open fields; ſhall I then goe into mine houſe, to eate and to drinke, and to lie with my wife? As thou liueſt, and as thy ſoule liueth, I will not doe this thing.12And Dauid ſaid to Uriah, Tary here to day alſo, and to morow I will let thee depart. So Uriah abode in Ieruſalem that day, and the morrow.13And when Dauid had called him, hee did eate and drinke before him, and he made him drunke: and at euen hee went out to lie on his bed with the ſeruants of his lord, but went not downe to his houſe.14And it came to paſſe in the morning, that Dauid wrote a letter to Ioab, and ſent it by the hand of Uriah.15And he wrote in the letter, ſaying, Set yee Uriah in the forefront of the hotteſt battel, and retire ye from him, that he may be ſmitten, and die.16And it came to paſſe when Ioab obſerued the citie, that he aſsigned Uriah vnto a place where hee knewe that valiant men were.17And the men of the city went out, and fought with Ioab: and there fell ſome of the people of the ſeruants of Dauid, and Uriah the Hittite died alſo.18Then Ioab ſent, and tolde Dauid all the things concerning the warre:19And charged the meſſenger, ſaying, When thou haſt made an ende of telling the matters of the warre vnto the King;20And if ſo be that the kings wrath Ariſe, and hee ſay vnto thee, Wherefore approched ye ſo nigh vnto the city when yee did fight? Knew yee not that they would ſhoot from the wall?21Who ſmote Abimelech the ſonne of Ierubeſheth? Did not a woman caſt a piece of a milſtone vpon him from the wall, that he died in Thebez? why went ye nigh the wall? Then ſay thou, Thy ſeruant Uriah the Hittite is dead alſo.22So the meſſenger went, and came and ſhewed Dauid all that Ioab had ſent him for.23And the meſſenger ſaid vnto Dauid, Surely the men preuailed againſt vs, and came out vnto vs into the field, and we were vpon them euen vnto the entring of the gate.24And the ſhooters ſhot from off the wall vpon thy ſeruants, and ſome of the Kings ſeruants be dead, and thy ſeruant Uriah the Hittite is dead alſo.25Then Dauid ſaid vnto the meſſenger, Thus ſhalt thou ſay vnto Ioab, Let not this thing diſpleaſe thee: for the ſword deuoureth one as well as another: Make thy battell more ſtrong againſt the citie, and ouerthrow it; and encourage thou him.26And when the wife of Uriah heard that Uriah her huſband was dead, ſhe mourned for her huſband.27And when the mourning was paſt, Dauid ſent, and fet her to his houſe, and ſhe became his wife, and bare him a ſonne: but the thing that Dauid had done, diſpleaſed the Lord.

CHAPTER 121And the Lord ſent Nathan vnto Dauid: and he came vnto him, and ſaid vnto him, There were two men in one citie; the one rich, and the other poore.2The rich man had exceeding many flockes and herds.3But the poore man had nothing ſaue one litle ewe lambe, which he had bought and nouriſhed vp: and it grew vp together with him, and with his children, it did eate of his owne meate, and dranke of his owne cup, and lay in his boſome, and was vnto him as a daughter.4And there came a traueller vnto the rich man, and he ſpared to take of his owne flocke, and of his owne herd, to dreſſe for the wayfaring man that was come vnto him, but tooke the poore mans lambe, and dreſſed it for the man that was come to him.5And Dauids anger was greatly kindled againſt the man, and he ſaid to Nathan, As the Lord liueth, the man that hath done this thing, ſhall ſurely die.6And he ſhall reſtore the Lambe fourefold, becauſe he did this thing, and becauſe he had no pittie.7And Nathan ſaid to Dauid, Thou art the man: thus ſaith the Lord God of Iſrael, I anointed thee king ouer Iſrael, and I deliuered thee out of the hand of Saul,8And I gaue thee thy Maſters houſe, and thy Maſters wiues into thy boſome, and gaue thee the houſe of Iſrael and of Iudah, and if that had bene too litle, I would moreouer haue giuen vnto thee ſuch and ſuch things.9Wherefore haſt thou deſpiſed the commandement of the Lord, to doe euill in his ſight? thou haſt killed Uriah the Hittite with the ſword, and haſt taken his wife to be thy wife, and haſt ſlaine him with the ſword of the children of Ammon.10Now therefore the ſword ſhall neuer depart from thine houſe, becauſe thou haſt deſpiſed me, and haſt taken the wife of Uriah the Hittite, to be thy wife.11Thus ſaith the Lord, Behold, I will raiſe vp euill againſt thee out of thine owne houſe, and I will take thy wiues before thine eyes, and giue them vnto thy neighbour, and he ſhall lie with thy wiues in the ſight of this Sunne.12For thou diddeſt it ſecretly: but I will do this thing before all Iſrael, and before the Sunne.13And Dauid ſaide vnto Nathan, I haue ſinned againſt the Lord. And Nathan ſaide vnto Dauid, The Lord alſo hath put away thy ſinne, thou ſhalt not die.14Howbeit, becauſe by this deede thou haſt giuen great occaſion to the enemies of the Lord to blaſpheme, the childe alſo that is borne vnto thee, ſhall ſurely die.15And Nathan departed vnto his houſe: and the Lord ſtrake the childe that Uriahs wife bare vnto Dauid, and it was very ſicke.16Dauid therfore beſought God for the childe, and Dauid faſted, and went in, and lay all night vpon the earth.17And the Elders of his houſe aroſe, and went to him, to raiſe him vp from the earth: but he would not, neither did he eate bread with them.18And it came to paſſe on the ſeuenth day, that the childe died: and the ſeruants of Dauid feared to tell him that the child was dead: for they ſaide, Behold, while the childe was yet aliue, we ſpake vnto him, and he would not hearken vnto our voice: how will he then vexe himſelfe, if we tell him that the childe is dead?19But when Dauid ſaw that his ſeruants whiſpered, Dauid perceiued that the childe was dead: therefore Dauid ſaid vnto his ſeruants, Is the child dead? and they ſaid, He is dead.20Then Dauid aroſe from the earth and waſhed, and anointed himſelfe, and changed his apparell, and came into the houſe of the Lord, and worſhipped: then hee came to his owne houſe, and when he required, they ſet bread before him, and he did eate.21Then ſaid his ſeruants vnto him, What thing is this that thou haſt done? thou didſt faſt and weepe for the childe, while it was aliue, but when the childe was dead, thou didſt riſe and eat bread.22And he ſaid, While the child was yet aliue, I faſted and wept: for I ſaid, Who can tell, whether God will be gracious to me, that the child may liue?23But now hee is dead, Wherefore ſhould I faſt? Can I bring him backe againe? I ſhall goe to him, but he ſhall not returne to me.24And Dauid comforted Bathſheba his wife, and went in vnto her, and lay with her: and ſhe bare a ſonne, and he called his name Solomon, and the Lord loued him.25And hee ſent by the hand of Nathan the Prophet, and hee called his name Iedidiah, becauſe of the Lord.26And Ioab fought againſt Rabbah of the children of Ammon, and tooke the royall citie.27And Ioab ſent meſſengers to Dauid, and ſaid, I haue fought againſt Rabbah, and haue taken the citie of waters.28Now therefore, gather the reſt of the people together, and encampe againſt the citie, and take it: leſt I take the citie, and it be called after my name.29And Dauid gathered all the people together, and went to Rabbah, and fought againſt it, and tooke it.30And he tooke their kings crowne from off his head (the weight whereof was a talent of gold, with the precious ſtoneſ) and it was ſet on Dauids head, and he brought forth the ſpoile of the citie in great abundance.31And he brought foorth the people that were therein, and put them vnder ſawes, and vnder harrowes of yron, and vnder axes of yron, and made them paſſe through the bricke-kilne: And thus did he vnto all the cities of the children of Ammon. So Dauid and all the people returned vnto Ieruſalem.

CHAPTER 131And it came to paſſe after this, that Abſalom the ſonne of Dauid had a faire ſiſter, whoſe name was Tamar: and Amnon the ſonne of Dauid loued her.2And Amnon was ſo vexed, that he fell ſicke for his ſiſter Tamar: for ſhe was a virgine, and Amnon thought it hard for him to doe any thing to her.3But Amnon had a friend, whoſe name was Ionadab, the ſonne of Shimeah, Dauids brother: and Ionadab was a very ſubtill man.4And he ſaide vnto him, Why art thou, being the Kings ſonne, leane from day to day? Wilt thou not tel me? and Amnon ſaid vnto him, I loue Tamar my brother Abſaloms ſiſter.5And Ionadab ſaid vnto him, Lay thee downe on thy bed, and make thy ſelfe ſicke: and when thy father commeth to ſee thee, ſay vnto him, I pray thee, let my ſiſter Tamar come, and giue me meat, and dreſſe the meat in my ſight, that I may ſee it, and eate it at her hand.6So Amnon lay downe, and made himſelfe ſicke: and when the king was come to ſee him, Amnon ſaid vnto the king, I pray thee, let Tamar my ſiſter come, & make me a couple of cakes in my ſight, that I may eat at her hand.7Then Dauid ſent home to Tamar, ſaying, Goe now to thy brother Amnons houſe, and dreſſe him meat.8So Tamar went to her brother Amnons houſe (and hee was laide downe) and ſhe tooke flowre, and kneaded it, and made cakes in his ſight, and did bake the cakes.9And ſhe tooke a pan, and powred them out before him, but hee refuſed to eate: and Amnon ſaid, Haue out all men from mee: And they went out euery man from him.10And Amnon ſaide vnto Tamar, Bring the meate into the chamber, that I may eate of thine hand. And Tamar tooke the cakes which ſhee had made, and brought them into the chamber to Amnon her brother.11And when ſhee had brought them vnto him to eate, hee tooke hold of her, and ſaid vnto her, Come lye with mee, my ſiſter.12And ſhe anſwered him, Nay, my brother, doe not force me: for no ſuch thing ought to bee done in Iſrael; doe not thou this folly.13And I, whither ſhall I cauſe my ſhame to goe? and as for thee, thou ſhalt be as one of the fooles in Iſrael: now therefore, I pray thee, ſpeake vnto the king, for he will not withhold me from thee.14Howbeit hee would not hearken vnto her voice, but being ſtronger then ſhee, forced her, and lay with her.15Then Amnon hated her exceedingly, ſo that the hatred wherwith he hated her, was greater then the loue wherewith hee had loued her: And Amnon ſaid vnto her, Ariſe, be gone.16And ſhe ſaid vnto him, There is no cauſe: this euill in ſending me away, is greater then the other that thou diddeſt vnto me: But he would not hearken vnto her.17Then hee called his ſeruant that miniſtred vnto him, and ſaid, Put now this woman out from mee, and bolt the doore after her.18And ſhee had a garment of diuers colours vpon her: for with ſuch robes were the Kings daughters, that were virgins, apparelled. Then his ſeruant brought her out, and bolted the doore after her.19And Tamar put aſhes on her head, and rent her garment of diuers colours that was on her, and layde her hand on her head, and went on, crying.20And Abſalom her brother ſayde vnto her, Hath Amnon thy brother beene with thee? But holde nowe thy peace, my ſiſter: he is thy brother, regard not this thing. So Tamar remained deſolate in her brother Abſaloms houſe.21But when King Dauid heard of all theſe things, he was very wroth.22And Abſalom ſpake vnto his brother Amnon neither good nor bad: for Abſalom hated Amnon, becauſe he had forced his ſiſter Tamar.23And it came to paſſe after two full yeeres, that Abſalom had ſheepeſhearers in Baal-Hazor, which is beſide Ephraim: and Abſalom inuited all the kings ſonnes.24And Abſalom came to the King, and ſaid, Behold now, thy ſeruant hath ſheepe-ſhearers, Let the King, I beſeech thee, and his ſeruants, goe with thy ſeruant.25And the King ſayde to Abſalom, Nay, my ſonne, let vs not all now goe, leſt we be chargeable vnto thee. And he preſſed him: howbeit he would not goe, but bleſſed him.26Then ſaid Abſalom, If not, I pray thee, let my brother Amnon goe with vs. And the King ſaid vnto him, Why ſhould he goe with thee?27But Abſalom preſſed him, that he let Amnon and all the kings ſonnes goe with him.28Now Abſalom had commanded his ſeruants, ſaying, Marke yee now when Amnons heart is merrie with wine, and when I ſay vnto you, Smite Amnon, then kill him, feare not: haue not I commanded you? be couragious, and be valiant.29And the ſeruants of Abſalom did vnto Amnon as Abſalom had commanded: then all the Kings ſonnes aroſe, and euery man gate him vp vpon his mule, and fled.30And it came to paſſe while they were in the way, that tidings came to Dauid, ſaying, Abſalom hath ſlaine all the Kings ſonnes, and there is not one of them left.31Then the king aroſe, and tare his garments, and lay on the earth: and all his ſeruants ſtoode by with their clothes rent.32And Ionadab the ſonne of Shimeah Dauids brother, anſwered and ſaid, Let not my lord ſuppoſe that they haue ſlaine all the yong men the Kings ſonnes; for Amnon onely is dead: for by the appointment of Abſalom this hath beene determined, from the day that he forced his ſiſter Tamar.33Now therefore let not my lord the King take the thing to his heart, to thinke that all the Kings ſonnes are dead: for Amnon onely is dead.34But Abſalom fled: and the yong man that kept the watch, lift vp his eyes, and looked, and behold, there came much people by the way of the hill ſide behind him.35And Ionadab ſaid vnto the king, Behold, the kings ſonnes come: as thy ſeruant ſaid, ſo it is.36And it came to paſſe aſsoone as hee had made an ende of ſpeaking, that behold, the kings ſonnes came, and lift vp their voice, and wept; and the King alſo and all his ſeruants wept very ſore.37But Abſalom fled, and went to Talmai the ſonne of Ammihud king of Geſhur: and Dauid mourned for his ſonne euery day.38So Abſalom fled, and went to Geſhur, and was there three yeeres.39And the ſoule of king Dauid longed to goe foorth vnto Abſalom: for he was comforted concerning Amnon, ſeeing he was dead.

CHAPTER 141Now Ioab the ſonne of Zeruiah, perceiued that the kings heart was toward Abſalom.2And Ioab ſent to Tekoah, and fetcht thence a wiſe woman, and ſaid vnto her, I pray thee, faine thy ſelfe to be a mourner, and put on now mourning apparel, and anoint not thy ſelfe with oile, but be as a woman that had a long time mourned for the dead:3And come to the king, and ſpeake on this maner vnto him: ſo Ioab put the words in her mouth.4And when the woman of Tekoah ſpake to the king, ſhee fell on her face to the ground, and did obeyſance, and ſaid, Helpe, O king.5And the king ſaid vnto her, What aileth thee? And ſhe anſwered, I am indeed a widow woman, and mine huſband is dead.6And thy handmayd had two ſonnes, and they two ſtroue together in the field, and there was none to part them, but the one ſmote the other, and ſlew him.7And behold, the whole family is riſen againſt thine handmayd, and they ſaid, Deliuer him that ſmote his brother, that we may kill him, for the life of his brother whom he ſlew, and we will deſtroy the heire alſo: and ſo they ſhall quench my cole which is left, and ſhall not leaue to my huſband neither name nor remainder vpon the earth.8And the king ſaide vnto the woman, Goe to thine houſe, and I will giue charge concerning thee.9And the woman of Tekoah ſaid vnto the king, My lord, O king, the iniquitie bee on mee, and on my fathers houſe: and the king and his throne bee guiltleſſe.10And the king ſaid, Whoſoeuer ſaith ought vnto thee, bring him to mee, and he ſhall not touch thee any more.11Then ſaid ſhe, I pray thee, let the king remember the Lord thy God, that thou wouldeſt not ſuffer the reuengers of blood to deſtroy any more, leſt they deſtroy my ſonne. And he ſaid, As the Lord liueth, there ſhall not one haire of thy ſonne fall to the earth.12Then the woman ſaid, Let thine handmayd, I pray thee, ſpeake one word vnto my lord the king. And hee ſaid, ſay on.13And the woman ſaid, Wherefore then haſt thou thought ſuch a thing againſt the people of God? For the king doeth ſpeake this thing as one which is faulty, in that the king doeth not fetch home againe his baniſhed.14For we muſt needs die, and are as water ſpilt on the ground, which cannot bee gathered vp againe: neither doeth God reſpect any perſon, yet doeth he deuiſe meanes, that his baniſhed bee not expelled from him.15Now therefore that I am come to ſpeake of this thing vnto my lord the king, it is becauſe the people haue made me afraid: and thy handmayd ſaid, I will now ſpeake vnto the king; it may bee that the king will performe the requeſt of his handmayd.16For the king wil heare, to deliuer his handmayd out of the hand of the man that would deſtroy mee, and my ſonne together out of the inheritance of God:17Then thine handmaid ſaid, The word of my lord the king ſhall now be comfortable: for as an Angel of God, ſo is my lord the king to diſcerne good and bad: therfore the Lord thy God will be with thee.18Then the king anſwered and ſaid vnto the woman, Hide not from me, I pray thee, the thing that I ſhall aſke thee. And the woman ſaid, Let my lord the king now ſpeake.19And the king ſaid, Is not the hand of Ioab with thee in all this? And the woman anſwered and ſaid, As thy ſoule liueth, my lord the king, none can turne to the right hand or to the left from ought that my lord the king hath ſpoken: for thy ſeruant Ioab, hee bade me, and he put all theſe wordes in the mouth of thine handmaid:20To fetch about this forme of ſpeech hath thy ſeruant Ioab done this thing: and my lord is wiſe, according to the wiſedome of an Angel of God, to know all things that are in the earth.21And the king ſaid vnto Ioab, Behold now, I haue done this thing: goe therefore, bring the yong man Abſalom againe.22And Ioab fell to the ground on his face, & bowed himſelfe, and thanked the king: and Ioab ſaid, To day thy ſeruant knoweth that I haue found grace in thy ſight, my lord O king, in that the king hath fulfilled the requeſt of his ſeruant.23So Ioab aroſe, and went to Geſhur, & brought Abſalom to Ieruſalem.24And the king ſaid, Let him turne to his owne houſe, & let him not ſee my face. So Abſalom returned to his owne houſe, and ſawe not the kings face.25But in all

Iſrael there was none to be ſo much praiſed as Abſalom, for his beautie:
from the ſole of his foot euen to the crowne of his head, there was no
blemiſh in him.26And when he polled his head, (for it was at euery yeres
end that he polled it: becauſe the haire was heauy on him, therefore he
polled it) hee weighed the haire of his head at two hundred ſhekels after
the kings weight.27And vnto Abſalom there were borne three ſonnes,
and one daughter, whoſe name was Tamar: ſhee was a woman of a faire
countenance.28So Abſalom dwelt two full yeeres in Ieruſalem, and ſaw
not the kings face.29Therefore Abſalom ſent for Ioab, to haue ſent him
to the king, but hee would not come to him: and when hee ſent againe
the ſecond time, hee would not come.30Therefore hee ſaid vnto his
ſeruants, See, Ioabs field is neere mine, and he hath barley there: goe,
and ſet it on fire: and Abſaloms ſeruants ſet the field on fire.31Then Ioab
aroſe, and came to Abſalom vnto his houſe, and ſaid vnto him,
Wherefore haue thy ſeruants ſet my field on fire?32And Abſalom
anſwered Ioab, Behold, I ſent vnto thee, ſaying, come hither, that I may
ſend thee to the king to ſay, Wherefore am I come from Geſhur? It had
bene good for mee to haue bene there ſtill: now therefore let me ſee the
kings face: and if there bee any iniquitie in me, let him kill me.33So Ioab
came to the King, and told him: and when hee had called for Abſalom,
he came to the king, and bowed himſelfe on his face to the ground
before the king, and the King kiſſed Abſalom.
CHAPTER 151And it came to paſſe after this, that Abſalom prepared
him charets and horſes, and fiftie men to runne before him.2And
Abſalom roſe vp earely, and ſtood beſide the way of the gate: and it was
ſo, that when any man that had a controuerſie, came to the king for
iudgment, then Abſalom called vnto him, and ſaid, Of what citie art
thou? And he ſaid, Thy ſeruant is of one of the tribes of Iſrael.3And
Abſalom ſaid vnto him, See, thy matters are good & right, but there is
no man deputed of the king to heare thee.4Abſalom ſaid moreouer, Oh
that I were made Iudge in the land, that euery man which hath any ſuit
or cauſe, might come vnto me, and I would do him iuſtice.5And it was
ſo, that when any man came nigh to him, to doe him obeiſance, he put
foorth his hand, and tooke him, and kiſſed him.6And on this maner did
Abſalom to all Iſrael, that came to the King for iudgement: ſo Abſalom
ſtole the hearts of the men of Iſrael.7And it came to paſſe after fourtie
yeeres, that Abſalom ſaid vnto the king, I pray thee, let mee goe and pay
my vow which I haue vowed vnto the Lord in Hebron.8For thy ſeruant
vowed a vowe while I abode at Geſhur in Syria, ſaying, If the Lord ſhall
bring mee againe in deed to Ieruſalem, then I will ſerue the Lord.9And
the king ſaid vnto him, Goe in peace. So he aroſe, and went to
Hebron.10But Abſalom ſent ſpies thorowout all the tribes of Iſrael,
ſaying, As ſoone as yee heare the ſound of the trumpet, then yee ſhall
ſay, Abſalom reigneth in Hebron.11And with Abſalom went two
hundred men out of Ieruſalem, that were called, and they went in their
ſimplicitie, and they knew not any thing.12And Abſalom ſent for
Ahithophel the Gilonite, Dauids counſeller, from his citie, euen from
Giloh, while he offered ſacrifices: and the conſpiracie was ſtrong, for
the people encreaſed continually with Abſalom.13And there came a
meſſenger to Dauid, ſaying, The hearts of the men of Iſrael are after
Abſalom.14And Dauid ſaid vnto all his ſeruants that were with him at
Ieruſalem, Ariſe, and let vs flee; for wee ſhall not elſe eſcape from
Abſalom: make ſpeede to depart, leſt hee ouertake vs ſuddenly, and
bring euill vpon vs, and ſmite the city with the edge of the ſword.15And
the kings ſeruants ſaid vnto the king, Behold, thy ſeruants are readie to
doe whatſoeuer my lord the king ſhall appoint.16And the king went
foorth, and all his houſhold after him: and the King left tenne women,
which were concubines, to keepe the houſe.17And the king went forth,
and all the people after him, and taried in a place that was farre off.18And
all his ſeruants paſſed on beſide him: and all the Cherethites, and all the
Pelethites, and all the Gittites, ſixe hundred men, which came after him
from Gath, paſſed on before the king.19Then ſaid the king to Ittai the
Gittite, Wherefore goeſt thou alſo with vs? Returne to thy place, and
abide with the King: for thou art a ſtranger, and alſo an exile.20Whereas
thou cameſt but yeſterday, ſhould I this day make thee goe vp and
downe with vs? Seeing I goe whither I may, returne thou, and take backe
thy brethren: mercie and trueth be with thee.21And Ittai anſwered the
King, and ſaid, As the Lord liueth, and as my lord the king liueth, ſurely
in what place my lord the king ſhall be, whether in death or life, euen
there alſo will thy ſeruant be.22And Dauid ſaid to Ittai, Goe, and paſſe
ouer. And Ittai the Gittite paſſed ouer, and all his men, and all the little
ones that were with him.23And all the countrey wept with a loude voice,
and all the people paſſed ouer: the King alſo himſelfe paſſed ouer the
brooke Kidron, and all the people paſſed ouer, toward the way of the
wilderneſſe.24And loe, Zadok alſo, and all the Leuites were with him,
bearing the Arke of the Couenant of God, and they ſet downe the Arke
of God; and Abiathar went vp, vntill all the people had done paſsing out
of the citie.25And the King ſaid vnto Zadok, Cary backe the Arke of
God into the citie: if I ſhall finde fauour in the eyes of the Lord, he wil
bring me againe, and ſhew me both it, and his habitation.26But if he thus
ſay, I haue no delight in thee: beholde, here am I, let him doe to me, as
ſeemeth good vnto him.27The king ſaid alſo vnto Zadok the Prieſt, Art
not thou a Seer? Returne into the citie in peace, and your two ſonnes
with you, Ahimaaz thy ſonne, and Ionathan the ſonne of Abiathar.28See,
I will tarie in the plaine of the wilderneſſe, vntill there come word from
you to certifie me.29Zadok therefore and Abiathar caried the Arke of
God againe to Ieruſalem; and they taried there.30And Dauid went vp by
the aſcent of mount Oliuet, and wept as he went vp, and had his head
couered, and he went barefoote, and all the people that was with him,
couered euery man his head, and they went vp, weeping as they went
vp.31And one tolde Dauid, ſaying, Ahithophel is among the conſpirators
with Abſalom. And Dauid ſayde, O Lord, I pray thee turne the counſell
of Ahithophel into fooliſhneſse.32And it came to paſſe, that when Dauid
was come to the top of the mount, where he worſhipped God, behold,
Huſhai the Archite came to meet him, with his coat rent, and earth vpon
his head:33Unto whom Dauid ſaid, If thou paſſeſt on with me, then thou
ſhalt be a burden vnto me.34But if thou returne to the citie, and ſay vnto
Abſalom, I wil be thy ſeruant, O king: as I haue bene thy fathers ſeruant
hitherto, ſo will I now alſo be thy ſeruant: then mayeſt thou for mee
defeat the counſell of Ahithophel.35And haſt thou not there with thee
Zadok, and Abiathar the Prieſts? therefore it ſhall be, that what thing
ſoeuer thou ſhalt heare out of the kings houſe, thou ſhalt tell it to Zadok
and Abiathar the Prieſts.36Behold, they haue there with them their two
ſonnes, Ahimaaz Zadoks ſonne, and Ionathan Abiathars ſonne: and by
them ye ſhall ſend vnto me euery thing that ye can heare.37So Huſhai
Dauids friend came into the citie, and Abſalom came into Ieruſalem.
CHAPTER 161And when Dauid was a little paſt the top of the hill,
Beholde, Ziba the ſeruant of Mephiboſheth met him with a couple of
aſſes ſadled, and vpon them two hundred loaues of bread, and an
hundred bunches of raiſins, and an hundred of ſummer fruits, and a
bottell of wine.2And the King ſaide vnto Ziba, What meaneſt thou by
theſe? And Ziba ſaide, The aſſes bee for the kings houſhold to ride on,
and the bread and ſummer fruit for the yong men to eate, and the wine,
that ſuch as be faint in the wilderneſſe, may drinke.3And the king ſaid,
And where is thy maſters ſonne? and Ziba ſaid vnto the king, Behold,
he abideth at Ieruſalem: for hee ſaid, To day ſhall the houſe of Iſrael
reſtore mee the kingdome of my father.4Then ſaid the king to Ziba,
Behold, thine are all that pertained vnto Mephiboſheth. And Ziba ſaide,
I humbly beſeech thee that I may finde grace in thy ſight, my lord, O
king.5And when king Dauid came to Bahurim, behold, thence came out
a man of the family of the houſe of Saul, whoſe name was Shimei the
ſonne of Gera: hee came foorth, and curſed ſtill as he came.6And he caſt
ſtones at Dauid, and at all the ſeruants of king Dauid: and all the people,
and all the mighty men were on his right hand, and on his left.7And thus
ſaid Shimei when hee curſed, Come out, come out thou bloody man,
and thou man of Belial:8The Lord hath returned vpon thee all the blood
of the houſe of Saul, in whoſe ſtead thou haſt raigned, and the Lord hath
deliuered the kingdome into the hand of Abſalom thy ſonne: and
behold, thou art taken to thy miſchiefe, becauſe thou art a bloody
man.9Then ſaid Abiſhai the ſonne of Zeruiah vnto the king, Why ſhould
this dead dogge curſe my lord the king? let mee goe ouer, I pray thee,
and take off his head.10And the king ſaid, What haue I to doe with you,
ye ſonnes of Zeruiah? So let him curſe, becauſe the Lord hath ſaid vnto
him, Curſe Dauid. Who ſhall then ſay, Wherefore haſt thou done
ſo?11And Dauid ſaid to Abiſhai, and to all his ſeruants, Beholde, my
ſonne which came foorth of my bowels, ſeeketh my life: how much
more now may this Beniamite doe it? let him alone, and let him curſe:
for the Lord hath bidden him.12It may bee that the Lord will looke on
mine affliction, and that the Lord will requite good for his curſing this
day.13And as Dauid and his men went by the way, Shimei went along on

the hilles ſide ouer againſt him, and curſed as hee went, and threw ſtones at him, and caſt duſt.14And the king, and all the people that were with him, came weary, and refreſhed themſelues there.15And Abſalom and al the people the men of Iſrael, came to Ieruſalem, and Ahithophel with him.16And it came to paſſe when Huſhai the Archite, Dauids friend, was come vnto Abſalom, that Huſhai ſaid vnto Abſalom, God ſaue the king, God ſaue the king.17And Abſalom ſaid to Huſhai, Is this thy kindneſſe to thy friend? Why wenteſt thou not with thy friend?18And Huſhai ſaid vnto Abſalom, Nay, but whom the Lord and this people, and all the men of Iſrael chuſe, his will I bee, and with him will I abide.19And againe, whom ſhould I ſerue? ſhould I not ſerue in the preſence of his ſonne? as I haue ſerued in thy fathers preſence, ſo will I be in thy preſence.20Then ſaid Abſalom to Ahithophel, Giue counſell among you what we ſhall doe.21And Ahithophel ſaid vnto Abſalom, Goe in vnto thy fathers concubines, which he hath left to keepe the houſe, and all Iſrael ſhall heare that thou art abhorred of thy father, then ſhall the hands of all that are with thee be ſtrong.22So they ſpread Abſalom a tent vpon the top of the houſe, and Abſalom went in vnto his fathers concubines, in the ſight of all Iſrael.23And the counſell of Ahithophel which he counſelled in thoſe dayes, was as if a man had enquired at the Oracle of God: ſo was all the counſell of Ahithophel, both with Dauid and with Abſalom.

CHAPTER 171Moreouer Ahithophel ſaid vnto Abſalom, Let mee nowe chuſe out twelue thouſand men, and I will Ariſe and purſue after Dauid this night.2And I wil come vpon him while hee is wearie and weake handed, and wil make him afraid: and all the people that are with him ſhall flee, and I will ſmite the king onely.3And I wil bring backe all the people vnto thee: the man whom thou ſeekeſt is as if all returned: ſo all the people ſhall be in peace.4And the ſaying pleaſed Abſalom well, and all the Elders of Iſrael.5Then ſaid Abſalom, Call now Huſhai the Archite alſo, and let vs heare likewiſe what he ſaith.6And when Huſhai was come to Abſalom, Abſalom ſpake vnto him, ſaying, Ahithophel hath ſpoken after this maner: ſhall we doe after his ſaying? if not, ſpeake thou.7And Huſhai ſaid vnto Abſalom, The counſell that Ahithophel hath giuen, is not good at this time.8For, (ſaid Huſhai,) thou knoweſt thy father and his men, that they bee mightie men, and they be chafed in their minds, as a beare robbed of her whelps in the field: and thy father is a man of warre, and will not lodge with the people.9Behold, he is hid now in ſome pit, or in ſome other place: and it wil come to paſſe when ſome of them bee ouerthrowen at the firſt, that whoſoeuer heareth it, wil ſay, There is a ſlaughter among the people that followe Abſalom.10And he alſo that is valiant, whoſe heart is as the heart of a Lyon, ſhall vtterly melt: for all Iſrael knoweth that thy father is a mightie man, and they which be with him are valiant men.11Therefore I counſell, that all Iſrael be generally gathered vnto thee, from Dan euen to Beer-ſheba, as the ſand that is by the ſea for multitude, and that thou goe to battell in thine owne perſon.12So ſhall wee come vpon him in ſome place where he ſhall be found, and we will light vpon him as the dew falleth on the ground: and of him and of all the men that are with him, there ſhall not be left ſo much as one.13Moreouer, if hee be gotten into a citie, then ſhall all Iſrael bring ropes to that city, and we will draw it into the riuer, vntill there be not one ſmall ſtone found there.14And Abſalom and all the men of Iſrael ſaid, The counſell of Huſhai the Archite, is better then the counſell of Ahithophel: For the Lord had appointed to defeate the good counſell of Ahithophel, to the intent that the Lord might bring euill vpon Abſalom.15Then ſaid Huſhai vnto Zadok and to Abiathar the Prieſtes, Thus and thus did Ahithophel counſell Abſalom and the Elders of Iſrael, and thus and thus haue I counſelled.16Now therefore ſend quickly, and tell Dauid, ſaying, Lodge not this night in the plaines of the wildernes, but ſpeedily paſſe ouer, leſt the King be ſwallowed vp, and all the people that are with him.17Now Ionathan and Ahimaaz ſtayed by En-rogel: (for they might not be ſeene to come into the citie) and a wench went and tolde them: and they went, and tolde king Dauid.18Neuertheleſſe, a ladde ſaw them, and tolde Abſalom: but they went both of them away quickely, and came to a mans houſe in Bahurim, which had a Well in his court, whither they went downe.19And the woman tooke and ſpread a couering ouer the welles mouth, and ſpread ground corne thereon; and the thing was not knowen.20And when Abſaloms ſeruants came to the woman to the houſe, they ſaid, Where is Ahimaaz and Ionathan? And the woman ſaid vnto them, They be gone ouer the brooke of water. And when they had ſought, and could not finde them, they returned to Ieruſalem.21And it came to paſſe after they were departed, that they came vp out of the Well, and went and tolde king Dauid, and ſaid vnto Dauid, Ariſe, and paſſe quickely ouer the water: for thus hath Ahithophel counſelled againſt you.22Then Dauid aroſe, and all the people that were with him, and they paſſed ouer Iordane: by the morning light there lacked not one of them that was not gone ouer Iordane.23And when Ahithophel ſawe that his counſell was not followed, he ſadled his aſſe, and aroſe, and gate him home to his houſe, to his citie, and put his houſhold in order, and hanged himſelfe, and died, and was buried in the ſepulchre of his father.24Then Dauid came to Mahanaim: and Abſalom paſſed ouer Iordane, he and all the men of Iſrael with him.25And Abſalom made Amaſa captaine of the hoſte in ſtead of Ioab: which Amaſa was a mans ſonne whoſe name was Ithra an Iſraelite, that went in to Abigal the daughter of Nahaſh, ſiſter to Zeruiah Ioabs mother.26So Iſrael and Abſalom pitched in the land of Gilead.27And it came to paſſe when Dauid was come to Mahanaim, that Shobi the ſonne of Nahaſh of Rabbah of the children of Ammon, and Machir the ſonne of Ammiel of Lodebar, and Barzillai the Gileadite, of Rogelim,28Brought beds, and baſins, and earthen veſſels, and wheat, and barley, and floure, and parched corne, & beanes, and lentiles, and parched pulſe,29And honie, and butter, and ſheepe, and cheeſe of kine for Dauid, and for the people that were with him, to eate: for they ſaid, The people is hungrie, and wearie, and thirſtie in the wilderneſſe.

CHAPTER 181And Dauid numbred the people that were with him, and ſet captaines of thouſands, and captaines of hundreds ouer them.2And Dauid ſent forth a third part of the people vnder the hand of Ioab, and a third part vnder the hand of Abiſhai the ſonne of Zeruiah Ioabs brother, and a third part vnder the hand of Ittai the Gittite: and the king ſaid vnto the people, I will ſurely goe foorth with you my ſelfe alſo.3But the people anſwered, Thou ſhalt not goe foorth: for if we flee away, they will not care for vs, neither if halfe of vs die will they care for vs: but now thou art worth ten thouſand of vs: therfore now it is better that thou ſuccour vs out of the citie.4And the King ſayde vnto them, What ſeemeth you beſt, I will doe. And the King ſtood by the gate ſide, and all the people came out by hundreds, and by thouſands.5And the king commanded Ioab, and Abiſhai, and Ittai, ſaying, Deale gently for my ſake with the yong man, euen with Abſalom. And all the people heard when the king gaue all the captaines charge concerning Abſalom.6So the people went out into the field againſt Iſrael: and the battell was in the wood of Ephraim,7Where the people of Iſrael were ſlaine before the ſeruants of Dauid, and there was there a great ſlaughter that day of twenty thouſand men.8For the battell was there ſcattered ouer the face of all the countrey: and the wood deuoured more people that day, then the ſword deuoured.9And Abſalom met the ſeruants of Dauid; and Abſalom rode vpon a mule, and the mule went vnder the thicke boughs of a great Oke, and his head caught hold of the Oke, and hee was taken vp betweene the heauen and the earth, and the mule that was vnder him, went away.10And a certaine man ſaw it, and told Ioab, and ſaid, Behold, I ſaw Abſalom hanged in an Oke.11And Ioab ſaid vnto the man that told him, And behold, thou ſaweſt him, and why didſt thou not ſmite him there to the ground, and I would haue giuen thee tenne ſhekels of ſiluer, and a girdle?12And the man ſaide vnto Ioab, Though I ſhould receiue a thouſand ſhekels of ſiluer in mine hand, yet would I not put foorth mine hand againſt the Kings ſonne: for in our hearing the King charged thee, and Abiſhai, and Ittai, ſaying, Beware that none touch the yong man Abſalom.13Otherwyſe, I ſhould haue wrought falſhood againſt mine owne life: for there is no matter hid from the King, and thou thy ſelfe wouldeſt haue ſet thy ſelfe againſt me.14Then ſaid Ioab, I may not tary thus with thee. And hee tooke three darts in his hand, and thruſt them thorow the heart of Abſalom, while hee was yet aliue in the midſt of the Oke.15And ten yong men that bare Ioabs armour, compaſſed about and ſmote Abſalom, and ſlew him.16And Ioab blew the trumpet, and the people returned from purſuingafter Iſrael: for Ioab helde backe the people.17And they tooke Abſalom, and caſt him into a great pit in the wood, and layd a very great heape of ſtones vpon him: and all Iſrael fled euery one to his tent.18Now Abſalom in his life time had taken and reared vp for himſelfe a pillar, which is in the Kings dale: for hee ſaid, I haue no ſonne to keepe my name in remembrance: And hee called the pillar after his owne name, and it is called vnto this day, Abſaloms place.19Then ſaid Ahimaaz the ſonne of Zadok, Let mee now runne, and beare the King tidings, how that the Lord hath auenged him of his enemies.20And Ioab ſaid vnto him, Thou ſhalt not beare tidings this day, but thou ſhalt beare tidings another day: but this day thou ſhalt beare no tidings, becauſe the Kings ſonne is dead.21Then ſaid Ioab to Cuſhi, Goe tell the King what thou haſt ſeene. And Cuſhi bowed himſelfe vnto Ioab, and ranne.22Then ſaid Ahimaaz the ſonne of Zadok yet againe to Ioab, But howſoeuer, let mee, I pray thee, alſo runne after Cuſhi. And Ioab ſaid, Wherefore wilt thou runne, my ſonne, ſeeing that thou haſt no tidings ready?23But howſoeuer, (ſaid he) let mee runne: And hee ſaid vnto him, Runne. Then Ahimaaz ranne by the way of the plaine, and ouerranne Cuſhi.24And Dauid ſate betweene the two gates: and the watchman went vp to the roofe ouer the gate vnto the wall, and lift vp his eyes, and looked, and behold, a man running alone.25And the watchman cried, and told the King. And the king ſaid, If he bee alone, there is tidings in his mouth. And he came apace, and drew neere.26And the watchman ſaw another man running, and the watchman called vnto the porter, and ſaid, Behold, another man running alone. And the King ſaid, He alſo bringeth tidings.27And the watchman ſaid, Mee thinketh the running of the foremoſt is like the running of Ahimaaz the ſonne of Zadok. And the King ſaid, Hee is a good man, and commeth with good tidings.28And Ahimaaz called, and ſaid vnto the King, All is well. And hee fell downe to the earth vpon his face before the King, and ſaide, Bleſſed bee the Lord thy God which hath deliuered vp the men that lift vp their hande againſt my lord the King.29And the king ſaid, Is the yong man Abſalom ſafe? And Ahimaaz anſwered, When Ioab ſent the kings ſeruant, and me thy ſeruant, I ſaw a great tumult, but I knew not what it was.30And the king ſaid vnto him, Turne aſide and ſtand here. And hee turned aſide, and ſtood ſtill.31And behold, Cuſhi came, and Cuſhi ſaid, Tidings my lord the king: for the Lord hath auenged thee this day of all them that roſe vp againſt thee.32And the king ſaid vnto Cuſhi, Is the yong man Abſalom ſafe? And Cuſhi anſwered, The enemies of my lord the king, and all that riſe againſt thee to doe thee hurt, be as that yong man is.33And the king was much moued, and went vp to the chamber ouer the gate, and wept: and as he went, thus hee ſaid, O my ſonne Abſalom, my ſonne, my ſonne Abſalom: would God I had died for thee, O Abſalom, my ſonne, my ſonne.

CHAPTER 191And it was told Ioab, Beholde, the king weepeth and mourneth for Abſalom.2And the victorie that day was turned into mourning vnto all the people: for the people heard ſay that day, how the king was grieued for his ſonne.3And the people gate them by ſtealth that day into the citie, as people beeing aſhamed ſteale away when they flee in battell.4But the king couered his face, and the king cried with a loud voyce, O my ſonne Abſalom, O Abſalom my ſonne, my ſonne.5And Ioab came into the houſe to the king, and ſaid, Thou haſt ſhamed this day the faces of all thy ſeruants, which this day haue ſaued thy life, and the liues of thy ſonnes, & of thy daughters, and the liues of thy wiues, and the liues of thy concubines,6In that thou loueſt thine enemies, and hateſt thy friends; for thou haſt declared this day, that thou regardeſt neither princes, nor ſeruants: for this day I perceiue, that if Abſalom had liued, and all we had died this day, then it had pleaſed thee well.7Now therefore Ariſe, goe foorth, and ſpeake comfortably vnto thy ſeruants: for I ſweare by the Lord, if thou goe not forth, there wil not tarie one with thee this night, and that will be worſe vnto thee then all the euill that befell thee from thy youth vntill now.8Then the King roſe, and ſate in the gate: and they told vnto all the people, ſaying, Behold, the king doth ſit in the gate: and all the people came before the king: for Iſrael had fled euery man to his tent.9And all the people were at ſtrife throughout all the tribes of Iſrael, ſaying, The king ſaued vs out of the hand of our enemies, and he deliuered vs out of the hand of the Philiſtines, and now he is fled out of the land for Abſalom.10And Abſalom whom wee anointed ouer vs, is dead in battell: nowe therefore why ſpeake ye not a word of bringing the king backe?11And King Dauid ſent to Zadok and to Abiathar the prieſts, ſaying, Speake vnto the Elders of Iudah, ſaying, Why are ye the laſt to bring the king backe to his houſe? (ſeeing the ſpeech of all Iſrael is come to the king, euen to his houſe.)12Yee are my brethren, Yee are my bones and my fleſh: wherfore then are ye the laſt to bring backe the king?13And ſay ye to Amaſa: Art thou not of my bone, and of my fleſh? God do ſo to me, and more alſo, if thou be not captaine of the hoſte before me continually in the roome of Ioab.14And he bowed the heart of all the men of Iudah, euen as the heart of one man, ſo that they ſent this word vnto the King, Returne thou and all thy ſeruants.15So the King returned, and came to Iordan: and Iudah came to Gilgal, to goe to meet the King, to conduct the king ouer Iordane.16And Shimei the ſonne of Gera, a Beniamite, which waſs of Bahurim, haſted, & came downe with the men of Iudah, to meet King Dauid.17And there were a thouſand men of Beniamin with him, and Ziba the ſeruant of the houſe of Saul, and his fifteene ſonnes and his twenty ſeruants with him, and they went ouer Iordane before the King.18And there went ouer a ferry-boat to cary ouer the kings houſhold, and to doe what he thought good: and Shimei the ſonne of Gera fell downe before the king as he was come ouer Iordane;19And ſaid vnto the king, Let not my lord impute iniquitie vnto me, neither do thou remember that which thy ſeruant did peruerſly the day that my lord the king went out of Ieruſalem, that the king ſhould take it to his heart.20For thy ſeruant doeth know that I haue ſinned: therefore behold, I am come the firſt this day of all the houſe of Ioſeph, to goe downe to meete my lord the king.21But Abiſhai the ſonne of Zeruiah anſwered, and ſayd, Shall not Shimei be put to death for this, becauſe hee curſed the Lords Anointed?22And Dauid ſaid, What haue I to doe with you, yee ſonnes of Zeruiah, that yee ſhould this day be aduerſaries vnto me? ſhall there any man be put to death this day in Iſrael? for doe not I know, that I am this day King ouer Iſrael?23Therfore the king ſaid vnto Shimei, Thou ſhalt not die: and the King ſware vnto him.24And Mephiboſheth the ſonne of Saul came downe to meet the king, and had neither dreſſed his feete, nor trimmed his beard, nor waſhed his clothes, from the day the King departed, vntill the day hee came againe in peace.25And it came to paſſe when he was come to Ieruſalem to meete the King, that the King ſayd vnto him, Wherefore wenteſt not thou with me, Mephiboſheth?26And hee anſwered, My lord O king, my ſeruant deceiued mee; for thy ſeruant ſayd, I will ſaddle me an aſſe that I may ride thereon, and goe to the king, becauſe thy ſeruant is lame:27And hee hath ſlandered thy ſeruant vnto my lord the king, but my lord the King is as an Angel of God: doe therefore what is good in thine eyes.28For all of my fathers houſe were but dead men before my lord the king: yet diddeſt thou ſet thy ſeruant among them that did eate at thine owne table: what right therefore haue I yet to crie any more vnto the king?29And the king ſaid vnto him, Why ſpeakeſt thou any more of thy matters? I haue ſaid, Thou and Ziba diuide the land.30And Mephiboſheth ſaid vnto the king, Yea, let him take all, foraſmuch as my lorde the king is come againe in peace vnto his owne houſe.31And Barzillai the Gileadite came downe from Rogelim, and went ouer Iordane with the king, to conduct him ouer Iordane.32Now Barzillai was a very aged man, euen foureſcore yeeres olde, and he had prouided the king of ſuſtenance while he lay at Mahanaim: for he was a very great man.33And the king ſaid vnto Barzillai, Come thou ouer with me, and I will feede thee with me in Ieruſalem.34And Barzillai ſayde vnto the king, How long haue I to liue, that I ſhould goe vp with the King vnto Ieruſalem?35I am this day foureſcore yeeres olde: and can I diſcerne betweene good and euill? Can thy ſeruant taſte what I eate, or what I drinke? can I heare any more the voice of ſinging men and ſinging women? wherfore then ſhould thy ſeruant bee yet a burden vnto my lord the king?36Thy ſeruant will goe a little way ouer Iordane with the king: and why ſhould the king recompenſe it me with ſuch a reward?37Let thy ſeruant, I pray thee, turne backe againe, that I may die in mine owne citie, and be buried by the graue of my father, and of my mother: but behold thy ſeruant Chimham, let him go ouer with my lord the king, and doe to him what ſhall ſeeme good vnto thee.38And the king anſwered, Chimham ſhal goe ouer with me, and I will doe to him that which ſhall ſeeme good vnto thee: and whatſoeuer thou ſhalt require of me, that will I doe for thee.39And all the people went ouer Iordane: and when the king was come ouer, the king kiſſed Barzillai, and bleſſed him, and he returned vnto his owne place.40Then the King went on to Gilgal, and Chimham went on with him: and all the people of Iudah conducted the king, and alſo halfe the people of Iſrael.41And behold, all the men of Iſrael came to the king, and ſaid vnto the king, Why haue our brethren the men of Iudah ſtollen thee away, and haue brought the King and his houſhold, and all Dauids men with him, ouer Iordane?42And all the men of Iudah anſwered the men of Iſrael, Becauſe the king is neere of kinne to vs: wherefore then be ye angrie for this matter? Haue we eaten at all of the kings coſt? or hath he giuen vs any gift?43And the men of Iſrael anſwered the men of Iudah, and ſaid, Wee haue ten parts in the king, and we haue alſo more right in Dauid then yee: why then did yee deſpiſe vs, that our aduice ſhould not be firſt had in bringing backe our king? And the wordes of the men of Iudah were fiercer then the words of the men of Iſrael.

CHAPTER 201And there happened to bee there a man of Belial, whoſe name was Sheba the ſonne of Bichri, a Beniamite, & hee blew a trumpet, and ſaid, Wee haue no part in Dauid, neither haue we inheritance in the ſonne of Ieſſe: euery man to his tents, O Iſrael.2So euery man of Iſrael went vp from after Dauid, and followed Sheba the ſonne of Bichri: but the men of Iudah claue vnto their king, from Iordane euen to Ieruſalem.3And Dauid came to his houſe at Ieruſalem, and the king tooke the ten women his concubines, whom he had left to keep the houſe, and put them in ward, and fed them, but went not in vnto them: ſo they were ſhut vp vnto the day of their death, liuing in widowhood.4Then ſaid the king to Amaſa, Aſsemble me the men of Iudah within three dayes, and be thou here preſent.5So Amaſa went to aſſemble the men of Iudah; but hee taried longer then the ſet time which he had appointed him.6And Dauid ſaid to Abiſhai, Now ſhall Sheba the ſonne of Bichri doe vs more harme then did Abſalom: take thou thy lords ſeruants, and purſue after him, leſt he get him fenced cities, and eſcape vs.7And there went out after him Ioabs men, and the Cherethites, and the Pelethites, and all the mighty men: and they went out of Ieruſalem, to purſue after Sheba the ſonne of Bichri.8When they were at the great ſtone which is in Gibeon, Amaſa went before them: and Ioabs garment that he had put on, was girded vnto him, and vpon it a girdle with a ſword faſtned vpon his loynes in the ſheath thereof, and as hee went forth, it fell out.9And Ioab ſaide to Amaſa, Art thou in health, my brother? And Ioab tooke Amaſa by the beard with the right hand to kiſſe him.10But Amaſa tooke no heed to the ſword that was in Ioabs hand: ſo hee ſmote him therewith in the fifth rib, and ſhed out his bowels to the ground, and ſtrake him not againe, and he died: ſo Ioab and Abiſhai his brother purſued after Sheba the ſonne of Bichri.11And one of Ioabs men ſtood by him, and ſaid, He that fauoureth Ioab, and hee that is for Dauid, let him goe after Ioab.12And Amaſa wallowed in blood in the mids of the high way: and when the man ſaw that all the people ſtood ſtill, he remoued Amaſa out of the high way into the field, and caſt a cloth vpon him, when hee ſaw that euery one that came by him, ſtood ſtill.13When he was remoued out of the high way, all the people went on after Ioab, to purſue after Sheba the ſonne of Bichri.14And hee went thorow all the tribes of Iſrael vnto Abel, and to Bethmaachah, and all the Berites: and they were gathered together, and went alſo after him.15And they came and beſieged him in Abel of Bethmaachah, and they caſt vp a banke againſt the citie, and it ſtood in the trench: and all the people that were with Ioab, battered the wall, to throw it downe.16Then cried a wiſe woman out of the citie, Heare, heare; ſay, I pray you, vnto Ioab, Come neere hither, that I may ſpeake with thee.17And when he was come neere vnto her, the woman ſaid, Art thou Ioab? And he anſwered, I am he: Then ſhee ſaid vnto him, Heare the words of thine handmaid. And he anſwered, I doe heare.18Then ſhe ſpake, ſaying, They were wont to ſpeake in old time, ſaying, They ſhall ſurely aſke counſell at Abel: and ſo they ended the matter.19I am one of them that are peaceable and faithfull in Iſrael: thou ſeekeſt to deſtroy a citie, and a mother in Iſrael: Why wilt thou ſwallow vp the inheritance of the Lord ?20And Ioab anſwered and ſaide, Farre be it, farre be it from me, that I ſhould ſwallow vp or deſtroy.21The matter is not ſo: but a man of mount Ephraim (Sheba the ſonne of Bichri by name) hath lift vp his hand againſt the king, euen againſt Dauid: deliuer him onely, and I will depart from the city. And the woman ſaid vnto Ioab, Behold, his head ſhall be throwen to thee ouer the wall.22Then the woman went vnto all the people in her wiſedome, and they cut off the head of Sheba the ſonne of Bichri, and caſt it out to Ioab: and hee blew a trumpet, and they retired from the citie, euery man to his tent: & Ioab returned to Ieruſalem vnto the king.23Now Ioab was ouer all the hoſte of Iſrael, and Benaiah the ſonne of Iehoiada was ouer the Cherethites, and ouer the Pelethites.24And Adoram was ouer the tribute, and Iehoſhaphat the ſonne of Ahilud was Recorder.25And Sheua was ſcribe, and Zadok, and Abiathar were the Prieſts.26And Ira alſo the Iairite, was a chiefe ruler about Dauid.

CHAPTER 211Then there was a famine in the dayes of Dauid three yeeres, yeere after yeere, and Dauid enquired of the Lord. And the Lord anſwered, It is for Saul, and for his bloodie houſe, becauſe he ſlew the Gibeonites.2And the king called the Gibeonites, and ſaid vnto them, (now the Gibeonites were not of the children of Iſrael, but of the remnant of the Amorites, and the children of Iſrael had ſworne vnto them: and Saul ſought to ſlay them, in his zeale to the children of Iſrael and Iudah)3Wherefore Dauid ſaid vnto the Gibeonites, What ſhall I doe for you? and wherwith ſhall I make the atonement, that ye may bleſſe the inheritance of the Lord ?4And the Gibeonites ſaide vnto him, We will haue no ſiluer nor golde of Saul, nor of his houſe, neither for vs ſhalt thou kill any man in Iſrael. And he ſaid, What you ſhall ſay, that will I doe for you.5And they anſwered the king, The man that conſumed vs, and that deuiſed againſt vs, that we ſhould be deſtroied from remaining in any of the coaſts of Iſrael,6Let ſeuen men of his ſonnes bee deliuered vnto vs, and wee will hang them vp vnto the Lord in Gibeah of Saul, whome the Lord did chuſe. And the king ſaid, I will giue them.7But the king ſpared Mephiboſheth the ſonne of Ionathan the ſonne of Saul, becauſe of the Lords othe that was between them, betweene Dauid, and Ionathan the ſonne of Saul.8But the king tooke the two ſons of Rizpah the daughter of Aiah, whom ſhe bare vnto Saul, Armoni and Mephiboſheth, and the fiue ſonnes of Michal the daughter of Saul, whome ſhe brought vp for Adriel the ſonne of Barzillai the Meholathite.9And hee deliuered them into the hands of the Gibeonites, and they hanged them in the hill before the Lord: and they fell all ſeuen together, and were put to death in the dayes of harueſt, in the firſt dayes, in the beginning of barley harueſt.10And Rizpah the daughter of Aiah tooke ſackecloth, and ſpread it for her vpon the rocke, from the beginning of harueſt, vntill water dropped vpon them out of heauen, and ſuffered neither the birds of the aire to reſt on them by day, nor the beaſtes of the fielde by night.11And it was tolde Dauid what Rizpah the daughter of Aiah the concubine of Saul had done.12And Dauid went and tooke the bones of Saul, and the bones of Ionathan his ſonne from the men of Iabeſh Gilead, which had ſtollen them from the ſtreet of Bethſhan where the Philiſtines had hanged them, when the Philiſtines had ſlaine Saul in Gilboa.13And hee brought vp from thence the bones of Saul, and the bones of Ionathan his ſonne, and they gathered the bones of them that were hanged.14And the bones of Saul and Ionathan his ſonne buried they in the countrey of Beniamin in Zelah, in the ſepulchre of Kiſh his father: and they perfourmed all that the king commanded: and after that, God was entreated for the land.15Moreouer, the Philiſtines had yet warre againe with Iſrael, and Dauid went down, and his ſeruants with him, and fought againſt the Philiſtines, and Dauid waxed faint.16And Iſhbi-benob which was of the ſonnes of the gyant, (the weight of whoſe ſpeare weighed three hundred ſhekels of braſſe in weight) he being girded with a new ſword, thought to haue ſlaine Dauid.17But Abiſhai the ſonne of Zeruiah ſuccoured him, and ſmote the Philiſtine, and killed him. Then the men of Dauid ſware vnto him, ſaying, Thou ſhalt goe no more out with vs to battell, that thou quench not the light of Iſrael.18And it came to paſſe after this, that there was againe a battell with the Philiſtines at Gob: then Sibbechai the Huſhathite ſlew Saph, which was of the ſonnes of the Gyant.19And there was againe a battell in Gob, with the Philiſtines, where Elhanan the ſonne of Iaare-Oregim a Bethlehemite, ſlewe the brother of Goliath the Gittite, the ſtaffe of whoſe ſpeare was like a weauers beame.20And there was yet a battell in Gath, where was a man of great ſtature, that had on euery hand ſixe fingers, and on euery foote ſixe toes, foure and twenty in number, and he alſo was borne to the Gyant.21And when he defied Iſrael, Ionathan the ſonne of Shimea the brother of Dauid, ſlew him.22Theſe foure were borne to the Gyant in Gath, and fell by the hand of Dauid, and by the hand of his ſeruants.

CHAPTER 221And Dauid ſpake vnto the Lord the wordes of this ſong, in the day that the Lord had deliuered him out of the hand of all his enemies, and out of the hand of Saul.2And he ſaid, The Lord is my rocke and my fortreſse, and my deliuerer:3The God of my rocke, in him will I truſt: hee is my ſhield, and the horne of my ſaluation, my high tower, and my refuge, my Sauiour; thou saueſt me from violence.4I will call on the Lord, who is worthy to be praiſed: ſo ſhall I be ſaued from mine enemies.5When the waues of death compaſſed me: the floods of vngodly men made me afraid.6The ſorowes of Hell compaſſed me

about: the ſnares of death preuented me.7In my diſtreſſe I called vpon
the Lord, and cryed to my God, and hee did heare my voice out of his
Temple, and my crie did enter into his eares.8Then the earth ſhooke and
trembled: the foundations of heauen mooued and ſhooke, becauſe hee
was wroth.9There went vp a ſmoake out of his noſtrils, and fire out of
his mouth deuoured: coales were kindled by it.10Hee bowed the heauens
alſo and came downe: and darkeneſſe was vnder his feete.11And he rode
vpon a Cherub, and did flie: and hee was ſeene vpon the wings of the
winde.12And hee made darkeneſſe pauilions round about him, darke
waters, and thicke clouds of the ſkies.13Through the brightneſse before
him, were coales of fire kindled.14The Lord thundred from heauen: and
the moſt high vttered his voice.15And he ſent out arrowes, and ſcattered
them; lightning, and diſcomfited them.16And the channels of the ſea
appeared, the foundations of the world were diſcouered, at the rebuking
of the Lord, at the blaſt of the breath of his noſtrils.17He ſent from
aboue, he tooke me: he drew me out of many waters.18He deliuered me
from my ſtrong enemy, and from them that hated mee: for they were
too ſtrong for me.19They preuented me in the day of my calamitie: but
the Lord was my ſtay.20Hee brought me forth alſo into a large place: he
deliuered me, becauſe hee delighted in me.21The Lord rewarded mee
according to my righteouſneſſe: according to the cleanneſſe of my
hands, hath hee recompenſed me.22For I haue kept the wayes of the
Lord, and haue not wickedly departed from my God.23For all his
iudgements were before me: and as for his Statutes, I did not depart
from them.24I was alſo vpright before him: and haue kept my ſelfe from
mine iniquitie.25Therefore the Lord hath recompenſed me, according to
my righteouſneſſe: according to my cleanneſſe in his eye ſight.26With
the merciful thou wilt ſhew thy ſelfe mercifull, and with the vpright man
thou wilt ſhew thy ſelfe vpright.27With the pure thou wilt ſhew thy ſelfe
pure: and with the froward, thou wilt ſhew thy ſelfe vnſauoury.28And
the afflicted people thou wilt ſaue: but thine eyes are vpon the hautie,
that thou mayeſt bring them downe.29For thou art my lampe, O Lord:
and the Lord wil lighten my darkeneſſe.30For by thee I haue run through
a troupe: by my God haue I leaped ouer a wall.31As for God, his way is
perfect, the word of the Lord is tried: he is a buckler to all them that
truſt in him.32For who is God, ſaue the Lord ? and who is a rocke, ſaue
our God?33God is my ſtrength and power: and he maketh my way
perfect.34Hee maketh my feet like hindes feet: and ſetteth mee vpon my
high places.35He teacheth my hands to warre: ſo that a bow of ſteele is
broken by mine armes.36Thou haſt alſo giuen mee the ſhield of thy
ſaluation: and thy gentleneſse hath made me great.37Thou haſt enlarged
my ſteps vnder me: ſo that my feet did not ſlip.38I haue purſued mine
enemies, and deſtroyed them: and turned not againe vntill I had
conſumed them.39And I haue conſumed them and wounded them, that
they could not Ariſe: yea, they are fallen vnder my feet.40For thou haſt
girded mee with ſtrength to battel: them that roſe vp againſt me, haſt
thou ſubdued vnder me.41Thou haſt alſo giuen mee the necks of mine
enemies, that I might deſtroy them that hate me.42They looked, but
there was none to ſaue: euen vnto the Lord, but he anſwered them
not.43Then did I beat them as ſmall as the duſt of the earth: I did ſtampe
them as the myre of the ſtreet, and did ſpread them abroad.44Thou alſo
haſt deliuered mee from the ſtriuings of my people, thou haſt kept mee
to be head of the heathen: a people which I knew not, ſhall ſerue
me.45Strangers ſhall ſubmit themſelues vnto me: as ſoone as they heare,
they ſhall be obedient vnto me.46Strangers ſhall fade away: and they ſhall
bee afraid out of their cloſe places.47The Lord liueth, and bleſſed be my
rocke: and exalted be the God of the rocke of my ſaluation.48It is God
that auengeth mee, and that bringeth downe the people vnder me:49And
that bringeth me forth from mine enemies: thou alſo haſt lifted mee vp
on high aboue them that roſe vp againſt me: thou haſt deliuered me
from the violent man.50Therefore I will giue thankes vnto thee, O Lord,
among the heathen: and I will ſing praiſes vnto thy Name.51He is the
towre of ſaluation for his king: and ſheweth mercy to his Anointed, vnto
Dauid, and to his ſeede for euermore.
CHAPTER 231Nowe theſe bee the laſt words of Dauid: Dauid the
ſonne of Ieſſe ſaide, and the man who was raiſed vp on high, the
Anointed of the God of Iacob, and the ſweet Pſalmiſt of Iſrael, ſaid,2The
ſpirit of the Lord ſpake by me, and his word was in my tongue.3The
God of Iſrael ſaid, the Rocke of Iſrael ſpake to me: he that ruleth ouer
men muſt be iuſt, ruling in the feare of God:4And he ſhall be as the light
of the morning, when the Sunne riſeth, euen a morning, without
cloudes; as the tender graſſe ſpringing out of the earth by cleare ſhining
after raine:5Although my houſe be not ſo with God: yet he hath made
with mee an euerlaſting couenant, ordred in al things and ſure: for this
is all my ſaluation, and all my deſire, although he make it not to
grow.6But the ſonnes of Belial ſhall bee all of them as thornes thruſt
away, becauſe they cannot be taken with hands,7But the man that ſhal
touch them, muſt be fenced with yron, and the ſtaffe of a ſpeare, and
they ſhall bee vtterly burnt with fire in the ſame place.8Theſe be the
names of the mightie men whome Dauid had: The Tachmonite that ſate
in the ſeat, chiefe among the captaines, (the ſame was Adino the Eznite:)
hee lift vp his ſpeare againſt eight hundred, whom he ſlew at one
time.9And after him was Eleazar the ſonne of Dodo the Ahohite, one
of the three mightie men with Dauid, when they defied the Philiſtines
that were there gathered together to battell, and the men of Iſrael were
gone away.10He aroſe, and ſmote the Philiſtines vntill his hand was
wearie, and his hand claue vnto the ſword: and the Lord wrought a great
victorie that day, and the people returned after him onely to ſpoile.11And
after him was Shammah the ſonne of Agee the Hararite: and the
Philiſtines were gathered together into a troupe, where was a piece of
ground full of lentiles: and the people fled from the Philiſtines.12But hee
ſtood in the midſt of the ground, and defended it, and ſlewe the
Philiſtines: and the Lord wrought a great victorie.13And three of the
thirtie chiefe went downe and came to Dauid in the harueſt time, vnto
the caue of Adullam: and the troupe of the Philiſtines pitched in the
valley of Rephaim.14And Dauid was then in an holde, and the gariſon
of the Philiſtines was then in Bethlehem.15And Dauid longed, and ſaid,
Oh that one would giue mee drinke of the water of the well of
Bethlehem which is by the gate.16And the three mightie men brake
through the hoſt of the Philiſtines, and drew water out of the Well of
Bethlehem, that was by the gate, and tooke it, and brought it to Dauid:
neuertheleſſe he would not drinke thereof, but powred it out vnto the
Lord.17And he ſaid, Be it farre from me, O Lord, that I ſhould doe this:
is not this the blood of the men that went in ieopardie of their liues?
therefore he would not drinke it. Theſe things did theſe three mightie
men.18And Abiſhai the brother of Ioab, the ſonne of Zeruiah, was
chiefe among three, and he lift vp his ſpeare againſt three hundred, and
ſlew them, and had the name among three.19Was hee not moſt
honourable of three? therefore he was their captaine: howbeit, hee
attained not vnto the firſt three.20And Benaiah the ſonne of Iehoiada
the ſonne of a valiant man, of Kabzeel, who had done many actes, he
ſlew two lion-like men of Moab: hee went downe alſo, and ſlewe a Lyon
in the middeſt of a pit in time of ſnow.21And he ſlew an Egyptian a
goodly man: and the Egyptian had a ſpeare in his hand; but he went
downe to him with a ſtaffe, and plucked the ſpeare out of the Egyptians
hand, and ſlewe him with his owne ſpeare.22Theſe things did Benaiah
the ſonne of Iehoiada, and had the name among three mightie
men.23Hee was more honourable then the thirtie, but hee attained not
to the firſt three: and Dauid ſet him ouer his guard.24Aſahel the brother
of Ioab was one of the thirtie: Elhanan the ſonne of Dodo of
Bethlehem,25Shammah the Harodite, Elika the Harodite,26Helez the
Paltite, Ira the ſonne of Ikkeſh the Tekoite,27Abiezer the Anethothite,
Mebunnai the Huſhathite,28Zalmon the Ahohite, Maharai the
Netophathite,29Heleb the ſonne of Baanah, a Netophathite, Ittai the
ſonne of Ribai out of Gibeah of the children of Beniamin.30Benaiah the
Pirathonite, Hiddai of the brookes of Gaaſh,31Abialbon the Arbathite,
Azmaueth the Barhumite,32Elihaba the Shaalbonite: of the ſonnes of
Iaſhen, Ionathan,33Shammah the Hararite, Ahiam the ſonne of Sharar
the Hararite,34Eliphelet the ſonne of Ahaſbai, the ſonne of the
Maachathite, Eliam the ſonne of Ahithophel the Gilonite,35Hezrai the
Carmelite, Paarai the Arbite,36Igal the ſonne of Nathan of Zobah, Bani
the Gadite,37Zelek the Ammonite, Naharai the Berothite, armour-
bearer to Ioab the ſonne of Zeruiah,38Ira an Ithrite, Gareb an
Ithrite,39Uriah the Hittite: thirtie and ſeuen in all.
CHAPTER 241And againe the anger of the Lord was kindled againſt
Iſrael, and hee mooued Dauid againſt them, to ſay, Goe, number Iſrael
and Iudah.2For the king ſaid to Ioab the captaine of the hoſte, which
was with him, Goe now through all the tribes of Iſrael, from Dan euen
to Beer-ſheba, and number ye the people, that I may know the number

of the people. 3 And Ioab ſayde vnto the King, Now the Lord thy God adde vnto the people (how many ſoeuer they be) an hundred folde, and that the eyes of my lorde the king may ſee it: but why doeth my lord the king delight in this thing? 4 Notwithſtanding, the kings word preuailed againſt Ioab, and againſt the captaines of the hoſte: and Ioab and the captaines of the hoſt went out from the preſence of the king, to number the people of Iſrael. 5 And they paſſed ouer Iordane, and pitched in Aroer, on the right ſide of the citie that lieth in the midſt of the riuer of Gad, and toward Iazer. 6 Then they came to Gilead, and to the land of Tahtim-Hodſhi; and they came to Dan-Iaan, and about to Zidon, 7 And came to the ſtrong holde of Tyre, and to all the cities of the Hiuites, and of the Canaanites: and they went out to the South of Iudah, euen to Beer-ſheba. 8 So when they had gone through all the land, they came to Ieruſalem at the ende of nine moneths, and twentie dayes. 9 And Ioab gaue vp the ſumme of the number of the people vnto the king, and there were in Iſrael eight hundred thouſand valiant men that drewe the ſword: and the men of Iudah were fiue hundred thouſand men. 10 And Dauids heart ſmote him, after that hee had numbred the people: and Dauid ſayde vnto the Lord, I haue ſinned greatly in that I haue done: and nowe I beſeech thee, O Lord, take away the iniquitie of thy ſeruant, for I haue done very fooliſhly. 11 For when Dauid was vp in the morning, the word of the Lord came vnto the Prophet Gad Dauids Seer, ſaying, 12 Goe and ſay vnto Dauid, Thus ſaith the Lord, I offer thee three things; chuſe thee one of them, that I may doe it vnto thee. 13 So Gad came to Dauid, and told him, and ſaid vnto him, Shall ſeuen yeeres of famine come vnto thee in thy land? or wilt thou flee three moneths before thine enemies, while they purſue thee? or that there be three dayes peſtilence in thy land? Now aduiſe, and ſee what anſwere I ſhall returne to him that ſent me. 14 And Dauid ſaide vnto Gad, I am in a great ſtrait: let vs fall now into the hand of the Lord (for his mercies are great,) and let me not fall into the hand of man. 15 So the Lord ſent a peſtilence vpon Iſrael, from the morning, euen to the time appointed: and there died of the people from Dan euen to Beerſheba, ſeuentie thouſand men. 16 And when the Angel ſtretched out his hand vpon Ieruſalem to deſtroy it, the Lord repented him of the euill, and ſaid to the Angel that deſtroyed the people, It is ynough: ſtay now thine hand. And the Angel of the Lord was by the threſhing place of Araunah the Iebuſite. 17 And Dauid ſpake vnto the Lord when he ſaw the Angel that ſmote the people, and ſaid, Loe, I haue ſinned, and I haue done wickedly: but theſe ſheepe, what haue they done? Let thine hand, I pray thee, be againſt mee, and againſt my fathers houſe. 18 And Gad came that day to Dauid, and ſaid vnto him, Goe vp, reare an Altar vnto the Lord, in the threſhing floore of Araunah the Iebuſite. 19 And Dauid, according to the ſaying of Gad, went vp, as the Lord commanded. 20 And Araunah looked, and ſaw the King and his ſeruants comming on toward him: and Araunah went out, and bowed himſelfe before the King on his face vpon the ground. 21 And Araunah ſaid, Wherefore is my lord the King come to his ſeruant? and Dauid ſaide, To buy the threſhing floore of thee, to build an Altar vnto the Lord, that the plague may be ſtayed from the people. 22 And Araunah ſaid vnto Dauid, Let my lord the King take and offer vp what ſeemeth good vnto him: Beholde, here be oxen for burnt ſacrifice, and threſhing inſtruments, and other inſtruments of the oxen for wood. 23 All theſe things did Araunah, as a king, giue vnto the King: and Araunah ſaide vnto the King, The Lord thy God accept thee. 24 And the King ſaid vnto Araunah, Nay, but I will ſurely buy it of thee at a price: neither will I offer burnt offerings vnto the Lord my God, of that which doeth coſt mee nothing. So Dauid bought the threſhing floore, and the oxen, for fiftie ſhekels of ſiluer. 25 Aud Dauid built there an Altar vnto the Lord, and offered burnt offerings, and peace offerings: ſo the Lord was intreated for the land, and the plague was ſtayed from Iſrael.

1 KINGS

CHAPTER 1 1 Now King Dauid was olde, and ſtriken in yeeres, and they couered him with clothes, but hee gate no heate. 2 Wherefore his ſeruants ſaid vnto him, Let there be ſought for my lord the king a yong virgin, and let her ſtand before the King, and let her cheriſh him, and let her lie in thy boſome, that my lord the King may get heate. 3 So they ſought for a faire damoſel throughout all the coaſts of Iſrael, and found Abiſhag a Shunammite, and brought her to the King. 4 And the damoſell was very faire, and cheriſhed the king, and miniſtred to him: but the king knew her not. 5 Then Adoniiah the ſonne of Haggith exalted himſelfe, ſaying, I wil be king: And he prepared him charets and horeſemen, and fiftie men to runne before him. 6 And his father had not diſpleaſed him at any time, in ſaying, Why haſt thou done ſo? And hee alſo was a very goodly man, and his mother bare him after Abſalom. 7 And hee conferred with Ioab the ſonne of Zeruiah, and with Abiathar the Prieſt: and they following Adoniiah, helped him. 8 But Zadok the Prieſt, and Benaiah the ſonne of Iehoiada, and Nathan the Prophet, and Shimei, and Rei, and the mightie men which belonged to Dauid, were not with Adoniiah. 9 And Adoniiah ſlew ſheepe, and oxen, and fat cattell, by the ſtone of Zoheleth, which is by En-Rogel, and called all his brethren the kings ſonnes, and all the men of Iudah the kings ſeruants. 10 But Nathan the Prophet, and Benaiah, and the mightie men, and Solomon his brother he called not. 11 Wherefore Nathan ſpake vnto Bath-ſheba the mother of Solomon, ſaying, Haſt thou not heard that Adoniiah the ſon of Haggith doth reigne, and Dauid our lord knoweth it not? 12 Now therefore come, let mee, I pray thee, giue thee counſell, that thou mayeſt ſaue thine owne life, and the life of thy ſonne Solomon. 13 Goe, and get thee in vnto King Dauid, and ſay vnto him, Diddeſt not thou, my lord, O king, ſweare vnto thine handmaid, ſaying, Aſſuredly Solomon thy ſonne ſhall reigne after mee, and he ſhall ſit vpon my throne? why then doth Adoniiah reigne? 14 Beholde, while thou yet talkeſt there with the king, I alſo will come in after thee, and confirme thy words. 15 And Bath-ſheba went in vnto the King into the chamber: and the king was very olde, and Abiſhag the Shunammite miniſtred vnto the king. 16 And Bathſheba bowed, and did obeyſance vnto the king: and the king ſaid, What wouldeſt thou? 17 And ſhe ſaid vnto him, My lord, thou ſwareſt by the Lord thy God vnto thine handmaid, ſaying, Aſſuredly Solomon thy ſonne ſhall reigne after me, and he ſhall ſit vpon my throne: 18 And now behold, Adoniiah reigneth; and now my lord the king, thou knoweſt it not. 19 And he hath ſlaine oxen, and fat cattell, and ſheepe in abundance, and hath called all the ſonnes of the king, and Abiathar the Prieſt, and Ioab the captaine of the hoſte: but Solomon thy ſeruant hath he not called. 20 And thou, my lord O king, the eyes of all Iſrael are vpon thee, that thou ſhouldeſt tell them who ſhall ſit on the throne of my lord the king after him. 21 Otherwiſe it ſhall come to paſſe, when my lord the king ſhal ſleepe with his fathers, that I and my ſonne Solomon ſhall be counted offenders. 22 And loe, while ſhee yet talked with the king, Nathan the Prophet alſo came in. 23 And they tolde the king, ſaying, Beholde Nathan the Prophet. And when hee was come in before the king, he bowed himſelfe before the king with his face to the ground. 24 And Nathan ſaid, My lord O king, haſt thou ſaid, Adoniiah ſhall reigne after mee, and hee ſhall ſit vpon my throne? 25 For hee is gone downe this day, and hath ſlaine oxen, and fat cattel, and ſheepe in abundance, and hath called all the kings ſonnes, and the captaines of the hoſt, and Abiathar the Prieſt: and behold, they eate and drinke before him, and ſay, God ſaue king Adoniiah. 26 But me, euen me thy ſeruant, and Zadok the Prieſt, and Benaiah the ſonne of Iehoiada, and thy ſeruant Solomon hath he not called. 27 Is this thing done by my lord the king, and thou haſt not ſhewed it vnto thy ſeruant, who ſhould ſit on the throne of my lord the king, after him? 28 Then king Dauid anſwered, and ſaid, Call me Bathſheba. And ſhe came into the kings preſence, and ſtood before the king. 29 And the king ſware, and ſaid, As the Lord liueth, that hath redeemed my ſoule out of all diſtreſſe, 30 Euen as I ſware vnto thee by the Lord God of Iſrael, ſaying, Aſſuredly Solomon thy ſonne ſhall reigne after me, and he ſhal ſit vpon my throne in my ſtead; euen ſo wil I certainly doe this day. 31 Then Bathſheba bowed with her face to the earth, and did reuerence to the king, and ſaid, Let my lord king Dauid liue for euer. 32 And king Dauid ſaid, Call me Zadok the Prieſt, and Nathan the Prophet, and Benaiah the ſonne of Iehoiada. And they came before the king. 33 The king alſo ſaide vnto them, Take with you the

ſeruants of your lord, and cauſe Solomon my ſonne to ride vpon mine
owne mule, and bring him downe to Gihon.[34]And let Zadok the Prieſt,
and Nathan the Prophet, anoint him there King ouer Iſrael: and blow
ye with the trumpet, and ſay, God ſaue King Solomon.[35]Then ye ſhall
come vp after him, that hee may come and ſit vpon my throne; for he
ſhall be king in my ſtead: and I haue appointed him to be ruler ouer
Iſrael, and ouer Iudah.[36]And Benaiah the ſonne of Iehoiada anſwered
the King, and ſaid, Amen: The Lord God of my lord the king ſay ſo
too.[37]As the Lord hath bene with my lord the King, euen ſo be he with
Solomon, and make his throne greater then the throne of my lord King
Dauid.[38]So Zadok the Prieſt, and Nathan the Prophet, and Benaiah the
ſonne of Iehoiada, and the Cherethites, and the Pelethites went downe,
and cauſed Solomon to ride vpon King Dauids mule, and brought him
to Gihon.[39]And Zadok the Prieſt tooke an horne of oile out of the
Tabernacle, and anointed Solomon: and they blew the trumpet, and all
the people ſaid, God ſaue King Solomon.[40]And all the people came vp
after him, and the people piped with pipes, and reioyced with great ioy,
ſo that the earth rent with the ſound of them.[41]And Adoniiah and all
the gheſts that were with him, heard it as they had made an end of eating:
and when Ioab heard the ſound of the trumpet, hee ſaid, Wherefore is
this noiſe of the citie, being in an vproare?[42]And while hee yet ſpake,
behold, Ionathan the ſonne of Abiathar the Prieſt came, and Adoniiah
ſayde vnto him, Come in, for thou art a valiant man, and bringeſt good
tidings.[43]And Ionathan anſwered, and ſaid to Adoniiah, Uerily our lorde
king Dauid hath made Solomon king.[44]And the king hath ſent with him
Zadok the Prieſt, and Nathan the Prophet, and Benaiah the ſonne of
Iehoiada, and the Cherethites, and the Pelethites, and they haue cauſed
him to ride vpon the kings mule.[45]And Zadok the Prieſt, and Nathan
the Prophet haue anointed him king in Gihon: and they are come vp
from thence reioycing, ſo that the citie rang againe: this is the noyſe that
yee haue heard.[46]And alſo Solomon ſitteth on the throne of the
kingdome.[47]And moreouer, the kings ſeruants came to bleſſe our lorde
king Dauid, ſaying, God make the name of Solomon better then thy
name, and make his throne greater then thy throne. And the king bowed
himſelfe vpon the bed.[48]And alſo thus ſayde the King, Bleſſed be the
Lord God of Iſrael, which hath giuen one to ſit on my throne this day,
mine eyes euen ſeeing it.[49]And all the gueſts that were with Adoniiah,
were afraid, and roſe vp, and went euery man his way.[50]And Adoniiah
feared becauſe of Solomon, and aroſe, and went, and caught hold on
the hornes of the Altar.[51]And it was tolde Solomon, ſaying, Behold,
Adoniiah feareth King Solomon: for loe, he hath caught hold on the
hornes of the Altar, ſaying, Let King Solomon ſweare vnto mee to day,
that hee will not ſlay his ſeruant with the ſword.[52]And Solomon ſayd, If
hee will ſhewe himſelfe a worthy man, there ſhall not an haire of him
fall to the earth: but if wickedneſſe ſhall be found in him, he ſhall
die.[53]So king Solomon ſent, and they brought him downe from the
Altar, and hee came and bowed himſelfe to king Solomou: and Solomon
ſayde vnto him, Goe to thine houſe.
CHAPTER 2[1]Now the dayes of Dauid drew nigh, that he ſhould die,
and he charged Solomon his ſonne, ſaying;[2]I goe the way of all the earth:
be thou ſtrong therefore, and ſhew thy ſelfe a man.[3]And keepe the
charge of the Lord thy God, to walke in his wayes, to keepe his Statutes,
and his Commandements, & his Iudgements, and his Teſtimonies, as it
is written in the Law of Moſes, that thou mayeſt proſper in all that thou
doeſt, and whitherſoeuer thou turneſt thy ſelfe:[4]That the Lord may
continue his word which hee ſpake concerning me, ſaying, If thy
children take heede to their way, to walke before mee in trueth, with all
their heart, and with all their ſoule, there ſhall not faile thee (ſayd hee) a
man on the throne of Iſrael.[5]Moreouer thou knoweſt alſo what Ioab the
ſonne of Zeruiah did to mee, and what he did to the two captaines of
the hoſtes of Iſrael, vnto Abner the ſonne of Ner, and vnto Amaſa the
ſonne of Iether, whom hee ſlewe, and ſhed the blood of warre in peace,
and put the blood of warre vpon his girdle that was about his loynes,
and in his ſhooes that were on his feet.[6]Doe therefore according to thy
wiſedome, and let not his hoare head goe downe to the graue in
peace.[7]But ſhewe kindneſſe vnto the ſonnes of Barzillai the Gileadite,
and let them be of thoſe that eate at thy table: for ſo they came to me
when I fled becauſe of Abſalom thy brother.[8]And behold, thou haſt
with thee Shimei the ſonne of Gera, a Beniamite of Bahurim, which
curſed mee with a grieuous curſe, in the day when I went to Mahanaim:
but hee came downe to meete me at Iordane, and I ſware to him by the
Lord, ſaying, I will not put thee to death with the ſword.[9]Nowe
therefore holde him not guiltleſſe: for thou art a wiſe man, and knoweſt
what thou oughteſt to doe vnto him, but his hoare head bring thou
downe to the graue with blood.[10]So Dauid ſlept with his fathers, and
was buried in the citie of Dauid.[11]And the dayes that Dauid raigned ouer
Iſrael, were fourty yeeres: ſeuen yeeres raigned hee in Hebron, and thirty
and three yeeres raigned hee in Ieruſalem.[12]Then ſate Solomon vpon the
throne of Dauid his father, and his kingdome was eſtabliſhed
greatly.[13]And Adoniiah the ſonne of Haggith came to Bathſheba the
mother of Solomon, and ſhe ſaid, Commeſt thou peaceably? And he
ſaid, Peaceably.[14]He ſaid moreouer, I haue ſomewhat to ſay vnto thee.
And ſhe ſaide, ſay on.[15]And he ſaid, Thou knoweſt that the kingdome
was mine, and that all Iſrael ſet their faces on me, that I ſhould raigne:
howbeit the kingdome is turned about, and is become my brothers: for
it was his from the Lord.[16]And now I aſke one petition of thee, deny
me not. And ſhe ſaide vnto him, ſay on.[17]And hee ſaide, Speake, I pray
thee, vnto Solomon the king (for hee will not ſay thee nay) that he giue
me Abiſhag the Shunammite to wife.[18]And Bathſheba ſaid, Wel, I will
ſpeake for thee vnto the king.[19]Bathſheba therefore went vnto king
Solomon, to ſpeake vnto him for Adoniiah: and the king roſe vp to
meete her, and bowed himſelfe vnto her, and ſate downe on his throne,
and cauſed a ſeate to bee ſet for the Kings mother, and ſhe ſate on his
right hand.[20]Then ſhe ſaid, I deſire one ſmall petition of thee, I pray thee
ſay me not nay: and the King ſaid vnto her, Aſke on, my mother, for I
will not ſay thee nay.[21]And ſhe ſaide, Let Abiſhag the Shunammite be
giuen to Adoniiah thy brother to wife.[22]And king Solomon anſwered,
and ſaid vnto his mother, And why doeſt thou aſke Abiſhag the
Shunammite for Adoniiah? Aſke for him the kingdome alſo (for he is
mine elder brother) euen for him, and for Abiathar the Prieſt, & for Ioab
the ſonne of Zeruiah.[23]Then king Solomon ſware by the Lord, ſaying,
God doe ſo to me, and more alſo, if Adoniiah haue not ſpoken this word
againſt his owne life.[24]Now therefore as the Lord liueth, which hath
eſtabliſhed mee, and ſet mee on the throne of Dauid my father, and who
hath made me an houſe as he promiſed, Adoniiah ſhall be put to death
this day.[25]And king Solomon ſent by the hand of Benaiah the ſonne of
Iehoiada, and he fell vpon him that he died.[26]And vnto Abiathar the
Prieſt ſaide the King, Get thee to Anathoth, vnto thine own fields, for
thou art worthy of death: but I will not at this time put thee to death,
becauſe thou bareſt the arke of the Lord God before Dauid my father,
and becauſe thou haſt bene afflicted in all wherein my father was
afflicted.[27]So Solomon thruſt out Abiathar from beeing Prieſt vnto the
Lord: that hee might fulfill the word of the Lord, which hee ſpake
concerning the houſe of Eli in Shiloh.[28]Then tidings came to Ioab (for
Ioab had turned after Adoniiah, though hee turned not after Abſalom)
and Ioab fled vnto the Tabernacle of the Lord, and caught hold on the
hornes of the Altar.[29]And it was told king Solomon that Ioab was fled
vnto the Tabernacle of the Lord, and behold, hee is by the Altar: Then
Solomon ſent Benaiah the ſonne of Iehoiada, ſaying, Goe fall vpon
him.[30]And Benaiah came to the Tabernacle of the Lord, and ſaid vnto
him, Thus ſaith the king, Come foorth. And he ſaid, Nay, but I will die
heere. And Benaiah brought the king word againe, ſaying, Thus ſaid
Ioab, and thus he anſwered me.[31]And the king ſaide vnto him, Doe as
he hath ſaid, and fall vpon him, and bury him, that thou mayeſt take
away the innocent blood which Ioab ſhed, from mee, and from the
houſe of my father.[32]And the Lord ſhall returne his blood vpon his owne
head, who fell vpon two men, more righteous and better then hee, and
ſlew them with the ſword, my father Dauid not knowing thereof, to wit,
Abner the ſonne of Ner, captaine of the hoſte of Iſrael, and Amaſa the
ſonne of Iether, captaine of the hoſte of Iudah.[33]Their blood ſhall
therefore returne vpon the head of Ioab, and vpon the head of his ſeed
for euer: but vpon Dauid, and vpon his ſeede, and vpon his houſe, and
vpon his throne, ſhall there bee peace for euer from the Lord.[34]So
Benaiah the ſonne of Iehoiada went vp, and fell vpon him, and ſlewe
him, and hee was buried in his owne houſe in the wilderneſſe.[35]And the
king put Benaiah the ſonne of Iehoiada in his roome ouer the hoſte, and
Zadok the Prieſt did the king put in the roume of Abiathar.[36]And the
king ſent, and called for Shimei, and ſaid vnto him, Build thee an houſe
in Ieruſalem, and dwell there, and goe not forth thence any
whither.[37]For it ſhall be, that on the day thou goeſt out, & paſſeſt ouer

the brooke Kidron, thou ſhalt know for certaine, that thou ſhalt ſurely
die: thy blood ſhal be vpon thine owne head.38And Shimei ſaid vnto the
King, The ſaying is good: as my lord the king hath ſaid, ſo will thy
ſeruant doe. And Shimei dwelt in Ieruſalem many dayes.39And it came
to paſſe at the end of three yeeres, that two of the ſeruants of Shimei
ranne away vnto Achiſh ſonne of Maachah king of Gath: and they told
Shimei, ſaying, Beholde, thy ſeruants be in Gath.40And Shimei aroſe,
and ſadled his aſſe, and went to Gath to Achiſh, to ſeeke his ſeruants:
and Shimei went and brought his ſeruants from Gath.41And it was told
Solomon, that Shimei had gone from Ieruſalem to Gath, and was come
againe.42And the king ſent and called for Shimei, and ſaid vnto him, Did
I not make thee to ſweare by the Lord, and proteſted vnto thee, ſaying,
Know for a certaine, that on the day thou goeſt out, and walkeſt abroad
any whither, that thou ſhalt ſurely die? And thou ſaideſt vnto me, The
word that I haue heard, is good.43Why then haſt thou not kept the Oath
of the Lord, and the commandement that I haue charged thee
with?44The king ſaid moreuer to Shimei, Thou knoweſt all the
wickedneſſe which thine heart is priuie to, that thou diddeſt to Dauid
my father: therefore the Lord ſhall returne thy wickedneſſe vpon thine
owne head.45And king Solomon ſhall be bleſſed, and the throne of
Dauid ſhall bee eſtabliſhed before the Lord for euer.46So the king
commaunded Benaiah the ſonne of Iehoiada, which went out, and fell
vpon him, that he died, and the kingdome was eſtabliſhed in the hand
of Solomon.
CHAPTER 31And Solomon made affinitie with Pharaoh king of
Egypt, and tooke Pharaohs daughter, and brought her into the citie of
Dauid, vntill he had made an end of building his owne houſe, and the
houſe of the Lord, and the wall of Ieruſalem round about.2Only the
people ſacrificed in high places, becauſe there was no houſe built vnto
the Name of the Lord vntill thoſe dayes.3And Solomon loued the Lord,
walking in the ſtatutes of Dauid his father: onely he ſacrificed and burnt
incenſe in high places.4And the king went to Gibeon to ſacrifice there;
for that was the great high place: a thouſand burnt offerings did
Solomon offer vp on that Altar.5In Gibeon the Lord appeared to
Solomon in a dreame by night: and God ſayd, Aſke what I ſhall giue
thee.6And Solomon ſaid, Thou haſt ſhewed vnto thy ſeruant Dauid my
father great mercy, according as he walked before thee in trueth, and in
righteouſneſſe, and in vprightneſse of heart with thee, and thou haſt
kept for him this great kindneſse, that thou haſt giuen him a ſonne to ſit
on his throne, as it is this day.7And now, O Lord my God, thou haſt
made thy ſeruant King in ſtead of Dauid my father: and I am but a litle
childe: I know not how to goe out or come in.8And thy ſeruant is in the
midſt of thy people which thou haſt choſen, a great people, that cannot
be numbred, nor counted for multitude.9Giue therefore thy ſeruant an
vnderſtanding heart, to iudge thy people, that I may diſcerne betweene
good and bad: for who is able to iudge this thy ſo great a people?10And
the ſpeach pleaſed the Lord, that Solomon had aſked this thing.11And
God ſaid vnto him, Becauſe thou haſt aſked this thing, and haſt not
aſked for thy ſelfe long life, neither haſt aſked riches for thy ſelfe, nor
haſt aſked the life of thine enemies, but haſt aſked for thy ſelfe
vnderſtanding to diſcerne iudgement;12Behold, I haue done according
to thy word: loe, I haue giuen thee a wiſe and an vnderſtanding heart, ſo
that there was none like thee before thee, neither after thee ſhall any
Ariſe like vnto thee.13And I haue alſo giuen thee that which thou haſt
not aſked, both riches, and honour: ſo that there ſhall not be any among
the Kings like vnto thee, all thy dayes.14And if thou wilt walke in my
wayes, to keepe my Statutes and my Commandements, as thy father
Dauid did walke, then I will lengthen thy dayes.15And Solomon awoke,
and behold, it was a dreame: and he came to Ieruſalem, and ſtood before
the Arke of the Couenant of the Lord, and offered vp burnt offerings,
and offered peace offerings, and made a feaſt to all his ſeruants.16Then
came there two women that were harlots, vnto the king, and ſtood
before him.17And the one woman ſaid, O my lord, I and this woman
dwell in one houſe, and I was deliuered of a childe, with her in the
houſe.18And it came to paſſe the third day after that I was deliuered, that
this woman was deliuered alſo: and wee were together; there was no
ſtranger with vs in the houſe, ſaue we two in the houſe.19And this
womans childe died in the night: becauſe ſhe ouerlaid it.20And ſhee aroſe
at midnight, and tooke my ſonne from beſide me, while thine handmaid
ſlept, and layd it in her boſome, and layd her dead childe in my
boſome.21And when I roſe in the morning to giue my childe ſucke,
behold, it was dead: but when I had conſidered it in the morning,
beholde, it was not my ſonne, which I did beare.22And the other woman
ſaid, Nay, but the liuing is my ſonne, and the dead is thy ſonne: And this
ſaid, No, but the dead is thy ſonne, and the liuing is my ſonne. Thus
they ſpake before the king.23Then ſaid the King, The one ſaith, This is
my ſonne, that liueth, and thy ſonne is the dead: and the other ſaith Nay:
but thy ſonne is the dead, and my ſonne is the liuing.24And the King
ſaid, Bring mee a ſword. And they brought a ſword before the
king:25And the king ſaid, Diuide the liuing childe in two, and giue halfe
to the one, and halfe to the other.26Then ſpake the woman whoſe the
liuing childe was, vnto the king, (for her bowels yerned vpon her ſonne)
and ſhe ſaid, O my lord, giue her the liuing childe, and in no wiſe ſlay it:
But the other ſaid, Let it be neither mine nor thine, but diuide it.27Then
the King anſwered and ſaid, Giue her the liuing child, and in no wiſe ſlay
it: ſhe is the mother thereof.28And all Iſrael heard of the Iudgement
which the king had iudged, and they feared the King: for they ſaw that
the wiſedome of God was in him, to doe Iudgement.
CHAPTER 41So King Solomon was king ouer all Iſrael.2And theſe
were the Princes which he had, Azariah the ſonne of Zadok, the
Prieſt,3Elihoreph, and Ahiah the ſonnes of Shiſha, Scribes: Iehoſhaphat
the ſonne of Ahilud the Recorder;4And Benaiah the ſonne of Iehoiada
was ouer the hoſt: And Zadok and Abiathar were the Prieſts:5And
Azariah the ſonne of Nathan was ouer the officers: and Zabud the ſonne
of Nathan was principall officer, and the kings friend.6And Ahiſhar was
ouer the houſhold: and Adoniram the ſonne of Abda was ouer the
tribute.7And Solomon had twelue officers ouer all Iſrael, which
prouided victuals for the king and his houſhold: each man his moneth
in a yeere made prouiſion.8And theſe are their names: the ſonne of Hur
in mount Ephraim,9The ſonne of Dekar in Makaz, and in Shaalbim, and
Bethſhemeſh, and Elon-Bethhanan.10The ſonne of Heſeb in Aruboth,
to him pertained Sochoh, and all the land of Hepher;11The ſonne of
Abinadab in all the region of Dor, which had Taphath the daughter of
Solomon to wife:12Baana the ſonne of Ahilud, to him pertained Taanach
and Megiddo, and all Beth-ſhean, which is by Zartanah beneath Iezreel,
from Beth-ſhean to Abel-Meholah, euen vnto the place that is beyond
Iokneam:13The ſonne of Geber in Ramoth Gilead, to him pertained the
townes of Iair the ſonne of Manaſſeh, which are in Gilead: to him alſo
pertained the region of Argob, which is in Baſhan, threeſcore great
cities, with walles, and braſen barres.14Ahinadab the ſonne of Iddo had
Mahanaim.15Ahimaaz was in Naphtali; he alſo tooke Baſmath the
daughter of Solomon to wife.16Baanah the ſonne of Huſhai was in Aſher
and in Aloth:17Iehoſhaphat the ſonne of Paruah in Iſſachar:18Shimei the
ſonne of Elah in Beniamin:19Geber the ſonne of Uri was in the countrey
of Gilead, in the countrey of Sihon king of the Amorites, and of Og king
of Baſhan; and hee was the onely officer which was in the land.20Iudah
and Iſrael were many, as the ſand which is by the ſea in multitude, eating
and drinking and making merrie.21And Solomon reigned ouer all
kingdoms from the riuer vnto the land of the Philiſtines, and vnto the
border of Egypt: they brought preſents, and ſerued Solomon all the
dayes of his life.22And Solomons prouiſion for one day, was thirtie
meaſures of fine floure, and threeſcore meaſures of meale,23Ten fat
oxen, and twentie oxen out of the paſtures, and an hundred ſheepe,
beſide Harts, and Roe-buckes, and fallow Deere, and fatted foule.24For
he had dominion ouer all the region on this ſide the Riuer, from Tiphſah
euen to Azzah ouer all the kings on this ſide the Riuer: and he had peace
on all ſides round about him.25And Iudah and Iſrael dwelt ſafely, euery
man vnder his Uine, and vnder his Figtree, from Dan euen to Beer-
ſheba, all the dayes of Solomon.26And Solomon had fourtie thouſand
ſtalles of horſes for his charets, and twelue thouſand horſemen.27And
thoſe officers prouided victuall for king Solomon, and for all that came
vnto king Solomons table, euery man in his moneth: they lacked
nothing.28Barley alſo and ſtraw for the horſes and dromedaries, brought
they vnto the place where the officers were, euery man according to his
charge.29And God gaue Solomon wiſdome, and vnderſtanding,
exceeding much, and largeneſse of heart, euen as the ſand that is on the
ſea ſhoare.30And Solomons wiſedome excelled the wiſedome of all the
children of the Eaſt countrey, and all the wiſedome of Egypt.31For hee
was wiſer then all men; then Ethan the Ezrahite, and Heman, and
Chalcol, and Darda the ſonnes of Mahol: and his fame was in all nations

round about.32And he ſpake three thouſand prouerbes: and his ſongs
were a thouſand and fiue.33And hee ſpake of trees, from the Cedar tree
that is in Lebanon, euen vnto the Hyſsope that ſpringeth out of the wall:
hee ſpake alſo of beaſts, and of foule, and of creeping things, and of
fiſhes.34And there came of all people to heare the wiſedome of
Solomon, from all kings of the earth, which had heard of his wiſedome.
CHAPTER 51And Hiram king of Tyre ſent his ſeruants vnto Solomon:
(for hee had heard that they had anointed him King in the roume of his
father,) for Hiram was euer a louer of Dauid.2And Solomon ſent to
Hiram, ſaying,3Thou knoweſt how that Dauid my father could not build
an houſe vnto the Name of the Lord his God, for the warres which were
about him on euery ſide, vntill the Lord put them vnder the ſoles of his
feet.4But now the Lord my God hath giuen me reſt on euery ſide, ſo
that there is neither aduerſary, nor euill occurrent.5And behold, I
purpoſe to build an houſe vnto the Name of the Lord my God, as the
Lord ſpake vnto Dauid my father, ſaying, Thy ſonne, whom I will ſet
vpon thy throne in thy roume, he ſhall build an houſe vnto my
Name.6Now therefore command thou, that they hew me Cedar trees
out of Lebanon, and my ſeruants ſhall bee with thy ſeruants: and vnto
thee will I giue hire for thy ſeruants, according to all that thou ſhalt
appoint: for thou knoweſt that there is not among vs, any that can ſkill
to hew timber, like vnto the Sidonians.7And it came to paſſe when
Hiram heard the wordes of Solomon, that hee reioyced greatly, and ſaid,
Bleſſed be the Lord this day, which hath giuen vnto Dauid a wiſe ſonne
ouer this great people.8And Hiram ſent to Solomon, ſaying, I haue
conſidered the things which thou ſenteſt to me for: and I will doe all thy
deſire concerning timber of Cedar, and concerning timber of firre.9My
ſeruants ſhall bring them downe from Lebanon vnto the ſea: and I wil
conuey them by ſea in flotes, vnto the place that thou ſhalt appoint me,
and will cauſe them to be diſcharged there, and thou ſhalt receiue them:
and thou ſhalt accompliſh my deſire, in giuing food for my
houſhold.10So Hiram gaue Solomon Cedar trees, and Firre trees,
according to all his deſire.11And Solomon gaue Hiram twentie thouſand
meaſures of wheate for food to his houſhold, and twentie meaſures of
pure oile: thus gaue Solomon to Hiram yeere by yeere.12And the Lord
gaue Solomon wiſedome, as hee promiſed him: and there was peace
betweene Hiram and Solomon, and they two made a league
together.13And King Solomon raiſed a leuie out of all Iſrael, and the
leuie was thirtie thouſand men.14And hee ſent them to Lebanon, ten
thouſand a moneth by courſes: a moneth they were in Lebanon, and two
moneths at home: and Adoniram was ouer the leuie.15And Solomon had
threeſcore and ten thouſand that bare burdens, and foureſcore thouſand
hewers in the mountaines:16Beſides the chiefe of Solomons officers
which were ouer the worke, three thouſand and three hundred, which
ruled ouer the people that wrought in the worke.17And the king
commanded, and they brought great ſtones, coſtly ſtones, and hewed
ſtones, to lay the foundation of the houſe.18And Solomons builders, and
Hirams builders, did hewe them, and the ſtone-ſquarers: ſo they
prepared timber and ſtones to build the houſe.
CHAPTER 61And it came to paſſe in the foure hundred and foureſcore
yeere after the children of Iſrael were come out of the land of Egypt, in
the fourth yere of Solomons reigne ouer Iſrael, in the moneth Zif, which
is the ſecond moneth, that he began to build the houſe of the Lord.2And
the houſe which king Solomon built for the Lord, the length thereof was
threeſcore cubites, and the breadth thereof twentie cubits, and the
height thereof thirtie cubites.3And the porch before the Temple of the
houſe: twentie cubites was the length thereof, according to the breadth
of the houſe, and tenne cubites was the breadth thereof before the
houſe.4And for the houſe he made windowes of narrow lights.5And
againſt the wall of the houſe he built chambers round about, againſt the
walles of the houſe round about, both of the Temple and of the Oracle:
and hee made chambers round about.6The nethermoſt chamber was
fiue cubites broad, and the middle was ſixe cubites broad, and the third
was ſeuen cubites broad: for without in the wall of the houſe hee made
narrowed reſts round about, that the beames ſhould not bee faſtened in
the walles of the houſe.7And the houſe when it was in building, was built
of ſtone, made ready before it was brought thither: ſo that there was
neither hammer nor axe, nor any toole of yron heard in the houſe, while
it was in building.8The doore for the middle chamber was in the right
ſide of the houſe: and they went vp with winding ſtaires into the middle
chamber, and out of the middle into the third.9So he built the houſe and
finiſhed it: and couered the houſe with beams and boards of
Cedar.10And then hee built chambers againſt all the houſe, fiue cubites
high: and they reſted on the houſe with timber of Cedar.11And the word
of the Lord came to Solomon, ſaying;12Concerning this Houſe which
thou art in building, if thou wilt walke in my Statutes, and execute my
Iudgments, and keepe all my Commandements to walke in them: then
will I performe my word with thee, which I ſpake vnto Dauid thy
father.13And I will dwell among the children of Iſrael, and will not
forſake my people Iſrael.14So Solomon built the houſe, and finiſhed
it.15And hee built the walles of the houſe within with boards of Cedar,
both the floore of the houſe, and the walles of the ſieling: and hee
couered them on the inſide with wood, and couered the floore of the
houſe with plankes of firre.16And hee built twentie cubites on the ſides
of the houſe, both the floore, and the walles with boards of Cedar: he
euen built them for it within, euen for the Oracle, euen for the moſt
holy place.17And the houſe, that is, the Temple before it, was fortie
cubites long.18And the Cedar of the houſe within was carued with
knops, and open flowres: all was Cedar, there was no ſtone ſeene.19And
the Oracle he prepared in the houſe within, to ſet there the Arke of the
Couenant of the Lord.20And the Oracle in the forepart, was twenty
cubits in length and twentie cubites in breadth, and twentie cubites in
the height thereof: and hee ouerlayd it with pure golde, and ſo couered
the Altar which was of Cedar.21So Solomon ouerlayd the houſe within
with pure golde: and he made a partition, by the chaines of golde before
the Oracle, and he ouerlaid it with gold.22And the whole houſe he
ouerlaid with golde vntill he had finiſhed all the houſe: alſo the whole
Altar that was by the Oracle he ouerlaide with golde.23And within the
Oracle he made two Cherubims of Oliue tree, each ten cubites
high.24And fiue cubits was the one wing of the Cherub, and fiue cubits
the other wing of the Cherub: from the vttermoſt part of the one wing,
vnto the vttermoſt part of the other, were ten cubites.25And the other
Cherub was tenne cubites: both the Cherubims were of one meaſure,
and one ſize.26The height of the one Cherub was ten cubites, and ſo was
it of the other Cherub.27And he ſet the Cherubims within the inner
houſe: and they ſtretched foorth the wings of the Cherubims, ſo that the
wing of the one touched the one wall, and the wing of the other Cherub
touched the other wall: & their wings touched one another in the midſt
of the houſe.28And he ouerlayd the Cherubims with golde.29And he
carued all the walles of the houſe round about with carued figures of
Cherubims, and palme trees, and open flowers, within & without.30And
the floore of the houſe hee ouerlayed with gold, within and
without.31And for the entring of the Oracle he made doores of Oliue
tree: the lintell and ſide poſts were a fifth part of the wall.32The two
doores alſo were of Oliue tree, and he carued vpon them caruings of
Cherubims, and palme trees, and open flowers, and ouerlayd them with
gold, and ſpread gold vpon the Cherubims, and vpon the palme
trees.33So alſo made hee for the doore of the Temple poſtes of Oliue
tree a fourth part of the wall.34And the two doores were of firre tree:
the two leaues of the one doore were folding, and the two leaues of the
other doore were folding.35And he carued thereon Cherubims, and
palme trees, and open flowers: and couered them with gold, fitted vpon
the carued worke.36And hee built the inner Court with three rowes of
hewed ſtone, and a row of Cedar beames.37In the fourth yeere was the
foundation of the houſe of the Lord layd, in the moneth Zif.38And in
the eleuenth yeere in the moneth Bul (which is the eight moneth) was
the houſe finiſhed throughout all the parts therof, and according to all
the faſhion of it: So was he ſeuen yeeres in building it.
CHAPTER 71But Solomon was building his owne houſe thirteene
yeres, and he finiſhed all his houſe.2Hee built alſo the houſe of the
forreſt of Lebanon; the length thereof was a hundred cubites, and the
breadth thereof fiftie cubites, and the height thereof thirtie cubites, vpon
foure rowes of Cedar pillars, with Cedar beames vpon the pillars.3And
it was couered with Cedar aboue vpon the beames, that lay on fortie fiue
pillars, fifteene in a row.4And there were windowes in three rowes, and
light was againſt light in three rankes.5And all the doores and poſtes
were ſquare, with the windowes: and light was againſt light in three
rankes.6And he made a porch of pillars, the length thereof was fiftie
cubites, and the breadth thereof thirtie cubites: and the porch was before
them: and the other pillars, and the thicke beame were before

them.7Then hee made a porch for the throne where he might iudge, euen the porch of Iudgement: and it was couered with Cedar from one ſide of the floore to the other.8And his houſe where he dwelt, had another court within the porch, which was of the like worke: Solomon made alſo an houſe for Pharaohs daughter, (whom he had taken to wife) like vnto this porch.9All theſe were of coſtly ſtones, according to the meaſures of hewed ſtones, ſawed with ſawes, within and without, euen from the foundation vnto the coping, and ſo on the outſide toward the great court.10And the foundation was of coſtly ſtones, euen great ſtones; ſtones of ten cubites, and ſtones of eight cubites.11And aboue were coſtly ſtones (after the meaſures of hewed ſtoneſ) and Cedars.12And the great court round about, was with three rowes of hewed ſtones, and a row of Cedar beames, both for the inner court of the houſe of the Lord, and for the porch of the houſe.13And king Solomon ſent and fet Hiram out of Tyre.14Hee was a widowes ſonne of the tribe of Naphtali, and his father was a man of Tyre, a worker in braſſe, and he was filled with wiſedome, and vnderſtanding, and cunning to worke all workes in braſſe: and hee came to king Solomon, and wrought all his worke.15For he caſt two pillars of braſſe of eighteene cubites high a piece: and a line of twelue cubites did compaſſe either of them about.16And hee made two Chapiters of molten braſſe, to ſet vpon the tops of the pillars: the height of the one chapiter was fiue cubites, and the height of the other chapiter was fiue cubites:17And nets of checker worke, and wreathes of chaine worke, for the chapiters which were vpon the top of the pillars: ſeuen for the one chapiter, and ſeuen for the other chapiter.18And he made the pillars, and two rowes round about vpon the one networke, to couer the chapiters that were vpon the top, with pomegranates: and ſo did he for the other chapiter.19And the chapiters that were vpon the top of the pillars, were of lillie worke in the porch, foure cubites.20And the chapiters vpon the two pillars had pomegranates alſo, aboue, ouer againſt the belly which was by the networke: and the pomegranates were two hundred in rowes round about, vpon the other chapiter.21And he ſet vp the pillars in the porch of the temple: and hee ſet vp the right pillar, and called the name therof Iachin: and he ſet vp the left pillar, and called the name thereof Boaz.22And vpon the top of the pillars was lillie worke: ſo was the worke of the pillars finiſhed.23And he made a moulten ſea, ten cubites from the one brim to the other: it was round all about, & his height was fiue cubits: and a line of thirtie cubites did compaſſe it round about.24And vnder the brimme of it round about there were knops compaſsing it, ten in a cubite, compaſsing the ſea round about: the knops were caſt in two rowes, when it was caſt.25It ſtood vpon twelue oxen, three looking toward the North, and three looking toward the Weſt, and three looking toward the South, and three looking toward the Eaſt: and the ſea was ſet aboue vpon them, and all their hinder parts were inward.26And it was an hand breadth thicke, and the brimme thereof was wrought like the brim of a cup, with flowres of lillies: it contained two thouſand Baths.27And he made ten baſes of braſſe; foure cubites was the length of one baſe, and foure cubites the breadth thereof, and three cubites the height of it.28And the worke of the baſes was on this maner: they had borders, and the borders were betweene the ledges:29And on the borders that were betweene the ledges were lyons, oxen, and Cherubims: and vpon the ledges there was a baſe aboue: and beneath the lyons and oxen were certaine additions made of thinne worke.30And euery baſe had foure braſen wheeles, and plates of braſſe: and the foure corners therof had vnderſetters: vnder the lauer were vnderſetters molten, at the ſide of euery addition.31And the mouth of it within the chapiter, and aboue, was a cubite: but the mouth thereof was round after the worke of the baſe, a cubite and an halfe: and alſo vpon the mouth of it were grauings with their borders, foure ſquare not round.32And vnder the borders were foure wheeles: & the axletrees of the wheeles were ioyned to the baſe, and the height of a wheele was a cubite and halfe a cubite.33And the worke of the wheeles was like the worke of a charet wheele: their axletrees and their naues, and their felloes, and their ſpokes were all molten.34And there were foure vnderſetters to the foure corners of one baſe: and the vnderſetters were of the very baſe it ſelfe.35And in the top of the baſe was there a round compaſſe of halfe a cubite high: and on the top of the baſe the ledges thereof, and the borders thereof were of the ſame.36For on the plates of the ledges thereof, and on the borders thereof, he graued Cherubims, lions, and palme trees, according to the proportion of euery one, and additions round about.37After this maner he made the ten baſes: all of them had one caſting, one meaſure, and one ſize.38Then made hee ten lauers of braſſe: one lauer conteined fourtie baths: and euery lauer was foure cubites, and vpon euery one of the ten baſes, one lauer.39And he put fiue baſes on the right ſide of the houſe, and fiue on the left ſide of the houſe: and he ſet the ſea on the right ſide of the houſe Eaſtward, ouer againſt the South.40And Hiram made the lauers, and the ſhouels, and the baſons: So Hiram made an ende of doing all the worke that hee made King Solomon, for the houſe of the Lord.41The two pillars, and the two bowles of the chapiters that were on the top of the two pillars: and the two networkes, to couer the two bowles of the chapiters which were vpon the top of the pillars:42And foure hundred Pomegranates for the two networkes, euen two rowes of Pomegranates for one networke, to couer the two bowles of the chapiters that were vpon the pillars:43And the ten baſes, and ten lauers on the baſes.44And one ſea, and twelue oxen vnder the ſea.45And the pots, and the ſhouels, and the baſons: and all theſe veſſels which Hiram made to King Solomon, for the houſe of the Lord, were of bright braſſe.46In the plaine of Iordane did the king caſt them in the clay ground, betweene Succoth and Zarthan.47And Solomon left all the veſſels vnweighed, becauſe they were exceeding many: neither was the weight of the braſſe found out.48And Solomon made all the veſſels that pertained vnto the houſe of the Lord: the Altar of gold, and the table of gold, whereupon the Shewbread was:49And the candleſticks of pure gold, fiue on the right ſide, and fiue on the left, before the Oracle, with the flowers, and the lampes, and the tongs of gold,50And the boules, and the ſnuffers, and the baſons, & the ſpoones, and the cenſers of pure gold: and the hindges of gold, both for the doores of the inner houſe the moſt Holy place, and for the doores of the houſe, to wit, of the temple.51So was ended all the worke that king Solomon made for the houſe of the Lord: and Solomon brought in the things which Dauid his father had dedicated, euen the ſiluer, and the gold, & the veſſels did he put among the treaſures of the houſe of the Lord.

CHAPTER 81Then Solomon aſſembled the Elders of Iſrael, and all the heads of the tribes, the chiefe of the fathers of the children of Iſrael, vnto king Solomon in Ieruſalem, that they might bring vp the Arke of the Couenant of the Lord, out of the citie of Dauid, which is Zion.2And all the men of Iſrael aſſembled themſelues vnto king Solomon, at the feaſt, in the moneth Ethanim, which is the ſeuenth moneth.3And all the Elders of Iſrael came, and the Prieſts tooke vp the Arke.4And they brought vp the Arke of the Lord, and the Tabernacle of the Congregation, and all the holy veſſels that were in the Tabernacle, euen thoſe did the Prieſts & the Leuites bring vp.5And king Solomon, and all the Congregation of Iſrael, that were aſſembled vnto him, were with him before the Arke, ſacrificing ſheepe, and oxen, that could not bee told nor numbred for multitude.6And the Prieſts brought in the Arke of the Couenant of the Lord vnto his place, into the Oracle of the houſe to the moſt holy place, euen vnder the wings of the Cherubims.7For the Cherubims ſpread forth their two wings ouer the place of the Arke, and the Cherubims couered the Arke, and the ſtaues thereof aboue.8And they drew out the ſtaues, that the ends of the ſtaues were ſeene out in the Holy place before the Oracle, and they were not ſeene without: and there they are vnto this day.9There was nothing in the Arke, ſaue the two Tables of ſtone, which Moſes put there at Horeb, when the Lord made a Couenant with the children of Iſrael, when they came out of the land of Egypt.10And it came to paſſe when the Prieſts were come out of the holy place, that the cloud filled the houſe of the Lord;11So that the Prieſts could not ſtand to miniſter, becauſe of the cloud: for the glory of the Lord had filled the houſe of the Lord.12Then ſpake Solomon; The Lord ſaid that hee would dwell in the thicke darkeneſſe.13I haue ſurely built thee an houſe to dwel in, a ſetled place for thee to abide in for euer.14And the King turned his face about, and bleſſed all the Congregation of Iſrael: (and all the Congregation of Iſrael ſtood.)15And he ſaid, Bleſſed be the Lord God of Iſrael, which ſpake with his mouth vnto Dauid my father, and hath with his hand fulfilled it, ſaying;16Since the day that I brought foorth my people Iſrael out of Egypt, I choſe no citie out of all the tribes of Iſrael to build an houſe that my Name might be therein; but I choſe Dauid to be ouer my people Iſrael.17And it was in the heart of Dauid my father, to builde an houſe for the Name of the Lord God of Iſrael.18And the Lord ſayd vnto Dauid my father, Whereas

it was in thine heart to build an houſe vnto my Name, thou diddeſt well
that it was in thine heart.19Neuertheleſſe, thou ſhalt not build the houſe,
but thy ſonne that ſhall come foorth out of thy loynes, hee ſhall build
the houſe vnto my Name.20And the Lord hath perfourmed his word
that he ſpake, and I am riſen vp in the roume of Dauid my father, and
ſit on the throne of Iſrael, as the Lord promiſed, and haue built an Houſe
for the Name of the Lord God of Iſrael.21And I haue ſet there a place
for the Arke, wherein is the Couenant of the Lord, which he made with
our fathers, when he brought them out of the land of Egypt.22And
Solomon ſtood before the Altar of the Lord, in the preſence of all the
Congregation of Iſrael, and ſpread foorth his handes toward
heauen:23And hee ſaid, Lord God of Iſrael, there is no God like thee, in
heauen aboue, or on earth beneath, who keepeſt couenant and mercy
with thy ſeruants, that walke before thee with all their heart:24Who haſt
kept with thy ſeruant Dauid my father that thou promiſedſt him: thou
ſpakeſt alſo with thy mouth, and haſt fulfilled it with thine hand, as it is
this day.25Therefore now Lord God of Iſrael, keepe with thy ſeruant
Dauid my father, that thou promiſedſt him, ſaying; There ſhall not faile
thee a man in my ſight to ſit on the Throne of Iſrael; ſo that thy children
take heede to their way, that they walke before me as thou haſt walked
before me:26And now, O God of Iſrael, let thy worde (I pray thee) bee
verified, which thou ſpakeſt vnto thy ſeruant Dauid my father.27But will
God indeede dwell on the earth? Behold, the heauen, and heauen of
heauens cannot conteine thee: how much leſſe this Houſe that I haue
builded?28Yet haue thou reſpect vnto the prayer of thy ſeruant, and to
his ſupplication, O Lord my God, to hearken vnto the crie and to the
prayer, which thy ſeruant prayeth before thee to day:29That thine eyes
may be open toward this houſe, night and day, euen toward the place of
which thou haſt ſaid, My Name ſhall be there: that thou mayeſt hearken
vnto the prayer which thy ſeruant ſhall make towards this place.30And
hearken thou to the ſupplication of thy ſeruant, and of thy people Iſrael,
when they ſhall pray towards this place: and heare thou in heauen thy
dwelling place, and when thou heareſt, forgiue.31If any man treſpaſſe
againſt his neighbour, and an oath be laid vpon him to cauſe him to
ſweare, and the oath come before thine Altar in this houſe:32Then heare
thou in heauen, and doe, and iudge thy ſeruants, condemning the wicked
to bring his way vpon his head, and iuſtifying the righteous, to giue him
according to his righteouſneſſe.33When thy people Iſrael bee ſmitten
downe before the enemie, becauſe they haue ſinned againſt thee, and
ſhall turne againe to thee, and confeſse thy Name, and pray, and make
ſupplication vnto thee in this houſe:34Then heare thou in heauen, and
forgiue the ſinne of thy people Iſrael, and bring them againe vnto the
land, which thou gaueſt vnto their fathers.35When heauen is ſhut vp,
and there is no raine, becauſe they haue ſinned againſt thee: if they pray
towards this place, and confeſse thy Name, and turne from their ſinne,
when thou afflicteſt them:36Then heare thou in heauen, and forgiue the
ſinne of thy ſeruants, and of thy people Iſrael, that thou teach them the
good way wherein they ſhould walke, and giue raine vpon thy land which
thou haſt giuen to thy people for an inheritance.37If there be in the land
famine, if there be peſtilence, blaſting, mildew, locuſt, or if there be
caterpiller: if their enemy beſiege them in the land of their cities,
whatſoeuer plague, whatſoeuer ſicknes there be;38What prayer and
ſupplication ſoeuer be made by any man, or by all thy people Iſrael,
which ſhall know euery man the plague of his owne heart, and ſpread
forth his handes towards this houſe:39Then heare thou in heauen thy
dwelling place, and forgiue, and do, and giue to euery man according to
his wayes, whoſe heart thou knoweſt; (for thou, euen thou onely
knoweſt the hearts of all the children of men,)40That they may feare
thee all the dayes that they liue, in the land which thou gaueſt vnto our
fathers.41Moreouer, concerning a ſtranger that is not of thy people
Iſrael, but commeth out of a farre countrey, for thy Names ſake;42(For
they ſhall heare of thy great Name, and of thy ſtrong hand, and of thy
ſtretched out arme) when hee ſhall come and pray towards this
houſe:43Heare thou in heauen thy dwelling place, and doe according to
all that the ſtranger calleth to thee for: that all people of the earth may
know thy Name, to feare thee, as doe thy people Iſrael, and that they
may know that this houſe which I haue builded, is called by thy
Name.44If thy people goe out to battell againſt their enemie,
whitherſoeuer thou ſhalt ſend them, and ſhall pray vnto the Lord toward
the city which thou haſt choſen, and toward the houſe that I haue built
for thy Name:45Then heare thou in heauen their prayer & their
ſupplication, and mainteine their cauſe.46If they ſinne againſt thee, (for
there is no man that ſinneth not,) and thou be angry with them, and
deliuer them to the enemy, ſo that they cary them away captiues, vnto
the land of the enemy, farre or neere;47Yet if they ſhall bethinke
themſelues, in the land whither they were caried captiues, and repent,
and make ſupplication vnto thee in the land of them that caried them
captiues, ſaying, Wee haue ſinned, and haue done peruerſly, we haue
committed wickednes;48And ſo returne vnto thee with all their heart,
and with all their ſoule, in the land of their enemies, which led them
away captiue, and pray vnto thee toward their land, which thou gaueſt
vnto their fathers, the city which thou haſt choſen, and the houſe which
I haue built for thy Name:49Then heare thou their prayer and their
ſupplication in heauen thy dwelling place, and mainteine their
cauſe,50And forgiue thy people that haue ſinned againſt thee, and all
their tranſgreſſions, wherein they haue tranſgreſſed againſt thee, and
giue them compaſſion before them who caried them captiue, that they
may haue compaſſion on them:51For they bee thy people and thine
inheritance, which thou broughteſt foorth out of Egypt, from the mids
of the furnace of iron:52That thine eyes may be open vnto the
ſupplication of thy ſeruant, and vnto the ſupplication of thy people
Iſrael, to hearken vnto them in all that they call for vnto thee.53For thou
didſt ſeparate them from among all the people of the earth, to be thine
inheritance, as thou ſpakeſt by the hand of Moſes thy ſeruant, when thou
broughteſt our fathers out of Egypt, O Lord God.54And it was ſo, that
when Solomon had made an end of praying all this prayer and
ſupplication vnto the Lord, he aroſe from before the Altar of the Lord,
from kneeling on his knees, with his handes ſpread vp to heauen.55And
he ſtood, and bleſſed all the Congregation of Iſrael, with a lowd voice,
ſaying;56Bleſſed be the Lord, that hath giuen reſt vnto his people Iſrael,
according to all that he promiſed: there hath not failed one word of all
his good promiſe, which he promiſed by the hand of Moſes his
ſeruant.57The Lord our God be with vs, as he was with our fathers: let
him not leaue vs, nor forſake vs:58That hee may encline our hearts vnto
him, to walke in all his wayes, and to keepe his Commaundements, and
his Statutes, and his Iudgements which hee commaunded our
fathers.59And let theſe my wordes wherewith I haue made ſupplication
before the Lord, be nigh vnto the Lord our God, day and night, that hee
maintaine the cauſe of his ſeruant, and the cauſe of his people Iſrael at
all times, as the matter ſhall require:60That all the people of the earth
may know that the Lord is God: and that there is none elſe.61Let your
heart therefore be perfect with the Lord your God, to walke in his
Statutes, and to keepe his Commandements, as at this day.62And the
king, and all Iſrael with him, offered ſacrifice before the Lord.63And
Solomon offered a ſacrifice of peace offerings, which he offered vnto
the Lord, two and twentie thouſand oxen, and an hundred and twentie
thouſand ſheepe: ſo the king and all the children of Iſrael dedicated the
houſe of the Lord.64The ſame day did the king hallow the middle of the
Court that was before the houſe of the Lord: for there hee offered burnt
offerings, and meat offerings, and the fat of the peace offerings: becauſe
the braſen Altar that was before the Lord, was too little to receiue the
burnt offerings, and meat offerings, and the fat of the peace
offerings.65And at that time Solomon held a feaſt, and all Iſrael with
him, a great Congregation, from the entring in of Hamath, vnto the riuer
of Egypt, before the Lord our God, ſeuen dayes and ſeuen dayes, euen
fourteene dayes.66On the eight day he ſent the people away: and they
bleſſed the King, and went vnto their tents ioyfull, and glad of heart, for
all the goodneſſe that the Lord had done for Dauid his ſeruant, and for
Iſrael his people.

CHAPTER 91And it came to paſſe, when Solomon had finiſhed the
building of the houſe of the Lord, and the kings houſe, and all Solomons
deſire which hee was pleaſed to doe,2That the Lord appeared to
Solomon the ſecond time, as hee had appeared vnto him at
Gibeon.3And the Lord ſaid vnto him, I haue heard thy prayer and thy
ſupplication that thou haſt made before me: I haue hallowed this houſe
which thou haſt built, to put my Name there for euer, and mine eyes
and mine heart ſhall be there perpetually.4And if thou wilt walke before
me, as Dauid thy father walked, in integritie of heart, and in
vprightneſse, to doe according to all that I haue commanded thee, and
wilt keepe my Statutes, and my Iudgements:5Then I will eſtabliſh the

throne of thy kingdome vpon Iſrael for euer, as I promiſed to Dauid thy
father, ſaying, There ſhall not faile thee a man vpon the throne of
Iſrael. 6 But if you ſhall at all turne from following me, you or your
children, and will not keepe my Commandements, and my Statutes,
which I haue ſet before you, but goe and ſerue other gods, and worſhip
them: 7 Then will I cut off Iſrael out of the land which I haue giuen them;
and this houſe which I haue hallowed for my Name, will I caſt out of
my ſight, and Iſrael ſhall bee a prouerbe, and a by-word among all
people: 8 And at this houſe which is high, euery one that paſſeth by it,
ſhalbe aſtoniſhed, and ſhall hiſse, and they ſhal ſay, Why hath the Lord
done thus vnto this land, and to this houſe? 9 And they ſhall anſwere,
Becauſe they forſooke the Lord their God, who brought forth their
fathers out of the land of Egypt, and haue taken hold vpon other gods,
and haue worſhipped them, and ſerued them: therefore hath the Lord
brought vpon them all this euill. 10 And it came to paſſe at the end of
twentie yeeres, when Solomon had built the two houſes, the houſe of
the Lord, and the Kings houſe, 11 (Now Hiram the king of Tyre had
furniſhed Solomon with Cedar trees, and firre trees, and with golde
according to al his deſire) that then Solomon gaue Hiram twentie cities
in the land of Galile. 12 And Hiram came out from Tyre to ſee the cities
which Solomon had giuen him, and they pleaſed him not. 13 And he ſaid,
What cities are theſe which thou haſt giuen me, my brother? And he
called them the land of Cabul vnto this day. 14 And Hiram ſent to the
king ſixe ſcore talents of gold. 15 And this is the reaſon of the leuie which
king Solomon raiſed, for to build the houſe of the Lord, and his owne
houſe, and Millo, and the wall of Ieruſalem, and Hazor, and Megiddo,
and Gezer. 16 For Pharaoh king of Egypt had gone vp, and taken Gezer,
and burnt it with fire, and ſlaine the Canaanites that dwelt in the citie,
and giuen it for a preſent vnto his daughter Solomons wife. 17 And
Solomon built Gezer, and Beth-horon the nether, 18 And Baalath, and
Tadmor in the wilderneſſe, in the land. 19 And all the cities of ſtore that
Solomon had, and cities for his charets, and cities for his horſemen, and
that which Solomon diſired to build in Ieruſalem, and in Lebanon, and
in all the land of his dominion. 20 And all the people that were left of the
Amorites, Hittittes, Perizzites, Hiuites, and Iebuſites, which were not of
the children of Iſrael, 21 Their children that were left after them in the
land, whom the children of Iſrael alſo were not able vtterly to deſtroy,
vpon thoſe did Solomon leuie a tribute of bond-ſeruice vnto this
day. 22 But of the children of Iſrael did Solomon make no bondmen: but
they were men of warre, and his ſeruants, and his princes, and his
captaines, and rulers of his charets, and his horſemen. 23 Theſe were the
chiefe of the officers that were ouer Solomons worke, fiue hundred and
fiftie, which bare rule ouer the people that wrought in the worke. 24 But
Pharaohs daughter came vp out of the citie of Dauid, vnto her houſe
which Solomon had built for her: then did he build Millo. 25 And three
times in a yeere did Solomon offer burnt offerings, and peace offerings
vpon the Altar which he built vnto the Lord, and he burnt incenſe vpon
the altar that was before the Lord: ſo he finiſhed the houſe. 26 And king
Solomon made a nauie of ſhips in Ezion Geber, which is beſide Eloth,
on the ſhoare of the red ſea, in the land of Edom. 27 And Hiram ſent in
the nauie his ſeruants, ſhipmen that had knowledge of the ſea, with the
ſeruants of Solomon. 28 And they came to Ophir, and fet from thence
gold foure hundred and twentie talents, and brought it to king Solomon.
CHAPTER 10 1 And when the Queene of Sheba heard of the fame of
Solomon, concerning the Name of the Lord; ſhee came to prooue him
with hard queſtions. 2 And ſhe came to Ieruſalem with a very great traine,
with camels that bare ſpices, and very much gold, and precious ſtones:
and when ſhee was come to Solomon, ſhe communed with him, of all
that was in her heart. 3 And Solomon tolde her all her queſtions: there
was not any thing hid from the king, which hee told her not. 4 And when
the Queene of Sheba had ſeene all Solomons wiſedome, and the houſe
that he had built, 5 And the meat of his table, and the ſitting of his
ſeruants, and the attendance of his miniſters, and their apparell, and his
cup bearers, and his aſcent by which hee went vp vnto the houſe of the
Lord: there was no more ſpirit in her. 6 And ſhe ſaid to the king, It was a
true report that I heard in mine owne land, of thy actes and of thy
wiſedome. 7 Howbeit, I beleeued not the words, vntill I came and mine
eyes had ſeene it: and beholde, the halfe was not told me: thy wiſedom
and proſperitie exceedeth the fame which I heard. 8 Happie are thy men,
happy are theſe thy ſeruants, which ſtand continually before thee, and
that heare thy wiſedom. 9 Bleſſed be the Lord thy God which delighted
in thee, to ſet thee on the throne of Iſrael; becauſe the Lord loued Iſrael
for euer, therefore made he thee King, to doe iudgement and
iuſtice. 10 And ſhe gaue the king an hundred and twentie talents of gold,
and of ſpices very great ſtore, & precious ſtones: there came no more
ſuch abundance of ſpices, as theſe, which the Queene of Sheba gaue to
king Solomon. 11 And the nauie alſo of Hiram that brought gold from
Ophir, brought in from Ophir, great plentie of Almug trees, and
precious ſtones. 12 And the king made of the Almug trees, pillars for the
houſe of the Lord, and for the Kings houſe, Harpes alſo and Pſalteries
for ſingers: there came no ſuch Almug trees, nor were ſeene vnto this
day. 13 And king Solomon gaue vnto the Queene of Sheba, al her deſire
whatſoeuer ſhe aſked, beſides that which Solomon gaue her of his royall
bountie: ſo ſhe turned and went to her owne countrey, ſhe and her
ſeruants. 14 Now the weight of gold that came to Solomon in one yere,
was ſixe hundred, threeſcore & ſix talents of gold, 15 Beſides that he had
of the merchant men, and of the traffique of the ſpicemerchants, and of
all the kings of Arabia, and of the gouernours of the countrey. 16 And
king Solomon made two hundred targets of beaten golde: ſixe hundred
ſhekels of golde went to one target. 17 And he made three hundred ſhields
of beaten gold, three pound of gold went to one ſhield; and the king put
them in the houſe of the forreſt of Lebanon. 18 Moreouer the king made
a great throne of yuorie, and ouerlaide it with the beſt gold. 19 The throne
had ſixe ſteps, and the top of the throne was round behind: and there
were ſtayes on either ſide on the place of the ſeate, and two lyons ſtood
beſide the ſtayes. 20 And twelue lions ſtood there on the one ſide and on
the other vpon the ſixe ſteps: there was not the like made in any
kingdome. 21 And all king Solomons drinking veſſels were of gold, and all
the veſſels of the houſe of the forreſt of Lebanon were of pure gold,
none were of ſiluer, it was nothing accounted of in the dayes of
Solomon. 22 For the king had at ſea a nauie of Tharſhiſh, with the nauie
of Hiram: once in three yeeres came the nauie of Tharſhiſh, bringing
golde and ſiluer, yuorie, and apes, and peacocks. 23 So king Solomon
exceeded all the kings of the earth, for riches and for wiſedome. 24 And
all the earth ſought to Solomon, to heare his wiſedom which God had
put in his heart. 25 And they brought euery man his preſent, veſſels of
ſiluer, and veſſels of gold, and garments, and armour, and ſpices, horſes,
and mules, a rate yeere by yeere. 26 And Solomon gathered together
charets and horſemen. And hee had a thouſand and foure hundred
charets, and twelue thouſand horſemen, whom he beſtowed in the cities
for charets, and with the king at Ieruſalem. 27 And the king made ſiluer
to be in Ieruſalem as ſtones, and Cedars made he to be as the Sycomore
trees, that are in the vale for abundance. 28 And Solomon had horſes
brought out of Egypt, and linen yarne: the kings merchants receiued the
linen yarne at a price. 29 And a charet came vp and went out of Egypt for
ſixe hundred ſhekels of ſiluer, and an horſe for an hundred and fiftie:
and ſo for all the kings of the Hittites, and for the kings of Syria, did
they bring them out by their meanes.
CHAPTER 11 1 But King Solomon loued many ſtrange women, (
together with þe daughter of Pharaoh) women of the Moabites,
Ammonites, Edomites, Sidonians & Hittites: 2 Of the nations concerning
which the Lord ſaid vnto the children of Iſrael, Yee ſhall not goe in to
them, neither ſhall they come in vnto you, for ſurely they will turne away
your heart after their gods: Solomon claue vnto theſe in loue. 3 And he
had ſeuen hundred wiues, Princeſses, and three hundred concubines:
and his wiues turned away his heart. 4 For it came to paſſe when Solomon
was old, that his wiues turned away his heart after other gods: and his
heart was not perfect with the Lord his God, as was the heart of Dauid
his father. 5 For Solomon went after Aſhtoreth the goddeſse of the
Zidonians, and after Milcom the abomination of the Amorites. 6 And
Solomon did euill in the ſight of the Lord, and went not fully after the
Lord, as did Dauid his father. 7 Then did Solomon build an hie place for
Chemoſh the abomination of Moab, in the hill that is before Ieruſalem,
and for Molech the abomination of the children of Ammon. 8 And
likewiſe did hee for all his ſtrange wiues, which burnt incenſe and
ſacrificed vnto their gods. 9 And the Lord was angry with Solomon,
becauſe his heart was turned from the Lord God of Iſrael which had
appeared vnto him twiſe, 10 And had commaunded him concerning this
thing, that hee ſhould not goe after other gods: but hee kept not that
which the Lord commanded. 11 Wherefore the Lord ſaid vnto Solomon;

Foraſmuch as this is done of thee, and thou haſt not kept my Couenant, and my Statutes which I haue commanded thee, I wil ſurely rend the kingdome from thee, and will giue it to thy ſeruant.12Notwithſtanding in thy dayes I wil not doe it, for Dauid thy fathers ſake: but I wil rend it out of the hand of thy ſonne.13Howbeit, I wil not rend away all the kingdome: but wil giue one tribe to thy ſonne, for Dauid my ſeruants ſake, and for Ieruſalems ſake, which I haue choſen.14And the Lord ſtirred vp an aduerſary vnto Solomon, Hadad the Edomite: hee was of the kings ſeed in Edom.15For it came to paſſe when Dauid was in Edom, and Ioab the captaine of the hoſt was gone vp to bury the ſlaine, after he had ſmitten euery male in Edom:16(For ſixe moneths did Ioab remaine there with all Iſrael, vntil hee had cut off euery male in Edom.)17That Hadad fled, he and certaine Edomites of his fathers ſeruants with him, to goe into Egypt: Hadad being yet a litle childe.18And they aroſe out of Midian, and came to Paran, and they tooke men with them out of Paran, and they came to Egypt, vnto Pharaoh king of Egypt, which gaue him an houſe, and appointed him vitailes, and gaue him land.19And Hadad found great fauour in the ſight of Pharaoh, ſo that he gaue him to wife the ſiſter of his owne wife, the ſiſter of Tahpenes the Queene.20And the ſiſter of Tahpenes bare him Genubath his ſonne, whom Tahpenes weaned in Pharaohs houſe: and Genubath was in Pharaohs houſhold among the ſonnes of Pharaoh.21And when Hadad heard in Egypt that Dauid ſlept with his fathers, and that Ioab the captaine of the hoſt was dead, Hadad ſaid to Pharaoh, Let me depart, that I may go to mine owne countrey.22Then Pharaoh ſaid vnto him, But what haſt thou lacked with mee, that, behold, thou ſeekeſt to goe to thine owne countrey? And hee anſwered, Nothing: Howbeit, let mee goe in any wiſe.23And God ſtirred him vp another aduerſary: Rezon, the ſonne of Eliadah, which fled from his lord Hadadezer king of Zobah:24And he gathered men vnto him, and became captaine ouer a band, when Dauid ſlew them of Zobah: and they went to Damaſcus, and dwelt therein, and reigned in Damaſcus.25And he was an aduerſarie to Iſrael all the dayes of Solomon, beſide the miſchiefe that Hadad did: and he abhorred Iſrael, and reigned ouer Syria.26And Ieroboam the ſonne of Nebat, an Ephrathite of Zereda, Solomons ſeruant, (whoſe mothers name was Zeruah a widow woman) euen he lift vp his hand againſt the king.27And this was the cauſe that hee lift vp his hand againſt the king: Solomon built Millo, and repaired the breaches of the citie of Dauid his father.28And the man Ieroboam was a mightie man of valour: and Solomon ſeeing the young man that he was induſtrious, hee made him ruler ouer all the charge of the houſe of Ioſeph.29And it came to paſſe at that time when Ieroboam went out of Ieruſalem, that the Prophet Ahiiah the Shilonite found him in the way: and hee had clad himſelfe with a new garment; and they two were alone in the field.30And Ahiiah caught the new garment that was on him, and rent it in twelue pieces.31And he ſaid to Ieroboam, Take thee tenne pieces: for thus ſayth the Lord the God of Iſrael, Behold, I will rent the kingdome out of the hand of Solomon, and will giue ten tribes to thee:32(But hee ſhall haue one tribe, for my ſeruant Dauids ſake, and for Ieruſalems ſake, the citie which I haue choſen out of all the tribes of Iſrael:)33Becauſe that they haue forſaken mee, and haue worſhipped Aſhtaroth the goddeſse of the Zidonians, Chemoſh the god of the Moabites, and Milcom the god of the children of Anunon, and haue not walked in my wayes, to doe that which is right in mine eyes, and to keepe my Statutes, and my Iudgements, as did Dauid his father.34Howbeit, I will not take the whole kingdome out of his hand: but I will make him Prince all the dayes of his life, for Dauid my ſeruants ſake, whom I choſe, becauſe hee kept my Commandements and my Statutes:35But I will take the kingdome out of his ſonnes hand, and will giue it vnto thee, euen ten tribes.36And vnto his ſonne will I giue one tribe, that Dauid my ſeruant may haue a light alway before me in Ieruſalem, the citie which I haue choſen me to put my Name there.37And I will take thee, and thou ſhalt reigne according to all that thy ſoule deſireth, and ſhalt be King ouer Iſrael.38And it ſhall be, if thou wilt hearken vnto all that I command thee, and wilt walke in my wayes, and doe that is right in my ſight, to keepe my Statutes and my Commandements, as Dauid my ſeruant did; that I will be with thee, and build thee a ſure houſe, as I built for Dauid, and will giue Iſrael vnto thee.39And I will for this afflict the ſeed of Dauid, but not for euer.40Solomon ſought therefore to kill Ieroboam, and Ieroboam aroſe, and fledde into Egypt, vnto Shiſhak king of Egypt, and was in Egypt vntill the death of Solomon.41And the reſt of the actes of Solomon, and all that he did, and his wiſedome, are they not written in the booke of the actes of Solomon?42And the time that Solomon reigned in Ieruſalem, ouer all Iſrael, was fourtie yeeres.43And Solomon ſlept with his fathers, and was buried in the citie of Dauid his father: and Rehoboam his ſonne reigned in his ſtead.

CHAPTER 121And Rehoboam went to Shechem: for all Iſrael were come to Shechem to make him king.2And it came to paſſe when Ieroboam the ſonne of Nebat, who was yet in Egypt, heard of it (for hee was fled from the preſence of king Solomon, and Ieroboam dwelt in Egypt:)3That they ſent, and called him: and Ieroboam and all the Congregation of Iſrael came, and ſpake vnto Rehoboam, ſaying;4Thy father made our yoke grieuous: now therefore, make thou the grieuous ſeruice of thy father, and his heauy yoke which he put vpon vs, lighter, and we will ſerue thee.5And hee ſaid vnto them, Depart yet for three daies, then come againe to me. And the people departed.6And king Rehoboam conſulted with the old men that ſtood before Solomon his father, while he yet liued, and ſaid, How doe you aduiſe, that I may anſwere this people?7And they ſpake vnto him, ſaying, If thou wilt be a ſeruant vnto this people this day, and wilt ſerue them, and anſwere them, and ſpeake good words to them, then they will be thy ſeruants for euer.8But hee forſooke the counſell of the old men, which they had giuen him, and conſulted with the yong men, that were growen vp with him, and which ſtood before him.9And hee ſaid vnto them, What counſell giue ye, that we may anſwere this people, who haue ſpoken to mee, ſaying, Make the yoke which thy father did put vpon vs, lighter?10And the young men that were growen vp with him, ſpake vnto him, ſaying, Thus ſhalt thou ſpeake vnto this people that ſpake vnto thee, ſaying, Thy father made our yoke heauy, but make thou it lighter vnto vs; thus ſhalt thou ſay vnto them, My litle finger ſhall bee thicker then my fathers loynes.11And now whereas my father did lade you with a heauy yoke, I wil adde to your yoke: my father hath chaſtiſed you with whippes, but I will chaſtiſe you with ſcorpions.12So Ieroboam and all the people came to Rehoboam the third day, as the king had appointed, ſaying, Come to me againe the third day.13And the king anſwered the people roughly, and forſooke the old mens counſell that they gaue him:14And ſpake to them after the counſell of the young men, ſaying, My father made your yoke heauy, and I will adde to your yoke; my father alſo chaſtiſed you with whips, but I will chaſtiſe you with ſcorpions.15Wherefore the king hearkened not vnto the people: for the cauſe was from the Lord, that hee might performe his ſaying, which the Lord ſpake by Ahiiah the Shilonite vnto Ieroboam the ſonne of Nebat.16So when all Iſrael ſaw that the king hearkned not vnto them, the people anſwered the king, ſaying, What portion haue we in Dauid? neither haue we inheritance in the ſonne of Ieſſe: to your tents, O Iſrael: nowe ſee to thine owne houſe, Dauid. So Iſrael departed vnto their tents.17But as for the children of Iſrael which dwelt in the cities of Iudah, Rehoboam reigned ouer them.18Then king Rehoboam ſent Adoram, who was ouer the tribute, and all Iſrael ſtoned him with ſtones that hee died: therefore king Rehoboam made ſpeed to get him vp to his charet, to flee to Ieruſalem.19So Iſrael rebelled againſt the houſe of Dauid vnto this day.20And it came to paſſe when all Iſrael heard that Ieroboam was come againe, that they ſent and called him vnto the Congregation, and made him king ouer all Iſrael: there was none that followed the houſe of Dauid, but the tribe of Iudah onely.21And when Rehoboam was come to Ieruſalem, hee aſſembled all the houſe of Iudah, with the tribe of Beniamin, an hundred and foureſcore thouſand choſen men which were warriers, to fight againſt the houſe of Iſrael, to bring the kingdome againe to Rehoboam the ſonne of Solomon.22But the word of God came vnto Shemaiah, the man of God, ſaying,23Speake vnto Rehoboam the ſonne of Solomon king of Iudah, and vnto all the houſe of Iudah and Beniamin, and to the remnant of the people, ſaying,24Thus ſaith the Lord, Ye ſhall not goe vp, nor fight againſt your brethren the children of Iſrael: returne euery man to his houſe, for this thing is from me. They hearkened therefore to the word of the Lord, and returned to depart, according to the word of the Lord.25Then Ieroboam built Shechem in mount Ephraim, and dwelt therein, and went out from thence, and built Penuel.26And Ieroboam ſaid in his heart, Now ſhall the kingdome returne to the houſe of Dauid:27If this people goe vp, to doe ſacrifice in the houſe of the Lord at Ieruſalem, then ſhall the heart of this people turne againe vnto their lorde, euen vnto Rehoboam king of Iudah, and they ſhall kill mee, and goe againe to Rehoboam king of Iudah.28Whereupon the king tooke counſell, and made two calues of gold, and ſaid vnto them, It is too much for you to goe vp to Ieruſalem: Behold thy gods, O Iſrael, which brought thee vp out of the land of Egypt.29And he ſet the one in Bethel, and the other put he in Dan.30And this thing became a ſinne: for the people went to worſhip before the one, euen vnto Dan.31And he made an houſe of hie places, and made prieſts of the loweſt of the people, which were not of the ſonnes of Leui.32And Ieroboam ordeined a feaſt in the eight moneth, on the fifteenth day of the moneth, like vnto the feaſt that is in Iudah, and he offered vpon the altar (ſo did he in Bethel,) ſacrificing vnto the calues that he had made: and he placed in Bethel the prieſts of the high places which he had made.33So hee offered vpon the altar, which hee had made in Bethel, the fifteenth day of the eighth moneth, euen in the moneth which he had deuiſed of his owne heart: and ordeined a feaſt vnto the children of Iſrael, and he offered vpon the altar, and burnt incenſe.

CHAPTER 131And behold, there came a man of God out of Iudah by the word of the Lord vnto Bethel: and Ieroboam ſtood by the altar to burne incenſe.2And hee cried againſt the altar in the word of the Lord, and ſaid, O altar, altar, thus ſaith the Lord, Behold, a child ſhalbe borne vnto the houſe of Dauid, Ioſiah by name, and vpon thee ſhall he offer the prieſts of the high places that burne incenſe vpon thee, and mens bones ſhall bee burnt vpon thee.3And he gaue a ſigne the ſame day, ſaying, This is the ſigne which the Lord hath ſpoken: Behold, the altar ſhall be rent, and the aſhes that are vpon it, ſhalbe powred out.4And it came to paſſe when king Ieroboam heard the ſaying of the man of God, which had cried againſt the altar in Bethel, that he put forth his hand from the altar, ſaying, Lay hold on him: And his hand which hee put foorth againſt him, dried vp, ſo that hee could not pull it in againe to him.5The altar alſo was rent, and the aſhes powred out from the altar, according to the ſigne which the man of God had giuen by the word of the Lord.6And the king anſwered, and ſaid vnto the man of God, Intreat now the face of the Lord thy God, and pray for mee, that my hand may be reſtored mee againe. And the man of God beſought the Lord, and the kings hand was reſtored againe, and became as it was before.7And the king ſaid vnto the man of God, Come home with mee, and refreſh thy ſelfe, and I wil giue thee a reward.8And the man of God ſaid vnto the king, If thou wilt giue mee halfe thine houſe, I will not goe in with thee, neither will I eat bread, nor drinke water in this place:9For ſo was it charged mee by the word of the Lord, ſaying, Eate no bread, nor drinke water, nor turne again by the ſame way that thou cameſt.10So he went another way, and returned not by the way that hee came to Bethel.11Now there dwelt an old Prophet in Bethel, and his ſonne came and told him all the workes that the man of God had done that day in Bethel: the words which hee had ſpoken vnto the king, them they tolde alſo to their father.12And their father ſaid vnto them, What way went he? for his ſonnes had ſeene what way the man of God went, which came from Iudah.13And hee ſaide vnto his ſonnes, Saddle me the aſſe. So they ſadled him the aſſe, and he rode thereon,14And went after the man of God, and found him ſitting vnder an oke; and he ſaid vnto him, Art thou the man of God that cameſt from Iudah? And he ſaid, I am.15Then hee ſaid vnto him, Come home with me, and eate bread.16And he ſaid, I may not returne with thee, nor goe in with thee: neither will I eat bread, nor drinke water with thee in this place.17For it was ſaid to mee by the word of the Lord, Thou ſhalt eate no bread, nor drinke water there, nor turne againe to go by the way that thou cameſt.18He ſaid vnto him, I am a prophet alſo as thou art, and an angel ſpake vnto me by the word of the Lord, ſaying, Bring him backe with thee into thine houſe, that he may eat bread, and drinke water: But he lied vnto him.19So he went backe with him, and did eate bread in his houſe, and dranke water.20And it came to paſſe as they ſate at the table, that the word of the Lord came vnto the prophet that brought him backe:21And he cried vnto the man of God that came from Iudah, ſaying, Thus ſaith the Lord, Foraſmuch as thou haſt diſobeied the mouth of the Lord, and haſt not kept the commandement which the Lord thy God commanded thee,22But cameſt backe, and haſt eaten bread, and drunke water, in the place, of the which the Lord did ſay to thee, Eate no bread, and drinke no water; thy carcaiſe ſhall not come vnto the ſepulchre of thy fathers.23And it came to paſſe after he had eaten bread, and after hee had drunke, that he ſadled for him the aſſe, to wit, for the Prophet, whome hee had brought backe.24And when he was gone, a lyon met him by the way, and ſlew him: and his carcaiſe was caſt in the way, and the aſſe ſtood by it, the lyon alſo ſtood by the carcaiſe.25And beholde, men paſſed by, and ſaw the carcaiſe caſt in the way, and the lyon ſtanding by the carcaiſe: and they came and told it in the citie where the old prophet dwelt.26And when the prophet that brought him back from the way, heard thereof, he ſaid, It is the man of God, who was diſobedient vnto the word of the Lord: therefore the Lord hath deliuered him vnto the lion, which hath torne him, and ſlaine him, according to the word of the Lord, which he ſpake vnto him.27And he ſpake to his ſonnes, ſaying, Saddle me the aſſe: and they ſadled him.28And he went and found his carcaiſe caſt in the way, and the aſſe and the lyon ſtanding by the carcaiſe: the lyon had not eaten the carcaiſe, nor torne the aſſe.29And the prophet tooke vp the carcaiſe of the man of God, and laid it vpon the aſſe, and brought it backe: and the old prophet came to the city, to mourne, and to burie him.30And hee laid his carcaiſe in his owne graue, and they mourned ouer him, ſaying, Alas my brother.31And it came to paſſe after hee had buried him, that he ſpake to his ſonnes, ſaying, When I am dead, then bury me in the ſepulchre, wherein the man of God is buried, lay my bones beſide his bones.32For the ſaying which hee cried by the word of the Lord againſt the altar in Bethel, and againſt all the houſes of the high places which are in the cities of Samaria, ſhall ſurely come to paſſe.33After this thing, Ieroboam returned not from his euill way, but made againe of the loweſt of the people prieſts of the high places: whoſoeuer would, he conſecrated him, and he became one of the prieſts of the high places.34And this thing became ſinne vnto the houſe of Ieroboam, euen to cut it off, and to deſtroy it from off the face of the earth.

CHAPTER 141At that time Abiiah the ſonne of Ieroboam fell ſicke.2And Ieroboam ſaid to his wife, Ariſe, I pray thee, and diſguiſe thy ſelfe, that thou be not knowen to be the wife of Ieroboam: and get thee to Shiloh: Behold, there is Ahiiah the Prophet, which told mee that I ſhould be king ouer this people.3And take with thee ten loaues, and cracknels, and a cruſe of honie, and goe to him: he ſhall tell thee what ſhall become of the childe.4And Ieroboams wife did ſo, and aroſe, and went to Shiloh, and came to the houſe of Ahiiah: but Ahiiah could not ſee, for his eyes were ſet by reaſon of his age.5And the Lord ſaid vnto Ahiiah, Behold, the wife of Ieroboam commeth to aſke a thing of thee for her ſonne, for hee is ſicke: thus and thus ſhalt thou ſay vnto her: for it ſhall be when ſhee commeth in, that ſhee ſhall faine her ſelfe to be another woman.6And it was ſo, when Ahiiah heard the ſound of her feet, as ſhe came in at the doore, that hee ſaid, Come in, thou wife of Ieroboam, why faineſt thou thy ſelfe to be another? for I am ſent to thee with heauie tidings.7Goe, tell Ieroboam, Thus ſaith the Lord God of Iſrael, Foraſmuch as I exalted thee from among the people, and made thee prince ouer my people Iſrael,8And rent the kingdome away from the houſe of Dauid, and gaue it thee: and yet thou haſt not beene as my ſeruant Dauid, who kept my Commandements, and who followed mee with all his heart, to doe that onely which was right in mine eyes,9But haſt done euill aboue all that were before thee: for thou haſt gone and made thee other gods, and molten images, to prouoke me to anger, and haſt caſt me behinde thy backe:10Therefore behold, I will bring euill vpon the houſe of Ieroboam, and will cut off from Ieroboam, him that piſseth againſt the wall, and him that is ſhut vp and left in Iſrael, and will take away the remnant of the houſe of Ieroboam, as a man taketh away dung, till it be all gone.11Him that dieth of Ieroboam in the citie, ſhall the dogs eate: and him that dieth in the field, ſhall the foules of the aire eate: for the Lord hath ſpoken it.12Ariſe thou therefore, get thee to thine owne houſe: and when thy feete enter into the citie, the child ſhall die.13And all Iſrael ſhall mourne for him, and bury him: for he onely of Ieroboam ſhal come to the graue, becauſe in him there is found ſome good thing toward the Lord God of Iſrael, in the houſe of Ieroboam.14Moreouer, the Lord ſhall raiſe him vp a king ouer Iſrael, who ſhal cut off the houſe of Ieroboam that day: but what? euen now.15For the Lord ſhall ſmite Iſrael, as a reede is ſhaken in the water, and hee ſhall root vp Iſrael out of this good land, which hee gaue to their fathers, and ſhall ſcatter them beyond the Riuer, becauſe they haue made their groues, prouoking the Lord to anger.16And hee ſhall giue Iſrael vp, becauſe of the ſinnes of Ieroboam, who did ſinne, & who made Iſrael to ſinne.[17]And Ieroboams wife aroſe, and departed, and came to Tirzah: and when ſhee came to the threſhold of the doore, the child died.[18]And they buried him, and all Iſrael mourned for him, according to the word of the Lord, which hee ſpake by the hand of his ſeruant Ahiiah the Prophet.[19]And the reſt of the actes of Ieroboam, how hee warred, and how hee reigned, behold, they are written in the booke of the Chronicles of the kings of Iſrael.[20]And the dayes which Ieroboam reigned, were two and twentie yeeres: and he ſlept with his fathers, and Nadab his ſonne reigned in his ſtead.[21]And Rehoboam the ſonne of Solomon reigned in Iudah: Rehoboam was fourtie and one yeeres olde when he began to reigne, and hee reigned ſeuenteene yeeres in Ieruſalem, the citie which the Lord did chuſe out of all the tribes of Iſrael, to put his Name there: and his mothers name was Naamah an Ammoniteſſe.[22]And Iudah did euill in the ſight of the Lord, and they prouoked him to iealouſie with their ſinnes which they had committed, aboue all that their fathers had done.[23]For they alſo built them high places, and images, and groues on euery high hill, and vnder euery greene tree.[24]And there were alſo Sodomites in the land, and they did according to all the abominations of the nations which the Lord caſt out before the children of Iſrael.[25]And it came to paſſe in the fift yeere of king Rehoboam, that Shiſhak king of Egypt came vp againſt Ieruſalem:[26]And he tooke away the treaſures of the houſe of the Lord, and the treaſures of the kings houſe, hee euen tooke away all: and he tooke away all the ſhields of gold which Solomon had made.[27]And king Rehoboam made in their ſtead braſen ſhields, and committed them vnto the hands of the chiefe of the guard, which kept the doore of the kings houſe.[28]And it was ſo, when the king went into the houſe of the Lord, that the guard bare them, and brought them backe into the guard-chamber.[29]Nowe the reſt of the actes of Rehoboam, and all that hee did, are they not written in the booke of the Chronicles of the kings of Iudah?[30]And there was warre betweene Rehoboam and Ieroboam all their dayes.[31]And Rehoboam ſlept with his fathers, and was buried with his fathers in the city of Dauid: and his mothers name was Naamah an Ammoniteſse. And Abijam his ſonne reigned in his ſtead.

CHAPTER 15[1]Nowe in the eighteenth yeere of king Ieroboam the ſonne of Nebat, reigned Abiiam ouer Iudah.[2]Three yeeres reigned hee in Ieruſalem: and his mothers name was Maachah, the daughter of Abiſhalom.[3]And he walked in all the ſinnes of his father, which hee had done before him: and his heart was not perfect with the Lord his God, as the heart of Dauid his father.[4]Neuertheleſſe, for Dauids ſake did the Lord his God giue him a lampe in Ieruſalem, to ſet vp his ſonne after him, and to eſtabliſh Ieruſalem:[5]Becauſe Dauid did that which was right in the eies of the Lord, and turned not aſide from any thing that he commanded him all the daies of his life, ſaue onely in the matter of Uriiah the Hittite.[6]And there was warre betweene Rehoboam and Ieroboam all the dayes of his life.[7]Now the reſt of the actes of Abiiam, and all that hee did, are they not written in the booke of the Chronicles of the Kings of Iudah? And there was warre betweene Abiiam and Ieroboam.[8]And Abiiam ſlept with his fathers, and they buried him in the citie of Dauid: and Aſa his ſonne reigned in his ſtead.[9]And in the twentieth yeere of Ieroboam king of Iſrael, reigned Aſa ouer Iudah.[10]And forty and one yeeres reigned hee in Ieruſalem: and his mothers name was Maachah, the daughter of Abiſhalom.[11]And Aſa did that which was right in the eies of the Lord, as did Dauid his father.[12]And hee tooke away the Sodomites out of the land, and remooued all the idoles that his fathers had made.[13]And alſo Maachah his mother, euen her hee remoued from being Queene, becauſe ſhe had made an idole in a groue, and Aſa deſtroyed her idole, and burnt it by the brooke Kidron.[14]But the high places were not remooued: neuertheleſſe, Aſa his heart was perfect with the Lord all his dayes.[15]And he brought in the things which his father had dedicated, and the things which himſelfe had dedicated, into the houſe of the Lord, ſiluer, and gold, and veſſels.[16]And there was war betweene Aſa and Baaſha King of Iſrael all their dayes.[17]And Baaſha king of Iſrael went vp againſt Iudah, and built Ramah, that he might not ſuffer any to goe out or come in to Aſa king of Iudah.[18]Then Aſa tooke all the ſiluer and the golde that were left in the treaſures of the houſe of the Lord, and the treaſures of the kings houſe, and deliuered them into the hand of his ſeruants: and king Aſa ſent them to Benhadad the ſonne of Tabrimon, the ſonne of Hezion king of Syria, that dwelt at Damaſcus, ſaying,[19]There is a league betweene me and thee, and betweene my father and thy father: behold, I haue ſent vnto thee a preſent of ſiluer and gold; come and breake the league with Baaſha king of Iſrael, that he may depart from me.[20]So Benhadad hearkened vnto king Aſa, and ſent the captaines of the hoſts, which he had, againſt the cities of Iſrael, and ſmote Iion, and Dan, and Abel-Bethmaachah, and all Cinneroth, with all the land of Naphtali.[21]And it came to paſſe when Baaſha heard thereof, that hee left off building of Ramah, and dwelt in Tirzah.[22]Then king Aſa made a Proclamation throughout all Iudah, (none was exempted:) and they tooke away the ſtones of Ramah, and the timber thereof wherewith Baaſha had builded, and king Aſa built with them Geba of Beniamin, and Mizpah.[23]The reſt of all the acts of Aſa, and all his might, and all that he did, and the cities which hee built, are they not written in the booke of the Chronicles of the Kings of Iudah? Neuertheleſſe in the time of his old age, hee was diſeaſed in his feete.[24]And Aſa ſlept with his fathers, and was buried with his fathers, in the citie of Dauid his father: and Iehoſhaphat his ſonne reigned in his ſtead.[25]And Nadab the ſonne of Ieroboam began to reigne ouer Iſrael, in the ſecond yeere of Aſa king of Iudah, and reigned ouer Iſrael two yeeres.[26]And he did euill in the ſight of the Lord, and walked in the way of his father, and in his ſinne wherewith hee made Iſrael to ſinne.[27]And Baaſha the ſonne of Ahiiah, of the houſe of Iſſachar, conſpired againſt him, and Baaſha ſmote him at Gibbethon, which belongeth to the Philiſtines, (for Nadab and all Iſrael layd ſiege to Gibbethon,)[28]Euen in the third yeere of Aſa king of Iudah, did Baaſha ſlay him, and reigned in his ſtead.[29]And it came to paſſe when hee raigned, that he ſmote all the houſe Ieroboam, hee left not to Ieroboam any that breathed, vntill hee had deſtroyed him, according vnto the ſaying of the Lord, which hee ſpake by his ſeruant Ahiiah the Shilonite:[30]Becauſe of the ſinnes of Ieroboam which he ſinned, and which hee made Iſrael ſinne, by his prouocation wherewith he prouoked the Lord God of Iſrael to anger.[31]Now the reſt of the acts of Nadab, and all that hee did, are they not written in the booke of the Chronicles of the Kings of Iſrael?[32]And there was warre betweene Aſa and Baaſha king of Iſrael al their dayes.[33]In the third yeere of Aſa King of Iudah, began Baaſha the ſonne of Ahiiah to reigne ouer all Iſrael in Tirzah, twentie and foure yeeres.[34]And hee did euill in the ſight of the Lord, and walked in the way of Ieroboam, and in his ſinne wherewith he made Iſrael to ſinne.

CHAPTER 16[1]Then the word of the Lord came to Iehu the ſonne of Hanani, againſt Baaſha, ſaying,[2]Foraſmuch as I exalted thee out of the duſt, and made thee Prince ouer my people Iſrael, and thou haſt walked in the way of Ieroboam, and haſt made my people Iſrael to ſinne, to prouoke mee to anger with their ſinnes:[3]Behold, I will take away the poſteritie of Baaſha, and the poſteritie of his houſe: and will make thy houſe like the houſe of Ieroboam the ſonne of Nebat.[4]Him that dieth of Baaſha in the citie, ſhall the dogs eate: and him that dieth of his in the fields, ſhall the foules of the aire eate.[5]Now the reſt of the actes of Baaſha, and what he did, and his might, are they not written in the booke of the Chronicles of the kings of Iſrael?[6]So Baaſha ſlept with his fathers, and was buried in Tirzah, and Elah his ſonne reigned in his ſtead.[7]And alſo by the hand of the prophet Iehu the ſonne of Hanani, came the word of the Lord againſt Baaſha, and againſt his houſe, euen for all the euill that hee did in the ſight of the Lord, in prouoking him to anger with the worke of his hands, in being like the houſe of Ieroboam, and becauſe he killed him.[8]In the twentieth and ſixt yeere of Aſa king of Iudah, began Elah the ſonne of Baaſha to reigne ouer Iſrael in Tirzah, two yeeres.[9]And his ſeruant Zimri (captaine of halfe his charetſ) conſpired againſt him as he was in Tirzah drinking himſelfe drunke in the houſe of Arza ſteward of his houſe in Tirzah.[10]And Zimri went in and ſmote him, and killed him, in the twentie and ſeuenth yeere of Aſa king of Iudah, and reigned in his ſtead.[11]And it came to paſſe when hee began to reigne, aſsoone as hee ſate on his throne, that he ſlew all the houſe of Baaſha: hee left him not one that piſseth againſt a wall, neither of his kinſfolkes, nor of his friends.[12]Thus did Zimri deſtroy all the houſe of Baaſha, according to the word of the Lord, which he ſpake againſt Baaſha by Iehu the prophet,[13]For all the ſinnes of Baaſha and the ſinnes of Elah his ſonne, by which they ſinned, and by which they made Iſrael to ſinne, in prouoking the Lord God of Iſrael to anger with their vanities.[14]Now the reſt of the actes of Elah, and all that he did, are they not written in the booke of the Chronicles of the kings of

Iſrael?15In the twentie and ſeuenth yeere of Aſa king of Iudah, did Zimri reigne ſeuen dayes in Tirzah: and the people were encamped againſt Gibbethon which belonged to the Philiſtines.16And the people that were encamped, heard ſay, Zimri hath conſpired, and hath alſo ſlaine the king: Wherfore all Iſrael made Omri the captaine of the hoſte, king ouer Iſrael that day, in the campe.17And Omri went vp from Gibbethon, and all Iſrael with him, and they beſieged Tirzah.18And it came to paſſe when Zimri ſaw that the citie was taken, that hee went into the palace of the kings houſe, and burnt the kings houſe ouer him with fire, and died,19For his ſinnes which he ſinned in doing euill in the ſight of the Lord, in walking in the way of Ieroboam, and in his ſinne which he did, to make Iſrael ſinne.20Now the reſt of the acts of Zimri, and his treaſon that hee wrought, are they not written in the booke of the Chronicles of the kings of Iſrael?21Then were the people of Iſrael diuided into two parts: halfe of the people followed Tibni the ſonne of Ginath, to make him king: and halfe followed Omri.22But the people that followed Omri preuailed againſt the people that followed Tibni the ſonne of Ginath: ſo Tibni died, and Omri reigned.23In the thirtie and one yeere of Aſa king of Iudah, began Omri to reigne ouer Iſrael twelue yeeres: ſixe yeeres reigned he in Tirzah.24And hee bought the hill Samaria of Shemer, for two talents of ſiluer, and built on the hill, and called the name of the citie which hee built, after the name of Shemer, owner of the hill, Samaria.25But Omri wrought euil in the eyes of the Lord, and did worſe then all that were before him.26For he walked in all the way of Ieroboam the ſon of Nebat, and in his ſinne wherewith hee made Iſrael to ſinne, to prouoke the Lord God of Iſrael to anger with their vanities.27Now the reſt of the acts of Omri, which he did, and his might that he ſhewed, are they not written in the booke of the Chronicles of the kings of Iſrael?28So Omri ſlept with his fathers, and was buried in Samaria, and Ahab his ſonne reigned in his ſtead.29And in the thirtie and eight yeere of Aſa king of Iudah, began Ahab the ſonne of Omri to reigne ouer Iſrael, and Ahab the ſonne of Omri reigned ouer Iſrael in Samaria, twentie and two yeeres.30And Ahab the ſonne of Omri did euill in the ſight of the Lord, aboue all that were before him.31And it came to paſſe, as if it had beene a light thing for him to walke in the ſinnes of Ieroboam the ſonne of Nebat; that hee tooke to wife Iezebel the daughter of Ethbaal king of the Zidonians, and went and ſerued Baal, and worſhipped him.32And hee reared vp an Altar for Baal, in the houſe of Baal, which hee had built in Samaria.33And Ahab made a groue, and Ahab did more to prouoke the Lord God of Iſrael to anger, then all the kings of Iſrael that were before him.34In his dayes did Hiel the Bethelite build Iericho: he laid the foundation therof in Abiram his firſt borne, and ſet vp the gates thereof in his yongeſt ſonne Segub, according to the word of the Lord, which hee ſpake by Ioſhua the ſonne of Nun.

CHAPTER 171And Eliiah the Tiſhbite, who was of the inhabitants of Gilead, ſaid vnto Ahab, As the Lord God of Iſrael liueth, before whome I ſtand, there ſhall not be deaw nor raine theſe yeres, but according to my word.2And the worde of the Lord came vnto him, ſaying,3Get thee hence, and turne thee Eaſtward, and hide thy ſelfe by the brooke Cherith, that is before Iordane.4And it ſhall bee, that thou ſhalt drinke of the brooke, and I haue commanded the rauens to feed thee there.5So hee went, and did according vnto the word of the Lord: for hee went and dwelt by the brooke Cherith, that is before Iordane.6And the rauens brought him bread and fleſh in the morning, and bread and fleſh in the euening: and hee dranke of the brooke.7And it came to paſſe after a while, that the brooke dryed vp, becauſe there had beene no raine in the land.8And the word of the Lord came vnto him, ſaying,9Ariſe, get thee to Zarephath, which belongeth to Zidon, and dwell there: behold, I haue commaunded a widow woman there to ſuſtaine thee.10So he aroſe, and went to Zarephath: and when he came to the gate of the citie, behold, the widow woman was there gathering of ſtickes: and he called to her, and ſaid, Fetch me, I pray thee, a little water in a veſſell, that I may drinke.11And as ſhee was going to fetch it, he called to her, and ſaid, Bring mee, I pray thee, a morſell of bread in thine hand.12And ſhe ſaid, As the Lord thy God liueth, I haue not a cake, but an handfull of meale in a barrell, and a little oyle in a cruſe: and behold, I am gathering two ſtickes, that I may goe in, and dreſſe it for me and my ſonne, that we may eate it, and die.13And Eliiah ſaid vnto her, Feare not, goe, and doe as thou haſt ſaid: but make mee thereof a little cake firſt, and bring it vnto mee, and after make for thee, and for thy ſonne.14For thus ſaith the Lord God of Iſrael, The barrell of meale ſhall not waſte, neither ſhall the cruſe of oile faile, vntill the day that the Lord ſendeth raine vpon the earth.15And ſhee went, and did according to the ſaying of Eliiah: and ſhe, and he, and her houſe did eate many dayes.16And the barrell of meale waſted not, neither did the cruſe of oyle faile, according to the word of the Lord, which he ſpake by Eliiah.17And it came to paſſe after theſe things, that the ſonne of the woman, the miſtreſſe of the houſe, fell ſicke, and his ſickeneſse was ſo ſore, that there was no breath left in him.18And ſhee ſayd vnto Eliiah, What haue I to doe with thee? O thou man of God! Art thou come vnto me to call my ſinne to remembrance, and to ſlay my ſonne?19And he ſaid vnto her, Giue me thy ſonne. And he tooke him out of her boſome, and caried him vp into a loft, where he abode, and laide him vpon his owne bed.20And hee cried vnto the Lord, and ſaid, O Lord my God, haſt thou alſo brought euill vpon the widow, with whom I ſoiourne, by ſlaying her ſonne?21And he ſtretched himſelfe vpon the child three times, and cried vnto the Lord, and ſaid; O Lord my God, I pray thee, let this childes ſoule come into him againe.22And the Lord heard the voice of Eliiah, and the ſoule of the child came into him againe, and he reuiued.23And Eliiah tooke the childe, and brought him downe out of the chamber into the houſe, and deliuered him vnto his mother: and Eliiah ſaid, See, thy ſonne liueth.24And the woman ſaid to Eliiah, Now by this I know, that thou art a man of God, and that the word of the Lord in thy mouth is trueth.

CHAPTER 181And it came to paſſe after many daies, that the word of the Lord came to Eliiah in the third yeere, ſaying, Goe ſhewe thy ſelfe vnto Ahab, and I will ſend raine vpon the earth.2And Eliiah went to ſhew himſelfe vnto Ahab, and there was a ſore famine in Samaria.3And Ahab called Obadiah which was the gouernour of his houſe: (now Obadiah feared the Lord greatly:4For it was ſo, when Iezebel cut off the Prophets of the Lord, that Obadiah tooke an hundred Prophets, and hid them by fiftie in a caue, and fed them with bread and water.)5And Ahab ſaid vnto Obadiah, Goe into the land, vnto all fountaines of water, and vnto all brookes: peraduenture we may finde graſſe to ſaue the horſes and mules aliue, that we leeſe not all the beaſts.6So they diuided the land betweene them to paſſe throughout it: Ahab went one way by himſelfe, and Obadiah went another way by himſelfe.7And as Obadiah was in the way, behold, Eliiah met him: and hee knew him, and fell on his face, and ſaid; Art thou that my lord Eliiah?8And he anſwered him, I am: goe, tell thy lord, Behold, Eliiah is here.9And he ſaid, What haue I ſinned, that thou wouldeſt deliuer thy ſeruant into the hand of Ahab, to ſlay mee?10As the Lord thy God liueth, there is no nation or kingdome, whither my lord hath not ſent to ſeeke thee: and when they ſaid, He is not there, hee tooke an oath of the kingdome and nation, that they found thee not.11And now thou ſayeſt, Goe, tell thy lord, Behold, Eliiah is here.12And it ſhall come to paſſe, as ſoone as I am gone from thee, that the ſpirit of the Lord ſhall cary thee whither I know not; and ſo when I come and tell Ahab, and he cannot finde thee, he ſhall ſlay mee: but I thy ſeruant feare the Lord from my youth.13Was it not told my lord, what I did when Iezebel ſlew the Prophets of the Lord ? How I hid an hundred men of the Lords Prophets, by fiftie in a caue, and fedde them with bread and water?14And now thou ſayeſt, Goe, tell thy lord, Behold, Eliiah is here: and hee ſhall ſlay me.15And Eliiah ſaid, As the Lord of hoſtes liueth, before whom I ſtand, I will ſurely ſhew my ſelfe vnto him to day.16So Obadiah went to meete Ahab, and told him: and Ahab went to meete Eliiah.17And it came to paſſe when Ahab ſaw Eliiah, that Ahab ſaide vnto him, Art thou hee that troubleth Iſrael?18And hee anſwered, I haue not troubled Iſrael, but thou and thy fathers houſe, in that yee haue forſaken the Commandements of the Lord, and thou haſt followed Baalim.19Now therefore ſend, and gather to mee all Iſrael vnto mount Carmel, and the prophets of Baal foure hundred and fiftie, and the prophets of the groues foure hundred, which eate at Iezebels table.20So Ahab ſent vnto all the children of Iſrael, and gathered the prophets together vnto mount Carmel.21And Eliiah came vnto all the people, and ſaid, how long halt yee betweene two opinions? If the Lord bee God, follow him: but if Baal, then follow him: and the people anſwered him not a word.22Then ſaid Eliiah vnto the people, I, euen I onely remaine a Prophet of the Lord: but Baals prophets are foure hundred and fiftie men.23Let them therefore giue vs two bullocks, and let them chuſe one bullocke for themſelues, and cut it in pieces, and lay it on wood, and put no fire vnder: and I will dreſſe the other bullocke, and lay it on wood, and put no fire vnder.24And call ye on the name of your gods, and I will call on the Name of the Lord: and the God that anſwereth by fire, let him be God. And all the people anſwered, and ſaid, It is well ſpoken.25And Eliiah ſaid vnto the prophets of Baal, Chuſe you one bullocke for your ſelues, and dreſſe it firſt, for yee are many: and call on the name of your gods, but put no fire vnder.26And they took the bullocke which was giuen them, and they dreſſed it, and called on the name of Baal from morning, euen vntil noone, ſaying, O Baal, heare vs. But there was no voyce, nor any that anſwered: And they leapt vpon the altar which was made.27And it came to paſſe at noone, that Eliiah mocked them, and ſaide, Crie aloud: for he is a god, either he is talking, or he is purſuing, or hee is in a iourney, or peraduenture he ſleepeth, and muſt be awaked.28And they cried loud, and cut themſelues after their maner, with kniues, and lancers, till the blood guſhed out vpon them.29And it came to paſſe when midday was paſt, and they propheſied vntil the time of the offering of the euening ſacrifice; that there was neither voice, nor any to anſwere, nor any that regarded.30And Eliiah ſaid vnto all the people, Come neere vnto me. And all the people came neere vnto him. And he repaired the Altar of the Lord that was broken downe.31And Eliiah tooke twelue ſtones, according to the number of the tribes of the ſonnes of Iacob, vnto whome the word of the Lord came, ſaying, Iſrael ſhall bee thy name.32And with the ſtones hee built an altar in the Name of the Lord, and hee made a trench about the altar, as great as would containe two meaſures of ſeed.33And he put the wood in order, and cut the bullocke in pieces, and laide him on the wood, and ſaid, Fill foure barrels with water, and powre it on the burnt ſacrifice, and on the wood.34And hee ſaid, Doe it the ſecond time. And they did it the ſecond time. And he ſaid, Doe it the third time. And they did it the third time.35And the water ran round about the altar, and hee filled the trench alſo with water.36And it came to paſſe at the time of the offering of the euening ſacrifice, that Eliiah the prophet came neere and ſaid, Lord God of Abraham, Iſaac, and of Iſrael, Let it bee knowen this day that thou art God in Iſrael, and that I am thy ſeruant, and that I haue done all theſe things at thy word.37Heare me, O Lord, heare me, that this people may know that thou art the Lord God, and that thou haſt turned their heart backe againe.38Then the fire of the Lord fell, and conſumed the burnt ſacrifice, and the wood, and the ſtones, and the duſt, and licked vp the water that was in the trench.39And when all the people ſawe it, they fell on their faces: and they ſaide, The Lord, he is the God, the Lord, he is the God.40And Eliiah ſaide vnto them, Take the prophets of Baal, let not one of them eſcape: And they tooke them, and Eliiah brought them downe to the brooke Kiſhon, and ſlewe them there.41And Eliiah ſaid vnto Ahab, Get thee vp, eate and drinke, for there is a ſound of abundance of raine.42So Ahab went vp to eate and to drinke, and Eliiah went vp to the top of Carmel, and he caſt himſelfe downe vpon the earth, and put his face betweene his knees,43And ſaid to his ſeruant, Goe vp now, looke toward the ſea. And hee went vp, and looked, and ſaide, There is nothing. And he ſaid, Goe againe ſeuen times.44And it came to paſſe at the ſeuenth time, that he ſaid, Behold, there Ariſeth a little cloud out of the ſea, like a mans hand. And he ſaid, Goe vp, ſay vnto Ahab, Prepare thy charet, and get thee downe, that the raine ſtop thee not.45And it came to paſſe in the meane while, that the heauen was blacke with cloudes and winde, and there was a great raine: and Ahab rode and went to Iezreel.46And the hand of the Lord was on Eliiah; and hee girded vp his loynes, and ranne before Ahab, to the entrance of Iezreel.

CHAPTER 191And Ahab told Iezebel all that Eliiah had done, and withall, how hee had ſlaine all the Prophets with the ſword.2Then Iezebel ſent a meſſenger vnto Eliiah, ſaying; So let the gods do to me, and more alſo, if I make not thy life as the life of one of them, by to morrow about this time.3And when he ſaw that, hee aroſe, and went for his life, and came to Beerſheba, which belongeth to Iudah, and left his ſeruant there.4But he himſelfe went a dayes iourney into the wilderneſſe, and came and ſate downe vnder a Iuniper tree: and hee requeſted for himſelfe that hee might die, and ſayd, It is enough, now O Lord, take away my life: for I am not better then my fathers.5And as hee lay and ſlept vnder a Iuniper tree, behold then, an Angel touched him, and ſayd vnto him, Ariſe, and eate.6And he looked, and behold, there was a cake baken on the coales, and a cruſe of water at his head: and hee did eate and drinke, and laide him downe againe.7And the Angel of the Lord came againe the ſecond time, and touched him, and ſayd, Ariſe, and eate, becauſe the iourney is too great for thee.8And hee aroſe, and did eate and drinke, and went in the ſtrength of that meate fourtie dayes and fourtie nights, vnto Horeb the mount of God.9And he came thither vnto a caue, and lodged there, and behold, the word of the Lord came to him, and he ſaid vnto him, What doeſt thou here, Eliiah?10And hee ſayd, I haue beene very iealous for the Lord God of hoſtes: for the children of Iſrael haue forſaken thy Couenant, throwen downe thine Altars, and ſlaine thy Prophets with the ſword: and I, euen I onely am left, and they ſeeke my life, to take it away.11And he ſayd, Goe forth, and ſtand vpon the mount before the Lord. And beholde, the Lord paſſed by, and a great and ſtrong winde rent the mountaines, and brake in pieces the rockes, before the Lord; but the Lord was not in the winde: and after the winde an earthquake, but the Lord was not in the earthquake.12And after the earthquake, a fire, but the Lord was not in the fire: and after the fire, a ſtill ſmall voice.13And it was ſo, when Eliiah heard it, that he wrapped his face in his mantle, and went out, and ſtood in the entring in of the caue: and behold, there came a voice vnto him, and ſayd, What doeſt thou here, Eliiah?14And he ſayd, I haue beene very iealous for the Lord God of hoſtes, becauſe the children of Iſrael haue forſaken thy Couenant, throwen downe thine Altars, and ſlaine thy Prophets with the ſword, and I, euen I onely am left, and they ſeeke my life, to take it away.15And the Lord ſayd vnto him, Goe, returne on thy way to the wilderneſſe of Damaſcus: and when thou commeſt, anoint Hazael to be King ouer Syria.16And Iehu the ſonne of Nimſhi ſhalt thou anoint to bee king ouer Iſrael: and Eliſha the ſonne of Shaphat of Abel Meholah, ſhalt thou annoint to be Prophet in thy roume.17And it ſhall come to paſſe, that him that eſcapeth the ſword of Hazael, ſhall Iehu ſlay: and him that eſcapeth from the ſword of Iehu, ſhall Eliſha ſlay.18Yet I haue left me ſeuen thouſand in Iſrael, all the knees which haue not bowed vnto Baal, and euery mouth which hath not kiſſed him.19So hee departed thence and found Eliſha the ſonne of Shaphat, who was plowing with twelue yoke of oxen before him, and hee with the twelfth: and Eliiah paſſed by him, and caſt his mantle vpon him.20And he left the oxen, and ranne after Eliiah, and ſaid, Let mee, I pray thee, kiſſe my father and my mother, and then I wil follow thee: and he ſaid vnto him, Goe backe againe; for what haue I done to thee?21And he returned backe from him, and tooke a yoke of oxen, & ſlew them, and boyled their fleſh with the inſtruments of the oxen, and gaue vnto the people, and they did eat: then he aroſe, and went after Eliiah, and miniſtred vnto him.

CHAPTER 201And Benhadad the King of Syria gathered all his hoſte together, and there were thirtie and two kings with him, and horſes, and charets: and hee went vp and beſieged Samaria, and warred againſt it.2And hee ſent meſſengers to Ahab king of Iſrael, into the city, and ſaide vnto him, Thus ſaith Benhadad,3Thy ſiluer and thy gold is mine, thy wiues alſo, and thy children, euen the goodlieſt, are mine.4And the king of Iſrael anſwered, and ſaid, My lord O king, according to thy ſaying, I am thine, and all that I haue.5And the meſſengers came againe, and ſaide, Thus ſpeaketh Benhadad, ſaying, Although I haue ſent vnto thee, ſaying, Thou ſhalt deliuer me thy ſiluer, and thy gold, and thy wiues, and thy children:6Yet I will ſend my ſeruants vnto thee to morrow about this time, and they ſhall ſearch thine houſe, and the houſes of thy ſeruants; and it ſhall be, that whatſoeuer is pleaſant in thine eies, they ſhall put it in their hand, and take it away.7Then the king of Iſrael called all the Elders of the land, and ſaide; Marke, I pray you, and ſee how this man ſeeketh miſchiefe: for hee ſent vnto me for my wiues, and for my children, and for my ſiluer, and for my gold, and I denied him not.8And all the Elders, and all the people ſaid vnto him; Hearken not vnto him, nor conſent.9Wherefore hee ſaid vnto the meſſengers of Benhadad, Tell my lord the king, All that thou diddeſt ſend for to thy ſeruant at the firſt, I will doe: but this thing I may not doe. And the meſſengers departed, and brought him word againe.10And Benhadad ſent vnto him, and ſaid, The gods doe ſo vnto me and more alſo, if the duſt of Samaria ſhall ſuffice for handfuls for all the people that follow me.11And the king of Iſrael anſwered, and ſaid, Tell him, Let not him that girdeth on his harneſe, boaſt himſelfe, as he that putteth it off.12And it came to paſſe, when Benhadad heard this meſsage (as hee was drinking, he and the kings in the pauilionſ) that hee ſaid vnto his ſeruants, Set yourſelues in aray. And they ſet themſelues in aray againſt the citie.13And behold, there came a Prophet vnto Ahab king of Iſrael, ſaying, Thus ſaith the Lord, Haſt thou ſeene all this great multitude? behold, I will deliuer it into thine hand this day, and thou ſhalt knowe that I am the Lord.14And Ahab ſaide, By whom? and he ſaide, Thus ſaith the Lord, Euen by the young men of the Princes of the prouinces: Then he ſaid, Who ſhall order the battell? And hee anſwered, Thou.15Then he numbred the young men of the Princes of the prouinces, and they were two hundred and thirty two: and after them hee numbred all the people, euen all the children of Iſrael, being ſeuen thouſand.16And they went out at noone: But Benhadad was drinking himſelfe drunke in the pauilions, hee and the kings, the thirty and two kings that helped him.17And the young men of the Princes of the Prouinces went out firſt, and Benhadad ſent out, and they told him, ſaying, There are men come out of Samaria.18And he ſaid, Whether they be come out for peace, take them aliue: or whether they be come out for warre, take them aliue.19So theſe yong men of the princes of the prouinces, came out of the citie, and the armie which followed them:20And they ſlew euery one his man: and the Syrians fled, and Iſrael purſued them: and Benhadad the king of Syria eſcaped on an horſe, with the horſemen.21And the king of Iſrael went out, and ſmote the horſes and charets, and ſlewe the Syrians with a great ſlaughter.22And the Prophet came to the king of Iſrael, and ſaid vnto him, Goe, ſtrengthen thy ſelfe, and marke and ſee what thou doeſt: for at the returne of the yeere, the king of Syria will come vp againſt thee.23And the ſeruants of the King of Syria ſaid vnto him, Their gods are gods of the hilles, therefore they were ſtronger then wee: but let vs fight againſt them in the plaine, and ſurely we ſhall be ſtronger then they.24And doe this thing, Take the kings away, euery man out of his place, and put captaines in their roumes.25And number thee an armie, like the armie that thou haſt loſt, horſe for horſe, and charet for charet: and wee will fight againſt them in the plaine, and ſurely wee ſhall be ſtronger then they. And hee hearkened vnto their voice, and did ſo.26And it came to paſſe at the returne of the yeere, that Benhadad numbred the Syrians, and went vp to Aphek, to fight againſt Iſrael.27And the children of Iſrael were numbred, and were all preſent, and went againſt them: and the children of Iſrael pitched before them, like two little flockes of kids: but the Syrians filled the countrey.28And there came a man of God, and ſpake vnto the king of Iſrael, and ſayd, Thus ſayth the Lord, Becauſe the Syrians haue ſayde, The Lord is God of the hilles, but hee is not God of the valleys: therefore will I deliuer all this great multitude into thine hand, and yee ſhall know that I am the Lord.29And they pitched one ouer againſt the other ſeuen daies, and ſo it was, that in the ſeuenth day the battell was ioyned: and the children of Iſrael ſlewe of the Syrians an hundred thouſand footmen in one day.30But the reſt fled to Aphek, into the citie, and there a wall fell vpon twentie and ſeuen thouſand of the men that were left: and Benhadad fled, and came into the citie, into an inner chamber.31And his ſeruants ſaid vnto him, Behold now, wee haue heard that the kings of the houſe of Iſrael are mercifull kings: let vs, I pray thee, put ſackcloth on our loines, and ropes vpon our heads, and goe out to the king of Iſrael; peraduenture he will ſaue thy life.32So they girded ſackcloth on their loynes, and put ropes on their heads, and came to the king of Iſrael, and ſaid, Thy ſeruant Benhadad ſaith, I pray thee, let me liue. And he ſaid, Is he yet aliue? he is my brother.33Now the men did diligently obſerue whether any thing would come from him, and did haſtily catch it: and they ſaide, Thy brother Benhadad. Then he ſaid, Goe ye, bring him: then Benhadad came forth to him: and hee cauſed him to come vp into the charet.34And Benhadad ſaid vnto him, The cities which my father tooke from thy father, I will reſtore, and thou ſhalt make ſtreets for thee in Damaſcus, as my father made in Samaria. Then, ſaid Ahab, I will ſend thee away with this couenant. So he made a couenant with him, and ſent him away.35And a certaine man of the ſonnes of the Prophets, ſaide vnto his neighbour in the word of the Lord, Smite me, I pray thee. And the man refuſed to ſmite him.36Then ſaid he vnto him, Becauſe thou haſt not obeyed the voyce of the Lord, beholde, aſsoone as thou art departed from me, a lyon ſhal ſlay thee. And aſsoone as hee was departed from him, a lyon found him, and ſlew him.37Then he found another man, and ſaid, Smite me, I pray thee. And the man ſmote him, ſo that in ſmiting hee wounded him.38So the prophet departed, and waited for the king by the way, and diſguiſed himſelfe with aſhes vpon his face.39And as the king paſſed by, he cried vnto the king: and he ſaide, Thy ſeruant went out into the mids of the battell, and behold, a man turned aſide, and brought a man vnto me, and ſaid, Keep this man: if by any meanes he be miſsing, then ſhall thy life be for his life, or elſe thou ſhalt pay a talent of ſiluer.40And as thy ſeruant was buſie here and there, he was gone. And the king of Iſrael ſaide vnto him, So ſhall thy iudgement bee, thy ſelfe haſt diſcided it.41And he haſted, and tooke the aſhes away from his face, and the king of Iſrael diſcernedhim that hee was of the Prophets.42And hee ſaid vnto him, Thus ſaith the Lord, Becauſe thou haſt let goe out of thy hand, a man whom I appointed to vtter deſtruction, therfore thy life ſhall goe for his life, and thy people for his people.43And the king of Iſrael went to his houſe, heauie, and diſpleaſed, and came to Samaria.

CHAPTER 211And it came to paſſe after theſe things, that Naboth the Iezreelite had a vineyard, which was in Iezreel, hard by the palace of Ahab king of Samaria.2And Ahab ſpake vnto Naboth, ſaying, Giue me thy vineyard, that I may haue it for a garden of herbes, becauſe it is neere vnto my houſe, and I will giue thee for it a better vineyard then it: or if it ſeeme good to thee, I will giue thee the worth of it in money.3And Naboth ſaid to Ahab, The Lord forbid it mee, that I ſhould giue the inheritance of my fathers vnto thee.4And Ahab came into his houſe, heauie, and diſpleaſed, becauſe of the word which Naboth the Iezreelite had ſpoken to him: for he had ſaide, I will not giue thee the inheritance of my fathers: and he laid him downe vpon his bed, and turned away his face, and would eate no bread.5But Iezebel his wife came to him, and ſaid vnto him, Why is thy ſpirit ſo ſad, that thou eateſt no bread?6And he ſaid vnto her, Becauſe I ſpake vnto Naboth the Iezreelite, and ſaid vnto him, Giue mee thy vineyard for money, or elſe if it pleaſe thee, I will giue thee another vineyard for it: And he anſwered, I wil not giue thee my vineyard.7And Iezebel his wife ſaide vnto him, Doeſt thou now gouerne the kingdome of Iſrael? Ariſe, and eate bread, and let thine heart bee merrie: I will giue thee the vineyard of Naboth the Iezreelite.8So ſhee wrote letters in Ahabs name, and ſealed them with his ſeale, and ſent the letters vnto the Elders, and to the Nobles that were in his citie dwelling with Naboth.9And ſhe wrote in the letters, ſaying, Proclaime a faſt, and ſet Naboth on high among the people:10And ſet two men, ſonnes of Belial before him, to beare witnes againſt him, ſaying, Thou diddeſt blaſpheme God and the king: and then carie him out, and ſtone him that he may die.11And the men of his citie, euen the Elders and the Nobles who were the inhabitants in his citie, did as Iezebel had ſent vnto them, and as it was written in the letters which ſhe had ſent vnto them.12They proclaimed a faſt, and ſet Naboth on high among the people.13And there came in two men, children of Belial, and ſate before him: and the men of Belial witneſſed againſt him, euen againſt Naboth, in the preſence of the people, ſaying, Naboth did blaſpheme God and the king. Then they caried him foorth out of the citie, and ſtoned him with ſtones, that hee died.14Then they ſent to Iezebel, ſaying, Naboth is ſtoned, and is dead.15And it came to paſſe when Iezebel heard that Naboth was ſtoned and was dead, that Iezebel ſaid to Ahab, Ariſe, take poſſeſſion of the Uineyard of Naboth the Iezreelite, which hee refuſed to giue thee for money: for Naboth is not aliue, but dead.16And it came to paſſe when Ahab heard that Naboth was dead, that Ahab roſe vp to goe downe to the Uineyard of Naboth the Iezreelite, to take poſſeſſion of it.17And the word of the Lord came to Eliiah the Tiſhbite, ſaying,18Ariſe, goe downe to meet Ahab king of Iſrael, which is in Samaria: behold, hee is in the Uineyard of Naboth, whither he is gone downe to poſſeſſe it.19And thou ſhalt ſpeake vnto him, ſaying, Thus ſaith the Lord, Haſt thou killed, and alſo taken poſſeſſion? And thou ſhalt ſpeake vnto him, ſaying, Thus ſaith the Lord; In the place where dogs licked the blood of Naboth, ſhall dogges licke thy blood, euen thine.20And Ahab ſaid to Eliiah, Haſt thou found me, O mine enemie? And he anſwered, I haue found thee: becauſe thou haſt ſold thy ſelfe to worke euill in the ſight of the Lord.21Behold, I will bring euill vpon thee, and will take away thy poſteritie, and will cut off from Ahab him that piſseth againſt the wall, and him that is ſhut vp, and left in Iſrael,22And will make thine houſe like the houſe of Ieroboam the ſonne of Nebat, and like the houſe of Baaſha the ſonne of Ahiiah, for the prouocation wherewith thou haſt prouoked mee to anger, and made Iſrael to ſinne.23And of Iezebel alſo ſpake the Lord, ſaying, The dogs ſhall eate Iezebel by the wall of Iezreel.24Him that dieth of Ahab in the citie, the dogs ſhall eate: and him that dieth in the field, ſhall the foules of the aire eat.25But there was none like vnto Ahab, which did ſell himſelfe to worke wickedneſſe in the ſight of the Lord, whom Iezebel his wife ſtirred vp.26And hee did very abominably in following Idoles, according to all things as did the Amorites, whom the Lord caſt out before the children of Iſrael.27And it came to paſſe when Ahab heard thoſe wordes, that hee rent his clothes, and put ſackecloth vpon his fleſh, and faſted, and lay in ſackcloth, and went ſoftly.28And the word of the Lord came to Eliiah the Tiſhbite, ſaying,29Seeſt thou how Ahab humbleth himſelfe before mee? becauſe hee humbleth himſelfe before mee, I will not bring the euill in his dayes: but in his ſonnes dayes will I bring the euill vpon his houſe.

CHAPTER 221And they continued three yeeres without warre betweene Syria and Iſrael.2And it came to paſſe on the third yere, that Iehoſhaphat the King of Iudah came downe to the king of Iſrael.3(And the king of Iſrael ſaid vnto his ſeruants, Know ye that Ramoth in Gilead is ours, and wee be ſtill, and take it not out of the hand of the king of Syria?)4And hee ſaid vnto Iehoſhaphat, Wilt thou goe with me to battel to Ramoth Gilead? And Iehoſhaphat ſaid to the king of Iſrael, I am as thou art, my people as thy people, my horſes as thy horſes.5And Iehoſhaphat ſaid vnto the king of Iſrael, Enquire, I pray thee, at the word of the Lord to day.6Then the king of Iſrael gathered the prophets together about foure hundred men, and ſaid vnto them, Shall I goe againſt Ramoth Gilead to battell, or ſhall I forbeare? And they ſaid, Goe vp, for the Lord ſhall deliuer it into the hand of the king.7And Iehoſhaphat ſaid, Is there not here a Prophet of the Lord beſides, that we might enquire of him?8And the king of Iſrael ſaid vnto Iehoſhaphat, There is yet one man, (Micaiah the ſonne of Imlah) by whom we may enquire of the Lord; but I hate him, for he doth not propheſie good concerning me, but euill. And Iehoſhaphat ſaid, Let not the King ſay ſo.9Then the king of Iſrael called an Officer, and ſaid, Haſten hither Micaiah the ſonne of Imlah.10And the King of Iſrael and Iehoſhaphat the King of Iudah ſate each on his throne, hauing put on their robes, in a voyd place in the entrance of the gate of Samaria, and all the Prophets prophecied before them.11And Zedekiah the ſonne of Chenaanah made him hornes of yron: and he ſayd, Thus ſaith the Lord, With theſe ſhalt thou puſh the Syrians, vntill thou haue conſumed them.12And all the Prophets prophecied ſo, ſaying; Goe vp to Ramoth Gilead, and proſper: for the Lord ſhall deliuer it into the kings hand.13And the meſſenger that was gone to call Micaiah, ſpake vnto him, ſaying, Behold now, the words of the prophets declare good vnto the King with one mouth: let thy word, I pray thee, bee like the word of one of them, and ſpeake that which is good.14And Micaiah ſayde, As the Lord liueth, what the Lord ſaith vnto me, that will I ſpeake.15So he came to the king, and the king ſayd vnto him, Micaiah, ſhall wee goe againſt Ramoth Gilead to battell, or ſhall we forbeare? And he anſwered him, Go, and proſper: for the Lord ſhall deliuer it into the hand of the king.16And the king ſaid vnto him, How many times ſhall I adiure thee, that thou tell me nothing but that which is true, in the Name of the Lord ?17And hee ſayd, I ſaw all Iſrael ſcattered vpon the hilles, as ſheepe that haue not a ſhepheard. And the Lord ſaid, Theſe haue no maſter, let them returne euery man to his houſe in peace.18And the King of Iſrael ſaid vnto Iehoſhaphat, Did I not tell thee, that he would prophecie no good concerning me, but euill?19And he ſaid, Heare thou therefore the word of the Lord: I ſawe the Lord ſitting on his Throne, and all the hoſte of heauen ſtanding by him, on his right hand and on his left.20And the Lord ſaid, Who ſhall perſwade Ahab, that hee may goe vp and fall at Ramoth Gilead? And one ſayd on this manner, and another ſaid on that manner.21And there came forth a ſpirit, and ſtood before the Lord, and ſaid, I will perſwade him.22And the Lord ſaid vnto him, Wherewith? And hee ſayd, I will goe foorth, and I will be a lying ſpirit in the mouth of all his prophets. And he ſaid, Thou ſhalt perſwade him, and preuaile alſo: Goe forth, and doe ſo.23Now therfore behold, the Lord hath put a lying ſpirit in the mouth of all theſe thy prophets, and the Lord hath ſpoken euill concerning thee.24But Zedekiah the ſonne of Chenaanah went neere, and ſmote Micaiah on the cheeke, and ſaid, Which way went the Spirit of the Lord from me, to ſpeake vnto thee?25And Micaiah ſayde, Beholde, thou ſhalt ſee in that day, when thou ſhalt goe into an inner chamber, to hide thy ſelfe.26And the King of Iſrael ſayde, Take Micaiah, and cary him backe vnto Amon the gouernour of the citie, and to Ioaſh the kings ſonne:27And ſay, Thus ſayth the King, Put this fellow in the priſon, and feede him with bread of affliction, and with water of afflictiō, vntil I come in peace.28And Micaiah ſaide, If thou returne at all in peace, the Lord hath not ſpoken by me. And he ſaid, Hearken, O people, euery one of you.29So the King of Iſrael, and Iehoſhaphat the king of Iudah, went vp to Ramoth Gilead.30And the king of Iſrael ſaid vnto Iehoſhaphat, I wil diſguiſe my ſelfe, & enter into the battell, but put thou on thy robes. And the King of Iſrael diſguiſed himſelfe, & went into the battell.31But the King of Syria commanded his thirtie and two Captaines that had rule ouer his charets, ſaying, Fight neither with ſmall nor great, ſaue only with the king of Iſrael.32And it came to paſſe, when the captaines of the charets ſaw Iehoſhaphat, that they ſaid, Surely it is the king of Iſrael. And they turned aſide to fight againſt him: and Iehoſhaphat cryed out.33And it came to paſſe, when the captaines of the charets perceiued that it was not the king of Iſrael, that they turned backe from purſuinghim.34And a certaine man drew a bow at a venture, and ſmote the king of Iſrael betweene the ioynts of the harneſse: wherefore hee ſayd vnto the driuer of his charet, Turne thine hand, and cary me out of the hoſte, for I am wounded.35And the battell increaſed that day: and the king was ſtayed vp in his charet againſt the Syrians, and died at euen: and the blood ranne out of the wound, into the mids of the charet.36And there went a proclamation throughout the hoſte, about the going downe of the Sunne, ſaying, Euery man to his citie, and euery man to his owne countrey.37So the King died, and was brought to Samaria, and they buried the king in Samaria.38And one waſhed the charet in the poole of Samaria, and the dogges licked vp his blood, and they waſhed his armour, according vnto the word of the Lord which he ſpake.39Now the reſt of the actes of Ahab, and all that he did, and the Iuory houſe which he made, and all the cities that he built, are they not written in the booke of the Chronicles of the Kings of Iſrael?40So Ahab ſlept with his fathers, and Ahaziah his ſonne reigned in his ſtead.41And Iehoſhaphat the ſonne of Aſa began to reigne ouer Iudah in the fourth yeere of Ahab King of Iſrael.42Iehoſhaphat was thirtie and fiue yeeres olde when hee began to reigne, and he reigned twentie and fiue yeeres in Ieruſalem: and his mothers name was Azubah the daughter of Shilhi.43And he walked in all the wayes of Aſa his father, hee turned not aſide from it, doing that which was right in the eyes of the Lord: neuertheleſſe, the high places were not taken away: for the people offered and burnt incenſe yet in the high places.44And Iehoſhaphat made peace with the king of Iſrael.45Now the reſt of the actes of Iehoſhaphat, and his might that hee ſhewed, and how he warred, are they not written in the booke of the Chronicles of the Kings of Iudah?46And the remnant of the Sodomites which remained in the dayes of his father Aſa, he tooke out of the land.47There was then no king in Edom: a deputie was king.48Iehoſhaphat made ſhippes of Tharſhiſh to goe to Ophir for golde: but they went not, for the ſhippes were broken at Ezion Geber.49Then ſaid Ahaziah the ſonne of Ahab vnto Iehoſhaphat, Let my ſeruants goe with thy ſeruants in the ſhips: But Iehoſhaphat would not.50And Iehoſhaphat ſlept with his fathers, and was buried with his fathers in the citie of Dauid his father: and Iehoram his ſonne reigned in his ſtead.51Ahaziah the ſonne of Ahab began to reigne ouer Iſrael in Samaria the ſeuenteenth yeere of Iehoſhaphat king of Iudah, and reigned two yeres ouer Iſrael.52And he did euill in the ſight of the Lord, and walked in the way of his father, and in the way of his mother, and in the way of Ieroboam the ſonne of Nebat, who made Iſrael to ſinne.53For he ſerued Baal, and worſhipped him, and prouoked to anger the Lord God of Iſrael, according vnto all that his father had done.

2 KINGS

CHAPTER 11Then Moab rebelled againſt Iſrael, after the death of Ahab.2And Ahaziah fel downe thorow a latteſse in his vpper chamber that was in Samaria, and was ſicke: and he ſent meſſengers, and ſaid vnto them, Goe, enquire of Baalzebub the god of Ekron, whether I ſhal recouer of this diſeaſe.3But the Angel of the Lord ſaid to Eliiah the Tiſhbite, Ariſe, goe vp to meete the meſſengers of the king of Samaria, and ſay vnto them, Is it not becauſe there is not a God in Iſrael, that ye goe to enquire of Baalzebub the god of Ekron?4Now therefore, thus ſayeth the Lord, Thou ſhalt not come downe from that bed on which thou art gone vp, but ſhalt ſurely die. And Eliiah departed.5And when the meſſengers turned backe vnto him, he ſaid vnto them, Why are ye now turned backe?6And they ſaid vnto him, There came a man vp to meet vs, and ſaid vnto vs, Goe, turne againe vnto the king that ſent you, and ſay vnto him, Thus ſaith the Lord, Is it not becauſe there is not a God in Iſrael, that thou ſendeſt to enquire of Baalzebub the god of Ekron? therefore thou ſhalt not come downe from that bedde on which thou art gone vp, but ſhalt ſurely die.7And hee ſaid vnto them, What maner of man was he which came vp to meet you, and told you theſe words?8And they anſwered him, He was an hairy man, and girt with a girdle of leather about his loynes: and he ſaid, It is Eliiah the Tiſhbite.9Then the King ſent vnto him a captaine of fiftie, with his fiftie: and he went vp to him, (and behold, he ſate on the top of an hill) and hee ſpake vnto him, Thou man of God, the king hath ſaid, Come downe.10And Eliiah anſwered, and ſaid to the captaine of fiftie, If I be a man of God, then let fire come downe from heauen, and conſume thee and thy fiftie. And there came downe fire from heauen, and conſumed him and his fiftie.11Againe alſo hee ſent vnto him another captaine of fiftie, with his fiftie: And hee anſwered, and ſaid vnto him, O man of God, Thus hath the king ſaid, Come downe quickly.12And Eliiah anſwered, and ſaide vnto them, If I be a man of God, let fire come downe from heauen, and conſume thee, and thy fiftie. And the fire of God came downe from heauen, and conſumed him, and his fiftie.13And hee ſent againe a captaine of the third fiftie, with his fiftie: and the third captaine of fiftie went vp, and came and fell on his knees before Eliiah, and beſought him, and ſaide vnto him, Oh man of God, I pray thee, let my life, and the life of theſe fiftie thy ſeruants, be precious in thy ſight.14Behold, there came fire downe from heauen, and burnt vp the two captaines of the former fifties, with their fifties: Therefore let my life now be precious in thy ſight.15And the Angel of the Lord ſaid vnto Elijah, Goe downe with him, be not afraid of him. And he aroſe, and went downe with him vnto the king.16And he ſaid vnto him, Thus ſaith the Lord, Foraſmuch as thou haſt ſent meſſengers to enquire of Baalzebub the god of Ekron (is it not becauſe there is no God in Iſrael, to enquire of his word?) therefore thou ſhalt not come downe off that bed on which thou art gone vp, but ſhalt ſurely die.17So he died, according to the worde of the Lord which Eliiah had ſpoken: and Iehoram reigned in his ſtead, in the ſecond yeere of Iehoram the ſonne of Iehoſhaphat king of Iudah, becauſe he had no ſonne.18Now the reſt of the actes of Ahaziah, which hee did, are they not written in the booke of the Chronicles of the kings of Iſrael?

CHAPTER 21And it came to paſſe when the Lord would take vp Elijah into heauen by a whirlewinde, that Elijah went with Eliſha from Gilgal.2And Elijah ſaid vnto Eliſha, Tarie here, I pray thee: for the Lord hath ſent me to Bethel: and Eliſha ſaid vnto him, As the Lord liueth, and as thy ſoule liueth, I wil not leaue thee. So they went downe to Bethel.3And the ſonnes of the Prophets that were at Bethel, came foorth to Eliſha, and ſaid vnto him, Knoweſt thou that the Lord will take away thy maſter from thy head to day? And he ſaid, Yea, I know it, hold you your peace.4And Elijah ſaid vnto him, Eliſha, tarie here, I pray thee: for the Lord hath ſent me to Iericho: And hee ſaid, As the Lord liueth, and as thy ſoule liueth, I will not leaue thee. So they came to Iericho.5And the ſonnes of the Prophets that were at Iericho came to Eliſha, and ſaid vnto him, Knoweſt thou that the Lord will take away thy maſter from thy head to day? And hee anſwered, Yea, I knowe it, holde you your peace.6And Elijah ſaid vnto him, Tarie, I pray thee, here: for the Lord hath ſent me to Iordan. And he ſaid, As the Lord liueth, and as thy ſoule liueth, I will not leaue thee. And they two went on.7And fiftie men of the ſonnes of the Prophets went, and ſtood to view afarre off: and they two ſtood by Iordan.8And Elijah tooke his mantle, and wrapt it together, and ſmote the waters, and they were diuided hither and thither, ſo that they two went ouer on drie ground.9And it came to paſſe when they were gone ouer, that Elijah ſaid vnto Eliſha, Aſke what I ſhall doe for thee, before I be taken away from thee. And Eliſha ſaid, I pray thee, let a double portion of thy ſpirit be vpon me.10And hee ſaid, Thou haſt aſked a hard thing: neuertheleſſe, if thou ſee me, when I am taken from thee, it ſhall be ſo vnto thee: but if not, it ſhall not be ſo.11And it came to paſſe as they ſtill went on and talked, that beholde, there appeared a charet of fire, and horſes of fire, and parted them both aſunder, and Elijah went vp by a whirlewind into heauen.12And Eliſha ſaw it, and he cried, My father, my father, the charet of Iſrael, and the horſemen thereof. And he ſaw him no more: and he tooke hold of his owne cloathes, and rent them in two pieces.13He tooke vp alſo the mantle of Elijah that fell from him, and went back, and ſtood by the banke of Iordan.14And he tooke the mantle of Eliiah that fell from him, and ſmote the waters, and ſaid, Where is the Lord God of Elijah? And when hee alſo had ſmitten the waters, they parted hither and thither: and Eliſha went ouer.15And when the ſonnes of the Prophets which were to view at Iericho, ſaw him, they ſaid, The ſpirit of Elijah doth reſt on Eliſha: And they came to meet him, and bowed themſelues to the ground before him.16And they ſaid vnto him, Behold now, there bee with thy ſeruants fiftie ſtrong men, let them goe, we pray thee, and ſeeke thy maſter: leſt peraduenture the Spirit of the Lord hath taken him vp, and caſt him vpon ſome mountaine, or into ſome valley. And he ſaid, Ye ſhall not ſend.17And when they vrged him, till he was aſhamed, he ſaid, Send. They ſent therefore fiftie men, and they ſought three dayes, but found him not.18And when they came againe to him (for he taried at Iericho) hee ſaid vnto them, Did I not ſay vnto you, Goe not?19And the men of the city ſaid vnto Eliſha, Behold, I pray thee, the ſituation of this city is pleaſant, as my lord ſeeth: but the water is nought, and the ground barren.20And hee ſaid, Bring mee a new cruſe, and put ſalt therein. And they brought it to him.21And he went forth vnto the ſpring of the waters, and caſt the ſalt in there, and ſaid, Thus ſaith the Lord, I haue healed theſe waters; there ſhall not be from thence any more death, or barren land.22So the waters were healed vnto this day, according to the ſaying of Eliſha, which he ſpake.23And he went vp from thence vnto Bethel: and as hee was going vp by the way, there came foorth little children out of the citie, and mocked him, and ſaid vnto him, Goe vp thou bald head, Goe vp thou bald head.24And hee turned backe, and looked on them, and curſed them in the Name of the Lord: and there came foorth two ſhee Beares out of the wood, and tare fortie and two children of them.25And hee went from thence to mount Carmel, and from thence he returned to Samaria.

CHAPTER 31Now Iehoram the ſonne of Ahab began to reigne ouer Iſrael in Samaria, the eighteenth yere of Iehoſhaphat king of Iudah, and reigned twelue yeeres.2And he wrought euill in the ſight of the Lord, but not like his father and like his mother; for hee put away the image of Baal that his father had made.3Neuertheleſſe, hee cleaued vnto the ſinnes of Ieroboam the ſonne of Nebat, which made Iſrael to ſinne; he departed not therefrom.4And Meſha king of Moab was a ſheepe-maſter, and rendred vnto the king of Iſrael an hundred thouſand lambes, and an hundred thouſand rammes, with the wooll.5But it came to paſſe when Ahab was dead, that the king of Moab rebelled againſt the king of Iſrael.6And king Iehoram went out of Samaria the ſame time, and numbred all Iſrael.7And he went, and ſent to Iehoſhaphat the King of Iudah, ſaying, The king of Moab hath rebelled againſt mee: Wilt thou goe with mee againſt Moab to battell? and he ſaid, I will goe vp: I am as thou art, my people as thy people, and my horſes as thy horſes.8And he ſaid, Which way ſhall we goe vp? And he anſwered, The way through the wilderneſſe of Edom.9So the king of Iſrael went, and the king of Iudah, and the king of Edom: and they fetcht a compaſſe of ſeuen dayes iourney: and there was no water for the hoſte, and for the cattell that followed them.10And the king of Iſrael ſaid, Alas, that the Lord hath called theſe three kings together, to deliuer them into the hand of Moab.11But Iehoſhaphat ſaid, Is there not here a Prophet of the Lord, that we may enquire of the Lord by him? And one of the king of Iſraels ſeruants anſwered, and ſaid, Here is Eliſha the ſonne of Shaphat, which powred water on the hands of Eliiah.12And Iehoſhaphat ſaide, The word of the Lord is with him. So the king of Iſrael, & Iehoſhaphat, and the king of Edom went downe to him.13And Eliſha ſaide vnto the king of Iſrael, What haue I to doe with thee? Get thee to the prophets of thy father, and to the prophets of thy mother. And the king of Iſrael ſaid vnto him, Nay: for the Lord hath called theſe three kings together, to deliuer them into the hand of Moab.14And Eliſha ſaid, As the Lord of hoſtes liueth, before whom I ſtand, Surely were it not that I regard the preſence of Iehoſhaphat the King of Iudah, I would not looke toward thee, nor ſee thee.15But now bring me a minſtrell. And it came to paſſe when the minſtrell played, that the hand of the Lord came vpon him.16And hee ſayde, Thus ſayth the Lord, Make this valley full of ditches.17For thus ſayth the Lord, Yee ſhall not ſee winde, neither ſhall ye ſee raine, yet that valley ſhall be filled with water, that ye may drinke, both ye, and your cattell, and your beaſts.[18]And this is but a light thing in the ſight of the Lord, he will deliuer the Moabites alſo into your hand.[19]And ye ſhall ſmite euery fenced citie, and euery choice citie, and ſhall fell euery good tree, and ſtop all welles of water, and marre euery good piece of land with ſtones.[20]And it came to paſſe in the morning when the meate offering was offered, that behold, there came water by the way of Edom, and the countrey was filled with water.[21]And when all the Moabites heard that the kings were come vp to fight againſt them, they gathered all that were able to put on armour, and vpward, and ſtood in the border.[22]And they roſe vp early in the morning, and the Sunne ſhone vpon the water, and the Moabites ſawe the water on the other ſide as red as blood.[23]And they ſaid, This is blood: the kings are ſurely ſlaine, and they haue ſmitten one another: now therefore, Moab, to the ſpoile.[24]And when they came to the campe of Iſrael, the Iſraelites roſe vp and ſmote the Moabites, ſo that they fledde before them: but they went forward ſmiting the Moabites, euen in their countrey.[25]And they beat downe the cities, and on euery good piece of land caſt euery man his ſtone, and filled it, and they ſtopped all the welles of water, and felled all the good trees: onely in Kirharaſeth left they the ſtones thereof: howbeit the ſlingers went about it, and ſmote it.[26]And when the king of Moab ſawe that the battell was too ſore for him, he tooke with him ſeuen hundred men that drewe ſwordes, to breake thorow euen vnto the king of Edom: but they could not.[27]Then hee tooke his eldeſt ſonne that ſhould haue reigned in his ſtead, and offered him for a burnt offering vpon the wall: and there was great indignation againſt Iſrael, and they departed from him, and returned to their owne land.

CHAPTER 4 [1]Now there cryed a certaine woman of the wiues of the ſonnes of the Prophets vnto Eliſha, ſaying, Thy ſeruant my huſband is dead, and thou knoweſt that thy ſeruant did feare the Lord: and the creditour is come to take vnto him my two ſonnes to be bondmen.[2]And Eliſha ſaid vnto her, What ſhall I doe for thee? Tell mee, what haſt thou in the houſe? And ſhee ſayd, Thine handmaid hath not any thing in the houſe, ſaue a pot of oyle.[3]Then hee ſaid, Goe, borrow thee veſſels abroad, of all thy neighbours; euen emptie veſſels, borrow not a few.[4]And when thou art come in, thou ſhalt ſhut the doore vpon thee, and vpon thy ſonnes, and ſhalt powre out into all thoſe veſſels, and thou ſhalt ſet aſide that which is full.[5]So ſhee went from him, and ſhut the doore vpon her, & vpon her ſonnes: who brought the veſſels to her, and ſhee powred out.[6]And it came to paſſe, when the veſſels were full, that ſhee ſaid vnto her ſonne, Bring me yet a veſſell. And hee ſaid vnto her, There is not a veſſel more. And the oyle ſtayed.[7]Then ſhe came, and told the man of God: and he ſaid, Goe, ſell the oyle, and pay thy debt, and liue thou and thy children of the reſt.[8]And it fell on a day, that Eliſha paſſed to Shunem, where was a great woman; and ſhee conſtrained him to eate bread: And ſo it was, that as oft as he paſſed by, hee turned in thither to eate bread.[9]And ſhee ſaid vnto her huſband, Behold now, I perceiue that this is an holy man of God, which paſſeth by vs continually.[10]Let vs make a litle chamber, I pray thee, on the wall, and let vs ſet for him there a bed, and a table, and a ſtoole, and a candleſticke: and it ſhall be when he commeth to vs, that hee ſhall turne in thither.[11]And it fell on a day that hee came thither, and hee turned into the chamber, and lay there.[12]And he ſaid to Gehazi his ſeruant, Call this Shunammite. And when hee had called her, ſhe ſtood before him.[13]And he ſaid vnto him, Say, now vnto her, Behold, thou haſt beene carefull for vs with all this care; What is to be done for thee? Wouldeſt thou be ſpoken for to the king, or to the captaine of the hoſte? And ſhe anſwered, I dwell among mine owne people.[14]And he ſaid, What then is to bee done for her? And Gehazi anſwered, Uerily ſhe hath no child, and her huſband is old.[15]And he ſaid, Call her. And when he had called her, ſhe ſtood in the doore.[16]And he ſaid, About this ſeaſon, according to the time of life, thou ſhalt imbrace a ſonne. And ſhe ſaid, Nay my lord, thou man of God, doe not lie vnto thine handmaid.[17]And the woman conceiued, and bare a ſonne at that ſeaſon, that Eliſha had ſaid vnto her, according to the time of life.[18]And when the child was growen, it fell on a day that hee went out to his father, to the reapers.[19]And he ſaid vnto his father, My head, my head: and he ſaid to a ladde, Carie him to his mother.[20]And when he had taken him, and brought him to his mother, hee ſate on her knees till noone, and then died.[21]And ſhe went vp, and laid him on the bed of the man of God, and ſhut the doore vpon him, and went out.[22]And ſhe called vnto her huſband, and ſaid, Send me, I pray thee, one of the yong men, and one of the aſſes, that I may runne to the man of God, and come againe.[23]And he ſaid, Wherefore wilt thou goe to him to day? it is neither newe moone nor Sabbath. And ſhee ſaid, It ſhalbe well.[24]Then ſhe ſadled an aſſe, and ſaid to her ſeruant, Driue, and goe forward: ſlacke not thy riding for mee, except I bid thee.[25]So ſhe went, and came vnto the man of God to mount Carmel: and it came to paſſe when the man of God ſaw her afarre off, that hee ſaid to Gehazi his ſeruant, Behold, yonder is that Shunammite:[26]Runne now, I pray thee, to meet her, and ſay vnto her, Is it wel with thee? is it wel with thy huſband? is it wel with the child? And ſhe anſwered, It is well.[27]And when ſhee came to the man of God to the hill, ſhee caught him by the feet: but Gehazi came neere to thruſt her away. And the man of God ſaide, Let her alone, for her ſoule is vexed within her: and the Lord hath hid it from me, and hath not told me.[28]Then ſhee ſaid, Did I deſire a ſonne of my Lord ? did I not ſay, Doe not deceiue me?[29]Then he ſaid to Gehazi, Gird vp thy loines, and take my ſtaffe in thine hand, and goe thy way: if thou meete any man, ſalute him not: and if any ſalute thee, anſwere him not againe: and lay my ſtaffe vpon the face of the childe.[30]And the mother of the childe ſaid, As the Lord liueth, and as thy ſoule liueth, I will not leaue thee. And he aroſe, and followed her.[31]And Gehazi paſſed on before them, and laid the ſtaffe vpon the face of the child, but there was neither voyce, nor hearing: wherefore he went againe to meete him, and tolde him, ſaying, The child is not awaked.[32]And when Eliſha was come into the houſe, behold, the child was dead, and laid vpon his bed.[33]He went in therefore, and ſhut the doore vpon them twaine, and prayed vnto the Lord.[34]And he went vp, and lay vpon the child, and put his mouth vpon his mouth, and his eyes vpon his eyes, and his hands vpon his hands, and he ſtretched himſelfe vpon the child, and the fleſh of the child waxed warme.[35]Then he returned, and walked in the houſe to and fro, and went vp, and ſtretched himſelfe vpon him: and the child neeſed ſeuen times, and the child opened his eyes.[36]And hee called Gehazi, and ſaid, Call this Shunammite. So hee called her: and when ſhee was come in vnto him, he ſaid, Take vp thy ſonne.[37]Then ſhe went in, and fell at his feet, and bowed her ſelfe to the ground, and tooke vp her ſonne, and went out.[38]And Eliſha came againe to Gilgal, and there was a dearth in the land, and the ſonnes of the Prophets were ſitting before him: and hee ſaid vnto his ſeruant, Set on the great pot, and ſeethe pottage for the ſonnes of the Prophets.[39]And one went out into the field to gather herbes, and found a wild vine, and gathered thereof wilde gourds his lap full, and came and ſhred them into the pot of pottage: for they knew them not.[40]So they powred out for the men to eat: and it came to paſſe as they were eating of the pottage, that they cried out, and ſaid, O thou man of God, there is death in the pot. And they could not eate thereof.[41]But he ſaid, Then bring meale. And he caſt it into the pot: And he ſaid, Powre out for the people, that they may eat. And there was no harme in the pot.[42]And there came a man from Baal-Shaliſha, and brought the man of God bread of the firſt fruits, twentie loaues of barley, and full eares of corne in the huſke thereof: and he ſaid, Giue vnto the people, that they may eate.[43]And his ſeruitour ſaide, What ſhould I ſet this before an hundred men? He ſaid againe, Giue the people, that they may eate: for thus ſaith the Lord, They ſhall eate, and ſhall leaue thereof.[44]So he ſet it before them, and they did eate, and left thereof, according to the word of the Lord.

CHAPTER 5 [1]Now Naaman captaine of the hoſt of the king of Syria, was a great man with his maſter, and honourable, becauſe by him the Lord had giuen deliuerance vnto Syria: He was alſo a mighty man in valour, but he was a leper.[2]And the Syrians had gone out by companies, and had brought away captiue out of the land of Iſrael a litle maid, & ſhe waited on Naamans wife.[3]And ſhee ſaide vnto her miſtreſſe, Would God my lord were with the Prophet that is in Samaria, for hee would recouer him of his leproſie.[4]And one went in, and tolde his lord, ſaying, Thus and thus ſaid the mayd that is of the land of Iſrael.[5]And the king of Syria ſaid, Goe to, Goe, and I will ſend a letter vnto the king of Iſrael. And hee departed, and tooke with him ten talents of ſiluer, and ſixe thouſand pieces of gold, and ten changes of raiment.[6]And hee brought the letter to the king of Iſrael, ſaying, Now when this letter is come vnto thee, behold, I haue therewith ſent Naaman my ſeruant to thee, that thou mayeſt recouer him of his leproſie.[7]And it came to paſſe when the king of Iſrael had read the letter, that he rent his clothes, and ſaid, Am I God, to kill and to make aliue, that this man doeth ſend vnto me, to recouer a man of his leproſie? Wherefore conſider, I pray you, and ſee how he ſeeketh a quarrell againſt me.8And it was ſo when Eliſha the man of God had heard, that the king of Iſrael had rent his clothes, that he ſent to the king, ſaying, Wherefore haſt thou rent thy clothes? Let him come now to mee, and he ſhall know that there is a Prophet in Iſrael.9So Naaman came with his horſes, and with his charet, and ſtood at the doore of the houſe of Eliſha.10And Eliſha ſent a meſſenger vnto him, ſaying, Goe and waſh in Iordane ſeuen times, and thy fleſh ſhall come againe to thee, and thou ſhalt be cleane.11But Naaman was wroth, and went away, and ſaide, Beholde, I thought, He will ſurely come out to me and ſtand, and call on the Name of the Lord his God, and ſtrike his hand ouer the place, and recouer the leper.12Are not Abana and Pharpar, riuers of Damaſcus, better then all the waters of Iſrael? May I not waſh in them, and be cleane? So he turned, and went away in a rage.13And his ſeruants came neere and ſpake vnto him, and ſaid, My father, If the Prophet had bid thee do ſome great thing, wouldeſt thou not haue done it? How much rather then, when hee ſaith to thee, Waſh and be cleane?14Then went he downe, and dipped himſelfe ſeuen times in Iordan, according to the ſaying of the man of God: and his fleſh came againe like vnto the fleſh of a litle childe, and he was cleane.15And he returned to the man of God, he and all his company, and came, and ſtood before him: and he ſaid, Behold, now I know that there is no God in all the earth, but in Iſrael: now therefore, I pray thee, take a bleſſing of thy ſeruant.16But he ſaid, As the Lord liueth, before whom I ſtand, I will receiue none: And hee vrged him to take it, but he refuſed.17And Naaman ſaid, Shall there not then, I pray thee, be giuen to thy ſeruant two mules burden of earth? for thy ſeruant wil henceforth offer neither burnt offering, nor ſacrifice vnto other gods, but vnto the Lord.18In this thing the Lord pardon thy ſeruant, that when my maſter goeth into the houſe of Rimmon to worſhip there, and hee leaneth on my hand, and I bow myſelfe in the houſe of Rimmon: when I bow downe my ſelfe in the houſe of Rimmon, the Lord pardon thy ſeruant in this thing.19And he ſaid vnto him, Go in peace. So he departed from him, a litle way.20But Gehazi the ſeruant of Eliſha the man of God, ſaid, Behold, my maſter hath ſpared Naaman this Syrian, in not receiuing at his hands that which hee brought: but as the Lord liueth, I wil runne after him, and take ſomewhat of him.21So Gehazi followed after Naaman: and when Naaman ſaw him running after him, hee lighted downe from the charet to meet him, and ſaid, Is all well?22And he ſaid, All is well: my maſter hath ſent me, ſaying, Behold, euen now there be come to mee from mount Ephraim two yong men, of the ſonnes of the Prophets: Giue them, I pray thee, a talent of ſiluer, and two changes of garments.23And Naaman ſaid, Bee content, take two talents: and hee vrged him, and bound two talents of ſiluer in two bags, with two changes of garments, and layde them vpon two of his ſeruants, and they bare them before him.24And when he came to the towre, he tooke them from their hand, and beſtowed them in the houſe, and hee let the men goe, and they departed.25But he went in, and ſtood before his maſter: and Eliſha ſaid vnto him, Whence commeſt thou, Gehazi? And hee ſaid, Thy ſeruant went no whither.26And he ſaid vnto him, Went not mine heart with thee, when the man turned againe from his charet to meete thee? Is it a time to receiue money, and to receiue garments, and Oliue yards, and Uineyards, and ſheepe, and oxen, and men ſeruants, and mayd ſeruants?27The leproſie therefore of Naaman ſhall cleaue vnto thee, and vnto thy ſeede for euer: And hee went out from his preſence a leper as white as ſnow.

CHAPTER 61And the ſonnes of the Prophets ſaide vnto Eliſha, Beholde now, the place where wee dwell with thee, is too ſtrait for vs:2Let vs goe, wee pray thee, vnto Iordane, and take thence euery man a beame, and let vs make vs a place there where we may dwell. And hee anſwered, Goe ye.3And one ſaid, Be content, I pray thee, and goe with thy ſeruants. And he anſwered, I will goe.4So hee went with them: and when they came to Iordane, they cut downe wood.5But as one was felling a beame, the axe head fell into the water: and hee cryed, and ſayd, Alas maſter, for it was borrowed.6And the man of God ſaid, Where fell it? and hee ſhewed him the place: and he cut downe a ſticke, and caſt it in thither, and the yron did ſwimme.7Therefore ſaid he, Take it vp to thee: And hee put out his hand, and tooke it.8Then the king of Syria warred againſt Iſrael, and tooke counſell with his ſeruants, ſaying, In ſuch and ſuch a place ſhall be my campe.9And the man of God ſent vnto the king of Iſrael, ſaying, Beware that thou paſſe not ſuch a place; for thither the Syrians are come downe.10And the king of Iſrael ſent to the place which the man of God tolde him, and warned him of, and ſaued himſelfe there, not once nor twiſe.11Therefore the heart of the king of Syria was ſore troubled for this thing, and he called his ſeruants, and ſaid vnto them, Will ye not ſhewe me which of vs is for the king of Iſrael?12And one of his ſeruants ſayde, None, my lord O king; but Eliſha the Prophet, that is in Iſrael, telleth the king of Iſrael, the wordes that thou ſpeakeſt in thy bed-chamber.13And he ſaid, Goe and ſpie where he is, that I may ſend and fetch him. And it was tolde him, ſaying, Behold, he is in Dothan.14Therefore ſent he thither horſes, and charets, and a great hoſte: and they came by night, and compaſſed the citie about.15And when the ſeruant of the man of God was riſen early and gone forth, behold, an hoſt compaſſed the citie, both with horſes and charets: and his ſeruant ſaid vnto him, Alas my maſter, how ſhall we doe?16And he anſwered, Feare not: for they that be with vs, are moe then they that be with them.17And Eliſha prayed, and ſayde, Lord, I pray thee, open his eyes that he may ſee. And the Lord opened the eyes of the young man, and hee ſaw: and behold, the mountaine was full of horſes, and charets of fire round about Eliſha.18And when they came downe to him, Eliſha prayed vnto the Lord, and ſaid, Smite this people, I pray thee, with blindneſse. And hee ſmote them with blindneſse, according to the word of Eliſha.19And Eliſha ſaide vnto them, This is not the way, neither is this the citie: follow me, and I will bring you to the man whom ye ſeeke. But hee led them to Samaria.20And it came to paſſe when they were come into Samaria, that Eliſha ſaid, Lord, open the eyes of theſe men, that they may ſee. And the Lord opened their eyes, and they ſaw, and beholde, they were in the mids of Samaria.21And the king of Iſrael ſaide vnto Eliſha, when he ſaw them, My father, ſhall I ſmite them? ſhall I ſmite them?22And he anſwered, Thou ſhalt not ſmite them: wouldeſt thou ſmite thoſe whom thou haſt taken captiue with thy ſword, and with thy bow? ſet bread and water before them, that they may eate, and drinke, and go to their maſter.23And hee prepared great prouiſion for them, and when they had eaten and drunke, hee ſent them away, and they went to their maſter: ſo the bands of Syria came no more into the lande of Iſrael.24And it came to paſſe after this, that Benhadad king of Syria gathered all his hoſte, and went vp, and beſieged Samaria.25And there was a great famine in Samaria: and behold, they beſieged it, vntill an aſſes head was ſolde for foureſcore pieces of ſiluer, and the fourth part of a kab of doues doung for fiue pieces of ſiluer.26And as the king of Iſrael was paſsing by vpon the wall, there cried a woman vnto him, ſaying, Helpe, my lord, O king.27And he ſaid, If the Lord do not helpe thee, whence ſhall I helpe thee? out of the barne floore, or out of the wine preſse?28And the king ſaid vnto her, What aileth thee? And ſhee anſwered, This woman ſaid vnto me, Giue thy ſonne, that we may eate him to day, and wee will eate my ſonne to morrow.29So we boyled my ſonne, and did eate him: and I ſaide vnto her on the next day, Giue thy ſonne, that we may eate him: and ſhe hath hid her ſonne.30And it came to paſſe when the king heard the words of the woman, that he rent his clothes, and hee paſſed by vpon the wall, and the people looked, and behold, hee had ſackcloth within, vpon his fleſh.31Then he ſaid, God doe ſo, and more alſo to mee, if the head of Eliſha the ſonne of Shaphat, ſhall ſtand on him this day.32But Eliſha ſate in his houſe (and the elders ſate with him) and the king ſent a man from before him: but yer the meſſenger came to him, hee ſaid to the Elders, ſee yee how this ſonne of a murderer hath ſent to take away mine head? Looke when the meſſenger commeth, ſhut the doore, and hold him faſt at the doore: Is not the ſound of his maſters feete behind him?33And while hee yet talked with them, beholde, the meſſenger came downe vnto him: and he ſaid, Behold, this euill is of the Lord, what ſhould I waite for the Lord any longer?

CHAPTER 71Then Eliſha ſaid, Heare yee the word of the Lord, Thus ſaith the Lord, To morrowe about this time ſhal a meaſure of fine flower be ſold for a ſhekell, and two meaſures of barley for a ſhekel, in the gate of Samaria.2Then a lord on whoſe hand the king leaned, anſwered the man of God, and ſaid, Behold, if the Lord would make windowes in heauen, might this thing bee? and he ſaide, Behold, thou ſhalt ſee it with thine eies, but ſhalt not eate thereof.3And there were foure leprous men at the entring in of the gate: and they ſaide one to another, Why ſit wee here vntill we die?4If we ſay, We will enter into the citie, then the famine is in the citie, and wee ſhall die there: and if we ſit ſtill here, we die alſo. Now therefore come, and let vs fall vnto the hoſt of the Syrians: if they ſaue vs aliue, we ſhall liue; and if they kill vs, we ſhall but die.5And they roſe vp in the twilight, to goe vnto the campe of the Syrians: and when they were come to the vttermoſt part of the campe of Syria, behold, there was no man there.6For the Lord had made the hoſt of the Syrians to heare a noiſe of charets, and a noiſe of horſes, euen the noiſe of a great hoſt: and they ſaid one to another, Loe, the king of Iſrael hath hired againſt vs the kings of the Hittites, and the kings of the Egyptians, to come vpon vs.7Wherefore they aroſe and fled in the twilight, and left their tents, and their horſes, and their aſſes, euen the campe as it was, and fled for their life.8And when theſe lepers came to the vttermoſt part of the campe, they went into one tent, and did eate, and drinke, and carried thence ſiluer, and gold, and raiment, and went and hid it, and came againe, and entred into another tent, and carried thence alſo, and went and hid it.9Then they ſaid one to another, We doe not well: this day is a day of good tydings, and we hold our peace: if we tarie till the morning light, ſome miſchiefe will come vpon vs: nowe therefore come, that we may goe, and tell the kings houſhold.10So they came, and called vnto the porter of the citie: and they told them, ſaying; We came to the campe of the Syrians, and behold, there was no man there, neither voice of man, but horſes tyed, and aſſes tyed, and the tents as they were.11And hee called the porters, and they told it to the kings houſe within.12And the king aroſe in the night, and ſaid vnto his ſeruants, I will now ſhew you what the Syrians haue done to vs: They know that we be hungrie, therefore are they gone out of the camp, to hide themſelues in the field, ſaying; When they come out of the citie, we ſhal catch them aliue, and get into the citie.13And one of his ſeruants anſwered, and ſaid, Let ſome take, I pray thee, fiue of the horſes that remaine, which are left in the citie: (behold, they are as all the multitude of Iſrael that are left in it: behold, I ſay, they are euen as all the multitude of the Iſraelites that are conſumed) and let vs ſend, and ſee.14They tooke therefore two charet horſes, and the king ſent after the hoſte of the Syrians, ſaying, Goe, and ſee.15And they went after them vnto Iordane, and loe, all the way was full of garments, and veſſels, which the Syrians had caſt away in their haſte: and the meſſengers returned, and told the king.16And the people went out, and ſpoiled the tents of the Syrians: So a meaſure of fine flowre was ſold for a ſhekell, and two meaſures of barley for a ſhekel, according to the word of the Lord.17And the king appointed the lord on whoſe hand he leaned, to haue the charge of the gate: and the people trode vpon him in the gate, and he died, as the man of God had ſaid, who ſpake when the king came downe to him.18And it came to paſſe, as the man of God had ſpoken to the king, ſaying, Two meaſures of barley for a ſhekel, and a meaſure of fine flowre for a ſhekel, ſhalbe to morrow about this time, in the gate of Samaria:19And that lord anſwered the man of God, and ſaid, Now behold, if the Lord ſhould make windowes in heauen, might ſuch a thing be? And he ſaid, Behold, thou ſhalt ſee it with thine eyes, but ſhalt not eate thereof.20And ſo it fell out vnto him: for the people trode vpon him in the gate, and he died.

CHAPTER 81Then ſpake Eliſha vnto the woman (whoſe ſonne he had reſtored to life) ſaying, Ariſe, and goe thou and thine houſholde, and ſoiourne wherſoeuer thou canſt ſoiourne: for the Lord hath called for a famin, and it ſhall alſo come vpon the land ſeuen yeeres.2And the woman aroſe, and did after the ſaying of the man of God: and ſhe went with her houſholde, and ſoiourned in the land of the Philiſtines ſeuen yeeres.3And it came to paſſe at the ſeuen yeeres ende, that the woman returned out of the land of the Philiſtines: and ſhe went foorth to crie vnto the king for her houſe, and for her land.4And the king talked with Gehazi the ſeruant of the man of God, ſaying, Tell mee, I pray thee, all the great things that Eliſha hath done.5And it came to paſſe as he was telling the King how hee had reſtored a dead body to life, that behold, the woman whoſe ſonne he had reſtored to life, cryed to the King for her houſe and for her land. And Gehazi ſaid, My lord O king, this is the woman, and this is her ſonne, whom Eliſha reſtored to life.6And when the king aſked the woman, ſhee tolde him. So the King appointed vnto her a certaine officer, ſaying, Reſtore all that was hers, and all the fruites of the field, ſince the day that ſhe left the land, euen till now.7And Eliſha came to Damaſcus, and Benhadad the king of Syria was ſicke, and it was tolde him, ſaying, The man of God is come hither.8And the king ſaid vnto Hazael, Take a preſent in thine hand, and goe meete the man of God, and enquire of the Lord by him, ſaying, Shall I recouer of this diſeaſe?9So Hazael went to meete him, and tooke a preſent with him, euen of euery good thing of Damaſcus, fourtie camels burden, and came, and ſtood before him, and ſaid, Thy ſonne Benhadad king of Syria hath ſent me to thee, ſaying, Shall I recouer of this diſeaſe?10And Eliſha ſaid vnto him, Goe, ſay vnto him, Thou mayeſt certeinly recouer: howbeit, the Lord hath ſhewed me, that he ſhall ſurely die.11And hee ſetled his countenance ſtedfaſtly, vntill he was aſhamed: and the man of God wept.12And Hazael ſaid, Why weepeth my lord? And he anſwered, Becauſe I know the euill that thou wilt doe vnto the children of Iſrael: their ſtrong holds wilt thou ſet on fire, and their young men wilt thou ſlay with the ſword, and wilt daſh their children, and rip vp their women with childe.13And Hazael ſaid, But what, is thy ſeruant a dogge, that he ſhould doe this great thing? And Eliſha anſwered, The Lord hath ſhewed mee that thou ſhalt be king ouer Syria.14So he departed from Eliſha, and came to his maſter, who ſaide to him, What ſaid Eliſha to thee? and hee anſwered, He told me that thou ſhouldſt ſurely recouer.15And it came to paſſe on the morrow, that he tooke a thicke cloth, and dipt it in water, and ſpread it on his face, ſo that he died, and Hazael reigned in his ſtead.16And in the fifth yeere of Ioram the ſonne of Ahab king of Iſrael, Iehoſhaphat being then king of Iudah, Iehoram the ſonne of Iehoſhaphat king of Iudah began to reigne.17Thirtie and two yeeres old was he when he began to reigne, and hee reigned eight yeeres in Ieruſalem.18And he walked in the way of the kings of Iſrael, as did the houſe of Ahab: for the daughter of Ahab was his wife, and hee did euill in the ſight of the Lord.19Yet the Lord would not deſtroy Iudah, for Dauid his ſeruants ſake, as hee promiſed to giue to him alway a light, and to his children.20In his dayes Edom reuolted from vnder the hand of Iudah, and made a king ouer themſelues.21So Ioram went ouer to Zair, and all the charets with him, and hee roſe by night, and ſmote the Edomites, which compaſſed him about: and the captaines of the charets, and the people fled into their tents.22Yet Edom reuolted from vnder the hand of Iudah vnto this day. Then Libnah reuolted at the ſame time.23And the reſt of the actes of Ioram, and all that hee did, are they not written in the booke of the Chronicles of the kings of Iudah?24And Ioram ſlept with his fathers, and was buried with his fathers in the citie of Dauid: And Ahaziah his ſonne reigned in his ſtead.25In the twelfth yeere of Ioram the ſonne of Ahab, king of Iſrael, did Ahaziah, the ſonne of Iehoram king of Iudah, begin to reigne.26Two and twentie yeeres old was Ahaziah when he began to reigne, and he reigned one yeere in Ieruſalem, and his mothers name was Athaliah the daughter of Omri king of Iſrael.27And he walked in the way of the houſe of Ahab, and did euill in the ſight of the Lord, as did the houſe of Ahab: for hee was the ſonne in law of the houſe of Ahab.28And he went with Ioram the ſonne of Ahab, to the warre againſt Hazael king of Syria in Ramoth Gilead, and the Syrians wounded Ioram.29And king Ioram went backe to be healed in Iezreel, of the woundes which the Syrians had giuen him at Ramah, when hee fought againſt Hazael king of Syria: And Ahaziah the ſon of Iehoram king of Iudah, went downe to ſee Ioram the ſonne of Ahab in Iezreel, becauſe he was ſicke.

CHAPTER 91And Eliſha the Prophet called one of the children of the Prophets, and ſaid vnto him, Gird vp thy loines, and take this boxe of oile in thine hand, and goe to Ramoth Gilead.2And when thou commeſt thither, looke out there Iehu the ſonne of Iehoſhaphat, the ſonne of Nimſhi, and goe in, and make him Ariſe vp from among his brethren, and carie him to an inner chamber.3Then take the boxe of oile, and powre it on his head, and ſay, Thus ſaith the Lord, I haue anointed thee king ouer Iſrael: then open the doore, and flee, and tary not.4So the yong man, euen the yong man the Prophet, went to Ramoth Gilead:5And when hee came, behold, the captaines of the hoſt were ſitting; and hee ſaid, I haue an errand to thee, O captaine: And Iehu ſaid, Unto which of all vs? And he ſaid, To thee, O captaine.6And hee aroſe, and went into the houſe, and hee powred the oyle on his head, and ſaid vnto him, Thus ſayth the Lord God of Iſrael, I haue anoynted thee king ouer the people of the Lord, euen ouer Iſrael.7And thou ſhalt ſmite the houſe of Ahab thy maſter, that I may auenge the blood of my ſeruants the Prophets, and the blood of all the ſeruants of the Lord, at the hand of Iezebel.8For the whole houſe of Ahab ſhal periſh, and I will cut off from

Ahab, him that piſseth againſt the wall, and him that is ſhut vp and left in Iſrael.9And I will make the houſe of Ahab, like the houſe of Ieroboam the ſonne of Nebat, and like the houſe of Baaſha the ſonne of Ahiiah.10And the dogges ſhal eate Iezebel in the portion of Iezreel, and there ſhal be none to burie her. And he opened the doore, and fled.11Then Iehu came foorth to the ſeruants of his lord, and one ſaid vnto him, Is all well? wherefore came this madde fellow to thee? And he ſaid vnto them, Yee know the man, and his communication.12And they ſaid, It is falſe, tell vs now: And hee ſayde, Thus and thus ſpake he to me, ſaying, Thus ſaith the Lord, I haue anoynted thee King ouer Iſrael.13Then they haſted, and tooke euery man his garment, and put it vnder him on the top of the ſtaires, and blewe with trumpets, ſaying, Iehu is king.14So Iehu the ſonne of Iehoſhaphat, the ſonne of Nimſhi, conſpired againſt Ioram: (now Ioram had kept Ramoth Gilead, hee, and all Iſrael, becauſe of Hazael king of Syria:15But king Ioram was returned to bee healed in Iezreel, of the wounds which the Syrians had giuen him, when he fought with Hazael king of Syria.) And Iehu ſaid, If it be your minds, then let none goe forth nor eſcape out of the citie, to goe to tell it in Iezreel.16So Iehu rode in a charet, and went to Iezreel, (for Ioram lay there:) and Ahaziah king of Iudah was come downe to ſee Ioram.17And there ſtood a watchman on the towre in Iezreel, and hee ſpied the company of Iehu as he came, and ſaid, I ſee a companie. And Ioram ſayd, Take an horſeman, and ſend to meete them, and let him ſay, Is it peace?18So there went one on horſebacke to meete him, and ſaid, Thus ſayth the king, Is it peace? And Iehu ſaid, What haſt thou to doe with peace? turne thee behinde me. And the watchman tolde, ſaying, The meſſenger came to them, but he commeth not againe.19Then he ſent out a ſecond on horſebacke, which came to them, and ſayd, Thus ſayth the king, Is it peace? And Iehu anſwered, What haſt thou to doe with peace? turne thee behinde me.20And the watchman tolde, ſaying, He came euen vnto them, and commeth not againe: and the driuing is like the driuing of Iehu the ſonne of Nimſhi; for he driueth furiouſly.21And Ioram ſaid, Make readie. And his charet was made ready. And Ioram king of Iſrael, and Ahaziah king of Iudah, went out, each in his charet, and they went out againſt Iehu, and met him in the portion of Naboth the Iezreelite.22And it came to paſſe when Ioram ſaw Iehu, that hee ſaid, Is it peace, Iehu? And he anſwered, What peace, ſo long as the whoredomes of thy mother Iezebel, and her witchcrafts are ſo many?23And Ioram turned his hand, and fled, and ſaid to Ahaziah, There is treachery, O Ahaziah.24And Iehu drew a bowe with his full ſtrength, and ſmote Iehoram betweene his armes, and the arrow went out at his heart, and hee ſunke downe in his charet.25Then ſaid Iehu to Bidkar his captaine, Take vp, and caſt him in the portion of the field of Naboth the Iezreelite: for remember, how that when I and thou rode together after Ahab his father, the Lord laide this burden vpon him:26Surely I haue ſeene yeſterday the blood of Naboth, and the blood of his ſonnes, ſayd the Lord, and I will requite thee in this plat, ſayth the Lord. Now therefore take and caſt him into the plat of ground, according to the word of the Lord.27But when Ahaziah the king of Iudah ſaw this, hee fled by the way of the garden houſe: and Iehu followed after him, and ſaid, Smite him alſo in the charet; and they did ſo, at the going vp to Gur, which is by Ibleam: And hee fled to Megiddo, and died there.28And his ſeruants caried him in a charet to Ieruſalem, and buried him in his ſepulchre with his fathers, in the citie of Dauid.29And in the eleuenth yeere of Ioram the ſonne of Ahab, began Ahaziah to reigne ouer Iudah.30And when Iehu was come to Iezreel, Iezebel heard of it, and ſhee painted her face, and tyred her head, and looked out at a window.31And as Iehu entred in at the gate, ſhe ſaid, Had Zimri peace, who ſlew his maſter?32And he lift vp his face to the window, and ſaid, Who is on my ſide, who? And there looked out to him two or three Eunuches.33And he ſaid, Throw her downe. So they threw her downe, and ſome of her blood was ſprinkled on the wall, and on the horſes: and he trode her vnder foote.34And when he was come in, hee did eate and drinke, and ſaide, Goe, ſee now this curſed woman, and burie her: for ſhe is a kings daughter.35And they went to burie her, but they found no more of her then the ſkul, and the feete, & the palmes of her hands.36Wherefore they came againe, and told him: and he ſaid, This is the word of the Lord, which he ſpake by his ſeruant Elijah the Tiſhbite, ſaying, In the portion of Iezreel ſhall dogs eate the fleſh of Iezebel:37And the carkeiſeof Iezebel ſhall be as doung vpon the face of the field in the portion of Iezreel, ſo that they ſhall not ſay, This is Iezebel.

CHAPTER 101And Ahab had ſeuentie ſonnes in Samaria: and Iehu wrote letters, and ſent to Samaria vnto the rulers of Iezreel, to the Elders, and to them that brought vp Ahabs children, ſaying,2Now aſsoone as this letter commeth to you, ſeeing your maſters ſons are with you, and there are with you charets and horſes, a fenced citie alſo, and armour:3Looke euen out the beſt and meeteſt of your maſters ſonnes, and ſet him on his fathers throne, and fight for your maſters houſe.4But they were exceedingly afraid, and ſaid, Behold, two kings ſtood not before him: how then ſhall we ſtand?5And he that was ouer the houſe, and he that was ouer the citie, the elders alſo, and the bringers vp of the children, ſent to Iehu, ſaying, Wee are thy ſeruants, and will doe all that thou ſhalt bid vs, we will not make any king: doe thou that which is good in thine eyes.6Then he wrote a letter the ſecond time to them, ſaying, If yee be mine, and if ye will hearken vnto my voyce, take ye the heads of the men your maſters ſonnes, and come to me to Iezreel by to morow this time: (now the kings ſonnes being ſeuenty perſons, were with the great men of the city, which brought them vp.)7And it came to paſſe when the letter came to them, that they tooke the kings ſonnes, and ſlewe ſeuentie perſons, and put their heads in baſkets, and ſent him them to Iezreel.8And there came a meſſenger, and tolde him, ſaying, They haue brought the heads of the kings ſonnes. And he ſaid, Lay ye them in two heaps at the entring in of the gate, vntill the morning.9And it came to paſſe in the morning, that he went out, & ſtood, and ſaid to all the people, Ye be righteous: behold, I conſpired againſt my maſter, and ſlew him: But who ſlew all theſe?10Know now, that there ſhall fall vnto the earth nothing of the worde of the Lord, which the Lord ſpake concerning the houſe of Ahab: for the Lord hath done that which he ſpake by his ſeruant Elijah.11So Iehu ſlew all that remained of the houſe of Ahab, in Iezreel, and all his great men, and his kinſefolkes, and his prieſts, vntill he left him none remaining.12And hee aroſe, and departed, and came to Samaria: And as he was at the ſhearing houſe in the way,13Iehu met with the brethren of Ahaziah king of Iudah, and ſaid, Who are ye? And they anſwered, Wee are the brethren of Ahaziah, and we go downe to ſalute the children of the King, and the children of the Queene.14And hee ſaid, Take them aliue. And they tooke them aliue, and ſlew them at the pit of the ſhearing houſe, euen two and fourty men; neither left he any of them.15And when hee was departed thence, he lighted on Iehonadab the ſonne of Rechab, comming to meet him: and he ſaluted him, & ſaid to him, Is thine heart right, as my heart is with thy heart? And Iehonadab anſwered, It is: If it be, giue mee thine hand. And hee gaue him his hand, and hee tooke him vp to him into the charet.16And he ſaid, Come with me, and ſee my zeale for the Lord: ſo they made him ride in his charet.17And when he came to Samaria, he ſlew all that remained vnto Ahab in Samaria, till he had deſtroyed him, according to the ſaying of the Lord, which he ſpake to Eliiah.18And Iehu gathered all the people together, and ſaid vnto them, Ahab ſerued Baal a litle, but Iehu ſhall ſerue him much.19Now therefore, call vnto me all the prophets of Baal, all his ſeruants, and all his prieſts, let none be wanting: for I haue a great ſacrifice to doe to Baal; whoſoeuer ſhall be wanting, he ſhall not liue. But Iehu did it in ſubtilitie, to the intent that hee might deſtroy the worſhippers of Baal.20And Iehu ſaid, Proclaime a ſolemne aſſembly for Baal. And they proclaimed it.21And Iehu ſent through all Iſrael, and all the worſhippers of Baal came, ſo that there was not a man left that came not: and they came into the houſe of Baal; and the houſe of Baal was full from one end to another.22And he ſaid vnto him that was ouer the veſtrie, Bring forth veſtments for all the worſhippers of Baal. And he brought them forth veſtments.23And Iehu went, and Iehonadab the ſonne of Rechab into the houſe of Baal, and ſaid vnto the worſhippers of Baal, ſearch, and looke that there be here with you none of the ſeruants of the Lord, but the worſhippers of Baal onely.24And when they went in to offer ſacrifices, and burnt offerings, Iehu appointed foureſcore men without, and ſaid, If any of the men whom I haue brought into your hands, eſcape, hee that letteth him goe, his life ſhall be for the life of him.25And it came to paſſe aſsoone as hee had made an end of offering the burnt offering, that Iehu ſaide to the guard, and to the captaines, Goe in, and ſlay them, let none come foorth. And they ſmote them with the edge of the ſword, and the guard, and the captaines caſt them out, and went to the citie of the houſe of

Baal. 26 And they brought foorth the Images out of the houſe of Baal,
and burnt them. 27 And they brake downe the image of Baal, and brake
downe the houſe of Baal, and made it a draughthouſe, vnto this
day. 28 Thus Iehu deſtroyed Baal out of Iſrael. 29 Howbeit, from the ſinnes
of Ieroboam the ſonne of Nebat, who made Iſrael to ſinne, Iehu
departed not from after them, to wit, the golden calues that were in
Bethel, and that were in Dan. 30 And the Lord ſaid vnto Iehu, Becauſe
thou haſt done well in executing that which is right in mine eyes, and
haſt done vnto the houſe of Ahab according to all that was in mine heart,
thy children of the fourth generation, ſhal ſit on the throne of
Iſrael. 31 But Iehu tooke no heede to walke in the Law of the Lord God
of Iſrael, with all his heart: for he departed not from the ſinnes of
Ieroboam, which made Iſrael to ſinne. 32 In thoſe dayes the Lord began
to cut Iſrael ſhort: and Hazael ſmote them in all the coaſts of
Iſrael: 33 From Iordan Eaſtward, all the land of Gilead, the Gadites, and
the Reubenites, and the Manaſsites, from Aroer, (which is by the riuer
Arnon) euen Gilead and Baſhan. 34 Now the reſt of the acts of Iehu, and
all that he did, & all his might, are they not written in the booke of the
Chronicles of the kings of Iſrael? 35 And Iehu ſlept with his fathers, and
they buried him in Samaria, and Iehoahaz his ſonne reigned in his
ſtead. 36 And the time that Iehu reigned ouer Iſrael in Samaria, was
twentie and eight yeeres.

CHAPTER 11 1 And when Athaliah the mother of Ahaziah ſawe that
her ſonne was dead, ſhe aroſe, and deſtroyed all the ſeed royall. 2 But
Iehoſheba the daughter of king Ioram, ſiſter of Ahaziah, tooke Ioaſh the
ſonne of Ahaziah, and ſtale him from among the Kings ſonnes which
were ſlaine; and they hid him, euen him and his nurſe in the bed-
chamber from Athaliah, ſo that he was not ſlaine. 3 And he was with her
hidde in the Houſe of the Lord, ſixe yeeres: and Athaliah did reigne ouer
the land. 4 And the ſeuenth yeere Iehoiada ſent and fet the rulers ouer
hundreds, with the captains, and the guard, and brought them to him
into the houſe of the Lord, and made a couenant with them, and tooke
an othe of them in the houſe of the Lord, and ſhewed them the Kings
ſonne. 5 And he commanded them, ſaying, This is the thing that yee ſhall
doe; A third part of you that enter in on the Sabbath, ſhall euen be
keepers of the watch of the kings houſe: 6 And a third part ſhall be at the
gate of Sur, and a third part at the gate behinde the guard: ſo ſhall yee
keepe the watch of the houſe, that it be not broken downe. 7 And two
parts of all you, that goe foorth on the Sabbath, euen they ſhall keepe
the watch of the houſe of the Lord about the King. 8 And yee ſhall
compaſſe the King round about, euery man with his weapons in his
hand: and he that commeth within the ranges, let him bee ſlaine: and be
yee with the king, as hee goeth out, and as he commeth in. 9 And the
captaines ouer the hundreds did according to all things that Iehoiada the
Prieſt commanded: and they tooke euery man his men that were to come
in on the Sabbath, with them that ſhould goe out on the Sabbath, and
came to Iehoiada the Prieſt. 10 And to the captaines ouer hundreds, did
the Prieſt giue king Dauids ſpeares and ſhields, that were in the
Temple. 11 And the guard ſtood, euery man with his weapons in his hand,
round about the king, from the right corner of the Temple, to the left
corner of the Temple, along by the Altar and the Temple. 12 And he
brought foorth the kings ſonne, and put the crowne vpon him, and gaue
him the Teſtimonie, and they made him King, and anointed him, and
they clapt their hands, and ſaid, God ſaue the King. 13 And when Athaliah
heard the noiſe of the guard, and of the people, ſhe came to the people,
into the Temple of the Lord. 14 And when ſhee looked, behold, the king
ſtood by a pillar, as the maner was, and the Princes, and the trumpetters
by the King, and all the people of the land reioyced, and blew with
trumpets: and Athaliah rent her clothes, and cryed, Treaſon,
treaſon. 15 But Iehoiada the Prieſt commanded the captaines of the
hundreds, the officers of the hoſte, and ſayde vnto them, Haue her
foorth without the ranges; and him that followeth her, kill with the
ſword: for the Prieſt had ſayd, Let her not be ſlaine in the houſe of the
Lord. 16 And they laid hands on her, and ſhe went by the way, by the
which the horſes came into the kings houſe, and there was ſhe
ſlaine. 17 And Iehoiada made a couenant betweene the Lord and the king,
and the people, that they ſhould be the Lords people; betweene the king
alſo and the people. 18 And all the people of the land went into the houſe
of Baal, and brake it down, his altars, and his images brake they in pieces
throughly, and ſlew Mattan the prieſt of Baal before the altars: and the
Prieſt appointed officers ouer the houſe of the Lord. 19 And hee tooke
the rulers ouer hundreds, and the captaines, and the guard, and all the
people of the land, and they brought downe the king from the houſe of
the Lord, and came by the way of the gate of the guard, to the kings
houſe, and he ſate on the throne of the kings. 20 And all the people of the
land reioyced, and the citie was in quiet, and they ſlew Athaliah with the
ſword, beſide the kings houſe. 21 Seuen yeeres old was Iehoaſh when he
began to reigne.

CHAPTER 12 1 In the ſeuenth yeere of Iehu, Iehoaſh began to reigne,
and fourtie yeeres reigned he in Ieruſalem, and his mothers name was
Zibiah of Beerſheba. 2 And Iehoaſh did that which was right in the ſight
of the Lord all his dayes, wherein Iehoiada the Prieſt inſtructed him. 3 But
the high places were not taken away: the people ſtill ſacrificed, and burnt
incenſe in the high places. 4 And Iehoaſh ſaid to the prieſts, All the money
of the dedicated things that is brought into the houſe of the Lord, euen
the money of euery one that paſſeth the account, the money that euery
man is ſet at, and all the money that commeth into any mans heart, to
bring into the houſe of the Lord, 5 Let the prieſts take it to them, euery
man of his acquaintance, and let them repaire the breaches of the houſe,
whereſoeuer any breach ſhalbe found. 6 But it was ſo that in the three
and twentieth yeere of king Iehoaſh, the prieſts had not repaired the
breaches of the houſe. 7 Then king Iehoaſh called for Iehoiada the prieſt,
and the other prieſts, and ſaide vnto them, Why repaire ye not the
breaches of the houſe? now therefore receiue no more money of your
acquaintance, but deliuer it for the breaches of the houſe. 8 And the
prieſts conſented to receiue no more money of the people, neither to
repaire the breaches of the houſe. 9 But Iehoiada the prieſt tooke a cheſt,
and bored a hole in the lid of it, and ſet it beſide the Altar, on the right
ſide, as one commeth into the houſe of the Lord, and the prieſts that
kept the doore, put therein all the money that was brought into the
houſe of the Lord. 10 And it was ſo when they ſaw that there was much
money in the cheſt, that the kings ſcribe, and the high prieſt came vp,
and they put vp in bags and told the money that was found in the houſe
of the Lord. 11 And they gaue the money, being told, into the handes of
them that did the worke, that had the ouerſight of the houſe of the Lord:
and they laid it out to the carpenters and builders, that wrought vpon
the houſe of the Lord, 12 And to Maſons, and hewers of ſtone, and to buy
timber, and hewed ſtone to repaire the breaches of the houſe of the
Lord, and for all that was laid out for the houſe to repaire it. 13 Howbeit,
there were not made for the houſe of the Lord, bowles of ſiluer, ſnuffers,
baſons, trumpets, any veſſels of gold, or veſſels of ſiluer, of the money
that was brought into the houſe of the Lord: 14 But they gaue that to the
workemen, and repaired therewith the houſe of the Lord. 15 Moreouer,
they reckned not with the men, into whoſe hand they deliuered the
money to be beſtowed on workmen: for they dealt faithfully. 16 The
treſpaſſe money, and ſinnemoney was not brought into the houſe of the
Lord: it was the Prieſts. 17 Then Hazael king of Syria went vp, and fought
againſt Gath, and tooke it: and Hazael ſet his face to goe vp to
Ieruſalem. 18 And Iehoaſh king of Iudah tooke all the hallowed things
that Iehoſhaphat, and Iehoram, and Ahaziah his fathers, kings of Iudah
had dedicate, and his owne hallowed things, and all the gold that was
found in the treaſures of the houſe of the Lord, and in the kings houſe,
and ſent it to Hazael king of Syria, and hee went away from
Ieruſalem. 19 And the reſt of the actes of Iehoaſh, and all that he did, are
they not written in the booke of the Chronicles of the kings of
Iudah? 20 And his ſeruants aroſe, and made a conſpiracie, and ſlew
Iehoaſh in the houſe of Millo, which goeth downe to Silla. 21 For Iozachar
the ſonne of Shimeath, and Iehozabad the ſonne of Shomer, his
ſeruants, ſmote him, and he died; and they buried him with his fathers
in the citie of Dauid, and Amaziah his ſonne reigned in his ſtead.

CHAPTER 13 1 In the three and twentieth yeere of Ioaſh the ſonne of
Ahaziah king of Iudah, Iehoahaz the ſonne of Iehu beganne to reigne
ouer Iſrael in Samaria, and reigned ſeuenteene yeeres. 2 And hee did that
which was euill in the ſight of the Lord, and followed the ſinnes of
Ieroboam the ſonne of Nebat, which made Iſrael to ſinne, he departed
not there from. 3 And the anger of the Lord was kindled againſt Iſrael,
and hee deliuered them into the hand of Hazael king of Syria, and into
the hand of Benhadad the ſonne of Hazael, all their dayes. 4 And
Iehoahaz beſought the Lord, and the Lord hearkened vnto him: for hee
ſaw the oppreſſion of Iſrael, becauſe the king of Syria oppreſſed

them.5(And the Lord gaue Iſrael a ſauiour, ſo that they went out from vnder the hand of the Syrians: and the children of Iſrael dwelt in their tents as before-time.6Neuertheleſſe, they departed not from the ſinnes of the houſe of Ieroboam, who made Iſrael ſinne, but walked therein: and there remained the groue alſo in Samaria.)7Neither did he leaue of the people to Iehoahaz, but fiftie horſemen, and tenne charets, and tenne thouſand footmen: for the king of Syria had deſtroyed them, and had made them like the duſt by threſhing.8Nowe the reſt of the actes of Iehoahaz, and all that he did, and his might, are they not written in the booke of the Chronicles of the kings of Iſrael?9And Iehoahaz ſlept with his fathers, and they buried him in Samaria, and Ioaſh his ſonne reigned in his ſtead.10In the thirty and ſeuenth yeere of Ioaſh king of Iudah, beganne Iehoaſh the ſonne of Iehoahaz to reigne ouer Iſrael in Samaria, and reigned ſixteene yeeres.11And hee did that which was euill in the ſight of the Lord; hee departed not from all the ſinnes of Ieroboam the ſonne of Nebat, who made Iſrael ſinne: but hee walked therein.12And the reſt of the actes of Ioaſh, and all that hee did, and his might, wherewith hee fought againſt Amaziah king of Iudah, are they not written in the booke of the chronicles of the kings of Iſrael?13And Ioaſh ſlept with his fathers, and Ieroboam ſate vpon his throne: and Ioaſh was buried in Samaria with the kings of Iſrael.14Nowe Eliſha was fallen ſicke, of his ſickneſse whereof he died, and Ioaſh the king of Iſrael came downe vnto him, and wept ouer his face, and ſaid, O my father, my father, the charet of Iſrael, and the horſemen thereof.15And Eliſha ſaid vnto him, Take bowe and arrowes. And he tooke vnto him bowe and arrowes.16And he ſaid to the king of Iſrael, Put thine hand vpon the bowe. And he put his hand vpon it: and Eliſha put his hands vpon the kings hands.17And he ſayd, Open the window Eaſtward. And hee opened it. Then Eliſha ſayd, Shoote. And he ſhot. And he ſaid; The arrowe of the Lords deliuerance, and the arrowe of deliuerance from Syria: for thou ſhalt ſmite the Syrians in Aphek, till thou haue conſumed them.18And he ſayd, Take the arrowes. And he tooke them. And hee ſaid vnto the king of Iſrael, Smite vpon the ground. And he ſmote thriſe, and ſtayed.19And the man of God was wroth with him, and ſaide, Thou ſhouldeſt haue ſmitten fiue or ſixe times, then haddeſt thou ſmitten Syria till thou haddeſt conſumed it: whereas now thou ſhalt ſmite Syria but thrice.20And Eliſha died, and they buried him: And the bands of the Moabites inuaded the land at the comming in of the yeere.21And it came to paſſe as they were burying a man, that behold, they ſpyed a band of men, and they caſt the man into the ſepulchre of Eliſha: and when the man was let downe, and touched the bones of Eliſha, he reuiued, and ſtood vp on his feete.22But Hazael king of Syria, oppreſſed Iſrael all the dayes of Iehoahaz.23And the Lord was gracious vnto them, and had compaſſion on them, and had reſpect vnto them, becauſe of his couenant with Abraham, Iſaac, and Iacob, and would not deſtroy them, neither caſt hee them from his preſence as yet.24So Hazael the king of Syria dyed, and Benhadad his ſonne reigned in his ſtead.25And Iehoaſh the ſonne of Iehoahaz tooke againe out of the hand of Benhadad the ſonne of Hazael, the cities which he had taken out of the hand of Iehoahaz his father, by warre: three times did Ioaſh beat him, and recouered the cities of Iſrael.

CHAPTER 141In the ſecond yeere of Ioaſh ſonne of Iehoahaz king of Iſrael, reigned Amaziah the ſonne of Ioaſh king of Iudah.2Hee was twentie and fiue yeeres olde when he began to reigne, and reigned twentie and nine yeeres in Ieruſalem: and his mothers name was Iehoaddan of Ieruſalem.3And he did that which was right in the ſight of the Lord, yet not like Dauid his father: hee did according to all things as Ioaſh his father did.4Howbeit, the high places were not taken away: as yet the people did ſacrifice, and burnt incenſe on the high places.5And it came to paſſe aſsoone as the kingdome was confirmed in his hand, that he ſlew his ſeruants which had ſlaine the king his father.6But the children of the murderers he ſlew not, according vnto that which is written in the booke of the Law of Moſes, wherein the Lord commanded, ſaying, The fathers ſhal not be put to death for the children, nor the children be put to death for the fathers: but euery man ſhall be put to death for his owne ſinne.7He ſlew of Edom in the valley of ſalt, ten thouſand, and tooke Selah by warre, and called the name of it, Ioktheel, vnto this day.8Then Amaziah ſent meſſengers to Iehoaſh the ſonne of Iehoahaz ſonne of Iehu king of Iſrael, ſaying, Come, let vs looke one another in the face.9And Iehoaſh the king of Iſrael ſent to Amaziah king of Iudah, ſaying, The thiſtle that was in Lebanon, ſent to the Cedar that was in Lebanon, ſaying, Giue thy daughter to my ſonne to wife. And there paſſed by a wilde beaſt that was in Lebanon, and trode downe the thiſtle.10Thou haſt indeed ſmitten Edom, and thine heart hath lifted thee vp: glory of this, and tary at home: for why ſhouldeſt thou meddle to thy hurt, that thou ſhouldeſt fall, euen thou, and Iudah with thee?11But Amaziah would not heare: therefore Iehoaſh king of Iſrael went vp, and hee, and Amaziah king of Iudah, looked one another in the face at Bethſhemeſh, which belongeth to Iudah.12And Iudah was put to the worſe before Iſrael, and they fled euery man to their tents.13And Iehoaſh king of Iſrael tooke Amaziah king of Iudah, the ſonne of Iehoaſh the ſonne of Ahaziah at Bethſhemeſh, and came to Ieruſalem, and brake downe the wall of Ieruſalem, from the gate of Ephraim, vnto the corner gate, foure hundred cubites.14And he tooke all the golde and ſiluer, and all the veſſels that were found in the houſe of the Lord, and in the treaſures of the kings houſe, and hoſtages, and returned to Samaria.15Now the reſt of the acts of Iehoaſh which he did, and his might, and how he fought with Amaziah king of Iudah, are they not written in the booke of the Chronicles of the kings of Iſrael?16And Iehoaſh ſlept with his fathers, and was buried in Samaria, with the kings of Iſrael, and Ieroboam his ſonne reigned in his ſtead.17And Amaziah the ſonne of Ioaſh king of Iudah, liued after the death of Iehoaſh ſonne of Iehoahaz king of Iſrael, fifteene yeeres.18And the reſt of the acts of Amaziah, are they not written in the booke of the Chronicles of the kings of Iudah?19Now they made a conſpiracie againſt him in Ieruſalem: and he fled to Lachiſh, but they ſent after him to Lachiſh, and ſlew him there.20And they brought him on horſes, and he was buried at Ieruſalem with his fathers, in the city of Dauid.21And all the people of Iudah tooke Azariah (which was ſixteene yeeres old) and made him king in ſtead of his father Amaziah.22He built Elath, and reſtored it to Iudah, after that the king ſlept with his fathers.23In the fifteenth yeere of Amaziah the ſonne of Ioaſh king of Iudah, Ieroboam the ſonne of Ioaſh king of Iſrael began to raigne in Samaria, and raigned forty and one yeeres:24And hee did that which was euill in the ſight of the Lord: hee departed not from all the ſinnes of Ieroboam the ſonne of Nebat, who made Iſrael to ſinne.25Hee reſtored the coaſt of Iſrael, from the entring of Hamath, vnto the ſea of the plaine, according to the word of the Lord God of Iſrael, which he ſpake by the hand of his ſeruant Ionah, the ſonne of Amittai the Prophet, which was of Gath Hepher.26For the Lord ſaw the affliction of Iſrael, that it was very bitter: for there was not any ſhut vp, nor any left, nor any helper for Iſrael.27And the Lord ſaid not, that hee would blot out the name of Iſrael from vnder heauen: but he ſaued them by the hand of Ieroboam the ſonne of Ioaſh.28Now the reſt of the actes of Ieroboam, and all that he did, and his might, how he warred, and how he recouered Damaſcus and Hamath, which belonged to Iudah, for Iſrael, are they not written in the booke of the Chronicles of the kings of Iſrael?29And Ieroboam ſlept with his fathers, euen with the kings of Iſrael, and Zachariah his ſonne reigned in his ſtead.

CHAPTER 151In the twenty and ſeuenth yeere of Ieroboam king of Iſrael, began Azariah ſonne of Amaziah king of Iudah to reigne.2Sixteene yeeres old was he when he began to reigne, and he reigned two aud fifty yeeres in Ieruſalem: and his mothers name was Iecholiah of Ieruſalem.3And he did that which was right in the ſight of the Lord, according to all that his father Amaziah had done;4Saue that the high places were not remoued: the people ſacrificed, and burnt incenſe ſtill on the high places.5And the Lord ſmote the king, ſo that hee was a Leper vnto the day of his death, and dwelt in a ſeuerall houſe, and Iotham the kings ſonne was ouer the houſe, iudging the people of the land.6And the reſt of the actes of Azariah, and all that hee did, are they not written in the booke of the Chronicles of the kings of Iudah?7So Azariah ſlept with his fathers, and they buried him with his fathers in the city of Dauid, and Iotham his ſonne reigned in his ſtead.8In the thirty and eight yeere of Azariah king of Iudah, did Zachariah the ſonne of Ieroboam reigne ouer Iſrael in Samaria ſixe moneths.9And hee did that which was euil in the ſight of the Lord, as his fathers had done: he departed not from the ſinnes of Ieroboam the ſonne of Nebat, who made Iſrael to ſinne.10And Shallum the ſonne of Iabeſh, conſpired againſt him, and ſmote him before the people, and ſlewe him, and reigned in his ſtead.11And the reſt of the actes of Zachariah, beholde, they are written in the booke of the chronicles of the kings of Iſrael.12This was the word of the Lord which he ſpake vnto Iehu, ſaying, Thy ſonnes ſhall ſit on the throne of Iſrael, vnto the fourth generation. And ſo it came to paſſe.13Shallum the ſonne of Iabeſh began to reigne in the nine and thirtieth yeere of Uzziah king of Iudah, and he reigned a full moneth in Samaria.14For Menahem the ſonne of Gadi, went vp from Tirzah, and came to Samaria, and ſmote Shallum the ſonne of Iabeſh, in Samaria, and ſlew him, and reigned in his ſtead.15And the reſt of the actes of Shallum, and the conſpiracy which he made, behold, they are written in the booke of the chronicles of the kings of Iſrael.16Then Menahem ſmote Tiphſah, and all that were therein, and the coaſts thereof from Tirzah: becauſe they opened not to him, therfore he ſmote it, and all the women therein that were with child, he ript vp.17In the nine and thirtieth yeere of Azariah king of Iudah, began Menahem the ſonne of Gadi to reigne ouer Iſrael, and reigned tenne yeres in Samaria.18And he did that which was euill in the ſight of the Lord: hee departed not all his dayes from the ſinnes of Ieroboam the ſonne of Nebat, who made Iſrael to ſinne.19And Pul the king of Aſſyria came againſt the land: and Menahem gaue Pul a thouſand talents of ſiluer, that his hand might be with him, to confirm the kingdome in his hand.20And Menahem exacted the mony of Iſrael, euen of all the mightie men of wealth, of each man fiftie ſhekels of ſiluer, to giue to the king of Aſſyria: ſo the king of Aſſyria turned backe, and ſtayed not there in the land.21And the reſt of the acts of Menahem, and all that he did, are they not written in the booke of the Chronicles of the kings of Iſrael?22And Menahem ſlept with his fathers, and Pekahiah his ſonne reigned in his ſtead.23In the fiftieth yere of Azariah king of Iudah, Pekahiah the ſonne of Menahem began to reigne ouer Iſrael in Samaria, and reigned two yeeres.24And he did that which was euill in the ſight of the Lord, hee departed not from the ſinnes of Ieroboam the ſonne of Nebat, who made Iſrael to ſinne.25But Pekah the ſonne of Remaliah, a captaine of his, conſpired againſt him, and ſmote him in Samaria, in the palace of the kings houſe, with Argob, and Arieh, and with him fiftie men of the Gileadites: and hee killed him, and reigned in his roume.26And the reſt of the actes of Pekahiah, and all that he did, beholde, they are written in the booke of the chronicles of the kings of Iſrael.27In the two and fiftieth yeere of Azariah king of Iudah, Pekah the ſonne of Remaliah began to reigne ouer Iſrael in Samaria, and reigned twentie yeeres.28And he did that which was euill in the ſight of the Lord, hee departed not from the ſinnes of Ieroboam the ſonne of Nebat, who made Iſrael to ſinne.29In the dayes of Pekah king of Iſrael, came Tiglath Pileſer king of Aſſyria, and tooke Iion, and Abel-Beth-maachah, and Ianoah, and Kedeſh, and Hazor, and Gilead, and Galilee, all the land of Naphtali, and caried them captiue to Aſſyria.30And Hoſhea the ſonne of Elah, made a conſpiracie againſt Pekah the ſonne of Remaliah, and ſmote him, and ſlew him, and reigned in his ſtead, in the twentieth yeere of Iotham the ſonne of Uzziah.31And the reſt of the actes of Pekah, and all that he did, behold, they are written in the booke of the Chronicles of the kings of Iſrael.32In the ſecond yeere of Pekah the ſonne of Remaliah king of Iſrael, began Iotham the ſonne of Uzziah king of Iudah to reigne.33Fiue and twentie yeeres olde was he when he began to reigne, and hee reigned ſixteene yeeres in Ieruſalem: and his mothers name was Ieruſha, the daughter of Zadok.34And he did that which was right in the ſight of the Lord: hee did according to all that his father Uzziah had done.35Howbeit, the high places were not remoued: the people ſacrificed and burnt incenſe ſtill in the high places: He built the higher gate of the houſe of the Lord.36Now the reſt of the actes of Iotham, and all that hee did, are they not written in the booke of the Chronicles of the kings of Iudah?37(In thoſe dayes the Lord began to ſend againſt Iudah, Rezin the king of Syria, and Pekah the ſonne of Remaliah)38And Iotham ſlept with his fathers, and was buried with his fathers in the citie of Dauid his father, and Ahaz his ſonne reigned in his ſtead.

CHAPTER 161In the ſeuenteenth yeere of Pekah the ſonne of Remaliah, Ahaz the ſonne of Iotham King of Iudah began to reigne.2Twentie yeeres olde was Ahaz when hee began to reigne, and reigned ſixteene yeeres in Ieruſalem, and did not that which was right in the ſight of the Lord his God, like Dauid his father:3But hee walked in the way of the kings of Iſrael, yea & made his ſonne to paſſe through the fire, according to the abominations of the heathen, whom the Lord caſt out from before the children of Iſrael.4And hee ſacrificed and burnt incenſe in the high places, and on the hils, and vnder euery greene tree.5Then Rezin king of Syria, and Pekah ſonne of Remaliah king of Iſrael, came vp to Ieruſalem to warre: and they beſieged Ahaz, but could not ouercome him.6At that time Rezin king of Syria, recouered Elath to Syria, & draue the Iewes from Elath: and the Syrians came to Elath, and dwelt there vnto this day.7So Ahaz ſent meſſengers to Tiglath Pileſer king of Aſſyria, ſaying, I am thy ſeruant, and thy ſonne: come vp, and ſaue me out of the hand of the king of Syria, and out of the hand of the king of Iſrael, which riſe vp againſt me.8And Ahaz tooke the ſiluer and gold that was found in the houſe of the Lord, and in the treaſures of the kings houſe, and ſent it for a preſent to the king of Aſſyria.9And the king of Aſſyria hearkened vnto him: for the king of Aſſyria went vp againſt Damaſcus, and tooke it, and caried the people of it captiue to Kir, and ſlew Rezin.10And King Ahaz went to Damaſcus, to meete Tiglath Pileſer king of Aſſyria, and ſaw an altar that was at Damaſcus: and king Ahaz ſent to Uriiah the Prieſt the faſhion of the altar, and the paterne of it, according to all the workemanſhip thereof.11And Uriiah the Prieſt built an altar: according to all that king Ahaz had ſent from Damaſcus, ſo Uriiah the Prieſt made it, againſt king Ahaz came from Damaſcus.12And when the king was come from Damaſcus, the King ſaw the altar: and the King approched to the altar, and offered thereon.13And he burnt his burnt offering, and his meate offering, and powred his drinke offering, and ſprinkled the blood of his peace offerings vpon the altar.14And hee brought alſo the braſen altar which was before the Lord, from the forefront of the houſe, from betweene the altar and the houſe of the Lord, and put it on the North ſide of the altar.15And king Ahaz commanded Uriiah the Prieſt, ſaying, Upon the great altar, burne the morning burnt offering, and the euening meate offering, and the Kings burnt ſacrifice, and his meate offering, with the burnt offering of all the people of the land, and their meate offering, and their drinke offerings, and ſprinkle vpon it all the blood of the burnt offering, and all the blood of the ſacrifice: and the braſen altar ſhall be for me to enquire by.16Thus did Uriiah the Prieſt, according to all that king Ahaz commaunded.17And king Ahaz cut off the borders of the baſes, and remooued the lauer from off them, and tooke downe the ſea from off the braſen oxen that were vnder it, and put it vpon a pauement of ſtones:18And the couert for the Sabbath that they had built in the houſe, and the kings entry without, turned hee from the houſe of the Lord, for the king of Aſſyria.19Now the reſt of the actes of Ahaz, which he did, are they not written in the booke of the Chronicles of the kings of Iudah?20And Ahaz ſlept with his fathers, and was buried with his fathers in the city of Dauid, and Hezekiah his ſonne reigned in his ſtead.

CHAPTER 171In the twelfth yeere of Ahaz, king of Iudah, began Hoſhea the ſonne of Elah to reigne in Samaria, ouer Iſrael nine yeeres.2And hee did that which was euill in the ſight of the Lord, but not as the kings of Iſrael that were before him.3Againſt him came vp Shalmaneſer king of Aſſyria, and Hoſhea became his ſeruant, and gaue him preſents.4An the king of Aſſyria found conſpiracie in Hoſhea: for hee had ſent meſſengers to So king of Egypt, and brought no preſent to the king of Aſſyria, as he had done yeere by yeere: therefore the king of Aſſyria ſhut him vp, and bound him in priſon.5Then the king of Aſſyria came vp thorowout all the land, and went vp to Samaria, and beſieged it three yeres.6In the ninth yeere of Hoſhea, the king of Aſſyria tooke Samaria, and caried Iſrael away into Aſſyria, and placed them in Halah, and in Habor by the riuer of Gozan, and in the cities of the Medes.7For ſo it was, that the children of Iſrael had ſinned againſt the Lord their God, which had brought them vp out of the land of Egypt, from vnder the hand of Pharaoh king of Egypt, and had feared other gods,8And walked in the ſtatutes of the heathen, (whom the Lord caſt out from before the children of Iſrael) and of the kings of Iſrael, which they had made.9And the children of Iſrael did ſecretly thoſe things that were not right, againſt the Lord their God: and they built them high places in all their cities, from the tower of the watchmen, to the fenced city.10And they ſet them vp images, and groues in euery high hill, and vnder euery greene tree.11And there they burnt incenſe in all the high places, as did the heathen whom the Lord caried away before them, and wrought wicked things to prouoke the Lord to anger.12For they ſerued idoles, whereof the Lord had ſaid vnto them, Yee ſhall not doe this thing.13Yet the Lord teſtified againſt Iſrael, and againſt Iudah, by all the Prophets, and by all the Seers, ſaying, Turne ye from your euill wayes, and keepe my commandements, and my ſtatutes, according to all the law which I

commanded your fathers, and which I ſent to you by my ſeruants the
Prophets.14Notwithſtanding, they would not heare, but hardened their
neckes, like to the necke of their fathers, that did not beleeue in the Lord
their God.15And they reiected his Statutes, and his Couenant that hee
made with their fathers, and his Teſtimonies which he teſtified againſt
them, and they followed vanitie, and became vaine, and went after the
heathen that were round about them, concerning whom the Lord had
charged them, that they ſhould not doe like them.16And they left all the
Commandements of the Lord their God, and made them molten
images, euen two calues, and made a groue, and worſhipped all the hoſte
of heauen, and ſerued Baal.17And they cauſed their ſonnes and their
daughters to paſſe through the fire, and vſed diuination, and
inchantments, and ſold themſelues to doe euill in the ſight of the Lord,
to prouoke him to anger.18Therefore the Lord was very angry with
Iſrael, and remoued them out of his ſight, there was none left, but the
tribe of Iudah onely.19Alſo Iudah kept not the Commandements of the
Lord their God, but walked in the Statutes of Iſrael which they
made.20And the Lord reiected all the ſeed of Iſrael, and afflicted them,
and deliuered them into the hand of ſpoilers, vntill he had caſt them out
of his ſight.21For he rent Iſrael from the houſe of Dauid, and they made
Ieroboam the ſonne of Nebat king, and Ieroboam draue Iſrael from
following the Lord, and made them ſinne a great ſinne.22For the children
of Iſrael walked in al the ſinnes of Ieroboam which he did, they departed
not from them:23Untill the Lord remoued Iſrael out of his ſight, as hee
had ſaid by all his ſeruants the Prophets: ſo was Iſrael caried away out
of their owne land to Aſſyria, vnto this day.24And the King of Aſſyria
brought men from Babylon, and from Cuthah, and from Aua, and from
Hamath, and from Sepharuaim, and placed them in the cities of Samaria,
in ſtead of the children of Iſrael; and they poſſeſſed Samaria, and dwelt
in the cities thereof.25And ſo it was at the beginning of their dwelling
there, that they feared not the Lord; therefore the Lord ſent Lions
among them, which ſlew ſome of them.26Wherefore they ſpake to the
king of Aſſyria, ſaying, The nations which thou haſt remoued, and
placed in the cities of Samaria, know not the maner of the God of the
land: therfore he hath ſent Lions among them, and beholde, they ſlay
them, becauſe they know not the maner of the God of the land.27Then
the king of Aſſyria commanded, ſaying, Carie thither one of the prieſts
whom ye brought from thence, and let them goe and dwell there, and
let him teach them the maner of the God of the land.28Then one of the
prieſts whom they had caried away from Samaria, came and dwelt in
Bethel, and taught them howe they ſhould feare the Lord.29Howbeit,
euery nation made gods of their owne, and put them in the houſes of
the high places which the Samaritanes had made, euery nation in their
cities wherein they dwelt:30And the men of Babylon made Succoth-
Benoth, and the men of Cuth made Nergal, and the men of Hamath
made Aſhima:31And the Auites made Nibhaz and Tartak; and the
Sepharuites burnt their children in fire to Adrammelech, and
Anammelech, the gods of Sepharuaim.32So they feared the Lord, and
made vnto themſelues of the loweſt of them prieſts of the high places,
which ſacrificed for them in the houſes of the high places.33They feared
the Lord, and ſerued their owne gods, after the maner of the nations
whom they caried away from thence.34Unto this day they doe after the
former maners: they feare not the Lord, neither doe they after their
Statutes, or after their Ordinances, or after the Law and
Commaundement which the Lord commaunded the children of Iacob,
whom hee named Iſrael,35With whom the Lord had made a Couenant,
and charged them, ſaying, Yee ſhall not feare other gods, nor bow your
ſelues to them, nor ſerue them, nor ſacrifice to them:36But the Lord,
who brought you vp out of the land of Egypt, with great power, and a
ſtretched out arme, him ſhall ye feare, and him ſhall ye worſhip, and to
him ſhall ye doe ſacrifice.37And the Statutes, and the Ordinances, and
the Law, and the Commandement which he wrote for you, ye ſhall
obſerue to doe for euermore, and ye ſhall not feare other gods:38And
the Couenant that I haue made with you, ye ſhall no forget, neither ſhall
ye feare other gods.39But the Lord your God yee ſhall feare, and he ſhall
deliuer you out of the hand of all your enemies.40Howbeit, they did not
hearken, but they did after their former maner.41So theſe nations feared
the Lord, and ſerued their grauen images, both their children, and their
childrens children: as did their fathers, ſo doe they vnto this day.

CHAPTER 181Now it came to paſſe in the third yere of Hoſhea ſonne
of Elah king of Iſrael, that Hezekiah the ſonne of Ahaz king of Iudah,
began to reigne.2Twentie and fiue yeeres old was he when hee began to
reigne, and hee reigned twentie and nine yeeres in Ieruſalem: His
mothers name alſo was Abi, the daughter of Zachariah.3And he did that
which was right in the ſight of the Lord, according to all that Dauid his
father did.4He remooued the high places, and brake the images, and cut
downe the groues, and brake in pieces the braſen ſerpent that Moſes had
made: for vnto thoſe dayes the children of Iſrael did burne incenſe to it:
and he called it Nehuſhtan.5He truſted in the Lord God of Iſrael, ſo that
after him was none like him among all the kings of Iudah, nor any that
were before him.6For he claue to the Lord, and departed not from
following him, but kept his commandements, which the Lord
commanded Moſes.7And the Lord was with him, and hee proſpered
whitherſoeuer hee went forth: and he rebelled againſt the king of
Aſſyria, and ſerued him not.8He ſmote the Philiſtines euen vnto Gaza,
and the borders thereof, from the towre of the watchmen to the fenced
cities.9And it came to paſſe in the fourth yeere of king Hezekiah, (which
was the ſeuenth yeere of Hoſhea, ſonne of Elah king of Iſrael) that
Shalmaneſer king of Aſſyria came vp againſt Samaria, and beſieged
it.10And at the end of three yeeres they tooke it: euen in the ſixt yeere of
Hezekiah (that is the ninth yeere of Hoſhea king of Iſrael) Samaria was
taken.11And the king of Aſſyria did carie away Iſrael vnto Aſſyria, and
put them in Halah and in Habor by the riuer of Gozan, & in the cities
of the Medes:12Becauſe they obeyed not the voice of the Lord their God,
but tranſgreſſed his Couenant, and all that Moſes the ſeruant of the Lord
commanded, and would not heare them, nor doe them.13Now in the
fourteenth yeere of king Hezekiah, did Sennacherib king of Aſſyria
come vp againſt all the fenced cities of Iudah, and tooke them.14And
Hezekiah king of Iudah ſent to the king of Aſſyria to Lachiſh, ſaying, I
haue offended, returne from me: that which thou putteſt on me, wil I
beare. And the king of Aſſyria appointed vnto Hezekiah king of Iudah,
three hundred talents of ſiluer, and thirtie talents of gold.15And
Hezekiah gaue him all the ſiluer that was found in the houſe of the Lord,
and in the treaſures of the kings houſe.16At that time did Hezekiah cut
off the gold from the doores of the temple of the Lord, and from the
pillars which Hezekiah king of Iudah had ouerlaid, and gaue it to the
king of Aſſyria.17And the king of Aſſyria ſent Tartan and Rabſaris, and
Rabſhakeh, from Lachiſh to king Hezekiah, with a great hoſte againſt
Ieruſalem: and they went vp, and came to Ieruſalem: and when they were
come vp, they came and ſtood by the conduit of the vpper poole, which
is in the high way of the fullers field.18And when they had called to the
king there came out to them Eliakim the ſonne of Helkiah, which was
ouer the houſhold, and Shebna the Scribe, and Ioah the ſonne of Aſaph
the Recorder.19And Rabſhakeh ſaid vnto them, Speake yee now to
Hezekiah, Thus ſaith the great king, the king of Aſſyria, What
confidence is this wherein thou truſteſt?20Thou ſayeſt, (but they are but
vaine wordſ) I haue counſell and ſtrength for the warre: now on whom
doeſt thou truſt, that thou rebelleſt againſt me?21Now behold, thou
truſteſt vpon the ſtaffe of this bruiſed reed, euen vpon Egypt, on which
if a man leane, it will goe into his hand, and pierce it: ſo is Pharaoh king
of Egypt vnto all that truſt on him.22But if ye ſay vnto me, We truſt in
the Lord our God: is not that hee whoſe high places, and whoſe altars
Hezekiah hath taken away, and hath ſaid to Iudah and Ieruſalem, Ye
ſhall worſhip before this altar in Ieruſalem?23Now therefore, I pray thee,
giue pledges to my lord the king of Aſſyria, and I will deliuer thee two
thouſand horſes, if thou be able on thy part to ſet riders vpon
them.24How then wilt thou turne away the face of one captaine of the
leaſt of my maſters ſeruants, and put thy truſt on Egypt for charets and
for horſemen?25Am I now come vp without the Lord againſt this place,
to deſtroy it? The Lord ſayd to me, Goe vp againſt this land, and deſtroy
it.26Then ſaid Eliakim the ſonne of Hilkiah, and Shebna, and Ioah, vnto
Rabſhakeh, Speake, I pray thee, to thy ſeruants in the Syrian language,
(for wee vnderſtand it) and talke not with vs in the Iewes language, in
the eares of the people that are on the wall.27But Rabſhakeh ſayd vnto
them, Hath my maſter ſent me to thy maſter, and to thee, to ſpeake theſe
wordes? hath he not ſent me to the men which ſit on the wall, that they
may eate their owne doung, and drinke their owne piſſe with
you?28Then Rabſhakeh ſtood and cried with a loude voice in the Iewes
language, and ſpake, ſaying, Heare the word of the great king, the king

of Aſſyria.29Thus ſayth the king, Let not Hezekiah deceiue you, for he
ſhall not be able to deliuer you out of his hand:30Neither let Hezekiah
make you truſt in the Lord, ſaying, The Lord will ſurely deliuer vs, and
this city ſhall not bee deliuered into the hand of the king of
Aſſyria.31Hearken not to Hezekiah: for thus ſayth the king of Aſſyria,
Make an agreement with me by a preſent, and come out to me, and then
eate yee euery man of his owne vine, and euery one of his figge tree, and
drinke yee euery one the waters of his ciſterne:32Untill I come and take
you away to a land like your owne land, a land of corne and wine, a land
of bread and vineyards, a land of oile Oliue, and of honie, that yee may
liue, and not die: and hearken not vnto Hezekiah, when hee perſwadeth
you, ſaying, The Lord will deliuer vs.33Hath any of the gods of the
nations deliuered at all his land out of the hand of the king of
Aſſyria?34Where are the gods of Hamath, and of Arpad? where are the
gods of Sepharuaim, Hena, and Iuah? haue they deliuered Samaria out
of mine hand?35Who are they among all the gods of the countreys, that
haue deliuered their countrey out of mine hand, that the Lord ſhould
deliuer Ieruſalem out of mine hand?36But the people helde their peace,
and anſwered him not a word: for the kings commaundement was,
ſaying, Anſwere him not.37Then came Eliakim the ſonne of Hilkiah,
which was ouer the houſhold, and Shebna the Scribe, and Ioah the
ſonne of Aſaph the Recorder, to Hezekiah with their clothes rent, and
tolde him the words of Rabſhakeh.
CHAPTER 19 1And it came to paſſe when King Hezekiah heard it, that
hee rent his clothes, and couered himſelfe with ſackecloth, and went into
the houſe of the Lord.2And hee ſent Eliakim, which was ouer the
houſhold, and Shebna the Scribe, and the Elders of the Prieſts, couered
with ſackcloth, to Eſai the Prophet the ſonne of Amoz.3And they ſayd
vnto him, Thus ſayth Hezekiah, This day is a day of trouble, and of
rebuke, and blaſphemie: for the children are come to the birth, and there
is not ſtrength to bring foorth.4It may be, the Lord thy God will heare
all the words of Rabſhakeh whome the king of Aſſyria his maſter hath
ſent to reproch the liuing God, and will reprooue the wordes which the
Lord thy God hath heard: wherefore lift vp thy prayer for the remnant
that are left.5So the ſeruants of king Hezekiah came to Iſaiah.6And
Iſaiah ſaid vnto them, Thus ſhal ye ſay to your maſter, Thus ſaith the
Lord, Be not afraid of the wordes which thou haſt heard, with which
the ſeruants of the king of Aſſyria haue blaſphemed me.7Behold, I will
ſend a blaſt vpon him, and he ſhall heare a rumour, and ſhall returne to
his owne land, and I will cauſe him to fall by the ſword in his owne
land.8So Rabſhakeh returned, and found the king of Aſſyria warring
againſt Libnah: for hee had heard that he was departed from
Lachiſh.9And when he heard ſay of Tirhakah king of Ethiopia, Behold,
hee is come out to fight againſt thee: hee ſent meſſengers againe vnto
Hezekiah, ſaying,10Thus ſhall ye ſpeake to Hezekiah king of Iudah,
ſaying, Let not thy God in whome thou truſteſt, deceiue thee, ſaying,
Ieruſalem ſhall not be deliuered into the hande of the king of
Aſſyria.11Behold, thou haſt heard what the kings of Aſſyria haue done
to all lands, by deſtroying them vtterly: and ſhalt thou be
deliuered?12Haue the gods of the nations deliuered them which my
fathers haue deſtroyed? As Gozan, and Haran, and Rezeph, and the
children of Eden which were in Thelaſar?13Where is the king of Hamath,
and the king of Arpad, and the king of the citie of Sepharuaim, of Hena,
and Iuah?14And Hezekiah receiued the letter of the hand of the
meſſengers, and read it: and Hezekiah went vp into the houſe of the
Lord, and ſpread it before the Lord.15And Hezekiah prayed before the
Lord, and ſaid, O Lord God of Iſrael, which dwelleſt between the
Cherubims, thou art the God, euen thou alone, of all the kingdomes of
the earth, thou haſt made heauen and earth.16Lord, bow downe thine
eare, and heare: open, Lord, thine eyes; and ſee: and heare the words of
Sennacherib which hath ſent him to reproch the liuing God.17Of a
trueth, Lord, the kings of Aſſyria haue deſtroyed the nations and their
lands,18And haue caſt their gods into the fire: for they were no gods, but
the work of mens hands, wood and ſtone: therfore they haue deſtroyed
them.19Now therefore, O Lord our God, I beſeech thee, ſaue thou vs
out of his hand, that all the kingdoms of the earth may know, that thou
art the Lord God, euen thou onely.20Then Iſaiah the ſonne of Amoz
ſent to Hezekiah, ſaying, Thus ſaith the Lord God of Iſrael, That which
thou haſt prayed to mee againſt Sennacherib king of Aſſyria, I haue
heard.21This is the word that the Lord hath ſpoken concerning him, The
Uirgin, the daughter of Zion hath deſpiſed thee, and laughed thee to
ſcorne, the daughter of Ieruſalem hath ſhaken her head at thee.22Whome
haſt thou reproched and blaſphemed? and againſt whome haſt thou
exalted thy voyce, and lift vp thine eyes on high? euen againſt the Holy
One of Iſrael.23By thy meſſengers thou haſt reproched the Lord, and
haſt ſaid, With the multitude of my charets, I am come vp to the height
of the mountaines, to the ſides of Lebanon, and will cut downe the tall
cedar trees thereof, and the choice firre trees thereof: and I will enter
into the lodgings of his borders, and into the forreſt of his Carmel.24I
haue digged & drunke ſtrange waters, and with the ſole of my feete haue
I dried vp all the riuers of beſieged places.25Haſt thou not heard long
agoe, how I haue done it, and of ancient times that I haue formed it?
now haue I brought it to paſſe, that thou ſhouldeſt be to lay waſte fenced
cities into ruinous heapes.26Therefore their Inhabitants were of ſmall
power, they were diſmayed and confounded, they were as the graſſe of
the field, and as the greene herbe, as the graſſe on the houſe tops, and
as corne blaſted before it be growen vp.27But I know thy abode, and thy
going out, and thy coming in, and thy rage againſt me.28Becauſe thy rage
againſt me, and thy tumult is come vp into mine eares, therefore I will
put my hooke in thy noſe, and my bridle in thy lips, and I will turne thee
backe by the way by which thou cameſt.29And this ſhalbe a ſigne vnto
thee, Yee ſhall eate this yeere ſuch things as grow of themſelues, and in
the ſecond yeere that which ſpringeth of the ſame, and in the third yeere
ſow ye and reape, and plant Uineyards, and eate the fruits thereof.30And
the remnant that is eſcaped of the houſe of Iudah, ſhall yet againe take
root downeward, and beare fruit vpward.31For out of Ieruſalem ſhall goe
forth a remnant, and they that eſcape out of mount Zion: the zeale of
the Lord of hoſtes ſhall doe this.32Therefore thus ſaith the Lord
concerning the king of Aſſyria, He ſhall not come into this city, nor
ſhoot an arrow there, nor come before it with ſhield, nor caſt a banke
againſt it:33By the way that hee came, by the ſame ſhal he returne, and
ſhal not come into this city, ſaith the Lord.34For I will defend this citie,
to ſaue it, for mine owne ſake, and for my ſeruant Dauids ſake.35And it
came to paſſe that night, that the Angel of the Lord went out, and ſmote
in the campe of the Aſſyrians, an hundred foure ſcore and fiue thouſand:
and when they aroſe earely in the morning, behold, they were all dead
corpſes.36So Sennacherib king of Aſſyria departed, and went and
returned, and dwelt at Nineueh.37And it came to paſſe as hee was
worſhipping in the houſe of Niſroch his god, that Adramelech, and
Sharezer his ſonnes, ſmote him with the ſword: and they eſcaped into
the land of Armenia, and Eſarhaddon his ſonne reigned in his ſtead.
CHAPTER 20 1In thoſe dayes was Hezekiah ſicke vnto death: and the
Prophet Iſaiah the ſonne of Amos came to him, and ſaide vnto him,
Thus ſaith the Lord, Set thine houſe in order: for thou ſhalt die, and not
liue.2Then hee turned his face to the wall, and prayed vnto the Lord,
ſaying;3I beſeech thee, O Lord, remember now how I haue walked
before thee in trueth, and with a perfect heart, and haue done that which
is good in thy ſight: and Hezekiah wept ſore.4And it came to paſſe afore
Iſaiah was gone out into the middle court, that the word of the Lord
came to him, ſaying:5Turne againe, and tell Hezekiah the captaine of my
people, Thus ſaith the Lord, the God of Dauid thy father, I haue heard
thy prayer, I haue ſeene thy teares: behold, I will heale thee; on the third
day thou ſhalt goe vp vnto the houſe of the Lord.6And I will adde vnto
thy dayes fifteene yeeres, and I will deliuer thee, and this city, out of the
hand of the king of Aſſyria, and I will defend this citie for mine owne
ſake, and for my ſeruant Dauids ſake.7And Iſaiah ſaid, Take a lumpe of
figs. And they tooke and layd it on the boile, and he recouered.8And
Hezekiah ſaid vnto Iſaiah, What ſhall bee the ſigne that the Lord wil
heale me, and that I ſhall goe vp into the houſe of the Lord the third
day?9And Iſaiah ſaid, This ſigne ſhalt thou haue of the Lord, that the
Lord will doe the thing that hee hath ſpoken: ſhall the ſhadow goe
forward ten degrees, or goe backe tenne degrees?10And Hezekiah
anſwered, It is a light thing for the ſhadow to go downe tenne degrees:
nay, but let the ſhadow returne backward tenne degrees.11And Iſaiah the
Prophet cryed vnto the Lord, and he brought the ſhadow tenne degrees
backeward, by which it had gone downe in the diall of Ahaz.12At that
time Berodach-Baladan the ſonne of Baladan King of Babylon, ſent
letters and a preſent vnto Hezekiah: for he had heard that Hezekiah had
beene ſicke.13And Hezekiah hearkened vnto them, and ſhewed them the
houſe of his precious things, the ſiluer, and the golde, and the ſpices,

and the precious oyntment, and all the houſe of his armour, and all that was found in his treaſures: there was nothing in his houſe, nor in all his dominion, that Hezekiah ſhewed them not.14Then came Iſaiah the Prophet vnto King Hezekiah, and ſayde vnto him, What ſayd theſe men? and from whence came they vnto thee? And Hezekiah ſayde, They are come from a farre countrey, euen from Babylon.15And he ſaid, What haue they ſeene in thine houſe? And Hezekiah anſwered, All the things that are in mine houſe haue they ſeene: there is nothing among my treaſures, that I haue not ſhewed them.16And Iſaiah ſaid vnto Hezekiah, Heare the word of the Lord.17Behold, the dayes come, that all that is in thine houſe, and that which thy fathers haue layde vp in ſtore vnto this day, ſhall be caried vnto Babylon: nothing ſhall be left, ſayth the Lord.18And of thy ſonnes that ſhall iſſue from thee, which thou ſhalt beget, ſhall they take away, and they ſhall bee Eunuches in the palace of the king of Babylon.19Then ſaid Hezekiah vnto Iſaiah, Good is the word of the Lord which thou haſt ſpoken. And he ſaid, Is it not good, if peace and trueth be in my dayes?20And the reſt of the actes of Hezekiah, and all his might, and how hee made a poole and a conduit, & brought water into the city, are they not written in the booke of the Chronicles of the Kings of Iudah?21And Hezekiah ſlept with his fathers, and Manaſſeh his ſonne reigned in his ſtead.

CHAPTER 211Manaſſeh was twelue yeres olde when hee beganne to reigne, and reigned fiftie and fiue yeeres in Ieruſalem: and his mothers name was Hephzibah.2And hee did that which was euill in the ſight of the Lord, after the abominations of the heathen, whom the Lord caſt out before the children of Iſrael.3For he built vp againe the high places, which Hezekiah his father had deſtroyed, and hee reared vp altars for Baal, and made a groue, as did Ahab king of Iſrael, and worſhipped all the hoſte of heauen, and ſerued them.4And he built altars in the houſe of the Lord, of which the Lord ſayd, In Ieruſalem will I put my Name.5And he built altars for all the hoſt of heauen, in the two courts of the houſe of the Lord.6And he made his ſonne paſſe thorow the fire, and obſerued times, and vſed enchantments, and dealt with familiar ſpirits, and wizards: he wrought much wickedneſſe in the ſight of the Lord, to prouoke him to anger.7And he ſet a grauen image of the groue that he had made, in the houſe, of which the Lord ſaid to Dauid, and to Solomon his ſonne, In this houſe and in Ieruſalem, which I haue choſen out of all tribes of Iſrael, wil I put my Name for euer:8Neither will I make the feete of Iſrael mooue any more out of the land, which I gaue their fathers: onely if they will obſerue to doe according to all that I haue commanded them, and according to all the Law, that my ſeruant Moſes commanded them.9But they hearkened not: and Manaſſeh ſeduced them to doe more euill then did the nations, whome the Lord deſtroyed before the children of Iſrael.10And the Lord ſpake by his ſeruants the Prophets, ſaying,11Becauſe Manaſſeh king of Iudah hath done theſe abominations, and hath done wickedly aboue all that the Amorites did, which were before him, and hath made Iudah alſo to ſinne with his idoles:12Therefore thus ſaith the Lord God of Iſrael, Behold, I am bringing ſuch euill vpon Ieruſalem and Iudah, that whoſoeuer heareth of it, both his eares ſhall tingle.13And I will ſtretch ouer Ieruſalem the line of Samaria, and the plummet of the houſe of Ahab: and I will wipe Ieruſalem as a man wipeth a diſh, wiping it and turning it vpſide downe.14And I will forſake the remnant of mine inheritance, and deliuer them into the hand of their enemies, and they ſhall become a pray and a ſpoile to all their enemies,15Becauſe they haue done that which was euill in my ſight, and haue prouoked me to anger ſince the day their fathers came forth out of Egypt, euen vnto this day.16Moreouer, Manaſſeh ſhed innocent blood very much, till he had filled Ieruſalem from one end to another, beſide his ſinne wherwith he made Iudah to ſinne, in doing that which was euill in the ſight of the Lord.17Now the reſt of the actes of Manaſſeh, and all that he did, and his ſinne that he ſinned, are they not written in the booke of the Chronicles of the kings of Iudah?18And Manaſſeh ſlept with his fathers, and was buried in the garden of his owne houſe, in the garden of Uzza: and Amon his ſonne reigned in his ſtead.19Amon was twentie and two yeres old when he began to reigne, and he reigned two yeeres in Ieruſalem: and his mothers name was Meſhullemeth, the daughter of Haruz of Iotbah.20And he did that which was euill in the ſight of the Lord, as his father Manaſſeh did.21And he walked in all the wayes that his father walked in, and ſerued the idoles that his father ſerued, and worſhipped them:22And he forſooke the Lord God of his fathers, and walked not in the way of the Lord.23And the ſeruants of Amon conſpired againſt him, and ſlew the king in his owne houſe.24And the people of the land ſlew al them that had conſpired againſt king Amon, and the people of the land made Ioſiah his ſonne king in his ſtead.25Now the reſt of the acts of Amon, which he did, are they not written in the booke of the chronicles of the kings of Iudah?26And he was buried in his ſepulchre, in the garden of Uzza, and Ioſiah his ſonne reigned in his ſtead.

CHAPTER 221Ioſiah was eight yeeres old when hee beganne to reigne, and hee reigned thirtie and one yeeres in Ieruſalem: and his mothers name was Iedidah, the daughter of Adaiah of Boſcath.2And he did that which was right in the ſight of the Lord, and walked in all the wayes of Dauid his father, and turned not aſide to the right hand, or to the left.3And it came to paſſe in the eighteenth yeere of king Ioſiah, that the king ſent Shaphan the ſonne of Azaliah, the ſonne of Meſhullam the Scribe to the houſe of the Lord, ſaying,4Goe vp to Hilkiah the high prieſt, that he may ſumme the ſiluer which is brought into the houſe of the Lord, which the keepers of the doore haue gathered of the people.5And let them deliuer it into the hand of the doers of the worke, that haue the ouerſight of the houſe of the Lord: and let them giue it to the doers of the worke, which is in the houſe of the Lord, to repaire the breaches of the houſe,6Unto carpenters, and builders, and maſons, and to buy timber and hewen ſtone, to repaire the houſe.7Howbeit, there was no reckoning made with them, of the money that was deliuered into their hand, becauſe they dealt faithfully.8And Hilkiah the high Prieſt ſaid vnto Shaphan the Scribe, I haue found the booke of the Law in the houſe of the Lord. And Hilkiah gaue the booke to Shaphan, and he read it.9And Shaphan the Scribe came to the king, and brought the king word againe, and ſaid, Thy ſeruants haue gathered the money that was found in the houſe, and haue deliuered it into the hand of them that doe the worke, that haue the ouerſight of the houſe of the Lord.10And Shaphan the Scribe ſhewed the king, ſaying, Hilkiah the Prieſt hath deliuered mee a booke: and Shaphan read it before the king.11And it came to paſſe when the king had heard the words of the booke of the Law, that he rent his clothes.12And the king commanded Hilkiah the Prieſt, and Ahikam the ſonne of Shaphan, and Achbor the ſonne of Michaiah, and Shaphan the Scribe, and Aſahiah a ſeruant of the Kings, ſaying,13Goe yee, enquire of the Lord for me, and for the people, and for all Iudah, concerning the wordes of this booke that is found: for great is the wrath of the Lord that is kindled againſt vs, becauſe our fathers haue not hearkened vnto the woordes of this booke, to doe according vnto all that which is written concerning vs.14So Hilkiah the Prieſt, and Ahikam, and Achbor, and Shaphan, and Aſahiah, went vnto Huldah the Prophetefse, the wife of Shallum the ſonne of Tikuah, the ſonne of Harhas, keeper of the wardrobe: now ſhe dwelt in Ieruſalem in the colledge: And they communed with her.15And ſhe ſaid vnto them, Thus ſaith the Lord God of Iſrael, Tell the man that ſent you to me;16Thus ſaith the Lord, Behold, I will bring euill vpon this place, and vpon the inhabitants thereof, euen all the words of the booke which the king of Iudah hath read.17Becauſe they haue forſaken me, and haue burnt incenſe vnto other gods, that they might prouoke mee to anger with all the woorkes of their handes: therefore my wrath ſhall bee kindled againſt this place, and ſhall not be quenched.18But to the king of Iudah which ſent you to enquire of the Lord, Thus ſhall yee ſay to him, Thus ſaith the Lord God of Iſrael, as touching the woordes which thou haſt heard:19Becauſe thine heart was tender, and thou haſt humbled thy ſelfe before the Lord, when thou heardeſt what I ſpake againſt this place, and againſt the inhabitants thereof, that they ſhould become a deſolation and a curſe, and haſt rent thy cloathes, and wept before me; I alſo haue heard thee, ſaith the Lord.20Behold therefore, I will gather thee vnto thy fathers, and thou ſhalt be gathered into thy graue in peace, and thine eyes ſhal not ſee all the euil which I will bring vpon this place. And they brought the king word againe.

CHAPTER 231And the king ſent, and they gathered vnto him all the Elders of Iudah, and of Ieruſalem.2And the king went vp into the houſe of the Lord, and all the men of Iudah, and all the inhabitants of Ieruſalem with him, and the Prieſtes, and the Prophets, and all the people both ſmall and great: and he read in their eares all the wordes of the booke of the Couenant which was found in the houſe of the Lord.3And the King ſtood by a pillar, and made a Couenant before the

Lord, to walke after the Lord, and to keepe his Commaundements, and his Teſtimonies, & his Statutes, with all their heart, and all their ſoule, to performe the words of this Couenant, that were written in this booke: and all the people ſtood to the Couenant.4And the king commanded Hilkiah the high Prieſt, and the prieſts of the ſecond order, and the keepers of the doore to bring forth out of the Temple of the Lord all the veſſels that were made for Baal, and for the groue, and for all the hoſte of heauen: and he burnt them without Ieruſalem in the fields of Kidron, and caried the aſhes of them vnto Bethel.5And hee put downe the idolatrous prieſts whome the kings of Iudah had ordeined to burne incenſe in the high places, in the cities of Iudah and in the places round about Ieruſalem: them alſo that burnt incenſe vnto Baal, to the Sunne, and to the Moone, and to the Planets, and to all the hoſte of heauen.6And he brought out the groue from the houſe of the Lord, without Ieruſalem, vnto the brooke Kidron, and burnt it at the brooke Kidron, and ſtampt it ſmall to powder, and caſt the powder thereof vpon the graues of the children of the people.7And he brake downe the houſes of the Sodomites that were by the houſe of the Lord, where the women woue hangings for the groue.8And he brought all the prieſts out of the cities of Iudah, and defiled the high places where the prieſts had burnt incenſe, from Geba to Beerſheba, and brake downe the hie places of the gates that were in the entring in of the gate of Ioſhua the gouernour of the citie, which were on a mans left hand at the gate of the citie.9Neuertheleſſe, the prieſts of the high places came not vp to the Altar of the Lord in Ieruſalem, but they did eate of the vnleauened bread among their brethren.10And he defiled Topheth which is in the valley of the children of Hinnom, that no man might make his ſonne or his daughter to paſſe through the fire to Molech.11And he tooke away the horſes that the kings of Iudah had giuen to the Sunne, at the entring in of the houſe of the Lord, by the chamber of Nathanmelech the chamberlaine, which was in the ſuburbs, and burnt the charets of the Sunne with fire,12And the altars that were on the top of the vpper chamber of Ahaz, which the kings of Iudah had made, and the altars which Manaſſeh had made in the two courts of the houſe of the Lord, did the king beat downe, and brake them downe from thence, and caſt the duſt of them into the brooke Kidron.13And the high places that were before Ieruſalem, which were on the right hand of the mount of corruption, which Solomon the king of Iſrael had builded for Aſhtoreth, the abomination of the Zidonians, and for Chemoſh the abomination of the Moabites, and for Milchom the abomination of the children of Ammon, did the king defile.14And he brake in pieces the images, and cut downe the groues, and filled their places with the bones of men.15Moreouer the altar that was at Bethel, and the high place which Ieroboam the ſonne of Nebat, who made Iſrael to ſinne, had made, both that altar, and the high place he brake downe, and burnt the high place, and ſtampt it ſmall to powder, and burnt the groue.16And as Ioſiah turned himſelfe, he ſpied the ſepulchres that were there in the mount, and ſent, & tooke the bones out of the ſepulchres, and burnt them vpon the altar, and polluted it, according to the word of the Lord which the man of God proclaimed, who proclaimed theſe words.17Then hee ſaid, What title is that that I ſee? and the men of the city told him, It is the ſepulchre of the man of God, which came from Iudah, and proclaimed theſe things that thou haſt done againſt the altar of Bethel.18And he ſaid, Let him alone: let no man moue his bones: ſo they let his bones alone, with the bones of the Prophet that came out of Samaria.19And all the houſes alſo of the hie places that were in the cities of Samaria, which the kings of Iſrael had made to prouoke the Lord to anger, Ioſiah tooke away, and did to them according to all the actes that hee had done in Bethel.20And he ſlew all the prieſts of the high places that were there, vpon the altars, and burnt mens bones vpon them, and returned to Ieruſalem.21And the King commanded all the people ſaying, Keepe the Paſſeouer vnto the Lord your God, as it is written in this booke of the Couenant.22Surely there was not holden ſuch a Paſſeouer, from the daies of the Iudges that iudged Iſrael, nor in all the dayes of the kings of Iſrael, nor of the kings of Iudah:23But in the eighteenth yeere of king Ioſiah, wherein this Paſſeouer was holden to the Lord in Ieruſalem.24Moreouer the workers with familiar ſpirits, and the wizards, and the images, and the idoles, and all the abominations that were ſpied in the land of Iudah, and in Ieruſalem, did Ioſiah put away, that he might performe the wordes of the lawe, which were written in the booke that Hilkiah the prieſt found in the houſe of the Lord.25And like vnto him was there no king before him, that turned to the Lord with all his heart, and with all his ſoule, and with all his might, according to all the Law of Moſes, neither after him aroſe there any like him.26Notwithſtanding, the Lord turned not from the fierceneſſe of his great wrath, wherwith his anger was kindled againſt Iudah, becauſe of all the prouocations that Manaſſeh had prouoked him withall.27And the Lord ſaid, I will remoue Iudah alſo out of my ſight, as I haue remoued Iſrael, and will caſt off this citie Ieruſalem, which I haue choſen, and the houſe of which I ſayd, My name ſhall be there.28Now the reſt of the actes of Ioſiah, and all that hee did, are they not written in the booke of the chronicles of the kings of Iudah?29In his dayes, Pharaoh Nechoh king of Egypt, went vp againſt the king of Aſſyria to the riuer Euphrates: and king Ioſiah went againſt him, and hee ſlew him at Megiddo, when he had ſeene him.30And his ſeruants caried him in a charet dead from Megiddo, & brought him to Ieruſalem, and buried him in his owne ſepulchre: and the people of the land tooke Iehoahaz the ſonne of Ioſiah, and anointed him, and made him king in his fathers ſtead.31Iehoahaz was twenty and three yeeres olde when he beganne to reigne, and hee reigned three moneths in Ieruſalem: and his mothers name was Hamital, the daughter of Ieremiah, of Libnah.32And hee did that which was euill in the ſight of the Lord, according to all that his fathers had done.33And Pharaoh Nechoh put him in bandes at Riblah in the land of Hamath, that he might not reigne in Ieruſalem, and put the land to a tribute of an hundred talents of ſiluer, and a talent of golde.34And Pharaoh Nechoh made Eliakim the ſonne of Ioſiah king, in the roume of Ioſiah his father, and turned his name to Iehoiakim, and tooke Iehoahaz away: and hee came to Egypt, and died there.35And Iehoiakim gaue the ſiluer, and the golde to Pharaoh, but he taxed the land to giue the money according to the commandement of Pharaoh: hee exacted the ſiluer and the golde of the people of the land, of euery one according to his taxation, to giue it vnto Pharaoh Nechoh.36Iehoiakim was twentie and fiue yeere olde when he began to reigne, and he reigned eleuen yeeres in Ieruſalem: and his mothers name was Zebudah, the daughter of Pedaiah of Rumah.37And he did that which was euill in the ſight of the Lord, according to all that his fathers had done.

CHAPTER 241In his dayes Nebuchadnezzar king of Babylon came vp, and Iehoiakim became his ſeruant three yeeres: then hee turned and rebelled againſt him.2And the Lord ſent againſt him bands of the Chaldees, and bandes of the Syrians, and bandes of the Moabites, and bands of the children of Ammon, and ſent them againſt Iudah to deſtroy it, according to the word of the Lord, which hee ſpake by his ſeruants the Prophets.3Surely at the commandement of the Lord came this vpon Iudah, to remooue them out of his ſight, for the ſinnes of Manaſſeh, according to all that he did:4And alſo for the innocent blood that hee ſhedde: (for hee filled Ieruſalem with innocent blood) which the Lord would not pardon.5Nowe the reſt of the actes of Iehoiakim, and all that he did, are they not written in the booke of the Chronicles of the Kings of Iudah?6So Iehoiakim ſlept with his fathers: and Iehoiachin his ſonne reigned in his ſtead.7And the king of Egypt came not againe any more out of his land: for the King of Babylon had taken from the riuer of Egypt, vnto the riuer Euphrates, all that pertained to the King of Egypt.8Iehoiachin was eighteene yeres old when he began to reigne, & he reigned in Ieruſalem three moneths: & his mothers name was Nehuſhta the daughter of Elnathan, of Ieruſalem.9And hee did that which was euill in the ſight of the Lord, according to all that his father had done.10At that time the ſeruants of Nebuchadnezzar King of Babylon came vp againſt Ieruſalem, and the citie was beſieged.11And Nebuchadnezzar king of Babylon came againſt the citie, and his ſeruants did beſiege it.12And Iehoiachin the King of Iudah went out to the king of Babylon, hee, and his mother, and his ſeruants, and his princes, and his officers: and the king of Babylon tooke him in the eight yeere of his reigne.13And hee caried out thence all the treaſures of the houſe of the Lord, and the treaſure of the kings houſe, and cut in pieces all the veſſels of gold which Solomon King of Iſrael had made in the Temple of the Lord, as the Lord had ſaid.14And hee caried away all Ieruſalem, and all the princes, & all the mighty men of valour, euen tenne thouſand captiues, and all the craftſmen, and ſmiths: none remained, ſaue the pooreſt ſort of the people of the land.15And he caried away Iehoiachin to Babylon, and the kings mother, and the kings wiues, and his officers, and the mighty of the land, thoſe caried hee into captiuitie, from Ieruſalem to Babylon.16And all the men of might, euen ſeuen thouſand, and crafteſmen, & ſmiths a thouſand, all that were ſtrong and apt for warre, euen them the king of Babylon brought captiue to Babylon.17And the king of Babylon made Mattaniah his fathers brother king in his ſtead, and changed his name to Zedekiah.18Zedekiah was twentie and one yeeres olde when hee began to reigne, and he reigned eleuen yeeres in Ieruſalem: and his mothers name was Hamutal, the daughter of Ieremiah of Libnah.19And hee did that which was euill in the ſight of the Lord, according to all that Iehoiachin had done.20For through the anger of the Lord it came to paſſe in Ieruſalem and Iudah, vntill he had caſt them out from his preſence, that Zedekiah rebelled againſt the king of Babylon.

CHAPTER 251And it came to paſſe in the ninth yeere of his reigne, in the tenth moneth, in the tenth day of the moneth, that Nebuchadnezzar king of Babylon came, hee, and all his hoſte, againſt Ieruſalem, and pitched againſt it, and they built fortes againſt it, round about.2And the citie was beſieged vnto the eleuenth yeere of king Zedekiah.3And on the ninth day of the fourth moneth, the famine preuailed in the city, and there was no bread for the people of the land.4And the citie was broken vp, and all the men of warre fled by night, by the way of the gate, betweene two walles, which is by the kings garden, (now the Caldees were againſt the citie round about) and the King went the way toward the plaine.5And the army of the Caldees purſued after the King, and ouertooke him in the plaines of Iericho: and all his armie were ſcattered from him.6So they tooke the King, and brought him vp to the King of Babylon, to Riblah, and they gaue iudgement vpon him.7And they ſlew the ſonnes of Zedekiah before his eyes, and put out the eyes of Zedekiah, and bound him with fetters of braſſe, and carried him to Babylon.8And in the fifth moneth, on the ſeuenth day of the moneth (which is the nineteenth yeere of King Nebuchadnezzar King of Babylon) came Nebuzaradan captaine of the guard, a ſeruant of the king of Babylon, vnto Ieruſalem:9And hee burnt the houſe of the Lord, and the kings houſe, and all the houſes of Ieruſalem, and euery great mans houſe burnt he with fire.10And all the army of the Caldees that were with the captaine of the guard, brake downe the walles of Ieruſalem round about.11Now the reſt of the people that were left in the citie, and the fugitiues that fell away to the king of Babylon, with the remnant of the multitude, did Nebuzaradan the captaine of the guard cary away.12But the captaine of the guard left of the poore of the land, to be Uine-dreſſers, and huſbandmen.13And the pillars of braſſe that were in the houſe of the Lord, and the baſes, and the braſen ſea that was in the houſe of the Lord, did the Caldees breake in pieces, and caried the braſſe of them to Babylon.14And the pots, and the ſhouels, and the ſnuffers, and the ſpoones, and all the veſſels of braſſe wherewith they miniſtred, tooke they away.15And the fire-pans, and the bowles, & ſuch things as were of golde, in golde, and of ſiluer, in ſiluer, the captaine of the guard tooke away.16The two pillars, one ſea, and the baſes which Solomon had made for the houſe of the Lord, the braſſe of al theſe veſſels was without weight.17The height of the one pillar was eighteene cubits, and the chapiter vpon it was braſſe: and the height of the chapiter three cubites; and the wreathen worke, and pomegranates vpon the chapiter round about, all of braſſe: and like vnto theſe had the ſecond pillar with wreathen worke.18And the captaine of the guard, tooke Seraiah the chiefe Prieſt, and Zephaniah the ſecond Prieſt, and the three keepers of the doore.19And out of the citie hee tooke an Officer, that was ſet ouer the men of warre, and fiue men of them that were in the kings preſence, which were found in the citie, and the principall Scribe of the hoſte, which muſtered the people of the land, and threeſcore men of the people of the land that were found in the citie.20And Nebuzaradan captaine of the guard tooke theſe, and brought them to the king of Babylon, to Riblah.21And the King of Babylon ſmote them, and ſlew them at Riblah in the land of Hamath: ſo Iudah was caried away out of their land.22And as for the people that remained in the land of Iudah, whom Nebuchadnezzar King of Babylon had left, euen ouer them he made Gedaliah the ſonne of Ahikam, the ſonne of Shaphan, ruler.23And when all the captaines of the armies, they, and their men, heard that the King of Babylon had made Gedaliah gouernour, there came to Gedaliah to Miſpah, euen Iſhmael the ſonne of Nethaniah, and Iohanan the ſonne of Careah, and Seraiah the ſonne of Tanhumeth the Netophathite, and Iaazaniah the ſonne of a Maachathite, they, and their men.24And Gedaliah ſware to them and to their men, and ſaid vnto them, Feare not to be the ſeruants of the Caldees: dwell in the land, and ſerue the King of Babylon; and it ſhall bee well with you.25But it came to paſſe in the ſeuenth moneth, that Iſhmael the ſonne of Nethaniah, the ſonne of Eliſhama, of the ſeed royal, came, and ten men with him, and ſmote Gedaliah, that he died, and the Iewes, and the Caldees that were with him at Mizpah.26And all the people both ſmall and great, and the captaines of the armies aroſe, and came to Egypt: for they were afraid of the Caldees.27And it came to paſſe in the ſeuen and thirtieth yeere of the captiuitie of Iehoiachin king of Iudah, in the twelfth moneth, on the ſeuen and twentieth day of the moneth, that Euilmerodach king of Babylon, in the yeere that he began to reigne, did lift vp the head of Iehoiachin king of Iudah out of priſon.28And he ſpake kindly to him, and ſet his throne aboue the throne of the kings that were with him in Babylon,29And changed his priſon garments: and he did eate bread continually before him all the dayes of his life.30And his allowance was a continuall allowance giuen him of the king, a dayly rate for euery day, all the dayes of his life.

1 CHRONICLES

CHAPTER 1 1Adam, Sheth, Enoſh,2Kenan, Mahalaleel, Iered,3Henoch, Methuſhelah, Lamech,4Noah, Shem, Ham, & Iapheth.5The ſonnes of Iapheth: Gomer, and Magog, and Madai, and Iauan, and Tubal, and Meſhech, and Tiras.6And the ſonnes of Gomer: Aſhchenaz, and Riphath, and Togarmah.7And the ſonnes of Iauan: Eliſhah, and Tarſhiſh, Kittim, and Dodanim.8The ſonnes of Ham: Cuſh, and Mizraim, Put, and Canaan.9And the ſonnes of Cuſh: Siba, and Hauilah, and Sabta, and Raamah, and Sabtecha: and the ſonnes of Raamah: Sheba, and Dedan.10And Cuſh begate Nimrod: hee began to be mightie vpon the earth.11And Mizraim begate Ludim, and Anamim, and Lehabim, and Naphtuhim,12And Pathruſim, and Caſluhim (of whome came the Philiſtineſ) and Caphthorim.13And Canaan begate Zidon his firſt borne, and Heth.14The Iebuſite alſo, and the Amorite, and the Girgaſhite,15And the Hiuite, and the Arkite, and the Sinite,16And the Aruadite, and the Zemarite, and the Hamathite.17The ſonnes of Shem: Elam, and Aſshur, and Arphaxad, and Lud, and Aram, and Uz, & Hul, and Gether, and Meſhech.18And Arphaxad begate Shelah, and Shelah begate Eber.19And vnto Eber were borne two ſonnes: the name of the one was Peleg, (becauſe in his dayes the earth was diuided) and his brothers name was Ioktan.20And Ioktan begate Almodad, and Sheleph, and Hazermaueth, and Ierah,21Hadoram alſo, and Uzal, and Diklah,22And Ebal, and Abimael, and Sheba,23And Ophir, and Hauilah, and Iobab: all theſe were the ſonnes of Ioktan.24Shem, Arphaxad, Shelah,25Eber, Peleg, Rehu,26Serug, Nahor, Terah,27Abram, the ſame is Abraham.28The ſonnes of Abraham: Iſaac, and Iſhmael.29Theſe are their generations: The firſt-borne of Iſhmael, Nebaioth, then Kedar, and Adbeel, and Mibſam,30Miſhma, and Dumah, Maſſa, Hadad, and Tema,31Ietur, Naphiſh, and Kedemah. Theſe are the ſonnes of Iſhmael.32Now the ſonnes of Keturah, Abrahams Concubine: ſhe bare Zimran, and Iokſhan, and Medan, and Midian, and Iſhbak, and Shuah. And the ſonnes of Iokſhan, Sheba, and Dedan.33And the ſonnes of Midian: Ephah, and Ephar, and Henoch, and Abida, and Eldaah. All theſe are the ſonnes of Keturah.34And Abraham begate Iſaac. The ſonnes of Iſaac: Eſau, and Iſrael.35The ſonnes of Eſau: Eliphaz, Reuel, and Ieuſh, and Iaalam, and Korah.36The ſonnes of Eliphaz: Teman, and Omar, Zephi, and Gatam, Kenaz, and Timna, and Amalek.37The ſonnes of Reuel: Nahath, Zerah, Shammah, and Mizzah.38And the ſonnes of Seir: Lotan, and Shobal, and Zibeon, and Anah, and Diſhon, and Ezer, and Diſhan.39And the ſonnes of Lotan: Hori, and Homam: and Timna was Lotans ſiſter.40The ſonnes of Shobal: Atian, and Manahath, and Ebal, Shephi, and Onam. And the ſonnes of Zibeon: Aiah, and Anah.41The ſonnes of Anah: Diſhon. And the ſonnes of Diſhon: Amram, and Eſhban, and Ithran, and Cheran.42The ſonnes of Ezer: Bilham, and Zauan, and Iakan. The ſonnes of Diſhon: Uz, and Aran.43Now theſe are the kings that reigned in the land of Edom, before

any king reigned ouer the children of Iſrael. Bela the ſonne of Beor; and
the name of his citie, was Dinhabah.44And when Bela was dead, Iobab
the ſonne of Zerah of Boſrah, reigned in his ſtead.45And when Iobab
was dead, Huſham of the land of the Temanits, reigned in his
ſtead.46And when Huſham was dead, Hadad, the ſonne of Bedad
(which ſmote Midian in the field of Moab) reigned in his ſtead: and the
name of his citie was Auith.47And when Hadad was dead, Samlah of
Maſrekah, reigned in his ſtead.48And when Samlah was dead, Shaul of
Rehoboth by the riuer, reigned in his ſtead.49And when Shaul was dead,
Baal-hanan the ſonne of Achbor, reigned in his ſtead.50And when Baal-
hanan was dead, Hadad reigned in his ſtead: and the name of his citie
was Pai: and his wiues name was Mehetabel the daughter of Matred, the
daughter of Mezahab.51Hadad dyed alſo. And the Dukes of Edom were:
Duke Timnah, Duke Aliah, Duke Ietheth,52Duke Aholibamah, Duke
Elah, Duke Pinon,53Duke Kenaz, Duke Teman, Duke Mibzar,54Duke
Magdiel, Duke Iram. Theſe are the Dukes of Edom.
CHAPTER 21Theſe are the ſonnes of Iſrael: Reuben, Simeon, Leui,
and Iudah, Iſſachar, and Zebulun,2Dan, Ioſeph, and Beniamin,
Naphtali, Gad, and Aſher.3The ſonnes of Iudah: Er, and Onan, and
Shelah. Which three were borne vnto him, of the daughter of Shua the
Canaanites. And Er the firſt-borne of Iudah, was euill in the ſight of the
Lord, and he ſlue him.4And Tamar his daughter-in law bare him Pharez,
and Zerah. All the ſonnes of Iudah were fiue.5The ſonnes of Pharez:
Hezron, and Hamul.6And the ſonnes of Zerah: Zimri, and Ethan, and
Heman, and Calcol, and Dara. Fiue of them in all.7And the ſonnes of
Carmi: Achar, the troubler of Iſrael, who tranſgreſſed in the thing
accurſed.8And the ſonnes of Ethan: Azariah.9The ſonnes alſo of
Hezron, that were borne vnto him: Ierahmeel, and Ram, and
Chelubai.10And Ram begate Aminadab, and Aminadab begat Nahſhon,
prince of the children of Iudah.11And Nahſhon begate Salma, and Salma
begate Boaz.12And Boaz begate Obed, and Obed begate Ieſſe.13And
Ieſſe begate his firſt-borne Eliab, and Abinadab the ſecond, and Shimma
the third,14Nathanael the fourth, Raddai the fifth,15Ozem the ſixth,
Dauid the ſeuenth:16Whoſe ſiſters were Zeruiah, and Abigail. And the
ſonnes of Zeruiah: Abiſhai, and Ioab, and Aſahel, three.17And Abigail
bare Amaſa. And the father of Amaſa, was Iether the Iſhmeelite.18And
Caleb the ſonne of Hezron, begate children of Azubah his wife, and of
Ierioth: her ſonnes are theſe: Ieſher, Shobab, and Ardon.19And when
Azubah was dead, Caleb tooke vnto him Ephrath, which bare him
Hur.20And Hur begate Uri, and Uri begate Bezaleel.21And afterward
Hezron went in to the daughter of Machir, the father of Gilead, whom
hee married when he was threeſcore yeeres old, and ſhe bare him
Segub.22And Segub begate Iair, who had three and twenty cities in the
land of Gilead.23And he tooke Geſhur, and Aram, with the townes of
Iair, from them, with Kenath, and the townes thereof, euen threeſcore
cities. All theſe belonged to the ſonnes of Machir, the father of
Gilead.24And after that Hezron was dead in Caleb Ephratah, then Abiah
Hezrons wife, bare him Aſhur, the father of Tekoa.25And the ſonnes of
Ierahmeel the firſt-borne of Hezron, were Ram the firſt-borne, and
Bunah, and Oren, and Ozen, and Ahiiah.26Ierahmeel had alſo an other
wife, whoſe name was Atarah, ſhe was the mother of Onam.27And the
ſonnes of Ram the firſt-borne of Ierahmeel, were Maaz, and Iamin, and
Ekar.28And the ſonnes of Onam were, Shammai, and Iada. And the
ſonnes of Shammai: Nadab, and Abiſhur.29And the name of the wife of
Abiſhur was Abihail, and ſhee bare him Ahban, and Molid.30And the
ſonnes of Nadab: Seled, and Appaim. But Seled died without
children.31And the ſonnes of Appaim, Iſhi: and the ſonnes of Iſhi,
Sheſhan: and the children of Sheſhan, Ahlai.32And the ſonnes of Iada
the brother of Shammai, Iether, and Ionathan: and Iether died without
children.33And the ſonnes of Ionathan, Peleth, and Zaza. Theſe were
the ſonnes of Ierahmeel.34Now Sheſhan had no ſonnes, but daughters:
and Sheſhan had a ſeruant, an Egyptian, whoſe name was Iarha.35And
Sheſhan gaue his daughter to Iarha his ſeruant to wife, and ſhe bare him
Attai.36And Attai begate Nathan, and Nathan begate Zabad,37And
Zabad begate Ephlal, and Ephlal begate Obed,38And Obed begate Iehu,
and Iehu begate Azariah,39And Azariah begate Helez, and Helez begate
Eleaſah,40And Eleaſah begate Siſamai, and Siſamai begate
Shallum,41And Shallum begate Iekamiah, and Iekamiah begate
Eliſhama.42Now the ſonnes of Caleb the brother of Ierahmeel were,
Meſha his firſt-borne, which was the father of Ziph: and the ſonnes of
Mareſha the father of Hebron.43And the ſonnes of Hebron: Korah, and
Tappuah, and Rekem, and Shema.44And Shema begat Raham, the father
of Iorkoam: and Rekem begate Shammai.45And the ſonne of Shammai
was Maon: and Maon was the father of Beth-zur.46And Ephah Calebs
concubine bare Haran, and Moza, and Gazez: and Haran begate
Gazez.47And the ſonnes of Iahdai: Regem, and Iotham, and Geſhan,
and Pelet, and Ephah, and Shaaph.48Maacha Calebs concubine, bare
Sheber, and Tirhanah.49Shee bare alſo Shaaph the father of
Madmannah, Sheua the father of Machbenah, & the father of Gibea:
And the daughter of Caleb was Achſah.50Theſe were the ſonnes of
Caleb, the ſonne of Hur, the firſt borne of Ephratah: Shobal the father
of Kiriath-iearim,51Salma the father of Bethlehem: Hareph the father of
Beth-gader.52And Shobal the father of Kiriath-iearim, had ſonnes,
Haroe, and halfe of the Manahethites.53And the families of Kiriath-
iearim, the Ithrites, and the Puhites, and the Shumathites, and the
Miſhraites: of them came the Zareathites, and the Eſhtaulites.54The
ſonnes of Salmah: Bethlehem, and the Netophathites, Ataroth, the
houſe of Ioab, and halfe of the Manahethites, the Zorites.55And the
families of the Scribes, which dwelt at Iabez: the Tirathites, the
Shimeathites, and Suchathites. Theſe are the Kenites that came of
Hemath, the father of the houſe of Rechab.
CHAPTER 31Now theſe were the ſonnes of Dauid, which were borne
vnto him in Hebron. The firſt borne Amnon, of Ahinoam the
Ieſreeliteſse: the ſecond Daniel, of Abigail the Carmeliteſse:2The third,
Abſalom the ſonne of Maacha, the daughter of Talmai king of Geſhur:
the fourth, Adoniah the ſonne of Haggith:3The fifth, Shephatia of
Abital: the ſixth, Ithream by Eglah his wife.4Theſe ſixe were borne vnto
him in Hebron, and there hee reigned ſeuen yeeres, and ſixe moneths:
and in Ieruſalem he reigned thirty and three yeres.5And theſe were borne
vnto him in Ieruſalem. Shimea, and Shobab, and Nathan, and Solomon,
foure, of Bathſhua the daughter of Ammiel.6Ibhar alſo, and Eliſhama,
and Eliphelet,7And Noga, and Nepheg, and Iaphia,8And Eliſhama, and
Eliada, and Eliphelet, nine.9Theſe were all the ſonnes of Dauid: beſide
the ſonnes of the concubines, and Tamar their ſiſter.10And Solomons
ſonne was Rehoboam: Abia his ſonne: Aſa his ſon: Iehoſhaphat his
ſonne:11Ioram his ſonne: Ahaziah his ſonne: Ioaſh his ſonne:12Amaziah
his ſonne: Azariah his ſonne: Iotham his ſonne:13Ahaz his ſonne:
Hezekiah his ſonne: Manaſſeh his ſonne:14Amon his ſonne: Ioſiah his
ſonne.15And the ſonnes of Ioſiah were: the firſt borne Iohanan, the
ſecond Ioakim, the third Zedekiah, the fourth Sallum.16And the ſonnes
of Ioakim: Ieconiah his ſonne, Zedekiah his ſonne.17And the ſonnes of
Ieconiah, Aſsir, Salathiel his ſonne,18Malchiram alſo, and Pedaiah, and
Shenazar, Iecamiah, Hoſama, and Nedabiah.19And the ſonnes of
Pedaiah were: Zerubbabel, and Shimei: And the ſonne of Zerubbabel,
Meſhullam, and Hananiah, and Shelomith their ſiſter.20And Hazubah,
and Ohel, and Berechiah, & Haſadiah, Iuſhabheſed, fiue.21And the
ſonnes of Hananiah, Pelatiah, and Ieſaiah: the ſonnes of Rephaiah, the
ſons of Arnan, the ſonnes of Obadiah, the ſonnes of Sechaniah.22And
the ſonnes of Sechaniah, Semaiah: and the ſonnes of Semaiah, Hattuſh,
and Igeal, and Bariah, and Neariah, and Shaphat, ſixe.23And the ſonnes
of Neariah: Elioenai, and Hezekiah, and Azrikam, three.24And the
ſonnes of Elioenai, were: Hodaiah, and Eliaſhib, and Pelaiah, and
Akkub, and Iohanan, and Dalaiah, and Anani, ſeuen.
CHAPTER 41The ſonnes of Iudah: Pharez, Hezron, and Carmi, and
Hur, and Shobal.2And Reaiah, the ſon of Shobal, begate Iahath, and
Iahath begate Ahumai, & Lahad. Theſe are the families of the
Zorathites.3And theſe were of the father of Etam: Iezreel & Iſhma, &
Idbaſh: and the name of their ſiſter was Hazelelponi.4And Penuel the
father of Gedor, and Ezer the father of Huſhah. Theſe are the ſonnes
of Hur, the firſt borne of Ephratah, the father of Bethlehem.5And Aſhur
the father of Tekoa, had two wiues: Helah, & Naarah.6And Naarah bare
him Ahuſam, and Hepher, and Temeni, and Ahaſhtari. Theſe were the
ſonnes of Naarah.7And the ſonnes of Helah were: Zereth, and Zoar,
and Ethnan.8And Coz begate Anub, and Zobebah, and the families of
Aharhel, the ſonne of Harum.9And Iabez was more honourable then
his brethren: and his mother called his name Iabez, ſaying, Becauſe I
bare him with ſorrow.10And Iabez called on the God of Iſrael, ſaying,
Oh that thou wouldeſt bleſſe mee indeede, and enlarge my coaſt, and

that thine hand might bee with me, and that thou wouldeſt keepe mee from euill, that it may not grieue me. And God granted him that which he requeſted.11And Chelub the brother of Shuah, begate Mehir, which was the father of Eſhton.12And Eſhton begate Beth-rapha, and Paſeah, and Tehinnah the father of Ir-nahaſh. Theſe are the men of Rechah.13And the ſonnes of Kenaz: Othniel, and Saraia: and the ſonnes of Othniel, Hathath.14And Meonothai begate Ophrah: and Seraiah begate Ioab, the father of the valley of Charaſim, for they were craftesmen.15And the ſonnes of Caleb the ſonne of Iephunneh: Iru, Elah, and Naam, and the ſonnes of Elah, euen Kenaz.16And the ſonnes of Iehaleleel: Ziph, and Ziphah, Tiria, and Aſareel.17And the ſonnes of Ezra were: Iether, and Mered, and Epher, and Ialon: and ſhe bare Miriam, and Shammai, & Iſhbah the father of Eſhtemoa.18And his wife Iehudiiah bare Iered the father of Gedor, and Heber the father of Socho, and Iekuthiel the father of Zanoah. And theſe are the ſonnes of Bithiah the daughter of Pharaoh, which Mered tooke.19And the ſonnes of his wife Hodiah, the ſiſter of Naham the father of Keilah, the Garmite, and Eſhtemoa the Maachathite.20And the ſonnes of Simeon were: Amnon, and Rinnah, Ben-hanan, and Tilon. And the ſonnes of Iſhi were: Zoheth, and Ben-zoheth.21The ſonnes of Shelah the ſonne of Iudah were: Er the father of Lecah, and Laadah the father of Mareſhah, and the families of the houſe of them that wrought fine linnen, of the houſe of Aſhbea.22And Iokim, and the men of Chozeba, and Ioaſh, and Saraph, who had the dominion in Moab, & Iaſhubi Lehem. And theſe are ancient things.23Theſe were the Potters, and thoſe that dwelt amongſt plants and hedges. There they dwelt with the king for his worke.24The ſonnes of Simeon were: Nemuel, and Iamin, Iarib, Zerah, and Shaul:25Shallum his ſonne: Mibſam his ſonne: Miſhma his ſonne.26And the ſonnes of Miſhma: Hamuel his ſonne, Zacchur his ſonne, Shimei his ſonne.27And Shimei had ſixteene ſonnes, and ſixe daughters, but his brethren had not many children, neither did all their family multiply like to the children of Iudah.28And they dwelt at Beer-ſheba, and Moladah, and Hazar-ſhual,29And at Bilha, and at Ezem, and at Tolad,30And at Bethuel, and at Hormah, and at Ziklag,31And at Beth-marcaboth, and Hazar-Suſim, and at Bethbirei, and at Shaaraim. Theſe were their cities, vnto the reigne of Dauid.32And their villages were: Etam, and Ain, Rimmon, and Tochen, and Aſhan, fiue cities.33And all their villages that were round about the ſame cities, vnto Baal. Theſe were their habitations, and their genealogie:34And Meſhobab, and Iamlech, and Ioſhah the ſonne of Amaſhiah,35And Ioel, and Iehu the ſonne of Ioſibia, the ſonne of Seraia, the ſonne of Aſiel,36And Elioenai, and Iaakobah, and Ieſohaiah, and Aſaiah, and Adiel, and Ieſimiel, and Benaiah,37And Ziza the ſonne of Shiphi, the ſonne of Allon, the ſonne of Iedaia, the ſonne of Shimri, the ſonne of Shemaiah.38Theſe mentioned by their names, were Princes in their families, and the houſe of their fathers increaſed greatly.39And they went to the entrance of Gedor, euen vnto the Eaſt ſide of the valley, to ſeeke paſture for their flocks.40And they found fat paſture and good, and the land was wide, and quiet, and peaceable: for they of Ham had dwelt there of old.41And theſe written by name, came in the dayes of Hezekiah king of Iudah, and ſmote their tents, and the habitations that were found there, and deſtroyed them vtterly vnto this day, and dwelt in their roomes: becauſe there was paſture there for their flocks.42And ſome of them, euen of the ſonnes of Simeon, fiue hundred men, went to mount Seir, hauing for their captaines Pelatiah, and Neariah, and Rephaiah, and Uzziel, the ſonnes of Iſhi.43And they ſmote the reſt of the Amalekites that were eſcaped, and dwelt there vnto this day.

CHAPTER 51Now the ſonnes of Reuben the firſt borne of Iſrael, (for hee was the firſt borne, but, foraſmuch as he defiled his fathers bed, his birthright was giuen vnto the ſonnes of Ioſeph the ſonne of Iſrael: and the genealogie is not to be reckoned after the birthright.2For Iudah preuailed aboue his brethren, and of him came the chiefe rulers, but the birthright was Ioſephs.3The ſonnes, I ſay, of Reuben the firſt borne of Iſrael were: Hanoch, and Pallu, Ezron, and Carmi.4The ſonnes of Ioel: Shemaiah his ſonne: Gog his ſonne: Shimei his ſonne:5Micah his ſon: Reaia his ſonne: Baal his ſonne.6Beerah his ſonne: whom Tilgath-pilneſer king of Aſſyria, carried away captiue: He was Prince of the Reubenites.7And his brethren by their families (when the genealogie of their generations was reckoned) were the chiefe, Ieiel, and Zechariah,8And Bela the ſonne of Azah, the ſonne of Shema, the ſonne of Ioel, who dwelt in Aroer, euen vnto Nebo, and Baalmeon.9And Eaſtward he inhabited vnto the entring in of the wildernes, from the riuer Euphrates: becauſe their cattell were multiplied in the land of Gilead.10And in the dayes of Saul, they made warre with the Hagarites, who fell by their hand: and they dwelt in their tents throughout all the Eaſt land of Gilead.11And the children of Gad dwelt ouer againſt them, in the land of Baſhan vnto Salchah.12Ioel the chiefe, and Shapham the next: and Iaanai, and Shaphat in Baſhan.13And their brethren of the houſe of their fathers, were: Michael, and Meſhullam, and Sheba, and Iorai, and Iachan, and Zia, and Heber, ſeuen.14Theſe are the children of Abihail the ſonne of Huri, the ſonne of Iaroah, the ſonne of Gilead, the ſonne of Michael, the ſonne of Ieſhiſhai, the ſonne of Iahdo, the ſonne of Buz:15Ahi the ſonne of Abdiel, the ſonne of Guni, chiefe of the houſe of their fathers.16And they dwelt in Gilead in Baſhan, and in her townes, and in all the Suburbs of Sharon, vpon their borders.17All theſe were reckoned by genealogies in the dayes of Iotham king of Iudah, and in the dayes of Ieroboam king of Iſrael.18The ſonnes of Reuben, and the Gadites, and halfe the tribe of Manaſſeh, of valiant men, men able to beare buckler and ſword, and to ſhoote with bow, and ſkilfull in warre, were foure and fourtie thouſand, ſeuen hundred and threeſcore, that went out to the warre.19And they made warre with the Hagarites, with Ietur, and Nephiſh, and Nodab.20And they were helped againſt them, and the Hagarites were deliuered into their hand, and all that were with them: for they cried to God in the battell, and he was intreated of them, becauſe they put their truſt in him.21And they tooke away their cattell: of their camels fiftie thouſand, and of ſheepe two hundred and fiftie thouſand, and of aſſes two thouſand, and of men an hundred thouſand.22For there fell downe many ſlaine, becauſe the warre was of God. And they dwelt in their ſteads vntil the captiuity.23And the children of the halfe tribe of Manaſſeh dwelt in the lande: they increaſed from Baſhan vnto Baal-hermon, and Senir, and vnto mount Hermon.24And theſe were the heads of the houſe of their fathers, euen Epher, and Iſhi, & Eliel, and Azriel, and Ieremiah, and Hodauiah, and Iahdiel, mightie men of valour, famous men, & heads of the houſe of their fathers.25And they tranſgreſſed againſt the God of their fathers, and went a whoring after the Gods of the people of the land, whome God deſtroyed before them.26And the God of Iſrael ſtirred vp the ſpirit of Pul king of Aſſyria, and the ſpirit of Tilgath-pilneſer king of Aſſyria, and he caried them away (euen the Reubenites, and the Gadites, and the halfe tribe of Manaſſeh:) & brought them vnto Halah, and Habor, and Hara, and to the riuer Gozan, vnto this day.

CHAPTER 61The ſonnes of Leui: Gerſhon, Kohath & Merari.2And the ſonnes of Kohath: Amram, Izahar, & Hebron, & Uzziel.3And the children of Amram: Aaron, and Moſes, and Miriam. The ſonnes alſo of Aaron: Nadab, and Abihu, Eleazar, and Ithamar.4Eleazar begate Phinehas, Phinehas begate Abiſhua.5And Abiſhua begate Bukki, and Bukki begate Uzzi,6And Uzzi begate Zerahiah, and Zerahiah begate Meraioth,7Meraioth begate Amariah, and Amariah begate Ahitub,8And Ahitub begate Zadok, and Zadok begate Ahimaaz,9And Ahimaaz begate Azariah, and Azariah begate Iohanan,10And Iohanan begate Azariah, (hee it is that executed the Prieſts office, in the temple that Solomon built in Ieruſalem)11And Azariah begate Amariah, and Amariah begate Ahitub,12And Ahitub begate Zadok, and Zadok begate Shallum,13And Shallum begate Hilkiah, and Hilkiah begate Azariah,14And Azariah begate Seraiah, and Seraiah begate Iehozadak,15And Iehozadak went into captiuitie, when the Lord caried away Iudah and Ieruſalem by the hand of Nebuchad-nezzar.16The ſonnes of Leui: Gerſhom, Kohath, and Merari.17And theſe be the names of the ſonnes of Gerſhom: Libni, & Shimei.18And the ſonnes of Kohath were: Amram, and Izhar, and Hebron, and Uzziel.19The ſonnes of Merari: Mahli, and Muſhi. And theſe are the families of the Leuites, according to their fathers.20Of Gerſhom: Libni his ſonne, Iahath his ſonne, Zimmah his ſonne,21Ioah his ſonne, Iddo his ſonne, Zerah his ſonne, Ieaterai his ſonne,22The ſonnes of Kohath: Amminadab his ſonne, Korah his ſonne, Aſſir his ſonne,23Elkanah his ſonne, and Ebiaſaph his ſonne, and Aſſir his ſonne,24Tahath his ſonne, Uriel his ſonne, Uzziah his ſonne, and Shaul his ſonne.25And the ſonnes of Elkanah: Amaſai, and Ahimoth.26As for Elkanah: the ſonnes of

Elkanah, Zophai his ſonne, and Nahath his ſonne,[27]Eliab his ſonne, Ieroham his ſonne, Elkanah his ſonne.[28]And the ſonnes of Samuel: the firſt borne Uaſhni, and Abiah.[29]The ſonnes of Merari: Mahli, Libni his ſonne, Shimei his ſonne, Uzza his ſonne,[30]Shimea his ſonne, Haggiah his ſonne, Aſaiah his ſonne.[31]And theſe are they, whom Dauid ſet ouer the ſeruice of ſong in the houſe of the Lord, after that the Arke had reſt.[32]And they miniſtred before the dwelling place of the Tabernacle of the Congregation, with ſinging, vntill Solomon had built the houſe of the Lord in Ieruſalem: and then they waited on their office, according to their order.[33]And theſe are they that waited with their children of the ſonnes of the Kohathites, Heman a ſinger: the ſonne of Ioel, the ſonne of Shemuel,[34]The ſonne of Elkanah, the ſonne of Ieroham, the ſonne of Eliel, the ſonne of Toah,[35]The ſonne of Zuph, the ſonne of Elkanah, the ſonne of Mahath, the ſonne of Amaſai,[36]The ſonne of Elkanah, the ſonne of Ioel, the ſonne of Azariah, the ſonne of Zephaniah,[37]The ſonne of Tahath, the ſonne of Aſsir, the ſonne of Ebiaſaph, the ſonne of Korah,[38]The ſonne of Izhar, the ſonne of Kohath, the ſonne of Leui, the ſonne of Iſrael.[39]And his brother Aſaph (who ſtood on his right hand) euen Aſaph the ſonne of Berachiah, the ſonne of Shimea,[40]The ſonne of Michael, the ſonne of Baaſiah, the ſonne of Melchiah,[41]The ſonne of Ethni, the ſonne of Zerah, the ſonne of Adaiah,[42]The ſonne of Ethan, the ſonne of Zimmah, the ſonne of Shimei,[43]The ſonne of Iahath, the ſonne of Gerſhom, the ſonne of Leui.[44]And their brethren the ſonnes of Merari, ſtood on the left hand: Ethan the ſonne of Kiſhi, the ſonne of Abdi, the ſonne of Malluch,[45]The ſonne of Haſhabiah, the ſonne of Amaziah, the ſonne of Hilkiah,[46]The ſonne of Amzi, the ſonne of Bani, the ſonne of Shamer,[47]The ſonne of Mahli, the ſonne of Muſhi, the ſonne of Merari, the ſonne of Leui.[48]Their brethren alſo the Leuits were appointed vnto all maner of ſeruice of the Tabernacle of the houſe of God.[49]But Aaron, and his ſonnes offered vpon the altar of the burnt offering, and on the altar of incenſe, and were appointed for all the worke of the place moſt holy, and to make an atonement for Iſrael, according to all that Moſes the ſeruant of God had commaunded.[50]And theſe are the ſonnes of Aaron: Eleazar his ſonne, Phinehas his ſonne, Abiſhua his ſonne,[51]Bukki his ſonne, Uzzi his ſonne, Zerahiah his ſonne,[52]Meraioth his ſonne, Amariah his ſonne, Ahitub his ſonne,[53]Zadok his ſonne, Ahimaaz his ſonne.[54]Now theſe are their dwelling places, throughout their caſtels in their coaſts, of the ſonnes of Aaron, of the families of the Kohathites: for theirs was the lot.[55]And they gaue them Hebron in the land of Iudah, and the ſuburbes thereof round about it.[56]But the fields of the citie, and the villages thereof, they gaue to Caleb the ſonne of Iephunneh.[57]And to the ſonnes of Aaron they gaue the cities of Iudah, namely Hebron the citie of refuge, and Libna with her ſuburbes, and Iattir and Eſhtemoa, with their ſuburbes,[58]And Hilen with her ſuburbes, Debir with her ſuburbes,[59]And Aſhan with her ſuburbes, and Beth-ſhemeſh with her ſuburbes.[60]And out of the tribe of Beniamin, Geba with her ſuburbes, and Alemeth with her ſuburbes, Anathoth with her ſuburbes. All their cities throughout their families were thirteene cities.[61]And vnto the ſonnes of Rohath, which were left of the family of that tribe, were cities giuen out of the halfe tribe, namely out of the halfe tribe of Manaſſeh, by lot, ten cities.[62]And to the ſonnes of Gerſhom throughout their families, out of the tribe of Iſſachar, and out of the tribe of Aſher, and out of the tribe of Naphtali, and out of the tribe of Manaſſeh in Baſhan, thirteene cities.[63]Unto the ſonnes of Merari were giuen by lot, throughout their families, out of the tribe of Reuben, and out of the tribe of Gad, and out of the tribe of Zebulun, twelue cities.[64]And the children of Iſrael gaue to the Leuites theſe cities, with their ſuburbs.[65]And they gaue by lot, out of the tribe of the children of Iudah, and out of the tribe of the children of Simeon, and out of the tribe of the children of Beniamin, theſe cities, which are called by their names.[66]And the reſidue of the families of the ſonnes of Kohath, had cities of their coaſts, out of the tribe of Ephraim.[67]And they gaue vnto them of the cities of refuge, Shechem in mount Ephraim, with her ſuburbs: they gaue alſo Gezer with her ſuburbs,[68]And Iokmeam with her ſuburbs, & Beth-horon with her ſuburbs,[69]And Aialon with her ſuburbs, and Gath-rimmon with her ſuburbs.[70]And out of the halfe tribe of Manaſſeh, Aner with her ſuburbs, and Bileam with her ſuburbs, for the family of the remnant of the ſonnes of Kohath.[71]Unto the ſonnes of Gerſhom, were giuen out of the family of the halfe tribe of Manaſſeh, Golan in Baſhan with her ſuburbs, and Aſhtaroth with her ſuburbs.[72]And out of the tribe of Iſſachar, Kedeſh with her ſuburbs, Daberath with her ſuburbs,[73]And Ramoth with her ſuburbs, and Anem with her ſuburbs.[74]And out of the tribe of Aſher, Maſhal with her ſuburbs, and Abdon with her ſuburbs,[75]And Hukok with her ſuburbs, and Rehob with her ſuburbs.[76]And out of the tribe of Naphtali, Kedeſh in Galilee, with her ſuburbs, and Hammon with her ſuburbs, and Kiriathaim with her ſuburbs.[77]Unto the reſt of the children of Merari were giuen out of the tribe of Zebulun, Rimmon with her ſuburbs, Tabor with her ſuburbs.[78]And on the other ſide Iorden by Iericho, on the Eaſt ſide of Iorden,were giuen them out of the tribe of Reuben, Bezer in the wilderneſſe with her ſuburbs, & Iahzah with her ſuburbs,[79]Kedemoth alſo with her ſuburbs, & Mephaath with her ſuburbs.[80]And out of the tribe of Gad, Ramoth in Gilead with her ſuburbs, and Mahanaim with her ſuburbs,[81]And Heſhbon with her ſuburbs, and Iazer with her ſuburbs.

CHAPTER 7[1]Now the ſonnes of Iſſachar were, Tola, and Puah, Iaſhub, and Shimron, foure.[2]And the ſonnes of Tola: Uzzi, and Rephaiah, and Ieriel, and Iahmai, and Iibſam, and Shemuel, heads of their fathers houſe, to wit, of Tola, they were valiant men of might in their generations, whoſe number was in the dayes of Dauid two and twentie thouſand and ſixe hundred.[3]And the ſonnes of Uzzi, Izrahiah: and the ſonnes of Izrahiah, Michael, and Obadiah, and Ioel, Iſhiah, fiue: all of them chiefe men.[4]And with them, by their generations, after the houſe of their fathers, were bands of ſouldiers for warre, ſixe and thirtie thouſand men: for they had many wiues and ſonnes.[5]And their brethren among all the families of Iſſachar, were men of might, reckoned in all by their genealogies, foureſcore and ſeuen thouſand.[6]The ſonnes of Beniamin: Bela, and Becher, and Iediael, three.[7]And the ſonnes of Bela: Ezbon, and Uzzi, and Uzziel, and Ierimoth, and Iri, fiue, heads of the houſe of their fathers, mightie men of valour, and were reckoned by their genealogies, twentie and two thouſand, and thirtie and foure.[8]And the ſonnes of Becher: Zemira, and Ioaſh, and Eliezer, and Elioenai, and Omri, and Ierimoth, and Abiah, and Anathoth, and Alameth. All theſe are the ſonnes of Becher.[9]And the number of them, after their genealogie by their generations, heads of the houſe of their fathers, mightie men of valour, was twentie thouſand and two hundred.[10]The ſonnes alſo of Iediael, Bilhan: and the ſonnes of Bilhan, Ieuſh, and Beniamin, and Ehud, and Chenaanah, and Zethan, and Tharſhiſh, and Ahiſhahar.[11]All theſe the ſonnes of Iediael, by the heads of their fathers, mighty men of valour, were ſeuenteene thouſand and two hundred ſouldiers, fit to goe out for warre and battaile.[12]Shuppim alſo, and Huppim, the children of Ir, and Huſhim, the ſonnes of Aher.[13]The ſonnes of Naphtali, Iahziel, and Guni, and Iezer, and Shallum, the ſonnes of Bilhah.[14]The ſonnes of Manaſſeh: Aſhriel, whom ſhee bare (but his concnbine the Aramiteſſe, bare Machir the father of Gilead.[15]And Machir tooke to wife the ſiſter of Huppim and Shuppim, whoſe ſiſters name was Maachah) and the name of the ſecond was Zelophehad: and Zelophehad had daughters.[16]And Maachah the wife of Machir bare a ſonne, and ſhee called his name Pereſh, and the name of his brother was Shereſh, and his ſonnes were Ulam and Rakem.[17]And the ſonnes of Ulam, Bedan. Theſe were the ſonnes of Gilead, the ſonne of Machir, the ſonne of Manaſſeh.[18]And his ſiſter Hammoleketh bare Iſhad, and Abiezer, and Mahalah.[19]And the ſonnes of Shemida were: Ahian, and Shechem, and Likhi, and Aniam.[20]And the ſonnes of Ephraim: Shuthelah: and Bered his ſonne, and Tahath his ſonne, and Eladah his ſonne, and Tahath his ſonne,[21]And Zabad his ſonne, and Shuthelah his ſonne, and Ezer, and Elead, whom the men of Gath, that were borne in that land ſlewe, becauſe they came downe to take away their cattell.[22]And Ephraim their father mourned many dayes, and his brethren came to comfort him.[23]And when hee went in to his wife, ſhee conceiued and bare a ſonne, and he called his name, Beriah, becauſe it went euill with his houſe.[24](And his daughter was Sherah, who built Bethoron the nether, and the vpper, and Uzzen Sherah.)[25]And Rephah was his ſonne, alſo Rezeph, and Telah his ſonne, and Tahan his ſonne,[26]Laadan his ſonne, Amihud his ſonne, Eliſhama his ſonne,[27]Non his ſonne, Iehoſhua his ſonne.[28]And their poſſeſſions and habitations were, Bethel, and the townes thereof, and Eaſtward Naaran, and Weſtward Gezer with the townes thereof, Shechem alſo and the townes thereof, vnto Gaza and the townes thereof.29And by the borders of the children of Manaſſeh, Bethſhean and her townes, Taanach and her townes, Megiddo and her townes, Dor and her townes. In theſe dwelt the children of Ioſeph the ſonne of Iſrael.30The ſonnes of Aſher: Imnah, and Iſuah, and Iſhuai, and Beriah, and Serah their ſiſter.31And the ſonnes of Beriah: Heber, and Malchiel, who is the father of Birzauith.32And Heber begate Iaphlet, and Shomer, and Hotham, and Shuah their ſiſter.33And the ſonnes of Iaphlet: Paſach, and Bimhal, and Aſhuath. Theſe are the children of Iaphlet.34And the ſonnes of Shamer: Ahi, and Rohgah, Iehubbah, and Aram.35And the ſonne of his brother, Helem: Zophah, and Imna, and Shelesh, and Amal.36The ſonnes of Zophah: Suah, and Harnepher, and Shual, and Beri, and Imrah:37Bezer, and Hod, and Shamma, and Shilſhah, and Ithran, and Beera.38And the ſonnes of Iether: Iephunneh, and Piſpa, and Ara.39And the ſonnes of Ulla: Arah, and Haniel, and Rezia.40All theſe were the children of Aſher, heads of their fathers houſe, choice and mightie men of valour, chiefe of the princes. And the number throughout the genealogie of them, that were apt to the warre and to battell, was twentie and ſixe thouſand men.

CHAPTER 81Now Beniamin begate Bela his firſt borne, Aſhbel the ſecond, and Aharah the third,2Nohah the fourth, and Rapha the fifth.3And the ſonnes of Bela were: Addar, and Gera, and Abihud,4And Abiſhua, and Naaman, and Ahoah,5And Gera, and Shephuphan, and Huram.6And theſe are the ſonnes of Ehud: theſe are the heads of the fathers of the inhabitants of Geba, and they remoued them to Manahath:7And Naaman, and Ahiah, and Gera, he remooued them, and begate Uzza, and Ahihud.8And Shaharaim begate children in the countrey of Moab. After hee had ſent them away: Huſhim, and Baara were his wiues.9And he begat of Hodeſh his wife, Iobab, and Zibia, and Meſha, and Malcham,10And Ieuz, and Shachia, and Mirma. Theſe were his ſonnes, heads of the fathers.11And of Huſhim he begate Ahitub, and Elpaal.12The ſonnes of Elpaal: Eber, and Miſham, & Shamed, who built Ono, and Lod with the townes thereof.13Beriah alſo and Shema, who were heads of the fathers of the inhabitants of Aialon, who droue away the inhabitants of Gath.14And Ahio, Shaſhak, and Ierimoth,15And Zebadiah, & Arad, & Ader,16And Michael, and Iſpah, and Ioha the ſonnes of Beriah,17And Zebadiah, and Meſhullam, and Hezeki, and Heber,18Iſhmerai alſo, and Iezliah, and Iobab the ſonnes of Elpaal.19And Iakim, and Zichri, & Zabdi,20And Elienai, and Zilthai, & Eliel,21And Adaiah, and Beraiah, and Shimrath, the ſonnes of Shimhi,22And Iſhpan, and Heber, & Eliel,23And Abdon, and Zichri, and Hanan,24And Hananiah, and Elam, and Antothiiah,25And Iphedeiah, and Penuel, the ſonnes of Shaſhak,26And Shamſherai, and Shehariah, and Athaliah,27And Iareſiah, and Eliah, and Zichri the ſonnes of Ieroham.28Theſe were heads of the fathers, by their generations, chiefe men. Theſe dwelt in Ieruſalem.29And at Gibeon dwelt the father of Gibeon, (whoſe wiues name was Maachah:)30And his firſt borne ſonne Abdon, and Zur, and Kiſh, and Baal, & Nadab,31And Gidor, & Ahio, and Zacher,32And Mikloth begate Shimeah. And theſe alſo dwelt with their brethren in Ieruſalem, ouer againſt them.33And Ner begate Kiſh, and Kiſh begate Saul, and Saul begate Ionathan, and Malchiſhua, and Abinadab, and Eſhbaal.34And the ſonne of Ionathan was Meribbaal, and Meribbaal begate Micah.35And the ſonnes of Micah were Pithon, and Melech, and Tarea, and Ahaz.36And Ahaz begat Iehoadah, and Iehoadah begate Alemeth, and Aſmaueth, and Zimri, and Zimri begate Moza,37And Moza begate Binea: Rapha was his ſonne, Elaſa his ſonne, Azel his ſonne:38And Azel had ſixe ſonnes, whoſe names are theſe, Azrikam, Bocheru, and Iſhmael, and Sheariah, and Obadiah, and Hanan. All theſe were the ſonnes of Azel.39And the ſonnes of Eſhek his brother were Ulam his firſt-borne, Iehuſh the ſecond, and Eliphelet the third.40And the ſonnes of Ulam were mighty men of valour, archers, and had many ſonnes, and ſonnes ſonnes, an hundred and fiftie. All theſe are of the ſonnes of Beniamin.

CHAPTER 91So all Iſrael were reckoned by genealogies, & behold, they were written in the booke of the Kings of Iſrael and Iudah, who were caried away to Babylon for their tranſgreſsion.2Now the firſt inhabitants that dwelt in their poſſeſſions, in their cities, were the Iſraelites, the Prieſts, Leuits, and the Nethinims.3And in Ieruſalem dwelt of the children of Iudah, and of the children of Beniamin, and of the children of Ephraim, and Manaſſeh.4Uthai the ſonne of Amihud, the ſonne of Omri, the ſonne of Imri, the ſonne of Bani, of the children of Pharez the ſonne of Iudah.5And of the Shilonites: Aſaiah the firſt borne, and his ſonnes.6And of the ſonnes of Zerah: Ieuel, and their brethren, ſixe hundred and ninetie.7And of the ſonnes of Beniamin: Sallu the ſonne of Meſhullam, the ſonne of Hodauiah, the ſonne of Haſenuah:8And Ibneiah the ſonne of Ieroham, and Elah the ſonne of Uzzi, the ſonne of Michri, and Meſhullam the ſonne of Shephatiah, the ſonne of Reuel, the ſonne of Ibniiah,9And their brethren, according to their generations, nine hundred and fiftie and ſixe. All theſe men were chiefe of the fathers in the houſe of their fathers.10And of the Prieſts: Iedaiah, and Iehoiarib, and Iachin,11And Azariah the ſonne of Hilkiah, the ſonne of Meſhullam, the ſonne of Zadok, the ſonne of Meraioth, the ſonne of Ahitub the ruler of the houſe of God.12And Adaiah the ſonne of Ieroham, the ſonne of Paſhur, the ſonne of Malchiiah, and Maaſia the ſonne of Adiel, the ſonne of Iahzerah, the ſonne of Meſhullam, the ſonne of Meſhillemith, the ſonne of Immer.13And their brethren, heads of the houſe of their fathers, a thouſand, and ſeuen hundred and threeſcore, very able men for the worke of the ſeruice of the houſe of God.14And of the Leuites: Shemaiah the ſonne of Haſſhub, the ſonne of Azrikam, the ſonne of Haſhabiah, of the ſonnes of Merari.15And Bakbakkar, Hereſh, and Galal: and Mattaniah the ſonne of Micah, the ſonne of Zichri, the ſonne of Aſaph.16And Obadiah the ſonne of Shemaiah, the ſonne of Galal, the ſonne of Ieduthun: and Berechiah the ſonne of Aſa, the ſonne of Elkanah, that dwelt in the villages of the Netophathites.17And the Porters were Shallum, and Akkub, and Talmon, and Ahiman, and their brethren: Shallum was the chiefe.18(Who hitherto waited in the kings gate Eaſtward) they were Porters in the companies of the children of Leui.19And Shallum the ſonne of Kore, the ſonne of Ebiaſaph, the ſonne of Korah, and his brethren (of the houſe of his father) the Korahites, were ouer the worke of the ſeruice, keepers of the gates of the Tabernacle: and their fathers being ouer the hoſte of the Lord, were keepers of the entrie.20And Phinehas the ſonne of Eleazar was the ruler ouer them in time paſt, and the Lord was with him.21And Zechariah the ſonne of Meſhelemiah, was porter of the doore of the Tabernacle of the Congregation.22All theſe which were choſen to be porters in the gates, were two hundred and twelue. Theſe were reckoned by their genealogie in their villages: whom Dauid and Samuel the Seer, did ordeine in their ſet office.23So they and their children had the ouerſight of the gates of the houſe of the Lord, namely, the houſe of the Tabernacle, by wards.24In foure quarters were the porters: toward the Eaſt, Weſt, North, and South.25And their brethren, which were in their villages, were to come after ſeuen dayes, from time to time with them.26For theſe Leuites, the foure chiefe porters, were in their ſet office, and were ouer the chambers and treaſuries of the houſe of God.27And they lodged round about the houſe of God, becauſe the charge was vpon them, and the opening thereof euery morning, perteined to them.28And certaine of them had the charge of the miniſtring veſſels, that they ſhould bring them in and out by tale.29Some of them alſo were appointed to ouerſee the veſſels, and all the inſtruments of the Sanctuarie, and the fine floure, and the wine, and the oyle, and the frankincenſe, and the ſpices.30And ſome of the ſonnes of the Prieſts made the oyntment of the ſpices.31And Mattithiah, one of the Leuites (who was the firſt borne of Shallum the Korahite) had the ſet office ouer the things that were made in the pannes.32And other of their brethren of the ſonnes of the Kohathites, were ouer the Shew-bread to prepare it euery Sabbath.33And theſe are the ſingers, chiefe of the fathers of the Leuites, who remayning in the chambers, were free: for they were imployed in that worke, day and night.34Theſe chiefe fathers of the Leuites, were chiefe throughout their generations; theſe dwelt at Ieruſalem.35And in Gibeon dwelt the father of Gibeon, Iehiel, whoſe wiues name was Maacha:36And his firſt borne ſonne Abdon, then Zur, and Kiſh, and Baal, and Ner, and Nadab,37And Gedor, and Ahio, and Zechariah, and Mikloth.38And Mikloth begate Shimeam: and they alſo dwelt with their brethren at Ieruſalem, ouer againſt their brethren.39And Ner begat Kiſh, and Kiſh begate Saul, and Saul begate Ionathan, and Malchiſhua, and Abinadab, and Eſhbaal.40And the ſonne of Ionathan was Meribbaal: and Meribbaal begate Micah.41And the ſonnes of Micah were Pithon, and Melech, and Tahrea, and Ahaz.42And Ahaz begate Iarah, and Iarah begate Alemeth, & Azmaueth, and Zimri: and Zimri begate Moza,43And Moza begate Binea: and Rephaiah his ſon, Eleaſah his ſonne, Azel his ſonne.44And Azel had ſixe ſonnes, whoſe names are theſe: Azrikam, Bocheru, and Iſmael, and Sheariah, and Obadiah, and Hanan. Theſe were the ſonnes of Azel.

CHAPTER 101Nowe the Philiſtines fought againſt Iſrael, and the men of Iſrael fled from before the Philiſtines, and fell downe ſlaine in mount Gilboa.2And the Philiſtines followed hard after Saul, and after his ſonnes, and the Philiſtines ſlew Ionathan, and Abinadab, and Malchiſhua, the ſonnes of Saul.3And the battell went ſore againſt Saul, and the archers hit him, and he was wounded of the archers.4Then ſaide Saul to his armour bearer, Draw thy ſword, and thruſt me through therewith, leſt theſe vncircumciſed come, and abuſe mee: but his armour bearer would not, for he was ſore afraid. So Saul tooke a ſword, and fell vpon it.5And when his armour bearer ſaw that Saul was dead, hee fell likewiſe on the ſword, and died.6So Saul died, and his three ſonnes, and all his houſe died together.7And when all the men of Iſrael that were in the valley, ſaw that they fled, and that Saul and his ſonnes were dead: then they forſooke their cities, and fled, and the Philiſtines came and dwelt in them.8And it came to paſſe on the morrow, when the Philiſtines came to ſtrip the ſlaine, that they found Saul and his ſonnes fallen in mount Gilboa.9And when they had ſtripped him, they tooke his head, and his armour, and ſent into the land of the Philiſtines round about, to cary tidings vnto their idoles, and to the people.10And they put his armour in the houſe of their gods, and faſtened his head in the temple of Dagon.11And when all Iabeſh Gilead heard all that the Philiſtines had done to Saul:12They aroſe, all the valiant men, and tooke away the body of Saul, and the bodies of his ſonnes, and brought them to Iabeſh, and buried their bones vnder the oke in Iabeſh, and faſted ſeuen dayes.13So Saul died for his tranſgreſſion which hee committed againſt the Lord, euen againſt the word of the Lord which he kept not, and alſo for aſking counſel of one that had a familiar ſpirit, to enquire of it:14And enquired not of the Lord: therefore he ſlew him, and turned the kingdome vnto Dauid the ſonne of Ieſſe.

CHAPTER 111Then all Iſrael gathered themſelues to Dauid vnHebron, ſaying, Behold, wee are thy bone and thy fleſh.2And moreouer in time paſt, euen when Saul was king, thou waſt he that leddeſt out and broughteſt in Iſrael: and the Lord thy God ſaid vnto thee, Thou ſhalt feede my people Iſrael, and thou ſhalt be ruler ouer my people Iſrael.3Therefore came all the Elders of Iſrael to the king to Hebron, and Dauid made a couenant with them in Hebron before the Lord, and they annointed Dauid king ouer Iſrael, according to the word of the Lord, by Samuel.4And Dauid & all Iſrael, went to Ieruſalem, which is Iebus, where the Iebuſites were the inhabitants of the land.5And the inhabitants of Iebus ſaid to Dauid, Thou ſhalt not come hither. Neuertheleſſe Dauid tooke the caſtle of Zion, which is the citie of Dauid.6And Dauid ſaid, Whoſoeuer ſmiteth the Iebuſites firſt, ſhall be chiefe, and captaine. So Ioab the ſonne of Zeruiah went firſt vp, and was chiefe.7And Dauid dwelt in the caſtell: therefore they called it the citie of Dauid.8And he built the citie round about, euen from Millo round about: and Ioab repaired the reſt of the citie.9So Dauid waxed greater and greater: for the Lord of hoſtes was with him.10Theſe alſo are the chiefe of the mightie men, whom Dauid had, who ſtrenthened themſelues with him in his kingdome, and with all Iſrael, to make him king according to the word of the Lord, concerning Iſrael.11And this is the number of the mightie men, whom Dauid had: Iaſhobeam an Hachmonite, the chiefe of the captaines: he lift vp his ſpeare againſt three hundred, ſlaine by him at one time.12And after him was Eleazar the ſonne of Dodo the Ahohite, who was one of the three mighties.13He was with Dauid at Paſdammim; and there the Philiſtines were gathered together to battell, where was a parcell of ground full of barley, and the people fled from before the Philiſtines.14And they ſet themſelues in the middeſt of that parcell, and deliuered it, and ſlue the Philiſtines, & the Lord ſaued them by a great deliuerance.15Now three of the thirtie captaines, went downe to the rocke of Dauid, into the caue of Adullam, and the hoſt of the Philiſtines encamped in the valley of Rephaim.16And Dauid was then in the hold, and the Philiſtines gariſon was then at Bethlehem.17And Dauid longed and ſaid, Oh that one would giue me drinke of the water of the well of Bethlehem, that is at the gate.18And the three brake through the hoſt of the Philiſtines, and drew water out of the well of Bethlehem, that was by the gate, and tooke it and brought it to Dauid. But Dauid would not drink of it, but powred it out to the Lord,19And ſaid, My God forbid it mee, that I ſhould doe this thing. Shall I drinke the blood of theſe men, that haue put their liues in ieopardie? for with the ieopardie of their liues, they brought it: therfore he would not drink it. Theſe things did theſe three mightieſt.20And Abiſhai the brother of Ioab, he was chiefe of the three. For lifting vp his ſpeare againſt three hundred, he ſlew them, and had a name among the three.21Of the three, hee was more honourable then the two, for he was their captaine; howbeit, he attained not to the firſt three.22Benaiah the ſonne of Iehoiada, the ſonne of a valiant man of Kabzeel, who had done many acts: he ſlue two Lyon-like men of Moab, alſo he went downe and ſlue a Lyon in a pit in a ſnowy day.23And he ſlue an Egyptian, a man of great ſtature, fiue cubits high, and in the Egyptians hand was a ſpeare like a weauers beame: and he went downe to him with a ſtaffe, and pluckt the ſpeare out of the Egyptians hand, and ſlue him with his owne ſpeare.24Theſe things did Benaiah the ſonne of Iehoiada, and had the name among the three mighties.25Behold, hee was honourable among the thirtie, but attained not to the firſt three: and Dauid ſet him ouer his guard.26Alſo the valiant men of the armies were Aſahel the brother of Ioab, Elhanan the ſonne of Dodo of Bethlehem.27Shammoth the Harorite, Helez the Pelonite,28Ira the ſonne of Ikkeſh the Tekoite, Abiezer the Antothite,29Sibbecai the Huſhathite, Ilai the Ahohite,30Maharai the Netophathite, Heled the ſonne of Baanah the Netophathite,31Ithai the ſonne of Ribai of Gibeah, that perteined to the children of Beniamin, Benaiah the Pirathonite,32Hurai of the brookes of Gaaſh, Abiel the Arbathite,33Azmaueth the Baharumite, Elihaba the Shaalbonite,34The ſonnes of Haſhem the Gizonite: Ionathan the ſonne of Shageh the Hararite,35Ahiham the ſonne of Sacar the Hararite, Eliphal the ſonne of Ur,36Hepher the Mecherathite, Ahiiah the Pelonite,37Hezro the Carmelite, Naarai the ſonne of Ezbai,38Ioel the brother of Nathan, Mibhar the ſonne of Haggeri,39Zelek the Ammonite, Naharai the Berothite, the armour bearer of Ioab the ſonne of Zeruiah,40Ira the Ithrite, Gareb the Ithrite,41Uriah the Hittite, Zabad the ſonne of Ahlai,42Adina the ſonne of Shiza the Reubenite, a captaine of the Reubenites, and thirtie with him,43Hanan the ſonne of Maacah, and Ioſhaphat the Mithnite,44Uzzia the Aſhterathite, Shama and Iehiel the ſonnes of Hothan the Aroerite,45Iediael the ſonne of Zimri, and Ioha his brother, the Tizite,46Eliel the Mahauite, and Ieribai, and Ioſhauiah the ſonnes of Elnaan, and Ithmah the Moabite,47Eliel, and Obed, and Iaſiel the Meſobaite.

CHAPTER 121Now theſe are they that came to Dauid to Ziklag while hee yet kept himſelfe cloſe, becauſe of Saul the ſonne of Kiſh: and they were among the mighty men, helpers of the warre.2They were armed with bowes, and could vſe both the right hand and the left, in hurling ſtones, and ſhooting arrowes out of a bow, euen of Sauls brethren of Beniamin.3The chiefe was Ahiezer, then Ioaſh the ſonnes of Shemaah the Gibeathite, and Ieziel, and Pelet, the ſonnes of Azmaueth, and Berachah, and Iehu the Antothite,4And Iſmaiah the Gibeonite, a mightie man among the thirtie, and ouer the thirtie, and Ieremiah, and Iahaziel, and Iohanan, and Ioſabad the Gederathite,5Eleuzai, and Ierimoth, and Bealiath, and Shemariah, and Shephatiah the Haruphite,6Elkanah, and Ieſiah, and Azariel, and Ioezer, and Iaſhobeam, the Korhites,7And Ioelah, and Zebadiah the ſonnes of Ieroam of Gedor.8And of the Gadites there ſeparated themſelues vnto Dauid, into the hold to the wilderneſſe, men of might, and men of warre, fit for the battel, that could handle ſhield and buckler, whoſe faces were like the faces of Lyons, and were as ſwift as the Roes vpon the mountaines:9Ezer the firſt, Obadiah the ſecond, Eliab the third,10Maſhmannah the fourth, Ieremiah the fift,11Atthai the ſixt, Eliel the ſeuenth,12Iohanan the eighth, Elzabad the ninth,13Ieremiah the tenth, Machbanai the eleuenth.14Theſe were of the ſonnes of Gad, captaines of the hoſte: one of the leaſt was ouer an hundred, and the greateſt, ouer a thouſand.15Theſe are they that went ouer Iorden in the firſt moneth, when it had ouerflowen all his bankes, and they put to flight all them of the valleis, both toward the Eaſt, and toward the Weſt.16And there came of the children of Beniamin, and Iudah, to the hold vnto Dauid.17And Dauid went out to meete them, and anſwered and ſayd vnto them: If yee bee come peaceably vnto me to helpe me, mine heart ſhall be knit vnto you: but if yee be come to betray me to mine enemies, ſeeing there is no wrong in mine hands: the God of our fathers looke thereon, and rebuke it.18Then the ſpirit came vpon Amaſai, who was chiefe of the captaines, and he ſayd, Thine are we, Dauid, and on thy ſide, thou ſonne of Ieſſe: Peace, peace be vnto thee, and peace be to thine helpers; for thy God helpeth thee. Then Dauid receiued them, and made them captaines of the band.19And there fell ſome of Manaſſeh to Dauid, when he came with the Philiſtines againſt Saul to battell, but they helped them not. For the Lords of the Philiſtines, vpon aduiſement, ſent him away, ſaying, Hee will fall to his maſter Saul, to the ieopardie of our heads.20As he went to Ziklag, there fell to him of Manaſſeh, Adnah, and Iozabad, and Iediel, and Michael, and Iozabad, and Elihu, and Zilthai, captaines of the thouſands that were of Manaſſeh.21And they helped Dauid againſt the band of the Rouers: for they were all mighty men of valour, and were captaines in the hoſte.22For at that time day by day, there came to Dauid to helpe him, vntill it was a great hoſte, like the hoſte of God.23And theſe are the numbers of the bands, that were ready armed to the warre, and came to Dauid to Hebron, to turne the kingdome of Saul to him, according to the word of the Lord.24The children of Iudah that bare ſhield, and ſpeare, were ſixe thouſand, and eight hundred, readie armed to the warre.25Of the children of Simeon, mighty men of valour for the warre, ſeuen thouſand and one hundred.26Of the children of Leui, foure thouſand and ſixe hundred.27And Iehoiada was the leader of the Aaronits, and with him were three thouſand, and ſeuen hundred.28And Zadok a young man mightie of valour, and of his fathers houſe twentie and two captaines.29And of the children of Beniamin the kinred of Saul three thouſand: for hitherto the greateſt part of them had kept the ward of the houſe of Saul.30And of the children of Ephraim, twentie thouſand, and eight hundred, mightie men of valour, famous throughout the houſe of their fathers.31And of the halfe tribe of Manaſſeh, eighteene thouſand, which were expreſſed by name, to come and make Dauid king.32And of the children of Iſſachar, which were men that had vnderſtanding of the times, to know what Iſrael ought to doe: the heads of them were two hundred, and all their brethren were at their commandement.33Of Zebulun, ſuch as went foorth to battell, expert in warre, with all inſtruments of warre, fifty thouſand, which could keepe ranke: They were not of double heart.34And of Naphtali a thouſand captaines, and with them, with ſhield and ſpeare, thirtie and ſeuen thouſand.35And of the Danites, expert in war, twentie and eight thouſand, and ſixe hundred.36And of Aſher, ſuch as went foorth to battell, expert in warre, fourtie thouſand.37And on the other ſide of Iorden, of the Reubenites, & the Gadites, and of the halfe tribe of Manaſſeh, with all maner of inſtruments of warre for the battell, an hundred and twentie thouſand.38All theſe men of warre, that could keepe ranke, came with a perfect heart to Hebron, to make Dauid king ouer all Iſrael: and all the reſt alſo of Iſrael, were of one heart to make Dauid king.39And there they were with Dauid three dayes, eating and drinking: for their brethren had prepared for them.40Moreouer, they that were nigh them, euen vnto Iſſachar, and Zebulun, and Naphtali brought bread on aſſes, and on camels, and on mules, and on oxen, and meat, meale, cakes of figs, and bunches of raiſins, and wine, and oyle, and oxen, and ſheepe abundantly: for there was ioy in Iſrael.

CHAPTER 131And Dauid conſulted with the captaines of thouſands, and hundreds, and with euery leader.2And Dauid ſaid vnto all the Congregation of Iſrael, If it ſeeme good vnto you, and that it be of the Lord our God, let vs ſend abroad vnto our brethren euery where, that are left in all the land of Iſrael, and with them alſo to the Prieſts and Leuites which are in their cities and ſuburbs, that they may gather themſelues vnto vs.3And let vs bring againe the Arke of our God to vs: for wee enquired not at it in the dayes of Saul.4And all the Congregation ſaide, that they would doe ſo: for the thing was right in the eyes of all the people.5So Dauid gathered all Iſrael together, from Shihor of Egypt, euen vnto the entring of Hemath, to bring the Arke of God from Kiriath-iearim.6And Dauid went vp, and all Iſrael, to Baalah, that is, to Kiriath-iearim, which belonged to Iudah, to bring vp thence the Arke of God the Lord, that dwelleth betweene the Cherubims, whoſe name is called on it.7And they caried the Arke of God in a new cart, out of the houſe of Abinadab: and Uzza, and Ahio draue the cart.8And Dauid and all Iſrael played before God with all their might, and with ſinging, and with harpes, and with pſalteries, and with tymbrels, and with cymbals, and with trumpets.9And when they came vnto the threſhing floore of Chidon, Uzza put foorth his hand to hold the Arke, for the oxen ſtumbled.10And the anger of the Lord was kindled againſt Uzza, and hee ſmote him, becauſe hee put his hand to the Arke: and there he died before God.11And Dauid was diſpleaſed, becauſe the Lord had made a breach vpon Uzza; wherefore that place is called Perez-Uzza, to this day.12And Dauid was afraide of God that day, ſaying, How ſhall I bring the Arke of God home to me?13So Dauid brought not the Arke home to himſelfe to the city of Dauid, but caried it aſide into the houſe of Obed-Edom the Gittite.14And the Arke of God remained with the family of Obed-Edom in his houſe three moneths. And the Lord bleſſed the houſe of Obed-Edom, and all that he had.

CHAPTER 141Now Hiram king of Tyre ſent meſſengers to Dauid, and timber of Cedars, with maſons, and carpenters to build him an houſe.2And Dauid perceiued that the Lord had confirmed him king ouer Iſrael, for his kingdome was lift vp on high, becauſe of his people Iſrael.3And Dauid tooke moe wiues at Ieruſalem: and Dauid begate moe ſonnes and daughters.4Now theſe are the names of his children which hee had in Ieruſalem: Shammua, and Shobab, Nathan, and Solomon,5And Ibhar, and Eliſhua, and Elpalet,6And Noga, and Nepheg, and Iaphia,7And Eliſhama, and Beeliada, and Elpalet.8And when the Philiſtines heard that Dauid was anoynted king ouer all Iſrael, all the Philiſtines went vp to ſeeke Dauid: and Dauid heard of it, and went out againſt them.9And the Philiſtines came & ſpread themſelues in the valley of Rephaim.10And Dauid enquired of God, ſaying, Shall I goe vp againſt the Philiſtines? and wilt thou deliuer them into mine hand? And the Lord ſaid vnto him, Go vp, for I will deliuer them into thine hand.11So they came vp to Baal-Perazim, and Dauid ſmote them there. Then Dauid ſaid, God hath broken in vpon mine enemies by mine hand, like the breaking foorth of waters: therefore they called the name of that place, Baal-Perazim.12And when they had left their gods there, Dauid gaue a commandement, and they were burnt with fire.13And the Philiſtines yet againe ſpread themſelues abroad in the valley.14Therfore Dauid enquired againe of God, and God ſaid vnto him, Goe not vp after them, turne away from them, and come vpon them ouer againſt the mulbery trees.15And it ſhall bee, when thou ſhalt heare a ſound of going in the tops of the mulbery trees, that then thou ſhalt goe out to battaile: for God is gone foorth before thee, to ſmite the hoſte of the Philiſtines.16Dauid therefore did as God commanded him: and they ſmote the hoſte of the Philiſtines from Gibeon euen to Gazer.17And the fame of Dauid went out into all lands, and the Lord brought the feare of him vpon all nations.

CHAPTER 151And Dauid made him houſes in the citie of Dauid, and prepared a place for the Arke of God, and pitched for it a tent.2Then Dauid ſayd, None ought to carie the Arke of God, but the Leuites: for them hath the Lord choſen to cary the Arke of God, and to miniſter vnto him for euer.3And Dauid gathered all Iſrael together to Ieruſalem, to bring vp the Arke of the Lord vnto his place, which hee had prepared for it.4And Dauid aſſembled the children of Aaron, and the Leuites.5Of the ſonnes of Kohath: Uriel the chiefe, and his brethren an hundred and twentie.6Of the ſonnes of Merari: Aſaiah the chiefe, and his brethren two hundred and twentie.7Of the ſonnes of Gerſhom: Ioel the chiefe, and his brethren an hundred and thirtie.8Of the ſonnes of Elizaphan: Shemaiah the chiefe, and his brethren two hundred.9Of the ſonnes of Hebron: Eliel the chiefe, and his brethren foureſcore.10Of the ſonnes of Uzziel: Amminadab the chiefe, and his brethren an hundred and twelue.11And Dauid called for Zadok and Abiathar the Prieſts, and for the Leuites, for Uriel, Aſaiah and Ioel, Shemaiah, and Eliel, and Amminadab,12And ſaid vnto them, Yee are the chiefe of the fathers of the Leuites: ſanctifie your ſelues both yee and your brethren, that you may bring vp the Arke of the Lord God of Iſrael, vnto the place that I haue prepared for it.13For becauſe ye did it not at the firſt, the Lord our God made a breach vpon vs, for that we ſought him not after the due order.14So the Prieſtes and the Leuites ſanctified themſelues to bring vp the Arke of the Lord God of Iſrael.15And the children of the Leuites bare the Arke of God vpon their ſhoulders , with the ſtaues thereon, as Moſes commanded, according to the word of the Lord.16And Dauid

ſpake to the chiefe of the Leuites, to appoint their brethren to be the
ſingers with inſtruments of muſicke, Pſalteries, and Harpes, and
Cymbales, ſounding, by lifting vp the voice with ioy.17So the Leuites
appointed Heman the ſonne of Ioel: and of his brethren. Aſaph the
ſonne of Berechiah: and of the ſonnes of Merari their brethren, Ethan
the ſonne of Kuſhaiah.18And with them their brethren of the ſecond
degree, Zachariah, Ben, and Iaziel, & Shemiramoth, and Iehiel, and
Unni, Eliab, and Benaiah, and Maaſiah, and Mattithiah, and Eliphaleh,
and Mikniah, and Obed Edom, and Iehiel the Porters.19So the Singers,
Heman, Aſaph, and Ethan, were appointed to ſound with cymbales of
braſſe.20And Zachariah, and Aziel, and Shemiramoth, and Iehiel, and
Unni, and Eliab, and Maaſiah, and Benaiah, with Pſalteries on
Alamoth.21And Mattithiah, and Eliphaleh, and Mikniah, and Obed
Edom, and Ieiel, and Azzaziah, with harpes on the Sheminith to
excell.22And Chenaniah chiefe of the Leuites was for ſong: he inſtructed
about the ſong, becauſe he was ſkilfull.23And Berechiah, and Elkanah
were doore keepers for the Arke.24And Shebaniah, and Iehoſhaphat,
and Nathaneel, and Amaſai, and Zachariah, and Benaiah, and Eliezer
the prieſts, did blow with the trumpets before the Arke of God: and
Obed Edom, and Iehiah were doore keepers for the Arke.25So Dauid
and the Elders of Iſrael, and the captaines ouer thouſands, went to bring
vp the Arke of the couenant of the Lord, out of the houſe of Obed
Edom with ioy.26And it came to paſſe when God helped the Leuites
that bare the Arke of the couenant of the Lord, that they offered ſeuen
bullocks, and ſeuen rammes.27And Dauid was clothed with a robe of
fine linnen, and all the Leuites that bare the Arke, and the ſingers, and
Chenaniah the maſter of the ſong, with the ſingers. Dauid alſo had vpon
him, an Ephod of linnen.28Thus all Iſrael brought vp the Arke of the
Couenant of the Lord with ſhouting, and with ſound of the cornet, and
with trumpets, and with cymbals, making a noiſe with pſalteries and
harpes.29And it came to paſſe as the Arke of the couenant of the Lord
came to the citie of Dauid, that Michal the daughter of Saul looking out
at a window, ſaw King Dauid dauncing and playing: and ſhee deſpiſed
him in her heart.

CHAPTER 161So they brought the Arke of God, and ſet it in the midſt
of the tent that Dauid had pitched for it: and they offered burnt
ſacrifices, and peace offerings before God.2And when Dauid had made
an end of offering the burnt offerings, and the peace offrings, he bleſſed
the people in the name of the Lord.3And hee dealt to euery one of Iſrael,
both man and woman, to euery one a loafe of bread, and a good piece
of fleſh, and a flagon of wine.4And he appointed certaine of the Leuites
to miniſter before the Arke of the Lord, and to record, and to thanke
and praiſe the Lord God of Iſrael,5Aſaph the chiefe, and next to him
Zachariah, Ieiel, and Shemiramoth, and Iehiel, and Mattithiah, and
Eliab, and Benaiah, and Obed Edom: and Ieiel with Pſalteries and with
harpes: but Aſaph made a ſound with cymbals.6Benaiah alſo and
Iahaziel the Prieſtes, with trumpets continually before the Arke of the
Couenant of God.7Then on that day, Dauid deliuered firſt this Pſalme
to thanke the Lord, into the hand of Aſaph and his brethren:8Giue
thankes vnto the Lord, call vpon his name, make knowen his deeds
among the people.9Sing vnto him, ſing pſalmes vnto him, talke you of
all his wonderous workes.10Glory yee in his holy Name, let the heart of
them reioyce that ſeeke the Lord.11Seeke the Lord, and his ſtrength,
ſeeke his face continually.12Remember his marueilous works that he
hath done, his wonders, and the iudgements of his mouth,13O ye ſeed
of Iſrael his ſeruant, ye children of Iacob his choſen ones.14He is the
Lord our God, his iudgements are in all the earth.15Be ye mindfull
alwayes of his Couenant: the worde which hee commanded to a
thouſand generations:16Euen of the Couenant which hee made with
Abraham, and of his othe vnto Iſaac:17And hath confirmed the ſame to
Iacob for a lawe, and to Iſrael for an euerlaſting Couenant,18Saying, vnto
thee will I giue the land of Canaan, the lot of your inheritance.19When
ye were but few, euen a few, and ſtrangers in it:20And when they went
from nation to nation, and from one kingdome to another people:21Hee
ſuffered no man to doe them wrong: yea, hee reprooued kings for their
ſakes,22Saying, Touch not mine anointed, and doe my Prophets no
harme.23Sing vnto the Lord all the earth: ſhew foorth from day to day
his ſaluation.24Declare his glory among the heathen: his marueilous
workes among all nations.25For great is the Lord, and greatly to be
praiſed: he alſo is to be feared aboue all gods.26For all the gods of the
people are idoles: but the Lord made the heauens.27Glory and honour
are in his preſence: ſtrength and gladneſſe are in his place.28Giue vnto
the Lord, yee kinreds of the people: giue vnto the Lord glory and
ſtrength.29Giue vnto the Lord the glory due vnto his Name: bring an
offering, and come before him, worſhip the Lord in the beautie of
holineſſe.30Feare before him all the earth: the world alſo ſhall be ſtable,
that it be not mooued.31Let the heauens be glad, and let the earth
reioyce: and let men ſay among the nations, The Lord reigneth.32Let the
ſea roare, and the fulneſe thereof: let the fieldes reioyce, and all that is
therein.33Then ſhall the trees of the wood ſing out at the preſence of the
Lord, becauſe hee commeth to iudge the earth.34O giue thanks vnto the
Lord, for hee is good: for his mercy endureth for euer.35And ſay yee,
Saue vs, O God of our ſaluation, and gather vs together, and deliuer vs
from the heathen, that we may giue thanks to thy holy Name, and glory
in thy praiſe.36Bleſſed be the Lord God of Iſrael for euer and euer: and
all the people ſaide, Amen, and praiſed the Lord.37So hee left there
before the Arke of the couenant of the Lord, Aſaph and his brethren,
to miniſter before the Arke continually, as euery dayes worke
required:38And Obed Edom with their brethren, threeſcore and eight:
Obed Edom alſo the ſonne of Ieduthun, and Hoſah to be porters:39And
Zadok the Prieſt, and his brethren the Prieſts, before the Tabernacle of
the Lord, in the high place that was at Gibeon,40To offer burnt offerings
vnto the Lord, vpon the Altar of the burnt offering continually morning
and euening, and to doe according to all that is written in the Lawe of
the Lord, which hee commanded Iſrael:41And with them Heman and
Ieduthun, and the reſt that were choſen, who were expreſſed by name,
to giue thankes to the Lord, becauſe his mercy endureth for euer.42And
with them Heman and Ieduthun with trumpets and cymbales, for thoſe
that ſhould make a ſound, and with muſicall inſtruments of God: and
the ſonnes of Ieduthun were Porters.43And all the people departed euery
man to his houſe, and Dauid returned to bleſſe his houſe.

CHAPTER 171Now it came to paſſe, as Dauid ſate in his houſe, that
Dauid ſayde to Nathan the Prophet, Loe, I dwell in an houſe of Cedars,
but the Arke of the Couenant of the Lord remaineth vnder
curtaines.2Then Nathan ſayd vnto Dauid, Doe all that is in thine heart,
for God is with thee.3And it came to paſſe the ſame night, that the word
of God came to Nathan, ſaying,4Goe and tell Dauid my ſeruant, Thus
ſaith the Lord, Thou ſhalt not build me an houſe to dwell in.5For I haue
not dwelt in a houſe ſince the day that I brought vp Iſrael, vnto this day,
but haue gone from tent to tent, and from one Tabernacle to
another.6Whereſoeuer I haue walked with all Iſrael, ſpake I a word to
any of the Iudges of Iſrael (whom I commanded to feed my people)
ſaying, Why haue ye not built me an houſe of Cedars?7Now therefore
thus ſhalt thou ſay vnto my ſeruant Dauid, Thus ſaith the Lord of hoſts,
I tooke thee from the Sheep-coat, euen from folowing the ſheep, that
thou ſhouldeſt be ruler ouer my people Iſrael:8And I haue bene with
thee whitherſoeuer thou haſt walked, and haue cut off all thine enemies
from before thee, and haue made thee a name, like the name of the great
men that are in the earth.9Alſo I will ordeine a place for my people Iſrael,
and will plant them, and they ſhall dwell in their place, and ſhall be
moued no more: neither ſhal the children of wickedneſſe waſte them
any more (as at the beginning,10And ſince the time that I commanded
Iudges to bee ouer my people Iſrael.) Moreouer, I will ſubdue all thine
enemies. Furthermore I tel thee, that the Lord will build thee an
houſe.11And it ſhall come to paſſe, when thy dayes be expired, that thou
muſt go to be with thy fathers, that I will raiſe vp thy ſeed after thee,
which ſhall bee of thy ſonnes, and I wil ſtabliſh his kingdome.12He ſhall
build me an houſe, and I will ſtabliſh his throne for euer.13I will be his
father, and he ſhall be my ſonne, and I will not take my mercie away
from him, as I tooke it from him that was before thee.14But I will ſettle
him in mine houſe, and in my kingdom for euer, and his throne ſhall
bee eſtabliſhed for euermore.15According to all theſe words, and
according to all this viſion, ſo did Nathan ſpeake vnto Dauid.16And
Dauid the king came, and ſate before the Lord, and ſaid, Who am I, O
Lord God, and what is mine houſe, that thou haſt brought mee
hitherto?17And yet this was a ſmall thing in thine eyes, O God: for thou
haſt alſo ſpoken of thy ſeruants houſe, for a great while to come, and
haſt regarded mee according to the eſtate of a man of high degree, O

Lord God.18What can Dauid ſpeake more to thee for the honour of thy
ſeruant? for thou knoweſt thy ſeruant.19O Lord, for thy ſeruants ſake,
and according to thine owne heart, haſt thou done all this greatneſſe in
making knowen all theſe great things.20O Lord, there is none like thee
neither is there any God beſides thee, according to all that we haue heard
with our eares.21And what one nation in the earth is like thy people
Iſrael, whome God went to redeeme to be his owne people, to make
thee a name of greatneſſe and terribleneſſe, by driuing out nations from
before thy people whom thou haſt redeemed out of Egypt?22For thy
people Iſrael didſt thou make thine owne people for euer, and thou,
Lord, becameſt their God.23Therefore now Lord, let the thing that thou
haſt ſpoken concerning thy ſeruant, and concerning his houſe, be
eſtabliſhed for euer, and doe as thou haſt ſaid.24Let it euen bee
eſtabliſhed, that thy name may bee magnified for euer, ſaying, The Lord
of hoſts is the God of Iſrael, euen a God to Iſrael: and let the houſe of
Dauid thy ſeruant be eſtabliſhed before thee.25For thou, O my God,
haſt tolde thy ſeruant that thou wilt build him an houſe: therefore thy
ſeruant hath found in his heart to pray before thee.26And now, Lord
(thou art God, and haſt promiſed this goodneſſe vnto thy
ſeruant.)27Now therefore let it pleaſe thee to bleſſe the houſe of thy
ſeruant, that it may bee before thee for euer: for thou bleſſeſt, O Lord,
and it ſhalbe bleſſed for euer.
CHAPTER 181Now after this, it came to paſſe, that Dauid ſmote the
Philiſtines & ſubdued them, and tooke Gath, and her townes out of the
hand of the Philiſtines.2And he ſmote Moab, and the Moabites became
Dauids ſeruants, and brought gifts.3And Dauid ſmote Hadarezer king
of Zobah vnto Hamath, as hee went to ſtabliſh his dominion by the
riuer Euphrates.4And Dauid tooke from him a thouſand charets, and
ſeuen thouſand horſemen, and twentie thouſand footmen: Dauid alſo
houghed all the charet horſes, but referuedof them an hundred
charets.5And when the Syrians of Damaſcus came to helpe Hadarezer
king of Zobah, Dauid ſlew of the Syrians two and twentie thouſand
men.6Then Dauid put gariſons in Syria Damaſcus, and the Syrians
became Dauids ſeruants, and brought giftes. Thus the Lord preſerued
Dauid, whitherſoeuer he went.7And Dauid tooke the ſhields of golde
that were on the ſeruants of Hadarezer, & brought them to
Ieruſalem.8Likewiſe from Tibhath, and from Chun, cities of Hadarezer,
broght Dauid very much braſſe, wherewith Solomon made the braſen
ſea, and the pillars, and the veſſels of braſſe.9Now when Tou king of
Hamath heard how Dauid had ſmitten all the hoſte of Hadarezer king
of Zobah:10Hee ſent Hadoram his ſonne to king Dauid, to enquire of
his welfare, and to congratulate him, becauſe hee had fought againſt
Hadarezer, and ſmitten him (for Hadarezer had warre with Tou) and
with him all manner of veſſels of golde and ſiluer, and braſſe.11Them
alſo king Dauid dedicated vnto the Lord, with the ſiluer and the golde
that he brought from all theſe nations: from Edom, and from Moab,
and from the children of Ammon, and from the Philiſtines, and from
Amalek.12Moreouer, Abiſhai the ſonne of Zeruiah, ſlew of the Edomites
in the valley of ſalt, eighteene thouſand.13And he put gariſons in Edom,
and all the Edomites became Dauids ſeruants. Thus the Lord preſerued
Dauid whitherſoeuer he went.14So Dauid reigned ouer all Iſrael, and
executed iudgement and iuſtice among all his people.15And Ioab the
ſonne of Zeruiah was ouer the hoſte, and Iehoſhaphat the ſonne of
Ahilud, Recorder.16And Zadok the ſonne of Ahitub, and Abimelech the
ſonne of Abiathar, were the Prieſts, and Shauſha was Scribe.17And
Benaiah the ſonne of Iehoiada was ouer the Cherethites, and the
Pelethites: and the ſonnes of Dauid were chiefe about the king.
CHAPTER 191Now it came to paſſe after this, that Nahaſh the King
of the children of Ammon dyed, & his ſonne reigned in his ſtead.2And
Dauid ſayde, I will ſhewe kindneſſe vnto Hanun the ſonne of Nahaſh,
becauſe his father ſhewed kindneſſe to mee. And Dauid ſent meſſengers
to comfort him concerning his father. So the ſeruants of Dauid came
into the land of the children of Ammon, to Hanun, to comfort him.3But
the Princes of the children of Ammon ſayde to Hanun, Thinkeſt thou
that Dauid doeth honour thy father, that he hath ſent comforters vnto
thee? Are not his ſeruants come vnto thee for to ſearch, and to
ouerthrow, and to ſpie out the land?4Wherefore Hanun tooke Dauids
ſeruants, and ſhaued them, and cut off their garments in the middeſt,
hard by their buttockes, and ſent them away.5Then there went certeine,
and told Dauid, how the men were ſerued, and hee ſent to meet them
(for the men were greatly aſhamed) and the King ſayde, Tary at Iericho
vntill your beards be growen, and then returne.6And when the children
of Ammon ſawe, that they had made themſelues odious to Dauid;
Hanun and the children of Ammon ſent a thouſand talents of ſiluer, to
hire them charets and horſemen out of Meſopotamia, and out of Syria-
Maachah, and out of Zobah.7So they hired thirtie and two thouſand
charets, and the king of Maachah and his people, who came and pitched
before Medeba. And the children of Ammon gathered themſelues
together from their cities, and came to battaile.8And when Dauid heard
of it, hee ſent Ioab, and all the hoſt of the mightie men.9And the children
of Ammon came out, and put the battell in aray before the gate of the
citie, and the kings that were come, were by themſelues in the
field.10Now when Ioab ſaw that the battell was ſet againſt him, before
and behinde: hee choſe out of all the choice of Iſrael, and put them in
aray againſt the Syrians.11And the reſt of the people hee deliuered vnto
the hand of Abiſhai his brother, and they ſet themſelues in aray againſt
the children of Ammon.12And he ſaid, If the Syrians bee too ſtrong for
me, then thou ſhalt helpe me: but if the children of Ammon be too
ſtrong for thee, then I wil helpe thee.13Be of good courage, and let vs
behaue our ſelues valiantly for our people, and for the Cities of our God:
and let the Lord do that which is good in his ſight.14So Ioab and the
people that were with him, drew nigh before the Syrians, vnto the battell;
and they fled before him.15And when the children of Ammon ſaw that
the Syrians were fled, they likewiſe fled before Abiſhai his brother, and
entred into the city. Then Ioab came to Ieruſalem.16And when the
Syrians ſaw that they were put to the worſe before Iſrael, they ſent
meſſengers, and drew forth the Syrians, that were beyond the Riuer: and
Shophach the captaine of the hoſte of Hadarezer, went before
them.17And it was tolde Dauid, and hee gathered all Iſrael, and paſſed
ouer Iordane, and came vpon them, and ſet the battell in aray againſt
them: ſo when Dauid had put the battell in aray againſt the Syrians, they
fought with him.18But the Syrians fled before Iſrael, and Dauid ſlew of
the Syrians ſeuen thouſand men, which fought in charets, and fourty
thouſand footmen, and killed Shophach the captaine of the hoſte.19And
when the ſeruants of Hadarezer ſaw that they were put to the worſe
before Iſrael, they made peace with Dauid, and became his ſeruants:
neither would the Syrians helpe the children of Ammon any more.
CHAPTER 201And it came to paſſe, that after the yeere was expired,
at the time that kings goe out to battell, Ioab led forth the power of the
armie, and waſted the countrey of the children of Ammon, and came
and beſieged Rabbah (but Dauid taried at Ieruſalem,) and Ioab ſmote
Rabbah, and deſtroyed it.2And Dauid tooke the crowne of their king
from off his head, and found it to weigh a talent of gold, and there were
precious ſtones in it, and it was ſet vpon Dauids head; and hee brought
alſo exceeding much ſpoile out of the city.3And hee brought out the
people that were in it, and cut them with ſawes, and with harrowes of
yron, and with axes: euen ſo dealt Dauid with all the cities of the children
of Ammon. And Dauid and all the people returned to Ieruſalem.4And
it came to paſſe after this, that there aroſe warre at Gezer with the
Philiſtines, at which time Sibbechai the Huſhathite, ſlew Sippai, that was
of the children of the giant: and they were ſubdued.5And there was
warre againe with the Philiſtines, and Elhanan the ſonne of Iair, ſlew
Lahmi the brother of Goliath the Gittite, whoſe ſpeareſtaffe was like a
weauers beame.6And yet againe there was warre at Gath, where was a
man of great ſtature, whoſe fingers and toes were foure and twentie, ſixe
on each hand, and ſixe on each foot. And he alſo was the ſonne of the
giant.7But when he defied Iſrael, Ionathan the ſonne of Shimea Dauids
brother, ſlew him.8Theſe were borne vnto the Giant in Gath, and they
fell by the hand of Dauid, and by the hand of his ſeruants.
CHAPTER 211And Satan ſtoode vp againſt Iſrael, and prouoked Dauid
to number Iſrael.2And Dauid ſaide to Ioab, and to the rulers of the
people, Goe, number Iſrael from Beer-ſheba eueu to Dan: and bring the
number of them to me, that I may know it.3And Ioab anſwered, The
Lord make his people an hundred times ſo many moe as they bee: but,
my lord the king, are they not al my lords ſeruants? why then doeth my
lord require this thing? why will hee bee a cauſe of treſpaſſe to
Iſrael?4Neuertheleſſe, the kings word preuailed againſt Ioab: wherefore
Ioab departed, and went throughout all Iſrael, and came to
Ieruſalem.5And Ioab gaue the ſumme of the number of the people vnto
Dauid: and all they of Iſrael were a thouſand thouſand, and an hundred

thouſand men that drew ſword: and Iudah was foure hundred threeſcore and ten thouſand men, that drew ſword.6But Leui and Beniamin counted hee not among them: for the kings word was abominable to Ioab.7And God was diſpleaſed with this thing, therefore he ſmote Iſrael.8And Dauid ſaide vnto God, I haue ſinned greatly, becauſe I haue done this thing: but now, I beſeech thee, doe away the iniquitie of thy ſeruant, for I haue done very fooliſhly.9And the Lord ſpake vnto Gad, Dauids Seer, ſaying,10Goe and tell Dauid, ſaying, Thus ſaith the Lord, I offer thee three things, chooſe thee one of them, that I may doe it vnto thee.11So Gad came to Dauid, and ſaid vnto him, Thus ſaith the Lord, Chooſe thee12Either three yeeres famine, or three moneths to bee deſtroyed before thy foes (while that the ſword of thine enemies ouertaketh thee) or elſe three dayes the ſword of the Lord, euen the peſtilence in the land, and the Angel of the Lord deſtroying throughout all the coaſts of Iſrael. Now therefore aduiſe thy ſelfe, what word I ſhall bring againe to him that ſent me.13And Dauid ſaid vnto Gad, I am in a great ſtrait. Let mee fall now into the hand of the Lord (for very great are his mercies,) but let me not fall into the hand of man.14So the Lord ſent peſtilence vpon Iſrael: and there fell of Iſrael, ſeuentie thouſand men.15And God ſent an Angel vnto Ieruſalem to deſtroy it: and as he was deſtroying, the Lord beheld, and he repented him of the euill, and ſaid to the Angel that deſtroyed, It is ynough, ſtay now thine hand. And the Angel of the Lord ſtood by the threſhing floore of Ornan the Iebuſite.16And Dauid lift vp his eyes, and ſaw the Angel of the Lord ſtand betweene the earth and the heauen, hauing a drawen ſword in his hand ſtretched out ouer Ieruſalem. Then Dauid and the Elders of Iſrael, who were clothed in ſackecloth, fell vpon their faces.17And Dauid ſaid vnto God, Is it not I that commanded the people to be numbred? euen I it is that haue ſinned, and done euill indeed, but as for theſe ſheepe, what haue they done? Let thine hand, I pray thee, O Lord my God, be on me, and on my fathers houſe, but not on thy people, that they ſhould bee plagued.18Then the Angel of the Lord commanded Gad to ſay to Dauid, that Dauid ſhould goe vp and ſet vp an Altar vnto the Lord, in the threſhing floore of Ornan the Iebuſite.19And Dauid went vp at the ſaying of Gad, which he ſpake in the Name of the Lord.20And Ornan turned backe and ſaw the Angel, and his foure ſonnes with him, hid themſelues. Now Ornan was threſhing wheat.21And as Dauid came to Ornan, Ornan looked and ſaw Dauid, and went out of the threſhing floore, and bowed himſelfe to Dauid with his face to the ground.22Then Dauid ſaide to Ornan, Grant mee the place of this threſhing floore, that I may build an Altar therein vnto the Lord: thou ſhalt grant it mee for the full price, that the plague may be ſtayed from the people.23And Ornan ſaide vnto Dauid, Take it to thee, and let my lord the king do that which is good in his eyes. Loe, I giue thee the oxen alſo for burnt offerings, and the threſhing inſtruments for wood, and the wheat for the meate offering, I giue it all.24And king Dauid ſaid to Ornan; Nay, but I wil verily buy it for the full price: for I will not take that which is thine for the Lord, nor offer burnt offerings without coſt.25So Dauid gaue to Ornan for the place, ſixe hundred ſhekels of gold by weight.26And Dauid built there an Altar vnto the Lord, and offered burnt offerings, and peace offerings, and called vpon the Lord, and hee anſwered him from heauen by fire vpon the Altar of burnt offering.27And the Lord commaunded the Angel, and hee put vp his ſword againe into the ſheath thereof.28At that time, when Dauid ſaw that the Lord had anſwered him in the threſhing floore of Ornan the Iebuſite, then he ſacrificed there.29For the tabernacle of the Lord which Moſes made in the wilderneſſe, and the Altar of the burnt offering were at that ſeaſon, in the high place at Gibeon:30But Dauid could not goe before it to euquire of God; for he was afraid, becauſe of the ſword of the Angel of the Lord.

CHAPTER 221Then Dauid ſaid, This is the houſe of the Lord God, and this is the Altar of the burnt offering for Iſrael.2And Dauid commanded to gather together the ſtrangers that were in the land of Iſrael: and hee ſet maſons to hew wrought ſtones to build the houſe of God.3And Dauid prepared yron in abundance for the nailes for the doores of the gates, and for the ioynings, and braſſe in abundance without weight;4Alſo Cedar trees in abundance: for the Zidonians, and they of Tyre, brought much Cedar wood to Dauid.5And Dauid ſaid, Solomon my ſonne is yong and tender, and the houſe that is to be builded for the Lord, muſt be exceeding magnificall, of fame and of glory throughout all countreys: I will therefore now make preparation for it. So Dauid prepared abundantly before his death.6Then hee called for Solomon his ſonne, and charged him to build an houſe for the Lord God of Iſrael.7And Dauid ſaide to Solomon; My ſonne, as for me, it was in my mind to build an houſe vnto the Name of the Lord my God.8But the word of the Lord came to mee, ſaying, Thou haſt ſhed blood abundantly, and haſt made great warres: thou ſhalt not build an houſe vnto my Name, becauſe thou haſt ſhed much blood vpon the earth in my ſight.9Behold, a ſonne ſhall bee borne to thee, who ſhall bee a man of reſt, and I will giue him reſt from all his enemies round about: for his name ſhalbe Solomon, and I wil giue peace and quietneſſe vnto Iſrael in his dayes.10Hee ſhall build an houſe for my Name, and he ſhal be my ſonne, and I will be his father, and I will eſtabliſh the throne of his kingdome ouer Iſrael for euer.11Now my ſonne, The Lord be with thee, and proſper thou, and build the houſe of the Lord thy God, as he hath ſaid of thee.12Onely the Lord giue thee wiſedome and vnderſtanding, and giue thee charge concerning Iſrael, that thou mayeſt keepe the Law of the Lord thy God.13Then ſhalt thou proſper, if thou takeſt heed to fulfill the Statutes and Iudgements which the Lord charged Moſes with, concerning Iſrael: be ſtrong, and of good courage, dread not, nor be diſmayed.14Now beholde, in my trouble I haue prepared for the houſe of the Lord an hundred thouſand talents of gold, and a thouſand thouſand talents of ſiluer, and of braſſe and yron without weight: (for it is in abundance) timber alſo and ſtone haue I prepared, and thou mayeſt adde thereto.15Moreouer, there are workmen with thee in abundance, hewers, and workers of ſtone and timber, and all maner of cunning men for euery maner of worke:16Of the gold, the ſiluer, and the braſſe, and the yron, there is no number. Ariſe therefore, and be doing, and the Lord be with thee.17Dauid alſo commanded all the Princes of Iſrael to helpe Solomon his ſonne, ſaying,18Is not the Lord your God with you? and hath he not giuen you reſt on euery ſide? for he hath giuen the inhabitants of the land into mine hand, and the land is ſubdued before the Lord, and before his people.19Now ſet your heart and your ſoule to ſeeke the Lord your God: Ariſe therfore, and build ye the Sanctuary of the Lord God, to bring the Arke of the Couenant of the Lord, & the holy veſſels of God, into the houſe that is to be built to the Name of the Lord.

CHAPTER 231So when Dauid was old and full of dayes, he made Solomon his ſonne king ouer Iſrael.2And he gathered together all the Princes of Iſrael, with the Prieſts and the Leuites.3Now the Leuites were numbred from the age of thirtie yeeres and vpward: and their number, by their polles, man by man, was thirtie and eight thouſand.4Of which, twentie and foure thouſand were to ſet forward the work of the houſe of the Lord: and ſixe thouſand were Officers and Iudges.5Moreouer, foure thouſand were porters, and foure thouſand praiſed the Lord with the inſtruments which I made (ſaid Dauid) to praiſe therewith.6And Dauid diuided them into courſes among the ſonnes of Leui, namely Gerſhon, Kohath, and Merari.7Of the Gerſhonites were Laadan, and Shimei.8The ſonnes of Laadan, the chiefe was Iehiel, and Zetham, and Ioel, three.9The ſonnes of Shimei: Shelomith, and Haziel, and Haran, three. Theſe were the chiefe of the fathers of Laadan.10And the ſonnes of Shimei were: Iahath, Zina, and Ieuſh, and Beriah. Theſe foure were the ſonnes of Shimei.11And Iahath was the chiefe, and Ziza the ſecond: but Ieuſh and Beriah had not many ſonnes: therefore they were in one reckoning, according to their fathers houſe.12The ſonnes of Kohath: Amram, Izhar, Hebron, and Uzziel, foure.13The ſonnes of Amram: Aaron and Moſes: and Aaron was ſeparated, that he ſhould ſanctifie the moſt holy things, he and his ſonnes for euer, to burne incenſe before the Lord, to miniſter vnto him, and to bleſſe in his Name for euer.14Now concerning Moſes the man of God, his ſonnes were named of the tribe of Leui.15The ſonnes of Moſes were: Gerſhom and Eliezer.16Of the ſonnes of Gerſhom Shebuel was the chiefe.17And the ſonnes of Eliezer were: Rehabiah the chiefe. And Eliezer had none other ſonnes: but the ſonnes of Rehabiah were very many.18Of the ſonnes of Izhar, Shelomith the chiefe.19Of the ſonnes of Hebron, Ieriah the firſt, Amariah the ſecond, Iahaziel the third, and Iekamiam the fourth.20Of the ſonnes of Uzziel: Michah the firſt, and Ieſiah the ſecond.21The ſonnes of Merari: Mahli and Muſhi. The ſonnes of Mahli: Eleazar and Kiſh.22And Eleazar died, and had no ſonnes but daughters: and their brethren the ſonnes of Kiſh tooke them.23The ſonnes of Muſhi: Mahli, and Eder, and Ierimoth, three.24Theſe were the ſonnes of Leui after the houſe of their fathers, euen the chiefe of the fathers, as they were counted by number of names by their polles, that did the worke for the ſeruice of the houſe of the Lord, from the age of twentie yeeres and vpward.25For Dauid ſayd, The Lord God of Iſrael hath giuen reſt vnto his people, that they may dwell in Ieruſalem for euer.26And alſo vnto the Leuites: they ſhall no more cary the Tabernacle, nor any veſſels of it for the ſeruice thereof.27For by the laſt words of Dauid, the Leuites were numbred from twentie yeeres olde, and aboue:28Becauſe their office was to wait on the ſonnes of Aaron, for the ſeruice of the houſe of the Lord, in the courts, and in the chambers, and in the purifying of all holy things, and the worke of the ſeruice of the houſe of God:29Both for the ſhew-bread, and for the fine floure for meat offering, and for the vnleauened cakes, and for that which is baked in the panne, and for that which is fried, and for all maner of meaſures and ſize:30And to ſtand euery morning to thanke and praiſe the Lord, and likewiſe at Euen:31And to offer all burnt ſacrifices vnto the Lord in the Sabbaths, in the new moones, and on the ſet feaſts, by number, according to the order commanded vnto them continually before the Lord:32And that they ſhould keepe the charge of the Tabernacle of the Congregation, and the charge of the holy place, and the charge of the ſonnes of Aaron their brethren, in the ſeruice of the houſe of the Lord.

CHAPTER 241Now theſe are the diuiſions of the ſonnes of Aaron. The ſonnes of Aaron: Nadab and Abihu, Eleazar and Ithamar.2But Nadab and Abihu died before their father, and had no children: Therefore Eleazar and Ithamar executed the Prieſts office.3And Dauid diſtributed them, both Zadok of the ſonnes of Eleazar, and Ahimelech of the ſonnes of Ithamar, according to their offices in their ſeruice.4And there were moe chiefe men found of the ſonnes of Eleazar, then of the ſonnes of Ithamar: and thus were they diuided. Among the ſonnes of Eleazar there were ſixteene chiefe men of the houſe of their fathers, and eight among the ſonnes of Ithamar according to the houſe of their fathers.5Thus were they diuided by lot, one ſort with another; for the gouernours of the Sanctuarie, and gouernours of the houſe of God, were of the ſonnes of Eleazar, and of the ſonnes of Ithamar.6And Shemaiah the ſonne of Nathanael the Scribe, one of the Leuites, wrote them before the King and the Princes, and Zadok the Prieſt, and Ahimelech the ſonne of Abiathar, and before the chiefe of the fathers of the prieſts and Leuites: one principall houſhold being taken for Eleazar, and one taken for Ithamar.7Now the firſt lot came foorth to Iehoiarib: the ſecond to Iedaiah,8The third to Harim, the fourth to Seorim,9The fifth to Malchiiah, the ſixth to Miiamin,10The ſeuenth to Hakkoz, the eight to Abiiah,11The ninth to Ieſhua, the tenth to Shecaniah,12The eleuenth to Eliaſhib, the twelfth to Iakim,13The thirteenth to Huppah, the fourteenth to Ieſhebeab,14The fifteenth to Bilgah, the ſixteenth to Immer,15The ſeuenteenth to Hezir, the eighteenth to Aphſes,16The ninteenth to Pethahiah, the twentieth to Iehezekel,17The one and twentieth to Iachin, the two and twentieth to Gamul,18The three and twentieth to Delaiah, the foure and twentieth to Maaziah.19Theſe were the orderings of them in their ſeruice to come into the houſe of the Lord according to their maner, vnder Aaron their father, as the Lord God of Iſrael had commanded him.20And the reſt of the ſonnes of Leui were theſe: of the ſons of Amram, Shubael: of the ſonnes of Shubael, Iedeiah.21Concerning Rehabiah, of the ſons of Rehabiah, the firſt was Iſshiah.22Of the Izharites, Shelomoth: of the ſonnes of Shelomoth, Iahath.23And the ſonnes of Hebron, Ieriah the firſt, Amariah the ſecond, Iahaziel the third, Iekameam the fourth.24Of the ſonnes of Uzziel, Michah: of the ſonnes of Michah, Shamir.25The brother of Michah was Iſshiah: of the ſonnes of Iſshiah, Zechariah.26The ſonnes of Merari were Mahli and Muſhi: the ſonnes of Iaaziah, Beno.27The ſonnes of Merari by Iaaziah, Beno, and Shoham, and Zaccur, and Ibri.28Of Mahli came Eleazar, who had no ſonnes.29Concerning Kiſh: the ſonne of Kiſh was Ierahmeel.30The ſonnes alſo of Muſhi, Mahli, and Eder, and Ierimoth. Theſe were the ſonnes of the Leuites after the houſe of their fathers.31Theſe likewiſe caſt lots ouer againſt their brethren the ſonnes of Aaron, in the preſence of Dauid the King, and Zadok and Ahimelech, and the chiefe of the fathers of the prieſts and Leuites, euen the principall fathers ouer againſt their yonger brethren.

CHAPTER 251Moreouer Dauid and the captaines of the hoſte ſeparated to the ſeruice of the ſonnes of Aſaph, and of Heman, and of Ieduthun, who ſhould propheſie with harps, with pſalteries, and with cymbals: and the number of the workmen, according to their ſeruice, was:2Of the ſonnes of Aſaph: Zaccur, and Ioſeph, and Nethaniah, and Aſarelah, the ſonnes of Aſaph vnder the hands of Aſaph, which propheſied according to the order of the king.3Of Ieduthun: the ſonnes of Ieduthun, Gedaliah, and Zeri, and Ieſhaiah, Haſhabiah, and Mattithiah, ſixe, vnder the handes of their father Ieduthun, who propheſied with a harpe, to giue thankes and to praiſe the Lord.4Of Heman: the ſonnes of Heman, Bukkiah, Mattaniah, Uzziel, Shebuel, and Ierimoth, Hananiah, Hanani, Eliatha, Giddalti, and Romamti-Ezer, Ioſhbekaſhah, Mallothi, Hothir, and Mahazioth:5All theſe were the ſonnes of Heman the kings Seer in the wordes of God, to lift vp the horne. And God gaue to Heman fourteene ſonnes and three daughters.6All theſe were vnder the hands of their father, for ſong in the houſe of the Lord with cymbals, pſalteries and harpes, for the ſeruice of the houſe of God, according to the kings order, to Aſaph, Ieduthun, and Heman.7So the number of them, with their brethren that were inſtructed in the ſongs of the Lord, euen all that were cunning, was two hundred, foure ſcore and eight.8And they caſt lots ward againſt ward, as well the ſmall as the great, the teacher as the ſcholler.9Now the firſt lot came foorth for Aſaph to Ioſeph, the ſecond to Gedaliah, who with his brethren and ſonnes were twelue:10The third to Zaccur, he, his ſons, and his brethren were twelue:11The fourth to Izri, he, his ſonnes and his brethren were twelue:12The fift to Nethaniah, hee, his ſonnes and his brethren were twelue:13The ſixt to Bukkiah, he, his ſons and his brethren were twelue.14The ſeuenth to Ieſharelah, hee, his ſonnes & his brethren were twelue:15The eight to Ieſhaiah, hee, his ſonnes and his brethren, were twelue:16The ninth to Mattaniah, he, his ſonnes and his brethren were twelue:17The tenth to Shimei, he, his ſons and his brethren were twelue:18The eleuenth to Azareel, hee, his ſonnes and his brethren were twelue:19The twelfth to Haſhabiah, he, his ſonnes and his brethren, were twelue:20The thirteenth to Shubael, hee, his ſonnes and his brethren were twelue:21The fourteenth to Mattithiah, hee, his ſonnes and his brethren, were twelue.22The fifteenth to Ierimoth, hee, his ſonnes & his brethren, were twelue:23The ſixteenth to Hananiah, hee, his ſonnes & his brethren, were twelue:24The ſeuenteenth to Ioſhbekaſhah, he, his ſonnes and his brethren, were twelue:25The eighteenth to Hanani: hee, his ſonnes & his brethren, were twelue:26The nineteenth to Mallothi, hee, his ſonnes & his brethren, were twelue:27The twentieth to Eliathah, hee, his ſonnes & his brethren, were twelue:28The one and twentieth to Hothir, he, his ſonnes and his brethren were twelue.29The two and twentieth to Giddalti, hee, his ſonnes and his brethren, were twelue.30The three and twentieth to Mahazioth, he, his ſonnes and his brethren, were twelue.31The foure and twentieth to Romamti-Ezer, he, his ſonnes and his brethren, were twelue.

CHAPTER 261Concerning the diuiſions of the porters: of the Korhites was Meſhelemiah the ſonne of Kore, of the ſonnes of Aſaph.2And the ſonnes of Meſhelemiah were Zechariah the firſt borne, Iediael the ſecond, Zebadiah the third, Iathniel the fourth,3Elam the fifth, Iehohanan the ſixth, Elioenai the ſeuenth.4Moreouer the ſonnes of Obed-Edom were Shemaiah the firſt borne, Iehozabad the ſecond, Ioah the thirde, and Sacar the fourth, and Nethaneel the fifth.5Ammiel the ſixth, Iſſachar the ſeuenth, Peulthai the eighth: for God bleſſed him.6Alſo vnto Shemaiah his ſonne were ſonnes borne, that ruled throughout the houſe of their father: for they were mighty men of valour.7The ſonnes of Shemaiah: Othni, and Rephael, and Obed, Elzabad, whoſe brethren were ſtrong men; Elihu, and Semachiah.8All theſe of the ſonnes of Obed-Edom: they and their ſonnes and their brethren, able men for ſtrength for the ſeruice, were threeſcore and two of Obed-Edom.9And Meſhelemiah had ſonnes and brethren, ſtrong men, eighteene.10Alſo Hoſah of the children of Merari, had ſonnes: Simri the chiefe, (for though he was not the firſt borne, yet his father made him the chiefe)11Hilkiah the ſecond, Tebaliah the thirde, Zechariah the fourth: all the ſonnes and brethren of Hoſah, were thirteene.12Among theſe were the diuiſions of the porters, euen among the chiefe men, hauing wards one againſt another, to miniſter in the houſe of the Lord.13And they caſt lots as well the ſmall as the great, according to the houſe of their fathers for euery gate.14And the lot Eaſtward fel to Shelemiah; then for Zechariah his ſonne (a wiſe

counſeller:) they caſt lots, and his lot came out Northward.[15]To Obed-
Edom Southward, and to his ſonnes, the houſe of Aſuppim.[16]To
Shuppim and Hoſa, the lot came foorth Weſtward with the gate
Shallecheth, by the cauſey of the going vp, ward againſt ward.[17]Eaſtward
were ſixe Leuites, Northward foure a day, Southward foure a day, and
toward Aſuppim two and two.[18]And Parbar Weſtward, foure at the
cauſey, and two at Parbar.[19]Theſe are the diuiſions of the porters among
the ſonnes of Kore, and among the ſonnes of Merari.[20]And of the
Leuites, Ahiiah was ouer the treaſures of the houſe of God, and ouer
the treaſures of the dedicate things.[21]As concerning the ſonnes of
Laadan: the ſonnes of the Gerſhonite Laadan, hiefe fathers; euen of
Laadan the Gerſhonite, were Iehieli.[22]The ſonnes of Iehieli, Zetham and
Ioel his brother, which were ouer the treaſures of the houſe of the
Lord.[23]Of the Amramites, and the Izharites, the Hebronites, and the
Uzzielites:[24]And Shebuel the ſonne of Gerſhom, the ſonne of Moſes,
was ruler of the treaſures.[25]And his brethren by Eliezer: Rehabiah his
ſonne, and Ieſhaiah his ſonne, and Ioram his ſonne, and Zichri his
ſonne, & Shelomith his ſonne.[26]Which Shelomith and his brethren,
were ouer all the treaſures of the dedicate things, which Dauid the king
and the chiefe fathers, the captaines ouer thouſands and hundreds, and
the captaines of the hoſte had dedicated.[27]Out of the ſpoyles wonne in
battels, did they dedicate to maintaine the houſe of the Lord.[28]And all
that Samuel the Seer, and Saul the ſonne of Kiſh, and Abner the ſonne
of Ner, and Ioab the ſonne of Zeruiah had dedicated, and whoſoeuer
had dedicated any thing, it was vnder the hand of Shelomith and of his
brethren.[29]Of the Izharites, Chenaniah and his ſonnes, were for the
outward buſines ouer Iſrael, for officers and Iudges.[30]And of the
Hebronits, Haſhabiah and his brethren, men of valour, a thouſand and
ſeuen hundred, were officers among them of Iſrael on this ſide Iorden
Weſtward, in all buſines of the Lord, and in the ſeruice of the
king.[31]Among the Hebronites was Ieriiah the chiefe, euen among the
Hebronits, according to the generations of his fathers: in the fourtieth
yeere of the reigne of Dauid, they were ſought for, and there were found
among them mightie men of valour, at Iazer of Gilead.[32]And his
brethren, men of valour, were two thouſand and ſeuen hundred chiefe
fathers, whom King Dauid made rulers ouer the Reubenites, the
Gadites, & the halfe tribe of Manaſſeh, for euery matter perteining to
God, and affaires of the king.

CHAPTER 27[1]Nowe the children of Iſrael after their number, to wit,
the chiefe fathers and captaines of thouſands and hundreds, and their
officers that ſerued the king in any matter of the courſes, which came
in, and went out moneth by moneth, throughout all the moneths of the
yeare, of euery courſe were twentie and foure thouſand.[2]Ouer the firſt
courſe for the firſt moneth was Iaſhobeam the ſonne of Zabdiel, and in
his courſe were twentie and foure thouſand.[3]Of the children of Perez,
was the chiefe of all the captaines of the hoſt, for the firſt moneth.[4]And
ouer the courſe of the ſecond moneth was Dodai an Ahohite, and of his
courſe was Mikloth alſo the ruler: In his courſe likewiſe were twentie
and foure thouſand.[5]The third captaine of the hoſt for the third month
was Benaiah the ſonne of Iehoiada a chiefe prieſt, and in his courſe were
twenty and foure thouſand.[6]This is that Benaiah, who was mightie
among the thirtie, and aboue the thirty: and in his courſe was Amizabad
his ſonne.[7]The fourth captaine for the fourth moneth was Aſahel the
brother of Ioab, and Zebadiah his ſonne after him: and in his courſe
were twentie and foure thouſand.[8]The fifth captaine for the fifth
moneth, was Shamhuth the Izrahite: and in his courſe were twentie and
foure thouſand.[9]The ſixt captaine for the ſixt moneth, was Ira the ſon
of Ikkeſh the Tekoite: and in his courſe were twentie and foure
thouſand.[10]The ſeuenth captaine for the ſeuenth moneth was Helez the
Pelonite, of the children of Ephraim: and in his courſe were twentie and
foure thouſand.[11]The eighth captaine for the eighth moneth, was
Sibbecai the Huſhathite, of the Zarhites: and in his courſe were twentie
and foure thouſand.[12]The ninth captaine for the ninth moneth, was
Abiezer the Anetothite, of the Beniamites: and in his courſe were
twentie and foure thouſand.[13]The tenth captaine for the tenth moneth,
was Maharai the Netophathite, of the Zarhites: and in his courſe were
twentie and foure thouſand.[14]The eleuenth captaine for the eleuenth
moneth was Benaiah the Pirathonite, of the children of Ephraim: and in
his courſe were twenty and foure thouſand.[15]The twelfth captaine for
the twelfth moneth, was Heldai the Netophathite, of Othniel: and in his
courſe were twentie and foure thouſand.[16]Furthermore, ouer the tribes
of Iſrael: The Ruler of the Reubenites was Eliezer the ſonne of Zichri:
of the Simeonites, Shephatiah the ſonne of Maachah.[17]Of the Leuites:
Haſhabiah the ſonne of Kemuel; of the Aaronites, Zadok.[18]Of Iudah,
Elihu, one of the brethren of Dauid: of Iſſachar, Omri the ſonne of
Michael.[19]Of Zebulun, Iſhmaiah the ſon of Obadiah: of Naphtali,
Ierimoth the ſonne of Azriel.[20]Of the children of Ephraim, Hoſhea the
ſonne of Azazziah: of the halfe tribe of Manaſſeh, Ioel the ſonne of
Pedaiah.[21]Of the halfe tribe of Manaſſeh in Gilead, Iddo the ſonne of
Zechariah: of Beniamin, Iaaſiel the ſon of Abner.[22]Of Dan, Azariel the
ſonne of Ieroham. Theſe were the princes of the tribes of Iſrael.[23]But
Dauid tooke not the number of them from twentie yeeres olde and
vnder: becauſe the Lord had ſaid, hee would increaſe Iſrael like to the
ſtarres of the heauens.[24]Ioab the ſonne of Zeruiah began to number,
but he finiſhed not, becauſe there fell wrath for it againſt Iſrael, neither
was the number put in the account of the Chronicles of King
Dauid.[25]And ouer the Kings treaſures, was Azmaueth the ſonne of
Adiel: and ouer the ſtore-houſes in the fields, in the cities, and in the
villages, and in the caſtles, was Iehonathan the ſonne of Uzziah.[26]And
ouer them that did the worke of the field, for tillage of the ground, was
Ezri the ſonne of Chelub.[27]And ouer the Uineyards, was Shimei the
Ramathite: ouer the increaſe of the vineyards for the wine cellars, was
Sabdi the Ziphmite.[28]And ouer the Oliue trees, and the Sycomore trees
that were in the lowe plaines, was Baal-hanan the Gederite: and ouer the
cellars of oyle was Ioaſh.[29]And ouer the herdes that fed in Sharon, was
Shetrai the Sharonite: and ouer the herds that were in the valleys, was
Shaphat the ſonne of Adlai.[30]Ouer the camels alſo, was Obil the
Iſhmaelite: and ouer the Aſſes, was Iehdeiah the Meronothite.[31]And
ouer the flockes, was Iaziz the Hagerite. All theſe were the rulers of the
ſubſtance which was king Dauids.[32]Alſo Ionathan Dauids uncle, was a
counſeller, a wiſe man, and a Scribe: and Iehiel the ſonne of Hachmoni,
was with the kings ſonnes.[33]And Ahitophel was the kings counſeller, and
Huſhai the Archite, was the kings companion.[34]And after Ahitophel,
was Iehoiada the ſonne of Benaiah, and Abiathar: and the general of the
Kings armie was Ioab.

CHAPTER 28[1]And Dauid aſſembled all the Princes of Iſrael, the
Princes of the tribes, and the captains of the companies that miniſtred
to the king by courſe: and the captaines ouer the thouſands, and
captaines ouer the hundreds, and the ſtewards ouer all the ſubſtance and
poſſeſſion of the King, and of his ſonnes, with the officers, and with the
mightie men, and with all the valiant men, vnto Ieruſalem.[2]Then Dauid
the king ſtood vp vpon his feete, and ſaid, Heare me, my brethren, and
my people: As for me, I had in mine heart to builde an houſe of reſt for
the Arke of the Couenant of the Lord, and for the footeſtoole of our
God, & had made ready for the building.[3]But God ſaid vnto me, Thou
ſhalt not builde an houſe for my Name, becauſe thou haſt been a man
of warre, and haſt ſhed blood.[4]Howbeit, the Lord God of Iſrael choſe
me before all the houſe of my father, to be king ouer Iſrael for euer: for
he hath choſen Iudah to be the ruler; & of the houſe of Iudah, the houſe
of my father; and among the ſonnes of my father, he liked me to make
me king ouer all Iſrael:[5]And of all my ſonnes (for the Lord hath giuen
me many ſonneſ) hee hath choſen Solomon my ſonne, to ſit vpon the
throne of the kingdome of the Lord ouer Iſrael.[6]And he ſaid vnto me,
Solomon thy ſonne, hee ſhall build my houſe and my courts: for I haue
choſen him to be my ſonne, and I will be his father.[7]Moreouer, I will
eſtabliſh his kingdome for euer, if he be conſtant to do my
commandements and my iudgements, as at this day.[8]Now therefore in
the ſight of all Iſrael, the congregation of the Lord, and in the audience
of our God, keepe, and ſeeke for all the commandements of the Lord
your God, that ye may poſſeſſe this good land, and leaue it for an
inheritance for your children after you, for euer.[9]And thou, Solomon
my ſonne, know thou the God of thy father, and ſerue him with a perfite
heart, and with a willing minde: for the Lord ſearcheth all hearts, and
vnderſtandeth all the imaginations of the thoughts: if thou ſeeke him, he
will be found of thee, but if thou forſake him, he will caſt thee off for
euer.[10]Take heed now, for the Lord hath choſen thee to builde an houſe
for the Sanctuarie: be ſtrong, and doe it.[11]Then Dauid gaue to Solomon
his ſonne the paterne of the porch, and of the houſes thereof, and of
the treaſuries thereof, and of the vpper chambers thereof, and of the
inner parlours thereof, and of the place of the Mercie-ſeate.[12]And the

paterne of all that hee had by the ſpirit, of the courts of the houſe of the Lord, and of all the chambers round about, of the treaſuries of the houſe of God, and of the treaſuries of the dedicate things:13Alſo for the courſes of the Prieſts and the Leuites, & for all the worke of the ſeruice of the houſe of the Lord, and for all the veſſels of ſeruice in the houſe of the Lord.14Hee gaue of golde by weight, for things of golde, for all inſtruments of all manner of ſeruice: ſiluer alſo for all inſtruments of ſiluer, by weight, for all inſtruments of euery kinde of ſeruice:15Euen the weight for the Candleſtickes of golde, and for their lampes of golde, by weight for euery candleſticke, and for the lampes thereof: and for the Candleſtickes of ſiluer by weight, both for the Candleſticke and alſo for the lampes thereof, according to the vſe of euery candleſticke.16And by weight hee gaue golde for the tables of ſhew-bread, for euery table, and likewiſe ſiluer for the tables of ſiluer.17Alſo pure golde for the fleſhhookes, and the bowles, and the cups: and for the golden baſins hee gaue golde by weight, for euery baſin; and likewiſe ſiluer by weight, for euery baſin of ſiluer.18And for the Altar of incenſe, refined golde by weight; and gold for the paterne of the charet of the Cherubims, that ſpread out their wings, and couered the Arke of the Couenant of the Lord.19All this, ſayd Dauid, the Lord made mee underſtand in writing by his hand vpon mee, euen all the workes of this paterne.20And Dauid ſaid to Solomon his ſonne, Be ſtrong, and of good courage, and doe it: feare not, nor be diſmayed, for the Lord God, euen my God, will be with thee; he will not faile thee, nor forſake thee, vntill thou haſt finiſhed all the worke for the ſeruice of the houſe of the Lord.21And behold, the courſes of the Prieſts and the Leuites, euen they ſhall be with thee for all the ſeruice of the houſe of God, and there ſhall be with thee for all manner of workemanſhip, euery willing ſkilfull man, for any maner of ſeruice: alſo the Princes and all the people will bee wholly at thy commandement.

CHAPTER 291Furthermore, Dauid the King ſaid vnto all the congregation, Solomon my ſonne, whome alone God hath choſen, is yet young and tender, and the worke is great: for the palace is not for man, but for the Lord God.2Now I haue prepared with all my might for the houſe of my God, the gold for things to be made of gold, the ſiluer for things of ſiluer, and the braſſe for things of braſſe, the yron for things of yron, and wood for things of wood, onix ſtones, and ſtones to be ſet, gliſtering ſtones, and of diuers colours, and all maner of precious ſtones, and marble ſtones in abundance.3Moreouer, becauſe I haue ſet my affection to the houſe of my God, I haue of mine owne proper good, of gold and ſiluer, which I haue giuen to the houſe of my God, ouer & aboue all that I haue prepared for the holy houſe:4Euen three thouſand talents of gold, of the gold of Ophir, and ſeuen thouſand talents of refined ſiluer, to ouerlay the walles of the houſes withall.5The gold for things of golde, and the ſiluer for things of ſiluer, and for all maner of worke to be made by the hands of Artificers. And who then is willing to conſecrate his ſeruice this day vnto the Lord?6Then the chiefe of the fathers and Princes of the tribes of Iſrael, and the captaines of thouſands and of hundreds, with the rulers ouer the Kings worke, offered willingly,7And gaue for the ſeruice of the houſe of God, of gold fiue thouſand talents, and ten thouſand drammes: and of ſiluer, ten thouſand talents: and of braſſe, eighteene thouſand talents: and one hundred thouſand talents of yron.8And they with whom precious ſtones were found, gaue them to the treaſure of the houſe of the Lord, by the hand of Iehiel the Gerſhonite.9Then the people reioyced, for that they offred willingly, becauſe with perfect heart they offered willingly to the Lord: and Dauid the King alſo reioyced with great ioy.10Wherefore Dauid bleſſed the Lord before all the Congregation: and Dauid ſaide, Bleſſed bee thou, Lord God of Iſrael our father, for euer and euer.11Thine, O Lord, is the greatnes, and the power, and the glory, & the victorie, and the maieſtie: for all that is in the heauen & in the earth, is thine: thine is the kingdome, O Lord, and thou art exalted as head aboue all.12Both riches, and honour come of thee, and thou reigneſt ouer all, and in thine hand is power and might, and in thine hand it is to make great, and to giue ſtrength vnto all.13Now therefore, our God, wee thanke thee, and praiſe thy glorious Name.14But who am I, and what is my people, that we ſhould be able to offer ſo willingly after this ſort? for all things come of thee, and of thine owne haue we giuen thee.15For we are ſtrangers before thee, and ſoiourners, as were all our fathers: Our dayes on the earth are as a ſhadow, and there is none abiding.16O Lord our God, all this ſtore that we haue prepared to build thee an houſe for thine holy Name, commeth of thine hand, and is all thine owne.17I know alſo, my God, that thou trieſt the heart, and haſt pleaſure in vprightneſſe. As for me, in the vprightnes of mine heart I haue willingly offered all theſe things: and now haue I ſeene with ioy, thy people which are preſent here, to offer willingly vnto thee.18O Lord God of Abraham, Iſaac and of Iſrael our fathers, keepe this for euer in the imagination of the thoughts of the heart of thy people, and prepare their heart vnto thee:19And giue vnto Solomon my ſonne a perfect heart to keepe thy Commaundements, thy teſtimonies, and thy ſtatutes, and to doe all theſe things, and to build the pallace, for the which I haue made prouiſion.20And Dauid ſaid to all the Congregation: Nowe bleſſe the Lord your God. And all the Congregation bleſſed the Lord God of their fathers, and bowed downe their heads, and worſhipped the Lord, and the King.21And they ſacrificed ſacrifices vnto the Lord, & offered burnt offerings vnto the Lord on the morrow after that day, euen a thouſand bullockes, a thouſand rams, and a thouſand lambes, with their drinke offerings, and ſacrifices in abundance for all Iſrael:22And did eate and drinke before the Lord on that day with great gladneſſe, and they made Solomon the ſonne of Dauid King the ſecond time, and anointed him vnto the Lord to be the chiefe gouernour, and Zadok to be Prieſt.23Then Solomon ſate on the throne of the Lord, as king in ſtead of Dauid his father, and proſpered, and all Iſrael obeyed him.24And all the princes and the mightie men, and all the ſonnes likewiſe of king Dauid, ſubmitted themſelues vnto Solomon the King.25And the Lord magnified Solomon exceedingly in the ſight of all Iſrael, and beſtowed vpon him ſuch royal maieſtie, as had not bene on any king before him in Iſrael.26Thus Dauid the ſonne of Ieſſe, reigned ouer all Iſrael.27And the time that he reigned ouer Iſrael, was fourtie yeeres. Seuen yeeres reigned hee in Hebron, and thirtie and three yeeres reigned hee in Ieruſalem.28And he died in a good old age, full of dayes, riches and honour: and Solomon his ſonne reigned in his ſtead.29Now the acts of Dauid the King firſt and laſt, behold, they are written in the booke of Samuel the Seer, and in the booke of Nathan the Prophet, and in the booke of Gad the Seer,30With all his reigne and his might, and the times that went ouer him, and ouer Iſrael, and ouer all the kingdomes of the countreys.

2 CHRONICLES

CHAPTER 11And Solomon the ſonne of Dauid was ſtrengthned in his kingdome, and the Lord his God was with him, & magnified him exceedingly.2Then Solomon ſpake vnto all Iſrael, to the captaines of thouſands, and of hundreds, and to the Iudges, and to euery gouernour in all Iſrael, the chiefe of the fathers.3So Solomon and all the Congregation with him, went to the high place that was at Gibeon, for there was the Tabernacle of the Congregation of God, which Moſes the ſeruant of the Lord had made in the wilderneſſe.4But the Arke of God had Dauid brought vp from Kiriath-iearim, to the place which Dauid had prepared for it: for he had pitched a tent for it at Ieruſalem.5Moreouer the braſen Altar that Bezaleel the ſonne of Uri, the ſonne of Hur, had made, hee put before the Tabernacle of the Lord: and Solomon and the Congregation ſought vnto it.6And Solomon went vp thither to the braſen Altar before the Lord, which was at the Tabernacle of the Congregation, and offered a thouſand burnt offerings vpon it.7In that night did God appeare vnto Solomon, and ſaide vnto him; Aſke what I ſhall giue thee.8And Solomon ſaide vnto God, Thou haſt ſhewed great mercy vnto Dauid my father, and haſt made me to reigne in his ſtead:9Now, O Lord God, let thy promiſe vnto Dauid my father be eſtabliſhed: for thou haſt made mee King ouer a people, like the duſt of the earth in multitude.10Giue mee now wiſedome and knowledge, that I may goe out and come in before this people. For who can iudge this thy people, that is ſo great?11And God ſaid to Solomon, Becauſe this was in thine heart, and thou haſt not aſked riches, wealth, or honour, nor the life of thine enemies, neither yet haſt aſked long life; but haſt aſked wiſedome and knowledge for thy ſelfe, that thou mayeſt iudge my people, ouer whom I haue made thee King:12Wiſedome and knowledge is granted vnto thee, and I will giue thee riches, and wealth, and honour, ſuch as none of the kings haue had, that haue beene before thee, neither ſhall there any after thee haue the like.[13]Then Solomon came from his iourney to the high place that was at Gibeon, to Ieruſalem, from before the Tabernacle of the Congregation, and reigned ouer Iſrael.[14]And Solomon gathered charets and horſemen: and hee had a thouſand and foure hundred charets, and twelue thouſand horſemen, which he placed in the charet-cities, and with the King at Ieruſalem.[15]And the King made ſiluer and gold at Ieruſalem as plenteous as ſtones, and Cedar trees made hee as the Sycomore trees, that are in the vale for abundance.[16]And Solomon had horſes brought out of Egypt, and linen yarne: the Kings merchants receiued the linnen yarne at a price.[17]And they fetcht vp and brought foorth out of Egypt, a charet for ſixe hundred ſhekels of ſiluer, and an horſe for an hundred and fiftie: and ſo brought they out horſes for all the kings of the Hittites, and for the kings of Syria, by their meanes.

CHAPTER 2[1]And Solomon determined to build an houſe for the Name of the Lord, and an houſe for his kingdome.[2]And Solomon told out threeſcore and tenne thouſand men to beare burdens, and foureſcore thouſand to hewe in the mountaine, and three thouſand and ſixe hundred to ouerſee them.[3]And Solomon ſent to Huram the king of Tyre, ſaying, As thou diddeſt deale with Dauid my father, and diddeſt ſend him Cedars to builde him an houſe to dwell therein, euen ſo deale with me.[4]Behold, I build an houſe to the name of the Lord my God, to dedicate it to him, and to burne before him ſweet incenſe, and for the continuall ſhew-bread, and for the burnt offrings morning and euening, on the Sabbaths, and on the new Moones, and on the ſolemne feaſts of the Lord our God. This is an ordinance for euer to Iſrael.[5]And the houſe which I build, is great: for great is our God aboue all gods.[6]But who is able to build him an houſe, ſeeing the heauen, and heauen of heauens cannot conteine him? who am I then that I ſhould build him an houſe? ſaue onely to burne ſacrifice before him?[7]Send me now therefore a man, cunning to worke in gold and in ſiluer, and in braſſe, and in yron, and in purple and crimſon, and blew, and that can ſkil to graue, with the cunning men that are with me in Iudah, and in Ieruſalem, whome Dauid my father did prouide.[8]Send me alſo Cedar trees, firre trees, and Algume trees, out of Lebanon: (for I know that thy ſeruants can ſkill to cut timber in Lebanon) and behold, my ſeruants ſhalbe with thy ſeruants,[9]Euen to prepare me timber in abundance: for the houſe which I am about to build, ſhalbe wonderfull great.[10]And behold, I will giue to thy ſeruants the hewers that cut timber, twentie thouſand meaſures of beaten wheat, and twentie thouſand meaſures of barley, and twentie thouſand baths of wine, and twentie thouſand baths of oyle.[11]Then Huram the king of Tyre anſwered in writing, which hee ſent to Solomon: Becauſe the Lord hath loued his people, hee hath made thee King ouer them.[12]Huram ſaid moreouer, Bleſſed be the Lord God of Iſrael that made heauen and earth, who hath giuen to Dauid the King a wiſe ſonne, indued with prudence and vnderſtanding, that might build an houſe for the Lord, and an houſe for his kingdome.[13]And now I haue ſent a cunning man (indued with vnderſtanding) of Huram my fathers:[14]The ſonne of a woman of the daughters of Dan, and his father was a man of Tyre, ſkilfull to worke in golde and in ſiluer, in braſſe, in yron, in ſtone and in timber, in purple, in blew, and in fine linen, and in crimſon: alſo to graue any maner of grauing, and to find out euery deuice which ſhall be put to him, with thy cunning men, and with the cunning men of my lord Dauid thy father.[15]Now therefore the wheate and the barley, the oyle and the wine, which my lord hath ſpoken of, let him ſend vnto his ſeruants:[16]And wee will cut wood out of Lebanon, as much as thou ſhalt need, and wee will bring it to thee in flotes by ſea to Ioppa, and thou ſhalt carie it vp to Ieruſalem.[17]And Solomon numbred all the ſtrangers that were in the lande of Iſrael, after the numbring wherewith Dauid his father had numbred them: and they were found an hundred and fiftie thouſand, and three thouſand and ſixe hundred.[18]And he ſet threeſcore and ten thouſand of them to be bearers of burdens, and foureſcore thouſand to be hewers in the mountaine, and three thouſand and ſixe hundred ouerſeers to ſet the people a worke.

CHAPTER 3[1]Then Solomon began to build the houſe of the Lord at Ieruſalem in Mount Moriah, where the Lord appeared vnto Dauid his father, in the place that Dauid had prepared in the threſhing floore of Ornan the Iebuſite.[2]And he began to build in the ſecond day of the ſecond moneth, in the fourth yeere of his reigne.[3]Now theſe are the things wherein Solomon was inſtructed for the building of the houſe of God. The length by cubites after the firſt meaſure was threeſcore cubits, and the breadth twentie cubites.[4]And the porch that was in the front of the houſe, the length of it was atcording to the breadth of the houſe, twentie cubites, and the height was an hundred and twenty: and he ouerlaid it within, with pure gold.[5]And the greater houſe hee ſieled with firre tree, which he ouerlaid with fine gold, and ſet thereon palme trees and chaines.[6]And he garniſhed the houſe with precious ſtones for beautie, and the gold was gold of Paruaim.[7]Hee ouerlaid alſo the houſe, the beames, the poſtes and the wals thereof, and the doores thereof with gold, and graued Cherubims on the walles.[8]And he made the moſt holy houſe, the length whereof was, according to the breadth of the houſe, twenty cubits, and the breadth thereof twentie cubits: and he ouerlaid it with fine gold amounting to ſixe hundred talents.[9]And the weight of the nailes was fiftie ſhekels of gold: and he ouerlaide the vpper chambers with gold.[10]And in the moſt holy place hee made two Cherubims of image work, and ouerlaid them with gold.[11]And the wings of the Cherubims were twentie cubites long: one wing of the one Cherub was fiue cubites, reaching to the wall of the houſe: and the other wing was likewiſe fiue cubites, reaching to the wing of the other Cherub:[12]And one wing of the other Cherub was fiue cubites, reaching to the wall of the houſe: and the other wing was fiue cubites alſo, ioyning to the wing of the other Cherub.[13]The wings of theſe Cherubims ſpread themſelues forth twentie cubits: and they ſtood on their feet, and their faces were inward.[14]And he made the vaile of blue and purple, and crimſon, and fine linen, and wrought Cherubims thereon.[15]Alſo hee made before the houſe, two pillars of thirtie and fiue cubites high, and the chapiter that was on the top of each of them, was fiue cubites.[16]And he made chaines, as in the Oracle, and put them on the heads of the pillars, and made an hundred pomegranates, and put them on the chaines.[17]And he reared vp the pillars before the temple, one on the right hand, and the other on the left, and called the name of that on the right hand, Iachin, and the name of that on the left, Boaz.

CHAPTER 4[1]Moreouer he made an Altar of braſſe, twentie cubites the length thereof, and twentie cubites the breadth thereof, and ten cubites the height therof.[2]Alſo he made a molten ſea of ten cubites, from brim to brim, round in compaſſe, and fiue cubites the height thereof, and a line of thirtie cubites did compaſſe it round about.[3]And vnder it was the ſimilitude of oxen, which did compaſſe it round about: tenne in a cubite compaſsing the ſea round about. Two rowes of oxen were caſt, when it was caſt.[4]It ſtood vpon twelue oxen: three looking toward the North, and three looking toward the Weſt, and three looking toward the South, and three looking toward the Eaſt: and the ſea was ſet aboue vpon them, and all their hinder parts were inward.[5]And the thicknes of it was an hand breadth, & the brim of it like the worke of the brim of a cup, with flowers of Lillies: and it receiued and held three thouſand baths.[6]He made alſo ten Lauers, and put fiue on the right hand, and fiue on the left, to waſh in them: ſuch things as they offered for the burnt offring, they waſhed in them, but the ſea was for the Prieſts to waſh in.[7]And hee made ten candleſticks of gold according to their forme, and ſet them in the Temple, fiue on the right hand, and fiue on the left.[8]He made alſo ten tables, and placed them in the Temple, fiue on the right ſide, and fiue on the left: and hee made an hundred baſens of gold.[9]Furthermore, hee made the court of the Prieſts, and the great court, and doores for the court, and ouerlayd the doores of them with braſſe.[10]And he ſet the ſea on the rightſide of the Eaſt end, ouer againſt the South.[11]And Huram made the pots, and the ſhouels, and the baſens, and Huram finiſhed the worke that he was to make for King Solomon for the houſe of God:[12]To wit, the two pillars, and the pommels, and the chapiters, which were on the top of the two pillars, and the two wreathes to couer the two pommels of the chapiters, which were on the top of the pillars:[13]And foure hundred Pomegranats on the two wreathes: two rowes of Pomegranats on each wreath, to couer the two pommels of the chapiters, which were vpon the pillars.[14]He made alſo baſes; and lauers made he vpon the baſes.[15]One ſea, & twelue oxen vnder it.[16]The pots alſo, and the ſhouels, and the fleſhhookes, and all their inſtruments, did Huram his father make to King Solomon for the houſe of the Lord, of bright braſſe.[17]In the plaine of Iordan did the King caſt them, in the clay-ground, betweene Succoth and Zeredathah.[18]Thus Solomon made all theſe veſſels in great abundance: for the weight of the braſſe could not be found out.19And Solomon made all the veſſels, that were for the houſe of God, the golden Altar alſo, and the tables whereon the Shew-bread was ſet.20Moreouer the candleſticks with their lampes, that they ſhould burne after the maner, before the Oracle, of pure gold:21And the flowers, and the lamps, and the tongs made he of golde, and that perfect gold.22And the ſnuffers, and the baſens, and the ſpoones, and the cenſers, of pure gold. And the entry of the houſe, the inner doores thereof for the moſt Holy place, and the doores of the houſe of the Temple, were of gold.

CHAPTER 51Thus al the worke that Solomon made for the houſe of the Lord, was finiſhed: & Solomon brought in all the things that Dauid his father had dedicated; and the ſiluer, and the gold, and all the inſtruments, put he among the treaſures of the houſe of God.2Then Solomon aſſembled the Elders of Iſrael, and all the heads of the Tribes, the chiefe of the fathers of the children of Iſrael vnto Ieruſalem, to bring vp the Arke of the Couenant of the Lord, out of the citie of Dauid, which is Zion.3Wherefore all the men of Iſrael aſſembled themſelues vnto the king in the feaſt, which was in the ſeuenth moneth.4And all the Elders of Iſrael came, and the Leuites tooke vp the Arke.5And they brought vp the Arke, and the tabernacle of the Congregation, and all the holy veſſels that were in the tabernacle, theſe did the Prieſts and the Leuites bring vp.6Alſo king Solomon and all the congregation of Iſrael that were aſſembled vnto him before the Arke, ſacrificed ſheepe and oxen, which could not be told nor numbred for multitude.7And the prieſts brought in the Arke of the Couenant of the Lord vnto his place, to the Oracle of the houſe, into the moſt holy place, euen vnder the wings of the Cherubims:8For the Cherubims ſpread foorth their wings ouer the place of the Arke, and the Cherubims couered the Arke and the ſtaues thereof, aboue.9And they drew out the ſtaues of the Arke, that the ends of the ſtaues were ſeene from the Arke before the Oracle, but they were not ſeene without. And there it is vnto this day.10There was nothing in the Arke ſaue the two tables which Moſes put therein at Horeb, when the Lord made a couenant with the children of Iſrael, when they came out of Egypt.11And it came to paſſe when the Prieſts were come out of the holy place (for all the prieſts that were preſent were ſanctified, and did not then wait by courſe:12Alſo the Leuites which were the ſingers, all of them of Aſaph, of Heman, of Ieduthun, with their ſonnes and their brethren, being arayed in white linnen hauing cymbals, and pſalteries, and harpes, ſtood at the Eaſt end of the altar, and with them an hundred and twentie Prieſts, ſounding with trumpets:)13It came euen to paſſe, as the trumpetters and ſingers were as one, to make one ſound to be heard in praiſing and thanking the Lord: and when they lift vp their voyce with the trumpets, and cymbals, and inſtruments of muſicke, and praiſed the Lord, ſaying, For he is good, for his mercie endureth for euer: that then the houſe was filled with a cloude, euen the houſe of the Lord.14So that the Prieſts could not ſtand to miniſter, by reaſon of the cloud: for the glory of the Lord had filled the houſe of God.

CHAPTER 61Then ſaid Solomon, The Lord hath ſaid that he would dwell in the thicke darkeneſſe.2But I haue built an houſe of habitation for thee, and a place for thy dwelling for euer.3And the King turned his face and bleſſed the whole Congregation of Iſrael, (and all the Congregation of Iſrael ſtood)4And he ſaid, Bleſſed be the Lord God of Iſrael, who hath with his handes fulfilled that which he ſpake with his mouth to my father Dauid, ſaying,5Since the day that I brought foorth my people out of the land of Egypt, I choſe no citie among all the tribes of Iſrael to builde an houſe in, that my Name might be there, neither choſe I any man to be a ruler ouer my people Iſrael:6But I haue choſen Ieruſalem, that my name might be there, and haue choſen Dauid to be ouer my people Iſrael.7Now it was in the heart of Dauid my father to build an houſe for the Name of the Lord God of Iſrael.8But the Lord ſaid to Dauid my father: Foraſmuch as it was in thine heart to builde an houſe for my Name, thou diddeſt well in that it was in thine heart.9Notwithſtanding thou ſhalt not build the houſe, but thy ſonne which ſhall come foorth out of thy loynes, he ſhall build the houſe for my Name.10The Lord therefore hath performed his word that he hath ſpoken: for I am riſen vp in the roome of Dauid my father, and am ſet on the throne of Iſrael, as the Lord promiſed, and haue built the houſe for the Name of the Lord God of Iſrael.11And in it haue I put the Arke, wherein is the Couenant of the Lord, that hee made with the children of Iſrael.12And he ſtood before the Altar of the Lord, in the preſence of all the Congregation of Iſrael, and ſpread foorth his hands:13(For Solomon had made a braſen ſcaffold of fiue cubites long, and fiue cubites broad, and three cubites high, and had ſet it in the midſt of the Court, and vpon it hee ſtood, and kneeled downe vpon his knees before all the Congregation of Iſrael, and ſpread foorth his hands towards heauen.)14And ſaid, O Lord God of Iſrael, there is no God like thee in the heauen, nor in the earth, which keepeſt couenant, and ſheweſt mercy vnto thy ſeruants, that walke before thee with all their hearts,15Thou which haſt kept with thy ſeruant Dauid my father, that which thou haſt promiſed him: and ſpakeſt with thy mouth, and haſt fulfilled it with thine hand, as it is this day.16Now therefore, O Lord God of Iſrael, keepe with thy ſeruant Dauid my father, that which thou haſt promiſed him, ſaying, There ſhall not faile thee a man in my ſight, to ſit vpon the throne of Iſrael: yet ſo, that thy children take heede to their way, to walke in my Law, as thou haſt walked before me.17Now then, O Lord God of Iſrael, let thy word be verified, which thou haſt ſpoken vnto thy ſeruant Dauid.18(But wil God in very deed dwell with men on the earth? Behold, heauen, and the heauen of heauens cannot conteine thee: how much leſſe this houſe which I haue built?)19Haue reſpect therfore to the prayer of thy ſeruant, and to his ſupplication, O Lord my God, to hearken vnto the cry, and the prayer which thy ſeruant prayeth before thee:20That thine eyes may bee open vpon this houſe day and night, vpon the place whereof thou haſt ſaide, that thou wouldeſt put thy Name there, to hearken vnto the prayer, which thy ſeruant prayeth towards this place.21Hearken therefore vnto the ſupplications of thy ſeruant, and of thy people Iſrael, which they ſhall make towards this place: heare thou from thy dwelling place, euen from heauen; and when thou heareſt, forgiue.22If a man ſinne againſt his neighbour, and an oath be layd vpon him, to make him ſweare, and the oath come before thine Altar in this houſe:23Then heare thou from heauen, and doe, and iudge thy ſeruants by requiting the wicked, by recompenſing his way vpon his owne head, and by iuſtifying the righteous, by giuing him according to his righteouſneſſe.24And if thy people Iſrael be put to the worſe before the enemy, becauſe they haue ſinned againſt thee, and ſhall returne and confeſſe thy Name, and pray and make ſupplication before thee in this houſe:25Then heare thou from the heauens, and forgiue the ſinne of thy people Iſrael, and bring them againe vnto the land which thou gaueſt to them, and to their fathers.26When the heauen is ſhut vp, and there is no raine, becauſe they haue ſinned againſt thee: yet if they pray towards this place, and confeſſe thy Name, and turne from their ſinne, when thou doeſt afflict them:27Then heare thou from heauen, and forgiue the ſinne of thy ſeruants, and of thy people Iſrael; when thou haſt taught them the good way, wherein they ſhould walke, and ſend raine vpon the land, which thou haſt giuen vnto thy people for an inheritance.28If there be dearth in the land, if there be peſtilence, if there be blaſting, or mil-dew, locuſts or caterpillers; if their enemies beſiege them in the cities of their land: whatſoeuer ſore, or whatſoeuer ſickneſſe there be:29Then what prayer, or what ſupplication ſoeuer ſhall bee made of any man, or of all thy people Iſrael, when euery one ſhal know his owne ſore and his owne griefe, and ſhall ſpread foorth his hands in this houſe:30Then heare thou from heauen thy dwelling place, and forgiue, and render vnto euery man according vnto all his wayes, whoſe heart thou knoweſt (for thou onely knoweſt the hearts of the children of men:)31That they may feare thee, to walke in thy waies ſo long as they liue in the land which thou gaueſt vnto our fathers.32Moreouer concerning the ſtranger which is not of thy people Iſrael, but is come from a farre countrey for thy great Names ſake, & thy mightie hand, and thy ſtretched out arme: if they come and pray in this houſe:33Then heare thou from the heauens, euen from thy dwelling place, and doe according to all that the ſtranger calleth to thee for; that all people of the earth may know thy Name, and feare thee, as doeth thy people Iſrael, and may know that this houſe which I haue built, is called by thy Name.34If thy people goe out to warre againſt their enemies by the way that thou ſhalt ſend them, and they pray vnto thee toward this citie which thou haſt choſen, and the houſe which I haue built for thy Name:35Then heare thou from the heauens their prayer and their ſupplication, and maintaine their cauſe.36If they ſinne againſt thee (for there is no man which ſinneth not) and thou be angry with them, and deliuer them ouer before their enemies, and they cary them away captiues vnto a land far off or neere:37Yet if they bethinke themſelues in the land whither they are caried captiue, and turne and pray vnto thee in the land of their captiuitie, ſaying, Wee haue ſinned, we haue done amiſse, and haue dealt wickedly: 38 If they returne to thee with all their heart, and with all their ſoule, in the land of their captiuitie, whither they haue caried them captiues, and pray toward their land which thou gaueſt vnto their fathers, and toward the citie which thou haſt choſen, and toward the houſe which I haue built for thy Name: 39 Then heare thou from the heauens, euen from thy dwelling place, their prayer and their ſupplications, and maintaine their cauſe, and forgiue thy people, which haue ſinned againſt thee. 40 Now, my God, let (I beſeech thee) thine eyes bee open, and let thine eares be attent vnto the prayer that is made in this place. 41 Now therefore Ariſe, O Lord God, into thy reſting place, thou, and the Arke of thy ſtrength: Let thy Prieſts, O Lord God, be clothed with ſaluation, and let thy Saints reioyce in goodneſse. 42 O Lord God, turne not away the face of thine anointed: remember the mercies of Dauid thy ſeruant.

CHAPTER 7 1 Now when Solomon had made an ende of praying, the fire came downe from heauen, and conſumed the burnt offering, and the ſacrifices, and the glory of the Lord filled the houſe. 2 And the Prieſts could not enter into the houſe of the Lord, becauſe the glory of the Lord had filled the Lords houſe. 3 And when all the children of Iſrael ſaw how the fire came downe, and the glory of the Lord vpon the houſe, they bowed themſelues with their faces to the ground vpon the pauement, and worſhipped, and praiſed the Lord, ſaying, For hee is good, for his mercy endureth for euer. 4 Then the King and all the people, offered ſacrifices before the Lord. 5 And King Solomon offered a ſacrifice of twentie and two thouſand oxen, and an hundred and twentie thouſand ſheepe. So the King and all the people, dedicated the houſe of God. 6 And the Prieſts waited on their offices: the Leuites alſo with inſtruments of muſicke of the Lord, which Dauid the King had made to praiſe the Lord, becauſe his mercy endureth for euer, when Dauid praiſed by their miniſterie: and the Prieſts ſounded trumpets before them, and all Iſrael ſtood. 7 Moreouer, Solomon hallowed the middle of the Court, that was before the houſe of the Lord: for there hee offered burnt offerings, and the fat of the peace offerings, becauſe the braſen Altar which Solomon had made, was not able to receiue the burnt offerings, and the meat offerings, and the fat. 8 Alſo at the ſame time Solomon kept the feaſt ſeuen dayes, and all Iſrael with him, a very great Congregation, from the entring in of Hamath, vnto the Riuer of Egypt. 9 And in the eight day they made a ſolemne aſſembly: for they kept the dedication of the Altar ſeuen dayes, and the feaſt ſeuen dayes. 10 And on the three and twentieth day of the ſeuenth moneth, he ſent the people away into their tents, glad and merry in heart for the goodneſſe that the Lord had ſhewed vnto Dauid, and to Solomon, and to Iſrael his people. 11 Thus Solomon finiſhed the houſe of the Lord, and the Kings houſe: and all that came into Solomons heart to make in the houſe of the Lord, and in his owne houſe, hee proſperouſly effected. 12 And the Lord appeared to Solomon by night, and ſaid vnto him, I haue heard thy prayer, and haue choſen this place to my ſelfe for an houſe of ſacrifice. 13 If I ſhut vp heauen that there bee no raine, or if I command the locuſts to deuoure the land, or if I ſend peſtilence among my people: 14 If my people which are called by my Name, ſhall humble themſelues and pray, and ſeeke my face, and turne from their wicked wayes: then will I heare from heauen, and will forgiue their ſinne, and will heale their land. 15 Now mine eyes ſhalbe open, and mine eares attent vnto the prayer that is made in this place. 16 For now haue I choſen, & ſanctified this houſe, that my Name may be there for euer: and mine eyes and mine heart ſhalbe there perpetually. 17 And as for thee, if thou wilt walke before me, as Dauid thy father walked, and doe according to all that I haue commanded thee, and ſhalt obſerue my Statutes, and my Iudgements: 18 Then wil I ſtabliſh the throne of thy kingdome, according as I haue couenanted with Dauid thy father, ſaying, There ſhall not faile thee a man to be ruler in Iſrael. 19 But if yee turne away and forſake my Statutes and my Commandements which I haue ſet before you, and ſhall goe and ſerue other gods, and worſhip them: 20 Then will I plucke them vp by the roots out of my land which I haue giuen them, and this houſe which I haue ſanctified for my Name, wil I caſt out of my ſight, and will make it to be a prouerbe, and a by-word among all nations. 21 And this houſe which is high, ſhall be an aſtoniſhment to euery one that paſſeth by it; ſo that hee ſhall ſay; Why hath the Lord done thus vnto this land, and vnto this houſe? 22 And it ſhalbe anſwered, Becauſe they forſooke the Lord God of their fathers, which brought them forth out of the land of Egypt, and layd hold on others gods, and worſhipped them, aud ſerued them: Therefore hath hee brought all this euil vpon them.

CHAPTER 8 1 And it came to paſſe (at the end of twentie yeeres, wherein Solomon had built the houſe of the Lord, & his own houſe) 2 That the cities which Huram had reſtored to Solomon, Solomon built them, and cauſed the children of Iſrael to dwell there. 3 And Solomon went to Hamath Zobah, and preuailed againſt it. 4 And he built Tadmor in the wilderneſſe, and all the ſtore-cities, which he built in Hamath. 5 Alſo he built Beth-horon the vpper, and Beth-horon the nether, fenſed cities with walles, gates and barres: 6 And Baalath, and all the ſtore-cities that Solomon had, and all the charet-cities, and the cities of the horſemen, and all that Solomon deſired to build in Ieruſalem, and in Lebanon, and throughout all the land of his dominion. 7 As for all the people that were left of the Hittites, and the Amorites, and the Perizzites, and the Hiuites, and the Iebuſites, which were not of Iſrael: 8 But of their children, who were left after them in the land, whom the children of Iſrael conſumed not; them did Solomon make to pay tribute, vntill this day. 9 But of the children of Iſrael did Solomon make no ſeruants for his worke: but they were men of warre, and chiefe of his captains, and captains of his charets and horſemen. 10 And theſe were the chiefe of king Solomons officers, euen two hundred and fifty, that bare rule ouer the people. 11 And Solomon brought vp the daughter of Pharaoh out of the citie of Dauid, vnto the houſe that he had built for her: for hee ſaid, My wife ſhall not dwell in the houſe of Dauid king of Iſrael, becauſe the places are holy, whereunto the Arke of the Lord hath come. 12 Then Solomon offered burnt offerings vnto the Lord on the Altar of the Lord, which he had built before the porch: 13 Euen after a certaine rate euery day, offering according to the commandement of Moſes, on the Sabbaths, and on the new Moones, and on the ſolemne Feaſts three times in the yeere, euen in the feaſt of Unleauened bread, and in the feaſt of Weekes, and in the feaſt of Tabernacles. 14 And he appointed, according to the order of Dauid his father, the courſes of the Prieſts to their ſeruice, and the Leuites to their charges, to praiſe and miniſter before the Prieſts, as the duety of euery day required: the porters alſo by their courſes, at euery gate: for ſo had Dauid the man of God commanded. 15 And they departed not from the commandement of the King vnto the Prieſts and Leuites, concerning any matter, or concerning the treaſures. 16 Now all the worke of Solomon was prepared vnto the day of the foundation of the houſe of the Lord, and vntill it was finiſhed: ſo the houſe of God was perfected. 17 Then went Solomon to Ezion Geber, and to Eloth, at the ſea ſide in the land of Edom. 18 And Huram ſent him by the hands of his ſeruants, ſhippes, and ſeruants that had knowledge of the ſea; and they went with the ſeruants of Solomon to Ophir, and tooke thence foure hundred and fiftie talents of golde, and brought them to king Solomon.

CHAPTER 9 1 And when the Queene of Sheba heard of the fame of Solomon, ſhee came to prooue Solomon with hard queſtions at Ieruſalem, with a very great companie, and camels that bare ſpices, and golde in abundance, and precious ſtones: and when ſhe was come to Solomon, ſhee communed with him of all that was in her heart. 2 And Solomon tolde her all her queſtions: and there was nothing hid from Solomon, which he told her not. 3 And when the Queene of Sheba had ſeene the wiſedome of Solomon, and the houſe that he had built, 4 And the meate of his table, and the ſitting of his ſeruants, and the attendance of his miniſters, and their apparell, his cup-bearers alſo, and their apparell, and his aſcent, by which hee went vp into the houſe of the Lord; there was no more ſpirit in her. 5 And ſhe ſaid to the King, It was a true report which I heard in mine owne land, of thine actes, and of thy wiſedome: 6 Howbeit, I beleeued not their wordes, vntill I came, and mine eyes had ſeene it: and behold, the one halfe of the greatneſſe of thy wiſedome was not tolde mee: for thou exceedeſt the fame that I heard. 7 Happy are thy men, and happy are theſe thy ſeruants, which ſtand continually before thee, and heare thy wiſedome. 8 Bleſſed be the Lord thy God, which delighted in thee to ſet thee on his throne, to be King for the Lord thy God: becauſe thy God loued Iſrael, to eſtabliſh them for euer, therefore made hee thee King ouer them, to doe iudgement and iuſtice. 9 And ſhe gaue the king an hundred and twentie talents of gold, and of ſpices great abundance, & precious ſtones: neither

was there any ſuch ſpice as the Queene of Sheba gaue King
Solomon.10And the ſeruants alſo of Huram, and the ſeruants of
Solomon, which brought gold from Ophir, brought Algume trees and,
precious ſtones.11And the king made of the Algume trees, terriſes to the
houſe of the Lord, and to the kings palace, and harpes and pſalteries for
ſingers: and there were none ſuch ſeene before in the laud of
Iudah.12And King Solomon gaue to the Queene of Sheba, all her deſire,
whatſoeuer ſhe aſked, beſides that which ſhe had brought vnto the king:
So ſhe turned, and went away to her owne land, ſhe, and her
ſeruants.13Now the weight of gold that came to Solomon in one yeere,
was ſixe hundred and threeſcore and ſixe talents of gold:14Beſides that
which chapmen and merchants brought: and all the kings of Arabia, and
gouernours of the countrie, brought gold and ſiluer to Solomon.15And
king Solomon made two hundred targets of beaten gold: ſixe hundred
ſhekels of beaten gold went to one target.16And three hundred ſhields
made he of beaten gold: three hundred ſhekels of gold went to one
ſhield: and the king put them in the houſe of the forreſt of
Lebanon.17Moreouer the king made a great throne of yuorie, and
ouerlaid it with pure gold.18And there were ſixe ſteps to the throne, with
a footſtoole of gold, which were faſtened to the throne, and ſtayes on
each ſide of the ſitting place, and two lyons ſtanding by the ſtayes.19And
twelue lyons ſtood there on the one ſide and on the other, vpon the ſixe
ſteps. There was not the like made in any kingdome.20And all the
drinking veſſels of King Solomon were of gold, and all the veſſels of the
houſe of the forreſt of Lebanon were of pure gold: none were of ſiluer;
it was not any thing accounted of in the dayes of Solomon.21For the
kings ſhips went to Tarſhiſh with the ſeruants of Huram: euerie three
yeeres once came the ſhips of Tarſhiſh bringing golde, and ſiluer, yuorie,
and apes, and peacocks.22And king Solomon paſſed all the kings of the
earth in riches and wiſedome.23And all the kings of the earth ſought the
preſence of Solomon, to heare his wiſedome, that God had put in his
heart.24And they brought euery man his preſent, veſſels of ſiluer, and
veſſels of gold, and raiment, harneſse, and ſpices, horſes, and mules, a
rate yeere by yeere.25And Solomon had foure thouſand ſtalles for horſes,
and charets, and twelue thouſand horſemen, whom hee beſtowed in the
charet cities, and with the king at Ieruſalem.26And hee reigned ouer all
the kings, from the riuer, euen vnto the land of the Philiſtines, and to
the border of Egypt.27And the king made ſiluer in Ieruſalem as ſtones,
and cedar trees made he as the Sycomore trees, that are in the low
plaines, in abundance.28And they brought vnto Solomon horſes out of
Egypt, and out of all lands.29Now the reſt of the actes of Solomon firſt
and laſt, are they not written in the booke of Nathan the Prophet, and
in the propheſie of Ahiiah the Shilonite, and in the viſions of Iddo the
Seer, againſt Ieroboam the ſonne of Nebat?30And Solomon reigned in
Ieruſalem ouer all Iſrael, fourtie yeeres.31And Solomon ſlept with his
fathers, and hee was buried in the citie of Dauid his father, and
Rehoboam his ſonne reigned in his ſtead.
CHAPTER 101And Rehoboam went to Shechem: for to Shechem were
all Iſrael come to make him king.2And it came to paſſe when Ieroboam
the ſonne of Nebat (who was in Egypt, whither hee had fled from the
preſence of Solomon the king) heard it, that Ieroboam returned out of
Egypt.3And they ſent and called him. So Ieroboam and all Iſrael came,
and ſpake to Rehoboam, ſaying,4Thy father made our yoke grieuous,
nowe therefore eaſe thou ſomewhat the grieuous ſeruitude of thy father,
and his heauy yoke that he put vpon vs, and we will ſerue thee.5And hee
ſaid vnto them, Come againe vnto me after three dayes. And the people
departed.6And king Rehoboam tooke counſel with the old men that had
ſtood before Solomon his father, while hee yet liued, ſaying, What
counſell giue ye me, to returne anſwere to this people?7And they ſpake
vnto him, ſaying, If thou bee kinde to this people, and pleaſe them, and
ſpeake good words to them, they will be thy ſeruants for euer.8But he
forſooke the counſel which the old men gaue him, and tooke counſell
with the yong men, that were brought vp with him, that ſtood before
him.9And he ſaid vnto them, What aduice giue ye, that wee may returne
anſwere to this people, which haue ſpoken to me, ſaying, Eaſe ſomewhat
the yoke that thy father did put vpon vs?10And the yong men that were
brought vp with him, ſpake vnto him, ſaying, Thus ſhalt thou anſwere
the people that ſpake vnto thee, ſaying, Thy father made our yoke heauy,
but make thou it ſomewhat lighter for vs: thus ſhalt thou ſay vnto them,
My litle finger ſhall be thicker then my fathers loynes.11For where as my
father put a heauy yoke vpon you, I will put more to your yoke: my
father chaſtiſed you with whips, but I will chaſtiſe you with
ſcorpions.12So Ieroboam and all the people came to Rehoboam on the
third day, as the King bade, ſaying, Come againe to me on the third
day.13And the king anſwered them roughly, and king Rehoboam
forſooke the counſell of the old men,14And anſwered them after the
aduice of the yong men, ſaying, My father made your yoke heauy, but I
will adde thereto: my father chaſtiſed you with whips, but I will chaſtiſe
you with ſcorpions.15So the king hearkened not vnto the people, for the
cauſe was of God, that the Lord might performe his word, which he
ſpake by the hand of Ahijah the Shilonite to Ieroboam the ſonne of
Nebat.16And when all Iſrael ſawe that the king would not hearken vnto
them, the people anſwered the king ſaying, What portion haue wee in
Dauid? and wee haue none inheritance in the ſonne of Ieſſe: Euery man
to your tents, O Iſrael: and now Dauid, ſee to thine owne houſe. So all
Iſrael went to their tents.17But as for the children of Iſrael that dwelt in
the cities of Iudah, Rehoboam reigned ouer them.18Then king
Rehoboam ſent Hadoram that was ouer the tribute, and the children of
Iſrael ſtoned him with ſtones, that he died: but king Rehoboam made
ſpeed to get him vp to his charet, to flee to Ieruſalem.19And Iſrael
rebelled againſt the houſe of Dauid vnto this day.
CHAPTER 111And when Rehoboam was come to Ieruſalem, he
gathered of the houſe of Iudah and Beniamin, an hundred and
foureſcore thouſand choſen men, which were warriers, to fight againſt
Iſrael, that hee might bring the kingdome againe to Rehoboam.2But the
worde of the Lord came to Shemaiah the man of God, ſaying,3Speake
vnto Rehoboam the ſon of Solomon, king of Iudah, and to all Iſrael in
Iudah & Beniamin, ſaying,4Thus ſaith the Lord; Ye ſhall not goe vp, nor
fight againſt your brethren: returne euery man to his houſe, for this thing
is done of me. And they obeyed the words of the Lord, and returned
from going againſt Ieroboam.5And Rehoboam dwelt in Ieruſalem, and
built cities for defence in Iudah.6He built euen Bethlehem, and Etam,
and Tekoa,7And Bethzur, and Shoco, and Adullam,8And Gath, and
Mareſha, and Ziph,9And Adoraim, and Lachiſh, and Azekah,10And
Zorah, and Aialon, and Hebron, which are in Iudah and in Beniamin,
fenced cities.11And he fortified the ſtrong holds, and put captaines in
them, and ſtore of vitaile, and of oyle and wine.12And in euery ſeuerall
citie he put ſhields and ſpeares, and made them exceeding ſtrong, hauing
Iudah and Beniamin on his ſide.13And the Prieſts and the Leuites that
were in all Iſrael, reſorted to him out of all their coaſts.14For the Leuites
left their ſuburbs, and their poſſeſſion, and came to Iudah and
Ieruſalem: for Ieroboam and his ſonnes had caſt them off from
executing the Prieſts office vnto the Lord.15And hee ordeined him
prieſts for the high places, and for the deuils, and for the calues which
he had made.16And after them out of all the tribes of Iſrael, ſuch as ſet
their hearts to ſeeke the Lord God of Iſrael, came to Ieruſalem, to
ſacrifice vnto the Lord God of their fathers.17So they ſtrengthened the
kingdome of Iudah, and made Rehoboam the ſonne of Solomon ſtrong,
three yeeres: for three yeeres they walked in the way of Dauid and
Solomon.18And Rehoboam tooke him Mahalath the daughter of
Ierimoth the ſonne of Dauid to wife, and Abihail the daughter of Eliab
the ſon of Ieſſe:19Which bare him children, Ieuſh, and Shamariah, and
Zaham.20And after her, hee tooke Maacah the daughter of Abſalom,
which bare him Abiiah, and Atthai, and Ziza, and Shelomith.21And
Rehoboam loued Maacah the daughter of Abſalom, aboue all his wiues
and his concubines: for he tooke eighteene wiues, and threeſcore
concubines, and begate twentie and eight ſonnes, and threeſcore
daughters.22And Rehoboam made Abiiah the ſonne of Maacah the
chiefe, to be ruler among his brethren: for he thought to make him
king.23And he dealt wiſely, and diſperſed of all his children throughout
all the countries of Iudah and Beniamin, vnto euery fenced citie: and he
gaue them vitaile in abundance: and hee deſired many wiues.
CHAPTER 121And it came to paſſe when Rehoboam had eſtabliſhed
the kingdome, and had ſtrengthened himſelfe, hee forſooke the Law of
the Lord, and all Iſrael with him.2And it came to paſſe, that in the fifth
yere of Rehoboam, Shiſhak king of Egypt came vp againſt Ieruſalem, (
becauſe they had tranſgreſſed againſt the Lord)3With twelue hundred
charets, and threeſcore thouſand horſemen: and the people were
without number that came with him out of Egypt: the Lubims, the
Sukkiims, & the Ethiopians.4And hee tooke the fenced cities which

perteined to Iudah, and came to Ieruſalem.5Then came Shemaiah the prophet to Rehoboam, and to the Princes of Iudah that were gathered together to Ieruſalem becauſe of Shiſhak, and ſaid vnto them, Thus ſaith the Lord, Ye haue forſaken me, and therfore haue I alſo left you in the hand of Shiſhak.6Whereupon, the Princes of Iſrael, and the king humbled themſelues and they ſaide, The Lord is righteous.7And when the Lord ſaw that they humbled themſelues, the word of the Lord came to Shemaiah, ſaying, They haue humbled themſelues, therefore I will not deſtroy them, but I will grant them ſome deliuerance, and my wrath ſhall not bee powred out vpon Ieruſalem, by the hand of Shiſhak.8Neuertheleſſe they ſhalbe his ſeruants, that they may know my ſeruice, and the ſeruice of the kingdomes of the countreys.9So Shiſhak king of Egypt came vp againſt Ieruſalem, and tooke away the treaſures of the houſe of the Lord, and the treaſures of the kings houſe, hee tooke all: he caried away alſo the ſhields of gold, which Solomon had made.10In ſtead of which, king Rehoboam made ſhields of braſſe, and committed them to the hands of the chiefe of the guard, that kept the entrance of the Kings houſe.11And when the king entred into the houſe of the Lord, the guard came and fet them, and brought them againe into the guard-chamber.12And when he humbled himſelfe, the wrath of the Lord turned from him, that hee would not deſtroy him altogether: and alſo in Iudah things went well.13So king Rehoboam ſtrengthened himſelfe in Ieruſalem, and reigned: for Rehoboam was one and fourty yeeres olde when hee began to reigne, and he reigned ſeuenteen yeeres in Ieruſalem, the citie which the Lord had choſen out of all the tribes of Iſrael, to put his Name there: and his mothers name was Naamah an Ammoniteſse.14And hee did euill, becauſe hee prepared not his heart to ſeeke the Lord.15Now the acts of Rehoboam firſt and laſt, are they not written in the booke of Shemaiah the Prophet, and of Iddo the Seer, concerning genealogies? and there were warres betweene Rehoboam & Ieroboam continually.16And Rehoboam ſlept with his fathers, and was buried in the citie of Dauid, and Abiiah his ſonne reigned in his ſtead.

CHAPTER 131Nowe in the eighteenth yeere of king Ieroboam, began Abiiah to reigne ouer Iudah.2He reigned three yeres in Ieruſalem: (his mothers name alſo was Michaiah the daughter of Uriel of Gibea:) and there was warre between Abiiah and Ieroboam.3And Abiiah ſet the battel in aray with an army of valiant men of warre, euen foure hundred thouſand choſen men: Ieroboam alſo ſet the battell in aray againſt him with eight hundred thouſand choſen men, being mightie men of valour.4And Abiiah ſtood vp vpon mount Zemaraim, which is in mount Ephraim, and ſayde, Heare mee thou Ieroboam, and all Iſrael:5Ought you not to know, that the Lord God of Iſrael gaue the kingdome ouer Iſrael to Dauid for euer, euen to him and to his ſonnes by a couenant of ſalt?6Yet Ieroboam the ſonne of Nebat, the ſeruant of Solomon the ſonne of Dauid, is riſen vp, and hath rebelled againſt his Lord.7And there are gathered vnto him vaine men the children of Belial, and haue ſtrengthened themſelues againſt Rehoboam the ſonne of Solomon, when Rehoboam was young, & tender hearted, and could not withſtand them.8And now ye thinke to withſtand the kingdome of the Lord, in the hand of the ſonnes of Dauid, and ye be a great multitude, and there are with you golden calues, which Ieroboam made you for gods.9Haue yee not caſt out the Prieſts of the Lord the ſonnes of Aaron, and the Leuites, and haue made you prieſts after the maner of the nations of other lands? ſo that whoſoeuer commeth to conſecrate himſelfe with a young bullocke and ſeuen rammes, the ſame may be a prieſt of them that are no gods.10But as for vs, the Lord is our God, and wee haue not forſaken him, and the Prieſts which miniſter vnto the Lord, are the ſonnes of Aaron, and the Leuites waite vpon their buſineſse.11And they burne vnto the Lord euery morning, and euery euening, burnt ſacrifices and ſweete incenſe: the ſhew-bread alſo ſet they in order vpon the pure table, and the Candleſticke of golde with the lampes therof, to burne euery euening: for we keepe the charge of the Lord our God, but yee haue forſaken him.12And behold, God himſelfe is with vs for our captaine, and his Prieſts with ſounding trumpets to cry alarme againſt you: O children of Iſrael, fight ye not againſt the Lord God of your fathers, for you ſhall not proſper.13But Ieroboam cauſed an ambuſhment to come about behinde them: ſo they were before Iudah, and the ambuſhment was behind them.14And when Iudah looked backe, behold, the battel was before and behind; and they cried vnto the Lord, and the Prieſts ſounded with the trumpets.15Then the men of Iudah gaue a ſhout: and as the men of Iudah ſhouted, it came to paſſe that God ſmote Ieroboam and all Iſrael, before Abiiah and Iudah.16And the children of Iſrael fled before Iudah: and God deliuered them into their hand.17And Abiiah and his people ſlew them with a great ſlaughter: ſo there fel downe ſlaine of Iſrael, fiue hundred thouſand choſen men.18Thus the children of Iſrael were brought vnder at that time, and the children of Iudah preuailed, becauſe they relied vpon the Lord God of their fathers.19And Abiiah purſued after Ieroboam, & tooke cities from him, Beth-el with the townes thereof, and Ieſhanah with the townes thereof, and Ephrain with the townes thereof.20Neither did Ieroboam recouer ſtrength againe in the dayes of Abiiah: and the Lord ſtrooke him, & he died.21But Abiiah waxed mighty, and married fourteene wiues, and begate twentie and two ſonnes, and ſixteene daughters.22And the reſt of the acts of Abiiah, and his waies, and his ſayings, are written in the ſtory of the Prophet Iddo.

CHAPTER 141So Abiiah ſlept with his fathers, and they buried him in the citie of Dauid, and Aſa his ſonne reigned in his ſtead: in his dayes the land was quiet ten yeeres.2And Aſa did that which was good and right in the eyes of the Lord his God.3For hee tooke away the altars of the ſtrange gods, and the high places, and brake downe the images, and cut downe the groues:4And commanded Iudah to ſeeke the Lord God of their fathers, and to do the Law, and the Commandement.5Alſo he tooke away out of all the cities of Iudah, the high places and the images: and the kingdome was quiet before him.6And hee built fenced cities in Iudah; for the land had reſt, and hee had no warre in thoſe yeeres; becauſe the Lord had giuen him reſt.7Therefore hee ſaid vnto Iudah, Let vs build theſe cities, & make about them walles, and towers, gates and barres, while the land is yet before vs: becauſe wee haue ſought the Lord our God, wee haue ſought him, and hee hath giuen vs reſt on euery ſide: ſo they built, and proſpered.8And Aſa had an armie of men that bare targets and ſpeares, out of Iudah three hundred thouſand, and out of Beniamin, that bare ſhields and drew bowes, two hundred and foureſcore thouſand: all theſe were mighty men of valour.9And there came out againſt them Zerah the Ethiopian, with an hoſt of a thouſand thouſand, and three hundred charets, and came vnto Mareſhah.10Then Aſa went out againſt him, and they ſet the battel in aray in the valley of Zephathah at Mareſhah.11And Aſa cried vnto the Lord his God, and ſaid, Lord, it is nothing with thee to helpe, whether with many, or with them that haue no power. Helpe vs, O Lord our God, for we reſt on thee, and in thy Name wee goe againſt this multitude: O Lord thou art our God, let not man preuaile againſt thee.12So the Lord ſmote the Ethiopians before Aſa, and before Iudah, and the Ethiopians fled.13And Aſa and the people that were with him, purſued them vnto Gerar: and the Ethiopians were ouerthrown, that they could not recouer themſelues, for they were deſtroyed before the Lord, and before his hoſte, and they caried away very much ſpoile.14And they ſmote all the cities round about Gerar, for the feare of the Lord came vpon them: and they ſpoiled all the cities, for there was exceeding much ſpoile in them.15They ſmote alſo the tents of cattell, and caried away ſheepe and camels inabundance, and returned to Ieruſalem.

CHAPTER 151And the Spirit of God came vpon Azariah the ſonne of Oded.2And he went out to meet Aſa, and ſaid vnto him, Heare ye me, Aſa, and all Iudah, and Beniamin, The Lord is with you, while yee be with him: and if yee ſeeke him, he will be found of you: but if ye forſake him, he will forſake you.3Now for a long ſeaſon Iſrael hath bene without the true God, and without a teaching prieſt, and without law.4But when they in their trouble did turne vnto the Lord God of Iſrael, and ſought him, hee was found of them.5And in thoſe times there was no peace to him that went out, nor to him that came in, but great vexations were vpon all the inhabitants of the countreys.6And nation was deſtroyed of nation, and citie of citie: for God did vexe them with all aduerſitie.7Be ye ſtrong therefore, and let not your hands bee weake: for your worke ſhall be rewarded.8And when Aſa heard theſe words, and the propheſie of Oded the prophet, he tooke courage, and put away the abominable idoles out of all the lande of Iudah and Beniamin, and out of the cities which hee had taken from mount Ephraim, and renewed the Altar of the Lord, that was before the porch of the Lord.9And he gathered all Iudah and Beniamin, and the ſtrangers with them out of Ephraim and Manaſſeh, and out of Simeon: (for they fell to him out of Iſrael in abundance when they ſaw that the Lord his God was with him.)10So they gathered themſelues together at Ieruſalem, in the third moneth, in the fifteenth yeere of the reigne of Aſa.11And they offered vnto the Lord the ſame time, of the ſpoile which they had brought, ſeuen hundred oxen, and ſeuen thouſand ſheepe.12And they entred into a couenant to ſeeke the Lord God of their fathers, with all their heart and with all their ſoule:13That whoſoeuer would not ſeeke the Lord God of Iſrael, ſhould be put to death, whether ſmall or great, whether man or woman.14And they ſware vnto the Lord with a loud voice, and with ſhouting, and with trumpets, and with cornets.15And all Iudah reioyced at the oath: for they had ſworne with all their heart, & ſought him with their whole deſire, and he was found of them: and the Lord gaue them reſt round about.16And alſo concerning Maachah the mother of Aſa the king, he remooued her from beeing Queene, becauſe ſhe had made an idole in a groue: and Aſa cut downe her idole, and ſtamped it, and burnt it at the brooke Kidron.17But the high places were not taken away out of Iſrael: neuertheleſſe the heart of Aſa was perfect all his dayes.18And he brought into the houſe of God the things that his father had dedicated, and that he himſelfe had dedicated, ſiluer, and gold, and veſſels.19And there was no more warre vnto the fiue and thirtieth yeere of the reigne of Aſa.

CHAPTER 161In the ſixe and thirtieth yeere of the reigne of Aſa, Baaſha king of Iſrael came vp againſt Iudah, and built Ramah, to the intent that hee might let none goe out or come in to Aſa king of Iudah.2Then Aſa brought out ſiluer and golde out of the treaſures of the houſe of the Lord, and of the kings houſe, and ſent to Benhadad King of Syria that dwelt at Damaſcus, ſaying;3There is a league betweene me and thee, as there was betweene my father and thy father: beholde, I haue ſent thee ſiluer and golde, goe, breake thy league with Baaſha king of Iſrael, that he may depart from me.4And Benhadad hearkened vnto king Aſa, and ſent the captaines of his armies againſt the cities of Iſrael; and they ſmote Iion, and Dan, and Abelmaim, & all the ſtore-cities of Naphtali.5And it came to paſſe, when Baaſha heard it, that hee left off building of Ramah, and let his worke ceaſe.6Then Aſa the king tooke all Iudah, and they caried away the ſtones of Ramah, and the timber thereof, wherewith Baaſha was a building, and hee built there with Geba and Mizpah.7And at that time Hanani the Seer came to Aſa king of Iudah, and ſaid vnto him, Becauſe thou haſt relyed on the king of Syria, and not relyed on the Lord thy God, therefore is the hoſte of the king of Syria eſcaped out of thine hand.8Were not the Ethiopians and the Lubims a huge hoſte, with very many charets and horſemen? Yet becauſe thou diddeſt relie on the Lord, he deliuered them into thine hand.9For the eyes of the Lord run to and fro throughout the whole earth, to ſhewe himſelfe ſtrong in the behalfe of them, whoſe heart is perfite towards him. Herein thou haſt done fooliſhly; therefore, from hencefoorth thou ſhalt haue warres.10Then Aſa was wroth with the Seer, and put him in a priſon-houſe; for he was in a rage with him becauſe of this thing. And Aſa oppreſſed ſome of the people the ſame time.11And behold, the actes of Aſa firſt and laſt, lo, they are written in the booke of the Kings of Iudah and Iſrael.12And Aſa in the thirtie and ninth yeere of his reigne, was diſeaſed in his feete, vntill his diſeaſe was exceeding great: yet in his diſeaſe hee ſought not to the Lord, but to the Phyſicians.13And Aſa ſlept with his fathers, and died in the one and fourtieth yeere of his reigne.14And they buried him in his owne ſepulchres which he had made for himſelfe in the citie of Dauid, and laide him in the bed, which was filled with ſweet odours, and diuers kindes of ſpices prepared by the Apothecaries arte: & they made a very great burning for him.

CHAPTER 171And Iehoſhaphat his ſonne reigned in his ſtead, and ſtrengthened himſelfe againſt Iſrael.2And he placed forces in all the fenced cities of Iudah, and ſet gariſons in the land of Iudah, and in the cities of Ephraim, which Aſa his father had taken.3And the Lord was with Iehoſhaphat, becauſe hee walked in the firſt wayes of his father Dauid, and ſought not vnto Baalim:4But ſought to the Lord God of his father, and walked in his commandements, and not after the doings of Iſrael:5Therefore the Lord ſtabliſhed the kingdome in his hand, and all Iudah brought to Iehoſhaphat preſents, and he had riches and honour in abundance.6And his heart was lift vp in the wayes of the Lord: moreouer hee tooke away the high places and groues out of Iudah.7Alſo in the third yeere of his reigne, hee ſent to his princes, euen to Benhail, and to Obadiah, and to Zechariah, and to Nethaneel, and to Michaiah, to teach in the cities of Iudah:8And with them hee ſent Leuites, euen Shemaiah, and Nethaniah, and Zebadiah, and Aſahel, and Shemiramoth, and Iehonathan, and Adoniiah, and Tobiiah, and Tob-adoniiah, Leuites: and with them, Eliſhama and Iehoram, Prieſts.9And they taught in Iudah, and had the book of the Law of the Lord with them, and went about throughout all the cities of Iudah, and taught the people.10And the feare of the Lord fell vpon all the kingdomes of the lands that were round about Iudah, ſo that they made no warre againſt Iehoſhaphat.11Alſo ſome of the Philiſtines brought Iehoſhaphat preſents, and tribute ſiluer, and the Arabians brought him flocks, ſeuen thouſand and ſeuen hundred rammes, and ſeuen thouſand and ſeuen hundred he goats.12And Iehoſhaphat waxed great exceedingly, and he built in Iudah caſtles, and cities of ſtore.13And he had much buſineſse in the cities of Iudah: and the men of warre, mightie men of valour, were in Ieruſalem.14And theſe are the numbers of them according to the houſe of their fathers: Of Iudah, the captaines of thouſands, Adnah the chiefe, and with him mighty men of valour, three hundred thouſand.15And next to him was Iehohanan the captaine, and with him two hundred and foureſcore thouſand.16And next him was Amaſiah the ſonne of Zichri, who willingly offered himſelfe vnto the Lord, and with him two hundred thouſand mightie men of valour.17And of Beniamin, Eliada a mightie man of valour, and with him, armed men with bow and ſhield two hundred thouſand.18And next him was Iehoſhabad, and with him an hundred and foure ſcore thouſand, ready prepared for the warre.19Theſe waited on the king, beſides thoſe whom the king put in the fenced cities throughout all Iudah.

CHAPTER 181Now Iehoſhaphat had riches and honour in abundance, and ioyned affinitie with Ahab.2And after certaine yeeres, he went downe to Ahab to Samaria: and Ahab killed ſheepe and oxen for him in abundance, and for the people that he had with him, and perſwaded him to goe vp with him to Ramoth Gilead.3And Ahab king of Iſrael ſaid vnto Iehoſhaphat king of Iudah, Wilt thou goe with me to Ramoth Gilead? And he anſwered him, I am as thou art, and my people as thy people, and we will be with thee in the warre.4And Iehoſhaphat ſaide vnto the king of Iſrael, Enquire, I pray thee, at the word of the Lord to day.5Therefore the king of Iſrael gathered together of prophets foure hundred men, and ſaid vnto them, ſhal we goe to Ramoth Gilead to battel, or ſhal I forbeare? And they ſaid, Goe vp, for God will deliuer it into the kings hand.6But Iehoſhaphat ſaide, Is there not here a Prophet of the Lord beſides, that we might enquire of him?7And the king of Iſrael ſaid vnto Iehoſhaphat, There is yet one man, by whom we may enquire of the Lord: but I hate him, for he neuer propheſied good vnto me, but alwayes euill: the ſame is Micaiah the ſonne of Iimla. And Iehoſhaphat ſaide, Let not the king ſay ſo.8And the king of Iſrael called for one of his officers, and ſaide, Fetch quickly Micaiah the ſonne of Iimla.9And the king of Iſrael and Iehoſhaphat king of Iudah ſate, either of them on his throne, clothed in their robes, and they ſate in a voide place at the entring in of the gate of Samaria, and all the prophets propheſied before them.10And Zedekiah the ſonne of Chenaanah, had made him hornes of yron, and ſaid, Thus ſaith the Lord, With theſe thou ſhalt puſh Syria, vntil they be conſumed.11And all the prophets propheſied ſo, ſaying, Goe vp to Ramoth Gilead, and proſper: for the Lord ſhall deliuer it into the hand of the king.12And the meſſenger that went to call Micaiah, ſpake to him, ſaying, Behold, the words of the prophets declare good to the king with one aſſent: let thy word therefore, I pray thee be like one of theirs, and ſpeake thou good.13And Micaiah ſaid, As the Lord liueth, euen what my God ſaith, that will I ſpeake.14And when hee was come to the king, the king ſayd vnto him, Micaiah, ſhall we goe to Ramoth Gilead to battell, or ſhall I fobreare? and he ſayd, Goe yee vp, and proſper, and they ſhall be deliuered into your hand.15And the king ſayd to him, Howe many times ſhall I adiure thee, that thou ſay nothing but the truth to me, in the name of the Lord?16Then he ſayd, I did ſee all Iſrael ſcattered vpon the mountaines, as ſheepe that haue no ſhepheard: and the Lord ſayd, Theſe haue no maſter, let them returne therefore, euery man to his houſe in peace.17(And the king of Iſrael ſayd to Iehoſhaphat, Did I not tell thee, that hee would not propheſie good vnto mee, but euill?)18Againe he ſayd; Therefore heare the word of the Lord: I ſawe the Lord ſitting vpon his throne, and all the hoſte of heauen ſtanding on his right hand, and on his left.19And the Lord ſayd, Who ſhall entiſe Ahab king of Iſrael, that hee may goe vp and fall at Ramoth Gilead? And one ſpake, ſaying after this maner, and another ſaying after that maner.20Then there came out a ſpirit, and ſtood before the Lord, and ſayd, I will entiſe him. And the Lord ſayd vnto him, Wherewith?[21]And hee ſayd, I will goe out, and be a lying ſpirit in the mouth of all his prophets. And the Lord ſayd, Thou ſhalt entiſe him, and thou ſhalt alſo preuaile: goe out, and doe euen ſo.[22]Nowe therefore behold, the Lord hath put a lying ſpirit in the mouth of theſe thy prophets, and the Lord hath ſpoken euill againſt thee.[23]Then Zedekiah the ſonne of Chenaanah, came neere, and ſmote Micaiah vpon the cheeke, and ſayd, Which way went the ſpirit of the Lord from mee, to ſpeake vnto thee?[24]And Micaiah ſayd, Behold, thou ſhalt ſee on that day, when thou ſhalt goe into an inner chamber to hide thy ſelfe.[25]Then the king of Iſrael ſayd, Take yee Micaiah, and carie him backe to Amon the gouernour of the citie, and to Ioaſh the kings ſonne:[26]And ſay, Thus ſaith the king, Put this fellow in the priſon, and feede him with bread of affliction, and with water of affliction, vntill I returne in peace.[27]And Micaiah ſayd, If thou certainly returne in peace, then hath not the Lord ſpoken by mee. And hee ſayd, Hearken all yee people.[28]So the king of Iſrael, and Iehoſhaphat the king of Iudah, went vp to Ramoth Gilead.[29]And the king of Iſrael ſayd vnto Iehoſhaphat, I will diſguiſe my ſelfe, and will goe to the battell, but put thou on thy robes. So the king of Iſrael diſguiſed himſelfe, and they went to the battell.[30]Now the king of Syria had commaunded the captaines of the charets that were with him, ſaying, Fight ye not with ſmall or great, ſaue onely with the king of Iſrael.[31]And it came to paſſe when the captaines of the charets ſaw Iehoſhaphat, that they ſayd, It is the king of Iſrael: therefore they compaſſed about him to fight. But Iehoſhaphat cryed out, and the Lord helped him, and God moued them to depart from him.[32]For it came to paſſe, that when the captaines of the charets perceiued that it was not the king of Iſrael, they turned backe againe from purſuinghim.[33]And a certaine man drew a bowe at a venture, and ſmote the king of Iſrael betweene the ioints of the harneſse: therefore hee ſayd to his charetman, Turne thine hand, that thou mayeſt carie me out of the hoſte, for I am wounded.[34]And the battell increaſed that day: howbeit the king of Iſrael ſtayed himſelfe vp in his charet againſt the Syrians, vntill the Euen: and about the time of the ſunne going downe, hee dyed.

CHAPTER 19[1]And Iehoſhaphat the king of Iudah returned to his houſe in peace to Ieruſalem.[2]And Iehu the ſonne of Hanani the ſeer, went out to meete him, and ſayd to king Iehoſhaphat, Shouldeſt thou helpe the vngodly, and loue them that hate the Lord ? Therefore is wrath vpon thee from before the Lord.[3]Neuertheleſſe, there are good things found in thee, in that thou haſt taken away the groues out of the land, and haſt prepared thine heart to ſeeke God.[4]And Iehoſhaphat dwelt at Ieruſalem: and hee went out againe through the people, from Beer-ſheba to mount Ephraim, and brought them backe vnto the Lord God of their fathers.[5]And he ſet Iudges in the land, throughout all the fenced cities of Iudah, city by city,[6]And ſaid to the Iudges, Take heed what ye doe: for yee iudge not for man, but for the Lord, who is with you in the iudgement.[7]Wherefore now, let the feare of the Lord be vpon you, take heed and doe it: for there is no iniquitie with the Lord our God, nor reſpect of perſons, nor taking of gifts.[8]Moreouer in Ieruſalem did Iehoſhaphat ſet of the Leuites, and of the Prieſts, and of the chiefe of the fathers of Iſrael, for the iudgement of the Lord, and for controuerſies, when they returned to Ieruſalem.[9]And hee charged them, ſaying, Thus ſhall yee doe in the feare of the Lord faithfully, and with a perfect heart.[10]And what cauſe ſoeuer ſhal come to you of your brethren that dwell in their cities, betweene blood and blood, betweene Law and Commandement, Statutes and Iudgements, yee ſhall euen warne them that they treſpaſſe not againſt the Lord, and ſo wrath come vpon you, and vpon your brethren: this doe, & ye ſhall not treſpaſſe.[11]And behold, Amariah the chiefe Prieſt is ouer you in all matters of the Lord, and Zebadiah the ſonne of Iſhmael, the ruler of the houſe of Iudah, for all the Kings matters: Alſo the Leuites ſhall be officers before you. Deale couragiouſly, and the Lord ſhalbe with the good.

CHAPTER 20[1]It came to paſſe after this alſo, that the children of Moab, and the children of Ammon, and with them, other beſide the Ammonites, came againſt Iehoſhaphat to battell.[2]Then there came ſome that tolde Iehoſhaphat, ſaying, There commeth a great multitude againſt thee from beyond the ſea on this ſide Syria, and behold, they bee in Hazazon-Tamar, which is En-gedi.[3]And Iehoſhaphat feared, and ſet himſelfe to ſeeke the Lord, and proclaimed a faſt throughout all Iudah.[4]And Iudah gathered themſelues together, to aſke helpe of the Lord: euen out of all the cities of Iudah they came to ſeeke the Lord.[5]And Iehoſhaphat ſtood in the Congregation of Iudah and Ieruſalem, in the houſe of the Lord before the new Court,[6]And ſaid, O Lord God of our fathers, art not thou God in heauen? and ruleſt not thou ouer all the kingdoms of the heathen? and in thine hand is there not power and might, ſo that none is able to withſtand thee?[7]Art not thou our God, who didſt driue out the inhabitants of this land before thy people Iſrael, and gaueſt it to the ſeed of Abraham thy friend for euer?[8]And they dwelt therein, and haue built thee a Sanctuarie therein for thy Name, ſaying,[9]If, when euill commeth vpon vs, as the ſword, iudgement, or peſtilence, or famine, wee ſtand before this houſe, and in thy preſence (for thy Name is in this houſe) and cry vnto thee in our affliction, then thou wilt heare & helpe.[10]And now behold, the children of Ammon, and Moab, and mount Seir, whom thou wouldeſt not let Iſrael inuade, when they came out of the land of Egypt, but they turned from them, and deſtroyed them not:[11]Beholde, I ſay, how they reward vs, to come to caſt vs out of thy poſſeſſion, which thou haſt giuen vs to inherit.[12]O our God, wilt thou not iudge them? for wee haue no might againſt this great company that commeth againſt vs? neither know wee what to doe; but our eyes are vpon thee.[13]And all Iudah ſtood before the Lord, with their litle ones, their wiues and their children.[14]Then vpon Iahaziel the ſonne of Zechariah, the ſonne of Benaiah, the ſonne of Iehiel, the ſonne of Mattaniah, a Leuite of the ſons of Aſaph, came the Spirit of the Lord in the midſt of the Congregation:[15]And he ſaid, Hearken yee, all Iudah, and ye inhabitants of Ieruſalem, and thou king Iehoſhaphat, Thus ſayth the Lord vnto you; Be not afraid, nor diſmayed by reaſon of this great multitude; for the battell is not yours, but Gods.[16]To morrow goe ye downe againſt them: behold, they come vp by the cliffe of Ziz, and ye ſhall finde them at the end of the brooke, before the wilderneſſe of Ieruel.[17]Yee ſhall not neede to fight in this battell; ſet your ſelues, ſtand yee ſtill, and ſee the ſaluation of the Lord with you, O Iudah and Ieruſalem: feare not, nor be diſmayed; to morow goe out againſt them, for the Lord will bee with you.[18]And Iehoſhaphat bowed his head, with his face to the ground: and all Iudah, and the inhabitants of Ieruſalem, fell before the Lord, worſhipping the Lord.[19]And the Leuites, of the children of the Kohathites, and of the children of the Korhites, ſtood vp to praiſe the Lord God of Iſrael, with a loude voice on high.[20]And they roſe early in the morning, and went foorth into the wilderneſſe of Tekoa: and as they went forth, Iehoſhaphat ſtood and ſaid, Heare me, O Iudah, and yee inhabitants of Ieruſalem; Beleeue in the Lord your God, ſo ſhall you be eſtabliſhed; beleeue his Prophets, ſo ſhall yee proſper.[21]And when he had conſulted with the people, he appointed Singers vnto the Lord, and that ſhould praiſe the beautie of holineſſe, as they went out before the armie; and to ſay, Praiſe the Lord, for his mercy endureth for euer.[22]And when they beganne to ſing and to praiſe, the Lord ſet ambuſhments againſt the children of Ammon, Moab, and mount Seir, which were come againſt Iudah, and they were ſmitten.[23]For the children of Ammon and Moab, ſtood vp againſt the inhabitants of mount Seir, vtterly to ſlay and deſtroy them: and when they had made an end of the inhabitants of Seir, euery one helped to deſtroy another.[24]And when Iudah came toward the watch-tower in the wilderneſſe, they looked vnto the multitude, and behold, they were dead bodies fallen to the earth, and none eſcaped.[25]And when Iehoſhaphat and his people came to take away the ſpoile of them, they found among them in abundance both riches with the dead bodies, and precious iewels (which they ſtript off for themſelueſ) more then they could cary away: and they were three dayes in gathering of the ſpoile, it was ſo much.[26]And on the fourth day they aſſembled themſelues in the valley of Berachah; for there they bleſſed the Lord: therfore the name of the ſame place was called the valley of Berachah vnto this day.[27]Then they returned, euery man of Iudah and Ieruſalem, and Iehoſhaphat in the forefront of them, to go againe to Ieruſalem with ioy: for the Lord had made them to reioyce ouer their enemies.[28]And they came to Ieruſalem with Pſalteries, and harpes, and trumpets, vnto the houſe of the Lord.[29]And the feare of God was on all the kingdoms of thoſe countreys, when they had heard that the Lord fought againſt the enemies of Iſrael.[30]So the Realme of Iehoſhaphat was quiet; for his God gaue him reſt round about.[31]And Iehoſhaphat reigned ouer Iudah: Hee was thirtie and fiue yeeres olde when hee began to reigne, and he reigned twentie and fiue yeeres in Ierusalem: and his mothers name was Azubah the daughter of Shilhi.32And he walked in the way of Aſa his father, and departed not from it, doing that which was right in the ſight of the Lord.33Howbeit the high places were not taken away: for as yet the people had not prepared their hearts vnto the God of their fathers.34Now the reſt of the actes of Iehoſhaphat firſt and laſt, behold, they are written in the booke of Iehu the ſonne of Hanani; who is mentioned in the booke of the Kings of Iſrael.35And after this did Iehoſhaphat king of Iudah ioine himſelfe with Ahaziah king of Iſrael, who did very wickedly:36And he ioyned himſelfe with him to make ſhips to goe to Tarſhiſh: and they made the ſhips in Ezion-Geber.37Then Eliezer the ſonne of Dodanah of Mareſhah, propheſied againſt Iehoſhaphat, ſaying; Becauſe thou haſt ioyned thy ſelfe with Ahaziah, the Lord hath broken thy workes: and the ſhips were broken, that they were not able to goe to Tarſhiſh.

CHAPTER 211Now Iehoſhaphat ſlept with his fathers, and was buried with his fathers in the citie of Dauid: and Iehoram his ſonne reigned in his ſtead.2And he had brethren the ſonnes of Iehoſhaphat, Azariah, and Iehiel, and Zechariah, and Azariah, and Michael, and Shephatiah: All theſe were the ſonnes of Iehoſhaphat king of Iſrael.3And their father gaue them great giftes of ſiluer and of golde, and of precious things, with fenced cities in Iudah: but the kingdome gaue hee to Iehoram, becauſe he was the firſt borne.4Now when Iehoram was riſen vp to the kingdome of his father, he ſtrengthened himſelfe, and ſlew all his brethren with the ſword, and diuers alſo of the Princes of Iſrael.5Iehoram was thirtie and two yeeres olde when hee began to reigne, and hee reigned eight yeeres in Ieruſalem.6And he walked in the way of the kings of Iſrael, like as did the houſe of Ahab: for hee had the daughter of Ahab to wife: and he wrought that which was euill in the eyes of the Lord.7Howbeit the Lord would not deſtroy the houſe of Dauid, becauſe of the couenant that hee had made with Dauid, and as hee promiſed, to giue a light to him and to his ſons for euer.8In his dayes the Edomites reuolted from vnder the dominion of Iudah, and made themſelues a king.9Then Iehoram went forth with his Princes, and all his charets with him: and he roſe vp by night, and ſmote the Edomites which compaſſed him in, and the captaines of the charets.10So the Edomites reuolted from vnder the hand of Iudah vnto this day. The ſame time alſo did Libnah reuolt from vnder his hand, becauſe he had forſaken the Lord God of his fathers.11Moreouer, he made high places in the mountaines of Iudah, and cauſed the inhabitants of Ieruſalem to commit fornication, and compelled Iudah thereto.12And there came a writing to him from Eliiah the Prophet, ſaying, Thus ſaith the Lord God of Dauid thy father, Becauſe thou haſt not walked in the wayes of Iehoſhaphat thy father, nor in the wayes of Aſa king of Iudah:13But haſt walked in the way of the kings of Iſrael, and haſt made Iudah and the inhabitants of Ieruſalem to goe a whoring, like to the whoredomes of the houſe of Ahab, and alſo haſt ſlaine thy brethren of thy fathers houſe, which were better then thy ſelfe:14Behold, with a great plague wil the Lord ſmite thy people, and thy children, and thy wiues, and all thy goods.15And thou ſhalt haue great ſicknefſe by diſeaſe of thy bowels, vntil thy bowels fall out, by reaſon of the ſickenefſe day by day.16Moreouer, the Lord ſtirred vp againſt Iehoram the ſpirit of the Philiſtines, and of the Arabians, that were neere the Ethiopians.17And they came vp into Iudah, and brake into it, and caried away all the ſubſtance that was found in the kings houſe, and his ſonnes alſo and his wiues; ſo that there was neuer a ſonne left him, ſaue Iehoahaz, the yongeſt of his ſonnes.18And after all this, the Lord ſmote him in his bowels, with an incurable diſeaſe.19And it came to paſſe, that in proceſſe of time, after the end of two yeres, his bowels fell out by reaſon of his ſickenefſe: ſo hee dyed of ſore diſeaſes. And his people made no burning for him, like the burning of his fathers.20Thirtie and two yeeres old was he when he began to reigne, and he reigned in Ieruſalem eight yeeres, and departed without being deſired: howbeit, they buried him in the citie of Dauid, but not in the ſepulchres of the kings.

CHAPTER 221And the inhabitants of Ieruſalem made Ahaziah his yongeſt ſonne, king in his ſtead: for the band of men that came with the Arabians to the campe, had ſlaine all the eldeſt. So Ahaziah the ſonne of Iehoram king of Iudah reigned.2Fourtie and two yeeres old was Ahaziah, when he began to reigne, and he reigned one yeere in Ieruſalem: his mothers name alſo was Athaliah the daughter of Omri.3Hee alſo walked in the wayes of the houſe of Ahab: for his mother was his counſeller to doe wickedly.4Wherefore he did euill in the ſight of the Lord, like the houſe of Ahab: for they were his counſellers after the death of his father, to his deſtruction.5He walked alſo after their counſell, and went with Iehoram the ſonne of Ahab king of Iſrael, to warre againſt Hazael king of Syria at Ramoth Gilead: and the Syrians ſmote Ioram.6And he returned to bee healed in Iezreel, becauſe of the wounds which were giuen him at Ramah when hee fought with Hazael king of Syria. And Azariah the ſonne of Iehoram king of Iudah, went downe to ſee Iehoram the ſonne of Ahab at Iezreel, becauſe he was ſicke.7And the deſtruction of Ahaziah was of God by comming to Ioram: For when he was come, hee went out with Iehoram againſt Iehu the ſonne of Nimſhi, whome the Lord had anointed to cut off the houſe of Ahab.8And it came to paſſe, that when Iehu was executing iudgement vpon the houſe of Ahab, and found the princes of Iudah, and the ſonnes of the brethren of Ahaziah, that miniſtred to Ahaziah, he ſlew them.9And he ſought Ahaziah: and they caught him (for he was hid in Samaria) and brought him to Iehu: and when they had ſlaine him, they buried him: becauſe, ſaid they, hee is the ſonne of Iehoſhaphat, who ſought the Lord with all his heart. So the houſe of Ahaziah had no power to keepe ſtill the kingdome.10But when Athaliah the mother of Ahaziah, ſawe that her ſonne was dead, ſhee aroſe, and deſtroyed all the ſeed royall of the houſe of Iudah.11But Iehoſhabeath the daughter of the king, tooke Ioaſh the ſonne of Ahaziah, and ſtole him from among the kings ſonnes, that were ſlaine, and put him and his nurſe in a bed chamber. So Iehoſhabeath the daughter of king Iehoram, the wife of Iehoiada the prieſt (for ſhe was the ſiſter of Ahaziah) hid him from Athaliah, ſo that ſhe ſlew him not.12And he was with them hid in the houſe of God ſixe yeeres, and Athaliah reigned ouer the land.

CHAPTER 231And in the ſeuenth yeere Iehoiada ſtrengthened himſelfe, and tooke the captaines of hundreds, Azariah the ſonne of Ieroham, and Iſhmael the ſonne of Iehohanan, and Azariah the ſonne of Obed, and Maaſiah the ſonne of Adaiah, and Eliſhaphat the ſonne of Zichri, into couenant with him.2And they went about in Iudah, and gathered the Leuites out of all the cities of Iudah, and the chiefe of the fathers of Iſrael, and they came to Ieruſalem.3And all the Congregation made a couenant with the king in the houſe of God: and he ſaid vnto them, Beholde, the kings ſonne ſhall reigne, as the Lord hath ſaid of the ſonnes of Dauid.4This is the thing that yee ſhall doe, A third part of you entring on the Sabbath, of the prieſts and of the Leuites, ſhalbe porters of the doores.5And a thirde part ſhall bee at the kings houſe, and a third part at the gate of the foundation: and all the people ſhall be in the Courts of the houſe of the Lord.6But let none come into the houſe of the Lord, ſaue the Prieſts, & they that miniſter of the Leuites, they ſhall go in, for they are holy: but all the people ſhall keepe the watch of the Lord.7And the Leuites ſhall compaſſe the king round about, euery man with his weapons in his hand, and whoſoeuer elſe commeth into the houſe, hee ſhalbe put to death: but be you with the King when he commeth in, and when he goeth out.8So the Leuites and all Iudah did according to all things that Iehoiada the Prieſt had commanded: and tooke euery man his men that were to come in on the Sabbath, with them that were to goe out on the Sabbath: for Iehoiada the Prieſt diſmiſsed not the courſes.9Moreouer, Iehoiada the Prieſt deliuered to the captaines of hundreds, ſpeares and bucklers, and ſhields, that had bene King Dauids, which were in the houſe of God.10And hee ſet all the people (euery man hauing his weapon in his hand) from the right ſide of the Temple, to the left ſide of the Temple, along by the Altar and the Temple, by the King, round about.11Then they brought out the kings ſonne, and put vpon him the Crowne, and gaue him the Teſtimony, and made him King: and Iehoiada and his ſonnes anointed him, and ſaid, God ſaue the King.12Now when Athaliah heard the noiſe of the people running and praiſing the King; ſhe came to the people into the houſe of the Lord.13And ſhe looked, and behold, the king ſtood at his pillar, at the entring in, and the Princes, and the trumpets by the King: and all the people of the land reioyced, and ſounded with trumpets; alſo the ſingers with inſtruments of muſicke; and ſuch as taught to ſing praiſe. Then Athaliah rent her clothes, and ſaid, Treaſon, treaſon.14Then Iehoiada the Prieſt brought out the captaines of hundreds, that were ſet ouer the hoſt, and ſaid vnto them, Haue her foorth of the ranges: and who ſo followeth her, let him bee ſlaine with the ſword. For the Prieſt ſaid; Slay her not in the houſe of the Lord.15So they layd handes on her, and when ſhee was come to the entring of the horſe gate, by the kings houſe, they ſlew her there.16And Iehoiada made a couenant betweene him, and betweene all the people, and betweene the king, that they ſhould be the Lords people.17Then all the people went to the houſe of Baal, and brake it downe, and brake his altars and his images in pieces, and ſlew Mattan the prieſt of Baal before the altars.18Alſo Iehoiada appointed the offices of the houſe of the Lord by the hand of the Prieſts the Leuites, whom Dauid had diſtributed in the houſe of the Lord, to offer the burnt offrings of the Lord, as it is written in the Law of Moſes, with reioycing and with ſinging, as it was ordeined by Dauid.19And he ſet the porters at the gates of the houſe of the Lord, that none which was vncleane in any thing, ſhould enter in.20And hee tooke the captaines of hundreds, and the nobles, and the gouernours of the people, and all the people of the land, and brought downe the king from the houſe of the Lord: and they came through the high gate into the kings houſe, and ſet the king vpon the throne of the kingdome.21And all the people of the land reioyced, and the city was quiet, after that they had ſlaine Athaliah *wt* the ſword.

CHAPTER 241Ioaſh was ſeuen yeeres old when he beganne to reigne; and he reigned fortie yeeres in Ieruſalem: his mothers name alſo was Zibiah, of Beer-ſheba.2And Ioaſh did that which was right in the ſight of the Lord, all the dayes of Iehoiada the Prieſt.3And Iehoiada tooke for him two wiues, and he begat ſonnes and daughters.4And it came to paſſe after this that Ioaſh was minded to repaire the houſe of the Lord.5And hee gathered together the prieſts and the Leuites, and ſaide to them, Go out vnto the cities of Iudah, and gather of all Iſrael money to repaire the houſe of your God from yeere to yere, and ſee that ye haſte the matter: howbeit the Leuites haſtened it not.6And the king called for Iehoiada the chiefe, and ſaide vnto him, Why haſt thou not required of the Leuites to bring in out of Iudah and out of Ieruſalem, the collection, according to the commandement of Moſes the ſeruant of the Lord, and of the Congregation of Iſrael, for the tabernacle of Witneſse?7For the ſonnes of Athaliah that wicked woman, had broken vp the houſe of God, and alſo all the dedicate things of the houſe of the Lord, did they beſtow vpon Baalim.8And at the kings commandement they made a cheſt, and ſet it without, at the gate of the houſe of the Lord.9And they made a proclamation through Iudah & Ieruſalem, to bring in to the Lord, the collection that Moſes the ſeruant of God laid vpon Iſrael in the wilderneſſe.10And all the Princes and all the people reioyced, and brought in, and caſt into the cheſt, vntill they had made an ende.11Now it came to paſſe that at what time the cheſt was brought vnto the kings office, by the hand of the Leuites: and when they ſawe that there was much money: the kings Scribe, and the high prieſts officer, came and emptied the cheſt, and tooke it, and caried it to his place againe. Thus they did day by day, and gathered money in abundance.12And the king and Iehoiada gaue it to ſuch as did the worke of the ſeruice of the houſe of the Lord, and hired Maſons and carpenters to repaire the houſe of the Lord, and alſo ſuch as wrought yron and braſſe to mend the houſe of the Lord.13So the workemen wrought, and the worke was perfected by them: and they ſet the houſe of God in his ſtate, and ſtrengthened it.14And when they had finiſhed it, they brought the reſt of the money before the king and Iehoiada, whereof were made veſſels for the houſe of the Lord, euen veſſels to miniſter and to offer withall, and ſpoones, and veſſels of golde and ſiluer: and they offered burnt offerings in the houſe of the Lord continually, all the dayes of Iehoiada.15But Iehoiada waxed old, and was full of dayes when hee died: an hundred and thirtie yeeres olde was hee when hee died.16And they buried him in the citie of Dauid among the kings, becauſe he had done good in Iſrael, both towards God, and towards his houſe.17Now after the death of Iehoiada, came the Princes of Iudah, and made obeyſance to the king: then the king hearkened vnto them.18And they left the houſe of the Lord God of their fathers, and ſerued groues and idols: and wrath came vpon Iudah and Ieruſalem for this their treſpaſſe.19Yet hee ſent prophets to them to bring them againe vnto the Lord, and they teſtified againſt them: but they would not giue eare.20And the ſpirit of God came vpon Zechariah the ſonne of Iehoiada the prieſt, which ſtood aboue the people, and ſaid vnto them: Thus ſaith God, Why tranſgreſse yee the commandements of the Lord, that yee cannot proſper? Becauſe yee haue forſaken the Lord, he hath alſo forſaken you.21And they conſpired againſt him, and ſtoned him with ſtones at the commandement of the king, in the court of the houſe of the Lord.22Thus Ioaſh the king remembred not the kindneſſe which Iehoiada his father had done to him, but ſlew his ſonne: and when he died, he ſaid, The Lord looke vpon it, and require it.23And it came to paſſe at the end of the yeere, that the hoſte of Syria came vp againſt him: and they came to Iudah and Ieruſalem, and deſtroyed all the Princes of the people from among the people, and ſent all the ſpoile of them vnto the king of Damaſcus.24For the armie of the Syrians came with a ſmall companie of men, and the Lord deliuered a very great hoſte into their hand, becauſe they had forſaken the Lord God of their fathers: ſo they executed iudgement againſt Ioaſh.25And when they were departed from him (for they left him in great diſeaſeſ) his owne ſeruants conſpired againſt him, for the blood of the ſonnes of Iehoiada the Prieſt, and ſlewe him on his bed, and he died: and they buried him in the citie of Dauid, but they buried him not in the ſepulchres of the Kings.26And theſe are they that conſpired againſt him; Zabad the ſonne of Shimeah an Ammoniteſse, and Iehozabad the ſonne of Shimrith a Moabiteſse.27Now concerning his ſonnes, and the greatneſſe of the burdens laide vpon him, and the repairing of the houſe of God, behold, they are written in the ſtory of the booke of the Kings. And Amaziah his ſonne reigned in his ſtead.

CHAPTER 251Amaziah was twentie and fiue yeeres olde when hee began to reigne, and hee reigned twentie and nine yeeres in Ieruſalem, and his mothers name was Iehoadan of Ieruſalem.2And hee did that which was right in the ſight of the Lord, but not with a perfite heart.3Now it came to paſſe when the kingdome was eſtabliſhed to him, that he ſlew his ſeruants, that had killed the king his father.4But hee ſlewe not their children, but did as it is written in the Law in the booke of Moſes, where the Lord commanded, ſaying, The fathers ſhall not die for the children, neither ſhall the children die for the fathers; but euery man ſhall die for his owne ſinne.5Moreouer, Amaziah gathered Iudah together, and made them Captaines ouer thouſands, and captaines ouer hundreds, according to the houſes of their fathers, throughout all Iudah and Beniamin: And he numbred them from twentie yeeres olde and aboue, and found them three hundred thouſand choice men, able to goe foorth to warre, that could handle ſpeare and ſhield.6Hee hired alſo an hundred thouſand mightie men of valour, out of Iſrael, for an hundred talents of ſiluer.7But there came a man of God to him, ſaying, O king, let not the armie of Iſrael goe with thee: for the Lord is not with Iſrael, to wit, with all the children of Ephraim.8But if thou wilt goe, doe it, bee ſtrong for the battell: God ſhall make thee fall before the enemy: for God hath power to helpe, and to caſt downe.9And Amaziah ſaid to the man of God, But what ſhall wee doe for the hundred talents which I haue giuen to the armie of Iſrael? And the man of God anſwered, The Lord is able to giue thee much more then this.10Then Amaziah ſeparated them, to wit, the armie that was come to him out of Ephraim, to goe home againe. Wherfore their anger was greatly kindled againſt Iudah, and they returned home in great anger.11And Amaziah ſtrengthened himſelfe, and ledde foorth his people, and went to the valley of ſalt, and ſmote of the children of Seir, ten thouſand.12And other ten thouſand left aliue, did the children of Iudah cary away captiue, and brought them vnto the top of the rocke, and caſt them downe from the top of the rocke, that they all were broken in pieces.13But the ſouldiers of the army which Amaziah ſent backe, that they ſhould not goe with him to battell, fell vpon the cities of Iudah, from Samaria euen vnto Beth-horon, and ſmote three thouſand of them, and took much ſpoile.14Now it came to paſſe, after that Amaziah was come from the ſlaughter of the Edomites, that hee brought the gods of the children of Seir, and ſet them vp to be his gods, and bowed down himſelfe before them, and burned incenſe vnto them.15Wherfore the anger of the Lord was kindled againſt Amaziah, and hee ſent vnto him a Prophet, which ſaid vnto him, Why haſt thou ſought after the gods of the people, which could not deliuer their owne people out of thine hand?16And it came to paſſe as hee talked with him, that the king ſaid vnto him, Art thou made of the Kings counſell? forbeare; why ſhouldeſt thou be ſmitten? Then the Prophet forbare, and ſaid, I know that God hath determined to deſtroy thee, becauſe thou haſt done this, and haſt not hearkened vnto my counſell.17Then Amaziah king of Iudah tooke aduice, and ſent to Ioaſh the ſonne of Iehoahaz the ſonne of Iehu, king of Iſrael, ſaying, Come, let vs ſee one another in the face.18And Ioaſh king of Iſrael ſent to

Amaziah king of Iudah, ſaying, The thiſtle that was in Lebanon, ſent to the Cedar that was in Lebanon, ſaying, Giue thy daughter to my ſonne to wife: and there paſſed by a wild beaſt that was in Lebanon, and trode downe the thiſtle.19Thou ſayeſt, Loe, thou haſt ſmitten the Edomites, and thine heart lifteth thee vp to boaſt. Abide now at home, why ſhouldeſt thou meddle to thine hurt, that thou ſhouldeſt fall, euen thou, and Iudah with thee?20But Amaziah would not heare: for it came of God, that he might deliuer them into the hand of their enemies, becauſe they ſought after the gods of Edom.21So Ioaſh the King of Iſrael went vp, and they ſaw one another in the face, both hee and Amaziah King of Iudah at Beth-ſhemeſh, which belongeth to Iudah.22And Iudah was put to the worſe before Iſrael, and they fled euery man to his tent.23And Ioaſh the king of Iſrael tooke Amaziah king of Iudah the ſon of Ioaſh, the ſon of Ioahaz, at Bethſhemeſh, and brought him to Ieruſalem, and brake downe the wall of Ieruſalem, from the gate of Ephraim to the corner gate, foure hundred cubits.24And hee tooke all the gold and the ſiluer, and all the veſſels that were found in the houſe of God with Obed-Edom, and the treaſures of the kings houſe, the hoſtages alſo, and returned to Samaria.25And Amaziah the ſonne of Ioaſh King of Iudah liued after the death of Ioaſh ſonne of Iehoahaz king of Iſrael, fifteene yeeres.26Now the reſt of the acts of Amaziah, firſt and laſt, behold, are they not written in the booke of the Kings of Iudah and Iſrael?27Now after the time that Amaziah did turne away from following the Lord, they made a conſpiracie againſt him in Ieruſalem, and he fled to Lachiſh: but they ſent to Lachiſh after him, and ſlew him there.28And they brought him vpon horſes, and buried him with his fathers in the citie of Iudah.

CHAPTER 261Then all the people of Iudah tooke Uzziah, who was ſixteene yeeres old, and made him King in the roome of his father Amaziah.2He built Eloth, and reſtored it to Iudah: after that the King ſlept with his fathers.3Sixteene yeeres old was Uzziah, when he began to reigne, and he reigned fiftie and two yeeres in Ieruſalem: his mothers name alſo was Iecoliah of Ieruſalem.4And hee did that which was right in the ſight of the Lord, according to all that his father Amaziah did.5And hee ſought God in the dayes of Zechariah, who had vnderſtanding in the viſions of God: and as long as he ſought the Lord, God made him to proſper.6And hee went foorth and warred againſt the Philiſtines, & brake downe the wall of Gath, and the wall of Iabneh, and the wall of Aſhdod, and built cities about Aſhdod, and among the Philiſtines.7And God helped him againſt the Philiſtines, and againſt the Arabians, that dwelt in Gur-baal, and the Mehunims.8And the Ammonites gaue gifts to Uzziah, and his name ſpread abroad euen to the entring in of Egypt: for hee ſtrengthened himſelfe exceedingly.9Moreouer Uzziah built towers in Ieruſalem at the corner gate, and at the valley gate, and at the turning of the wall, and fortified them.10Alſo he built towers in the deſert, and digged many welles, for hee had much cattell, both in the low countrey, and in the plaines: huſbandmen alſo, and vine dreſſers in the mountaines, and in Carmel: for hee loued huſbandrie.11Moreouer, Uzziah had an hoſt of fighting men, that went out to warre by bands, according to the number of their account, by the hand of Ieiel the Scribe, and Maaſiah the ruler, vnder the hand of Hananiah, one of the kings captaines.12The whole number of the chiefe of the fathers of the mightie men of valour, were two thouſand and ſixe hundred.13And vnder their hand was an armie, three hundred thouſand, and ſeuen thouſand, and fiue hundred, that made warre with mightie power, to helpe the king againſt the enemie.14And Uzziah prepared for them throughout all the hoſte, ſhields, and ſpeares, and helmets, and habergions, and bowes, and ſlings to caſt ſtones.15And hee made in Ieruſalem engines inuented by cunning men, to bee on the towers, & vpon the bulwarks, to ſhoote arrowes and great ſtones withall: and his name ſpread farre abroad, for he was marueilouſly helped, till he was ſtrong.16But when he was ſtrong, his heart was lifted vp to his deſtruction: for he tranſgreſſed againſt the Lord his God, and went into the temple of the Lord, to burne incenſe vpon the altar of incenſe.17And Azariah the prieſt went in after him, and with him foureſcore prieſts of the Lord, that were valiant men.18And they withſtood Uzziah the king, and ſaid vnto him, It perteineth not vnto thee, Uzziah, to burne incenſe vnto the Lord, but to the prieſtes the ſonnes of Aaron, that are conſecrated to burne incenſe. Goe out of the Sanctuarie; for thou haſt treſpaſſed, neither ſhall it be for thine honour from the Lord God.19Then Uzziah was wroth, and had a cenſer in his hand, to burne incenſe, and while he was wroth with the prieſts, the leproſie euen roſe vp in his forehead, before the prieſts, in the houſe of the Lord, from beſide the incenſe altar.20And Azariah the chiefe prieſt, and all the prieſts looked vpon him, and behold, he was leprous in his forehead, and they thruſt him out from thence, yea himſelfe haſted alſo to goe out, becauſe the Lord had ſmitten him.21And Uzziah the king was a leper vnto the day of his death, and dwelt in a ſeuerall houſe being a leper, for he was cut off from the houſe of the Lord: and Iotham his ſonne was ouer the kings houſe, iudging the people of the land.22Now the reſt of the actes of Uzziah firſt and laſt, did Iſaiah the prophet the ſonne of Amoz write.23So Uzziah ſlept with his fathers, and they buried him with his fathers in the field of the buriall which belonged to the kings: for they ſaide, He is a leper: And Iotham his ſonne reigned in his ſtead.

CHAPTER 271Iotham was twenty and fiue yeeres olde, when hee began to reigne, and hee reigned ſixteene yeeres in Ieruſalem: his mothers name alſo was Ieruſhah, the daughter of Zadok.2And he did that which was right in the ſight of the Lord, according to all that his father Uzziah did: howbeit hee entred not into the temple of the Lord. And the people did yet corruptly.3He built the high gate of the houſe of the Lord, and on the wall of Ophel, he built much.4Moreouer hee built cities in the mountaines of Iudah, and in the forreſts he built caſtles and towers.5He fought alſo with the king of the Ammonites, and preuailed againſt them. And the children of Ammon gaue him the ſame yeere an hundred talents of ſiluer, and ten thouſand meaſures of wheate, and tenne thouſand of barley. So much did the children of Ammon pay vnto him, both the ſecond yeere, and the third.6So Iotham became mightie, becauſe he prepared his wayes before the Lord his God.7Now the reſt of the actes of Iotham and all his warres, and his wayes, lo, they are written in the booke of the Kings of Iſrael and Iudah.8Hee was fiue and twentie yeeres olde when he began to reigne, and reigned ſixteene yeeres in Ieruſalem.9And Iotham ſlept with his fathers, and they buried him in the city of Dauid: and Ahaz his ſonne reigned in his ſtead.

CHAPTER 281Ahaz was twentie yeeres olde when hee beganne to reigne, and he reigned ſixteene yeres in Ieruſalem: but hee did not that which was right in the ſight of the Lord, like Dauid his father.2For he walked in the wayes of the Kings of Iſrael, and made alſo molten images for Baalim.3Moreouer, he burnt incenſe in the valley of the ſonne of Hinnom, & burnt his children in the fire, after the abominations of the heathen, whome the Lord had caſt out before the children of Iſrael.4Hee ſacrificed alſo, and burnt incenſe in the high places, and on the hils, and vnder euery greene tree.5Wherefore the Lord his God deliuered him into the hand of the king of Syria, and they ſmote him, and caried away a great multitude of them captiues, and brought them to Damaſcus: And he was alſo deliuered into the hand of the king of Iſrael, who ſmote him wich a great ſlaughter.6For Pekah the ſonne of Remaliah ſlew in Iudah an hundred & twentie thouſand in one day, which were all valiant men: becauſe they had forſaken the Lord God of their fathers.7And Zichri a mightie man of Ephraim, ſlue Maaſeiah the kings ſonne, and Azrikam the gouernour of the houſe, and Elkanah that was next to the King.8And the children of Iſrael caried away captiue of their brethren, two hundred thouſand, women, ſonnes and daughters, and tooke alſo away much ſpoile from them, and brought the ſpoile to Samaria.9But a Prophet of the Lord was there, whoſe name was Oded: and hee went out before the hoſte that came to Samaria, and ſaid vnto them, Behold, becauſe the Lord God of your fathers was wroth with Iudah, he hath deliuered them into your hand, and yee haue ſlaine them in a rage that reacheth vp vnto heauen.10And now ye purpoſe to keepe vnder the children of Iudah and Ieruſalem for bondmen, and bondwomen vnto you: But are there not with you, euen with you, ſinnes againſt the Lord your God?11Now heare me therefore, and deliuer the captiues againe, which ye haue taken captiue of your brethren: for the fierce wrath of God is vpon you.12Then certeine of the heads of the children of Ephraim, Azariah the ſonne of Iohanan, Berechiah the ſonne of Meſhillemoth, and Iehizkiah the ſon of Shallum, and Amaſa the ſonne of Hadlai, ſtood vp againſt them that came from the warre,13And ſaid vnto them, Ye ſhall not bring in the captiues hither: for whereas wee haue offended againſt the Lord already, ye intend to adde more to our ſinnes and to our treſpaſſe: for our treſpaſſe is great, and there is fierce wrath againſt Iſrael.14So the armed men left the captiues, and the ſpoile before the Princes, and all the congregation.15And the men which were expreſſed by name, roſe vp and tooke the captiues, and with the ſpoile clothed all that were naked among them, and arayed them, and ſhod them, and gaue them to eate and to drinke, and anointed them, and caried all the feeble of them vpon aſſes, and brought them to Iericho, the city of palme-trees, to their brethren: then they returned to Samaria.16At that time did king Ahaz ſend vnto the kings of Aſſyria to helpe him.17For againe the Edomites had come and ſmitten Iudah, and caried away captiues.18The Philiſtines alſo had inuaded the cities of the low-countrey, and of the South of Iudah, and had taken Beth-ſhemeſh, and Aialon, and Gedetoth, and Shocho with the villages thereof, and Timnah with the villages thereof, Gimzo alſo, and the villages thereof: and they dwelt there.19For the Lord brought Iudah low, becauſe of Ahaz king of Iſrael; for he made Iudah naked, and tranſgreſſed ſore againſt the Lord.20And Tilgath-Pilneſer king of Aſſyria came vnto him, and diſtreſſed him, but ſtrengthened him not.21For Ahaz tooke away a portion out of the houſe of the Lord, and out of the houſe of the King, and of the Princes, and gaue it vnto the King of Aſſyria: but he helped him not.22And in the time of this diſtreſſe did hee treſpaſſe yet more againſt the Lord: This is that king Ahaz.23For he ſacrificed vnto the gods of Damaſcus, which ſmote him: and he ſaid, Becauſe the gods of the kings of Syria helpe them, therefore will I ſacrifice to them, that they may helpe me: but they were the ruine of him, and of all Iſrael.24And Ahaz gathered together the veſſels of the houſe of God, and cut in pieces the veſſels of the houſe of God, and ſhut vp the doores of the houſe of the Lord, and hee made him altars in euery corner of Ieruſalem.25And in euery ſeuerall city of Iudah hee made high places to burne incenſe vnto other gods, and prouoked to anger the Lord God of his fathers.26Now the reſt of his acts, and of all his wayes, firſt and laſt, behold, they are written in the booke of the kings of Iudah and Iſrael.27And Ahaz ſlept with his fathers, and they buried him in the citie, euen in Ieruſalem: but they brought him not into the ſepulchres of the kings of Iſrael: and Hezekiah his ſonne reigned in his ſtead.

CHAPTER 291Hezekiah began to reigne when hee was fiue and twentie yeeres old, and he reigned nine and twentie yeeres in Ieruſalem: and his mothers name was Abiiah the daughter of Zechariah.2And hee did that which was right in the ſight of the Lord, according to all that Dauid his father had done.3He, in the firſt yere of his reigne, in the firſt moneth, opened the doores of the houſe of the Lord, and repaired them.4And hee brought in the Prieſts, and the Leuites, and gathered them together into the Eaſt ſtreet,5And ſaid vnto them, Heare me, ye Leuites, ſanctifie now your ſelues, and ſanctifie the houſe of the Lord God of your fathers, and cary foorth the filthineſse out of the holy place.6For our fathers haue treſpaſſed, and done that which was euill in the eyes of the Lord our God, and haue forſaken him, and haue turned away their faces from the habitation of the Lord, and turned their backs.7Alſo they haue ſhut vp the doores of the Porch, and put out the lampes, and haue not burnt incenſe, nor offered burnt offerings in the holy place, vnto the God of Iſrael.8Wherfore the wrath of the Lord was vpon Iudah and Ieruſalem, and he hath deliuered them to trouble, to aſtoniſhment, and to hiſsing, as yee ſee with your eyes.9For loe, our fathers haue fallen by the ſword, and our ſonnes and our daughters, and our wiues, are in captiuitie for this.10Now it is in mine heart to make a couenant with the Lord God of Iſrael, that his fierce wrath may turne away from vs.11My ſonnes, bee not now negligent: for the Lord hath choſen you to ſtand before him, to ſerue him, and that you ſhould miniſter vnto him, and burne incenſe.12Then the Leuites aroſe, Mahath the ſonne of Amaſhai, and Ioel the ſonne of Azariah, of the ſonnes of the Kohathites: and of the ſonnes of Merari, Kiſh the ſonne of Abdi, and Azariah the ſonne of Iahalelel: and of the Gerſhonites Ioah, the ſonne of Zimmah, and Eden the ſonne of Ioah:13And of the ſonnes of Elizaphan, Shimri, and Iehiel: and of the ſonnes of Aſaph, Zechariah and Mattaniah:14And of the ſonnes of Heman, Iehiel, and Shimei: and of the ſonnes of Ieduthun, Shemaiah and Uzziel.15And they gathered their brethren, and ſanctified themſelues, and came according to the commandement of the king, by the words of the Lord, to cleanſe the houſe of the Lord.16And the prieſts went into the inner part of the houſe of the Lord, to cleanſe it, and brought out all the vncleannes that they found in the temple of the Lord, into the court of the houſe of the Lord. And the Leuites tooke it, to carie it out abroad into the brooke Kidron.17Now they began on the firſt day of the firſt moneth to ſanctifie, and on the eight day of the moneth, came they to the porch of the Lord. So they ſanctified the houſe of the Lord in eight dayes, and in the ſixteenth day of the firſt moneth, they made an end.18Then they went in to Hezekiah the king, and ſaid, We haue cleanſed all the houſe of the Lord, and the altar of burnt offering, with all the veſſels thereof, and the ſhew-bread table, with all the veſſels thereof.19Moreouer all the veſſels which king Ahaz in his reigne did caſt away in his tranſgreſsion, haue we prepared and ſanctified, and behold, they are before the altar of the Lord.20Then Hezekiah the king roſe earely, and gathered the rulers of the citie, and went vp to the houſe of the Lord.21And they brought ſeuen bullocks and ſeuen rammes, and ſeuen lambes, and ſeuen hee goats for a ſinne offring for the kingdome, and for the Sanctuarie, and for Iudah: and he commaunded the prieſts the ſonnes of Aaron to offer them on the Altar of the Lord.22So they killed the bullockes, and the prieſtes receiued the blood, and ſprinkled it on the altar: like wiſe when they had killed the rams, they ſprinkled the blood vpon the altar: they killed alſo the lambes, and they ſprinkled the blood vpon the altar.23And they brought foorth the hee goats for the ſinne offering, before the king and the congregation, and laide their hands vpon them:24And the prieſts killed them, and they made reconciliation with their blood vpon the altar, to make an atonement for all Iſrael: for the king commanded that the burnt offring and the ſin offering ſhould be made for all Iſrael.25And hee ſet the Leuites in the houſe of the Lord with cymbals, with pſalteries, and with harpes, according to the commandement of Dauid, and of Gad the kings Seer, and Nathan the prophet: for ſo was the commandement of the Lord by his prophets.26And the Leuites ſtood with the inſtruments of Dauid, and the prieſtes with the trumpets.27And Hezekiah commaunded to offer the burnt offering vpon the altar: and when the burnt offering began, the ſong of the Lord began alſo with the trumpets, and with the inſtruments ordeined by Dauid king of Iſrael.28And all the congregation worſhipped, and the ſingers ſang, and the trumpetters ſounded: and all this continued vntill the burnt offering was finiſhed.29And when they had made an end of offering, the king and all that were preſent with him, bowed themſelues and worſhipped.30Moreouer Hezekiah the king and the Princes, commanded the Leuites to ſing praiſe vnto the Lord, with the words of Dauid, and of Aſaph the Seer: and they ſang praiſes with gladnes, and they bowed their heads and worſhipped.31Then Hezekiah anſwered and ſaid, Now ye haue conſecrated your ſelues vnto the Lord: come neere and bring ſacrifices, and thanke-offerings into the houſe of the Lord. And the congregation brought in ſacrifices, and thank-offrings, and as many as were of a free heart, burnt offerings.32And the number of the burnt offerings which the congregation brought, was threeſcore and ten bullockes, an hundred rammes, and two hundred lambs: all theſe were for a burnt offring to the Lord.33And the conſecrated things were, ſixe hundred oxen, and three thouſand ſheepe.34But the Prieſts were too few, ſo that they could not flay all the burnt offerings: wherefore their brethren the Leuites did helpe them, till the worke was ended, and vntill the other Prieſtes had ſanctified themſelues: for the Leuites were more vpright in heart, to ſanctifie themſelues, then the Prieſts.35And alſo the burnt offerings were in abundance, with the fat of the peace offerings, & the drinke offrings, for euery burnt offering. So the ſeruice of the houſe of the Lord was ſet in order.36And Hezekiah reioyced, and all the people, that God had prepared the people: for the thing was done ſuddenly.

CHAPTER 301And Hezekiah ſent to all Iſrael and Iudah, and wrote letters alſo to Ephraim and Manaſſeh, that they ſhould come to the houſe of the Lord at Ieruſalem, to keepe the Paſſeouer vnto the Lord God of Iſrael.2For the king had taken counſell, and his Princes, and all the congregation in Ieruſalem, to keepe the Paſſeouer in the ſecond moneth.3For they could not keepe it at that time, becauſe the Prieſts had not ſanctified themſelues ſufficiently, neither had the people gathered themſelues together to Ieruſalem.4And the thing pleaſed the king, and all the Congregation.5So they eſtabliſhed a decree, to make proclamation throughout all Iſrael, from Beerſheba euen to Dan, that they ſhould come to keep the Paſſeouer vnto the Lord God of Iſrael at Ieruſalem: for they had not done it of a long time in ſuch ſort, as it was written.6So the Poſtes went with the letters from the King and his Princes, throughout all Iſrael and Iudah, and according to the commandement of the king, ſaying; Yee children of Iſrael, turne againe vnto the Lord God of Abraham, Iſaac and Iſrael, and hee wil returne to the remnant of you, that are eſcaped out of the hand of the kings of Aſſyria.7And be not ye like your fathers, and like your brethren, which treſpaſſed againſt the Lord God of their fathers, who therefore gaue them vp to deſolation, as ye ſee.8Now be yee not ſtiffe-necked as your fathers were, but yeeld your ſelues vnto the Lord, and enter into his Sanctuarie, which he hath ſanctified for euer: and ſerue the Lord your God, that the fiercenesſe of his wrath may turne away from you.9For if yee turne againe vnto the Lord, your brethren and your children ſhall finde compaſſion before them that leade them captiue, ſo that they ſhall come againe into this land: for the Lord your God is gracious and mercifull, and will not turne away his face from you, if ye returne vnto him.10So the Poſts paſſed from citie to citie, through the countrey of Ephraim and Manaſſeh, euen vnto Zebulun: but they laughed them to ſcorne, and mocked them.11Neuertheleſſe, diuers of Aſher, and Manaſſeh, and of Zebulun, humbled themſelues, and came to Ieruſalem.12Alſo in Iudah, the hand of God was to giue them one heart to doe the commandement of the king and of the Princes, by the word of the Lord.13And there aſſembled at Ieruſalem much people, to keepe the feaſt of vnleauened bread in the ſecond moneth, a very great congregation.14And they aroſe and tooke away the altars that were in Ieruſalem, and all the altars for incenſe tooke they away, and caſt them into the brooke Kidron.15Then they killed the Paſſeouer on the fourteenth day of the ſecond moneth: and the Prieſts and the Leuites were aſhamed, and ſanctified themſelues, and brought in the burnt offerings into the houſe of the Lord.16And they ſtood in their place after their maner, according to the Law of Moſes the man of God: The prieſts ſprinckled the blood, which they receiued of the hand of the Leuites.17For there were many in the Congregation that were not ſanctified: therefore the Leuites had the charge of the killing of the Paſſeouers for euery one that was not cleane, to ſanctifie them vnto the Lord.18For a multitude of the people, euen many of Ephraim and Manaſſeh, Iſſachar and Zebulun, had not cleanſed themſelues: yet did they eate the Paſſeouer otherwiſe then it was written. But Hezekiah prayed for them, ſaying; The good Lord pardon euery one,19That prepareth his heart to ſeeke God, the Lord God of his fathers, though hee be not cleanſed according to the purification of the Sanctuary.20And the Lord hearkened to Hezekiah, and healed the people.21And the children of Iſrael that were preſent at Ieruſalem, kept the feaſt of vnleauened bread ſeuen dayes with great gladneſſe: and the Leuites and the Prieſts praiſed the Lord day by day, ſinging with lowd inſtruments vnto the Lord.22And Hezekiah ſpake comfortably vnto all the Leuites, that taught the good knowledge of the Lord: and they did eate throughout the feaſt, ſeuen dayes, offering peace-offerings, and making confeſsion to the Lord God of their fathers.23And the whole aſſembly tooke counſel to keepe other ſeuen dayes: and they kept other ſeuen dayes with gladneſſe.24For Hezekiah king of Iudah did giue to the Congregation, a thouſand bullockes, and ſeuen thouſand ſheep: and the Princes gaue to the Congregation a thouſand bullocks, and ten thouſand ſheepe, and a great number of Prieſts ſanctified themſelues.25And all the Congregation of Iudah, with the Prieſts and the Leuites, and all the Congregation that came out of Iſrael, and the ſtrangers that came out of the land of Iſrael, and that dwelt in Iudah, reioyced.26So there was great ioy in Ieruſalem: for ſince the time of Solomon the ſonne of Dauid King of Iſrael, there was not the like in Ieruſalem.27Then the Prieſts the Leuites aroſe, and bleſſed the people: and their voice was heard, and their prayer came vp to his holy dwelling place, euen vnto heauen.

CHAPTER 311Now when all this was finiſhed, all Iſrael that were preſent, went out to the cities of Iudah, and brake the images in pieces, and cut downe the groues, and threw downe the high places and the altars out of all Iudah and Beniamin, in Ephraim alſo and Manaſſeh, vntill they had vtterly deſtroyed them all. Then all the children of Iſrael returned euery man to his poſſeſſion into their owne cities.2And Hezekiah appointed the courſes of the Prieſts and the Leuites after their courſes, euery man according to his ſeruice, the Prieſts and Leuites for burnt offerings, and for peace offerings, to miniſter and to giue thankes, and to praiſe in the gates of the tents of the Lord.3He appointed alſo the kings portion of his ſubſtance, for the burnt offrings, to wit, for the morning and euening burnt offrings; and the burnt offrings for the Sabbaths, and for the Newmoones, and for the ſet feaſts, as it is written in the Law of the Lord.4Moreouer, he commaunded the people that dwelt in Ieruſalem, to giue the portion of the Prieſts, and the Leuites, that they might be incouraged in the Law of the Lord.5And aſsoone as the commaundement came abroad, the children of Iſrael brought in abundance the firſt fruits of corne, wine and oile, & hony, and of all the increaſe of the field, and the tithe of all things brought they in abundantly.6And concerning the children of Iſrael and Iudah, that dwelt in the cities of Iudah, they alſo brought in the tithes of oxen and ſheepe, and the tithe of holy things, which were conſecrated vnto the Lord their God, and layd them by heapes.7In the third moneth they began to lay the foundation of the heapes, and finiſhed them in the ſeuenth moneth.8And when Hezekiah and the princes came, and ſaw the heapes, they bleſſed the Lord, and his people Iſrael.9Then Hezekiah queſtioned with the prieſts and the Leuites concerning the heapes.10And Azariah the chiefe prieſt of the houſe of Zadok, anſwered him & ſaid: Since the people began to bring the offerings into the houſe of the Lord, wee haue had enough to eate, and haue left plentie: for the Lord hath bleſſed his people; and that which is left, is this great ſtore.11Then Hezekiah commanded to prepare chambers in the houſe of the Lord, and they prepared them,12And brought in the offerings and the tithes, and the dedicate things, faithfully: ouer which Cononiah the Leuite was ruler, and Shimei his brother was the next.13And Iehiel, and Azaziah, and Nahath, and Aſahel, and Ierimoth, and Iozabad, and Eliel, and Iſmachiah, and Mahath, and Benaiah were ouerſeers vnder the hande of Cononiah, and Shimei his brother, at the commandement of Hezekiah the king, and Azariah the ruler of the houſe of God.14And Kore the ſonne of Immah the Leuite the porter toward the Eaſt, was ouer the free will offerings of God, to diſtribute the oblations of the Lord, and the moſt holy things.15And next him were Eden, and Miniamin, and Ieſhua, and Shemaiah, Amariah, and Shechaniah, in the cities of the prieſts, in their ſet office, to giue to their brethren by courſes, as wel to the great as to the ſmall:16Beſide their genealogie of males, from three yeeres old and vpward, euen vnto euery one that entreth into the houſe of the Lord, his dayly portion for their ſeruice in their charges, according to their courſes:17Both to the genealogie of the prieſts by the houſe of their fathers, and the Leuites from twenty yeeres olde and vpward, in their charges by their courſes:18And to the genealogie of all their litle ones, their wiues, and their ſonnes, and their daughters, through all the congregation: for in their ſet office they ſanctified themſelues in holineſſe.19Alſo of the ſonnes of Aaron the prieſts, which were in the fields of the ſuburbs of their cities, in euery ſeuerall citie, the men that were expreſſed by name, to giue portions to all the males among the prieſts, and to all that were reckoned by genealogies, among the Leuites.20And thus did Hezekiah throughout al Iudah, and wrought that which was good and right, and trueth before the Lord his God.21And in euery worke that he began in the ſeruice of the houſe of God, and in the law, and in the commandements to ſeeke his God, he did it with all his heart, and proſpered.

CHAPTER 321After theſe things and the eſtabliſhment therof, Sennacherib king of Aſſyria came, and entred into Iudah, & encamped againſt the fenced cities, and thought to winne them for himſelfe.2And when Hezekiah ſawe that Sennacherib was come, and that hee was purpoſed to fight againſt Ieruſalem,3He tooke counſel with his princes, and his mightie men, to ſtop the waters of the fountaines, which were without the citie: and they did helpe him.4So there was gathered much people together, who ſtopt all the fountaines, and the brooke that ranne through the midſt of the land, ſaying, Why ſhould the kings of Aſſyria come, and finde much water?5Alſo he ſtrengthened himſelfe, and built vp all the wall that was broken, and raiſed it vp to the towers, and another wall without, and prepared Millo in the citie of Dauid, and made darts and ſhields in abundance.6And hee ſet captaines of warre ouer the people, and gathered them together to him in the ſtreete of the gate of the city, and ſpake comfortably to them, ſaying;7Be ſtrong and couragious, be not afraid nor diſmayed for the king of Aſſyria, nor for all the multitude that is with him: for there bee moe with vs, then with him.8With him is an arme of fleſh, but with vs is the Lord our God to helpe vs, and to fight our battels. And the people reſted themſelues vpon the words of Hezekiah king of Iudah.9After this did Sennacherib king of Aſſyria ſend his ſeruants to Ieruſalem (but he himſelfe laide ſiege againſt Lachiſh, and all his power with him) vnto Hezekiah king of

Iudah, and vnto all Iudah that were at Ieruſalem, ſaying; 10 Thus ſayth Semacherib king of Aſſyria, Whereon doe ye truſt, that yee abide in the ſiege in Ieruſalem? 11 Doeth not Hezekiah perſwade you to giue ouer your ſelues to die by famine and by thirſt, ſaying, The Lord our God ſhall deliuer vs out of the hand of the king of Aſſyria? 12 Hath not the ſame Hezekiah taken away his high places, and his altars, and commanded Iudah and Ieruſalem, ſaying; Yee ſhall worſhip before one altar, & burne incenſe vpon it? 13 Know ye not what I and my fathers haue done vnto all the people of other lands? were the gods of the nations of thoſe landes any wayes able to deliuer their lands out of mine hand? 14 Who was there among all the gods of thoſe nations, that my fathers vtterly deſtroyed, that could deliuer his people out of mine hand, that your God ſhould bee able to deliuer you out of mine hand? 15 Now therefore let not Hezekiah deceiue you, nor perſwade you on this manner, neither yet beleeue him: for no god of any nation or kingdome was able to deliuer his people out of mine hand, & out of the hand of my fathers: how much leſſe ſhall your God deliuer you out of mine hand? 16 And his ſeruants ſpake yet more againſt the Lord God, and againſt his ſeruant Hezekiah. 17 Hee wrote alſo letters to raile on the Lord God of Iſrael, & to ſpeake againſt him, ſaying, As the gods of the nations of other lands haue not deliuered their people out of mine hand: ſo ſhall not the God of Hezekiah deliuer his people out of mine hand. 18 Then they cryed with a loude voice in the Iewes ſpeech vnto the people of Ieruſalem that were on the wal, to affright them, and to trouble them, that they might take the city. 19 And they ſpake againſt the God of Ieruſalem, as againſt the gods of the people of the earth which were the worke of the hands of man. 20 For this cauſe Hezekiah the king, and the Prophet Iſaiah the ſonne of Amoz, prayed and cryed to heauen. 21 And the Lord ſent an Angel, which cut off all the mightie men of valour, and the leaders and captains in the campe of the king of Aſſyria: ſo hee returned with ſhame of face to his owne land. And when hee was come into the houſe of his god, they that came foorth of his owne bowels, ſlew him there with the ſword. 22 Thus the Lord ſaued Hezekiah, and the inhabitants of Ieruſalem, from the hand of Sennacherib the king of Aſſyria, and from the hand of all other, and guided them on euery ſide. 23 And many brought gifts vnto the Lord to Ieruſalem, and preſents to Hezekiah king of Iudah: ſo that hee was magnified in the ſight of all nations, from thenceforth. 24 In thoſe dayes Hezekiah was ſicke to the death, and prayed vnto the Lord: and he ſpake vnto him, and he gaue him a ſigne. 25 But Hezekiah rendred not againe, according to the benefit done vnto him: for his heart was lifted vp, therefore there was wrath vpon him, and vpon Iudah and Ieruſalem. 26 Notwithſtanding, Hezekiah humbled himſelfe for the pride of his heart, (both hee and the inhabitants of Ieruſalem) ſo that the wrath of the Lord came not vpon them in the dayes of Hezekiah. 27 And Hezekiah had exceeding much riches, and honour: and he made himſelfe treaſuries for ſiluer, and for golde, and for precious ſtones, and for ſpices, and for ſhields, and for all maner of pleaſant iewels; 28 Store-houſes alſo for the increaſe of corne, and wine and oile; and ſtalles for all maner of beaſts, and coates for flocks. 29 Moreouer, hee prouided him cities, and poſſeſſions of flockes & heards in abundance: for God had giuen him ſubſtance very much. 30 This ſame Hezekiah alſo ſtopped the vpper water-courſe of Gihon, and brought it ſtraight downe to the Weſtſide of the City of Dauid. And Hezekiah proſpered in all his workes. 31 Howbeit, in the buſineſse of the Embaſſadours of the Princes of Babylon, who ſent vnto him to enquire of the wonder that was done in the land, God left him, to try him, that he might know all that was in his heart. 32 Now, the reſt of the acts of Hezekiah, and his goodneſse, behold, they are written in the viſion of Iſaiah the Prophet, the ſonne of Amoz, and in the booke of the kings of Iudah and Iſrael. 33 And Hezekiah ſlept with his fathers, and they buried him in the chiefeſt of the Sepulchres of the ſonnes of Dauid: and all Iudah and the inhabitants of Ieruſalem did him honour at his death: and Manaſſeh his ſonne reigned in his ſtead.

CHAPTER 33 1 Manaſſeh was twelue yeeres old when he began to reigne, and he reigned fiftie and fiue yeres in Ieruſalem: 2 But did that which was euil in the ſight of the Lord, like vnto the abominations of the heathen, whom the Lord had caſt out before the children of Iſrael. 3 For hee built againe the high places, which Hezekiah his father had broken downe, and he reared vp altars for Baalim, and made groues, and worſhipped all the hoſt of heauen, and ſerued them. 4 Alſo hee built altars in the houſe of the Lord, whereof the Lord had ſaide, In Ieruſalem ſhall my Name be for euer. 5 And he built altars for all the hoſt of heauen, in the two Courts of the houſe of the Lord. 6 And he cauſed his children to paſſe through the fire in the valley of the ſon of Hinnom: alſo he obſerued times, and vſed inchantments, and vſed witchcraft, and dealt with a familiar ſpirit, and with wizards: he wrought much euill in the ſight of the Lord, to prouoke him to anger. 7 And hee ſet a carued image (the idole which he had made) in the houſe of God, of which God had ſaid to Dauid, and to Solomon his ſonne: In this houſe, and in Ieruſalem which I haue choſen before all the tribes of Iſrael, will I put my Name for euer. 8 Neither will I any more remoue the foot of Iſrael from out of the land which I haue appointed for your fathers; ſo that they will take heed to doe all that I haue commanded them, according to the whole Law, and the ſtatutes, and the ordinances by the hand of Moſes. 9 So Manaſſeh made Iudah, and the inhabitants of Ieruſalem to erre, and to doe worſe then the heathen, whom the Lord had deſtroyed before the children of Iſrael. 10 And the Lord ſpake to Manaſſeh, and to his people: but they would not hearken. 11 Wherfore the Lord brought vpon them the captaines of the hoſt of the king of Aſſyria, which took Manaſſeh among the thornes, & bound him with fetters, & caried him to Babylon. 12 And when hee was in affliction, he beſought the Lord his God, and humbled himſelfe greatly before the God of his fathers, 13 And prayed vnto him, and he was intreated of him, and heard his ſupplication, and brought him againe to Ieruſalem into his kingdome. Then Manaſſeh knew that the Lord hee was God. 14 Now after this, hee built a wall without the citie of Dauid, on the Weſtſide of Gihon, in the valley, euen to the entring in at the fiſh-gate, and compaſſed about Ophel, and raiſed it vp a very great height, and put captaines of warre in all the fenced cities of Iudah. 15 And hee tooke away the ſtrange gods and the idol out of the houſe of the Lord, and all the altars that he had built in the mount of the houſe of the Lord, and in Ieruſalem, and caſt them out of the citie. 16 And hee repaired the altar of the Lord, and ſacrificed thereon peace offerings, and thanke offerings, and commaunded Iudah to ſerue the Lord God of Iſrael. 17 Neuertheleſſe, the people did ſacrifice ſtill in the high places, yet vnto the Lord their God only. 18 Nowe the reſt of the actes of Manaſſeh, & his prayer vnto his God, and the words of the ſeers that ſpake to him in the name of the Lord God of Iſrael, behold, they are written in the booke of the kings of Iſrael: 19 His prayer alſo, and how God was intreated of him, and all his ſinne, and his treſpaſſe, and the places wherein he built high places, and ſet vp groues and grauen images before hee was humbled: behold, they are written among the ſayings of the Seers. 20 So Manaſſeh ſlept with his fathers, and they buried him in his owne houſe: and Amon his ſonne reigned in his ſtead. 21 Amon was two and twentie yeeres old, when he beganne to reigne, and reigned two yeares in Ieruſalem. 22 But he did that which was euill in the ſight of the Lord, as did Manaſſeh his father: for Amon ſacrificed vnto all the carued images, which Manaſſeh his father had made, and ſerued them; 23 And humbled not himſelfe before the Lord, as Manaſſeh his father had humbled himſelfe: but Amon treſpaſſed more and more. 24 And his ſeruants conſpired againſt him, and ſlew him in his owne houſe. 25 But the people of the land ſlew all them that had conſpired againſt king Amon, and the people of the land made Ioſiah his ſonne, king in his ſtead.

CHAPTER 34 1 Ioſiah was eight yeeres old when hee beganne to reigne, and he reigned in Ieruſalem one and thirty yeeres. 2 And he did that which was right in the ſight of the Lord, and walked in the wayes of Dauid his father, and declined neither to the right hand nor to the left. 3 For in the eight yeare of his reigne, while he was yet young, hee beganne to ſeeke after the God of Dauid his father: and in the twelfth yeere hee beganne to purge Iudah and Ieruſalem from the high places and the groues, and the carued images, and the molten images. 4 And they brake downe the altars of Baalim in his preſence, and the images that were on high aboue them, he cut downe, and the groues, and the carued images, and the molten images he brake in peeces, and made duſt of them, and ſtrowed it vpon the graues of them, that had ſacrificed vnto them. 5 And hee burnt the bones of the prieſts vpon their altars, and cleanſed Iudah and Ieruſalem. 6 And ſo did he in the cities of Manaſſeh, and Ephraim, and Simeon, euen vnto Naphtali, with their mattockes, round about. 7 And when he had broken downe the altars and the groues, and had beaten the grauen images into pouder, and cut downe all the idoles throughout

all the land of Iſrael, hee returned to Ieruſalem.8Now in the eighteenth
yeere of his reigne, when hee had purged the land, and the houſe; he
ſent Shaphan the ſonne of Azaliah, and Maaſiah the gouernour of the
citie, and Ioah the ſonne of Ioahaz the recorder, to repaire the houſe of
the Lord his God.9And when they came to Hilkiah the high prieſt, they
deliuered the money that was brought into the houſe of God, which the
Leuites that kept the doores, had gathered of the hand of Manaſſeh, and
Ephraim, and of all the remnant of Iſrael, and of all Iudah, and
Beniamin, and they returned to Ieruſalem.10And they put it in the hand
of the workemen that had the ouerſight of the houſe of the Lord, and
they gaue it to the workemen that wrought in the houſe of the Lord, to
repaire and mend the houſe.11Euen to the artificers and builders gaue
they it, to buy hewen ſtone, and timber for couplings, and to floore the
houſes, which the kings of Iudah had deſtroyed.12And the men did the
worke faithfully, and the ouerſeers of them were Iahath, and Obadiah,
the Leuites, of the ſonnes of Merari, and Sechariah, and Meſhullam, of
the ſonnes of the Kohathites, to ſet it forward: and other of the Leuites,
all that could ſkill of inſtruments of muſicke.13Alſo they were ouer the
bearers of burdens, and were ouerſeers of all that wrought the worke in
any manner of ſeruice: and of the Leuites there were Scribes, and
officers, and porters.14And when they brought out the money that was
brought into the houſe of the Lord, Hilkiah the prieſt found a booke of
the lawe of the Lord, giuen by Moſes.15And Hilkiah anſwered and ſaide
to Shaphan the ſcribe: I haue found the booke of the law in the houſe
of the Lord. And Hilkiah deliuered the booke to Shaphan:16And
Shaphan caried the booke to the king, and brought the king word backe
againe, ſaying, All that was committed to thy ſeruants, they doe it.17And
they haue gathered together the money that was found in the houſe of
the Lord, and haue deliuered it into the hand of the ouerſeers, and to
the hand of the workemen.18Then Shaphan the ſcribe tolde the king,
ſaying, Hilkiah the prieſt hath giuen me a booke. And Shaphan read it
before the king.19And it came to paſſe when the king had heard the
words of the lawe, that he rent his clothes.20And the king commanded
Hilkiah, and Ahikam the ſonne of Shaphan, and Abdon the ſonne of
Mirah, and Shaphan the ſcribe, and Aſaiah a ſeruant of the kings,
ſaying,21Goe, enquire of the Lord for me, and for them that are left in
Iſrael and in Iudah, concerning the wordes of the booke that is found:
for great is the wrath of the Lord that is powred out vpon vs, becauſe
our fathers haue not kept the word of the Lord, to doe after all that is
written in this booke.22And Hilkiah and they that the king had appointed
went to Huldah the propheteſse, the wife of Shallum the ſonne of
Tikuath, the ſonne of Haſrah, keeper of the wardrobe (now ſhe dwelt in
Ieruſalem in the colledge,) and they ſpake to her to that effect.23And ſhe
anſwered them, Thus ſaith the Lord God of Iſrael: Tell ye the man that
ſent you to me,24Thus ſaith the Lord, behold, I will bring euill vpon this
place, and vpon the inhabitants thereof, euen all the curſes that are
written in the booke which they haue read before the king of
Iudah:25Becauſe they haue forſaken mee, and haue burned incenſe vnto
other gods, that they might prouoke mee to anger with all the workes of
their hands, therefore my wrath ſhall bee powred out vpon this place,
and ſhall not be quenched.26And as for the king of Iudah, who ſent you
to enquire of the Lord, ſo ſhal ye ſay vnto him: Thus ſaith the Lord God
of Iſrael, concerning the words which thou haſt heard:27Becauſe thine
heart was tender, and thou didſt humble thy ſelfe before God, when
thou heardeſt his words againſt this place, and againſt the inhabitants
thereof, and humbledſt thy ſelfe before me, and diddeſt rend thy clothes,
and weepe before me, I haue euen heard thee alſo, ſaith the
Lord.28Behold, I will gather thee to thy fathers, and thou ſhalt bee
gathered to thy graue in peace, neither ſhall thine eyes ſee all the euill
that I will bring vpon this place, and vpon the inhabitants of the ſame.
So they brought the king word againe.29Then the king ſent, and gathered
together all the Elders of Iudah and Ieruſalem.30And the king went vp
into the houſe of the Lord, and all the men of Iudah, and the inhabitants
of Ieruſalem, and the prieſts and the Leuites, and all the people great
and ſmall: and he read in their eares all the words of the booke of the
couenant, that was found in the houſe of the Lord.31And the King ſtood
in his place, & made a Couenant before the Lord, to walke after the
Lord, and to keep his Commandements, and his Teſtimonies, and his
Statutes, with all his heart, & with all his ſoule, to performe the words
of the Couenant which are written in this booke.32And he cauſed all that
were preſent in Ieruſalem and Beniamin, to ſtand to it. And the
inhabitants of Ieruſalem did according to the couenant of God, the God
of their fathers.33And Ioſiah tooke away all the abominations out of all
the countreys that perteined to the children of Iſrael, and made all that
were preſent in Iſrael to ſerue, euen to ſerue the Lord their God. And
all his dayes they departed not from folowing the Lord the God of their
fathers.

CHAPTER 351Moreouer Ioſiah kept a Paſſeouer vnto þe Lord4 in
Ieruſalem: and they killed the Paſſeouer on the fourteenth day of the
firſt moneth.2And hee ſet the Prieſtes in their charges, and encouraged
them to the ſeruice of the houſe of the Lord,3And ſaid vnto the Leuites,
that taught all Iſrael, which were holy vnto the Lord, Put the holy Arke
in the houſe, which Solomon the ſonne of Dauid king of Iſrael did build;
it ſhall not be a burden vpon your ſhoulders : ſerue now the Lord your
God, and his people Iſrael.4And prepare your ſelues by the houſes of
your fathers, after your courſes, according to the writing of Dauid king
of Iſrael, and according to the writing of Solomon his ſonne.5And ſtand
in the holy place according to the diuiſions of the families of the fathers
of your brethren the people, and after the diuiſion of the families of the
Leuites.6So kill the Paſſeouer, and ſanctifie your ſelues, and prepare your
brethren, that they may doe according to the word of the Lord, by the
hand of Moſes.7And Ioſiah gaue to the people, of the flocke, lambes
and kiddes, all for the Paſſeouer-offerings, for all that were preſent, to
the number of thirtie thouſand, and three thouſand bullocks: theſe were
of the kings ſubſtance.8And his Princes gaue willingly vnto the people,
to the Prieſts and to the Leuites: Hilkiah, and Zachariah, and Iehiel,
rulers of the houſe of God, gaue vnto the Prieſts for the Paſſeouer-
offerings, two thouſand and ſixe hundred ſmall cattell, and three
hundred oxen.9Conaniah alſo, and Shemaiah, and Nethaneel, his
brethren, & Haſhabiah, and Iehiel, and Ioſhabad chiefe of the Leuites,
gaue vnto the Leuites for Paſſeouer-offerings, fiue thouſand ſmall
cattell, and fiue hundred oxen.10So the ſeruice was prepared, and the
Prieſts ſtood in their place, and the Leuites in their courſes, according
to the kings commandement.11And they killed the Paſſeouer, and the
Prieſtes ſprinckled the blood from their handes, and the Leuites flayed
them.12And they remooued the burnt offerings, that they might giue
according to the diuiſions of the families of the people, to offer vnto the
Lord, as it is written in the booke of Moſes: and ſo did they with the
oxen.13And they roſted the Paſſeouer with fire, according to the
ordinance: but the other holy offerings ſod they in pots, and in
cauldrons, and in pannes, and diuided them ſpeedily among all the
people.14And afterward they made ready for themſelues, and for the
Prieſts: becauſe the Prieſts the ſonnes of Aaron were buſied in offring
of burnt offrings, and the fat vntill night: therefore the Leuites prepared
for themſelues, and for the Prieſts the ſonnes of Aaron.15And the
ſingers the ſonnes of Aſaph, were in their place according to the
commandement of Dauid, and Aſaph, and Heman, and Ieduthun the
kings Seer: and the Porters waited at euery gate: they might not depart
from their ſeruice; for their brethren the Leuites prepared for them.16So
all the ſeruice of the Lord was prepared the ſame day, to keepe the
Paſſeouer, and to offer burnt offerings vpon the altar of the Lord,
according to the commaundement of king Ioſiah.17And the children of
Iſrael that were preſent, kept the Paſſeouer at that time, and the feaſt of
vnleauened bread ſeuen dayes.18And there was no Paſſeouer like to that,
kept in Iſrael, from the dayes of Samuel the Prophet: neither did all the
Kings of Iſrael keepe ſuch a Paſſeouer, as Ioſiah kept, and the Prieſts
and the Leuites, and all Iudah and Iſrael that were preſent, and the
inhabitants of Ieruſalem.19In the eighteenth yeere of the reigne of
Ioſiah, was this Paſſeouer kept.20After all this, when Ioſiah had prepared
the Temple, Necho king of Egypt came vp to fight againſt Carchemiſh
by Euphrates: and Ioſiah went out againſt him.21But hee ſent
Embaſſadours to him, ſaying, What haue I to doe with thee, thou king
of Iudah? I come not againſt thee this day, but againſt the houſe,
wherewith I haue warre: for God commaunded mee to make haſte:
forbeare thee from medling with God, who is with mee, that hee deſtroy
thee not.22Neuertheleſſe Ioſiah would not turne his face from him, but
diſguiſed himſelfe that he might fight with him, and hearkened not vnto
the wordes of Necho from the mouth of God, and came to fight in the
valley of Megiddo.23And the archers ſhot at king Ioſiah: and the King
ſaide to his ſeruants, Haue mee away, for I am ſore wounded.24His

ſeruants therefore tooke him out of that charet, and put him in the ſecond charet that hee had: and they brought him to Ieruſalem, and hee died, and was buried in one of the Sepulchres of his fathers. And all Iudah and Ieruſalem mourned for Ioſiah.25And Ieremiah lamented for Ioſiah, and all the ſinging men and the ſinging women ſpake of Ioſiah in their lamentations to this day, and made them an ordinance in Iſrael; and beholde, they are written in the Lamentations.26Now the reſt of the acts of Ioſiah, and his goodnes, according to that which was written in the Law of the Lord,27And his deedes firſt and laſt; behold, they are written in the booke of the kings of Iſrael and Iudah.

CHAPTER 361Then the people of the land tooke Iehoahaz the ſon of Ioſiah, and made him King in his fathers ſtead in Ieruſalem.2Iehoahaz was twentie and three yeeres old, when hee began to reigne, and hee reigned three moneths in Ieruſalem.3And the king of Egypt put him downe at Ieruſalem, and condemned the land in an hundred talents of ſiluer, and a talent of gold.4And the king of Egypt made Eliakim his brother, king ouer Iudah and Ieruſalem, and turned his name to Iehoiakim. And Necho tooke Iehoahaz his brother, and caried him to Egypt.5Iehoiakim was twentie and fiue yeres old when he began to reigne, and he reigned eleuen yeeres in Ieruſalem: and hee did that which was euill in the ſight of the Lord his God.6Againſt him came vp Nebuchadnezzar King of Babylon, and bound him in fetters to cary him to Babylon.7Nebuchadnezzar alſo caried of the veſſels of the houſe of the Lord to Babylon, and put them in his temple at Babylon.8Now the reſt of the acts of Iehoiakim, and his abominations which he did, and that which was found in him, behold, they are written in the booke of the Kings of Iſrael and Iudah: and Iehoiachin his ſonne reigned in his ſtead.9Iehoiachin was eight yeeres old when hee began to reigne, and hee reigned three moneths and ten dayes in Ieruſalem, and hee did that which was euill in the ſight of the Lord.10And when the yeere was expired, King Nebuchadnezzar ſent, and brought him to Babylon, with the goodly veſſels of the houſe of the Lord, and made Zedekiah his brother, king ouer Iudah and Ieruſalem.11Zedekiah was one and twentie yeres old, when he began to reigne, and reigned eleuen yeeres in Ieruſalem.12And hee did that which was euill in the ſight of the Lord his God, and humbled not himſelfe before Ieremiah the Prophet, ſpeaking from the mouth of the Lord.13And he alſo rebelled againſt king Nebuchadnezzar, who had made him ſweare by God: but he ſtiffened his necke, and hardened his heart from turning vnto the Lord God of Iſrael.14Moreouer all the chiefe of the prieſts, and the people tranſgreſſed very much, after all the abominations of the heathen, and polluted the houſe of the Lord which hee had hallowed in Ieruſalem.15And the Lord God of their fathers ſent to them by his meſſengers, riſing vp betimes, and ſending: becauſe he had compaſſion on his people, and on his dwelling place:16But they mocked the meſſengers of God, and deſpiſed his wordes, and miſuſed his prophets, vntill the wrath of the Lord aroſe againſt his people, till there was no remedie.17Therefore hee brought vpon them the king of the Caldees, who ſlew their yong men with the ſword, in the houſe of their ſanctuarie, and had no compaſſion vpon yong man or maiden, olde man, or him that ſtouped for age: he gaue them all into his hand.18And all the veſſels of the houſe of God great and ſmall, and the treaſures of the houſe of the Lord, and the treaſures of the king, and of his princes: all theſe he brought to Babylon.19And they burnt the houſe of God, and brake downe the wall of Ieruſalem, and burnt all the palaces thereof with fire, and deſtroyed all the goodly veſſels thereof.20And them that had eſcaped from the ſword, caried he away to Babylon: where they were ſeruants to him and his ſonnes, vntil the reigne of the kingdome of Perſia:21To fulfill the word of the Lord by the mouth of Ieremiah, vntill the land had enioyed her Sabbaths: for as long as ſhee lay deſolate, ſhee kept Sabbath, to fulfill threeſcore and tenne yeeres.22Now in the firſt yeere of Cyrus king of Perſia (that the word of the Lord ſpoken by the mouth of Ieremiah, might bee accompliſhed) the Lord ſtirred vp the ſpirit of Cyrus king of Perſia, that hee made a proclamation throughout all his kingdome, and put it alſo in writing, ſaying,23Thus ſaith Cyrus king of Perſia, All the kingdomes of the earth hath the Lord God of heauen giuen mee, and he hath charged me to build him an houſe in Ieruſalem, which is in Iudah: Who is there among you of all his people? the Lord his God be with him, and let him goe vp.

EZRAH (EZRA)

CHAPTER 11Now in the firſt yeere of Cyrus King of Perſia, (that the word of the Lord by the mouth of Ieremiah, might be fulfilled) þe Lord ſtirred vp the ſpirit of Cyrus king of Perſia, that he made a proclamation throughout all his kingdome, and put it alſo in writing, ſaying;2Thus ſayth Cyrus king of Perſia, The Lord God of heauen hath giuen mee all the kingdomes of the earth, and he hath charged me to build him an houſe at Ieruſalem, which is in Iudah.3Who is there among you of all his people? his God be with him, and let him goe vp to Ieruſalem, which is in Iudah, and build the houſe of the Lord God of Iſrael (He is the God) which is in Ieruſalem.4And whoſoeuer remaineth in any place where hee ſoiourneth, let the men of his place helpe him with ſiluer, and with golde, and with goods, and with beaſts, beſides the free-will offering for the houſe of God that is in Ieruſalem.5Then roſe vp the chiefe of the fathers of Iudah and Beniamin, and the Prieſts, and the Leuites, with all them whoſe ſpirit God had raiſed to goe vp, to build the houſe of the Lord which is in Ieruſalem.6And all they that were about them, ſtrengthened their hands with veſſels of ſiluer, with golde, with goods, and with beaſts, and with precious things; beſides all that was willingly offered.7Alſo Cyrus the king brought foorth the veſſels of the houſe of the Lord, which Nebuchadnezzar had brought foorth out of Ieruſalem, and had put them in the houſe of his gods:8Euen thoſe did Cyrus king of Perſia bring foorth, by the hand of Mithredath the treaſurer, and numbred them vnto Sheſhbazzar the Prince of Iudah.9And this is the number of them: thirtie chargers of golde, a thouſand chargers of ſiluer, nine and twentie kniues:10Thirtie baſins of golde: ſiluer baſins of a ſecond ſort, foure hundred and ten: and other veſſels a thouſand.11All the veſſels of golde and of ſiluer, were fiue thouſand and foure hundred. All theſe did Sheſhbazzar bring vp with them of the captiuitie, that were brought vp from Babylon vnto Ieruſalem.

CHAPTER 21Now theſe are the children of the prouince, that went vp out of the captiuitie, of thoſe which had beene caried away, whom Nebuchadnezzar the King of Babylon had caried away vnto Babylon, and came againe vnto Ieruſalem and Iudah, euery one vnto his citie;2Which came with Zerubbabel, Ieſhua, Nehemiah, Saraiah, Reelaiah, Mordecai, Bilſhan, Miſpar, Biguai, Rehum, Baanah: The number of the men of the people of Iſrael.3The children of Paroſh, two thouſand, an hundred ſeuentie and two.4The children of Shephatiah, three hundred ſeuentie and two.5The children of Arah, ſeuen hundred, ſeuentie and fiue.6The children of Pahath-Moab, of the children of Ieſhua and Ioab, two thouſand, eight hundred and twelue.7The children of Elam, a thouſand, two hundred fiftie and foure.8The children of Zattu, nine hundred fourtie and fiue.9The children of Zaccai, ſeuen hundred and threeſcore.10The children of Bani, ſixe hundred, fourtie and two.11The children of Bebai, ſixe hundred, twentie and three.12The children of Azgad, a thouſand, two hundred, twentie and two.13The children of Adonikam, ſixe hundred, ſixtie and ſixe.14The children of Biguai, two thouſand fiftie and ſixe.15The children of Adin, foure hundred, fiftie and foure.16The children of Ater of Hezekiah, ninetie and eight.17The children of Bezai, three hundred twenty and three.18The children of Iorah, an hundred and twelue.19The children of Haſhum, two hundred twentie and three.20The children of Gibbar, ninetie and fiue.21The children of Bethlehem, an hundred twentie and three.22The children of Netophah, fiftie and ſixe.23The men of Anathoth, an hundred twentie and eight.24The children of Azmaueth, fortie and two.25The children of Kiriath-arim, Chephirah, and Beeroth, ſeuen hundred, and fourtie and three.26The children of Ramah and Gaba, ſixe hundred, twentie and one.27The men of Michmas, an hundred, twentie and two.28The men of Bethel and Ai, two hundred, twentie and three.29The children of Nebo, fiftie and two.30The children of Magbiſh, an hundred fiftie and ſixe.31The children of the other Elam, a thouſand, two hundred, fiftie and foure.32The children of Harim, three hundred and twentie.33The children of Lod Hadid, and Ono, ſeuen hundred, twentie and fiue.34The children of Iericho, three hundred fourtie and fiue.35The children of Senaah, three thouſand and ſixe hundred and thirtie.36The Prieſts. The children of Iedaiah, of the houſe of Ieſhua, nine hundred, ſeuentie and three.37The children of Immer, a thouſand, fiftie and two.38The children of Paſhur, a thouſand, two hundred, fourtie and ſeuen.39The children of Harim, a thouſand and

ſeuenteene.40The Leuites. The children of Ieſhua, and Kadmiel, of the
children of Hodauia, ſeuentie and foure.41The ſingers. The children of
Aſaph, an hundred twentie and eight.42The children of the porters. The
children of Shallum, the children of Ater, the children of Talmon, the
children of Akkub, the children of Hatita, the children of Shobai, in all,
an hundred thirtie and nine.43The Nethinims. The children of Ziha, the
children of Haſupha, the children of Tabbaoth,44The children of Keros,
the children of Siaha, the children of Padon,45The children of Lebanah,
the children of Hagabah, the children of Akkub,46The children of
Hagab, the children of Shalmai, the children of Hanan.47The children
of Giddel, the children of Gahar, the children of Reaiah,48The children
of Rezin, the children of Nekoda, the children of Gazzam,49The
children of Uzza, the children of Paſeah, the children of Beſai,50The
children of Aſnah, the children of Mehunim, the children of
Nephuſhim,51The children of Bakbuk, the children of Hakupha, the
children of Harhur,52The children of Bazluth, the children of Mehida,
the children of Harſha,53The children of Barkos, the children of Siſera,
the children of Thamah,54The children of Neziah, the children of
Hatipha.55The children of Solomons ſeruants. The children of Sotai, the
children of Sophereth, the children of Peruda,56The children of Iaalah,
the children of Darkon, the children of Giddel,57The children of
Shephatiah, the children of Hattil, the children of Pochereth of Zebaim,
the children of Ami.58All the Nethinims, and the children of Solomons
ſeruants, were three hundred ninetie and two.59And theſe were they
which went vp from Tel-melah, Tel-Harſa, Cherub, Addan, and Immer:
but they could not ſhewe their fathers houſe, and their ſeed, whether
they were of Iſrael.60The children of Delaiah, the children of Tobiah,
the children of Nekoda: ſixe hundred fiftie and two.61And of the
children of the prieſts: the children of Habaiah, the children of Koz, the
children of Barzillai, (which tooke a wife of the daughters of Barzillai
the Gileadite, and was called after their name.)62Theſe ſought their
regiſter among thoſe that were reckoned by genealogie, but they were
not found: therefore were they as polluted, put from the
prieſthood.63And the Tirſhatha ſaid vnto them, that they ſhould not eate
of the moſt holy things, till there ſtood vp a prieſt with Urim & with
Thummim.64The whole Congregation together, was fourtie and two
thouſand, three hundred and threeſcore:65Beſide their ſeruants and their
maids, of whom there were ſeuen thouſand, three hundred thirtie and
ſeuen: and there were among them two hundred ſinging men, and
ſinging women.66Their horſes were ſeuen hundred, thirtie and ſixe: their
mules, two hundred fourtie and fiue:67Their camels, foure hundred,
thirty and fiue: their aſſes, ſixe thouſand, ſeuen hundred and
twentie.68And ſome of the chiefe of the fathers, when they came to the
houſe of the Lord which is at Ieruſalem, offered freely for the houſe of
God, to ſet it vp in his place:69They gaue after their abilitie, vnto the
treaſure of the worke, threeſcore and one thouſand drammes of golde,
and fiue thouſand pound of ſiluer, and one hundred prieſts
garments.70So the prieſts and the Leuites, and ſome of the people, and
the ſingers, and the porters, and the Nethinims, dwelt intheir cities, and
all Iſrael in their cities.
CHAPTER 31And when the ſeuenth moneth was come, and the
children of Iſrael were in the cities: the people gathered themſelues
together, as one man to Ieruſalem.2Then ſtood vp Ieſhua the ſonne of
Iozadak, & his brethren the prieſts, and Zerubbabel the ſonne of
Shealtiel, and his brethren, and builded the Altar of the God of Iſrael,
to offer burnt offrings thereon, as it is written in the law of Moſes the
man of God.3And they ſet the altar vpon his baſes, (for feare was vpon
them, becauſe of the people of thoſe countreyſ) and they offered burnt
offerings thereon vnto the Lord, euen burnt offerings, morning and
euening.4They kept alſo the feaſt of tabernacles, as it is written, and
offred the dayly burnt offrings, by number, according to the cuſtome,
as the duetie of euery day required:5And afterward offered the continuall
burnt offering, both of the new moones, and of all the ſet feaſts of the
Lord, that were conſecrated, and of euery one that willingly offred,
offered a free will offering vnto the Lord.6From the firſt day of the
ſeuenth moneth, began they to offer burnt offerings vnto the Lord: but
the foundation of the temple of the Lord was not yet laid.7They gaue
money alſo vnto the maſons, and to the carpenters, and meate, and
drinke, and oyle, vnto them of Zidon, and to them of Tyre, to bring
Cedar trees from Lebanon to the ſea of Ioppa: according to the grant
that they had of Cyrus king of Perſia.8Now in the ſecond yere of their
coming vnto the houſe of God at Ieruſalem, in the ſecond moneth,
began Zerubbabel the ſonne of Shealtiel, and Ieſhua the ſonne of
Iozadak, and the remnant of their brethren, the Prieſts and the Leuites,
and all they that were come out of the captiuitie vnto Ieruſalem: and
appointed the Leuites, from twentie yeeres olde and vpward, to ſet
forward the worke of the houſe of the Lord.9Then ſtood Ieſhua, with
his ſons and his brethren, Kadmiel and his ſonnes, the ſonnes of Iudah
together, to ſet forward the workemen in the houſe of God: the ſonnes
of Henadad, with their ſonnes and their brethren the Leuites.10And
when the builders laide the foundation of the Temple of the Lord, they
ſet the Prieſts in their apparell with Trumpets, and the Leuites the
ſonnes of Aſaph, with Cymbales, to praiſe the Lord, after the ordinance
of Dauid king of Iſrael.11And they ſung together by courſe, in praiſing,
and giuing thanks vnto the Lord; Becauſe hee is good, for his mercy
endureth for euer towards Iſrael. And all the people ſhouted with a great
ſhoute, when they praiſed the Lord; becauſe the foundation of the houſe
of the Lord was laide.12But many of the Prieſts and Leuites, and chiefe
of the fathers, who were ancient men, that had ſeene the firſt houſe;
when the foundation of this houſe was laide before their eyes, wept with
a loude voice, and many ſhouted aloude for ioy:13So that the people
could not diſcerne the noyſe of the ſhout of ioy, from the noyſe of the
weeping of the people: for the people ſhouted with a loude ſhout, and
the noyſe was heard afarre off.
CHAPTER 41Now when the aduerſaries of Iudah and Beniamin, heard
that the children of the captiuitie builded the Temple vnto the Lord God
of Iſrael:2Then they came to Zerubbabel, and to the chiefe of the
fathers, and ſaid vnto them, Let vs build with you, for wee ſeeke your
God, as yee doe, and we doe ſacrifice vnto him, ſince the dayes of Eſar-
Haddon king of Aſſur, which brought vs vp hither.3But Zerubbabel and
Ieſhua, and the reſt of the chiefe of the fathers of Iſrael, ſaid vnto them,
You haue nothing to doe with vs, to build an houſe vnto our God, but
we our ſelues together will build vnto the Lord God of Iſrael, as king
Cyrus the King of Perſia hath commanded vs.4Then the people of the
land weakened the handes of the people of Iudah, and troubled them in
building,5And hired counſellers againſt them, to fruſtrate their purpoſe,
all the dayes of Cyrus king of Perſia, euen vntill the reigne of Darius king
of Perſia.6And in the reigne of Ahaſuerus, in the beginning of his reigne,
wrote they vnto him an accuſation againſt the inhabitants of Iudah and
Ieruſalem.7And in the dayes of Artaxerxes wrote Biſhlam, Mithredath,
Tabeel, and the reſt of their companions, vnto Artaxerxes king of Perſia;
and the writing of the letter was written in the Syrian tongue, and
interpreted in the Syrian tongue.8Rehum the Chancellour, and Shimſhai
the Scribe, wrote a letter againſt Ieruſalem, to Artaxerxes the king, in
this ſort:9Then, wrote Rehum the Chancellour, and Shimſhai the Scribe,
and the reſt of their companions; the Dinaites, the Apharſathkites, the
Tarpelites, the Apharſites, the Archeuites, the Babylonians, the
Suſanchites, the Dehauites, and the Elamites,10And the reſt of the
nations whom the great and noble Aſnappar brought ouer, and ſet in
the cities of Samaria, and the reſt that are on this ſide the Riuer, and at
ſuch a time.11This is the copy of the Letter, that they ſent vnto him, euen
vnto Artaxerxes the king: Thy ſeruants on this ſide the Riuer, and at ſuch
a time,12Be it knowen vnto the king, that the Iewes which came vp from
thee to vs, are come vnto Ieruſalem, building the rebellious and the bad
citie, and haue ſet vp the walles thereof, and ioyned the foundations.13Be
it knowen now vnto the king, that if this city be builded, and the wals
ſet vp againe, then will they not pay tolle, tribute, and cuſtome, and ſo
thou ſhalt endammage the reuenue of the kings.14Now becauſe we haue
maintenance from the Kings palace, and it was not meete for vs to ſee
the kings diſhonour: therefore haue we ſent, and certified the
king,15That ſearch may be made in the booke of the Records of thy
fathers: ſo ſhalt thou finde in the booke of the Records, and know, that
this City is a rebellious city, and hurtfull vnto Kings and prouinces, and
that they haue moued ſedition within the ſame of olde time: for which
cauſe was this citie deſtroyed.16We certifie the king, that if this citie be
builded againe, & the walles thereof ſet vp: by this meanes, thou ſhalt
haue no portion on this ſide the Riuer.17Then ſent the king an anſwere
vnto Rehum the Chancellour, and to Shimſhai the ſcribe, and to the reſt
of their companions, that dwell in Samaria, and vnto the reſt beyond the

Riuer, Peace, and at ſuch a time.[18]The letter, which ye ſent vnto vs, hath bene plainly read before me.[19]And I commaunded, and ſearch hath bene made, and it is found, that this citie of old time hath made inſurrection againſt Kings, and that rebellion & ſedition haue bene made therein.[20]There haue bene mighty Kings alſo ouer Ieruſalem, which haue ruled ouer all countreys beyond the Riuer, and tolle, tribute, and cuſtome, was payd vnto them.[21]Giue ye now commandement, to cauſe theſe men to ceaſe, and that this citie be not builded, vntill another commandement ſhall be giuen from me.[22]Take heed now that ye faile not to doe this: why ſhould damage grow to the hurt of the kings?[23]Now when the copy of King Artaxerxes letter was read before Rehum and Shimſhai the ſcribe, and their companions, they went vp in haſte to Ieruſalem, vnto the Iewes, and made them to ceaſe, by force and power.[24]Then ceaſed the woorke of the houſe of the God, which is at Ieruſalem. So it ceaſed, vnto the ſecond yeere of the reigne of Darius king of Perſia.

CHAPTER 5[1]Then the Prophets, Haggai the Prophet, and Zechariah the ſonne of Iddo, propheſied vnto the Iewes that were in Iudah and Ieruſalem, in the Name of the God of Iſrael, euen vnto them.[2]Then roſe vp Zerubbabel the ſonne of Shealtiel, and Ieſhua the ſonne of Iozadak, and began to build the houſe of God which is at Ieruſalem: and with them were the Prophets of God helping them.[3]At the ſame time came to them Tatnai, gouernour on this ſide the Riuer, and Shethar-Boznai, and their companions, and ſaid thus vnto them; Who hath commaunded you to build this houſe, and to make vp this wall?[4]Then ſaid wee vnto them after this maner, What are the names of the men that make this building?[5]But the eye of their God was vpon the Elders of the Iewes, that they could not cauſe them to ceaſe, till the matter came to Darius: and then they returned anſwere by letter concerning this matter.[6]The copy of the letter that Tatnai, gouernour on this ſide the Riuer, and Shethar-Boznai, and his companions the Apharſachites, which were on this ſide the Riuer, ſent vnto Darius the King:[7]They ſent a letter vnto him, wherein was written thus: Unto Darius the king, all peace.[8]Be it knowen vnto the king, that we went into the prouince of Iudea, to the houſe of the great God, which is builded with great ſtones, & timber is laied in the wals, and this worke goeth faſt on, and proſpereth in their hands.[9]Then aſked we thoſe Elders, and ſaid vnto them thus, Who commanded you to build this houſe, and to make vp theſe walles?[10]We aſked their names alſo, to certifie thee, that we might write the names of the men that were the chiefe of them.[11]And thus they returned vs anſwere, ſaying, We are the ſeruants of the God of heauen and earth, and build the houſe that was builded theſe many yeeres agoe, which a great King of Iſrael builded, and ſet vp.[12]But after that our fathers had prouoked the God of heauen vnto wrath: he gaue them into the hande of Nebuchadnezzar the king of Babylon, the Caldean, who deſtroyed this houſe, and caried the people away into Babylon.[13]But in the firſt yere of Cyrus the king of Babylon, the ſame king Cyrus made a decree to build this houſe of God.[14]And the veſſels alſo of golde and ſiluer of the houſe of God, which Nebuchadnezzar tooke out of the Temple that was in Ieruſalem, and brought them into the temple of Babylon, thoſe did Cyrus the king take out of the temple of Babylon, and they were deliuered vnto one, whoſe name was Sheſhbazzar, whome he had made gouernour:[15]And ſaid vnto him, Take theſe veſſels, goe, carie them into the temple that is in Ieruſalem, and let the houſe of God be builded in his place.[16]Then came the ſame Sheſhbazzar, and laid the foundation of the houſe of God, which is in Ieruſalem. And ſince that time, euen vntill now, hath it bin in building, & yet it is not finiſhed.[17]Now therefore, if it ſeeme good to the king, let there be ſearch made in the kings treaſure houſe which is there at Babylon, whether it be ſo that a decree was made of Cyrus the king, to build this houſe of God at Ieruſalem: and let the king ſend his pleaſure to vs concerning this matter.

CHAPTER 6[1]Then Darius the King made a decree, and ſearch was made in the houſe of the rolles, where the treaſures were laide vp in Babylon.[2]And there was found at Achmetha, in the palace that is in the prouince of the Medes, a rolle, and therein was a record thus written:[3]In the firſt yeere of Cyrus the king, the ſame Cyrus the king made a decree concerning the houſe of God at Ieruſalem: Let the houſe be builded, the place where they offered ſacrifices, and let the foundations thereof of be ſtrongly laid, the height therof threeſcore cubits, and the breadth thereof threeſcore cubites:[4]With three rowes of great ſtones, and a row of new timber: and let the expences bee giuen out of the kings houſe.[5]And alſo let the golden, and ſiluer veſſels of the houſe of God, which Nebuchadnezzar tooke foorth out of the temple which is at Ieruſalem, and brought vnto Babylon, be reſtored, and brought againe vnto the temple which is at Ieruſalem, euery one to his place, and place them in the houſe of God.[6]Now therefore Tatnai, gouernour beyond the riuer, Shethar-Boznai, and your companions the Apharſachites, which are beyond the riuer, be ye farre from thence:[7]Let the worke of this houſe of God alone, let the gouernour of the Iewes, and the elders of the Iewes, build this houſe of God in his place.[8]Moreouer I make a decree, what ye ſhall doe to the Elders of theſe Iewes, for the building of this houſe of God: that of the kings goods, euen of the tribute beyond the riuer, forthwith expences be giuen vnto theſe men, that they be not hindered.[9]And that which they haue need of, both yong bullocks, and rammes, and lambes, for the burnt offerings of the God of heauen, wheat, ſalt, wine, and oyle, according to the appoyment of the prieſts which are at Ieruſalem, let it be giuen them, day by day without faile:[10]That they may offer ſacrifices of ſweet ſauours vnto the God of heauen, and pray for the life of the king, and of his ſonnes.[11]Alſo I haue made a decree, that whoſoeuer ſhall alter this word, let timber be pulled down from his houſe, and being ſet vp, let him bee hanged thereon, and let his houſe bee made a doung hill for this.[12]And the God that hath cauſed his name to dwell there, deſtroy all kings and people that ſhall put to their hand, to alter and to deſtroy this houſe of God which is at Ieruſalem. I Darius haue made a decree, let it be done with ſpeed.[13]Then Tatnai gouernour on this ſide the riuer, Shethar-Boznai, & their companions, according to that which Darius the king had ſent, ſo they did ſpeedily.[14]And the elders of the Iewes builded, and they proſpered, through the prophecying of Haggai the Prophet, and Zechariah the ſonne of Iddo, and they builded, and finiſhed it, according to the commandement of the God of Iſrael, and according to the commandement of Cyrus and Darius, and Artaxerxes king of Perſia.[15]And this honſe was finiſhed on the third day of the month Adar, which was in the ſixt yere of the reigne of Darius the king.[16]And the children of Iſrael, the Prieſts and the Leuites, and the reſt of the children of the captiuitie, kept the dedicatiō of this houſe of God, with ioy,[17]And offered at the dedication of this houſe of God, an hundred bullockes, two hundred rammes, foure hundred lambes; and for a ſinne offering for all Iſrael, twelue hee goates, according to the number of the tribes of Iſrael.[18]And they ſet the Prieſts in their diuiſions, and the Leuites in their courſes, for the ſeruice of God, which is at Ieruſalem, as it is written in the booke of Moſes.[19]And the children of the captiuitie kept the Paſſeouer, vpon the fourteenth day of the firſt moneth:[20]For the Prieſtes and the Leuites were purified together, all of them were pure, and killed the Paſſeouer for all the children of the captiuitie, and for their brethren the Prieſts, and for themſelues.[21]And the children of Iſrael, which were come againe out of captiuitie, and all ſuch as had ſeparated themſelues vnto them, from the filthineſse of the heathen of the land, to ſeeke the Lord God of Iſrael, did eate,[22]And kept the feaſt of vnleauened bread ſeuen dayes, with ioy: for the Lord had made them ioyfull, and turned the heart of the king of Aſſyria vnto them, to ſtrengthen their handes in the worke of the houſe of God, the God of Iſrael.

CHAPTER 7[1]Now after theſe things, in the reigne of Artaxerxes king of Perſia, Ezra the ſon of Seraiah, the ſonne of Azariah, the ſonne of Hilkiah,[2]The ſonne of Shallum, the ſonne of Zadok, the ſonne of Ahitub,[3]The ſonne of Amariah, the ſonne of Azariah, the ſonne of Meraioth,[4]The ſonne of Zeraiah, the ſonne of Uzzi, the ſonne of Bukki,[5]The ſonne of Abiſhua, the ſonne of Phinehas, the ſonne of Eleazar, the ſonne of Aaron the chiefe Prieſt:[6]This Ezra went vp from Babylon, and hee was a ready Scribe in the law of Moſes, which the Lord God of Iſrael had giuen: and the king granted him all his requeſt, according to the hand of the Lord his God vpon him.[7]And there went vp ſome of the children of Iſrael, and of the Prieſts, and the Leuites, and the Singers, and the Porters, and the Nethinims, vnto Ieruſalem, in the ſeuenth yeere of Artaxerxes the king.[8]And he came to Ieruſalem in the fifth moneth, which was in the ſeuenth yeere of the king.[9]For vpon the firſt day of the firſt moneth, began he to go vp frō Babylon, and on the firſt day of the fifth moneth, came he to Ieruſalem, according to the good hand of his God vpon him.[10]For Ezra had prepared his heart to ſeeke the Law of the Lord, and to doe it, and to teach in Iſrael, Statutes and Iudgements.[11]Now this is the copy of the letter that the king Artaxerxes gaue vnto Ezra the Prieſt, the Scribe, euen a Scribe of the words of the commandements of the Lord, and of his Statutes to Iſrael.[12]Artaxerxes king of kings, Unto Ezra the Prieſt, a Scribe of the Law of the God of heauen, Perfect peace, and at ſuch a time.[13]I make a decree, that all they of the people of Iſrael, and of his Prieſts, and Leuites in my Realme, which are minded of their owne free-will to goe vp to Ieruſalem, goe with thee.[14]Foraſmuch as thou art ſent of the king, and of his ſeuen counſellers, to enquire concerning Iudah and Ieruſalem, according to the Lawe of thy God, which is in thine hand;[15]And to cary the ſiluer and gold, which the king and his counſellers haue freely offered vnto the God of Iſrael, whoſe habitation is in Ieruſalem.[16]And all the ſiluer and gold, that thou canſt find in all the prouince of Babylon, with the free-will offering of the people, and of the prieſts, offering willingly for the houſe of their God, which is in Ieruſalem:[17]That thou maieſt buy ſpeedily with this money, bullockes, rammes, lambes, with their meate offerings, and their drinke offerings, and offer them vpon the altar of the houſe of your God, which is in Ieruſalem.[18]And whatſoeuer ſhall ſeeme good to thee, and to thy brethren, to doe with the reſt of the ſiluer and gold; that doe, after the will of your God.[19]The veſſels alſo that are giuen thee, for the ſeruice of the houſe of thy God, thoſe deliuer thou before the God of Ieruſalem.[20]And whatſoeuer more ſhall be needfull for the houſe of thy God, which thou ſhalt haue occaſion to beſtowe; beſtowe it out of the kings treaſure houſe.[21]And I, euen I Artaxerxes the king, doe make a decree to all the treaſurers which are beyond the riuer, that whatſoeuer Ezra the prieſt, the ſcribe of the law of the God of heauen, ſhall require of you, it be done ſpeedily,[22]Unto an hundred talents of ſiluer, and to an hundred meaſures of wheate, and to an hundred bathes of wine, and to an hundred bathes of oyle, and ſalt, without preſcribing how much.[23]Whatſoeuer is commanded by the God of heauen, let it be diligently done, for the houſe of the God of heauen: for why ſhould there be wrath againſt the realme of the king and his ſonnes?[24]Alſo we certifie you, that touching any of the prieſts, and Leuites, ſingers, porters, Nethinims, or miniſters of this houſe of God, it ſhall not be lawfull to impoſe tolle, tribute, or cuſtome vpon them.[25]And thou, Ezra, after the wiſdome of thy God, that is in thine hand, ſet magiſtrates and iudges, which may iudge all the people, that are beyond the riuer, all ſuch as know the lawes of thy God, and teach yee them that knowe them not.[26]And whoſoeuer will not doe the law of thy God, and the law of the king, let iudgement be executed ſpeedily vpon him, whether it be vnto death, or to baniſhment, or to confiſcation of goods, or to impriſonment.[27]Bleſſed be the Lord God of our fathers, which hath put ſuch a thing as this, in the kings heart, to beautifie the houſe of the Lord which is in Ieruſalem:[28]And hath extended mercy vnto me, before the king and his counſellers, and before all the kings mighty princes, and I was ſtrengthned as the hand of the Lord my God was vpon me, and I gathered together out of Iſrael, chiefe men to goe vp with me.

CHAPTER 8[1]Theſe are now the chiefe of their fathers, and this is the genealogie of them that went vp with mee from Babylon, in the reigne of Artaxerxes the king.[2]Of the ſonnes of Phinehas, Gerſhom: of the ſonnes of Ithamar, Daniel: of the ſonnes of Dauid, Hattuſh.[3]Of the ſonnes of Shechaniah, of the ſonnes of Pharoſh, Zechariah, and with him were reckoned, by genealogie of the males, an hundred and fiftie.[4]Of the ſonnes of Pahath Moab, Elihoenai the ſonne of Zerahiah: and with him, two hundred males.[5]Of the ſonnes of Shechaniah, the ſonne of Iahaziel, and with him three hundred males.[6]Of the ſonnes alſo of Adin, Ebed the ſonne of Ionathan, and with him fiftie males.[7]And of the ſonnes of Elam, Ieſhaiah the ſonne of Athaliah, and with him ſeuentie males.[8]And of the ſonnes of Shephatiah, Zebadiah the ſonne of Michael, and with him foureſcore males.[9]Of the ſonnes of Ioab, Obadiah the ſonne of Iehiel: and with him two hundred and eighteene males.[10]And of the ſonnes of Shelomith, the ſonne of Ioſiphiah, and with him an hundred and threeſcore males.[11]And of the ſonnes of Bebai, Zechariah the ſonne of Bebai, and with him twenty and eight males.[12]And of the ſonnes of Azgad, Iohanan the ſonne of Hakkatan, and with him an hundred and ten males.[13]And of the laſt ſonnes of Adonikam, whoſe names are theſe: Eliphelet, Iehiel, and Shemaiah, and with them threeſcore males.[14]Of the ſonnes alſo of Biguai, Uthai, and Zabbud, and with them ſeuentie males.[15]And I gathered them together to the riuer, that runneth to Ahaua, and there abode wee in tents three dayes: and I viewed the people, and the Prieſts, and found there none of the ſonnes of Leui.[16]Then ſent I for Eliezer, for Ariel, for Shemaiah, and for Elnathan, and for Iarib, and for Elnathan, and for Nathan, and for Zechariah, and for Meſhullam, chiefe men; alſo for Iarib, and for Elnathan, men of vnderſtanding.[17]And I ſent them with commandement vnto Iddo the chiefe at the place Caſiphia, and I told them what they ſhould ſay vnto Iddo, and to his brethren the Nethinims, at the place Caſiphia, that they ſhould bring vnto vs miniſters for the houſe of our God.[18]And by the good hand of our God vpon vs, they brought vs a man of vnderſtanding, of the ſonnes of Mahli the ſonne of Leui, the ſonne of Iſrael, and Sherebiah, with his ſonnes, and his brethren, eighteene.[19]And Haſhabiah, and with him Ieſhaiah of the ſonnes of Merari, his brethren, and their ſonnes, twentie.[20]Alſo of the Nethinims, whom Dauid, and the Princes had appointed for the ſeruice of the Leuites, two hundred and twentie Nethinims: all of them were expreſſed by name.[21]Then I proclaimed a faſt there, at the riuer Ahaua, that we might afflict our ſelues before our God, to ſeeke of him a right way for vs, and for our little ones, and for all our ſubſtance.[22]For I was aſhamed to require of the king a band of ſouldiers and horſmen, to helpe vs againſt the enemie in the way: becauſe wee had ſpoken vnto the king, ſaying, The hand of our God is vpon all them for good, that ſeeke him, but his power and his wrath is againſt all them that forſake him.[23]So we faſted, and beſought our God for this, and hee was intreated of vs.[24]Then I ſeparated twelue of the chiefe of the Prieſts, Sherebiah, Haſhabiah, and ten of their brethren with them,[25]And weighed vnto them the ſiluer and the gold, and the veſſels, euen the offering of the houſe of our God, which the king and his counſellours, and his lords, and all Iſrael there preſent, had offered:[26]I euen weighed vnto their hand, ſixe hundred and fifty talents of ſiluer, and ſiluer veſſels an hundred talents, and of gold an hundred talents:[27]Alſo twenty baſons of gold, of a thouſand drammes, and two veſſels of fine copper, precious as gold.[28]And I ſaid vnto them, Yee are holy vnto the Lord, the veſſels are holy alſo, and the ſiluer and the gold are a free-will offring vnto the Lord God of your fathers.[29]Watch ye, and keepe them, vntill yee weigh them before the chiefe of the Prieſts, and the Leuites, and chiefe of the fathers of Iſrael at Ieruſalem, in the chambers of the houſe of the Lord.[30]So tooke the Prieſts and the Leuites the weight of the ſiluer and the gold, and the veſſels, to bring them to Ieruſalem, vnto the houſe of our God.[31]Then wee departed from the riuer of Ahaua, on the twelfth day of the firſt moneth, to goe vnto Ieruſalem; and the hand of our God was vpon vs, and hee deliuered vs from the hand of the enemie, and of ſuch as lay in wait by the way.[32]And we came to Ieruſalem, and abode there three dayes.[33]Now on the fourth day was the ſiluer and the gold, and the veſſels weighed in the houſe of our God, by the hand of Meremoth the ſonne of Uriah the Prieſt, and with him was Eleazar the ſonne of Phinehas, and with them was Iozabad the ſonne of Ieſhua, and Noadiah the ſonne of Binnui, Leuites:[34]By number, and by weight of uery one: and all the weight was written at that time.[35]Alſo the children of thoſe that had bene caried away which were come out of the captiuitie, offered burnt offrings vnto the God of Iſrael, twelue bullocks for all Iſrael, ninetie and ſixe rammes, ſeuentie and ſeuen lambes, twelue hee goates for a ſinne offering: All this was a burnt offering vnto the Lord.[36]And they deliuered the Kings commiſsions vnto the kings lieuteuants, and to the gouernours on this ſide the riuer, and they furthered the people, and the houſe of God.

CHAPTER 9[1]Nowe when theſe things were done, the Princes came to me, ſaying, The people of Iſrael, and the prieſts and the Leuites, haue not ſeparated themſelues from the people of the lands, doing according to their abominations, euen of the Canaanites, the Hittites, the Perizzites, the Iebuſites, the Ammonites, the Moabites, the Egyptians, and the Amorites.[2]For they haue taken of their daughters for themſelues, and for their ſonnes: ſo that the holy ſeed haue mingled themſelues with the people of thoſe lands, yea the hand of the princes and rulers hath bin chiefe in this treſpaſſe.[3]And when I heard this thing, I rent my garment and my mantle, and pluckt off the haire of my head, and of my beard, and ſate downe aſtonied.[4]Then were aſſembled vnto me euery one that trembled at the words of the God of Iſrael, becauſe of the tranſgreſſion of thoſe that had bene caried away, and I ſate aſtonied, vntill the euening ſacrifice.5And at the euening ſacrifice, I aroſe vp from my heauineſse, and hauing rent my garment and my mantle, I fell vpon my knees, and ſpread out my hands vnto the Lord my God,6And ſaid, O my God, I am aſhamed, and bluſh to lift vp my face to thee, my God: for our iniquities are increaſed ouer our head, and our treſpaſſe is growen vp vnto the heauens.7Since the dayes of our fathers, haue wee beene in a great treſpaſſe vnto this day, & for our iniquities haue we, our kings and our prieſts, bin deliuered into the hand of the kings of the lands, to the ſword, to captiuitie, and to a ſpoile, and to confuſion of face, as it is this day.8And now for a litle ſpace grace hath bene ſhewed from the Lord our God, to leaue vs a remnant to eſcape, and to giue vs a naile in his holy place, that our God may lighten our eyes, and giue vs a litle reuiuing in our bondage:9For wee were bondmen, yet our God hath not forſaken vs in our bondage, but hath extended mercie vnto vs in the ſight of the kings of Perſia, to giue vs a reuiuing to ſet vp the houſe of our God, and to repaire the deſolations thereof, and to giue vs a wall in Iudah and in Ieruſalem.10And now, O our God, what ſhal we ſay after this? for we haue forſaken thy commandements,11Which thou haſt commanded by thy ſeruants the prophets, ſaying, The land vnto which ye go to poſſeſſe it, is an vncleane land, with the filthineſse of the people of the lands, with their abominations, which haue filled it from one end to another, with their vncleanneſſe.12Nowe therefore giue not your daughters vnto their ſonnes, neither take their daughters vnto your ſonnes, nor ſeeke their peace or their wealth for euer: that ye may bee ſtrong, and eate the good of the land, and leaue it for an inheritance to your children for euer.13And after all that is come vpon vs, for our euill deeds, and for our great treſpaſſe, ſeeing that thou, our God, haſt puniſhed vs leſſe, then our iniquities deſerue, and haſt giuen vs ſuch deliuerance as this:14Should wee againe breake thy commandements, and ioyne in affinitie with the people of theſe abominations? wouldeſt thou not be angry with vs, til thou haddeſt conſumed vs, ſo that there ſhould be no remnant, nor eſcaping?15O Lord God of Iſrael, thou art righteous, for wee remaine yet eſcaped, as it is this day: Behold, we are before thee in our treſpaſſes: for wee can not ſtand before thee, becauſe of this.

CHAPTER 9 1Nowe when theſe things were done, the Princes came to me, ſaying, The people of Iſrael, and the prieſts and the Leuites, haue not ſeparated themſelues from the people of the lands, doing according to their abominations, euen of the Canaanites, the Hittites, the Perizzites, the Iebuſites, the Ammonites, the Moabites, the Egyptians, and the Amorites.2For they haue taken of their daughters for themſelues, and for their ſonnes: ſo that the holy ſeed haue mingled themſelues with the people of thoſe lands, yea the hand of the princes and rulers hath bin chiefe in this treſpaſſe.3And when I heard this thing, I rent my garment and my mantle, and pluckt off the haire of my head, and of my beard, and ſate downe aſtonied.4Then were aſſembled vnto me euery one that trembled at the words of the God of Iſrael, becauſe of the tranſgreſſion of thoſe that had bene caried away, and I ſate aſtonied, vntill the euening ſacrifice.5And at the euening ſacrifice, I aroſe vp from my heauineſse, and hauing rent my garment and my mantle, I fell vpon my knees, and ſpread out my hands vnto the Lord my God,6And ſaid, O my God, I am aſhamed, and bluſh to lift vp my face to thee, my God: for our iniquities are increaſed ouer our head, and our treſpaſſe is growen vp vnto the heauens.7Since the dayes of our fathers, haue wee beene in a great treſpaſſe vnto this day, & for our iniquities haue we, our kings and our prieſts, bin deliuered into the hand of the kings of the lands, to the ſword, to captiuitie, and to a ſpoile, and to confuſion of face, as it is this day.8And now for a litle ſpace grace hath bene ſhewed from the Lord our God, to leaue vs a remnant to eſcape, and to giue vs a naile in his holy place, that our God may lighten our eyes, and giue vs a litle reuiuing in our bondage:9For wee were bondmen, yet our God hath not forſaken vs in our bondage, but hath extended mercie vnto vs in the ſight of the kings of Perſia, to giue vs a reuiuing to ſet vp the houſe of our God, and to repaire the deſolations thereof, and to giue vs a wall in Iudah and in Ieruſalem.10And now, O our God, what ſhal we ſay after this? for we haue forſaken thy commandements,11Which thou haſt commanded by thy ſeruants the prophets, ſaying, The land vnto which ye go to poſſeſſe it, is an vncleane land, with the filthineſse of the people of the lands, with their abominations, which haue filled it from one end to another, with their vncleanneſſe.12Nowe therefore giue not your daughters vnto their ſonnes, neither take their daughters vnto your ſonnes, nor ſeeke their peace or their wealth for euer: that ye may bee ſtrong, and eate the good of the land, and leaue it for an inheritance to your children for euer.13And after all that is come vpon vs, for our euill deeds, and for our great treſpaſſe, ſeeing that thou, our God, haſt puniſhed vs leſſe, then our iniquities deſerue, and haſt giuen vs ſuch deliuerance as this:14Should wee againe breake thy commandements, and ioyne in affinitie with the people of theſe abominations? wouldeſt thou not be angry with vs, til thou haddeſt conſumed vs, ſo that there ſhould be no remnant, nor eſcaping?15O Lord God of Iſrael, thou art righteous, for wee remaine yet eſcaped, as it is this day: Behold, we are before thee in our treſpaſſes: for wee can not ſtand before thee, becauſe of this.

CHAPTER 10 1Now when Ezra had praiſed, and when he had confeſsed, weeping, and caſting himſelfe downe before the houſe of God, there aſſembled vnto him out of Iſrael, a very great congregation of men, and women, and children: for the people wept very ſore.2And Shechaniah the ſonne of Iehiel, one of the ſonnes of Elam, anſwered and ſaid vnto Ezra, Wee haue treſpaſſed againſt our God, and haue taken ſtrange wiues, of the people of the land: yet now there is hope in Iſrael concerning this thing.3Now therefore let vs make a couenant with our God, to put away all the wiues, & ſuch as are borne of them, according to the counſell of my lord, and of thoſe that tremble at the commandement of our God, and lee it be done according to the Law.4Ariſe, for this matter belongeth vnto thee, wee alſo will be with thee: be of good courage, and doe it.5Then aroſe Ezra, and made the chiefe Prieſts, the Leuites, and all Iſrael to ſweare, that they ſhould doe according to this word: and they ſware.6Then Ezra roſe vp from before the houſe of God, and went into the chamber of Iohanan, the ſonne of Eliaſhib: and when hee came thither, hee did eate no bread, nor drinke water: for hee mourned becauſe of the tranſgreſſion of them that had bene caried away.7And they made Proclamation throughout Iudah and Ieruſalem, vnto all the children of the captiuitie, that they ſhould gather themſelues together vnto Ieruſalem;8And that whoſoeuer would not come within three dayes, according to the counſell of the Princes, and the Elders, all his ſubſtance ſhould be forfeited, and himſelfe ſeparated from the congregation of thoſe that had beene caried away.9Then all the men of Iudah and Beniamin, gathered themſelues together vnto Ieruſalem, within three dayes: it was the ninth moneth, on the twentieth day of the moneth, and all the people ſate in the ſtreete of the houſe of God, trembling becauſe of this matter, and for the great raine.10And Ezra the Prieſt ſtood vp, and ſaid vnto them, Yee haue tranſgreſſed, and haue taken ſtrange wiues, to encreaſe the treſpaſſe of Iſrael.11Now therefore make confeſsion vnto the Lord God of your fathers, and doe his pleaſure: and ſeparate your ſelues from the people of the land, and from the ſtrange wiues.12Then all the congregation anſwered, and ſaid with a loude voice, As thou haſt ſaid, ſo muſt we doe:13But the people are many, and it is a time of much raine, and we are not able to ſtand without; neither is this a worke of one day or two: for wee are many that haue tranſgreſſed in this thing.14Let now our rulers of all the congregation ſtand, and let all them which haue taken ſtrange wiues in our cities, come at appointed times, & with them the Elders of euery citie, and the Iudges thereof; vntill the fierce wrath of our God for this matter, be turned from vs.15Onely Ionathan the ſonne of Aſahel, and Iahaziah the ſonne of Tikuah, were employed about this matter: and Meſhullam, and Shabbethai the Leuite, helped them.16And the children of the captiuitie did ſo: and Ezra the Prieſt, with certaine chiefe of the fathers, after the houſe of their fathers, and all of them by their names, were ſeparated, and ſate downe in the firſt day of the tenth moneth to examine the matter.17And they made an ende, with all the men that had taken ſtrange wiues, by the firſt day of the firſt moneth.18And among the ſonnes of the Prieſtes, there were found that had taken ſtrange wiues: namely, of the ſons of Ieſhua the ſonne of Iozadak, and his brethren, Maaſiah, and Eliezer, and Iarib, and Gedaliah.19And they gaue their hands, that they would put away their wiues: and being guiltie, they offered a ramme of the flocke for their treſpaſſe.20And of the ſonnes of Immer, Hanani, and Zebadiah:21And of the ſonnes of Harim, Maaſiah, and Eliiah, and Shemaiah, and Iehiel, and Uzziah.22And of the ſonnes of Paſhur: Elioenai, Maaſiah, Iſhmael, Nethaneel, Iozabad and Elaſah.23Alſo of the Leuites: Iozabad, and Shimei, and Kelaiah (the ſame is Kelitah) Pethahiah, Iudah, and Eliezer. 24 Of the ſingers alſo, Eliaſhib; and of the porters, Shallum, and Telem, and Uri. 25 Moreouer of Iſrael, of the ſonnes of Paroſh, Ramiah, and Ieſiah, and Malchiah, and Miamin, and Eleazar, and Malchiiah, and Benaiah. 26 And of the ſonnes of Elam: Mattaniah, Zechariah, and Iehiel, and Abdi, and Ieremoth, and Eliah. 27 And of the ſonnes of Zattu: Elioenai, Eliaſhib, Mattaniah, and Ieremoth, and Zabad, and Aziza. 28 Of the ſonnes alſo of Bebai: Iehohanan, Hananiah, Zabbai, & Athlai. 29 And of the ſonnes of Bani: Meſhullam, Malluch, and Adaiah, Iaſhub, and Sheal, and Ramoth. 30 And of the ſonnes of Pahath Moab: Adna, and Chelal, Benaiah, Maaſiah, Mattaniah, Bezaleel, and Binnui, and Manaſſeh. 31 And of the ſonnes of Harim: Eliezer, Iſhiiah, Malchiah, Shemaiah, Shimeon, 32 Beniamin, Malluch, and Shemariah. 33 Of the ſonnes of Haſhum: Mattenai, Mattatha, Zabad, Eliphelet, Ieremai, Manaſſeh, and Shimei. 34 Of the ſonnes of Bani: Maadai, Amram, and Uel, 35 Benaiah, Bedaiah, Chelluh, 36 Uaniah, Meremoth, Eliaſhib, 37 Mattaniah, Mattenai, and Iaaſau, 38 And Bani, and Bennui, Shimei, 39 And Shelemiah, and Nathan, and Adaiah, 40 Machnadebai, Shaſhai, Sharai, 41 Azareel, and Shelemiah, Shemariah, 42 Shallum, Amariah, and Ioſeph. 43 Of the ſonnes of Nebo, Iehiel, Mattithiah, Zabad, Zebina, Iadau, and Ioel, Benaiah. 44 All theſe had taken ſtrange wiues: and ſome of them had wiues, by whom they had children.

NEHEMIAH

CHAPTER 1 1 The words of Nehemiah the ſonne of Hachaliah. And it came to paſſe in the moneth Chiſleu, in the twentieth yeere, as I was in Shuſhan the palace; 2 That Hanani, one of my brethren came, he and certaine men of Iudah, and I aſked them concerning the Iewes that had eſcaped, which were left of the captiuitie, and concerning Ieruſalem. 3 And they ſaid vnto me, The remnant that are left of the captiuitie there in the prouince, are in great affliction and reproch: the wall of Ieruſalem alſo is broken downe, and the gates thereof are burnt with fire. 4 And it came to paſſe when I heard theſe words, that I ſate downe and wept, and mourned certaine dayes, and faſted, and prayed before the God of heauen, 5 And ſaid, I beſeech thee, O Lord God of heauen, the great and terrible God, that keepeth couenant and mercie for them that loue him, and obſerue his commandements: 6 Let thine eare now be attentiue, and thine eyes open, that thou mayeſt heare the prayer of thy ſeruant, which I pray before thee now, day and night, for the children of Iſrael thy ſeruants, and confeſse the ſinnes of the children of Iſrael, which wee haue ſinned againſt thee: both I, and my fathers houſe haue ſinned. 7 We haue dealt very corruptly againſt thee, and haue not kept the commandements, nor the ſtatutes, nor the iudgements, which thou commandedſt thy ſeruant Moſes. 8 Remember, I beſeech thee, the word that thou commandedſt thy ſeruant Moſes, ſaying, If yee tranſgreſse, I will ſcatter you abroad among the nations: 9 But if ye turne vnto me, and keepe my commandements, and doe them: though there were of you caſt out vnto the vttermoſt part of the heauen, yet will I gather them from thence, and will bring them vnto the place that I haue choſen, to ſet my Name there. 10 Now theſe are thy ſeruants, and thy people, whom thou haſt redeemed by thy great power, and by thy ſtrong hand. 11 O Lord, I beſeech thee, let now thine eare be attentiue to the prayer of thy ſeruant, and to the prayer of thy ſeruants, who deſire to feare thy name: and proſper, I pray thee, thy ſeruant this day, and grant him mercie in the ſight of this man. For I was the kings cup-bearer.

CHAPTER 2 1 And it came to paſſe, in the moneth Niſan, in the twentieth yeere of Artaxerxes the king, that wine was before him: and I tooke vp the wine, and gaue it vnto the King: now I had not bene beforetime ſad in his preſence. 2 Wherefore the king ſaid vnto me, Why is thy countenance ſadde, ſeeing thou art not ſicke? this is nothing elſe but ſorrow of heart. Then I was very ſore afraid, 3 And ſaid vnto the king, Let the king liue for euer: why ſhould not my countenance be ſad, when the city, the place of my fathers Sepulchres, lyeth waſte, and the gates thereof are conſumed with fire? 4 Then the king ſaid vnto me, For what doeſt thou make requeſt? So I prayed to the God of heauen. 5 And I ſaid vnto the king, If it pleaſe the king, and if thy ſeruant haue found fauour in thy ſight, that thou wouldeſt ſend me vnto Iudah vnto the City of my fathers ſepulchres, that I may build it. 6 And the king ſaide vnto mee (the Queene alſo ſitting by him) For how long ſhall thy iourney bee? and when wilt thou returne? So it pleaſed the king to ſend me, and I ſet him a time. 7 Moreouer I ſaide vnto the king, If it pleaſe the king, let letters be giuen mee to the gouernours beyond the Riuer, that they may conuey me ouer, till I come into Iudah; 8 And a letter vnto Aſaph the keeper of the kings forreſt, that he may giue me timber to make beames for the gates of the palace which appertained to the houſe, and for the wall of the Citie, and for the houſe that I ſhall enter into: And the king granted me, according to the good hand of my God vpon me. 9 Then I came to the gouernours beyond the riuer, and gaue them the kings letters: (now the king had ſent captaines of the army, and horſemen with me.) 10 When Sanballat the Horonite, and Tobiah the ſeruant, the Ammonite, heard of it, it grieued them exceedingly, that there was come a man, to ſeeke the welfare of the children of Iſrael. 11 So I came to Ieruſalem, and was there three dayes. 12 And I aroſe in the night, I, and ſome few men with mee, neither tolde I any man what God had put in my heart to doe at Ieruſalem: neither was there any beaſt with mee, ſaue the beaſt that I rode vpon. 13 And I went out by night, by the gate of the valley, euen before the dragon well, and to the doung-port, and viewed the walls of Ieruſalem, which were broken downe, and the gates thereof were conſumed with fire. 14 Then I went on to the gate of the fountaine, and to the kings poole: but there was no place for the beaſt that was vnder me, to paſſe. 15 Then went I vp in the night by the brooke, and viewed the wall, and turned backe, and entred by the gate of the valley, and ſo returned. 16 And the rulers knew not whither I went, or what I did, neither had I as yet tolde it to the Iewes, nor to the Prieſts, nor to the nobles, nor to the rulers, nor to the reſt that did the worke. 17 Then ſaid I vnto them, Yee ſee the diſtreſſe that we are in, how Ieruſalem lieth waſte, and the gates therof are burnt with fire: come, and let vs builde vp the wall of Ieruſalem, that we be no more a reproch. 18 Then I told them of the hand of my God, which was good vpon me; as alſo the kings wordes that he had ſpoken vnto me. And they ſaid, Let vs riſe vp and builde. So they ſtrengthened their hands for this good worke. 19 But when Sanballat the Horonite, and Tobiah the ſeruant the Ammonite, and Geſhem the Arabian heard it, they laughed vs to ſcorne, and deſpiſed vs, and ſaid, What is this thing that yee doe? will ye rebell againſt the king? 20 Then anſwered I them, and ſaid vnto them, The God of heauen, he will proſper vs, therefore wee his ſeruants will Ariſe and build: But you haue no portion, nor right, nor memoriall in Ieruſalem.

CHAPTER 3 1 Then Eliaſhib the hie prieſt, roſe vp with his brethren the Prieſts, and they built the ſheepe-gate, they ſanctified it, & ſet vp the doores of it, euen vnto the towre of Meah they ſanctified it, vnto the towre of Hananeel. 2 And next vnto him builded the men of Iericho: and next to them builded Zaccur the ſonne of Imri. 3 But the fiſh-gate did the ſonnes of Haſſenaah build, who alſo laide the beames thereof, and ſet vp the doores thereof, the locks thereof, and the barres thereof. 4 And next vnto them repaired Merimoth the ſon of Uriah, the ſonne of Koz: and next vnto them repaired Meſhullam the ſonne of Berechiah, the ſonne of Meſhezabeel: and next vnto them repaired Zadok the ſonne of Baana. 5 And uext vnto them, the Tekoites repaired; but their nobles put not their neckes to the worke of their Lord. 6 Moreouer the olde gate repaired Iehoiada the ſonne of Paſeah, and Meſhullam the ſonne of Beſodaiah; they laid the beames thereof, and ſet vp the doores thereof, and the lockes thereof, and the barres thereof. 7 And next vnto them repaired Melatiah the Gibeonite, and Iadon the Meronothite, the men of Gibeon, and of Mizpah, vnto the throne of the gouernour on this ſide the Riuer. 8 Next vnto him repaired Uzziel the ſonne of Harhaiah, of the goldſmiths: next vnto him alſo repaired Hananiah, the ſonne of one of the Apothecaries, and they fortified Ieruſalem vnto the broad wall. 9 And next vnto them repaired Rephaiah the ſonne of Hur, the ruler of the halfe part of Ieruſalem. 10 And next vnto them repaired Iedaiah the ſonne of Harumaph, euen ouer againſt his houſe: and next vnto him repaired Hattuſh the ſonne of Haſhabniah. 11 Malchiiah the ſonne of Harim, and Haſhub the ſon of Pahath Moab, repaired the other piece, & the towre of the furnaces. 12 And next vnto him repaired Shallum the ſonne of Halloeſh the ruler of the halfe part of Ieruſalem, hee, and his daughters. 13 The valley-gate repaired Hanun, and the inhabitants of Zanoah; they built it, and ſet vp the doores thereof, the lockes thereof, and the bars thereof, and a thouſand cubits on the wall, vnto the doung-gate.14But the doung-gate repaired Malchiah the ſonne of Rechab, the ruler of part of Beth-haccerem: hee built it, and ſet vp the doores thereof, the lockes thereof, and the barres thereof.15But the gate of the fountaine repaired Shallum the ſonne of Col-hozeh, the ruler of part of Mizpah: hee built it, and couered it, and ſet vp the doores thereof, the lockes thereof, and the barres thereof, and the wall of the poole of Siloah by the kings garden, and vnto the ſtaires that goe downe from the citie of Dauid.16After him repaired Nehemiah the ſonne of Azbuk, the ruler of the halfe part of Beth-zur, vnto the place ouer againſt the ſepulchres of Dauid, and to the poole that was made, and vnto the houſe of the mightie.17After him repaired the Leuites, Rehum the ſonne of Bani: next vnto him repaired Haſhabiah the ruler of the halfe part of Keilah in his part.18After him repaired their brethren, Bauai, the ſonne of Henadad the ruler of the halfe part of Keilah.19And next to him repaired Ezer the ſonne of Ieſhua, the ruler of Mizpah, another piece, ouer againſt the going vp to the armorie, at the turning of the wall.20After him Baruch the ſonne of Zabbai, earneſtly repaired the other piece, from the turning of the wall vnto the doore of the houſe of Eliaſhib the high Prieſt.21After him repaired Merimoth the ſonne of Uriiah, the ſonne of Koz, another piece, from the doore of the houſe of Eliaſhib, euen to the end of the houſe of Eliaſhib.22And after him repaired the Prieſts, the men of the plaine.23After him repaired Beniamin, and Haſhub, ouer againſt their houſe: after him repaired Azariah the ſonne of Maaſeiah, the ſonne of Ananiah, by his houſe.24After him repaired Binnui the ſonne of Henadad, another piece from the houſe of Azariah, vnto the turning of the wall, euen vnto the corner.25Palal the ſonne of Uzai, ouer againſt the turning of the wall, and the tower which lyeth out, from the kings hie houſe, that was by the court of the priſon: after him, Pedaiah the ſonne of Paroſh.26Moreouer the Nethinims dwelt in Ophel, vnto the place ouer againſt the water gate, toward the Eaſt, and the tower that lieth out.27After them the Tekoites repaired another piece, ouer againſt the great tower that lieth out, euen vnto the wall of Ophel.28From aboue the horſegate repaired the Prieſts, euery one ouer againſt his houſe.29After them repaired Zadok the ſonne of Immer, ouer againſt his houſe: after him repaired alſo Shemaiah, the ſon of Shechaniah, the keeper of the Eaſt-gate.30After him repaired Hananiah the ſonne of Shelemiah, and Hanun the ſixth ſonne of Zalaph, another piece: after him repaired Meſhullam, the ſonne of Berechiah ouer againſt his chamber.31After him repaired Malchiah, the goldſmiths ſonne, vnto the place of the Nethinims, and of the merchants, ouer againſt the gate Miphkad, and to the going vp of the corner.32And betweene the going vp of the corner vnto the ſheepe-gate, repaired the gold-ſmithes and the merchants.

CHAPTER 41But it came to paſſe, that when Sanballat heard, that we builded the wall, he was wroth, and tooke great indignation, and mocked the Iewes.2And he ſpake before his brethren, and the army of Samaria, and ſaid, What doe theſe feeble Iewes? wil they fortifie themſelues? will they ſacrifice? wil they make an end in a day? wil they reuiue the ſtones, out of the heapes of the rubbiſh, which are burnt?3Now Tobiah the Ammonite was by him, and he ſaid, Euen that which they build, if a foxe goe vp, he ſhall euen breake downe their ſtone wall.4Heare, O our God, for we are deſpiſed: and turne their reproch vpon their owne head, and giue them for a pray, in the land of captiuitie.5And couer not their iniquitie, and let not their ſinne bee blotted out from before thee: for they haue prouoked thee to anger before the builders.6So built we the wall, and all the wall was ioyned together vnto the halfe therof: for the people had a minde to worke.7But it came to paſſe that when Sanballat and Tobiah, and the Arabians, and the Ammonites, and the Aſhdodites, heard that the walles of Ieruſalem were made vp, and that the breaches began to bee ſtopped, then they were very wroth,8And conſpired all of them together, to come and to fight againſt Ieruſalem, and to hinder it.9Neuertheles, we made our prayer vnto our God, and ſet a watch againſt them, day and night, becauſe of them.10And Iudah ſaid, The ſtrength of the bearers of burdens is decayed, and there is much rubbiſh, ſo that we are not able to build the wall.11And our aduerſaries ſaid, They ſhall not know, neither ſee, till wee come in the midſt among them, and ſlay them, and cauſe the worke to ceaſe.12And it came to paſſe that when the Iewes which dwelt by them, came, they ſaid vnto vs ten time, From all places, whence yee ſhall returne vnto vs, they will be vpon you.13Therefore ſet I in the lower places behind the wall, and on the higher places, I euen ſet the people, after their families, with their ſwords, their ſpeares, and their bowes.14And I looked, and roſe vp, and ſaid vnto the Nobles, and to the rulers, and to reſt of the people, Bee not ye afraid of them: Remember the Lord which is great and terrible, and fight for your brethren, your ſonnes and your daughters, your wiues & your houſes.15And it came to paſſe when our enemies heard that it was knowen vnto vs, and God had brought their counſell to nought, that we returned all of vs to the wall, euery one vnto his worke.16And it came to paſſe from that time forth, that the halfe of my ſeruants wrought in the worke, and the other halfe of them held both the ſpeares, the ſhields and the bowes, and the habergeons, and the rulers were behind all the houſe of Iudah.17They which builded on the wall, and they that bare burdens, with thoſe that laded, euery one with one of his hands wrought in the worke, and with the other hand held a weapon.18For the builders, euery one had his ſword girded by his ſide, and ſo builded: and he that ſounded the trumpet was by mee.19And I ſaid vnto the Nobles, and to the rulers, and to the reſt of the people, The worke is great and large, and wee are ſeparated vpon the wall, one farre from another:20In what place therefore ye heare the ſound of the trumpet, reſort ye thither vnto vs: our God ſhal fight for vs.21So wee laboured in the worke: and halfe of them held the ſpeares, from the riſing of the morning, til the ſtarres appeared.22Likewiſe at the ſame time ſaid I vnto the people, Let euery one, with his ſeruant, lodge within Ieruſalem, that in the night they may be a guard to vs, and labour on the day.23So neither I, nor my brethren, nor my ſeruants, nor the men of the guard which followed me, none of vs put off our clothes, ſauing that euery one put them off for waſhing.

CHAPTER 51And there was a great crie of the people, and of their wiues, againſt their brethren the Iewes.2For there were that ſaid, We, our ſonnes, and our daughters are many: therefore wee take vp corne for them, that we may eat, and liue.3Some alſo there were that ſaide, We haue morgaged our landes, vineyards and houſes, that we might buy corne, becauſe of the dearth.4There were alſo that ſaid, Wee haue borrowed money for the kings tribute, and that vpon our lands and vineyards.5Yet now our fleſh is as the fleſh of our brethren, our children as their children: and loe, wee bring into bondage our ſonnes and our daughters, to bee ſeruants, and ſome of our daughters are brought vnto bondage already, neither is it in our power to redeeme them: for other men haue our lands and vineyards.6And I was very angry, when I heard their crie, and theſe words.7Then I conſulted with my ſelfe, and I rebuked the Nobles, and the rulers, and ſaid vnto them, You exact vſurie, euery one of his brother. And I ſet a great aſſembly againſt them:8And I ſaid vnto them, We, after our abilitie, haue redeemed our brethren the Iewes, which were ſold vnto the heathen; and will you euen ſell your brethren? or ſhall they be ſold vnto vs? Then held they their peace, and found nothing to anſwere.9Alſo I ſaid, It is not good that yee doe: ought yee not to walke in the feare of our God, becauſe of the reproch of the heathen our enemies?10I likewiſe, and my brethren, and my ſeruants, might exact of them money and corne: I pray you let vs leaue off this vſurie.11Reſtore, I pray you, to them, euen this day, their lands, their vineyards, their oliue-yards, and their houſes, alſo the hundreth part of the money, and of the corne, the wine, and the oyle, that ye exact of them.12Then ſaid they, Wee will reſtore them, and will require nothing of them; ſo will we doe, as thou ſayeſt. Then I called the Prieſts, and tooke an oath of them, that they ſhould doe according to this promiſe.13Alſo I ſhooke my lap, and ſaid, So God ſhake out euery man from his houſe, and from his labour, that performeth not this promiſe, euen thus be he ſhaken out, and emptied. And all the Congregation ſaid, Amen, and praiſed the Lord. And the people did according to this promiſe.14Moreouer, from the time that I was appointed to be their gouernor in the land of Iudah, from the twentieth yeere euen vnto the two and thirtieth yere of Artaxerxes the king, that is, twelue yeres, I and my brethren, haue not eaten the bread of the gouernour:15But the former gouernours that had bene before me, were chargeable vnto the people, and had taken of them bread, and wine, beſide fourtie ſhekels of ſiluer, yea euen their ſeruants bare rule ouer the people: but ſo did not I, becauſe of the feare of God.16Yea alſo I continued in the worke of this wall, neither bought wee any land: and all my ſeruants were gathered thither vnto the worke.17Moreouer, there were at my table, an hundred and fiftie of the Iewes and rulers, beſides thoſe that came vnto vs from among the heathen that are about vs.[18]Now that which was prepared for me daily, was one oxe, and ſixe choice ſheepe; alſo foules were prepared for mee, and once in ten dayes, ſtore of all ſorts of wine: yet for all this required not I the bread of the gouernour, becauſe the bondage was heauy vpon this people.[19]Thinke vpon mee, my God, for good, according to all that I haue done for this people.

CHAPTER 6[1]Now it came to paſſe when Sanballat, and Tobiah, and Geſhem the Arabian, and the reſt of our enemies heard, that I had builded the wall, and that there was no breach left therein: (though at that time I had not ſet vp the doores vpon the gates,)[2]That Sanballat, and Geſhem ſent vnto me, ſaying, Come, let vs meet together in ſome one of the villages in the plaine of Ono: But they thought to doe me miſchiefe.[3]And I ſent meſſengers vnto them, ſaying, I am doing a great worke, ſo that I can not come down: why ſhould the worke ceaſe, whileſt I leaue it, and come downe to you?[4]Yet they ſent vnto me foure times, after this ſort; and I anſwered them after the ſame maner.[5]Then ſent Sanballat his ſeruant vnto me, in like manner, the fifth time, with an open letter in his hand:[6]Wherein was written; It is reported among the heathen, and Gaſhmu ſayth it, that thou and the Iewes thinke to rebell: for which cauſe thou buildeſt the wall, that thou mayeſt be their King, according to theſe words.[7]And thou haſt alſo appointed Prophets to preach of thee at Ieruſalem, ſaying, There is a King in Iudah. And now ſhall it be reported to the king, according to theſe wordes. Come now therefore, and let vs take counſell together.[8]Then I ſent vnto him, ſaying, There are no ſuch things done as thou ſayeſt, but thou feigneſt them out of thine owne heart.[9]For they all made vs afraid, ſaying, Their handes ſhall be weakened from the worke that it bee not done. Now therefore, O God, ſtrengthen my hands.[10]Afterward I came vnto the houſe of Shemaiah the ſonne of Delaiah, the ſonne of Mehetabel, who was ſhut vp, and he ſaid, Let vs meet together in the houſe of God, within the Temple, and let vs ſhut the doores of the Temple; for they will come to ſlay thee, yea in the night wil they come to ſlay thee.[11]And I ſaid, Should ſuch a man as I, flee? and who is there, that being as I am, would goe into the Temple to ſaue his life? I will not goe in.[12]And loe, I perceiued that God had not ſent him, but that he pronounced this prophecie againſt mee: for Tobiah, and Sanballat had hired him.[13]Therefore was hee hired, that I ſhould be afraid, and doe ſo, and ſinne, and that they might haue matter for an euill report, that they might reproch mee.[14]My God, thinke thou vpon Tobiah, and Sanballat, according to theſe their workes, and on the prophetesſe Noadiah, and the reſt of the prophets, that would haue put me in feare.[15]So the wall was finiſhed, in the twentie and fifth day of the moneth Elul, in fiftie and two dayes.[16]And it came to paſſe that when all our enemies heard thereof, and all the heathen, that were about vs, ſaw theſe things, they were much caſt downe in their owne eyes: for they perceiued that this worke was wrought of our God.[17]Moreouer, in thoſe dayes the nobles of Iudah ſent many letters vnto Tobiah, and the letters of Tobiah came vnto them.[18]For there were many in Iudah ſworne vnto him: becauſe hee was the ſonne in law of Shechaniah the ſonne of Arah, and his ſonne Iohanan had taken the daughter of Meſhullam, the ſonne of Berechiah.[19]Alſo they reported his good deeds before me, and vttered my wordes to him: and Tobiah ſent letters to put me in feare.

CHAPTER 7[1]Now it came to paſſe when the wall was built, and I had ſet vp the doores; and the porters, and the ſingers, and the Leuites were appointed,[2]That I gaue my brother Hanani, and Hananiah the ruler of the palace, charge ouer Ieruſalem (for hee was a faithfull man, and feared God aboue many.)[3]And I ſaid vnto them, Let not the gates of Ieruſalem be opened, vntill the Sunne bee hot; and while they ſtand by, let them ſhut the doores, and barre them. And appoint watches of the inhabitants of Ieruſalem, euery one in his wateh, and euery one to bee ouer againſt his houſe.[4]Now the city was large and great, but the people were few therein, and the houſes were not builded.[5]And my God put into mine heart, to gather together the nobles, and the rulers, & the people, that they might be reckoned by genealogie. And I found a regiſter of the genealogie of them which came vp at the firſt, and found written therein;[6]Theſe are the children of the prouince, that went vp out of the captiuitie, of thoſe that had beene caried away whom Nebuchadnezzar the King of Babylon had caried away, and came againe to Ieruſalem and to Iudah, euery one vnto his citie:[7]Who came with Zerubbabel, Ieſhua, Nehemiah, Azariah, Raamiah, Nahamani, Mordecai, Bilſhan, Miſpereth, Biguai, Nahum, Baanah. The number, I ſay, of the men of the people of Iſrael, was this:[8]The children of Paroſh, two thouſand, an hundred, ſeuentie and two.[9]The children of Shephatiah, three hundred, ſeuentie and two.[10]The children of Arah, ſixe hundred, fiftie and two.[11]The children of Pahath-Moab, of the children of Ieſhua, and Ioab, two thouſand, and eight hundred, and eighteene.[12]The children of Elam, a thouſand, two hundred, fiftie and foure.[13]The children of Zattu, eight hundred fourtie and fiue.[14]The children of Zaccai, ſeuen hundred and threeſcore.[15]The children of Binnui, ſixe hundred, fourty and eight.[16]The children of Bebai, ſixe hundred, twentie and eight.[17]The children of Azgad, two thouſand, three hundred, twentie and two.[18]The children of Adonikam, ſixe hundred, threeſcore and ſeuen.[19]The children of Biguai, two thouſand, threeſcore and ſeuen.[20]The children of Adin, ſixe hundred, fiftie and fiue.[21]The children of Ater of Hezekiah, ninetie and eight.[22]The children of Haſhum, three hundred, twentie and eight.[23]The children of Bezai, three hundred twentie and foure.[24]The children of Hariph, an hundred and twelue.[25]The children of Gibeon, ninetie and fiue.[26]The men of Bethlehem, and Netophah, an hundred, foureſcore and eight.[27]The men of Anathoth, an hundred, twentie and eight.[28]The men of Bethazmaueth, fourtie and two.[29]The men of Kiriath-iearim, Chephirah and Beeroth, ſeuen hundred fourtie and three.[30]The men of Ramah and Geba, ſixe hundred, twentie and one.[31]The men of Michmaſh, an hundred and twenty and two.[32]The men of Bethel and Ai, an hundred, twentie and three.[33]The men of the other Nebo, fiftie and two.[34]The children of the other Elam, a thouſand, two hundred, fiftie & foure.[35]The children of Harim, three hundred and twentie.[36]The children of Iericho, three hundred, fourtie and fiue.[37]The children of Lod, Hadid, and Ono, ſeuen hundred, twentie and one.[38]The children of Senaa, three thouſand, nine hundred, and thirty.[39]The Prieſts. The children of Iedaia, of the houſe of Ieſhua, nine hundred, ſeuentie and three.[40]The children of Immer, a thouſand, fifty and two.[41]The children of Paſhur, a thouſand, two hundred, fourtie and ſeuen.[42]The children of Harim, a thouſand, and ſeuenteene.[43]The Leuites. The children of Ieſhua, of Kadmiel, and of the children of Hodeuah, ſeuentie and foure.[44]The ſingers. The children of Aſaph, an hundred, fourtie and eight.[45]The porters. The children of Shallum, the children of Ater, the children of Talmon, the children of Akkub, the children of Hatita, the children of Shobai, an hundred, thirtie and eight.[46]The Nethinims. The children of Ziha, the children of Haſhupha, the children of Tabaoth,[47]The children of Keros, the children of Sia, the children of Padon,[48]The children of Lebana, the children of Hagaba, the children of Shalmai,[49]The children of Hanan, the children of Giddel, the children of Gahar,[50]The children of Reaiah, the children of Rezin, the children of Nekoda,[51]The children of Gazzam, the children of Uzza, the children of Phaſeah,[52]The children of Beſai, the children of Meunim, the children of Nephiſheſim,[53]The children of Bakbuk, the children of Hakupha, the children of Harhur,[54]The children of Baſlith, the children of Mehida, the children of Harſha,[55]The children of Barkos, the children of Siſera, the children of Tamiah,[56]The children of Neziah, the children of Hatipha.[57]The children of Solomons ſeruants: The children of Sotai, the children of Sophereth, the children of Perida,[58]The children of Iaala, the children of Darkon, the children of Giddel,[59]The children of Shephatiah, the children of Hattil, the children of Pochereth Zebaim, the children of Amon,[60]All the Nethinims, and the children of Solomons ſeruants, were three hundred ninetie and two.[61]And theſe were they which went vp alſo from Tel-Melah, Tel-Hareſha, Cherub, Addon, and Immer: but they could not ſhewe their fathers houſe, nor their ſeede, whether they were of Iſrael.[62]The children of Delaiah, the children of Tobiah, the children of Nekoda, ſixe hundred fourtie and two.[63]And of the prieſts: the children of Habaiah, the children of Koz, the children of Barzillai, which tooke one of the daughters of Barzillai the Gileadite to wife, and was called after their name.[64]Theſe ſought their regiſter, among thoſe that were reckoned by genealogie, but it was not found: therfore were they, as polluted, put from the prieſthood.[65]And the Tirſhatha ſaid vnto them, that they ſhould not eate of the moſt holy things, till there ſtood vp a prieſt with

Urim and Thummim.66The whole congregation together, was fourtie and two thouſand, three hundred and threeſcore:67Beſide their man ſeruants, and their maid ſeruants, of whome there were ſeuen thouſand, three hundred, thirtie and ſeuen: and they had two hundred fourtie and fiue ſinging men and ſinging women.68Their horſes, ſeuen hundred, thirtie and ſixe: their mules, two hundred fourtie and fiue:69Their camels, foure hundred thirtie and fiue: ſixe thouſand, ſeuen hundred and twentie aſſes.70And ſome of the chiefe of the fathers, gaue vnto the worke: The Tirſhatha gaue to the treaſure, a thouſand drammes of gold, fiftie baſons, fiue hundred and thirtie prieſts garments.71And ſome of the chiefe of the fathers gaue to the treaſure of the worke twentie thouſand drammes of golde, and two thouſand and two hundred pound of ſiluer.72And that which the reſt of the people gaue, was twentie thouſand drammes of gold, and two thouſand pound of ſiluer, and threeſcore and ſeuen prieſts garments.73So the prieſts, and the Leuites, and the porters, and the ſingers, and ſome of the people, and the Nethinims, and all Iſrael, dwelt in their cities: And when the ſeuenth moneth came, the children of Iſrael were in their cities.

CHAPTER 8 1And all the people gathered themſelues together, as one man, into the ſtreet that was before the water gate, and they ſpake vnto Ezra the ſcribe, to bring the booke of the Law of Moſes, which the Lord had commanded to Iſrael.2And Ezra the prieſt brought the Law before the Congregation, both of men and women, and all that could heare with vnderſtanding, vpon the firſt day of the ſeuenth moneth.3And hee read therein before the ſtreet that was before the water gate, from the morning vntill midday, before the men and the women, and thoſe that could vnderſtand: And the eares of all the people were attentiue vnto the booke of the law.4And Ezra the ſcribe, ſtood vpon a pulpit of wood, which they had made for the purpoſe, and beſide him ſtood Mattithiah, and Shema, and Anaiah, and Urijah, and Hilkiah, and Maaſeiah, on his right hand: and on his left hand, Pedaiah, and Miſhael, and Malchiah, and Haſhum, and Haſhbadana, Zechariah, and Meſhullam.5And Ezra opened the booke in the ſight of all the people (for hee was aboue al the people) and when he opened it, all the people ſtood vp:6And Ezra bleſſed the Lord the great God: and al the people anſwered, Amen, Amen, with lifting vp their hands: and they bowed their heads, and worſhipped the Lord, with their faces to the ground.7Alſo Ieſhua and Bani, and Sherebiah, Iamin, Akkub, Shabbethai, Hodijah, Maaſeiah, Kelita, Azariah, Iozabad, Hanan, Pelaiah, and the Leuites, cauſed the people to vnderſtand the law: and the people ſtood in their place.8So they read in the booke, in the Law of God diſtinctly, and gaue the ſenſe, and cauſed them to vnderſtand the reading.9And Nehemiah, which is the Tirſhatha, and Ezra the Prieſt the Scribe, and the Leuites that taught the people, ſaid vnto all the people, This day is holy vnto the Lord your God, mourne not, nor weepe: for all the people wept, when they heard the words of the Law.10Then hee ſayd vnto them, Goe your way, eat the fat, & drinke the ſweet, and ſend portions vnto them, for whom nothing is prepared: for this day is holy vnto our Lord: neither be ye ſory, for the ioy of the Lord is your ſtrength.11So the Leuites ſtilled all the people, ſaying, Holde your peace, for the day is holy, neither be ye grieued.12And all the people went their way to eate, and to drinke, and to ſend portions, and to make great mirth, becauſe they had vnderſtood the wordes that were declared vnto them.13And on the ſecond day were gathered together the chiefe of the fathers of all the people, the Prieſtes and the Leuites, vnto Ezra the Scribe, euen to vnderſtand the wordes of the Law.14And they found written in the Law whith the Lord had commanded by Moſes, that the children of Iſrael ſhould dwell in boothes, in the feaſt of the ſeuenth moneth:15And that they ſhould publiſh and proclaime in all their cities, and in Ieruſalem, ſaying, Goe foorth vnto the mount, and fetch Oliue branches, and Pine branches, and Myrtle branches, and Palme branches, and branches of thicke trees, to make boothes, as it is written.16So the people went foorth, and brought them, and made themſelues boothes, euery one vpon the roofe of his houſe, and in their courts, and in the courts of the houſe of God, and in the ſtreete of the water-gate, and in the ſtreete of the gate of Ephraim.17And all the congregation of them that were come againe out of the captiuitie, made boothes, and ſate vnder the boothes: for ſince the dayes of Ieſhua the ſonne of Nun, vnto that day, had not the children of Iſrael done ſo: and there was very great gladneſſe.18Alſo day by day from the firſt day vnto the laſt day, he read in the booke of the Law of God: and they kept the feaſt ſeuen dayes, and on the eight day was a ſolemne aſſembly according vnto the maner.

CHAPTER 9 1Now in the twentie and fourth day of this moneth, the children of Iſrael were aſſembled with faſting, & with ſackclothes, and earth vpon them.2And the ſeede of Iſrael ſeparated themſelues from all ſtrangers, and ſtood and confeſsed their ſinnes, and the iniquities of their fathers.3And they ſtood vp in their place, and read in the booke of the Law of the Lord their God, one fourth part of the day, and another fourth part they confeſsed and worſhipped the Lord their God.4Then ſtoode vp, vpon the ſtaires of the Leuites, Ieſhua and Bani, Kadmiel, Shebaniah, Bunni, Sherebiah, Bani, and Chenani, and cryed with a loude voice vnto the Lord their God.5Then the Leuites, Ieſhua and Kadmiel, Bani, Haſhabniah, Sherebiah, Hodiiah, Shebaniah, and Pethahiah, ſayde, ſtand vp, and bleſſe the Lord your God for euer and euer, and bleſſed bee thy glorious Name, which is exalted aboue all bleſſing and praiſe.6Thou, euen thou art Lord alone, thou haſt made heauen, the heauen of heauens, with all their hoſte, the earth, and all things that are therein, the ſeas, and all that is therin, and thou preſerueſt them all, and the hoſte of heauen worſhippeth thee.7Thou art the Lord the God, who diddeſt chooſe Abram, and broughteſt him forth out of Ur of the Caldees, and gaueſt him the name of Abraham:8And foundeſt his heart faithfull before thee, & madeſt a couenant with him, to giue the land of the Canaanites, the Hittites, the Amorites, and the Perizzites, and the Iebuſites, and the Girgaſhites, to giue it, I ſay, to his ſeed, and haſt performed thy words, for thou art righteous,9And didſt ſee the affliction of our fathers in Egypt, and heardeſt their cry by the red ſea,10And ſhewedſt ſignes and wonders vpon Pharaoh, and on all his ſeruants, and on all the people of his land: for thou kneweſt that they dealt proudlie againſt them: ſo didſt thou get thee a name, as it is this day.11And thou didſt diuide the ſea before them, ſo that they went through the midſt of the ſea on the drie land, and their perſecutours thou threweſt into the deepes, as a ſtone into the mightie waters.12Moreouer thou leddeſt them in the day by a cloudy pillar, and in the night, by a pillar of fire, to giue them light in the way wherin they ſhould go.13Thou cameſt downe alſo vpon mount Sinai, and ſpakeſt with them from heauen, and gaueſt them right iudgements, and true lawes, good ſtatutes and commandements:14And madeſt knowen vnto them thy holy Sabbath, and commandedſt them precepts, ſtatutes, and lawes, by the hand of Moſes thy ſeruant:15And gaueſt them bread from heauen for their hunger, and broughteſt forth water for them out of the rocke, for their thirſt, and promiſedſt them that they ſhould goe in to poſſeſſe the land, which thou hadſt ſworne to giue them.16But they and our fathers dealt proudly, and hardened their necks, and hearkned not to thy commandements:17And refuſed to obey, neither were mindful of the wonders that thou didſt among them: but hardened their necks, and in their rebellion appointed a captaine to returne to their bondage: but thou art a God ready to pardon, gracious and mercifull, ſlow to anger, and of great kindnes, & forſookeſt them not.18Yea when they had made them a molten calfe, and ſaid, This is thy God, that brought thee vp out of Egypt, and had wrought great prouocations:19Yet thou, in thy manifold mercies, forſookeſt them not in the wilderneſſe: the pillar of the cloude departed not from them by day, to leade them in the way, neither the pillar of fire by night, to ſhew them light, and the way wherin they ſhould goe.20Thou gaueſt alſo thy good ſpirit, to inſtruct them, and withheldeſt not thy Manna from their mouth, and gaueſt them water for their thirſt.21Yea fourtie yeeres diddeſt thou ſuſtaine them in the wilderneſſe, ſo that they lacked nothing; their clothes wared not old, and their feet ſwelled not.22Moreouer, thou gaueſt them kingdomes and nations, and didſt diuide them into corners: ſo they poſſeſſed the land of Sihon, and the land of the king of Heſhbon, and the land of Og king of Baſhan.23Their children alſo multipliedſt thou as the ſtarres of heauen, and broughteſt them into the land, concerning which thou hadſt promiſed to their fathers, that they ſhould goe in to poſſeſſe it.24So the children went in, and poſſeſſed the land, and thou ſubduedſt before them the inhabitants of the lande, the Canaanites, and gaueſt them into their hands, with their kings, and the people of the land, that they might doe with them, as they would.25And they tooke ſtrong cities, and a fat land, and poſſeſſed houſes ful of all goods, welles digged, vineyards, and Olive yards, and fruit trees in abundance: So they did eat and were filled, and became fat, and delighted themſelues in thy great goodneſse.26Neuertheleſſe, they were diſobedient, and rebelled againſt thee, and caſt thy law behind their backes, and ſlewe thy prophets, which teſtified againſt them to turne them to thee, and they wrought great prouocations.27Therefore thou deliueredſt them into the hande of their enemies, who vexed them, & in the time of their trouble, when they cried vnto thee, thou heardeſt them from heauen: and according to thy manifold mercies, thou gaueſt them ſauiours, who ſaued them out of the hand of their enemies.28But after they had reſt, they did euill againe before thee: therefore lefteſt thou them in the hand of their enemies, ſo that they had the dominion ouer them: yet when they returned and cried vnto thee, thou heardeſt them from heauen, and many times didſt thou deliuer them, according to thy mercies:29And teſtifiedſt againſt them, that thou mighteſt bring them againe vnto thy lawe: yet they dealt proudly, and hearkened not vnto thy commaundements, but ſinned againſt thy iudgements, (which if a man doe, he ſhal liue in them) and withdrew the ſhoulder, and hardened their necke, and would not heare.30Yet many yeres diddeſt thou forbeare them, and teſtifiedſt againſt them by the Spirit in thy Prophets: yet would they not giue eare: therefore gaueſt thou them into the hand of the people of the lands.31Neuertheleſſe, for thy great mercies ſake, thou diddeſt not vtterly conſume them, nor forſake them; for thou art a gracious and mercifull God.32Now therefore, our God, the great, the mightie, and the terrible God, who keepeſt couenant and mercie: let not all the trouble ſeeme little before thee, that hath come vpon vs, on our Kings, on our Princes, & on our Prieſts, and on our Prophets, & on our fathers, & on al thy people, ſince the time of the Kings of Aſſyria, vnto this day.33Howbeit, thou art iuſt in all that is brought vpon vs, for thou haſt done right, but we haue done wickedly:34Neither haue our kings, our Princes, our Prieſts, nor our fathers kept thy Law, nor hearkened vnto thy Commandements, and thy Teſtimonies, wherewith thou didſt teſtifie againſt them.35For they haue not ſerued thee in their kingdome, and in thy great goodneſſe that thou gaueſt them, and in the large and fat land which thou gaueſt before them, neither turned they from their wicked workes.36Behold, we are ſeruants this day; and for the land that thou gaueſt vnto our fathers, to eat the fruit thereof, and the good thereof, behold, wee are ſeruants in it.37And it yeeldeth much increaſe vnto the kings, whom thou haſt ſet ouer vs, becauſe of our ſinnes: alſo they haue dominion ouer our bodies, and ouer our cattell, at their pleaſure; and wee are in great diſtreſſe.38And becauſe of all this, wee make a ſure couenant, and write it, and our Princes, Leuites, and Prieſtes, ſeale vnto it.

CHAPTER 10 1Now thoſe that ſealed were, Nehemiah the Tirſhatha the ſonne of Hachaliah, and Zidkiiah,2Seraiah, Azariah, Ieremiah,3Paſhur, Amariah, Malchiah,4Hattuſh, Shebaniah, Malluch,5Harim, Merimoth, Obadiah,6Daniel, Ginnethon, Baruch,7Meſhullam, Abiiah, Miiamin,8Maaziah, Bilgai, Shemaiah: theſe were the Prieſts.9And the Leuites: both Ieſhua the ſonne of Azaniah, Binnui, of the ſonnes of Henadad, Kadmiel;10And their brethren, Shebaniah, Hodiiah, Kelita, Pelaiah, Hanan,11Micah, Rehob, Haſhabiah,12Zaccur, Sherebiah, Shebaniah,13Hodiiah, Bani, Beninu,14The chiefe of the people. Paroſh, Pahath-Moab, Elam, Zatthu, Bani,15Bunni, Azgad, Bebai,16Adoniiah, Biguai, Adin,17Ater, Hizkiiah, Azzur,18Hodiah, Haſhum, Bezai,19Hariph, Anathoth, Nebai,20Magpiaſh, Meſhullam, Hezir,21Meſhezabeel, Zadok, Iaddua,22Pelatiah, Hanan, Anaiah,23Hoſhea, Hananiah, Haſhub,24Halloheſh, Pileha, Shobek,25Rehum, Haſhabnah, Maaſeiah,26And Ahiiah, Hanan, Anan,27Malluch, Harim, Baanah.28And the reſt of the people, the Prieſts, the Leuites, the Porters, the ſingers, the Nethinims, and all they that had ſeparated themſelues from the people of the lands, vnto the Law of God, their wiues, their ſonnes, and their daughters, euery one hauing knowledge, and hauing vnderſtanding.29They claue to their brethren their nobles, and entred into a curſe, and into an oath to walke in Gods law, which was giuen by Moſes the ſeruant of God, and to obſerue and doe all the commandements of the Lord our Lord, and his Iudgements, and his ſtatutes:30And that we would not giue our daughters vnto the people of the land, nor take their daughters for our ſonnes.31And if the people of the land bring ware or any victuals on the Sabbath day, to ſell, that we would not buy it of them on the Sabbath, or on the holyday, and that wee would leaue the ſeuenth yeere, and the exaction of euerie debt.32Alſo we made ordinances for vs, to charge our ſelues yeerely, with the third part of a ſhekel, for the ſeruice of the houſe of our God,33For the ſhew-bread, and for the continuall meate-offering, and for the continuall burnt offering, of the Sabbaths, of the new moones, for the ſet-feaſtes, and for the holy things, and for the ſin-offerings, to make an atonement for Iſrael, and for all the worke of the houſe of our God.34And we caſt the lots among the prieſts, the Leuites, and the people, for the wood offering, to bring it into the houſe of our God, after the houſes of our fathers, at times appointed, yeere by yeere, to burne vpon the altar of the Lord our God, as it is written in the law:35And to bring the firſt fruits of our ground, and the firſt fruites of all fruit of all trees, yeere by yeere, vnto the houſe of the Lord.36Alſo the firſt-borne of our ſonnes, and of our cattell (as it is written in the lawe) and the firſtlings of our heards, and of our flockes, to bring to the houſe of our God, vnto the prieſts that miniſter in the houſe of our God:37And that we ſhould bring the firſt fruits of our dough, and our offerings, and the fruit of all maner of trees, of wine and of oile, vnto the prieſts, to the chambers of the houſe of our God, and the tithes of our ground vnto the Leuites, that the ſame Leuites might haue the tithes, in all the cities of our tillage.38And the prieſt the ſonne of Aaron, ſhall be with the Leuites, when the Leuites take tithes, and the Leuites ſhal bring vp the tithe of the tithes vnto the houſe of our God, to the chambers into the treaſure houſe.39For the children of Iſrael, and the children of Leui, ſhall bring the offering of the corne, of the new wine, and the oyle, vnto the chambers, where are the veſſels of the ſanctuarie, and the prieſts that miniſter, and the porters, and the ſingers, and we will not forſake the houſe of our God.

CHAPTER 11 1And the rulers of the people dwelt at Ieruſalem: the reſt of the people alſo caſt lots, to bring one of tenne, to dwell in Ieruſalem, the holy citie, and nine parts to dwell in other cities.2And the people bleſſed all the men, that willingly offered themſelues, to dwell at Ieruſalem.3Now theſe are the chiefe of the prouince that dwelt in Ieruſalem: but in the cities of Iudah dwelt euerie one in his poſſeſſion in their cities, to wit, Iſrael, the prieſts, and the Leuites, and the Nethinims, and the children of Solomons ſeruants.4And at Ieruſalem dwelt certaine of the children of Iudah, and of the children of Beniamin. Of the children of Iudah: Athaiah the ſonne of Uzziah, the ſonne of Zechariah, the ſonne of Amariah, the ſonne of Shephatiah, the ſonne of Mahalaleel, of the children of Perez.5And Maaſeiah the ſonne of Baruch the ſonne of Col-Hozeh, the ſonne of Hazaiah the ſonne of Adaiah, the ſonne of Ioiarib, the ſonne of Zechariah, the ſonne of Shiloni.6All the ſonnes of Perez that dwelt at Ieruſalem, were foure hundred threeſcore and eight valiant men.7And theſe are the ſonnes of Beniamin: Sallu the ſonne of Meſhullam, the ſonne of Ioed, the ſonne of Pedaiah, the ſonne of Kolaiah, the ſonne of Maaſeiah, the ſonne of Ithiel, the ſonne of Ieſaiah.8And after him Gabai, Sallai, nine hundred twentie and eight.9And Ioel the ſonne of Zichri was their ouerſeer: and Iudah the ſonne of Senuah, was ſecond ouer the city.10Of the Prieſts: Iedaiah the ſonne of Ioiarib, Iachin;11Seraiah the ſonne of Hilkiah, the ſonne of Meſhullam, the ſonne of Zadok, the ſonne of Meraioth, the ſonne of Ahitub, was the ruler of the houſe of God.12And their brethren that did the worke of the houſe, were eight hundred twentie and two: and Adaiah the ſonne of Ieroham, the ſonne of Pelaliah, the ſonne of Amzi, the ſonne of Zechariah, the ſonne of Paſhur, the ſonne of Malchiah,13And his brethren, chiefe of the fathers, two hundred fourty and two: and Amaſhai the ſonne of Azareel, the ſonne of Ahaſai, the ſonne of Meſhilemoth, the ſonne of Immer.14And their brethren mighty men of valour, an hundred twenty and eight; and their ouerſeer was Zaddiel, the ſonne of one of the great men.15Alſo of the Leuites: Shemaiah the ſonne of Haſhub, the ſonne of Azrikam, the ſonne of Haſhabiah, the ſonne of Bunni.16And Shabbethai, and Iozabad, of the chiefe of the Leuits, had the ouerſight of the outward buſineſe of the houſe of God.17And Mattaniah the ſonne of Micha, the ſonne of Zabdi, the ſonne of Aſaph, was the principall to beginne the thankeſgiuing in prayer: and Bakbukiah the ſecond among his brethren, and Abda the ſonne of Shammua, the ſonne of Galal, the ſonne of Ieduthun.18All the Leuites in the holy City, were two hundred, foureſcore and foure.19Moreouer, the porters, Akkub, Talmon, and their brethren that kept the gates, were an hundred ſeuenty and two.20And the reſidue of Iſrael, of the Prieſts and the Leuites, were in all the cities of Iudah, euery one in his inheritance.21But

the Nethinims dwelt in Ophel: and Ziha, and Giſpa were ouer the
Nethinims.22The ouerſeer alſo of the Leuites at Ieruſalem, was Uzzi the
ſonne of Bani, the ſon of Haſhabiah, the ſonne of Mattaniah, the ſonne
of Micha: Of the ſonnes of Aſaph, the ſingers were ouer the buſineſse
of the houſe of God.23For it was the kings commandement concerning
them, that a certaine portion ſhould be for the ſingers, due for euery
day.24And Pethahiah the ſonne of Meſhezabel, of the children of Zerah
the ſonne of Iudah, was at the kings hand in all matters concerning the
people.25And for the villages, with their fields, ſome of the children of
Iudah dwelt at Kiriath-arba, and in the villages thereof; and at Dibon,
and in the villages thereof, and at Iekabzeel, and in the villages
thereof:26And at Ieſhua, and at Moladah, and at Beth-phelet,27And at
Hazer-Shual, and at Beer-ſheba and in the villages thereof:28And at
Ziglag, and at Mekonah, and in the villages thereof:29And at En-
Rimmon, and at Zareah, and at Iarmuth,30Zanoah, Adullam, and in their
villages, at Lachiſh, and the fieldes thereof: at Azekah, and in the villages
thereof. And they dwelt from Beer-ſheba, vnto the valley of
Hinnom.31The children alſo of Beniamin, from Geba, dwelt at
Michmaſh, and Aiia, and Beth-el, and in their villages:32And at
Anathoth, Nob, Ananiah,33Hazor, Ramah, Gittaim,34Hadid, Zeboim,
Neballat,35Lod, and Ono, the valley of crafteſ-men.36And of the
Leuites, were diuiſions in Iudah, and in Beniamin.
CHAPTER 121Now theſe are the Prieſts and the Leuits that went vp
with Zerubbabel the ſonne of Shealtiel, and Ieſhua: Seraiah, Ieremiah,
Ezra,2Amariah, Malluch, Hattuſh,3Shecaniah, Rehum, Merimoth,4Iddo,
Ginnetho, Abiiah,5Miamin, Madiſh, Bilgah,6Shemaiah, & Ioiarib,
Iedaiah,7Sallu, Amok, Hilkiah, Iedaiah: theſe were the chiefe of the
Prieſts, and of their brethren in the dayes of Ieſhua.8Moreouer the
Leuites: Ieſhua, Binnui, Kadmiel, Sherebiah, Iudah, and Mattaniah,
which was ouer the thankeſgiuing, he and his brethren.9Alſo Bakbukiah,
and Unni; their brethren, were ouer againſt them in the watches.10And
Ieſhua begate Ioiakim, Ioiakim alſo begate Eliaſhib, and Eliaſhib begate
Ioiada,11And Ioiada begate Ionathan, and Ionathan begate Iaddua.12And
in the dayes of Ioiakim, were Prieſts the chiefe of the fathers: of Seraiah,
Meraiah: of Ieremiah, Hananiah:13Of Ezra, Meſhullam: of Amariah,
Iehohanan:14Of Melicu, Ionathan: of Shebaniah, Ioſeph:15Of Harim,
Adna: of Meraioth, Helkai:16Of Iodo, Zechariah: of Ginnethon,
Meſhullam:17Of Abijah, Zichri: of Miniamin, of Moadiah, Piltai:18Of
Bilgah, Shammua: of Shemaiah, Iehonathan:19And of Ioiarib, Mattenai:
of Iedaiah, Uzzi:20Of Sallai, Kallai: of Amok, Eber:21Of Hilkiah,
Haſhabiah: of Iedaiah, Nethanael.22The Leuites in the dayes of Eliaſhib,
Ioiada, and Iohanan, and Iaddua, were recorded chiefe of the fathers:
alſo the Prieſts, to the reigne of Darius the Perſian.23The ſonnes of Leui,
the chiefe of the fathers, were written in the booke of the Chronicles,
euen vntill the dayes of Iohanan the ſonne of Eliaſhib.24And the chiefe
of the Leuites: Haſhabiah, Sherebiah, and Ieſhua the ſonne of Kadmiel,
with their brethren ouer againſt them, to praiſe and to giue thankes,
according to the commandement of Dauid the man of God, ward ouer
againſt ward.25Mattaniah, and Bakbukiah, Obadiah, Meſhullam,
Talmon, Akkub, were porters keeping the ward, at the threſholds of the
gates.26Theſe were in the dayes of Ioiakim, the ſonne of Ieſhua, the
ſonne of Iozadak, and in the dayes of Nehemiah the gouernour, and of
Ezra the Prieſt, the Scribe.27And at the dedication of the wall of
Ieruſalem, they ſought the Leuites out of all their places, to bring them
to Ieruſalem, to keepe the dedication with gladneſſe, both with
thankeſgiuings and with ſinging, with cymbals, pſalteries, and with
harpes.28And the ſonnes of the Singers gathered themſelues together,
both out of the plaine countrey round about Ieruſalem, and from the
villages of Netophathi.29Alſo from the houſe of Gilgal, and out of the
fields of Geba, and Azmaueth: for the Singers had builded them villages
round about Ieruſalem.30And the Prieſts and the Leuites purified
themſelues, and purified the people, and the gates, and the wall.31Then
I brought vp the princes of Iudah vpon the wall, and appointed two
great companies of them that gaue thankes, whereof one went on the
right hand vpon the wall toward the dounggate:32And after them went
Hoſhaiah, and halfe of the Princes of Iudah,33And Azariah, Ezra, and
Meſhullam,34Iudah, and Beniamin, and Shemaiah, and Ieremiah,35And
certaine of the Prieſts ſonnes with trumpets: namely, Zechariah the
ſonne of Ionathan, the ſonne of Shemaiah, the ſonne of Mattaniah, the
ſonne of Michaiah, the ſonne of Zaccur, the ſonne of Aſaph:36And his
brethren, Shemaiah, and Aſarael, Milalai, Gilalai, Maai, Nethanael, and
Iudah, Hanani, with the muſicall inſtruments of Dauid the man of God;
and Ezra the Scribe before them.37And at the fountaine-gate, which was
ouer againſt them, they went vp by the ſtaires of the citie of Dauid, at
the going vp of the wall, aboue the houſe of Dauid, euen vnto the water-
gate, Eaſtward.38And the other company of them that gaue thankes,
went ouer againſt them, and I after them, and the halfe of the people
vpon the wall, from beyond the towre of the fornaces, euen vnto the
broad wall,39And from aboue the gate of Ephraim, and aboue the olde
gate, and aboue the fiſh-gate, and the towre of Hananeel, and the towre
of Meah, euen vnto the ſheepegate; and they ſtood ſtill in the priſon
gate.40So ſtood the two companies of them that gaue thankes in the
houſe of God, and I, and the halfe of the rulers with me:41And the
Prieſts: Eliakim, Maaſeiah, Miniamin, Michaiah, Elioenai, Zachariah,
and Hananiah with trumpets:42And Maaſeiah, and Shemaiah, and
Eleazar, and Uzzi, and Iehohanan, and Malchiiah, and Elam, and Ezer.
And the Singers ſang loud, with Iezrahiah their ouerſeer.43Alſo that day
they offered great ſacrifices, and reioyced; for God had made them
reioyce with great ioy: the wiues alſo and the children reioyced: ſo that
the ioy of Ieruſalem was heard euen afarre off.44And at that time were
ſome appointed ouer the chambers for the treaſures, for the offerings,
for the firſt fruits, and for the tithes, to gather into them out of the fields
of the cities the portions of the law for the prieſts and Leuites: for Iudah
reioyced for the Prieſts, & for the Leuites that waited.45And both the
ſingers and the porters kept the ward of their God, and the ward of the
purification, according to the commandement of Dauid, and of
Solomon his ſonne.46For in the dayes of Dauid and Aſaph of old, there
were chiefe of the ſingers, and ſongs of praiſe and thankſgiuing vnto
God.47And all Iſrael in the dayes of Zerubbabel, and in the dayes of
Nehemiah, gaue the portions of the ſingers, and the porters, euery day
his portion, and they ſanctified holy things vnto the Leuites, and the
Leuites ſanctified them vnto the children of Aaron.
CHAPTER 131On that day they read in the booke of Moſes in the
audience of the people, and therein was found written, that the
Ammonite and the Moabite ſhould not come into the Congregation of
God for euer,2Becauſe they met not the children of Iſrael with bread,
and with water, but hired Balaam againſt them, that he ſhould curſe
them: howbeit our God turned the curſe into a bleſſing.3Now it came
to paſſe when they had heard the law, that they ſeparated from Iſrael all
the mixed multitude.4And before this Eliaſhib the prieſt hauing the
ouerſight of the chamber of the houſe of our God, was allied vnto
Tobiah:5And hee had prepared for him a great chamber, where
aforetime they laid the meat offrings, the frankincenſe and the veſſels,
and the tithes of the corne, the new wine, and the oile, which was
commanded to be giuen to the Leuites, and the ſingers, and the porters,
and the offerings of the prieſts.6But in all this time was not I at
Ieruſalem: for in the two and thirtieth yeere of Artaxerxes king of
Babylon, came I vnto the king, and after certaine dayes, obtained I leaue
of the King:7And I came to Ieruſalem, and vnderſtood of the euil that
Eliaſhib did for Tobiah, in preparing him a chamber in the courts of the
houſe of God.8And it grieued me ſore, therefore I caſt foorth all the
houſhold ſtuffe of Tobiah out of the chamber:9Then I commanded, and
they cleanſed the chambers, and thither brought I againe the veſſels of
the houſe of God, with the meate offering, and the frankincenſe.10And
I perceiued that the portions of the Leuites had not beene giuen them:
for the Leuites and the ſingers that did the worke, were fled euery one
to his field.11Then contended I with the rulers, and ſaid, Why is the
houſe of God forſaken? And I gathered them together, and ſet them in
their place.12Then brought all Iudah the tithe of the corne, and the new
wine, and the oyle, vnto the treaſuries.13And I made treaſurers ouer the
treaſuries, Shelemiah the prieſt, and Zadok the ſcribe, and of the Leuites,
Pedaiah: and next to them was Hanan the ſonne of Zaccur, the ſonne
of Mattaniah: for they were counted faithfull, and their office was to
diſtribute vnto their brethren.14Remember me, O my God, concerning
this, and wipe not out my good deeds, that I haue done for the houſe of
my God, and for the offices thereof.15In thoſe dayes ſawe I in Iudah,
ſome treading wine preſses on the Sabbath, and bringing in ſheaues, and
lading aſſes, as alſo wine, grapes, and figs, and all maner of burdens,
which they brought into Ieruſalem on the Sabbath day: and I teſtified

againſt them in the day wherein they ſolde victuals.16There dwelt men
of Tyre alſo therein, which brought fiſh and all maner of ware, and ſolde
on the Sabbath vnto the children of Iudah, and in Ieruſalem.17Then I
contended with the Nobles of Iudah, and ſayd vnto them, What euill
thing is this that ye doe, and profane the Sabbath day?18Did not your
fathers thus, and did not our God bring all this euill vpon vs, and vpon
this citie? yet ye bring more wrath vpon Iſrael, by profaning the
Sabbath.19And it came to paſſe, that when the gates of Ieruſalem
beganne to be darke before the Sabbath, I commanded that the gates
ſhould be ſhut, and charged that they ſhould not be opened till after the
Sabbath: and ſome of my ſeruants ſet I at the gates, that there ſhould no
burden be brought in on the Sabbath day.20So the merchants, and ſellers
of all kinde of ware, lodged without Ieruſalem once or twice.21Then I
teſtified againſt them, and ſaid vnto them, Why lodge yee about the wall?
If ye doe ſo againe, I will lay hands on you. From that time forth came
they no more on the Sabbath.22And I commanded the Leuites, that they
ſhould cleanſe themſelues, and that they ſhould come and keepe the
gates, to ſanctifie the Sabbath day: Remember me, O my God,
concerning this alſo, and ſpare me, according to the greatneſſe of thy
mercie.23In thoſe dayes alſo ſawe I Iewes that had maried wiues of
Aſhdod, of Ammon, and of Moab:24And their children ſpake halfe in
the ſpeech of Aſhdod, and could not ſpeake in the Iewes language, but
according to the language of ech people.25And I contended with them,
and curſed them, and ſmote certeine of them, and pluckt off their haire,
and made them ſweare by God, ſaying, Yee ſhall not giue your daughters
vnto their ſonnes, nor take their daughters vnto your ſonnes, or for your
ſelues.26Did not Solomon king of Iſrael ſinne by theſe things? yet among
many nations was there no king like him, who was beloued of his God,
and God made him king ouer all Iſrael: neuertheleſſe, euen him did
outlandiſh women cauſe to ſinne.27Shall wee then hearken vnto you, to
doe all this great euill, to tranſgreſse againſt our God, in marrying ſtrange
wiues?28And one of the ſonnes of Ioiada, the ſonne of Eliaſhib the high
Prieſt, was ſonne in law to Sanballat the Horonite: therfore I chaſed him
from me.29Remember them, O my God, becauſe they haue defiled the
Prieſthood, and the couenant of the Prieſthood, and of the
Leuites.30Thus cleanſed I them from all ſtrangers, and appointed the
wards of the Prieſts and the Leuites, euery one in his buſineſse:31And
for the wood-offering, at times appointed, and for the firſt fruits.
Remember me, O my God, for good.

EſTER (ESTHER)

CHAPTER 1 1Now it came to paſſe in the dayes of Ahaſuerus, (this is
Ahaſuerus which reigned from India, euen vnto Ethiopia, ouer an
hundred, and ſeuen and twentie prouinces.)2That in thoſe dayes, when
the King Ahaſuerus ſate on the throne of his kingdome, which was in
Shuſhan the palace:3In the third yeere of his reigne, he made a feaſt vnto
all his Princes, and his ſeruants, the power of Perſia and Media, the
Nobles and Princes of the prouinces being before him.4When he
ſhewed the riches of his glorious kingdome, and the honour of his
excellent maieſtie, many dayes, euen an hundred and foureſcore
dayes.5And when theſe dayes were expired, the king made a feaſt vnto
all the people that were preſent in Shuſhan the palace, both vnto great
and ſmall, ſeuen dayes, in the court of the garden of the kings
palace,6Where were white, greene and blew hangings, faſtened with
cords of fine linnen, and purple, to ſiluer rings, and pillers of marble: the
beds were of gold and ſiluer, vpon a pauement of red, and blewe, and
white, and blacke marble.7And they gaue them drinke in veſſels of gold,
(the veſſels being diuers one from another) and royall wine in
abundance, according to the ſtate of the king.8And the drinking was
according to the law, none did compell: for the king had appointed to
all the officers of his houſe, that they ſhould doe according to euery
mans pleaſure.9Alſo Uaſthi the Queene made a feaſt for the women, in
the royall houſe which belonged to king Ahaſuerus.10On the ſeuenth
day, when the heart of the King was merry with wine, he commanded
Mehuman, Biztha, Harbona, Bigtha, and Abagtha, Zethar, and Carcas,
the ſeuen chamberlens that ſerued in the preſence of Ahaſuerus the
king,11To bring Uaſthi the Queene before the king, with the Crowne
royall, to ſhew the people, and the Princes her beautie: for ſhe was faire
to looke on.12But the Queene Uaſthi refuſed to come at the Kings
commandement by his chamberlens: therefore was the King very wroth,
and his anger burned in him.13Then the king ſaide to the wiſe men,
which knew the times (for ſo was the Kings maner towards all that knew
law, and iudgement:14And the next vnto him, was Carſhena, Shethar,
Admatha, Tarſhis, Meres, Marſena, and Memucan, the ſeuen Princes of
Perſia, and Media, which ſaw the Kings face, and which ſate the firſt in
the kingdome.)15What ſhall wee doe vnto the Queene Uaſthi, according
to law, becauſe ſhe hath not performed the commandement of the king
Ahaſuerus, by the chamberlens?16And Memucan anſwered before the
king and the Princes; Uaſthi the Queene hath not done wrong to the
king onely, but alſo to all the Princes, and to all the people that are in all
the prouinces of the king Ahaſuerus.17For this deed of the queene ſhall
come abroad vnto all women, ſo that they ſhal deſpiſe their huſbands in
their eyes, when it ſhall bee reported; The king Ahaſuerus commanded
Uaſthi the queene to be brought in before him, but ſhe came
not.18Likewiſe ſhall the Ladies of Perſia and Media ſay this day vnto all
the kings princes, which haue heard of the deed of the Queene. Thus
ſhall there Ariſe too much contempt and wrath.19If it pleaſe the king, let
there go a royall commandement from him, and let it bee written among
the lawes of the Perſians, and the Medes, that it be not altered, that
Uaſthi come no more before king Ahaſuerus, and let the king giue her
royall eſtate vnto another that is better then ſhe.20And when the kings
decree, which he ſhal make, ſhalbe publiſhed throughout all his empire,
(for it is great:) all the wiues ſhall giue to their huſbands honour, both
to great and ſmall.21And the ſaying pleaſed the king and the princes, and
the king did according to the word of Memucan:22For he ſent letters
into all the kings prouinces, into euery prouince, according to the writing
thereof, and to euery people after their language, that euery man ſhould
beare rule in his owne houſe, and that it ſhould be publiſhed according
to the language of euerie people.

CHAPTER 2 1After theſe things, when the wrath of king Ahaſuerus
was appeaſed, hee remembred Uaſthi, and what ſhee had done, and what
was decreed againſt her.2Then ſaide the kings ſeruants, that miniſtred
vnto him, Let there bee faire yong virgins ſought for the king:3And let
the king appoint officers in all the prouinces of his kingdome, that they
may gather together all the faire yong virgins vnto Shuſhan the palace,
to the houſe of the women vnto the cuſtodie of Hege the kings
chamberlaine, keeper of the women, and let their things for purification
bee giuen them:4And let the maiden which pleaſeth the king, bee
Queene in ſtead of Uaſthi. And the thing pleaſed the king, and he did
ſo.5Now in Shuſhan the palace, there was a certaine Iew, whoſe name
was Mordecai, the ſonne of Iair, the ſonne of Shimei, the ſonne of Kiſh,
a Beniamite,6Who had bene caried away from Ieruſalem, with the
captiuitie which had bene caried away with Ieconiah king of Iudah,
whom Nebuchadnezzar the King of Babylon had caried away.7And hee
brought vp Hadaſſah (that is Eſther) his vncles daughter, for ſhe had
neither father nor mother, and the maid was faire and beautiful, whom
Mordecai (when her father and mother were dead) tooke for his owne
daughter.8So it came to paſſe, when the kings commandement and his
decree was heard, and when many maidens were gathered together vnto
Shuſhan the palace, to the cuſtodie of Hegai, that Eſther was brought
alſo vnto the kings houſe, to the cuſtodie of Hegai, keeper of the
women.9And the maiden pleaſed him, and ſhe obtained kindneſſe of
him, and hee ſpeedily gaue her her things for purification, with ſuch
things as belonged to her, and ſeuen maidens, which were meet to be
giuen her, out of the Kings houſe, and hee preferred her and her maids,
vnto the beſt place of the houſe of the women.10Eſther had not ſhewed
her people, nor her kinred: for Mordecai had charged her, that ſhe
ſhould not ſhew it.11And Mordecai walked euery day before the court of
the womens houſe, to know how Eſther did, and what ſhould become
of her.12Now when euery maids turne was come, to goe in to King
Ahaſnerus, after that ſhee had bene twelue moneths, according to the
maner of the women (for ſo were the dayes of their purifications
accompliſhed, to wit, ſixe moneths with oile of myrrhe, and ſixe
moneths with ſweet odours, and with other things for the purifying of
the women.)13Then thus came euery maiden vnto the king, whatſoeuer
ſhe deſired, was giuen her, to goe with her out of the houſe of the

women, vnto the kings houſe.14In the euening ſhe went, and on the morrowe ſhe returned into the ſecond houſe of the women, to the cuſtodie of Shaaſhgaz the kings chamberlen, which kept the concubines: ſhee came in vnto the king no more, except the king delighted in her, and that ſhee were called by name.15Now when the turne of Eſther, the daughter of Abihail, the vncle of Mordecai (who had taken her for his daughter) was come, to goe in vnto the king: ſhe required nothing, but what Hegai the kings chamberlen the keeper of the women, appointed: And Eſther obtained fauour in the ſight of all them that looked vpon her.16So Eſther was taken vnto king Ahaſuerus, into his houſe royall, in the tenth moneth (which is the moneth Tebeth) in the ſeuenth yeere of his reigne.17And the king loued Eſther aboue all the women, and ſhe obtained grace and fauour in his ſight, more then all the virgins; ſo that hee ſet the royall crowne vpon her head, and made her queene, in ſtead of Uaſthi.18Then the king made a great feaſt vnto all his princes and his ſeruants, euen Eſthers feaſt, and hee made a releaſe to the prouinces, and gaue gifts, according to the ſtate of the king.19And when the virgins were gathered together the ſecond time, then Mordecai ſate in the kings gate.20Eſther had not yet ſhewed her kindred, nor her people, as Mordecai had charged her: For Eſther did the commandement of Mordecai, like as when ſhe was brought vp with him.21In thoſe dayes, (while Mordecai ſate in the kings gate) two of the kings chamberlens, Bigthan and Tereſh, of thoſe which kept the doore, were wroth, and ſought to lay hand on the king Ahaſuerus:22And the thing was knowen to Mordecai, who told it vnto Eſther the Queene, and Eſther certified the king thereof, in Mordecais name.23And when inquiſition was made of the matter, it was found out; therfore they were both hanged on a tree: and it was written in the booke of the chronicles before the king.

CHAPTER 31After theſe things did king Ahaſuerus promote Haman, the ſonne of Amedatha the Agagite, and aduanced him, and ſet his ſeate aboue all the princes that were with him.2And all the kings ſeruants, that were in the kings gate, bowed, and reuerenced Haman, for the king had ſo commanded concerning him: but Mordecai bowed not, nor did him reuerence.3Then the kings ſeruants, which were in the kings gate, ſayd vnto Mordecai, Why tranſgreſseſt thou the kings commandement?4Now it came to paſſe, when they ſpake daily vnto him, and he hearkened not vnto them; that they told Haman, to ſee whether Mordecai his matters would ſtand, for he had told them that he was a Iewe.5And when Haman ſaw that Mordecai bowed not, nor did him reuerence, then was Haman full of wrath.6And hee thought ſcorne to lay hands on Mordecai alone, for they had ſhewed him the people of Mordecai: wherefore Haman ſought to deſtroy all the Iewes, that were throughout the whole kingdome of Ahaſuerus, euen the people of Mordecai.7In the firſt moneth (that is, the moneth Niſan) in the twelfth yeere of king Ahaſuerus, they caſt Pur, that is, the lot, before Haman, from day to day, and from moneth to moneth, to the twelfth moneth, that is the moneth Adar.8And Haman ſaide vnto king Ahaſuerus: There is a certaine people ſcattered abroad, and diſperſed among the people, in all the prouinces of thy kingdome, and their lawes are diuerſe from all people, neither keepe they the kings lawes; therefore it is not for the kings profit to ſuffer them.9If it pleaſe the king, let it be written, that they may be deſtroyed: and I will pay ten thouſand talents of ſiluer to the handes of thoſe that haue the charge of the buſineſse, to bring it into the kings treaſuries.10And the king tooke his ring from his hand, and gaue it vnto Haman the ſonne of Ammedatha the Agagite, the Iewes enemie.11And the king ſaide vnto Haman, The ſiluer is giuen to thee, the people alſo, to doe with them, as it ſeemeth good to thee.12Then were the kings ſcribes called on the thirteenth day of the firſt moneth, and there was written, according to all that Haman had commanded, vnto the kings Lieutenants, and to the gouernours, that were ouer euery prouince, and to the rulers of euery people of euery prouince, according to the writing thereof, and to euery people, after their language, in the name of king Ahaſuerus was it written, and ſealed with the kings ring.13And the letters were ſent by poſts into all the kings prouinces, to deſtroy, to kill, and to cauſe to periſh all Iewes, both yong and olde, litle children and women, in one day, euen vpon the thirteenth day of the twelfth moneth (which is the moneth Adar) and to take the ſpoile of them for a pray.14The copie of the writing for a commandement to bee giuen in euery prouince, was publiſhed vnto all people, that they ſhould bee ready againſt that day.15The poſtes went out, being haſtened by the kings commandement, and the decree was giuen in Shuſhan the palace: and the king and Haman ſate downe to drinke, but the citie Shuſhan was perplexed.

CHAPTER 41When Mordecai perceiued all that was done, Mordecai rent his clothes, and put on ſackcloth with aſhes, and went out into the midſt of the citie, and cried with a loud and a bitter crie:2And came euen before the kings gate: for none might enter into the kings gate clothed with ſackcloth.3And in euery prouince, whitherſoeuer the kings commaundement, and his decree came, there was great mourning among the Iewes, and faſting, and weeping, and wailing, and many lay in ſackcloth and aſhes.4So Eſthers maides and her chamberlaines came, and told it her: then was the Queene exceedingly grieued, and ſhe ſent raiment to clothe Mordecai, and to take away the ſackcloth from him: but he receiued it not.5Then called Eſther for Hatach, one of the kings chamberlaines, whom he had appointed to attend vpon her, and gaue him a commaundement to Mordecai, to know what it was, and why it was.6So Hatach went forth to Mordecai, vnto the ſtreet of the citie, which was before the kings gate:7And Mordecai tolde him of all that had happened vnto him, and of the ſumme of the money that Haman had promiſed to pay to the Kings treaſuries for the Iewes, to deſtroy them.8Alſo he gaue him the copie of the writing of the decree, that was giuen at Shuſhan to deſtroy them, to ſhewe it vnto Eſther, and to declare it vnto her, and to charge her that ſhe ſhould goe in vnto the king, to make ſupplication vnto him, and to make requeſt before him, for her people.9And Hatach came and told Eſther the words of Mordecai.10Againe Eſther ſpake vnto Hatach, and gaue him commaundement vnto Mordecai;11All the Kings ſeruants, and the people of the kings prouinces do know, that whoſoeuer, whether man or woman, ſhall come vnto the King into the inner court, who is not called, there is one lawe of his to put him to death, except ſuch to whom the King ſhall hold out the golden ſcepter, that he may liue: but I haue not beene called to come in vnto the King, theſe thirtie dayes.12And they tolde to Mordecai Eſthers words.13Then Mordecai commanded to anſwere Eſther; Thinke not with thy ſelfe that thou ſhalt eſcape in the kings houſe, more then all the Iewes.14For if thou altogether holdeſt thy peace at this time, then ſhall there enlargement and deliuerance Ariſe to the Iewes from another place, but thou and thy fathers houſe ſhall be deſtroyed: And who knoweth, whether thou art come to the kingdome for ſuch a time as this?15Then Eſther bade them returne Mordecai this anſwere:16Goe, gather together all the Iewes that are preſent in Shuſhan, and faſt yee for me, and neither eate nor drinke three dayes, night or day: I alſo and my maidens will faſt likewiſe, and ſo will I goe in vnto the king, which is not according to the Law, and if I periſh, I periſh.17So Mordecai went his way, and did according to all that Eſther had commanded him.

CHAPTER 51Now it came to paſſe on the third day, that Eſther put on her royall apparell, and ſtood in the inner court of the kings houſe, ouer againſt the kings houſe: and the King ſate vpon his royall throne in the royall houſe, ouer againſt the gate of the houſe.2And it was ſo, when the king ſaw Eſther the Queene ſtanding in the court, that ſhee obtained fauour in his ſight: and the king helde out to Eſther the golden ſcepter that was in his hand: So Eſther drew neere, and touched the top of the ſcepter.3Then ſayd the King vnto her, What wilt thou, Queene Eſther? and what is thy requeſt? it ſhall bee euen giuen thee to the halfe of the kingdome.4And Eſther anſwered, If it ſeeme good vnto the King, let the King and Haman come this day vnto the banquet that I haue prepared for him.5Then the King ſayd, Cauſe Haman to make haſte, that he may doe as Eſther hath ſaid: So the king and Haman came to the banquet that Eſther had prepared.6And the king ſaid vnto Eſther at the banquet of wine, What is thy petition, and it ſhall be granted thee? and what is thy requeſt? euen to the halfe of the kingdome it ſhall be performed.7Then anſwered Eſther, and ſaid, My petition, and my requeſt is,8If I haue found fauour in the ſight of the king, and if it pleaſe the king to grant my petition, and to performe my requeſt, let the king, and Haman, come to the banquet that I ſhall prepare for them, and I wil do to morow, as the king hath ſaid.9Then went Haman foorth that day, ioyfull, and with a glad heart: but when Haman ſaw Mordecai in the kings gate, that hee ſtood not vp, nor mooued for him, hee was full of indignation againſt Mordecai.10Neuertheleſſe Haman refrained himſelfe, and when he came home, hee ſent and called for his friends, and Zereſh his wife.11And Haman told them of the glory of his riches, and the multitude of his children, and all the things wherein the king had promoted him, and how he had aduanced him aboue the Princes, and ſeruants of the king.12Haman ſaid moreouer, Yea Eſther the Queene did let no man come in with the king vnto the banquet that ſhe had prepared, but my ſelfe; and to morrow am I inuited vnto her alſo with the king.13Yet all this auaileth me nothing, ſo long as I ſee Mordecai the Iew ſitting at the kings gate.14Then ſaide Zereſh his wife, and all his friends vnto him, Let a gallous be made of fifty cubits hie, and to morrow ſpeake thou vnto the king, that Mordecai may be hanged thereon: then goe thou in merily with the king vnto the banquet. And the thing pleaſed Haman, and hee cauſed the gallous to be made.

CHAPTER 61On that night could not the King ſleepe, and hee commaunded to bring the booke of Records of the chronicles; and they were read before the king.2And it was found written, that Mordecai had told of Bigthana, and Tereſh, two of the kings chamberleus, the keepers of the doore, who ſought to lay hand on the king Ahaſuerus.3And the king ſaid, What honour and dignitie hath bene done to Mordecai for this? Then ſaid the kings ſeruants that miniſtred vnto him, There is nothing done for him.4And the king ſaid, Who is in the court? (now Haman was come into the outward court of the kings houſe, to ſpeake vnto the king, to hang Mordecai on the gallons that hee had prepared for him.)5And the kings ſeruants ſaid vnto him, Behold, Haman ſtandeth in the court. And the King ſaide, Let him come in.6So Haman came in, and the king ſaid vnto him, What ſhall be done vnto the man whom the king delighteth to honour? (now Haman thought in his heart, To whom would the king delight to doe honour, more then to my ſelfe?)7And Haman anſwered the king, For the man whom the king delighteth to honour,8Let the royall apparell bee brought, which the King vſeth to weare, and the horſe that the King rideth vpon, and the crowne royal which is ſet vpon his head:9And let this apparell and horſe bee deliuered to the hand of one of the kings moſt noble Princes, that they may aray the man withall, whom the king delighteth to honour, and bring him on horſebacke through the ſtreete of the city, and proclaime before him, Thus ſhal it be done to the man whom the king delighteth to honour.10Then the king ſaide to Haman, Make haſte, and take the apparell, and the horſe, as thou haſt ſaid, and doe euen ſo to Mordecai the Iew, that ſitteth at the Kings gate: let nothing faile of all that thou haſt ſpoken.11Then tooke Haman the apparell, and the horſe, & arayed Mordecai, and brought him on horſ-backe through the ſtreete of the city, and proclaimed before him: Thus ſhall it bee done vnto the man whom the King delighteth to honour.12And Mordecai came againe to the kings gate: but Haman haſted to his houſe, mourning, and hauing his head couered.13And Haman told Zereſh his wife, and all his friends, euery thing that had befallen him. Then ſaide his wiſe men, and Zereſh his wife vnto him, If Mordecai be of the ſeed of the Iewes, before whom thou haſt begun to fall, thou ſhalt not preuaile againſt him, but ſhalt ſurely fall before him.14And while they were yet talking with him, came the kings chamberlens, and haſted to bring Haman vnto the banquet that Eſther had prepared.

CHAPTER 71So the King and Haman came to banquet with Eſther the Queene.2And the king ſaid againe vnto Eſther, on the ſecond day at the banquet of wine, What is thy petition, Queene Eſther, and it ſhalbe granted thee? and what is thy requeſt? and it ſhall bee performed, euen to the halfe of the kingdome.3Then Eſther the Queene anſwered, and ſaid; If I haue found fauour in thy ſight, O King, and if it pleaſe the King, let my life be giuen me at my petition, and my people at my requeſt.4For we are ſold, I, and my people, to be deſtroyed, to be ſlaine, and to periſh: but if we had bene ſold for bondmen, and bondwomen, I had held my tongue, although the enemy could not counteruaile the kings dammage.5Then the king Ahaſuerus anſwered, & ſaid vnto Eſther the Queene: Who is he? and where is he, that durſt preſume in his heart to do ſo?6And Eſther ſaid, The aduerſary and enemie, is this wicked Haman. Then Haman was afraid before the King and the Queene.7And the king ariſing from the banquet of wine in his wrath, went into the palace garden: and Haman ſtood vp to make requeſt for his life to Eſther the Queene: for he ſaw that there was euill determined againſt him by the King.8Then the king returned out of the palace garden, into the place of the banquet of wine, and Haman was fallen vpon the bed whereon Eſther was. Then ſaid the King, Will hee force the Queene alſo before me in the houſe? As the word went out of the Kings mouth, they couered Hamans face.9And Harbonah one of the chamberlaines, ſaid before the king; Behold alſo the gallowes, fiftie cubites high, which Haman had made for Mordecai, who had ſpoken good for the king, ſtandeth in the houſe of Haman. Then the king ſaid, Hang him thereon.10So they hanged Haman on the gallows that he had prepared for Mordecai. Then was the Kings wrath pacified.

CHAPTER 81On that day did the King Ahaſuerus giue the houſe of Haman, the Iewes enemy, vnto Eſther the Queene; and Mordecai came before the King; for Eſther hade told what he was vnto her.2And the king tooke off his Ring which he had taken from Haman, and gaue it vnto Mordecai. And Eſther ſet Mordecai ouer the houſe of Haman.3And Eſther ſpake yet againe before the king, and fell downe at his feet, and beſought him with teares, to put away the miſchiefe of Haman the Agagite, and his deuice, that he had deuiſed againſt the Iewes.4Then the king helde out the golden ſcepter toward Eſther. So Eſther aroſe, and ſtood before the king,5And ſaid, If it pleaſe the king, and if I haue found fauour in his ſight, and the thing ſeeme right before the king, and I bee pleaſing in his eyes, let it be written to reuerſe the letters deuiſed by Haman the ſonne of Hammedatha the Agagite, which hee wrote to deſtroy the Iewes, which are in all the kings prouinces.6For how can I endure to ſee the euill that ſhall come vnto my people? or how can I endure to ſee the deſtruction of my kinred?7Then the king Ahaſuerus ſaid vnto Eſther the Queene, and to Mordecai the Iewe, Behold, I haue giuen Eſther the houſe of Haman, and him they haue hanged vpon the gallowes, becauſe hee layde his hand vpon the Iewes.8Write ye alſo for the Iewes, as it liketh you, in the Kings name, and ſeale it with the Kings ring: for the writing which is written in the Kings name, and ſealed with the Kings ring, may no man reuerſe.9Then were the kings ſcribes called at that time, in the third moneth, (that is, the month Siuan) on the three and twentieth day thereof, and it was written (according to all that Mordecai commanded) vnto the Iewes, and to the Lieutenants, and the deputies and rulers of the prouinces, which are from India vnto Ethiopia, an hundred, twentie and ſeuen prouinces, vnto euery prouince according to the writing thereof, and vnto euery people after their language, and to the Iewes, according to their writing, and according to their language.10And he wrote in the king Ahaſuerus name, and ſealed it with the kings Ring, and ſent letters by Poſtes, on horſebacke, and riders on mules, camels, and yong dromedaries:11Wherein the King granted the Iewes, which were in euery citie, to gather themſelues together, and to ſtand for their life, to deſtroy, to ſlay, and to cauſe to periſh all the power of the people and prouince that would aſsault them, both little ones, and women, and to take the ſpoile of them for a pray:12Upon one day, in all the prouinces of king Ahaſuerus, namely vpon the thirteenth day of the twelfth moneth, which is the moneth Adar.13The copy of the writing, for a commandement to bee giuen in euery prouince, was publiſhed vnto all people, and that the Iewes ſhould be readie againſt that day, to auenge themſelues on their enemies.14So the poſts that rode vpon mules and camels went out, being haſtened, and preſſed on by the kings commandement, and the decree was giuen at Shuſhan the palace.15And Mordecai went out from the preſence of the king, in royall apparell, of blew and white, and with a great crowne of gold, and with a garment of fine linnen, and purple, and the citie of Shuſhan reioyced, and was glad:16The Iewes had light and gladneſſe, and ioy and honour.17And in euery prouince, and in euery city, whitherſoeuer the kings commandement, and his decree came, the Iewes had ioy and gladnes, a feaſt and a good day: And many of the people of the land became Iewes; for the feare of the Iewes fell vpon them.

CHAPTER 91Now in the twelfth month (that is the moneth Adar) on the thirteenth day of the ſame, when the Kings commaundement and his decree drew neere to bee put in execution, in the day that the enemies of the Iewes hoped to haue power ouer them: (though it was turned to the contrary, that the Iewes had rule ouer them that hated them.)2The Iewes gathered themſelues together in their cities, throughout all the prouinces of the king Ahaſuerus, to lay hand on ſuch as ſought their hurt, and no man could withſtand them: for the feare of them fell vpon all people.3And all the rulers of the prouinces, and the Lieutenants, and the deputies, and officers of the king, helped the Iewes: becauſe the feare of Mordecai fell vpon them.4For Mordecai was great in the kings houſe, and his fame went out, throughout all the prouinces: for this man

Mordecai waxed greater and greater.[5]Thus the Iewes ſmote all their enemies with the ſtroke of the ſword, and ſlaughter, and deſtruction, and did what they would vnto thoſe that hated them.[6]And in Shuſhan the palace the Iewes ſlew and deſtroyed fiue hundred men:[7]And Parſhandatha, and Dalphon, and Aſpatha,[8]And Poratha, and Adalia, and Aridatha,[9]And Parmaſhta, and Ariſai, and Aridai, and Uaiezatha,[10]The ten ſonnes of Haman the ſonne of Hammedatha, the enemie of the Iewes, ſlew they, but on the ſpoile laid they not their hand.[11]On that day, the number of thoſe that were ſlaine in Shuſhan the palace, was brought before the king.[12]And the king ſaid vnto Eſther the Queene; The Iewes haue ſlaine and deſtroied fiue hundred men in Shuſhan the palace, & the ten ſonnes of Haman; what haue they done in the reſt of the kings prouinces? now what is thy petition? and it ſhalbe granted thee: or what is thy requeſt further? and it ſhall be done.[13]Then ſaid Eſther, If it pleaſe the king, Let it bee granted to the Iewes which are in Shuſhan, to doe to morow alſo, according vnto this dayes decree, and let Hamans ten ſonnes be hanged vpon the gallous.[14]And the king commanded it ſo to be done; and the decree was giuen at Shuſhan, and they hanged Hamans ten ſonnes.[15]For the Iewes that were in Shuſhan, gathered themſelues together on the fourteenth day alſo of the moneth Adar, and ſlewe three hundred men at Shuſhan: but on the pray they laid not their hand.[16]But the other Iewes that were in the kings prouinces, gathered themſelues together, & ſtood for their liues, and had reſt from their enemies, and ſlew of their foes ſeuenty and fiue thouſand, but they laid not their handes on the pray.[17]On the thirteenth day of the moneth Adar, and on the fourteenth day of the ſame, reſted they, and made it a day of feaſting and gladnes.[18]But the Iewes that were at Shuſhan, aſſembled together on the thirteenth day therof, and on the fourteenth thereof; and on the fifteenth day of the ſame, they reſted, and made it a day of feaſting and gladneſſe.[19]Therefore the Iewes of the villages, that dwelt in the vnwalled townes, made the foureteenth day of the moneth Adar, a day of gladneſſe and feaſting, and a good day, and of ſending portions one to another.[20]And Mordecai wrote theſe things, and ſent letters vnto all the Iewes, that were in all the prouinces of the king Ahaſuerus, both nigh & farre,[21]To ſtabliſh this among them, that they ſhould keepe the fourteenth day of the moneth Adar, and the fifteenth day of the ſame, yeerely:[22]As the dayes wherein the Iewes reſted from their enemies, & the moneth which was turned vnto them, from ſorrow to ioy, and from mourning into a good day: that they ſhould make them daies of feaſting and ioy, and of ſending portions one to another, and gifts to the poore.[23]And the Iewes vndertooke to doe, as they had begun, and as Mordecai had written vnto them:[24]Becauſe Haman the ſonne of Hammedatha the Agagite, the enemie of all the Iewes, had deuiſed againſt the Iewes to deſtroy them, and had caſt Pur (that is, the lot) to conſume them, and to deſtroy them.[25]But when Eſther came before the king, he commanded by letters, that his wicked deuice which he deuiſed againſt the Iewes, ſhould returne vpon his owne head, and that he and his ſonnes, ſhould be hanged on the gallous.[26]Wherefore they called theſe dayes Purim, after the name of Pur: therefore for all the words of this letter, and of that which they had ſeene concerning this matter, and which had come vnto them,[27]The Iewes ordeined, and tooke vpon them, and vpon their ſeed, and vpon all ſuch as ioyned themſelues vnto them, ſo as it ſhould not faile, that they would keepe theſe two dayes, according to their writing, and according to their appointed time, euery yeere:[28]And that theſe dayes ſhould be remembred, and kept throughout euery generation, euery family, euery prouince, and euery citie, and that theſe dayes of Purim ſhould not faile from among the Iewes, nor the memoriall of them periſh from their ſeed.[29]Then Eſther the Queene, the daughter of Abihail, and Mordecai the Iew, wrote with all authoritie, to confirme this ſecond letter of Purim.[30]And hee ſent the letters vnto all the Iewes, to the hundred, twentie and ſeuen prouinces of the kingdome of Ahaſuerus, with wordes of peace and trueth:[31]To confirme theſe dayes of Purim, in their times appointed, according as Mordecai the Iew, and Eſther the Queene had enioyned them, and as they had decreed for themſelues and for their ſeed, the matters of the faſtings and their cry.[32]And the decree of Eſther confirmed theſe matters of Purim, and it was written in the booke.

CHAPTER 10[1]And the king Ahaſuerus layde a tribute vpon the land, and vpon the Iſles of the ſea.[2]And all the actes of his power, and of his might, and the declaration of the greatneſſe of Mordecai, whereunto the king aduanced him, are they not written in the booke of the Chronicles of the kings of Media and Perſia?[3]For Mordecai the Iew was next vnto King Ahaſuerus, and great among the Iewes, and accepted of the multitude of his brethren, ſeeking the wealth of his people, and ſpeaking peace to all his ſeed.

IOB (JOB)

CHAPTER 1[1]There was a man in the land of Uz, whoſe name was Iob, and that man was perfect and vpright, and one that feared God, and eſchewed euill.[2]And there were borne vnto him ſeuen ſonnes, and three daughters.[3]His ſubſtance alſo was ſeuen thouſand ſheepe, and three thouſand camels, and fiue hundred yoke of oxen, and fiue hundred ſhee aſſes, and a very great houſhold; ſo that this man was the greateſt of all the men of the Eaſt.[4]And his ſonnes went and feaſted in their houſes, euery one his day, and ſent and called for their three ſiſters, to eate and to drinke with them.[5]And it was ſo, when the dayes of their feaſting were gone about, that Iob ſent and ſanctified them, and roſe vp early in the morning, and offered burnt offerings according to the number of them all: For Iob ſaid, It may be that my ſonnes haue ſinned, and curſed God in their hearts: Thus did Iob continually.[6]Now there was a day, when the ſons of God came to preſent themſelues before the Lord, and Satan came alſo among them.[7]And the Lord ſaid vnto Satan, Whence commeſt thou? Then Satan anſwered the Lord, and ſayde, From going to and fro in the earth, and from walking vp and downe in it.[8]And the Lord ſayd vnto Satan, Haſt thou conſidered my ſeruant Iob, that there is none like him in the earth? a perfect and an vpright man, one that feareth God, and eſcheweth euill?[9]Then Satan anſwered þe Lord, and ſayd, Doeth Iob feare God for nought?[10]Haſt not thou made an hedge about him, and about his houſe, and about all that he hath on euery ſide? thou haſt bleſſed the worke of his hands, and his ſubſtance is increaſed in the land.[11]But put foorth thine hand now, and touch all that he hath, and he will curſe thee to thy face.[12]And the Lord ſaid vnto Satan, Behold, all that hee hath is in thy power, onely vpon himſelfe put not foorth thine hand. So Satan went forth from the preſence of the Lord.[13]And there was a day, when his ſonnes and his daughters were eating and drinking wine in their eldeſt brothers houſe:[14]And there came a meſſenger vnto Iob, and ſaid, The oxen were plowing, and the aſſes feeding beſide them,[15]And the Sabeans fell vpon them, and tooke them away: yea they haue ſlaine the ſeruants with the edge of the ſword, and I onely am eſcaped alone, to tell thee.[16]While he was yet ſpeaking, there came alſo another, and ſaid, The fire of God is fallen from heauen, and hath burnt vp the ſheepe, and the ſeruants, and conſumed them, and I onely am eſcaped alone, to tell thee.[17]While he was yet ſpeaking, there came alſo another, and ſaid, The Caldeans made out three bands, and fell vpon the camels, and haue caried them away, yea, and ſlaine the ſeruants with the edge of the ſword, and I onely am eſcaped alone, to tell thee.[18]While he was yet ſpeaking, there came alſo another, & ſaid, Thy ſonnes, and thy daughters, were eating and drinking wine in their eldeſt brothers houſe.[19]And beholde, there came a great winde from the wildernes, and ſmote the foure corners of the houſe, and it fell vpon the yong men, and they are dead, and I onely am eſcaped alone to tell thee.[20]Then Iob aroſe, and rent his mantle, and ſhaued his head, and fell downe vpon the ground and worſhipped,[21]And ſaid, Naked came I out of my mothers wombe, and naked ſhall I returne thither: the Lord gaue, and the Lord hath taken away, bleſſed be the Name of the Lord.[22]In all this Iob ſinned not, nor charged God fooliſhly.

CHAPTER 2[1]Againe there was a day when the ſonnes of God came to preſent themſelues before the Lord, and Satan came alſo among them to preſent himſelfe before the Lord.[2]And the Lord ſaid vnto Satan, From whence commeſt thou? And Satan anſwered the Lord, and ſaid, From going to & fro in the earth, and from walking vp and downe in it.[3]And the Lord ſaid vnto Satan, Haſt thou conſidered my ſeruant Iob, that there is none like him in the earth; a perfect and an vpright man, one that feareth God, and eſcheweth euill? and ſtill hee holdeth faſt his integritie, although thou moouedſt mee againſt him, to deſtroy him without cauſe.[4]And Satan anſwered the Lord, and ſaid, Skinne for ſkinne, yea all that a man hath, wil he giue for his life.5But put foorth thine hand now, and touch his bone and his fleſh, and he will curſe thee to thy face.6And the Lord ſaid vnto Satan, Behold, hee is in thine hand, but ſaue his life.7So went Satan foorth from the preſence of the Lord, and ſmote Iob with ſore biles, from the ſole of his foote vnto his crowne.8And hee tooke him a potſheard to ſcrape himſelfe withall; and hee ſate downe among the aſhes.9Then ſaide his wife vnto him, Doeſt thou ſtill reteine thine integritie? Curſe God, and die.10But he ſaid vnto her, Thou ſpeakeſt as one of the fooliſh women ſpeaketh; what? ſhall wee receiue good at the hand of God, and ſhall wee not receiue euill? In all this did not Iob ſinne with his lippes.11Now when Iobs three friends heard of all this euill, that was come vpon him, they came euery one from his owne place: Eliphaz the Temanite, and Bildad the Shuhite, and Zophar the Naamathite; for they had made an appointment together to come to mourne with him, and to comfort him.12And when they lift vp their eyes afarre off, and knew him not, they lifted vp their voice, and wept; and they rent euery one his mantle, and ſprinckled duſt vpon their heades toward heauen.13So they ſate downe with him vpon the ground ſeuen dayes, and ſeuen nights, and none ſpake a word vnto him; for they ſaw that his griefe was very great.

CHAPTER 31After this, opened Iob his mouth, and curſed his day.2And Iob ſpake, and ſaid,3Let the day periſh, wherein I was borne, and the night in which it was ſaid, There is a man-childe conceiued.4Let that day bee darkeneſſe, let not God regard it from aboue, neither let the light ſhine vpon it.5Let darkenes and the ſhadowe of death ſtaine it, let a cloud dwell vpon it, let the blacknes of the day terrifie it.6As for that night, let darkeneſſe ſeaze vpon it, let it not be ioyned vnto the dayes of the yeere, let it not come into the number of the moneths.7Loe, let that night be ſolitarie, let no ioyfull voice come therein.8Let them curſe it that curſe the day, who are ready to raiſe vp their mourning.9Let the ſtarres of the twilight thereof be darke, let it looke for light, but haue none, neither let it ſee the dawning of the day:10Becauſe it ſhut not vp the doores of my mothers wombe, nor hid ſorrowe from mine eyes.11Why died I not from the wombe? why did I not giue vp the ghoſt when I came out of the bellie?12Why did the knees preuent mee? or why the breaſts, that I ſhould ſucke?13For now ſhould I haue lien ſtill and beene quiet, I ſhould haue ſlept; then had I bene at reſt,14With Kings and counſellers of the earth, which built deſolate places for themſelues,15Or with Princes that had golde, who filled their houſes with ſiluer:16Or as an hidden vntimely birth, I had not bene; as infants which neuer ſaw light.17There the wicked ceaſe from troubling: and there the wearie be at reſt.18There the priſoners reſt together, they heare not the voice of the oppreſsour.19The ſmall and great are there, and the ſeruant is free from his maſter.20Wherefore is light giuen to him that is in miſery, and life vnto the bitter in ſoule?21Which long for death, but it commeth not, and dig for it more then for hid treaſures:22Which reioice exceedingly, and are glad when they can finde the graue?23Why is light giuen to a man, whoſe way is hid, and whom God hath hedged in?24For my ſighing commeth before I eate, and my roarings are powred out like the waters.25For the thing which I greatly feared is come vpon me, and that which I was afraid of, is come vnto me.26I was not in ſafetie, neither had I reſt, neither was I quiet: yet trouble came.

CHAPTER 41Then Eliphaz the Temanite anſwered, and ſaid,2If we aſſay to commune with thee, wilt thou be grieued? But who can withhold himſelfe from ſpeaking?3Beholde, Thou haſt inſtructed many, and thou haſt ſtrengthened the weake hands.4Thy words haue vpholden him that was falling, and thou haſt ſtrengthened the feeble knees.5But now it is come vpon thee, and thou fainteſt, it toucheth thee, and thou art troubled.6Is not this thy feare, thy confidence; the vprightneſse of thy wayes and thy hope?7Remember, I pray thee, who euer periſhed, being innocent? or where were the righteous cut off?8Euen as I haue ſeene, they that plow iniquity, and ſow wickednſse, reape the ſame.9By the blaſt of God they periſh, and by the breath of his noſtrils are they conſumed.10The roaring of the Lyon, and the voice of the fierce Lyon, and the teeth of the yong Lyons are broken.11The old Lyon periſheth for lacke of pray, and the ſtout Lyons whelpes are ſcattered abroad.12Nowe a thing was ſecretly brought to me, and mine eare receiued a litle thereof.13In thoughts from the viſions of the night, when deepe ſleepe falleth on men:14Feare came vpon me, and trembling, which made all my bones to ſhake.15Then a ſpirit paſſed before my face: the haire of my fleſh ſtood vp.16It ſtood ſtill, but I could not diſcerne the forme thereof: an image was before mine eyes, there was ſilence, and I heard a voyce, ſaying,17Shall mortall man be more iuſt then God? ſhall a man bee more pure then his maker?18Behold, hee put no truſt in his ſeruants; and his Angels hee charged with folly:19Howe much leſſe on them that dwell in houſes of clay, whoſe foundation is in the duſt, which are cruſhed before the moth.20They are deſtroyed from morning to euening: they periſh for euer, without any regarding it.21Doeth not their excellencie which is in them, goe away? they die, euen without wiſedome.

CHAPTER 51Call now, if there be any that wil anſwere thee, and to which of the Saints wilt thou turne?2For wrath killeth the fooliſh man, and enuy ſlayeth the ſilly one.3I haue ſeene the fooliſh taking roote: but ſuddenly I curſed his habitation.4His children are farre from ſafetie, and they are cruſhed in the gate, neither is there any to deliuer them.5Whoſe harueſt the hungry eateth vp, and taketh it euen out of the thorns, and the robber ſwalloweth vp their ſubſtance.6Although affliction commeth not forth of the duſt, neither doeth trouble ſpring out of the ground:7Yet man is borne vnto trouble, as the ſparkes flie vpward.8I would ſeeke vnto God, and vnto God would I commit my cauſe:9Which doth great things & vnſearchable: marueilous things without number.10Who giueth raine vpon the earth, and ſendeth waters vpon the fields:11To ſet vp on high thoſe that be low; that thoſe which mourne, may be exalted to ſafetie.12Hee diſappointeth the deuices of the craftie, ſo that their hands cannot performe their enterpriſe.13He taketh the wiſe in their owne craftineſse: and the counſell of the froward is caried headlong.14They meete with darkeneſſe in the day time, and grope in the noone day as in the night.15But he ſaueth the poore from the ſword, from their mouth, and from the hand of the mightie.16So the poore hath hope, and iniquitie ſtoppeth her mouth.17Behold, happy is the man whom God correcteth: therefore deſpiſe not thou the chaſtening of the Almightie.18For he maketh ſore, and bindeth vp: he woundeth, and his hands make whole.19Hee ſhall deliuer thee in ſixe troubles, yea in ſeuen there ſhall no euill touch thee.20In famine he ſhall redeeme thee from death: and in warre from the power of the ſword.21Thou ſhalt be hidde from the ſcourge of the tongue: neither ſhalt thou be afraid of deſtruction, when it commeth.22At deſtruction and famine thou ſhalt laugh: neither ſhalt thou be afraid of the beaſts of the earth.23For thou ſhalt be in league with the ſtones of the field: and the beaſts of the field ſhall be at peace with thee.24And thou ſhalt know that thy tabernacle ſhall bee in peace; and thou ſhalt viſite thy habitation, and ſhalt not ſinne.25Thou ſhalt know alſo that thy ſeede ſhalbe great, and thine offſpring as the graſſe of the earth.26Thou ſhalt come to thy graue in a full age, like as a ſhocke of corne commeth in, in his ſeaſon.27Loe this, wee haue ſearched it, ſo it is; heare it, and know thou it for thy good.

CHAPTER 61But Iob anſwered, and ſayd,2Oh that my griefe were throughly weighed, and my calamitie layd in the balances together.3For now it would be heauier then the ſand of the ſea, therefore my words are ſwallowed vp.4For the arrowes of the Almightie are within me, the poyſon whereof drinketh vp my ſpirit: the terrors of God doe ſet themſelues in aray againſt mee.5Doeth the wilde aſſe bray when he hath graſſe? or loweth the oxe ouer his fodder?6Can that which is vnſauery, bee eaten without ſalt? or is there any taſte in the white of an egge?7The things that my ſoule refuſed to touch, are as my ſorrowfull meat.8O that I might haue my requeſt! and that God would graunt mee the thing that I long for!9Euen that it would pleaſe God to deſtroy mee, that he would let looſe his hand, and cut me off.10Then ſhould I yet haue comfort, yea I would harden my ſelfe in ſorrow; let him not ſpare, for I haue not concealed the words of the holy One.11What is my ſtrength, that I ſhould hope? and what is mine ende, that I ſhould prolong my life?12Is my ſtrength the ſtrength of ſtones? or is my fleſh of braſſe?13Is not my helpe in me? and is wiſedome driuen quite from me?14To him that is afflicted, pitie ſhould be ſhewed from his friend; But he forſaketh the feare of the Almighty.15My brethren haue delt deceitfully as a brooke, & as the ſtreame of brookes they paſſe away,16Which are blackiſh by reaſon of the yce, and wherein the ſnow is hid:17What time they waxe warme, they vaniſh: when it is hot, they are conſumed out of their

place.18The pathes of their way are turned aſide; they goe to nothing,
and periſh.19The troupes of Tema looked, the companies of Sheba
waited for them.20They were confounded becauſe they had hoped; they
came thither, and were aſhamed.21For now ye are nothing; ye ſee my
caſting downe, and are afraid.22Did I ſay, Bring vnto mee? or giue a
reward for me of your ſubſtance?23Or deliuer me from the enemies
hand, or redeeme me from the hand of the mighty?24Teach me, and I
will hold my tongue: and cauſe mee to vnderſtand wherein I haue
erred.25How forcible are right wordes? but what doeth your arguing
reproue?26Do ye imagine to reproue words, and the ſpeeches of one
that is deſperate, which are as winde?27Yea, ye ouerwhelme the
fatherleſſe, and you digge a pit for your friend.28Now therefore be
content, looke vpon mee, for it is euident vnto you, if I lie.29Returne, I
pray you, let it not be iniquitie; yea returne againe: my righteouſneſſe is
in it.30Is there iniquitie in my tongue? cannot my taſte diſcerne peruerſe
things?
CHAPTER 71Is there not an appointed time to man vpon earth? are
not his dayes alſo like the dayes of an hireling?2As a ſeruant earneſtly
deſireth the ſhadow, and as an hireling looketh for the reward of his
worke:3So am I made to poſſeſſe moneths of vanitie, and weariſome
nights are appointed to me.4When I lie downe, I ſay, When ſhall I Ariſe,
and the night be gone? and I am full of toſsings to and fro, vnto the
dawning of the day.5My fleſh is cloathed with wormes and clods of duſt,
my ſkinne is broken, and become loathſome.6My dayes are ſwifter then
a weauers ſhuttle, and are ſpent without hope.7O remember that my life
is winde: mine eye ſhall no more ſee good.8The eye of him that hath
ſeene me, ſhall ſee mee no more: thine eyes are vpon me, and I am
not.9As the cloud is conſumed and vaniſheth away: ſo he that goeth
downe to the graue, ſhall come vp no more.10Hee ſhall returne no more
to his houſe: neither ſhall his place know him any more.11Therefore I
will not refraine my mouth, I wil ſpeake in the anguiſh of my ſpirit, I
will complaine in the bitterneſse of my ſoule.12Am I a ſea, or a whale,
that thou ſetteſt a watch ouer me?13When I ſay, My bed ſhal comfort
me, my couch ſhall eaſe my complaint:14Then thou ſkareſt mee with
dreames, and terrifieſt me through viſions.15So that my ſoule chooſeth
ſtrangling: and death rather then my life.16I loath it, I would not liue
alway: let me alone, for my dayes are vanitie.17What is man, that thou
ſhouldeſt magnifie him? and that thou ſhouldeſt ſet thine heart vpon
him?18And that thou ſhouldeſt viſite him euery morning, and trie him
euery moment?19How long wilt thou not depart from me? nor let me
alone till I ſwallow downe my ſpittle?20I haue ſinned, what ſhall I doe
vnto thee, O thou preſeruer of men? why haſt thou ſet me as a mark
againſt thee, ſo that I am a burden to my ſelfe?21And why doeſt thou
not pardon my tranſgreſsion, and take away mine iniquitie? for now ſhall
I ſleepe in the duſt, and thou ſhalt ſeeke me in the morning, but I ſhall
not be.
CHAPTER 81Then anſwered Bildad the Shuhite, and ſaid,2How long
wilt thou ſpeake theſe things? and how long ſhall the wordes of thy
mouth be like a ſtrong wind?3Doth God peruert iudgement? or doth the
Almightie peruert iuſtice?4If thy children haue ſinned againſt him, and
he haue caſt them away for their tranſgreſsion:5If thou wouldeſt ſeeke
vnto God betimes, and make thy ſupplication to the Almightie:6If thou
wert pure and vpright, ſurely now he would awake for thee, and make
the habitation of thy righteouſnes proſperous.7Though thy beginning
was ſmall, yet thy latter end ſhould greatly increaſe.8For enquire, I pray
thee, of the former age, and prepare thy ſelfe to the ſearch of their
fathers.9(For we are but of yeſterday, and know nothing, becauſe our
dayes vpon earth are a ſhadow.)10Shall not they teach thee, and tell thee,
& vtter words out of their heart?11Can the ruſh growe vp without myre?
can the flag growe without water?12Whileſt it is yet in his greenneſse,
and not cut downe, it withereth before any other herbe.13So are the
paths of all that forget God, and the hypocrites hope ſhall
periſh:14Whoſe hope ſhall be cut off, and whoſe truſt ſhall be a ſpiders
web.15He ſhall leane vpon his houſe, but it ſhall not ſtand: he ſhal hold
it faſt, but it ſhall not endure.16He is greene before the ſunne, and his
branch ſhooteth forth in his garden.17His roots are wrapped about the
heape, and ſeeth the place of ſtones.18If he deſtroy him from his place,
then it ſhal denie him, ſaying, I haue not ſeene thee.19Beholde, this is
the ioy of his way, and out of the earth ſhall others grow.20Behold, God
will not caſt away a perfect man, neither will hee helpe the euill
doers:21Till he fill thy mouth with laughing, and thy lips with
reioycing.22They that hate thee ſhall be cloathed with ſhame, and the
dwelling place of the wicked ſhall come to nought.
CHAPTER 91Then Iob anſwered, and ſaid,2I know it is ſo of a trueth:
but howe ſhould man be iuſt with God.3If he will contend with him, he
cannot anſwere him one of a thouſand.4He is wiſe in heart, and mightie
in ſtrength: who hath hardened himſelfe againſt him, and hath
proſpered?5Which remoueth the mountains, and they know not: which
ouerturneth them in his anger:6Which ſhaketh the earth out of her place,
& the pillars thereof tremble:7Which commandeth the Sunne, and it
riſeth not: and ſealeth vp the ſtarres.8Which alone ſpreadeth out the
heauens, and treadeth vpon the waues of the ſea.9Which maketh
Arcturus, Orion and Pleiades, and the chambers of the South.10Which
doeth great things paſt finding out, yea and wonders without
number.11Loe, hee goeth by me, and I ſee him not: he paſſeth on alſo,
but I perceiue him not.12Behold, he taketh away, who can hinder him?
who will ſay vnto him, What doeſt thou?13If God will not withdraw his
anger, the proud helpers doe ſtoupe vnder him.14How much leſſe ſhall
I anſwere him, and chooſe out my words to reaſon with him?15Whom,
though I were righteous, yet would I not anſwere, but I would make
ſupplication to my Iudge.16If I had called, and had anſwered me, yet
would I not beleeue that he had hearkened vnto my voice:17For he
breaketh me with a tempeſt, and multiplieth my wounds without
cauſe.18Hee will not ſuffer me to take my breath, but filleth me with
bitterneſse.19If I ſpeake of ſtrength, loe, hee is ſtrong: and if of
iudgement, who ſhall ſet me a time to pleade?20If I iuſtifie my ſelfe, mine
owne mouth ſhall condemne me: If I ſay, I am perfect, it ſhall alſo
prooue me peruerſe.21Though I were perfect, yet would I not know my
ſoule: I would deſpiſe my life.22This is one thing, therefore I ſaid it; he
deſtroyeth the perfect and the wicked.23If the ſcourge ſlay ſuddenly, hee
will laugh at the triall of the innocent.24The earth is giuen into the hand
of the wicked: he coureth the faces of the Iudges thereof; if not, where,
and who is hee?25Now my dayes are ſwifter then a Poſte: they flee away,
they ſee no good.26They are paſſed away as the ſhips: as the Eagle that
haſteth to the pray.27If I ſay, I will forget my complaint, I will leaue off
my heauineſse, and comfort my ſelfe.28I am afraid of all my ſorrowes, I
know that thou wilt not holde me innocent.29If I be wicked, why then
labour I in vaine?30If I waſh my ſelfe with ſnow water, and make my
handes neuer ſo cleane:31Yet ſhalt thou plunge me in the ditch, and mine
owne clothes ſhall abhorre me.32For he is not a man as I am, that I
ſhould anſwere him, and we ſhould come together in
iudgement.33Neither is there any dayeſ-man betwixt vs, that might lay
his hand vpon vs both.34Let him take his rodde away from me, & let
not his feare terrifie me:35Then would I ſpeake, and not feare him; but
it is not ſo with me.
CHAPTER 101My ſoule is weary of my life, I will leaue my complaint
vpon my ſelfe; I will ſpeake in the bitterneſse of my ſoule.2I will ſay vnto
God, Doe not condemne mee; ſhewe me wherefore thou contendeſt
with me.3Is it good vnto thee, that thou ſhouldeſt oppreſse? that thou
ſhouldeſt deſpiſe the worke of thine hands? and ſhine vpon the counſell
of the wicked?4Haſt thou eyes of fleſh? or ſeeſt thou as man ſeeth?5Are
thy dayes as the dayes of man? are thy yeeres as mans dayes,6That thou
enquireſt after mine iniquitie, and ſearcheſt after my ſinne?7Thou
knoweſt that I am not wicked, and there is none that can deliuer out of
thine hand.8Thine hands haue made me and faſhioned me together
round about yet thou doeſt deſtroy me.9Remember, I beſeech thee, that
thou haſt made me as the clay, and wilt thou bring me into duſt
againe?10Haſt thou not powred me out as milke, and cruddled me like
cheeſe?11Thou haſt cloathed me with ſkin and fleſh, and haſt fenced me
with bones and ſinewes.12Thou haſt granted me life and fauour, and thy
viſitation hath preſerued my ſpirit.13And theſe things haſt thou hid in
thine heart; I know that this is with thee.14If I ſinne, then thou markeſt
me, and thou wilt not acquite me from mine iniquitie.15If I be wicked,
woe vnto me; and if I be righteous, yet will I not lift vp my head: I am
full of confuſion, therefore ſee thou mine affliction:16For it increaſeth:
thou hunteſt me as a fierce Lion: and againe thou ſheweſt thy ſelfe
maruelous vpon me.17Thou renueſt thy witneſſes againſt me, and
increaſeſt thine indignation vpon me; Changes and warre are againſt

me. 18 Wherfore then haſt thou brought me forth out of the wombe? Oh
that I had giuen vp the ghoſt, and no eye had ſeene me! 19 I ſhould haue
bene as though I had not bene, I ſhould haue bene caried from the
wombe to the graue. 20 Are not my dayes few? ceaſe then, and let me
alone that I may take comfort a litle, 21 Before I goe whence I ſhall not
returne, euen to the land of darknes and the ſhadow of death, 22 A land
of darknes, as darknes it ſelfe, and of the ſhadow of death, without any
order, and where the light is as darkenes.
CHAPTER 11 1 Then anſwered Zophar the Naamathite, and
ſaid, 2 Should not the multitude of words be anſwered? and ſhould man
ful of talke be iuſtified? 3 Should thy lies make men hold their peace? and
when thou mockeſt, ſhall no man make thee aſhamed? 4 For thou haſt
ſaid, My doctrine is pure, and I am cleane in thine eyes. 5 But, O that God
would ſpeake, and open his lippes againſt thee, 6 And that he would ſhew
thee the ſecrets of wiſedome, that they are double to that which is: know
therefore that God exacteth of thee leſſe then thine iniquitie
deſerueth. 7 Canſt thou by ſearching finde out God? canſt thou finde out
the Almightie vnto perfection? 8 It is as high as heauen, what canſt thou
doe? deeper then hell, what canſt thou know? 9 The meaſure therof is
longer then the earth, and broader then the ſea. 10 If he cut off, and ſhut
vp, or gather together, then who can hinder him? 11 For, he knoweth
vaine men: hee ſeeth wickedneſſe alſo, will he not then conſider it? 12 For
vaine man would be wiſe; though man be borne like a wilde aſſes
coult. 13 If thou prepare thine heart, and ſtretch out thine hands toward
him: 14 If iniquitie be in thine hand, put it farre away, and let not
wickednes dwell in thy tabernacles. 15 For then ſhalt thou lift vp thy face
without ſpot, yea thou ſhalt be ſtedfaſt, and ſhalt not feare: 16 Becauſe
thou ſhalt forget thy miſery, and remember it as waters that paſſe
away: 17 And thine age ſhalbe clearer then the noone day; thou ſhalt ſhine
foorth, thou ſhalt be as the morning. 18 And thou ſhalt be ſecure becauſe
there is hope, yea thou ſhalt digge about thee, and thou ſhalt take thy
reſt in ſafety. 19 Alſo thou ſhalt lye downe, and none ſhall make thee
afraid; yea many ſhall make ſuite vnto thee. 20 But the eyes of the wicked
ſhall faile, and they ſhall not eſcape, and their hope ſhall be as the giuing
vp of the ghoſt.
CHAPTER 12 1 And Iob anſwered, and ſayd, 2 No doubt but ye are the
people, and wiſedome ſhall die with you. 3 But I haue vnderſtanding as
well as you, I am not inferiour to you: yea, who knoweth not ſuch things
as theſe? 4 I am as one mocked of his neighbour, who calleth vpon God,
and he anſwereth him: the iuſt vpright man is laughed to ſcorne. 5 He
that is ready to ſlippe with his feet, is as a lamp deſpiſed in the thought
of him that is at eaſe. 6 The tabernacles of robbers proſper, and they that
prouoke God are ſecure, into whoſe hand God bringeth
abundantly. 7 But aſke now the beaſts, and they ſhall teach thee; and the
foules of the aire, and they ſhall tell thee. 8 Or ſpeake to the earth, and it
ſhall teach thee; and the fiſhes of the ſea ſhall declare vnto thee. 9 Who
knoweth not in all theſe, that the hand of the Lord hath wrought
this? 10 In whoſe hand is the ſoule of euery liuing thing, and the breath of
all mankinde. 11 Doeth not the eare trie wordes? and the mouth taſte his
meate? 12 With the ancient is wiſedome, and in length of dayes,
vnderſtanding. 13 With him is wiſedome & ſtrength, he hath counſell and
vnderſtanding. 14 Behold, he breaketh downe, and it cannot be built
againe: hee ſhutteth vp a man, and there can be no opening. 15 Behold,
hee withholdeth the waters, and they drie vp: alſo hee ſendeth them out,
and they ouerturne the earth. 16 With him is ſtrength & wiſedome: the
deceiued, and the deceiuer, are his. 17 He leadeth counſellers away
ſpoiled, and maketh the Iudges fooles. 18 He looſeth the bond of kings,
and girdeth their loines with a girdle. 19 He leadeth Princes away ſpoiled,
and ouerthroweth the mightie. 20 He remoooueth away the ſpeech of the
truſtie, and taketh away the vnderſtanding of the aged. 21 He powreth
contempt vpon princes, and weakeneth the ſtrength of the
mightie. 22 Hee diſcouereth deepe things out of darkeneſſe, and bringeth
out to light the ſhadow of death. 23 He increaſeth the nations, and
deſtroyeth them: hee inlargeth the nations, and ſtraiteneth them
againe. 24 He taketh away the heart of the chiefe of the people of the
earth, and cauſeth them to wander in a wildernes where there is no
way. 25 They grope in the darke without light, and hee maketh them to
ſtagger like a drunken man.
CHAPTER 13 1 Loe, mine eye hath ſeene all this, mine eare hath heard
and vnderſtood it. 2 What yee know, the ſame doe I know alſo, I am not
inferiour vnto you. 3 Surely I would ſpeake to the Almighty, & I deſire to
reaſon with God. 4 But ye are forgers of lies, yee are all Phyſicians of no
value. 5 O that you would altogether hold your peace, & it ſhould be your
wiſdome. 6 Heare now my reaſoning, and hearken to the pleadings of my
lips. 7 Wil you ſpeake wickedly for God? and talke deceitfully for
him? 8 Will ye accept his perſon? Will yee contend for God? 9 Is it good
that hee ſhould ſearch you out? or as one man mocketh another, doe ye
ſo mocke him? 10 He will ſurely reprooue you, if yee doe ſecretly accept
perſons. 11 Shall not his excellencie make you afraid? and his dread fall
vpon you? 12 Your remembrances are like vnto aſhes, your bodies to
bodies of clay. 13 Hold your peace, let me alone that I may ſpeake, and let
come on me what will. 14 Wherefore doe I take my fleſh in my teeth, and
put my life in mine hand? 15 Though hee ſlay mee, yet will I truſt in him:
but I will maintaine mine owne wayes before him. 16 Hee alſo ſhall be my
ſaluation: for an hypocrite ſhall not come before him. 17 Heare diligently
my ſpeach, and my declaration with your eares. 18 Behold now, I haue
ordered my cauſe, I know that I ſhall be iuſtified. 19 Who is hee that will
plead with me? for now if I hold my tongue, I ſhall giue vp the
ghoſt. 20 Only doe not two things vnto me: then will I not hide my ſelfe
from thee. 21 Withdrawe thine hand far from me: and let not thy dread
make mee afraid. 22 Then call thou, and I will anſwere: or let me ſpeake,
and anſwere thou mee. 23 How many are mine iniquities and ſinnes? make
mee to knowe my tranſgreſsion, and my ſinne. 24 Wherefore hideſt thou
thy face, and holdeſt me for thine enemie? 25 Wilt thou breake a leafe
driuen to and fro? and wilt thou purſue the drie ſtubble? 26 For thou
writeſt bitter things againſt mee, and makeſt me to poſſeſſe the iniquities
of my youth. 27 Thou putteſt my feete alſo in the ſtockes, and lookeſt
narrowly vnto all my pathes; thou ſetteſt a print vpon the heeles of my
feete. 28 And hee, as a rotten thing conſumeth, as a garment that is moth-
eaten.
CHAPTER 14 1 Man that is borne of a woman, is of few dayes, and full
of trouble. 2 Hee commeth forth like a flower, and is cut downe: he fleeth
alſo, as a ſhaddow and continueth not. 3 And doeſt thou open thine eies
vpon ſuch an one, and bringeſt me into iudgment with thee? 4 Who can
bring a cleane thing out of an vncleane? not one. 5 Seeing his daies are
determined, the number of his moneths are with thee, thou haſt
appointed his bounds that he cannot paſſe. 6 Turne from him that hee
may reſt, till he ſhall accompliſh, as an hircling, his day. 7 For there is
hope of a tree, if it be cut downe, that it will ſprout againe, and that the
tender branch thereof will not ceaſe. 8 Though the roote thereof waxe
old in the earth, and the ſtocke thereof die in the ground: 9 Yet through
the ſent of water it will bud, and bring forth boughes like a plant. 10 But
man dyeth, and waſteth away; yea, man giueth vp the ghoſt, and where
is hee? 11 As the waters faile from the ſea, and the floud decayeth and
dryeth vp: 12 So man lyeth downe, and riſeth not, till the heauens be no
more, they ſhall not awake; nor bee raiſed out of their ſleepe. 13 O that
thou wouldeſt hide mee in the graue, that thou wouldeſt keepe me
ſecret, vntill thy wrath bee paſt, that thou wouldeſt appoint me a ſet
time, and remember me. 14 If a man die, ſhall he liue againe? All the dayes
of my appointed time will I waite, till my change come. 15 Thou ſhalt call,
and I will anſwer thee: thou wilt haue a deſire to the worke of thine
hands. 16 For nowe thou numbreſt my ſteppes, doeſt thou not watch ouer
my ſinne? 17 My tranſgreſſion is ſealed vp in a bagge, and thou ſoweſt vp
mine iniquitie. 18 And ſurely the mountaine falling commeth to nought:
and the rocke is remoued out of his place. 19 The waters weare the ſtones,
thou waſheſt away the things which growe out of the duſt of the earth,
and thou deſtroyeſt the hope of man. 20 Thou preuaileſt for euer againſt
him, and hee paſſeth: thou changeſt his countenance, and ſendeſt him
away. 21 His ſonnes come to honour, and he knoweth it not; and they are
brought lowe, but he perceiueth it not of them. 22 But his fleſh vpon him
ſhall haue paine, and his ſoule within him ſhall mourne
CHAPTER 15 1 Then anſwered Eliphaz the Temanite, and ſaid, 2 Should
a wiſe man vtter vaine knowledge, and fill his belly with the Eaſt
winde? 3 Should hee reaſon with vnprofitable talke? or with ſpeeches
wherewith he can doe no good? 4 Yea thou caſteſt off feare, and
reſtraineſt prayer before God. 5 For thy mouth vttereth thine iniquitie,
and thou chooſeſt the tongue of the craftie. 6 Thine owne mouth

condemneth thee, and not I: yea thine owne lippes teſtifie againſt thee.7Art thou the firſt man that was borne? or waſt thou made before the hilles?8Haſt thou heard the ſecret of God? and doeſt thou reſtraine wiſedome to thy ſelfe?9What knoweſt thou that we know not? what vnderſtandeſt thou, which is not in vs?10With vs are both the gray headed, and very aged men, much elder then thy father.11Are the conſolations of God ſmall with thee? is there any ſecret thing with thee?12Why doeth thine heart carie thee away? and what doe thine eyes winke at,13That thou turneſt thy ſpirit againſt God, and letteſt ſuch words goe out of thy mouth?14What is man, that he ſhould be cleane? and he which is borne of a woman, that he ſhould be righteous?15Beholde, he putteth no truſt in his Saints, yea, the heauens are not cleane in his ſight.16How much more abominable and filthie is man, which drinketh iniquitie like water?17I will ſhew thee, heare me, and that which I haue ſeene, I wil declare,18Which wiſe men haue tolde from their fathers, and haue not hid it:19Unto whom alone the earth was giuen, and no ſtranger paſſed among them.20The wicked man trauaileth with paine all his dayes, and the number of yeeres is hidden to the oppreſsour.21A dreadfull ſound is in his eares; in proſperitie the deſtroyer ſhall come vpon him.22He beleeueth not that he ſhall returne out of darkeneſſe, and he is waited for, of the ſword.23He wandereth abroad for bread, ſaying, Where is it? he knoweth that the day of darkenes is ready at his hand.24Trouble and anguiſh ſhall make him afraid; they ſhall preuaile againſt him, as a king ready to the battell.25For he ſtretcheth out his hand againſt God, and ſtrengtheneth himſelfe againſt the Almightie.26He runneth vpon him, euen on his necke, vpon the thicke boſses of his bucklers:27Becauſe he couereth his face with his fatneſſe, and maketh collops of fat on his flankes.28And he dwelleth in deſolate cities, and in houſes which no man inhabiteth, which are ready to become heapes.29He ſhall not be rich, neither ſhall his ſubſtance continue, neither ſhall he prolong the perfection thereof vpon the earth.30He ſhall not depart out of darkeneſſe, the flame ſhall drie vp his branches, and by the breath of his mouth ſhall he goe away.31Let not him that is deceiued, truſt in vanitie: for vanitie ſhalbe his recompence.32It ſhall be accompliſhed before his time, and his branch ſhall not bee greene.33He ſhal ſhake off his vnripe grape as the Uine, and ſhall caſt off his flowre as the Oliue.34For the congregation of hypocrites ſhall be deſolate, and fire ſhall conſume the tabernacles of briberie.35They conceiue miſchiefe, and bring forth vanitie, and their belly prepareth deceit.

CHAPTER 161Then Iob anſwered, and ſaid,2I haue heard many ſuch things: miſerable comforters are ye all.3Shall vaine words haue an ende? or what emboldeneth thee, that thou anſwereſt?4I alſo could ſpeake as yee doe: if your ſoule were in my ſoules ſtead, I could heape vp words againſt you, and ſhake mine head at you.5But I would ſtrengthen you with my mouth, and the mouing of my lips ſhould aſswage your griefe.6Though I ſpeake, my griefe is not aſſwaged: and though I forbeare; what am I eaſed?7But now he hath made me weary: thou haſt made deſolate al my companie.8And thou haſt filled mee with wrinckles, which is a witneſſe againſt me: and my leanneſſe riſing vp in me, beareth witneſſe to my face.9He teareth me in his wrath, who hateth me: he gnaſheth vpon me with his teeth; mine enemy ſharpeneth his eyes vpon me.10They haue gaped vpon me with their mouth, they haue ſmitten me vpon the cheeke reprochfully, they haue gathered themſelues together againſt mee.11God hath deliuered me to the vngodly, and turned me ouer into the hands of the wicked.12I was at eaſe, but he hath broken me aſunder: he hath alſo taken me by my necke, and ſhaken me to pieces, and ſet me vp for his marke.13His archers compaſſe me round about, he cleaueth my reines aſunder, and doeth not ſpare; he powreth out my gall vpon the ground.14He breaketh me with breach vpon breach, he runneth vpon me like a giant.15I haue ſowed ſackcloth vpon my ſkin, and defiled my horne in the duſt.16My face is fowle with weeping, and on mine eye-lids is the ſhadow of death;17Not for any iniuſtice in mine hands: alſo my prayer is pure.18O earth couer not thou my blood, and let my cry haue no place.19Alſo now, behold my witneſſe is in heauen, and my record is on high.20My friends ſcorne me: but mine eye powreth out teares vnto God.21O that one might plead for a man with God, as a man pleadeth for his neighbour.22When a few yeeres are come, then I ſhall goe the way whence I ſhall not returne.

CHAPTER 171My breath is corrupt, my dayes are extinct, the graues are ready for me.2Are there not mockers with mee? and doeth not mine eye continue in their prouocation?3Lay downe now, put me in a ſuretie with thee; who is he that will ſtrike hands with me?4For thou haſt hid their heart from vnderſtanding: therefore ſhalt thou not exalt them.5Hee that ſpeaketh flattery to his friends, euen the eyes of his children ſhall faile.6He hath made me alſo a by-word of the people, and afore time I was as a tabret.7Mine eye alſo is dimme by reaſon of ſorrow, and all my members are as a ſhadow.8Upright men ſhall be aſtonied at this, and the innocent ſhall ſtirre vp himſelfe againſt the hypocrite.9The righteous alſo ſhall hold on his way, and he that hath cleane hands ſhalbe ſtronger, and ſtronger.10But as for you all, doe you returne, and come now, for I cannot find one wiſe man among you.11My dayes are paſt, my purpoſes are broken off, euen the thoughts of my heart:12They change the night into day: the light is ſhort, becauſe of darknes.13If I waite, the graue is mine houſe: I haue made my bedde in the darkneſſe.14I haue ſaid to corruption, Thou art my father: to the worme, Thou art my mother, and my ſiſter.15And where is now my hope? as for my hope, who ſhall ſee it?16They ſhall goe downe to the barres of the pit, when our reſt together is in the duſt.

CHAPTER 181Then anſwered Bildad the Shuhite and ſaid,2How long will it bee, ere you make an ende of words? Marke, and afterwards we will ſpeake.3Wherefore are wee counted as beaſts, and reputed vile in your ſight?4He teareth himſelfe in his anger: ſhall the earth be forſaken for thee? and ſhall the rocke bee remooued out of his place?5Yea, the light of the wicked ſhalbe put out, and the ſparke of his fire ſhall not ſhine.6The light ſhalbe darke in his tabernacle, and his candle ſhalbe put out with him.7The ſteps of his ſtrength ſhall be ſtraitened, and his owne counſell ſhall caſt him downe.8For hee is caſt into a net by his owne feete, & he walketh vpon a ſnare.9The grinne ſhall take him by the heele, and the robber ſhall preuaile againſt him.10The ſnare is laide for him in the ground, and a trap for him in the way.11Terrours ſhall make him afraid on euery ſide, and ſhall driue him to his feete.12His ſtrength ſhalbe hunger-bitten, and deſtruction ſhall be ready at his ſide.13It ſhall deuoure the ſtrength of his ſkinne: euen the firſt borne of death ſhall deuoure his ſtrength.14His confidence ſhalbe rooted out of his tabernacle, and it ſhall bring him to the king of terrours.15It ſhall dwell in his tabernacle, becauſe it is none of his: brimſtone ſhall be ſcattered vpon his habitation.16His rootes ſhall be dryed vp beneath: and aboue ſhall his branch be cut off.17His remembrance ſhall periſh from the earth, and hee ſhall haue no name in the ſtreete.18He ſhall be driuen from light into darkeneſſe, and chaſed out of the world.19Hee ſhall neither haue ſonne nor nephew among his people, nor any remaining in his dwellings.20They that come after him ſhalbe aſtonied at his day, as they that went before, were affrighted.21Surely ſuch are the dwellings of the wicked, and this is the place of him that knoweth not God.

CHAPTER 191Then Iob anſwered, and ſayd,2How long will yee vexe my ſoule, and breake me in pieces with words?3Theſe tenne times haue ye reproched me: you are not aſhamed that you make your ſelues ſtrange to me.4And be it indeed that I haue erred, mine errour remaineth with my ſelfe.5If indeed yee will magnifie your ſelues againſt me, and plead againſt me my reproch:6Know now that God hath ouerthrowen me, and hath compaſſed me with his net.7Behold, I cry out of wrong, but I am not heard: I cry aloude, but there is no iudgement.8Hee hath fenced vp my way that I cannot paſſe; and hee hath ſet darkeneſſe in my pathes.9Hee hath ſtript me of my glory, and taken the crowne from my head.10He hath deſtroyed me on euery ſide, and I am gone: and mine hope hath he remooued like a tree.11He hath alſo kindled his wrath againſt me, and hee counteth me vnto him as one of his enemies.12His troupes come together, and raiſe vp their way againſt me, and encampe round about my tabernacle.13Hee hath put my brethren farre from me, and mine acquaintance are verely eſtranged from me.14My kinſefolke haue failed, and my familiar friends haue forgotten me.15They that dwell in mine houſe, and my maides count me for a ſtranger: I am an aliant in their ſight.16I called my ſeruant, and he gaue me no anſwere: I intreated him with my mouth.17My breath is ſtrange to my wife, though I entreated for the childrens ſake of mine owne body.18Yea, yong children deſpiſed me; I aroſe, and they ſpake againſt me.19All my inward friends abhorred me: and they whom I loued, are turned againſt me.20My bone

cleaueth to my ſkinne, and to my fleſh, and I am eſcaped with the ſkinne
of my teeth.21Haue pity vpon me, haue pitie vpon me, O ye my friends;
for the hand of God hath touched me.22Why doe ye perſecute me as
God, and are not ſatiſfied with my fleſh?23Oh that my wordes were now
written, oh that they were printed in a booke!24That they were grauen
with an iron pen and lead, in the rocke for euer.25For I know that my
Redeemer liueth, and that he ſhall ſtand at the latter day, vpon the
earth:26And though after my ſkin, wormes deſtroy this body, yet in my
fleſh ſhall I ſee God:27Whom I ſhal ſee for my ſelfe, and mine eyes ſhall
beholde, and not another, though my reines bee conſumed within
me.28But ye ſhould ſay, Why perſecute we him? ſeeing the root of the
matter is found in me.29Bee ye afraid of the ſword: for wrath bringeth
the puniſhments of the ſword, that yee may know there is a iudgement.
CHAPTER 201Then anſwered Zophar the Naamathite, and
ſaide,2Therefore doe my thoughts cauſe mee to anſwere, and for this I
make haſte.3I haue heard the checke of my reproach, and the ſpirit of
my vnderſtanding cauſeth me to anſwere.4Knoweſt thou not this of old,
ſince man was placed vpon earth,5That the triumphing of the wicked is
ſhort, and the ioy of the hypocrite but for a moment?6Though his
excellencie mount vp to the heauens, and his head reach vnto the
clouds:7Yet he ſhall periſh for euer, like his owne doung: they which
haue ſeene him, ſhall ſay, Where is he?8He ſhall flie away as a dreame,
and ſhall not be found: yea he ſhalbe chaſed away as a viſion of the
night.9The eye alſo which ſaw him, ſhall ſee him no more; neither ſhall
his place any more behold him.10His children ſhall ſeeke to pleaſe the
poore, and his hands ſhall reſtore their goods.11His bones are ful of the
ſinne of his youth, which ſhall ye downe with him in the duſt.12Though
wickednes be ſweet in his mouth, though hee hide it vnder his
tongue;13Though he ſpare it, and forſake it not, but keepe it ſtil within
his mouth:14Yet his meate in his bowels is turned, it is the gall of Aſpes
within him.15He hath ſwallowed downe riches, and hee ſhall vomite
them vp againe: God ſhall caſt them out of his belly.16He ſhall ſucke the
poiſon of Aſpes: the vipers tongue ſhall ſlay him.17Hee ſhall not ſee the
riuers, the floods, the brookes of hony and butter.18That which he
laboured for, ſhall he reſtore, & ſhall not ſwallow it downe: according
to his ſubſtance ſhall the reſtitution bee, and hee ſhall not reioyce
therein.19Becauſe hee hath oppreſſed, and hath forſaken the poore;
becauſe he hath violently taken away an houſe which he builded
not:20Surely he ſhall not feele quietneſse in his belly, hee ſhall not ſaue
of that which he deſired.21There ſhall none of his meat be left, therefore
ſhall no man looke for his goods.22In the fulneſse of his ſufficiencie, he
ſhalbe in ſtraites: euery hand of the wicked ſhall come vpon him.23When
he is about to fill his belly, God ſhall caſt the furie of his wrath vpon
him, and ſhall raine it vpon him while he is eating.24He ſhall flee from
the iron weapon, and the bow of ſteele ſhall ſtrike him through.25It is
drawen, and commeth out of the body; yea the gliſtering ſword
commeth out of his gall; terrours are vpon him.26All darkneſſe ſhalbe
hid in his ſecret places: a fire not blowen ſhall conſume him; it ſhall goe
ill with him that is left in his tabernacle.27The heauen ſhall reueale his
iniquitie: and the earth ſhall riſe vp againſt him.28The increaſe of his
houſe ſhall depart, and his goods ſhall flow away in the day of his
wrath.29This is the portion of a wicked man from God, and the heritage
appointed vnto him by God.
CHAPTER 211But Iob anſwered, and ſayd,2Heare diligently my
ſpeech, and let this be your conſolations.3Suffer me that I may ſpeake,
and after that I haue ſpoken, mocke on.4As for mee, is my complaint to
man? and if it were ſo, why ſhould not my ſpirit be troubled?5Marke
mee, and be aſtoniſhed, and lay your hand vpon your mouth.6Euen
when I remember, I am afraid, and trembling taketh holde on my
fleſh.7Wherefore doe the wicked liue, become old, yea, are mightie in
power?8Their ſeede is eſtabliſhed in their ſight with them, and their
offſpring before their eyes.9Their houſes are ſafe from feare, neither is
the rod of God vpon them.10Their bull gendreth and faileth not, their
cow calueth, and caſteth not her calfe.11They ſend foorth their little ones
like a flocke, and their children dance.12They take the timbrell and harpe,
and reioyce at the ſound of the organe.13They ſpend their daies in
wealth, and in a moment goe downe to the graue.14Therefore they ſay
vnto God, Depart from vs: for we deſire not the knowledge of thy
wayes.15What is the Almightie, that wee ſhould ſerue him? and what
profite ſhould we haue, if we pray vnto him?16Loe, their good is not in
their hand, the counſell of the wicked is farre from me.17How oft is the
candle of the wicked put out? and how oft commeth their deſtruction
vpon them? God diſtributeth ſorrowes in his anger.18They are as ſtubble
before the winde, and as chaffe that the ſtorme carieth away.19God
layeth vp his iniquitie for his children: he rewardeth him, and he ſhall
know it.20His eyes ſhall ſee his deſtruction, and he ſhall drinke of the
wrath of the Almightie.21For what pleaſure hath he in his houſe after
him, when the number of his moneths is cut off in the middeſt?22Shall
any teach God knowledge? ſeeing he iudgeth thoſe that are high.23One
dieth in his full ſtrength, being wholly at eaſe and quiet.24His breaſts are
full of milke, and his bones are moiſtened with marrow.25And another
dieth in the bitterneſse of his ſoule, and neuer eateth with
pleaſure.26They ſhall lie downe alike in the duſt, and the wormes ſhall
couer them.27Behold, I know your thoughts, and the deuices which yee
wrongfully imagine againſt me.28For ye ſay, where is the houſe of the
prince? and where are the dwelling places of the wicked?29Haue ye not
aſked them that goe by the way? and doe ye not know their
tokens?30That the wicked is reſeruedto the day of deſtruction; they ſhall
bee brought foorth to the day of wrath.31Who ſhall declare his way to
his face? and who ſhall repay him what he hath done?32Yet ſhall hee be
brought to the graue, & ſhall remaine in the tombe.33The cloudes of the
valley ſhalbe ſweete vnto him, and euery man ſhall draw after him, as
there are innumerable before him.34How then comfort ye me in vaine,
ſeeing in your anſweres there remaineth falſhood?
CHAPTER 221Then Eliphaz the Temanite anſwered, and ſaid,2Can a
man be profitable vnto God? as hee that is wiſe may be profitable vnto
himſelfe.3Is it any pleaſure to the Almighty, that thou art righteous? or
is it gaine to him, that thou makeſt thy waies perfite?4Will hee reproue
thee for feare of thee? will he enter with thee into iudgment?5Is not thy
wickedneſſe great? and thine iniquities infinite?6For thou haſt taken a
pledge from thy brother for nought, and ſtripped the naked of their
clothing.7Thou haſt not giuen water to the wearie to drinke, and thou
haſt withholden bread from the hungry.8But as for the mightie man, hee
had the earth, and the honourable man dwelt in it.9Thou haſt ſent
widowes away emptie, and the armes of the fatherleſſe haue bene
broken.10Therefore ſnares are round about thee, and ſudden feare
troubleth thee,11Or darkenes that thou canſt not ſee, and abundance of
waters couer thee.12Is not God in the height of heauen? and behold the
height of the ſtarres how high they are.13And thou ſayeſt, How doth
God know? can he iudge through the darke cloude?14Thicke cloudes are
a couering to him that he ſeeth not, and hee walketh in the circuit of
heauen.15Haſt thou marked the olde way which wicked men haue
troden?16Which were cut downe out of time, whoſe foundation was
ouerflowen with a flood.17Which ſaid vnto God, Depart from vs, and
what can the Almightie doe for them?18Yet he filled their houſes with
good things: but the counſell of the wicked is farre from me.19The
righteous ſee it, and are glad, and the innocent laugh them to
ſcorne.20Whereas our ſubſtance is not cut downe, but the remnant of
them the fire conſumeth.21Acquaint now thy ſelfe with him, and be at
peace: thereby good ſhal come vnto thee.22Receiue, I pray thee, the
Lawe from his mouth, and lay vp his words in thine heart.23If thou
returne to the Almightie, thou ſhalt be built vp, thou ſhalt put away
iniquitie farre from thy tabernacles.24Then ſhalt thou lay vp golde as
duſt, and the gold of Ophir as the ſtones of the brookes.25Yea the
Almightie ſhall bee thy defence, and thou ſhalt haue plenty of
ſiluer.26For then ſhalt thou haue thy delight in the Almightie, and ſhalt
lift vp thy face vnto God.27Thou ſhalt make thy prayer vnto him, and
he ſhall heare thee, and thou ſhalt pay thy vowes.28Thou ſhalt alſo decree
a thing, and it ſhal be eſtabliſhed vnto thee: and the light ſhall ſhine vpon
thy wayes.29When men are caſt downe, then thou ſhalt ſay, There is
lifting vp: and he ſhall ſaue the humble perſon.30He ſhall deliuer the
Iland of the innocent: and it is deliuered by the pureneſse of thine hands.
CHAPTER 231Then Iob anſwered, and ſaid,2Euen to day is my
complaint bitter: my ſtroke is heauier then my groning.3O that I knewe
where I might find him! that I might come euen to his ſeate!4I would
order my cauſe before him, and fill my mouth with arguments.5I would
know the words which he would anſwere me, and vnderſtand what he
would ſay vnto me.6Will he plead againſt me with his great power? No,

but hee would put ſtrength in me.7There the righteous might diſpute
with him; ſo ſhould I be deliuered for euer from my Iudge.8Behold, I
goe forward, but he is not there, and backward, but I cannot perceiue
him:9On the left hand where hee doeth worke, but I cannot behold him:
he hideth himſelfe on the right hand, that I cannot ſee him.10But he
knoweth the way that I take: when he hath tried me, I ſhall come forth
as gold.11My foot hath held his ſteps, his way haue I kept, and not
declined.12Neither haue I gone backe from the commaundement of his
lippes, I haue eſteemed the words of his mouth more then my neceſsary
food.13But hee is in one minde, and who can turne him? and what his
ſoule deſireth, euen that he doeth.14For he performeth the thing that is
appointed for mee: and many ſuch things are with him.15Therefore am
I troubled at his preſence: when I conſider, I am afraid of him.16For
God maketh my heart ſoft, and the Almighty troubleth me:17Becauſe I
was not cut off before the darknes, neither hath he couered the darknes
from my face.
CHAPTER 241Why, ſeeing Times are not hidden from the Almightie,
doe they, that know him not, ſee his dayes?2Some remooue the land-
markes; they violently take away flocks, and feed thereof.3They driue
away the aſſe of the fatherleſſe, they take the widowes oxe for a
pledge.4They turne the needy out of the way: the poore of the earth hide
themſelues together.5Behold, as wilde aſſes in the deſart, goe they foorth
to their worke, riſing betimes for a pray: the wildernes yeeldeth food for
them, and for their children.6They reape euery one his corne in the
fielde: and they gather the vintage of the wicked.7They cauſe the naked
to lodge without clothing, that they haue no couering in the cold.8They
are wet with the ſhowres of the mountaines, and imbrace the rocke for
want of a ſhelter.9They plucke the fatherleſſe from the breſt, and take a
pledge of the poore.10They cauſe him to go naked without clothing: and
they take away the ſheafe from the hungry,11Which make oyle within
their walles, and tread their winepreſſe s, and ſuffer thirſt.12Men groane
from out of the city, and the ſoule of the wounded crieth out: yet God
layeth not folly to them.13They are of thoſe that rebell againſt the light,
they know not the wayes thereof, nor abide in the pathes thereof.14The
murderer riſing with the light, killeth the poore and needy, and in the
night is as a thiefe.15The eye alſo of the adulterer waiteth for the twilight,
ſaying, No eye ſhall ſee me: and diſguiſeth his face.16In the darke they
digge through houſes which they had marked for themſelues in the day
time: they know not the light.17For the morning is to them euen as the
ſhadow of death: if one know them, they are in the terrours of the
ſhadow of death.18Hee is ſwift as the waters, their portion is curſed in
the earth: he beholdeth not the way of the Uineyards.19Drought and
heate conſume the ſnow waters: ſo doeth the graue thoſe which haue
ſinned.20The wombe ſhall forget him, the worme ſhall feed ſweetly on
him, hee ſhall be no more remembred, and wickednes ſhalbe broken as
a tree.21He euill intreateth the barren, that beareth not: and doeth not
good to the widow.22He draweth alſo the mighty with his power: he
riſeth vp, and no man is ſure of life.23Though it be giuen him to be in
ſafety, whereon he reſteth; yet his eyes are vpon their wayes.24They are
exalted for a litle while, but are gone and brought low, they are taken
out of the way as al other, and cut off as the tops of the eares of
corne.25And if it be not ſo now, who will make mee a liar, and make my
ſpeach nothing worth?
CHAPTER 251Then anſwered Bildad the Shuhite, and ſaid:2Dominion
and feare are with him, hee maketh peace in his high places.3Is there any
number of his armies? and vpon whom doeth not his light Ariſe?4How
then can man bee iuſtified with God? or how can he be cleane that is
borne of a woman?5Behold euen to the moone, and it ſhineth not, yea
the ſtarres are not pure in his ſight.6How much leſſe man, that is a
worme: and the ſonne of man which is a worme?
CHAPTER 261But Iob anſwered and ſayd,2Howe haſt thou helped
him that is without power? how ſaueſt thou the arme that hath no
ſtrength?3How haſt thou counſelled him that hath no wiſedome? and
how haſt thou plentifully declared the thing, as it is?4To whom haſt thou
vttered words? and whoſe ſpirit came from thee?5Dead things are
formed from vnder the waters, and the inhabitants thereof.6Hell is
naked before him, and deſtruction hath no couering.7He ſtretcheth out
the North ouer the emptie place, and hangeth the earth vpon
nothing.8Hee bindeth vp the waters in his thicke clouds, and the cloud
is not rent vnder them.9Hee holdeth backe the face of his throne, and
ſpreadeth his cloud vpon it.10Hee hath compaſſed the waters with
bounds, vntill the day and night come to an end.11The pillars of heauen
tremble, and are aſtoniſhed at his reproofe.12Hee diuideth the ſea with
his power, and by his vnderſtanding he ſmiteth through the proud.13By
his ſpirit he hath garniſhed the heauens; his hand hath formed the
crooked ſerpent.14Loe, theſe are parts of his waies, but how little a
portion is heard of him? but the thunder of his power who can
vnderſtand?
CHAPTER 271Moreouer Iob continued his parable, and ſayd,2As God
liueth, who hath taken away my iudgment, and the Almighty, who hath
vexed my ſoule;3All the while my breath is in mee, and the ſpirit of God
is in my noſtrils;4My lips ſhall not ſpeake wickedneſſe, nor my tongue
vtter deceit.5God forbid that I ſhould iuſtifie you: till I die, I will not
remoue my integritie from me.6My righteouſneſſe I hold faſt, and will
not let it goe: my heart ſhall not reproach me ſo long as I liue.7Let mine
enemie be as the wicked, and he that riſeth vp againſt me, as the
vnrighteous.8For what is the hope of the hypocrite, though he hath
gained, when God taketh away his ſoule?9Will God heare his cry, when
trouble commeth vpon him?10Will he delight himſelfe in the Almightie?
will hee alwayes call vpon God?11I will teach you by the hand of God:
that which is with the Almightie, will I not conceale.12Behold, all ye your
ſelues haue ſeene it, why then are yee thus altogether vaine?13This is the
portion of a wicked man with God, and the heritage of oppreſsours
which they ſhall receiue of the Almightie.14If his children be multiplied,
it is for the ſword: and his offpring ſhall not be ſatiſfied with
bread.15Thoſe that remaine of him ſhall bee buried in death: and his
widowes ſhall not weepe.16Though he heape vp ſiluer as the duſt, and
prepare rayment as the clay:17He may prepare it, but the iuſt ſhall put it
on, and the innocent ſhall diuide the ſiluer.18He buildeth his houſe as a
moth, and as a booth that the keeper maketh.19The rich man ſhall lie
downe, but he ſhall not be gathered: he openeth his eyes, and he is
not:20Terrours take hold on him as waters, a tempeſt ſtealeth him away
in the night.21The Eaſt winde carieth him away, and he departeth: and
as a ſtorme hurleth him out of his place.22For God ſhall caſt vpon him,
and not ſpare: hee would faine flee out of his hand.23Men ſhall clap their
handes at him, and ſhall hiſse him out of his place.
CHAPTER 281Surely there is a veine for the ſiluer, and a place for
golde where they fine it.2Iron is taken out of the earth, and braſſe is
molten out of the ſtone.3Hee ſetteth an ende to darkeneſſe, and
ſearcheth out all perfection: the ſtones of darkeneſſe and the ſhadow of
death.4The floud breaketh out from the inhabitant; euen the waters
forgotten of the foote: they are dried vp, they are gone away from
men.5As for the earth, out of it commeth bread: and vnder it, is turned
vp as it were fire.6The ſtones of it are the place of Saphires: and it hath
duſt of golde.7There is a path which no foule knoweth, and which the
vulturs eye hath not ſeene.8The lyons whelps haue not troden it, nor the
fierce lyon paſſed by it.9Hee putteth foorth his hand vpon the rocke;
hee ouerturneth the mountaines by the rootes.10Hee cutteth out riuers
among the rockes, and his eye ſeeth euery precious thing.11He bindeth
the floods from ouerflowing, and the thing that is hid, bringeth he
foorth to light.12But where ſhall wiſedome bee found? and where is the
place of vnderſtanding?13Man knoweth not the price thereof neither is
it found in the land of the liuing.14The depth ſaith, It is not in me: and
the ſea ſaith, It is not with me.15It cannot be gotten for golde, neither
ſhall ſiluer be weighed for the price thereof.16It cannot be valued with
the golde of Ophir, with the precious Onix, or the Saphire.17The golde
and the chryſtall cannot equall it: and the exchange of it ſhall not be for
iewels of fine golde.18No mention ſhalbe made of Corall, or of Pearles:
for the price of wiſedome is aboue Rubies.19The Topaze of Ethiopia
ſhall not equall it, neither ſhall it be valued with pure golde.20Whence
then commeth wiſedome? and where is the place of
vnderſtanding?21Seeing it is hid from the eyes of all liuing, and kept cloſe
from the foules of the ayre.22Deſtruction and death ſay, Wee haue heard
the fame thereof with our eares.23God vnderſtandeth the way thereof,
and he knoweth the place thereof.24For hee looketh to the endes of the
earth, and ſeeth vnder the whole heauen:25To make the weight for the
windes, and he weigheth the waters by meaſure.26When hee made a
decree for the raine, and a way for the lightning of the thunder:27Then

did he ſee it, and declare it, he prepared it, yea and ſearched it out.28And
vnto man he ſaid, Behold, the feare of the Lord, that is wiſedome, and
to depart from euill, is vnderſtanding.
CHAPTER 291Moreouer Iob continued his parable, and ſaid,2O that I
were as in moneths paſt, as in the dayes when God preſerued me.3When
his candle ſhined vpon my head, and when by his light I walked through
darkeneſſe:4As I was in the dayes of my youth, when the ſecret of God
was vpon my tabernacle:5When the Almightie was yet with me, when
my children were about me:6When I waſhed my ſteps with butter, and
the rocke powred me out riuers of oyle:7When I went out to the gate,
through the citie, when I prepared my ſeate in the ſtreet.8The yong men
ſaw me, and hid themſelues: and the aged aroſe, and ſtood vp.9The
princes refrained talking, and laid their hand on their mouth.10The
Nobles held their peace, and their tongue cleaued to the roofe of their
mouth.11When the eare heard mee, then it bleſſed me, and when the eye
ſaw me, it gaue witneſſe to me:12Becauſe I deliuered the poore that cried,
and the fatherleſſe, and him that had none to helpe him.13The bleſſing
of him that was readie to periſh, came vpon me: and I cauſed the
widowes heart to ſing for ioy.14I put on righteouſneſſe, and it clothed
me: my iudgement was as a robe and a diademe.15I was eyes to the blind,
and feet was I to the lame.16I was a father to the poore: and the cauſe
which I knewe not, I ſearched out.17And I brake the iawes of the wicked,
and pluckt the ſpoile out of his teeth.18Then I ſaid, I ſhall die in my neſt,
and I ſhall multiplie my dayes as the ſand.19My roote was ſpread out by
the waters, and the dew lay all night vpon my branch.20My glory was
freſh in mee, and my bow was renewed in my hand.21Unto me men gaue
eare, and waited, and kept ſilence at my counſell.22After my words they
ſpake not againe, & my ſpeach dropped vpon them,23And they waited
for me as for the raine, and they opened their mouth wide as for the
latter raine.24If I laughed on them, they beleeued it not, and the light of
my countenance they caſt not downe.25I choſe out their way, and ſate
chiefe, and dwelt as a king in the army, as one that comforteth the
mourners.
CHAPTER 301But nowe they that are yonger then I, haue mee in
deriſion, whoſe fathers I would haue diſdained to haue ſet with the dogs
of my flocke.2Yea whereto might the ſtrength of their hands profit me,
in whom olde age was periſhed?3For want and famine they were
ſolitarie: flying into the wilderneſſe in former time deſolate and
waſte:4Who cut vp mallowes by the buſhes, and Iuniper rootes for their
meate.5They were driuen foorth from among men, (they cried after
them, as after a thiefe.)6To dwell in the clifts of the valleys, in caues of
the earth, and in the rockes.7Among the buſhes they brayed: vnder the
nettles they were gathered together.8They were children of fooles, yea
children of baſe men: they were viler then the earth.9And now am I their
ſong, yea I am their by-word.10They abhorre me, they flee farre from
me, and ſpare not to ſpit in my face.11Becauſe hee hath looſed my cord
and afflicted me, they haue alſo let looſe the bridle before me.12Upon
my right hand riſe the youth, they puſh away my feete, and they raiſe vp
againſt mee the wayes of their deſtruction.13They marre my path, they
ſet forward my calamitie, they haue no helper.14They came vpon me as
a wide breaking in of waters: in the deſolation they rolled themſelues
vpon me.15Terrours are turned vpon mee: they purſue my ſoule as the
wind: and my welfare paſſeth away as a cloude.16And now my ſoule is
powred out vpon me: the dayes of affliction haue taken hold vpon
me.17My bones are pierced in mee in the night ſeaſon: and my ſinewes
take no reſt.18By the great force of my diſeaſe, is my garment changed:
it bindeth mee about as the collar of my coat.19He hath caſt mee into
the myre, and I am become like duſt and aſhes.20I crie vnto thee, and
thou doeſt not heare me: I ſtand vp, and thou regardeſt me not.21Thou
art become cruell to me: with thy ſtrong hand thou oppoſeſt thy ſelfe
againſt me.22Thou lifteſt me vp to the wind: thou cauſeſt me to ride
vpon it, and diſsolueſt my ſubſtance.23For I know that thou wilt bring
me to death, and to the houſe appointed for all liuing.24Howbeit he will
not ſtretch out his hand to the graue, though they cry in his
deſtruction.25Did not I weepe for him that was in trouble? was not my
ſoule grieued for the poore?26When I looked for good, then euill came
vnto mee: and when I waited for light, there came darkenes.27My bowels
boyled and reſted not: the dayes of affliction preuented mee.28I went
mourning without the Sunne: I ſtood vp, and I cried in the
Congregation.29I am a brother to dragons, and a companion to
owles.30My ſkinne is blacke vpon mee, and my bones are burnt with
heat.31My harpe alſo is turned to mourning, and my organe into the
voyce of them that weepe.
CHAPTER 311I made a couenant with mine eyes; why then ſhould I
thinke vpon a mayd?2For what portion of God is there from aboue? and
what inheritance of the Almighty from on high?3Is not deſtruction to
the wicked? and a ſtrange puniſhment to the workers of
iniquitie?4Doeth not he ſee my wayes, and count all my ſteps?5If I haue
walked with vanitie, or if my foot hath haſted to deceit;6Let me bee
weighed in an euen ballance, that God may know mine integritie.7If my
ſtep hath turned out of the way, and mine heart walked after mine eyes,
and if any blot hath cleaued to my hands:8Then let mee ſow, and let
another eate, yea let my off-ſpring be rooted out.9If mine heart haue
bene deceiued by a woman, or if I haue layde wait at my neighbours
doore:10Then let my wife grind vnto another, and let others bow downe
vpon her.11For this is an heinous crime, yea, it is an iniquitie to bee
puniſhed by the Iudges.12For it is a fire that conſumeth to deſtruction,
and would roote out all mine encreaſe.13If I did deſpiſe the cauſe of my
man-ſeruant, or of my mayd-ſeruant, when they contended with
me:14What then ſhall I do, when God riſeth vp? and when hee viſiteth,
what ſhall I anſwere him?15Did not hee that made mee in the wombe,
make him? and did not one faſhion vs in the wombe?16If I haue
withhelde the poore from their deſire, or haue cauſed the eyes of the
widow to faile:17Or haue eaten my morſell my ſelfe alone, and the
fatherleſſe hath not eaten thereof:18(For from my youth hee was
brought vp with me as with a father, and I haue guided her from my
mothers wombe.)19If I haue ſeene any periſh for want of cloathing, or
any poore without couering:20If his loynes haue not bleſſed me, and if
hee were not warmed with the fleece of my ſheepe:21If I haue lift vp my
hand againſt the fatherleſſe, when I ſaw my helpe in the gate:22Then let
mine arme fall from my ſhoulder-blade, and mine arme be broken from
the bone.23For deſtruction from God was a terrour to mee: and by
reaſon of his highneſse, I could not endure.24If I haue made golde my
hope, or haue ſaid to the fine gold, Thou art my confidence:25If I
reioyced becauſe my wealth was great, and becauſe mine hand had
gotten much:26If I beheld the Sunne when it ſhined, or the Moone
walking in brightneſse:27And my heart hath bene ſecretly enticed, or my
mouth hath kiſſed my hand:28This alſo were an iniquitie to be puniſhed
by the Iudge: For I ſhould haue denied the God that is aboue.29If I
reioyced at the deſtruction of him that hated me, or lift vp my ſelfe when
euill found him:30(Neither haue I ſuffered my mouth to ſinne by wiſhing
a curſe to his ſoule.)31If the men of my tabernacle ſaid not, Oh that we
had of his fleſh! wee cannot be ſatiſfied.32The ſtranger did not lodge in
the ſtreet: but I opened my doores to the trauailer.33If I couered my
tranſgreſſions, as Adam: by hiding mine iniquitie in my boſome:34Did I
feare a great multitude, or did the contempt of families terrifie me: that
I kept ſilence, and went not out of the doore?35O that one would heare
me! beholde, my deſire is, that the Almightie would anſwere me, and
that mine aduerſary had written a booke.36Surely I would take it vpon
my ſhoulder, and bind it as a crowne to me.37I would declare vnto him
the number of my ſteps, as a prince would I goe neere vnto him.38If my
land cry againſt me, or that the furrowes likewiſe thereof complaine:39If
I haue eaten the fruits thereof without money, or haue cauſed the
owners thereof to looſe their life:40Let thiſtles grow in ſtead of wheat,
and cockle in ſtead of barley. The words of Iob are ended.
CHAPTER 321So theſe three men ceaſed to anſwere Iob, becauſe he
was righteous in his owne eyes.2Then was kindled the wrath of Elihu,
the ſonne of Barachel the Buzite, of the kinred of Ram: againſt Iob was
his wrath kindled, becauſe he iuſtified himſelfe rather then God.3Alſo
againſt his three friends was his wrath kindled: becauſe they had found
no anſwere, and yet had condemned Iob.4Now Elihu had waited till Iob
had ſpoken: becauſe they were elder then he.5When Elihu ſaw that there
was no anſwere in the mouth of theſe three men, then his wrath was
kindled.6And Elihu the ſonne of Barachel the Buzite anſwered and ſayd:
I am yong, and yee are very old, wherefore I was afraid, and durſt not
ſhew you mine opinion.7I ſaid, Dayes ſhould ſpeake, and multitude of
yeeres ſhould teach wiſedome.8But there is a ſpirit in man: and the
inſpiration of the Almightie giueth them vnderſtanding.9Great men are

not alwayes wiſe: neither doe the aged vnderſtand iudgement.10Therfore I ſayd, Hearken to me: I alſo will ſhew mine opinion.11Behold, I waited for your words: I gaue eare to your reaſons, whileſt you ſearched out what to ſay.12Yea, I attended vnto you: and beholde, there was none of you that conuinced Iob, or that anſwered his words:13Leſt ye ſhould ſay, We haue found out wiſdom: God thruſteth him down, not man.14Now he hath not directed his words againſt me: neither will I anſwere him with your ſpeeches.15They were amaſed, they anſwered no more, they left off ſpeaking.16When I had waited, (for they ſpake not, but ſtood ſtill and anſwered no more.)17I ſayd, I will anſwere alſo my part, I alſo will ſhew mine opinion.18For I am full of matter, the ſpirit within me conſtraineth me.19Behold, my belly is as wine, which hath no vent, it is ready to burſt like new bottles.20I will ſpeake, that I may be refreſhed: I will open my lippes, and anſwere.21Let me not, I pray you, accept any mans perſon: neither let me giue flattering titles vnto man.22For I know not to giue flattering titles: in ſo doing my maker would ſoone take me away.

CHAPTER 331Wherefore, Iob, I pray thee, heare my ſpeeches, and hearken to all my wordes.2Behold, now I haue opened my mouth, my tongue hath ſpoken in my mouth.3My words ſhalbe of the vprightneſse of my heart: and my lippes ſhall vtter knowledge clearely.4The Spirit of God hath made me, and the breath of the Almightie hath giuen me life.5If thou canſt, anſwere me, ſet thy wordes in order before me, ſtand vp.6Behold, I am according to thy wiſh in Gods ſtead: I alſo am formed out of the clay.7Behold, my terrour ſhall not make thee afraid, neither ſhall my hand be heauie vpon thee.8Surely thou haſt ſpoken in mine hearing, and I haue heard the voice of thy words, ſaying,9I am cleane without tranſgreſsion, I am innocent; neither is there iniquitie in me.10Behold, hee findeth occaſions againſt mee, hee counteth mee for his enemie.11He putteth my feete in the ſtockes, he marketh all my pathes.12Behold, in this thou art not iuſt: I will anſwere thee, That God is greater then man.13Why doeſt thou ſtriue againſt him? for he giueth not account of any of his matters.14For God ſpeaketh once, yea twice, yet man perceiueth it not.15In a dreame, in a viſion of the night, when deepe ſleepe falleth vpon men, in ſlumbrings vpon the bed:16Then hee openeth the eares of men, and ſealeth their inſtruction,17That hee may withdraw man from his purpoſe, and hide pride from man.18Hee keepeth backe his ſoule from the pit, and his life from periſhing by the ſword.19Hee is chaſtened alſo with paine vpon his bed, and the multitude of his bones with ſtrong paine.20So that his life abhorreth bread, and his ſoule daintie meate.21His fleſh is conſumed away that it cannot be ſeene; and his bones that were not ſeene, ſticke out.22His ſoule draweth neere vnto the graue, and his life to the deſtroyers.23If there be a meſſenger with him, an interpreter, one among a thouſand, to ſhew vnto man his vprightneſse:24Then hee is gracious vnto him, and ſayth, Deliuer him from going downe to the pit; I haue found a ranſome.25His fleſh ſhall be freſher then a childes: he ſhall returne to the dayes of his youth.26He ſhall pray vnto God, and hee will be fauourable vnto him, and hee ſhall ſee his face with ioy: for hee will render vnto man his righteouſneſſe.27He looketh vpon men, and if any ſay, I haue ſinned, and peruerted that which was right, and it profited mee not:28Hee will deliuer his ſoule from going into the pit, and his life ſhall ſee the light.29Loe, all theſe things worketh God oftentimes with man,30To bring backe his ſoule from the pit, to be enlightened with the light of the liuing.31Marke well, O Iob, hearken vnto me, hold thy peace, and I wil ſpeake.32If thou haſt any thing to ſay, anſwere me: ſpeake, for I deſire to iuſtifie thee.33If not, hearken vnto me: holde thy peace, and I ſhall teach thee wiſedome.

CHAPTER 341Furthermore Elihu anſwered, and ſaid,2Heare my wordes, O yee wiſe men, and giue eare vnto me, ye that haue knowledge.3For the eare trieth words, as the mouth taſteth meate.4Let vs chuſe to vs iudgement: let vs know among our ſelues what is good.5For Iob hath ſaid, I am righteous: and God hath taken away my iudgement.6Should I lye againſt my right? my wound is incurable without tranſgreſsion.7What man is like Iob, who drinketh vp ſcorning like water?8Which goeth in company with the workers of iniquitie, and walketh with wicked men.9For hee hath ſaid, It profiteth a man nothing, that he ſhould delight himſelfe with God.10Therefore hearken vnto me, ye men of vnderſtanding: farre bee it from God, that he ſhould doe wickednes, and from the Almighty, that hee ſhould commit iniquitie.11For the worke of a man ſhall he render vnto him, and cauſe euery man to finde according to his wayes.12Yea ſurely God will not doe wickedly, neither will the Almighty peruert iudgement.13Who hath giuen him a charge ouer the earth? or who hath diſpoſed the whole world?14If he ſet his heart vpon man, if he gather vnto himſelfe his ſpirit and his breath;15All fleſh ſhall periſh together, and man ſhall turne againe vnto duſt.16If now thou haſt vnderſtanding, heare this: hearken to the voyce of my words.17Shall euen he that hateth right, gouerne? and wilt thou condemne him that is moſt iuſt?18Is it fit to ſay to a King, Thou art wicked? and to Princes, Ye are vngodly?19How much leſſe to him that accepteth not the perſons of Princes, nor regardeth the rich more then the poore? for they all are the woorke of his hands.20In a moment ſhall they die, and the people ſhalbe troubled at midnight, and paſſe away: and the mighty ſhall be taken away without hand.21For his eyes are vpon the wayes of man, and he ſeeth all his goings.22There is no darkenes, nor ſhadow of death, where the workers of iniquitie may hide themſelues.23For hee will not lay vpon man more then right; that he ſhould enter into iudgement with God.24He ſhall breake in pieces mighty men without number, and ſet others in their ſtead.25Therefore hee knoweth their workes, and he ouerturneth them in the night, ſo that they are deſtroyed.26He ſtriketh them as wicked men, in the open ſight of others:27Becauſe they turned backe from him, and would not conſider any of his wayes.28So that they cauſe the cry of the poore to come vnto him, and he heareth the cry of the afflicted.29When he giueth quietneſse, who then can make trouble? and when hee hideth his face, who then can beholde him? whether it be done againſt a nation, or againſt a man onely:30That the hypocrite raigne not, leſt the people be enſnared.31Surely it is meete to be ſaid vnto God, I haue borne chaſtiſement, I will not offend any more.32That which I ſee not, teach thou me; If I haue done iniquitie, I will doe no more.33Should it bee according to thy minde? he will recompenſe it, whether thou refuſe, or whether thou chuſe, and not I: therefore ſpeake what thou knoweſt.34Let men of vnderſtanding tell mee, and let a wiſe man hearken vnto mee.35Iob hath ſpoken without knowledge, and his words were without wiſdome.36My deſire is that Iob may bee tried vnto the ende, becauſe of his anſweres for wicked men.37For he addeth rebellion vnto his ſinne, hee clappeth his handes amongſt vs, and multiplieth his words againſt God.

CHAPTER 351Elihu ſpake moreouer, and ſaid,2Thinkeſt thou this to bee right, that thou ſaydeſt, My righteouſneſſe is more then Gods?3For thou ſaydſt, what aduantage will it bee vnto thee, and, what profite ſhall I haue, if I bee cleanſed from my ſinne?4I will anſwere thee, and thy companions with thee.5Looke vnto the heauens and ſee, and behold the clouds which are higher then thou.6If thou ſinneſt, what doeſt thou againſt him? or if thy tranſgreſſions be multiplied, what doeſt thou vnto him?7If thou be righteous, what giueſt thou him? or what receiueth hee of thine hand?8Thy wickedneſſe may hurt a man as thou art, and thy righteouſneſſe may profit the ſonne of man.9By reaſon of the multitude of oppreſſions they make the oppreſſed to crie: they crie out by reaſon of the arme of the mightie.10But none ſaith, where is God my maker, who giueth ſongs in the night?11Who teacheth vs more then the beaſts of the earth, and maketh vs wiſer then the foules of heauen.12There they crie, (but none giueth anſwere) becauſe of the pride of euill men.13Surely God wil not heare vanitie, neither wil the Almightie regard it.14Although thou ſayeſt thou ſhalt not ſee him, yet iudgement is before him, therefore truſt thou in him.15But now becauſe it is not ſo, hee hath viſited in his anger, yet he knoweth it not in great extremitie:16Therefore doeth Iob open his mouth in vaine: he multiplieth words without knowledge.

CHAPTER 361Elihu alſo proceeded, and ſaid,2Suffer mee a little, and I will ſhewe thee, that I haue yet to ſpeake on Gods behalfe.3I will fetch my knowledge from afarre, and will aſcribe righteouſneſſe to my Maker.4For truely my words ſhall not be falſe: he that is perfect in knowledge, is with thee.5Behold, God is mightie, and deſpiſeth not any: he is mightie in ſtrength and wiſedome.6He preſerueth not the life of the wicked: but giueth right to the poore.7Hee withdraweth not his eyes from the righteous: but with kings are they on the throne, yea he doth eſtabliſh them for euer, and they are exalted.8And if they bee bound in

fetters, and be holden in cords of affliction:9Then hee ſheweth them
their worke, and their tranſgreſſions, that they haue exceeded.10He
openeth alſo their eare to diſcipline, and commandeth that they returne
from iniquitie.11If they obey and ſerue him, they ſhall ſpend their dayes
in proſperitie, and their yeeres in pleaſures.12But if they obey not, they
ſhall periſh by the ſword, and they ſhall die without knowledge.13But the
hypocrites in heart heape vp wrath: they crie not when he bindeth
them.14They die in youth, and their life is among the vncleane.15He
deliuereth the poore in his affliction, and openeth their eares in
oppreſſion.16Euen ſo would he haue remooued thee out of the ſtrait
into a broad place, where there is no ſtraitneſse, and that which ſhould
be ſet on thy table, ſhould be full of fatneſſe.17But thou haſt fulfilled the
iudgement of the wicked: iudgement and iuſtice take hold on
thee.18Becauſe there is wrath, beware leſt he take thee away with his
ſtroke: then a great ranſome cannot deliuer thee.19Will he eſteeme thy
riches? no not gold, nor all the forces of ſtrength.20Deſire not the night,
when people are cut off in their place.21Take heed, regard not iniquitie:
for this haſt thou choſen rather then affliction.22Beholde, God exalteth
by his power: who teacheth like him?23Who hath inioyned him his way?
or who can ſay, Thou haſt wrought iniquitie?24Remember that thou
magnifie his worke, which men behold.25Euery man may ſee it, man
may behold it afarre off.26Behold, God is great, and we know him not,
neither can the number of his yeeres be ſearched out.27For hee maketh
ſmall the drops of water: they powre downe raine according to the
vapour thereof:28Which the clouds doe drop, and diſtill vpon man
abundantly.29Alſo can any vnderſtand the ſpreadings of the clouds, or
the noiſe of his tabernacle?30Behold, he ſpreadeth his light vpon it, and
couereth the bottome of the ſea.31For by them iudgeth he the people,
he giueth meate in abundance.32With clouds he couereth the light, and
commaundeth it not to ſhine, by the cloud that commeth betwixt.33The
noiſe thereof ſheweth concerning it, the cattel alſo concerning the
Uapour.

CHAPTER 37 1At this alſo my heart trembleth, and is moued out of
his place.2Heare attentiuely the noiſe of his voice, and the ſound that
goeth out of his mouth.3Hee directeth it vnder the whole heauen, and
his lightning vnto the ends of the earth.4After it a voyce roareth: he
thundreth with the voice of his excellencie, and hee will not ſtay them
when his voice is heard.5God thundereth maruellouſly with his voice:
great things doth hee, which we cannot comprehend.6For he ſaith to
the ſnow, Be thou on the earth: likewiſe to the ſmall raine, and to the
great raine of his ſtrength.7He ſealeth vp the hand of euery man; that all
men may knowe his worke.8Then the beaſtes goe into dennes: and
remaine in their places.9Out of the South commeth the whirlewinde:
and cold out of the North.10By the breath of God, froſt is giuen: and
the breadth of the waters is ſtraitned.11Alſo by watring he wearieth the
thicke cloud: hee ſcattereth his bright cloud.12And it is turned round
about by his counſels: that they may doe whatſoeuer hee commaundeth
them vpon the face of the world in the earth.13He cauſeth it to come,
whether for correction, or for his land, or for mercy.14Hearken vnto
this, O Iob: ſtand ſtill, and conſider the wondrous workes of
God.15Doeſt thou knowe when God diſpoſed them, and cauſed the
light of his cloud to ſhine?16Doeſt thou know the ballancings of the
clouds, the wondrous workes of him which is perfect in
knowledge?17How thy garments are warme, when hee quieteth the earth
by the South wind?18Haſt thou with him ſpread out the ſkie, which is
ſtrong, and as a molten looking glaſſe?19Teach vs what we ſhall ſay vnto
him; for we cannot order our ſpeach by reaſon of darknes.20Shall it bee
told him that I ſpeake? if a man ſpeake, ſurely he ſhalbe ſwallowed
vp.21And nowe men ſee not the bright light which is in the clouds: but
the wind paſſeth and cleanſeth them.22Faire weather commeth out of
the North: with God is terrible maieſtie.23Touching the Almighty, we
cannot find him out: he is excellent in power, and in iudgement, and in
plenty of iuſtice: he will not afflict.24Men doe therefore feare him: he
reſpecteth not any that are wiſe of heart.

CHAPTER 38 1Then the Lord anſwered Iob out of the whirlewind, and
ſayd,2Who is this that darkneth counſell by words without
knowledge?3Gird vp nowe thy loines like a man; for I will demaund of
thee, and anſwere thou me.4Where waſt thou when I layd the
foundations of the earth? declare, if thou haſt vnderſtanding.5Who hath
layd the meaſures thereof, if thou knoweſt? or who hath ſtretched the
line vpon it?6Wherepuon are the foundations thereof faſtened? or who
layd the corner ſtone thereof?7When the morning ſtarres ſang together,
and all the ſonnes of God ſhouted for ioy.8Or who ſhut vp the ſea with
doores, when it brake foorth as if it had iſſued out of the wombe?9When
I made the cloud the garment thereof, and thicke darkneſſe a ſwadling
band for it,10And brake vp for it my decreed place, and ſet barres and
doores,11And ſaid, Hitherto ſhalt thou come, but no further: and heere
ſhall thy proud waues be ſtayed.12Haſt thou commaunded the morning
ſince thy daies? and cauſed the day-ſpring to know his place,13That it
might take hold of the endes of the earth, that the wicked might be
ſhaken out of it?14It is turned as clay to the ſeale, and they ſtand as a
garment.15And from the wicked their light is withholden, and the high
arme ſhalbe broken.16Haſt thou entred into the ſprings of the ſea? or
haſt thou walked in the ſearch of the depth?17Haue the gates of death
bene opened vnto thee? or haſt thou ſeene the doores of the ſhadow of
death?18Haſt thou perceiued the breadth of the earth? Declare if thou
knoweſt it all.19Where is the way where light dwelleth? And as for
darkneſſe, where is the place thereof?20That thou ſhouldeſt take it to the
bound thereof, and that thou ſhouldeſt know the pathes to the houſe
thereof.21Knoweſt thou it, becauſe thou waſt then borne? or becauſe the
number of thy daies is great?22Haſt thou entred into the treaſures of the
ſnowe? or haſt thou ſeene the treaſures of the haile,23Which I haue
reſeruedagainſt the time of trouble, againſt the day of battaile and
warre?24By what way is the light parted? which ſcattereth the Eaſt wind
vpon the earth.25Who hath diuided a water-courſe for the ouerflowing
of waters? or a way for the lightning of thunder,26To cauſe it to raine on
the earth, where no man is: on the wilderneſſe wherein there is no
man?27To ſatiſfie the deſolate and waſte ground, and to cauſe the bud
of the tender herbe to ſpring forth.28Hath the raine a father? or who
hath begotten the drops of dew?29Out of whoſe wombe came the yce?
and the hoary froſt of heauen, who hath gendred it?30The waters are hid
as with a ſtone, and the face of the deepe is frozen.31Canſt thou bind the
ſweete influences of Pleiades? or looſe the bands of Orion?32Canſt thou
bring forth Mazzaroth in his ſeaſon, or canſt thou guide Arcturus with
his ſonnes?33Knoweſt thou the ordinances of heauen? canſt thou ſet the
dominion thereof in the earth?34Canſt thou lift vp thy voice to the
cloudes, that abundance of waters may couer thee?35Canſt thou ſend
lightnings, that they may goe, and ſay vnto thee, Here we are?36Who
hath put wiſedome in the inward parts? or who hath giuen
vnderſtanding to the heart?37Who can number the cloudes in
wiſedome? or who can ſtay the bottles of heauen,38When the duſt
groweeh into hardneſse, and the clods cleaue faſt together?39Wilt thou
hunt the pray for the lyon? or fill the appetite of the young lyons,40When
they couch in their dennes, and abide in the couert to lie in waite?41Who
prouideth for the rauen his foode? when his young ones cry vnto God,
they wander for lacke of meate.

CHAPTER 39 1Knoweſt thou the time when the wild goates of the
rocke bring forth? or canſt thou marke when the hindes doe
calue?2Canſt thou number the moneths that they fulfill? or knoweſt thou
the time when they bring forth?3They bowe themſelues, they bring forth
their young ones, they caſt out their ſorrowes.4Their yong ones are in
good liking, they grow vp with corne: they go forth, and returne not
vnto them.5Who hath ſent out the wild aſſe free? or who hath loooſed
the bands of the wild aſſe?6Whoſe houſe I haue made the wilderneſſe,
and the barren lande his dwellings.7He ſcorneth the multitude of the
citie, neither regardeth he the crying of the driuer.8The range of the
mountaines is his paſture, and hee ſearcheth after euery greene
thing.9Will the Unicorne be willing to ſerue thee? or abide by thy
cribbe?10Canſt thou binde the Unicorne with his band in the furrow? or
will he harrow the valleyes after thee?11Wilt thou truſt him becauſe his
ſtrength is great? or wilt thou leaue thy labour to him?12Wilt thou
beleeue him that hee will bring home thy ſeed? and gather it into thy
barne?13Gaueſt thou the goodly wings vnto the peacocks, or wings and
feathers vnto the Oſtrich?14Which leaueth her egges in the earth, and
warmeth them in duſt,15And forgetteth that the foot may cruſh them,
or that the wilde beaſt may breake them.16She is hardened againſt her
yong ones, as though they were not hers: her labour is in vaine without
feare.17Becauſe God hath depriued her of wiſedome, neither hath he

imparted to her vnderſtanding.18What time ſhe lifteth vp her ſelfe on
high, ſhe ſcorneth the horſe and his rider.19Haſt thou giuen the horſe
ſtrength? haſt thou clothed his necke with thunder?20Canſt thou make
him afraid as a graſhopper? the glory of his noſtrils is terrible.21He
paweth in the valley, and reioyceth in his ſtrength: hee goeth on to meet
the armed men.22He mocketh at feare, and is not affrighted: neither
turneth he backe from the ſword.23The quiuer ratleth againſt him, the
glittering ſpeare and the ſhield.24He ſwalloweth the ground with
fiercenefse and rage: neither beleeueth he that it is the ſound of the
trumpet.25Hee ſaith among the trumpets, Ha, ha: and he ſmelleth the
battaile afarre off, the thunder of the captaines, and the
ſhouting.26Doeth the hawke flie by thy wiſedome, and ſtretch her wings
toward the South?27Doeth the Eagle mount vp at thy commaund? and
make her neſt on high?28She dwelleth and abideth on the rocke, vpon
the cragge of the rocke, and the ſtrong place.29From thence ſhe ſeeketh
the pray, and her eyes behold a farre off.30Her yong ones alſo ſuck vp
blood: and where the ſlaine are, there is he.

CHAPTER 401Moreouer the Lord anſwered Iob, and ſaid,2Shall hee
that contendeth with the Almightie, inſtruct him? he that reproueth
God, let him anſwere it.3Then Iob anſwered the Lord, and ſaid,4Behold,
I am vile, what ſhall I anſwere thee? I wil lay my hand vpon my
mouth.5Once haue I ſpoken, but I will not anſwere: yea twiſe, but I will
proceed no further.6Then anſwered the Lord vnto Iob out of the
whirlewinde, and ſaid:7Gird vp thy loynes now like a man: I will
demaund of thee, and declare thou vnto me.8Wilt thou alſo diſanul my
iudgement? Wilt thou condemne mee, that thou mayeſt be
righteous?9Haſt thou an arme like God? or canſt thou thunder with a
voyce like him?10Decke thy ſelfe now with Maieſtie, and excellencie, and
aray thy ſelfe with glory, and beautie.11Caſt abroad the rage of thy wrath:
and behold euery one that is proud, and abaſe him.12Looke on euery one
that is proud, and bring him low: and tread downe the wicked in their
place.13Hide them in the duſt together, and binde their faces in
ſecret.14Then will I alſo confeſse vnto thee, that thine owne right hand
can ſaue thee.15Beholde now Behemoth which I made with thee, hee
eateth graſſe as an oxe.16Loe now, his ſtrength is in his loynes, and his
force is in the nauell of his belly.17Hee moueth his taile like a Cedar: the
ſinewes of his ſtones are wrapt together.18His bones are as ſtrong pieces
of braſſe: his bones are like barres of iron.19Hee is the chiefe of the
wayes of God: he that made him, can make his ſword to approach vnto
him.20Surely the mountaines bring him foorth foode: where all the
beaſts of the field play.21He lieth vnder the ſhady trees in the couert of
the reede, and fennes.22The ſhady trees couer him with their ſhaddow:
the willowes of the brooke compaſſe him about.23Behold, he drinketh
vp a riuer, and haſteth not: he truſteth that he can draw vp Iordan into
his mouth.24He taketh it with his eyes: his noſe pearceth through ſnares.

CHAPTER 411Canſt thou draw out Leuiathan with an hooke? or his
tongue with a corde which thou letteſt downe?2Canſt thou put an hooke
into his noſe? or bore his iawe through with a thorne?3Will he make
many ſupplications vnto thee? will he ſpeake ſoft words vnto thee?4Will
he make a couenant with thee? wilt thou take him for a ſeruant for
euer?5Wilt thou play with him as with a birde? wilt thou binde him for
thy maydens?6Shall the companions make a banquet of him? ſhall they
part him among the merchants?7Canſt thou fill his ſkinne with barbed
irons? or his head with fiſhſpeares?8Lay thine hand vpon him,
remember the battell: doe no more.9Behold, the hope of him is in vaine:
ſhall not one be caſt downe euen at the ſight of him?10None is ſo fierce
that dare ſtirre him vp: who then is able to ſtand before me?11Who hath
preuented me that I ſhould repay him? whatſoeuer is vnder the whole
heauen, is mine.12I will not conceale his parts, nor his power, nor his
comely proportion.13Who can diſcouer the face of his garment? or who
can come to him, with his double bridle?14Who can open the doores of
his face? his teeth are terrible round about.15His ſcales are his pride, ſhut
vp together as with a cloſe ſeale.16One is ſo neere to another, that no
ayre can come betweene them.17They are ioyned one to another, they
ſticke together, that they cannot be ſundred.18By his neeſings a light
doth ſhine, and his eyes are like the eye-liddes of the morning.19Out of
his mouth goe burning lampes, and ſparkes of fire leape out.20Out of
his noſtrels goeth ſmoke, as out of a ſeething pot or caldron.21His breath
kindleth coales, and a flame goeth out of his mouth.22In his necke
remaineth ſtrength, and ſorrowe is turned into ioy before him.23The
flakes of his fleſh are ioyned together: they are firme in themſelues, they
cannot be moued.24His heart is as firme as a ſtone, yea as hard as a peece
of the nether mil-ſtone.25When he rayſeth vp himſelfe, the mightie are
afraid: by reaſon of breakings they purifie themſelues.26The ſword of
him that layeth at him cannot hold. the ſpeare, the dart, nor the
habergeon.27He eſteemeth iron as ſtraw, and braſſe as rotten
wood.28The arrow cannot make him flee: ſling-ſtones are turned with
him into ſtubble.29Darts are counted as ſtubble: he laugheth at the
ſhaking of a ſpeare.30Sharpe ſtones are vnder him: he ſpreadeth ſharpe
pointed things vpon the mire.31He maketh the deepe to boyle like a pot:
hee maketh the ſea like a pot of oyntment.32Hee maketh a path to ſhine
after him; one would thinke the deepe to bee hoarie.33Upon earth there
is not his like: who is made without feare.34He beholdeth all high things:
he is a king ouer all the children of pride.

CHAPTER 421Then Iob anſwered the Lord, and ſaid,2I know that
thou canſt doe euery thing, and that no thought can bee withholden
from thee.3Who is he that hideth counſel without knowledge? therefore
haue I vttered that I vnderſtood not, things too wonderfull for me,
which I knew not.4Heare, I beſeech thee, and I will ſpeake: I will
demand of thee, and declare thou vnto me.5I haue heard of thee by the
hearing of the eare: but now mine eye ſeeth thee.6Wherefore I abhorre
my ſelfe, and repent in duſt and aſhes.7And it was ſo, that after the Lord
had ſpoken theſe words vnto Iob, the Lord ſaid to Eliphaz the
Temanite, My wrath is kindled againſt thee, & againſt thy two friends:
for ye haue not ſpoken of mee the thing that is right, as my ſeruant Iob
hath.8Therefore take vnto you now ſeuen bullocks, and ſeuen rammes,
and goe to my ſeruant Iob, and offer vp for your ſelues a burnt offring,
and my ſeruant Iob ſhal pray for you, for him wil I accept: leſt I deale
with you after your folly, in that ye haue not ſpoken of mee the thing
which is right, like my ſeruant Iob.9So Eliphaz the Temanite, and Bildad
the Shuhite, and Zophar the Naamathite went, and did according as the
Lord commanded them: the Lord alſo accepted Iob.10And the Lord
turned the captiuitie of Iob, when he prayed for his friends: alſo the
Lord gaue Iob twice as much as he had before.11Then came there vnto
him all his brethren, and all his ſiſters, and all they that had bin of his
acquaintance before, and did eat bread with him in his houſe: and they
bemoned him, and comforted him ouer all the euill that the Lord had
brought vpon him: euery man alſo gaue him a piece of money, and euery
one an eare-ring of gold.12So the Lord bleſſed the latter end of Iob, more
then his beginning: for he had fourteene thouſand ſheepe, and ſixe
thouſand camels, and a thouſand yoke of oxen, and a thouſand ſhee
aſſes.13He had alſo ſeuen ſonnes, and three daughters.14And he called
the name of the firſt, Iemima, and the name of the ſecond, Kezia, and
the name of the third, Keren-happuch.15And in all the land were no
women found ſo faire as the daughters of Iob: and their father gaue
them inheritance among their brethren.16After this liued Iob an hundred
and fourtie yeeres, and ſaw his ſonnes, and his ſonnes ſonnes, euen foure
generations.17So Iob died being old, and full of dayes.

PſALMES (PSALMS)

CHAPTER 11Bleſſed is the man that walketh not in the counſell of the
vngodly, nor ſtandeth in the way of ſinners, nor ſitteth in the ſeat of the
ſcornefull.2But his delight is in the Law of the Lord, and in his Law
doeth he meditate day and night.3And he ſhalbe like a tree planted by
the riuers of water, that bringeth foorth his fruit in his ſeaſon, his leafe
alſo ſhall not wither, and whatſoeuer he doeth, ſhall proſper.4The
vngodly are not ſo: but are like the chaffe, which the winde driueth
away.5Therefore the vngodly ſhall not ſtand in the iudgement, nor
ſinners in the Congregation of the righteous.6For the Lord knoweth the
way of the righteous: but the way of the vngodly ſhall periſh.

CHAPTER 21Why do the heathen rage, and the people imagine a vaine
thing?2The Kings of the earth ſet themſelues, and the rulers take
counſell together, againſt the Lord, and againſt his Anoynted, ſaying,3Let
vs breake their bandes aſunder, and caſt away their cords from vs.4Hee
that ſitteth in the heauens ſhal laugh: the Lord ſhall haue them in

deriſion.5Then ſhall hee ſpeake vnto them in his wrath, and vexe them in his ſore diſpleaſure.6Yet haue I ſet my King vpon my holy hill of Sion.7I will declare the decree: the Lord hath ſaid vnto mee, Thou art my ſonne, this day haue I begotten thee.8Aſke of me, and I ſhall giue thee the heathen for thine inheritance, and the vttermoſt parts of the earth for thy poſſeſſion.9Thou ſhalt breake them with a rod of iron, thou ſhalt daſh them in pieces like a potters veſſell.10Bee wiſe now therefore, O yee Kings: be inſtructed ye Iudges of the earth.11Serue the Lord with feare, and reioyce with trembling.12Kiſſe the Sonne leſt he be angry, and ye periſh from the way, when his wrath is kindled but a little: Bleſſed are all they that put their truſt in him.

CHAPTER 31*A Pſalme of Dauid when he fled from Abſalom his ſonne.* Lord, how are they increaſed that trouble mee? many are they that riſe vp againſt me.2Many there bee which ſay of my ſoule, There is no helpe for him in God. Selah.3But thou, O Lord, art a ſhield for me; my glory, and the lifter vp of mine head.4I cryed vnto the Lord with my voyce, and he heard me out of his holy hill. Selah.5I layd me downe and ſlept; I awaked, for the Lord ſuſtained me.6I will not be afraid of ten thouſands of people, that haue ſet themſelues againſt me round about.7Ariſe, O Lord, ſaue mee, O my God; for thou haſt ſmitten all mine enemies vpon the cheeke bone: thou haſt broken the teeth of the vngodly.8Saluation belongeth vnto the Lord: thy bleſſing is vpon thy people. Selah.

CHAPTER 41*To the chiefe Muſician on Neginoth, A Pſalme of Dauid.* Heare me, when I call, O God of my righteouſneſſe: thou haſt inlarged mee when I was in diſtreſſe, haue mercy vpon me, and heare my prayer.2O ye ſonnes of men, how long will yee turne my glory into ſhame? how long will yee loue vanitie, and ſeeke after leaſing? Selah.3But know that the Lord hath ſet apart him that is godly, for himſelfe: the Lord will heare when I call vnto him.4ſtand in awe, and ſinne not: commune with your owne heart vpon your bed, and be ſtill. Selah.5Offer the ſacrifices of righteouſneſſe, and put your truſt in the Lord.6There be many that ſay, Who wil ſhew vs any good? Lord lift thou vp the light of thy countenance vpon vs.7Thou haſt put gladneſſe in my heart, more then in the time that their corne and their wine increaſed.8I will both lay mee downe in peace, and ſleepe: for thou Lord only makeſt me dwell in ſafetie.

CHAPTER 51*To the chiefe muſician vpon Nehiloth, A Pſalme of Dauid.* Giue eare to my words, O Lord, conſider my meditation.2Hearken vnto the voice of my crie, my King, and my God: for vnto thee will I pray.3My voyce ſhalt thou heare in the morning, O Lord; in the morning will I direct my prayer vnto thee, and will looke vp.4For thou art not a God that hath pleaſure in wickedneſſe: neither ſhall euill dwell with thee.5The fooliſh ſhall not ſtand in thy ſight: thou hateſt al workers of iniquity6Thou ſhalt deſtroy them that ſpeake leaſing: the Lord will abhorre the bloodie and deceitfull man.7But as for me, I will come into thy houſe in the multitude of thy mercy: and in thy feare will I worſhip toward thy holy temple.8Lead me O Lord, in thy righteouſneſſe, becauſe of mine enemies; make thy way ſtraight before my face.9For there is no faithfulnes in their mouth, their inward part is very wickedneſſe: their throat is an open ſepulchre, they flatter with their tongue.10Deſtroy thou them, O God, let them fall by their owne counſels: caſt them out in the multitude of their tranſgreſſions, for they haue rebelled againſt thee.11But let all thoſe that put their truſt in thee, reioyce: let them euer ſhout for ioy; becauſe thou defendeſt them: let them alſo that loue thy name, be ioyfull in thee.12For thou, Lord, wilt bleſſe the righteous: with fauour wilt thou compaſſe him as with a ſhield.

CHAPTER 61*To the chiefe muſician on Neginoth vpon Sheminith, A Pſalme of Dauid.* O Lord, rebuke me not in thine anger, neither chaſten me in thy hot diſpleaſure.2Haue mercy vpon me, O Lord, for I am weake: O Lord heale mee, for my bones are vexed.3My ſoule is alſo ſore vexed: but thou, O Lord, how long?4Returne, O Lord, deliuer my ſoule: oh ſaue mee, for thy mercies ſake.5For in death there is no remembrance of thee: in the graue who ſhall giue thee thankes?6I am weary with my groning, all the night make I my bed to ſwim: I water my couch with my teares.7Mine eie is conſumed becauſe of griefe; it waxeth olde becauſe of all mine enemies.8Depart from me, all yee workers of iniquitie: for the Lord hath heard the voice of my weeping.9The Lord hath heard my ſupplication; the Lord will receiue my prayer.10Let all mine enemies be aſhamed and ſore vexed: let them returne and be aſhamed ſuddainly.

CHAPTER 71*Shiggaion of Dauid; which he ſang vnto the Lord concerning the words of Cuſh the Beniamite.* O Lord, my God, in thee doe I put my truſt: ſaue me from all them that perſecute me, and deliuer me.2Leaſt hee teare my ſoule like a lyon, renting it in pieces, while there is none to deliuer.3O Lord my God, if I haue done this; if there be iniquitie in my hands:4If I haue rewarded euill vnto him that was at peace with me: (yea I haue deliuered him that without cauſe is mine enemie.)5Let the enemie perſecute my ſoule, and take it, yea let him tread downe my life vpon the earth, and lay mine honour in the duſt. Selah.6Ariſe, O Lord, in thine anger, lift vp thy ſelfe, becauſe of the rage of mine enemies: and awake for me to the iudgement that thou haſt commanded.7So ſhall the congregation of the people compaſſe thee about: for their ſakes therefore returne thou on high.8The Lord ſhal iudge the people: iudge me, O Lord, according to my righteouſneſſe, and according to mine integritie that is in me.9Oh let the wickednes of the wicked come to an end, but eſtabliſh the iuſt: for the righteous God trieth the hearts and reines.10My defence is of God, which ſaueth the vpright in heart.11God iudgeth the righteous, and God is angrie with the wicked euery-day.12If he turne not, he will whet his ſword; he hath bent his bowe, and made it ready.13He hath alſo prepared for him the inſtruments of death; he ordaineth his arrowes againſt the perſecutors.14Behold, he trauelleth with iniquitie, and hath conceiued miſchiefe, and brought forth falſhood.15He made a pit and digged it, and is fallen into the ditch which he made.16His miſchiefe ſhall returne vpon his owne head, and his violent dealing ſhall come downe vpon his owne pate.17I will praiſe the Lord according to his righteouſneſſe: and will ſing praiſe to the name of the Lord moſt high.

CHAPTER 81*To the chiefe Muſicion vpon Gittith, a Pſalme of Dauid.* O Lord our Lord, how excellent is thy name in all the earth! who haſt ſet thy glory aboue the heauens.2Out of the mouth of babes and ſucklings haſt thou ordained ſtrength, becauſe of thine enemies, that thou mighteſt ſtill the enemie and the auenger.3When I conſider thy heauens, the worke of thy fingers, the moone and the ſtarres which thou haſt ordained;4What is man, that thou art mindfull of him? and the ſonne of man, that thou viſiteſt him?5For thou haſt made him a little lower then the Angels; and haſt crowned him with glory and honour.6Thou madeſt him to haue dominion ouer the workes of thy hands; thou haſt put all things vnder his feete.7All ſheepe and oxen, yea and the beaſts of the field.8The foule of the aire, and the fiſh of the ſea, and whatſoeuer paſſeth through the paths of the ſeas.9O Lord our Lord, how excellent is thy name in all the earth!

CHAPTER 91*To the chiefe muſician vpon MuthLabben. A Pſalme of Dauid.* I wil praiſe thee, O Lord, with my whole heart: I will ſhewe foorth all thy maruellous workes.2I will bee glad and reioyce in thee: I will ſing prayſe to thy name, O thou moſt High.3When mine enemies are turned backe, they ſhall fall and periſh at thy preſence.4For thou haſt maintained my right, and my cauſe: thou ſateſt in the throne iudging right.5Thou haſt rebuked the heathen, thou haſt deſtroyed the wicked; thou haſt put out their name for euer and euer.6O thou enemie, deſtructions are come to a perpetuall end; and thou haſt deſtroyed cities, their memoriall is periſhed with them.7But the Lord ſhall endure for euer: he hath prepared his throne for iudgement.8And hee ſhall iudge the world in righteouſneſſe; he ſhall miniſter iudgement to the people in vprightneſse.9The Lord alſo will bee a refuge for the oppreſſed: a refuge, in times of trouble.10And they that know thy name will put their truſt in thee: for thou Lord haſt not forſaken them that ſeeke thee.11Sing praiſes to the Lord, which dwelleth in Sion: declare among the people his doings.12When he maketh inquiſition for blood, he remembreth them: he forgetteth not the crie of the humble.13Haue mercie vpon me O Lord, conſider my trouble which I ſuffer of them that hate me, thou that lifteſt mee vp from the gates of death:14That I may ſhew foorth all thy prayſe in the gates of the daughter of Sion: I will reioyce in thy ſaluation.15The heathen are ſunke downe in the pit that they made: in the net which they hid, is their own foot taken.16The Lord is knowen by the iudgement which he executeth: the wicked is ſnared in the worke of his owne hands. Higgaion. Selah.17The wicked ſhall be turned into hell, and all the nations that forget God.18For the needie ſhall not alway be forgotten: the expectation of the poore ſhall not periſh for euer.19Ariſe, O Lord, let not man preuaile: let the heathen bee iudged in thy ſight.20Put them in feare, O Lord: that the nations may know themſelues to be but men. Selah.

CHAPTER 10 1Why ſtandeſt thou afarre off, O Lord? why hideſt thou thy ſelfe in times of trouble?2The wicked in his pride doeth perſecute the poore: let them be taken in the deuices that they haue imagined.3For the wicked boaſteth of his hearts deſire, and bleſſeth the couetous, whom the Lord abhorreth.4The wicked through the pride of his countenance will not ſeeke after God: God is not in all his thoughts.5His wayes are alwayes grieuous, thy iudgements are farre aboue out of his ſight: as for all his enemies, he puffeth at them.6He hath ſaid in his heart, I ſhall not be moued: for I ſhall neuer be in aduerſitie.7His mouth is full of curſing, and deceit, and fraud: vnder his tongue is miſchiefe and vanitie.8He ſitteth in the lurking places of the villages: in the ſecret places doeth he murder the innocent: his eyes are priuily ſet againſt the poore.9He lieth in waite ſecretly as a lyon in his denne, he lieth in wait to catch the poore: he doth catch the poore when he draweth him into his net.10He croucheth, and humbleth himſelfe, that the poore may fall by his ſtrong ones.11Hee hath ſaid in his heart, God hath forgotten: he hideth his face, hee will neuer ſee it.12Ariſe, O Lord, O God lift vp thine hand: forget not the humble.13Wherefore doeth the wicked contemne God? he hath ſaid in his heart, Thou wilt not require it.14Thou haſt ſeene it, for thou beholdeſt miſchiefe and ſpite to requite it with thy hand: the poore committeth himſelfe vnto thee, thou art the helper of the fatherleſſe.15Breake thou the arme of the wicked, and the euill man: ſeeke out his wickednes, till thou finde none.16The Lord is King for euer and euer: the heathen are periſhed out of his land.17Lord, thou haſt heard the deſire of the humble: thou wilt prepare their heart, thou wilt cauſe thine eare to heare,18To iudge the fatherleſſe and the oppreſſed, that the man of the earth may no more oppreſse.

CHAPTER 11 1*To the chiefe Muſician. A Pſalme of Dauid.* In the Lord put I my truſt: how ſay yee to my ſoule, Flee as a bird to your mountaine?2For loe, the wicked bende their bow, they make ready their arrow vpon the ſtring: that they may priuily ſhoote at the vpright in heart.3If the foundations bee deſtroyed: what can the righteous doe?4The Lord is in his holy Temple, the Lords Throne is in heauen: his eyes beholde, his eye lids trie the children of men.5The Lord trieth the righteous: but the wicked and him that loueth violence, his ſoule hateth.6Upon the wicked hee ſhall raine ſnares, fire and brimſtone, and an horrible tempeſt: this ſhall be the portion of their cup.7For the righteous Lord loueth righteouſneſſe: his countenance doeth behold the vpright.

CHAPTER 12 1*To the chiefe Muſician vpon Sheminith. A Pſalme of Dauid.* Helpe Lord, for the godly man ceaſeth; for the faithfull faile from among the children of men.2They ſpeake vanitie euery one with his neighbour: with flattering lips, and with a double heart do they ſpeake.3The Lord ſhall cut off all flattering lips, and the tongue that ſpeaketh proud things.4Who haue ſaid, with our tongue wil we preuaile, our lips are our owne: who is Lord ouer vs?5For the oppreſſion of the poore, for the ſighing of the needy, now will I Ariſe (ſaith the Lord,) I will ſet him in ſafetie from him that puffeth at him.6The wordes of the Lord are pure wordes: as ſiluer tried in a fornace of earth purified ſeuen times.7Thou ſhalt keepe them, (O Lord,) thou ſhalt preſeruethem, from this generation for euer.8The wicked walke on euery ſide, when the vileſt men are exalted.

CHAPTER 13 1*To the chiefe Muſician. A Pſalme of Dauid.* How long wilt thou forget mee (O Lord) for euer? how long wilt thou hide thy face from me?2How long ſhall I take counſel in my ſoule, hauing ſorrow in my heart dayly? how long ſhall mine enemie be exalted ouer me?3Conſider and heare me, O Lord my God: lighten mine eyes, leſt I ſleep the ſleepe of death.4Leaſt mine enimie ſay, I haue preuailed againſt him: and thoſe that trouble mee, reioyce, when I am moued.5But I haue truſted in thy mercy, my heart ſhall reioyce in thy ſaluation.6I will ſing vnto the Lord, becauſe hee hath dealt bountifully with mee.

CHAPTER 14 1*To the chiefe muſician, A Pſalme of Dauid.* The foole hath ſayd in his heart, There is no God: they are corrupt, they haue done abominable workes, there is none that doeth good.2The Lord looked downe from heauen vpon the children of men; to ſee if there were any that did vnderſtand and ſeeke God.3They are all gone aſide, they are all together become filthy: there is none that doeth good, no not one.4Haue all the workers of iniquity no knowledge? who eate vp my people as they eate bread, and call not vpon the Lord.5There were they in great feare; for God is in the generation of the righteous.6You haue ſhamed the counſell of the poore; becauſe the Lord is his refuge.7O that the ſaluation of Iſrael were come out of Sion! when the Lord bringeth backe the captiuitie of his people, Iacob ſhall reioyce, and Iſrael ſhalbe glad.

CHAPTER 15 1*A Pſalme of Dauid.* Lord, who ſhall abide in thy tabernacle? who ſhall dwell in thy holy hill?2Hee that walketh vprightly, and worketh righteouſneſſe, and ſpeaketh the trueth in his heart.3Hee that backbiteth not with his tongue, nor doth euill to his neighbour, nor taketh vp a reproach againſt his neighbour.4In whoſe eies a vile perſon is contemned; but he honoureth them that feare the Lord: he that ſweareth to his owne hurt, and changeth not.5He that putteth not out his money to vſury, nor taketh reward againſt the innocent: he that doth theſe things, ſhall neuer be moued.

CHAPTER 16 1*Michtam of Dauid.* Preſerueme, O God: for in thee doe I put my truſt.2O my ſoule, thou haſt ſayd vnto the Lord, Thou art my Lord: my goodnes extendeth not to thee:3But to the Saints, that are in the earth, and to the excellent, in whom is all my delight.4Their ſorrowes ſhalbe multiplied, that haſten after another God: their drinke offerings of blood will I not offer, nor take vp their names into my lippes.5The Lord is the portion of mine inheritance, and of my cup: thou maintaineſt my lot.6The lines are fallen vnto mee in pleaſant places; yea, I haue a goodly heritage.7I will bleſſe the Lord, who hath giuen me counſell: my reines alſo inſtruct me in the night ſeaſons.8I haue ſet the Lord alwaies before me: becauſe hee is at my right hand, I ſhall not be moued.9Therefore my heart is glad, and my glory reioyceth: my fleſh alſo ſhall reſt in hope.10For thou wilt not leaue my ſoule in hell; neither wilt thou ſuffer thine holy one to ſee corruption.11Thou wilt ſhewe me the path of life: in thy preſence is fulneſse of ioy, at thy right hand there are pleaſures for euermore.

CHAPTER 17 1*A prayer of Dauid.* Heare the right, O Lord, attend vnto my crie, giue eare vnto my prayer, that goeth not out of fained lips.2Let my ſentence come forth from thy preſence: let thine eyes beholde the things that are equall.3Thou haſt prooued mine heart, thou haſt viſited me in the night, thou haſt tried me, and ſhalt find nothing: I am purpoſed that my mouth ſhall not tranſgreſse.4Concerning the workes of men, by the word of thy lips, I haue kept me from the paths of the deſtroyer.5Hold vp my goings in thy paths, that my footſteps ſlip not.6I haue called vpon thee, for thou wilt heare me, O God: incline thine eare vnto me, and heare my ſpeach.7Shewe thy marueilous louing kindneſse, O thou that ſaueſt by thy right hand, them which put their truſt in thee, frō thoſe that riſe vp againſt them.8Keepe me as the apple of the eye: hide mee vnder the ſhadowe of thy wings,9From the wicked that oppreſſe me, from my deadly enemies, who compaſſe me about.10They are incloſed in their owne fat: with their mouth they ſpeake proudly.11They haue now compaſſed vs in our ſteps: they haue ſet their eyes bowing downe to the earth:12Like as a lyon that is greedie of his pray, and as it were a yong lyon lurking in ſecret places.13Ariſe, O Lord, diſappoint him, caſt him downe: deliuer my ſoule from the wicked, which is thy ſword:14From men which are thy hand, O Lord, from men of the world, which haue their portion in this life, and whoſe belly thou filleſt with thy hid treaſure: They are full of children, and leaue the reſt of their ſubſtance to their babes.15As for me, I will behold thy face in righteouſneſſe: I ſhall bee ſatiſfied, when I awake, with thy likeneſſe.

CHAPTER 18 1*To the chiefe muſicion, a pſalme of Dauid, the ſeruant of the Lord, who ſpake vnto the Lord the words of this ſong, in the day that the Lord deliuered him from the hand of all his enemies, and from the hand of Saul: And he ſaid,* I will loue thee, O Lord, my ſtrength.2The Lord is my rocke, and my fortreſse, and my deliuerer: my God, my ſtrength in whome I will truſt, my buckler, and the horne of my ſaluation, and my high tower.3I will call vpon the Lord, who is worthy to be praiſed: ſo ſhall I be ſaued from mine enemies.4The ſorrowes of death compaſſed me, and the floods of vngodly men made me afraid.5The ſorrowes of hell compaſſed me about: the ſnares of death preuented me.6In my diſtreſſe I called vpon the Lord, and cryed vnto my God: hee heard my voyce out of his temple, and my crie came before him, euen into his eares.7Then the earth ſhooke and trembled; the foundations alſo of the hilles mooued and were ſhaken, becauſe hee was wroth.8There went vp a ſmoke out of his noſtrils, and fire out of his mouth deuoured, coales were kindled by it.9He bowed the heauens alſo, and came downe: and darkeneſſe was

vnder his feet. 10 And he rode vpon a Cherub, and did flie: yea he did flie
vpon the wings of the wind. 11 He made darkenes his ſecret place: his
pauilion round about him, were darke waters, and thicke cloudes of the
ſkies. 12 At the brightnes that was before him his thicke clouds paſſed,
haile ſtones and coales of fire. 13 The Lord alſo thundered in the heauens,
and the higheſt gaue his voyce; haileſtones and coales of fire. 14 Yea, he
ſent out his arrowes, and ſcattered them; and he ſhot out lightnings, and
diſcomfited them. 15 Then the chanels of waters were ſeene, and the
foundations of the world were diſcouered: at thy rebuke, O Lord, at the
blaſt of the breath of thy noſtrils. 16 He ſent from aboue, he tooke me,
he drew me out of many waters. 17 He deliuered me from my ſtrong
enemie, and from them which hated me: for they were too ſtrong for
me. 18 They preuented me in the day of my calamitie: but the Lord was
my ſtay. 19 He brought me forth alſo into a large place: he deliuered me,
becauſe he delighted in me. 20 The Lord rewarded me according to my
righteouſneſſe, according to the cleanneſſe of my hands hath hee
recompenſed me. 21 For I haue kept the wayes of the Lord, and haue not
wickedly departed from my God. 22 For all his iudgements were before
me, and I did not put away his ſtatutes from me. 23 I was alſo vpright
before him: and I kept my ſelfe from mine iniquity. 24 Therefore hath the
Lord recompenſed me according to my righteouſneſſe, according to the
cleanneſſe of my hands in his eye-ſight. 25 With the mercifull thou wilt
ſhew thy ſelfe mercifull, with an vpright man thou wilt ſhew thy ſelfe
vpright. 26 With the pure thou wilt ſhewe thy ſelfe pure, and with the
froward thou wilt ſhew thy ſelfe froward. 27 For thou wilt ſaue the
afflicted people: but wilt bring downe high lookes. 28 For thou wilt light
my candle: the Lord my God will enlighten my darkeneſſe. 29 For by thee
I haue run through a troupe? and by my God haue I leaped ouer a
wall. 30 As for God, his way is perfect: the word of the Lord is tried: he
is a buckler to all thoſe that truſt in him. 31 For who is God ſaue the Lord?
or who is a rocke ſaue our God? 32 It is God that girdeth mee with
ſtrength, and maketh my way perfect. 33 Hee maketh my feete like hindes
feete, and ſetteth me vpon my high places. 34 He teacheth my hands to
warre, ſo that a bow of ſteele is broken by mine armes. 35 Thou haſt alſo
giuen me the ſhield of thy ſaluation: and thy right hand hath holden me
vp, and thy gentleneſse hath made me great. 36 Thou haſt enlarged my
ſteppes vnder me; that my feete did not ſlippe. 37 I haue purſued mine
enemies, and ouertaken them: neither did I turne againe till they were
conſumed. 38 I haue wounded them that they were not able to riſe: they
are fallen vnder my feete. 39 For thou haſt girded mee with ſtrength vnto
the battell: thou haſt ſubdued vnder me, thoſe that roſe vp againſt
me. 40 Thou haſt alſo giuen mee the neckes of mine enemies: that I might
deſtroy them that hate me. 41 They cried, but there was none to ſaue
them: euen vnto the Lord, but he anſwered them not. 42 Then did I beate
them ſmall as the duſt before the winde: I did caſt them out, as the dirt
in the ſtreetes. 43 Thou haſt deliuered me from the ſtriuings of the people,
and thou haſt made mee the head of the heathen: a people whom I haue
not knowen, ſhall ſerue me. 44 As ſoone as they heare of mee, they ſhall
obey me: the ſtrangers ſhall ſubmit themſelues vnto me. 45 The ſtrangers
ſhall fade away, and be afraid out of their cloſe places. 46 The Lord liueth,
and bleſſed be my rocke: and let the God of my ſaluation be exalted. 47 It
is God that auengeth mee, and ſubdueth the people vnder me. 48 He
deliuereth me from mine enemies: yea thou lifteſt mee vp aboue thoſe
that riſe vp againſt me; thou haſt deliuered me from the violent
man. 49 Therfore will I giue thankes vnto thee, (O Lord) among the
heathen: and ſing prayſes vnto thy name. 50 Great deliuerance giueth he
to his King: and ſheweth mercy to his Annointed, to Dauid, and to his
ſeede for euermore.
CHAPTER 19 1 *To the chiefe Muſician, A Pſalme of Dauid.* The heauens
declare the glory of God: and the firmament ſheweth his handy
worke. 2 Day vnto day vttereth ſpeach, and night vnto night ſheweth
knowledge. 3 There is no ſpeach nor language, where their voyce is not
heard. 4 Their line is gone out through all the earth, and their words to
the end of the world: In them hath he ſet a tabernacle for the
Sunne. 5 Which is as a bridegrome comming out of his chamber, and
reioyceth as a ſtrong man to runne a race. 6 His going forth is from the
end of the heauen, and his circuite vnto the ends of it: and there is
nothing hidde from the heat thereof. 7 The Law of the Lord is perfect,
conuerting the ſoule: the teſtimonie of the Lord is ſure, making wiſe the
ſimple. 8 The Statutes of the Lord are right, reioycing the heart: the
Commandement of the Lord is pure, inlightning the eyes. 9 The feare of
the Lord is cleane, enduring for euer: the Iudgements of the Lord are
true, and righteous altogether. 10 More to bee deſired are they then gold,
yea, then much fine gold: ſweeter alſo then hony, and the hony
combe. 11 Moreouer by them is thy ſeruant warned: and in keeping of
them there is great reward. 12 Who can vnderſtand his errours? cleanſe
thou me from ſecret faults. 13 Keepe back thy ſeruant alſo from
preſumptuous ſinnes, let them not haue dominion ouer me: then ſhall I
be vpright, and I ſhalbe innocent from the great tranſgreſsion. 14 Let the
words of my mouth, and the meditation of my heart, bee acceptable in
thy ſight, O Lord my ſtrength, and my redeemer.
CHAPTER 20 1 *To the chiefe Muſician. A Pſalme of Dauid.* The Lord heare
thee in the day of trouble, the Name of the God of Iacob defend
thee. 2 Send thee helpe from the Sanctuary: and ſtrengthen thee out of
Sion. 3 Remember all thy offerings, and accept thy burnt ſacrifice.
Selah. 4 Graunt thee according to thine owne heart, and fulfill all thy
counſell. 5 We will reioyce in thy ſaluation, and in the Name of our God
we will ſet vp our banners: the Lord fulfill all thy petitions. 6 Now know
I, that the Lord ſaueth his Anointed: he wil heare him from his holy
heauen, with the ſauing ſtrength of his right hand. 7 Some truſt in charets,
and ſome in horſes: but wee will remember the Name of the Lord our
God. 8 They are brought downe and fallen: but we are riſen, and ſtand
vpright. 9 Saue Lord, let the King heare vs when we call.
CHAPTER 21 1 *To the chiefe Muſician. A Pſalme of Dauid.* The King ſhall
ioy in thy ſtrength, O Lord: and in thy ſaluation how greatly ſhall he
reioyce? 2 Thou haſt giuen him his hearts deſire; and haſt not withholden
the requeſt of his lips. Selah. 3 For thou preuenteſt him with the bleſſings
of goodneſse: thou ſetteſt a Crowne of pure gold on his head. 4 He aſked
life of thee, and thou gaueſt it him, euen length of dayes for euer and
euer. 5 His glory is great in thy ſaluation: honour and Maieſtie haſt thou
layde vpon him. 6 For thou haſt made him moſt bleſſed for euer: thou
haſt made him exceeding glad with thy countenance. 7 For the King
truſteth in the Lord, and through the mercy of the moſt High, he ſhall
not be moued. 8 Thine hand ſhall finde out all thine enemies, thy right
hand ſhal finde out thoſe that hate thee. 9 Thou ſhalt make them as a fiery
ouen in the time of thine anger: the Lord ſhall ſwallow them vp in his
wrath, and the fire ſhall deuoure them. 10 Their fruit ſhalt thou deſtroy
from the earth, and their ſeed from among the children of men. 11 For
they intended euill againſt thee: they imagined a miſchieuous deuice,
which they are not able to performe. 12 Therefore ſhalt thou make them
turne their back, when thou ſhalt make ready thine arrowes vpon thy
ſtrings, againſt the face of them. 13 Be thou exalted, Lord, in thine owne
ſtrength: ſo will wee ſing, aud praiſe thy power.
CHAPTER 22 1 *To the chiefe Muſician vpon Aijeleth Shahar. A Pſalme of
Dauid.* My God, my God, why haſt thou forſaken mee? Why art thou ſo
far from helping me, and from the words of my roaring? 2 O my God, I
crie in the day time, but thou heareſt not; and in the night ſeaſon, and
am not ſilent. 3 But thou art holy, O thou that inhabiteſt the praiſes of
Iſrael! 4 Our fathers truſted in thee: they truſted, and thou didſt deliuer
them. 5 They cryed vnto thee, and were deliuered: they truſted in thee,
and were not confounded. 6 But I am a worme, and no man; a reproach
of men, and deſpiſed of the people. 7 All they that ſee me, laugh me to
ſcorne: they ſhoote out the lippe, they ſhake the head, ſaying, 8 He truſted
on the Lord, that he would deliuer him: let him deliuer him, ſeeing he
delighted in him. 9 But thou art hee that tooke mee out of the wombe;
thou didſt make me hope, when I was vpon my mothers breaſts. 10 I was
caſt vpon thee from the wombe: thou art my God from my mothers
belly. 11 Be not farre from me, for trouble is neere; for there is none to
helpe. 12 Many bulles haue compaſſed me: ſtrong bulles of Baſhan haue
beſet me round. 13 They gaped vpon me with their mouthes, as a rauening
and a roaring Lyon. 14 I am powred out like water, and all my bones are
out of ioynt: my heart is like waxe, it is melted in the middeſt of my
bowels. 15 My ſtrength is dried vp like a potſheard: and my tongue
cleaueth to my iawes; and thou haſt brought me into the duſt of
death. 16 For dogges haue compaſſed me: the aſſembly of the wicked
haue incloſed me: they pierced my hands and my feete. 17 I may tell all
my bones: they looke and ſtare vpon me. 18 They part my garments
among them, and caſt lots vpon my veſture. 19 But be not thou farre from

mee, O Lord; O my ſtrength, haſt thee to helpe me.20Deliuer my ſoule from the ſword: my darling from the power of the dogge.21Saue me from the lyons mouth: for thou haſt heard me from the hornes of the vnicornes.22I will declare thy name vnto my brethren: in the midſt of the congregation will I praiſe thee.23Yee that feare the Lord, praiſe him; all yee the ſeede of Iacob glorifie him, and feare him all yee the ſeede of Iſrael.24For he hath not deſpiſed, nor abhorred the affliction of the afflicted; neither hath he hid his face from him, but when he cried vnto him, he heard.25My praiſe ſhalbe of thee, in the great congregation: I will pay my vowes, before them that feare him.26The meeke ſhall eate and be ſatiſfied: they ſhall praiſe the Lord that ſeeke him; your heart ſhall liue for euer.27All the ends of the world ſhall remember, and turne vnto the Lord: and all the kinreds of the nations ſhall worſhip before thee.28For the kingdome is the Lords: and he is the gouernour among the nations.29All they that be fat vpon earth ſhall eate and worſhip: all they that goe downe to the duſt ſhall bow before him, and none can keepe aliue his owne ſoule.30A ſeed ſhall ſerue him; it ſhalbe accounted to the Lord for a generation.31They ſhall come, and ſhall declare his righteouſnes vnto a people that ſhalbe borne, that he hath done this.

CHAPTER 231*A Pſalme of Dauid.* The Lord is my ſhepheard, I ſhall not want.2He maketh me to lie downe in greene paſtures: he leadeth mee beſide the ſtill waters.3He reſtoreth my ſoule: he leadeth me in the pathes of righteouſnes, for his names ſake.4Yea though I walke through the valley of the ſhadowe of death, I will feare no euill: for thou art with me, thy rod and thy ſtaffe, they comfort me.5Thou prepareſt a table before me, in the preſence of mine enemies: thou anointeſt my head with oyle, my cuppe runneth ouer.6Surely goodnes and mercie ſhall followe me all the daies of my life: and I will dwell in the houſe of the Lord for euer.

CHAPTER 241*A Pſalme of Dauid.* The earth is the Lords, and the fulneſse thereof; the world, and they that dwell therein.2For he hath founded it vpon the ſeas, and eſtabliſhed it vpon the floods.3Who ſhall aſcend into the hill of the Lord? and who ſhall ſtand in his holy place?4He that hath cleane hands, and a pure heart; who hath not lift vp his ſoule vnto vanitie, nor ſworne deceitfully.5Hee ſhall receiue the bleſſing from the Lord, and righteouſneſſe from the God of his ſaluation.6This is the generation of them that ſeeke him: that ſeeke thy face, O Iacob. Selah.7Lift vp your heads, O yee gates, and be ye lift vp ye euerlaſting doores; and the King of glory ſhall come in.8Who is this king of glory? the Lord ſtrong & mightie, the Lord mighty in battell.9Lift vp your heads, O ye gates, euen lift them vp, ye euerlaſting doores; and the king of glory ſhall come in.10Who is this king of glory? the Lord of hoſtes, he is the king of glory. Selah.

CHAPTER 251*A Pſalme of Dauid.* Vnto thee, O Lord, doe I lift vp my ſoule.2O my God, I truſt in thee, let me not be aſhamed: let not mine enemies triumph ouer me.3Yea let none that waite on thee, be aſhamed: let them bee aſhamed which tranſgreſse without cauſe.4Shewe mee thy wayes, O Lord: teach me thy pathes.5Lead me in thy trueth, and teach me: for thou art the God of my ſaluation, on thee doe I waite all the day.6Remember, O Lord, thy tender mercies, and thy louing kindneſses: for they haue beene euer of old.7Remember not the ſinnes of my youth, nor my tranſgreſſions: according to thy mercie remember thou me, for thy goodneſſe ſake, O Lord.8Good and vpright is the Lord: therefore will hee teach ſinners in the way.9The meeke will he guide in iudgement: and the meeke will he teach his way.10All the pathes of the Lord are mercy and truth: vnto ſuch as keepe his couenant, and his teſtimonies.11For thy names ſake, O Lord, pardon mine iniquitie: for it is great.12What man is he that feareth the Lord? him ſhall he teach in the way that he ſhall chuſe.13His ſoule ſhall dwell at eaſe: and his ſeede ſhall inherite the earth.14The ſecret of the Lord is with them that feare him: and he will ſhew them his couenant.15Mine eyes are euer towards the Lord: for hee ſhall plucke my feete out of the net.16Turne thee vnto me, and haue mercy vpon me: for I am deſolate and afflicted.17The troubles of my heart are inlarged: O bring thou me out of my diſtreſſes.18Looke vpon mine affliction, aud my paine, and forgiue all my ſinnes.19Conſider mine enemies: for they are many, and they hate me with cruell hatred.20O keepe my ſoule and deliuer me: let me not bee aſhamed, for I put my truſt in thee.21Let integritie and vprightneſse preſerueme: for I wait on thee.22Redeeme Iſrael, O God, out of all his troubles.

CHAPTER 261*A Pſalme of Dauid.* Iudge me, O Lord, for I haue walked in mine integritie: I haue truſted alſo in the Lord: therfore I ſhall not ſlide.2Examine me, O Lord, and proue me; try my reines and my heart.3For thy louing kindneſſe is before mine eyes: and I haue walked in thy trueth.4I haue not ſate with vaine perſons, neither will I goe in with diſſemblers.5I haue hated the congregation of euill doers: and will not ſit with the wicked.6I will waſh mine hands in innocencie: ſo will I compaſſe thine Altar, O Lord:7That I may publiſh with the voyce of thankeſgiuing, and tell of all thy wonderous workes.8Lord, I haue loued the habitation of thy houſe, and the place where thine honour dwelleth.9Gather not my ſoule with ſinners, nor my life with bloody men.10In whoſe hands is miſchiefe: and their right hand is full of bribes.11But as for mee, I will walke in mine integritie: redeeme me, and bee mercifull vnto me.12My foot ſtandeth in an euen place: in the congregations will I bleſſe the Lord.

CHAPTER 271*A Pſalme of Dauid.* The Lord is my light, and my ſaluation, whome ſhal I feare? the Lord is the ſtrength of my life, of whō ſhall I be afraid?2When the wicked, euen mine enemies and my foes came vpon me to eat vp my fleſh, they ſtumbled and fell.3Though an hoſt ſhould encampe againſt me, my heart ſhall not feare: though warre ſhould riſe againſt me, in this will I be confident.4One thing haue I deſired of the Lord, that will I ſeeke after: that I may dwel in the houſe of the Lord, all the dayes of my life, to behold the beautie of the Lord, and to inquire in his temple.5For in the time of trouble he ſhall hide me in his pauilion: in the ſecret of his tabernacle ſhall he hide me, hee ſhall ſet me vp vpon a rocke.6And now ſhall mine head be lifted vp aboue mine enemies round about me: therefore will I offer in his tabernacle ſacrifices of ioy, I will ſing, yea, I will ſing praiſes vnto the Lord.7Heare, O Lord, when I crie with my voice: haue mercie alſo vpon mee, and anſwere me.8When thou ſaidſt, Seeke ye my face, my heart ſaid vnto thee, Thy face, Lord, will I ſeeke.9Hide not thy face farre frō me, put not thy ſeruant away in anger: thou haſt bin my helpe, leaue me not, neither forſake me, O God of my ſaluation.10When my father and my mother forſake me, then the Lord will take me vp.11Teach me thy way, O Lord, and leade me in a plaine path, becauſe of mine enemies.12Deliuer me not ouer vnto the will of mine enemies: for falſe witneſſes are riſen vp againſt me, and ſuch as breath out crueltie.13I had fainted, vnleſſe I had beleeued to ſee the goodneſſe of the Lord in the land of the liuing.14Wait on the Lord: be of good courage, and he ſhall ſtrengthen thine heart: wait, I ſay, on the Lord.

CHAPTER 281*A Pſalme of Dauid.* Vnto thee will I cry, O Lord, my rocke, be not ſilent to mee: leſt if thou be ſilent to me, I become like them that goe downe into the pit.2Heare the voyce of my ſupplications, when I cry vnto thee: when I lift vp my handes toward thy holy Oracle.3Draw me not away with the wicked, and with the workers of iniquitie: which ſpeake peace to their neighbors, but miſchiefe is in their hearts.4Giue them according to their deedes, and according to the wickednes of their endeuours: giue them after the worke of their handes, render to them their deſert.5Becauſe they regard not the workes of the Lord, nor the operation of his hands, he ſhal deſtroy them, and not build them vp.6Bleſſed be the Lord, becauſe he hath heard the voyce of my ſupplications.7The Lord is my ſtrength, and my ſhield, my heart truſted in him, and I am helped: therefore my heart greatly reioyceth, and with my ſong will I praiſe him.8The Lord is their ſtrength, and hee is the ſauing ſtrength of his Anointed.9Saue thy people, and bleſſe thine inheritance, feede them alſo, and lift them vp for euer.

CHAPTER 291*A Pſalme of Dauid.* Giue vnto the Lord (O ye mighty) giue vnto the Lord glory and ſtrength.2Giue vnto the Lord the glory due vnto his Name; worſhip the Lord in the beautie of holineſſe.3The voice of the Lord is vpon the waters: the God of glory thundreth, the Lord is vpon many waters.4The voice of the Lord is powerfull; the voyce of the Lord is full of Maieſtie.5The voyce of the Lord breaketh the Cedars: yea, the Lord breaketh the Cedars of Lebanon.6He maketh them alſo to ſkip like a calfe: Lebanon, and Sirion like a yong Unicorne.7The voyce of the Lord diuideth the flames of fire.8The voyce of the Lord ſhaketh the wildernes: the Lord ſhaketh the wilderneſſe of Kadeſh.9The voice of the Lord maketh the hindes to calue, and diſcouereth the forreſts: and in his Temple doeth euery one ſpeake of his glory.10The Lord ſitteth vpon the flood: yea the Lord ſitteth King for euer.11The Lord will giue ſtrength vnto his people; the Lord will bleſſe his people with peace.

CHAPTER 301*A Pſalme, and ſong at the dedication of the houſe of Dauid.* I wil extol thee, O Lord, for thou haſt lifted me vp; and haſt not made my foes to reioyce ouer me.2O Lord my God, I cried vnto thee, and thou haſt healed me.3O Lord, thou haſt brought vp my ſoule from the graue: thou haſt kept me aliue, that I ſhould not goe downe to the pit.4Sing vnto the Lord, (O yee Saints of hiſ) and giue thanks at the remembrance of his holineſſe.5For his anger endureth but a moment; in his fauour is life: weeping may endure for a night, but ioy commeth in the morning.6And in my proſperitie I ſaid, I ſhall neuer be mooued.7Lord, by thy fauour thou haſt made my mountaine to ſtand ſtrong: Thou didſt hide thy face, and I was troubled.8I cried to thee, O Lord: and vnto the Lord I made ſupplication.9What profit is there in my blood, when I goe downe to the pit? Shall the duſt praiſe thee? ſhall it declare thy trueth?10Heare, O Lord, and haue mercie vpon me: Lord be thou my helper.11Thou haſt turned for mee my mourning into dauncing: thou haſt put off my ſackecloth, and girded mee with gladneſſe:12To the end that my glory may ſing prayſe to thee, and not be ſilent: O Lord my God, I will giue thankes vnto thee for euer.

CHAPTER 311*To the chiefe Muſician, A Pſalme of Dauid.* In thee, O Lord, doe I put my truſt, let me neuer be aſhamed: deliuer me in thy righteouſneſſe.2Bowe downe thine eare to me, deliuer me ſpeedily: be thou my ſtrong rocke, for an houſe of defence to ſaue me.3For thou art my rocke and my fortreſe: therfore for thy names ſake lead me, and guide me.4Pull me out of the net, that they haue layd priuily for me: for thou art my ſtrength.5Into thine hand I commit my ſpirit: thou haſt redeemed mee, O Lord God of trueth.6I haue hated them that regard lying vanities: but I truſt in the Lord.7I will be glad, and reioyce in thy mercie: for thou haſt conſidered my trouble; thou haſt knowen my ſoule in aduerſities;8And haſt not ſhut me vp into the hand of the enemie: thou haſt ſet my feete in a large roome.9Haue mercy vpon me, O Lord, for I am in trouble; mine eie is conſumed with griefe, yea my ſoule and my belly.10For my life is ſpent with griefe, and my yeeres with ſighing: my ſtrength faileth, becauſe of mine iniquitie, and my bones are conſumed.11I was a reproch among all mine enemies, but eſpecially among my neighbours, and a feare to mine acquaintance: they that did ſee me without, fled from me.12I am forgotten as a dead man out of minde: I am like a broken veſſell.13For I haue heard the ſlaunder of many, feare was on euery ſide: while they tooke counſell together againſt me, they deuiſed to take away my life.14But I truſted in thee, O Lord: I ſayd, Thou art my God.15My times are in thy hand: deliuer me from the hand of mine enemies, and from them that perſecute me.16Make thy face to ſhine vpon thy ſeruant: ſaue me for thy mercies ſake.17Let mee not be aſhamed, O Lord, for I haue called vpon thee: let the wicked be aſhamed, and let them be ſilent in the graue.18Let the lying lippes be put to ſilence: which ſpeake grieuous things proudly and contemptuouſly againſt the righteous.19O how great is thy goodneſe, which thou haſt layd vp for them that feare thee: which thou haſt wrought for them that truſt in thee, before the ſonnes of men!20Thou ſhalt hide them in the ſecret of thy preſence, from the pride of man: thou ſhalt keepe them ſecretly in a pauilion, from the ſtrife of tongues.21Bleſſed be the Lord; for hee hath ſhewed me his maruellous kindneſe, in a ſtrong citie.22For I ſayd in my haſte, I am cut off from before thine eies: Neuertheleſſe thou heardeſt the voice of my ſupplications, when I cryed vnto thee.23O loue the Lord, all yee his Saints: for the Lord preſerueth the faithfull, and plentifully rewardeth the proud doer.24Be of good courage, and hee ſhall ſtrenghten your heart: all ye that hope in the Lord.

CHAPTER 321*A Pſalme of Dauid, Maſchil.* Bleſſed is he whoſe tranſgreſſion is forgiuen, whoſe ſinne is couered.2Bleſſed is the man vnto whom the Lord imputeth not iniquitie: and in whoſe ſpirit there is no guile.3When I kept ſilence, my bones waxed old; through my roaring all the day long.4For day and night thy hand was heauy vpon me: my moiſture is turned into the drought of ſummer. Selah.5I acknowledged my ſin vnto thee, and mine iniquitie haue I not hid: I ſaid, I will confeſe my tranſgreſſions vnto the Lord; and thou forgaueſt the iniquitie of my ſinne. Selah.6For this ſhall euery one that is godly pray vnto thee, in a time when thou mayeſt bee found: ſurely in the floods of great waters, they ſhall not come nigh vnto him.7Thou art my hiding place, thou ſhalt preſeruemee from trouble: thou ſhalt compaſſe me about with ſongs of deliuerance. Selah.8I will inſtruct thee, and teach thee in the way which thou ſhalt goe: I will guide thee with mine eye.9Be yee not as the horſe, or as the mule which haue no vnderſtanding: whoſe mouth muſt be held in with bit and bridle, leaſt they come neere vnto thee.10Many ſorrowes ſhall be to the wicked: but he that truſteth in the Lord, mercy ſhall compaſſe him about.11Be glad in the Lord, and reioyce yee righteous: and ſhout for ioy all ye that are vpright in heart.

CHAPTER 331Reioyce in the Lord, O yee righteous: for prayſe is comely for the vpright.2Praiſe the Lord with harp: ſing vnto him with the Pſalterie, and an inſtrument of ten ſtrings.3Sing vnto him a new ſong; play ſkilfully with a loud noiſe.4For the word of the Lord is right: and all his workes are done in trueth.5Hee loueth righteouſneſſe and iudgement: the earth is ful of the goodneſſe of the Lord.6By the word of the Lord were the heauens made: and all the hoſt of them, by the breath of his mouth.7He gathereth the waters of the ſea together, as an heape: he layeth vp the depth in ſtorehouſes.8Let all the earth feare the Lord: let all the inhabitants of the world ſtand in awe of him.9For he ſpake, and it was done: he commanded, and it ſtood faſt.10The Lord bringeth the counſell of the heathen to nought: he maketh the deuices of the people, of none effect.11The counſaile of the Lord ſtandeth for euer, the thoughts of his heart to all generations.12Bleſſed is the nation, whoſe God is the Lord: and the people, whom he hath choſen for his owne inheritance.13The Lord looketh from heauen: he beholdeth all the ſonnes of men.14From the place of his habitation, he looketh vpon all the inhabitants of the earth.15He faſhioneth their hearts alike: he conſidereth all their workes.16There is no king ſaued by the multitude of an hoſte: a mightie man is not deliuered by much ſtrength.17An horſe is a vaine thing for ſafetie: neither ſhall he deliuer any by his great ſtrength.18Behold, the eye of the Lord is vpon them that feare him: vpon them that hope in his mercy:19To deliuer their ſoule from death, and to keepe them aliue in famine.20Our ſoule waiteth for the Lord: he is our helpe, and our ſhield.21For our heart ſhall reioyce in him: becauſe we haue truſted in his holy name.22Let thy mercy (O Lord) be vpon vs: according as we hope in thee.

CHAPTER 341*A Pſalme of Dauid, when he changed his behauiour before Abimelech: who droue him away & he departed.* I will bleſſe the Lord at all times: his prayſe ſhall continually bee in my mouth.2My ſoule ſhall make her boaſt in the Lord: the humble ſhall heare thereof, and be glad.3O magnifie the Lord with me, and let vs exalt his name together.4I ſought the Lord, and hee heard me; and deliuered mee from all my feares.5They looked vnto him, and were lightned: and their faces were not aſhamed.6This poore man cried, and the Lord heard him; and ſaued him out of all his troubles.7The Angel of the Lord encampeth round about them that feare him, and deliuereth them.8O taſte and ſee that the Lord is good: bleſſed is the man that truſteth in him.9O feare the Lord yee his Saints: for there is no want to them that feare him.10The young lyons doe lacke, and ſuffer hunger: but they that ſeeke the Lord, ſhall not want any good thing.11Come yee children, hearken vnto me: I will teach you the feare of the Lord.12What man is hee that deſireth life; and loueth many dayes, that he may ſee good?13Keepe thy tongue from euill, and thy lippes from ſpeaking guile.14Depart from euill, and doe good: ſeeke peace and purſue it.15The eies of the Lord are vpon the righteous; and his eares are open vnto their crie.16The face of the Lord is againſt them that doe euill; to cut off the remembrance of them from the earth.17The righteous crie, and the Lord heareth; and deliuereth them out of all their troubles.18The Lord is nigh vnto them that are of a broken heart: and ſaueth ſuch as be of a contrite ſpirit.19Many are the afflictions of the righteous: but the Lord deliuereth him out of them all.20He keepeth all his bones: not one of them is broken.21Euill ſhall ſlay the wicked: and they that hate the righteous ſhalbe deſolate.22The Lord redeemech the ſoule of his ſeruants: and none of them that truſt in him, ſhalbe deſolate.

CHAPTER 351*A Pſalme of Dauid.* Plead my cauſe (O Lord) with them that ſtriue with mee: fight againſt them that fight againſt me.2Take hold of ſhield and buckler, and ſtand vp for mine helpe.3Draw out alſo the ſpeare, and ſtop the way againſt them that perſecute me: ſay vnto my ſoule, I am thy ſaluation.4Let them be confounded and put to ſhame that ſeeke after my ſoule: let them be turned backe and brought to confuſion, that deuiſe my hurt.5Let them be as chaffe before the wind: and let the Angel of the Lord chaſe them.6Let their way be darke and ſlippery, and let the Angel of the Lord perſecute them.7For without cauſe haue they hid for me their net in a pit, which without cauſe they haue digged for my ſoule.8Let deſtruction come vpon him at vnawares, and let his net that hee hath hid, catch himſelfe: into that very deſtruction let him fall.9And my ſoule ſhalbe ioyfull in the Lord: it ſhall reioyce in his ſaluation.10All my bones ſhall ſay, Lord, who is like vnto thee which deliuereſt the poore from him that is too ſtrong for him, yea the poore and the needy, from him that ſpoileth him?11Falſe witneſſes did riſe vp they layd to my charge things that I knew not.12They rewarded mee euill for good, to the ſpoiling of my ſoule.13But as for me, when they were ſicke, my clothing was ſack-cloth: I humbled my ſoule with faſting, and my prayer returned into mine owne boſome.14I behaued my ſelfe as though he had bene my friend, or brother: I bowed downe heauily, as one that mourneth for his mother.15But in mine aduerſitie they reioyced, and gathered themſelues together: yea, the abiects gathered themſelues together againſt me, & I knew it not, they did teare me, and ceaſed not,16With hypocriticall mockers in feaſts: they gnaſhed vpon mee with their teeth.17Lord, how long wilt thou looke on? reſcue my ſoule from their deſtructions, my darling from the lyons.18I will giue thee thankes in the great congregation: I will praiſe thee among much people.19Let not them that are mine enemies wrongfully, reioyce ouer me: neither let them winke with the eye, that hate me without a cauſe.20For they ſpeake not peace: but they deuiſe deceitfull matters againſt them that are quiet in the land.21Yea they opened their mouth wide againſt me, and ſaide, Aha, Aha, our eye hath ſeene it.22This thou haſt ſeene (O Lord) keepe not ſilence: O Lord be not farre from me.23Stirre vp thy ſelfe and awake to my iudgement, euen vnto my cauſe, my God and my Lord.24Iudge me O Lord my God, according to thy righteouſneſſe, and let them not reioyce ouer me.25Let them not ſay in their hearts, Ah, ſo would we haue it: let them not ſay, We haue ſwallowed him vp.26Let them be aſhamed and brought to confuſion together, that reioyce at mine hurt: let them bee cloathed with ſhame and diſhonour, that magnifie themſelues againſt me.27Let them ſhoute for ioy, and bee glad that fauour my righteous cauſe: yea let them ſay continually, Let the Lord bee magnified, which hath pleaſure in the proſperity of his ſeruant28And my tongue ſhall ſpeake of thy righteouſneſſe, and of thy praiſe all the day long.

CHAPTER 361*To the chiefe muſician, A Pſalme of Dauid, the ſeruant of the Lord.* The tranſgreſſion of the wicked ſaith within my heart, that there is no feare of God before his eyes.2For he flatterech himſelfe in his owne eyes, vntill his iniquitie be found to be hatefull.3The words of his mouth are iniquitie and deceit: he hath left off to bee wiſe, and to doe good.4Hee deuiſeth miſchiefe vpon his bed, he ſetteth himſelfe in a way that is not good; he abhorreth not euill.5Thy mercie (O Lord) is in the heauens; and thy faithfulneſse reacheth vnto the cloudes.6Thy righteouſneſſe is like the great mountaines; thy iudgements are a great deepe; O Lord, thou preſerueſt man and beaſt.7How excellent is thy louing kindneſse, O God! therefore the children of men put their truſt vnder the ſhadowe of thy wings.8They ſhall be abundantly ſatiſfied with the fatneſſe of thy houſe: and thou ſhalt make them drinke of the riuer of thy pleaſures.9For with thee is the fountaine of life: in thy light ſhall we ſee light.10O continue thy louing kindneſſe vnto them that know thee; and thy righteouſneſſe to the vpright in heart.11Let not the foot of pride come againſt me, and let not the hand of the wicked remoue me.12There are the workers of iniquitie fallen: they are caſt downe, and ſhal not be able to riſe.

CHAPTER 371*A Pſalme of Dauid.* Fret not thy ſelfe becauſe of euill doers, neither bee thou enuious againſt the workers of iniquitie.2For they ſhall ſoone be cut downe like the graſſe; and wither as the greene herbe.3Truſt in the Lord, and do good, ſo ſhalt thou dwell in the land, and verely thou ſhalt be fed.4Delight thy ſelfe alſo in the Lord; and he ſhall giue thee the deſires of thine heart.5Commit thy way vnto the Lord: truſt alſo in him, and he ſhall bring it to paſſe.6And he ſhall bring forth thy righteouſnes as the light, and thy iudgement as the noone day.7Reſt in the Lord, and wait patiently for him: fret not thy ſelfe becauſe of him who proſpereth in his way, becauſe of the man who bringeth wicked deuices to paſſe.8Ceaſe from anger, and forſake wrath: fret not thy ſelfe in any wiſe to doe euill.9For euil doers ſhall be cut off: but thoſe that waite vpon the Lord, they ſhall inherite the earth.10For yet a little while, and the wicked ſhall not bee: yea, thou ſhalt diligently conſider his place, and it ſhall not be.11But the meeke ſhall inherite the earth: and ſhall delight themſelues in the abundance of peace.12The wicked plotteth againſt the iuſt, and gnaſheth vpon him with his teeth.13The Lord ſhall laugh at him: for he ſeeth that his day is comming.14The wicked haue drawen out the ſword, and haue bent their bow to caſt downe the poore and needy, and to ſlay ſuch as be of vpright conuerſation.15Their ſword ſhall enter into their owne heart, and their bowes ſhall be broken.16A little that a righteous man hath, is better then the riches of many wicked.17For the armes of the wicked ſhall be broken: but the Lord vpholdeth the righteous.18The Lord knoweth the dayes of the vpright: and their inheritance ſhall be for euer.19They ſhall not be aſhamed in the euill time: and in the dayes of famine they ſhalbe ſatiſfied.20But the wicked ſhall periſh, and the enemies of the Lord ſhall be as the fat of lambes: they ſhall conſume: into ſmoke ſhall they conſume away.21The wicked borroweth, and payeth not againe: but the righteous ſheweth mercy, and giueth.22For ſuch as be bleſſed of him, ſhall inherite the earth: and they that be curſed of him, ſhalbe cut off.23The ſteps of a good man are ordered by the Lord: and he delighteth in his way.24Though hee fall, he ſhall not be vtterly caſt downe: for the Lord vpholdeth him with his hand.25I haue bene yong, and now am old; yet haue I not ſeene the righteous forſaken, nor his ſeede begging bread.26He is euer mercifull, and lendeth: and his ſeede is bleſſed.27Depart from euill, and doe good; and dwell for euermore.28For the Lord loueth iudgement, and forſaketh not his Saints, they are preſerued for euer: but the ſeed of the wicked ſhall be cut off.29The righteous ſhall inherite the land, and dwell therein for euer.30The mouth of the righteous ſpeaketh wiſedome; and his tongue talketh of iudgement.31The Law of his God is in his heart: none of his ſteps ſhall ſlide.32The wicked watcheth the righteous, and ſeeketh to ſlay him.33The Lord will not leaue him in his hand, nor condemne him when he is iudged.34Wait on the Lord, and keepe his way, and he ſhall exalt thee to inherit the land: when the wicked are cut off, thou ſhalt ſee it.35I haue ſeene the wicked in great power: and ſpreading himſelfe like a greene bay tree.36Yet he paſſed away, and loe he was not: yea, I ſought him, but hee could not be found.37Marke the perfect man, and behold the vpright: for the end of that man is peace.38But the tranſgreſsours ſhall be deſtroyed together: the end of the wicked ſhalbe cut off.39But the ſaluation of the righteous is of the Lord: he is their ſtrength in the time of trouble.40And the Lord ſhall helpe them and deliuer them: he ſhall deliuer them from the wicked, and ſaue them becauſe they truſt in him.

CHAPTER 381*A Pſalme of Dauid, to bring to remembrance.* O Lord, rebuke me not in thy wrath: neither chaſten me in thy hot diſpleaſure.2For thine arrowes ſticke faſt in me; and thy hand preſseth me ſore.3There is no ſoundneſse in my fleſh, becauſe of thine anger: neither is there any reſt in my bones, becauſe of my ſinne.4For mine iniquities are gone ouer mine head: as an heauy burden, they are too heauie for me.5My wounds ſtinke, and are corrupt: becauſe of my fooliſhneſse.6I am troubled, I am bowed downe greatly; I goe mourning all the day long.7For my loynes are filled with a loathſome diſeaſe: and there is no ſoundneſse in my fleſh.8I am feeble and ſore broken; I haue roared by reaſon of the diſquietneſse of my heart.9Lord, all my deſire is before thee: and my groning is not hid from thee.10My heart panteth, my ſtrength faileth me: as for the light of mine eies, it alſo is gone from me.11My louers and my friends ſtand a loofe from my ſore: and my kinſmen ſtand a farre off.12They alſo that ſeeke after my life, lay ſnares for me: and they that ſeeke my hurt, ſpeake miſchieuous things, and imagine deceits all the day long.13But I, as a deafe man, heard not; and I was as a dumbe man that openeth not his mouth.14Thus I was as a man that heareth not; and in whoſe mouth are no reproofes.15For in thee, O Lord, doe I hope: thou wilt heare, O Lord my God.16For I ſaid, heare me, leaſt otherwiſe they ſhould reioyce ouer me: when my foot ſlippeth, they magnifie themſelues againſt me.17For I am ready to halt, and my ſorrow is continually before me.18For I will declare mine iniquitie; I will be ſory for my ſinne.19But mine enemies are liuely, and they are ſtrong: and they that hate mee wrongfully, are multiplied.20They alſo that render euill for good, are mine aduerſaries: becauſe I follow the thing that good is.21Forſake me not, O Lord: O my God, be not farre from me.22Make haſte to helpe mee, O Lord my ſaluation.

CHAPTER 391*To the chiefe Muſician, euen to Ieduthun, A Pſalme of Dauid.* I ſayd, I will take heede to my waies, that I ſinne not with my tongue: I will keepe my mouth with a bridle, while the wicked is before me.2I was dumbe with ſilence, I held my peace, euen from good, and my ſorrow was ſtirred.3My heart was hot within mee, while I was muſing the fire burned: then ſpake I with my tongue.4Lord, make me to know mine end, and the meaſure of my dayes, what it is: that I may know how fraile I am.5Behold, thou haſt made my dayes as an hand breadth, and mine age is as nothing before thee: verily euery man at his beſt ſtate is altogether vanitie. Selah.6Surely euery man walketh in a vaine ſhew: ſurely they are diſquieted in vaine: he heapeth vp riches, and knoweth not who ſhall gather them.7And now Lord, what wait I for? my hope is in thee.8Deliuer me from all my tranſgreſſions: make mee not the reproch of the fooliſh.9I was dumbe, I opened not my mouth; becauſe thou diddeſt it.10Remooue thy ſtroke away from mee: I am conſumed by the blowe of thine hand.11When thou with rebukes doeſt correct man for iniquitie, thou makeſt his beautie to conſume away like a moth: ſurely euery man is vanitie. Selah.12Heare my prayer, O Lord, and giue eare vnto my crie, hold not thy peace at my teares: for I am a ſtraunger with thee, and a ſoiourner, as all my fathers were.13O ſpare me, that I may recouer ſtrength: before I goe hence, and be no more.

CHAPTER 401*To the chiefe Muſician, A Pſalme of Dauid.* I waited patiently for the Lord, and he inclined vnto me, and heard my crie.2He brought me vp alſo out of an horrible pit, out of the mirie clay, and ſet my feete vpon a rock, and eſtabliſhed my goings.3And he hath put a new ſong in my mouth, euen praiſe vnto our God: many ſhall ſee it, and feare, and ſhall truſt in the Lord.4Bleſſed is that man that maketh the Lord his truſte: and reſpecteth not the proud, nor ſuch as turne aſide to lies.5Many, O Lord my God; are thy wonderfull workes which thou haſt done, and thy thoughts, which are to vs ward: they cannot be reckoned vp in order vnto thee: if I would declare and ſpeake of them, they are moe then can be numbred.6Sacrifice and offering thou didſt not deſire, mine eares haſt thou opened: burnt offering and ſinne-offering haſt thou not required.7Then ſayd I, Loe, I come: in the volume of the booke it is written of me:8I delight to doe thy will, O my God: yea thy lawe is within my heart.9I haue preached righteouſneſſe in the great congregation: loe, I haue not refrained my lippes, O Lord, thou knoweſt.10I haue not hid thy righteouſneſſe within my heart, I haue declared thy faithfulneſse and thy ſaluation: I haue not concealed thy louing kindneſse, and thy truth, from the great congregation.11With-hold not thou thy tender mercies from me, O Lord: let thy louing kindneſse, and thy trueth continually preſerueme.12For innumerable euils haue compaſſed me about, mine iniquities haue taken hold vpon me, ſo that I am not able to looke vp: they are moe then the haires of mine head, therefore my heart faileth me.13Be pleaſed, O Lord, to deliuer me: O Lord, make haſte to helpe me.14Let them be aſhamed and confounded together, that ſeeke after my ſoule to deſtroy it: let them be driuen backward, and put to ſhame, that wiſh me euill.15Let them be deſolate, for a reward on their ſhame, that ſay vnto me, Aha, aha!16Let all thoſe that ſeeke thee, reioyce and bee glad in thee: let ſuch as loue thy ſaluation, ſay continually, The Lord be magnified.17But I am poore and needy, yet the Lord thinketh vpon me: thou art my helpe and my deliuerer, make no tarrying, O my God.

CHAPTER 411*To the chiefe Muſician. A Pſalme of Dauid.* Bleſſed is he that conſidereth the poore; the Lord will deliuer him in time of trouble.2The Lord will preſeruehim, and keepe him aliue, and he ſhall be bleſſed vpon the earth; and thou wilt not deliuer him vnto the will of his enemies.3The Lord will ſtrengthen him vpon the bed of languiſhing: thou wilt make all his bed in his ſickneſse.4I ſayd, Lord be mercifull vnto me, heale my ſoule, for I haue ſinned againſt thee.5Mine enemies ſpeake euill of me: when ſhall hee die, and his name periſh?6And if hee come to ſee me, he ſpeaketh vanity: his heart gathereth iniquitie to it ſelfe, when he goeth abroad, he telleth it.7All that hate me, whiſper together againſt me; againſt me doe they deuiſe my hurt.8An euill diſeaſe, ſay they, cleaueth faſt vnto him; and now that he lyeth, he ſhall riſe vp no more.9Yea mine owne familiar friend in whom I truſted, which did eate of my bread, hath lift vp his heele againſt me.10But thou, O Lord, be mercifull vnto mee, and raiſe me vp that I may requite them.11By this I know that thou fauoureſt me: becauſe mine enemie doeth not triumph ouer me.12And as for me, thou vpholdeſt me in mine integritie; and ſetteſt me before thy face for euer.13Bleſſed bee the Lord God of Iſrael, from euerlaſting, and to euerlaſting. Amen, and Amen.

CHAPTER 421*To the chiefe Muſician, Maſchil, for the ſonnes of Korah.* As the Hart panteth after the water brookes, ſo panteth my ſoule after thee, O God.2My ſoule thirſteth for God, for the liuing God: when ſhall I come and appeare before God?3My teares haue bene my meate day and night; while they continually ſay vnto me, Where is thy God?4When I remember theſe things, I powre out my ſoule in mee; for I had gone with the multitude, I went with them to the houſe of God; with the voyce of ioy and praiſe, with a multitude that kept holy day.5Why art thou caſt downe, O my ſoule, and why art thou diſquieted in me? hope thou in God, for I ſhall yet praiſe him for the helpe of his countenance.6O my God, my ſoule is caſt downe within me: therefore will I remember thee from the land of Iordane, and of the Hermonites, from the hill Miſar.7Deepe calleth vnto deepe at the noyſe of thy water-ſpouts: all thy waues, and thy billowes are gone ouer me.8Yet the Lord will command his louing kindnes in the day time, and in the night his ſong ſhalbe with me, and my prayer vnto the God of my life.9I will ſay vnto God, My rocke, why haſt thou forgotten me? why goe I mourning, becauſe of the oppreſſion of the enemy?10As with a ſword in my bones, mine enemies reproch mee: while they ſay dayly vnto me, Where is thy God?11Why art thou caſt downe, O my ſoule? and why art thou diſquieted within me? hope thou in God, for I ſhall yet praiſe him, who is the health of my countenance, and my God.

CHAPTER 431Iudge mee, O God, and plead my cauſe againſt an vngodly nation; O deliuer me from the deceitfull and vniuſt man.2For thou art the God of my ſtrength, why doeſt thou caſt me off? why goe I mourning becauſe of the oppreſſion of the enemy?3O ſend out thy light & thy trueth; let them leade mee, let them bring mee vnto thy holy hill, and to thy Tabernacles.4Then will I goe vnto the Altar of God, vnto God my exceeding ioy: yea vpon the harpe will I praiſe thee, O God, my God.5Why art thou caſt downe, O my ſoule? and why art thou diſquieted within me? hope in God, for I ſhall yet praiſe him, who is the health of my countenance, and my God.

CHAPTER 441*To the chiefe Muſician for the ſonnes of Korah.* Wee haue heard with our eares, O God, our fathers haue told vs, what worke thou didſt in their dayes, in the times of old.2How thou didſt driue out the heathen with thy hand, & plantedſt them; how thou didſt afflict the people, and caſt them out.3For they got not the land in poſſeſſion by their owne ſword, neither did their owne arme ſaue them: but thy right hand, and thine arme, and the light of thy countenance, becauſe thou hadſt a fauour vnto them.4Thou art my King, O God: command deliuerances for Iacob.5Through thee will wee puſh downe our enemies: through thy Name will wee tread them vnder that riſe vp againſt vs.6For I will not truſt in my bow, neither ſhall my ſword ſaue me.7But thou haſt ſaued vs from our enemies, and haſt put them to ſhame that hated vs.8In God we boaſt all the day long: and praiſe thy Name for euer. Selah.9But thou haſt caſt off and put vs to ſhame; and goeſt not forth with our armies.10Thou makeſt vs to turne backe from the enemie: and they which hate vs, ſpoile for themſelues.11Thou haſt giuen vs like ſheepe appointed for meate: and haſt ſcattered vs among the heathen.12Thou ſelleſt thy people for nought, and doeſt not increaſe thy wealth by their price.13Thou makeſt vs a reproch to our neighbours, a ſcorne and a deriſion to them that are round about vs.14Thou makeſt vs a by-word among the heathen: a ſhaking of the head among the people.15My confuſion is continually before me, and the ſhame of my face hath couered me.16For the voice of him that reproacheth, and blaſphemeth: by reaſon of the enemie and auenger.17All this is come vpon vs; yet haue wee not forgotten thee, neither haue we dealt falſly in thy couenant.18Our heart is not turned backe: neither haue our ſteps declined from thy way,19Though thou haſt ſore broken vs in the place of dragons, and couered vs with the ſhadow of death.20If wee haue forgotten the name of our God, or ſtretched out our hands to a ſtrange God:21Shall not God ſearch this out? for he knoweth the ſecrets of the heart.22Yea for thy ſake are wee killed all the day long: wee are counted as ſheepe for the ſlaughter.23Awake, why ſleepeſt thou, O Lord? Ariſe, caſt vs not off for euer.24Wherefore hideſt thou thy face? and forgetteſt our affliction, and our oppreſſion?25For our ſoule is bowed downe to the duſt; our belly cleaueth vnto the earth.26Ariſe for our helpe, and redeeme vs for thy mercies ſake.

CHAPTER 451*To the chiefe Muſician vpon Shoſhannim, for the ſonnes of Korah, Maſchil: a ſong of loues.* My heart is inditing a good matter: I ſpeake of the things which I haue made, touching the King: my tongue is the penne of a ready writer.2Thou art fairer then the children of men: grace is powred into thy lips: therfore God hath bleſſed thee for euer.3Gird thy ſword vpon thy thigh, O moſt mightie: with thy glory and thy maieſtie.4And in thy maieſtie ride proſperouſly, becauſe of trueth and meekenes, and righteouſneſſe: and thy right hand ſhall teach thee terrible things.5Thine arrowes are ſharpe in the heart of the Kings enemies; whereby the people fall vnder thee.6Thy throne (O God) is for euer and euer: the ſcepter of thy kingdome is a right ſcepter.7Thou loueſt righteouſneſſe, and hateſt wickedneſſe: therefore God, thy God, hath anointed thee with the oyle of gladneſſe aboue thy fellowes.8All thy garments ſmell of myrrhe, and aloes, and caſsia: out of the Iuorie palaces, whereby they haue made thee glad.9Kings daughters were among thy honourable women: vpon thy right hand did ſtand the Queene in golde of Ophir.10Hearken (O daughter) and conſider, and incline thine eare; forget alſo thine owne people, and thy fathers houſe.11So ſhall the king greatly deſire thy beautie: for he is thy Lord, and worſhip thou him.12And the daughter of Tyre ſhall be there with a gift, euen the rich among the people ſhall intreate thy fauour.13The kings daughter is all glorious within; her clothing is of wrought gold.14She ſhall bee brought vnto the king in raiment of needle worke: the virgins her companions that followe her, ſhall be brought vnto thee.15With gladneſſe and reioycing ſhall they be brought: they ſhall enter into the kings palace.16In ſtead of thy fathers ſhall bee thy children, whom thou mayeſt make princes in all the earth.17I will make thy name to bee remembred in all generations: therefore ſhall the people praiſe thee for euer and euer.

CHAPTER 461*To the chiefe Muſician for the ſonnes of Korah, a ſong vpon Alamoth.* God is our refuge and ſtrength: a very preſent helpe in trouble.2Therfore will not we feare, though the earth be remoued: and though the mountaines be caried into the midſt of the ſea.3Though the waters thereof roare, and be troubled, though the mountaines ſhake with the ſwelling thereof. Selah.4There is a riuer, the ſtreames wherof ſhall make glad the citie of God: the holy place of the Tabernacles of the moſt High.5God is in the midſt of her: ſhe ſhal not be moued; God ſhall helpe her, and that right early.6The heathen raged, the kingdomes were mooued: he vttered his voyce, the earth melted.7The Lord of hoſts is with vs; the God of Iacob is our refuge. Selah.8Come, behold the workes of the Lord, what deſolations hee hath made in the earth.9He maketh warres to ceaſe vnto the end of the earth: hee breaketh the bow, and cutteth the ſpeare in ſunder, he burneth the chariot in the fire.10Be ſtil, and know that I am God: I will bee exalted among the heathen, I will be exalted in the earth.11The Lord of hoſts is with vs; the God of Iacob is our refuge. Selah.

CHAPTER 471*To the chiefe muſician, a pſalme for the ſonnes of Korah.* O Clap your hands (all ye people:) ſhoute vnto God with the voyce of triumph:2For the Lord moſt high is terrible; he is a great King ouer all the earth.3Hee ſhall ſubdue the people vnder vs, and the nations vnder our feet.4He ſhall chuſe our inheritance for vs, the excellencie of Iacob whom hee loued. Selah.5God is gone vp with a ſhout, the Lord with the ſound of a trumpet.6Sing praiſes to God, ſing praiſes: ſing praiſes vnto our King, ſing praiſes.7For God is the King of all the earth, ſing ye praiſes with vnderſtanding.8God reigneth ouer the heathen: God ſitteth vpon the throne of his holineſſe.9The princes of the people are gathered together, euen the people of the God of Abraham: for the ſhields of the earth belong vnto God: hee is greatly exalted.

CHAPTER 481*A ſong, and Pſalme for the ſonnes of Korah.* Great is the Lord, and greatly to bee praiſed in the citie of our God, in the mountaine of his holineſſe.2Beautifull for ſituation, the ioy of the whole earth is mount Sion, on the ſides of the North, the citie of the great King.3God is knowen in her palaces for a refuge.4For loe, the kings were aſſembled: they paſſed by together.5They ſawe it, and ſo they marueiled, they were troubled and haſted away.6Feare tooke holde vpon them there, and paine, as of a woman in trauaile.7Thou breakeſt the ſhips of Tarſhiſh with an Eaſt wind.8As we haue heard, ſo haue wee ſeene in the citie of the Lord of hoſts, in the citie of our God, God will eſtabliſh it for euer. Selah,9Wee haue thought of thy louing kindneſe, O God, in the middeſt of thy Temple.10According to thy Name, O God, ſo is thy praiſe vnto the endes of the earth: thy right hand is full of righteouſneſſe.11Let mount Sion reioyce, let the daughters of Iudah be glad, becauſe of thy iudgements.12Walke about Sion, and goe round about her: tell the towres thereof.13Marke yee well her bulwarkes, conſider her palaces; that yee may tell it to the generation following.14For this God is our God for euer, and euer; he will be our guide euen vnto death.

CHAPTER 491*To the chiefe Muſician, a Pſalme for the ſonnes of Korah.* Heare this, all yee people, giue eare all yee inhabitants of the world:2Both low, and high, rich and poore together.3My mouth ſhall ſpeake of wiſedome: and the meditation of my heart ſhalbe of vnderſtanding.4I will incline mine eare to a parable; I will open my darke ſaying vpon the harpe.5Wherefore ſhould I feare in the daies of euill, when the iniquitie of my heeles ſhall compaſſe me about?6They that truſt in their wealth, and boaſt themſelues in the multitude of their riches:7None of them can by any meanes redeeme his brother, nor giue to God a ranſome for him:8(For the redemption of their ſoule is precious, and it ceaſeth for euer.)9That he ſhould ſtill liue for euer, and not ſee corruption.10For he ſeeth that wiſe men die, likewiſe the foole, and the brutiſh perſon periſh, and leaue their wealth to others.11Their inward thought is, that their houſes ſhall continue for euer, and their dwelling places to all generations; they call their lands after their owne names.12Neuertheleſſe man being in honour abideth not: he is like the beaſtes that periſh.13This their way is their follie; yet their poſteritie approue their ſayings. Selah.14Like ſheepe they are layd in the graue, death ſhall feede on them; and the vpright ſhall haue dominion ouer them in the morning, and their beauty ſhall conſume in the graue, from their dwelling.15But God will redeeme my ſoule from the power of the graue; for he ſhall receiue me. Selah.16Be not thou afraid when one is made rich, when the glory of his houſe is increaſed.17For when he dieth, he ſhall carry nothing away: his glory ſhall not deſcend after him.18Though whiles he liued, he bleſſed his ſoule: and men will praiſe thee, when thou doeſt well to thy ſelfe.19Hee ſhall goe to the generation of his fathers, they ſhall neuer ſee light.20Man that is in honour and vnderſtandeth not, is like the beaſts that periſh.

CHAPTER 501*A Pſalme of Aſaph.* The mightie God, euen the Lord hath ſpoken, and called the earth from the riſing of the ſunne, vnto the going downe thereof.2Out of Sion the perfection of beautie, God hath ſhined.3Our God ſhall come, and ſhall not keepe ſilence: a fire ſhall deuoure before him, and it ſhalbe very tempeſtuous round about him.4He ſhall call to the heauens from aboue, and to the earth, that hee may iudge his people.5Gather my Saints together vnto mee: thoſe that haue made a couenant with me, by ſacrifice.6And the heauens ſhall declare his righteouſnes; for God is iudge himſelfe. Selah.7Heare, O my people, and I will ſpeake, O Iſrael, and I will teſtifie againſt thee; I am God, euen thy God.8I will not reproue thee for thy ſacrifices, or thy burnt offerings, to haue bene continually before me.9I will take no bullocke out of thy houſe, nor hee goates out of thy folds.10For euery beaſt of the forreſt is mine, and the cattell vpon a thouſand hilles.11I know all the foules of the mountaines: and the wild beaſts of the field are mine.12If I were hungry, I would not tell thee, for the world is mine, and the fulneſe thereof.13Will I eate the fleſh of bulles, or drinke the blood of goats?14Offer vnto God thankeſgiuing, and pay thy vowes vnto the moſt high.15And call vpon mee in the day of trouble; I will deliuer thee, and thou ſhalt glorifie me.16But vnto the wicked God ſaith, What haſt thou to doe, to declare my Statutes, or that thou ſhouldeſt take my Couenant in thy mouth?17Seeing thou hateſt inſtruction, and caſteſt my words behinde thee.18When thou ſaweſt a thiefe, then thou conſentedſt with him, and haſt bene partaker with adulterers.19Thou giueſt thy mouth to euill, and thy tongue frameth deceit.20Thou ſitteſt and ſpeakeſt againſt thy brother; thou ſlandereſt thine owne mothers ſonne.21Theſe things haſt thou done, and I kept ſilence: thou thoughteſt that I was altogether ſuch a one as thy ſelfe: but I will reproue thee, and ſet them in order before thine eyes.22Now conſider this, ye that forget God, leſt I teare you in pieces, and there be none to deliuer.23Who ſo offereth praiſe, glorifieth me: and to him that ordereth his conuerſation aright, will I ſhew the ſaluation of God.

CHAPTER 511*To the chiefe Muſician. A Pſalme of Dauid, when Nathan the Prophet came vnto him, after hee had gone in to Bath-ſheba.* Haue mercie vpon mee, O God, according to thy louing kindneſse: according vnto the multitude of thy tender mercies blot out my tranſgreſſions.2Waſh mee throughly from mine iniquitie, and clenſe me from my ſinne.3For I acknowledge my tranſgreſſions: and my ſinne is euer before mee.4Againſt thee, thee onely haue I ſinned, and done this euill in thy ſight: that thou mighteſt bee iuſtified when thou ſpeakeſt, and be cleare when thou iudgeſt.5Behold, I was ſhapen in iniquitie: and in ſinne did my mother conceiue me.6Behold, thou deſireſt trueth in the inward parts: and in the hidden part thou ſhalt make me to know wiſedome.7Purge me with hyſſope, and I ſhalbe cleane: waſh me, and I ſhall be whiter then ſnow.8Make mee to heare ioy and gladneſſe: that the bones which thou haſt broken, may reioyce.9Hide thy face from my ſinnes; and blot out all mine iniquities.10Create in mee a cleane heart, O God; and renew a right ſpirit within mee.11Caſt mee not away from thy preſence; and take not thy holy Spirit from me.12Reſtore vnto me the ioy of thy ſaluation: and vphold mee with thy free Spirit.13Then will I teach tranſgreſsours thy wayes, and ſinners ſhalbe conuerted vnto thee.14Deliuer mee from blood-guiltineſſe, O God, thou God of my ſaluation: and my tongue ſhall ſing alowd of thy righteouſneſſe.15O Lord open thou my lips, and my mouth ſhall ſhew foorth thy praiſe.16For thou deſireſt not ſacrifice: elſe would I giue it: thou delighteſt not in burnt offering.17The ſacrifices of God are a broken ſpirit: a broken and a contrite heart, O God, thou wilt not deſpiſe.18Doe good in thy good pleaſure vnto Sion: build thou the walles of Ieruſalem.19Then ſhalt thou be pleaſed with the ſacrifices of righteouſneſſe, with burnt offering and whole burnt offering: then ſhall they offer bullockes vpon thine altar.

CHAPTER 52

1*To the chiefe Muſician, Maſchil, A Pſalme of Dauid: When Doeg the Edomite came and told Saul, and ſaid vnto him, Dauid is come to the houſe of Ahimelech.* Why boaſteſt thou thy ſelfe in miſchiefe, O mightie man? the goodneſſe of God indureth continually.2Thy tongue deuiſeth miſchiefes: like a ſharpe raſor, working deceitfully.3Thou loueſt euill more then good; and lying rather then to ſpeake righteouſneſſe. Selah.4Thou loueſt all deuouring words, O thou deceitfull tongue.5God ſhall likewiſe deſtroy thee for euer, hee ſhall take thee away and plucke thee out of thy dwelling place, and roote thee out of the land of the liuing. Selah.6The righteous alſo ſhall ſee, and feare, and ſhall laugh at him.7Loe, this is the man that made not God his ſtrength: but truſted in the abundance of his riches, and ſtrengthened himſelfe in his wickedneſſe.8But I am like a greene oliue tree in the houſe of God: I truſt in the mercy of God for euer and euer.9I will prayſe thee for euer, becauſe thou haſt done it: and I will wait on thy name, for it is good before thy Saints.

CHAPTER 531*To the chiefe muſician vpon Mahalath, Maſchil, A Pſalme of Dauid.* The foole hath ſayde in his heart, There is no god; Corrupt are they, and haue done abhominable iniquitie; there is none that doth good.2God looked downe from heauen vpon the children of men, to ſee if there were any that did vnderſtand, that did ſeeke God.3Euery one of them is gone backe, they are altogether become filthy: there is none that doth good, no not one.4Haue the workers of iniquitie no knowledge? who eate vp my people, as they eate bread; they haue not called vpon God.5There were they in great feare, where no feare was: for God hath ſcattered the bones of him that incampeth againſt thee, thou haſt put them to ſhame, becauſe God hath deſpiſed them.6O that the ſaluation of Iſrael were come out of Sion! when God bringeth backe the captiuitie of his people, Iaakob ſhall reioyce, and Iſrael ſhall be glad.

CHAPTER 541*To the chiefe muſician on Neginoth, Maſchil, A Pſalme of Dauid. When the Ziphims came and ſayde to Saul: doeth not Dauid hide himſelfe with vs?* Saue me, O God, by thy name, and iudge me by thy ſtrength.2Heare my prayer, O God; giue eare to the words of my mouth.3For ſtrangers are riſen vp againſt me, and oppreſsors ſeeke after my ſoule; they haue not ſet God before them. Selah.4Behold, God is mine helper: the Lord is with them that vphold my ſoule.5He ſhall reward euill vnto mine enemies: cut them off in thy trueth.6I will freely ſacrifice vnto thee; I will praiſe thy name (O Lord:) for it is good.7For hee hath deliuered me out of all trouble: and mine eye hath ſeene his deſire vpon mine enemies.

CHAPTER 551*To the chiefe muſician on Neginoth, Maſchil. A Pſalme of Dauid.* Giue eare to my prayer, O God: and hide not thy ſelfe from my ſupplication.2Attend vnto me, and heare me: I mourne in my complaint, and make a noiſe.3Becauſe of the voyce of the enemie, becauſe of the oppreſſion of the wicked: for they caſt iniquitie vpon me, and in wrath they hate me.4My heart is ſore pained within me: and the terrours of death are fallen vpon me.5Fearefulneſse and trembling are come vpon me, and horrour hath ouerwhelmed me.6And I ſaid, O that I had wings like a doue; for then would I flee away and be at reſt.7Loe, then would I wander farre off, and remaine in the wilderneſſe. Selah.8I would haſten my eſcape from the windie ſtorme, and tempeſt.9Deſtroy, O Lord, and diuide their tongues: for I haue ſeene violence and ſtrife in the citie.10Day and night they goe about it vpon the walles thereof: miſchiefe alſo and ſorrow are in the midſt of it.11Wickedneſſe is in the midſt thereof: deceite and guile depart not from her ſtreets.12For it was not an enemie that reproached me, then I could haue borne it, neither was it hee that hated me, that did magnifie himſelfe againſt me, then I would haue hid my ſelfe from him.13But it was thou, a man, mine equal, my guide, and mine acquaintance.14Wee tooke ſweet counſell together, and walked vnto the houſe of God in companie.15Let death ſeaze vpon them, and let them goe downe quicke into hell: for wickednes is in their dwellings, and among them.16As for me, I will call vpon God: and the Lord ſhall ſaue me.17Euening and morning, and at noone will I pray, and crie aloud: and he ſhall heare my voyce.18He hath deliuered my ſoule in peace from the battell that was againſt me: for there were many with me.19God ſhall heare and afflict them, euen he that abideth of old, Selah: becauſe they haue no changes, therefore they feare not God.20He hath put foorth his handes againſt ſuch as be at peace with him: he hath broken his couenant.21The words of his mouth were ſmoother then butter, but warre was in his heart: his words were ſofter then oyle, yet were they drawen ſwords.22Caſt thy burden vpon the Lord, and he ſhall ſuſtaine thee: hee ſhall neuer ſuffer the righteous to bee moued.23But thou, O God, ſhalt bring them downe into the pit of deſtruction: Bloody and deceitfull men ſhall not liue out halfe their dayes, but I will truſt in thee.

CHAPTER 561*To the chiefe muſician vpon Ionath Elem Rechokim, Michtam of Dauid, when the Philiſtines tooke him in Gath.* Be mercifull vnto mee, O God, for man would ſwallow me vp: he fighting daily, oppreſseth me.2Mine enemies would dayly ſwallow me vp: for they bee many that fight againſt me, O thou moſt high.3What time I am afraide, I will truſt in thee.4In God I will praiſe his worde, In God I haue put my truſt, I will not feare what fleſh can doe vnto me.5Euery day they wreſt my words: all their thoughts are againſt mee for euill.6They gather themſelues together; they hide themſelues, they marke my ſteps when they wait for my ſoule.7Shall they eſcape by iniquitie? in thine anger caſt downe the people, O God.8Thou telleſt my wanderings, put thou my teares into thy bottle: are they not in thy booke?9When I crie vnto thee, then ſhall mine enemies turne backe: this I know, for God is for me.10In God will I praiſe his word: in the Lord will I praiſe his word.11In God haue I put my truſt: I will not bee afraid what man can doe vnto me.12Thy vowes are vpon me, O God: I will render praiſes vnto thee.13For thou haſt deliuered my ſoule from death: wilt not thou deliuer my feet from falling? that I may walke before God in the light of the liuing.

CHAPTER 571*To the chiefe muſician Al-taſchith, Michtam of Dauid, when hee fled from Saul in the caue.* Be mercifull vnto mee, O God, be merciful vnto me, for my ſoule truſteth in thee: yea in the ſhadow of thy wings will I make my refuge, vntill theſe calamities bee ouerpaſt.2I will crie vnto God moſt high: vnto God that perfourmeth all things for mee.3Hee ſhall ſend from heauen, and ſaue me from the reproch of him, that would ſwallow me vp; Selah. God ſhall ſend forth his mercy and his trueth.4My ſoule is among lyons, and I lie euen among them that are ſet on fire: euen the ſonnes of men, whoſe teeth are ſpeares and arrowes, and their tongue a ſharpe ſword.5Be thou exalted, O God, aboue the heauens: let thy glory be aboue all the earth.6They haue prepared a net for my ſteppes, my ſoule is bowed downe: they haue digged a pit before me, into the midſt whereof they are fallen themſelues. Selah.7My heart is fixed, O God, my heart is fixed: I will ſing, and giue praiſe.8Awake vp my glory, awake pſalterie and harpe; I my ſelfe will awake early.9I will praiſe thee, O Lord, among the people; I will ſing vnto thee among the nations.10For thy mercy is great vnto the heauens, and thy trueth vnto the clouds.11Be thou exalted, O God, aboue the heauens: let thy glory be aboue all the earth.

CHAPTER 581*To the chiefe muſician Al-taſchith, Michtam of Dauid.* Doe yee indeed ſpeake righteouſneſſe, O congregation? doe ye iudge vprightly, O ye ſonnes of men?2Yea, in heart you worke wickedneſſe; you waigh the violence of your hands in the earth.3The wicked are eſtranged from the wombe, they goe aſtray as ſoone as they be borne, ſpeaking lies.4Their poiſon is like the poyſon of a ſerpent; they are like the deafe adder that ſtoppeth her eare:5Which will not hearken to the voyce of charmers, charming neuer ſo wiſely.6Breake their teeth, O God, in their mouth: breake out the great teeth of the young lyons, O Lord.7Let them melt away as waters, which runne continually: When he bendeth his bow to ſhoote his arrowes, let them be as cut in pieces.8As a ſnaile which melteth, let euery one of them paſſe away: like the vntimely birth of a woman, that they may not ſee the ſunne.9Before your pots can feele the thornes, he ſhall take them away as with a whirlewind, both liuing, and in his wrath.10The righteous ſhall reioyce when he ſeeth the vengeance: he ſhall waſh his feete in the blood of the wicked.11So that a man ſhall ſay, Uerily there is a reward for the righteous: verily hee is a God that iudgeth in the earth.

CHAPTER 591*To the chiefe muſician Al-taſchith, Michtam of Dauid: when Saul ſent, and they watcht the houſe to kill him.* Deliuer me from mine enemies, O my God: defend mee from them that riſe vp againſt me.2Deliuer mee from the workers of iniquitie, and ſaue me from bloodie men.3For loe, they lye in waite for my ſoule; the mighty are gathered againſt me, not for my tranſgreſsion, nor for my ſinne, O Lord.4They runne and prepare themſelues without my fault: awake to helpe me, and behold.5Thou therefore, O Lord God of hoſtes, the God of Iſrael, awake to viſite all the heathen: be not mercifull to any wicked tranſgreſsours. Selah.6They returne at euening: they make a noiſe like a dogge, and go round about the citie.7Behold, they belch out with their mouth: ſwords are in their lippes; for who, ſay they, doeth heare?8But thou, O Lord, ſhalt laugh at them; thou ſhalt haue all the heathen in deriſion.9Becauſe of his ſtrength will I wait vpon thee: for God is my defence.10The God of my mercy ſhall preuent me; God ſhall let mee ſee my deſire vpon mine enemies.11Slay them not, leſt my people forget: ſcatter them by thy power; and bring them downe, O Lord our ſhield.12For the ſinne of their mouth, and the words of their lips, let them euen be taken in their pride: and for curſing and lying which they ſpeake.13Conſume them in wrath, conſume them, that they may not be: and let them know that God ruleth in Iacob, vnto the ends of the earth. Selah.14And at euening let them returne, and let them make a noiſe like a dogge, and goe round about the citie.15Let them wander vp and downe for meate, and grudge if they be not ſatiſfied.16But I will ſing of thy power; yea I will ſing alowd of thy mercy in the morning: for thou haſt bene my defence and refuge, in the day of my trouble.17Vnto thee, O my ſtrength, wil I ſing: for God is my defence, and the God of my mercy.

CHAPTER 601*To the chiefe Muſician vpon Shuſhan-Eduth Michtam of Dauid, to teach. When hee ſtroue with Aram Naharaim, and with Aram Zobah, when Ioab returned, and ſmote of Edom in the valley of ſalt, twelue thouſand.* O God, thou haſt caſt vs off; thou haſt ſcattered vs, thou haſt bene diſpleaſed, O turne thy ſelfe to vs againe.2Thou haſt made the earth to tremble; thou haſt broken it: heale the breaches thereof, for it ſhaketh.3Thou haſt ſhewed thy people hard things: thou haſt made vs to drinke the wine of aſtoniſhment.4Thou haſt giuen a banner to them that feare thee: that it may be diſplayed becauſe of the trueth. Selah.5That thy beloued may be deliuered; ſaue with thy right hand, and heare mee.6God hath ſpoken in his holineſſe, I wil reioyce: I will diuide Shechem, and mete out the valley of Succoth.7Gilead is mine, and Manaſſeh is mine; Ephraim alſo is the ſtrength of mine head; Iudah is my Lawgiuer.8Moab is my waſh-pot, ouer Edom wil I caſt out my ſhooe: Philiſtia, triumph thou becauſe of me.9Who wil bring me into the ſtrong citie? who will lead me into Edom?10Wilt not thou, O God, which hadſt caſt vs off? and thou, O God, which didſt not goe out with our armies.11Giue vs helpe from trouble: for vaine is the helpe of man.12Through God wee ſhall doe valiantly: for he it is that ſhall tread downe our enemies.

CHAPTER 611*To the chiefe Muſician vpon Neginah. A Pſalme of Dauid.* Heare my cry, O God, attend vnto my prayer.2From the end of the earth wil I cry vnto thee, when my heart is ouerwhelmed: leade me to the rocke, that is higher then I.3For thou haſt bene a ſhelter for me, and a ſtrong tower from the enemy.4I will abide in thy Tabernacle for euer: I will truſt in the couert of thy wings. Selah.5For thou, O God, haſt heard my vowes: thou haſt giuen me the heritage of thoſe that feare thy name.6Thou wilt prolong the kings life: and his yeeres as many generations.7He ſhall abide before God for euer: O prepare mercy and trueth which may preſeruehim.8So will I ſing praiſe vnto thy name for euer, that I may daily performe my vowes.

CHAPTER 621*To the chiefe muſician, to Ieduthun, A Pſalme of Dauid.* Truely my ſoule waiteth vpon God: from him commeth my ſaluation.2He onely is my rocke and my ſaluation: he is my defence, I ſhall not be greatly moued.3How long wil ye imagine miſchiefe againſt a man? ye ſhall be ſlaine all of you: as a bowing wall ſhall ye be, and as a tottering fence.4They onely conſult to caſt him downe from his excellency, they delight in lies: they bleſſe with their mouth, but they curſe inwardly. Selah.5My ſoule, wait thou onely vpon God: for my expectation is from him.6He onely is my rocke and my ſaluation; he is my defence; I ſhall not bee moued.7In God is my ſaluation, and my glorie: the rocke of my ſtrength, and my refuge is in God.8Truſt in him at all times; ye people, powre out your heart before him: God is a refuge for vs. Selah.9Surely men of low degree are vanitie, and men of high degree are a lie: to be laid in the ballance, they are altogether lighter then vanitie.10Truſt not in oppreſſion, become not vaine in robberie: if riches increaſe, ſet not your heart vpon them.11God hath ſpoken once; twice haue I heard this, that power belongeth vnto God.12Alſo vnto thee, O Lord, belongeth mercie: for thou rendereſt to euery man according to his worke.

CHAPTER 631*A Pſalme of Dauid, when hee was in the wilderneſſe of Iudah.* O God, thou art my God, earely will I ſeeke thee: my ſoule thirſteth for thee, my fleſh longeth for thee, in a drie and thirſtie lande, where no water is:2To ſee thy power and thy glory, ſo as I haue ſeen thee in the Sanctuary.3Becauſe thy louing kindnes is better then life: my lips ſhal praiſe thee.4Thus will I bleſſe thee, while I liue: I will lift vp my handes in thy Name.5My ſoule ſhall be ſatiſfied as with marrow and fatneſſe: and my mouth ſhall praiſe thee with ioyfull lips:6When I remember thee vpon my bed, and meditate on thee in the night watches.7Becauſe thou haſt bene my helpe; therefore in the ſhadow of thy wings will I reioyce.8My ſoule followeth hard after thee: thy right hand vpholdeth me.9But thoſe that ſeeke my ſoule to deſtroy it, ſhall goe into the lower parts of the earth.10They ſhall fall by the ſword: they ſhall be a portion for foxes.11But the King ſhal reioyce in God; euery one that ſweareth by him ſhall glorie: but the mouth of them that ſpeake lies, ſhall be ſtopped.

CHAPTER 641*To the chiefe muſician, a Pſalme of Dauid.* Heare my voice, O God, in my praier; preſeruemy life from feare of the enemie.2Hide me from the ſecret counſel of the wicked: from the inſurrection of the workers of iniquitie:3Who whet their tongue like a ſword, and bend their bowes to ſhoote their arrowes, euen bitter words:4That they may ſhoote in ſecret at the perfect: ſuddenly doe they ſhoote at him, and feare not.5They incourage themſelues in an euill matter: they commune of laying ſnares priuily; they ſay, Who ſhall ſee them?6They ſearch out iniquities, they accompliſh a diligent ſearch: both the inward thought of euery one of them, and the heart, is deepe.7But God ſhall ſhoote at them: with an arrowe, ſodenly ſhall they be wounded.8So they ſhall make their owne tongue to fall vpon themſelues: all that ſee them, ſhall flee away.9And all men ſhall feare, and ſhall declare the worke of God; for they ſhall wiſely conſider of his doing.10The righteous ſhalbe glad in the Lord, and ſhall truſt in him; and all the vpright in heart ſhall glory.

CHAPTER 651*To the chiefe muſician, a Pſalme and ſong of Dauid.* Praiſe waiteth for thee, O God, in Sion: and vnto thee ſhall the vowe be performed.2O thou that heareſt prayer, vnto thee ſhall all fleſh come.3Iniquities preuaile againſt me: as for our tranſgreſſions, thou ſhalt purge them away.4Bleſſed is the man whom thou chooſeſt and cauſeſt to approach vnto thee, that hee may dwell in thy Courts: we ſhalbe ſatiſfied with the goodneſſe of thy houſe, euen of thy holy temple.5By terrible things in righteouſneſſe, wilt thou anſwere vs, O God of our ſaluation: who art the confidence of all the ends of the earth, and of them that are a farre off vpon the ſea.6Which by his ſtrength ſetteth faſt the mountaines; being girded with power.7Which ſtilleth the noiſe of the ſeas; the noiſe of their waues, and the tumult of the people.8They alſo that dwell in the vttermoſt parts are afraid at thy tokens: thou makeſt the outgoings of the morning, and euening to reioyce.9Thou viſiteſt the earth and watereſt it: thou greatly inricheſt it with the riuer of God which is full of water; thou prepareſt them corne, when thou haſt ſo prouided for it.10Thou watereſt the ridges thereof abundantly: thou ſettleſt the furrowes thereof: thou makeſt it ſoft with ſhowres, thou bleſſeſt the ſpringing thereof.11Thou crowneſt the yeere with thy goodneſse; and thy paths drop fatneſſe.12They drop vpon the paſtures of the wilderneſſe; and the little hilles reioyce on euery ſide.13The paſtures are cloathed with flockes; the valleis alſo are couered ouer with corne; they ſhout for ioy, they alſo ſing.

CHAPTER 661*To the chiefe muſician, a ſong or Pſalme.* Make a ioyfull noiſe vnto God, all yee lands.2Sing forth the honour of his name: make his praiſe glorious.3ſay vnto God, How terrible art thou in thy workes? through the greatneſſe of thy power ſhall thine enemies ſubmit themſelues vnto thee.4All the earth ſhall worſhip thee; and ſhall ſing vnto thee, they ſhall ſing to thy name; Selah.5Come and ſee the workes of God: he is terrible in his doing toward the children of men.6He turned the ſea into dry land: they went through the flood on foote, there did we reioyce in him.7He ruleth by his power for euer, his eyes behold the nations: let not the rebellious exalt themſelues. Selah.8O bleſſe our God, yee people, and make the voice of his praiſe to be heard.9Which holdeth our ſoule in life, and ſuffereth not our feete to be moued.10For thou, O God, haſt proued vs: thou haſt tried vs, as ſiluer is tryed.11Thou broughteſt vs into the net; thou layedſt affliction vpon our loynes.12Thou haſt cauſed men to ride ouer our heads, we went through fire, and through water: but thou broughteſt vs out into a wealthy place.13I will goe into thy houſe, with burnt offerings: I will pay thee my vowes,14Which my lips haue vttered, and my mouth hath ſpoken, when I was in trouble.15I will offer vnto thee burnt ſacrifices of fatlings, with the incenſe of rammes: I will offer bullockes with goates. Selah.16Come and heare all ye that feare God, and I will declare what he hath done for my ſoule.17I cried vnto him with my mouth: and he was extolled with my tongue.18If I regard iniquitie in my heart: the Lord will not heare me.19But verily God hath heard mee; hee hath attended to the voice of my prayer.20Bleſſed bee God, which hath not turned away my prayer, nor his mercie from me.

CHAPTER 671*To the chiefe Muſician on Neginoth. A Pſalme or ſong.* God be mercifull vnto vs, and bleſſe vs: and cauſe his face to ſhine vpon vs. Selah.2That thy way may bee knowen vpon earth, thy ſauing health among all nations.3Let the people praiſe thee, O God; let all the people praiſe thee.4O let the nations be glad, and ſing for ioy: for thou ſhalt iudge the people righteouſly; and gouerne the nations vpon earth. Selah.5Let the people praiſe thee, O God, let all the people praiſe thee.6Then ſhall the earth yeeld her increaſe; and God, euen our owne God, ſhall bleſſe vs.7God ſhall bleſſe vs; and all the ends of the earth ſhall feare him.

CHAPTER 681*To the chiefe Muſician. A Pſalme or ſong of Dauid.* Let God Ariſe, let his enemies be ſcattered: let them alſo that hate him, flee before him.2As ſmoke is driuen away, ſo driue them away: as waxe melteth before the fire, ſo let the wicked periſh at the preſence of God.3But let the righteous be glad: let them reioyce before God, yea let them exceedingly reioyce.4Sing vnto God, ſing praiſes to his Name: extoll him that rideth vpon the heauens, by his Name Iah, and reioyce before him.5A father of the fatherleſſe, and a iudge of the widowes, is God in his holy habitation.6God ſetteth the ſolitary in a families: hee bringeth out thoſe which are bound with chaines, but the rebellious dwell in a dry land.7O God, when thou wenteſt forth before thy people; when thou didſt march through the wildernes, Selah.8The earth ſhooke, the heauens alſo dropped at the preſence of God: euen Sinai it ſelfe was mooued at the preſence of God, the God of Iſrael.9Thou, O God, didſt ſend a plentifull raine, whereby thou didſt confirme thine inheritance, when it was weary.10Thy Congregation hath dwelt therein: thou, O God, haſt prepared of thy goodneſſe for the poore.11The Lord gaue the word: great was the company of thoſe that publiſhed it.12Kings of armies did flee apace: and ſhe that taried at home, diuided the ſpoile.13Though ye haue lien among the pots, yet ſhall yee bee as the wings of a doue, couered with ſiluer, and her feathers with yellow gold.14When the Almighty ſcattered Kings in it, it was white as ſnow in Salmon.15The hil of God is as the hill of Baſhan, an high hill as the hill of Baſhan.16Why leape ye, ye high hilles? this is the Hil which God deſireth to dwell in, yea the Lord will dwel in it for euer.17The chariots of God are twentie thouſand, euen thouſands of Angels: the Lord is among them as in Sinai, in the holy place.18Thou haſt aſcended on high, thou haſt ledde captiuitie captiue, thou haſt receiued giftes for men; yea, for the rebellious alſo, that the Lord God might dwell among them.19Bleſſed be the Lord, who daily loadeth vs with benefits, euen the God of our ſaluation. Selah.20Hee that is our God, is the God of ſaluation; and vnto God the Lord belong the iſſues from death.21But God ſhall wound the head of his enemies: and the hairy ſcalpe of ſuch a one as goeth on ſtill in his treſpaſſes.22The Lord ſaid, I will bring againe from Baſhan, I will bring my people againe from the depthes of the ſea:23That thy foote may be dipped in the blood of thine enemies, and the tongue of thy dogges in the ſame.24They haue ſeene thy goings, O God, euen the goings of my God, my King, in the Sanctuarie.25The ſingers went before, the players on inſtruments followed after; amongſt them were the damoſels playing with timbrels.26Bleſſe yee God, in the Congregations, euen the Lord, from the fountaine of Iſrael.27There is little Beniamin with their ruler, the princes of Iudah and their Councill, the princes of Zebulun, and the princes of Naphtali.28Thy God hath commanded thy ſtrength: ſtrengthen, O God, that which thou haſt wrought for vs.29Becauſe of thy Temple at Ieruſalem, ſhall kings bring preſents vnto thee.30Rebuke the company of ſpearemen, the multitude of the bulles, with the calues of the people, till euery one ſubmit himſelfe with pieces of ſiluer: ſcatter thou the people that delite in warre.31Princes ſhall come out of Egypt, Ethiopia ſhall ſoone ſtretch out her hands vnto God.32Sing vnto God, yee kingdomes of the earth: O ſing praiſes vnto the Lord, Selah:33To him that rideth vpon the heauens of heauens, which were of olde: loe, hee doeth ſend out his voice, and that a mightie voice.34Aſcribe yee ſtrength vnto God: his excellencie is ouer Iſrael, and his ſtrength is in the cloudes.35O God, thou art terrible out of thy holy places: the God of Iſrael is he that giueth ſtrength, and power vnto his people: bleſſed be God.

CHAPTER 691*To the chiefe muſician vpon Shoſhannim, A Pſalme of Dauid.* Saue mee, O God, for the waters are come in vnto my ſoule.2I ſinke in deepe mire, where there is no ſtanding: I am come into deepe waters, where the flouds ouerflow me.3I am weary of my crying, my throate is dried: mine eyes faile while I waite for my God.4They that hate mee without a cauſe, are moe then the haires of mine head: they that would deſtroy me, being mineenemies wrongfully, are mightie: then I reſtored that which I tooke not away.5O God, thou knoweſt my fooliſhneſse; and my ſinnes are not hidde from thee.6Let not them that waite on thee, O Lord God of hoſtes, be aſhamed for my ſake: let not thoſe that ſeeke thee, beconfounded for my ſake, O God of Iſrael.7Becauſe for thy ſake I haue borne reproch: ſhame hath couered my face.8I am become a ſtranger vnto my brethren, and an aliant vnto my mothers children.9For the zeale of thine houſe hath eaten mee vp; and the reproches of them that reproched thee, are fallen vpon me.10When I wept, and chaſtened my ſoule with faſting, that was to my reproch.11I made ſackecloth alſo my garment: & I became a prouerbe to them.12They that ſit in the gate, ſpeake againſt mee; and I was the ſong of the drunkards.13But as for mee, my prayer is vnto thee, O Lord, in an acceptable time: O God, in the multitude of thy mercie heareme, in the trueth of thy ſaluation.14Deliuer me out of the mire, and let me not ſinke: let me bee deliuered from them that hate me, and out of thedeepe waters.15Let not the water flood ouerflow me, neither let the deepe ſwallow mee vp, and let not the pit ſhut her mouth vponme.16Heare me, O Lord, for thy louing kindneſſe is good: turne vnto mee according to the multitude of thy tendermercies.17And hide not thy face from thy ſeruant, for I am in trouble: heare me ſpeedily.18Draw nigh vnto my ſoule, and redeeme it: deliuer me becauſe of mine enemies.19Thou haſt knowen my reproch and my ſhame and my diſhonor: mine aduerſaries are all before thee.20Reproch hath broken my heart, and I am full of heauines: and I looked for ſome to take pitie, but there was none;and for comforters, but I found none.21They gaue mee alſo gall for my meat, and in my thirſt they gaue mee vineger to drinke.22Let their table become a ſnare before them: and that which ſhould haue bene for their welfare, let it become atrap.23Let their eyes be darkened that they ſee not; and make their loines continually to ſhake.24Powre out thine indignation vpon them, and let thy wrathfull anger take hold of them.25Let their habitation be deſolate, and let none dwell in their tents.26For they perſecute him whõ thou haſt ſmitten, and they talke to the griefe of thoſe whom thou haſt wounded.27Adde iniquitie vnto their iniquitie: and let them not come into thy righteouſneſſe.28Let them bee blotted out of the booke of the liuing, and not be written with the righteous.29But I am poore, and ſorowfull: let thy ſaluation (O God) ſet me vp on high.30I will praiſe the name of God with a ſong, and will magnifie him with thankeſgiuing.31This alſo ſhall pleaſe the Lord better then an oxe or bullocke that hath hornes and hoofes.32The humble ſhall ſee this, and be glad: and your heart ſhall liue that ſeeke good.33For the Lord heareth the poore, and deſpiſeth not his priſoners.34Let the heauen and earth praiſe him, the ſeas, and euery thing that moueth therein.35For God will ſaue Sion, and will build the cities of Iudah, that they may dwell there, and haue it in poſſeſſion.36The ſeede alſo of his ſeruants ſhall inherit it: and they that loue his name ſhall dwell therein.

CHAPTER 701*To the chiefe muſician, a pſalme of Dauid, to bring to remembrance.* Make haſte, O God, to deliuer mee, make haſte to helpe me, O Lord.2Let them be aſhamed and confounded that ſeeke after my ſoule: let them be turned backward, and put to confuſion, that deſire my hurt.3Let them be turned backe for a reward of their ſhame, that ſay, Aha, aha.4Let all thoſe that ſeeke thee, reioyce, and be glad in thee: and let ſuch as loue thy ſaluation, ſay continually, Let God be magnified.5But I am poore and needy, make haſte vnto me, O God: Thou art my helpe and my deliuerer, O Lord make no tarrying.

CHAPTER 711In thee, O Lord, doe I put my truſt, let me neuer be put to confuſion.2Deliuer mee in thy righteouſneſſe, and cauſe me to eſcape: incline thine eare vnto me, and ſaue me.3Bee thou my ſtrong habitation, whereunto I may continually reſort: thou haſt giuen commandement to ſaue mee, for thou art my rocke, and my fortreſse.4Deliuer me, O my God, out of the hand of the wicked, out of the hand of the vnrighteous, and cruel man.5For thou art my hope, O Lord God: thou art my truſt from my youth.6By thee haue I bene holden vp from the wombe: thou art hee that tooke mee out of my mothers vowels, my praiſe ſhalbe continually of thee.7I am as a wonder vnto many, but thou art my ſtrong refuge.8Let my mouth bee filled with thy praiſe, and with thy honour all the day.9Caſt me not off in the time of old age; forſake me not when my ſtrength faileth.10For mine enemies ſpeake againſt mee: and they that lay waite for my ſoule, take counſell together,11Saying, God hath forſaken him: perſecute and take him, for there is none to deliuer him.12O God, be not farre from mee: O my God, make haſte for my helpe.13Let them be confounded and conſumed, that are aduerſaries to my ſoule: let them bee couered with reproch and diſhonour, that ſeeke my hurt.14But I wil hope continually, and will yet praiſe thee more and more.15My mouth ſhall ſhew foorth thy righteouſneſſe, and thy ſaluation all the day: for I know not the numbers thereof.16I will goe in the ſtrength of the Lord God: I will make mention of thy righteouſneſſe, euen of thine onely.17O God, thou haſt taught me from my youth: and hitherto haue I declared thy wonderous workes.18Now alſo when I am old and gray headed, O God, forſake me not: vntill I haue ſhewed thy ſtrength vnto this generation, and thy power to euery one that is to come.19Thy righteouſnes alſo, O God, is very high, who haſt done great things: O God, who is like vnto thee?20Thou which haſt ſhewed mee great, and ſore troubles, ſhalt quicken mee againe, and ſhalt bring mee vp againe from the depthes of the earth.21Thou ſhalt increaſe my greatneſse, and comfort me on euery ſide.22I will alſo praiſe thee with the pſalterie, euen thy trueth, O my God: vnto thee will I ſing withthe harpe, O thou Holy one of Iſrael.23My lippes ſhall greatly reioyce when I ſing vnto thee: and my ſoule, which thou haſt redeemed.24My tongue alſo ſhall talke of thy righteouſneſſe all the day long: for they are confounded, forthey are brought vnto ſhame, that ſeeke my hurt.

CHAPTER 721*A Pſalme for Solomon.* Giue the King thy Iudgements, O God, and thy Righteouſneſſe vnto the Kings ſonne.2Hee ſhall iudge thy people with righteouſneſſe, and thy poore with iudgement.3The mountaines ſhal bring peace to the people, and the litle hils, by righteouſneſſe.4Hee ſhall iudge the poore of the people, he ſhall ſaue the children of the needie, and ſhallbreake in pieces the oppreſsour.5They ſhall feare thee as long as the Sunne & Moone indure, throughout all generations.6Hee ſhall come downe like raine vpon the mowen graſſe: as ſhowres that water the earth.7In his dayes ſhall the righteous flouriſh: and abundance of peace ſo long as the Moone endureth.8He ſhall haue dominion alſo from ſea to ſea, and from the riuer, vnto the ends of the earth.9They that dwell in the wilderneſſe ſhall bowe before him: and his enemies ſhall licke the duſt.10The kings of Tarſhiſh and of the Iſles ſhall bring preſents: the Kings of Sheba and Seba ſhalloffer gifts.11Yea, all Kings ſhall fall downe before him: all nations ſhall ſerue him.12For hee ſhall deliuer the needy when he crieth: the poore alſo, and him that hath no helper.13He ſhal ſpare the poore and needy, and ſhall ſaue the ſoules of the needy.14He ſhall redeeme their ſoule from deceit and violence: and precious ſhall their blood be in hiſſight.15And he ſhall liue, and to him ſhalbe giuen of the gold of Sheba; prayer alſo ſhalbe made for himcontinually, and daily ſhall he be praiſed.16There ſhalbe an handfull of corne in the earth vpon the top of the mountaines; the fruit thereofſhall ſhake like Lebanon, and they of the citie ſhall flouriſh like graſſe of the earth.17His name ſhall endure for euer: his name ſhalbe continued as long as the ſunne: and men ſhalbebleſſed in him; all nations ſhall call him bleſſed.18Bleſſed be the Lord God, the God of Iſrael, who only doth wonderous things.19And bleſſed be his glorious name for euer, and let the whole earth be filled with his glory. Amen,and Amen.20The prayers of Dauid the ſonne of Ieſſe, are ended.

CHAPTER 731*A Pſalme of Aſaph.* Truely God is good to Iſrael, euen to ſuch as are of a cleane heart.2But as for mee, my feete were almoſt gone: my ſteps had well-nigh ſlipt.3For I was enuious at the fooliſh, when I ſawe the proſperity of the wicked.4For there are no bands in their death: but their ſtrength is firme.5They are not in trouble as other men: neither are they plagued like other men.6Therefore pride compaſſeth them about as a chaine: violence couereth them as a garment.7Their eies ſtand out with fatnes: they haue more then heart could wiſh.8They are corrupt, and ſpeake wickedly concerning oppreſſion: they ſpeake loftily.9They ſet their mouth againſt the heauens; and their tongue walketh through the earth.10Therefore his people returne hither: and waters of a full cup are wrung out to them.11And they ſay, How doth God know? and is there knowledge in the moſt High?12Behold, theſe are the vngodly: who proſper in the world, they increaſe in riches.13Uerily I haue cleanſed my heart in vaine, and waſhed my hands in innocencie.14For all the day long haue I bene plagued, and chaſtened euery morning.15If I ſay, I will ſpeake thus: behold, I ſhould offend againſt the generation of thy children.16When I thought to know this, it was too painfull for me,17Untill I went into the Sanctuarie of God; then vnderſtood I their end.18Surely thou didſt ſet them in ſlippery places: thou caſtedſt them downe into deſtruction.19How are they brought into deſolation as in a moment? they are vtterly conſumed with terrours.20As a dreame when one awaketh; ſo, O Lord, when thou awakeſt thou ſhalt deſpiſe their image.21Thus my heart was greeued, and I was pricked in my reines.22So fooliſh was I, and ignorant: I was as a beaſt before thee.23Neuertheleſſe I am continually with thee: thou haſt holden me by my right hand.24Thou ſhalt guide me with thy counſell; and afterward receiue me to glory.25Whom haue I in heauen but thee? and there is none vpon earth that I deſire beſides thee.26My fleſh and my heart faileth: but God is the ſtrength of my heart, and my portion for euer.27For loe, they that are farre from thee, ſhall periſh: thou haſt deſtroyed all them that goe awhoring from thee.28But it is good for me, to drawe neere to God: I haue put my truſt in the Lord God, that I maydeclare all thy workes.

CHAPTER 741*Maſchil of Aſaph.* O God, why haſt thou caſt vs off for euer? why doeth thine anger ſmoke againſt the ſheepe of thy paſture?2Remember thy Congregation which thou haſt purchaſed of olde: the rod of thine inheritance which thou haſt redeemed, this mount Sion, wherein thou haſt dwelt.3Lift vp thy feete vnto the perpetuall deſolations: euen all that the enemie hath done wickedly in the Sanctuarie.4Thine enemies roare in the midſt of thy congregations: they ſet vp their enſignes for ſignes.5A man was famous according as he had lifted vp axes vpon the thicke trees.6But now they breake downe the carued worke thereof at once, with axes and hammers.7They haue caſt fire into thy Sanctuary, they haue defiled by caſting downe, the dwelling place of thy Nawe to the ground.8They ſaid in their hearts, Let vs deſtroy them together: they haue burnt vp all the Synagogues of God in the land.9We ſee not our ſignes, there is no more any prophet, neither is there among vs any that knoweth howe long.10O God, how long ſhall the aduerſarie reproach? ſhall the enemie blaſpheme thy Name for euer?11Why withdraweſt thou thy hand, euen thy right hand? plucke it out of thy boſome.12For God is my King of old working ſaluation in the midſt of the earth.13Thou didſt diuide the ſea by thy ſtrength: thou brakeſt the heads of the dragons in the waters.14Thou brakeſt the heads of Leuiathan in pieces, and gaueſt him to bee meat to the people inhabiting the wilderneſſe.15Thou didſt cleaue the fountaine and the flood: thou driedſt vp mightie riuers.16The day is thine, the night alſo is thine: thou haſt prepared the light and the ſunne.17Thou haſt ſet all the borders of the earth: Thou haſt made Summer and Winter.18Remember this, that the enemie hath reproached, O Lord, and that the fooliſh people haue blaſphemed thy Name.19O deliuer not the ſoule of thy turtle doue vnto the multitude of the wicked forget not the Congregation of thy poore for euer.20Haue reſpect vnto the couenant: for the darke places of the earth are full of the habitations of crueltie.21O let not the oppreſſed returne aſhamed: let the poore and needie praiſe thy name.22Ariſe, O God, plead thine owne cauſe: remember how the fooliſh man reprocheth thee daily.23Forget not the voyce of thine enemies: the tumult of thoſe that riſe vp againſt thee, increaſeth continually.

CHAPTER 751*To the chiefe muſician Al-taſchith, A Pſalme or ſong of Aſaph.* Unto thee, O God, doe we giue thankes, vnto thee doe we giue thanks: for that thy name is nere, thy wonderous works declare.2When I ſhall receiue the congregation, I will iudge vprightly.3The earth and all the inhabitants thereof are diſſolued: I beare vp the pillars of it. Selah.4I ſaid vnto the fooles, Deale not fooliſhly: and to the wicked, Lift not vp the horne.5Lift not vp your horne on high: ſpeake not with a ſtiffe necke.6For promotion commeth neither from the Eaſt, nor from the Weſt, nor from the South.7But God is the iudge: he putteth downe one, and ſetteth vp another.8For in the hand of the Lord there is a cup, and the wine is red: it is full of mixture, and he powreth out of the ſame: but the dregges thereof all the wicked of the earth ſhall wring them out, and drinke them.9But I will declare for euer; I will ſing praiſes to the God of Iacob.10All the hornes of the wicked alſo will I cut off; but the hornes of the righteous ſhall be exalted.

CHAPTER 761*To the chiefe muſician on Neginoth, a Pſalme or ſong of Aſaph.* In Iudah is God knowen: his name is great in Iſrael.2In Salem alſo is his tabernacle, and his dwelling place in Sion.3There brake he the arrowes of the bowe, the ſhield, and the ſword, and the battell. Selah.4Thou art more glorious and excellent then the mountaines of pray.5The ſtout hearted are ſpoiled, they haue ſlept their ſleepe: and none of the men of might haue found their hands.6At thy rebuke, O God of Iacob, both the chariot and horſe are caſt into a dead ſleepe.7Thou, euen thou art to be feared; and who may ſtand in thy ſight when once thou art angry?8Thou didſt cauſe iudgement to be heard from heauen: the earth feared and was ſtill,9When God aroſe to iudgement, to ſaue all the meeke of the earth. Selah.10Surely the wrath of man ſhall praiſe thee: the remainder of wrath ſhalt thou reſtraine.11Uowe, and pay vnto the Lord your God; let all that be round about him bring preſents vnto him that ought to be feared.12Hee ſhall cut off the ſpirit of princes: hee is terrible to the kings of the earth.

CHAPTER 771I cryed vnto God with my voice: euen vnto God with my voice, and he gaue eare vnto me.2In the day of my trouble, I ſought the Lord; my ſore ranne in the night, and ceaſed not: my ſoule refuſed to be comforted.3I remembred God, and was troubled: I complained, and my ſpirit was ouerwhelmed. Selah.4Thou holdeſt mine eyes waking: I am ſo troubled that I cannot ſpeake.5I haue conſidered the dayes of old, the yeeres of auncient times.6I call to remembrance my ſong in the night: I commune with mine owne heart, and my ſpirit made diligent ſearch.7Will the Lord caſt off for euer? and will hee be fauourable no more?8Is his mercy cleane gone for euer? doth his promiſe faile for euermore?9Hath God forgotten to be gracious? hath he in anger ſhut vp his tender mercies? Selah.10And I ſayd, This is my infirmitie: but I will remember the yeeres of the right hand of the moſt high.11I will remember the workes of the Lord: ſurely I will remember thy wonders of old.12I will meditate alſo of all thy worke, and talke of thy doings.13Thy way, O God, is in the Sanctuarie: who is ſo great a God, as our God?14Thou art the God that doeſt wonders; thou haſt declared thy ſtrength among the people.15Thou haſt with thine arme redeemed thy people, the ſonnes of Iacob and Ioſeph. Selah.16The waters ſaw thee, O God, the waters ſaw thee: they were afraid; the depths alſo were troubled.17The cloudes powred out water, the ſkies ſent out a ſound; thine arrowes alſo went abroad.18The voice of thy thunder was in the heauen: the lightnings lightned the world, the earth trembled and ſhooke.19Thy way is in the ſea, and thy path in the great waters: and thy foot-ſteps are not knowen.20Thou leddeſt thy people like a flock, by the hand of Moſes and Aaron.

CHAPTER 781Giue eare, O my people, to my Lawe: incline your eares to the wordes of my mouth.2I will open my mouth in a parable: I wil vtter darke ſayings of old:3Which we haue heard, & knowen: and our fathers haue told vs.4We will not hide them from their children, ſhewing to the generation to come, the praiſes of the Lord: and his ſtrength, and his wonderful works that he hath done.5For he eſtabliſhed a Teſtimony in Iacob, and appointed a Law in Iſrael, which he commaunded our fathers: that they ſhould make them knowen to their children.6That the generation to come might know them, euen the children which ſhould be borne: who ſhould Ariſe and declare them to their children:7That they might ſet their hope in God, and not forget the works of God: but keepe his Commandements,8And might not bee as their fathers, a ſtubborne and rebellious generation, a generation that ſet not their heart aright: and whoſe ſpirit was not ſtedfaſt with God.9The children of Ephraim being armed, and carying bowes, turned backe in the day of battell.10They kept not the couenant of God: and refuſed to walke in his Law:11And forgat his workes: and his wonders that he had ſhewed them.12Marueilous things did he in the ſight of their fathers: in the land of Egypt, in the field of Zoan.13Hee diuided the ſea, and cauſed them to paſſe through: and he made the waters to ſtand as an heape.14In the day time alſo he led them with a cloud: and all the night with a light of fire.15Hee claue the rockes in the wildernes: and gaue them drinke as out of the great depthes.16Hee brought ſtreames alſo out of the rocke, and cauſed waters to runne downe like riuers.17And they ſinned yet more againſt him: by prouoking the moſt High in the wildernes.18And they tempted God in their heart: by aſking meat for their luſt.19Yea, they ſpake againſt God: they ſaid, Can God furniſh a table in the wildernes?20Behold, he ſmote the rocke, that the waters guſhed out, & the ſtreames ouerflowed; can he giue bread alſo? can he prouide fleſh for his people?21Therefore the Lord heard this, and was wroth, ſo a fire was kindled againſt Iacob: and anger alſo came vp againſt Iſrael.22Becauſe they beleeued not in God: and truſted not in his ſaluation:23Though he had commanded the cloudes from aboue: and opened the doores of heauen:24And had rained downe Manna vpon them to eate, and had giuen them of the corne of heauen.25Man did eate Angels food: hee ſent them meat to the full.26He cauſed an Eaſt wind to blow in the heauen: and by his power hee brought in the South wind.27He rained fleſh alſo vpon them as duſt: and feathered ſoules like as the ſand of the ſea.28And hee let it fall in the midſt of their campe, round about their habitations.29So they did eate, & were well filled: for he gaue them their owne deſire.30They were not eſtranged from their luſt: but while their meate was yet in their mouthes,31The wrath of God came vpon them, and ſlew the fatteſt of them: and ſmote downe the choſen men of Iſrael.32For all this they ſinned ſtill: and beleeued not for his wondrous works.33Therefore their dayes did he conſume in vanitie, and their yeeres in trouble.34When hee ſlew them, then they ſought him: and they returned, and inquired early after God.35And they remembred that God was their rocke: and the high God, their redeemer.36Neuertheleſſe they did flatter him with their mouth: and they lyed vnto him with their tongues.37For their heart was not right with him: neither were they ſtedfaſt in his couenant.38But hee being full of compaſſion, forgaue their iniquity, and deſtroyed them not; yea many a time turned he his anger away, and did not ſtirre vp all his wrath.39For he remembred that they were but fleſh; a wind that paſſeth away, and commeth not againe.40How oft did they prouoke him in the wilderneſſe: and grieue him in the deſert?41Yea they turned backe and tempted God: and limited the holy one of Iſrael.42They remembred not his hand: nor the day when hee deliuered them from the enemie:43How he had wrought his ſignes in Egypt: and his wonders in the field of Zoan:44And had turned their riuers into blood: and their floods, that they could not drinke. 45 Hee ſent diuers ſorts of flies among them, which deuoured them: and frogges which deſtroyed them. 46 He gaue alſo their increaſe vnto the caterpiller: and their labour vnto the locuſt. 47 He deſtroyed their vines with haile: and their Sycomore trees with froſt. 48 He gaue vp their cattel alſo to the haile: and their flockes to hot thunder-bolts. 49 He caſt vpon them the fierceneſse of his anger, wrath and indignation, and trouble: by ſending euill angels among them. 50 He made a way to his anger, hee ſpared not their ſoule from death: but gaue their life ouer to the peſtilence. 51 And ſmote all the firſt borne in Egypt: the chiefe of their ſtrength in the tabernacles of Ham: 52 But made his owne people to goe forth like ſheepe: and guided them in the wilderneſſe like a flocke. 53 And he led them on ſafely, ſo that they feared not: but the ſea ouerwhelmed their enemies. 54 And he brought them to the border of his ſanctuarie: euen to this mountaine which his right hand had purchaſed. 55 He caſt out the heathen alſo before them, and diuided them an inheritance by line: and made the tribes of Iſrael to dwell in their tents. 56 Yet they tempted and prouoked the moſt high God: and kept not his teſtimonies: 57 But turned backe, and dealt vnfaithfully like their fathers: they were turned aſide like a deceitfull bowe. 58 For they prouoked him to anger with their high places: and moued him to ielouſie with their grauen images. 59 When God heard this, hee was wroth, and greatly abhorred Iſrael: 60 So that he forſooke the tabernacle of Shiloh: the tent which he placed among men, 61 And deliuered his ſtrength into captiuitie: and his glory into the enemies hand. 62 He gaue his people ouer alſo vnto the ſword: and was wroth with his inheritance. 63 The fire conſumed their young men: and their maidens were not giuen to mariage. 64 Their prieſts fell by the ſword: and their widowes made no lamentation. 65 Then the Lord awaked as one out of ſleepe: and like a mighty man that ſhouteth by reaſon of wine. 66 And he ſmote his enemies in the hinder parts: he put them to a perpetuall reproch. 67 Moreouer he refuſed the tabernacle of Ioſeph: and choſe not the tribe of Ephraim. 68 But choſe the tribe of Iudah: the mount Sion which he loued. 69 And he built his ſanctuarie like high palaces: like the earth which he hath eſtabliſhed for euer. 70 He choſe Dauid alſo his ſeruant, and tooke him from the ſheepe-folds: 71 From following the ewes great with young, hee brought him to feed Iacob his people, and Iſrael his inheritance. 72 So he fed them according to the integritie of his heart: and guided them by the ſkilfulneſse of his hands.

CHAPTER 79 1 *A pſalme of Aſaph.* O God, the heathen are come into thine, inheritance, thy holy temple haue they defiled: they haue layd Ieruſalem on heapes. 2 The dead bodies of thy ſeruants haue they giuen to bee meate vnto the foules of the heauen: the fleſh of thy Saints vnto the beaſts of the earth. 3 Their blood haue they ſhed like water round about Ieruſalem: and there was none to burie them. 4 We are become a reproach to our neighbours: a ſcorne and deriſion to them that are round about vs. 5 How long, Lord, wilt thou be angry, for euer? ſhall thy ielouſie burne like fire? 6 Powre out thy wrath vpon the heathen that haue not knowen thee, and vpon the kingdomes that haue not called vpon thy name. 7 For they haue deuoured Iacob: and laid waſte his dwelling place. 8 O remember not againſt vs former iniquities, let thy tender mercies ſpeedily preuent vs: for we are brought very low. 9 Helpe vs, O God of our ſaluation, for the glory of thy Name: and deliuer vs, and purge away our ſinnes for thy Names ſake. 10 Wherfore ſhould the heathen ſay, Where is their God? let him be knowen among the heathen in our ſight by the reuenging of the blood of thy ſeruants which is ſhed. 11 Let the ſighing of the priſoner come before thee, according to the greatneſſe of thy power: preſeruethou thoſe that are appointed to die. 12 And render vnto our neighbours ſeuen fold into their boſome, their reproach wherewith they haue reproched thee, O Lord. 13 So we thy people and ſheepe of thy paſture, will giue thee thankes for euer: we will ſhew forth thy praiſe to all generations.

CHAPTER 80 1 *To the chiefe Muſician vpon Shoſhannim Eduth, A Pſalme of Aſaph.* Giue eare, ſhepheard of Iſrael, thou that leadeſt Ioſeph like a flocke, thou that dwelleſt betweene the Cherubims, ſhine forth. 2 Before Ephraim and Beniamin, and Manaſſeh, ſtirre vp thy ſtrength: and come and ſaue vs. 3 Turne vs againe, O God: and cauſe thy face to ſhine, and we ſhall bee ſaued. 4 O Lord God of hoſts, how long wilt thou bee angry againſt the prayer of thy people? 5 Thou feedeſt them with the bread of teares: and giueſt them teares to drinke in great meaſure. 6 Thou makeſt vs a ſtrife vnto our neighbours: and our enemies laugh among themſelues. 7 Turne vs againe, O God of hoſts, and cauſe thy face to ſhine, and we ſhall be ſaued. 8 Thou haſt brought a vine out of Egypt: thou haſt caſt out the heathen, and planted it. 9 Thou preparedſt roome before it: and didſt cauſe it to take deepe root, and it filled the land. 10 The hilles were coucred with the ſhadow of it, and the boughs thereof were like the goodly cedars. 11 She ſent out her boughs vnto the ſea: and her branches vnto the riuer. 12 Why haſt thou then broken downe her hedges: ſo that all they which paſſe by the way, doe plucke her? 13 The boare out of the wood doth waſte it: and the wild beaſt of the field doth deuoure it. 14 Returne, we beſeech thee, O God of hoſts: looke downe from heauen, and behold, and viſit this vine: 15 And the vineyard which thy right hand hath planted: and the branch that thou madeſt ſtrong for thy ſelfe. 16 It is burnt with fire, it is cut downe: they periſh at the rebuke of thy countenance. 17 Let thy hand be vpon the man of thy right hand: vpon the ſonne of man, whom thou madeſt ſtrong for thy ſelfe. 18 So will not wee goe backe from thee: quicken vs, and we will call vpon thy Name. 19 Turne vs againe, O Lord God of hoſts, cauſe thy face to ſhine, and wee ſhall be ſaued.

CHAPTER 81 1 *To the chiefe Muſician vpon Gittith. A Pſalme of Aſaph.* Sing alowd vnto God our ſtrength: make a ioyfull noiſe vnto the God of Iacob. 2 Take a Pſalme, and bring hither the timbrell: the pleaſant harpe with the pſalterie. 3 Blow vp the trumpet in the new Moone: in the time appointed on our ſolemne feaſt day. 4 For this was a ſtatute for Iſrael: and a Law of the God of Iacob. 5 This he ordained in Ioſeph for a teſtimonie, when he went out through the land of Egypt: where I heard a language, that I vnderſtood not. 6 I remoued his ſhoulder from the burden: his handes were deliuered from the pots. 7 Thou calledſt in trouble, and I deliuered thee, I anſwered thee in the ſecret place of thunder: I proued thee at the waters of Meribah. Selah. 8 Heare, O my people, and I will teſtifie vnto thee: O Iſrael, if thou wilt hearken vnto me: 9 There ſhall no ſtrange God be in thee: neither ſhalt thou worſhip any ſtrange God. 10 I am the Lord thy God, which brought thee out of the land of Egypt: open thy mouth wide, and I will fill it. 11 But my people would not hearken to my voice: and Iſrael would none of me. 12 So I gaue them vp vnto their owne hearts luſt: and they walked in in their owne counſels. 13 O that my people had hearkned vnto me: and Iſrael had walked in my wayes! 14 I ſhould ſoone haue ſubdued their enemies, and turned my hand againſt their aduerſaries. 15 The haters of the Lord ſhould haue ſubmitted themſelues vnto him: but their time ſhould haue endured for euer. 16 Hee ſhould haue fedde them alſo with the fineſt of the wheat: and with honie out of the rocke, ſhould I haue ſatiſfied thee.

CHAPTER 82 1 *A Pſalme of Aſaph.* God ſtandeth in the Congregation of the mightie: hee iudgeth among the gods. 2 How long will yee iudge vniuſtly: and accept the perſons of the wicked? Selah. 3 Defend the poore and fatherleſſe: doe iuſtice to the afflicted and needie. 4 Deliuer the poore and needy: rid them out of the hand of the wicked. 5 They know not, neither wil they vnderſtand; they walke on in darknes: all the foundations of the earth are out of courſe. 6 I haue ſaid, Ye are gods: and all of you are children of the moſt High: 7 But ye ſhall die like men, and fall like one of the Princes. 8 Ariſe, O God, iudge the earth: for thou ſhalt inherite all nations.

CHAPTER 83 1 *A ſong or Pſalme of Aſaph.* Keepe not thou ſilence, O God: hold not thy peace, and be not ſtill, O God. 2 For loe, thine enemies make a tumult: and they that hate thee, haue lift vp the head. 3 They haue taken craftie counſell againſt thy people, and conſulted againſt thy hidden ones. 4 They haue ſaid, Come, and let vs cut them off from being a nation: that the name of Iſrael may bee no more in remembrance. 5 For they haue conſulted together with one conſent: they are confederate againſt thee. 6 The tabernacles of Edom, and the Iſhmaelites: of Moab, and the Hagarens. 7 Gebal and Ammon, and Amalek: the Philiſtines, with the inhabitants of Tyre. 8 Aſſur alſo is ioyned with them: they haue holpen the children of Lot. Selah. 9 Doe vnto them as vnto the Midianites: as to Siſera, as to Iabin, at the brooke of Kiſon: 10 Which periſhed at En-dor: they became as dung for the earth. 11 Make their nobles like Oreb, and like Zeeb: yea all their princes as Zebah, and as Zalmunna: 12 Who ſayd, Let vs take to our ſelues, the houſes of God in poſſeſſion. 13 O my God, make them like a wheele: as the ſtubble before the wind. 14 As the fire burneth a wood: and as the flame ſetteth the mountaines on fire:15So perſecute them with thy tempeſt: and make them afraid with thy ſtorme.16Fill their faces with ſhame: that they may ſeeke thy name, O Lord.17Let them be confounded and troubled for euer: yea let them be put to ſhame, and periſh:18That men may knowe, that thou, whoſe name alone is IEHOVAH: art the moſt High ouer all the earth.

CHAPTER 841*To the chiefe muſician vpon Gittith, a Pſalme for the ſonnes of Korah.* How amiable are thy tabernacles, O Lord of hoſtes!2My ſoule longeth, yea euen fainteth for the courts of the Lord: my heart and my fleſh cryeth out for the liuing God.3Yea the ſparrowe hath found an houſe, and the ſwallow a neſt for her ſelfe, where ſhe may lay her young, euen thine altars, O Lord of hoſtes, my king and my God.4Bleſſed are they that dwell in thy houſe: they wilbe ſtill prayſing thee. Selah.5Bleſſed is the man whoſe ſtrength is in thee: in whoſe heart are the wayes of them:6Who paſsing through the valley of Baca, make it a well: the raine alſo filleth the pooles.7They goe from ſtrength to ſtrength: euery one of them in Zion appeareth before God.8O Lord God of hoſtes, heare my prayer: giue eare, O God of Iacob. Selah.9Behold, O God our ſhield: and looke vpon the face of thine anointed.10For a day in thy courts, is better then a thouſand: I had rather be a doore keeper in the houſe of my God, then to dwell in the tents of wickedneſſe.11For the Lord God is a ſunne and ſhield: the Lord will giue grace and glory: no good thing will he withhold from them that walke vprightly.12O Lord of hoſtes: bleſſed is the man that truſteth in thee.

CHAPTER 851*To the chiefe muſician, a Pſalme for the ſonnes of Korah.* Lord, thou haſt bene fauourable vnto thy land: thou haſt brought backe the captiuity of Iacob.2Thou haſt forgiuen the iniquitie of thy people, thou haſt couered all their ſinne. Selah.3Thou haſt taken away all thy wrath: thou haſt turned thy ſelfe from the fierceneſse of thine anger.4Turne vs, O God of our ſaluation: and cauſe thine anger towards vs to ceaſe.5Wilt thou be angry with vs for euer? wilt thou drawe out thine anger to all generations?6Wilt thou not reuiue vs againe: that thy people may reioyce in thee?7ſhew vs thy mercy, O Lord; and graunt vs thy ſaluation.8I will heare what God the Lord will ſpeake: for hee will ſpeake peace vnto his people, and to his Saints: but let them not turne againe to folly.9Surely his ſaluation is nigh them that feare him; that glory may dwell in our land.10Mercy and truth are met together: righteouſneſſe and peace haue kiſſed each other.11Truth ſhall ſpring out of the earth: and righteouſneſſe ſhall looke downe from heauen.12Yea the Lord ſhall giue that which is good: and our land ſhall yeeld her increaſe.13Righteouſnes ſhall go before him: and ſhall ſet vs in the way of his ſteps.

CHAPTER 861*A prayer of Dauid.* Bow downe thine eare, O Lord, heare me: for I am poore & needy.2Preſeruemy ſoule, for I am holy: O thou my God, ſaue thy ſeruant, that truſteth in thee.3Be merciful vnto me, O Lord: for I cry vnto thee daily.4Reioyce the ſoule of thy ſeruant: for vnto thee (O Lord) doe I lift vp my ſoule.5For thou Lord art good, and ready to forgiue: and plenteous in mercie vnto all them that call vpon thee.6Giue eare O Lord, vnto my prayer: and attend to the voice of my ſupplications.7In the day of my trouble I will call vpon thee: for thou wilt anſwere mee.8Among the gods there is none like vnto thee (O Lord:) neither are there any workes like vnto thy workes.9All nations whom thou haſt made, ſhall come and worſhip before thee, O Lord: and ſhall glorifie thy Name.10For thou art great, and doeſt wonderous things: thou art God alone.11Teach me thy way, O Lord, I will walke in thy trueth: vnite my heart to feare thy Name.12I will praiſe thee, O Lord my God, with all my heart: and I wil glorifie thy Name for euermore.13For great is thy mercy toward me: and thou haſt deliuered my ſoule from the loweſt hell.14O God, the proud are riſen againſt mee, and the aſſemblies of violent men haue ſought after my ſoule: and haue not ſet thee before them.15But thou, O Lord, art a God full of compaſſion, and gracious: long ſuffering, and plenteous in mercy and trueth.16O turne vnto me, and haue mercie vpon me, giue thy ſtrength vnto thy ſeruant: and ſaue the ſonne of thine handmaid.17ſhew me a token for good, that they which hate me may ſee it, and bee aſhamed: becauſe thou, Lord, haſt holpen me, and comforted me.

CHAPTER 871*A Pſalme or ſong for the ſonnes of Korah.* His foundation is in the holy mountaines.2The Lord loueth the gates of Zion: more then all the dwellings of Iacob.3Glorious things are ſpoken of thee, O Citie of God. Selah.4I will make mention of Rahab, and Babylon, to them that know mee; behold Philiſtia, and Tyre, with Ethiopia: this man was borne there.5And of Zion it ſhalbe ſaid, This and that man was borne in her: and the higheſt himſelfe ſhall eſtabliſh her.6The Lord ſhall count when he writeth vp the people: that this man was borne there. Selah.7As wel the ſingers as the players on inſtruments ſhall bee there: all my ſprings are in thee.

CHAPTER 881*A ſong or Pſalme for the ſonnes of Korah, to the chiefe Muſician vpon Mahalath Leannoth, Maſchil of Heman the Ezrahite.* O Lord God of my ſaluation, I haue cried day and night before thee.2Let my prayer come before thee: incline thine eare vnto my cry.3For my ſoule is full of troubles: and my life draweth nigh vnto the graue.4I am counted with them that go downe into the pit: I am as a man that hath no ſtrength.5Free among the dead, like the ſlaine that lie in the graue, whom thou remembreſt no more: and they are cut off from thy hand.6Thou haſt laid me in the loweſt pit: in darkeneſſe, in the deepes.7Thy wrath lieth hard vpon me: and thou haſt afflicted me with all thy waues. Selah.8Thou haſt put away mine acquaintance farre from mee: thou haſt made me an abomination vnto them: I am ſhut vp, and I cannot come forth.9Mine eye mourneth by reaſon of affliction, Lord, I haue called daily vpon thee: I haue ſtretched out my hands vnto thee.10Wilt thou ſhew wonders to the dead? ſhal the dead Ariſe and praiſe thee? Selah.11Shall thy louing kindneſſe be declared in the graue? or thy faithfulneſse in deſtruction?12Shall thy wonders be knowen in the darke? and thy righteouſneſſe in the land of forgetfulneſse?13But vnto thee haue I cried, O Lord, and in the morning ſhall my prayer preuent thee.14Lord, why caſteſt thou off my ſoule? why hideſt thou thy face from me?15I am afflicted and ready to die, from my youth vp: while I ſuffer thy terrours, I am diſtracted.16Thy fierce wrath goeth ouer me: thy terrours haue cut me off.17They came round about mee daily like water: they compaſſed mee about together.18Louer and friend haſt thou put farre from me: and mine acquaintance into darkeneſſe.

CHAPTER 891*Maſchil of Ethan the Ezrahite.* I will ſing of the mercies of the Lord for euer: with my mouth will I make knowen thy faithfulneſse to all generations.2For I haue ſaid, Mercie ſhall bee built vp for euer: thy faithfulneſse ſhalt thou eſtabliſh in the very heauens.3I haue made a couenant with my choſen: I haue ſworne vnto Dauid my ſeruant.4Thy ſeed will I ſtabliſh for euer: and build vp thy throne to all generations. Selah.5And the heauens ſhall praiſe thy wonders, O Lord: thy faithfulnes alſo in the congregation of the Saints.6For who in the heauen can be compared vnto the Lord? who among the ſonnes of the mightie can be likened vnto the Lord?7God is greatly to be feared in the aſſembly of the Saints: and to bee had in reuerence of all them that are about him.8O Lord God of hoſts, who is a ſtrong Lord like vnto thee? or to thy faithfulneſse round about thee?9Thou ruleſt the raging of the ſea: when the waues thereof Ariſe; thou ſtilleſt them.10Thou haſt broken Rahab in pieces, as one that is ſlaine: thou haſt ſcattered thine enemies with thy ſtrong arme.11The heauens are thine, the earth alſo is thine: as for the world and the fulnes thereof, thou haſt founded them.12The North and the South, thou haſt created them: Tabor and Hermon ſhall reioyce in thy Name.13Thou haſt a mighty arme: ſtrong is thy hand, and high is thy right hand.14Iuſtice and iudgement are the habitation of thy throne: mercie and trueth ſhall goe before thy face.15Bleſſed is the people that knowe the ioyfull ſound: they ſhall walke O Lord in the light of thy countenance.16In thy name ſhall they reioyce all the day: and in thy righteouſnes ſhall they be exalted.17For thou art the glory of their ſtrength: and in thy fauour our horne ſhall be exalted.18For the Lord is our defence: and the holy One of Iſrael is our king.19Then thou ſpakeſt in viſion to thy holy one, and ſaidſt, I haue laid helpe vpon one that is mightie: I haue exalted one choſen out of the people.20I haue found Dauid my ſeruant: with my holy oile haue I anointed him.21With whome my hand ſhall bee eſtabliſhed: mine arme alſo ſhall ſtrengthen him.22The enemie ſhall not exact vpon him: nor the ſonne of wickedneſſe afflict him.23And I will beate downe his foes before his face: and plague them that hate him.24But my faithfulneſse and my mercy ſhalbe with him: and in my name ſhall his horne be exalted.25I will ſet his hand alſo in the ſea: and his right hand in the riuers.26He ſhall crie vnto mee, Thou art my father: my God, and the rocke of my ſaluation.27Alſo I will make him my firſt borne: higher then the kings of the earth.28My mercy will I keepe for him for euermore: and my couenant ſhall ſtand faſt with him.29His ſeed alſo will I make to indure for euer: and his throne as the dayes of heauen.[30]If his children forſake my lawe, and walke not in my iudgements;[31]If they breake my ſtatutes, and keepe not my commandements:[32]Then will I viſite their tranſgreſſion with the rod, and their iniquitie with ſtripes.[33]Neuertheleſſe, my louing kindneſſe will I not vtterly take from him: nor ſuffer my faithfulneſse to faile.[34]My couenant will I not breake: nor alter the thing that is gone out of my lippes.[35]Once haue I ſworne by my holineſſe; that I will not lye vnto Dauid.[36]His ſeede ſhall endure for euer; and his throne as the ſunne before me.[37]It ſhalbe eſtabliſhed for euer as the Moone: and as a faithfull witneſſe in heauen. Selah.[38]But thou haſt caſt off and abhorred: thou haſt bene wroth with thine anointed.[39]Thou haſt made voyd the couenant of thy ſeruant: thou haſt profaned his crowne, by caſting it to the ground.[40]Thou haſt broken downe all his hedges: thou haſt brought his ſtrong holds to ruine.[41]All that paſſe by the way; ſpoile him: hee is a reproach to his neighbours.[42]Thou haſt ſet vp the right hand of his aduerſaries: thou haſt made all his enemies to reioyce.[43]Thou haſt alſo turned the edge of his ſword: and haſt not made him to ſtand in the battaile.[44]Thou haſt made his glory to ceaſe: and caſt his throne downe to the ground.[45]The dayes of his youth haſt thou ſhortned: thou haſt couered him with ſhame. Selah.[46]How long, Lord, wilt thou hide thy ſelfe, for cuer? ſhall thy wrath burne like fire?[47]Remember how ſhort my time is: wherefore haſt thou made all men in vaine?[48]What man is he that liueth, and ſhall not ſee death? ſhall he deliuer his ſoule from the hand of the graue? Selah.[49]Lord, where are thy former louing kindneſses, which thou ſwareſt vnto Dauid in thy trueth?[50]Remember (Lord) the reproach of thy ſeruants: how I doe beare in my boſome the reproache of all the mighty people.[51]Wherewith thine enemies haue reproached, O Lord: wherewith they haue reproached the foote-ſteppes of thine Annointed.[52]Bleſſed be the Lord for euermore, Amen, and Amen.

CHAPTER 90[1]*A prayer of Moſes the man of God.* Lord, thou haſt bene our dwelling place in all generations.[2]Before the mountaines were broughtforth, or euer thou hadſt formed the earth and the world: euen from euerlaſting to euerlaſting thou art God.[3]Thou turneſt man to deſtruction: and ſayeſt, Returne yee children of men.[4]For a thouſand yeeres in thy ſight are but as yeſterday when it is paſt: and as a watch in the night.[5]Thou carrieſt them away as with a flood, they are as a ſleepe: in the morning they are like graſſe which groweth vp.[6]In the morning it flouriſheth, and groweth vp: in the euening it is cut downe, and withereth.[7]For we are conſumed by thine anger: and by thy wrath are we troubled.[8]Thou haſt ſet our iniquities before thee: our ſecret ſinnes in the light of thy countenance.[9]For all our dayes are paſſed away in thy wrath: we ſpend our yeeres as a tale that is told.[10]The dayes of our yeres are threeſcore yeeres and ten, and if by reaſon of ſtrength they be foureſcore yeeres, yet is their ſtrength labour and ſorrow: for it is ſoone cut off, and we flie away.[11]Who knoweth the power of thine anger? euen according to thy feare, ſo is thy wrath.[12]So teach vs to number our daies: that wee may apply our hearts vnto wiſedome.[13]Returne (O Lord) how long? and let it repent thee concerning thy ſeruants.[14]O ſatiſfie vs early with thy mercie: that we may reioyce, and be glad all our dayes.[15]Make vs glad according to the dayes wherein thou haſt afflicted vs: and the yeeres wherein we haue ſeene euil.[16]Let thy worke appeare vnto thy ſeruants: and thy glory vnto their children.[17]And let the beautie of the Lord our God be vpon vs, and eſtabliſh thou the worke of our hands vpon vs: yea, the work of our hands eſtabliſh thou it.

CHAPTER 91[1]He that dwelleth in the ſecret place of the moſt high: ſhall abide vnder the ſhadow of the Almightie.[2]I will ſay of the Lord, He is my refuge, and my fortreſse: my God, in him will I truſt.[3]Surely he ſhall deliuer thee from the ſnare of the fouler: and from the noiſome peſtilence.[4]Hee ſhall couer thee with his feathers, and vnder his wings ſhalt thou truſt: his trueth ſhall bee thy ſhield and buckler.[5]Thou ſhalt not bee afraid for the terrour by night: nor for the arrow that flieth by day:[6]Nor for the peſtilence that walketh in darknes: nor for the deſtruction, that waſteth at noone-day.[7]A thouſand ſhall fall at thy ſide, and ten thouſand at thy right hand: but it ſhall not come nigh thee.[8]Onely with thine eyes ſhalt thou behold: & ſee the reward of the wicked.[9]Becauſe thou haſt made the Lord, which is my refuge, euen the moſt High, thy habitation:[10]There ſhall no euill befall thee: neither ſhall any plague come nigh thy dwelling.[11]For hee ſhall giue his Angels charge ouer thee: to keepe thee in all thy wayes.[12]They ſhall beare thee vp in their hands: leſt thou daſh thy foot againſt a ſtone.[13]Thou ſhalt tread vpon the Lion, and adder: the yong Lion and the dragon ſhalt thou trample vnder feete.[14]Becauſe he hath ſet his loue vpon me, therefore will I deliuer him: I wil ſet him on high, becauſe hee hath knowen my Name.[15]He ſhall call vpon me, and I will anſwere him. I will bee with him in trouble, I will deliuer him, and honour him.[16]With long life wil I ſatiſfie him: and ſhew him my ſaluation.

CHAPTER 92[1]*A Pſalme or ſong for the Sabbath day.* It is a good thing to giue thanks vnto the Lord, and to ſing praiſes vnto thy Name, O moſt High:[2]To ſhew foorth thy louing kindneſſe in the morning: and thy faithfulneſse euery night:[3]Upon an inſtrument of tenne ſtrings, and vpon the pſalterie: vpon the harpe with a ſolemne ſound.[4]For thou, Lord, haſt made me glad through thy worke: I will triumph in the workes of thy hands.[5]O Lord, how great are thy workes! and thy thoughts are very deepe.[6]A brutiſh man knoweth not: neither doeth a foole vnderſtand this.[7]When the wicked ſpring as the graſſe, and when all the workers of iniquitie doe flouriſh: it is that they ſhall be deſtroyed for euer.[8]But thou, Lord, art moſt high for euermore.[9]For loe, thine enemies, O Lord, for loe, thine enemies ſhall periſh: all the workers of iniquity ſhalbe ſcattred.[10]But my horne ſhalt thou exalt like the horne of an vnicorne: I ſhalbe anointed with freſh oyle.[11]Mine eye alſo ſhall ſee my deſire on mine enemies: and mine eares ſhall heare my deſire of the wicked that riſe vp againſt me.[12]The righteous ſhal flouriſh like the palme tree: hee ſhall growe like a cedar in Lebanon.[13]Thoſe that be planted in the houſe of the Lord, ſhall flouriſh in the courts of our God.[14]They ſhal ſtill bring forth fruit in old age: they ſhalbe fat, & flouriſhing:[15]To ſhew that the Lord is vpright: hee is my rocke, and there is no vnrighteouſneſſe in him.

CHAPTER 93[1]The Lord reigneth, he is clothed with Maieſtie, the Lord is clothed with ſtrength, wherewith hee hath girded himſelfe: the world alſo is ſtabliſhed, that it cannot be moued.[2]Thy throne is eſtabliſhed of old: thou art from euerlaſting.[3]The floods haue lifted vp, O Lord, the floods haue lifted vp their voice: the floods lift vp their waues.[4]The Lord on high is mightier then the noiſe of many waters, yea then the mightie waues of the ſea.[5]Thy teſtimonies are very ſure: holineſſe becommeth thine houſe, O Lord, for euer.

CHAPTER 94[1]O Lord God, to whome vengeance belongeth: O God to whome vengeance belongeth, ſhew thy ſelfe.[2]Lift vp thy ſelfe, thou iudge of the earth: render a reward to the proud.[3]Lord, how long ſhall the wicked? how long ſhall the wicked triumph?[4]How long ſhal they vtter, and ſpeake hard things? and all the workers of iniquitie boaſt themſelues?[5]They breake in pieces thy people, O Lord: and afflict thine heritage.[6]They ſlay the widowe and the ſtranger: and murder the fatherleſſe.[7]Yet they ſay, The Lord ſhall not ſee: neither ſhall the God of Iacob regard it.[8]Underſtand, yee brutiſh among the people: and ye fooles, when will ye be wiſe?[9]He that planted the eare, ſhall he not heare? he that formed the eye, ſhall he not ſee?[10]He that chaſtiſeth the heathen, ſhall not he correct? hee that teacheth man knowledge, ſhall not he know?[11]The Lord knoweth the thoughts of man: that they are vanitie.[12]Bleſſed is the man whome thou chaſteneſt, O Lord: and teacheſt him out of thy Law:[13]That thou mayeſt giue him reſt from the dayes of aduerſitie: vntill the pit be digged for the wicked.[14]For the Lord will not caſt off his people: neither will he forſake his inheritance.[15]But iudgement ſhall returne vnto righteouſneſſe: and all the vpright in heart ſhall follow it.[16]Who will riſe vp for mee againſt the euill doers? or who will ſtand vp for me againſt the workers of iniquitie?[17]Unleſſe the Lord had bene my helpe: my ſoule had almoſt dwelt in ſilence.[18]When I ſaid, My foote ſlippeth: thy mercie, O Lord, held me vp.[19]In the multitude of my thoughts within me, thy comforts delight my ſoule.[20]ſhal the throne of iniquitie haue fellowſhip with thee: which frameth miſchiefe by a lawe?[21]They gather themſelues together againſt the ſoule of the righteous: and condemne the innocent blood.[22]But the Lord is my defence: and my God is the rocke of my refuge.[23]And hee ſhall bring vpon them their owne iniquitie, and ſhall cut them off in their owne wickedneſſe: yea the Lord our God ſhall cut them off.

CHAPTER 95[1]O come, let vs ſing vnto the Lord: let vs make a ioyfull noiſe to the rocke of our ſaluation.[2]Let vs come before his preſence with thankſgiuing: and make a ioyfull noiſe vnto him with pſalmes.[3]For the

Lord is a great God: and a great king aboue all Gods.4In his hand are the deepe places of the earth: the ſtrength of the hilles is his alſo.5The ſea is his, and he made it: and his hands formed the dry land.6O come, let vs worſhip and bowe downe: let vs kneele before the Lord our maker.7For he is our God, and we are the people of his paſture, and the ſheepe of his hand: to day if yee will heare his voyce,8Harden not your heart, as in the prouocation: and as in the day of temptation, in the wilderneſſe:9When your fathers tempted me: proued me, and ſawe my worke.10Fortie yeeres long was I grieued with this generation: and ſayd, It is a people that doe erre in their heart: and they haue not knowen my wayes.11Unto whom I ſware in my wrath: that they ſhould not enter into my reſt.

CHAPTER 961O ſing vnto the Lord a new ſong: ſing vnto the Lord all the earth.2Sing vnto the Lord, bleſſe his name: ſhew forth his ſaluation from day to day.3Declare his glory among the heathen: his wonders among all people.4For the Lord is great, and greatly to be praiſed: hee is to be feared aboue all Gods.5For all the gods of the nations are idoles: but the Lord made the heauens.6Honour and maieſtie are before him: ſtrength and beauty are in his ſanctuary.7Giue vnto the Lord (O yee kinreds of the people:) giue vnto the Lord glory and ſtrength.8Giue vnto the Lord the glory due vnto his name: bring an offering, and come into his courts.9O worſhip the Lord, in the beautie of holineſſe: feare before him all the earth.10ſay among the heathen, that the Lord reigneth: the world alſo ſhalbe eſtabliſhed that it ſhall not be moued: he ſhall iudge the people righteouſly.11Let the heauens reioyce, and let the earth be glad: let the ſea roare, and the fulneſse thereof.12Let the field be ioyfull, and all that is therein: then ſhall all the trees of the wood reioyce13Before the Lord, for hee commeth, for hee commeth to iudge the earth: hee ſhall iudge the world with righteouſneſſe, and the people with his trueth.

CHAPTER 971The Lord raigneth, let the earth reioyce: let the multitude of Iſles bee glad thereof.2Clouds and darkeneſſe are round about him: righteouſneſſe and iudgement are the habitation of his throne.3A fire goeth before him: and burneth vp his enemies round about.4His lightnings inlightned the world: the earth ſawe, and trembled.5The hilles melted like waxe at the preſence of the Lord: at the preſence of the Lord of the whole earth.6The heauens declare his righteouſneſſe: and all the people ſee his glory.7Confounded be all they that ſerue grauen images, that boaſt themſelues of idoles: worſhip him all yee gods.8Sion heard, and was glad, and the daughters of Iudah reioyced: becauſe of thy iudgements, O Lord.9For thou, Lord, art high aboue all the earth: thou art exalted farre aboue all gods.10Yee that loue the Lord, hate euil; hee preſerueth the ſoules of his Saints: hee deliuereth them out of the hand of the wicked.11Light is ſowen for the righteous: and gladneſſe for the vpright in heart.12Reioyce in the Lord, ye righteous: and giue thanks at the remembrance of his holineſſe.

CHAPTER 981*A Pſalme.* O ſing vnto the Lord a New ſong, for hee hath done marueilous things: his right hand, and his holy arme hath gotten him the victorie.2The Lord hath made knowen his ſaluation: his righteouſneſſe hath hee openly ſhewed in the ſight of the heathen.3Hee hath remembred his mercie and his trueth toward the houſe of Iſrael: all the ends of the earth haue ſeene the ſaluation of our God.4Make a ioyfull noiſe vnto the Lord, all the earth: make a lowd noiſe, and reioyce, and ſing praiſe.5Sing vnto the Lord with the harpe: with the harpe, and the voice of a Pſalme.6With trumpets and ſound of cornet: make a ioyfull noiſe before the Lord, the King.7Let the ſea roare, and the fulneſse thereof: the world, and they that dwell therein.8Let the floods clap their handes: let the hilles be ioyfull together9Before the Lord, for he commeth to iudge the earth: with righteouſneſſe ſhall hee iudge the world, and the people with equitie.

CHAPTER 991The Lord raigneth, let the people tremble: he ſitteth betweene the Cherubims, let the earth bee mooued.2The Lord is great in Zion: and he is high aboue all people.3Let them praiſe thy great and terrible Name: for it is holy.4The Kings ſtrength alſo loueth iudgement, thou doeſt eſtabliſh equitie: thou executeſt iudgement and righteouſnes in Iacob.5Exalt yee the Lord our God, and worſhip at his footſtoole: for he is holy.6Moſes and Aaron among his Prieſts, and Samuel among them that call vpon his Name: they called vpon the Lord, and he anſwered them.7He ſpake vnto them in the cloudie pillar: they kept his Teſtimonies, and the Ordinance that he gaue them.8Thou anſweredſt them, O Lord our God: thou waſt a God that forgaueſt them, though thou tookeſt vengeance of their inuentions.9Exalt the Lord our God, and worſhip at his holy hill: for the Lord our God is holy.

CHAPTER 1001*A Pſalme of praiſe.* Make a ioyfull noiſe vnto the Lord, all ye lands.2Serue the Lord with gladnes: come before his preſence with ſinging.3Know ye that the Lord, hee is God, it is he that hath made vs, and not we our ſelues: wee are his people, and the ſheepe of his paſture.4Enter into his gates with thankſgiuing, and into his Courts with praiſe: bee thankfull vnto him, and bleſſe his Name.5For the Lord is good, his mercy is euerlaſting: and his trueth endureth to all generations.

CHAPTER 1011*A Pſalme of Dauid.* I will ſing of Mercie and Iudgement: vnto thee, O Lord, wil I ſing.2I will behaue my ſelfe wiſely in a perfect way, O when wilt thou come vnto me? I will walke within my houſe with a perfect heart.3I will ſet no wicked thing before mine eyes: I hate the worke of them that turne aſide, it ſhal not cleaue to me.4A froward heart ſhall depart from me, I will not knowe a wicked perſon.5Whoſo priuily ſlandereth his neighbour, him will I cut off: him that hath an high looke, and a proud heart, will not I ſuffer.6Mine eyes ſhall be vpon the faithfull of the land, that they may dwell with me: he that walketh in a perfect way, he ſhall ſerue me.7He that worketh deceit, ſhall not dwell within my houſe: he that telleth lies ſhall not tarie in my ſight.8I will earely deſtroy all the wicked of the land: that I may cut off all wicked doers from the citie of the Lord.

CHAPTER 1021*A prayer of the afflicted when he is ouerwhelmed, and powreth out his complaint before the Lord.* Heare my prayer, O Lord: and let my crie come vnto thee.2Hide not thy face from me in the day when I am in trouble, incline thine eare vnto me: in the day when I call, anſwere mee ſpeedily.3For my dayes are conſumed like ſmoke: and my bones are burnt as an hearth.4My heart is ſmitten, and withered like graſſe: ſo that I forget to eate my bread.5By reaſon of the voice of my groning, my bones cleaue to my ſkinne.6I am like a Pelican of the wildernes: I am like an owle of the deſert.7I watch, and am as a ſparowe alone vpon the houſe top.8Mine enemies reproch me all the day: and they that are mad againſt me, are ſworne againſt me.9For I haue eaten aſhes like bread: and mingled my drinke with weeping.10Becauſe of thine indignation and thy wrath: for thou haſt lifted me vp, and caſt me downe.11My dayes are like a ſhadow, that declineth: & I am withered like graſſe.12But thou, O Lord, ſhalt endure for euer: and thy remembrance vnto all generations.13Thou ſhalt Ariſe, and haue mercie vpon Zion: for the time to fauour her, yea the ſet time is come.14For thy ſeruants take pleaſure in her ſtones: and fauour the duſt therof.15So the heathen ſhall feare the Name of the Lord: and all the kings of the earth thy glory.16When the Lord ſhall build vp Zion: he ſhall appeare in his glory.17He will regard the prayer of the deſtitute, and not deſpiſe their prayer.18This ſhall be written for the generation to come: and the people which ſhall be created, ſhall praiſe the Lord.19For hee hath looked downe from the height of his Sanctuarie: from heauen did the Lord beholde the earth:20To heare the groning of the priſoner: to looſe thoſe that are appointed to death:21To declare the Name of the Lord in Zion: and his praiſe in Ieruſalem:22When the people are gathered together: and the kingdomes to ſerue the Lord.23He weakened my ſtrength in the way: he ſhortened my dayes.24I ſaid, O my God, take me not away in the midſt of my dayes: thy yeres are throughout all generations.25Of old haſt thou laid the foundation of the earth: and the heauens are the worke of thy hands.26They ſhall periſh, but thou ſhalt indure, yea all of them ſhall waxe old like a garment: as a veſture ſhalt thou change them, and they ſhalbe changed.27But thou art the ſame: and thy yeeres ſhall haue no end.28The children of thy ſeruants ſhal continue: and their ſeed ſhall be eſtabliſhed before thee.

CHAPTER 1031*A Pſalme of Dauid.* Bleſſe the Lord, O my ſoule: and all that is within me, bleſſe his holy Name.2Bleſſe the Lord, O my ſoule: & forget not all his benefits.3Who forgiueth all thine iniquities: who healeth all thy diſeaſes.4Who redeemeth thy life from deſtruction: who crowneth thee with louing kindneſſe and tender mercies.5Who ſatiſfieth thy mouth with good things: ſo that thy youth is renewed like the Eagles.6The Lord executeth righteouſneſſe: and iudgement for all that are oppreſſed.7He made knowen his wayes vnto Moſes: his actes vnto the children of Iſrael.8The Lord is mercifull and gracious: ſlow to anger, and plenteous in mercy.9Hee will not alwayes chide: neither will he keepe his anger for euer.10Hee hath not dealt with vs after our ſinnes: nor rewarded vs according to our iniquities.11For as the heauen is high aboue the earth: ſo great is his mercy toward them that feare him.12As farre as the Eaſt is from the Weſt: ſo farre hath hee remooued our tranſgreſſions from vs.13Like as a father pitieth his children: ſo the Lord pitieth them that feare him.14For he knoweth our frame: hee remembreth that we are duſt.15As for man, his dayes are as graſſe: as a flower of the field, ſo he flouriſheth.16For the winde paſſeth ouer it, and it is gone; and the place thereof ſhall know it no more.17But the mercy of the Lord is from euerlaſting to euerlaſting vpon them that feare him: and his righteouſneſſe vnto childrens children:18To ſuch as keepe his couenant: and to thoſe that remember his commandements to doe them.19The Lord hath prepared his throne in the heauens: and his kingdome ruleth ouer all.20Bleſſe the Lord yee his Angels, that excell in ſtrength, that do his commandements: hearkening vnto the voice of his word.21Bleſſe ye the Lord all yee his hoſtes: ye miniſters of his that doe his pleaſure.22Bleſſe the Lord all his works in all places of his dominion: bleſſe the Lord, O my ſoule.

CHAPTER 1041Bleſſe the Lord, O my ſoule, O Lord my God, thou art very great: thou art clothed with honour and maieſtie.2Who couereſt thy ſelfe with light, as with a garment: who ſtretcheſt out the heauens like a curtaine.3Who layeth the beames of his chambers in the waters, who maketh the cloudes his charet: who walketh vpon the wings of the wind.4Who maketh his Angels ſpirits: his miniſters a flaming fire.5Who laid the foundations of the earth: that it ſhould not be remoued for euer.6Thou coueredſt it with the deepe as with a garment: the waters ſtood aboue the mountaines.7At thy rebuke they fled: at the voice of thy thunder they haſted away.8They go vp by the mountaines: they goe downe by the valleys vnto the place which thou haſt founded for them.9Thou haſt ſet a bound that they may not paſſe ouer: that they turne not againe to couer the earth.10He ſendeth the ſprings into the valleys: which runne among the hilles.11They giue drinke to euery beaſt of the field: the wild aſſes quench their thirſt.12By them ſhall the foules of the heauen haue their habitation: which ſing among the branches.13He watereth the hilles from his chambers: the earth is ſatiſfied with the fruit of thy workes.14He cauſeth the graſſe to grow for the cattell, and herbe for the ſeruice of man: that he may bring forth food out of the earth:15And wine that maketh glad the heart of man, and oile to make his face to ſhine: and bread which ſtrengtheneth mans heart.16The trees of the Lord are full of ſappe: the cedars of Lebanon which he hath planted.17Where the birds make their neſts: as for the Storke, the firre trees are her houſe.18The hie hilles are a refuge for the wilde goates: and the rockes for the conies.19He appointed the moone for ſeaſons; the ſunne knoweth his going downe.20Thou makeſt darkneſſe, and it is night: wherein all the beaſts of the forreſt doe creepe forth.21The young lyons roare after their pray: and ſeeke their meate from God.22The ſunne Ariſeth, they gather themſelues together: and lay them downe in their dennes.23Man goeth forth vnto his worke: and to his labour, vntill the euening.24O Lord, how manifold are thy workes! in wiſedome haſt thou made them all: the earth is full of thy riches.25So is this great and wide ſea, wherein are things creeping innumerable: both ſmall and great beaſts.26There goe the ſhippes; there is that Leuiathan, whom thou haſt made to play therein.27Theſe waite all vpon thee: that thou mayeſt giue them their meate in due ſeaſon.28That thou giueſt them, they gather: thou openeſt thine hand, they are filled with good.29Thou hideſt thy face, they are troubled, thou takeſt away their breath, they die: and returne to their duſt.30Thou ſendeſt forth thy ſpirit, they are created: and thou reneweſt the face of the earth.31The glory of the Lord ſhall endure for euer: the Lord ſhall reioyce in his workes.32Hee looketh on the earth, and it trembleth; he toucheth the hilles, and they ſmoke.33I will ſing vnto the Lord as long as I liue: I will ſing praiſe to my God, while I haue my being.34My meditation of him ſhalbe ſweete: I will be glad in the Lord.35Let the ſinners be conſumed out of the earth, and let the wicked bee no more: bleſſe thou the Lord, O my ſoule. Praiſe yee the Lord.

CHAPTER 1051O giue thankes vnto the Lord, call vpon his name: make knowen his deeds among the people.2Sing vnto him; ſing Pſalmes vnto him: talke yee of all his wondrous workes.3Glory yee in his holy name: let the heart of them reioyce, that ſeeke the Lord.4Seeke the Lord, and his ſtrength: ſeeke his face euermore.5Remember his maruellous workes, that hee hath done: his wonders, and the iudgements of his mouth,6O yee ſeede of Abraham his ſeruant: yee children of Iacob his choſen.7He is the Lord our God: his iudgements are in all the earth.8He hath remembred his couenant for euer: the word which he commanded to a thouſand generations.9Which couenant he made with Abraham, and his oath vnto Iſaac:10And confirmed the ſame vnto Iacob for a law: and to Iſrael for an euerlaſting couenant:11Saying, Unto thee will I giue the land of Canaan: the lot of your inheritance.12When they were but a few men in number: yea very few, & ſtrangers in it.13When they went from one nation to another: from one kingdome to another people.14He ſuffred no man to doe them wrong: yea he reproued kings for their ſakes:15Saying, Touch not mine anointed; and doe my Prophets no harme.16Moreouer hee called for a famine vpon the land: he brake the whole ſtaffe of bread.17Hee ſent a man before them: euen Ioſeph, who was ſold for a ſeruant.18Whoſe feete they hurt with fetters: he was layd in iron.19Untill the time that his word came: the word of the Lord tried him.20The king ſent and looſed him: euen the ruler of the people, and let him goe free.21Hee made him lord of his houſe: and ruler of all his ſubſtance:22To binde his princes at his pleaſure: and teach his Senatours wiſedome.23Iſrael alſo came into Egypt: and Iacob ſoiourned in the land of Ham.24And hee increaſed his people greatly: and made them ſtronger then their enemies.25He turned their heart to hate his people: to deale ſubtilly with his ſeruants.26Hee ſent Moſes his ſeruant: and Aaron whom he had choſen.27They ſhewed his ſignes among them: and wonders in the land of Ham.28Hee ſent darkneſſe, and made it darke: and they rebelled not againſt his word.29Hee turned their waters into blood: and ſlew their fiſh.30The land brought foorth frogs in abundance: in the chambers of their kings.31He ſpake, and there came diuers ſorts of flies: and lice in all their coaſts.32Hee gaue them haile for raine: and flaming fire in their laud.33Hee ſmote their Uines alſo, and their figge trees: and brake the trees of their coaſtes.34He ſpake, and the locuſts came: and catterpillers, and that without number,35And did eate vp all the herbes in their land: and deuoured the fruite of their ground.36Hee ſmote alſo all the firſt borne in their land: the chiefe of all their ſtrength.37Hee brought them foorth alſo with ſiluer and gold: and there was not one feeble perſon among their tribes.38Egypt was glad when they departed: for the feare of them fell vpon them.39He ſpread a cloud for a couering: and fire to giue light in the night.40The people aſked, and he brought quailes: and ſatiſfied them with the bread of heauen.41He opened the rocke, and the waters guſhed out: they ranne in the dry places like a riuer.42For he remembred his holy promiſe: and Abraham his ſeruant.43And he brought forth his people with ioy: and his choſen with gladneſſe:44And gaue them the lands of the heathen: and they inherited the labour of the people:45That they might obſerue his ſtatutes, and keepe his Lawes, Praiſe ye the Lord.

CHAPTER 1061Praiſe ye the Lord. O giue thankes vnto the Lord, for he is good: for his mercie endureth for euer.2Who can vtter the mighty acts of the Lord? who can ſhew foorth all his praiſe?3Bleſſed are they that keepe iudgement: and he that doeth righteouſneſſe at all times.4Remember me, O Lord, with the fauour that thou beareſt vnto thy people: O viſite me with thy ſaluation:5That I may ſee the good of thy choſen, that I may reioyce in the gladneſſe of thy nation: that I may glory with thine inheritance.6Wee haue ſinned with our fathers: we haue committed iniquitie, we haue done wickedly.7Our fathers vnderſtood not thy wonders in Egypt, they remembred not the multitude of thy mercies: but prouoked him at the ſea, euen at the Red-ſea.8Neuertheleſſe hee ſaued them for his Names ſake: that hee might make his mighty power to be knowen.9He rebuked the Red ſea alſo, and it was dried vp: ſo hee led them through the depthes, as through the wildernes.10And he ſaued them from the hand of him that hated them: and redeemed them from the hand of the enemie.11And the waters couered their enemies: there was not one of them left.12Then beleeued they his words: they ſang his praiſe.13They ſoone forgate his works: they waited not for his counſell:14But luſted exceedingly in the wildernes: & tempted God in the deſert.15And he gaue them their requeſt: but ſent leanneſſe into their ſoule.16They enuied Moſes alſo in the campe: and Aaron the Saint of the Lord.17The earth opened and ſwallowed vp

Dathan: and couered the company of Abiram.18And a fire was kindled
in their company: the flame burnt vp the wicked.19They made a calfe in
Horeb: and worſhipped the molten image.20Thus they changed their
glory, into the ſimilitude of an oxe that eateth graſſe.21They forgate God
their Sauiour: which had done great things in Egypt:22Wonderous
workes in the lande of Ham: and terrible things by the red
ſea.23Therefore he ſaid that he would deſtroy them, had not Moſes his
choſen ſtood before him in the breach: to turne away his wrath, leſt hee
ſhould deſtroy them.24Yea, they deſpiſed the pleaſant land: they
beleeued not his word:25But murmured in their tents: and hearkened
not vnto the voyce of the Lord.26Therefore he lifted vp his hande againſt
them: to ouerthrow them in the wilderneſſe:27To ouerthrow their ſeed
alſo among the nations, and to ſcatter them in the lands.28They ioyned
themſelues alſo vnto Baal-Peor: and ate the ſacrifices of the dead.29Thus
they prouoked him to anger with their inuentions: and the plague brake
in vpon them.30Then ſtood vp Phinehas, and executed iudgement: and
ſo the plague was ſtayed.31And that was counted vnto him for
righteouſneſſe: vnto all generations for euermore.32They angred him
alſo at the waters of ſtrife: ſo that it went ill with Moſes for their
ſakes:33Becauſe they prouoked his ſpirit: ſo that hee ſpake vnaduiſedly
with his lippes.34They did not deſtroy the nations, concerning whom the
Lord commanded them:35But were mingled among the heathen, and
learned their workes.36And they ſerued their idoles: which were a ſnare
vnto them.37Yea they ſacrificed their ſonnes, and their daughters vnto
deuils,38And ſhed innocent blood, euen the blood of their ſons and of
their daughters, whome they ſacrificed vnto the idoles of Canaan: and
the land was polluted with blood.39Thus were they defiled with their
owne works: and went a whoring with their owne
inuentions.40Therefore was the wrath of the Lord kindled againſt his
people: inſomuch that he abhorred his owne inheritance.41And he gaue
them into the hand of the heathen: and they that hated them, ruled ouer
them.42Their enemies alſo oppreſſed them: and they were brought into
ſubiection vnder their hand.43Many times did he deliuer them: but they
prouoked him with their counſell, and were brought low for their
iniquitie.44Neuertheles he regarded their affliction: when he heard their
crie.45And hee remembred for them his couenant: and repented
according to the multitude of his mercies.46He made them alſo to be
pitied, of all thoſe that caried them captiues.47Saue vs, O Lord our God,
and gather vs from among the heathen to giue thankes vnto thy holy
Name: and to triumph in thy praiſe.48Bleſſed bee the Lord God of Iſrael
from euerlaſting to euerlaſting: and let all the people ſay, Amen. Praiſe
ye the Lord.

CHAPTER 1071O giue thankes vnto the Lord, for hee is good: for his
mercie endureth for euer.2Let the redeemed of the Lord ſay ſo: whome
he hath redeemed from the hand of the enemie:3And gathered them out
of the lands, from the Eaſt and from the Weſt: from the North and from
the South.4They wandred in the wildernes, in a ſolitary way: they found
no citie to dwell in.5Hungry and thirſtie: their ſoule fainted in
them.6Then they cryed vnto the Lord in their trouble: and he deliuered
them out of their diſtreſſes.7And hee led them forth by the right way:
that they might goe to a citie of habitation.8Oh that men would praiſe
the Lord, for his goodneſse: and for his wonderfull workes to the
children of men.9For he ſatiſfieth the longing ſoule: and filleth the
hungry ſoule with goodneſse.10ſuch as ſit in darkneſſe and in the
ſhadowe of death: being bound in affliction and yron:11Becauſe they
rebelled againſt the words of God: and contemned the counſell of the
moſt high:12Therefore hee brought downe their heart with labour: they
fel downe, and there was none to helpe.13Then they cryed vnto the Lord
in their trouble: and he ſaued them out of their diſtreſſes.14Hee brought
them out of darkeneſſe, and the ſhadowe of death: and brake their bands
inſunder.15Oh that men would praiſe the Lord for his goodneſse: and
for his wonderfull workes to the children of men.16For he hath broken
the gates of braſſe: and cut the barres of yron in ſunder.17Fooles,
becauſe of their tranſgreſsion, and becauſe of their iniquities, are
afflicted.18Their ſoule abhorreth all manner of meate: and they drawe
neere vnto the gates of death.19Then they crie vnto the Lord in their
trouble: he ſaueth them out of their diſtreſſes.20Hee ſent his word, and
healed them: and deliuered them from their deſtructions.21Oh that men
would praiſe the Lord for his goodneſse: and for his wonderfull workes,
to the children of men.22And let them ſacrifice the ſacrifices of
thankeſgiuing: and declare his workes with reioycing.23They that goe
downe to the ſea in ſhippes: that doe buſineſse in great waters:24Theſe
ſee the workes of the Lord: and his wonders in the deepe.25For he
commandeth, and raiſeth the ſtormy winde: which lifteth vp the waues
thereof.26They mount vp to the heauen: they goe downe againe to the
depthes: their ſoule is melted becauſe of trouble.27They reele to and fro,
and ſtagger like a drunken man; and are at their wits end.28Then they
cry vnto the Lord in their trouble: and hee bringeth them out of their
diſtreſſes.29He maketh the ſtorme a calme: ſo that the waues thereof are
ſtill.30Then are they glad, becauſe they be quiet: ſo he bringeth them
vnto their deſired hauen.31Oh that men would praiſe the Lord for his
goodneſse; and for his wonderfull workes to the children of men:32Let
them exalt him alſo in the congregation of the people, and praiſe him in
the aſſembly of the Elders.33Hee turneth riuers into a wilderneſſe: and
the water ſprings into dry ground:34A fruitfull land into barrenneſse; for
the wickedneſſe of them that dwell therein.35He turneth the wilderneſſe
into a ſtanding water: and dry ground into water-ſprings.36And there he
maketh the hungry to dwell; that they may prepare a citie for
habitation,37And ſowe the fields, and plant vineyards; which may yeeld
fruits of increaſe.38He bleſſeth them alſo, ſo that they are multiplied
greatly: and ſuffreth not their cattell to decreaſe.39Againe, they are
miniſhed and brought lowe through oppreſſion, affliction and
ſorrow.40Hee powreth contempt vpon princes: and cauſeth them to
wander in the wilderneſſe, where there is no way.41Yet ſetteth he the
poore on high from affliction: and maketh him families like a
flocke.42The righteous ſhall ſee it, and reioyce; and all iniquitie ſhall ſtop
her mouth.43Who ſo is wiſe, and will obſerue thoſe things; euen they
ſhall vnderſtand the louing kindeneſse of the Lord.

CHAPTER 1081*A ſong or Pſalme of Dauid.* O God, my heart is fixed: I
will ſing & giue praiſe, euen with my glory.2Awake pſaltery and harpe: I
my ſelfe will awake early.3I will praiſe thee, O Lord, among the people:
and I wil ſing praiſes vnto thee among the nations.4For thy mercy is
great aboue the heauens: and thy trueth reacheth vnto the clouds.5Be
thou exalted, O God, aboue the heauens: and thy glory aboue all the
earth:6That thy beloued may bee deliuered: ſaue with thy right hand, and
anſwere me.7God hath ſpoken in his holineſſe, I wil reioyce, I will diuide
Shechem: and mete out the valley of Succoth.8Gilead is mine, Manaſſeh
is mine, Ephraim alſo is the ſtrength of mine head: Iudah is my
Lawgiuer.9Moab is my waſh pot, ouer Edom wil I caſt out my ſhooe:
ouer Philiſtia will I triumph.10Who wil bring me into the ſtrong citie?
who will leade me into Edom?11Wilt not thou, O God, who haſt caſt vs
off? and wilt not thou, O God, goe foorth with our hoſtes?12Giue vs
helpe from trouble: for vaine is the helpe of man.13Through God wee
ſhall doe valiantly: for hee it is that ſhall tread downe our enemies.

CHAPTER 1091*To the chiefe Muſician, A Pſalme of Dauid.* Hold not thy
peace, O God of my praiſe.2For the mouth of the wicked, and the mouth
of the deceitfull are opened againſt mee: they haue ſpoken againſt me
with a lying tongue.3They compaſſed mee about alſo with wordes of
hatred: and fought againſt me without a cauſe.4For my loue, they are my
aduerſaries: but I giue my ſelfe vnto prayer.5And they haue rewarded me
euill for good: and hatred for my loue.6Set thou a wicked man ouer him:
and let Satan ſtand at his right hand.7When he ſhall be iudged, let him
be condemned: and let his prayer become ſinne.8Let his dayes be few:
and let another take his office.9Let his children bee fatherleſſe: and his
wife a widow.10Let his children bee continually vagabonds, & begge: let
them ſeeke their bread alſo out of their deſolate places.11Let the
extortioner catch all that he hath: and let the ſtrangers ſpoile his
labour.12Let there be none to extend mercy vnto him: neither let there
be any to fauour his fatherleſſe children.13Let his poſteritie be cut off:
and in the generation folowing let their name be blotted out.14Let the
iniquitie of his fathers be remembred with the Lord: and let not the ſinne
of his mother be blotted out.15Let them be before the Lord continually:
that he may cut off the memory of them from the earth.16Becauſe that
he remembred not to ſhew mercy, but perſecuted the poore and needy
man: that he might euen ſlay the broken in heart.17As he loued curſing,
ſo let it come vnto him: as hee delighted not in bleſſing, ſo let it be farre
from him.18As he clothed himſelfe with curſing like as with his garment:
ſo let it come into his bowels like water, and like oyle into his

bones.[19]Let it be vnto him as the garment which coucreth him: and for a girdle wherewith he is girded continually.[20]Let this be the reward of mine aduerſaries from the Lord: and of them that ſpeake euill againſt my ſoule.[21]But do thou for me, O God the Lord, for thy Names ſake: becauſe thy mercie is good: deliuer thou me.[22]For I am poore and needie: and my heart is wounded within me.[23]I am gone like the ſhadow, when it declineth: I am toſsed vp and downe as the locuſt.[24]My knees are weake through faſting: and my fleſh faileth of fatneſſe.[25]I became alſo a reproch vnto them: when they looked vpon me, they ſhaked their heads.[26]Helpe me, O Lord my God: O ſaue me according to thy mercie.[27]That they may know, that this is thy hand: that thou, Lord, haſt done it.[28]Let them curſe, but bleſſe thou: when they Ariſe, let them be aſhamed, but let thy ſeruant reioyce.[29]Let mine aduerſaries be clothed with ſhame: and let them couer them ſelues with their owne confuſion, as with a mantle.[30]I will greatly praiſe the Lord with my mouth: yea I will praiſe him among the multitude.[31]For he ſhal ſtand at the right hand of the poore: to ſaue him from thoſe that condemne his ſoule.

CHAPTER 110[1]*A Pſalme of Dauid.* The Lord ſaid vnto my Lord, Sit thou at my right hand: vntil I make thine enemies thy footeſtoole.[2]The Lord ſhall ſend the rod of thy ſtrength out of Zion: rule thou in the midſt of thine enemies.[3]Thy people ſhalbe willing in the day of thy power, in the beauties of holineſſe from the wombe of the morning: thou haſt the dew of thy youth.[4]The Lord hath ſworne, and will not repent, thou art a Prieſt for euer: after the order of Melchizedek.[5]The Lord at thy right hand ſhall ſtrike through kings in the day of his wrath.[6]He ſhal iudge among the heathen, he ſhal fil the places with the dead bodies: he ſhall wound the heads ouer many countries.[7]He ſhall drinke of the brooke in the way: therefore ſhall hee lift vp the head.

CHAPTER 111[1]Praiſe yee the Lord. I will praiſe the Lord with my whole heart: in the aſſembly of the vpright, and in the Congregation.[2]The workes of the Lord are great: ſought out of all them that haue pleaſure therein.[3]His worke is honourable and glorious: and his righteouſneſſe endureth for euer.[4]Hee hath made his wonderfull works to be remembred: the Lord is gracious, and full of compaſſion.[5]He hath giuen meate vnto them that feare him: he will euer be mindfull of his couenant.[6]He hath ſhewed his people the power of his workes: that he may giue them the heritage of the heathen.[7]The works of his hands are veritie and iudgment: all his commandements are ſure.[8]They ſtand faſt for euer and euer: and are done in trueth and vprightnes.[9]He ſent redemption vnto his people, hee hath commanded his couenant for euer: holy and reuerend is his Name.[10]The feare of the Lord is the beginning of wiſedome, a good vnderſtanding haue all they that doe his commandements: his praiſe endureth for euer.

CHAPTER 112[1]Praiſe ye the Lord. Bleſſed is the man that feareth the Lord, that delighteth greatly in his Commaundements.[2]His ſeed ſhall bee mightie vpon earth: the generation of the vpright ſhalbe bleſſed.[3]Wealth and riches ſhalbe in his houſe: and his righteouſneſſe endureth for euer.[4]Unto the vpright there Ariſeth light in the darkneſſe: hee is gracious, and full of compaſſion, and righteous.[5]A good man ſheweth fauour and lendeth: he will guide his affaires with diſcretion.[6]Surely he ſhall not be moued for euer: the righteous ſhalbe in euerlaſting remembrance.[7]He ſhall not be afraid of euill tidings: his heart is fixed, truſting in the Lord.[8]His heart is eſtabliſhed, hee ſhall not be afraid, vntill he ſee his deſire vpon his enemies.[9]He hath diſperſed, he hath giuen to the poore: his righteouſneſſe endureth for euer; his horne ſhalbe exalted with honour.[10]The wicked ſhall ſee it, and be grieued; he ſhall gnaſh with his teeth, and melt away: the deſire of the wicked ſhall periſh.

CHAPTER 113[1]Praiſe yee the Lord. Praiſe, O yee ſeruants of the Lord: praiſe the name of the Lord.[2]Bleſſed be the name of the Lord: from this time forth and for euermore.[3]From the riſing of the ſunne vnto the going downe of the ſame: the Lords name is to be praiſed.[4]The Lord is high aboue all nations: and his glory aboue the heauens.[5]Who is like vnto the Lord our God: who dwelleth on high:[6]Who humbleth himſelfe to behold the things that are in heauen, and in the earth?[7]He raiſeth vp the poore out of the duſt: and lifteth the needie out of the dung-hill:[8]That he may ſet him with princes: euen with the princes of his people.[9]He maketh the barren woman to keepe houſe; to be a ioyfull mother of children: Praiſe yee the Lord.

CHAPTER 114[1]When Iſrael went out of Egypt, the houſe of Iacob from a people of ſtrange language:[2]Iudah was his ſanctuarie: and Iſrael his dominion.[3]The ſea ſawe it, and fled: Iordan was driuen backe.[4]The mountaines ſkipped like rammes: and the little hilles like lambes.[5]What ailed thee, O thou ſea, that thou fleddeſt? thou Iordan, that thou waſt driuen backe?[6]Yee mountaines, that yee ſkipped like rammes: and yee little hilles like lambes?[7]Tremble thou earth at the preſence of the Lord: at the preſence of the God of Iacob:[8]Which turned the rocke into a ſtanding water: the flint into a fountaine of waters.

CHAPTER 115[1]Not vnto vs, O Lord, not vnto vs, but vnto thy name giue glory: for thy mercy, and for thy truthes ſake.[2]Wherefore ſhould the heathen ſay: Where is now their God?[3]But our God is in the heauens: he hath done whatſoeuer he pleaſed.[4]Their idoles are ſiluer and gold: the worke of mens hands.[5]They haue mouths, but they ſpeake not; eies haue they, but they ſee not.[6]They haue eares, but they heare not: noſes haue they, but they ſmell not.[7]They haue hands, but they handle not, feete haue they, but they walke not: neither ſpeake they through their throat.[8]They that make them are like vnto them: ſo is euery one that truſteth in them.[9]O Iſrael, truſt thou in the Lord: he is their helpe and their ſhield.[10]O houſe of Aaron, truſt in the Lord: he is their helpe & their ſhield.[11]Ye that feare the Lord truſt in the Lord: he is their helpe and their ſhield.[12]The Lord hath bene mindfull of vs, he will bleſſe vs, he will bleſſe the houſe of Iſrael: he will bleſſe the houſe of Aaron.[13]Hee will bleſſe them that feare the Lord: both ſmall and great.[14]The Lord ſhall increaſe you more and more: you and your children.[15]You are bleſſed of the Lord: which made heauen and earth.[16]The heauen, euen the heauens are the Lords: but the earth hath hee giuen to the children of men.[17]The dead praiſe not the Lord: neither any that go downe into ſilence.[18]But we will bleſſe the Lord, from this time foorth and for euermore. Praiſe the Lord.

CHAPTER 116[1]I loue the Lord: becauſe hee hath heard my voice, & my ſupplications.[2]Becauſe hee hath inclined his eare vnto mee: therefore will I call vpon him as long as I liue.[3]The ſorrowes of death compaſſed me, and the paines of hell gate hold vpon me: I found trouble and ſorrow.[4]Then called I vpon the Name of the Lord: O Lord, I beſeech thee deliuer my ſoule.[5]Gracious is the Lord, and righteous: yea our God is mercifull.[6]The Lord preſerueth the ſimple: I was brought low, and hee helped me.[7]Returne vnto thy reſt, O my ſoule: for the Lord hath dealt bountifully with thee.[8]For thou haſt deliuered my ſoule from death, mine eyes from teares, and my feete from falling.[9]I wil walke before the Lord: in the land of the liuing.[10]I beleeued, therfore haue I ſpoken: I was greatly afflicted.[11]I ſaid in my haſte: All men are lyers.[12]What ſhall I render vnto the Lord: for all his benefits towards mee?[13]I will take the cup of ſaluation: and call vpon the Name of the Lord.[14]I will pay my vowes vnto the Lord: now in the preſence of all his people.[15]Precious in þe ſight of the Lord: is the death of his Saints.[16]Oh Lord, truely I am thy ſeruant, I am thy ſeruant, and the ſonne of thy handmayde: thou haſt looſed my bonds.[17]I will offer to thee the ſacrifice of thankeſ-giuing: and will call vpon the Name of the Lord.[18]I will pay my vowes vnto the Lord: now in the preſence of all his people:[19]In the Courts of the Lords houſe, in the middes of thee, O Ieruſalem. Praiſe ye the Lord.

CHAPTER 117[1]O praiſe the Lord, all ye nations: praiſe him all ye people.[2]For his merciful kindneſſe is great toward vs: and the trueth of the Lord endureth for euer. Praiſe ye the Lord.

CHAPTER 118[1]O giue thankes vnto the Lord, for hee is good: becauſe his mercie endureth for euer.[2]Let Iſrael now ſay: that his mercy endureth for euer.[3]Let the houſe of Aaron now ſay: that his mercy endureth for euer.[4]Let them now that feare the Lord, ſay: that his mercy endureth for euer.[5]I called vpon the Lord in diſtreſſe: the Lord anſwered me, and ſet me in a large place.[6]The Lord is on my ſide, I will not feare: What can man doe vnto mee?[7]The Lord taketh my part with them that helpe me: therfore ſhall I ſee my deſire vpon them that hate me.[8]It is better to truſt in the Lord: then to put confidence in man.[9]It is better to truſt in the Lord: then to put confidence in Princes.[10]All nations compaſſed me about: but in the Name of the Lord, will I deſtroy them.[11]They compaſſed mee about, yea they compaſſed mee about: but in the Name of the Lord, I will deſtroy them.[12]They compaſſed mee about like Bees, they are quenched as the fire of thornes: for in the Name of the Lord I wil deſtroy them.[13]Thou haſt thruſt ſore at mee that I might fall: but the

Lord helped mee.14The Lord is my ſtrength and ſong: and is become
my ſaluation.15The voice of reioycing and ſaluation is in the tabernacles
of the righteous: the Right hand of the Lord doeth valiantly.16The Right
hand of the Lord is exalted: the Right hand of the Lord doeth
valiantly.17I ſhall not die, but liue: and declare the workes of the
Lord.18The Lord hath chaſtened me ſore: but he hath not giuen me ouer
vnto death.19Open to mee the gates of righteouſneſſe: I will goe into
them, and I will praiſe the Lord:20This gate of the Lord: into which the
righteous ſhall enter.21I will praiſe thee, for thou haſt heard mee: and art
become my ſaluation.22The ſtone which the builders refuſed: is become
the head ſtone of the corner.23This is the Lords doing: it is marueilous
in our eyes.24This is the day which the Lord hath made: we will reioyce,
and be glad in it.25Saue now, I beſeech thee, O Lord: O Lord, I beſeech
thee, ſend now proſperitie.26Bleſſed be he that commeth in the Name
of the Lord: wee haue bleſſed you out of the houſe of the Lord.27God
is the Lord, which hath ſhewed vs light, bind the ſacrifice with cords:
euen vnto the horns of the Altar.28Thou art my God, and I will praiſe
thee: thou art my God, I will exalt thee.29O giue thanks vnto the Lord,
for he is good: for his mercy endureth for euer.

CHAPTER 119 1*ALEPH.* Bleſſed are the vndefiled in the way: who
walke in the Law of the Lord.2Bleſſed are they that keepe his
teſtimonies: and that ſeeke him with the whole heart.3They alſo doe no
iniquitie: they walke in his wayes.4Thou haſt commaunded vs to keepe
thy precepts diligently.5O that my wayes were directed to keepe thy
ſtatutes!6Then ſhall I not bee aſhamed: when I haue reſpect vnto all thy
commandements.7I will praiſe thee with vprightneſse of heart: when I
ſhall haue learned thy righteous iudgements.8I will keepe thy ſtatutes: O
forſake me not vtterly.9*BETH.* Wherewithall ſhall a yong man cleanſe
his way? by taking heede thereto according to thy word.10With my whole
heart haue I ſought thee: O let me not wander from thy
Commandements.11Thy word haue I hidde in mine heart: that I might
not ſinne againſt thee.12Bleſſed art thou, O Lord: teach me thy
ſtatutes.13With my lips haue I declared all the iudgements of thy
mouth.14I haue reioyced in the way of thy teſtimonies: as much as in all
riches.15I will meditate in thy precepts: and haue reſpect vnto thy
wayes.16I will delight my ſelfe in thy ſtatutes: I will not forget thy
word.17*GIMEL.* Deale bountifully with thy ſeruant; that I may liue, and
keepe thy word.18Open thou mine eyes, that I may behold wonderous
things out of thy Law.19I am a ſtranger in the earth: hide not thy
commandements from me.20My ſoule breaketh for the longing: that it
hath vnto thy iudgements at all times.21Thou haſt rebuked the proud
that are curſed: which doe erre from thy Commandements.22Remooue
from me reproch and contempt: for I haue kept thy
teſtimonies.23Princes alſo did ſit and ſpeake againſt me: but thy ſeruant
did meditate in thy ſtatutes.24Thy teſtimonies alſo are my delight: and
my counſellers.25*DALETH.* My ſoule cleaueth vnto the duſt: quicken
thou mee according to thy word.26I haue declared my wayes, and thou
heardeſt me: teach me thy Statutes.27Make me to vnderſtand the way of
thy precepts: ſo ſhall I talke of thy wonderous workes.28My ſoule
melteth for heauines: ſtrengthen thou me according vnto thy
word.29Remoue from mee the way of lying: and grant me thy Law
graciouſly.30I haue choſen the way of trueth: thy iudgements haue I laid
before me.31I haue ſtucke vnto thy Teſtimonies: O Lord put me not to
ſhame.32I will runne the way of thy Commandements: when thou ſhalt
enlarge my heart.33*HE.* Teach me, O Lord, the way of thy Statutes: and
I ſhall keepe it vnto the end.34Giue me vnderſtanding, and I ſhall keepe
thy Law: yea I ſhall obſerue it with my whole heart.35Make me to goe in
the path of thy commandements: for therein doe I delight.36Incline my
heart vnto thy teſtimonies: and not to couetouſneſſe.37Turne away mine
eyes from beholding vanitie: and quicken thou me in thy way.38Stabliſh
thy word vnto thy ſeruant: who is deuoted to thy feare.39Turne away my
reproch which I feare: for thy iudgements are good.40Behold, I haue
longed after thy precepts: quicken me in thy righteouſneſſe.41*VAV.* Let
thy mercies come alſo vnto me, O Lord: euen thy ſaluation, according
to thy word.42So ſhall I haue wherewith to anſwere him that reprocheth
me: for I truſt in thy word.43And take not the word of trueth vtterly out
of my mouth: for I haue hoped in thy iudgements.44So ſhall I keepe thy
Law continually: for euer and euer.45And I wil walke at libertie: for I
ſeeke thy precepts.46I will ſpeake of thy teſtimonies alſo before kings, &
wil not be aſhamed.47And I will delight my ſelfe in thy commandements,
which I haue loued.48My hands alſo will I lift vp vnto thy
commandements, which I haue loued: and I will meditate in thy
ſtatutes.49*ZAIN.* Remember the word vnto thy ſeruant: vpon which
thou haſt cauſed me to hope.50This is my comfort in my affliction: for
thy word hath quickened me.51The proud haue had mee greatly in
deriſion: yet haue I not declined from thy Law.52I remembred thy
iudgements of old, O Lord: and haue comforted my ſelfe.53Horrour
hath taken holde vpon me, becauſe of the wicked that forſake thy
Law.54Thy ſtatutes haue bin my ſongs in the houſe of my pilgrimage.55I
haue remembred thy name, O Lord, in the night, and haue kept thy
Law.56This I had: becauſe I kept thy precepts.57*CHETH.* Thou art my
portion, O Lord, I haue ſaid, that I would keepe thy words.58I intreated
thy fauour with my whole heart: be mercifull vnto mee according to thy
word.59I thought on my wayes: and turned my feete vnto thy
Teſtimonies.60I made haſte; and delayed not to keepe thy
commandements.61The bands of the wicked haue robbed me: but I
haue not forgotten thy lawe.62At mid-night I will riſe to giue thankes
vnto thee: becauſe of thy righteous iudgements.63I am a companion of
all them that feare thee: and of them that keepe thy precepts.64The
earth, O Lord, is full of thy mercy: teach me thy ſtatutes.65*TETH.* Thou
haſt dealt well with thy ſeruant, Oh Lord, according vnto thy
word.66Teach me good iudgement and knowledge: for I haue beleeued
thy commandements.67Before I was afflicted, I went aſtray: but now
haue I kept thy word.68Thou art good, and doeſt good; teach me thy
ſtatutes.69The proud haue forged a lie againſt me: but I will keepe thy
precepts with my whole heart.70Their heart is as fat as greaſe: but I
delight in thy law.71It is good for me that I haue bene afflicted: that I
might learne thy ſtatutes.72The law of thy mouth is better vnto me: then
thouſands of gold and ſiluer.73*IOD.* Thy hands haue made me and
faſhioned me: giue me vnderſtanding, that I may learne thy
commandements.74They that feare thee will bee glad when they ſee
mee: becauſe I haue hoped in thy word.75I knowe, O Lord, that thy
iudgements are right: and that thou in faithfulneſse haſt afflicted
me.76Let, I pray thee, thy mercifull kindneſſe be for my comfort;
according to thy word vnto thy ſeruant.77Let thy tender mercies come
vnto me, that I may liue: for thy lawe is my delight.78Let the proud be
aſhamed, for they dealt peruerſly with me without a cauſe: but I will
meditate in thy precepts.79Let thoſe that feare thee turne vnto me: and
thoſe that haue knowen thy teſtimonies.80Let my heart be ſound in thy
ſtatutes; that I be not aſhamed.81*CAPH.* My ſoule fainteth for thy
ſaluation: but I hope in thy word.82Mine eyes faile for thy word: ſaying,
When wilt thou comfort me?83For I am become like a bottle in the
ſmoke: yet doe I not forget thy ſtatutes.84How many are the dayes of
thy ſeruant? when wilt thou execute iudgement on them that perſecute
me?85The proud haue digged pittes for me: which are not after thy
law.86All thy commaundements are faithfull: they perſecute me
wrongfully; helpe thou me.87They had almoſt conſumed mee vpon
earth: but I forſooke not thy precepts.88Quicken mee after thy louing
kindneſse: ſo ſhall I keepe the teſtimonie of thy
mouth.89*LAMED.* Foreuer, O Lord, thy word is ſetled, in
heauen.90Thy faithfulneſse is vnto all generations: thou haſt eſtabliſhed
the earth, and it abideth.91They continue this day according to thine
ordinances: for all are thy ſeruants.92Unleſſe thy lawe had bene my
delights: I ſhould then haue periſhed in mine affliction.93I will neuer
forget thy precepts: for with them thou haſt quickened me.94I am thine,
ſaue me: for I haue ſought thy precepts.95The wicked haue waited for
me to deſtroy me: but I will conſider thy teſtimonies.96I haue ſeene an
end of all perfection: but thy commandement is exceeding
broad.97*MEM.* O How loue I thy Law! it is my meditation all the
day.98Thou through thy Commandements haſt made me wiſer then
mine enemies: for they are euer with mee.99I haue more vnderſtanding
then all my teachers: for thy Teſtimonies are my meditation.100I
vnderſtand more then the ancients: becauſe I keepe thy precepts.101I
haue refrained my feete from euery euill way: that I may keepe thy
word.102I haue not departed from thy Iudgements: for thou haſt taught

me.[103]How ſweet are thy words vnto my taſte! yea, ſweeter then hony to my mouth.[104]Through thy precepts I get vnderſtanding: therefore I hate euery falſe way.[105]*NVN.* Thy word is a lampe vnto my feete: and a light vnto my path.[106]I haue ſworne, and I will performe it: that I will keepe thy righteous iudgements.[107]I am afflicted very much: quicken mee, O Lord, according vnto thy word.[108]Accept, I beſeech thee, the freewil offrings of my mouth, O Lord: and teach me thy iudgements.[109]My ſoule is continually in my hand: yet doe I not forget thy Law.[110]The wicked haue layde a ſnare for mee: yet I erred not from thy precepts.[111]Thy Teſtimonies haue I taken as an heritage for euer: for they are the reioycing of my heart.[112]I haue inclined mine heart to performe thy Statutes, alway, euen vnto the end.[113]*SAMECH.* I hate vaine thoughts: but thy Law doe I loue.[114]Thou art my hiding place, and my ſhield: I hope in thy word.[115]Depart from me, ye euil doers: for I will keepe the Commandements of my God.[116]Vphold mee according vnto thy word, that I may liue: and let mee not be aſhamed of my hope.[117]Hold thou me vp, and I ſhall be ſafe: and I will haue reſpect vnto thy Statutes continually.[118]Thou haſt troden downe all them that erre from thy Statutes: for their deceit is falſhood.[119]Thou putteſt away all the wicked of the earth like droſse: therefore I loue thy Teſtimonies.[120]My fleſh trembleth for feare of thee: and I am afraide of thy Iudgements.[121]*AIN.* I Haue done Iudgement and iuſtice: leaue mee not to mine oppreſsours.[122]Bee ſuretie for thy ſeruant for good: let not the proud oppreſſe me.[123]Mine eyes faile for thy ſaluation: and for the word of thy righteouſneſſe.[124]Deale with thy ſeruant according vnto thy mercie: and teach me thy Statutes.[125]I am thy ſeruant, giue me vnderſtanding: that I may know thy Teſtimonies.[126]It is time for thee, Lord, to worke: for they haue made voyde thy Law.[127]Therefore I loue thy Commandements: aboue gold, yea aboue fine gold.[128]Therefore I eſteeme all thy precepts concerning all things to be right: and I hate euery falſe way.[129]*PE.* Thy Teſtimonies are wonderfull: therefore doeth my ſoule keepe them.[130]The entrance of thy wordes giueth light: it giueth vnderſtanding vnto the ſimple.[131]I opened my mouth, and panted: for I longed for thy Commandements.[132]Looke thou vpon mee, and be mercifull vnto me: as thou vſeſt to do vnto thoſe that loue thy Name.[133]Order my ſteps in thy word: and let not any iniquitie haue dominion ouer me.[134]Deliuer me from the oppreſſion of man: ſo will I keepe thy precepts.[135]Make thy face to ſhine vpon thy ſeruant: and teach me thy Statutes.[136]Riuers of waters runne downe mine eyes: becauſe they keepe not thy Law.[137]*TSADDI.* Righteous art thou, O Lord: and vpright are thy iudgements.[138]Thy teſtimonies that thou haſt commaunded, are righteous: and very faithfull.[139]My zeale hath conſumed me: becauſe mine enemies haue forgotten thy words.[140]Thy word is very pure: therefore thy ſeruant loueth it.[141]I am ſmall and deſpiſed: yet doe not I forget thy precepts.[142]Thy righteouſneſſe is an euerlaſting righteouſneſſe: and thy law is the trueth.[143]Trouble and anguiſh haue taken hold on me: yet thy commaundements are my delights.[144]The righteouſneſſe of thy Teſtimonies is euerlaſting: giue me vnderſtanding, and I ſhall liue.[145]*KOPH.* I Cried with my whole heart: heare me, O Lord, I will keepe thy ſtatutes.[146]I cried vnto thee, ſaue me: and I ſhall keepe thy teſtimonies.[147]I preuented the dawning of the morning, and cried: I hoped in thy word.[148]Mine eyes preuent the night watches: that I might meditate in thy word.[149]Heare my voice according vnto thy louing kindneſse: O Lord quicken me according to thy iudgement.[150]They draw nigh that follow after miſchiefe: they are farre from thy Law.[151]Thou art neere, O Lord: and all thy commandements are trueth.[152]Concerning thy teſtimonies, I haue knowen of old: that thou haſt founded them for euer.[153]*RESH.* Conſider mine affliction, and deliuer me: for I doe not forget thy Law.[154]Plead my cauſe, and deliuer me: quicken me according to thy word.[155]Saluation is farre from the wicked: for they ſeeke not thy ſtatutes.[156]Great are thy tender mercies, O Lord: quicken me according to thy iudgements.[157]Many are my perſecutors, and mine enemies: yet doe I not decline from thy teſtimonies.[158]I beheld the tranſgreſsours, and was grieued: becauſe they kept not thy word.[159]Conſider how I loue thy precepts: quicken me, O Lord, according to thy louing kindneſse.[160]Thy word is true from the beginning: and euery one of thy righteous iudgements endureth for euer.[161]*SCHIN.* Princes haue perſecuted mee without a cauſe: but my heart ſtandeth in awe of thy word.[162]I reioyce at thy word: as one that findeth great ſpoile.[163]I hate and abhorre lying: but thy Law doe I loue.[164]Seuen times a day doe I praiſe thee: becauſe of thy righteous iudgements.[165]Great peace haue they which loue thy law: & nothing ſhall offend them.[166]Lord, I haue hoped for thy ſaluation: and done thy commandements.[167]My ſoule hath kept thy teſtimonies: and I loue them exceedingly.[168]I haue kept thy precepts and thy teſtimonies: for all my wayes are before thee.[169]*TAV.* Let my crie come neere before thee, O Lord: giue mee vnderſtanding according to thy worde.[170]Let my ſupplication come before thee: deliuer me according to thy word.[171]My lips ſhall vtter praiſe: when thou haſt taught me thy Statutes.[172]My tongue ſhall ſpeake of thy word: for all thy commandements are righteouſneſſe.[173]Let thine hand helpe me: for I haue choſen thy precepts.[174]I haue longed for thy ſaluation, O Lord: and thy Lawe is my delight.[175]Let my ſoule liue, and it ſhall praiſe thee: and let thy iudgments helpe me.[176]I haue gone aſtray like a loſt ſheepe, ſeeke thy ſeruant: for I doe not forget thy commandements.

CHAPTER 120[1]*A ſong of degrees.* In my diſtreſſe I cried vnto the Lord: and hee heard me.[2]Deliuer my ſoule, O Lord, from lying lips: and from a deceitfull tongue.[3]What ſhall be giuen vnto thee? or what ſhalbe done vnto thee, thou falſe tongue?[4]Sharpe arrowes of the mightie: with coales of iuniper.[5]Woe is me, that I ſoiourne in Meſech: that I dwell in the tents of Kedar.[6]My ſoule hath long dwelt with him that hateth peace.[7]I am for peace: but when I ſpeak, they are for warre.

CHAPTER 121[1]*A ſong of degrees.* I will lift vp mine eyes vnto the hilles: from whence commeth my helpe.[2]My helpe commeth from the Lord: which made heauen and earth.[3]He will not ſuffer thy foote to bee moued: he that keepeth thee will not ſlumber.[4]Behold, he that keepeth Iſrael; ſhall neither ſlumber nor ſleepe.[5]The Lord is thy keeper: the Lord is thy ſhade, vpon thy right hand.[6]The ſunne ſhall not ſmite thee by day; nor the moone by night.[7]The Lord ſhall preſeruethee from all euill: hee ſhall preſeruethy ſoule.[8]The Lord ſhall preſeruethy going out, and thy comming in: from this time foorth and euen for euermore.

CHAPTER 122[1]*A ſong of degrees of Dauid.* I was glad when they ſayd vnto me: Let vs goe into the houſe of the Lord.[2]Our feete ſhall ſtand within thy gates, O Ieruſalem.[3]Ieruſalem is builded as a citie, that is compact together:[4]Whither the tribes goe vp, the tribes of the Lord, vnto the teſtimonie of Iſrael: to giue thankes vnto the name of the Lord.[5]For there are ſet thrones of iudgment: the thrones of the houſe of Dauid.[6]Pray for the peace of Ieruſalem: they ſhall proſper that loue thee.[7]Peace be within thy walles: and proſperitie within thy palaces.[8]For my brethren and companions ſakes: I will now ſay, Peace be within thee.[9]Becauſe of the houſe of the Lord our God: I will ſeeke thy good.

CHAPTER 123[1]*A ſong of degrees.* Vnto thee lift I vp mine eyes: O thou that dwelleſt in the heauens.[2]Beholde, as the eyes of ſeruants looke vnto the hand of their Maſters, and as the eyes of a maiden, vnto the hand of her miſtreſſe: ſo our eyes waite vpon the Lord our God, vntill that he haue mercy vpon vs.[3]Haue mercy vpon vs, O Lord, haue mercy vpon vs: for we are exceedingly filled with contempt.[4]Our ſoule is exceedingly filled with the ſcorning of thoſe that are at eaſe: and with the contempt of the proud.

CHAPTER 124[1]*A ſong of degrees of Dauid.* If it had not bene the Lord who was on our ſide: nowe may Iſrael ſay:[2]If it had not bene the Lord, who was on our ſide, when men roſe vp againſt vs:[3]Then they had ſwallowed vs vp quicke: when their wrath was kindled againſt vs.[4]Then the waters had ouerwhelmed vs; the ſtreame had gone ouer our ſoule.[5]Then the proud waters had gone ouer our ſoule.[6]Bleſſed be the Lord: who hath not giuen vs as a pray to their teeth.[7]Our ſoule is eſcaped as a bird out of the ſnare of the foulers; the ſnare is broken, and we are eſcaped.[8]Our helpe is in the name of the Lord: who made heauen and earth.

CHAPTER 125[1]*A ſong of degrees.* They that truſt in the Lord, ſhalbe as mount Zion, which cannot be remooued, but abideth for euer.[2]As the mountaines are round about Ieruſalem, ſo the Lord is round about his people: from hencefoorth euen for euer.[3]For the rod of the wicked ſhall not reſt vpon the lot of the righteous: leſt the righteous put forth their hands vnto iniquitie.[4]Doe good, O Lord, vnto thoſe that be good: and to them that are vpright in their hearts.[5]As for ſuch as turne aſide vnto their crooked wayes, the Lord ſhall lead them foorth with the workers of iniquitie: but peace ſhalbe vpon Iſrael.

CHAPTER 126 1*A ſong of degrees.* When the Lord turned againe the captiuitie of Zion: wee were like them that dreame.2Then was our mouth filled with laughter, and our tongue with ſinging, then ſaid they among the heathen: The Lord hath done great things for them.3The Lord hath done great things for vs: whereof we are glad.4Turne againe our captiuitie, O Lord: as the ſtreames in the South.5They that ſow in teares: ſhall reape in ioy.6He that goeth forth and weepeth, bearing precious ſeed, ſhall doubtleſſe come againe with reioycing: bringing his ſheaues with him.

CHAPTER 127 1*A ſong of degrees for Solomon.* Except the Lord build the houſe, they labour in vaine that build it: except the Lord keepe the citie, the watchman waketh but in vaine.2It is vaine for you to riſe vp early, to ſit vp late, to eate the bread of ſorrowes: for ſo hee giueth his beloued ſleepe.3Loe, children are an heritage of the Lord: and the fruit of the wombe is his reward.4As arrowes are in the hand of a mightie man: ſo are children of the youth.5Happie is the man that hath his quiuer full of them, they ſhall not be aſhamed: but they ſhall ſpeake with the enemies in the gate.

CHAPTER 128 1*A ſong of degrees.* Bleſſed is euery one that feareth the Lord: that walketh in his wayes.2For thou ſhalt eat the labour of thine handes: happie ſhalt thou bee, and it ſhall be well with thee.3Thy wife ſhalbe as a fruitful Uine by the ſides of thine houſe, thy children like Oliue plants: round about thy table.4Beholde that thus ſhall the man be bleſſed; that feareth the Lord.5The Lord ſhall bleſſe thee out of Zion: and thou ſhalt ſee the good of Ieruſalem, all the dayes of thy life.6Yea, thou ſhalt ſee thy childrens children: and peace vpon Iſrael.

CHAPTER 129 1*A ſong of degrees.* Many a time haue they afflicted me from my youth: may Iſrael now ſay.2Many a time haue they afflicted me from my youth: yet they haue not preuailed againſt mee.3The plowers plowed vpon my backe: they made long their furrowes.4The Lord is righteous: hee hath cut aſunder the cordes of the wicked.5Let them all be confounded and turned backe, that hate Zion.6Let them bee as the graſſe vpon the houſe tops: which withereth afore it groweth vp:7Wherewith the mower filleth not his hand: nor hee that bindeth ſheaues, his boſome.8Neither doe they which goe by, ſay, The bleſſing of the Lord be vpon you: wee bleſſe you in the Name of the Lord.

CHAPTER 130 1*A ſong of degrees.* Out of the depths haue I cryed vnto thee, O Lord.2Lorde, heare my voice: let thine eares be attentiue to the voice of my ſupplications.3If thou, Lord, ſhouldeſt marke iniquities: O Lord, who ſhal ſtand?4But there is forgiueneſse with thee: that thou mayeſt be feared.5I wait for the Lord, my ſoule doeth waite: and in his worde doe I hope.6My ſoule waiteth for the Lord, more then they that watch for the morning: I ſay, more then they that watch for the morning.7Let Iſrael hope in the Lord, for with the Lord there is mercy: and with him is plenteous redemption.8And hee ſhall redeeme Iſrael, from all his iniquities.

CHAPTER 131 1*A ſong of degrees of Dauid.* Lord, my heart is not haughtie, nor mine eyes loftie: neither doe I exerciſe my ſelfe in great matters, or in things too high for mee.2Surely I haue behaued and quieted my ſelfe as a child that is weaned of his mother: my ſoule is euen as a weaned childe.3Let Iſrael hope in the Lord, from henceforth and for euer.

CHAPTER 132 1*A ſong of degrees.* Lord remember Dauid, and all his afflictions:2How he ſware vnto the Lord, and vowed vnto the mightie God of Iacob.3Surely I will not come into the tabernacle of my houſe: nor goe vp into my bed.4I will not giue ſleepe to mine eyes: or ſlumber to mine eyelids,5Untill I finde out a place for the Lord: an habitation for the mightie God of Iacob.6Loe, wee heard of it at Ephrata: we found it in the fields of the wood.7We will goe into his tabernacles: we will worſhip at his footſtoole.8Ariſe, O Lord, into thy reſt: thou, and the Arke of thy ſtrength.9Let thy Prieſtes be clothed with righteouſneſſe: and let thy ſaints ſhout for ioy.10For thy ſeruant Dauids ſake: turne not away the face of thine Anointed.11The Lord hath ſworne in trueth vnto Dauid, hee will not turne from it; of the fruit of thy body will I ſet vpon thy throne.12If thy children will keepe my couenant and my teſtimonie, that I ſhall teach them; their children alſo ſhall ſit vpon thy throne for euermore.13For the Lord hath choſen Zion: he hath deſired it for his habitation.14This is my reſt for euer: here will I dwell, for I haue deſired it.15I will abundantly bleſſe her prouiſion: I will ſatiſfie her poore with bread.16I will alſo clothe her prieſts with ſaluation: and her Saints ſhall ſhout aloud for ioy.17There will I make the horne of Dauid to budde: I haue ordained a lampe for mine Anointed.18His enemies will I clothe with ſhame: but vpon himſelfe ſhall his crowne flouriſh.

CHAPTER 133 1*A ſong of degrees of Dauid.* Behold how good and how pleaſant it is: for brethren to dwell together in vnitie.2It is like the precious oyntment vpon the head, that ranne downe vpon the beard, euen Aarons beard: that went downe to the ſkirts of his garments.3As the dew of Hermon, and as the dewe that deſcended vpon the mountaines of Zion, for there the Lord commanded the bleſſing: euen life for euermore.

CHAPTER 134 1*A ſong of degrees.* Beholde, bleſſe yee the Lord, all yee ſeruants of the Lord: which by night ſtand in the houſe of the Lord.2Lift vp your hands in the Sanctuary: & bleſſe the Lord.3The Lord that made heauen and earth: bleſſe thee out of Zion.

CHAPTER 135 1Praiſe ye the Lord, Praiſe ye the Name of the Lord: prayſe him, O ye ſeruants of the Lord.2Yee that ſtand in the Houſe of the Lord: in the courts of the houſe of our God.3Praiſe the Lord, for the Lord is good: ſing praiſes vnto his Name, for it is pleaſant.4For the Lord hath choſen Iacob vnto himſelfe: and Iſrael for his peculiar treaſure.5For I know that the Lord is great: and that our Lord is aboue all gods.6Whatſoeuer the Lord pleaſed, that did he in heauen and in earth: in the ſeas, and all deepe places.7Hee cauſeth the vapours to aſcend from the ends of the earth, he maketh lightnings for the raine: he bringeth the winde out of his treaſuries.8Who ſmote the firſt borne of Egypt: both of man and beaſt.9Who ſent tokens and woonders into the midſt of thee, O Egypt: vpon Pharaoh, and vpon all his ſeruants.10Who ſmote great nations: and ſlew mightie kings:11Sihon king of the Amorites, and Og king of Baſhan: and all the kingdomes of Canaan,12And gaue their land for an heritage: an heritage vnto Iſrael his people.13Thy Name, O Lord, endureth for euer: and thy memoriall, O Lord, throughout all generations.14For the Lord will iudge his people: and he will repent himſelfe concerning his ſeruants.15The idoles of the heathen are ſiluer and golde: the worke of mens hands.16They haue mouthes, but they ſpeake not: eyes haue they, but they ſee not:17They haue eares, but they heare not: neither is there any breath in their mouthes.18They that make them are like vnto them: ſo is euery one that truſteth in them.19Bleſſe the Lord, O houſe of Iſrael: bleſſe the Lord, O houſe of Aaron.20Bleſſe the Lord, O houſe of Leui: ye that feare the Lord, bleſſe the Lord.21Bleſſed be the Lord out of Zion; which dwelleth at Ieruſalem. Praiſe ye the Lord.

CHAPTER 136 1O giue thankes vnto the Lord, for hee is good: for his mercy endureth for euer.2O giue thankes vnto the God of gods: for his mercy endureth for euer.3O giue thankes to the Lord of lords: for his mercy endureth for euer.4To him who alone doth great wonders: for his mercy endureth for euer.5To him that by wiſedome made the heauens: for his mercy endureth for euer.6To him that ſtretched out the earth aboue the waters: for his mercy endureth for euer.7To him that made great lights: for his mercy endureth for euer.8The ſunne to rule by day: for his mercy endureth for euer.9The moone and ſtarres to rule by night: for his mercy endureth for euer.10To him that ſmote Egypt in their firſt borne: for his mercy endureth for euer.11And brought out Iſrael from among them: for his mercy endureth for euer.12With a ſtrong hand and with a ſtretched out arme: for his mercy endureth for euer.13To him which diuided the red ſea into parts: for his mercy endureth for euer.14And made Iſrael to paſſe through the midſt of it: for his mercy endureth for euer.15But ouerthrewe Pharaoh and his hoſte in the red ſea: for his mercy endureth for euer.16To him which led his people through the wilderneſſe: for his mercy endureth for euer.17To him which ſmote great kings: for his mercy endureth for euer.18And ſlue famous kings: for his mercy endureth for euer.19Sihon king of the Amorites: for his mercy endureth for euer.20And Og the king of Baſhan: for his mercy endureth for euer.21And gaue their land for an heritage: for his mercy endureth for euer.22Euen an heritage vnto Iſrael his ſeruant: for his mercy endureth for euer.23Who remembred vs in our lowe eſtate: for his mercy endureth for euer.24And hath redeemed vs from our enemies: for his mercy endureth for euer.25Who giueth foode to all fleſh: for his mercy endureth for euer.26O giue thankes vnto the God of heauen: for his mercy endureth for euer.

CHAPTER 1371By the riuers of Babylon, there wee ſate downe, yea we wept: when we remembred Zion.2Wee hanged our harpes vpon the willowes, in the midſt thereof.3For there they that carried vs away captiue, required of vs a ſong, and they that waſted vs, required of vs mirth: ſaying, Sing vs one of the ſongs of Zion.4How ſhall we ſing the Lords ſong: in a ſtrange land?5If I forget thee, O Ieruſalem: let my right hand forget her cunning.6If I doe not remember thee, let my tongue cleaue to the roofe of my mouth; if I preferre not Ieruſalem aboue my chiefe ioy.7Remember, O Lord, the children of Edom, in the day of Ieruſalem; who ſayd, raſe it, raſe it: euen to the foundation thereof.8O daughter of Babylon, who art to be deſtroyed: happy ſhall he be that rewardeth thee, as thou haſt ſerued vs.9Happy ſhall he be that taketh and daſheth thy little ones againſt the ſtones.

CHAPTER 1381*A Pſalme of Dauid.* I will praiſe thee with my whole heart: before the gods will I ſing praiſe vnto thee.2I will worſhip towards thy holy temple, and praiſe thy name, for thy louing kindneſſe and for thy trueth: for thou haſt magnified thy word aboue all thy name.3In the day when I cried, thou anſweredſt me: and ſtrengthenedſt me with ſtrength in my ſoule.4All the kings of the earth ſhall praiſe thee, O Lord: when they heare the words of thy mouth.5Yea they ſhall ſing in the wayes of the Lord: for great is the glory of the Lord.6Though the Lord be high, yet hath he reſpect vnto the lowly: but the proud he knoweth afarre off.7Though I walke in the mids of trouble, thou wilt reuiue me, thou ſhalt ſtretch foorth thine hand againſt the wrath of mine enemies: and thy right hand ſhall ſaue me.8The Lord wil perfit that which concerneth me: thy mercie, O Lord, endureth for euer: forſake not the works of thine owne hands.

CHAPTER 1391*To the chiefe Muſician, A Pſalme of Dauid.* O Lord, thou haſt ſearched mee, and knowen me.2Thou knoweſt my downe ſitting, and mine vpriſing: thou vnderſtandeſt my thought afarre off.3Thou compaſſeſt my path, and my lying downe, and art acquainted with all my wayes.4For there is not a worde in my tongue: but lo, O Lord, thou knoweſt it altogether.5Thou haſt beſet me behind, and before: and laid thine hand vpon me.6ſuch knowledge is too wonderfull for me: it is high, I cannot attaine vnto it.7Whither ſhall I goe from thy ſpirit? or whither ſhall I flie from thy preſence?8If I aſcend vp into heauen, thou art there: if I make my bed in hell, behold, thou art there.9If I take the wings of the morning: and dwell in the vttermoſt parts of the ſea:10Euen there ſhall thy hand leade me: and thy right hand ſhall hold me.11If I ſay, Surely the darkenes ſhall couer me: euen the night ſhall bee light about me.12Yea the darkeneſſe hideth not from thee, but the night ſhineth as the day: the darknes and the light are both alike to thee.13For thou haſt poſſeſſed my reines: thou haſt couered me in my mothers wombe.14I will praiſe thee, for I am fearefully and wonderfully made, marueilous are thy works: and that my ſoule knoweth right well.15My ſubſtance was not hid from thee, when I was made in ſecret: and curiouſly wrought in the loweſt parts of the earth.16Thine eyes did ſee my ſubſtance yet being vnperfect, and in thy booke all my members were written, which in continuance were faſhioned: when as yet there was none of them.17Howe precious alſo are thy thoughts vnto me, O God: how great is the ſumme of them?18If I ſhould count them, they are moe in number then the ſand: when I awake, I am ſtill with thee.19Surely thou wilt ſlay the wicked, O God: depart from me therefore, ye bloody men.20For they ſpeake againſt thee wickedly: and thine enemies take thy name in vaine.21Doe not I hate them, O Lord, that hate thee? and am not I grieued with thoſe that riſe vp againſt thee?22I hate them with perfect hatred: I count them mine enemies.23ſearch me, O God, and knowe my heart: trie mee, and knowe my thoughts:24And ſee if there bee any wicked way in me: and leade me in the way euerlaſting.

CHAPTER 1401*To the chiefe Muſician, A Pſalme of Dauid.* Deliuer me, O Lord, from the euill man: preſerueme from the violent man.2Which imagine miſchiefes in their heart: continually are they gathered together for warre.3They haue ſharpned their tongues like a ſerpent: adders poiſon is vnder their lips. Selah.4Keepe me, O Lord, from the hands of the wicked, preſerueme from the violent man: who haue purpoſed to ouerthrow my goings.5The proude haue hid a ſnare for me and cords, they haue ſpread a net by the way ſide: they haue ſet grinnes for me. Selah.6I ſaid vnto the Lord, Thou art my God: heare the voyce of my ſupplications, O Lord.7O God the Lord, the ſtrength of my ſaluation: thou haſt couered my head in the day of battell.8Grant not, O Lord, the deſires of the wicked: further not his wicked deuice, leſt they exalt themſelues. Selah.9As for the head of thoſe that compaſſe me about: let the miſchiefe of their owne lips couer them.10Let burning coales fall vpon them, let them be caſt into the fire: into deepe pits, that they riſe not vp againe.11Let not an euill ſpeaker bee eſtabliſhed in the earth: euill ſhall hunt the violent man to ouerthrow him.12I know that the Lord will maintaine the cauſe of the afflicted: and the right of the poore.13Surely the righteous ſhall giue thankes vnto thy Name: the vpright ſhall dwell in thy preſence.

CHAPTER 1411*A Pſalme of Dauid.* Lord, I crie vnto thee, make haſte vnto mee: giue eare vnto my voice, when I crie vnto thee.2Let my prayer bee ſet foorth before thee as incenſe: and the lifting vp of my hands as the Euening ſacrifice.3Set a watch (O Lord) before my mouth: keepe the doore of my lips.4Incline not my heart to any euill thing, to practiſe wicked workes with men that worke iniquitie: and let mee not eate of their dainties.5Let the righteous ſmite mee, it ſhalbe a kindneſse: and let him reprooue me, it ſhalbe an excellent oile, which ſhall not breake my head: for yet my prayer alſo ſhalbe in their calamities.6When their Iudges are ouerthrowen in ſtonie places, they ſhall heare my words, for they are ſweet.7Our bones are ſcattered at the graues mouth: as when one cutteth and cleaueth wood vpon the earth.8But mine eyes are vnto thee, O God the Lord: in thee is my truſt, leaue not my ſoule deſtitute.9Keepe mee from the ſnare which they haue laide for me, and the grinnes of the workers of iniquitie.10Let the wicked fall into their owne nets: whileſt that I withal eſcape.

CHAPTER 1421*Maſchil of Dauid; A prayer when he was in the caue.* I cried vnto the Lord with my voice: with my voice vnto the Lord did I make my ſupplication.2I powred out my complaint before him: I ſhewed before him my trouble.3When my ſpirit was ouerwhelmed within mee, then thou kneweſt my path: in the way wherein I walked, haue they priuily laid a ſnare for me.4I looked on my right hand, and beheld, but there was no man that would know me, refuge failed me: no man cared for my ſoule.5I cried vnto thee, O Lord, I ſaid, Thou art my refuge, and my portion in the land of the liuing.6Attend vnto my crie, for I am brought very low, deliuer mee from my perſecuters: for they are ſtronger then I.7Bring my ſoule out of priſon, that I may praiſe thy Name: the righteous ſhall compaſſe me about: for thou ſhalt deale bountifully with me.

CHAPTER 1431*A Pſalme of Dauid.* Heare my prayer, O Lord, giue eare to my ſupplications: in thy faithfulneſse anſwere me, and in thy righteouſnes.2And enter not into iudgement with thy ſeruant: for in thy ſight ſhall no man liuing be iuſtified.3For the enemie hath perſecuted my ſoule, he hath ſmitten my life downe to the ground: hee hath made mee to dwell in darkeneſſe, as thoſe that haue bene long dead.4Therefore is my ſpirit ouerwhelmed within me: my heart within me is deſolate.5I remember the dayes of old, I meditate on all thy workes: I muſe on the worke of thy hands.6I ſtretch forth my hands vnto thee: my ſoule thirſteth after thee, as a thirſtie land, Selah.7Heare me ſpeedily, O Lord, my ſpirit faileth, hide not thy face from mee: leſt I be like vnto them that goe downe into the pit.8Cauſe mee to heare thy louing kindneſſe in the morning, for in thee doe I truſt, cauſe mee to knowe the way wherein I ſhould walke: for I lift vp my ſoule vnto thee.9Deliuer mee, O Lord, from mine enemies: I flie vnto thee to hide me.10Teach me to doe thy will, for thou art my God, thy ſpirit is good: leade me into the land of vprightneſse.11Quicken me, O Lord, for thy names ſake: for thy righteouſneſſe ſake bring my ſoule out of trouble.12And of thy mercy cut off mine enemies, and deſtroy all them that afflict my ſoule: for I am thy ſeruant.

CHAPTER 1441*A Pſalme of Dauid.* Bleſſed be the Lord my ſtrength, which teacheth my hands to warre, and my fingers to fight.2My goodnes and my fortreſse, my high tower and my deliuerer, my ſhield, and he in whome I truſt: who ſubdueth my people vnder me.3Lord, what is man, that thou takeſt knowledge of him? or the ſonne of man, that thou makeſt account of him?4Man is like to vanity: his dayes are as a ſhadow that paſſeth away.5Bow thy heauens, O Lord, and come downe: touch the mountaines, and they ſhall ſmoke.6Caſt forth lightning, and ſcatter

them: ſhoote out thine arrowes, and deſtroy them.[7]Send thine hand
from aboue, rid me, and deliuer me out of great waters: from the hand
of ſtrange children,[8]Whoſe mouth ſpeaketh vanitie: and their right hand
is a right hand of falſhood.[9]I will ſing a new ſong vnto thee, O God:
vpon a pſalterie, and an inſtrument of ten ſtrings will I ſing praiſes vnto
thee.[10]It is he that giueth ſaluation vnto kings: who deliuereth Dauid his
ſeruant from the hurtfull ſword.[11]Rid me, and deliuer me from the hand
of ſtrange children, whoſe mouth ſpeaketh vanitie: and their right hand
is a right hand of falſhood.[12]That our ſonnes may be as plants growen
vp in their youth; that our daughters may be as corner ſtones, poliſhed
after the ſimilitude of a palace:[13]That our garners may bee full,
affoording all maner of ſtore; that our ſheepe may bring forth thouſands,
and tenne thouſands in our ſtreetes.[14]That our oxen may be ſtrong to
labour, that there be no breaking in, nor going out; that there be no
complaining in our ſtreetes.[15]Happy is that people that is in ſuch a caſe:
yea, happy is that people, whoſe God is the Lord.
CHAPTER 145[1]*Dauids Pſalme of praiſe.* I will extoll thee, my God, O
King: and I will bleſſe thy name for euer and euer.[2]Euery day wil I bleſſe
thee: and I will praiſe thy Name for euer and euer.[3]Great is the Lord,
and greatly to be praiſed: and his greatnes is vnſearchable.[4]One
generation ſhall praiſe thy works to another, and ſhal declare thy mightie
actes.[5]I will ſpeake of the glorious honour of thy maieſtie: and of thy
wonderous workes.[6]And men ſhall ſpeake of the might of thy terrible
acts: and I wil declare thy greatneſse.[7]They ſhall abundantly vtter the
memory of thy great goodneſse: and ſhall ſing of thy
righteouſneſſe.[8]The Lord is gracious and full of compaſſion: ſlow to
anger, and of great mercy.[9]The Lord is good to all: and his tender
mercies are ouer all his workes.[10]All thy workes ſhall praiſe thee, O
Lord: and thy Saints ſhal bleſſe thee.[11]They ſhall ſpeake of the glory of
thy kingdome: and talke of thy power.[12]To make knowen to the ſonnes
of men his mightie actes: and the glorious Maieſtie of his
kingdome.[13]Thy kingdome is an euerlaſting kingdome: and thy
dominion endureth throughout all generations.[14]The Lord vpholdeth all
that fall: and raiſeth vp all thoſe that bee bowed downe.[15]The eyes of all
waite vpon thee: and thou giueſt them their meat in due ſeaſon.[16]Thou
openeſt thine hand: and ſatiſfieſt the deſire of euery liuing thing.[17]The
Lord is righteous in all his wayes: and holy in all his works.[18]The Lord
is nigh vnto all them that call vpon him: to all that call vpon him in
trueth.[19]Hee will fulfill the deſire of them that feare him: he alſo will
heare their cry, and will ſaue them.[20]The Lord preſerueth all them that
loue him: but all the wicked will he deſtroy.[21]My mouth ſhall ſpeake the
praiſe of the Lord: and let all fleſh bleſſe his holy Name for euer and
euer.
CHAPTER 146[1]Praiſe yee the Lord: prayſe the Lord, O my
ſoule.[2]While I liue, will I praiſe the Lord: I will ſing praiſes vnto my God,
while I haue any being.[3]Put not your truſt in Princes: nor in the ſonne
of man, in whom there is no helpe.[4]His breath goeth foorth, he
returneth to his earth: in that very day his thoughts periſh.[5]Happy is he
that hath the God of Iacob for his helpe: whoſe hope is in the Lord his
God:[6]Which made heauen and earth, the ſea, and all that therein is:
which keepeth trueth for euer:[7]Which executeth iudgement for the
oppreſſed, which giueth food to the hungry: the Lord looſeth the
priſoners.[8]The Lord openeth the eyes of the blinde, the Lord raiſeth
them that are bowed downe: the Lord loueth the righteous.[9]The Lord
preſerueth the ſtrangers, he relieueth the fatherleſſe and widow: but the
way of the wicked he turneth vpſide downe.[10]The Lord ſhall reigne for
euer, euen thy God, O Zion, vnto all generations: Praiſe ye the Lord.
CHAPTER 147[1]Praiſe ye the Lord: for it is good to ſing praiſes vnto
our God: for it is pleaſant, and praiſe is comely.[2]The Lord doeth build
vp Ieruſalem: he gathereth together the out-caſts of Iſrael.[3]Hee healeth
the broken in heart: and bindeth vp their wounds.[4]He telleth the
number of the ſtars: he calleth them all by their names.[5]Great is our
Lord, and of great power: his vnderſtanding is infinite.[6]The Lord lifteth
vp the meeke: hee caſteth the wicked downe to the ground.[7]Sing vnto
the Lord with thankeſgiuing: ſing prayſe vpon the harpe vnto our
God:[8]Who coucreth the heauen with cloudes, who prepareth raine for
the earth: who maketh graſſe to growe vpon the mountaines.[9]He giueth
to the beaſt his foode: and to the yong rauens which crie.[10]Hee
delighteth not in the ſtrength of the horſe: he taketh not pleaſure in the
legs of a man.[11]The Lord taketh pleaſure in them that feare him: in thoſe
that hope in his mercie.[12]Praiſe the Lord, O Ieruſalem: praiſe thy God,
O Zion.[13]For hee hath ſtrengthened the barres of thy gates: hee hath
bleſſed thy children within thee.[14]He maketh peace in thy borders: and
filleth thee with the fineſt of the wheate.[15]He ſendeth forth his
commandement vpon earth: his word runneth very ſwiftly.[16]He giueth
ſnow like wooll: he ſcattereth the hoare froſt like aſhes.[17]He caſteth
forth his yce like morſels: who can ſtand before his cold?[18]He ſendeth
out his word, and melteth them: he cauſeth his wind to blow, and the
waters flow.[19]He ſheweth his word vnto Iacob: his ſtatutes and his
iudgements vnto Iſrael.[20]He hath not dealt ſo with any nation: and as
for his iudgements, they haue not knowen them. Praiſe yee the Lord.
CHAPTER 148[1]Praiſe yee the Lord. Praiſe ye the Lord from the
heauens: praiſe him in the heights.[2]Praiſe yee him all his Angels: praiſe
ye him all his hoſts.[3]Praiſe ye him Sunne and Moone: praiſe him all ye
ſtarres of light.[4]Praiſe him ye heauens of heauens: and ye waters that be
aboue the heauens.[5]Let them praiſe the Name of the Lord: for he
commanded, and they were created.[6]Hee hath alſo ſtabliſhed them for
euer and euer: he hath made a decree which ſhall not paſſe.[7]Praiſe the
Lord from the earth: ye dragons and all deepes.[8]Fire and haile, ſnow and
vapour: ſtormie wind fulfilling his word.[9]Mountaines and all hilles:
fruitfull trees, and all cedars.[10]Beaſtes and all cattell: creeping things, and
flying foule.[11]Kings of the earth, and all people: Princes, and all Iudges
of the earth.[12]Both young men and maidens: olde men and
children.[13]Let them praiſe the Name of the Lord, for his Name alone is
excellent: his glory is aboue the earth and heauen.[14]Hee alſo exalteth the
horne of his people, the praiſe of all his Saints; euen of the children of
Iſrael, a people neere vnto him. Praiſe ye the Lord.
CHAPTER 149[1]Praiſe yee the Lord: Sing vnto the Lord a new ſong:
and his prayſe in the Congregation of Saints.[2]Let Iſrael reioyce in him
that made him: let the children of Zion bee ioyfull in their King.[3]Let
them praiſe his Name in the dance: let them ſing praiſes vnto him with
the timbrell and harpe.[4]For the Lord taketh pleaſure in his people: hee
will beautifie the meeke with ſaluation.[5]Let the Saints be ioyfull in glory:
let them ſing aloude vpon their beddes.[6]Let the high praiſes of God be
in their mouth: and a two edged ſword in their hand:[7]To execute
vengeance vpon the heathen: and puniſhments vpon the people.[8]To
binde their Kings with chaines: and their Nobles with fetters of
yron.[9]To execute vpon them the iudgement written: This honour haue
all his Saints. Praiſe ye the Lord.
CHAPTER 150[1]Praiſe ye the Lord. Praiſe God in his Sanctuarie: Praiſe
him in the firmament of his power.[2]Praiſe him for his mightie actes:
Praiſe him according to his excellent greatneſse.[3]Praiſe him with the
ſound of the Trumpet: Prayſe him with the Pſalterie and Harpe.[4]Praiſe
him with the timbrell and dance: praiſe him with ſtringed inſtruments,
and Organes.[5]Praiſe him vpon the loud cymbals: praiſe him vpon the
high ſounding cymbals.[6]Let euery thing that hath breath, praiſe the
Lord. Praiſe yee the Lord.

PROUERBS (PROVERBS)

CHAPTER 1[1]The Prouerbes of Solomon the ſonne of Dauid, King of
Iſrael,[2]To knowe wiſedome and inſtruction, to perceiue the words of
vnderſtanding,[3]To receiue the inſtruction of wiſdome, iuſtice, and
iudgement & equitie,[4]To giue ſubtiltie to the ſimple, to the yong man
knowledge and diſcretion.[5]A wiſe man wil heare, and wil increaſe
learning: and a man of vnderſtanding ſhall attaine vnto wiſe
counſels:[6]To vnderſtand a prouerbe, and the interpretation; the wordes
of the wiſe, and their darke ſayings.[7]The feare of the Lord is the
beginning of knowledge: but fooles deſpiſe wiſedome and
inſtruction.[8]My ſonne, heare the inſtruction of thy father, and forſake
not the law of thy mother.[9]For they ſhall be an ornament of grace vnto
thy head, and chaines about thy necke.[10]My ſonne, if ſinners entiſe thee,
conſent thou not.[11]If they ſay, Come with vs, let vs lay wait for blood,
let vs lurke priuily for the innocent without cauſe:[12]Let vs ſwallow them
vp aliue, as the graue, and whole, as thoſe that goe downe into the

pit:13Wee ſhall finde all precious ſubſtance, wee ſhall fill our houſes with ſpoile:14Caſt in thy lot among vs, let vs all haue one purſe:15My ſonne, walke not thou in the way with them; refraine thy foot from their path:16For their feete runne to euil, and make haſte to ſhed blood.17Surely in vaine the net is ſpread in the ſight of any bird.18And they lay wait for their owne blood, they lurke priuily for their owne liues.19So are the waies of euery one that is greedie of gaine: which taketh away the life of the owners thereof.20Wiſedome crieth without, ſhe vttereth her voice in the ſtreets:21Shee crieth in the chiefe place of concourſe, in the openings of the gates: in the city ſhe vttereth her words, ſaying,22How long, ye ſimple ones, will ye loue ſimplicitie? and the ſcorners delight in their ſcorning, and fooles hate knowledge?23Turne you at my reproofe: behold, I will powre out my ſpirit vnto you, I will make knowen my wordes vnto you.24Becauſe I haue called, and yee refuſed, I haue ſtretched out my hand, and no man regarded:25But ye haue ſet at nought all my counſell, & would none of my reproofe:26I alſo will laugh at your calamitie, I wil mocke when your feare commeth.27When your feare commeth as deſolation, and your deſtruction commeth as a whirlewinde; when diſtreſſe and anguiſh commeth vpon you:28Then ſhall they call vpon mee, but I will not anſwere; they ſhall ſeeke me early, but they ſhall not finde me:29For that they hated knowledge, and did not chooſe the feare of the Lord.30They would none of my counſel: they deſpiſed all my reproofe.31Therefore ſhall they eate of the fruite of their owne way, and be filled with their owne deuices.32For the turning away of the ſimple ſhall ſlay them, and the proſperity of fooles ſhall deſtroy them.33But who ſo hearkneth vnto mee, ſhall dwell ſafely, and ſhall be quiet from feare of euill.

CHAPTER 21My ſonne, if thou wilt receiue my words, and hide my commaundements with thee;2So that thou incline thine eare vnto wiſedome, and apply thine heart to vnderſtanding:3Yea if thou cryeſt after knowledge, and lifteſt vp thy voyce for vnderſtanding:4If thou ſeekeſt her as ſiluer, and ſearcheſt for her, as for hid treaſures:5Then ſhalt thou vnderſtand the feare of the Lord, and find the knowledge of God.6For the Lord giueth wiſedome: out of his mouth commeth knowledge, and vnderſtanding.7He layeth vp ſound wiſedome for the righteous: he is a buckler to them that walke vprightly.8He keepeth the pathes of iudgement, and preſerueth the way of his Saints.9Then ſhalt thou vnderſtand righteouſneſſe, and iudgement, and equity; yea euery good path.10When wiſedome entreth into thine heart, and knowledge is pleaſant vnto thy ſoule;11Diſcretion ſhall preſeruethee, vnderſtanding ſhall keepe thee:12To deliuer thee from the way of the euill man, from the man that ſpeaketh froward things.13Who leaue the pathes of vprightneſse, to walke in the wayes of darkeneſſe:14Who reioyce to doe euill, and delight in the frowardneſse of the wicked.15Whoſe wayes are crooked, and they froward in their pathes.16To deliuer thee from the ſtrange woman, euen from the ſtranger, which flattereth with her words:17Which forſaketh the guide of her youth, and forgetteth the couenant of her God.18For her houſe inclineth vnto death, and her pathes vnto the dead:19None that goe vnto her, returne againe, neither take they hold of the pathes of life.20That thou mayeſt walke in the way of good men, and keepe the pathes of the righteous.21For the vpright ſhall dwell in the land, and the perfect ſhall remaine in it.22But the wicked ſhall be cut off from the earth, and the tranſgreſsours ſhalbe rooted out of it.

CHAPTER 31My ſonne, forget not my lawe; but let thine heart keepe my commaundements:2For length of dayes, and long life, and peace ſhall they adde to thee.3Let not mercy and trueth forſake thee: bind them about thy necke, write them vpon the table of thine heart.4So ſhalt thou find fauour, and good vnderſtanding in the ſight of God, and man.5Truſt in the Lord with all thine heart; and leaue not vnto thine owne vnderſtanding.6In all thy wayes acknowledge him, and he ſhall direct thy pathes.7Be not wiſe in thine owne eyes: feare the Lord, and depart from euill.8It ſhalbe health to thy nauill, and marrow to thy bones.9Honour the Lord with thy ſubſtance, and with the firſt fruits of all thine increaſe.10So ſhall thy barnes be filled with plenty, and thy preſses ſhall burſt out with new wine.11My ſonne, deſpiſe not the chaſtening of the Lord: neither be weary of his correction.12For whom the Lord loueth, he correcteth, euen as a father the ſonne, in whom he delighteth.13Happy is the man that findeth wiſedome, and the man that getteth vnderſtanding.14For the merchandiſe of it is better then the merchandiſe of ſiluer, and the gaine thereof, then fine gold.15She is more precious then Rubies: and all the things thou canſt deſire, are not to be compared vnto her.16Length of dayes is in her right hand: and in her left hand, riches and honour.17Her wayes are wayes of pleſantneſse: and all her pathes are peace.18She is a tree of life, to them that lay hold vpon her: and happy is euery one that retaineth her.19The Lord by wiſedome hath founded the earth; by vnderſtanding hath he eſtabliſhed the heauens.20By his knowledge the depthes are broken vp; and the cloudes droppe downe the dew.21My ſonne, let not them depart from thine eyes: keepe ſound wiſedome and diſcretion.22So ſhall they bee life vnto thy ſoule, and grace to thy necke.23Then ſhalt thou walke in thy way ſafely, & thy foot ſhall not ſtumble.24When thou lyeſt downe, thou ſhalt not be afraide: yea, thou ſhalt lye downe, and thy ſleepe ſhalbe ſweet.25Be not afraid of ſudden feare, neither of the deſolation of the wicked, when it commeth.26For the Lord ſhalbe thy confidence, and ſhall keepe thy foote from being taken.27Withhold not good from them to whom it is due, when it is in the power of thine hand to doe it.28ſay not vnto thy neighbour, Goe, and come againe, and to morrow I will giue, when thou haſt it by thee.29Deuiſe not euil againſt thy neighbour, ſeeing hee dwelleth ſecurely by thee.30Striue not with a man without cauſe, if hee haue done thee no harme.31Enuie thou not the oppreſsour, and chooſe none of his wayes.32For the froward is abomination to the Lord: but his ſecret is with the righteous.33The curſe of the Lord is in the houſe of the wicked: but he bleſſeth the habitation of the iuſt.34Surely he ſcorneth the ſcorners: but he giueth grace vnto the lowly.35The wiſe ſhall inherite glory, but ſhame ſhalbe the promotion of fooles.

CHAPTER 41Heare, ye children, the inſtruction of a father, and attend to know vnderſtanding.2For I giue you good doctrine: forſake you not my law.3For I was my fathers ſonne, tender and onely beloued in the ſight of my mother.4He taught me alſo, and ſaid vnto me, Let thine heart reteine my wordes: keepe my commandements, and liue.5Get wiſedome, get vnderſtanding: forget it not, neither decline from the wordes of my mouth.6Forſake her not, and ſhe ſhall preſeruethee: loue her, and ſhe ſhall keepe thee.7Wiſedome is the principall thing, therefore get wiſedome: and with all thy getting, get vnderſtanding.8Exalt her, and ſhee ſhall promote thee: ſhee ſhall bring thee to honour, when thou doeſt imbrace her.9She ſhall giue to thine head an ornament of grace, a crowne of glory ſhall ſhe deliuer to thee.10Heare, O my ſonne, and receiue my ſayings: and the yeeres of thy life ſhalbe many.11I haue taught thee in the way of wiſedome: I haue lead thee in right pathes.12When thou goeſt, thy ſteps ſhall not be ſtraitned, and when thou runneſt, thou ſhalt not ſtumble.13Take faſt hold of inſtruction, let her not goe; keepe her, for ſhe is thy life.14Enter not into the path of the wicked, and goe not in the way of euill men.15Auoid it, paſſe not by it, turne from it, and paſſe away.16For they ſleepe not except they haue done miſchiefe: and their ſleepe is taken away vnleſſe they cauſe ſome to fall.17For they eate the bread of wickedneſſe, and drinke the wine of violence.18But the path of the iuſt is as the ſhining light that ſhineth more and more vnto the perfect day.19The way of the wicked is as darknes: they know not at what they ſtumble.20My ſonne, attend to my words, incline thine eare vnto my ſayings.21Let them not depart from thine eyes: keepe them in the midſt of thine heart.22For they are life vnto thoſe that find them, and health to all their fleſh.23Keepe thy heart with all diligence: for out of it are the iſsues of life.24Put away from thee a froward mouth, and peruerſe lips put farre from thee.25Let thine eyes looke right on, and let thine eye lids looke ſtraight before thee.26Ponder the path of thy feet, and let all thy wayes be eſtabliſhed.27Turne not to the right hande nor to the left: remoue thy foot frō euil.

CHAPTER 51My ſonne, attend vnto my wiſedome, and bowe thine eare to my vnderſtanding.2That thou mayeſt regard diſcretion, and that thy lips may keepe knowledge.3For the lips of a ſtrange woman drop as an hony combe, and her mouth is ſmoother then oyle.4But her end is bitter as wormewood, ſharpe as a two edged ſword.5Her feete goe downe to death: her ſteps take hold on hell.6Leſt thou ſhouldeſt ponder the path of life, her wayes are moueable, that thou canſt not know them.7Heare me now therefore, O yee children: & depart not from the words of my mouth.8Remoue thy way farre from her, and come not nie

the doore of her houſe:9Leſt thou giue thine honour vnto others, and
thy yeeres vnto the cruell:10Leſt ſtrangers be filled with thy wealth, and
thy labors be in the houſe of a ſtranger,11And thou mourne at the laſt,
when thy fleſh and thy body are conſumed,12And ſay, How haue I hated
inſtruction, and my heart deſpiſed reproofe?13And haue not obeyed the
voyce of my teachers, nor inclined mine eare to them that inſtructed
me?14I was almoſt in all euill, in the midſt of the congregation &
aſſembly.15Drinke waters out of thine owne ciſterne, and running waters
out of thine owne well.16Let thy fountaines bee diſperſed abroad, and
riuers of waters in the ſtreets.17Let them be onely thine owne, and not
ſtrangers with thee.18Let thy fountaine be bleſſed: and reioyce with the
wife of thy youth.19Let her bee as the louing Hinde and pleaſant Roe,
let her breaſts ſatiſfie thee at all times, and be thou rauiſht alwayes with
her loue.20And why wilt thou, my ſonne, be rauiſht with a ſtrange
woman, and imbrace the boſome of a ſtranger?21For the wayes of man
are before the eyes of the Lord, and he pondereth all his goings.22His
owne iniquities ſhall take the wicked himſelfe, and he ſhall be holden
with the coards of his ſinnes.23He ſhall die without inſtruction, and in
the greatneſſe of his folly he ſhal goe aſtray.
CHAPTER 61My ſonne, if thou bee ſurety for thy friend, it thou haſt
ſtricken thy hand with a ſtranger,2Thou art ſnared with the words of thy
mouth, thou art taken with the wordes of thy mouth.3Doe this now, my
ſonne, and deliuer thy ſelfe, when thou art come into the hand of thy
friend: goe, humble thy ſelfe, and make ſure thy friend.4Giue not ſleepe
to thine eyes, nor ſlumber to thine eyelids.5Deliuer thy ſelfe as a Roe
from the hand of the hunter, and as a bird from the hand of the
fowler.6Goe to the Ant, thou ſluggard, conſider her wayes, and be
wiſe.7Which hauing no guide, ouerſeer, or ruler,8Prouideth her meat in
the Summer, and gathereth her food in the harueſt.9How long wilt thou
ſleepe, O ſluggard? when wilt thou Ariſe out of thy ſleepe?10Yet a little
ſleepe, a little ſlumber, a little folding of the hands to ſleepe.11So ſhall
thy pouertie come as one that trauaileth, and thy want as an armed
man.12A naughtie perſon, a wicked man walketh with a froward
mouth.13He winketh with his eyes, he ſpeaketh with his feete, hee
teacheth with his fingers.14Frowardneſe is in his heart, he deuiſeth
miſchiefe continually, he ſoweth diſcord.15Therefore ſhall his calamitie
come ſuddenly; ſuddenly ſhall hee be broken without remedie.16Theſe
ſixe things doeth the Lord hate; yea ſeuen are an abomination vnto
him:17A proude looke, a lying tongue, and hands that ſhed innocent
blood:18An heart that deuiſeth wicked imaginations, feet that be ſwift in
running to miſchiefe:19A falſe witneſſe that ſpeaketh lies; and him that
ſoweth diſcord among brethren.20My ſonne, keepe thy fathers
commandement, and forſake not the law of thy mother.21Binde them
continually vpon thine heart, and tie them about thy necke.22When thou
goeſt, it ſhall leade thee; when thou ſleepeſt, it ſhall keepe thee; and when
thou awakeſt, it ſhall talke with thee.23For the Commandement is a
lampe, and the Lawe is light: and reproofes of inſtruction are the way of
life:24To keepe thee from the euill woman, from the flatterie of the
tongue of a ſtrange woman.25Luſt not after her beautie in thine heart;
neither let her take thee with her eyelids.26For by meanes of a whoriſh
woman, a man is brought to a piece of bread: and the adultereſe will
hunt for the precious life.27Can a man take fire in his boſome, and his
clothes not be burnt?28Can one goe vpon hote coales, and his feete not
be burnt?29So he that goeth in to his neighbours wife; whoſoeuer
toucheth her, ſhall not be innocent.30Men doe not deſpiſe a thiefe, if he
ſteale to ſatiſfie his ſoule, when hee is hungry:31But if he be found, he
ſhall reſtore ſeuenfold, he ſhall giue all the ſubſtance of his houſe.32But
who ſo committeth adultery with a woman, lacketh vnderſtanding: hee
that doeth it, deſtroyeth his owne ſoule.33A wound and diſhonour ſhall
he get, and his reproch ſhall not be wiped away.34For iealouſie is the
rage of a man: therefore he will not ſpare in the day of vengeance.35He
will not regard any ranſome; neither will hee reſt content, though thou
giueſt many giftes.
CHAPTER 71My ſonne, keepe my words, and lay vp my
commaundements with thee.2Keepe my commandements, and liue: and
my law as the apple of thine eye.3Bind them vpon thy fingers, write them
vpon the table of thine heart.4ſay vnto Wiſedome, Thou art my ſiſter,
and call Underſtanding thy kinſe woman,5That they may keepe thee
from the ſtrange woman, from the ſtranger which flattereth with her
words.6For at the windowe of my houſe I looked through my
caſement,7And behelde among the ſimple ones, I diſcernedamong the
youths, a yong man void of vnderſtanding,8Paſsing through the ſtreete
neere her corner, and he went the way to her houſe,9In the twilight in
the euening, in the blacke and darke night:10And behold, there met him
a woman, with the attire of an harlot, and ſubtill of heart.11(She is loud
and ſtubburne, her feet abide not in her houſe:12Now is ſhee without,
now in the ſtreetes, and lieth in waite at euery corner.)13So ſhe caught
him, and kiſſed him, and with an impudent face, ſaid vnto him,14I haue
peace offerings with me: this day haue I paid my vowes.15Therefore
came I forth to meete thee, diligently to ſeeke thy face, and I haue found
thee.16I haue deckt my bed with couerings of tapeſtrie, with carued
workes, with fine linnen of Egypt.17I haue perfumed my bed with
myrrhe, aloes, and cynamom.18Come, let vs take our fill of loue vntill
the morning, let vs ſolace our ſelues with loues.19For the good-man is
not at home, he is gone a long iourney.20He hath taken a bag of money
with him, and will come home at the day appointed.21With much faire
ſpeech ſhe cauſed him to yeeld, with the flattering of her lips ſhe forced
him.22He goeth after her ſtraightway, as an oxe goeth to the ſlaughter,
or as a foole to the correction of the ſtocks,23Til a dart ſtrike through
his liuer, as a bird haſteth to the ſnare, and knoweth not that it is for his
life.24Hearken vnto me now therefore, O ye children, and attend to the
words of my mouth.25Let not thine heart decline to her wayes, goe not
aſtray in her paths.26For ſhee hath caſt downe many wounded: yea many
ſtrong men haue bene ſlaine by her.27Her houſe is the way to hell, going
downe to the chambers of death.
CHAPTER 81Doeth not Wiſedome crie? & Underſtanding put foorth
her voice?2Shee ſtandeth in the top of high places, by the way in the
places of the pathes.3She cryeth at the gates, at the entrie of the citie, at
the comming in at the doores.4Unto you, O men, I call, and my voice is
to the ſonnes of man.5O yee ſimple, vnderſtand wiſedome: and yee
fooles, be yee of an vnderſtanding heart.6Heare, for I will ſpeake of
excellent things: and the opening of my lippes ſhalbe right things.7For
my mouth ſhall ſpeake truth, and wickedneſſe is an abomination to my
lippes.8All the words of my mouth are in righteouſnes, there is nothing
froward or peruerſe in them.9They are all plaine to him that
vnderſtandeth: and right to them that find knowledge.10Receiue my
inſtruction, and not ſiluer: and knowledge rather then choiſe gold.11For
wiſedome is better then rubies: and all the things that may be deſired,
are not to be compared to it.12I wiſedome dwell with prudence, and find
out knowledge of witty inuentions.13The feare of the Lord is to hate
euill: pride and arrogancie, and the euill way, and the froward mouth doe
I hate.14Counſell is mine, and ſound wiſedome: I am vnderſtanding, I
haue ſtrength.15By me kings reigne, and princes decree iuſtice.16By me
Princes rule, and Nobles, euen all the Iudges of the earth.17I loue them
that loue me, and thoſe that ſeeke me early, ſhall find me.18Riches and
honour are with me, yea durable riches and righteouſneſſe.19My fruite is
better then gold, yea then fine gold, and my reuenue then choiſe
ſiluer.20I leade in the way of righteouſneſſe, in the midſt of the pathes
of iudgment.21That I may cauſe thoſe that loue me, to inherite ſubſtance:
and I will fill their treaſures.22The Lord poſſeſſed me in the beginning
of his way, before his works of old.23I was ſet vp from euerlaſting, from
the beginning, or euer the earth was.24When there were no depthes, I
was brought forth: when there were no fountaines abounding with
water.25Before the mountaines were ſetled: before the hilles, was I
brought foorth:26While as yet he had not made the earth, nor the fields,
nor the higheſt part of the duſt of the world.27When hee prepared the
heauens, I was there: when he ſet a compaſſe vpon the face of the
depth.28When he eſtabliſhed the cloudes aboue: when he ſtrengthned
the fountaines of the deepe.29When he gaue to the ſea his decree, that
the waters ſhould not paſſe his commandement: when he appointed the
foundations of the earth:30Then I was by him, as one brought vp with
him: and I was daily his delight, reioycing alwayes before
him:31Reioycing in the habitable part of his earth, and my delights were
with the ſonnes of men.32Nowe therefore hearken vnto me, O yee
children: for bleſſed are they that keepe my wayes.33Heare inſtruction,
and bee wiſe, and refuſe it not.34Bleſſed is the man that heareth me:
watching daily at my gates, waiting at the poſtes of my doores.35For
whoſo findeth mee, findeth life, and ſhall obtaine fauour of the

Lord.36But hee that ſinneth againſt me, wrongeth his owne ſoule; all they that hate me, loue death.

CHAPTER 9 1Wiſedome hath builded her houſe: ſhe hath hewen out her ſeuen pillars.2She hath killed her beaſtes; ſhe hath mingled her wine: ſhe hath alſo furniſhed her table.3She hath ſent forth her maidens; ſhe cryeth vpon the higheſt places of the citie.4Who ſo is ſimple, let him turne in hither: as for him that wanteth vnderſtanding, ſhe ſayth to him:5Come, eate of my bread, and drinke of the wine, which I haue mingled.6Forſake the fooliſh, and liue; and goe in the way of vnderſtanding.7He that reproueth a ſcorner, getteth to himſelfe ſhame: and he that rebuketh a wicked man, getteth himſelfe a blot.8Reproue not a ſcorner, leſt hee hate thee: rebuke a wiſe man, and hee will loue thee.9Giue inſtruction to a wiſe man, and he will be yet wiſer: teach a iuſt man, and he will increaſe in learning.10The feare of the Lord is the beginning of wiſedome: and the knowledge of the holy is vnderſtanding.11For by me thy dayes ſhall be multiplied: and the yeeres of thy life ſhalbe increaſed.12If thou be wiſe, thou ſhalt be wiſe for thy ſelfe: but if thou ſcorneſt, thou alone ſhalt beare it.13A fooliſh woman is clamorous: ſhe is ſimple, & knoweth nothing.14For ſhe ſitteth at the doore of her houſe on a ſeate, in the high places of the Citie:15To call paſſengers who go right on their wayes:16Who ſo is ſimple, let him turne in hither: and as for him that wanteth vnderſtanding, ſhe ſaith to him;17Stollen waters are ſweet, and bread eaten in ſecret is pleaſant.18But hee knoweth not that the dead are there, and that her gueſts are in the depths of hell.

CHAPTER 10 1The Prouerbes of Solomon: A wiſe ſonne maketh a glad father: but a fooliſh ſonne is the heauineſse of his mother.2Treaſures of wickedneſſe profit nothing: but righteouſnes deliuereth from death.3The Lord will not ſuffer the ſoule of the righteous to famiſh: but he caſteth away the ſubſtance of the wicked.4Hee becommeth poore that dealeth with a ſlacke hand: but the hand of the diligent, maketh rich.5Hee that gathereth in Summer, is a wiſe ſonne: but hee that ſleepeth in harueſt, is a ſonne that cauſeth ſhame.6Bleſſings are vpon the head of the iuſt: but violence couereth the mouth of the wicked.7The memorie of the iuſt is bleſſed: but the name of the wicked ſhall rot.8The wiſe in heart will receiue commaundements: but a prating foole ſhall fall.9He that walketh vprightly, walketh ſurely: but he that peruerteth his wayes, ſhalbe knowen.10Hee that winketh with the eye, cauſeth ſorrow: but a prating foole ſhall fall.11The mouth of a righteous man is a well of life: but violence couereth the mouth of the wicked.12Hatred ſtirreth vp ſtrifes: but loue couereth all ſinnes.13In the lips of him that hath vnderſtanding, wiſedome is found: but a rod is for the backe of him that is voyd of vnderſtanding.14Wiſe men lay vp knowledge: but the mouth of the fooliſh is neere deſtruction.15The rich mans wealth is his ſtrong citie: the deſtruction of the poore is their pouertie.16The labour of the righteous tendeth to life: the fruite of the wicked to ſinne.17He is in the way of life that keepeth inſtruction: but hee that refuſeth reproofe, erreth.18Hee that hideth hatred with lying lippes, and he that vttereth a ſlander, is a foole.19In the multitude of words there wanteth not ſinne: but he that refraineth his lippes, is wiſe.20The tongue of the iuſt is as choiſe ſiluer: the heart of the wicked is little worth.21The lippes of the righteous feed many: but fooles die for want of wiſedome.22The bleſſing of the Lord, it maketh rich, and hee addeth no ſorrow with it.23It is as a ſport to a foole to doe miſchiefe: but a man of vnderſtanding hath wiſedome.24The feare of the wicked, it ſhall come vpon him: but the deſire of the righteous ſhalbe granted.25As the whirlewinde paſſeth, ſo is the wicked no more: but the righteous is an euerlaſting foundation.26As vineger to the teeth, and as ſmoke to the eyes, ſo is the ſluggard to them that ſend him.27The feare of the Lord prolongeth dayes: but the yeeres of the wicked ſhalbe ſhortened.28The hope of the righteous ſhall bee gladneſſe: but the expectation of the wicked ſhall periſh.29The way of the Lord is ſtrength to the vpright: but deſtruction ſhall bee to the workers of iniquitie.30The righteous ſhall neuer bee remooued: but the wicked ſhall not inhabite the earth.31The mouth of the iuſt bringeth foorth wiſedome: but the froward tongue ſhalbe cut out.32The lips of the righteous know what is acceptable: but the mouth of the wicked ſpeaketh frowardneſse.

CHAPTER 11 1A falſe ballance is abomination to the Lord: but a iuſt weight is his delight.2When pride commeth, then commeth ſhame: but with the lowly is wiſedome.3The integritie of the vpright ſhall guide them: but the peruerſeneſse of tranſgreſsours ſhall deſtroy them.4Riches profite not in the day of wrath: but righteouſneſſe deliuereth from death.5The righteouſneſſe of the perfect ſhall direct his way: but the wicked ſhall fall by his owne wickedneſſe.6The righteouſneſſe of the vpright ſhall deliuer them: but tranſgreſsours ſhall be taken in their owne naughtineſse.7When a wicked man dieth, his expectation ſhall periſh: and the hope of vniuſt men periſheth.8The righteous is deliuered out of trouble, and the wicked commeth in his ſtead.9An hypocrite with his mouth deſtroyeth his neighbour: but through knowledge ſhall the iuſt be deliuered.10When it goeth well with the righteous, the citie reioyceth: and when the wicked periſh, there is ſhouting.11By the bleſſing of the vpright the citie is exalted; but it is ouerthrowen by the mouth of the wicked.12He that is void of wiſedome, deſpiſeth his neighbour: but a man of vnderſtanding holdeth his peace.13A tale-bearer reuealeth ſecrets: but hee that is of a faithfull ſpirit, concealeth the matter.14Where no counſell is, the people fall: but in the multitude of counſellers there is ſafetie.15Hee that is ſuretie for a ſtranger, ſhall ſmart for it: and hee that hateth ſuretiſhip, is ſure.16A gracious woman retaineth honour: and ſtrong men retaine riches.17The mercifull man doeth good to his owne ſoule: but he that is cruell, troubleth his owne fleſh.18The wicked worketh a deceitfull worke: but to him that ſoweth righteouſneſſe, ſhall be a ſure reward.19As righteouſneſſe tendeth to life: ſo he that purſueth euill, purſueth it to his owne death.20They that are of a froward heart, are abomination to the Lord: but ſuch as are vpright in their way, are his delight.21Though hand ioyne in hand, the wicked ſhall not be vnpuniſhed: but the ſeede of the righteous ſhall be deliuered.22As a iewell of golde in a ſwines ſnowt; ſo is a faire woman which is without diſcretion.23The deſire of the righteous is onely good: but the expectation of the wicked is wrath.24There is that ſcattereth, and yet increaſeth; and there is that withholdeth more then is meete, but it tendeth to pouertie.25The liberall ſoule ſhalbe made fat: and he that watereth, ſhall be watered alſo himſelfe.26Hee that withholdeth corne, the people ſhall curſe him: but bleſſing ſhall be vpon the head of him that ſelleth it.27He that diligently ſeeketh good, procureth fauour: but hee that ſeeketh miſchiefe, it ſhall come vnto him.28He that truſteth in his riches, ſhall fall: but the righteous ſhall flouriſh as a branch.29He that troubleth his owne houſe, ſhall inherite the winde: and the foole ſhall be ſeruant to the wiſe of heart.30The fruit of the righteous is a tree of life: and hee that winneth ſoules, is wiſe.31Behold, the righteous ſhalbe recompenſed in the earth: much more the wicked and the ſinner.

CHAPTER 12 1Whoſo loueth inſtruction, loueth knowledge: but he that hateth reproofe, is brutiſh.2A good man obtaineth fauour of the Lord: but a man of wicked deuices will he condemne.3A man ſhall not bee eſtabliſhed by wickedneſſe: but the roote of the righteous ſhall not be mooued.4A vertuous woman is a crowne to her huſband: but ſhe that maketh aſhamed, is as rottenneſse in his bones.5The thoughts of the righteous are right: but the counſels of the wicked are deceit.6The words of the wicked are to lie in waite for blood: but the mouth of the vpright ſhall deliuer them.7The wicked are ouerthrowen, and are not: but the houſe of the righteous ſhall ſtand.8A man ſhall be commended according to his wiſedome: but hee that is of a peruerſe heart, ſhall be deſpiſed.9Hee that is deſpiſed and hath a ſeruant, is better then he that honoureth himſelfe, and lacketh bread.10A righteous man regardeth the life of his beaſt: but the tender mercies of the wicked are cruell.11Hee that tilleth his land, ſhall bee ſatiſfied with bread: but he that followeth vaine perſons, is void of vnderſtanding.12The wicked deſireth the net of euill men: but the roote of the righteous yeeldeth fruit.13The wicked is ſnared by the tranſgreſſion of his lippes: but the iuſt ſhall come out of trouble.14A man ſhall bee ſatiſfied with good by the fruit of his mouth, and the recompence of a mans hands ſhall bee rendred vnto him.15The way of a foole is right in his owne eyes: but he that hearkeneth vnto counſell, is wiſe.16A fooles wrath is preſently knowen: but a prudent man couereth ſhame.17He that ſpeaketh trueth, ſheweth foorth righteouſneſſe: but a falſe witneſſe, deceit.18There is that ſpeaketh like the pearcings of a ſword: but the tongue of the wiſe is health.19The lippe of trueth ſhall bee eſtabliſhed for euer: but a lying tongue is but for a moment.20Deceit is in the heart of them that imagine euill: but to the counſellours of peace, is ioy.21There ſhall no euill happen to the iuſt: but the wicked ſhall bee filled with miſchiefe.22Lying lippes are abomination to the Lord: but they that deale truely, are his delight.23A prudent man concealeth knowledge: but the heart of fooles proclaimeth fooliſhneſse.24The hand of the diligent ſhall beare rule: but the ſlouthfull ſhall bee vnder tribute.25Heauineſse in the heart of man maketh it ſtoope: but a good word maketh it glad.26The righteous is more excellent then his neighbour: but the way of the wicked ſeduceth them.27The ſlouthfull man roſteth not that which he tooke in hunting: but the ſubſtance of a diligent man is precious.28In the way of righteouſneſſe is life, and in the path-way thereof there is no death.

CHAPTER 131A wiſe ſonne heareth his fathers inſtruction: but a ſcorner heareth not rebuke.2A man ſhall eate good by the fruit of his mouth: but the ſoule of the tranſgreſsours, ſhall eate violence.3He that keepeth his mouth, keepeth his life: but hee that openeth wide his lips, ſhall haue deſtruction.4The ſoule of the ſluggard deſireth, and hath nothing: but the ſoule of the diligent ſhall be made fat.5A righteous man hateth lying: but a wicked man is loathſome, and commeth to ſhame.6Righteouſneſſe keepeth him that is vpright in the way: but wickedneſſe ouerthroweth the ſinner.7There is that maketh himſelfe rich, yet hath nothing: there is that maketh himſelfe poore, yet hath great riches.8The ranſome of a mans life are his riches: but the poore heareth not rebuke.9The light of the righteous reioyceth: but the lampe of the wicked ſhall be put out.10Onely by pride commeth contention: but with the well aduiſed is wiſedome.11Wealth gotten by vanitie ſhall be diminiſhed: but he that gathereth by labour, ſhall increaſe.12Hope deferred maketh the heart ſicke: but when the deſire commeth, it is a tree of life.13Whoſo deſpiſeth the word, ſhall be deſtroyed: but he that feareth the commaundement, ſhall be rewarded.14The lawe of the wiſe is a fountaine of life, to depart from the ſnares of death.15Good vnderſtanding giueth fauour: but the way of tranſgreſsours is hard.16Euery prudent man dealeth with knowledge: but a foole layeth open his folly.17A wicked meſſenger falleth into miſchiefe: but a faithfull ambaſsadour is health.18Pouerty and ſhame ſhall be to him that refuſeth inſtruction: but he that regardeth reproofe, ſhall be honoured.19The deſire accompliſhed is ſweet to the ſoule: but it is abomination to fooles to depart from euill.20He that walketh with wiſe men, ſhall be wiſe: but a companion of fooles ſhall be deſtroyed.21Euill purſueth ſinners: but to the righteous, good ſhall be repayd.22A good man leaueth an inheritance to his childrens children: and the wealth of the ſinner is layd vp for the iuſt.23Much food is in the tillage of the poore: but there is that is deſtroyed for want of iudgement.24He that ſpareth his rod, hateth his ſonne: but he that loueth him, chaſteneth him betimes.25The righteous eateth to the ſatiſfying of his ſoule: but the belly of the wicked ſhall want.

CHAPTER 141Euery wiſe woman buildeth her houſe; but the fooliſh plucketh it downe with her hands.2He that walketh in his vprightneſse, feareth the Lord: but he that is peruerſe in his wayes, deſpiſeth him.3In the mouth of the fooliſh is a rod of pride: but the lippes of the wiſe ſhall preſeruethem.4Where no Oxen are, the crib is cleane: but much increaſe is by the ſtrength of the Oxe.5A faithfull witneſſe will not lye: but a falſe witneſſe will vtter lyes.6A ſcorner ſeeketh wiſedome, and findeth it not: but knowledge is eaſie vnto him that vnderſtandeth.7Goe from the preſence of a fooliſh man, when thou perceiueſt not in him the lippes of knowledge.8The wiſedome of the prudent is to vnderſtand his way: but the folly of fooles is deceit.9Fooles make a mocke at ſinne: but among the righteous there is fauour.10The heart knoweth his owne bitterneſse; and a ſtranger doth not intermeddle with his ioy.11The houſe of the wicked ſhall bee ouerthrowen: but the tabernacle of the vpright ſhall flouriſh.12There is a way which ſeemeth right vnto a man: but the end thereof are the wayes of death.13Euen in laughter the heart is ſorrowfull; and the end of that mirth is heauineſse.14The backſlider in heart ſhall be filled with his owne wayes: and a good man ſhall be ſatiſfied from himſelfe.15The ſimple beleeueth euery word: but the prudent man looketh well to his going.16A wiſe man feareth, and departeth from euill: but the foole rageth, and is confident.17Hee that is ſoone angry, dealeth fooliſhly: and a man of wicked deuices is hated.18The ſimple inherite folly: but the prudent are crowned with knowledge.19The euill bowe before the good: and the wicked at the gates of the righteous.20The poore is hated euen of his owne neighbour: but the rich hath many friends.21He that deſpiſeth his neighbour, ſinneth: but he that hath mercy on the poore, happy is he.22Doe they not erre that deuiſe euil? but mercy and trueth ſhall be to them that deuiſe good.23In all labour there is profit: but the talke of the lippes tendeth onely to penury.24The crowne of the wiſe is their riches: but the fooliſhneſse of fooles is folly.25A true witneſſe deliuereth ſoules: but a deceitfull witneſſe ſpeaketh lyes.26In the feare of the Lord is ſtrong confidence: and his children ſhall haue a place of refuge.27The feare of the Lord, is a fountaine of life, to depart from the ſnares of death.28In the multitude of people is the kings honour: but in the want of people is the deſtruction of the prince.29Hee that is ſlow to wrath, is of great vnderſtanding: but hee that is haſty of ſpirit, exalteth folly.30A ſound heart, is the life of the fleſh: but enuie, the rottenneſse of the bones.31Hee that oppreſseth the poore, reprocheth his Maker: but hee that honoureth him, hath mercy on the poore.32The wicked is driuen away in his wickednes: but the righteous hath hope in his death.33Wiſedome reſteth in the heart of him that hath vnderſtanding: but that which is in the midſt of fooles, is made knowen.34Righteouſnes exalteth a nation: but ſinne is a reproch to any people.35The Kings fauour is toward a wiſe ſeruant: but his wrath, is againſt him that cauſeth ſhame.

CHAPTER 151A ſoft anſwere turneth away wrath: but grieuous words ſtirre vp anger.2The tongue of the wiſe, vſeth knowledge aright: but the mouth of fooles, powreth out fooliſhnes.3The eyes of the Lord are in euery place, beholding the euill & the good.4A wholeſome tongue is a tree of life: but peruerſneſse therein is a breach in the ſpirit.5A foole deſpiſeth his fathers inſtruction: but hee that regardeth reproofe, is prudent.6In the houſe of the righteous is much treaſure: but in the reuenues of the wicked is trouble.7The lippes of the wiſe diſperſe knowledge: but the heart of the fooliſh, doeth not ſo.8The ſacrifice of the wicked is an abomination to the Lord: but the prayer of the vpright is his delight.9The way of the wicked is an abomination vnto the Lord: but he loueth him that followeth after righteouſnes.10Correction is grieuous vnto him that forſaketh the way: and he that hateth reproofe, ſhall die.11Hell and deſtruction are before the Lord: how much more then, the hearts of the children of men?12A ſcorner loueth not one that reproueth him: neither will he goe vnto the wiſe.13A merry heart maketh a cheerefull countenance: but by ſorrow of the heart, the ſpirit is broken.14The heart of him that hath vnderſtanding, ſeeketh knowledge: but the mouth of fooles feedeth on fooliſhneſse.15All the dayes of the afflicted are euill: but he that is of a merry heart, hath a continuall feaſt.16Better is little with the feare of the Lord, then great treaſure, and trouble therewith.17Better is a dinner of herbes where loue is, then a ſtalled oxe, and hatred therewith.18A wrathfull man ſtirreth vp ſtrife: but he that is ſlow to anger, appeaſeth ſtrife.19The way of the ſlouthfull man is as an hedge of thornes: but the way of the righteous is made plaine.20A wiſe ſonne maketh a glad father: but a fooliſh man deſpiſeth his mother.21Folly is ioy to him that is deſtitute of wiſedome: but a man of vnderſtanding walketh vprightly.22Without counſell, purpoſes are diſappointed: but in the multitude of counſellours they are eſtabliſhed.23A man hath ioy by the anſwere of his mouth: and a word ſpoken in due ſeaſon, how good is it?24The way of life is aboue to the wiſe, that he may depart from hell beneath.25The Lord will deſtroy the houſe of the proud: but he will eſtabliſh the border of the widow.26The thoughts of the wicked are an abomination to the Lord: but the wordes of the pure, are pleaſant words.27Hee that is greedy of gaine, troubleth his owne houſe: but he that hateth gifts, ſhall liue.28The heart of the righteous ſtudieth to anſwere: but the mouth of the wicked, powreth out euil things.29The Lord is farre from the wicked: but hee heareth the prayer of the righteous.30The light of the eyes reioyceth the heart: and a good report maketh the bones fat.31The eare that heareth the reproofe of life, abideth among the wiſe.32He that refuſeth inſtruction, deſpiſeth his owne ſoule: but he that heareth reproofe, getteth vnderſtanding.33The feare of the Lord is the inſtruction of wiſedome; and before honour is humilitie.

CHAPTER 161The preparations of the heart in man, and the anſwere of the tongue, is from the Lord.2All the wayes of a man are cleane in his owne eyes: but the Lord weigheth the ſpirits.3Commit thy workes vnto the Lord, and thy thoughts ſhalbe eſtabliſhed.4The Lord hath made all things for himſelfe: yea, euen the wicked for the day of euill.5Euery one that is proud in heart, is an abomination to the Lord: though hand ioyne in hand, he ſhall not be vnpuniſhed.6By mercy and trueth iniquitie is purged: and by the feare of the Lord, men depart from euill.7When a mans wayes pleaſe the Lord, he maketh euen his enemies to be at peace with him.8Better is a little with righteouſneſſe, then great reuenewes without right.9A mans heart deuiſeth his way: but the Lord directeth his ſteps.10A diuine ſentence is in the lips of the king: his mouth tranſgreſseth not in iudgement.11A iuſt weight and ballance are the Lords: all the weights of the bagge are his worke.12It is an abomination to kings to commit wickedneſſe: for the throne is eſtabliſhed by righteouſneſſe.13Righteous lips are the delight of kings: and they loue him that ſpeaketh right.14The wrath of a king is as meſſengers of death: but a wiſe man will pacifie it.15In the light of the kings countenance is life, and his fauour is as a cloude of the latter raine.16How much better is it to get wiſedome, then gold? and to get vnderſtanding, rather to be choſen then ſiluer?17The high way of the vpright is to depart from euill: hee that keepeth his way, preſerueth his ſoule.18Pride goeth before deſtruction: and an hautie ſpirit before a fall.19Better it is to be of an humble ſpirit with the lowly, then to diuide the ſpoile with the proud.20He that handleth a matter wiſely, ſhall finde good: and who ſo truſteth in the Lord, happy is hee.21The wiſe in heart ſhall be called prudent; and the ſweetneſse of the lips increaſeth learning.22Underſtanding is a well-ſpring of life vnto him that hath it: but the inſtruction of fooles is folly.23The heart of the wiſe teacheth his mouth, and addeth learning to his lippes.24Pleaſant words are as an honycombe, ſweete to the ſoule, and health to the bones.25There is a way that ſeemeth right vnto a man; but the end thereof are the wayes of death.26Hee that laboureth, laboureth for himſelfe; for his mouth craueth it of him.27An vngodly man diggeth vp euill: and in his lips there is as a burning fire.28A froward man ſoweth ſtrife; & a whiſperer ſeparateth chiefe friends.29A violent man enticeth his neighbour, and leadeth him into the way that is not good.30He ſhutteth his eyes to deuiſe froward things: moouing his lips he bringeth euill to paſſe.31The hoary head is a crowne of glory, if it be found in the way of righteouſneſſe.32He that is ſlow to anger, is better then the mighty: and he that ruleth his ſpirit, then he that taketh a citie.33The lot is caſt into the lap: but the whole diſpoſing thereof is of the Lord.

CHAPTER 171Better is a drie morſell, and quietneſse therewith; then an houſe full of ſacrifices with ſtrife.2A wiſe ſeruant ſhall haue rule ouer a ſon that cauſeth ſhame: and ſhall haue part of the inheritance among the brethren.3The fining pot is for ſiluer, and the furnace for gold: but the Lord trieth the hearts.4A wicked doer giueth heed to falſe lips: and a liar giueth eare to a naughtie tongue.5Whoſo mocketh the poore, reproacheth his maker: and he that is glad at calamities, ſhall not be vnpuniſhed.6Childrens children are the crowne of old men: and the glory of children are their fathers.7Excellent ſpeech becommeth not a foole: much leſſe doe lying lippes a prince.8A gift is as a precious ſtone in the eyes of him that hath it: whitherſoeuer it turneth, it proſpereth.9He that coureth a tranſgreſsion, ſeeketh loue; but he that repeateth a matter, ſeparateth very friends.10A reproofe entreth more into a wiſe man, then an hundred ſtripes into a foole.11An euill man ſeeketh onely rebellion; therefore a cruell meſſenger ſhall be ſent againſt him.12Let a beare robbed of her whelps meet a man, rather then a foole in his folly.13Whoſo rewardeth euill for good, euill ſhall not depart from his houſe.14The beginning of ſtrife is as when one letteth out water: therfore leaue off contention, before it be medled with.15He that iuſtifieth the wicked, and he that condemneth the iuſt: euen they both are abomination to the Lord.16Wherfore is there a price in the hand of a foole to get wiſedome, ſeeing he hath no heart to it?17A friend loueth at all times, and a brother is borne for aduerſitie.18A man void of vnderſtanding ſtriketh hands, and becommeth ſuretie in the preſence of his friend.19He loueth tranſgreſsion, that loueth ſtrife: and he that exalteth his gate, ſeeketh deſtruction.20He that hath a froward heart, findeth no good, and he that hath a peruerſe tongue, falleth into miſchiefe.21He that begetteth a foole, doth it to his ſorrow: and the father of a foole hath no ioy.22A merrie heart doth good like a medicine: but a broken ſpirit drieth the bones.23A wicked man taketh a gift out of the boſome, to peruert the wayes of iudgement.24Wiſedome is before him that hath vnderſtanding: but the eyes of a foole are in the ends of the earth.25A fooliſh ſonne is a griefe to his father, & bitternes to her that bare him.26Alſo to puniſh the iuſt is not good, nor to ſtrike princes for equitie.27He that hath knowledge, ſpareth his words: and a man of vnderſtanding is of an excellent ſpirit.28Euen a foole, when he holdeth his peace, is counted wiſe: and he that ſhutteth his lips, is eſteemed a man of vnderſtanding.

CHAPTER 181Through deſire a man hauing ſeparated himſelfe, ſeeketh and intermedleth with all wiſedome.2A foole hath no delight in vnderſtanding, but that his heart may diſcouer it ſelfe.3When the wicked commeth, then commeth alſo contempt, and with ignominie, reproch.4The words of a mans mouth, are as deepe waters, and the well-ſpring of wiſedome as a flowing brooke.5It is not good to accept the perſon of the wicked, to ouerthrowe the righteous in iudgement.6A fooles lips enter into contention, and his mouth calleth for ſtrokes.7A fooles mouth is his deſtruction, and his lips are the ſnare of his ſoule.8The words of a tale bearer are as wounds, and they goe downe into the innermoſt parts of the belly.9Hee alſo that is ſlouthful in his worke, is brother to him that is a great waſter.10The name of the Lord is a a ſtrong tower: the righteous runneth into it, and is ſafe.11The rich mans wealth is his ſtrong citie: and as an high wall in his owne conceit.12Before deſtruction the heart of man is haughtie, and before honour is humilitie.13He that anſwereth a matter before he heareth it, it is folly and ſhame vnto him.14The ſpirit of a man will ſuſtaine his infirmitie: but a wounded ſpirit who can beare?15The heart of the prudent getteth knowledge; and the eare of the wiſe ſeeketh knowledge.16A mans gift maketh roome for him, & bringeth him before great men.17He that is firſt in his owne cauſe, ſeemeth iuſt; but his neighbour commeth and ſearcheth him.18The lot cauſeth contentions to ceaſe, and parteth betweene the mighty.19A brother offended is harder to be wonne then a ſtrong citie: and their contentions are like the barres of a caſtle.20A mans belly ſhall be ſatiſfied with the fruite of his mouth; and with the increaſe of his lippes ſhall he be filled.21Death and life are in the power of the tongue; and they that loue it ſhall eate the fruite thereof.22Who ſo findeth a wife, findeth a good thing, and obtaineth fauour of the Lord.23The poore vſeth intreaties, but the rich anſwereth roughly.24A man that hath friends muſt ſhewe himſelfe friendly: and there is a friend that ſticketh cloſer then a brother.

CHAPTER 191Better is the poore that walketh in his integrity, then he that is peruerſe in his lippes, and is a foole.2Alſo, that the ſoule be without knowledge, it is not good, and hee that haſteth with his feete, ſinneth.3The fooliſhneſse of man peruerteth his way: and his heart fretteth againſt the Lord.4Wealth maketh many friends: but the poore is ſeparated from his neighbour.5A falſe witneſſe ſhall not be vnpuniſhed: and he that ſpeaketh lyes, ſhal not eſcape.6Many will entreate the fauour of the Prince: and euery man is a friend to him that giueth gifts.7All the brethren of the poore doe hate him: howe much more doe his friends goe farre from him? Hee purſueth them with words, yet they are wanting to him.8He that getteth wiſedome loueth his owne ſoule: he that keepeth vnderſtanding ſhall find good.9A falſe witneſſe ſhall not be vnpuniſhed, and hee that ſpeaketh lyes, ſhall periſh.10Delight is not ſeemely for a foole: much leſſe for a ſeruant to haue rule ouer princes.11The diſcretion of a man deferreth his anger: and it is his glory to paſſe ouer a tranſgreſsion.12The kings wrath is as the roaring of a lyon: but his fauour is as dewe vpon the graſſe.13A fooliſh ſonne is the calamity of his father; and the contentions of a wife are a continuall dropping.14Houſe and riches, are the inheritance of fathers; and a prudent wife is from the Lord.15Slouthfulneſse caſteth into a deep ſleepe: and an idle ſoule ſhall ſuffer hunger.16He that keepeth the commandement, keepeth his owne ſoule: but hee that deſpiſeth his wayes, ſhall die.17Hee that hath pity vpon the poore, lendeth vnto the Lord; and that which he hath giuen, will he pay him againe.18Chaſten thy ſonne while there is hope; and let not thy ſoule ſpare for his crying.19A man of great wrath ſhall ſuffer puniſhment: for if thou deliuer him, yet thou muſt doe it againe.20Heare counſell, and receiue inſtruction, that thou mayeſt be wiſe in thy latter end.21There are many deuices in a mans heart: neuertheleſſe the counſell of the Lord, that ſhall ſtand.22The deſire of a man is his kindneſse: and a poore man is better then a lyar.23The feare of the Lord tendeth to life, and he that hath it ſhall abide ſatiſfied: he ſhall not be viſited with euill.24A ſlouthfull man hideth his hand in his boſome, and wil not ſo much as bring it to his mouth againe.25Smite a ſcorner, and the ſimple will beware; and reprooue one that hath vnderſtanding, and he will vnderſtand knowledge.26He that waſteth his father, and chaſeth away his mother, is a ſonne that cauſeth ſhame, and bringeth reproch.27Ceaſe, my ſonne, to heare the inſtruction, that cauſeth to erre from the words of knowledge.28An vngodly witneſſe ſcorneth iudgement: and the mouth of the wicked deuoureth iniquitie.29Iudgements are prepared for ſcorners, and ſtripes for the backe of fooles.

CHAPTER 201Wine is a mocker, ſtrong drinke is raging: and whoſoeuer is deceiued thereby, is not wiſe.2The feare of a king, is as the roaring of a Lion: who ſo prouoketh him to anger, ſinneth againſt his owne ſoule.3It is an honour for a man to ceaſe from ſtrife: but euery foole will be medling.4The ſluggard will not plow by reaſon of the cold; therefore ſhall he begge in harueſt, and haue nothing.5Counſell in the heart of man is like deepe water: but a man of vnderſtanding will draw it out.6Moſt men will proclaime euery one his owne goodnes: but a faithfull man who can finde?7The iuſt man walketh in his integritie: his children are bleſſed after him.8A king that ſitteth in the throne of iudgement, ſcattereth away all euill with his eyes.9Who can ſay, I haue made my heart cleane, I am pure from my ſinne?10Diuers weights, and diuers meaſures, both of them are alike abomination to the Lord.11Euen a childe is knowen by his doings, whether his worke be pure, and whether it be right.12The hearing eare, and the ſeeing eye, the Lord hath made euen both of them.13Loue not ſleepe, leſt thou come to pouertie: open thine eyes, and thou ſhalt be ſatiſfied with bread.14It is nought, it is nought (ſaith the buyer:) but when he is gone his way, then he boaſteth.15There is gold, and a multitude of Rubies: but the lips of knowledge are a precious iewell.16Take his garment that is ſuerty for a ſtranger: and take a pledge of him for a ſtrange woman.17Bread of deceit is ſweet to a man: but afterwards his mouth ſhall be filled with grauell.18Euery purpoſe is eſtabliſhed by counſell: and with good aduice make warre.19He that goeth about as a tale-bearer, reueileth ſecrets; therefore meddle not with him that flattereth with his lippes.20Who ſo curſeth his father or his mother, his lampe ſhall be put out in obſcure darkeneſſe.21An inheritance may be gotten haſtily at the beginning: but the ende thereof ſhall not be bleſſed.22ſay not thou, I will recompence euil: but wait on the Lord, and he ſhall ſaue thee.23Diuers waights are an abomination vnto the Lord: and a falſe ballance is not good.24Mans goings are of the Lord; how can a man then vnderſtand his owne way?25It is a ſnare to the man who deuoureth that which is holy: and after vowes, to make inquirie.26A wiſe king ſcattereth the wicked, & bringeth the wheele ouer them.27The ſpirit of man is the candle of the Lord, ſearching all the inward parts of the belly.28Mercy and trueth preſerue the king: and his throne is vpholden by mercy.29The glory of yong men is their ſtrength: and the beautie of old men is the gray head.30The blewnes of a wound cleanſeth away euill: ſo doe ſtripes the inward parts of the belly.

CHAPTER 211The kings heart is in the hand of the Lord, as the riuers of water: hee turneth it whitherſoeuer he will.2Euery way of a man is right in his owne eyes: but the Lord pondereth the hearts.3To doe iuſtice and iudgement, is more acceptable to the Lord, then ſacrifice.4An high looke, and a proud heart, and the plowing of the wicked, is ſinne.5The thoughts of the diligent tend onely to plenteouſnes: but of euery one that is haſtie, onely to want.6The getting of treaſures by a lying tongue, is a vanitie toſsed to and fro of them that ſeeke death.7The robbery of the wicked ſhall deſtroy them; becauſe they refuſe to doe iudgement.8The way of man is froward and ſtrange: but as for the pure; his worke is right.9It is better to dwell in a corner of the houſe top; then with a brawling woman in a wide houſe.10The ſoule of the wicked deſireth euill: his neighbour findeth no fauour in his eyes.11When the ſcorner is puniſhed, the ſimple is made wiſe: and when the wiſe is inſtructed, he receiueth knowledge.12The righteous man wiſely conſidereth the houſe of the wicked: but God ouerthroweth the wicked for their wickedneſſe.13Whoſo ſtoppeth his eares at the cry of the poore, hee alſo ſhall cry himſelfe, but ſhall not be heard.14A gift in ſecret pacifieth anger; and a reward in the boſome, ſtrong wrath.15It is ioy to the iuſt to doe iudgement: but deſtruction ſhalbe to the workers of iniquitie.16The man that wandreth out of the way of vnderſtanding, ſhall remaine in the congregation of the dead.17He that loueth pleaſure, ſhall be a poore man: hee that loueth wine and oyle, ſhall not be rich.18The wicked ſhalbe a ranſome for the righteous; and the tranſgreſsour for the vpright.19It is better to dwell in the wilderneſſe, then with a contentious and an angry woman.20There is treaſure to be deſired, and oyle in the dwelling of the wiſe: but a fooliſh man ſpendeth it vp.21Hee that followeth after righteouſneſſe and mercy, findeth life, righteouſneſſe and honour.22A wiſe man ſcaleth the citie of the mightie, and caſteth downe the ſtrength of the confidence thereof.23Whoſo keepeth his mouth and his tongue, keepeth his ſoule from troubles.24Proud and haughtie ſcorner, is his name, who dealeth in proud wrath.25The deſire of the ſlouthfull killeth him: for his hands refuſe to labour.26Hee coueteth greedily all the day long: but the righteous giueth and ſpareth not.27The ſacrifice of the wicked is abomination: how much more, when he bringeth it with a wicked minde?28A falſe witneſſe ſhall periſh: but the man that heareth, ſpeaketh conſtantly.29A wicked man hardeneth his face: but as for the vpright, he directeth his way.30There is no wiſedome, nor vnderſtanding, nor counſell againſt the Lord.31The horſe is prepared againſt the day of battell: but ſafetie is of the Lord.

CHAPTER 221A Good name is rather to be choſen then great riches, and louing fauour rather then ſiluer & golde.2The rich and poore meet together: the Lord is the maker of them all.3A prudent man foreſeeth the euill, and hideth himſelfe: but the ſimple paſſe on, and are puniſhed.4By humilitie and the feare of the Lord, are riches, and honour, and life.5Thornes and ſnares are in the way of the froward: he that doeth keepe his ſoule, ſhalbe farre from them.6Traine vp a childe in the way he ſhould goe: and when he is olde, hee will not depart from it.7The rich ruleth ouer the poore, and the borrower is ſeruant to the lender.8Hee that ſoweth iniquitie, ſhall reape vanitie: and the rodde of his anger ſhall faile.9Hee that hath a bountifull eye, ſhall bee bleſſed: for hee giueth of his bread to the poore.10Caſt out the ſcorner, and contention ſhall goe out; yea ſtrife, and reproch ſhall ceaſe.11He that loueth pureneſse of heart, for the grace of his lips the king ſhall be his friend.12The eyes of the Lord preſerueknowledge, and he ouerthroweth the words of the tranſgreſsour.13The ſlothfull man ſayth, There is a lyon without, I ſhall be ſlaine in the ſtreetes.14The mouth of ſtrange women is a deepe pit: he that is abhorred of the Lord ſhall fall therein.15Fooliſhneſse is bound in the heart of a child: but the rod of correction ſhal driue it farre from him.16Hee that oppreſseth the poore to increaſe his riches, and he that giueth to the rich, ſhall ſurely come to want.17Bow downe thine eare, and heare the words of the wiſe, and apply thine heart vnto my knowledge.18For it is a pleaſant thing, if thou keepe them within thee; they ſhall withall be fitted in thy lippes.19That thy truſt may bee in the Lord, I haue made knowen to thee this day, euen to thee.20Haue not I written to thee excellent things in counſailes and knowledge:21That I might make thee knowe the certainty of the words of truth; that thou mighteſt anſwere the words of trueth to them that ſend vnto thee?22Rob not the poore becauſe he is poore, neither oppreſſe the afflicted in the gate.23For the Lord will plead their cauſe, and ſpoile the ſoule of thoſe that ſpoiled them.24Make no friendſhip with an angrie man: and with a furious man thou ſhalt not goe;25Leſt thou learne his wayes, and get a ſnare to thy ſoule.26Be not thou one of them that ſtrike hands, or of them that are ſureties for debts.27If thou haſt nothing to pay, why ſhould he take away thy bed from vnder thee?28Remoue not the ancient land marke, which thy fathers haue ſet.29Seeſt thou a man diligent in his buſineſse? hee ſhall ſtand before kings, he ſhall not ſtand before meane men.

CHAPTER 231When thou ſitteſt to eate with a ruler, conſider diligently what is before thee.2And put a knife to thy throate, if thou be a man giuen to appetite.3Be not deſirous of his dainties: for they are deceitfull meate.4Labour not to bee rich: ceaſe from thine owne wiſedome.5Wilt thou ſet thine eyes vpon that which is not? for riches certainly make themſelues wings, they fly away as an Eagle toward heauen.6Eate thou not the bread of him that hath an euill eye, neither deſire thou his dainty meates.7For as he thinketh in his heart, ſo is he: Eate, and drinke, ſayth he to thee, but his heart is not with thee.8The morſell which thou haſt eaten, ſhalt thou vomite vp, and looſe thy ſweete words.9Speake not in the eares of a foole: for hee will deſpiſe the wiſedome of thy words.10Remoue not the old landmarke; and enter not into the fields of the fatherleſſe.11For their redeemer is mighty; he ſhall plead their cauſe with thee.[12]Apply thine heart vnto inſtruction, and thine eares to the words of knowledge.[13]Withhold not correction from the child: for if thou beateſt him with the rod, he ſhall not die.[14]Thou ſhalt beate him with the rod, and ſhalt deliuer his ſoule from hell.[15]My ſonne, if thine heart be wiſe, my heart ſhall reioyce, euen mine.[16]Yea my reines ſhall reioyce, when thy lippes ſpeake right things.[17]Let not thine heart enuy ſinners, but be thou in the feare of the Lord all the day long.[18]For ſurely there is an end, and thine expectation ſhall not be cut off.[19]Heare thou, my ſonne, and be wiſe, and guide thine heart in the way.[20]Be not amongſt wine-bibbers; amongſt riotous eaters of fleſh.[21]For the drunkard and the glutton ſhall come to pouerty; and drouſineſse ſhall cloath a man with ragges.[22]Hearken vnto thy father that begate thee, and deſpiſe not thy mother when ſhe is old.[23]Buy the trueth, and ſell it not; alſo wiſedome and inſtruction and vnderſtanding.[24]The father of the righteous ſhall greatly reioyce: and he that begetteth a wiſe child, ſhall haue ioy of him.[25]Thy father and thy mother ſhall be glad, and ſhe that bare thee ſhall reioyce.[26]My ſonne, giue me thine heart, and let thine eyes obſerue my wayes.[27]For an whore is a deepe ditch; and a ſtrange woman is a narrow pit.[28]She alſo lyeth in wait as for a pray, and increaſeth the tranſgreſsours among men.[29]Who hath woe? who hath ſorrow? who hath contentions? who hath babbling? who hath wounds without cauſe? who hath redneſse of eyes?[30]They that tarry long at the wine, they that goe to ſeeke mixt wine.[31]Looke not thou vpon the wine when it is red, when it giueth his colour in the cup, when it moueth it ſelfe aright.[32]At the laſt it biteth like a ſerpent, and ſtingeth like an adder.[33]Thine eyes ſhall behold ſtrange women, and thine heart ſhall vtter peruerſe things.[34]Yea thou ſhalt be as he that lyeth downe in the midſt of the ſea, or as he that lyeth vpon the top of a maſt.[35]They haue ſtriken me, ſhalt thou ſay, and I was not ſicke: they haue beaten me, and I felt it not: when ſhall I awake? I will ſeeke it yet againe.

CHAPTER 24[1]Be not thou enuious againſt euill men, neither deſire to be with them.[2]For their heart ſtudieth deſtruction, and their lippes talke of miſchiefe.[3]Through wiſedome is an houſe builded, and by vnderſtanding it is eſtabliſhed.[4]And by knowledge ſhall the chambers bee filled with all precious and pleaſant riches.[5]A wiſe man is ſtrong, yea a man of knowledge encreaſeth ſtrength.[6]For by wiſe counſell thou ſhalt make thy warre: and in multitude of counſellers there is ſafetie.[7]Wiſedome is too high for a foole: he openeth not his mouth in the gate.[8]He that deuiſeth to doe euill, ſhall be called a miſchieuous perſon.[9]The thought of fooliſhneſse is ſinne: and the ſcorner is an abomination to men.[10]If thou faint in the day of aduerſitie, thy ſtrength is ſmall:[11]If thou forbeare to deliuer them that are drawen vnto death, and thoſe that are ready to be ſlaine:[12]If thou ſayeſt, Behold, we knew it not: doth not he that pondereth the heart, conſider it? and he that keepeth thy ſoule, doth not he know it? and ſhall not hee render to euery man according to his workes?[13]My ſonne, eate thou honie, becauſe it is good, and the honie combe, which is ſweete to thy taſte.[14]So ſhall the knowledge of wiſedome be vnto thy ſoule: when thou haſt found it, then there ſhall be a reward, and thy expectation ſhall not be cut off.[15]Lay not waite, (O wicked man) againſt the dwelling of the righteous: ſpoile not his reſting place.[16]For a iuſt man falleth ſeuen times, and riſeth vp againe: but the wicked ſhall fall into miſchiefe.[17]Reioyce not when thine enemie falleth: and let not thine heart be glad when he ſtumbleth:[18]Leſt the Lord ſee it, and it diſpleaſe him, and hee turne away his wrath from him.[19]Fret not thy ſelfe becauſe of euill men; neither be thou enuious at the wicked.[20]For there ſhall be no reward to the euill man: the candle of the wicked ſhall be put out.[21]My ſonne, feare thou the Lord, and the king: and medle not with them that are giuen to change.[22]For their calamity ſhall riſe ſuddenly, and who knoweth the ruine of them both?[23]Theſe things alſo belong to the wiſe: It is not good to haue reſpect of perſons in iudgement.[24]He that ſayth vnto the wicked, Thou art righteous, him ſhall the people curſe; nations ſhall abhorre him:[25]But to them that rebuke him ſhall be delight, and a good bleſſing ſhall come vpon them.[26]Euery man ſhall kiſſe his lippes that giueth a right anſwere.[27]Prepare thy worke without, and make it fit for thy ſelfe in the field; and afterwards build thine houſe.[28]Be not a witneſſe againſt thy neighbour without cauſe: and deceiue not with thy lippes.[29]ſay not, I will doe ſo to him as he hath done to mee: I will render to the man according to his worke.[30]I went by the field of the ſlouthfull, and by the vineyard of the man voyd of vnderſtanding:[31]And loe, it was all growen ouer with thornes, and nettles had couered the face thereof, and the ſtone wall therof was broken downe:[32]Then I ſaw, and conſidered it well, I looked vpon it, and receiued inſtruction.[33]Yet a little ſleepe, a little ſlumber, a little folding of the handes to ſleepe:[34]So ſhall thy pouertie come, as one that traueileth, and thy want, as an armed man.

CHAPTER 25[1]Theſe are alſo Prouerbes of Solomon, which the men of Hezekiah king of Iudah copied out.[2]It is the glory of God to conceale a thing: but the honour of Kings is to ſearch out a matter.[3]The heauen for height, and the earth for depth, and the heart of Kings is vnſearchable.[4]Take away the droſse from the ſiluer, and there ſhall come foorth a veſſell for the finer.[5]Take away the wicked from before the king, and his throne ſhalbe eſtabliſhed in righteouſnes.[6]Put not forth thy ſelfe in the preſence of the king, and ſtand not in the place of great men.[7]For better it is that it be ſaid vnto thee, Come vp hither; then that thou ſhouldeſt be put lower in the preſence of the Prince whom thine eies haue ſeene.[8]Goe not forth haſtily to ſtriue, leſt thou know not what to doe in the ende thereof, when thy neighbour hath put thee to ſhame.[9]Debate thy cauſe with thy neighbour himſelfe; and diſcouer not a ſecret to another:[10]Leſt he that heareth it, put thee to ſhame, and thine infamie turne not away.[11]A word fitly ſpoken is like apples of gold in pictures of ſiluer.[12]As an eare-ring of gold, and an ornament of fine gold, ſo is a wiſe reprouer vpon an obedient eare.[13]As the cold of ſnow in the time of harueſt, ſo is a faithfull meſſenger to them that ſend him: for hee refreſheth the ſoule of his maſters.[14]Who ſo boaſteth himſelfe of a falſe gift, is like cloudes and winde without raine.[15]By long forbearing is a Prince perſwaded, and a ſoft tongue breaketh the bone.[16]Haſt thou found hony? eate ſo much as is ſufficient for thee: leſt thou be filled therewith, and vomit it.[17]Withdraw thy foote from thy neighbours houſe: leſt he be weary of thee, and ſo hate thee.[18]A man that beareth falſe witnes againſt his neighbour, is a maule, and a ſword, and a ſharpe arrow.[19]Confidence in an vnfaithfull man in time of trouble, is like a broken tooth, and a foot out of ioynt.[20]As hee that taketh away a garment in cold weather; and as vineger vpon nitre; ſo is he that ſingeth ſongs to an heauy heart.[21]If thine enemie be hungry, giue him bread to eate: and if hee be thirſtie, giue him water to drinke.[22]For thou ſhalt heape coales of fire vpon his head, and the Lord ſhall reward thee.[23]The North winde driueth away raine: ſo doeth an angrie countenance a backbiting tongue.[24]It is better to dwell in a corner of the houſe top, then with a brawling woman, and in a wide houſe.[25]As cold waters to a thirſtie ſoule: ſo is good newes from a farre countrey.[26]A righteous man falling downe before the wicked, is as a troubled fountaine, aud a corrupt ſpring.[27]It is not good to eat much hony: ſo for men to ſearch their owne glory, is not glory.[28]Hee that hath no rule ouer his owne ſpirit, is like a citie that is broken downe, and without walles.

CHAPTER 26[1]As ſnow in ſummer, and as raine in harueſt: ſo honour is not ſeemely for a foole.[2]As the bird by wandring, as the ſwallow by flying: ſo the curſe cauſeleſſe ſhall not come.[3]A whip for the horſe, a bridle for the aſſe; and a rod for the fooles backe.[4]Anſwere not a foole according to his folly, leſt thou alſo be like vnto him.[5]Anſwere a foole according to his folly, leſt hee be wiſe in his owne conceit.[6]He that ſendeth a meſsage by the hand of a foole, cutteth off the feete, and drinketh dammage.[7]The legges of the lame are not equall: ſo is a parable in the mouth of fooles.[8]As hee that bindeth a ſtone in a ſling; ſo is hee that giueth honour to a foole.[9]As a thorne goeth vp into the hand of a drunkard; ſo is a parable in the mouth of fooles.[10]The great God that formed all things, both rewardeth the foole, and rewardeth tranſgreſsours.[11]As a dogge returneth to his vomite: ſo a foole returneth to his folly.[12]Seeſt thou a man wiſe in his owne conceit? there is more hope of a foole then of him.[13]The ſlothfull man ſayth, There is a lion in the way, a lion is in the ſtreets.[14]As the doore turneth vpon his hinges: ſo doeth the ſlothfull vpon his bedde.[15]The ſlothfull hideth his hand in his boſome, it grieueth him to bring it againe to his mouth.[16]The ſluggard is wiſer in his owne conceit, then ſeuen men that can render a reaſon.[17]He that paſſeth by, and medleth with ſtrife belonging not to him, is like one that taketh a dog by the eares.[18]As a mad man, who caſteth firebrands, arrowes, and death:[19]So is the man that deceiueth his neighbour, & ſayth, Am not I in ſport?[20]Where no wood is, there the fire goeth out: ſo where there is no tale-bearer, the ſtrife ceaſeth.[21]As

coales are to burning coales, and wood to fire; ſo is a contentious man
to kindle ſtrife.22The words of a tale-bearer are as woundes, and they
goe downe into the innermoſt parts of the belly.23Burning lips, and a
wicked heart, are like a potſheard couered with ſiluer droſse.24Hee that
hateth, diſsembleth with his lips, and layeth vp deceit within
him.25When he ſpeaketh faire, beleeue him not: for there are ſeuen
abominations in his heart.26Whoſe hatred is couered by deceit, his
wickedneſſe ſhall be ſhewed before the whole congregation.27Whoſo
diggeth a pit, ſhall fall therein: and he that rolleth a ſtone, it will returne
vpon him.28A lying tongue hateth thoſe that are afflicted by it, and a
flattering mouth worketh ruine.
CHAPTER 271Boaſt not thy ſelfe of to morrow: for thou knoweſt not
what a day may bring foorth.2Let another man praiſe thee, and not thine
owne mouth; a ſtranger, and not thine owne lips.3A ſtone is heauie, and
the ſand weightie: but a fooles wrath is heauier then them both.4Wrath
is cruell, and anger is outragious: but who is able to ſtand before
enuie?5Open rebuke is better then ſecret loue.6Faithfull are the
woundes of a friend: but the kiſſes of an enemy are deceitfull.7The full
ſoule loatheth an honie combe: but to the hungry ſoule euery bitter thing
is ſweete.8As a bird that wandreth from her neſt: ſo is a man that
wandreth from his place.9Oyntment and perfume reioyce the heart: ſo
doeth the ſweetneſse of a mans friend by heartie counſell.10Thine owne
friend and thy fathers friend forſake not; neither goe in to thy brothers
houſe in the day of thy calamitie: for better is a neighbour that is neere,
then a brother farre off.11My ſonne, be wiſe, and make my heart glad,
that I may anſwere him that reprocheth me.12A prudent man foreſeeth
the euil, and hideth himſelfe: but the ſimple paſſe on, and are
puniſhed.13Take his garment that is ſurety for a ſtranger, and take a
pledge of him for a ſtrange woman.14He that bleſſeth his friend with a
loud voice, riſing earely in the morning, it ſhall be counted a curſe to
him.15A continuall dropping in a very rainie day, and a contentious
woman, are alike.16Whoſoeuer hideth her, hideth the wind, and the
ointment of his right hand which be wrayeth it ſelfe.17Iron ſharpeneth
iron: ſo a man ſharpeneth the countenance of his friend.18Whoſo
keepeth the figtree, ſhall eate the fruit therof: ſo he that waiteth on his
maſter, ſhall be honoured.19As in water face anſwereth to face: ſo the
heart of man to man.20Hell and deſtruction are neuer full: ſo the eyes of
man are neuer ſatiſfied.21As the fining pot for ſiluer, and the furnace for
gold: ſo is a man to his praiſe.22Though thou ſhouldeſt bray a foole in a
morter among wheate with a peſtell, yet will not his fooliſhneſse depart
from him.23Be thou diligent to knowe the ſtate of thy flocks, and looke
well to thy herds.24For riches are not for euer: and doth the crowne
endure to euery generation?25The hay appeareth, and the tender graſſe
ſheweth it ſelfe, and herbes of the mountaines are gathered.26The
lambes are for thy clothing, and the goates are the price of thy
field.27And thou ſhalt haue goats milke enough for thy food, for the
food of thy houſhold, and for the maintenance for thy maidens.
CHAPTER 281The wicked flee when no man purſueth: but the
righteous are bolde as a lyon.2For the tranſgreſſion of a land, many are
the princes thereof: but by a man of vnderſtanding and knowledge the
ſtate thereof ſhall bee prolonged.3A poore man that oppreſseth the
poore, is like a ſweeping raine which leaueth no food.4They that forſake
the law, praiſe the wicked: but ſuch as keepe the Law, contend with
them.5Euill men vnderſtand not iudgement: but they that ſeeke the
Lord, vnderſtand all things.6Better is the poore that walketh in his
vprightneſse, then he that is peruerſe in his wayes, though he be
rich.7Whoſo keepeth the law, is a wiſe ſonne: but he that is a companion
of riotous men, ſhameth his father.8He that by vſurie and vniuſt gaine
increaſeth his ſubſtance, he ſhall gather it for him that wil pity the
poore.9He that turneth away his eare from hearing the law, euen his
prayer ſhalbe abomination.10Who ſo cauſeth the righteous to goe aſtray
in an euill way, he ſhall fall himſelfe into his owne pit: but the vpright
ſhall haue good things in poſſeſſion.11The rich man is wiſe in his owne
conceit: but the poore that hath vnderſtanding ſearcheth him
out.12When righteous men do reioyce, there is great glory: but when the
wicked riſe, a man is hidden.13He that couereth his ſinnes, ſhall not
proſper: but who ſo confeſseth and forſaketh them, ſhall haue
mercie.14Happy is the man that feareth always: but he that hardeneth his
heart, ſhall fall into miſchiefe.15As a roaring lyon and a ranging beare: ſo
is a wicked ruler ouer the poore people.16The prince that wanteth
vnderſtanding, is alſo a great oppreſsour: but he that hateth
couetouſneſſe, ſhall prolong his dayes.17A man that doth violence to the
blood of any perſon, ſhall flie to the pit, let no man ſtay him.18Whoſo
walketh vprightly, ſhall be ſaued: but he that is peruerſe in his wayes,
ſhall fall at once.19He that tilleth his land, ſhal haue plentie of bread: but
he that followeth after vaine perſons, ſhall haue pouerty enough.20A
faithfull man ſhall abound with bleſſings: but hee that maketh haſte to
be rich, ſhall not be innocent.21To haue reſpect of perſons, is not good:
for, for a piece of bread that man will tranſgreſse.22He that haſteth to
bee rich, hath an euill eye, and conſidereth not that pouerty ſhall come
vpon him.23He that rebuketh a man, afterwards ſhall find more fauour,
then he that flattereth with the tongue.24Who ſo robbeth his father or
his mother, and ſaith, it is no tranſgreſsion, the ſame is the companion
of a deſtroyer.25He that is of a proud heart, ſtirreth vp ſtrife: but he that
putteth his truſt in the Lord, ſhalbe made fat.26Hee that truſteth in his
owne heart, is a foole: but who ſo walketh wiſely, he ſhall be
deliuered.27He that giueth vnto the poore, ſhall not lacke: but he that
hideth his eyes, ſhall haue many a curſe.28When the wicked riſe, men
hide themſelues: but when they periſh, the righteous increaſe.
CHAPTER 291He that being often reproued, hardeneth his necke, ſhal
ſuddenly be deſtroied, and that without remedy.2When the righteous are
in authoritie, the people reioyce: but when the wicked beareth rule, the
people mourne.3Whoſo loueth wiſedome, reioyceth his father: but hee
that keepeth company with harlots, ſpendeth his ſubſtance.4The king by
iudgement ſtabliſheth the land: but he that receiueth gifts, ouerthroweth
it.5A man that flattereth his neighbour, ſpreadeth a net for his feet.6In
the tranſgreſſion of an euill man there is a ſnare: but the righteous doth
ſing and reioyce.7The righteous conſidereth the cauſe of the poore: but
the wicked regardeth not to know it.8Scornefull men bring a citie into a
ſnare: but wiſe men turne away wrath.9If a wiſe man contendeth with a
fooliſh man, whether hee rage or laugh, there is no reſt.10The
bloodthirſtie hate the vpright: but the iuſt ſeeke his ſoule.11A foole
vttereth all his mind: but a wiſe man keepeth it in till afterwards.12If a
ruler hearken to lies, all his ſeruants are wicked.13The poore and the
deceitful man meet together: the Lord lightneth both their eyes.14The
King that faithfully iudgeth the poore, his throne ſhall be eſtabliſhed for
euer.15The rod and reproofe giue wiſedome: but a child left to himſelfe
bringeth his mother to ſhame.16When the wicked are multiplied,
tranſgreſſion increaſeth: but the righteous ſhall ſee their fall.17Correct
thy ſonne, and hee ſhall giue thee reſt: yea he ſhall giue delight vnto thy
ſoule.18Where there is no viſion, the people periſh: but he that keepeth
the Law, happy is he.19A ſeruant will not be corrected by words: for
though hee vnderſtand, hee will not anſwere.20Seeſt thou a man that is
haſty in his words? there is more hope of a foole then of him.21He that
delicately bringeth vp his ſeruant from a child, ſhall haue him become
his ſonne at the length.22An angry man ſtirreth vp ſtrife, and a furious
man aboundeth in tranſgreſsion.23A mans pride ſhall bring him lowe:
but honour ſhall vpholde the humble in ſpirit.24Who ſo is partner with
a thiefe, hateth his owne ſoule: hee heareth curſing, and bewrayeth it
not.25The feare of man bringeth a ſnare: but who ſo putteth his truſt in
the Lord, ſhall be ſafe.26Many ſeeke the rulers fauour, but euery mans
iudgement commeth from the Lord.27An vniuſt man is an abomination
to the iuſt: and he that is vpright in the way, is abomination to the
wicked.
CHAPTER 301The words of Agur the ſonne of Iakeh, euen the
prophecy: The man ſpake vnto Ithiel, euen vnto Ithiel and Ucal.2Surely
I am more brutiſh then any man, and haue not the vnderſtanding of a
man.3I neither learned wiſedome, nor haue the knowledge of the
holy.4Who hath aſcended vp into heauen, or deſcended? who hath
gathered the wind in his fiſts? who hath bound the waters in a garment?
who hath eſtabliſhed all the ends of the earth? what is his name, and
what is his ſonnes name, if thou canſt tell?5Euery word of God is pure:
he is a ſhield vnto them that put their truſt in him.6Adde thou not vnto
his words, leſt he reproue thee, and thou be found a lyar.7Two things
haue I required of thee, deny me them not before I die.8Remoue farre
from mee vanity, and lyes; giue me neither pouerty, nor riches, feede me
with food conuenient for me.9Leſt I be full, and deny thee, and ſay, Who
is the Lord? or leſt I be poore, and ſteale, and take the name of my God

in vaine.10Accuſe not a ſeruant vnto his maſter; leſt he curſe thee, and
thou be found guilty.11There is a generation that curſeth their father, and
doth not bleſſe their mother.12There is a generation that are pure in their
owne eyes, and yet is not waſhed from their filthineſse.13There is a
generation, O howe lofty are their eyes! and their eye-lids are lifted
vp.14There is a generation, whoſe teeth are as ſwords, and their iaw-
teeth as kniues, to deuoure the poore from off the earth, and the needy
from among men.15The horſe-leach hath two daughters, crying, Giue,
giue. There are three things that are neuer ſatiſfied, yea foure things ſay
not, It is enough:16The graue; and the barren wombe; the earth that is
not filled with water; and the fire that ſaith not, It is enough.17The eye
that mocketh at his father, and deſpiſeth to obey his mother; the rauens
of the valley ſhall picke it out, and the young Eagles ſhall eate it.18There
be three things which are too wonderfull for me; yea foure, which I
know not:19The way of an Eagle in the ayre; the way of a ſerpent vpon
a rocke; the the way of a ſhip in the midſt of the ſea; and the way of a
man with a maid.20ſuch is the way of an adulterous woman: ſhe eateth,
and wipeth her mouth, and ſaith, I haue done no wickedneſſe.21For
three things the earth is diſquieted, and for foure which it cannot
beare:22For a ſeruant when he reigneth, and a foole when hee is filled
with meate:23For an odious woman when ſhee is married, and an
handmayd that is heire to her miſtreſſe.24There be foure things which
are little vpon the earth; but they are exceeding wiſe:25The Ants are a
people not ſtrong, yet they prepare their meate in the ſummer.26The
conies are but a feeble folke, yet make they their houſes in the
rockſ?27The locuſtes haue no king, yet goe they forth all of them by
bands.28The ſpider taketh hold with her hands, and is in kings
palaces.29There be three things which goe well, yea foure are comely in
going:30A lyon which is ſtrongeſt among beaſtes, and turneth not away
for any:31A gray-hound; an hee-goate alſo; and a king, againſt whom
there is no riſing vp.32If thou haſt done fooliſhly in lifting vp thy ſelfe,
or if thou haſt thought euill, lay thine hand vpon thy mouth.33Surely the
churning of milke bringeth forth butter; and the wringing of the noſe
bringeth forth blood: ſo the forcing of wrath bringeth forth ſtrife.
CHAPTER 311The wordes of King Lemuel, the prophecie that his
mother taught him.2What, my ſonne! and what, the ſonne of my wombe!
and what, the ſonne of my vowes!3Giue not thy ſtrength vnto women,
nor thy wayes to that which deſtroyeth kings.4It is not for kings, O
Lemuel, it is not for kings to drinke wine, nor for Princes, ſtrong
drinke:5Leſt they drinke, and forget the Law, and peruert the iudgement
of any of the afflicted.6Giue ſtrong drinke vnto him that is ready to
periſh, and wine vnto thoſe that be of heauie hearts.7Let him drinke,
and forget his pouertie, and remember his miſery no more.8Open thy
mouth for the dumbe in the cauſe of all ſuch as are appointed to
deſtruction.9Open thy mouth, iudge righteouſly, and plead the cauſe of
the poore and needy.10Who can finde a vertuous woman? for her price
is farre aboue Rubies.11The heart of her huſband doeth ſafely truſt in
her, ſo that he ſhall haue no need of ſpoile.12She will doe him good, and
not euill, all the dayes of her life.13She ſeeketh wooll and flaxe, and
worketh willingly with her hands.14She is like the merchants ſhips, ſhe
bringeth her food from afarre.15Shee riſeth alſo while it is yet night, and
giueth meate to her houſehold, and a portion to her maydens.16She
conſidereth a field, and buyeth it: with the fruit of her handes ſhe
planteth a Uineyard.17She girdeth her loynes with ſtrength, and
ſtrengtheneth her armes.18She perceiueth that her merchandiſe is good;
her candle goeth not out by night.19She layeth her handes to the ſpindle,
and her handes hold the diſtaffe.20She ſtretcheth out her hand to the
poore, yea ſhe reacheth foorth her handes to the needy.21She is not
afraid of the ſnow for her houſhold: for all her houſhold are cloathed
with ſcarlet.22She maketh herſelfe couerings of tapeſtrie; her cloathing is
ſilke and purple.23Her huſband is knowen in the gates, when he ſitteth
among the Elders of the land.24She maketh fine linnen, and ſelleth it,
and deliuereth girdles vnto the merchant.25Strength and honour are her
cloathing; and ſhe ſhall reioyce in time to come.26She openeth her
mouth with wiſedome; and in her tongue is the law of kindneſse.27She
looketh well to the wayes of her houſholde, and eateth not the bread of
idleneſse.28Her children Ariſe vp, and call her bleſſed; her huſband alſo,
and he praiſeth her.29Many daughters haue done vertuouſly, but thou
excelleſt them all.30Fauour is deceitfull, and beautie is vaine: but a
woman that feareth the Lord, ſhe ſhalbe praiſed.31Giue her of the fruit
of her hands, and let her owne workes praiſe her in the gates.

ECCLEſIAſTES (ECCLESIASTES)

CHAPTER 11The wordes of the Preacher, the ſon of Dauid, King in
Ieruſalem.2Uanitie of vanities, ſaith the Preacher, vanitie of vanities, all
is vanitie.3What profite hath a man of all his labour which hee taketh
vnder the Sunne?4One generation paſſeth away, and another generation
commeth: but the earth abideth for euer.5The Sunne alſo Ariſeth, and
the Sunne goeth downe, and haſteth to the place where he aroſe.6The
winde goeth toward the South, and turneth about vnto the North; it
whirleth about continually, and the winde returneth againe according to
his circuits.7All the riuers runne into the ſea, yet the ſea is not full: vnto
the place from whence the riuers come, thither they returne againe.8All
things are full of labour, man cannot vtter it: the eye is not ſatiſfied with
ſeeing, nor the eare filled with hearing.9The thing that hath beene, it is
that which ſhall be: and that which is done, is that which ſhall be done;
and there is no new thing vnder the ſunne.10Is there any thing, whereof
it may be ſayd, See, this is new? it hath beene already of olde time, which
was before vs.11There is no remembrance of former things; neither ſhall
there bee any remembrance of things that are to come, with thoſe that
ſhall come after.12I the Preacher was king ouer Iſrael in Ieruſalem.13And
I gaue my heart to ſeeke and ſearch out by wiſedome, concerning all
things that are done vnder heauen: this ſore trauell hath God giuen to
the ſonnes of man, to be exerciſed therewith.14I haue ſeene all the
workes that are done vnder the Sunne, and behold, all is vanitie, and
vexation of ſpirit.15That which is crooked, cannot be made ſtraight: and
that which is wanting cannot be numbred.16I communed with mine
owne heart, ſaying, Loe, I am come to great eſtate, and haue gotten more
wiſedome then all they that haue beene before me in Ieruſalem: yea my
heart had great experience of wiſedome & knowledge.17And I gaue my
heart to know wiſedome, and to know madneſse and folly: I perceiued
that this alſo is vexation of ſpirit.18For in much wiſedome is much griefe:
and hee that increaſeth knowledge, increaſeth ſorrow.
CHAPTER 21I ſaid in mine heart, Goe to now, I wil prooue thee with
mirth, therfore enioy pleaſure: and behold, this alſo is vanitie.2I ſaide of
laughter, It is mad: and of mirth, What doeth it?3I ſought in mine heart
to giue my ſelfe vnto wine, (yet acquainting mine heart with wiſedome)
and to lay hold on folly, till I might ſee what was that good for the ſonnes
of men, which they ſhould doe vnder the heauen all the dayes of their
life.4I made me great workes, I builded mee houſes, I planted mee
Uineyards.5I made mee gardens & orchards, and I planted trees in them
of all kinde of fruits.6I made mee pooles of water, to water therewith
the wood that bringeth foorth trees:7I got me ſeruants and maydens,
and had ſeruants borne in my houſe; alſo I had great poſſeſſions of great
and ſmall cattell, aboue all that were in Ieruſalem before me.8I gathered
mee alſo ſiluer and gold, and the peculiar treaſure of kings and of the
prouinces: I gate mee men ſingers and women ſingers, and the delights
of the ſonnes of men, as muſical inſtruments, and that of all ſorts.9So I
was great, and increaſed more then all that were before mee in Ieruſalem;
alſo my wiſedome remained with me.10And whatſoeuer mine eyes
deſired, I kept not from them; I withheld not my heart from any ioy: for
my heart reioyced in all my labour; and this was my portion of all my
labour.11Then I looked on all the workes that my hands had wrought,
and on the labour that I had laboured to doe: and behold, all was vanitie,
and vexation of ſpirit, and there was no profit vnder the Sunne.12And I
turned my ſelfe to behold wiſedome, and madneſse and folly: for what
can the man doe, that commeth after the king? euen that which hath
bene already done.13Then I ſaw that wiſedome excelleth folly, as farre as
light excelleth darkeneſſe.14The wiſe mans eyes are in his head, but the
foole walketh in darknes: and I my ſelfe perceiued alſo that one euent
happeneth to them all.15Then ſaid I in my heart, As it happeneth to the
foole, ſo it happeneth euen to me, and why was I then more wiſe? then
I ſaid in my heart, That this alſo is vanitie.16For there is no remembrance
of the wiſe, more then of the foole for euer; ſeeing that which now is,
in the dayes to come ſhall be forgotten; and how dieth the wiſe man? as

the foole.[17]Therefore I hated life, becauſe the worke that is wrought
vnder the Sunne is grieuous vnto mee: for all is vanitie, and vexation of
ſpirit.[18]Yea I hated all my labour which I had taken vnder the Sunne:
becauſe I ſhould leaue it vnto the man that ſhalbe after mee.[19]And who
knoweth whether he ſhall be a wiſe man or a foole? yet ſhall he haue
rule ouer all my labour, wherein I haue laboured, and wherein I haue
ſhewed my ſelfe wiſe vnder the Sunne. This is alſo vanitie.[20]Therefore I
went about to cauſe my heart to deſpaire of all the labour which I tooke
vnder the Sunne.[21]For there is a man whoſe labour is in wiſedome and
in knowledge, and in equitie: yet to a man that hath not laboured therein,
ſhall hee leaue it for his portion; This alſo is vanitie, and a great
euill.[22]For what hath man of all his labour, and of the vexation of his
heart wherein hee hath laboured vnder the Sunne?[23]For all his dayes are
ſorrowes, and his traueile, griefe; yea his heart taketh not reſt in the
night. This is alſo vanitie.[24]There is nothing better for a man, then that
he ſhould eat and drinke, and that he ſhould make his ſoule enioy good
in his labour. This alſo I ſaw, that it was from the hand of God.[25]For
who can eate? or who elſe can haſten hereunto more then I?[26]For God
giueth to a man that is good in his ſight, wiſedome, and knowledge, and
ioy: but to the ſinner hee giueth traueile, to gather and to heape vp that
he may giue to him that is good before God: This alſo is vanitie and
vexation of ſpirit.
CHAPTER 3[1]To euery thing there is a ſeaſon, and a time to euery
purpoſe vnder the heauen.[2]A time to be borne, and a time to die: a time
to plant, and a time to pluck vp that which is planted.[3]A time to kill, and
a time to heale: a time to breake downe, and a time to build vp.[4]A time
to weepe, and a time to laugh: a time to mourne, and a time to dance.[5]A
time to caſt away ſtones, and a time to gather ſtones together: a time to
imbrace, and a time to refraine from imbracing.[6]A time to get, and a
time to loſe: a time to keepe, and a time to caſt away.[7]A time to rent,
and a time to ſow: a time to keepe ſilence, and a time to ſpeake.[8]A time
to loue, and a time to hate: a time of warre, and a time of peace.[9]What
profite hath hee that worketh, in that wherein he laboureth?[10]I haue
ſeene the trauaile which God hath giuen to the ſonnes of men, to be
exerciſed in it.[11]He hath made euery thing beautifull in his time: alſo hee
hath ſet the world in their heart, ſo that no man can finde out the worke
that God maketh from the beginning to the end.[12]I know that there is
no good in them, but for a man to reioyce, and to doe good in his
life.[13]And alſo that euery man ſhould eate and drinke, and enioy the
good of all his labour: it is the gift of God.[14]I know that whatſoeuer
God doeth, it ſhalbe for euer: nothing can be put to it, nor any thing
taken from it: and God doth it, that men ſhould feare before him.[15]That
which hath beene, is now: and that which is to be, hath alreadie beene,
and God requireth that which is paſt.[16]And moreouer, I ſawe vnder the
Sunne the place of iudgement, that wickedneſſe was there; and the place
of righteouſneſſe, that iniquitie was there.[17]I ſaid in mine heart, God
ſhall iudge the righteous and the wicked: for there is a time there, for
euery purpoſe and for euery worke.[18]I ſaid in my heart concerning the
eſtate of the ſonnes of men, that God might manifeſt them, and that
they might ſee that they themſelues are beaſts.[19]For that which befalleth
the ſonnes of men, befalleth beaſtes, euen one thing befalleth them: as
the one dieth, ſo dieth the other; yea they haue all one breath, ſo that a
man hath no preheminence aboue a beaſt; for all is vanitie.[20]All goe vnto
one place, all are of the duſt, and all turne to duſt againe.[21]Who knoweth
the ſpirit of man that goeth vpward; and the ſpirit of the beaſt that goeth
downeward to the earth?[22]Wherefore I perceiue that there is nothing
better, then that a man ſhould reioyce in his owne workes: for that is his
portion; for who ſhall bring him to ſee what ſhalbe after him?
CHAPTER 4[1]So I returned, and conſidered all the oppreſſions that are
done vnder the ſunne; & behold the teares of ſuch as were oppreſſed,
and they had no comforter: and on the ſide of their oppreſsours there
was power, but they had no comforter.[2]Wherefore I praiſed the dead
which are already dead, more then the liuing which are yet aliue.[3]Yea
better is he then both they, which hath not yet been, who hath not ſeene
the euill worke that is done vnder the Sunne.[4]Againe I conſidered all
trauaile, and euery right worke, that for this a man is enuied of his
neighbour: this is alſo vanitie, and vexation of ſpirit.[5]The foole foldeth
his hands together, and eateth his owne fleſh.[6]Better is an handfull with
quietneſse, then both the hands full with trauell and vexation of
ſpirit.[7]Then I returned, and I ſaw vanitie vnder the Sunne.[8]There is one
alone, and there is not a ſecond; yea, he hath neither childe nor brother:
yet is there no end of all his labour, neither is his eye ſatiſfied with riches,
neither ſayth hee, For whom doe I labour, and bereaue my ſoule of
good? this is alſo vanitie, yea it is a ſore trauell.[9]Two are better then one;
becauſe they haue a good reward for their labour.[10]For if they fall, the
one will lift vp his fellow; but woe to him that is alone, when he falleth:
for he hath not another to helpe him vp.[11]Againe, if two lye together,
then they haue heate; but howe can one be warme alone?[12]And if one
preuaile againſt him, two ſhall withſtand him; and a threefold coard is
not quickly broken.[13]Better is a poore and a wiſe child, then an old and
fooliſh king who will no more be admoniſhed.[14]For out of priſon hee
commeth to raigne, whereas alſo he that is borne in his kingdome,
becommeth poore.[15]I conſidered all the liuing which walke vnder the
ſunne, with the ſecond child that ſhall ſtand vp in his ſtead.[16]There is
no end of all the people, euen of all that haue beene before them: they
alſo that come after, ſhall not reioyce in him: ſurely this alſo is vanitie,
and vexation of ſpirit.
CHAPTER 5[1]Kepe thy foote when thou goeſt to the houſe of God,
and be more ready to heare, then to giue the ſacrifice of fooles: for they
conſider not that they doe euill.[2]Be not raſh with thy mouth, and let not
thine heart be haſty to vtter any thing before God: for God is in heauen,
and thou vpon earth: therefore let thy words be few.[3]For a dreame
commeth through the multitude of buſineſse, and a fooles voyce is
knowen by multitude of words.[4]When thou voweſt a vow vnto God,
deferre not to pay it: for he hath no pleaſure in fooles; pay that which
thou haſt vowed.[5]Better is it that thou ſhouldeſt not vowe, then that
thou ſhouldeſt vowe and not pay.[6]Suffer not thy mouth to cauſe thy
fleſh to ſinne, neither ſay thou before the Angel, that it was an errour:
wherefore ſhould God be angrie at thy voyce, and deſtroy the worke of
thine hands?[7]For in the multitude of dreames and many words, there
are alſo diuers vanities: but feare thou God.[8]If thou ſeeſt the oppreſſion
of the poore, and violent peruerting of iudgement, and iuſtice in a
prouince, maruell not at the matter: for he that is higher then the higheſt,
regardeth, and there be higher then they.[9]Moreouer the profit of the
earth is for all: the king himſelfe is ſerued by the field.[10]Hee that loueth
ſiluer ſhall not be ſatiſfied with ſiluer; nor he that loueth abundance, with
increaſe: this is alſo vanitie.[11]When goods increaſe, they are increaſed
that eate them: and what good is there to the owners thereof, ſauing the
beholding of them with their eyes?[12]The ſleepe of a labouring man is
ſweete, whether he eate little or much: but the abundance of the rich
will not ſuffer him to ſleepe.[13]There is a ſore euill which I haue ſeene
vnder the Sun, namely riches kept for the owners therof to their
hurt.[14]But thoſe riches periſh by euill trauell; and he begetteth a ſonne,
and there is nothing in his hand.[15]As he came forth of his mothers
wombe, naked ſhall he returne to goe as he came, and ſhall take nothing
of his labour, which he may carry away in his hand.[16]And this alſo is a
ſore euill, that in all points as he came, ſo ſhall hee goe: and what profit
hath he that hath laboured for the winde?[17]All his dayes alſo hee eateth
in darkeneſſe, and he hath much ſorrowe, and wrath with his
ſickneſse.[18]Behold that which I haue ſeene: It is good and comely for
one to eate and to drinke, and to enioy the good of all his labour that he
taketh vnder the ſunne, all the dayes of his life, which God giueth him:
for it is his portion.[19]Euery man alſo to whom God hath giuen riches
and wealth, and hath giuen him power to eate thereof, and to take his
portion, and to reioyce in his labour; this is the gift of God.[20]For he ſhall
not much remember the dayes of his life: becauſe God anſwereth him
in the ioy of his heart.
CHAPTER 6[1]There is an euill which I haue ſeen vnder the Sun, and it
is common among men:[2]A man to whom God hath giuen riches, wealth
and honour, ſo that he wanteth nothing for his ſoule of all that he
deſireth, yet God giueth him not power to eate thereof, but a ſtranger
eateth it: This is vanitie, and it is an euill diſeaſe.[3]If a man beget an
hundred children, and liue many yeeres, ſo that the dayes of his yeeres
bee many: and his ſoule be not filled with good, and alſo that he haue
no buriall, I ſay, that an vntimely birth is better then he.[4]For he
commeth in with vanitie, and departeth in darkeneſſe, and his name ſhall
be couered with darkeneſſe.[5]Moreouer hee hath not ſeene the Sunne,
nor knowen any thing: this hath more reſt then the other.[6]Yea though
he liue a thouſand yeeres twice told, yet hath he ſeene no good: Doe not
all goe to one place?[7]All the labour of man is for his mouth, and yet the

appetite is not filled.8For what hath the wiſe more then the foole? what hath the poore, that knoweth to walke before the liuing?9Better is the ſight of the eyes, then the wandering of the deſire: this is alſo vanitie and vexation of ſpirit.10That which hath bene, is named already, and it is knowen that it is man: neither may he contend with him that is mightier then he.11Seeing there be many things that increaſe vanitie, what is man the better?12For who knoweth what is good for man in this life, all the dayes of his vaine life, which he ſpendeth as a ſhadow? for who can tell a man what ſhal be after him vnder the ſunne?

CHAPTER 71A Good name is better then precious ointment: and the day of death, then the day of ones birth.2It is better to goe to the houſe of mourning, then to goe to the houſe of feaſting: for that is the end of all men, and the liuing will lay it to his heart.3ſorrow is better then laughter: for by the ſadneſse of the countenance the heart is made better.4The heart of the wiſe is in the houſe of mourning: but the heart of fooles is in the houſe of mirth.5It is better to heare the rebuke of the wiſe, then for a man to heare the ſong of fooles.6For as the crackling of thornes vnder a pot, ſo is the laughter of the foole: this alſo is vanitie.7Surely oppreſſion maketh a wiſe man mad: and a gift deſtroyeth the heart.8Better is the ende of a thing then the beginning thereof: and the patient in ſpirit is better then the proude in ſpirit.9Be not haſtie in thy ſpirit to bee angry: for anger reſteth in the boſome of fooles.10ſay not thou, What is the cauſe that the former dayes were better then theſe? For thou doeſt not enquire wiſely concerning this.11Wiſcdome is good with an inheritance: and by it there is profite to them that ſee the ſunne.12For wiſedome is a defence, and money is a defence: but the excellencie of knowledge is, that wiſedome giueth life to them that haue it.13Conſider the worke of God: for who can make that ſtraight, which hee hath made crooked?14In the day of proſperitie be ioyfull, but in the day of aduerſitie conſider: God alſo hath ſet the one ouer againſt the other, to the end that man ſhould find nothing after him.15All things haue I ſeene in the dayes of my vanitie: there is a iuſt man that periſheth in his righteouſnes, and there is a wicked man that prolongeth his life in his wickednes.16Be not righteous ouer much, neither make thy ſelfe ouer wiſe: why ſhouldeſt thou deſtroy thy ſelfe?17Be not ouermuch wicked, neither be thou fooliſh: why ſhouldeſt thou die before thy time?18It is good that thou ſhouldeſt take holde of this, yea alſo from this withdraw not thine hand: for hee that feareth God, ſhall come foorth of them all.19Wiſedome ſtrengtheneth the wiſe, more then ten mightie men which are in the citie.20For there is not a iuſt man vpon earth, that doeth good, and ſinneth not.21Alſo take no heede vnto all words that are ſpoken; leſt thou heare thy ſeruant curſe thee.22For often times alſo thine owne heart knoweth, that thou thy ſelfe likewiſe haſt curſed others.23All this haue I prooued by wiſedome: I ſaid, I will be wiſe, but it was farre from me.24That which is farre off, and exceeding deepe, who can finde it out?25I applyed mine heart to know, and to ſearch, and to ſeeke out wiſdome, and the reaſon of things, aud to know the wickednes of folly, euen of fooliſhneſse and madneſse.26And I finde more bitter then death, the woman whoſe heart is ſnares & nets, and her handes as bands: who ſo pleaſeth God, ſhall eſcape from her, but the ſinner ſhall be taken by her.27Behold, this haue I found (ſaith the Preacher) counting one by one to finde out the account:28Which yet my ſoule ſeeketh, but I finde not: one man among a thouſand haue I found, but a woman among all thoſe haue I not found.29Loe, this onely haue I found, that God hath made man vpright: but they haue ſought out many inuentions.

CHAPTER 81Who is as the Wiſe man? and who knoweth the interpretation of a thing? a mans wiſedome maketh his face to ſhine, and the boldnes of his face ſhalbe changed.2I counſell thee, to keepe the kings commandement, and that in regard of the oath of God.3Bee not haſtie to goe out of his ſight: ſtand not in an euill thing, for he doeth whatſoeuer pleaſeth him.4Where the word of a king is, there is power: and who may ſay vnto him, What doeſt thou?5Whoſo keepeth the commandement, ſhall feele no euill thing: and a wiſe mans heart diſcerneth both time and iudgement.6Becauſe to euery purpoſe there is time, and iudgement; therefore the miſery of man is great vpon him.7For hee knoweth not that which ſhall be: for who can tell him, when it ſhall be?8There is no man that hath power ouer the ſpirit to retaine the ſpirit; neither hath he power in the day of death: and there is no diſcharge in that warre, neither ſhall wickedneſſe deliuer thoſe that are giuen to it.9All this haue I ſeene, and applied my heart vnto euery worke that is done vnder the Sunne: there is a time wherein one man ruleth ouer another to his owne hurt.10And ſo I ſaw the wicked buried, who had come, and gone from the place of the Holy, and they were forgotten in the city, where they had ſo done: this is alſo vanitie.11Becauſe ſentence againſt an euill worke is not executed ſpeedily; therefore the heart of the ſonnes of men is fully ſet in them to doe euill.12Though a ſinner doe euill an hundred times, and his dayes be prolonged; yet ſurely I know that it ſhall be well with them that feare God, which feare before him.13But it ſhall not be well with the wicked, neither ſhall hee prolong his dayes which are as a ſhadow; becauſe he feareth not before God.14There is a vanitie which is done vpon the earth, that there be iuſt men vnto whom it happeneth according to the worke of the wicked: againe, there be wicked men, to whom it happeneth according to the worke of the righteous: I ſaid, that this alſo is vanitie.15Then I commended mirth, becauſe a man hath no better thing vnder the Sunne, then to eate and to drinke, and to be merrie: for that ſhall abide with him of his labour, the dayes of his life, which God giueth him vnder the Sunne.16When I applied mine heart to know wiſedome, and to ſee the buſines that is done vpon the earth: (for alſo there is that neither day nor night ſeeth ſleepe with his eyes.)17Then I behelde all the worke of God, that a man cannot finde out the worke that is done vnder the Sunne: becauſe though a man labour to ſeeke it out, yea further though a wiſe man thinke to know it, yet ſhall hee not be able to finde it.

CHAPTER 91For all this I conſidered in my heart, euen to declare all this, that the righteous, and the wiſe, and their workes, are in the hand of God: no man knoweth either loue, or hatred, by all that is before them.2All things come alike to all: there is one euent to the righteous and to the wicked, to the good and to the cleane, and to the vncleane; to him that ſacrificeth, and to him that ſacrificeth not: as is the good, ſo is the ſinner, and hee that ſweareth, as he that feareth an oath.3This is an euill among all things that are done vnder the Sunne, that there is one euent vnto all: yea alſo the heart of the ſonnes of men is full of euill, and madneſse is in their heart while they liue, and after that they goe to the dead.4For to him that is ioyned to all the liuing, there is hope: for a liuing dogge is better then a dead Lion.5For the liuing know that they ſhall die: but the dead know not any thing, neither haue they any more a reward, for the memorie of them is forgotten.6Alſo their loue, and their hatred, and their enuy is now periſhed; neither haue they any more a portion for euer in any thing that is done vnder the Sunne.7Goe thy way, eate thy bread with ioy, and drinke thy wine with a merry heart; for God now accepteth thy workes.8Let thy garments bee alwayes white; and let thy head lacke no oyntment.9Liue ioyfully with the wiſe, whom thou loueſt, all the dayes of the life of thy vanitie, which he hath giuen thee vnder the Sunne, all the dayes of thy vanitie: for that is thy portion in this life, and in thy labour which thou takeſt vnder the Sunne.10Whatſoeuer thy hand findeth to doe, doe it with thy might: for there is no worke, nor deuice, nor knowledge, nor wiſedome in the graue, whither thou goeſt.11I returned, and ſaw vnder the Sunne, That the race is not to the ſwift, nor the battell to the ſtrong, neither yet bread to the wiſe, nor yet riches to men of vnderſtanding, nor yet fauour to men of ſkil; but time and chance happeneth to them all.12For man alſo knoweth not his time, as the fiſhes that are taken in an euil net, and as the birds that are caught in the ſnare; ſo are the ſonnes of men ſnared in an euill time, when it falleth ſuddenly vpon them.13This wiſedome haue I ſeene alſo vnder the Sunne, and it ſeemed great vnto me:14There was a little citie, and few men within it; and there came a great King againſt it, and beſieged it, & built great bulwarks againſt it:15Now there was found in it a poore wiſe man, and hee by his wiſedome deliuered the citie; yet no man remembred that ſame poore man.16Then ſaid I, Wiſedome is better then ſtrength: neuertheleſſe, the poore mans wiſedome is deſpiſed, and his words are not heard.17The words of wiſe men are heard in quiet, more then the cry of him that ruleth among fooles.18Wiſedome is better then weapons of warre: but one ſinner deſtroyeth much good.

CHAPTER 101Dead flies cauſe the oyntment of the Apothecarie to ſend foorth a ſtinking ſauour: ſo doeth a little folly him that is in reputation for wiſedome and honour.2A wiſe mans heart is at his right hand: but a fooles heart at his left.3Yea alſo when hee that is a foole walketh by the way, his wiſedome faileth him, and hee ſaith to euery one that he is a foole.4If the ſpirit of the ruler riſe vp againſt thee, leaue not thy place; for yeelding pacifieth great offences.5There is an euill which I haue ſeene vnder the Sunne, as an errour, which proceedeth from the ruler.6Folly is ſet in great dignitie; and the rich ſit in lowe place.7I haue ſeene ſeruants vpon horſes, and princes walking as ſeruants vpon the earth.8He that diggeth a pit, ſhall fall into it; and who ſo breaketh an hedge, a ſerpent ſhall bite him.9Who ſo remoueth ſtones, ſhall be hurt therewith: and hee that cleaueth wood, ſhalbe endangered thereby.10If the yron be blunt, and he doe not whet the edge, then muſt he put to more ſtrength: but wiſedome is profitable to direct.11Surely the ſerpent will bite without inchauntment, and a babbler is no better.12The words of a wiſe mans mouth are gratious: but the lips of a foole will ſwallow vp himſelfe.13The beginning of the words of his mouth is fooliſhneſse: and the end of his talke is miſchieuous madneſse.14A foole alſo is full of words; a man cannot tell what ſhall be; and what ſhall bee after him who can tell him?15The labour of the fooliſh wearyeth euery one of them; becauſe hee knoweth not how to goe to the citie.16Woe to thee, O land, when thy king is a child, and thy princes eate in the morning.17Bleſſed art thou, O land, when thy king is the ſonne of nobles, and thy princes eate in due ſeaſon, for ſtrength, and not for drunkenneſse.18By much ſlouthfulneſse the building decayeth; and through idleneſse of the hands the houſe droppeth through.19A feaſt is made for laughter, and wine maketh merry: but money anſwereth all things.20Curſe not the king, no not in thy thought, and curſe not the rich in thy bed-chamber: for a bird of the aire ſhall carry the voyce, and that which hath wings ſhall tell the matter.

CHAPTER 111Caſt thy bread vpon the waters: for thou ſhalt find it after many dayes.2Giue a portion to ſeuen and alſo to eight; for thou knoweſt noc what euill ſhall be vpon the earth.3If the clouds be full of raine, they emptie themſelues vpon the earth: and if the tree fall toward the South, or toward the North, in the place where the tree falleth, there it ſhall be.4He that obſerueth the wind, ſhall not ſow: and hee that regardeth the clouds, ſhall not reape.5As thou knoweſt not what is the way of the ſpirit, nor how the bones doe growe in the wombe of her that is with child: euen ſo thou knoweſt not the workes of God who maketh all.6In the morning ſowe thy ſeede, and in the euening withhold not thine hand: for thou knoweſt not whether ſhall proſper, either this or that, or whether they both ſhall be alike good.7Truly the light is ſweet, and a pleaſant thing is it for the eyes to behold the ſunne.8But if a man liue many yeeres, and reioyce in them all; yet let him remember the dayes of darkeneſſe, for they ſhall be many. All that commeth is vanitie.9Reioyce, O young man, in thy youth, and let thy heart cheere thee in the dayes of thy youth, and walke in the wayes of thine heart, and in the ſight of thine eyes: but know thou, that for all theſe things, God will bring thee into iudgement.10Therefore remoue ſorrow from thy heart, and put away euill from thy fleſh; for child-hood & youth are vanitie.

CHAPTER 121Remember now thy Creatour in the dayes of thy youth, while the euil daies come not, nor the yeeres drawe nigh, when thou ſhalt ſay, I haue no pleaſure in them:2While the Sunne, or the light, or the moone, or the ſtarres be not darkened, nor the cloudes returne after the raine:3In the day when the keepers of the houſe ſhall tremble, and the ſtrong men ſhall bowe themſelues, and the grinders ceaſe, becauſe they are fewe, and thoſe that looke out of the windowes be darkened:4And the doores ſhal be ſhut in the ſtreets, when the ſound of the grinding is low, and he ſhall riſe vp at the voice of the bird, and all the daughters of muſicke ſhall be brought low.5Alſo when they ſhalbe afraid of that which is high, and feares ſhall bee in the way, and the Almond tree ſhall flouriſh, and the graſhopper ſhall be a burden, and deſire ſhall faile: becauſe man goeth to his long home, and the mourners goe about the ſtreets:6Or euer the ſiluer corde be looſed, or the golden bowle be broken, or the pitcher be broken at the fountaine, or the wheele broken at the ciſterne.7Then ſhall the duſt returne to the earth as it was: and the ſpirit ſhall returne vnto God who gaue it.8Uanitie of vanities (ſaith the preacher) all is vanitie.9And moreouer becauſe the preacher was wiſe, he ſtill taught the people knowledge, yea he gaue good heed, and ſought out, and ſet in order many prouerbes.10The preacher ſought to finde out acceptable words, and that which was written was vpright, euen wordes of trueth.11The wordes of the wiſe are as goads, and as nailes faſtened by the maſters of aſſemblies, which are giuen from one ſhepheard.12And further, by theſe, my ſonne, be admoniſhed: of making many bookes there is no end, and much ſtudie is a wearineſse of the fleſh.13Let vs heare the concluſion of the whole matter: Feare God, and keepe his commandements, for this is the whole duetie of man.14For God ſhal bring euery worke into iudgement, with euer ſecret thing, whether it bee good, or whether it bee euill.

THE SONG OF SOLOMON

CHAPTER 11The ſong of ſongs, which is Solomons.2Let him kiſſe mee with the kiſſes of his mouth: for thy Loue is better then wine.3Becauſe of the ſauour of thy good ointments, thy name is as ointment powred forth, therefore doe the virgins loue thee.4Draw me, we will runne after thee: the king hath brought me into his chambers: we will be glad and reioyce in thee, we wil remember thy loue more then wine: the vpright loue thee.5I am blacke, but comely, (O ye daughters of Ieruſalem) as the tents of Kedar, as the curtaines of Solomon.6Looke not vpon me becauſe I am blacke, becauſe the Sunne hath looked vpon me: my mothers children were angry with me, they made me the keeper of the vineyards, but mine owne vineyard haue I not kept.7Tell me, (O thou whom my ſoule loueth) where thou feedeſt, where thou makeſt thy flocke to reſt at noone: for why ſhould I be as one that turneth aſide by the flockes of thy companions?8If thou know not (O thou faireſt among women) goe thy way forth by the footſteps of the flocke, and feede thy kiddes beſide the ſhepheards tents.9I haue compared thee, O my loue, to a company of horſes in Pharaohs chariots.10Thy cheekes are comely with rowes of iewels, thy necke with chaines of golde.11Wee will make thee borders of golde, with ſtuddes of ſiluer.12While the king ſitteth at his table, my ſpikenard ſendeth foorth the ſmell thereof.13A bundle of myrrhe is my welbeloued vnto me; he ſhall lie all night betwixt my breaſts.14My beloued is vnto me, as a cluſter of Camphire in the vineyards of Engedi.15Behold, thou art faire, my loue: behold, thou art faire, thou haſt doues eyes.16Behold, thou art faire, my beloued; yea pleaſant: alſo our bedde is greene.17The beames of our houſe are Cedar, and our rafters of firre.

CHAPTER 21I Am the roſe of Sharon, and the lillie of the valleys.2As the lillie among thornes, ſo is my loue among the daughters.3As the apple tree among the trees of the wood, ſo is my beloued among the ſonnes. I ſate downe vnder his ſhadow with great delight, and his fruit was ſweete to my taſte.4Hee brought me to the banketting houſe, and his banner ouer mee, was loue.5Stay me with flagons, comfort me with apples, for I am ſicke of loue.6His left hand is vnder my head, and his right hand doeth imbrace me.7I charge you, O ye daughters of Ieruſalem, by the Roes, and by the hindes of the field, that ye ſtirre not vp, nor awake my loue, till ſhe pleaſe.8The voice of my beloued! behold! hee commeth leaping vpon the mountaines, ſkipping vpon the hils.9My beloued is like a Roe, or a yong Hart: behold, he ſtandeth behind our wall, he looketh foorth at the windowe, ſhewing himſelfe through the latteſse.10My beloued ſpake, and ſaid vnto me, Riſe vp, my Loue, my faire one, and come away.11For loe, the winter is paſt, the raine is ouer, and gone.12The flowers appeare on the earth, the time of the ſinging of birds is come, and the voice of the turtle is heard in our land.13The fig tree putteth foorth her greene figs, and the vines with the tender grape giue a good ſmell. Ariſe, my loue, my faire one, and come away.14O my doue! that art in the clefts of the rocke, in the ſecret places of the ſtaires: let me ſee thy countenance, let me heare thy voice, for ſweet is thy voice, and thy countenance is comely.15Take vs the foxes, the litle foxes, that ſpoile the vines: for our vines haue tender grapes.16My beloued is mine, and I am his: he feedeth among the lillies.17Untill the day breake, and the ſhadowes flee away: turne my beloued and be thou like a Roe, or a yong Hart, vpon the mountaines of Bether.

CHAPTER 31By night on my bed I ſought him whome my ſoule loueth. I ſought him, but I found him not.2I will riſe now, and goe about the citie in the ſtreets, and in the broad wayes I will ſeeke him whom my ſoule loueth: I ſought him, but I found him not.3The watchmen that goe about the citie, found me: to whom I ſaid, Saw ye him whom my ſoule loueth?4It was but a litle that I paſſed from them, but I found him whome my ſoule loueth: I helde him, and would not let him goe, vntill

I had brought him into my mothers houſe, and into the chamber of her that conceiued me. 5 I charge you, O ye daughters of Ieruſalem, by the Roes and by the Hindes of the field, that ye ſtirre not vp, nor awake my loue, till he pleaſe. 6 Who is this that commeth out of the wildernes like pillars of ſmoke, perfumed with myrrhe and frankincenſe, with all powders of the merchant? 7 Behold his bed, which is Solomons: threeſcore valiant men are about it, of the valiant of Iſrael: 8 They all hold ſwords, being expert in warre: Euery man hath his ſword vpon his thigh, becauſe of feare in the night. 9 King Solomon made himſelfe a charet of the wood of Lebanon. 10 He made the pillars thereof of ſiluer, the bottome thereof of gold, the couering of it, of purple; the midſt thereof being paued with loue, for the daughters of Ieruſalem. 11 Goe foorth, O yee daughters of Zion, and behold king Solomon with the Crowne wherewith his mother crowned him in the day of his eſpouſals, and in the day of the gladneſſe of his heart.

CHAPTER 4 1 Behold, thou art faire, my loue, behold thou art faire, thou haſt doues eyes within thy lockes: thy haire is as a flocke of goats, that appeare from mount Gilead. 2 Thy teeth are like a flocke of ſheepe that are euen ſhorne, which came vp from the waſhing: whereof euery one beare twinnes, and none is barren among them. 3 Thy lips are like a threed of ſcarlet, and thy ſpeach is comely: thy temples are like a piece of a pomegranate within thy lockes. 4 Thy necke is like the tower of Dauid builded for an armorie, whereon there hang a thouſand bucklers, all ſhields of mightie men. 5 Thy two breaſts, are like two yong Roes, that are twinnes, which feed among the lillies. 6 Untill the day breake, and the ſhadowes flee away, I will get mee to the mountaines of myrrhe, and to the hill of frankincenſe. 7 Thou art all faire, my loue, there is no ſpot in thee. 8 Come with me from Lebanon (my ſpouſe,) with me from Lebanon: looke from the top of Amana, from the top of Shenir and Hermon, from the Lions dennes, from the mountaines of the Leopards. 9 Thou haſt rauiſhed my heart, my ſiſter, my ſpouſe; thou haſt rauiſhed my heart, with one of thine eyes, with one chaine of thy necke. 10 How faire is thy loue, my ſiſter, my ſpouſe! how much better is thy loue then wine! and the ſmell of thine oyntments then all ſpices! 11 Thy lips, O my ſpouſe! drop as the hony combe: hony and milke are vnder thy tongue, and the ſmell of thy garments is like the ſmell of Lebanon. 12 A garden incloſed is my ſiſter, my ſpouſe: a ſpring ſhut vp, a fountaine ſealed. 13 Thy plants are an orchard of pomegranates, with pleaſant fruits, Camphire, with Spikenaed, 14 Spikenard and Saffron, Calamus and Cynamom, with all trees of Frankincenſe, Mirrhe and Aloes, with all the chiefe ſpices. 15 A fountaine of gardens, a well of liuing waters, and ſtreames from Lebanon. 16 Awake, O Northwinde, and come thou South, blow vpon my garden, that the ſpices thereof may flow out: let my beloued come into his garden, and eate his pleaſant fruits.

CHAPTER 5 1 I am come into my garden, my ſiſter, my ſpouſe, I haue gathered my Myrrhe with my ſpice, I haue eaten my honie combe with my hony, I haue drunke my wine with my milke: eate, O friends, drinke, yea drinke abundantly, O beloued! 2 I ſleepe, but my heart waketh: it is the voyce of my beloued that knocketh, ſaying, Open to me, my ſiſter, my loue, my doue, my vndefiled: for my head is filled with dewe, and my lockes with the drops of the night. 3 I haue put off my coate, how ſhall I put it on? I haue waſhed my feete, how ſhall I defile them? 4 My beloued put in his hand by the hole of the dore, and my bowels were moued for him. 5 I roſe vp to open to my beloued, and my hands dropped with myrrhe, and my fingers with ſweete ſmelling myrrhe, vpon the handles of the locke. 6 I opened to my beloued, but my beloued had with drawen himſelfe, and was gone: my ſoule failed when hee ſpake: I ſought him, but I could not find him: I called him, but he gaue me no anſwere. 7 The watchmen that went about the citie, found me, they ſmote me, they wounded me, the keepers of the walles tooke away my vaile from me. 8 I charge you, O daughters of Ieruſalem, if ye find my beloued, that yee tell him, that I am ſicke of loue. 9 What is thy beloued more then another beloued, O thou faireſt among women? what is thy beloued more then another beloued, that thou doeſt ſo charge vs? 10 My beloued is white and ruddy, the chiefeſt among tenne thouſand. 11 His head is as the moſt fine gold, his locks are buſhy, and blacke as a Rauen. 12 His eyes are as the eyes of doues by the riuers of water, waſhed with milk, and fitly ſet. 13 His cheekes are as a bed of ſpices, as ſweete flowers: his lippes like lillies, dropping ſweete ſmelling myrrhe. 14 His hands are as gold rings ſet with the Berill: His belly is as bright iuorie, ouerlayd with Saphires. 15 His legges are as pillars of marble, ſet vpon ſockets of fine gold: his countenance is as Lebanon, excellent as the Cedars. 16 His mouth is moſt ſweete, yea he is altogether louely. This is my beloued, and this is my friend, O daughters of Ieruſalem.

CHAPTER 6 1 Whither is thy beloued gone? O thou faireſt among women, whither is thy beloued turned aſide? that we may ſeeke him with thee. 2 My beloued is gone downe into his garden, to the beds of ſpices, to feede in the gardens, and to gather lillies. 3 I am my belloueds, & my beloued is mine: he feedeth among the lillies. 4 Thou art beautifull, O my loue, as Tirzah, comely as Ieruſalem, terrible as an armie with banners. 5 Turne away thine eyes from me, for they haue ouercome me: thy haire is a flocke of goates, that appeare from Gilead. 6 Thy teeth are as a flocke of ſheepe which goe vp from the waſhing, wherof euery one beareth twinnes, and there is not one barren among them. 7 As a piece of a pomegranat are thy temples within thy lockes. 8 There are threeſcore Queenes, and foureſcore concubines, and virgins without number. 9 My doue, my vndefiled is but one; ſhe is the only one of her mother, ſhe is the choice one of her that bare her: The daughters ſawe her, and bleſſed her; yea the Queenes and the concubins, and they prayſed her. 10 Who is ſhe that looketh forth as the morning, faire as the moone, cleare as the ſunne, and terrible as an armie with banners? 11 I went downe into the garden of nuts to ſee the fruits of the valley, and to ſee whether the vine flouriſhed, and the pomegranats budded. 12 Or euer I was aware, my ſoule made me like the chariots of Amminadib. 13 Returne, returne, O Shulamite; returne, returne, that we may looke vpon thee: what will yee ſee in the Shulamite? as it were the company of two armies.

CHAPTER 7 1 Howe beautifull are thy feete with ſhooes, O princes daughter! the ioynts of thy thighs are like iewels, the worke of the hands of a cunning workman. 2 Thy nauell is like a round goblet, which wanteth not licour: thy belly is like an heape of wheate, ſet about with lillies. 3 Thy two breaſts are like two yong Roes that are twinnes. 4 Thy necke is as a towre of yuory: thine eyes like the fiſh pooles in Heſhbon, by the gate of Bathrabbim: thy noſe is as the towre of Lebanon, which looketh toward Damaſcus. 5 Thine head vpon thee is like Carmel, and the haire of thine head like purple, the king is held in the galleries. 6 How faire, and how pleaſant art thou, O Loue, for delights! 7 This thy ſtature is like to a palme tree, and thy breaſts to cluſters of grapes. 8 I ſaid, I will goe vp to the palme tree, I will take hold of the boughes thereof: now alſo thy breaſts ſhall be as cluſters of the vine, and the ſmell of thy noſe, like apples. 9 And the roofe of thy mouth like the beſt wine, for my beloued, that goeth downe ſweetely, cauſing the lippes of thoſe that are aſleepe, to ſpeake. 10 I am my belloueds, and his deſire is towards me. 11 Come, my beloued, let vs goe forth into the field: let vs lodge in the villages. 12 Let vs get vp earely to the vineyards, let vs ſee if the vine flouriſh, whether the tender grape appeare, and the pomegranates bud forth: there will I giue thee my loues. 13 The mandrakes giue a ſmell, and at our gates are all maner of pleaſant fruits, new and olde, which I haue laid vp for thee, O my beloued.

CHAPTER 8 1 O that thou wert as my brother that ſucked the breſts of my mother, when I ſhould find thee without, I would kiſſe thee, yet I ſhould not be deſpiſed. 2 I would leade thee, and bring thee into my mothers houſe, who would inſtruct me: I would cauſe thee to drinke of ſpiced wine, of the iuice of my pomegranate. 3 His left hand ſhould be vnder my head, and his right hand ſhould embrace me. 4 I charge you, O daughters of Ieruſalem, that ye ſtirre not vp, nor awake my loue vntill he pleaſe. 5 (Who is this that commeth vp from the wilderneſſe, leaning vpon her beloued?) I raiſed thee vp vnder the apple tree: there thy mother brought thee forth, there ſhe brought thee forth, that bare thee. 6 Set mee as a ſeale vpon thine heart, as a ſeale vpon thine arme: for loue is ſtrong as death, iealouſie is cruel as the graue: the coales thereof are coales of fire, which hath a moſt vehement flame. 7 Many waters cannot quench loue, neither can the floods drowne it: if a man would giue all the ſubſtance of his houſe for loue, it would vtterly be contemned. 8 We haue a litle ſiſter, and ſhee hath no breaſts: what ſhall we doe for our ſiſter, in the day when ſhe ſhall bee ſpoken for? 9 If ſhe be a wall, we will build vpon her a palace of ſiluer: and if ſhe bee a dore, we will incloſe her with boards of Cedar. 10 I am a wall, and my breaſts like towers: then was I in his eyes as one that found fauour. 11 Solomon had a vineyard at Baalhamon, hee let out the vineyard vnto keepers: euery one for the fruit thereof was to bring a thouſand pieces of ſiluer.12My vineyard which is mine, is before me: thou (O Solomon) muſt haue a thouſand, and thoſe that keepe the fruit thereof, two hundred.13Thou that dwelleſt in the gardens, the companions hearken to thy voice: cauſe me to heare it.14Make haſte, my beloued, and be thou like to a Roe, or to a yong Hart vpon the mountaines of ſpices.

IſAIAH (ISAIAH)

CHAPTER 11The Uiſion of Iſaiah the ſonne of Amoz, which hee ſawe concerning Iudah and Ieruſalem, in the dayes of Uzziah, Iotham, Ahaz, & Hezekiah kings of Iudah.2Heare, O heauens, and giue eare, O earth: for the Lord hath ſpoken; I haue nouriſhed and brought vp children, and they haue rebelled againſt me.3The oxe knoweth his owner, and the aſſe his maſters cribbe: but Iſrael doeth not know, my people doeth not conſider.4Ah ſinnefull nation, a people laden with iniquitie, a ſeede of euill doers, children that are corrupters: they haue forſaken the Lord, they haue prouoked the Holy one of Iſrael vnto anger, they are gone away backward.5Why ſhould yee be ſtricken any more? yee will reuolt more and more: the whole head is ſicke, and the whole heart faint.6From the ſole of the foote, euen vnto the head, there is no ſoundneſſe in it; but wounds, and bruiſes, and putrifying ſores: they haue not beene cloſed, neither bound vp, neither mollified with oyntment.7Your countrey is deſolate, your cities are burnt with fire: your land, ſtrangers deuoure it in your preſence, and it is deſolate as ouerthrowen by ſtrangers.8And the daughter of Zion is left as a cottage in a vineyard, as a lodge in a garden of cucumbers, as a beſieged citie.9Except the Lord of hoſtes had left vnto vs a very ſmall remnant, we ſhould haue beene as Sodom, and we ſhould haue bene like vnto Gomorrah.10Heare the word of the Lord, ye rulers of Sodom, giue eare vnto the Law of our God, yee people of Gomorrah.11To what purpoſe is the multitude of your ſacrifices vnto me, ſayth the Lord? I am full of the burnt offerings of rammes, and the fat of fedde beaſts, and I delight not in the blood of bullockes, or of lambes, or of hee goates.12When ye come to appeare before mee, who hath required this at your hand, to tread my courts?13Bring no more vaine oblations, incenſe is an abomination vnto me: the new Moones, and Sabbaths, the calling of aſſemblies I cannot away with; it is iniquitie, euen the ſolemne meeting.14Your new Moones, and your appointed Feaſts my ſoule hateth: they are a trouble vnto me, I am weary to beare them.15And when ye ſpread foorth your handes, I will hide mine eyes from you; yea, when yee make many prayers I will not heare: your hands are full of blood.16Waſh yee, make you cleane, put away the euill of your doings from before mine eyes, ceaſe to doe euill,17Learne to doe well, ſeeke iudgement, relieue the oppreſſed, iudge the fatherleſſe, plead for the widow.18Come now and let vs reaſon together, ſaith the Lord: though your ſinnes be as ſcarlet, they ſhall be as white as ſnow; though they be red like crimſin, they ſhall be as wooll.19If yee be willing and obedient, yee ſhall eate the good of the land.20But if yee refuſe and rebell, yee ſhalbe deuoured with the ſword: for the mouth of the Lord hath ſpoken it.21Howe is the faithfull citie become an harlot? it was full of iudgement, righteouſneſſe lodged in it; but now murtherers.22Thy ſiluer is become droſſe, thy wine mixt with water.23Thy princes are rebellious and companions of theeues: euery one loueth gifts, and followeth after rewards: they iudge not the fatherleſſe, neither doth the cauſe of the widowe come vnto them.24Therefore, ſaith the Lord, the Lord of hoſtes, the mighty one of Iſrael; Ah, I will eaſe me of mine aduerſaries, and auenge me of mine enemies.25And I will turne my hand vpon thee, and purely purge away thy droſſe, and take away all thy tinne.26And I will reſtore thy iudges as at the firſt, and thy counſellers as at the beginning: afterward thou ſhalt be called the citie of righteouſneſſe, the faithfull citie.27Zion ſhall be redeemed with iudgement, and her conuerts with righteouſneſſe.28And the deſtruction of the tranſgreſſours and of the ſinners ſhall be together: and they that forſake the Lord ſhall be conſumed.29For they ſhall be aſhamed of the okes which yee haue deſired, and yee ſhalbe confounded for the gardens that yee haue choſen.30For yee ſhall be as an oke whoſe leafe fadeth, and as a garden that hath no water.31And the ſtrong ſhall be as towe, and the maker of it as a ſparke, and they ſhall both burne together, and none ſhall quench them.

CHAPTER 21The word that Iſaiah, the ſonne of Amoz, ſawe concerning Iudah and Ieruſalem.2And it ſhall come to paſſe in the laſt dayes, that the mountaine of the Lords houſe ſhall be eſtabliſhed in the top of the mountaines, and ſhall be exalted aboue the hilles; and all nations ſhall flow vnto it.3And many people ſhall goe & ſay; Come yee and let vs go vp to the mountaine of the Lord, to the houſe of the God of Iacob, and he will teach vs of his wayes, and we will walke in his pathes: for out of Zion ſhall goe forth the lawe, and the word of the Lord from Ieruſalem.4And hee ſhall iudge among the nations, and ſhall rebuke many people: and they ſhall beate their ſwords into plow-ſhares, and their ſpeares into pruning hookes: nation ſhall not lift vp ſword againſt nation, neither ſhall they learne warre any more.5O houſe of Iacob, come yee, and let vs walke in the light of the Lord.6Therefore thou haſt forſaken thy people the houſe of Iacob; becauſe they be repleniſhed from the Eaſt, and are ſoothſayers like the Philiſtines, and they pleaſe themſelues in the children of ſtrangers.7Their land alſo is full of ſiluer and gold, neither is there any end of their treaſures: their land is alſo full of horſes; neither is there any end of their charets.8Their land alſo is full of idoles: they worſhip the worke of their owne hands, that which their owne fingers haue made.9And the meane man boweth downe, and the great man humbleth himſelfe; therefore forgiue them not.10Enter into the rocke, and hide thee in the duſt, for feare of the Lord, and for the glory of his Maieſtie.11The loftie lookes of man ſhalbe humbled, and the hautines of men ſhalbe bowed downe: and the Lord alone ſhalbe exalted in that day.12For the day of the Lord of hoſtes ſhall bee vpon euery one that is proud and loftie, and vpon euery one that is lifted vp, and he ſhalbe brought low;13And vpon all the Cedars of Lebanon, that are high and lifted vp; and vpon all the okes of Baſhan,14And vpon all the high mountaines, and vpon all the hilles that are lifted vp,15And vpon euery high tower, and vpon euery fenced wall,16And vpon all the ſhips of Tarſhiſh, and vpon all pleaſant pictures.17And the loftineſſe of man ſhall be bowed downe, and the hautineſſe of men ſhalbe made low: and the Lord alone ſhalbe exalted in that day.18And the idoles hee ſhall vtterly aboliſh.19And they ſhall goe into the holes of the rocks, and into the caues of the earth for feare of the Lord, and for the glory of his Maieſtie; when hee Ariſeth to ſhake terribly the earth.20In that day a man ſhall caſt his idoles of ſiluer, and his idoles of golde which they made each one for himſelfe to worſhip, to the moules and to the battes:21To go into the clefts of the rocks, and into the tops of the ragged rockes, for feare of the Lord, and for the glorie of his Maieſtie; when hee Ariſeth to ſhake terribly the earth.22Ceaſe ye from man whoſe breath is in his noſtrels: for wherein is hee to be accounted of?

CHAPTER 31For behold, the Lord, the Lord of hoſtes doeth take away from Ieruſalem, and from Iudah, the ſtay and the ſtaffe, the whole ſtay of bread, and the whole ſtay of water,2The mighty man, and the man of warre; the Iudge and the Prophet, and the prudent, and the ancient,3The captaine of fiftie, and the honourable man, and the counſeller, and the cunning artificer, and the eloquent oratour.4And I will giue children to bee their Princes, and babes ſhall rule ouer them.5And the people ſhall be oppreſſed, euery one by another, and euery one by his neighbour: the childe ſhall behaue himſelfe proudly againſt the ancient, and the baſe againſt the honourable.6When a man ſhall take hold of his brother of the houſe of his father, ſaying, Thou haſt clothing, be thou our ruler, and let this ruine bee vnder thy hand:7In that day ſhall he ſweare, ſaying, I will not be an healer: for in my houſe is neither bread nor clothing: make me not a ruler of the people.8For Ieruſalem is ruined, & Iudah is fallen: becauſe their tongue and their doings are againſt the Lord, to prouoke the eyes of his glorie.9The ſhew of their countenance doeth witneſſe againſt them, and they declare their ſinne as Sodom, they hide it not: woe vnto their ſoule, for they haue rewarded euill vnto themſelues.10ſay yee to the righteous, that it ſhall be well with him: for they ſhall eate the fruit of their doings.11Woe vnto the wicked, it ſhall be ill with him: for the reward of his handes ſhalbe giuen him.12As for my people, children are their oppreſſours, and women rule ouer them: O my people, they which lead thee, cauſe thee to erre, and deſtroy the way of thy paths.13The Lord ſtandeth vp to plead, and ſtandeth to iudge the people.14The Lord will enter into iudgement with the ancients of his people, and the Princes thereof: for ye haue eaten vp the Uineyard; the ſpoile of the poore is in your houſes.15What meane yee that yee beat my people to pieces, and grinde the faces of the poore, ſaith the Lord God of hoſts? 16 Moreouer the Lord ſaith; Becauſe the daughters of Zion are hautie, and walke with ſtretched forth necks, and wanton eyes, walking and mincing as they goe, and making a tinkeling with their feet: 17 Therefore the Lord will ſmite with a ſcab the crowne of the head of the daughters of Zion, and the Lord will diſcouer their ſecret parts. 18 In that day the Lord will take away the brauery of their tinckling ornaments about their feete, and their caules, and their round tyres like the Moone. 19 The chaines, and the bracelets, and the mufflers, 20 The bonnets, and the ornaments of the legges, and the headbands, and the tablets, and the earerings, 21 The rings, and noſe-iewels, 22 The changeable ſutes of apparell, and the mantles, and the wimples, and the criſping pinnes, 23 The glaſſes, and the fine linnen, and the hoods, and the vailes. 24 And it ſhall come to paſſe, that in ſteade of ſweete ſmell, there ſhall bee ſtinke; and in ſtead of a girdle, a rent; and in ſtead of well ſet haire, baldneſse; and in ſtead of a ſtomacher, a girding of ſackecloth; and burning, in ſtead of beautie. 25 Thy men ſhall fall by the ſword, and thy mightie in the warre. 26 And her gates ſhall lament and mourne; and ſhe being deſolate, ſhall ſit vpon the ground.

CHAPTER 4 1 And in that day ſeuen women ſhall take hold of one man, ſaying, We will eate our owne bread, & weare our owne apparell: onely let vs be called by thy name, to take away our reproch. 2 In that day ſhall the Branch of the Lord be beautifull and glorious, and the fruit of the earth ſhalbe excellent and comely for them that are eſcaped of Iſrael. 3 And it ſhall come to paſſe, that hee that is left in Zion, and hee that remaineth in Ieruſalem, ſhall be called Holy, euen euery one that is written among the liuing in Ieruſalem, 4 When the Lord ſhall haue waſhed away the filth of the daughters of Zion, and ſhall haue purged the blood of Ieruſalem from the middeſt thereof, by the ſpirit of iudgement, and by the ſpirit of burning. 5 And the Lord will create vpon euery dwelling place of mount Zion, and vpon her aſſemblies a cloude, and ſmoke by day, and the ſhining of a flaming fire by night; for vpon all the glory ſhall be a defence. 6 And there ſhalbe a tabernacle for a ſhadow in the day time from the heat, and for a place of refuge, and for a couert from ſtorme and from raine.

CHAPTER 5 1 Now will I ſing to my welbeloued, a ſong of my beloued touching his vineyard: my wellbeloued hath a vineyard in a very fruitfull hill. 2 And hee fenced it, and gathered out the ſtones thereof, and planted it with the choiceſt vine, and built a towre in the middeſt of it, and alſo made a winepreſſe therein: and he looked that it ſhould bring foorth grapes, and it brought foorth wilde grapes. 3 And now, O inhabitants of Ieruſalem, and men of Iudah, Iudge, I pray you, betwixt me and my Uineyard. 4 What could haue beene done more to my Uineyard, that I haue not done in it? wherefore when I looked that it ſhould bring foorth grapes, brought it foorth wilde grapes? 5 And now goe to; I will tell you what I will doe to my Uineyard, I will take away the hedge thereof, and it ſhall be eaten vp; and breake downe the wall thereof, and it ſhall be troden downe. 6 And I will lay it waſte; it ſhall not be pruned, nor digged, but there ſhall come vp briars and thornes: I will alſo command the cloudes, that they raine no raine vpon it. 7 For the Uineyard of the Lord of hoſtes is the houſe of Iſrael, and the men of Iudah his pleaſant plant: and he looked for iudgement, but beholde oppreſſion; for righteouſneſſe, but behold a crie. 8 Woe vnto them that ioyne houſe to houſe, that lay field to field, till there be no place, that they may be placed alone in the midſt of the earth. 9 In mine eares ſaid the Lord of hoſtes, Of a trueth many houſes ſhall be deſolate, euen great and faire without inhabitant. 10 Yea ten acres of vineyard ſhall yeeld one Bath, and the ſeed of an Homer ſhall yeeld an Ephah. 11 Woe vnto them that riſe vp earely in the morning, that they may follow ſtrong drink, that continue vntill night, till wine enflame them. 12 And the harpe and the viole, the tabret and pipe, and wine are in their feaſts: but they regard not the worke of the Lord, neither conſider the operation of his hands. 13 Therefore my people are gone into captiuitie, becauſe they haue no knowledge: and their honourable men are famiſhed, aud their multitude dried vp with thirſt. 14 Therefore hell hath enlarged her ſelfe, and opened her mouth without meaſure: and their glory, and their multitude, and their pompe, and hee that reioyceth, ſhall deſcend into it. 15 And the meane man ſhall bee brought downe, and the mightie man ſhall be humbled, and the eyes of the loftie ſhall be humbled. 16 But the Lord of hoſts ſhalbe exalted in iudgement, and God that is holy, ſhall bee ſanctified in righteouſneſſe. 17 Then ſhall the lambes feed after their maner, and the waſte places of the fat ones ſhall ſtrangers eate. 18 Woe vnto them that draw iniquitie with cords of vanitie, and ſinne, as it were with a cart rope: 19 That ſay, Let him make ſpeede, and haſten his worke, that we may ſee it: and let the counſell of the holy one of Iſrael draw nigh and come, that wee may know it. 20 Woe vnto them that call euill good, and good euill, that put darkenes for light, and light for darkeneſſe, that put bitter for ſweete, and ſweete for bitter. 21 Woe vnto them that are wiſe in their owne eyes, and prudent in their owne ſight. 22 Woe vnto them that are mightie to drinke wine, and men of ſtrength to mingle ſtrong drinke. 23 Which iuſtifie the wicked for reward, and take away the righteouſnes of the righteous from him. 24 Therfore as the fire deuoureth the ſtubble, and the flame conſumeth the chaffe, ſo their root ſhall be rottennes, and their bloſſome ſhall goe vp as duſt: becauſe they haue caſt away the Lawe of the Lord of hoſts, and deſpiſed the worde of the Holy One of Iſrael. 25 Therefore is the anger of the Lord kindled againſt his people, and he hath ſtretched foorth his hande againſt them, and hath ſmitten them: and the hilles did tremble, and their carkeiſes were torne in the midſt of the ſtreets: for all this, his anger is not turned away, but his hand is ſtretched out ſtill. 26 And he will lift vp an enſigne to the nations from farre, and wil hiſse vnto them from the end of the earth: and behold, they ſhall come with ſpeed ſwiftly. 27 None ſhalbe weary, nor ſtumble amongſt them: none ſhall ſlumber nor ſleepe, neither ſhall the girdle of their loynes be looſed, nor the latchet of their ſhooes be broken. 28 Whoſe arrowes are ſharpe, and all their bowes bent, their horſes hoofs ſhall bee counted like flint, and their wheeles like a whirlewind. 29 Their roaring ſhalbe like a lyon, they ſhall roare like yong lions: yea they ſhal roare and lay hold of the pray, and ſhall carie it away ſafe, and none ſhall deliuer it. 30 And in that day they ſhall roare againſt them, like the roaring of the ſea: and if one looke vnto the land, behold darkeneſſe and ſorrow, and the light is darkened in the heauens therof.

CHAPTER 6 1 In the yeere that King Uzziah died, I ſaw alſo the Lord ſitting vpon a throne, high and lifted vp, and his traine filled the Temple. 2 Aboue it ſtood the Seraphims: each one had ſixe wings, with twaine he couered his face, and with twaine hee couered his feete, and with twaine hee did flie. 3 And one cryed vnto another, and ſayd; Holy, holy, holy, is the Lord of hoſtes, the whole earth is full of his glory. 4 And the poſts of the doore moued at the voyce of him that cryed, and the houſe was filled with ſmoke. 5 Then ſayd I; woe is me; for I am vndone, becauſe I am a man of vncleane lippes, and I dwell in the midſt of a people of vncleane lippes: for mine eyes haue ſeene the king, the Lord of hoſtes. 6 Then flew one of the Seraphims vnto mee, hauing a liue-cole in his hand, which hee had taken with the tongs from off the altar. 7 And he laide it vpon my mouth, and ſayd, Loe, this hath touched thy lippes, and thine iniquitie is taken away, and thy ſinne purged. 8 Alſo I heard the voyce of the Lord, ſaying; Whom ſhall I ſend, and who will goe for vs? Then I ſaide; Heere am I, ſend me. 9 And he ſayd, Goe and tell this people; Heare yee indeede, but vnderſtand not: and ſee yee indeed, but perceiue not. 10 Make the heart of this people fat, and make their eares heauy, and ſhut their eyes: leſt they ſee with their eyes, and heare with their eares, and vnderſtand with their heart, and conuert and be healed. 11 Then ſayd I; Lord, how long? And hee anſwered, Untill the cities be waſted without inhabitant, and the houſes without man, and the land be vtterly deſolate, 12 And the Lord haue remoued men farre away, and there be a great forſaking in the midſt of the land. 13 But yet in it ſhalbe a tenth, and it ſhall returne, and ſhall be eaten: as a Teyle tree, and as an Oke whoſe ſubſtance is in them, when they caſt their leaues: ſo the holy ſeede ſhall be the ſubſtance thereof.

CHAPTER 7 1 And it came to paſſe in the dayes of Ahaz the ſonne of Iotham, the ſonne of Uzziah king of Iudah, that Rezin the king of Syria, and Pekah, the ſonne of Remaliah king of Iſrael, went vp towards Ieruſalem to warre againſt it, but could not preuaile againſt it. 2 And it was told the houſe of Dauid, ſaying, Syria is confederate with Ephraim: and his heart was moued, and the heart of his people as the trees of the wood are mooued with the wind. 3 Then ſayd the Lord vnto Iſaiah; Goe forth now to meete Ahaz, thou, & Shear-iaſhub thy ſonne, at the end of the conduit of the vpper poole in the high way of the fullers field. 4 And ſay vnto him; Take heede and be quiet: feare not, neither be faint hearted for the two tailes of theſe ſmoking firebrands, for the fierce anger of Rezin with Syria, and of the ſonne of Remaliah. 5 Becauſe Syria, Ephraim, and the ſonne of Remaliah haue taken euill counſell againſt thee, ſaying;6Let vs goe vp againſt Iudah and vexe it, and let vs make a breach therein for vs, and ſet a king in the midſt of it, euen the ſonne of Tabeal.7Thus ſaith the Lord God; It ſhall not ſtand, neither ſhall it come to paſſe.8For the head of Syria is Damaſcus, and the head of Damaſcus is Rezin, and within threeſcore and fiue yeeres ſhall Ephraim be broken, that it be not a people.9And the head of Ephraim is Samaria, and the head of Samaria is Remaliahs ſonne: if yee will not beleeue, ſurely yee ſhall not be eſtabliſhed.10Moreouer the Lord ſpake againe vnto Ahaz, ſaying;11Aſke thee a ſigne of the Lord thy God; aſke it either in the depth, or in the height aboue.12But Ahaz ſayd, I will not aſke, neither will I tempt the Lord.13And he ſayd; Heare yee now, O houſe of Dauid; Is it a ſmall thing for you to wearie men, but will yee wearie my God alſo?14Therefore the Lord himſelfe ſhal giue you a ſigne: Behold, a Uirgine ſhall conceiue and beare a Sonne, and ſhall call his name Immanuel.15Butter and hony ſhall he eat, that hee may know to refuſe the euill, and chooſe the good.16For before the childe ſhall know to refuſe the euill and chooſe the good; the land that thou abhorreſt, ſhalbe forſaken of both her kings.17The Lord ſhall bring vpon thee and vpon thy people, and vpon thy fathers houſe, dayes that haue not come, from the day that Ephraim departed from Iudah; euen the King of Aſſyria.18And it ſhall come to paſſe in that day, that the Lord ſhall hiſſe for the flie, that is in the vttermoſt part of the riuers of Egypt, and for the Bee that is in the land of Aſſyria.19And they ſhall come, and ſhall reſt all of them in the deſolate valleys, and in the holes of the rockes, and vpon all thornes, and vpon all buſhes.20In the ſame day ſhall the Lord ſhaue with a raſor that is hired, namely by them beyond the riuer, by the king of Aſſyria, the head, and the haire of the feet: and it ſhal alſo conſume the beard.21And it ſhall come to paſſe in that day, that a man ſhal nouriſh a yong cow and two ſheepe.22And it ſhall come to paſſe, for the abundance of milke that they ſhall giue, he ſhal eate butter: for butter and hony ſhall euery one eate, that is left in the land.23And it ſhall come to paſſe in that day, that euery place ſhalbe, where there were a thouſand Uines at a thouſand ſiluerlings, it ſhall euen be for briers and thornes.24With arrowes and with bowes ſhall men come thither; becauſe all the land ſhall become briars and thornes.25And on all hilles that ſhalbe digged with the mattocke, there ſhall not come thither the feare of briars and thornes: but it ſhall bee for the ſending foorth of oxen, and for the treading of leſſer cattell.

CHAPTER 81Moreouer the Lord ſaid vnto mee, Take thee a great roule, and write in it with a mans penne, concerning Maher-ſhalal-haſh-baz.2And I tooke vnto mee faithfull witneſſes to record, Uriah the Prieſt, and Zechariah the ſonne of Ieberechiah.3And I went vnto the Propheteſse, and ſhee conceiued and bare a ſonne, then ſaid the Lord to mee, Call his name Maher-ſhalal-haſh-baz.4For before the childe ſhall haue knowledge to cry, My father and my mother, the riches of Damaſcus, and the ſpoile of Samaria ſhalbe taken away before the king of Aſſyria.5The Lord ſpake alſo vnto me againe, ſaying,6For ſo much as this people refuſeth the waters of Shiloah that goe ſoftly, and reioyce in Rezin, and Remaliahs ſonne:7Now therefore behold, the Lord bringeth vp vpon them the waters of the riuer ſtrong and many, euen the king of Aſſyria, and all his glory: and he ſhall come vp ouer all his channels, and goe ouer all his bankes.8And hee ſhall paſſe through Iudah, he ſhall ouerflow and goe ouer, he ſhall reach euen to the necke; and the ſtretching out of his wings ſhall fill the breadth of thy land, O Immanuel.9Aſsociate your ſelues, O ye people, and yee ſhalbe broken in pieces; and giue eare all ye of farre countreys: gird your ſelues, and ye ſhalbe broken in pieces; gird your ſelues, and ye ſhalbe broken in pieces.10Take counſell together, and it ſhall come to nought: ſpeake the word, and it ſhall not ſtand; for God is with vs.11For the Lord ſpake thus to me with a ſtrong hand, and inſtructed me that I ſhould not walke in the way of this people, ſaying,12ſay ye not, A confederacie to all them, to whom this people ſhall ſay, A confederacie; neither feare yee their feare, nor be afraid.13ſanctifie the Lord of hoſtes himſelfe, and let him bee your feare, and let him be your dread.14And he ſhalbe for a ſanctuary; but for a ſtone of ſtumbling and for a rocke of offence to both the houſes of Iſrael, for a ginne, and for a ſnare to the inhabitants of Ieruſalem.15And many among them ſhall ſtumble and fall, and be broken, and be ſnared, and be taken.16Binde vp the Teſtimonie, ſeale the Law among my diſciples.17And I wil wait vpon the Lord that hideth his face from the houſe of Iacob, and I will looke for him.18Behold, I, and the children whom the Lord hath giuen me, are for ſignes, and for wonders in Iſrael: from the Lord of hoſtes, which dwelleth in mount Zion.19And when they ſhall ſay vnto you; Seeke vnto them that haue familiar ſpirits, and vnto wizards that peepe and that mutter: ſhould not a people ſeeke vnto their God? for the liuing, to the dead?20To the Law and to the Teſtimonie: if they ſpeake not according to this word, it is becauſe there is no light in them.21And they ſhall paſſe through it, hardly beſtead and hungry: and it ſhall come to paſſe, that when they ſhall be hungry, they ſhall fret themſelues, and curſe their King, and their God, and looke vpward.22And they ſhall looke vnto the earth: and behold trouble and darkeneſſe, dimneſse of anguiſh; and they ſhall be driuen to darkeneſſe.

CHAPTER 91Neuertheleſſe the dimneſse ſhall not be ſuch as was in her vexation; when at the firſt he lightly afflicted the land of Zebulun, and the land of Naphtali, and afterward did more grieuouſly afflict her by the way of the ſea, beyond Iordan in Galile of the nations.2The people that walked in darkneſſe, haue ſeene a great light: they that dwel in the land of the ſhadow of death, vpon them hath the light ſhined.3Thou haſt multiplied the nation, and not increaſed the ioy: they ioy before thee, according to the ioy in harueſt, and as men reioyce when they diuide the ſpoile.4For thou haſt broken the yoke of his burden, and the ſtaffe of his ſhoulder, the rod of his oppreſsour, as in the day of Midian.5For euery battell of the warriour is with confuſed noiſe, and garments rolled in blood; but this ſhall be with burning and fewell of fire.6For vnto vs a child is borne, vnto vs a Sonne is giuen, and the gouernment ſhalbe vpon his ſhoulder: and his name ſhalbe called, Wonderfull, Counſeller, The mightie God, The euerlaſting Father, The Prince of peace.7Of the increaſe of his gouernment and peace there ſhall be no end, vpon the throne of Dauid & vpon his kingdome, to order it, and to ſtabliſh it with iudgement and with iuſtice, from henceforth euen for euer: the zeale of the Lord of hoſtes will performe this.8The Lord ſent a word into Iacob, and it hath lighted vpon Iſrael.9And all the people ſhal know, euen Ephraim and the inhabitant of Samaria, that ſay in the pride and ſtoutneſse of heart;10The brickes are fallen downe, but we will build with hewen ſtones: the Sycomores are cut downe, but we will change them into Cedars.11Therefore the Lord ſhall ſet vp the aduerſaries of Rezin againſt him, and ioyne his enemies together.12The Syrians before, and the Philiſtines behinde, and they ſhall deuoure Iſrael with open mouth: for all this his anger is not turned away, but his hand is ſtretched out ſtill.13For the people turneth not vnto him that ſmiteth them, neither doe they ſeeke the Lord of hoſtes.14Therefore the Lord will cut off from Iſrael head and taile, branch and ruſh in one day.15The ancient and honourable, hee is the head: and the prophet that teacheth lies, he is the taile.16For the leaders of this people cauſe them to erre, and they that are ledde of them, are deſtroyed.17Therfore the Lord ſhall haue no ioy in their yong men, neither ſhall haue mercy on their fatherleſſe & widowes: for euery one is an hypocrite, and an euil doer, and euery mouth ſpeaketh folly: for all this his anger is not turned away, but his hand is ſtretched out ſtill.18For wickednes burneth as the fire: it ſhall deuoure the briers and thornes, and ſhall kindle in the thickets of the forreſt, and they ſhall mount vp like the lifting vp of ſmoke.19Through the wrath of the Lord of hoſts is the land darkened, and the people ſhall be as the fuell of the fire: no man ſhall ſpare his brother.20And he ſhall ſnatch on the right hand, and be hungry, and he ſhall eate on the left hand, and they ſhall not bee ſatiſfied: they ſhall eate euery man the fleſh of his owne arme.21Manaſſeh, Ephraim: and Ephraim, Manaſſeh: and they together ſhalbe againſt Iudah: for all this his anger is not turned away, but his hand is ſtretched out ſtill.

CHAPTER 101Woe vnto them that decree vnrighteous decrees, and that write grieuouſneſse which they haue preſcribed:2To turne aſide the needy from iudgement, and to take away the right from the poore of my people, that widdowes may be their pray, and that they may robbe the fatherles.3And what wil ye doe in the day of viſitation, and in the deſolation which ſhall come from farre? To whom wil ye flee for helpe? And where will yee leaue your glory?4Without mee they ſhall bowe downe vnder the priſoners, and they ſhall fall vnder the ſlaine: for all this his anger is not turned away, but his hand is ſtretched out ſtill.5O Aſſyrian, the rod of mine anger, and the ſtaffe in their hand is mine indignation.6I will ſend him againſt an hypocriticall nation, and againſt

the people of my wrath will I giue him a charge to take the ſpoile, and
to take the praye, and to tread them downe like the mire of the
ſtreets.7Howbeit he meaneth not ſo, neither doth his heart thinke ſo,
but it is in his heart to deſtroy, and cut off nations not a few.8For he
ſaith, Are not my princes altogether kings?9Is not Calno, as Carchemiſh?
Is not Hamath, as Arpad? Is not Samaria, as Damaſcus?10As my hand
hath found the kingdomes of the idoles, and whoſe grauen images did
excell them of Ieruſalem and of Samaria:11Shall I not, as I haue done
vnto Samaria and her idoles, ſo doe to Ieruſalem and her
idoles?12Wherefore it ſhall come to paſſe, that when the Lord hath
performed his whole worke vpon mount Zion, and on Ieruſalem, I will
puniſh the fruit of the ſtout heart of the king of Aſſyria, and the glory
of his high lookes.13For hee ſaith, By the ſtrength of my hand I haue
done it, and by my wiſedome, for I am prudent: and I haue remooued
the bounds of the people, and haue robbed their treaſures, and I haue
put downe the inhabitants like a valiant man.14And my hand hath found
as a neſt the riches of the people: and as one gathereth egges that are
left, haue I gathered all the earth, and there was none that moued the
wing, or opened the mouth, or peeped.15Shall the axe boaſt it ſelfe
againſt him that heweth therewith? Or ſhal the ſawe magnifie it ſelfe
againſt him that ſhaketh it? as if the rod ſhould ſhake it ſelfe againſt them
that lift it vp, or as if the ſtaffe ſhould lift vp it ſelfe, as if it were no
wood.16Therefore ſhall the Lord, the Lord of hoſts, ſend among his fat
ones leanneſſe, and vnder his glory hee ſhall kindle a burning, like the
burning of a fire.17And the light of Iſrael ſhall bee for a fire, and his
Holy One for a flame: and it ſhall burne and deuoure his thornes and
his briers in one day:18And ſhall conſume the glory of his forreſt, and of
his fruitfull field both ſoule and body: and they ſhall bee as when a
ſtanderd bearer fainteth.19And the reſt of the trees of his forreſt ſhall be
few, that a child may write them.20And it ſhal come to paſſe in that day,
that the remnant of Iſrael, and ſuch as are eſcaped of the houſe of Iacob,
ſhall no more againe ſtay vpon him that ſmote them: but ſhall ſtay vpon
the Lord, the Holy One of Iſrael in trueth.21The remnant ſhall returne,
euen the remnant of Iacob, vnto the mightie God.22For though thy
people Iſrael be as the ſand of the ſea, yet a remnant of them ſhall
returne: the conſumption decreed ſhall ouerflow with
righteouſneſſe.23For the Lord God of hoſtes ſhall make a conſumption,
euen determined in the middeſt of all the land.24Therfore thus ſaith the
Lord God of hoſtes, O my people that dwelleſt in Zion, be not afraide
of the Aſſyrian: he ſhall ſmite thee with a rod, and ſhall lift vp his ſtaffe
againſt thee, after the maner of Egypt.25For yet a very litle while, and
the indignation ſhall ceaſe, and mine anger in their deſtruction.26And
the Lord of hoſtes ſhall ſtirre vp a ſcourge for him, according to the
ſlaughter of Midian at the rocke Oreb: and as his rod was vpon the ſea,
ſo ſhall he lift it vp after the manner of Egypt.27And it ſhall come to
paſſe in that day, that his burden ſhalbe taken away from off thy
ſhoulder, and his yoke from off thy necke, and the yoke ſhalbe deſtroyed
becauſe of the anointing.28He is come to Aiath, hee is paſſed to Migron:
at Michmaſh he hath laid vp his cariages.29They are gone ouer the
paſsage: they haue taken vp their lodging at Geba, Ramah is afraid,
Gebeah of Saul is fled.30Lift vp thy voice, O daughter of Gallim: cauſe
it to bee heard vnto Laiſh, O poore Anathoth.31Madmenah is remooued,
the inhabitants of Gebim gather themſelues to flee.32As yet ſhall hee
remaine at Nob that day: he ſhall ſhake his hand againſt the mount of
the daughter of Zion, the hill of Ieruſalem.33Behold, the Lord, the Lord
of hoſtes ſhall lop the bough with terrour: and the high ones of ſtature
ſhal be hewen downe, and the haughtie ſhalbe humbled.34And he ſhall
cut downe the thickets of the forreſts with yron, and Lebanon ſhall fall
by a mightie one.

CHAPTER 111And there ſhall come forth a rod out of the ſtemme of
Ieſſe, and a branch ſhal grow out of his rootes.2And the Spirit of the
Lord ſhall reſt vpon him, the ſpirit of wiſedome and vnderſtanding, the
ſpirit of counſell and might, the ſpirit of knowledge, and of the feare of
the Lord:3And ſhal make him of quicke vnderſtanding in the feare of
the Lord, and he ſhall not iudge after the ſight of his eyes, neither
reproue after the hearing of his eares.4But with righteouſneſſe ſhall he
iudge the poore, and reprooue with equitie, for the meeke of the earth:
and he ſhall ſmite the earth with the rodde of his mouth, and with the
breath of his lips ſhall he ſlay the wicked.5And righteouſneſſe ſhalbe the
girdle of his loines, and faithfulneſse the girdle of his reines.6The wolfe
alſo ſhall dwell with the lambe, and the leopard ſhall lie downe with the
kid: and the calfe and the yong lion, and the fatling together, and a litle
child ſhall lead them.7And the cow and the beare ſhall feed, their yong
ones ſhall lie downe together: and the lyon ſhall eate ſtraw like the
oxe.8And the ſucking childe ſhall play on the hole of the aſpe, and the
weaned childe ſhall put his hand on the cockatrice denne.9They ſhall not
hurt nor deſtroy in all my holy mountaine: for the earth ſhall bee full of
the knowledge of the Lord, as the waters couer the ſea.10And in that day
there ſhall bee a roote of Ieſſe, which ſhall ſtand for an enſigne of the
people; to it ſhall the Gentiles ſeeke, and his reſt ſhall bee glorious.11And
it ſhall come to paſſe in that day, that the Lord ſhall ſet his hande againe
the ſecond time, to recouer the remnant of his people which ſhalbe left,
from Aſſyria, and from Egypt, & from Pathros, and from Cuſh, and
from Elam, and from Shinar, and from Hamath, and from the ylands of
the ſea.12And he ſhall ſet vp an enſigne for the nations, and ſhall
aſſemble the outcaſts of Iſrael, and gather together the diſperſed of
Iudah, from the foure corners of the earth.13The enuie alſo of Ephraim
ſhal depart, and the aduerſaries of Iudah ſhalbe cut off: Ephraim ſhall
not enuie Iudah, and Iudah ſhall not vexe Ephraim.14But they ſhall fly
vpon the ſhoulderſof the Philiſtines toward the Weſt, they ſhall ſpoile
them of the Eaſt together: they ſhall lay their hand vpon Edom and
Moab, and the children of Ammon ſhall obey them.15And the Lord ſhall
vtterly deſtroy the tongue of the Egyptian ſea, and with his mighty wind
ſhall hee ſhake his hand ouer the riuer, and ſhall ſmite it in the ſeuen
ſtreames, and make men goe ouer dry-ſhod.16And there ſhalbe an high
way for the remnant of his people, which ſhalbe left from Aſſyria; like
as it was to Iſrael in the day that hee came vp out of the land of Egypt.

CHAPTER 121And in that day thou ſhalt ſay, O Lord, I will praiſe thee:
though thou waſt angrie with mee, thine anger is turned away, and thou
comfortedſt me.2Behold, God is my ſaluation: I will truſt, and not be
afraid; for the Lord IEHOVAH is my ſtrength and my ſong, he alſo is
become my ſaluation.3Therefore with ioy ſhall yee draw water out of the
wels of ſaluation.4And in that day ſhall yee ſay; Praiſe the Lord, call vpon
his name, declare his doings among the people, make mention that his
name is exalted.5Sing vnto the Lord; for hee hath done excellent things:
this is knowen in all the earth.6Cry out and ſhout thou inhab

CHAPTER 131The burden of Babylon, which Iſaiah the ſonne of
Amoz did ſee.2Lift yee vp a banner vpon the high mountaine, exalt the
voice vnto them, ſhake the hand, that they may goe into the gates of the
nobles.3I haue commanded my ſanctified ones: I haue alſo called my
mightie ones for mine anger, euen them that reioyce in my
highneſse.4The noiſe of a multitude in the mountaines, like as of a great
people: a tumultuous noiſe of the kingdomes of nations gathered
together: the Lord of hoſtes muſtereth the hoſte of the battell.5They
come from a farre countrey from the end of heauen, euen the Lord and
the weapons of his indignation, to deſtroy the whole land.6Howle yee;
for the day of the Lord is at hand; it ſhall come as a deſtruction from
the Almighty.7Therefore ſhall all hands bee faint, and euery mans heart
ſhall melt.8And they ſhalbe afraid: pangs and ſorrowes ſhall take hold of
them, they ſhalbe in paine as a woman that trauelleth: they ſhalbe
amazed one at another, their faces ſhalbe as flames.9Behold, the day of
the Lord commeth, cruell both with wrath and fierce anger, to lay the
land deſolate; and he ſhall deſtroy the ſinners thereof out of it.10For the
ſtarres of heauen, and the conſtellations thereof ſhall not giue their light:
the ſunne ſhalbe darkened in his going forth, and the moone ſhall not
cauſe her light to ſhine.11And I will puniſh the world for their euill, and
the wicked for their iniquitie; and I will cauſe the arrogancie of the proud
to ceaſe, and will lay low the hautineſse of the terrible.12I will make a
man more pretious then fine gold; euen a man then the golden wedge
of Ophir.13Therefore I will ſhake the heauens, and the earth ſhall
remoue out of her place in the wrath of the Lord of hoſtes, and in the
day of his fierce anger.14And it ſhalbe as the chaſed Roe, and as a ſheepe
that no man taketh vp: they ſhall euery man turne to his owne people,
and flee euery one into his owne land.15Euery one that is found ſhall be
thruſt through: and euery one that is ioyned vnto them, ſhall fall by the
ſword.16Their children alſo ſhalbe daſhed to pieces before their eyes,
their houſes ſhalbe ſpoiled, & their wiues rauiſhed.17Beholde, I will ſtirre
vp the Medes againſt them, which ſhall not regard ſiluer, and as for gold,
they ſhall not delight in it.18Their bowes alſo ſhall daſh the yong men to
pieces, and they ſhall haue no pitie on the fruit of the wombe; their eye

ſhall not ſpare children.19And Babylon the glory of kingdomes, the beautie of the Chaldees excellencie, ſhall be as when God ouerthrew Sodom and Gomorrah.20It ſhall neuer be inhabited, neither ſhall it be dwelt in from generation to generation: neither ſhall the Arabian pitch tent there, neither ſhal the ſhepheards make their fold there.21But wilde beaſtes of the deſert ſhall lye there, and their houſes ſhalbe full of dolefull creatures, and owles ſhall dwell there, and Satyres ſhall daunce there.22And the wilde beaſtes of the Ilands ſhal cry in their deſolate houſes, and dragons in their pleaſant palaces: and her time is neere to come, and her dayes ſhall not be prolonged.

CHAPTER 141For the Lord wil haue mercie on Iacob, and wil yet chooſe Iſrael, and ſet them in their owne land: and the ſtrangers ſhalbe ioyned with them, and they ſhal cleaue to the houſe of Iacob.2And the people ſhall take them, and bring them to their place: and the houſe of Iſrael ſhall poſſeſſe them in the land of the Lord, for ſeruants and handmaides: and they ſhall take them captiues, whoſe captiues they were, and they ſhall rule ouer their oppreſsours.3And it ſhall come to paſſe in the day that the Lord ſhal giue thee reſt from thy ſorrow, and from thy feare, and from the hard bondage wherein thou waſt made to ſerue,4That thou ſhalt take vp this prouerbe againſt the king of Babylon, and ſay; How hath the oppreſsour ceaſed? the golden citie ceaſed?5The Lord hath broken the ſtaffe of the wicked, and the ſcepter of the rulers.6He who ſmote the people in wrath with a continuall ſtroke; hee that ruled the nations in anger, is perſecuted and none hindereth.7The whole earth is at reſt and is quiet: they breake foorth into ſinging.8Yea the firre trees reioyce at thee, and the cedars of Lebanon, ſaying, Since thou art layd downe, no feller is come vp againſt vs.9Hell from beneath is mooued for thee to meet thee at thy comming: it ſtirreth vp the dead for thee, euen all the chiefe ones of the earth; it hath raiſed vp from their thrones, all the kings of the nations.10All they ſhall ſpeake and ſay vnto thee; Art thou alſo become weake as we? art thou become like vnto vs?11Thy pompe is brought downe to the graue, and the noyſe of thy violes: the worme is ſpread vnder thee, and the wormes couer thee.12How art thou fallen from heauen, O Lucifer, ſonne of the morning? how art thou cut downe to the ground, which didſt weaken the nations?13For thou haſt ſaid in thine heart; I wil aſcend into heauen, I wil exalt my throne aboue the ſtarres of God: I wil ſit alſo vpon the mount of the congregation, in the ſides of the North.14I wil aſcend aboue the heights of the cloudes, I wil bee like the moſt High.15Yet thou ſhalt be brought downe to hel, to the ſides of the pit.16They that ſee thee ſhal narrowly looke vpon thee, and conſider thee, ſaying; Is this the man that made the earth to tremble, that did ſhake kingdomes?17That made the world as a wilderneſſe, and deſtroyed the cities thereof that opened not the houſe of his priſoners?18All the kings of the nations, euen all of them lie in glory, euery one in his owne houſe.19But thou art caſt out of thy graue, like an abominable branch: and as the raiment of thoſe that are ſlaine, thruſt through with a ſword, that goe downe to the ſtones of the pit, as a carkeis troden vnder feete.20Thou ſhalt not be ioyned with them in buriall, becauſe thou haſt deſtroyed thy land, and ſlaine thy people: the ſeede of euill doers ſhall neuer be renowmed.21Prepare ſlaughter for his children for the iniquitie of their fathers, that they doe not riſe nor poſſeſſe the land, nor fill the face of the world with cities.22For I will riſe vp againſt them, ſayth the Lord of hoſtes, and cut off from Babylon the name, and remnant, and ſonne and nephew, ſayth the Lord.23I will alſo make it a poſſeſſion for the Bitterne, and pooles of water: and I will ſweepe it with the beſome of deſtruction, ſayth the Lord of hoſtes.24The Lord of hoſtes hath ſworne, ſaying; Surely as I haue thought, ſo ſhall it come to paſſe; and as I haue purpoſed, ſo ſhall it ſtand:25That I will breake the Aſſyrian in my land, and vpon my mountaines tread him vnder foote: then ſhall his yoke depart from off them, and his burden depart from off their ſhoulders .26This is the purpoſe, that is purpoſed vpon the whole earth: and this is the hand that is ſtretched out vpon all the nations.27For the Lord of hoſtes hath purpoſed, and who ſhall diſanull it? and his hand is ſtretched out, and who ſhall turne it backe?28In the yeere that king Ahaz died, was this burden.29Reioyce not thou whole Paleſtina, becauſe the rod of him that ſmote thee is broken: for out of the ſerpents roote ſhall come foorth a cockatrice, and his fruite ſhall be a fierie flying ſerpent.30And the firſt borne of the poore ſhall feed, and the needy ſhall lie downe in ſafetie: and I will kill thy root with famine, and he ſhall ſlay thy remnant.31Howle, O gate, crie, O citie, thou whole Paleſtina art diſſolued, for there ſhal come from the North a ſmoke, and none ſhall bee alone in his appointed times.32What ſhall one then anſwere the meſſengers of the nation? that the Lord hath founded Zion, and the poore of his people ſhall truſt in it.

CHAPTER 151The burden of Moab: becauſe in the night Ar of Moab is laide waſte and brought to ſilence; becauſe in the night Kir of Moab is laide waſte, and brought to ſilence:2Hee is gone vp to Baijth, and to Dibon, the high places, to weepe: Moab ſhall howle ouer Nebo, and ouer Medeba, on all their heads ſhalbe baldneſse, and euery beard cut off.3In their ſtreetes they ſhall girde themſelues with ſackecloth: on the toppes of their houſes, and in their ſtreetes euery one ſhall howle, weeping abundantly.4And Heſhbon ſhall cry, and Elealeh: their voice ſhalbe heard euen vnto Iahaz: therefore the armed ſouldiers of Moab ſhall crie out, his life ſhall be grieuous vnto him.5My heart ſhall cry out for Moab; his fugitiues ſhall flee vnto Zoar, an heifer of three yeeres olde: for by the mounting vp of Luhith with weeping ſhall they goe it vp: for in the way of Horonaim, they ſhall raiſe vp a crie of deſtruction.6For the waters of Nimrim ſhall be deſolate: for the hay is withered away, the graſſe faileth, there is no greene thing.7Therefore the abundance they haue gotten, and that which they haue laide vp, ſhall they cary away to the brooke of the willowes.8For the cry is gone round about the borders of Moab: the howling thereof vnto Eglaim, and the howling thereof vnto Beer-Elim.9For the waters of Dimon ſhalbe full of blood: for I will bring more vpon Dimon, lyons vpon him that eſcapeth of Moab, and vpon the remnant of the land.

CHAPTER 161Send ye the lambe to the ruler of the land from Sela to the wilderneſſe, vnto the mount of the daughter of Zion.2For it ſhalbe that as a wandering bird caſt out of the neſt: ſo the daughters of Moab ſhalbe at the fordes of Arnon.3Take counſell, execute Iudgement, make thy ſhadow as the night in the middeſt of the nooneday, hide the outcaſtes, bewray not him that wandereth.4Let mine outcaſts dwel with thee, Moab, be thou a couert to them from the face of the ſpoiler: for the extortioner is at an end, the ſpoiler ceaſeth, the oppreſsours are conſumed out of the land.5And in mercy ſhall the throne be eſtabliſhed, and hee ſhal ſit vpon it in trueth, in the tabernacle of Dauid, iudging and ſeeking iudgement, and haſting righteouſneſſe.6We haue heard of the pride of Moab (hee is very proud) euen of his hautines, and his pride, and his wrath: but his lies ſhall not be ſo.7Therefore ſhall Moab howle for Moab, euery one ſhal howle: for the foundations of Kir-hareſeth ſhall yee mourne, ſurely they are ſtricken.8For the fieldes of Heſhbon languiſh, and the vine of Sibmah, the lords of the heathen haue broken downe the principall plants thereof, they are come euen vnto Iazer, they wandred through the wilderneſſe, her branches are ſtretched out, they are gone ouer the ſea.9Therefore I wil bewaile with the weeping of Iazer, the Uine of Sibmah I wil water thee with my teares, O Heſhbon, and Elealeh: for the ſhouting for thy Summer fruits, and for thy harueſt, is fallen.10And gladneſſe is taken away, and ioy out of the plentifull field, and in the Uineyards there ſhalbe no ſinging, neither ſhal there be ſhouting: the treaders ſhall tread out no wine in their preſses; I haue made their vintage ſhouting to ceaſe.11Wherefore my bowels ſhal ſound like an harpe for Moab, and mine inward parts for Kir-hareſh.12And it ſhal come to paſſe, when it is ſeene that Moab is weary on the high place, that hee ſhall come to his Sanctuary to pray: but hee ſhall not preuaile.13This is the word that the Lord hath ſpoken concerning Moab ſince that time.14But now the Lord hath ſpoken, ſaying, Within three yeeres, as the yeeres of an hireling, and the glory of Moab ſhalbe contemned, with all that great multitude; and the remnant ſhall be very ſmall and feeble.

CHAPTER 171The burden of Damaſcus: Behold, Damaſcus is taken away from being a citie, and it ſhalbe a ruinous heape.2The cities of Aroer are forſaken: they ſhall bee for flockes, which ſhall lye downe, and none ſhall make them afraid.3The fortreſse alſo ſhall ceaſe from Ephraim, and the kingdome from Damaſcus, and the remnant of Syria: they ſhall bee as the glorie of the children of Iſrael, ſaith the Lord of hoſtes.4And in that day it ſhall come to paſſe, that the glory of Iacob ſhall bee made thinne, and the fatneſſe of his fleſh ſhall waxe leane.5And it ſhall be as when the harueſt-man gathereth the corne, and reapeth the eares with his arme; and it ſhalbe as he that gathereth eares in the valley of Rephaim.6(Yet gleaning-grapes ſhall be left in it, as the ſhaking of an

Oliue tree, two or three berries in the toppe of the vppermoſt bough:
foure or fiue in the out-moſt fruitfull branches thereof, ſaith the Lord
God of Iſrael.7At that day ſhall a man looke to his Maker, and his eyes
ſhall haue reſpect to the Holy one of Iſrael.8And hee ſhall not looke to
the altars, the worke of his handes, neither ſhall reſpect that which his
fingers haue made, either the groues or the images.)9In that day ſhall his
ſtrong cities be as a forſaken bough, and an vppermoſt branch, which
they left, becauſe of the children of Iſrael: and there ſhalbe
deſolation.10Becauſe thou haſt forgotten the God of thy ſaluation, and
haſt not beene mindfull of the rocke of thy ſtrength: therefore ſhalt thou
plant pleaſant plants, and ſhalt ſet it with ſtrange ſlips.11In the day ſhalt
thou make thy plant to grow, and in the morning ſhalt thou make thy
ſeede to flouriſh: but the harueſt ſhall be a heape in the day of griefe,
and of deſperate ſorrow.12Woe to the multitude of many people, which
make a noiſe, like the noiſe of the ſeas; and to the ruſhing of nations,
that make a ruſhing, like the ruſhing of mighty waters.13The nations ſhall
ruſh like the ruſhing of many waters: but God ſhall rebuke them, and
they ſhall flee farre off, and ſhalbe chaſed as the chaffe of the
mountaines before the wind, and like a rolling thing before the
whirlewind.14And behold at euening tide trouble, and before the
morning he is not: this is the portion of them that ſpoile vs, and the lot
of them that robbe vs.
CHAPTER 181Woe to the land ſhadowing with wings, which is beyond
the riuers of Ethiopia:2That ſendeth ambaſſadours by the ſea, euen in
veſſels of bulruſhes vpon the waters, ſaying; Goe yee ſwift meſſengers
to a nation ſcattered and peeled, to a people terrible from their beginning
hitherto, a nation meted out and troden downe; whoſe land the riuers
haue ſpoiled.3All yee inhabitants of the world, and dwellers on the earth,
ſee yee, when hee lifteth vp an enſigne on the mountaines; and when he
bloweth a trumpet, heare yee.4For ſo the Lord ſayd vnto me: I will take
my reſt, and I will conſider in my dwelling place like a cleare heate vpon
herbes, and like a cloud of dew in the heate of harueſt.5For afore the
harueſt when the bud is perfect, and the ſowre grape is ripening in the
flowre; hee ſhall both cut off the ſprigges with pruning hookes, and take
away and cut downe the branches.6They ſhalbe left together vnto the
foules of the mountaines, and to the beaſts of the earth: and the foules
ſhall ſummer vpon them, and all the beaſtes of the earth ſhall winter
vpon them.7In that time ſhall the preſent be brought vnto the Lord of
hoſtes, of a people ſcattered and peeled, and from a people terrible from
their beginning hitherto; a nation meted out and troden vnder foote,
whoſe land the riuers haue ſpoiled, to the place of the name of the Lord
of hoſtes, the mount Zion.
CHAPTER 191The burden of Egypt: Behold, the Lord rideth vpon a
ſwift cloude, and ſhall come into Egypt, and the idoles of Egypt ſhalbe
moued at his preſence, and the heart of Egypt ſhall melt in the midſt of
it.2And I will ſet the Egyptians againſt the Egyptians: and they ſhall fight
euery one againſt his brother, and euery one againſt his neighbour; citie
againſt citie, and kingdome againſt kingdome.3And the ſpirit of Egypt
ſhall faile in the midſt thereof, and I will deſtroy the counſell thereof:
and they ſhall ſeeke to the idoles, and to the charmers, and to them that
haue familiar ſpirits, and to the wizards.4And the Egyptians will I giue
ouer into the hand of a cruell Lord; and a fierce king ſhall rule ouer
them, ſaith the Lorde, the Lord of hoſtes.5And the waters ſhall faile
from the ſea, and the riuer ſhalbe waſted, and dried vp.6And they ſhall
turne the riuers farre away, and the brookes of defence ſhall be emptied
and dried vp: the reeds and flagges ſhall wither.7The paper reeds by the
brookes, by the mouth of the brookes, and euery thing ſowen by the
brooks ſhal wither, be driuen away, and be no more.8The fiſhers alſo
ſhall mourne, and all they that caſt angle into the brookes ſhall lament,
and they that ſpread nets vpon the waters ſhall languiſh.9Moreouer they
that worke in fine flaxe, and they that weaue net-works ſhall be
confounded.10And they ſhall be broken in the purpoſes thereof, all that
make ſluces and ponds for fiſh.11Surely the princes of Zoan are fooles,
the counſell of the wiſe counſellers of Pharaoh is become brutiſh: How
ſay ye vnto Pharaoh, I am the ſonne of the wiſe, the ſonne of ancient
kings?12Where are they? Where are thy wiſe men? and let them tell thee
now, and let them know, what the Lord of hoſts hath purpoſed vpon
Egypt.13The princes of Zoan are become fooles, the princes of Noph
are deceiued, they haue alſo ſeduced Egypt, euen they that are the ſtay
of the tribes thereof.14The Lord hath mingled a peruerſe ſpirit in the
midſt thereof: and they haue cauſed Egypt to erre in euery worke
thereof, as a drunken man ſtaggereth in his vomit.15Neither ſhall there
be any worke for Egypt, which the head or taile, branch or ruſh may
doe.16In that day ſhall Egypt bee like vnto women: and it ſhall be afraid
and feare, becauſe of the ſhaking of the hand of the Lord of hoſts, which
he ſhaketh ouer it.17And the land of Iudah ſhall bee a terrour vnto
Egypt, euery one that maketh mention thereof, ſhal be afraid in himſelfe,
becauſe of the counſell of the Lord of hoſts, which he hath determined
againſt it.18In that day ſhall fiue cities in the land of Egypt ſpeake the
language of Canaan, and ſweare to the Lord of hoſtes: one ſhalbe called
the citie of deſtruction.19In that day ſhall there be an Altar to the Lord
in the midſt of the land of Egypt, and a pillar at the border thereof to
the Lord.20And it ſhall be for a ſigne, and for a witneſſe vnto the Lord
of hoſts in the land of Egypt: for they ſhall crie vnto the Lord, becauſe
of the oppreſſours, and he ſhal ſend them a Sauiour and a great One,
and he ſhall deliuer them.21And the Lord ſhalbe knowen to Egypt, and
the Egyptians ſhal know the Lord in that day, and ſhal do ſacrifice and
oblation, yea they ſhall vow a vowe vnto the Lord, and performe
it.22And the Lord ſhall ſmite Egypt, he ſhall ſmite and heale it, and they
ſhall returne euen to the Lord, and he ſhalbe intreated of them, and ſhall
heale them.23In that day ſhall there be a hie way out of Egypt to Aſſyria,
and the Aſſyrian ſhall come into Egypt, and the Egyptian into Aſſyria,
and the Egyptians ſhall ſerue with the Aſſyrians.24In that day ſhall Iſrael
bee the third with Egypt, and with Aſſyria, euen a bleſſing in the midſt
of the land:25Whom the Lord of hoſts ſhal bleſſe, ſaying, Bleſſed be
Egypt my people, and Aſſyria the work of my hands, and Iſrael mine
inheritance.
CHAPTER 201In the yeere that Tartan came vnto Aſhdod (when
Sargon the king of Aſſyria ſent him) and fought againſt Aſhdod and
tooke it:2At the ſame time ſpake the Lord by Iſaiah the ſonne of Amoz,
ſaying, Go and looſe the ſackcloth from off thy loynes, and put off thy
ſhooe from thy foot: and he did ſo, walking naked and bare foot.3And
the Lord ſaid, Like as my ſeruant Iſaiah hath walked naked and bare
foote three yeeres for a ſigne and wonder vpon Egypt and vpon
Ethiopia:4So ſhall the king of Aſſyria lead away the Egyptians priſoners,
and the Ethiopians captiues, yong and old, naked and bare foote, euen
with their buttocks vncouered, to the ſhame of Egypt.5And they ſhall
be afraid and aſhamed of Ethiopia their expectation, and of Egypt their
glory.6And the inhabitant of this yle ſhall ſay in that day; Behold, ſuch
is our expectation whither we flee for helpe to be deliuered from the
king of Aſſyria: and how ſhall we eſcape?
CHAPTER 211The burden of the deſert of the ſea. As whirlewinds in
the South paſſe thorough; ſo it commeth from the deſert, from a terrible
land.2A grieuous viſion is declared vnto me; The treacherous dealer
dealeth treacherouſly, and the ſpoiler ſpoileth: Goe, vp O Elam: beſiege,
O Media: all the ſighing thereof haue I made to ceaſe.3Therefore are my
loynes filled with paine, pangs haue taken hold vpon me, as the pangs
of a woman that trauelleth: I was bowed downe at the hearing of it, I
was diſmayed at the ſeeing of it.4My heart panted, fearefulneſſe
affrighted me: the night of my pleaſure hath he turned into feare vnto
me.5Prepare the table, watch in the watch-tower, eate, drinke: Ariſe yee
princes, and anoint the ſhield.6For thus hath the Lord ſayd vnto me;
Goe, ſet a watchman, let him declare what he ſeeth.7And he ſaw a charet
with a couple of horſemen, a charet of aſſes, and a charet of camels; and
hee hearkened diligently with much heede.8And he cryed; A lyon: my
Lord, I ſtand continually vpon the watch-tower in the day time, and I
am ſet in my ward whole nights.9And behold, heere commeth a charet
of men with a couple of horſemen: and he anſwered and ſayd; Babylon
is fallen, is fallen, and all the grauen images of her Gods he hath broken
vnto the ground.10O my threſhing and the corne of my floore: that
which I haue heard of the Lord of hoſtes the God of Iſrael, haue I
declared vnto you.11The burden of Dumah. Hee calleth to me out of
Seir: Watchman, what of the night? Watchman, what of the night?12The
watchman ſayd; The morning commeth, and alſo the night: if yee will
enquire, enquire yee: returne, come.13The burden vpon Arabia. In the
foreſt in Arabia ſhall yee lodge, O yee trauelling companies of
Dedanim.14The inhabitants of the land of Tema brought water to him
that was thirſty, they preuented with their bread him that fled.15For they
fled from the ſwords, from the drawen ſword, and from the bent bow,
and from the grieuouſneſſe of warre.16For thus hath the Lord ſayd vnto

me: Within a yeere, according to the yeeres of an hireling, and all the
glory of Kedar ſhall faile.17And the reſidue of the number of archers,
the mighty men of the children of Kedar ſhalbe diminiſhed: for the Lord
God of Iſrael hath ſpoken it.
CHAPTER 221The burden of the valley of viſion. What ayleth thee
now, that thou art wholly gone vp to the houſe toppes?2Thou that art
full of ſtirres, a tumultuous citie, a ioyous citie: thy ſlaine men are not
ſlaine with the ſword, nor dead in battell.3All thy rulers are fled together,
they are bound by the archers: all that are found in thee are bound
together, which haue fled from farre.4Therefore ſayd I; Looke away
from me, I will weepe bitterly, labour not to comfort me; becauſe of the
ſpoiling of the daughter of my people.5For it is a day of trouble, and of
treading downe, and of perplexitie by the Lord God of hoſtes in the
valley of viſion, breaking downe the walles, and of crying to the
mountaines.6And Elam bare the quiuer with charets of men and
horſemen, and Kir vncouered the ſhield.7And it ſhall come to paſſe that
thy choiceſt valleys ſhall be full of charets, and the horſemen ſhall ſet
themſelues in aray at the gate.8And he diſcouered the couering of Iudah,
and thou diddeſt looke in that day to the armour of the houſe of the
forreſt.9Ye haue ſeene alſo the breaches of the citie of Dauid, that they
are many: and ye gathered together the waters of the lower poole.10And
ye haue numbred the houſes of Ieruſalem, and the houſes haue yee
broken downe to fortifie the wall.11Ye made alſo a ditch betweene the
two walles, for the water of the olde poole: but ye haue not looked vnto
the maker thereof, neither had reſpect vnto him that faſhioned it long
agoe.12And in that day did the Lord God of hoſtes call to weeping and
to mourning, and to baldneſse, and to girding with ſackecloth.13And
behold ioy and gladneſſe, ſlaying oxen and killing ſheep, eating fleſh, and
drinking wine; let vs eate and drinke, for to morrow we ſhall die.14And
it was reuealed in mine eares by the Lord of hoſtes; ſurely this iniquitie
ſhall not be purged from you, till yee die, ſayth the Lord God of
hoſtes.15Thus ſayth the Lord God of hoſtes, Goe, get thee vnto this
treaſurer, euen vnto Shebna, which is ouer the houſe, and ſay;16What
haſt thou here? And whom haſt thou here, that thou haſt hewed thee
out a ſepulchre here, as hee that heweth him out a ſepulchre on high,
and that graueth an habitation for himſelfe in a rocke?17Behold; the
Lord will cary thee away with a mightie captiuitie, and will ſurely couer
thee.18He will ſurely violently turne and toſſe thee, like a ball into a large
countrey: there ſhalt thou die, and there the charets of thy glory ſhall be
the ſhame of thy Lords houſe.19And I will driue thee from thy ſtation,
and from thy ſtate ſhall he pull thee downe.20And it ſhall come to paſſe
in that day, that I will call my ſeruant Eliakim the ſonne of Hilkiah:21And
I will clothe him with thy robe, and ſtrengthen him with thy girdle, and
I wil commit thy gouernment into his hand, and he ſhalbe a father to
the inhabitants of Ieruſalem, and to the houſe of Iudah.22And the key
of the houſe of Dauid will I lay vpon his ſhoulder: ſo he ſhall open and
none ſhall ſhut, and he ſhall ſhut and none ſhall open.23And I will faſten
him as a naile in aſure place, and he ſhalbe for a glorious throne to his
fathers houſe.24And they ſhall hang vpon him all the glory of his fathers
houſe, the offſpring and the iſsue, all veſſels of ſmall quantitie: from the
veſſels of cups, euen to all the veſſels of flagons.25In that day, ſayth the
Lord of hoſtes, ſhall the naile that is faſtened in the ſure place, be
remooued, and be cut downe and fall: and the burden that was vpon it
ſhall bee cut off: for the Lord hath ſpoken it.
CHAPTER 231The burden of Tyre. Howle yee ſhips of Tarſhiſh, for it
is laide waſte, ſo that there is no houſe, no entring in: from the land of
Chittim it is reuealed to them.2Be ſtill, yee inhabitants of the yle, thou
whom the merchants of Zidon, that paſſe ouer the ſea, haue
repleniſhed.3And by great waters the ſeede of Sihor, the harueſt of the
riuer is her reuenew, and ſhe is a mart of nations.4Be thou aſhamed, O
Zidon; for the ſea hath ſpoken, euen the ſtrength of the ſea, ſaying; I
trauell not, nor bring foorth children, neither doe I nouriſh vp yong
men, nor bring vp virgines.5As at the report concerning Egypt, ſo ſhal
they be ſorely pained at the report of Tyre.6Paſſe ye ouer to Tarſhiſh,
howle ye inhabitants of the yle.7Is this your ioyous citie, whoſe antiquitie
is of ancient dayes? her owne feete ſhall cary her afarre off to
ſoiourne.8Who hath taken this counſell againſt Tyre the crowning citie,
whoſe merchants are princes, whoſe traffiquers are the honourable of
the earth?9The Lord of hoſtes hath purpoſed it, to ſtaine the pride of all
glory, and to bring into contempt all the honorable of the earth.10Paſſe
through thy land as a riuer O daughter of Tarſhiſh: there is no more
ſtrength.11He ſtretched out his hand ouer the ſea, hee ſhooke the
kingdomes: the Lord hath giuen a commandement againſt the merchant
citie, to deſtroy the ſtrong holdes thereof.12And he ſaid, Thou ſhalt no
more reioice, O thou oppreſſed virgin, daughter of Zidon: Ariſe, paſſe
ouer to Chittim, there alſo ſhalt thou haue no reſt.13Behold, the land of
the Caldeans, this people was not till the Aſſyrian founded it for them
that dwel in the wilderneſſe: they ſet vp the towers thereof, they raiſed
vp the palaces thereof, and he brought it to ruine.14Howle ye ſhips of
Tarſhiſh: for your ſtrength is laid waſte.15And it ſhall come to paſſe in
that day, that Tyre ſhall be forgotten ſeuentie yeeres according to the
dayes of one king: after the end of ſeuentie yeeres ſhall Tyre ſing as an
harlot.16Take an harpe, goe about the city thou harlot, that haſt beene
forgotten, make ſweet melody, ſing many ſongs, that thou mayeſt be
remembred.17And it ſhall come to paſſe after the ende of ſeuentie
yeeres, that the Lord will viſite Tyre, and ſhee ſhall turne to her hire, and
ſhall commit fornication with all the kingdomes of the world vpon the
face of the earth.18And her merchandize and her hire ſhall be holineſſe
to the Lord: it ſhall not be treaſured nor laid vp: for her merchandize
ſhalbe for them that dwell before the Lord, to eate ſufficiently, and for
durable clothing.
CHAPTER 241Behold, the Lord maketh the earth emptie, and maketh
it waſte, and turneth it vpſide downe, and ſcattereth abroad the
inhabitants thereof.2And it ſhall be as with the people, ſo with the prieſt,
as with the ſeruant, ſo with his maſter, as with the maid, ſo with her
miſtreſſe, as with the buyer, ſo with the ſeller, as with the lender, ſo with
the borower, as with the taker of vſurie, ſo with the giuer of vſurie to
him.3The land ſhall be vtterly emptied, and vtterly ſpoiled: for the Lord
hath ſpoken this word.4The earth mourneth and fadeth away, the world
languiſheth and fadeth away, the haughtie people of the earth doe
languiſh.5The earth alſo is defiled vnder the inhabitants thereof: becauſe
they haue tranſgreſſed the lawes, changed the ordinance, broken the
euerlaſting couenant.6Therefore hath the curſe deuoured the earth, and
they that dwell therin are deſolate: therefore the inhabitants of the earth
are burned, and few men left.7The new wine mourneth, the vine
languiſheth, all the merrie hearted doe ſigh.8The mirth of tabrets
ceaſeth, the noiſe of them that reioyce, endeth, the ioy of the harpe
ceaſeth.9They ſhall not drinke wine with a ſong, ſtrong drinke ſhall bee
bitter to them that drinke it.10The city of confuſion is broken downe:
euery houſe is ſhut vp, that no man may come in.11There is a crying for
wine in the ſtreets, all ioy is darkened, the mirth of the land is gone.12In
the citie is left deſolation, and the gate is ſmitten with
deſtruction.13When thus it ſhalbe in the midſt of the land among the
people: there ſhall be as the ſhaking of an oliue tree, and as the gleaning
grapes when the vintage is done.14They ſhal lift vp their voice, they ſhal
ſing, for the maieſty of the Lord, they ſhall crie aloud from the
ſea.15Wherefore, glorifie ye the Lord in the fires, euen the Name of the
Lord God of Iſrael in the yles of the ſea.16From the vttermoſt part of
the earth haue we heard ſongs, euen glory to the righteous: but I ſaid,
My leanneſſe, my leanneſſe, woe vnto me: the treacherous dealers haue
dealt treacherouſly, yea the treacherous dealers haue dealt very
treacherouſly.17Feare, and the pit, & the ſnare are vpon thee, O
inhabitant of the earth.18And it ſhall come to paſſe, that he who fleeth
from the noiſe of the feare, ſhall fall into the pit; and he that commeth
vp out of the midſt of the pit, ſhalbe taken in the ſnare: for the windowes
from on high are open, and the foundations of the earth doe
ſhake.19The earth is vtterly broken downe, the earth is cleane diſſolued,
the earth is moued exceedingly.20The earth ſhall reele to and fro, like a
drunkard, and ſhall be remooued like a cottage, and the tranſgreſſion
thereof ſhall be heauie vpon it, and it ſhall fall, and not riſe againe.21And
it ſhall come to paſſe in that day, that the Lord ſhall puniſh the hoſte of
the high ones that are on high, and the kings of the earth vpon the
earth.22And they ſhalbe gathered together as priſoners are gathered in
the pit, and ſhall be ſhut vp in the priſon, and after many dayes ſhall they
bee viſited.23Then the Moone ſhall be confounded, and the Sunne
aſhamed, when the Lord of hoſts ſhall reigne in mount Zion and in
Ieruſalem, and before his ancients gloriouſly.
CHAPTER 251O Lord, thou art my God, I will exalt thee, I will praiſe
thy Name; for thou haſt done wonderfull things; thy counſels of old are
faithfulneſse and trueth.2For thou haſt made of a citie, an heape; of a

defenced city, a ruine: a palace of ſtrangers, to be no citie, it ſhall neuer be built.3Therefore ſhall the ſtrong people glorifie thee, the city of the terrible nations ſhall feare thee.4For thou haſt bene a ſtrength to the poore, a ſtrength to the needy in his diſtreſſe, a refuge from the ſtorme, a ſhadow from the heat, when the blaſt of the terrible ones is as a ſtorme againſt the wall.5Thou ſhalt bring downe the noiſe of ſtrangers, as the heat in a dry place; euen the heat with the ſhadow of a cloud: the branch of the terrible ones ſhalbe brought low.6And in this mountaine ſhall the Lord of hoſtes make vnto all people a feaſt of fat things, a feaſt of wines on the lees, of fat things full of marrow, of wines on the lees well refined.7And he wil deſtroy in this mountaine the face of the couering caſt ouer all people, and the vaile that is ſpread ouer all nations.8He will ſwallow vp death in victorie, and the Lord God wil wipe away teares from off al faces, and the rebuke of his people ſhall he take away from off all the earth: for the Lord hath ſpoken it.9And it ſhalbe ſaid in that day, Loe, this is our God, we haue waited for him, and he will ſaue vs: this is the Lord, we haue waited for him, we wil be glad, and reioyce in his ſaluation.10For in this mountaine ſhall the hand of the Lord reſt, and Moab ſhalbe troden downe vnder him, euen as ſtraw is troden downe for the doungHill.11And hee ſhall ſpread foorth his hands in the midſt of them, as hee that ſwimmeth ſpreadeth foorth his hands to ſwimme: and hee ſhall bring downe their pride together with the ſpoiles of their hands.12And the fortreſse of the high fort of thy walles ſhall hee bring downe, lay low, and bring to the ground, euen to the duſt.

CHAPTER 261In that day ſhall this ſong bee ſung in the land of Iudah; Wee haue a ſtrong citie, ſaluation will God appoint for walles and bulwarkes.2Open ye the gates, that the righteous nation which keepeth the trueth may enter in.3Thou wilt keepe him in perfect peace, whoſe minde is ſtayed on thee; becauſe he truſteth in thee.4Truſt ye in the Lord for euer: for in the Lord Iehouah is euerlaſting ſtrength.5For hee bringeth downe them that dwell on high, the loftie citie he layeth it low; he layeth it low, euen to the ground, he bringeth it euen to the duſt.6The foote ſhall treade it downe, euen the feete of the poore, and the ſteps of the needie.7The way of the iuſt is vprightneſse: thou moſt vpright, doeſt weigh the path of the iuſt.8Yea in the way of thy Iudgements, O Lord, haue we waited for thee; the deſire of our ſoule is to thy Name, and to the remembrance of thee.9With my ſoule haue I deſired thee in the night, yea with my ſpirit within me will I ſeeke thee early: for when thy iudgements are in the earth, the inhabitants of the world will learne righteouſneſſe.10Let fauour be ſhewed to the wicked, yet will hee not learne righteouſneſſe: in the land of vprightneſse will he deale vniuſtly, and will not behold the maieſtie of the Lord.11Lord, when thy hand is lifted vp, they will not ſee: but they ſhall ſee, and be aſhamed for their enuie at the people, yea the fire of thine enemies ſhall deuoure them.12Lord, thou wilt ordaine peace for vs: for thou alſo haſt wrought all our workes in vs.13O Lord our God, other lordes beſides thee haue had dominion ouer vs: but by thee only will we make mention of thy Name.14They are dead, they ſhall not liue; they are deceaſed, they ſhall not riſe: therefore haſt thou viſited and deſtroyed them, and made all their memory to periſh.15Thou haſt increaſed the nation, O Lord, thou haſt increaſed the nation, thou art glorified; thou hadſt remooued it farre vnto all the ends of the earth.16Lord, in trouble haue they viſited thee: they powred out a prayer when thy chaſtening was vpon them.17Like as a woman with childe that draweth neere the time of her deliuerie, is in paine and cryeth out in her pangs; ſo haue wee beene in thy ſight, O Lord.18Wee haue beene with childe, wee haue beene in paine, we haue as it were brought foorth winde, wee haue not wrought any deliuerance in the earth, neither haue the inhabitants of the world fallen.19Thy dead men ſhall liue, together with my dead body ſhall they Ariſe: awake and ſing yee that dwell in duſt: for thy dewe is as the dewe of herbes, and the earth ſhall caſt out the dead.20Come, my people, enter thou into thy chambers, and ſhut thy doores about thee; hide thy ſelfe as it were for a little moment, vntill the indignation be ouerpaſt.21For behold, the Lord commeth out of his place to puniſh the inhabitants of the earth for their iniquitie: the earth alſo ſhall diſcloſe her blood, and ſhall no more couer her ſlaine.

CHAPTER 271In that day the Lord with his ſore and great and ſtrong ſworde ſhall puniſh Leuiathan the piercing ſerpent, euen Leuiathan that crooked ſerpent, and hee ſhall ſlay the dragon that is in the ſea.2In that day, ſing yee vnto her; A vineyard of red wine.3I the Lord doe keepe it; I will water it euery moment: leſt any hurt it, I will keepe it night and day.4Furie is not in mee: who would ſet the briars and thornes againſt me in battell? I would goe through them, I would burne them together.5Or let him take holde of my ſtrength, that he may make peace with me, and he ſhall make peace with me.6Hee ſhall cauſe them that come of Iacob to take roote: Iſrael ſhall bloſſome and budde, and fill the face of the world with fruite.7Hath hee ſmitten him, as hee ſmote thoſe that ſmote him? or is hee ſlaine according to the ſlaughter of them that are ſlaine by him?8In meaſure when it ſhooteth foorth, thou wilt debate with it: hee ſtayeth his rough winde in the day of the Eaſt winde.9By this therefore ſhall the iniquitie of Iacob be purged, and this is all the fruit, to take away his ſinne: when he maketh all the ſtones of the Altar as chalke ſtones, that are beaten in ſunder, the groues and images ſhall not ſtand vp.10Yet the defenced citie ſhall be deſolate, and the habitation forſaken, and left like a wilderneſſe: there ſhall the calfe feede, and there ſhall he lie downe, and conſume the branches thereof.11When the boughes thereof are withered, they ſhall be broken off: the women come and ſet them on fire: for it is a people of no vnderſtanding: therefore hee that made them will not haue mercie on them, and hee that formed them, will ſhewe them no fauour.12And it ſhall come to paſſe in that day, that the Lord ſhall beate off from the chanell of the riuer vnto the ſtreame of Egypt, and ye ſhall bee gathered one by one, O ye children of Iſrael.13And it ſhall come to paſſe in that day, that the great trumpet ſhall bee blowen, and they ſhall come which were ready to periſh in the land of Aſſyria, and the outcaſts in the land of Egypt, and ſhall worſhip the Lord in the holy mount at Ieruſalem.

CHAPTER 281Woe to the crowne of pride, to the drunkards of Ephraim, whoſe glorious beauty is a fading flowre, which are on the head of the fat valleys of them that are ouercome with wine.2Behold, the Lord hath a mightie and ſtrong one, which as a tempeſt of haile and a deſtroying ſtorme, as a flood of mightie waters ouerflowing, ſhall caſt downe to the earth with the hand.3The crowne of pride, the drunkards of Ephraim ſhall be troden vnder feete.4And the glorious beautie which is on the head of the fat valley, ſhall bee a fading flowre, and as the haſtie fruite before the ſummer: which when he that looketh vpon it, ſeeth it, while it is yet in his hand, he eateth it vp.5In that day ſhall the Lord of hoſts be for a crowne of glory, and for a diademe of beautie vnto the reſidue of his people:6And for a ſpirit of iudgement to him that ſitteth in iudgement, and for ſtrength to them that turne the battell to the gate.7But they alſo haue erred through wine, and through ſtrong drinke are out of the way: the prieſt and the prophet haue erred through ſtrong drinke, they are ſwallowed vp of wine: they are out of the way through ſtrong drinke, they erre in viſion, they ſtumble in iudgement.8For all tables are full of vomite and filthineſse, ſo that there is no place cleane.9Whome ſhall he teach knowledge? and whom ſhall he make to vnderſtand doctrine? them that are weaned from the milke, and drawen from the breaſts.10For precept muſt be vpon precept, precept vpon precept, line vpon line, line vpon line, here a litle, and there a litle.11For with ſtammering lips and another tongue will he ſpeake to this people.12To whom he ſaid, This is the reſt wherwith ye may cauſe the weary to reſt, and this is the refreſhing, yet they would not heare.13But the word of the Lord was vnto them, precept vpon precept, precept vpon precept, line vpon line, line vpon line, here a litle and there a litle: that they might goe and fall backward, and be broken, and ſnared, and taken.14Wherefore heare the worde of the Lord, yee ſcornefull men, that rule this people which is in Ieruſalem.15Becauſe ye haue ſaid, Wee haue made a couenant with death, and with hell are we at agreement, when the ouerflowing ſcourge ſhall paſſe thorow, it ſhall not come vnto vs: for wee haue made lies our refuge, and vnder falſehood haue we hid our ſelues:16Therefore thus ſaith the Lord God, Beholde, I lay in Zion for a foundation, a ſtone, a tryed ſtone, a precious corner ſtone, a ſure foundation: hee that beleeueth, ſhall not make haſte.17Iudgement alſo will I lay to the line, and righteouſneſſe to the plummet: and the haile ſhall ſweepe away the refuge of lyes, and the waters ſhall ouerflow the hiding place.18And your couenant with death ſhalbe diſanulled, and your agreement with hell ſhall not ſtand; when the ouerflowing ſcourge ſhall paſſe thorough, then yee ſhalbe troden downe by it.19From the time that it goeth forth, it ſhall take you: for morning by morning ſhall it paſſe ouer, by day and by night, and it ſhalbe a vexation, onely to vnderſtand the report.20For the bed is ſhorter, then that a man can ſtretch himſelfe

on it: and the couering narrower, then that he can wrap himſelfe in
it.21For the Lord ſhall riſe vp as in mount Perazim, he ſhalbe wroth as
in the valley of Gibeon, that he may doe his worke, his ſtrange worke;
and bring to paſſe his act, his ſtrange act.22Now therefore be yee not
mockers, leſt your bands be made ſtrong: for I haue heard from the Lord
God of hoſtes a conſumption euen determined vpon the whole
earth.23Giue yee eare, and heare my voyce, hearken and heare my
ſpeach.24Doth the plowman plow all day to ſow? doth he open and
breake the clods of his ground?25When hee hath made plaine the face
thereof, doth he not caſt abroad the fitches, and ſcatter the cummin, and
caſt in the principall wheate, and the appointed barly and the rye in their
place?26For his God doth inſtruct him to diſcretion, and doth teach
him.27For the fitches are not threſhed with a threſhing inſtrument,
neither is a cart wheele turned about vpon the cummin: but the fitches
are beaten out with a ſtaffe, and the cummin with a rodde.28Bread corne
is bruiſed; becauſe he will not euer be threſhing it, nor breake it with the
wheele of his cart, nor bruiſe it with his horſemen.29This alſo commeth
forth from the Lord of hoſtes, which is wonderfull in counſell, and
excellent in working.
CHAPTER 291Woe to Ariel, to Ariel the citie where Dauid dwelt: adde
yee yeere to yeere; let them kill ſacrifices.2Yet I will diſtreſſe Ariel, and
there ſhalbe heauineſse and ſorrow; and it ſhall be vnto mee as
Ariel.3And I will campe againſt thee round about, and will lay ſiege
againſt thee with a mount, and I will raiſe forts againſt thee.4And thou
ſhalt bee brought downe, and ſhalt ſpeake out of the ground, and thy
ſpeach ſhall be low out of the duſt, and thy voyce ſhalbe as of one that
hath a familiar ſpirit, out of the ground, and thy ſpeach ſhall whiſper out
of the duſt.5Moreouer the multitude of thy ſtrangers ſhalbe like ſmall
duſt, and the multitude of the terrible ones ſhalbe as chaffe, that paſſeth
away; yea it ſhalbe at an inſtant ſuddenly.6Thou ſhalt bee viſited of the
Lord of hoſtes with thunder, and with earthquake, and great noiſe, with
ſtorme and tempeſt, and the flame of deuouring fire.7And the multitude
of all the nations that fight againſt Ariel, euen all that fight againſt her
and her munition, and that diſtreſſe her, ſhalbe as a dreame of a night
viſion.8It ſhall euen be as when a hungry man dreameth, and behold he
eateth; but he awaketh, and his ſoule is emptie: or as when a thirſtie man
dreameth, and behold he drinketh; but hee awaketh, and behold he is
faint, and his ſoule hath appetite: ſo ſhall the multitude of all the nations
bee, that fight againſt mount Zion.9Stay your ſelues and wonder, cry yee
out, and cry: they are drunken, but not with wine, they ſtagger, but not
with ſtrong drinke.10For the Lord hath powred out vpon you the ſpirit
of deepe ſleepe, and hath cloſed your eyes: the Prophets and your rulers,
the Seers hath hee coured.11And the vſion of all is become vnto you,
as the wordes of a booke that is ſealed, which men deliuer to one that is
learned, ſaying, Reade this, I pray thee: and hee ſaith, I cannot, for it is
ſealed.12And the booke is deliuered to him that is not learned, ſaying,
Reade this, I pray thee: and he ſaith, I am not learned.13Wherefore the
Lord ſaid, Foraſmuch as this people draw neere mee with their mouth,
and with their lips doe honour me, but haue remoued their heart farre
from me, and their feare towards mee is taught by the precept of
men:14Therefore behold, I will proceed to do a marueilous worke
amongſt this people, euen a marueilous worke and a wonder: for the
wiſedome of their wiſe men ſhall periſh, and the vnderſtanding of their
prudent men ſhall be hid.15Woe vnto them that ſeeke deepe to hide their
counſell from the Lord, and their workes are in the darke, and they ſay,
Who ſeeth vs? and who knoweth vs?16Surely your turning of things
vpſide downe ſhall be eſteemed as the potters clay: for ſhall the worke
ſay of him that made it, He made me not? or ſhall the thing framed, ſay
of him that framed it, He had no vnderſtanding?17Is it not yet a very litle
while, and Lebanon ſhall be turned into a fruitful field, and the fruitfull
field ſhall be eſteemed as a forreſt?18And in that day ſhall the deafe heare
the words of the booke, and the eyes of the blind ſhall ſee out of
obſcuritie, and out of darkeneſſe.19The meeke alſo ſhall increaſe their
ioy in the Lord, and the poore among men ſhall reioice in the holy One
of Iſrael.20For the terrible one is brought to nought, and the ſcorner is
conſumed, and all that watch for iniquitie are cut off:21That make a man
an offendour for a word, and lay a ſnare for him that reproueth in the
gate, and turne aſide the iuſt for a thing of nought.22Therefore thus ſaith
the Lord who redeemed Abraham, concerning the houſe of Iacob: Iacob
ſhall not now be aſhamed, neither ſhall his face now waxe pale.23But
when hee ſeeth his children the worke of mine hands in the midſt of
him, they ſhall ſanctifie my Name, and ſanctifie the Holy One of Iacob,
and ſhall feare the God of Iſrael.24They alſo that erred in ſpirit ſhall
come to vnderſtanding, and they that murmured, ſhall learne doctrine.
CHAPTER 301Woe to the rebellious children, ſayth the Lord, that take
counſell, but not of mee; and that couer with a couering, but not of my
Spirit, that they may adde ſinne to ſinne:2That walke to goe downe into
Egypt, (and haue not aſked at my mouth) to ſtrengthen themſelues in
the ſtrength of Pharaoh, and to truſt in the ſhadow of Egypt.3Therefore
ſhall the ſtrength of Pharaoh be your ſhame, and the truſt in the ſhadow
of Egypt, your confuſion.4For his princes were at Zoan, and his
ambaſsadors came to Hanes.5They were all aſhamed of a people that
could not profit them, nor be an helpe nor profite, but a ſhame and alſo
a reproch.6The burden of the beaſtes of the South: into the lande of
trouble and anguiſh, from whence come the yong and old lyon, the
viper, and fierie flying ſerpent, they will carie their riches vpon the
ſhoulderſof yong aſſes, and their treaſures vpon the bunches of camels,
to a people that ſhall not profite them.7For the Egyptians ſhall helpe in
vaine, and to no purpoſe: Therefore haue I cried concerning this: Their
ſtrength is to ſit ſtill.8Now goe, write it before them in a table, and note
it in a booke, that it may bee for the time to come for euer and
euer:9That this is a rebellious people, lying children, children that will
not heare the Law of the Lord:10Which ſay to the ſeers, ſee not; and to
the prophets, Prophecie not vnto vs right things: ſpeake vnto vs ſmooth
things, prophecie deceits.11Get ye out of the way: turne aſide out of the
path: cauſe the Holy one of Iſrael to ceaſe from before vs.12Wherefore,
thus ſaith the Holy one of Iſrael: Becauſe ye deſpiſe this word, and truſt
in oppreſſion and peruerſneſse, and ſtay thereon:13Therefore this
iniquitie ſhalbe to you as a breach ready to fall, ſwelling out in a high
wall, whoſe breaking commeth ſuddenly at an inſtant.14And he ſhall
breake it as the breaking of the potters veſſell, that is broken in pieces,
he ſhall not ſpare; ſo that there ſhall not be found in the burſting of it, a
ſheard to take fire from the hearth, or to take water withall out of the
pit.15For thus ſaith the Lord God, the Holy one of Iſrael, In returning
and reſt ſhall ye be ſaued, in quietneſse and in confidence ſhalbe your
ſtrength, and ye would not:16But ye ſaid; No, for we will flee vpon
horſes; therefore ſhall ye flee. And we will ride vpon the ſwift; therefore
ſhall they that purſue you, be ſwift.17One thouſand ſhall flee at the
rebuke of one: at the rebuke of fiue, ſhall ye flee, till ye be left as a beacon
vpon the top of a mountaine, and as an enſigne on a hill.18And therefore
wil the Lord wait that he may be gracious vnto you, and therefore wil
he be exalted that he may haue mercy vpon you: for the Lord is a God
of Iudgment. Bleſſed are all they that wait for him.19For the people ſhall
dwel in Zion at Ieruſalem: thou ſhalt weepe no more: hee will be very
gracious vnto thee, at the voice of thy cry; when he ſhall heare it, he will
anſwere thee.20And though the Lord giue you the bread of aduerſitie,
and the water of affliction, yet ſhall not thy teachers be remooued into
a corner any more: but thine eyes ſhall ſee thy teachers.21And thine eares
ſhall heare a word behinde thee, ſaying; This is the way, walke ye in it,
when ye turne to the right hand, and when ye turne to the left.22Ye ſhall
defile alſo the couering of thy grauen images of ſiluer, and the ornament
of thy moulten images of gold: thou ſhalt caſt them away as a
menſtruous cloth, thou ſhalt ſay vnto it; Get thee hence.23Then ſhall he
giue the raine of thy ſeed that thou ſhalt ſow the ground withall; and
bread of the increaſe of the earth, and it ſhalbe fat and plenteous: in that
day ſhall thy cattell feed in large paſtures.24The oxen likewiſe and the
yong aſſes that eare the ground, ſhall eate cleane prouender which hath
bene winnowed with the ſhouell and with the fanne.25And there ſhall be
vpon euery high mountaine, and vpon euery high hill, riuers and
ſtreames of waters, in the day of the great ſlaughter when the towers
fall.26Moreouer the light of the Moone ſhalbe as the light of the Sunne,
and the light of the Sunne ſhall be ſeuenfold, as the light of ſeuen dayes,
in the day that the Lord bindeth vp the breach of his people, and healeth
the ſtroke of their wound.27Beholde, the Name of the Lord commeth
from farre, burning with his anger, and the burden thereof is heauy: his
lips are full of indignation, and his tongue as a deuouring fire.28And his
breath as an ouerflowing ſtreame, ſhall reach to the midſt of the necke,
to ſift the nations with the ſieue of vanitie: and there ſhalbe a bridle in
the iawes of the people cauſing them to erre.29Yee ſhall haue a ſong as
in the night, when a holy ſolemnitie is kept, and gladneſſe of heart, as

when one goeth with a pipe to come into the mountaine of the Lord, to the mighty one of Iſrael.[30]And the Lord ſhall cauſe his glorious voice to be heard, and ſhall ſhew the lighting downe of his arme, with the indignation of his anger, and with the flame of a deuouring fire, with ſcattering and tempeſt and haileſtones.[31]For through the voyce of the Lord ſhall the Aſſyrian be beaten downe, which ſmote with a rod.[32]And in euery place where the grounded ſtaffe ſhall paſſe, which the Lord ſhall lay vpon him, it ſhall be with tabrets and harpes: and in battels of ſhaking will he fight with it.[33]For Tophet is ordained of olde; yea, for the king it is prepared, he hath made it deepe and large: the pile thereof is fire and much wood, the breath of the Lord, like a ſtreame of brimſtone, doeth kindle it.

CHAPTER 31[1]Woe to them that go down to Egypt for helpe, and ſtay on horſes, and truſt in charets, becauſe they are many; and in horſemen, becauſe they are very ſtrong: but they looke not vnto the Holy one of Iſrael, neither ſeeke the Lord.[2]Yet he alſo is wiſe, and will bring euill, and wil not call backe his words: but will Ariſe againſt the houſe of the euill doers, and againſt the helpe of them that worke iniquitie.[3]Now the Egyptians are men and not God, and their horſes fleſh and not ſpirit: when the Lord ſhall ſtretch out his hand, both he that helpeth ſhall fall, and hee that is holpen ſhall fall downe, and they all ſhall faile together.[4]For thus hath the Lord ſpoken vnto me; Like as the lyon and the yong lyon roaring on his pray, when a multitude of ſhepheards is called foorth againſt him, he will not be afraid of their voice, nor abaſe himſelfe for the noyſe of them: ſo ſhall the Lord of hoſtes come downe to fight for mount Zion, and for the hill thereof.[5]As birds flying, ſo wil the Lord of hoſtes defend Ieruſalem, defending alſo hee will deliuer it, and paſsing ouer, he will preſerueit.[6]Turne yee vnto him from whom the children of Iſrael haue deeply reuolted.[7]For in that day euery man ſhall caſt away his idoles of ſiluer, and his idoles of gold, which your owne hands haue made vnto you for a ſinne.[8]Then ſhall the Aſſyrian fall with the ſword, not of a mightie man; and the ſword, not of a meane man, ſhal deuoure him: but hee ſhall flee from the ſword, and his young men ſhall be diſcomfited.[9]And hee ſhall paſſe ouer to his ſtrong holde for feare, and his princes ſhall be afraid of the enſigne, ſayth the Lord, whoſe fire is in Zion, and his fornace in Ieruſalem.

CHAPTER 32[1]Behold, a King ſhal reigne in righteouſnes, and princes ſhal rule in iudgement.[2]And a man ſhall be as an hiding place from the winde, and a couert from the tempeſt: as riuers of water in a drie place, as the ſhadow of a great rocke in a wearie land.[3]And the eyes of them that ſee, ſhall not be dimme; and the eares of them that heare, ſhall hearken.[4]The heart alſo of the raſh ſhall vnderſtand knowledge, and the tongue of the ſtammerers ſhall bee readie to ſpeake plainely.[5]The vile perſon ſhall be no more called liberall, nor the churle ſayd to be bountifull.[6]For the vile perſon wil ſpeake villenie, and his heart will worke iniquitie, to practiſe hypocriſie, and to vtter errour againſt the Lord, to make emptie the ſoule of the hungry, and hee will cauſe the drinke of the thirſtie to faile.[7]The inſtruments alſo of the churle are euill: he deuiſeth wicked deuices, to deſtroy the poore with lying wordes, euen when the needie ſpeaketh right.[8]But the liberall deuiſeth liberall things, and by liberall things ſhall hee ſtand.[9]Riſe vp ye women that are at eaſe: heare my voice, ye careleſſe daughters, giue eare vnto my ſpeech.[10]Many dayes and yeeres ſhall ye be troubled, yee careleſſe women: for the vintage ſhall faile, the gathering ſhall not come.[11]Tremble yee women that are at eaſe: be troubled, ye careleſſe ones, ſtrip ye and make ye bare, and gird ſackecloth vpon your loynes.[12]They ſhall lament for the teats, for the pleaſant fieldes, for the fruitfull vine.[13]Upon the land of my people ſhall come vp thornes, and briars, yea vpon all the houſes of ioy in the ioyous citie.[14]Becauſe the palaces ſhall be forſaken, the multitude of the citie ſhall be left, the forts and towres ſhall be for dennes for euer, a ioy of wild aſſes, a paſture of flockes;[15]Untill the ſpirit be powred vpon vs from on high, and the wilderneſſe be a fruitfull field, and the fruitfull field be counted for a forreſt.[16]Then iudgement ſhall dwell in the wilderneſſe, and righteouſneſſe remaine in the fruitfull field.[17]And the worke of righteouſneſſe ſhalbe peace, and the effect of righteouſneſſe, quietneſse and aſsurance for euer.[18]And my people ſhall dwell in a peaceable habitation, and in ſure dwellings, and in quiet reſting places:[19]When it ſhall haile, comming downe on the forreſt; and the citie ſhall be low in a low place.[20]Bleſſed are yee that ſow beſide all waters, that ſend forth thither the feete of the oxe and the aſſe.

CHAPTER 33[1]Woe to thee that ſpoileſt, and thou waſt not ſpoiled; and dealeſt treacherouſly, and they dealt not treacherouſly with thee: when thou ſhalt ceaſe to ſpoile, thou ſhalt bee ſpoiled; and when thou ſhalt make an end to deale treacherouſly, they ſhall deale treacherouſly with thee.[2]O Lord, be gratious vnto vs, we haue waited for thee: be thou their arme euery morning, our ſaluation alſo in the time of trouble.[3]At the noiſe of the tumult the people fled: at the lifting vp of thy ſelfe the nations were ſcattered.[4]And your ſpoile ſhall be gathered like the gathering of the caterpiller: as the running to and fro of Locuſts ſhall he runne vpon them.[5]The Lord is exalted: for hee dwelleth on high, he hath filled Zion with iudgement and righteouſneſſe.[6]And wiſedome and knowledge ſhall be the ſtabilitie of thy times, and ſtrength of ſaluation: the feare of the Lord is his treaſure.[7]Behold, their valiant ones ſhall cry without: the ambaſsadours of peace ſhall weepe bitterly.[8]The high wayes lye waſte; the way faring man ceaſeth: he hath broken the couenant, he hath deſpiſed the cities, he regardeth no man.[9]The earth mourneth and languiſheth: Lebanon is aſhamed and hewen downe: Sharon is like a wildernes, and Baſhan and Carmel ſhake off their fruits.[10]Now will I riſe, ſaith the Lord: now will I be exalted, now will I lift vp my ſelfe.[11]Yee ſhall conceiue chaffe, yee ſhall bring forth ſtubble: your breath as fire ſhall deuoure you.[12]And the people ſhalbe as the burnings of lyme: as thornes cut vp ſhall they be burnt in the fire.[13]Heare yee that are farre off, what I haue done; and yee that are neere, acknowledge my might.[14]The ſinners in Zion are afraid, fearefulneſse hath ſurpriſed the hypocrites: who among vs ſhall dwell with the deuouring fire? who amongſt vs ſhall dwell with euerlaſting burnings?[15]He that walketh righteouſly, and ſpeaketh vprightly, hee that deſpiſeth the gaine of oppreſſions, that ſhaketh his hands from holding of bribes, that ſtoppeth his eares from hearing of blood, and ſhutteth his eyes from ſeeing euill:[16]He ſhall dwell on high: his place of defence ſhalbe the munitions of rocks, bread ſhalbe giuen him, his waters ſhall be ſure.[17]Thine eyes ſhall ſee the king in his beauty: they ſhall behold the land that is very farre off.[18]Thine heart ſhall meditate terrour; Where is the ſcribe? where is the receiuer? where is he that counted the towres?[19]Thou ſhalt not ſee a fierce people, a people of a deeper ſpeech then thou canſt perceiue; of a ſtammering tongue, that thou canſt not vnderſtand.[20]Looke vpon Zion, the city of our ſolemnities: thine eyes ſhall ſee Ieruſalem a quiet habitation, a tabernacle that ſhall not be taken downe, not one of the ſtakes thereof ſhall euer be remoued, neither ſhall any of the coardes thereof be broken.[21]But there the glorious Lord will be vnto vs a place of broad riuers and ſtreames; wherein ſhall goe no galley with oares, neither ſhall gallant ſhip paſſe thereby.[22]For the Lord is our Iudge, the Lord is our Lawgiuer, the Lord is our King, he wil ſaue vs.[23]Thy tacklings are looſed: they could not well ſtrengthen their maſt, they could not ſpread the ſaile: then is the praye of a great ſpoile diuided, the lame take the praye.[24]And the inhabitant ſhall not ſay; I am ſicke: the people that dwel therein ſhalbe forgiuen their iniquitie.

CHAPTER 34[1]Come neere ye nations to heare, and hearken ye people: let the earth heare, and all that is therein, the world, and all things that come forth of it.[2]For the indignation of the Lord is vpon all nations, and his furie vpon all their armies: hee hath vtterly deſtroyed them, he hath deliuered them to the ſlaughter.[3]Their ſlaine alſo ſhalbe caſt out, and their ſtinke ſhall come vp out of their carkeiſes, and the mountaines ſhalbe melted with their blood.[4]And all the hoſte of heauen ſhalbe diſſolued, and the heauens ſhalbe rouled together as a ſcrole: and all their hoſte ſhall fall downe as the leafe falleth off from the Uine, and as a falling figge from the figge tree.[5]For my ſword ſhall bee bathed in heauen: beholde, it ſhall come downe vpon Idumea, and vpon the people of my curſe to iudgement.[6]The ſword of the Lord is filled with blood, it is made fat with fatneſſe, and with the blood of lambes and goates, with the fat of the kidneys of rammes: for the Lord hath a ſacrifice in Bozrah, and a great ſlaughter in the land of Idumea.[7]And the Unicornes ſhall come downe with them, and the bullockes with the bulles, and their land ſhall be ſoaked with blood, and their duſt made fat with fatneſſe.[8]For it is the day of the Lords vengeance, and the yeere of recompences for the controuerſie of Zion.[9]And the ſtreames thereof ſhalbe turned into pitch, and the duſt thereof into brimſtone, and the land thereof ſhall become burning pitch.[10]It ſhal not be quenched night nor day, the ſmoke thereof ſhall goe vp for euer: from generation to generation it ſhall lye waſte, none ſhal paſſe through it for euer and euer.[11]The cormorant and the bitterne ſhall poſſeſſe it, the owle alſo and the rauen ſhall dwell in it, and he ſhall ſtretch out vpon it the line of confuſion, and the ſtones of emptineſſe.[12]They ſhall call the nobles thereof to the kingdome, but none ſhall bee there, and all her Princes ſhall bee nothing.[13]And thornes ſhall come vp in her palaces, nettles and brambles in the fortreſſes thereof: and it ſhalbe an habitation of dragons, and a court for owles.[14]The wilde beaſts of the deſert ſhall alſo meete with the wilde beaſts of the Iland and the ſatyre ſhall cry to his felow, the ſhrichowle alſo ſhall reſt there, & finde for her ſelfe a place of reſt.[15]There ſhall the great owle make her neſt, and lay and hatch, and gather vnder her ſhadow: there ſhall the vultures alſo be gathered, euery one with her mate.[16]Seeke ye out of the booke of the Lord, and reade: no one of theſe ſhall faile, none ſhall want her mate: for my mouth, it hath commaunded, and his ſpirit, it hath gathered them.[17]And he hath caſt the lot for them, and his hand hath diuided it vnto them by line: they ſhall poſſeſſe it for euer, from generation to generation ſhall they dwell therein.

CHAPTER 35[1]The wilderneſſe and the ſolitarie place ſhall be glad for them: and the deſert ſhall reioyce and bloſſome as the roſe.[2]It ſhall bloſſome abundantly, and reioyce euen with ioy and ſinging: the glory of Lebanon ſhal be giuen vnto it, the excellencie of Carmel and Sharon: they ſhall ſee the glory of the Lord, and the excellencie of our God.[3]Strengthen yee the weake hands, and confirme the feeble knees.[4]ſay to them that are of a fearefull heart; Be ſtrong, feare not: behold, your God will come with vengeance, euen God with a recompence, he will come and ſaue you.[5]Then the eyes of the blind ſhall be opened, and the eares of the deafe ſhalbe vnſtopped.[6]Then ſhall the lame man leape as an Hart, and the tongue of the dumbe ſing: for in the wilderneſſe ſhall waters breake out, and ſtreames in the deſert.[7]And the parched ground ſhall become a poole, and the thirſtie land ſprings of water: in the habitation of dragons, where each lay, ſhalbe graſſe with reeds and ruſhes.[8]And an high way ſhalbe there, and away, and it ſhall be called the way of holineſſe, the vncleane ſhall not paſſe ouer it, but it ſhall be for thoſe: the wayfaringmen, though fooles, ſhall not erre therein.[9]No lyon ſhalbe there; nor any rauenous beaſt ſhall goe vp thereon, it ſhall not be found there: but the redeemed ſhall walke there.[10]And the ranſomed of the Lord ſhall returne and come to Zion with ſongs, and euerlaſting ioy vpon their heads: they ſhall obtaine ioy and gladneſſe, and ſorrow and ſighing ſhall flee away.

CHAPTER 36[1]Nowe it came to paſſe in the fourteenth yeere of king Hezekiah, that Sennacherib king of Aſſyria came vp againſt all the defenced cities of Iudah, and tooke them.[2]And the king of Aſſyria ſent Rabſhakeh, from Lachiſh to Ieruſalem, vnto king Hezekiah, with a great armie: and he ſtood by the conduit of the vpper poole in the high way of the fullers field.[3]Then came forth vnto him Eliakim Hilkiahs ſonne, which was ouer the houſe, and Shebna the ſcribe, and Ioah Aſaphs ſonne the Recorder.[4]And Rabſhakeh ſayd vnto them; ſay yee now to Hezekiah; Thus ſaith the great king, the king of Aſſyria; What confidence is this wherein thou truſteſt?[5]I ſay, (ſayeſt thou) (but they are but vaine wordſ) I haue counſell and ſtrength for warre: Now on whom doeſt thou truſt, that thou rebelleſt againſt me?[6]Loe, thou truſteſt in the ſtaffe of this broken reede, on Egypt; whereon if a man leane, it will goe into his hand and pierce it: ſo is Pharaoh king of Egypt to all that truſt in him.[7]But if thou ſay to me; We truſt in the Lord our God: Is it not he, whoſe high places and whoſe altars Hezekiah hath taken away, and ſayd to Iudah and to Ieruſalem; Yee ſhall worſhip before this altar?[8]Now therefore giue pledges, I pray thee, to my maſter the king of Aſſyria, and I will giue thee two thouſand horſes, if thou be able on thy part to ſet riders vpon them.[9]How then wilt thou turne away the face of one captaine of the leaſt of my maſters ſeruants: and put thy truſt on Egypt for charets and for horſemen?[10]And am I now come vp without the Lord againſt this land to deſtroy it? the Lord ſayd vnto me; Goe vp againſt this land and deſtroy it.[11]Then ſayd Eliakim and Shebna & Ioah vnto Rabſhakeh; Speake, I pray thee, vnto thy ſeruants in the Syrian language; for we vnderſtand it: and ſpeake not to vs in the Iewes language, in the eares of the people that are on the wall.[12]But Rabſhakeh ſayd; Hath my maſter ſent me to thy maſter and to thee, to ſpeake theſe words? Hath he not ſent me to the men that ſit vpon the wall, that they may eate their owne dongue, and drinke their owne piſse with you?[13]Then Rabſhakeh ſtood, and cryed with a loud voice in the Iewes language, and ſayd; Heare ye the words of the great king, the king of Aſſyria.[14]Thus ſaith the king; Let not Hezekiah deceiue you, for he ſhall not be able to deliuer you.[15]Neither let Hezekiah make you truſt in the Lord, ſaying; The Lord will ſurely deliuer vs: this citie ſhall not be deliuered into the hand of the King of Aſſyria.[16]Hearken not to Hezekiah: for thus ſayth the King of Aſſyria, Make an agreement with mee by a preſent, and come out to mee: and eate yee euery one of his vine, and euery one of his figgetree, and drinke yee euery one the waters of his owne ciſterne:[17]Until I come and take you away to a land like your owne land, a land of corne and wine, a land of bread and vineyards:[18]Beware leſt Hezekiah perſwade you, ſaying; The Lord will deliuer vs. Hath any of the gods of the nations deliuered his land out of the hand of the king of Aſſyria?[19]Where are the gods of Hamath, and Arphad? where are the gods of Sepharuaim? and haue they deliuered Samaria out of my hand?[20]Who are they amongſt all the gods of theſe landes, that haue deliuered their land out of my hand, that the Lord ſhould deliuer Ieruſalem out of my hand?[21]But they held their peace, and anſwered him not a word: for the Kings commandement was, ſaying; Anſwere him not.[22]Then came Eliakim the ſonne of Hilkiah, that was ouer the houſhold, and Shebna the Scribe, and Ioah the ſonne of Aſaph the Recorder, to Hezekiah with their clothes rent, and tolde him the wordes of Rabſhakeh.

CHAPTER 37[1]And it came to paſſe when King Hezekiah heard it, that hee rent his clothes, and couered himſelfe with ſackecloth, and went into the houſe of the Lord.[2]And hee ſent Eliakim, who was ouer the houſhold, and Shebna the Scribe, and the Elders of the Prieſtes couered with ſackecloth, vnto Iſaiah the Prophet the ſonne of Amoz.[3]And they ſayd vnto him; Thus ſayth Hezekiah, This day is a day of trouble, and of rebuke, and of blaſphemie: for the children are come to the birth, and there is not ſtrength to bring foorth.[4]It may be the Lord thy God will heare the words of Rabſhakeh, whom the king of Aſſyria his maſter hath ſent to reproch the liuing God, and will reprooue the words which the Lord thy God hath heard: wherefore lift vp thy prayer for the remnant that is left.[5]So the ſeruants of King Hezekiah came to Iſaiah.[6]And Iſaiah ſayd vnto them; Thus ſhall yee ſay vnto your maſter, Thus ſayth the Lord, Be not afraid of the wordes that thou haſt heard, wherewith the ſeruants of the king of Aſſyria haue blaſphemed me.[7]Behold, I will ſend a blaſt vpon him, and hee ſhall heare a rumour, and returne to his owne land, and I will cauſe him to fall by the ſword in his owne land.[8]So Rabſhakeh returned and found the king of Aſſyria warring againſt Libnah: for hee had heard that he was departed from Lachiſh.[9]And he heard ſay concerning Tirhakah king of Ethiopia, Hee is come foorth to make warre with thee: and when he heard it, he ſent meſſengers to Hezekiah, ſaying;[10]Thus ſhall ye ſpeake to Hezekiah King of Iudah, ſaying, Let not thy God in whom thou truſteſt deceiue thee, ſaying, Ieruſalem ſhall not bee giuen into the hand of the king of Aſſyria.[11]Behold, thou haſt heard what the kings of Aſſyria haue done to all lands by deſtroying them vtterly, and ſhalt thou be deliuered?[12]Haue the gods of the nations deliuered them which my fathers haue deſtroyed, as Gozan, and Haran, and Rezeph, and the children of Eden which were in Telaſsar?[13]Where is the king of Hamath, and the king of Arphad, and the king of the citie of Sepharuaim, Hena and Iuah?[14]And Hezekiah receiued the letter from the hand of the meſſengers, and read it, and Hezekiah went vp vnto the houſe of the Lord, and ſpread it before the Lord.[15]And Hezekiah prayed vnto the Lord, ſaying,[16]O Lord of hoſtes, God of Iſrael, that dwelleſt betweene the Cherubims, thou art the God, euen thou alone, of all the kingdomes of the earth, thou haſt made heauen and earth.[17]Encline thine eare, O Lord, and heare, Open thine eyes, O Lord, and ſee, and heare all the wordes of Sennacherib, which hath ſent to reproch the liuing God.[18]Of a trueth, Lord, the kings of Aſſyria haue laid waſte all the nations and their countreys,[19]And haue caſt their gods into the fire: for they were no gods, but the work of mens hands, wood and ſtone: therfore they haue deſtroyed them.[20]Now therefore, O Lord our God, ſaue vs from his hand, that all the kingdomes of the earth may knowe, that thou art the Lord, euen thou onely.[21]Then Iſaiah the ſonne of Amoz ſent vnto Hezekiah, ſaying, Thus ſaith the Lord God of Iſrael, Wheras thou haſt prayed to me againſt Sennacherib king of Aſſyria:[22]This is the worde which the Lord hath ſpoken concerning him: The virgin, the daughter of Zion hath deſpiſed thee, and laughed thee to ſcorne, the daughter of

Ieruſalem hath ſhaken her head at thee.[23]Whom haſt thou reproched and blaſphemed? and againſt whome haſt thou exalted thy voice, and lifted vp thine eyes on high? euen againſt the Holy One of Iſrael.[24]By thy ſeruants haſt thou reproched the Lord, and haſt ſaid, By the multitude of my charets am I come vp to the height of the mountaines, to the ſides of Lebanon, and I wil cut downe the tall cedars thereof, and the choiſe firre trees thereof: and I will enter into the height of his border, and the forreſt of his Carmel.[25]I haue digged and drunke water, and with the ſole of my feete haue I dried vp all the riuers of the beſieged places.[26]Haſt thou not heard long agoe, how I haue done it, and of ancient times, that I haue formed it? now haue I brought it to paſſe, that thou ſhouldeſt be to lay waſte defenced cities into ruinous heapes.[27]Therefore their inhabitants were of ſmall power, they were diſmayed and confounded: they were as the graſſe of the field, and as the greene herbe, as the graſſe on the houſe tops, and as corne blaſted before it be growen vp.[28]But I know thy abode, and thy going out, and thy comming in, and thy rage againſt me.[29]Becauſe thy rage againſt me, and thy tumult is come vp into mine eares: therefore will I put my hooke in thy noſe, and my bridle in thy lips, and I will turne thee backe by the way by which thou cameſt.[30]And this ſhall be a ſigne vnto thee, Ye ſhall eate this yeere ſuch as groweth of it ſelfe: and the ſecond yeere that which ſpringeth of the ſame: and in the third yeere ſow ye and reape, and plant vineyards, and eate the fruit thereof.[31]And the remnant that is eſcaped of the houſe of Iudah, ſhal againe take roote downeward, and beare fruite vpward.[32]For out of Ieruſalem ſhall goe forth a remnant, and they that eſcape out of mount Zion: the zeale of the Lord of hoſtes ſhall doe this.[33]Therefore thus ſaith the Lord concerning the king of Aſſyria, He ſhall not come into this citie, nor ſhoot an arrow there, nor come before it with ſhields, nor caſt a banke againſt it.[34]By the way that he came, by the ſame ſhall he returne, and ſhall not come into this citie, ſaith the Lord.[35]For I will defend this citie to ſaue it, for mine owne ſake, and for my ſeruant Dauids ſake.[36]Then the Angel of the Lord went forth, and ſmote in the campe of the Aſſyrians a hundred and foureſcore and fiue thouſand: and when they aroſe earely in the morning, behold, they were all dead corpſes.[37]So Sennacherib king of Aſſyria departed, and went, and returned, and dwelt at Nineueh.[38]And it came to paſſe as hee was worſhipping in the houſe of Niſroch his god, that Adramelech and Sharezer his ſons ſmote him with the ſword, and they eſcaped into the land of Armenia: and Eſarhaddon his ſonne reigned in his ſtead.

CHAPTER 38[1]In thoſe daies was Hezekiah ſicke vnto death: and Iſaiah the Prophet the ſonne of Amoz came vnto him, and ſaid vnto him; Thus ſaith the Lord, Set thine houſe in order: for thou ſhalt die, and not liue.[2]Then Hezekiah turned his face toward the wall, and prayed vnto the Lord,[3]And ſaid, Remember now, O Lord, I beſeech thee, how I haue walked before thee in trueth, and with a perfect heart, and haue done that which is good in thy ſight: and Hezekiah wept ſore.[4]Then came the word of the Lord to Iſaiah, ſaying,[5]Goe and ſay to Hezekiah, Thus ſaith the Lord, the God of Dauid thy father; I haue heard thy prayer, I haue ſeene thy teares: behold, I will adde vnto thy dayes fifteene yeeres.[6]And I will deliuer thee and this citie, out of the hand of the king of Aſſyria: and I will defend this citie.[7]And this ſhall be a ſigne vnto thee from the Lord, that the Lord will doe this thing that he hath ſpoken.[8]Behold, I will bring againe the ſhadow of the degrees which is gone downe in the Sunne-diall of Ahaz ten degrees backward: ſo the Sunne returned ten degrees, by which degrees it was gone downe.[9]The writing of Hezekiah king of Iudah, when he had bene ſicke, and was recouered of his ſickneſe:[10]I ſaide in the cutting off of my dayes; I ſhall goe to the gates of the graue: I am depriued of the reſidue of my yeeres.[11]I ſaid, I ſhal not ſee the Lord, euen the Lord in the land of the liuing: I ſhal behold man no more with the inhabitants of the world.[12]Mine age is departed, and is remoued from me as a ſhepheards tent: I haue cut off like a weauer my life: he will cut mee off with pining ſickneſe: from day euen to night wilt thou make an end of me.[13]I reckoned till morning, that as a Lyon ſo will hee breake all my bones: from day euen to night wilt thou make an end of me.[14]Like a crane or a ſwallow, ſo did I chatter; I did mourne as a doue: mine eyes faile with looking vpward: O Lord, I am oppreſſed, vndertake for me.[15]What ſhall I ſay? hee hath both ſpoken vnto mee, and himſelfe hath done it: I ſhall goe ſoftly, all my yeeres in the bitterneſe of my ſoule.[16]O Lord, by theſe things men liue: and in all theſe things is the life of my ſpirit, ſo wilt thou recouer me, and make me to liue.[17]Behold, for peace I had great bitterneſe, but thou haſt in loue to my ſoule deliuered it from the pit of corruption: for thou haſt caſt all my ſinnes behinde thy backe.[18]For the graue cannot praiſe thee, death cannot celebrate thee: they that goe downe into the pit cannot hope for thy trueth.[19]The liuing, the liuing, hee ſhall praiſe thee, as I doe this day: the father to the children ſhall make knowen thy trueth.[20]The Lord was ready to ſaue me: therefore we will ſing my ſongs to the ſtringed inſtruments, all the dayes of our life, in the houſe of the Lord.[21]For Iſaiah had ſaid, Let them take a lumpe of figges, and lay it for a plaiſter vpon the boile, and he ſhall recouer.[22]Hezekiah alſo had ſaid, what is the ſigne, that I ſhall goe vp to the houſe of the Lord ?

CHAPTER 39[1]At that time Merodach Baladan the ſonne of Baladan king of Babylon, ſent letters and a preſent to Hezekiah: for hee had heard that he had bene ſicke, and was recouered.[2]And Hezekiah was glad of them, and ſhewed them the houſe of his precious things, the ſiluer, and the golde, and the ſpices, and the precious oyntment, and all the houſe of his armour, and all that was found in his treaſures: there was nothing in his houſe, nor in all his dominion, that Hezekiah ſhewed them not.[3]Then came Iſaiah the Prophet vnto King Hezekiah, and ſayde vnto him, What ſayd theſe men? and from whence came they vnto thee? And Hezekiah ſaid, They are come from a farre countrey vnto me, euen from Babylon.[4]Then ſaid hee, What haue they ſeene in thine houſe? And Hezekiah anſwered, All that is in mine houſe haue they ſeene: there is nothing among my treaſures, that I haue not ſhewed them.[5]Then ſayde Iſaiah to Hezekiah, Heare the word of the Lord of hoſtes.[6]Behold, the dayes come, that all that is in thine houſe, and that which thy fathers haue laide vp in ſtore, vntill this day, ſhalbe caried to Babylon: nothing ſhalbe left, ſaith the Lord.[7]And of thy ſonnes that ſhall iſſue from thee, which thou ſhalt beget, ſhall they take away; and they ſhall bee Eunuches in the palace of the king of Babylon.[8]Then ſayde Hezekiah to Iſaiah, Good is the word of the Lord which thou haſt ſpoken: hee ſayd moreouer, For there ſhalbe peace and trueth in my dayes.

CHAPTER 40[1]Comfort ye, comfort ye my people, ſayth your God.[2]Speake ye comfortably to Ieruſalem, and cry vnto her, that her warrefare is accompliſhed, that her iniquitie is pardoned: for ſhee hath receiued of the Lords hand double for all her ſinnes.[3]The voyce of him that cryeth in the wilderneſſe, Prepare yee the way of the Lord, make ſtraight in the deſert a high way for our God.[4]Euery valley ſhalbe exalted, and euery mountaine and hill ſhalbe made low: and the crooked ſhall be made ſtraight, and the rough places plaine.[5]And the glory of the Lord ſhall be reuealed, and all fleſh ſhall ſee it together: for the mouth of the Lord hath ſpoken it.[6]The voyce ſayd; Cry. And hee ſayd; What ſhall I cry? All fleſh is graſſe, and all the goodlineſſe thereof is as the flowre of the field.[7]The graſſe withereth, the flowre fadeth; becauſe the ſpirit of the Lord bloweth vpon it: ſurely the people is graſſe.[8]The graſſe withereth, the flowre fadeth: but the word of our God ſhall ſtand for euer.[9]O Zion, that bringeſt good tydings, get thee vp into the high mountaine: O Ieruſalem, that bringeſt good tidings, lift vp thy voyce with ſtrength, lift it vp, be not afraid: ſay vnto the cities of Iudah; Behold your God.[10]Behold, the Lord God will come with ſtrong hand, and his arme ſhall rule for him: behold, his reward is with him, and his worke before him.[11]He ſhall feede his flocke like a ſhepheard: he ſhall gather the lambes with his arme; and carie them in his boſome, and ſhall gently lead thoſe that are with yoong.[12]Who hath meaſured the waters in the hollow of his hand? and meted out heauen with the ſpanne, and comprehended the duſt of the earth in a meaſure, and weighed the mountaines in ſcales, and the hilles in a balance?[13]Who hath directed the ſpirit of the Lord, or, being his counſeller, hath taught him?[14]With whom tooke he counſell, and who inſtructed him, and taught him in the path of iudgement? and taught him knowledge, and ſhewed to him the way of vnderſtanding?[15]Behold, the nations are as a drop of a bucket, and are counted as the ſmall duſt of the balance: behold, hee taketh vp the yles as a very litle thing.[16]And Lebanon is not ſufficient to burne, nor the beaſts thereof ſufficient for a burnt offring.[17]All nations before him are as nothing, and they are counted to him leſſe then nothing, and vanitie.[18]To whom then will ye liken God? or what likeneſſe will ye compare vnto him?[19]The workeman melteth a grauen image, and the goldſmith ſpreadeth it ouer with golde, and caſteth ſiluer chaines.[20]He that is ſo impoueriſhed that he hath no oblation, chooſeth a tree that will not rot; he ſeeketh vnto him a cunning workeman, to prepare a grauen image that ſhall not be mooued.[21]Haue yee not knowen? haue yee not heard? hath it not beene tolde you from the beginning? haue yee not vnderſtood from the foundations of the earth?[22]It is he that ſitteth vpon the circle of the earth, and the inhabitants thereof are as graſhoppers; that ſtretcheth out the heauens as a curtaine, and ſpreadeth them out as a tent to dwel in:[23]That bringeth the princes to nothing; hee maketh the Iudges of the earth as vanitie.[24]Yea they ſhal not be planted, yea they ſhall not be ſowen, yea their ſtocke ſhall not take roote in the earth: and he ſhall alſo blow vpon them, & they ſhall wither, and the whirlewinde ſhall take them away as ſtubble.[25]To whom then will ye liken me, or ſhal I be equall, ſaith the Holy One?[26]Lift vp your eyes on high, and behold who hath created theſe things, that bringeth out their hoſt by number: he calleth them all by names, by the greatneſſe of his might, for that hee is ſtrong in power, not one faileth.[27]Why ſayeſt thou, O Iacob, and ſpeakeſt O Iſrael, My way is hid from the Lord, and my iudgement is paſſed ouer from my God?[28]Haſt thou not knowen? haſt thou not heard, that the euerlaſting God, the Lord, the Creatour of the ends of the earth, fainteth not, neither is wearie? there is no ſearching of his vnderſtanding.[29]He giueth power to the faint, and to them that haue no might, he increaſeth ſtrength.[30]Euen the youths ſhall faint, and be weary, and the yong men ſhall vtterly fall.[31]But they that waite vpon the Lord, ſhall renew their ſtrength: they ſhall mount vp with wings as Eagles, they ſhal runne and not be weary, and they ſhall walke, and not faint.

CHAPTER 41[1]Keepe ſilence before me, O ylands, and let the people renew their ſtrength: let them come neere, then let them ſpeake: let vs come neere together to iudgement.[2]Who raiſed vp the righteous man from the Eaſt, called him to his foote, gaue the nations before him, and made him rule ouer kings? Hee gaue them as the duſt to his ſword, and as driuen ſtuble to his bow.[3]He purſued them, and paſſed ſafely; euen by the way, that hee had not gone with his feete.[4]Who hath wrought and done it, calling the generations from the beginning? I the Lord the firſt, and with the laſt, I am he.[5]The yles ſaw it and feared, the ends of the earth were afraid, drew neere, and came.[6]They helped euery one his neighbour, and euery one ſayd to his brother, Be of good courage.[7]So the carpenter encouraged the goldſmith, and he that ſmootheth with the hammer him that ſmote the anuill, ſaying; It is ready for the ſodering: and he faſtened it with nayles that it ſhould not be moued.[8]But thou Iſrael, art my ſeruant, Iacob whom I haue choſen, the ſeede of Abraham my friend.[9]Thou whom I haue taken from the ends of the earth, and called thee from the chiefe men thereof, and ſayd vnto thee; Thou art my ſeruant, I haue choſen thee, and not caſt thee away.[10]Feare thou not, for I am with thee: be not diſmaied, for I am thy God: I will ſtrengthen thee, yea I will helpe thee, yea I will vphold thee with the right hand of my righteouſneſſe.[11]Behold, all they that were incenſed againſt thee, ſhalbe aſhamed and confounded: they ſhall be as nothing, and they that ſtriue with thee, ſhall periſh.[12]Thou ſhalt ſeeke them, and ſhalt not find them, euen them that contended with thee: they that warre againſt thee ſhalbe as nothing, and as a thing of nought.[13]For I the Lord thy God will hold thy right hand, ſaying vnto thee, Feare not, I will helpe thee.[14]Feare not, thou worme Iacob, and ye men of Iſrael: I will helpe thee, ſaith the Lord, and thy Redeemer, the Holy One of Iſrael.[15]Behold, I will make thee a new ſharpe threſhing inſtrument hauing teeth: thou ſhalt threſh the mountaines, and beate them ſmall, and ſhalt make the hilles as chaffe.[16]Thou ſhalt fanne them, and the winde ſhall carie them away, and the whirlewinde ſhall ſcatter them: and thou ſhalt reioyce in the Lord, and ſhalt glory in the Holy One of Iſrael.[17]When the poore and needie ſeeke water and there is none, and their tongue faileth for thirſt, I the Lord will heare them, I the God of Iſrael will not forſake them.[18]I will open riuers in hie places, and fountaines in the midſt of the valleys: I will make the wilderneſſe a poole of water, and the dry land ſprings of water.[19]I will plant in the wildernes the Cedar, the Shittah tree, and the Myrtle, and the Oyle tree: I will ſet in the deſert the Firre tree, and the Pine and the Boxe tree together:[20]That they may ſee, and knowe, and conſider, and vnderſtand together, that the hand of the Lord hath done this, and the Holy One of Iſrael hath created it.[21]Produce your cauſe, ſaith the Lord, bring foorth your ſtrong reaſons, ſaith the King of Iacob.[22]Let them bring them foorth, and ſhew vs what ſhall happen: let them ſhew the former things what they bee, that we may conſider them, and know the latter end of them, or declare vs things for to come.[23]Shewe the things that are to come hereafter, that wee may knowe that ye are gods: yea doe good or doe euill, that we may be diſmayed, and behold it together.[24]Behold, ye are of nothing, and your worke of nought: an abomination is he that chooſeth you.[25]I haue raiſed vp one from the North, and he ſhall come: from the riſing of the Sunne ſhall he call vpon my name, and he ſhall come vpon princes as vpon morter, and as the potter treadeth clay.[26]Who hath declared from the beginning, that we may know? and before time, that we may ſay, He is righteous? yea there is none that ſheweth, yea there is none that declareth, yea there is none that heareth your words.[27]The firſt ſhall ſay to Zion, Behold, behold them, and I will giue to Ieruſalem one that bringeth good tidings.[28]For I beheld, and there was no man, euen amongſt them, and there was no counſeller, that when I aſked of them, could anſwere a word.[29]Behold, they are all vanitie, their works are nothing: their moulten images are winde and confuſion.

CHAPTER 42[1]Behold my ſeruant whome I vphold, mine elect in whom my ſoule delighteth: I haue put my Spirit vpon him, he ſhall bring forth iudgement to the Gentiles.[2]Hee ſhall not crie, nor lift vp, nor cauſe his voyce to bee heard in the ſtreete.[3]A bruiſed reed ſhall he not breake, and the ſmoking flaxe ſhall hee not quench: he ſhall bring forth iudgment vnto trueth.[4]He ſhall not faile nor be diſcouraged, till he haue ſet iudgement in the earth: and the yles ſhall waite for his lawe.[5]Thus ſaith God the Lord, he that created the heauens, and ſtretched them out, he that ſpread foorth the earth and that which commeth out of it, he that giueth breath vnto the people vpon it, and ſpirit to them that walke therein:[6]I the Lord haue called thee in righteouſnes, and wil hold thine hand, and will keepe thee, and giue thee for a couenant of the people, for a light of the Gentiles:[7]To open the blind eyes, to bring out the priſoners from the priſon, and them that ſit in darkeneſſe out of the priſon houſe.[8]I am the Lord; that is my name, and my glory will I not giue to another, neither my praiſe to grauen images.[9]Behold, the former things are come to paſſe, and new things doe I declare: before they ſpring forth I tell you of them.[10]Sing vnto the Lord a newe ſong, and his praiſe from the end of the earth: yee that goe downe to the ſea, and all that is therein; the yles, and the inhabitants thereof.[11]Let the wildernes and the cities thereof lift vp their voyce, the villages that Kedar doeth inhabite: let the inhabitants of the rocke ſing, let them ſhoute from the top of the mountaines.[12]Let them giue glory vnto the Lord, and declare his praiſe in the Ilands.[13]The Lord ſhall goe foorth as a mighty man, he ſhall ſtirre vp iealouſie like a man of warre: he ſhall cry, yea roare; hee ſhall preuaile againſt his enemies.[14]I haue long time holden my peace, I haue bene ſtill and refrained my ſelfe: now wil I cry like a trauailing woman, I will deſtroy and deuoure at once.[15]I will make waſte mountaines and hilles, and dry vp all their herbes, and I will make the riuers Ilands, and I will dry vp the pooles.[16]And I will bring the blinde by a way that they knew not, I will lead them in pathes that they haue not knowen: I wil make darkeneſſe light before them, and crooked things ſtraight. Theſe things will I doe vnto them, and not forſake them.[17]They ſhall be turned backe, they ſhalbe greatly aſhamed, that truſt in grauen images, that ſay to the moulten images; Ye are our gods.[18]Heare ye deafe, and looke ye blinde that ye may ſee.[19]Who is blinde, but my ſeruant? or deafe, as my meſſenger that I ſent? who is blinde as he that is perfit, and blinde as the Lords ſeruant?[20]Seeing many things, but thou obſerueſt not: opening the eares, but he heareth not.[21]The Lord is well pleaſed for his righteouſnes ſake, he will magnifie the Law, and make it honourable.[22]But this is a people robbed and ſpoiled, they are all of them ſnared in holes, and they are hid in priſon houſes: they are for a praye, & none deliuereth; for a ſpoile, and none ſaith, Reſtore.[23]Who among you will giue eare to this? who will hearken, and heare for the time to come?[24]Who gaue Iacob for a ſpoile, and Iſrael to the robbers? Did not the Lord, hee, againſt whom wee haue ſinned? For they would not walke in his wayes, neither were they obedient vnto his Law.[25]Therefore he hath powred vpon him the furie of his anger, and the ſtrength of battell: and it hath ſet him on fire round about, yet hee knew not; and it burned him, yet hee layed it not to heart.

CHAPTER 43[1]But now thus ſayeth the Lord that created thee, O Iacob, and hee that formed thee, O Iſrael; Feare not: for I haue redeemed thee, I haue called thee by thy name, thou art mine.[2]When thou paſſeſt through the waters, I wil be with thee; and through the riuers, they ſhal not ouerflow thee: when thou walkeſt through the fire, thou ſhalt not be burnt; neither ſhall the flame kindle vpon thee.3For I am the Lord thy God, the Holy one of Iſrael, thy Sauiour: I gaue Egypt for thy ranſome, Ethiopia and Seba for thee.4Since thou waſt precious in my ſight, thou haſt bene honourable, and I haue loued thee: therefore will I giue men for thee, and people for thy life.5Feare not, for I am with thee: I will bring thy ſeed from the Eaſt, and gather thee from the Weſt.6I wil ſay to the North, Giue vp; and to the South, Keepe not backe: bring my ſonnes from farre, and my daughters from the ends of the earth;7Euen euery one that is called by my Name: for I haue created him for my glory, I haue formed him, yea I haue made him.8Bring foorth the blinde people, that haue eyes; and the deafe that haue eares.9Let all the nations be gathered together, and let the people be aſſembled: who among them can declare this, and ſhew vs former things? let them bring foorth their witneſſes, that they may be iuſtified: or let them heare, and ſay, It is trueth.10Yee are my witneſſes, ſaith the Lord, and my ſeruant whom I haue choſen: that ye may know and beleeue me, and vnderſtand that I am he: before me there was no God formed, neither ſhall there be after me.11I, euen I am the Lord, and beſide me there is no Sauiour.12I haue declared, and haue ſaued, and I haue ſhewed, when there was no ſtrange God among you: therefore yee are my witneſſes, ſaith the Lord, that I am God.13Yea before the day was, I am hee; and there is none that can deliuer out of my hand: I will worke, and who ſhall let it?14Thus ſayth the Lord your Redeemer, the Holy one of Iſrael; For your ſake I haue ſent to Babylon, and haue brought downe all their nobles, and the Caldeans, whoſe crie is in the ſhippes.15I am the Lord, your Holy one, the Creatour of Iſrael, your King.16Thus ſayth the Lord, which maketh a way in the ſea, and a path in the mightie waters:17Which bringeth foorth the charet and horſe, the armie and the power: they ſhall lie downe together, they ſhall not riſe: they are extinct, they are quenched as towe.18Remember yee not the former things, neither conſider the things of olde.19Behold, I will doe a new thing: now it ſhall ſpring foorth, ſhall yee not know it? I will euen make a way in the wilderneſſe, and riuers in the deſert.20The beaſt of the field ſhall honor mee, the dragons and the owles, becauſe I giue waters in the wilderneſſe, and riuers in the deſert, to giue drinke to my people, my choſen.21This people haue I formed for my ſelfe, they ſhall ſhewe foorth my praiſe.22But thou haſt not called vpon me, O Iacob, but thou haſt beene wearie of me, O Iſrael.23Thou haſt not brought mee the ſmall cattell of thy burnt offrings, neither haſt thou honoured mee with thy ſacrifices. I haue not cauſed thee to ſerue with an offring, nor wearied thee with incenſe.24Thou haſt bought mee no ſweete cane with money, neither haſt thou filled mee with the fat of thy ſacrifices: but thou haſt made mee to ſerue with thy ſins, thou haſt wearied mee with thine iniquities.25I, euen I am hee that blotteth out thy tranſgreſſions for mine owne ſake, and will not remember thy ſinnes.26Put mee in remembrance: let vs plead together: declare thou, that thou mayeſt bee iuſtified.27Thy firſt father hath ſinned, and thy teachers haue tranſgreſſed againſt mee.28Therefore I haue profaned the princes of the Sanctuarie, and haue giuen Iacob to the curſe, and Iſrael to reproches.

CHAPTER 441Yet now heare, O Iacob my ſeruant, and Iſrael whom I haue choſen.2Thus ſayeth the Lord that made thee, and formed thee from the wombe, which wil helpe thee: Feare not, O Iacob, my ſeruant, and thou Ieſurun, whom I haue choſen.3For I will powre water vpon him that is thirſtie, and floods vpon the dry ground: I will powre my ſpirit vpon thy ſeede, and my bleſſing vpon thine offſpring:4And they ſhall ſpring vp as among the graſſe, as willowes by the water courſes.5One ſhall ſay, I am the Lords: and another ſhall call himſelfe by the name of Iacob: and another ſhall ſubſcribe with his hand vnto the Lord, and ſurname himſelfe by the name of Iſrael.6Thus ſaith the Lord the king of Iſrael and his redeemer the Lord of hoſtes, I am the firſt, and I am the laſt, and beſides me there is no God.7And who, as I, ſhall call, and ſhall declare it, and ſet it in order for me, ſince I appointed the ancient people? and the things that are comming, and ſhall come? let them ſhew vnto them.8Feare yee not, neither be afraid: haue not I told thee from that time, and haue declared it? yee are euen my witneſſes. Is there a God beſides me? yea there is no God, I know not any.9They that make a grauen image are all of them vanitie, and their delectable things ſhall not profit, and they are their owne witneſſes, they ſee not, nor know; that they may be aſhamed.10Who hath formed a God, or moulten a grauen image that is profitable for nothing?11Behold, all his fellowes ſhall be aſhamed: and the workemen, they are of men: let them all be gathered together, let them ſtand vp; yet they ſhal feare, and they ſhalbe aſhamed together.12The ſmith with the tonges both worketh in the coales, and faſhioneth it with hammers, and worketh it with the ſtrength of his armes: yea he is hungrie, and his ſtrength faileth; hee drinketh no water, and is faint.13The carpenter ſtretcheth out his rule: he maketh it out with the line: he fitteth it with planes, and he marketh it out with the compaſſe, and maketh it after the figure of a man, according to the beautie of a man; that it may remaine in the houſe.14He heweth him downe cedars, and taketh the Cypreſse and the Oke, which he ſtrengthneth for himſelfe among the trees of the forreſt: he planteth an Aſhe, and the raine doth nouriſh it.15Then ſhall it bee for a man to burne: for hee will take thereof and warme himſelfe; yea he kindleth it and baketh bread; yea he maketh a God, and worſhippeth it: he maketh it a grauen image, and falleth downe thereto.16He burneth part thereof in the fire: with part thereof he eateth fleſh: he roſteth roſt, and is ſatiſfied: yea hee warmeth himſelfe, and ſaith; Aha, I am warme, I haue ſeene the fire.17And the reſidue thereof he maketh a God, euen his grauen image: hee falleth downe vnto it, and worſhippeth it, and prayeth vnto it, and ſaith; Deliuer me, for thou art my God.18They haue not knowen, nor vnderſtood: for he hath ſhut their eyes, that they cannot ſee; and their hearts, that they cannot vnderſtand.19And none conſidereth in his heart, neither is there knowledge nor vnderſtanding to ſay; I haue burnt part of it in the fire, yea alſo I haue baked bread vpon the coales thereof: I haue roſted fleſh and eaten it; and ſhall I make the reſidue thereof an abomination? ſhall I fall downe to the ſtocke of a tree?20He feedeth of aſhes: a deceiued heart hath turned him aſide, that he cannot deliuer his ſoule, nor ſay; Is there not a lie in my right hand?21Remember theſe (O Iacob and Iſrael) for thou art my ſeruant: I haue formed thee: thou art my ſeruant, O Iſrael; thou ſhalt not be forgotten of me.22I haue blotted out, as a thicke cloude, thy tranſgreſſions, and as a a cloud, thy ſinnes: returne vnto me, for I haue redeemed thee.23Sing, O yee heauens; for the Lord hath done it: ſhout yee lower parts of the earth: breake forth into ſinging yee mountaines, O forreſt and euery tree therein: for the Lord hath redeemed Iacob, and glorified himſelfe in Iſrael.24Thus ſaith the Lord thy redeemer, and he that formed thee from the wombe; I am the Lord that maketh all things, that ſtretcheth forth the heauens alone, that ſpreadeth abroad the earth by my ſelfe:25That fruſtrateth the tokens of the lyers, and maketh diuiners mad, that turneth wiſemen backward, and maketh their knowledge fooliſh:26That confirmeth the word of his ſeruant, and performeth the counſell of his meſſengers, that ſaith to Ieruſalem, Thou ſhalt be inhabited; and to the cities of Iudah, Yee ſhall be built, and I will raiſe vp the decayed places thereof.27That ſaith to the deepe; Be dry, and I will drie vp thy riuers.28That ſaith of Cyrus, Hee is my ſhepheard, and ſhall performe all my pleaſure, euen ſaying to Ieruſalem, Thou ſhalt be built, and to the Temple, Thy foundation ſhalbe laid.

CHAPTER 451Thus ſaith the Lord to his Anointed, to Cyrus whoſe right hande I haue holden, to ſubdue nations before him: and I will looſe the loines of kings to open before him the two leaued gates, and the gates ſhall not be ſhut.2I will goe before thee, and make the crooked places ſtraight, I wil break in pieces the gates of braſſe, and cut in ſunder the barres of yron.3And I will giue thee the treaſures of darkeneſſe, & hidden riches of ſecret places, that thou mayeſt know, that I the Lord which call thee by thy name, am the God of Iſrael.4For Iacob my ſeruants ſake, and Iſrael mine elect, I haue euen called thee by thy name: I haue ſurnamed thee, though thou haſt not knowen me.5I am the Lord, and there is none els, there is no God beſides me: I girded thee, though thou haſt not knowen me:6That they may knowe from the riſing of the Sun, and from the Weſt, that there is none beſides me, I am the Lord, and there is none elſe.7I forme the light, and create darkeneſſe: I make peace, and create euill: I the Lord do all theſe things.8Drop downe, ye heauens, from aboue, and let the ſkies powre downe righteouſneſſe: let the earth open, and let them bring forth ſaluation, and let righteouſneſſe ſpring vp together: I the Lord haue created it.9Woe vnto him that ſtriueth with his maker: Let the potſheard ſtriue with the potſheards of the earth: ſhal the clay ſay to him that faſhioneth it, What makeſt thou? or thy worke, he hath no hands?10Woe vnto him that ſaith vnto his father, What begetteſt thou? or to the woman, What haſt thou brought

forth?11Thus ſaith the Lord, the Holy One of Iſrael, and his maker, Aſke
me of things to come concerning my ſonnes, and concerning the worke
of my hands command ye me.12I haue made the earth, and created man
vpon it: I, euen my handes haue ſtretched out the heauens, and all their
hoſte haue I commanded.13I haue raiſed him vp in righteouſneſſe, and I
will direct all his wayes: he ſhall build my citie, and hee ſhall let goe my
captiues, not for price nor reward, ſaith the Lord of hoſts.14Thus ſaith
the Lord, The labour of Egypt, and merchandiſe of Ethiopia, and of the
Sabeans, men of ſtature ſhall come ouer vnto thee, and they ſhall be
thine, they ſhall come after thee, in chaines they ſhall come ouer: and
they ſhal fall downe vnto thee, they ſhal make ſupplication vnto thee,
ſaying, Surely God is in thee, and there is none elſe, there is no
god.15Uerely thou art a God that hideſt thy ſelfe, O God of Iſrael the
Sauiour.16They ſhall be aſhamed, and alſo confounded all of them: they
ſhall goe to confuſion together that are makers of idoles.17But Iſrael
ſhall bee ſaued in the Lord with an euerlaſting ſaluation: ye ſhall not be
aſhamed nor confounded world without end.18For thus ſaith the Lord
that created the heauens, God himſelfe that formed the earth and made
it, hee hath eſtabliſhed it, he created it not in vaine, he formed it to be
inhabited, I am the Lord, and there is none elſe.19I haue not ſpoken in
ſecret, in a darke place of the earth: I ſaid not vnto the ſeed of Iacob,
Seeke ye mee in vaine: I the Lord ſpeake righteouſneſſe, I declare things
that are right.20Aſſemble your ſelues and come: draw neere together ye
that are eſcaped of the nations: they haue no knowledge that ſet vp the
wood of their grauen image, and pray vnto a god that cannot ſaue.21Tell
ye and bring them neere, yea let them take counſell together, who hath
declared this from ancient time? who hath told it from that time? Haue
not I the Lord ? and there is no God elſe beſide me, a iuſt God and a
Sauiour, there is none beſide me.22Looke vnto mee, and be ye ſaued all
the endes of the earth: for I am God, and there is none elſe.23I haue
ſworne by my ſelfe: the word is gone out of my mouth in righteouſnes,
and ſhall not returne, that vnto me euery knee ſhall bowe, euery tongue
ſhall ſweare.24Surely, ſhall one ſay, In the Lord haue I righteouſneſſe and
ſtrength: euen to him ſhall men come, and all that are incenſed againſt
him, ſhalbe aſhamed.25In the Lord ſhall all the ſeed of Iſrael be iuſtified,
and ſhall glory.
CHAPTER 461Bel boweth downe, Nebo ſtoupeth, their idoles were
vpon the beaſts, and vpon the cattell: your carriages were heauie loaden,
they are a burden to the wearie beaſt.2They ſtoupe, they bow downe
together, they could not deliuer the burden, but themſelues are gone
into captiuitie.3Hearken vnto me, O houſe of Iacob, and al the remnant
of the houſe of Iſrael, which are borne by me, from the belly, which are
caried from the wombe.4And euen to your old age I am he, and euen to
hoare haires will I cary you: I haue made, and I will beare, euen I wil
cary and wil deliuer you.5To whom wil ye liken me, and make me equall,
and compare me, that we may be like?6They lauiſh gold out of the bagge,
and weigh ſiluer in the balance, and hire a goldſmith, and hee maketh it
a god: they fall downe, yea they worſhip.7They beare him vpon the
ſhoulder, they cary him and ſet him in his place, and hee ſtandeth; from
his place ſhall he not remooue: yea one ſhall cry vnto him, yet can he
not anſwere, nor ſaue him out of his trouble.8Remember this, and ſhew
your ſelues men: bring it againe to minde, O ye
tranſgreſsours.9Remember the former things of old, for I am God, and
there is none elſe, I am God, and there is none like me,10Declaring the
end from the beginning, and from ancient times the things that are not
yet done, ſaying, My counſell ſhall ſtand, and I wil doe all my
pleaſure:11Calling a rauenous bird from the Eaſt, the man that executeth
my counſell from a farre countrey; yea I haue ſpoken it, I will alſo bring
it to paſſe, I haue purpoſed it, I will alſo doe it.12Hearken vnto me, ye
ſtout hearted, that are farre from righteouſneſſe.13I bring neere my
righteouſneſſe: it ſhall not bee farre off, and my ſaluation ſhall not tarie;
and I wil place ſaluation in Zion for Iſrael my glorie.
CHAPTER 471Come downe and ſit in the duſt: O virgin daughter of
Babylon, ſit on the ground: there is no throne, O daughter of the
Caldeans: for thou ſhalt no more be called tender and delicate.2Take the
milſtones and grinde meale, vncouer thy lockes: make bare the legge:
vncouer the thigh, paſſe ouer the riuers.3Thy nakednes ſhalbe
vncouered, yea thy ſhame ſhalbe ſeene: I will take vengeance, and I will
not meet thee as a man.4As for our redeemer, the Lord of hoſtes is his
Name, the Holy one of Iſrael.5Sit thou ſilent, and get thee into darknes,
O daughter of the Caldeans: for thou ſhalt no more be called the Ladie
of kingdomes.6I was wroth with my people: I haue polluted mine
inheritance, and giuen them into thine hand: thou didſt ſhew them no
mercy; vpon the ancient haſt thou very heauily layed the yoke.7And thou
ſaydſt, I ſhall bee a Ladie for euer: ſo that thou didſt not lay theſe things
to thy heart, neither didſt remember the later end of it.8Therefore heare
now this, thou that art giuen to pleaſures, that dwelleſt careleſly, that
ſayeſt in thine heart, I am, and none elſe beſides mee, I ſhall not ſit as a
widow, neither ſhall I know the loſſe of children.9But theſe two things
ſhall come to thee in a moment in one day; the loſſe of children, and
widowhood; they ſhall come vpon thee in their perfection, for the
multitude of thy ſorceries, and for the great abundance of thine
inchantments.10For thou haſt truſted in thy wickedneſſe: thou haſt ſaid,
None ſeeth me. Thy wiſedome and thy knowledge, it hath peruerted
thee, and thou haſt ſaid in thine heart, I am, and none elſe beſides
me.11Therefore ſhall euill come vpon thee, thou ſhalt not know from
whence it riſeth: and miſchiefe ſhall fall vpon thee, thou ſhalt not be able
to put it off: and deſolation ſhall come vpon thee ſuddenly, which thou
ſhalt not know.12ſtand now with thine inchantments, and with the
multitude of thy ſorceries, wherein thou haſt laboured from thy youth;
if ſo be thou ſhalt be able to profite, if ſo be thou mayeſt preuaile.13Thou
art wearied in the multitude of thy counſels: let now the aſtrologers, the
ſtarre-gazers, the monethly prognoſticators ſtand vp, and ſaue thee from
theſe things that ſhall come vpon thee.14Behold, they ſhall be as ſtubble:
the fire ſhall burne them, they ſhall not deliuer themſelues from the
power of the flame: there ſhall not bee a coale to warme at, nor fire to
ſit before it.15Thus ſhal they be vnto thee with whom thou haſt
laboured, euen thy merchants from thy youth, they ſhall wander euery
one to his quarter: none ſhall ſaue thee.
CHAPTER 481Heare yee this, O houſe of Iacob, which are called by
the name of Iſrael, and are come foorth out of the waters of Iudah;
which ſweare by the Name of the Lord, and make mention of the God
of Iſrael, but not in trueth nor in righteouſnes.2For they call themſelues
of the holy city, and ſtay themſelues vpon the God of Iſrael, the Lord
of hoſtes is his Name.3I haue declared the former things from the
beginning: and they went foorth out of my mouth, and I ſhewed them,
I did them ſuddenly, and they came to paſſe.4Becauſe I knew that thou
art obſtinate, and thy necke is an yron ſinew, and thy brow braſſe:5I haue
euen from the beginning declared it to thee; before it came to paſſe I
ſhewed it thee: leſt thou ſhouldeſt ſay, Mine idole hath done them, and
my grauen image, and my molten image hath commanded them.6Thou
haſt heard, ſee all this, and will not yee declare it? I haue ſhewed thee
new things from this time, euen hidden things, and thou didſt not know
them.7They are created now, and not from the beginning, euen before
the day when thou heardeſt them not; leſt thou ſhouldeſt ſay, Behold, I
knew them.8Yea thou heardeſt not, yea thou kneweſt not, yea from that
time that thine eare was not opened: for I knew that thou wouldeſt deale
very treacherouſly, and waſt called a tranſgreſsour from the wombe.9For
my names ſake will I deferre mine anger, and for my praiſe will I refraine
for thee, that I cut thee not off.10Behold, I haue refined thee, but not
with ſiluer; I haue choſen thee in the fornace of affliction.11For mine
owne ſake, euen for mine owne ſake will I doe it; for how ſhould my
Name bee polluted? And I will not giue my glory vnto
another.12Hearken vnto me, O Iacob, and Iſrael my called; I am hee, I
am the firſt, I alſo am the laſt.13Mine hand alſo hath laid the foundation
of the earth, and my right hand hath ſpanned the heauens: when I call
vnto them, they ſtand vp together.14All yee aſſemble your ſelues and
heare: which among them hath declared theſe things? the Lord hath
loued him: hee will doe his pleaſure on Babylon, and his arme ſhall be
on the Caldeans.15I, euen I haue ſpoken, yea I haue called him: I haue
brought him, and he ſhall make his way proſperous.16Come ye neere
vnto me; heare ye this; I haue not ſpoken in ſecret from the beginning;
from the time that it was, there am I; and now the Lord God and his
Spirit hath ſent me.17Thus ſaith the Lord thy redeemer, the holy one of
Iſrael; I am the Lord thy God which teacheth thee to profit, which
leadeth thee by the way that thou ſhouldeſt goe.18O that thou haddeſt
hearkened to my commandements! then had thy peace beene as a riuer,
and thy righteouſneſſe as the waues of the ſea.19Thy ſeede alſo had
beene as the ſand, and the offpring of thy bowels like the grauell thereof:
his name ſhould not haue beene cut off, nor deſtroyed from before

me.[20]Goe yee forth of Babylon: flee yee from the Caldeans, with a voyce of ſinging, declare yee, tell this, vtter it euen to the end of the earth: ſay yee; The Lord hath redeemed his ſeruant Iacob.[21]And they thirſted not when he led them through the deſerts; he cauſed the waters to flow out of the rocke for them: he claue the rocke alſo, and the waters guſhed out.[22]There is no peace, ſaith the Lord, vnto the wicked.

CHAPTER 49[1]Liſten, O yles, vnto me, and hearken yee people from farre. The Lord hath called mee from the wombe, from the bowels of my mother hath he made mention of my name.[2]And he hath made my mouth like a ſharpe ſword, in the ſhadow of his hand hath he hid me, and made mee a poliſhed ſhaft; in his quiuer hath hee hid me,[3]And ſayd vnto me; Thou art my ſeruant, O Iſrael, in whom I will be glorified.[4]Then I ſaid; I haue laboured in vaine, I haue ſpent my ſtrength for nought, and in vaine, yet ſurely my iudgement is with the Lord, and my worke with my God.[5]And now, ſaith the Lord that formed me from the wombe to be his ſeruant, to bring Iacob againe to him; Though Iſrael be not gathered, yet ſhall I be glorious in the eyes of the Lord, and my God ſhall bee my ſtrength.[6]And he ſaid, It is a light thing that thou ſhouldeſt be my ſeruant to raiſe vp the tribes of Iacob, and to reſtore the preſerued of Iſrael: I will alſo giue thee for a light to the Gentiles, that thou mayeſt be my ſaluation, vnto the end of the earth.[7]Thus ſaith the Lord the redeemer of Iſrael, and his holy one, to him whom man diſpiſeth, to him whom the nation abhorreth, to a ſeruant of rulers; Kings ſhall ſee and Ariſe, princes alſo ſhall worſhip, becauſe of the Lord, that is faithfull, and the holy one of Iſrael, and he ſhall chooſe thee.[8]Thus ſaith the Lord, In an acceptable time haue I heard thee, and in a day of ſaluation haue I helped thee: and I will preſeruethee, and giue thee for a couenant of the people, to eſtabliſh the earth, to cauſe to inherite the deſolate heritages:[9]That thou mayeſt ſay to the priſoners, Goe forth; to them that are in darkeneſſe, Shewe your ſelues: they ſhall feede in the wayes, and their paſtures ſhalbe in all high places.[10]They ſhall not hunger nor thirſt, neither ſhall the heate nor ſunne ſmite them: for he that hath mercy on them ſhall lead them, euen by the ſprings of water ſhall he guide them.[11]And I will make all my mountaines a way, and my high wayes ſhall be exalted.[12]Behold, theſe ſhall come from far: and loe, theſe from the North and from the Weſt, and theſe from the land of Sinim.[13]Sing, O heauen, and be ioyfull, O earth, and breake forth into ſinging, O mountaines: for God hath comforted his people, and will haue mercy vpon his afflicted.[14]But Zion ſaid, The Lord hath forſaken me, and my Lord hath forgotten me.[15]Can a woman forget her ſucking child, that ſhe ſhould not haue compaſſion on the ſonne of her wombe? yea they may forget, yet will I not forget thee.[16]Behold, I haue grauen thee vpon the palmes of my hands: thy walles are continually before mee.[17]Thy children ſhal make haſte, thy deſtroyers, and they that made thee waſte, ſhall goe forth of thee.[18]Lift vp thine eyes round about, and behold: all theſe gather themſelues together and come to thee: as I liue, ſaith the Lord, thou ſhalt ſurely clothe thee with them all, as with an ornament, and bind them on thee as a bride doeth.[19]For thy waſte and thy deſolate places, and the land of thy deſtruction ſhall euen now be too narrow by reaſon of the inhabitants, and they that ſwallowed thee vp, ſhall bee farre away.[20]The children which thou ſhalt haue, after thou haſt loſt the other, ſhall ſay againe in thine eares, The place is too ſtraight for me: giue place to mee that I may dwell.[21]Then ſhalt thou ſay in thine heart, Who hath begotten me theſe, ſeeing I haue loſt my children and am deſolate, a captiue and remouing to and fro? and who hath brought vp theſe? Beholde, I was left alone, theſe where had they beene?[22]Thus ſaith the Lord God, Behold, I will lift vp mine hand to the Gentiles, and ſet vp my ſtanderd to the people: and they ſhall bring thy ſonnes in their armes: and thy daughters ſhal be caried vpon their ſhoulders .[23]And kings ſhall be thy nurſing fathers, and their queenes thy nurſing mothers: they ſhall bow downe to thee with their face toward the earth, and licke vp the duſt of thy feete, and thou ſhalt know that I am the Lord: for they ſhall not be aſhamed that waite for me.[24]Shall the pray be taken from the mightie, or the lawfull captiue deliuered?[25]But thus ſaith the Lord, Euen the captiues of the mightie ſhall be taken away, and the pray of the terrible ſhall be deliuered: for I will contend with him that contendeth with thee, and I will ſaue thy children.[26]And I will feede them that oppreſſe thee, with their owne fleſh, and they ſhall be drunken with their owne blood, as with ſweet wine: and all fleſh ſhall know that I the Lord am thy Sauiour and thy Redeemer, the mightie One of Iacob.

CHAPTER 50[1]Thus ſaith the Lord, Where is the bill of your mothers diuorcement, whom I haue put away? or which of my creditours is it to whom I haue ſold you? Behold, for your iniquities haue you ſolde your ſelues, and for your tranſgreſſions is your mother put away.[2]Wherefore when I came was there no man? when I called, was there none to anſwere? Is my hand ſhortened at all, that it cannot redeeme? or haue I no power to deliuer? Beholde, at my rebuke I drie vp the ſea: I make the riuers a wildernes: their fiſh ſtinketh, becauſe there is no water, and dieth for thirſt.[3]I clothe the heauens with blackeneſse, and I make ſackcloth their couering.[4]The Lord God hath giuen me the tongue of the learned, that I ſhould know how to ſpeake a worde in ſeaſon to him that is wearie: hee wakeneth morning by morning, hee wakeneth mine eare to heare as the learned.[5]The Lord God hath opened mine eare, and I was not rebellious, neither turned away backe.[6]I gaue my backe to the ſmiters, and my cheeks to them that plucked off the haire: I hidde not my face from ſhame and ſpitting.[7]For the Lord God will helpe me, therefore ſhall I not be confounded: therefore haue I ſet my face like a flint, and I know that I ſhall not bee aſhamed.[8]He is neere that iuſtifieth me, who will contend with me? let vs ſtand together: who is mine aduerſarie? let him come neere to me.[9]Behold, the Lord God wil helpe me, who is he that ſhall condemne mee? Loe, they all ſhall waxe olde as a garment: the moth ſhall eate them vp.[10]Who is among you that feareth the Lord, that obeyeth the voyce of his ſeruant, that walketh in darkeneſſe and hath no light? let him truſt in the Name of the Lord, and ſtay vpon his God.[11]Behold, all ye that kindle a fire, that compaſſe your ſelues about with ſparks: walke in the light of your fire, and in the ſparkes that ye haue kindled. This ſhall ye haue of mine hand, yee ſhall lie downe in ſorrow.

CHAPTER 51[1]Hearken to me, ye that follow after righteouſneſſe, ye that ſeeke the Lord: looke vnto the rocke whence yee are hewen, and to the hole of the pitte whence ye are digged.[2]Looke vnto Abraham your father, and vnto Sarah that bare you: for I called him alone, and bleſſed him, and increaſed him.[3]For the Lord ſhall comfort Zion: he wil comfort all her waſte places, and he wil make her wildernes like Eden, and her deſert like the garden of the Lord: ioy and gladneſſe ſhalbe found therein, thankeſgiuing, and the voice of melody.[4]Hearken vnto me, my people, and giue eare vnto me, O my nation: for a Law ſhall proceed from mee, and I will make my iudgement to reſt for a light of the people.[5]My righteouſnes is neere: my ſaluation is gone foorth, and mine armes ſhall iudge the people: the Iles ſhall wait vpon me, and on mine arme ſhall they truſt.[6]Lift vp your eyes to the heauens, and looke vpon the earth beneath: for the heauens ſhall vaniſh away like ſmoke, and the earth ſhall waxe old like a garment, and they that dwel therein ſhall die in like maner: but my ſaluation ſhal be for euer, and my righteouſnes ſhall not be aboliſhed.[7]Hearken vnto me ye that know righteouſneſſe, the people in whoſe heart is my Law: Feare ye not the reproch of men, neither be yee afraid of their reuilings.[8]For the moth ſhall eate them vp like a garment, and the worme ſhal eate them like wooll: but my righteouſnes ſhalbe for euer; and my ſaluation from generation to generation.[9]Awake, awake, put on ſtrength, O arme of the Lord, awake as in the ancient dayes, in the generations of old. Art thou not it that hath cut Rahab, and wounded the dragon?[10]Art thou not it which hath dried the ſea, the waters of the great deepe, that hath made the depthes of the ſea a way for the ranſomed to paſſe ouer?[11]Therefore the redeemed of the Lord ſhall returne, and come with ſinging vnto Zion, and euerlaſting ioy ſhalbe vpon their head: they ſhall obtaine gladneſſe and ioy, and ſorrow and mourning ſhall flee away.[12]I, euen I am hee that comforteth you, who art thou that thou ſhouldeſt be afraid of a man that ſhall die, and of the ſonne of man which ſhall bee made as graſſe?[13]And forgetteſt the Lord thy maker that hath ſtretched foorth the heauens, and layed the foundations of the earth? and haſt feared continually euery day, becauſe of the furie of the oppreſsour, as if hee were ready to deſtroy? and where is the furie of the oppreſsour?[14]The captiue exile haſteneth that he may be looſed, and that hee ſhould not die in the pit, nor that his bread ſhould faile.[15]But I am the Lord thy God, that diuided the ſea, whoſe waues roared: the Lord of hoſts is his Name.[16]And I haue put my wordes in thy mouth, and haue couered thee in the ſhadow of mine hand, that I may plant the heauens, and lay the foundations of the earth, and ſay vnto Zion, Thou art my people.[17]Awake, awake, ſtand vp, O Ieruſalem, which haſt drunke at the hand of the Lord the cup of his furie; thou haſt drunken the dregges of the cup of trembling, and wrung them out.18There is none to guide her among all the ſonnes whom ſhee hath brought foorth: neither is there any that taketh her by the hand, of all the ſonnes that ſhe hath brought vp.19Theſe two things are come vnto thee; who ſhall be ſorie for thee? deſolation and deſtruction, and the famine and the ſword: by whom ſhall I comfort thee?20Thy ſonnes haue fainted, they lie at the head of all the ſtreetes as a wilde bull in a net; they are full of the furie of the Lord, the rebuke of thy God.21Therefore heare now this thou afflicted and drunken, but not with wine.22Thus ſaith thy Lord, the Lord and thy God that pleadeth the cauſe of his people, Behold, I haue taken out of thine hand the cup of trembling, euen the dregges of the cup of my furie: thou ſhalt no more drinke it againe.23But I will put it into the hand of them that afflict thee: which haue ſaid to thy ſoule, Bow downe that wee may goe ouer: and thou haſt laide thy body as the ground, and as the ſtreete to them that went ouer.

CHAPTER 521Awake, awake, put on thy ſtrength, O Zion, put on thy beautifull garments, O Ieruſalem the holy citie: for hencefoorth there ſhall no more come into thee the vncircumciſed, and the vncleane.2Shake thy ſelfe from the duſt: Ariſe, and ſit downe, O Ieruſalem: looſe thy ſelfe from the bandes of thy necke, O captiue daughter of Zion.3For thus ſayth the Lord, Yee haue ſolde your ſelues for nought: and ye ſhall be redeemed without money.4For thus ſaith the Lord God, My people went downe aforetime into Egypt to ſoiourne there, and the Aſſyrian oppreſſed them without cauſe.5Now therefore, what haue I here, ſayth the Lord, that my people is taken away for nought? they that rule ouer them, make them to howle, ſayth the Lord, and my Name continually euery day is blaſphemed.6Therefore my people ſhall know my Name: therefore they ſhall know in that day, that I am he that doth ſpeake. Behold, it is I.7How beautifull vpon the mountaines are the feete of him that bringeth good tidings, that publiſheth peace, that bringeth good tidings of good, that publiſheth ſaluation, that ſayth vnto Zion, Thy God reigneth?8Thy watchmen ſhall lift vp the voice, with the voice together ſhall they ſing: for they ſhall ſee eye to eye when the Lord ſhall bring againe Zion.9Breake foorth into ioy, ſing together, yee waſte places of Ieruſalem: for the Lord hath comforted his people, he hath redeemed Ieruſalem.10The Lord hath made bare his holy arme in the eyes of all the nations, and all the endes of the earth ſhall ſee the ſaluation of our God.11Depart ye, depart ye, goe ye out from thence, touch no vncleane thing; goe ye out of the middeſt of her; be yee cleane, that beare the veſſels of the Lord.12For ye ſhall not go out with haſte, nor goe by flight: for the Lord will goe before you: and the God of Iſrael will be your rereward.13Behold, my ſeruant ſhal deale prudently, he ſhall be exalted and extolled, and be very high.14As many were aſtonied at thee (his viſage was ſo marred more then any man, and his forme more then the ſonnes of men:)15So ſhall hee ſprinckle many nations, the kings ſhall ſhut their mouthes at him: for that which had not beene told them, ſhall they ſee, and that which they had not heard, ſhall they conſider.

CHAPTER 531Who hath beleeued our report? and to whom is the arme of the Lord reuealed?2For he ſhall grow vp before him as a tender plant, and as a root out of a drie ground: hee hath no forme nor comelineſse: and when wee ſhall ſee him, there is no beautie that we ſhould deſire him.3He is deſpiſed and reiected of men, a man offorrows, and acquainted with griefe: and we hid as it were our faces from him; hee was deſpiſed, and wee eſteemed him not.4Surely he hath borne our griefes, and caried our ſorrowes: yet we did eſteeme him ſtriken, ſmitten of God, and afflicted.5But he was wounded for our tranſgreſſions, he was bruiſed for our iniquities: the chaſtiſement of our peace was vpon him, and with his ſtripes we are healed.6All we like ſheepe haue gone aſtray: we haue turned euery one to his owne way, and the Lord hath layd on him the iniquitie of vs all.7He was oppreſſed, and he was afflicted, yet he opened not his mouth: he is brought as a lambe to the ſlaughter, and as a ſheepe before her ſhearers is dumme, ſo he openeth not his mouth.8He was taken from priſon, and from iudgement: and who ſhall declare his generation? for he was cut off out of the land of the liuing, for the tranſgreſſion of my people was he ſtricken.9And he made his graue with the wicked, and with the rich in his death, becauſe he had done no violence, neither was any deceit in his mouth.10Yet it pleaſed the Lord to bruiſe him, he hath put him to griefe: when thou ſhalt make his ſoule an offring for ſinne, he ſhall ſee his ſeede, hee ſhall prolong his daies, and the pleaſure of the Lord ſhall proſper in his hand.11He ſhall ſee of the trauell of his ſoule, and ſhalbe ſatiſfied: by his knowledge ſhall my righteous ſeruant iuſtifie many: for hee ſhall beare their iniquities.12Therefore will I diuide him a portion with the great, and he ſhall diuide the ſpoile with the ſtrong: becauſe hee hath powred out his ſoule vnto death: and he was numbred with the tranſgreſsours, and he bare the ſinne of many, and made interceſsion for the tranſgreſsours.

CHAPTER 541Sing O barren thou that didſt not beare; breake forth into ſinging, and crie aloud thou that didſt not trauell with child: for more are the children of the deſolate then the children of the maried wife, ſaith the Lord.2Enlarge the place of thy tent, and let them ſtretch forth the curtaines of thine habitations: ſpare not, lengthen thy cords, and ſtrengthen thy ſtakes.3For thou ſhalt breake forth on the right hand, and on the left; and thy ſeed ſhall inherite the Gentiles, and make the deſolate cities to be inhabited.4Feare not: for thou ſhalt not be aſhamed: neither be thou confounded, for thou ſhalt not be put to ſhame: for thou ſhalt forget the ſhame of thy youth, and ſhalt not remember the reproach of thy widowhood any more.5For thy maker is thine huſband, (the Lord of hoſtes is his name;) and thy redeemer the holy one of Iſrael, the God of the whole earth ſhall he be called.6For the Lord hath called thee as a woman forſaken, and grieued in ſpirit, and a wife of youth, when thou waſt refuſed, ſaith thy God.7For a ſmall moment haue I forſaken thee, but with great mercies will I gather thee.8In a litle wrath I hid my face from thee, for a moment; but with euerlaſting kindneſſe will I haue mercie on thee, ſaith the Lord thy redeemer.9For this is as the waters of Noah vnto me: for as I haue ſworne that the waters of Noah ſhould no more goe ouer the earth; ſo haue I ſworne that I would not be wroth with thee, nor rebuke thee.10For the mountaines ſhall depart, and the hilles be remoued, but my kindneſſe ſhall not depart from thee, neither ſhall the couenant of my peace be remoued, ſaith the Lord, that hath mercie on thee.11Oh thou afflicted, toſsed with tempeſt and not comforted, behold, I will lay thy ſtones with faire colours, and lay thy foundations with Saphires.12And I will make thy windowes of Agates, and thy gates of Carbuncles, and all thy borders of pleaſant ſtones.13And all thy children ſhalbe taught of the Lord, and great ſhalbe the peace of thy children.14In righteouſneſſe ſhalt thou be eſtabliſhed: thou ſhalt be farre from oppreſſion, for thou ſhalt not feare; & from terrour, for it ſhall not come neere thee.15Behold, they ſhall ſurely gather together, but not by me: whoſoeuer ſhal gather together againſt thee, ſhall fall for thy ſake.16Behold, I haue created the ſmith that bloweth the coales in the fire, and that bringeth foorth an inſtrument for his worke, and I haue created the waſter to deſtroy.17No weapon that is formed againſt thee, ſhall proſper, and euery tongue that ſhall riſe againſt thee in iudgement, thou ſhalt condemne. This is the heritage of the ſeruants of the Lord, and their righteouſneſſe is of me, ſaith the Lord.

CHAPTER 551Ho, euery one that thirſteth, come ye to the waters, and he that hath no money: come ye, buy and eate, yea come, buy wine and milke without money, and without price.2Wherefore doe yee ſpend money for that which is not bread? and your labour for that which ſatiſfieth not? hearken diligently vnto me, and eate ye that which is good, and let your ſoule delight it ſelfe in fatneſſe.3Incline your eare, and come vnto me: heare, and your ſoule ſhall liue, and I will make an euerlaſting couenant with you, euen the ſure mercies of Dauid.4Behold, I haue giuen him for a witneſſe to the people, a leader and commander to the people.5Behold, thou ſhalt call a nation that thou knoweſt not, and nations that knew not thee, ſhall runne vnto thee, becauſe of the Lord thy God, and for the Holy One of Iſrael, for he hath glorified thee.6Seeke ye the Lord, while he may be found, call ye vpon him while he is neere.7Let the wicked forſake his way, & the vnrighteous man his thoughts: and let him returne vnto the Lord, and he will haue mercie vpon him, and to our God, for hee will abundantly pardon.8For my thoughts are not your thoughts, neither are your wayes my wayes, ſaith the Lord.9For as the heauens are higher then the earth, ſo are my wayes higher then your wayes, and my thoughts then your thouhts.10For as the raine commeth down, and the ſnow from heauen, and returneth not thither, but watereth the earth, and maketh it bring foorth and bud, that it may giue ſeed to the ſower, and bread to the eater:11So ſhall my word bee that goeth forth out of my mouth: it ſhall not returne vnto me void, but it ſhall accompliſh that which I pleaſe, and it ſhall proſper in the thing whereto I ſent it.12For ye ſhall goe out with ioy, and bee led foorth with peace: the mountaines and the hilles ſhall breake forth before you into ſinging, and al the trees of the field ſhall clap their hands.13In ſtead of the thorne ſhall come vp the Firre tree, and in ſtead of the brier ſhall come vp the Myrtle tree, and it ſhall be to the Lord for a name, for an euerlaſting ſigne that ſhall not bee cut off.

CHAPTER 561Thus ſaith the Lord, Keepe yee iudgement, and doe iuſtice: for my ſaluation is neere to come, and my righteouſneſſe to bee reuealed.2Bleſſed is the man that doeth this, and the ſonne of man that layeth holde on it: that keepeth the Sabbath from polluting it, and keepeth his hand from doing any euill.3Neither let the ſonne of the ſtranger, that hath ioyned himſelfe to the Lord, ſpeake, ſaying, The Lord hath vtterly ſeparated mee from his people: neither let the Eunuch ſay, Behold, I am a drie tree.4For thus ſaith the Lord vnto the Eunuches that keep my Sabbaths, and chooſe the things that pleaſe mee, and take hold of my couenant:5Euen vnto them will I giue in mine houſe, and within my walles, a place and a name better then of ſonnes and of daughters: I wil giue them an euerlaſting name, that ſhal not be cut off.6Alſo the ſonnes of the ſtranger that ioyne themſelues to the Lord, to ſerue him, and to loue the Name of the Lord, to be his ſeruants, euery one that keepeth the Sabbath from polluting it, and taketh hold of my Couenant:7Euen them will I bring to my holy mountaine, and make them ioyfull in my houſe of prayer: their burnt offerings and their ſacrifices ſhall be accepted vpon mine Altar: for mine houſe ſhalbe called an houſe of prayer for all people.8The Lord God which gathereth the outcaſts of Iſrael, ſaith, Yet will I gather others to him, beſides thoſe that are gathered vnto him.9All ye beaſts of the field, come to deuoure, yea all ye beaſts in the foreſt.10His watchmen are blinde: they are all ignorant, they are all dumbe dogs, they cannot barke; ſleeping, lying downe, louing to ſlumber.11Yea they are greedy dogges which can neuer haue ynough, and they are ſhepheards that cannot vnderſtand: they all looke to their owne way, euery one for his gaine, from his quarter.12Come ye, ſay they, I wil fetch wine, and we will fill our ſelues with ſtrong drinke, and to morrow ſhal be as this day, and much more abundant.

CHAPTER 571The righteous periſheth, and no man layeth it to heart; and mercifull men are taken away none conſidering that the righteous is taken away from the euill to come.2Hee ſhall enter into peace: they ſhall reſt in their beds, each one walking in his vprightneſse.3But draw neere hither, yee ſonnes of the ſorcereſse, the ſeed of the adulterer, and the whore.4Againſt whom doe ye ſport your ſelues? againſt whom make ye a wide mouth, and draw out the tongue? are ye not children of tranſgreſsion, a ſeede of falſehood?5Inflaming your ſelues with idoles vnder euery greene tree, ſlaying the children in the valleys vnder the cliftes of the rockes?6Among the ſmooth ſtones of the ſtreame is thy portion; they, they are thy lot: euen to them haſt thou powred a drinke offering, thou haſt offered a meate offering. Should I receiue comfort in theſe?7Upon a loftie and high mountaine haſt thou ſet thy bed: euen thither wenteſt thou vp to offer ſacrifice.8Behinde the doores alſo and the poſts haſt thou ſet vp thy remembrance: for thou haſt diſcouered thy ſelfe to an other then mee, and art gone vp: thou haſt enlarged thy bed, and made a couenant with them: thou louedſt their bed where thou ſaweſt it.9And thou wenteſt to the king with oyntment, and didſt increaſe thy perfumes, and didſt ſend thy meſſengers farre off, and didſt debaſe thy ſelfe euen vnto hell.10Thou art wearied in the greatneſſe of thy way; yet ſaydſt thou not, There is no hope: thou haſt found the life of thine hand; therefore thou waſt not grieued.11And of whom haſt thou bene afraid or feared, that thou haſt lyed, and haſt not remembred me, nor layed it to thy heart? haue not I held my peace euen of old, and thou feareſt me not?12I will declare thy righteouſnes; and thy workes, for they ſhall not profit thee.13When thou crieſt, let thy companies deliuer thee: but the winde ſhall cary them all away; Uanitie ſhall take them: but hee that putteth his truſt in me, ſhall poſſeſſe the land, and ſhall inherit my holy mountaine.14And ſhall ſay, Caſt yee vp, caſt yee vp; prepare the way, take vp the ſtumbling blocke out of the way of my people.15For thus ſaith the High and loftie One that inhabiteth eternitie, whoſe Name is Holy; I dwell in the high and holy place: with him alſo that is of a contrite and humble ſpirit, to reuiue the ſpirit of the humble, and to reuiue the heart of the contrite ones.16For I will not contend for euer, neither will I be alwayes wroth: for the ſpirit ſhould faile before me, and the ſoules which I haue made.17For the iniquitie of his couetouſneſſe was I wroth, and ſmote him: I hid me, and was wroth, and hee went on frowardly in the way of his heart.18I haue ſeene his wayes, and will heale him: I will leade him alſo, and reſtore comforts vnto him, and to his mourners.19I create the fruite of the lippes; peace, peace to him that is farre off, and to him that is neere, ſayth the Lord, and I will heale him.20But the wicked are like the troubled ſea, when it cannot reſt, whoſe waters caſt vp myre and dirt.21There is no peace, ſayth my God, to the wicked.

CHAPTER 581Crie aloude, ſpare not, lift vp thy voice like a trumpet, and ſhewe my people their tranſgreſsion, & the houſe of Iacob their ſins.2Yet they ſeeke mee daily, and delight to know my wayes, as a nation that did righteouſneſſe, and forſooke not the ordinance of their God: they aſke of me the ordinances of iuſtice: they take delight in approching to God.3Wherefore haue wee faſted, ſay they, and thou ſeeſt not? wherefore haue wee afflicted our ſoule, & thou takeſt no knowledge? Behold, in the day of your faſt you find pleaſure, and exact all your labours.4Behold, yee faſt for ſtrife and debate; and to ſmite with the fiſt of wickedneſſe, yee ſhall not faſt as yee doe this day, to make your voice to be heard on high.5Is it ſuch a faſt that I haue choſen? a day for a man to afflict his ſoule? Is it to bow down his head as a bulruſh, and to ſpread ſackecloth and aſhes vnder him? wilt thou call this a faſt, and an acceptable day to the Lord ?6Is not this the faſt that I haue choſen? to looſe the bandes of wickedneſſe, to vndoe the heauie burdens, and to let the oppreſſed goe free, and that ye breake euery yoke?7Is it not, to deale thy bread to the hungry, and that thou bring the poore that are caſt out, to thy houſe? when thou ſeeſt the naked, that thou couer him, and that thou hide not thy ſelfe from thine owne fleſh?8Then ſhall thy light breake foorth as the morning, and thine health ſhall ſpring foorth ſpeedily: and thy righteouſneſſe ſhall goe before thee, the glory of the Lord ſhall be thy rereward.9Then ſhalt thou call, and the Lord ſhall anſwere; thou ſhalt cry, and he ſhal ſay, Here I am: if thou take away from the midſt of thee the yoke, the putting forth of the finger, and ſpeaking vanitie:10And if thou draw out thy ſoule to the hungry, and ſatiſfie the afflicted ſoule: then ſhall thy light riſe in obſcuritie, and thy darkeneſſe be as the noone day.11And the Lord ſhal guide thee continually, and ſatiſfie thy ſoule in drought, and make fat thy bones: and thou ſhalt be like a watered garden, and like a ſpring of water, whoſe waters faile not.12And they that ſhall be of thee, ſhall builde the olde waſte places: thou ſhalt raiſe vp the foundations of many generations; and thou ſhalt be called, the repairer of the breach, the reſtorer of paths to dwell in.13If thou turne away thy foote from the Sabbath, from doing thy pleaſure on my Holy day, and call the Sabbath a delight, the holy of the Lord, honourable, and ſhalt honour him, not doing thine owne wayes, nor finding thine owne pleaſure, nor ſpeaking thine owne wordes:14Then ſhalt thou delight thy ſelfe in the Lord, and I will cauſe thee to ride vpon the high places of the earth, and feede thee with the heritage of Iacob thy father; for the mouth of the Lord hath ſpoken it.

CHAPTER 591Beholde, the Lords hand is not ſhortened, that it cannot ſaue: neither his eare heauie, that it cannot heare.2But your iniquities haue ſeparated betweene you and your God, and your ſinnes haue hid his face from you, that he will not heare.3For your hands are defiled with blood, and your fingers with iniquitie, your lippes haue ſpoken lies, your tongue hath muttered peruerſneſse.4None calleth for iuſtice, nor any pleadeth for trueth: they truſt in vanity and ſpeake lies; they conceiue miſchiefe, and bring forth iniquitie.5They hatch cockatrice egges, and weaue the ſpiders web: he that eateth of their egges dieth, and that which is cruſhed breaketh out into a viper.6Their webbes ſhall not become garments, neither ſhall they couer themſelues with their workes: their workes are workes of iniquitie, and the act of violence is in their hands.7Their feete runne to euill, and they make haſte to ſhed innocent blood: their thoughts are thoughts of iniquity, waſting & deſtruction are in their paths.8The way of peace they know not, and there is no iudgement in their goings: they haue made them crooked pathes; whoſoeuer goeth therein, ſhall not know peace.9Therefore is iudgement farre from vs, neither doth iuſtice ouertake vs: we waite for light, but behold obſcuritie, for brightneſse, but we walke in darkneſſe.10We grope for the wall like the blind, and we grope as if we had no eies: we ſtumble at noone day as in the night, we are in deſolate places as dead men.11We roare all like beares, and mourne ſore like doues: we looke for

iudgement, but there is none; for ſaluation, but it is farre off from
vs.[12]For our tranſgreſſions are multiplied before thee, and our ſinnes
teſtifie againſt vs: for our tranſgreſſions are with vs, and as for our
iniquities, we know them:[13]In tranſgreſsing and lying againſt the Lord,
and departing away from our God, ſpeaking oppreſſion and reuolt,
conceiuing and vttering from the heart words of falſhood.[14]And
iudgement is turned away backward, and iuſtice ſtandeth a farre off: for
truth is fallen in the ſtreete, and equitie cannot enter.[15]Yea truth faileth,
and he that departeth from euill maketh himſelfe a pray: and the Lord
ſaw it, and it diſpleaſed him, that there was no iudgement.[16]And hee ſaw
that there was no man, and wondered that there was no interceſsour.
Therefore his arme brought ſaluation vnto him, and his righteouſneſſe,
it ſuſtained him.[17]For he put on righteouſneſſe as a breſtplate, and an
helmet of ſaluation vpon his head; and he put on the garments of
vengeance for clothing, and was clad with zeale as a cloake.[18]According
to their deedes accordingly he will repay, furie to his aduerſaries,
recompence to his enemies, to the ylands he will repay recompence.[19]So
ſhall they feare the name of the Lord from the Weſt, and his glory from
the riſing of the ſunne: when the enemie ſhall come in like a flood, the
ſpirit of the Lord ſhall lift vp a ſtandard againſt him.[20]And the redeemer
ſhall come to Zion, and vnto them that turne from tranſgreſſion in
Iacob, ſaith the Lord.[21]As for me, this is my couenant with them, ſaith
the Lord; My ſpirit that is vpon thee, and my words which I haue put in
thy mouth, ſhall not depart out of thy mouth, nor out of the mouth of
the ſeede, nor out of the mouth of thy ſeedes ſeed, ſaith the Lord, from
henceforth, and for euer.

CHAPTER 60[1]Ariſe, ſhine, for thy light is come, and the glory of the
Lord is riſen vpon thee.[2]For behold, the darkneſſe ſhall couer the earth,
and groſse darkneſſe the people: but the Lord ſhall Ariſe vpon thee, and
his glory ſhall be ſeene vpon thee.[3]And the Gentiles ſhall come to thy
light, and kings to the brightneſse of thy riſing.[4]Lift vp thine eyes round
about, and ſee: all they gather themſelues together, they come to thee:
thy ſonnes ſhall come from farre, and thy daughters ſhalbe nourced at
thy ſide.[5]Then thou ſhalt ſee, and flow together, and thine heart ſhall
feare and be inlarged, becauſe the abundance of the ſea ſhalbe conuerted
vnto thee, the forces of the Gentiles ſhall come vnto thee.[6]The
multitude of camels ſhall couer thee, the dromedaries of Midian and
Ephah: all they from Sheba ſhall come: they ſhal bring gold and incenſe,
and they ſhall ſhew forth the praiſes of the Lord.[7]All the flockes of
Kedar ſhall be gathered together vnto thee, the rams of Nebaioth ſhall
miniſter vnto thee: they ſhall come vp with acceptance on mine altar,
and I wil glorifie the houſe of my glory.[8]Who are theſe that flie as a
cloude, and as the doues to their windowes?[9]Surely the yles ſhall wait
for me, and the ſhips of Tarſhiſh firſt, to bring thy ſonnes from farre,
their ſiluer and their gold with them, vnto the Name of the Lord thy
God, and to the Holy One of Iſrael, becauſe he hath glorified thee.[10]And
the ſonnes of ſtrangers ſhall build vp thy walles, and their kings ſhal
miniſter vnto thee: for in my wrath I ſmote thee, but in my fauour haue
I had mercie on thee.[11]Therefore thy gates ſhal be open continually, they
ſhall not bee ſhut day nor night, that men may bring vnto thee the forces
of the Gentiles, and that their kings may be brought.[12]For the nation
and kingdome that will not ſerue thee, ſhall periſh, yea thoſe nations
ſhall be vtterly waſted.[13]The glory of Lebanon ſhal come vnto thee, the
Firre tree, the Pine tree, and the Boxe together, to beautifie the place of
my Sanctuarie, and I will make the place of my feete glorious.[14]The
ſonnes alſo of them that afflicted thee, ſhall come bending vnto thee:
and all they that deſpiſed thee ſhal bow themſelues downe at the ſoles
of thy feet, and they ſhall call thee the citie of the Lord, the Zion of the
Holy One of Iſrael.[15]Whereas thou haſt bene forſaken and hated, ſo that
no man went thorow thee, I will make thee an eternall excellencie, a ioy
of many generations.[16]Thou ſhalt alſo ſucke the milke of the Gentiles,
and ſhalt ſucke the breſt of kings, and thou ſhalt know that I the Lord
am thy Sauiour and thy Redeemer, the mightie One of Iacob.[17]For
braſſe I will bring gold, and for yron I will bring ſiluer, and for wood
braſſe, and for ſtones yron: I will alſo make thy officers peace, and thine
exactours righteouſneſſe.[18]Uiolence ſhall no more be heard in thy land,
waſting nor deſtruction within thy borders, but thou ſhalt call thy walles
ſaluation, and thy gates praiſe.[19]The Sunne ſhall be no more thy light by
day, neither for brightneſse ſhall the moone giue light vnto thee: but the
Lord ſhall be vnto thee an euerlaſting light, & thy God thy glory.[20]Thy
Sunne ſhall no more goe downe, neither ſhall thy moone withdraw it
ſelfe: for the Lord ſhall bee thine euerlaſting light, and the dayes of thy
mourning ſhall be ended.[21]Thy people alſo ſhall be all righteous: they
ſhal inherit the land for euer, the branch of my planting, the worke of
my hands, that I may be glorified.[22]A litle one ſhall become a thouſand,
and a ſmall one a ſtrong nation: I the Lord will haſten it in his time.

CHAPTER 61[1]The Spirit of the Lord God is vpon me, becauſe the
Lord hath anointed me, to preach good tidings vnto the meeke, hee hath
ſent me to binde vp the broken hearted, to proclaime libertie to the
captiues, and the opening of the priſon to them that are bound:[2]To
proclaime the acceptable yere of the Lord, and the day of vengeance of
our God, to comfort all that mourne:[3]To appoint vnto them that
mourne in Zion, to giue vnto them beautie for aſhes, the oyle of ioy for
mourning, the garment of praiſe for the ſpirit of heauineſse, that they
might be called trees of righteouſneſſe, the planting of the Lord, that he
might be glorified.[4]And they ſhall build the olde waſtes, they ſhall raiſe
vp the former deſolations, and they ſhall repaire the waſte cities, the
deſolations of many generations.[5]And ſtrangers ſhall ſtand and feed
your flockes, and the ſonnes of the alient ſhalbe your plowmen, and
your Uine-dreſſers.[6]But ye ſhalbe named the Prieſts of the Lord: men
ſhall call you the miniſters of our God: ye ſhall eat the riches of the
Gentiles, and in their glory ſhall you boaſt your ſelues.[7]For your ſhame
you ſhall haue double; and for confuſion they ſhall reioyce in their
portion: therefore in their land they ſhal poſſeſſe the double: euerlaſting
ioy ſhalbe vnto them.[8]For I the Lord loue Iudgement, I hate robbery
for burnt offering, and I will direct their worke in trueth, and I will make
an euerlaſting Couenant with them.[9]And their ſeed ſhalbe knowen
among the Gentiles, and their offſpring among the people: All that ſee
them, ſhall acknowledge them, that they are the ſeed which the Lord
hath bleſſed.[10]I will greatly reioyce in the Lord, my ſoule ſhalbe ioyfull
in my God: for he hath clothed me with the garments of ſaluation, he
hath couered me with the robe of righteouſnes, as a bridegrome decketh
himſelfe with ornaments, and as a bride adorneth herſelfe with her
iewels.[11]For as the earth bringeth foorth her bud, and as the garden
cauſeth the things that are ſowen in it, to ſpring foorth: ſo the Lord God
will cauſe righteouſnes and praiſe to ſpring forth before all the nations.

CHAPTER 62[1]For Zions ſake, wil I not hold my peace, and for
Ieruſalems ſake I will not reſt, vntill the righteouſneſſe thereof goe forth
as brightneſse, and the ſaluation thereof as a lampe that burneth;[2]And
the Gentiles ſhall ſee thy righteouſnes, and all Kings thy glory: and thou
ſhalt be called by a new name, which the mouth of the Lord ſhall
name.[3]Thou ſhalt alſo be a crowne of glory in the hand of the Lord, and
a royall diademe in the hand of thy God.[4]Thou ſhalt no more bee
termed, Forſaken; neither ſhall thy land any more be termed, Deſolate:
but thou ſhalt be called Hephzi-bah, and thy land, Beulah: for the Lord
delighteth in thee, and thy land ſhalbe maried.[5]For as a yong man
marrieth a virgine, ſo ſhall thy ſonnes marry thee: and as the bridegrome
reioyceth ouer the bride, ſo ſhall thy God reioyce ouer thee.[6]I haue ſet
watchmen vpon thy walles, O Ieruſalem, which ſhall neuer hold their
peace day nor night: ye that make mention of the Lord, keepe not
ſilence:[7]And giue him no reſt till he eſtabliſh, and till hee make Ieruſalem
a praiſe in the earth.[8]The Lord hath ſworne by his Right hand, and by
the arme of his ſtrength, Surely, I will no more giue thy corne to be meat
for thine enemies, and the ſonnes of the ſtranger ſhall not drinke thy
wine, for the which thou haſt laboured:[9]But they that haue gathered it
ſhall eat it, and praiſe the Lord, and they that haue brought it together,
ſhal drinke it in the Courts of my Holineſse.[10]Goe through, goe through
the gates: prepare you the way of the people: caſt vp, caſt vp the high
way, gather out the ſtones, lift vp a ſtandard for the people.[11]Behold, the
Lord hath proclaimed vnto the end of the world, ſay ye to the daughter
of Zion, Behold, thy ſaluation commeth; behold, his reward is with him,
and his worke before him.[12]And they ſhall call them, The holy people:
the redeemed of the Lord: and thou ſhalt be called, Sought out, a citie
not forſaken.

CHAPTER 63[1]Who is this that commeth from Edom, with died
garments from Bozrah? this that is glorious in his apparel, trauelling in
the greatneſſe of his ſtrength? I that ſpeake in righteouſneſſe, mightie to
ſaue.[2]Wherefore art thou red in thine apparell, and thy garments like him
that treadeth in the winefat?[3]I haue troden the winepreſſe alone, and of
the people there was none with me: for I will tread them in mine anger,
and trample them in my furie, and their blood ſhall be ſprinkled vpon

my garments, and I will ſtaine all my raiment. 4 For the day of vengeance is in mine heart, and the yeere of my redeemed is come. 5 And I looked, and there was none to helpe; and I wondered that there was none to vphold: therefore mine owne arme brought ſaluation vnto me, and my furie, it vpheld me. 6 And I will tread downe the people in mine anger, & make them drunke in my furie, and I will bring downe their ſtrength to the earth. 7 I will mention the louing kindneſses of the Lord, and the praiſes of the Lord, according to all that the Lord hath beſtowed on vs; and the great goodnes towards the houſe of Iſrael, which he hath beſtowed on them, according to his mercies, and according to the multitude of his louing kindneſses. 8 For hee ſaid, Surely they are my people, children that will not lie: ſo hee was their ſauiour. 9 In all their affliction he was afflicted, and the Angel of his preſence ſaued them: in his loue and in his pitie hee redeemed them, and he bare them, and caried them all the dayes of olde. 10 But they rebelled, and vexed his holy ſpirit: therefore hee was turned to be their enemie, and he fought againſt them. 11 Then he remembred the dayes of old, Moſes and his people, ſaying; Where is hee that brought them vp out of the ſea, with the ſhepheard of his flocke? where is hee that put his holy Spirit within him? 12 That led them by the right hand of Moſes with his glorious arme, diuiding the water before them, to make himſelfe an euerlaſting name? 13 That led them through the deepe as an horſe in the wilderneſſe, that they ſhould not ſtumble? 14 As a beaſt goeth downe into the valley, the Spirit of the Lord cauſed him to reſt: ſo diddeſt thou leade thy people, to make thy ſelfe a glorious Name. 15 Looke downe from heauen, and behold from the habitation of thy holineſſe, and of thy glory: where is thy zeale and thy ſtrength, the ſounding of thy bowels, and of thy mercies towards me? are they reſtrained? 16 Doubtleſſe thou art our father, though Abraham be ignorant of vs, and Iſrael acknowledge vs not: thou, O Lord art our Father, our Redeemer, thy Name is from euerlaſting. 17 O Lord, why haſt thou made vs to erre from thy wayes? and hardened our heart from thy feare? Returne for thy ſeruants ſake, the tribes of thine inheritance. 18 The people of thy holineſſe haue poſſeſſed it but a little while: our aduerſaries haue troden downe thy Sanctuarie. 19 Wee are thine, thou neuer bareſt rule ouer them, they were not called by thy Name.

CHAPTER 64 1 Oh that thou wouldeſt rent the heauens, that thou wouldeſt come down, that the mountaines might flowe downe at thy preſence, 2 As when the melting fire burneth, the fire cauſeth the waters to boyle: to make thy Name knowen to thine aduerſaries, that the nations may tremble at thy preſence. 3 When thou diddeſt terrible things which wee looked not for, thou cameſt downe, the mountaines flowed downe at thy preſence. 4 For ſince the beginning of the world men haue not heard, nor perceiued by the eare, neither hath the eye ſeene, O God, beſides thee, what hee hath prepared for him that waiteth for him. 5 Thou meeteſt him that reioyceth, and worketh righteouſneſſe, thoſe that remember thee in thy wayes: behold, thou art wroth, for we haue ſinned: in thoſe is continuance, and we ſhall be ſaued. 6 But we are al as an vncleane thing, and all our righteouſneſſes are as filthy ragges, and we all doe fade as a leafe, and our iniquities like the wind haue taken vs away. 7 And there is none that calleth vpon thy name, that ſtirreth vp himſelfe to take hold of thee: for thou haſt hid thy face from vs, and haſt conſumed vs becauſe of our iniquities. 8 But now, O Lord, thou art our father: we are the clay, and thou our potter, and we all are the worke of thine hand. 9 Be not wroth very ſore, O Lord, neither remember iniquitie for euer: behold, ſee we beſeech thee, we are all thy people. 10 Thy holy cities are a wilderneſſe, Zion is a wilderneſſe, Ieruſalem a deſolation. 11 Our holy and our beautifull houſe, where our fathers praiſed thee, is burnt vp with fire, and all our pleaſant things are layed waſte: 12 Wilt thou refraine thy ſelfe for theſe things, O Lord? wilt thou hold thy peace, and afflict vs very ſore?

CHAPTER 65 1 I am ſought of them that aſked not for me: I am found of them that ſought me not: I ſaid, Behold me, behold me, vnto a nation that was not called by my name. 2 I haue ſpread out my hands all the day vnto a rebellious people, which walketh in a way that was not good, after their owne thoughts: 3 A people that prouoketh mee to anger continually to my face, that ſacrificeth in gardens, and burneth incenſe vpon altars of bricke: 4 Which remaine among the graues, and lodge in the monuments, which eate ſwines fleſh, and broth of abominable things is in their veſſels: 5 Which ſay; ſtand by thy ſelfe, come not neere to me; for I am holier then thou: theſe are a ſmoke in my noſe, a fire that burneth all the day. 6 Behold, it is written before me: I will not keepe ſilence, but will recompence, euen recompence into their boſome, 7 Your iniquities, and the iniquities of your fathers together, (ſaith the Lord) which haue burnt incenſe vpon the mountaines, & blaſphemed mee vpon the hils: therfore will I meaſure their former worke into their boſome. 8 Thus ſaith the Lord, As the new wine is found in the cluſter, and one ſaith, Deſtroy it not, for a bleſſing is in it: ſo wil I doe for my ſeruants ſakes, that I may not deſtroy them all. 9 And I will bring forth a ſeede out of Iacob, and out of Iudah an inheritour of my mountains: and mine elect ſhall inherit it, and my ſeruants ſhall dwell there. 10 And Sharon ſhall be a fold of flockes, and the valley of Achor a place for the herds to lie downe in, for my people that haue ſought me. 11 But yee are they that for ſake the Lord, that forget my holy mountaine, that prepare a table for that troope, and that furniſh the drinke offring vnto that number. 12 Therefore will I number you to the ſword, and yee ſhall all bow downe to the ſlaughter: becauſe when I called, yee did not anſwere; when I ſpake, yee did not heare, but did euill before mine eyes, and did chooſe that wherein I delighted not: 13 Therefore thus ſaith the Lord God; Behold, my ſeruants ſhall eate, but ye ſhall be hungry: behold, my ſeruants ſhall drinke, but yee ſhall be thirſtie: behold, my ſeruants ſhall reioyce, but yee ſhall be aſhamed. 14 Behold, my ſeruants ſhall ſing for ioy of heart, but yee ſhall cry for ſorrow of heart, and ſhall howle for vexation of ſpirit. 15 And yee ſhall leaue your name for a curſe vnto my choſen: for the Lord God ſhall ſlay thee, and call his ſeruants by another name: 16 That he who bleſſeth himſelfe in the earth, ſhall bleſſe himſelfe in the God of trueth; and he that ſweareth in the earth, ſhall ſweare by the God of trueth; becauſe the former troubles are forgotten, and becauſe they are hid from mine eyes. 17 For behold, I create new heauens, and a new earth: & the former ſhal not be remembred, nor come into mind. 18 But bee you glad and reioyce for euer in that which I create: for beholde, I create Ieruſalem a reioycing, and her people a ioy. 19 And I wil reioyce in Ieruſalem, and ioy in my people, and the voice of weeping ſhall be no more heard in her, nor the voice of crying. 20 There ſhalbe no more thence an infant of dayes, nor an olde man, that hath not filled his dayes: for the childe ſhall die an hundreth yeeres olde: but the ſinner being an hundreth yeres old, ſhalbe accurſed. 21 And they ſhall builde houſes, and inhabite them, and they ſhall plant vineyards, and eate the fruit of them. 22 They ſhal not build, and another inhabit: they ſhall not plant, and another eat: for as the daies of a tree, are the dayes of my people, and mine elect ſhal long enioy the worke of their hands. 23 They ſhall not labour in vaine, nor bring forth for trouble: for they are the ſeede of the bleſſed of the Lord, and their offſpring with them. 24 And it ſhal come to paſſe, that before they call, I will anſwere, & whiles they are yet ſpeaking, I will heare. 25 The wolfe and the lambe ſhall feede together, and the lyon ſhall eate ſtraw like the bullocke: and duſt ſhalbe the ſerpents meat. They ſhall not hurt nor deſtroy in all my holy mountaine, ſayth the Lord.

CHAPTER 66 1 Thus ſayth the Lord, The heauen is my throne, and the earth is my footeſtoole: where is the houſe that yee builde vnto mee? and where is the place of my reſt? 2 For all thoſe things hath mine hand made, and all thoſe things haue beene, ſaith the Lord: but to this man wil I looke, euen to him that is poore and of a contrite ſpirit, and trembleth at my word. 3 He that killeth an oxe is as if he ſlue a man: he that ſacrificeth a lambe, as if he cut off a dogs necke: he that offereth an oblation, as if he offered ſwines blood: he that burneth incenſe, as if he bleſſed an idole: yea, they haue choſen their owne wayes, and their ſoule delighteth in their abominations. 4 I alſo will chuſe their deluſions, and will bring their feares vpon them; becauſe when I called, none did anſwere, when I ſpake they did not heare: but they did euill before mine eyes, and choſe that in which I delighted not. 5 Heare the word of the Lord, ye that tremble at his word: Your brethren that hated you, that caſt you out for my Names ſake, ſayd, Let the Lord be glorified: but he ſhal appeare to your ioy, and they ſhalbe aſhamed. 6 A voice of noyſe from the city, a voice from the Temple, a voice of the Lord, that rendreth recompenſe to his enemies. 7 Before ſhe trauailed, ſhe brought foorth: before her paine came, ſhee was deliuered of a man childe. 8 Who hath heard ſuch a thing? who hath ſeene ſuch things? ſhall the earth be made to bring forth in one day, or ſhall a nation be borne at once? for as ſoone as Zion traueiled, ſhee brought foorth her children. 9 Shall I bring to the birth, & not cauſe to bring forth, ſaith the Lord ? ſhall I cauſe to bring foorth, and ſhut the wombe, ſayth thy God?10Reioyce ye with Ieruſalem, and be glad with her, all yee that loue her: reioyce for ioy with her, all yee that mourne for her:11That ye may ſucke and be ſatiſfied with the breaſts of her conſolations: that ye may milke out, and be delighted with the abundance of her glory.12For thus ſayth the Lord, Behold, I will extend peace to her like a riuer, and the glory of the Gentiles like a flowing ſtreame: then ſhall ye ſucke, ye ſhalbe borne vpon her ſides, and be dandled vpon her knees.13As one whom his mother comforteth, ſo wil I comfort you: and ye ſhall be comforted in Ieruſalem.14And when yee ſee this, your heart ſhall reioyce, and your bones ſhall flouriſh like an herbe: and the hand of the Lord ſhall be knowen towards his ſeruants, and his indignation towards his enemies.15For behold, the Lord wil come with fire, and with his charets like a whirlewinde, to render his anger with furie, and his rebuke with flames of fire.16For by fire and by his ſword, will the Lord plead with all fleſh: and the ſlaine of the Lord ſhalbe many.17They that ſanctifie themſelues, and purifie themſelues in the gardens, behinde one tree in the midſt, eating ſwines fleſh, and the abomination, and the mouſe, ſhall be conſumed together, ſaith the Lord.18For I know their works and their thoughts: it ſhall come that I will gather all nations and tongues, and they ſhall come and ſee my glorie.19And I will ſet a ſigne among them, and I will ſend thoſe that eſcape of them vnto the nations, to Tarſhiſh, Pul and Lud, that draw the bow, to Tubal and Iauan, to the Iles afarre off, that haue not heard my fame, neither haue ſeene my glory, and they ſhall declare my glory among the Gentiles.20And they ſhall bring all your brethren for an offering vnto the Lord, out of all nations, vpon horſes and in charets, and in litters, and vpon mules, and vpon ſwift beaſts to my holie mountaine Ieruſalem, ſaith the Lord; as the children of Iſrael bring an offering in a cleane veſſell, into the houſe of the Lord.21And I will alſo take of them for Prieſtes and for Leuites, ſaith the Lord.22For as the new heauens, and the new earth which I wil make, ſhall remaine before me, ſaith the Lord, ſo ſhall your ſeed and your name remaine.23And it ſhall come to paſſe, that from one new Moone to an other, and from one Sabbath to an other, ſhall all fleſh come to worſhip before me, ſaith the Lord.24And they ſhall goe foorth, and looke vpon the carkeiſes of the men that haue tranſgreſſed againſt me: for their worme ſhall not die, neither ſhall their fire be quenched, and they ſhall be an abhorring vnto all fleſh.

IEREMIAH (JEREMIAH)

CHAPTER 11The wordes of Ieremiah the ſonne of Hilkiah, of the Prieſts that were in Anathoth in the land of Beniamin:2To whom the word of the Lord came in the dayes of Ioſiah the ſonne of Amon king of Iudah, in the thirteenth yeere of his reigne.3It came alſo in the dayes of Iehoiakim the ſonne of Ioſiah king of Iudah, vnto the ende of the eleuenth yeere of Zedekiah the ſonne of Ioſiah king of Iudah, vnto the carrying away of Ieruſalem captiue in the fift moneth.4Then the word of the Lord came vnto me, ſaying,5Before I formed thee in the bellie, I knew thee; and before thou cameſt forth out of the wombe, I ſanctified thee, and I ordeined thee a Prophet vnto the nations.6Then ſaid I, Ah Lord God, behold, I cannot ſpeake, for I am a childe.7But the Lord ſayd vnto me, ſay not, I am a childe: for thou ſhalt goe to all that I ſhall ſend thee, and whatſoeuer I command thee, thou ſhalt ſpeake.8Be not afraid of their faces: for I am with thee to deliuer thee, ſayth the Lord.9Then the Lord put foorth his hand, and touched my mouth, and the Lord ſaid vnto me, Behold, I haue put my words in thy mouth.10See, I haue this day ſet thee ouer the nations, and ouer the kingdomes, to roote out, and to pull downe, and to deſtroy, and to throw down, to build and to plant.11Moreouer, the word of the Lord came vnto me, ſaying; Ieremiah, what ſeeſt thou? And I ſaid, I ſee a rodde of an almond tree.12Then ſaid the Lord vnto me, Thou haſt well ſeene: for I will haſten my word to performe it.13And the worde of the Lord came vnto mee the ſecond time, ſaying; What ſeeſt thou? And I ſaid; I ſee a ſeething pot, and the face thereof was towards the North.14Then the Lord ſaid vnto me; Out of the North an euill ſhal breake foorth vpon all the inhabitants of the land.15For loe, I will call all the families of the kingdoms of the North, ſaith the Lord, and they ſhall come, and they ſhall ſet euery one his throne at the entring of the gates of Ieruſalem, and againſt all the walles thereof round about, & againſt all the cities of Iudah.16And I will vtter my iudgements againſt them touching all their wickedneſſe, who haue forſaken me, and haue burnt incenſe vnto other gods, and worſhipped the workes of their owne hands.17Thou therefore gird vp thy loynes, and Ariſe and ſpeake vnto them all that I commaund thee: be not diſmayed at their faces, leſt I confound thee before them.18For behold, I haue made thee this day a defenced citie, and an yron pillar, and braſen walles againſt the whole land, againſt the kings of Iudah, againſt the princes thereof, againſt the Prieſts thereof, and againſt the people of the land.19And they ſhall fight againſt thee, but they ſhall not preuaile againſt thee: for I am with thee, ſayth the Lord, to deliuer thee.

CHAPTER 21Moreouer, the word of the Lord came to me, ſaying;2Goe, and crie in the eares of Ieruſalem, ſaying; Thus ſayth the Lord, I remember thee, the kindneſſe of thy youth, the loue of thine eſpouſals, when thou wenteſt after me in the wilderneſſe, in a land that was not ſowen.3Iſrael was holineſſe vnto the Lord, and the firſt fruites of his increaſe: all that deuoure him, ſhall offend, euill ſhall come vpon them, ſayth the Lord.4Heare ye the word of the Lord, O houſe of Iacob, and all the families of the houſe of Iſrael.5Thus ſayth the Lord, What iniquitie haue your fathers found in me, that they are gone farre from mee, and haue walked after vanitie, and are become vaine?6Neither ſayd they, Where is the Lord that brought vs vp out of the land of Egypt? that led vs through the wilderneſſe, through a land of deſerts and of pittes, through a land of drought, and of the ſhadow of death, through a land that no man paſſed thorow, and where no man dwelt.7And I brought you into a plentifull countrey, to eate the fruit thereof, and the goodneſſe thereof; but when ye entred yee defiled my land, and made mine heritage an abomination.8The Prieſts ſaid not, Where is the Lord ? and they that handle the Law knew me not: the paſtours alſo tranſgreſſed againſt mee, and the Prophets prophecied by Baal, and walked after things that doe not profit.9Wherefore, I will yet pleade with you, ſayth the Lord, and with your childrens children will I pleade.10For paſſe ouer the yles of Chittim, and ſee; and ſend vnto Kedar and conſider diligently, and ſee if there be ſuch a thing.11Hath a nation changed their Gods, which are yet no Gods? but my people haue changed their glory, for that which doth not profit.12Be aſtoniſhed, O yee heauens, at this, and be horribly afraid, be yee very deſolate, ſaith the Lord.13For my people haue committed two euils: they haue forſaken me, the fountaine of liuing waters, and hewed them out ciſternes, broken ciſternes that can hold no water.14Is Iſrael a ſeruant? is he a home-borne ſlaue? why is he ſpoiled?15The young lyons roared vpon him and yelled, and they made his land waſte: his cities are burnt without inhabitant.16Alſo the children of Noph and Tahapanes haue broken the crowne of thy head.17Haſt thou not procured this vnto thy ſelfe, in that thou haſt forſaken the Lord thy God, when he led thee by the way?18And now what haſt thou to doe in the way of Egypt, to drinke the waters of Sihor? Or what haſt thou to doe in the way of Aſſyria, to drinke the waters of the riuer?19Thine owne wickedneſſe ſhall correct thee, and thy backſlidings ſhall reproue thee: know therefore and ſee, that it is an euill thing and bitter that thou haſt forſaken the Lord thy God, and that my feare is not in thee, ſaith the Lord GOD of Hoſtes.20For of old time I haue broken thy yoke, and burſt thy bands, and thou ſaidſt; I will not tranſgreſe: when vpon euery high hill, and vnder euery greene tree thou wandreſt, playing the harlot.21Yet I had planted thee a noble vine, wholy a right ſeede: How then art thou turned into the degenerate plant of a ſtrange vine vnto me?22For though thou waſh thee with nitre, and take thee much ſope, yet thine iniquitie is marked before me, ſaith the Lord GOD.23How canſt thou ſay, I am not polluted, I haue not gone after Baalim? ſee thy way in the valley, know what thou haſt done: thou art a ſwift dromedarie trauerſing her wayes.24A wild aſſe vſed to the wilderneſſe, that ſnuffeth vp the wind at her pleaſure, in her occaſion who can turne her away? all they that ſeeke her will not wearie themſelues, in her moneth they ſhall find her.25Withhold thy foote from being vnſhod, and thy throte from thirſt: but thou ſaidſt, There is no hope. No, for I haue loued ſtrangers, and after them will I goe.26As the thiefe is aſhamed, when he is found: ſo is the houſe of Iſrael aſhamed, they, their kings, their princes, and their prieſts, & their prophets,27Saying to a ſtocke; Thou art my father, and to a ſtone; Thou haſt brought me forth: for they haue turned their backe vnto me, and not their face: but in the time of their trouble, they will ſay; Ariſe and ſaue vs.28But where are thy Gods that thou haſt made thee? let them Ariſe if they can ſaue thee in the time of thy trouble: for according to the number of thy cities, are thy Gods, O Iudah.29Wherefore will yee plead with me? yee all haue tranſgreſſed againſt me, ſaith the Lord.30In vaine haue I ſmitten your children, they receiued no correction: your owne ſword hath deuoured your prophets, like a deſtroying lyon.31O generation, ſee yee the word of the Lord: haue I beene a wilderneſſe vnto Iſrael? a land of darkeneſſe? wherefore ſay my people; We are Lords, we will come no more vnto thee?32Can a maide forget her ornaments, or a bride her attire? yet my people haue forgotten me dayes without number.33Why trimmeſt thou thy way to ſeeke loue? therefore haſt thou alſo taught the wicked ones thy wayes.34Alſo in thy ſkirts is found the blood of the ſoules of the poore innocents: I haue not found it by ſecret ſearch, but vpon all theſe.35Yet thou ſayeſt; Becauſe I am innocent, ſurely his anger ſhall turne from me: behold, I will plead with thee, becauſe thou ſayeſt, I haue not ſinned.36Why gaddeſt thou about ſo much to change thy way? thou alſo ſhalt bee aſhamed of Egypt, as thou waſt aſhamed of Aſſyria.37Yea thou ſhalt goe forth from him, and thine hands vpon thine head: for the Lord hath reiected thy confidences, and thou ſhalt not proſper in them.

CHAPTER 31They ſay; If a man put away his wife, and ſhe goe from him, and become another mans, ſhall hee returne vnto her againe? ſhall not that land be greatly polluted? but thou haſt played the harlot with many louers; yet returne againe to me, ſaith the Lord.2Lift vp thine eyes vnto the high places, and ſee where thou haſt not bene lien with: in the wayes haſt thou ſate for them, as the Arabian in the wilderneſſe, and thou haſt polluted the land with thy whoredomes, and with thy wickednes.3Therefore the ſhowres haue bin withholden, and there hath bene no latter raine, and thou haddeſt a whores forehead, thou refuſedſt to be aſhamed.4Wilt thou not from this time cry vnto me; My father, thou art the guide of my youth?5Will he reſerue his anger for euer? wil he keepe it to the end? Behold, thou haſt ſpoken and done euill things as thou couldeſt.6The Lord ſaid alſo vnto me, in the daies of Ioſiah the king, Haſt thou ſeene that which backſliding Iſrael hath done? ſhe is gone vp vpon euery high mountaine, and vnder euery greene tree, and there hath plaied the harlot.7And I ſaid after ſhe had done all theſe things; Turne thou vnto me: but ſhee returned not, and her treacherous ſiſter Iudah ſaw it.8And I ſaw, when for all the cauſes whereby backſliding Iſrael committed adulterie, I had put her away and giuen her a bill of diuorce: yet her treacherous ſiſter Iudah feared not, but went and played the harlot alſo.9And it came to paſſe thorow the lightnes of her whoredome, that ſhee defiled the land, and committed adultery with ſtones and with ſtockes.10And yet for all this her treacherous ſiſter Iudah hath not turned vnto mee with her whole heart, but fainedly, ſaith the Lord.11And the Lord ſaid vnto mee, The backeſliding Iſrael hath iuſtified her ſelfe more then treacherous Iudah.12Go and proclaime theſe words toward the North, and ſay, Returne thou backeſliding Iſrael, ſayeth the Lord, and I will not cauſe mine anger to fall vpon you: for I am mercifull, ſaith the Lord, and I will not keepe anger for euer.13Only acknowledge thine iniquity that thou haſt tranſgreſſed againſt the Lord thy God, and haſt ſcattered thy wayes to the ſtrangers vnder euery greene tree, and ye haue not obeyed my voice, ſaith the Lord.14Turne, O backeſliding children, ſaith the Lord, for I am maried vnto you: and I will take you one of a city, and two of a family, and I wil bring you to Zion.15And I will giue you Paſtours according to mine heart, which ſhall feede you with knowledge and vnderſtanding.16And it ſhall come to paſſe when yee bee multiplied and increaſed in the land; in thoſe dayes, ſaith the Lord, they ſhal ſay no more; The Arke of the Couenant of the Lord: neither ſhal it come to minde, neither ſhall they remember it, neither ſhall they viſit it, neither ſhall that be done any more.17At that time they ſhall call Ieruſalem the Throne of the Lord, and all the nations ſhalbe gathered vnto it, to the Name of the Lord, to Ieruſalem: neither ſhall they walke any more after the imagination of their euill heart.18In thoſe dayes the houſe of Iudah ſhall walke with the houſe of Iſrael, and they ſhall come together out of the land of the North to the land that I haue giuen for an inheritance vnto your fathers.19But I ſaid; How ſhall I put thee among the children, and giue thee a pleaſant land, a goodly heritage of the hoſtes of nations? and I ſaid, Thou ſhalt call me; My father, and ſhalt not turne away from me.20Surely as a wife treacherouſly departeth from her huſband: ſo haue you dealt treacherouſly with mee, O houſe of Iſrael, ſaith the Lord.21A voice was heard vpon the high places, weeping and ſupplications of the children of Iſrael: for they haue peruerted their way, and they haue forgotten the Lord their God.22Returne ye backſliding children, and I wil heale your backſlidings: Beholde, wee come vnto thee, for thou art the Lord our God.23Truely in vaine is ſaluation hoped for from the hilles, and from the multitude of mountaines: truely in the Lord our God is the ſaluation of Iſrael.24For ſhame hath deuoured the labour of our fathers from our youth: their flockes and their heards, their ſonnes and their daughters.25We lie downe in our ſhame, and our confuſion coueretħ vs: for we haue ſinned againſt the Lord our God, wee and our fathers from our youth euen vnto this day, and haue not obeied the voice of the Lord our God.

CHAPTER 41If thou wilt returne, O Iſrael, ſaith the Lord, returne vnto mee: and if thou wilt put away thine abominations out of my ſight, then ſhalt thou not remoue.2And thou ſhalt ſweare, The Lord liueth, in Trueth, in Iudgement, and in Righteouſnes, and the nations ſhall bleſſe themſelues in him, and in him ſhall they glorie.3For thus ſaith the Lord to the men of Iudah and Ieruſalem, Breake vp your fallow ground, and ſow not among thornes.4Circumciſe your ſelues to the Lord, and take away the foreſkinnes of your heart, ye men of Iudah, and inhabitants of Ieruſalem, leſt my furie come forth like fire, and burne that none can quench it, becauſe of the euill of your doings.5Declare ye in Iudah, and publiſh in Ieruſalem, and ſay, Blow yee the Trumpet in the land: cry, gather together, and ſay, Aſſemble your ſelues, and let vs goe into the defenced cities.6Set vp the ſtandards toward Zion: retyre, ſtay not; for I will bring euil from the North, and a great deſtruction.7The Lion is come vp from his thicket, and the deſtroyer of the Gentiles is on his way; hee is gone foorth from his place to make thy land deſolate, and thy cities ſhall be layed waſte, without an inhabitant.8For this gird you with ſackcloth; lament and howle: for the fierce anger of the Lord is not turned backe from vs.9And it ſhall come to paſſe at that day, ſaith the Lord, that the heart of the King ſhall periſh, and the heart of the Princes: and the Prieſts ſhalbe aſtoniſhed, & the prophets ſhall wonder.10Then ſaid I, Ah Lord God, ſurely thou haſt greatly deceiued this people, and Ieruſalem, ſaying, Ye ſhall haue peace, whereas the ſword reacheth vnto the ſoule.11At that time ſhall it bee ſaid to this people, and to Ieruſalem; A dry winde of the high places in the wildernes toward the daughter of my people, not to fanne, nor to cleanſe.12Euen a full winde from thoſe places ſhall come vnto mee: now alſo will I giue ſentence againſt them.13Behold, hee ſhall come vp as cloudes, and his charets ſhall bee as a whirlewinde: his horſes are ſwifter then Eagles: woe vnto vs, for wee are ſpoiled.14O Ieruſalem, waſh thine heart from wickedneſſe, that thou mayeſt bee ſaued: how long ſhall thy vaine thoughts lodge within thee?15For a voice declareth from Dan, and publiſheth affliction from mount Ephraim.16Make ye mention to the nations, behold, publiſh againſt Ieruſalem, that watchers come from a farre countrey, and giue out their voice againſt the cities of Iudah.17As keepers of a fielde are they againſt her round about; becauſe ſhee hath bene rebellious againſt mee, ſaith the Lord.18Thy way and thy doings haue procured theſe things vnto thee, this is thy wickednes becauſe it is bitter, becauſe it reacheth vnto thine heart.19My bowels, my bowels, I am pained at my very heart, my heart maketh a noiſe in mee, I cannot hold my peace, becauſe thou haſt heard, O my ſoule, the ſound of the Trumpet, the alarme of warre.20Deſtruction vpon deſtruction is cried, for the whole land is ſpoiled: ſuddenly are my tents ſpoiled, and my curtaines in a moment.21How long ſhal I ſee the ſtandard and heare the ſound of the Trumpet?22For my people is fooliſh, they haue not knowen me, they are ſottiſh children, and they haue none vnderſtanding: they are wiſe to doe euill, but to doe good they haue no knowledge.23I beheld the earth, and loe, it was without forme and void: and the heauens, and they had no light.24I beheld the mountaines, and loe they trembled, and all the hilles mooued lightly.25I beheld, and loe, there was no man, and all the birdes of the heauens were fled.26I beheld, and loe, the fruitfull place was a wilderneſſe, and all the cities thereof were broken downe at the preſence of the Lord, and by his fierce anger.27For thus hath the Lord ſaid; The whole land ſhall be deſolate; yet will I not make a full ende.28For this ſhall the earth mourne, and the heauens aboue be blacke: becauſe I haue ſpoken it, I haue purpoſed it, and will not repent, neither will I turne backe from it. 29 The whole citie ſhall flee, for the noiſe of the horſemen and bowmen, they ſhall goe into thickets, and climbe vp vpon the rockes: euery city ſhall be forſaken, and not a man dwell therein. 30 And when thou art ſpoiled, what wilt thou doe? though thou clotheſt thy ſelfe with crimſin, though thou deckeſt thee with ornaments of golde, though thou renteſt thy face with painting, in vaine ſhalt thou make thy ſelfe faire, thy louers will deſpiſe thee, they will ſeeke thy life. 31 For I haue heard a voice as of a woman in trauel, and the anguiſh as of her that bringeth foorth her firſt childe, the voice of the daughter of Zion, that bewaileth her ſelfe, that ſpreadeth her hands, ſaying; Woe is me now, for my ſoule is wearied becauſe of murderers.

CHAPTER 5 1 Runne yee to and fro thorow the ſtreetes of Ieruſalem, and ſee now and knowe, and ſeeke in the broad places thereof, if ye can finde a man, if there be any that executeth iudgement, that ſeeketh the trueth, and I will pardon it. 2 And though they ſay, The Lord liueth, ſurely they ſweare falſely. 3 O Lord, are not thine eyes vpon the trueth? thou haſt ſtricken them, but they haue not grieued; thou haſt conſumed them, but they haue refuſed to receiue correction: they haue made their faces harder then a rocke, they haue refuſed to returne. 4 Therefore I ſaid, Surely theſe are poore, they are fooliſh: for they know not the way of the Lord, nor the iudgement of their God. 5 I wil get me vnto the great men, and will ſpeake vnto them, for they haue knowen the way of the Lord, and the iudgement of their God: but theſe haue altogether broken the yoke, and burſt the bondes. 6 Wherfore a lyon out of the forreſt ſhall ſlay them, and a wolfe of the euenings ſhall ſpoile them, a leopard ſhall watch ouer their cities: euery one that goeth out thence ſhalbe torne in pieces, becauſe their tranſgreſſions are many, and their backeſlidings are increaſed. 7 How ſhall I pardon thee for this? thy children haue forſaken mee, and ſworne by them that are no gods: when I had fed them to the full, they then committed adulterie, and aſſembled themſelues by troupes in the harlots houſes. 8 They were as fed horſes in the morning: euery one neighed after his neighbours wife: 9 Shall I not viſit for theſe things, ſayth the Lord, and ſhall not my ſoule bee auenged on ſuch a nation as this? 10 Goe yee vp vpon her walles, and deſtroy, but make not a full ende: take away her battlements, for they are not the Lords. 11 For the houſe of Iſrael, and the houſe of Iudah haue dealt very treacherouſly againſt me, ſaith the Lord. 12 They haue belyed the Lord, and ſaid; It is not he, neither ſhall euill come vpon vs, neither ſhal we ſee ſword nor famine. 13 And the prophets ſhall become wind, and the word is not in them: thus ſhall it be done vnto them. 14 Wherfore thus ſaith the Lord God of Hoſtes; Becauſe yee ſpeake this word, behold, I will make my words in thy mouth, fire, and this people wood, and it ſhall deuoure them. 15 Loe, I will bring a nation vpon you from farre, O houſe of Iſrael, ſaith the Lord: it is a mighty nation, it is an ancient nation, a nation whoſe language thou knoweſt not, neither vnderſtandeſt what they ſay. 16 Their quiuer is as an open ſepulchre, they are all mighty men. 17 And they ſhall eate vp thine harueſt and thy bread, which thy ſonnes and thy daughters ſhould eate: they ſhall eate vp thy flockes and thine heards: they ſhall eate vp thy vines and thy figtrees: they ſhall impoueriſh thy fenced cities wherein thou truſtedſt, with the ſword. 18 Neuertheleſſe in thoſe daies, ſaith the Lord, I will not make a full end with you. 19 And it ſhall come to paſſe when yee ſhall ſay; Wherefore doth the Lord our God all theſe things vnto vs? then ſhalt thou anſwere them; Like as ye haue forſaken me, & ſerued ſtrange Gods in your land; ſo ſhall yee ſerue ſtrangers in a land that is not yours. 20 Declare this in the houſe of Iacob, and publiſh it in Iudah ſaying; 21 Heare now this, O fooliſh people, and without vnderſtanding, which haue eyes and ſee not, which haue eares and heare not. 22 Feare yee not mee, ſaith the Lord ? Will yee not tremble at my preſence, which haue placed the ſand for the bound of the ſea, by a perpetuall decree that it cannot paſſe it, and though the waues thereof toſſe themſelues, yet can they not preuaile, though they roare, yet can they not paſſe ouer it? 23 But this people hath a reuolting and a rebellious heart: they are reuolted and gone. 24 Neither ſay they in their heart; Let vs now feare the Lord our God, that giueth raine, both the former and the later in his ſeaſon: he reſerueth vnto vs the appointed weekes of the harueſt. 25 Your iniquities haue turned away theſe things, & your ſinnes haue withholden good things from you. 26 For among my people are found wicked men: they lay waite as hee that ſetteth ſnares, they ſet a trap, they catch men. 27 As a cage is full of birds, ſo are their houſes full of deceit: therefore they are become great, and waxen rich. 28 They are waxen fat, they ſhine: yea they ouerpaſſe the deedes of the wicked: they iudge not the cauſe, the cauſe of the fatherleſſe, yet they proſper: and the right of the needy doe they not iudge. 29 Shall I not viſit for theſe things, ſaith the Lord ? ſhall not my ſoule be auenged on ſuch a nation as this? 30 A wonderfull and horrible thing is committed in the land. 31 The prophets prophecie falſely, and the prieſts beare rule by their meanes, and my people loue to haue it ſo: and what will yee doe in the end therof?

CHAPTER 6 1 O yee children of Beniamin, gather your ſelues to flee out of the middeſt of Ieruſalem, and blow the trumpet in Tekoa: and ſet vp a ſigne of fire in Beth-haccerem: for euill appeareth out of the North, and great deſtruction. 2 I haue likened the daughter of Zion to a comely and delicate woman. 3 The ſhepheards with their flocks ſhall come vnto her: they ſhall pitch their tents againſt her round about: they ſhall feede, euery one in his place. 4 Prepare yee warre againſt her: Ariſe, and let vs goe vp at noone: woe vnto vs, for the day goeth away, for the ſhadowes of the euening are ſtretched out. 5 Ariſe, and let vs goe by night, and let vs deſtroy her palaces. 6 For thus hath the Lord of hoſtes ſaid; Hew yee downe trees and caſt a mount againſt Ieruſalem: this is the citie to be viſited, ſhe is wholly oppreſſion in the midſt of her. 7 As a fountaine caſteth out her waters, ſo ſhe caſteth out her wickedneſſe: violence and ſpoile is heard in her, before me continually is griefe and wounds. 8 Be thou inſtructed, O Ieruſalem, leſt my ſoule depart from thee: leſt I make thee deſolate, a lande not inhabited. 9 Thus ſaith the Lord of hoſts, They ſhall throughly gleane the remnant of Iſrael as a vine: turne backe thine hand as a grape gatherer into the baſkets. 10 To whome ſhall I ſpeake and giue warning, that they may heare? Behold, their eare is vncircumciſed, and they cannot hearken: beholde, the word of the Lord is vnto them a reproch: they haue no delight in it. 11 Therefore I am full of the furie of the Lord: I am weary with holding in: I will powre it out vpon the children abroad, and vpon the aſſembly of yong men together: for euen the huſband with the wife ſhall be taken, the aged with him that is full of dayes. 12 And their houſes ſhall be turned vnto others, with their fields and wiues together: for I wil ſtretch out my hand vpon the inhabitants of the land, ſaith the Lord. 13 For from the leaſt of them euen vnto the greateſt of them, euery one is giuen to couetouſneſſe, and from the prophet euen vnto the prieſt, euery one dealeth falſly. 14 They haue healed alſo the hurt of the daughter of my people ſleightly, ſaying, Peace, peace, when there is no peace. 15 Were they aſhamed when they had committed abomination? nay they were not at all aſhamed, neither could they bluſh: therefore they ſhall fall among them that fall: at the time that I viſit them, they ſhall bee caſt downe, ſaith the Lord. 16 Thus ſaith the Lord, ſtand ye in the wayes and ſee, and aſke for the old paths, where is the good way, and walke therein, and ye ſhall finde reſt for your ſoules: but they ſaid, We will not walke therein. 17 Alſo I ſet watchmen ouer you, ſaying, Hearken to the ſound of the trumpet: but they ſaid, We wil not hearken. 18 Therefore heare ye nations, and know, O Congregation what is among them. 19 Heare, O earth, behold, I will bring euill vpon this people, euen the fruit of their thoughts, becauſe they haue not hearkened vnto my wordes, nor to my law, but reiected it. 20 To what purpoſe cōmeth there to me incenſe from Sheba? and the ſweet cane from a farre countrey? your burnt offerings are not acceptable, nor your ſacrifices ſweet vnto me. 21 Therefore thus ſaith the Lord, Behold, I will lay ſtumbling blockes before this people, and the fathers and the ſons together ſhall fall vpon them: the neighbor and his friend ſhall periſh. 22 Thus ſaith the Lord, Behold, a people commeth from the North countrey, and a great nation ſhall bee raiſed from the ſides of the earth. 23 They ſhall lay hold on bowe and ſpeare: they are cruell, and haue no mercie: their voice roareth like the ſea, and they ride vpon horſes, ſet in aray as men for warre againſt thee, O daughter of Zion. 24 We haue heard the fame thereof, our hands waxe feeble, anguiſh hath taken hold of vs, and paine as of a woman in trauaile. 25 Goe not forth into the field, nor walke by the way: for the ſword of the enemie and feare is on euery ſide. 26 O daughter of my people, gird thee with ſackcloth, and wallowe thy ſelfe in aſhes: make thee mourning, as for an onely ſonne, moſt bitter lamentation: for the ſpoiler ſhall ſuddenly come vpon vs. 27 I haue ſet thee for a towre, and a fortreſse among my people: that thou mayeſt know and trie their way. 28 They are all grieuous reuolters, walking with ſlanders: they are braſſe and yron, they are all corrupters. 29 The bellowes are burnt, the lead is conſumed of the fire: the founder melteth in vaine:

for the wicked are not plucked away.[30]Reprobate ſiluer ſhall men call them, becauſe the Lord hath reiected them.

CHAPTER 7[1]The word that came to Ieremiah from the Lord, ſaying,[2]ſtand in the gate of the Lords houſe, and proclaime there this word, and ſay, Heare the word of the Lord, all ye of Iudah, that enter in at theſe gates to worſhip the Lord.[3]Thus ſaith the Lord of hoſtes the God of Iſrael; Amend your wayes, and your doings, and I will cauſe you to dwell in this place.[4]Truſt ye not in lying words, ſaying, The Temple of the Lord, the Temple of the Lord, the Temple of the Lord are theſe.[5]For if ye throughly amend your waies and your doings, if you throughly execute iudgement betweene a man and his neighbour:[6]If ye oppreſſe not the ſtranger, the fatherleſſe and the widow, and ſhed not innocent blood in this place, neither walke after other gods to your hurt:[7]Then will I cauſe you to dwell in this place, in the land that I gaue to your fathers, for euer and euer.[8]Behold, ye truſt in lying words, that cannot profit.[9]Will ye ſteale, murther, and commit adulterie, and ſweare falſly, and burne incenſe vnto Baal, and walke after other gods, whom ye know not;[10]And come and ſtand before me in this houſe, which is called by my Name, and ſay, We are deliuered, to do all theſe abominations?[11]Is this houſe, which is called by my Name, become a denne of robbers in your eies? Behold, euen I haue ſeen it, ſaith the Lord.[12]But goe yee now vnto my place which was in Shiloh, where I ſet my Name at the firſt, and ſee what I did to it, for the wickedneſſe of my people Iſrael.[13]And now becauſe ye haue done all theſe workes, ſaith the Lord, and I ſpake vnto you, riſing vp earely, and ſpeaking, but ye heard not; and I called you, but ye anſwered not:[14]Therefore will I doe vnto this houſe, which is called by my Name, wherein yee truſt, and vnto the place which I gaue to you, and to your fathers, as I haue done to Shiloh.[15]And I will caſt you out of my ſight, as I haue caſt out all your brethren, euen the whole ſeed of Ephraim.[16]Therefore pray not thou for this people, neither lift vp cry nor prayer for them, neither make intercesſion to me, for I will not heare thee.[17]Seeſt thou not what they doe in the cities of Iudah, and in the ſtreets of Ieruſalem?[18]The children gather wood, and the fathers kindle the fire, & the women knead their dough to make cakes to the Queene of heauen, and to powre out drinke offerings vnto other gods, that they may prouoke me to anger.[19]Doe they prouoke mee to anger, ſaith the Lord ? Doe they not prouoke themſelues to the confuſion of their owne faces?[20]Therefore thus ſaith the Lord God, Behold, mine anger and my furie ſhalbe powred out vpon this place, vpon man & vpon beaſt, and vpon the trees of the field, and vpon the fruit of the ground, and it ſhall burne, and ſhall not be quenched.[21]Thus ſaith the Lord of hoſts the God of Iſrael, Put your burnt offrings vnto your ſacrifices, & eate fleſh.[22]For I ſpake not vnto your fathers, nor commanded them in the day that I brought them out of the land of Egypt, concerning burnt offerings or ſacrifices.[23]But this thing commaunded I them, ſaying, Obey my voice, and I wil be your God, and ye ſhalbe my people: and walke ye in all the wayes that I haue commanded you, that it may be well vnto you.[24]But they hearkened not, nor inclined their eare, but walked in the counſels and in the imagination of their euill heart, and went backward, and not forward.[25]Since the day that your fathers came forth out of the land of Egypt vnto this day, I haue euen ſent vnto you all my ſeruants the Prophets, daily riſing vp early, and ſending them.[26]Yet they hearkned not vnto me, nor inclined their eare, but hardened their neck, they did worſe then their fathers.[27]Therefore thou ſhalt ſpeake all theſe wordes vnto them, but they will not hearken to thee: thou ſhalt alſo call vnto them, but they will not anſwere thee.[28]But thou ſhalt ſay vnto them; This is a nation, that obeyeth not the voyce of the Lord their God, nor receiueth correction: trueth is periſhed, and is cut off from their mouth.[29]Cut off thine haire, O Ieruſalem, and caſt it away, and take vp a lamentation on high places, for the Lord hath reiected, and forſaken the generation of his wrath.[30]For the children of Iudah haue done euill in my ſight, ſaith the Lord: they haue ſet their abominations in the houſe which is called by my Name, to pollute it.[31]And they haue built the high places of Tophet which is in the valley of the ſonne of Hinnom, to burne their ſonnes and their daughters in the fire, which I commanded them not, neither came it into my heart.[32]Therefore behold, the dayes come, ſaith the Lord, that it ſhall no more be called Tophet, nor the valley of the ſonne of Hinnom, but the valley of ſlaughter: for they ſhall bury in Tophet, till there be no place.[33]And the carkeiſes of this people ſhall be meate for the fowles of the heauen, and for the beaſts of the earth, and none ſhall fray them away.[34]Then will I cauſe to ceaſe from the cities of Iudah, and from the ſtreets of Ieruſalem, the voice of mirth and the voice of gladneſſe, the voice of the bridegroome, and the voice of the bride: for the land ſhall be deſolate.

CHAPTER 8[1]At that time, ſayeth the Lord, they ſhall bring out the bones of the kings of Iudah, and the bones of his princes, and the bones of the Prieſts, and the bones of the Prophets, and the bones of the inhabitants of Ieruſalem out of their graues.[2]And they ſhall ſpread them before the Sunne, and the Moone, and all the hoſte of heauen whom they haue loued, and whom they haue ſerued, and after whom they haue walked, and whom they haue ſought, and whom they haue worſhipped: they ſhall not be gathered, nor be buried, they ſhall be for doung, vpon the face of the earth.[3]And death ſhall bee choſen rather then life, by all the reſidue of them that remaine of this euill family, which remaine in all the places whither I haue driuen them, ſaith the Lord of hoſts.[4]Moreouer thou ſhalt ſay vnto them, Thus ſaith the Lord, Shall they fall, and not Ariſe? ſhall hee turne away, and not returne?[5]Why then is this people of Ieruſalem ſlidden backe, by a perpetual backeſliding? they hold faſt deceit, they refuſe to returne.[6]I hearkened and heard, but they ſpake not aright: no man repented him of his wickedneſſe, ſaying, What haue I done? euery one turned to his courſe, as the horſe ruſheth into the battell.[7]Yea the Storke in the heauen knoweth her appointed times, and the turtle, and the crane, and the ſwallow obſerue the time of their coming; but my people know not the iudgement of the Lord.[8]How doe ye ſay, We are wiſe, and the Law of the Lord is with vs? Loe, certainly, in vaine made he it, the pen of the ſcribes is in vaine.[9]The wiſe men are aſhamed, they are diſmayed and taken; loe, they haue reiected the word of the Lord, and what wiſedome is in them?[10]Therfore will I giue their wiues vnto others, & their fields to them that ſhall inherite them: for euery one from the leaſt euen vnto the greateſt is giuen to couetouſnes, from the Prophet euen vnto the prieſt, euery one dealeth falſly.[11]For they haue healed the hurt of the daughter of my people ſlightly, ſaying, Peace, peace, when there is no peace.[12]Were they aſhamed when they had committed abomination? nay, they were not at all aſhamed, neither could they bluſh: therefore ſhall they fall among them that fal, in the time of their viſitation they ſhall be caſt downe, ſaith the Lord.[13]I will ſurely conſume them, ſaith the Lord; there ſhalbe no grapes on the vine, nor figges on the figtree, and the leafe ſhall fade, and the things that I haue giuen them, ſhall paſſe away from them.[14]Why doe wee ſit ſtill? aſſemble your ſelues, and let vs enter into the defenced cities, and let vs be ſilent there: for the Lord our God hath put vs to ſilence, and giuen vs waters of gall to drink, becauſe we haue ſinned againſt the Lord.[15]We looked for peace, but no good came: and for a time of health, and behold trouble.[16]The ſnorting of his horſes was heard from Dan: the whole land trembled at the ſound of the neighing of his ſtrong ones, for they are come and haue deuoured the land, and all that is in it, the citie, and thoſe that dwell therein.[17]For behold, I wil ſend ſerpents, cockatrices among you, which will not be charmed, and they ſhall bite you; ſaith the Lord.[18]When I would comfort my ſelfe againſt ſorrow, my heart is faint in me.[19]Behold the voice of the crie of the daughter of my people becauſe of them that dwel in a farre countrey: Is not the Lord in Zion? is not her king in her? why haue they prouoked me to anger with their grauen images, and with ſtrange vanities?[20]The harueſt is paſt, the ſummer is ended, and we are not ſaued.[21]For the hurt of the daughter of my people am I hurt, I am blacke: aſtoniſhment hath taken hold on me.[22]Is there no balme in Gilead? is there no phyſician there? why then is not the health of the daughter of my people recouered?

CHAPTER 9[1]Oh that my head were waters, and mine eyes a fountaine of teares, that I might weepe day and night for the ſlaine of the daughter of my people.[2]Oh that I had in the wilderneſſe a lodging place of wayfaring men, that I might leaue my people, and goe from them: for they be all adulterers, an aſſembly of treacherous men.[3]And they bend their tongue like their bow for lies: but they are not valiant for the trueth vpon the earth: for they proceed from euil to euill, and they know not me, ſaith the Lord.[4]Take yee heede euery one of his neighbour, and truſt yee not in any brother: for euery brother will vtterly ſupplant, and euery neighbour will walke with ſlanders.[5]And they will deceiue euery one his neighbour, and will not ſpeake the trueth, they haue taught their tongue

to ſpeake lies, and weary themſelues to commit iniquity.6Thine
habitation is in the middeſt of deceit, through deceit they refuſe to know
me, ſayth the Lord.7Therfore thus ſaith the Lord of hoſtes; Behold, I
will melt them, and trie them: for how ſhall I doe for the daughter of
my people?8Their tongue is as an arrowe ſhot out, it ſpeaketh deceit:
one ſpeaketh peaceably to his neighbour with his mouth, but in heart he
layeth his waite.9Shall I not viſit them for theſe things, ſaith the Lord ?
ſhall not my ſoule be auenged on ſuch a nation as this?10For the
mountaines will I take vp a weeping and wayling, and for the habitations
of the wilderneſſe a lamentation, becauſe they are burnt vp, ſo that none
can paſſe through them, neither can men heare the voyce of the cattell,
both the foule of the heauens, and the beaſt are fled, they are gone.11And
I will make Ieruſalem heapes, and a denne of dragons, and I wil make
the cities of Iudah deſolate, without an inhabitant.12Who is the wiſe man
that may vnderſtand this, and who is he to whom the mouth of the Lord
hath ſpoken, that hee may declare it; for what the land periſheth, and is
burnt vp like a wilderneſſe that none paſſeth through?13And the Lord
ſaith; Becauſe they haue forſaken my law, which I ſet before them, and
haue not obeyed my voyce, neither walked therein;14But haue walked
after the imagination of their owne heart, & after Baalim, which their
fathers taught them:15Therefore thus ſaith the Lord of hoſts, the God
of Iſrael, Behold, I will feed them, euen this people with wormewood,
and giue them water of gall to drinke.16I will ſcatter them alſo among
the heathen, whome neither they nor their fathers haue knowen: and I
wil ſend a ſword after them, til I haue conſumed them.17Thus ſaith the
Lord of hoſts, Conſider yee, and call for the mourning women, that they
may come, and ſend for cunning women, that they may come.18And let
them make haſte, and take vp a wailing for vs, that our eyes may run
down with teares, and our eyelids guſh out with waters.19For a voyce of
wayling is heard out of Zion, How are we ſpoiled? wee are greatly
confounded, becauſe wee haue forſaken the land, becauſe our dwellings
haue caſt vs out.20Yet heare the word of the Lord, O ye women, & let
your eare receiue the word of his mouth, and teach your daughters
wailing, and euery one her neighbour lamentation.21For death is come
vp into our windowes, and is entred into our palaces, to cut off the
children from without and the yong men from the ſtreetes.22Speake,
Thus ſaith the Lord, Euen the carkeiſes of men ſhall fall as dung vpon
the open field, and as the handfull after the harueſt man, and none ſhall
gather them.23Thus ſaith the Lord, Let not the wiſe man glory in his
wiſdom, neither let the mighty man glory in his might, let not the rich
man glory in his riches.24But let him that glorieth, glory in this, that hee
vnderſtandeth and knoweth me, that I am the Lord which exerciſe
louing kindneſse, iudgement and righteouſneſſe in the earth: for in theſe
things I delight, ſaith the Lord.25Behold, the dayes come, ſaith the Lord,
that I will puniſh all them which are circumciſed, with the
vncircumciſed,26Egypt, and Iudah, and Edom, and the children of
Ammon, and Moab, and all that are in the vtmoſt corners, that dwell in
the wilderneſſe: for all theſe nations are vncircumciſed, and all the houſe
of Iſrael are vncircumciſed in the heart.

CHAPTER 101Heare ye the word which the Lord ſpeaketh vnto you,
O houſe of Iſrael.2Thus ſayeth the Lord, Learne not the way of the
heathen, and be not diſmayed at the ſignes of heauen, for the heathen
are diſmayed at them.3For the cuſtomes of the people are vaine: for one
cutteth a tree out of the forreſt (the worke of the handes of the
workeman) with the axe.4They decke it with ſiluer and with golde, they
faſten it with nayles, and with hammers that it mooue not.5They are
vpright as the palme tree, but ſpeake not: they muſt needes bee borne,
becauſe they cannot goe: be not afraid of them, for they cannot doe euil,
neither alſo is it in them to doe good.6Foraſmuch as there is none like
vnto thee, O Lord, thou art great, and thy Name is great in might.7Who
would not feare thee, O King of nations? for to thee doeth it appertaine:
foraſmuch as among all the wiſe men of the nations, and in all their
kingdomes, there is none like vnto thee.8But they are altogether brutiſh
and fooliſh: the ſtocke is a doctrine of vanities.9ſiluer ſpread into plates
is brought from Tarſhiſh, and gold from Uphaz, the worke of the
workeman, and of the hands of the founder: blue and purple is their
clothing: they are all the worke of cunning men.10But the Lord is the
true God, he is the liuing God, and an euerlaſting King: at his wrath the
earth ſhal tremble, and the nations ſhall not be able to abide his
indignation.11Thus ſhal ye ſay vnto them, The Gods that haue not made
the heauens, & the earth, euen they ſhall periſh from the earth, & from
vnder theſe heauens.12Hee hath made the earth by his power, he hath
eſtabliſhed the world by his wiſedome, and hath ſtretched out the
heauens by his diſcretion.13When he vttereth his voice, there is a
multitude of waters in the heauens, and hee cauſeth the vapours to
aſcend from the ends of the earth: hee maketh lightnings with raine, and
bringeth forth the wind out of his treaſures.14Euery man is brutiſh in his
knowledge, euery founder is confounded by the grauen image: for his
moulten image is falſehood, and there is no breath in them.15They are
vanity, and the worke of errours: in the time of their viſitation they ſhall
periſh.16The portion of Iacob is not like them: for he is the fourmer of
all things, and Iſrael is the rod of his inheritance: the Lord of hoſtes is
his Name.17Gather vp thy wares out of the land, O inhabitant of the
fortreſse.18For thus ſaith the Lord, Behold, I will ſling out the
inhabitants of the land at this once, and will diſtreſſe them, that they
may find it ſo.19Woe is mee for my hurt, my wound is grieuous: but I
ſayd, Truely this is a griefe, and I muſt beare it.20My Tabernacle is
ſpoyled, and all my cordes are broken: my children are gone foorth of
me, and they are not: there is none to ſtretch foorth my tent any more,
and to ſet vp my curtaines.21For the Paſtours are become brutiſh, and
haue not ſought the Lord: therefore they ſhall not proſper, and all their
flockes ſhall be ſcattered.22Behold, the noiſe of the bruit is come, and a
great commotion out of the North countrey, to make the cities of Iudah
deſolate, and a denne of dragons.23O Lord, I know that the way of man
is not in himſelfe: it is not in man that walketh, to direct his ſteps.24O
Lord, correct mee, but with iudgement, not in thine anger, leſt thou
bring me to nothing.25Powre out thy fury vpon the heathen that know
thee not, and vpon the families that call not on thy Name: for they haue
eaten vp Iacob, and deuoured him, and conſumed him, and haue made
his habitation deſolate.

CHAPTER 111The word that came to Ieremiah from the Lord,
ſaying,2Heare yee the words of this Couenant, and ſpeake vnto the men
of Iudah, and to the inhabitants of Ieruſalem.3And ſay thou vnto them,
Thus ſaith the Lord God of Iſrael, Curſed bee the man that obeyeth not
the words of this Couenant,4Which I commaunded your fathers in the
day that I brought them foorth out of the land of Egypt, from the yron
furnace, ſaying, Obey my voyce, and doe them, according to all which I
command you: ſo ſhall yee be my people, and I will be your God.5That
I may performe the othe which I haue ſworne vnto your fathers, to giue
them a land flowing with milke and honie, as it is this day: then anſwered
I, and ſaid, So bee it, O Lord.6Then the Lord ſaid vnto me, Proclaime
all theſe wordes in the cities of Iudah, and in the ſtreets of Ieruſalem,
ſaying, Heare ye the words of this Couenant, and doe them.7For I
earneſtly proteſted vnto your fathers, in the day that I brought them vp
out of the land of Egypt, euen vnto this day, riſing earely and proteſting,
ſaying, Obey my voice.8Yet they obeyed not, nor inclined their eare: but
walked euery one in the imagination of their euill heart: therefore I will
bring vpon them all the words of this Couenant, which I commaunded
them to doe; but they did them not.9And the Lord ſaid vnto me, A
conſpiracie is found among the men of Iudah, and among the
inhabitants of Ieruſalem.10They are turned backe to the iniquities of
their forefathers, which refuſed to heare my wordes: and they went after
other gods to ſerue them: the houſe of Iſrael, and the houſe of Iudah
haue broken my Couenant, which I made with their fathers.11Therefore
thus ſayeth the Lord, Behold, I will bring euill vpon them which they
ſhall not be able to eſcape; and though they ſhall crie vnto mee, I will
not hearken vnto them.12Then ſhall the cities of Iudah, and inhabitants
of Ieruſalem goe, and crie vnto the gods vnto whom they offer incenſe;
but they ſhall not ſaue them at all in the time of their trouble.13For
according to the number of thy cities were thy gods, O Iudah, and
according to the number of the ſtreetes of Ieruſalem haue ye ſet vp altars
to that ſhamefull thing, euen altars to burne incenſe vnto
Baal.14Therefore pray not thou for this people, neither lift vp a cry or
prayer for them: for I will not heare them in the time that they crie vnto
mee for their trouble.15What hath my beloued to doe in mine houſe,
ſeeing ſhee hath wrought lewdneſse with many? and the holy fleſh is
paſſed from thee: when thou doeſt euill, then thou reioyceſt.16The Lord
called thy name, A greene oliue tree, faire and of goodly fruite: with the
noiſe of a great tumult hee hath kindled fire vpon it, and the branches
of it are broken.17For the Lord of hoſtes that planted thee, hath

pronounced euill againſt thee, for the euill of the houſe of Iſrael, and of the houſe of Iudah, which they haue done againſt themſelues to prouoke mee to anger in offering incenſe vnto Baal.18And the Lord hath giuen mee knowledge of it, and I knowe it, then thou ſhewedſt me their doings.19But I was like a lambe or an oxe that is brought to the ſlaughter, and I knew not that they had deuiſed deuices againſt me, ſaying; Let vs deſtroy the tree with the fruit thereof, and let vs cut him off from the land of the liuing, that his name may be no more remembred.20But, O Lord of hoſtes, that iudgeſt righteouſly, that tryeſt the reines, and the heart; let me ſee thy vengeance on them, for vnto thee haue I reuealed my cauſe.21Therefore thus ſaith the Lord of the men of Anathoth, that ſeeke thy life, ſaying; Prophecie not in the Name of the Lord, that thou die not by our hand:22Therefore thus ſaith the Lord of hoſts, Behold, I wil puniſh them: the young men ſhall die by the ſword, their ſonnes and their daughters ſhall die by famine.23And there ſhall be no remnant of them, for I will bring euill vpon the men of Anathoth, euen the yere of their viſitation.

CHAPTER 11Righteous art thou, O Lord, when I pleade with thee: yet let mee talke with thee of thy iudgements: Wherefore doeth the way of the wicked proſper? Wherefore are all they happie that deale very treacherouſly?2Thou haſt planted them, yea they haue taken root: they grow, yea they bring foorth fruit, thou art neere in their mouth, and farre from their reines.3But thou, O Lord, knoweſt me; thou haſt ſeene me, and tried mine heart towards thee: pull them out like ſheep for the ſlaughter, and prepare them for the day of ſlaughter.4How long ſhall the land mourne, and the herbes of euery field wither, for the wickedneſſe of them that dwell therein? the beaſts are conſumed, and the birds, becauſe they ſaid; He ſhall not ſee our laſt end.5If thou haſt runne with the footmen, and they haue wearied thee, then how canſt thou contend with horſes? And if in the land of peace, wherein thou truſtedſt, they wearied thee, then how wilt thou doe in the ſwelling of Iordan?6For euen thy brethren and the houſe of thy father, euen they haue dealt treacherouſly with thee, yea they haue called a multitude after thee; beleeue them not, though they ſpeake faire words vnto thee.7I haue forſaken mine houſe: I haue left mine heritage: I haue giuen the dearely beloued of my ſoule into the hand of her enemies.8Mine heritage is vnto me as a lyon in the forreſt: it cryeth out againſt me, therefore haue I hated it.9Mine heritage is vnto mee as a ſpeckled bird, the birdes round about are againſt her; come yee, aſſemble all the beaſts of the field, come to deuoure.10Many paſtors haue deſtroyed my vineyard; they haue troden my portion vnder foote: they haue made my pleaſant portion a deſolate wilderneſſe.11They haue made it deſolate, and being deſolate it mourneth vnto me; the whole land is made deſolate, becauſe no man layeth it to heart.12The ſpoilers are come vpon all high places through the wilderneſſe: for the ſword of the Lord ſhall deuoure from the one end of the land euen to the other end of the land: no fleſh ſhall haue peace.13They haue ſowen wheate, but ſhall reape thornes: they haue put themſelues to paine, but ſhall not profit: and they ſhall be aſhamed of your reuenues, becauſe of the fierce anger of the Lord.14Thus ſaith the Lord againſt all mine euill neighbours, that touch the inheritance, which I haue cauſed my people Iſrael to inherit; Behold, I will plucke them out of their land, and plucke out the houſe of Iudah from among them.15And it ſhall come to paſſe after that I haue plucked them out, I will returne, and haue compaſſion on them, and will bring againe euery man to his heritage, and euery man to his land.16And it ſhall come to paſſe, if they will diligently learne the wayes of my people to ſweare by my name (The Lord liueth, as they taught my people to ſweare by Baal:) then ſhall they be built in the middeſt of my people.17But if they will not obey, I will vtterly plucke vp, and deſtroy that nation, ſaith the Lord.

CHAPTER 131Thus ſaith the Lord vnto me; Goe and get thee a linen girdle, and put it vpon thy loynes, and put it not in water.2So I got a girdle, according to the word of the Lord, and put it on my loines.3And the word of the Lord came vnto me the ſecond time, ſaying;4Take the girdle that thou haſt got, which is vpon thy loines, and Ariſe, goe to Euphrates, and hide it there in a hole of the rocke.5So I went and hid it by Euphrates, as the Lord commaunded mee.6And it came to paſſe after many daies, that the Lord ſaide vnto me; Ariſe, goe to Euphrates, and take the girdle from thence, which I commaunded thee to hide there.7Then I went to Euphrates and digged, and tooke the girdle from the place where I had hid it, and behold, the girdle was marred, it was profitable for nothing.8Then the word of the Lord came vnto me, ſaying;9Thus ſaith the Lord; After this maner will I marre the pride of Iudah, and the great pride of Ieruſalem.10This euill people which refuſe to heare my words, which walke in the imagination of their heart, and walke after other Gods to ſerue them and to worſhip them, ſhall euen be as this girdle, which is good for nothing.11For as the girdle cleaueth to the loines of a man: ſo haue I cauſed to cleaue vnto me the whole houſe of Iſrael, and the whole houſe of Iudah, ſaith the Lord; that they might bee vnto me for a people, and for a name, and for a praiſe, and for a glory: but they would not heare.12Therefore thou ſhalt ſpeake vnto them this word; Thus ſaith the Lord God of Iſrael; Euerie botle ſhalbe filled with wine: and they ſhall ſay vnto thee; Doe we not certainly know, that euery botle ſhall be filled with wine?13Then ſhalt thou ſay vnto them; Thus ſaith the Lord; Behold, I will fill all the inhabitants of this land, euen the kings that ſit vpon Dauids throne, and the prieſts and the prophets, and all the inhabitants of Ieruſalem with drunkenneſse.14And I will daſh them one againſt another, euen the fathers and the ſonnes together, ſaith the Lord: I wil not pitie nor ſpare, nor haue mercie, but deſtroy them.15Heare ye and giue eare, bee not proud: for the Lord hath ſpoken.16Giue glory to the Lord your God before he cauſe darkneſſe, and before your feet ſtumble vpon the darke mountaines, and while yee looke for light, he turne it into the ſhadowe of death, and make it groſse darkeneſſe.17But if ye will not heare it, my ſoule ſhall weepe in ſecret places for your pride, and mine eye ſhall weepe ſore, and run downe with teares, becauſe the Lords flocke is caried away captiue.18ſay vnto the king, and to the queene, Humble your ſelues, ſit downe, for your principalities ſhall come downe, euen the crowne of your glory.19The cities of the South ſhall bee ſhut vp, and none ſhall open them, Iudah ſhall be caried away captiue all of it, it ſhall bee wholly caried away captiue.20Lift vp your eyes, and beholde them that come from the North, where is the flocke that was giuen thee, thy beautifull flocke?21What wilt thou ſay when he ſhall puniſh thee (for thou haſt taught them to be captaines and as chiefe ouer thee) ſhall not ſorrowes take thee as a woman in trauaile?22And if thou ſay in thine heart, Wherefore come theſe things vpon me? for the greatneſſe of thine iniquitie are thy ſkirts diſcouered, and thy heeles made bare.23Can the Ethiopian change his ſkinne? or the leopard his ſpots? then may ye alſo doe good, that are accuſtomed to doe euill.24Therefore will I ſcatter them as the ſtubble that paſſeth away by the winde of the wilderneſſe.25This is thy lot, the portion of thy meaſures from me, ſaith the Lord, becauſe thou haſt forgotten mee, and truſted in falſhood.26Therefore will I diſcouer thy ſkirts vpon thy face, that thy ſhame may appeare.27I haue ſeene thine adulteries, and thy neighings, the lewdneſe of thy whordome, and thine abominations on the hils in the fields: woe vnto thee, O Ieruſalem, wilt thou not bee made cleane? when ſhall it once be?

CHAPTER 141The word of the Lord that came to Ieremiah concerning the dearth.2Iudah mourneth, and the gates thereof languiſh, they are blacke vnto the ground, and the crie of Ieruſalem is gone vp.3And their nobles haue ſent their litle ones to the waters, they came to the pits and found no water, they returned with the veſſels emptie: they were aſhamed and confounded, and couered their heads.4Becauſe the ground is chapt, for there was no raine in the earth, the plowmen were aſhamed, they couered their heads.5Yea the hinde alſo calued in the field, and forſooke it, becauſe there was no graſſe.6And the wilde aſſes did ſtand in the hie places, they ſnuffed vp the winde like dragons: their eyes did faile becauſe there was no graſſe.7O Lord, though our iniquities teſtifie againſt vs, doe thou it for thy Names ſake: for our backſlidings are many, we haue ſinned againſt thee.8O the hope of Iſrael, the Sauiour thereof in time of trouble, why ſhouldeſt thou be as a ſtranger in the land, and as a wayfaring man, that turneth aſide to tarie for a night?9Why ſhouldeſt thou bee as a man aſtonied, as a mightie man that cannot ſaue? yet thou, O Lord, art in the midſt of vs, and we are called by thy Name, leaue vs not.10Thus ſaith the Lord vnto this people, Thus haue they loued to wander, they haue not refrained their feete, therefore the Lord doeth not accept them, hee will now remember their iniquitie, and viſite their ſinnes.11Then ſaid the Lord vnto mee, Pray not for this people, for their good.12When they faſt I will not heare their crie, and when they offer burnt offering and an oblation I wil not accept them: but I will conſume them by the ſword, and by the famine, and by the

peſtilence.13Then ſaid I Ah Lord God, behold, the prophets ſay vnto
them; Ye ſhall not ſee the ſword, neither ſhall ye haue famine, but I will
giue you aſsured peace in this place.14Then the Lord ſaid vnto me, The
prophets prophecie lies in my Name, I ſent them not, neither haue I
commanded them, neither ſpake vnto them: they prophecie vnto you a
falſe viſion and diuination, and a thing of nought, and the deceit of their
heart.15Therefore thus ſaith the Lord concerning the prophets that
prophecie in my Name, and I ſent them not, yet they ſay, Sword and
famine ſhall not be in this land, By ſword and famine ſhall thoſe
prophets be conſumed.16And the people to whom they prophecie, ſhall
be caſt out in the ſtreets of Ieruſalem, becauſe of the famine and the
ſword, and they ſhall haue none to burie them, them, their wiues, nor
their ſonnes, nor their daughters: for I will powre their wickedneſſe
vpon them.17Therefore thou ſhalt ſay this word vnto them, Let mine
eies runne downe with teares night and day, and let them not ceaſe, for
the virgin daughter of my people is broken with a great breach, with a
very grieuous blow.18If I goe forth into the field, then behold the ſlaine
with the ſword, and if I enter into the citie, then behold them that are
ſicke with famine, yea both the prophet and the prieſt goe about into a
land that they know not.19Haſt thou vtterly reiected Iudah? hath thy
ſoule loathed Zion? why haſt thou ſmitten vs, and there is no healing
for vs? we looked for peace, and there is no good, and for the time of
healing, and behold trouble.20We acknowledge, O Lord, our wickednes,
and the iniquitie of our fathers: for wee haue ſinned againſt thee.21Do
not abhorre vs, for thy Names ſake, doe not diſgrace the Throne of thy
glorie: remember, breake not thy Couenant with vs.22Are there any
among the vanities of the Gentiles that can cauſe raine? or can the
heauens giue ſhowres, Art not thou he, O Lord our God? therefore we
will waite vpon thee: for thou haſt made all theſe things.

CHAPTER 151Then ſaid the Lord vnto me, Though Moſes and Samuel
ſtood before me, yet my minde could not be toward this people, caſt
them out of my ſight, and let them goe foorth.2And it ſhall come to
paſſe if they ſay vnto thee, Whither ſhall wee goe foorth? then thou ſhalt
tell them; Thus ſaith the Lord, ſuch as are for death to death; and ſuch
as are for the ſword, to the ſword; and ſuch as are for the famine, to the
famine; and ſuch as are for the captiuitie, to the captiuitie.3And I will
appoint ouer them foure kindes, ſaith the Lord, the ſword to ſlay, and
the dogs to teare, and the foules of the heauen, and the beaſts of the
earth to deuoure and deſtroy.4And I will cauſe them to be remoued into
all kingdomes of the earth, becauſe of Manaſſeh the ſonne of Hezekiah
king of Iudah, for that which hee did in Ieruſalem.5For who ſhall haue
pitie vpon thee, O Ieruſalem? or who ſhall bemoane thee? or who ſhall
goe aſide to aſke how thou doeſt?6Thou haſt forſaken me, ſaith the
Lord, thou art gone backward: therefore will I ſtretch out my hand
againſt thee, and deſtroy thee, I am wearie with repenting.7And I will
fanne them with a fanne in the gates of the land: I will bereaue them of
children, I wil deſtroy my people, ſith they returne not from their
waies.8Their widowes are increaſed to me aboue the ſand of the ſeas: I
haue brought vpon them againſt the mother of the yongmen, a ſpoiler
at noone day: I haue cauſed him to fall vpon it ſuddenly, and terrors
vpon the citie.9She that hath borne ſeuen, languiſheth: ſhe hath giuen
vp the ghoſt: her ſunne is gone down while it was yet day: ſhee hath
bene aſhamed and confounded, and the reſidue of them will I deliuer to
the ſword before their enemies, ſaith the Lord.10Woe is mee, my
mother, that that thou haſt borne me a man of ſtrife, and a man of
contention to the whole earth: I haue neither lent on vſurie, nor men
haue lent to me on vſurie, yet euery one of them doeth curſe me.11The
Lord ſaid, Uerely it ſhall be well with thy remnant, verely I will cauſe the
enemie to intreat thee well in the time of euill, and in the time of
affliction.12Shall yron breake the Northren yron, and the ſteele?13Thy
ſubſtance and thy treaſures will I giue to the ſpoile without price, and
that for all thy ſinnes, euen in all thy borders.14And I will make thee to
paſſe with thine enemies, into a land which thou knoweſt not: for a fire
is kindled in mine anger, which ſhall burne vpon you.15O Lord, thou
knoweſt, remember me, and viſit me, and reuenge me of my perſecutors,
take mee not away in thy long ſuffering: know that for thy ſake I haue
ſuffered rebuke.16Thy wordes were found, and I did eate them, and thy
word was vnto mee, the ioy and reioycing of mine heart: for I am called
by thy Name, O Lord God of hoſtes.17I ſate not in the aſſembly of the
mockers, nor reioyced: I ſate alone becauſe of thy hand: for thou haſt
filled me with indignation.18Why is my paine perpetuall? and my wound
incurable which refuſeth to be healed? wilt thou be altogether vnto me
as a lyar, and as waters that faile?19Therfore thus ſaith the Lord; If thou
returne, then will I bring thee againe, and thou ſhalt ſtand before me:
and if thou take forth the precious from the vile, thou ſhalt be as my
mouth: let them returne vnto thee, but returne not thou vnto
them.20And I will make thee vnto this people a fenced braſen wall, and
they ſhall fight againſt thee, but they ſhall not preuaile againſt thee: for
I am with thee to ſaue thee, and to deliuer thee, ſayth the Lord.21And I
will deliuer thee out of the hand of the wicked, and I will redeeme thee
out of the hand of the terrible.

CHAPTER 161The word of the Lord came alſo vnto me, ſaying;2Thou
ſhalt not take thee a wife, neither ſhalt thou haue ſonnes nor daughters
in this place.3For thus ſayth the Lord concerning the ſonnes and
concerning the daughters that are borne in this place, and concerning
their mothers that bare them, and concerning their fathers that begate
them in this land:4They ſhal die of grieuous deaths, they ſhall not bee
lamented, neither ſhall they be buried: but they ſhall be as doung vpon
the face of the earth, and they ſhalbe conſumed by the ſword, and by
famine, and their carkeiſes ſhall be meate for the foules of heauen, and
for the beaſts of the earth.5For thus ſayth the Lord, Enter not into the
houſe of mourning, neither goe to lament nor bemoane them: for I haue
taken away my peace from this people, ſayth the Lord, euen louing
kindneſſe and mercies.6Both the great and the ſmall ſhall die in this land:
they ſhall not be buried, neither ſhall men lament for them, nor cut
themſelues, nor make themſelues balde for them.7Neither ſhall men
teare themſelues for them in mourning to comfort them for the dead,
neither ſhall men giue them the cuppe of conſolation to drinke for their
father, or for their mother.8Thou ſhalt not alſo goe into the houſe of
feaſting, to ſit with them to eat and to drinke.9For thus ſayth the Lord
of hoſtes, the God of Iſrael: Behold, I will cauſe to ceaſe out of this
place in your eyes, and in your dayes, the voice of mirth, and the voice
of gladneſſe, the voice of the bridegroome, and the voice of the
bride.10And it ſhal come to paſſe when thou ſhalt ſhewe this people all
theſe wordes, and they ſhall ſay vnto thee; Wherefore hath the Lord
pronounced all this great euill againſt vs? or what is our iniquitie? or
what is our ſinne, that we haue committed againſt the Lord our
God?11Then ſhalt thou ſay vnto them; Becauſe your fathers haue
forſaken me, ſaith the Lord, and haue walked after other Gods, and haue
ſerued them, and haue worſhipped them, and haue forſaken mee, and
haue not kept my law:12And yee haue done worſe then your fathers, (for
behold, yee walke euerie one after the imagination of his euill heart, that
they may not hearken vnto me.)13Therefore will I caſt you out of this
land into a land that yee knowe not, neither yee, nor your fathers, and
there ſhall yee ſerue other Gods day and night, where I will not ſhewe
you fauour.14Therefore behold, the dayes come, ſaith the Lord, that it
ſhall no more be ſaid; The Lord liueth that brought vp the children of
Iſrael out of the land of Egypt;15But, The Lord liueth, that brought vp
the children of Iſrael from the land of the North, and from all the lands
whither hee had driuen them: and I will bring them againe into their
land, that I gaue vnto their fathers.16Behold, I will ſend for many fiſhers,
ſaith the Lord, and they ſhal fiſh them, and after will I ſend for manie
hunters, and they ſhall hunt them from euery mountaine, and from
euery hill, and out of the holes of the rockes.17For mine eyes are vpon
all their waies: they are not hid from my face, neither is their iniquitie
hid from mine eies.18And firſt I will recompenſe their iniquitie, and their
ſinne double, becauſe they haue defiled my land, they haue filled mine
inheritance with the carkeiſes of their deteſtable and abominable
things.19O Lord, my ſtrength and my fortreſe, and my refuge in the day
of affliction; the Gentiles ſhall come vnto thee from the ends of the
earth, and ſhall ſay; Surely our fathers haue inherited lyes, vanitie, and
things wherein there is no profit.20Shall a man make Gods vnto
himſelfe, and they are no Gods?21Therefore behold, I will this once
cauſe them to know: I will cauſe them to knowe mine hand and my
might, and they ſhall know that my name is the Lord.

CHAPTER 171The ſinne of Iudah is written with a pen of yron, and
with the point of a diamond; it is grauen vpon the table of their heart,
and vpon the hornes of your altars:2Whileſt their children remember
their altars and their groues by the greene trees vpon the high hilles.3O
my mountaine, in the field I will giue thy ſubſtance, and all thy treaſures

to the ſpoile, and thy high places for ſinne, throughout all thy borders.4And thou, euen thy ſelfe ſhalt diſcontinue from thine heritage that I gaue thee, and I will cauſe thee to ſerue thine enemies in the land which thou knoweſt not: for yee haue kindled a fire in mine anger, which ſhall burne for euer.5Thus ſaith the Lord; Curſed be the man that truſteth in man, and maketh fleſh his arme, and whoſe heart departeth from the Lord.6For hee ſhall be like the heath in the deſert, and ſhall not ſee when good commeth, but ſhall inhabite the parched places in the wilderneſſe, in a ſalt land and not inhabited.7Bleſſed is the man that truſteth in the Lord, and whoſe hope the Lord is.8For he ſhall be as a tree planted by the waters, and that ſpreadeth out her rootes by the riuer, and ſhall not ſee when heate commeth, but her leafe ſhall be greene, and ſhall not be carefull in the yeere of drought, neither ſhall ceaſe from yeelding fruit.9The heart is deceitfull aboue all things, and deſperately wicked, who can know it?10I the Lord ſearch the heart, I try the reines, euen to giue euery man according to his waies, and according to the fruit of his doings.11As the partrich ſitteth on egges, and hatcheth them not: ſo he that getteth riches and not by right, ſhall leaue them in the midſt of his dayes, and at his end ſhall be a foole.12A glorious high throne from the beginning, is the place of our Sanctuarie.13O Lord, the hope of Iſrael, all that forſake thee ſhall be aſhamed, and they that depart from me ſhall bee written in the earth, becauſe they haue forſaken the Lord the fountaine of liuing waters.14Heale me, O Lord, and I ſhall be healed: ſaue me, and I ſhalbe ſaued: for thou art my praiſe.15Behold, they ſay vnto mee, Where is the word of the Lord ? let it come now.16As for me, I haue not haſtened from being a paſtour to follow thee, neither haue I deſired the wofull day, thou knoweſt: that which came out of my lips, was right before thee.17Be not a terrour vnto me, thou art my hope in the day of euill.18Let them bee confounded that perſecute me, but let not me be confounded: let them be diſmayed, but let not me be diſmayed: bring vpon them the day of euill, and deſtroy them with double deſtruction.19Thus ſayd the Lord vnto me, Go and ſtand in the gate of the children of the people, whereby the kings of Iudah come in, and by the which they goe out, and in all the gates of Ieruſalem.20And ſay vnto them, Heare ye the word of the Lord, ye kings of Iudah, and all Iudah, and all the inhabitants of Ieruſalem, that enter in by theſe gates.21Thus ſaith the Lord, Take heed to your ſelues, and beare no burden on the Sabbath day, nor bring it in by the gates of Ieruſalem.22Neither carie forth a burden out of your houſes on the Sabbath day, neither doe ye any worke, but hallowe ye the Sabbath day, as I commanded your fathers.23But they obeyed not, neither inclined their eare, but made their necke ſtiffe, that they might not heare nor receiue inſtruction.24And it ſhall come to paſſe, if yee diligently hearken vnto me, ſaith the Lord, to bring in no burden through the gates of this citie on the Sabbath day, but hallow the Sabbath day, to doe no worke therein:25Then ſhall there enter into the gates of this citie kings and princes ſitting vpon the throne of Dauid, riding in charets and on horſes, they and their princes, the men of Iudah and the inhabitants of Ieruſalem: and this citie ſhall remaine for euer.26And they ſhall come from the cities of Iudah, and from the places about Ieruſalem, and from the lande of Beniamin, and from the plaine and from the mountaines, and from the South, bringing burnt offerings, and ſacrifices, and meate offerings, and incenſe, and bringing ſacrifices of praiſe vnto the houſe of the Lord.27But if you will not hearken vnto me to hallow the Sabbath day, and not to beare a burden, euen entring in at the gates of Ieruſalem on the Sabbath day: then will I kindle a fire in the gates thereof, and it ſhall deuoure the palaces of Ieruſalem, and it ſhall not be quenched.

CHAPTER 181The word which came to Ieremiah from þe Lord ſaying,2Ariſe and go downe to the potters houſe, & there I will cauſe thee to heare my words.3Then I went downe to the potters houſe, and behold, hee wrought a worke on the wheeles.4And the veſſell that he made of clay, was marred in the hand of the potter; ſo he made it againe another veſſell as ſeemed good to the potter to make it.5Then the word of the Lord came to me, ſaying,6O houſe of Iſrael, cannot I doe with you as this potter, ſaith the Lord ? Behold, as the clay is in the potters hand, ſo are ye in mine hand, O houſe of Iſrael.7At what inſtant I ſhall ſpeake concerning a nation, and concerning a kingdome, to plucke vp and to pull downe, and to deſtroy it.8If that nation againſt whom I haue pronounced, turne from their euill, I will repent of the euill that I thought to doe vnto them.9And at what inſtant I ſhall ſpeake concerning a nation, and concerning a kingdome to build and to plant it;10If it doe euill in my ſight, that it obey not my voice, then I will repent of the good; wherewith I ſaide I would benefite them.11Now therefore goe to, ſpeake to the men of Iudah, and to the inhabitants of Ieruſalem, ſaying, Thus ſaith the Lord; Behold, I frame euill againſt you, and deuiſe a deuice againſt you: returne ye now euery one from his euill way, and make your waies and your doings good.12And they ſaid, There is no hope, but wee will walke after our owne deuices, and wee will euery one doe the imagination of his euil heart.13Therefore thus ſaith the Lord, Aſke ye now among the heathen, who hath heard ſuch things? the Uirgin of Iſrael hath done a very horrible thing.14Will a man leaue the ſnow of Lebanon which commeth from the rocke of the fielde? or ſhall the colde flowing waters that come from another place, be forſaken?15Becauſe my people hath forgotten mee, they haue burnt incenſe to vanitie, and they haue cauſed them to ſtumble in their waies from the ancient paths, to walke in paths, in a way not caſt vp,16To make their land deſolate and a perpetuall hiſſing: euery one that paſſeth thereby ſhall bee aſtoniſhed, and wagge his head.17I will ſcatter them as with an Eaſt winde before the enemie: I will ſhew them the backe, and not the face, in the day of their calamitie.18Then ſaid they, Come, and let vs deuiſe deuices againſt Ieremiah: for the Law ſhall not periſh from the Prieſt, nor counſell from the wiſe, nor the word from the prophet: Come and let vs ſmite him with the tongue, and let vs not giue heede to any of his wordes.19Giue heed to me, O Lord, and hearken to the voice of them that contend with me.20Shall euill bee recompenſed for good? for they haue digged a pit for my ſoule: remember that I ſtood before thee to ſpeake good for them, and to turne away thy wrath from them.21Therefore deliuer vp their children to the famine, and powre out their blood by the force of the ſword, and let their wiues be bereaued of their children and be widowes, and let their men be put to death, let their yong men be ſlaine by the ſword in battell.22Let a crie bee heard from their houſes, when thou ſhalt bring a troupe ſuddenly vpon them, for they haue digged a pit to take me, and hid ſnares for my feet.23Yet Lord thou knoweſt all their counſell againſt me to ſlay mee: forgiue not their iniquitie, neither blot out their ſinne from thy ſight, but let them bee ouerthrowen before thee, deale thus with them in the time of thine anger.

CHAPTER 191Thus ſaith the Lord, Goe and get a potters earthen bottell, and take of the ancients of the people, and of the ancients of the Prieſtes.2And goe forth vnto the valley of the ſonne of Hinnom, which is by the entrie of the Eaſtgate, and proclaime there the words that I ſhall tell thee:3And ſay, Heare ye the word of the Lord, O kings of Iudah, and inhabitants of Ieruſalem; Thus ſaith the Lord of hoſtes, the God of Iſrael; Behold, I will bring euill vpon this place, the which whoſoeuer heareth, his eares ſhall tingle.4Becauſe they haue forſaken mee, and haue eſtranged this place, and haue burnt incenſe in it vnto other gods, whom neither they, nor their fathers haue knowen, nor the kings of Iudah, and haue filled this place with the blood of innocents.5They haue built alſo the high places of Baal, to burne their ſonnes with fire for burnt offerings vnto Baal, which I commanded not, nor ſpake it, neither came it into my minde.6Therefore behold, the daies come, ſaith the Lord, that this place ſhall no more bee called Tophet, nor the valley of the ſonne of Hinnom, but the valley of ſlaughter.7And I will make void the counſell of Iudah and Ieruſalem in this place, and I will cauſe them to fall by the ſword before their enemies, and by the hands of them that ſeek their liues: and their carkeiſes will I giue to be meat for the foules of the heauen, and for the beaſts of the earth.8And I will make this citie deſolate and an hiſſing: euery one that paſſeth thereby ſhalbe aſtoniſhed and hiſſe, becauſe of all the plagues thereof.9And I will cauſe them to eate the fleſh of their ſonnes and the fleſh of their daughters, and they ſhal eate euery one the fleſh of his friend in the ſiege and ſtraitneſſe, wherewith their enemies, and they that ſeeke their liues, ſhall ſtraiten them.10Then ſhalt thou breake þe bottle in the ſight of the men that goe with thee,11And ſhalt ſay vnto them; Thus ſaith the Lord of hoſtes, Euen ſo will I breake this people and this citie as one breaketh a potters veſſell that cannot bee made whole againe, and they ſhall bury them in Tophet, till there be no place elſe to bury.12Thus will I doe vnto this place, ſayth the Lord, and to the inhabitants thereof, and euen make their citie as Tophet.13And the houſes of Ieruſalem, and the houſes of the kings of Iudah ſhall bee defiled as the place of Tophet, becauſe of all the houſes vpon whoſe roofes they haue burnt incenſe vnto all the hoſte of heauen,

& haue powred out drinke offrings vnto other gods.[14]Then came Ieremiah from Tophet, whither the Lord had ſent him to prophecie, and hee ſtood in the court of the Lords houſe, and ſaid to all the people,[15]Thus ſaith the Lord of hoſtes the God of Iſrael, Behold, I wil bring vpon this city, and vpon all her townes all the euill that I haue pronounced againſt it, becauſe they haue hardened their neckes, that they might not heare my wordes.

CHAPTER 20[1]Now Paſhur the ſonne of Immer the Prieſt, who was alſo chiefe gouernor in the houſe of the Lord, heard that Ieremiah prophecied theſe things.[2]Then Paſhur ſmote Ieremiah the Prophet, and put him in the ſtockes that were in the high gate of Beniamin, which was by the houſe of the Lord.[3]And it came to paſſe on the morrow, that Paſhur brought foorth Ieremiah out of the ſtockes. Then ſayd Ieremiah vnto him, The Lord hath not called thy name Paſhur, but Magor-miſsabib.[4]For thus ſayth the Lord, Behold, I will make thee a terrour to thy ſelfe, and to all thy friends, and they ſhall fall by the ſword of their enemies, and thine eyes ſhall behold it, and I will giue all Iudah into the hand of the king of Babylon, and hee ſhall cary them captiue into Babylon, and ſhall ſlay them with the ſword.[5]Moreouer, I will deliuer all the ſtrength of this city, and all the labours thereof, and all the precious things thereof, and all the treaſures of the kings of Iudah will I giue into the hand of their enemies which ſhal ſpoile them, and take them and cary them to Babylon.[6]And thou Paſhur, and all that dwell in thine houſe, ſhall goe into captiuitie, and thou ſhalt come to Babylon, and there thou ſhalt die, and ſhalt be buried there, thou and all thy friends to whom thou haſt prophecied lies.[7]O Lord, thou haſt deceiued me, and I was deceiued, thou art ſtronger then I, and haſt preuailed: I am in deriſion daily, euery one mocketh me.[8]For ſince I ſpake I cryed out, I cried violence and ſpoyle; becauſe the word of the Lord was made a reproch vnto me, and a deriſion daily?[9]Then I ſaid; I will not make mention of him, nor ſpeake any more in his name. But his word was in mine heart, as a burning fire ſhut vp in my bones, and I was weary with forbearing, and I could not ſtay.[10]For I heard the defaming of many, feare on euery ſide. Report, ſay they, and wee will report it: all my familiars watched for my halting, ſaying; Peraduenture he will be enticed: and we ſhall preuaile againſt him, and we ſhall take our reuenge on him.[11]But the Lord is with me as a mighty terrible one: therefore my perſecutours ſhall ſtumble, and they ſhall not preuaile, they ſhall be greatly aſhamed, for they ſhall not proſper, their euerlaſting confuſion ſhall neuer be forgotten.[12]But O Lord of hoſtes, that tryeſt the righteous, and ſeeſt the reines and the heart, let me ſee thy vengeance on them: for vnto thee haue I opened my cauſe.[13]Sing vnto the Lord, praiſe yee the Lord: for hee hath deliuered the ſoule of the poore from the hand of euill doers.[14]Curſed be the day wherein I was borne: let not the day wherein my mother bare mee, be bleſſed.[15]Curſed be the man who brought tidings to my father, ſaying: A man child is borne vnto thee, making him very glad.[16]And let that man be as the cities which the Lord ouerthrew and repented not: and let him heare the cry in the morning, and the ſhouting at noonetide,[17]Becauſe he ſlew me not from the wombe: or that my mother might haue beene my graue, and her wombe to be alwaies great with me.[18]Wherefore came I forth out of the wombe to ſee labour and ſorrow, that my daies ſhould be conſumed with ſhame?

CHAPTER 21[1]The word which came vnto Ieremiah from the Lord, when king Zedekiah ſent vnto him Paſhur the ſonne of Melchiah, and Zephaniah the ſonne of Maaſeiah the prieſt, ſaying;[2]Enquire, I pray thee, of the Lord for vs (for Nebuchad-rezzar king of Babylon maketh warre againſt vſ) if ſo be that the Lord will deale with vs, according to all his wondrous workes, that he may goe vp from vs.[3]Then ſaide Ieremiah vnto them. Thus ſhall yee ſay to Zedekiah,[4]Thus ſaith the Lord God of Iſrael; Behold, I will turne backe the weapons of warre that are in your hands, wherewith yee fight againſt the king of Babylon, and againſt the Caldeans, which beſiege you without the walles, and I will aſſemble them into the middeſt of this citie.[5]And I myſelfe will fight againſt you with an out ſtretched hand, and with a ſtrong arme, euen in anger, and in furie, and in great wrath.[6]And I will ſmite the inhabitants of this citie both man and beaſt: they ſhall die of a great peſtilence.[7]And afterward, ſaith the Lord, I will deliuer Zedekiah king of Iudah, and his ſeruants, and the people, and ſuch as are left in this citie from the peſtilence, from the ſword, and from the famine, into the hand of Nebuchadrezzar king of Babylon, and into the hand of their enemies, and into the hand of thoſe that ſeeke their life, and and he ſhall ſmite them with the edge of the ſword: hee ſhall not ſpare them, neither haue pitie, nor haue mercy.[8]And vnto this people thou ſhalt ſay; Thus ſaith the Lord; Behold, I ſet before you the way of life, and the way of death.[9]He that abideth in this citie, ſhall die by the ſword, and by the famine, and by the peſtilence: but he that goeth out, and falleth to the Caldeans, that beſiege you, he ſhall liue, and his life ſhall be vnto him, for a pray.[10]For I haue ſet my face againſt this citie for euill and not for good, ſaith the Lord; it ſhall be giuen into the hand of the king of Babylon, and he ſhall burne it with fire.[11]And touching the houſe of the king of Iudah, ſay; Heare yee the word of the Lord.[12]Oh houſe of Dauid, thus ſaith the Lord, Execute iudgement in the morning, and deliuer him that is ſpoiled, out of the hand of the oppreſsour, leſt my furie goe out like fire, and burne, that none can quench it, becauſe of the euill of your doings.[13]Behold, I am againſt thee, O inhabitant of the valley, and rocke of the plaine, ſaith the Lord, which ſay, Who ſhall come downe againſt vs? or who ſhall enter into our habitations?[14]But I will puniſh you according to the fruit of your doings, ſaith the Lord: and I will kindle a fire in the forreſt thereof, and it ſhall deuoure all things round about it.

CHAPTER 22[1]Thus ſaith the Lord, Goe downe to the houſe of the king of Iudah, and ſpeake there this word,[2]And ſay, Heare the word of the Lord, O king of Iudah, that ſitteſt vpon the throne of Dauid, thou, and thy ſeruants, and thy people that enter in by theſe gates.[3]Thus ſaith the Lord, Execute ye iudgement and righteouſneſſe, and deliuer the ſpoiler out of the hand of the oppreſsour: and doe no wrong, doe no violence to the ſtranger, the fatherleſſe, nor the widow, neither ſhed innocent blood in this place.[4]For if ye doe this thing indeede, then ſhall there enter in by the gates of this houſe, Kings ſitting vpon the throne of Dauid, riding in charets and on horſes, he, and his ſeruants, and his people.[5]But if yee will not heare theſe words, I ſweare by my ſelfe, ſaith the Lord, that this houſe ſhall become a deſolation.[6]For thus ſaith the Lord vnto the kings houſe of Iudah, Thou art Gilead vnto me, and the head of Lebanon: yet ſurely I will make thee a wilderneſſe, and cities which are not inhabited.[7]And I will prepare deſtroyers againſt thee, euery one with his weapons, and they ſhall cut downe thy choiſe cedars, and caſt them into the fire.[8]And many nations ſhall paſſe by this citie, and they ſhall ſay euery man to his neighbour, Wherefore hath the Lord done thus vnto this great citie?[9]Then they ſhall anſwere, Becauſe they haue forſaken the couenant of the Lord their God, and worſhipped other gods, and ſerued them.[10]Weepe ye not for the dead, neither bemoane him, but weepe ſore for him that goeth away: for he ſhall returne no more, nor ſee his natiue countrey.[11]For thus ſaith the Lord touching Shallum, the ſonne of Ioſiah king of Iudah which reigned in ſtead of Ioſiah his father, which went forth out of this place, He ſhall not returne thither any more.[12]But he ſhall die in the place whither they haue led him captiue, and ſhal ſee this land no more.[13]Woe vnto him that buildeth his houſe by vnrighteouſneſſe, and his chambers by wrong: that vſeth his neighbours ſeruice without wages, and giueth him not for his worke:[14]That ſaith, I will build mee a wide houſe and large chambers, and cutteth him out windowes, and it is ſieled with cedar, and painted with vermilion.[15]Shalt thou reigne becauſe thou cloſeſt thy ſelfe in cedar? did not thy father eate and drinke, and doe iudgment and iuſtice, and then it was wel with him?[16]He iudged the cauſe of the poore and needy, then it was well with him: was not this to know me, ſaith the Lord ?[17]But thine eyes and thine heart are not but for thy couetouſneſſe, and for to ſhed innocent blood, and for oppreſſion, and for violence to doe it.[18]Therefore thus ſaith the Lord concerning Iehoiakim the ſonne of Ioſiah king of Iudah, They ſhall not lament for him, ſaying, Ah my brother, or ah ſiſter: they ſhall not lament for him, ſaying, Ah Lord, or ah his glory.[19]He ſhall be buried with the buriall of an aſſe, drawen and caſt forth beyond the gates of Ieruſalem.[20]Goe vp to Lebanon, and crie, and lift vp thy voice in Baſhan, and crie from the paſsages: for all thy louers are deſtroyed.[21]I ſpake vnto thee in thy proſperitie, but thou ſaideſt, I will not heare: this hath bin thy maner from thy youth, that thou obeyedſt not my voice.[22]The winde ſhall eate vp all thy paſtors, and thy louers ſhall goe into captiuitie, ſurely then ſhalt thou be aſhamed and confounded for all thy wickedneſſe.[23]O inhabitant of Lebanon, that makeſt thy neſt in the Cedars, how gracious ſhalt thou bee when pangs come vpon thee, the paine as of a woman in trauell?[24]As I liue, ſaith the Lord, though Coniah the ſonne of Iehoiakim king of Iudah were the ſignet vpon my right hand, yet would I plucke thee thence.25And I will giue thee into the hand of them that ſeeke thy life, and into the hand of them whoſe face thou feareſt, euen into the hand of Nebuchad-rezzar king of Babylon, and into the hand of the Caldeans.26And I will caſt thee out, and thy mother that bare thee, into another countrey where ye were not borne, and there ſhall ye die.27But to the land whereunto they deſire to returne, thither ſhall they not returne.28Is this man Coniah a deſpiſed broken idole? is hee a veſſell wherein is no pleaſure? wherefore are they caſt out, he and his ſeed, and are caſt into a land which they know not?29O earth, earth, earth, heare the word of the Lord:30Thus ſaith the Lord, Write ye this man childleſſe, a man that ſhall not proſper in his dayes: for no man of his ſeed ſhall proſper, ſitting vpon the throne of Dauid, and ruling any more in Iudah.

CHAPTER 231Woe bee vnto the paſtors that deſtroy and ſcatter the ſheepe of my paſture, ſaith the Lord.2Therefore thus ſaith the Lord God of Iſrael againſt the paſtors that feed my people; Yee haue ſcattered my flocke and driuen them away, and haue not viſited them; behold I will viſite vpon you the euill of your doings, ſaith the Lord.3And I wil gather the remnant of my flocke, out of all countreis whither I haue driuen them, and will bring them againe to their foldes, and they ſhalbe fruitfull and increaſe.4And I will ſet vp ſhepheards ouer them which ſhall feed them, and they ſhal feare no more nor be diſmaied, neither ſhall they bee lacking, ſaith the Lord.5Behold, the daies come, ſaith the Lord, that I wil raiſe vnto Dauid a righteous branch, and a King ſhall reigne and proſper, and ſhall execute iudgement and iuſtice in the earth.6In his dayes Iudah ſhalbe ſaued, and Iſrael ſhall dwell ſafely, and this is his Name whereby hee ſhall be called, The Lord Our Righteouſnes.7Therefore behold, the dayes come, ſaith the Lord, that they ſhall no more ſay; The Lord liueth, which brought vp the children of Iſrael out of the land of Egypt:8But, The Lord liueth, which brought vp, and which led the ſeed of the houſe of Iſrael out of the North countrey, and from all countreis whither I had driuen them, and they ſhall dwell in their owne land.9Mine heart within me is broken becauſe of the prophets, all my bones ſhake: I am like a drunken man (and like a man whom wine hath ouercome) becauſe of the Lord, and becauſe of the words of his Holineſse.10For the land is full of adulterers, for becauſe of ſwearing the land mourneth: the pleaſant places of the wildernes are dried vp, and their courſe is euil, and their force is not right.11For both prophet and prieſt are prophane, yea in my houſe haue I found their wickedneſſe, ſaith the Lord.12Wherefore their way ſhalbe vnto them as ſlippery wayes in the darkenes: they ſhalbe driuen on and fall therein: for I will bring euill vpon them, euen the yeere of their viſitation, ſaith the Lord.13And I haue ſeene folly in the prophets of Samaria; they prophecied in Baal, and cauſed my people Iſrael to erre.14I haue ſeene alſo in the prophets of Ieruſalem an horrible thing: they commit adultery, and walke in lies: they ſtrengthen alſo the hands of euill doers, that none doeth returne from his wickedneſſe: they are all of them vnto me as Sodom, and the inhabitants thereof as Gomorrah.15Therefore thus ſaith the Lord of hoſts concerning the Prophets; Behold, I will feede them with wormewood, and make them drinke the water of gall: for from the Prophets of Ieruſalem is profaneneſse gone forth into all the land.16Thus ſaith the Lord of hoſts, Hearken not vnto the wordes of the prophets that prophecie vnto you; they make you vaine: they ſpeake a viſion of their owne heart, and not out of the mouth of the Lord.17They ſay ſtill vnto them that deſpiſe me; The Lord hath ſayde, Yee ſhall haue peace; and they ſay vnto euery one that walketh after the imagination of his owne heart, No euill ſhall come vpon you.18For who hath ſtood in the counſell of the Lord, and hath perceiued, and heard his word? who hath marked his word, and heard it?19Behold, a whirlewinde of the Lord is gone foorth in furie, euen a grieuous whirlewinde, it ſhall fall grieuouſly vpon the head of the wicked.20The anger of the Lord ſhall not returne, vntill hee haue executed, and til he haue performed the thoughts of his heart: in the latter dayes ye ſhall conſider it perfectly.21I haue not ſent theſe prophets, yet they ranne: I haue not ſpoken to them, yet they prophecied.22But if they had ſtood in my counſell, and had cauſed my people to heare my wordes, then they ſhould haue turned them from their euil way, and from the euill of their doings.23Am I a God at hand, ſayth the Lord, and not a God afarre off?24Can any hide himſelfe in ſecret places that I ſhall not ſee him, ſaith the Lord ? doe not I fill heauen and earth, ſayth the Lord ?25I haue heard what the prophets ſaid, that prophecie lyes in my Name, ſaying; I haue dreamed, I haue dreamed.26How long ſhall this bee in the heart of the prophets that prophecie lies? yea they are prophets of the deceit of their owne heart;27Which thinke to cauſe my people to forget my Name by their dreames which they tell euery man to his neighbour, as their fathers haue forgotten my Name, for Baal.28The prophet that hath a dreame, let him tell a dreame; and hee that hath my word, let him ſpeake my word faithfully: what is the chaffe to the wheat, ſayth the Lord ?29Is not my word like as a fire, ſaith the Lord ? and like a hammer that breaketh the rocke in pieces?30Therefore, behold, I am againſt the prophets, ſayth the Lord, that ſteale my worde euery one from his neighbour.31Beholde, I am againſt the prophets, ſaith the Lord, that vſe their tongues, and ſay; He ſayth.32Behold, I am againſt them that prophecie falſe dreames, ſayeth the Lord, and doe tell them, and cauſe my people to erre by their lyes and by their lightneſse, yet I ſent them not, nor commanded them: therefore they ſhall not profite this people at all, ſayth the Lord.33And when this people, or the prophet, or a prieſt ſhall aſke thee, ſaying; What is the burden of the Lord ? thou ſhalt then ſay vnto them; What burden? I will euen forſake you, ſaith the Lord.34And as for the prophet, and the prieſt, and the people that ſhal ſay, The burden of the Lord, I will euen puniſh that man and his houſe.35Thus ſhall yee ſay euery one to his neighbour, and euery one to his brother, What hath the Lord anſwered? and what hath the Lord ſpoken?36And the burden of the Lord ſhall yee mention no more: for euery mans word ſhall be his burden: for yee haue peruerted the words of the liuing God, of the Lord of hoſtes our God.37Thus ſhalt thou ſay to the prophet, What hath the Lord anſwered thee? and what hath the Lord ſpoken?38But ſith ye ſay, The burden of the Lord; therefore thus ſayeth the Lord, Becauſe you ſay this word, The burden of the Lord, and I haue ſent vnto you, ſaying; Ye ſhall not ſay, The burden of the Lord:39Therefore beholde, I, euen I will vtterly forget you, and I will forſake you, and the citie that I gaue you and your fathers, and caſt you out of my preſence.40And I will bring an euerlaſting reproch vpon you, and a perpetuall ſhame, which ſhall not be forgotten.

CHAPTER 241The Lord ſhewed mee, and behold, two baſkets of figges were ſet before the temple of the Lord, after that Nebuchad-rezzar king of Babylon had caried away captiue Ieconiah the ſonne of Iehoiakim king of Iudah, and the princes of Iudah, with the carpenters and ſmiths from Ieruſalem, and had brought them to Babylon.2One baſket had very good figges, euen like the figges that are firſt ripe: and the other baſket had very naughty figges, which could not be eaten, they were ſo bad.3Then ſaid the Lord vnto me; What ſeeſt thou Ieremiah? and I ſaid: Figges: the good figges, very good and the euill, very euill, that cannot be eaten, they are ſo euill.4Againe, the word of the Lord came vnto me, ſaying;5Thus ſaith the Lord, the God of Iſrael, Like theſe good figges, ſo will I acknowledge them that are caried away captiue of Iudah, whom I haue ſent out of this place into the land of the Caldeans for their good.6For I will ſet mine eyes vpon them for good, and I will bring them againe to this land, and I will build them, and not pull them downe, and I will plant them, and not plucke them vp.7And I will giue them an heart to know me, that I am the Lord, and they ſhall be my people, and I will be their God: for they ſhall returne vnto me with their whole heart.8And as the euill figges which cannot be eaten, they are ſo euill; (Surely thus ſaith the Lord) ſo will I giue Zedekiah the king of Iudah, and his princes, and the reſidue of Ieruſalem, that remaine in this land, and them that dwell in the land of Egypt.9And I will deliuer them to be remoued into all the kingdomes of the earth for their hurt, to be a reproch and a prouerbe, a taunt and a curſe in all places whither I ſhall driue them.10And I will ſend the ſword, the famine, and the peſtilence among them, till they be conſumed from off the land, that I gaue vnto them, and to their fathers.

CHAPTER 251The word that came to Ieremiah concerning all the people of Iudah, in the fourth yeere of Iehoiakim the ſonne of Ioſiah king of Iudah, that was the firſt yeere of Nebuchad-rezzar king of Babylon:2The which Ieremiah the prophet ſpake vnto all the people of Iudah, and to all the inhabitants of Ieruſalem, ſaying;3From the thirteenth yere of Ioſiah the ſonne of Amon king of Iudah, euen vnto this day (that is the three and twentith yeere) the word of the Lord hath come vnto me, and I haue ſpoken vnto you, riſing early and ſpeaking, but yee haue not hearkened.4And the Lord hath ſent vnto you all his

ſeruants the prophets, riſing early and ſending them, but yee haue not
hearkened, nor inclined your eare to heare.5They ſayd, Turne yee againe
now euery one from his euill way, and from the euil of your doings, and
dwell in the land that the Lord hath giuen vnto you, and to your fathers
for euer and euer.6And goe not after other Gods to ſerue them, and to
worſhip them, and prouoke mee not to anger with the workes of your
hands, and I will doe you no hurt.7Yet yee haue not hearkened vnto me,
ſaith the Lord, that yee might prouoke me to anger with the workes of
your hands, to your owne hurt.8Therefore thus ſaith the Lord of hoſtes;
Becauſe yee haue not heard my words:9Behold, I will ſend and take all
the families of the North, ſaith the Lord, and Nebuchad-rezzar the king
of Babylon my ſeruant, and will bring them againſt this land, and againſt
the inhabitants thereof, and againſt all theſe nations round about, and
will vtterly deſtroy them, and make them an aſtoniſhment, and an
hiſsing, and perpetuall deſolations.10Moreouer, I will take from them the
voyce of myrth, and the voice of gladnes, the voice of the bridegrome,
and the voice of the bride, the ſound of the milſtones, & the light of the
candle.11And this whole land ſhall be a deſolation, and an aſtoniſhment,
and theſe nations ſhal ſerue the king of Babylon ſeuentie yeeres.12And it
ſhall come to paſſe when ſeuentie yeeres are accompliſhed, that I will
puniſh the king of Babylon and that nation, ſaith the Lord, for their
iniquitie, and the land of the Caldeans, and will make it perpetuall
deſolations.13And I will bring vpon that land all my words which I haue
pronounced againſt it, euen all that is written in this booke, which
Ieremiah hath prophecied againſt all the nations.14For many nations and
great kings ſhall ſerue themſelues of them alſo: and I will recompenſe
them according to their deeds, and according to the workes of their
owne hands.15For thus ſaith the Lord God of Iſrael vnto me, Take the
wine cup of this furie at my hand, and cauſe all the nations, to whom I
ſend thee, to drinke it.16And they ſhall drinke, and be moued, and be
mad, becauſe of the ſworde that I will ſend among them.17Then tooke
I the cuppe at the Lords hand, and made all the nations to drinke, vnto
whom the Lord had ſent me:18To wit Ieruſalem, and the cities of Iudah,
and the kings thereof, and the princes thereof, to make them a
deſolation, an aſtoniſhment, an hiſsing, and a curſe (as it is this
day:)19Pharaoh king of Egypt, and his ſeruants, and his princes, and all
his people:20And all the mingled people, & all the kings of the land of
Uz: and all the kings of the land of the Philiſtines, and Aſhkelon, and
Azzah, and Ekron, and the remnant of Aſhdod:21Edom, and Moab, and
the children of Ammon:22And all the kings of Tyrus, and all the kings
of Zidon, and the kings of the yles which are beyond the ſea:23Dedan,
and Tema, and Buz, and all that are in the vtmoſt corners:24And all the
kings of Arabia, and all the kings of the mingled people that dwell in the
deſert:25And all the kings of Zimri, and all the kings of Elam, and all the
kings of the Medes:26And all the kings of the North, farre and neere,
one with another, and all the kingdomes of the world, which are vpon
the face of the earth, and the king of Sheſhach ſhall drinke after
them.27Therefore thou ſhalt ſay vnto them, Thus ſaith the Lord of hoſts,
the God of Iſrael, Drinke ye and bee drunken, and ſpue and fall, and riſe
no more, becauſe of the ſword which I wil ſend among you.28And it
ſhall bee, if they refuſe to take the cup at thine hand to drinke, then ſhalt
thou ſay vnto them, Thus ſaith the Lord of hoſts, Yee ſhall certainely
drinke.29For loe, I begin to bring euill on the citie, which is called by my
name, and ſhould yee be vtterly vnpuniſhed? ye ſhall not be vnpuniſhed:
for I will cal for a ſword vpon all the inhabitants of the earth, ſaith the
Lord of hoſts.30Therefore prophecie thou againſt them all theſe wordes,
and ſay vnto them, The Lord ſhall roare from an high, and vtter his voice
from his holy habitation, he ſhall mightily roare vpon his habitation, hee
ſhall giue a ſhout, as they that treade the grapes, againſt all the
inhabitants of the earth.31A noiſe ſhall come euen to the ends of the
earth; for the Lord hath a controuerſie with the nations: hee will pleade
with all fleſh, he will giue them that are wicked to the ſword, ſaith the
Lord.32Thus ſaith the Lord of hoſts, Behold, euill ſhall goe forth from
nation to nation, and a great whirlewinde ſhall be raiſed vp from the
coaſts of the earth.33And the ſlaine of the Lord ſhall be at that day from
one end of the earth euen vnto the other ende of the earth: they ſhall
not be lamented, neither gathered nor buried, they ſhall be doung vpon
the ground.34Howle yee ſhepheards and cry, and wallow your ſelues in
the aſhes ye principall of the flocke: for the dayes of your ſlaughter, and
of your diſperſions are accompliſhed, and yee ſhall fall like a pleaſant
veſſell.35And the ſhepheards ſhall haue no way to flee, nor the principall
of the flocke to eſcape.36A voyce of the cry of the ſhepheards, and an
howling of the principall of the flocke ſhall be heard: for the Lord hath
ſpoiled their paſture.37And the peaceable habitations are cut downe
becauſe of the fierce anger of the Lord.38He hath forſaken his couert,
as the Lyon: for their land is deſolate, becauſe of the fierceneſſe of the
oppreſsour, and becauſe of his fierce anger.

CHAPTER 261In the beginning of the reigne of Iehoiakim the ſonne
of Ioſiah king of Iudah, came this word from the Lord, ſaying;2Thus
ſaith the Lord, ſtand in the Court of the Lords houſe, and ſpeake vnto
all the cities of Iudah, which come to worſhip in the Lords houſe, all the
wordes that I command thee to ſpeake vnto them: diminiſh not a
word;3If ſo bee they will hearken, and turne euery man from his euill
way, that I may repent me of the euil which I purpoſe to doe vnto them,
becauſe of the euil of their doings.4And thou ſhalt ſay vnto them, Thus
ſaith the Lord; If yee will not hearken to mee to walke in my Law, which
I haue ſet before you,5To hearken to the wordes of my ſeruants the
Prophets, whom I ſent vnto you, both riſing vp early and ſending them,
(but ye haue not hearkned:)6Then wil I make this houſe like Shiloh, and
wil make this city a curſe to all the nations of the earth.7So the prieſts
and the prophets, and all the people heard Ieremiah ſpeaking theſe
wordes in the houſe of the Lord.8Now it came to paſſe when Ieremiah
had made an ende of ſpeaking all that the Lord had commanded him to
ſpeake vnto all the people, that the prieſts and the prophets, and all the
people tooke him, ſaying; Thou ſhalt ſurely die.9Why haſt thou
prophecied in the Name of the Lord, ſaying, This houſe ſhalbe like
Shiloh, and this city ſhalbe deſolate without an inhabitant? And all the
people were gathered againſt Ieremiah in the houſe of the Lord.10When
the Princes of Iudah heard theſe things, then they came vp from the
kings houſe vnto the houſe of the Lord, and ſate downe in the entrie of
the new gate of the Lords houſe.11Then ſpake the prieſts and the
prophets vnto the Princes, and to all the people, ſaying; This man is
worthy to die, for he hath prophecied againſt this citie, as yee haue heard
with your eares.12Then ſpake Ieremiah vnto all the Princes, and to all
the people, ſaying, The Lord ſent me to prophecie againſt this houſe,
and againſt this citie, all the wordes that yee haue heard.13Therefore
nowe amend your wayes, and your doings, and obey the voice of the
Lord your God, and the Lord will repent him of the euill that he hath
pronounced againſt you.14As for mee, behold, I am in your hand: doe
with mee as ſeemeth good and meet vnto you.15But know ye for
certaine, That if ye put mee to death, ye ſhall ſurely bring innocent blood
vpon your ſelues, and vpon this citie, and vpon the inhabitants thereof:
for of a trueth the Lord hath ſent mee vnto you, to ſpeake all theſe words
in your eares.16Then ſaid the Princes, and all the people, vnto the prieſts,
and to the prophets; This man is not worthy to die: for hee hath ſpoken
to vs in the Name of the Lord our God.17Then roſe vp certaine of the
Elders of the land, and ſpake to all the aſſembly of the people,
ſaying;18Micah the Moraſhite prophecied in the dayes of Hezekiah king
of Iudah, and ſpake to all the people of Iudah, ſaying; Thus ſaith the
Lord of hoſtes, Zion ſhall be plowed like a field, and Ieruſalem ſhall
become heapes, and the mountaine of the houſe, the hie places of a
forreſt.19Did Hezekiah King of Iudah and all Iudah put him at all to
death? did hee not feare the Lord, and beſought the Lord, and the Lord
repented him of the euill which he had pronounced againſt them? thus
might wee procure great euill againſt our ſoules.20And there was alſo a
man that prophecied in the Name of the Lord, Urijah the ſonne of
Shemaiah of Kiriath-iearim, who prophecied againſt this citie and
againſt this land, according to all the words of Ieremiah.21And when
Iehoiakim the king with all his mightie men, and all the princes heard
his wordes, the king ſought to put him to death; but when Urijah heard
it, he was afraid and fled, and went into Egypt.22And Iehoiakim the king
ſent men into Egypt, namely Elnathan the ſonne of Achbor, and
certeine men with him, into Egypt.23And they fet foorth Urijah out of
Egypt, and brought him vnto Iehoiakim the king, who ſlewe him with
the ſword, and caſt his dead body into the graues of the common
people.24Neuertheleſſe, the hand of Ahikam, the ſonne of Shaphan, was
with Ieremiah, that they ſhould not giue him into the hand of the people,
to put him to death.

CHAPTER 271In the beginning of the reigne of Iehoiakim the ſonne
of Ioſiah King of Iudah, came this worde vnto Ieremiah from the Lord,

ſaying,2Thus ſayth the Lord to me, Make thee bonds and yokes, and put them vpon thy necke.3And ſend them to the king of Edom, and to the king of Moab, and to the king of the Ammonites, and to the king of Tyrus, and to the king of Zidon, by the hand of the meſſengers which come to Ieruſalem vnto Zedekiah king of Iudah.4And command them to ſay vnto their maſters, Thus ſaith the Lord of hoſts the God of Iſrael, Thus ſhall ye ſay vnto your maſters:5I haue made the earth, the man and the beaſt that are vpon the ground, by my great power, and by my outſtretched arme, and haue giuen it vnto whom it ſeemed meet vnto me.6And now haue I giuen all theſe landes into the hand of Nebuchadnezzar the king of Babylon my ſeruant, and the beaſts of the field haue I giuen him alſo to ſerue him.7And all nations ſhall ſerue him and his ſonne, and his ſonnes ſonne, vntill the very time of his land come: and then many nations and great kings ſhall ſerue themſelues of him.8And it ſhall come to paſſe, that the nation and kingdome which will not ſerue the ſame Nebuchad-nezzar the king of Babylon, and that will not put their necke vnder the yoke of the king of Babylon, that nation will I puniſh, ſayth the Lord, with the ſword, and with the famine, and with the peſtilence, vntill I haue conſumed them by his hand.9Therefore hearken not ye to your prophets, nor to your diuiners, nor to your dreamers, nor to your inchanters, nor to your ſorcerers, which ſpeak vnto you, ſaying; Ye ſhall not ſerue the king of Babylon:10For they prophecie a lie vnto you, to remooue you farre from your land, and that I ſhould driue you out, and ye ſhould periſh.11But the nations that bring their necke vnder the yoke of the king of Babylon, and ſerue him, thoſe will I let remaine ſtill in their owne land, ſayth the Lord, and they ſhall till it, and dwell therein.12I ſpake alſo to Zedekiah king of Iudah according to all theſe wordes, ſaying, Bring your neckes vnder the yoke of the king of Babylon, and ſerue him and his people, and liue.13Why will yee die, thou and thy people, by the ſword, by the famine, and by the peſtilence, as the Lord hath ſpoken againſt the nation that will not ſerue the king of Babylon?14Therefore hearken not vnto the words of the prophets, that ſpeake vnto you, ſaying; Yee ſhall not ſerue the king of Babylon: for they prophecie a lie vnto you.15For I haue not ſent them, ſaith the Lord, yet they prophecie a lye in my name, that I might driue you out, & that yee might periſh, ye, and the prophets that prophecie vnto you.16Alſo I ſpake to the prieſts, and to all this people, ſaying; Thus ſaith the Lord, Hearken not to the words of your prophets, that prophecie vnto you, ſaying; Behold, the veſſels of the Lords houſe ſhall now ſhortly be brought againe from Babylon; for they prophecie a lie vnto you.17Hearken not vnto them: ſerue the king of Babylon, and liue: wherefore ſhould this citie be laid waſte?18But if they be prophets, and if the word of the Lord be with them, let them nowe make interceſsion to the Lord of hoſtes, that the veſſels which are left in the houſe of the Lord, and in the houſe of the king of Iudah, and at Ieruſalem, goe not to Babylon.19For thus ſaith the Lord of hoſtes concerning the pillars, and concerning the ſea, and concerning the baſes, and concerning the reſidue of the veſſels that remaine in this citie,20Which Nebuchadnezzar king of Babylon tooke not, when he caried away captiue Ieconiah the ſonne of Iehoiakim king of Iudah, from Ieruſalem to Babylon, and all the nobles of Iudah and Ieruſalem:21Yea thus ſaith the Lord of hoſtes the God of Iſrael, concerning the veſſels that remaine in the houſe of the Lord, and in the houſe of the king of Iudah and of Ieruſalem;22They ſhall be caried to Babylon, and there ſhall they be vntill the day that I viſit them, ſaith the Lord: then will I bring them vp, and reſtore them to this place.

CHAPTER 281And it came to paſſe the ſame yeere, in the beginning of the reigne of Zedekiah king of Iudah, in the fourth yeere, and in the fift moneth, that Hananiah the ſonne of Azur the prophet, which was of Gibeon, ſpake vnto mee in the houſe of the Lord, in the preſence of the prieſts and of all the people, ſaying;2Thus ſpeaketh the Lord of hoſtes, the God of Iſrael, ſaying; I haue broken the yoke of the king of Babylon.3Within two full yeeres will I bring againe into this place all the veſſels of the Lords houſe, that Nebuchadnezzar king of Babylon tooke away from this place, and caried them to Babylon.4And I will bring againe to this place Ieconiah the ſonne of Iehoiakim king of Iudah, with all the captiues of Iudah, that went into Babylon, ſaith the Lord, for I will breake the yoke of the king of Babylon.5Then the prophet Ieremiah ſaid vnto the prophet Hananiah in the preſence of the prieſts, and in the preſence of all the people, that ſtood in the houſe of the Lord,6Euen the prophet Ieremiah ſaid; Amen: the Lord doe ſo, the Lord performe the words which thou haſt prophecied, to bring againe the veſſels of the Lords houſe, and all that is caried away captiue from Babylon into this place.7Neuertheleſſe, heare thou now this word that I ſpeake in thine eares, and in the eares of all the people.8The prophets that haue beene before mee, and before thee of old, prophecied both againſt many countries, and againſt great kingdoms, of warre, and of euill, and of peſtilence.9The prophet which prophecieth of peace, when the word of the prophet ſhall come to paſſe, then ſhall the prophet be knowen, that the Lord hath truely ſent him.10Then Hananiah the prophet tooke the yoke from off the prophet Ieremiahs necke, and brake it.11And Hananiah ſpake in the preſence of all the people, ſaying; Thus ſaith the Lord, Euen ſo will I breake the yoke of Nebuchadnezzer king of Babylon from the necke of all nations within the ſpace of two full yeeres: and the Prophet Ieremiah went his way.12Then the word of the Lord came vnto Ieremiah the Prophet (after that Hananiah the prophet had broken the yoke from off the necke of the Prophet Ieremiah) ſaying,13Goe, and tell Hananiah, ſaying, Thus ſaith the Lord, Thou haſt broken the yokes of wood, but thou ſhalt make for them yokes of yron.14For thus ſaith the Lord of hoſts, the God of Iſrael, I haue put a yoke of yron vpon the neck of all theſe nations, that they may ſerue Nebuchad-nezzar king of Babylon, and they ſhall ſerue him, and I haue giuen him the beaſts of the field alſo.15Then ſaid the Prophet Ieremiah vnto Hananiah the prophet, Heare nowe Hananiah: the Lord hath not ſent thee, but thou makeſt this people to truſt in a lye.16Therefore thus ſaith the Lord, Beholde, I will caſt thee from off the face of the earth: this yeere thou ſhalt die, becauſe thou haſt taught rebellion againſt the Lord.17So Hananiah the prophet died the ſame yeere, in the ſeuenth moneth.

CHAPTER 291Now theſe are the words of the letter, that Ieremiah the prophet ſent from Ieruſalem vnto the reſidue of the elders which were caried away captiues, and to the prieſts, and to the prophets, and to all the people whom Nebuchad-nezzar had caried away captiue from Ieruſalem to Babylon,2(After that Ieconiah the king, and the queene, and the eunuches, the princes of Iudah and Ieruſalem, and the carpenters and the ſmithes were departed from Ieruſalem)3By the hand of Elaſah the ſonne of Shaphan, and Gemariah the ſonne of Hilkiah, whome Zedekiah king of Iudah ſent vnto Babylon to Nebuchad-nezzar king of Babylon, ſaying,4Thus ſaith the Lord of hoſts the God of Iſrael vnto all that are caried away captiues, whom I haue cauſed to be caried away from Ieruſalem vnto Babylon:5Build ye houſes and dwell in them, and plant gardens, and eate the fruit of them.6Take ye wiues, and beget ſonnes and daughters, and take wiues for your ſonnes, and giue your daughters to huſbands, that they may beare ſonnes and daughters, that ye may bee increaſed there, and not diminiſhed.7And ſeeke the peace of the citie, whither I haue cauſed you to be caried away captiues, & pray vnto the Lord for it: for in the peace thereof ſhall yee haue peace.8For thus ſaith the Lord of hoſts, the God of Iſrael, Let not your prophets and your diuiners, that bee in the midſt of you, deceiue you, neither hearken to your dreames which yee cauſe to be dreamed.9For they prophecie falſly vnto you in my name: I haue not ſent them, ſaith the Lord.10For thus ſaith the Lord, That after ſeuentie yeeres be accompliſhed at Babylon, I will viſite you, and performe my good word towards you, in cauſing you to returne to this place.11For I knowe the thoughts that I thinke towards you, ſaith the Lord, thoughts of peace, and not of euill, to giue you an expected end.12Then ſhall ye call vpon me, and ye ſhall goe and pray vnto mee, and I will hearken vnto you.13And ye ſhall ſeeke me, and finde me, when ye ſhall ſearch for me with all your heart.14And I will be found of you, ſaith the Lord, and I will turne away your captiuitie, and I will gather you from all the nations, and from all the places whither I haue driuen you, ſaith the Lord, and I will bring you againe into the place whence I cauſed you to be caried away captiue.15Becauſe yee haue ſaid, The Lord hath raiſed vs vp prophets in Babylon:16Know that thus ſaith the Lord, of the king that ſitteth vpon the throne of Dauid, and of all the people that dwelleth in this citie, and of your brethren that are not gone foorth with you into captiuitie.17Thus ſaith the Lord of hoſts, Beholde, I will ſend vpon them the ſword, the famine, and the peſtilence, and will make them like vile figges, that cannot be eaten, they are ſo euill.18And I will perſecute them with the ſword, with the famine, and with the peſtilence, and will deliuer them to be remooued to all the kingdomes of the earth, to be a curſe and an aſtoniſhment, and an hiſsing, and a reproch among all the nations, whither I haue driuen them.19Becauſe they haue not hearkened to my words, ſaith the Lord, which I ſent vnto them by my ſeruants the Prophets, riſing vp early, and ſending them, but ye would not heare, ſaith the Lord.20Heare yee therefore the word of the Lord, all ye of the captiuitie, whom I haue ſent from Ieruſalem to Babylon.21Thus ſaith the Lord of hoſts the God of Iſrael, of Ahab the ſonne of Kolaiah, and of Zedekiah the ſonne of Maaſeiah, which prophecie a lye vnto you in my Name, Behold, I will deliuer them into the hand of Nebuchadrezzar king of Babylon, and hee ſhall ſlay them before your eyes.22And of them ſhall bee taken vp a eurſe by all the captiuitie of Iudah which are in Babylon, ſaying, The Lord make thee like Zedekiah, and like Ahab, whom the king of Babylon roſted in the fire.23Becauſe they haue committed villanie in Iſrael, and haue committed adulterie with their neighbors wiues, and haue ſpoken lying wordes in my Name, which I haue not commanded them, euen I know, and am a witneſſe, ſaith the Lord.24Thus ſhalt thou alſo ſpeake to Shemaiah the Nehelamite, ſaying:25Thus ſpeaketh the Lord of hoſtes the God of Iſrael, ſaying, Becauſe thou haſt ſent letters in thy name vnto all the people that are at Ieruſalem, and to Zephaniah the ſonne of Maaſeiah the Prieſt, and to all the prieſts, ſaying;26The Lord hath made thee Prieſt in the ſtead of Iehoiada the Prieſt, that ye ſhould be Officers in the houſe of the Lord, for euery man that is madde, and maketh himſelfe a Prophet, that thou ſhouldeſt put him in priſon, and in the ſtockes:27Now therefore why haſt thou not reproued Ieremiah of Anathoth, which maketh himſelfe a Prophet to you?28For therefore he ſent vnto vs in Babylon, ſaying, This captiuitie is long, build ye houſes and dwell in them, and plant gardens, and eate the fruit of them.29And Zephaniah the Prieſt read this letter in the eares of Ieremiah the Prophet.30Then came the word of the Lord vnto Ieremiah, ſaying;31Send to all them of the captiuitie, ſaying, Thus ſaith the Lord, concerning Shemaiah the Nehelamite, Becauſe that Shemaiah hath prophecied vnto you, and I ſent him not, and he cauſed you to truſt in a lye.32Therefore thus ſaith the Lord, Behold, I will puniſh Shemaiah the Nehelamite and his ſeed: he ſhall not haue a man to dwell among this people, neither ſhall hee behold the good that I will doe for my people, ſaith the Lord, becauſe he hath taught rebellion againſt the Lord.

CHAPTER 301The word that came to Ieremiah from the Lord, ſaying,2Thus ſpeaketh the Lord God of Iſrael, ſaying; Write thee all the wordes that I haue ſpoken vnto thee, in a booke.3For loe, the dayes come, ſaith the Lord, that I will bring againe the captiuitie of my people Iſrael and Iudah, ſaith the Lord, and I wil cauſe them to returne to the land, that I gaue to their fathers, and they ſhall poſſeſſe it.4And theſe are the words that the Lord ſpake concerning Iſrael, and concerning Iudah.5For thus ſayth the Lord, Wee haue heard a voice of trembling, of feare, and not of peace.6Aſke yee now and ſee whether a man doeth trauaile with child? wherefore doe I ſee euery man with his handes on his loynes, as a woman in trauaile, and all faces are turned into palenefse?7Alas, for that day is great, ſo that none is like it: it is euen the time of Iacobs trouble, but he ſhall be ſaued out of it.8For it ſhall come to paſſe in that day, ſaith the Lord of hoſtes, that I will breake his yoke from off thy necke, and will burſt thy bondes, and ſtrangers ſhall no more ſerue themſelues of him.9But they ſhall ſerue the Lord their God, and Dauid their King whom I will raiſe vp vnto them.10Therefore feare thou not, O my ſeruant Iacob, ſaith the Lord, neither be diſmayed, O Iſrael; for loe, I will ſaue thee from afarre, and thy ſeede from the land of their captiuitie, and Iacob ſhall returne, and ſhall be in reſt, and be quiet, and none ſhall make him afraid.11For I am with thee, ſayeth the Lord, to ſaue thee: though I make a full end of all nations whither I haue ſcattered thee, yet will I not make a full ende of thee: but I will correct thee in meaſure, and will not leaue thee altogether vnpuniſhed.12For thus ſaith the Lord, Thy bruiſe is incurable, and thy wound is grieuous.13There is none to pleade thy cauſe, that thou mayeſt bee bonnd vp: thou haſt no healing medicines.14All thy louers haue forgotten thee: they ſeeke thee not, for I haue wounded thee with the wound of an enemy, with the chaſtiſement of a cruell one, for the multitude of thine iniquitie: becauſe thy ſinnes were increaſed.15Why cryeſt thou for thine affliction? thy ſorrow is incurable, for the multitude of thine iniquitie: becauſe thy ſinnes were increaſed, I haue done theſe things vnto thee.16Therefore all they that deuoure thee ſhalbe deuoured, and all thine aduerſaries euery one of them ſhall goe into captiuitie: and they that ſpoile thee ſhall be a ſpoile, and all that pray vpon thee, will I giue for a pray.17For I will reſtore health vnto thee, and I will heale thee of thy wounds, ſayth the Lord, becauſe they called thee an outcaſt, ſaying; This is Zion whom no man ſeeketh after.18Thus ſaith the Lord, Behold, I will bring againe the captiuitie of Iacobs tents, and haue mercie on his dwelling places: and the citie ſhall be builded vpon her owne heape, and the palace ſhall remaine after the manner thereof.19And out of them ſhall proceede thankeſgiuing, and the voice of them that make merry; and I will multiply them, and they ſhall not be few: I will alſo glorifie them, and they ſhall not be ſmall.20Their children alſo ſhall be as aforetime, and their congregation ſhalbe eſtabliſhed before me, and I will puniſh all that oppreſſe them.21And their nobles ſhall be of themſelues, and their gouernour ſhall proceede from the middeſt of them, and I will cauſe him to draw neere, and hee ſhall approch vnto me: for who is this that engaged his heart to approch vnto me, ſayth the Lord ?22And yee ſhall be my people, and I will be your God.23Behold, the whirlewinde of the Lord goeth foorth with furie, a continuing whirlewinde, it ſhall fall with paine vpon the head of the wicked.24The fierce anger of the Lord ſhall not returne, vntill hee haue done it, and vntill he haue performed the intents of his heart: in the latter dayes ye ſhall conſider it.

CHAPTER 311At the ſame time, ſaith the Lord, wil I be the God of all the families of Iſrael, & they ſhalbe my people.2Thus ſaith the Lord; The people which were left of the ſword found grace in the wilderneſſe, euen Iſrael, when I went to cauſe him to reſt.3The Lord hath appeared of old vnto mee, ſaying; Yea I haue loued thee with an euerlaſting loue: therefore with louing kindneſſe haue I drawen thee.4Againe I will build thee, and thou ſhalt be built, O virgine of Iſrael, thou ſhalt againe be adorned with thy tabrets, and ſhalt goe forth in the daunces of them that make merry.5Thou ſhalt yet plant vines vpon the mountaines of Samaria, the planters ſhall plant, and ſhall eate them as common things.6For there ſhall be a day, that the watchmen vpon the mount Ephraim ſhall cry; Ariſe yee, and let vs goe vp to Zion vnto the Lord our God.7For thus ſaith the Lord, Sing with gladneſſe for Iacob, and ſhout among the chiefe of the nations: publiſh yee, praiſe yee, and ſay; O Lord ſaue thy people the remnant of Iſrael.8Behold, I will bring them from the North countrey, and gather them from the coaſts of the earth, and with them the blind and the lame, the woman with child, and her that trauelleth with child together, a great company ſhall returne thither.9They ſhall come with weeping, and with ſupplications will I leade them: I will cauſe them to walke by the riuers of waters, in a ſtraight way wherein they ſhall not ſtumble: for I am a father to Iſrael, and Ephraim is my firſt borne.10Heare the word of the Lord, O yee nations, and declare it in the iles afarre off, and ſay; Hee that ſcattered Iſrael will gather him, and keepe him as a ſhepheard doth his flocke.11For the Lord hath redeemed Iacob, and ranſomed him from the hand of him that was ſtronger then hee.12Therefore they ſhall come and ſing in the height of Zion, and ſhall flow together to the goodneſſe of the Lord, for wheate, and for wine, and for oyle, and for the young of the flocke and of the herd: and their ſoule ſhall be as a watered garden, and they ſhall not ſorrow any more at all.13Then ſhall the virgine reioyce in the daunce, both yoong men and old together: for I will turne their mourning into ioy, and will comfort them, and make them reioyce from their ſorrow.14And I will ſatiate the ſoule of the prieſts with fatneſſe, and my people ſhall be ſatiſfied with goodneſse, ſaith the Lord.15Thus ſaith the Lord; A voyce was heard in Ramah, lamentation and bitter weeping: Rahel weeping for her children, refuſed to be comforted for her children, becauſe they were not.16Thus ſaith the Lord; Refraine thy voice from weeping, and thine eyes from teares: for thy worke ſhall be rewarded, ſaith the Lord, and they ſhall come againe from the land of the enemie.17And there is hope in thine end, ſaith the Lord, that thy children ſhall come againe to their owne border.18I haue ſurely heard Ephraim bemoaning himſelfe thus, Thou haſt chaſtiſed me, and I was chaſtiſed, as a bullocke vnaccuſtomed to the yoke: turne thou me, and I ſhall be turned; thou art the Lord my God.19Surely after that I was turned, I repented; and after that I was inſtructed, I ſmote vpon my thigh: I was aſhamed, yea euen confounded, becauſe I did beare the reproch of my youth.20Is Ephraim my deare ſonne? is he a pleaſant child? for ſince I ſpake againſt him, I doe earneſtly remember him ſtill:

therefore my bowels are troubled for him; I will ſurely haue mercy vpon
him, ſaith the Lord.21Set thee vp way-markes; make thee high heaps: ſet
thine heart toward the high way, euen the way which thou wenteſt: turne
againe, O virgine of Iſrael, turne againe to theſe thy cities.22How long
wilt thou go about, O thou backſliding daughter? for the Lord hath
created a new thing in the earth: A woman ſhall compaſſe a man.23Thus
ſaith the Lord of hoſts the God of Iſrael, As yet they ſhall vſe this ſpeech
in the land of Iudah, and in the cities thereof, when I ſhall bring againe
their captiuitie, The Lord bleſſe thee, O habitation of iuſtice, and
mountaine of holineſſe.24And there ſhall dwell in Iudah it ſelfe, and in
all the cities thereof together, huſbandmen, and they that goe forth with
flocks.25For I haue ſatiated the wearie ſoule, and I haue repleniſhed
euery ſorowfull ſoule.26Upon this I awaked and beheld, and my ſleepe
was ſweete vnto me.27Behold, the dayes come, ſaith the Lord, that I will
ſow the houſe of Iſrael, and the houſe of Iudah with the ſeed of man,
and with the ſeed of beaſt.28And it ſhall come to paſſe, that like as I haue
watched ouer them, to plucke vp and to breake downe, and to throw
downe, and to deſtroy, and to afflict: ſo will I watch ouer them, to build
and to plant, ſaith the Lord.29In thoſe dayes they ſhall ſay no more, The
fathers haue eaten a ſowre grape, and the childrens teeth are ſet on
edge.30But euery one ſhall die for his owne iniquitie, euery man that
eateth the ſowre grape, his teeth ſhall be ſet on edge.31Behold, the dayes
come, ſaith the Lord, that I will make a newe couenant with the houſe
of Iſrael, and with the houſe of Iudah.32Not according to the couenant
that I made with their fathers in the day that I tooke them by the hand,
to bring them out of the land of Egypt, which my couenant they brake,
although I was an huſband vnto them, ſaith the Lord.33But this ſhall be
the couenant, that I will make with the houſe of Iſrael, After thoſe dayes,
ſaith the Lord, I will put my law in their inward parts, and write it in
their hearts, and wil be their God, and they ſhall be my people.34And
they ſhall teach no more euery man his neighbour, and euery man his
brother, ſaying, Know the Lord: for they ſhall all know mee, from the
leaſt of them vnto the greateſt of them, ſaith the Lord; for I will forgiue
their iniquitie, and I will remember their ſinne no more.35Thus ſaith the
Lord which giueth the Sunne for a light by day, and the ordinances of
the moone and of the ſtarres for a light by night, which diuideth the ſea
when the waues thereof roare, the Lord of hoſts is his name.36If thoſe
ordinances depart from before me, ſaith the Lord, then the ſeed of Iſrael
alſo ſhall ceaſe from being a nation before me for euer.37Thus ſaith the
Lord, If heauen aboue can bee meaſured, and the foundations of the
earth ſearched out beneath, I will alſo caſt off all the ſeed of Iſrael for
all that they haue done, ſaith the Lord.38Behold, the dayes come, ſaith
the Lord, that the citie ſhall be built to the Lord from the tower of
Hananeel vnto the gate of the corner.39And the meaſuring line ſhall yet
goe forth ouer againſt it, vpon the hill Gareb, and ſhall compaſſe about
to Goath.40And the whole valley of the dead bodies, and of the aſhes,
and all the fields vnto the brooke of Kidron, vnto the corner of the
horſe gate towards the Eaſt, ſhalbe holy vnto the Lord, it ſhall not be
plucked vp, nor throwen downe any more for euer.

CHAPTER 321The worde that came to Ieremiah from the Lord in the
tenth yeere of Zedekiah king of Iudah, which was the eighteenth yeere
of Nebuchad-rezzar.2For then the king of Babylons armie beſieged
Ieruſalem: and Ieremiah the prophet was ſhut vp in the court of the
priſon which was in the king of Iudahs houſe.3For Zedekiah king of
Iudah had ſhut him vp, ſaying, Wherefore doeſt thou prophecie and ſay,
Thus ſaith the Lord, Behold, I will giue this citie into the hand of the
king of Babylon, and hee ſhall take it?4And Zedekiah king of Iudah, ſhal
not eſcape out of the hand of the Caldeans, but ſhall ſurely be deliuered
into the hand of the king of Babylon, and ſhal ſpeake with him mouth
to mouth, and his eyes ſhall behold his eyes.5And he ſhall lead Zedekiah
to Babylon, and there ſhall he be vntill I viſit him, ſaith the Lord: though
ye fight with the Caldeans, yee ſhall not proſper.6And Ieremiah ſaid; The
word of the Lord came vnto me, ſaying;7Behold, Hanameel the ſonne
of Shallum thine vncle, ſhall come vnto thee, ſaying; Buy thee my field
that is in Anathoth: for the right of redemption is thine to buy it.8So
Hanameel mine vncles ſonne came to me in the court of the priſon,
according to the word of the Lord, and ſaid vnto me; Buy my field, I
pray thee, that is in Anathoth, which is in the countrey of Beniamin: for
the right of inheritance is thine, and the redemption is thine, buy it for
thy ſelfe. Then I knew that this was the word of the Lord.9And I bought
the field of Hanameel my vncles ſonne, that was in Anathoth, and
weighed him the money, euen ſeuenteene ſhekels of ſiluer.10And I
ſubſcribed the euidence, and ſealed it, and tooke witneſſes, and weighed
him the money in the ballances.11So I tooke the euidence of the
purchaſe, both that which was ſealed according to the law and cuſtome,
and that which was open.12And I gaue the euidence of the purchaſe vnto
Baruch the ſonne of Neriah, the ſonne of Maaſeiah, in the ſight of
Hanameel mine vncles ſonne, and in the preſence of the witneſſes, that
ſubſcribed the booke of the purchaſe, before all the Iewes that ſate in
the court of the priſon.13And I charged Baruch before them,
ſaying,14Thus ſaith the Lord of hoſts the God of Iſrael; Take theſe
euidences, this euidence of the purchaſe, both which is ſealed, and this
euidence which is open, and put them in an earthen veſſell, that they
may continue many daies.15For thus ſaith the Lord of hoſtes the God
of Iſrael; Houſes and fields, and Uineyards ſhalbe poſſeſſed againe in
this land.16Now when I had deliuered the euidence of the purchaſe vnto
Baruch the ſonne of Neriah, I prayed vnto the Lord, ſaying,17Ah Lord
God, beholde, thou haſt made the heauen and the earth by thy great
power & ſtretched out arme, and there is nothing too hard for
thee.18Thou ſheweſt louing kindneſſe vnto thouſands, and
recompenſeſt the iniquitie of the fathers into the boſome of their
children after them: the great, the mightie God, the Lord of hoſts is his
Name,19Great in counſell, and mightie in worke, (for thine eyes are open
vpon all the wayes of the ſonnes of men, to giue euery one according to
his wayes, and according to the fruit of his doingſ)20Which haſt ſet
ſignes and wonders in the land of Egypt, euen vnto this day, and in
Iſrael, and amongſt other men, and haſt made thee a Name, as at this
day,21And haſt brought foorth thy people Iſrael out of the land of Egypt,
with ſignes and with wonders, and with a ſtrong hand, and with a
ſtretched out arme, and with great terrour,22And haſt giuen them this
land which thou didſt ſweare to their fathers to giue them a land flowing
with milke and honie.23And they came in and poſſeſſed it, but they
obeied not thy voice, neither walked in thy Law, they haue done nothing
of all that thou commaundedſt them to doe: therefore thou haſt cauſed
all this euill to come vpon them.24Beholde the mounts, they are come
vnto the citie to take it, and the citie is giuen into the hand of the
Caldeans that fight againſt it, becauſe of the ſword, and of the famine,
and of the peſtilence, and what thou haſt ſpoken is come to paſſe, and
behold, thou ſeeſt it.25And thou haſt ſaid vnto mee, O Lord God, buy
thee the field for money, and take witneſſes: for the citie is giuen into
the hand of the Caldeans.26Then came the word of the Lord vnto
Ieremiah, ſaying,27Behold, I am the Lord, the God of all fleſh: Is there
any thing too hard for me?28Therfore thus ſaith the Lord, Behold, I will
giue this citie into the hand of the Caldeans, and into the hand of
Nebuchad-rezzar king of Babylon, and he ſhall take it.29And the
Caldeans that fight againſt this citie, ſhall come and ſet fire on this citie,
and burne it with the houſes vpon whoſe roofes they haue offered
incenſe vnto Baal, and powred out drinke offerings vnto other Gods to
prouoke me to anger.30For the children of Iſrael, and the children of
Iudah, haue onely done euill before me from their youth: for the
children of Iſrael haue onely prouoked mee to anger with the worke of
their hands, ſayth the Lord.31For this citie hath beene to me, as a
prouocation of mine anger, and of my furie, from the day that they built
it, euen vnto this day; that I ſhould remooue it from before my
face:32Becauſe of all the euill of the children of Iſrael, and of the children
of Iudah, which they haue done to prouoke mee to anger, they, their
kings, their Princes, their Prieſtes, and their Prophets, and the men of
Iudah, and the inhabitants of Ieruſalem.33And they haue turned vnto
mee the backe, and not the face, though I taught them riſing vp early,
and teaching them, yet they haue not hearkened to receiue
inſtruction,34But they ſet their abominations in the houſe (which is
called by my Name) to defile it.35And they built the high places of Baal,
which are in the valley of the ſonne of Hinnom, to cauſe their ſonnes
and their daughters to paſſe through the fire vnto Molech, which I
commanded them not, neither came it into my minde, that they ſhould
doe this abomination, to cauſe Iudah to ſinne.36And now therefore, thus
ſayth the Lord the God of Iſrael concerning this citie, whereof ye ſay, It
ſhall be deliuered into the hand of the king of Babylon, by the ſword,
and by the famine, and by the peſtilence:37Behold, I wil gather them out
of all countreys, whither I haue driuen them in mine anger, and in my

furie, and in great wrath, and I will bring them againe vnto this place; and I will cauſe them to dwell ſafely.[38]And they ſhalbe my people, and I will be their God.[39]And I will giue them one heart, and one way, that they may feare mee for euer, for the good of them, and of their children after them.[40]And I will make an euerlaſting couenant with them, that I will not turne away from them, to doe them good, but I will put my feare in their hearts, that they ſhall not depart from mee.[41]Yea, I will reioyce oner them to doe them good, and I will plant them in this land aſsuredly, with my whole heart, and with my whole ſoule.[42]For thus ſayth the Lord, Like as I haue brought all this great euill vpon this people, ſo will I bring vpon them all the good that I haue promiſed them.[43]And fields ſhalbe bought in this land whereof ye ſay, It is deſolate without man or beaſt, it is giuen into the hand of the Caldeans.[44]Men ſhall buy fields for money, and ſubſcribe euidences, and ſeale them, and take witneſſes in the land of Beniamin, and in the places about Ieruſalem, and in the cities of Iudah, and in the cities of the mountaines, and in the cities of the valley, and in the cities of the South: for I will cauſe their captiuitie to returne, ſaith the Lord.

CHAPTER 33[1]Moreouer, the word of the Lord came vnto Ieremiah the ſecond time (while hee was yet ſhut vp in the court of the priſon) ſaying;[2]Thus ſaith the Lord the maker thereof, the Lord that formed it, to eſtabliſh it, the Lord is his Name.[3]Call vnto me, and I will anſwere thee, and ſhew thee great and mightie things, which thou knoweſt not.[4]For thus ſayth the Lord the God of Iſrael concerning the houſes of this citie, and concerning the houſes of the kings of Iudah, which are throwen downe by the mounts, and by the ſword.[5]They come to fight with the Caldeans, but it is to fill them with the dead bodies of men, whome I haue ſlaine in mine anger, and in my fury, and for all whoſe wickedneſſe I haue hid my face from this citie.[6]Behold, I will bring it health and cure, and I will cure them, and wil reueale vnto them the abundance of peace, and trueth.[7]And I will cauſe the captiuitie of Iudah, and the captiuitie of Iſrael to returne, and will build them as at the firſt.[8]And I will clenſe them from all their iniquitie, whereby they haue ſinned againſt mee: and I will pardon all their iniquities whereby they haue ſinned, and whereby they haue tranſgreſſed againſt me.[9]And it ſhall be to me a name of ioy, a praiſe and an honour before all the nations of the earth, which ſhall heare all the good that I doe vnto them: and they ſhall feare and tremble for all the goodneſse, and for all the proſperitie that I procure vnto it.[10]Thus ſaith the Lord; Againe there ſhall be heard in this place (which yee ſay ſhalbe deſolate without man and without beaſt, euen in the cities of Iudah, and in the ſtreetes of Ieruſalem that are deſolate without man and without inhabitant, & without beaſt.)[11]The voyce of ioy and the voyce of gladneſſe, the voyce of the bridegroome, and the voyce of the bride, the voyce of them that ſhall ſay; Praiſe the Lord of hoſtes, for the Lord is good, for his mercy endureth for euer, and of them that ſhall bring the ſacrifice of praiſe into the houſe of the Lord; for I will cauſe to returne the captiuitie of the land, as at the firſt, ſaith the Lord.[12]Thus ſaith the Lord of hoſtes; Againe in this place which is deſolate without man and without beaſt, and in all the cities thereof ſhalbe a habitation of ſhepheards cauſing their flockes to lie downe.[13]In the cities of the mountaines, in the cities of the vale, and in the cities of the South, and in the land of Beniamin, and in the places about Ieruſalem, and in the cities of Iudah, ſhall the flockes paſſe againe vnder the hands of him that telleth them, ſaith the Lord.[14]Behold, the dayes come, ſaith the Lord, that I will performe that good thing which I haue promiſed vnto the houſe of Iſrael, and to the houſe of Iudah.[15]In thoſe dayes, and at that time will I cauſe the branch of righteouſneſſe to grow vp vnto Dauid, and he ſhall execute iudgement and righteouſneſſe in the land.[16]In thoſe dayes ſhall Iudah be ſaued, and Ieruſalem ſhall dwell ſafely, and this is the name wherewith ſhe ſhall be called, The Lord our righteouſneſſe.[17]For thus ſaith the Lord; Dauid ſhall neuer want a man to ſit vpon the throne of the houſe of Iſrael.[18]Neither ſhall the prieſts the Leuites want a man before me to offer burnt offrings, and to kindle meate offrings, and to doe ſacrifice continually.[19]And the word of the Lord came vnto Ieremiah, ſaying,[20]Thus ſaith the Lord; If you can breake my couenant of the day, and my couenant of the night, and that there ſhould not be day, and night in their ſeaſon:[21]Then may alſo my couenant bee broken with Dauid my ſeruant, that he ſhould not haue a ſonne to reigne vpon his throne; and with the Leuites the prieſts my miniſters.[22]As the hoſte of heauen cannot be numbred, neither the ſand of the ſea meaſured: ſo will I multiply the ſeede of Dauid my ſeruant, and the Leuites that miniſter vnto me.[23]Moreouer, the word of the Lord came to Ieremiah, ſaying;[24]Conſidereſt thou not what this people haue ſpoken, ſaying; The two families, which the Lord hath choſen, he hath euen caſt them off? thus they haue diſpiſed my people, that they ſhould be no more a nation before them.[25]Thus ſaith the Lord; If my couenant be not with day and night, and if I haue not appointed the ordinances of heauen and earth:[26]Then will I caſt away the ſeede of Iacob and Dauid my ſeruant, ſo that I will not take any of his ſeede to be rulers ouer the ſeede of Abraham, Iſaac and Iacob: for I will cauſe their captiuitie to returne, and haue mercie on them.

CHAPTER 34[1]The word which came vnto Ieremiah frō the Lord (when Nebuchad-nezzar king of Babylon and all his armie, and all the kingdomes of the earth of his dominion, and all the people fought againſt Ieruſalem and againſt all the cities thereof) ſaying,[2]Thus ſaith the Lord, the God of Iſrael, Go, and ſpeake to Zedekiah king of Iudah, and tell him, Thus ſaith the Lord, Behold, I will giue this citie into the hand of the king of Babylon, and he ſhal burne it with fire.[3]And thou ſhalt not eſcape out of his hand, but ſhalt ſurely be taken, and deliuered into his hand, and thine eyes ſhall behold the eyes of the king of Babylon, and he ſhall ſpeake with thee mouth to mouth, and thou ſhalt goe to Babylon.[4]Yet heare the word of the Lord, O Zedekiah king of Iudah: Thus ſaith the Lord of thee, Thou ſhalt not die by the ſword:[5]But thou ſhalt die in peace, and with the burnings of thy fathers the former kings which were before thee, ſo ſhall they burne odours for thee, and they will lament thee, ſaying, Ah Lord; for I haue pronounced the word, ſaith the Lord.[6]Then Ieremiah the Prophet ſpake all theſe words vnto Zedekiah king of Iudah in Ieruſalem;[7]When the king of Babylons armie fought againſt Ieruſalem, and againſt all the cities of Iudah that were left, againſt Lachiſh, and againſt Azekah: for theſe defenced cities remained of the cities of Iudah.[8]This is the word that came vnto Ieremiah from the Lord, after that the king Zedekiah had made a couenant with all the people which were at Ieruſalem to proclaime liberty vnto them,[9]That euery man ſhould let his man ſeruant, and euery man his maide ſeruant, being an Hebrewe, or an Hebreweſse, goe free, that none ſhould ſerue himſelfe of them, to wit, of a Iew his brother.[10]Now when all the princes and all the people which had entred into the couenant, heard that euery one ſhould let his man ſeruant, and euery one his maid ſeruant goe free, that none ſhould ſerue themſelues of them any more, then they obeyed and let them goe.[11]But afterwards they turned, and cauſed the ſeruants and the handmaids whom they had let goe free, to returne, and brought them into ſubiection for ſeruants and for handmaids.[12]Therefore the worde of the Lord came to Ieremiah, from the Lord, ſaying,[13]Thus ſaith the Lord the God of Iſrael, I made a couenant with your fathers in the day that I brought them forth out of the land of Egypt, out of the houſe of bondmen, ſaying,[14]At the end of ſeuen yeeres, let ye go euery man his brother an Hebrew which hath bene ſold vnto thee: and when he hath ſerued thee ſixe yeeres, thou ſhalt let him goe free from thee, but your fathers hearkened not vnto me, neither inclined their eare.[15]And ye were now turned, and had done right in my ſight, in proclaiming libertie euery man to his neighbour, and ye had made a couenant before me in the houſe, which is called by my Name.[16]But yee turned and polluted my Name, and cauſed euery man his ſeruant, and euery man his handmaide, whome yee had ſet at libertie at their pleaſure, to returne; and brought them into ſubiection, to bee vnto you for ſeruants and for handmaids.[17]Therfore thus ſaith the Lord, Ye haue not hearkened vnto me, in proclaiming libertie euery one to his brother, and euery man to his neighbour: behold, I proclaime a libertie for you, ſaith the Lord, to the ſword, to the peſtilence, and to the famine, and I wil make you to be remoued into all the kingdomes of the earth.[18]And I wil giue the men that haue tranſgreſſed my couenant, which haue not performed the wordes of the couenant which they had made before mee, when they cut the calfe in twaine, and paſſed betweene the parts thereof,[19]The princes of Iudah and the princes of Ieruſalem, the eunuches, and the prieſts, and all the people of the land which paſſed betweene the parts of the calfe,[20]I will euen giue them into the hande of their enemies, and into the hand of them that ſeeke their life, and their dead bodies ſhall bee for meate vnto the foules of the heauen, and to the beaſts of the earth.[21]And Zedekiah king of Iudah, and his Princes will I giue into the hand of their enemies, and into the hand of them that ſeeke their life and into the hand of the king of Babylons armie, which are gone vp from you.[22]Behold, I will command, ſaith the Lord, and cauſe them to returne to this citie, and they ſhall fight againſt it, and take it, and burne it with fire, and I will make the cities of Iudah a deſolation without an inhabitant.

CHAPTER 35[1]The word which came vnto Ieremiah from the Lord, in the daies of Iehoiakim the ſonne of Ioſiah King of Iudah, ſaying,[2]Goe vnto the houſe of the Rechabites, and ſpeake vnto them, and bring them into the houſe of the Lord, into one of the chambers, and giue them wine to drinke.[3]Then I tooke Iaazaniah the ſonne of Ieremiah the ſonne of Habazimah and his brethren, and all his ſonnes, and the whole houſe of the Rechabites.[4]And I brought them into the houſe of the Lord, into the chamber of the ſonnes of Hanan, the ſonne of Igdaliah a man of God, which was by the chamber of the Princes, which was aboue the chamber of Maaſeiah, the ſonne of Shallum, the keeper of the doore.[5]And I ſet before the ſonnes of the houſe of the Rechabites, pottes, full of wine, and cups, and I ſaid vnto them, Drinke ye wine.[6]But they ſaid, We will drinke no wine: for Ionadab the ſonne of Rechab our father, commanded vs, ſaying; Ye ſhall drinke no wine, neither ye, nor your ſonnes for euer.[7]Neither ſhall ye build houſe, nor ſow ſeed, nor plant Uineyard, nor haue any: but all your dayes ye ſhall dwell in tents, that ye may liue many dayes in the land where ye be ſtrangers.[8]Thus haue we obeyed the voice of Ionadab the ſonne of Rechab our father, in all that he hath charged vs, to drinke no wine all our dayes, we, our wiues, our ſonnes, nor our daughters:[9]Nor to build houſes for vs to dwel in, neither haue we Uineyard, nor field, nor ſeed.[10]But wee haue dwelt in tents, and haue obeyed, and done according to all that Ionadab our father commanded vs.[11]But it came to paſſe when Nebuchadrezzar king of Babylon came vp into the land, that we ſaid, Come, and let vs goe to Ieruſalem for feare of the armie of the Caldeans, and for feare of the armie of the Syrians: ſo we dwell at Ieruſalem.[12]Then came the word of the Lord vnto Ieremiah, ſaying,[13]Thus ſaith the Lord of hoſts, the God of Iſrael, Goe and tel the men of Iudah, and inhabitants of Ieruſalem, Will yee not receiue inſtruction to hearken to my words, ſaith the Lord ?[14]The wordes of Ionadab the ſonne of Rechab, that hee commanded his ſonnes, not to drinke wine, are performed; for vnto this day they drinke none, but obey their fathers commandement: notwithſtanding I haue ſpoken vnto you, riſing early, and ſpeaking, but ye hearkened not vnto me.[15]I haue ſent alſo vnto you all my ſeruants the Prophets, riſing vp early and ſending them, ſaying, Returne ye now euery man from his euil way, and amend your doings, and goe not after other gods to ſerue them, and ye ſhall dwell in the land, which I haue giuen to you, and to your fathers: but yee haue not enclined your eare, nor hearkned vnto me.[16]Becauſe the ſonnes of Ionadab, the ſonne of Rechab, haue performed the commaundement of their father, which he commaunded them, but this people hath not hearkened vnto me;[17]Therefore thus ſaith the Lord God of hoſtes, the God of Iſrael, Behold, I will bring vpon Iudah, and vpon all the inhabitants of Ieruſalem, all the euill that I haue pronounced againſt them: becauſe I haue ſpoken vnto them, but they haue not heard, and I haue called vnto them, but they haue not anſwered.[18]And Ieremiah ſayd vnto the houſe of the Rechabites, Thus ſayth the Lord of hoſts the God of Iſrael, Becauſe ye haue obeyed the commandement of Ionadab your father, and kept all his precepts, and done according vnto all that he hath commanded you:[19]Therefore thus ſayth the Lord of hoſtes, the God of Iſrael, Ionadab the ſon of Rechab ſhall not want a man to ſtand before me for euer.

CHAPTER 36[1]And it came to paſſe in the fourth yeere of Iehoiakim the ſonne of Ioſiah king of Iudah, that this word came vnto Ieremiah from the Lord, ſaying;[2]Take thee a roule of a booke, and write therein all the words that I haue ſpoken vnto thee againſt Iſrael, and againſt Iudah, & againſt all the nations, from the day I ſpake vnto thee, frō the dayes of Ioſiah, euen vnto this day.[3]It may be that the houſe of Iudah will heare all the euil which I purpoſe to doe vnto them; that they may returne euery man from his euill way, that I may forgiue their iniquitie, and their ſinne.[4]Then Ieremiah called Baruch the ſonne of Neriah, and Baruch wrote from the mouth of Ieremiah all the words of the Lord, which he had ſpoken vnto him, vpon a roule of a booke.[5]And Ieremiah commanded Baruch, ſaying, I am ſhut vp, I cannot goe into the houſe of the Lord.[6]Therefore goe thou and reade in the roule, which thou haſt written from my mouth, the wordes of the Lord in the eares of the people in the Lords houſe vpon the faſting day: and alſo thou ſhalt reade them in the eares of all Iudah, that come out of their cities.[7]It may bee they will preſent their ſupplication before the Lord, and will returne euery one from his euill way; for great is the anger and the furie that the Lord hath pronounced againſt this people.[8]And Baruch the ſonne of Neriah did according to all that Ieremiah the Prophet commanded him, reading in the booke the wordes of the Lord, in the Lords houſe.[9]And it came to paſſe in the fifth yeere of Iehoiakim the ſonne of Ioſiah king of Iudah, in the ninth moneth, that they proclaimed a faſt before the Lord to all the people in Ieruſalem, & to all the people that came from the cities of Iudah vnto Ieruſalem.[10]Then read Baruch in the booke, the wordes of Ieremiah in the houſe of the Lord, in the chamber of Gemariah the ſonne of Shaphan the ſcribe, in the higher court at the entry of the newe gate of the Lords houſe, in the eares of all the people.[11]When Michaiah the ſonne of Gemariah the ſonne of Shaphan had heard out of the booke, all the words of the Lord;[12]Then hee went downe into the kings houſe into the ſcribes chamber, and loe, all the princes ſate there, euen Eliſhama the ſcribe, and Delaiah the ſonne of Shemaiah, and Elnathan the ſonne of Achbor, and Gemariah the ſonne of Shaphan, and Zedekiah the ſonne of Hananiah, and all the princes.[13]Then Michaiah declared vnto them all the words that hee had heard when Baruch read the booke in the eares of the people.[14]Therefore all the princes ſent Iehudi the ſonne of Nethaniah, the ſonne of Shelemiah, the ſonne of Cuſhi, vnto Baruch, ſaying; Take in thine hand the roule wherein thou haſt read in the eares of the people, and come. So Baruch the ſonne of Neriah took the roule in his hand, and came vnto them.[15]And they ſayde vnto him, Sit downe now and read it in our eares. So Baruch read it in their eares.[16]Now it came to paſſe when they had heard all the words, they were afraid both one and other, and ſayd vnto Baruch, Wee will ſurely tell the King of all theſe words.[17]And they aſked Baruch, ſaying, Tell vs now, How diddeſt thou write all theſe words at his mouth?[18]Then Baruch anſwered them, Hee pronounced all theſe words vnto me with his mouth, and I wrote them with inke in the Booke.[19]Then ſaid the Princes vnto Baruch, Go hide thee, thou and Ieremiah, and let no man know where yee bee.[20]And they went in to the King into the Court, bnt they layed vp the roule in the chamber of Eliſhama the Scribe, and told all the words in the eares of the king.[21]So the king ſent Iehudi to fet the roule, and hee tooke it out of Eliſhama the ſcribes chamber, and Iehudi read it in the eares of the king, and in the eares of all the princes which ſtood beſide the king.[22]Now the king ſate in the winter houſe, in the ninth moneth, & there was a fire on the hearth burning before him.[23]And it came to paſſe that when Iehudi had read three or foure leaues, he cut it with the penknife, and caſt it into the fire that was on the hearth, vntill all the roule was conſumed in the fire that was on the hearth.[24]Yet they were not afraid, nor rent their garments, neither the king, nor any of his ſeruants that heard all theſe words.[25]Neuertheleſſe Elnathan, and Delaiah & Gemariah had made interceſsion to the king that he would not burne the roule, but he would not heare them.[26]But the king commaunded Ierahmeel the ſonne of Hammelech, and Seraiah the ſonne of Azriel, & Shelennah the ſonne of Abdiel, to take Baruch the ſcribe, and Ieremiah the Prophet: but the Lord hid them.[27]Then the word of the Lord came to Ieremiah (after that the king had burnt the roule and the words which Baruch wrote at the mouth of Ieremiah) ſaying;[28]Take thee againe another roule, and write in it all the former words that were in the firſt roule, which Iehoiakim the king of Iudah hath burnt.[29]And thou ſhalt ſay to Iehoiakim king of Iudah, Thus ſayth the Lord, Thou haſt burnt this roule, ſaying, Why haſt thou written therein, ſaying, The king of Babylon ſhall certainely come and deſtroy this land, and ſhall cauſe to ceaſe from thence man and beaſt?[30]Therefore thus ſaith the Lord of Iehoiakim king of Iudah; He ſhall haue none to ſit vpon the throne of Dauid, and his dead body ſhall be caſt out in the day to the heate, and in the night to the froſt.[31]And I will puniſh him and his ſeede, and his ſeruants for their iniquitie, and I will bring vpon them, and vpon the inhabitants of Ieruſalem, and vpon the men of Iudah all the euill that I haue pronounced againſt them: but they hearkened not.[32]Then tooke Ieremiah another roule, and gaue it to Baruch the ſcribe the ſonne of Neriah, who wrote therein from the mouth of Ieremiah, all the words of the booke which Iehoiakim king of

Iudah had burnt in the fire, and there were added beſides vnto them, many like words.

CHAPTER 371And king Zedekiah the ſonne of Ioſiah reigned in ſtead of Coniah the ſon of Iehoiakim, whō Nebuchad-rezzar king of Babylon made king in the land of Iudah.2But neither he, nor his ſeruants, nor the people of the land, did hearken vnto the words of the Lord, which he ſpake by the prophet Ieremiah.3And Zedekiah the king ſent Iehucal the ſonne of Shelemiah, and Zephaniah the ſon of Maaſeiah the prieſt to the prophet Ieremiah, ſaying, Pray now vnto the Lord our God for vs.4Nowe Ieremiah came in and went out among the people: for they had not put him into priſon.5Then Pharaohs armie was come forth out of Egypt: and when the Caldeans that beſieged Ieruſalem, heard tidings of them, they departed from Ieruſalem.6Then came the word of the Lord vnto the Prophet Ieremiah, ſaying,7Thus ſaith the Lord, the God of Iſrael, Thus ſhall ye ſay to the king of Iudah, that ſent you vnto me to enquire of me, Behold, Pharaohs armie which is come forth to helpe you, ſhall returne to Egypt into their owne land.8And the Caldeans ſhall come againe, and fight againſt this citie and take it, and burne it with fire.9Thus ſaith the Lord, Deceiue not your ſelues, ſaying, The Caldeans ſhall ſurely depart from vs: for they ſhall not depart.10For though yee had ſmitten the whole armie of the Caldeans that fight againſt you, and there remained but wounded men among them, yet ſhould they riſe vp euery man in his tent, and burne this citie with fire.11And it came to paſſe that when the armie of the Caldeans was broken vp from Ieruſalem for feare of Pharaohs armie,12Then Ieremiah went forth out of Ieruſalem to goe into the lande of Beniamin, to ſeparate himſelfe thence in the mids of the people.13And when he was in the gate of Beniamin, a captaine of the warde was there, whoſe name was Irijah, the ſon of Shelemiah, the ſonne of Hananiah, & he tooke Ieremiah the Prophet, ſaying, Thou falleſt away to the Caldeanſ14Then ſaid Ieremiah, It is falſe, I fall not away to the Caldeans: but he hearkened not to him: ſo Irijah tooke Ieremiah, and brought him to the princes.15Wherfore the princes were wroth with Ieremiah, and ſmote him, and put him in priſon, in the houſe of Ionathan the ſcribe, for they had made that the priſon.16When Ieremiah was entred into the dungeon, and into the cabbins, and Ieremiah had remained there many dayes:17Then Zedekiah the king ſent and tooke him out, and the king aſked him ſecretly in his houſe, and ſaid, Is there any word from the Lord ? and Ieremiah ſaid, There is: for, ſaid he, thou ſhalt be deliuered into the hand of the king of Babylon.18Moreouer Ieremiah ſayd vnto king Zedekiah, What haue I offended againſt thee, or againſt thy ſeruants, or againſt this people, that yee haue put me in priſon?19Where are now your prophets, which prophecied vnto you, ſaying, The king of Babylon ſhall not come againſt you, nor againſt this land?20Therefore heare now, I pray thee, O my Lord the king; let my ſupplication, I pray thee, be accepted before thee, that thou cauſe me not to returne to the houſe of Ionathan the ſcribe, leſt I die there.21Then Zedekiah the king commanded that they ſhould commit Ieremiah into the court of the priſon, and that they ſhould giue him daily a piece of bread out of the bakers ſtreete, vntill all the bread in the citie were ſpent. Thus Ieremiah remained in the court of the priſon.

CHAPTER 381Then Shephatiah the ſonne of Mattan, and Gedaliah the ſonne of Paſhur and Iucal the ſonne of Shelemiah, & Paſhur the ſonne of Malchiah heard the words that Ieremiah had ſpoken vnto all the people, ſaying,2Thus ſaith the Lord, He that remaineth in this citie, ſhall die by the ſword, by the famine, and by the peſtilence, but he that goeth forth to the Caldeans, ſhall liue: for he ſhall haue his life for a pray, and ſhall liue.3Thus ſaith the Lord, This citie ſhall ſurely be giuen into the hand of the king of Babylons armie, which ſhall take it.4Therefore the princes ſayd vnto the king, We beſeech thee let this man be put to death: for thus he weakeneth the hands of the men of warre that remaine in this citie, and the hands of all the people, in ſpeaking ſuch words vnto them: for this man ſeeketh not the welfare of this people, but the hurt.5Then Zedekiah the king ſayd, Behold, he is in your hand; for the king is not he that can do any thing againſt you.6Then tooke they Ieremiah, and caſt him into the dungeon of Malchiah the ſonne of Hammelech that was in the court of the priſon: and they let downe Ieremiah with cords: and in the dungeon there was no water, but mire: ſo Ieremiah ſunke in the mire.7Now when Ebed-melech the Ethiopian, one of þe eunuches which was in the kings houſe, heard that they had put Ieremiah in the dungeon (the king then ſitting in the gate of Beniamin)8Ebed-melech went foorth out of the kings houſe, and ſpake to the king, ſaying,9My lord the king, theſe men haue done euill in all that they haue done to Ieremiah the Prophet, whom they haue caſt into the dungeon, and he is like to die for hunger in the place where he is, for there is no more bread in the city.10Then the king commanded Ebed-melech the Ethiopian, ſaying, Take from hence thirtie men with thee, and take vp Ieremiah the Prophet out of the dungeon before he die.11So Ebed-melech tooke the men with him, and went into the houſe of the king vnder the treaſurie, and tooke thence old caſt cloutes, and old rotten ragges, and let them downe by cordes into the dungeon to Ieremiah.12And Ebed-melech the Ethiopian ſaid vnto Ieremiah, Put now theſe old caſt cloutes and rotten ragges vnder thine arme-holes, vnder the cordes. And Ieremiah did ſo.13So they drew vp Ieremiah with cordes, and tooke him vp out of the dungeon, and Ieremiah remained in the court of the priſon.14Then Zedekiah the king ſent, and tooke Ieremiah the Prophet vnto him into the third entrie that is in the houſe of the Lord, and the king ſaid vnto Ieremiah, I will aſke thee a thing: hide nothing from me.15Then Ieremiah ſaid vnto Zedekiah, If I declare it vnto thee, wilt thou not ſurely put me to death? and if I giue thee counſell, wilt thou not hearken vnto me?16So the king ſware ſecretly vnto Ieremiah, ſaying, As the Lord liueth that made vs this ſoule, I wil not put thee to death, neither will I giue thee into the hand of theſe men that ſeeke thy life.17Then ſaid Ieremiah vnto Zedekiah, Thus ſaith the Lord the God of hoſtes, the God of Iſrael, If thou wilt aſſuredly goe foorth vnto the king of Babylons Princes, then thy ſoule ſhall liue, and this Citie ſhall not be burnt with fire, and thou ſhalt liue, and thine houſe.18But if thou wilt not goe foorth to the king of Babylons Princes, then ſhall this City be giuen into the hand of the Caldeans, and they ſhall burne it with fire, and thou ſhalt not eſcape out of their hand.19And Zedekiah the king ſaid vnto Ieremiah, I am afraid of the Iewes that are fallen to the Caldeans, leſt they deliuer mee into their hand, and they mocke me.20But Ieremiah ſaid, They ſhall not deliuer thee: obey, I beſeech thee, the voyce of the Lord, which I ſpeake vnto thee: ſo it ſhall be well vnto thee, and thy ſoule ſhall liue.21But if thou refuſe to goe foorth, this is the word that the Lord hath ſhewed me.22And behold, all the women that are left in the king of Iudahs houſe, ſhalbe brought forth to the king of Babylons Princes, and thoſe women ſhall ſay, Thy friends haue ſet thee on, and haue preuailed againſt thee: thy feet are ſunke in the mire, and they are turned away backe.23So they ſhall bring out all thy wiues, and thy children to the Caldeans, and thou ſhalt not eſcape out of their hand, but ſhalt be taken by the hand of the King of Babylon: and thou ſhalt cauſe this citie to be burnt with fire.24Then ſaid Zedekiah vnto Ieremiah, Let no man know of theſe words, and thou ſhalt not die.25But if the Princes heare that I haue talked with thee, and they come vnto thee, and ſay vnto thee, Declare vnto vs now what thou haſt ſaid vnto the king; hide it not from vs, and wee wil not put thee to death; alſo what the king ſaid vnto thee:26Then thou ſhalt ſay vnto them, I preſented my ſupplication before the king, that he would not cauſe me to returne to Ionathans houſe to die there.27Then came all the Princes vnto Ieremiah, and aſked him, and he told them according to all theſe words, that the king had commanded: ſo they left off ſpeaking with him, for the matter was not perceiued.28So Ieremiah abode in the court of the priſon, vntill the day that Ieruſalem was taken, and hee was there when Ieruſalem was taken.

CHAPTER 391In the ninth yeere of Zedekiah king of Iudah, in the tenth moneth, came Nebuchad rezzar king of Babylon, and all his armie againſt Ieruſalem, and they beſieged it.2And in the eleuenth yeere of Zedekiah, in the fourth moneth, the ninth day of the moneth, the citie was broken vp.3And all the princes of the king of Babylon came in, and ſate in the middle gate, euen Nergal-Sharezer, Samgar-Nebo, Sarſechim, Rabſaris, Nergal-Sharezer, Rabmag, with all the reſidue of the princes of the king of Babylon.4And it came to paſſe, that when Zedekiah the king of Iudah ſaw them and all the men of warre, then they fled and went forth out of the citie by night, by the way of the kings garden, by the gate betwixt the two walles, and hee went out the way of the plaine.5But the Caldeans armie purſued after them, and ouertooke Zedekiah in the plaines of Iericho: and when they had taken him, they brought him vp to Nebuchad-nezzar king of Babylon to Riblah in the land of Hamath, where he gaue iudgement vpon him.6Then the king of Babylon ſlewe

the ſonnes of Zedekiah in Riblah before his eyes: alſo the king of
Babylon ſlew all the nobles of Iudah.7Moreouer he put out Zedekiahs
eyes, and bound him with chaines, to cary him to Babylon.8And the
Caldeans burnt the kings houſe, and the houſes of the people with fire,
and brake downe the wals of Ieruſalem.9Then Nebuzaradan the
captaine of the guard caried away captiue into Babylon the remnant of
the people that remained in the citie, and thoſe that fell away, that fell
to him, with the reſt of the people that remained.10But Nebuzaradan the
captaine of the guard left of the poore of the people which had nothing,
in the land of Iudah, and gaue them vineyards and fieldes at the ſame
time.11Now Nebuchad-rezzar king of Babylon gaue charge coucerning
Ieremiah to Nebuzaradan the captaine of the guard, ſaying;12Take him,
and looke well to him, and doe him no harme, but doe vnto him euen
as he ſhall ſay vnto thee.13So Nebuzaradan the captaine of the guard
ſent, and Nebuſhaſban, Rabſaris, and Nergal-Sharezer, Rabmag, and all
the King of Babylons Princes:14Euen they ſent, and tooke Ieremiah out
of the court of the priſon, and committed him vnto Gedaliah the ſon of
Ahikam, the ſonne of Shaphan, that hee ſhould carie him home: ſo hee
dwelt among the people.15Now the word of the Lord came vnto
Ieremiah, while hee was ſhut vp in the court of the priſon, ſaying;16Goe
and ſpeake to Ebed-melech the Ethiopian, ſaying, Thus ſayth the Lord
of hoſtes the God of Iſrael, Behold, I will bring my words vpon this citie
for euill, and not for good, and they ſhall be accompliſhed in that day
before thee.17But I will deliuer thee in that day, ſayth the Lord, and thou
ſhalt not be giuen into the hand of the men of whom thou art
afraid.18For I wil ſurely deliuer thee, and thou ſhalt not fall by the ſword,
but thy life ſhall be for a pray vnto thee, becauſe thou haſt put thy truſt
in me, ſayth the Lord.

CHAPTER 401The word which came to Ieremiah frō the Lord after
that Nebuzaradan the captaine of the guard had let him goe from
Ramath, when hee had taken him being bound in chaines among all that
were caried away captiue of Ieruſalem and Iudah, which were caried
away captiue vnto Babylon.2And the captaine of the gard took Ieremiah,
and ſayd vnto him, The Lord thy God hath pronounced this euill vpon
this place.3Now the Lord hath brought it, and done according as he hath
ſayd: becauſe yee haue ſinned againſt the Lord, and haue not obeyed his
voyce, therefore this thing is come vpon you.4And now behold, I looſe
thee this day from the chaines which were vpon thine hand: if it ſeeme
good vnto thee to come with me into Babylon, come, and I will looke
well vnto thee: but if it ſeeme ill vnto thee to come with me into
Babylon, forbeare: behold, all the land is before thee: whither it ſeemeth
good and conuenient for thee to goe, thither goe.5Now while he was
not yet gone backe, he ſayd, Goe backe alſo to Gedaliah the ſonne of
Ahikam the ſonne of Shaphan, whom the king of Babylon hath made
gouernour ouer all the cities of Iudah, and dwell with him among the
people: or goe whereſoeuer it ſeemeth conuenient vnto thee to goe. So
the captaine of the gard gaue him vitailes and a reward, and let him
goe.6Then went Ieremiah vnto Gedaliah the ſonne of Ahikam to
Mizpah, and dwelt with him among the people, that were left in the
land.7Now when all the captaines of the forces which were in the fields,
euen they and their men, heard that the king of Babylon had made
Gedaliah the ſonne of Ahikam gouernour in the land, and had
committed vnto him men, and women and children, and of the poore
of the land, of them that were not caried away captiue to Babylon;8Then
they came to Gedaliah to Mizpah, euen Iſhmael the ſonne of Nethaniah,
and Iohanan, and Ionathan the ſonnes of Kareah, and Seraiah the ſonne
of Tanhumeth, and the ſonnes of Ephai the Netophathite, and Iezaniah
the ſonne of a Maachathite, they and their men.9And Gedaliah the ſonne
of Ahikam the ſonne of Shaphan, ſware vnto them and to their men,
ſaying, Feare not to ſerue the Caldeans: dwell in the land and ſerue the
king of Babylon, and it ſhalbe well with you.10As for me, behold, I will
dwell at Mizpah to ſerue the Caldeans, which will come vnto vs: but yee,
gather yee wine, and ſummer fruits, and oyle, and put them in your
veſſels, and dwell in your cities, that yee haue taken.11Likewiſe when all
the Iewes that were in Moab, and among the Ammonites, and in Edom,
and that were in all the countries, heard that the king of Babylon had
left a remnant of Iudah, and that he had ſet ouer them Gedaliah the
ſonne of Ahikam the ſonne of Shaphan;12Euen all the Iewes returned
out of all places whither they were driuen, and came to the land of Iudah,
to Gedaliah vnto Mizpah, and gathered wine and ſummer fruits, very
much.13Moreouer Iohanan the ſonne of Kareah, and all the captaines of
the forces that were in the fields, came to Gedaliah to Mizpah,14And
ſayd vnto him, Doeſt thou certainly know, that Baalis the king of the
Ammonites hath ſent Iſhmael the ſonne of Nethaniah to ſlay thee? But
Gedaliah the ſonne of Ahikam beleeued them not.15Then Iohanan the
ſonne of Kareah, ſpake to Gedaliah in Mizpah ſecretly, ſaying, Let me
goe, I pray thee, and I will ſlay Iſhmael the ſonne of Nethaniah, and no
man ſhall know it. Wherefore ſhould he ſlay thee, that all the Iewes
which are gathered vnto thee ſhould be ſcattered, and the remnant in
Iudah periſh?16But Gedaliah the ſonne of Ahikam ſayd vnto Iohanan
the ſonne of Kareah; Thou ſhalt not do this thing, for thou ſpeakeſt
falſely of Iſhmael.

CHAPTER 411Now it came to paſſe in the ſeuenth moneth, that
Iſhmael the ſonne of Nethaniah the ſonne of Eliſhamah of the ſeede
royall, and the princes of the king, euen tenne men with him, came vnto
Gedaliah the ſonne of Ahikam to Mizpah, and there they did eate bread
together in Mizpah.2Then aroſe Iſhmael the ſonne of Nethaniah, and
the ten men that were with him, and ſmote Gedaliah the ſon of Ahikam
the ſonne of Shaphan with the ſword, and ſlew him, whome the king of
Babylon had made gouernour ouer the land.3Iſhmael alſo ſlew all the
Iewes that were with him, euen with Gedaliah at Mizpah, and the
Caldeans that were found there, and the men of warre.4And it came to
paſſe the ſecond day after he had ſlaine Gedaliah, and no man knew
it,5That there came certaine from Shechem, from Shiloh, and from
Samaria, euen foureſcore men, hauing their beards ſhauen, and their
clothes rent, and hauing cut themſelues, with offerings and incenſe in
their hand, to bring them to the houſe of the Lord.6And Iſhmael the
ſonne of Nethaniah went foorth from Mizpah to meete them, weeping
all along as hee went: and it came to paſſe as hee met them, he ſaid vnto
them, Come to Gedaliah the ſonne of Ahikam.7And it was ſo when they
came into the midſt of the citie, that Iſhmael the ſonne of Nethaniah
ſlew them, and caſt them into the midſt of the pit, he, and the men that
were with him.8But ten men were found among them, that ſaid vnto
Iſhmael, Slay vs not: for we haue treaſures in the field, of wheate, and
of barley, and of oyle, and of hony: ſo he forbare, and ſlewe them not
among their brethren.9Now the pit wherein Iſhmael had caſt all the dead
bodies of the men (whom he had ſlaine becauſe of Gedaliah) was it,
which Aſa the king had made, for feare of Baaſha king of Iſrael, and
Iſhmael the ſonne of Nethaniah filled it with them that were
ſlaine.10Then Iſhmael caried away captiue all the reſidue of the people,
that were in Mizpah, euen the kings daughters, and al the people that
remained in Mizpah, whom Nebuzaradan the captaine of the guard had
committed to Gedaliah the ſonne of Ahikam, and Iſhmael the ſonne of
Nethaniah caried them away captiue, and departed to goe ouer to the
Ammonites.11But when Iohanan the ſonne of Kareah, and all the
captaines of the forces that were with him, heard of all the euill that
Iſhmael the ſonne of Nethaniah had done,12Then they tooke all the men,
and went to fight with Iſhmael the ſonne of Nethaniah, and found him
by the great waters that are in Gibeon.13Now it came to paſſe that when
al the people which were with Iſhmael, ſawe Iohanan the ſonne of
Kareah, and all the captaines of the forces, that were with him, then they
were glad.14So all the people that Iſhmael had caried away captiue from
Mizpah caſt about and returned, and went vnto Iohanan the ſonne of
Kareah.15But Iſhmael the ſonne of Nethaniah eſcaped from Iohanan
with eight men, and went to the Ammonites.16Then tooke Iohanan the
ſonne of Kareah, and all the captaines of the forces that were with him,
all the remnant of the people whom he had recouered from Iſhmael the
ſonne of Nethaniah, from Mizpah (after that he had ſlaine Gedaliah the
ſonne of Ahikam,) euen mighty men of warre, and the women, and the
children, and the eunuches whom he had brought againe from
Gibeon.17And they departed and dwelt in the habitation of Chimham,
which is by Bethlehem, to goe to enter into Egypt,18Becauſe of the
Caldeans: for they were afraid of them, becauſe Iſhmael the ſonne of
Nethaniah had ſlaine Gedaliah the ſonne of Ahikam, whom the king of
Babylon made gouernour in the land.

CHAPTER 421Then all the captaines of the forces, and Iohanan the
ſonne of Kareah, and Iezaniah the ſonne of Hoſhaiah, and all the people
from the leaſt euen vnto the greateſt, came neere,2And ſaid vnto
Ieremiah the prophet, Let, we beſeech thee, our ſupplication be
accepted before thee, and pray for vs vnto the Lord thy God, euen for

all this remnant (for we are left but a few of many, as thine eies do
behold vs)3That the Lord thy God may ſhew vs the way wherein we may
walke, and the thing that we may doe.4Then Ieremiah the prophet ſayd
vnto them, I haue heard you; behold, I will pray vnto the Lord your
God, according to your words, and it ſhall come to paſſe that whatſoeuer
thing the Lord ſhall anſwere you, I will declare it vnto you: I will keepe
nothing backe from you.5Then they ſayd to Ieremiah, The Lord be a
true and faithfull witneſſe betweene vs, if we doe not, euen according to
all things for the which the Lord thy God ſhall ſend thee to vs.6Whether
it be good, or whether it be euill, we will obey the voice of the Lord our
God, to whom we ſend thee, that it may be well with vs, when we obey
the voice of the Lord our God.7And it came to paſſe after tenne dayes,
that the word of the Lord came vnto Ieremiah.8Then called hee Iohanan
the ſonne of Kareah, and all the captaines of the forces which were with
him, and all the people, from the leaſt, euen to the greateſt,9And ſaid
vnto them, Thus ſaith the Lord, the God of Iſrael, vnto whom ye ſent
me to preſent your ſupplication before him:10If ye will ſtill abide in this
land, then will I build you, and not pull you downe, and I will plant you,
and not plucke you vp: for I repent mee of the euill, that I haue done
vnto you.11Be not afraid of the king of Babylon, of whom yee are afraid:
be not afraid of him, ſaith the Lord: for I am with you to ſaue you, and
to deliuer you from his hand.12And I will ſhew mercies vnto you, that
he may haue mercy vpon you; and cauſe you to returne to your owne
land.13But if ye ſay, We will not dwell in this land, neither obey the voice
of the Lord your God,14Saying, No, but we will goe into the land of
Egypt, where we ſhall ſee no warre, nor heare the ſound of the Trumpet,
nor haue hunger of bread, and there will we dwell:15(And now therefore
heare the word of the Lord, yee remnant of Iudah, Thus ſaith the Lord
of hoſtes the God of Iſrael, If ye wholly ſet your faces to enter into
Egypt, and goe to ſoiourne there:)16Then it ſhall come to paſſe, that the
ſword which yee feared, ſhall ouertake you there in the land of Egypt,
and the famine whereof yee were afraid, ſhall follow cloſe after you in
Egypt, and there ye ſhall die.17So ſhall it bee with all the men that ſet
their faces to goe into Egypt to ſoiourne there, they ſhall die by the
ſword, by the famine, and by the peſtilence: and none of them ſhall
remaine or eſcape from the euil that I will bring vpon them.18For thus
ſaith the Lord of hoſts the God of Iſrael, As mine anger and my furie
hath bene powred foorth vpon the inhabitants of Ieruſalem: ſo ſhall my
furie bee powred foorth vpon you, when yee ſhall enter into Egypt: and
ye ſhall be an execration, and an aſtoniſhment, and a curſe, and a
reproch, and ye ſhall ſee this place no more.19The Lord hath ſaid
concerning you, O ye remnant of Iudah, Goe ye not into Egypt: know
certainly, that I haue admoniſhed you this day.20For ye diſsembled in
your hearts when ye ſent me vnto the Lord your God, ſaying, Pray for
vs vnto the Lord our God, and according vnto all that the Lord our God
ſhall ſay, ſo declare vnto vs, and we wil doe it.21And now I haue this day
declared it to you, but ye haue not obeied the voice of the Lord your
God, nor any thing for the which he hath ſent me vnto you.22Now
therefore know certainly, that ye ſhall die by the ſword, by the famine,
and by the peſtilence, in the place whither ye deſire to go and to
ſoiourne.

CHAPTER 431And it came to paſſe that whē Ieremiah had made an
end of ſpeaking vnto all the people, al the words of the Lord their God,
for which the Lord their God had ſent him to them, euen all theſe
words;2Then ſpake Azariah the ſonne of Hoſhaiah, and Iohanan the
ſonne of Kareah, and all the proud men, ſaying vnto Ieremiah, Thou
ſpeakeſt falſly: the Lord our God hath not ſent thee to ſay, Goe not into
Egypt, to ſoiourne there.3But Baruch the ſonne of Neriah ſetteth thee
on againſt vs, for to deliuer vs into the hand of the Caldeans, that they
might put vs to death, and carie vs away captiues into Babylon.4So
Iohanan the ſonne of Kareah, and all the captaines of the forces, and all
the people, obeied not the voice of the Lord, to dwell in the land of
Iudah.5But Iohanan the ſonne of Kareah, and all the captaines of the
forces, tooke all the remnant of Iudah, that were returned from all
nations whither they had bene driuen, to dwell in the land of
Iudah,6Euen men, and women, and children, and the kings daughters,
and euery perſon that Nebuzaradan the captaine of the guard had left
with Gedaliah the ſonne of Ahikam, the ſonne of Shaphan, and
Ieremiah the Prophet, and Baruch the ſonne of Neriah.7So they came
into the land of Egypt: for they obeyed not the voyce of the Lord, thus
came they euen to Tahpanhes.8Then came the word of the Lord vnto
Ieremiah in Tahpanhes, ſaying;9Take great ſtones in thine hand, and
hide them in the clay in the bricke kill, which is at the entry of Pharaohs
houſe in Tahpanhes, in the ſight of the men of Iudah:10And ſay vnto
them, Thus ſaieth the Lord of hoſts the God of Iſrael; Beholde, I will
ſend and take Nebuchadrezzar the king of Babylon my ſeruant, and will
ſet his throne vpon theſe ſtones that I haue hidde, and hee ſhall ſpread
his royall pauilion ouer them.11And when he commeth, hee ſhall ſmite
the land of Egypt, and deliuer ſuch as are for death, to death; and ſuch
as are for captiuitie to captiuitie; and ſuch as are for the ſword, to the
ſword.12And I wil kindle a fire in the houſes of the gods of Egypt, and
hee ſhall burne them, and carry them away captiues, and hee ſhall aray
himſelfe with the land of Egypt, as a ſhepheard putteth on his garment,
and hee ſhall goe forth from thence in peace.13He ſhall breake alſo the
images of Beth-ſhemeſh that is in the land of Egypt, and the houſes of
the gods of the Egyptians ſhall he burne with fire.

CHAPTER 441The word that came to Ieremiah concerning all the
Iewes which dwel in the land of Egypt, which dwell at Migdol, and at
Tahpanhes, and at Noph, and in the countrey of Pathros, ſaying,2Thus
ſaith the Lord of hoſts, the God of Iſrael; Ye haue ſeene all the euill that
I haue brought vpon Ieruſalem, and vpon all the cities of Iudah: and
behold, this day they are a deſolation, and no man dwelleth
therein,3Becauſe of their wickednes which they haue committed, to
prouoke me to anger, in that they went to burne incenſe, and to ſerue
other gods, whom they knew not, neither they, you, nor your
fathers.4Howbeit I ſent vnto you all my ſeruants the Prophets, riſing
early and ſending them, ſaying, Oh doe not this abominable thing that I
hate.5But they hearkened not, nor enclined their eare to turne from their
wickednes, to burne no incenſe vnto other gods.6Wherefore my furie
and mine anger was powred forth, and was kindled in the cities of Iudah,
and in the ſtreets of Ieruſalem, and they are waſted and deſolate, as at
this day.7Therefore now thus ſaith the Lord the God of hoſtes, the God
of Iſrael, Wherefore commit ye this great euill againſt your ſoules, to cut
off from you man and woman, childe and ſuckling out of Iudah, to leaue
you none to remaine.8In that yee prouoke mee vnto wrath with the
workes of your hands, burning incenſe vnto other gods in the land of
Egypt whither ye bee gone to dwell, that yee might cut your ſelues off,
and that ye might be a curſe, and a reproch among all the nations of the
earth?9Haue ye forgotten the wickednes of your fathers, and the
wickedneſſe of the kings of Iudah, and the wickednes of their wiues, and
your owne wickedneſſe, and the wickedneſſe of your wiues, which they
haue committed in the land of Iudah, and in the ſtreets of
Ieruſalem?10They are not humbled euen vnto this day, neither haue they
feared, nor walked in my Law, nor in my Statutes that I ſet before you,
and before your fathers.11Therefore thus ſayeth the Lord of hoſtes, the
God of Iſrael, Behold, I will ſet my face againſt you for euill, and to cut
off all Iudah.12And I will take the remnant of Iudah, that haue ſet their
faces to goe into the land of Egypt to ſoiourne there, and they ſhall all
be conſumed and fall in the land of Egypt: they ſhall euen bee conſumed
by the ſword, and by the famine: they ſhall die, from the leaſt euen vnto
the greateſt, by the ſword and by the famine: and they ſhalbe an
execration and an aſtoniſhment, and a curſe, and a reproch.13For I will
puniſh them that dwell in the land of Egypt, as I haue puniſhed
Ieruſalem, by the ſword, by the famine, and by the peſtilence;14So that
none of the remnant of Iudah which are gone into the land of Egypt to
ſoiourne there, ſhall eſcape or remaine, that they ſhould returne into the
land of Iudah to the which they haue a deſire to returne to dwell there:
for none ſhall returne but ſuch as ſhall eſcape.15Then all the men which
knew that their wiues had burnt incenſe vnto other Gods, and all the
women that ſtood by, a great multitude, euen all the people that dwelt
in the land of Egypt in Pathros, anſwered Ieremiah, ſaying,16As for the
word that thou haſt ſpoken vnto vs in the name of the Lord, we will not
hearken vnto thee.17But we will certainly doe whatſoeuer thing goeth
forth out of our owne mouth, to burne incenſe vnto the queene of
heauen, and to powre out drinke offrings vnto her, as we haue done, we
and our fathers, our kings and our princes in the cities of Iudah, and in
the ſtreetes of Ieruſalem: for then had we plentie of vitailes, and were
well, and ſaw no euill.18But ſince we left off to burne incenſe to the
queene of heauen, and to powre out drinke offrings vnto her, we haue
wanted all things, and haue beene conſumed by the ſword, and by the

famine.19And when we burnt incenſe to the queene of heauen, and
powred out drinke offrings vnto her, did we make her cakes to worſhip
her, and powre out drinke offrings vnto her without our men?20Then
Ieremiah ſayd vnto all the people, to the men and to the women, and to
all the people which had giuen him that anſwere, ſaying;21The incenſe
that yee burnt in the cities of Iudah, and in the ſtreetes of Ieruſalem, yee
and your fathers, your kings and your princes, and the people of the
land, did not the Lord remember them, and came it not into his
minde?22So that the Lord could no longer beare, becauſe of the euill of
your doings, and becauſe of the abominations, which yee haue
committed: therefore is your land a deſolation, and an aſtoniſhment, and
a curſe without an inhabitant, as at this day.23Becauſe you haue burnt
incenſe, and becauſe yee haue ſinned againſt the Lord, and haue not
obeyed the voyce of the Lord, nor walked in his law, nor in his ſtatutes,
nor in his teſtimonies: therefore this euill is happened vnto you, as at
this day.24Moreouer Ieremiah ſayd vnto all the people, and to all the
women; Heare the word of the Lord, all Iudah, that are in the land of
Egypt.25Thus ſaith the Lord of hoſtes the God of Iſrael, ſaying: Yee and
your wiues haue both ſpoken with your mouths, and fulfilled with your
hand, ſaying; We will ſurely performe our vowes that we haue vowed,
to burne incenſe to the queene of heauen, and to powre out drinke
offrings vnto her: yee will ſurely accompliſh your vowes, and ſurely
performe your vowes.26Therefore heare yee the word of the Lord, all
Iudah that dwell in the land of Egypt, Behold, I haue ſworne by my great
Name, ſaith the Lord, that my Name ſhal no more be named in the
mouth of any man of Iudah, in all the land of Egypt, ſaying, The Lord
God liueth.27Behold, I will watch ouer them for euill, and not for good,
and all the men of Iudah that are in the land of Egypt ſhalbe conſumed
by the ſword, & by the famin, vntil there be an end of them.28Yet a ſmall
number that eſcape the ſword, ſhall returne out of the land of Egypt
into the land of Iudah: and all the remnant of Iudah that are gone into
the land of Egypt to ſoiourne there, ſhall know whoſe wordes ſhall
ſtand, mine or theirs.29And this ſhalbe a ſigne vnto you, ſaith the Lord,
that I will puniſh you in this place, that ye may knowe that my words
ſhal ſurely ſtand againſt you for euill.30Thus ſaith the Lord, Behold, I
will giue Pharaoh-Hophra king of Egypt into the hand of his enemies,
and into the hande of them that ſeeke his life, as I gaue Zedekiah king
of Iudah into the hand of Nebuchadrezzar king of Babylon his enemy,
and that ſought his life.

CHAPTER 451The word that Ieremiah the Prophet ſpake vnto Baruch
the ſonne of Neriah, when he had written theſe words in a booke at the
mouth of Ieremiah, in the fourth yeere of Iehoiakim the ſonne of Ioſiah
king of Iudah, ſaying,2Thus ſaith the Lord the God of Iſrael vnto thee,
O Baruch,3Thou didſt ſay, Woe is me now, for the Lord hath added
griefe to my ſorow, I fainted in my ſighing, and I find no reſt.4Thus ſhalt
thou ſay vnto him, The Lord ſaith thus, Behold, that which I haue built
will I breake downe, and that which I haue planted I will plucke vp, euen
this whole land:5And ſeekeſt thou great things for thy ſelfe? ſeeke them
not: for behold, I wil bring euill vpon all fleſh, ſaith the Lord: but thy
life will I giue vnto thee for a pray in all places whither thou goeſt.

CHAPTER 461The word of the Lord which came to Ieremiah the
Prophet, againſt the Gentiles,2Againſt Egypt, againſt the armie of
Pharaoh Necho king of Egypt, which was by the riuer Euphrates in
Carchemiſh, which Nebuchad-rezzar king of Babylon ſmote in the
fourth yeere of Iehoiakim the ſon of Ioſiah king of Iudah.3Order ye the
buckler and ſhield, and draw neere to battell.4Harneſse the horſes, and
get vp ye horſemen, and ſtand forth with your helmets, furbiſh the
ſpeares, and put on the brigandines.5Wherefore haue I ſeene them
diſmaid, and turned away backe? and their mightie ones are beaten
downe, & are fled apace, and looke not back: for feare was round about,
ſaith the Lord.6Let not the ſwift flee away, nor the mightie man eſcape:
they ſhal ſtumble and fall toward the North by the riuer
Euphrates.7Who is this that cōmeth vp as a flood, whoſe waters are
moued as yͤ riuers?8Egypt riſeth vp like a flood, and his waters are
moued like the riuers, and he ſaith, I wil goe vp, and will couer the earth,
I will deſtroy the citie and the inhabitants thereof.9Come vp ye horſes,
and rage yee charets, and let the mightie men come forth, the Ethiopians
and the Libyans that handle the ſhield, and the Lydians that handle and
bend the bow.10For this is the day of the Lord God of hoſtes, a day of
vengeance, that he may auenge him of his aduerſaries: and the ſword
ſhal deuoure, and it ſhall be ſatiate, and made drunke with their blood:
for the Lord God of hoſts hath a ſacrifice in the North countrey by the
riuer Euphrates.11Goe vp into Gilead, and take balme, O virgine, the
daughter of Egypt: in vaine ſhalt thou vſe many medicines: for thou ſhalt
not be cured.12The nations haue heard of thy ſhame, and thy crie hath
filled the land: for the mightie man hath ſtumbled againſt the mightie,
and they are fallen both together.13The word that the Lord ſpake to
Ieremiah the Prophet, how Nebuchadrezzar King of Babylon ſhould
come & ſmite the land of Egypt.14Declare ye in Egypt, and publiſh in
Migdol, and publiſh in Noph, and in Tahpanhes: ſay ye, ſtand faſt, and
prepare thee; for the ſword ſhal deuoure round about thee.15Why are
thy valiant men ſwept away? they ſtood not, becauſe the Lord did driue
them.16He made many to fall, yea one fell vpon another, and they ſaid,
Ariſe, and let vs goe againe to our owne people, and to the land of our
natiuitie, from the oppreſsing ſword.17They did crie there, Pharaoh king
of Egypt is but a noiſe, he hath paſſed the time appointed.18As I liue,
ſaith the King, whoſe Name is the Lord of hoſtes, Surely as Tabor is
among the mountaines, and as Carmel by the ſea, ſo ſhall hee come.19Oh
thou daughter dwelling in Egypt, furniſh thy ſelfe to goe into captiuitie:
for Noph ſhalbe waſte and deſolate without an inhabitant.20Egypt is like
a very faire heifer, but deſtruction commeth: it commeth out of the
North.21Alſo her hired men are in the midſt of her, like fatted bullocks,
for they alſo are turned backe, and are fled away together; they did not
ſtand, becauſe the day of their calamitie was come vpon them, and the
time of their viſitation.22The voice thereof ſhall goe like a ſerpent, for
they ſhall march with an armie, and come againſt her with axes, as
hewers of wood.23They ſhall cut downe her forreſt, ſaith the Lord,
though it cannot be ſearched, becauſe they are more then the
graſhoppers, and are innumerable.24The daughter of Egypt ſhalbe
confounded, ſhe ſhalbe deliuered into the hand of the people of the
North.25The Lord of hoſtes the God of Iſrael ſaith, Behold, I will puniſh
the multitude of No, and Pharaoh, and Egypt, with their gods, and their
kings, euen Pharaoh, and all them that truſt in him.26And I will deliuer
them into the hand of thoſe that ſeeke their liues, and into the hand of
Nebuchadrezzar king of Babylon, and into the hand of his ſeruants, and
afterwards it ſhalbe inhabited, as in the dayes of old, ſaith the Lord.27But
feare not thou, O my ſeruant Iacob, and be not diſmaied, O Iſrael: for
behold, I will ſaue thee from afarre off, and thy ſeed from the land of
their captiuitie, and Iacob ſhall returne and be in reſt and at eaſe, and
none ſhall make him afraid.28Feare thou not, O Iacob my ſeruant, ſaith
the Lord, for I am with thee, for I will make a full end of all the nations
whither I haue driuen thee, but I will not make a full end of thee, but
correct thee in meaſure, yet will I not leaue thee wholly vnpuniſhed.

CHAPTER 471The word of the Lord that came to Ieremiah the
Prophet againſt the Philiſtines, before that Pharaoh ſmote Gaza.2Thus
ſaith the Lord, Behold, waters riſe vp out of the North, and ſhall be an
ouerflowing flood, and ſhall ouerflow the land, and all that is therein,
the citie, and them that dwell therein: then the men ſhall crie, and all the
inhabitants of the land ſhall howle.3At the noiſe of the ſtamping of the
hoofes of his ſtrong horſes, at the ruſhing of his charets, and at the
rumbling of his wheeles, the fathers ſhall not looke backe to their
children for feebleneſse of handes.4Becauſe of the day that commeth to
ſpoile all the Philiſtines, and to cut off from Tyrus and Zidon euery
helper that remaineth: for the Lord will ſpoile the Philiſtines, the
remnant of the countrey of Caphtor.5Baldneſse is come vpon Gaza.
Aſhkelon is cut off with the remnant of their valley: how long wilt thou
cut thy ſelfe?6O thou ſword of the Lord, how long will it be ere thou be
quiet? put vp thy ſelfe into thy ſcabberd, reſt and be ſtill.7How can it
bee quiet, ſeeing the Lord hath giuen it a charge againſt Aſhkelon, and
againſt the ſea ſhoare? there hath he appointed it.

CHAPTER 481Againſt Moab thus ſayth the Lord of hoſtes, the God
of Iſrael, Woe vnto Nebo, for it is ſpoiled: Kiriathaim is confounded
and taken. Miſgab is confounded and diſmayed.2There ſhall bee no more
prayſe of Moab: in Heſhbon they haue deuiſed euill againſt it; come and
let vs cut it off from being a nation; alſo thou ſhalt bee cut downe, O
Madmen, the ſword ſhall purſue thee.3A voice of crying ſhall be from
Horonaim; Spoiling & great deſtruction.4Moab is deſtroyed, her little
ones haue cauſed a crie to be heard.5For in the going vp of Luhith
continuall weeping ſhall go vp; for in the going downe of Horonaim the
enemies haue heard a crie of deſtruction.6Flee, ſaue your liues, and be

like the heath in the wilderneſſe.7For becauſe thou haſt truſted in thy
workes, and in thy treaſures, thou ſhalt alſo be taken, and Chemoſh ſhall
goe foorth into captiuitie with his prieſts and his princes together.8And
the ſpoyler ſhall come vpon euery citie, and no citie ſhall eſcape: the
valley alſo ſhal periſh, & the plaine ſhall be deſtroyed, as þe Lord hath
ſpoken.9Giue wings vnto Moab, that it may flee and get away: for the
cities thereof ſhalbe deſolate, without any to dwell therein.10Curſed be
he that doeth the worke of the Lord deceitfully, and curſed be he that
keepeth backe his ſword from blood.11Moab hath bene at eaſe from his
youth, and hee hath ſetled on his lees, and hath not been emptied from
veſſell to veſſell, neither hath he gone into captiuitie: therefore his taſte
remained in him, and his ſent is not changed.12Therfore behold, the
dayes come, ſayth the Lord, that I will ſend vnto him wanderers that
ſhall cauſe him to wander, and ſhall emptie his veſſels, and breake their
bottles.13And Moab ſhall bee aſhamed of Chemoſh, as the houſe of
Iſrael was aſhamed of Bethel their confidence.14How ſay yee, We are
mightie and ſtrong men for the warre?15Moab is ſpoiled and gone vp
out of her cities, and his choſen yong men are gone downe to the
ſlaughter, ſayth the King, whoſe Name is the Lord of hoſtes.16The
calamitie of Moab is neere to come, and his affliction haſteth faſt.17All
yee that are about him bemoane him, and all yee that know his Name,
ſay, How is the ſtrong ſtaffe broken, and the beautifull rod!18Thou
daughter that doeſt inhabit Dibon, come downe from thy glory, and ſit
in thirſt; for the ſpoiler of Moab ſhall come vpon thee, and he ſhall
deſtroy thy ſtrong holdes.19O inhabitant of Aroer, ſtand by the way and
eſpie, aſke him that fleeth, and her that eſcapeth, and ſay, What is
done?20Moab is confounded, for it is broken downe: howle and cry, tell
ye it in Arnon, that Moab is ſpoiled,21And iudgement is come vpon the
plaine countrey, vpon Holon, and vpon Iahazah, and vpon
Mephaath,22And vpon Dibon, and vpon Nebo, and vpon Beth-
diblathaim,23And vpon Kiriathaim, and vpon Beth-Gamul, and vpon
Beth-meon,24And vpon Kerioth, and vpon Bozrah, and vpon all the
cities of the land of Moab farre or neere.25The horne of Moab is cut off,
& his arme is broken, ſaith the Lord.26Make ye him drunken: for hee
magnified himſelfe againſt the Lord: Moab alſo ſhall wallow in his vomit,
and he alſo ſhalbe in deriſion.27For was not Iſrael a deriſion vnto thee?
was hee found among theeues? for ſince thou ſpakeſt of him, thou
ſkippedſt for ioy.28O yee that dwell in Moab, leaue the cities and dwell
in the rocke, and be like the doue that maketh her neſt in the ſides of
the holes mouth.29We haue heard the pride of Moab, (he is exceeding
proud) his loftineſe and his arrogancie, and his pride, and the hautineſe
of his heart.30I knowe his wrath, ſayeth the Lord, but it ſhall not be ſo,
his lyes ſhall not ſo effect it.31Therefore will I howle for Moab, and I
will cry out for all Moab, mine heart ſhall mourne for the men of Kir-
heres.32O vine of Sibmah, I wil weepe for thee, with the weeping of
Iazer; thy plants are gone ouer the ſea, they reach euen to the ſea of
Iazer, the ſpoiler is fallen vpon thy ſummer fruits, and vpon thy
vintage.33And ioy and gladneſſe is taken from the plentifull field, and
from the land of Moab, and I haue cauſed wine to faile from the
winepreſſe s, none ſhall tread with ſhouting, their ſhowting ſhall be no
ſhowting.34From the cry of Heſhbon euen vnto Elealeh, and euen vnto
Iahaz haue they vttered their voyce, from Zoar euen vnto Horonaim as
an heifer of three yeeres old: for the waters alſo of Nimrim ſhall be
deſolate.35Moreouer, I will cauſe to ceaſe in Moab, ſaith the Lord, him
that offereth in the high places, and him that burneth incenſe to his
Gods.36Therefore mine heart ſhall ſound for Moab like pipes, and mine
heart ſhall ſound like pipes for the men of Kir-heres: becauſe the riches
that hee hath gotten is periſhed.37For euery head ſhall be bald, and euery
beard clipt: vpon all the hands ſhall be cuttings, and vpon the loines
ſackcloth.38There ſhall be lamentation generally vpon all the houſe
toppes of Moab, and in the ſtreetes thereof: for I haue broken Moab
like a veſſell, wherin is no pleaſure, ſaith the Lord.39They ſhall howle,
ſaying; How is it broken downe? how hath Moab turned the backe with
ſhame? ſo ſhall Moab be a deriſion, and a diſmaying to all them about
him.40For thus ſaith the Lord, Behold, hee ſhall fly as an eagle, and ſhall
ſpread his wings ouer Maob.41Kerioth is taken, and the ſtrong holds are
ſurpriſed, & the mighty mens hearts in Moab at that day ſhall be as the
heart of a woman in her pangs.42And Moab ſhall be deſtroyed from
being a people, becauſe he hath magnified himſelfe againſt the
Lord.43Feare, and the pit, and the ſnare ſhall be vpon thee, O inhabitant
of Moab, ſaith the Lord.44Hee that fleeth from the feare ſhall fall into
the pit, and he that getteth vp out of the pit ſhall be taken in the ſnare:
for I will bring vpon it, euen vpon Moab, the yeere of their viſitation,
ſaith the Lord.45They that fled, ſtood vnder the ſhadow of Heſhbon,
becauſe of the force: but a fire ſhall come forth out of Heſhbon, and a
flame from the middeſt of Sihon, and ſhall deuoure the corner of Moab,
and the crowne of the head of the tumultuous ones.46Woe be vnto thee,
O Moab, the people of Chemoſh periſheth: for thy ſonnes are taken
captiues, and thy daughters captiues.47Yet will I bring againe the
captiuitie of Moab in the later dayes, ſaith the Lord. Thus farre is the
iudgement of Moab.

CHAPTER 491Concerning the Ammonites, thus ſayth the Lord; hath
Iſrael no ſonnes? Hath he no heire? Why then doth their king inherit
God, and his people dwell in his cities?2Therfore behold, the dayes
come, ſaith the Lord, that I will cauſe an alarme of warre to be heard in
Rabbah of the Ammonites, and it ſhall be a deſolate heape, and her
daughters ſhall be burnt with fire: then ſhall Iſrael be heire vnto them
that were his heires, ſaith the Lord.3Howle, O Heſhbon, for Ai is ſpoiled:
cry yee daughters of Rabbah, gird yee with ſackcloth: lament and runne
to and fro by the hedges: for their king ſhall goe into captiuitie: and his
prieſts and his princes together.4Wherfore glorieſt thou in the valleys,
thy flowing valley, O backſliding daughter? That truſted in her treaſures,
ſaying; Who ſhall come vnto mee?5Behold, I will bring a feare vpon
thee, ſaith the Lord God of hoſtes, from all thoſe that be about thee,
and yee ſhall be driuen out euery man right forth, and none ſhal gather
vp him that wandereth.6And afterward I will bring againe the captiuitie
of the children of Ammon, ſaith the Lord.7Concerning Edom thus ſaith
the Lord of hoſts, Is wiſedome no more in Teman? is counſell periſhed
from the prudent? is their wiſedom vaniſhed?8Flee ye, turne backe,
dwell deepe, O inhabitants of Dedan: for I will bring the calamitie of
Eſau vpon him, the time that I will viſite him.9If grape gatherers come
to thee, would they not leaue ſome gleaning grapes? If theeues by night,
they will deſtroy till they haue enough.10But I haue made Eſau bare, I
haue vncouered his ſecret places, and he ſhall not be able to hide
himſelfe: his ſeed is ſpoiled, and his brethren and his neighbours, and
he is not.11Leaue thy fatherleſſe children, I will preſeruethem aliue: and
let thy widowes truſt in me.12For thus ſaith the Lord, Behold, they whoſe
iudgement was not to drinke of the cup, haue aſsuredly drunken, and art
thou he that ſhall altogether go vnpuniſhed? thou ſhalt not go
vnpuniſhed, but thou ſhalt ſurely drinke of it.13For I haue ſworne by my
ſelfe, ſaith the Lord, that Bozrah ſhall become a deſolation, a reproch, a
waſte, and a curſe, and all the cities thereof ſhall be perpetuall waſtes.14I
haue heard a rumor from the Lord, & an ambaſsadour is ſent vnto the
heathen, ſaying, Gather ye together & come againſt her, & riſe vp to the
battell.15For lo, I wil make thee ſmal among the heathen, and deſpiſed
among men.16Thy terribleneſſe hath deceiued thee, and the pride of
thine heart, O thou that dwelleſt in the clefts of the rocke, that holdeſt
the height of the hill: thogh thou ſhouldeſt make thy neſt as high as the
eagle, I will bring thee downe from thence, ſaith the Lord.17Alſo Edom
ſhalbe a deſolation: euery one þt goeth by it ſhalbe aſtoniſhed, and ſhall
hiſse at all the plagues thereof,18As in the ouerthrow of Sodom and
Gomorrah, and the neighbour cities thereof, ſaith the Lord: no man ſhall
abide there, neither ſhall a ſonne of man dwell in it.19Behold, he ſhal
come vp like a lyon from the ſwelling of Iordane againſt the habitation
of the ſtrong: but I wil ſuddenly make him runne away from her, and
who is a choſen man that I may appoynt ouer her? For who is like mee?
And who will appoint me the time? Who is that ſhepheard that will ſtand
before mee?20Therfore heare the counſell of the Lord, that he hath
taken againſt Edom, & his purpoſes that hee hath purpoſed againſt the
inhabitants of Teman: ſurely the leaſt of the flocke ſhall draw them out:
ſurely hee ſhall make their habitations deſolate with them.21The earth is
moued at the noiſe of their fall: at the crie, the noiſe thereof was heard
in the red ſea.22Behold, he ſhall come vp and flie as the eagle, and ſpread
his wings ouer Bozrah: and at that day ſhall the heart of the mightie men
of Edom, be as the heart of a woman in her pangs.23Concerning
Damaſcus, Hamath is confounded, & Arpad, for they haue heard euil
tidings, they are faint hearted, there is ſorrow on the ſea, it can not be
quiet.24Damaſcus is waxed feeble, and turneth her ſelfe to flee, and feare
hath ſeiſed on her: anguiſh and ſorrowes haue taken her as a woman in

trauell.25How is the citie of praiſe not left, the citie of my ioy?26Therefore her yong men ſhal fall in her ſtreets, and all the men of warre ſhall bee cut off in that day, ſaith the Lord of hoſts.27And I will kindle a fire in the wall of Damaſcus, and it ſhal conſume the palaces of Ben-hadad.28Concerning Kedar, and concerning the kingdoms of Hazor, which Nebuchad-rezzar king of Babylon ſhall ſmite, Thus ſaith the Lord: Ariſe ye, goe vp to Kedar, and ſpoile the men of the Eaſt.29Their tents and their flocks ſhall they take away: they ſhal take to themſelues their curtaines and all their veſſels, and their camels, and they ſhal crie vnto them, Feare is on euery ſide.30Flee, get you farre off, dwell deepe, O ye inhabitants of Hazor, ſaith the Lord: for Nebuchad-rezzar king of Babylon hath taken counſel againſt you, and hath conceiued a purpoſe againſt you.31Ariſe, get you vp vnto the wealthy nation that dwelleth without care, ſaith the Lord, which haue neither gates nor barres, which dwell alone.32And their camels ſhall be a bootie, and the multitude of their cattell a ſpoile, and I will ſcatter into all winds them that are in the vtmoſt corners, and I will bring their calamitie from all ſides thereof, ſaith the Lord.33And Hazor ſhall be a dwelling for dragons, and a deſolation for euer; there ſhall no man abide there, nor any ſonne of man dwell in it.34The word of the Lord that came to Ieremiah the Prophet againſt Elam in the beginning of the reigne of Zedekiah king of Iudah, ſaying,35Thus ſaith the Lord of hoſts, Behold, I will breake the bow of Elam, the chiefe of their might.36And vpon Elam will I bring the foure windes from the foure quarters of heauen, and will ſcatter them towards all thoſe windes, and there ſhall be no nation, whither the outcaſts of Elam ſhall not come.37For I will cauſe Elam to bee diſmayed before their enemies, and before them that ſeeke their life: and I will bring euill vpon them, euen my fierce anger, ſaith the Lord, and I will ſend the ſword after them, till I haue conſumed them.38And I will ſet my throne in Elam, and will deſtroy from thence the king and the princes, ſaith the Lord.39But it ſhall come to paſſe in the later daies, that I wil bring againe the captiuitie of Elam, ſaith the Lord.

CHAPTER 501The word that the Lord ſpake againſt Babylon, and againſt the land of the Caldeans by Ieremiah the Prophet.2Declare yee among the nations, and publiſh, and ſet vp a ſtandart, publiſh and conceale not: ſay, Babylon is taken, Bel is confounded, Merodach is broken in pieces, her idols are confounded, her Images are broken in pieces.3For out of the North there commeth vp a nation againſt her, which ſhall make her land deſolate, and none ſhall dwell therein: they ſhall remoue, they ſhall depart both man and beaſt.4In thoſe daies, and in that time, ſaith the Lord, the children of Iſrael ſhall come, they, and the children of Iudah together, going and weeping: they ſhall goe, and ſeeke the Lord their God.5They ſhall aſke the way to Zion with their faces thitherward, ſaying, Come, and let vs ioyne our ſelues to the Lord, in a perpetuall Couenant that ſhall not be forgotten.6My people hath bene loſt ſheepe: their ſhepheards haue cauſed them to goe aſtray, they haue turned them away on the mountaines: they haue gone from mountaine to hill, they haue forgotten their reſting place.7All that found them haue deuoured them, and their aduerſaries ſaid, We offend not, becauſe they haue ſinned againſt the Lord, the habitation of iuſtice, euen the Lord, the hope of their fathers.8Remoue out of the midſt of Babylon, and goe foorth out of the land of the Caldeans, and be as the hee goats before the flocks.9For loe, I will raiſe and cauſe to come vp againſt Babylon, an aſſembly of great nations from the North countrey, and they ſhall ſet themſelues in aray againſt her, from thence ſhee ſhalbe taken: their arrowes ſhalbe as of a mightie expert man: none ſhall returne in vaine.10And Caldea ſhall bee a ſpoile: all that ſpoile her ſhall be ſatiſfied, ſaith the Lord.11Becauſe ye were glad, becauſe yee reioyced, O ye deſtroyers of mine heritage, becauſe ye are growen fat, as the heifer at graſſe, and bellow as bulles:12Your mother ſhalbe ſore confounded, ſhe that bare you ſhalbe aſhamed: beholde, the hindermoſt of the nations ſhalbe a wildernes, a dry land, & a deſert.13Becauſe of the wrath of the Lord, it ſhall not be inhabited, but it ſhalbe wholly deſolate: euery one that goeth by Babylon ſhall be aſtoniſhed, and hiſse at all her plagues.14Put your ſelues in aray againſt Babylon round about: all ye that bend the bow, ſhoot at her; ſpare no arrows: for ſhe hath ſinned againſt the Lord,15Shout againſt her round about: ſhee hath giuen her hand: her foundations are fallen, her walls are throwen downe: for it is the vengeance of the Lord: take vengeance vpon her; as ſhe hath done, doe vnto her.16Cut off the ſower from Babylon, and him that handleth the ſickle in the time of harueſt: for feare of the oppreſsing ſword, they ſhall turne euery one to his people, and they ſhall flee euery one to his owne lande.17Iſrael is a ſcattered ſheepe, the lyons haue driuen him away: firſt the king of Aſſyria hath deuoured him, and laſt this Nebuchad-rezzar king of Babylon hath broken his bones.18Therefore thus ſaith the Lord of hoſtes the God of Iſrael; Behold, I will puniſh the king of Babylon and his land, as I haue puniſhed the king of Aſſyria.19And I will bring Iſrael againe to his habitation, and he ſhal feed on Carmel and Baſhan, and his ſoule ſhall be ſatiſfied vpon mount Ephraim and Gilead.20In thoſe dayes, and in that time, ſayth the Lord, the iniquitie of Iſrael ſhall be ſought for, and there ſhall be none; and the ſinnes of Iudah, and they ſhall not be found: for I will pardon them whom I reſerue.21Goe vp againſt the land of Merathaim, euen againſt it, and againſt the inhabitants of Pekod: waſte and vtterly deſtroy after them, ſayeth the Lord, and doe according to all that I haue commanded thee.22A ſound of battell is in the land, and of great deſtruction.23How is the hammer of the whole earth cut aſunder and broken? how is Babylon become a deſolation among the nations?24I haue laide a ſnare for thee, and thou art alſo taken, O Babylon, and thou waſt not aware: thou art found and alſo caught, becauſe thou haſt ſtriuen againſt the Lord.25The Lord hath opened his armorie, and hath brought foorth the weapons of his indignation: for this is the worke of the Lord God of hoſts, in the land of the Caldeans.26Come againſt her from the vtmoſt border, open her ſtore-houſes: caſt her vp as heapes, and deſtroy her vtterly: let nothing of her be left.27Slay all her bullocks: let them goe downe to the ſlaughter: woe vnto them, for their day is come, the time of their viſitation.28The voice of them that flee & eſcape out of the land of Babylon to declare in Zion the vengeance of the Lord our God, the vengeance of his Temple.29Call together the archers againſt Babylon: all yee that bend the bow, campe againſt it round about; let none thereof eſcape: recompenſe her according to her worke; according to all that ſhee hath done vnto her: for ſhee hath bene proud againſt the Lord, againſt the Holy one of Iſrael.30Therefore ſhall her yong men fall in the ſtreets, & all her men of war ſhall be cut off in that day, ſaith the Lord.31Behold, I am againſt thee, O thou moſt proud, ſayth the Lord God of hoſtes: for thy day is come, the time that I will viſit thee.32And the moſt proude ſhall ſtumble and fall, and none ſhal raiſe him vp: and I will kindle a fire in his cities, and it ſhall deuoure all round about him.33Thus ſaith the Lord of hoſts; The children of Iſrael and the children of Iudah were oppreſſed together, and all that tooke them captiues, held them faſt, they refuſed to let them goe.34Their Redeemer is ſtrong, the Lord of hoſts is his Name, he ſhall throughly pleade their cauſe, that hee may giue reſt to the land, and diſquiet the inhabitants of Babylon.35A ſword is vpon the Caldeans, ſaith the Lord, and vpon the inhabitants of Babylon, and vpon her princes, and vpon her wiſe men.36A ſword is vpon the lyers, and they ſhall dote: a ſword is vpon her mighty men, and they ſhalbe diſmayed.37A ſword is vpon their horſes, and vpon their charets, and vpon all the mingled people that are in the middeſt of her, and they ſhall become as women: a ſword is vpon her treaſures, and they ſhall be robbed.38A drought is vpon her waters, and they ſhalbe dried vp: for it is the land of grauen images, and they are madde vpon their idoles.39Therefore the wilde beaſts of the deſert with the wilde beaſtes of the Ilands ſhall dwel there, and the owles ſhall dwell therein: & it ſhalbe no more inhabited for euer: neither ſhall it bee dwelt in frō generation to generation.40As God ouerthrew Sodom and Gomorrah, and the neighbour cities thereof, ſayth the Lord: ſo ſhall no man abide there, neither ſhal any ſonne of man dwell therein.41Behold, a people ſhall come from the North, and a great nation, and many kings ſhall bee raiſed vp from the coaſts of the earth.42They ſhall holde the bow and the lance: they are cruell and will not ſhewe mercy: their voice ſhall roare like the ſea, and they ſhall ride vpon horſes, euery one put in aray like a man to the battell, againſt thee, O daughter of Babylon.43The king of Babylon hath heard the report of them, and his hands waxed feeble; anguiſh tooke hold of him, and pangs as of a woman in trauell.44Behold, he ſhall come vp like a lyon from the ſwelling of Iordan, vnto the habitation of the ſtrong: but I will make them ſuddenly runne away from her: and who is a choſen man that I may appoint ouer her? for who is like me, and who will appoint me the time? and who is that ſhepheard that will ſtand before me?45Therefore heare yee the counſell of the Lord that hee hath taken againſt Babylon, and his purpoſes that he hath purpoſed againſt the land of the Caldeans: ſurely the leaſt of the flocke ſhall drawe them out: ſurely he ſhall make their habitation deſolate with them.[46]At the noiſe of the taking of Babylon the earth is moued, and the cry is heard among the nations.

CHAPTER 51[1]Thus ſaith the Lord; Behold, I will raiſe vp againſt Babylon, and againſt them that dwell in the middeſt of them that riſe vp againſt me, a deſtroying wind;[2]And will ſend vnto Babylon fanners, that ſhall fanne her, and ſhall emptie her land: for in the day of trouble they ſhall be againſt her round about.[3]Againſt him that bendeth let the archer bend his bow, and againſt him that lifteth himſelfe vp in his brigandine; and ſpare yee not her young men, deſtroy yee vtterly all her hoſte.[4]Thus the ſlaine ſhall fall in the land of the Caldeans, and they that are thruſt through in her ſtreetes.[5]For Iſrael hath not beene forſaken, nor Iudah of his God, of the Lord of hoſtes; though their land was filled with ſinne againſt the holy one of Iſrael.[6]Flee out of the middeſt of Babylon, and deliuer euery man his ſoule: bee not cut off in her iniquitie: for this is the time of the Lords vengeance: he will render vnto her a recompence.[7]Babylon hath beene a golden cup in the Lords hand, that made all the earth drunken: the nations haue drunken of her wine, therefore the nations are mad.[8]Babylon is ſuddenly fallen and deſtroyed: howle for her, take balme for her paine, if ſo be ſhe may be healed.[9]We would haue healed Babylon, but ſhe is not healed: forſake her, and let vs goe euery one into his owne countrey: for her iudgement reacheth vnto heauen, and is lifted vp euen to the ſkies.[10]The Lord hath brought forth our righteouſneſſe: come and let vs declare in Zion the worke of the Lord our God.[11]Make bright the arrowes: gather the ſhields: the Lord hath raiſed vp the ſpirit of the kings of the Medes: for his deuice is againſt Babylon, to deſtroy it; becauſe it is the vengeance of the Lord, the vengeance of his temple.[12]Set vp the ſtandart vpon the walles of Babylon, make the watch ſtrong: ſet vp the watchman: prepare the ambuſhes: for the Lord hath both deuiſed and done that, which hee ſpake againſt the inhabitants of Babylon.[13]O thou that dwelleſt vpon many waters, abundant in treaſures; thine end is come, and the meaſure of thy couetouſneſſe.[14]The Lord of hoſtes hath ſworne by himſelfe, ſaying, Surely I will fill thee with men, as with caterpillers; and they ſhall lift vp a ſhoute againſt thee.[15]Hee hath made the earth by his power, he hath eſtabliſhed the world by his wiſedome, and hath ſtretched out the heauen by his vnderſtanding.[16]When he vttereth his voyce, there is a multitude of waters in the heauens, and he cauſeth the vapours to aſcend from the ends of the earth, he maketh lightnings with raine, and bringeth forth the wind out of his treaſures.[17]Euery man is brutiſh by his knowledge: euery founder is confounded by the grauen image: for his moulten image is falſehood, and there is no breath in them.[18]They are vanitie, the worke of errours: in the time of their viſitation they ſhall periſh.[19]The portion of Iacob is not like them, for he is the former of all things, and Iſrael is the rod of his inheritance: the Lord of hoſtes is his Name.[20]Thou art my battel-axe and weapons of warre: for with thee will I breake in pieces the nations, and with thee will I deſtroy kingdomes;[21]And with thee will I breake in pieces the horſe and his rider, and with thee will I breake in pieces the charet, and his rider;[22]With thee alſo will I breake in pieces man and woman, and with thee will I breake in pieces old and yong, and with thee will I breake in pieces the yong man and the maide.[23]I will alſo breake in pieces with thee, the ſhepheard and his flocke, and with thee will I breake in pieces the huſbandman, and his yoke of oxen, and with thee will I breake in pieces Captaines and rulers.[24]And I will render vnto Babylon, and to all the inhabitants of Caldea, all their euil that they haue done in Zion in your ſight, ſaith the Lord.[25]Behold, I am againſt thee, O deſtroying mountaine, ſaith the Lord, which deſtroieſt all the earth, and I wil ſtretch out mine hand vpon thee, and roule thee downe from the rockes, and will make thee a burnt mountaine.[26]And they ſhall not take of thee a ſtone for a corner, nor a ſtone for foundations, but thou ſhalt be deſolate for euer, ſaith the Lord.[27]Set ye vp a ſtandart in the land, blow the trumpet among the nations: prepare the nations againſt her: call together againſt her the kingdomes of Ararat, Minni, & Aſhchenaz: appoint a captaine againſt her: cauſe her horſes to come vp as the rough caterpillers.[28]Prepare againſt her the nations with the kings of the Medes, the captaines thereof, and all the rulers thereof, and all the land of his dominion.[29]And the land ſhall tremble and ſorrow: for euery purpoſe of the Lord ſhalbe performed againſt Babylon, to make the land of Babylon a deſolation without an inhabitant.[30]The mightie men of Babylon haue forborne to fight: they haue remained in their holdes: their might hath failed, they became as women: they haue burnt their dwelling places: her barres are broken.[31]One poſte ſhall runne to meet another, and one meſſenger to meete another, to ſhew the king of Babylon that his citie is taken at one end,[32]And that the paſsages are ſtopped, and the reedes they haue burnt with fire, and the men of warre are afrighted.[33]For thus ſaith the Lord of hoſtes, the God of Iſrael; The daughter of Babylon is like a threſhing floore; it is time to threſh her: yet a little while, and the time of her harueſt ſhall come.[34]Nebuchadrezzar the king of Babylon hath deuoured me, he hath cruſhed me; he hath made me an emptie veſſell: hee hath ſwallowed mee vp like a dragon; he hath filled his bellie with my delicates, he hath caſt me out.[35]The violence done to me and to my fleſh, be vpon Babylon, ſhall the inhabitant of Zion ſay; and my blood vpon the inhabitants of Caldea, ſhall Ieruſalem ſay.[36]Therefore thus ſaith the Lord, Behold, I wil plead thy cauſe, and take vengeance for thee, and I will drie vp her ſea, and make her ſprings drie.[37]And Babylon ſhal become heaps, a dwelling place for dragons, an aſtoniſhment, and an hiſsing without an inhabitant.[38]They ſhall roare together like lions; they ſhall yell as lions whelps.[39]In their heat I will make their feaſts, and I will make them drunken, that they may reioyce, and ſleepe a perpetuall ſleepe, and not wake, ſaith the Lord.[40]I will bring them downe like lambes to the ſlaughter, like rammes with hee goates.[41]How is Sheſhach taken? and how is the praiſe of the whole earth ſurpriſed? how is Babylon become an aſtoniſhment among the nations?[42]The ſea is come vp vpon Babylon: ſhe is couered with the multitude of the waues thereof.[43]Her cities are a deſolation, a dry land and a wildernes, a land wherein no man dwelleth, neither doeth any ſonne of man paſſe thereby.[44]And I will puniſh Bel in Babylon, and I will bring forth out of his mouth that which he hath ſwallowed vp, and the nations ſhall not flow together any more vnto him, yea, the wall of Babylon ſhall fall.[45]My people, goe ye out of the midſt of her, and deliuer ye euery man his ſoule frō the fierce anger of the Lord,[46]And leſt your heart faint, and ye feare for the rumour that ſhall be heard in the land: a rumour ſhall both come one yeere, and after that in another yeere ſhall come a rumour, and violence in the land, ruler againſt ruler.[47]Therefore behold, the dayes come, that I will doe iudgment vpon the grauen images of Babylon, and her whole land ſhall bee confounded, and all her ſlaine ſhall fall in the midſt of her.[48]Then the heauen and the earth, and all that is therein, ſhall ſing for Babylon: for the ſpoilers ſhall come vnto her from the North, ſaith the Lord.[49]As Babylon hath cauſed the ſlaine of Iſrael to fall: ſo at Babylon ſhall fall the ſlaine of all the earth.[50]Ye that haue eſcaped the ſword, go away, ſtand not ſtill: remember the Lord afarre off: and let Ieruſalem come into your mind.[51]We are confounded, becauſe wee haue heard reproch, ſhame hath couered our faces: for ſtrangers are come into the Sanctuaries of the Lords houſe.[52]Wherfore behold, the dayes come, ſaith the Lord, that I will do iudgment vpon her grauen images, and through all her land the wounded ſhall grone.[53]Though Babylon ſhould mount vp to heauen, and though ſhee ſhould fortifie the height of her ſtrength, yet from me ſhall ſpoilers come vnto her, ſaith the Lord.[54]A ſound of a crie commeth from Babylon, and great deſtruction from the land of the Caldeans.[55]Becauſe the Lord hath ſpoiled Babylon, and deſtroyed out of her the great voyce when her waues doe roare like great waters, a noiſe of their voice is vttered.[56]Becauſe the ſpoiler is come vpon her, euen vpon Babylon, and her mightie men are taken, euery one of their bowes is broken, for the Lord God of recompenſes ſhall ſurely requite.[57]And I will make drunke her princes and her wiſe men, her captaines and her rulers, and her mightie men: and they ſhall ſleepe a perpetuall ſleepe, and not wake, ſaith the king, whoſe Name is the Lord of hoſts.[58]Thus ſaith the Lord of hoſts, The broad walles of Babylon ſhalbe vtterly broken, and her high gates ſhal be burnt with fire, and the people ſhall labour in vaine, and the folke in the fire, and they ſhall be weary.[59]The word which Ieremiah the prophet commanded Seraiah the ſonne of Neriah, the ſonne of Maaſeiah, when he went with Zedekiah the king of Iudah into Babylon, in the fourth yeere of his reigne, and this Seraiah was a quiet prince.[60]So Ieremiah wrote in a booke all the euill that ſhould come vpon Babylon: euen all theſe wordes that are written againſt Babylon.[61]And Ieremiah ſaid to Seraiah, When thou

commeſt to Babylon, and ſhalt ſee, and ſhalt read all theſe words,62Then
ſhalt thou ſay, O Lord, thou haſt ſpoken againſt this place, to cut it off,
that none ſhall remaine in it, neither man nor beaſt, but that it ſhalbe
deſolate for euer.63And it ſhall bee when thou haſt made an end of
reading this booke, that thou ſhalt binde a ſtone to it, and caſt it into the
midſt of Euphrates.64And thou ſhalt ſay, Thus ſhall Babylon ſinke, and
ſhall not riſe from the euill that I will bring vpon her: and they ſhall be
wearie. Thus farre are the words of Ieremiah.
CHAPTER 521Zedekiah was one and twentie yeere olde when he
began to reigne, and he reigned eleuen yeeres in Ieruſalem, and his
mothers name was Hamutal the daughter of Ieremiah of Libnah.2And
hee did that which was euill in the eyes of the Lord, according to all that
Iehoiakim had done.3For through the anger of the Lord it came to paſſe
in Ieruſalem and Iudah, till hee had caſt them out from his preſence,
that Zedekiah rebelled againſt the king of Babylon.4And it came to paſſe
in the ninth yere of his reigne, in the tenth moneth, in the tenth day of
the moneth, that Nebuchad rezzar king of Babylon came, hee, and all
his armie againſt Ieruſalem, and pitched againſt it, and built fortes againſt
it round about.5So the citie was beſieged vnto the eleuenth yeere of king
Zedekiah.6And in the fourth moneth, in the ninth day of the moneth,
the famine was ſore in the citie, ſo that there was no bread for the people
of the land.7Then the city was broken vp, and all the men of warre fled,
and went foorth out of the citie by night, by the way of the gate between
the two wals, which was by the kings garden (now the Caldeans were by
the city round about) and they went by the way of the plaine.8But the
armie of the Caldeans purſued after the king, and ouertooke Zedekiah
in the plaines of Iericho, & all his armie was ſcattered from him.9Then
they tooke the king, and caried him vp vnto the king of Babylon to
Riblah in the land of Hamath: where he gaue iudgement vpon
him.10And the king of Babylon ſlew the ſonnes of Zedekiah before his
eyes: he ſlewe alſo all the princes of Iudah in Riblah.11Then he put out
the eyes of Zedekiah, and the king of Babylon bound him in chaines,
and caried him to Babylon, and put him in priſon till the day of his
death.12Now in the fifth moneth, in the tenth day of the moneth (which
was the nineteenth yeere of Nebuchad-rezzar king of Babylon) came
Nebuzaradan captaine of the guard, which ſerued the king of Babylon,
into Ieruſalem;13And burnt the houſe of the Lord, and the kings houſe,
and all the houſes of Ieruſalem, and all the houſes of the great men burnt
he with fire.14And all the armie of the Caldeans that were with the
captaine of the guard, brake downe all the walles of Ieruſalem round
about.15Then Nebuzaradan the captaine of the guard, caried away
captiue certaine of the poore of the people, and the reſidue of the people
that remained in the citie, and thoſe that fell away, that fell to the king
of Babylon, and the reſt of the multitude.16But Nebuzaradan the
captaine of the guard, left certaine of the poore of the land for Uine-
dreſſers and for huſbandmen.17Alſo the pillars of braſſe that were in the
houſe of the Lord, and the baſes, and the braſen ſea that was in the
houſe of the Lord, the Caldeans brake, and caried all the braſſe of them
to Babylon.18The cauldrons alſo, and the ſhouels, and the ſnuffers, and
the bolles, and the ſpoones, and all the veſſels of braſſe wherewith they
miniſtred, tooke they away.19And the baſons, and the firepans, and the
bolles, and the cauldrons, and the candleſtickes, and the ſpoones, and
the cuppes; that which was of golde, in golde, and that which was of
ſiluer, in ſiluer, tooke the captaine of the guard away:20The two pillars,
one ſea, and twelue braſen bulles, that were vnder the baſes, which king
Solomon had made in the houſe of the Lord: the braſſe of all theſe
veſſels was without weight.21And concerning the pillars, the height of
one pillar was eighteene cubites, and a fillet of twelue cubites did
compaſſe it, and the thickeneſſe thereof was foure fingers: it was
hollow.22And a chapiter of braſſe was vpon it, and the height of one
chapiter was fiue cubites, with networke and pomegranates vpon the
chapiters round about, all of braſſe: the ſecond pillar alſo and the
pomegranates were like vnto theſe.23And there were ninetie and ſixe
pomegranates on a ſide, and all the pomegranates vpon the networke
were an hundreth round about.24And the captaine of the guard tooke
Seraiah the chiefe Prieſt, and Zephaniah the ſecond Prieſt, and the three
keepers of the doore.25Hee tooke alſo out of the citie an Eunuch, which
had the charge of the men of warre, and ſeuen men of them that were
neere the kings perſon which were found in the citie, and the principall
Scribe of the hoſt, who muſtered the people of the land, and threeſcore
men of the people of the land, that were found in the middeſt of the
citie.26So Nebuzar-adan the captaine of the guard tooke them, and
brought them to the king of Babylon to Riblah.27And the king of
Babylon ſmote them, and put them to death in Riblah, in the land of
Hamath: thus Iudah was caried away captiue out of his owne land.28This
is the people whom Nebuchad-rezzar caried away captiue in the ſeuenth
yeere, three thouſand Iewes and three and twentie.29In the eighteenth
yeere of Nebuchad-rezzar hee caried away captiue from Ieruſalem eight
hundredth, thirtie and two perſons.30In the three and twentith yeere of
Nebuchad-rezzar, Nebuzar-adan the captaine of the guard, caried away
captiue of the Iewes ſeuen hundreth fortie and fiue perſons: all the
perſons were foure thouſand and ſixe hundreth.31And it came to paſſe
in the ſeuen and thirtieth yeere of the captiuitie of Iehoiakin king of
Iudah, in the twelfth moneth, in the fiue and twentieth day of the
moneth, that Euil-merodach king of Babylon, in the firſt yeere of his
reigne, lifted vp the head of Iehoiakin king of Iudah, and brought him
forth out of priſon,32And ſpake kindly vnto him, and ſet his throne
aboue the throne of the kings that were with him in Babylon,33And
changed his priſon garments: and hee did continually eate bread before
him all the dayes of his life.34And for his diet, there was a continuall diet
giuen him of the king of Babylon, euery day a portion vntill the day of
his death, all the dayes of his life.

LAMENTATIONS

CHAPTER 11How doeth the citie ſit ſolitarie that was full of people?
How is ſhe become as a widow? She that was great among the nations,
and princeſſe among the prouinces, how is ſhe become tributarie?2Shee
weepeth ſore in the night, and her teares are on her cheekes: among all
her louers ſhe hath none to comfort her, all her friends haue dealt
treacherouſly with her, they are become her enemies.3Iudah is gone into
captiuitie, becauſe of affliction, and becauſe of great ſeruitude: ſhe
dwelleth among the heathen, ſhe findeth no reſt: all her perſecutors
ouertook her betweene the ſtraits.4The wayes of Zion do mourne,
becauſe none come to the ſolemne feaſts: all her gates are deſolate: her
prieſts ſigh: her virgins are afflicted, and ſhe is in bitterneſſe.5Her
aduerſaries are the chiefe, her enemies proſper: for the Lord hath
afflicted her; for the multitude of her tranſgreſſions, her children are
gone into captiuitie before the enemie.6And from the daughter of Zion
all her beautie is departed: her princes are become like Harts that find
no paſture, & they are gone without ſtrength before the
purſuer.7Ieruſalem remembred in the dayes of her affliction, and of her
miſeries, all her pleaſant things that ſhe had in the dayes of old, when
her people fell into the hand of the enemie, and none did helpe her, the
aduerſaries ſaw her, and did mocke at her Sabbaths.8Ieruſalem hath
grieuouſly ſinned, therefore ſhe is remoued: all that honoured her,
deſpiſe her, becauſe they haue ſeene her nakedneſſe: yea, ſhee ſigheth
and turneth backward.9Her filthines is in her ſkirts, ſhe remembreth not
her laſt end, therfore ſhe came downe wonderfully: ſhee had no
comforter: O Lord, behold my affliction: for þe enemie hath magnified
himſelfe.10The aduerſarie hath ſpread out his hand vpon all her pleaſant
things: for ſhe hath ſeene that the heathen entred into her Sanctuarie,
whom thou didſt command that they ſhould not enter into thy
congregation.11All her people ſigh, they ſeek bread, they haue giuen their
pleaſant things for meate to relieue the ſoule: ſee, O Lord, & conſider:
for I am become vile.12Is it nothing to you, all ye that paſſe by? Behold
and ſee, if there be any ſorow like vnto my ſorowe, which is done vnto
me, wherewith the Lord hath afflicted me, in the day of his fierce
anger.13From aboue hath he ſent fire into my bones, and it preuaileth
againſt them: he hath ſpread a net for my feete, he hath turned me backe:
he hath made me deſolate, and faint all the day.14The yoke of my
tranſgreſſions is bound by his hand: they are wreathed, and come vp
vpon my necke: he hath made my ſtrength to fall, the Lord hath
deliuered me into their hands, from whom I am not able to riſe vp.15The
Lord hath troden vnder foot all my mightie men in the midſt of me: he
hath called an aſſembly againſt mee, to cruſh my yong men. The Lord
hath troden the virgine, the daughter of Iudah, as in a wine preſſe.16For
theſe things I weepe, mine eye, mine eye runneth downe with water,

becauſe the comforter that ſhould relieue my ſoule is farre from me: my
children are deſolate, becauſe the enemy preuailed.17Zion ſpreadeth
forth her hands, and there is none to comfort her: the Lord hath
commanded concerning Iacob, that his aduerſaries ſhould bee round
about him: Ieruſalem is as a menſtruous woman among them.18The
Lord is righteous, for I haue rebelled againſt his commandement: heare,
I pray you, all people, and behold my ſorow: my virgins and my yong
men are gone into captiuitie.19I called for my louers, but they deceiued
me: my prieſts and mine elders gaue vp the ghoſt in the citie, while they
ſought their meat to relieue their ſouleſ20Behold, O Lord: for I am in
diſtreſſe: my bowels are troubled: mine heart is turned within mee, for I
haue grieuouſly rebelled: abroad the ſword bereaueth, at home there is
as death.21They haue heard that I ſigh, there is none to comfort me: all
mine enemies haue heard of my trouble, they are glad that thou haſt
done it: thou wilt bring the day that thou haſt called, and they ſhall be
like vnto me.22Let all their wickednes come before thee: and doe vnto
them, as thou haſt done vnto me for all my tranſgreſſions: for my ſighes
are many, and my heart is faint.
CHAPTER 21How hath the Lord couered the daughter of Zion with
a cloud, in his anger, and caſt downe from heauen vnto the earth the
beautie of Iſrael, and remembred not his footſtoole in the day of his
anger?2The Lord hath ſwallowed vp all the habitations of Iacob, and
hath not pitied: he hath throwen downe in his wrath the ſtrong holds of
the daughter of Iudah: he hath brought them down to the ground: hee
hath polluted the kingdome and the princes thereof.3He hath cut off in
his fierce anger all the horne of Iſrael: he hath drawen backe his right
hand from before the enemy, and he burned againſt Iacob like a flaming
fire which deuoureth round about.4He hath bent his bow like an enemy:
he ſtood with his right hand as an aduerſary, and ſlew all that were
pleaſant to the eye, in the tabernacle of the daughter of Zion: he powred
out his furie like fire.5The Lord was an enemie: he hath ſwallowed vp
Iſrael, hee hath ſwallowed vp all her palaces: he hath deſtroyed his ſtrong
holds, and hath increaſed in the daughter of Iudah mourning and
lamentation.6And he hath violently taken away his tabernacle, as if it
were of a garden, hee hath deſtroyed his places of the aſſembly: the Lord
hath cauſed the ſolemne feaſts and Sabbaths to be forgotten in Zion,
and hath deſpiſed in the indignation of his anger the King and the
Prieſt.7The Lord hath caſt off his Altar: hee hath abhorred his
Sanctuarie: he hath giuen vp into the hand of the enemie the walles of
her palaces: they haue made a noiſe in the houſe of the Lord, as in the
day of a ſolemne Feaſt.8The Lord hath purpoſed to deſtroy the wall of
the daughter of Zion: he hath ſtretched out a line: he hath not
withdrawen his hand from deſtroying: therefore hee made the rampart
and the wall to lament: they languiſhed together.9Her gates are ſunke
into the ground: he hath deſtroyed and broken her barres: her King and
her Princes are among the Gentiles: the Law is no more, her prophets
alſo finde no viſion from the Lord.10The Elders of the daughter of Zion
ſit vpon the ground and keepe ſilence: they haue caſt vp duſt vpon their
heads: they haue girded themſelues with ſackcloth: the virgins of
Ieruſalem hang downe their heades to the ground.11Mine eyes doe faile
with teares: my bowels are troubled: my liuer is powred vpon the earth,
for the deſtruction of the daughter of my people, becauſe the children
and the ſucklings ſwoone in the ſtreets of the citie.12They ſay to their
mothers, Where is corne and wine? when they ſwooned as the wounded
in the ſtreets of the citie, when their ſoule was powred out into their
mothers boſome.13What thing ſhall I take to witneſſe for thee? what
thing ſhall I liken to thee, O daughter of Ieruſalem? what ſhall I equal
to thee, that I may comfort thee, O Uirgin daughter of Zion? for thy
breach is great like the ſea: who can heale thee?14Thy Prophets haue
ſeene vaine and fooliſh things for thee, and they haue not diſcouered
thine iniquitie, to turne away thy captiuitie: but haue ſeene for thee falſe
burdens, and cauſes of baniſhment.15All that paſſe by, clap their hands
at thee: they hiſse and wagge their head at the daughter of Ieruſalem,
ſaying, Is this the citie that men call the perfection of beauty, the ioy of
the whole earth?16All thine enemies haue opened their mouth againſt
thee: they hiſse and gnaſh the teeth: they ſay, We haue ſwallowed her
vp: certainly this is the day that we looked for: we haue found, we haue
ſeene it.17The Lord hath done that which he had deuiſed: he hath
fulfilled his word that he had commanded in the dayes of old: hee hath
throwen downe and hath not pitied: and he hath cauſed thine enemie to
reioyce ouer thee, hee hath ſet vp the horne of thine aduerſaries.18Their
heart cried vnto the Lord, O wall of the daughter of Zion, let teares
runne downe like a riuer, day and night: giue thy ſelfe no reſt, let not the
apple of thine eyes ceaſe.19Ariſe, cry out in the night: in the beginning
of the watches powre out thine heart like water before the face of the
Lord: lift vp thy handes toward him, for the life of thy yong children,
that faint for hunger in the top of euery ſtreete.20Behold, O Lord, and
conſider to whom thou haſt done this: ſhal the women eat their fruit,
and children of a ſpanne long? ſhall the prieſt and the prophet be ſlaine
in the Sanctuary of the Lord?21The yong and the old lye on the ground
in the ſtreets: my virgins and my yong men are fallen by the ſword: thou
haſt ſlaine them in the day of thy anger: thou haſt killed, and not
pitied.22Thou haſt called as in a ſolemne day my terrours round about,
ſo that in the day of the Lords anger, none eſcaped nor remained: thoſe
that I haue ſwadled and brought vp, hath mine enemy conſumed.
CHAPTER 31I Am the man that hath ſeene affliction by the rod of his
wrath.2He hath led me and brought mee into darkeneſſe, but not into
light.3Surely againſt me is he turned, he turneth his hand againſt me all
the day.4My fleſh and my ſkinne hath he made old, he hath broken my
bones.5He hath builded againſt me, and compaſſed me with gall and
trauel.6He hath ſet me in darke places, as they that be dead of old.7He
hath hedged me about, that I cannot get out: hee hath made my chaine
heauie.8Alſo when I cry and ſhout, he ſhutteth out my prayer.9Hee hath
incloſed my wayes with hewen ſtone: he hath made my pathes
crooked.10He was vnto me as a Beare lying in waite, and as a Lion in
ſecret places.11Hee hath turned aſide my wayes, and pulled me in pieces:
hee hath made me deſolate.12He hath bent his bow, and ſet me as a
marke for the arrow.13Hee hath cauſed the arrowes of his quiuer to enter
into my reines.14I was a deriſion to all my people, and their ſong all the
day.15Hee hath filled me with bitterneſse, hee hath made me drunken
with wormewood.16He hath alſo broken my teeth with grauell ſtones,
hee hath couered me with aſhes.17And thou haſt remoued my ſoule farre
off from peace: I forgate proſperitie.18And I ſaid, My ſtrength and my
hope is periſhed from the Lord:19Remembring mine affliction and my
miſerie, the wormewood & the gall.20My ſoule hath them ſtill in
remembrance, and is humbled in me.21This I recall to my mind,
therefore haue I hope.22It is of the Lords mercies that wee are not
conſumed, becauſe his compaſſions faile not.23They are newe euery
morning: great is thy faithfulneſse.24The Lord is my portion, ſayth my
ſoule, therefore will I hope in him.25The Lord is good vnto them that
waite for him, to the ſoule that ſeeketh him.26It is good that a man
ſhould both hope and quietly wait for the ſaluation of the Lord.27It is
good for a man that he beare the yoke in his youth.28Hee ſitteth alone
and keepeth ſilence, becauſe hee hath borne it vpon him.29He putteth
his mouth in the duſt, if ſo be there may be hope.30Hee giueth his cheeke
to him that ſmiteth him, hee is filled full with reproch.31For the Lord
will not caſt off for euer.32But though hee cauſe griefe, yet will hee haue
compaſſion according to the multitude of his mercies.33For he doth not
afflict willingly, nor grieue the children of men.34To cruſh vnder his
feete all the priſoners of the earth,35To turne aſide the right of a man
before the face of the moſt high,36To ſubuert a man in his cauſe, the
Lord approoueth not.37Who is hee that ſayth, and it commeth to paſſe,
when the Lord commandeth it not?38Out of the mouth of the moſt hie
proceedeth not euill and good?39Wherefore doeth a liuing man
complaine, a man for the puniſhment of his ſinnes?40Let vs ſearch and
try our waies, and turne againe to the Lord.41Let vs lift vp our heart with
our hands vnto God in the heauens.42We haue tranſgreſſed, and haue
rebelled, thou haſt not pardoned.43Thou haſt couered with anger, and
perſecuted vs: thou haſt ſlaine, thou haſt not pitied.44Thou haſt couered
thy ſelfe with a cloud, that our prayer ſhould not paſſe through.45Thou
haſt made vs as the offſcouring and refuſe in the middeſt of the
people.46All our enemies haue opened their mouthes againſt vs.47Feare
and a ſnare is come vpon vs, deſolation and deſtruction.48Mine eye
runneth downe with riuers of water, for the deſtruction of the daughter
of my people.49Mine eye trickleth downe and ceaſeth not, without any
intermiſsion:50Till the Lord looke downe, and behold from
heauen.51Mine eye affecteth mine heart, becauſe of all the daughters of
my city.52Mine enemies chaſed me ſore like a bird, without cauſe.53They

haue cut off my life in the dungeon, and caſt a ſtone vpon me.[54]Waters flowed ouer mine head, then I ſayd, I am cut off.[55]I called vpon thy name, O Lord, out of the low dungeon.[56]Thou haſt heard my voice, hide not thine eare at my breathing, at my crie.[57]Thou dreweſt neere in the day that I called vpon thee: thou ſaidſt, Feare not.[58]O Lord, thou haſt pleaded the cauſes of my ſoule, thou haſt redeemed my life.[59]O Lord, thou haſt ſeene my wrong, iudge thou my cauſe.[60]Thou haſt ſeene all their vengeance; and all their imaginations againſt me.[61]Thou haſt heard their reproch, O Lord, and all their imaginations againſt me:[62]The lippes of thoſe that roſe vp againſt me, and their deuice againſt me all the day.[63]Behold, their ſitting downe and their riſing vp, I am their muſicke.[64]Render vnto them a recompenſe, O Lord, according to the worke of their hands.[65]Giue them ſorrow of heart, thy curſe vnto them.[66]Perſecute and deſtroy them in anger, from vnder the heauens of the Lord.

CHAPTER 4[1]How is the gold become dimme! how is the moſt fine gold changed! the ſtones of the ſanctuarie are powred out in the top of euery ſtreete.[2]The precious ſonnes of Zion, comparable to fine gold, how are they eſteemed as earthen pitchers, the worke of the hands of the potter![3]Euen the ſea-monſters draw out the breaſt, they giue ſucke to their young ones: the daughter of my people is become cruell, like the oſtriches in the wilderneſſe.[4]The tongue of the ſucking child cleaueth to the roofe of his mouth for thirſt: the young children aſke bread, and no man breaketh it vnto them.[5]They that did feede delicatly, are deſolate in the ſtreetes: they that were brought vp in ſcarlet, embrace dounghilles.[6]For the puniſhment of the iniquitie of the daughter of my people, is greater then the puniſhment of the ſinne of Sodom, that was ouerthrowen as in a moment, and no hands ſtayed on her.[7]Her Nazarites were purer then ſnow, they were whiter then milke, they were more ruddie in body then rubies, their poliſhing was of Saphir.[8]Their viſage is blacker then a cole: they are not knowen in the ſtreets: their ſkinne cleaueth to their bones: it is withered, it is become like a ſticke.[9]They that bee ſlaine with the ſword, are better then they that be ſlain with hunger: for theſe pine away, ſtricken through for want of the fruits of the field.[10]The hands of the pitifull women haue ſodden their owne children, they were their meate in the deſtruction of the daughter of my people.[11]The Lord hath accompliſhed his furie, he hath powred out his fierce anger, and hath kindled a fire in Zion, and it hath deuoured the foundations thereof.[12]The kings of the earth, and all the inhabitants of the world would not haue beleeued, that the aduerſarie and the enemie ſhould haue entred into the gates of Ieruſalem.[13]For the ſinnes of her prophets, and the iniquities of her prieſts, that haue ſhed the blood of the iuſt in the middeſt of her:[14]They haue wandred as blind men in the ſtreetes, they haue polluted themſelues with blood, ſo that men could not touch their garments.[15]They cryed vnto them; Depart yee, it is vncleane, depart, depart, touch not, when they fled away and wandred: they ſaid among the heathen, They ſhall no more ſoiourne there.[16]The anger of the Lord hath diuided them, he will no more regard them: they reſpected not the perſons of the prieſts, they fauoured not the elders.[17]As for vs, our eyes as yet failed for our vaine helpe: in our watching we haue watched for a nation that could not ſaue vs.[18]They hunt our ſteps that we cannot goe in our ſtreets: our end is neere, our dayes are fulfilled, for our ende is come.[19]Our perſecutours are ſwifter then the eagles of the heauen: they purſued vs vpon the mountaines, they laide waite for vs in the wilderneſſe.[20]The breath of our noſtrels, the anointed of the Lord was taken in their pits, of whom we ſaid, Under his ſhadowe we ſhall liue among the heathen.[21]Reioyce and be glad, O daughter of Edom, that dwelleſt in the lande of Uz, the cup alſo ſhall paſſe through vnto thee: thou ſhalt be drunken, and ſhalt make thy ſelfe naked.[22]The puniſhment of thine iniquitie is accompliſhed, O daughter of Zion, he will no more carie thee away into captiuitie: hee will viſit thine iniquitie, O daughter of Edom, hee will diſcouer thy ſinnes.

CHAPTER 5[1]Remember, O Lord, what is come vpon vs: conſider and beholde our reproch.[2]Our inheritance is turned to ſtrangers, our houſes to aliants.[3]We are orphanes and fatherleſſe, our mothers are as widowes.[4]We haue drunken our water for money, our wood is ſold vnto vs.[5]Our neckes are vnder perſecution: we labour and haue no reſt.[6]We haue giuen the hand to the Egyptians, and to the Aſſyrians, to be ſatiſfied with bread.[7]Our fathers haue ſinned and are not, and wee haue borne their iniquities.[8]Seruants haue ruled ouer vs: there is none that doeth deliuer vs out of their hand.[9]We gate our bread with the perill of our liues, becauſe of the ſword of the wilderneſſe.[10]Our ſkinne was blacke like an ouen, becauſe of the terrible famine.[11]They rauiſhed the women in Zion, and the maides in the cities of Iudah.[12]Princes are hanged vp by their hand: the faces of Elders were not honoured.[13]They tooke the young men to grinde, and the children fell vnder the wood.[14]The Elders haue ceaſed from the gate, the young men from their muſicke.[15]The ioy of our heart is ceaſed, our daunce is turned into mourning.[16]The crowne is fallen from our head: Woe vnto vs, that wee haue ſinned.[17]For this our heart is faint, for theſe things our eyes are dimme.[18]Becauſe of the mountaine of Zion, which is deſolate, the foxes walke vpon it.[19]Thou, O Lord, remaineſt for euer: thy throne from generation to generation.[20]Wherefore doeſt thou forget vs for euer, and forſake vs ſo long time?[21]Turne thou vs vnto thee, O Lord, and we ſhall be turned: renew our dayes as of old.[22]But thou haſt vtterly reiected vs: thou art very wroth againſt vs.

EZEKIEL

CHAPTER 1[1]Now it came to paſſe in the thirtieth yeere, in the fourth moneth, in the fifth day of the moneth, (as I was among the captiues by the riuer of Chebar) that the heauens were opened, and I ſaw viſions of God.[2]In the fifth day of the moneth, (which was the fifth yeere of king Iehoiakins captiuitie,)[3]The word of the Lord came expreſly vnto Ezekiel the Prieſt, the ſonne of Buzi, in the land of the Caldeans, by the riuer Chebar, and the hand of the Lord was there vpon him.[4]And I looked, and behold, a whirlewinde came out of the North, a great cloude, and a fire infoulding it ſelfe, and a brightneſse was about it, and out of the midſt thereof as the colour of amber, out of the midſt of the fire.[5]Alſo out of the midſt thereof came the likeneſſe of foure liuing creatures, and this was their appearance: they had the likeneſſe of a man.[6]And euery one had foure faces, and euery one had foure wings.[7]And their feet were ſtraight feet, and the ſole of their feet was like the ſole of a calues foot, and they ſparkled like the colour of burniſhed braſſe.[8]And they had the handes of a man vnder their wings on their foure ſides, and they foure had their faces and their wings.[9]Their wings were ioyned one to another, they turned not when they went: they went euery one ſtraight forward.[10]As for the likeneſſe of their faces, they foure had the face of a man, and the face of a lyon on the right ſide, and they foure had the face of an oxe on the left ſide: they foure alſo had the face of an eagle.[11]Thus were their faces: and their wings were ſtretched vpward, two wings of euery one were ioyned one to an other, and two couered their bodies.[12]And they went euery one ſtraight forward: whither the ſpirit was to goe, they went: and they turned not when they went.[13]As for the likeneſſe of the liuing creatures, their appearance was like burning coles of fire, and like the appearance of lamps: it went vp and downe among the liuing creatures, and the fire was bright, and out of the fire went foorth lightning.[14]And the liuing creatures ranne, and returned as the appearance of a flaſh of lightning.[15]Now as I behelde the liuing creatures: behold one wheele vpon the earth by the liuing creatures, with his foure faces.[16]The appearance of the wheeles, and their worke was like vnto the colour of a Berill: and they foure had one likeneſſe, and their appearance and their worke was as it were a wheele in the middle of a wheele.[17]When they went, they went vpon their foure ſides: and they returned not when they went.[18]As for their rings, they were ſo high, that they were dreadful, and their rings were full of eyes round about them foure.[19]And when the liuing creatures went, the wheeles went by them: and when the liuing creatures were lift vp from the earth, the wheels were lift vp.[20]Whitherſoeuer the ſpirit was to goe, they went, thither was their ſpirit to goe, and the wheeles were lifted vp ouer againſt them: for the ſpirit of the liuing creature was in the wheeles.[21]When thoſe went, theſe went, and when thoſe ſtood, theſe ſtood; and when thoſe were lifted vp from the earth, the wheeles were lifted vp ouer againſt them: for the ſpirit of the liuing creature was in the wheeles.[22]And the likeneſſe of the firmament vpon the heads of the liuing creature was as the colour of the terrible chryſtall, ſtretched foorth ouer their heads aboue.23And vnder the firmament were their wings ſtraight, the one toward the other, euery one had two which couered on this ſide, & euery one had two, which couered on that ſide their bodies.24And when they went, I heard the noiſe of their wings, like the noiſe of great waters, as the voice of the Almightie, the voice of ſpeech, as the noiſe of an hoſte: when they ſtood, they let downe their wings.25And there was a voice from the firmament, that was ouer their heads, when they ſtood, and had let downe their wings.26And aboue the firmament that was ouer their heads, was the likeneſſe of a Throne, as the appearance of a Saphyre ſtone, and vpon the likeneſſe of the Throne was the likeneſſe as the appearance of a man aboue vpon it.27And I ſaw as the colour of amber, as the appearance of fire round about within it: from the appearance of his loynes euen vpward, and from the appearance of his loynes euen downeward, I ſaw as it were the appearance of fire, & it had brightneſse round about.28As the appearance of the bow that is in the cloude in the day of raine, ſo was the appearance of the brightneſse round about. This was the appearance of the likeneſſe of the glory of the Lord: and when I ſaw it, I fell vpon my face, and I heard a voice of one that ſpake.

CHAPTER 21And he ſaid vnto me, Son of man, ſtand vpon thy feete, and I will ſpeake vnto thee.2And the ſpirit entred into me, when hee ſpake vnto me, and ſet me vpon my feete, that I heard him that ſpake vnto me:3And hee ſaid vnto me, Sonne of man, I ſend thee to the children of Iſrael, to a rebellious nation that hath rebelled againſt mee: they and their fathers haue tranſgreſſed againſt mee, euen vnto this very day.4For they are impudent children and ſtiffe hearted: I doe ſend thee vnto them, and thou ſhalt ſay vnto them, Thus ſayth the Lord God.5And they, whether they wil heare or whether they will forbeare, (for they are a rebellious houſe) yet ſhall know that there hath bene a Prophet among them.6And thou ſonne of man, be not afraid of them, neither be afraid of their wordes, though bryars and thornes be with thee, and thou doeſt dwell among ſcorpions: be not afraid of their words, nor be diſmayed at their lookes, though they be a rebellious houſe.7And thou ſhalt ſpeake my words vnto them, whether they will heare or whether they will forbeare, for they are moſt rebellious.8But thou, ſonne of man, heare what I ſay vnto thee; Be not thou rebellious like that rebellious houſe: open thy mouth and eate that I giue thee.9And when I looked, behold, an hand was ſent vnto mee, and loe, a roule of a booke was therein.10And he ſpread it before me, and it was written within and without, and there was written therein lamentations, and mourning, and woe.

CHAPTER 31Moreouer he ſaid vnto me, Sonne of man, eate that thou findeſt: eate this roule, and goe, ſpeake vnto the houſe of Iſrael.2So I opened my mouth, and hee cauſed me to eate that roule.3And he ſaid vuto mee; Sonne of man, cauſe thy belly to eate, and fill thy bowels with this roule that I giue thee. Then did I eate it, and it was in my mouth as honie for ſweetneſse.4And he ſaid vnto me, Sonne of man, goe, get thee vnto the houſe of Iſrael, and ſpeake with my words vnto them.5For thou art not ſent to a people of a ſtrange ſpeech, and of an hard language, but to the houſe of Iſrael.6Not to many people of a ſtrange ſpeech and of an hard language, whoſe words thou canſt not vnderſtand: ſurely had I ſent thee to them, they would haue hearkened vnto thee:7But the houſe of Iſrael will not hearken vnto thee; for they will not hearken vnto me: for all the houſe of Iſrael are impudent and hard hearted.8Behold, I haue made thy face ſtrong againſt their faces, and thy forehead ſtrong againſt their foreheads.9As an adamant harder then flint haue I made thy forehead: feare them not, neither be diſmayed at their lookes, though they be a rebellious houſe.10Moreouer he ſaid vnto me, Sonne of man, all my words that I ſhall ſpeake vnto thee, receiue in thine heart, and heare with thine eares.11And goe, get thee to them of the captiuity, vnto thy people, and ſpeake vnto them and tell them, Thus ſaith the Lord God, whether they will heare, or whether they will forbeare.12Then the ſpirit tooke me vp, and I heard behind me a voyce of a great ruſhing, ſaying Bleſſed be the glory of the Lord from his place.13I heard alſo the noiſe of the wings of the liuing creatures that touched one another, and the noiſe of the wheeles ouer againſt them, and a noiſe of a great ruſhing.14So the ſpirit lifted me vp, and tooke me away, and I went in bitterneſse, in the heate of my ſpirit, but the hand of the Lord was ſtrong vpon mee.15Then I came to them of the captiuity at Tel-abib, that dwelt by the riuer of Chebar, and I ſate where they ſate, and remained there aſtoniſhed among them ſeuen daies.16And it came to paſſe at the end of ſeuen dayes, that the word of the Lord came vnto me, ſaying;17Sonne of man, I haue made thee a watchman vnto the houſe of Iſrael: therefore heare the word at my mouth, & giue them warning from me.18When I ſay vnto the wicked; Thou ſhalt ſurely die, and thou giueſt him not warning, nor ſpeakeſt to warne the wicked from his wicked way to ſaue his life; the ſame wicked man ſhall die in his iniquitie: but his blood will I require at thine hand.19Yet if thou warne the wicked, and he turne not from his wickedneſſe, nor from his wicked way, he ſhall die in his iniquity, but thou haſt deliuered thy ſoule.20Againe, when a righteous man doth turne from his righteouſneſſe and commit iniquity, and I lay a ſtumbling blocke before him, he ſhall die: becauſe thou haſt not giuen him warning, he ſhall die in his ſinne, and his righteouſneſſe which he hath done ſhal not be remembred: but his blood will I require at thine hand.21Neuertheleſſe if thou warne the righteous man, that the righteous ſinne not, and he doth not ſinne; he ſhall ſurely liue, becauſe he is warned: alſo thou haſt deliuered thy ſoule.22And the hand of the Lord was there vpon me, and he ſaid vnto me; Ariſe, goe forth into the plaine, and I will there talke with thee.23Then I aroſe and went forth into the plaine, and behold, the glory of the Lord ſtood there as the glory which I ſaw by the riuer of Chebar, and I fell on my face.24Then the ſpirit entred into me, and ſet me vpon my feet, and ſpake with me, and ſaid vnto me, Goe ſhut thy ſelfe within thine houſe.25But thou, O ſonne of man, behold, they ſhall put bands vpon thee, and ſhall bind thee with them, and thou ſhalt not goe out among them.26And I will make thy tongue cleaue to the roofe of thy mouth, that thou ſhalt be dumme and ſhalt not be to them a reprouer: for they are a rebellious houſe.27But when I ſpeake with thee, I will open thy mouth, and thou ſhalt ſay vnto them; Thus ſaith the Lord God, He that heareth, let him heare, and he that forbeareth, let him forbeare: for they are a rebellious houſe.

CHAPTER 41Thou alſo ſonne of man, take thee a tile, and lay it before thee, and pourtray vpon it the citie, euen Ieruſalem,2And lay ſiege againſt it, and build a fort againſt it, and caſt a mount againſt it: ſet the campe alſo againſt it, and ſet battering rammes againſt it round about.3Moreouer take thou vnto thee an yron panne, and ſet it for a wall of yron betweene thee and the city, and ſet thy face againſt it, and it ſhalbe beſieged, and thou ſhalt lay ſiege againſt it: this ſhalbe a ſigne to the houſe of Iſrael.4Lie thou alſo vpon thy left ſide, and lay the iniquitie of the houſe of Iſrael vpon it: according to the number of the dayes that thou ſhalt lie vpon it, thou ſhalt beare their iniquitie.5For I haue layed vpon thee the yeeres of their iniquitie, according to the number of the dayes, three hundreth and ninetie daies. So ſhalt thou beare the iniquitie of the houſe of Iſrael.6And when thou haſt accompliſhed them, lie againe on thy right ſide, and thou ſhalt beare the iniquitie of the houſe of Iudah fourtie dayes: I haue appointed thee each day for a yeere.7Therefore thou ſhalt ſet thy face toward the ſiege of Ieruſalem, and thine arme ſhalbe vncouered, and thou ſhalt prophecie againſt it.8And behold, I wil lay bands vpon thee, and thou ſhalt not turne thee from one ſide to an other, till thou haſt ended the dayes of thy ſiege.9Take thou alſo vnto thee wheat, and barley, and beanes, and lentils, and millet, and fitches, and put them in one veſſell, and make thee bread thereof according to the number of the dayes that thou ſhalt lie vpon thy ſide; three hundreth and ninetie dayes ſhalt thou eate thereof.10And thy meate which thou ſhalt eat, ſhalbe by weight twentie ſhekels a day: from time to time ſhalt thou eat it.11Thou ſhalt drinke alſo water by meaſure, the ſixt part of an hin: from time to time ſhalt thou drinke.12And thou ſhalt eate it as barley cakes, & thou ſhalt bake it with doung that commeth out of man in their ſight.13And the Lord ſaid, Euen thus ſhall the children of Iſrael eat their defiled bread among the Gentiles, whither I will driue them.14Then ſaid I, Ah Lord God, behold, my ſoule hath not bene polluted: for from my youth vp euen til now, haue I not eaten of that which dieth of it ſelfe, or is torne in pieces, neither came there abominable fleſh into my mouth.15Then he ſaid vnto me, Loe, I haue giuen thee cowes doung for mans doung and thou ſhalt prepare thy bread therewith.16Moreouer he ſaid vnto me, Sonne of man, behold, I wil breake the ſtaffe of bread in Ieruſalem, and they ſhall eat bread by weight, and with care, and they ſhal drinke water by meaſure, and with aſtoniſhment:17That they may want bread and water, & be aſtonied one with an other, and conſume away for their iniquitie.

CHAPTER 51And thou ſonne of man, take thee a ſharpe knife, take
thee a barbours raſor, and cauſe it to paſſe vpon thine head and vpon
thy beard: then take the ballances to weigh, and diuide the haire.2Thou
ſhalt burne with fire a third part in the midſt of the city, when the dayes
of the ſiege are fulfilled, and thou ſhalt take a third part, and ſmite about
it with a knife, and a third part thou ſhalt ſcatter in the winde, and I will
draw out a ſword after them.3Thou ſhalt alſo take thereof a few in
number, and bind them in thy ſkirts.4Then take of them againe, and caſt
them into the midſt of the fire, and burne them in the fire: for thereof
ſhall a fire come foorth into all the houſe of Iſrael.5Thus ſaith the Lord
God; This is Ieruſalem: I haue ſet it in the midſt of the nations and
countreys that are round about her.6And ſhe hath changed my
iudgements into wickedneſſe more then the nations, and my ſtatutes
more then the countreyes that are round about her: for they haue refuſed
my iudgements and my ſtatutes, they haue not walked in
them.7Therefore thus ſaith the Lord God, Becauſe yee multiplied more
then the nations that are round about you, and haue not walked in my
Statutes, neither haue kept my iudgments, neither haue done according
to the iudgements of the nations that are round about you:8Therefore
thus ſaith the Lord God, Behold, I, euen I am againſt thee, and will
execute iudgements in the midſt of thee in the ſight of the nations.9And
I will doe in thee that which I haue not done, and whereunto I will not
doe any more the like, becauſe of all thine abominations.10Therefore the
fathers ſhall eate the ſonnes in the midſt of thee, and the ſonnes ſhall
eate their fathers, and I will execute iudgements in thee, and the whole
remnant of thee will I ſcatter into all the windes.11Wherefore, as I liue,
ſaith the Lord God, Surely becauſe thou haſt defiled my Sanctuary with
all thy deteſtable things, and with all thine abominations, therefore will
I alſo diminiſh thee, neither ſhall mine eye ſpare, neither will I haue any
pitie.12A third part of thee ſhall die with the peſtilence, and with famine
ſhall they be conſumed in the middeſt of thee: and a third part ſhall fall
by the ſword round about thee: and I will ſcatter a third part into all the
windes, and I wil draw out a ſword after them.13Thus ſhall mine anger
be accompliſhed, and I will cauſe my fury to reſt vpon them, and I will
be comforted: and they ſhal know that I the Lord haue ſpoken it in my
zeale, when I haue accompliſhed my fury in them.14Moreouer I will
make thee waſte, and a reproch among the nations that are round about
thee, in the ſight of all that paſſe by.15So it ſhall bee a reproch and a
taunt, an inſtruction and an aſtoniſhment vnto the nations that are
round about thee, when I ſhall execute iudgments in thee in anger and
in furie, and in furious rebukes: I the Lord haue ſpoken it.16When I ſhall
ſend vpon them the euill arrowes of famine, which ſhall be for their
deſtruction, and which I will ſend to deſtroy you: and I wil increaſe the
famine vpon you, and will breake your ſtaffe of bread.17So will I ſend
vpon you famine, and euill beaſts, and they ſhall bereaue thee, and
peſtilence and blood ſhal paſſe through thee, and I will bring the ſword
vpon thee: I the Lord haue ſpoken it.
CHAPTER 61And the worde of the Lord came vnto mee,
ſaying,2Sonne of man, ſet thy face towardes the mountaines of Iſrael,
and prophecie againſt them,3And ſay, Ye mountaines of Iſrael, Heare
the word of the Lord God, Thus ſaith the Lord God to the mountaines
and to the hilles, to the riuers and to the valleys, Behold, I, euen I will
bring a ſword vpon you, and I will deſtroy your high places.4And your
altars ſhalbe deſolate, and your images ſhall be broken: and I will caſt
downe your ſlaine men before your idoles.5And I will lay the dead
carkeiſes of the children of Iſrael before their idoles, and I will ſcatter
your bones round about your altars.6In all your dwelling places the cities
ſhall be laid waſte, and the high places ſhalbe deſolate, that your altars
may be laid waſte and made deſolate, and your idols may be broken and
ceaſe, and your images may bee cut downe, and your workes may be
aboliſhed.7And the ſlaine ſhall fall in the midſt of you, and ye ſhall
knowe that I am the Lord.8Yet will I leaue a remnant, that he may haue
ſome, that ſhall eſcape the ſword among the nations, when ye ſhalbe
ſcattered through the countreys.9And they that eſcape of you ſhall
remember me among the nations, whither they ſhalbe caried captiues,
becauſe I am broken with their whoriſh heart which hath departed from
me, and with their eyes which goe a whoring after their idoles: and they
ſhall loathe themſelues for the euils which they haue committed in all
their abominations.10And they ſhall know that I am the Lord, and that
I haue not ſaid in vaine, that I would doe this euill vnto them.11Thus
ſayth the Lord God; Smite with thine hand, and ſtampe with thy foot,
and ſay, Alas, for all the euill abominations of the houſe of Iſrael: for
they ſhall fall by the ſword, by the famine, and by the peſtilence.12He
that is farre off ſhall die of the peſtilence, and he that is neere ſhall fall
by the ſword, and hee that remaineth and is beſieged, ſhall die by the
famine: thus will I accompliſh my furie vpon them.13Then ſhal ye know
that I am the Lord, when their ſlaine men ſhalbe among their idoles
round about their altars, vpon euery high hill in all the tops of the
mountaines, and vnder euery greene tree, and vnder euery thicke oke,
the place where they did offer ſweet ſauour to all their idoles.14So will I
ſtretch out my hand vpon them, and make the land deſolate, yea more
deſolate then the wilderneſſe towards Diblath, in all their habitations,
and they ſhall know that I am the Lord.
CHAPTER 71Moreouer the word of the Lord came vnto mee,
ſaying;2Alſo thou ſonne of man, thus ſaith the Lord God vnto the land
of Iſrael, An end, the ende is come vpon the foure corners of the
land.3Now is the ende come vpon thee, and I will ſend mine anger vpon
thee, and will iudge thee according to thy wayes, and will recompenſe
vpon thee all thine abominations.4And mine eye ſhal not ſpare thee,
neither will I haue pitie: but I will recompenſe thy wayes vpon thee, and
thine abominations ſhalbe in the midſt of thee, and yee ſhall know that
I am the Lord.5Thus ſayth the Lord God, An euill, an onely euill, behold,
is come.6An end is come, the end is come, it watcheth for thee, behold,
it is come.7The morning is come vnto thee, O thou that dwelleſt in the
land: the time is come, the day of trouble is neere, and not the ſounding
againe of the mountaines.8Now will I ſhortly powre out my furie vpon
thee, and accompliſh mine anger vpon thee: and I wil iudge thee
according to thy wayes, and will recompenſe thee for all thine
abominations.9And mine eye ſhall not ſpare, neither will I haue pitie: I
will recompenſe thee according to thy wayes, and thine abominations
that are in the middeſt of thee, and yee ſhall know that I am the Lord
that ſmiteth.10Behold the day, behold, it is come, the morning is gone
foorth, the rodde hath bloſsomed, pride hath budded.11Uiolence is riſen
vp into a rod of wickedneſſe: none of them ſhall remaine, nor of their
multitude, nor of any of theirs, neither ſhall there be wailing for
them.12The time is come, the day draweth neere, let not the buyer
reioyce, nor the ſeller mourne: for wrath is vpon all the multitude
thereof.13For the ſeller ſhall not returne to that which is ſolde, although
they were yet aliue: for the viſion is touching the whole multitude
thereof which ſhal not returne: neither ſhall any ſtrengthen himſelfe in
the iniquity of his life.14They haue blowen the trumpet, euen to make all
ready, but none goeth to the battell: for my wrath is vpon all the
multitude thereof.15The ſword is without, and the peſtilence and the
famine within: he that is in the field ſhall die with the ſword, and hee
that is in the city, famine and peſtilence ſhall deuoure him.16But they
that eſcape of them, ſhall eſcape, and ſhall be on the mountaines like
doues of the valleys, all of them mourning, euery one for his
iniquitie.17All hands ſhall be feeble, and all knees ſhalbe weake as
water.18They ſhall alſo girde themſelues with ſackcloth, and horrour
ſhall couer them, and ſhame ſhall be vpon all faces, and baldneſse vpon
all their heads.19They ſhall caſt their ſiluer in the ſtreets, and their golde
ſhalbe remooued: their ſiluer and their golde ſhall not be able to deliuer
them in the day of the wrath of the Lord: they ſhall not ſatiſfie their
ſoules, neither fill their bowels: becauſe it is the ſtumbling blocke of their
iniquitie.20As for the beautie of his ornament, he ſet it in maieſtie: but
they made the images of their abominations, and of their deteſtable
things therein: therefore haue I ſet it farre from them.21And I will giue
it into the hands of the ſtrangers for a pray, and to the wicked of the
earth for a ſpoile, and they ſhall pollute it.22My face will I turne alſo from
them, and they ſhall pollute my ſecret place: for the robbers ſhall enter
into it and defile it.23Make a chaine: for the land is full of bloody crimes,
the citie is full of violence.24Wherfore I will bring the worſt of the
heathen, and they ſhall poſſeſſe their houſes: I will alſo make the pompe
of the ſtrong to ceaſe, and their holy places ſhall be defiled.25Deſtruction
commeth, and they ſhall ſeeke peace, and there ſhall be none.26Miſchiefe
ſhall come vpon miſchiefe, and rumour ſhall be vpon rumour, then ſhall
they ſeeke a viſion of the prophet: but the law ſhall periſh from the
prieſt, and counſell from the ancients.27The king ſhall mourne, and the
prince ſhall be clothed with deſolation, and the hands of the people of
the land ſhall be troubled: I will doe vnto them after their way, and

according to their deſerts will I iudge them, and they ſhall know that I
am the Lord.
CHAPTER 8 1And it came to paſſe in the ſixt yeere, in the ſixt moneth,
in the fift day of the month, as I ſate in mine houſe, and the elders of
Iudah ſate before me; that the hand of the Lord God fell there vpon
me.2Then I beheld, and loe, a likeneſſe as the appearance of fire: from
the appearance of his loines euen downeward, fire: and from his loines
euen vpward, as the appearance of brightneſse, as the colour of
amber.3And he put forth the forme of an hand, and tooke me by a locke
of mine head, and the ſpirit lift me vp betweene the earth and the
heauen, and brought me in the viſions of God to Ieruſalem, to the doore
of the inner gate, that looketh toward the North, where was the ſeate of
the image of ielouſie, which prouoketh to ielouſie.4And behold, the
glory of the God of Iſrael was there according to the viſion that I ſaw in
the plaine.5Then ſaid he vnto me, Sonne of man, lift vp thine eyes now
the way towards the North: ſo I lift vp mine eyes the way toward the
North, and behold, Northward at the gate of the altar, this image of
ielouſie in the entry.6He ſaid furthermore vnto me, Sonne of man, ſeeſt
thou what they doe? euen the great abominations that the houſe of Iſrael
committeth heere, that I ſhould goe farre off from my ſanctuarie? but
turne thee yet againe, and thou ſhalt ſee greater abominations.7And hee
brought me to the doore of the court, and when I looked, behold a hole
in the wall.8Then ſaid he vnto me, Sonne of man, digge now in the wall:
and when I had digged in the wall, behold a doore.9And he ſaid vnto
me, Goe in, and behold the wicked abominations that they doe
heere.10So I went in and ſaw, and behold euery forme of creeping things,
and abominable beaſts, and all the idols of the houſe of Iſrael purtrayed
vpon the wall round about.11And there ſtood before them ſeuentie men
of the ancients of the houſe of Iſrael, and in the middeſt of them ſtood
Iaazaniah the ſonne of Shaphan, with euery man his cenſer in his hand,
and a thicke cloud of incenſe went vp.12Then ſaid he vnto me, Sonne of
man, haſt thou ſeene what the ancients of the houſe of Iſrael doe in the
darke, euery man in the chambers of his imagery? for they ſay, The Lord
ſeeth vs not, the Lord hath forſaken the earth.13Hee ſaid alſo vnto me,
Turne thee yet againe, and thou ſhalt ſee greater abominations that they
doe.14Then he brought me to the doore of the gate of the Lords houſe
which was towards the North, and behold, there ſate women weeping
for Tammuz.15Then ſaid hee vnto me, Haſt thou ſeene this, O ſonne of
man? Turne thee yet againe, and thou ſhalt ſee greater abominations
then theſe.16And he brought me into the inner court of the Lords houſe,
and behold at the doore of the Temple of the Lord, betweene the porch
and the altar, were about fiue and twentie men, with their backes toward
the temple of the Lord, and their faces towards the Eaſt, and they
worſhipped the ſunne towards the Eaſt.17Then he ſaid vnto me, Haſt
thou ſeene this, O ſonne of man? Is it a light thing to the houſe of Iudah,
that they commit the abominations, which they commit heere? for they
haue filled the land with violence, and haue returned to prouoke me to
anger: and loe, they put the branch to their noſe.18Therefore will I alſo
deale in furie: mine eye ſhall not ſpare, neither will I haue pitie: and
though they crie in mine eares with a loud voyce, yet will I not heare
them.
CHAPTER 9 1Hee cryed alſo in mine eares, with a loude voyce, ſaying;
Cauſe them that hauecharge ouer the citie, to draw neere, euen euery
man with his deſtroying weapon in his hand.2And behold, ſixe men
came from the way of the higher gate, which lyeth toward the North,
and euery man a ſlaughter weapon in his hand: and one man among
them was clothed with linnen, with a writers inkehorne by his ſide, and
they went in and ſtood beſide the braſen altar.3And the glory of the God
of Iſrael was gone vp from the Cherub whereupon hee was, to the
threſhold of the houſe, and he called to the man clothed with linnen,
which had the writers inkehorne by his ſide.4And the Lord ſayd vnto
him, Goe through the middeſt of the citie, through the middeſt of
Ieruſalem, and ſet a marke vpon the foreheads of the men that ſigh, and
that cry for all the abominations, that bee done in the middeſt
thereof.5And to the others he ſaid in mine hearing, Goe ye after him
through the citie, and ſmite: let not your eye ſpare, neither haue ye
pitie.6Slay vtterly olde and yong; both maides, and litle children, and
women: but come not neere any man vpon whom is the marke, and
begin at my ſanctuary: then they began at the ancient men which were
before the houſe.7And hee ſayd vnto them, Defile the houſe, and fill the
courts with the ſlaine, goe ye forth: and they went forth and ſlew in the
citie.8And it came to paſſe while they were ſlaying them, and I was left,
that I fell vpon my face, and cryed and ſaid, Ah, Lord God, wilt thou
deſtroy all the reſidue of Iſrael, in thy powring out of thy fury vpon
Ieruſalem?9Then ſayd he vnto me; The iniquity of the houſe of Iſrael
and Iudah is exceeding great, and the land is full of blood, and the citie
full of peruerſeneſse: for they ſay; The Lord hath forſaken the earth, and
the Lord ſeeth not.10And as for me alſo, mine eye ſhal not ſpare, neither
will I haue pitie, but I will recompence their way vpon their head.11And
behold, the man clothed with linnen, which had the inkehorne by his
ſide, reported the matter, ſaying; I haue done as thou haſt commanded
me.
CHAPTER 10 1Then I looked, and beholde, in the firmament that was
aboue the head of the Cherubims, there appeared ouer them as it were
a Saphir ſtone, as the appearance of the likeneſſe of a throne.2And hee
ſpake vnto the man clothed with linnen, and ſayd, Goe in between the
wheeles, euen vnder the Cherub, and fill thine hand with coales of fire
from betweene the Cherubims, and ſcatter them ouer the city. And he
went in my ſight.3Now the Cherubims ſtood on the right ſide of the
houſe, when the man went in, and the cloud filled the inner court.4Then
the glory of the Lord went vp from the Cherub, and ſtood ouer the
threſhold of the houſe, and the houſe was filled with the cloud, and the
court was full of the brightneſse of the Lords glory.5And the ſound of
the Cherubims wings was heard euen to the vtter court, as the voice of
the Almighty God when he ſpeaketh.6And it came to paſſe that when
he had commanded the man clothed with linnen, ſaying; Take fire from
betweene the wheeles, from betweene the Cherubims; then he went in
and ſtood beſide the wheeles.7And one Cherub ſtretched forth his hand
from betweene the Cherubims vnto the fire that was betweene the
Cherubims: and tooke thereof, and put it into the handes of him that
was clothed with linnen, who tooke it, and went out.8And there
appeared in the Cherubims, the forme of a mans hand vnder their
wings.9And when I looked, behold the foure wheeles by the Cherubims,
one wheele by one Cherub, and an other wheele by an other Cherub:
and the appearance of the wheeles was as the colour of a Berill
ſtone.10And as for their appearances, they foure had one likenes as if a
wheele had bene in the midſt of a wheele.11When they went, they went
vpon their foure ſides; they turned not as they went, but to the place
whither the head looked, they followed it; they turned not as they
went.12And their whole body, and their backes, and their handes, and
their wings, and the wheeles, were ful of eyes round about, euen the
wheeles that they foure had.13As for the wheeles, it was cried vnto them
in my hearing, O wheele.14And euery one had foure faces: the firſt face
was the face of a Cherub, and the ſecond face was the face of a man,
and the third the face of a lion, and the fourth the face of an eagle.15And
the Cherubims were lifted vp, this is the liuing creature that I ſaw by the
riuer of Chebar.16And when the Cherubims went, the wheeles went by
them: and when the Cherubims lift vp their wings, to mount vp from
the earth, the ſame wheels alſo turned not frō beſide them.17When they
ſtood, theſe ſtood, and when they were lifted vp, theſe lift vp themſelues
alſo: for the ſpirit of the liuing creature was in them.18Then the glory of
the Lord departed from off the threſhold of the houſe, and ſtood ouer
the Cherubims.19And the Cherubims lift vp their wings, and mounted
vp from the earth in my ſight: when they went out, the wheeles alſo were
beſides them, and euery one ſtood at the doore of the Eaſt gate of the
Lords houſe, and the glorie of the God of Iſrael was ouer them
aboue.20This is the liuing creature that I ſaw vnder the God of Iſrael, by
the riuer of Chebar, and I knew that they were the Cherubims.21Euery
one had foure faces a piece, and euery one foure wings, and the likeneſſe
of the handes of a man was vnder their wings.22And the likeneſſe of
their faces was the ſame faces which I ſaw by the riuer of Chebar, their
appearances and themſelues: they went euery one ſtraight forward.
CHAPTER 11 1Moreouer the Spirit lift me vp, and brought me vnto
the Eaſt gate of the Lords houſe, which looketh Eaſtward: and behold
at the doore of the gate fiue and twenty men; among whom I ſaw
Iaazaniah the ſonne of Azur, and Pelatiah the ſonne of Benaiah, Princes
of the people.2Then ſaid he vnto me; Sonne of man, theſe are the men
that deuiſe miſchiefe, & giue wicked counſel in this city.3Which ſay, It is
not neere, let vs build houſes: this citie is the caldron, and we be the
fleſh.4Therefore prophecie againſt them, prophecie, O ſonne of

man. 5 And the Spirit of the Lord fell vpon me, and ſaid vnto me, Speake,
thus ſaith the Lord; Thus haue ye ſaid, O houſe of Iſrael: for I know the
things that come into your minde, euery one of them. 6 Ye haue
multiplyed your ſlaine in this citie, and yee haue filled the ſtreetes thereof
with the ſlaine. 7 Therefore thus ſayth the Lord God; Your ſlaine whom
ye haue laid in the middeſt of it, they are the fleſh, and this citie is the
cauldron: but I wil bring you foorth out of the middeſt of it. 8 Ye haue
feared the ſword, and I will bring a ſword vpon you, ſaith the Lord
God. 9 And I will bring you out of the middeſt thereof, and deliuer you
into the hands of ſtrangers, and will execute iudgements among
you. 10 Yee ſhall fall by the ſword, I will iudge you in the border of Iſrael,
and ye ſhall know that I am the Lord. 11 This citie ſhall not be your
cauldron, neither ſhall ye be the fleſh in the middeſt thereof, but I will
iudge you in the border of Iſrael. 12 And ye ſhall know that I am the Lord:
for yee haue not walked in my ſtatutes, neither executed my iudgements,
but haue done after the maners of the heathen that are round about
you. 13 And it came to paſſe, when I prophecied, that Pelatiah the ſonne
of Benaiah died: then fell I downe vpon my face, and cried with a loud
voice, and ſaid; Ah Lord God, wilt thou make a full end of the remnant
of Iſrael? 14 Againe the word of the Lord came vnto me, ſaying; 15 Sonne
of man, thy brethren, euen thy brethren, the men of thy kinred, and all
the houſe of Iſrael wholly are they, vnto whom the inhabitants of
Ieruſalem haue ſayd; Get yee farre from the Lord: vnto vs is this land
giuen in poſſeſſion. 16 Therefore ſay, Thus ſayth the Lord God; Although
I haue caſt them farre off among the heathen, and although I haue
ſcattered them among the countreys, yet will I be to them as a little
Sanctuarie in the countreys where they ſhall come. 17 Therefore ſay, Thus
ſaith the Lord God; I will euen gather you from the people, and aſſemble
you out of the countreys where ye haue beene ſcattered, and I will giue
you the land of Iſrael. 18 And they ſhall come thither, and they ſhall take
away all the deteſtable things thereof, and all the abominations thereof
from thence. 19 And I wil giue them one heart, and I wil put a new ſpirit
within you: and I will take the ſtonie heart out of their fleſh, and will
giue them an heart of fleſh, 20 That they may walke in my ſtatutes, and
keepe mine ordinances, and doe them: and they ſhall be my people, and
I will be their God. 21 But as for them whoſe heart walketh after the heart
of their deteſtable things, and their abominations, I wil recompenſe their
way vpon their owne heads, ſaith the Lord God. 22 Then did the
Cherubims lift vp their wings, and the wheeles beſides them, and the
glory of the God of Iſrael was ouer them aboue. 23 And the glory of the
Lord went vp from the middeſt of the citie, and ſtood vpon the
mountaine, which is on the Eaſt ſide of the citie. 24 Afterwards the ſpirit
tooke me vp, and brought me in viſion by the ſpirit of God into Caldea
to them of the captiuity: ſo the viſion that I had ſeene, went vp from
me. 25 Then I ſpake vnto them of the captiuity, all the things that the
Lord had ſhewed me.
CHAPTER 12 1 The word of the Lord alſo came vnto me, ſaying; 2 Sonne
of man, thou dwelleſt in the middeſt of a rebellious houſe, which haue
eyes to ſee, and ſee not: they haue eares to heare, and heare not: for they
are a rebellious houſe. 3 Therefore thou ſonne of man, prepare thee ſtuffe
for remoouing, and remooue by day in their ſight, and thou ſhalt remoue
from thy place to another place in their ſight; it may be they will
conſider, though they bee a rebellious houſe. 4 Then ſhalt thou bring
foorth thy ſtuffe by day in their ſight, as ſtuffe for remoouing: and thou
ſhalt goe foorth at euen in their ſight, as they that goe foorth into
captiuitie. 5 Digge thou through the wall in their ſight, and cary out
thereby. 6 In their ſight ſhalt thou beare it vpon thy ſhoulders , and cary
it foorth in the twy light: thou ſhalt couer thy face, that thou ſee not the
ground: for I haue ſet thee for a ſigne vnto the houſe of Iſrael. 7 And I
did ſo as I was commanded: I brought forth my ſtuffe by day, as ſtuffe
for captiuity, and in the euen I digged through the wall with mine hand,
I brought it foorth in the twy light, and I bare it vpon my ſhoulder in
their ſight. 8 And in the morning came the word of the Lord vnto me,
ſaying, 9 Sonne of man, hath not the houſe of Iſrael, the rebellious houſe,
ſayd vnto thee, What doeſt thou? 10 ſay thou vnto them; Thus ſaith the
Lord God; This burden concerneth the Prince in Ieruſalem, and all the
houſe of Iſrael that are among them. 11 Say, I am your ſigne: like as I haue
done, ſo ſhall it be done vnto them: they ſhall remooue and goe into
captiuitie. 12 And the Prince that is among them, ſhall beare vpon his
ſhoulder in the twylight, and ſhall goe forth: they ſhall digge through the
wall to cary out thereby: he ſhall couer his face, that he ſee not the
ground with his eyes. 13 My net alſo will I ſpread vpon him, and he ſhall
be taken in my ſnare, and I wil bring him to Babylon to the land of the
Caldeans, yet ſhall hee not ſee it, though he ſhall die there. 14 And I will
ſcatter toward euery winde all that are about him to helpe him, and all
his bands, and I wil draw out the ſword after them. 15 And they ſhall
know that I am the Lord, when I ſhal ſcatter them among the nations,
and diſperſe them in the countreys. 16 But I will leaue a few men of them
from the ſword, from the famine, and from the peſtilence, that they may
declare all their abominations among the heathen whither they come,
and they ſhall know that I am the Lord. 17 Moreouer, the worde of the
Lord came to me, ſaying; 18 Sonne of man, eate thy bread with quaking,
and drinke thy water with trembling and with carefulneſse, 19 And ſay
vnto the people of the land; Thus ſayth the Lord God, of the inhabitants
of Ieruſalem, and of the land of Iſrael; They ſhall eat their bread with
carefulnes, and drinke their water with aſtoniſhment, that her land may
be deſolate from all that is therein, becauſe of the violence of them that
dwell therein. 20 And the cities that are inhabited, ſhall be laid waſte, and
the land ſhall be deſolate, and yee ſhall know that I am the Lord. 21 And
the word of the Lord came vnto me, ſaying; 22 Sonne of man, what is that
prouerbe, that ye haue in the land of Iſrael, ſaying; The dayes are
prolonged, and euery viſion faileth? 23 Tell them therefore, Thus ſayth the
Lord God; I will make this prouerbe to ceaſe, and they ſhall no more
vſe it as a prouerbe in Iſrael: but ſay vnto them, The dayes are at hand,
and the effect of euery viſion. 24 For there ſhall bee no more any vaine
viſion, nor flattering diuination, within the houſe of Iſrael. 25 For I am
the Lord: I will ſpeake, & the word that I ſhall ſpeake, ſhall come to
paſſe: it ſhall be no more prolonged: for in your dayes, O rebellious
houſe, will I ſay the word, and will performe it, ſayth the Lord
God. 26 Againe the word of the Lord came to me, ſaying; 27 Sonne of man,
behold, they of the houſe of Iſrael ſay; The viſion that he ſeeth is for
many dayes to come, and he prophecieth of the times that are far
off. 28 Therefore ſay vnto them, Thus ſaith the Lord God, There ſhal
none of my words be prolonged any more, but the worde which I haue
ſpoken, ſhall be done, ſayth the Lord God.
CHAPTER 13 1 And the worde of the Lord came vnto mee,
ſaying; 2 Sonne of man, prophecie againſt the Prophets of Iſrael that
prophecie, and ſay thou vnto them that prophecie out of their owne
hearts, Heare ye the word of the Lord. 3 Thus ſaith the Lord God; Woe
vnto the fooliſh prophets, that follow their owne ſpirit, and haue ſeene
nothing. 4 O Iſrael, thy prophets are like the foxes in the deſerts. 5 Yee
haue not gone vp into the gaps, neither made vp the hedge for the houſe
of Iſrael, to ſtand in the battell in the day of the Lord. 6 They haue ſeene
vanity, and lying diuination, ſaying; The Lord ſaith, and the Lord hath
not ſent them: and they haue made others to hope, that they would
confirme the word. 7 Haue ye not ſeene a vaine viſion, and haue ye not
ſpoken a lying diuination, whereas yee ſay, The Lord ſayth it, albeit I
haue not ſpoken? 8 Therefore thus ſaith the Lord God; Becauſe ye haue
ſpoken vanity and ſeene lyes, therefore behold, I am againſt you, ſaith
the Lord God. 9 And mine hand ſhall be vpon the Prophets that ſee
vanitie, and that diuine lyes: they ſhall not bee in the aſſembly of my
people, neither ſhall they be written in the writing of the houſe of Iſrael,
neither ſhall they enter into the land of Iſrael, and ye ſhall know that I
am the Lord God. 10 Becauſe, euen becauſe they haue ſeduced my people,
ſaying; Peace, and there was no peace: and one built vp a wall, and loe,
others dawbed it with vntempered morter, 11 ſay vnto them which dawbe
it with vntempered morter, that it ſhall fall: there ſhall bee an
ouerflowing ſhowre, and yee, O great haile ſtones, ſhal fall, and a ſtormie
wind ſhal rent it. 12 Loe, when the wall is fallen, ſhall it not bee ſayde vnto
you; Where is the dawbing wherwith ye haue dawbed it? 13 Therefore thus
ſayth the Lord God; I will euen rent it with a ſtormie wind in my fury:
and there ſhall be an ouerflowing ſhowre in mine anger, and great
haileſtones in my fury, to conſume it. 14 So wil I breake downe the wall
that ye haue dawbed with vntempered morter, & bring it downe to the
ground, ſo that the foundation thereof ſhall be diſcouered, and it ſhall
fall, and ye ſhall be conſumed in the middeſt thereof: and ye ſhall know
that I am the Lord. 15 Thus will I accompliſh my wrath vpon the wall,
and vpon them that haue dawbed it with vntempered morter, and will
ſay vnto you; The wall is no more, neither they that dawbed it: 16 To wit,
the Prophets of Iſrael which prophecie concerning Ieruſalem, and which

ſee viſions of peace for her, and there is no peace, ſayth the Lord God.17Likewiſe thou ſonne of man, ſet thy face againſt the daughters of thy people; which prophecie out of their owne heart, and prophecie thou againſt them,18And ſay, Thus ſaith the Lord God; Woe to the women that ſow pillowes to all arme holes, and make kerchiefes vpon the head of euery ſtature to hunt ſoules: Will ye hunt the ſoules of my people, and will yee ſaue the ſoules aliue that come vnto you?19And will yee pollute me among my people for handfuls of barley, and for pieces of bread, to ſlay the ſoules that ſhould not die, and to ſaue the ſoules aliue that ſhould not liue, by your lying to my people that heare your lyes?20Wherefore thus ſayth the Lord God, Behold, I am againſt your pillowes, wherewith yee there hunt the ſoules to make them flie, and I will teare them from your armes, and will let the ſoules goe, euen the ſoules that ye hunt to make them flie.21Your kerchiefes alſo will I teare, and deliuer my people out of your hand, and they ſhalbe no more in your hand to be hunted, and yee ſhall know that I am the Lord.22Becauſe with lyes yee haue made the heart of the righteous ſad whom I haue not made ſad; and ſtrengthened the hands of the wicked, that hee ſhould not returne from his wicked way by promiſing him life:23Therefore yee ſhall ſee no more vanitie, nor diuine diuinations, for I will deliuer my people out of your hand, and ye ſhall knowe that I am the Lord. par

CHAPTER 141Then came certaine of the Elders of Iſrael vnto me, and ſate before me.2And the word of the Lord came vnto me, ſaying,3Sonne of man, theſe men haue ſet vp their idoles in their heart, and put the ſtumbling blocke of their iniquitie before their face: ſhould I be enquired of at all by them?4Therefore ſpeake vnto them, and ſay vnto them, Thus ſaith the Lord God; Euery man of the houſe of Iſrael that ſetteth vp his idoles in his heart, and putteth the ſtumbling blocke of his iniquitie before his face, and commeth to the Prophet, I the Lord will anſwere him that commeth, according to the multitude of his idoles,5That I may take the houſe of Iſrael in their owne heart, becauſe they are all eſtranged from mee through their idoles.6Therefore ſay vnto the houſe of Iſrael, Thus ſaith the Lord God, Repent, and turne your ſelues from your idoles, and turne away your faces from all your abominations.7For euery one of the houſe of Iſrael, or of the ſtranger that ſoiourneth in Iſrael, which ſeparateth himſelfe from me, and ſetteth vp his idols in his heart, and putteth the ſtumbling blocke of his iniquitie before his face, and commeth to a prophet to enquire of him concerning me, I the Lord will anſwere him by my ſelfe.8And I wil ſet my face againſt that man, and will make him a ſigne and a prouerbe, and I will cut him off from the midſt of my people, and yee ſhall know that I am the Lord.9And if the prophet bee deceiued when hee hath ſpoken a thing, I the Lord haue deceiued that prophet, and I will ſtretch out my hand vpon him, and will deſtroy him from the midſt of my people Iſrael.10And they ſhall beare the puniſhment of their iniquitie: the puniſhment of the prophet ſhall bee euen as the puniſhment of him that ſeeketh vnto him:11That the houſe of Iſrael may goe no more aſtray from me, neither be polluted any more with all their tranſgreſſions; but that they may be my people, and I may bee their God, ſayeth the Lord God.12The word of the Lord came againe to me, ſaying,13Sonne of man, when the land ſinneth againſt mee by treſpaſsing grieuouſly, then will I ſtretch out mine hand vpon it, and will breake the ſtaffe of the bread thereof, and will ſend famine vpon it, and will cut off man and beaſt from it.14Though theſe three men, Noah, Daniel and Iob were in it, they ſhould deliuer but their owne ſoules by their righteouſnes, ſaith the Lord God.15If I cauſe noiſome beaſtes to paſſe through the land, and they ſpoile it, ſo that it bee deſolate, that no man may paſſe through becauſe of the beaſts:16Though theſe three men were in it, as I liue, ſaith the Lord God, they ſhall deliuer neither ſonnes nor daughters: they onely ſhalbe deliuered, but the land ſhalbe deſolate.17Or if I bring a ſword vpon that land, and ſay, Sword, goe through the lande, ſo that I cut off man and beaſt from it:18Though theſe three men were in it, as I liue, ſaith the Lord God, they ſhall deliuer neither ſonnes nor daughter, but they onely ſhall bee deliuered themſelues.19Or if I ſend a peſtilence into that land, and powre out my fury vpon it in blood, to cut off from it man and beaſt:20Though Noah, Daniel and Iob were in it, as I liue, ſaith the Lord God, they ſhal deliuer neither ſon nor daughter: they ſhall but deliuer their owne ſoules by their righteouſnes.21For thus ſaith the Lord God, How much more when I ſend my foure ſore iudgements vpon Ieruſalem; the ſword, and the famine, and the noiſome beaſt, and the peſtilence, to cut off from it man and beaſt?22Yet behold, therein ſhalbe left a remnant that ſhalbe brought foorth, both ſonnes and daughters: behold, they ſhall come foorth vnto you, and ye ſhall ſee their way and their doings: and ye ſhalbe comforted concerning the euill that I haue brought vpon Ieruſalem, euen concerning all that I haue brought vpon it.23And they ſhall comfort you when yee ſee their wayes and their doings: and ye ſhal know that I haue not done without cauſe, all that I haue done in it, ſaith the Lord God.

CHAPTER 151And the word of þe Lord came vnto me, ſaying.2Sonne of man, What is the Uine tree more then any tree, or then a branch which is among the trees of the forreſt?3Shall wood bee taken thereof to doe any worke? or, will men take a pin of it, to hang any veſſell thereon?4Behold, it is caſt into the fire for fewell: the fire deuoureth both the ends of it, and the middeſt of it is burnt. Is it meete for any worke?5Behold, when it was whole it was meete for no worke: how much leſſe ſhall it be meete yet for any worke, when the fire hath deuoured it, and it is burned?6Therefore thus ſaith the Lord God; As the Uine tree among the trees of the forreſt, which I haue giuen to the fire for fewell, ſo will I giue the inhabitants of Ieruſalem.7And I will ſet my face againſt them, they ſhall goe out from one fire, and another fire ſhall deuoure them, and ye ſhall know that I am the Lord, when I ſet my face againſt them.8And I will make the land deſolate, becauſe they haue committed a treſpaſſe, ſaith the Lord God.

CHAPTER 161Againe the worde of the Lord came vnto me, ſaying;2Son of man, cauſe Ieruſalem to know her abominations,3And ſay, Thus ſaith the Lord God vnto Ieruſalem; Thy birth and thy natiuitie is of the land of Canaan, thy father was an Amorite, and thy mother an Hittite.4And as for thy natiuity in the day thou waſt borne, thy nauell was not cut, neither waſt thou waſhed in water to ſupple thee: thou waſt not ſalted at all, nor ſwadled at all.5None eye pitied thee to doe any of theſe vnto thee, to haue compaſſion vpon thee, but thou waſt caſt out in the open field, to the lothing of thy perſon, in the day that thou waſt borne.6And when I paſſed by thee, and ſaw thee polluted in thine owne blood, I ſaid vnto thee when thou waſt in thy blood, Liue: yea I ſaid vnto thee when thou waſt in thy blood, Liue.7I haue cauſed thee to multiply as the bud of the field, and thou haſt increaſed and waxen great, and thou art come to excellent ornaments: thy breaſts are faſhioned, and thine haire is growen, whereas thou waſt naked and bare.8Now when I paſſed by thee, and looked vpon thee, behold, thy time was the time of loue, and I ſpread my ſkirt ouer thee, and couered thy nakedneſse: yea, I ſware vnto thee, and entred into a couenant with thee, ſayth the Lord God, and thou becameſt mine.9Then waſhed I thee with water: yea, I throughly waſhed away thy blood from thee, and I anointed thee with oyle.10I clothed thee alſo with broidred worke, & ſhod thee with badgers ſkin, and I girded thee about with fine linen, and I couered thee with ſilke.11I decked thee alſo with ornaments, and I put bracelets vpon thine hands, and a chaine on thy necke.12And I put a iewell on thy forehead, and eare-rings in thine eares, and a beautifull crowne vpon thine head.13Thus waſt thou decked with gold and ſiluer, and thy raiment was of fine linen & ſilke, and broidered worke, thou didſt eate fine floure and honie and oyle, and thou waſt exceeding beautiful, and thou didſt proſper into a kingdome.14And thy renowme went foorth among the heathen for thy beautie: for it was perfect through my comelineſse which I had put vpon thee, ſayth the Lord God.15But thou diddeſt truſt in thine owne beauty, and playedſt the harlot, becauſe of thy renowne, and powredſt out thy fornications on euery one that paſſed by; his it was.16And of thy garments thou diddeſt take, and deckedſt thy high places with diuers colours, and playedſt the harlot thereupon: the like things ſhall not come, neither ſhall it be ſo.17Thou haſt alſo taken thy faire iewels of my gold and of my ſiluer, which I had giuen thee, and madeſt to thy ſelfe images of men, and diddeſt commit whoredome with them,18And tookeſt thy broidered garments and coueredſt them: and thou haſt ſet mine oyle and mine incenſe before them.19My meate alſo which I gaue thee, fine flowre, and oyle, and honie wherewith I fed thee, thou haſt euen ſet it before them for a ſweete ſauour: and thus it was, ſaith the Lord God.20Moreouer thou haſt taken thy ſonnes and thy daughters, whom thou haſt borne vnto me, and theſe haſt thou ſacrificed vnto them to be deuoured: is this of thy whoredomes a ſmall matter,21That thou haſt ſlaine my children, and deliuered them to cauſe them to paſſe through the fire for them?22And in all thine abominations and thy whooredomes, thou haſt not remembred the dayes of thy youth,

when thou waſt naked and bare, and waſt polluted in thy blood.23And it
came to paſſe after all thy wickedneſſe (woe, woe vnto thee, ſaith the
Lord God.)24That thou haſt alſo built vnto thee an eminent place, and
haſt made thee an high place in euery ſtreete.25Thou haſt built thy high
place at euery head of the way, and haſt made thy beauty to be abhorred,
and haſt opened thy feete to euery one that paſſed by, and multiplied
thy whooredomes.26Thou haſt alſo committed fornication with the
Egyptians thy neighbours great of fleſh, & haſt increaſed thy
whooredomes, to prouoke me to anger.27Behold therefore, I haue
ſtretched out my hand ouer thee, and haue diminiſhed thine ordinarie
foode, and deliuered thee vnto the will of them that hate thee, the
daughters of the Philiſtines, which are aſhamed of thy lewd way.28Thou
haſt played the whoore alſo with the Aſſyrians, becauſe thou waſt
vnſatiable: yea thou haſt played the harlot with them, and yet couldeſt
not be ſatiſfied.29Thou haſt moreouer multiplied thy fornication in the
land of Canaan vnto Caldea, and yet thou waſt not ſatiſfied
heerewith.30How weake is thine heart, ſaith the Lord God, ſeeing thou
doeſt all theſe things, the work of an imperious whoriſh woman?31In
that thou buildeſt thine eminent place in the head of euery way, and
makeſt thine high place in euery ſtreete, and haſt not beene as an harlot,
in that thou ſcorneſt hire:32But as a wife that committeth adulterie,
which taketh ſtrangers in ſteede of her huſband.33They giue gifts to all
whores, but thou giueſt thy gifts to all thy louers, and hyreſt them, that
they may come vnto thee on euery ſide for thy whoredome.34And the
contrary is in thee from other women in thy whoredomes, whereas none
followeth thee to commit whoredomes: and in that thou giueſt a reward,
and no reward is giuen vnto thee: therefore thou art
contrary.35Wherefore, O harlot, heare the word of the Lord.36Thus ſaith
the Lord God; Becauſe thy filthineſse was powred out, and thy
nakedneſſe diſcouered through thy whoredomes with thy louers, and
with all the idols of thy abominations, and by the blood of thy children,
which thou diddeſt giue vnto them,37Behold therefore, I will gather all
thy louers, with whom thou haſt taken pleaſure, and all them that thou
haſt loued, with all them that thou haſt hated: I will euen gather them
round about againſt thee, and will diſcouer thy nakedneſſe vnto them,
that they may ſee all thy nakedneſse.38And I will iudge thee, as women
that breake wedlocke and ſhead blood are iudged, and I will giue thee
blood in fury and iealouſie.39And I will alſo giue thee into their hand,
and they ſhal throw downe thine eminent place, and ſhall breake downe
thy high places: they ſhall ſtrip thee alſo of thy clothes, and ſhall take thy
faire iewels, and leaue thee naked and bare.40They ſhall alſo bring vp a
companie againſt thee, and they ſhall ſtone thee with ſtones, and thruſt
thee thorough with their ſwords.41And they ſhall burne thine houſes
with fire, and execute iudgements vpon thee in the ſight of many
women: and I wil cauſe thee to ceaſe from playing the harlot, and thou
alſo ſhalt giue no hire any more.42So will I make my fury towards thee
to reſt, and my iealouſie ſhall depart from thee, and I will be quiet, and
will be no more angry.43Becauſe thou haſt not remembred the dayes of
thy youth, but haſt fretted mee in all theſe things; behold therefore, I
alſo will recompence thy way vpon thine head, ſaith the Lord God: and
thou ſhalt not commit this lewdneſse, aboue all thine
abominations.44Behold, euery one that vſeth prouerbs, ſhall vſe this
prouerbe againſt thee, ſaying, As is the mother, ſo is her
daughter.45Thou art thy mothers daughter, that lotheth her huſband and
her children, and thou art the ſiſter of thy ſiſters which lothed their
huſbands, and their children: your mother was an Hittite, and your
father an Amorite.46And thine elder ſiſter is Samaria, ſhe and her
daughters, that dwell at thy left hand: and thy younger ſiſter that dwelleth
at thy right hand, is Sodom and her daughters.47Yet haſt thou not
walked after their wayes, nor done after their abominations: but as if
that were a very litle thing, thou waſt corrupted more then they in all thy
wayes.48As I liue, ſaith the Lord God, Sodom thy ſiſter hath not done,
ſhe nor her daughters, as thou haſt done, thou and thy
daughters.49Behold, this was the iniquitie of thy ſiſter Sodom; Pride,
fulneſse of bread, and aboundance of idleneſse was in her and in her
daughters, neither did ſhe ſtrengthen the hand of the poore and
needy.50And they were hautie, and committed abomination before me:
therefore I tooke them away, as I ſaw good.51Neither hath Samaria
committed halfe of thy ſinnes, but thou haſt multiplied thine
abominations more then they, and haſt iuſtified thy ſiſters in all thine
abominations, which thou haſt done.52Thou alſo which haſt iudged thy
ſiſters, beare thine owne ſhame for thy ſinnes, that thou haſt committed
more abominable then they: they are more righteous then thou: yea be
thou confounded alſo, and beare thy ſhame, in that thou haſt iuſtified
thy ſiſters.53When I ſhall bring againe their captiuitie, the captiuitie of
Sodom and her daughters, and the captiuitie of Samaria and her
daughters, then will I bring againe the captiuity of thy captiues in the
midſt of them;54That thou mayeſt beare thine owne ſhame, and mayeſt
be confounded in all that thou haſt done, in that thou art a comfort vnto
them.55When thy ſiſters, Sodom and her daughters ſhal returne to their
former eſtate, and Samaria and her daughters ſhall returne to their
former eſtate, then thou and thy daughters ſhall returne to your former
eſtate.56For thy ſiſter Sodom was not mentioned by thy mouth in the
day of thy pride;57Before thy wickedneſſe was diſcouered, as at the time
of thy reproch of the daughters of Syria, and all that are round about
her, the daughters of the Philiſtines which deſpiſe thee round
about.58Thou haſt borne thy lewdneſse, and thine abominations, ſaith
the Lord.59For thus ſaith the Lord God; I will euen deale with thee as
thou haſt done, which haſt deſpiſed the oath in breaking the
couenant.60Neuertheleſſe I will remember my couenant with thee in the
dayes of thy youth, and I will eſtabliſh vnto thee an euerlaſting
couenant.61Then thou ſhalt remember thy wayes and be aſhamed, when
thou ſhalt receiue thy ſiſters, thine elder and thy younger, and I will giue
them vnto thee for daughters, but not by thy couenant.62And I will
eſtabliſh my couenant with thee, and thou ſhalt know that I am the
Lord:63That thou mayeſt remember, and bee confounded, and neuer
open thy mouth any more: becauſe of thy ſhame, when I am pacified
toward thee, for all that thou haſt done, ſayeth the Lord God.
CHAPTER 171And the word of the Lord came vnto mee,
ſaying,2Sonne of man, put foorth a riddle, and ſpeake a parable vnto the
houſe of Iſrael,3And ſay, Thus ſaith the Lord God, A great eagle with
great wings, long wing'd, full of feathers, which had diuers colours,
camevnto Lebanon, and tooke the higheſt branch of the Cedar.4Hee
cropt off the top of his yong twigs, and caried it into a land of traffique;
he ſet it in a city of merchants.5Hee tooke alſo of the ſeed of the land,
and planted it in a fruitfull field, he placed it by great waters, and ſet it
as a willow tree.6And it grew, and became a ſpreading Uine of low
ſtature, whoſe branches turned toward him, and the roots thereof were
vnder him: ſo it became a Uine, and brought forth branches, and ſhot
foorth ſprigges.7There was alſo an other great eagle, with great wings
and many feathers, and behold, this Uine did bend her rootes towards
him, and ſhot forth her branches toward him, that hee might water it by
the furrowes of her plantation.8It was planted in a good ſoile by great
waters, that it might bring forth branches, and that it might beare fruit,
that it might be a goodly Uine.9ſay thou, Thus ſaith the Lord God; Shall
it proſper? ſhall he not pull vp the rootes thereof, and cut off the fruit
thereof, that it wither? it ſhall wither in all the leaues of her ſpring, euen
without great power, or many people to plucke it vp by the rootes
thereof.10Yea behold, being planted, ſhall it proſper? ſhall it not vtterly
wither, when the Eaſt wind toucheth it? it ſhal wither in the furrowes
where it grew.11Moreouer the word of the Lord came vnto me,
ſaying,12ſay now to the rebellious houſe, Know ye not what theſe things
meane? tell them, behold, the king of Babylon is come to Ieruſalem, and
hath taken the King thereof, and the Princes thereof, and ledde them
with him to Babylon,13And hath taken of the kings ſeed, and made a
couenant with him, and hath taken an oath of him: he hath alſo taken
the mighty of the land,14That the kingdome might bee baſe, that it might
not lift it ſelfe vp, but that by keeping of his Couenant it might
ſtand.15But he rebelled againſt him in ſending his ambaſsadours into
Egypt, that they might giue him horſes and much people: ſhall he
proſper? ſhall he eſcape that doeth ſuch things? or ſhall hee breake the
Couenant, and bee deliuered?16As I liue, ſaith the Lord God, ſurely in
the place where the king dwelleth that made him king, whoſe oath he
deſpiſed, and whoſe couenant he brake, euen with him, in the midſt of
Babylon he ſhall die.17Neither ſhall Pharaoh with his mightie armie and
great companie make for him in the warre by caſting vp mounts, and
building forts, to cut off many perſons.18Seeing hee deſpiſed the oath
by breaking the couenant (when loe, he had giuen his hand) and hath
done all theſe things, he ſhall not eſcape.19Therefore thus ſaith the Lord
God, As I liue, ſurely mine oath that he hath deſpiſed, and my Couenant

that he hath broken, euen it will I recompenſe vpon his owne
head.20And I will ſpread my net vpon him, & he ſhalbe taken in my
ſnare, and I will bring him to Babylon, and will plead with him there for
his treſpaſſe, that he hath treſpaſſed againſt me.21And all his fugitiues,
with all his bands, ſhall fall by the ſword, and they that remaine ſhalbe
ſcattered towards all windes: and ye ſhall know that I the Lord haue
ſpoken it.22Thus ſaith the Lord God, I wil alſo take of the higheſt branch
of the high Cedar, and will ſet it, I will croppe off from the top of his
yong twigges a tender one, and will plant it vpon an high mountaine and
eminent.23In the mountaine of the height of Iſrael will I plant it: and it
ſhall bring foorth boughes, and beare fruite, and be a goodly Cedar, and
vnder it ſhall dwell all foule of euery wing: in the ſhadow of the branches
thereof ſhal they dwell.24And all the trees of the field ſhall know that I
the Lord haue brought downe the high tree, haue exalted the low tree,
haue dried vp the greene tree, and haue made the drie tree to flouriſh: I
the Lord haue ſpoken, and haue done it.
CHAPTER 18 1And the word of þe Lord came vnto me againe,
ſaying;2What meane ye that yee vſe this prouerbe concerning the land
of Iſrael, ſaying, The fathers haue eaten ſowre grapes, and the childrens
teeth are ſet on edge?3As I liue, ſaith the Lord God, yee ſhall not haue
occaſion any more to vſe this prouerbe in Iſrael.4Behold, all ſoules are
mine, as the ſoule of the father, ſo alſo the ſoule of the ſonne is mine:
the ſoule that ſinneth, it ſhall die.5But if a man be iuſt, and do that which
is lawfull and right:6And hath not eaten vpon the mountaines, neither
hath lift vp his eyes to the idoles of the houſe of Iſrael, neither hath
defiled his neighbours wife, neither hath come neere to a menſtruous
woman,7And hath not oppreſſed any, but hath reſtored to the
debtourhis pledge, hath ſpoiled none by violence, hath giuen his bread
to the hungrie, and hath couered the naked with a garment,8He that
hath not giuen foorth vpon vſurie, neither hath taken any increaſe, that
hath withdrawen his hand from iniquitie, hath executed true iudgement
betweene man and man,9Hath walked in my Statutes, and hath kept my
Iudgements to deale truely; hee is iuſt, hee ſhall ſurely liue, ſaith the Lord
God.10If hee beget a ſonne that is a robber, a ſhedder of blood, and that
doth the like to any one of theſe things,11And that doeth not any of
thoſe duties, bnt euen hath eaten vpon the mountains, and defiled his
neighbours wife,12Hath oppreſſed the poore and needie, hath ſpoiled by
violence, hath not reſtored the pledge, and hath lift vp his eyes to the
idoles, hath committed abomination,13Hath giuen foorth vpon vſurie,
and hath taken encreaſe: ſhall he then liue? hee ſhall not liue: hee hath
done all theſe abominations, hee ſhall ſurely die, his blood ſhalbe vpon
him.14Now loe, if hee beget a ſonne that ſeeth all his fathers ſinnes
which he hath done, and conſidereth, and doth not ſuch like,15That hath
not eaten vpon the mountaines, neither hath lift vp his eyes to the idoles
of the houſe of Iſrael, hath not defiled his neighbours wife,16Neither
hath oppreſſed any, hath not withholden the pledge, neither hath ſpoiled
by violence, but hath giuen his bread to the hungry, and hath couered
the naked with a garment,17That hath taken off his hand from the poore,
that hath not receiued vſurie nor increaſe, hath executed my
Iudgements, hath walked in my Statutes, he ſhall not die for the iniquitie
of his father, he ſhall ſurely liue.18As for his father, becauſe hee cruelly
oppreſſed, ſpoiled his brother by violence, and did that which is not
good among his people, loe, euen he ſhall die in his iniquitie.19Yet ſay
yee, Why? doeth not the ſonne beare the iniquitie of the father? when
the ſonne hath done that which is lawfull and right, and hath kept all my
Statutes, and hath done them, he ſhall ſurely liue.20The ſoule that
ſinneth, it ſhal die: the ſonne ſhall not beare the iniquitie of the father,
neither ſhal the father beare the iniquitie of the ſonne; the righteouſneſſe
of the righteous ſhall bee vpon him, and the wickedneſſe of the wicked
ſhalbe vpon him.21But if the wicked will turne from all his ſinnes that he
hath committed and keepe all my ſtatutes, and doe that which is lawful
and right, he ſhall ſurely liue, he ſhall not die.22All his tranſgreſſions that
he hath committed, they ſhall not be mentioned vnto him: in his
righteouſneſſe, that he hath done, he ſhall liue.23Haue I any pleaſure at
all that the wicked ſhould die, ſaith the Lord God ? And not that he
ſhould returne from his wayes, and liue?24But when the righteous
turneth away frō his righteouſnes, & committeth iniquitie, and doth
according to all the abominations that the wicked man doth, ſhall he
liue? all his righteouſneſſe that he hath done, ſhall not be mentioned: in
his treſpaſſe that he hath treſpaſſed, and in his ſinne that he hath ſinned,
in them ſhall he die.25Yet yee ſay; The way of the Lord is not equall.
Heare now, O houſe of Iſrael; Is not my way equall? are not your wayes
vnequall?26When a righteous man turneth away from his righteouſneſſe,
& committeth iniquitie, and dieth in them; for his iniquitie that he hath
done, ſhall he die.27Againe, when the wicked man turneth away from his
wickedneſſe that he hath committed, and doth that which is lawfull and
right, he ſhall ſaue his ſoule aliue.28Becauſe he conſidereth and turneth
away from all his tranſgreſſions that he hath committed, he ſhall ſurely
liue, he ſhall not die.29Yet ſaith the houſe of Iſrael; The way of the Lord
is not equall. O houſe of Iſrael, are not my wayes equall? are not your
wayes vnequall?30Therefore I will iudge you, O houſe of Iſrael, euery
one according to his wayes, ſaith the Lord God; repent, and turne your
ſelues from all your tranſgreſſions: ſo iniquitie ſhall not be your
ruine.31Caſt away from you all your tranſgreſſions, wherby yee haue
tranſgreſſed, and make you a new heart and a new ſpirit: for why will
yee die, O houſe of Iſrael?32For I haue no pleaſure in þe death of him
that dieth, ſaith the Lord God: wherefore turne your ſelues, & liue ye.
CHAPTER 19 1Moreouer, take thou vp a lamentation for the princes
of Iſrael,2And ſay, What is thy mother? a lyoneſſe: ſhee lay downe
among lions, ſhe nouriſhed her whelpes among yong lions.3And ſhee
brought vp one of her whelps: it became a yong lion, & it learned to
catch the pray, it deuoured men.4The nations alſo heard of him, hee was
taken in their pit, and they brought him with chaines vnto the land of
Egypt.5Now when ſhe ſaw that ſhee had waited, and her hope was loſt,
then ſhe tooke another of her whelps, and made him a yong lion.6And
he went vp and downe among the lions, he became a yong lion, and
learned to catch the pray, and deuoured men.7And he knew there
deſolate palaces, and he laied waſte their cities, and the land was deſolate,
and the fulneſſe thereof by the noiſe of his roaring.8Then the nations
ſet againſt him on euery ſide from the prouinces, and ſpread their net
ouer him: he was taken in their pit.9And they put him in ward in chaines,
and brought him to the king of Babylon, they brought him into holds,
that his voyce ſhould no more be heard vpon the mountaines of
Iſrael.10Thy mother is like a vine in thy blood, planted by the waters, ſhe
was fruitfull and full of branches by reaſon of many waters,11And ſhe
had ſtrong rods for the ſcepters of them that beare rule, and her ſtature
was exalted among the thicke branches, & ſhe appeared in her height
with the multitude of her branches.12But ſhe was plucked vp in fury: ſhe
was caſt downe to the ground, and the Eaſt wind dryed vp her fruite:
her ſtrong rods were broken and withered, the fire conſumed
them.13And now ſhe is planted in the wilderneſſe, in a dry and thirſty
ground.14And fire is gone out of a rod of her branches, which hath
deuoured her fruite, ſo that ſhe hath no ſtrong rod to be a ſcepter to
rule: this is a lamentation, and ſhall be for a lamentation.
CHAPTER 20 1And it came to paſſe in the ſeuenth yeere, in the fift
moneth, the tenth day of the moneth, that certaine of the elders of Iſrael
came to enquire of the Lord, and ſate before me.2Then came the word
of the Lord vnto me, ſaying,3Sonne of man, ſpeake vnto the elders of
Iſrael, and ſay vnto them, Thus ſaith the Lord God, Are yee come to
enquire of me? As I liue, ſaith the Lord God, I will not be enquired of
by you.4Wilt thou iudge them, ſonne of man, wilt thou iudge them?
cauſe them to know the abominations of their fathers:5And ſay vnto
them, Thus ſaith the Lord God, In the day when I choſe Iſrael, and lifted
vp mine hand vnto the ſeed of the houſe of Iacob, and made my ſelfe
knowen vnto them in the land of Egypt, when I lifted vp mine hand
vnto them, ſaying, I am the Lord your God,6In the day that I lifted vp
mine hand vnto them to bring them foorth of the land of Egypt, into a
lande that I had eſpied for them, flowing with milke and hony, which is
the glory of all lands:7Then ſaid I vnto them, Caſt ye away euery man
the abominations of his eyes, and defile not your ſelues with the idoles
of Egypt: I am the Lord your God.8But they rebelled againſt me, and
would not hearken vnto mee: they did not euery man caſt away the
abominations of their eyes, neither did they forſake the idoles of Egypt:
then I ſaid, I will powre out my furie vpon them, to accompliſh my anger
againſt them in the middeſt of the land of Egypt.9But I wrought for my
names ſake that it ſhould not be polluted before the heathen, among
whom they were, in whoſe ſight I made my ſelfe knowen vnto them, in
bringing them foorth out of the land of Egypt.10Wherefore I cauſed
them to goe foorth out of the land of Egypt, and brought them into the
wilderneſſe.11And I gaue them my ſtatutes, and ſhewed them my

iudgements, which if a man doe, he ſhall euen liue in them.12Moreouer alſo, I gaue them my Sabbaths, to be a ſigne betweene mee and them, that they might know that I am the Lord that ſanctifie them.13But the houſe of Iſrael rebelled againſt me in the wilderneſſe: they walked not in my ſtatutes, and they deſpiſed my iudgements, which if a man doe, hee ſhall euen liue in them, and my ſabbaths they greatly polluted: then I ſaid I would powre out my furie vpon them in the wilderneſſe, to conſume them:14But I wrought for my names ſake, that it ſhould not bee polluted before the heathen, in whoſe ſight I brought them out.15Yet alſo I lifted vp my hand vnto them in the wilderneſſe, that I would not bring them into the land which I had giuen them, flowing with milke and hony, which is the glory of all lands,16Becauſe they deſpiſed my iudgements, and walked not in my ſtatutes, but polluted my Sabbaths: for their heart went after their idoles.17Neuertheleſſe, mine eye ſpared them from deſtroying them, neither did I make an end of thē in the wildernes.18But I ſaid vnto their children in the wilderneſſe; Walke ye not in the ſtatutes of your fathers, neither obſerue their iudgements, nor defile your ſelues with their idoles.19I am the Lord your God: walke in my ſtatutes, and keepe my iudgements and doe them:20And hallow my Sabbaths, and they ſhall be a ſigne betweene mee and you, that yee may know that I am the Lord your God.21Notwithſtanding the children rebelled againſt me: they walked not in my ſtatutes, neither kept my iudgements to doe them, which if a man doe, hee ſhall euen liue in them; they polluted my Sabbaths: then I ſaid I would powre out my furie vpon them, to accompliſh my anger againſt them in the wilderneſſe.22Neuertheleſſe I withdrew mine hand and wrought for my names ſake, that it ſhould not be polluted in the ſight of the heathen, in whoſe ſight I brought them foorth.23I lifted vp mine hand vnto them alſo in the wilderneſſe, that I would ſcatter them among the heathen, and diſperſe them through the countreys;24Becauſe they had not executed my iudgements, but had deſpiſed my Statutes, and had polluted my Sabbaths, and their eyes were after their fathers idoles.25Wherefore I gaue them alſo ſtatutes that were not good, and iudgements whereby they ſhould not liue.26And I polluted them in their owne gifts, in that they cauſed to paſſe through the fire all that openeth the wombe, that I might make them deſolate, to the end, that they might know that I am the Lord.27Therefore ſonne of man, ſpeake vnto the houſe of Iſrael, and ſay vnto them, Thus ſaith the Lord God, Yet in this your fathers haue blaſphemed me, in that they haue committed a treſpaſſe againſt me.28For when I had brought them into the land, for the which I lifted vp mine hand to giue it to them, then they ſaw euery high hill, and all the thicke trees, and they offered there their ſacrifices, and there they preſented the prouocation of their offering: there alſo they made their ſweet ſauour, and powred out there their drinke offerings.29Then I ſaid vnto them, What is the high place whereunto ye goe? and the name thereof is called Bamah vnto this day.30Wherefore ſay vnto the houſe of Iſrael, Thus ſaith the Lord God, Are ye polluted after the maner of your fathers? and commit ye whoredome after their abominations?31For when yee offer your gifts, when yee make your ſonnes to paſſe through the fire, ye pollute your ſelues with all your idoles euen vnto this day: and ſhall I be inquired of by you, O houſe of Iſrael? As I liue, ſaith the Lord God, I will not be inquired of by you.32And that which cōmeth into your minde, ſhall not be at all, that ye ſay, We wil be as the heathen, as the families of the countreys, to ſerue wood and ſtone.33As I liue, ſayeth the Lord God, ſurely with a mighty hand, and with a ſtretched out arme, and with furie powred out, will I rule ouer you.34And I will bring you out from the people, and will gather you out of the countreys wherein ye are ſcattered, with a mighty hand, & with a ſtretched out arme, and with fury powred out.35And I wil bring you into the wildernes of the people, and there will I plead with you face to face.36Like as I pleaded with your fathers in the wildernes of the land of Egypt, ſo wil I plead with you, ſaith the Lord God.37And I will cauſe you to paſſe vnder the rod, and I will bring you into the bond of the Couenant.38And I will purge out from among you the rebels, and them that tranſgreſse againſt mee: I will bring them foorth out of the countrey where they ſoiourne, and they ſhall not enter into the land of Iſrael, and yee ſhall know that I am the Lord.39As for you, O houſe of Iſrael, thus ſaith the Lord God, Goe yee, ſerue ye euery one his idoles, and hereafter alſo, if ye wil not hearken vnto me: but pollute ye my holy Name no more with your gifts, and with your idoles.40For in mine holy mountaine, in the mountaine of the height of Iſrael, ſaith the Lord God, there ſhall all the houſe of Iſrael, all of them in the land ſerue me: there will I accept them, and there wil I require your offerings, and the firſt fruits of your oblations, with all your holy things.41I will accept you with your ſweet ſauour, when I bring you out from the people, and gather you out of the countreys wherein yee haue bene ſcattered, and I wil be ſanctified in you before the heathen.42And ye ſhall know that I am the Lord, when I ſhall bring you into the land of Iſrael, into the countrey for the which I lifted vp mine hand, to giue it to your fathers.43And there ſhall yee remember your wayes, & all your doings, wherein ye haue bene defiled, and ye ſhal lothe your ſelues in your owne ſight, for all your euils that ye haue committed.44And ye ſhal know that I am the Lord, when I haue wrought with you for my Names ſake, not according to your wicked wayes, nor according to your corrupt doings, O yee houſe of Iſrael, ſaith the Lord God.45Moreouer, the worde of the Lord came vnto me, ſaying,46Sonne of man, ſet thy face toward the South, and drop thy word toward the South, and propheſie againſt the forreſt of the South field.47And ſay to the foreſt of þe South, Heare the word of the Lord: Thus ſaith the Lord God; Behold, I will kindle a fire in thee, and it ſhall deuoure euery greene tree in thee, and euery dry tree: the flaming flame ſhal not be quenched, and all faces from the South to the North ſhalbe burnt therein.48And all fleſh ſhall ſee that I the Lord haue kindled it: it ſhall not be quenched.49Then ſaid I, Ah Lord God, they ſay of me, Doeth he not ſpeake parables?

CHAPTER 211And the word of þe Lord came vnto me, ſaying,2Sonne of man, ſet thy face toward Ieruſalem, and drop thy word toward the holy places, and prophecie againſt the land of Iſrael,3And ſay to þe land of Iſrael, Thus ſaith the Lord, Behold, I am againſt thee, and will draw forth my ſword out of his ſheath, and will cut off from thee the righteous and the wicked.4Seeing then that I will cut off from thee the righteous and the wicked, therefore ſhall my ſword goe forth out of his ſheath againſt all fleſh from the South to the North:5That all fleſh may know, that I the Lord haue drawen foorth my ſword out of his ſheath: it ſhall not returne any more.6Sigh therefore thou ſonne of man with the breaking of thy loynes, and with bitterneſse ſigh before their eyes.7And it ſhall be, when they ſay vnto thee; Wherefore ſigheſt thou? that thou ſhalt anſwere, For the tidings, becauſe it commeth: and euery heart ſhall melt, and all hands ſhalbe feeble, and euery ſpirit ſhal faint, and all knees ſhal be weake as water: behold, it commeth, and ſhalbe brought to paſſe, ſayth the Lord God.8Againe, the word of the Lord came vnto me, ſaying,9Sonne of man, prophecie and ſay, Thus ſayth the Lord, Say, A ſword, a ſword is ſharpened, and alſo fourbiſhed.10It is ſharpened to make a ſore ſlaughter; it is fourbiſhed, that it may glitter: ſhould we then make mirth? It contemneth the rod of my ſonne, as euery tree.11And he hath giuen it to be fourbiſhed, that it may be handled: this ſword is ſharpened, and it is fourbiſhed to giue it into the hand of the ſlayer.12Cry and howle, ſonne of man, for it ſhalbe vpon my people, it ſhalbe vpon all the princes of Iſrael: terrours, by reaſon of the ſword, ſhall be vpon my people: ſmite therefore vpon thy thigh.13Becauſe it is a tryall, and what if the ſword contemne euen the rodde? it ſhall be no more, ſayth the Lord God.14Thou therefore ſonne of man, prophecie and ſmite thine hands together, and let the ſword bee doubled the third time, the ſword of the ſlaine, it is the ſword of the great men, that are ſlaine, which entreth into their priuie chambers.15I haue ſet the point of the ſword againſt all their gates, that their heart may faint, and their ruines be multiplied. Ah, it is made bright, it is wrapt vp for the ſlaughter.16Goe thee one way or other, either on the right hand, or on the left, whitherſoeuer thy face is ſet.17I will alſo ſmite mine hands together, and I wil cauſe my furie to reſt: I the Lord haue ſayd it.18The word of the Lord came vnto me againe, ſaying,19Alſo thou ſonne of man, appoint thee two wayes, that the ſword of the king of Babylon may come: both twaine ſhall come forth out of one land: and chooſe thou a place, chooſe it at the head of the way to the citie.20Appoint a way, that the ſword may come to Rabbath of the Ammonites, and to Iudah in Ieruſalem the defenced.21For the king of Babylon ſtood at the parting of the way, at the head of the two wayes, to vſe diuination: he made his arrowes bright, he conſulted with images, he looked in the liuer.22At his right hand was the diuination for Ieruſalem to appoint captaines, to open the mouth in the ſlaughter, to lift vp the voice with ſhouting, to appoint battering-rammes againſt the gates, to caſt a mount and to build a fort.23And it ſhall be vnto them as a falſe diuination in their ſight, to them that haue ſworne oathes: but he will call to remembrance the iniquitie, that they may be taken.[24]Therefore thus ſaith the Lord God, Becauſe yee haue made your iniquitie to be remembred, in that your tranſgreſſions are diſcouered, ſo that in all your doings your ſinnes doe appeare: becauſe, I ſay, that yee are come to remembrance, yee ſhall be taken with the hand.[25]And thou prophane wicked prince of Iſrael, whoſe day is come, when iniquitie ſhall haue an end,[26]Thus ſaith the Lord God, Remoue the diademe, and take off the crowne: this ſhall not be the ſame: exalt him that is low, and abaſe him that is high.[27]I will ouerturne, ouerturne, ouerturne it, and it ſhall be no more, vntill he come, whoſe right it is, and I wil giue it him.[28]And thou ſonne of man, prophecie, and ſay, Thus ſaith the Lord God concerning the Ammonites, and concerning their reproch: Euen ſay thou; The ſword, the ſword is drawen, for the ſlaughter it is fourbiſhed, to conſume becauſe of the glittering:[29]Whiles they ſee vanitie vnto thee, whiles they diuine a lie vnto thee, to bring thee vpon the necks of them that are ſlaine, of the wicked whoſe day is come, when their iniquitie ſhall haue an end.[30]Shall I cauſe it to returne into his ſheath? I will iudge thee in the place where thou waſt created, in the land of thy natiuitie.[31]And I will powre out mine indignation vpon thee, I will blow againſt thee in the fire of my wrath, and deliuer thee into the hand of brutiſh men and ſkilfull to deſtroy.[32]Thou ſhalt be for fuell to the fire: thy blood ſhall be in the middeſt of the land, thou ſhalt be no more remembred: for I the Lord haue ſpoken it.

CHAPTER 22[1]Moreouer the word of the Lord came vnto me, ſaying;[2]Now thou ſonne of man, wilt thou iudge, wilt thou iudge the bloodie citie? yea thou ſhalt ſhew her all her abominations.[3]Then ſay thou, Thus ſaith the Lord God; The citie ſheadeth blood in the middeſt of it, that her time may come, and maketh idoles againſt herſelfe to defile herſelfe.[4]Thou art become guilty in thy blood that thou haſt ſhed, and haſt defiled thy ſelfe in thine idoles, which thou haſt made, and thou haſt cauſed thy daies to draw neere, and art come euen vnto thy yeeres; therfore haue I made thee a reproch vnto the heathen, and a mocking to all countries.[5]Thoſe that be neere, and thoſe that be farre from thee, ſhall mocke thee which art infamous, and much vexed.[6]Behold the princes of Iſrael, euerie one were in thee to their power to ſhead blood.[7]In thee haue they ſet light by father and mother: in the middeſt of thee haue they dealt by oppreſſion with the ſtranger: in thee haue they vexed the fatherleſſe and the widow:[8]Thou haſt deſpiſed mine holy things, & haſt prophaned my ſabbaths:[9]In thee are men that carie tales to ſhead blood: and in thee they eate vpon the mountaines: in the middeſt of thee they commit lewdneſſe.[10]In thee haue they diſcouered their fathers nakedneſſe: in thee haue they humbled her that was ſet apart for pollution.[11]And one hath committed abomination with his neighbours wife, and an other hath lewdly defiled his daughter in law, and an other in thee hath humbled his ſiſter, his fathers daughter.[12]In thee haue they taken gifts to ſhead blood: thou haſt taken vſury and increaſe, and thou haſt greedily gained of thy neighbours by extortion, and haſt forgotten me, ſaith the Lord God.[13]Behold therefore, I haue ſmitten mine hand at thy diſhoneſt gaine which thou haſt made, and at thy blood which hath bene in the midſt of thee.[14]Can thine heart indure, or can thine hands be ſtrong in the dayes that I ſhall deale with thee? I the Lord haue ſpoken it, and will doe it.[15]And I will ſcatter thee among the heathen, and diſperſe thee in the countreys, and will conſume thy filthineſſe out of thee.[16]And thou ſhalt take thine inheritance in thy ſelfe in the ſight of the heathen, and thou ſhalt know that I am the Lord.[17]And the word of the Lord came vnto me, ſaying,[18]Sonne of man, the houſe of Iſrael is to me become droſſe: all they are braſſe, and tinne, and yron, and lead in the midſt of the furnace: they are euen the droſſe of ſiluer.[19]Therefore thus ſaith the Lord God, Becauſe ye are all become droſſe, behold therefore I will gather you into the midſt of Ieruſalem.[20]As they gather ſiluer, and braſſe, and yron, and lead, and tinne into the midſt of the furnace, to blow the fire vpon it, to melt it: ſo will I gather you in mine anger, and in my fury, and I will leaue you there, and melt you.[21]Yea, I will gather you, and blow vpon you in the fire of my wrath, and ye ſhalbe melted in the midſt thereof.[22]As ſiluer is melted in the midſt of the furnace, ſo ſhall ye be melted in the middeſt thereof, and ye ſhall know that I the Lord haue powred out my furie vpon you.[23]And the word of the Lord came vnto me, ſaying,[24]Son of man, ſay vnto her, Thou art the land that is not cleanſed, nor rained vpon in the day of indignation.[25]There is a conſpiracie of her prophets in the middeſt thereof like a roaring lyon, rauening the praye: they haue deuoured ſoules: they haue taken the treaſure and precious things: they haue made her many widowes in the midſt thereof.[26]Her prieſts haue violated my law, and haue prophaned mine holy things: they haue put no difference betweene the holy and prophane, neither haue they ſhewed difference between the vncleane and the cleane, and haue hid their eyes from my Sabbaths, and I am prophaned among them.[27]Her princes in the midſt thereof are like wolues rauening the praye, to ſhed blood, and to deſtroy ſoules, to get diſhoneſt gaine.[28]And her prophets haue dawbed them with vntempered morter, ſeeing vanity, and diuining lies vnto them, ſaying, Thus ſaith the Lord God, when the Lord hath not ſpoken.[29]The people of the land haue vſed oppreſſion, and exerciſed robbery, and haue vexed the poore and needie: yea, they haue oppreſſed the ſtranger wrongfully.[30]And I ſought for a man among them, that ſhould make vp the hedge, and ſtand in the gap before me for the land, that I ſhould not deſtroy it: but I found none.[31]Therefore haue I powred out mine indignation vpon them, I haue conſumed them with the fire of my wrath: their owne way haue I recompenſed vpon their heads, ſaith the Lord God.

CHAPTER 23[1]The word of the Lord came againe vnto me, ſaying,[2]Sonne of man, there were two women, the daughters of one mother.[3]And they committed whordomes in Egypt, they committed whordomes in their youth: there were their breſts preſſed, and there they bruiſed the teats of their virginitie.[4]And the names of them were Aholah the elder, and Aholibah her ſiſter: and they were mine, & they bare ſonnes and daughters: thus were their names: Samaria is Aholah, and Ieruſalem Aholibah.[5]And Aholah played the harlot, when ſhe was mine, & ſhe doted on her louers, on the Aſſyrians her neighbors,[6]Which were clothed with blew, captaines and rulers, all of them deſireable yong men, horſemen riding vpon horſes.[7]Thus ſhe committed her whordomes with them, with all them that were the choſen men of Aſſyria, and with all on whom ſhe doted, with all their idoles ſhe defiled her ſelfe.[8]Neither left ſhe her whoredomes brought from Egypt: for in her youth they lay with her, and they bruiſed the breaſts of her virginitie, and powred their whoredome vpon her.[9]Wherefore I haue deliuered her into the hand of her louers, into the hand of the Aſſyrians, vpon whom ſhe doted.[10]Theſe diſcouered her nakednes, they tooke her ſonnes and her daughters, and ſlew her with the ſword: and ſhe became famous among women, for they had executed iudgement vpon her.[11]And when her ſiſter Aholibah ſaw this, ſhe was more corrupt in her inordinate loue then ſhe, and in her whoredoms more then her ſiſter in her whoredomes.[12]She doted vpon the Aſſyrians her neighbours, captaines and rulers clothed moſt gorgeouſly, horſemen riding vpon horſes, all of them deſireable young men.[13]Then I ſaw that ſhe was defiled, that they tooke both one way;[14]And that ſhe increaſed her whoredomes: for when ſhee ſaw men pourtrayed vpon the wall, the images of the Caldeans pourtrayed with vermilion,[15]Girded with girdles vpon their loynes, exceeding in dyed attire vpon their heads, all of them princes to looke to, after the maner of the Babylonians of Caldea, the land of their natiuitie:[16]And aſſoone as ſhee ſaw them with her eyes, ſhe doted vpon them, and ſent meſſengers vnto them into Caldea.[17]And the Babylonians came to her into the bed of loue, and they defiled her with their whoredome, and ſhee was polluted with them, and her mind was alienated from them.[18]So ſhee diſcouered her whoredomes, and diſcouered her nakedneſſe; then my mind was alienated from her, like as my minde was alienated from her ſiſter.[19]Yet ſhee multiplied her whoredomes, in calling to remembrance the dayes of her youth, wherein ſhe had played the harlot in the land of Egypt.[20]For ſhe doted vpon their paramours, whoſe fleſh is as the fleſh of aſſes, and whoſe iſſue is like the iſſue of horſes.[21]Thus thou calledſt to remembrance the lewdneſſe of thy youth, in bruiſing thy teates by the Egyptians, for the paps of thy youth.[22]Therefore, O Aholibah, thus ſaith the Lord God, Behold, I will raiſe vp thy louers againſt thee, from whom thy minde is alienated, and I will bring them againſt thee on euery ſide;[23]The Babylonians, and all the Caldeans, Pekod, and Shoah, and Koa, all the the Aſſyrians with them, all of them deſireable young men, captaines and rulers, great lords and renowmed, all of them riding vpon horſes.[24]And they ſhall come againſt thee with charets, wagons and wheeles, and with an aſſemblie of people which ſhall ſet againſt thee buckler, and ſhield, and helmet round about: and I will ſet iudgement before them, and they ſhal iudge thee according to their iudgements. 25 And I will ſet my ielouſie againſt thee, and they ſhall deale furiouſly with thee: they ſhall take away thy noſe and thine eares, and thy remnant ſhall fall by the ſword: they ſhall take thy ſonnes and thy daughters, and thy reſidue ſhal be deuoured by the fire. 26 They ſhall alſo ſtrippe thee out of thy clothes, and take away thy faire iewels. 27 Thus will I make thy lewdneſse to ceaſe from thee, and thy whoredome brought from the land of Egypt: ſo that thou ſhalt not lift vp thine eyes vnto them, nor remember Egypt any more. 28 For thus ſaith the Lord God; Beholde, I will deliuer thee into the hand of them whom thou hateſt; into the hand of them from whom thy mind is alienated. 29 And they ſhall deale with thee hatefully, and ſhall take away all thy labour, and ſhall leaue thee naked and bare, and the nakedneſſe of thy whoredomes ſhall bee diſcouered, both thy lewdneſse and thy whoredomes. 30 I wil doe theſe things vnto thee, becauſe thou haſt gone a whoring after the heathen, and becauſe thou art polluted with their idoles. 31 Thou haſt walked in the way of thy ſiſter, therefore will I giue her cup into thine hand. 32 Thus ſayth the Lord God, Thou ſhalt drinke of thy ſiſters cuppe deepe and large: thou ſhalt be laughed to ſcorne and had in deriſion; it containeth much. 33 Thou ſhalt be filled with drunkenneſse and ſorrow, with the cup of aſtoniſhment and deſolation, with the cup of thy ſiſter Samaria. 34 Thou ſhalt euen drinke it and ſucke it out, and thou ſhalt breake the ſheards thereof, and plucke off thine owne breaſts: for I haue ſpoken it, ſaith the Lord God. 35 Therefore thus ſayth the Lord God, Becauſe thou haſt forgotten me, and caſt me behinde thy backe, therfore beare thou alſo thy lewdneſse, and thy whoredomes. 36 The Lord ſaid moreouer vnto mee, Sonne of man, wilt thou iudge Aholah and Aholibah? yea declare vnto them their abominations; 37 That they haue committed adulterie, and blood is in their handes, and with their idoles haue they committed adulterie, and haue alſo cauſed their ſonnes, whom they bare vnto me, to paſſe for them through the fire to deuoure them. 38 Moreouer this they haue done vnto me: they haue defiled my Sanctuarie in the ſame day, and haue profaned my Sabbaths. 39 For when they had ſlaine their children to their idoles, then they came the ſame day into my Sanctuarie to profane it, and loe, thus haue they done in the middeſt of mine houſe. 40 And furthermore that yee haue ſent for men to come from farre, vnto whom a meſſenger was ſent, and loe they came; for whom thou didſt waſh thy ſelfe, paintedſt thy eyes, and deckedſt thy ſelfe with ornaments, 41 And ſateſt vpon a ſtately bedde, and a table prepared before it, whereupon thou haſt ſet mine incenſe and mine oile. 42 And a voice of a multitude being at eaſe was with her, and with the men of the common ſort were brought Sabeans from the wilderneſſe, which put bracelets vpon their hands, and beautifull crownes vpon their heads. 43 Then ſaid I vnto her that was olde in adulteries; Will they now commit whoredomes with her, and ſhee with them? 44 Yet they went in vnto her, as they goe in vnto a woman that playeth the harlot: ſo went they in vnto Aholah & vnto Aholibah the lewd women. 45 And the righteous men, they ſhall iudge them after the manner of adultereſses, and after the manner of women that ſhed blood; becauſe they are adultereſses, and blood is in their handes. 46 For thus ſayth the Lord God, I will bring vp a company vpon them, and will giue them to be remoued and ſpoiled. 47 And the companie ſhall ſtone them with ſtones, and diſpatch them with their ſwords: they ſhall ſlay their ſonnes and their daughters, and burne vp their houſes with fire. 48 Thus will I cauſe lewdneſse to ceaſe out of the land, that all women may be taught not to doe after your lewdneſse. 49 And they ſhall recompenſe your lewdneſse vpon you, and ye ſhall beare the ſinnes of your idoles, and yee ſhall know that I am the Lord God.

CHAPTER 24 1 Againe in the ninth yeere, in the tenth moneth, in the tenth day of the moneth, the word of the Lord came vnto me, ſaying; 2 Sonne of man, Write thee the name of the day, euen of this ſame day: the king of Babylon ſet himſelfe againſt Ieruſalem this ſame day. 3 And vtter a parable vnto the rebellious houſe, and ſay vnto them, Thus ſayth the Lord God, Set on a pot, ſet it on, and alſo powre water into it. 4 Gather the pieces thereof into it, euen euery good piece, the thigh, and the ſhoulder; fill it with the choice bones. 5 Take the choice of the flocke, and burne alſo the bones vnder it, and make it boyle well, and let him ſeethe the bones of it therein. 6 Wherefore thus ſayth the Lord God, Woe to the bloodie citie, to the pot whoſe ſcumme is therein, and whoſe ſcumme is not gone out of it; bring it out piece by piece, let no lot fall vpon it. 7 For her blood is in the middeſt of her: ſhe ſet it vpon the toppe of a rocke, ſhe powred it vpon the ground to couer it with duſt: 8 That it might cauſe furie to come vp to take vengeance: I haue ſet her blood vpon the top of a rocke, that it ſhould not be couered. 9 Therefore thus ſaith the Lord God; Woe to the bloody citie, I will euen make the pile for fire, great. 10 Heape on wood, kindle the fire, conſume the fleſh, and ſpice it well, and let the bones be burnt. 11 Then ſet it empty vpon the coales thereof, that the braſſe of it may be hot and may burne, and that the filthineſse of it may be molten in it, that the ſcum of it may be conſumed. 12 She hath wearied herſelfe with lies, and her great ſcumme went not forth out of her: her ſcumme ſhall be in the fire. 13 In thy filthineſse is lewdneſse, becauſe I haue purged thee, and thou waſt not purged, thou ſhalt not be purged from thy filthineſse any more, till I haue cauſed my fury to reſt vpon thee. 14 I the Lord haue ſpoken it, it ſhall come to paſſe, and I will doe it, I will not goe backe, neither will I ſpare, neither will I repent, according to thy wayes and according to thy doings, ſhall they iudge thee, ſaith the Lord God. 15 Alſo the word of the Lord came vnto me, ſaying; 16 Sonne of man, behold, I take away from thee the deſire of thine eyes with a ſtroke: yet neither ſhalt thou mourne, nor weepe, neither ſhall thy teares runne downe. 17 Forbeare to crie, make no mourning for the dead, bind the tire of thine head vpon thee, and put on thy ſhooes vpon thy feete, and couer not thy lips, and eate not the bread of men. 18 So I ſpake vnto the people in the morning, and at euen my wife died, and I did in the morning as I was commanded. 19 And the people ſaid vnto me; Wilt thou not tell vs what theſe things are to vs, that thou doeſt ſo? 20 Then I anſwered them, The word of the Lord came vnto me, ſaying; 21 Speake vnto the houſe of Iſrael; Thus ſaith the Lord God; Behold, I will prophane my ſanctuarie, the excellencie of your ſtrength, the deſire of your eyes, and that which your ſoule pitieth; and your ſonnes and your daughters, whom yee haue left, ſhall fall by the ſword. 22 And yee ſhall doe as I haue done: yee ſhall not couer your lips, nor eate the bread of men. 23 And your tires ſhall be vpon your heads, and your ſhooes vpon your feet: yee ſhall not mourne nor weepe, but yee ſhall pine away for your iniquities, and mourne one towards an other. 24 Thus Ezekiel is vnto you a ſigne: according to all that he hath done, ſhall yee doe: and when this commeth, yee ſhall know that I am the Lord God. 25 Alſo thou ſonne of man, ſhall it not be in the day when I take from them their ſtrength, the ioy of their glorie, the deſire of their eyes, and that whereupon they ſet their minds, their ſonnes and their daughters; 26 That he that eſcapeth in that day, ſhall come vnto thee, to cauſe thee to heare it with thine eares? 27 In that day ſhall thy mouth be opened to him which is eſcaped, and thou ſhalt ſpeake & be no more dumbe, and thou ſhalt be a ſigne vnto them, and they ſhall know that I am the Lord.

CHAPTER 25 1 The word of the Lord came againe vnto me, ſaying; 2 Sonne of man, ſet thy face againſt the Ammonites, and prophecie againſt them, 3 And ſay vnto the Ammonites; Heare the word of the Lord God, Thus ſaith the Lord God; Becauſe thou ſaidſt, Aha, againſt my ſanctuarie, when it was prophaned, and againſt the land of Iſrael, when it was deſolate, & againſt the houſe of Iudah, when they went into captiuitie; 4 Behold therefore, I will deliuer thee to the men of the Eaſt for a poſſeſſion, and they ſhall ſet their palaces in thee, and make their dwellings in thee: they ſhall eate thy fruit, and they ſhall drinke thy milke. 5 And I will make Rabbah a ſtable for camels, and the Ammonites a couching place for flocks: and ye ſhal know that I am the Lord. 6 For thus ſaith the Lord God, Becauſe thou haſt clapped thine hands and ſtamped with the feete, and reioyced in heart with all thy deſpite againſt the land of Iſrael: 7 Behold therefore, I will ſtretch out mine hand vpon thee, and will deliuer thee for a ſpoile to the heathen, and I will cut thee off from the people, and I wil cauſe thee to periſh out of the countreys: I will deſtroy thee, and thou ſhalt know that I am the Lord. 8 Thus ſaith the Lord God, Becauſe that Moab and Seir doe ſay, Behold, the houſe of Iudah is like vnto all the heathen: 9 Therefore beholde, I will open the ſide of Moab from the cities, from his cities which are on his frontiers, the glory of the countrey Beth-ieſhimoth, Baal-meon and Kiriathaim, 10 Unto the men of the Eaſt with the Ammonites, and will giue them in poſſeſſion, that the Ammonites may not be remembred among the nations. 11 And I will execute iudgments vpon Moab, and they ſhall know that I am the Lord. 12 Thus ſaith the Lord God, Becauſe that Edom hath dealt againſt the houſe of Iudah by taking vengeance, and hath greatly offended, and reuenged himſelfe vpon them:13Therefore thus ſaith the Lord God, I will alſo ſtretch out mine hand vpon Edom, and will cut off man and beaſt from it, and I will make it deſolate from Teman, and they of Dedan ſhall fall by the ſword.14And I will lay my vengeance vpon Edom by the hand of my people Iſrael, and they ſhall doe in Edom according to mine anger, and according to my furie, and they ſhall know my vengeance, ſaith the Lord God.15Thus ſaith the Lord God, Becauſe the Philiſtines haue dealt by reuenge, and haue taken vengeance with a deſpiteful heart, to deſtroy it for the old hatred:16Therefore thus ſaith the Lord God, Behold, I will ſtretch out mine hand vpon the Philiſtines, and I will cut off the Cherethims, and deſtroy the remnant of the ſeacoaſt.17And I wil execute great vengeance vpon them with furious rebukes, and they ſhall knowe that I am the Lord, when I ſhall lay my vengeance vpon them.

CHAPTER 261And it came to paſſe in the eleuenth yeere, in the firſt day of the moneth, that the word of the Lord came vnto me, ſaying,2Sonne of man, becauſe that Tyrus hath ſaid againſt Ieruſalem, Aha, ſhe is broken that was the gates of the people, ſhe is turned vnto me, I ſhalbe repleniſhed now ſhe is laid waſte:3Therefore thus ſaith the Lord God, Behold, I am againſt thee, O Tyrus, and will cauſe many nations to come vp againſt thee, as the ſea cauſeth his waues to come vp.4And they ſhall deſtroy the walles of Tyrus, and breake downe her towres: I will alſo ſcrape her duſt from her, and make her like the top of a rocke.5It ſhall be a place for the ſpreading of nets in the middeſt of the ſea: for I haue ſpoken it, ſaith the Lord God, and it ſhall become a ſpoile to the nations.6And her daughters which are in the field ſhall be ſlaine by the ſword, and they ſhall know that I am the Lord.7For thus ſaith the Lord God; Behold, I will bring vpon Tyrus, Nebuchadrezzar king of Babylon, a king of kings, from the North, with horſes, and with charets, and with horſemen, and companies, and much people.8Hee ſhall ſlay with the ſword thy daughters in the field, and he ſhal make a fort againſt thee, and caſt a mount againſt thee, and lift vp the buckler againſt thee.9Hee ſhall ſet engines of warre againſt thy walles, and with his axes he ſhall breake downe thy towres.10By reaſon of the abundance of his horſes, their duſt ſhall couer thee: thy walles ſhall ſhake at the noiſe of the horſemen, and of the wheeles, and of the charets, when he ſhall enter into thy gates, as men enter into a citie wherein is made a breach.11With the hoofes of his horſes ſhall he tread downe all thy ſtreets: he ſhall ſlay thy people by the ſword, and thy ſtrong gariſons ſhall goe downe to the ground.12And they ſhall make a ſpoile of thy riches, and make a pray of thy merchandiſe, and they ſhall breake downe thy walles, and deſtroy thy pleaſant houſes, and they ſhall lay thy ſtones, and thy timber, and thy duſt in the midſt of the water.13And I wil cauſe the noiſe of thy ſongs to ceaſe, and the ſound of thy harpes ſhalbe no more heard.14And I will make thee like the top of a rocke: they ſhall bee a place to ſpread nets vpon: thou ſhalt bee built no more: for I the Lord haue ſpoken it, ſaith the Lord God.15Thus ſaith the Lord God to Tyrus; Shall not the Iles ſhake at the ſound of thy fall, when the wounded crie, when the ſlaughter is made in the midſt of thee?16Then all the Princes of the ſea ſhall come downe from their thrones, and lay away their robes, and put off their broidred garments: they ſhall cloth themſelues with trembling, they ſhall ſit vpon the ground, and ſhall tremble at euery moment, and be aſtoniſhed at thee.17And they ſhall take vp a lamentation for thee, and ſay to thee, How art thou deſtroyed that waſt inhabited of ſea-faring men, the renowned citie, which waſt ſtrong in the ſea, ſhe and her inhabitants, which cauſe their terrour to be on all that haunt it?18Now ſhall the Iles tremble in the day of thy fall, yea the Iles that are in the ſea, ſhall bee troubled at thy departure.19For thus ſaith the Lord God; When I ſhal make thee a deſolate citie, like the cities that are not inhabited, when I ſhall bring vp the deepe vpon thee, and great waters ſhall couer thee;20When I ſhall bring thee downe, with them that deſcend into the pit, with the people of old time, and ſhall ſet thee in the low parts of the earth, in places deſolate of olde, with them that goe downe to the pit, that thou bee not inhabited, and I ſhall ſet glorie in the land of the liuing:21I will make thee a terrour, and thou ſhalt bee no more: though thou be ſought for, yet ſhalt thou neuer bee found againe, ſaith the Lord God.

CHAPTER 271The word of the Lord came againe vnto mee, ſaying,2Now thou ſonne of man, take vp a lamentation for Tyrus;3And ſay vnto Tyrus, O thou that art ſituate at the entrie of the ſea, which art a merchant of the people for many Iles, Thus ſaith the Lord God; O Tyrus, thou haſt ſaid, I am of perfit beautie.4Thy borders are in the midſt of the ſeas, thy builders haue perfected thy beautie.5They haue made all thy ſhippe bords of firre trees of Senir: they haue taken Cedars from Lebanon, to make maſtes for thee.6Of the okes of Baſhan haue they made thine oares: the companie of the Aſhurites haue made thy benches of Yuorie, brought out of the Iles of Chittim.7Fine linnen with broidred worke from Egypt, was that which thou ſpreddeſt forth to be thy ſaile, blew and purple from the Iles of Eliſhah was that which couered thee.8The inhabitants of Zidon and Aruad were thy mariners: thy wiſe men, O Tyrus, that were in thee, were thy pilots.9The ancients of Gebal, and the wiſe men thereof were in thee thy calkers, all the ſhips of the ſea with their mariners were in thee, to occupie thy merchandiſe.10They of Perſia, and of Lud, and of Phut were in thine army, thy men of warre: they hanged the ſhield and helmet in thee: they ſet forth thy comelines.11The men of Aruad with thine armie were vpon thy wals round about, and the Gammadims were in thy towres: they hanged their ſhields vpon thy wals round about: they haue made thy beautie perfect.12Tarſhiſh was thy merchant by reaſon of the multitude of all kinde of riches: with ſiluer, yron, tinne, and lead they traded in thy faires.13Iauan, Tubal and Meſhech, they were thy merchants: they traded the perſons of men, and veſſels of braſſe in thy market.14They of the houſe of Togarmah traded in thy faires with horſes, and horſemen, and mules.15The men of Dedan were thy merchants, many Iles were the merchandiſe of thine hand: they brought thee for a preſent, hornes of Iuorie, and Ebenie.16Syria was thy merchant by reaſon of the multitude of the wares of thy making: they occupied in thy faires with Emeraulds, purple, and broidered worke, and fine linen, and Corall, and Agate.17Iudah and the land of Iſrael they were thy merchants: they traded in thy market wheate of Minnith, and Pannag, and honie, and oyle, & balme.18Damaſcus was thy merchant in the multitude of the wares of thy making, for the multitude of all riches: in the wine of Helbon, and white wooll.19Dan alſo and Iauan going to and fro, occupyed in thy faires: bright yron, Caſſia and Calamus were in thy market.20Dedan was thy merchant in precious clothes for charets.21Arabia and all the princes of Kedar, they occupied with thee in lambes and rammes and goats: in theſe were they thy merchants.22The merchants of Shebah and Raamah, they were thy merchants: they occupied in thy faires with chiefe of all ſpices, and with all precious ſtones and golde.23Haran, and Canneh, and Eden, the merchants of Shebah, Aſshur and Chilmad were thy merchants.24Theſe were thy merchants in all ſorts of things, in blewe clothes and broidered worke, and in cheſts of rich apparell, bound with cordes and made of Cedar among thy merchandiſe.25The ſhips of Tarſhiſh did ſing of thee in thy market, and thou waſt repleniſhed, and made very glorious in the middeſt of the ſeas.26Thy rowers haue brought thee into great waters: the Eaſt winde hath broken thee in the middeſt of the ſeas.27Thy riches and thy faires, thy merchandiſe, thy mariners, and thy pilots, thy calkers, and the occupiers of thy merchandiſe, and all thy men of warre that are in thee, and in all thy company, which is in the midſt of thee, ſhall fall into the middeſt of the ſeas, in the day of thy ruine.28The ſuburbs ſhall ſhake at the ſound of the crie of thy pilots.29And all that handle the oare; the mariners, and all the pilots of the ſea, ſhal come downe from their ſhips, they ſhall ſtand vpon the land;30And ſhall cauſe their voice to be heard againſt thee, and ſhall crie bitterly, and ſhall caſt vp duſt vpon their heads, they ſhall wallow themſelues in the aſhes.31And they ſhall make themſelues vtterly balde for thee, and girde them with ſackecloth, and they ſhall weepe for thee with bitterneſse of heart and bitter wailing.32And in their wailing, they ſhall take vp a lamentation for thee, and lament ouer thee, ſaying; What citie is like Tyrus, like the deſtroyed in the middeſt of the ſea?33When thy wares went foorth out of the ſeas, thou filledſt many people, thou didſt enrich the kings of the earth, with the multitude of thy riches, and of thy merchandiſe.34In the time when thou ſhalt be broken by the ſeas in the depths of the waters, thy merchandiſe and all thy companie in the middeſt of thee ſhal fall.35All the inhabitants of the Iles ſhall bee aſtoniſhed at thee, and their kings ſhall be ſore afraid, they ſhall be troubled in their countenance.36The merchants among the people ſhall hiſse at thee, thou ſhalt bee a terrour, and neuer ſhalt be any more.

CHAPTER 281The word of the Lord came againe vnto me,
ſaying,2Sonne of man, ſay vnto the prince of Tyrus, Thus ſaith the Lord
God; Becauſe thine heart is lifted vp, and thou haſt ſaid, I am a God, I
ſit in the ſeate of God in the middeſt of the ſeas; yet thou art a man and
not God, though thou ſet thine heart as the heart of God.3Behold, thou
art wiſer then Daniel: there is no ſecret that they can hide from
thee.4With thy wiſedome and with thine vnderſtanding thou haſt gotten
thee riches, and haſt gotten gold and ſiluer into thy treaſures.5By thy
great wiſedome, and by thy traffique haſt thou increaſed thy riches, and
thine heart is lifted vp becauſe of thy riches.6Therefore thus ſaith the
Lord God; Becauſe thou haſt ſet thine heart as the heart of God;7Behold
therefore, I will bring ſtrangers vpon thee, the terrible of the nations:
and they ſhall draw their ſwords againſt the beautie of thy wiſedome, &
they ſhall defile thy brightneſſe.8They ſhall bring thee downe to the pit,
and thou ſhalt die the deaths of them, that are ſlaine in the middeſt of
the ſeas.9Wilt thou yet ſay before him that ſlayeth thee, I am God? but
thou ſhalt be a man, and no God in the hand of him that ſlayeth
thee.10Thou ſhalt die the deaths of the vncircumciſed, by the hand of
ſtrangers: for I haue ſpoken it, ſaith the Lord God.11Moreouer the word
of the Lord came vnto me, ſaying;12Sonne of man, take vp a lamentation
vpon the king of Tyrus, and ſay vnto him, Thus ſaith the Lord God;
Thou ſealeſt vp the ſumme, full of wiſedome and perfect in
beautie.13Thou haſt beene in Eden the garden of God; euery precious
ſtone was thy couering, the Sardius, Topaze, and the Diamond, the Beril,
the Onyx, and the Iaſper, the Saphir, the Emeraude, and the Carbuncle
and gold: the workmanſhip of thy tabrets and of thy pipes was prepared
in thee, in the day that thou waſt created.14Thou art the annointed
Cherub that couereth: and I haue ſet thee ſo; thou waſt vpon the holy
mountaine of God; thou haſt walked vp and downe in the middeſt of
the ſtones of fire.15Thou waſt perfect in thy wayes from the day that
thou waſt created, till iniquitie was found in thee.16By the multitude of
thy merchandiſe they haue filled the middeſt of thee with violence, and
thou haſt ſinned: therefore I will caſt thee as prophane out of the
mountaine of God: and I wil deſtroy thee, O couering Cherub, from the
middeſt of the ſtones of fire.17Thine heart was lifted vp becauſe of thy
beautie, thou haſt corrupted thy wiſedome by reaſon of thy brightneſſe:
I will caſt thee to the ground: I will lay thee before kings, that they may
behold thee.18Thou haſt defiled thy ſanctuaries by the multitude of thine
iniquities, by the iniquitie of thy traffique: therefore will I bring forth a
fire from the middeſt of thee, it ſhall deuoure thee: and I will bring thee
to aſhes vpon the earth in the ſight of all them that behold thee.19All
they that know thee among the people, ſhall be aſtoniſhed at thee: thou
ſhalt be a terrour, and neuer ſhalt thou be any more.20Againe the word
of the Lord came vnto me, ſaying;21Sonne of man, ſet thy face againſt
Zidon, and prophecie againſt it,22And ſay, Thus ſaith the Lord God;
Behold, I am againſt thee, O Zidon, and I will be glorified in the middeſt
of thee: and they ſhall know that I am the Lord, when I ſhall haue
executed iudgements in her, and ſhall be ſanctified in her.23For I will
ſend into her, peſtilence, and blood into her ſtreetes, and the wounded
ſhall be iudged in the middeſt of her by the ſword vpon her on euery
ſide, and they ſhall know that I am the Lord.24And there ſhall be no
more a pricking briar vnto the houſe of Iſrael, nor any grieuing thorne
of all that are round about them that deſpiſed them, and they ſhal know
that I am the Lord God.25Thus ſaith the Lord God; When I ſhall haue
gathered the houſe of Iſrael frõ the people among whom they are
ſcattered, and ſhall be ſanctified in them in the ſight of the heathen, then
ſhall they dwell in their land, that I haue giuen to my ſeruant
Iacob.26And they ſhal dwell ſafely therein, and ſhall build houſes, and
plant vineyards: yea, they ſhall dwell with confidence when I haue
executed iudgments vpon all thoſe that deſpiſe them round about them,
and they ſhal know that I am the Lord their God.
CHAPTER 291In the tenth yeere, in the tenth moneth, in the twelft
day of the moneth, the word of the Lord came vnto me, ſaying,2Sonne
of man, ſet thy face againſt Pharaoh king of Egypt, and prophecie
againſt him, and againſt all Egypt.3Speake and ſay, Thus ſaith the Lord
God, Behold, I am againſt thee, Pharaoh king of Egypt, the great dragon
that lieth in the middeſt of his riuers, which hath ſaide, My riuer is mine
owne, and I haue made it for my ſelfe.4But I will put hookes in thy
chawes, and I will cauſe the fiſh of thy riuers to ſticke vnto thy ſcales,
and I will bring thee vp out of the middeſt of thy riuers, and all the fiſh
of thy riuers ſhall ſticke vnto thy ſcales.5And I will leaue thee throwen
into the wildernes, thee and all the fiſh of thy riuers: thou ſhalt fall vpon
the open fields, thou ſhalt not be brought together, nor gathered: I haue
giuen thee for meat to the beaſtes of the field, and to the foules of the
heauen.6And all the inhabitants of Egypt ſhall know that I am the Lord,
becauſe they haue bene a ſtaffe of reede to the houſe of Iſrael.7When
they tooke hold of thee by thy hand, thou didſt breake, and rent all their
ſhoulder: and when they leaned vpon thee, thou brakeſt, and madeſt all
their loynes to be at a ſtand.8Therefore thus ſaith the Lord God, Behold,
I will bring a ſword vpon thee, and cut off man and beaſt out of
thee.9And the land of Egypt ſhalbe deſolate and waſte, and they ſhall
knowe that I am the Lord: becauſe he hath ſaide, The riuer is mine, and
I haue made it.10Beholde therefore, I am againſt thee, and againſt thy
riuers, and I wil make the land of Egypt vtterly waſte and deſolate, from
the towre of Syene euen vnto the border of Ethiopia.11No foot of man
ſhal paſſe through it, nor foote of beaſt ſhall paſſe through it, neither
ſhall it bee inhabited fourtie yeeres.12And I will make the land of Egypt
deſolate in the midſt of the countreys that are deſolate, and her cities
among the cities that are layed waſte, ſhall be deſolate fourtie yeeres: and
I will ſcatter the Egyptians among the nations, and wil diſperſe them
through the countreys.13Yet thus ſaith the Lord God, At the end of
fourtie yeeres will I gather the Egyptians from the people whither they
were ſcattered.14And I will bring againe the captiuitie of Egypt, and will
cauſe them to returne into the land of Pathros, into the land of their
habitation, and they ſhall be there a baſe kingdome.15It ſhall be the
baſeſt of the kingdomes, neither ſhall it exalt it ſelfe any more aboue the
nations: for I will diminiſh them, that they ſhall no more rule ouer the
nations.16And it ſhall be no more the confidence of the houſe of Iſrael,
which bringeth their iniquity to remembrance, when they ſhall looke
after them: but they ſhall know that I am the Lord God.17And it came
to paſſe in the ſeuen and twentieth yeere, in the firſt moneth, in the firſt
day of the moneth, the worde of the Lord came vnto me, ſaying,18Sonne
of man, Nebuchad-rezzar king of Babylon cauſed his armie to ſerue a
great ſeruice againſt Tyrus: euery head was made balde, and euery
ſhoulder was peeled: yet had he no wages, nor his armie for Tyrus, for
the ſeruice that he had ſerued againſt it.19Therefore thus ſaith the Lord
God, Behold, I will giue the land of Egypt vnto Nebuchad-rezzar king
of Babylon, and he ſhall take her multitude, and take her ſpoile, and take
her praye, and it ſhall be the wages for his armie.20I haue giuen him the
land of Egypt for his labour wherewith he ſerued againſt it, becauſe they
wrought for me, ſaith the Lord God.21In that day will I cauſe the horne
of the houſe of Iſrael to budde forth, and I will giue thee the opening of
the mouth in the midſt of them, and they ſhal know that I am the Lord.
CHAPTER 301The word of the Lord came againe vnto me,
ſaying,2Sonne of man, prophecie and ſay, Thus ſaith the Lord God,
Howle ye, woe worth the day.3For the day is neere, euen the day of the
Lord is neere, a cloudie day; it ſhalbe the time of the heathen.4And the
ſword ſhall come vpon Egypt, and great paine ſhalbe in Ethiopia, when
the ſlaine ſhall fall in Egypt, and they ſhall take away her multitude, and
her foundations ſhalbe broken downe.5Ethiopia, and Libya, and Lydia,
and all the mingled people, and Chub, and the men of the land that is in
league, ſhal fal with them by the ſword.6Thus ſaith the Lord, They alſo
that vphold Egypt ſhall fall, and the pride of her power ſhall come
downe: from the towre of Syene ſhall they fall in it by the ſword, ſaith
the Lord God.7And they ſhall bee deſolate in the midſt of the countries
that are deſolate, and her cities ſhalbe in the midſt of the cities that are
waſted.8And they ſhall know that I am the Lord, when I haue ſet a fire
in Egypt, and when all her helpers ſhall be deſtroied.9In that day ſhall
meſſengers goe foorth from me in ſhippes, to make the careleſſe
Ethiopians afraid, and great paine ſhall come vpon them, as in the day
of Egypt: for loe, it commeth.10Thus ſaith the Lord God, I will alſo
make the multitude of Egypt to ceaſe by the hand of Nebuchad-rezzar,
king of Babylon.11He and his people with him, the terrible of the nations
ſhall be brought to deſtroy the land: and they ſhall draw their ſwords
againſt Egypt, and fill the land with the ſlaine.12And I will make the
riuers drie, and ſell the land into the hand of the wicked, and I wil make
the land waſt, and all that is therein, by the hand of ſtrangers: I the Lord
haue ſpoken it.13Thus ſaith the Lord God, I will alſo deſtroy the idoles,
and I will cauſe their images to ceaſe out of Noph: and there ſhalbe no
more a Prince of the land of Egypt, and I will put a feare in the land of

Egypt.14And I wil make Pathros deſolate, and wil ſet fire in Zoan, and will execute iudgements in No.15And I wil powre my furie vpon Sin, the ſtrength of Egypt, and I wil cut off the multitude of No.16And I will ſet fire in Egypt, Sin ſhall haue great paine, and No ſhall be rent aſunder, and Noph ſhall haue diſtreſſes daily.17The yong men of Auen and of Phibeſeth, ſhall fall by the ſword: and theſe cities ſhall goe into captiuitie.18At Tehaphnehes alſo the day ſhalbe darkened when I ſhall breake there the yokes of Egypt: & the pompe of her ſtrength ſhall ceaſe in her: as for her, a cloud ſhall couer her, and her daughters ſhall goe into captiuitie.19Thus will I execute iudgements in Egypt, and they ſhall know that I am the Lord.20And it came to paſſe in the eleuenth yeere, in the firſt moneth, in the ſeuenth day of the moneth, that the word of the Lord came vnto me, ſaying,21Sonne of man, I haue broken the arme of Pharaoh king of Egypt, and loe, it ſhall not be bound vp to be healed, to put a rouler to binde it, to make it ſtrong to hold the ſword.22Therefore thus ſaith the Lord God, Behold, I am againſt Pharaoh king of Egypt, and will breake his armes, the ſtrong, and that which was broken; and I wil cauſe the ſword to fall out of his hand.23And I wil ſcatter the Egyptians among the nations, and wil diſperſe them through the countries.24And I wil ſtrengthen the armes of the king of Babylon, and put my ſword in his hand: but I will breake Pharaohs armes, and he ſhall grone before him, with the groanings of a deadly wounded man.25But I wil ſtrengthen the armes of the king of Babylon, and the armes of Pharaoh ſhall fall downe, and they ſhall knowe that I am the Lord, when I ſhall put my ſword into the hand of the king of Babylon, & he ſhall ſtretch it out vpon the land of Egypt.26And I wil ſcatter the Egyptians among the nations, and diſperſe them among the countreys, and they ſhall know that I am the Lord.

CHAPTER 311And it came to paſſe in the eleuenth yeere, in the third moneth, in the firſt day of the moneth, that the word of the Lord came vnto mee, ſaying;2Sonne of man, ſpeake vnto Pharaoh king of Egypt, and to his multitude, Whom art thou like in thy greatneſſe?3Behold, the Aſſyrian was a Cedar in Lebanon with faire branches, and with a ſhadowing ſhrowd, and of an hie ſtature, and his top was among the thicke boughes.4The waters made him great, the deepe ſet him vp on high with her riuers running round about his plants, and ſent out her little riuers vnto all the trees of the field.5Therefore his height was exalted aboue all the trees of the field, and his boughes were multiplied, and his branches became long becauſe of the multitude of waters, when he ſhot foorth.6All the foules of heauen made their neſts in his boughes, and vnder his branches did all the beaſtes of the field bring foorth their yong, and vnder his ſhadow dwelt all great nations.7Thus was hee faire in his greatneſſe, in the length of his branches: for his roote was by great waters.8The Cedars in the garden of God could not hide him: the Firre trees were not like his boughes, and the cheſnut trees were not like his branches: not any tree in the garden of God, was like vnto him in his beautie.9I haue made him faire by the multitude of his branches: ſo that all the trees of Eden, that were in the garden of God, enuied him.10Therefore thus ſaith the Lord God, Becauſe thou haſt lifted vp thy ſelfe in height, and hee hath ſhot vp his top among the thicke boughes, and his heart is lifted vp in his height;11I haue therefore deliuered him into the hand of the mightie one of the heathen: hee ſhall ſurely deale with him, I haue driuen him out for his wickedneſſe.12And ſtrangers, the terrible of the nations haue cut him off, and haue left him: vpon the mountaines and in all the valleys his branches are fallen, and his boughes are broken by all the riuers of the land, and all the people of the earth are gone downe from his ſhadow, and haue left him.13Upon his ruine ſhal all the foules of the heauen remaine, & all the beaſts of the field ſhalbe vpon his branches,14To the ende that none of all the trees by the waters exalt themſelues for their height, neither ſhoot vp their top among the thicke boughes, neither their trees ſtand vp in their height, all that drinke water: for they are all deliuered vnto death, to the nether parts of the earth in the middeſt of the children of men, with them that go downe to the pit.15Thus ſaith the Lord God, In the day when hee went downe to the graue, I cauſed a mourning, I couered the deepe for him, and I reſtrained the floods therof, and the great waters were ſtayed; and I cauſed Lebanon to mourne for him, and all the trees of the field fainted for him.16I made the nations to ſhake at the ſound of his fall, when I caſt him downe to hell with them that deſcend into the pit: and all the trees of Eden, the choice and beſt of Lebanon, all that drinke water, ſhall be comforted in the nether parts of the earth.17They alſo went downe into hell with him vnto them that be ſlaine with the ſword, and they that were his arme, that dwelt vnder his ſhadow in the middeſt of the heathen.18To whom art thou thus like in glory & in greatneſſe among the trees of Eden? yet ſhalt thou be brought downe with the trees of Eden vnto the nether parts of the earth: thou ſhalt lie in the middeſt of the vncircumciſed, with them that be ſlaine by the ſword: this is Pharaoh and all his multitude, ſaith the Lord God.

CHAPTER 321And it came to paſſe in the twelfth yeere, in the twelft moneth, in the firſt day of the moneth, that the word of the Lord came vnto me, ſaying;2Sonne of man, take vp a lamentation for Pharaoh king of Egypt, and ſay vnto him; Thou art like a young lyon of the nations, & thou art as a whale in the ſeas: and thou cameſt forth with thy riuers, and troubledſt the waters with thy feet, and fouledſt their riuers.3Thus ſaith the Lord God; I will therefore ſpread out my net ouer thee, with a company of many people, and they ſhall bring thee vp in my net.4Then will I leaue thee vpon the land, I will caſt thee forth vpon the open field, and will cauſe all the foules of the heauen to remaine vpon thee, and I will fill the beaſts of the whole earth with thee.5And I will lay thy fleſh vpon the mountaines, and fill the valleis with thy height.6I will alſo water with thy blood the land wherein thou ſwimmeſt, euen to the mountaines, and the riuers ſhall be full of thee.7And when I ſhall put thee out, I wil couer the heauen, and make the ſtarres thereof darke: I will couer the ſunne with a cloud, and the moone ſhall not giue her light.8All the bright lights of heauen will I make darke ouer thee, and ſet darkeneſſe vpon thy land, ſaith the Lord God.9I wil alſo vex the hearts of many people, when I ſhall bring thy deſtruction among the nations, into the countries which thou haſt not knowen.10Yea I will make many people amazed at thee, and their kings ſhall be horribly afraide for thee, when I ſhall brandiſh my ſword before them, and they ſhall tremble at euery moment; euerie man for his owne life, in the day of thy fall.11For thus ſaith the Lord God, The ſword of the king of Babylon ſhal come vpon thee.12By the ſwords of the mighty will I cauſe thy multitude to fall, the terrible of the nations all of them: and they ſhall ſpoile the pompe of Egypt, and all the multitude therof ſhall be deſtroyed.13I will deſtroy alſo all the beaſts thereof from beſides the great waters, neither ſhall the foote of man trouble them any more, nor the hoofes of beaſts trouble them.14Then will I make their waters deepe, and cauſe their riuers to runne like oyle, ſaith the Lord God.15When I ſhall make the land of Egypt deſolate, and the countrey ſhall be deſtitute of that wherof it was full; when I ſhall ſmite all them that dwell therein, then ſhal they know that I am the Lord.16This is the lamentation wherewith they ſhall lament her: the daughters of the nations ſhall lament her: they ſhall lament for her, euen for Egypt and for al her multitude, ſaith the Lord God.17It came to paſſe alſo in the twelfth yeere, in the fifteenth day of the moneth, that the word of the Lord came vnto me, ſaying;18Sonne of man, waile for the multitude of Egypt, & caſt them downe, euen her, and the daughters of the famous nations, vnto the nether parts of the earth, with them that goe downe into the pit.19Whom doeſt thou paſſe in beautie? goe downe, and be thou layed with the vncircumciſed.20They ſhall fall in the middeſt of them that are ſlaine by the ſword: ſhe is deliuered to the ſword; draw her and all her multitudes.21The ſtrong among the mighty ſhall ſpeake to him out of the middeſt of hell with them that helpe him: they are gone downe, they lie vncircumciſed, ſlaine by the ſword.22Aſhur is there, and all her companie: his graues are about him: al of them ſlaine, fallen by the ſword.23Whoſe graues are ſet in the ſides of the pit, and her company is round about her graue: all of them ſlaine, fallen by the ſword, which cauſed terrour in the land of the liuing.24There is Elam and all her multitude round about her graue, all of them ſlaine, fallen by the ſword, which are gone downe vncircumciſed into the nether parts of the earth, which cauſed their terrour in the lande of the liuing, yet haue they borne their ſhame with them that goe downe to the pit.25They haue ſet her a bed in the midſt of the ſlaine with all her multitudes: her graues are round about him, all of them vncircumciſed, ſlaine by the ſword: though their terrour was cauſed in the land of the liuing, yet haue they borne their ſhame with them that goe downe to the pit: he is put in the midſt of them that be ſlaine.26There is Meſhech, Tubal, and all her multitude: her graues are round about him: all of them vncircumciſed, ſlaine by the ſword, though they cauſed their terrour in the land of the liuing.27And they ſhall not lie with the mightie, that are

fallen of the vncircumciſed, which are gone downe to hell with their
weapons of warre: and they haue laid their ſwords vnder their heads, but
their iniquities ſhalbe vpon their bones, though they were the terrour of
the mightie in the land of the liuing.28Yea thou ſhalt be broken in the
midſt of the vncircumciſed, and ſhalt lie with them that are ſlaine with
þͤ ſword.29There is Edom, her kings and all her princes, which with
their might are laid by them that were ſlaine by the ſword: they ſhall lie
with the vncircumciſed, and with them that go downe to the pit.30There
be the princes of the North all of them, and all the Zidomans: which are
gone downe with the ſlaine, with their terrour they are aſhamed of their
might, and they lie vncircumciſed with them that be ſlaine by the ſword,
and beare their ſhame with them that goe downe to the pit.31Pharaoh
ſhall ſee them, and ſhall bee comforted ouer all his multitude, euen
Pharaoh and all his armie ſlaine by the ſword, ſaith the Lord God.32For
I haue cauſed my terrour in the land of the liuing: and he ſhall bee laid
in the midſt of the vncircumciſed with them that are ſlaine with the
ſword, euen Pharaoh and all his multitude, ſaith the Lord God.
CHAPTER 331Againe the worde of the Lord came vnto mee,
ſaying,2Sonne of man, ſpeake to the children of thy people, and ſay vnto
them, When I bring the ſword vpon a land, if the people of the land take
a man of their coaſts, and ſet him for their watchman,3If when he ſeeth
the ſword come vpon the land, hee blow the trumpet, and warne the
people,4Then whoſoeuer heareth the ſound of the trumpet, and taketh
not warning, if the ſword come, and take him away, his blood ſhall be
vpon his owne head.5Hee heard the ſound of the trumpet, and tooke
not warning, his blood ſhall be vpon him: but he that taketh warning,
ſhall deliuer his ſoule.6But if the watchman ſee the ſword come, and
blow not the trumpet, and the people be not warned: if the ſword come
and take any perſon from among them, he is taken away in his iniquitie:
but his blood will I require at the watchmans hand.7So thou, O ſonne
of man, I haue ſet thee a watchman vnto the houſe of Iſrael: therefore
thou ſhalt heare the worde at my mouth, and warne them from
me.8When I ſay vnto the wicked, O wicked man, thou ſhalt ſurely die,
if thou doeſt not ſpeake to warne the wicked from his way, that wicked
man ſhall die in his iniquitie: but his blood will I require at thine
hand.9Neuertheleſſe if thou warne the wicked of his way to turne from
it: if he do not turne from his way, he ſhal die in his iniquitie: but thou
haſt deliuered thy ſoule.10Therefore, O thou ſonne of man, ſpeake vnto
the houſe of Iſrael, Thus ye ſpeake, ſaying, If our tranſgreſſions and our
ſinnes be vpon vs, & we pine away in them, how ſhould we then
liue?11ſay vnto them, As I liue, ſaith the Lord God, I haue no pleaſure
in the death of the wicked, but that the wicked turne from his way &
liue: turne ye, turne ye from your euill wayes, for why wil ye die, O houſe
of Iſrael?12Therefore thou ſonne of man, ſay vnto the children of thy
people, The righteouſnes of the righteous ſhal not deliuer him in the day
of his tranſgreſsion: as for the wickednes of the wicked, he ſhall not fall
thereby in the day that hee turneth from his wickednes, neither ſhall the
righteous bee able to liue for his righteouſnes in the day that he
ſinneth.13When I ſhal ſay to the righteous, that he ſhall ſurely liue if he
truſt to his owne righteouſnes and commit iniquitie, all his
righteouſneſſes ſhall not be remembred; but for his iniquitie that he hath
committed, he ſhall die for it.14Againe, when I ſay vnto the wicked,
Thou ſhalt ſurely die, if hee turne from his ſinne, and do that which is
lawfull and right;15If the wicked reſtore the pledge, giue againe that he
had robbed, walke in the Statutes of life without committing iniquitie,
hee ſhall ſurely liue, hee ſhall not die.16None of his ſinnes that hee hath
committed, ſhall be mentioned vnto him: he hath done that which is
lawfull and right; he ſhall ſurely liue.17Yet the children of thy people ſay,
The way of the Lord is not equall: but as for them, their way is not
equall.18When the righteous turneth from his righteouſnes, and
committeth iniquitie, he ſhall euen die thereby.19But if the wicked turne
from his wickednes, and doe that which is lawfull and right, he ſhall liue
thereby.20Yet yee ſay, The way of the Lord is not equall, O yee houſe of
Iſrael; I will iudge you euery one after his wayes.21And it came to paſſe
in the twelfth yeere of our captiuitie, in the tenth moneth, in the fifth
day of the moneth, that one that had eſcaped out of Ieruſalem, came
vnto mee, ſaying, The city is ſmitten.22Now the hand of the Lord was
vpon mee in the euening, afore hee that was eſcaped came, and had
opened my mouth vntill hee came to mee in the morning, and my mouth
was opened, and I was no more dumbe.23Then the word of the Lord
came vnto me, ſaying,24Sonne of man, they that inhabite thoſe waſtes
of the land of Iſrael, ſpeake, ſaying, Abraham was one, and he inherited
the land: but we are many, the land is giuen vs for
inheritance.25Wherefore ſay vnto them, Thus ſaith the Lord God, Ye
eate with the blood, and lift vp your eyes toward your idoles, and ſhed
blood; and ſhal ye poſſeſſe the land?26Yee ſtand vpon your ſword; yee
worke abomination, and ye defile euery one his neighbours wife, and
ſhall ye poſſeſſe the land?27ſay thou thus vnto them, Thus ſaith the Lord
God, As I liue, ſurely they that are in the waſtes, ſhall fall by the ſword,
and him that is in the open field will I giue to the beaſts to be deuoured:
and they that be in the forts and in the caues, ſhall die of the
peſtilence.28For I will lay the land moſt deſolate, and the pompe of her
ſtrength ſhall ceaſe: and the mountaines of Iſrael ſhall bee deſolate, that
none ſhall paſſe through.29Then ſhall they know that I am the Lord,
when I haue layed the land moſt deſolate, becauſe of all their
abominations which they haue committed.30Alſo thou ſonne of man,
the children of thy people ſtill are talking againſt thee by the walles, and
in the doores of the houſes, and ſpeake one to another, euery one to his
brother, ſaying, Come, I pray you, and heare what is the word that
commeth foorth from the Lord.31And they come vnto thee as the
people commeth, and they ſit before thee as my people, and they heare
thy words, but they will not doe them: for with their mouth they ſhew
much loue, but their heart goeth after their couetouſneſſe.32And loe,
thou art vnto them as a very louely ſong of one that hath a pleaſant
voyce, and can play well on an inſtrument: for they heare thy wordes,
but they doe them not.33And when this commeth to paſſe, (loe it will
come) then ſhall they know that a Prophet hath bene among them.
CHAPTER 341And the word of þͤ Lord came vnto me, ſaying;2Sonne
of man, prophecie againſt the ſhepheards of Iſrael, prophecie and ſay
vnto them, Thus ſaith the Lord God vnto the ſhepheards, Woe be to
the ſhepheards of Iſrael that doe feede themſelues: ſhould not the
ſhepheards feede the flockes?3Yee eate the fat, and ye clothe you with
the wooll, yee kill them that are fed: but ye feede not the flocke.4The
diſeaſed haue ye not ſtrengthened, neither haue yee healed that which
was ſicke, neither haue ye bound vp that which was broken, neither haue
yee brought againe that which was driuen away, neither haue yee ſought
that which was loſt; but with force and with crueltie haue yee ruled
them.5And they were ſcattered becauſe there is no ſhepheard: and they
became meate to all the beaſts of the field, when they were ſcattered.6My
ſheepe wandered through all the mountaines, and vpon euery high hill:
yea my flocke was ſcattered vpon all the face of the earth, and none did
ſearch or ſeeke after them.7Therefore, yee ſhepheards, heare the word
of the Lord.8As I liue, ſaith the Lord God, ſurely becauſe my flocke
became a pray, and my flocke became meate to euery beaſt of the field,
becauſe there was no ſhepheard, neither did my ſhepheards ſearch for
my flocke, but the ſhepheards fed themſelues, and fed not my
flocke:9Therefore, O yee ſhepheards, heare the word of the Lord.10Thus
ſaith the Lord God, Behold, I am againſt the ſhepheards, and I will
require my flocke at their hand, and cauſe them to ceaſe from feeding
the flocke, neither ſhall the ſhepheards feede themſelues any more: for
I will deliuer my flock from their mouth, that they may not be meat for
them.11For thus ſaith the Lord God, Behold, I, euen I will both ſearch
my ſheepe, and ſeeke them out.12As a ſhepheard ſeeketh out his flocke
in the day that hee is among his ſheepe that are ſcattered: ſo wil I ſeeke
out my ſheep, and will deliuer them out of all places, where they haue
bene ſcattered in the cloudie and darke day.13And I will bring them out
from the people, and gather them from the countreys, and will bring
them to their owne land, and feede them vpon the mountaines of Iſrael
by the riuers, and in all the inhabited places of the countrey,14I will feede
them in a good paſture, and vpon the high mountaines of Iſrael ſhall
their folde be: there ſhall they lie in a good folde, and in a fat paſture
ſhall they feede vpon the mountaines of Iſrael.15I will feed my flocke,
and I will cauſe them to lie downe, ſaith the Lord God.16I will ſeeke that
which was loſt, and bring againe that which was driuen away, and will
bind vp that which was broken, and will ſtrengthen that which was ſicke:
but I will deſtroy the fat and the ſtrong, I will feed them with
iudgement.17And as for you, O my flocke, thus ſaith the Lord God,
Behold, I iudge betweene cattell and cattell, betweene the rammes and
the hee goates.18Seemeth it a ſmall thing vnto you, to haue eaten vp the
good paſture, but ye muſt tread downe with your feet the reſidue of your

paſtures? and to haue drunke of the deepe waters, but yee muſt fonle the reſidue with your feete?19And as for my flocke, they eate that which yee haue troden with your feete: and they drinke that which yee haue fouled with your feete.20Therefore thus ſaith the Lord God vnto them, Behold, I, euen I will iudge betweene the fat cattell, and betweene the leane cattell.21Becauſe yee haue thruſt with ſide and with ſhoulder, and puſht all the diſeaſed with your hornes, till yee haue ſcattered them abroad:22Therefore will I ſaue my flocke, and they ſhall no more be a pray, and I will iudge betweene cattell and cattell.23And I will ſet vp one ſhepheard ouer them, and hee ſhall feede them, euen my ſeruant Dauid; he ſhall feede them, and hee ſhall be their ſhepheard.24And I the Lord will be their God, and my ſeruant Dauid a prince among them, I the Lord haue ſpoken it.25And I will make with them a couenant of peace, and will cauſe the euill beaſts to ceaſe out of the land: and they ſhall dwell ſafely in the wilderneſſe, and ſleepe in the woods.26And I will make them and the places round about my hill, a bleſſing; and I will cauſe the ſhowre to come downe in his ſeaſon: there ſhall bee ſhowres of bleſſing.27And the tree of the field ſhal yeeld her fruite, and the earth ſhall yeeld her increaſe, and they ſhall be ſafe in their land, and ſhall know that I am the Lord, when I haue broken the bands of their yoke, and deliuered them out of the hand of thoſe that ſerued themſelues of them.28And they ſhall no more be a pray to the heathen, neither ſhall the beaſts of the land deuoure them; but they ſhall dwell ſafely, and none ſhall make them afraide.29And I will raiſe vp for them a plant of renowne, and they ſhall be no more conſumed with hunger in the land, neither beare the ſhame of the heathen any more.30Thus ſhall they know that I the Lord their God am with them, and that they, euen the houſe of Iſrael, are my people, ſaith the Lord God.31And yee my flocke of my paſture, are men, and I am your God, ſaith the Lord God.

CHAPTER 351Moreouer the word of the Lord came vnto mee, ſaying;2Sonne of man, ſet thy face againſt mount Seir, and prophecie againſt it,3And ſay vnto it, Thus ſaith the Lord God; Behold, O mount Seir, I am againſt thee, and I will ſtretch out mine hand againſt thee, and I will make thee moſt deſolate.4I will lay thy cities waſte, and thou ſhalt be deſolate, and thou ſhalt know that I am the Lord.5Becauſe thou haſt had a perpetuall hatred, and haſt ſhed the blood of the children of Iſrael by the force of the ſword in the time of their calamitie, in the time that their iniquitie had an end;6Therefore, as I liue, ſaith the Lord God, I will prepare thee vnto blood, and blood ſhall purſue thee: ſith thou haſt not hated blood, euen blood ſhall purſue thee.7Thus will I make mount Seir moſt deſolate, and cut off from it him that paſſeth out, & him that returneth.8And I will fill his mountaines with his ſlaine men: in thy hilles, and in thy valleis, and in all thy riuers ſhall they fall that are ſlaine with the ſword.9I will make thee perpetuall deſolations, & thy cities ſhall not returne, and ye ſhal know that I am the Lord10Becauſe thou haſt ſaid; Theſe two nations, and theſe two countries ſhall be mine, and we will poſſeſſe it, whereas the Lord was there:11Therefore, as I liue, ſaith the Lord God, I will euen doe according to thine anger, and according to thine enuie, which thou haſt vſed out of thy hatred againſt them: and I will make my ſelfe knowen amongſt them, when I haue iudged thee.12And thou ſhalt know, that I am the Lord, and that I haue heard all thy blaſphemies which thou haſt ſpoken againſt the mountaines of Iſrael, ſaying; They are layed deſolate, they are giuen vs to conſume.13Thus with your mouth yee haue boaſted againſt me, & haue multiplied your words againſt me: I haue heard them.14Thus ſaith the Lord God; When the whole earth reioyceth, I will make thee deſolate.15As thou didſt reioyce at the inheritance of the houſe of Iſrael, becauſe it was deſolate, ſo will I doe vnto thee: thou ſhalt be deſolate, O mount Seir, and all Idumea, euen all of it, and they ſhall know that I am the Lord.

CHAPTER 361Alſo thou ſonne of man, prophecie vnto the mountaines of Iſrael, and ſay; Ye mountaines of Iſrael, Heare the word of the Lord.2Thus ſaith the Lord God, Becauſe the enemy had ſaid againſt you, Aha, euen the ancient high places are ours in poſſeſſion:3Therfore prophecie and ſay, Thus ſaith the Lord God, Becauſe they haue made you deſolate, and ſwallowed you vp on euery ſide, that ye might be a poſſeſſion vnto the reſidue of the heathen, and ye are taken vp in the lips of talkers, and are an infamy of the people:4Therefore ye mountaines of Iſrael, heare the word of the Lord God, Thus ſaith the Lord God to the mountaines and to the hilles, to the riuers and to the valleys, to the deſolate waſtes, and to the cities that are forſaken, which became a pray and deriſion to the reſidue of the heathen that are round about:5Therefore thus ſaith the Lord God, Surely in the fire of my ielouſie haue I ſpoken againſt the reſidue of the heathen, and againſt al Idumea, which haue appointed my land into their poſſeſſion, with the ioy of all their heart, with deſpitefull minds to caſt it out for a praye.6Prophecie therefore concerning the land of Iſrael, and ſay vnto the mountaines and to the hilles, to the riuers and to the valleys, Thus ſaith the Lord God, Behold, I haue ſpoken in my iealouſie and in my furie, becauſe ye haue borne the ſhame of the heathen,7Therefore thus ſaith the Lord God, I haue lifted vp mine hand, Surely the heathen that are about you, they ſhall beare their ſhame.8But ye, O mountaines of Iſrael, ye ſhall ſhoot forth your branches, and yeeld your fruit to my people of Iſrael, for they are at hand to come.9For behold, I am for you, and I will turne vnto you, and ye ſhall be tilled and ſowen.10And I will multiplie men vpon you, all the houſe of Iſrael, euen all of it, and the cities ſhall be inhabited, and the waſtes ſhall be builded.11And I will multiply vpon you man and beaſt, and they ſhall increaſe and bring fruite, and I will ſettle you after your olde eſtates: and will doe better vnto you, then at your beginnings, and ye ſhall know that I am the Lord.12Yea I will cauſe men to walke vpon you, euen my people Iſrael, and they ſhall poſſeſſe thee, and thou ſhalt be their inheritance, and thou ſhalt no more henceforth bereaue them of men.13Thus ſaith the Lord God, Becauſe they ſay vnto you, Thou land deuoureſt vp men, and haſt bereaued thy nations,14Therefore thou ſhalt deuoure men no more, neither bereaue thy nations any more, ſaith the Lord God.15Neither will I cauſe men to heare in thee the ſhame of the heathen any more, neither ſhalt thou beare the reproch of the people any more, neither ſhalt thou cauſe the nations to fall any more, ſaith the Lord God.16Moreouer the worde of the Lord came vnto me, ſaying,17Sonne of man, when the houſe of Iſrael dwelt in their own land, they defiled it by their owne way, and by their doings: their way was before me as the vncleanneſſe of a remooued woman.18Wherefore I powred my furie vpon them for the blood that they had ſhed vpon the land, and for their idoles wherewith they had polluted it.19And I ſcattered them among the heathen, and they were diſperſed through the countreys: according to their way and according to their doings I iudged them.20And when they entred vnto the heathen whither they went, they prophaned my holy Name, when they ſaid to them, Theſe are the people of the Lord, and are gone forth out of his land.21But I had pitie for mine holy Name, which the houſe of Iſrael had prophaned among the heathen, whither they went.22Therefore ſay vnto the houſe of Iſrael, Thus ſaith the Lord God, I doe not this for your ſakes, O houſe of Iſrael, but for mine holy Names ſake, which ye haue prophaned among the heathen, whither ye went.23And I will ſanctifie my great Name which was prophaned among the heathen, which ye haue prophaned in the midſt of them, and the heathen ſhall know, that I am the Lord, ſaith the Lord God, when I ſhall be ſanctified in you before their eyes.24For I will take you from among the heathen, and gather you out of all countreys, and will bring you into your owne land.25Then will I ſprinckle cleane water vpon you, and ye ſhalbe cleane: from all your filthineſse, and from all your idoles wil I cleanſe you.26A new heart alſo will I giue you, and a new ſpirit will I put within you, and I will take away the ſtonie heart out of your fleſh, and I will giue you an heart of fleſh.27And I wil put my Spirit within you, and cauſe you to walke in my Statutes, and ye ſhall keepe my iudgements, and doe them.28And ye ſhall dwel in the land that I gaue to your fathers, and ye ſhall be my people, and I wil be your God.29I wil alſo ſaue you from all your vncleanneſſes, and I will call for the corne, and will increaſe it, and lay no famine vpon you.30And I will multiply the fruit of the tree, and the increaſe of the field, that yee ſhall receiue no more reproch of famine among the heathen.31Then ſhall yee remember your owne euil waies, and your doings that were not good, and ſhall lothe your ſelues in your owne ſight for your iniquities, and for your abominations.32Not for your ſakes doe I this, ſaith the Lord God, be it knowen vnto you: be aſhamed and confounded for your owne wayes, O houſe of Iſrael.33Thus ſaith the Lord God, In the day that I ſhall haue cleanſed you from all your iniquities, I will alſo cauſe you to dwell in the cities, and the waſtes ſhalbe builded.34And the deſolate land ſhalbe tilled, whereas it lay deſolate in the ſight of all that paſſed by.35And they ſhall ſay, This land that was deſolate, is become like the garden of Eden, and the waſte and deſolate and ruined cities, are become fenced, and are inhabited.[36]Then the heathen that are left round about you, ſhall know that I the Lord build the ruined places, and plant that that was deſolate: I the Lord haue ſpoken it, and I wil doe it.[37]Thus ſaith the Lord God, I wil yet for this bee enquired of by the houſe of Iſrael, to doe it for them: I will increaſe them with men like a flocke.[38]As the holy flocke, as the flocke of Ieruſalem in her ſolemne feaſtes, ſo ſhal the waſte cities be filled with flocks of men, and they ſhall know that I am the Lord.

CHAPTER 37[1]The hand of the Lord was vpon mee, and caried mee out in the Spirit of the Lord, and ſet mee downe in the middeſt of the valley which was full of bones,[2]And cauſed mee to paſſe by them round about, and beholde, there were very many in the open valley, and loe, they were very drie.[3]And hee ſaid vnto mee, Sonne of man, can theſe bones liue? and I anſwered, O Lord God, thou knoweſt.[4]Againe he ſaid vnto me, Prophecie vpon theſe bones, and ſay vnto them; O yee drie bones, heare the word of the Lord.[5]Thus ſaith the Lord God vnto theſe bones, Behold, I wil cauſe breath to enter into you, and ye ſhall liue.[6]And I wil lay ſinewes vpon you, and wil bring vp fleſh vpon you, and couer you with ſkinne, and put breath in you, and ye ſhall liue, and ye ſhall know that I am the Lord.[7]So I prophecied as I was commanded: and as I prophecied, there was a noiſe, and beholde a ſhaking, and the bones came together, bone to his bone.[8]And when I beheld, loe, the ſinews and the fleſh came vp vpon them, and the ſkin couered them aboue; but there was no breath in them.[9]Then ſaid he vnto mee, Prophecie vnto the winde, prophecie ſonne of man, and ſay to the winde, Thus ſaith the Lord God; Come from the foure windes, O breath, and breathe vpon theſe ſlaine, that they may liue.[10]So I prophecied as he commanded mee, and the breath came into them, and they liued, and ſtood vp vpon their feet, an exceeding great armie.[11]Then he ſaid vnto me, Sonne of man, theſe bones are the whole houſe of Iſrael: behold, they ſay; Our bones are dried, and our hope is loſt, wee are cut off for our parts.[12]Therefore prophecie and ſay vnto them, Thus ſaith the Lord God, Behold, O my people, I wil open your graues, and cauſe you to come vp out of your graues, and bring you into the land of Iſrael.[13]And ye ſhall know that I am the Lord, when I haue opened your graues, O my people, and brought you vp out of your graues,[14]And ſhall put my ſpirit in you, and yee ſhall liue, and I ſhall place you in your owne land: then ſhall ye know that I the Lord haue ſpoken it, and perfourmed it, ſaith the Lord.[15]The word of the Lord came againe vnto me, ſaying;[16]Moreouer thou ſonne of man, take thee one ſticke, and write vpon it, For Iudah and for the children of Iſrael his companions: then take another ſticke, and write vpon it; For Ioſeph the ſticke of Ephraim, and for all the houſe of Iſrael his companions.[17]And ioyne them one to another into one ſticke, and they ſhall become one in thine hand.[18]And when the children of thy people ſhall ſpeake vnto thee, ſaying, Wilt thou not ſhew vs what thou meaneſt by theſe?[19]ſay vnto them, Thus ſaith the Lord God, Behold, I will take the ſticke of Ioſeph which is in the hand of Ephraim, and the tribes of Iſrael his fellowes, and will put them with him, euen with the ſticke of Iudah, and make them one ſticke, and they ſhall be one in mine hand.[20]And the ſtickes whereon thou writeſt, ſhalbe in thine hand before their eyes.[21]And ſay vnto them, Thus ſaith the Lord God, Behold, I will take the children of Iſrael from among the heathen whither they be gone, and will gather them on euery ſide, and bring them into their owne land.[22]And I will make them one nation in the land vpon the mountaines of Iſrael, and one King ſhall be king to them all: and they ſhalbe no more two nations, neither ſhall they bee diuided into two kingdomes any more at all.[23]Neither ſhall they defile themſelues any more with their idoles, nor with their deteſtable things, nor with any of their tranſgreſſions: but I will ſaue them out of all their dwelling places, wherein they haue ſinned, and will cleanſe them: ſo ſhall they be my people, and I will be their God.[24]And Dauid my ſeruant ſhall be King ouer them, and they all ſhall haue one ſhepheard: they ſhall alſo walke in my iudgements, and obſerue my ſtatutes, and doe them.[25]And they ſhall dwell in the land that I haue giuen vnto Iacob my ſeruant, wherin your fathers haue dwelt, and they ſhall dwell therein, euen they and their children, and their childrens children for euer, and my ſeruant Dauid ſhalbe their prince for euer.[26]Moreouer I will make a couenant of peace with them, it ſhall be an euerlaſting couenant wich them, and I will place them and multiply them, and will ſet my Sanctuary in the middeſt of them for euermore.[27]My Tabernacle alſo ſhalbe with them: yea, I will be their God, and they ſhalbe my people.[28]And the heathen ſhal know that I the Lord doe ſanctifie Iſrael, when my Sanctuarie ſhalbe in the middeſt of them for euermore.

CHAPTER 38[1]And the word of þe Lord came vnto me, ſaying;[2]Sonne of man, ſet thy face againſt Gog, the land of Magog the chiefe prince of Meſhech and Tubal, and prophecie againſt him,[3]And ſay, Thus ſaith the Lord God; Behold, I am againſt thee, O Gog, the chiefe prince of Meſhech and Tubal.[4]And I will turne thee backe, and put hookes into thy chawes, and I will bring thee foorth, and all thine armie, horſes and horſemen, all of them clothed with all ſorts of armour, euen a great company with bucklers & ſhields, all of them handling ſwordes.[5]Perſia, Ethiopia and Libya with them; all of them with ſhield & helmet:[6]Gomer and all his bandes, the houſe of Togarmah of the North quarters, and all his bands, and many people with thee.[7]Be thou prepared, and prepare for thy ſelfe, thou and all thy company, that are aſſembled vnto thee, and be thou a guard vnto them.[8]After many daies thou ſhalt be viſited: in the latter yeeres thou ſhalt come into the land, that is brought back from the ſword, and is gathered out of many people againſt the mountaines of Iſrael, which haue beene alwayes waſte: but it is brought forth out of the nations, and they ſhall dwell ſafely all of them.[9]Thou ſhalt aſcend and come like a ſtorme, thou ſhalt be like a cloud to couer the land, thou and all thy bands, and many people with thee.[10]Thus ſaith the Lord God; It ſhall alſo come to paſſe, that at the ſame time ſhall things come into thy minde, and thou ſhalt thinke an euill thought.[11]And thou ſhalt ſay: I will goe vp to the land of vnwalled villages; I will goe to them that are at reſt, that dwell ſafely all of them dwelling without walles, and hauing neither barres nor gates;[12]To take a ſpoile, and to take a praye, to turne thine hand vpon the deſolate places that are now inhabited, and vpon the people that are gathered out of the nations which haue gotten cattel and goods, that dwell in the middeſt of the land.[13]Sheba, and Dedan, and the marchants of Tarſhiſh, with all the young lyons thereof, ſhall ſay vnto thee, Art thou come to take a ſpoile? haſt thou gathered thy company to take a praye? to carie away ſiluer and gold, to take away cattell and goods, to take a great ſpoile?[14]Therefore, ſonne of man, prophecie and ſay vnto Gog, Thus ſaith the Lord God; In that day when my people of Iſrael dwelleth ſafely, ſhalt thou not know it?[15]And thou ſhalt come from thy place out of the North parts, thou and many people with thee, all of them riding vpon horſes, a great company, and a mighty armie.[16]And thou ſhalt come vp againſt my people of Iſrael, as a cloud to couer the land; it ſhall be in the latter dayes, and I will bring thee againſt my land, that the heathen may know me, when I ſhall be ſanctified in thee, O Gog, before their eyes.[17]Thus ſaith the Lord God; Art thou hee, of whom I haue ſpoken in old time by my ſeruants the prophets of Iſrael, which prophecied in thoſe dayes many yeeres, that I would bring thee againſt them?[18]And it ſhall come to paſſe at the ſame time, when Gog ſhal come againſt the land of Iſrael, ſaith the Lord God, that my furie ſhall come vp in my face.[19]For in my iealouſie, and in the fire of my wrath haue I ſpoken: ſurely in that day, there ſhall be a great ſhaking in the land of Iſrael.[20]So that the fiſhes of the ſea, and the foules of the heauen, and the beaſts of the field, and all creeping things that creepe vpon the earth, and all the men that are vpon the face of the earth, ſhall ſhake at my preſence, and the mountaines ſhall be throwen downe, and the ſteepe places ſhall fall, and euery wall ſhall fall to the ground.[21]And I will call for a ſword againſt him throughout all my mountaines, ſaith the Lord God: euery mans ſword ſhalbe againſt his brother.[22]And I will plead againſt him with peſtilence and with blood, and I will raine vpon him and vpon his bands, and vpon the many people that are with him, an ouerflowing raine, and great haileſtones, fire, and brimſtone.[23]Thus will I magnifie my ſelfe, and ſanctifie my ſelfe, and I will be knowen in the eyes of many nations, and they ſhall know that I am the Lord.

CHAPTER 39[1]Therefore thou ſonne of man, prophecie againſt Gog, and ſay, Thus ſaith the Lord God; Behold, I am againſt thee O Gog, the chiefe prince of Meſhech & Tubal.[2]And I will turne thee backe, and leaue but the ſixt part of thee, and will cauſe thee to come vp from the North parts, and will bring thee vpon the mountaines of Iſrael:[3]And I will ſmite thy bow out of thy left hand, and will cauſe thine arrowes to fall out of thy right hand.[4]Thou ſhalt fall vpon the mountaines of Iſrael, thou & all thy bands, and the people that is with thee: I will giue thee vnto the rauenous birds of euery ſort, and to the beaſts of the field to be deuoured.5Thou ſhalt fall vpon the open field, for I haue ſpoken it, ſaith the Lord God.6And I will ſend a fire on Magog, and among them that dwell careleſly in the yles, and they ſhall know that I am the Lord.7So will I make my holy Name knowen in the midſt of my people Iſrael, and I will not let them pollute my holy Name any more, and the heathen ſhall know that I am the Lord, the holy One in Iſrael.8Behold, it is come, and it is done, ſaith the Lord God, this is the day whereof I haue ſpoken.9And they that dwell in the cities of Iſrael, ſhall goe forth, and ſhall ſet on fire, and burne the weapons, both the ſhields and the bucklers, the bowes and the arrowes, and the handſtaues and the ſpeares, and they ſhall burne them with fire ſeuen yeeres.10So that they ſhall take no wood out of the field, neither cut downe any out of the forreſts: for they ſhall burne the weapons with fire, and they ſhall ſpoile thoſe that ſpoiled them, and rob thoſe that robbed them, ſaith the Lord God.11And it ſhal come to paſſe at that day, that I will giue vnto Gog a place there of graues in Iſrael, the valley of the paſſengers on the Eaſt of the ſea: and it ſhall ſtop the noſes of the paſſengers, and there ſhall they burie Gog, and all his multitude, and they ſhal call it, the valley of Hamon-gog.12And ſeuen moneths ſhall the houſe of Iſrael bee burying of them, that they may cleanſe the land.13Yea all the people of the land ſhall burie them, and it ſhall be to them a renowne the day that I ſhall be glorified, ſaith the Lord God.14And they ſhall ſeuer out men of continual emploiment, paſsing through the land, to burie with the paſſengers thoſe that remaine vpon the face of the earth to clenſe it: after the end of ſeuen moneths ſhall they ſearch.15And the paſſengers that paſſe through the lande, when any ſeeth a mans bone, then ſhall he ſet vp a ſigne by it, till the buriers haue buried it in the valley of Hamon-gog.16And alſo the name of the citie ſhall be Hamonah: thus ſhal they clenſe the land.17And thou ſonne of man, Thus ſaith the Lord God, Speake vnto euery feathered foule, and to euery beaſt of the field, Aſsemble your ſelues, and come, gather your ſelues on euery ſide to my ſacrifice that I doe ſacrifice for you, euen a great ſacrifice vpon the mountaines of Iſrael, that ye may eat fleſh and drinke blood.18Ye ſhall eate the fleſh of the mightie, and drinke the blood of the princes of the earth, of rammes, of lambes and of goats, of bullocks, all of them fatlings of Baſhan.19And yee ſhall eate fat till yee be full, and drinke blood till yee be drunken, of my ſacrifice which I haue ſacrificed for you.20Thus yee ſhall be filled at my table with horſes and charets, with mightie men, and with all men of warre, ſaith the Lord God.21And I will ſet my glory among the heathen, and all the heathen ſhal ſee my iudgement that I haue executed, and my hande that I haue laid vpon them.22So the houſe of Iſrael ſhall know that I am the Lord their God from that day and forward.23And the heathen ſhall knowe that the houſe of Iſrael went into captiuitie for their iniquitie: becauſe they treſpaſſed againſt me, therefore hid I my face from them, and gaue them into the hand of their enemies; ſo fell they all by the ſword.24According to their vncleanneſſe, and according to their tranſgreſſions haue I done vnto them, and hid my face from them.25Therefore thus ſaith the Lord God, Now will I bring againe the captiuitie of Iacob, and haue mercie vpon the whole houſe of Iſrael, and will be ielous for my holy Name:26After that they haue borne their ſhame, and all their treſpaſſes, wherby they haue treſpaſſed againſt me, when they dwelt ſafely in their lande, and none made them afraid.27When I haue brought them againe from the people, and gathered them out of their enemies lands, and am ſanctified in them in the ſight of many nations;28Then ſhall they know that I am the Lord their God, which cauſed them to be led into captiuitie among the heathen: but I haue gathered them vnto their owne land, and haue left none of them any more there.29Neither will I hide my face any more from them: for I haue powred out my Spirit vpon the houſe of Iſrael, ſaith the Lord God.

CHAPTER 401In the fiue and twentieth yeere of our captiuitie, in the beginning of the yere, in the tenth day of the moneth, in the fourteenth yeere after that the citie was ſmitten, in the ſelfe ſame day, the hand of the Lord was vpon mee, and brought me thither.2In the viſions of God brought he me into the land of Iſrael, and ſet mee vpon a very high mountaine, by which was as the frame of a citie on the South.3And he brought mee thither, and behold, there was a man, whoſe appearance was like the appearance of braſſe, with a line of flaxe in his hand, & a meaſuring reed; and he ſtood in the gate.4And the man ſaide vnto mee; Sonne of man, behold with thine eyes, and heare with thine eares, & ſet thine heart vpon all that I ſhall ſhew thee: for to the intent that I might ſhew them vnto thee, art thou brought hither: declare all that thou ſeeſt, to the houſe of Iſrael.5And behold a wall on the outſide of the houſe round about: and in the mans hand a meaſuring reed of ſixe cubites long, by the cubite, and an hand breadth: ſo hee meaſured the breadth of the building, one reed, and the height one reed.6Then came hee vnto the gate which looketh toward the Eaſt, and went vp the ſtaires thereof, and meaſured the threſhold of the gate, which was one reed broad, and the other threſhold of the gate, which was one reed broad.7And euery little chamber was one reed long, and one reed broad, and betweene the litle chambers were fiue cubites, & the threſhold of the gate, by the porch of the gate within was one reed.8He meaſured alſo the porch of the gate within, one reed.9Then meaſured hee the porch of the gate, eight cubites, and the poſtes thereof two cubits, and the porch of the gate was inward.10And the litle chambers of the gate Eaſtward, were three on this ſide, and three on that ſide, they three were of one meaſure, and the poſtes had one meaſure on this ſide, and on that ſide.11And hee meaſured the breadth of the entrie of the gate, ten cubits, and the length of the gate, thirteene cubites.12The ſpace alſo before the litle chambers was one cubite on this ſide, and the ſpace was one cubite on that ſide, and the litle chambers were ſixe cubites on this ſide, and ſixe cubits on that ſide.13Hee meaſured then the gate from the roofe of the one litle chamber to the roofe of another: the breadth was fiue and twentie cubits, doore againſt doore.14He made alſo poſtes of threeſcore cubites, euen vnto the poſte of the court round about the gate.15And from the face of the gate of the entrance, vnto the face of the porch of the inner gate, were fiftie cubites.16And there were narrow windows to the litle chambers, and to their poſts within the gate round about, and likewiſe to the arches: and windowes were round about inward: and vpon ech poſt were palme-trees.17Then brought he me into the outward court, and loe there were chambers, and a pauement, made for the court round about: thirtie chambers were vpon the pauement.18And the pauement by the ſide of the gates ouer againſt the length of the gates, was the lower pauement.19Then hee meaſured the breadth from the forefront of the lower gate, vnto the forefront of the inner court without, an hundred cubits Eaſtward and Northward.20And the gate of the outward court, that looked toward the North, he meaſured the length thereof, and the breadth thereof.21And the little chambers thereof were three on this ſide, and three on that ſide, and the poſtes thereof, and the arches thereof were after the meaſure of the firſt gate: the length thereof was fiftie cubites, and the breadth fiue and twentie cubites.22And their windowes, and their arches, and their palme trees, were after the meaſure of the gate that looketh towards the Eaſt, and they went vp vnto it by ſeuen ſteps, and the arches thereof were before them.23And the gate of the inner court was ouer againſt the gate toward the North and toward the Eaſt, and hee meaſured from gate to gate an hundreth cubites.24After that hee brought me toward the South, and behold a gate toward the South, and he meaſured the poſtes thereof, and the arches thereof according to theſe meaſures.25And there were windowes in it, and in the arches thereof round about, like thoſe windowes, the length was fiftie cubites, and the breadth fiue and twentie cubites.26And there were ſeuen ſteps to goe vp to it, and the arches thereof were before them, and it had palme trees, one on this ſide, and another on that ſide vpon the poſtes thereof.27And there was a gate in the inner court toward the South, and he meaſured from gate to gate toward the South an hundred cubites.28And hee brought me to the inner court by the South gate, and he meaſured the South gate according to theſe meaſures,29And the little chambers thereof, and the poſtes thereof, and the arches thereof according to theſe meaſures, and there were windowes in it, and in the arches thereof round about: it was fiftie cubites long, and fiue and twentie cubites broad.30And the arches round about were fiue and twenty cubits long, and fiue cubites broad.31And the arches thereof were toward the vtter court, and palme trees were vpon the poſtes thereof, and the going vp to it had eight ſteps.32And hee brought me into the inner court toward the Eaſt, and hee meaſured the gate according to theſe meaſures.33And the little chambers thereof, and the poſtes thereof, and the arches thereof were according to theſe meaſures, and there were windowes therein, and in the arches thereof round about, it was fiftie cubites long, and fiue and twentie cubits broad.34And the arches thereof were toward the outward court, and palme trees were vpon the poſtes thereof on this ſide, and on that ſide, and the going vp to it had eight ſteps.35And hee brought me to the North gate, and meaſured it according to theſe meaſures.36The little chambers thereof, the poſtes thereof, and the arches thereof and the windowes to it round about: the length was fiftie cubites, and the breadth fiue and twentie cubites.37And the poſtes thereof were toward the vtter court, and palme trees were vpon the poſts thereof on this ſide, and on that ſide, and the going vp to it had eight ſteps.38And the chambers, and the entries thereof were by the poſtes of the gates, where they waſhed the burnt offering.39And in the porch of the gate were two tables on this ſide, and two tables on that ſide, to ſlay thereon the burnt offering, and the ſinne offering, and the treſpaſſe offering.40And at the ſide without, as one goeth vp to the entry of the North gate, were two tables, and on the other ſide, which was at the porch of the gate, were two tables.41Foure tables were on this ſide, and foure tables on that ſide, by the ſide of the gate; eight tables, whereupon they ſlew their ſacrifices.42And the foure tables were of hewen ſtone for the burnt offering, of a cubite and an halfe long, and a cubite & a halfe broad, and one cubit high: whereupon alſo they laide the inſtruments wherewith they ſlewe the burnt offering and the ſacrifice.43And within were hooks, an hand broad, faſtened round about, and vpon the tables was the fleſh of the offering.44And without the inner gate were the chambers of the ſingers in the inner court, which was at the ſide of the North gate: and their proſpect was toward the South, one at the ſide of the Eaſt gate, hauing the proſpect toward the North.45And hee ſaid vnto me; This chamber whoſe proſpect is toward the South, is for the prieſts, the keepers of the charge of the houſe.46And the chamber whoſe proſpect is toward the North, is for the prieſts the keepers of the charge of the altar: theſe are the ſonnes of Zadok among the ſonnes of Leui, which come neere to the Lord to miniſter vnto him.47So he meaſured the court, an hundreth cubites long, and an hundreth cubites broad foure ſquare, and the altar that was before the houſe.48And he brought me to the porch of the houſe, and meaſured each poſt of the porch, fiue cubites on this ſide, and fiue cubites on that ſide: and the bredth of the gate was three cubites on this ſide, and three cubites on that ſide.49The length of the porch was twentie cubites, and the bredth eleuen cubites, and he brought me by the ſteps, whereby they went vp to it, and there were pillars by the poſts, one on this ſide, and another on that ſide.

CHAPTER 411Afterward he brought me to the Temple, and meaſured the poſts, ſix cubites broad on the one ſide, and ſixe cubites broad on the other ſide, which was the bredth of the Tabernacle.2And the bredth of the doore was tenne cubites, and the ſides of the doore were fiue cubites on the one ſide, and fiue cubites on the other ſide, and he meaſured the length thereof fortie cubites, and the bredth twentie cubites.3Then went he inward, and meaſured the poſt of the doore two cubites, and the doore ſixe cubites, and the bredth of the doore ſeuen cubites.4So he meaſured the length therof twentie cubites, and the bredth twentie cubites before the temple, and he ſaid vnto me; This is the moſt holy place.5After he meaſured the wall of the houſe ſixe cubites, and the bredth of euerie ſide-chamber foure cubites round about the houſe on euery ſide.6And the ſide-chambers were three, one ouer an other, and thirtie in order, and they entred into the wall which was of the houſe for the ſide chambers round about, that they might haue hold, but they had not hold in the wall of the houſe.7And there was an enlarging and a winding about ſtill vpward to the ſide-chambers, for the winding about of the houſe went ſtill vpward round about the houſe: therefore the bredth of the houſe was ſtill vpward, and ſo increaſed from the loweſt chamber to the higheſt by the middeſt.8I ſaw alſo the height of the houſe round about; the foundations of the ſide-chambers were a full reede of ſixe great cubites.9The thickneſse of the wall which was for the ſide chamber without, was fiue cubites, and that which was left, was the place of the ſide-chambers that were within.10And betweene the chambers was the wideneſse of twentie cubites round about the houſe on euery ſide.11And the doores of the ſide-chambers were toward the place that was left, one doore toward the North, and an other doore toward the South, and the bredth of the place that was left, was fiue cubites round about.12Now the building that was before the ſeperate place, at the end toward the Weſt, was ſeuenty cubites broad, and the wall of the building was fiue cubites thicke round about, and the length thereof ninety cubites.13So he meaſured the houſe, an hundreth cubites long, and the ſeparate place and the building with the walles thereof, an hundreth cubites long.14Alſo the bredth of the face of the houſe, and of the ſeparate place toward the Eaſt, an hundreth cubites.15And he meaſured the length of the building ouer againſt the ſeparate place which was behind it, and the galleries thereof on the one ſide, and on the other ſide an hundreth cubites with the inner temple, and the porches of the court.16The doore-poſts and the narrow windows, and the galleries round about on their three ſtories, ouer againſt the doore ſieled with wood round about, and from the ground vp to the windows, & the windows were couered.17To that aboue the doore, euen vnto the inner houſe and without, and by all the wall round about within and without by meaſure.18And it was made with Cherubims and Palme trees, ſo that a Palme tree was betweene a Cherub and a Cherub, and euery Cherub had two faces.19So that the face of a man was toward the Palme-tree on the one ſide, and the face of a yong lyon toward the Palme-tree on the other ſide: it was made through all the houſe round about.20From the ground vnto aboue the doore were Cherubims and Palme-trees made, & on the wall of the temple.21The poſtes of the Temple were ſquared, and the face of the Sanctuary, the appearance of the one as the appearance of the other.22The altar of wood was three cubits high, and the length thereof two cubits; and the corners thereof and the length thereof and the walles thereof were of wood: and hee ſaid vnto mee; This is the Table that is before the Lord.23And the Temple and the Sanctuarie had two doores.24And the doores had two leaues a piece, two turning leaues, two leaues for the one doore, and two leaues for the other doore.25And there were made on them, on the doores of the Temple, Cherubims and Palme-trees, like as were made vpon the walles, and there were thicke planckes vpon the face of the porch without.26And there were narrow windowes and Palme-trees on the one ſide and on the other ſide, on the ſides of the porch, and vpon the ſide chambers of the houſe, and thicke plankes.

CHAPTER 421Then he brought me foorth into the vtter court, the way toward the North, and hee brought mee into the chamber, that was ouer againſt the ſeparate place, & which was before the building toward the North.2Before the length of an hundreth cubites was the North doore, and the breadth was fiftie cubits.3Ouer againſt the twentie cubites which were for the inner court, and ouer againſt the pauement which was for the vtter court, was gallerie againſt gallery in three ſtories.4And before the chambers was a walke of ten cubites breadth inward, a way of one cubite, and their doores toward the North.5Now the vpper-chambers were ſhorter: for the galleries were higher then theſe, then the lower, and then the middlemoſt of the building.6For they were in three ſtories, but had not pillars as the pillars of the courts: therefore the building was ſtraitned more then the loweſt, and the middlemoſt from the ground.7And the wall that was without ouer againſt the chambers towards the vtter court on the forepart of the chambers, the length thereof was fiftie cubites.8For the length of the chambers that were in the vtter court was fiftie cubites: and loe, before the Temple were an hundreth cubites.9And from vnder theſe chambers was the entrie on the Eaſt ſide, as one goeth into them from the vtter court.10The chambers were in the thickenes of the wall of the court toward the Eaſt, ouer againſt the ſeparate place, and ouer againſt the building.11And the way before them was like the appearance of the chambers, which were toward the North, as long as they and as broad as they, and all their goings out were both according to their faſhions, and according to their doores.12And according to the doores of the chambers that were toward the South, was a doore in the head of the way, euen the way directly before þe wall toward the Eaſt, as one entreth into them.13Then ſayd hee vnto mee, The North chambers, and the South chambers, which are before the ſeparate place, they be holy chambers, where þe Prieſts that approach vnto the Lord ſhall eate the moſt holy things: there ſhall they lay the moſt holy things, and the meat offering, & the ſinne offering, and the treſpaſſe offring, for the place is holy.14When the Prieſts enter therein, then ſhall they not goe out of the holy place into the vtter court, but there they ſhall lay their garments, wherein they miniſter: for they are holy, and ſhall put on other garments, and ſhall approch to thoſe things which are for the people.15Now when hee had made an end of meaſuring the inner houſe, hee brought mee foorth toward the gate, whoſe proſpect is toward the Eaſt, and meaſured it round about.16He meaſured the Eaſt ſide with the meaſuring reede, fiue hundreth reedes, with the meaſuring reed round about.[17]Hee meaſured the North ſide fiue hundreth reedes, with a meaſuring reed round about.[18]Hee meaſured the South ſide fiue hundreth reedes, with the meaſuring reede.[19]Hee turned about to the Weſt ſide, and meaſured fiue hundreth reedes with the meaſuring reed.[20]He meaſured it by the foure ſides: it had a wall round about fiue hundreth reedes long, and fiue hundreth broad, to make a ſeparation betweene the Sanctuary and the prophane place.

CHAPTER 43[1]Afterward he brought me to the gate, euen the gate that looketh toward the Eaſt.[2]And behold, the glory of the God of Iſrael came from the way of the Eaſt: and his voice was like a noiſe of many waters, and the earth ſhined with his glory.[3]And it was according to the appearance of the viſion which I ſaw, euen according to the viſion that I ſaw, when I came to deſtroy the citie: and the viſions were like the viſion that I ſaw by the riuer Chebar: and I fell vpon my face.[4]And the glorie of the Lord came into the houſe by the way of the gate, whoſe proſpect is toward the Eaſt.[5]So the Spirit tooke me vp, and brought mee into the inner court, and behold, the glory of the Lord filled the houſe.[6]And I heard him ſpeaking vnto me out of the houſe, & the man ſtood by me.[7]And he ſaid vnto me, Sonne of man, the place of my throne, and the place of the ſoles of my feete, where I will dwell in the midſt of the children of Iſrael for euer, and my holy Name, ſhall the houſe of Iſrael no more defile, neither they, nor their kings, by their whoredome, nor by the carkeiſes of their kings in their high places.[8]In their ſetting of their threſhold by my threſholds, and their poſt by my poſtes, and the wall betweene me and them, they haue euen defiled my holy Name by their abominations that they haue committed: wherefore I haue conſumed them in mine anger.[9]Now let them put away their whoredome, and the carkeiſes of their kings farre from me, and I wil dwell in the middeſt of them for euer.[10]Thou ſonne of man, ſhew the houſe to the houſe of Iſrael, that they may be aſhamed of their iniquities, and let them meaſure the patterne.[11]And if they be aſhamed of all that they haue done; ſhew them the forme of the houſe, and the faſhion thereof, and the goings out thereof, and the commings in thereof, and all the formes thereof, and all the ordinances thereof, and all the formes thereof, and all the lawes thereof: & write it in their ſight, that they may keepe the whole forme thereof, and all the Ordinances therof, and doe them.[12]This is the law of the houſe; Upon the top of the mountaine, the whole limit thereof round about ſhall be moſt holy: behold, this is the law of the houſe.[13]And theſe are the meaſures of the Altar after the cubites; the cubite is a cubite and an hand breadth, euen the bottom ſhalbe a cubite, and the breadth a cubite, and the border thereof by the edge therof round about ſhalbe a ſpanne, and this ſhalbe the higher place of the Altar.[14]And from the bottom vpon the ground, euen to the lower ſettle, ſhalbe two cubits, and the breadth one cubite, and from the leſſer ſettle euen to the greater ſettle ſhalbe foure cubites, and the breadth one cubite.[15]So the Altar ſhalbe foure cubites, and from the altar and vpward ſhalbe foure hornes.[16]And the altar ſhalbe twelue cubites long, twelue broad, ſquare in the foure ſquares thereof.[17]And the ſettle ſhall bee fourteene cubites long, and fourteene broad in the foure ſquares thereof, and the border about it ſhalbe halfe a cubite, and the bottome thereof ſhall be a cubite about, and his ſtaires ſhall looke toward the Eaſt.[18]And he ſaid vnto me, Sonne of man, thus ſaith the Lord God, Theſe are the ordinances of the Altar in the day when they ſhall make it to offer burnt offrings thereon, and to ſprinkle blood thereon.[19]And thou ſhalt giue to the Prieſts the Leuites that be of the ſeede of Zadok, which approch vnto me, to miniſter vnto me, ſaith the Lord God, a yong bullocke for a ſinne offering.[20]And thou ſhalt take of the blood thereof, and put it on the foure hornes of it, and on the foure corners of the ſettle, and vpon the border round about: thus ſhalt thou cleanſe and purge it.[21]Thou ſhalt take the bullocke alſo of the ſinne offering, and he ſhall burne it in the appointed place of the houſe without the Sanctuary.[22]And on the ſecond day thou ſhalt offer a kidde of the goats without blemiſh for a ſinne offering, and they ſhall cleanſe the Altar, as they did cleanſe it with the bullocke.[23]When thou haſt made an ende of cleanſing it, thou ſhalt offer a yong bullocke without blemiſh, and a ramme out of the flocke, without blemiſh.[24]And thou ſhalt offer them before the Lord, and the Prieſts ſhall caſt ſalt vpon them, and they ſhall offer them vp for a burnt offering vnto the Lord.[25]Seuen dayes ſhalt thou prepare euery day a goate for a ſinne offering: they ſhall alſo prepare a yong bullocke, and a ramme out of the flocke, without blemiſh.[26]Seuen dayes ſhal they purge the Altar and purifie it, and they ſhall conſecrate themſelues.[27]And when theſe dayes are expired, it ſhall be that vpon the eight day and ſo forward, the Prieſts ſhall make your burnt offerings vpon the Altar, and your peace offerings; and I will accept you, ſaith the Lord God.

CHAPTER 44[1]Then he brought me backe the way of the gate of the outward Sanctuarie which looketh toward the Eaſt, and it was ſhut.[2]Then ſaid the Lord vnto me, This gate ſhall be ſhut, it ſhall not be opened, and no man ſhall enter in by it; becauſe the Lord the God of Iſrael hath entred in by it, therefore it ſhall be ſhut.[3]It is for the Prince; the Prince, hee ſhall ſit in it to eate bread before the Lord: hee ſhall enter by the way of the porch of that gate, and ſhall goe out by the way of the ſame.[4]Then brought he me the way of the North gate before the houſe, and I looked, and behold, the glory of the Lord filled the houſe of the Lord, and I fell vpon my face.[5]And the Lord ſaid vnto me; Sonne of man, marke well, and behold with thine eyes, and heare with thine eares, all that I ſay vnto thee, concerning all the ordinances of the houſe of ehe Lord, and all the lawes thereof, and marke well the entring in of the houſe, with euery going foorth of the Sanctuary.[6]And thou ſhalt ſay to the rebellious, euen to the houſe of Iſrael, Thus ſayth the Lord God; O yee houſe of Iſrael, let it ſuffice you, of all your abominations;[7]In that ye haue brought into my Sanctuarie ſtrangers vncircumciſed in heart, and vncircumciſed in fleſh, to be in my Sanctuarie to pollute it, euen my Houſe, when ye offer my bread, the fat and the blood, and they haue broken my Couenant, becauſe of all your abominations.[8]And yee haue not kept the charge of mine holy things: but ye haue ſet keepers of my charge in my Sanctuarie for your ſelues.[9]Thus ſayth the Lord God, No ſtranger vncircumciſed in heart, nor vncircumciſed in fleſh, ſhall enter into my Sanctuarie, of any ſtranger that is among the children of Iſrael.[10]And the Leuites that are gone away farre from me, when Iſrael went aſtray, which went aſtray away from me after their idoles, they ſhall euen beare their iniquitie.[11]Yet they ſhall be miniſters in my Sanctuary, hauing charge at the gates of the houſe, and miniſtring to the houſe: they ſhall ſlay the burnt offring, and the ſacrifice for the people, and they ſhall ſtand before them to miniſter vnto them:[12]Becauſe they miniſtred vnto them before their idoles, and cauſed the houſe of Iſrael to fall into iniquitie; therefore haue I lift vp mine hand againſt them, ſaith the Lord God, and they ſhall beare their iniquitie.[13]And they ſhall not come neere vnto me to doe the office of a prieſt vnto me, nor to come neere to any of my holy things, in the moſt holy place: but they ſhall beare their ſhame, and their abominations which they haue committed.[14]But I will make them keepers of the charge of the houſe for all the ſeruice thereof, and for all that ſhalbe done therein.[15]But the prieſts the Leuites, the ſonnes of Zadok, that kept the charge of my ſanctuarie, when the children of Iſrael went aſtray from me, they ſhall come neere to me to miniſter vnto me, and they ſhall ſtand before me to offer vnto me the fat and the blood, ſaith the Lord God.[16]They ſhall enter into my ſanctuarie, and they ſhall come neere to my table to miniſter vnto mee, and they ſhall keepe my charge.[17]And it ſhall come to paſſe that when they enter in at the gates of the inner court, they ſhall be clothed with linnen garments, and no wooll ſhall come vpon them, whiles they miniſter in the gates of the inner court and within.[18]They ſhall haue linnen bonets vpon their heads, and ſhall haue linnen breeches vpon their loynes: they ſhall not girde themſelues with any thing that cauſeth ſweat.[19]And when they goe forth into the vtter court, euen into the vtter court to the people, they ſhall put off their garments wherein they miniſtred, and lay them in the holy chambers, and they ſhall put on other garments, and they ſhall not ſanctifie the people with their garments.[20]Neither ſhall they ſhaue their heads, nor ſuffer their lockes to grow long, they ſhall only polle their heads.[21]Neither ſhall any prieſt drinke wine, when they enter into the inner court.[22]Neither ſhall they take for their wiues a widow, or her that is put away: but they ſhall take maidens of the ſeede of the houſe of Iſrael, or a widow that had a prieſt before.[23]And they ſhall teach my people the difference betweene the holy and prophane, and cauſe men to diſcerne betweene the vncleane and the cleane.[24]And in controuerſie they ſhall ſtand in iudgement, and they ſhall iudge it according to my iudgements: and they ſhall keepe my lawes and my ſtatutes in all mine aſſemblies, and they ſhall halow my Sabbaths.[25]And they ſhall come at no dead perſon to defile themſelues:

but for father or for mother, or for ſonne or for daughter, for brother or for ſiſter, that hath had no huſband, they may defile themſelues.26And after he is cleanſed, they ſhal reckon vnto him ſeuen dayes.27And in the day that he goeth into the ſanctuarie, vnto the inner court to miniſter in the ſanctuarie, he ſhall offer his ſinne offring, ſaith the Lord God.28And it ſhall be vnto them for an inheritance; I am their inheritance: and yee ſhall giue them no poſſeſſion in Iſrael; I am their poſſeſſion.29They ſhal eate the meate offring, and the ſinne offring, and the treſpaſſe offring, and euery dedicate thing in Iſrael ſhall be theirs.30And the firſt of all the firſt fruits of all things, and euery oblation of all of euery ſort of your oblations ſhall be the prieſts: yee ſhall alſo giue vnto the prieſt the firſt of your dough, that he may cauſe the bleſſing to reſt in thine houſe.31The prieſts ſhall not eate of any thing that is dead of it ſelfe or torne, whether it be foule or beaſt.

CHAPTER 451Moreouer, when yee ſhall diuide by lot the land for inheritance, yee ſhall offer an oblation vnto the Lord, an holy portion of the land: the length ſhall be the length of fiue and twentie thouſand reedes, and the bredth ſhalbe ten thouſand: this ſhall be holy in all the borders thereof round about.2Of this there ſhal be for the Sanctuarie fiue hundreth in length, with fiue hundreth in bredth, ſquare round about, and fiftie cubites round about, for the ſuburbs thereof.3And of this meaſure ſhalt thou meaſure the length of fiue and twentie thouſand, and the bredth of ten thouſand: and in it ſhall be the Sanctuarie and the moſt holy place.4The holy portion of the land ſhal bee for the prieſts the miniſters of the Sanctuarie, which ſhall come neere to miniſter vnto the Lord, and it ſhall be a place for their houſes, and an holy place for the Sanctuarie.5And the fiue and twenty thouſand of length, and the tenne thouſand of breadth, ſhall alſo the Leuites the miniſters of the houſe haue for themſelues, for a poſſeſſion for twentie chambers.6And ye ſhall appoint the poſſeſſion of the citie fiue thouſand broad, and fiue and twentie thouſand long ouer againſt the oblation of the holy portion: it ſhall be for the whole houſe of Iſrael.7And a portion ſhalbe for the prince on the one ſide, and on the other ſide of the oblation of the holy portion, and of the poſſeſſion of the citie, before the oblation of the holy portion, and before the poſſeſſion of the citie from the Weſt ſide Weſtward, and from the Eaſt ſide Eaſtward, and the length ſhalbe ouer againſt one of the portions from the Weſt border vnto the Eaſt border.8In the land ſhall be his poſſeſſion in Iſrael, and my princes ſhall no more oppreſſe my people, and the reſt of the land ſhall they giue to the houſe of Iſrael according to their tribes.9Thus ſaith the Lord God, Let it ſuffice you, O princes of Iſrael: remoue violence and ſpoile, and execute iudgement and iuſtice, take away your exactions from my people, ſaith the Lord God.10Ye ſhall haue iuſt ballances, and a iuſt Ephah, and a iuſt Bath.11The Ephah and the Bath ſhal be of one meaſure, that the Bath may containe the tenth part of an Homer, and the Ephah the tenth part of an Homer: the meaſure thereof ſhall be after the Homer.12And the ſhekell ſhall be twentie Gerahs: twenty ſhekels, fiue and twentie ſhekels, fifteene ſhekels ſhall be your Maneh.13This is the oblation that ye ſhal offer, the ſixt part of an Ephah of an Homer of wheat, & ye ſhal giue the ſixt part of an Ephah of an Homer of barley.14Concerning the ordinance of oile, the Bath of oyle, ye ſhall offer the tenth part of a Bath out of the Cor, which is an Homer of ten Baths, for ten Baths are an Homer.15And one lambe out of the flocke, out of two hundred, out of the fat paſtures of Iſrael for a meate offering, and for a burnt offering, and for peace offerings to make reconciliation for them, ſaith the Lord God.16All the people of the land ſhall giue this oblation for the prince in Iſrael.17And it ſhall be the princes part to giue burnt offerings, and meat offrings, and drinke offerings, in the feaſts, and in the new moones, and in the Sabbaths, in all ſolemnities of the houſe of Iſrael: he ſhall prepare the ſinne offering, and the meate offering, and the burnt offering, and the peace offrings, to make reconciliation for the houſe of Iſrael.18Thus ſaith the Lord God, In the firſt moneth, in the firſt day of the moneth, thou ſhalt take a yong bullock without blemiſh, and clenſe the Sanctuarie.19And the prieſt ſhall take of the blood of the ſinne offering, and put it vpon the poſtes of the houſe, and vpon the foure corners of the ſettle of the Altar, and vpon the poſtes of the gate of the inner court.20And ſo thou ſhalt doe the ſeuenth day of the moneth, for euery one that erreth, and for him that is ſimple: ſo ſhall ye reconcile the houſe.21In the firſt moneth, in the fourteenth day of the moneth, ye ſhall haue the paſſeouer a feaſt of ſeuen dayes, vnleauened bread ſhall be eaten.22And vpon that day ſhall the prince prepare for himſelfe, and for all the people of the land, a bullocke for a ſinne offering.23And ſeuen dayes of the feaſt he ſhall prepare a burnt offering to the Lord, ſeuen bullockes, and ſeuen rammes without blemiſh dayly the ſeuen dayes, and a kidde of the goats daily for a ſinne offering.24And hee ſhall prepare a meat offering of an Ephah for a bullocke, and an Ephah for a ramme, and an Hin of oyle for an Ephah.25In the ſeuenth moneth, in the fifteenth day of the moneth ſhall he doe the like in the feaſt of the ſeuen dayes, according to the ſinne offring, according to the burnt offering, & according to the meat offering, and according to the oile.

CHAPTER 461Thus ſaith the Lord God, The gate of the inner court, that looketh toward the Eaſt, ſhalbe ſhut the ſixe working dayes: but on the Sabbath it ſhall be opened, and in the day of the New moone it ſhalbe opened.2And the Prince ſhall enter by the way of the porch of that gate without, and ſhall ſtand by the poſt of the gate, and the Prieſts ſhall prepare his burnt offering, and his peace offerings, and he ſhall worſhip at the threſhold of the gate: then he ſhall goe foorth, but the gate ſhall not be ſhut vntil the euening.3Likewiſe the people of the land ſhall worſhip at the doore of this gate before the Lord, in the Sabbaths, and in the New moones.4And the burnt offering that the Prince ſhall offer vnto the Lord in the Sabbath day, ſhall be ſixe lambes without blemiſh, and a ramme without blemiſh.5And the meat offring ſhalbe an Ephah for a ramme, and the meate offering for the lambes as he ſhalbe able to giue, and an Hin of oile to an Ephah.6And in the day of the New moone it ſhall be a yong bullocke without blemiſh, and ſixe lambes, and a ramme: they ſhalbe without blemiſh.7And hee ſhall prepare a meat offering, an Ephah for a bullocke, and an Ephah for a ramme, and for the lambs, according as his hand ſhall attaine vnto, and an Hin of oile to an Ephah.8And when the Prince ſhall enter, he ſhall goe in by the way of the porch of that gate, and he ſhall goe foorth by the way thereof.9But when the people of the land ſhall come before the Lord, in the ſolemne feaſts, he that entreth in by the way of the North gate to worſhip, ſhall goe out by the way of the South gate: and he that entreth by the way of the South gate, ſhall goe forth by the way of the North gate: he ſhall not returne by the way of the gate whereby he came in, but ſhall goe foorth ouer againſt it.10And the Prince in the midſt of them when they goe in, ſhal goe in, and when they goe foorth, ſhall goe forth.11And in the feaſts, and in the ſolemnities, the meat offering ſhalbe an Ephah to a bullocke, and an Ephah to a ramme, and to the lambes, as he is able to giue, and an Hin of oile to an Ephah.12Now when the Prince ſhall prepare a voluntary burnt offering or peace offerings, voluntarily vnto the Lord, one ſhall then open him the gate that looketh toward the Eaſt, and he ſhall prepare his burnt offering, and his peace offerings, as hee did on the Sabbath day, then he ſhall goe foorth, and after his going foorth, one ſhall ſhut the gate.13Thou ſhalt daily prepare a burnt offering vnto the Lord, of a lambe of the firſt yeere, without blemiſh thou ſhalt prepare it euery morning.14And thou ſhalt prepare a meat offering for it euery morning; the ſixt part of an Ephah, and the third part of an Hin of oyle, to temper with the fine flowre; a meat offering continually, by a perpetual ordinance vnto the Lord.15Thus ſhall they prepare the lambe, and the meat offering, and the oyle, euery morning, for a continuall burnt offering.16Thus ſaith the Lord God, If the prince giue a gift vnto any of his ſonnes, the inheritance thereof ſhall be his ſonnes, it ſhall be their poſſeſſion by inheritance:17But if hee giue a gift of his inheritance to one of his ſeruants, then it ſhalbe his to the yeere of libertie: after, it ſhall returne to the Prince, but his inheritance ſhalbe his ſonnes for them.18Moreouer, the Prince ſhall not take of the peoples inheritance by oppreſſion, to thruſt them out of their poſſeſſion: but hee ſhall giue his ſonnes inheritance out of his owne poſſeſſion, that my people be not ſcattered euery man from his poſſeſſion.19After, he brought me through the entry, which was at the ſide of the gate, into the holy chambers of the Prieſts which looked toward yͤ North: and behold, there was a place on the two ſides Weſtward.20Then ſaid hee vnto me, This is the place where the Prieſts ſhall boyle the treſpaſſe offring, and the ſinne offering, where they ſhall bake the meate offering: that they beare them not out into the vtter court, to ſanctifie the people.21Then hee brought me foorth into the vtter court, and cauſed me to paſſe by the foure corners of the court, and behold, in euery corner of the court there was a court.22In the foure corners of the court there were courts ioyned of fourtie cubits long, and thirtie broad: theſe foure corners were of one meaſure.23And there was a new building round about in them, round about them foure and it was made with boyling places vnder the rowes round about.24Then ſaid he vnto me, Theſe are the places of them that boyle, where the miniſters of the houſe ſhall boyle the ſacrifice of the people.

CHAPTER 471Afterward hee brought me againe vnto the doore of the houſe, and behold, waters iſſued out from vnder the threſhold of the houſe Eaſtward: for the forefront of the houſe ſtood toward the Eaſt, and the waters came downe from vnder from the right ſide of the houſe, at the South ſide of the Altar.2Then brought hee me out of the way of the gate Northward, and ledde me about the way without vnto the vtter gate by the way that looketh Eaſtward, and behold, there ranne out waters on the right ſide.3And when the man that had the line in his hand, went forth Eaſtward, he meaſured a thouſand cubites, and he brought me through the waters: the waters were to the ancles.4Againe he meaſured a thouſand, and brought me through the waters; the waters were to the knees: againe he meaſured a thouſand, and brought mee through; the waters were to the loynes.5Afterward hee meaſured a thouſand, and it was a riuer, that I could not paſſe ouer: for the waters were riſen, waters to ſwimme in, a riuer that could not be paſſed ouer.6And hee ſaid vnto me, Sonne of man, haſt thou ſeene this? Then hee brought me, and cauſed me to returne to the brinke of the riuer.7Now when I had returned, behold, at the banke of the riuer were very many trees on the one ſide and on the other.8Then ſaid he vnto me, Theſe waters iſſue out toward the Eaſt country, and go downe into the deſert, and goe into the ſea: which being brought foorth into the ſea, the waters ſhalbe healed.9And it ſhall come to paſſe, that euery thing that liueth, which mooueth, whitherſoeuer the riuers ſhall come, ſhall liue, and there ſhall be a very great multitude of fiſh, becauſe theſe waters ſhall come thither: for they ſhall be healed, and euery thing ſhall liue whither the riuer commeth.10And it ſhall come to paſſe that the fiſhers ſhall ſtand vpon it, from Engedi euen vnto En-eglaim; they ſhall be a place to ſpread foorth nets, their fiſh ſhall bee according to their kindes, as the fiſh of the great ſea, exceeding many.11But the myrie places thereof, and the mariſhes thereof, ſhall not be healed, they ſhall be giuen to ſalt.12And by the riuer vpon the banke thereof on this ſide, and on that ſide, ſhall grow all trees for meat, whoſe leafe ſhal not fade, neither ſhal the fruit thereof be conſumed: it ſhall bring forth new fruit, according to his moneths, becauſe their waters they iſſued out of the Sanctuarie, and the fruite thereof ſhall be for meate, and the leafe thereof for medicine.13Thus ſayth the Lord God, This ſhall be the border, whereby yee ſhall inherite the land, according to the twelue tribes of Iſrael: Ioſeph ſhall haue two portions.14And yee ſhall inherite it, one as well as an other: concerning the which I lifted vp mine hand to giue it vnto your fathers, and this land ſhal fall vnto you for inheritance.15And this ſhall be the border of the land toward the North ſide from the great ſea, the way of Hethlon, as men goe to Zedad:16Hamath, Berothah, Sibraim, which is betweene the border of Damaſcus, and the border of Hamath: Hazar Hatticon, which is by the coaſt of Hauran.17And the border from the ſea ſhall be Hazar-enan, the border of Damaſcus, and the North northward, and the border of Hamath: and this is the North ſide.18And the Eaſt ſide yee ſhall meaſure from Hauran, and from Damaſcus, and from Gilead, and from the land of Iſrael by Iordan, from the border vnto the Eaſt ſea: & this is the Eaſt ſide.19And the South ſide Southward from Tamar, euen to the waters of ſtrife in Kadeſh, the riuer, to the great ſea; and this is the South ſide Southward.20The Weſt ſide alſo ſhall be the great ſea from the border, till a man come ouer againſt Hamath: this is the Weſt ſide.21So ſhall yee diuide this land vnto you according to the Tribes of Iſrael.22And it ſhall come to paſſe, that yee ſhall diuide it by lot for an inheritance vnto you, and to the ſtrangers that ſoiourne among you, which ſhall beget children among you, and they ſhall be vnto you as borne in the countrey among the children of Iſrael; they ſhall haue inheritance with you among the Tribes of Iſrael.23And it ſhall come to paſſe that in what Tribe the ſtranger ſoiourneth, there ſhall yee giue him his inheritance, ſaith the Lord God.

CHAPTER 481Now theſe are the names of the Tribes, from the North end to the coaſt of the way of Hathlon, as one goeth to Hamath, Hazarenan, the border of Damaſcus Northward, to þe coaſt of Hamath (for theſe are his ſides Eaſt & Weſt) a portion for Dan.2And by the border of Dan, from the Eaſt ſide vnto the Weſt, a portion for Aſher.3And by the border of Aſher, from the Eaſt ſide euen vnto the Weſt ſide, a portion for Naphtali.4And by the border of Naphtali, from the Eaſt ſide vnto the Weſt ſide, a portion for Manaſſeh.5And by the border of Manaſſeh, from the Eaſt ſide vnto the Weſt ſide, a portion for Ephraim.6And by the border of Ephraim, from the Eaſt ſide euen vnto the Weſt ſide, a portion for Reuben.7And by the border of Reuben, from the Eaſt ſide vnto the Weſt ſide, a portion for Iudah.8And by the border of Iudah, from the Eaſt ſide vnto the Weſt ſide, ſhall be the offring which they ſhall offer of fiue and twentie thouſand reedes in bredth, and in length as one of the other parts, from the Eaſt ſide vnto the Weſt ſide, and the Sanctuarie ſhall be in the midſt of it.9The oblation that yee ſhall offer vnto the Lord, ſhall be of fiue and twentie thouſand in length, and of ten thouſand in bredth.10And for them, euen for the prieſts ſhall be this holy oblation, toward the North, fiue and twentie thouſand in length, and toward the Weſt ten thouſand in bredth, and toward the Eaſt ten thouſand in bredth, and toward the South fiue and twentie thouſand in length, & the ſanctuarie of the Lord ſhall be in the midſt thereof.11It ſhall be for the Prieſts that are ſanctified, of the ſonnes of Zadok, which haue kept my charge, which went not aſtray when the children of Iſrael went aſtray, as the Leuites went aſtray.12And this oblation of the land that is offred, ſhalbe vnto them a thing moſt holy by the border of the Leuites.13And ouer againſt the border of the Prieſts, the Leuites ſhall haue fiue and twentie thouſand in length, and tenne thouſand in bredth: all the length ſhalbe fiue and twentie thouſand, and the bredth tenne thouſand.14And they ſhall not ſell of it, neither exchange, nor alienate the firſt fruits of the land: for it is holy vnto the Lord.15And the fiue thouſand that are left in the breadth ouer againſt the fiue and twentie thouſand, ſhall bee a prophane place for the citie, for dwelling, and for ſuburbs, and the citie ſhall be in the midſt thereof.16And theſe ſhall bee the meaſures thereof, the North ſide foure thouſand and fiue hundred, and the South ſide foure thouſand and fiue hundred, and on the Eaſt ſide foure thouſand, and fiue hundred, and the Weſt ſide foure thouſand and fiue hundred.17And the ſuburbs of the city ſhall be toward the North two hundred and fiftie, and toward the South two hundred and fifty, and toward the Eaſt two hundred and fiftie, and toward the Weſt two hundred and fiftie.18And the reſidue in length ouer againſt the oblation of the holy portion, ſhalbe ten thouſand Eaſtward, and ten thouſand Weſtward: and it ſhall be ouer againſt the oblation of the holy portion, and the increaſe thereof ſhall bee for food vnto them that ſerue the citie.19And they that ſerue the citie, ſhall ſerue it out of all the tribes of Iſrael.20All the oblation ſhall bee fiue and twentie thouſand, by fiue and twentie thouſand: ye ſhall offer the holy oblation foure ſquare, with the poſſeſſion of the citie.21And the reſidue ſhall bee for the prince on the one ſide, and on the other of the holy oblation, and of the poſſeſſion of the citie ouer againſt the fiue and twentie thouſand, of the oblation toward the Eaſt border, and Weſtward ouer againſt the fiue and twentie thouſand toward the Weſt border, ouer againſt the portions for the prince, and it ſhall be the holy oblation, and the Sanctuarie of the houſe ſhall be in the middeſt thereof.22Moreouer, from the poſſeſſion of the Leuites, and from the poſſeſſion of the citie, being in the midſt of that which is the princes, betweene the border of Iudah, and the border of Beniamin, ſhall bee for the prince.23As for the reſt of the tribes, from the Eaſt ſide vnto the Weſt ſide, Beniamin ſhall haue a portion:24And by the border of Beniamin, from the Eaſt ſide vnto the Weſt ſide, Simeon ſhall haue a portion:25And by the border of Simeon, from the Eaſt ſide vnto the Weſt ſide, Iſſachar a portion:26And by the border of Iſſachar, from the Eaſt ſide vnto the Weſt ſide, Zebulun a portion:27And by the border of Zebulun from the Eaſt ſide vnto the Weſt ſide, Gad a portion:28And by the border of Gad, at the South ſide Southward, the border ſhall be euen from Tamar, vnto the waters of ſtrife in Kadeſh, and to the riuer toward the great ſea.29This is the land which ye ſhal diuide by lot vnto the tribes of Iſrael for inheritance, and theſe are their portions, ſaith the Lord God.30And theſe are the goings out of the citie, on the North ſide foure thouſand and fiue hundred meaſures.31And the gates of the citie ſhall bee after the names of the tribes of Iſrael, three gates Northward, one gate of Reuben, one gate of Iudah, one gate of Leui.32And at the Eaſt ſide foure thouſand and fiue hundred: and three gates; and one gate of Ioſeph, one gate of Beniamin, one gate of Dan.33And at the South ſide foure thouſand and fiue hundred meaſures,

and three gates: one gate of Simeon, one gate of Iſſachar, one gate of
Zebulun.[34]At the Weſt ſide foure thouſand and fiue hundred, with their
three gates: one gate of Gad, one gate of Aſher, one gate of Naphtali.[35]It
was round about eighteene thouſand meaſures, and the name of the citie
from that day ſhall be, The Lord is there.

DANIEL

CHAPTER 1[1]In the thirde yere of the reigne of Iehoiakim King of
Iudah, came Nebuchad-nezzar King of Babylon, vnto Ieruſalem, and
beſieged it.[2]And the Lord gaue Iehoiakim king of Iudah into his hand,
with part of the veſſels of the houſe of God, which he caried into the
land of Shinar to the houſe of his god, and he brought the veſſels into
the treaſure houſe of his god.[3]And the king ſpake vnto Aſhpenaz the
maſter of his Eunuches, that he ſhould bring certaine of the children of
Iſrael, and of the kings ſeed, and of the Princes:[4]Children in whom was
no blemiſh, but well fauoured, and ſkilfull in all wiſedome, and cunning
in knowledge, and vnderſtanding ſcience, and ſuch as had abilitie in
them to ſtand in the Kings palace, and whom they might teach the
learning, and the tongue of the Caldeans.[5]And the King appointed them
a daily prouiſion of the kings meat, and of the wine which he dranke: ſo
nouriſhing them three yeeres, that at the ende thereof they might ſtand
before the king.[6]Now among theſe were of the children of Iudah,
Daniel, Hananiah, Miſhael, and Azariah:[7]Unto whom the Prince of the
Eunuches gaue names: for he gaue vnto Daniel the name of
Belteſhazzar; and to Hananiah, of Shadrach; and to Miſhael, of Meſhach;
and to Azariah of Abednego.[8]But Daniel purpoſed in his heart, that he
would not defile himſelfe with the portion of the kings meat, nor with
the wine which he dranke: therefore hee requeſted of the Prince of the
Eunuches, that hee might not defile himſelfe.[9]Now God had brought
Daniel into fauour and tender loue with the Prince of the
Eunuches.[10]And the Prince of the Eunuches ſaid vnto Daniel, I feare
my lord the king, who hath appointed your meat, and your drinke: for
why ſhould he ſee your faces worſe liking then the children which are
of your ſort? then ſhall yee make mee indanger my head to the
King.[11]Then ſaid Daniel to Melzar, whom the Prince of the Eunuches
had ſet ouer Daniel, Hananiah, Miſhael, and Azariah,[12]Proue thy
ſeruants, I beſeech thee, ten dayes, and let them giue pulſe to eat, and
water to drinke.[13]Then let our countenances be looked vpon before
thee, and the countenance of the children that eat of the portion of the
Kings meate: and as thou ſeeſt, deale with thy ſeruants.[14]So hee
conſented to them in this matter, and proued them ten dayes.[15]And at
the end often dayes, their countenances appeared fairer, and fatter in
fleſh, then all the children, which did eate the portion of the kings
meat.[16]Thus Melzar tooke away the portion of their meat, and the wine
that they ſhould drink: and gaue them pulſe.[17]As for theſe foure
children, God gaue them knowledge, and ſkil in all learning and
wiſedome, and Daniel had vnderſtanding in all viſions and
dreames.[18]Now at the end of the dayes that the King had ſaid he ſhould
bring them in, then the Prince of the Eunuches brought them in before
Nebuchadnezzar.[19]And the King communed with them: and among
them all was found none like Daniel, Hananiah, Miſhael, and Azariah:
therefore ſtood they before the King.[20]And in all matters of wiſedome
and vnderſtanding that the king enquired of them, hee found them ten
times better then all the Magicians and Aſtrologers that were in all his
Realme.[21]And Daniel continued euen vnto the firſt yeere of king Cyrus.
CHAPTER 2[1]And in the ſecond yeere of the reigne of
Nebuchadnezzar, Nebuchad-nezzar dreamed dreames, wherewith his
ſpirit was troubled, and his ſleepe brake from him.[2]Then the King
commanded to call the Magicians, and the Aſtrologers, and the
Sorcerers, and the Caldeans, for to ſhew the King his dreames: ſo they
came and ſtood before the king.[3]And the King ſaid vnto them, I haue
dreamed a dreame, and my ſpirit was troubled to know the
dreame.[4]Then ſpake the Caldeans to the King in Syriacke; O king, liue
for euer: tell thy ſeruants the dreame, and we will ſhew the
interpretation.[5]The King anſwered, and ſaid to the Caldeans, The thing
is gone from mee: if ye will not make knowen vnto me the dreame, with
the interpretation thereof, yee ſhall be cut in pieces, and your houſes
ſhalbe made a dunghill.[6]But if yee ſhewe the dreame, and the
interpretation thereof, yee ſhall receiue of me giftes and rewards, and
great honour: therefore ſhewe me the dreame, and the interpretation
thereof.[7]They anſwered againe, and ſaid, Let the King tell his ſeruants
the dreame, and we will ſhew the interpretation of it.[8]The King
anſwered, and ſaid, I know of certeinty that ye would gaine the time,
becauſe ye ſee the thing is gone from me.[9]But if yee will not make
knowen vnto me the dreame, there is but one decree for you: for ye
haue prepared lying, and corrupt words to ſpeake before me, till the time
be changed: therefore tell me the dreame, and I ſhall know that yee can
ſhewe mee the interpretation thereof.[10]The Caldeans anſwered before
the King, and ſaid, There is not a man vpon the earth that can ſhew the
kings matter: therefore there is no King, lord, nor ruler, that aſked ſuch
things at any Magician, or Aſtrologer, or Caldean.[11]And it is a rare thing
that the king requireth, and there is none other that can ſhew it before
the King, except the gods, whoſe dwelling is not with fleſh.[12]For this
cauſe the King was angry and very furious, and commanded to deſtroy
all the wiſe men of Babylon.[13]And the decree went foorth that the wiſe
men ſhould be ſlaine, and they ſought Daniel and his fellowes to be
ſlaine.[14]Then Daniel anſwered with counſell and wiſedome to Arioch
the captaine of the Kings guard, which was gone foorth to ſlay the wiſe
men of Babylon.[15]Hee anſwered and ſaid to Arioch the Kings captaine,
Why is the decree ſo haſtie from the King? Then Arioch made the thing
knowen to Daniel.[16]Then Daniel went in and deſired of the King, that
hee would giue him time, and that he would ſhew the king the
interpretation.[17]Then Daniel went to his houſe, and made the thing
knowen to Hananiah, Miſhael, and Azariah his companions:[18]That they
would deſire mercies of the God of heauen concerning this ſecret, that
Daniel and his fellowes ſhould not periſh with the reſt of the Wiſe men
of Babylon.[19]Then was the ſecret reuealed vnto Daniel in a night viſion:
then Daniel bleſſed the God of heauen.[20]Daniel anſwered and ſaid;
Bleſſed be the name of God for euer and euer: for wiſedome and might
are his:[21]And he changeth the times and the ſeaſons: he remoueth Kings,
and ſetteth vp Kings: he giueth wiſedome vnto the wiſe, and knowledge
to them that know vnderſtanding.[22]He reuealeth the deepe and ſecret
things: hee knoweth what is in the darknes, & the light dwelleth with
him.[23]I thanke thee and praiſe thee, O thou God of my fathers, who haſt
giuen me wiſedome and might, and haſt made knowen vnto me now
what we deſired of thee: for thou haſt now made knowen vnto vs the
kings matter.[24]Therefore Daniel went in vnto Arioch whom the king
had ordained to deſtroy the wiſe men of Babylon: he went and ſaid thus
vnto him, Deſtroy not the wiſe men of Babylon: bring me in before the
king, and I will ſhew vnto the king the interpretation.[25]Then Arioch
brought in Daniel before the king in haſte, & ſaid thus vnto him, I haue
found a man of the captiues of Iudah, that will make knowen vnto the
king the interpretation.[26]The King anſwered and ſaid to Daniel whoſe
name was Belteſhazzar, Art thou able to make knowen vnto me the
dreame which I haue ſeene, and the interpretation thereof?[27]Daniel
anſwered in the preſence of the King, and ſaid, The ſecret which the
King hath demanded, cannot the wiſe men, the aſtrologians, the
magicians, þe ſouthſaiers ſhew vnto the king:[28]But there is a God in
heauen that reuealeth ſecrets, and maketh knowen to the king
Nebuchad-nezzar, what ſhalbe in the latter dayes. Thy dreame, and the
viſions of thy head vpon thy bed, are theſe.[29]As for thee, O King, thy
thoughts came into thy minde vpon thy bed, what ſhould come to paſſe
hereafter: and he that reuealeth ſecrets, maketh knowen to thee, what
ſhall come to paſſe.[30]But as for me, this ſecret is not reuealed to me, for
any wiſdome that I haue more then any liuing, but for their ſakes that
ſhall make knowen the interpretation to the King, and that thou
mighteſt know the thoughts of thy heart.[31]Thou, O King, ſaweſt, and
behold a great image: this great image whoſe brightneſſe was excelleut,
ſtood before thee, and the forme thereof was terrible.[32]This images head
was of fine gold, his breaſt and his armes of ſiluer, his belly and his
thighes of braſſe:[33]His legs of yron, his feete part of yron, and part of
clay.[34]Thou ſaweſt till that a ſtone was cut out without hands, which
ſmote the image vpon his feete that were of yron and clay, and brake
them to pieces.[35]Then was the yron, the clay, the braſſe, the ſiluer, and
the golde broken to pieces together, and became like the chaffe of the
ſummer threſhing floores, and the wind caried them away, that no place
was found for them: & the ſtone that ſmote the image became a great

mountaine, and filled the whole earth.36This is the dreame, and we will tell the interpretation thereof before the King.37Thou, O King, art a king of Kings: for the God of heauen hath giuen thee a kingdome, power, and ſtrength, and glory.38And whereſoeuer the children of men dwel, the beaſts of the field, and the foules of the heauen hath he giuen into thine hand, and hath made thee ruler ouer them all: thou art this head of gold.39And after thee ſhall Ariſe an other kingdome inferiour to thee, and another third kingdome of braſſe, which ſhall beare rule ouer all the earth.40And the fourth kingdome ſhall be ſtrong as yron: foraſmuch as yron breaketh in pieces and ſubdueth all things; and as yron that breaketh all theſe, ſhall it breake in pieces and bruiſe.41And whereas thou ſaweſt the feete and toes, part of potters clay, and part of yron: the kingdome ſhalbe diuided, but there ſhalbe in it of the ſtrength of the yron, foraſmuch as thou ſaweſt the yron mixt with myrie clay.42And as the toes of the feete were part of yron, and part of clay; ſo the kingdome ſhall be partly ſtrong, and partly broken.43And whereas thou ſaweſt yron mixt with myrie clay, they ſhall mingle themſelues with the ſeede of men: but they ſhall not cleaue one to an other, euen as yron is not mixed with clay.44And in the daies of theſe Kings ſhall the God of heauen ſet vp a kingdome, which ſhall neuer be deſtroyed: and the Kingdome ſhall not be left to other people, but it ſhall breake in pieces, and conſume all theſe kingdomes, and it ſhall ſtand for euer.45Foraſmuch as thou ſaweſt that the ſtone was cut out of the mountaine without hands, and that it brake in pieces the yron, the braſſe, the clay, the ſiluer, and the gold: the great God hath made knowen to the King what ſhall come to paſſe hereafter, & the dreame is certaine, and the interpretation thereof ſure.46Then the King Nebuchadnezzar fell vpon his face, and worſhipped Daniel, and commanded that they ſhould offer an oblation, and ſweet odours vnto him.47The King anſwered vnto Daniel and ſaid, Of a trueth it is, that your God is a God of gods, and a Lord of Kings, and a reuealer of ſecrets, ſeeing thou couldeſt reueale this ſecret.48Then the King made Daniel a great man, and gaue him many great gifts, & made him ruler ouer the whole prouince of Babylon, and chiefe of the gouernours ouer all the wiſe men of Babylon.49Then Daniel requeſted of the King, and he ſet Shadrach, Meſhach, and Abednego ouer the affaires of the prouince of Babylon: but Daniel ſate in the gate of the King.

CHAPTER 31Nebuchad-nezzar the king made an image of gold, whoſe height was threeſcore cubits, and þe breadth thereof ſixe cubites: he ſet it vp in the plaine of Dura, in the prouince of Babylon.2Then Nebuchad-nezzar the king ſent to gather together the Princes, the Gouernours, and the Captaines, the Iudges, the Treaſurers, the Counſellers, the Sherifes, and all the rulers of the Prouinces, to come to the dedication of the image which Nebuchad-nezzar the King had ſet vp.3Then the Princes, the Gouernours and Captaines, the Iudges, the Treaſurers, the Counſellers, the Sherifes, and all the rulers of the Prouinces were gathered together vnto the dedicatiō of the image, that Nebuchadnezzar the King had ſet vp, and they ſtood before the image that Nebuchadnezzar had ſet vp.4Then an herauld cryed aloud, To you it is commaunded, O people, nations, and languages,5That at what time yee heare the ſound of the cornet, flute, harpe, ſackbut, pſalterie, dulcimer, and all kinds of muſicke, yee fall downe, and worſhip the golden image that Nebuchad-nezzar the King hath ſet vp:6And who ſo falleth not down and worſhippeth, ſhall the ſame houre bee caſt into the middeſt of a burning fierie furnace.7Therefore at that time, when all the people heard the ſound of the cornet, flute, harpe, ſackbut, pſalterie, and all kindes of muſicke, all the people, the nations, and the languages fell downe and worſhipped the golden image, that Nebuchad-nezzar the King had ſet vp.8Wherefore at that time certaine Caldeans came neere, and accuſed the Iewes.9They ſpake and ſayd to the King Nebuchad-nezzar, O King, liue for euer.10Thou, O King, haſt made a decree, that euery man that ſhal heare the ſound of the cornet, flute, harpe, ſackbut, pſalterie, and dulcimer, and all kinds of muſicke, ſhall fall downe and worſhip the golden image:11And who ſo falleth not downe & worſhippeth, that he ſhould be caſt into the midſt of a burning fierie furnace.12There are certain Iewes whom thou haſt ſet ouer the affaires of the prouince of Babylon, Shadrach, Meſhach, and Abednego: theſe men, O King, haue not regarded thee, they ſerue not thy gods, nor worſhip the golden image, which thou haſt ſet vp.13Then Nebuchad-nezzar in his rage and furie commaunded to bring Shadrach, Meſhach, and Abednego: then they brought theſe men before the King.14Nebuchad-nezzar ſpake and ſaid vnto them, Is it true, O Shadrach, Meſhach and Abednego? doe not yee ſerue my gods, nor worſhip the golden image which I haue ſet vp?15Now if ye be ready that at what time yee heare the ſound of the cornet, flute, harpe, ſackbut, pſalterie, and dulcimer, and all kindes of muſicke, ye fall downe, and worſhip the image which I haue made, well: but if yee worſhip not, ye ſhall be caſt the ſame houre into the midſt of a fierie furnace, and who is that God that ſhall deliuer you out of my handes?16Shadrach, Meſhach, and Abednego anſwered and ſaid to the king; O Nebuchad-nezzar, we are not carefull to anſwere thee in this matter.17If it be ſo, our God whom wee ſerue, is able to deliuer vs from the burning fierie furnace, and he will deliuer vs out of thine hand, O king.18But if not, bee it knowen vnto thee, O king, that we will not ſerue thy gods, nor worſhip thy golden image, which thou haſt ſet vp.19Then was Nebuchad-nezzar full of furie, and the forme of his viſage was changed againſt Shadrach, Meſhach and Abednego: therefore he ſpake and commanded, that they ſhould heat the furnace one ſeuen times more then it was wont to be heat.20And hee commaunded the moſt mighty men that were in his armie, to binde Shadrach, Meſhach and Abednego, and to caſt them into the burning fierie furnace.21Then theſe men were bound in their coates, their hoſen, and their hats, and their other garments, and were caſt into the midſt of the burning fierie furnace.22Therefore becauſe the Kings commandement was vrgent, and the furnace exceeding hot, the flame of the fire ſlew thoſe men that tooke vp Shadrach, Meſhach and Abednego.23And theſe three men, Shadrach, Meſhach, and Abednego, fell downe bound into the midſt of the burning fierie furnace.24Then Nebuchad-nezzar the king was aſtonied, and roſe vp in haſte, and ſpake and ſaid vnto his counſellers, Did not wee caſt three men bound into the midſt of the fire? They anſwered and ſaid vnto the king; True, O king.25He anſwered and ſaid, Loe, I ſee foure men looſe, walking in the midſt of the fire, and they haue no hurt, and the forme of the fourth is like the ſonne of God.26Then Nebuchad-nezzar came neere to the mouth of the burning fierie furnace, and ſpake and ſaid, Shadrach, Meſhach and Abednego, ye ſeruants of the moſt High God, come forth, and come hither. Then Shadrach, Meſhach, and Abednego came forth of the midſt of the fire.27And the princes, gouernours, and captaines, and the kings counſellers, being gathered together, ſaw theſe men, vpon whoſe bodies the fire had no power, nor was an haire of their head ſinged, neither were their coats changed, nor the ſmell of fire had paſſed on them.28Then Nebuchad-nezzar ſpake and ſaid; Bleſſed bee the God of Shadrach, Meſhach, and Abednego, who hath ſent his Angel, and deliuered his ſeruants that truſted in him, and haue changed the Kings word, and yeelded their bodies, that they might not ſerue nor worſhip any God, except their owne God.29Therefore I make a decree, That euery people, nation, and language, which ſpeake any thing amiſse againſt the God of Shadrach, Meſhach, and Abednego, ſhall be cut in pieces, and their houſes ſhall be made a dunghill, becauſe there is no other God, that can deliuer after this ſort.30Then the King promoted Shadrach, Meſhach, and Abednego in the prouince of Babylon.

CHAPTER 41Nebuchad-nezzar the king, vnto all people, nations, and languages that dwell in all the earth, Peace be multiplied vnto you.2I thought it good to ſhew the ſignes, and wonders, that the high God hath wrought toward me.3How great are his ſignes? and how mighty are his wonders? his kingdome is an euerlaſting kingdome, and his dominion is frō generation to generation.4I Nebuchadnezzar was at reſt in mine houſe, and flouriſhing in my palace.5I ſaw a dreame which made me afraid, and the thoughts vpon my bed, and the viſions of my head troubled me.6Therefore made I a decree, to bring in all the wiſe men of Babylon before mee, that they might make knowen vnto me the interpretation of the dreame.7Then came in the Magicians, the Aſtrologers, the Caldeans, and the Southſayers: and I tolde the dreame before them; but they did not make knowen vnto mee the interpretation thereof.8But at the laſt Daniel came in before me, (whoſe name was Belteſhazzar, according to the name of my God, and in whom is the ſpirit of the holy Godſ) & before him I told the dreame, ſaying,9O Belteſhazzar, maſter of the Magicians, becauſe I know that the ſpirit of the holy Gods is in thee, and no ſecret troubleth thee, tell me the viſions of my dreame that I haue ſeene, and the interpretation thereof.10Thus were the viſions of mine head in my bed: I ſaw, and behold, a tree in the middeſt of the earth, and the height thereof was great.11The tree grew, and was ſtrong, and the height thereof reached vnto heauen, and the ſight thereof to the end of all the earth.12The leaues thereof were faire, and the fruite thereof much, and in it was meate for all: the beaſts of the field had ſhadow vnder it, and the foules of the heauen dwelt in the boughes thereof, and all fleſh was fed of it.13I ſawe in the viſions of my head vpon my bed, & behold, a watcher and an holy one came downe from heauen.14He cryed aloude, and ſaid thus; Hew downe the tree, and cut off his branches; ſhake off his leaues, and ſcatter his fruite; let the beaſts get away from vnder it, and the foules from his branches.15Neuertheleſſe leaue the ſtumpe of his rootes in the earth, euen with a band of yron and braſſe, in the tender graſſe of the field, and let it be wet with the dew of heauen, and let his portion be with the beaſtes in the graſſe of the earth.16Let his heart bee changed from mans, and let a beaſts heart be giuen vnto him, and let ſeuen times paſſe ouer him.17This matter is by the decree of the watchers, and the demaund by the word of the Holy ones: to the intent that the liuing may know, that the moſt High ruleth in the kingdome of men, and giueth it to whomſoeuer hee will, and ſetteth vp ouer it the baſeſt of men.18This dreame, I king Nebuchadnezzar haue ſeene: Now thou, O Belteſhazzar, declare the interpretation thereof, foraſmuch as all the Wiſe men of my kingdome are not able to make knowen vnto mee the interpretation: but thou art able, for the ſpirit of the holy Gods is in thee.19Then Daniel (whoſe name was Belteſhazzar) was aſtonied for one houre, and his thoughts troubled him: The King ſpake, and ſaid, Belteſhazzar, let not the dreame, or the interpretation thereof trouble thee. Belteſhazzar anſwered; and ſaid; My lord, the dreame be to them that hate thee, and the interpretation thereof to thine enemies.20The tree that thou ſaweſt, which grew, and was ſtrong, whoſe height reached vnto the heauen, and the ſight thereof to all the earth:21Whoſe leaues were faire, and the fruit thereof much, and in it was meate for all, vnder which the beaſts of the field dwelt, and vpon whoſe branches the foules of the heauen had their habitation:22It is thou, O King, that art growen and become ſtrong: for thy greatneſſe is growen and reacheth vnto heauen, and thy dominion to the end of the earth.23And whereas the King ſaw a watcher, and an holy one comming downe from heauen, and ſaying, Hew the tree downe, and deſtroy it, yet leaue the ſtumpe of the rootes thereof in the earth, euen with a band of yron and braſſe in the tender graſſe of the field, and let it be wet with the dewe of heauen, and let his portion be with the beaſts of the field, till ſeuen times paſſe ouer him:24This is the interpretation, O king, & this is the decree of the moſt Hie, which is come vpon my lord the king:25That they ſhall driue thee from men, and thy dwelling ſhall be with the beaſts of the field, and they ſhall make thee to eate graſſe as oxen, and they ſhall wet thee with the dew of heauen, and ſeuen times ſhall paſſe ouer thee, till thou know that the moſt high ruleth in the kingdome of men, and giueth it to whomſoeuer he will.26And whereas they commanded to leaue the ſtumpe of the tree rootes; thy kingdome ſhall be ſure vnto thee, after that thou ſhalt haue knowen that the heauens doe rule.27Wherefore, O King, let my counſell be acceptable vnto thee, and breake off thy ſinnes by righteouſneſſe, and thine iniquities by ſhewing mercy to the poore; if it may be a lengthening of thy tranquillitie.28All this came vpon the King Nebuchad-nezzar.29At the end of twelue moneths he walked in the palace of the kingdome of Babylon.30The King ſpake, and ſaid, Is not this great Babylon, that I haue built for the houſe of the kingdome, by the might of my power, and for the honour of my maieſtie?31While the word was in the Kings mouth, there fell a voice from heauen, ſaying, O King Nebuchad-nezzar, to thee it is ſpoken; The kingdome is departed from thee.32And they ſhall driue thee from men, and thy dwelling ſhall be with the beaſts of the field; they ſhall make thee to eate graſſe as oxen, and ſeuen times ſhall paſſe ouer thee, vntill thou know that the moſt high ruleth in the kingdome of men, and giueth it to whomſoeuer he will.33The ſame houre was the thing fulfilled vpon Nebuchad-nezzar, and he was driuen from men, and did eate graſſe as oxen, and his body was wet with the dew of heauen, till his haires were growen like Egles feathers, and his nailes like birds clawes.34And at the end of the dayes, I Nebuchad-nezzar lift vp mine eyes vnto heauen, and mine vnderſtanding returned vnto me, and I bleſſed the moſt high, and I praiſed, and honoured him that liueth for euer, whoſe dominion is an euerlaſting dominion, and his kingdome is from generation to generation.35And all the inhabitants of the earth are reputed as nothing: and hee doth according to his will in the armie of heauen, and among the inhabitants of the earth: and none can ſtay his hand, or ſay vnto him, What doeſt thou?36At the ſame time my reaſon returned vnto me, and for the glory of my kingdome, mine honour, and brightnes returned vnto me, and my counſellers, and my Lords ſought vnto me, and I was eſtabliſhed in my kingdome, and excellent Maieſtie was added vnto me.37Now I Nebuchad-nezzar praiſe, and extoll and honour the King of heauen, all whoſe workes are truth, and his waies iudgement, and thoſe that walke in pride he is able to abaſe.

CHAPTER 51Belſhazzar the King made a great feaſt to a thouſand of his Lords, and dranke wine before the thouſand.2Belſhazzar, whiles he taſted the wine, commaunded to bring the golden and ſiluer veſſels, which his father Nebuchad-nezzar had taken out of the temple which was in Ieruſalem, that the king and his princes, his wiues, and his concubines might drinke therein.3Then they brought the golden veſſels that were taken out of the temple of the houſe of God, which was at Ieruſalem, and the king and his princes, his wiues, and his concubines dranke in them.4They drunke wine, and praiſed the gods of gold and of ſiluer, of braſſe, of yron, of wood, and of ſtone.5In the ſame houre came forth fingers of a mans hand, and wrote ouer againſt the candleſticke vpon the plaiſter of the wall of the Kings palace, and the king ſaw the part of the hand that wrote.6Then the kings countenance was changed, and his thoughts troubled him, ſo that the ioints of his loines were looſed, and his knees ſmote one againſt another.7The king cried aloud to bring in the Aſtrologers, the Caldeans, and the ſoothſayers: and the king ſpake and ſaid to the wiſe men of Babylon, Whoſoeuer ſhall reade this writing, and ſhewe me the interpretation thereof, ſhall bee clothed with ſcarlet, and haue a chaine of gold about his necke, and ſhall be the third ruler in the kingdome.8Then came in all the kings wiſe men, but they could not reade the writing, nor make knowen to the king the interpretation thereof.9Then was King Belſhazzar greatly troubled, and his countenance was changed in him, and his lordes were aſtonied.10Now the queene, by reaſon of the wordes of the king and his lords, came into the banquet houſe, and the queene ſpake and ſaid, O king, liue for euer: let not thy thoughts trouble thee, nor let thy countenance be changed.11There is a man in thy kingdom, in whome is the ſpirit of the holy gods, and in the dayes of thy father light and vnderſtanding and wiſedome like the wiſedome of the gods, was found in him: whom the king Nebuchad-nezzar thy father, the king, I ſay, thy father made maſter of the magicians, aſtrologers, Caldeans, and ſoothſayers,12Foraſmuch as an excellent ſpirit and knowledge and vnderſtanding, interpreting of dreames, and ſhewing of hard ſentences, & diſſoluing of doubts were found in the ſame Daniel, whom the king named Belteſhazzar: now let Daniel be called, and he will ſhewe the interpretation.13Then was Daniel brought in before the king, and the king ſpake and ſaid vnto Daniel, Art thou that Daniel, which art of the children of the captiuity of Iudah, whom the king my father brought out of Iewrie?14I haue euen heard of thee, that the ſpirit of the gods is in thee, and that light, and vnderſtanding, and excellent wiſedome is found in thee.15And now the wiſe men, the aſtrologers haue bene brought in before me, that they ſhould reade this writing, and make knowen vnto me the interpretation thereof: but they could not ſhewe the interpretation of the thing.16And I haue heard of thee, that thou canſt make interpretations, and diſſolue doubts: now if thou canſt read the writing, and make knowen to mee the interpretation thereof, thou ſhalt be clothed with ſcarlet, & haue a chaine of gold about thy necke, and ſhalt bee the third ruler in the kingdome.17Then Daniel anſwered and ſaid before the king, Let thy gifts be to thy ſelfe, and giue thy rewards to an other, yet I will reade the writing vnto the king, and make knowen to him the interpretation.18O thou king, the moſt high God gaue Nebuchad-nezzar thy father a kingdome, and maieſtie, and glory, and honour.19And for the maieſtie that hee gaue him, all people, nations, and languages trembled and feared before him: whom he would, he ſlew, & whom he would, he kept aliue, and whom he would hee ſet vp, and whom he would hee put downe.20But when his heart was lifted vp, and his minde hardened in pride: hee was depoſed from his kingly throne, and they tooke his glory from him.21And hee was driuen from the ſonnes of men, and his heart was made like the beaſts, and his dwelling was with the wilde aſſes: they fed him with graſſe like oxen, and his body was wet with the dew of heauen, till hee knew that the moſt high God ruled in the kingdome of men, and that hee appointeth ouer it whomſoeuer he will. 22 And thou his ſonne, O Belſhazzar, haſt not humbled thine heart, though thou kneweſt all this: 23 But haſt lifted vp thy ſelfe againſt the Lord of heauen, and they haue brought the veſſels of his houſe before thee, and thou and thy lords, thy wiues and thy concubines haue drunke wine in them, and thou haſt praiſed the gods of ſiluer, and golde, of braſſe, yron, wood and ſtone, which ſee not, nor heare, nor knowe: and the God in whoſe hande thy breath is, and whoſe are all thy wayes, haſt thou not glorified. 24 Then was the part of the hand ſent from him, and this writing was written. 25 And this is the writing that was written, MENE, MENE, TEKEL VPHARSIN. 26 This is the interpretation of the thing, MENE, God hath numbred thy kingdome, and finiſhed it. 27 TEKEL, thou art weighed in the balances, and art found wanting. 28 PERES, thy kingdome is diuided, and giuen to the Medes and Perſians. 29 Then commanded Belſhazzar, and they clothed Daniel with ſcarlet, and put a chaine of gold about his necke, and made a Proclamation concerning him, that he ſhould be the third ruler in the kingdome. 30 In that night was Belſhazzar the king of the Caldeans ſlaine. 31 And Darius the Median tooke the kingdome, being about threeſcore and two yeere old.

CHAPTER 6 1 It pleaſed Darius to ſet ouer the kingdome an hundred and twenty Princes, which ſhould be ouer the whole kingdome. 2 And ouer theſe, three Preſidents, (of whom Daniel was firſt) that the Princes might giue accompts vnto them, and the King ſhould haue no damage. 3 Then this Daniel was preferred aboue the Preſidents, and Princes, becauſe an excellent ſpirit was in him, and the king thought to ſet him ouer the whole realme. 4 Then the Preſidents and Princes ſought to finde occaſion againſt Daniel concerning the kingdome, but they could finde none occaſion, nor fault: foraſmuch as he was faithfull, neither was there any errour or fault found in him. 5 Then ſaid theſe men, We ſhall not finde any occaſion againſt this Daniel, except wee finde it againſt him concerning the Law of his God. 6 Then theſe Preſidents and Princes aſſembled together to the king, and ſaid thus vnto him, King Darius, liue foreuer. 7 All the Preſidents of the kingdome, the gouernours, and the Princes, the counſellers and the captaines haue conſulted together to eſtabliſh a royall ſtatute, and to make a firme decree, that whoſoeuer ſhall aſke a petition of any God or man for thirty dayes, ſaue of thee, O King, hee ſhall be caſt into the denne of Lions. 8 Now, O king, eſtabliſh the decree, and ſigne the writing, that it be not changed, according to the law of the Medes & Perſians, which altereth not. 9 Wherefore King Darius ſigned the writing and the decree. 10 Now when Daniel knew that the writing was ſigned, hee went into his houſe, and his windowes being open in his chamber toward Ieruſalem, hee kneeled vpon his knees three times a day, and prayed, and gaue thankes before his God, as hee did afore time. 11 Then theſe men aſſembled, and found Daniel praying, and making ſupplication before his God. 12 Then they came neere, and ſpake before the king concerning the kings decree; Haſt thou not ſigned a decree, that euery man that ſhall aſke a petition of any God or man, within thirty dayes, ſaue of thee, O king, ſhalbe caſt into the denne of Lions? The king anſwered and ſaid, The thing is true, according to the law of the Medes and Perſians, which altereth not. 13 Then anſwered they and ſaid before the king; That Daniel which is of the captiuity of the children of Iudah, regardeth not thee, O king, nor the decree that thou haſt ſigned, but maketh his petition three times a day. 14 Then the king, when hee heard theſe wordes, was ſore diſpleaſed with himſelfe, and ſet his heart on Daniel to deliuer him: and he laboured till the going downe of the ſunne, to deliuer him. 15 Then theſe men aſſembled vnto the king, and ſaid vnto the king, Know O king, that the law of the Medes and Perſians is, that no decree nor ſtatute which the king eſtabliſheth, may bee changed. 16 Then the king commanded, and they brought Daniel, and caſt him into the denne of Lions: now the king ſpake and ſaide vnto Daniel; Thy God, whom thou ſerueſt continually, he will deliuer thee. 17 And a ſtone was brought and laid vpon the mouth of the denne, and the King ſealed it with his owne ſignet, and with the ſignet of his lords; that the purpoſe might not be changed concerning Daniel. 18 Then the king went to his palace, and paſſed the night faſting: neither were inſtruments of muſicke brought before him, and his ſleepe went from him. 19 Then the king aroſe very early in the morning, and went in haſte vnto the den of Lyons. 20 And when he came to the den, he cryed with a lamentable voice vnto Daniel, and the king ſpake and ſaid to Daniel: O Daniel, ſeruant of the liuing God, Is thy God whom thou ſerueſt continually, able to deliuer thee from the Lyons? 21 Then ſaid Daniel vnto the king, O king, liue for euer. 22 My God hath ſent his Angel, and hath ſhut the lyons mouthes that they haue not hurt me: foraſmuch as before him, innocencie was found in me; and alſo before thee, O king, haue I done no hurt. 23 Then was the king exceeding glad for him, and commanded that they ſhould take Daniel vp out of the denne: ſo Daniel was taken vp out of the den, and no maner of hurt was found vpon him, becauſe he beleeued in his God. 24 And the king commanded, and they brought thoſe men which had accuſed Daniel, and they caſt them into the den of Lyons, them, their children, and their wiues: and the Lyons had the maſtery of them, and brake all their bones in pieces or euer they came at the bottome of the den. 25 Then king Darius wrote vnto all people, nations, and languages that dwell in all the earth; Peace be multiplied vnto you. 26 I make a decree, That in euery dominion of my kingdome, men tremble and feare before the God of Daniel: for he is the liuing God, and ſtedfaſt for euer, and his kingdome that, which ſhal not be deſtroyed, and his dominion ſhall be euen vnto the end. 27 He deliuereth and reſcueth, and he worketh ſignes and wonders in heauen and in earth: who hath deliuered Daniel from the power of the lyons. 28 So this Daniel proſpered in the reigne of Darius, and in the reigne of Cyrus the Perſian.

CHAPTER 7 1 In the firſt yeere of Belſhazzar king of Babylon, Daniel had a dreame, and viſions of his head vpon his bed: then he wrote the dreame, and tolde the ſumme of the matters. 2 Daniel ſpake, and ſaid, I ſaw in my viſion by night, & behold, the foure windes of the heauen ſtroue vpon the great ſea. 3 And foure great beaſtes came vp from the ſea, diuers one from another. 4 The firſt was like a Lyon, and had Eagles wings: I beheld till the wings thereof were pluckt, and it was lifted vp from the earth, and made ſtand vpon the feete as a man, and a mans heart was giuen to it. 5 And behold, another beaſt, a ſecond, like to a Beare, and it raiſed vp it ſelfe on one ſide, and it had three ribbes in the mouth of it betweene the teeth of it, and they ſaid thus vnto it, Ariſe, deuoure much fleſh. 6 After this I beheld, and loe, another like a Leopard, which had vpon the backe of it foure wings of a foule, the beaſt had alſo foure heads, and dominion was giuen to it. 7 After this I ſaw in the night viſions, and behold, a fourth beaſt, dreadfull and terrible, and ſtrong exceedingly; and it had great yron teeth: it deuoured and brake in pieces, and ſtamped the reſidue with the feete of it, and it was diuers from all the beaſts that were before it, and it had ten hornes. 8 I conſidered the hornes, and behold, there came vp among them another little horne, before whom there were three of the firſt hornes pluckt vp by the roots: and behold, in this horne were eyes like the eyes of man, and a mouth ſpeaking great things. 9 I beheld till the thrones were caſt downe, and the Ancient of dayes did ſit, whoſe garment was white as ſnow, and the haire of his head like the pure wooll: his throne was like the fierie flame, and his wheeles as burning fire. 10 A fierie ſtreame iſſued, and came foorth from before him: thouſand thouſands miniſtred vnto him, and ten thouſand times ten thouſand ſtood before him: the iudgement was ſet, and the bookes were opened. 11 I beheld then, becauſe of the voice of the great words which the horne ſpake: I beheld euen till the beaſt was ſlaine, and his body deſtroyed, and giuen to the burning flame. 12 As concerning the reſt of the beaſts, they had their dominion taken away: yet their liues were prolonged for a ſeaſon and time. 13 I ſaw in the night viſions, and behold, one like the ſonne of man, came with the clouds of heauen, and came to the Ancient of daies, and they brought him neere before him. 14 And there was giuen him dominion and glory, and a kingdome, that all people, nations, and languages ſhould ſerue him: his dominion is an euerlaſting dominion, which ſhall not paſſe away; and his kingdome that, which ſhall not be deſtroyed. 15 I Daniel was grieued in my ſpirit in the midſt of my body, and the viſions of my head troubled me. 16 I came neere vnto one of them that ſtood by, and aſked him the truth of all this: ſo he told mee, and made me know the interpretation of the things. 17 Theſe great beaſts, which are foure, are foure Kings, which ſhall Ariſe out of the earth. 18 But the Saints of the moſt high ſhall take the kingdome, & poſſeſſe the kingdome for euer, euen for euer & euer. 19 Then I would know the truth of the fourth beaſt, which was diuerſe from al the others, exceeding dreadful, whoſe teeth were of yron, and his nailes of braſſe, which deuoured, brake in pieces, and ſtamped the reſidue with his feete,20And of the ten hornes that were in his head, and of the other, which came vp, and before whom three fell, euen of that horne that had eyes, and a mouth that ſpake very great things, whoſe looke was more ſtout then his fellowes.21I beheld, and the ſame horne made warre with the Saints, and preuailed againſt them;22Untill the Ancient of daies came, and iudgment was giuen to the Saints of the moſt high: and the time came that the Saints poſſeſſed the kingdome.23Thus he ſaid, The fourth beaſt ſhall be the fourth kingdome vpon earth, which ſhall be diuerſe from all kingdomes, & ſhall deuoure the whole earth, and ſhall tread it downe, and breake it in pieces.24And the tenne hornes out of this kingdome are tenne Kings that ſhall Ariſe: and an other ſhall riſe after them, and he ſhall be diuerſe from the firſt, and he ſhall ſubdue three Kings.25And he ſhall ſpeake great words againſt the moſt high, and ſhall weare out the Saints of the moſt high, and thinke to change times, and lawes: and they ſhall be giuen into his hand, vntill a time and times, & the diuiding of time.26But the iudgement ſhall ſit, and they ſhall take away his dominion, to conſume, and to deſtroy it vnto the end.27And the kingdome and dominion, and the greatneſſe of the kingdome vnder the whole heauen, ſhall be giuen to the people of the Saints of the moſt high, whoſe kingdome is an euerlaſting kingdome, and all dominions ſhall ſerue and obey him.28Hitherto is the end of the matter. As for me Daniel, my cogitations much troubled me, and my countenance changed in me: but I kept the matter in my heart.

CHAPTER 81In the third yeere of the reigne of King Belſhazzar, a viſion appeared vnto mee, euen vnto me Daniel, after that which appeared vnto me at the firſt.2And I ſaw in a viſion (and it came to paſſe when I ſaw, that I was at Shuſhan in the palace, which is in the prouince of Elam) and I ſaw in a viſion, and I was by the riuer of Ulai.3Then I lifted vp mine eyes, and ſaw, and behold, there ſtood before the riuer, a ramme which had two hornes, and the two hornes were high: but one was higher then the other, and the higher came vp laſt.4I ſaw the ramme puſhing Weſtward, & Northward, and Southward: ſo that no beaſts might ſtand before him, neither was there any that could deliuer out of his hand, but he did according to his will, and became great.5And as I was conſidering, behold, an he goat came frō the weſt on the face of the whole earth, & touched not the ground: and the goate had a notable horne betweene his eyes.6And he came to the ramme that had two hornes, which I had ſeene ſtanding before the riuer, and ranne vnto him in the furie of his power.7And I ſaw him come cloſe vnto the ramme, and he was mooued with choler againſt him, and ſmote the ramme, and brake his two hornes, and there was no power in the ramme to ſtand before him, but he caſt him downe to the ground, and ſtamped vpon him, and there was none that could deliuer the ramme out of his hand.8Therefore the hee goate waxed very great, and when he was ſtrong, the great horne was broken: and for it came vp foure notable ones, toward the foure windes of heauen.9And out of one of them came forth a litle horne, which waxed exceeding great, toward the South, and toward the Eaſt, and toward the pleaſant land.10And it waxed great euen to the hoſte of heauen, and it caſt downe ſome of the hoſte, and of the ſtarres to the ground, and ſtamped vpon them.11Yea he magnified himſelfe euen to the prince of the hoſte, and by him the dayly ſacrifice was taken away, and the place of his Sanctuary was caſt down.12And an hoſte was giuen him againſt the daily ſacrifice by reaſon of tranſgreſsion, and it caſt downe the trueth to the ground, and it practiſed, and proſpered.13Then I heard one Saint ſpeaking, and another Saint ſaide vnto that certaine Saint which ſpake, How long ſhall bee the viſion concerning the daily ſacrifice, and the tranſgreſſion of deſolation, to giue both the Sanctuary, and the hoſte to be troden vnder foot?14And he ſaid vnto me, Unto two thouſand and three hundred dayes: then ſhall the Sanctuary be clenſed.15And it came to paſſe, when I, euen I Daniel had ſeene the viſion, and ſought for the meaning, then beholde, there ſtood before me as the appearance of a man.16And I heard a mans voyce betweene the bankes of Ulai, which called and ſaid, Gabriel, make this man to vnderſtand the viſion.17So he came neere where I ſtood: and when he came, I was afraid, and fell vpon my face: but he ſaid vnto mee, Underſtand, O ſonne of man: for at the time of the end ſhalbe the viſion.18Now as he was ſpeaking with me, I was in a deepe ſleepe on my face toward the ground: but he touched me, and ſet me vpright.19And he ſaid, Behold, I wil make thee know what ſhall be in the laſt end of the indignation: for at the time appointed the end ſhalbe.20The ramme which thou ſaweſt hauing two hornes, are the kings of Media, and Perſia.21And the rough goat is the king of Grecia, and the great horne that is betweene his eyes, is the firſt king.22Now that being broken, whereas foure ſtood vp for it, foure kingdomes ſhall ſtand vp out of the nation, but not in his power.23And in the latter time of their kingdome, when the tranſgreſsours are come to the full, a king of fierce countenance, and vnderſtanding darke ſentences, ſhall ſtand vp.24And his power ſhall be mighty, but not by his owne power: and hee ſhall deſtroy wonderfully, and ſhall proſper, and practiſe, and ſhall deſtroy the mightie, and the holy people.25And through his policie alſo hee ſhall cauſe craft to proſper in his hand, and hee ſhall magnifie himſelfe in his heart, and by peace ſhal deſtroy many: he ſhall alſo ſtand vp againſt the prince of princes, but he ſhalbe broken without hand.26And the viſion of the euening, and the morning, which was tolde, is true: wherfore ſhut thou vp the viſion, for it ſhalbe for many dayes.27And I Daniel fainted and was ſicke certaine dayes: afterward I roſe vp and did the kings buſineſse, and I was aſtoniſhed at the viſion, but none vnderſtood it.

CHAPTER 91In the firſt yeere of Darius the ſonne of Ahaſuerus, of the ſeede of the Medes, which was made King ouer the realme of the Caldeans,2In the firſt yeere of his reigne, I Daniel vnderſtood by bookes the number of the yeeres, whereof the word of the Lord came to Ieremiah the Prophet, that he would accompliſh ſeuentie yeeres in the deſolations of Ieruſalem.3And I ſet my face vnto the Lord God to ſeeke by prayer, and ſupplications, with faſting, and ſackcloth, and aſhes.4And I prayed vnto the Lord my God, and made my confeſsion, and ſaid; O Lord, the great and dreadfull God, keeping the couenant, and mercy to them that loue him, and to them that keepe his Commandements:5We haue ſinned, and haue committed iniquitie, and haue done wickedly, and haue rebelled, euen by departing from thy precepts, and from thy iudgements.6Neither haue we hearkened vnto thy ſeruants the Prophets, which ſpake in thy Name to our kings, our princes, and our fathers, and to all the people of the land.7O Lord, righteouſnes belongeth vnto thee, but vnto vs confuſion of faces, as at this day: to the men of Iudah, and to the inhabitants of Ieruſalem, and vnto all Iſrael that are neere, and that are farre off, through all the countreys whither thou haſt driuen them, becauſe of their treſpaſſe, that they haue treſpaſſed againſt thee.8O Lord, to vs belongeth confuſion of face, to our kings, to our princes, and to our fathers; becauſe we haue ſinned againſt thee.9To the Lord our God belong mercies and forgiueneſses, though we haue rebelled againſt him.10Neither haue we obeyed the voice of the Lord our God, to walke in his Lawes which he ſet before vs, by his ſeruants the Prophets.11Yea, all Iſrael haue tranſgreſſed thy Law, euen by departing, that they might not obey thy voice, therefore the curſe is powred vpon vs, and the othe that is written in the Law of Moſes the ſeruant of God, becauſe we haue ſinned againſt him.12And he hath confirmed his words which he ſpake againſt vs, and againſt our Iudges that iudged vs, by bringing vpon vs a great euill: for vnder the whole heauen hath not bene done, as hath bene done vpon Ieruſalem.13As it is written in the Law of Moſes, all this euill is come vpon vs: yet made we not our prayer before the Lord our God, that we might turne from our iniquities, and vnderſtand thy trueth.14Therefore hath the Lord watched vpon the euil, and brought it vpon vs: for the Lord our God is righteous in all his workes, which he doeth: for we obeyed not his voice.15And now O Lord our God, that haſt brought thy people forth out of the land of Egypt with a mighty hand, and haſt gotten thee renowne, as at this day, wee haue ſinned, wee haue done wickedly.16O Lord, according to all thy righteouſnes, I beſeech thee, let thine anger and thy furie bee turned away from thy citie Ieruſalem, thy holy Mountaine: becauſe for our ſinnes, and for the iniquities of our fathers, Ieruſalem and thy people are become a reproch to all that are about vs.17Now therefore, O our God, heare the prayer of thy ſeruant, and his ſupplications, and cauſe thy face to ſhine vpon thy Sanctuary that is deſolate, for the Lords ſake.18O my God, encline thine eare and heare: open thine eyes, and behold our deſolations, & the city, which is called by thy name: for we do not preſent our ſupplications before thee for our righteouſneſſes, but for thy great mercies.19O Lord heare, O Lord forgiue, O Lord hearken and doe: deferre not for thine owne ſake, O my God: for thy citie, & thy people are called by thy Name.20And whiles I was ſpeaking, and praying, and confeſsing my ſinne, and the ſinne of my people Iſrael, and preſenting my ſupplication before the Lord my God, for the holy Mountaine of my God:21Yea whiles I was ſpeaking in praier, euen the man Gabriel, whom I had ſeene in the viſion at the beginning, being cauſed to flie ſwiftly, touched me about the time of the euening oblation.22And he informed mee, and talked with mee, and ſaid; O Daniel, I am now come foorth to giue thee ſkill and vnderſtanding.23At the beginning of thy ſupplications the commandement came forth, and I am come to ſhew thee: for thou art greatly beloued: therefore vnderſtand the matter, & conſider the viſion.24Seuentie weekes are determined vpon thy people, and vpon thy holy citie, to finiſh the tranſgreſsion, and to make an ende of ſinnes, and to make reconciliation for iniquitie, and to bring in euerlaſting righteouſnes, and to ſeale vp the viſion and prophecie, and to anoynt the moſt Holy.25Know therefore and vnderſtand, that from the going foorth of the commandement to reſtore and to build Ieruſalem, vnto the Meſsiah the Prince, ſhall be ſeuen weekes; and threeſcore and two weekes, the ſtreet ſhall be built againe, and the wall, euen in troublous times.26And after threeſcore and two weekes, ſhall Meſsiah be cut off, but not for himſelfe, and the people of the Prince that ſhall come, ſhall deſtroy the citie, and the Sanctuarie, and the ende thereof ſhall be with a flood, and vnto the ende of the warre deſolations are determined.27And hee ſhall confirme the couenant with many for one weeke: and in the midſt of the weeke he ſhall cauſe the ſacrifice and the oblation to ceaſe, and for the ouerſpreading of abominations hee ſhall make it deſolate, euen vntill the conſummation, & that determined, ſhalbe powred vpon the deſolate.

CHAPTER 101In the third yere of Cyrus King of Perſia, a thing was reuealed vnto Daniel (whoſe name was called Belteſhazzar) and the thing was true, but the time appointed was long, and he vnderſtood the thing, and had vnderſtanding of the viſion.2In thoſe dayes, I Daniel was mourning three full weekes.3I ate no pleaſant bread, neither came fleſh, nor wine in my mouth, neither did I anoynt my ſelfe at all, till three whole weekes were fulfilled.4And in the foure and twentieth day of the firſt moneth, as I was by the ſide of the great riuer, which is Hiddekel:5Then I lift vp mine eyes and looked, and behold, a certaine man clothed in linen, whoſe loynes were girded with fine gold of Uphaz.6His body alſo was like the Berill, and his face as the appearance of lightning, and his eyes as lampes of fire, and his armes, and his feete like in colour to poliſhed braſſe, and the voice of his words like the voice of a multitude.7And I Daniel alone ſaw the viſion: for the men that were with mee ſaw not the viſion: but a great quaking fell vpon them, ſo that they fled to hide themſelues.8Therefore I was left alone, and ſaw this great viſion, and there remained no ſtrength in me: for my comelineſse was turned in me into corruption, and I retained no ſtrength.9Yet heard I the voice of his words: and when I heard the voice of his wordes, then was I in a deepe ſleepe on my face, and my face toward the ground.10And behold, an hand touched me, which ſet me vpon my knees, and vpon the palmes of my hands.11And hee ſaid vnto me, O Daniel, a man greatly beloued, vnderſtand the wordes that I ſpeake vnto thee, and ſtand vpright: for vnto thee am I now ſent; and when he had ſpoken this word vnto me, I ſtood trembling.12Then ſayd hee vnto me; Feare not, Daniel: for from the firſt day that thou diddeſt ſet thine heart to vnderſtand, and to chaſten thy ſelfe before thy God, thy wordes were heard, and I am come for thy words.13But the prince of the kingdome of Perſia withſtood mee one and twentie dayes: but loe, Michael one of the chiefe Princes came to helpe mee, and I remained there with the Kings of Perſia.14Now I am come to make thee vnderſtand what ſhall befall thy people, in the latter dayes: for yet the viſion is for many dayes.15And when hee had ſpoken ſuch words vnto me, I ſet my face toward the ground, and I became dumbe.16And behold, one like the ſimilitude of the ſonnes of men touched my lippes: then I opened my mouth, and ſpake, and ſayd vnto him that ſtoode before me; O my Lord, by the viſion my ſorrowes are turned vpon me, and I haue retained no ſtrength.17For how can the ſeruant of this my Lord, talke with this my Lord? for as for me, ſtraightway there remained no ſtrength in mee, neither is there breath left in me.18Then there came againe and touched me one like the appearance of a man, and he ſtrengthned me,19And ſaid; O man greatly beloued, feare not: peace be vnto thee, be ſtrong, yea be ſtrong; and when he had ſpoken vnto me, I was ſtrengthened, and ſaid; Let my Lord ſpeake; for thou haſt ſtrengthened me.20Then ſaid hee, Knoweſt thou wherefore I come vnto thee? and now will I returne to fight with the prince of Perſia: and when I am gone forth, loe, the prince of Grecia ſhall come.21But I will ſhew thee that which is noted in the Scripture of trueth: and there is none that holdeth with me in theſe things, but Michael your prince.

CHAPTER 111Alſo I, in the firſt yeere of Darius the Mede, euen I ſtood to confirme and to ſtrengthen him.2And now will I ſhew thee the trueth. Behold, there ſhall ſtand vp yet three Kings in Perſia, & the fourth ſhalbe farre richer then they all: and by his ſtrength through his riches he ſhall ſtirre vp all againſt the realme of Grecia.3And a mighty King ſhal ſtand vp, that ſhall rule with great dominion, and doe according to his will.4And when he ſhall ſtand vp, his kingdome ſhall be broken, and ſhall be diuided toward the foure winds of heauen; and not to his poſteritie, nor according to his dominion which he ruled: for his kingdome ſhall be pluckt vp, euen for others beſides thoſe.5And the King of the South ſhall be ſtrong, and one of his princes, and he ſhall be ſtrong aboue him, and haue dominion: his dominion ſhall be a great dominion.6And in the end of yeeres they ſhall ioyne themſelues together: for the Kings daughter of the South ſhall come to the King of the North to make an agreement, but ſhe ſhall not retaine the power of the arme, neither ſhall he ſtand, nor his arme: but ſhe ſhall be giuen vp, and they that brought her, and he that begate her, and he that ſtrengthened her in theſe times.7But out of a branch of her rootes ſhall one ſtand vp in his eſtate, which ſhall come with an armie, and ſhall enter into the fortreſse of the King of the North, and ſhall deale againſt them, and ſhall preuaile:8And ſhall alſo carie captiues into Egypt their gods with their princes, and with their precious veſſels of ſiluer and of gold, and he ſhall continue moe yeeres then the King of the North.9So the King of the South ſhall come into his kingdome, and ſhall returne into his owne land.10But his ſonnes ſhall be ſtirred vp, and ſhall aſſemble a multitude of great forces: and one ſhall certainly come and ouerflow and paſſe through: then ſhall he returne, and be ſtirred vp euen to his fortreſse.11And the King of the South ſhall be moued with choler, and ſhall come forth and fight with him, euen with the King of the North: and hee ſhall ſet forth a great multitude, but the multitude ſhall be giuen into his hand.12And when he hath taken away the multitude, his heart ſhall be lifted vp: and he ſhall caſt downe many tenne thouſands: but he ſhall not be ſtrengthened by it.13For the King of the North ſhall returne, and ſhall ſet forth a multitude greater then the former, and ſhall certainly come (after certaine yeereſ) with a great armie & with much riches.14And in thoſe times there ſhall many ſtand vp againſt the King of the South: alſo the robbers of thy people ſhall exalt themſelues to eſtabliſh the viſion, but they ſhall fall.15So the King of the North ſhall come, and caſt vp a mount, and take the moſt fenced cities, and the armes of the South ſhall not withſtand, neither his choſen people, neither ſhall there be any ſtrength to withſtand.16But he that commeth againſt him, ſhall doe according to his owne will, and none ſhall ſtand before him: and he ſhall ſtand in the glorious land, which by his hand ſhall be conſumed.17He ſhall alſo ſet his face to enter with the ſtrength of his whole kingdome and vpright ones with him: thus ſhall he doe, and he ſhall giue him the daughter of women corrupting her: but ſhe ſhall not ſtand on his ſide, neither be for him.18After this ſhall he turne his face vnto the yles, and ſhall take many, but a prince for his own behalfe ſhall cauſe the reproch offred by him to ceaſe without his owne reproch: he ſhall cauſe it to turne vpon him.19Then he ſhall turne his face towards the fort of his owne lande: but he ſhall ſtumble and fall, and not bee found.20Then ſhall ſtand vp in his eſtate a raiſer of taxes in the glory of the kingdome, but within few dayes he ſhall be deſtroyed, neither in anger, nor in battell.21And in his eſtate ſhall ſtand vp a vile perſon, to whom they ſhal not giue the honour of the kingdome: but hee ſhall come in peaceably, and obtaine the kingdome by flatteries.22And with the armes of a flood ſhall they bee ouerflowen from before him, and ſhall be broken: yea alſo the prince of the couenant.23And after the league made with him he ſhall worke deceitfully, for hee ſhall come vp, and ſhall become ſtrong with a ſmall people.24He ſhall enter peaceably euen vpon the fatteſt places of the prouince, and he ſhall doe that which his fathers haue not done, nor his fathers fathers, he ſhall ſcatter among them the praye and ſpoile, and riches: yea and he ſhall forecaſt his deuices againſt the ſtrong holdes, euen for a time.25And he ſhall ſtirre vp his power, and his courage againſt the king of the South with a great army, and the king of the South ſhall bee ſtirred vp to battell with a very great and mightie armie: but he ſhall not ſtand: for they ſhall forecaſt deuices againſt him.26Yea they that feede of the portion of his meate, ſhall deſtroy him, and his armie ſhall ouerflow: and many ſhall fall downe ſlaine.27And both theſe kings hearts ſhall be to doe miſchiefe, and they ſhall ſpeake lies at one table: but it ſhall not proſper: for yet the end ſhall bee at the time appointed.28Then ſhall hee returne into his land with great riches, and his heart ſhall be againſt the holy couenant: and he ſhall doe exploits, and returne to his owne land.29At the time appointed he ſhall returne, and come toward the South: but it ſhall not be as the former, or as the latter.30For the ſhips of Chittim ſhall come againſt him: therefore he ſhall be grieued and returne, and haue indignation againſt the holy Couenant: ſo ſhal he doe, he ſhall euen returne, and haue intelligence with them that forſake the holy Couenant.31And armes ſhal ſtand on his part, and they ſhall pollute the Sanctuarie of ſtrength, and ſhall take away the daily ſacrifice, and they ſhal place the abomination that maketh deſolate.32And ſuch as doe wickedly againſt the couenant, ſhall he corrupt by flatteries: but the people that do know their God, ſhall be ſtrong and doe exploits.33And they that vnderſtand among the people ſhall inſtruct many: yet they ſhall fall by the ſword, and by flame, by captiuitie, and by ſpoile many dayes.34Now when they ſhall fall, they ſhalbe holpen with a litle help: but many ſhall cleaue to them with flatteries.35And ſome of them of vnderſtanding ſhall fall, to trie them, and to purge, and to make them white, euen to the time of the end: becauſe it is yet for a time appointed.36And the king ſhall doe according to his will, and he ſhall exalt himſelfe, and magnifie himſelfe aboue euery god, and ſhall ſpeake marueilous things againſt the God of gods, & ſhall proſper till the indignation be accompliſhed: for that that is determined, ſhall be done.37Neither ſhall hee regard the god of his fathers, nor the deſire of women, nor regard any god: for he ſhall magnifie himſelfe aboue all.38But in his eſtate ſhall he honour the god of forces: and a God whome his fathers knew not, ſhall hee honour with gold, and ſiluer, and with precious ſtones, and pleaſant things.39Thus ſhall hee doe in the moſt ſtrong holds with a ſtrange god, whom he ſhall acknowledge and increaſe with glory: and he ſhall cauſe them to rule ouer many, and ſhall diuide the land for gaine.40And at the time of the end ſhall the king of the South puſh at him, and the king of the North ſhal come againſt him like a whirlewind with charets, and with horſemen, and with many ſhips, and he ſhall enter into the countreys, and ſhall ouerflow and paſſe ouer.41He ſhall enter alſo into the glorious land, and many countreys ſhall be ouerthrowen: but theſe ſhall eſcape out of his hand, euen Edom, and Moab, and the chiefe of the children of Ammon.42He ſhall ſtretch foorth his hand alſo vpon the countreys, and the land of Egypt ſhall not eſcape.43But he ſhall haue power ouer the treaſures of gold and of ſiluer, and ouer all the precious things of Egypt: and the Libyans and the Ethiopians ſhalbe at his ſteps.44But tidings out of the Eaſt, and out of the North ſhall trouble him: therefore he ſhall goe foorth with great fury to deſtroy, and vtterly to make away many.45And hee ſhall plant the tabernacles of his palace betweene the ſeas in the glorious holy mountaine, yet he ſhall come to his end, and none ſhall helpe him.

CHAPTER 121And at that time ſhall Michael ſtand vp, the great Prince which ſtandeth for the children of thy people, and there ſhalbe a time of trouble, ſuch as neuer was ſince there was a nation, euen to that ſame time: and at that time thy people ſhalbe deliuered, euery one that ſhalbe found written in the booke.2And many of them that ſleepe in the duſt of the earth ſhall awake, ſome to euerlaſting life, and ſome to ſhame and euerlaſting contempt.3And they that be wiſe ſhall ſhine as the brightneſse of the firmament, and they that turne many to righteouſneſſe, as the ſtarres for euer and euer.4But thou, O Daniel, ſhut vp the wordes, and ſeale the booke euen to the time of the ende: many ſhall runne to and fro, and knowledge ſhall bee increaſed.5Then I Daniel looked, and behold, there ſtood other two, the one on this ſide of the banke of the riuer, and the other on that ſide of the banke of the riuer.6And one ſaid to the man clothed in linnen, which was vpon the waters of the riuer; How long ſhall it bee to the end of theſe wonders?7And I heard the man clothed in linnen, which was vpon the waters of the riuer, when he held vp his right hand, and his left hand vnto heauen, and ſware by him that liueth for euer, that it ſhalbe for a time, times, and an halfe: and when hee ſhall haue accompliſhed to ſcatter the power of the holy people, all theſe things ſhall bee finiſhed.8And I heard, but I vnderſtood not: then ſaid I, O my Lord, what ſhalbe the end of theſe things?9And he ſaid, Goe thy way, Daniel: for the wordes are cloſed vp and ſealed till the time of the end.10Many ſhalbe purified, and made white and tried: but the wicked ſhall doe wickedly: and none of the wicked ſhall vnderſtand, but the wiſe ſhall vnderſtand.11And from the time that the dayly ſacrifice ſhalbe taken away, and the abomination that maketh deſolate ſet vp, there ſhalbe a thouſand two hundred and ninetie dayes.12Bleſſed is he that waiteth, and commeth to the thouſand, three hundred and fiue and thirtie dayes.13But goe thou thy way till the end be: for thou ſhalt reſt, and ſtand in the lot at the end of the dayes.

HOſEA (HOſEA)

CHAPTER 11The word of the Lord that came vnto Hoſea, the ſonne of Beeri, in the dayes of Uzziah, Iotham, Ahaz, and Hezekiah kings of Iudah, and in the dayes of Ieroboam the ſonne of Ioaſh king of Iſrael.2The beginning of the word of the Lord by Hoſea: and the Lord ſayd to Hoſea, Goe, take vnto thee a wife of whoredomes, and children of whoredomes: for the land hath committed great whoredome, departing from the Lord.3So he went and tooke Gomer the daughter of Diblaim, which conceiued and bare him a ſonne.4And the Lord ſaid vnto him, Call his name Iezreel; for yet a little while, and I will auenge the blood of Iezreel vpon the houſe of Iehu, and will cauſe to ceaſe the kingdome of the houſe of Iſrael.5And it ſhall come to paſſe at that day, that I will breake the bow of Iſrael in the valley of Iezreel.6And ſhee conceiued againe and bare a daughter, and God ſayd vnto him, Call her name Lo-ruhamah: for I will no more haue mercy vpon the houſe of Iſrael: but I will vtterly take them away.7But I will haue mercy vpon the houſe of Iudah, and will ſaue them by the Lord their God, and will not ſaue them by vow, nor by ſword, nor by battell, by horſes nor by horſemen.8Now when ſhee had weaned Lo-ruhamah, ſhe couceiued and bare a ſonne.9Then ſayde God, Call his name Lo-ammi: for yee are not my people, and I will not be your God.10Yet the number of the children of Iſrael ſhall be as the ſand of the ſea, which cannot bee meaſured nor numbred, and it ſhall come to paſſe, that in the place where it was ſaid vnto them, Yee are not my people, there it ſhall be ſaid vnto them, Ye are the ſonnes of the liuing God.11Then ſhall the children of Iudah and the children of Iſrael be gathered together, and appoint themſelues one head, and they ſhall come vp out of the land: for great ſhalbe the day of Iezreel.

CHAPTER 21ſay ye vnto your brethren, Ammi, & to your ſiſters, Ruhamah:2Plead with your mother, plead: for ſhe is not my wife, neither am I her huſband: let her therefore put away her whordomes out of her ſight, and her adulteries from betweene her breaſts;3Leſt I ſtrip her naked, and ſet her as in the day that ſhee was borne, and make her as a wilderneſſe, and ſet her like a drie land, and ſlay her with thirſt.4And I will not haue mercy vpon her children, for they be the children of whordomes.5For their mother hath played the harlot: ſhee that conceiued them hath done ſhamefully: for ſhee ſayd, I will goe after my louers, that giue me my bread and my water, my wooll and my flaxe, mine oyle, and my drinke.6Therefore behold, I will hedge vp thy way with thornes, and make a wall, that ſhe ſhall not find her pathes.7And ſhe ſhall follow after her louers, but ſhe ſhall not ouertake them, and ſhe ſhall ſeeke them, but ſhall not find them: then ſhall ſhe ſay, I will goe and returne to my firſt huſband, for then was it better with me then now.8For ſhe did not know that I gaue her corne, and wine, and oyle, and multiplied her ſiluer and gold, which they prepared for Baal.9Therefore will I returne, and take away my Corne in the time thereof, and my wine in the ſeaſon thereof, and wil recouer my wooll and my flaxe giuen to couer her nakedneſse.10And now will I diſcouer her lewdneſse in the ſight of her louers, and none ſhall deliuer her out of mine hand.11I will alſo cauſe all her mirth to ceaſe, her feaſt daies, her new moones, and her Sabbaths, and all her ſolemne feaſts.12And I will deſtroy her vines and her figge trees, whereof ſhe hath ſaid; Theſe are my rewards that my louers haue giuen me: and I will make them a forreſt, and the beaſts of the field ſhall eate them.13And I will viſite vpon her the daies of Baalim, wherein ſhe burnt incenſe to them, and ſhe decked her ſelfe with her eare-rings, and her Iewels, and ſhe went after her louers, and forgate me, ſaith the Lord. 14 Therefore behold, I will allure her, and bring her into the wilderneſſe, and ſpeake comfortably vnto her. 15 And I wil giue her, her vineyards from thence, and the valley of Achor for a doore of hope, and ſhe ſhall ſing there, as in the dayes of her youth, and as in the day when ſhe came vp out of the land of Egypt. 16 And it ſhall be at that day, ſaith the Lord, that thou ſhalt call mee Iſhi; and ſhalt call mee no more Baali. 17 For I will take away the names of Baalim out of her mouth, & they ſhal no more be remembred by their name. 18 And in that day will I make a couenant for them with the beaſts of the field, and with the foules of heauen, and with the creeping things of the ground: and I will breake the bow and the ſword, and the battell out of the earth, and will make them to lie downe ſafely. 19 And I will betroth thee vnto me for euer; yea, I will betroth thee vnto me in righteouſneſſe, and in iudgement, and in louing kindneſse, and in mercies. 20 I will euen betroth thee vnto me in faithfulneſse, and thou ſhalt know the Lord. 21 And it ſhall come to paſſe in that day, I will heare, ſaith the Lord, I will heare the heauens, and they ſhall heare the earth, 22 And the earth ſhall heare the corne, and the wine, and the oyle, and they ſhall heare Iezreel. 23 And I will ſow her vnto me in the earth, and I will haue mercy vpon her that had not obtained mercy, and I will ſay to them which were not my people; Thou art my people, and they ſhallſay, Thou art my God.

CHAPTER 3 1 Then ſaid the Lord vnto me, Goe yet, loue a woman (beloued of her friend, yet an adultereſse) according to the loue of the Lord toward the children of Iſrael, who looke to other gods, and loue flagons of wine. 2 So I bought her to me for fifteene pieces of ſiluer, and for an homer of barley and an halfe homer of barley. 3 And I ſaid vnto her, Thou ſhalt abide for me many dayes, thou ſhalt not play the harlot, & thou ſhalt not be for an other man, ſo will I alſo be for thee. 4 For the children of Iſrael ſhall abide many dayes without a King, and without a Prince, and without a ſacrifice, and without an image, and without an Ephod, and without Teraphim. 5 Afterward ſhall the children of Iſrael returne, and ſeeke the Lord their God, and Dauid their King, and ſhall feare the Lord, and his goodneſſe in the latter dayes.

CHAPTER 4 1 Heare the worde of the Lord, yee children of Iſrael: for the Lord hath a controuerſie with the inhabitants of the land, becauſe there is no trueth, nor mercie, nor knowledge of God in the land. 2 By ſwearing, and lying, and killing, and ſtealing, and committing adulterie, they breake out, and blood toucheth blood. 3 Therefore ſhall the land mourne, and euery one that dwelleth therein ſhall languiſh, with the beaſtes of the field, and with the foules of heauen, yea the fiſhes of the ſea alſo ſhall be taken away. 4 Yet let no man ſtriue, nor reproue another: for this people are as they that ſtriue with the prieſt. 5 Therefore ſhalt thou fall in the day, and the prophet alſo ſhall fall with thee in the night, and I will deſtroy thy mother. 6 My people are deſtroyed for lacke of knowledge: becauſe thou haſt reiected knowledge, I will alſo reiect thee, that thou ſhalt be no prieſt to me: ſeeing thou haſt forgotten the lawe of thy God, I wil alſo forget thy children. 7 As they were increaſed, ſo they ſinned againſt me: therfore wil I change their glory into ſhame. 8 They eate vp the ſinne of my people, and they ſet their heart on their iniquitie. 9 And there ſhall be like people, like prieſt: and I will puniſh them for their wayes, and reward them their doings. 10 For they ſhall eate, and not haue enough: they ſhall commit whordome, and ſhall not increaſe, becauſe they haue left off to take heed to the Lord. 11 Whoredome, and wine, and newe wine take away the heart. 12 My people aſke counſel at their ſtocks, and their ſtaffe declareth vnto them: for the ſpirit of whordomes hath cauſed them to erre, and they haue gone a whoring from vnder their God. 13 They ſacrifice vpon the tops of the mountaines, and burne incenſe vpon the hilles vnder okes and poplars, and elmes, becauſe the ſhadowe thereof is good: therefore your daughters ſhall commit whoredome, and your ſpouſes ſhall commit adulterie. 14 I will not puniſh your daughters when they commit whordome, nor your ſpouſes when they commit adulterie: for themſelues are ſeparated with whores, and they ſacrifice with harlots: therfore the people that doth not vnderſtand, ſhall fall. 15 Though thou Iſrael play the harlot, yet let not Iudah offend, and come not ye vnto Gilgal, neither goe ye vp to Beth-auen, nor ſweare, The Lord liueth: 16 For Iſrael ſlideth backe, as a backe ſliding heifer: now the Lord will feede them as a lambe in a large place. 17 Ephraim is ioyned to idoles: let him alone. 18 Their drinke is ſowre: they haue committed whordome continually: her rulers with ſhame doe loue, Giue ye. 19 The wind hath bound her vp in her wings, and they ſhall be aſhamed becauſe of their ſacrifices.

CHAPTER 5 1 Heare yee this, O prieſts, and hearken, ye houſe of Iſrael, and giue yee eare, O houſe of the king: for iudgement is toward you, becauſe yee haue beene a ſnare on Mizpah, and a net ſpread vpon Tabor. 2 And the reuolters are profound to make ſlaughter, though I haue bene a rebuker of them all. 3 I know Ephraim, and Iſrael is not hid from me: for now, O Ephraim, thou committeſt whordome, and Iſrael is defiled. 4 They will not frame their doings to turne vnto their God: for the ſpirit of whoredomes is in the midſt of them, and they haue not knowen the Lord. 5 And the pride of Iſrael doth teſtifie to his face: therefore ſhall Iſrael and Ephraim fall in their iniquity: Iudah alſo ſhall fall with them. 6 They ſhall goe with their flocks, and with their heards to ſeeke the Lord: but they ſhall not finde him, he hath withdrawen himſelfe from them. 7 They haue dealt treacherouſly againſt the Lord: for they haue begotten ſtrange children, now ſhall a moneth deuoure them with their portions. 8 Blow yee the cornet in Gibeah, and the trumpet in Ramah: cry alowd at Beth-auen: after thee, O Beniamin. 9 Ephraim ſhall be deſolate in the day of rebuke: among the tribes of Iſrael haue I made knowen that which ſhall ſurely be. 10 The Princes of Iudah were like them that remooue the bound: therefore I will powre out my wrath vpon them like water. 11 Ephraim is oppreſſed, and broken in iudgement: becauſe he willingly walked after the commandement. 12 Therefore wil I be vnto Ephraim as a moth: and to the houſe of Iudah as rottenneſse. 13 When Ephraim ſaw his ſickneſse, and Iudah ſaw his wound: then went Ephraim to the Aſſyrian, and ſent to king Iareb; yet could he not heale you, nor cure you of your wound. 14 For I will bee vnto Ephraim as a Lion, and as a yong Lion to the houſe of Iudah: I, euen I wil teare and goe away: I will take away, and none ſhall reſcue him. 15 I will goe and returne to my place, till they acknowledge their offence, and ſeeke my face: in their affliction they will ſeeke me early.

CHAPTER 6 1 Come, and let vs returne vnto the Lord: for hee hath torne, and hee will heale vs: he hath ſmitten, and he will binde vs vp. 2 After two daies will he reuiue vs, in the third day he will raiſe vs vp, and we ſhall liue in his ſight. 3 Then ſhal we know, if we follow on to know the Lord: his going forth is prepared, as the morning; & he ſhall come vnto vs, as the raine; as the latter and former raine vnto the earth. 4 O Ephraim, what ſhall I doe vnto thee? O Iudah, what ſhall I do vnto thee? for your goodneſſe is as a morning cloud, and as the early dew it goeth away. 5 Therefore haue I ſhewed them by the Prophets: I haue ſlaine them by the wordes of my mouth, and thy iudgements are as the light that goeth foorth. 6 For I deſired mercie, and not ſacrifice; and the knowledge of God more then burnt offerings. 7 But they like men haue tranſgreſſed the Couenant: there haue they dealt treacherouſly againſt me. 8 Gilead is a city of them that worke iniquitie; and is polluted with blood. 9 And as troupes of robbers waite for a man, ſo the company of prieſtes murther in the way by conſent: for they commit lewdneſse. 10 I haue ſeene an horrible thing in the houſe of Iſrael: there is the whoredome of Ephraim, Iſrael is defiled. 11 Alſo O Iudah, hee hath ſet an harueſt for thee, when I returned the captiuitie of my people.

CHAPTER 7 1 When I would haue healed Iſrael, then the iniquitie of Ephraim was diſcouered, and the wickedneſſe of Samaria: for they commit falſehood: and the thiefe commeth in, and the troupe of robbers ſpoileth without. 2 And they conſider not in their hearts that I remember al their wickedneſſe: now their owne doings haue beſet them about, they are before my face. 3 They make the king glad with their wickedneſſe, and the princes with their lies. 4 They are al adulterers, as an ouen heated by the baker: who ceaſeth from raiſing after he hath kneaded the dough, vntill it be leauened. 5 In the day of our King, the princes haue made him ſicke with bottels of wine, he ſtretched out his hand with ſcorners. 6 For they haue made ready their heart like an ouen, whiles they lie in wait: their baker ſleepeth all the night, in the morning it burneth as a flaming fire. 7 They are all hot as an ouen, and haue deuoured their Iudges; all their Kings are fallen, there is none among them that calleth vnto me. 8 Ephraim, he hath mixed himſelfe among the people, Ephraim is a cake not turned. 9 Strangers haue deuoured his ſtrength, and hee knoweth it not: yea, gray haires are here and there vpon him, yet he knoweth

not.10And the pride of Iſrael teſtifieth to his face, and they doe not
returne to the Lord their God, nor ſeeke him for all this.11Ephraim alſo
is like a ſilly doue, without heart: they call to Egypt; they goe to
Aſſyria.12When they ſhall goe, I wil ſpread my net vpon them, I will
bring them downe as the foules of the heauen: I will chaſtiſe them as
their congregation hath heard.13Woe vnto them, for they haue fled from
me: deſtruction vnto them, becauſe they haue tranſgreſſed againſt me,
though I haue redeemed them, yet they haue ſpoken lies againſt
me.14And they haue not cryed vnto me with their heart, when they
howled vpon their beds: they aſſemble themſelues for corne and wine,
and they rebell againſt me.15Though I haue bound, and ſtrengthened
their armes, yet doe they imagine miſchiefe againſt me.16They returne,
but not to the moſt High: they are like a deceitfull bow: their princes
ſhall fall by the ſword, for the rage of their tongue: this ſhall be their
deriſion in the land of Egypt.
CHAPTER 81Set the Trumpet to thy mouth: hee ſhall come as an
Eagle againſt the houſe of the Lord, becauſe they haue tranſgreſſed my
Couenant, and treſpaſſed againſt my Lawe.2Iſrael ſhall crie vnto me, My
God, we know thee.3Iſrael hath caſt off the thing that is good: the
enemie ſhall purſue him.4They haue ſet vp Kings, but not by me: they
haue made Princes, and I knew it not: of their ſiluer and their golde haue
they made them idoles, that they may be cut off.5Thy calfe, O Samaria,
hath caſt thee off: mine anger is kindled againſt them: how long will it
bee ere they attaine to innocencie?6For from Iſrael was it alſo, the
workeman made it, therefore it is not God: but the calfe of Samaria ſhall
be broken in pieces.7For they haue ſowen the winde, and they ſhall reape
the whirlewinde: it hath no ſtalke: the budde ſhall yeeld no meale: if ſo
be it yeeld, the ſtrangers ſhall ſwallow it vp.8Iſrael is ſwallowed vp, now
ſhal they be among the Gentiles, as a veſſell wherein is no pleaſure.9For
they are gone vp to Aſſyria, a wilde Aſse alone by himſelfe; Ephraim
hath hired louers.10Yea, though they haue hired among the nations, now
will I gather them, and they ſhall ſorrow a little for the burden of the
King of princes.11Becauſe Ephraim hath made many altars to ſinne,
altars ſhall be vnto him to ſinne.12I haue written to him the great things
of my Law, but they were counted as a ſtrange thing.13They ſacrifice
fleſh for the ſacrifices of mine offerings, and eate it; but the Lord
accepteth them not: now will he remember their iniquitie, and viſite their
ſinnes: they ſhal returne to Egypt.14For Iſrael hath forgotten his maker,
and buildeth temples; and Iudah hath multiplied fenced cities: but I will
ſend a fire vpon his cities, and it ſhall deuoure the palaces thereof.
CHAPTER 91Reioyce not, O Iſrael, for ioy as other people: for thou
haſt gone a whoring from thy God, thou haſt loued a reward vpon euery
corne floore.2The floore and the winepreſſe ſhall not feede them, and
the new wine ſhall faile in her.3They ſhal not dwel in þe Lords land: but
Ephraim ſhall returne to Egypt, and they ſhall eat vncleane things in
Aſſyria.4They ſhall not offer wine offrings to the Lord: neither ſhall they
be pleaſing vnto him: their ſacrifices ſhalbe vnto them as the bread of
mourners: all that eate thereof ſhall be polluted: for their bread for their
ſoule ſhall not come into the houſe of the Lord.5What will yee doe in
the ſolemne day, and in the day of the feaſt of the Lord ?6For loe they
are gone, becauſe of deſtruction: Egypt ſhall gather them vp, Memphis
ſhall burie them: the pleaſant places for their ſiluer, netles ſhal poſſeſſe
them: thornes ſhall be in their Tabernacles.7The dayes of viſitation are
come, the dayes of recompence are come, Iſrael ſhall know it; the
Prophet is a foole, the ſpirituall man is madde, for the multitude of thine
iniquitie and the great hatred.8The watchman of Ephraim was with my
God: but the Prophet is a ſnare of a fouler in all his wayes, and hatred
in the houſe of his God.9They haue deeply corrupted themſelues as in
the dayes of Gibeah: therefore he will remember their iniquitie, he will
viſite their ſinnes.10I found Iſrael like grapes in the wilderneſſe: I ſaw
your fathers as the firſt ripe in the fig tree at her firſt time: but they went
to Baalpeor, and ſeparated themſelues vnto that ſhame, and their
abominations were according as they loued.11As for Ephraim, their glory
ſhall flee away like a bird: from the birth and from the wombe, and from
the conception.12Though they bring vp their children, yet wil I bereaue
them that there ſhall not be a man left: yea, woe alſo to them when I
depart from them.13Ephraim, as I ſaw Tyrus, is planted in a pleaſant
place: but Ephraim ſhall bring foorth his children to the
murderer.14Giue them, O Lord: what wilt thou giue? giue them a
miſcarying wombe, and drie breaſts.15All their wickedneſſe is in Gilgal:
for there I hated them: for the wickedneſſe of their doings I will driue
them out of mine houſe, I will loue them no more: all their princes are
reuolters.16Ephraim is ſmitten, their roote is dried vp, they ſhall beare
no fruite: yea though they bring foorth, yet wil I ſlay euen the beloued
fruite of their wombe.17My God will caſt them away, becauſe they did
not hearken vnto him: and they ſhalbe wanderers among the nations.
CHAPTER 101Iſrael is an empty vine, he bringeth forth fruite vnto
himſelfe: according to the multitude of his fruite, he hath increaſed the
altars, according to the goodneſſe of his land, they haue made goodly
images.2Their heart is diuided: now ſhall they be found faultie: hee ſhall
breake downe their altars: he ſhall ſpoile their images.3For now they ſhall
ſay, We haue no King, becauſe we feared not the Lord, What then
ſhould a King doe to vs?4They haue ſpoken words, ſwearing falſely in
making a couenant: thus iudgement ſpringeth vp as hemlocke in the
furrowes of the field.5The inhabitants of Samaria ſhall feare, becauſe of
the calues of Bethauen: for the people thereof ſhall mourne ouer it, and
the prieſts thereof that reioyced on it, for the glory thereof, becauſe it is
departed from it.6It ſhall be alſo caried vnto Aſſyria for a preſent to
King Iareb: Ephraim ſhall receiue ſhame, and Iſrael ſhall be aſhamed of
his owne counſell.7As for Samaria, her King is cut off as the ſome vpon
the water.8The high places alſo of Auen, the ſinne of Iſrael, ſhall be
deſtroyed: the thorne and the thiſtle ſhall come vp on their altars; and
they ſhall ſay to the mountaines, Couer vs; and to the hilles, Fall on
vs.9O Iſrael, thou haſt ſinned from the dayes of Gibeah: there they
ſtood: the battell in Gibeah againſt the children of iniquitie did not
ouertake them.10It is in my deſire that I ſhould chaſtiſe them, and the
people ſhall be gathered againſt them, when they ſhall bind themſelues
in their two furrowes.11And Ephraim is as an heifer that is taught and
loueth to tread out the corne, but I paſſed ouer vpon her faire necke: I
will make Ephraim to ride: Iudah ſhall plow, and Iacob ſhall breake his
clods.12Sow to your ſelues in righteouſneſſe, reape in mercie: breake vp
your fallow ground: for it is time to ſeeke the Lord, till he come and
raine righteouſneſſe vpon you.13Ye haue plowed wickedneſſe, yee haue
reaped iniquitie, ye haue eaten the fruite of lies: becauſe thou didſt truſt
in thy way, in the multitude of thy mightie men.14Therefore ſhall a
tumult Ariſe among thy people, and all thy fortreſſes ſhall bee ſpoiled,
as Shalman ſpoiled Beth-arbel in the day of battell: the mother was
daſhed in pieces vpon her children.15So ſhall Bethel doe vnto you,
becauſe of your great wickedneſſe: in a morning ſhall the king of Iſrael
be vtterly cut off.
CHAPTER 111When Iſrael was a childe, then I loued him, and called
my ſonne out of Egypt.2As they called them, ſo they went from them:
they ſacrificed vnto Baalim, and burnt incenſe to grauen images.3I taught
Ephraim alſo to goe, taking them by their armes: but they knew not that
I healed them.4I drew them with cords of a man, with bands of loue,
and I was to them as they that take off the yoke on their iawes, and I
laid meat vnto them.5He ſhall not returne into the land of Egypt; but
the Aſſyrian ſhall be his king, becauſe they refuſed to returne6And the
ſword ſhall abide on his cities, and ſhall conſume his branches, and
deuoure them, becauſe of their own counſels.7And my people are bent
to backeſliding from mee: though they called them to the moſt High,
none at all would exalt him.8How ſhall I giue thee vp, Ephraim? how
ſhall I deliuer thee, Iſrael? how ſhall I make thee as Admah? how ſhall I
ſet thee as Zeboim? mine heart is turned within mee, my repentings are
kindled together.9I will not execute the fiercenes of mine anger, I will
not returne to deſtroy Ephraim, for I am God, and not man, the Holy
One in the midſt of thee, and I will not enter into the citie.10They ſhal
walke after the Lord: he ſhall roare like a lyon: when he ſhall roare, then
the children ſhall tremble from the Weſt.11They ſhall tremble as a bird
out of Egypt, and as a doue out of the land of Aſſyria: and I will place
them in their houſes, ſaith the Lord.12Ephraim compaſſeth mee about
with lies, and the houſe of Iſrael with deceit: but Iudah yet ruleth with
God, and is faithfull with the Saints.
CHAPTER 121Ephraim feedeth on winde, and followeth after the Eaſt
winde: hee daily increaſeth lies and deſolation, and they doe make a
couenant with the Aſſyrians, and oyle is caried into Egypt.2The Lord
hath alſo a controuerſie with Iudah, and will puniſh Iacob according to
his wayes, according to his doings will he recompenſe him.3Hee tooke
his brother by the heele in the wombe, and by his ſtrength he had power
with God.4Yea, he had power ouer the Angel and preuailed: hee wept

and made ſupplication vnto him: he found him in Bethel, and there he
ſpake with vs. 5 Euen the Lord God of hoſts, the Lord is his
memoriall. 6 Therefore turne thou to thy God: keepe mercie and
iudgement, and wait on thy God continually. 7 He is a merchant, the
balances of deceit are in his hand: hee loueth to oppreſse. 8 And Ephraim
ſaid, Yet I am become rich, I haue found mee out ſubſtance: in all my
labours they ſhall finde none iniquitie in mee, that were ſinne. 9 And I
that am the Lord thy God from the lande of Egypt, will yet make thee
to dwell in tabernacles, as in the dayes of the ſolemne feaſt. 10 I haue alſo
ſpoken by the prophets, and I haue multiplied viſions, and vſed
ſimilitudes, by the miniſterie of the prophets. 11 Is there iniquitie in
Gilead? ſurely they are vanitie, they ſacrifice bullocks in Gilgal, yea their
altars are as heapes in the furrowes of the fields. 12 And Iacob fled into
the countrey of Syria, and Iſrael ſerued for a wife, and for a wife he kept
ſheepe. 13 And by a Prophet the Lord brought Iſrael out of Egypt, and by
a Prophet was he preſerued. 14 Ephraim prouoked him to anger, moſt
bitterly: therefore ſhall he leaue his blood vpon him, and his reproch
ſhall his Lord returne vnto him.
CHAPTER 13 1 When Ephraim ſpake, trembling, he exalted himſelfe in
Iſrael, but, when he offended in Baal, he died. 2 And now they ſinne more
and more, and haue made them molten images of their ſiluer, and idoles
according to their owne vnderſtanding, all of it the worke of the
crafteſmen: they ſay of them, Let the men that ſacrifice, kiſſe the
calues. 3 Therefore they ſhalbe as the morning cloud, and as the early dew
it paſſeth away, as the chaffe that is driuen with a whirlewinde out of the
floore, and as the ſmoke out of the chimney. 4 Yet I am the Lord thy God
from the land of Egypt, and thou ſhalt know no God, but me: for there
is no ſauiour beſide me. 5 I did know thee in the wilderneſſe, in the land
of great drought. 6 According to their paſture, ſo were they filled: they
were filled, and their heart was exalted: therefore haue they forgotten
me. 7 Therefore I will bee vnto them as a Lion, as a Leopard by the way
will I obſerue them. 8 I will meet them as a beare that is bereaued of her
whelpes, and will rent the kall of their heart, and there will I deuoure
them like a Lion: the wilde beaſt ſhall teare them. 9 O Iſrael, thou haſt
deſtroied thy ſelfe, but in me is thine helpe. 10 I will be thy King: where
is any other that may ſaue thee in all thy cities? and thy Iudges of whom
thou ſaidſt, Giue me a King and Princes? 11 I gaue thee a king in mine
anger, and tooke him away in my wrath. 12 The iniquitie of Ephraim is
bound vp: his ſinne is hid. 13 The ſorrowes of a traueiling woman ſhall
come vpon him, he is an vnwiſe ſonne, for he ſhould not ſtay long in
the place of the breaking foorth of children. 14 I will ranſome them from
the power of the graue: I will redeeme them from death: O death, I will
be thy plagues, O graue, I will be thy deſtruction; repentance ſhall be hid
from mine eyes. 15 Though he be fruitfull among his brethren, an Eaſt
winde ſhall come, the winde of the Lord ſhall come vp from the
wilderneſſe, and his ſpring ſhall become drie, and his fountaine ſhalbe
dried vp: he ſhall ſpoile the treaſure of all pleaſant veſſels. 16 Samaria ſhall
become deſolate, for ſhe hath rebelled againſt her God: they ſhall fall by
the ſword: their infants ſhalbe daſhed in pieces, and their women with
childe ſhalbe ript vp.
CHAPTER 14 1 O Iſrael, returne vnto the Lord thy God; for thou haſt
fallen by thine iniquitie. 2 Take with you words, and turne to the Lord, ſay
vnto him, Take away all iniquitie, and receiue vs graciouſly: ſo will wee
render the calues of our lips. 3 Aſshur ſhall not ſaue vs, we will not ride
vpon horſes, neither will wee ſay any more to the work of our hands,
Yee are our gods: for in thee the fatherleſſe findeth mercie. 4 I will heale
their backſliding, I will loue them freely: for mine anger is turned away
from him. 5 I wil be as the dew vnto Iſrael: hee ſhall grow as the lillie, and
caſt foorth his rootes as Lebanon. 6 His branches ſhall ſpread, and his
beautie ſhalbe as the oliue tree, and his ſmell as Lebanon. 7 They that
dwell vnder his ſhadow ſhall returne: they ſhall reuiue as the corne, &
grow as the vine, the ſent thereof ſhalbe as the wine of
Lebanon. 8 Ephraim ſhall ſay, What haue I to doe any more with idoles?
I haue heard him, and obſerued him: I am like a greene firre tree, from
me is thy fruite found. 9 Who is wiſe, and hee ſhall vnderſtand theſe
things? prudent, and hee ſhall know them? for the wayes of the Lord are
right, and the iuſt ſhall walke in them: but the tranſgreſsours ſhall fall
therein.

IOEL (JOEL)

CHAPTER 1 1 The word of the Lord that came to Ioel the ſonne of
Pethuel. 2 Heare this, yee olde men, and giue eare, all yee inhabitants of
the lande: Hath this been in your dayes, or euen in the dayes of your
fathers? 3 Tell ye your children of it, and let your children tell their
children, and their children another generation. 4 That which the palmer
worme hath left, hath the locuſt eaten; and that which the locuſt hath
left, hath the canker-worme eaten; and that which the canker-worme
hath left, hath the caterpillar eaten. 5 Awake ye drunkards, and weepe,
and howle all yee drinkers of wine, becauſe of the new wine, for it is cut
off from your mouth. 6 For a nation is come vp vpon my lande, ſtrong,
and without number, whoſe teeth are the teeth of a lyon, and he hath
the cheeke-teeth of a great lyon. 7 He hath laide my vine waſte: and
barked my figge-tree: hee hath made it cleane bare, and caſt it away, the
branches thereof are made white. 8 Lament like a virgine girded with
ſackecloth for the huſband of her youth. 9 The meate offring and the
drinke offering is cut off from the houſe of the Lord, the Prieſtes the
Lords miniſters mourne. 10 The field is waſted, the lande mourneth; for
the corne is waſted: the new wine is dried vp, the oyle languiſheth. 11 Be
yee aſhamed, O yee huſbandmen: howle, O yee vine-dreſſers, for the
wheate and for the barley; becauſe the harueſt of the field is
periſhed. 12 The vine is dried vp, and the figgetree languiſheth, the
pomegranate tree, the palme tree alſo and the apple tree, euen all the
trees of the field are withered: becauſe ioy is withered away from the
ſonnes of men. 13 Gird your ſelues, and lament, yee Prieſts: howle, ye
miniſters of the Altar: come, lie all night in ſackecloth, ye miniſters of
my God: for the meat offering and the drinke offering is withholden
from the houſe of your God. 14 ſanctifie yee a faſt: call a ſolemne
aſſembly: gather the Elders, and all the inhabitants of the land into the
houſe of the Lord your God, and cry vnto the Lord: 15 Alas for the day:
for the day of the Lord is at hand, and as a deſtruction from the
Almightie ſhall it come. 16 Is not the meate cut off before your eyes, yea
ioy and gladneſſe from the houſe of our God? 17 The ſeede is rotten
vnder their clods: the garners are laide deſolate: the barnes are broken
downe, for the corne is withered. 18 How doe the beaſtes grone? the
heards of cattell are perplexed, becauſe they haue no paſture, yea the
flockes of ſheepe are made deſolate. 19 O Lord, to thee will I crie: for the
fire hath deuoured the paſtures of the wilderneſſe, and the flame hath
burnt all the trees of the field. 20 The beaſts of the field crie alſo vnto
thee: for the riuers of waters are dried vp, and the fire hath deuoured
the paſtures of the wilderneſſe.
CHAPTER 2 1 Blow yee the trumpet in Zion, & ſound an alarme in my
holy mountaine: let all the inhabitants of the land tremble: for the day
of the Lord cōmeth, for it is nie at hand; 2 A day of darkeneſſe and of
gloomineſse, a day of clouds and of thicke darkeneſſe, as the morning
ſpread vpon the mountaines: a great people and a ſtrong, there hath not
beene euer the like, neither ſhall be any more after it, euen to the yeres
of many generations. 3 A fire deuoureth before them, and behind them a
flame burneth: the land is as the garden of Eden before them, and
behind them a deſolate wildernes, yea and nothing ſhall eſcape
them. 4 The appearance of them is as the appearance of horſes; and as
horſe men, ſo ſhall they runne. 5 Like the noiſe of charets on the tops of
mountaines ſhall they leape, like the noiſe of a flame of fire that
deuoureth the ſtubble, as a ſtrong people, ſet in battell aray. 6 Before their
face the people ſhall be much pained: all faces ſhall gather
blackneſse. 7 They ſhall runne like mighty men, they ſhall clime the wall
like men of warre, and they ſhall march euery one on his wayes, and they
ſhall not breake their rankes. 8 Neither ſhall one thruſt another, they ſhall
walke euery one in his path: and when they fall vpon the ſword, they
ſhall not be wounded. 9 They ſhall runne to and fro in the citie: they ſhall
runne vpon the wall: they ſhall clime vp vpon the houſes: they ſhall enter
in at the windowes, like a theefe. 10 The earth ſhall quake before them,
the heauens ſhall tremble, the Sun & the Moone ſhall be darke, & the
ſtarres ſhall withdrawe their ſhining. 11 And the Lord ſhall vtter his voyce
before his armie, for his campe is very great: for he is ſtrong that
executeth his word: for the day of the Lord is great and very terrible,
and who can abide it? 12 Therefore alſo now, ſaith the Lord, turne yee
euen to me with all your heart, and with faſting, and with weeping, and
with mourning. 13 And rent your heart and not your garments; and turne
vnto the Lord your God: for he is gracious and mercifull, ſlow to anger,

and of great kindneſse, and repenteth him of the euill.14Who knoweth if he will returne and repent, and leaue a bleſſing behind him, euen a meate offring and a drinke offring vnto the Lord your God?15Blow the trumpet in Zion, ſanctifie a faſt, call a ſolemne aſſembly.16Gather the people: ſanctifie the congregation: aſſemble the elders: gather the children, and thoſe that ſucke the breaſts: let the bridegroome goe forth of his chamber, and the bride out of her cloſet.17Let the prieſts, the miniſters of the Lord, weepe betweene the porch and the altar, & let them ſay; Spare thy people O Lord, and giue not thine heritage to reproch; that the heathen ſhould rule ouer them: Wherefore ſhould they ſay among the people, Where is their God?18Then will the Lord be iealous for his land, and pitie his people.19Yea the Lord will anſwere and ſay vnto his people; Behold, I will ſend you corne and wine, and oyle, and yee ſhall be ſatiſfied therewith: and I will no more make you a reproch among the heathen.20But I will remoue farre off from you the northren armie, & will driue him into a land barren and deſolate, with his face toward the Eaſt ſea, and his hinder part towards the vtmoſt ſea, and his ſtinke ſhall come vp, and his ill fauour ſhall come vp, becauſe he hath done great things.21Feare not, O land, be glad and reioyce: for the Lord will doe great things.22Be not afraid, yee beaſts of the field: for the paſtures of the wilderneſſe doe ſpring, for the tree beareth her fruit, the fig tree and the vine doe yeeld their ſtrength.23Be glad then, ye children of Zion, and reioyce in the Lord your God: for he hath giuen you the former raine moderately, and he will cauſe to come downe for you the raine, the former raine, & the latter raine in the firſt month.24And the floores ſhall bee full of wheate, and the fats ſhall ouerflowe with wine and oyle.25And I will reſtore to you the yeeres that the locuſt hath eaten, the canker worme, and the caterpiller, and the palmer worme, my great armie which I ſent among you.26And ye ſhall eate in plentie, and be ſatiſfied, and praiſe the Name of the Lord your God, that hath dealt wonderouſly with you: and my people ſhall neuer be aſhamed.27And ye ſhal know that I am in the midſt of Iſrael, and that I am the Lord your God, and none elſe: and my people ſhall neuer be aſhamed.28And it ſhall come to paſſe afterward, that I will powre out my Spirit vpon all fleſh, and your ſonnes and your daughters ſhall prophecie, your old men ſhall dreame dreames, your yong men ſhall ſee viſions.29And alſo vpon the ſeruants, and vpon the handmaids in thoſe dayes will I powre out my Spirit.30And I will ſhew wonders in the heauens, and in the earth, blood and fire, and pillars of ſmoke.31The Sunne ſhall be turned into darkeneſſe, and the Moone into blood, before the great and the terrible day of the Lord come.32And it ſhall come to paſſe that whoſoeuer ſhall call on the Name of the Lord, ſhall bee deliuered: for in mount Zion and in Ieruſalem ſhalbe deliuerance, as the Lord hath ſaid, and in the remnant, whom the Lord ſhall call.

CHAPTER 31For behold, in thoſe dayes and in that time, when I ſhall bring againe the captiuitie of Iudah and Ieruſalem,2I wil alſo gather all nations, and will bring them downe into the valley of Iehoſhaphat, and wil plead with them there for my people, and for my heritage Iſrael, whom they haue ſcattered among the nations, and parted my land.3And they haue caſt lots for my people, and haue giuen a boy for a harlot, and ſolde a girle for wine, that they might drinke.4Yea and what haue ye to do with me, O Tyre and Zidon, and all the coaſts of Paleſtine? will ye render mee a recompence? and if ye recompenſe me, ſwiftly and ſpeedily will I returne your recompenſe vpon your owne head.5Becauſe yee haue taken my ſiluer and my gold, and haue caried into your temples my goodly pleaſant things.6The children alſo of Iudah and the children of Ieruſalem haue ye ſold vnto the Grecians, that yee might remoue them farre from their border.7Behold, I will raiſe them out of the place whither yee haue ſold them, and wil returne your recompence vpon your owne head.8And I will ſell your ſonnes and your daughters into the hande of the children of Iudah, and they ſhall ſell them to the Sabeans, to a people farre off, for the Lord hath ſpoken it.9Proclaime ye this among the gentiles: prepare warre, wake vp the mightie men, let all the men of warre draw neere, let them come vp.10Beate your plowe ſhares into ſwords, and your pruning hookes into ſpeares, let the weake ſay, I am ſtrong.11Aſſemble your ſelues, and come all ye heathen, and gather your ſelues together round about: thither cauſe thy mightie ones to come downe, O Lord.12Let the heathen be wakened, and come vp to the valley of Iehoſhaphat: for there will I ſit to iudge all the heathen round about.13Put ye in the ſickle, for the harueſt is ripe, come, get you downe, for the preſſe is full, the fats ouerflowe, for the wickedneſſe is great.14Multitudes, multitudes in the valley of deciſion: for þe day of the Lord is neere in the valley of deciſion.15The Sunne and the Moone ſhall be darkened, and the ſtarres ſhall withdraw their ſhining.16The Lord alſo ſhal roare out of Zion, and vtter his voice from Ieruſalem, and the heauens and the earth ſhall ſhake, but the Lord will be the hope of his people, and the ſtrength of the children of Iſrael.17So ſhall ye know that I am the Lord your God, dwelling in Zion, my holy Mountaine: then ſhall Ieruſalem be holy, and there ſhall no ſtrangers paſſe through her any more.18And it ſhall come to paſſe in that day, that the mountaines ſhal drop downe new wine, and the hils ſhall flow with milke, and all the riuers of Iudah ſhall flow with waters, and a fountaine ſhall come forth of the houſe of the Lord, and ſhall water the valley of Shittim.19Egypt ſhall be a deſolation, and Edom ſhall be a deſolate wildernes, for the violence againſt the children of Iudah, becauſe they haue ſhed innocent blood in their land.20But Iudah ſhall dwell for euer, and Ieruſalem from generation to generation.21For I wil cleanſe their blood, that I haue not cleanſed, for the Lord dwelleth in Zion.

AMOS

CHAPTER 11The wordes of Amos, who was among the heardmen of Tekoa, which hee ſawe concerning Iſrael, in the daies of Uzziah King of Iudah, and in the dayes of Ieroboam the ſonne of Ioaſh king of Iſrael, two yere before the earthquake.2And he ſaid, The Lord will roare from Zion, and vtter his voice from Ieruſalem: and the habitations of the ſhepheards ſhall mourne, and the top of Carmel ſhall wither.3Thus ſaith the Lord; For three tranſgreſſions of Damaſcus, and for foure I wil not turne away the puniſhment thereof, becauſe they haue threſhed Gilead, with threſhing inſtruments of yron.4But I will ſend a fire into the houſe of Hazael, which ſhall deuoure the palaces of Benhadad.5I wil breake alſo the barre of Damaſcus, and cut off the inhabitant from the plaine of Auen: and him that holdeth the ſcepter from the houſe of Eden, and the people of Syria ſhall goe into captiuitie, vnto Kir, ſaith the Lord.6Thus ſaith the Lord, For three tranſgreſſions of Gaza, and for foure I will not turne away the puniſhment thereof: becauſe they caried away captiue the whole captiuitie, to deliuer them vp to Edom.7But I wil ſend a fire on the wall of Gaza, which ſhall deuoure the palaces thereof.8And I wil cut off the inhabitant from Aſhdod, and him that holdeth the ſcepter from Aſhkelon, and I wil turne mine hand againſt Ekron; and the remnant of the Philiſtines ſhall periſh, ſaith the Lord God.9Thus ſaith the Lord, For three tranſgreſſions of Tyrus, and for foure I wil not turne away the puniſhment thereof, becauſe they deliuered vp the whole captiuitie to Edom, and remembred not the brotherly couenant.10But I wil ſend a fire on the wall of Tyrus, which ſhall deuoure the palaces thereof.11Thus ſaith the Lord, For three tranſgreſſions of Edom, and for foure, I will not turne away the puniſhment thereof, becauſe he did purſue his brother with the ſword, and did caſt off all pitie, and his anger did teare perpetually, and kept his wrath for euer.12But I will ſend a fire vpon Teman, which ſhall deuoure the palaces of Bozrah.13Thus ſayth the Lord, For three tranſgreſſions of the children of Ammon, and for foure, I wil not turne away the puniſhment thereof; becauſe they haue ript vp the women with childe of Gilead, that they might enlarge their border.14But I will kindle a fire in the wall of Rabbah, and it ſhall deuoure the palaces thereof, with ſhowting in the day of battell, with a tempeſt in the day of the whirlewinde.15And their king ſhall goe into captiuitie, hee, and his princes together, ſayth the Lord.

CHAPTER 21Thus ſayth the Lord, For three tranſgreſſions of Moab, and for foure, I wil not turne away the puniſhment thereof, becauſe hee burnt the bones of the King of Edom into lime.2But I will ſend a fire vpon Moab, and it ſhall deuoure the palaces of Kerioth, and Moab ſhall die with tumult, with ſhouting, and with the ſound of the trumpet:3And I will cut off the iudge from the middeſt thereof, and wil ſlay all the princes thereof with him, ſayeth the Lord.4Thus ſayth the Lord, For three tranſgreſſions of Iudah, and for foure, I will not turne away the puniſhment thereof; becauſe they haue deſpiſed the Law of the Lord, and haue not kept his Commandements, and their lies cauſed them to erre, after the which their fathers haue walked.5But I will ſend a fire vpon Iudah, and it ſhall deuoure the palaces of Ieruſalem.6Thus ſayth the Lord, For three tranſgreſſions of Iſrael, and for foure, I will not turne away the puniſhment thereof; becauſe they ſolde the righteous for ſiluer, and the poore for a paire of ſhooes:7That pant after the duſt of the earth on the head of the poore, and turne aſide the way of the meeke; and a man and his father will goe in vnto the ſame maid, to profane my holy Name.8And they lay themſelues downe vpon clothes laide to pledge, by euery Altar, and they drinke the wine of the condemned in the houſe of their God.9Yet deſtroyed I the Amorite before them, whoſe height was like the height of the Cedars, and hee was ſtrong as the okes, yet I deſtroyed his fruite from aboue, and his rootes from beneath.10Alſo I brought you vp from the land of Egypt, and ledde you fourtie yeeres through the wilderneſſe, to poſſeſſe the land of the Amorite.11And I raiſed vp of your ſonnes for Prophets, and of your young men for Nazarites. Is it not euen thus, O ye children of Iſrael, ſaith the Lord ?12But ye gaue the Nazarites wine to drinke, and commaunded the Prophets, ſaying, Prophecie not.13Behold, I am preſſed vnder you, as a cart is preſſed that is ful of ſheaues.14Therefore the flight ſhall periſh from the ſwift, and the ſtrong ſhall not ſtrengthen his force, neither ſhall the mightie deliuer himſelfe:15Neither ſhall hee ſtand that handleth the bow, and hee that is ſwift of foote, ſhall not deliuer himſelfe, neither ſhall hee that rideth the horſe, deliuer himſelfe.16And hee that is couragious among the mighty, ſhall flee away naked in that day, ſaith the Lord.

CHAPTER 31Heare this word that the Lord hath ſpoken againſt you, O children of Iſrael, againſt the whole family, which I brought vp from the land of Egypt, ſaying;2You onely haue I knowen of all the families of the earth: therefore I will puniſh you for all your iniquities.3Can two walke together, except they be agreed?4Will a lyon roare in the forreſt, when he hath no pray? will a young lyon cry out of his den, if he haue taken nothing?5Can a bird fall in a ſnare vpon the earth, where no ginne is for him? ſhall one take vp a ſnare from the earth, and haue taken nothing at all?6Shall a trumpet be blowen in the citie, and the people not be afraid? ſhall there be euill in a citie, and the Lord hath not done it?7Surely the Lord God will doe nothing, but he reuealeth his ſecret vnto his ſeruants the Prophets.8The lyon hath roared, Who will not feare? the Lord God hath ſpoken, Who can but prophecie?9Publiſh in the palaces at Aſhdod, and in the palaces in the land of Egypt, and ſay; Aſsemble your ſelues vpon the mountaines of Samaria: and behold the great tumults in the midſt thereof, and the oppreſſed in the midſt thereof.10For they know not to doe right, ſaith the Lord; who ſtore vp violence, and robberie in their palaces.11Therefore thus ſaith the Lord God, An aduerſarie there ſhall be euen round about the land: and he ſhal bring downe thy ſtrength from thee, and thy palaces ſhall be ſpoiled.12Thus ſaith the Lord, As the ſhepheard taketh out of the mouth of the lyon two legges or a piece of an eare; ſo ſhall the children of Iſrael be taken out that dwell in Samaria, in the corner of a bed, and in Damaſcus in a couch.13Heare yee and teſtifie in the houſe of Iacob, ſaith the Lord God, the God of hoſtes;14That in the day that I ſhall viſite the tranſgreſſions of Iſrael vpon him, I will alſo viſite the altars of Bethel, and the hornes of the altar ſhall be cut off, and fall to the ground.15And I will ſmite the winter houſe with the ſummer houſe; and the houſes of yuorie ſhall periſh, and the great houſes ſhall haue an end, ſaith the Lord.

CHAPTER 41Heare this word yea kine of Baſhan, that are in the mountaine of Samaria, which oppreſſe the poore, which cruſh the needy, which ſay to their maſters; Bring, and let vs drinke.2The Lord God hath ſworne by his holineſſe, that loe, the dayes ſhall come vpon you, that he will take you away with hookes, and your poſteritie with fiſh-hookes.3And yee ſhall goe out at the breaches, euery Cow at that which is before her, and yee ſhall caſt them into the palace, ſaith the Lord.4Come to Bethel and tranſgreſse, at Gilgal multiplie tranſgreſsion; and bring your ſacrifices euery morning, and your tithes after three yeeres.5And offer a ſacrifice of thankſgiuing with leauen, and proclaime and publiſh the free offrings; for this liketh you, O yee children of Iſrael, ſaith the Lord God.6And I alſo haue giuen you cleanneſſe of teeth in all your cities, and want of bread in all your places: yet haue yee not returned vnto me, ſaith the Lord.7And alſo I haue withholden the raine from you, when there were yet three moneths to the harueſt, and I cauſed it to raine vpon one citie, and cauſed it not to raine vpon an other city: one piece was rained vpon, & the piece wherupon it rained not, withered.8So two or three cities wandered vnto one citie, to drinke water; but they were not ſatiſfied: yet haue yee not returned vnto me, ſaith the Lord.9I haue ſmitten you with blaſting and mildew; when your gardens and your vineyards, and your fig trees, and your oliue trees increaſed, the palmer worme deuoured them: yet haue yee not returned vnto me, ſaith the Lord.10I haue ſent among you the peſtilence, after the maner of Egypt: your yongmen haue I ſlain with the ſword, and haue taken away your horſes, & I haue made the ſtinke of your campes to come vp vnto your noſtrils, yet haue ye not returned vnto me, ſaith the Lord.11I haue ouerthrowen ſome of you, as God ouerthrew Sodome & Gomorrah, and yee were as a firebrand pluckt out of the burning: yet haue yee not returned vnto me, ſaith the Lord.12Therefore thus will I doe vnto thee, O Iſrael: and becauſe I will doe this vnto thee, prepare to meete thy God, O Iſrael.13For loe, he that formeth the mountaines, and createth the wind, and declareth vnto man, what is his thought, that maketh the morning darkeneſſe, and treadeth vpon the high places of the earth: the Lord, the God of hoſtes is his Name.

CHAPTER 51Heare ye this word which I take vp againſt you, euen a lamentation, O houſe of Iſrael.2The virgin of Iſrael is fallen, ſhe ſhall no more riſe: ſhe is forſaken vpon her land, there is none to raiſe her vp.3For thus ſaith the Lord God, The citie that went out by a thouſand, ſhall leaue an hundred, and that which went foorth by an hundred, ſhall leaue ten to the houſe of Iſrael.4For thus ſaith the Lord vnto the houſe of Iſrael, Seeke ye mee, and ye ſhall liue.5But ſeeke not Bethel, nor enter into Gilgal and paſſe not to Beer-ſheba: for Gilgal ſhall ſurely goe into captiuitie, and Bethel ſhal come to nought.6Seeke the Lord, and ye ſhall liue, leſt hee breake out like fire in the houſe of Ioſeph and deuoure it, and there be none to quench it in Bethel,7Ye who turne iudgment to wormwood, and leaue off righteouſneſſe in the earth:8Seeke him that maketh the ſeuen ſtarres and Orion, and turneth the ſhadow of death into the morning, and maketh the day darke with night: that calleth for the waters of the ſea, and powreth them out vpon the face of the earth: the Lord is his Name.9That ſtrengtheneth the ſpoiled againſt the ſtrong: ſo that the ſpoiled ſhall come againſt the fortreſse.10They hate him that rebuketh in the gate: and they abhorre him that ſpeaketh vprightly.11Foraſmuch therfore as your treading is vpon the poore, and ye take from him burdens of wheate, ye haue built houſes of hewen ſtone, but ye ſhall not dwell in them: yee haue planted pleaſant vineyards, but ye ſhall not drinke wine of them.12For I know your manifold tranſgreſſions, and your mighty ſinnes: they afflict the iuſt, they take a bribe, and they turne aſide the poore in the gate from their right.13Therefore the prudent ſhall keepe ſilence in that time, for it is an euill time.14Seeke good and not euill, that ye may liue: and ſo the Lord, the God of hoſts ſhall be with you, as yee haue ſpoken.15Hate the euill, and loue the good, and eſtabliſh iudgement in the gate: it may be that the Lord God of hoſtes will bee gracious vnto the remnant of Ioſeph.16Therefore the Lord, the God of hoſtes, the Lord ſaith thus: Wailing ſhall be in all ſtreets, and they ſhall ſay in all the high wayes, Alas, Alas: and they ſhall call the huſbandman to mourning, and ſuch as are ſkilful of lamentation, to wailing.17And in all vineyards ſhall be wailing: for I will paſſe through thee, ſaith the Lord.18Woe vnto you that deſire the day of the Lord: to what ende is it for you? the day of the Lord is darknes and not light.19As if a man did flee from a lyon, and a beare met him, or went into the houſe, and leaned his hand on the wall, and a ſerpent bit him.20Shall not the day of the Lord be darkenes, and not light? euen very darke, and no brightneſse in it?21I hate, I deſpiſe your feaſt dayes, and I will not ſmell in your ſolemne aſſemblies.22Though ye offer me burnt offerings, and your meat offerings, I will not accept them: neither will I regard the peace offerings of your fat beaſts.23Take thou away from mee the noiſe of thy ſongs: for I will not heare the melodie of thy violes.24But let iudgement run downe as waters, and righteouſneſſe as a mightie ſtreame.25Haue yee offered vnto mee ſacrifices and offerings in the wilderneſſe fourtie yeeres, O houſe of Iſrael?26But yee haue borne the tabernacle of your Moloch, and Chiun your images, the ſtarre of your god, which ye made to your ſelues.27Therefore wil I cauſe you to go into captiuitie beyond Damaſcus, ſaith the Lord, whoſe Name is the God of hoſtes.

CHAPTER 61Woe to them that are at eaſe in Zion, and truſt in the mountaine of Samaria, which are named chiefe of the nations, to whom

the houſe of Iſrael came. 2 Paſſe ye vnto Calneh, and ſee, and from thence
go ye to Hemath the great: then goe downe to Gath of the Philiſtines:
bee they better then theſe kingdomes? or their border greater then your
border? 3 Ye that put farre away the euil day, and cauſe the ſeat of
violence to come neere: 4 That lie vpon beds of Yuorie, and ſtretch
themſelues vpon their couches, and eate the lambes out of the flocke,
and the calues out of the midſt of the ſtall: 5 That chaunt to the ſound of
the Uiole, and inuent to themſelues inſtruments of muſicke, like
Dauid: 6 That drinke wine in bowles, and anoint themſelues with the
chiefe ointments: but they are not grieued for the affliction of
Ioſeph. 7 Therefore now ſhall they goe captiue, with the firſt that goe
captiue, and the banquet of them that ſtretched themſelues, ſhalbe
remoued. 8 The Lord God hath ſworne by himſelfe, ſaith the Lord the
God of hoſtes, I abhorre the excellencie of Iacob, and hate his palaces:
therefore wil I deliuer vp the citie, with all that is therein. 9 And it ſhall
come to paſſe, if there remaine tenne men in one houſe, that they ſhall
die. 10 And a mans vncle ſhall take him vp, and he that burneth him, to
bring out the bones out of the houſe, and ſhall ſay vnto him that is by
the ſides of the houſe; Is there yet any with thee? and hee ſhall ſay, No.
Then ſhall he ſay, Holde thy tongue: for wee may not make mention of
the Name of the Lord. 11 For beholde, the Lord commandeth, and hee
will ſmite the great houſe with breaches, and the little houſe with
clefts. 12 Shall horſes runne vpon the rocke? wil one plow there with
oxen? for ye haue turned iudgement into gall, and the fruite of
righteouſneſſe into hemlocke. 13 Yee which reioyce in a thing of nought,
which ſay, Haue we not taken to vs hornes by our owne ſtrength? 14 But
beholde, I wil raiſe vp againſt you a nation, O houſe of Iſrael, ſaith the
Lord, the God of hoſtes, and they ſhall afflict you from the entring in
of Hemath, vnto the riuer of the wilderneſſe.

CHAPTER 7 1 Thus hath the Lord God ſhewed vnto me, and behold,
he formed graſſehoppers in the beginning of the ſhooting vp of the
latter grouth: and loe, it was the latter grouth after the kings
mowings. 2 And it came to paſſe, that when they had made an ende of
eating the graſſe of the land, then I ſaid; O Lord God, forgiue, I beſeech
thee, by whom ſhal Iacob Ariſe? for he is ſmall. 3 The Lord repented for
this. It ſhall not be, ſaith the Lord. 4 Thus hath the Lord God ſhewed
vnto me; and behold, the Lord God called to contend by fire, and it
deuoured the great deepe, and did eate vp a part. 5 Then ſaid I, O Lord
God , ceaſe, I beſeech thee, by whom ſhal Iacob Ariſe? for he is
ſmall. 6 The Lord repented for this. This alſo ſhall not bee, ſaith the Lord
God. 7 Thus hee ſhewed mee, and behold, the Lord ſtood vpon a wall
made by a plumbline, with a plumbline in his hand. 8 And the Lord ſaid
vnto mee, Amos, what ſeeſt thou? And I ſayd, A plumb-line. Then ſayd
the Lord, Behold, I will ſet a plumb-line in the midſt of my people Iſrael,
I will not againe paſſe by them any more. 9 And the high places of Iſaac
ſhall be deſolate, and the Sanctuaries of Iſrael ſhalbe laide waſte: and I
will riſe againſt the houſe of Ieroboam with the ſword. 10 Then Amaziah
the Prieſt of Beth-el ſent to Ieroboam king of Iſrael, ſaying; Amos hath
conſpired againſt thee in the midſt of the houſe of Iſrael: the land is not
able to beare all his words. 11 For thus Amos ſaith, Ieroboam ſhall die by
the ſword, and Iſrael ſhall ſurely be led away captiue, out of their owne
land. 12 Alſo Amaziah ſaid vnto Amos, O thou Seer, goe, flee thee away
into the land of Iudah, and there eate bread, and prophecie there. 13 But
prophecie not againe any more at Beth-el: for it is the Kings Chappell,
and it is the Kings Court. 14 Then anſwered Amos, and ſayde to Amaziah;
I was no Prophet, neither was I a Prophets ſonne, but I was an
heardman, and a gatherer of Sycomore fruit. 15 And the Lord tooke me
as I followed the flocke, and the Lord ſaid vnto me, Goe, prophecie
vnto my people Iſrael. 16 Now therefore heare thou the worde of the
Lord; Thou ſayeſt, Prophecie not againſt Iſrael, and drop not thy word
againſt the houſe of Iſaac. 17 Therfore thus ſayth the Lord; Thy wife ſhall
be an harlot in the city, and thy ſonnes and thy daughters ſhall fall by
the ſword, and thy land ſhall be diuided by line: and thou ſhalt die in a
polluted land, and Iſrael ſhall ſurely goe into captiuitie foorth of his land.

CHAPTER 8 1 Thus hath the Lord God ſhewed vnto me, and beholde,
a baſket of Summer fruit. 2 And he ſaid, Amos, what ſeeſt thou? And I
ſayde, A baſket of Summer fruite. Then ſaid the Lord vnto mee, The
ende is come vpon my people of Iſrael; I will not againe paſſe by them
anymore. 3 And the ſongs of the Temples ſhalbe howlings in that day,
ſayth the Lord God: there ſhall be many dead bodies in euery place, they
ſhall caſt them foorth with ſilence. 4 Heare this, O ye that ſwallow vp the
needy, euen to make the poore of the land to faile, 5 Saying, When will
the newe Moone be gone, that we may ſell corne? and the Sabbath, that
wee may ſet forth wheat, making the Ephah ſmall, and the ſhekel great,
and falſifying the balances by deceit? 6 That wee may buy the poore for
ſiluer, & the needie for a paire of ſhoes; yea, and ſell the refuſe of the
wheate? 7 The Lord hath ſworne by the excellencie of Iacob, Surely I will
neuer forget any of their workes. 8 Shall not the land tremble for this, and
euery one mourne that dwelleth therein? and it ſhall riſe vp wholly as a
flood; and it ſhall be caſt out and drowned, as by the flood of
Egypt. 9 And it ſhall come to paſſe in that day, ſaith the Lord God, that
I will cauſe the Sunne to go downe at noone, and I will darken the earth
in the cleare day. 10 And I will turne your feaſts into mourning, and all
your ſongs into lamentation, and I will bring vp ſackcloth vpon all
loynes, and baldneſſe vpon euery head: and I will make it as the
mourning of an onely ſonne, and the end thereof as a bitter
day. 11 Behold, the daies come, ſaith the Lord God, that I will ſend a
famine in the land, not a famine of bread, nor a thirſt for water, but of
hearing the words of the Lord. 12 And they ſhall wander from ſea to ſea,
and from the North euen to the Eaſt they ſhall runne to and fro, to ſeeke
the worde of the Lord, and ſhall not finde it. 13 In that day ſhall the faire
virgines and young men faint for thirſt. 14 They that ſweare by the ſinne
of Samaria, and ſay, Thy God, O Dan, liueth, and the manner of Beer-
ſheba liueth, euen they ſhall fall, and neuer riſe vp againe.

CHAPTER 9 1 I ſaw the Lord ſtanding vpon the altar, and he ſaid, Smite
the lintell of the doore, that the poſts may ſhake: and cut them in the
head all of them, and I will ſlay the laſt of them with the ſword: hee that
fleeth of them, ſhall not flee away, and he that eſcapeth of them, ſhall
not be deliuered. 2 Though they digge into hell, thence ſhall mine hand
take them: though they clime vp to heauen, thence will I bring them
downe. 3 And though they hide themſelues in the top of Carmel, I will
ſearch and take them out thence, and though they be hid from my ſight
in the bottome of the ſea, thence will I commaund the ſerpent, and he
ſhall bite them. 4 And though they goe into captiuitie before their
enemies, thence will I commaund the ſword, and it ſhall ſlay them: and
I will ſet mine eyes vpon them for euill, and not for good. 5 And the Lord
God of hoſtes is he that toucheth the land, and it ſhall melt, and all that
dwelleth therein ſhall mourne, and it ſhall riſe vp wholly like a flood, and
ſhall be drowned as by the flood of Egypt. 6 It is he that buildeth his
ſtories in the heauen, and hath founded his troupe in the earth, he that
calleth for the waters of the ſea, and powreth them out vpon the face of
the earth: the Lord is his name. 7 Are yee not as children of the
Ethiopians vnto me, O children of Iſrael, ſaith the Lord ? haue not I
brought vp Iſrael out of the land of Egypt? and the Philiſtines from
Caphtor, and the Syrians from Kir? 8 Behold, the eyes of the Lord God
are vpon the ſinfull kingdome, and I will deſtroy it from off the face of
the earth; ſauing that I will not vtterly deſtroy the houſe of Iacob, ſaith
the Lord. 9 For loe, I will commaund, and I will ſift the houſe of Iſrael
among all nations, like as corne is ſifted in a ſieue, yet ſhall not the leaſt
graine fall vpon the earth. 10 All the ſinners of my people ſhall die by the
ſword, which ſay: The euill ſhall not ouertake nor preuent vs. 11 In that
day will I raiſe vp the tabernacle of Dauid, that is fallen, and cloſe vp the
breaches thereof, and I will raiſe vp his ruines, and I will build it as in
the dayes of old; 12 That they may poſſeſſe the remnant of Edom, and of
all the heathen; which are called by my name, ſaith the Lord that doth
this. 13 Behold, the daies come, ſaith the Lord, that the plowman ſhall
ouertake the reaper, & the treader of grapes him that ſoweth ſeede, and
the mountaines ſhall drop ſweete wine, and all the hils ſhall melt. 14 And
I will bring againe the captiuitie of my people of Iſrael: and they ſhall
build the waſte cities, and inhabit them; and they ſhall plant vineyards,
and drinke the wine thereof: they ſhall alſo make gardens, and eate the
fruite of them. 15 And I will plant them vpon their land, and they ſhall no
more be pulled vp out of their land, which I haue giuen them, ſaith the
Lord thy God.

OBADIAH

CHAPTER 11The viſion of Obadiah: Thus ſaith the Lord God, concerning Edom; Wee haue heard a rumour from the Lord, and an ambaſsador is ſent among the heathen: Ariſe yee, and let vs riſe vp againſt her in battell.2Behold, I haue made thee ſmall among the heathen: thou art greatly deſpiſed.3The pride of thine heart hath deceiued thee: thou that dwelleſt in the clefts of the rocke, Whoſe habitation is high, that ſaith in his heart: Who ſhall bring me downe to the ground?4Though thou exalt thy ſelfe as the eagle, and though thou ſet thy neſt among the ſtarres, thence will I bring thee downe, ſaith the Lord.5If theeues came to thee, if robbers by night (how art thou cut off?) would they not haue ſtollen til they had enough? if the grape gatherers came to thee, would they not leaue ſome grapes?6How are the things of Eſau ſearched out? how are his hid things ſought vp?7All the men of thy confederacie haue brought thee euen to the border: the men that were at peace with thee, haue deceiued thee, and preuailed againſt thee: they that eate thy bread haue laide a wound vnder thee: there is none vnderſtanding in him.8ſhal I not in that day, ſaith the Lord, euen deſtroy the wiſe men out of Edom, and vnderſtanding out of the mount of Eſau?9And thy mightie men, O Teman, ſhall be diſmayed, to the end that euery one of the mount of Eſau may be cut off by ſlaughter.10For thy violence againſt thy brother Iacob ſhame ſhall couer thee, and thou ſhalt be cut off for euer.11In the day that thou ſtoodeſt on the other ſide, in the day that the ſtrangers caried away captiue his forces, and forreiners entred into his gates, and caſt lots vpon Ieruſalem, euen thou waſt as one of them.12But thou ſhouldeſt not haue looked on the day of thy brother in the day that hee became a ſtranger, neither ſhouldeſt thou haue reioyced ouer the children of Iudah in the day of their deſtruction: neither ſhouldeſt thou haue ſpoken proudly in the day of diſtreſſe.13Thou ſhouldeſt not haue entred into the gate of my people in the day of their calamitie: yea, thou ſhouldeſt not haue looked on their affliction in the day of their calamitie, nor haue laid hands on their ſubſtance in the day of their calamitie.14Neither ſhouldeſt thou haue ſtood in the croſse way to cut off thoſe of his that did eſcape, neither ſhouldeſt thou haue deliuered vp thoſe of his that did remaine in the day of diſtreſſe.15For the day of the Lord is neere vpon all the heathen: as thou haſt done, it ſhall bee done vnto thee, thy reward ſhall returne vpon thine owne head.16For as ye haue drunke vpon my holy mountaine, ſo ſhall all the heathen drinke continually: yea, they ſhall drinke, and they ſhall ſwallow downe, and they ſhall bee as though they had not bene.17But vpon mount Zion ſhall be deliuerance, and there ſhall be holineſſe, and the houſe of Iacob ſhall poſſeſſe their poſſeſſions.18And the houſe of Iacob ſhall bee a fire, and the houſe of Ioſeph a flame, and the houſe of Eſau for ſtubble, and they ſhall kindle in them and deuoure them, and there ſhall not be any remaining of the houſe of Eſau, for the Lord hath ſpoken it.19And they of the South ſhall poſſeſſe the mount of Eſau, and they of the plaine, the Philiſtines: and they ſhall poſſeſſe the fields of Ephraim, and the fields of Samaria, and Beniamin ſhall poſſeſſe Gilead.20And the captiuitie of this hoſte of the children of Iſrael ſhall poſſeſſe that of the Canaanites euen vnto Zarephath, and the captiuitie of Ieruſalem which is in Sepharad, ſhall poſſeſſe the cities of the South.21And Sauiours ſhall come vp on mount Zion to iudge the mount of Eſau, and the kingdome ſhall be the Lords.

IONAH (JONAH)

CHAPTER 11Now the word of the Lord came vnto Ionah the ſonne of Amittai, ſaying,2Ariſe, goe to Nineueh that great citie, and cry againſt it: for their wickednes is come vp before me.3But Ionah roſe vp to flee vnto Tarſhiſh, from the preſence of the Lord, and went downe to Ioppa, and he found a ſhip going to Tarſhiſh: ſo he payed the fare thereof, and went downe into it, to goe with them vnto Tarſhiſh from the preſence of the Lord.4But the Lord ſent out a great winde into the ſea, and there was a mightie tempeſt in the ſea, ſo that the ſhip was like to be broken.5Then the Mariners were afraid, and cried euery man vnto his god, and caſt foorth the wares that were in the ſhip, into the ſea, to lighten it of them: but Ionah was gone downe into the ſides of the ſhip, and hee lay, and was faſt aſleepe.6So the ſhipmaſter came to him, and ſaid vnto him; What meaneſt thou, O ſleeper? Ariſe, call vpon thy God, if ſo be that God wil thinke vpon vs, that we periſh not.7And they ſaid euery one to his fellow; Come, and let vs caſt lots, that we may know for whoſe cauſe this euil is vpon vs. So they caſt lots, and the lot fell vpon Ionah.8Then ſaid they vnto him, Tel vs, we pray thee, for whoſe cauſe this euill is vpon vs: What is thine occupation? and whence commeſt thou? What is thy countrey? and of what people art thou?9And hee ſaid vnto them, I am an Hebrew, and I feare the Lord the God of heauen, which hath made the ſea, and the dry land.10Then were the men exceedingly afraid, and ſaide vnto him; Why haſt thou done this? (for the men knew that he fled from the preſence of the Lord, becauſe he had told them.)11Then ſaid they vnto him, What ſhall we doe vnto thee, that the ſea may be calme vnto vs? (for the ſea wrought and was tempeſtuous.)12And he ſaid vnto them, Take me vp, and caſt mee foorth into the ſea; ſo ſhall the ſea be calme vnto you: for I know that for my ſake this great tempeſt is vpon you.13Neuertheleſſe the men rowed hard to bring it to the land, but they could not: for the ſea wrought, and was tempeſtuous againſt them.14Wherefore they cried vnto the Lord, and ſaid, We beſeech thee, O Lord, We beſeech thee, let vs not periſh for this mans life, and lay not vpon vs, innocent blood: for thou, O Lord, haſt done as it pleaſed thee.15So they tooke vp Ionah, and caſt him foorth into the ſea, and the ſea ceaſed from her raging.16Then the men feared the Lord exceedingly, and offered a ſacrifice vnto the Lord, and made vowes.17Now the Lord had prepared a great fiſh to ſwallow vp Ionah, and Ionah was in the belly of the fiſh three dayes, and three nights.

CHAPTER 21Then Ionah prayed vnto the Lord his God, out of the fiſhes belly,2And ſaid, I cried by reaſon of mine affliction vnto the Lord, and hee heard mee; out of the belly of hell cried I, and thou heardeſt my voyce.3For thou hadſt caſt mee into the deepe, in the middeſt of the ſeas, and the floods compaſſed me about: all thy billowes & thy waues paſſed ouer me.4Then I ſaid, I am caſt out of thy ſight; yet I will looke againe toward thy holy Temple.5The waters compaſſed mee about euen to the ſoule; the depth cloſed mee round about; the weedes were wrapt about my head.6I went downe to the bottomes of the mountaines: the earth with her barres was about me for euer: yet haſt thou brought vp my life from corruption, O Lord my God.7When my ſoule fainted within mee, I remembred the Lord, and my prayer came in vnto thee, into thine holy Temple.8They that obſerue lying vanities, forſake their owne mercy.9But I wil ſacrifice vnto thee with the voice of thankſgiuing, I will pay that that I haue vowed: ſaluation is of the Lord.10And the Lord ſpake vnto the fiſh, and it vomited out Ionah vpon the drie land.

CHAPTER 31And the word of þe Lordcame vnto Ionah the ſecond time, ſaying;2Ariſe, goe vnto Nineueh that great citie, and preach vnto it the preaching that I bid thee.3So Ionah aroſe and went vnto Nineueh, according to the word of the Lord: now Nineueh was an exceeding great citie of three dayes iourney.4And Ionah began to enter into the citie a dayes iourney, and hee cryed, and ſaid; Yet fourtie dayes, and Niniueh ſhalbe ouerthrowen.5So the people of Nineueh beleeued God, and proclaimed a faſt, and put on ſackecloth from the greateſt of them euen to the leaſt of them.6For word came vnto the King of Nineueh, and he aroſe from his throne, and he laid his robe from him and couered him with ſackcloth, & ſate in aſhes.7And he cauſed it to be proclaimed and publiſhed through Nineueh (by the decree of the King and his nobleſ) ſaying; Let neither man nor beaſt, herd nor flocke taſte any thing; let them not feede, nor drinke water.8But let man and beaſt be couered with ſackecloth, and cry mightily vnto God: yea, let them turne euery one from his euill way, and from the violence that is in their hands.9Who can tell if God will turne and repent, and turne away from his fierce anger, that we periſh not?10And God ſaw their workes, that they turned from their euill way, and God repented of the euill that hee had ſayd, that he would doe vnto them, and he did it not.

CHAPTER 41But it diſpleaſed Ionah exceedingly, and he was very angry.2And he prayed vnto the Lord, and ſayd, I pray thee, O Lord, was not this my ſaying, when I was yet in my countrey? Therefore I fledde before vnto Tarſhiſh: for I knew that thou art a gracious God, and mercifull, ſlow to anger, and of great kindneſse, and repenteſt thee of the euill.3Therefore now, O Lord, Take, I beſeech thee, my life from me; for it is better for me to die then to liue.4Then ſaid the Lord, Doeſt thou well to be angry?5So Ionah went out of the citie, and ſate on the Eaſt ſide of the city, and there made him a boothe, and ſate vnder it in the ſhadow, till hee might ſee what would become of the citie.6And the Lord God prepared a gourd, and made it to come vp ouer Ionah, that it might be a ſhadow ouer his head, to deliuer him from his griefe. So Ionah was exceeding glad of the gourd.7But God prepared a worme when the morning roſe the next day, and it ſmote the gourd that it withered.8And it came to paſſe when the Sunne did Ariſe, that God prepared a vehement Eaſt wind; and the Sunne beat vpon the head of Ionah, that hee fainted, and wiſhed in himſelfe to die, and ſaid, It is better for me to die, then to liue.9And God ſaid to Ionah, Doeſt thou well to be angry for the gourd? and he ſaid, I doe well to be angry, euen vnto death.10Then ſaid the Lord, Thou haſt had pitie on the gourde, for the which thou haſt not laboured, neither madeſt it grow, which came vp in a night, and periſhed in a night:11And ſhould not I ſpare Nineueh that great citie, wherein are more then ſixſcore thouſand perſons, that cannot diſcerne betweene their right hand and their left hand, and alſo much cattell?

MICAH

CHAPTER 11The word of the Lord that came to Micah the Moraſthite in the dayes of Iotham, Ahaz, and Hezekiah Kings of Iudah, which hee ſaw concerning Samaria and Ieruſalem.2Heare all ye people, hearken O earth, and all that therein is, and let the Lord God be witneſſe againſt you, the Lord from his holy temple.3For behold, the Lord commeth forth out of his place, and will come downe and tread vpon the high places of the earth.4And the mountaines ſhall be molten vnder him, and the valleis ſhall be cleft: as waxe before the fire, and as the waters that are powred downe a ſteepe place.5For the tranſgreſſion of Iacob is all this, and for the ſinnes of the houſe of Iſrael: What is the tranſgreſſion of Iacob? Is it not Samaria? and what are the high places of Iudah? are they not Ieruſalem?6Therfore I will make Samaria as an heape of the field, and as plantings of a vineyard; and I will powre downe the ſtones therof into the valley, and I will diſcouer the foundations thereof.7And all the grauen images thereof ſhall be beaten to pieces, and all the hires thereof ſhall be burnt with the fire, and all the idoles therof will I lay deſolate: for ſhe gathered it of the hire of an harlot, and they ſhall returne to the hire of an harlot.8Therfore I wil waile and houle, I will goe ſtript and naked: I will make a wailing like the dragons, and mourning as the owles.9For her wound is incurable, for it is come vnto Iudah: he is come vnto the gate of my people, euen to Ieruſalem.10Declare yee it not at Gath, weepe yee not at all: In the houſe of Aphrah rowle thy ſelfe in the duſt.11Paſſe yee away thou inhabitant of Saphir, hauing thy ſhame naked; the inhabitant of Zaanan came not forth in the mourning of Beth-ezel, he ſhall receiue of you his ſtanding.12For the inhabitant of Maroth waited carefully for good, but euill came downe from the Lord vnto the gate of Ieruſalem.13O thou inhabitant of Lachiſh, bind the charet to the ſwift beaſt: ſhe is the beginning of the ſinne to the daughter of Zion: for the tranſgreſſions of Iſrael were found in thee.14Therfore ſhalt thou giue preſents to Moreſheth-Gath: the houſes of Achzib ſhalbe a lie to þe kings of Iſrael.15Yet wil I bring an heire vnto thee, O inhabitant of Mareſhah: he ſhall come vnto Adullam, the glory of Iſrael16Make thee bald, and polle thee for thy delicate children, enlarge thy baldneſse as the Eagle, for they are gone into captiuitie from thee.

CHAPTER 21Woe to them that deuiſe iniquitie, and worke euill vpon their beds: when the morning is light, they practiſe it, becauſe it is in the power of their hand.2And they couet fields and take them by violence: and houſes, and take them away: ſo they oppreſſe a man and his houſe, euen a man and his heritage.3Therefore thus ſaith the Lord, Behold, againſt this familie doe I deuiſe an euill, from which ye ſhall not remoue your necks, neither ſhall ye goe haughtily: for this time is euill.4In that day ſhall one take vp a parable againſt you, and lament with a dolefull lamentation, and ſay, We be vtterly ſpoiled: hee hath changed the portion of my people: how hath he remoued it from me? turning away hee hath diuided our fields.5Therefore thou ſhalt haue none that ſhall caſt a cord by lot in the Congregation of the Lord.6Prophecie ye not, ſay they, to them that prophecie: they ſhall not prophecie to them, that they ſhall not take ſhame.7O thou that art named the houſe of Iacob, is the Spirit of the Lord ſtraitned? are theſe his dongs? doe not my words do good to him that walketh vprightly?8Euen of late, my people is riſen vp as an enemie: ye pull off the robe with the garment, frō them that paſſe by ſecurely, as men auerſe from warre.9The women of my people haue ye caſt out from their pleaſant houſes, from their children haue ye taken away my glory for euer.10Ariſe ye and depart, for this is not your reſt: becauſe it is polluted, it ſhall deſtroy you euen with a ſore deſtruction.11If a man walking in the ſpirit and falſhood, doe lie, ſaying, I will prophecie vnto thee of wine and of ſtrong drinke, he ſhall euen bee the prophet of this people.12I will ſurely aſſemble, O Iacob, all of thee: I will ſurely gather the remnant of Iſrael, I will put them together as the ſheepe of Bozrah, as the flocke in the midſt of their fold: they ſhall make great noiſe by reaſon of the multitude of men.13The breaker is come vp before them: they haue broken vp and haue paſſed through the gate, and are gone out by it, and their king ſhal paſſe before them, & the Lord on the head of them.

CHAPTER 31And I ſaid, Heare, I pray you, O heads of Iacob, and ye princes of the houſe of Iſrael: is it not for you to know iudgement?2Who hate the good and loue the euill, who plucke off their ſkinne from off them, and their fleſh from off their bones.3Who alſo eate the fleſh of my people, and flay their ſkinne from off them, and they breake their bones, and chop them in pieces, as for the pot, and as fleſh within the cauldron.4Then ſhall they cry vnto the Lord, but he will not heare them: he will euen hide his face from them at that time, as they haue behaued themſelues ill in their doings.5Thus ſaith the Lord concerning the Prophets that make my people erre, that bite with their teeth and crie; Peace: and he that putteth not into their mouths, they euen prepare warre againſt him:6Therefore night ſhall be vnto you, that yee ſhall not haue a viſion, and it ſhall be darke vnto you, that yee ſhall not diuine, and the Sunne ſhall goe downe ouer the Prophets, and the day ſhall be darke ouer them.7Then ſhall the ſeers be aſhamed, and the diuiners confounded: yea, they ſhall all couer their lips; for there is no anſwere of God.8But truely I am full of power by the ſpirit of the Lord, and of iudgment and of might, to declare vnto Iacob his tranſgreſsion, and to Iſrael his ſinne.9Heare this, I pray you, yee heads of the houſe of Iacob, and princes of the houſe of Iſrael, that abhorre iudgement and peruert all equitie.10They build vp Zion with blood, and Ieruſalem with iniquitie.11The heads thereof iudge for reward, and the prieſts thereof teach for hyre, and the Prophets thereof diuine for money: yet will they leane vpon the Lord, and ſay; Is not the Lord among vs? none euill can come vpon vs.12Therefore ſhall Zion for your ſake be plowed as a field, and Ieruſalem ſhal become heapes, and the mountaine of the houſe, as the high places of the forreſt.

CHAPTER 41But in the laſt dayes it ſhal come to paſſe, that the mountaine of the houſe of the Lord ſhall be eſtabliſhed in the top of the mountaines, and it ſhalbe exalted aboue the hilles, and people ſhall flow vnto it.2And many nations ſhall come, and ſay; Come, and let vs goe vp to the mountaine of the Lord, and to the houſe of the God of Iacob, and he will teach vs of his wayes, and wee will walke in his pathes: for the Law ſhall goe foorth of Zion, and the word of the Lord from Ieruſalem.3And he ſhall iudge among many people, and rebuke ſtrong nations afarre off, and they ſhall beate their ſwords into plowſhares, and their ſpeares into pruning hookes: nation ſhall not lift vp a ſword againſt nation, neither ſhall they learne warre any more.4But they ſhall ſit euery man vnder his Uine, and vnder his figgetree, and none ſhal make them afraid: for the mouth of the Lord of hoſtes hath ſpoken it.5For all people will walke euery one in the name of his god, and we will walke in the Name of the Lord our God for euer and euer.6In that day, ſaith the Lord, will I aſſemble her that halteth, and I will gather her that is driuen out, and her that I haue afflicted.7And I will make her that halted, a remnant; and her that was caſt farre off, a ſtrong nation; and the Lord ſhall reigne ouer them, in Mount Zion from hencefoorth, euen for euer.8And thou, O towre of the flock, the ſtrong hold of the daughter of Zion, vnto thee ſhall it come, euen the firſt dominion, the kingdome ſhall come to the daughter of Ieruſalem.9Now why doeſt thou cry out alowd? is there no king in thee? is thy counſeller periſhed? for pangs haue taken thee, as a woman in trauell.10Bee in paine and labour to bring forth, O daughter of Zion, like a woman in trauell: for now ſhalt thou goe foorth out of the citie, and thou ſhalt dwel in the field, and thou ſhalt go euen to Babylon: there ſhalt thou be deliuered: there the Lord ſhall redeeme thee from the hand of thine enemies.11Now alſo many nations are gathered againſt thee, that ſay, Let her be defiled, & let our eye look vpon Zion.12But they know not the thoughts of the Lord, neither vnderſtand they his counſell: for hee ſhall gather them as the ſheaues into the floore.13Ariſe and threſh, O daughter of Zion: for I will make thine horne yron, & I will make thy hooues braſſe, and thou ſhalt beat in pieces many people: and I will conſecrate their gaine vnto the Lord, and their ſubſtance vnto the Lord of the whole earth.

CHAPTER 51Now gather thy ſelfe in troupes, O daughter of troupes: he hath laid ſiege againſt vs: they ſhal ſmite the Iudge of Iſrael with a rod vpon the cheeke.2But thou Beth-leem Ephratah, though thou bee little among the thouſands of Iudah, yet out of thee ſhall he come foorth vnto mee, that is to be ruler in Iſrael: whoſe goings foorth haue bene from of old, from euerlaſting.3Therefore will hee giue them vp, vntill the time that ſhee which trauaileth, hath brought forth: then the remnant of his brethren ſhall returne vnto the children of Iſrael.4And he ſhall ſtand and feed in the ſtrength of the Lord, in the Maieſtie of the Name of the Lord his God, and they ſhall abide: for now ſhall he be great vnto the ends of the earth.5And this man ſhall bee the peace when the Aſſyrian ſhall come into our land: and when hee ſhall tread in our palaces, then ſhall we raiſe againſt him ſeuen Shepheards, and eight principall men.6And they ſhall waſte the land of Aſſyria with the ſword, and the land of Nimrod in the entrances thereof: thus ſhall hee deliuer vs from the Aſſyrian, when he commeth into our land, and when hee treadeth within our borders.7And the remnant of Iacob ſhall be in the midſt of many people, as a dew from the Lord, as the ſhowres vpon the graſſe that tarieth not for man, nor waiteth for the ſonnes of men.8And the remnant of Iacob ſhal be among the Gentiles in the middeſt of many people, as a Lyon among the beaſts of the forreſt, as a yong Lyon among the flockes of ſheepe: who if he goe through, both treadeth downe, and teareth in pieces, and none can deliuer.9Thine hand ſhall be lift vp vpon thine aduerſaries, and all thine enemies ſhalbe cut off.10And it ſhall come to paſſe in that day, ſayth the Lord, that I will cut off thy horſes out of the midſt of thee, and I will deſtroy thy charets.11And I will cut off the cities of thy land, and throw downe all thy ſtrong holdes.12And I will cut off witchcrafts out of thine hand, and thou ſhalt haue no more Southſayers.13Thy grauen images alſo will I cut off, and thy ſtanding images out of the midſt of thee: & thou ſhalt no more worſhip the worke of thine hands.14And I will plucke vp thy groues out of the middeſt of thee: ſo will I deſtroy thy cities.15And I will execute vengeance in anger, and furie vpon the heathen, ſuch as they haue not heard.

CHAPTER 61Heare yee now what the Lord ſaith, Ariſe, contend thou before the mountaines, and let the hilles heare thy voice.2Heare yee, O mountaines, the Lords controuerſie, and ye ſtrong foundations of the earth: for the Lord hath a controuerſie with his people, and he will pleade with Iſrael.3O my people, what haue I done vnto thee, and wherein haue I wearied thee? teſtifie againſt me.4For I brought thee vp out of the land of Egypt, and redeemed thee out of the houſe of ſeruants, and I ſent before thee Moſes, Aaron and Miriam.5O my people, remember now what Balak king of Moab conſulted, and what Balaam the ſonne of Beor anſwered him from Shittim vnto Gilgal, that yee may know the righteouſneſſe of the Lord.6Wherewith ſhall I come before the Lord, and bow my ſelfe before the high God? ſhall I come before him with burnt offerings, with calues of a yeere olde?7Will the Lord be pleaſed with thouſands of rammes, or with tenne thouſands of riuers of oyle? ſhall I giue my firſt borne for my tranſgreſsion, the fruit of my body for the ſinne of my ſoule?8Hee hath ſhewed thee, O man, what is good; and what doeth the Lord require of thee, but to do iuſtly, and to loue mercy, and to walke humbly with thy God?9The Lords voice cryeth vnto the citie, and the man of wiſedome ſhall ſee thy Name: heare ye the rodde, and who hath appointed it.10Are there yet the treaſures of wickedneſſe in the houſe of the wicked, and the ſcant meaſure that is abominable.11Shall I count them pure with the wicked balances, and with the bag of deceitfull weights?12For the rich men thereof are full of violence, and the inhabitants thereof haue ſpoken lies, and their tongue is deceitfull in their mouth.13Therefore alſo will I make thee ſicke in ſmiting thee, in making thee deſolate, becauſe of thy ſinnes.14Thou ſhalt eate, but not be ſatiſfied, and thy caſting downe ſhall be in the midſt of thee, and thou ſhalt take holde, but ſhalt not deliuer: & that which thou deliuereſt, will I giue vp to the ſword.15Thou ſhalt ſow, but thou ſhalt not reape: thou ſhalt tread the oliues, but thou ſhalt not anoint thee with oile; & ſweet wine, but ſhalt not drinke wine.16For the ſtatutes of Omri are kept, and all the workes of the houſe of Ahab, and ye walke in their counſels, that I ſhould make thee a deſolation, and the inhabitants thereof an hiſsing: therefore yee ſhall beare the reproch of my people.

CHAPTER 71Woe is mee, for I am as when they haue gathered the ſummer fruits, as the grape gleanings of the vintage: there is no cluſter to eate: my ſoule deſired the firſt ripe fruit.2The good man is periſhed out of the earth, and there is none vpright among men: they all lie in waite for blood: they hunt euery man his brother with a net.3That they may doe euill with both hands earneſtly, the prince aſketh, and the iudge aſketh for a reward: and the great man, he vttereth his miſchieuous deſire: ſo they wrap it vp.4The beſt of them is as a brier: the moſt vpright is ſharper then a thorne hedge: the day of thy watchmen, and thy viſitation commeth; now ſhall be their perplexitie.5Truſt yee not in a friend, put ye not confidence in a guide: keepe the doores of thy mouth from her that lyeth in thy boſome.6For the ſonne diſhonoureth the father: the daughter riſeth vp againſt her mother: the daughter in law againſt her mother in law; a mans enemies are the men of his owne houſe.7Therefore I will looke vnto you the Lord: I will waite for the God of my ſaluation: my God will heare me.8Reioyce not againſt mee, O mine enemie: When I fall, I ſhall Ariſe; when I ſit in darknes, the Lord ſhall be a light vnto me.9I will beare the indignation of the Lord, becauſe I haue ſinned againſt him, vntill he plead my cauſe, and execute iudgement for me: he will bring me forth to the light, and I ſhall behold his righteouſneſſe.10Then ſhe that is mine enemie ſhall ſee it, and ſhame ſhall couer her which ſaid vnto mee; Where is the Lord thy God? mine eyes ſhall behold her: now ſhall ſhe bee troden downe, as the myre of the ſtreets.11In the day that thy walles are to be built, in that day ſhall the decree bee farre remoued.12In that day alſo he ſhal come euen to thee from Aſſyria, and from the fortified cities, and from the fortreſse euen to the riuer, and from ſea to ſea, and from mountaine to mountaine;13Notwithſtanding the land ſhall be deſolate becauſe of them that dwell therein, for the fruite of their doings.14Feede thy people with thy rod, the flocke of thine heritage, which dwell ſolitarily in the wood, in the midſt of Carmel: let them feede in Baſhan and Gilead, as in the dayes of old.15According to the dayes of thy comming out of the land of Egypt will I ſhew vnto him meruailous things.16The nations ſhall ſee, and be confounded at all their might: they ſhall lay their hand vpon their mouth: their eares ſhall be deafe.17They ſhall licke the duſt like a ſerpent, they ſhall moue out of their holes like wormes of the earth: they ſhall be afraid of the Lord our God, and ſhall feare becauſe of thee.18Who is a God like vnto thee, that pardoneth iniquitie, and paſſeth by the tranſgreſſion of the remnant of his heritage? hee retaineth not his anger for euer, becauſe he delighteth in mercy.19He wil turne againe, he will haue compaſſion vpon vs: he will ſubdue our iniquities, and thou wilt caſt all their ſinnes into the depths of the ſea.20Thou wilt performe the trueth to Iacob, and the mercy to Abraham, which thou haſt ſworne vnto our fathers from the dayes of old.

NAHUM

CHAPTER 11The burden of Nineueh. The book of the viſion of Nahum the Elkoſhite.2God is ielous, and the Lord reuengeth: the Lord reuengeth, and is furious, the Lord wil take vengeance on his aduerſaries, and he reſerueth wrath for his enemies.3The Lord is ſlow to anger, and great in power, and will not at all acquit the wicked: the Lord hath his way in the whirlewind, and in the ſtorme, and the clouds are the duſt of his feete.4He rebuketh the ſea, and maketh it drie, and drieth vp all the riuers: Baſhan languiſheth, and Carmel, and the floure of Lebanon languiſheth.5The mountaines quake at him, and the hilles melt, and the earth is burnt at his preſence, yea the world and all that dwell therein.6Who can ſtand before his indignation? and who can abide in the fierceneſse of his anger? his furie is powred out like fire, and the rocks are throwen downe by him.7The Lord is good, a ſtrong hold in the day of trouble, & he knoweth them that truſt in him.8But with an ouer-running flood he will make an vtter ende of the place thereof, and darkeneſſe ſhall purſue his enemies.9What doe ye imagine againſt the Lord ? he will make an vtter ende: affliction ſhall not riſe vp the ſecond time.10For while they be folden together as thornes, and while they are drunken as drunkards, they ſhall be deuoured as ſtubble fully drie.11There is one come out of thee, that imagineth euill againſt the Lord: a wicked counſeller.12Thus ſaith the Lord, Though they be quiet, and likewiſe many, yet thus ſhall they be cut downe, when he ſhall paſſe through: though I haue afflicted thee, I will afflict thee no more.13For now will I breake his yoke from off thee, and will burſt thy bonds in ſunder.14And the Lord hath giuen a commandement concerning thee, that no more of thy name be ſowen: out of the houſe of thy gods will I cut off the grauen image, and the molten image, I wil make thy graue, for thou art vile.15Behold vpon the mountaines the feete of him that bringeth good tidings, that publiſheth peace. O Iudah keepe thy ſolemne feaſts, performe thy vowes: for the wicked ſhall no more paſſe through thee, he is vtterly cut off.

CHAPTER 21He that daſheth in pieces is come up before thy face: keep the munition, watch the way: make thy loines ſtrong: fortifie thy power mightily.2For the Lord hath turned away the excellencie of Iacob, as the excellencie of Iſrael: for the emptiers haue emptied them out, and marred their vine branches.3The ſhield of his mightie men is made red, the valiant men are in ſcarlet: the charets ſhall bee with flaming torches in the day of his preparation, and the firre trees ſhall bee terribly ſhaken.4The charets ſhall rage in the ſtreets, they ſhall iuſtle one againſt another in the broad wayes: they ſhall ſeeme like torches, they ſhall runne like the lightnings.5Hee ſhall recount his worthies: they ſhall ſtumble in their walke: they ſhall make haſte to the wal thereof, and the defence ſhall bee prepared.6The gates of the riuers ſhall bee opened, and the palace ſhall bee diſſolued.7And Huzzab ſhall be led away captiue, ſhe ſhall be brought vp, and her maids ſhall leade her as with the voyce of doues, tabring vpon their breaſts.8But Nineueh is of olde like a poole of water: yet they ſhall flee away. Stand, ſtand ſhall they cry: but none ſhal looke backe.9Take ye the ſpoyle of ſiluer, take the ſpoile of golde: for there is none end of the ſtore, and glory out of all the pleaſant furniture.10Shee is emptie, and voide, and waſte, and the heart melteth, and the knees ſmite together, and much paine is in all loynes, and the faces of them all gather blacknefse.11Where is the dwelling of the Lions, and the feeding place of the yong Lions? where the Lion, euen the olde Lion walked, and the Lions whelpe, and none made them afraid.12The Lion did teare in pieces enough for his whelpes, and ſtrangled for his Lionefses, and filled his holes with pray, and his dens with rauine.13Behold, I am againſt thee, ſaith the Lord of hoſts, and I will burne her charets in the ſmoke, and the ſword ſhall deuoure thy yong Lions, and I wil cut off thy pray from the earth, and the voice of thy meſſengers ſhall no more be heard.

CHAPTER 31Woe to the bloody City, it is all full of lyes and robberie, the pray departeth not.2The noiſe of a whip, and the noiſe of the rattling of the wheeles, and of the praunſing horſes, and of the iumping charets.3The horſeman lifteth vp both the bright ſword, & the glittering ſpeare, and there is a multitude of ſlaine, and a great number of carkeiſes: and there is none ende of their corpſes: they ſtumble vpon their corpſes,4Becauſe of the multitude of the whoredomes of the wel-fauoured harlot, the miſtreſſe of witchcrafts, that ſelleth nations through her whoredomes, and families through her witchcrafts.5Behold, I am againſt thee, ſaith the Lord of hoſtes, and I will diſcouer thy ſkirtes vpon thy face, and I will ſhew the nations thy nakednefse, and the kingdomes thy ſhame.6And I will caſt abominable filth vpon thee, and make thee vile, and will ſet thee as a gazing ſtocke.7And it ſhall come to paſſe, that all they that looke vpon thee, ſhall flee from thee, and ſay; Nineueh is layde waſte, who will bemoane her? whence ſhall I ſeeke comforters for thee?8Art thou better then populous No, that was ſcituate among the riuers that had the waters round about it, whoſe rampart was the ſea, and her wall was from the ſea?9Ethiopia and Egypt were her ſtrength, and it was infinit, Put and Lubim were thy helpers.10Yet was ſhe caried away, ſhe went into captiuitie: her yong children alſo were daſhed in pieces at the top of all the ſtreetes: and they caſt lots for her honourable men, and all her great men were bound in chaines.11Thou alſo ſhalt be drunken: thou ſhalt bee hid, thou alſo ſhalt ſeeke ſtrength becauſe of the enemie.12All thy ſtrong holds ſhall be like fig trees with the firſt ripe figs: if they bee ſhaken, they ſhall euen fall into the mouth of the eater.13Beholde, thy people in the midſt of thee are women: the gates of thy land ſhall be ſet wide open vnto thine enemies, the fire ſhall deuoure thy barres.14Draw thee waters for the ſiege: fortifie thy ſtrong holdes, goe into clay, and tread the morter: make ſtrong the bricke-kill.15There ſhall the fire deuoure thee: the ſword ſhall cut thee off: it ſhall eate thee vp like the cankerworme: make thy ſelfe many as the cankerworme, make thy ſelfe many as the locuſts.16Thou haſt multiplied thy merchants aboue the ſtarres of heauen; the cankerworme ſpoileth & flieth away.17The crowned are as the locuſts, and thy captains as the great graſhoppers which campe in the hedges in the cold day: but when the Sunne Ariſeth, they flee away, and their place is not knowen where they are.18Thy ſhepheards ſlumber, O king of Aſſyria: thy nobles ſhall dwell in the duſt: thy people is ſcattered vpon the mountaines, & no man gathereth them.19There is no healing of thy bruiſe: thy wound is grieuous: all that heare the bruit of thee, ſhall clap the hands ouer thee; for vpon whom hath not thy wickedneſſe paſſed continually?

HABAKKUK

CHAPTER 11The burden which Habakkuk þe Prophet did ſee.2O Lord, howe long ſhall I crie, and thou wilt not heare! euen cry out vnto thee of violence, and thou wilt not ſaue?3Why doeſt thou ſhew me iniquity, & cauſe me to behold grieuance? for ſpoiling and violence are before me: & there are that raiſe vp ſtrife and contention.4Therefore the Lawe is ſlacked, and iudgement doeth neuer goe foorth: for the wicked doeth compaſſe about the righteous: therfore wrong iudgement proceedeth.5Behold ye among the heathen, and regard, and wonder marueilouſly: for I wil worke a worke in your daies, which yee will not beleeue, though it be tolde you.6For loe, I raiſe vp the Caldeans, that bitter and haſtie nation, which ſhall march through the breadth of the land, to poſſeſſe the dwelling places that are not theirs.7They are terrible and dreadfull: their iudgement and their dignity ſhal proceed of themſelues.8Their horſes alſo are ſwifter then the leopards, and are more fierce then the euening wolues: & their horſemen ſhall ſpread themſelues, and their horſemen ſhall come from farre, they ſhall flie as the Eagle that haſteth to eate.9They ſhall come all for violence: their faces ſhall ſup vp as the Eaſt winde, and they ſhall gather the captiuitie as the ſand.10And they ſhal ſcoffe at the Kings, and the Princes ſhall bee a ſcorne vnto them: they ſhall deride euery ſtrong holde, for they ſhall heape duſt & take it.11Then ſhall his minde change, and he ſhall paſſe ouer, and offend, imputing this his power vnto his God.12Art thou not from euerlaſting, O Lord my God, mine Holy one? we ſhall not die: O Lord, thou haſt ordained them for iudgement, and O mightie God, thou haſt eſtabliſhed them for correction.13Thou art of purer eyes then to beholde euill, and canſt not looke on ininquitie: wherefore lookeſt thou vpon them that deale treacherouſly, and holdeſt thy tongue when the wicked deuoureth the man that is more righteous then hee?14And makeſt men as the fiſhes of the ſea, as the creeping things, that haue no ruler ouer them.15They take vp all of them with the angle: they catch them in their net, and gather them in their dragge; therefore they reioyce and are glad.16Therefore they ſacrifice vnto their net, and burne incenſe vnto their drag: becauſe by them their portion is fat, and their meat plenteous.17Shall they therefore emptie their net, and not ſpare continually to ſlay the nations?

CHAPTER 21I will ſtand vpon my watch, & ſet mee vpon the towre, and will watch to ſee what he will ſay vnto me, and what I ſhall anſwere when I am reproued.2And the Lord anſwered me and ſaid, write the viſion, and make it plaine vpon tables, that he may runne that readeth it.3For the viſion is yet for an appointed time, but at the the end it ſhall ſpeak, and not lie: though it tary, wait for it, becauſe it will ſurely come, it wil not tary.4Behold, his ſoule which is lifted vp, is not vpright in him; but the iuſt ſhall liue by his faith.5Yea alſo, becauſe he tranſgreſseth by wine, he is a proud man, neither keepeth at home, who enlargeth his deſire as hell, and is as death, and cannot be ſatiſfied, but gathereth vnto him all nations, & heapeth vnto him all people:6ſhal not all theſe take vp a parable againſt him, and a tanting prouerbe againſt him, and ſay; Woe to him that increaſeth that which is not his: how long? and to him that ladeth himſelfe with thicke clay.7Shall they not riſe vp ſuddenly that ſhall bite thee? and awake, that ſhall vexe thee? and thou ſhalt be for booties vnto them?8Becauſe thou haſt ſpoiled many nations, all the remnant of the people ſhal ſpoile thee: becauſe of mens blood, and for the violence of the land, of the citie, and of all that dwell therein.9Woe to him that coueteth an euill couetouſneſſe to his houſe, that he may ſet his neſt on high, that hee may be deliuered from the power of euill.10Thou haſt conſulted ſhame to thy houſe, by cutting off many people, and haſt ſinned againſt thy ſoule.11For the ſtone ſhall crie out of the wall, and the beame out of the timber ſhall anſwere it.12Woe to him that buildeth a towne with blood, and ſtabliſheth a citie by iniquitie.13Behold, is it not of the Lord of hoſtes, that the people ſhall labour in the very fire, and the people ſhal wearie themſelues for very vanitie?14For the earth ſhall be filled with the knowledge of the glory of the Lord, as the waters couer the ſea.15Woe vnto him that giueth his neighbour drinke: that putteſt thy bottell to him, and makeſt him drunken alſo; that thou mayeſt looke on their nakedneſse.16Thou art filled with ſhame for glory: drinke thou alſo, and let thy foreſkin bee vncouered: the cup of the Lords right hand ſhall be turned vnto thee, and ſhamefull ſpewing ſhalbe on thy glory.17For the violence of Lebanon ſhall couer thee: and the ſpoile of beaſts, which made them afraide, becauſe of mens blood, and for the violence of the land, of the city, & of al that dwel therin.18What profiteth the grauen image, that the maker thereof hath grauen it; the molten image, and a teacher of lies, that the maker of his worke, truſteth therin, to make dumbe idoles.19Woe vnto him that ſaith to the wood, Awake: to the dumbe ſtone, Ariſe, it ſhall teach: behold, it is layed ouer with gold and ſiluer, and there is no breath at all in the middeſt of it.20But the Lord is in his holy temple: let all the earth keepe ſilence before him.

CHAPTER 31A prayer of Habakkuk the prophet vpon Sigionoth.2O Lord, I haue heard thy ſpeach, and was afraide: O Lord, reuiue thy worke in the midſt of the yeeres, in the midſt of the yeeres make knowen; in wrath remember mercy.3God came from Teman, and the holy on from mount Paran Selah. His glory couered the heauens and the earth was full of his praiſe.4And his brightneſse was as the light: he had hornes comming out of his hand, and there was the hiding of his power:5Before him went the peſtilence, and burning coales went forth at his feete.6He ſtood and meaſured the earth: hee beheld and droue aſunder the nations, and the euerlaſting mountaines were ſcattered, the perpetuall hilles did bowe: his wayes are euerlaſting.7I ſaw the tents of Cuſhan in affliction: and the curtaines of the land of Midian did tremble.8Was the Lord diſpleaſed againſt the riuers? was thine anger againſt the riuers? was thy wrath againſt the ſea, that thou didſt ride vpon thine horſes, and thy charets of ſaluation?9Thy bow was made quite naked according to the oathes of the tribes, euen thy word. Selah. Thou didſt cleaue the earth with riuers.10The mountaines ſawe thee, and they trembled: the ouerflowing of the water paſſed by: the deepe vttered his voyce, and lift vp his hands on high.11The Sunne and Moone ſtood ſtill in their habitation: at the light of thine arrowes they went, and at the ſhining of thy glittering ſpeare.12Thou didſt march through the land in indignation, thou didſt threſh the heathen in anger.13Thou wenteſt forth for the ſaluation of thy people, euen for ſaluation with thine Anointed, thou woundedſt the head out of the houſe of the wicked, by diſcouering the foundation vnto the necke. Selah.14Thou didſt ſtrike through with his ſtaues the head of his villages: they came out as a whirle-winde to ſcatter me: their reioycing was as to deuoure the poore ſecretly.15Thou didſt walke through the ſea with thine horſes, through the heape of great waters.16When I heard, my belly trembled: my lips quiuered at the voice: rottenneſse entred into my bones, and I trembled in my ſelfe, that I might reſt in the day of trouble: when hee commeth vp vnto the people, he wil inuade them with his troupes.17Although the fig tree ſhall not bloſsome, neither ſhall fruite bee in the vines: the labour of the Oliue ſhall faile, and the fields ſhal yeeld no meat, the flocke ſhall be cut off from the folde, and there ſhalbe no heard in the ſtalles:18Yet I will reioyce in the Lord: I will ioy in the God of my ſaluation.19The Lord God is my ſtrength, and he will make my feet like hindes feet, and he will make me to walke vpon mine high places. To the chiefe ſinger on my ſtringed inſtruments.

ZEPHANIAH

CHAPTER 11The worde of the Lord which came vnto Zephaniah the ſon of Cuſhi, the ſon of Gedaliah, the ſonne of Amariah, the ſonne of Hizkiah, in the dayes of Ioſiah, the ſonne of Amon king of Iudah.2I will vtterly conſume all things from off the land, ſaith the Lord.3I will conſume man and beaſt: I will conſume the foules of the heauen and the fiſhes of the ſea, and the ſtumbling blocks with the wicked, and I will cut off man from off the land, ſaith the Lord.4I will alſo ſtretch out mine hand vpon Iudah, and vpon all the inhabitants of Ieruſalem, and I will cut off the remnant of Baal from this place, and the name of the Chemarims with the prieſts:5And them that worſhip the hoſte of heauen vpon the houſe tops, & them that worſhip, and that ſweare by the Lord, and that ſweare by Malcham:6And them that are turned backe from the Lord, & thoſe that haue not ſought þe Lord, nor enquired for him.7Hold thy peace at the preſence of the Lord God: for the day of the Lord is at hand: for the Lord hath prepared a ſacrifice: he hath bid his gheſts.8And it ſhall come to paſſe in the day of the Lords Sacrifice, that I will puniſh the princes, and the kings children, and al ſuch as are clothed with ſtrange apparell.9In the ſame day alſo wil I puniſh all thoſe that leape on the threſhold, which fill their maſters houſes with violence and deceit.10And it ſhall come to paſſe in that day, ſaith the Lord, that there ſhall be the noiſe of a cry from the fiſh gate, and an howling from the ſecond, and a great craſhing from the hils.11Howle yee inhabitants of Makteſh, for all the merchant people are cut downe: all they that beare ſiluer are cut off.12And it ſhall come to paſſe at that time, that I wil ſearch Ieruſalem with candles, and puniſh the men that are ſetled on their lees, that ſay in their heart, The Lord will not doe good, neither will he doe euill.13Therefore their goods ſhall become a booty, and their houſes a deſolation: they ſhall alſo build houſes, but not inhabite them, and they ſhall plant Uineyards, but not drinke the wine thereof.14The great day of the Lord is neere, it is neere, and haſteth greatly, euen the voice of the day of the Lord: the mighty man ſhall cry there bitterly.15That day is a day of wrath, a day of trouble and diſtreſſe, a day of waſteneſse and deſolation, a day of darkneſſe and gloomineſse, a day of cloudes and thicke darkeneſſe;16A day of the trumpet and alarme againſt the fenced cities, and againſt the high towres.17And I will bring diſtreſſe vpon men, that they ſhall walke like blinde men, becauſe they haue ſinned againſt the Lord, and their blood ſhall bee powred out as duſt, and their fleſh as the doung.18Neither their ſiluer nor their golde ſhall be able to deliuer them in the day of the Lords wrath; but the whole land ſhall bee deuoured by the fire of his iealouſie: for hee ſhall make euen a ſpeedy riddance of all them that dwell in the land.

CHAPTER 21Gather your ſelues together, yea gather together, O nation not deſired.2Before the decree bring foorth, before the day paſſe as the chaffe, before the fierce anger of the Lord come vpon you, before the day of the Lords anger come vpon you.3Seeke ye the Lord all ye meeke of the earth, which haue wrought his iudgement, ſeeke righteouſneſſe, ſeeke meekneſse: it may be, ye ſhall be hid in the day of the Lords anger.4For Gaza ſhall bee forſaken, and Aſhkelon a deſolation: they ſhall driue out Aſhdod at the noone day, and Ekron ſhall be rooted vp.5Woe vnto the inhabitants of the ſea coaſt: the nation of the Cherethites, the word of the Lord is againſt you: O Canaan, the land of the Philiſtines, I will euen deſtroy thee, that there ſhal be no inhabitant.6And the ſea coaſt ſhall bee dwellings and cottages for ſhepheards, and foldes for flockes.7And the coaſt ſhall bee for the remnant of the houſe of Iudah, they ſhall feede thereupon, in the houſes of Aſhkelon ſhall they lie downe in the euening: for the Lord their God ſhall viſite them, and turne away their captiuitie.8I haue heard the reproach of Moab, and the reuilings of the children of Ammon, whereby they haue reproched my people, and magnified themſelues againſt their border.9Therefore, as I liue, ſaith the Lord of hoſtes the God of Iſrael, ſurely Moab ſhalbe as Sodom, and the children of Ammon as Gomorrah, euen the breeding of netles, and ſalt pits, and a perpetuall deſolation, the reſidue of my people ſhall ſpoile them, and the remnant of my people ſhall poſſeſſe them.10This ſhall they haue for their pride, becauſe they haue reproched and magnified themſelues againſt the people of the Lord of hoſtes.11The Lord will be terrible vnto them: for he will famiſh all the gods of the earth, and men ſhall worſhip him, euery one from his place, euen all the Iles of the heathen.12Ye Ethiopians alſo, ye ſhalbe ſlaine by my ſword.13And he wil ſtretch out his hand againſt the North, and deſtroy Aſſyria, and wil make Nineueh a deſolation, and dry like a wildernes.[14]And flocks ſhall lie downe in the midſt of her, all the beaſts of the nations: both the Cormorant, and the Bitterne, ſhall lodge in the vpper lintels of it: their voice ſhal ſing in the windowes, deſolation ſhall be in the threſholds: for he ſhall vncouer the Cedar worke.[15]This is the reioycing citie that dwelt careleſſely, that ſaid in her heart, I am, and there is none beſide me: how is ſhee become a deſolation, a place for beaſts to lie downe in! euery one that paſſeth by her, ſhall hiſse and wagge his hand.

CHAPTER 3[1]Woe to her that is filthie and polluted, to the oppreſsing citie.[2]She obeyed not the voice: ſhe receiued not correction: ſhe truſted not in the Lord: ſhe drew not neere to her God.[3]Her princes within her are roaring lyons; her Iudges are euening wolues, they gnaw not the bones till the morrow.[4]Her prophets are light and treacherous perſons: her prieſts haue polluted the Sanctuarie, they haue done violence to the Law.[5]The iuſt Lord is in the middeſt thereof: he will not doe iniquitie: euery morning doeth hee bring his iudgement to light, he faileth not: but the vniuſt knoweth no ſhame.[6]I haue cut off the nations: their towres are deſolate, I made their ſtreetes waſte, that none paſſeth by: their cities are deſtroied, ſo that there is no man, that there is none inhabitant.[7]I ſaid, Surely thou wilt feare mee: thou wilt receiue inſtruction: ſo their dwelling ſhould not bee cut off, howſoeuer I puniſhed them: but they roſe early, & corrupted all their doings.[8]Therefore waite ye vpon mee, ſayth the Lord, vntill the day that I riſe vp to the pray: for my determination is to gather the nations, that I may aſſemble the kingdomes to powre vpon them mine indignation, euen all my fierce anger: for all the earth ſhalbe deuoured with the fire of my iealouſie.[9]For then will I turne to the people a pure language, that they may all call vpon the Name of the Lord, to ſerue him with one conſent.[10]From beyond the riuers of Ethiopia, my ſuppliants, euen the daughter of my diſperſed ſhal bring mine offring.[11]In that day ſhalt thou not be aſhamed for all thy doings, wherein thou haſt tranſgreſſed againſt me: for then I will take away out of the midſt of thee them that reioyce in thy pride, and thou ſhalt no more be haughty becauſe of mine holy mountaine.[12]I will alſo leaue in the middeſt of thee an afflicted and poore people: and they ſhall truſt in the Name of the Lord.[13]The remnant of Iſrael ſhall not doe iniquitie, nor ſpeake lies: neither ſhall a deceitful tongue be found in their mouth: for they ſhall feede, and lie downe, and none ſhall make them afraid.[14]Sing, O daughter of Zion: ſhout, O Iſrael: be glad and reioyce with all the heart, O daughter of Ieruſalem.[15]The Lord hath taken away thy iudgements, he hath caſt out thine enemy: the King of Iſrael, euen the Lord is in the middeſt of thee: thou ſhalt not ſee euill any more.[16]In that day it ſhall be ſaid to Ieruſalem, Feare thou not: and to Zion, Let not thine hands be ſlacke.[17]The Lord thy God in the midſt of thee is mightie: hee will ſaue, he will reioyce ouer thee with ioy: hee will reſt in his loue, hee will ioy ouer thee with ſinging.[18]I will gather them that are ſorrowfull for the ſolemne aſſembly, who are of thee, to whom the reproch of it was a burden.[19]Behold, at that time I will vndoe all that afflict thee, and I will ſaue her that halteth, and gather her that was driuen out, and I will get them praiſe and fame in euery land, where they haue beene put to ſhame.[20]At that time will I bring you againe euen in the time that I gather you: for I will make you a name and a praiſe among all people of the earth, when I turne backe your captiuitie before your eyes, ſaith the Lord.

HAGGAI

CHAPTER 1[1]In the ſecond yeere of Darius the king, in the ſixt moneth, in the firſt day of the moneth came the worde of the Lord by Haggai the Prophet vnto Zerubbabel the ſonne of Shealtiel, gouernour of Iudah, and to Ioſuah the ſonne of Ioſedech the high prieſt, ſaying;[2]Thus ſpeaketh the Lord of hoſtes, ſaying; This people ſay, The time is not come, the time that the Lords houſe ſhould be built.[3]Then came the word of the Lord by Haggai the prophet, ſaying;[4]Is it time for you, O yee, to dwell in your ſieled houſes, and this houſe lie waſte?[5]Nowe therefore thus ſaith the Lord of hoſtes; Conſider your wayes.[6]Yee haue ſowen much and bring in litle: ye eate, but ye haue not inough: yee drinke, but yee are not filled with drinke: yee cloth you, but there is none warme: and hee that earneth wages, earneth wages to put it into a bag with holes.[7]Thus ſaith the Lord of hoſtes, Conſider your wayes.[8]Goe vp to the mountaine, and bring wood, and build the houſe; and I will take pleaſure in it, and I will be glorified, ſaith the Lord.[9]Ye looked for much, and loe it came to litle: and when yee brought it home, I did blow vpon it: Why, ſaith the Lord of hoſtes? becauſe of mine houſe that is waſte, and yee runne euery man vnto his owne houſe.[10]Therefore the heauen ouer you is ſtayed from dew, and the earth is ſtaied from her fruite.[11]And I called for a drought vpon the land and vpon the mountaines, and vpon the corne, and vpon the new wine, and vpon the oyle, and vpon that which the ground bringeth forth, & vpon men, and vpon cattell, and vpon all the labour of the hands.[12]Then Zerubbabel the ſonne of Shealtiel, and Ioſuah the ſonne of Ioſedech the high prieſt, with all the remnant of the people obeyed the voyce of the Lord their God, and the words of Haggai the Prophet (as the Lord their God had ſent him) and the people did feare before the Lord.[13]Then ſpake Haggai the Lords meſſenger in the Lords meſsage vnto the people, ſaying; I am with you, ſaith the Lord.[14]And the Lord ſtirred vp the ſpirit of Zerubbabel the ſonne of Shealtiel gouernour of Iudah, and the ſpirit of Ioſuah the ſonne of Ioſedech the high prieſt, and the ſpirit of all the remnant of the people, and they came and did worke in the houſe of the Lord of hoſtes their God:[15]In the foure and twentieth day of the ſixt moneth, in the ſecond yeere of Darius the King.

CHAPTER 2[1]In the ſeuenth moneth, in the one and twentith day of the moneth, came the word of the Lord by the Prophet Haggai, ſaying;[2]Speake now to Zerubbabel the ſonne of Shealtiel, gouernour of Iudah, and to Ioſuah the ſonne of Ioſedech the high prieſt, and to the reſidue of the people, ſaying,[3]Who is left among you that ſawe this houſe in her firſt glory? and how do ye ſee it now? Is it not in your eyes in compariſon of it, as nothing?[4]Yet now be ſtrong, O Zerubbabel, ſaith the Lord, and bee ſtrong, O Ioſhua, ſonne of Ioſedech the high Prieſt, and be ſtrong all ye people of the land, ſaith the Lord, and worke: (for I am with you, ſaith the Lord of hoſts,)[5]According to the word that I couenanted with you, when ye came out of Egypt, ſo my Spirit remaineth among you, Feare ye not.[6]For thus ſaith the Lord of hoſts, Yet once, it is a litle while, and I will ſhake the heauens, and the earth, and the ſea, and the drie land.[7]And I will ſhake all nations, and the deſire of all nations ſhall come, and I will fill this houſe with glory, ſaith the Lord of hoſts.[8]The ſiluer is mine, and the gold is mine, ſaith the Lord of hoſts.[9]The glory of this latter houſe ſhal be greater then of the former, ſaith the Lord of hoſtes: and in this place will I giue peace, ſaith the Lord of hoſtes.[10]In the foure and twentieth day of the ninth moneth, in the ſecond yeere of Darius, came þe word of the Lord by Haggai the Prophet, ſaying,[11]Thus ſaith the Lord of hoſts, Aſke now the prieſts concerning the law, ſaying,[12]If one beare holy fleſh in the ſkirt of his garment, and with his ſkirt doe touch bread or pottage, or wine, or oile, or any meate, ſhall it be holy? and the prieſts anſwered and ſaid, No.[13]Then ſaid Haggai, If one that is vncleane by a dead body, touch any of theſe, ſhal it be vncleane? and the prieſts anſwered and ſaid, It ſhalbe vncleane.[14]Then anſwered Haggai, and ſaid, So is this people, and ſo is this nation before me, ſaith the Lord, and ſo is euery worke of their hands, and that which they offer there, is vncleane.[15]And now I pray you conſider from this day and vpward, from before a ſtone was laid vpon a ſtone in the Temple of the Lord.[16]Since thoſe dayes were, when one came to an heape of twentie meaſures, there were but ten: when one came to the preſse-fatte for to draw out fiftie veſſels out of the preſse, there were but twentie.[17]I ſmote you with blaſting, and with mildew, and with haile in all the labours of your hands: yet yee turned not to me, ſaith the Lord.[18]Conſider now from this day, and vpward from the foure and twentieth day of the ninth moneth, euen from the day that the foundatio of the Lords Temple was laid, conſider it.[19]Is the ſeed yet in the barne? yea, as yet the vine and the fig tree, & the pomegranate, and the Oliue tree hath not brought foorth: from this day will I bleſſe you.[20]And againe the worde of the Lord came vnto Haggai in the foure and twentieth day of the moneth, ſaying,[21]Speake to Zerubbabel gouernor of Iudah, ſaying, I wil ſhake the heauens and the earth.[22]And I will ouerthrow the throne of kingdomes, and I will deſtroy the ſtrength of the kingdomes of the heathen, and I will ouerthrow the charets, and thoſe that ride in them, and the horſes and their riders ſhall come downe, euery one by the ſword of his brother.[23]In that day, ſaith the Lord of hoſts, will I take thee, O Zerubbabel, my ſeruant, the ſon of Shealtiel, ſaith the Lord, and will make thee as a ſignet: for I haue choſen thee, ſaith the Lord of hoſts.

ZECHARIAH

CHAPTER 1 1In the eight moneth, in the ſeconde yeere of Darius, came the word of the Lord vnto Zechariah, the ſonne of Barachiah, the ſonne of Iddo the Prophet, ſaying,2The Lord hath bene ſore diſpleaſed with your fathers.3Therefore ſay thou vnto them, Thus ſaith the Lord of hoſtes; Turne ye vnto me, ſaith the Lord of hoſtes, and I will turne vnto you, ſaith the Lord of hoſtes.4Be ye not as your fathers, vnto whom the former Prophets haue cried, ſaying, Thus ſaith the Lord of hoſtes, Turne ye now from your euill wayes, and from your euil doings: but they did not heare, nor hearken vnto me, ſaith the Lord.5Your fathers, where are they? and the Prophets, doe they liue for euer?6But my words and my ſtatutes, which I commanded my ſeruants the Prophets, did they not take holde of your fathers? and they returned and ſaide; Like as the Lord of hoſtes thought to doe vnto vs, according to our wayes, and according to our doings, ſo hath he dealt with vs.7Upon the foure and twentieth day of the eleuenth moneth, which is the moneth Sebat, in the ſecond yere of Darius, came the word of the Lord vnto Zechariah, the ſonne of Barachiah, the ſonne of Iddo the Prophet, ſaying:8I ſaw by night, and behold a man riding vpon a red horſe, and he ſtood among the mirtle trees that were in the bottome, and behinde him were there red horſes, ſpeckled and white.9Then ſaid I, O my Lord, what are theſe? And the Angel that talked with me, ſaid vnto me, I wil ſhew thee what theſe be.10And the man that ſtood among the myrtle trees anſwered, and ſaid, Theſe are they, whom the Lord hath ſent to walke to and fro through the earth.11And they anſwered the Angel of the Lord that ſtood among the mirtle trees, and ſaid, Wee haue walked to and fro through the earth: and behold, all the earth ſitteth ſtill, and is at reſt.12Then the Angel of the Lord anſwered, and ſaid, O Lord of hoſts, how long wilt thou not haue mercie on Ieruſalem, and on the cities of Iudah, againſt which thou haſt had indignation theſe threeſcore and ten yeeres?13And the Lord anſwered the Angel that talked with me, with good words, and comfortable words.14So the Angel that communed with me, ſaid vnto me; Cry thou, ſaying; Thus ſaith the Lord of hoſts, I am iealous for Ieruſalem, and for Zion, with a great iealouſie.15And I am very ſore diſpleaſed with the heathen that are at eaſe: for I was but a little diſpleaſed, and they helped forward the affliction.16Therefore thus ſaith the Lord, I am returned to Ieruſalem with mercies: my houſe ſhall bee built in it, ſaith the Lord of hoſtes, and a line ſhalbe ſtretched forth vpon Ieruſalem.17Cry yet, ſaying, Thus ſaith the Lord of hoſtes, My cities through proſperitie ſhall yet be ſpread abroad, and the Lord ſhall yet comfort Zion, and ſhall yet chooſe Ieruſalem.18Then lift I vp mine eyes, and ſaw, and behold foure hornes.19And I ſaid vnto the Angel that talked with me; What be theſe? and he anſwered mee, Theſe are the hornes which haue ſcattered Iudah, Iſrael, and Ieruſalem.20And the Lord ſhewed mee foure carpenters.21Then ſaid I, What come theſe to doe? And hee ſpake, ſaying, Theſe are the hornes which haue ſcattered Iudah, ſo that no man did lift vp his head: but theſe are come to fray them, to caſt out the hornes of the Gentiles, which lift vp their horne ouer the land of Iudah to ſcatter it.

CHAPTER 2 1I lift vp mine eyes againe, and looked, and behold, a man with a meaſuring line in his hand.2Then ſaid I, Whither goeſt thou? And hee ſaid vnto me, To meaſure Ieruſalem, to ſee what is the breadth thereof, and what is the length thereof.3And behold, the Angel that talked with me, went foorth, and another Angel went out to meete him:4And ſaid vnto him, Run, ſpeake to this young man, ſaying; Ieruſalem ſhall be inhabited as townes without walles, for the multitude of men and cattell therein.5For I, ſaith the Lord, will be vnto her a wall of fire round about, and will be the glory in the midſt of her.6Ho, ho, come foorth, and flee from the land of the North, ſaith the Lord: for I haue ſpread you abroad as the foure windes of the heauen, ſayth the Lord.7Deliuer thy ſelfe, O Zion, that dwelleſt with the daughter of Babylon.8For thus ſayth the Lord of hoſtes, After the glory hath he ſent me vnto the nations which ſpoiled you: for he that toucheth you, toucheth the apple of his eye.9For behold, I will ſhake mine hand vpon them, and they ſhall bee a ſpoile to their ſeruants: and yee ſhall know that the Lord of hoſtes hath ſent me.10Sing and reioyce, O daughter of Zion: for loe, I come, and I will dwell in the middeſt of thee, ſayth the Lord.11And many nations ſhalbe ioyned to the Lord in that day, and ſhall be my people: and I will dwel in the middeſt of thee, and thou ſhalt know that the Lord of hoſtes hath ſent me vnto thee.12And the Lord ſhall inherite Iudah his portion in the holy land, and ſhall chooſe Ieruſalem againe.13Be ſilent, O all fleſh, before the Lord: for he is raiſed vp out of his holy habitation.

CHAPTER 3 1And he ſhewed me Ioſhua the high Prieſt, ſtanding before the Angel of the Lord, and Satan ſtanding at his right hand to reſiſt him.2And the Lord ſaid vnto Satan; The Lord rebuke thee, O Satan, euen the Lord that hath choſen Ieruſalem rebuke thee. Is not this a brand pluckt out of the fire?3Now Ioſhua was clothed with filthie garments, and ſtood before the Angel.4And he anſwered, and ſpake vnto thoſe that ſtood before him, ſaying, Take away the filthie garments from him. And vnto him he ſaid, Behold, I haue cauſed thine iniquity to paſſe from thee, and I wil clothe thee with change of raiment.5And I ſaid, Let them ſet a faire mitre vpon his head. So they ſet a faire mitre vpon his head, and clothed him with garments, and the Angel of the Lord ſtood by.6And the Angel of the Lord proteſted vnto Ioſhua, ſaying;7Thus ſayth the Lord of hoſts, If thou wilt walke in my wayes, and if thou wilt keepe my charge, then thou ſhalt alſo iudge my Houſe, and ſhalt alſo keepe my Courts, and I will giue thee places to walke among theſe that ſtand by.8Heare now, O Ioſhua the high Prieſt, thou and thy fellowes that ſit before thee: for they are men wondred at: for behold, I will bring foorth my ſeruant the Branch.9For behold the ſtone that I haue layd before Ioſhua: vpon one ſtone ſhall be ſeuen eyes, behold, I will engraue the grauing thereof, ſaith the Lord of hoſtes, and I will remoue the iniquitie of that land in one day.10In that day, ſaith the Lord of hoſtes, ſhal ye call euery man his neighbour vnder the vine and vnder the figge tree.

CHAPTER 4 1And the Angell that talked with me, came againe and waked me, as a man that is wakened out of his ſleepe:2And ſaid vnto mee, What ſeeſt thou? and I ſaid, I haue looked, and behold a candleſticke all of gold, with a bowle vpon the top of it, and his ſeuen lampes thereon, and ſeuen pipes to the ſeuen lampes, which were vpon the top thereof.3And two Oliue trees by it, one vpon the right ſide of the bowle, and the other vpon the left ſide thereof.4So I anſwered and ſpake to the Angell that talked with mee, ſaying: What are theſe, my Lord?5Then the Angel that talked with me, anſwered and ſaid vnto me; Knoweſt thou not what theſe be? and I ſaid; No, my Lord.6Then hee anſwered and ſpake vnto mee, ſaying; This is the word of the Lord vnto Zerubbabel, ſaying; Not by might, nor by power, but by my ſpirit, ſaith the Lord of hoſtes.7Who art thou, O great mountaine? before Zerubbabel thou ſhalt become a plaine, and he ſhall bring forth the head ſtone thereof with ſhoutings, crying; Grace, grace vnto it.8Moreouer the word of the Lord came vnto me, ſaying;9The hands of Zerubbabel haue layed the foundation of this houſe: his hands ſhall alſo finiſh it, and thou ſhalt know that the Lord of hoſtes hath ſent me vnto you.10For who hath deſpiſed the day of ſmall things? for they ſhall reioyce and ſhall ſee the plummet in the hand of Zerubbabel with thoſe ſeuen: they are the eyes of the Lord, which run to and fro through the whole earth.11Then anſwered I, and ſaid vnto him; What are theſe two oliue trees vpon the right ſide of the candleſticke, and vpon the left ſide thereof?12And I anſwered againe and ſaid vnto him, What be theſe two oliue branches, which through the two golden pipes emptie the golden oyle out of themſelues?13And hee anſwered mee and ſaid; Knoweſt thou not what theſe be? and I ſaid, No, my Lord.14Then ſaid he; Theſe are the two annointed ones, that ſtand by the Lord of the whole earth.

CHAPTER 5 1Then I turned, and lift vp mine eyes, and looked, and behold, a flying roule.2And hee ſaid vnto mee, What ſeeſt thou? and I anſwered, I ſee a flying roule, the length thereof is twentie cubites, and the breadth thereof tenne cubites.3Then ſaid hee vnto mee; This is the curſe, that goeth forth ouer the face of the whole earth: for euery one that ſtealeth ſhall be cut off as on this ſide, according to it; and euery one that ſweareth ſhall be cut off as on that ſide, according to it.4I will bring it forth, ſaith the Lord of hoſtes, and it ſhall enter into the houſe of the theefe, and into the houſe of him that ſweareth falſely by my

name: and it ſhall remaine in the midſt of his houſe, and ſhall conſume
it, with the timber thereof, and the ſtones thereof.[5]Then the Angell that
talked with me, went forth and ſaid vnto me, Lift vp now thine eyes,
and ſee what is this that goeth forth.[6]And I ſaid, What is it? and hee ſaid,
This is an Ephah that goeth forth. Hee ſaid moreouer, This is their
reſemblance through all the earth.[7]And behold, there was lift vp a talent
of lead: and this is a woman that ſitteth in the midſt of the Ephah.[8]And
he ſaid, This is wickedneſſe, and he caſt it into the midſt of the Ephah,
and he caſt the weight of lead vpon the mouth thereof.[9]Then lift I vp
mine eyes, and looked, & behold, there came out two women, and the
winde was in their wings (for they had wings like the wings of a ſtorke)
and they lift vp the Ephah betweene the earth and the heauen.[10]Then
ſaide I to the Angel that talked with me, Whither do theſe beare the
Ephah?[11]And he ſaid vnto mee, To build it an houſe in the land of
Shinar, and it ſhall be eſtabliſhed, and ſet there vpon her owne baſe.

CHAPTER 6[1]And I turned, and lift vp mine eyes, and looked, and
beholde, there came foure charets out from betweene two mountaines,
and the mountaines were mountaines of braſſe.[2]In the firſt charet were
red horſes, and in the ſecond charet, blacke horſes.[3]And in the third
charet white horſes, and in the fourth charet griſled and bay
horſes.[4]Then I anſwered, and ſaid vnto the Angel that talked with mee,
What are theſe, my Lord ?[5]And the Angel anſwered and ſaid vnto me,
Theſe are the foure ſpirits of the heauens, which go forth from ſtanding
before the Lord of all the earth.[6]The blacke horſes which are therin, goe
forth into the North countrey, and the white goe forth after them, and
the griſled goe forth toward the South countrey.[7]And the baye went
foorth, and ſought to goe, that they might walke to and fro through the
earth: and he ſaid, Get ye hence, walke to and fro through the earth. So
they walked to and fro through the earth.[8]Then cried he vpon me, and
ſpake vnto me, ſaying, Behold, theſe that goe toward the North
countrey, haue quieted my ſpirit, in the North countrey.[9]And the word
of the Lord came vnto me, ſaying,[10]Take of them of the captiuitie, euen
of Heldai, of Tobijah, and of Iedaiah, which are come from Babylon,
and come thou the ſame day, and go into the houſe of Ioſiah the ſon of
Zephaniah.[11]Then take ſiluer, and golde, and make crownes, and ſet
them vpon the head of Ioſhua the ſonne of Ioſedech, the high
prieſt.[12]And ſpeake vnto him, ſaying, Thus ſpeaketh the Lord of hoſtes,
ſaying, Behold, the man whoſe name is the Branch, and he ſhall growe
vp out of his place, and he ſhall build the Temple of the Lord:[13]Euen he
ſhall build the temple of the Lord, and he ſhal beare the glory, and ſhall
ſit and rule vpon his throne, and he ſhall be a prieſt vpon his throne,
and the counſell of peace ſhall bee betweene them both.[14]And the
crownes ſhall bee to Helem, and to Tobijah, and to Iedaiah, and to Hen
the ſonne of Zephaniah for a memoriall, in the Temple of the
Lord.[15]And they that are farre off, ſhall come and build in the Temple
of the Lord, and ye ſhall knowe that the Lord of hoſts hath ſent me vnto
you. And this ſhall come to paſſe, if ye will diligently obey the voyce of
the Lord your God.

CHAPTER 7[1]And it came to paſſe in the fourth yeere of King Darius,
that the word of the Lord came vnto Zechariah in the fourth day of the
ninth moneth, euen in Chiſleu.[2]When they had ſent vnto the houſe of
God, Sherezer and Regem-melech, and their men to pray before the
Lord,[3]And to ſpeake vnto the prieſtes, which were in the houſe of the
Lord of hoſts, and to the prophets, ſaying, Should I weepe in the fift
moneth, ſeparating my ſelfe, as I haue done theſe ſo many yeeres?[4]Then
came the word of the Lord of hoſts vnto me, ſaying,[5]Speake vnto all the
people of the land, and to the prieſts, ſaying, When ye faſted and
mourned in the fift and ſeuenth moneth, euen thoſe ſeuenty yeeres; did
ye at all faſt vnto me, euen to me?[6]And when ye did eat, and when ye
did drinke, did not ye eat for your ſelues, and drinke for your
ſelues?[7]Should yee not heare the wordes, which the Lord hath cried by
the former Prophets, when Ieruſalem was inhabited, and in proſperitie,
and the cities thereof round about her, when men inhabited the South
of the plaine?[8]And the word of the Lord came vnto Zechariah,
ſaying;[9]Thus ſpeaketh the Lord of hoſtes, ſaying, Execute true
iudgement, and ſhew mercie and compaſſions euery man to his
brother.[10]And oppreſſe not the widow, nor the fatherleſſe, the ſtranger,
nor the poore, and let none of you imagine euill againſt his brother in
your heart.[11]But they refuſed to hearken, and pulled away the ſhoulder,
and ſtopped their eares, that they ſhould not heare.[12]Yea, they made
their hearts as an adamant ſtone, leſt they ſhould heare the Law, and the
wordes which the Lord of hoſtes hath ſent in his ſpirit by the former
Prophets: therefore came a great wrath from the Lord of
hoſtes.[13]Therefore it is come to paſſe, that as he cried, and they would
not heare, ſo they cried, and I would not heare, ſaith the Lord of
hoſtes.[14]But I ſcattered them with a whirlewinde among all the nations,
whom they knew not: thus the land was deſolate after them, that no man
paſſed through, nor returned: for they layed the pleaſant land deſolate.

CHAPTER 8[1]Againe the word of the Lord of hoſtes came to me,
ſaying;[2]Thus ſayeth the Lord of hoſtes, I was iealous for Zion, with great
iealouſie; and I was iealous for her with great furie.[3]Thus ſaith the Lord,
I am returned vnto Zion, and will dwell in the midſt of Ieruſalem, and
Ieruſalem ſhall be called a Citie of trueth, and the Mountaine of the Lord
of hoſtes, the holy Mountaine.[4]Thus ſaith the Lord of hoſts; There ſhall
yet old men, and old women, dwell in the ſtreets of Ieruſalem, and euery
man with his ſtaffe in his hand for very age.[5]And the ſtreets of the citie
ſhall be full of boyes and girles playing in the ſtreets thereof.[6]Thus ſaith
the Lord of hoſts, If it bee marueilous in the eyes of the remnant of this
people in theſe dayes, ſhould it alſo bee marueilous in my eyes, ſaith the
Lord of hoſtes?[7]Thus ſaith the Lord of hoſts, Beholde, I will ſaue my
people from the Eaſt countrey, and from the Weſt countrey.[8]And I will
bring them, and they ſhall dwell in the midſt of Ieruſalem, and they
ſhalbe my people, and I will bee their God, in Trueth and in
Righteouſneſſe.[9]Thus ſaith the Lord of hoſtes, Let your handes be
ſtrong, ye that heare in theſe dayes, theſe wordes by the mouth of the
Prophets, which were in the day that the foundation of the houſe of the
Lord of hoſts was laied, that the Temple might be built.[10]For before
theſe daies there was no hire for man, nor any hire for beaſt, neither was
there any peace to him that went out, or came in, becauſe of the
affliction: for I ſet all men, euery one againſt his neighbour.[11]But now I
will not bee vnto the reſidue of this people, as in the former daies, ſaith
the Lord of hoſtes.[12]For the ſeed ſhalbe proſperous: the Uine ſhall giue
her fruit, and the ground ſhall giue her increaſe, and the heauens ſhall
giue their dew, and I will cauſe the remnant of this people to poſſeſſe all
theſe things.[13]And it ſhall come to paſſe, that as yee were a curſe among
the heathen, O houſe of Iudah, and houſe of Iſrael; ſo will I ſaue you,
and ye ſhalbe a bleſſing: feare not, but let your handes bee ſtrong.[14]For
thus ſaith the Lord of hoſtes, As I thought to puniſh you, when your
fathers prouoked mee to wrath, ſaith the Lord of hoſtes, and I repented
not:[15]So againe haue I thought in theſe dayes to doe well vnto Ieruſalem,
and to the houſe of Iudah: feare ye not.[16]Theſe are the things that yee
ſhall doe; Speake yee euery man the truth to his neighbor: execute the
iudgment of trueth and peace in your gates.[17]And let none of you
imagine euill in your hearts againſt his neighbour, and loue no falſe oath:
for all theſe are things that I hate, ſaith the Lord.[18]And the word of the
Lord of hoſtes came vnto me, ſaying,[19]Thus ſaith the Lord of hoſts; The
faſt of the fourth moneth, and the faſt of the fift, and the faſt of the
ſeuenth, and the faſt of the tenth ſhall be to the houſe of Iudah ioy and
gladneſſe, and cheerefull feaſts: therefore loue the trueth and
peace.[20]Thus ſaith the Lord of hoſts, It ſhall yet come to paſſe, that there
ſhall come people, and the inhabitants of many cities.[21]And the
inhabitants of one citie ſhall goe to another, ſaying, Let vs goe ſpeedily
to pray before the Lord, and to ſeeke the Lord of hoſtes: I will goe
alſo.[22]Yea many people and ſtrong nations ſhall come to ſeeke the Lord
of hoſtes in Ieruſalem, and to pray before the Lord.[23]Thus ſaith the Lord
of hoſts, In thoſe daies it ſhall come to paſſe, that ten men ſhall take
holde out of all languages of the nations, euen ſhall take hold of the ſkirt
of him that is a Iew, ſaying, Wee will goe with you: for we haue heard
that God is with you.

CHAPTER 9[1]The burden of the word of the Lord in the land of
Hadrach, and Damaſcus ſhall bee the reſt thereof: when the eyes of man,
as of all the tribes of Iſrael ſhalbe toward the Lord.[2]And Hamath alſo
ſhall border thereby; Tyrus and Zidon, though it be very wiſe.[3]And
Tyrus did builde her ſelfe a ſtrong hold, and heaped vp ſiluer as the duſt,
and fine golde as the myre of the ſtreets.[4]Behold, the Lord wil caſt her
out, and he will ſmite her power in the ſea, and ſhe ſhalbe deuoured with
fire.[5]Aſhkelon ſhall ſee it, and feare, Gaza alſo ſhall ſee it and be very
ſorrowfull, and Ekron: for her expectation ſhalbe aſhamed, and the king
ſhall periſh from Gaza, and Aſhkelon ſhal not be inhabited.[6]And a
baſtard ſhall dwell in Aſhdod, and I will cut off the pride of the

Philiſtines.7And I wil take away his blood out of his mouth, and his abominations from betweene his teeth: but he that remaineth, euen hee ſhalbe for our God, and he ſhall be as a gouernour in Iudah, and Ekron as a Iebuſite.8And I will encampe about mine houſe becauſe of the armie, becauſe of him that paſſeth by, and becauſe of him that returneth: and no oppreſsour ſhall paſſe through them any more: for now haue I ſeene with mine eyes.9Reioyce greatly, O daughter of Zion; ſhout O daughter of Ieruſalem: beholde, thy King commeth vnto thee: hee is iuſt, and hauing ſaluation, lowly, and riding vpon an aſſe, and vpon a colt, the foale of an aſſe.10And I wil cut off the charet from Ephraim, and the horſe from Ieruſalem: and the battell bow ſhalbe cut off, and he ſhall ſpeake peace vnto the heathen, and his dominion ſhalbe from ſea euen to ſea, and from the Riuer, euen to the ends of the earth.11As for thee alſo, by the blood of thy Couenant, I haue ſent foorth thy priſoners out of the pit, wherein is no water.12Turne ye to the ſtrong hold, ye priſoners of hope, euen to day doe I declare that I will render double vnto thee:13When I haue bent Iudah for me, filled the bow with Ephraim, and raiſed vp thy ſonnes O Zion, againſt thy ſonnes, O Greece, and made thee as the ſword of a mightie man.14And the Lord ſhalbe ſeene ouer them, and his arrow ſhall goe forth as the lightning: and the Lord God ſhall blow the trumpet, and ſhall goe with whirlewinds of the South.15The Lord of hoſtes ſhall defend them, and they ſhall deuoure, and ſubdue with ſling ſtones, and they ſhal drinke and make a noiſe, as through wine, and they ſhall bee filled like bowles, and as the corners of the Altar.16And the Lord their God ſhall ſaue them in that day as the flock of his people, for they ſhall be as the ſtones of a crowne lifted vp as an enſigne vpon his land.17For how great is his goodneſse, and how great is his beautie? corne ſhal make the yong men cheerefull, and new wine the maides.

CHAPTER 101Aſke yee of the Lord raine in the time of the latter raine, ſo the Lord ſhal make bright clouds, and giue them ſhowres of raine, to euery one graſſe in the field.2For the idoles haue ſpoken vanitie, and the diuiners haue ſeene a lye, and haue told falſe dreames; they comfort in vaine: therefore they went their way as a flocke, they were troubled becauſe there was no ſhepheard.3Mine anger was kindled againſt the ſhepheards, and I puniſhed the goats: for the Lord of hoſtes hath viſited his flocke the houſe of Iudah, and hath made them as his goodly horſe in the battell.4Out of him came forth the corner, out of him the naile, out of him the battell bow, out of him euery oppreſsour together.5And they ſhall bee as mightie men which tread downe their enemies in the myre of the ſtreets in the battell, and they ſhall fight becauſe the Lord is with them, and the riders on horſes ſhall be confounded.6And I will ſtrengthen the houſe of Iudah, and I will ſaue the houſe of Ioſeph, and I will bring them againe to place them, for I haue mercie vpon them: and they ſhall be as though I had not caſt them off: for I am the Lord their God, & will heare them.7And they of Ephraim ſhall be like a mightie man, and their heart ſhall reioyce as through wine: yea, their children ſhall ſee it, and be glad, their heart ſhall reioyce in the Lord.8I will hiſse for them and gather them, for I haue redeemed them: and they ſhall increaſe as they haue increaſed.9And I will ſow them among the people, and they ſhall remember me in farre countries, and they ſhall liue with their children, and turne againe.10I will bring them againe alſo out of the land of Egypt, and gather them out of Aſſyria, and I will bring them into the land of Gilead and Lebanon, and place ſhall not be found for them.11And he ſhall paſſe through the ſea with affliction, & ſhall ſmite the waues in the ſea, and all the deepes of the riuer ſhall dry vp: and the pride of Aſſyria ſhall be brought downe, and the ſcepter of Egypt ſhall depart away.12And I will ſtrengthen them in the Lord, and they ſhall walke vp and downe in his name, ſaith the Lord.

CHAPTER 111Open thy doores, O Lebanon, that the fire may deuoure thy cedars.2Howle firre tree, for the cedar is fallen; becauſe all the mighty are ſpoiled; howle O yee okes of Baſhan, for the forreſt of the vintage is come downe.3There is a voyce of the howling of the ſhepheards; for their glory is ſpoiled: a voyce of the roaring of young lyons; for the pride of Iordan is ſpoiled.4Thus ſaith the Lord my God; Feede the flocke of the ſlaughter;5Whoſe poſſeſſours ſlay them, and hold themſelues not guiltie: and they that ſell thē ſay, Bleſſed be the Lord; for I am rich: and their owne ſhepheards pitie them not.6For I will no more pitie the inhabitants of the land, ſaith the Lord: but loe, I will deliuer the men euery one into his neighbours hand, and into the hand of his King, and they ſhall ſmite the land, and out of their hand I will not deliuer them.7And I will feede the flocke of ſlaughter, euen you, O poore of the flock: and I tooke vnto me two ſtaues; the one I called Beautie, and the other I called Bandes, and I fed the flocke.8Three ſhepheards alſo I cut off in one moneth, and my ſoule loathed them, and their ſoule alſo abhorred mee.9Then ſaid I, I will not feede you: that that dieth, let it die: and that that is to be cut off, let it be cut off, and let the reſt eate, euery one the fleſh of another.10And I tooke my ſtaffe, euen Beautie, and cut it aſunder, that I might breake my couenant which I had made with all the people.11And it was broken in that day: and ſo the poore of the flocke that waited vpon me, knew that it was the word of the Lord.12And I ſaid vnto them, If yee thinke good, giue me my price: and if not, forbeare: ſo they weighed for my price thirtie pieces of ſiluer.13And the Lord ſaid vnto mee, Caſt it vnto the potter: a goodly price, that I was priſed at of them. And I tooke the thirtie pieces of ſiluer, and caſt them to the potter in the houſe of the Lord.14Then I cut aſunder mine other ſtaffe, euen Bands, that I might break the brotherhood betweene Iudah and Iſrael.15And the Lord ſaid vnto me, Take vnto thee yet the inſtruments of a fooliſh ſhepheard.16For loe, I wil raiſe vp a ſhepherd in the land, which ſhall not viſit thoſe that bee cut off, neither ſhall ſeeke the yong one, nor heale that that is broken, nor feed that that ſtandeth ſtill: but he ſhal eate the fleſh of the fat, and teare their clawes in pieces.17Woe to the idoll ſhepheard that leaueth the flocke: the ſword ſhall be vpon his arme, and vpon his right eye: his arme ſhall be cleane dryed vp, and his right eye ſhall be vtterly darkened.

CHAPTER 121The burden of the word of the Lord for Iſrael, ſaith the Lord, which ſtretcheth foorth the Heauens, and laith the foundation of the earth, and formeth the ſpirit of man within him.2Behold, I will make Ieruſalem a cup of trembling vnto all the people round about, when they ſhall be in the ſiege both againſt Iudah and againſt Ieruſalem.3And in that day will I make Ieruſalem a burdenſome ſtone for all people: all that burden themſelues with it, ſhall be cut in pieces; though all the people of the earth bee gathered together againſt it.4In that day, ſaith the Lord, I will ſmite euery horſe with aſtoniſhment, and his rider with madneſse, and I will open mine eyes vpon the houſe of Iudah, and will ſmite euery horſe of the people with blindneſse.5And the gouernours of Iudah ſhall ſay in their heart, The inhabitants of Ieruſalem ſhall be my ſtrength in the Lord of hoſtes their God.6In that day will I make the gouernours of Iudah like a harth of fire among the wood, and like a torch of fire in a ſheafe; and they ſhall deuoure all the people round about, on the right hand and on the left: and Ieruſalem ſhall bee inhabited againe in her owne place, euen in Ieruſalem.7The Lord alſo ſhall ſaue the tents of Iudah firſt, that the glory of the houſe of Dauid, and the glory of the inhabitants of Ieruſalem do not magnifie themſelues againſt Iudah.8In that day ſhall the Lord defend the inhabitants of Ieruſalem, and he that is feeble among them at that day ſhall be as Dauid; and the houſe of Dauid ſhall be as God, as the Angel of the Lord before them.9And it ſhall come to paſſe in that day, that I will ſeeke to deſtroy all the nations that come againſt Ieruſalem.10And I wil powre vpon the houſe of Dauid, and vpon the inhabitants of Ieruſalem the ſpirit of grace and of ſupplications, and they ſhall looke vpon me whom they haue pearced, and they ſhal mourne for him, as one mourneth for his onely ſonne, and ſhall be in bitterneſse for him, as one that is in bitterneſse for his firſt borne.11In that day ſhall there bee a great mourning in Ieruſalem, as the mourning of Hadadrimmon in the valley of Megiddon.12And the land ſhal mourne, euery familie apart, the familie of the houſe of Dauid apart, and their wiues apart, the familie of the houſe of Nathan apart, and their wiues apart:13The familie of the houſe of Leui apart, and their wiues apart: the familie of Shimei apart, and their wiues apart:14All the families that remaine, euery family apart, & their wiues apart.

CHAPTER 131In that day there ſhalbe a fountaine opened to the houſe of Dauid, and to the inhabitants of Ieruſalem, for ſinne, and for vncleanneſſe.2And it ſhal come to paſſe in that day, ſaith the Lord of hoſtes, that I will cut off the names of the idoles out of the land: and they ſhal no more be remembred: and alſo I wil cauſe the prophets, and the vncleane ſpirit to paſſe out of the land.3And it ſhal come to paſſe that when any ſhall yet prophecie, then his father and his mother that begate him, ſhall ſay vnto him, Thou ſhalt not liue: for thou ſpeakeſt lies in the Name of the Lord: and his father and his mother, that begate him, ſhall thruſt him through when he prophecieth.4And it ſhall come to paſſe in that day, that the prophets ſhalbe aſhamed euery one of his viſion, when hee hath prophecied: neither ſhall they weare a rough garment to deceiue.5But he ſhal ſay, I am no prophet, I am an huſbandman: for man taught me to keepe cattell from my youth.6And one ſhal ſay vnto him, What are theſe wounds in thine hands? Then hee ſhall anſwere: Thoſe with which I was wounded in the houſe of my friends.7Awake, O ſword, againſt my ſhepheard, and againſt the man that is my fellow, ſaith the Lord of hoſtes: ſmite the Shepheard, and the ſheepe ſhalbe ſcattered: and I wil turne mine hand vpon the litle ones.8And it ſhall come to paſſe, that in all the land, ſaith the Lord, two parts therein ſhall be cut off, and die, but the third ſhall be left therein.9And I will bring the thirde part through the fire, and wil refine them as ſiluer is refined, & will try them as gold is tried: they ſhall call on my Name, and I wil heare them: I wil ſay, It is my people: and they ſhall ſay, The Lord is my God.

CHAPTER 141Beholde, the day of the Lord commeth, and thy ſpoile ſhall be diuided in the midſt of thee.2For I wil gather all nations againſt Ieruſalem to battell, and the citie ſhall be taken, & the houſes rifeled, and the women rauiſhed, and halfe of the citie ſhall goe forth into captiuitie, and the reſidue of the people ſhal not be cut off from the citie.3Then ſhall the Lord goe forth and fight againſt thoſe nations, as when he fought in the day of battel.4And his feet ſhall ſtand in that day vpon the mount of Oliues, which is before Ieruſalem on the Eaſt, and the mount of Oliues ſhall cleaue in the midſt thereof toward the Eaſt, and toward the Weſt, and there ſhall bee a very great valley, and halfe of the Mountaine ſhall remoue toward the North, and halfe of it toward the South.5And ye ſhal flee to the valley of the mountaines: for the valley of the mountaines ſhal reach vnto Azal: yea, ye ſhall flee like as yee fled from before the earthquake in the dayes of Uzziah king of Iudah: and the Lord my God ſhall come, and all the Saints with thee.6And it ſhall come to paſſe in that day, that the light ſhall not be cleare, nor darke.7But it ſhall be one day, which ſhalbe knowen to the Lord, not day nor night: but it ſhal come to paſſe that at euening time it ſhalbe light.8And it ſhal be in that day, that liuing waters ſhall goe out from Ieruſalem: halfe of them toward the former ſea, and halfe of them toward the hinder ſea: in Summer and in winter ſhall it be.9And the Lord ſhall be King ouer all the earth: in that day ſhal there be one Lord, and his Name one.10All the land ſhall be turned as a plaine from Geba to Rimmon, South of Ieruſalem: and it ſhall be lifted vp and inhabited in her place: from Beniamins gate vnto the place of the firſt gate, vnto the corner gate, and from the towre of Hananiel vnto the Kings winepreſſe s.11And men ſhall dwell in it, and there ſhalbe no more vtter deſtruction: but Ieruſalem ſhalbe ſafely inhabited.12And this ſhall be the plague, wherewith the Lord will ſmite all the people, that haue fought againſt Ieruſalem: their fleſh ſhall conſume away, while they ſtand vpon their feete, and their eyes ſhall conſume away in their holes, and their tongue ſhall conſume away in their mouth.13And it ſhall come to paſſe in that day, that a great tumult from the Lord ſhalbe among them, and they ſhall lay holde euery one on the hand of his neighbour, and his hand ſhall riſe vp againſt the hand of his neighbour.14And Iudah alſo ſhall fight at Ieruſalem; and the wealth of all the heathen round about ſhall be gathered together, golde and ſiluer, and apparell in great abundance.15And ſo ſhall be the plague of the horſe, of the mule, of the camell, and of the aſſe, and of all the beaſts that ſhall be in theſe tents, as this plague.16And it ſhall come to paſſe that euery one that is left of all the nations which came againſt Ieruſalem, ſhall euen goe vp from yeere to yeere to worſhip the King the Lord of hoſtes, and to keepe the feaſt of Tabernacles.17And it ſhall be, that who ſo will not come vp of all the families of the earth vnto Ieruſalem, to worſhip the King the Lord of hoſtes, euen vpon them ſhall be no raine.18And if the family of Egypt goe not vp, and come not, that haue no raine: there ſhall bee the plague wherewith the Lord will ſmite the heathen that come not vp to keepe the feaſt of Tabernacles.19This ſhall be the puniſhment of Egypt, and the puniſhment of all nations that come not vp to keepe the feaſt of Tabernacles.20In that day ſhall there be vpon the bels of the horſes, Holines Unto The Lord, and the pots in the Lords houſe ſhall bee like the bowles before the Altar.21Yea, euery pot in Ieruſalem and in Iudah ſhall bee Holineſse vnto the Lord of hoſtes, and all they that ſacrifice, ſhall come and take of them, and ſeethe therein: and in that day there ſhall be no more the Canaanite in the houſe of the Lord of hoſtes.

MALACHI

CHAPTER 11The burden of the word of þe Lord to Iſrael by Malachi.2I haue loued you, ſayth the Lord: yet yee ſay, Wherein haſt thou loued vs? was not Eſau Iacobs brother, ſayth the Lord ? yet I loued Iacob,3And I hated Eſau, and layde his mountaines, and his heritage waſte, for the dragons of the wilderneſſe.4Whereas Edom ſayth, Wee are impoueriſhed, but we will returne and build the deſolate places; Thus ſayth the Lord of hoſtes, They ſhal build, but I will throw downe; and they ſhal call them, The border of wickedneſſe, & the people againſt whom the Lord hath indignation for euer.5And your eyes ſhall ſee, and yee ſhall ſay; The Lord will be magnified from the border of Iſrael.6A ſonne honoureth his father, and a ſeruant his Maſter. If then I be a father, where is mine honour? and if I be a Maſter, where is my feare, ſaith the Lord of hoſtes, vnto you O prieſts, that deſpiſe my name? and yee ſay, Wherein haue we deſpiſed thy name?7Yee offer polluted bread vpon mine altar; and yee ſay, Wherein haue we polluted thee? In that yee ſay, The table of the Lord is contemptible.8And if hee offer the blind for ſacrifice, is it not euill? and if yee offer the lame and ſicke, is it not euill? offer it now vnto thy gouernour: will he be pleaſed with thee, or accept thy perſon, ſaith the Lord of hoſtes?9And now I pray you, beſeech God, that hee will be gracious vnto vs: this hath beene by your meanes: will he regard your perſons, ſaith the Lord of hoſtes?10Who is there euen among you that would ſhut the doores for nought? neither doe yee kindle fire on mine altar for nought. I haue no pleaſure in you, ſaith the Lord of hoſtes, neither will I accept an offring at your hand.11For from the riſing of the Sunne, euen vnto the going downe of the ſame my name ſhall be great among the Gentiles, and in euery place incenſe ſhall be offered vnto my name, and a pure offring: for my name ſhall be great among the heathen, ſaith the Lord of hoſtes.12But yee haue prophaned it, in that yee ſay; The table of the Lord is polluted, and the fruite thereof, euen his meate, is contemptible.13Yee ſaid alſo; Behold what a wearineſse is it, and yee haue ſnuffed at it, ſaith the Lord of hoſtes, and yee brought that which was torne, and the lame, and the ſicke: thus yee brought an offring: ſhould I accept this of your hand, ſaith the Lord ?14But curſed be the deceiuer, which hath in his flocke a male, and voweth and ſacrificeth vnto the Lord a corrupt thing: for I am a great King, ſaith the Lord of hoſtes, and my name is dreadfull among the heathen.

CHAPTER 21And now, O yee Prieſts, this commaundement is for you.2If ye will not heare, and if yee will not lay it to heart, to giue glory vnto my name, ſaith the Lord of hoſtes; I will euen ſend a curſe vpon you, and will curſe your bleſſings: yea, I haue curſed them already, becauſe yee doe not lay it to heart.3Behold, I will corrupt your ſeed, and ſpread doung vpon your faces, euen the doung of your ſolemne feaſts, and one ſhall take you away with it.4And yee ſhall know that I haue ſent this commaundement vnto you, that my couenant might be with Leui, ſaith the Lord of hoſtes.5My couenant was with him of life and peace, and I gaue them to him, for the feare, wherewith he feared mee, and was afraid before my name.6The law of truth was in his mouth, and iniquitie was not found in his lips: he walked with me in peace and equitie, and did turne many away from iniquitie.7For the prieſts lips ſhould keepe knowledge, and they ſhould ſeeke the law at his mouth: for he is the meſſenger of the Lord of hoſtes.8But yee are departed out of the way: ye haue cauſed many to ſtumble at the law: ye haue corrupted the couenant of Leui, ſaith the Lord of hoſtes.9Therefore haue I alſo made you contemptible and baſe before al the people, according as yee haue not kept my wayes, but haue bin partiall in þe law.10Haue we not all one father? hath not one God created vs? Why doe we deale treacherouſly euery man againſt his brother, by prophaning the couenant of our fathers?11Iudah hath dealt treacherouſly, and an abomination is committed in Iſrael and in Ieruſalem: for Iudah hath prophaned the holineſſe of the Lord which he loued, and hath maried the daughter of a ſtrange God.12The Lord will cut off the man that doth this: the Maſter and the ſcholler out of the tabernacles of Iacob, and him that offereth an offring vnto the Lord of hoſtes.13And this haue yee done againe, couering the Altar of the Lord with teares, with weeping and with crying out, in ſo much that hee regardeth not the offering any more, or receiueth it with good will at your hand.14Yet ye ſay, Wherefore? Becauſe the Lord hath bene witnes betweene thee and the wife of thy youth, againſt whome thou haſt dealt treacherouſly: yet is ſhe thy companion, and the wife of thy couenant.15And did not he make one? yet had he the reſidue of the ſpirit: and wherefore one? that hee might ſeeke a godly ſeed: therefore take heed to your ſpirit, and let none deale treacherouſly againſt the wife of his youth.16For the Lord the God of Iſrael ſaith, that he hateth putting away: for one couereth violence with his garment, ſaith the Lord of hoſts, therfore take heed to your ſpirit, that ye deale not treacherouſly.17Ye haue wearied the Lord with your words: yet ye ſay, Wherein haue we wearied him? when ye ſay, Euery one that doeth euill, is good in the ſight of the Lord, and he delighteth in them, or where is the God of iudgement?

CHAPTER 31Beholde, I will ſend my meſſenger, and he ſhal prepare the way before mee: and the Lord whom ye ſeeke, ſhall ſuddenly come to his Temple: euen þe meſſenger of the Couenant, whom ye delight in: behold, he ſhall come, ſaith the Lord of hoſts.2But who may abide the day of his comming? and who ſhall ſtand when he appeareth? for he is like a refiners fire, and like fullers ſope.3And he ſhall ſit as a refiner and purifier of ſiluer: and he ſhall purifie the ſonnes of Leui, and purge them as gold & ſiluer, that they may offer vnto the Lord an offring in righteouſnes.4Then ſhall the offerings of Iudah and Ieruſalem bee pleaſant vnto the Lord, as in the dayes of old, and as in former yeeres.5And I will come neere to you to iudgement, and I will bee a ſwift witneſſe againſt the ſorcerers, and againſt the adulterers, and againſt falſe ſwearers, and againſt thoſe that oppreſſe the hireling in his wages, the widowe, and the fatherleſſe, and that turne aſide the ſtranger from his right, and feare not me, ſaith the Lord of hoſts.6For I am the Lord, I change not: therefore ye ſonnes of Iacob are not conſumed.7Euen from the dayes of your fathers yee are gone away from mine ordinances, and haue not kept them: returne vnto me, and I will returne vnto you, ſaith the Lord of hoſts: But ye ſaid, Wherein ſhall we returne?8Wil a man rob God? yet ye haue robbed me. But ye ſay, Wherein haue we robbed thee? In tithes & offerings.9Ye are curſed with a curſe: for ye haue robbed me, euen this whole nation.10Bring ye all the tithes into the ſtore-houſe, that there may be meate in mine houſe, & proue me now herewith, ſaith the Lord of hoſtes, if I will not open you the windowes of heauen, and powre you out a bleſſing, that there ſhall not be roome enough to receiue it.11And I wil rebuke the deuourer for your ſakes: and he ſhal not deſtroy the fruits of your ground, neither ſhal your vine caſt her fruit before the time in the field, ſaith the Lord of hoſts.12And all nations ſhall call you bleſſed: for ye ſhall be a delightſome land, ſaith the Lord of hoſts.13Your words haue bin ſtout againſt me, ſaith the Lord, yet ye ſay, What haue we ſpoken ſo much againſt thee?14Ye haue ſaid, It is vaine to ſerue God: and what profit is it, that we haue kept his ordinance, and that wee haue walked mournfully before the Lord of hoſts?15And now we call the proud happy: yea, they that worke wickednes are ſet vp, yea they that tempt God, are euen deliuered.16Then they that feared the Lord, ſpake often one to another, and the Lord hearkened and heard it, & a booke of remembrance was written before him, for them that feared the Lord, & that thought vpon his name.17And they ſhall be mine, ſaith the Lord of hoſts, in that day when I make vp my iewels, and I wil ſpare them as a man ſpareth his owne ſonne that ſerueth him.18Then ſhall yee returne and diſcerne betweene the righteous and the wicked, betweene him that ſerueth God, and him that ſerueth him not.

CHAPTER 41For beholde, the day commeth, that ſhall burne as an ouen, and all the proud, yea and all that doe wickedly ſhalbe ſtubble: and the day that commeth, ſhal burne them vp, ſaith the Lord of hoſtes, that it ſhall leaue them neither roote nor branch.2But vnto you that feare my Name, ſhall the Sunne of righteouſneſſe Ariſe with healing in his wings, and ſhall goe foorth and grow vp as calues of the ſtaule.3And yee ſhall treade downe the wicked: for they ſhall bee aſhes vnder the ſoles of your feet, in the day that I ſhall doe this, ſaith the Lord of hoſts.4Remember yee the Law of Moſes my ſeruant, which I commanded vnto him in Horeb for all Iſrael, with the Statutes and iudgements.5Beholde, I will ſend you Eliiah the Prophet, before the comming of the great and dreadfull day of the Lord.6And hee ſhall turne the heart of the fathers to the children, and the heart of the children to their fathers, leſt I come and ſmite the earth with a curſe.

THE APOCRYPHA

1 EſDRAS

CHAPTER 11And Ioſias helde the Feaſt of the Paſſeouer in Ieruſalem vnto his Lord, and offered the Paſſeouer the fourteenth day of the firſt moneth:2Hauing ſet the Prieſts according to their daily courſes, being arayed in long garments, in the Temple of the Lord.3And hee ſpake vnto the Leuites the holy miniſters of Iſrael, that they ſhould hallow themſelues vnto the Lord, to ſet the holy Arke of the Lord, in the houſe that king Solomon the ſonne of Dauid had built:4And ſaid, Ye ſhall no more beare the Arke vpon your ſhoulders : now therefore ſerue the Lord your God, and miniſter vnto his people Iſrael, and prepare you after your families and kinreds.5According as Dauid the king of Iſrael preſcribed, & according to the magnificence of Solomon his ſonne: & ſtanding in the Temple according to the ſeuerall dignitie of the families of you the Leuites, who miniſter in the preſence of your brethren the children of Iſrael.6Offer the Paſſeouer in order, and make ready the ſacrifices for your brethren, and keepe the Paſſeouer according to the commaundement of the Lord, which was giuen vnto Moyſes.7And vnto the people that was found there, Ioſias gaue thirtie thouſand lambes, and kids, and three thouſand calues: theſe things were giuen of the kings allowance, according as hee promiſed to the people, to the Prieſtes, and to the Leuites.8And Helkias, Zacharias, and Sielus the gouernours of the Temple, gaue to the Prieſts for the Paſſeouer, two thouſand and ſixe hundred ſheepe, and three hundreth calues.9And Iechonias, and Samaias, and Nathanael his brother, and Aſsabias, and Ochiel, and Ioram captaines ouer thouſands, gaue to the Leuites for the Paſſeouer fiue thouſand ſheepe, and ſeuen hundreth calues.10And when theſe things were done, the Prieſts and Leuites hauing the vnleauened bread, ſtood in very comely order according to the kinreds,11And according to the ſeuerall dignities of the fathers, before the people, to offer to the Lord, as it is written in the booke of Moyſes: And thus did they in the morning.12And they roſted the Paſſeouer with fire, as appertaineth: as for the ſacrifices, they ſodde them in braſſe pots, and pannes with a good ſauour.13And ſet them before all the people, and afterward they prepared for themſelues, and for the Prieſts their brethren the ſonnes of Aaron.14For the Prieſts offered the fat vntill night: and the Leuites prepared for themſelues, and the Prieſts their brethren the ſonnes of Aaron.15The holy Singers alſo, the ſonnes of Aſaph, were in their order, according to the appointment of Dauid, to wit, Aſaph, Zacharias, and Ieduthun, who was of the kings retinue.16Moreouer the porters were at euery gate: it was not lawfull for any to goe from his ordinary ſeruice: for their brethren the Leuites prepared for them.17Thus were the things that belonged to the ſacrifices of the Lord accompliſhed in that day, that they might hold the Paſſeouer,18And offer ſacrifices vpon the altar of the Lord, according to the commandement of king Ioſias.19So the children of Iſrael which were preſent, held the Paſſeouer at that time, and the feaſt of ſweet bread ſeuen dayes.20And ſuch a Paſſeouer was not kept in Iſrael ſince the time of the Prophet Samuel.21Yea all the kings of Iſrael held not ſuch a Paſſeouer as Ioſias, and the Prieſts and the Leuites, & the Iewes held with all Iſrael that were found dwelling at Ieruſalem.22In the eighteenth yeere of the reigne of Ioſias was this Paſſeouer kept.23And the workes of Ioſias were vpright before his Lord with an heart full of godlineſse.24As for the things that came to paſſe in his time, they were written in former times, concerning thoſe that ſinned, and did wickedly againſt the Lord aboue all people and kingdomes, and how they grieued him exceedingly, ſo that the words of the Lord roſe vp againſt Iſrael.25Now after all theſe acts of Ioſias, it came to paſſe that Pharao the king of Egypt came to raiſe warre at Carchamis vpon Euphrates: and Ioſias went out againſt him.26But the king of Egypt ſent to him ſaying, What haue I to doe with thee, O king of Iudea?27I am not ſent out from the Lord God againſt thee: for my warre is vpon Euphrates, and now the Lord is with mee, yea the Lord is with mee haſting me forward: Depart from me and be not againſt the Lord.28Howbeit Ioſias did not turne backe his chariot from him, but vndertooke to fight with him, not regarding the words of the Prophet Ieremie, ſpoken by the mouth of the Lord:29But ioyned battell with him in the plaine of Magiddo, and the princes came againſt king

Ioſias.30Then ſaid the king vnto his ſeruants, carry me away out of the
battell for I am very weake: and immediately his ſeruants tooke him away
out of the battell.31Then gate he vp vpon his ſecond chariot, and being
brought backe to Ieruſalem, dyed, and was buried in his fathers
ſepulchre.32And in all Iury they mourned for Ioſias, yea Ieremie the
Prophet lamented for Ioſias, and the cheefe men with the women made
lamentation for him vnto this day: and this was giuen out for an
ordinance to be done continually in all the nation of Iſrael.33Theſe things
are written in the booke of the ſtories of the kings of Iudah, and euery
one of the acts that Ioſias did, and his glory, and his vnderſtanding in
the law of the Lord, and the things that he had done before, and the
things now recited, are reported in the bookes of the Kings of Iſrael and
Iudea.34And the people tooke Ioachaz the ſonne of Ioſias, and made
him king in ſtead of Ioſias his father, when hee was twentie and three
yeeres old.35And he reigned in Iudea and in Ieruſalem three moneths:
and then the King of Egypt depoſed him from reigning in
Ieruſalem.36And he ſet a taxe vpon the land of an hundreth talents of
ſiluer, and one talent of gold.37The king of Egypt alſo made king Ioacim
his brother king of Iudea and Ieruſalem.38And hee bound Ioacim and
the nobles: but Zaraces his brother he apprehended, and brought him
out of Egypt.39Fiue and twentie yeere old was Ioacim when he was made
king in the land of Iudea and Ieruſalem, and he did euill before the
Lord.40Wherefore againſt him Nabuchodonoſor the King of Babylon
came vp, and bound him with a chaine of braſſe, and carried him vnto
Babylon.41Nabuchodonoſor alſo tooke of the holy veſſels of the Lord,
and carried them away, and ſet them in his owne temple at
Babylon.42But thoſe things that are recorded of him, and of his
vncleannes, and impietie, are written in the Chronicles of the
kings.43And Ioacim his ſonne reigned in his ſtead: he was made king
being eighteene yeeres old,44And reigned but three moneths and ten
dayes in Ieruſalem, and did euill before the Lord.45So after a yere
Nabuchodonoſor ſent, and cauſed him to be brought into Babylon with
þe holy veſſels of þe Lord,46And made Zedechias king of Iudea and
Ieruſalem, when he was one and twentie yeeres old, and he reigned
eleuen yeeres:47And he did euill alſo in the ſight of the Lord, & cared
not for the words that were ſpoken vnto him, by the Prophet Ieremie
from the mouth of the Lord.48And after that king Nabuchodonoſor had
made him to ſweare by the Name of the Lord, he forſwore himſelfe, and
rebelled, and hardening his necke, and his heart, hee tranſgreſſed the
lawes of the Lord God of Iſrael.49The gouernours alſo of the people
and of the prieſts did many things againſt the lawes, and paſſed al the
pollutions of all nations, and defiled the Temple of the Lord which was
ſanctified in Ieruſalem.50Neuertheleſſe, the God of their fathers ſent by
his meſſenger to call them backe, becauſe he ſpared them and his
tabernacle alſo:51But they had his meſſengers in deriſion, and looke
when the Lorde ſpake vnto them, they made a ſport of his prophets,52So
farre foorth that he being wroth with his people for their great
vngodlineſse, commanded the kings of the Caldees to come vp againſt
them.53Who ſlew their yong men with the ſword, yea euen within the
compaſſe of their holy Temple, & ſpared neither yong man nor maid,
old man nor child among them, for hee deliuered all into their
hands.54And they tooke all the holy veſſels of the Lord, both great and
ſmall, with the veſſels of the Ark of God, and the kings treaſures, and
caried them away into Babylon.55As for the houſe of the Lord they
burnt it, brake downe the walles of Ieruſalem, ſet fire vpon her
towres.56And as for her glorious things, they neuer ceaſed til they had
conſumed and brought them all to nought, and the people that were not
ſlaine with the ſword, he caried vnto Babylon:57Who became ſeruants
to him and his children, till the Perſians reigned, to fulfill the word of
the Lord ſpoken by the mouth of Ieremie:58Untill the land had enioyed
her Sabbaths, the whole time of her deſolation ſhal ſhe reſt, vntill the
full terme of ſeuentie yeeres.

CHAPTER 21In the firſt yeere of Cyrus king of the Perſians, that the
worde of the Lorde might bee accompliſhed, that hee had promiſed by
the mouth of Ieremie:2The Lord raiſed vp the ſpirit of Cyrus the king of
the Perſians, and he made proclamation thorow al his kingdome, and
alſo by writing,3Saying, Thus ſaith Cyrus king of the Perſians, The Lord
of Iſrael the moſt high Lord, hath made me king of the whole
world,4And commanded me to build him an houſe at Ieruſalem in
Iurie.5If therefore there bee any of you that are of his people, let the
Lord, euen his Lord be with him, and let him goe vp to Ieruſalem that
is in Iudea, and build the houſe of the Lord of Iſrael: for he is the Lord
that dwelleth in Ieruſalem.6Whoſoeuer then dwell in the places about,
let them helpe him, thoſe I ſay that are his neighbours, with gold and
with ſiluer,7With gifts, with horſes, and with cattell, and other things,
which haue bene ſet forth by vowe, for the Temple of the Lord at
Ieruſalem.8Then the chiefe of the families of Iudea, and of the tribes of
Beniamin ſtood vp: the prieſts alſo and the Leuites, and all they whoſe
minde the Lord had moued to goe vp, and to build an houſe for the
Lord at Ieruſalem,9And they that dwelt round about them, and helped
them in all things with ſiluer and gold, with horſes and cattell, and with
very free gifts of a great number whoſe mindes were ſtirred vp
thereto.10King Cyrus alſo brought foorth the holy veſſels which
Nabuchodonoſor had caried away from Ieruſalem, and had ſet vp in his
temple of idoles.11Now when Cyrus king of the Perſians had brought
them foorth, hee deliuered them to Mithridates his treaſurer:12And by
him they were deliuered to Sanabaſſar þe gouernour of Iudea.13And this
was the number of them, a thouſand golden cuppes, and a thouſand of
ſiluer, cenſers of ſiluer twentie nine, vials of gold thirtie, and of ſiluer
two thouſand foure hundred and ten, and a thouſand other veſſels.14So
all the veſſels of gold, and of ſiluer which were caried away, were fiue
thouſand, foure hundred, threeſcore and nine.15Theſe were brought
back by Sanabaſſar, together with them of the captiuity, from Babylon
to Ieruſalem.16But in the time of Artaxerxes king of the Perſians,
Belemus, and Mithridates, and Tabellius, and Rathumus, and
Beeltethmus, and Semellius the Secretarie, with others that were in
commiſſion with them, dwelling in Samaria and other places, wrote vnto
him againſt them that dwelt in Iudea and Ieruſalem, theſe letters
following.17To King Artaxerxes our lord, Thy ſeruants Rathumus the
ſtory writer, and Semellius the ſcribe, and the reſt of their counſell, and
the Iudges that are in Coeloſyria and Phenice.18Be it now knowen to the
lord the king, that the Iewes that are come vp from you to vs, being
come into Ieruſalem (that rebellious and wicked citie,) doe build the
market places, and repaire the walles of it, and doe lay the foundation of
the Temple.19Now if this citie, and the walles thereof be made vp againe,
they will not onely refuſe to giue tribute, but alſo rebell againſt
kings.20And foraſmuch as the things pertaining to the Temple, are now
in hand, we thinke it meete not to neglect ſuch a matter,21But to ſpeake
vnto our lord the king, to the intent that if it be thy pleaſure, it may be
ſought out in the bookes of thy fathers:22And thou ſhalt finde in the
Chronicles, what is written concerning theſe things, and ſhalt vnderſtand
that that citie was rebellious, troubling both kings and cities:23And that
the Iewes were rebellious, and raiſed alwayes warres therin, for the
which cauſe euen this citie was made deſolate.24Wherefore now wee doe
declare vnto thee, (O lord the king) that if this citie bee built againe, and
the walles thereof ſet vp anew, thou ſhalt from hencefoorth haue no
paſsage into Corloſyria and Phenice.25Then the King wrote backe againe
to Rathumus the ſtorie-writer, to Beeltethmus, to Semellius the ſcribe,
and to the reſt that were in commiſſion, and dwellers in Samaria and
Syria, and Phenice, after this maner.26I haue read the Epiſtle which ye
haue ſent vnto mee: therefore I commanded to make diligent ſearch,
and it hath bene found, that that city was from the beginning practiſing
againſt Kings.27And the men therein were giuen to rebellion, and warre,
and that mightie Kings and fierce were in Ieruſalem, who reigned and
exacted tributes in Coeloſyria and Phenice.28Now therefore I haue
commanded to hinder thoſe men from building the citie, and heed to be
taken that there be no more done in it,29And that thoſe wicked workers
proceed no further to the annoyance of Kings.30Then king Artaxerxes
his letters being read, Rathumus and Semellius the ſcribe, and the reſt
that were in commiſſion with them, remoouing in haſt towards
Ieruſalem with a troupe of horſemen, and a multitude of people in
battell aray, began to hinder the builders, and the building of the Temple
in Ieruſalem ceaſed vntill the ſecond yeere of the reigne of Darius King
of the Perſians.

CHAPTER 31Now when Darius reigned, hee made a great feaſt vnto
all his Subiects and vnto all his houſhold, and vnto all the princes of
Media and Perſia,2And to all the gouernours and captaines, and
lieutenants that were vnder him, from Iudia vnto Ethiopia, of an
hundreth twenty and ſeuen prouinces.3And when they had eaten and

drunken, and being ſatiſfied were gone home, then Darius the king went
into his bed chamber, and ſlept, and ſoone after awaked.4Then three
yong men that were of the guard, that kept the kings body, ſpake one to
another:5Let euery one of vs ſpeake a ſentence: hee that ſhall ouercome,
& whoſe ſentence ſhall ſeeme wiſer then the others, vnto him ſhall the
king Darius giue great gifts, and great things in token of victory:6As to
be clothed in purple, to drink in golde, and to ſleepe vpon golde, and a
chariot with bridles of golde, and an head-tyre of fine linen, and a chaine
about his necke:7And hee ſhall ſit next to Darius, becauſe of his
wiſedome, and ſhalbe called, Darius his couſin.8And then euery one
wrote his ſentence, ſealed it, and laide it vnder king Darius his
pillow,9And ſayd, that when the king is riſen, ſome will giue him the
writings, and of whoſe ſide the king, and the three princes of Perſia ſhall
iudge, that his ſentence is the wiſeſt, to him ſhall the victory be giuen as
was appointed.10The firſt wrote: Wine is the ſtrongeſt.11The ſecond
wrote: The King is ſtrongeſt.12The third wrote; Women are ſtrongeſt,
but aboue all things trueth beareth away the victory.13Now when the
king was riſen vp, they tooke their writings, and deliuered them vnto
him, and ſo hee read them.14And ſending foorth, hee called all the
Princes of Perſia and Media, and the gouernours, and the captaines, and
the lieutenants, and the chiefe officers,15And ſate him downe in the
royall ſeate of Iudgement, and the writings were read before them:16And
he ſaid, Call the young men, and they ſhall declare their owne ſentences:
ſo they were called, and came in.17And hee ſaid vnto them, Declare vnto
vs your minde, concerning the writings. Then began the firſt, who had
ſpoken of the ſtrength of wine;18And he ſaid thus: O ye men, how
exceeding ſtrong is wine! it cauſeth all men to erre that drinke it:19It
maketh the minde of the king, and of the fatherleſſe childe to be all one
of the bondman and of the freeman, of the poore man and of the
rich:20It turneth alſo euery thought into iollitie and mirth, ſo that a man
remembreth neither ſorow nor debt:21And it maketh euery heart rich, ſo
that a man remembreth neither king nor gouernour, and it maketh to
ſpeake all things by talents:22And when they are in their cups, they forget
their loue both to friends and brethren, and a litle after draw out
ſwords:23But when they are from the wine, they remember not what
they haue done.24O ye men, is not wine the ſtrongeſt, that enforceth to
doe thus? And when hee had ſo ſpoken, hee helde his peace.

CHAPTER 41Then the ſecond that had ſpoken of the ſtrength of the
King, began to ſay;2O yee men, doe not men excel in ſtrength, that beare
rule ouer ſea and land, and all things in them?3But yet the King is more
mighty: for hee is lord of all theſe things, and hath dominion ouer them,
and whatſoeuer he commandeth them, they doe:4If thee bid them make
warre the one againſt the other, they doe it: if hee ſend them out againſt
the enemies, they goe, and breake downe mountaines, walles and
towres.5They ſlay and are ſlaine, and tranſgreſse not the Kings
commandement: if they get the victory, they bring all to the King, as
well the ſpoile as all things elſe.6Likewiſe for thoſe that are no ſouldiers,
and haue not to doe with warres, but vſe huſbandrie; when they haue
reaped againe, that which they had ſowen, they bring it to the King, and
compell one another to pay tribute vnto the King.7And yet he is but one
man; if hee commaund to kill, they kill, if he command to ſpare, they
ſpare.8If he command to ſmite, they ſmite; if he command to make
deſolate, they make deſolate; if hee command to build, they build:9If he
command to cut downe, they cut downe; if he command to plant, they
plant.10So all his people and his armies obey him; furthermore he lieth
downe, he eateth and drinketh, & taketh his reſt.11And theſe keepe
(watch) round about him, neither may any one depart, and doe his owne
buſineſse, neither diſobey they him in any thing.12O yee men, how
ſhould not the King be mightieſt, when in ſuch ſort he is obeyed? and
he held his tongue.13Then the third, who had ſpoken of women, and of
the truth (this was Zorobabel) beganne to ſpeake.14O yee men, it is not
the great King, nor the multitude of men, neither is it wine that excelleth;
who is it then that ruleth them, or hath the lordſhip ouer them, are they
not women?15Women haue borne the King and all the people, that
beare rule by ſea and land.16Euen of thē came they: & they nouriſhed
them vp that planted the vineyards from whence the wine
commeth.17Theſe alſo make garments for men; theſe bring glory vnto
men, and without women cannot men be.18Yea and if men haue
gathered together gold and ſiluer, or any other goodly thing, doe they
not loue a woman, which is comely in fauour and beautie?19And letting
all thoſe things goe, doe they not gape, and euen with open mouth fixe
their eyes faſt on her; and haue not all men more deſire vnto her, then
vnto ſiluer or gold, or any goodly thing whatſoeuer?20A man leaueth his
owne father that brought him vp, and his owne countrie, and cleaueth
vnto his wife.21He ſtickes not to ſpend his life with his wife, and
remembreth neither father, nor mother, nor countrey.22By this alſo you
muſt know, that women haue dominion ouer you: doe yee not labour
and toyle, and giue and bring all to the woman?23Yea a man taketh his
ſword, and goeth his way to rob, and to ſteale, to ſaile vpon the ſea, and
vpon riuers,24And looketh vpon a lyon, and goeth in the darkneſſe, and
when he hath ſtolen, ſpoiled and robbed, he bringeth it to his
loue.25Wherefore a man loueth his wife better then father and
mother.26Yea many there be that haue run out of their wits for women,
and become ſeruants for their ſakes:27Many alſo haue periſhed, haue
erred, and ſinned for women.28And now doe yee not belieue me? is not
the King great in his power? doe not all regions feare to touch him?29Yet
did I ſee him and Apame the Kings concubine, the daughter of the
admirable Bartacus, ſitting at the right hand of the King,30And taking
the crowne from the Kings head, and ſetting it vpon her owne head; ſhe
alſo ſtrooke the King with her left hand.31And yet for all this, the King
gaped and gazed vpon her with open mouth: if ſhe laughed vpon him,
hee laughed alſo: but if ſhe tooke any diſpleaſure at him, the King was
faine to flatter, that ſhe might be reconciled to him againe.32O ye men,
how can it be but women ſhould be ſtrong, ſeeing they doe thus?33Then
the king & the princes looked one vpon another: ſo he began to ſpeake
of the trueth.34O ye men, are not women ſtrong? great is the earth, high
is the heauen, ſwift is the Sunne in his courſe, for he compaſſeth the
heauens round about, and fetcheth his courſe againe to his owne place
in one day.35Is he not great that maketh theſe things? therefore great is
the truth, and ſtronger then all things.36All the earth calleth vpon the
truth, & the heauen bleſſeth it, all works ſhake and tremble at it, and
with it is no vnrighteous thing.37Wine is wicked, the king is wicked,
women are wicked, all the children of men are wicked, and ſuch are all
their wicked workes, and there is no trueth in them. In their
vnrighteouſnes alſo they ſhall periſh.38As for the trueth it endureth, and
is alwayes ſtrong, it liueth and conquereth for euermore.39With her there
is no accepting of perſons, or rewards, but ſhe doeth the things that are
iuſt, and refraineth from all vniuſt and wicked things, and all men doe
well like of her workes.40Neither in her iudgement is any
vnrighteouſneſſe, & ſhe is the ſtrength, kingdome, power and maieſtie
of all ages. Bleſſed be the God of trueth.41And with that he held his
peace, and al the people then ſhouted and ſaid, Great is trueth, and
mightie aboue all things.42Then ſaide the king vnto him, Aſke what thou
wilt, more then is appointed in the writing, and we wil giue it thee,
becauſe thou art found wiſeſt, and thou ſhalt ſit next me, and ſhalt bee
called my couſin.43Then ſaid hee vnto the king, Remember thy vow
which thou haſt vowed to build Ieruſalem in the day when thou cameſt
to the kingdome,44And to ſend away all the veſſels that were taken away
out of Ieruſalem, which Cyrus ſet apart, when hee vowed to deſtroy
Babylon, and to ſend them againe thither.45Thou alſo haſt vowed to
build vp the Temple, which the Edomites burnt when Iudea was made
deſolate by the Chaldees.46And now, O lord the king, this is that which
I require, and which I deſire of thee, and this is the princely liberalitie
proceeding from thy ſelfe: I deſire therefore that thou make good the
vow, the performance wherof with thine owne mouth thou haſt vowed
to the king of heauen.47Then Darius the king ſtood vp and kiſſed him,
and wrote letters for him vnto all the treaſurers and lieutenants, and
captaines and gouernours that they ſhould ſafely conuey on their way,
both him, and all thoſe that go vp with him to build Ieruſalem.48Hee
wrote letters alſo vnto the lieutenants that were in Coeloſyria and
Phenice, and vnto them in Libanus, that they ſhould bring Cedar wood
from Libanus vnto Ieruſalem, and that they ſhould build the city with
him49Moreouer he wrote for all the Iewes that went out of his realme
vp into Iurie, concerning their freedome, that no officer, no ruler, no
lieutenant, nor treaſurer, ſhould forcibly enter into their dores,50And
that all the countrey which they hold, ſhould be free without tribute, &
that the Edomites ſhould giue ouer the villages of the Iewes which then
they held,51Yea that there ſhould be yereely giuen twentie talents to

þͤ building of the Temple, vntill ye time that it were built,52And other tenne talents yeerely, to maintaine the burnt offerings vpon the Altar euery day (as they had a commandement to offer ſeuenteene)53And that all they that went from Babylon to build the citie, ſhould haue free liberty as well they as their poſteritie, and all the prieſts that went away.54He wrote alſo concerning the charges, and the prieſts veſtments wherein they miniſter:55And likewiſe for the charges of the Leuites, to be giuen them, vntill the day that the houſe were finiſhed, and Ieruſalem builded vp.56And he commanded to giue to all that kept the city, penſions and wages.57He ſent away alſo all the veſſels frō Babylon that Cyrus had ſet apart, and all that Cyrus had giuen in commandement, the ſame charged hee alſo to be done, and ſent vnto Ieruſalem.58Now when this yong man was gone forth, he lifted vp his face to heauen toward Ieruſalem, and praiſed the king of heauen,59And ſaid, From thee commeth victory, from thee commeth wiſedom, and thine is the glory, & I am thy ſeruant.60Bleſſed art thou who haſt giuen me wiſedom: for to thee I giue thanks, O Lord of our fathers.61And ſo he tooke the letters, and went out, and came vnto Babylon, and told it all his brethren.62And they praiſed the God of their fathers: becauſe he had giuen them freedome and libertie63To goe vp, and to build Ieruſalem, and the Temple which is called by his Name, and they feaſted with inſtruments of muſick, & gladnes ſeuen dayes.

CHAPTER 5 1After this were the principall men of the families choſen according to their tribes, to go vp with their wiues, and ſonnes, and daughters, with their men-ſeruants and maid-ſeruants, and their cattel.2And Darius ſent with them a thouſand horſmen, til they had brought them backe to Ieruſalem ſafely, and with muſicall *inſtruments,* tabrets and flutes:3And all their brethren played, and hee made them goe vp together with them.4And theſe are the names of the men which went vp, according to their families, amongſt their tribes, after their ſeuerall heads.5The Prieſtes the ſonnes of Phinees, the ſonne of Aaron: Ieſus the ſonne of Ioſedec, the ſonne of Saraias, and Ioachim the ſonne of Zorobabel, the ſonne of Salathiel of the houſe of Dauid, out of the kindred of Phares, of the tribe of Iuda;6Who ſpake wiſe ſentences before Darius the king of Perſia, in the ſecond yeere of his reigne, in the moneth Niſan, which is the firſt moneth.7And theſe are they of Iewrie that came vp from the captiuitie, where they dwelt as ſtrangers, whom Nabuchodonoſor the king of Babylon had carried away vnto Babylon:8And they returned vnto Ieruſalem, and to the other parts of Iurie euery man to his owne city, who came with Zorobabel, with Ieſus, Nehemias, and Zacharias, and Reeſaias, Enenius, Mardocheus, Beelſarus, Aſpharaſus, Reelius, Roimus, and Baana their guides.9The number of them of the nation, and their gouernours: ſonnes of Phoros two thouſand an hundred ſeuentie and two: the ſonnes of Saphat foure hundred ſeuentie and two;10The ſonnes of Ares ſeuen hundred fiftie and ſixe:11The ſonnes of Phaath Moab, two thouſand eight hundred & twelue:12The ſonnes of Elam, a thouſand two hundred fifty and foure: the ſonnes of Zathui, nine hundred fourtie and fiue: the ſonnes of Corbe ſeuen hundred and fiue: the ſonnes of Bani, ſixe hundred fourtie and eight:13The ſonnes of Bebai, ſixe hundred twentie and three: the ſonnes of Sadas, three thouſand two hundred twentie and two:14The ſonnes of Adonican, ſixe hundred ſixtie and ſeuen: the ſonnes of Bagoi, two thouſand ſixtie and ſixe: the ſonnes of Adin, foure hundred fiftie and foure:15The ſonnes of Aterezias, ninetie and two: the ſonnes of Ceilan and Azetas, threeſcore and ſeuen: the ſonnes of Azuran, foure hundred thirtie & two.16The ſonnes of Ananias, an hundred and one: the ſonnes of Arom thirtie two, and the ſonnes of Baſſa, three hundred twentie and three: the ſonnes of Azephurith, an hundred and two:17The ſonnes of Meterus, three thouſand and fiue: the ſonnes of Bethlomon, an hundred twentie and three.18They of Netophah fiftie and fiue: they of Anathoth, an hundred fiftie and eight: they of Bethſamos, fourtie and two:19They of Kiriathiarius, twentie and fiue: they of Caphira and Beroth, ſeuen hundred fourtie and three: they of Pyra, ſeuen hundred:20They of Chadias and Ammidioi, foure hundred twenty and two: they of Cyrama, and Gabdes, ſixe hundred twentie and one:21They of Macalon, an hundred twentie and two: they of Betolius fiftie and two: the ſonnes of Nephis, an hundred fiftie and ſixe.22The ſonnes of Calamolalus, and Onus, ſeuen hundred twentie and fiue: the ſonnes of Ierechus, two hundred fourtie and fiue:23The ſonnes of Annaas, three thouſand three hundred and thirtie:24The Prieſts, the ſonnes of Ieddu, the ſonne of Ieſus, among the ſonnes of Sanaſib, nine hundred ſeuentie and two: the ſonnes of Meruth, a thouſand fiftie and two:25The ſonnes of Phaſſaron, a thouſand fourtie and ſeuen: the ſonnes of Carme a thouſand and ſeuenteene.26The Leuites: the ſonnes of Ieſsue, and Cadmiel, and Banuas, and Sudias, ſeuentie and foure.27The holy ſingers: the ſonnes of Aſaph an hundred twentie and eight.28The porters: the ſonnes of Salum, the ſonnes of Iatal, the ſonnes of Talmon, the ſonnes of Dacobi, the ſonnes of Teta, the ſonnes of Sami, in all an hundred thirty and nine.29The ſeruants of the Temple: the ſonnes of Eſau, the ſonnes of Aſipha, the ſonnes of Tabaoth, the ſonnes of Ceras: the ſonnes of Sud, the ſonnes of Phaleas, the ſonnes of Labana, the ſonnes of Graba:30The ſonnes of Acua, the ſonnes of Uta, the ſonnes of Cetab, the ſons of Agaba, the ſonnes of Subai, the ſonnes of Anan, the ſonnes of Cathua, the ſonnes of Geddur:31The ſonnes of Airus, the ſonnes of Daiſan, the ſonnes of Noeba, the ſonnes of Chaſeba, the ſonnes of Gazera, the ſonnes of Azia, the ſonnes of Phinees, the ſonnes of Azara, the ſonnes of Baſtai, the ſonnes of Aſana the ſonnes of Meani, the ſonnes of Naphiſi, the ſonnes of Acub, the ſons of Aſipha, the ſonnes of Aſsur, the ſonnes of Pharacim, the ſons of Baſaloth.32The ſonnes of Meeda: the ſons of Coutha, the ſonnes of Charea, the ſonnes of Chareus, the ſonnes of Aſerer, the ſonnes of Thomoi, the ſonnes of Naſith, the ſons of Atipha.33The ſons of the ſeruants of Solomon: the ſonnes of Azaphion, the ſonnes of Pharira, the ſonnes of Ioeli, the ſonnes of Lozon, the ſonnes of Iſdael, the ſonnes of Sapheth:34The ſonnes of Hagia, the ſons of Phacareth, the ſonnes of Sabie, the ſonnes of Sarothie, the ſonnes of Maſias, the ſonnes of Gar, the ſons of Addus, the ſonnes of Suba, the ſonnes of Apherra, the ſonnes of Barodis, the ſonnes of Sabat, the ſonnes of Allom.35All the miniſters of the Temple, and the ſonnes of the ſeruants of Solomon, were three hundred ſeuenty & two.36Theſe came vp from Thermeleth, and Thelerſas, Charaathalar leading them and Aalar.37Neither could they ſhewe their families, nor their ſtock, how they were of Iſrael: the ſonnes of Ladan, the ſonnes of Ban, the ſonnes of Necodan, ſixe hundred fiftie and two.38And of the Prieſts that vſurped the office of the Prieſthood, and were not found, the ſonnes of Obdia: the ſonnes of Accoz, the ſonnes of Addus, who married Augia one of the daughters of Berzelus, and was named after his name.39And when the deſcription of the kinred of theſe men was ſought in the Regiſter, and was not found, they were remooued from executing the office of the Prieſthood.40For vnto them ſaid Nehemias, and Atharias, that they ſhould not be partakers of the holy things, till there aroſe vp an high Prieſt, clothed with Doctrine and Trueth.41So of Iſrael from them of twelue yeeres olde and vpward, they were all in number fourtie thouſand, beſides men ſeruants and women ſeruants, two thouſand three hundred and ſixtie.42Their men ſeruants and handmaids were ſeuen thouſand three hundred fourtie and ſeuen: the ſinging men and ſinging women, two hundred fortie and fiue.43Foure hundred thirtie and fiue camels, ſeuen thouſand thirtie and ſixe horſes, two hundred fourtie and fiue mules, fiue thouſand fiue hundred twentie & fiue beaſts vſed to the yoke.44And certaine of the chiefe of their families, when they came to the Temple of God that is in Ieruſalem, vowed to ſet vp the houſe againe in his owne place according to their abilitie:45And to giue into the holy treaſurie of the workes, a thouſand pounds of golde, fiue thouſand of ſiluer, and an hundred prieſtly veſtments.46And ſo dwelt the Prieſts, and the Leuites, and the people in Ieruſalem, and in the countrey: the Singers alſo, and the Porters, and all Iſrael in their villages.47But when the ſeuenth moneth was at hand, and when the children of Iſrael were euery man in his owne place, they came all together with one conſent into the open place of the firſt gate, which is towards the Eaſt.48Then ſtood vp Ieſus the ſonne of Ioſedec, and his brethren the Prieſts, and Zorobabel the ſonne of Salathiel, and his brethren, and made ready the Altar of the God of Iſrael,49To offer burnt ſacrifices vpon it, according as it is expreſly commanded in the booke of Moſes the man of God.50And there were gathered vnto them out of the other nations of the land, and they erected the Altar vpon his owne place, becauſe all the nations of the land were at enmitie with them, and oppreſſed them, and they offered ſacrifices according to the time, and burnt offerings to the Lord both morning, and euening.51Alſo they held the feaſt of Tabernacles, as it is commanded in the law, and offered ſacrifices daily as was meet:52And after, that the continuall oblations,

and the ſacrifice of the Sabbaths, and of the new Moones, and of all holy
feaſts.53And all they that had made any vow to God, beganne to offer
ſacrifices to God from the firſt day of the ſeuenth moneth, although the
Temple of the Lord was not yet built.54And they gaue vnto the Maſons
and Carpenters, money, meate and drinke with cheerefulneſse.55Unto
them of Sidon alſo and Tyre, they gaue carres that they ſhould bring
Cedar trees from Libanus, which ſhould bee brought by flotes to the
hauen of Ioppe, according as it was commanded them by Cyrus King
of the Perſians.56And in the ſecond yeere and ſecond moneth, after his
comming to the Temple of God at Ieruſalem, beganne Zorobabel the
ſonne of Salathiel, and Ieſus the ſonne of Ioſedec, and their brethren
and the prieſts, and the Leuites, and all they that were come vnto
Ieruſalem out of the captiuity:57And they layd the foundation of the
houſe of God, in the firſt day of the ſecond moneth, in the ſecond yeere
after they were come to Iury & Ieruſalem.58And they appointed the
Lenites from twenty yeeres old, ouer the workes of the Lord. Then ſtood
vp Ieſus and his ſonnes, and brethren, and Cadmiel his brother, & the
ſonnes of Madiabun, with the ſonnes of Ioda the ſonne of Eliadun, with
their ſonnes and brethren, all Leuites, with one accord ſeters forward of
the buſineſse, labouring to aduance the workes in the houſe of God. So
the workmen built the temple of the Lord.59And the Prieſts ſtood
arayed in their veſtiments with muſicall inſtruments, and trumpets, and
the Leuites the ſonnes of Aſaph had Cymbals,60Singing ſongs of
thankſgiuing, and praiſing the Lord according as Dauid the king of Iſrael
had ordained.61And they ſung with loud voices ſongs to the praiſe of
the Lord: becauſe his mercy and glory is for euer in all Iſrael.62And all
the people ſounded trumpets, and ſhouted with a loud voyce, ſinging
ſongs of thankeſgiuing vnto the Lord for the rearing vp of the houſe of
the Lord.63Alſo of the Prieſts and Leuites, and of the chiefe of their
families the ancients who had ſeene the former houſe, came to the
building of this with weeping and great crying.64But many with trumpets
and ioy ſhouted with loud voyce.65Inſomuch that the trumpets might
not be heard for the weeping of the people: yet the multitude ſounded
marueilouſly, ſo that it was heard a farre off.66Wherefore when the
enemies of the Tribe of Iuda and Beniamin heard it, they came to know
what that noiſe of trumpets ſhould meane.67And they perceiued, that
they that were of the captiuity did build the temple vnto the Lord God
of Iſrael.68So they went to Zorobabel and Ieſus, and to the chiefe of the
families, and ſaid vnto them, We will build together with you.69For we
likewiſe, as you, doe obey your Lord, and doe ſacrifice vnto him from
the dayes of Aſbazareth the king of the Aſſyrians who brought vs
hither70Then Zorobabel and Ieſus, and the chiefe of the families of
Iſrael ſaid vnto them, It is not for vs and you to build together an houſe
vnto the Lord our God.71We our ſelues alone will build vnto the Lord
of Iſrael, according as Cyrus the King of the Perſians hath commanded
vs.72But the heathen of the land lying heauy vpon the inhabitants of
Iudea, and holding them ſtraite, hindred their building:73And by their
ſecret plots, and popular perſwaſions, and commotions, they hindred
the finiſhing of the building, all the time that king Cyrus liued, ſo they
were hindered from building for the ſpace of two yeeres, vntill the reigne
of Darius.
CHAPTER 6 1Now in the ſecond yeere of the reigne of Darius, Aggeus,
and Zacharias the ſonne of Addo, the prophets propheſied vnto the
Iewes, in Iurie and Ieruſalem in the Name of the Lord God of Iſrael
which was vpon them.2Then ſtood vp Zorobabel the ſonne of Salathiel,
and Ieſus the ſon of Ioſedec, and beganne to build the houſe of the Lord
at Ieruſalem, the prophets of the Lord being with them,and helping
them.3At the ſame time came vnto them Siſinnes the gouernor of Syria,
and Phenice, with Sathrabuzanes, and his companions, and ſaid vnto
them,4By whoſe appointment doe you build this houſe, and this roofe,
and performe all the other things? and who are the workemen that
performe theſe things?5Neuertheleſſe the Elders of the Iewes obtained
fauour: becauſe the Lord had viſited the captiuitie.6And they were not
hindred from building vntil ſuch time as ſignification was giuen vnto
Darius concerning them, and an anſwere receiued.7The copie of the
letters which Siſinnes goucrnour of Syria, and Phenice, and
Sathrabuzanes with their companions rulers in Syria and Phenice, wrote
and ſent vnto Darius, To king Darius, greeting.8Let all things bee
knowen vnto our lord the King, that being come into the countrey of
Iudea, and entred into the citie of Ieruſalem, we found in the citie of
Ieruſalem the ancients of the Iewes that were of the captiuitie;9Building
an houſe vnto the Lord, great, and newe, of hewen and coſtly ſtones,
and the timber already laid vpon the walles.10And thoſe workes are done
with great ſpeede, and the worke goeth on proſperouſly in their handes,
and with all glory and diligence is it made.11Then aſked wee theſe Elders,
ſaying, By whoſe commaundement builde you this houſe, and lay the
foundations of theſe workes?12Therefore to the intent that wee might
giue knowledge vnto thee by writing, we demanded of them who were
the chiefe doers, and we required of them the names in writing of their
principall men.13So they gaue vs this anſwere: We are the ſeruants of the
Lord which made heauen and earth.14And as for this houſe, it was
builded many yeeres agoe, by a king of Iſrael great and ſtrong, and was
finiſhed.15But when our fathers prouoked God vnto wrath, and ſinned
againſt the Lord of Iſrael which is in heauen, hee gaue them ouer into
the power of Nabuchodonoſor king of Babylon of the Chaldees:16Who
pulled downe the houſe and burnt it, and caried away the people
captiues vnto Babylon.17But in the firſt yeere that King Cyrus reigned
ouer the country of Babylon, Cyrus the king wrote to build vp this
houſe.18And the holy veſſels of gold and of ſiluer, that Nabuchodonoſor
had caried away out of the houſe at Ieruſalem, and had ſet them in his
owne temple, thoſe Cyrus the king brought forth againe out of the
temple at Babylon, and they were deliuered to Zorobabel and to
Sanabaſsarus the ruler,19With commaundement that hee ſhould carrie
away the ſame veſſels, and put them in the Temple at Ieruſalem, and
that the Temple of þe Lord ſhould be built in his place.20Then the ſame
Sanabaſsarus being come hither, laid the foundations of the houſe of
the Lord at Ieruſalem, and from that time to this, being ſtill a building,
it is not yet fully ended.21Now therefore if it ſeeme good vnto the king,
let ſearch be made among the records of King Cyrus,22And if it be
found, that the building of the houſe of the Lord at Ieruſalem hath bene
done with the conſent of King Cyrus, and if our lord the king be ſo
minded, let him ſignifie vnto vs thereof.23Then commanded king Darius
to ſeeke among the records at Babylon: and ſo at Ecbatana the palace
which is in the countrey of Media, there was found a roule wherein theſe
things were recorded.24In the firſt yeere of the reigne of Cyrus, king
Cyrus commaunded that the houſe of the Lord at Ieruſalem ſhould bee
built againe where they doe ſacrifice with continuall fire.25Whoſe height
ſhalbe ſixtie cubits, and the breadth ſixtie cubits, with three rowes of
hewen ſtones, and one row of new wood of that countrey, and the
expenſes thereof to bee giuen out of the houſe of king Cyrus.26And that
the holy veſſels of the houſe of the Lord, both of gold and ſiluer that
Nabuchodonoſor tooke out of the houſe at Ieruſalem, and brought to
Babylon, ſhould be reſtored to the houſe at Ieruſalem, and bee ſet in the
place where they were before.27And alſo he commanded that Siſinnes
the gouernour of Syria and Phenice, and Sathrabuzanes, and their
companions, and thoſe which were appointed rulers in Syria, and
Phenice ſhould be carefull not to meddle with the place, but ſuffer
Zorobabel the ſeruant of the Lord, and gouernour of Iudea, and the
Elders of the Iewes, to build the houſe of the Lord in that place.28I haue
commanded alſo to haue it built vp whole againe, and that they looke
diligently to helpe thoſe that be of the captiuitie of the Iewes, till the
houſe of the Lord be finiſhed.29And out of the tribute of Coeloſyria,
and Phenice, a portion carefully to be giuen theſe men, for the ſacrifices
of the Lord that is, to Zorobabel the gouernour, for bullocks, and
rammes, and lambes;30And alſo corne, ſalt, wine and oile, and that
continually euery yeere without further queſtion, according as the Prieſts
that be in Ieruſalem ſhall ſignifie, to be daily ſpent:31That offrings may
be made to the moſt high God, for the king and for his children, and
that they may pray for their liues.32And he commanded, that whoſoeuer
ſhould tranſgreſse, yea, or make light of any thing afore ſpoken or
written, out of his owne houſe ſhould a tree be taken, and he thereon
be hanged, and all his goods ſeized for the king.33The Lord therfore
whoſe Name is there called vpon, vtterly deſtroy euery king and nation,
that ſtretcheth out his hand to hinder or endammage that houſe of the
Lord in Ieruſalem.34I Darius the king haue ordeined, that according
vnto theſe things it be done with diligence.
CHAPTER 7 1Then Siſinnes the gouernour of Coeloſyria, and Phenice,
and Sathrabuzanes, with their companions, following the
commandements of king Darius,2Did very carefully ouerſee the holy
workes, aſsiſting the ancients of the Iewes, & gouernours of the

Temple.3And ſo the holy workes proſpered, when Aggeus, and Zacharias the Prophets prophecied.4And they finiſhed theſe things, by the commandement of the Lord God of Iſrael, and with the conſent of Cyrus, Darius, and Artaxerxes, kings of Perſia.5And thus was the holy houſe finiſhed, in the three and twentieth day of the moneth Adar, in the ſixt yeere of Darius king of the Perſians.6And the children of Iſrael: the Prieſts, and the Leuites, and other that were of the captiuitie, that were added vnto them, did according to the things written in the booke of Moſes.7And to the dedication of the Temple of the Lord, they offered an hundred bullockes, two hundred rammes, foure hundred lambes;8And twelue goats for the ſinne of all Iſrael, according to the number of the chiefe of the tribes of Iſrael.9The Prieſts alſo and the Leuites, ſtood arayed in their veſtments according to their kinreds, in the ſeruices of the Lord God of Iſrael, according to the booke of Moſes: and the porters at euery gate.10And the children of Iſrael that were of the captiuitie, held the Paſſeouer the fourteenth day of the firſt moueth, after that the Prieſts and the Leuites were ſanctified.11They that were of the captiuitie were not all ſanctified together: but the Leuites were all ſanctified together,12And ſo they offered the Paſſeouer for all them of the captiuitie, and for their brethren the Prieſtes, and for themſelues.13And the children of Iſrael that came out of the captiuitie, did eate, euen all they that had ſeparated themſelues from the abominations of the people of the land, and ſought the Lord.14And they kept the feaſt of vnleauened bread ſeuen dayes, making mercy before the Lord,15For that he had turned the counſell of the King of Aſſyria towards them to ſtrengthen their hands in the workes of the Lord God of Iſrael.

CHAPTER 81And after theſe things, when Artaxerxes the king of the Perſians reigned, came Eſdras the ſonne of Saraias, the ſonne of Ezerias, the ſonne of Helchiah, the ſonne of Salum,2The ſonne of Sadduc, the ſonne of Achitob, the ſonne of Amarias, the ſonne of Ozias, the ſonne of Memeroth, the ſonne of Zaraias, the ſonne of Sauias, the ſonne of Boccas, the ſonne of Abiſum, the ſonne of Phinees, the ſonne of Eleaſar, the ſonne of Aaron the chiefe Prieſt.3This Eſdras went vp from Babylon, as a Scribe being very ready in the Law of Moyſes, that was giuen by the God of Iſrael,4And the king did him honour: for he found grace in his ſight in all his requeſts.5There went vp with him alſo certaine of the children of Iſrael, of the Prieſts, of the Leuites, of the holy Singers, Porters, and Miniſters of the Temple, vnto Ieruſalem,6In the ſeuenth yere of the reigne of king Artaxerxes, in the fifth moneth, (this was the kings ſeuenth yeere) for they went from Babylon in the firſt day of the firſt moneth, and came to Ieruſalem, according to the proſperous iourney which the Lord gaue them.7For Eſdras had very great ſkill, ſo that he omitted nothing of the Law and Commaundements of the Lord, but taught all Iſrael the Ordinances and Iudgements.8Now the copy of the Commiſsion which was written from Artaxerxes the King, and came to Eſdras the prieſt and reader of the Law of the Lord, is this that followeth.9King Artaxerxes vnto Eſdras the Prieſt and reader of the Law of the Lord, ſendeth greeting.10Hauing determined to deale graciouſly, I haue giuen order, that ſuch of the nation of the Iewes, and of the Prieſts and Leuites being within our Realme, as are willing and deſirous, ſhould goe with thee vnto Ieruſalem.11As many therefore as haue a minde thereunto, let them depart with thee, as it hath ſeemed good both to me, & my ſeuen friends the counſellors,12That they may looke vnto the affaires of Iudea and Ieruſalem, agreeably to that which is in the Law of the Lord.13And cary the gifts vnto the Lord of Iſrael to Ieruſalem, which I and my friends haue vowed, and all the golde and ſiluer that in the countrey of Babylon can be found, to the Lord in Ieruſalem,14With that alſo which is giuen of the people, for the Temple of the Lord their God at Ieruſalem: and that ſiluer and golde may be collected for bullocks, rammes and lambes, and things thereunto appertaining,15To the end that they may offer ſacrifices vnto the Lord, vpon the Altar of the Lord their God, which is in Ieruſalem.16And whatſoeuer thou and thy brethren will doe with the ſiluer and golde, that doe according to the will of thy God.17And the holy veſſels of the Lord which are giuen thee, for the vſe of the Temple of thy God which is in Ieruſalem, thou ſhalt ſet before thy God in Ieruſalem.18And whatſoeuer thing elſe thou ſhalt remember for the vſe of the Temple of thy God, thou ſhalt giue it out of the kings treaſury.19And I, king Artaxerxes, haue alſo commaunded the keepers of the treaſures in Syria and Phenice, that whatſoeuer Eſdras the prieſt, and the reader of the law of the moſt high God ſhall ſend for, they ſhould giue it him with ſpeed,20To the ſumme of an hundred talents of ſiluer: likewiſe alſo of wheat euen to an hundred cores, and an hundred pieces of wine, and other things in abundance.21Let all things be performed after the law of God diligently vnto the moſt high God, that wrath come not vpon the kingdome of the King and his ſonnes.22I command you alſo that yee require no taxe, nor any other impoſition of any of the Prieſts or Leuites, or holy ſingers, or porters, or miniſters of the temple, or of any that haue doings in this temple, and that no man haue authority to impoſe any thing vpon them.23And thou, Eſdras, according to the wiſedome of God, ordaine iudges, and iuſtices, that they may iudge in all Syria and Phenice, all thoſe that know the law of thy God, and thoſe that know it not thou ſhalt teach.24And whoſoeuer ſhal tranſgreſse the law of thy God, and of the king, ſhall be puniſhed diligently, whether it be by death or other puniſhment, by penalty of money, or by impriſonment.25Then ſaid Eſdras the Scribe, Bleſſed be the onely Lord God of my fathers, who hath put theſe things into the heart of the king, to glorifie his houſe that is in Ieruſalem;26And hath honoured mee in the ſight of the king and his counſellers, and all his friends and Nobles.27Therefore was I encouraged, by the helpe of the Lord my God, and gathered together men of Iſrael to goe vp with me:28And theſe are the chiefe according to their families and ſeuerall dignities, that went vp with me from Babylon in the reigne of king Artaxerxes.29Of the ſonnes of Phinees, Gerſon: of the ſonnes of Ithamar, Gamael: of the ſonnes of Dauid; Lettus the ſonne of Sechenias:30Of the ſonnes of Pharez, Zacharias, and with him were counted, an hundred and fifty men:31Of the ſonnes of Pahath, Moab; Eliaonias, the ſonne of Zaraias, and with him two hundred men:32Of the ſonnes of Zathoe, Sechenias, the ſonne of Iezelus, and with him three hundred men, Of the ſonnes of Adin, Obeth the ſonne of Ionathan, and with him two hundred and fifty men.33Of the ſonnes of Elam, Ioſias ſonne of Gotholias, and with him ſeuenty men:34Of the ſonnes of Saphatias, Zaraias ſonne of Michael, and with him threeſcore and ten men:35Of the ſonnes of Ioab, Abadias ſonne of Iezelus, and with him two hundred and twelue men:36Of the ſonnes of Banid, Aſsalimoth ſonne of Ioſaphias, and with him an hundred and threeſcore men:37Of the ſonnes of Babi, Zacharias ſonne of Bebai, and with him twentie and eight men:38Of the ſonnes of Aſtath, Iohanneſſonne of Acatan, and with him an hundred and ten men:39Of the ſonnes of Adonicam the laſt, and theſe are the names of them, Eliphalet, Ieuel, and Samaias and with them ſeuenty men:40Of the ſonnes of Bago, Uthi, the ſonne of Iſtalcurus, and with him ſeuenty men:41And theſe I gathered together to the riuer, called Theras, where we pitched our tents three dayes, and then I ſuruayed them.42But when I had found there, none of the prieſts and Leuites,43Then ſent I vnto Eleazar and Iduel, and Maſman,44And Alnathan, and Mamaias, and Ioribas, and Nathan, Eunatan, Zacharias, and Moſollamon principal men and learned.45And I bad them that they ſhould goe vnto Saddeus the captaine, who was in the place of the treaſury:46And commanded them that they ſhould ſpeake vnto Daddeus, and to his brethren, and to the treaſurers in that place, to ſend vs ſuch men as might execute the Prieſts office in the houſe of the Lord.47And by the mighty hand of our Lord they brought vnto vs ſkilful men of the ſonnes of Moli, the ſonne of Leui, the ſonne of Iſrael, Aſebebia and his ſonnes and his brethren, who were eighteene.48And Aſebia, and Annuus, and Oſaias his brother of the ſonnes of Channuneus, and their ſonnes were twentie men.49And of the ſeruants of the Temple whom Dauid had ordeined, and the principall men, for the ſeruice of the Leuites (to wit) the ſeruants of the Temple, two hundred and twentie, the catalogue of whoſe names were ſhewed.50And there I vowed a faſt vnto the yong men before our Lord, to deſire of him a proſperous iourney, both for vs, and them that were with vs: for our children and for the cattell:51For I was aſhamed to aſke the king footmen, & horſemen, and conduct for ſafegard againſt our aduerſaries:52For wee had ſaid vnto the king, that the power of the Lord our God, ſhould be with them that ſeeke him, to ſupport them in all wayes.53And againe wee beſought our Lord, as touching theſe things, & found him fauourable vnto vs.54Then I ſeparated twelue of the chiefe of the prieſts, Eſebrias, & Aſsanias, and ten men of their brethren with them.55And I weighed them the golde, and the ſiluer, and the holy veſſels of the houſe of our Lord, which the king and his counſell, and the princes, and all Iſrael had giuen. 56 And when I had weighed it, I deliuered vnto them ſixe hundred and fiftie talents of ſiluer, and ſiluer veſſels of an hundred talents, and an hundred talents of gold, 57 And twentie golden veſſels, and twelue veſſels of braſſe, euen of fine braſſe, glittering like gold. 58 And I ſaid vnto them, Both you are holy vnto the Lord, and the veſſels are holy, and the golde, and the ſiluer iſa vowe vnto the Lord, the Lord of our fathers. 59 Watch ye, and keepe them till yee deliuer them to the chiefe of the prieſtes and Leuites, and to the principall men of the families of Iſrael in Ieruſalem into the chambers of the houſe of our God. 60 So the prieſts and the Leuites who had receiued the ſiluer & the golde, and the veſſels, brought them vnto Ieruſalem into the Temple of the Lord. 61 And from the riuer Theras wee departed the twelft day of the firſt moneth, and came to Ieruſalem by the mightie hand of our Lord, which was with vs: and from the beginning of our iourney, the Lord deliuered vs from euery enemy, and ſo wee came to Ieruſalem. 62 And when wee had bene there three dayes, the golde and ſiluer that was weighed, was deliuered in the houſe of our Lord on the fourth day vnto Marmoth the prieſt, the ſonne of Iri. 63 And with him was Eleazar the ſonne of Phinees, and with them were Ioſabad the ſonne of Ieſu, and Moeth the ſonne of Sabban, Leuites: all was deliuered them by number and weight. 64 And all the weight of them was written vp the ſame houre. 65 Moreouer they that were come out of the captiuitie offered ſacrifice vnto the Lord God of Iſrael, euen twelue bullocks for all Iſrael, foureſcore and ſixteene rammes, 66 Threeſcore and twelue lambes, goates for a peace offering, twelue, all of them a ſacrifice to the Lord. 67 And they deliuered the kings commandements vnto the kings ſtewards, and to the gouernours of Coeloſyria, and Phenice, and they honoured the people, and the Temple of God. 68 Now when theſe things were done, the rulers came vnto me, and ſaid: 69 The nation of Iſrael, the princes, the prieſts, and Leuites haue not put away from them the ſtrange people of the land: nor the pollutions of the Gentiles, to wit, of the Chanaanites, Hittites, Phereſites, Iebuſites, and the Moabites, Egyptians, and Edomites. 70 For both they, and their ſonnes, haue maried with their daughters, and the holy ſeed is mixed with the ſtrange people of the land, and from the beginning of this matter, the rulers and the great men haue bene partakers of this iniquitie. 71 And aſsoone as I had heard theſe things, I rent my clothes, and the holy garment, and pulled off the haire from off my head, and beard, and ſate me downe ſad, and very heauy. 72 So all they that were then mooued at the word of the Lord God of Iſrael, aſſembled vnto me, whileſt I mourned for the iniquitie: but I ſate ſtill full of heauineſse, vntill the euening ſacrifice. 73 Then riſing vp from the faſt with my clothes and the holy garment rent, and bowing my knees, and ſtretching foorth my hands vnto the Lord: 74 I ſaid, O Lord, I am confounded, and aſhamed before thy face; 75 For our ſinnes are multiplied aboue our heads, and our ignorances haue reached vp vnto heauen. 76 For euer ſince the time of our fathers wee haue bene and are in great ſinne, euen vnto this day: 77 And for our ſinnes and our fathers, we with our brethren, and our kings, and our prieſts, were giuen vp vnto the Kings of the earth, to the ſword, and to captiuitie, and for a pray with ſhame, vnto this day. 78 And now in ſome meaſure hath mercy bene ſhewed vnto vs, from thee, O Lord, that there ſhould be left vs a roote, and a name, in the place of thy Sanctuary. 79 And to diſcouer vnto vs a light in the houſe of the Lord our God, and to giue vs foode in the time of our ſeruitude. 80 Yea, when we were in bondage, we were not forſaken of our Lord; but he made vs gracious before the Kings of Perſia, ſo that they gaue vs food; 81 Yea, and honoured the Temple of our Lord, and raiſed vp the deſolate Sion, that they haue giuen vs a ſure abiding in Iurie, and Ieruſalem. 82 And now, O Lord, what ſhall wee ſay hauing theſe things? for wee haue tranſgreſſed thy Commaundements, which thou gaueſt by the hand of thy ſeruants the Prophets, ſaying, 83 That the land which ye enter into to poſſeſſe as an heritage, is a land polluted with the pollutions of the ſtrangers of the land, and they haue filled it with their vncleanneſſe. 84 Therefore now ſhal ye not ioyne your daughters vnto their ſonnes, neither ſhall ye take their daughters vnto your ſonnes. 85 Moreouer you ſhall neuer ſeeke to haue peace with them, that yee may be ſtrong, and eate the good things of the land, and that ye may leaue the inheritance of the land vnto your children for euermore. 86 And all that is befallen, is done vnto vs for our wicked workes, and great ſinnes: for thou, O Lord, didſt make our ſinnes light: 87 And didſt giue vnto vs ſuch a roote: but we haue turned backe againe to tranſgreſse thy Law, and to mingle our ſelues with the vncleanneſſe of the nations of the land. 88 Mighteſt not thou be angry with vs to deſtroy vs, till thou hadſt left vs neither root, ſeed, nor name? 89 O Lord of Iſrael, thou art true: for we are left a root this day. 90 Behold, now are we before thee in our iniquities, for wee cannot ſtand any longer by reaſon of theſe things before thee. 91 And as Eſdras in his praier made his confeſsion, weeping, and lying flat vpon the ground before the Temple, there gathered vnto him from Ieruſalem, a very great multitude of men, and women, & children: for there was great weeping among the multitude. 92 Then Iechonias the ſonne of Ieelus, one of the ſonnes of Iſrael called out and ſaide, O Eſdras, wee haue ſinned againſt the Lord God, wee haue maried ſtrange women of the nations of the land, & now is all Iſrael aloft. 93 Let vs make an oath to the Lord, that wee will put away all our wiues, which we haue taken of the heathen, with their children, 94 Like as thou haſt decreed, and as many as doe obey the Law of the Lord. 95 Ariſe, and put in execution: for to thee doeth this matter appertaine, and wee will bee with thee: doe valiantly. 96 So Eſdras aroſe, and tooke an oath of the chiefe of the Prieſtes, and Leuites of all Iſrael, to do after theſe things, and ſo they ſware.

CHAPTER 9 1 Then Eſdras riſing from the court of the Temple, went to the chamber of Ioanan the ſonne of Eliaſib, 2 And remained there, and did eate no meate nor drinke water, mourning for the great iniquities of the multitude. 3 And there was a proclamation in all Iury and Ieruſalem, to all them that were of the captiuitie, that they ſhould be gathered together at Ieruſalem: 4 And that whoſoeuer met not there within two or three dayes according as the Elders that bare rule, appointed, their cattell ſhould be ſeized to the vſe of the Temple, and himſelfe caſt out from them that were of the captiuitie. 5 And in three dayes were all they of the tribe of Iuda and Beniamin gathered together at Ieruſalem the twentieth day of the ninth moneth. 6 And all the multitude ſate trembling in the broad court of the Temple, becauſe of the preſent foule weather. 7 So Eſdras aroſe vp, and ſaid vnto them, Ye haue tranſgreſſed the law in marrying ſtrange wiues, thereby to increaſe the ſinnes of Iſrael. 8 And now by confeſsing giue glory vnto the Lord God of our fathers, 9 And doe his will, and ſeparate your ſelues from the heathen of the land, and from the ſtrange women. 10 Then cryed the whole multitude, and ſayd with a loude voice; Like as thou haſt ſpoken, ſo will we doe. 11 But foraſmuch as the people are many, and it is foule weather, ſo that wee cannot ſtand without, and this is not a worke of a day or two, ſeeing our ſinne in theſe things is ſpread farre: 12 Therefore let the rulers of the multitude ſtay, and let all them of our habitations that haue ſtrange wiues, come at the time appointed, 13 And with them the Rulers and Iudges of euery place, till we turne away the wrath of the Lord from vs, for this matter. 14 Then Ionathan the ſonne of Azael, and Ezechias the ſonne of Theocanus, accordingly tooke this matter vpon them: and Moſollam, and Leuis, and Sabbatheus helped them. 15 And they that were of the captiutie, did according to all theſe things. 16 And Eſdras the Prieſt choſe vnto him the principal men of their families, all by name: and in the firſt day of the tenth moneth, they ſate together to examine the matter. 17 So their cauſe that helde ſtrange wiues, was brought to an ende in the firſt day of the firſt moneth. 18 And of the Prieſts that were come together, and had ſtrange wiues, there were found: 19 Of the ſonnes of Ieſus the ſonne of Ioſedec, and his brethren, Matthelas, and Eleazar, and Ioribus, and Ioadanus. 20 And they gaue their hands to put away their wiues, & to offer rammes, to make reconcilement for their errors. 21 And of the ſonnes of Emmer, Ananias, and Zabdeus, and Eanes, and Sameius, and Hierel, and Azarias. 22 And of the ſonnes of Phaiſur, Ellionas, Maſsias, Iſmael, and Nathanael, and Oridelus, and Talſas. 23 And of the Leuites: Ioſabad, and Semis, and Colius who was called Calitas, and Patheus, and Iudas, and Ionas. 24 Of the holy Singers: Eleazurus, Bacchurus. 25 Of the Porters: Sallumus, and Tolbanes. 26 Of them of Iſrael, of the ſonnes of Phoros, Hiermas, and Eddias, and Melchias, and Maelus, and Eleazar, and Aſibias, and Baanias. 27 Of the ſonnes of Ela, Matthanias, Zacharias, and Hierielus, and Hieremoth, and Aedias. 28 And of the ſonnes of Zamoth, Eliadas, Eliſimus, Othonias, Iarimoth, and Sabatus, and Sardeus. 29 Of the ſonnes of Bebai, Iohannes, and Ananias, and Ioſabad, and Amatheis. 30 Of the ſonnes of Many,

Olamus, Mamuchus, Iedeus, Iaſubus, Iaſael, and Hieremoth. 31 And of the ſonnes of Addi, Naathus, and Mooſias, Lacunus, and Naidus, and Mathanias, and Seſthel, Balunus, and Manaſſeas. 32 And of the ſonnes of Annas, Elionas, and Aſeas, and Milchias, and Sabbeus, and Simon Choſameus. 33 And of the ſonnes of Aſom, Altaneus, and Matthias, and Bannaia, Eliphalat, and Manaſſes, and Semei. 34 And of the ſonnes of Maani, Ieremias, Momdis, Omaerus, Iuel, Mabdai, and Pelias, and Anos, Carabaſion, and Enaſibus, & Mamnitanaimus, Eliaſis, Bannus, Eliali, Samis, Selenias, Nathanias: And of the ſons of Ozora, Seſis, Eſril, Azailus, Samatus, Zambis, Ioſiphus, 35 And of the ſonnes of Ethma, Mazitias, Zabadaias, Edes, Iuel, Banaias. 36 All theſe had taken ſtrange wiues, and they put them away with their children. 37 And the prieſts, and Leuites, and they that were of Iſrael dwelt in Ieruſalem, and in the countrey, in the firſt day of þe ſeuenth month: ſo the children of Iſrael were in their habitations. 38 And the whole multitude came together with one accord, into the broad place of the holy porch toward the Eaſt. 39 And they ſpake vnto Eſdras the prieſt and reader, that he would bring the law of Moſes, that was giuen of the Lord God of Iſrael. 40 So Eſdras the chiefe prieſt, brought the law vnto the whole multitude from man to woman, and to all the prieſts, to heare the law in the firſt day of the ſeuenth moneth. 41 And hee read in the broad court before the holy porch from morning vnto midday, before both men and women; and all the multitude gaue heed vnto the law. 42 And Eſdras the prieſt, and reader of the law ſtood vp, vpon a pulpit of wood which was made for that purpoſe. 43 And there ſtood vp by him Matathias, Sammus, Ananias, Azarias, Urias, Ezecias, Balaſamus, vpon the right hand. 44 And vpon his left hand ſtood Phaldaius, Miſael, Melchias, Lothaſubus and Nabarias. 45 Then tooke Eſdras the booke of the law before the multitude: for he ſate honourably in the firſt place in the ſight of them all. 46 And when hee opened the law, they ſtood all ſtreight vp. So Eſdras bleſſed the Lord God moſt high, the God of hoſtes Almighty. 47 And all the people anſwered Amen, and lifting vp their hands they fell to the ground, & worſhipped the Lord. 48 Alſo Ieſus, Anus, Sarabias, Adinus, Iacubus, Sabateus, Auteas, Maianeas, and Calitas, Azarias, and Ioazabdus, and Ananias, Biatas, the Leuites taught the law of the Lord, making them withall to vnderſtand it. 49 Then ſpake Attharates vnto Eſdras the chiefe prieſt, and reader, and to the Leuites that taught the multitude, euen to all, ſaying, 50 This day is holy vnto þe Lord; for they all wept when they heard the law. 51 Goe then and eate the fat, and drinke the ſweet, and ſend part to them that haue nothing. 52 For this day is holy vnto the Lord, and be not ſorrowfull; for the Lord will bring you to honour. 53 So the Leuites publiſhed all things to the people, ſaying: This day is holy to the Lord, be not ſorrowfull. 54 Then went they their way, euery one to eate and drinke, & make mery, and to giue part to them that had nothing, and to make great cheere, 55 Becauſe they vnderſtood the words wherein they were inſtructed, and for þe which they had bin aſſembled.

2 EſDRAS (2 ESDRAS)

CHAPTER 1 1 The ſecond booke of the Prophet Eſdras the ſonne of Saraias, the ſonne of Azarias, the ſonne of Helchias, the ſonne of Sadamias, the ſonne of Sadoc, the ſonne of Achitob, 2 The ſonne of Achias, the ſonne of Phinees, the ſonne of Heli, the ſonne of Amarias, the ſonne of Aziei, the ſonne of Marimoth, the ſonne of Arna, the ſonne of Ozias, the ſonne of Borith, the ſonne of Abiſei, the ſonne of Phinees, the ſonne of Eleazar, 3 The ſonne of Aaron, of the Tribe of Leui, which was captiue in the land of the Medes, in the reigne of Artaxerxes king of the Perſians. 4 And the word of the Lord came vnto me, ſaying, 5 Goe thy way, and ſhew my people their ſinfull deeds, and their children their wickednes which they haue done againſt me, that they may tell their childrens children, 6 Becauſe the ſinnes of their fathers are increaſed in them: for they haue forgotten me, & haue offered vnto ſtrange gods. 7 Am not I euen hee that brought them out of the land of Egypt, from the houſe of bondage? but they haue prouoked me vnto wrath, and deſpiſed my counſels. 8 Pull thou off then the haire of thy head, and caſt all euill vpon them, for they haue not beene obedient vnto my law, but it is a rebellious people. 9 How long ſhall I forbeare them vnto whō I haue done ſo much good? 10 Many kings haue I deſtroyed for their ſakes, Pharao with his ſeruants, and all his power haue I ſmitten downe. 11 All the nations haue I deſtroyed before them, & in the Eaſt I haue ſcattered the people of two prouinces, euen of Tyrus and Sidon, and haue ſlaine all their enemies. 12 Speake thou therefore vnto them ſaying, Thus ſaith the Lord, 13 I led you through the ſea, and in the beginning gaue you a large and ſafe paſsage, I gaue you Moyſes for a leader, and Aaron for a prieſt, 14 I gaue you light in a pillar of fire, and great wonders haue I done among you, yet haue you forgotten me, ſaith the Lord. 15 Thus ſaith the Almightie Lord, The quailes were as a token for you, I gaue you tents for your ſafegard, neuertheleſſe you murmured there, 16 And triumphed not in my name for the deſtruction of your enemies, but euer to this day doe ye yet murmure. 17 Where are the benefits that I haue done for you? when you were hungry and thirſtie in the wilderneſſe, did you not crie vnto me? 18 Saying, Why haſt thou brought vs into this wilderneſſe to kill vs? It had bin better for vs to haue ſerued the Egyptians, then to die in this wilderneſſe. 19 Then had I pity vpon your mournings, and gaue you Manna to eat, ſo ye did eate Angels bread. 20 When ye were thirſtie, did I not cleaue the rocke, and waters flowed out to your fill? for the heate I couered you with the leaues of the trees. 21 I diuided amongſt you a fruitfull land, I caſt out the Canaanites, the Pherezites, and the Philiſtines before you: what ſhall I yet doe more for you: ſaith the Lord? 22 Thus ſaith the Almighty Lord, when you were in the wildernes in the riuer of the Amorites, being athirſt, and blaſpheming my Name, 23 I gaue you not fire for your blaſphemies, but caſt a tree in the water, and made the riuer ſweet. 24 What ſhall I doe vnto thee, O Iacob? thou Iuda wouldeſt not obey me: I will turne me to other nations, and vnto thoſe will I giue my Name, that they may keepe my Statutes. 25 Seeing yee haue forſaken mee, I will forſake you alſo: when yee deſire me to be gracious vnto you, I ſhall haue no mercy vpon you. 26 Whenſoeuer you ſhall call vpon me, I will not heare you: for yee haue defiled your hands with blood, and your feete are ſwift to commit manſlaughter. 27 Yee haue not as it were forſaken me, but your owne ſelues, ſaith the Lord. 28 Thus ſaith the Almighty Lord, Haue I not prayed you as a father his ſonnes, as a mother her daughters, and a nurſe her young babes, 29 That yee would be my people, and I ſhoud be your God, that ye would be my children, and I ſhould be your father? 30 I gathered you together, as a henne gathereth her chickens vnder her wings: but now, what ſhall I doe vnto you? I will caſt you out from my face. 31 When you offer vnto me, I will turne my face from you: for your ſolemne feaſt dayes, your newe Moone, and your circumciſions haue I forſaken. 32 I ſent vnto you my ſeruants the Prophets, whom yee haue taken and ſlaine, and torne their bodies in pieces, whoſe blood I will require of your hands, ſaith the Lord. 33 Thus ſaith the Almighty Lord, Your houſe is deſolate, I will caſt you out, as the wind doth ſtubble. 34 And your children ſhall not bee fruitful: for they haue deſpiſed my Commandement, and done the thing that is euill before me. 35 Your houſes wil I giue to a people that ſhall come, which not hauing heard of mee, yet ſhall beleeue mee, to whom I haue ſhewed no ſignes, yet they ſhall doe that I haue commaunded them. 36 They haue ſeene no Prophets, yet they ſhall call their ſinnes to remembrance, and acknowledge them. 37 I take to witneſſe the grace of the people to come, whoſe little ones reioyce in gladneſſe: and though they haue not ſeene me with bodily eyes, yet in ſpirit they beleeue the thing that I ſay. 38 And now brother, behold what glory: and ſee the people that commeth from the Eaſt. 39 Unto whom I will giue for leaders, Abraham, Iſaac, and Iacob, Oſeas, Amos, and Micheas, Ioel, Abdias, and Ionas, 40 Nahum, and Abacuc, Sophonias, Aggeus, Zacharie, and Malachie, which is called alſo an Angel of the Lord.

CHAPTER 2 1 Thus ſaith the Lord, I brought this people out of bondage, and I gaue them my Commaundements by my ſeruants the prophets, whom they would not heare, but deſpiſed my counſailes. 2 The mother that bare them, ſaith vnto them, Goe your way ye children, for I am a widow, and forſaken. 3 I brought you vp with gladneſſe, but with ſorrow and heauineſse haue I loſt you: for yee haue ſinned before the Lord your God, and done that thing that is euil before him. 4 But what ſhall I now doe vnto you? I am a widow and forſaken: goe your way, O my children, and aſke mercy of the Lord. 5 As for mee, O father, I call vpon thee for a witneſſe ouer the mother of theſe children, which would not keepe my Couenant,6That thou bring them to confuſion, and their mother to a ſpoile, that there may be no off ſpring of them.7Let them bee ſcattered abroad among the heathen, let their names bee put out of the earth: for they haue deſpiſed my Couenant.8Woe be vnto thee Aſsur, thou that hideſt the vnrighteous in thee, O thou wicked people, remember what I did vnto Sodome and Gomorrhe.9Whoſe land lieth in clods of pitch and heapes of aſhes: euen ſo alſo wil I doe vnto them that heare me not, ſaith the Almightie Lord.10Thus ſaith the Lord vnto Eſdras, Tell my people that I will giue them the kingdome of Hieruſalem, which I would haue giuen vnto Iſrael.11Their glory alſo wil I take vnto mee, and giue theſe the euerlaſting Tabernacles, which I had prepared for them.12They ſhall haue the tree of Life for an oyntment of ſweet ſauour, they ſhall nether labour, nor be weary.13Goe and yee ſhall receiue: pray for few dayes vnto you, that they may be ſhortned: the kingdome is already prepared for you: Watch.14Take heauen and earth to witneſſe; for I haue broken the euill in pieces, and created the good; for I liue, ſaith the Lord.15Mother, embrace thy children, and bring them vp with gladneſſe, make their feet as faſt as a pillar: for I haue choſen thee, ſaith the Lord.16And thoſe that be dead wil I raiſe vp againe from their places, and bring them out of the graues: for I haue knowen my Name in Iſrael.17Feare not thou mother of the children: for I haue choſen thee, ſaith the Lord.18For thy helpe I will ſend my ſeruants Eſay and Ieremie, after whoſe counſaile I haue ſanctified and prepared for thee twelue trees, laden with diuers fruits;19And as many fountaines flowing with milke and hony: and ſeuen mightie mountaines, whereupon there grow roſes and lillies, whereby I will fill thy children with ioy.20Doe right to the widow, iudge for the fatherleſſe, giue to the poore, defend the orphane, clothe the naked,21Heale the broken and the weake, laugh not a lame man to ſcorne, defend the maimed, and let the blind man come into the ſight of my cleareneſſe.22Keepe the olde and yong within thy walles.23Whereſouer thou findeſt the dead, take them and bury them, and I will giue thee the firſt place in my reſurrection.24Abide ſtill, O my people, and take thy reſt, for thy quietneſse ſhall come.25Nouriſh thy children, O thou good nource, ſtabliſh their feete.26As for the ſeruants whom I haue giuen thee, there ſhall not one of them periſh; for I will require them from among thy number.27Be not weary, for when the day of trouble and heauineſse commeth, others ſhal weepe and be ſorrowfull, but thou ſhalt be merry, and haue abundance.28The heathen ſhall enuie thee, but they ſhall be able to doe nothing againſt thee, ſayth the Lord.29My hands ſhal couer thee, ſo that thy children ſhall not ſee hell.30Be ioyfull, O thou mother, with thy children, for I will deliuer thee, ſayth the Lord.31Remember thy children that ſleep, for I ſhall bring them out of the ſides of the earth, and ſhew mercy vnto them: for I am mercifull, ſayth the Lord Almightie.32Embrace thy children vntill I come and ſhew mercy vnto them: for my welles runne ouer, and my grace ſhall not faile.33I Eſdras receiued a charge of the Lord vpon the mount Oreb, that I ſhould goe vnto Iſrael; but when I came vnto them, they ſet me at nought, and deſpiſed the commandement of the Lord.34And therefore I ſay vnto you, O yee heathen, that heare and vnderſtand, Looke for your ſhepheard, hee ſhall giue you euerlaſting reſt; for he is nigh at hand, that ſhall come in the end of the world.35Be ready to the reward of the kingdome, for the euerlaſting light ſhal ſhine vpon you for euermore.36Flee the ſhadow of this world, receiue the ioyfulneſse of your glory: I teſtifie my Sauiour openly.37O receiue the gift that is giuen you, and be glad, giuing thankes vnto him that hath called you to the heauenly kingdome.38Ariſe vp and ſtand, behold the number of thoſe that be ſealed in the feaſt of the Lord:39Which are departed from the ſhadow of the world, and haue receiued glorious garments of the Lord.40Take thy number, O Sion, and ſhut vp thoſe of thine that are clothed in white, which haue fulfilled the Law of the Lord.41The number of thy children whom thou longedſt for, is fulfilled: beſeech the power of the Lord, that thy people which haue been called from the beginning, may be hallowed.42I Eſdras ſaw vpon the mount Sion a great people, whom I could not number, and they all praiſed the Lord with ſongs.43And in the middeſt of them there was a young man of a high ſtature, taller then all the reſt, and vpon euery one of their heads he ſet crownes, and was more exalted, which I marueiled at greatly.44So I aſked the Angel, and ſaid, Sir, what are theſe?45Hee anſwered, and ſaid vnto me, Theſe be they that haue put off the mortall clothing, and put on the immortall, and haue confeſsed the Name of God: now are they crowned, and receiue palmes.46Then ſayd I vnto the Angel, What yong perſon is it that crowneth them, and giueth them palmes in their handes?47So hee anſwered, and ſaid vnto me, It is the ſonne of God, whom they haue confeſsed in the world. Then began I greatly to commend them, that ſtood ſo ſtiffely for the Name of the Lord.48Then the Angel ſayd vnto me, Goe thy way, and tell my people what maner of things, and how great wonders of the Lord thy God thou haſt ſeene.

CHAPTER 31In the thirtieth yeere after the ruine of the citie, I was in Babylon, and lay troubled vpon my bed, and my thoughts came vp ouer my heart.2For I ſaw the deſolation of Sion, and the wealth of them that dwelt at Babylon.3And my ſpirit was ſore moued, ſo that I began to ſpeake words full of feare to the moſt High, and ſaid,4O Lord, who beareſt rule, thou ſpakeſt at the beginning, when thou didſt plant the earth (and that thy ſelfe alone) and commandedſt the people,5And gaueſt a body vnto Adam without ſoule, which was the workemanſhip of thine hands, & didſt breathe into him the breath of life, and he was made liuing before thee.6And thou leddeſt him into paradiſe, which thy right hand had planted, before euer the earth came forward.7And vnto him thou gaueſt commandement to loue thy way, which he tranſgreſſed, and immediatly thou appointedſt death in him, and in his generations, of whom came nations, tribes, people, and kinreds out of number.8And euery people walked after their owne will, and did wonderfull things before thee, and deſpiſed thy commandements.9And againe in proceſſe of time thou broughteſt the flood vpon thoſe that dwelt in the world, and deſtroyedſt them.10And it came to paſſe in euery of them, that as death was to Adam, ſo was the flood to theſe.11Neuertheleſſe one of them thou lefteſt, namely Noah with his houſehold, of whom came all righteous men.12And it happened, that when they that dwelt vpō the earth began to multiply, and had gotten them many children, and were a great people, they beganne againe to be more vngodly then the firſt.13Now when they liued ſo wickedly before thee, thou diddeſt chooſe thee a man from among them, whoſe name was Abraham.14Him thou louedſt, and vnto him onely thou ſhewedſt thy will:15And madeſt an euerlaſting couenant with him, promiſing him that thou wouldeſt neuer forſake his ſeede.16And vnto him, thou gaueſt Iſahac, and vnto Iſahac alſo thou gaueſt Iacob and Eſau. As for Iacob thou didſt chooſe him to thee, and put by Eſau: and ſo Iacob became a great multitude.17And it came to paſſe, that when thou leddeſt his ſeede out of Egypt, thou broughteſt them vp to the mount Sina.18And bowing the heauens, thou dideſt ſet faſt the earth, mouedſt the whole world, and madeſt the depth to tremble, and troubledſt the men of that age.19And thy glory went through foure gates, of fire, and of earthquake, and of wind, and of cold, that thou mighteſt giue the law vnto the ſeed of Iacob, and diligence vnto the generation of Iſrael.20And yet tookeſt thou not away from them a wicked heart, that thy law might bring forth fruite in them.21For the firſt Adam bearing a wicked heart tranſgreſſed, and was ouercome; and ſo be all they that are borne of him.22Thus infirmity was made permanent; and the law (alſo) in the heart of the people with the malignity of the roote, ſo that the good departed away, and the euill abode ſtill.23So the times paſſed away, and the yeeres were brought to an end: then diddeſt thou raiſe thee vp a ſeruant, called Dauid,24Whom thou commandedſt to build a citie vnto thy name, and to offer incenſe and oblations vnto thee therein.25When this was done many yeeres, then they that inhabited the citie forſooke thee,26And in all things did euen as Adam, and all his generations had done, for they alſo had a wicked heart.27And ſo thou gaueſt the citie ouer into the hands of thine enemies.28Are their deeds then any better that inhabite Babylon, that they ſhould therefore haue the dominion ouer Sion?29For when I came thither, and had ſeene impieties without number, then my ſoule ſaw many euill doers in this thirtieth yeere, ſo that my heart failed me.30For I haue ſeene how thou ſuffereſt them ſinning, and haſt ſpared wicked doers: and haſt deſtroyed thy people, and haſt preſerued thine enemies, and haſt not ſignified it.31I doe not remember how this way may be left: Are they then of Babylon better then they of Sion?32Or is there any other people that knoweth thee beſides Iſrael? or what generation hath ſo beleeued thy Couenants as Iacob?33And yet their reward appeareth not, and their labour hath no fruite: for I haue gone here and there through the heathen, and I ſee that they flowe in wealth, and think not vpon thy commandements.[34]Weigh thou therfore our wickedneſſe now in the ballance, and theirs alſo that dwell in the world: and ſo ſhall thy Name no where be found, but in Iſrael.[35]Or when was it that they which dwell vpon the earth, haue not ſinned in thy ſight? or what people hath ſo kept thy commandements?[36]Thou ſhalt find that Iſrael by name hath kept thy precepts: but not the heathen.

CHAPTER 4[1]And the Angel that was ſent vnto me, whoſe name was Uriel, gaue mee an anſwere,[2]And ſaid, Thy heart hath gone too farre in this world, and thinkeſt thou to comprehend the way of the moſt High?[3]Then ſaid I, Yea my Lord: and he anſwered me and ſaid, I am ſent to ſhew thee three wayes, and to ſet forth three ſimilitudes before thee.[4]Whereof if thou canſt declare me one, I will ſhew thee alſo the way that thou deſireſt to ſee, & I ſhall ſhew thee from whence the wicked heart cōmeth.[5]And I ſaid, Tel on my Lord. Then ſaid he vnto me, Goe thy way, weigh me the weight of the fire, or meaſure me the blaſt of the wind, or call me againe the day that is paſt.[6]Then anſwered I and ſaid, What man is able to doe that, that thou ſhouldeſt aſke ſuch things of mee?[7]And he ſaid vnto me, If I ſhould aſke thee how great dwellings are in the midſt of þe ſea, or how many ſprings are in the beginning of the deepe, or how many ſprings are aboue the firmament, or which are the outgoings of Paradiſe:[8]Peraduenture thou wouldeſt ſay vnto me, I neuer went downe into the deepe, nor as yet into hell, neither did I euer climbe vp into heauen.[9]Neuertheleſſe, now haue I aſked thee but onely of the fire and winde, and of the day where through thou haſt paſſed, and of things frō which thou canſt not be ſeparated, and yet canſt thou giue me uo anſweere of them.[10]He ſaid moreouer vnto me, Thine owne things, and ſuch as are growen vp with thee, canſt thou not know.[11]How ſhould thy veſsel then bee able to comprehend the way of the higheſt, and the world being now outwardly corrupted, to vnderſtand the corruption that is euident in my ſight?[12]Then ſaid I vnto him, It were better that we were not at all, then that we ſhould liue ſtill in wickedneſſe, and to ſuffer, and not to know wherefore.[13]He anſwered me and ſaid, I went into a foreſt into a plaine, and the trees tooke counſell,[14]And ſaid, Come, let vs goe and make warre againſt the ſea, that it may depart away before vs, and that we may make vs more woods.[15]The floods of the ſea alſo in like maner tooke counſell, and ſaid, Come, let vs goe vp and ſubdue the woods of the plaine, that there alſo we may make vs another countrey.[16]The thought of the wood was in vaine, for the fire came and conſumed it.[17]The thought of the floods of the ſea came likewiſe to nought, for the ſand ſtood vp and ſtopped them.[18]If thou wert iudge now betwixt theſe two, whom wouldeſt thou begin to iuſtifie, or whom wouldeſt thou condemne?[19]I anſwered and ſaid, Uerily it is a fooliſh thought that they both haue deuiſed: for the ground is giuen vnto the wood, and the ſea alſo hath his place to beare his floods.[20]Then anſwered he me and ſaid, Thou haſt giuen a right iudgment, but why iudgeſt thou not thy ſelfe alſo?[21]For like as the ground is giuen vnto the wood, & the ſea to his floods: euen ſo they that dwell vpon the earth may vnderſtand nothing, but that which is vpon the earth: and hee that dwelleth aboue the heauens, may onely vnderſtand the things that are aboue the height of the heauens.[22]Then anſwered I, and ſaid, I beſeech thee, O Lord, let me haue vnderſtanding.[23]For it was not my minde to be curious of the high things, but of ſuch as paſſe by vs dayly, namely wherefore Iſrael is giuen vp as a reproch to the heathen, and for what cauſe the people whom thou haſt loued, is giuen ouer vnto vngodly nations, and why the Lawe of our forefathers is brought to nought, and the written Couenants come to none effect.[24]And wee paſſe away out of the world as graſſehoppers, and our life is aſtoniſhment and feare, and we are not worthy to obtaine mercie.[25]What will he then doe vnto his Name, whereby we are called? of theſe things haue I aſked.[26]Then anſwered he me, and ſaid, The more thou ſearcheſt, the more thou ſhalt marueile, for the world haſteth faſt to paſſe away,[27]And cannot comprehend the things that are promiſed to the righteous in time to come: for this world is ful of vnrighteouſneſſe and infirmities.[28]But as concerning the things whereof thou aſkeſt me, I wil tell thee; for the euil is ſowen, but the deſtruction thereof is not yet come.[29]If therefore that which is ſowen, be not turned vpſide downe; and if the place where the euil is ſowen paſſe not away, then cannot it come that is ſowen with good.[30]For the graine of euill ſeed hath bene ſowen in the heart of Adam from the beginning, and how much vngodlineſse hath it brought vp vnto this time? and how much ſhall it yet bring foorth vntill the time of threſhing come.[31]Ponder now by thy ſelfe, how great fruit of wickedneſſe the graine of euil ſeed hath brought forth.[32]And when the eares ſhall bee cut downe, which are without number, how great a floore ſhall they fill?[33]Then I anſwered and ſaid, How and when ſhall theſe things come to paſſe? wherefore are our yeeres few and euill?[34]And he anſwered me, ſaying, Do not thou haſten aboue the moſt Higheſt: for thy haſte is in vaine to be aboue him, for thou haſt much exceeded.[35]Did not the ſoules alſo of the righteous aſke queſtion of theſe things in their chambers, ſaying, How long ſhall I hope on this faſhion? when commeth the fruit of the floore of our reward?[36]And vnto theſe things Uriel the Archangel gaue them anſwere, and ſaid, Euen when the number of ſeedes is filled in you: for he hath weighed the world in the ballance.[37]By meaſure hath hee meaſured the times, and by number hath he numbred the times; and he doeth not mooue nor ſtirre them, vntill the ſaid meaſure be fulfilled.[38]Then anſwered I, and ſaid, O Lord that beareſt rule, euen we all are full of impietie.[39]And for our ſakes peraduenture it is that the floores of the righteous are not filled, becauſe of the ſinnes of them that dwell vpon the earth.[40]So he anſwered me, and ſaid, Go thy way to a wman with childe, and aſke of her, when ſhe hath fulfilled her nine moneths, if her wombe may keepe the birth any longer within her?[41]Then ſaid I, No Lord, that can ſhe not. And he ſaid vnto mee, In the graue, the chambers of ſoules are like the wombe of a woman:[42]For like as a woman that trauaileth, maketh haſte to eſcape the neceſsitie of the trauaile: euen ſo doe theſe places haſte to deliuer thoſe things that are committed vnto them.[43]From the beginning looke what thou deſireſt to ſee, it ſhalbe ſhewed thee.[44]Then anſwered I, and ſaid, If I haue found fauour in thy ſight, and if it be poſsible, and if I be meet therefore,[45]ſhew me then whether there be more to come then is paſt, or more paſt then is to come.[46]What is paſt I know; but what is for to come I know not.[47]And he ſaid vnto me, ſtand vp vpon the right ſide, and I ſhal expound the ſimilitude vnto you.[48]So I ſtood and ſaw, and behold an hot burning ouen paſſed by before mee: and it happened that when the flame was gone by, I looked, and behold, the ſmoke remained ſtill.[49]After this there paſſed by before me a watrie cloude, and ſent downe much raine with a ſtorme, and when the ſtormie raine was paſt, the drops remained ſtill.[50]Then ſaid he vnto me, Conſider with thy ſelfe: as the raine is more then the drops, and as the fire is greater then the ſmoke: but the drops and the ſmoke remaine behind: ſo the quantity which is paſt, did more exceede.[51]Then I prayed, and ſayd, May I liue, thinkeſt thou, vntill that time? or what ſhall happen in thoſe dayes?[52]He anſwered me, and ſayd, As for the tokens whereof thou aſkeſt me, I may tell thee of them in part; but as touching thy life, I am not ſent to ſhew thee, for I doe not know it.

CHAPTER 5[1]Neuertheles as concerning the tokens, beholde, the dayes ſhall come that they which dwell vpon earth, ſhall bee taken in a great number, and the way of trueth ſhall be hidden, and the land ſhall be barren of faith.[2]But iniquitie ſhalbe increaſed aboue that which now thou ſeeſt, or that thou haſt heard long agoe.[3]And the land that thou ſeeſt now to haue roote, ſhalt thou ſee waſted ſuddenly.[4]But if the moſt high graunt thee to liue, thou ſhalt ſee after the third trumpet, that the Sunne ſhall ſuddenly ſhine againe in the night, and the Moone thrice in the day.[5]And blood ſhal drop out of wood, and the ſtone ſhall giue his voice, and the people ſhalbe troubled.[6]And enen he ſhal rule whom they looke not for that dwel vpon the earth, and the foules ſhall take their flight away together.[7]And the Sodomitiſh ſea ſhall caſt out fiſh, and make a noyſe in the night, which many haue not knowen: but they ſhall all heare the voice thereof.[8]There ſhall be a confuſion alſo in many places, and the fire ſhalbe oft ſent out againe, and the wilde beaſts ſhall change their places, and menſtruous women ſhall bring foorth monſters.[9]And ſalt waters ſhall be found in the ſweete, and all friends ſhall deſtroy one another: then ſhall wit hide it ſelfe, and vnderſtanding withdraw it ſelfe into his ſecret chamber,[10]And ſhall be ſought of many, and yet not be found: then ſhall vnrighteouſneſſe and incontinencie be multiplyed vpon earth.[11]One land alſo ſhall aſke another, and ſay, Is righteouſnes that maketh a man righteous, gone through thee? And it ſhall ſay, No.[12]At the ſame time ſhall men hope, but nothing obtaine: they ſhall labour, but their wayes ſhall not proſper.[13]To ſhew thee ſuch tokens I haue leaue: and if thou wilt pray againe, and weepe as now, and

faſt ſeuen dayes, thou ſhalt heare yet greater things. 14 Then I awaked, &
an extreme fearefulneſse went through all my body, and my minde was
troubled, ſo that it fainted. 15 So the Angel that was come to talke with
me, helde me, comforted me, and ſet me vp vpon my feete. 16 And in the
ſecond night it came to paſſe, that Salathiel the captaine of the people
came vnto mee, ſaying, Where haſt thou beene? and why is thy
countenance ſo heauie? 17 Knoweſt thou not that Iſrael is committed
vnto thee, in the land of their captiuitie? 18 Up then, and eate bread, and
forſake vs not as the ſhepheard that leaueth his flocke in the handes of
cruell wolues. 19 Then ſayd I vnto him, Goe thy waies from me, and come
not nigh me: And he heard what I ſaid, and went from me. 20 And ſo I
faſted ſeuen dayes, monrning and weeping, like as Uriel the Angel
commanded me. 21 And after ſeuen dayes, ſo it was that the thoughts of
my heart were very grieuous vnto me againe. 22 And my ſoule recouered
the ſpirit of vnderſtanding, and I began to talke with the moſt high
againe, 23 And ſaid, O Lord, that beareſt rule of euery wood of the earth,
and of all the trees thereof, thou haſt choſen thee one onely vine. 24 And
of all lands of the whole world thou haſt choſen thee one pit: and of all
the flowers thereof, one Lillie. 25 And of all the depths of the ſea, thou
haſt filled thee one riuer: and of all builded cities, thou haſt hallowed
Sion vnto thy ſelfe. 26 And of all the foules that are created, thou haſt
named thee one Doue: and of all the cattell that are made, thou haſt
prouided thee one ſheepe. 27 And among all the multitudes of peoples,
thou haſt gotten thee one people: and vnto this people whom thou
louedſt, thou gaueſt a law that is approued of all. 28 And now O Lord,
why haſt thou giuen this one people ouer vnto many? and vpon the one
roote haſt thou prepared others, and why haſt thou ſcattered thy onely
one people among many? 29 And they which did gaineſay thy promiſes,
and beleeued not thy couenants, haue trodden them downe. 30 If thou
didſt ſo much hate thy people, yet ſhouldeſt thou puniſh them with thine
owne hands. 31 Now when I had ſpoken theſe words, the Angell that
came to me the night afore, was ſent vnto me, 32 And ſaid vnto me, Heare
me, and I will inſtruct thee, hearken to the thing that I ſay, & I ſhal tell
thee more. 33 And I ſaid, Speake on, my Lord: then ſaid he vnto me, thou
art ſore troubled in minde for Iſraels ſake: loueſt thou that people better
then hee that made them? 34 And I ſaid, No Lord, but of very griefe haue
I ſpoken: For my reines paine me euery houre, while I labour to
comprehend the way of the moſt High, and to ſeeke out part of his
iudgement. 35 And he ſaid vnto me, Thou canſt not: and I ſaid, wherfore
Lord? wherunto was I borne then? or why was not my mothers wombe
then my graue, that I might not haue ſeene the trauell of Iacob, and the
weariſome toyle of the ſtocke of Iſrael? 36 And he ſaid vnto me, Number
me the things that are not yet come, gather me together the droppes that
are ſcattered abroad, make mee the flowres greene againe that are
withered. 37 Open me the places that are cloſed, and bring me forth the
winds that in them are ſhut vp, ſhew me the image of a voyce: and then
I will declare to thee the thing that thou laboureſt to knowe. 38 And I ſaid,
O Lord, that beareſt rule, who may know theſe things, but hee that hath
not his dwelling with men? 39 As for me, I am vnwiſe: how may I then
ſpeake of theſe things whereof thou aſkeſt me? 40 Then ſaid he vnto me,
Like as thou canſt doe none of theſe things that I haue ſpoken of, euen
ſo canſt thou not find out my iudgement, or in the end the loue that I
haue promiſed vnto my people. 41 And I ſaid, behold, O Lord, yet art
thou nigh vnto them that be reſeruedtill the end; and what ſhall they doe
that haue beene before me, or we (that be now) or they that ſhall come
after vs? 42 And he ſaid vnto me, I wil liken my iudgement vnto a ring:
like as there is no ſlackneſse of the laſt, euen ſo there is no ſwiftneſse of
the firſt. 43 So I anſwered and ſaid, Couldſt thou not make thoſe that haue
beene made, and be now, and that are for to come, at once, that thou
mighteſt ſhewe thy iudgement the ſooner? 44 Then anſwered he me, and
ſaid, The creature may not haſt aboue the maker, neither may the world
hold them at once that ſhalbe created therin. 45 And I ſaid, As thou haſt
ſaid vnto thy ſeruant, that thou which giueſt life to all, haſt giuen life at
once to the creature that thou haſt created, and the creature bare it: euen
ſo it might now alſo beare them that now be preſent at once. 46 And he
ſaid vnto me, Aſke the wombe of a woman, & ſay vnto her, If thou
bringeſt forth children, why doeſt thou it not together, but one after
another? pray her therefore to bring forth tenne children at once. 47 And
I ſaid, She cannot: but muſt doe it by diſtance of time. 48 Then ſaid he
vnto me, Euen ſo haue I giuen the wombe of the earth to thoſe that be
ſowen in it, in their times. 49 For like as a young child may not bring forth
the things that belong to the aged, euen ſo haue I diſpoſed the world
which I created. 50 And I aſked and ſaid, Seeing thou haſt now giuen me
the way, I will proceed to ſpeak before thee: for our mother of whom
thou haſt told me that ſhe is yong, draweth now nigh vnto age. 51 He
anſwered me and ſaid, Aſke a woman that beareth children, and ſhee
ſhall tell thee. 52 ſay vnto her, Wherefore are not they whome thou haſt
now brought forth, like thoſe that were before, but leſſe of
ſtature? 53 And ſhe ſhall anſwere thee, They that be borne in the ſtrength
of youth, are of one faſhion, and they that are borne in the time of age
(when the wombe faileth) are otherwiſe. 54 Conſider thou therfore alſo,
how that yee are leſſe of ſtature then thoſe that were before you. 55 And
ſo are they that come after you leſſe then ye, as the creatures which now
begin to be old, and haue paſſed ouer the ſtrength of youth. 56 Then ſaide
I, Lord, I beſeech thee, if I haue found fauor in thy ſight, ſhew thy
ſeruant by whom thou viſiteſt thy creature.
CHAPTER 6 1 And he ſaid vnto me, in the beginning when þe earth was
made, before the borders of the world ſtood, or euer the windes
blew, 2 Before it thundred and lightned, or euer the foundations of
Paradiſe were laide, 3 Before the faire flowers were ſeene, or euer the
moueable powers were eſtabliſhed, before þe innumerable multitude of
Angels were gathered together, 4 Or euer the heights of the aire were
lifted vp, before the meaſures of the firmament were named, or euer the
chimnies in Sion were hot, 5 And ere the preſent yeeres were ſought out,
and or euer the inuentions of them that now ſinne were turned, before
they were ſealed that haue gathered faith for a treaſure: 6 Then did I
conſider theſe things, and they all were made through mee alone, and
through none other: by mee alſo they ſhall be ended, & by none
other. 7 Then anſwered I and ſaid, What ſhall bee the parting aſunder of
the times? or when ſhall be the ende of the firſt, and the beginning of it
that followeth? 8 And he ſaid vnto me, From Abraham vnto Iſaac, when
Iacob and Eſau were borne of him, Iacobs hand held firſt the heele of
Eſau. 9 For Eſau is the end of the world, and Iacob is the beginning of it
that followeth. 10 The hand of man is betwixt the heele and the hand:
other queſtion, Eſdras, aſke thou not. 11 I anſwered then and ſaid, O Lord
that beareſt rule, if I haue found fauour in thy ſight, 12 I beſeech thee,
ſhew thy ſeruant the end of thy tokens, whereof thou ſhewedſt me part
the laſt night. 13 So he anſwered and ſaid vnto me, ſtand vp vpon thy
feete, and heare a mightie ſounding voyce. 14 And it ſhall be as it were a
great motion, but the place where thou ſtandeſt, ſhall not be
moued. 15 And therefore when it ſpeaketh be not afraid: for the word is
of the end, and the foundation of the earth is vnderſtood. 16 And why?
becauſe the ſpeech of theſe things trembleth and is mooued: for it
knoweth that the ende of theſe things muſt be changed. 17 And it
happened that when I had heard it, I ſtood vp vpon my feet, and
hearkened, & behold, there was a voice that ſpake, and the ſound of it
was like the ſound of many waters. 18 And it ſaid, Behold, the dayes come,
that I will begin to draw nigh, and to viſit them that dwell vpon the
earth, 19 And will begin to make inquiſition of them, what they be that
haue hurt vniuſtly with their vnrighteouſneſſe, and when the affliction
of Sion ſhalbe fulfilled. 20 And when the world that ſhal begin to vaniſh
away ſhall bee finiſhed: then will I ſhew theſe tokens, the books ſhalbe
opened before the firmament, and they ſhall ſee all together. 21 And the
children of a yeere olde ſhall ſpeake with their voyces, the women with
childe ſhall bring foorth vntimely children, of three or foure moneths
old: and they ſhall liue, and bee raiſed vp. 22 And ſuddenly ſhal the ſowen
places appeare vnſowen, the full ſtorehouſes ſhall ſuddenly be found
empty. 23 And the trumpet ſhall giue a ſound, which when euery man
heareth they ſhalbe ſuddenly afraid. 24 At that time ſhall friendes fight one
againſt another like enemies, and the earth ſhall ſtand in feare with thoſe
that dwell therein, the ſprings of the fountaines ſhall ſtand ſtill, and in
three houres they ſhall not runne. 25 Whoſoeuer remaineth from all theſe
that I haue told thee, ſhall eſcape, and ſee my ſaluation, and the ende of
your world. 26 And the men that are receiued, ſhall ſee it, who haue not
taſted death from their birth: and the heart of the inhabitants ſhalbe
changed, and turned into another meaning. 27 For euil ſhalbe put out, and
deceit ſhalbe quenched. 28 As for faith, it ſhall flouriſh, corruption ſhalbe
ouercome, & the trueth which hath bene ſo long without fruit, ſhalbe

declared.29And when hee talked with mee, behold, I looked by little and
little vpon him before whom I ſtood.30And theſe words ſaid he vnto
me, I am come to ſhew thee the time of the night to come.31If thou wilt
pray yet more, & faſt ſeuen daies againe, I ſhal tel thee greater things by
day, then I haue heard.32For thy voice is heard before the moſt High:
for the mighty hath ſeene thy righteous dealing, he hath ſeene alſo thy
chaſtitie, which thou haſt had euer ſince thy youth.33And therefore hath
he ſent mee to ſhew thee al theſe things, and to ſay vnto thee, Be of
good comfort, & feare not.34And haſten not with the times that are paſt,
to thinke vaine things, that thou mayeſt not haſten from the latter
times.35And it came to paſſe after this, that I wept againe, and faſted
ſeuen dayes in like maner, that I might fulfill the three weekes which he
told me.36And in the eight night was my heart vexed within mee againe,
and I began to ſpeake before the moſt High.37For my ſpirit was greatly
ſet on fire, and my ſoule was in diſtreſſe.38And I ſaid, O Lord, thou
ſpakeſt from the beginning of the creation, euen the firſt day, & ſaideſt
thus, Let heauen and earth bee made: and thy word was a perfect
worke.39And then was the ſpirit, and darkeneſſe, and ſilence were on
euery ſide; the ſound of mans voice was not yet formed.40Then
commandedſt thou a faire light to come foorth of thy treaſures, that thy
worke might appeare.41Upon the ſecond day thou madeſt the ſpirit of
the firmament, and commandedſt it to part aſunder, and to make a
diuiſion betwixt the waters, that the one part might goe vp, and the other
remaine beneath.42Upon the thirde day thou didſt commaund that the
waters ſhould bee gathered in the ſeuenth part of the earth: ſixe parts
haſt thou dried vp and kept them, to the intent that of theſe ſome being
planted of God and tilled, might ſerue thee.43For as ſoone as thy word
went foorth, the worke was made.44For immediatly there was great and
innumerable fruit, and many and diuers pleaſures for the taſte, & flowers
of vnchangeable colour, and odours of wonderfull ſmell: and this was
done the third day.45Upon the fourth day thou commandedſt that the
Sunne ſhould ſhine, and the Moone giue her light, and the ſtarres ſhould
be in order,46And gaueſt them a charge to do ſeruice vnto man, that was
to be made.47Upon the fift day, thou ſaydſt vnto the ſeuenth part, where
the waters were gathered, that it ſhould bring foorth liuing creatures,
foules and fiſhes: and ſo it came to paſſe.48For the dumbe water, and
without life, brought foorth liuing things at the commandement of God,
that al people might praiſe thy wondrous works.49Then didſt thou
ordeine two liuing creatures, the one thou calledſt Enoch, and the other
Leuiathan,50And didſt ſeparate the one from the other: for the ſeuenth
part (namely where the water was gathered together) might not hold
them both.51Unto Enoch thou gaueſt one part which was dried vp the
third day, that he ſhould dwel in the ſame part, wherein are a thouſand
hilles.52But vnto Leuiathan thou gaueſt the ſeuenth part, namely the
moiſt, and haſt kept him to be deuoured of whom thou wilt, and
when.53Upon the ſixt day thou gaueſt commaundement vnto the earth,
that before thee it ſhould bring foorth beaſts, cattell, and creeping
things:54And after theſe, Adam alſo whom thou madeſt lord of all thy
creatures, of him come wee all, and the people alſo whom thou haſt
choſen.55All this haue I ſpoken before thee, O Lord, becauſe thou
madeſt the world for our ſakes.56As for the other people which alſo
come of Adam, thou haſt ſaid that they are nothing, but be like vnto
ſpittle, and haſt likened the abundance of them vnto a drop that falleth
from a veſſell.57And now, O Lord, behold, theſe heathen, which haue
euer been reputed as nothing, haue begun to be lordes ouer vs, and to
deuoure vs:58But wee thy people (whom thou haſt called thy firſt borne,
thy onely begotten, and thy feruent louer) are giuen into their hands.59If
the world now be made for our ſakes, why doe we not poſſeſſe an
inheritance with the world? how long ſhall this endure?

CHAPTER 71And when I had made an ende of ſpeaking theſe words,
there was ſent vnto mee the Angel which had beene ſent vnto mee the
nights afore.2And he ſaid vnto me, Up Eſdras, and heare the wordes
that I am come to tell thee.3And I ſaid, Speake on, my God. Then ſaid
he vnto me, The ſea is ſet in a wide place, that it might be deepe and
great.4But put the caſe the entrance were narrow, and like a riuer,5Who
then could goe into the ſea to looke vpon it, and to rule it? If hee went
not through the narrow, how could he come into the broad?6There is
alſo another thing. A city is builded, and ſet vpon a broad field, and is
full of all good things.7The entrance thereof is narrow, and is ſet in a
dangerous place to fall, like as if there were a fire on the right hand, and
on the left a deepe water.8And one only path between them both, euen
betweene the fire and the water, ſo ſmall that there could but one man
goe there at once.9If this city now were giuen vnto a man for an
inheritance, if he neuer ſhall paſſe the danger ſet before it, how ſhall he
receiue this inheritance?10And I ſaid, It is ſo, Lord. Then ſaid he vnto
me, Euen ſo alſo is Iſraels portion:11Becauſe for their ſakes I made the
world: and when Adam tranſgreſſed my Statutes, then was decreed that
now is done.12Then were the entrances of this world made narrow, full
of ſorrow and trauaile: they are but few and euill, full of perils, and very
painefull.13For the entrances of the elder world were wide and ſure, and
brought immortall fruit.14If then they that liue, labour not to enter theſe
ſtrait and vaine things, they can neuer receiue thoſe that are laide vp for
them.15Now therefore why diſquieteſt thou thy ſelfe, ſeeing thou art but
a corruptible man? and why art thou mooued, whereas thou art but
mortall?16Why haſt thou not conſidered in thy minde this thing that is
to come, rather then that which is preſent?17Then anſwered I, and ſayd,
O Lord, that beareſt rule, thou haſt ordained in thy Law, that the
righteous ſhould inherite theſe things, but that the vngodly ſhould
periſh:18Neuertheleſſe, the righteous ſhal ſuffer ſtrait things, and hope
for wide: for they that haue done wickedly, haue ſuffered the ſtrait
things, and yet ſhall not ſee the wide.19And he ſaid vnto me, There is no
iudge aboue God, and none that hath vnderſtanding aboue the
higheſt.20For there be many that periſh in this life, becauſe they deſpiſe
the Lawe of God that is ſet before them.21For God hath giuen ſtrait
commandement to ſuch as came, what they ſhould doe to liue, euen as
they came, and what they ſhould obſerue to auoid
puniſhment.22Neuertheleſſe they were not obedient vnto him, but ſpake
againſt him, and imagined vaine things:23And deceiued themſelues by
their wicked deeds, and ſayd of the moſt Hie, that he is not, and knew
not his waies.24But his Law haue they deſpiſed, and denied his
couenants in his ſtatutes haue they not beene faithfull, and haue not
performed his workes.25And therfore Eſdras, for the emptie, are emptie
things, and for the ful, are the full things.26Behold, the time ſhall come,
that theſe tokens which I haue told thee, ſhall come to paſſe, and the
bride ſhall appeare, and ſhe comming forth ſhall be ſeene, that now is
withdrawen from the earth.27And whoſoeuer is deliuered from the
foreſaid euils, ſhall ſee my wonders.28For my ſonne Ieſus ſhall be
reuealed with thoſe that be with him, and they that remaine ſhall reioyce
within foure hundred yeeres.29After theſe yeeres ſhall my ſonne Chriſt
die, and all men that haue life.30And the world ſhall be turned into the
old ſilence ſeuen dayes, like as in the former iudgements: ſo that no man
ſhall remaine.31And after ſeuen dayes, the world that yet awaketh not
ſhall be raiſed vp, and that ſhall die, that is corrupt.32And the earth ſhall
reſtore thoſe that are aſleepe in her, and ſo ſhall the duſt thoſe that dwell
in ſilence, and the ſecret places ſhall deliuer thoſe ſoules that were
committed vnto them.33And the moſt high ſhall appeare vpon the ſeate
of iudgement, and miſerie ſhall paſſe away, and the long ſuffering ſhall
haue an end.34But iudgement onely ſhall remaine, trueth ſhall ſtand, and
faith ſhall waxe ſtrong.35And the worke ſhall follow, and the reward ſhall
be ſhewed, and the good deeds ſhall be of force, and wicked deeds ſhall
beare no rule.36Then ſaid I, Abraham prayed firſt for the Sodomites,
and Moſes for the fathers that ſinned in the wilderneſſe:37And Ieſus
after him for Iſrael in the time of Achan,38And Samuel; and Dauid for
the deſtruction: and Solomon for them that ſhould come to the
ſanctuary.39And Helias for thoſe that receiued raine, & for the dead that
hee might liue.40And Ezechias for the people in the time of
Sennacherib: and many for many.41Euen ſo now ſeeing corruption is
growen vp, and wickedneſſe increaſed, and the righteous haue prayed
for the vngodly: wherefore ſhall it not be ſo now alſo?42He anſwered
me and ſaid, This preſent life is not the end where much glory doth
abide; therefore haue they prayed for the weake.43But the day of doome
ſhall be the end of this time, and the beginning of the immortality for to
come, wherein corruption is paſt.44Intemperancie is at an end, infidelity
is cut off, righteouſneſſe is growen, and trueth is ſprung vp.45Then ſhall
no man be able to ſaue him that is deſtroyed, nor to oppreſſe him that
hath gotten the victory.46I anſwered then and ſaid, This is my firſt and
laſt ſaying; that it had beene better not to haue giuen the earth vnto
Adam: or elſe when it was giuen him, to haue reſtrained him from

ſinning. 47 For what profit is it for men now in this preſent time to liue in heauineſse, and after death to looke for puniſhment? 48 O thou Adam, what haſt thou done? for though it was thou that ſinned, thou art not fallen alone, but we all that come of thee. 49 For what profit is it vnto vs, if there be promiſed vs an immortall time, wheras we haue done the works that bring death? 50 And that their is promiſed vs an euerlaſting hope, whereas our ſelues being moſt wicked are made vaine? 51 And that there are layd vp for vs dwellings of health and ſafety, whereas we haue liued wickedly? 52 And that the glory of the moſt high is kept to defend them which haue led a wary life, whereas we haue walked in the moſt wicked wayes of all? 53 And that there ſhould be ſhewed a paradiſe whoſe fruite endureth for euer, wherein is ſecuritie and medicine, ſith we ſhall not enter into it? 54 For we haue walked in vnpleaſant places. 55 And that the faces of them which haue vſed abſtinence, ſhall ſhine aboue the ſtarres, whereas our faces ſhall bee blacker then darkeneſſe? 56 For while we liued and committed iniquitie, we conſidered not that we ſhould begin to ſuffer for it after death. 57 Then anſwered he me and ſaide, This is the condition of the battell, which man that is borne vpon the earth ſhall fight, 58 That if he be ouercome, he ſhall ſuffer as thou haſt ſaid, but if he get the victorie, he ſhall receiue the thing that I ſay. 59 For this is the life whereof Moſes ſpake vnto the people while hee liued, ſaying, Chooſe thee life that thou mayeſt liue. 60 Neuertheleſſe they beleeued not him, nor yet the prophets after him, no nor me which haue ſpoken vnto them, 61 That there ſhould not be ſuch heauineſse in their deſtruction, as ſhall bee ioy ouer them that are perſwaded to ſaluation. 62 I anſwered then and ſaide, I know, Lord, that the moſt Hie is called mercifull, in that he hath mercy vpon them, which are not yet come into the world, 63 And vpon thoſe alſo that turne to his Law, 64 And that he is patient, and long ſuffereth thoſe that haue ſinned, as his creatures, 65 And that he is bountifull, for hee is ready to giue where it needeth, 66 And that is of great mercie, for he multiplieth more and more mercies to them that are preſent, and that are paſt, & alſo to them which are to come. 67 For if he ſhall not multiplie his mercies, the world would not continue with them that inherit therein. 68 And he pardoneth; for if hee did not ſo of his goodneſse, that they which haue committed iniquities might be eaſed of them, the ten thouſand part of men ſhould not remaine liuing. 69 And being Iudge, if he ſhould not forgiue them that are cured with his word, and put out the multitude of contentions, 70 There ſhould bee very fewe left peraduenture in an innumerable multitude.

CHAPTER 8 1 And he anſwered me, ſaying, The moſt High hath made this world for many, but the world to come for fewe. 2 I will tell thee a ſimilitude, Eſdras, As when thou aſkeſt the earth, it ſhall ſay vnto thee, that it giueth much mold wherof earthen veſſels are made, but litle duſt that golde commeth of: euen ſo is þe courſe of this preſent world. 3 There be many created, but few ſhall be ſaued. 4 So anſwered I and ſaid, Swallow then downe O my ſoule, vnderſtanding, and deuoure wiſedome. 5 For thou haſt agreed to giue eare, and art willing to propheſie: for thou haſt no longer ſpace then onely to liue. 6 O Lord, if thou ſuffer not thy ſeruant that we may pray before thee, and thou giue vs ſeed vnto our heart, and culture to our vnderſtanding, that there may come fruit of it, howe ſhall each man liue that is corrupt, who beareth the place of a man? 7 For thou art alone, and we all one workemanſhip of thine hands, like as thou haſt ſaid. 8 For when the body is faſhioned now in the mothers wombe, and thou giueſt it members, thy creature is preſerued in fire & water, and nine months doeth thy workemanſhip endure thy creature which is created in her. 9 But that which keepeth, and is kept, ſhall both be preſerued: and when the time commeth, the wombe preſerued, deliuereth vp the things that grew in it. 10 For thou haſt commanded out of the parts of the body, that is to ſay, out of the breaſts milke to be giuen, which is the fruit of the breaſts, 11 That the thing which is faſhioned, may bee nouriſhed for a time, till thou diſpoſeſt it to thy mercy. 12 Thou broughteſt it vp with thy righteouſneſſe, and nourturedſt it in thy Law, and reformedſt it with thy iudgement. 13 And thou ſhalt mortifie it as thy creature, and quicken it as thy worke. 14 If therefore thou ſhalt deſtroy him which with ſo great labour was faſhioned, it is an eaſie thing to be ordeined by thy Commaundement, that the thing which was made might be preſerued. 15 Now therefore, Lord, I will ſpeake (touchiug man in generall, thou knoweſt beſt) but touching thy people, for whoſe ſake I am ſory, 16 And for thine inheritance, for whoſe cauſe I mourne, and for Iſrael, for whom I am heauy, and for Iacob, for whoſe ſake I am troubled: 17 Therefore will I begin to pray before thee, for my ſelfe, and for them: for I ſee the falles of vs that dwell in the land. 18 But I haue heard the ſwiftneſse of the Iudge which is to come. 19 Therefore heare my voyce, and vnderſtand my wordes, and I ſhall ſpeake before thee: this is the beginning of the words of Eſdras, before he was taken vp: and I ſaid; 20 O Lord, Thou that dwelleſt in euerlaſtingnes, which beholdeſt from aboue, things in the heauen, & in the aire, 21 Whoſe Throne is ineſtimable, whoſe glory may not be comprehended, before whom the hoſts of Angels ſtand with trembling, 22 (Whoſe ſeruice is conuerſant in wind and fire,) whoſe word is true, and ſayings conſtant, whoſe Commandement is ſtrong, and ordinance fearefull, 23 Whoſe looke drieth vp the depths, and indignation maketh the mountaines to melt away, which the trueth witneſſeth: 24 O heare the prayer of thy ſeruant, and giue eare to the petition of thy creature. 25 For while I liue, I will ſpeake, and ſo long as I haue vnderſtanding, I wil anſwere. 26 O looke not vpon the ſinnes of thy people: but on them which ſerue thee in trueth. 27 Regard not the wicked inuentions of the heathen: but the deſire of thoſe that keepe thy Teſtimonies in afflictions. 28 Thinke not vpon thoſe that haue walked fainedly before thee: but remember them, which according to thy will haue knowen thy feare. 29 Let it not bee thy will to deſtroy them, which haue liued like beaſts: but to looke vpon them that haue clearely taught thy Law. 30 Take thou no indignation at them which are deemed worſe then beaſts: but loue them that alway put their truſt in thy righteouſneſſe, and glory. 31 For we and our fathers doe languiſh of ſuch diſeaſes; but becauſe of vs ſinners, thou ſhalt be called mercifull. 32 For if thou haſt a deſire to haue mercy vpon vs, thou ſhalt bee called mercifull, to vs namely, that haue no workes of righteouſneſſe. 33 For the iuſt which haue many good workes layed vp with thee, ſhall out of their owne deedes receiue reward. 34 For what is man that thou ſhouldeſt take diſpleaſure at him? or what is a corruptible generation, that thou ſhouldeſt be ſo bitter toward it? 35 For in trueth there is no man among them that be borne, but he hath dealt wickedly, and among the faithfull, there is none which hath not done amiſse. 36 For in this, O Lord, thy righteouſneſſe, and thy goodneſſe ſhalbe declared, if thou be mercifull vnto them which haue not the confidence of good workes. 37 Then anſwered he mee, and ſaid, Some things haſt thou ſpoken aright, and according vnto thy words it ſhalbe. 38 For indeed I will not thinke on the diſpoſition of them which haue ſinned before death, before iudgement, before deſtruction. 39 But I will reioyce ouer the diſpoſition of the righteous, and I wil remember alſo their pilgrimage, and the ſaluation, and the reward that they ſhall haue. 40 Like as I haue ſpoken now, ſo ſhall it come to paſſe. 41 For as the huſbandmau ſoweth much ſeed vpon the ground, and planteth many trees, and yet the thing that is ſowen good in his ſeaſon, commeth not vp, neither doeth all that is planted take root: euen ſo is it of them that are ſowen in the world, they ſhall not all be ſaued. 42 I anſwered then, and ſaid, If I haue found grace, let me ſpeake. 43 Like as the huſbandmans ſeede periſheth, if it come not vp, and receiue not the raine in due ſeaſon, or if there come too much raine and corrupt it: 44 Euen ſo periſheth man alſo which is formed with thy hands, and is called thine owne image, becauſe thou art like vnto him, for whoſe ſake thou haſt made all things, and likened him vnto the huſbandmans ſeede. 45 Be not wroth with vs, but ſpare thy people, and haue mercy vpon thine owne inheritance: for thou art mercifull vnto thy creature. 46 Then anſwered he me, and ſaid, Things preſent are for the preſent, and things to come, for ſuch as be to come. 47 For thou commeſt farre ſhort, that thou ſhouldeſt be able to loue my creature more then I: but I haue oft times drawen nigh vnto thee, and vnto it, but neuer to the vnrighteous. 48 In this alſo thou art marueilous before the moſt high; 49 In that thou haſt humbled thy ſelfe as it becommeth thee, and haſt not iudged thy ſelfe worthy to be much glorified among the righteous. 50 For many great miſeries ſhall be done to them, that in the latter time ſhal dwell in the world, becauſe they haue walked in great pride. 51 But vnderſtand thou for thy ſelfe, and ſeeke out the glory for ſuch as be like thee. 52 For vnto you is Paradiſe opened, the tree of life is planted, the time to come is prepared, plenteouſneſse is made ready, a citie is builded, and reſt is allowed, yea perfect goodneſſe and wiſedome. 53 The root of euil is ſealed vp from you, weakeneſse and the moth is hidde from you, and corruption is fled into hell to be

forgotten. 54 Sorrows are paſſed, & in the end is ſhewed the treaſure of
immortalitie. 55 And therefore aſke thou no more queſtions concerning
the multitude of them that periſh. 56 For when they had taken liberty,
they deſpiſed the moſt High, thought ſcorne of his Lawe, and forſooke
his wayes. 57 Moreouer, they haue troden downe his righteous, 58 And ſaid
in their heart, that there is no God, yea and that knowing they muſt
die. 59 For as the things aforeſaid ſhall receiue you, ſo thirſt and paine are
prepared for them; for it was not his will that men ſhould come to
nought. 60 But they which be created, haue defiled the Name of him that
made them, and were vnthankefull vnto him which prepared life for
them. 61 And therefore is my iudgement now at hand. 62 Theſe things haue
I not ſhewed vnto all men, but vnto thee, and a fewe like thee. Then
anſwered I, and ſaid, 63 Behold, O Lord, now haſt thou ſhewed me the
multitude of the wonders which thou wilt begin to doe in the laſt times:
but at what time, thou haſt not ſhewed me.
CHAPTER 9 1 Hee anſwered me then, and ſayde, Meaſure thou the time
diligently in it ſelfe: and when thou ſeeſt part of the ſignes paſt, which I
haue tolde thee before, 2 Then ſhalt thou vnderſtand, that it is the very
ſame time, wherein the higheſt will begin to viſite the world which he
made. 3 Therefore when there ſhall bee ſeene earthquakes and vprores of
the people in the world: 4 Then ſhalt thou wel vnderſtand, that the moſt
high ſpake of thoſe things from the dayes that were before thee, euen
from the beginning. 5 For like as all that is made in the world hath a
beginning, and an ende, and the end is manifeſt: 6 Euen ſo the times alſo
of the higheſt, haue plaine beginnings in wonders and powerfull workes,
and endings in effects and ſignes. 7 And euery one that ſhalbe ſaued, and
ſhalbe able to eſcape by his works, and by faith, whereby ye haue
beleeued, 8 Shall be preſerued from the ſayd perils, and ſhall ſee my
ſaluation, in my land, and within my borders: for I haue ſanctified them
for me, from the beginning. 9 Then ſhall they be in pitifull caſe which
now haue abuſed my wayes: and they that haue caſt them away
deſſpitefully, ſhall dwell in torments. 10 For ſuch, as in their life haue
receiued benefits, & haue not knowen me: 11 And they that haue loathed
my law, while they had yet liberty, and when as yet place of repentance
was open vnto them, vnderſtood not, but deſpiſed it: 12 The ſame muſt
know it after death by paine. 13 And therefore be thou not curious, how
the vngodly ſhalbe puniſhed and when: but enquire how the righteous
ſhall be ſaued, whoſe the world is, and for whom the world is
created. 14 Then anſwered I, and ſaid, 15 I haue ſaid before, and now doe
ſpeake, and will ſpeake it alſo heereafter: that there be many moe of
them which periſh, then of them which ſhall be ſaued, 16 Like as a waue
is greater then a droppe. 17 And he anſwered me, ſaying: like as the field
is, ſo is alſo the ſeed: as the flowres be, ſuch are the colours alſo: ſuch
as the workeman is, ſuch alſo is the worke: and as the huſbandman is
himſelfe, ſo is his huſbandry alſo: for it was the time of the world. 18 And
now when I prepared the world, which was not yet made, euen for them
to dwell in that now liue, no man ſpake againſt me. 19 For then euery one
obeyed, but now the maners of them which are created in this world
that is made, are corrupted by a perpetuall ſeed, & by a law which is
vnſearchable, rid themſelues. 20 So I conſidered the world, and behold
there was perill, becauſe of the deuices that were come into it. 21 And I
ſaw and ſpared it greatly, and haue kept me a grape of the cluſter, and a
plant of a great people. 22 Let the multitude periſh then, which was borne
in vaine, and let my grape be kept and my plant: for with great labour
haue I made it perfect. 23 Neuertheleſſe if thou wilt ceaſe yet ſeuen dayes
moe (but thou ſhalt not faſt in them.) 24 But goe into a field of flowres,
where no houſe is builded, and eate only the flowres of the field, Taſt
no fleſh, drinke no wine, but eate flowres onely. 25 And pray vnto the
Higheſt continually, then wil I come and talke with thee. 26 So I went my
way into the field which is called Ardath, like as he commanded me, and
there I ſate amongſt the flowres, and did eate of the herbes of the field,
and the meate of the ſame ſatiſfied me. 27 After ſeuen dayes I ſate vpon
the graſſe, and my heart was vexed within me, like as before. 28 And I
opened my mouth, and beganne to talke before the moſt High and
ſaid, 29 O Lord, thou that ſheweſt thy ſelfe vnto vs, thou waſt ſhewed
vnto our fathers in the wilderneſſe, in a place where no man treadeth, in
a barren place when they came out of Egypt. 30 And thou ſpakeſt, ſaying,
Heare me, O Iſrael, and marke my words, thou ſeed of Iacob. 31 For
behold I ſow my law in you, and it ſhall bring fruite in you, and yee ſhall
be honoured in it for euer. 32 But our fathers which receiued the law, kept
it not, and obſerued not thy ordinances, and though the fruite of thy law
did not periſh, neither could it, for it was thine: 33 Yet they that receiued
it, periſhed, becauſe they kept not the thing that was ſowen in
them. 34 And loe, it is a cuſtome when the ground hath receiued ſeed, or
the ſea a ſhip, or any veſſel, meate or drinke, that, that being periſhed
wherein it was ſowen, or caſt into, 35 That thing alſo which was ſowen or
caſt therein, or receiued, doth periſh, and remaineth not with vs: but
with vs it hath not happened ſo. 36 For we that haue receiued the law
periſh by ſinne, and our heart alſo which receiued it. 37 Notwithſtanding
the law periſheth not, but remaineth in his force. 38 And when I ſpake
theſe things in my heart, I looked backe with mine eyes, & vpon the
right ſide I ſaw a woman, and behold, ſhe mourned, & wept with a loud
voyce, and was much grieued in heart, and her clothes were rent, and
ſhe had aſhes vpon her head. 39 Then let I my thoughts goe that I was in,
and turned me vnto her, 40 And ſaid vnto her, Wherefore weepeſt thou?
why art thou ſo grieued in thy minde? 41 And ſhe ſaid vnto me, Sir, let me
alone, that I may bewaile my ſelfe, and adde vnto my ſorow, for I am
ſore vexed in my minde, and brought very low. 42 And I ſaid vnto her,
What aileth thee? Tell me. 43 She ſaid vnto me, I thy ſeruant haue bene
barren, and had no childe, though I had an huſband thirty yeres. 44 And
thoſe thirtie yeeres I did nothing elſe day and night, and euery houre,
but make my prayer to þͤ higheſt. 45 After thirtie yeeres, God heard me
thine handmaid, looked vpon my miſery, conſidered my trouble, and
gaue me a ſonne: and I was very glad of him, ſo was my huſband alſo,
and all my neighbours, and we gaue great honour vnto the
Almightie. 46 And I nouriſhed him with great trauaile. 47 So when he grew
vp, and came to the time that he ſhould haue a wife, I made a feaſt.
CHAPTER 10 1 And it ſo came to paſſe, that when my ſonne was entred
into his wedding chamber, he fell downe and died. 2 Then we all
ouerthrew the lights, and all my neighbours roſe vp to comfort me, ſo I
tooke my reſt vnto the ſecond day at night. 3 And it came to paſſe when
they had all left off to comfort me, to the end I might be quiet: then roſe
I vp by night and fled, and came hither into this field, as thou ſeeſt. 4 And
I doe now purpoſe not to returne into the citie, but here to ſtay, and
neither to eate nor drinke, but continually to mourne, & to faſt vntil I
die. 5 Then left I the meditations wherein I was, and ſpake to her in anger,
ſaying, 6 Thou fooliſh woman aboue all other, ſeeſt thou not our
mourning, and what happeneth vnto vs? 7 How that Sion our mother is
full of all heauineſſe, and much humbled, mourning very ſore? 8 And
now ſeeing we all mourne, and are ſad, for we are all in heauineſſe, art
thou grieued for one ſonne? 9 For aſke the earth, and ſhe ſhall tell thee,
that it is ſhe, which ought to mourne, for the fall of ſo many that grow
vpon her. 10 For out of her came all at the firſt, and out of her ſhal all
others come: and behold they walke almoſt all into deſtruction, and a
multitude of them is vtterly rooted out. 11 Who then ſhould make more
mourning, then ſhe that hath loſt ſo great a multitude, and not thou
which art ſory but for one? 12 But if thou ſayeſt vnto me, My lamentation
is not like the earths, becauſe I haue loſt the fruit of my womb, which I
brought foorth with paines, and bare with ſorrowes. 13 But the earth not
ſo: for the multitude preſent in it, according to the courſe of the earth,
is gone, as it came. 14 Then ſay I vnto thee, Like as thou haſt brought
foorth with labour: euen ſo the earth alſo hath giuen her fruit, namely
man, euer ſithence the beginning, vnto him that made her. 15 Now
therefore keepe thy ſorrow to thy ſelfe, and beare with a good courage
that which hath befallen thee. 16 For if thou ſhalt acknowledge the
determination of God to be iuſt, thou ſhalt both receiue thy ſonne in
time, and ſhalt be commended amongſt women. 17 Goe thy way then into
the citie, to thine huſband. 18 And ſhe ſaid vnto me, That will I not doe:
I will not goe into the city, but here will I die. 19 So I proceeded to ſpeake
further vnto her, and ſaid, 20 Doe not ſo, but bee counſelled by me: for
how many are the aduerſities of Sion? Bee comforted in regard of the
ſorow of Ieruſalem. 21 For thou ſeeſt that our Sanctuary is laid waſte, our
Altar broken downe, our Temple deſtroyed. 22 Our Pſaltery is laid on
þͤ ground, our ſong is put to ſilence, our reioycing is at an end, the light
of our candleſticke is put out, the Arke of our Couenant is ſpoiled, our
holy things are defiled, and the Name that is called vpon vs, is almoſt
prophaned: our children are put to ſhame, our prieſts are burnt, our
Leuites are gone into captiuitie, our virgines are defiled, and our wiues

rauiſhed, our righteous men caried away, our litle ones deſtroyed, our
yong men are brought in bondage, and our ſtrong men are become
weake.23And which is the greateſt of all, the ſeale of Sion hath now loſt
her honour: for ſhe is deliuered into the hands of them that hate
vs.24And therefore ſhake off thy great heauineſse, and put away the
multitude of ſorrowes, that the mighty may be mercifull vnto thee
againe, and the higheſt ſhal giue thee reſt, and eaſe from thy
labour.25And it came to paſſe while I was talking with her, behold her
face vpon a ſudden ſhined exceedingly, & her countenance gliſtered, ſo
that I was afraid of her, and muſed what it might be.26And behold
ſuddenly, ſhe made a great cry very fearful: ſo that the earth ſhooke at
the noiſe of the woman.27And I looked, and beholde, the woman
appeared vnto me no more, but there was a city builded, and a large
place ſhewed it ſelfe from the foundations: then was I afraid, and cried
with a lowd voice, and ſaid,28Where is Uriel the Angel, who came vnto
mee at the firſt? for hee hath cauſed me to fall into many traunces, and
mine end is turned into corruption, and my prayer to rebuke.29And as I
was ſpeaking theſe wordes, behold, he came vnto me, and looked vpon
me.30And loe, I lay as one that had bene dead, & mine vnderſtanding
was taken from me, and he tooke me by the right hand, and comforted
mee, and ſet me vpon my feet, and ſaid vnto me,31What aileth thee? and
why art thou ſo diſquieted, and why is thine vnderſtanding troubled, &
the thoughts of thine heart?32And I ſaid, becauſe thou haſt forſaken me,
and yet I did according to thy words, and I went into the field, and loe
I haue ſeene, and yet ſee, that I am not able to expreſse.33And hee ſaid
vnto me, ſtand vp manfully, and I wil aduiſe thee.34Then ſaid I, Speake
on, my lord in me, onely forſake me not, leſt I die fruſtrate of my
hope.35For I haue ſeene, that I knew not, and heare that I do not
know.36Or, is my ſenſe deceiued, or my ſoule in a dreame?37Now
therfore, I beſeech thee, that thou wilt ſhew thy ſeruant of this viſiō.38He
anſwered me then, & ſaid, Heare me, and I ſhall enforme thee, and tell
thee wherefore thou art afraid: for the higheſt will reueile many ſecret
things vnto thee.39Hee hath ſeene that thy way is right: for that thou
ſorroweſt continually for thy people, and makeſt great lamentation for
Sion.40This therefore is the meaning of the viſion which thou lately
ſaweſt.41Thou ſaweſt a woman mourning, and thou beganſt to comfort
her:42But now ſeeſt thou the likeneſſe of the woman no more, but there
appeared vnto thee a city builded.43And whereas ſhe told thee of the
death of her ſonne, this is the ſolution.44This woman whom thou
ſaweſt, is Sion: and whereas ſhe ſaid vnto thee (euen ſhe whom thou
ſeeſt as a city builded.)45Whereas I ſay, ſhe ſaid vnto thee, that ſhe hath
bene thirty yeres barren: thoſe are the thirty yeeres wherein there was no
offering made in her.46But after thirtie yeeres, Solomon builded the city,
& offered offrings: and then bare the barren a ſonne.47And whereas ſhe
told thee that ſhee nouriſhed him with labour: that was the dwelling in
Hieruſalem.48But whereas ſhe ſaid vnto thee, That my ſonne comming
into his marriage chamber, happened to haue a fall, and died, this was
the deſtruction that came to Hieruſalem.49And behold, thou ſaweſt her
likeneſſe, and becauſe ſhe mourned for her ſonne, thou beganſt to
comfort her, and of theſe things which haue chaunced, theſe are to be
opened vnto thee.50For now the moſt High ſeeth, that thou art grieued
vnfainedly, & ſuffereſt from thy whole heart for her, ſo hath he ſhewed
thee the brightnes of her glory, and the comelineſse of her beautie.51And
therfore I bad thee remaine in þe field, where no houſe was
builded.52For I knew that the Higheſt would ſhew this vnto
thee.53Therefore I commanded thee to goe into the field, where no
foundation of any building was.54For in the place wherein the Higheſt
beginneth to ſhew his city, ther can no mans building be able to
ſtand.55And therfore feare not, let not thy heart be afrighted, but goe
thy way in, and ſee the beautie and greatneſſe of the building, as much
as thine eyes be able to ſee:56And then ſhalt thou heare as much as thine
eares may comprehend.57For thou art bleſſed aboue many other, and
art called with the higheſt, and ſo are but few.58But to morrow at night
thou ſhalt remaine here.59And ſo ſhall the higheſt ſhew thee viſions of
the high things, which the moſt high will do vnto them, that dwel vpon
earth in the laſt dayes. So I ſlept that night and another, like as he
commanded me.
CHAPTER 111Then ſaw I a dreame, and beholde, there came vp from
the ſea an Eagle, which had twelue feathered wings, & three heads.2And
I ſaw, and behold, ſhe ſpred her wings ouer all the earth, and all the
windes of the ayre blewe on her, and were gathered together.3And I
beheld, and out of her feathers there grewe other contrary feathers, and
they became little feathers, and ſmall.4But her heads were at reſt: the
head in the middeſt was greater then the other, yet reſted it with the
reſidue.5Moreouer I beheld, and loe, the Eagle flew with her feathers,
and reigned vpon earth, and ouer them that dwelt therein.6And I ſaw
that all things vnder heauen were ſubiect vnto her, and no man ſpake
againſt her, no not one creature vpon earth.7And I beheld, and loe, the
Eagle roſe vpon her talents, and ſpake to her feathers, ſaying,8Watch
not all at once, ſleepe euery one in his own place, & watch by
courſe.9But let the heads be preſerued for the laſt.10And I beheld, and
loe, the voice went not out of her heads, but from the middeſt of her
body.11And I numbred her contrary feathers, and behold, there were
eight of them.12And I looked, and behold, on the right ſide there aroſe
one feather, and reigned ouer all the earth.13And ſo it was, that when it
reigned, the ende of it came, and the place thereof appeared no more:
ſo the next following ſtood vp and reigned, and had a great time.14And
it happened, that when it reigned, the end of it came alſo, like as the firſt,
ſo that it appeared no more.15Then came there a voice vnto it, and
ſayd,16Heare, thou that haſt borne rule ouer the earth ſo long: this I ſay
vnto thee, before thou beginneſt to appeare no more.17There ſhall none
after thee attaine vnto thy time, neither vnto the halfe thereof.18Then
aroſe the third, and reigned as the other before: and appeared no more
alſo.19So went it with all the reſidue one after another, as that euery one
reigned, and then appeared no more.20Then I beheld, & loe, in proceſſe
of time, the feathers that folowed, ſtood vp vpon the right ſide, that they
might rule alſo, and ſome of them ruled, but within a while they
appeared no more:21For ſome of them were ſet vp, but ruled not.22After
this I looked, and behold, the twelue feathers appeared no more, nor
the two little feathers:23And there was no more vpon the Eagles body,
but three heads that reſted, and ſixe little wings.24Then ſaw I alſo that
two little feathers diuided themſelues from the ſixe, and remained vnder
the head, that was vpon the right ſide: for the foure continued in their
place.25And I beheld, & loe, the feathers that were vnder the wing,
thought to ſet vp themſelues, and to haue the rule.26And I beheld, &
loe, there was one ſet vp, but ſhortly it appeared no more.27And the
ſecond was ſooner away then the firſt.28And I beheld, and loe, the two
that remained, thought alſo in themſelues to reigne.29And when they ſo
thought, behold, there awaked one of the heads that were at reſt, namely
it that was in the middeſt, for that was greater then the two other
heads.30And then I ſaw, that the two other heads were ioyned with
it.31And behold, the head was turned with them that were with it, and
did eate vp the two feathers vnder the wing that would haue
reigned.32But this head put the whole earth in feare, and bare rule in it
ouer all thoſe that dwelt vpon the earth, with much oppreſſion, and it
had the gouernance of the world more then all the wings that had
beene.33And after this I beheld, and loe the head that was in the midſt,
ſuddenly appeared no more, like as the wings.34But there remained the
two heads, which alſo in like ſort ruled vpon the earth, and ouer thoſe
that dwelt therein.35And I beheld, and loe, the head vpon the right ſide,
deuoured it, that was vpon the left ſide.36Then I heard a voyce, which
ſaid vnto me, Looke before thee, and conſider the thing that thou
ſeeſt.37And I beheld, and loe, as it were a roaring Lyon, chaſed out of
the wood: and I ſaw that hee ſent out a mans voyce vnto the Eagle, and
ſaid,38Heare thou, I will talke with thee, and the higheſt ſhall ſay vnto
thee,39Art not thou it that remaineſt of the foure beaſts, whom I made
to raigne in my world, that the end of their times might come through
them?40And the fourth came and ouercame all the beaſts that were paſt,
and had power ouer the world with great fearefulneſse, and ouer the
whole compaſſe of the earth with much wicked oppreſſion, and ſo long
time dwelt he vpon the earth with deceit.41For the earth haſt thou not
iudged with trueth.42For thou haſt afflicted the meeke, thou haſt hurt
the peaceable, thou haſt loued lyers, and deſtroyed the dwellings of them
that brought forth fruite, and haſt caſt downe the walles of ſuch, as did
thee no harme.43Therefore is thy wrongfull dealing come vp vnto the
Higheſt, and thy pride vnto the Mighty.44The Higheſt alſo hath looked
vpon the proud times, and behold, they are ended, and his abominations
are fulfilled.45And therefore appeare no more thou Eagle, nor thy

horrible wings, nor thy wicked feathers, nor thy malitious heads, nor thy hurtfull clawes, nor all thy vaine body:[46]That all the earth may be refreſhed, and may returne, being deliuered from thy violence, and that ſhe may hope for the iudgement, and mercy of him that made her.

CHAPTER 12[1]And it came to paſſe whiles the Lyon ſpake theſe words vnto the Eagle, I ſaw:[2]And behold, the head that remained, and the foure wings appeared no more, and the two went vnto it, and ſet themſelues vp to raigne, and their kingdome was ſmall and full of vprore.[3]And I ſaw, and behold, they appeared no more, and the whole body of the Eagle was burnt, ſo that the earth was in great feare: then awaked I out of the trouble and traunce of my minde, and from great feare, and ſaid vnto my ſpirit,[4]Loe, this haſt thou done vnto me, in that thou ſearcheſt out the wayes of the Higheſt.[5]Loe, yet am I weary in my mind, and very weake in my ſpirit: and litle ſtrength is there in me; for the great feare, wherewith I was affrighted this night.[6]Therefore wil I now beſeech the Higheſt, that hee will comfort me vnto the end.[7]And I ſaid, Lord, that beareſt rule, If I haue found grace before thy ſight, and if I am iuſtified with thee, before many others, and if my prayer indeed be come vp before thy face,[8]Comfort me then, and ſhew me thy ſeruant the interpretation, and plaine difference of this fearefull viſion, that thou maiſt perfectly comfort my ſoule.[9]For thou haſt iudged me worthy, to ſhew me the laſt times.[10]And he ſaid vnto me, This is the interpretation of the viſion.[11]The Eagle whom thou ſaweſt come vp from the ſea, is the kingdome which was ſeene, in the viſion of thy brother Daniel.[12]But it was not expounded vnto him, therefore now I declare it vnto thee.[13]Behold, the dayes will come, that there ſhall riſe vp a kingdome vpon earth, and it ſhall be feared aboue all the kingdomes that were before it.[14]In the ſame ſhall twelue kings reigne, one after another.[15]Whereof the ſecond ſhall begin to reigne, and ſhall haue more time then any of the twelue.[16]And this doe the twelue wings ſignifie which thou ſaweſt.[17]As for the voice which thou heardeſt ſpeake, and that thou ſaweſt not to goe out from the heads, but from the mids of the body thereof, this is the interpretation:[18]That after the time of that kingdome, there ſhall Ariſe great ſtriuings, and it ſhall ſtand in perill of falling: neuertheleſſe it ſhall not then fall, but ſhal be reſtored againe to his beginning.[19]And whereas thou ſaweſt the eight ſmall vnder feathers ſticking to her wings, this is the interpretation:[20]That in him there ſhal Ariſe eight kings, whoſe time ſhall bee but ſmall, and their yeeres ſwift.[21]And two of them ſhall periſh: the middle time approching, foure ſhall bee kept vntill their end begin to approch: but two ſhall be kept vnto the end.[22]And whereas thou ſaweſt three heads reſting, this is the interpretation[23]In his laſt dayes ſhall the moſt High raiſe vp three kingdomes, and renew many things therein, and they ſhal haue the dominion of the earth,[24]And of thoſe that dwell therein with much oppreſſion, aboue all thoſe that were before them: therefore are they called the heads of the Eagle.[25]For theſe are they that ſhal accompliſh his wickedneſſe, and that ſhall finiſh his laſt end.[26]And whereas thou ſaweſt that the great head appeared no more, it ſignifieth that one of them ſhall die vpon his bed, and yet with paine.[27]For the two that remaine, ſhall be ſlaine with the ſword.[28]For the ſword of the one ſhall deuoure the other: but at the laſt ſhall he fall through the ſword himſelfe.[29]And whereas thou ſaweſt two feathers vnder the wings paſsing ouer the head, that is on the right ſide:[30]It ſignifieth that theſe are they whom the Higheſt hath kept vnto their end: this is the ſmall kingdom and full of trouble, as thou ſaweſt.[31]And the Lyon whom thou ſaweſt riſing vp out of the wood, and roaring, and ſpeaking to the Eagle, and rebuking her for her vnrighteouſneſſe, with all the words which thou haſt heard,[32]This is the Anointed which the Higheſt hath kept for them, and for their wickedneſſe vnto the end: he ſhall reprooue them, and ſhall vpbraid them with their crueltie.[33]For hee ſhall ſet them before him aliue in iudgement, and ſhall rebuke them and correct them.[34]For the reſt of my people ſhall he deliuer with mercie, thoſe that haue bin preſerued vpon my borders, and he ſhal make them ioyfull vntill the comming of the day of iudgement, whereof I haue ſpoken vnto thee from the beginning.[35]This is the dreame that thou ſaweſt, and theſe are the interpretations.[36]Thou onely haſt bene meete to know this ſecret of the Higheſt.[37]Therefore write all theſe things that thou haſt ſeene, in a booke, and hide them.[38]And teach them to the wiſe of the people, whoſe hearts thou knoweſt may comprehend, & keepe theſe ſecrets.[39]But wait thou here thy ſelfe yet ſeuen dayes moe, that it may be ſhewed thee whatſoeuer it pleaſeth the Higheſt to declare vnto thee: And with that he went his way.[40]And it came to paſſe when all the people ſaw that the ſeuen dayes were paſt, and I not come againe into the citie, they gathered them all together, from the leaſt vnto the greateſt, and came vnto me, and ſaid,[41]What haue we offended thee? and what euill haue we done againſt thee, that thou forſakeſt vs, and ſitteſt here in this place?[42]For of all the prophets thou only art left vs, as a cluſter of the vintage, and as a candle in a darke place, and as a hauen or ſhip preſerued from the tempeſt:[43]Are not the euils which are come to vs, ſufficient?[44]If thou ſhalt forſake vs, how much better had it bene for vs, if we alſo had bene burnt in the midſt of Sion.[45]For we are not better then they that died there. And they wept with a loud voice: then anſwered I them, and ſaid,[46]Be of good comfort, O Iſrael, and be not heauy thou houſe of Iacob.[47]For the Higheſt hath you in remembrance, and the mighty hath not forgotten you in temptation.[48]As for mee, I haue not forſaken you, neither am I departed from you: but am come into this place, to pray for the deſolation of Sion, and that I might ſeeke mercy for the low eſtate of your Sanctuary.[49]And now goe your way home euery man, and after theſe dayes will I come vnto you.[50]So the people went their way into the city, like as I commanded them:[51]But I remained ſtill in the field ſeuen dayes, as the Angel commanded me, and did eate onely in thoſe dayes, of the flowers of the fielde, and had my meat of the herbes.

CHAPTER 13[1]And it came to paſſe after ſeuen dayes, I dreamed a dreame by night.[2]And loe, there aroſe a winde from the ſea that it mooued all the waues thereof.[3]And I beheld, and loe, that man waxed ſtrong with the thouſands of heauen: and when he turned his countenance to looke, all the things trembled that were ſeene vnder him.[4]And whenſoeuer the voyce went out of his mouth, all they burnt, that heard his voyce, like as the earth faileth when it feeleth the fire.[5]And after this I beheld, and loe, there was gathered together a multitude of men out of number, from the foure windes of the heauen, to ſubdue the man that came out of the ſea.[6]But I beheld, and loe, hee had graued himſelfe a great mountaine, and flew vp vpon it.[7]But I would haue ſeene the region, or place, whereout the hill was grauen, and I could not.[8]And after this I beheld, and loe, all they which were gathered together to ſubdue him, were ſore afraid, and yet durſt fight.[9]And loe, as hee ſaw the violence of the multitude that came, hee neither lift vp his hand, nor held ſword, nor any inſtrument of warre.[10]But onely I ſaw that he ſent out of his mouth, as it had bene a blaſt of fire, and out of his lippes a flaming breath, and out of his tongue he caſt out ſparkes and tempeſts,[11]And they were all mixt together; the blaſt of fire, the flaming breath, and the great tempeſt, and fel with violence vpon the multitude, which was prepared to fight, and burnt them vp euery one, ſo that vpon a ſudden, of an innumerable multitude, nothing was to be perceiued, but onely duſt and ſmell of ſmoke: whē I ſaw this, I was afraid.[12]Afterward ſaw I the ſame man come downe from the mountaine, and call vnto him an other peaceable multitude.[13]And there came much people vnto him, whereof ſome were glad, ſome were ſory, ſome of them were bound, and other ſome brought of them that were offred: then was I ſicke through great feare, and I awaked and ſaid,[14]Thou haſt ſhewed thy ſeruant wonders from the beginning, and haſt counted me worthy that thou ſhouldeſt receiue my prayer:[15]ſhew mee now yet the interpretation of this dreame.[16]For as I conceiue in mine vnderſtanding, woe vnto them that ſhall be left in thoſe dayes; and much more woe vnto them that are not left behinde.[17]For they that were not left, were in heauineſse.[18]Now vnderſtand I the things that are layde vp in the latter dayes, which ſhall happen vnto them, and to thoſe that are left behinde.[19]Therefore are they come into great perils, and many neceſsities, like as theſe dreames declare.[20]Yet is it eaſier for him that is in danger, to come into theſe things, then to paſſe away as a cloud out of the world, and not to ſee the things that happen in the laſt dayes. And he anſwered vnto me, and ſaid,[21]The interpretation of the viſion ſhal I ſhew thee, and I wil open vnto thee, the thing that thou haſt required.[22]Wheras thou haſt ſpoken of them that are left behinde, this is the interpretation.[23]He that ſhall endure the perill in that time, hath kept himſelfe: they that be fallen into danger, are ſuch as haue workes, and faith towards the Almightie.[24]Know this therefore, that they which be left behinde, are more bleſſed then they that be dead. 25 This is the meaning of the viſion: Whereas thou ſaweſt a man comming vp from the middeſt of the ſea: 26 The ſame is hee whom God the higheſt hath kept a great ſeaſon, which by his owne ſelfe ſhall deliuer his creature: and hee ſhall order them that are left behinde. 27 And whereas thou ſaweſt, that out of his mouth there came as a blaſt of winde, and fire, and ſtorme: 28 And that he helde neither ſword, nor any inſtrument of warre, but that the ruſhing in of him deſtroyed the whole multitude that came to ſubdue him, this is the interpretation. 29 Behold, the dayes come, when the moſt high wil begin to deliuer them that are vpon the earth. 30 And he ſhall come to the aſtoniſhment of them that dwell on the earth. 31 And one ſhall vndertake to fight againſt another, one city againſt another, one place againſt another, one people againſt another, and one realme againſt another. 32 And the time ſhalbe, when theſe things ſhall come to paſſe, and the ſignes ſhall happen which I ſhewed thee before, and then ſhall my ſonne be declared, whom thou ſaweſt as a man aſcending. 33 And when all the people heare his voice, euery man ſhall in their owne land, leaue the battaile they haue one againſt another. 34 And an innumerable multitude ſhalbe gathered together, as thou ſaweſt them willing to come, and to ouercome him by fighting. 35 But hee ſhall ſtand vpon the top of the mount Sion. 36 And Sion ſhall come and ſhall be ſhewed to all men, being prepared and builded, like as thou ſaweſt the hill grauen without hands. 37 And this my ſonne ſhall rebuke the wicked inuentions of thoſe nations, which for their wicked life are fallen into the tempeſt, 38 And ſhall lay before them their euill thoughts, and the torments wherwith they ſhall begin to be tormented, which are like vnto a flame: and hee ſhall deſtroy them without labour, by the law which is like vnto fire. 39 And whereas thou ſaweſt that hee gathered another peaceable multitude vnto him; 40 Thoſe are the ten tribes, which were caried away priſoners out of their owne land, in the time of Oſea the king, whom Salmanaſar the king of Aſſyria ledde away captiue, and hee caried them ouer the waters, and ſo came they into another land. 41 But they tooke this counſaile amongſt themſelues, that they would leaue the multitude of the heathen, and goe foorth into a further countrey, where neuer mankind dwelt, 42 That they might there keepe their ſtatutes, which they neuer kept in their owne land. 43 And they entred into Euphrates by the narrow paſsages of the Riuer. 44 For the moſt high then ſhewed ſignes for them, and held ſtill the flood, till they were paſſed ouer. 45 For through that countrey there was a great way to goe; namely, of a yeere and a halfe: and the ſame region is called Arſareth. 46 Then dwelt they there vntill the latter time; and now when they ſhall begin to come, 47 The higheſt ſhall ſtay the ſprings of the ſtreame againe, that they may go through: therefore ſaweſt thou the multitude with peace. 48 But thoſe that be left behinde of thy people, are they that are found within my borders. 49 Now when hee deſtroyeth the multitude of the nations that are gathered together, he ſhal defend his people that remaine. 50 And then ſhall hee ſhewe them great wonders. 51 Then ſaid I, O Lord, that beareſt rule, ſhew me this: Wherefore haue I ſeene the man comming vp from the midſt of the ſea? 52 And he ſaid vnto me, Like as thou canſt neither ſeeke out, nor know the things that are in the deepe of the ſea: euen ſo can no man vpon earth ſee my ſonne, or thoſe that be with him, but in the day time. 53 This is the interpretation of the dreame which thou ſaweſt, and whereby thou onely art here lightened. 54 For thou haſt forſaken thine owne way, and applied thy diligence vnto my law, and ſought it. 55 Thy life haſt thou ordered in wiſdome, and haſt called vnderſtanding thy mother. 56 And therefore haue I ſhewed thee the treaſures of the Higheſt: After other three dayes, I will ſpeake other things vnto thee, and declare vnto thee mightie and wonderous things. 57 Then went I forth into the field giuing praiſe and thanks greatly vnto the moſt High, becauſe of his wonders which he did in time, 58 And becauſe hee gouerneth the ſame, and ſuch things as fall in their ſeaſons, and there I ſate three dayes.

CHAPTER 14 1 And it came to paſſe, vpon the third day I ſate vnder an oke, and behold, there came a voyce out of a buſh ouer againſt me, and ſaid, Eſdras, Eſdras. 2 And I ſaid, Here am I Lord, and I ſtood vp vpon my feet. 3 Then ſaid he vnto me, In the buſh I did manifeſtly reueale my ſelfe vnto Moſes, and talked with him, when my people ſerued in Egypt. 4 And I ſent him, and led my people out of Egypt, and brought him vp to the mount of Sinai, where I held him by me, a long ſeaſon, 5 And told him many wonderous things, and ſhewed him the ſecrets of the times, and the end, and commanded him, ſaying, 6 Theſe wordes ſhalt thou declare, and theſe ſhalt thou hide. 7 And now I ſay vnto thee, 8 That thou lay vp in thy heart the ſignes that I haue ſhewed, and the dreames that thou haſt ſeene, and the interpretations which thou haſt heard: 9 For thou ſhalt be taken away from all, and from henceforth thou ſhalt remaine with my ſonne, and with ſuch as be like thee, vntill the times be ended. 10 For the world hath loſt his youth, and the times begin to waxe old. 11 For the world is diuided into twelue parts, and the ten parts of it are gone already, and halfe of a tenth part. 12 And there remaineth that which is after the halfe of the tenth part. 13 Now therefore ſet thine houſe in order, and reproue thy people, comfort ſuch of them as be in trouble, and now renounce corruption. 14 Let go frō thee mortall thoughts, caſt away the burdens of man, put off now the weake nature, 15 And ſet aſide the thoughts that are moſt heauy vnto thee, and haſte thee to flie from theſe times. 16 For yet greater euils then thoſe which thou haſt ſeene happen, ſhall bee done hereafter. 17 For looke how much the world ſhall be weaker through age: ſo much the more ſhall euils increaſe vpon them that dwell therein. 18 For the trueth is fled farre away, and leaſing is hard at hand: For now haſteth the viſion to come, which thou haſt ſeene. 19 Then anſwered I before thee, and ſaid, 20 Behold, Lord, I will go as thou haſt commanded me, and reprooue the people which are preſent, but they that ſhall be borne afterward, who ſhall admoniſh them? thus the world is ſet in darkenes, and they that dwell therein, are without light. 21 For thy law is burnt, therefore no man knoweth the things that are done of thee, or the works that ſhal begin. 22 But if I haue found grace before thee, ſend the holy Ghoſt into me, and I ſhall write all that hath bene done in the world, ſince the beginning, which were written in thy Lawe, that men may find thy path, and that they which will liue in the latter dayes, may liue. 23 And he anſwered me, ſaying, Goe thy way, gather the people together, and ſay vnto them, that they ſeeke thee not for fourtie dayes. 24 But looke thou prepare thee many boxe trees, and take with thee Sarea, Dabria, Selemia, Eranus and Aſiel, theſe fiue which are ready to write ſwiftly. 25 And come hither, and I ſhall light a candle of vnderſtanding in thine heart, which ſhall not be put out, till the things be performed which thou ſhalt beginne to write. 26 And when thou haſt done, ſome things ſhalt thou publiſh, and ſome things ſhalt thou ſhew ſecretly to the wiſe: to morrowe this houre ſhalt thou beginne to write. 27 Then went I foorth as he commanded, and gathered all the people together, and ſaid, 28 Heare theſe words, O Iſrael. 29 Our fathers at the beginning were ſtrangers in Egypt, from whence they were deliuered: 30 And receiued the law of life which they kept not, which ye alſo haue tranſgreſſed after them. 31 Then was the land, euen the land of Sion, parted among you by lot, but your fathers, and yee your ſelues haue done vnrighteouſneſſe, and haue not kept the wayes which the Higheſt commanded you. 32 And for as much as he is a righteous iudge, hee tooke from you in time, the thing that he had giuen you. 33 And now are you heere, and your brethren amongſt you. 34 Therefore if ſo be that you will ſubdue your owne vnderſtanding, and reforme your hearts, yee ſhall be kept aliue, and after death yee ſhall obtaine mercy. 35 For after death, ſhall the iudgement come, when we ſhall liue againe: and then ſhall the names of the righteous be manifeſt, and the workes of the vngodly ſhall be declared. 36 Let no man therefore come vnto me now, nor ſeeke after me theſe fourty dayes. 37 So I tooke the fiue men as hee commanded me, and we went into the field, and remained there. 38 And the next day behold a voyce called mee ſaying, Eſdras, open thy mouth and drinke that I giue thee to drinke. 39 Then opened I my mouth, and behold, he reached me a full cup, which was full as it were with water, but the colour of it was like fire. 40 And I tooke it, and dranke: and when I had drunke of it, my heart vttered vnderſtanding: and wiſedome grew in my breſt, for my ſpirit ſtrengthened my memory. 41 And my mouth was opened and ſhut no more. 42 The higheſt gaue vnderſtanding vnto the fiue men, and they wrote the wonderfull viſions of the night, that were told, which they knew not: And they ſate fourty dayes, and they wrote in the day, and at night they ate bread. 43 As for me I ſpake in the day, and held not my tongue by night: 44 In fourty dayes they wrote two hundred and foure bookes. 45 And it came to paſſe when the fourty dayes were fulfilled, that the Higheſt ſpake, ſaying, The firſt that thou haſt written, publiſh

openly, that the worthy and vnworthy may read it.46But keepe the
ſeuenty laſt, that thou mayeſt deliuer them onely to ſuch as be wiſe,
among the people.47For in them is the ſpring of vnderſtanding, the
fountains of wiſedome, and the ſtreame of knowledge.48And I did ſo.

CHAPTER 151Behold, ſpeake thou in the eares of my people the
words of propheſie, which I will put in thy mouth, ſaith the Lord.2And
cauſe them to be written in paper: for they are faithfull and true.3Feare
not the imaginations againſt thee, let not the incredulity of them trouble
thee, that ſpeake againſt thee.4For all the vnfaithfull ſhall die in their
vnfaithfulneſse.5Behold, ſaith the Lord, I will bring plagues vpon the
world; the ſword, famine, death, and deſtruction.6For wickedneſſe hath
exceedingly polluted the whole earth, and their hurtfull workes are
fulfilled.7Therefore ſaith the Lord,8I will hold my tongue no more as
touching their wickedneſſe, which they prophanely commit, neither wil
I ſuffer them in thoſe things, in which they wickedly exerciſe themſelues:
behold, the innocent & righteous blood cryeth vnto me, and the ſoules
of the iuſt complaine continually.9And therefore ſaith the Lord, I wil
ſurely auenge them, and receiue vnto me, all the innocent blood from
among them.10Beholde, my people is ledde as a flocke to the ſlaughter:
I wil not ſuffer them now to dwel in the land of Egypt.11But I will bring
them with a mighty hand, and a ſtretched out arme, and ſmite Egypt
with plagues as before, and wil deſtroy al the land thereof.12Egypt ſhal
mourne, and the foundation of it ſhall bee ſmitten with the plague and
puniſhment, that God ſhall bring vpon it.13They that till the ground ſhall
mourne: for their ſeedes ſhall faile, through the blaſting, and haile, and
with a fearefull conſtellation.14Woe to the world, and them that dwell
therein.15For the ſword and their deſtruction draweth nigh, and one
people ſhall ſtand vp to fight againſt another, and ſwords in their
hands.16For there ſhalbe ſedition among men, and inuading one
another, they ſhal not regard their kings, nor princes, and the courſe of
their actions ſhall ſtand in their power.17A man ſhall deſire to goe into a
citie, and ſhall not be able.18For becauſe of their pride, the cities ſhalbe
troubled, the houſes ſhalbe deſtroyed, and men ſhalbe afraid.19A man
ſhall haue no pitie vpon his neighbour, but ſhall deſtroy their houſes
with the ſword, and ſpoile their goods, becauſe of the lacke of bread,
and for great tribulation.20Behold, ſaith God, I will call together all the
Kings of the earth to reuerence me, which are from the riſing of the
Sunne, from the South, from the Eaſt, and Libanus: to turne themſelues
one againſt another, and repay the things that they haue done to
them.21Like as they doe yet this day vnto my choſen, ſo will I doe alſo
and recompenſe in their boſome, Thus ſaith the Lord God;22My right
hand ſhall not ſpare the ſinners, and my ſword ſhal not ceaſe ouer them,
that ſhed innocent blood vpon earth.23The fire is gone foorth from his
wrath, and hath conſumed the foundations of the earth, and the ſinners
like the ſtraw that is kindled.24Wo to them that ſinne and keepe not my
cōmandements, ſaith the Lord.25I will not ſpare them: goe your way ye
children from the power, defile not my Sanctuary:26For the Lord
knoweth all them that ſinne againſt him, and therefore deliuereth he
them vnto death and deſtruction.27For now are the plagues come vpon
the whole earth, and ye ſhall remaine in them, for God ſhal not deliuer
you, becauſe ye haue ſinned againſt him.28Behold an horrible viſion, and
the appearance thereof from the Eaſt.29Where the nations of the
dragons of Arabia ſhall come out with many charets, and the multitude
of them ſhalbe caried as the winde vpon earth, that all they which heare
them, may feare and tremble.30Alſo the Carmanians raging in wrath,
ſhall go forth as the wilde bores of the wood, and with great power ſhall
they come, and ioyne battell with them, and ſhall waſte a portion of the
land of the Aſſyrians.31And then ſhall the dragons haue the vpper hand,
remembring their nature, and if they ſhall turne themſelues, conſpiring
together in great power to perſecute them,32Then theſe ſhalbe troubled,
and keepe ſilence through their power, and ſhall flee.33And from the
land of the Aſſyrians, ſhall the enemy beſiege them, and conſume ſome
of them, and in their hoſt ſhall be feare, and dread and ſtrife among their
kings.34Behold clouds from the Eaſt, and from the North, vnto the
South, and they are very horrible to looke vpon; full of wrath and
ſtorme.35They ſhall ſmite one vpon another, & they ſhall ſmite downe a
great multitude of ſtarres vpon the earth, euen their owne ſtarre; and
blood ſhalbe from the ſword vnto the belly.36And doung of men vnto
the camels hough.37And there ſhalbe great fearefulneſse and trembling
vpon earth: and they that ſee the wrath, ſhall be afraid, and trembling
ſhall come vpon them.38And then ſhall there come great ſtormes, from
the South, and from the North, & another part from the Weſt.39And
ſtrong winds ſhal Ariſe from the Eaſt, and ſhall open it, and the cloud
which hee raiſed vp in wrath, and the ſtarre ſtirred to cauſe feare toward
the Eaſt and Weſt winde, ſhalbe deſtroyed.40The great and mightie
cloudes ſhall be lifted vp full of wrath, and the ſtarre, that they may make
all the earth afraid, and them that dwel therein, and they ſhall powre out
ouer euery high and eminent place, an horrible ſtarre.41Fire and haile,
and fleeing ſwords, and many waters, that all fields may be full, and all
riuers with the abundance of great waters.42And they ſhal breake downe
the cities, and walls, mountaines and hils, trees of the wood, and graſſe
of the medowes, and their corne.43And they ſhal goe ſtedfaſtly vnto
Babylon, and make her afraid.44They ſhall come to her, and beſiege her,
the ſtarre and all wrath ſhall they powre out vpon her, then ſhall the duſt
and ſmoke goe vp vnto the heauen: and all they that be about her, ſhall
bewaile her.45And they that remaine vnder her, ſhall doe ſeruice vnto
them that haue put her in feare.46And thou Aſia that art partaker of the
hope of Babylon, and art the glory of her perſon:47Woe be vnto thee
thou wretch, becauſe thou haſt made thy ſelfe like vnto her, and haſt
deckt thy daughters in whoredome, that they might pleaſe and glory in
thy louers, which haue alway deſired to commit whordome with
thee.48Thou haſt followed her, that is hated in all her works and
inuentions: therefore ſayth God,49I will ſend plagues vpon thee:
widowhood, pouertie, famine, ſword, and peſtilence, to waſte thy houſes
with deſtruction and death.50And the glory of the power ſhall be dried
vp as floure, when the heate ſhall Ariſe that is ſent ouer thee.51Thou
ſhalt bee weakened as a poore woman with ſtripes, and as one chaſtiſed
with woundes, ſo that the mightie and louers ſhall not be able to receiue
thee.52Would I with iealouſie haue ſo proceeded againſt thee, ſaith the
Lord,53If thou haddeſt not alway ſlaine my choſen, exalting the ſtroke
of thine hands, & ſaying ouer their dead, when thou waſt drunken,54Set
foorth the beauty of thy countenance.55The reward of thy whoredome
ſhall be in thy boſome, therefore ſhalt thou receiue recompenſe.56Like
as thou haſt done vnto my choſen, ſayth the Lord; euen ſo ſhall God
doe vnto thee, and ſhall deliuer thee into miſchiefe.57Thy children ſhall
die of hunger, and thou ſhalt fall through the ſword: thy cities ſhalbe
broken downe, and all thine ſhall periſh with the ſword in the
field.58They that be in the mountaines ſhall die of hunger, and eate their
owne fleſh, and drinke their owne blood, for very hunger of bread, &
thirſt of water.59Thou, as vnhappy, ſhalt come through the ſea, and
receiue plagues againe.60And in the paſsage, they ſhall ruſh on the idle
citie, and ſhall deſtroy ſome portion of thy land, and conſume part of
thy glory, and ſhall returne to Babylon that was deſtroyed.61And thou
ſhalt be caſt downe by them, as ſtubble, and they ſhall be vnto thee as
fire,62And ſhall conſume thee and thy cities, thy land and thy
mountaines, all thy woods and thy fruitfull trees ſhall they burne vp with
fire.63Thy children ſhall they cary away captiue, and looke what thou
haſt, they ſhall ſpoile it, and marre the beauty of thy face.

CHAPTER 161Woe be vnto thee, Babylon and Aſia, woe be vnto thee
Egypt and Syria.2Gird vp your ſelues with clothes of ſacke and haire,
bewaile your children, and be ſory, for your deſtruction is at hand.3A
ſword is ſent vpon you, and who may turne it backe?4A fire is ſent
among you, and who may quench it?5Plagues are ſent vnto you, and
what is he that may driue them away?6May any man driue away a hungry
Lion in the wood? or may any one quench the fire in ſtubble, when it
hath begun to burne?7May one turne againe the arrow that is ſhot of a
ſtrong archer?8The mightie Lord ſendeth the plagues, and who is hee
that can driue them away?9A fire ſhall goe foorth from his wrath: & who
is he that may quench it?10He ſhall caſt lightnings, and who ſhall not
feare? he ſhall thunder, and who ſhall not be afraid?11The Lord ſhall
threaten, and who ſhall not be vtterly beaten to powder at his
preſence?12The earth quaketh and the foundations thereof, the ſea
Ariſeth vp with waues from the deepe, and the waues of it are troubled,
and the fiſhes thereof alſo before the Lord, and before the glorie of his
power.13For ſtrong is his right hand that bendeth the bow, his arrowes
that hee ſhooteth are ſharpe, and ſhall not miſse when they begin to bee
ſhot into the ends of the world.14Behold, the plagues are ſent, and ſhall
not returne againe, vntill they come vpon the earth.15The fire is kindled,

and ſhall not be put out, till it conſume the foundation of the earth. 16 Like as an arrow which is ſhot of a mightie archer returneth not backward: euen ſo the plagues that ſhall be ſent vpon earth, ſhall not returne againe. 17 Woe is me, woe is me, who will deliuer me in thoſe dayes? 18 The beginning of ſorrowes, and great mournings, the beginning of famine, and great death: the beginning of warres, and the powers ſhall ſtand in feare, the beginning of euils, what ſhall I doe when theſe euils ſhal come? 19 Behold, famine, and plague, tribulation and anguiſh, are ſent as ſcourges for amendment. 20 But for all theſe things they ſhall not turne from their wickednes, nor be alway mindfull of the ſcourges. 21 Behold, victuals ſhall be ſo good cheape vpon earth, that they ſhal think themſelues to be in good caſe, and euen then ſhall euils growe vpon earth, ſword, famine, and great confuſion. 22 For many of them that dwell vpon earth, ſhall periſh of famine, and the other that eſcape the hunger, ſhall the ſword deſtroy. 23 And the dead ſhall be caſt out as doung, and there ſhalbe no man to comfort them, for the earth ſhall be waſted, and the cities ſhall be caſt downe. 24 There ſhall be no man left to till the earth, and to ſow it. 25 The trees ſhall giue fruite, and who ſhall gather them? 26 The grapes ſhall ripe, and who ſhall treade them? for all places ſhall be deſolate of men. 27 So that one man ſhall deſire to ſee another, and to heare his voyce. 28 For of a citie there ſhalbe ten left, and two of the field which ſhall hide themſelues in the thicke groues, and in the clefts of rockes. 29 As in an orchard of oliues, vpon euery tree there are left three or foure oliues: 30 Or, when as a vineyard is gathered, there are left ſome cluſters of them that diligently ſeek through þe vineyard: 31 Euen ſo in thoſe dayes there ſhalbe three or foure left by them that ſearch their houſes with the ſword. 32 And the earth ſhall be laid waſte, and the fields therof ſhal waxe old, and her wayes and all her paths ſhall grow full of thornes, becauſe no man ſhal trauaile therethrough. 33 The virgins ſhall mourne hauing no bridegromes, þe women ſhal mourne hauing no huſbands, their daughters ſhall mourne hauing no helpers. 34 In the warres ſhall their bridegromes bee deſtroyed, and their huſbands ſhall periſh of famine. 35 Heare now theſe things, and vnderſtand them, ye ſeruants of the Lord. 36 Behold the word of the Lord, receiue it, beleeue not the gods of whom the Lord ſpake. 37 Behold, the plagues draw nigh, and are not ſlacke. 38 As when a woman with childe in the ninth month bringeth forth her ſon, within two or three houres of her birth great paines compaſſe her wombe, which paines, when the child commeth forth, they ſlacke not a moment, 39 Euen ſo ſhall not the plagues bee ſlacke to come vpon the earth, and the world ſhall mourne, and ſorrowes ſhal come vpon it on euery ſide. 40 O my people, Heare my word: make you ready to the battell, and in thoſe euils, be euen as pilgrimes vpon the earth. 41 He that ſelleth let him be as hee that fleeth away: and he that buyeth, as one that will looſe. 42 He that occupieth merchandize, as he that had no profit by it: and he that buildeth, as hee that ſhall not dwell therein. 43 He that ſoweth, as if he ſhould not reape: ſo alſo he that planteth the vineyard, as he that ſhal not gather the grapes. 44 They that marry, as they that ſhall get no children: and they that marrie not, as the widowers. 45 And therefore they that labour, labour in vaine. 46 For ſtrangers ſhall reape their fruits, and ſpoile their goods, ouerthrowe their houſes; and take their children captiues, for in captiuity and famine ſhall they get children. 47 And they that occupy their merchandize with robbery, the more they decke their citties, their houſes, their poſſeſſions and their owne perſons: 48 The more will I be angry with them for their ſinne, ſaith the Lord. 49 Like as an whore enuieth a right honeſt and vertuous woman: 50 So ſhall righteouſneſſe haue iniquity, when ſhe decketh herſelfe, and ſhall accuſe her, to her face, when he commeth that ſhall defend him that diligently ſearcheth out euery ſinne vpon earth. 51 And therfore be yee not like therunto, nor to the workes thereof. 52 For yet a little iniquitie ſhall be taken away out of the earth, and righteouſneſſe ſhall reigne among you. 53 Let not the ſinner ſay that he hath not ſinned: for God ſhall burne coales of fire vpon his head, which ſaith before the Lord God and his glory, I haue not ſinned. 54 Behold, the Lord knoweth all the workes of men, their imaginations, their thoughts, and their hearts: 55 Which ſpake but the word, let the earth be made, and it was made: let the heauen be made, and it was created. 56 In his word were the ſtarres made, and he knoweth the number of them. 57 He ſearcheth the deepe, and the treaſures thereof, he hath meaſured the ſea, and what it containeth. 58 He hath ſhut the ſea in the midſt of the waters, and with his word hath he hanged the earth vpon the waters. 59 He ſpreadeth out the heauens like a vault, vpon the waters hath he founded it. 60 In the deſart hath hee made ſprings of water, and pooles vpon the tops of the mountaines, that the floods might powre downe from the high rockes to water the earth. 61 He made man, and put his heart in the midſt of the body, and gaue him breath, life, and vnderſtanding. 62 Yea and the ſpirit of Almighty God, which made all things, and ſearcheth out all hidden things in the ſecrets of the earth. 63 Surely he knoweth your inuentions, and what you thinke in your hearts, euen them that ſinne, and would hide their ſinne. 64 Therefore hath the Lord exactly ſearched out all your workes, and he will put you all to ſhame. 65 And when your ſinnes are brought foorth yee ſhalbe aſhamed before men, and your owne ſinnes ſhall be your accuſers in that day. 66 What will yee doe? or how will yee hide your ſinnes before God and his Angels? 67 Behold, God himſelfe is the iudge, feare him: leaue off from your ſinnes, and forget your iniquities to medle no more with them for euer, ſo ſhall God lead you forth, and deliuer you from all trouble. 68 For behold, the burning wrath of a great multitude is kindled ouer you, and they ſhall take away certaine of you, and feede you being idle with things offered vnto idoles. 69 And they that conſent vnto them ſhall be had in deriſion, and in reproch, and troden vnder foote. 70 For there ſhall be in euery place, and in the next cities a great inſurrection vpon thoſe that feare the Lord. 71 They ſhall be like mad men, ſparing none, but ſtill ſpoiling and deſtroying thoſe that feare the Lord. 72 For they ſhal waſte and take away their goods, and caſt them out of their houſes. 73 Then ſhall they be knowen who are my choſen, and they ſhall be tried, as the gold in the fire: 74 Heare, O yee my beloued, ſaith the Lord: behold, the dayes of trouble are at hand, but I will deliuer you from the ſame. 75 Be yee not afraid, neither doubt, for God is your guide, 76 And the guide of them who keepe my commaundements, and precepts, ſaith the Lord God; Let not your ſinnes weigh you downe, and let not your iniquities lift vp themſelues. 77 Woe bee vnto them that are bound with their ſinnes, and couered with their iniquities: like as a field is couered ouer with buſhes, and the path thereof couered with thornes, that no man may trauell through. 78 It is left vndreſſed, and is caſt into the fire, to bee conſumed therewith.

TOBIT

CHAPTER 1 1 The Booke of the wordes of Tobit, ſonne of Tobiel, the ſon of Ananiel, the ſonne of Aduel, the ſonne of Gabael, of the ſeed of Aſael, of the Tribe of Nephthali, 2 Who in the time of Enemeſſar king of the Aſſyrians, was led captiue out of This be which is at the right hand of that citie, which is called properly Nephthali in Galile aboue Aſer. 3 I Tobit haue walked all the dayes of my life in the way of trueth, and iuſtice, and I did many almes deeds to my brethren, and my nation, who came with me to Nineue into the land of the Aſſyrians. 4 And when I was in mine owne countrey, in the land of Iſrael, being but yong, all the tribe of Nephthali my father, fell from the houſe of Ieruſalem, which was choſen out of all the tribes of Iſrael, that all the tribes ſhould ſacrifice there where the Temple of the habitation of the moſt High was conſecrated, and built for all ages. 5 Now all the tribes which together reuolted, and the houſe of my father Nephthali ſacrificed vnto the heifer Baal. 6 But I alone went often to Ieruſalem at the Feaſts, as it was ordeined vnto al the people of Iſrael by an euerlaſting decree, hauing the firſt fruits, and tenths of encreaſe, with that which was firſt ſhorne, and them gaue I at the Altar to the Prieſtes the children of Aaron. 7 The firſt tenth part of al increaſe, I gaue to the ſonnes of Aaron, who miniſtred at Ieruſalem: another tenth part I ſold away, and went, and ſpent it euery yeere at Ieruſalem. 8 And the third, I gaue vnto them to whom it was meet, as Debora my fathers mother had commanded mee, becauſe I was left an orphane by my father. 9 Furthermore when I was come to the age of a man, I married Anna of mine owne kinred, and of her I begate Tobias. 10 And when we were caried away captiues to Nineue, all my brethren, and thoſe that were of my kinred, did eate of the bread of the Gentiles. 11 But I kept my ſelfe from eating 12 Becauſe I remembred God with all my heart. 13 And the moſt High gaue me grace, and fauour before

Enemeſsar, ſo that I was his purueyour.14And I went into Media, and
left in truſt with Gabael, the brother of Gabrias at Rages a citie of Media,
ten talents of ſiluer.15Now when Enemeſsar was dead, Sennacherib his
ſonne reigned in his ſtead, whoſe eſtate was troubled, that I could not
goe into Media.16And in the time of Enemeſsar, I gaue many almes to
my brethren, and gaue my bread to the hungry,17And my clothes to the
naked: and if I ſaw any of my nation dead, or caſt about the walles of
Nineue, I buried him.18And if the king Sennacherib had ſlaine any, when
hee was come, and fledde from Iudea, I buried them priuily, (for in his
wrath hee killed many) but the bodies were not found, when they were
ſought for of the king.19And when one of the Nineuites went, and
complained of me to the king that I buried them, and hid my ſelfe:
vnderſtanding that I was ſought for to be put to death, I withdrew my
ſelfe for feare.20Then all my goods were forcibly taken away, neither was
there any thing left me, beſides my wife Anna, and my ſonne
Tobias.21And there paſſed not fiue and fiftie dayes before two of his
ſonnes killed him, and they fled into the mountaines of Ararath, and
Sarchedonus his ſonne reigned in his ſtead, who appointed ouer his
fathers accounts, and ouer all his affaires, Achiacharus my brother
Anaels ſonne.22And Achiacharus entreating for me, I returned to
Nineue: now Achiacharus was Cup-bearer, and keeper of the Signet, and
Steward, and ouerſeer of the accounts: and Sarchedonus appointed him
next vnto him: and hee was my brothers ſonne.
CHAPTER 2 1Now when I was come home againe, and my wife Anna
was reſtored vnto me, with my ſonne Tobias, in the feaſt of Pentecoſt,
which is the holy Feaſt of the ſeuen weekes, there was a good dinner
prepared me, in the which I ſate down to eate.2And when I ſaw
abundance of meate, I ſayd to my ſonne, Goe and bring what poore
man ſoeuer thou ſhalt finde out of our brethren, who is mindfull of the
Lord, and loe, I tarie for thee.3But he came againe and ſaid, Father, one
of our nation is ſtrangled, and is caſt out in the market place.4Then
before I had taſted of any meate, I ſtart vp and tooke him vp into a
roume, vntill the going downe of the Sunne.5Then I returned and
waſhed my ſelfe, and ate my meate in heauineſse,6Remembring that
propheſie of Amos, as hee ſaid; Your feaſts ſhall be turned into
mourning, and all your mirth into lamentation.7Therefore I wept: and
after the going downe of the Sunne, I went and made a graue, and buried
him.8But my neighbours mocked me, and ſaid, This man is not yet
afraide to be put to death for this matter, who fledde away, and yet loe,
he burieth the dead againe.9The ſame night alſo I returned from the
buriall, and ſlept by the wall of my court yard, being polluted, and my
face was vncouered:10And I knewe not that there were Sparrowes in the
wall, and mine eyes being open, the Sparrowes muted warme doung into
mine eyes, and a whiteneſse came in mine eyes, and I went to the
Phyſicians, but they helped me not: moreouer Achiacharus did nouriſh
mee, vntill I went into Elymais.11And my wife Anna did take womens
workes to doe.12And when ſhee had ſent them home to the owners, they
payd her wages, and gaue her alſo beſides a kid.13And when it was in
mine houſe, and beganne to crie, I ſaid vnto her, From whence is this
kidde? is it not ſtollen? render it to the owners, for it is not lawfull to
eate any thing that is ſtollen.14But ſhee replyed vpon me, It was giuen
for a gift more then the wages: Howbeit I did not beleeue her, but bade
her render it to the owners: and I was abaſhed at her. But ſhe replyed
vpon me, Where are thine almes, and thy righteous deedes? behold, thou
and all thy workes are knowen.
CHAPTER 3 1Then I being grieued, did weepe, and in my ſorrowe
prayed, ſaying,2O Lord, thou art iuſt and all thy workes, and all thy wayes
are mercie and trueth, and thou iudgeſt truely & iuſtly for
euer.3Remember me, and looke on me, puniſh me not for my ſinnes and
ignorances, and the ſinnes of my fathers, who haue ſinned before
thee.4For they obeyed not thy commandements, wherefore thou haſt
deliuered vs for a ſpoile, and vnto captiuitie, and vnto death, and for a
prouerbe of reproch to all the nations among whom we are
diſperſed.5And now thy iudgments are many and true: Deale with me
according to my ſinnes, and my fathers: becauſe we haue not kept thy
commandements, neither haue walked in trueth before thee.6Now
therefore deale with me as ſeemeth beſt vnto thee, and command my
ſpirit to be taken from me, that I may be diſſolued, and become earth:
for it is profitable for me to die, rather then to liue, becauſe I haue heard
falſe reproches, and haue much ſorow: command therfore that I may
now be deliuered out of this diſtreſſe, and goe into the euerlaſting place:
turne not thy face away from me.7It came to paſſe the ſame day, that in
Ecbatane a citie of Media, Sara the daughter of Raguel, was alſo
reproched by her fathers maides,8Becauſe that ſhe had bin maried to
ſeuen huſbands, whom Almodeus the euill ſpirit had killed, before they
had lien with her. Doeſt thou not knowe, ſaid they, that thou haſt
ſtrangled thine huſbands? thou haſt had already ſeuen huſbands, neither
waſt thou named after any of them.9Wherefore doeſt thou beate vs for
them? If they be dead, goe thy wayes after them, let vs neuer ſee of thee
either ſonne or daughter.10When ſhe heard theſe things, ſhe was very
ſorowful, ſo that ſhe thought to haue ſtrangled her ſelfe, and ſhe ſaid, I
am the onely daughter of my father, and if I doe this, it ſhall bee a
reproch vnto him, and I ſhall bring his old age with ſorow vnto the
graue.11Then ſhe prayed toward the window, & ſaid, Bleſſed art thou, O
Lord my God, and thine holy and glorious Name is bleſſed, and
honourable foreuer, let al thy works praiſe thee for euer.12And now, O
Lord, I ſet mine eyes and my face toward thee,13And ſay, take me out of
the earth, that I may heare no more the reproch.14Thou knoweſt, Lord,
that I am pure from all ſinne with man,15And that I neuer polluted my
name, nor the name of my father in the land of my captiuitie: I am the
onely daughter of my father, neither hath he any child to bee his heire,
neither any neere kinſeman, nor any ſonne of his aliue, to whome I may
keepe my ſelfe for a wife: my ſeuen huſbands are already dead, and why
ſhould I liue? but if it pleaſe not thee that I ſhould die, command ſome
regard to be had of me, and pitie taken of me, that I heare no more
reproch.16So the prayers of them both were heard before the Maieſty of
the great God.17And Raphael was ſent to heale them both, that is, to
ſcale away the whiteneſse of Tobits eyes, and to giue Sara the daughter
of Raguel, for a wife to Tobias the ſonne of Tobit, and to bind
Aſmodeus the euill ſpirit, becauſe ſhe belongeth to Tobias by right of
inheritance. The ſelfe ſame time came Tobit home, and entred into his
houſe, and Sara, the daughter of Raguel came downe from her vpper
chamber.
CHAPTER 4 1In that day Tobit remembred the money, which he had
committed to Gabael in Rages of Media,2And ſaid with himſelfe, I haue
wiſhed for death, wherefore doe I not call for my ſonne Tobias, that I
may ſignifie to him of the money before I die.3And when he had called
him, he ſaid; My ſonne, when I am dead, bury me, and deſpiſe not thy
mother, but honour her all the dayes of thy life, and doe that which ſhall
pleaſe her, and greiue her not.4Remember, my ſonne, that ſhee ſaw
many dangers for thee, when thou waſt in her wombe, and when ſhee is
dead, bury her by me in one graue.5My ſonne, be mindfull of the Lord
our God all thy dayes, and let not thy will be ſet to ſinne, or to tranſgreſse
his Commandements: doe vprightly all thy life long, and follow not the
wayes of vnrighteouſneſſe.6For if thou deale truely, thy doings ſhall
proſperouſly ſucceed to thee, and to all them that liue iuſtly.7Giue almes
of thy ſubſtance, and when thou giueſt almes, let not thine eye be
enuious, neither turne thy face from any poore, and the face of God
ſhall not be turned away from thee.8If thou haſt abundance, giue almes
accordingly: if thou haue but a litle, be not afraid to giue according to
that litle.9For thou layeſt vp a good treaſure for thy ſelfe againſt the day
of neceſsitie.10Becauſe that almes doth deliuer from death, and ſuffereth
not to come into darkneſſe.11For almes is a good gift vnto all that giue
it, in the ſight of the moſt High.12Beware of all whoredome, my ſonne,
and chiefely take a wife of the ſeed of thy fathers, and take not a ſtrange
woman to wife, which is not of thy fathers tribe: for we are the children
of the Prophets, Noe, Abraham, Iſaak, and Iacob: remember, my ſonne,
that our fathers from the beginning, euen that they all maried wiues of
their owne kinred, and were bleſſed in their children, and their ſeede
ſhall inherite the land.13Now therefore my ſonne, loue thy brethren, and
deſpiſe not in thy heart thy brethren, the ſonnes and daughters of thy
people, in not taking a wife of them: for in pride is deſtruction and much
trouble, and in lewdneſse is decay, and great want: for lewdneſse is the
mother of famine.14Let not the wages of any man, which hath wrought
for thee, tary with thee, but giue him it out of hand: for if thou ſerue
God he will alſo repay thee: be circumſpect, my ſonne, in all things thou
doeſt, and be wiſe in all thy conuerſation.15Doe that to no man which
thou hateſt: drinke not wine to make thee drunken; neither let
drunkenneſse goe with thee in thy iourney.16Giue of thy bread to the
hungry, and of thy garments to them that are naked, and according to

thine abundance giue almes, and let not thine eye be enuious, when thou
giueſt almes. 17 Powre out thy bread on the buriall of the iuſt, but giue
nothing to the wicked. 18 Aſke counſell of all that are wiſe, and deſpiſe
not any counſell that is profitable. 19 Bleſſe the Lord thy God alway, and
deſire of him that thy wayes may be directed, and that all thy pathes, and
counſels may proſper: for euery nation hath not counſell, but the Lord
himſelfe giueth all good things, and hee humbleth whom he will, as he
will; now therefore my ſonne, remember my commandements, neither
let them be put out of thy minde. 20 And now I ſignifie this to thee, that
I committed tenne talents to Gabael the ſonne of Gabrias at Rages in
Media. 21 And feare not my ſonne, that we are made poore, for thou haſt
much wealth, if thou feare God, and depart from all ſinne, and doe that
which is pleaſing in his ſight.
CHAPTER 5 1 Tobias then anſwered and ſaid, Father, I will doe all
things, which thou haſt commanded me. 2 But how can I receiue the
money, ſeeing, I know him not? 3 Then he gaue him the handwriting, and
ſaid vnto him, Seeke thee a man which may goe with thee whiles I yet
liue, and I will giue him wages, and goe, and receiue the
money. 4 Therefore when he went to ſeeke a man, he found Raphael that
was an Angell. 5 But he knew not; and he ſaid vnto him, Canſt thou goe
with me to Rages? & knoweſt thou thoſe places well? 6 To whom the
Angel ſaid, I will goe with thee, and I know the way well: for I haue
lodged with our brother Gabael. 7 Then Tobias ſaid vnto him, Tary for
me till I tell my father. 8 Then he ſaid vnto him, Goe and tary not; ſo he
went in, and ſaid to his father; Behold, I haue found one, which wil goe
with me. Then he ſaid, Call him vnto me, that I may know of what tribe
he is, and whether hee be a truſtie man to goe with thee. 9 So he called
him, and he came in, and they ſaluted one another. 10 Then Tobit ſaid
vnto him, Brother, ſhew me of what tribe and family thou art. 11 To
whom hee ſaid, Doeſt thou ſeeke for a tribe or family, or an hired man
to goe with thy ſonne? Then Tobit ſaid vnto him, I would know,
brother, thy kinred, and name. 12 Then he ſaid, I am Azarias, the ſonne
of Ananias the great, and of thy brethren. 13 Then Tobit ſaid, Thou art
welcome brother, be not now angry with mee, becauſe I haue enquired
to know thy tribe, and thy family, for thou art my brother, of an honeſt
& good ſtocke: for I know Ananias, and Ionathas ſonnes of that great
Samaias: as we went together to Ieruſalem to worſhip, and offered the
firſt borne, and the tenths of the fruits, and they were not ſeduced with
the errour of our brethren: my brother, thou art of a good ſtocke. 14 But
tell me, what wages ſhall I giue thee? wilt thou a drachme a day? and
things neceſsary as to my owne ſonne? 15 Yea moreouer, if ye returne
ſafe, I will adde ſome thing to the wages. 16 So they were well pleaſed.
Then ſaid he to Tobias; Prepare thy ſelfe for the iourney, and God ſend
you a good iourney. And when his ſonne had prepared all things for the
iourney, his father ſaid; Goe thou with this man, and God which
dwelleth in heauen proſper your iourney, & the Angel of God keepe you
company. So they went foorth both, and the yong mans dogge with
them. 17 But Anna his mother wept, and ſaid to Tobit, Why haſt thou
ſent away our ſonne? is hee not the ſtaffe of our hand, in going in and
out before vs? 18 Be not greedy (to adde) money to money: but let it bee
as refuſe in reſpect of our childe. 19 For that which the Lord hath giuen
vs to liue with, doeth ſuffice vs. 20 Then ſaid Tobit to her, Take no care
my ſiſter he ſhal returne in ſafety, and thine eyes ſhall ſee him. 21 For the
good Angel will keepe him company, and his iourney ſhall be
proſperous, and he ſhall returne ſafe. 22 Then ſhe made an end of
weeping.
CHAPTER 6 1 And as they went on their iourney, they came in the
euening to the riuer Tigris, & they lodged there. 2 And when the yong
man went downe to waſh himſelfe, a fiſh leaped out of the riuer, and
would haue deuoured him. 3 Then the Angel ſaid vnto him, Take the fiſh;
and the yong man layd hold of the fiſh, and drew it to land. 4 To whom
the Angel ſaid, Open the fiſh, and take the heart, and the liuer and the
gall, and put them vp ſafely. 5 So the yong man did as the Angel
commaunded him, and when they had roſted the fiſh, they did eate it:
then they both went on their way, till they drew neere to
Ecbatane. 6 Then the yong man ſaide to the Angel; Brother Azarias, to
what vſe is the heart, and the liuer, and the gall of the fiſh? 7 And he ſaid
vnto him, Touching the heart and the liuer, if a deuil, or an euil ſpirit
trouble any, we muſt make a ſmoke thereof before the man or the
woman, and the party ſhalbe no more vexed. 8 As for the gall it is good
to anoint a man that hath whitteneſſe in his eyes, and he ſhalbe
healed. 9 And when they were come neere to Rages; 10 The Angel ſaid to
the yong man, Brother, to day wee ſhall lodge with Raguel, who is thy
couſin; hee alſo hath one onely daughter, named Sara, I wil ſpeake for
her, that ſhe may be giuen thee for a wife. 11 For to thee doth the right of
her appertaine, ſeeing thou onely art of her kinred. 12 And the maide is
faire and wiſe, now therefore heare me, & I wil ſpeake to her father, and
when wee returne from Rages, we will celebrate the mariage: for I know
that Raguel cannot marry her to another according to the Law of Moſes,
but he ſhalbe guiltie of death, becauſe the right of inheritance doeth
rather appertaine to thee, then to any other. 13 Then the yong man
anſwered the Angel, I haue heard, brother Azarias, that this maide hath
beene giuen to ſeuen men, who all died in the marriage chamber: 14 And
now I am the onely ſonne of my father, and I am afraid, leſt if I goe in
vnto her, I die, as the other before; for a wicked ſpirit loueth her, which
hurteth no body, but thoſe which come vnto her; wherefore I alſo feare,
leſt I die, and bring my fathers and my mothers life (becauſe of me) to
the graue with ſorrow, for they haue no other ſonne to bury
them. 15 Then the Angel ſaid vnto him, Doeſt thou not remember the
precepts, which thy father gaue thee, that thou ſhouldeſt marrie a wife
of thine owne kindred? wherefore heare me, O my brother, for ſhe ſhall
be giuen thee to wife, and make thou no reckoning of the euil ſpirit, for
this ſame night ſhall ſhee be giuen thee in mariage. 16 And when thou
ſhalt come into the mariage chamber, thou ſhalt take the aſhes of
perfume, and ſhalt lay vpon them, ſome of the heart, and liuer of the
fiſh, and ſhalt make a ſmoke with it. 17 And the deuill ſhall ſmell it, and
flee away, and neuer come againe any more: but when thou ſhalt come
to her, riſe vp both of you, and pray to God, which is mercifull, who
will haue pity on you, and ſaue you: feare not, for ſhee is appointed vnto
thee from the beginning; and thou ſhalt preſerueher, and ſhee ſhall goe
with thee. Moreouer I ſuppoſe that ſhee ſhall beare thee children. Now
when Tobias had heard theſe things, he loued her, and his heart was
effectually ioyned to her.
CHAPTER 7 1 And when they were come to Ecbatane, they came to
the houſe of Raguel; and Sara met them: and after that they had ſaluted
one another, ſhee brought them into the houſe. 2 Then ſayd Raguel to
Edna his wife, How like is this yong man to Tobit my couſin? 3 And
Raguel aſked them, From whence are you, brethren? To whom they ſaid,
We are of the ſonnes of Nephthali, which are captiues in Nineue. 4 Then
hee ſaid to them, Doe yee know Tobit our kinſeman? And they ſaid, We
know him. Then ſaid hee, Is he in good health? 5 And they ſaid, Hee is
both aliue, and in good health: And Tobias ſayd, He is my father. 6 Then
Raguel leaped vp, and kiſſed him, and wept, 7 And bleſſed him; and ſaid
vnto him, Thou art the ſonne of an honeſt and good man: but when he
had heard that Tobit was blinde, he was ſorowfull, and wept. 8 And
likewiſe Edna his wife, and Sara his daughter wept. Moreouer, they
entertained them cheerefully, and after that they had killed a ramme of
the flocke, they ſet ſtore of meat on the table. Then ſaid Tobias to
Raphael, Brother Azarias, ſpeak of thoſe things, of which thou diddeſt
talke in the way, and let this buſineſſe be diſpatched. 9 So he
communicated the matter with Raguel, and Raguel ſaid to Tobias, Eate
and drink, and make merry: 10 For it is meet that thou ſhouldeſt marry
my daughter: neuertheleſſe I will declare vnto thee the trueth. 11 I haue
giuen my daughter in mariage to ſeuen men, who died that night they
came in vnto her: neuertheleſſe for the preſent be merry: But Tobias
ſaid, I will eate nothing here, till we agree and ſweare one to
another. 12 Raguel ſaid, Then take her from hencefoorth according to the
manner, for thou art her couſin, and ſhe is thine, and the mercifull God
giue you good ſucceſſe in all things. 13 Then he called his daughter Sara,
and ſhe came to her father, and hee tooke her by the hand, and gaue her
to be wife to Tobias, ſaying, Behold, take her after the Law of Moſes,
and leade her away to thy father: And he bleſſed them, 14 And called Edna
his wife, & tooke paper, and did write an inſtrument of couenants, and
ſealed it. 15 Then they began to eate. 16 After Raguel called his wife Edna,
and ſaid vnto her, Siſter, prepare another chamber, & bring her in
thither. 17 Which when ſhe had done as hee had bidden her, ſhe brought
her thither, and ſhe wept, & ſhe receiued the teares of her daughter, and
ſaid vnto her, 18 Be of good comfort, my daughter, the Lord of heauen
and earth giue thee ioy for this thy ſorow: be of good comfort, my
daughter.

CHAPTER 8 1And when they had ſupped, they brought Tobias in vnto her.2And as he went, he remembred the wordes of Raphael, and tooke the aſhes of the perfumes, and put the heart, and the liuer of the fiſh thereupon, and made a ſmoke therewith.3The which ſmell, when the euill ſpirit had ſmelled, hee fled into the outmoſt parts of Egypt, and the Angel bound him.4And after that they were both ſhut in together, Tobias roſe out of the bed and ſaid, Siſter, Ariſe, and let vs pray, that God would haue pitie on vs.5Then began Tobias to ſay, Bleſſed art thou, O God of our fathers, and bleſſed is thy holy and glorious Name for euer, let the heauens bleſſe thee, and all thy creatures.6Thou madeſt Adam, and gaueſt him Eue his wife for an helper & ſtay: of them came mankind: thou haſt ſaid, It is not good that man ſhould bee alone, let vs make vnto him an aide like to himſelfe.7And now, O Lord, I take not this my ſiſter for luſt, but vprightly: therefore mercifully ordeine, that wee may become aged together.8And ſhe ſaid with him, Amen.9So they ſlept both that night, and Raguel aroſe, and went & made a graue10Saying, I feare leſt he be dead.11But when Raguel was come into his houſe,12He ſaid vnto his wife Edna, Send one of the maids, and let her ſee, whether he be aliue: if he be not, that we may bury him, and no man know it.13So the maid opened the doore and went in, and found them both aſleepe,14And came forth, and told them, that he was aliue.15Then Raguel praiſed God, and ſaid, O God, thou art worthy to be praiſed with all pure and holy praiſe: therefore let thy Saints praiſe thee with all thy creatures, and let all thine Angels and thine elect praiſe thee for euer.16Thou art to be praiſed, for thou haſt made mee ioyfull, and that is not come to me, which I ſuſpected: but thou haſt dealt with vs according to thy great mercie.17Thou art to be praiſed, becauſe thou haſt had mercie of two, that were the onely begotten children of their fathers, grant them mercy, O Lord, and finiſh their life in health, with ioy and mercie.18Then Raguel bade his ſeruants to fill the graue.19And hee kept the wedding feaſt fourteene dayes.20For before the dayes of the mariage were finiſhed, Raguel had ſaid vnto him by an othe, that he ſhould not depart, till the fourteene dayes of the mariage were expired,21And then he ſhould take the halfe of his goods, and goe in ſafetie to his father, and ſhould haue the reſt when I and my wife be dead.

CHAPTER 9 1Then Tobias called Raphael, and ſaid vnto him,2Brother Azarias, Take with thee a ſeruant, and two camels, and go to Rages of Media to Gabael, & bring me the money, & bring him to the wedding.3For Raguel hath ſworne that I ſhall not depart.4But my father counteth the dayes, and if I tarie long, he will be very ſorie.5So Raphael went out and lodged with Gabael, and gaue him the handwriting, who brought forth bags, which were ſealed vp, and gaue them to him.6And earely in the morning they went forth both together, and came to the wedding, and Tobias bleſſed his wife.

CHAPTER 10 1Nowe Tobit his father counted euery day, and when the dayes of the iourney were expired, and they came not:2Then Tobit ſaid, Are they detained? or is Gabael dead? and there is no man to giue him the money?3Therefore he was very ſory.4Then his wife ſaid to him, My ſonne is dead, ſeeing hee ſtayeth long, and ſhe beganne to bewaile him, and ſaid,5Now I care for nothing, my ſonne, ſince I haue let thee goe, the light of mine eyes.6To whom Tobit ſaid, Hold thy peace, take no care; for he is ſafe.7But ſhe ſaid, Hold thy peace, and deceiue me not: my ſonne is dead, and ſhe went out euery day into the way which they went, and did eate no meat on the day time, and ceaſed not whole nights, to bewaile her ſonne Tobias, vntill the foureteene dayes of the wedding were expired, which Raguel had ſworne, that he ſhould ſpend there: Then Tobias ſaid to Raguel, Let me goe, for my father, and my mother look no more to ſee me.8But his father in law ſaid vnto him, Tary with me, and I will ſend to thy father, and they ſhall declare vnto him, how things goe with thee.9But Tobias ſaid, No: but let me goe to my father.10Then Raguel aroſe and gaue him Sara his wife, and halfe his goods, ſeruants, & cattell, and money.11And hee bleſſed them, and ſent them away, ſaying, The God of heauen giue you a proſperous iourney, my children.12And he ſaid to his daughter, Honour thy father and thy mother in law, which are now thy parents, that I may heare good report of thee: and hee kiſſed her. Edna alſo ſaid to Tobias, The Lord of heauen reſtore thee, my deare brother, and grant that I may ſee thy children of my daughter Sara before I die, that I may reioyce before the Lord: behold, I commit my daughter vnto thee of ſpeciall truſt, wherefore doe not entreate her euill.

CHAPTER 11 1After theſe things Tobias went his way, praiſing God that he had giuen him a proſperous iourney, and bleſſed Raguel, and Edna his wife, and went on his way till they drew neere vnto Nineue.2Then Raphael ſaid to Tobias, Thou knoweſt brother, how thou didſt leaue thy father.3Let vs haſte before thy wife, and prepare the houſe.4And take in thine hand the gall of the fiſh: ſo they went their way, and the dog went after them.5Now Anna ſate looking about towards the way for her ſonne.6And when ſhe eſpied him comming, ſhe ſaid to his father, Behold, thy ſonne commeth, and the man that went with him.7Then ſaid Raphael, I know, Tobias, that thy father will open his eyes.8Therefore annoint thou his eies with the gall, and being pricked therewith he ſhall rub, and the whitenefse ſhall fall away, and he ſhall ſee thee.9Then Anna ran forth, and fell vpon the necke of her ſonne, and ſaid vnto him, ſeeing I haue ſeene thee my ſonne, from henceforth, I am content to die, and they wept both.10Tobit alſo went forth toward the doore, and ſtumbled: but his ſonne ran vnto him,11And tooke hold of his father, and he ſtrake of the gall on his fathers eyes, ſaying, Be of good hope, my father.12And when his eyes beganne to ſmart, he rubbed them.13And the whitenefse pilled away from the corners of his eyes, and when he ſaw his ſonne, he fell vpon his necke.14And he wept, and ſaid, Bleſſed art thou, O God, and bleſſed is thy Name for euer, and bleſſed are all thine holy Angels:15For thou haſt ſcourged, and haſt taken pitie on me: for behold, I ſee my ſonne Tobias. And his ſonne went in reioycing, and told his father the great things that had happened to him in Media.16Then Tobit went out to meete his daughter in law at the gate of Niniue, reioycing and prayſing God: and they which ſaw him goe, marueiled becauſe he had receiued his ſight.17But Tobit gaue thankes before them: becauſe God had mercy on him. And when hee came neere to Sara his daughter in Law, hee bleſſed her, ſaying, Thou art welcome daughter: God be bleſſed which hath brought thee vnto vs, and bleſſed be thy father and thy mother; And there was ioy amongſt all his brethren which were at Nineue.18And Achiacharus, and Naſbas his brothers ſonne came.19And Tobias wedding was kept ſeuen dayes with great ioy.

CHAPTER 12 1Then Tobit called his ſon Tobias, and ſaid vnto him, My ſonne, ſee that the man haue his wages, which went with thee, and thou muſt giue him more.2And Tobias ſaid vnto him, O father, it is no harme to me to giue him halfe of thoſe things which I haue brought.3For he hath brought me againe to thee in ſafety, and made whole my wife, and brought mee the money, and likewiſe healed thee.4Then the old man ſaid: It is due vnto him.5So he called the Angell, and he ſaid vnto him, Take halfe of all that yee haue brought, and goe away in ſafety.6Then he tooke them both apart, and ſayd vnto them, Bleſſe God, praiſe him, and magnifie him, and praiſe him for the things which he hath done vnto you in the ſight of all that liue. It is good to praiſe God and exalt his name, & honorably to ſhew forth the works of God, therfore be not ſlacke to praiſe him.7It is good to keepe cloſe the ſecret of a King, but it is honorable to reueale the works of God: do that which is good, and no euill ſhall touch you.8Praier is good with faſting, and almes and righteouſneſſe: a little with righteouſnes is better then much with vnrighteouſneſſe: it is better to giue almes then to lay vp gold.9For almes doth deliuer from death, and ſhall purge away all ſinne. Thoſe that exerciſe almes, and righteouſneſſe, ſhall be filled with life.10But they that ſinne are enemies to their owne life.11Surely I will keep cloſe nothing from you. For I ſaid, it was good to keepe cloſe the ſecret of a King, but that it was honorable to reueale the works of God.12Now therefore, when thou didſt pray, and Sara thy daughter in Law, I did bring the remembrance of your prayers before the holy one, and when thou didſt bury the dead, I was with thee likewiſe.13And when thou didſt not delay to riſe vp, and leaue thy dinner to go and couer the dead, thy good deede was not hidde from me: but I was with thee.14And now God hath ſent mee to heale thee, & Sara thy daughter in law.15I am Raphael one of the ſeuen holy Angels, which preſent the prayers of the Saints, and which go in and out before the glory of the Holy one.16Then they were both troubled, and fel vpon their faces: for they feared.17But he ſaid vnto them, feare not, for it ſhall go well with you, praiſe God therefore.18For not of any fauour of mine, but by the will of our God I came, wherefore praiſe him for euer.19All theſe daies I did appeare vnto you, but I did neither eat nor drinke, but you did ſee a viſion.20Now therefore giue God thanks: for I go vp to him þt ſent me, but write all things which are done, in a booke.21And when they roſe, they ſaw him no more.22Then they confeſsed the great and wonderfull workes of God, and how the Angel of the Lord had appeared vnto them.

CHAPTER 131Then Tobit wrote a prayer of reioycing, and ſaid, Bleſſed be God that liueth for euer, and bleſſed be his kingdome:2For he doeth ſcourge, and hath mercy: hee leadeth downe to hell, and bringeth vp againe: neither is there any that can auoid his hand.3Confeſse him before the Gentiles, ye children of Iſrael: for he hath ſcattered vs among them.4There declare his greatneſse, and extoll him before all the liuing, for he is our Lord, and he is the God our father for euer:5And he wil ſcourge vs for our iniquities, and will haue mercy againe, and will gather vs out of all nations, among whom he hath ſcattered vs.6If you turne to him with your whole heart, and with your whole minde, and deale vprightly before him, then will hee turne vnto you, and will not hide his face from you: Therefore ſee what he will doe with you, and confeſse him with your whole mouth, and praiſe the Lord of might, and extoll the euerlaſting King: in the land of my captiuitie doe I praiſe him, and declare his might and maieſty to a ſinnefull nation: O yee ſinners turne, and doe iuſtice before him: who can tell if he will accept you, and haue mercy on you?7I wil extoll my God, and my ſoule ſhal praiſe the King of heauen, and ſhal reioyce in his greatneſse.8Let all men ſpeake, and let all praiſe him for his righteouſneſſe.9O Ieruſalem the holy Citie, he will ſcourge thee for thy childrens workes, and will haue mercy againe on the ſonnes of the righteous.10Giue praiſe to the Lord, for hee is good: and praiſe the euerlaſting King, that his Tabernacle may bee builded in thee againe with ioy: and let him make ioyfull there in thee, thoſe that are captiues, and loue in thee for euer thoſe that are miſerable.11Many nations ſhall come from farre to the Name of the Lord God, with gifts in their hands, euen giftes to the King of heauen: all generations ſhall praiſe thee with great ioy.12Curſed are all they which hate thee, and bleſſed ſhall all be, which loue thee for euer.13Reioyce & be glad for the children of the iuſt: for they ſhall be gathered together, & ſhall bleſſe the Lord of the iuſt.14O bleſſed are they which loue thee, for they ſhall reioyce in thy peace: bleſſed are they which haue been ſorowfull for all thy ſcourges, for they ſhal reioyce for thee, when they haue ſeene all thy glory, and ſhalbe glad for euer.15Let my ſoule bleſſe God the great King.16For Ieruſalem ſhall be built vp with Saphires, and Emerauds, and precious ſtone: thy walles and towres, and battlements with pure golde.17And the ſtreets of Ieruſalem ſhal be paued with Berill, and Carbuncle, and ſtones of Ophir.18And all her ſtreets ſhall ſay, Halleluiah, and they ſhall praiſe him, ſaying, Bleſſed be God which hath extolled it for euer.

CHAPTER 141So Tobit made an ende of praiſing God.2And he was eight and fifty yeeres olde when hee loſt his ſight, which was reſtored to him after eight yeeres, and he gaue almes, and he increaſed in the feare of the Lord God, and praiſed him.3And when he was very aged, hee called his ſonne, and the ſixe ſons of his ſonne, and ſaid to him, My ſonne, take thy children; for behold, I am aged, and am ready to depart out of this life.4Goe into Media, my ſonne, for I ſurely beleeue thoſe things which Ionas the Prophet ſpake of Nineue, that it ſhall be ouerthrowen, and that for a time peace ſhal rather be in Media, and that our brethren ſhall lie ſcattered in the earth from that good land, and Ieruſalem ſhall be deſolate, and the houſe of God in it ſhalbe burned, and ſhall be deſolate for a time:5And that againe God will haue mercie on them, and bring them againe into the land where they ſhall build a Temple, but not like to the firſt, vntill the time of that age be fulfilled, and afterward they ſhall returne from all places of their captiuitie, and build vp Ieruſalem gloriouſly, and the houſe of God ſhall be built in it for euer, with a glorious building, as the prophets haue ſpoken thereof.6And all nations ſhall turne, and feare the Lord God truely, and ſhall burie their idoles.7So ſhall all nations praiſe the Lord, and his people ſhal confeſse God, and the Lord ſhall exalt his people, and all thoſe which loue the Lord God in trueth and iuſtice, ſhall reioyce, ſhewing mercie to our brethren.8And now, my ſonne, depart out of Nineue, becauſe that thoſe things which the Prophet Ionas ſpake, ſhall ſurely come to paſſe.9But keepe thou the Law and the Commandements, and ſhew thy ſelfe mercifull and iuſt, that it may goe well with thee.10And burie me decently, and thy mother with me, but tarie no longer at Nineue. Remember, my ſonne, how Aman handled Achiacharus þt brought him vp, how out of light he brought him into darkenes, and how he rewarded him againe: yet Ahiacharus was ſaued, but the other had his reward, for hee went downe into darkeneſſe. Manaſſes gaue almes, and eſcaped the ſnares of death which they had ſet for him: but Aman fell into the ſnare and periſhed.11Wherefore now, my ſonne, conſider what almes doeth, and how righteouſneſſe doth deliuer. When he had ſaid theſe things, he gaue vp the ghoſt in the bed, being an hundred, and eight and fiftie yeeres old, and he buried him honourably.12And when Anna his mother was dead, he buried her with his father: but Tobias departed with his wife and children to Ecbatane, to Raguel his father in law:13Where hee became old with honour, and hee buried his father and mother in lawe honourably, and hee inherited their ſubſtance, and his father Tobits.14And he died at Ecbatane in Media, being an hundred and ſeuen and twentie yeeres old.15But before he died, he heard of the deſtruction of Nineue, which was taken by Nabuchodonoſor & Aſsuerus: and before his death hee reioyced ouer Nineue.

IUDETH (JUDITH)

CHAPTER 11In the twelfth yeere of þe reigne of Nabuchodonoſor, who reigned in Nineue the great citie, (in the dayes of Arphaxad, which reigned ouer the Medes in Ecbatane,2And built in Ecbatane walles round about of ſtones hewen, three cubites broad, and ſixe cubites long, and made the height of the wall ſeuenty cubites, and the breadth thereof fiftie cubites:3And ſet the towers thereof vpon the gates of it, an hundred cubites high, and the breadth thereof in the foundation threeſcore cubites.4And he made the gates thereof, euen gates that were raiſed to the height of ſeuentie cubites, & the breadth of them was fourtie cubites, for the going foorth of his mightie armies, and for the ſetting in aray of his footmen.)5Euen in thoſe dayes, king Nabuchodonoſor made warre with king Arphaxad in the great plaine, which is the plaine in the borders of Ragau.6And there came vnto him, all they that dwelt in the hill countrey, and all that dwelt by Euphrates, and Tigris, and Hydaſpes, and the plaine of Arioch the king of the Elimeans, and very many nations of the ſonnes of Chelod, aſſembled themſelues to the battell.7Then Nabuchodonoſor king of the Aſſyrians, ſent vnto all that dwelt in Perſia, and to all that dwelt Weſtward, and to thoſe that dwelt in Cilicia, and Damaſcus and Libanus, and Antilibanus, and to all that dwelt vpon the ſea coaſt,8And to thoſe amongſt the nations that were of Carmel, and Galaad, and the higher Galile, and the great plaine of Eſdrelon,9And to all that were in Samaria, and the cities thereof: and beyond Iordan vnto Ieruſalem, and Betane, and Chellus, and Kades, and the riuer of Egypt, and Taphnes, and Rameſse, and all the land of Geſem,10Untill you come beyond Tanis, and Memphis, and to all the inhabitants of Egypt, vntill you come to the borders of Ethiopia.11But all the inhabitants of the land made light of the commandement of Nabuchodonoſor king of the Aſſyrians, neither went they with him to the battell: for they were not afraid of him: yea he was before them as one man, and they ſent away his Ambaſsadours from them without effect, and with diſgrace.12Therefore Nabuchodonoſor was very angry with all this countrey, and ſware by his throne and kingdome, that hee would ſurely be auenged vpon all thoſe coaſts of Cilicia, and Damaſcus, and Syria, and that he would ſlay with the ſword all the inhabitants of the land of Moab, and the children of Ammon, and all Iudea, and all that were in Egypt, till you come to the borders of the two ſeas.13Then he marched in battell aray with his power againſt king Arphaxad in the ſeuenteenth yeere, and he preuailed in his battell: for he ouerthrew all the power of Arphaxad, and all his horſemen and all his chariots,14And became Lord of his cities, and came vnto Ecbatane, and tooke the towers, and ſpoiled the ſtreetes thereof, and turned the beauty thereof into ſhame.15Hee tooke alſo Arphaxad in the mountaines of Ragau, and ſmote him through with his dartes, and deſtroyed him vtterly that day.16So he returned afterward to Nineue, both he and all his company of ſundry nations: being a very great multitude of men of warre, and there he tooke his eaſe and banketted, both he and his armie an hundred and twenty dayes.

CHAPTER 2 1And in the eighteenth yeere, the two and twentieth day of the firſt month, there was talke in the houſe of Nabuchodonoſor king of the Aſſyrians, that he ſhould as he ſaid auenge himſelfe on all the earth.2So he called vnto him all his officers, and all his nobles, and communicated with them his ſecret counſell, and concluded the afflicting of the whole earth out of his owne mouth.3Then they decreed to deſtroy all fleſh that did not obey the commaundement of his mouth.4And when he had ended his counſell, Nabuchodonoſor king of the Aſſyrians called Olofernes the chiefe captaine of his army, which was next vnto him, and ſaid vnto him,5Thus ſaith the great king, the Lord of the whole earth: behold, thou ſhalt goe forth from my preſence, and take with thee men that truſt in their owne ſtrength, of footemen an hundred and twenty thouſand, and the number of horſes with their riders twelue thouſand.6And thou ſhalt goe againſt all the Weſt countrey, becauſe they diſobeyed my commandement.7And thou ſhalt declare vnto them that they prepare for me earth and water: for I will goe forth in my wrath againſt them, and will couer the whole face of the earth with the feete of mine armie, and I will giue them for a ſpoile vnto them.8So that their ſlaine ſhall fill their vallies, and brookes, and the riuer ſhall be filled with their dead, til it ouerflow.9And I will lead them captiues to the vtmoſt parts of all the earth.10Thou therefore ſhalt goe foorth, and take before hand for me all their coaſts, and if they will yeeld themſelues vnto thee, thou ſhalt reſerue them for me till the day of their puniſhment.11But concerning them that rebell, let not thine eye ſpare them: but put them to the ſlaughter, and ſpoile them whereſoeuer thou goeſt.12For as I liue, and by the power of my kingdome, whatſoeuer I haue ſpoken, that will I doe by mine hand.13And take thou heede that thou tranſgreſse none of the Commaundements of thy Lord, but accompliſh them fully, as I haue commaunded thee, and deferre not to doe them.14Then Olofernes went foorth from the preſence of his Lord, and called all the gouernours and Captaines, and the officers of the army of Aſsur.15And he muſtered the choſen men for the battell, as his Lord had commaunded him, vnto an hundred and twenty thouſand, & twelue thouſand archers on Horſebacke.16And he ranged them as a great army is ordered for the warre.17And he tooke Camels, and Aſſes for their cariages a very great number, and ſheepe, and Oxen, & Goates without number, for their prouiſion,18And plenty of vittaile for euery man of the army, and very much gold, and ſiluer, out of the Kings houſe.19Then he went foorth and all his power to go before King Nabuchodonoſor in the voyage, and to couer al the face of the earth Weſtward with their charets, and horſemen, and their choſen footmen.20A great multitude alſo of ſundry countries came with them, like locuſts, and like the ſand of the earth: for the multitude was without number.21And they went foorth of Nineue, three dayes iourney toward the plaine of Bectileth, and pitched from Bectileth neere the mountaine, which is at the left hand of the vpper Cilicia.22Then he tooke all his armie, his footmen, and horſemen and chariots, and went from thence into the hill countrey,23And deſtroyed Phud, and Lud: and ſpoiled all the children of Raſſes, and the children of Iſmael, which were toward the wilderneſſe at the South of the land of the Chellians.24Then he went ouer Euphrates, and went through Meſopotamia, and deſtroyed all the high cities that were vpon the riuer Arbonai, till you come to the ſea.25And hee tooke the borders of Cilicia, and killed all that reſiſted him, and came to the borders of Iapheth, which were toward the South, ouer againſt Arabia.26He compaſſed alſo all the children of Madian, and burnt vp their tabernacles, and ſpoiled their ſheepcoats.27Then hee went downe into the plaine of Damaſcus in the time of wheat harueſt, and burnt vp all their fieldes, and deſtroyed their flockes, and heards, alſo he ſpoiled their cities, and vtterly waſted their countreys, and ſmote all their yong men with the edge of the ſword.28Therefore the feare and dread of him, fell vpon all the inhabitants of the ſea coaſtes, which were in Sidon and Tyrus, and them that dwelt in Sur, and Ocina, and all that dwelt in Ienmaan, and they that dwelt in Azotus, and Aſchalon feared him greatly.

CHAPTER 3 1So they ſent Embaſſadours vnto him, to treat of peace, ſaying,2Behold, we the ſeruants of Nabuchodonoſor the great king lie before thee; vſe vs as ſhall be good in thy ſight.3Behold, our houſes, and all our places, and all our fieldes of wheat, and flockes, and heards, and all the lodges of our tents, lie before thy face: vſe them as it pleaſeth thee.4Behold, euen our cities and the inhabitants thereof are thy ſeruants, come and deale with them, as ſeemeth good vnto thee.5So the men came to Holofernes, & declared vnto him after this maner.6Then came hee downe toward the ſea coaſt, both hee and his armie, and ſet gariſons in the high cities, and tooke out of them choſen men for aide.7So they and all the countrey round about, receiued them with garlands, with dances, and with timbrels.8Yet hee did caſt downe their frontiers, and cut downe their groues: for hee had decreed to deſtroy all the gods of the land, that all nations ſhould worſhip Nabuchodonoſor onely, and that all tongues and tribes ſhould call vpon him as God.9Alſo he came ouer againſt Eſdraelon neere vnto Iudea, ouer againſt the great ſtrait of Iudea.10And hee pitched betweene Geba, and Scythopolis, and there hee taried a whole moneth, that he might gather together all the cariages of his armie.

CHAPTER 4 1Now the children of Iſrael that dwelt in Iudea, heard all that Holofernes the chiefe captaine of Nabuchodonoſor king of the Aſſyrians had done to the nations, and after what manner hee had ſpoiled all their Temples, and brought them to nought.2Therefore they were exceedingly afraid of him, and were troubled for Ieruſalem, and for the Temple of the Lord their God.3For they were newly returned from the captiuitie, and all the people of Iudea were lately gathered together: and the veſſels, and the Altar, and the houſe, were ſanctified after the profanation.4Therefore they ſent into all the coaſts of Samaria, and the villages, and to Bethoron, and Belmen, and Iericho, and to Choba, and Eſora, and to the valley of Salem,5And poſſeſſed themſelues beforehand of all the tops of the high mountaines, and fortified the villages that were in them, and laid vp victuals for the prouiſion of warre: for their fieldes were of late reaped.6Alſo Ioacim the hie Prieſt which was in thoſe daies in Ieruſalem, wrote to them that dwelt in Bethulia, and Betomeſtham which is ouer againſt Eſdraelon toward the open countrey neere to Dothaim,7Charging them to keepe the paſsages of the hill countrey: for by them there was an entrance into Iudea, and it was eaſie to ſtoppe them that would come vp, becauſe the paſsage was ſtrait for two men at the moſt.8And the children of Iſrael did as Ioacim the hie Prieſt had commanded them, with the ancients of all the people of Iſrael, which dwelt at Ieruſalē.9Then euery man of Iſrael cryed to God with great feruencie, and with great vehemency did they humble their ſoules:10Both they and their wiues, and their children, and their cattell, and euery ſtranger and hireling, and their ſeruants bought with money, put ſackecloth vpon their loynes.11Thus euery man and woman, and the little children, & the inhabitants of Ieruſalem fell before the temple, and caſt aſhes vpon their heads, and ſpread out their ſackcloth before the face of the Lord: alſo they put ſackecloth about the Altar,12And cryed to the God of Iſrael all with one conſent earneſtly, that hee would not giue their children for a pray, and their wiues for a ſpoile, and the cities of their inheritance to deſtruction, and the Sanctuary to profanation and reproch, & for the nations to reioyce at.13So God heard their prayers, and looked vpon their afflictions: for the people faſted many dayes in all Iudea, and Ieruſalem, before the Sanctuary of the Lord Almighty.14And Ioacim the high Prieſt, and all the Prieſtes that ſtood before the Lord, and they which miniſtred vnto the Lord, had their loines girt with ſackecloth, and offered the daily burnt offerings, with the vowes and free gifts of the people,15And had aſhes on their miters, and cried vnto the Lord with all their power, that hee would looke vpon all the houſe of Iſrael graciouſly.

CHAPTER 5 1Then was it declared to Holofernes the chief captaine of the armie of Aſsur that the children of Iſrael had prepared for warre, and had ſhut vp the paſsages of the hill countrey, and had fortified all the tops of the high hilles, and had laide impediments in the champion countreys.2Wherewith he was very angry, and called all the princes of Moab, and the captaines of Ammon, and all the gouernours of the ſea coaſt.3And he ſaid vnto them, Tell mee now, ye ſonnes of Canaan, who this people is that dwelleth in the hill countrey? and what are the cities that they inhabite? and what is the multitude of their armie? and wherein is their power and ſtrength, and what king is ſet ouer them, or captaine of their armie?4And why haue they determined not to come and meet me, more then all the inhabitants of the Weſt?5Then ſaid Achior, the captaine of all the ſonnes of Ammon: Let my lord now heare a word from the mouth of thy ſeruant, and I will declare vnto thee the trueth, concerning this people which dwelleth neere thee, and inhabiteth the hill countreys: and there ſhall no lie come out of the mouth of thy ſeruant.6This people are deſcended of the Caldeans,7And they ſoiourned heretofore in Meſopotamia, becauſe they would not follow the gods of their fathers, which were in the land of Caldea.8For they left the way of their anceſtours, and worſhipped the God of heauen, the God whom they knew: ſo they caſt them out from the face of their gods, and they fled into Meſopotamia, and ſoiourned there many dayes.9Then their God commaunded them to depart from the place where they ſoiourned, and to goe into the land of Chanaan, where they dwelt, and were increaſed with gold and ſiluer, and with very much cattell.10But when a famine couered all the land of Chanaan, they went downe into Egypt, and ſoiourned there, while they were nouriſhed, and became there a great multitude, ſo that one could not number their nation.11Therefore the king of Egypt roſe vp againſt them, and dealt ſubtilly with them, and brought them low, with labouring in bricke, & made them ſlaues.12Then they cried vnto their God, and he ſmote all the land of Egypt with incurable plagues, ſo the Egyptians caſt them out of their ſight.13And God dried the red ſea before them:14And brought them to mount Sina, and Cades Barne, and caſt forth all that dwelt in the wilderneſſe.15So they dwelt in the land of the Amorites, and they deſtroyed by their ſtrength all them of Eſebon, and paſsing ouer Iordan they poſſeſſed all the hill countrey.16And they caſt forth before them, the Chanaanite, the Phereſite, the Iebuſite, and the Sychemite, and all the Gergeſites, and they dwelt in that countrey many dayes.17And whileſt they ſinned not before their God, they proſpered, becauſe the God that hateth iniquitie, was with them.18But when they departed from the way which he appointed them, they were deſtroyed in many battels very ſore, and were led captiues into a land that was not theirs, and the Temple of their God was caſt to the ground, and their cities were taken by the enemies.19But nowe are they returned to their God, and are come vp from the places, where they were ſcattered, and haue poſſeſſed Ieruſalem, where their Sanctuary is, and are ſeated in the hill countrey, for it was deſolate.20Now therefore, my lord and gouernour, if there be any errour in this people, & they ſinne againſt their God, let vs conſider that this ſhal be their ruine, and let vs goe vp, and we ſhal ouercome them.21But if there be no iniquitie in their nation, let my lord now paſſe by, leſt their Lord defend them, and their God be for them, and wee become a reproch before all the world.22And when Achior had finiſhed theſe ſayings, all the people ſtanding round about the tent, murmured, and the chiefe men of Holofernes, and all that dwelt by the ſea ſide, and in Moab, ſpake that he ſhould kill him.23For, ſay they, we will not be afraid of the face of the children of Iſrael, for loe, it is a people that haue no ſtrength, nor power for a ſtrong battell.24Now therefore, Lord Holofernes, we will goe vp, and they ſhall be a pray, to be deuoured of all thine armie.

CHAPTER 61And when the tumult of men that were about the councell was ceaſed, Holofernes the chiefe captaine of the armie of Aſsur, ſaid vnto Achior and all the Moabites, before all the company of other nations,2And who art thou Achior and the hirelings of Ephraim, that thou haſt propheſied amongſt vs as to day, and haſt ſaid, that we ſhould not make warre with the people of Iſrael, becauſe their God will defend them? and who is God but Nabuchodonoſor?3He will ſend his power, and will deſtroy them from the face of the earth, and their God ſhall not deliuer them: but we his ſeruants will deſtroy them as one man, for they are not able to ſuſtaine the power of our horſes.4For with them we will tread them vnder foote, and their mountains ſhall be drunken with their blood, and their fields ſhall be filled with their dead bodies, and their footeſteps ſhall not be able to ſtand before vs, for they ſhal vtterly periſh, ſaith king Nabuchodonoſor Lord of all the earth; for hee ſaid, none of my words ſhall be in vaine.5And thou Achior, an hireling of Ammon, which haſt ſpoken theſe words in the day of thine iniquity, ſhalt ſee my face no more, from this day vntill I take vengeance of this nation that came out of Egypt.6And then ſhall the ſword of mine armie, and the multitude of them that ſerue me, paſſe through thy ſides, and thou ſhalt fal among their ſlaine, when I returne.7Now therefore my ſeruants ſhall bring thee backe into the hill countrey, and ſhall ſet thee in one of the cities of the paſsages.8And thou ſhalt not periſh till thou be deſtroyed with them.9And if thou perſwade thy ſelfe in thy minde, that they ſhall not be taken, let not thy countenance fall: I haue ſpoken it, and none of my words ſhall be in vaine.10Then Holofernes commanded his ſeruants that waited in his tent, to take Achior and bring him to Bethulia, and deliuer him into the hands of the children of Iſrael.11So his ſeruants tooke him, and brought him out of the campe into the plaine, and they went from the midſt of the plaine into the hill countrey, and came vnto the fountaines that were vnder Bethulia.12And when the men of the citie ſaw them, they tooke vp their weapons, and went out of the citie to the toppe of the hill, and euery man that vſed a ſling from comming vp by caſting of ſtones againſt them.13Neuertheleſſe hauing gotten priuily vnder the hill, they bound Achior and caſt him downe, and left him at the foote of the hill, and returned to their Lord.14But the Iſraelites deſcended from their citie, and came vnto him, and looſed him, and brought him into Bethulia, and preſented him to the gouernours of the citie,15Which were in thoſe dayes Ozias the ſonne of Micha of the tribe of Simeon, and Chabris the ſonne of Gothoniel, and Charmis the ſonne of Melchiel.16And they called together all the ancients of the citie, and all their youth ranne together, and their women to the aſſembly, and they ſet Achior in the midſt of all their people. Then Ozias aſked him of that which was done.17And he anſwered and declared vnto them the words of the counſell of Holofernes, and all the words that he had ſpoken in the midſt of the princes of Aſsur, and whatſoeuer Holofernes had ſpoken proudly againſt the houſe of Iſrael.18Then the people fell downe, and worſhipped God, and cryed vnto God, ſaying,19O Lord God of heauen, behold their pride, and pity the low eſtate of our nation, and looke vpon the face of thoſe that are ſanctified vnto thee this day.20Then they comforted Achior and praiſed him greatly.21And Ozias tooke him out of the aſſembly vnto his houſe, and made a feaſt to the Elders, & they called on the God of Iſrael all that night for helpe.

CHAPTER 71The next day Holofernes commanded all his army, and all his people which were come to take his part, that they ſhould remooue their campe againſt Bethulia, to take aforehand the aſcents of the hill countrey, and to make warre againſt the children of Iſrael.2Then their ſtrong men remoued their campes in that day, and the armie of the men of warre was, an hundred and ſeuenty thouſand footmen, and twelue thouſand horſemen, beſide the baggage, & other men that were afoot amongſt them, a very great multitude.3And they camped in the valley neere vnto Bethulia, by the fountaine, and they ſpred themſelues in breadth ouer Dothaim, euen to Belmaim, and in length from Bethulia vnto Cyamon which is ouer againſt Eſdraelon.4Now the children of Iſrael when they ſaw the multitude of them, were greatly troubled, and ſaid euery one to his neighbour: Now will theſe men licke vp the face of the earth; for neither the high mountaines, nor the valleys, nor the hils, are able to beare their waight.5Then euery man tooke vp his weapons of warre, and when they had kindled fires vpon their towers, they remained and watched all that night.6But in the ſecond day Holofernes brought foorth all his horſemen, in the ſight of the children of Iſrael which were in Bethulia,7And viewed the paſsages vp to the city, and came to the fountaine of their waters, and tooke them, and ſet garriſons of men of warre ouer them, and he himſelfe remooued towards his people.8Then came vnto him all the chiefe of the children of Eſau, and al the gouernours of the people of Moab, and the captaines of the ſea coaſt, and ſaid,9Let our lord now heare a word, that there be not an ouerthrow in thine armie.10For this people of the children of Iſrael do not truſt in their ſpeares, but in the height of the mountaines wherein they dwell, becauſe it is not eaſie to come vp to the tops of their mountains.11Now therefore my lord, fight not againſt them in battell aray, and there ſhall not ſo much as one man of thy people periſh.12Remaine in thy campe, and keepe all the men of thine army, and let thy ſeruants get into their hands the fountaine of water which iſsueth foorth of the foot of the mountaine.13For all the inhabitants of Bethulia haue their water thence: ſo ſhall thirſt kil them, & they ſhall giue vp their citie, and we and our people ſhal goe vp to the tops of the mountaines that are neere, and will campe vpon them, to watch that none goe out of the city.14So they and their wiues, and their children ſhalbe conſumed with famine, and before the ſword come againſt them, they ſhall be ouerthrowen in the ſtreets where they dwel.15Thus ſhalt thou render them an euil reward: becauſe they rebelled and met not thy perſon peaceably.16And theſe words pleaſed Holofernes, and al his ſeruants, and he appointed to doe as they had ſpoken.17So the campe of the children of Ammon departed, and with them fiue thouſand of the Aſſyrians, and they pitched in the valley, and tooke the waters, and the fountaines of the waters of the children

of Iſrael.18Then the children of Eſau went vp, with the children of
Ammon, and camped in the hil countrey ouer againſt Dotha-em: and
they ſent ſome of them toward the South, & toward the Eaſt ouer
againſt Ekrebel, which is neere vnto Chuſi, that is vpon the brooke
Mochmur, and the reſt of the army of the Aſſyrians camped in the
plaine, and couered the face of the whole land, and their tents and
cariages were pitched to a very great multitude.19Then the children of
Iſrael cried vnto the Lord their God, becauſe their heart failed, for all
their enemies had compaſſed them round about, & there was no way to
eſcape out from among them.20Thus all the company of Aſsur remained
about them, both their footmen, charets and horſemen, foure and thirtie
dayes, ſo that all their veſſels of water failed all the inhabitants of
Bethulia.21And the ciſternes were emptied, and they had not water to
drinke their fill, for one day; for they gaue them drinke by
meaſure.22Therefore their young children were out of heart, and their
women and yong men fainted for thirſt, and fell downe in the ſtreetes
of the city, and by the paſsages of the gates, and there was no longer any
ſtrength in them.23Then all the people aſſembled to Ozias, and to the
chiefe of the city, both young men, and women, and children, and cryed
with a loude voice, and ſaide before all the Elders;24God be Iudge
betweene vs and you: for you haue done vs great iniury in that you haue
not required peace of the children of Aſsur.25For now we haue no
helper: but God hath ſold vs into their hands, that wee ſhould be
throwen downe before them with thirſt, and great deſtruction.26Now
therefore call them vnto you, and deliuer the whole citie for a ſpoile to
the people of Olofernes, and to all his armie.27For it is better for vs to
be made a ſpoile vnto them, then to die for thirſt: for wee will be his
ſeruants, that our ſoules may liue, and not ſee the death of our infants
before our eyes, nor our wiues nor our children to die.28We take to
witneſſe againſt you, the heauen and the earth, and our God, and Lord
of our fathers, which puniſheth vs according to our ſinnes, and the
ſinnes of our fathers, that hee doe not according as we haue ſaid this
day.29Then there was great weeping with one conſent in the middeſt of
the aſſembly, and they cryed vnto the Lord God with a loude
voice.30Then ſaid Ozias to them, Brethren, be of good courage, let vs
yet endure fiue dayes, in the which ſpace the Lord our God may turne
his mercy toward vs, for he will not forſake vs vtterly.31And if theſe
dayes paſſe, and there come no helpe vnto vs, I wil doe according to
your word.32And he diſperſed the people euery one to their owne
charge, and they went vnto the walles and towres of their citie, and ſent
the women and children into their houſes, and they were very low
brought in the city.

CHAPTER 81Now at that time Iudeth heard thereof, which was the
daughter of Merari the ſonne of Ox, the ſonne of Ioſeph, the ſonne of
Oziel, the ſonne of Elcia, the ſonne of Ananias, the ſonne of Gedeon,
the ſonne of Raphaim, the ſon of Acitho, the ſonne of Eliu, the ſonne
of Eliab, the ſonne of Nathanael, the ſonne of Samael, the ſonne of
Salaſadai, the ſon of Iſrael.2And Manaſſes was her huſband of her tribe
and kinred, who died in the barley haruеſt.3For as hee ſtood ouerſeeing
them that bound ſheaues in the field, the heat came vpon his head, and
hee fell on his bed, and died in the city of Bethulia, and they buried him
with his fathers, in the field betweene Dothaim and Balamo.4So Iudeth
was a widow in her houſe three yeeres, and foure moneths.5And ſhe
made her a tent vpon the top of her houſe, and put on ſackecloth on
her loynes, and ware her widowes apparell.6And ſhe faſted all the dayes
of her widowhood, ſaue the eues of the Sabbath, and the Sabbaths, and
the eues of the newe Moones, and the newe Moones, and the Feaſts,
and ſolemne dayes of the houſe of Iſrael.7Shee was alſo of a goodly
countenance, and very beautifull to behold: and her huſband Manaſſes
had left her golde and ſiluer, and men ſeruants and maide ſeruants, and
cattell, and lands, and ſhe remained vpon them.8And there was none
that gaue her an ill worde; for ſhee feared God greatly.9Now when ſhee
heard the euill wordes of the people againſt the gouernor, that they
fainted for lacke of water (for Iudeth had heard all the wordes that Ozias
had ſpoken vnto them, and that he had ſworne to deliuer the citie vnto
the Aſſyrians after fiue dayeſ)10Then ſhee ſent her waiting woman that
had the gouernment of all things that ſhe had, to call Ozias, and Chabris,
and Charmis, the ancients of the citie.11And they came vnto her, and ſhe
ſaid vnto them, Heare me now, O yee gouernours of the inhabitants of
Bethulia: for your wordes that you haue ſpoken before the people this
day are not right, touching this othe which ye made, and pronounced
betweene God and you, and haue promiſed to deliuer the citie to our
enemies, vnleſſe within theſe daies the Lord turne to helpe you.12And
now who are you, that haue tempted God this day, & ſtand in ſtead of
God amongſt the children of men?13And now trie the Lord Almighty,
but you ſhall neuer know any thing.14For you cannot find the depth of
the heart of man, neither can ye perceiue the things that he thinketh:
then how can you ſearch out God, that hath made all theſe things, and
knowe his minde, or comprehend his purpoſe? Nay my brethren,
prouoke not the Lord our God to anger.15For if he will not helpe vs
within theſe few dayes, he hath power to defend vs when he will, euen
euery day, or to deſtroy vs before our enemies.16Doe not binde the
counſels of the Lord our God, for God is not as man, that he may be
threatned, neither is he as the ſonne of man that he ſhould bee
wauering.17Therefore let vs waite for ſaluation of him, and call vpon
him to helpe vs, and he will heare our voyce if it pleaſe him.18For there
aroſe none in our age, neither is there any now in theſe daies, neither
tribe, nor familie, nor people, nor city among vs, which worſhip gods
made with hands, as hath bene aforetime.19For the which cauſe our
fathers were giuen to the ſword, & for a ſpoile, and had a great fall before
our enemies.20But we know none other god: therefore we truſt that he
will not deſpiſe vs, nor any of our nation.21For if we be taken ſo, all
Iudea ſhall lie waſte, and our Sanctuarie ſhal be ſpoiled, and he will
require the prophanation thereof, at our mouth.22And the ſlaughter of
our brethren, and the captiuitie of the countrey, and the deſolation of
our inheritance, will he turne vpon our heads among the Gentiles,
whereſoeuer we ſhall bee in bondage, and we ſhall be an offence and a
reproch to all them that poſſeſſe vs.23For our ſeruitude ſhall not be
directed to fauour: but the Lord our God ſhall turne it to
diſhonour.24Now therefore, O brethren, let vs ſhew an example to our
brethren, becauſe their hearts depend vpon vs, and the Sanctuary, and
the houſe, and the Altar reſt vpon vs.25Moreouer, let vs giue thankes to
the Lord our God, which trieth vs, euen as he did our
fathers.26Remember what things he did to Abraham, and how he tried
Iſaac, and what happened to Iacob in Meſopotamia of Syria, when he
kept the ſheepe of Laban his mothers brother.27For, hee hath not tried
vs in the fire as he did them, for the examination of their hearts, neither
hath hee taken vengeance on vs: but the Lord doeth ſcourge them that
come neere vnto him to admoniſh them.28Then ſaid Ozias to her, All
that thou haſt ſpoken, haſt thou ſpoken with a good heart, and there is
none that may gaineſay thy words.29For this is not the firſt day wherin
thy wiſedome is manifeſted, but from the beginning of thy dayes all thy
people haue knowen thy vnderſtanding, becauſe the diſpoſition of thine
heart is good.30But the people were very thirſty, and compelled vs to
doe vnto them as we haue ſpoken, and to bring an othe vpon our ſelues,
which wee will not breake.31Therefore now pray thou for vs, becauſe
thou art a godly woman, and the Lord will ſend vs raine to fill our
ciſternes, and we ſhall faint no more.32Then ſaid Iudeth vnto them,
Heare me, and I wil doe a thing, which ſhall goe throughout all
generations, to the children of our nation.33You ſhall ſtand this night in
the gate, and I will goe foorth with my waiting woman: and within the
dayes that you haue promiſed to deliuer the citie to our enemies, the
Lord will viſit Iſrael by mine hand.34But inquire not you of mine act: for
I will not declare it vnto you, til the things be finiſhed that I doe.35Then
ſaid Ozias and the princes vnto her, Goe in peace, and the Lord God be
before thee, to take vengeance on our enemies.36So they returned from
the tent, and went to their wards.

CHAPTER 9 1Then Iudeth fell vpon her face, and put aſhes vpon her
head, and vncouered the ſackcloth wherewith ſhe was clothed, and
about the time, that the incenſe of that euening was offered in Ieruſalem,
in the houſe of the Lord, Iudeth cryed with a loud voyce, and ſaid,2O
Lord God of my father Simeon, to whom thou gaueſt a ſword to take
vengeance of the ſtrangers, who looſened the girdle of a maide to defile
her, and diſcouered the thigh to her ſhame, and polluted her virginity to
her reproch, (for thou ſaidſt it ſhall not be ſo, and yet they did
ſo.)3Wherefore thou gaueſt their rulers to be ſlaine, ſo that they died
their bed in blood, being deceiued, and ſmoteſt the ſeruants with their
Lords, and the Lords vpon their thrones:4And haſt giuen their wiues for
a pray, and their daughters to bee captiues, and all their ſpoiles to be
diuided amongſt thy deere children: which were mooued with thy zeale,

and abhorred the pollution of their blood, and called vpon thee for aide: O God, O my God, heare me alſo a widow.5For thou haſt wrought not onely thoſe things, but alſo the things which fell out before, and which enſewed after, thou haſt thought vpon the things which are now, and which are to come.6Yea what things thou didſt determine were redy at hand, and ſaid, loe we are heere; for all thy wayes are prepared, and thy iudgements are in thy foreknowledge.7For behold, the Aſſyrians are multiplyed in their power: they are exalted with horſe and man: they glory in the ſtrength of their footemen: they truſt in ſhield and ſpeare, and bow, and ſling, and know not that thou art the Lord that breakeſt the battels: the Lord is thy name.8Throw downe their ſtrength in thy power, and bring downe their force in thy wrath; for they haue purpoſed to defile thy Sanctuary, and to pollute the Tabernacle, where thy glorious name reſteth, and to caſt downe with ſword the horne of thy altar.9Behold their pride, and ſend thy wrath vpon their heads: giue into mine hand which am a widow, the power that I haue conceiued.10Smite by the deceit of my lips the ſeruant with the prince, and the prince with the ſeruant: breake downe their ſtatelineſse by the hand of a woman.11For thy power ſtandeth not in multitude, nor thy might in ſtrong men, for thou art a God of the afflicted, an helper of the oppreſſed, an vpholder of the weake, a protector of the forelorne, a ſauiour of them that are without hope.12I pray thee, I pray thee, O God of my father, and God of the inheritance of Iſrael, Lord of the heauens, and earth, creator of the waters, king of euery creature: heare thou my prayer:13And make my ſpeech and deceit to be their wound & ſtripe, who haue purpoſed cruell things againſt thy couenant, and thy hallowed houſe, and againſt the top of Sion, and againſt the houſe of the poſſeſſion of thy children.14And make euery nation and tribe to acknowledge that thou art the God of all power and might, and that there is none other that protecteth the people of Iſrael but thou.

CHAPTER 101Now after that ſhe had ceaſed to cry vnto the God of Iſrael, and had made an end of all theſe words,2She roſe where ſhe had fallen downe, and called her maide, and went downe into the houſe, in the which ſhe abode in the Sabbath dayes and in her feaſt dayes,3And pulled off the ſackcloth which ſhe had on, and put off the garments of her widowhood, and waſhed her body all ouer with water, and annointed herſelfe with precious ointment, and braided the haire of her head, and put on a tire vpon it, and put on her garments of gladneſſe, wherewith ſhe was clad during the life of Manaſſes her huſband.4And ſhe tooke ſandals vpon her feete, and put about her, her bracelets and her chaines, and her rings, and her earerings, and all her ornaments, and decked her ſelfe brauely to allure the eyes of all men that ſhould ſee her.5Then ſhe gaue her mayd a bottle of wine, and a cruſe of oyle, and filled a bagge with parched corne, and lumpes of figs, and with fine bread, ſo ſhe folded all theſe things together, and layd them vpon her.6Thus they went forth to the gate of the citie of Bethulia, and found ſtandiug there Ozias, and the ancients of the city Chabris, and Charmis.7And when they ſaw her, that her countenance was altered, and her apparel was changed, they wondered at her beautie very greatly, and ſaid vnto her,8The God, the God of our fathers giue thee fauour, and accompliſh thine enterpriſes to the glory of the children of Iſrael, and to the exaltation of Ieruſalem: then they worſhipped God.9And ſhe ſaid vnto them, Command the gates of the city to be opened vnto me, that I may goe forth to accompliſh the things, whereof you haue ſpoken with me; ſo they commanded the yong men to open vnto her, as ſhee had ſpoken.10And when they had done ſo, Iudeth went out, ſhe and her mayd with her, and the men of the citie looked after her, vntill ſhee was gone downe the mountaine, and till ſhe had paſſed the valley, and could ſee her no more.11Thus they went ſtraight foorth in the valley: and the firſt watch of the Aſſyrians met her;12And tooke her, and aſked her, Of what people art thou? and whence cōmeſt thou? and whither goeſt thou? And ſhe ſaid, I am a woman of the Hebrewes, and am fled from them: for they ſhalbe giuen you to be conſumed:13And I am comming before Olofernes the chiefe captaine of your army, to declare words of trueth, and I will ſhew him a way, whereby he ſhall goe, and winne all the hil countrey, without looſing the body or life of any one of his men.14Now when the men heard her wordes, and beheld her countenance, they wondered greatly at her beautie, and ſaid vnto her;15Thou haſt ſaued thy life, in that thou haſt haſted to come downe to the preſence of our lord: now therfore come to his tent, and ſome of vs ſhall conduct thee, vntill they haue deliuered thee to his hands.16And when thou ſtandeſt before him, bee not afraid in thine heart: but ſhew vnto him according to thy word, and he will intreat thee well.17Then they choſe out of them an hundred men, to accompany her and her mayd, and they brought her to the tent of Olofernes.18Then was there a concourſe throughout all the campe: for her comming was noiſed among the tents, and they came about her, as ſhe ſtood without the tent of Olofernes, till they told him of her.19And they wondered at her beautie, and admired the children of Iſrael becauſe of her, and euery one ſaid to his neighbour; Who would deſpiſe this people, that haue among them ſuch women, ſurely it is not good that one man of them be left, who being let goe, might deceiue the whole earth.20And they that lay neere Olofernes, went out, and all his ſeruants, and they brought her into the tent.21Now Olofernes reſted vpon his bed vnder a canopie which was wouen with purple, and gold, and emeraudes, and precious ſtones.22So they ſhewed him of her, and he came out before his tent, with ſiluer lampes going before him.23And when Iudeth was come before him and his ſeruants, they all marueiled at the beautie of her countenance; and ſhe fel downe vpon her face, and did reuerence vnto him; and his ſeruants tooke her vp.

CHAPTER 111Then ſaid Olofernes vnto her, Woman, bee of good comfort, feare not in thine heart: for I neuer hurt any, that was willing to ſerue Nabuchodonoſor the king of all the earth.2Now therefore if thy people that dwelleth in the mountaines, had not ſet light by me, I would not haue lifted vp my ſpeare againſt them: but they haue done theſe things to themſelues.3But now tell me wherefore thou art fled from them, and art come vnto vs: for thou art come for ſafeguard, be of good comfort, thou ſhalt liue this night, and hereafter.4For none ſhall hurt thee, but intreat thee well, as they doe the ſeruants of king Nabuchodonoſor my lord.5Then Iudeth ſaid vnto him, Receiue the words of thy ſeruant, and ſuffer thine handmaid to ſpeake in thy preſence, and I will declare no lie to my lord this night.6And if thou wilt follow the words of thine handmaid, God will bring the thing perfectly to paſſe by thee, and my lord ſhall not faile of his purpoſes,7As Nabuchodonoſor king of all the earth liueth, and as his power liueth, who hath ſent thee for the vpholding of euery liuing thing: for not only men ſhall ſerue him by thee, but alſo the beaſts of the field, and the cattell, and the foules of the aire ſhall liue by thy power, vnder Nabuchodonoſor and all his houſe.8For wee haue heard of thy wiſedome, and thy policies, and it is reported in all the earth, that thou onely art excellent in all the kingdome, and mightie in knowledge, and wonderfull in feates of warre.9Now as concerning the matter which Achior did ſpeake in thy counſell, we haue heard his words; for the men of Bethulia ſaued him, and hee declared vnto them all that hee had ſpoken vnto thee.10Therefore, O lord and gouernor, reiect not his word, but lay it vp in thine heart, for it is true, for our nation ſhall not be puniſhed, neither can the ſword preuaile againſt them, except they ſinne againſt their God.11And now, that my lord be not defeated, and fruſtrate of his purpoſe, euen death is now fallen vpon them, and their ſinne hath ouertaken them, wherewith they will prouoke their God to anger, whenſoeuer they ſhall doe that which is not fit to be done.12For their victuals faile them, and all their water is ſcant, and they haue determined to lay hands vpon their cattell, and purpoſed to conſume all thoſe things, that God hath forbidden them to eate by his Lawes,13And are reſolued to ſpend the firſt fruits of the corne, & the tenths of wine and oyle, which they had ſanctified, and reſeruedfor the Prieſts that ſerue in Ieruſalem, before the face of our God, the which things it is not lawfull for any of the people ſo much as to touch with their hands.14For they haue ſent ſome to Ieruſalem, becauſe they alſo that dwelt there haue done the like, to bring them a licenſe from the Senate.15Now when they ſhall bring them word, they will forthwith doe it, and they ſhall be giuen thee to be deſtroyed the ſame day.16Wherefore I thine handmaide knowing all this, am fledde from their preſence, & God hath ſent me to worke things with thee, whereat all the earth ſhalbe aſtoniſhed, and whoſoeuer ſhall heare it.17For thy ſeruant is religious, and ſerueth the God of heauen day & night: now therefore, my lord, I will remaine with thee, and thy ſeruant will goe out by night into the valley, and I will pray vnto God, and he wil tel me when they haue committed their ſinnes.18And I will come, and ſhew it vnto thee: then thou ſhalt goe forth with all thine army, and there ſhall be none of them that ſhall reſiſt thee.19And I will leade thee through the midſt of Iudea, vntill thou come

before Ieruſalem, and I will ſet thy throne in the midſt thereof, and thou
ſhalt driue them as ſheep that haue no ſhepheard, and a dogge ſhall not
ſo much as open his mouth at thee: for theſe things were tolde mee,
according to my foreknowledge, and they were declared vnto me, and I
am ſent to tell thee.20Then her wordes pleaſed Olofernes, and all his
ſeruants, and they marueiled at her wiſedome, and ſaid,21There is not
ſuch a woman from one end of the earth to the other, both for beautie
of face, and wiſedome of wordes.22Likewiſe Olofernes ſaid vnto her,
God hath done well to ſend thee before the people, that ſtrength might
be in our hands, and deſtruction vpon them that lightly regard my
lord:23And now thou art both beautifull in thy countenance, and wittie
in thy wordes; ſurely if thou doe as thou haſt ſpoken, thy God ſhall be
my God, and thou ſhalt dwel in the houſe of king Nabuchodonoſor, and
ſhalt be renowmed through the whole earth.
CHAPTER 121Then hee commaunded to bring her in, where his plate
was ſet, and bad that they ſhould prepare for her of his owne meats, and
that ſhe ſhould drinke of his owne wine.2And Iudeth ſaid, I will not eat
thereof, leſt there bee an offence: but prouiſion ſhall be made for mee
of the things that I haue brought.3Then Olofernes ſaid vnto her, If thy
prouiſion ſhould faile, howe ſhould we giue thee the like? for there be
none with vs of thy nation.4Then ſaid Iudeth vnto him, As thy ſoule
liueth, my lord, thine handemaid ſhall not ſpend thoſe things that I haue,
before the Lord worke by mine hand, the things þt he hath
determined.5Then the ſeruants of Olofernes brought her into the tent,
and ſhee ſlept til midnight, and ſhe aroſe when it was towards the
morning watch,6And ſent to Olofernes, ſaying, Let my lord now
command, that thine handmaid may goe forth vnto prayer.7Then
Olofernes commaunded his guard that they ſhould not ſtay her: thus ſhe
abode in the camp three dayes, and went out in the night into the valley
of Bethulia, and waſhed her ſelfe in a fountaine of water by the
campe.8And when ſhe came out, ſhee beſought the Lord God of Iſrael
to direct her way, to the raiſing vp of the children of her people.9So ſhe
came in cleane, and remained in the tent, vntill ſhee did eate her meat at
euening.10And in the fourth day Olofernes made a feaſt to his owne
ſeruants only, and called none of the officers to the banquet.11Then ſaid
he to Bagoas the Eunuch, who had charge ouer all that he had: Goe
now, and perſwade this Ebrewe woman which is with thee, that ſhe
come vnto vs, and eate and drinke with vs.12For loe, it will be a ſhame
for our perſon, if we ſhall let ſuch a woman go, not hauing had her
company: for if we draw her not vnto vs, ſhe will laugh vs to
ſcorne.13Then went Bagoas from the preſence of Olofernes, and came
to her, and he ſaid, Let not this faire damoſell feare to come to my lord,
and to bee honoured in his preſence, and drink wine, and be merry with
vs, and be made this day as one of the daughters of the Aſſyrians, which
ſerue in the houſe of Nabuchodonoſor.14Then ſaid Iudeth vnto him,
Who am I now, that I ſhould gaineſay my lord? ſurely whatſoeuer
pleaſeth him, I will doe ſpeedily, and it ſhall bee my ioy vnto the day of
my death.15So ſhe aroſe, and decked her ſelfe with her apparell, and all
her womans attire, and her maid went and laid ſoft ſkinnes on the
ground for her, ouer againſt Olofernes, which ſhe had receiued of
Bagoas for her daily vſe, that ſhe might ſit, and eate vpon them.16Now
when Iudeth came in, and ſate downe, Olofernes his heart was rauiſhed
with her, and his minde was moued, and he deſired greatly her company,
for hee waited a time to deceiue her, from the day that he had ſeene
her.17Then ſaid Olofernes vnto her, Drinke now, and be merry with
vs.18So Iudeth ſaide, I will drinke now my lord, becauſe my life is
magnified in me this day, more then all the dayes ſince I was
borne.19Then ſhe tooke and ate and dranke before him what her maide
had prepared.20And Olofernes tooke great delight in her, & dranke
much more wine, then he had drunke at any time in one day, ſince he
was borne.
CHAPTER 131Now when the euening was come, his ſeruants made
haſte to depart, and Bagoas ſhut his tent without, and diſmiſsed the
waiters from the preſence of his lord, and they went to their beds: for
they were all weary, becauſe the feaſt had bene long.2And Iudeth was
left alone in the tent, and Olofernes lying along vpon his bed, for hee
was filled with wine.3Now Iudeth had commanded her maide to ſtand
without her bedchamber, and to waite for her comming forth as ſhe did
daily: for ſhe ſaid, ſhe would goe forth to her prayers, and ſhe ſpake to
Bagoas, according to the ſame purpoſe.4So all went forth, and none was
left in the bedchamber, neither little, nor great. Then Iudeth ſtanding by
his bed, ſaid in her heart: O Lord God of all power, looke at this preſent
vpon the workes of mine hands for the exaltation of Ieruſalem.5For now
is the time to helpe thine inheritance, and to execute mine enterpriſes,
to the deſtruction of the enemies, which are riſen againſt vs.6Then ſhe
came to the pillar of the bed, which was at Olofernes head, and tooke
downe his fauchin from thence,7And approched to his bed, and tooke
hold of the haire of his head, and ſaid, Strengthen mee, O Lord God of
Iſrael, this day.8And ſhe ſmote twiſe vpon his necke with all her might,
and ſhe tooke away his head from him,9And tumbled his body downe
from the bed, and pulled downe the canopy from the pillars, and anon
after ſhe went forth, and gaue Olofernes his head to her maide.10And
ſhe put it in her bag of meate, ſo they twaine went together according
to their cuſtome vnto prayer, and when they paſſed the campe, they
compaſſed the valley, and went vp the mountaine of Bethulia, and came
to the gates thereof.11Then ſaid Iudeth a farre off to the watchmen at
the gate, Open, open now the gate: God, euen our God is with vs, to
ſhew his power yet in Ieruſalem, and his forces againſt the enemie, as he
hath euen done this day.12Now when the men of her citie heard her
voyce, they made haſte to goe downe to the gate of their citie, and they
called the Elders of the citie.13And then they ranne altogether both ſmall
and great, for it was ſtrange vnto them that ſhe was come: ſo they
opened the gate, and receiued them, and made a fire for a light, and
ſtood round about them.14Then ſhe ſaid to them with a loud voyce,
Praiſe, praiſe God, praiſe God, (I ſay) for hee hath not taken away his
mercy from the houſe of Iſrael, but hath deſtroyed our enemies by mine
hands this night.15So ſhe tooke the head out of the bag, and ſhewed it,
and ſaid vnto them, Behold the head of Olofernes the chiefe captaine
of the armie of Aſsur, and behold the canopy wherein he did lie in his
drunkenneſse, and the Lord hath ſmitten him by the hand of a
woman.16As the Lord liueth, who hath kept me in my way that I went,
my countenance hath deceiued him to his deſtruction, and yet hath hee
not committed ſinne with mee, to defile and ſhame mee.17Then all the
people were wonderfully aſtoniſhed, and bowed themſelues, and
worſhipped God, and ſaid with one accord: Bleſſed be thou, O our God,
which haſt this day brought to nought the enemies of thy people.18Then
ſaid Ozias vnto her, O daughter, bleſſed art thou of the moſt high God,
aboue all the women vpon the earth, and bleſſed be the Lord God,
which hath created the heauens, and the earth, which hath directed thee
to the cutting off of the head of the chiefe of our enemies.19For this thy
confidence ſhall not depart from the heart of men, which remember the
power of God for euer.20And God turne theſe things to thee for a
perpetuall praiſe, to viſite thee in good things, becauſe thou haſt not
ſpared thy life for þe affliction of our nation, but haſt reuenged our
ruine, walking a ſtraight way before our God: and all the people ſaid, So
be it, ſo be it.
CHAPTER 141Then ſaide Iudeth vnto them, Heare me now, my
brethren, & take this head, and hang it vpon the higheſt place of your
walles.2And ſo ſoone as the morning ſhall appeare and the Sunne ſhal
come forth vpon the earth, take you euery one his weapons, and goe
forth euery valiant man out of the city, & ſet you a captaine ouer them,
as though you would goe downe into the field toward the watch of the
Aſſyrians, but goe not downe.3Then they ſhal take their armour, and ſhal
goe into their campe, and raiſe vp the captaines of the armie of Aſsur,
and they ſhall runne to the tent of Olofernes, but ſhall not finde him,
then feare ſhall fall vpon them, and they ſhall flee before your face.4So
you, and all that inhabite the coaſt of Iſrael, ſhall purſue them, and
ouerthrow them as they goe.5But before you doe theſe things, call me
Achior the Ammonite, that hee may ſee and know him that deſpiſed the
houſe of Iſrael, and that ſent him to vs as it were to his death.6Then they
called Achior out of the houſe of Ozias, and when hee was come, and
ſaw the head of Olofernes in a mans hand, in the aſſembly of the people,
he fell downe on his face, and his ſpirit failed.7But when they had
recouered him, hee fell at Iudeths feete, and reuerenced her, and ſaid:
Bleſſed art thou in all the tabernacle of Iuda, and in all nations, which
hearing thy name ſhall be aſtoniſhed.8Now therefore tell mee all the
things that thou haſt done in theſe dayes: Then Iudeth declared vnto
him in the midſt of the people, all that ſhee had done from the day that
ſhee went foorth, vntill that houre ſhe ſpake vnto them.9And when ſhee
had left off ſpeaking, the people ſhouted with a lowd voice, & made a

ioyful noiſe in their citie.10And when Achior had ſeene all that the God of Iſrael had done, hee beleeued in God greatly, and circumciſed the foreſkinne of his fleſh, and was ioyned vnto the houſe of Iſrael vnto this day.11And aſsoone as the morning aroſe, they hanged the head of Olofernes vpon the wall, and euery man took his weapons, and they went foorth by bandes vnto the ſtraits of the mountaine.12But when the Aſſyrians ſawe them, they ſent to their leaders, which came to their Captaines, and tribunes, and to euery one of their rulers.13So they came to Olofernes tent, and ſaid to him that had the charge of all his things, Waken now our lord: for the ſlaues haue beene bold to come downe againſt vs to battell, that they may be vtterly deſtroyed.14Then went in Bagoas, and knocked at the doore of the tent: for he thought that he had ſlept with Iudeth.15But becauſe none anſwered, he opened it, and went into the bedchamber, and found him caſt vpon the floore dead, & his head was taken from him.16Therefore he cried with a lowd voice, with weeping, and ſighing, and a mighty cry, and rent his garments.17After, hee went into the tent, where Iudeth lodged, and when hee found her not, he leaped out to the people, and cried,18Theſe ſlaues haue dealt treacherouſly, one woman of the Hebrewes hath brought ſhame vpon the houſe of king Nabuchodonoſor: for behold, Olofernes lieth vpon the ground without a head.19When the captaines of the Aſſyrians armie heard theſe words, they rent their coats, and their minds were wonderfully troubled, and there was a cry, and a very great noiſe throughout the campe.

CHAPTER 151And when they that were in the tents heard, they were aſtoniſhed at the thing that was done.2And feare and trembling fell vpon them, ſo that there was no man that durſt abide in the ſight of his neighbour, but ruſhing out altogether, they fled into euery way of the plaine, and of the hill countrey.3They alſo that had camped in the mountaines, round about Bethulia, fled away. Then the children of Iſrael euery one that was a warriour among them, ruſhed out vpon them.4Then ſent Ozias to Bethomaſthem, and to Bebai, and Chobai, and Cola, and to all the coaſts of Iſrael, ſuch as ſhould tell the things that were done, and that all ſhould ruſh forth vpon their enemies to deſtroy them.5Now when the children of Iſrael heard it, they all fell vpon them with one conſent, and ſlewe them vnto Choba: likewiſe alſo they that came from Ieruſalem, and from all the hill country, for men had told them what things were done in the campe of their enemies, and they that were in Galaad and in Galile chaſed them with a great ſlaughter, vntill they were paſt Damaſcus, and the borders thereof.6And the reſidue that dwelt at Bethulia, fell vpon the campe of Aſsur, and ſpoiled them, & were greatly enriched.7And the children of Iſrael that returned from the ſlaughter, had that which remained, and the villages, and the cities that were in the mountaines, and in the plaine, gate many ſpoiles: for the multitude was very great.8Then Ioacim the high Prieſt, and the Ancients of the children of Iſrael that dwelt in Ieruſalem, came to behold the good things that God had ſhewed to Iſrael, and to ſee Iudeth, and to ſalute her.9And when they came vnto her, they bleſſed her with one accord, and ſaid vnto her, Thou art the exaltation of Ieruſalem: thou art the great glory of Iſrael: thou art the great reioycing of our nation.10Thou haſt done all theſe things by thine hand: thou haſt done much good to Iſrael, and God is pleaſed therewith: bleſſed bee thou of the Almightie Lord for euermore: and all the people ſaid, So be it.11And the people ſpoiled the campe, the ſpace of thirty dayes, and they gaue vnto Iudeth Olofernes his tent, and all his plate, and beds, and veſſels, and all his ſtuffe: and ſhe tooke it, and laide it on her mule, and made ready her carts, and laid them thereon.12Then all the women of Iſrael ran together to ſee her, and bleſſed her, and made a dance among them for her: and ſhee tooke branches in her hand, & gaue alſo to the women that were with her.13And they put a garland of oliue vpon her, and her maid that was with her, and ſhee went before the people in the dance, leading all the women: and all the men of Iſrael followed in their armor with garlands, and with ſongs in their mouthes.

CHAPTER 161Then Iudeth began to ſing this thankeſgiuing in all Iſrael, and all the people ſang after her this ſong of praiſe.2And Iudeth ſaid, Begin vnto my God with timbrels, ſing vnto my Lord with cymbals: tune vnto him a newe Pſalme: exalt him, & cal vpon his name.3For God breaketh the battels: for amongſt the campes in the midſt of the people hee hath deliuered me out of the hands of them that perſecuted me.4Aſsur came out of the mountains from the North, he came with ten thouſands of his army, the multitude wherof ſtopped the torrents, and their horſemen haue couered the hilles.5He bragged that he would burne vp my borders, and kill my young men with the ſword, and daſh the ſucking children againſt the ground, and make mine infants as a pray, and my virgins as a ſpoile.6But the Almighty Lord hath diſappointed them by the hand of a woman.7For the mighty one did not fall by the yong men, neither did the ſonnes of the Titans ſmite him, nor high gyants ſet vpon him: but Iudeth the daughter of Merari weakned him with the beautie of her countenance.8For ſhe put off the garment of her widowhood, for the exaltation of thoſe that were oppreſſed in Iſrael, and anointed her face with oyntment, & bound her haire in a tyre, and tooke a linnen garment to deceiue him.9Her ſandals rauiſhed his eyes, her beautie tooke his minde priſoner, and the fauchin paſſed through his necke.10The Perſians quaked at her boldneſse, and the Medes were daunted at her hardineſse.11Then my afflicted ſhouted for ioy, and my weake ones cryed aloude; but they were aſtoniſhed: theſe lifted vp their voices, but they were ouerthrowen.12The ſonnes of the damoſels haue pierced them through, and wounded them as fugitiues children: they periſhed by the battell of the Lord.13I will ſing vnto the Lord a new ſong, O Lord thou art great and glorious, wonderful in ſtrength & inuincible.14Let all creatures ſerue thee: for thou ſpakeſt, and they were made, thou didſt ſend forth thy ſpirit, and it created them, and there is none that can reſiſt thy voyce.15For the mountaines ſhall be mooued from their foundations with the waters, the rockes ſhall melt as waxe at thy preſence: yet thou art mercifull to them that feare thee.16For all ſacrifice is too little for a ſweete ſauour vnto thee, and all the fat is not ſufficient, for thy burnt offering: but he that feareth the Lord is great at all times.17Woe to the nations that riſe vp againſt my kinred: the Lord almighty will take vengeance of them in the day of iudgement in putting fire & wormes in their fleſh, and they ſhall feele them and weepe for euer.18Now aſsoone as they entred into Ieruſalem, they worſhipped the Lord, and aſsoone as the people were purified, they offered their burnt offerings, and their free offerings, and their gifts.19Iudeth alſo dedicated all the ſtuffe of Olofernes, which the people had giuen her, and gaue the canopy which ſhe had taken out of his bed chamber, for a gift vnto the Lord.20So the people continued feaſting in Ieruſalem before the Sanctuarie, for the ſpace of three moneths, and Iudeth remained with them.21After this time, euery one returned to his owne inheritance, and Iudeth went to Bethulia, and remained in her owne poſſeſſion, and was in her time honourable in all the countrey.22And many deſired her, but none knew her all the dayes of her life, after that Manaſſes her huſband was dead, and was gathered to his people.23But ſhe encreaſed more and more in honour, and waxed olde in her huſbands houſe, being an hundred and fiue yeeres olde, and made her maide free, ſo ſhee died in Bethulia: and they buried her in the caue of her huſband Manaſſes.24And the houſe of Iſrael lamented her ſeauen dayes, and before ſhee dyed, ſhe did diſtribute her goods to all them that are neereſt of kinred to Manaſſes her huſband: and to them that were the neereſt of her kinred.25And there was none that made the children of Iſrael any more afraide, in the dayes of Iudeth, nor a long time after her death.

THE REſT OF EſTHER (ADDITIONS TO ESTHER)

CHAPTER 104Then Mardocheus ſaide, God hath done theſe things.5For I remember a dreame, which I ſawe concerning theſe matters, and nothing thereof hath failed.6A little fountaine became a riuer, and there was light, & the Sunne, and much water: this riuer is Eſther, whō the King married and made Queene.7And the two Dragons are I, and Aman.8And the nations were thoſe that were aſſembled, to deſtroy the name of the Iewes.9And my nation is this Iſrael, which cryed to God and were ſaued: for the Lord hath ſaued his people, and the Lord hath deliuered vs from all thoſe euils, and God hath wrought ſignes, and great wonders, which haue not bin done among the Gentiles.10Therefore hath hee made two lots, one for the people of God, and another for all the Gentiles.11And theſe two lots came at the houre, and time, and day of iudgement before God amongſt all nations.12So God remembred his people, and iuſtified his inheritance.13Therefore thoſe dayes ſhall be vnto them in the moneth Adar, the foureteenth and fifteenth day of the ſame moneth, with an aſſembly, and ioy, and with gladneſſe, before God, according to the generations for euer among his people.

CHAPTER 111In the fourth yeere of the raigne of Ptolomeus, and Cleopatra, Doſitheus, who ſaid hee was a prieſt and Leuite, and Ptolomeus his ſonne brought this Epiſtle of Phurim, which they ſaid was the ſame, and that Lyſimachus the ſonne of Ptolomeus, that was in Ieruſalem, had interpreted it.2In the ſecond yeere of the raigne of Artaxerxes the great: in the firſt day of the moneth Niſan, Mardocheus the ſonne of Iairus, the ſonne of Semei, the ſonne of Ciſai of the tribe of Beniamin, had a dreame.3Who was a Iew and dwelt in the citie of Suſa, a great man, being a ſeruitour in the kings court.4He was alſo one of the captiues, which Nabuchodonoſor the king of Babylon caried from Ieruſalem, with Iechonias king of Iudea; and this was his dreame.5Behold a noiſe of a tumult with thunder, and earthquakes, and vproare in the land.6And behold, two great dragons came forth ready to fight, and their crie was great.7And at their cry all nations were prepared to battel, that they might fight againſt the righteous people.8And loe a day of darkneſſe and obſcurity: tribulation, and anguiſh, affliction, and great vproare vpon the earth.9And the whole righteous nation was troubled, fearing their owne euils, and were ready to periſh.10Then they cryed vnto God, and vpon their cry, as it were from a little fountaine, was made a great flood, euen much water.11The light and the Sunne roſe vp, and the lowly were exalted, and deuoured the glorious.12Now when Mardocheus, who had ſeene this dreame, and what God had determined to doe, was awake: he bare this dreame in minde, and vntill night by all meanes was deſirous to know it.

CHAPTER 121And Mardocheus tooke his reſt in the court with Gabatha, and Tharra, the two Eunuches of the king, and keepers of the palace.2And he heard their deuices, and ſearched out their purpoſes, and learned that they were about to lay hands vpon Artaxerxes the king, and ſo he certified the king of them.3Then the king examined the two Eunuches, and after that they had confeſsed it, they were ſtrangled.4And the king made a record of theſe things, and Mardocheus alſo wrote thereof.5So the king commaunded Mardocheus to ſerue in the court, and for this he rewarded him.6Howbeit Aman the ſonne of Amadathus the Agagite, who was in great honour with the king, ſought to moleſt Mardocheus and his people, becauſe of the two Eunuches of the king.

CHAPTER 131The copy of the letters was this. The great king Artaxerxes, writeth theſe things to the princes, and gouernours that are vnder him from India vnto Ethiopia, in an hundred and ſeuen and twentie prouinces.2After that I became Lord ouer many nations, and had dominion ouer the whole world, not lifted vp with preſumption of my authoritie, but carying my ſelfe alway with equitie and mildeneſse, I purpoſed to ſettle my ſubiects continually in a quiet life, and making my kingdome peaceable, and open for paſsage to the vtmoſt coaſtes, to renue peace which is deſired of all men.3Now when I aſked my counſellers how this might bee brought to paſſe, Aman that excelled in wiſedome among vs, and was approoued for his conſtant good will, and ſtedfaſt fidelitie, and had the honour of the ſecond place in the kingdome,4Declared vnto vs, that in all nations throughout the world, there was ſcattered a certaine malitious people, that had Lawes contrary to all nations, and continually deſpiſed the commandements of Kings, ſo as the vniting of our kingdomes honourably intended by vs, cannot goe forward.5Seeing then we vnderſtand that this people alone is continually in oppoſition vnto all men, differing in the ſtrange maner of their Lawes, and euill affected to our ſtate, working all the miſchiefe they can, that our kingdome may not be firmely ſtabliſhed:6Therefore haue we commanded that al they that are ſignified in writing vnto you by Aman (who is ordained ouer the affaires, and is next vnto vſ) ſhall all with their wiues and children bee vtterly deſtroyed, by the ſword of their enemies, without all mercie and pitie, the fourteenth day of the twelfth moneth Adar of this preſent yeere:7That they, who of old, and now alſo are malitious, may in one day with violence goe into the graue, and ſo euer hereafter, cauſe our affaires to be well ſettled, and without trouble.8Then Mardocheus thought vpon all the works of the Lord, and made his prayer vnto him,9Saying, O Lord, Lord, the king Almightie: for the whole world is in thy power; and if thou haſt appointed to ſaue Iſrael, there is no man that can gaineſay thee.10For thou haſt made heauen and earth, and all the wonderous things vnder the heauen.11Thou art Lord of all things, and there is no man that can reſiſt thee, which art the Lord.12Thou knoweſt all things, and thou knoweſt Lord, that it was neither in contempt nor pride, nor for any deſire of glory, that I did not bow downe to proud Aman.13For I could haue bene content with good will for the ſaluation of Iſrael, to kiſſe the ſoles of his feet.14But I did this, that I might not preferre the glory of man aboue the glory of God: neither will I worſhip any but thee, O God, neither wil I doe it in pride.15And now, O Lord God, and King, ſpare thy people: for their eyes are vpon vs, to bring vs to nought, yea they deſire to deſtroy the inheritance that hath beene thine from the beginning.16Deſpiſe not the portion which thou haſt deliuered out of Egypt for thine owne ſelfe:17Heare my prayer, and be mercifull vnto thine inheritance: turne our ſorrow into ioy, that wee may liue, O Lord, and praiſe thy Name: and deſtroy not the mouthes of them that praiſe thee, O Lord.18All Iſrael in like maner cried moſt earneſtly vnto the Lord, becauſe their death was before their eyes.

CHAPTER 141Queene Eſther alſo being in feare of death, reſorted vnto the Lord,2And layd away her glorious apparel, and put on the garments of anguiſh, & mourning: and in ſtead of pretious oyntments, ſhe couered her head with aſhes, & doung, and ſhe humbled her body greatly, and all the places of her ioy ſhe filled with her torne haire.3And ſhee prayed vnto the Lord God of Iſrael, ſaying, O my Lord, thou onely art our king: helpe me deſolate woman, which haue no helper but thee:4For my danger is in mine hand.5From my youth vp I haue heard in the tribe of my family, that thou, O Lord, tookeſt Iſrael from among all people, and our fathers from all their predeceſsours, for a perpetuall inheritance, and thou haſt performed whatſoeuer thou didſt promiſe them.6And now we haue ſinned before thee: therefore haſt thou giuen vs into the hands of our enemies,7Becauſe wee worſhipped their gods: O Lord, thou art righteous.8Neuertheles it ſatiſfieth them not, that we are in bitter captiuitie, but they haue ſtriken hands with their idols,9That they will aboliſh the thing, that thou with thy mouth haſt ordained, and deſtroy thine inheritance, and ſtop the mouth of them that praiſe thee, and quench the glory of thy houſe, and of thine Altar,10And open the mouthes of the heathen to ſet foorth the praiſes of the Idoles, and to magnifie a fleſhly king for euer.11O Lord, giue not thy ſcepter vnto them that be nothing, and let them not laugh at our fall, but turne their deuice vpon themſelues, and make him an example that hath begunne this againſt vs.12Remember, O Lord, make thy ſelfe knowen in time of our affliction, and giue mee boldneſse, O King of the nations, and Lord of all power.13Giue me eloquent ſpeech in my mouth before the lyon: turne his heart to hate him that fighteth againſt vs, that there may be an end of him, and of all that are like minded to him:14But deliuer vs with thine hand, and helpe me that am deſolate, & which haue no other helper but thee.15Thou knoweſt all things, O Lord, thou knoweſt that I hate the glory of the vnrighteous, and abhorre the bed of the vncircumciſed, and of all the heathen.16Thou knoweſt my neceſsitie: for I abhorre the ſigne of my high eſtate, which is vpon mine head, in the dayes wherein I ſhewe my ſelfe, and that I abhorre it as a menſtruous ragge, and that I weare it not when I am priuate by my ſelfe.17And that thine handmaid hath not eaten at Amans table, and that I haue not greatly eſteemed the Kings feaſt, nor drunke the wine of the drinke offerings:18Neither had thine handmaid any ioy, ſince the day that I was brought hither to this preſent, but in thee, O Lord God of Abraham.19O thou mightie God aboue all, heare the voice of the forlorne, and deliuer vs out of the handes of the miſchieuous, and deliuer me out of my feare.

CHAPTER 151And vpon the third day when ſhee had ended her prayer, ſhe laide away her mourning garments, and put on her glorious apparell.2And being gloriouſly adorned, after ſhe had called vpon God, who is the beholder, and Sauiour of all things, ſhe tooke two maids with her.3And vpon the one ſhee leaned as carying her ſelfe daintily.4And the other followed bearing vp her traine.5And ſhe was ruddy through the perfection of her beautie, and her countenance was cheerefull, and very amiable: but her heart was in anguiſh for feare.6Then hauing paſſed through all the doores, ſhee ſtood before the King, who ſate vpon his royall throne, and was clothed with all his robes of maieſtie, all glittering with golde and precious ſtones, and he was very dreadfull.7Then lifting vp his countenance that ſhone with maieſtie, he looked very fiercely

vpon her: and the Queene fell downe and was pale, and fainted, and
bowed her ſelfe vpon the head of the maide that went before her.8Then
God changed the ſpirit of the king into mildneſse, who in a feare leaped
from his throne, and tooke her in his armes till ſhe came to her ſelfe
againe, and comforted her with louing words, and ſayd vnto her:9Eſther,
what is the matter? I am thy brother, be of good cheere.10Thou ſhalt not
die, though our cōmandement be generall: come neere.11And ſo he held
vp his golden ſcepter, and laid it vpon her necke,12And embraced her,
& ſaid, Speake vnto me.13Then ſaid ſhee vnto him, I ſaw thee, my lord,
as an Angel of God, and my heart was troubled for feare of thy
maieſtie.14For wonderfull art thou, lord, and thy countenance is full of
grace.15And as ſhe was ſpeaking, ſhe fell downe for faintneſse.16Then
the king was troubled, and all his ſeruants comforted her.
CHAPTER 161The great king Artaxerxes vnto the princes and
gouernours of an hundreth and ſeuen and twenty prouinces, from India
vnto Ethiopia, and vnto all our faithfull Subiects, greeting.2Many, the
more often they are honoured with the great bountie of their gracious
princes, the more proud they are waxen,3And endeauour to hurt not our
Subiects onely, but not being able to beare abundance, doe take in hand
to practiſe alſo againſt thoſe that doe them good:4And take not only
thankfulneſse away from among men, but alſo lifted vp with the glorious
words of lewde perſons that were neuer good, they thinke to eſcape the
iuſtice of God, that ſeeth all things, and hateth euill.5Often times alſo
faire ſpeech of thoſe that are put in truſt to manage their friends affaires,
hath cauſed many that are in authority to be partakers of innocent blood,
and hath enwrapped them in remedileſſe calamities:6Beguiling with the
falſhood and deceit of their lewd diſpoſition, the innocencie and
goodneſſe of princes.7Now yee may ſee this as we haue declared, not ſo
much by ancient hiſtories, as yee may, if ye ſearch what hath beene
wickedly done of late through the peſtilent behauiour of them that are
vnworthily placed in authoritie.8And we muſt take care for the time to
come, that our kingdome may bee quiet and peaceable for all men,9Both
by changing our purpoſes, and alwayes iudging things that are euident,
with more equall proceeding.10For Aman a Macedonian the ſon of
Amadatha, being indeed a ſtranger from the Perſian blood, and far
diſtant from our goodneſse, and as a ſtranger receiued of vs:11Had ſo
farre forth obtained the fauour that wee ſhew toward euery nation, as
that he was called our father, and was continually honoured of all men,
as the next perſon vnto the king.12But he not bearing his great dignitie,
went about to depriue vs of our kingdome and life:13Hauing by manifold
and cunning deceits ſought of vs the deſtruction as well of Mardocheus,
who ſaued our life, and continually procured our good, as alſo of
blameleſſe Eſther partaker of our kingdome, with their whole
nation.14For by theſe meanes he thought, finding vs deſtitute of friends,
to haue tranſlated the kingdome of the Perſians to the
Macedonians.15But wee finde that the Iewes, whom this wicked wretch
hath deliuered to vtter deſtruction, are no euill doers, but liue by moſt
iuſt lawes:16And that they be children of the moſt high and moſt mighty
liuing God, who hath ordered the kingdome both vnto vs, and to our
progenitors in the moſt excellent maner.17Wherefore ye ſhall doe well
not to put in execution the Letters ſent vnto you by Aman the ſonne of
Amadatha.18For hee that was the worker of theſe things, is hanged at
the gates of Suſa with all his family: God, who ruleth all things, ſpeedily
rendring vengeance to him according to his deſerts.19Therefore ye ſhall
publiſh the copy of this Letter in all places, that the Iewes may freely
liue after their owne lawes.20And ye ſhall aide them, that euen the ſame
day, being the thirteenth day of the twelfth moneth Adar, they may be
auenged on them, who in the time of their affliction ſhall ſet vpon
them.21For Almightie God hath turned to ioy vnto them the day,
wherein the choſen people ſhould haue periſhed.22You ſhall therefore
among your ſolemne feaſts keepe it an high day with all feaſting,23That
both now and hereafter there may be ſafetie to vs, and the well affected
Perſians: but to thoſe which doe conſpire againſt vs, a memoriall of
deſtruction.24Therefore euery citie and countrey whatſoeuer, which ſhall
not doe according to theſe things, ſhall bee deſtroyed without mercy,
with fire and ſword, and ſhall be made not onely vnpaſsable for men,
but alſo moſt hatefull to wilde beaſts and foules for euer.

WIſEDOME (WISDOM OF SOLOMON)

CHAPTER 11Loue righteouſneſſe, yee that be iudges of the earth:
thinke of the Lord with a good (heart) and in ſimplicitie of heart ſeeke
him.2For hee will bee found of them that tempt him not: and ſheweth
himſelfe vnto ſuch as doe not diſtruſt him.3For froward thoughts
ſeparate from God: and his power when it is tryed, reprooueth the
vnwiſe.4For into a malitious ſoule wiſedome ſhall not enter: nor dwell
in the body that is ſubiect vnto ſinne.5For the holy ſpirit of diſcipline
will flie deceit, & remoue from thoughts that are without vnderſtanding:
and will not abide when vnrighteouſneſſe commeth in.6For wiſedome
is a louing ſpirit: and will not acquite a blaſphemour of his words: for
God is witneſſe of his reines, and a true beholder of his heart, and a
hearer of his tongue.7For the ſpirit of the Lord filleth the world: and
that which containeth all things hath knowledge of the voice.8Therefore
he that ſpeaketh vnrighteous things, cannot be hid: neither ſhal
vengeance, when it puniſheth. paſſe by him.9For inquiſition ſhall be
made into the counſels of the vngodly: and the ſound of his words, ſhall
come vnto the Lord, for the manifeſtation of his wicked deedes.10For
the eare of iealouſie heareth al things: and the noiſe of murmurings is
not hid.11Therefore beware of murmuring, which is vnprofitable, and
refraine your tongue from backbiting: for there is no word ſo ſecret that
ſhall goe for nought: and the mouth that belieth, ſlayeth the
ſoule.12Seeke not death in the errour of your life: and pull not vpon your
ſelues deſtruction, with the workes of your hands.13For God made not
death: neither hath he pleaſure in the deſtruction of the liuing.14For he
created all things, that they might haue their being: and the generations
of the world were healthfull: and there is no poyſon of deſtruction in
them: nor the kingdome of death vpon the earth.15For righteouſneſſe is
immortall.16But vngodly men with their workes, and words called it to
them: for when they thought to haue it their friend, they conſumed to
nought, and made a couenant with it, becauſe they are worthy to take
part with it.
CHAPTER 21For the vngodly ſaid, reaſoning with themſelues, but not
aright: Our life is ſhort and tedious, and in the death of a man there is
no remedie: neither was there any man knowen to haue returned from
the graue.2For wee are borne at all aduenture: & we ſhalbe heereafter as
though we had neuer bene: for the breath in our noſtrils is as ſmoke,
and a litle ſparke in the mouing of our heart.3Which being extinguiſhed,
our body ſhall be turned into aſhes, and our ſpirit ſhall vaniſh as the ſoft
aire:4And our name ſhalbe forgotten in time, and no man ſhall haue our
works in remembrance, and our life ſhall paſſe away as the trace of a
cloud: and ſhall be diſperſed as a miſt that is driuen away with the
beames of the Sunne, and ouercome with the heat thereof.5For our time
is a very ſhadow that paſſeth away: and after our end there is no
returning: for it is faſt ſealed, ſo that no man commeth againe.6Come
on therefore, let vs enioy the good things that are preſent: and let vs
ſpeedily vſe the creatures like as in youth.7Let vs fill our ſelues with
coſtly wine, and ointments: and let no flower of the Spring paſſe by
vs.8Let vs crowne our ſelues with Roſe buds, before they be
withered.9Let none of vs goe without his part of our voluptuouſneſse:
let vs leaue tokens of our ioyfulneſſe in euery place: for this is our
portion, and our lot is this.10Let vs oppreſſe the poore righteous man,
let vs not ſpare the widow, nor reuerence the ancient gray haires of the
aged.11Let our ſtrength bee the Lawe of iuſtice: for that which is feeble
is found to be nothing worth.12Therefore let vs lye in wait for the
righteous: becauſe he is not for our turne, and he is cleane contrary to
our doings: he vpbraideth vs with our offending the Law, and obiecteth
to our infamy the tranſgreſsings of our education.13Hee profeſseth to
haue the knowledge of God: and hee calleth himſelfe the childe of the
Lord.14Hee was made to reprooue our thoughts.15Hee is grieuous vnto
vs euen to beholde: for his life is not like other mens, his waies are of
another faſhion.16We are eſteemed of him as counterfeits: he abſtaineth
from our wayes as from filthineſse: he pronounceth the end of the iuſt
to be bleſſed, and maketh his boaſt that God is his father.17Let vs ſee if
his wordes be true: and let vs proue what ſhall happen in the end of
him.18For if the iuſt man be the ſonne of God, he will helpe him, and
deliuer him from the hand of his enemies.19Let vs examine him with
deſpitefulneſse and torrture, that we may know his meekeneſse, and
prooue his patience.20Let vs condemne him with a ſhamefull death: for
by his owne ſaying, he ſhall be reſpected.21ſuch things they did imagine,

and were deceiued: for their owne wickedneſſe hath blinded them.22As
for the myſteries of God, they knew them not: neither hoped they for
the wages of righteouſneſſe: nor diſcerneda reward for blameleſſe
ſoules.23For God created man to bee immortall, and made him to be an
image of his owne eternitie.24Neuertheleſſe through enuie of the deuill
came death into the world: and they that doe holde of his ſide doe finde
it.
CHAPTER 31But the ſoules of the righteous are in the hand of God,
and there ſhall no torment touch them.2In the ſight of the vnwiſe they
ſeemed to die: and their departure is taken for miſery,3And their going
from vs to be vtter deſtruction: but they are in peace.4For though they
bee puniſhed in the ſight of men: yet is their hope full of
immortalitie.5And hauing bene a little chaſtiſed, they ſhalbe greatly
rewarded: for God proued them, and found them worthy for
himſelfe.6As gold in the furnace hath hee tried them, and receiued them
as a burnt offering.7And in the time of their viſitation, they ſhall ſhine
and runne to and fro, like ſparkes among the ſtubble.8They ſhall iudge
the nations, and haue dominion ouer the people, and their Lord ſhall
raigne for euer.9They that put their truſt in him, ſhall vnderſtand the
trueth: and ſuch as be faithfull in loue, ſhall abide with him: for grace &
mercy is to his ſaints, and he hath care for his elect.10But the vngodly
ſhalbe puniſhed according to their owne imaginations, which haue
neglected the righteous, and forſaken the Lord.11For who ſo deſpiſeth
wiſedome, and nurture, he is miſerable, and their hope is vaine, their
labours vnfruitfull, and their works vnprofitable.12Their wiues are
fooliſh, and their children wicked.13Their of-ſpring is curſed: wherefore
bleſſed is the barren that is vndefiled, which hath not knowen the ſinfull
bed: ſhe ſhall haue fruit in the viſitation of ſoules.14And bleſſed is the
Eunuch which with his hands hath wrought no iniquitie: nor imagined
wicked things againſt God: for vnto him ſhall be giuen the ſpeciall gift
of faith, and an inheritance in the Temple of the Lord more acceptable
to his minde.15For glorious is the fruit of good labours: and the root of
wiſedom ſhall neuer fall away.16As for the children of adulterers, they
ſhall not come to their perfection, and the ſeed of an vnrighteous bed
ſhal be rooted out.17For though they liue long, yet ſhall they bee nothing
regarded: and their laſt age ſhall be without honour.18Or if they die
quickly, they haue no hope, neither comfort in the day of triall.19For
horrible is the end of the vnrighteous generation.
CHAPTER 41Better it is to haue no children, and to haue vertue: for
the memoriall thereof is immortal: becauſe it is knowen with God and
with men.2When it is preſent, men take example at it, and when it is
gone they deſire it: it weareth a crown, and triumpheth for euer, hauing
gotten the victorie, ſtriuing for vndefiled rewards.3But the multiplying
brood of the vngodly ſhall not thriue, nor take deepe rooting from
baſtard ſlips, nor lay any faſt foundation.4For though they flouriſh in
branches for a time: yet ſtanding not faſt, they ſhall be ſhaken with the
winde: and through the force of windes they ſhall be rooted out.5The
vnperfect branches ſhall bee broken off, their fruit vnprofitable, not ripe
to eate: yea meet for nothing.6For children begotten of vnlawfull beds,
are witneſſes of wickednes againſt their parents in their triall.7But
though the righteous be preuented with death: yet ſhal he be in reſt.8For
honourable age is not that which ſtandeth in length of time, nor that is
meaſured by number of yeeres.9But wiſedome is the gray haire vnto
men, & an vnſpotted life is old age.10He pleaſed God, and was beloued
of him: ſo that liuing amongſt ſinners, he was tranſlated.11Yea, ſpeedily
was he taken away, leſt that wickednes ſhould alter his vnderſtanding, or
deceit beguile his ſoule.12For the bewitching of naughtines doth obſcure
things that are honeſt: and the wandring of concupiſcence, doth
vndermine the ſimple mind.13He being made perfect in a ſhort time,
fulfilled a long time.14For his ſoule pleaſed the Lord: therefore haſted
he to take him away, from among the wicked.15This the people ſaw, and
vnderſtood it not: neither laid they vp this in their mindes, That his grace
and mercie is with his Saints, and that he hath reſpect vnto his
choſen.16Thus the righteous that is dead, ſhall condemne the vngodly,
which are liuing, and youth that is ſoone perfected, the many yeeres and
old age of the vnrighteous.17For they ſhall ſee the end of the wiſe, &
ſhall not vnderſtand what God in his counſell hath decreed of him, and
to what end the Lord hath ſet him in ſafetie.18They ſhal ſee him and
deſpiſe him, but God ſhall laugh them to ſcorne, and they ſhal hereafter
be a vile carkeis, and a reproch among the dead for euermore.19For he
ſhall rend them, and caſt them downe headlong, that they ſhalbe
ſpeechles: and he ſhal ſhake them from the foundation: and they ſhall
bee vtterly laid waſte, and be in ſorow: and their memoriall ſhall
periſh.20And when they caſt vp the accounts of their ſinnes, they ſhall
come with feare: and their owne iniquities ſhall conuince them to their
face.
CHAPTER 51Then ſhal the righteous man ſtand in great boldneſse,
before the face of ſuch as haue afflicted him, and made no account of
his labours.2When they ſee it, they ſhalbe troubled with terrible feare, &
ſhall be amazed at the ſtrangeneſse of his ſaluation, ſo farre beyond all
that they looked for.3And they repenting, and groning for anguiſh of
ſpirit, ſhall ſay within themſelues, This was he whom wee had ſometimes
in deriſion, and a prouerbe of reproch.4We fooles accounted his life
madnes, and his end to be without honour.5How is hee numbred among
the children of God, and his lot is among the Saints?6Therefore haue
wee erred from the way of trueth, and the light of righteouſneſſe hath
not ſhined vnto vs, and the Sunne of righteouſneſſe roſe not vpon
vs.7We wearied ourſelues in the way of wickedneſſe, and deſtruction:
yea, we haue gone through deſerts, where there lay no way: but as for
the way of the Lord, we haue not knowen it.8What hath pride profited
vs? or what good hath riches with our vaunting brought vs?9All thoſe
things are paſſed away like a ſhadow, and as a Poſte that haſted by.10And
as a ſhip that paſſeth ouer the waues of the water, which when it is gone
by, the trace thereof cannot bee found: neither the path way of the keele
in the waues.11Or as when a bird hath flowen thorow the aire, there is
no token of her way to be found, but the light aire being beaten with the
ſtroke of her wings, and parted with the violent noiſe and motion of
them, is paſſed thorow, and therin afterwards no ſigne where ſhe went,
is to be found.12Or like as when an arrow is ſhot at a marke, it parteth
the aire, which immediatly commeth together againe: ſo that a man
cannot know where it went thorow:13Euen ſo we in like maner, aſsoone
as we were borne, began to draw to our end, and had no ſigne of vertue
to ſhew: but were conſumed in our owne wickedneſſe.14For the hope
of the vngodly is like duſt that is blowen away with þe wind, like a thinne
froth that is driuen away with þe ſtorme: like as the ſmoke which is
diſperſed here and there with a tempeſt, and paſſeth away as the
remembrance of a gueſt that tarieth but a day.15But þe righteous liue for
euermore, their reward alſo is with the Lord, and the care of them is
with the moſt High.16Therfore ſhall they receiue a glorious kingdome,
& a beautiful crowne from the Lords hande: for with his right hand ſhall
he couer them, and with his arme ſhall he protect them.17He ſhall take
to him his ielouſie for cōplete armour, & make the creature his weapon
for the reuenge of his enemies.18He ſhal put on righteouſneſſe as a
breſtplate, and true iudgement in ſtead of an helmet.19He ſhall take
holineſſe for an inuincible ſhield.20His ſeuere wrath ſhall he ſharpen for
a ſword, and the world ſhall fight with him againſt the vnwiſe.21Then
ſhal the right-aiming thunder bolts goe abroad, and from the cloudes, as
from a well-drawen bow, ſhall they flie to the marke.22And haileſtones
full of wrath ſhal be caſt as out of a ſtonebow, and the water of the ſea
ſhall rage againſt them, & the floods ſhall cruelly drowne them.23Yea a
mightie wind ſhall ſtand vp againſt them, & like a ſtorme ſhall blow them
away: thus iniquity ſhal lay waſt the whole earth, and ill dealing ſhall
ouerthrow the thrones of the mightie.
CHAPTER 61Heare therefore, O yee kings, and vnderſtand, learne yee
that be iudges of the ends of the earth.2Giue eare you that rule the
people, and glory in the multitude of nations.3For power is giuen you of
the Lord, & ſoueraigntie from the Higheſt, who ſhall try your workes;
and ſearch out your counſels.4Becauſe being Miniſters of his kingdome,
you haue not iudged aright, nor kept the law, nor walked after the
counſell of God,5Horribly and ſpeedily ſhall he come vpon you: for a
ſharpe iudgement ſhall be to them that be in high places.6For mercy will
ſoone pardon the meaneſt: but mighty men ſhall be mightily
tormented.7For he which is Lord ouer all, ſhall feare no mans perſon:
neither ſhall he ſtand in awe of any mans greatneſse: for he hath made
the ſmall and great, and careth for all alike.8But a ſore triall ſhall come
vpon the mighty.9Unto you therefore, O kings, doe I ſpeake, that yee
may learne wiſedome, and not fall away.10For they that keepe holineſſe
holily, ſhall be iudged holy: and they that haue learned ſuch things, ſhall
find what to anſwere.11Wherefore ſet your affection vpon my words,

deſire them, and yee ſhall be inſtructed.12Wiſedome is glorious and
neuer fadeth away: yea ſhe is eaſily ſeene of them that loue her, and
found of ſuch as ſeeke her.13She preuenteth them that deſire her, in
making herſelfe firſt knowen vnto them.14Whoſo ſeeketh her earely,
ſhall haue no great trauaile: for he ſhall find her ſitting at his doores.15To
thinke therefore vpon her is perfection of wiſedome: and who ſo
watcheth for her, ſhall quickly be without care.16For ſhe goeth about
ſeeking ſuch as are worthy of her, ſheweth herſelfe fauourably vnto
them in the wayes, and meeteth them in euery thought.17For the very
true beginning of her, is the deſire of diſcipline, and the care of diſcipline
is loue:18And loue is the keeping of her lawes; and the giuing heed vnto
her lawes, is the aſsurance of incorruption.19And incorruption maketh
vs neere vnto God.20Therefore the deſire of wiſedome bringeth to a
kingdome.21If your delight be then in thrones and ſcepters, O ye kings
of the people, honour wiſedome that yee may raigne for euermore.22As
for wiſedome what ſhe is, and how ſhe came vp, I will tell you, and will
not hide myſteries from you: but will ſeeke her out from the beginning
of her natiuity, & bring the knowledge of her into light, and will not
paſſe ouer the trueth.23Neither will I goe with conſuming enuy: for ſuch
a man ſhall haue no fellowſhip with wiſedome.24But the multitude of
the wiſe is the welfare of the world: and a wiſe king is the vpholding of
the people.25Receiue therefore inſtruction thorough my words, and it
ſhall doe you good.
CHAPTER 71I my ſelfe alſo am a mortall man, like to all, and the
offpring of him that was firſt made of the earth,2And in my mothers
wombe was faſhioned to be fleſh in the time of tenne moneths being
compacted in blood, of the ſeed of man, and the pleaſure that came with
ſleepe.3And when I was borne, I drew in the common aire, and fell vpon
the earth which is of like nature, and the firſt voice which I vttered, was
crying as all others doe.4I was nurſed in ſwadling clothes, and that with
cares.5For there is no king that had any other beginning of birth.6For
all men haue one entrance vnto life, and the like going out.7Wherefore
I prayed, and vnderſtanding was giuen mee: I called vpon God, and the
ſpirit of wiſedome came to me.8I preferred her before ſcepters, and
thrones, and eſteemed riches nothing in compariſon of her.9Neither
compared I vnto her any precious ſtone, becauſe all gold in reſpect of
her is as a little ſand, and ſiluer ſhalbe counted as clay before her.10I
loued her aboue health and beautie, and choſe to haue her in ſtead of
light: for the light that commeth from her neuer goeth out.11All good
things together came to me with her, and innumerable riches in her
hands.12And I reioyced in them all, becauſe wiſedome goeth before
them: and I knew not that ſhee was the mother of them.13I learned
diligently, and doe communicate her liberally: I doe not hide her
riches.14For ſhee is a treaſure vnto men that neuer faileth: which they
that vſe, become the friends of God: being commended for the gifts
that come from learning.15God hath granted me to ſpeake as I would,
and to conceiue as is meet for the things that are giuen mee: becauſe it
is hee that leadeth vnto wiſedome, and directeth the wiſe.16For in his
hand are both we and our wordes: all wiſedome alſo and knowledge of
workemanſhip.17For hee hath giuen mee certaine knowledge of the
things that are, namely to know how the world was made, & the
operation of the elements:18The beginning, ending, and midſt of the
times: the alterations of the turning of the Sunne, and the change of
ſeaſons:19The circuits of yeres, and the poſitions of ſtarres:20The natures
of liuing creatures, and the furies of wilde beaſts: the violence of windes,
and the reaſonings of men: the diuerſities of plants, and the vertues of
rootes:21And all ſuch things as are either ſecret or manifeſt: them I
know.22For wiſedome which is the worker of all things, taught mee: for
in her is an vnderſtanding ſpirit holy, one onely, manifold, ſubtile, liuely,
cleare, vndefiled, plaine, not ſubiect to hurt, louing the thing that is
good, quicke, which cãnot be letted, ready to do good:23Kinde to man,
ſtedfaſt, ſure, free from care, hauing all power, ouerſeeing all things, and
going through all vnderſtanding, pure, and moſt ſubtile ſpirits.24For
wiſedome is more moouing then any motion: ſhe paſſeth and goeth
through all things by reaſon of her pureneſse.25For ſhe is the breath of
the power of God, and a pure influence flowing from the glory of the
Almighty: therefore can no vndefiled thing fall into her.26For ſhee is the
brightneſse of the euerlaſting light: the vnſpotted mirrour of the power
of God, and the Image of his goodneſse.27And being but one ſhe can
doe all things: and remayning in her ſelfe, ſhe maketh all things new: and
in all ages entring into holy ſoules, ſhe maketh them friends of God, &
Prophets.28For God loueth none but him, that dwelleth with
wiſedome.29For ſhe is more beautiful then the Sunne, and aboue all the
order of ſtarres, being compared with the light, ſhe is found before
it.30For after this commeth night: but vice ſhall not preuaile againſt
wiſdome.
CHAPTER 81Wiſdome reacheth from one ende to another mightily:
and ſweetly doeth ſhe order all things.2I loued her and ſought her out,
from my youth I dedeſired to make her my ſpouſe, and I was a louer of
her beautie.3In that ſhe is conuerſant with God, ſhe magnifieth her
nobilitie: yea, the Lord of all things himſelfe loued her.4For ſhe is priuy
to the myſteries of the knowledge of God, and a louer of his workes.5If
riches be a poſſeſſion to be deſired in this life: what is richer then
wiſedome that worketh all things?6And if prudence worke; who of all
that are, is a more cunning workeman then ſhe?7And if a man loue
righteouſneſſe, her labours are vertues: for ſhe teacheth temperance and
prudence: iuſtice and fortitude, which are ſuch things as men can haue
nothing more profitable in their life.8If a man deſire much experience:
ſhe knoweth things of old, and coniectureth aright what is to come: ſhee
knoweth the ſubtilties of ſpeaches, and can expound darke ſentences:
ſhe foreſeeth ſignes and wonders, and the euents of ſeaſons and
times.9Therefore I purpoſed to take her to me to liue with mee, knowing
that ſhee would be a counſellour of good things, and a comfort in cares
& griefe.10For her ſake I ſhall haue eſtimation among the multitude, and
honour with the Elders, though I be yong.11I ſhall be found of a quicke
conceit in iudgement, and ſhall be admired in the ſight of great
men.12When I hold my tongue they ſhal bide my leiſure, and when I
ſpeake they ſhall giue good eare vnto me: if I talke much, they ſhall lay
their handes vpon their mouth.13Moreouer, by the meanes of her, I ſhall
obtaine immortalitie, and leaue behind me an euerlaſting memoriall to
them that come after me.14I ſhall ſet the people in order, and the nations
ſhalbe ſubiect vnto me.15Horrible tyrants ſhall be afraide when they doe
but heare of me, I ſhall be found good among the multitude, and valiant
in warre.16After I am come into mine houſe, I will repoſe my ſelfe with
her: for her conuerſation hath no bitternes, and to liue with her, hath no
ſorrow, but mirth and ioy.17Now when I conſidered theſe things in my
ſelfe, and pondered them in mine heart, how that to be allyed vnto
wiſedome, is immortalitie,18And great pleaſure it is to haue her
friendſhip, and in the workes of her hands are infinite riches, and in the
exerciſe of conference with her, prudence: and in talking with her a good
report: I went about ſeeking how to take her to me.19For I was a wittie
child, and had a good ſpirit.20Yea rather being good, I came into a body
vndefiled.21Neuertheleſſe when I perceiued that I could not otherwiſe
obtaine her, except God gaue her me (and that was a point of wiſdome
alſo to know whoſe gift ſhe waſ) I prayed vnto the Lord, and beſought
him, and with my whole heart I ſaid:
CHAPTER 9 1O God of my fathers, and Lord of mercy, who haſt
made all things with thy word,2And ordained man through thy
wiſedome, that he ſhould haue dominion ouer the creatures, which thou
haſt made,3And order the world according to equitie and righteouſneſſe,
and execute iudgement with an vpright heart:4Giue me wiſedome that
ſitteth by thy Throne, and reiect me not from among thy children:5For
I thy ſeruant and ſonne of thine handmaide, am a feeble perſon, and of
a ſhort time, and too young for the vnderſtanding of iudgement and
lawes.6For though a man be neuer ſo perfect among the children of
men, yet if thy wiſedome be not with him, hee ſhall be nothing
regarded.7Thou haſt choſen me to be a king of thy people, and a Iudge
of thy ſons and daughters:8Thou haſt commaunded me to build a
Temple vpon thy holy mount, and an Altar in the city wherein thou
dwelleſt, a reſemblance of the holy Tabernacle which thou haſt prepared
from the beginning:9And wiſedome was with thee: which knoweth thy
workes, and was preſent when thou madeſt the world, and knew what
was acceptable in thy ſight, and right in thy Commaundements.10O ſend
her out of thy holy heauens, and from the Throne of thy glory, that
being preſent ſhee may labour with mee, that I may know what is
pleaſing vnto thee.11For ſhe knoweth and vnderſtandeth all things, and
ſhee ſhall leade me ſoberly in my doings, and preſerueme in her
power.12So ſhall my workes be acceptable, and then ſhall I iudge thy
people righteouſly, and be worthy to ſit in my fathers ſeate.13For what
man is hee that can know the counſell of God? or who can thinke what

the will of the Lord is?14For the thoughts of mortall men are miſerable, and our deuices are but vncertaine.15For the corruptible body preſseth downe the ſoule, and the earthy tabernacle weigheth downe the minde that muſeth vpon many things.16And hardly doe we geſse aright at things that are vpon earth, and with labour doe wee find the things that are before vs: but the things that are in heauen, who hath ſearched out?17And thy counſell who hath knowen, except thou giue wiſedome, and ſend thy holy ſpirit from aboue?18For ſo the wayes of them which liued on the earth were reformed, and men were taught the things that are pleaſing vnto thee, and were ſaued through wiſedome.

CHAPTER 101She preſerued the firſt formed father of the world that was created alone, and brought him out of his fall,2And gaue him power to rule all things.3But when the vnrighteous went away from her in his anger, he periſhed alſo in the fury wherwith he murdered his brother.4For whoſe cauſe the earth being drowned with the flood, Wiſedome againe preſerued it, & directed the courſe of the righteous, in a piece of wood, of ſmall value.5Moreouer, the nations in their wicked conſpiracie being confounded, ſhe found out the righteous, and preſerued him blameleſſe vnto God, and kept him ſtrong againſt his tender compaſſion towards his ſonne.6When the vngodly periſhed, ſhee deliuered the righteous man, who fled from the fire which fell downe vpon the fiue cities.7Of whoſe wickedneſſe euen to this day the waſte land that ſmoketh, is a teſtimonie, and plants bearing fruite that neuer come to ripeneſse: and a ſtanding pillar of ſalt is a monument of an vnbeleeuing ſoule.8For regarding not wiſedome, they gate not only this hurt, that they knew not the things which were good: but alſo left behind them to the world a memoriall of their fooliſhnes: ſo that in the things wherein they offended, they could not ſo much as be hid.9But Wiſedome deliuered from paine thoſe that attended vpon her.10When the righteous fled from his brothers wrath, ſhe guided him in right paths: ſhewed him the kingdome of God: and gaue him knowledge of holy things, made him rich in his trauailes, and multiplied the fruit of his labours.11In the couetouſneſſe of ſuch as oppreſſed him, ſhe ſtood by him, and made him rich.12She defended him from his enemies, and kept him ſafe from thoſe that lay in wait, and in a ſore conflict ſhe gaue him the victory, that he might knowe that godlineſse is ſtronger then all.13When the righteous was ſolde, ſhe forſooke him not, but deliuered him from ſinne: ſhe went downe with him into the pit,14And left him not in bonds till ſhe brought him the ſcepter of the kingdom and power againſt thoſe that oppreſſed him: as for them that had accuſed him, ſhe ſhewed them to be liers, and gaue them perpetuall glory.15She deliuered the righteous people, and blameleſſe ſeed from the nation that oppreſſed them.16She entred into the ſoule of the ſeruant of the Lord, and withſtood dreadfull kings in wonders and ſignes,17Rendred to the righteous a reward of their labours, guided them in a marueilous way, and was vnto them for a couer by day, and a light of ſtarres in the night ſeaſon:18Brought them through the red ſea, and led them thorow much water.19But ſhe drowned their enemies, and caſt them vp out of the bottome of the deepe.20Therefore the righteous ſpoiled the vngodly, & praiſed thy holy Name, O Lord, and magnified with one accord thine hand that fought for them.21For wiſedome opened the mouth of the dumbe, and made the tongues of them that cannot ſpeake, eloquent.

CHAPTER 111She proſpered their works in the hand of the holy Prophet.2They went thorough the wilderneſſe that was not inhabited, and pitched tents in places where there lay no way.3They ſtood againſt their enemies, and were auenged of their aduerſaries.4When they were thirſty they called vpon thee, and water was giuen them out of the flinty rocke, and their thirſt was quenched out of the hard ſtone.5For by what things their enemies were puniſhed, by the ſame they in their neede were benefited.6For in ſtead of a fountaine of a perpetuall running riuer, troubled with foule blood,7For a manifeſt reproofe of that commandement, whereby the infants were ſlaine, thou gaueſt vnto them abundance of water by a meanes which they hoped not for,8Declaring by that thirſt then, how thou hadſt puniſhed their aduerſaries.9For when they were tryed, albeit but in mercy chaſtiſed, they knew how the vngodly were iudged in wrath and tormented thirſting in another maner then the Iuſt.10For theſe thou didſt admoniſh, and trie as a father: but the other as a ſeuere king thou didſt condemne and puniſh.11Whether they were abſent, or preſent, they were vexed alike.12For a double griefe came vpon them, and a groaning for the remembrance of things paſt.13For when they heard by their owne puniſhments the other to be benefited, they had ſome feeling of the Lord.14For whom they reiected with ſcorne when hee was long before throwen out at the caſting forth of the infants, him in the end, when they ſaw what came to paſſe, they admired.15But for the fooliſh deuiſes of their wickedneſſe, wherewith being deceiued, they worſhipped ſerpents voyd of reaſon, and vile beaſts: thou didſt ſend a multitude of vnreaſonable beaſts vpon them for vengeance,16That they might knowe that wherewithall a man ſinneth, by the ſame alſo ſhall he be puniſhed.17For thy Almighty hand that made the world of matter without forme, wanted not meanes to ſend among them a multitude of Beares, or fierce Lyons,18Or vnknowen wild beaſts full of rage newly created, breathing out either a fiery vapour, or filthy ſents of ſcattered ſmoake, or ſhooting horrible ſparkles out of their eyes:19Whereof not onely the harme might diſpatch them at once: but alſo the terrible ſight vtterly deſtroy them.20Yea and without theſe might they haue fallen downe with one blaſt, being perſecuted of vengeance, and ſcattered abroad thorough the breath of thy power, but thou haſt ordered all things in meaſure, and number, and weight.21For thou canſt ſhew thy great ſtrength at all times when thou wilt, and who may withſtand the power of thine arme?22For the whole world before thee is as a litle graine of the ballance, yea as a drop of the morning dew that falleth downe vpon the earth.23But thou haſt mercy vpon all: for thou canſt doe all things, and winkeſt at the ſinnes of men: becauſe they ſhould amend.24For thou loueſt all the things that are, and abhorreſt nothing which thou haſt made: for neuer wouldeſt thou haue made any thing, if thou hadſt hated it.25And how could any thing haue endured if it had not beene thy will? or beene preſerued, if not called by thee?26But thou ſpareſt all: for they are thine, O Lord, thou louer of ſoules.

CHAPTER 121For thine vncorruptible ſpirit is in all things.2Therefore chaſtneſt thou them by little, and little, that offend, and warneſt them by putting them in remembrance, wherin they haue offended, that leauing their wickedneſſe they may beleeue on thee O Lord.3For it was thy will to deſtroy by the handes of our fathers, both thoſe old inhabitants of thy holy land,4Whom thou hatedſt for doing moſt odious workes of witchcrafts, and wicked ſacrifices;5And alſo thoſe mercileſſe murderers of children, & deuourers of mans fleſh, and the feaſts of blood;6With their Prieſts out of the midſt of their idolatrous crew, and the parents that killed with their owne hands, ſoules deſtitute of helpe:7That the land which thou eſteemedſt aboue all other, might receiue a worthy colonie of Gods children.8Neuertheleſſe, euen thoſe thou ſparedſt as men, and didſt ſend waſpes forerunners of thine hoſte, to deſtroy them by little and little.9Not that thou waſt vnable to bring the vngodly vnder the hand of the righteous in battell, or to deſtroy them at once with cruel beaſtes, or with one rough word:10But executing thy iudgements vpon them by little and little, thou gaueſt them place of repentance, not being ignorant that they were a naughtie generation, and that their malice, was bred in them, and that their cogitation would neuer be changed.11For it was a curſed ſeed, from the beginning, neither didſt thou for feare of any man giue them pardon for thoſe things wherein they ſinned.12For who ſhall ſay, What haſt thou done? or who ſhall withſtand thy iudgement, or who ſhall accuſe thee for the nations that periſh whom thou haſt made? or who ſhall come to ſtand againſt thee, to be reuenged for the vnrighteous men?13For neither is there any God but thou, that careth for all, to whom thou mighteſt ſhew that thy iudgement is not vnright.14Neither ſhall king or tyrant bee able to ſet his face againſt thee, for any whom thou haſt puniſhed.15For ſo much then as thou art righteous thy ſelfe, thou ordereſt all things righteouſly: thinking it not agreeable with thy power to condemne him þt hath not deſerued to be puniſhed.16For thy power is the beginning of righteouſneſſe, and becauſe thou art the Lord of all, it maketh thee to be gracious vnto all.17For when men will not beleeue, that thou art of a full power, thou ſheweſt thy ſtrength, and among them that know it, thou makeſt their boldneſse manifeſt.18But thou, maſtering thy power, iudgeſt with equitie, and ordereſt vs with great fauour: for thou mayeſt vſe power when thou wilt.19But by ſuch workes haſt thou taught thy people, that the iuſt man ſhould be mercifull, and haſt made thy children to be of a good hope, that thou giueſt repentance for ſinnes.20For if thou didſt puniſh the enemies of thy children, and the condemned to death with ſuch deliberation, giuing them time and place, wherby they might be deliuered from their malice.21With how great circumſpection

diddeſt thou iudge thine owne ſonnes, vnto whoſe fathers thou haſt
ſworne, and made couenants of good promiſes?22Therefore whereas
thou doeſt chaſten vs, thou ſcourgeſt our enemies a thouſand times
more, to the intent that when wee iudge, wee ſhould carefully thinke of
thy goodneſse, and when we our ſelues are iudged, wee ſhould looke for
mercy.23Wherefore, whereas men haue liued diſsolutely and
vnrighteouſly, thou haſt tormented them with their owne
abominations.24For they went aſtray very farre in the wayes of errour,
& held them for gods (which euen amongſt the beaſts of their enemies
were deſpiſed) being deceiued as children of no
vnderſtanding.25Therefore vnto them, as to children without the vſe of
reaſon, thou didſt ſend a iudgement to mocke them.26But they that
would not bee refourmed by that correction wherein he dallied with
them, ſhall feele a iudgement worthy of God.27For looke, for what
things they grudged when they were puniſhed, (that iſ) for them whom
they thought to be gods, *now* being puniſhed in them; when they ſaw it,
they acknowledged him to be the true God, whome before they denyed
to know: and therefore came extreme damnation vpon them.
CHAPTER 131Surely vaine are all men by nature, who are ignorant of
God, and could not out of the good things that are ſeene, know him
that is: neither by conſidering the workes, did they acknowledge the
worke-maſter;2But deemed either fire, or wind, or the ſwift aire, or the
circle of the ſtars, or the violent water, or the lights of heauen to be the
gods which gouerne the world:3With whoſe beautie, if they being
delighted, tooke them to be gods: let them know how much better the
Lord of them is; for the firſt Author of beautie hath created them.4But
if they were aſtoniſhed at their power and vertue, let them vnderſtand
by them, how much mightier he is that made them.5For by the
greatneſſe and beautie of the creatures, proportionably the Maker of
them is ſeene.6But yet for this they are the leſſe to bee blamed: for they
peraduenture erre ſeeking God, and deſirous to finde him.7For being
conuerſant in his workes, they ſearch him diligently, and beleeue their
ſight: becauſe the things are beautifull that are ſeene.8Howbeit, neither
are they to bee pardoned.9For if they were able to know ſo much, that
they could aime at the world; how did they not ſooner finde out the
Lord thereof?10But miſerable are they, and in dead things is their hope,
who called them gods which are the workes of mens hands, golde and
ſiluer, to ſhewe arte in, and reſemblances of beaſts, or a ſtone good for
nothing, the worke of an ancient hand.11Now a carpenter that felleth
timber, after hee hath ſawen downe a tree meet for the purpoſe, and
taken off all the barke ſkilfully round about, and hath wrought it
handſomely, & made a veſſell thereof fit for the ſeruice of mans
life:12And after ſpending the refuſe of his worke to dreſſe his meat, hath
filled himſelfe:13And taking the very refuſe among thoſe which ſerued
to no vſe (being a crooked piece of wood, and ful of knotſ) hath carued
it diligently when hee had nothing elſe to doe, and formed it by the ſkill
of his vnderſtanding, and faſhioned it to the image of a man:14Or made
it like ſome vile beaſt, laying it ouer with vermilion, and with paint,
colouring it red, and couering euery ſpot therein:15And when he had
made a conuenient roume for it, ſet it in a wall, and made it faſt with
yron:16For he prouided for it, that it might not fall: knowing that it was
vnable to helpe it ſelfe, (for it is an image and hath neede of
helpe:)17Then maketh hee prayer for his goods, for his wife and
children, and is not aſhamed to ſpeake to that which hath no life.18For
health, hee calleth vpon that which is weake: for life, prayeth to that
which is dead: for aide, humbly beſeecheth that which hath leaſt meanes
to helpe: and for a good iourney, hee aſketh of that which cannot ſet a
foot forward:19And for gaining and getting, and for good ſuccesſe of his
hands, aſketh abilitie to doe, of him that is moſt vnable to doe any thing.
CHAPTER 141Againe, one preparing himſelfe to ſaile, and about to
paſſe through the raging waues, calleth vpon a piece of wood more
rotten then the veſell that carieth him.2For verely deſire of gaine deuiſed
that, and the workeman built it by his ſkill:3But thy prouidence, O
Father, gouerneth it: for thou haſt made a way in the ſea, and a ſafe path
in the waues:4Shewing that thou canſt ſaue from all danger: yea though
a man went to ſea without arte.5Neuertheleſſe thou wouldeſt not that
the works of thy wiſedome ſhould be idle, and therefore doe men
commit their liues to a ſmall piece of wood, and paſsing the rough ſea
in a weake veſſell, are ſaued.6For in the old time alſo when the proud
gyants periſhed, the hope of the world gouerned by thy hand, eſcaped
in a weake veſſell, and left to all ages a ſeed of generation.7For bleſſed
is the wood, whereby righteouſneſſe commeth.8But that which is made
with hands, is curſed, aſwell it, as hee that made it: he, becauſe he made
it, and it, becauſe being corruptible it was called God.9For the vngodly
and his vngodlines are both alike hatefull vnto God.10For that which is
made, ſhall bee puniſhed together with him that made it.11Therfore euen
vpon the idoles of the Gentiles ſhall there be a viſitation: becauſe in the
creature of God they are become an abomination and ſtumbling blocks
to the ſoules of men, and a ſnare to the feet of the vnwiſe.12For the
deuiſing of idoles was the beginning of ſpiritual fornication, and the
inuention of them the corruption of life.13For neither were they from
the beginning, neither ſhall they be for euer.14For by the vaine glory of
men they entred into the world, and therefore ſhall they come ſhortly to
an end.15For a father afflicted with vntimely mourning, when he hath
made an image of his childe ſoone taken away, now honoured him as a
god, which was then a dead man, and deliuered to thoſe that were vnder
him, ceremonies and ſacrifices.16Thus in proceſſe of time an vngodly
cuſtome growen ſtrong, was kept as a law, and grauen images were
worſhipped by the commandements of kings,17Whom men could not
honour in preſence, becauſe they dwelt farre off, they tooke the
counterfeit of his viſage from farre, and made an expreſse image of a
king whom they honoured, to the end that by this their forwardnes, they
might flatter him that was abſent, as if he were preſent.18Alſo the
ſingular diligence of the artificer did helpe to ſet forward the ignorant to
more ſuperſtition.19For he peraduenture willing to pleaſe one in
authoritie, forced all his ſkill to make the reſemblance of the beſt
faſhion.20And ſo the multitude allured by the grace of the worke, tooke
him now for a god, which a litle before was but honoured as a
man.21And this was an occaſion to deceiue the world: for men ſeruing
either calamitie or tyrannie, did aſcribe vnto ſtones, and ſtockes, the
incommunicable Name.22Moreouer this was not enough for them, that
they erred in the knowledge of God, but whereas they liued in the great
warre of ignorance, thoſe ſo great plagues called they peace.23For whileſt
they ſlew their children in ſacrifices, or vſed ſecret ceremonies, or made
reuellings of ſtrange riteſ24They kept neither liues nor mariages any
longer vndefiled: but either one ſlew another traiterouſly, or grieued him
by adulterie:25So that there reigned in all men without exception, blood,
manſlaughter, theft, and diſsimulation, corruption, vnfaithfulneſse,
tumults, periurie,26Diſquieting of good men, forgetfulneſse of good
turnes, defiling of ſoules, changing of kinde, diſorder in mariages,
adulterie, and ſhameles vncleanneſſe.27For the worſhipping of idoles
not to be named, is the beginning, the cauſe, and the end of all euill.28For
either they are mad when they be merry, or propheſie lies, or liue
vniuſtly, or elſe lightly forſweare themſelues.29For inſomuch as their
truſt is in idoles which haue no life, though they ſweare falſly, yet they
looke not to bee hurt.30Howbeit for both cauſes ſhal they be iuſtly
puniſhed: both becauſe they thought not well of God, giuing heed vnto
idols, and alſo vniuſtly ſwore in deceit, deſpiſing holineſſe.31For it is not
the power of them by whom they ſweare: but it is the iuſt vengeance of
ſinners, that puniſheth alwayes the offence of the vngodly.
CHAPTER 151But thou O God, art gracious and true: long ſuffering,
and in mercy ordering all things.2For if we ſinne we are thine, knowing
thy power: but we will not ſinne, knowing that we are counted thine.3For
to know thee is perfect righteouſneſſe: yea to know thy power is the
roote of immortality.4For neither did the miſchieuous inuention of men
deceiue vs: nor an image ſpotted with diuers colours, the painters
fruitleſſe labour.5The ſight wherof entiſeth fooles to luſt after it, and ſo
they deſire the forme of a dead image that hath no breath.6Both they
that make them, they that deſire them, and they that worſhip them, are
louers of euill things, and are worthy to haue ſuch things to truſt
vpon.7For the potter tempering ſoft earth faſhioneth, euery veſſell with
much labour for our ſeruice: yea of the ſame clay hee maketh both the
veſſels that ſerue for cleane vſes: and likewiſe alſo all ſuch as ſerue to the
contrary: but what is the vſe of either ſort, the potter himſelfe is the
iudge.8And employing his labours lewdly, he maketh a vaine God of the
ſame clay, euen he which a little before was made of earth himſelfe, and
within a little while after returneth to the ſame out of the which he was
taken: when his life which was lent him ſhall be
demanded.9Notwithſtanding his care is, not that hee ſhall haue much
labour, nor that his life is ſhort: but ſtriueth to excel goldſmiths, and

ſiluerſmiths, and endeuoureth to doe like the workers in braſſe, and
counteth it his glory to make counterfeit things. 10 His heart is aſhes, his
hope is more vile then earth, and his life of leſſe value then
clay: 11 Foraſmuch as hee knew not his maker, and him that inſpired into
him an actiue ſoule, and breathed in a liuing ſpirit. 12 But they counted
our life a paſtime, & our time here a market for gaine: for, ſay they, we
muſt be getting euery way, though it be by euil meanes. 13 For this man
that of earthly matter maketh brickle veſſels, and grauen images,
knoweth himſelfe to offend aboue all others. 14 And all the enemies of
thy people, that hold them in ſubiection are moſt fooliſh and are more
miſerable then very babes. 15 For they counted all the idoles of the
heathen to be gods: which neither haue the vſe of eyes to ſee, nor noſes
to draw breath, nor eares to heare, nor fingers of hands to handle, and
as for their feete they are ſlow to goe. 16 For man made them, and he that
borrowed his owne ſpirit faſhioned them, but no man can make a god
like vnto himſelfe. 17 For being mortall he worketh a dead thing with
wicked hands: for hee himſelfe is better then the things which he
worſhippeth: whereas he liued once, but they neuer. 18 Yea they
worſhipped thoſe beaſts alſo that are moſt hatefull: for being compared
together, ſome are worſe then others. 19 Neither are they beautifull, ſo
much, as to bee deſired in reſpect of beaſts, but they went without the
praiſe of God and his bleſſing.

CHAPTER 16 1 Therefore by the like were they puniſhed worthily, and
by the multitude of beaſts tormented. 2 In ſtead of which puniſhment,
dealing graciouſly with thine owne people thou preparedſt for them
meate of a ſtrange taſte: euen quailes to ſtirre vp their appetite: 3 To the
end that they deſiring food might for the ougly ſight of the beaſts ſent
among them, loath euen that which they muſt needs deſire: but theſe
ſuffering penury for a ſhort ſpace, might be made partakers of a ſtrange
taſte. 4 For it was requiſite, that vpon them excerciſing tyranny ſhould
come penury which they could not auoyde: but to theſe it ſhould onely
be ſhewed how their enemies were tormented. 5 For when the horrible
fierceneſse of beaſts came vpon theſe, and they periſhed with the ſtings
of crooked ſerpents, thy wrath endured not for euer. 6 But they were
troubled for a ſmal ſeaſon that they might be admoniſhed, hauing a ſigne
of ſaluation, to put them in remembrance of the commandement of thy
Law. 7 For hee that turned himſelfe towards it, was not ſaued by the thing
that he ſaw: but by thee that art the ſauiour of all. 8 And in this thou
madeſt thine enemies confeſse, that it is thou who deliuereſt from all
euill: 9 For them the bitings of graſſehoppers and flies killed, neither was
there found any remedy for their life: for they were worthy to bee
puniſhed by ſuch. 10 But thy ſonnes, not the very teeth of venemous
dragons ouercame: for thy mercy was euer by them, and healed
them. 11 For they were pricked, that they ſhould remember thy words,
and were quickly ſaued, that not falling into deep forgetfulneſse, they
might be continually mindefull of thy goodneſse. 12 For it was neither
herbe, nor mollifying plaiſter that reſtored them to health: but thy word,
O Lord, which healeth all things. 13 For thou haſt power of life and death:
thou leadeſt to the gates of hell, and bringeſt vp againe. 14 A man indeed
killeth through his malice: and the ſpirit when it is gone foorth returneth
not; neither the ſoule receiued vp, commeth againe. 15 But it is not
poſsible to eſcape thine hand. 16 For the vngodly that denied to know
thee, were ſcourged by the ſtrength of thine arme: with ſtrange raines,
hailes, and ſhowers were they perſecuted, that they could not auoyd, and
through fire were they conſumed. 17 For, which is moſt to be wondered
at, the fire had more force in the water that quencheth all things: for the
world fighteth for the righteous. 18 For ſometimes the flame was
mitigated, that it might not burne vp the beaſts that were ſent againſt
the vngodly: but themſelues might ſee and perceiue that they were
perſecuted with the iudgement of God. 19 And at another time it burneth
euen in the midſt of water, aboue the power of fire, that it might deſtroy
the fruits of an vniuſt land. 20 In ſtead whereof thou feddeſt thine owne
people, with Angels food, and didſt ſend them from heauen bread
prepared without their labour, able to content euery mans delight, and
agreeing to euery taſte. 21 For thy ſuſtenance declared thy ſweetneſse vnto
thy children, and ſeruing to the appetite of the eater tempered it ſelfe to
euery mans liking. 22 But ſnow and yce endured the fire and melted not,
that they might know that fire burning the haile, and ſparkling in the
raine, did deſtroy the fruits of the enemies. 23 But this againe did euen
forget his owne ſtrength, that the righteous might be nouriſhed. 24 For
the creature that ſerueth thee who art the maker, encreaſeth his ſtrength
againſt the vnrighteous for their puniſhment, and abateth his ſtrength
for the benefit of ſuch as put their truſt in thee. 25 Therefore euen then
was it altered into all faſhions, and was obedient to thy grace that
nouriſheth all things, according to the deſire of them that had
need: 26 That thy children, O Lord, whom thou loueſt, might know that
it is not the growing of fruits that nouriſheth man: but that it is thy word
which preſerueth them that put their truſt in thee. 27 For that which was
not deſtroied of the fire, being warmed with a litle Sunne beame, ſoone
melted away, 28 That it might bee knowen, that wee muſt preuent the
Sunne, to giue thee thanks, and at the day-ſpring pray vnto thee. 29 For
the hope of the vnfaithfull, ſhal melt away as the Winters hoarefroſt,
and ſhall runne away as vnprofitable water.

CHAPTER 17 1 For great are thy Iudgements, and cannot be expreſſed:
therefore vnnourtured ſoules haue erred. 2 For when vnrighteous men
thought to oppreſſe the holy nation: they being ſhut vp in their houſes,
the priſoners of darkeneſſe, and fettered with the bondes of a long night,
lay *there* exiled from the eternall prouidence. 3 For while they ſuppoſed to
lie hid in their ſecret ſinnes, they were ſcattered vnder a darke vaile of
forgetfulneſse, being horribly aſtoniſhed, and troubled with (ſtrange)
apparitions. 4 For neither might the corner that helde them keepe them
from feare: but noiſes (as of waterſ) falling downe, ſounded about them,
and ſadde viſions appeared vnto them with heauie countenances. 5 No
power of the fire might giue them light: neither could the bright flames
of the ſtarres endure to lighten that horrible night. 6 Onely there appeared
vnto them a fire kindled of it ſelfe, very dreadfull: for being much
terrified, they thought the things which they ſaw to be worſe then the
ſight they ſaw not. 7 As for the illuſions of arte Magicke, they were put
downe, and their vaunting in wiſedome was reproooued with
diſgrace. 8 For they that promiſed to driue away terrours, and troubles
from a ſicke ſoule, were ſicke themſelues of feare worthy to be laughed
at. 9 For though no terrible thing did feare them: yet being ſkared with
beaſts that paſſed by, and hiſsing of ſerpents, 10 They died for feare,
denying that they ſaw the ayre, which could of no ſide be auoided. 11 For
wickedneſſe condemned by her owne witneſſe, is very timorous, and
being preſſed with conſcience, alwayes forecaſteth grieuous things. 12 For
feare is nothing elſe, but a betraying of the ſuccours which reaſon
offereth. 13 And the expectation from within being leſſe, counteth the
ignorance more then the cauſe which bringeth the torment. 14 But they
ſleeping the ſame ſleepe that night which was indeed intolerable, and
which came vpon them out of the bottomes of ineuitable hell: 15 Were
partly vexed with monſtrous apparitions, and partly fainted, their heart
failing them: for a ſuddaine feare and not looked for, came vpon
them. 16 So then, whoſoeuer there fell downe, was ſtraitly kept, ſhut vp
in a priſon without yron barres. 17 For whether hee were huſbandman, or
ſhepheard, or a labourer in the field, he was ouertaken, and endured that
neceſsitie, which could not be auoided: for they were all bound with one
chaine of darkeneſſe. 18 Whether it were a whiſtling winde, or a
melodious noiſe of birdes among the ſpreading branches, or a pleaſing
fall of water running violently: 19 Or a terrible ſound of ſtones caſt
downe, or a running that could not be ſeene of ſkipping beaſts, or a
roaring voice of moſt ſauage wilde beaſts, or a rebounding Eccho from
the hollow mountaines: theſe things made them to ſwoone for
feare. 20 For the whole world ſhined with cleare light, and none were
hindered in their labour. 21 Ouer them onely was ſpread an heauie night,
an image of that darkeneſſe which ſhould afterwards receiue them: but
yet were they vnto themſelues more grieuous then the darkeneſſe.

CHAPTER 18 1 Neuertheleſſe, thy Saints had a very great light, whoſe
voice they hearing and not ſeeing their ſhape, becauſe they alſo had not
ſuffered the ſame things, they counted them happy. 2 But for that they
did not hurt them now, of whom they had beene wronged before, they
thanked them, and beſought them pardon, for that they had beene
enemies. 3 In ſtead whereof thou gaueſt them a burning pillar of fire, both
to be a guide of the vnknowen iourney, and an harmeleſſe Sunne to
entertaine them honourably. 4 For they were worthy to be depriued of
light, and impriſoned in darkneſſe, who had kept thy ſonnes ſhut vp, by
whom the vncorrupt light of the law was to be giuen vnto the
world. 5 And when they had determined to ſlay the babes of the Saints,
one child being caſt forth, and ſaued: to reproue them, thou tookeſt
away the multitude of their children, and deſtroyedſt them altogether in

a mightie water.6Of that night were our fathers certified afore, that
aſsuredly knowing vnto what oathes they had giuen credence, they might
afterwards bee of good cheere.7So of thy people was accepted both the
ſaluation of the righteous, and deſtruction of the enemies.8For
wherewith thou didſt puniſh our aduerſaries, by the ſame thou didſt
glorifie vs whom thou hadſt called.9For the righteous children of good
men did ſacrifice ſecretly, and with one conſent made a holy lawe, that
the Saints ſhould bee alike partakers of the ſame good and euill, the
fathers now ſinging out the ſongs of praiſe.10But on the other ſide there
ſounded an ill-according crie of the enemies, and a lamentable noiſe was
caried abroad for children that were bewailed.11The maſter and the
ſeruaunt were puniſhed after one maner, and like as the king, ſo ſuffered
the common perſon.12So they altogether had innumerable dead with one
kind of death, neither were the liuing ſufficient to burie them: for in one
moment the nobleſt offpring of them was deſtroyed.13For whereas they
would not beleeue any thing by reaſon of the enchantments, vpon the
deſtruction of the firſt borne, they acknowledged this people to be the
ſonnes of God.14For while all things were in quiet ſilence, and that night
was in the midſt of her ſwift courſe,15Thine almighty word leapt downe
from heauen, out of thy royall throne, as a fierce man of warre into the
midſt of a land of deſtruction,16And brought thine vnfained
commandement as a ſharpe ſword, and ſtanding vp filled all things with
death, and it touched the heauen, but it ſtood vpon the earth.17Then
ſuddenly viſions of horrible dreames troubled them ſore, and terrours
came vpon them vnlooked for.18And one throwen here, another there
halfe dead, ſhewed the cauſe of his death.19For the dreames that
troubled them, did foreſhew this, leſt they ſhould periſh, and not know
why they were afflicted.20Yea, the taſting of death touched the righteous
alſo, and there was a deſtruction of the multitude in the wildernes: but
the wrath endured not long.21For then the blameleſſe man made haſte,
and ſtood foorth to defend them, and bringing the ſhield of his proper
miniſterie, euen prayer and the propitiation of incenſe, ſet himſelfe
againſt the wrath, and ſo brought the calamity to an end, declaring that
hee was thy ſeruant.22So hee ouercame the deſtroyer, not with ſtrength
of body, nor force of armes, but with a word ſubdued he him that
puniſhed, alleaging the oathes and couenants made with the
fathers.23For when the dead were now fallen downe by heaps one vpon
another, ſtanding betweene, he ſtaied the wrath, and parted the way to
the liuing.24For in the long garment was the whole world, & in the foure
rowes of the ſtones was the glory of the fathers grauen, and thy maieſtie
vpon the diademe of his head.25Vnto theſe the deſtroyer gaue place, and
was afraid of them: for it was enough that they onely taſted of the wrath.
CHAPTER 19 1As for the vngodly, wrath came vpon them without
mercie vnto the end: for he knew before what they would doe;2Howe
that hauing giuen them leaue to depart, and ſent them haſtily away, they
would repent and purſue them.3For whileſt they were yet mourning, and
making lamentation at the graues of the dead, they added another fooliſh
deuice, and purſued them as fugitiues, whom they had entreated to be
gone.4For the deſtiny, whereof they were worthy, drew them vnto this
end, and made them forget the things that had already happened, that
they might fulfill the puniſhment which was wanting to their
torments,5And that thy people might paſſe a wonderfull way: but they
might find a ſtrange death.6For the whole creature in his proper kind
was faſhioned againe anew, ſeruing the peculiar commandements that
were giuen vnto them, that thy children might be kept without hurt.7As
namely, a cloud ſhadowing the campe, and where water ſtood before
drie land appeared, and out of the red ſea a way without impediment,
and out of the violent ſtreame a greene field:8Where-thorough all the
people went that were defended with thy hand, ſeeing thy marueilous
ſtrange wonders.9For they went at large like horſes, and leaped like
lambes, praiſing thee O Lord, who hadſt deliuered them.10For they were
yet mindefull of the things that were done while they ſoiourned in the
ſtrange land, how the ground brought forth flies in ſtead of cattell, and
how the riuer caſt vp a multitude of frogs in ſtead of fiſhes.11But
afterwards they ſaw a new generation of foules, when being led with
their appetite they aſked delicate meates.12For quailes came vp vnto
them from the ſea, for their contentment.13And puniſhments came
vpon the ſinners not without former ſignes by the force of thunders: for
they ſuffered iuſtly, according to their owne wickedneſſe, inſomuch as
they vſed a more hard and hatefull behauiour towards ſtrangers:14For
the Sodomits did not receiue thoſe whom they knew not when they
came: but theſe brought friends into bondage, that had well deſerued of
them.15And not onely ſo: but peraduenture ſome reſpect ſhall be had of
thoſe, becauſe they vſed ſtrangers not friendly.16But theſe very
grieuouſly afflicted them, whom they had receiued with feaſtings, and
were already made partakers of the ſame lawes with them.17Therefore
euen with blindneſse were theſe ſtricken, as thoſe were at the doores of
the righteous man: when being compaſſed about with horrible great
darkneſſe, euery one ſought the paſsage of his owne doores.18For the
elements were changed in themſelues by a kind of harmonie, like as in a
Pſaltery notes change the name of the tune, and yet are alwayes ſounds,
which may well be perceiued by the ſight of the things that haue beene
done.19For earthly things were turned into watry, and the things that
before ſwamme in the water, now went vpon the ground.20The fire had
power in the water, forgetting his owne vertue: and the water forgat his
owne quenching nature.21On the other ſide, the flames waſted not the
fleſh of the corruptible liuing things, though they walked therin, neither
melted they the ycie kind of heauenly meate, that was of nature apt to
melt.22For in all things, O Lord, thou didſt magnifie thy people, and
glorifie them, neither didſt thou lightly regard them: but didſt aſsiſt them
in euery time and place.

ECCLEſIAſTICUS (ECCLESIASTICUS)

CHAPTER 1 1*A Prologue made by an vncertaine Authour.* This Ieſus was
the ſonne of Sirach, and grand-childe to Ieſus of the ſame name with
him; This man therefore liued in the latter times, after the people had
bene led away captiue, and called home againe, and almoſt after all the
Prophets. Now his grandfather Ieſus (as he himſelfe witneſſeth) was a
man of great diligence and wiſedome among the Hebrewes, who did not
onely gather the graue and ſhort Sentences of wiſe men, that had bene
before him, but himſelfe alſo vttered ſome of his owne, full of much
vnderſtanding and wiſedome. When as therefore the firſt Ieſus died,
leauing this booke almoſt perfected, Si rach his ſonne receiuing it after
him, left it to his owne ſonne Ieſus, who hauing gotten it into his hands,
compiled it all orderly into one Volume, and called it Wiſdome,
Intituling it, both by his owne name, his fathers name, and his
grandfathers, alluring the hearer by the very name of Wiſedome, to haue
a greater loue to the ſtudie of this Booke. It conteineth therefore wiſe
Sayings, darke Sentences, and Parables, and certaine particular ancient
godly ſtories of men that pleaſed God. Alſo his Prayer and ſong.
Moreouer, what benefits God had vouchſafed his people, and what
plagues he had heaped vpon their enemies. This Ieſus did imitate
Solomon, and was no leſſe famous for Wiſedome, and learning, both
being indeed a man of great learning, and ſo reputed alſo. *The Prologue of
the Wiſdome of Ieſus the ſonne of Sirach* Whereas many and great things haue
bene deliuered vnto vs by the Law and the Prophets, and by others that
haue followed their ſteps, for the which things Iſrael ought to be
commended for learning and Wiſedome, and whereof not onely the
Readers muſt needs become ſkilful themſelues, but alſo they that deſire
to learne, be able to profit them which are without, both by ſpeaking
and writing : My grandfather Ieſus, when he had much giuen himſelfe
to the reading of the Law, and the Prophets, and other Bookes of our
fathers, and had gotten therein good iudgement, was drawen on alſo
himſelfe, to write ſomething pertayning to learning and Wiſedome, to
the intent that thoſe which are deſirous to learne, and are addicted to
theſe things, might profit much more in liuing according to the Law.
Wherefore, let me intreat you to reade it with fauour and attention, and
to pardon Vs, wherein wee may ſecme to come ſhort of ſome words
which we haue laboured to interprete. For the ſame things vttered in
Hebrew, and tranſlated into an other tongue, haue not the ſame force in
them : and not onely theſe things, but the Law it ſelfe, and the Prophets,
and the reſt of the Bookes, haue no ſmall difference, when they are
ſpoken in their owne language. For in the eight and thirtieth yeere
comming into Egypt, when Euergetes was King, and continuing there
ſome time, I found a Booke of no ſmall learning, therefore I thought it
moſt neceſsary for mee, to beſtow ſome diligence and trauaile to
interprete it: Vſing great watchfulneſse, and ſkill in that ſpace, to bring
the Booke to an end, and ſet it foorth for them alſo, which in a ſtrange

countrey are willing to learne, being prepared before in maners to liue after the Law. [1] All wiſedome commeth from the Lord, and is with him for euer.[2]Who can number the ſand of the ſea, and the drops of raine, and the dayes of eternity?[3]Who can finde out the height of heauen, and the breadth of the earth, and the deepe, and wiſedome?[4]Wiſedome hath beene created before all things, and the vnderſtanding of prudence from euerlaſting.[5]The word of God moſt high, is the fountaine of wiſdome, & her wayes are euerlaſting commandements.[6]To whom hath the root of wiſdome beene reuealed? or who hath knowen her wiſe counſels?[7] *Unto whom hath the knowledge of wiſedome beene made manifeſt? and who hath vnderſtood her great experience?*[8]There is one wiſe and greatly to bee feared; the Lord ſitting vpon his Throne.[9]He created her, and ſaw her, and numbred her, and powred her out vpon all his workes.[10]Shee *is* with all fleſh according to his gift, and hee hath giuen her to them that loue him.[11]The feare of the Lord is honour, and glory, and gladneſſe, and a crowne of reioycing.[12]The feare of the Lord maketh a merrie heart, and giueth ioy and gladneſſe, and a long life.[13]Who ſo feareth the Lord, it ſhall goe well with him at the laſt, & he ſhall finde fauour in the day of his death.[14]To feare the Lord, is the beginning of wiſedome: and it was created with the faithfull in the wombe.[15]Shee hath built an euerlaſting foundation with men, and ſhe ſhal continue with their ſeede.[16]To feare the Lord, is fulneſse of wiſedome, and filleth men with her fruits.[17]Shee filleth all their houſe with things deſireable, and the garners with her increaſe.[18]The feare of the Lord is a crowne of wiſedome, making peace and perfect health to flouriſh, both which are the gifts of God: and it enlargeth their reioycing that loue him.[19]Wiſedome raineth downe ſkill and knowledge of vnderſtanding, and exalteth them to honour that holde her faſt.[20]The root of wiſedome is to feare the Lord, and the branches thereof are long life.[21]The feare of the Lord driueth away ſinnes: and where it is preſent, it turneth away wrath.[22]A furious man cannot be iuſtified, for the ſway of his fury ſhalbe his deſtruction.[23]A patient man will beare for a time, and afterward ioy ſhall ſpring vp vnto him.[24]He wil hide his words for a time, and the lippes of many ſhall declare his wiſedome.[25]The parables of knowledge are in the treaſures of wiſedome: but godlines is an abomination to a ſinner.[26]If thou deſire wiſedome, keepe the commaundements, and the Lord ſhall giue her vnto thee.[27]For the feare of the Lord is wiſdome, and inſtruction: and faith and meekeneſse are his delight.[28]Diſtruſt not the feare of the Lord when thou art poore: and come not vnto him with a double heart.[29]Be not an hypocrite in the ſight of men, and take good heede what thou ſpeakeſt.[30]Exalt not thy ſelfe, leſt thou fall, and bring diſhonor vpon thy ſoule, and ſo God diſcouer thy ſecrets, and caſt thee downe in the midſt of the congregation, becauſe thou cameſt not in trueth, to the feare of the Lord: but thy heart is full of deceit.

CHAPTER 2 [1]My ſonne, if thou come to ſerue the Lorde, prepare thy ſoule for temptation.[2]Set thy heart aright, and conſtantly endure, and make not haſte in time of trouble.[3]Cleaue vnto him, and depart not away, that thou mayeſt be increaſed at thy laſt end.[4]Whatſoeuer is brought vpon thee, take cheerefully, and bee patient when thou art changed to a lowe eſtate.[5]For gold is tried in the fire, and acceptable men in the furnace of aduerſitie.[6]Beleeue in him, and he will helpe thee, order thy way aright, and truſt in him.[7]Ye that feare the Lord, waite for his mercie, and goe not aſide, leſt ye fall.[8]Yee that feare the Lord, beleeue him, and your reward ſhall not faile.[9]Ye that feare the Lord, hope for good, and for euerlaſting ioy and mercy.[10]Looke at the generations of old, and ſee, did euer any truſt in the Lord, and was confounded? or did any abide in his feare, & was forſaken? or whom did hee euer deſpiſe, that called vpon him?[11]For the Lord is full of compaſſion, and mercie, longſuffering, and very pitifull, and forgiueth ſinnes, and ſaueth in time of affliction.[12]Woe be to fearefull hearts, and faint hands, and the ſinner that goeth two wayes.[13]Woe vnto him that is faint hearted, for he beleeueth not, therefore ſhall he not be defended.[14]Woe vnto you that haue loſt patience: and what will ye doe when the Lord ſhall viſite you?[15]They that feare the Lord, will not diſobey his word, and they that loue him, will keepe his wayes.[16]They that feare the Lord, will ſeeke that which is well pleaſing vnto him, and they that loue him, ſhall bee filled with the Law.[17]They that feare the Lord, will prepare their hearts, and humble their ſoules in his ſight:[18]Saying, We will fal into the hands of the Lord, and not into the hands of men: for as his maieſtie is, ſo is his mercie.

CHAPTER 3 [1]Heare mee your father, O children, and doe thereafter, that ye may be ſafe.[2]For the Lord hath giuen the father honour ouer the children, and hath confirmed the authoritie of the mother ouer the ſonnes.[3]Who ſo honoureth his father, maketh an atonement for his ſinnes.[4]And he that honoureth his mother, is as one that layeth vp treaſure.[5]Who ſo honoureth his father, ſhal haue ioy of his owne children, and when he maketh his prayer, hee ſhall bee heard.[6]He that honoureth his father, ſhal haue a long life, and he that is obedient vnto the Lord, ſhall bee a comfort to his mother.[7]He that feareth the Lord, will honour his father, and will doe ſeruice vnto his parents, as to his maſters.[8]Honour thy father and mother, both in word and deed, that a bleſſing may come vpon thee from them.[9]For the bleſſing of the father eſtabliſheth the houſes of children, but the curſe of the mother rooteth out foundations.[10]Glory not in the diſhonour of thy father, for thy fathers diſhonour is no glory vnto thee.[11]For the glory of a man, is from the honour of his father, and a mother in diſhonour, is a reproch to the children.[12]My ſonne, helpe thy father in his age, and grieue him not as long as hee liueth.[13]And if his vnderſtanding faile, haue patience with him, and deſpiſe him not, when thou art in thy ful ſtrength.[14]For the relieuing of thy father ſhall not be forgotten: and in ſtead of ſinnes it ſhall be added to build thee vp.[15]In the day of thine affliction it ſhall be remembred, thy ſinnes alſo ſhal melt away, as the yce in þe faire warme weather.[16]He that forſaketh his father, is as a blaſphemer, and he that angreth his mother, is curſed of God.[17]My ſonne, goe on with thy buſineſse in meekeneſse, ſo ſhalt thou be beloued of him that is approued.[18]The greater thou art, the more humble thy ſelfe, and thou ſhalt find fauour before the Lord.[19]Many are in high place and of renowne: but myſteries are reueiled vnto the meeke.[20]For the power of the Lord is great, and hee is honoured of the lowly.[21]Seeke not out the things that are too hard for thee, neither ſearch the things that are aboue thy ſtrength.[22]But what is commaunded thee, thinke thereupon with reuerence, for it is not needfull for thee, to ſee with thine eyes, the things that are in ſecret.[23]Be not curious in vnneceſsarie matters: for moe things are ſhewed vnto thee, then men vnderſtand.[24]For many are deceiued by their owne vaine opinion, and an euill ſuſpition hath ouerthrowen their iudgement.[25]Without eyes thou ſhalt want light: profeſse not the knowledge therfore that thou haſt not.[26]A ſtubborne heart ſhall fare euill at the laſt, and he that loueth danger ſhall periſh therein.[27]An obſtinate heart ſhall be laden with ſorrowes, and the wicked man ſhall heape ſinne vpon ſinne.[28]In the puniſhment of the proud there is no remedie: for the plant of wickedneſſe hath taken roote in him.[29]The heart of the prudent will vnderſtand a parable, and an attentiue eare is the deſire of a wiſe man.[30]Water will quench a flaming fire, and almes maketh an attonement for ſinnes.[31]And hee that requiteth good turnes, is mindfull of that which may come heereafter: and when he falleth he ſhall find a ſtay.

CHAPTER 4 [1]My ſonne, defraude not the poore of his liuing, and make not the needy eies to waite long.[2]Make not an hungry ſoule ſorrowfull, neither prouoke a man in his diſtreſſe.[3]Adde not more trouble to an heart that is vexed, and deferre not to giue to him that is in neede.[4]Reiect not the ſupplication of the afflicted, neither turne away thy face from a poore man.[5]Turne not away thine eye from the needy, and giue him none occaſion to curſe thee:[6]For if he curſe thee in the bitterneſse of his ſoule, his prayer ſhall be heard of him that made him.[7]Get thy ſelfe the loue of the congregation, and bow thy head to a great man.[8]Let it not grieue thee to bowe downe thine eare to the poore, and giue him a friendly anſwere with meekeneſse.[9]Deliuer him that ſuffreth wrong, from the hand of the oppreſsour, and be not faint hearted when thou ſitteſt in iudgement.[10]Be as a father vnto the fatherleſſe, and in ſtead of a huſband vnto their mother, ſo ſhalt thou be as the ſonne of the moſt high, and he ſhall loue thee more then thy mother doeth.[11]Wiſedome exalteth her children, and layeth hold of them that ſeeke her.[12]He that loueth her, loueth life, and they that ſeeke to her earely, ſhall be filled with ioy.[13]He that holdeth her faſt ſhall inherit glory, and whereſoeuer ſhe entreth, the Lord will bleſſe.[14]They that ſerue her ſhall miniſter to the Holy one, and them that loue her, the Lord doth loue.[15]Who ſo giueth eare vnto her, ſhall iudge the nations,

and he that attendeth vnto her, ſhall dwell ſecurely.16If a man commit
himſelfe vnto her, he ſhall inherite her, and his generation ſhall hold her
in poſſeſſion.17For at the firſt ſhe will walke with him by crooked wayes,
and bring feare and dread vpon him, and torment him with her
diſcipline, vntill ſhe may truſt his ſoule, and try him by her Lawes.18Then
wil ſhe returne the ſtraight way vnto him, and comfort him, and ſhew
him her ſecrets.19But if he goe wrong, ſhe will forſake him, and giue him
ouer to his owne ruine.20Obſerue the opportunitie, and beware of euill,
and be not aſhamed when it concerneth thy ſoule.21For there is a ſhame
that bringeth ſinne, and there is a ſhame which is glorie and
grace.22Accept no perſon againſt thy ſoule, and let not the reuerence of
any man cauſe thee to fall:23And refraine not to ſpeake, when there is
occaſion to doe good, and hide not thy wiſedome in her beautie.24For
by ſpeach wiſedome ſhall be knowen, and learning by the word of the
tongue.25In no wiſe ſpeake againſt the trueth, but be abaſhed of the
errour of thine ignorance.26Bee not aſhamed to confeſse thy ſinnes, and
force not the courſe of the riuer.27Make not thy ſelfe an vnderling to a
fooliſh man, neither accept the perſon of the mighty.28Striue for the
trueth vnto death, and the Lord ſhall fight for thee.29Be not haſtie in thy
tongue, and in thy deeds ſlacke and remiſse.30Bee not as a Lion in thy
houſe, nor franticke among thy ſeruants.31Let not thine hand bee
ſtretched out to receiue, and ſhut when thou ſhouldeſt repay.
CHAPTER 5 1Set not thy heart vpon thy goods, and ſay not, I haue
ynough for my life.2Folow not thine owne minde, and thy ſtrength, to
walke in the wayes of thy heart:3And ſay not, Who ſhall controll mee for
my workes? for the Lord will ſurely reuenge thy pride.4ſay not, I haue
ſinned, and what harme hath happened vnto mee? for the Lord is long
ſuffering, he wil in no wiſe let thee goe.5Concerning propitiation, bee
not without feare to adde ſinne vnto ſinne.6And ſay not, His mercy is
great, hee will be pacified for the multitude of my ſinnes: for mercy and
wrath come from him, and his indignation reſteth vpon ſinners.7Make
no tarying to turne to the Lord, and put not off from day to day: for
ſuddenly ſhal the wrath of the Lord come foorth, and in thy ſecuritie
thou ſhalt be deſtroyed, and periſh in the day of vengeance.8Set not thy
heart vpon goods vniuſtly gotten: for they ſhall not profit thee in the
day of calamitie.9Winnow not with euery winde, and goe not into euery
way: for ſo doth the ſinner that hath a double tongue.10Be ſtedfaſt in thy
vnderſtanding, and let thy word be the ſame.11Be ſwift to heare, and let
thy life be ſincere, & with patience giue anſwere.12If thou haſt
vnderſtanding, anſwer thy neighbour, if not, lay thy hand vpon thy
mouth.13Honour and ſhame is in talke; and the tongue of man is his
fall.14Be not called a whiſperer, and lye not in wait with thy tongue: for
a foule ſhame is vpon the thiefe, and an euill condemnation vpon the
double tongue.15Be not ignorant of any thing, in a great matter or a
ſmall.
CHAPTER 6 1In ſtead of a friend, become not an enemie;
for *thereby* thou ſhalt inherite an ill name, ſhame, and reproch: euen ſo
ſhall a ſinner that hath a double tongue.2Extoll not thy ſelfe in the
counſell of thine owne heart, that thy ſoule bee not torne in pieces as a
bull *ſtraying alone.*3Thou ſhalt eat vp thy leaues, and looſe thy fruit, and
leaue thy ſelfe as a dry tree.4A wicked ſoule ſhall deſtroy him that hath
it, and ſhall make him to be laughed to ſcorne of his enemies.5ſweet
language will multiply friends: and a faire ſpeaking tongue will increaſe
kinde greetings.6Be in peace with many: neuertheleſſe haue but one
counſeller of a thouſand.7If thou wouldſt get a friend, proue him firſt,
and be not haſty to credit him.8For ſome man is a friend for his owne
occaſion, and will not abide in the day of thy trouble.9And there is a
friend, who being turned to enmitie, and ſtrife, will diſcouer thy
reproch.10Againe ſome friend is a companion at the table, and will not
continue in the day of thy affliction.11But in thy proſperitie hee will be
as thy ſelfe, and will be bould ouer thy ſeruants.12If thou be brought low,
he will be againſt thee, and will hide himſelfe from thy face.13Separate
thy ſelfe from thine enemies, and take heed of thy friends.14A faithfull
friend is a ſtrong defence: and hee that hath found ſuch an one, hath
found a treaſure.15Nothing doeth counteruaile a faithful friend, and his
excellencie is vnualuable.16A faithfull friend is the medicine of life, and
they that feare the Lord ſhal finde him.17Who ſo feareth the Lord ſhall
direct his friendſhip aright, for as he is, ſo ſhall his neighbour be
alſo.18My ſonne, gather inſtruction from thy youth vp: ſo ſhalt thou
finde wiſedome till thine old age.19Come vnto her as one that ploweth,
and ſoweth, and wait for her good fruits, for thou ſhalt not toile much
in labouring about her, but thou ſhalt eat of her fruits right ſoone.20She
is very vnpleaſant to the vnlearned: he that is without vnderſtanding,
will not remaine with her.21She wil lye vpon him as a mightie ſtone of
triall, and hee will caſt her from him ere it be long.22For wiſedome is
according to her name, and ſhe is not manifeſt vnto many.23Giue eare,
my ſonne, receiue my aduice, and refuſe not my counſell,24And put thy
feet into her fetters, and thy necke into her chaine.25Bow downe thy
ſhoulder, and beare her, and be not grieued with her bonds.26Come vnto
her with thy whole heart, and keepe her wayes with all thy
power.27ſearch and ſeeke, and ſhee ſhall bee made knowen vnto thee,
and when thou haſt got hold of her, let her not goe.28For at the laſt thou
ſhalt finde her reſt, and that ſhalbe turned to thy ioy.29Then ſhall her
fetters be a ſtrong defence for thee, and her chaines a robe of glory.30For
there is a golden ornament vpon her, and her bandes are purple
lace.31Thou ſhalt put her on as a robe of honour: and ſhalt put her about
thee as a crowne of ioy.32My ſonne, if thou wilt, thou ſhalt bee taught:
and if thou wilt apply thy minde, thou ſhalt be prudent.33If thou loue to
heare, thou ſhalt receiue vnderſtanding: and if thou bow thine eare, thou
ſhalt be wiſe.34ſtand in the multitude of the elders, and cleaue vnto him
that is wiſe.35Be willing to heare euery godly diſcourſe, and let not the
parables of vnderſtanding eſcape thee.36And if thou ſeeſt a man of
vnderſtanding, get thee betimes vnto him, and let thy foote weare the
ſteps of his doore.37Let thy minde be vpon the ordinances of the Lord,
& meditate continually in his commandements: he ſhal eſtabliſh thine
heart, and giue thee wiſedome at thine owne deſire.
CHAPTER 7 1Doe no euill, ſo ſhall no harme come vnto thee.2Depart
from the vniuſt, and iniquitie ſhall turne away from thee.3My ſonne, ſow
not vpon the furrowes of vnrighteouſneſſe, and thou ſhalt not reape
them ſeuen folde.4Seeke not of the Lord preheminence, neither of the
King the ſeate of honour.5Iuſtifie not thy ſelfe before the Lord, and
boaſt not of thy wiſedome before the king.6Seeke not to be iudge, being
not able to take away iniquitie, leſt at any time thou feare the perſon of
the mightie, and lay a ſtumbling blocke in the way of thy
vprightneſse.7Offend not againſt the multitude of a city, and then thou
ſhalt not caſt thy ſelfe downe among the people.8Bind not one ſinne
vpon another, for in one thou ſhalt not be vnpuniſhed.9ſay not, God wil
looke vpon the multitude of my oblations, and when I offer to the moſt
High God, he will accept it.10Be not faint hearted when thou makeſt thy
prayer, and neglect not to giue almes.11Laugh no man to ſcorne in the
bitterneſse of his ſoule: for there is one which humbleth and
exalteth.12Deuiſe not a lie againſt thy brother: neither doe the like to thy
friend.13Uſe not to make any maner of lie: for the cuſtome thereof is not
good.14Uſe not many words in a multitude of Elders, and make not
much babling when thou prayeſt.15Hate not laborious worke, neither
huſbandrie, which the moſt High hath ordeined.16Number not thy ſelfe
among the multitude of ſinners, but remember that wrath will not tary
long.17Humble thy ſoule greatly: for the vengeance of the vngodly is fire
and wormes.18Change not a friend for any good by no meanes: neither
a faithfull brother for the gold of Ophir.19Forgoe not a wiſe and good
woman: for her grace is aboue gold.20Whereas thy ſeruant worketh
truely, entreate him not euill, nor the hireling that beſtoweth himſelfe
wholly for thee.21Let thy ſoule loue a good ſeruant, and defraud him not
of liberty.22Haſt thou cattell? haue an eye to them, and if they be for thy
profit, keepe them with thee.23Haſt thou children? inſtruct them, and
bow downe their necke from their youth.24Haſt thou daughters? haue
care of their body, and ſhewe not thy ſelfe cheerefull toward
them.25Marrie thy daughter, and ſo ſhalt thou haue performed a
weightie matter: but giue her to a man of vnderſtanding.26Haſt thou a
wife after thy minde? forſake her not, but giue not thy ſelfe ouer to a
light woman.27Honour thy father with thy whole heart, and forget not
the ſorrowes of thy mother.28Remember that thou waſt begot of them,
and how canſt thou recompenſe them the things that they haue done
for thee?29Feare the Lord with all thy ſoule, and reuerence his
prieſts.30Loue him that made thee with all thy ſtrength, and forſake not
his miniſters.31Feare the Lord, and honour the prieſt: and giue him his
portion, as it is commanded thee, the firſt fruits, and the treſpaſſe
offering, & the gift of the ſhoulders , and the ſacrifice of ſanctification,

and the firſt fruits of the holy things.32And ſtretch thine hand vnto the poore, that thy bleſſing may be perfected33A gift hath grace in the ſight of euery man liuing, and for the dead deteine it not.34Faile not to bee with them that weepe, and mourne with them that mourne.35Be not ſlow to viſit the ſicke: for that ſhall make thee to be beloued.36Whatſoeuer thou takeſt in hand, remember the end, and thou ſhalt neuer doe amiſse.

CHAPTER 8 1Striue not with a mighty man, leſt thou fall into his hands.2Bee not at variance with a rich man, leſt he ouerweigh thee: for gold hath deſtroyed many, and peruerted the hearts of kings.3Striue not with a man that is full of tongue, and heape not wood vpon his fire.4Ieſt not with a rude man, leſt thy anceſtours be diſgraced.5Reproch not a man that turneth from ſinne, but remember that we are all worthy of puniſhment.6Diſhonour not a man in his old age: for euen ſome of vs waxe old.7Reioice not ouer thy greateſt enemie being dead, but remember that we die all.8Deſpiſe not the diſcourſe of the wiſe, but acquaint thy ſelfe with their prouerbs; for of them thou ſhalt learne inſtruction, & how to ſerue great men with eaſe.9Miſse not the diſcourſe of the Elders: for they alſo learned of their fathers, and of them thou ſhalt learne vnderſtanding, and to giue anſwere as need requireth.10Kindle not the coales of a ſinner, leſt thou be burnt with the flame of his fire.11Riſe not vp (in anger) at the preſence of an iniurious perſon, leaſt he lie in waite to entrap thee in thy words.12Lend not vnto him that is mightier then thy ſelfe; for if thou lendeſt him, count it but loſt.13Be not ſurety aboue thy power: for if thou be ſurety, take care to pay it.14Goe not to law with a iudge, for they will iudge for him according to his honour.15Trauaile not by the way with a bold fellow, leaſt he become grieuous vnto thee: for he will doe according to his owne will, and thou ſhalt periſh with him through his folly.16Striue not with an angry man, and goe not with him into a ſolitary place: for blood is as nothing in his ſight, and where there is no helpe, he will ouerthrow thee.17Conſult not with a foole; for he cannot keepe counſell.18Doe no ſecret thing before a ſtranger, for thou knoweſt not what he will bring forth.19Open not thine heart to euery man, leaſt he requite thee with a ſhrewd turne.

CHAPTER 9 1Be not iealous ouer the wife of thy boſome, and teach her not an euil leſson againſt thy ſelfe.2Giue not thy ſoule vnto a woman, to ſet her foot vpon thy ſubſtance.3Meete not with an harlot, leaſt thou fall into her ſnares.4Uſe not much the companie of a woman that is a ſinger, leaſt thou be taken with her attempts.5Gaze not on a maide, that thou fall not by thoſe things, that are pretious in her.6Giue not thy ſoule vnto harlots, that thou looſe not thine inheritance.7Looke not round about thee, in the ſtreets of the citie, neither wander thou in the ſolitary places thereof.8Turne away thine eye from a beautifull woman, and looke not vpon anothers beautie: for many haue beene deceiued by the beautie of a woman, for heerewith loue is kindled as a fire.9Sit not at all with another mans wife, nor ſit downe with her in thine armes, and ſpend not thy money with her at the wine, leaſt thine heart incline vnto her, and ſo thorough thy deſire thou fall into deſtruction.10Forſake not an old friend, for the new is not comparable to him: a new friend is as new wine: when it is old, thou ſhalt drinke it with pleaſure.11Enuy not the glory of a ſinner: for thou knoweſt not what ſhall be his end.12Delight not in the thing that the vngodly haue pleaſure in, but remember they ſhall not goe vnpuniſhed vnto their graue.13Keepe thee farre from the man that hath power to kill, ſo ſhalt thou not doubt the feare of death: and if thou come vnto him, make no fault, leaſt he take away thy life preſently: remember that thou goeſt in the midſt of ſnares, and that thou walkeſt vpon the battlements of the citie.14As neere as thou canſt, gheſse at thy neighbour, and conſult with the wiſe.15Let thy talke be with the wiſe, and all thy communication in the law of the moſt high.16And let iuſt men eate and drinke with thee, and let thy glorying be in the feare of the Lord.17For the hand of the artificer, the worke ſhall be commended: and the wiſe ruler of the people, for his ſpeech.18A man of an ill tongue is dangerous in his citie, and he that is raſh in his talke ſhall be hated.

CHAPTER 10 1A wiſe iudge will inſtruct his people, & the gouernement of a prudent man is well ordered.2As the iudge of the people is himſelfe, ſo are his officers, and what maner of man the ruler of the citie is, ſuch are all they that dwell therein.3An vnwiſe king deſtroyeth his people, but through the prudence of them which are in authoritie, the citie ſhalbe inhabited.4The power of the earth is in the hand of the Lord, and in due time hee will ſet ouer it one that is profitable.5In the hand of God is the proſperitie of man: and vpon the perſon of the ſcribe ſhall he lay his honour.6Beare not hatred to thy neighbour for euery wrong, and do nothing at all by iniurious practiſes.7Pride is hatefull before God, and man: and by both doeth one commit iniquitie.8Becauſe of vnrighteous dealings, iniuries, and riches got by deceit, the kingdome is tranſlated from one people to another.9Why is earth and aſhes proude? There is not a more wicked thing, then a couetous man: for ſuch an one ſetteth his owne ſoule to ſale, becauſe while he liueth, he caſteth away his bowels.10The Phiſition cutteth off a long diſeaſe, and he that is to day a King, to morrow ſhall die.11For when a man is dead, hee ſhall inherite creeping things, beaſtes and wormes.12The beginning of pride is, when one departeth from God, and his heart is turned away from his maker.13For pride is the beginning of ſinne, and hee that hath it, ſhall powre out abomination: and therefore the Lord brought vpon them ſtrange calamities, and ouerthrew them vtterly.14The Lord hath caſt downe the thrones of proud Princes, and ſet vp the meeke in their ſtead.15The Lord hath plucked vp the rootes of the proud nations: and planted the lowly in their place.16The Lord ouerthrew countreys of the heathen: and deſtroyed them to the foundations of the earth.17He tooke ſome of them away, and deſtroyed them, and hath made their memoriall to ceaſe from the earth.18Pride was not made for men, nor furious anger for them that are borne of a woman.19They that feare the Lord are a ſure ſeed, and they that loue him, an honourable plant: they that regard not the Law, are a diſhonourable ſeed, they that tranſgreſse the commandements, are a deceiuable ſeed.20Among brethren he that is chiefe is honourable, ſo are they that feare the Lord in his eyes.21The feare of the Lord goeth before the obtayning of authoritie: but roughneſse and pride, is the looſing thereof.22Whether hee bee rich, noble, or poore, their glorie is the feare of the Lord.23It is not meet to deſpiſe the poore man that hath vnderſtanding, neither is it conuenient to magnifie a ſinnefull man.24Great men, and Iudges, and Potentates ſhall bee honoured, yet is there none of them greater then he that feareth the Lord.25Unto the ſeruant that is wiſe, ſhall they that are free doe ſeruice: and hee that hath knowledge, will not grudge when he is reformed.26Be not ouerwiſe in doing thy buſines, and boaſt not thy ſelfe in the time of thy diſtreſſe.27Better is he that laboureth and aboundeth in all things, then hee that boaſteth himſelfe, and wanteth bread.28My ſonne, glorifie thy ſoule in meekeneſse, and giue it honour according to the dignitie thereof.29Who wil iuſtifie him that ſinneth againſt his owne ſoule? and who will honour him that diſhonoureth his owne life?30The poore man is honoured for his ſkill, and the rich man is honoured for his riches.31Hee that is honoured in pouertie, how much more in riches? And he that is diſhonourable in riches, how much more in pouertie?

CHAPTER 111Wiſedome lifteth vp the head of him that is of low degree, and maketh him to ſit among great men.2Commend not a man for his beautie, neither abhorre a man for his outward appearance.3The Bee is little among ſuch as flie, but her fruite is the chiefe of ſweete things.4Boaſt not of thy cloathing and raiment, and exalt not thy ſelfe in the day of honour: for the workes of the Lord are wonderfull, and his workes among men are hidden.5Many kings haue ſit downe vpon the ground, and one that was neuer thought of, hath worne the crowne.6Many mightie men haue beene greatly diſgraced: and the honourable deliuered into other mens hands.7Blame not before thou haſt examined the trueth: vnderſtand firſt, and then rebuke.8Anſwere not, before thou haſt heard the cauſe: neither interrupt men in the midſt of their talke.9Striue not in a matter that concerneth thee not: and ſit not in iudgement with ſinners.10My ſonne, meddle not with many matters: for if thou meddle much, thou ſhalt not be innocent: and if thou follow after, thou ſhalt not obtaine, neither ſhalt thou eſcape by flying.11There is one that laboureth and taketh paines, and maketh haſte, and is ſo much the more behinde.12Againe, there is another that is ſlow, and hath neede of helpe, wanting abilitie, and full of pouertie, yet the eye of the Lord looked vpon him for good, and ſet him vp from his low eſtate,13And lifted vp his head from miſerie, ſo that many that ſaw it, marueiled at him.14Proſperitie and aduerſitie, life and death, pouerty and

riches, come of the Lord.15Wiſedome, knowledge, and vnderſtanding of
the Lawe, are of the Lord: loue, & the way of good workes, are from
him.16Errour and darkeneſſe had their beginning together with ſinners:
and euill ſhall waxe old with them that glory therein.17The gift of the
Lord remaineth with the godly, and his fauour bringeth proſperitie for
euer.18There is that waxeth rich by his warineſse, and pinching, and this
is the portion of his reward:19Whereas he ſayth, I haue found reſt, and
now will eate continually of my goods, and yet hee knoweth not what
time ſhall come vpon him, and that hee muſt leaue thoſe things to
others, and die.20Be ſtedfaſt in thy couenant, and be conuerſant therein,
and waxe olde in thy worke.21Marueile not at the workes of ſinners, but
truſt in the Lord, and abide in thy labour: for it is an eaſie thing in the
ſight of the Lord, on the ſudden to make a poore man rich.22The bleſſing
of the Lord is in the reward of the godly, and ſuddenly he maketh his
bleſſing to flouriſh.23ſay not, what profit is there of my ſeruice? and what
good things ſhal I haue hereafter?24Againe, ſay not, I haue enough, and
poſſeſſe many things; and what euill can come to me hereafter?25In the
day of proſperitie, there is a forgetfulneſse of affliction: and in the day
of affliction, there is no remembrance of proſperitie.26For it is an eaſie
thing vnto the Lord in the day of death, to reward a man according to
his wayes.27The affliction of an houre, maketh a man forget pleaſure:
and in his end, his deeds ſhalbe diſcouered.28Iudge none bleſſed before
his death: for a man ſhall bee knowen in his children.29Bring not euery
man into thine houſe, for the deceitfull man hath many traines.30Like as
a Partrich taken *and kept* in a cage, ſo is the heart of the proud; and like
as a ſpie, watcheth hee for thy fall.31For hee lieth in wait, and turneth
good into euill, and in things worthy praiſe, will lay blame vpon
thee.32Of a ſparke of fire, a heape of coales is kindled: and a ſinnefull
man layeth waite for blood.33Take heed of a miſchieuous man, (for hee
worketh wickedneſſe) leſt hee bring vpon thee a perpetuall
blot.34Receiue a ſtranger into thine houſe, and hee will diſturbe thee,
and turne thee out of thine owne.

CHAPTER 12 1When thou wilt doe good, know to whō thou doeſt it,
ſo ſhalt thou be thanked for thy benefites.2Do good to the godly man,
and thou ſhalt find a recompence, and if not from him, yet from the
moſt high.3There can no good come to him that is alwayes occupied in
euill: nor to him that giueth no almes.4Giue to the godly man, and helpe
not a ſinner.5Doe well vnto him that is lowly, but giue not to the
vngodly: hold backe thy bread, and giue it not vnto him, leſt he
ouermaſter thee thereby. For *elſe* thou ſhalt receiue twice as much euill,
for all the good thou ſhalt haue done vnto him.6For the moſt High
hateth ſinners, and will repay vengeance vnto the vngodly, and keepeth
them againſt the mightie day of their puniſhment.7Giue vnto the good,
and helpe not the ſinner.8A friend cannot be knowen in proſperitie, and
an enemy cannot be hidden in aduerſitie.9In the proſperitie of a man,
enemies will be grieued, but in his aduerſitie, euen a friend will
depart.10Neuer truſt thine enemie: for like as yron ruſteth, ſo is his
wickedneſſe.11Though he humble himſelfe, and goe crouching, yet take
good heed, and beware of him, and thou ſhalt bee vnto him, as if thou
hadſt wiped a looking glaſſe, and thou ſhalt knowe that his ruſt hath not
beene altogether wiped away.12Set him not by thee, leſt when he hath
ouerthrowen thee, he ſtand vp in thy place, neither let him ſit at thy right
hand, leſt he ſeeke to take thy ſeat, and thou at the laſt remember my
wordes, and be pricked therewith.13Who will pitie a charmer that is
bitten with a ſerpent, or any ſuch as come nigh wilde beaſts?14So one
that goeth to a ſinner, and is defiled with him in his ſinnes, who will
pitie?15For a while hee will abide with thee, but if thou begin to fall, he
wil not tarie.16An enemie ſpeaketh ſweetly with his lippes, but in his
heart he imagineth how to throw thee into a pit: hee will weepe with his
eyes, but if he find opportunitie, hee will not be ſatiſfied with blood.17If
aduerſitie come vpon thee, thou ſhalt find him there firſt, & though he
pretend to helpe thee, yet ſhal he vndermine thee.18He will ſhake his
head and clap his handes, and whiſper much, and change his
countenance.

CHAPTER 13 1He that toucheth pitch, ſhal be defiled therewith, and
hee that hath fellowſhip with a proude man, ſhall be like vnto
him.2Burthen not thy ſelfe aboue thy power, while thou liueſt, and haue
no fellowſhip with one that is mightier, and richer then thy ſelfe. For
how agree the kettle and the earthen pot together? for if the one be
ſmitten againſt the other, it ſhall be broken.3The rich man hath done
wrong, and yet he threatneth withall: the poore is wronged, and he muſt
intreat alſo.4If thou be for his profit, he will vſe thee: but if thou haue
nothing, he will forſake thee.5If thou haue any thing, he will liue with
thee, yea he will make thee bare, and will not be ſorie for it.6If he haue
need of thee, hee will deceiue thee, and ſmile vpon thee, and put thee in
hope, he will ſpeake thee faire, and ſay, What wanteſt thou?7And hee
will ſhame thee by his meates, vntill he haue drawen thee drie twice or
thrice, and at the laſt hee will laugh thee to ſcorne: afterward when he
ſeeth thee, he will forſake thee, and ſhake his head at thee.8Beware that
thou bee not deceiued, and brought downe in thy iolitie.9If thou be
inuited of a mighty man, withdraw thy ſelfe, and ſo much the more will
he inuite thee.10Preſse thou not vpon him, leſt thou be put backe, ſtand
not farre off, leſt thou be forgotten.11Affect not to be made equall vnto
him in talke, and beleeue not his many words: for with much
communication will he tempt thee, and ſmiling vpon thee will get out
thy ſecrets.12But cruelly he will lay vp thy words, and will not ſpare to
doe thee hurt, and to put thee in priſon.13Obſerue and take good heed,
for thou walkeſt in peril of thy ouerthrowing: when thou heareſt theſe
things, awake in thy ſleepe.14Loue the Lord all thy life, and call vpon
him for thy ſaluation.15Euery beaſt loueth his like, and euery man loueth
his neighbour.16All fleſh conſorteth according to kind, and a man will
cleaue to his like:17What fellowſhip hath the wolfe with the lambe? ſo
the ſinner with the godly.18What agreement is there betweene the Hyena
and a dogge? and what peace betweene the rich and the poore?19As the
wilde aſſe is the lyons pray in the wilderneſſe: ſo the rich eate vp the
poore.20As the proud hate humilitie: ſo doth the rich abhorre the
poore.21A rich man beginning to fall, is held vp of his friends: but a
poore man being downe, is thruſt alſo away by his friends.22When a rich
man is fallen, he hath many helpers: he ſpeaketh things not to be ſpoken,
and yet men iuſtifie him: the poore man ſlipt, and yet they rebuked him
too: he ſpake wiſely, and could haue no place.23When a rich man
ſpeaketh, euery man holdeth his tongue, and looke what hee ſayeth, they
extoll it to the clouds: but if the poore man ſpeake, they ſay, What fellow
is this? and if he ſtumble, they will helpe to ouerthrowe him.24Riches are
good vnto him that hath no ſinne, and pouerty is euill in the mouth of
the vngodly.25The heart of a man changeth his countenance, whether it
be for good or euill: and a merry heart maketh a cheerefull
countenance.26A cheerefull countenance is a token of a heart that is in
proſperity, and the finding out of parables, is a weariſome labour of the
minde.

CHAPTER 14 1Bleſſed is the man that hath not ſlipt with his mouth,
and is not pricked with the multitude of ſinnes.2Bleſſed is hee whoſe
conſcience hath not condemned him, and who is not fallen from his
hope in the Lord.3Riches are not comely for a niggard: and what ſhould
an enuious man doe with money?4He that gathereth by defrauding his
owne ſoule, gathereth for others, that ſhall ſpend his goods
riotouſly.5Hee that is euill to himſelfe, to whom will he be good? he ſhall
not take pleaſure in his goods.6There is none worſe then he that enuieth
himſelfe; and this is a recompence of his wickedneſſe.7And if he doth
good, he doth it vnwillingly, and at the laſt he will declare his
wickedneſſe.8The enuious man hath a wicked eye, he turneth away his
face and deſpiſeth men.9A couetous mans eye is not ſatiſfied with his
portion, and the iniquity of the wicked dryeth vp his ſoule.10A wicked
eye enuieth *hiſ* bread, and he is a niggard at his table.11My ſonne,
according to thy habilitie doe good to thy ſelfe, and giue the Lord his
due offering.12Remember that death will not be long in comming, and
that the couenant of the graue is not ſhewed vnto thee.13Doe good vnto
thy friend before thou die, and according to thy abilitie, ſtretch out thy
hand and giue to him.14Defraud not thy ſelfe of the good day, and let
not the part of a good deſire ouerpaſſe thee.15Shalt thou not leaue thy
trauailes vnto another? and thy labours to be diuided by lot?16Giue, and
take, and ſanctifie thy ſoule, for there is no ſeeking of dainties in the
graue.17All fleſh waxeth old as a garment: for the couenant from the
beginning is; thou ſhalt die the death.18As of the greene leaues on a
thicke tree, ſome fall, and ſome grow; ſo is the generation of fleſh and
blood, one commeth to an end, and another is borne.19Euery worke
rotteth and conſumeth away, and the worker therof ſhal goe
withall.20Bleſſed is the man that doeth meditate good things in wiſdome,
and that reaſoneth of holy things by his vnderſtanding.21He that

conſidereth her wayes in his heart, ſhall alſo haue vnderſtanding in her ſecrets.22Goe after her as one that traceth, and lie in wait in her wayes.23Hee that prieth in at her windowes, ſhal alſo hearken at her doores.24Hee that doeth lodge neere her houſe, ſhall alſo faſten a pin in her walles.25He ſhall pitch his tent nigh vnto her, and ſhall lodge in a lodging where good things are.26He ſhal ſet his children vnder her ſhelter, and ſhall lodge vnder her branches.27By her he ſhall be couered from heat, and in her glory ſhall he dwell.

CHAPTER 15 1He that feareth the Lord will doe good, and he that hath the knowledge of the Law ſhal obtaine her.2And as a mother ſhall ſhe meet him, and receiue him as a wife maried of a virgin.3With the bread of vnderſtanding ſhall ſhe feed him, and giue him the water of wiſedome to drinke.4Hee ſhall be ſtayed vpon her, and ſhall not be moued, and ſhall rely vpon her, and ſhall not be confounded.5Shee ſhall exalt him aboue his neighbours, and in the midſt of the congregation ſhall ſhe open his mouth.6He ſhall finde ioy, and a crowne of gladneſſe, and ſhe ſhall cauſe him to inherit an euerlaſting name.7But fooliſh men ſhall not attaine vnto her, and ſinners ſhall not ſee her.8For ſhe is farre from pride, and men that are liers cannot remember her.9Praiſe is not ſeemly in the mouth of a ſinner, for it was not ſent him of the Lord:10For praiſe ſhalbe vttered in wiſdome, and the Lord wil proſper it.11ſay not thou, It is through the Lord, that I fell away, for thou oughteſt not to doe the things that he hateth.12ſay not thou, He hath cauſed mee to erre, for hee hath no need of the ſinfull man.13The Lord hateth all abomination, and they that feare God loue it not.14Hee himſelfe made man from the beginning, and left him in the hand of his counſell,15If thou wilt, to keepe the Commandements, and to performe acceptable faithfulneſse.16He hath ſet fire and water before thee: ſtretch forth thy hand vnto whether thou wilt.17Before man is life and death, and whether him liketh ſhalbe giuen him.18For the wiſedome of the Lord is great, and he is mighty in power, and beholdeth all things,19And his eyes are vpon them that feare him, & hee knoweth euery worke of man.20Hee hath commanded no man to do wickedly, neither hath he giuen any man licenſe to ſinne.

CHAPTER 16 1Deſire not a multitude of vnprofitable children, neither delight in vngodly ſonnes.2Though they multiply, reioyce not in them, except the feare of the Lord be with them.3Truſt not thou in their life, neither reſpect their multitude: for one that is iuſt, is better then a thouſand, and better it is to die without children, then to haue them that are vngodly.4For by one that hath vnderſtanding, ſhall the city be repleniſhed, but the kindred of the wicked, ſhall ſpeedily become deſolate.5Many ſuch things haue I ſeene with mine eyes, and mine eare hath heard greater things then theſe.6In the congregation of the vngodly, ſhall a fire be kindled, and in a rebellious nation, wrath is ſet on fire.7Hee was not pacified towards the olde giants, who fell away in the ſtrength of their fooliſhneſse.8Neither ſpared he the place where Lot ſoiourned, but abhorred them for their pride.9Hee pitied not the people of perdition, who were taken away in their ſinnes.10Nor the ſixe hundreth thouſand footmen, who were gathered together in the hardneſse of their hearts.11And if there be one ſtiffe-necked among the people, it is marueile, if he eſcape vnpuniſhed; for mercy and wrath are with him, hee is mighty to forgiue, and to powre out diſpleaſure.12As his mercy is great, ſo is his correction alſo: he iudgeth a man according to his workes.13The ſinner ſhall not eſcape with his ſpoiles, and the patience of the godly ſhall not be fruſtrate.14Make way for euery worke of mercy: for euery man ſhall finde according to his workes.15The Lord hardened Pharaoh, that hee ſhould not know him, that his powerfull workes might be knowen to the world.16His mercy is manifeſt to euery creature, and hee hath ſeparated his light from the darkeneſſe with an Adamant.17ſay not thou, I will hide my ſelfe from the Lord: ſhall any remember me from aboue? I ſhall not be remembred among ſo many people: for what is my ſoule among ſuch an infinite number of creatures?18Behold, the heauen, and the heauen of heauens, the deepe and the earth, and all that therein is, ſhall be mooued when he ſhall viſit.19The mountaines alſo, and foundations of the earth ſhall bee ſhaken with trembling, when the Lord looketh vpon them.20No heart can thinke vpon theſe things worthily: and who is able to conceiue his wayes?21It is a tempeſt, which no man can ſee: for the moſt part of his workes are hidde.22Who can declare the workes of his iuſtice? or who can endure them? for his Couenant is afarre off, and the triall of all things is in the ende.23He that wanteth vnderſtanding, will thinke vpon vaine things: and a fooliſh man erring, imagineth follies.24My ſonne, hearken vnto mee, and learne knowledge, and marke my words with thy heart.25I will ſhewe foorth doctrine in weight, and declare his knowledge exactly.26The works of the Lord are done in iudgement from the beginning: and from the time he made them, hee diſpoſed the parts thereof.27Hee garniſhed his workes for euer, and in his hand are the chiefe of them vnto all generations: they neither labour, nor are weary, nor ceaſe from their workes.28None of them hindreth another, and they ſhall neuer diſobey his word.29After this, the Lord looked vpon the earth, and filled it with his bleſſings.30With all maner of liuing things hath hee couered the face thereof, and they ſhall returne into it againe.

CHAPTER 17 1The Lord created man of the earth, and turned him into it againe.2He gaue them few dayes, and a ſhort time, and power alſo ouer the things therein.3He endued them with ſtrength by themſelues, and made them according to his image,4And put the feare of man vpon all fleſh, and gaue him dominion ouer beaſts and foules.5*They receiued the vſe of the fiue operations of the Lord, and in the ſixt place he imparted them vnderſtanding, and in the ſeuenth, ſpeech, an interpreter of the cogitations thereof.*6Counſell, and a tongue, and eyes, eares, and a heart, gaue he them to vnderſtand.7Withall, hee filled them with the knowledge of vnderſtanding, & ſhewed them good and euill.8Hee ſet his eye vpon their hearts, that he might ſhew them the greatneſſe of his workes.9He gaue them to glory in his marueilous actes for euer, that they might declare his works with vnderſtanding.10And the elect ſhall praiſe his holy Name.11Beſide this he gaue them knowledge, and the law of life for an heritage.12He made an euerlaſting couenant with them, and ſhewed them his iudgements.13Their eyes ſaw the maieſtie of his glory, and their eares heard his glorious voyce.14And he ſaid vnto them, Beware of all vnrighteouſnes, and he gaue euery man commandement concerning his neighbour,15Their wayes are euer before him, and ſhall not be hid from his eyes.16Euery man from his youth is giuen to euil, neither could they make to themſelues fleſhie hearts for ſtonie.17For in the diuiſion of the nations of the whole earth, he ſet a ruler ouer euery people, but Iſrael is the Lords portion.18Whom being his firſt borne, hee nouriſheth with diſcipline, and giuing him the light of his loue, doth not forſake him.19Therefore all their workes are as the Sunne before him, and his eyes are continually vpon their wayes.20None of their vnrighteous deeds are hid from him, but all their ſinnes are before the Lord:21But the Lord being gracious, and knowing his workemanſhip, neither left nor forſooke them, but ſpared them.22The almes of a man is as a ſignet with him, and he will keep the good deedes of man, as the apple of the eye, and giue repentance to his ſonnes and daughters.23Afterward he will riſe vp and reward them, and render their recompenſe vpon their heads.24But vnto them that repent, he granted them returne, and comforted thoſe that faile in patience.25Returne vnto the Lord, and forſake thy ſinnes, make thy prayer before his face, and offend leſſe.26Turne againe to the moſt High, and turne away from iniquitie: for he will leade thee out of darkeneſſe into the light of health, and hate thou abomination vehemently.27Who ſhall praiſe the moſt High in the graue, in ſtead of them which liue and giue thanks?28Thankeſgiuing periſheth from the dead, as from one that is not: the liuing and ſound in heart, ſhall praiſe the Lord.29How great is the louing kindnes of the Lord our God, and his compaſſion vnto ſuch as turne vnto him in holineſſe?30For all things cannot bee in men, becauſe þe ſonne of man is not immortal.31What is brighter then the Sun? yet the light thereof faileth: and fleſh and blood will imagine euill.32Hee vieweth the power of the height of heauen, and all men are but earth and aſhes.

CHAPTER 18 1Hee that liueth for euer, created all things in generall.2The Lord onely is righteous, and there is none other but he.3Who gouerneth the world with the palme of his hand, and all things obey his will, for he is the king of all, by his power diuiding holy things among them from prophane.4To whom hath he giuen power to declare his works? and who ſhall finde out his noble actes?5Who ſhall number the ſtrength of his maieſtie? and who ſhall alſo tel out his mercies?6As for the wonderous workes of the Lord, there may nothing bee taken from them, neither may any thing bee put vnto them, neither can the ground of them be found out.7When a man hath done, then he beginneth, and when hee leaueth off, then he ſhall be doubtfull. 8 What is man, and whereto ſerueth he? what is his good, & what is his euil? 9 The number of a mans dayes at the moſt are an hundred yeeres. 10 As a drop of water vnto the ſea, and a grauell ſtone in compariſon of the ſand, ſo are a thouſand yeeres to the dayes of eternitie. 11 Therfore is God patient with them, & powreth forth his mercy vpon them. 12 He ſaw and perceiued their end to be euill, therefore he multiplied his compaſſion. 13 The mercy of man is toward his neighbour, but the mercy of the Lord is vpon all fleſh: he reprooueth and nurtureth, and teacheth, & bringeth againe as a ſhepheard his flocke. 14 He hath mercy on them that receiue diſcipline, and that diligently ſeeke after his iudgements. 15 My ſonne, blemiſh not thy good deeds, neither vſe vncomfortable words when thou giueſt any thing. 16 Shall not the deaw aſswage the heate? ſo is a word better then a gift. 17 Loe is not a word better then a gift? but both are with a gracious man. 18 A foole will vpbraide churliſhly, and a gift of the enuious conſumeth the eyes. 19 Learne before thou ſpeake, and vſe phiſicke, or euer thou be ſicke. 20 Before iudgement examine thy ſelfe, and in the day of viſitation thou ſhalt find mercy. 21 Humble thy ſelfe before thou be ſicke, and in the time of ſinnes ſhew repentance. 22 Let nothing hinder thee to pay thy vowe in due time, and deferre not vntill death to be iuſtified. 23 Before thou prayeſt, prepare thy ſelfe, and be not as one that tempteth the Lord. 24 Thinke vpon the wrath that ſhall be at the end; and the time of vengeance when he ſhall turne away his face. 25 When thou haſt enough remember the time of hunger, and when thou art rich thinke vpon pouerty and need. 26 From the morning vntill the euening the time is changed, and all things are ſoone done before the Lord. 27 A wiſe man will feare in euery thing, and in the day of ſinning he will beware of offence: but a foole will not obſerue time. 28 Euery man of vnderſtanding knoweth wiſedome, and wil giue praiſe vnto him that found her. 29 They that were of vnderſtanding in ſayings, became alſo wiſe themſelues, and powred forth exquiſite parables. 30 Goe not after thy luſtes, but refraine thy ſelfe from thine appetites. 31 If thou giueſt thy ſoule the deſires that pleaſe her, ſhe will make thee a laughing ſtocke to thine enemies, that maligne thee. 32 Take not pleaſure in much good cheere, neither be tyed to the expence thereof. 33 Be not made a begger by banquetting vpon borrowing, when thou haſt nothing in thy purſe, for thou ſhalt lie in waite for thy owne life: and be talked on.

CHAPTER 19 1 A labouring man that is giuen to drunkenneſse ſhal not be rich, and hee that contemneth ſmall things ſhall fall by little & little. 2 Wine and women will make men of vnderſtanding to fall away, and he that cleaueth to harlots will become impudent. 3 Mothes and wormes ſhall haue him to heritage, and a bold man ſhall be taken away. 4 He that is haſty to giue credit is light minded, and he that ſinneth ſhall offend againſt his owne ſoule. 5 Who ſo taketh pleaſure in wickedneſſe ſhall be condemned, but he that reſiſteth pleaſures, crowneth his life. 6 He that can rule his tongue ſhall liue without ſtrife, and he that hateth babbling, ſhall haue leſſe euill. 7 Rehearſe not vnto another that which is told vnto thee, and thou ſhalt fare neuer the worſe. 8 Whether it be to friend or foe, talk not of other mens liues, and if thou canſt without offence reueale them not. 9 For he heard and obſerued thee, and when time commeth he will hate thee. 10 If thou haſt heard a word, let it die with thee, and be bold it will not burſt thee. 11 A foole trauaileth with a word, as a woman in labour of a child. 12 As an arrowe that ſticketh in a mans thigh, ſo is a word within a fooles belly. 13 Admoniſh a friend, it may be he hath not done it, and if he haue *done it* that he doe it no more. 14 Admoniſh thy friend, it may be he hath not ſaid it, and if he haue, that he ſpeake it not againe. 15 Admoniſh a friend: for many times it is a ſlander, & beleeue not euery tale. 16 There is one that ſlippeth in his ſpeach, but not from his heart, and who is he that hath not offended with his tongue? 17 Admoniſh thy neighbour before thou threaten him, and not being angry giue place to the Law of the moſt high. 18 The feare of the Lord is the firſt ſtep to be accepted *of him,* and wiſedome obtaineth his loue. 19 The knowledge of the Commandements of the Lord, is the doctrine of life, and they that do things that pleaſe him, ſhall receiue the fruit of the tree of immortalitie. 20 The feare of the Lord is all wiſedome, and in all wiſedome is the performance of the Law, and the knowledge of his omnipotencie. 21 If a ſeruant ſay to his maſter, I will not doe as it pleaſeth thee, though afterward hee doe it, hee angereth him that nouriſheth him. 22 The knowledge of wickednes is not wiſedome, neither at any time the counſell of ſinners, prudence. 23 There is a wickedneſſe, and the ſame an abomination, and there is a foole wanting in wiſedome. 24 He that hath ſmal vnderſtanding and feareth God, is better then one that hath much wiſedome, and tranſgreſseth the Law of the moſt High. 25 There is an exquiſite ſubtilty, and the ſame is vniuſt, and there is one that turneth aſide to make iudgement appeare: and there is a wiſe man that iuſtifieth in iudgement. 26 There is a wicked man that hangeth downe his head ſadly; but inwardly he is full of deceit, 27 Caſting downe his countenance, and making as if he heard not: where he is not knowen, he will do thee a miſchiefe before thou be aware. 28 And if for want of power hee be hindered from ſinning, yet when he findeth opportunitie he wil doe euil. 29 A man may bee knowen by his looke, and one that hath vnderſtanding, by his countenance, when thou meeteſt him. 30 A mans attire, and exceſsiue laughter, and gate, ſhew what he is.

CHAPTER 20 1 There is a reproofe that is not comely: againe ſome man holdeth his tongue, and he is wiſe. 2 It is much better to reprooue, then to be angry ſecretly, and he that confeſseth his fault, ſhall be preſerued from hurt. 3 How good is it when thou art reproued, to ſhew repentance? for ſo ſhalt thou eſcape wilfull ſinne. 4 As is the luſt of an Eunuch to defloure a virgine; ſo is he that executeth iudgement with violence. 5 There is one that keepeth ſilence and is found wiſe: and another by much babling becommeth hatefull. 6 Some man holdeth his tongue, becauſe hee hath not to anſwere, and ſome keepeth ſilence, knowing his time. 7 A wiſe man wil hold his tongue till he ſee opportunitie: but a babler and a foole will regard no time. 8 He that vſeth many words ſhalbe abhorred; and hee that taketh to himſelfe authoritie therein, ſhalbe hated. 9 There is a ſinner that hath good ſucceſse in euill things; and there is a gaine that turneth to loſse. 10 There is a gift that ſhall not profit thee; and there is a gift whoſe recompence is double. 11 There is an abaſement becauſe of glory; and there is that lifteth vp his head from a low eſtate. 12 There is that buyeth much for a little, and repayeth it ſeuen fold. 13 A wiſe man by his words maketh himſelfe beloued: but the graces of fooles ſhalbe powred out. 14 The gift of a foole ſhall doe thee no good when thou haſt it; neither yet of the enuious for his neceſsitie: for hee looketh to receiue many things for one. 15 Hee giueth little and vpbraideth much; hee openeth his mouth like a crier; to day he lendeth, and to morrow will he aſke it againe: ſuch an one is to be hated of God and man. 16 The foole ſaith, I haue no friends, I haue no thanke for all my good deeds: and they that eate my bread ſpeake euill of me. 17 How oft, and of how many ſhall he be laughed to ſcorne? for hee knoweth not aright what it is to haue; and it is all one vnto him, as if he had it not. 18 To ſlip vpon a pauement, is better then to ſlip with the tongue: ſo, the fall of the wicked ſhall come ſpeedily. 19 An vnſeaſonable tale will alwayes be in the mouth of the vnwiſe. 20 A wiſe ſentence ſhall be reiected when it commeth out of a fools mouth: for he will not ſpeake it in due ſeaſon. 21 There is that is hindred from ſinning through want: and when hee taketh reſt, he ſhall not be troubled. 22 There is that deſtroyeth his owne ſoule through baſhfulneſse, and by accepting of perſons ouerthroweth himſelfe. 23 There is that for baſhfulnes promiſeth to his friend, and maketh him his enemy for nothing. 24 A lie is a foule blot in a man, yet it is continually in the mouth of the vntaught. 25 A thiefe is better then a man that is accuſtomed to lie: but they both ſhall haue deſtruction to heritage. 26 The diſpoſition of a liar is diſhonourable, and his ſhame is euer with him. 27 A wiſe man ſhall promote himſelfe to honour with his words: and hee that hath vnderſtanding, will pleaſe great men. 28 He that tilleth his land, ſhall increaſe his heape: and he that pleaſeth great men, ſhal get pardon for iniquity. 29 Preſents and gifts blind the eyes of the wiſe, and ſtoppe vp his mouth that he cannot reprooue. 30 Wiſedome that is hidde, and treaſure that is hoarded vp, what profit is in them both? 31 Better is he that hideth his folly, then a man that hideth his wiſedome. 32 Neceſsary patience in ſeeking the Lord, is better then he that leadeth his life without a guide.

CHAPTER 21 1 My ſonne, haſt thou ſinned? doe ſo no more, but aſke pardon for thy former ſinnes. 2 Flee from ſinne as from the face of a Serpent: for if thou commeſt too neere it, it will bite thee: the teeth thereof, are as the teeth of a lyon, ſlaying the ſoules of men. 3 All iniquitie is as a two edged ſword, the wounds whereof cannot be healed. 4 To

terrifie and doe wrong, will waſte riches: thus the houſe of proude men
ſhalbe made deſolate.5A prayer out of a poore mans mouth reacheth to
the eares of God, and his iudgement commeth ſpeedily.6He that hateth
to be reprooued, is in the way of ſinners: but hee that feareth the Lord,
will repent from his heart.7An eloquent man is knowen farre and neere,
but a man of vnderſtanding knoweth when he ſlippeth.8He that buildeth
his houſe with other mens money, is like one that gathereth himſelfe
ſtones for the tombe of his buriall.9The congregation of the wicked is
like tow wrapped together: and the end of them is a flame of fire to
deſtroy them.10The way of ſinners is made plaine with ſtones, but at the
ende thereof is the pit of hell.11Hee that keepeth the Law of the Lord,
getteth the vnderſtanding thereof: and the perfection of the feare of the
Lord, is wiſedome.12He that is not wiſe, will not be taught: but there is
a wiſedome which multiplieth bitterneſse.13The knowledge of a wiſe
man ſhall abound like a flood: and his counſell is like a pure fountaine
of life.14The inner parts of a foole, are like a broken veſſell, and he will
holde no knowledge as long as he liueth.15If a ſkilfull man heare a wiſe
word, hee will commend it, and adde vnto it: but aſsoone as one of no
vnderſtanding heareth it, it diſpleaſeth him, and he caſteth it behinde his
backe.16The talking of a foole is like a burden in the way: but grace ſhall
be found in the lips of the wiſe.17They inquire at the mouth of the wiſe
man in the congregation, and they ſhall ponder his words in their
heart.18As is a houſe that is deſtroyed, ſo is wiſedome to a foole: and the
knowledge of the vnwiſe, is as talke without ſenſe.19Doctrine vnto
fooles, is as fetters on the feete, and like manacles on the right hand.20A
foole lifteth vp his voyce with laughter, but a wiſe man doeth ſcarce
ſmile a litle.21Learning is vnto a wiſe man, as an ornament of gold, and
like a bracelet vpon his right arme.22A fooliſh mans foote is ſoone in
hiſ *neighbourſ* houſe: but a man of experience is aſhamed of him.23A foole
will peepe in at the doore into the houſe, but he that is well nurtured,
will ſtand without.24It is the rudeneſse of a man to hearken at the doore:
but a wiſe man will be grieued with the diſgrace.25The lips of talkers will
bee telling ſuch things as pertaine not vnto them: but the words of ſuch
as haue vnderſtanding, are weighed in the ballance.26The heart of fooles
is in their mouth, but the mouth of the wiſe is in their heart.27When the
vngodly curſeth Satan, he curſeth his owne ſoule.28A whiſperer defileth
his owne ſoule, and is hated whereſoeuer hee dwelleth.
CHAPTER 22 1A ſlouthful man is compared to a filthy ſtone, and euery
one will hiſse him out to his diſgrace.2A ſlouthfull man is compared to
the filth of a dunghill: euery man that takes it vp, will ſhake his hand.3An
euill nurtured ſonne is the diſhonour of his father that begate him: and
a *fooliſh* daughter is borne to his loſse.4A wiſe daughter ſhall bring an
inheritance to her huſband: but ſhee that liueth diſhoneſtly, is her fathers
heauineſse.5Shee that is bold, diſhonoureth both her father and her
huſband, but they both ſhall deſpiſe her.6A tale out of ſeaſon *is aſ* muſick
in mourning: but ſtripes and correction of wiſedome are neuer out of
time.7Who ſo teacheth a foole, is as one that gleweth a potſheard
together, and as hee that waketh one from a ſound ſleepe.8Hee that
telleth a tale to a foole, ſpeaketh to one in a ſlumber: when hee hath told
his tale, he will ſay, What is the matter?9If children liue honeſtly, and
haue wherwithall, they ſhall couer the baſeneſse of their parents.10But
children being haughtie through diſdaine, and want of nurture, doe
ſtaine the nobilitie of their kinred.11Weepe for the dead, for hee hath
loſt the light: and weepe for the foole, for he wanteth vnderſtanding:
make litle weeping for the dead, for hee is at reſt: but the life of the foole
is worſe then death.12Seuen dayes doe men mourne for him that is dead;
but for a foole, and an vngodly man, all the dayes of his life.13Talke not
much with a foole, and goe not to him that hath no vnderſtanding,
beware of him leſt thou haue trouble, and thou ſhalt neuer be defiled
with his fooleries: depart from him, and thou ſhalt find reſt, and neuer
bee diſquieted with madneſse.14What is heauier then lead? and what is
the name thereof, but a foole?15Sand, and ſalt, and a maſſe of yron is
eaſier to beare then a man without vnderſtanding.16As timber girt and
bound together in a building, cannot be looſed with ſhaking: ſo the heart
that is ſtabliſhed by aduiſed counſel, ſhal feare at no time.17A heart ſetled
vpon a thought of vnderſtanding, is as a faire plaiſtering on the wall of
a gallerie.18Pales ſet on an high place will neuer ſtand againſt the wind:
ſo a feareful heart in the imagination of a foole, can not ſtand againſt
any feare.19He that pricketh the eye, wil make teares to fall: and he that
pricketh the heart, maketh it to ſhewe her knowledge.20Who ſo caſteth
a ſtone at the birds, frayeth them away, and he that vpbraideth his friend,
breaketh friendſhip.21Though thou dreweſt a ſword at thy friend, yet
deſpaire not, for there way be a returning (to fauour.)22If thou haſt
opened thy mouth againſt thy friend, feare not, for there may be a
reconciliation: except for vpbraiding, or pride, or diſcloſing of ſecrets,
or a treacherous wound, for, for theſe things euery friend will
depart.23Be faithfull to thy neighbour in his pouertie, that thou mayeſt
reioyce in his proſperitie: abide ſtedfaſt vnto him in the time of his
trouble, that thou mayeſt bee heire with him in his heritage: for a meane
eſtate is not alwayes to be contemned, nor the rich that is fooliſh, to be
had in admiration.24As the vapour and ſmoke of a furnace goeth before
the fire: ſo reuiling before blood.25I will not be aſhamed to defend a
friend: neither will I hide my ſelfe from him.26And if any euill happen
vnto me by him, euery one that heareth it will beware of him.27Who
ſhall ſet a watch before my mouth, and a ſeale of wiſedome vpon my
lippes, that I fall not ſuddenly by them, & that my tongue deſtroy me
not?
CHAPTER 23 1O Lord, father and gouernour of all my whole life, leaue
me not to their counſels, and let me not fall by them.2Who will ſet
ſcourges ouer my thoughts, and the diſcipline of wiſedome ouer mine
heart? that they ſpare me not for mine ignorances and it paſſe not by my
ſinnes:3Leaſt mine ignorances increaſe, and my ſinnes abound to my
deſtruction, and I fall before mine aduerſaries, and mine enemie reioyce
ouer mee, whoſe hope is farre from thy mercy.4O Lord, father and God
of my life, giue me not a proud looke, but turne away from thy ſeruants
alwaies a haughty minde:5Turne away from mee vaine hopes, and
concupiſcence, and thou ſhalt hold him vp that is deſirous alwaies to
ſerue thee.6Let not the greedineſse of the belly, nor luſt of the fleſh take
hold of me, and giue not ouer me thy ſeruant into an impudent
minde.7Heare, O yee children, the diſcipline of the mouth: He that
keepeth it, ſhall neuer be taken in his lippes.8The ſinner ſhall be left in
his fooliſhneſse: both the euill ſpeaker and the proud ſhall fall
thereby.9Accuſtome not thy mouth to ſwearing: neither vſe thy ſelfe to
the naming of the holy one.10For as a ſeruant that is continually beaten,
ſhall not be without a blew marke: ſo hee that ſweareth and nameth God
continually, ſhal not be faultleſſe.11A man that vſeth much ſwearing ſhall
be filled with iniquity, and the plague ſhall neuer depart from his houſe:
If he ſhall offend, his ſinne ſhall be vpon him: and if he acknowledge
not his ſinne, hee maketh a double offence, and if he ſweare in vaine, he
ſhall not be innocent, but his houſe ſhall be full of calamities.12There is
a word that is clothed about with death: God graunt that it be not found
in the heritage of Iacob, for all ſuch things ſhall be farre from the godly,
and they ſhall not wallow in their ſinnes.13Uſe not thy mouth to
vntemperate ſwearing, for therein is the word of ſinne.14Remember thy
father and thy mother, when thou ſitteſt among great men. Be not
forgetfull before them, and ſo thou by thy cuſtome become a foole, and
wiſh that thou hadſt not beene borne, and curſe the day of thy
natiuitie.15The man that is accuſtomed to opprobrious words, will neuer
be reformed all the daies of his life.16Two ſorts of men multiply ſinne,
and the third will bring wrath: a hot minde is as a burning fire, it will
neuer be quenched till it be conſumed: a fornicatour in the body of his
fleſh, will neuer ceaſe till he hath kindled a fire.17All bread is ſweete to a
whoremonger, he will not leaue off till he die.18A man that breaketh
wedlocke, ſaying thus in his heart, Who ſeeth me? I am compaſſed about
with darkneſſe: the walles couer me; & no body ſeeth me, what neede I
to feare? The moſt high wil not remember my ſinnes:19ſuch a man only
feareth the eies of men, and knoweth not that the eies of the Lord are
tenne thouſand times brighter then the Sunne, beholding all the waies
of men, and conſidering the moſt ſecret parts.20He knew all things ere
euer they were created, ſo alſo after they were perfited, he looked vpon
them all:21This man ſhall bee puniſhed in the ſtreets of the citie, and
where he ſuſpecteth not, he ſhall be taken.22Thus ſhall it goe alſo with
the wife, that leaueth her huſband, and bringeth in an heire by
another:23For firſt ſhe hath diſobeyed the Law of the moſt High: and
ſecondly, ſhe hath treſpaſſed againſt her owne huſband, and thirdly, ſhe
hath played the whore in adultery, and brought children by another
man.24Shee ſhall be brought out into the congregation, and inquiſition
ſhalbe made of her children.25Her children ſhall not take root, and her
branches ſhall bring foorth no fruit.26She ſhall leaue her memorie to be

curſed, and her reproch ſhall not be blotted out.27And they that remaine, ſhall know that there is nothing better then the feare of the Lord, and that there is nothing ſweeter then to take heed vnto the Commandement of the Lord.28It is great glory to follow the Lord, & to be receiued of him is long life.

CHAPTER 24 1Wiſedome ſhall praiſe her ſelfe, and ſhall glory in the midſt of her people.2In the Congregation of the moſt high, ſhall ſhe open her mouth, and triumph before his power.3I came out of the mouth of the moſt High, and couered the earth as a cloud.4I dwelt in high places, and my throne is in a cloudy pillar.5I alone compaſſed the circuit of heauen, and walked in the bottome of the deepe.6In the waues of the ſea, and in all the earth, and in euery people, and nation, I got a poſſeſſion.7With all theſe I ſought reſt: and in whoſe inheritance ſhall I abide?8So the creatour of all things gaue mee a commandement, and hee that made me, cauſed my tabernacle to reſt: and ſaid, Let thy dwelling be in Iacob, and thine inheritance in Iſrael.9Hee created mee from the beginning before the world, and I ſhall neuer faile.10In the holy Tabernacle I ſerued before him: and ſo was I eſtabliſhed in Sion.11Likewiſe in the beloued citie he gaue mee reſt, and in Ieruſalem was my power.12And I tooke roote in an honourable people, euen in the portion of the Lords inheritance.13I was exalted like a Cedar in Libanus, and as a Cypreſe tree vpon the mountaines of Hermon.14I was exalted like a palme tree in Engaddi, and as a roſe-plant in Iericho, as a faire oliue tree in a pleaſant fielde, and grew vp as a planetree by the water.15I gaue a ſweete ſmell like cinamon, and aſpalathus, and I yeelded a pleaſant odour like the beſt mirrhe, as Galbanum and Onix, and ſweet Storax, and as the ſume of franckincenſe in the Tabernacle.16As the Turpentine tree, I ſtretched out my branches, and my branches are the branches of honour and grace.17As the Uine brought I foorth pleaſant ſauour, and my flowers are the fruit of honour and riches.18I am the mother of faire loue, and feare, and knowledge, and holy hope, I therefore being eternall, am giuen to all my children which are named of him.19Come vnto me all ye that be deſirous of mee, and fill your ſelues with my fruits.20For my memorial is ſweeter then hony, and mine inheritance then the hony combe.21They that eate mee ſhall yet be hungry, and they that drinke me ſhall yet be thirſtie.22He that obeyeth me, ſhall neuer be confounded, and they that worke by me, ſhall not doe amiſse.23All theſe things are the booke of the Couenant of the moſt high God, euen the Law which Moſes commanded for an heritage vnto the Congregations of Iacob.24Faint not to bee ſtrong in the Lord; that he may confirme you, cleaue vnto him: for the Lord Almightie is God alone, and beſides him there is no other Sauiour.25He filleth all things with his wiſdome, as Phyſon, and as Tigris in the time of the new fruits.26He maketh the vnderſtanding to abound like Euphrates, and as Iorden in the time of the harueſt.27He maketh the doctrine of knowledge appeare as the light, and as Geon in the time of vintage.28The firſt man knew her not perfectly: no more ſhall the laſt finde her out.29For her thoughts are more then the ſea, and her counſels profounder then the great deepe.30I alſo came out as a brooke from a riuer, and as a conduit into a garden.31I ſaid, I will water my beſt garden, and will water abundantly my garden bedde: and loe, my brooke became a riuer, and my riuer became a ſea.32I will yet make doctrine to ſhine as the morning, and will ſend forth her light afarre off.33I will yet powre out doctrine as prophecie, and leaue it to all ages for euer.34Behold that I haue not laboured for my ſelfe onely, but for all them that ſeeke wiſedome.

CHAPTER 25 1In three things I was beautified, and ſtoode vp beautiful, both before God and men: the vnitie of brethren, the loue of neighbours, a man and a wife that agree together.2Three ſorts of men my ſoule hateth, and I am greatly offended at their life: a poore man that is proud, a rich man that is a lyar, and an olde adulterer that doteth.3If thou haſt gathered nothing in thy youth, how canſt thou finde any thing in thine age?4Oh how comely a thing is iudgement for gray haires, and for ancient men to know counſell?5Oh how comely is the wiſedome of olde men, and vnderſtanding and counſell to men of honour?6Much experience is the crowne of olde men, and the feare of God is their glory.7There be nine things which I haue iudged in mine heart to be happy, and the tenth I will vtter with my tongue: a man that hath ioy of his children, and he that liueth to ſee the fall of his enemie.8Well is him that dwelleth with a wife of vnderſtanding, and that hath not ſlipped with his tongue, and that hath not ſerued a man more vnworthy then himſelfe.9Well is him that hath found prudence, and he that ſpeaketh in the eares of him that will heare.10Oh how great is he that findeth wiſedome! yet is there none aboue him that feareth the Lord.11But the loue of the Lord paſſeth all things for illumination: he that holdeth it, whereto ſhall he be likened?12The feare of the Lord is the beginning of his loue: and faith is the beginning of cleauing vnto him.13*Giue mee* any plague, but the plague of the heart: and any wickedneſſe, but the wickedneſſe of a woman.14And any affliction, but the affliction from them that hate me: and any reuenge, but the reuenge of enemies.15There is no head aboue the head of a ſerpent, and there is no wrath aboue the wrath of an enemie.16I had rather dwell with a lyon and a dragon, then to keepe houſe with a wicked woman.17The wickedneſſe of a woman changeth her face, and darkeneth her countenance like ſackecloth.18Her huſband ſhall ſit among his neighbours: and when hee heareth it, ſhall ſigh bitterly.19All wickedneſſe is but little to the wickedneſſe of a woman: let the portion of a ſinner fall vpon her.20As the climbing vp a ſandie way is to the feete of the aged, ſo is a wife full of words to a quiet man.21Stumble not at the beautie of a woman, and deſire her not for pleaſure.22A woman, if ſhee maintaine her huſband, is full of anger, impudencie, and much reproch.23A wicked woman abateth the courage, maketh a heauie countenance, and a wounded heart: a woman that will not comfort her huſband in diſtreſſe maketh weake hands, and feeble knees.24Of the woman came the beginning of ſinne, & through her wee all die.25Giue the water no paſsage: neither a wicked woman libertie to gad abroad.26If ſhe goe not as thou wouldeſt haue her, cut her off from thy fleſh, and giue her a bill of diuorce, and let her goe.

CHAPTER 26 1Bleſſed is the man that hath a vertuous wife, for the number of his dayes ſhall be double.2A vertuous woman reioyceth her huſband, and he ſhall fulfill the yeeres of his life in peace.3A good wife is a good portion, which ſhall be giuen in the portion of them that feare the Lord.4Whether a man be rich or poore, if he haue a good heart towards the Lord, he ſhall at all times reioyce with a cheerefull countenance.5There bee three things that mine heart feareth: and for the fourth I was ſore afraid: the ſlander of a citie, the gathering together of an vnruly multitude, and a falſe accuſation: all theſe are worſe then death.6But a griefe of heart and ſorrow, is a woman that is ielous ouer another woman, and a ſcourge of the tongue which communicateth withall.7An euil wife is a yoke ſhaken to and fro: he that hath hold of her, is as though he held a ſcorpion.8A drunken woman and a gadder abroad, cauſeth great anger, and ſhee will not couer her owne ſhame.9The whordome of a woman may be knowen in her haughtie lookes, and eye lids.10If thy daughter be ſhameleſſe, keepe her in ſtraitly: leſt ſhe abuſe her ſelfe through ouermuch libertie.11Watch ouer an impudent eye: and marueile not, if ſhee treſpaſſe againſt thee.12Shee will open her mouth as a thirſtie traueiler, when he hath found a fountaine: and drinke of euery water neere her: by euery hedge will ſhe ſit downe, and open her quiuer againſt euery arrow.13The grace of a wife delighteth her huſband, and her diſcretion will fat his bones.14A ſilent and louing woman is a gift of the Lord, and there is nothing ſo much worth, as a mind well inſtructed.15A ſhamefaſt and faithfull woman is a double grace, and her continent mind cannot be valued.16As the Sunne when it Ariſeth in the high heauen: ſo is the beautie of a good wife in the ordering of her houſe.17As the cleare light is vpon the holy candleſticke: ſo is the beautie of the face in ripe age.18As the golden pillars are vpon the ſockets of ſiluer: ſo are the faire feete with a conſtant heart.19My ſonne, keepe the flowre of thine age ſound: and giue not thy ſtrength to ſtrangers.20When thou haſt gotten a fruitfull poſſeſſion through all the field: ſowe it with thine owne ſeede, truſting in the goodneſſe of thy ſtocke.21So thy race which thou leaueſt ſhalbe magnified, hauing the confidence of their good deſcent.22An harlot ſhall bee accounted as ſpittle: but a maried woman is a towre againſt death to her huſband.23A wicked woman is giuen as a portion to a wicked man: but a godly woman is giuen to him that feareth the Lord.24A diſhoneſt woman contemneth ſhame, but an honeſt woman will reuerence her huſband.25A ſhameleſſe woman ſhalbe counted as a dog: but ſhe that is ſhamefaſt will feare the Lord.26A woman that honoureth her huſband, ſhall bee iudged wiſe of all: but ſhe that diſhonoureth him in her pride, ſhall be counted vngodly of all.[27]A loude crying woman, and a ſcolde, ſhall be ſought out to driue away the enemies.[28]There be two things that grieue my heart: and the third maketh me angry: a man of warre that ſuffereth pouerty, and men of vnderſtanding that are not ſet by: and one that returneth from righteouſneſſe to ſinne: the Lord prepareth ſuch a one for the ſword.[29]A merchant ſhall hardly keepe himſelfe from doing wrong: and an huckſter ſhall not be freed from ſinne.

CHAPTER 27 [1]Many haue ſinned for a ſmal matter: & he that ſeeketh for abundance will turne his eies away.[2]As a naile ſticketh faſt betweene the ioynings of the ſtones: ſo doth ſinne ſticke cloſe betweene buying and ſelling.[3]Unleſſe a man hold himſelfe diligently in the feare of the Lord, his houſe ſhall ſoone be ouerthrowen.[4]As when one ſifteth with a ſieue, the refuſe remaineth, ſo the filth of man in his talke.[5]The furnace prooueth the potters veſſell: ſo the triall of man is in his reaſoning.[6]The fruite declareth if the tree haue beene dreſſed: ſo is the vtterance of a conceit in the heart of man.[7]Praiſe no man before thou heareſt him ſpeake, for this is the triall of men.[8]If thou followeſt righteouſneſſe, thou ſhalt obtaine her, and put her on, as a glorious long robe.[9]The birds will reſort vnto their like, ſo will truth returne vnto them that practiſe in her.[10]As the Lyon lieth in waite for the pray: ſo ſinne for them that worke iniquity.[11]The diſcourſe of a godly man is alwaies with wiſedome: but a foole changeth as the Moone.[12]If thou be among the vndiſcreet, obſerue the time: but be continually among men of vnderſtanding.[13]The diſcourſe of fooles is irkſome, and their ſport is in the wantonneſse of ſinne.[14]The talke of him that ſweareth much, maketh the haire ſtand vpright: and their braules make one ſtop his eares.[15]The ſtrife of the proud is blood-ſhedding, and their reuilings are grieuous to the eare.[16]Who ſo diſcouereth ſecrets, looſeth his credit: and ſhall neuer find friend to his minde.[17]Loue thy friend, and be faithfull vnto him: but if thou bewrayeſt his ſecrets, follow no more after him.[18]For as a man hath deſtroyed his enemie: ſo haſt thou loſt the loue of thy neighbour.[19]As one that letteth a bird goe out of his hand, ſo haſt thou let thy neighbour goe; and ſhalt not get him againe.[20]Follow after him no more, for he is too far off, he is as a roe eſcaped out of the ſnare.[21]As for a wound it may be bound vp, and after reuiling there may be reconcilement: but he that bewrayeth ſecrets is without hope.[22]He that winketh with the eies worketh euil, and he that knoweth him will depart from him.[23]When thou art preſent he will ſpeake ſweetly, and will admire thy words: but at the laſt he will writhe his mouth, and ſlander thy ſayings.[24]I haue hated many things, but nothing like him, for the Lord will hate him.[25]Who ſo caſteth a ſtone on high, caſteth it on his owne head, and a deceitfull ſtroke ſhall make wounds.[26]Who ſo diggeth a pit ſhall fall therein: and he that ſetteth a trap ſhall be taken therein.[27]He that worketh miſchiefe, it ſhall fall vpon him, and he ſhall not know whence it commeth.[28]Mockery and reproach are from the proud: but vengeance as a Lyon ſhall lie in waite for them.[29]They that reioyce at the fall of the righteous ſhalbe taken in the ſnare, and anguiſh ſhall conſume them before they die.[30]Malice and wrath, euen theſe are abhominations, and the ſinfull man ſhall haue them both.

CHAPTER 28 [1]He that reuengeth ſhall find vengeance from the Lord, and he will ſurely keepe his ſinnes (in remembrance.)[2]Forgiue thy neighbour the hurt that he hath done vnto thee, ſo ſhall thy ſinnes alſo be forgiuen when thou prayeſt.[3]One man beareth hatred againſt another, and doeth he ſeeke pardon from the Lord?[4]Hee ſheweth no mercy to a man, which is like himſelfe: and doeth hee aſke forgiueneſse of his owne ſinnes?[5]If he that is but fleſh nouriſh hatred, who will intreat for pardon of his ſinnes?[6]Remember thy end, and let enimitie ceaſe, *remember* corruption and death, and abide in the Commandements.[7]Remember the Commaundements, & beare no malice to thy neighbour: *remember* the Couenant of the higheſt, and winke at ignorance.[8]Abſtaine from ſtrife, and thou ſhalt diminiſh thy ſinnes: for a furious man will kindle ſtrife.[9]A ſinfull man diſquieteth friends, and maketh debate among them that be at peace.[10]As the matter of the fire is, ſo it burneth: and as a mans ſtrength is, ſo is his wrath, and according to his riches his anger riſeth, and the ſtronger they are which contend, the more they will be inflamed.[11]An haſtie contention kindleth a fire, and an haſty fighting ſheddeth blood.[12]If thou blow the ſparke, it ſhall burne: if thou ſpit vpon it, it ſhall bee quenched, and both theſe come out of thy mouth.[13]Curſe the whiſperer, and double tongued: for ſuch haue deſtroyed many that were at peace.[14]A backbiting tongue hath diſquieted many, and driuen them from nation to nation, ſtrong cities hath it pulled down, and ouerthrowen the houſes of great men.[15]A backbiting tongue hath caſt out vertuous women, and depriued them of their labours.[16]Who ſo hearkeneth vnto it, ſhall neuer finde reſt, and neuer dwel quietly.[17]The ſtroke of the whip maketh markes in the fleſh, but the ſtroke of the tongue breaketh the bones.[18]Many haue fallen by the edge of the ſword: but not ſo many as haue fallen by the tongue.[19]Well is hee that is defended from it, and hath not paſſed through the venime thereof: who hath not drawen the yoke thereof, nor hath bene bound in her bands.[20]For the yoke thereof is a yoke of yron, and the bands thereof are bandes of braſſe.[21]The death therof is an euil death, the graue were better then it.[22]It ſhall not haue rule ouer them that feare God, neither ſhall they be burnt with the flame thereof.[23]ſuch as forſake the Lord ſhall fall into it, and it ſhall burne in them, and not be quenched, it ſhalbe ſent vpon them as a Lion, and deuoure them as a Leopard.[24]Looke that thou hedge thy poſſeſſion about with thornes, and binde vp thy ſiluer and gold:[25]And weigh thy words in a ballance, and make a doore and barre for thy mouth.[26]Beware thou ſlide not by it, leſt thou fall before him that lieth in wait.

CHAPTER 29 [1]Hee that is mercifull, will lende vnto his neighbour, and hee that ſtrengthneth his hande, keepeth the Commandements.[2]Lend to thy neighbour in time of his need, and pay thou thy neighbour againe in due ſeaſon.[3]Keepe thy word & deale faithfully with him, and thou ſhalt alwaies finde the thing that is neceſsary for thee.[4]Many when a thing was lent them, reckoned it to be found, and put them to trouble that helped them.[5]Till he hath receiued, he will kiſſe a mans hand: and for his neighbours money he will ſpeake ſubmiſsely: but when he ſhould repay, he will prolong the time, and returne words of griefe, and complaine of the time.[6]If he preuaile, he ſhall hardly receiue the halfe, and he will count as if he had found it: if not; he hath depriued him of his money, and he hath gotten him an enemy without cauſe: he payeth him with curſings, and raylings: and for honour he will pay him diſgrace.[7]Many therefore haue refuſed to lend for other mens ill dealing, fearing to be defrauded.[8]Yet haue thou patience with a man in poore eſtate, and delay not to ſhew him mercy.[9]Helpe the poore for the commandements ſake, and turne him not away becauſe of his pouertie.[10]Loſe thy money for thy brother and thy friend, and let it not ruſt vnder a ſtone to be loſt.[11]Lay vp thy treaſure according to the commandements of the moſt high, and it ſhall bring thee more profite then golde.[12]ſhut vp almes in thy ſtorehouſes: and it ſhall deliuer thee from all affliction.[13]It ſhal fight for thee againſt thine enemies, better then a mightie ſhield and ſtrong ſpeare.[14]An honeſt man is ſuretie for his neighbour: but hee that is impudent, will forſake him.[15]Forget not the friendſhip of thy ſuretie: for hee hath giuen his life for thee.[16]A ſinner will ouerthrow the good eſtate of his ſuretie:[17]And he that is of an vnthankfull minde, will leaue him in *danger* that deliuered him.[18]Suretiſhip hath vndone many of good eſtate, and ſhaked them as a waue of the ſea: mightie men hath it driuen from their houſes, ſo that they wandred among ſtrange nations.[19]A wicked man tranſgreſsing the commandements of the Lord, ſhall fall into ſuretiſhip: and hee that vndertaketh and followeth other mens buſineſse for gaine, ſhall fall into ſuits.[20]Helpe thy neighbour according to thy power, and beware that thou thy ſelfe fall not into the ſame.[21]The chiefe thing for life is water and bread, and clothing, and an houſe to couer ſhame.[22]Better is the life of a poore man in a meane cottage, then delicate fare in another mans houſe.[23]Be it little or much, holde thee contented, that thou heare not the reproch of thy houſe.[24]For it is a miſerable life to goe from houſe to houſe: for where thou art a ſtranger, thou dareſt not open thy mouth.[25]Thou ſhalt entertaine and feaſt, and haue no thankes: moreouer, thou ſhalt heare bitter words.[26]Come thou ſtranger, and furniſh a table, and feede me of that thou haſt ready.[27]Giue place thou ſtranger to an honourable man, my brother commeth to be lodged, and I haue neede of mine houſe.[28]Theſe things are grieuous to a man of vnderſtanding: the vpbraiding of houſe-roome, and reproching of the lender.

CHAPTER 30 [1]Hee that loueth his ſonne, cauſeth him oft to feele the rodde, that hee may haue ioy of him in the end.[2]He that chaſtiſeth his ſonne, ſhall haue ioy in him, and ſhall reioyce of him among his

acquaintance.3He that teacheth his ſonne, grieueth the enemie: and
before his friends he ſhall reioyce of him.4Though his father die, yet he
is as though hee were not dead: for hee hath left one behinde him that
is like himſelfe.5While he liued, he ſaw and reioyced in him: and when
he died hee was not ſorrowfull.6He left behinde him an auenger againſt
his enemies, and one that ſhall requite kindneſſe to his friends.7He that
maketh too much of his ſonne, ſhall binde vp his wounds, and his
bowels wil be troubled at euery cry.8An horſe not broken becommeth
headſtrong: and a childe left to himſelfe will be wilfull.9Cocker thy
childe, and hee ſhall make thee afraid: play with him, and he will bring
thee to heauineſse.10Laugh not with him, leſt thou haue ſorrow with
him, and leſt thou gnaſh thy teeth in the end.11Giue him no liberty in his
youth, and winke not at his follies.12Bow downe his necke while hee is
young, and beate him on the ſides while he is a childe, leſt hee waxe
ſtubborne, and be diſobedient vnto thee, and ſo bring ſorrow to thine
heart.13Chaſtiſe thy ſonne, and hold him to labour, leſt his lewd
behauiour be an offence vnto thee.14Better is the poore being ſound and
ſtrong of conſtitution, then a rich man that is afflicted in his
body.15Health and good ſtate of body are aboue all gold, and a ſtrong
body aboue infinite wealth.16There is no riches aboue a ſound body, and
no ioy aboue the ioy of the heart.17Death is better then a bitter life, or
continuall ſickeneſse.18Delicates powred vpon a mouth ſhut vp, are as
meſses of meat ſet vpon a graue.19What good doth the offering vnto an
idole? for neither can it eat nor ſmell: ſo is he that is perſecuted of the
Lord.20Hee ſeeth with his eyes and groneth, as an Eunuch that
embraceth a virgine, and ſigheth.21Giue not ouer thy mind to heauineſse,
and afflict not thy ſelfe in thine owne counſell.22The gladneſſe of the
heart is the life of man, and the ioyfulnes of a man prolongeth his
dayes.23Loue thine owne ſoule, and comfort thy heart, remoue ſorrow
far from thee: for ſorrow hath killed many, and there is no profit
therein.24Enuie and wrath ſhorten the life, and carefulneſse bringeth age
before the time.25A cherefull and good heart will haue a care of his meat
and diet.

CHAPTER 31 1Watching for riches, conſumeth the fleſh, and the care
therof driueth away ſleepe.2Watching care will not let a man ſlumber, as
a ſore diſeaſe breaketh ſleepe.3The rich hath great labour in gathering
riches together, and when he reſteth, he is filled with his delicates.4The
poore laboureth in his poore eſtate, and when he leaueth off, hee is ſtill
needie.5He that loueth gold ſhall not bee iuſtified, and he that followeth
corruption, ſhall haue enough thereof.6Gold hath bin the ruine of many,
and their deſtruction was preſent.7It is a ſtumbling block vnto them that
ſacrifice vnto it, and euery foole ſhall be taken therewith.8Bleſſed is the
rich that is found without blemiſh, and hath not gone after gold:9Who
is he? and we will call him bleſſed: for wonderfull things hath hee done
among his people.10Who hath bene tried thereby, and found perfit? then
let him glory. Who might offend and hath not offended, or done euill,
and hath not done it?11His goods ſhall be eſtabliſhed, and the
congregatiō ſhall declare his almes.12If thou ſit at a bountifull table, bee
not greedy vpon it, and ſay not, There is much meate on it.13Remember
that a wicked eye is an euill thing: and what is created more wicked then
an eye? therefore it weepeth vpon euery occaſion.14Stretch not thine
hand whitherſoeuer it looketh, and thruſt it not with him into the
diſh.15Iudge of thy neighbour by thy ſelfe: and be diſcreet in euery
point.16Eate as it becommeth a man thoſe things which are ſet before
thee: and deuoure not, leſt thou be hated.17Leaue off firſt for maners
ſake, and be not vnſatiable, leſt thou offend.18When thou ſitteſt among
many, reach not thine hand out firſt of all.19A very litle is ſufficient for
a man well nurtured, and he fetcheth not his wind ſhort vpon his
bed.20Sound ſleepe commeth of moderate eating: he riſeth early, and his
wits are with him, but the paine of watching and choller, and pangs of
the bellie are with an vnſatiable man.21And if thou haſt bin forced to
eate, Ariſe, goe forth, vomit, and thou ſhalt haue reſt.22My ſonne, heare
me, and deſpiſe me not, and at the laſt thou ſhalt finde as I told thee: in
all thy workes bee quicke, ſo ſhall there no ſickeneſse come vnto
thee.23Who ſo is liberall of his meat, men ſhall ſpeake well of him, and
the report of his good houſekeeping will be beleeued.24But againſt him
that is a niggard of his meate, the whole citie ſhall murmure; and the
teſtimonies of his niggardneſse ſhall not be doubted of.25ſhew not thy
valiantneſse in wine, for wine hath deſtroyed many.26The furnace
prooueth the edge by dipping: ſo doth wine the hearts of the proud by
drunkenneſse.27Wine is as good as life to a man if it be drunke
moderatly: what life is then to a man that is without wine? for it was
made to make men glad.28Wine meaſurably drunke, and in ſeaſon,
bringeth gladneſſe of the heart and cheerefulneſse of the minde.29But
wine drunken with exceſse, maketh bitterneſse of the minde, with
brawling and quarreling.30Drunkenneſse increaſeth the rage of a foole
till he offend, it diminiſheth ſtrength, and maketh wounds.31Rebuke not
thy neighbour at the wine, and deſpiſe him not in his mirth: giue him no
deſpitefull words, and preſse not vpon him with vrging him (to drinke.)

CHAPTER 32 1If thou be made the maſter (of the feaſt) lift not thy
ſelfe vp, but bee among them as one of the reſt, take diligent care for
them, and ſo ſit downe.2And when thou haſt done all thy office, take
thy place that thou mayeſt be merry with them, and receiue a crowne
for thy well ordering of the feaſt.3Speake thou that art the elder, for it
becometh thee, but with ſound iudgement, and hinder not
muſicke.4Powre not out words where there is a muſitian, and ſhew not
forth wiſedome out of time.5A conſort of muſicke in a banket of wine,
is as a ſignet of Carbuncle ſet in gold.6As a ſignet of an Emeraud ſet in
a worke of gold, ſo is the melodie of muſicke with pleaſant wine.7Speake
yong man, if there be need of thee: and yet ſcarſely when thou art twiſe
aſked:8Let thy ſpeach be ſhort, comprehending much in few words, be
as one that knoweth, and yet holdeth his tongue.9If thou be among great
men, make not thy ſelfe equall with them, and when ancient men are in
place, vſe not many words.10Before the thunder goeth lightening: and
before a ſhamefaſt man ſhall goe fauour.11Riſe vp betimes, and be not
the laſt: but get thee home without delay.12There take thy paſtime, & do
what thou wilt: but ſinne not by proud ſpeach13And for theſe things
bleſſe him that made thee, and hath repleniſhed thee with his good
things.14Who ſo feareth the Lord, will receiue his diſcipline, and they
that ſeeke him early, ſhall find fauour.15He that ſeeketh the law, ſhall be
filled therewith: but the hypocrite will be offended thereat.16They that
feare the Lord ſhall find iudgement, and ſhall kindle iuſtice as a light.17A
ſinfull man will not be reproued, but findeth an excuſe according to his
will.18A man of counſell will be conſiderate, but a ſtrange and proud
man is not daunted with feare, euen when of himſelfe he hath done
without counſell.19Doe nothing without aduice, and when thou haſt
once done, repent not.20Goe not in a way wherein thou maieſt fall, and
ſtumble not among the ſtones.21Be not confident in a plaine way.22And
beware of thine owne children.23In euery good worke truſt thy owne
ſoule: for this is the keeping of the commandements.24He that beleeueth
in the Lord, taketh heed to the commandement, and he that truſted in
him, ſhall fare neuer the worſe.

CHAPTER 33 1There ſhall no euill happen vnto him that feareth the
Lord, but in temptation euen againe he will deliuer him.2A wiſe man
hateth not the Law, but he that is an hypocrite therein, is as a ſhip in a
ſtorme.3A man of vnderſtanding truſteth in the Law, and the Law is
faithfull vnto him, as an oracle.4Prepare what to ſay, and ſo thou ſhalt
be heard, and binde vp inſtruction, and then make anſwere.5The heart
of the fooliſh is like a cartwheele: and his thoughts are like a rolling
axeltree.6A ſtallion horſe is as a mocking friend, hee neigheth vnder
euery one that ſitteth vpon him.7Why doth one day excell another?
when as all the light of euery day in the yeere is of the Sunne.8By the
knowledge of the Lord they were diſtinguiſhed: and he altered ſeaſons
and feaſts.9Some of them hath hee made high dayes, and hallowed them,
and ſome of them hath hee made ordinary dayes.10And all men are from
the ground, and Adam was created of earth.11In much knowledge the
Lord hath diuided them, and made their wayes diuers.12Some of them
hath hee bleſſed, and exalted, and ſome of them hath hee ſanctified, and
ſet neere himſelfe: but ſome of them hath hee curſed, and brought low,
and turned out of their places.13As the clay is in the potters hand to
faſhion it at his pleaſure: ſo man is in the hand of him that made him,
to render to them as liketh him beſt.14Good is ſet againſt euill, and life
againſt death: ſo is the godly againſt the ſinner, and the ſinner againſt
the godly.15So looke vpon all the workes of the moſt High, and there
are two and two, one againſt another.16I awaked vp laſt of all, as one
that gathereth after the grape-gatherers: by the bleſſing of the Lord I
profited, and filled my wine-preſse, like a gatherer of grapes.17Conſider
that I laboured not for my ſelfe onely, but for all them that ſeeke

learning;18Heare me, O ye great men of the people, and hearken with your eares ye rulers of the Congregation:19Giue not thy ſonne, and wife, thy brother and friend power ouer thee while thou liueſt, and giue not thy goods to another, leſt it repent thee: and thou intreat for the ſame againe.20As long as thou liueſt and haſt breath in thee, giue not thy ſelfe ouer to any.21For better it is that thy children ſhould ſeeke to thee, then that thou ſhouldſt ſtand to their courteſie.22In all thy workes keepe to thy ſelfe the preheminence, leaue not a ſtaine in thine honour.23At the time when thou ſhalt end thy dayes, and finiſh thy life, diſtribute thine inheritance.24Fodder, a wand, and burdens, are for the aſſe: and bread, correction, and worke for a ſeruant.25If thou ſet thy ſeruant to labour, thou ſhalt finde reſt: but if thou let him goe idle, he ſhall ſeeke libertie.26A yoke and a collar doe bow the necke: ſo are tortures and torments for an euill ſeruant.27Sende him to labour that hee be not idle: for idleneſse teacheth much euill.28Set him to worke, as is fit for him; if he be not obedient, put on more heauy fetters.29But be not exceſsiue toward any, and without diſcretion doe nothing.30If thou haue a ſeruant, let him bee vnto thee as thy ſelfe, becauſe thou haſt bought him with a price.31If thou haue a ſeruant, intreate him as a brother: for thou haſt neede of him, as of thine owne ſoule: if thou intreate him euill, and he runne from thee, which way wilt thou goe to ſeeke him?

CHAPTER 34 1The hopes of a man voyd of vnderſtanding are vaine, and falſe: and dreames lift vp fooles.2Who ſo regardeth dreames, is like him that catcheth at a ſhadow, and followeth after the winde.3The viſion of dreames is the reſemblance of one thing to another, euen as the likeneſſe of a face to a face.4Of an vncleane thing, what can be cleanſed? and from that thing which is falſe, what trueth can come?5Diuinations, and ſoothſayings, and dreames are vaine: and the heart fancieth as a womans heart in trauell.6If they be not ſent from the moſt high in thy viſitation, ſet not thy heart vpon them.7For dreames haue deceiued many, and they haue failed that put their truſt in them.8The Law ſhall be found perfect without lies: and wiſedome is perfection to a faithfull mouth.9A man that hath trauailed knoweth many things: and hee that hath much experience, wil declare wiſedome.10He that hath no experience, knoweth little: but he that hath trauailed, is full of prudence.11When I trauailed, I ſaw many things: and I vnderſtand more, then I can expreſse.12I was oft times in danger of death, yet I was deliuered becauſe of theſe things.13The ſpirit of thoſe that feare the Lord ſhall liue, for their hope is in him that ſaueth them.14Who ſo feareth the Lord, ſhall not feare nor be afraid, for hee is his hope.15Bleſſed is the ſoule of him that feareth the Lord: to whom doeth hee looke? and who is his ſtrength?16For the eyes of the Lord are vpon them that loue him, he is their mightie protection, and ſtrong ſtay, a defence from heat, and a couer from the Sunne at noone, a preſeruation from ſtumbling, and a helpe from falling.17He raiſeth vp the ſoule, and lighteneth the eyes: hee giueth health, life, and bleſſing.18Hee that ſacrificeth of a thing wrongfully gotten, his offering is ridiculous, and the giftes of vniuſt men are not accepted.19The moſt high is not pleaſed with the offerings of the wicked, neither is he pacified for ſinne by the multitude of ſacrifices.20Who ſo bringeth an offering of the goods of the poore, doeth as one that killeth the ſonne before his fathers eyes.21The bread of the needie, is their life: he that defraudeth him thereof, is a man of blood.22Hee that taketh away his neighbours liuing, ſlayeth him: and hee that defraudeth the labourer of his hire, is a bloodſhedder.23When one buildeth, and another pulleth downe, what profite haue they then but labour?24When one prayeth, and another curſeth, whoſe voice will the Lorde heare?25He that waſheth himſelfe after the touching of a dead body, if he touch it againe, what auaileth his waſhing?26So is it with a man that faſteth for his ſinnes, and goeth againe and doeth the ſame: who will heare his prayer, or what doeth his humbling profit him?

CHAPTER 351Hee that keepeth the law, bringeth offerings enow: he that taketh heed to the commandement, offereth a peace offering.2He that requiteth a good turne, offereth fine floure: and he that giueth almes, ſacrificeth praiſe.3To depart from wickedneſſe is a thing pleaſing to the Lord: and to forſake vnrighteouſneſſe, is a propitiation.4Thou ſhalt not appeare emptie before the Lord:5For all theſe thingſ *are to bee done* becauſe of the commandement.6The offering of the righteous maketh the Altar fat, and the ſweete ſauour thereof is before the moſt high.7The ſacrifice of a iuſt man is acceptable, and the memoriall thereof ſhall neuer be forgotten.8Giue the Lord his honour with a good eye, and diminiſh not the firſt fruits of thine hands.9In all thy gifts ſhew a cheerefull countenance, and dedicate thy tithes with gladneſſe.10Giue vnto the moſt high, according as hee hath enriched thee, and as thou haſt gotten, giue with a cheerefull eye.11For the Lord recompenſeth, and will giue thee ſeuen times as much.12Doe not thinke to corrupt with gifts, for ſuch he will not receiue: and truſt not to vnrighteous ſacrifices, for the Lord is iudge, and with him is no reſpect of perſons.13Hee will not accept any perſon againſt a poore man: but will heare the prayer of the oppreſſed.14He will not deſpiſe the ſupplication of the fatherleſſe: nor the widowe when ſhe powreth out her complaint.15Doeth not the teares run downe the widowes cheeks? and is not her crie againſt him that cauſeth them to fall?16He that ſerueth the Lord, ſhall be accepted with fauour, and his prayer ſhall reach vnto the cloudes.17The prayer of the humble pierceth the clouds: and till it come nigh he will not be comforted: and will not depart till the moſt High ſhall beholde to iudge righteouſly, and execute iudgement.18For the Lord wil not be ſlacke, neither will the mightie be patient towards them, till he hath ſmitten in ſunder the loines of the vnmercifull, and repaid vengeance to the heathen: till he haue taken away the multitude of the proud, and broken the ſcepter of the vnrighteous:19Till he haue rendred to euery man according to his deeds, and to the works of men according to their deuiſes, till he haue iudged the cauſe of his people: and made them to reioyce in his mercie,20Mercie is ſeaſonable in the time of affliction, as cloudes of raine in the time of drought.

CHAPTER 36 1Haue mercie vpon vs, O Lord God of all, and behold vs:2And ſend thy feare vpon all the nations that ſeeke not after thee.3Lift vp thy hand againſt the ſtrange nations, and let them ſee thy power.4As thou waſt ſanctified in vs before them: ſo be thou magnified among them before vs.5And let them know thee, as we haue knowen thee, that there is no God, but onely thou, O God.6ſhew new ſignes, and make other ſtrange wonders: glorifie thy hand and thy right arme, that they may ſet forth thy wonderous workes.7Raiſe vp indignation, and powre out wrath: take away the aduerſarie and deſtroy the enemie.8Make the time ſhort, remember the couenant, and let them declare thy wonderfull works.9Let him that eſcapeth, be conſumed by the rage of the fire, and let them periſh that oppreſſe the people.10Smite in ſunder the heads of the rulers of the heathen, that ſay, There is none other but we.11Gather all the tribes of Iacob together, and inherit thou them, as from the beginning.12O Lord haue mercie vpon the people, that is called by thy name, and vpon Iſrael, whom thou haſt named thy firſt borne.13O bee mercifull vnto Ieruſalem thy holy citie, the place of thy reſt.14Fill Sion with thine vnſpeakable oracles, and thy people with thy glory.15Giue teſtimonie vnto thoſe that thou haſt poſſeſſed from the beginning, and raiſe vp prophets that haue bin in thy name.16Reward them that wait for thee, and let thy prophets be found faithfull.17O Lord heare the prayer of thy ſeruants, according to the bleſſing of Aaron ouer thy people, that all they which dwel vpon the earth, may know that thou art the Lord, the eternall God.18The belly deuoureth all meates, yet is one meat better then another.19As the palate taſteth diuers kinds of veniſon: ſo doth an heart of vnderſtanding falſe ſpeeches.20A froward heart cauſeth heauineſse: but a man of experience will recompenſe him.21A woman will receiue euery man, yet is one daughter better then another22The beautie of a woman cheareth the countenance, and a man loueth nothing better.23If there be kindneſse, meekenes, and comfort in her tongue, then is not her huſband like other men.24He that getteth a wife, beginneth a poſſeſſion, a helpe like vnto himſelfe, and a pillar of reſt.25Where no hedge is, there the poſſeſſion is ſpoiled: and he that hath no wife will wander vp and downe mourning.26Who will truſt a thiefe well appointed, that ſkippeth from citie to citie? ſo *who will beleeue* a man that hath no houſe? and lodgeth whereſoeuer the night taketh him?

CHAPTER 37 1Euery friend ſaieth, I am his friend alſo: but there is a friend which is onely a friend in name.2Is it not a griefe vnto death, when a companion and friend is turned to an enemie?3O wicked imagination, whence cameſt thou in to couer the earth with deceit?4There is a companion, which reioyceth in the proſperity of a friend: but in the time of trouble will be againſt him.5There is a companion which helpeth his friend for the belly, and taketh vp the buckler againſt the enemie.6Forget not thy friend in thy minde, and be not vnmindfull of him in thy

riches.7Euery counſeller extolleth counſell; but there is ſome that
counſelleth for himſelfe.8Beware of a counſeller, and know before what
neede he hath (for he will counſell for himſelfe) leſt hee caſt the lot vpon
thee:9And ſay vnto thee, Thy way is good: and afterward he ſtand on
the other ſide, to ſee what ſhall befall thee.10Conſult not with one that
ſuſpecteth thee: and hide thy counſell from ſuch as enuie thee.11Neither
conſult with a woman touching her of whom ſhe is iealous; neither with
a coward in matters of warre, nor with a merchant concerning exchange;
nor with a buyer of ſelling; nor with an enuious man of thankfulneſse;
nor with an vnmercifull man touching kindneſse; nor with the ſlouthfull
for any worke; nor with an hireling for a yeere, of finiſhing worke; nor
with an idle ſeruant of much buſineſse: Hearken not vnto theſe in any
matter of counſell.12But be continually with a godly man, whom thou
knoweſt to keepe the commandements of the Lord, whoſe minde is
according to thy minde, and will ſorrow with thee, if thou ſhalt
miſcarry.13And let the counſell of thine owne heart ſtand: for there is no
man more faithfull vnto thee then it.14For a mans minde is ſometime
wont to tell him more then ſeuen watchmen, that ſit aboue in an high
towre.15And aboue all this pray to the moſt high, that he will direct thy
way in trueth.16Let reaſon goe before euery enterpriſe, & counſell before
euery action.17The countenance is a ſigne of changing of the
heart.18Foure maner of things appeare: good and euill, life and death:
but the tongue ruleth ouer them continually.19There is one that is wiſe
and teacheth many, and yet is vnprofitable to himſelfe.20There is one
that ſheweth wiſedome in words, and is hated: he ſhall be deſtitute of all
foode.21For grace is not giuen him from the Lord: becauſe he is depriued
of all wiſedome.22Another is wiſe to himſelfe: and the fruits of
vnderſtanding are commendable in his mouth.23A wiſe man inſtructeth
his people, and the fruits of his vnderſtanding faile not.24A wiſe man
ſhall be filled with bleſſing, and all they that ſee him, ſhall count him
happy.25The daies of the life of man may be numbred: but the daies of
Iſrael are innumerable.26A wiſe man ſhall inherite glory among his
people, and his name ſhalbe perpetuall.27My ſonne prooue thy ſoule in
thy life, and ſee what is euill for it, and giue not that vnto it.28For all
things are not profitable for all men, neither hath euery ſoule pleaſure in
euery thing.29Be not vnſatiable in any dainty thing: nor too greedy vpon
meates.30For exceſse of meates, bringeth ſickneſse, and ſurfetting will
turne into choler.31By ſurfetting haue many periſhed, but hee that taketh
heed, prolongeth his life.
CHAPTER 38 1Honour a Phiſitian with the honour due vnto him, for
the vſes which you may haue of him: for the Lord hath created him.2For
of the moſt High commeth healing, and he ſhall receiue honour of the
King.3The ſkill of the Phiſitian ſhall lift vp his head: and in the ſight of
great men he ſhalbe in admiration.4The Lord hath created medicines out
of the earth; and he that is wiſe will not abhorre them.5Was not the
water made ſweet with wood, that the vertue thereof might be
knowen?6And he hath giuen men ſkill, that hee might be honoured in
his marueilous workes.7With ſuch doeth he heale *men,* and taketh away
their paines.8Of ſuch doeth the Apothecarie make a confection; and of
his workes there is no end, and from him is peace ouer all the earth.9My
ſonne, in thy ſickeneſse be not negligent: but pray vnto the Lord, and
he will make thee whole.10Leaue off from ſinne, and order thy hands
aright, and cleanſe thy heart from all wickedneſſe.11Giue a ſweet ſauour,
and a memoriall of fine flowre: and make a fat offering, as not
being.12Then giue place to the phiſitian, for the Lord hath created him:
let him not go from thee, for thou haſt need of him.13There is a time
when in their hands there is good ſucceſse.14For they ſhall alſo pray vnto
the Lord, that hee would proſper that, which they giue, for eaſe and
remedy to prolong life.15He that ſinneth before his maker, let him fal
into the hand of the Phiſitian.16My ſonne, let teares fall downe ouer the
dead, and begin to lament, as if thou hadſt ſuffered great harme thy ſelfe:
and then couer his body according to the cuſtome, & neglect not his
buriall.17Weepe bitterly, and make great moane, and vſe lamentation, as
hee is worthy, and that a day or two, leſt thou be euill ſpoken of: and
then comfort thy ſelfe for thy heauineſse.18For of heauineſse commeth
death, and the heauineſse of the heart, breaketh ſtrength.19In affliction
alſo ſorrow remaineth: and the life of the poore, is the curſe of the
heart.20Take no heauines to heart: driue it away, and remember the laſt
end.21Forget it not, for there is no turning againe: thou ſhalt not doe him
good, but hurt thy ſelfe.22Remember my iudgement: for thine alſo ſhall
be ſo; yeſterday for me, and to day for thee.23When the dead is at reſt,
let his remembrance reſt, & be comforted for him, when his ſpirit is
departed from him.24The wiſedome of a learned man cōmeth by
opportunitie of leaſure: & he that hath litle buſines ſhal become
wiſe.25How can he get wiſdome that holdeth the plough, and that
glorieth in the goad; that driueth oxen, and is occupied in their labours,
and whoſe talke is of bullocks?26He giueth his minde to make furrowes:
and is diligent to giue the kine fodder.27So euery carpenter, and
workemaſter, that laboureth night and day: and they that cut and graue
ſeales, and are diligent to make great variety, and giue themſelues to
counterfait imagerie, and watch to finiſh a worke.28The ſmith alſo ſitting
by the anuill, & conſidering the iron worke; the vapour of the fire
waſteth his fleſh, and he fighteth with the heat of the furnace: the noiſe
of the hammer & the anuill is euer in his eares, and his eies looke ſtill
vpon the patterne of the thing that he maketh, he ſetteth his mind to
finiſh his worke, & watcheth to poliſh it perfitly.29So doeth the potter
ſitting at his worke, and turning the wheele about with his feet, who is
alway carefully ſet at his worke: and maketh all his worke by
number.30He faſhioneth the clay with his arme, and boweth downe his
ſtrength before his feet: he applieth himſelfe to lead it ouer; and he is
diligent to make cleane the furnace.31All theſe truſt to their hands: and
euery one is wiſe in his worke.32Without theſe cannot a citie be
inhabited: and they ſhall not dwell where they will, nor goe vp and
downe.33They ſhall not be ſought for in publike counſaile; nor ſit high
in the congregation: they ſhal not ſit on the Iudges ſeate, nor vnderſtand
the ſentence of iudgement: they cannot declare iuſtice, and iudgement,
and they ſhall not be found where parables are ſpoken.34But they will
maintaine the ſtate of the world, and *all* their deſire is in the worke of
their craft.
CHAPTER 39 1But hee that giueth his minde to the Law of the moſt
high, and is occupied in the meditation thereof, wil ſeeke out the
wiſdome of all the ancient, and be occupied in prophecies.2Hee will
keepe the ſayings of the renowmed men: and where ſubtile parables are,
he will be there alſo.3Hee will ſeeke out the ſecrets of graue ſentences,
and be conuerſant in darke parables.4He ſhall ſerue among great men,
and appeare before princes: he will trauaile through ſtrange countreys,
for hee hath tried the good, and the euill among men.5Hee will giue his
heart to reſort early to the Lord that made him, and will pray before the
moſt high, and will open his mouth in prayer, and make ſupplication for
his ſinnes.6When the great Lord will, he ſhall bee filled with the ſpirit of
vnderſtanding: he ſhal powre out wiſe ſentences, and giue thankes vnto
the Lord in his prayer.7Hee ſhall direct his counſell and knowledge, and
in his ſecrets ſhall hee meditate.8Hee ſhall ſhew foorth that which he
hath learned, and ſhall glory in the Law of the couenant of the
Lord.9Many ſhall commend his vnderſtanding, and ſo long as the world
endureth, it ſhall not be blotted out, his memoriall ſhall not depart away,
and his name ſhall liue from generation to generation.10Nations ſhall
ſhewe foorth his wiſedome, and the congregation ſhall declare his
praiſe.11If hee die, he ſhall leaue a greater name then a thouſand: and if
he liue, he ſhall increaſe it.12Yet I haue more to ſay which I haue thought
vpon, for I am filled as the Moone at the full.13Hearken vnto me, ye holy
children, and budde foorth as a roſe growing by the brooke of the
field:14And giue yee a ſweete ſauour as frankincenſe, and flouriſh as a
lilly, ſend foorth a ſmell, and ſing a ſong of praiſe, bleſſe the Lord in all
his workes.15Magnifie his Name, and ſhewe foorth his praiſe with the
ſongs of your lips, and with harpes, and in praiſing him you ſhall ſay
after this maner:16Al the works of the Lord are exceeding good, &
whatſoeuer hee commandeth, ſhalbe accompliſhed in due ſeaſon.17And
none may ſay, What is this? wherefore is that? for at time conuenient
they ſhall all be ſought out: at his commaundement the waters ſtood as
an heape, & at the wordes of his mouth the receptacles of waters.18At
his commandement is done whatſoeuer pleaſeth him, and none can
hinder when he will ſaue.19The workes of all fleſh are before him, &
nothing can be hid from his eyes.20He ſeeth from euerlaſting to
euerlaſting, and there is nothing wonderfull before him.21A man neede
not to ſay, What is this? wherefore is that? for hee hath made all things
for their vſes.22His bleſſing couered the dry land as a riuer, and watered
it as a flood.23As hee hath turned the waters into ſaltneſse: ſo ſhall the
heathen inherite his wrath.24As his wayes are plaine vnto the holy, ſo are

they ſtumbling blockes vnto the wicked.25For the good, are good things created from the beginning: ſo euill things for ſinners.26The principall things for the whole vſe of mans life, are water, fire, yron, and ſalt, floure of wheate, honie, milke, and the blood of the grape, and oyle, and clothing.27All theſe things are for good to the godly: ſo to the ſinners they are turned into euill.28There be ſpirits that are created for vengeance, which in their furie lay on ſore ſtrokes, in the time of deſtruction they powre out their force, and appeaſe the wrath of him that made them.29Fire, and haile, and famine, and death: all theſe were created for vengeance:30Teeth of wild beaſts, and ſcorpions, ſerpents, & the ſword, puniſhing the wicked to deſtruction.31They ſhall reioice in his commandement, and they ſhall bee ready vpon earth when neede is, and when their time is come, they ſhall not tranſgreſse his word.32Therefore from the beginning I was reſolued, and thought vpon theſe things, and haue left them in writing.33All the workes of the Lord are good: and he will giue euery needefull thing in due ſeaſon.34So that a man cannot ſay, This is worſe then that: for in time they ſhall all be well approued.35And therefore praiſe ye the Lord with the whole heart and mouth, and bleſſe the Name of the Lord.

CHAPTER 40 1Great trauaile is created for euery man, and an heauy yoke is vpon the ſons of Adam, from the day that they goe out of their mothers wombe, till the day that they returne to the mother of all things.2Their imagination of things to come, & the day of death *trouble* their thoughts, and *cauſe* feare of heart:3From him that ſitteth on a throne of glory, vnto him that is humbled in earth and aſhes.4From him that weareth purple, and a crown, vnto him that is clothed with a linnen frocke.5Wrath, and enuie, trouble and vnquietneſse, feare of death, and anger, and ſtrife, and in the time of reſt vpon his bed, his night ſleepe doe change his knowledge.6A litle or nothing is his reſt, and afterward he is in his ſleepe, as in a day of keeping watch, troubled in the viſion of his heart, as if he were eſcaped out of a battell:7When all is ſafe, he awaketh, and marueileth that the feare was nothing.8*ſuch things happen* vnto all fleſh, both man and beaſt, and that is ſeuen fold more vpon ſinners.9Death and bloodſhed, ſtrife and ſword, calamities, famine, tribulation, and the ſcourge:10Theſe things are created for the wicked, and for their ſakes came the flood.11All things that are of the earth ſhal turne to the earth againe: and that which is of the waters doeth returne into the ſea.12All briberie and iniuſtice ſhall be blotted out: but true dealing ſhall endure for euer.13The goods of the vniuſt ſhall bee dried vp like a riuer, and ſhall vaniſh with noiſe, like a great thunder in raine.14While he openeth his hand he ſhal reioyce: ſo ſhall tranſgreſsours come to nought.15The children of the vngodly ſhall not bring forth many branches: but are as vncleane roots vpon a hard rocke.16The weed growing vpon euery water, and banke of a riuer, ſhall bee pulled vp before all graſſe.17Bountifulnes is as a moſt fruitfull garden, and mercifulneſse endureth for euer.18To labour & to be content with that a man hath, is a ſweet life: but hee that findeth a treaſure, is aboue them both.19Children and the building of a citie continue a mans name: but a blameleſſe wife is counted aboue them both.20Wine & muſicke reioyce the heart: but the loue of wiſedome is aboue them both.21The pipe and the pſalterie make ſweet melodie: but a pleaſant tongue is aboue them both.22Thine eye deſireth fauour and beautie: but more then both, corne while it is greene.23A friend and companion neuer meet amiſse: but aboue both is a wife with her huſband.24Brethren and helpe are againſt time of trouble: but almes ſhall deliuer more then them both.25Golde and ſiluer make the foote ſtand ſure: but counſell is eſteemed aboue them both.26Riches and ſtrength lift vp the heart: but the feare of the Lord is aboue them both: there is no want in the feare of the Lord, and it needeth not to ſeeke helpe.27The feare of the Lord is a fruitfull garden, and couereth him aboue all glory.28My ſonne, lead not a beggers life: for better it is to die then to beg.29The life of him that dependeth on another mans table, is not to be counted for a life: for he polluteth himſelfe with other mens meate, but a wiſe man well nurtured will beware thereof.30Begging is ſweet in the mouth of the ſhameleſſe: but in his belly there ſhall burne a fire.

CHAPTER 41 1O death, how bitter is the remembrance of thee to a man that liueth at reſt in his poſſeſſions, vnto the man that hath nothing to vexe him, and that hath proſperity in all things: yea vnto him that is yet able to receiue meate?2O death, acceptable is thy ſentence vnto the needy, and vnto him whoſe ſtrength faileth, that is now in the laſt age, and is vexed with all things, and to him that deſpaireth and hath loſt patience.3Feare not the ſentence of death, remember them that haue beene before thee, and that come after, for this is the ſentence of the Lord ouer all fleſh.4And why art thou againſt the pleaſure of the moſt High? there is no inquiſition in the graue, whether thou haue liued ten, or a hundred, or a thouſand yeeres.5The children of ſinners, are abhominable children: and they that are conuerſant in the dwelling of the vngodly.6The inheritance of ſinners children ſhal periſh, and their poſterity ſhal haue a perpetuall reproch.7The children will complaine of an vngodly father, becauſe they ſhall be reproched for his ſake.8Woe be vnto you vngodly men which haue forſaken the law of the moſt high God: for if you encreaſe, it ſhall be to your deſtruction.9And if you be borne, you ſhall be borne to a curſe: and if you die, a curſe ſhall be your portion.10All that are of the earth ſhall turne to earth againe: ſo the vngodly ſhall goe from a curſe to deſtruction.11The mourning of men is about their bodies: but an ill name of ſinners ſhall be blotted out.12Haue regard to thy name: for that ſhall continue with thee aboue a thouſand great treaſures of gold.13A good life hath but few daies: but a good name endureth for euer.14My children, keepe diſcipline in peace: for wiſedome that is hid, and a treaſure that is not ſeene, what profit is in them both?15A man that hideth his fooliſhneſse is better then a man that hideth his wiſedome.16Therefore be ſhamefaſt according to my word: for it is not good to retaine all ſhamefaſtneſse, neither is it altogether approoued in euery thing.17Be aſhamed of whoredome before father and mother, and of a lie before a prince and a mighty man:18Of an offence before a iudge and ruler, of iniquitie before a congregation and people, of vniuſt dealing before thy partner and friend:19And of theft in regard of the place where thou ſoiourneſt, and in regard of the trueth of God and his couenant, and to leane with thine elbow vpon the meate, and of ſcorning to giue and take:20And of ſilence before them that ſalute thee, and to look vpon an harlot:21And to turne away thy face from thy kinſman, or to take away a portion or a gift, or to gaze vpon another mans wife,22Or to bee ouerbuſie with his maide, and come not neere her bed, or of vpbraiding ſpeaches before friends; and after thou haſt giuen, vpbraide not:23Or of iterating and ſpeaking againe that which thou haſt heard, and of reuealing of ſecrets.24So ſhalt thou be truely ſhamefaſt, and finde fauour before all men.

CHAPTER 421Of theſe things be not thou aſhamed, and accept no perſon to ſinne thereby.2Of the Law of the moſt High, and his Couenant, and of iudgement to iuſtifie the vngodly:3Of reckoning with thy partners, and traueilers: or of the gift of the heritage of friends:4Of exactneſse of ballance, and waights: or of getting much or little:5And of merchants indifferent ſelling, of much correction of children, and to make the ſide of an euill ſeruant to bleed.6Sure keeping is good where an euill wife is, and ſhut vp where many hands are.7Deliuer all things in number and waight, and put al in writing that thou giueſt out, or receiueſt in.8Be not aſhamed to informe the vnwiſe and fooliſh, and the extreeme aged that contendeth with thoſe that are yong, thus ſhalt thou bee truely learned and approued of all men liuing.9The father waketh for the daughter when no man knoweth, and the care for her taketh away ſleepe; when ſhee is yong leſt ſhee paſſe away the flowre of her age, and being married, leſt ſhe ſhould be hated:10In her virginitie leſt ſhe ſhould be defiled, and gotten with childe in her fathers houſe; and hauing an huſband, leſt ſhe ſhould miſbehaue herſelfe: and when ſhee is married, leſt ſhee ſhould be barren.11Keepe a ſure watch ouer a ſhameleſſe daughter, leſt ſhee make thee a laughing ſtocke to thine enemies, and a by-word in the citie, and a reproch among the people, and make thee aſhamed before the multitude.12Behold not euery bodies beauty, and ſit not in the midſt of women.13For from garments commeth a moth, and from women wickedneſſe.14Better is the churliſhneſse of a man, then a courteous woman, a woman I ſay, which bringeth ſhame and reproch.15I will now remember the works of the Lord, and declare the things that I haue ſeene: in the words of the Lord are his workes.16The Sunne that giueth light, looketh vpon all things: and the worke thereof is full of the glory of the Lord.17The Lord hath not giuen power to the Saints to declare all his marueilous workes, which the Almightie Lord firmely ſetled, that whatſoeuer is, might be eſtabliſhed for his glory.18He ſeeketh out the deepe and the heart, and

confidereth their crafty deuices: for the Lord knoweth all that may be
knowen, and he beholdeth the ſignes of the world.19Hee declareth the
things that are paſt, and for to come, and reueileth the ſteps of hidden
things.20No thought eſcapeth him, neither any word is hidden from
him.21Hee hath garniſhed the excellent workes of his wiſedome, and hee
is from euerlaſting to euerlaſting, vnto him may nothing be added,
neither can he be diminiſhed, and he hath no need of any counſeller.22O
how deſireable are all his workes: and that a man may ſee euen to a
ſparke.23All theſe things liue and remaine for euer, for all vſes, and they
are all obedient.24All things are double one againſt another: and hee hath
made nothing vnperfit.25One thing eſtabliſheth the good of another:
and who ſhalbe filled with beholding his glory?

CHAPTER 431The pride of the height, the cleare firmament, the
beautie of heauen, with his glorious ſhew;2The Sunne when it appeareth,
declaring at his riſing, a marueilous inſtrument, the worke of the moſt
High.3At noone it parcheth the country, and who can abide the burning
heate thereof?4A man blowing a furnace is in works of heat, but the
Sunne burneth the mountaines three times more; breathing out fiery
vapours, and ſending foorth bright beames, it dimmeth the eyes.5Great
is the Lord that made it, and at his commandement it runneth
haſtily.6He made the Moone alſo to ſerue in her ſeaſon, for a declaration
of times, and a ſigne of the world.7From the Moone is the ſigne of
Feaſts, a light that decreaſeth in her perfection.8The moneth is called
after her name, encreaſing wonderfully in her changing, being an
inſtrument of the armies aboue, ſhining in the firmament of
heauen,9The beautie of heauen, the glory of the ſtarres, an ornament
giuing light in the higheſt places of the Lord.10At the commandement
of the holy One, they will ſtand in their order, and neuer faint in their
watches.11Looke vpon the rainebow, and praiſe him that made it, very
beautifull it is in the brightneſse thereof.12It compaſſeth the heauen
about with a glorious circle, and the hands of the moſt high haue bended
it.13By his commandement hee maketh the ſnow to fall apace, and
ſendeth ſwiftly the lightnings of his iudgment.14Through this the
treaſures are opened, and clouds flie forth as foules.15By his great power
hee maketh the cloudes firme, and the haileſtones are broken ſmall.16At
his ſight the mountaines are ſhaken, and at his will the South wind
bloweth.17The noiſe of the thunder maketh the earth to tremble: ſo doth
the Northren ſtorme, and the whirlewinde: as birds flying he ſcattereth
the ſnow, and the falling downe thereof, is as the lighting of
graſhoppers.18The eye marueileth at the beauty of the whiteneſse
thereof, and the heart is aſtoniſhed at the raining of it.19The hoare froſt
alſo as ſalt hee powreth on the earth, and being congealed, it lieth on the
toppe of ſharpe ſtakes.20Wheu the colde North-winde bloweth, and the
water is congealed into yce, it abideth vpon euery gathering together of
water, and clotheth the water as with a breſtplate.21It deuoureth the
mountaines, and burneth the wilderneſſe, and conſumeth the graſſe as
fire.22A preſent remedy of all is a miſte comming ſpeedily: a dew
comming after heate, refreſheth.23By his counſell he appeaſeth the
deepe, and planteth Ilands therein.24They that ſaile on the ſea, tell of the
danger thereof, and when wee heare it with our eares, wee marueile
thereat.25For therein be ſtrange and wonderous workes, varietie of all
kindes of beaſts, and whales created.26By him the ende of them hath
proſperous ſucceſse, and by his word all things conſiſt.27We may ſpeake
much, & yet come ſhort: wherefore in ſumme, he is all.28How ſhall wee
be able to magnifie him? for hee is great aboue all his workes.29The Lord
is terrible and very great, and marueilous is his power.30When you
glorifie the Lord exalt him as much as you can: for euen yet wil he farre
exceed, and when you exalt him, put foorth all your ſtrength, and be not
weary: for you can neuer goe farre enough.31Who hath ſeene him, that
hee might tell vs? and who can magnifie him as he is?32There are yet hid
greater things then theſe be, for wee haue ſeene but a few of his
workes:33For the Lord hath made all things, and to the godly hath hee
giuen wiſedome.

CHAPTER 441Let vs now praiſe famous men, and our Fathers that
begat vs.2The Lorde hath wrought great glory by them, through his great
power from the beginning.3ſuch as did beare rule in their kingdomes,
men renowmed for their power, giuing counſell by their vnderſtanding,
and declaring prophecies:4Leaders of the people by their counſels, and
learning meet for the people, wiſe and eloquent in their
inſtructions.5ſuch as found out muſical tunes, and reiected verſes in
writing.6Rich men furniſhed with abilitie, liuing peaceably in their
habitations.7All theſe were honoured in their generations, and were the
glory of their times.8There be of them, that haue left a name behind
them, that their praiſes might be reported.9And ſome there be, which
haue no memorial, who are periſhed as though they had neuer bene, and
are become as though they had neuer bene borne, and their children
after them.10But theſe were mercifull men, whoſe righteouſneſſe hath
not beene forgotten.11With their ſeed ſhall continually remaine a good
inheritance, and their children are within the couenant.12Their ſeed
ſtands faſt, and their children for their ſakes.13Their ſeed ſhall remaine
for euer, and their glory ſhall not be blotted out.14Their bodies are
buried in peace, but their name liueth for euermore.15The people will
tell of their wiſdome, and the congregation will ſhew forth their
praiſe.16Enoch pleaſed the Lord, and was tranſlated, being an example
of repentance, to all generations.17Noah was found perfect and
righteous, in the time of wrath, he was taken in exchange (for the world)
therefore was he left as a remnant vnto the earth, when the flood
came.18An euerlaſting Couenant was made with him, that all fleſh
ſhould periſh no more by the flood.19Abraham was a great father of
many people: in glory was there none like vnto him:20Who kept the Law
of the moſt High, and was in couenant with him, hee eſtabliſhed the
Couenant in his fleſh, and when he was proued, he was found
faithfull.21Therefore he aſsured him by an othe, that he would bleſſe the
nations in his ſeed, and that he would multiply him, as the duſt of the
earth, and exalt his ſeed as the ſtarres, and cauſe them to inherit from
ſea to ſea, & from the riuer vnto the vtmoſt part of the land.22With Iſaac
did he eſtabliſh likewiſe *for Abraham his fathers ſake* the bleſſing of all men
and the couenant,23And made it reſt vpon the head of Iacob. Hee
acknowledged him in his bleſſing, and gaue him an heritage, and diuided
his portions, among the twelue tribes did he part them.

CHAPTER 45 1And he brought out of him a mercifull man, which
found fauour in the ſight of all fleſh, euen Moſes beloued of God and
men, whoſe memoriall is bleſſed:2He made him like to the glorious
Saints, and magnified him, ſo that his enemies ſtood in feare of him.3By
his words he cauſed the wonders to ceaſe, and he made him glorious in
the ſight of kings, and gaue him a commaundement for his people, and
ſhewed him part of his glory.4He ſanctified him in his faithfulneſse, and
meekeneſse, and choſe him out of all men.5He made him to heare his
voyce, and brought him into the darke cloud, and gaue him
commandements before his face, euen the law of life and knowledge,
that hee might teach Iacob his Couenants, and Iſrael his iudgments.6He
exalted Aaron an holy man like vnto him, euen his brother, of the tribe
of Leui.7An euerlaſting couenant he made with him, and gaue him the
prieſthood among the people, he beautified him with comely
ornaments, and clothed him with a robe of glory.8Hee put vpon him
perfect glory: and ſtrengthened him with rich garments, with breeches,
with a long robe, and the Ephod:9And he compaſſed him with
pomegranates, and with many golden bels round about, that as he went,
there might be a ſound, and a noiſe made that might be heard in the
Temple, for a memoriall to the children of his people.10With an holy
garment, with gold and blew ſilke, and purple the worke of the
embroiderer; with a breſtplate of iudgement, and with Urim &
Thummim.11With twiſted ſcarlet, the worke of the cunning workeman,
with precious ſtones grauen like ſeales, and ſet in gold, the worke of the
Ieweller, with a writing engraued for a memoriall, after the number of
the tribes of Iſrael.12He ſet a crowne of gold vpon the miter, wherein
was engraued holineſſe an ornament of honour, a coſtly worke, the
deſires of the eies goodly & beautiful.13Before him there were none ſuch,
neither did euer any ſtranger put them on, but onely his children, and
his childrens children perpetually.14Their ſacrifices ſhall be wholy
conſumed euery day twiſe continually.15Moiſes conſecrated him, and
annointed him with holy oile, this was appointed vnto him by an
euerlaſting couenant, and to his ſeed ſo long as the heauens ſhould
remaine, that they ſhould miniſter vnto him, and execute the office of
the prieſthood, and bleſſe the people in his name.16He choſe him out of
all men liuing to offer ſacrifices to the Lord, incenſe and a ſweet ſauour,
for a memoriall, to make reconciliation for his people.17He gaue vnto
him his commandements, and authority in the ſtatutes of iudgements,
that he ſhould teach Iacob the teſtimonies, and informe Iſrael in his

lawes.[18]Strangers conſpired together againſt him, and maligned him in the wilderneſſe, euen the men that were of Dathans, and Abirons ſide, and the congregation of Core with fury and wrath.[19]This the Lord ſaw and it diſpleaſed him, and in his wrathfull indignation, were they conſumed: he did wonders vpon them, to conſume them with the fiery flame.[20]But he made Aaron more honourable, and gaue him an heritage, and diuided vnto him the firſt fruits of the encreaſe, eſpecially he prepared bread in abundance:[21]For they eate of the ſacrifices of the Lord, which he gaue vnto him and his ſeed:[22]Howbeit in the land of the people he had no inheritance, neither had he any portion among the people, for the Lord himſelfe is his portion and inheritance.[23]The third in glory is Phinees the ſonne of Eleazar, becauſe he had zeale in the feare of the Lord, and ſtood vp with good courage of heart, when the people were turned backe, and made reconciliation for Iſrael.[24]Therfore was there a couenant of peace made with him, that he ſhould be the cheefe of the ſanctuary, and of his people, and that he, and his poſteritie ſhould haue the dignitie of the Prieſthood for euer.[25]According to the couenant made with Dauid ſonne of Ieſſe, of the tribe of Iuda, that the inheritance of the king ſhould be to his poſterity alone: ſo the inheritance of Aaron ſhould alſo be vnto his ſeed.[26]God giue you wiſedome in your heart to iudge his people in righteouſneſſe, that their good things be not aboliſhed, and that their glory may endure for euer.

CHAPTER 46 [1]Ieſus the ſonne of Naue was valiant in the wars, and was the ſucceſſor of Moſes in propheſies, who according to his name was made great for the ſauing of the elect of God, and taking vengeance of the enemies that roſe vp againſt them, that he might ſet Iſrael in their inheritance.[2]How great glory gat he when he did lift vp his hands, and ſtretched out his ſword againſt the cities?[3]Who before him ſo ſtood to it? for the Lord himſelfe brought his enemies vnto him.[4]Did not the Sunne goe backe by his meanes? and was not one day as long as two?[5]He called vpon the moſt high Lord, when the enemies preſſed vpon him on euery ſide, & the great Lord heard him.[6]And with haileſtones of mighty power he made the battell to fall violently vpon the nations, and in the deſcent (of Bethoron) hee deſtroyed them that reſiſted, that the nations might know all their ſtrength, becauſe hee fought in the ſight of the Lord, and he followed the mightie one.[7]In the time of Moſes alſo, he did a worke of mercie, hee and Caleb the ſonne of Iephunne, in that they withſtood the Congregation, and withheld the people from ſinne, and appeaſed the wicked murmuring.[8]And of ſixe hundred thouſand people on foot, they two were preſerued to bring them into the heritage, euen vnto the land that floweth with milk & hony.[9]The Lord gaue ſtrength alſo vnto Caleb, which remained with him vnto his old age, ſo that he entred vpon the high places of the land, and his ſeed obtained it for an heritage.[10]That all the children of Iſrael might ſee that it is good to follow the Lord.[11]And concerning the Iudges, euery one by name, whoſe heart went not a whoring, nor departed from the Lord, let their memory be bleſſed.[12]Let their bones flouriſh out of their place, and let the name of them that were honoured, be continued vpon their children.[13]Samuel the Prophet of the Lord, beloued of his Lord, eſtabliſhed a kingdom, & anointed princes ouer his people.[14]By the Law of the Lord hee iudged the Congregation, and the Lord had reſpect vnto Iacob.[15]By his faithfulnes he was found a true Prophet, and by his word he was knowen to be faithfull in viſion.[16]He called vpon the mighty Lord, when his enemies preſſed vpon him on euery ſide, when he offered the ſucking lambe.[17]And the Lord thundered from heauen, and with a great noiſe made his voice to be heard.[18]And he deſtroyed the rulers of the Tyrians, and all the princes of the Philiſtines.[19]And before his long ſleepe hee made proteſtations in the ſight of the Lord, and his anoynted, I haue not taken any mans goods, ſo much as a ſhoe, and no man did accuſe him.[20]And after his death he propheſied, and ſhewed the King his end, and lift vp his voyce from the earth in propheſie, to blot out the wickedneſſe of the people.

CHAPTER 47 [1]And after him roſe vp Nathan to propheſie in the time of Dauid.[2]As is the fat taken away from the peace offering, ſo was Dauid choſen out of the children of Iſrael.[3]Hee played with Lions as with kids, and with beares as with lambs.[4]Slew he not a gyant when hee was yet but yong? and did he not take away reproch from the people, when he lifted vp his hand with the ſtone in the ſling, and beat downe the boaſting of Goliah?[5]For he called vpon the moſt high Lord, and he gaue him ſtrength in his right hand to ſlay that mighty warriour, and ſet vp the horne of his people:[6]So the people honoured him with ten thouſands, and praiſed him in the bleſſings of the Lord, in that hee gaue him a crowne of glory.[7]For hee deſtroyed the enemies on euery ſide, and brought to nought the Philiſtines his aduerſaries, and brake their horne in ſunder vnto this day.[8]In all his workes hee praiſed the holy one moſt High, with words of glory, with his whole heart he ſung ſongs, and loued him that made him.[9]He ſet ſingers alſo before the Altar, that by their voyces they might make ſweet melody, and daily ſing praiſes in their ſongs.[10]He beautified their feaſts, and ſet in order the ſolemne times, vntill the ende, that they might praiſe his holy Name, and that the Temple might ſound from morning.[11]The Lord tooke away his ſinnes, and exalted his horne for euer: he gaue him a couenant of kings, and a throne of glory in Iſrael.[12]After him roſe vp a wiſe ſonne, and for his ſake he dwelt at large.[13]Salomon reigned in a peaceable time, and was honoured; for God made all quiet round about him, that hee might build an houſe in his Name, and prepare his Sanctuary for euer.[14]How wiſe waſt thou in thy youth, & as a flood filled with vnderſtanding.[15]Thy ſoule couered the whole earth, and thou filledſt it with dark parables.[16]Thy name went farre vnto the Ilands, and for thy peace thou waſt beloued.[17]The countreys marueiled at thee for thy ſongs, and Prouerbs, and Parables, and interpretations.[18]By the Name of the Lord God, which is called the Lord God of Iſrael, thou didſt gather gold as tinne, and didſt multiply ſiluer as lead.[19]Thou didſt bow thy loines vnto women, and by thy body thou waſt brought into ſubiection.[20]Thou diſt ſtaine thy honour, and pollute thy ſeed, ſo that thou broughteſt wrath vpon thy children, and waſt grieued for thy folly.[21]So the kingdome was diuided, and out of Ephraim ruled a rebellious kingdome.[22]But the Lord will neuer leaue off his mercy, neither ſhall any of his workes periſh, neither will hee aboliſh the poſterity of his elect, and the ſeed of him that loueth him he will not take away: wherefore he gaue a remnant vnto Iacob, and out of him a roote vnto Dauid.[23]Thus reſted Solomon with his fathers, and of his ſeede he left behinde him Roboam, euen the fooliſhneſse of the people, and one that had no vnderſtanding; who turned away the people through his counſell: there was alſo Ieroboam the ſonne of Nabat, who cauſed Iſrael to ſinne, and ſhewed Ephraim the way of ſinne:[24]And their ſinnes were multiplied exceedingly, that they were driuen out of the land.[25]For they ſought out all wickednes, till the vengeance came vpon them.

CHAPTER 48 [1]Then ſtood vp Elias the Prophet as fire, and his word burnt like a lampe.[2]He brought a ſore famine vpon them, and by his zeale he diminiſhed their number.[3]By the word of the Lord he ſhut vp the heauen, and alſo three times brought downe fire.[4]O Elias, how waſt thou honoured in thy wondrous deedes! and who may glory like vnto thee![5]Who didſt raiſe vp a dead man from death, & his ſoule from the place of the dead by the word of the moſt Hie.[6]Who broughteſt kings to deſtruction, and honourable men from their bedde.[7]Who heardeſt the rebuke of the Lord in Sinai, and in Horeb the iudgment of vengeance.[8]Who anointed kings to take reuenge, & Prophets to ſucceed after him:[9]Who waſt taken vp in a whirlewinde of fire, and in a charet of fierie horſes:[10]Who waſt ordained for reproofes in their times, to pacifie the wrath of the Lordes iudgement before it brake foorth into fury, and to turne the heart of the father vnto the ſonne, and to reſtore the tribes of Iacob.[11]Bleſſed are they that ſaw thee, and ſlept in loue, for we ſhal ſurely liue.[12]Elias it was, who was couered with a whirlewinde: and Elizeus was filled with his ſpirit: whileſt he liued he was not mooued *with the preſence* of any prince, neither could any bring him into ſubiection.[13]No word could ouercome him, & after his death his body prophecied.[14]He did wonders in his life, and at his death were his works marueilous.[15]For all this the people repented not, neither departed they from their ſinnes, till they were ſpoiled and caried out of their land, and were ſcattered through all the earth: yet there remained a ſmall people, and a ruler in the houſe of Dauid:[16]Of whom, ſome did that which was pleaſing to God, and ſome multiplied ſinnes.[17]Ezekias fortified his citie, and brought in water into the midſt thereof: he digged the hard rocke with yron, and made welles for waters.[18]In his time Sennacherib came vp, and ſent Rabſaces, and lift vp his hand againſt Sion, & boaſted proudly.[19]Then trembled their hearts and handes, and they were in paine as women in trauell.[20]But they called vpon the Lord which is mercifull, and ſtretched out their hands towards him, and immediatly the holy One heard them out of heauen, and deliuered them by the miniſtery of Eſay.21He ſmote the hoſte of the Aſſyrians, and his Angel deſtroyed them.22For Ezekias had done the thing that pleaſed the Lord, and was ſtrong in the wayes of Dauid his father, as Eſay the Prophet, who was great and faithfull in his viſion, had commaunded him.23In his time the Sunne went backeward, and hee lengthened the kings life.24Hee ſawe by an excellent ſpirit what ſhould come to paſſe at the laſt, and hee comforted them that mourned in Sion.25He ſhewed what ſhould come to paſſe for euer, and ſecret things or euer they came.

CHAPTER 49 1The remembrance of Ioſias is like the compoſition of the perfume þt is made by the arte of the Apothecarie: it is ſweete as hony in all mouthes, and as muſicke at a banquet of wine.2He behaued himſelfe vprightly in the conuerſion of the people, and tooke away the abominations of iniquitie.3He directed his heart vnto the Lord, and in the time of the vngodly he eſtabliſhed the worſhip of God.4All, except Dauid and Ezechias, and Ioſias, were defectiue: for they forſooke the Law of the moſt High, (euen) the kings of Iudah failed:5Therefore he gaue their power vnto others, & their glory to a ſtrange nation.6They burnt the choſen citie of the Sanctuarie, and made the ſtreets deſolate according to the prophecie of Ieremias:7For they entreated him euil, who neuertheleſſe was a prophet ſanctified in his mothers wombe, that he might root out and afflict & deſtroy, and that he might build vp alſo and plant.8It was Ezechiel who ſawe the glorious viſion, which was ſhewed him vpon the chariot of the Cherubimſ9For he made mention of the enemies vnder *the figure of* the raine, and directed them that went right.10And of the twelue prophets let the memorial be bleſſed, and let their bones flouriſh againe out of their place: for they comforted Iacob, and deliuered them by aſsured hope.11How ſhall we magnifie Zorobabel? euen he was as a ſignet on the right hand.12So was Ieſus the ſonne of Ioſedec: who in their time builded the houſe, and ſet vp an holy Temple to the Lord, which was prepared for euerlaſting glory.13And among the elect was Neemias whoſe renowme is great, who raiſed vp for vs, the walles that were fallen, and ſet vp the gates & the barres, and raiſed vp our ruines againe.14But vpon the earth was no man created like Enoch, for he was taken from the earth.15Neither was there a man borne like vnto Ioſeph, a gouernour of his brethren, a ſtay of the people, whoſe bones were regarded of the Lord.16Sem and Seth were in great honour among men, and ſo was Adam aboue euery liuing thing in the creation.

CHAPTER 50 1Simon the high prieſt the ſonne of Onias, who in his life repaired the houſe againe, and in his dayes fortified the Temple:2And by him was built from the foundation the double height, the high fortreſe of the wall about the Temple.3In his dayes the ciſterne to receiue water being in compaſſe as the ſea, was couered with plates of braſſe.4He tooke care of the Temple that it ſhould not fall, and fortified the citie againſt beſieging.5How was he honoured in the midſt of the people, in his comming out of the Sanctuarie?6He was as the morning ſtarre in the midſt of a cloud: and as the moone at the full.7As the Sunne ſhining vpon the Temple of the moſt High, and as the rainebow giuing light in the bright cloudes.8And as the flowre of roſes in the ſpring of the yeere, as lillies by the riuers of waters, and as the branches of the frankincenſe tree in the time of ſummer.9As fire and incenſe in the cenſer, and as a veſſell of beaten gold ſet with all maner of precious ſtones,10And as a faire oliue tree budding forth fruit, and as a Cypreſe tree which groweth vp to the cloudes.11When he put on the robe of honour, and was clothed with the perfection of glory, when he went vp to the holy altar, he made the garment of holineſſe honourable.12When he tooke the portions out of the prieſts hands, hee himſelfe ſtood by the hearth of the altar, compaſſed with his brethren round about, as a yong cedar in Libanus, and as palme trees compaſſed they him round about.13So were all the ſonnes of Aaron in their glory, and the oblations of the Lord in their hands, before all the congregation of Iſrael.14And finiſhing the ſeruice at the altar, that he might adorne the offring of the moſt high Almighty,15He ſtretched out his hand to the cup, and powred of the blood of the grape, he powred out at the foote of the altar, a ſweet ſmelling ſauour vnto the moſt high King of all.16Then ſhouted the ſonnes of Aaron, and ſounded the ſiluer trumpets, and made a great noiſe to be heard, for a remembrance before the moſt High.17Then all the people together haſted, and fell downe to the earth vpon their faces to worſhip their Lord God almighty the moſt High.18The ſingers alſo ſang praiſes with their voices, with great variety of ſounds was there made ſweete melodie.19And the people beſought the Lord the moſt High by prayer before him that is mercifull, till the ſolemnity of the Lord was ended, and they had finiſhed his ſeruice.20Then he went downe, and lifted vp his hands ouer the whole congregation of the children of Iſrael, to giue the bleſſing of the Lord with his lips, and to reioyce in his name.21And they bowed themſelues downe to worſhip the ſecond time, that they might receiue a bleſſing from the moſt High.22Now therefore bleſſe yee the God of all, which onely doth wonderous things euery where, which exalteth our daies from the wombe, and dealeth with vs according to his mercy.23He grant vs ioyfulneſse of heart, and that peace may be in our daies in Iſrael for euer.24That hee would confirme his mercy with vs, and deliuer vs at his time.25There be two maner of nations which my heart abhorreth, and the third is no nation.26They that ſit vpon the mountaine of Samaria, and they that dwell amongſt the Philiſtines, and that fooliſh people that dwell in Sichem.27Ieſus the ſonne of Sirach of Hieruſalem hath written in this booke, the inſtruction of vnderſtanding and knowledge, who out of his heart powred forth wiſedome.28Bleſſed is he that ſhall be exerciſed in theſe things, and hee that layeth them vp in his heart, ſhall become wiſe.29For if he doe them, hee ſhall be ſtrong to all things, for the light of the Lord leadeth him, who giueth wiſedome to the godly: bleſſed be the Lord for euer. Amen. Amen.

CHAPTER 511I will thanke thee, O Lord and king, and praiſe thee O God my Sauiour, I doe giue praiſe vnto thy name:2For thou art my defeuder, and helper, and haſt preſerued my body from deſtruction, and from the ſnare of the ſlanderous tongue, and from the lippes that forge lies, and haſt beene my helper againſt mine aduerſaries.3And haſt deliuered me according to the multitude of thy mercies, and greatneſſe of thy name, from the teeth of them that were ready to deuoure me, and out of the hands of ſuch as ſought after my life, and from the manifold afflictions which I had:4From the choking of fire on euery ſide, and from the mids of the fire, which I kindled not:5From the depth of the belly of hel, from an vncleane tongue, and from lying words.6By an accuſation to the king from an vnrighteous tongue, my ſoule drew neere euen vnto death, my life was neere to the hell beneath:7They compaſſed me on euery ſide, and there was no man to helpe me: I looked for the ſuccour of men, but there was none:8Then thought I vpon thy mercy, O Lord, and vpon thy acts of old, how thou deliuereſt ſuch as waite for thee, and ſaueſt them out of the hands of the enemies:9Then lifted I vp my ſupplication from the earth, and prayed for deliuerance from death.10I called vpon the Lord the father of my Lord, that he would not leaue me in the dayes of my trouble, & in the time of the proud when there was no helpe.11I will praiſe thy Name continually, and will ſing praiſe with thankeſgiuing, and ſo my prayer was heard:12For thou ſauedſt me from deſtruction, and deliuereſt mee from the euill time: therefore will I giue thankes and praiſe thee, and bleſſe thy Name, O Lord.13When I was yet yong, or euer I went abroad, I deſired wiſedome openly in my prayer.14I prayed for her before the Temple, & will ſeeke her out euen to the end:15Euen from the flowre till the grape was ripe, hath my heart delighted in her, my foot went the right way, from my youth vp ſought I after her.16I bowed downe mine eare a litle and receiued her, & gate much learning.17I profited therein, *therefore* will I aſcribe the glory vnto him that giueth me wiſedome:18For I purpoſed to doe after her, and earneſtly I followed that which is good, ſo ſhall I not be confounded:19My ſoule hath wreſtled with her, and in my doings I was exact, I ſtretched foorth my hands to the heauen aboue, & bewailed my ignorances of her.20I directed my ſoule vnto her, and I found her in pureneſe, I haue had my heart ioyned with her from the beginning, therefore ſhall I not bee forſaken.21My heart was troubled in ſeeking her: therefore haue I gotten a good poſſeſſion.22The Lord hath giuen mee a tongue for my reward, and I wil praiſe him therewith.23Draw neere vnto me you vnlearned, and dwell in the houſe of learning.24Wherefore are you ſlow, and what ſay you of theſe things, ſeeing your ſoules are very thirſtie?25I opened my mouth, and ſaid, buy her for your ſelues without money.26Put your necke vnder the yoke, and let your ſoule receiue inſtruction, ſhe is hard at hand to finde.27Behold with your eies, how that I haue had but little labour, and haue gotten vnto me much reſt.28Get learning with a great ſumme of money, and get much gold by her. 29 Let your ſoule reioyce in his mercy, and be not aſhamed of his praiſe. 30 Worke your worke betimes, & in his time he will giue you your reward.

BARUCH

CHAPTER 1 1 And theſe are the wordes of the booke, which Baruch the ſonne of Nerias, the ſonne of Maaſias, the ſonne of Sedecias, the ſonne of Aſadias, the ſon of Chelcias, wrote in Babylon, 2 In the fift yere, and in the ſeuenth day of the moneth, what time as the Caldeans tooke Ieruſalem, and burnt it with fire. 3 And Baruch did reade the words of this booke, in the hearing of Iechonias, the ſonne of Ioachim king of Iuda, and in the eares of all the people, that came to *heare* the booke. 4 And in the hearing of the nobles, and of the kings ſonnes, and in the hearing of the Elders, and of all the people from the loweſt vnto the higheſt, euen of all them that dwelt at Babylon, by the riuer Sud. 5 Whereupon they wept, faſted, and prayed before the Lord. 6 They made alſo a collection of money, according to euery mans power. 7 And they ſent it to Ieruſalem vnto Ioachim the hie Prieſt the ſonne of Chelcias, ſonne of Salom, and to the Prieſtes, and to all the people which were found with him at Ieruſalem, 8 At the ſame time, when he receiued the veſſels of the houſe of the Lord that were caried out of the Temple, to returne them into the land of Iuda the tenth day of the moneth Siuan, *namely* ſiluer veſſels, which Sedecias the ſonne of Ioſias king of Iuda had made, 9 After that Nabuchodonoſor king of Babylon had caried away Iechonias, and the Princes, and the captiues, and the mightie men, and the people of the land from Ieruſalem, and brought them vnto Babylon: 10 And they ſaid, Behold, we haue ſent you money, to buy you burnt offerings, and ſinne offerings, and incenſe, and prepare yee Manna, and offer vpon the Altar of the Lord our God, 11 And pray for the life of Nabuchodonoſor king of Babylon, and for the life of Balthaſar his ſonne, that their dayes may be vpon earth as the dayes of heauen. 12 And the Lord wil giue vs ſtrength, and lighten our eyes, and we ſhall liue vnder the ſhadow of Nabuchodonoſor king of Babylon, and vnder the ſhadow of Balthaſar his ſonne, and wee ſhall ſerue them many dayes, and finde fauour in their ſight. 13 Pray for vs alſo vnto the Lord our God, (for wee haue ſinned againſt the Lord our God, and vnto this day the fury of the Lord, and his wrath is not turned from vſ) 14 And yee ſhall reade this booke, which we haue ſent vnto you, to make confeſsion in the houſe of the Lord, vpon the feaſts and ſolemne dayes. 15 And yee ſhall ſay, To the Lord our God belongeth righteouſneſſe, but vnto vs the confuſion of faces, as it is come to paſſe this day vnto them of Iuda, & to the inhabitants of Ieruſalem, 16 And to our kings, and to our princes, and to our Prieſts, and to our Prophets, and to our fathers. 17 For wee haue ſinned before the Lord, 18 And diſobeyed him, and haue not hearkened vnto the voice of the Lord our God, to walke in the commaundements that he gaue vs openly: 19 Since the day that the Lorde brought our forefathers out of the land of Egypt, vnto this preſent day, wee haue beene diſobedient vnto the Lord our God, and we haue beene negligent in not hearing his voice. 20 Wherefore the euils cleaued vnto vs, and the curſe which the Lord appointed by Moſes his ſeruant, at the time that he brought our fathers out of the land of Egypt, to giue vs a land that floweth with milke and honie, like as it is to ſee this day. 21 Neuertheleſſe we haue not hearkened vnto the voice of the Lord our God, according vnto all the wordes of the Prophets, whom he ſent vnto vs. 22 But euery man followed the imagination of his owne wicked heart, to ſerue ſtrange gods, and to doe euill in the ſight of the Lord our God.

CHAPTER 2 1 Therefore the Lord hath made good his worde, which hee pronounced againſt vs, and againſt our Iudges that iudged Iſrael, and againſt our kings, and againſt our princes, and againſt the men of Iſrael and Iuda, 2 To bring vpon vs great plagues, ſuch as neuer happened vnder the whole heauen, as it came to paſſe in Ieruſalem, according to the things that were written in the Law of Moſes, 3 That a man ſhould eat the fleſh of his owne ſonne, and the fleſh of his owne daughter. 4 Moreouer, he hath deliuered them to be in ſubiection to all the kingdomes that are round about vs, to be as a reproch and deſolation among all the people round about, where the Lord hath ſcattered them. 5 Thus wee were caſt downe and not exalted, becauſe wee haue ſinned againſt the Lord our God, and haue not beene obedient vnto his voice. 6 To the Lord our God appertaineth righteouſneſſe: but vnto vs and to our fathers open ſhame, as appeareth this day. 7 For all theſe plagues are come vpon vs, which the Lord hath pronounced againſt vs, 8 Yet haue we not prayed before the Lord, þt we might turne euery one from the imaginations of his wicked heart. 9 Wherefore the Lord watched ouer vs for euill, and the Lord hath brought it vpon vs: for the Lord is righteous in all his works, which he hath commanded vs. 10 Yet we haue not hearkened vnto his voice, to walk in the cōmandements of the Lord, that he hath ſet before vs. 11 And now O Lord God of Iſrael, that haſt brought thy people out of the land of Egypt with a mighty hand, and high arme, and with ſignes & with wonders, & with great power, and haſt gotten thy ſelfe a name, as appeareth this day: 12 O Lord our God, we haue ſinned, we haue done vngodly, wee haue dealt vnrighteouſly in all thine ordinances. 13 Let thy wrath turne from vs: for we are but a few left among the heathen, where thou haſt ſcattered vs. 14 Heare our prayers, O Lord, and our petitions, and deliuer vs for thine owne ſake, and giue vs fauour in the ſight of them which haue led vs away: 15 That all the earth may know that thou art þe Lord our God, becauſe Iſrael & his poſterity is called by thy name. 16 O Lord looke downe from thy holy houſe, & conſider vs: bow downe thine eare, O Lord, to heare vs. 17 Open thine eyes and behold: for the dead that are in the graues, whoſe ſoules are taken from their bodies, wil giue vnto the Lord neither praiſe nor righteouſneſſe. 18 But þe ſoule that is greatly vexed, which goeth ſtouping & feeble, and the eyes that faile, and the hungry ſoule wil giue thee praiſe & righteouſnes O Lord. 19 Therfore wee doe not make our humble ſupplication before thee, O Lord our God, for the righteouſnes of our fathers, and of our kings. 20 For thou haſt ſent out thy wrath & indignation vpon vs, as thou haſt ſpoken by thy ſeruants þe prophets, ſaying, 21 Thus ſaith the Lord, bow down your ſhoulderſto ſerue the king of Babylon: ſo ſhall ye remaine in the lande that I gaue vnto your fathers. 22 But if ye will not heare the voice of the Lord to ſerue þe king of Babylon, 23 I will cauſe to ceaſe out of the cities of Iuda, and from without Ieruſalem the voice of mirth, and the voice of ioy: the voice of the bridegrome, and the voice of the bride, and the whole land ſhall be deſolate of inhabitants. 24 But we would not hearken vnto thy voyce, to ſerue the king of Babylon: therefore haſt thou made good the wordes that thou ſpakeſt by thy ſeruants the prophets, namely that the bones of our kings, and the bones of our fathers ſhould be taken out of their places. 25 And loe, they are caſt out to the heat of the day, and to the froſt of the night, and they died in great miſeries, by famine, by ſword, and by peſtilence. 26 And the houſe which is called by thy name (haſt thou laid waſte) as it is to be ſeene this day, for the wickedneſſe of the houſe of Iſrael, and the houſe of Iuda. 27 O Lord our God, thou haſt dealt with vs after all thy goodneſse, and according to all that great mercie of thine. 28 As thou ſpakeſt by thy ſeruant Moſes in the day when thou didſt command him to write thy Law, before the children of Iſrael, ſaying, 29 If ye will not heare my voyce, ſurely this very great multitude ſhalbe turned into a ſmal *number* among the nations, where I will ſcatter them. 30 For I knew that they would not heare me: becauſe it is a ſtiffenecked people: but in the land of their captiuities, they ſhall remember themſelues, 31 And ſhall know that I am the Lord their God: For I giue them an heart, and eares to heare. 32 And they ſhal praiſe me in the land of their captiuitie, and thinke vpon my name, 33 And returne from their ſtiffe neck, and from their wicked deeds: for they ſhal remember the way of their fathers which ſinned before the Lord. 34 And I will bring them againe into the land which I promiſed with an oath vnto their fathers, Abraham, Iſaac, and Iacob, and they ſhall bee lords of it, and I will increaſe them, and they ſhall not be diminiſhed. 35 And I will make an euerlaſting couenant with them, to be their God, and they ſhall be my people: and I will no more driue my people of Iſrael out of the land that I haue giuen them.

CHAPTER 3 1 O Lord almighty, God of Iſrael, the ſoule in anguiſh, the troubled ſpirit crieth vnto thee. 2 Heare O Lord, and haue mercy: for thou art mercifull, and haue pitty vpon vs, becauſe we haue ſinned before thee. 3 For thou endureſt for euer, and we periſh vtterly. 4 O Lord almighty, thou God of Iſrael, heare now the prayers of the dead Iſraelites, and of their children, which haue ſinned before thee, and not

hearkened vnto the voice of thee their God: for the which cauſe theſe
plagues cleaue vnto vs.[5]Remember not the iniquities of our forefathers:
but thinke vpon thy power and thy name, now at this time.[6]For thou art
the Lord our God, and thee, O Lord, will we praiſe.[7]And for this cauſe
thou haſt put thy feare in our hearts, to the intent that we ſhould call
vpon thy name, and praiſe thee in our captiuity: for we haue called to
minde all the iniquity of our forefathers that ſinned before thee.[8]Behold,
we are yet this day in our captiuity, where thou haſt ſcattered vs, for a
reproch and a curſe, and to be ſubiect to payments, according to all the
iniquities of our fathers which departed from the Lord our God.[9]Heare,
Iſrael, the commandements of life, giue eare to vnderſtand
wiſedome.[10]How happeneth it, Iſrael, that thou art in thine enemies
land, that thou art waxen old in a ſtrange countrey, that thou art defiled
with the dead?[11]That thou art counted with them that goe downe into
the graue?[12]Thou haſt forſaken the fountaine of wiſedome.[13]For if thou
hadſt walked in the way of God, thou ſhouldeſt haue dwelled in peace
for euer.[14]Learne where is wiſedome, where is ſtrength, where is
vnderſtanding, that thou mayeſt know alſo where is length of daies, and
life, where is the light of the eyes and peace.[15]Who hath found out her
place? or who hath come into her treaſures?[16]Where are the princes of
the heathen become, and ſuch as ruled the beaſts vpon the earth.[17]They
that had their paſtime with the foules of the aire, and they that hoorded
vp ſiluer and gold wherein men truſt, and made no end of their
getting?[18]For they that wrought in ſiluer, and were ſo carefull, and whoſe
workes are vnſearchable,[19]They are vaniſhed, and gone downe to the
graue, and others are come vp in their ſteads.[20]Young men haue ſeene
light, and dwelt vpon the earth: but the way of knowledge haue they not
knowen,[21]Nor vnderſtood the pathes thereof; nor laid hold of it: their
children were farre off from that way.[22]It hath not beene heard of in
Chanaan: neither hath it beene ſeene in Theman.[23]The Agarenes that
ſeek wiſdome vpon earth, the marchants of Merran, and of Theman, the
authors of fables, and ſearchers out of vnderſtanding: none of theſe
haue knowen the way of wiſedome, or remember her pathes.[24]O Iſrael,
how great is the houſe of God? and how large is the place of his
poſſeſſion?[25]Great, and hath none end: high, and vnmeaſurable.[26]There
were the gyants, famous from the beginning, that were of ſo great
ſtature, and ſo expert in warre.[27]Thoſe did not the Lord chuſe, neither
gaue he the way of knowledge vnto them.[28]But they were deſtroyed,
becauſe they had no wiſedome, and periſhed through their owne
fooliſhneſse.[29]Who hath gone vp into heauen and taken her, and
brought her downe from the clouds?[30]Who hath gone ouer the ſea, and
found her, & wil bring her for pure gold?[31]No man knoweth her way,
nor thinketh of her path.[32]But he that knoweth all things, knoweth her,
and hath found her out with his vnderſtanding: he that prepared the
earth for euermore, hath filled it with fourefooted beaſts.[33]He that
ſendeth forth light, and it goeth: calleth it againe, and it obeyeth him
with feare.[34]The ſtarres ſhined in their watches, and reioyced: when he
calleth them, they ſay, Here we be, and ſo with cheerefulneſse they
ſhewed light vnto him that made them.[35]This is our God, and there ſhall
none other be accounted of in compariſon of him.[36]He hath found out
all the way of knowledge, and hath giuen it vnto Iacob his ſeruant, & to
Iſrael his beloued.[37]Afterward did he ſhew himſelfe vpon earth, and
conuerſed with men.
CHAPTER 4[1]This is the Booke of the commandements of God: and
the Law that endureth for euer: all they that keepe it ſhall come to life:
but ſuch as leaue it, ſhall die.[2]Turne thee, O Iacob, & take heed of it:
walke in the preſence of the light therof, that thou mayeſt be
illuminated.[3]Giue not thine honour to another, nor the things that are
profitable vnto thee, to a ſtrange nation.[4]O Iſrael, happie are wee: for
things that are pleaſing to God, are made knowen vnto vs.[5]Be of good
cheare, my people, the memoriall of Iſrael.[6]Ye were ſold to the nations,
not for *your* deſtruction: but becauſe you moued God to wrath, ye were
deliuered vnto the enemies.[7]For yee prouoked him that made you, by
ſacrificing vnto deuils, and not to God.[8]Ye haue forgotten the
euerlaſting God, that brought you vp, and ye haue grieued Ieruſalem
that nourſed you.[9]For when ſhee ſaw the wrath of God cōming vpon
you, ſhe ſaid; Hearken, O ye that dwell about Sion: God hath brought
vpō me great mourning.[10]For I ſaw the captiuitie of my ſonnes and
daughters, which the euerlaſting brought vpon them.[11]With ioy did I
nouriſh them: but ſent them away with weeping and mourning.[12]Let no
man reioyce ouer me a widow, and forſaken of many, who for the ſinnes
of my children, am left deſolate: becauſe they departed from the Law of
God.[13]They knew not his ſtatutes, nor walked in the waies of his
Commandements, nor trode in the pathes of diſcipline in his
righteouſneſſe.[14]Let them that dwell about Sion come, and remember
ye the captiuity of my ſonnes and daughters, which the euerlaſting hath
brought vpon them.[15]For he hath brought a nation vpon them from far:
a ſhameleſſe nation, and of a ſtrange language, who neither reuerenced
old man, nor pitied childe.[16]Theſe haue caried away the deare beloued
children of the widow, and left her that was alone, deſolate without
daughters.[17]But what can I helpe you?[18]For he that brought theſe
plagues vpon you, will deliuer you from the hands of your
enemies.[19]Goe your way, O my children, goe your way: for I am left
deſolate.[20]I haue put off the clothing of peace, and put vpon me the
ſackcloth of my prayer. I will cry vnto the euerlaſting in my dayes.[21]Be
of good cheare, O my children, cry vnto the Lord: & he ſhal deliuer you
from the power & hand of the enemies.[22]For my hope is in the
Euerlaſting that hee will ſaue you, and ioy is come vnto me from the
Holy one, becauſe of the mercy which ſhall ſoone come vnto you from
the euerlaſting our Sauiour.[23]For I ſent you out with mourning and
weeping: but God will giue you to mee againe, with ioy and gladneſſe
for euer.[24]Like as now the neighbours of Sion haue ſeene your captiuity:
ſo ſhall they ſee ſhortly your ſaluation from our God, which ſhall come
vpon you with great glory, and brightneſse of the euerlaſting.[25]My
children, ſuffer patiently the wrath that is come vpon you from God: for
thine enemy hath perſecuted thee: but ſhortly thou ſhalt ſee his
deſtruction, & ſhalt tread vpon his necke.[26]My delicate ones haue gone
rough wayes, and were taken away as a flocke caught of the
enemies.[27]Be of good comfort, O my children, and cry vnto God: for
you ſhall be remembred of him that brought theſe things vpon
you.[28]For as it was your minde to goe aſtray from God: ſo being
returned ſeeke him ten times more.[29]For he that hath brought theſe
plagues vpon you, ſhall bring you euerlaſting ioy againe with your
ſaluation.[30]Take a good heart, O Ieruſalem: for hee that gaue thee that
name, will comfort thee.[31]Miſerable are they that afflicted thee, and
reioyced at thy fall.[32]Miſerable are the cities which thy children ſerued:
miſerable is ſhe that receiued thy ſonnes.[33]For as ſhee reioyced at thy
ruine, and was glad of thy fall: ſo ſhall ſhe be grieued for her owne
deſolation.[34]For I will take away the reioycing of her great multitude,
and her pride ſhalbe turned into mourning.[35]For fire ſhal come vpon
her frō the euerlaſting, long to endure: and ſhe ſhal be inhabited of deuils
for a great time.[36]O Ieruſalem, looke about thee toward the Eaſt, and
behold the ioy that commeth vnto thee from God.[37]Loe, thy ſonnes
come whom thou ſenteſt away: they come gathered together from the
Eaſt to the Weſt, by the word of the holy One, reioycing in the glory of
God.
CHAPTER 5[1]Put off, O Ieruſalem, the garment of thy mourning and
affliction, and put on the comelineſse of the glory that commeth from
God for euer.[2]Caſt about thee a double garment of the righteouſneſſe
which commeth from God, and ſet a diademe on thine head of the glory
of the euerlaſting.[3]For God wil ſhew thy brightneſse vnto euery
countrey vnder heauen.[4]For thy name ſhall bee called of God for euer,
The peace of righteouſneſſe, and the glory of Gods worſhip.[5]Ariſe, O
Ieruſalem, and ſtand on high, and looke about toward the Eaſt, and
behold thy children gathered from the Weſt vnto the Eaſt by the word
of the holy One, reioycing in the remembrance of God.[6]For they
departed from thee on foote, and were ledde away of their enemies: but
God bringeth them vnto thee exalted with glory, as children of the
kingdome.[7]For God hath appointed that euery high hill, and banks of
long continuance ſhould be caſt downe, and valleys filled vp, to make
euen the ground, that Iſrael may goe ſafely in the glory of
God.[8]Moreouer, euen the woods, & euery ſweet ſmelling tree, ſhall
ouerſhadow Iſrael by the commandement of God.[9]For God ſhall leade
Iſrael with ioy, in the light of his glory, with the mercy and righteouſnes
that commeth from him.

EPIſTLE OF IEREMIAH (LETTER OF JEREMIAH)

CHAPTER 1 1A copy of an Epiſtle which Ieremie ſent vnto them
which were to be led captiues into Babylon, by the king of the
Babylonians, to certifie them as it was commanded him of God.2Becauſe
of þe ſinnes which ye haue committed before God, ye ſhall be led away
captiues vnto Babylon by Nabuchodonoſor king of the Babylonians.3So
when ye be come vnto Babylon, ye ſhal remaine there many yeeres, and
for a long ſeaſon, namely ſeuen generations: and after that I will bring
you away peaceably from thence.4Now ſhal ye ſee in Babylon gods of
ſiluer, and of gold, and of wood, borne vpon ſhoulders , which cauſe
the nations to feare.5Beware therefore that yee in no wiſe be like to
ſtrangers, neither be yee afraid of them, when yee ſee the multitude
before them, and behinde them, worſhipping them.6But ſay yee in your
hearts, O Lord, we muſt worſhip thee.7For mine Angel is with you, and
I my ſelfe caring for your ſoules.8As for their tongue, it is poliſhed by
the workeman, and they themſelues are guilded and laid ouer with ſiluer,
yet are they but falſe and cannot ſpeake.9And taking golde, as it were
for a virgine that loues to go gay, they make crownes for the heads of
their gods.10Sometimes alſo the Prieſts conuey from their gods golde
and ſiluer, and beſtow it vpon themſelues.11Yea they will giue thereof to
the common harlots, and decke them as men with garmentſ *being* gods
of ſiluer, and gods of gold, and wood.12Yet cannot theſe gods ſaue
themſelues from ruſt and moths, though they be couered with purple
raiment.13They wipe their faces becauſe of the duſt of the Temple, when
there is much vpon them.14And he that cannot put to death one that
offendeth him, holdeth a ſcepter as though hee were a iudge of the
countrey.15Hee hath alſo in his right hand a dagger, and an axe: but
cannot deliuer himſelfe from warre and theeues.16Whereby they are
knowen not to bee gods, therefore feare them not.17For like as a veſſell
that a man vſeth, is nothing worth when it is broken: euen ſo it is with
their gods: when they be ſet vp in the Temple, their eyes be full of duſt,
thorow the feet of them that come in.18And as the doores are made ſure
on euery ſide, vpon him that offendeth the king, as being committed to
ſuffer death: euen ſo the prieſts make faſt their temples, with doores,
with lockes and barres, leſt their gods bee ſpoiled with robbers.19They
light them candles, yea, more then for themſelues, whereof they cannot
ſee one.20They are as one of the beames of the temple, yet they ſay, their
hearts are gnawed vpon by things creeping out of the earth, & when
they eate them and their clothes, they feele it not.21Their faces are
blacked, thorow the ſmoke that comes out of the temple.22Upon their
bodies and heads, ſit battes, ſwallowes, and birds, and the cats alſo.23By
this you may know that they are no gods: therefore feare them
not.24Notwithſtanding the gold that is about them, to make them
beautifull, except they wipe off the ruſt they will not ſhine: for neither
when they were molten did they feele it.25The things wherein there is
no breath, are bought for a moſt hie price.26They are borne vpon
ſhoulders , hauing no feete, whereby they declare vnto men that they be
nothing worth.27They alſo that ſerue them, are aſhamed: for if they fall
to the ground at any time, they cannot riſe vp againe of themſelues:
neither if one ſet them upright can they moue of themſelues: neither if
they be bowed downe, can they make themſelues ſtreight: but they ſet
gifts before them as vnto dead men.28As for the things that are ſacrificed
vnto them, their prieſts ſell and abuſe: in like maner their wiues lay vp
part thereof in ſalt: but vnto the poore and impotent, they giue nothing
of it.29Menſtruous women, and women in childbed eate their ſacrifices:
by theſe things ye may know that they are no gods: feare them not.30For
how can they be called gods? becauſe women ſet meate before the gods
of ſiluer, gold, and wood.31And the prieſts ſit in their temples, hauing
their clothes rent, and their heads and beards ſhauen, and nothing vpon
their heads.32They roare and crie before their gods: as men doe at the
feaſt when one is dead.33The prieſtes alſo take off their garments, and
clothe their wiues and children.34Whether it be euill that one doth vnto
them, or good: they are not able to recompenſe it: they can neither ſet
vp a king, nor put him downe.35In like maner, they can neither giue
riches nor money: though a man make a vowe vnto them, and keepe it
not, they will not require it.36They can ſaue no man from death, neither
deliuer the weake from the mightie.37They cannot reſtore a blind man
to his ſight, nor helpe any man in his diſtreſſe.38They can ſhew no mercie
to the widow: nor doe good to the fatherleſſe.39Their gods of wood, and
which are ouerlaid with gold, and ſiluer, are like the ſtones that be hewen
out of the mountaine: they that worſhip them ſhall be
confounded.40How ſhould a man then thinke and ſay that they are
gods? when euen the Chaldeans thēſelues diſhonor them.41Who if they
ſhall ſee one dumbe that cannot ſpeake, they bring him and intreate Bel
that he may ſpeake, as though he were able to vnderſtand.42Yet they
cannot vnderſtand this themſelues, and leaue them: for they haue no
knowledge.43The women alſo with cordes aboue them, ſitting in the
wayes, burne branne for perfume: but if any of them drawen by ſome
that paſſeth by, lie with him, ſhe reproacheth her fellow that ſhe was not
thought as worthy as her ſelfe, nor her cord broken.44Whatſoeuer is
done among them is falſe: how may it then be thought or ſaid that they
are gods?45They are made of carpenters, and goldſmiths, they can be
nothing elſe, then the workman will haue them to be.46And they
themſelues that made them, can neuer continue long, how ſhould then
the things that are made of them, be gods?47For they left lies and
reproaches to them that come after.48For when there commeth any
warre or plague vpon them, the prieſts conſult with themſelues, where
they may be hidden with them.49How then cannot men perceiue, that
they be no gods, which can neither ſaue themſelues from warre nor from
plague?50For ſeeing they be but of wood, and ouerlaide with ſiluer and
gold: it ſhall be knowen heereafter that they are falſe.51And it ſhall
manifeſtly appeare to all nations and kings, that they are no gods: but
the workes of mens hands, and that there is no worke of God in
them.52Who then may not know that they are no gods?53For neither can
they ſet vp a king in the land, nor giue raine vnto men.54Neither can
they iudge their owne cauſe, nor redreſſe a wrong being vnable: for they
are as crowes between heauen and earth.55Whereupon when fire falleth
vpon the houſe of gods of wood, or layd ouer with gold or ſiluer, their
prieſts will fly away, & eſcape: but they themſelues ſhall be burnt aſunder
like beames.56Moreouer they cannot withſtand any king or enemies:
how can it then be thought or ſaid that they be gods?57Neither are thoſe
gods of wood, and layd ouer with ſiluer or gold able to eſcape either
from theeues or robbers.58Whoſe gold, and ſiluer, and garments
wherwith they are clothed, they that are ſtrong doe take, and goe away
withall: neither are they able to helpe themſelues.59Therefore it is better
to be a king that ſheweth his power, or elſe a profitable veſſell in an
houſe, which the owner ſhall haue vſe of, then ſuch falſe gods: or to be
a doore in an houſe to keepe ſuch things ſafe as be therein, then ſuch
falſe gods: or a pillar of wood in a palace, then ſuch falſe gods.60For
Sunne, Moone, and ſtarres, being bright and ſent to doe their offices,
are obedient.61In like maner the lightning when it breaketh forth is eaſie
to bee ſeene, and after the ſame maner the wind bloweth in euery
country.62And when God commandeth the clouds to goe ouer the
whole world: they doe as they are bidden:63And the fire ſent from aboue
to conſume hilles and woods, doth as it is commanded: but theſe are
like vnto them neither in ſhew, nor power.64Wherefore it is neither to
be ſuppoſed nor ſaid, that they are gods, ſeeing they are able, neither to
iudge cauſes, nor to doe good vnto men.65Knowing therefore that they
are no gods, feare them not.66For they can neither curſe nor bleſſe
kings.67Neither can they ſignes in the heauens among the heathen: nor
ſhine as the Sunne, nor giue light as the Moone.68The beaſts are better
then they: for they can get vnder a couert, and helpe themſelues.69It is
then by no meanes manifeſt vnto vs that they are gods: therefore feare
them not.70For as a ſcarcrow in a garden of Cucumbers keepeth
nothing: ſo are their gods of wood, and laid ouer with ſiluer and
gold.71And likewiſe their gods of wood, and laid ouer with ſiluer and
gold, are like to a white thorne in an orchard that euery bird ſitteth vpon:
as alſo to a dead body, that is caſt into the darke.72And you ſhall know
them to be no gods, by the bright purple that rotteth vpon them: and
they themſelues afterward ſhall be eaten, and ſhall be a reproach in the
country.73Better therefore is the iuſt man that hath none idoles: for he
ſhall be farre from reproach.

THE ſONG OF THE THREE CHILDREN (PRAYER OF AZARIAH)

CHAPTER 1 1*And they walked in the midſt of the fire, praiſing God, and bleſſing
the Lord.* Then Azarias ſtood vp & prayed on this manner, and opening
his mouth in the midſt of the fire, ſaid,2Bleſſed art thou, O Lord God
of our fathers: thy Name is worthy to be praiſed, and glorified for
euermore.3For thou art righteous in all the things that thou haſt done to
vs: yea, true are all thy workes: thy wayes are right, and all thy iudgements
trueth.4In all the things that thou haſt brought vpon vs, and vpon the
holy citie of our fathers, euen Ieruſalem, thou haſt executed true
iudgement: for according to trueth and iudgement, didſt thou bring all
theſe things vpon vs, becauſe of our ſinnes.5For wee haue ſinned and
committed iniquitie, departing from thee.6In all things haue we
treſpaſſed, and not obeyed thy Commandements, nor kept them, neither
done as thou haſt commanded vs, that it might goe well with
vs.7Wherefore all that thou haſt brought vpon vs, and euery thing that
thou haſt done to vs, thou haſt done in true iudgement.8And thou didſt
deliuer vs into the hands of lawleſſe enemies, moſt hatefull forſakerſ *of
God* and to an vniuſt King, and the moſt wicked in all the world.9And
now wee can not open our mouthes, we are become a ſhame, and
reproch to thy ſeruants, and to them that worſhip thee.10Yet deliuer vs
not vp wholy for thy Names ſake, neither diſanull thou thy
Couenant:11And cauſe not thy mercy to depart from vs: for thy beloued
Abrahams ſake: for thy ſeruant Iſaacs ſake, and for thy holy Iſraels
ſake.12To whom thou haſt ſpoken and promiſed, That thou wouldeſt
multiply their ſeed as the ſtarres of heauen, and as the ſand that lyeth
vpon the ſea ſhore.13For we, O Lord, are become leſſe then any nation,
and bee kept vnder this day in all the world, becauſe of our
ſinnes.14Neither is there at this time, Prince, or Prophet, or leader, or
burnt offering, or ſacrifice, or oblation, or incenſe, or place to ſacrifice
before thee, and to finde mercie.15Neuertheleſſe in a contrite heart, and
an humble ſpirit, let vs be accepted.16Like as in the burnt offering of
rammes and bullockes, and like as in ten thouſands of fat lambes: ſo let
our ſacrifice bee in thy ſight this day, and *grant* that wee may wholy goe
after thee: for they ſhall not bee confounded that put their truſt in
thee.17And now wee follow thee, with all our heart, wee feare thee, and
ſeeke thy face.18Put vs not to ſhame: but deale with vs after thy louing
kindeneſse, and according to the multitude of thy mercies.19Deliuer vs
alſo according to thy marueilous workes, and giue glory to thy Name, O
Lord, and let all them that doe thy ſeruants hurt be aſhamed.20And let
them be confounded in all their power and might, and let their ſtrength
be broken.21And let them know that thou art Lord, the onely God, and
glorious ouer the whole world.22And the kings ſeruants that put them
in, ceaſed not to make the ouen hote with roſin, pitch, towe, and ſmall
wood.23So that the flame ſtreamed forth aboue the fornace, fourtie and
nine cubites:24And it paſſed through, and burnt thoſe Caldeans it found
about the fornace.25But the Angel of the Lord came downe into the
ouen, together with Azarias and his fellowes, and ſmote the flame of the
fire out of the ouen:26And made the mids of the fornace, as it had bene
a moiſt whiſtling wind, ſo that the fire touched them not at all, neither
hurt nor troubled them.27Then the three, as out of one mouth, praiſed,
glorified, and bleſſed God in the fornace, ſaying;28Bleſſed art thou, O
Lord God of our fathers: and to be praiſed and exalted aboue all for
euer.29And bleſſed is thy glorious and holy Name: and to be praiſed and
exalted aboue all for euer.30Bleſſed art thou in the Temple of thine holy
glory: and to be praiſed and glorified aboue all for euer.31Bleſſed art thou
that beholdeſt the depths, and ſitteſt vpon the Cherubims, and to be
praiſed and exalted aboue all for euer.32Bleſſed art thou on the glorious
Throne of thy kingdome: and to bee praiſed and glorified aboue all for
euer.33Bleſſed art thou in the firmament of heauen: and aboue all to be
praiſed and glorified for euer.34O all yee workes of the Lorde, bleſſe ye
the Lord: praiſe and exalt him aboue all for euer.35O ye heauens, bleſſe
ye the Lord: praiſe and exalt him aboue all for euer.36O yee Angels of
the Lord, bleſſe ye the Lord: praiſe and exalt him aboue all for euer.37O
all ye waters that be aboue the heauen, bleſſe yee the Lord: praiſe and
exalt him aboue all for euer.38O all yee powers of the Lord, bleſſe ye the
Lord: praiſe and exalt him aboue all for euer.39O yee Sunne and Moone,
bleſſe ye the Lord: praiſe and exalt him aboue all for euer.40O ye ſtarres
of heauen, bleſſe ye the Lord: praiſe and exalt him aboue all for euer.41O
euery ſhowre and dew, bleſſe ye the Lord: praiſe and exalt him aboue all
for euer.42O all ye windes, bleſſe yee the Lord: praiſe and exalt him
aboue all for euer.43O yee fire and heate, bleſſe ye the Lord: praiſe and
exalt him aboue all for euer.44O yee Winter and Summer, bleſſe ye the
Lord: praiſe and exalt him aboue all for euer.45O ye dewes and ſtormes
of ſnow, bleſſe ye the Lord: praiſe and exalt him aboue all for euer.46O
ye nights and dayes, bleſſe ye the Lord: praiſe and exalt him aboue all
for euer.47O ye light and darkeneſſe, bleſſe ye the Lord: praiſe and exalt
him aboue all for euer.48O yee yce and colde, bleſſe ye the Lord: praiſe
and exalt him aboue all for euer.49O ye froſt and ſnow, bleſſe ye the
Lord: praiſe and exalt him aboue all for euer.50O ye lightnings and
clouds, bleſſe ye the Lord: praiſe and exalt him aboue all for euer.51O
let the earth bleſſe the Lord: praiſe and exalt him aboue all for euer.52O
ye mountaines and little hils, bleſſe ye the Lord: praiſe and exalt him
aboue all for euer.53O all ye things that grow on the earth, bleſſe ye the
Lord: praiſe and exalt him aboue all for euer.54O yee fountaines, bleſſe
yee the Lord: praiſe and exalt him aboue all for euer.55O ye ſeas and
riuers, bleſſe ye the Lord: praiſe and exalt him aboue all for euer.56O ye
whales and all that mooue in the waters, bleſſe ye the Lord: praiſe and
exalt him aboue all for euer.57O all ye foules of the aire, bleſſe ye the
Lord: praiſe and exalt him aboue all for euer.58O all ye beaſts and cattell,
bleſſe ye the Lord: praiſe and exalt him aboue all for euer.59O ye
children of men, bleſſe yee the Lord: praiſe and exalt him aboue all for
euer.60O Iſrael bleſſe ye the Lord: praiſe and exalt him aboue all for
euer.61O ye prieſts of the Lord, bleſſe ye the Lord: praiſe and exalt him
aboue all for euer.62O ye ſeruants of the Lord, bleſſe ye the Lord: praiſe
and exalt him aboue all for euer.63O ye ſpirits and ſoules of the
righteous, bleſſe ye the Lord, praiſe and exalt him aboue all for euer.64O
ye holy and humble men of heart, bleſſe ye the Lord: praiſe and exalt
him aboue all for euer.65O Ananias, Azarias, and Miſael, bleſſe ye the
Lord, praiſe and exalt him aboue all for euer: for hee hath deliuered vs
from hell, and ſaued vs from the hand of death, and deliuered vs out of
the mids of the furnace, *and* burning flame: euen out of the mids of the
fire hath he deliuered vs.66O giue thanks vnto the Lord, becauſe he is
gracious: for his mercie endureth for euer.67O all ye that worſhip the
Lord, bleſſe the God of gods, praiſe him, and giue him thankes: for his
mercie endureth for euer.

THE ſTORY OF SUſANNA (SUSANNA)

CHAPTER 1 1There dwelt a man in Babylon, called Ioacim.2And hee
tooke a wife, whoſe name was Suſanna, the daughter of Chelcias, a very
faire woman, and one that feared the Lord.3Her parents alſo were
righteous, and taught their daughter according to the Law of
Moſes.4Now Ioacim was a great rich man, and had a faire garden ioyning
vnto his houſe, and to him reſorted the Iewes: becauſe he was more
honourable then all others.5The ſame yeere were appointed two of the
Ancients of the people to be iudges, ſuch as the Lord ſpake of, that
wickedneſſe came from Babylon from ancient iudges, who ſeemed to
gouerne the people.6Theſe kept much at Ioacims houſe: and all that had
any ſuits in lawe, came vnto them.7Now when the people departed away
at noone, Suſanna went into her huſbands garden to walke.8And the
two Elders ſaw her going in euery day and walking: ſo that their luſt was
inflamed toward her.9And they peruerted their owne mind, and turned
away their eyes, that they might not looke vnto heauen, nor remember
iuſt iudgements.10And albeit they both were wounded with her loue: yet
durſt not one ſhew another his griefe.11For they were aſhamed to declare
their luſt, that they deſired to haue to doe with her.12Yet they watched
diligently from day to day to ſee her.13And the one ſaid to the other, Let
vs now goe home: for it is dinner time.14So when they were gone out,
they parted the one from the other, and turning backe againe they came
to the ſame place, and after that they had aſked one another the cauſe,
they acknowledged their luſt: then appointed they a time both together,
when they might find her alone.15And it fell out as they watched a fit
time, ſhe went in as before, with two maids onely, and ſhe was deſirous
to waſh her ſelfe in the garden: for it was hot.16And there was no body
there ſaue the two Elders, that had hid themſelues, and watched

her.17Then ſhe ſaid to her maids, Bring me oile and waſhing bals, and ſhut the garden doores, that I may waſh me.18And they did as ſhe bad them, and ſhut the garden doores, and went out themſelues at priuie doores to fetch the things that ſhe had commaunded them: but they ſaw not the Elders, becauſe they were hid.19Now when the maids were gone forth, the two Elders roſe vp, and ran vnto her, ſaying,20Behold, the garden doores are ſhut, that no man can ſee vs, and we are in loue with thee: therefore conſent vnto vs, and lie with vs.21If thou wilt not, we will beare witneſſe againſt thee, that a young man was with thee: and therefore thou didſt ſend away thy maides from thee.22Then Suſanna ſighed and ſaid, I am ſtraited on euery ſide: for if I doe this thing, it is death vnto me: and if I doe it not, I cannot eſcape your hands.23It is better for me to fall into your hands, and not doe it: then to ſinne in the ſight of the Lord.24With that Suſanna cried with a loud voice: and the two Elders cried out againſt her.25Then ranne the one, and opened the garden doore.26So when the ſeruants of the houſe heard the crie in the garden, they ruſhed in at a priuie doore to ſee what was done vnto her.27But when the Elders had declared their matter, the ſeruants were greatly aſhamed: for there was neuer ſuch a report made of Suſanna.28And it came to paſſe the next day, when the people were aſſembled to her huſband Ioacim, the two Elders came alſo full of miſchieuous imagination againſt Suſanna to put her to death,29And ſaid before the people, Send for Suſanna, the daughter of Chelcias, Ioacims wife. And ſo they ſent.30So ſhe came with her father and mother, her children and all her kinred.31Now Suſanna was a very delicate woman and beauteous to behold.32And theſe wicked men commanded to vncouer her face (for ſhe was couered) that they might be filled with her beautie.33Therefore her friends, and all that ſaw her, wept.34Then the two Elders ſtood vp in the mids of the people, and laid their hands vpon her head.35And ſhe weeping looked vp towards heauen: for her heart truſted in the Lord.36And the Elders ſaid, As we walked in the garden alone, this woman came in, with two maides, and ſhut the garden doores, & ſent the maides away.37Then a young man who there was hid, came vnto her & lay with her.38Then we that ſtood in a corner of the garden, ſeeing this wickedneſſe, ran vnto them.39And when we ſaw them together, the man we could not hold: for he was ſtronger then we, and opened the doore, and leaped out.40But hauing taken this woman, we aſked who the young man was: but ſhe would not tell vs: theſe things doe we teſtifie.41Then the aſſembly beleeued them, as thoſe that were the Elders and Iudges of the people: ſo they condemned her to death.42Then Suſanna cried out with a loud voice and ſaid: O euerlaſting God that knoweſt the ſecrets, and knoweſt all things before they be:43Thou knoweſt that they haue borne falſe witneſſe againſt me, and behold I muſt die: whereas I neuer did ſuch things, as theſe men haue malicioully inuented againſt me.44And the Lord heard her voice.45Therefore when ſhe was led to be put to death: the Lord raiſed vp the holy ſpirit of a young youth, whoſe name was Daniel,46Who cried with a loud voice: I am cleare frō the blood of this woman.47Then all the people turned them towards him, & ſaid: what meane theſe words that thou haſt ſpoken?48So he ſtanding in the mids of them, ſaid, Are ye ſuch fooles ye ſonnes of Iſrael, that without examination or knowledge of the truth, ye haue condemned a daughter of Iſrael?49Returne againe to the place of iudgement: for they haue borne falſe witneſſe againſt her50Wherefore all the people turned againe in haſt, and the Elders ſaid vnto him, Come ſit downe among vs, and ſhew it vs, ſeeing God hath giuen thee the honour of an Elder.51Then ſaid Daniel vnto them, Put theſe two aſide one farre from another, and I will examine them.52So when they were put aſunder one from another, hee called one of them, and ſaid vnto him, O thou that art waxen old in wickedneſſe: now thy ſinnes which thou haſt committed aforetime, are come *to light*.53For thou haſt pronounced falſe iudgement, and haſt condemned the innocent, and haſt let the guiltie goe free, albeit the Lord ſaith, The innocent and righteous ſhalt thou not ſlay.54Now then if thou haſt ſeene her: tell me, Under what tree ſaweſt thou them companying together? who anſwered, Under a maſticke tree.55And Daniel ſaid, Uery wel; Thou haſt lied againſt thine owne head: for euen now the Angel of God hath receiued the ſentence of God, to cut thee in two.56So hee put him aſide, and commanded to bring the other, & ſaid vnto him, O thou ſeed of Chanaan, and not of Iuda, beauty hath deceiued thee, and luſt hath peruerted thine heart.57Thus haue yee dealt with the daughters of Iſrael, and they for feare companied with you: but the daughter of Iuda would not abide your wickedneſſe.58Now therefore tell mee, Under what tree didſt thou take them companying together? who anſwered, Under a holme tree.59Then ſaid Daniel vnto him, Well: thou haſt alſo lied againſt thine owne head: for the Angel of God waiteth with the ſword to cut thee in two, that he may deſtroy you.60With that all the aſſembly cried out with a lowd voice, and praiſed God who ſaueth them that truſt in him.61And they aroſe againſt the two Elders, (for Daniel had conuicted them of falſe witneſſe by their owne mouth)62And according to the Law of Moſes, they did vnto them in ſuch ſort as they malitiouſly intended to doe to their neighbour: And they put them to death. Thus the innocent blood was ſaued the ſame day.63Therefore Chelcias and his wife praiſed God for their daughter Suſanna, with Ioacim her huſband, and all the kinred: becauſe there was no diſhoneſtie found in her.64From that day foorth was Daniel had in great reputation in the ſight of the people.

THE IDOLE BEL AND THE DRAGON (BEL AND THE DRAGON)

CHAPTER 11And King Aſtyages was gathered to his fathers, and Cyrus of Perſia receiued his kingdome.2And Daniel conuerſed with the king, and was honored aboue all his friends.3Now the Babylonians had an Idol called Bel, and there were ſpent vpon him euery day twelue great meaſures of fine flowre, and fourtie ſheepe, and ſixe veſſels of wine.4And the king worſhipped it, and went daily to adore it: but Daniel worſhipped his owne God. And the king ſaid vnto him, Why doeſt not thou worſhip Bel?5Who anſwered and ſaid, Becauſe I may not worſhip idols made with hands, but the liuing God, who hath created the heauen, and the earth, and hath ſoueraigntie ouer all fleſh.6Then ſaide the King vnto him, Thinkeſt thou not that Bel is a liuing god? ſeeſt thou not how much he eateth and drinketh euery day?7Then Daniel ſmiled, and ſaid, O king, be not deceiued: for this is but clay within, and braſſe without, and did neuer eate or drinke any thing.8So the king was wroth, and called for his Prieſts, and ſaid vnto them, If yee tell me not who this is that deuoureth theſe expenſes, ye ſhall die.9But if ye can certifie me that Bel deuoureth them, then Daniel ſhall die: for hee hath ſpoken blaſphemie againſt Bel. And Daniel ſayd vnto the king, Let it be according to thy word.10(Now the Prieſts of Bel were threeſcore and tenne, beſide their wiues and children) and the king went with Daniel into the temple of Bel.11So Bels Prieſts ſaid, Loe, wee goe out: but thou, O king, ſet on the meate, and make ready the wine, and ſhut the doore faſt, and ſeale it with thine owne ſignet:12And to morrow, when thou commeſt in, if thou findeſt not that Bel hath eaten vp all, wee will ſuffer death; or elſe Daniel, that ſpeaketh falſely againſt vs.13And they little regarded it: for vnder the table they had made a priuie entrance, whereby they entred in continually, and conſumed thoſe things.14So when they were gone forth, the king ſet meates before Bel. Now Daniel had commanded his ſeruants to bring aſhes, and thoſe they ſtrewed throughout all the temple, in the preſence of the king alone: then went they out and ſhut the doore, & ſealed it with the kings ſignet, and ſo departed.15Now in the night came the Prieſts with their wiues and children (as they were woont to doe) and did eate and drinke vp all.16In the morning betime the king aroſe, and Daniel with him.17And the king ſaid, Daniel, are the ſeales whole? And he ſaid, Yea, O king, they be whole.18And aſſoone as he had opened the doore, the king looked vpon the table, and cried with a loude voice, Great art thou, O Bel, and with thee is no deceit at all.19Then laughed Daniel, and helde the king that he ſhould not goe in, and ſayd, Behold now the pauement, and marke well whoſe footſteps are theſe.20And the king ſaid, I ſee the footſteps of men, women and children: and then the king was angry,21And tooke the Prieſts, with their wiues and children, who ſhewed him the priuy doores, where they came in, and conſumed ſuch things as were vpon the table.22Therefore the king ſlewe them, and deliuered Bel into Daniels power, who deſtroyed him and his temple.23And in that ſame place there was a great Dragon, which they of Babylon worſhipped.24And the king ſaid vnto Daniel, Wilt thou alſo ſay that this is of braſſe? loe, he liueth, he eateth and drinketh, thou canſt not ſay, that he is no liuing God: therefore worſhip him.25Then ſaid Daniel vnto the king, I will worſhip the Lord my God: for he is the liuing God.26But giue me leaue, O king, and I ſhall ſlay this dragon without ſword or ſtaffe. The king ſayde, I giue thee leaue.27Then Daniel tooke pitch, fat, and haire, and did ſeethe them together, and made lumpes thereof: this hee put in the Dragons mouth, and ſo the Dragon burſt in ſunder: and Daniel ſaid, Loe, theſe are the gods you worſhip.28When they of Babylon heard that, they tooke great indignation, and conſpired againſt the king, ſaying, The king is become a Iew, and he hath deſtroyed Bel, he hath ſlaine the Dragon, and put the Prieſts to death.29So they came to the king, and ſaid, Deliuer vs Daniel, or elſe we will deſtroy thee and thine houſe.30Now when the king ſawe that they preſſed him ſore, being conſtrained, he deliuered Daniel vnto them:31Who caſt him into the lions den, where he was ſixe dayes.32And in the den there were ſeuen lyons, and they had giuen them euery day two carkeiſes, and two ſheepe: which then were not giuen to them, to the intent they might deuoure Daniel.33Now there was in Iury a Prophet called Habacuc, who had made pottage, & had broken bread in a boule, and was going into the field, for to bring it to the reapers.34But the Angel of the Lord ſaid vnto Habacuc, Goe carrie the dinner that thou haſt into Babylon vnto Daniel, who is in the lions denne.35And Habacuc ſaid, Lord, I neuer ſaw Babylon: neither do I know where the denne is.36Then the Angel of the Lord tooke him by the crown, and bare him by the haire of his head, and through the vehemencie of his ſpirit, ſet him in Babylon ouer the den.37And Habacuc cryed, ſaying, O Daniel, Daniel, take the dinner which God hath ſent thee.38And Daniel ſaide, Thou haſt remembred mee, O God: neither haſt thou forſaken them that ſeeke thee, and loue thee.39So Daniel aroſe and did eate: and the Angel of the Lord ſet Habacuc in his owne place againe immediatly.40Upon the ſeuenth day the king went to bewaile Daniel: and when he came to the den, he looked in, and behold, Daniel was ſitting.41Then cried the king with a loud voyce, ſaying, Great art thou, O Lord God of Daniel, and there is none other beſides thee.42And he drew him out: and caſt thoſe that were the cauſe of his deſtruction into the den: and they were deuoured in a moment before his face.

THE PRAYER OF MANAſſEH (PRAYER OF MANASSEH)

CHAPTER 1 1*The prayer of Manaſſes King of Iuda, when he was holden captiue in Babylon.* O Lord, Almightie God of our Fathers, Abraham, Iſaac, and Iacob, and of their righteous ſeed: who haſt made heauen and earth, with all the ornament thereof: who haſt bound the ſea by the word of thy Commandement: who haſt ſhut vp the deepe, and ſealed it by thy terrible and glorious Name, whome all men feare, and tremble before thy power: for the Maieſtie of thy glory cannot bee borne, and thine angry threatning towards ſinners is importable: but thy mercifull promiſe is vnmeaſurable and vnſearchable: for thou art the moſt High Lord, of great compaſſion, long ſuffering, very mercifull, and repenteſt of the euils of men. Thou, O Lord, according to thy great goodneſſe haſt promiſed repentance, and forgiueneſse to them that haue ſinned againſt thee: and of thine infinite mercies haſt appointed repentance vnto ſinners that they may be ſaued. Thou therefore, O Lord, that art the God of the iuſt, haſt not appointed repentance to the iuſt, as to Abraham, and Iſaac, and Iacob, which haue not ſinned againſt thee: but thou haſt appointed repentance vnto me that am a ſinner: for I haue ſinned aboue the number of the ſands of the ſea. My tranſgreſſions, O Lord, are multiplied: my tranſgreſſions are multiplied, and I am not worthy to behold and ſee the height of heauen, for the multitude of mine iniquitie. I am bowed downe with many yron bands, that I cannot lift vp mine head, neither haue any releaſe: For I haue prouoked thy wrath, and done euill before thee, I did not thy will, neither kept I thy Commandements: I haue ſet vp abominations, and haue multiplied offences. Now therefore I bow the knee of mine heart, beſeeching thee of grace: I haue ſinned, O Lord, I haue ſinned and I acknowledge mine iniquities: wherefore I humbly beſeech thee, forgiue me, O Lord, forgiue me, and deſtroy me not with mine iniquities. Be not angry with me for euer, by reſeruing euill for me, neither condemne mee into the lower parts of the earth. For thou art the God, euen the God of them that repent: and in me thou wilt ſhew all thy goodneſse: for thou wilt ſaue me that am vnworthy, according to thy great mercie. Therefore I will praiſe thee for euer all the dayes of my life: for all the powers of the heauens doe praiſe thee, and thine is the glory for euer and euer, Amen.

1 MACCABEES

CHAPTER 1 1And it happened, after that Alexander ſonne of Philip, the Macedonian, who came out of the land of Chettum, had ſmitten Darius king of the Perſians and Medes, that hee reigned in his ſtead, the firſt ouer Greece,2And made many wars, and wan many ſtrong holds, and ſlew the kings of the earth,3And went through to the ends of the earth, and tooke ſpoiles of many nations, inſomuch, that the earth was quiet before him, whereupon he was exalted, and his heart was lifted vp.4And he gathered a mighty ſtrong hoſte, and ruled ouer countries, and nations and kings, who became tributaries vnto him.5And after theſe things he fell ſicke, and perceiued that he ſhould die.6Wherefore he called his ſeruants, ſuch as were honourable, and had bin brought vp with him from his youth, and parted kis kingdome among them, while he was yet aliue:7So Alexander reigned twelue yeeres, and (then) died.8And his ſeruants bare rule euery one in his place.9And after his death they all put crowneſ *vpon themſelueſ* ſo did their ſonnes after them, many yeeres, and euils were multiplied in the earth.10And there came out of them a wicked roote, Antiochuſ *ſurnamed* Epiphanes, ſonne of Antiochus the king, who had beene an hoſtage at Rome, and he reigned in the hundreth and thirty and ſeuenth yeere of the kingdome of the Greekes.11In thoſe daies went there out of Iſrael wicked men, who perſwaded many, ſaying, Let vs goe, and make a couenant with the heathen, that are round about vs: for ſince we departed from them, we haue had much ſorrow.12So this deuiſe pleaſed them well.13Then certaine of the people were ſo forward heerein, that they went to the king, who gaue them licence to doe after the ordinances of the heathen.14Whereupon they built a place of exerciſe at Ieruſalem, according to the cuſtomes of the heathen,15And made themſelues, vncircumciſed, and forſooke the holy couenant, and ioyned themſelues to the heathen, and were ſold to doe miſchiefe.16Now when the kingdome was eſtabliſhed, before Antiochus, hee thought to reigne ouer Egypt, that he might haue yͤ dominion of two realms:17Wherefore he entred into Egypt with a great multitude, with chariots, and elephants, and horſemen, and a great nauie,18And made warre againſt Ptolomee king of Egypt, but Ptolomee was afraide of him, and fled: and many were wounded to death.19Thus they got the ſtrong cities in the land of Egypt, and hee tooke the ſpoiles thereof.20And after that Antiochus had ſmitten Egypt, he returned againe in the hundreth fortie and third yeere, and went vp againſt Iſrael and Ieruſalem with a great multitude,21And entred proudly into the ſanctuarie, and tooke away the golden altar, and the candleſticke of light, and all the veſſels thereof,22And the table of the ſhewbread, and the powring veſſels, and the vials, and the cenſers of gold, & the vaile, and the crownes, & the golden ornaments that were before the temple, all which he pulled off.23Hee tooke alſo the ſiluer and the gold, and the pretious veſſels: alſo he tooke the hidden treaſures which hee found:24And when hee had taken all away, he went into his owne land, hauing made a great maſsacre, and ſpoken very proudly.25Therfore there was great mourning in Iſrael, in euery place where they were;26So that the Princes and Elders mourned, the virgines and yong men were made feeble, and the beautie of women was changed.27Euery bridegrome tooke vp lamentation, and ſhe that ſate in the marriage chamber, was in heauineſse.28The land alſo was moued for the inhabitants thereof, and all the houſe of Iacob was couered with confuſion.29And after two yeeres fully expired, the king ſent his chiefe collectour of tribute vnto the cities of Iuda, who came vnto Ieruſalem with a great multitude,30And ſpake peaceable wordes vnto them, but *all waſ* deceit: for when they had giuen him credence, he fell ſuddenly vpon the citie, and ſmote it very ſore, & deſtroyed much people of

Iſrael.31And when hee had taken the ſpoiles of the citie, hee ſet it on fire,
and pulled downe the houſes, and walles thereof on euery ſide.32But the
women & children tooke they captiue, and poſſeſſed the cattell.33Then
builded they the citie of Dauid with a great and ſtrong wall, *and* with
mightie towers, and made it a ſtrong hold for them,34And they put
therein a ſinfull nation, wicked men, and
fortified *themſelueſ* therein.35They ſtored it alſo with armour and victuals,
and when they had gathered together the ſpoiles of Ieruſalem, they layd
them vp there, and ſo they became a ſore ſnare:36For it was a place to
lie in wait againſt the Sanctuary, and an euill aduerſary to Iſrael.37Thus
they ſhed innocent blood on euery ſide of the Sanctuary, and defiled
it.38In ſo much that the inhabitants of Ieruſalem fledde becauſe of them,
whereupon *the citie* was made an habitation of ſtrangers, & became
ſtrange to thoſe that were borne in her, and her owne children left
her:39Her Sanctuary was laid waſte like a wilderneſſe, her feaſts were
turned into mourning, her Sabbaths into reproch, her honour into
contempt.40As had bene her glory, ſo was her diſhonour encreaſed, and
her excellencie was turned into mourning.41Moreouer king Antiochus
wrote to his whole kingdome, that all ſhould be one people,42And euery
one ſhould leaue his lawes: ſo all the heathen agreed, according to the
commandement of the king.43Yea many alſo of the Iſraelites conſented
to his religion, and ſacrificed vnto idols, and prophaned the
Sabbath.44For the king had ſent letters by meſſengers vnto Ieruſalem,
and the cities of Iuda, that they ſhould follow the ſtrange lawes of the
land,45And forbid burnt offerings, and ſacrifice, and drinke offerings in
the temple; and that they ſhould prophane the Sabbaths, and feſtiuall
dayes:46And pollute the Sanctuarie and holy people:47Set vp altars, and
groues, and chappels of idols, and ſacrifice ſwines fleſh, and vncleane
beaſts:48That they ſhould alſo leaue their children vncircumciſed, and
make their ſoules abominable with all maner of vncleanneſſe, and
prophanation:49To the end they might forget the Law, and change all
the ordinances.50And whoſoeuer would not doe according to the
commandement of the king *he ſaid* he ſhould die.51In the ſelfe ſame
maner wrote he to his whole kingdome, and appointed ouerſeers ouer
all the people, commanding the cities of Iuda to ſacrifice, citie by
citie.52Then many of the people were gathered vnto them, to wit, euery
one that forſooke the Lawe, and ſo they committed euils in the
land:53And droue the Iſraelites into ſecret places, euen whereſoeuer they
could flie for ſuccour.54Now the fifteenth day of the moneth Caſleu, in
the hundreth fourtie and fift yeere, they ſet vp the abomination of
deſolation vpon the Altar, and builded idole altars throughout the cities
of Iuda, on euery ſide:55And burnt incenſe at the doores of their houſes,
and in the ſtreetes.56And when they had rent in pieces the bookes of
the Lawe which they found, they burnt them with fire.57And
whereſoeuer was found with any, the booke of the Teſtament, or if any
conſented to the Lawe, the kings commandement was, that they ſhould
put him to death.58Thus did they by their authority, vnto the Iſraelites
euery moneth, to as many as were found in the cities.59Now the fiue
and twentieth day of the moneth, they did ſacrifice vpon the idole altar,
which was vpon the Altar of God.60At which time, according to the
commandement, they put to death certaine women that had cauſed their
children to be circumciſed.61And they hanged the infants about their
neckes, and rifled their houſes, and ſlewe them that had circumciſed
them.62Howbeit, many in Iſrael were fully reſolued and confirmed in
themſelues, not to eate any vncleane thing.63Wherfore they choſe rather
to die, that they might not be defiled with meats, and that they might
not profane the holy Couenant: So then they died.64And there was very
great wrath vpon Iſrael.

CHAPTER 21In thoſe daies aroſe Mattathias the ſon of Iohn, the
ſonne of Simeon, a Prieſt of the ſonnes of Ioarib, from Ieruſalem, and
dwelt in Modin.2And he had fiue ſonnes, Ioannan called Caddis:3Simon,
called Thaſsi:4Iudas, who was called Maccabeus:5Eleazar, called Auaran,
and Ionathan, whoſe ſurname was Apphus.6And when hee ſaw the
blaſphemies that were committed in Iuda and Ieruſalem,7He ſaid, Woe
is me, wherfore was I borne to ſee this miſery of my people, and of the
holy citie, and to dwell there, when it was deliuered into the hand of the
enemie, and the Sanctuary into the hand of ſtrangers?8Her Temple is
become as a man without glory.9Her glorious veſſels are caried away
into captiuitie, her infants are ſlaine in the ſtreets, her yong men with
the ſword of the enemie.10What nation hath not had a part in her
kingdome, and gotten of her ſpoiles?11All her ornaments are taken away,
of a free-woman ſhee is become a bondſlaue.12And behold, our
Sanctuarie, euen our beautie, aud our glory is laid waſte, & the Gentiles
haue profaned it.13To what ende therefore ſhall we liue any
longer?14Then Mattathias and his ſons rent their clothes, and put on
ſackcloth, and mourned very ſore.15In the meane while the kings
officers, ſuch as compelled the people to reuolt, came into the city
Modin to make them ſacrifice.16And when many of Iſrael came vnto
them, Mattathias alſo and his ſonnes came together.17Then anſwered
the kings officers, and ſaid to Mattathias on this wiſe; Thou art a ruler,
and an honourable and great man in this citie, and ſtrengthened with
ſons and brethren:18Now therefore come thou firſt and fulfill the kings
commandement, like as all the heathen haue done; yea and the men of
Iuda alſo, and ſuch as remaine at Ieruſalem: ſo ſhalt thou and thine houſe
be in the number of the kings friends, and thou and thy children ſhall
be honoured with ſiluer, and golde, and many rewards.19Then
Mattathias anſwered, and ſpake with a loude voice, Though all the
nations that are vnder the kings dominion obey him, and fall away euery
one from the religion of their fathers, and giue conſent to his
commandements:20Yet will I, and my ſonnes, and my brethren walke in
the couenant of our fathers.21God forbid that we ſhould forſake the
Law, and the ordinances:22We will not hearken to the kings words, to
goe from our religion, either on the right hand, or the left.23Now when
he had left ſpeaking theſe words, there came one of the Iewes in the
ſight of all, to ſacrifice on the altar, which was at Modin, according to
the kings commandement.24Which thing when Mattathias ſaw, he was
inflamed with zeale, and his reines trembled, neither could hee forbeare
to ſhew his anger according to iudgement: wherefore he ranne, and ſlew
him vpon the altar.25Alſo the kings commiſsioner who compelled men
to ſacrifice, he killed at that time, & the altar he pulled downe.26Thus
dealt he zealouſly for the Law of God, like as Phineas did vnto Zambri
the ſonne of Salom.27And Mattathias cried throughout the citie with a
loud voyce, ſaying, Whoſoeuer is zealous of the law, and maintaineth
the couenant, let him follow me.28So he and his ſonnes fled into the
mountaines, and left all that euer they had in the citie.29Then many that
ſought after iuſtice and iudgement, went downe into the wilderneſſe to
dwell there.30Both they and their children, and their wiues, and their
cattell, becauſe afflictions increaſed ſore vpon them.31Now when it was
told the kings ſeruants, and the hoſte that was at Ieruſalem, in the citie
of Dauid, that certaine men, who had broken the kings commandement,
were gone downe into the ſecret places in the wilderneſſe.32They
purſued after them, a great number, and hauing ouertaken them, they
camped againſt them, and made war againſt them on the Sabbath
day.33And they ſaid vnto them, Let that which you haue done hitherto,
ſuffice: Come foorth, and doe according to the commandement of the
king, and you ſhall liue.34But they ſaid, We will not come forth, neither
will we do the kings commandement to profane the Sabbath day.35So
then they gaue them the battell with all ſpeed.36Howbeit, they anſwered
them not, neither caſt they a ſtone at them, nor ſtopped the places where
they lay hid,37But ſaid, Let vs die all in our innocencie: heauen and earth
ſhall teſtifie for vs, that you put vs to death wrongfully.38So they roſe vp
againſt them in battell on the Sabbath, and they ſlew them with their
wiues & children, and their cattell, to the number of a thouſand
people.39Now when Mattathias and his friends vnderſtood hereof, they
mourned for them right ſore.40And one of them ſaid to another: If we
all do as our brethren haue done, and fight not for our liues, and lawes
againſt the heathen, they wil now quickly root vs out of the earth.41At
that time therfore they decreed, ſaying, Whoſoeuer ſhall come to make
battell with vs on the Sabbath day, we will fight againſt him, neither will
wee die all, as our brethren that were murdered in the ſecret
places.42Then came there vnto him a company of Aſſideans, who were
mightie men of Iſrael, euen all ſuch as were voluntarily deuoted vnto the
Lawe.43Alſo all they that fled for perſecution ioyned themſelues vnto
them, and were a ſtay vnto them.44So they ioyned their forces, and
ſmote ſinfull men in their anger, and wicked men in their wrath: but the
reſt fled to the heathen for ſuccour.45Then Mattathias & his friends
went round about, and pulled downe the altars.46And what children
ſoeuer they found within the coaſt of Iſrael vncircumciſed, thoſe they

circumciſed valiantly.47They purſued alſo after þe proud men, & the work proſpered in their hand.48So they recouered the Law out of the hand of the Gentiles, and out of the hande of Kings, neither ſuffered they the ſinner to triumph.49Now when the time drew neere, that Mattathias ſhould die, he ſaid vnto his ſonnes, Now hath pride & rebuke gotten ſtrength, and the time of deſtruction, and the wrath of indignation:50Now therefore, my ſonnes, be ye zealous for the Law, & giue your liues for the couenant of your fathers.51Call to remembrance what actes our fathers did in their time, ſo ſhall ye receiue great honour, & an euerlaſting name.52Was not Abraham found faithfull in tentation, and it was imputed vnto him for righteouſneſſe?53Ioſeph in the time of his diſtreſſe kept the commaundement, and was made Lord of Egypt.54Phineas our father in being zealous and feruent, obtained the couenant of an euerlaſting prieſthood.55Ieſus for fulfilling the word, was made a iudge in Iſrael.56Caleb for bearing witneſſe, before the congregation, receiued the heritage of the land.57Dauid for being mercifull, poſſeſſed the throne of an euerlaſting kingdome.58Elias for being zealous and feruent for the law, was taken vp into heauen.59Ananias, Azarias, and Miſael, by beleeuing were ſaued out of the flame60Daniel for his innocencie was deliuered from the mouth of Lyons.61And thus conſider ye throughout all ages, that none that put their truſt in him ſhall be ouercome.62Feare not then the words of a ſinfull man: for his glory ſhall bee dung and wormes.63To day he ſhall be lifted vp, and to morrow hee ſhall not be found, becauſe he is returned into his duſt, and his thought is come to nothing.64Wherefore you my ſonnes be valiant, and ſhew your ſelues men in the behalfe of the law, for by it ſhall you obtaine glory.65And behold, I know that your brother Simon is a man of counſell, giue eare vnto him alway: he ſhall be a father vnto you.66As for Iudas Maccabeus hee hath bin mighty and ſtrong, euen from his youth vp, let him be your captaine, and fight the battaile of the people.67Take alſo vnto you, all thoſe that obſerue the law, and auenge ye the wrong of your people.68Recompence fully the heathen, and take heed to the commandements of the law.69So he bleſſed them, and was gathered to his fathers.70And he died in the hundreth fortie, and ſixth yeere, and his ſonnes buried him in the Sepulchre of his fathers, at Modin, and all Iſrael made great lamentation for him.

CHAPTER 31Then his ſonne Iudas, called Maccabeus, roſe vp in his ſtead.2And all his brethren helped him, and ſo did all they that held with his father, and they fought with cheerefulneſe, the battaile of Iſrael.3So he gate his people great honor, and put on a breſtplate as a giant, and girt his warlike harneſe about him, and he made battels, protecting the hoſt with his ſword.4In his acts he was like a lyon, and like a lyons whelp roaring for his pray.5For hee purſued the wicked, and ſought them out, and burnt vp thoſe that vexed his people.6Wherefore the wicked ſhrunke for feare of him, and all the workers of iniquity were troubled, becauſe ſaluation proſpered in his hand.7He grieued alſo many kings, and made Iacob glad with his acts, and his memoriall is bleſſed for euer.8Moreouer he went through the citties of Iuda, deſtroying the vngodly out of them, and turning away wrath from Iſrael.9So that he was renowned vnto the vtmoſt part of the earth, & he receiued vnto him ſuch as were ready to periſh.10Then Apollonius gathered the Gentiles together, and a great hoſt out of Samaria to fight againſt Iſrael.11Which thing when Iudas perceiued he went forth to meete him, and ſo he ſmote him, and ſlew him, many alſo fell downe ſlaine, but the reſt fled.12Wherefore Iudas tooke their ſpoiles, and Apollonius ſword alſo, and therewith he fought, all his life long.13Now when Seron a prince of the armie of Syria, heard ſay that Iudas had gathered vnto him a multitude and company of the faithfull, to goe out with him to warre.14He ſaid, I will get me a name and honour in the kingdome, for I will goe fight with Iudas, and them that are with him, who deſpiſe the kings commandement.15So he made him ready to goe vp, and there went with him a mighty hoſt of the vngodly to helpe him, and to be auenged of the children of Iſrael.16And when hee came neere to the going vp of Bethoron, Iudas went forth to meet him with a ſmal company.17Who when they ſaw the hoſt comming to meet them, ſaid vnto Iudas; How ſhall wee be able, being ſo few to fight againſt ſo great a multitude, and ſo ſtrong, ſeeing wee are ready to faint with faſting all this day?18Unto whom Iudas anſwered: It is no hard matter for many to bee ſhut vp in the hands of a few; and with the God of heauen it is all one, to deliuer with a great multitude, or a ſmall company:19For the victory of battell ſtandeth not in the multitude of an hoſte, but ſtrength commeth from heauen.20They come againſt vs in much pride and iniquitie to deſtroy vs, and our wiues & children, and to ſpoile vs:21But wee fight for our liues, and our Lawes.22Wherefore the Lord himſelfe will ouerthrow them before our face: and as for you, be ye not afraid of them.23Now as ſoone as hee had left off ſpeaking, he lept ſuddenly vpon them, and ſo Seron and his hoſt was ouerthrowen before him.24And they purſued them from the going downe of Bethoron, vnto the plaine, where were ſlaine about eight hundred men of them; and the reſidue fledde into the land of the Philiſtines.25Then began the feare of Iudas and his brethren, & an exceeding great dread to fall vpon the nations round about them:26In ſo much, as his fame came vnto the king, and all nations talked of the battels of Iudas.27Now when King Antiochus heard theſe things, he was full of indignation: wherefore hee ſent and gathered together all the forces of his realme *euen* a very ſtrong armie.28He opened alſo his treaſure, and gaue his ſouldiers pay for a yeere, commanding them to be ready, whenſoeuer he ſhould need them.29Neuertheleſſe, when he ſaw that the money of his treaſures failed, and that the tributes in the countrey were ſmall, becauſe of the diſſention, and plague which he had brought vpon the land, in taking away the Lawes which had bene of old time,30Hee feared that he ſhould not be able to beare the charges any longer, nor to haue ſuch gifts to giue ſo liberally, as he did before: for hee had abounded aboue the Kings that were before him.31Wherefore, being greatly perplexed in his minde, hee determined to goe into Perſia, there to take the tributes of the countreys, and to gather much money.32So hee left Lyſias a noble man, and one of the blood royall, to ouerſee the affaires of the King, from the riuer Euphrates, vnto the borders of Egypt:33And to bring vp his ſonne Antiochus, vntill he came againe.34Moreouer he deliuered vnto him the halfe of his forces, and the Elephants, and gaue him charge of all things that he would haue done, as alſo concerning them that dwelt in Iuda and Ieruſalem.35To wit, that he ſhould ſend an armie againſt them, to deſtroy and root out the ſtrength of Iſrael, and the remnant of Ieruſalem, and to take away their memoriall from that place:36And that he ſhould place ſtrangers in all their quarters, and diuide their land by lot.37So the king tooke the halfe of the forces that remained, and departed from Antioch his royall city, the hundreth fourtie and ſeuenth yeere, and hauing paſſed the riuer Euphrates, hee went through the high countreys.38Then Lyſias choſe Ptoleme, the ſon of Dorymenes and Nicanor, & Gorgias, mighty men of the kings friends:39And with them hee ſent fourtie thouſand footmen, and ſeuen thouſand horſemen to goe into the land of Iuda, and to deſtroy it as the king cōmanded.40So they went forth with all their power, and came and pitched by Emmaus in the plaine countrey.41And the merchants of the countrey, hearing the fame of them, tooke ſiluer, & gold very much, with ſeruants, and came into the campe to buy the children of Iſrael for ſlaues; A power alſo of Syria, and of the land of the Philiſtines, ioyned themſelues vnto them.42Now when Iudas and his brethren ſaw that miſeries were multiplied, & that the forces did encampe themſelues in their borders, (for they knewe how the king had giuen commaundement to deſtroy the people, and vtterly aboliſh them.)43They ſaid one to another, Let vs reſtore the decayed eſtate of our people, and let vs fight for our people and the Sanctuarie.44Then was the Congregation gathered together, that they might be ready for battell, and that they might pray, and aſke mercy and compaſſion.45Now Ieruſalem lay voide as a wilderneſſe, there was none of her children that went in or out: the Sanctuarie alſo was troden downe, and aliens kept the ſtrong holde: the heathen had their habitation in that place, and ioy was taken from Iacob, and the pipe with the harpe ceaſed.46Wherefore the Iſraelites aſſembled themſelues together, and came to Maſpha ouer-againſt Ieruſalem; for in Maſpha was the place where they prayed aforetime in Iſrael.47Then they faſted that day, and put on ſackecloth, and caſt aſhes vpon their heads, and rent their clothes:48And laide open the booke of the Law, wherein þe heathen had ſought to paint the likeneſſe of their images.49They brought alſo the Prieſtes garments, and the firſt fruits, and the tithes, and the Nazarites they ſtirred vp, who had accompliſhed their dayes.50Then cried they with a loud voice toward heauen, ſaying, What ſhall we doe with theſe, and whither ſhall wee cary them away?51For thy Sanctuarie is troden downe and profaned, and thy Prieſtes are in heauineſse, and brought low.52And loe, the heathen are aſſembled together againſt vs, to deſtroy vs: what things they imagine againſt vs, thou knoweſt.53How ſhall wee be able to ſtand againſt them, except thou (O God) be our helpe?54Then ſounded they with trumpets, and cryed with a loude voice.55And after this, Iudas ordained captains ouer the people, euen captains ouer thouſands, and ouer hundreds, and ouer fifties, and ouer tennes.56But as for ſuch as were building houſes, or had betrothed wiues, or were planting vineyards, or were fearefull, thoſe hee commanded that they ſhould returne, euery man to his owne houſe, according to the Law.57So the campe remooued, and pitched vpon the South ſide of Emmaus.58And Iudas ſayde, Arme your ſelues, and be valiant men, and ſee that ye be in readineſse againſt the morning, that yee may fight with theſe nations, that are aſſembled together againſt vs, to deſtroy vs and our Sanctuarie.59For it is better for vs to die in battell, then to behold the calamities of our people, and our Sanctuarie.60Neuertheleſſe, as the will *of God* is in heauen, ſo let him doe.

CHAPTER 41Then tooke Gorgias fiue thouſand footmen, and a thouſand of the beſt horſemen, and remoooued out of the campe by night:2To the end he might ruſh in vpon the camp of the Iewes, and ſmite them ſuddenly. And the men of the fortreſse were his guides.3Now when Iudas heard thereof, hee himſelfe remooued, and the valiant men with him, that hee might ſmite the Kings armie which was at Emmaus,4While as yet the forces were diſperſed from the campe.5In the meane ſeaſon came Gorgias by night into the campe of Iudas: and when hee found no man there, hee ſought them in the mountaines: for ſaid hee, theſe fellowes flee from vs.6But aſsoone as it was day, Iudas ſhewed himſelfe in the plaine with three thouſand men, who neuertheleſſe had neither armour, nor ſwordes to their mindes.7And they ſawe the campe of the heathen, that it was ſtrong, and well harneſsed, and compaſſed round about with horſemen; and theſe were expert of warre.8Then ſaid Iudas to the men that were with him: feare ye not their multitude, neither be ye afraid of their aſsault9Remember how our fathers were deliuered in the red ſea, when Pharao purſued them with an armie.10Now therfore let vs crie vnto heauen, if peraduenture the Lord wil haue mercie vpon vs, and remember the couenant of our fathers, and deſtroy this hoſte before our face this day.11That ſo all the heathen may know that there is one, who deliuereth and ſaueth Iſrael.12Then the ſtrangers lift vp their eyes, & ſaw them comming ouer againſt them.13Wherefore they went out of the campe to battell, but they that were with Iudas ſounded their trumpets.14So they ioyned battell, and the heathen being diſcomfited, fled into the plaine.15Howbeit all the hindmoſt of them were ſlaine with the ſword: for they purſued them vnto Gazera, and vnto the plaines of Idumea, and Azotus, and Iamnia, ſo that there were ſlaine of them, vpon a three thouſand men.16This done, Iudas returned againe with his hoſte frõ purſuingthem,17And ſaid to the people, Bee not greedie of the ſpoiles, in as much as there is a battell before vs,18And Gorgias and his hoſte are here by vs in the mountaine, but ſtand ye now againſt your enemies, and ouercome them, & after this you may boldly take the ſpoiles.19As Iudas was yet ſpeaking theſe words, there appeared apart of them looking out of the mountaine.20Who when they perceiued that the Iewes had put their hoſte to flight, and were burning the tents: (for the ſmoke that was ſeene declared what was done)21When therefore they perceiued theſe things, they were ſore afraid, and ſeeing alſo the hoſte of Iudas in the plaine ready to fight:22They fled euery one into the land of ſtrangers.23Then Iudas returned to ſpoile the tents, where they got much golde, and ſiluer, and blew ſilke, and purple of the ſea, and great riches.24After this, they went home, and ſung a ſong of thankeſgiuing, & praiſed the Lord in heauen: becauſe it is good, becauſe his mercie endureth for euer.25Thus Iſrael had a great deliuerance that day.26Now all the ſtrangers that had eſcaped, came and told Lyſias what had happened.27Who when hee heard thereof, was confounded, and diſcouraged, becauſe neither ſuch things as he would, were done vnto Iſrael, nor ſuch things as the king commanded him were come to paſſe.28The next yeere therefore following, Lyſias gathered together threeſcore thouſand choice men of foote, and fiue thouſand horſemen, that he might ſubdue them.29So they came into Idumea, and pitched their tents at Bethſura, and Iudas met with them ten thouſand men.30And when he ſaw that mighty armie, he prayed, and ſaid, Bleſſed art thou, O ſauiour of Iſrael, who diddeſt quaile the violence of the mighty man by the hand of thy ſeruant Dauid, and gaueſt, the hoſt of ſtrangers into the hands of Ionathan the ſonne of Saul, and his armour bearer.31Shut vp this armie in the hand of thy people Iſrael, and let them be confounded in their power and horſemen.32Make them to be of no courage, and cauſe the boldneſse of their ſtrength to fall away, & let them quake at their deſtruction.33Caſt them downe with the ſword of them that loue thee, and let all thoſe that know thy name, praiſe thee with thankſgiuing.34So they ioyned battaile, and there were ſlaine of the hoſt of Lyſias about fiue thouſand men, euen before them were they ſlaine.35Now when Lyſias ſaw his armie put to flight, and the manlineſse of Iudas ſouldiers, and how they were ready, either to liue or die valiantly, he went into Antiochia, and gathered together a company of ſtrangers, and hauing made his armie greater then it was, he purpoſed to come againe into Iudea.36Then ſaide Iudas and his brethren, behold our enemies are diſcomfited: let vs goe vp to cleanſe, and dedicate the Sanctuarie.37Upon this all the hoſt aſſembled themſelues together, and went vp into mount Sion.38And when they ſaw the ſanctuarie deſolate, and the altar prophaned, and the gates burnt vp, and ſhrubs growing in the courts, as in a forreſt, or in one of the mountaines, yea and the prieſts chambers pulled downe,39They rent their clothes, and made great lamentation, and caſt aſhes vpon their heads,40And fell downe flat to the ground vpon their faces, and blew an alarme with the trumpets, and cried towards heauen.41Then Iudas appointed certaine men to fight againſt thoſe that were in the fortreſse, vntill he had clenſed the Sanctuarie.42So he choſe prieſts of blameleſſe conuerſation, ſuch as had pleaſure in the law.43Who cleanſed the Sanctuarie, and bare out the defiled ſtones into an vncleane place.44And when as they conſulted what to doe with the altar of burnt offrings which was prophaned,45They thought it beſt to pull it downe, leſt it ſhould be a reproch to them, becauſe the heathen had defiled it; wherefore they pulled it downe,46And laide vp the ſtones in the mountaine of the temple in a conuenient place, vntill there ſhould come a Prophet, to ſhew what ſhould be done with them.47Then they tooke whole ſtones according to the law, and built a new altar, according to the former:48And made vp the Sanctuarie, and the things that were within the temple, and hallowed the courts.49They made alſo new holy veſſels, and into the temple they brought the candleſticke, and the altar of burnt offerings, and of incenſe, and the table.50And vpon the altar they burnt incenſe, and the lamps that were vpon the candleſticke they lighted, that they might giue light in the temple.51Furthermore they ſet the loaues vpon the table, and ſpread out the veiles, and finiſhed all the workes which they had begunne to make.52Now on the fiue and twentieth day of the ninth moneth, (which is called the moneth Caſleu) in the hundreth fourty and eight yeere they roſe vp betimes in the morning,53And offered ſacrifice according to the law vpon the new altar of burnt offerings, which they had made.54Looke at what time, and what day the heathen had prophaned it, euen in that was it dedicated with ſongs, and cittherns, and harpes, & cimbals.55Then all the people fell vpon their faces, worſhipping and praiſing the God of heauen, who had giuen them good ſucceſse.56And ſo they kept the dedication of the altar eight dayes, and offered burnt offerings with gladneſſe, and ſacrificed the ſacrifice of deliuerance and praiſe.57They deckt alſo the forefront of the temple with crownes of gold; and with ſhields, and the gates, and the chambers they renewed and hanged doores vpon them.58Thus was there very great gladneſſe among the people, for that the reproch of the heathen was put away.59Moreouer Iudas and his brethren with the whole congregation of Iſrael ordained that the daies of the dedication of the altar, ſhould be kept in their ſeaſon from yeere to yeere by the ſpace of eight dayes, from the fiue and twentieth day of the moneth Caſleu, with mirth and gladneſſe.60At that time alſo they builded vp the mount Sion with high walles, and ſtrong towres round about, leſt the Gentiles ſhould come & tread it downe, as they had done before.61And they ſet there a gariſon to keepe it: and fortified Bethſura to preſerueit, that the people might haue a defence againſt Idumea.

CHAPTER 5 1Now when the nations round about heard that the Altar
was built, & the Sanctuarie renewed as before, it diſpleaſed them very
much.2Wherfore they thought to deſtroy the generation of Iacob that
was among them, and thereupon they began to ſlay and deſtroy the
people.3Then Iudas fought againſt the children of Eſau in Idumea at
Arabattine, becauſe they beſieged Iſrael: and hee gaue them a great
ouerthrow, and abated their courage, and tooke their ſpoiles.4Alſo he
remembred the iniurie of the children of Bean, who had bene a ſnare
and an offence vnto the people, in that they lay in waite for them in the
wayes.5Hee ſhut them vp therefore in the towres, and incamped againſt
them, and deſtroyed them vtterly, and burnt the towers of that place
with fire, and all that were therein.6Afterward he paſſed ouer to the
children of Ammon, where he found a mighty power, and much people,
with Timotheus their captaine.7So he fought many battels with them,
till at length they were diſcomfited before him; and he ſmote them.8And
when hee had taken Iazar, with the townes belonging thereto, he
returned into Iudea.9Then the heathen that were at Galead, aſſembled
themſelues together againſt the Iſraelites that were in their quarters to
deſtroy them: but they fled to the fortreſse of Dathema;10And ſent
letters vnto Iudas and his brethren: The heathen that are round about
vs, are aſſembled together againſt vs to deſtroy vs;11And they are
preparing to come and take the fortreſse whereunto wee are fled,
Timotheus being captaine of their hoſt.12Come now therefore and
deliuer vs from their handes, for many of vs are ſlaine.13Yea all our
brethren that were in the places of Tobie, are put to death, their wiues
and their children; Alſo they haue caried away captiues, and borne away
their ſtuffe, and they haue deſtroied there about a thouſand men.14While
theſe letters were yet reading, behold there came other meſſengers from
Galilee with their clothes rent, who reported on this wiſe,15And ſaid:
They of Ptolemais, and of Tyrus, and Sidon, and all Galilee of the
Gentiles are aſſembled together againſt vs to conſume vs.16Now when
Iudas and the people heard theſe wordes, there aſſembled a great
congregation together, to conſult what they ſhould doe for their
brethren, that were in trouble and aſsaulted of them.17Then ſaid Iudas
vnto Simon his brother, Chooſe thee out men, and goe, and deliuer thy
brethren that are in Galilee, for I and Ionathan my brother, will goe into
the countrey of Galaad.18So hee left Ioſeph the ſonne of Zacharias, and
Azarias captaines of the people, with the remnant of the hoſte in Iudea
to keepe it,19Unto whom he gaue commandement, ſaying, Take yee the
charge of this people, and ſee that you make not warre againſt the
heathen, vntill the time that we come againe.20Now vnto Simon were
giuen three thouſand men to goe into Galilee, and vnto Iudas eight
thouſand men for the countrey of Galaad.21Then went Simon into
Galilee, where hee fought many battels with the heathen, ſo that the
heathen were diſcomfited by him.22And hee purſued them vnto the gate
of Ptolemais; And there were ſlaine of the heathen about three thouſand
men, whoſe ſpoiles he tooke.23And thoſe that were in Galilee and in
Arbattis, with their wiues and their children, and all that they had, tooke
he away *with him* and brought them into Iudea, with great ioy.24Iudas
Maccabeus alſo and his brother Ionathan, went ouer Iordan, and
trauailed three dayes iourney in the wilderneſſe,25Where they met with
the Nabathites, who came vnto them in peaceable maner, and told them
euery thing that had happened to their brethren in the land of
Galaad,26And how that many of them were ſhut vp in Boſora, and
Boſor, in Alema, Caſphor, Maked & Carnaim (all theſe cities are ſtrong
and great.)27And that they were ſhut vp in the reſt of the cities of the
countrey of Galaad, and that againſt to morrow they had appointed to
bring their hoſt againſt the forts, and to take them, and to deſtroy them
all in one day.28Hereupon Iudas and his hoſt turned ſuddenly by the way
of the wilderneſſe vnto Boſorra, and when he had wonne the citie, hee
ſlew all the males with the edge of the ſword, and tooke all their ſpoiles,
and burnt the citie with fire.29From whence hee remooued by night, and
went till he came to the fortreſse.30And betimes in the morning they
looked vp, & behold, there was an innumerable people bearing ladders,
and other engines of warre, to take the fortreſse: for they aſsaulted
them.31When Iudas therefore ſaw that the battaile was begun, and that
the cry of the citie went vp to heauen, with trumpets, and a great
ſound,32He ſaid vnto his hoſte, Fight this day for your brethren.33So he
went foorth behinde them in three companies, who ſounded their
trumpets, and cryed with prayer.34Then the hoſte of Timotheus
knowing that it was Maccabeus, fled from him: wherefore hee ſmote
them with a great ſlaughter: ſo that there were killed of them that day
about eight thouſand men.35This done, Iudas turned aſide to Maſpha,
and after he had aſsaulted it, hee tooke it, and ſlewe all the males therein,
and receiued the ſpoiles therof, and burnt it with fire.36From thence
went he, and tooke Caſphon, Maged, Boſor, and the other cities of the
countrey of Galaad.37After theſe things, gathered Timotheus another
hoſte, and encamped againſt Raphon beyond the brooke.38So Iudas
ſent *men* to eſpie the hoſte, who brought him word, ſaying; All the
heathen that be round about vs, are aſſembled vnto them, euen a very
great hoſte.39Hee hath alſo hired the Arabians to helpe them, and they
haue pitched their tents beyond the brooke, readie to come and fight
againſt thee: vpon this Iudas went to meet them.40Then Timotheus ſaid
vnto the captaines of his hoſte, When Iudas and his hoſte come neere
the brooke, if he paſſe ouer firſt vnto vs, we ſhall not be able to
withſtand him, for hee will mightily preuaile againſt vs.41But if he be
afraid, and campe beyond the riuer, we ſhall goe ouer vnto him, and
preuaile againſt him.42Now when Iudas came neere the brooke, he
cauſed the Scribes of the people to remaine by the brooke: vnto whom
hee gaue commandement, ſaying, Suffer no man to remaine in the
campe, but let all come to the battell.43So he went firſt ouer vnto them,
and all the people after him: then all the heathen being diſcomfited
before him, caſt away their weapons, and fled vnto the Temple that was
at Carnaim.44But they tooke the citie, and burnt the Temple, with all
that were therein. Thus was Carnaim ſubdued, neither could they ſtand
any longer before Iudas.45Then Iudas gathered together all the Iſraelites
that were in the countrey of Galaad from the leaſt vnto the greateſt,
euen their wiues and their children, and their ſtuffe, a very great hoſte,
to the ende they might come into the land of Iudea.46Now when they
came vnto Ephron (this was a great city in the way as they ſhould goe,
very well fortified) they could not turne from it, either on the right hand
or the left, but muſt needs paſſe through the midſt of it.47Then they of
the city ſhut them out, and ſtopped vp the gates with
ſtones.48Whereupon Iudas ſent vnto them in peaceable maner, ſaying;
Let vs paſſe through your land to goe into our owne countrey, and none
ſhall doe you any hurt, we will onely paſſe thorow on foote: howbeit
they would not open vnto him.49Wherefore Iudas commaunded a
proclamation to be made throughout the hoſte, that euery man ſhould
pitch his tent in the place where he was.50So the ſouldiers pitched, and
aſsaulted the city all that day, and all that night, till at the length the city
was deliuered into his hands:51Who then ſlew all the males with the edge
of the ſword, and raſed the city, and tooke the ſpoiles therof, and paſſed
through the city ouer them that were ſlaine.52After this went they ouer
Iordan, into the great plaine before Bethſan.53And Iudas gathered
together thoſe that came behind, and exhorted the people all the way
through, till they came into the land of Iudea.54So they went vp to
mount Sion with ioy and gladneſſe, where they offered burnt offerings,
becauſe not one of them were ſlaine, vntill they had returned in
peace.55Now what time as Iudas and Ionathan were in the land of
Galaad, and Simon his brother in Galilee before Ptolemais,56Ioſeph the
ſonne of Zacharias, and Azarias, captaines of the gariſons, heard of the
valiant actes and warlike deeds which they had done.57Wherefore they
ſaid, Let vs alſo get vs a name, and goe fight againſt the heathen that are
round about vs.58So when they had giuen charge vnto the gariſon that
was with them, they went towards Iamnia.59Then came Gorgias and his
men out of the citie to fight againſt them.60And ſo it was, that Ioſeph
and Azarias were put to flight, and purſued vnto the borders of Iudea,
and there were ſlaine that day of the people of Iſrael about two thouſand
men.61Thus was there a great ouerthrow among the children of Iſrael,
becauſe they were not obedient vnto Iudas, and his brethren, but
thought to doe ſome valiant act.62Moreouer theſe men came not of the
ſeed of thoſe, by whoſe hand deliuerance was giuen vnto
Iſrael.63Howbeit the man Iudas and his brethren were greatly renowned
in the ſight of all Iſrael, and of all the heathen whereſoeuer their name
was heard of,64Inſomuch as the people aſſembled vnto them with
ioyfull acclamations.65Afterward went Iudas foorth with his brethren,
and fought againſt the children of Eſau in the land toward the South,
where he ſmote Hebron, and the townes thereof, and pulled downe the
fortreſse of it, and burnt the townes thereof round about.66From thence

he remoued to goe into the land of the Philiſtines, and paſſed through Samaria. 67 At that time certaine prieſts deſirous to ſhew their valour, were ſlaine in battell, for that they went out to fight vnaduiſedly. 68 So Iudas turned to Azotus in the land of the Philiſtines, and when he had pulled downe their altars, and burnt their carued images with fire, and ſpoiled their cities, he returned into the land of Iudea.

CHAPTER 6 1 About that time king Antiochus trauailing through the high countreys, heard ſay that Elimais in the countrey of Perſia, was a citie greatly renowned for riches, ſiluer, and gold, 2 And that there was in it a very rich temple, wherein were couerings of gold, and breſtplates, and ſhields which Alexander ſonne of Philippe the Macedonian King, who reigned firſt among the Grecians, had left there. 3 Wherefore he came and ſought to take the citie, and to ſpoile it, but he was not able, becauſe they of the citie hauing had warning thereof, 4 Roſe vp againſt him in battell: So he fled and departed thence with great heauineſſe, and returned to Babylon. 5 Moreouer there came one, who brought in tidings into Perſia, that the armies which went againſt the land of Iudea, were put to flight: 6 And that Lyſias who went forth firſt with a great power, was driuen away of the Iewes, and that they were made ſtrong by the armour, and power, and ſtore of ſpoiles, which they had gotten of the armies, whom they had deſtroyed. 7 Alſo that they had pulled downe the abomination which hee had ſet vp vpon the altar in Ieruſalem, and that they had compaſſed about the Sanctuarie with high wals as before, and his citie Bethſura. 8 Now when the king heard theſe words, he was aſtoniſhed, and ſore moued, whereupon hee laide him downe vpon his bedde, and fell ſicke for griefe, becauſe it had not befallen him, as hee looked for. 9 And there hee continued many dayes: for his griefe was euer more and more, and he made account that he ſhould die. 10 Wherefore he called for all his friends, and ſaid vnto them, The ſleepe is gone from mine eyes, and my heart faileth for very care. 11 And I thought with my ſelfe: Into what tribulation am I come, and how great a flood *of miſerie* is it wherein now I am? for I was bountifull, and beloued in my power. 12 But now I remember the euils that I did at Ieruſalem, and that I tooke all the veſſels of gold and ſiluer that were therein, and ſent to deſtroy the inhabitants of Iudea without a cauſe. 13 I perceiue therefore that for this cauſe theſe troubles are come vpon me, and behold I periſh through great griefe in a ſtrange land. 14 Then called he for Philip one of his friends whom he made ruler ouer all his realme: 15 And gaue him the crowne and his robe, and his ſignet, to the end hee ſhould bring vp his ſonne Antiochus, and nouriſh him vp for the kingdome. 16 So king Antiochus died there in the hundreth forty and ninth yeere. 17 Now when Lyſias knew that the king was dead, he ſet vp Antiochus his ſonne (whom he had brought vp being yong) to reigne in his ſtead, and his name he called Eupator. 18 About this time they that were in the towre ſhut vp the Iſraelites round about the Sanctuarie, and ſought alwayes their hurt, and the ſtrengthening of the heathen. 19 Wherefore Iudas purpoſing to deſtroy them, called all the people together to beſiege them. 20 So they came together, and beſieged them in the hundred and fiftith yeere, and he made mounts for ſhot againſt them, and *other* engines: 21 Howbeit certaine of them that were beſieged got forth, vnto whom ſome vngodly men of Iſrael ioyned themſelues. 22 And they went vnto the king and ſaid, How long will it be ere thou execute iudgement, and auenge our brethren? 23 We haue beene willing to ſerue thy father, and to doe as he would haue vs, and to obey his commandements. 24 For which cauſe they of our nation beſiege the towre, and are alienated from vs: Moreouer as many of vs as they could light on, they ſlew, and ſpoiled our inheritance. 25 Neither haue they ſtretched out their hand againſt vs only, but alſo againſt all their borders. 26 And behold this day are they beſieging the towre at Ieruſalem to take it: the Sanctuary alſo, and Bethſura haue they fortified. 27 Wherefore if thou doeſt not preuent them quickly, they wil doe greater things then theſe, neither ſhalt thou be able to rule them. 28 Now when the king heard this, he was angry, and gathered together all his friends, and the captaines of his armie, and thoſe that had charge of the horſe. 29 There came alſo vnto him from other kingdomes, and from Iſles of the ſea bands of hired ſouldiers. 30 So that the number of his armie was an hundred thouſand foote men, and twentie thouſand horſemen, and two and thirty Elephants exerciſed in battell. 31 Theſe went through Idumea, and pitched againſt Bethſura which they aſſaulted many daies, making engines of warre: but they *of Bethſura* came out, and burnt them with fire, and fought valiantly. 32 Upon this Iudas remoued from the towre, and pitched in Bathzacharias, ouer againſt the kings campe. 33 Then the king riſing very earely marched fiercely with his hoſt toward Bathzacharias, where his armies made them ready to battell, and ſounded the trumpets. 34 And to the end they might prouoke the elephants to fight, they ſhewed them the blood of grapes & mulberies. 35 Moreouer, they diuided the beaſts among the armies, and for euery elephant they appointed a thouſand men, armed with coats of male, and with helmets of braſſe on their heads, and beſides this, for euery beaſt were ordained fiue hundred horſemen of the beſt. 36 Theſe were ready at euery occaſion: whereſoeuer the beaſt was, and whitherſoeuer þ^e^ beaſt went, they went alſo, neither departed they from him. 37 And vpon the beaſtes were there ſtrong towres of wood, which couered euery one of them, and were girt faſt vnto them with deuices: there were alſo vpon euery one two and thirtie ſtrong men that fought vpon them, beſides the Indian that ruled him. 38 As for the remnant of the horſemen they ſet them on this ſide, and that ſide, at the two parts of the hoſt giuing them ſignes what to do, and being harneſſed all ouer amidſt the rankes. 39 Now when the Sunne ſhone vpon the ſhields of golde, and braſſe, the mountaines gliſtered therewith, and ſhined like lampes of fire. 40 So part of the kings armie being ſpred vpon the high mountaines, and part on the valleyes below, they marched on ſafely, and in order. 41 Wherefore all that heard the noiſe of their multitude, and the marching of the company, and the ratling of the harneſſe, were moued: for the army was very great and mighty. 42 Then Iudas and his hoſt drew neere, and entred into battell, and there were ſlaine of the kings army, ſixe hundred men. 43 Eleazar alſo (ſyrnamed) Sauaran, perceiuing that one of the beaſts, armed with royall harneſſe, was higher then all the reſt, and ſuppoſing that the king was vpon him, 44 Put himſelfe in ieopardie, to the end hee might deliuer his people, and get him a perpetuall name: 45 Wherefore hee ranne vpon him courageouſly through the midſt of the battell, ſlaying on the right hand, and on the left, ſo that they were diuided from him on both ſides. 46 Which done, he crept vnder the Elephant, and thruſt him vnder and ſlew him: whereupon the Elephant fell downe vpon him, and there he died. 47 How be it *the reſt of the Iewes* ſeeing the ſtrength of the king, and the violence of his forces, turned away from them. 48 Then the kings armie went vp to Ieruſalem to meet them, and the king pitched his tents againſt Iudea, and againſt mount Sion. 49 But with them that were in Bethſura hee made peace: for they came out of the citie, becauſe they had no victuals there, to endure the ſiege, it being a yeere of reſt to the land. 50 So the King tooke Bethſura, and ſet a gariſon there to keepe it. 51 As for the Sanctuarie hee beſieged it many dayes: and ſet there artillerie with engins, and inſtruments to caſt fire and ſtones, and pieces to caſt darts, and ſlings. 52 Whereupon they alſo made engins, againſt their engins, and helde them battell a long ſeaſon. 53 Yet at the laſt their veſſels being without victuals, (for that it was the ſeuenth yeere, and they in Iudea that were deliuered from the Gentiles, had eaten vp the reſidue of the ſtore) 54 There were but a few left in the Sanctuary, becauſe the famine did ſo preuaile againſt them, that they were faine to diſperſe themſelues, euery man to his owne place. 55 At that time Lyſias heard ſay, that Philip (whom Antiochus the King whiles hee liued had appointed to bring vp his ſonne Antiochus, that he might be king) 56 Was returned out of Perſia, and Media, and the Kings hoſt alſo that went with him, and that hee ſought to take vnto him the ruling of the affaires. 57 Wherefore hee went in all haſte, and ſaid to the King, and the captaines of the hoſt, and the company, Wee decay dayly, and our victuals are but ſmall, and the place wee lay ſiege vnto is ſtrong: and the affaires of the kingdome lie vpon vs. 58 Now therefore let vs be friends with theſe men, and make peace with them, and with all their nation. 59 And couenant with them, that they ſhall liue after their Lawes, as they did before: for they are therefore diſpleaſed, & haue done all theſe things becauſe wee aboliſhed their Lawes. 60 So the King and the Princes were content: wherefore hee ſent vnto them to make peace, and they accepted thereof. 61 Alſo the King and the Princes made an oath vnto them: whereupon they went out of the ſtrong hold. 62 Then the King entred into mount Sion, but when hee ſaw the ſtrength of the place, hee brake his oath that hee had made, and gaue commandement to pull downe the wall round about. 63 Afterward departed hee in all haſte, and returned vnto

Antiochia, where hee found Philip to bee maſter of the citie; So he fought againſt him, and tooke the citie by force.

CHAPTER 7 [1]In the hundreth and one and fiftieth yeere, Demetrius the ſonne of Seleucus departed from Rome, and came vp with a fewe men vnto a citie of the ſea coaſt, and reigned there.[2]And as he entred into the palace of his anceſtors, ſo it was, that his forces had taken Antiochus and Lyſias to bring them vnto him.[3]Wherefore when he knew it, hee ſaid; Let me not ſee their faces.[4]So his hoſte ſlewe them. Now when Demetrius was ſet vpon the throne of his kingdome,[5]There came vnto him all the wicked and vngodly men of Iſrael, hauing Alcimus (who was deſirous to be high Prieſt) for their captaine.[6]And they accuſed the people to the king, ſaying; Iudas and his brethren haue ſlaine all thy friends, and driuen vs out of our owne land.[7]Now therefore ſend ſome man whom thou truſteſt, and let him goe and ſee what hauocke he hath made amongſt vs, and in the kings land, and let him puniſh them with all them that aide them.[8]Then the king choſe Bacchides a friend of the king, who ruled beyond the flood, and was a great man in the kingdome, and faithfull to the king.[9]And him hee ſent with that wicked Alcimus, whom hee made high Prieſt, and commanded that he ſhould take vengeance of the children of Iſrael.[10]So they departed, and came with a great power into the land of Iudea, where they ſent meſſengers to Iudas and his brethren with peaceable words deceitfully.[11]But they gaue no heede to their words, for they ſawe that they were come with a great power.[12]Then did there aſſemble vnto Alcimus and Bacchides, a company of Scribes, to require iuſtice.[13]Now the Aſſideans were the firſt among the children of Iſrael, that ſought peace of them:[14]For, ſaid they, one that is a Prieſt of the ſeede of Aaron, is come with this armie, and he will doe vs no wrong.[15]So he ſpake vnto them peaceably, and ſware vnto them, ſaying; We will procure the harme neither of you nor your friends.[16]Whereupon they beleeued him: howbeit hee tooke of them threeſcore men, and ſlewe them in one day, according to the words which he wrote:[17]The fleſh of thy Saintſ *haue they caſt out* and their blood haue they ſhed round about Ieruſalem, and there was none to bury them.[18]Wherefore the feare and dread of them fell vpon all the people, who ſaid, There is neither trueth, nor righteouſneſſe in them; for they haue broken the couenant and othe that they made.[19]After this remoooued Bacchides from Ieruſalem, and pitched his tents in Bezeth, where he ſent and tooke many of the men that had forſaken him, and certaine of the people alſo, and when he had ſlaine them, *he caſt them* into the great pit.[20]Then committed he the countrey to Alcimus, and left with him a power to aide him: ſo Bacchides went vnto the king.[21]But Alcimus contended for the high Prieſthood.[22]And vnto him reſorted all ſuch as troubled the people, who after they had gotten the land of Iuda into their power, did much hurt in Iſrael.[23]Now when Iudas ſaw all the miſchiefe that Alcimus and his company had done among the Iſraelites, euen aboue the heathen,[24]He went out into all the coaſt of Iudea round about, and tooke vengeance of them that had reuolted from him, ſo that they durſt no more goe foorth into the countrey.[25]On the other ſide, when Alcimus ſaw that Iudas and his company had gotten the vpper hand, and knew that he was not able to abide their force, he went againe to the king, and ſaid all the worſt of them that he could.[26]Then the king ſent Nicanor one of his honourable princes, a man that bare deadly hate vnto Iſrael, with commandement to deſtroy the people.[27]So Nicanor came to Ieruſalem with a great force: and ſent vnto Iudas and his brethren deceitfully with friendly words, ſaying,[28]Let there be no battell betweene me and you, I will come with a fewe men, that I may ſee you in peace.[29]He came therefore to Iudas, and they ſaluted one another peaceably. Howbeit the enemies were prepared to take away Iudas by violence.[30]Which thing after it was knowen to Iudas (to wit) that he came vnto him with deceit, he was ſore afraid of him, and would ſee his face no more.[31]Nicanor alſo when he ſaw that his counſell was diſcouered, went out to fight againſt Iudas beſides Capharſalama.[32]Where there were ſlaine of Nicanors ſide, about fiue thouſand men, and *the reſt* fled into the citie of Dauid.[33]After this went Nicanor vp to mount Sion, and there came out of the Sanctuarie certaine of the prieſtes, and certaine of the elders of the people to ſalute him peaceably, and to ſhewe him the burnt ſacrifice that was offred for the king.[34]But he mocked them, and laughed at them, and abuſed them ſhamefully, and ſpake proudly,[35]And ſwore in his wrath, ſaying, vnleſſe Iudas and his hoſte be now deliuered into my hands, if euer I come againe in ſafetie, I will burne vp this houſe: and with that he went out in a great rage.[36]Then the prieſts entred in, and ſtood before the altar, and the Temple, weeping, and ſaying,[37]Thou O Lord didſt chooſe this houſe, to be called by thy Name, and to be a houſe of prayer and petition for thy people.[38]Be auenged of this man and his hoſte, and let them fall by the ſword: Remember their blaſphemies, and ſuffer them not to continue any longer.[39]So Nicanor went out of Ieruſalem, & pitched his tents in Bethoron, where an hoſte out of Syria met him.[40]But Iudas pitched in Adaſa with three thouſand men, and there he prayed, ſaying,[41]O Lord, when they that were ſent from the king of the Aſſyrians blaſphemed, thine Angel went out, and ſmote a hundred, foureſcore, and fiue thouſand of them.[42]Euen ſo deſtroy thou this hoſt before vs this day, that the reſt may know that he hath ſpoken blaſphemouſly againſt thy Sanctuary, and iudge thou him according to his wickedneſſe.[43]So the thirteenth day of the moneth Adar, the hoſtes ioyned battell, but Nicanors hoſt was diſcomfited, & he himſelfe was firſt ſlaine in the battell.[44]Now when Nicanors hoſt ſaw that he was ſlaine, they caſt away their weapons, and fled.[45]Then they purſued after them a dayes iourney from Adaſa, vnto Gaſera, ſounding an alarme after them with their trumpets.[46]Whereupon they came forth out of all the townes of Iudea round about, and cloſed them in, ſo that they turning backe vpon them that purſued them, were all ſlaine with the ſword, and not one of them was left.[47]Afterwards they tooke þe ſpoiles, and the pray, and ſmote off Nicanors head, & his right hand, which he ſtretched out ſo proudly, and brought them away; and hanged them vp, towards Ieruſalem.[48]For this cauſe the people reioyced greatly, and they kept that day, a day of great gladneſſe.[49]Moreouer they ordeined to keepe yeerely this day, being the thirteenth of Adar.[50]Thus the land of Iuda was in reſt a litle while.

CHAPTER 8 [1]Now Iudas had heard of the fame of the Romanes, that they were mighty and valiant men, and ſuch as would louingly accept all that ioyned themſelues vnto them, and make a league of amitie with all that came vnto them,[2]And that they were men of great valour: It was told him alſo of their warres and noble acts which they had done amongſt the Galatians, and how they had conquered them, and brought them vnder tribute.[3]And what they had done in þe countrey of Spaine, for the winning of the mines of the ſiluer & gold which is there[4]And that by their policie and patience, they had conquered all that place (though it were very farre from them) and the kings alſo that came againſt them from the vttermoſt part of the earth, till they had diſcomfited them, & giuen them a great ouerthrow, ſo that the reſt did giue them tribute euery yere.[5]Beſides this, how they had diſcomfited in battell Philip, and Perſeus king of the Citims, with others that lift vp themſelues againſt them, and had ouercome them.[6]How alſo Antiochus the great king of Aſia that came againſt them in battaile, hauing an hundred and twentie Elephants with horſemen and chariots, and a very great armie, was diſcomfited by them.[7]And how they tooke him aliue, and couenanted that hee and ſuch as reigned after him, ſhould pay a great tribute, and giue hoſtages, and that which was agreed vpon,[8]And the country of India, and Media, and Lidia, and of the goodlieſt countries: which they tooke of him, and gaue to king Eumenes.[9]Moreouer how the Grecians had determined to come and deſtroy them.[10]And that they hauing knowledge thereof ſent againſt them a certaine captaine, and fighting with them ſlew many of them, and caried away captiues, their wiues, and their children, and ſpoiled them, and tooke poſſeſſion of their lands, and pulled downe their ſtrong holds, and brought them to be their ſeruants vnto this day.[11]*It was told him beſideſ* how they deſtroyed and brought vnder their dominion, all other kingdomes and iſles that at any time reſiſted them.[12]But with their friends, and ſuch as relied vpon them they kept amitie: and that they had conquered kingdomes both farre and nigh, inſomuch as all that heard of their name were afraid of them.[13]Alſo that whom they would helpe to a kingdome, thoſe raigne, and whom againe they would, they diſplace: finally that they were greatly exalted.[14]Yet for all this, none of them wore a crowne, or was clothed in purple to be magnified thereby.[15]Moreouer how they had made for themſelues a ſenate houſe, wherin three hundred and twentie men ſate in counſell daily, conſulting alway for the people, to the end they might be wel ordered[16]And that they committed their gouernment to one man euery yeere, who ruled ouer all their countrie, and that all were obedient to that one, and that there was neither enuy, nor emulation amongſt them.17In conſideration of theſe things Iudas choſe Eupolemus the ſonne of Iohn, the ſonne of Accas, and Iaſon the ſonne of Eleazar, and ſent them to Rome to make a league of amitie and confederacie with them,18*And to intreate them* that they would take the yoke from them, for they ſaw that the kingdome of the Grecians did oppreſſe Iſrael with ſeruitude19They went therefore to Rome (which was a very great iourney) and came into the Senate, where they ſpake and ſaid,20Iudas Maccabeus with his brethren, and the people of the Iewes, haue ſent vs vnto you, to make a confederacie, and peace with you, and that we might be regiſtred, your confederats and friends.21So that matter pleaſed the Romanes well.22And this is the copie of the Epiſtle which (the Senate) wrote backe againe, in tables of braſſe: and ſent to Ieruſalem, that there they might haue by them a memorial of peace & confederacy.23Good ſucceſse be to the Romans and to the people of the Iewes, by ſea, and by land for euer: the ſword alſo and enemie, be farre from them.24If there come firſt any warre vpon the Romans or any of their confederats throughout all their dominion,25The people of the Iewes ſhall helpe them, as the time ſhall be appointed, with all their heart.26Neither ſhal they giue any thing, vnto them that make war vpon them, or aide them with victuals, weapons, money, or ſhips, as it hath ſeemed good vnto the Romans, but they ſhall keepe their couenant without taking any thing therefore.27In the ſame maner alſo, if warre come firſt vpon the nation of the Iewes, the Romans ſhall helpe them with all their heart, according as the time ſhall be appointed them.28Neither ſhal victuals be giuen to thē that take part againſt thē, or weapons, or money, or ſhips, as it hath ſeemed good to the Romanes; but they ſhall keepe their couenants, and that without deceit.29According to theſe articles did the Romanes make a couenant with the people of the Iewes.30Howbeit, if hereafter the one partie or the other, ſhall thinke meete to adde or diminiſh any thing, they may doe it at their pleaſures, and whatſoeuer they ſhall adde or take away, ſhalbe ratified.31And as touching the euils that Demetrius doeth to the Iewes, wee haue written vnto him, ſaying, Wherefore haſt thou made thy yoke heauie vpon our friends, and confederats the Iewes?32If therefore they complaine any more againſt thee: wee will doe them iuſtice, and fight with thee by ſea and by land.

CHAPTER 9 1Furthermore, when Demetrius heard that Nicanor and his hoſte were ſlaine in battell, hee ſent Bacchides and Alcimus into the land of Iudea the ſecond time, and with them the chiefe ſtrength of his hoſte.2Who went forth by the way that leadeth to Galgala, and pitched their tents before Maſaloth, which is in Arbela, and after they had wonne it, they ſlew much people.3Alſo the firſt moneth of the hundred fiftie and ſecond yeere, they encamped before Ieruſalem.4From whence they remoued and went to Berea, with twentie thouſand footmen, and two thouſand horſemen.5Now Iudas had pitched his tents at Eleaſa, and three thouſand choſen men with him.6Who ſeeing the multitude of the other army to be ſo great, were ſore afraide, whereupon many conueyed themſelues out of the hoſte, inſomuch as there abode of them no moe but eight hundred men.7When Iudas therefore ſaw that his hoſte ſlipt away, and that the battell preſſed vpon him, he was ſore troubled in mind, and much diſtreſſed for that he had no time to gather them together.8Neuertheleſſe vnto them that remained, he ſaid; Let vs Ariſe and goe vp againſt our enemies, if peraduenture we may be able to fight with them.9But they dehorted him, ſaying, Wee ſhall neuer be able: Let vs now rather ſaue our liues, and hereafter we will returne with our brethren, and fight againſt them: for we are but few.10Then Iudas ſaid, God forbid that I ſhould doe this thing, and flee away from them: If our time be come, let vs die manfully for our brethren, and let vs not ſtaine our honour.11With that the hoſte *of Bacchideſ* remoued out of their tents, and ſtood ouer againſt them, their horſemen being diuided into two troupes, and their ſlingers and archers going before the hoſte, and they that marched in the foreward were all mighty men.12As for Bacchides, hee was in the right wing, ſo the hoſte drew neere on the two parts, and ſounded their trumpets.13They alſo of Iudas ſide, euen they ſounded their trumpets alſo, ſo that the earth ſhooke at the noiſe of the armies, and the battell continued from morning till night.14Now when Iudas perceiued that Bacchides and the ſtrength of his armie were on the right ſide, he tooke with him all the hardy men,15Who diſcomfited the right wing, and purſued them vnto the mount Azotus.16But when they of the left wing, ſaw that they of the right wing were diſcomfited, they followed vpon Iudas and thoſe that were with him hard at the heeles from behinde:17Whereupon there was a ſore battell, inſomuch as many were ſlaine on both parts.18Iudas alſo was killed, and the remnant fled.19Then Ionathan and Simon tooke Iudas their brother, and buried him in the ſepulchre of his fathers in Modin.20Moreouer they bewailed him, and all Iſrael made great lamentation for him, and mourned many dayes, ſaying;21How is the valiant man fallen, that deliuered Iſrael?22As for the other things concerning Iudas and his warres, and the noble actes which he did, and his greatneſse, they are not written: for they were very many.23Now after the death of Iudas, the wicked began to put foorth their heads in all the coaſts of Iſrael, and there roſe vp all ſuch as wrought iniquitie.24In thoſe dayes alſo was there a very great famine, by reaſon whereof the countrey reuolted, and went with them.25Then Bacchides choſe the wicked men, and made them lordes of the countrey.26And they made enquirie & ſearch for Iudas friends, and brought them vnto Bacchides, who tooke vengeance of them, and vſed them deſpitefully.27So was there a great affliction in Iſrael, the like whereof was not ſince the time that a Prophet was not ſeene amongſt them.28For this cauſe all Iudas friends came together, & ſaid vnto Ionathan,29Since thy brother Iudas died, we haue no man like him to goe foorth againſt our enemies, and Bacchides, and againſt them of our nation that are aduerſaries to vs.30Now therefore wee haue choſen thee this day to be our prince, and captaine in his ſtead, that thou mayeſt fight our battels.31Upon this, Ionathan tooke the gouernance vpon him at that time, and roſe vp in ſtead of his brother Iudas.32But when Bacchides gat knowledge thereof, he ſought for to ſlay him.33Then Ionathan and Simon his brother, and all that were with him, perceiuing that, fled into the wildernes of Thecoe, and pitched their tents by the water of the poole Aſphar.34Which when Bacchides vnderſtood, he came neere to Iordan with all his hoſte vpon the Sabbath day.35Now Ionathan had ſent his brother *Iohn* a captaine of the people, to pray his friendes the Nabbathites that they might leaue with them their cariage, which was much.36But the children of Iambri came out of Medaba, and tooke Iohn and all that hee had, and went their way with it.37After this came word to Ionathan and Simon his brother, that the children of Iambri made a great mariage, and were bringing the bride from Nadabatha with a great traine, as being the daughter of one of the great princes of Canaan.38Therfore they remembred Iohn their brother, and went vp and hidde themſelues vnder the couert of the mountaine.39Where they lift vp their eyes, and looked, & behold, there was much adoe and great cariage: and the bridegrome came foorth, and his friends & brethren to meet them with drums and inſtruments of muſicke, and many weapons.40Then Ionathan and they that were with him, roſe vp againſt them from the place where they lay in ambuſh, and made a ſlaughter of them in ſuch ſort, as many fell downe dead, and the remnant fledde into the mountaine, and they tooke all their ſpoiles.41Thus was the mariage turned into mourning, and the noiſe of their melody into lamentation.42So when they had auenged fully the blood of their brother, they turned againe to the mariſh of Iordan.43Now when Bacchides heard hereof, hee came on the Sabbath day vnto the banks of Iordan with a great power.44Then Ionathan ſayde to his company, Let vs goe vp now and fight for our liues, for it ſtandeth not with vs to day, as in time paſt:45For behold, the battell is before vs and behinde vs, and the water of Iordan on this ſide and that ſide, the mariſh likewiſe and wood, neither is there place for vs to turne aſide.46Wherefore cry ye now vnto heauen, that ye may be deliuered from the hand of your enemies.47With that they ioyned battel, and Ionathan ſtretched foorth his hand to ſmite Bacchides, but hee turned backe from him.48Then Ionathan and they that were with him, leapt into Iordan, and ſwamme ouer vnto the farther banke: howbeit the other paſſed not ouer Iordan vnto them.49So there were ſlaine of Bacchides ſide that day about a thouſand men50Afterward returned *Bacchideſ* to Ieruſalem, and repaired the ſtrong cities in Iudea: the fort in Iericho, and Emmaus, and Bethoron, and Bethel, and Thamnatha, Pharathoni, and Taphon (theſe did he ſtrengthen with high wals, with gates, & with barres.)51And in them he ſet a gariſon, that they might worke malice vpon Iſrael.52He fortified alſo the citie Bethſura, and Gazara, and the towre, and put forces in them, and prouiſion of victuals.53Beſides, he tooke the chiefe mens ſonnes in the country for hoſtages, and put them into the towre at Ierufalem to be kept. 54 Moreouer, in the hundred, fiftie and third yere, in the fecond moneth, Alcimus commanded that the wall of the inner court of the Sanctuarie fhould be pulled downe, he pulled downe alfo the works of the prophets. 55 And as he began to pull downe, euen at that time was Alcimus plagued, and his enterprifes hindered: for his mouth was ftopped, and he was taken with a palfie, fo that hee could no more fpeake any thing, nor giue order concerning his houfe. 56 So Alcimus died at that time with great torment. 57 Now when Bacchides faw that Alcimus was dead, he returned to the king, wherupon the land of Iudea was in reft two yeere. 58 Then all the vngodly men held a counfell, faying, Behold, Ionathan and his companie are at eafe, and dwell without care: now therefore wee will bring Bacchides hither, who fhall take them all in one night. 59 So they went, and confulted with him. 60 Then remoued he, and came with a great hofte, and fent letters priuily to his adherents in Iudea, that they fhould take Ionathan, and thofe that were with him: Howbeit they could not, becaufe their counfell was knowen vnto them. 61 Wherefore they tooke of the men of the countrey that were authours of that mifchiefe, about fiftie perfons, and flew them. 62 Afterward Ionathan and Simon, and they that were with him, got them away to Bethbafi, which is in the wilderneffe, and they repaired the decayes thereof, and made it ftrong. 63 Which thing when Bacchides knew, he gathered together all his hoft, and fent word to them that were of Iudea. 64 Then went he and laid fiege againft Bethbafi, & they fought againft it a long feafon, and made engines of warre. 65 But Ionathan left his brother Simon in the citie, and went forth himfelfe into the countrey, and with a certaine number went he forth. 66 And he fmote Odonarkes and his brethren, and the children of Phafiron in their tent. 67 And when he began to fmite them, and came vp with his forces, Simon and his company went out of the citie, and burnt vp the engines of warre, 68 And fought againft Bacchides, who was difcomfited by them, and they afflicted him fore. For his counfell and trauaile was in vaine. 69 Wherefore he was very wroth at the wicked men that gaue him counfell to come into the countrey, infomuch as he flew many of them, and purpofed to returne into his owne countrey. 70 Whereof when Ionathan had knowledge, he fent ambafsadours vnto him, to the end he fhould make peace with him, & deliuer them the prifoners. 71 Which thing hee accepted, and did according to his demaunds, and fware vnto him that hee would neuer doe him harme all the dayes of his life. 72 When therefore hee had reftored vnto him the prifoners that he had taken aforetime out of the land of Iudea, he returned and went his way into his owne land, neither came he any more into their borders. 73 Thus the fword ceafed from Ifrael: but Ionathan dwelt at Machmas, and began to gouerne the people, and he deftroyed the vngodly men out of Ifrael.

CHAPTER 10 1 In the hundreth & fixtieth yere, Alexander the fonne of Antiochus furnamed Epiphanes, went vp and tooke Ptolemais: for the people had receiued him, by meanes whereof he reigned there. 2 Now when king Demetrius heard thereof, he gathered together an exceeding great hoft, and went foorth againft him to fight. 3 Moreouer Demetrius fent letters vnto Ionathan with louing wordes, fo as he magnified him. 4 For, faid hee, Let vs firft make peace with him before he ioyne with Alexander againft vs. 5 Elfe he wil remember all the euils that we haue done againft him, and againft his brethren and his people. 6 Wherefore he gaue him authority to gather together an hoft, and to prouide weapons that hee might aide him in battell: he commaunded alfo that the hoftages that were in the towre, fhould be deliuered him. 7 Then came Ionathan to Ierufalem, and read the letters in the audience of all the people, and of them that were in the towre. 8 Who were fore afraid when they heard that the king had giuen him authoritie to gather together an hoft. 9 Whereupon they of the towre deliuered their hoftages vnto Ionathan, & he deliuered them vnto their parents. 10 This done, Ionathan fetled himfelfe in Ierufalem, and began to build and repaire the citie. 11 And he commaunded the workemen to build the wals, and the mount Sion round about with fquare ftones, for fortification, and they did fo. 12 Then the ftrangers that were in the fortreffes which Bacchides had built, fled away: 13 Infomuch as euery man left his place, and went into his owne country. 14 Onely at Bethfura certaine of thofe that had forfaken the law, and the commaundements remained ftill: for it was their place of refuge. 15 Now when king Alexander had heard what promifes Demetrius had fent vnto Ionathan: when alfo it was told him of the battels and noble acts which he & his brethren had done, and of the paines that they had indured, 16 He faid, fhal we find fuch another man? Now therefore we will make him our friend, and confederate. 17 Upon this he wrote a letter and fent it vnto him according to thefe words, faying: 18 King Alexander to his brother Ionathan, fendeth greeting: 19 We haue heard of thee, that thou art a man of great power, and meete to be our friend. 20 Wherefore now this day we ordaine thee to bee the high prieft of thy nation, and to be called the kings friend, (and there withall he fent him a purple robe and a crowne of gold) to take our part, and keepe friendfhip with vs. 21 So in the feuenth moneth of the hundreth and fixtieth yere, at the feaft of the Tabernacles, Ionathan put on the holy robe, and gathered together forces, and prouided much armour. 22 Wherof when Demetrius heard, he was very fory, and faid, 23 What haue we done that Alexander hath preuented vs, in making amity with the Iewes to ftrengthen himfelf? 24 I alfo will write vnto them words of encouragement *and promife them* dignities and gifts, that I may haue their ayde. 25 He fent vnto him therefore, to this effect: King Demetrius vnto the people of the Iewes, fendeth greeting: 26 Whereas you haue kept couenants with vs, & continued in our friendfhip, not ioyning your felues with our enemies, we haue heard hereof, & are glad: 27 Wherefore now continue yee ftill to be faithful vnto vs, and we will well recompence you for the things you doe in our behalfe, 28 And will grant you many immunities, and giue you rewards. 29 And now I doe free you, and for your fake I releafe all the Iewes from tributes, and from the cuftomes of falt, and from crowne taxes, 30 And frō that which appertaineth vnto me to receiue for the third part of the feed, and the halfe of the fruit of the trees, I releafe it from this day forth, fo that they fhall not be taken of the land of Iudea, nor of the three gouernments which are added thereunto out of the country of Samaria and Galile, from this day forth for euermore. 31 Let Ierufalem alfo bee holy and free, with the borders thereof, both from tenths and tributes. 32 And as for the towre which is at Ierufalem, I yeeld vp my authoritie ouer it, and giue it to the high Prieft, that he may fet in it fuch men as he fhall choofe to keepe it. 33 Moreouer I freely fet at libertie euery one of the Iewes that were carried captiues out of the land of Iudea, into any part of my kingdome, and I will that all my officers remit the tributes, euen of their cattell. 34 Furthermore, I will that all the Feafts and Sabbaths, & New moones and folemne dayes, and the three dayes before the Feaft, and the three dayes after the Feaft, fhall be all dayes of immunitie and freedom for all the Iewes in my realme. 35 Alfo no man fhall haue authoritie to meddle with them, or to moleft any of them in any matter. 36 *I will further* that there be enrolled amongft the kings forces about thirtie thoufand men of the Iewes, vnto whom pay fhall be giuen as belongeth to all the kings forces. 37 And of them fome fhalbe placed in the kings ftrong holds, of whom alfo fome fhall be fet ouer the affaires of the kingdome, which are of truft: and I will that their ouerfeers and gouernours be of themfelues, and that they liue after their owne lawes, euen as the King hath commanded in the land of Iudea. 38 And concerning the three gouernments that are added to Iudea from the countrey of Samaria, let them be ioyned with Iudea, that they may be reckoned to be vnder one, nor bound to obey other authoritie then þe high prieft. 39 As for Ptolemais and the land pertaining thereto, I giue it as a free gift to the Sanctuary at Ierufalem, for the necefsary expences of the Sanctuary. 40 Moreouer, I giue euery yeere fifteene thoufand fhekels of filuer, out of the Kings accompts from the places appertaining. 41 And all the ouerplus which the officers payed not in as in former time, from henceforth fhalbe giuen towards the workes of the Temple. 42 And befides this, the fiue thoufand fhekels of filuer, which they tooke from the vfes of the Temple out of the accompts yeere by yeere, euen thofe things fhall be releafed, becaufe they appertaine to the Priefts that minifter. 43 And whofoeuer they be that flee vnto the Temple at Ierufalem, or be within the liberties thereof, being indebted vnto the King, or for any other matter, let them be at libertie, and all that they haue in my realme. 44 For the building alfo and repairing of the workes of the Sanctuary, expences fhalbe giuen of the Kings accompts. 45 Yea, and for the building of the walles of Ierufalem, and the fortifying thereof round about, expences fhall bee giuen out of the Kings accompts, as alfo for building of the walles in Iudea. 46 Now when Ionathan and the people heard thefe words, they gaue no credite vnto them, nor receiued them, becaufe they remembred the great euill that he had done in Ifrael;

for hee had afflicted them very ſore.47But with Alexander they were well pleaſed, becauſe hee was the firſt that entreated of peace with them, and they were confederate with him alwayes.48Then gathered king Alexander great forces, and camped ouer againſt Demetrius.49And after the two Kings had ioyned battell, Demetrius hoſte fled: but Alexander followed after him, and preuailed againſt them.50And he continued the battell very ſore vntill the Sunne went downe, and that day was Demetrius ſlaine.51Afterward Alexander ſent Embaſsadors to Ptoleme king of Egypt, with a meſsage to this effect;52Forſomuch as I am come againe to my realme, and am ſet in the throne of my progenitors, and haue gotten the dominion, and ouerthrowen Demetrius, and recouered our countrey,53(For after I had ioyned battell with him, both he, and his hoſte was diſcomfited by vs, ſo that we ſit in the throne of his kingdome)54Now therefore let vs make a league of amitie together, and giue me now thy daughter to wife: & I will be thy ſon in law, and will giue both thee and her, gifts according to thy dignity.55Then Ptoleme the king gaue anſwere, ſaying, Happy be the day wherein thou diddeſt returne into the land of thy fathers, and ſateſt in the throne of their kingdome.56And now will I doe to thee, as thou haſt written: meet me therefore at Ptolemais, that wee may ſee one another, for I will marry my daughter to thee according to thy deſire.57So Ptolome went out of Egypt with his daughter Cleopatra, and they came vnto Ptolemais in the hundred threeſcore and ſecond yeere.58Where king Alexander meeting him, gaue vnto him his daughter Cleopatra, and celebrated her marriage at Ptolemais with great glory, as the maner of kings is.59Now king Alexander had written vnto Ionathan, that hee ſhould come and meete him.60Who thereupon went honourably to Ptolemais, where he met the two kings, and gaue them and their friends ſiluer and golde, and many preſents, and found fauour in their ſight.61At that time certaine peſtilent fellowes of Iſrael, men of a wicked life, aſſembled themſelues againſt him, to accuſe him: but the king would not heare them.62Yea more then that, the king commanded to take off his garments, and clothe him in purple: and they did ſo.63Alſo he made him ſit by himſelfe, and ſaid vnto his princes, Goe with him into the midſt of the city, and make proclamation, that no man complaine againſt him of any matter, and that no man troble him for any maner of cauſe.64Now when his accuſers ſawe that he was honoured according to the proclamation, and clothed in purple, they fled all away.65So the king honoured him, and wrote him amongſt his chiefe friends, and made him a duke, and partaker of his dominion.66Afterward Ionathan returned to Ieruſalem with peace and gladnes.67Furthermore, in the hundreth threeſcore and fifth yeere, came Demetrius ſonne of Demetrius, out of Crete into the land of his fathers.68Whereof when king Alexander heard tell, he was right ſory, and returned into Antioch.69Then Demetrius made Apollonius the gouernour of Coeloſyria his general, who gathered together a great hoſte, and camped in Iamnia and ſent vnto Ionathan the high Prieſt, ſaying,70Thou alone lifteſt vp thy ſelfe againſt vs, and I am laughed to ſcorne for thy ſake, and reproched, and why doeſt thou vaunt thy power againſt vs in the mountaines?71Now therefore if thou truſteſt in thine owne ſtrength, come downe to vs into the plaine field, and there let vs trie the matter together, for with me is the power of the cities.72Aſke and learne who I am, and the reſt that take our part, and they ſhal tel thee that thy foot is not able to ſtand before our face; for thy fathers haue bene twice put to flight in their owne land.73Wherefore now thou ſhalt not be able to abide the horſemen and ſo great a power in the plaine, where is neither ſtone nor flint, nor place to flee vnto.74So when Ionathan heard theſe words of Apollonius, he was moued in his mind, & chooſing ten thouſand men, he went out of Ieruſalē, where Simon his brother met him for to helpe him.75And hee pitched his tents againſt Ioppe: but they of Ioppe ſhut him out of the citie, becauſe Apollonius had a gariſon there.76Then Ionathan laid ſiege vnto it: whereupon they of the city let him in for feare: & ſo Ionathan wan Ioppe.77Whereof when Apollonius heard, he tooke three thouſand horſemen with a great hoſte of footmen, and went to Azotus as one that iourneyed, & therewithal drew him forth into the plaine, becauſe he had a great number of horſemen, in whom he put his truſt.78Then Ionathan followed after him to Azotus, where the armies ioyned battell.79Now Apollonius had left a thouſand horſemen in ambuſh.80And Ionathan knew that there was an ambuſhment behinde him; for they had compaſſed in his hoſt, and caſt darts at the people, from morning till euening.81But the people ſtood ſtill, as Ionathan had commanded them: and ſo the enemies horſes were tired.82Then brought Simon forth his hoſte, and ſet them againſt the footmen, (for the horſmen were ſpent) who were diſcomfited by him, and fled.83The horſemen alſo being ſcattered in the field, fled to Azotus, and went into Bethdagō their idols temple for ſafety.84But Ionathan ſet fire on Azotus, and the cities round about it, and tooke their ſpoiles, and the temple of Dagon, with them that were fled into it, he burnt with fire.85Thus there were burnt and ſlaine with the ſword, well nigh eight thouſand men.86And from thence Ionathan remoued his hoſte, and camped againſt Aſcalon, where the men of the city came forth, and met him with great pompe.87After this, returned Ionathan and his hoſte vnto Ieruſalem, hauing many ſpoiles.88Now when king Alexander heard theſe things, he honoured Ionathan yet more,89And ſent him a buckle of golde, as the vſe is to be giuen to ſuch as are of the kings blood: he gaue him alſo Accaron with the borders thereof in poſſeſſion.

CHAPTER 111And the king of Egypt gathered together a great hoſt like the ſand that lieth vpon the ſea ſhore, and many ſhips, and went about through deceit to get Alexanders kingdome, and ioyne it to his owne.2Whereupon he tooke his iourney into Syria in peaceable maner, ſo as they of the cities opened vnto him, and met him: for king Alexander had commanded them ſo to doe, becauſe he was his father in law.3Now as Ptolomee entred into the cities, he ſet in euery one of them a gariſon of ſouldiers to kepe it.4And when he came neere to Azotus, they ſhewed him the temple of Dagon that was burnt, and Azotus, and the ſuburbs thereof that were deſtroyed, and the bodies that were caſt abroad, and them that he had burnt in the battell, for they had made heapes of them by the way where he ſhould paſſe.5Alſo they told the king whatſoeuer Ionathan had done, to the intent he might blame him: but the king helde his peace.6Then Ionathan met the king with great pompe at Ioppa, where they ſaluted one another, and lodged.7Afterward Ionathan when he had gone with the king to the riuer called Eleutherus, returned againe to Ieruſalem.8King Ptolomee therefore hauing gotten the dominion of the cities by the ſea, vnto Seleucia vpon the ſea coaſt, imagined wicked counſels againſt Alexander.9Whereupon he ſent embaſſadours vnto king Demetrius, ſaying, Come, let vs make a league betwixt vs, and I will giue thee my daughter whome Alexander hath, and thou ſhalt reigne in thy fathers kingdome:10For I repent þt I gaue my daughter vnto him, for he ſought to ſlay me.11Thus did he ſlander him, becauſe he was deſirous of his kingdome.12Wherefore he tooke his daughter from him, and gaue her to Demetrius, and forſooke Alexander, ſo that their hatred was openly knowen.13Then Ptolomee entred into Antioch, where he ſet two crownes vpō his head, the crowne of Aſia, and of Egypt.14In the meane ſeaſon was king Alexander in Cilicia, becauſe thoſe þt dwelt in thoſe parts, had reuolted from him.15But when Alexander heard of this, hee came to warre againſt him, whereupon king Ptolomee brought forth his hoſte, and met him with a mightie power, and put him to flight.16So Alexander fled into Arabia, there to be defended, but king Ptolomee was exalted.17For Zabdiel the Arabian tooke off Alexanders head, and ſent it vnto Ptolomee.18King Ptolemee alſo died the third day after, & they that were in the ſtrong holds, were ſlaine one of another.19By this meanes Demetrius reigned in the hundreth, threeſcore and ſeuenth yeere.20At the ſame time Ionathan gathered together them that were in Iudea, to take the towre that was in Ieruſalem, and he made many engines of warre againſt it.21Then certaine vngodly perſons who hated their owne people, went vnto the king, and told him that Ionathan beſieged the towre.22Whereof when he heard, he was angry, and immediately remouing, he can to Ptolemais, and wrote vnto Ionathan, that he ſhould not lay ſiege to the towre, but come and ſpeake with him at Ptolemais in great haſte.23Neuertheleſſe Ionathan when he heard this, commanded to beſiege it *ſtill* and he choſe certaine of the Elders of Iſrael, and the prieſts, and put himſelfe in perill.24And tooke ſiluer and gold, and rayment, and diuers preſents beſides, and went to Ptolemais, vnto the king, where he found fauour in his ſight.25And though certaine vngodly men of the people, had made complaints againſt him,26Yet the king entreated him as his predeceſsors had done before, & promoted him in the ſight of all his friends,27And confirmed him in the high prieſthood, and in all the honours that hee had before, and gaue him preeminence among his chiefe friends.28Then Ionathan deſired the king, that hee would make Iudea free from tribute, as alſo the three gouernments with the countrey of Samaria, & he promiſed him three hundred talentſ29So the king conſented and wrote letters vnto Ionathan, of all theſe things after this maner.30King Demetrius vnto his brother Ionathan, and vnto the nation of the Iewes, ſendeth greeting.31We ſend you heere a copie of the letter, which we did write vnto our couſin Laſthenes, concerning you, that you might ſee it.32King Demetrius vnto his father Laſthenes, ſendeth greeting:33We are determined to doe good to the people of the Iewes, who are our friends, and keepe couenants with vs, becauſe of their good will towards vs.34Wherefore we haue ratified vnto them the borders of Iudea, with the three gouernments of Apherema, and Lidda, and Ramathem, that are added vnto Iudea, from the countrie of Samaria, and all things appertaining vnto them, for all ſuch, as doe ſacrifice in Ieruſalem, in ſtead of the paiments, which the king receiued of them yeerely aforetime out of the fruits of the earth, and of trees.35And as for other things that belong vnto vs of the tithes and cuſtomes pertaining vnto vs, as alſo the ſalt pits, and the crowne taxes, which are due vnto vs, we diſcharge them of them all for their reliefe.36And nothing heereof ſhall be reuoked from this time foorth for euer.37Now therefore ſee that thou make a copie of theſe things, and let it be deliuered vnto Ionathan, and ſet vpon the holy mount in a conſpicuous place.38After this, when king Demetrius ſaw that the land was quiet before him, and that no reſiſtance was made againſt him, he ſent away all his forces euery one to his owne place, except certaine bands of ſtrangers, whom he had gathered from the iles of the heathen, wherefore all the forces of his fathers hated him.39Moreouer there was one Tryphon, that had beene of Alexanders part afore, who ſeeing that all the hoſte murmured againſt Demetrius, went to Simalcue the Arabian, that brought vp Antiochus þe yong ſonne of Alexander,40And lay ſore vpon him, to deliuer him *this young Antiochuſ* that he might raigne in his fathers ſtead: he told him therefore all that Demetrius had done, and how his men of warre were at enmitie with him, and there he remained a long ſeaſon.41In the meane time Ionathan ſent vnto king Demetrius, that hee would caſt thoſe of the towre out of Ieruſalem, and thoſe alſo in the fortreſses. For they fought againſt Iſrael.42So Demetrius ſent vnto Ionathan, ſaying, I will not onely doe this for thee, and thy people, but I will greatly honour thee and thy nation, if opportunitie ſerue.43Now therefore thou ſhalt do wel if thou ſend me men to helpe me; for all my forces are gone from me.44Upon this Ionathan ſent him three thouſand ſtrong men vnto Antioch, and when they came to þe king, the king was very glad of their comming.45Howbeit, they that were of the citie, gathered themſelues together into the midſt of the citie, to the number of an hundreth and twentie thouſand men, and would haue ſlaine the king.46Wherefore the king fled into the court, but they of the citie kept the paſsages of the citie, and began to fight.47Then the king called to the Iewes for helpe, who came vnto him all at once, and diſperſing themſelues through the city, ſlew that day in the citie to the number of an hundred thouſand.48Alſo they ſet fire on the citie, and gat many ſpoiles that day, and deliuered the king.49So when they of the city ſaw, that the Iewes had got the city as they would, their courage was abated, wherefore they made ſupplication to the king, and cried, ſaying:50Graunt vs peace, and let the Iewes ceaſe from aſsaulting vs and the citie.51With that they caſt away their weapons, and made peace, and the Iewes were honoured in the ſight of the king, and in the ſight of all that were in his realme, and they returned to Ieruſalem hauing great ſpoiles.52So king Demetrius ſate on the throne of his kingdome, and the land was quiet before him.53Neuertheleſſe hee diſsembled in all that euer hee ſpake, and eſtranged himſelfe from Ionathan, neither rewarded he him, according to the benefits which hee had receiued of him, but troubled him very ſore.54After this returned Tryphon, and with him the yong childe Antiochus, who reigned and was crowned.55Then there gathered vnto him all the men of warre whom Demetrius had put away, and they fought againſt Demetrius, who turned his backe and fled.56Moreouer Triphon tooke the Elephants, and wonne Antioch.57At that time yong Antiochus wrote vnto Ionathan, ſaying; I confirme thee in the high Prieſthood, and appoint thee ruler ouer the foure gouernments, and to be one of the kings friends.58Upon this he ſent him golden veſſels to be ſerued in, and gaue him leaue to drinke in gold, and to bee clothed in purple, and to weare a golden buckle.59His brother Simon alſo he made captaine from the place called the ladder of Tyrus, vnto the borders of Egypt.60Then Ionathan went foorth and paſſed through the cities beyond the water, and all the forces of Syria, gathered themſelues vnto him for to helpe him: and when he came to Aſcalon, they of the city met him honorably.61From whence he went to Gaza, but they of Gaza ſhut him out; wherefore hee layd ſiege vnto it, and burned the ſuburbs thereof with fire, and ſpoiled them.62Afterward when they of Gaza made ſupplication vnto Ionathan, he made peace with them, and tooke the ſonnes of the chiefe men for hoſtages, and ſent them to Ieruſalem, and paſſed through the countrey vnto Damaſcus.63Now when Ionathan heard that Demetrius Princes were come to Cades which is in Galilee, with a great power, purpoſing to remoue him out of the countrey,64Hee went to meet them, and left Simon his brother in the countrey.65Then Simon encamped againſt Bethſura, and fought againſt it a long ſeaſon, and ſhut it vp:66But they deſired to haue peace with him, which he granted them, and then put them out from thence, and tooke the city, and ſet a garriſon in it.67As for Ionathan and his hoſte, they pitched at the water of Genneſar, from whence betimes in the morning they gate them to the plaine of Naſor.68And behold, the hoſte of ſtrangers met them in the plaine, who hauing layed men in ambuſh for him in the mountaines, came themſelues ouer againſt him.69So when they that lay in ambuſh roſe out of their places, and ioyned battel, al that were of Ionathans ſide fled.70In ſo much as there was not one of them left, except Mattathias the ſonne of Abſolon, and Iudas the ſonne of Calphi the captaines of the hoſte.71Then Ionathan rent his clothes, and caſt earth vpon his head, and prayed.72Afterwards turning againe to battell, he put them to flight, and ſo they ranne away.73Now when his owne men that were fled ſaw this, they turned againe vnto him, and with him purſued them to Cades, euen vnto their owne tents, and there they camped.74So there were ſlaine of the heathen that day, about three thouſand men, but Ionathan returned to Ieruſalem.

CHAPTER 12 1Nowe when Ionathan ſaw that the time ſerued him, he choſe certaine men and ſent them to Rome, for to confirme and renew the friendſhip that they had with them.2He ſent letters alſo to the Lacedemonians, and to other places, for the ſame purpoſe.3So they went vnto Rome, and entred into the Senate, and ſaid, Ionathan the high Prieſt, and the people of the Iewes ſent vs vnto you, to the end you ſhould renew the friendſhip which you had with them, and league, as in former time.4Upon this the Romanes gaue them letters vnto the gouernours of euery place, that they ſhould bring them into the land of Iudea peaceably.5And this is the copy of the letters which Ionathan wrote to the Lacedemonians:6Ionathan the hie Prieſt, and the Elders of the nation, and the Prieſtes and the other people of the Iewes, vnto the Lacedemonians their brethren, ſend greeting.7There were letters ſent in times paſt vnto Onias the high Prieſt from Darius, who reigned then among you, to ſignifie that you are our brethren, as the copy here vnderwritten doeth ſpecifie.8At which time Onias intreated the Embaſsador that was ſent, honourably, and receiued the letters, wherein declaration was made of the league and friendſhip.9Therefore we alſo, albeit we need none of theſe things, for that wee haue the holy bookes of Scripture in our hands to comfort vs,10Haue neuertheleſſe attempted to ſend vnto you, for the renewing of brotherhood and friendſhip, leſt we ſhould become ſtrangers vnto you altogether: for there is a long time paſſed ſince you ſent vnto vs.11We therefore at all times without ceaſing, both in our Feaſts, and other conuenient dayes, doe remember you in the ſacrifices which we offer, and in our prayers, as reaſon is, and as it becommeth vs to thinke vpon our brethren:12And wee are right glad of your honour.13As for our ſelues, wee haue had great troubles and warres on euery ſide, forſomuch as the kings that are round about vs haue fought againſt vs.14Howbeit wee would not be troubleſome vnto you, nor to others of our confederates & friends in theſe warres:15For wee haue helpe from heauen that ſuccoureth vs, ſo as we are deliuered from our enemies, and our enemies are brought vnder foote.16For this cauſe we choſe Numenius the ſon of Antiochus, and Antipater the ſonne of Iaſon, and ſent them vnto the Romanes, to renew the amitie that we had with them, and the former league.17We commanded them alſo to goe vnto you, and to ſalute you, and to deliuer you our letters, concerning the renewing of our brotherhood.18Wherefore now ye ſhall doe well to giue vs an anſwere thereto.19And this is the copy of the letters which Omiares ſent:20Areus king of the Lacedemonians, to Onias the hie Prieſt, greeting.21It is found in writing, that the Lacedemonians and Iewes are brethren, and that they are of the ſtocke of Abraham:22Now therefore, ſince this is come to our knowledge, you ſhall doe well to write vnto vs of your proſperitie.23We doe write backe againe to you, that your cattell and goods are ours, and ours are yours. We doe command therefore *our Embaſſadourſ* to make report vnto you on this wiſe.24Now when Ionathan heard that Demetrius princes were come to fight againſt him with a greater hoſte then afore,25Hee remooued from Ieruſalem, and met them in the land of Amathis: for he gaue them no reſpite to enter his countrey.26He ſent ſpies alſo vnto their tents, who came againe, and tolde him, that they were appointed to come vpon them in the night ſeaſon.27Wherefore ſo ſoone as the Sunne was downe, Ionathan commaunded his men to watch, and to be in armes, that all the night long they might bee ready to fight: Alſo he ſent foorth ſentinels round about the hoſte.28But when the aduerſaries heard that Ionathan and his men were ready for battell, they feared, and trembled in their hearts, and they kindled fires in their campe.29Howbeit Ionathan and his company knew it not till the morning: for they ſaw the lights burning.30Then Ionathan purſued after them, but ouertooke them not: for they were gone ouer the riuer Eleutherus.31Wherefore Ionathan turned to the Arabians, who were called Zabadeans, and ſmote them, and tooke their ſpoiles.32And remouing thence, he came to Damaſcus, and ſo paſſed through all the countrey.33Simon alſo went foorth, and paſſed through the countrey vnto Aſcalon, and the holds there adioyning, from whence he turned aſide to Ioppe, and wanne it.34For he had heard that they would deliuer the hold vnto them that tooke Demetrius part, wherefore he ſet a gariſon there to keepe it.35After this came Ionathan home againe, and calling the Elders of the people together, hee conſulted with them about building ſtrong holdes in Iudea,36And making the walles of Ieruſalem higher, and raiſing a great mount betweene the towre and the city, for to ſeparate it from the city, that ſo it might be alone, that men might neither ſell nor buy in it.37Upon this they came together, to build vp the citie foraſmuch aſ *part of* the wall toward the brooke on the Eaſt ſide was fallen down, & they repaired that which was called Caphenatha38Simon alſo ſet vp Adida, in Sephela, and made it ſtrong with gates and barres.39Now Tryphon went about to get the kingdome of Aſia, and to kill Antiochus the king, that hee might ſet the crowne vpon his owne head.40Howbeit, he was afraid that Ionathan would not ſuffer him, and that he would fight againſt him, wherefore he ſought a way, howe to take Ionathan, that he might kill him. So he remoued, and came to Bethſan.41Then Ionathan went out to meet him with fourtie thouſand men, choſen for the battell, and came to Bethſan.42Now when Tryphon ſaw that Ionathan came with ſo great a force, hee durſt not ſtretch his hande againſt him,43But receiued him honourably, and cōmended him vnto all his friends, and gaue him gifts, and commaunded his men of warre to be as obedient vnto him, as to himſelfe.44Unto Ionathan alſo hee ſaid, Why haſt thou put all this people to ſo great trouble, ſeeing there is no warre betwixt vs?45Therefore ſend them now home againe, and chuſe a few men to waite on thee, and come thou with me to Ptolemais, for I will giue it thee and the reſt of the ſtrong holds and forces, and all that haue any charge: as for me, I will returne and depart: for this is the cauſe of my comming.46So Ionathan beleeuing him, did as he bade him, and ſent away his hoſt, who went into the land of Iudea.47And with himſelfe hee retained but three thouſand men, of whome he ſent two thouſand into Galile, and one thouſand went with him.48Now aſſoone as Ionathan entred into Ptolemais, they of Ptolemais ſhut the gates, and tooke him, and all them that came with him, they ſhewe with the ſword.49Then ſent Tryphon an hoſte of footmen, and horſemen into Galile, and into the great plaine, to deſtroy all Ionathans company.50But when they knew that Ionathan and they that were with him were taken and ſlaine, they encouraged one another, and went cloſe together, prepared to fight.51They therfore that followed vpon them, perceiuing þt they were ready to fight for their liues, turned back againe.52Whereupon they all came into the land of Iudea peaceably, and there they bewailed Ionathan & them that were with him, & they were ſore afraid, wherfore all Iſrael made great lamentation.53Then all the heathen that were round about them, ſought to deſtroy them. For, ſaid they, they haue no captaine, nor any to helpe them. Now therfore let vs make war vpon them, & take away their memorial frō amongſt men.

CHAPTER 13 1Now when Simon heard that Tryphon had gathered together a great hoſte to inuade the land of Iudea, and deſtroy it,2And ſaw that the people was in great trembling and feare, he went vp to Ieruſalem, and gathered the people together,3And gaue them exhortation, ſaying: Yee your ſelues know, what great things I and my brethren, and my fathers houſe haue done for the lawes, and the Sanctuarie, the battels alſo, and troubles which we haue ſeene,4By reaſon whereof all my brethren are ſlaine for Iſraels ſake, and I am left alone.5Now therefore be it farre from me, that I ſhould ſpare mine owne life in any time of trouble: for I am no better then my brethren.6Doubtleſſe I will auenge my nation and the Sanctuarie, & our wiues, and our children: for all the heathen are gathered to deſtroy vs, of very malice.7Now as ſoone as the people heard theſe words, their ſpirit reuiued.8And they anſwered with a loud voice, ſaying, Thou ſhalt bee our leader in ſtead of Iudas and Ionathan thy brother.9Fight thou our battels, & what ſoeuer thou commandeſt vs, that will we doe.10So then he gathered together all the men of warre, and made haſt to finiſh the walles of Ieruſalem, and he fortified it round about.11Alſo he ſent Ionathan, the ſonne of Abſolom, & with him a great power to Ioppe, who caſting out them that were therein, remained there in it.12So Tryphon remoued from Ptolemais, with a great power to inuade the land of Iudea, and Ionathan was with him in warde.13But Simon pitched his tents at Adida, ouer againſt the plaine.14Now when Tryphon knew that Simon, was riſen vp in ſtead of his brother Ionathan, and meant to ioyne battell with him, he ſent meſſengers vnto him, ſaying,15Whereas we haue Ionathan thy brother in hold, it is for money that he is owing vnto the kings treaſure, concerning the buſineſſe that was committed vnto him.16Wherefore, now ſend an hundred talents of ſiluer, and two of his ſonnes for hoſtages, that when he is at liberty he may not reuolt from vs, and we will let him goe.17Heereupon Simon, albeit he perceiued that they ſpake deceiptfully vnto him, yet ſent he the money, and the children, leſt peraduenture he ſhould procure to himſelfe great hatred of the people:18Who might haue ſaid, Becauſe I ſent him not the money, and the children, therefore iſ *Ionathan* dead.19So he ſent them the children, and the hundred talents: Howbeit *Tryphon* diſsembled, neither would he let Ionathan goe.20And after this came Tryphon to inuade the land, and deſtroy it, going round about by the way that leadeth vnto Adora, but Simon and his hoſt marched againſt him in euery place whereſoeuer he went.21Now they that were in the towre, ſent meſſengers vnto Tryphon, to the end that he ſhould haſten his comming vnto them by the wilderneſſe, and ſend them victuals.22Wherefore Tryphon made readie all his horſemen to come that night, but there fell a very great ſnow, by reaſon whereof he came not: So he departed & came into the countrey of Galaad.23And when he came neere to Baſcama, he ſlew Ionathan, who was buried there.24Afterward Tryphon returned, and went into his owne land.25Then ſent Simon and tooke the bones of Ionathan his brother, and buried them in Modin the citie of his fathers.26And all Iſrael made great lamentation for him, and bewailed him many daies.27Simon alſo built a monument vpon the Sepulchre of his father and his brethren, and raiſed it aloft to the ſight, with hewen ſtone behind and before.28Moreouer hee ſet vp ſeuen pyramides one againſt another, for his father and his mother, and his foure brethren.29And in theſe he made running deuices, about the which he ſet great pillars, and vpon the pillars he made all their armour for a perpetuall memory, and by the armour, ſhips carued, that they might be ſeene of all that ſaile on the ſea.30This is the Sepulchre which he made at Modin, and it ſtandeth yet vnto this day.31Now Tryphon dealt deceitfully with the yong king Antiochus, and ſlew him,32And he raigned in his ſtead, and crowned himſelfe king of Aſia, and brought a great calamitie vpō the land.33Then Simon built vp the ſtrong holds in Iudea, and fenſed them about with high towres, and great walles and gates and barres, and layd vp victuals therein.34Moreouer Simon choſe men, and ſent to king Demetrius, to the end he ſhould giue the land an immunitie, becauſe all that Tryphon did, was to ſpoyle.35Unto whom king Demetrius anſwered and wrote after this maner.36King Demetrius vnto

Simon the high Prieſt, and friend of kings, as alſo vnto the Elders and nation of the Iewes, ſendeth greeting.37The golden crowne, and the ſcarlet robe which ye ſent vnto vs, we haue receiued, and wee are ready to make a ſtedfaſt peace with you, yea and to write vnto our officers to confirme the immunities which we haue granted.38And whatſoeuer couenants we haue made with you, ſhall ſtand, and the ſtrong holdes which yee haue builded ſhalbe your owne.39As for any ouerſight or fault committed vnto this day, we forgiue it, and the crowne taxe alſo which yee owe vs, if there were any other tribute paide in Ieruſalem, it ſhall no more be paide.40And looke who are meet among you to be in our court, let them be inrolled, and let there be peace betwixt vs.41Thus the yoke of the heathen was taken away from Iſrael, in the hundred and ſeuentieth yeere.42Then the people of Iſrael began to write in their inſtruments, and contracts, in the firſt yeere of Simon the high Prieſt, the gouernour, and leader of the Iewes.43In thoſe dayes Simon camped againſt Gaza, and beſieged it round about; he made alſo an engine of warre, and ſet it by the city, and battered a certaine towre, and tooke it.44And they that were in the Engine leapt into the citie, whereupon there was a great vproare in the citie:45Inſomuch as the people of the citie rent their clothes, and climed vpon the walles, with their wiues and children, and cried with a lowd voice, beſeeching Simon to grant them peace.46And they ſaid, Deale not with vs according to our wickedneſſe, but according to thy mercy.47So Simon was appeaſed towards them, and fought no more againſt them, but put them out of the citie, and cleanſed the houſes wherein the idols were: and ſo entred into it, with ſongs, and thankeſgiuing.48Yea, he put all vncleanneſſe out of it, and placed ſuch men there, as would keepe the Law, and made it ſtronger then it was before, and built therein a dwelling place for himſelfe.49They alſo of the towre in Ieruſalem were kept ſo ſtrait, that they could neither come foorth, nor goe into the countrey, nor buy, nor ſell, wherefore they were in great diſtreſſe for want of victuals, and a great number of them periſhed through famine.50Then cried they to Simon, beſeeching him to bee at one with them, which thing hee graunted them, and when he had put them out from thence, he cleanſed the towre from pollutions:51And entred into it the three and twentieth day of the ſecond moneth, in the hundred ſeuentie and one yere, with thankeſgiuing, and branches of palme trees, and with harpes, and cymbals, and with viols and hymnes, and ſongs: becauſe there was deſtroyed a great enemy out of Iſrael.52Hee ordained alſo that that day ſhould be kept euery yeere with gladnes. Moreouer, the hill of the Temple that was by the towre he made ſtronger then it was, and there hee dwelt himſelfe with his company.53And when Simon ſawe that Iohn his ſonne was a valiant man, he made him captaine of all the hoſtes and dwelt in Gazara.

CHAPTER 14 1Now in the hundred threeſcore and twelfth yeere, king Demetrius gathered his forces together, and went into Media, to get him helpe to fight againſt Tryphon.2But when Arſaces the king of Perſia & Media, heard that Demetrius was entred within his borders, he ſent one of his princes to take him aliue.3Who went and ſmote the hoſte of Demetrius, and tooke him and brought him to Arſaces, by whom hee was put in warde.4As for the land of Iudea, that was quiet all the dayes of Simon: for he ſought the good of his nation, in ſuch wiſe, as that euermore his authoritie and honour pleaſed them well.5And as he was honourable (in all his actſ) ſo in this, that he tooke Ioppe for an hauen, and made an entrance to the yles of the ſea,6And enlarged the boundes of his nation, and recouered the countrey,7And gathered together a great number of captiues, and had the dominion of Gazara and Bethſura, and the towre, out of the which he tooke all vncleanneſſe, neither was there any that reſiſted him.8Then did they till their ground in peace, and the earth gaue her increaſe, and the trees of the field their fruit.9The ancient men ſate all in the ſtreetes, communing together of good things, and the young men put on glorious and warrelike apparell.10He prouided victuals for the cities, and ſet in them all maner of munition, ſo that his honourable name was renowmed vnto the end of the world.11He made peace in the land, and Iſrael reioyced with great ioy:12For euery man ſate vnder his vine, and his figgetree, and there was none to fray them:13Neither was there any left in the lande to fight againſt them: yea, the Kings themſelues were ouerthrowen in thoſe dayes.14Moreouer hee ſtrengthened all thoſe of his people that were brought low: the Law he ſearched out, and euery contemner of the Law, and wicked perſon, he tooke away.15He beautified the Sanctuary, and multiplied the veſſels of the Temple.16Now when it was heard at Rome, & as far as Sparta, that Ionathan was dead, they were very ſorie.17But aſsoone as they heard that his brother Simon was made high Prieſt in his ſtead, and ruled the countrey, and the cities therein,18They wrote vnto him in tables of braſſe, to renew the friendſhip & league which they had made with Iudas and Ionathan his brethren:19Which writings were read before the Congregation at Ieruſalem.20And this is the copy of the letters that the Lacedemonians ſent: The rulers of the Lacedemonians, with the city, vnto Simon the high Prieſt, and the Elders and Prieſtes, and reſidue of the people of the Iewes, our brethren, ſend greeting.21The Embaſsadors that were ſent vnto our people, certified vs of your glory and honour, wherefore we were glad of their comming,22And did regiſter the things that they ſpake, in the counſell of the people, in this maner: Numenius ſonne of Antiochus, and Antipater ſonne of Iaſon, the Iewes Embaſſadours, came vnto vs, to renew the friendſhip they had with vs.23And it pleaſed the people to entertaine the men honourably, and to put the copy of their embaſsage in publike records, to the end the people of the Lacedemonians might haue a memoriall therof: furthermore we haue written a copy thereof vnto Simon the hie Prieſt.24After this, Simon ſent Numenius to Rome, with a great ſhield of golde of a thouſand pound weight, to confirme the league with them.25Whereof when the people heard, they ſaid, What thankes ſhall wee giue to Simon and his ſonnes?26For hee and his brethren, and the houſe of his father, haue eſtabliſhed Iſrael, and chaſed away in fight their enemies from them, and confirmed their libertie.27So then they wrote *it* in tables of braſſe, which they ſet vpon pillars in mount Sion, and this is the copie of the writing. The eighteenth day of the moneth Elul, in the hundred threeſcore and twelft yeere, being the third yeere of Simon the hie prieſt,28At Saramel in the great congregation of the prieſts and people, and rulers of the nation, & elders of the country, were theſe things notified vnto vs.29Forſomuch as often times there haue bin warres in the countrey, wherin for the maintenance of their Sanctuarie, and the law, Simon the ſonne of Mattathias of the poſteritie of Iarib, together with his brethren, put themſelues in ieopardie, and reſiſting the enemies of their nation, did their nation great honour.30(For after that Ionathan hauing gathered his nation together, and bene their hie prieſt, was added to his people,31Their enemies purpoſed to inuade their countrey that they might deſtroy it, and lay hands on the Sanctuary.32At which time Simon roſe vp, and fought for his nation, and ſpent much of his own ſubſtance, & armed the valiant men of his nation, & gaue them wages,33And fortified the cities of Iudea, together with Bethſura that lieth vpon the borders of Iudea, where the armour of the enemies had bin before, but he ſet a gariſon of Iewes there.34Moreouer, hee fortified Ioppe which lieth vpon the ſea, and Gazara that bordereth vpon Azotus, where the enemies had dwelt before: but hee placed Iewes there, and furniſhed them with all things conuenient for the reparation thereof.)35The people therefore ſeeing the acts of Simon, and vnto what glory he thought to bring his nation, made him their gouernor and chiefe prieſt, becauſe he had done all theſe things, and for the iuſtice and faith which hee kept to his nation, and for that hee ſought by all meanes to exalt his people.36For in his time things proſpered in his hands, ſo that the heathen were taken out of their countrey, and they alſo that were in the citie of Dauid in Ieruſalem, who had made themſelues a towre, out of which they iſsued, and polluted all about the Sanctuarie, and did much hurt in the holy place.37But he placed Iewes therein, and fortified it for the ſafetie of the countrey, and the city, and raiſed vp the wals of Ieruſalem.38King Demetrius alſo confirmed him in the high prieſthood, according to thoſe things,39And made him one of his friends, and honoured him with great honour.40For he had heard ſay, that the Romanes had called the Iewes their friends, and confederates, and brethren, and that they had entertained the Embaſſadours of Simon honourably.41Alſo that the Iewes & prieſts were wel pleaſed that Simon ſhould be their gouernour, and high prieſt for euer vntil there ſhould Ariſe a faithfull prophet.42Moreouer, that he ſhould be their captaine, and ſhould take charge of the Sanctuarie, to ſet them ouer their workes, and ouer the countrey, and ouer the armour, and ouer the fortreſses, that (I ſay) he ſhould take charge of the Sanctuarie.43Beſides this, that he ſhould be obeyed of euery man, and that all the writings in the countrey ſhould be made in his name, and that he ſhould be clothed in purple, and weare gold.44Alſo that it ſhould be lawfull for none of the

people or prieſts, to breake any of theſe things, or to gaineſay his words,
or to gather an aſſembly in the countrey without him, or to bee clothed
in purple, or weare a buckle of gold. 45 And whoſoeuer ſhould do
otherwiſe, or breake any of theſe things, he ſhould be puniſhed. 46 Thus
it liked all þe people to deale with Simon, & to do as hath bene
ſaid. 47 Then Simon accepted hereof, and was well pleaſed to be high
Prieſt, and captaine, and gouernour of the Iewes, & prieſts, & to defend
them all. 48 So they commanded that this writing ſhould be put in tables
of braſſe, and that they ſhould be ſet vp within the compaſſe of the
Sanctuary in a conſpicuous place. 49 Alſo þt the copies therof ſhould be
laid vp in the treaſurie, to the ende that Simon & his ſonnes might haue
them.

CHAPTER 15 1 Moreouer Antiochus ſonne of Demetrius the king, ſent
letters from the iſles of the ſea, vnto Simon the prieſt, and prince of the
Iewes, and to all the people. 2 The contents whereof were theſe: King
Antiochus, to Simon the high Prieſt, and prince of his nation, and to the
people of the Iewes, greeting, 3 For as much as certaine peſtilent men,
haue vſurped the kingdome of our fathers, and my purpoſe is to
chalenge it againe, that I may reſtore it to the old eſtate, and to that end
haue gathered a multitude of forraine ſouldiers together, and prepared
ſhippes of warre, 4 My meaning alſo being to goe through the countrey,
that I may be auenged of them that haue deſtroyed it, and made many
cities in the kingdome deſolate: 5 Now therefore I confirme vnto thee, all
the oblations which the kings before me granted thee, and whatſoeuer
gifts beſides they granted. 6 I giue thee leaue alſo to coine money for thy
countrey with thine owne ſtampe. 7 And as concerning Ieruſalem, and
the Sanctuarie, let them be free, and al the armour that thou haſt made,
and fortreſſes that thou haſt built, and keepeſt in thy hands, let them
remaine vnto thee. 8 And if any thing bee, or ſhall be owing to the king,
let it be forgiuen thee, from this time forth for euermore. 9 Furthermore,
when we haue obtained our kingdome, we will honour thee, and thy
nation, and thy temple with great honour, ſo that your honour ſhall bee
knowen throughout the world. 10 In the hundred threeſcore and
fourteenth yeere, went Antiochus into the land of his fathers, at which
time all the forces came together vnto him, ſo that few were left with
Tryphon. 11 Wherefore being purſued by king Antiochus, he fled vnto
Dora, which lieth by the ſeaſide. 12 For he ſaw, that troubles came vpon
him all at once, and that his forces had forſaken him. 13 Then camped
Antiochus againſt Dora, hauing with him, an hundred and twentie
thouſand men of warre, and eight thouſand horſemen. 14 And when he
had compaſſed the citie round about, and ioyned ſhips cloſe to the
towne on the ſea ſide, hee vexed the citie by land, and by ſea, neither
ſuffered he any to goe out or in. 15 In the meane ſeaſon came Numenius,
& his company from Rome hauing letters to the kings and countries,
wherein were written theſe things. 16 Lucius, Conſul of the Romanes,
vnto king Ptolomee greeting. 17 The Iewes Embaſsadors our friends and
confederates, came vnto vs to renew the old friendſhip and league, being
ſent from Simon the high Prieſt, and from the people of the
Iewes. 18 And they brought a ſhield of gold, of a thouſand pound: 19 We
thought it good therefore, to write vnto the kings and countries, that
they ſhould doe them no harme, nor fight againſt them, their cities, or
countries, nor yet aide their enemies againſt them. 20 It ſeemed alſo good
to vs, to receiue the ſhield of them. 21 If therefore there be any peſtilent
fellowes, that haue fled from their countrie vnto you, deliuer them vnto
Simon the high prieſt, that hee may puniſh them according to their owne
lawe. 22 The ſame thing wrote hee likewiſe vnto Demetrius the king, and
Attalus, to Ariarathes, and Arſaces, 23 And to all the countries, and to
Sampſames, & the Lacedemonians, and to Delus, and Myndus, and
Sycion, and Caria, and Samos, and Pamphylia, and Lycia, and
Halicarnaſsus, and Rhodus, and Phaſeilis, and Cos, and Sidee, and
Aradus, and Gortina, and Cnidus, and Cyprus, and Cyrene. 24 And the
copy heereof they wrote, to Simon the high Prieſt. 25 So Antiochus the
king camped againſt Dora, the ſecond day, aſsaulting it continually, and
making engins, by which meanes he ſhut vp Tryphon, that he could
neither goe out nor in. 26 At that time Simon ſent him two thouſand
choſen men to aide him: ſiluer alſo, and gold, and much
armour. 27 Neuertheleſſe, he would not receiue them, but brake all the
couenants which he had made with him afore, and became ſtrange vnto
him. 28 Furthermore hee ſent vnto him Athenobius, one of his friends to
commune with him and ſay: you withhold Ioppe and Gazara with the
towre that is in Ieruſalem, which are cities of my realme. 29 The borders
thereof yee haue waſted and done great hurt in the land, and got the
dominion of many places within my kingdome. 30 Now therefore deliuer
the cities which ye haue taken, and the tributes of the places whereof
yee haue gotten dominion without the borders of Iudea. 31 Or elſe giue
me for them fiue hundred talents of ſiluer, and for the harme that you
haue done, and the tributes of the cities other fiue hundred talents: if
not, we wil come and fight againſt you. 32 So Athenobius the kings friend
came to Ieruſalem, and when hee ſaw the glory of Simon, and the
cupboard of gold, and ſiluer plate, and his great attendance, he was
aſtoniſhed and told him the kings meſsage. 33 Then anſwered Simon, and
ſaid vnto him, We haue neither taken other mens land, nor holden that
which apperteineth to others, but the inheritance of our fathers, which
our enemies had wrongfully in poſſeſſion a certaine time. 34 Wherefore
we hauing opportunitie, hold the inheritance of our fathers. 35 And
whereas thou demaundeſt Ioppe and Gazara; albeit they did great harme
vnto the people in our countrey, yet will we giue an hundred talents for
them. Hereunto Athenobius anſwered him not a word, 36 But returned in
a rage to the king, and made report vnto him of theſe ſpeaches, and of
the glory of Simon, and of all that hee had ſeene: whereupon the king
was exceeding wroth. 37 In the meane time fled Tryphon by ſhip vnto
Orthoſias. 38 Then the king made Cendebeus captaine of the ſea coaſt,
and gaue him an hoſte of footmen and horſemen, 39 And commanded
him to remoue his hoſte toward Iudea: alſo hee commanded him to
build vp Cedron, and to fortifie the gates, & to warre againſt the people,
but as for the king *himſelfe* he purſued Tryphon. 40 So Cendebeus came to
Iamnia, and began to prouoke the people, and to inuade Iudea, and to
take the people priſoners, and ſlay them. 41 And when hee had built vp
Cedron, he ſet horſemen there, and an hoſt *of footmen* to the end that
iſsuing out, they might make outroades vpon the wayes of Iudea, as the
king had commanded him.

CHAPTER 16 1 Then came vp Iohn from Gazara, and told Simon his
father, what Cendebeus had done. 2 Wherefore Simon called his two
eldeſt ſonnes, Iudas and Iohn, and ſaid vnto them, I and my brethren,
and my fathers houſe haue euer from our youth vnto this day fought
againſt the enemies of Iſrael, and things haue proſpered ſo well in our
hands, that wee haue deliuered Iſrael oftentimes. 3 But now I am old, and
yee *by Gods mercy* are of a ſufficient age: Be ye in ſtead of mee, and my
brother, and goe and fight for our nation, and the helpe from heauen be
with you. 4 So hee choſe out of the countrey twentie thouſand men of
warre with horſemen, who went out againſt Cendebeus, and reſted that
night at Modin. 5 And when as they roſe in the morning, and went into
the plaine, behold, a mighty great hoſte both of footmen, and horſmen,
came againſt them: Howbeit there was a water brooke betwixt them. 6 So
hee and his people pitched ouer againſt them, and when hee ſaw that
the people were afraid to goe ouer the water brooke, hee went firſt ouer
himſelfe, and then the men ſeeing him, paſſed through after him. 7 *That
done* he diuided his men, and ſet the horſemen in the midſt of the
footemen: for the enemies horſemen were very many. 8 Then ſounded
they with the holy Trumpets: whereupon Cendebeus and his hoſte were
put to flight, ſo that many of them were ſlaine, and the remnant gat them
to the ſtrong hold. 9 At that time was Iudas Iohns brother wounded: But
Iohn ſtill followed after them, vntill he came to Cedron
which *Cendebeuſ* had built. 10 So they fled euen vnto the towres in the
fields of Azotus, wherefore hee burnt it with fire: So that there were
ſlaine of them about two thouſand men. Afterward hee returned into
the land of Iudea in peace. 11 Moreouer, in the plaine of Iericho was
Ptolomeus the ſonne of Abubus made captaine, and hee had abundance
of ſiluer and golde. 12 For he was the hie Prieſts ſonne in
lawe. 13 Wherefore his heart being lifted vp, hee thought to get the
countrey to himſelfe, and thereupon conſulted deceitfully againſt Simon
and his ſons, to deſtroy them. 14 Now Simon was viſiting the cities that
were in the countrey, and taking care for the good ordering of them, at
which time hee came downe himſelfe to Iericho with his ſons,
Mattathias and Iudas, in the hundreth threeſcore and ſeuenth yeere, in
the eleuenth moneth called Sabat. 15 Where the ſonne of Abubus
receiuing them deceitfully into a little holde called Docus, which he had
built, made them a great banquet: howbeit he had hidde men there. 16 So
when Simon and his ſonnes had drunke largely, Ptolome and his men
roſe vp, and tooke their weapons, and came vpon Simon into the

banketting place, and ſlewe him and his two ſonnes, and certaine of his ſeruants.17In which doing, he committed a great treachery, and recompenſed euill for good.18Then Ptolome wrote theſe things, and ſent to the king, that he ſhould ſend him an hoſte to aide him, and he would deliuer him the countrey and cities.19He ſent others alſo to Gazara to kill Iohn, & vnto the tribunes he ſent letters to come vnto him, that he might giue them ſiluer, and golde, & rewards.20And others he ſent to take Ieruſalem, and the mountaine of the temple.21Now one had runne afore to Gazara, and tolde Iohn that his father and brethren were ſlaine, and *quoth he* Ptolome hath ſent to ſlay thee alſo.22Hereof when he heard, hee was ſore aſtoniſhed: So he laide hands on them that were come to deſtroy him, and ſlew them, for hee knew that they ſought to make him away.23As concerning the reſt of the actes of Iohn, and his wars & worthy deeds which hee did, and the building of the walles which he made, and his doings,24Behold, theſe are written in the Chronicles of his Prieſthood, from the time he was made high Prieſt after his father.

2 MACCABEES

CHAPTER 11The brethren the Iewes that bee at Ieruſalem, and in the lande of Iudea, wiſh vnto the brethren the Iewes that are throughout Egypt, health and peace.2God be gracious vnto you, and remember his Couenant that hee made with Abraham, Iſaac, and Iacob, his faithfull ſeruants:3And giue you all an heart to ſerue him, and to doe his will, with a good courage, and a willing minde:4And open your hearts in his law and commandements, & ſend you peace:5And heare your prayers, and be at one with you, and neuer forſake you in time of trouble.6And now wee be here praying for you.7What time as Demetrius reigned, in the hundred threeſcore and ninth yeere, wee the Iewes wrote vnto you, in the extremitie of trouble, that came vpon vs in thoſe yeeres, from the time that Iaſon and his company reuolted from the holy land, and kingdome,8And burnt the porch, and ſhed innocent blood. Then we prayed vnto the Lord, and were heard: we offered alſo ſacrifices, and fine flowre, and lighted the lampes, and ſet forth the loaues.9And now ſee that ye keepe the feaſt of Tabernacles in the moneth Caſleu.10In the hundreth, foureſcore, and eight yeere, the people that were at Ieruſalem, and in Iudea, and the counſel, and Iudas, ſent greeting and health vnto Ariſtobulus, king Ptolomeus maſter, who was of the ſtock of the anointed prieſts, and to the Iewes that were in Egypt.11Inſomuch as God hath deliuered vs from great perils, wee thanke him highly, as hauing bin in battell againſt a king.12For he caſt them out that fought within the holy citie.13For when the leader was come into Perſia, and the armie with him that ſeemed inuincible, they were ſlaine in the temple of Nanea, by the deceit of Naneas prieſts.14For Antiochus, as though hee would marrie her, came into the place, and his friends that were with him, to receiue money in name of a dowrie.15Which when the prieſts of Nanea had ſet forth, and he was entred with a ſmall company into the compaſſe of the temple, they ſhut the temple aſſoone as Antiochus was come in.16And opening a priuie doore of the roofe, they threw ſtones like thunderbolts, and ſtroke downe the captaine, hewed them in pieces, ſmote off their heads, and caſt them to thoſe that were without.17Bleſſed be our God in all things, who hath deliuered vp the vngodly.18Therefore whereas we are nowe purpoſed to keep the purification of the Temple vpon the fiue & twentieth day of the moneth Caſleu, we thought it neceſsary to certifie you thereof, that ye alſo might keepe it, as the *feaſt* of the tabernacles, and of the fire *which was giuen vs* when Neemias offered ſacrifice, after that he had builded the Temple, and the Altar.19For when our fathers were led into Perſia, the Prieſts that were then deuout, took the fire of the Altar priuily, & hid it in a hollow place of a pit without water, where they kept it ſure, ſo that the place was vnknowen to all men.20Now after many yeeres, when it pleaſed God, Neemias being ſent from the king of Perſia, did ſend of the poſteritie of thoſe Prieſts that had hid it, to the fire: but when they tolde vs they found no fire, but thicke water,21Then cōmanded he them to draw it vp, and to bring it: and when the ſacrifices were laid on, Neemias cōmanded the Prieſts to ſprinkle þe wood, and the things laid thereupon with þe water.22When this was done, and the time came that the Sun ſhone which afore was hid in the cloude, there was a great fire kindled, ſo that euery man marueiled.23And the Prieſts made a prayer whileſt the ſacrifice was conſuming, *I ſay* both the Prieſts, and all the reſt, Ionathan beginning, and the reſt anſwering thereunto, as Neemias did.24And the prayer was after this maner, O Lord, Lord God, Creatour of all things, who art fearefull, and ſtrong, and righteous, and mercifull, and the onely, and gracious king,25The onely giuer of all things, the onely iuſt, almightie & euerlaſting, thou that deliuereſt Iſrael from al trouble, & didſt chooſe the fathers, & ſanctifie them:26Receiue the ſacrifice for thy whole people Iſrael, and preſeruethine owne portion, and ſanctifie it.27Gather thoſe together that are ſcattered frō vs, deliuer them that ſerue among the heathen, looke vpon them that are deſpiſed & abhorred, and let the heathen know that thou art our God.28Puniſh them that oppreſſe vs, and with pride doe vs wrong.29Plant thy people againe in thy holy place, as Moiſes hath ſpoken.30And the Prieſts ſung pſalmes of thankeſgiuing.31Now when the ſacrifice was conſumed, Neemias commanded the water that was left, to bee powred on the great ſtones.32When this was done, there was kindled a flame: but it was conſumed by the light that ſhined from the Altar.33So when this matter was knowen, it was told the king of Perſia, that in the place, where the Prieſts that were led away, had hid the fire, there appeared water, and that Neemias had purified the ſacrifices therewith.34Then the king incloſing the place, made it holy after he had tried þe matter.35And the king tooke many gifts, and beſtowed thereof, on thoſe whom he would gratifie.36And Neemias called this thing Naphthar, which is as much to ſay as a cleanſing: but many men call it Nephi.

CHAPTER 21It is alſo found in the records, that Ieremie the Prophet, commaunded them that were caried away, to take of the fire as it hath beene ſignified,2And how that the Prophet hauing giuen them the law, charged them not to forget the commaundements of the Lord, and that they ſhould not erre in their minds, when they ſee images of ſiluer, and gold, with their ornaments.3And with other ſuch ſpeeches exhorted he them, that the law ſhould not depart from their hearts.4It was alſo contained in the ſame writing, that the Prophet being warned of God, commanded the Tabernacle, and the Arke to goe with him, as he went forth into the mountaine, where Moiſes climed vp, and ſawe the heritage of God.5And when Ieremie came thither, he found an hollow caue wherin he laid the Tabernacle, and the Arke, and the altar of incenſe, & ſo ſtopped the doore.6And ſome of thoſe that followed him, came to marke the way, but they could not find it.7Which when Ieremie perceiued, hee blamed them, ſaying, As for that place, it ſhall be vnknowen vntill the time that God gather his people againe together, and receiue them vnto mercy.8Then ſhall the Lord ſhew them theſe things, and the glory of the Lord ſhall appeare, and the cloud alſo as it was ſhewed vnder Moiſes, and as when Solomon deſired that the place might be honourably ſanctified.9It was alſo declared that he being wiſe, offered the ſacrifice of dedication, and of the finiſhing of the Temple.10And as when Moiſes prayed vnto the Lord, the fire came down from heauen, and conſumed the ſacrifices: euen ſo prayed Solomon alſo, and the fire came downe from heauen, and conſumed the burnt offerings.11And Moiſes ſaid, becauſe the ſinne offering was not to be eaten, it was conſumed.12So Solomon kept thoſe eight dayes.13The ſame things alſo were reported in the writings, and commentaries of Neemias, and how he founding a librarie, gathered together the acts of the Kings, and the Prophets, and of Dauid, and the Epiſtles of the Kings concerning the holy gifts.14In like maner alſo, Iudas gathered together all thoſe things that were loſt, by reaſon of the warre we had, and they remaine with vs.15Wherefore if yee haue neede thereof, ſend ſome to fetch them vnto you.16Whereas we then are about to celebrate the purification, we haue written vnto you, and yee ſhall doe well if yee keepe the ſame dayes.17We hope alſo that the God, that deliuered all his people, and gaue them all an heritage, and the kingdome, and the prieſthood, and the Sanctuarie,18As he promiſed in the lawe, will ſhortly haue mercy vpon vs, and gather vs together out of euery land vnder heauen into the holy place: for he hath deliuered vs out of great troubles, and hath purified the place.19Now as concerning Iudas Maccabeus, and his brethren, and the purification of the great Temple, and the dedication of the altar,20And the warres againſt Antiochus Epiphanes, & Eupator his ſonne,21And the manifeſt ſignes that came from heauen, vnto thoſe that behaued themſelues manfully to their honour for Iudaiſme: ſo that being but a few, they ouercame the whole country, and

chaſed barbarous multitudes,22And recouered againe the Temple
renowned all the world ouer, and freed the citie, and vpheld the lawes,
which were going downe, the Lord being gracious vnto them with al
fauour:23All theſe things (I ſay) being declared by Iaſon of Cyrene in fiue
books, we will aſſay to abridge in one volume.24For conſidering the
infinite number, and the difficulty, which they find that deſire to looke
into the narrations of the ſtory, for the variety of þe matter,25We haue
beene carefull, that they that will read might haue delight, and that they
that are deſirous to commit to memorie, might haue eaſe, and that all,
into whoſe hands it comes might haue profit.26Therefore to vs that haue
taken vpon vs this paineful labour of abridging, it was not eaſie, but a
matter of ſweat, and watching.27Euen as it is no eaſe vnto him, that
prepareth a banquet, and ſeeketh the benefit of others: yet for the
pleaſuring of many we will vndertake gladly this great paines:28Leauing
to the authour the exact handling of euery particular, and labouring to
follow the rules of an abridgement.29For as the maſter builder of a new
houſe, muſt care for the whole building: but hee that vndertaketh to ſet
it out, and paint it, muſt ſeeke out fit things for the adorning thereof:
euen ſo I thinke it is with vs.30To ſtand vpon euery point, and goe ouer
things at large, and to be curious in particulars, belongeth to the firſt
authour of the ſtorie.31But to vſe breuitie, and auoyde much labouring
of the worke, is to bee granted to him that will make an
abridgement.32Here then will we begin the ſtory: onely adding thus
much to that which hath bene ſaid, That it is a fooliſh thing to make a
long prologue, and to be ſhort in the ſtory it ſelfe.
CHAPTER 3 1Now when the holy Citie was inhabited with all peace,
and the Lawes were kept very well, becauſe of the godlineſse of Onias
the high Prieſt, and his hatred of wickedneſſe,2It came to paſſe that euen
the Kings themſelues did honour the place, and magnifie the Temple
with their beſt gifts;3Inſomuch that Seleucus king of Aſia, of his owne
reuenues, bare all the coſtes belonging to the ſeruice of the
ſacrifices.4But one Simon of the tribe of Beniamin, who was made
gouernour of the Temple, fell out with the high Prieſt about diſorder in
the citie.5And when he could not ouercome Onias, he gate him to
Apollonius the ſonne of Thraſeas, who then was gouernour of
Coeloſyria, and Phenice,6And told him that the treaſurie in Ieruſalem
was full of infinite ſummes of money, ſo that the multitude of their
riches which did not pertaine to the account of the ſacrifices, was
innumerable, and that it was poſsible to bring all into the kings
hand.7Now when Apollonius came to the king, and had ſhewed him of
the money, whereof he was told, the king choſe out Heliodorus his
treaſurer, and ſent him with a commaundement, to bring him the
foreſaid money.8So foorthwith Heliodorus tooke his iourney vnder a
colour of viſiting the cities of Coeloſyria, and Phenice, but indeed to
fulfill the kings purpoſe.9And when he was come to Ieruſalem, & had
bene courteouſly receiued of the high Prieſt of the citie, hee told him
what intelligence was giuen of the money, & declared wherefore hee
came, and and aſked if theſe things were ſo in deed.10Then the high
Prieſt tolde him that there was ſuch money layde vp for the reliefe of
widowes, and fatherleſſe children,11And that ſome of it belonged to
Hircanus, ſonne of Tobias, a man of great dignitie, and not as that
wicked Simon had miſinformed: the ſumme whereof in all was foure
hundred talents of ſiluer, and two hundred of gold,12And that it was
altogether impoſsible that ſuch wrong ſhould be done vnto them, that
had committed it to the holineſſe of the place, and to the maieſtie and
inuiolable ſanctitie of the Temple, honoured ouer all the world.13But
Heliodorus becauſe of the kings commandement giuen him, ſaid, That
in any wiſe it muſt be brought into the kings treaſury.14So at the day
which hee appointed, hee entred in to order this matter, wherefore,
there was no ſmall agonie throughout the whole citie.15But the Prieſts
proſtrating themſelues before the Altar in their Prieſts Ueſtments, called
vnto heauen vpon him that made a Lawe concerning things giuen to bee
kept, that they ſhould ſafely bee preſerued for ſuch as had committed
them to be kept.16Then whoſo had looked the hie Prieſt in the face, it
would haue wounded his heart: for his countenance, and the changing
of his colour, declared the inward agonie of his minde:17For the man
was ſo compaſſed with feare, and horror of the body, that it was
manifeſt to them that looked vpon him, what ſorrow hee had now in
his heart.18Others ran flocking out of their houſes to the generall
Supplication, becauſe the place was like to come into contempt.19And
the women girt with ſackecloth vnder their breaſts, abounded in the
ſtreetes, and the virgins that were kept in, ran ſome to the gates, and
ſome to the walles, and others looked out of the windowes:20And all
holding their handes towards heauen, made ſupplication.21Then it would
haue pitied a man to ſee the falling downe of the multitude of all ſorts,
and the feare of the hie Prieſt, being in ſuch an agony.22They then called
vpon the Almightie Lord, to keepe the things committed of truſt, ſafe
and ſure, for thoſe that had committed them.23Neuertheleſſe Heliodorus
executed that which was decreed.24Now as hee was there preſent
himſelfe with his guard about the treaſurie, the Lord of ſpirits, & the
Prince of all power cauſed a great apparition, ſo that all that preſumed
to come in with him, were aſtoniſhed at the power of God, and fainted,
and were ſore afraid.25For there appeared vnto them a horſe, with a
terrible rider vpon him, and adorned with a very faire couering, and he
ranne fiercely, and ſmote at Heliodorus with his forefeet, and it ſeemed
that hee that ſate vpon the horſe, had complete harneſse of
golde.26Moreouer two other yong men appeared before him, notable in
ſtrength, excellent in beautie, and comely in apparell, who ſtood by him
on either ſide, and ſcourged him continually, and gaue him many ſore
ſtripes.27And Heliodorus fell ſuddenly vnto the ground, and was
compaſſed with great darkeneſſe: but they that were with him, tooke
him vp, and put him into a litter.28Thus him that lately came with a great
traine, and with all his guard into the ſaid treaſury, they caried out, being
vnable to helpe himſelfe with his weapons: and manifeſtly they
acknowledged the power of God.29For hee by the hand of God was caſt
downe, and lay ſpeechleſſe without all hope of life.30But they praiſed the
Lord that had miraculouſly honoured his owne place: for the Temple
which a little afore was full of feare and trouble, when the Almightie
Lord appeared, was filled with ioy and gladneſſe.31Then ſtraightwayes
certaine of Heliodorus friends, prayed Onias that hee would call vpon
the moſt High to graunt him his life, who lay ready to giue vp the
ghoſt.32So the high Prieſt ſuſpecting leſt the king ſhould miſconceiue
that ſome treachery had beene done to Heliodorus by the Iewes, offered
a ſacrifice for the health of the man.33Now as the high Prieſt was making
an atonement, the ſame yong men, in the ſame clothing, appeared and
ſtood beſide Heliodorus, ſaying, Giue Onias the high Prieſt great
thankes, inſomuch as for his ſake the Lord hath granted thee life.34And
ſeeing that thou haſt beene ſcourged from heauen, declare vnto all men
the mightie power of God: and when they had ſpoken theſe wordes,
they appeared no more.35So Heliodorus after he had offered ſacrifice
vnto the Lord, and made great vowes vnto him that had ſaued his life,
and ſaluted Onias, returned with his hoſte to the king.36Then teſtified
hee to all men, the workes of the great God, which he had ſeene with
his eyes.37And when the king aſked Heliodorus, who might be a fit man
to be ſent yet once againe to Ieruſalem, he ſaid,38If thou haſt any enemy
or traitor, ſend him thither, and thou ſhalt receiue him well ſcourged, if
he eſcape with his life: for in that place, no doubt, there is an eſpeciall
power of God.39For hee that dwelleth in heauen hath his eye on that
place, and defendeth it, and hee beateth and deſtroyeth them that come
to hurt it.40And the things concerning Heliodorus, and the keeping of
the treaſurie, fell out on this ſort.
CHAPTER 4 1This Simon now (of whō wee ſpake afore) hauing bin a
bewrayer of the money, and of his countrey, ſlandered Onias, as if he
had terrified Heliodorus, and bene the worker of theſe euils.2Thus was
hee bold to call him a traitour, that had deſerued well of the citie, and
tendred his owne nation, and was ſo zealous of the lawes.3But when
their hatred went ſo farre, that by one of Simons faction murthers were
committed,4Onias ſeeing the danger of this contention, and that
Appollonius, as being the gouernour of Coeloſyria and Phenice, did
rage, and increaſe Simons malice,5He went to the king, not to be an
accuſer of his countrey men, but ſeeking the good of all, both publike,
& priuate.6For he ſaw that it was impoſsible, that the ſtate ſhould
continue quiet, and Simon leaue his folly, vnleſſe the king did looke
thereunto.7But after the death of Seleucus, when Antiochus called
Epiphanes, tooke the kingdom, Iaſon the brother of Onias, laboured
vnder hand to bee hie Prieſt,8Promiſing vnto the king by interceſsion,
three hundred and threeſcore talents of ſiluer, and of another reuenew,
eightie talents:9Beſides this, he promiſed to aſsigne an hundred and fiftie
more, if he might haue licence to ſet him vp a place for exerciſe, and for
the training vp of youth in the faſhions of the heathen, and to write

them of Ieruſalem *by the name of* Antiochians.10Which when the king had
granted, and hee had gotten into his hand the rule, he foorthwith
brought his owne nation to the Greekiſh faſhion.11And the royal
priuiledges granted of ſpeciall fauour to the Iewes, by the meanes of
Iohn the father of Eupolemus, who went Embaſsador to Rome, for
amitie and aid, he tooke away, and putting down the gouernments which
were according to the law, he brought vp new cuſtomes againſt the
law.12For he built gladly a place of exerciſe vnder the towre it ſelfe, and
brought the chiefe yong men vnder his ſubiection, and made them weare
a hat.13Now ſuch was the height of Greek faſhions, and increaſe of
heatheniſh maners, through the exceeding profanenes of Iaſon that
vngodly wretch, and no high prieſt:14That the prieſts had no courage to
ſerue any more at the altar, but deſpiſing the Temple, and neglecting the
ſacrifices, haſtened to be partakers of the vnlawfull allowance in the
place of exerciſe, after the game of Diſcus called them forth.15Not
ſetting by the honours of their fathers, but liking the glory of the
Grecians beſt of all.16By reaſon whereof ſore calamity came vpon them:
for they had them to be their enemies and auengers, whoſe cuſtome they
followed ſo earneſtly, and vnto whom they deſired to be like in all
things.17For it is not a light thing to doe wickedly againſt the lawes of
God, but the time following ſhall declare theſe things.18Now when the
game that was vſed euery fift yere was kept at Tyrus, the king being
preſent,19This vngracious Iaſon ſent ſpeciall meſſengers from Ieruſalem,
who were Antiochians, to carie three hundred drachmes of ſiluer to the
ſacrifice of Hercules, which euen the bearers therof thought fit not to
beſtow vpon the ſacrifice, becauſe it was not conuenient, but to be
reſeruedfor other charges.20This money then in regard of the ſender,
was appointed to Hercules ſacrifice, but becauſe of the bearers thereof,
it was imployed to the making of gallies.21Now when Apollonius the
ſonne of Manaſtheus was ſent vnto Egypt, for the coronation of king
Ptolomeus Philometor, Antiochus vnderſtanding him not to bee well
affected to his affaires, prouided for his owne ſafetie: whereupon he
came to Ioppe, & from thence to Ieruſalem.22Where he was honourably
receiued of Iaſon, and of the citie, and was brought in with torchlight,
and with great ſhoutings: and ſo afterward went with his hoſte vnto
Phenice.23Three yeere afterward, Iaſon ſent Menelaus the foreſaid
Simons brother, to beare the money vnto the king, and to put him in
minde of certaine neceſsary matters.24But he being brought to the
preſence of the king, when he had magnified him, for the glorious
appearance of his power, got the prieſthood to himſelfe, offering more
then Iaſon by three hundred talents of ſiluer.25So he came with the kings
Mandate, bringing nothing worthy the high prieſthood, but hauing the
fury of a cruell Tyrant, and the rage of a ſauage beaſt.26Then Iaſon, who
had vndermined his owne brother, being vndermined by another, was
cõpelled to flee into the countrey of the Ammonites.27So Menelaus got
the principalitie: but as for the money that he had promiſed vnto the
king, hee tooke no good order for it, albeit Soſtratus the ruler of the
caſtle required it.28For vnto him appertained the gathering of the
cuſtomes. Wherefore they were both called before the king.29Now
Menelaus left his brother Lyſimachus in his ſtead in the prieſthood, and
Soſtratus left Crates, who was gouernour of the Cyprians.30While thoſe
things were in doing, they of Tharſus and Mallos made inſurrection,
becauſe they were giuen to the kings concubine called Antiochis.31Then
came the king in all haſte to appeaſe matters, leauing Andronicus a man
in authority, for his deputy.32Now Menelaus ſuppoſing that he had
gotten a conuenient time, ſtole certaine veſſels of gold, out of the
temple, and gaue ſome of them to Andronicus, and ſome he ſold into
Tyrus, and the cities round about.33Which when Onias knew of a ſurety,
he reprooued him, and withdrew himſelfe into a Sanctuarie at Daphne,
that lieth by Antiochia.34Wherefore Menelaus, taking Andronicus apart,
prayed him to get Onias into his hands, who being perſwaded thereunto,
and comming to Onias in deceit, gaue him his right hand with othes,
and though hee were ſuſpected (by him) yet perſwaded he him to come
forth of the Sanctuarie: whom forthwith he ſhut vp without regard of
Iuſtice.35For the which cauſe not onely the Iewes, but many alſo of other
nations tooke great indignation, and were much grieued for the vniuſt
murder of the man.36And when the king was come againe from the
places about Cilicia, the Iewes that were in the citie, and certaine of the
Greekes, that abhorred the fact alſo, complained becauſe Onias was
ſlaine without cauſe.37Therefore Antiochus was heartily ſorry, and
mooued to pity, and wept, becauſe of the ſober and modeſt behauiour
of him that was dead.38And being kindled with anger, forthwith he
tooke away Andronicus his purple, and rent off his clothes, and leading
him through the whole city vnto that very place, where he had
committed impietie againſt Onias, there ſlew he the curſed murtherer.
Thus the Lord rewarded him his puniſhment, as he had deſerued.39Now
when many ſacriledges had beene committed in the citie by Lyſimachus,
with the conſent of Menelaus, and the bruit therof was ſpread abroad,
the multitude gathered themſelues together againſt Lyſimachus, many
veſſels of gold being already caried away.40Whereupon the common
people riſing, and being filled with rage, Lyſimachus armed about three
thouſand men, and beganne firſt to offer violence on Auranus, being
the leader, a man farre gone in yeeres, & no leſſe in folly.41They then
ſeeing the attempt of Lyſimachus, ſome of them caught ſtones, ſome
clubs, others taking handfuls of duſt, that was next at hand, caſt them
all together vpon Lyſimachus, and thoſe that ſet vpon them.42Thus
many of them they wounded, & ſome they ſtroke to the ground, and
all *of them* they forced to flee: but as for the Churchrobber himſelfe, him
they killed beſides the treaſury.43Of theſe matters therefore there was an
accuſation laide againſt Menelaus.44Now when the king came to Tyrus,
three men that were ſent from the Senate, pleaded the cauſe before
him:45But Menelaus being now conuicted, promiſed Ptolomee the
ſonne of Dorymenes, to giue him much money, if hee would pacifie the
King towards him.46Whereupon Ptolomee taking the king aſide into a
certaine gallerie, as it were to take the aire, brought him to be of another
minde;47Inſomuch that hee diſcharged Menelaus from the accuſations,
who notwithſtanding was cauſe of all the miſchiefe: and thoſe poore
men, who if they had told their cauſe, yea, before the Scythians, ſhould
haue bene iudged innocent, them he condemned to death.48Thus they
that followed the matter for the citie, and for the people, and for the
holy veſſels, did ſoone ſuffer vniuſt puniſhment.49Wherefore euen they
of Tyrus mooued with hatred of that wicked deed, cauſed them to bee
honourably buried.50And ſo through the couetouſneſſe of them that
were in power, Menelaus remained ſtill in authority, increaſing in malice,
and being a great traitour to the citizens.
CHAPTER 5 1About the ſame time Antiochus prepared his ſecond
voyage into Egypt:2And then it happened, that through all the citie, for
the ſpace almoſt of fourtie dayes, there were ſeene horſemen running in
the aire, in cloth of golde, and armed with lances, like a band of
ſouldiers,3And troupes of horſemen in aray, incountring, and running
one againſt another with ſhaking of ſhieldes, and multitude of pikes, and
drawing of ſwords, and caſting of darts, and glittering of golden
ornaments, and harneſse of all ſorts.4Wherefore euery man praied that
that apparition might turne to good.5Now when there was gone forth a
falſe rumour, as though Antiochus had bene dead, Iaſon tooke at the
leaſt a thouſand men, and ſuddenly made an aſsault vpon the citie, and
they that were vpon the walles, being put backe, and the citie at length
taken, Menelaus fled into the caſtle:6But Iaſon ſlew his owne citizens
without mercy, (not conſidering that to get the day of them of his owne
nation, would be a moſt vnhappy day for him: but thinking they had
bene his enemies, and not his countrey men whom he
conquered.)7Howbeit, for all this hee obtained not the principalitie, but
at the laſt receiued ſhame for the reward of his treaſon, and fled againe
into the countrey of the Ammonites.8In the end therefore hee had an
vnhappy returne, being accuſed before Aretas the king of the Arabians,
fleeing from city to city, purſued of all men, hated as a forſaker of the
Lawes, and being had in abomination, as an open enemie of his
countrey, and countreymen, he was caſt out into Egypt.9Thus hee that
had driuen many out of their countrey, periſhed in a ſtrange land, retiring
to the Lacedemonians, and thinking there to finde ſuccour by reaſon of
his kindred.10And hee that had caſt out many vnburied, had none to
mourne for him, nor any ſolemne funerals at all, nor ſepulchre with his
fathers.11Now when this that was done came to the kings eare, he
thought that Iudea had reuolted, whereupon remouing out of Egypt in
a furious minde, he tooke the citie by force of armes,12And
commaunded his men of warre not to ſpare ſuch as they met, and to
ſlay ſuch as went vp vpon the houſes.13Thus there was killing of yong
and old, making away of men, women and children, ſlaying of virgins
and infants.14And there were deſtroyed within the ſpace of three whole
daies, foureſcore thouſand, whereof fourty thouſand were ſlaine in the

conflict; and no fewer ſold, then ſlaine.[15]Yet was he not content with this, but preſumed to goe into the moſt holy Temple of all the world: Menelaus that traitour to the Lawes, and to his owne countrey, being his guide.[16]And taking the holy veſſels with polluted handes, and with prophane handes, pulling downe the things that were dedicated by other kings, to the augmentation and glory and honour of the place, he gaue them away.[17]And ſo haughtie was Antiochus in minde, that hee conſidered not that the Lord was angry for a while for the ſinnes of them that dwelt in the citie, and therefore his eye was not vpon the place.[18]For had they not beene formerly wrapped in many ſinnes, this man as ſoone as hee had come, had foorthwith beene ſcourged, and put backe from his preſumption, as Heliodorus was, whom Seleucus the king ſent to view the treaſurie.[19]Neuertheleſſe God did not chooſe the people for the places ſake, but the place for the peoples ſake.[20]And therefore the place it ſelfe that was partaker with them of the aduerſities that happened to the nation, did afterward communicate in the benefits ſent from the Lord: and as it was forſaken in the wrath of the Almighty, ſo againe the great Lord being reconciled, it was ſet vp with all glory.[21]So when Antiochus had caried out of the Temple, a thouſand and eight hundred talents, hee departed in all haſte into Antiochia, weening in his pride to make the land nauigable, and the ſea paſſable by foot: ſuch was the haughtineſse of his minde.[22]And he left gouernours to vexe the nation: at Ieruſalem Philip, for his countrey a Phrygian, and for manners more barbarous then hee that ſet him there:[23]And at Garizim, Andronicus; and beſides, Menelaus, who worſe then all the reſt, bare an heauie hand ouer the citizens, hauing a malicious minde againſt his countreymen the Iewes.[24]He ſent alſo that deteſtable ringleader Apollonius, with an armie of two and twentie thouſand, commaunding him to ſlay all thoſe that were in their beſt age, and to ſell the women and the yonger ſort:[25]Who comming to Ieruſalem, and pretending peace, did forbeare till the holy day of the Sabbath, when taking the Iewes keeping holy day, hee commanded his men to arme themſelues.[26]And ſo hee ſlewe all them that were gone to the celebrating of the Sabbath, and running through the city with weapons, ſlewe great multitudes.[27]But Iudas Maccabeus, with nine others, or thereabout, withdrew himſelfe into the wilderneſſe, and liued in the mountaines after the maner of beaſts, with his company, who fed on herbes continually, leſt they ſhould be partakers of the pollution.

CHAPTER 6 [1]Not long after this, the king ſent an olde man of Athens, to compell the Iewes to depart from the lawes of their fathers, and not to liue after the Lawes of God:[2]And to pollute alſo the Temple in Ieruſalem, and to call it the Temple of Iupiter Olympius: and that in Garizim, of Iupiter the defender of ſtrangers, as they did deſire that dwelt in the place.[3]The comming in of this miſchiefe was ſore and grieuous to the people:[4]For the Temple was filled with riot and reuelling, by the Gentiles, who dallied with harlots, and had to doe with women within the circuit of the holy places, and beſides that, brought in things that were not lawfull.[5]The Altar alſo was filled with profane things, which the Law forbiddeth.[6]Neither was it lawfull for a man to keepe Sabbath dayes, or ancient Feaſts, or to profeſse himſelfe at all to be a Iewe.[7]And in the day of the kings birth, euery moneth they were brought by bitter conſtraint to eate of the ſacrifices; and when the Feaſt of Bacchus was kept, the Iewes were compelled to goe in proceſsion to Bacchus, carying Iuie.[8]Moreouer there went out a decree to the neighbour cities of the heathen, by the ſuggeſtion of Ptolomee, againſt the Iewes, that they ſhould obſerue the ſame faſhions, and be partakers of their ſacrifices.[9]And whoſo would not conforme themſelues to the maners of the Gentiles, ſhould be put to death: then might a man hane ſeene the preſent miſery.[10]For there were two women brought, who had circumciſed their children, whom when they had openly led round about the citie, the babes hanging at their breaſts, they caſt them downe headlong from the wall.[11]And others that had run together into caues neere by, to keepe the Sabbath day ſecretly, being diſcouered to Philip, were all burnt together, becauſe they made a conſcience to helpe themſelues, for the honour of the moſt ſacred day.[12]Now I beſeech thoſe that reade this booke, that they be not diſcouraged for theſe calamities, but that they iudge thoſe puniſhments not to be for deſtruction, but for a chaſtening of our nation.[13]For it is a token of his great goodneſse, when wicked doers are not ſuffered any longtime, but forthwith puniſhed.[14]For not as with other nations whom the Lord patiently forbeareth to puniſh, till they be come to the fulneſse of their ſinnes, ſo dealeth he with vs,[15]Leſt that being come to the height of ſinne, afterwards hee ſhould take vengeance of vs.[16]And therfore he neuer withdraweth his mercie from vs: and though he puniſh with aduerſitie, yet doeth he neuer forſake his people.[17]But let this that we haue ſpoken be for a warning vnto vs: And nowe will wee come to the declaring of the matter in few words.[18]Eleazar one of the principall Scribes, an aged man, and of a well fauoured countenance, was conſtrained to open his mouth, and to eate ſwines fleſh.[19]But he chuſing rather to die glorioully, then to liue ſtained with ſuch an abomination, ſpit it forth, and came of his owne accord to the torment,[20]As it behoued them to come, that are reſolute to ſtand out againſt ſuch things, as are not lawfull for loue of life to be taſted.[21]But they that had the charge of that wicked feaſt, for the olde acquaintance they had with the man, taking him aſide, beſought him to bring fleſh of his owne prouiſion, ſuch as was lawfull for him to vſe, and make as if he did eate of the fleſh, taken from the ſacrifice commanded by the king,[22]That in ſo doing hee might bee deliuered from death, and for the olde friendſhip with them, find fauour.[23]But he began to conſider diſcreetly, and as became his age, and the excellencie of his ancient yeeres, and the honour of his gray head, whereunto hee was come, and his moſt honeſt education from a child, or rather the holy lawe made, and giuen by God: therefore hee anſwered accordingly, and willed them ſtraightwaies to ſend him to the graue.[24]For it becommeth not our age, ſaid he, in any wiſe to diſsemble, whereby many yong perſons might thinke, that Eleazar being foureſcore yeres old and ten, were now gone to a ſtrange religion.[25]And ſo they through mine hypocriſie, and deſire to liue a litle time, and a moment longer, ſhould bee deceiued by me, and I get a ſtaine to mine olde age, and make it abominable.[26]For though for the preſent time I ſhould be deliuered from the puniſhment of men: yet ſhould I not eſcape the hand of the Almightie, neither aliue nor dead.[27]Wherefore now manfully changing this life, I will ſhew my ſelfe ſuch an one, as mine age requireth,[28]And leaue a notable example to ſuch as bee yong, to die willingly, and couragiouſly, for the honourable and holy lawes: and when he had ſaid theſe words, immediatly he went to the torment,[29]They that led him, changing the good will they bare him a litle before, into hatred, becauſe the foreſaid ſpeaches proceeded as they thought, from a deſperate minde.[30]But when hee was readie to die with ſtripes, he groned, and ſaid, It is manifeſt vnto the Lord, that hath the holy knowledge, that wheras I might haue bin deliuered from death, I *now* endure ſore paines in body, by being beaten: but in ſoule am well content to ſuffer theſe things, becauſe I feare him.[31]And thus this man died, leauing his death for an example of a noble courage, and a memoriall of vertue not only vnto yong men, but vnto all his nation.

CHAPTER 7 [1]It came to paſſe alſo that ſeuen brethren with their mother were taken, and compelled by the king againſt the lawe to taſte ſwines fleſh, and were tormented with ſcourges, and whips:[2]But one of them that ſpake firſt ſaid thus: What wouldeſt thou aſke, or learne of vs? we are ready to die, rather then to tranſgreſse the lawes of our fathers.[3]Then the king being in a rage, commanded pannes, and caldrons to be made whot.[4]Which forthwith being heated, he commanded to cut out the tongue of him that ſpake firſt, and to cut off the vtmoſt parts of his body, the reſt of his brethren, and his mother looking on.[5]Now when he was thus maimed in all his members, he commanded him being yet aliue, to be brought to the fire, and to be fried in the panne: and as the vapour of the panne was for a good ſpace diſperſed, they exhorted one another, with the mother, to die manfully, ſaying thus:[6]The Lord God looketh vpon vs, and in trueth hath comfort in vs, as Moiſes in his ſong, which witneſſed to their faces declared, ſaying, And he ſhall be comforted in his ſeruants.[7]So when the firſt was dead, after this maner, they brought the ſecond to make him a mocking ſtocke: and when they had pulled off the ſkin of his head with the haire, they aſked him, Wilt thou eate before thou bee puniſhed throughout euery member of thy body?[8]But hee anſwered in his owne language, and ſaid, No. Wherefore hee alſo receiued the next torment in order, as the former did.[9]And when hee was at the laſt gaſpe, hee ſaid, Thou like a fury takeſt vs out of this preſent life, but the king of the world ſhall raiſe vs vp, who haue died for his lawes, vnto euerlaſting life.[10]After him was the third made a mocking ſtocke, and when he was required, he put out his tongue, and that right ſoone, holding forth his hands manfully,[11]And ſaid

courageiouſly, Theſe I had from heauen, and for his lawes I deſpiſe them,
and from him I hope to receiue them againe.12Inſomuch that the king,
and they that were with him marueiled at the yong mans courage, for
that he nothing regarded the paines.13Now when this man was dead alſo,
they tormented and mangled the fourth in like maner.14So when he was
ready to die, he ſaid thus, It is good, being put to death by men, to looke
for hope from God to be raiſed vp againe by him: as for thee thou ſhalt
haue no reſurrection to life.15Afterward they brought the fift alſo, and
mangled him.16Then looked hee vnto the king and ſaid, Thou haſt
power ouer men, thou art corruptible, thou doeſt what thou wilt, yet
thinke not that our nation is forſaken of God.17But abide a while, and
behold his great power, how he will torment thee, and thy ſeed.18After
him alſo they brought the ſixt, who being ready to die, ſaid, Be not
deceiued without cauſe: for we ſuffer theſe things for our ſelues, hauing
ſinned againſt our God. Therefore marueilous things are done (vnto
vs.)19But thinke not thou that takeſt in hand to ſtriue againſt God, that
thou ſhalt eſcape vnpuniſhed.20But the mother was marueilous aboue
all, and worthy of honorable memorie: for when ſhee ſawe her ſeuen
ſonnes ſlaine within the ſpace of one day, ſhe bare it with a good
courage, becauſe of the hope that ſhe had in þe Lord21Yea ſhe exhorted
euery one of them in her owne language, filled with couragious ſpirits,
and ſtirring vp her womaniſh thoughts, with a manly ſtomacke, ſhe ſaid
vnto them,22I cannot tell how you came into my wombe: for I neither
gaue you breath, nor life, neither was it I that formed the mēbers of
euery one of you.23But doubtleſſe the Creator of the world, who formed
the generation of man, and found out the beginning of all things, wil
alſo of his owne mercy giue you breath, and life againe, as you now
regard not your owne ſelues for his Lawes ſake.24Now Antiochus
thinking himſelfe deſpiſed, and ſuſpecting it to be a reprochfull ſpeach,
whiles the yongeſt was yet aliue, did not onely exhort him by wordes,
but alſo aſsured him with oathes, that he would make him both a rich,
and a happy man, if hee would turne from the Lawes of his fathers, and
that alſo he would take him for his friend, and truſt him with
affaires.25But when the yong man would in no caſe hearken vnto him,
the king called his mother, and exhorted her, that ſhe would counſell the
yong man to ſaue his life.26And when hee had exhorted her with many
words, ſhe promiſed him that ſhe would counſell her ſonne.27But ſhee
bowing her ſelfe towards him, laughing the cruell tyrant to ſcorne, ſpake
in her countrey language on this maner; O my ſonne, haue pitie vpon
mee that bare thee nine moneths in my wombe, and gaue thee ſucke
three yeeres, and nouriſhed thee, and brought thee vp vnto this age, and
endured the troubles of education.28I beſeech thee, my ſonne, looke
vpon the heauen, and the earth, and all that is therein, and conſider that
God made them of things that were not, and ſo was mankinde made
likewiſe;29Feare not this tormentour, but being worthy of thy brethren,
take thy death, that I may receiue thee againe in mercy with thy
brethren.30Whiles ſhe was yet ſpeaking theſe words, the yong man ſaid,
Whom wait ye for? I will not obey the kings commandement: but I will
obey the commandement of the Law that was giuen vnto our fathers,
by Moſes.31And thou that haſt bene the authour of all miſchiefe againſt
the Hebrewes, ſhalt not eſcape the handes of God.32For wee ſuffer
becauſe of our ſinnes.33And though the liuing Lord bee angrie with vs a
little while for our chaſtening and correction, yet ſhall hee be at one
againe, with his ſeruants.34But thou, O godleſſe man, and of all other
moſt wicked, be not lifted vp without a cauſe, nor puffed vp with
vncertaine hopes, lifting vp thy hand againſt the ſeruants of God:35For
thou haſt not yet eſcaped the iudgement of Almightie God, who ſeeth
all things.36For our brethren who now haue ſuffered a ſhort paine, are
dead vnder Gods Couenant of euerlaſting life: but thou through the
iudgement of God, ſhalt receiue iuſt puniſhment for thy pride.37But I,
as my brethren, offer vp my body, and life for the Lawes of our fathers,
beſeeching God that he would ſpeedily bee mercifull vnto our nation,
and that thou by torments & plagues mayeſt confeſse, that he alone is
God;38And that in me, and my brethren, the wrath of the Almighty,
which is iuſtly brought vpon all our nation, may ceaſe.39Then the King
being in a rage, handled him worſe then all the reſt, and took it grieuouſly
that he was mocked.40So this man died vndefiled, and put his whole
truſt in the Lord.41Laſt of all after the ſonnes, the mother died.42Let this
be ynough now to haue ſpoken cōcerning the idolatrous feaſts, and the
extreme tortures.

CHAPTER 8 1Then Iudas Maccabeus and they that were with him,
went priuily into the townes, and called their kinſefolkes together, and
tooke vnto them all ſuch as continued in the Iewes religion, and
aſſembled about ſixe thouſand men.2And they called vpon the Lord, that
hee would looke vpon the people that was troden downe of all, and alſo
pitie the Temple, prophaned of vngodly men,3And that he would haue
compaſſion vpon the city ſore defaced and ready to be made euen with
the ground, and heare the blood that cried vnto him,4And remember
the wicked ſlaughter of harmeleſſe infants, and the blaſphemies
committed againſt his Name, and that hee would ſhew his hatred againſt
the wicked.5Now when Maccabeus had his company about him, hee
could not be withſtood by the heathen: for the wrath of the Lord was
turned into mercy.6Therefore he came at vnawares, and burnt vp
townes and cities, and got into his hands the moſt commodious places,
and ouercame & put to flight no ſmall number of his enemies.7But
ſpecially tooke he aduantage of the night, for ſuch priuie attempts,
inſomuch that the bruite of his manlineſse was ſpread euery where.8So
when Philip ſawe that this man encreaſed by little and little, & that things
proſpered with him ſtill more and more, hee wrote vnto Ptolemeus, the
gouernour of Coeloſyria & Phenice, to yeeld more aide to the kings
affaires.9Then forthwith chooſing Nicanor the ſon of Patroclus, one of
his ſpeciall friends, he ſent him with no fewer then twentie thouſand of
all nations vnder him, to root out the whole generation of the Iewes;
and with him he ioyned alſo Gorgias a captaine, who in matters of warre
had great experience.10So Nicanor vndertooke to make ſo much money
of the captiue Iewes, as ſhould defray the tribute of two thouſand
talents, which the king was to pay to the Romanes.11Wherefore
immediatly he ſent to the cities vpon the ſea coaſt, proclaiming a ſale of
the captiue Iewes, and promiſing that they ſhould haue foureſcore and
ten bodies for one talent, not expecting the vengeance that was to follow
vpon him from the Almighty God.12Now when word was brought vnto
Iudas of Nicanors cōming, and he had imparted vnto thoſe that were
with him, that the army was at hand,13They that were fearefull, and
diſtruſted the iuſtice of God, fled, and conueyed themſelues
away.14Others ſold all that they had left, and withall beſought the Lord
to deliuer them, being ſolde by the wicked Nicanor before they met
together:15And if not for their owne ſakes, yet for þe couenants he had
made with their fathers, and for his holy and glorious Names ſake, by
which they were called16So Maccabeus called his men together vnto the
number of ſixe thouſand, and exhorted them not to be ſtricken with
terrour of the enemie, nor to feare the great multitude of the heathen
who came wrongfully againſt them, but to fight manfully,17And to ſet
before their eyes, the iniury that they had vniuſtly done to the holy place,
and the cruell handling of the city, whereof they made a mockery, and
alſo the taking away of the gouernment of their forefathers:18For they,
ſaid he, truſt in their weapons and boldneſse, but our confidence is in
the Almightie God, who at a becke can caſt downe both them that come
againſt vs, and alſo all the world.19Moreouer, hee recounted vnto them
what helps their forefathers had found, and how they were deliuered,
when vnder Sennacherib an hundred foureſcore and fiue thouſand
periſhed.20And he told them of þe battel that they had in Babylon with
the Galatians, how they came but eight thouſand in all to þe buſines,
with foure thouſand Macedonians, and that the Macedonians being
perplexed, the eight thouſand deſtroyed an hundred and twenty
thouſand, becauſe of the helpe that they had from heauen, & ſo receiued
a great booty.21Thus when hee had made them bold with theſe words,
and ready to die for the Lawes, and the countrey, he diuided his army
into foure parts:22And ioyned with himſelfe his owne brethren, leaders
of each band, to wit, Simon, and Ioſeph, & Ionathan, giuing each one
fifteene hundred men.23Alſo (hee appointed) Eleazar to reade the holy
booke: and when he had giuen them this watchword, The help of God;
himſelfe leading the firſt band, he ioyned battell with Nicanor:24And by
the helpe of the Almightie, they ſlew aboue nine thouſand of their
enemies, and wounded and maimed the moſt part of Nicanors hoſte,
and ſo put all to flight:25And tooke their money that came to buy them,
and purſued them farre: but lacking time, they returned.26For it was the
day before the Sabbath, and therefore they would no longer purſue
them.27So when they had gathered their armour together, and ſpoiled
their enemies, they occupied themſelues about the Sabbath, yeelding
exceeding praiſe, & thanks to the Lord, who had preſerued them vnto

þe day, which was the beginning of mercy, diſtilling vpon them.28And
after the Sabbath, when they had giuen part of the ſpoiles to the maimed,
and the widdowes, and Orphanes, the reſidue they diuided among
themſelues, and their ſeruants.29When this was done, and they had made
a common ſupplication, they beſought the mercifull Lord to be
reconciled with his ſeruants for euer.30Moreouer of thoſe that were with
Timotheus & Bacchides, who fought againſt them, they ſlewe aboue
twentie thouſand, and very eaſily got high and ſtrong holds, & diuided
amongſt them ſelues many ſpoiles more, and made the maimed,
orphanes, widowes, yea, & the aged alſo, equal in
ſpoileſ *wt* themſelueſ31And when they had gathered their armour
together, they laid them vp all carefully in couenient places, and the
remnant of the ſpoiles they brought to Ieruſalem.32They ſlew alſo
Philarches that wicked perſō who waſ *wt* Timotheus, & had annoied the
Iewes many waies.33Furthermore at ſuch time as they kept the feaſt for
the victorie in their coūtry, they burnt Caliſthenes that had ſet fire vpon
the holy gates, who was fled into a litle houſe, and ſo he receiued a
reward meet for his wickedneſſe.34As for that moſt vngracious Nicanor,
who had brought a thouſand merchants to buy the Iewes,35He was
through the helpe of the Lord brought downe by them, of whō he made
leaſt account, & putting off his glorious apparell, and diſcharging his
company, he came like a fugitiue ſeruant through the mid land vnto
Antioch, hauing very great diſhonour for that his hoſte was
deſtroyed.36Thus he that tooke vpon him to make good to the Romanes,
their tribute by meanes of the captiues in Ieruſalem, told abroad, that
the Iewes had God to fight for them, and therfore they could not be
hurt, becauſe they followed the lawes that he gaue them.
CHAPTER 9 1About that time came Antiochus with diſhonor out of
the countrey of Perſia.2For he had entred the citie called Perſepolis, and
went about to rob the Temple, and to hold the citie, whereupon the
multitude running to defend thēſelues with their weapons, put them to
flight, & ſo it happened þt Antiochus being put to flight of the
inhabitants, returned with ſhame.3Now when he came to Ecbatana,
newes was brought him what had happened vnto Nicanor &
Timotheus.4Then ſwelling with anger, hee thought to auenge vpon the
Iewes the diſgrace done vnto him by thoſe that made him flie. Therfore
commanded he his chariot man to driue without ceaſing, and to diſpatch
the iourney, the iudgement of God now following him. For he had
ſpoken proudly in this ſort, þt he would come to Ieruſalem, & make it a
common burying place of þe Iewes.5But the Lord almightie, the God of
Iſrael ſmote him with an incurable and inuiſible plague: for aſsoone as
hee had ſpoken theſe words, a paine of the bowels that was remediles,
came vpon him, & ſore torments of the inner parts.6And that moſt
iuſtly: for hee had tormented other mens bowels with many and ſtrange
torments.7Howbeit hee nothing at all ceaſed from his bragging, but ſtill
was filled with pride, breathing out fire in his rage againſt the Iewes, and
commanding to haſte the iourney: but it came to paſſe that he fel downe
frō his chariot, caried violently, ſo that hauing a ſore fal, al the mēbers
of his body were much pained.8And thus hee that a little afore thought
he might command the waues of the ſea (ſo proud was hee beyond the
condition of man) and weigh the high mountaines in a ballance, was
now caſt on the ground, and carried in an horſelitter, ſhewing foorth
vnto all, the manifeſt power of God.9So that the wormes roſe vp out of
the body of this wicked man, & whiles hee liued in ſorrow and paine,
his fleſh fell away, and the filthineſe of his ſmell was noyſome to all his
army.10And the man that thought a little afore he could reach to the
ſtarres of heauen, no man could endure to carry for his intollerable
ſtinke.11Here therefore being plagued, hee began to leaue off his great
pride, and to come to the knowledge *of himſelfe* by the ſcourge of God,
his paine encreaſing euery moment.12And when hee himſelfe could not
abide his owne ſmell; hee ſaide theſe wordes: It is meete to bee ſubiect
vnto God, and that a man that is mortall, ſhould not proudly thinke of
himſelfe, as if he were God.13This wicked perſon vowed alſo vnto the
Lord, (who now no more would haue mercy vpon him) ſaying
thus:14That the holy citie (to the which hee was going in haſte to lay it
euen with the ground, & to make it a common burying place) he would
ſet at liberty.15And as touching the Iewes, whom hee had iudged not
worthy ſo much as to be buried, but to be caſt out with their children to
be deuoured of the foules, and wild beaſts, he would make them al
equals to þe citizens of Athens,16And the holy Temple, which before he
had ſpoiled, hee would garniſh with goodly gifts, and reſtore all the holy
veſſels with many more, and out of his owne reuenew defray the charges
belonging to the ſacrifices:17Yea, and that alſo hee would become a Iew
himſelfe, and goe through all the world that was inhabited, and declare
the power of God.18But for all this his paines would not ceaſe: for the
iuſt iudgement of God was come vpō him: therfore deſpairing of his
health, he wrote vnto the Iewes the letter vnderwritten, containing the
forme of a ſupplicatiō, after this maner.19Antiochus king and gouernour,
to the good Iewes his Citizens, wiſheth much ioy, health, and
proſperity.20If ye, and your children fare well, and your affaires be to
your contentment, I giue very great thankes to God, hauing my hope in
heauen.21As for mee I was weake, or elſe I would haue remembred
kindly your honour, and good will. Returning out of Perſia, and being
taken with a grieuous diſeaſe, I thought it neceſsary to care for the
common ſafety of all:22Not diſtruſting mine health, but hauing great
hope to eſcape this ſickneſ23But conſidering that euen my father, at what
time he led an armie into the hie countries, appointed a ſucceſsor,24To
the end, that if any thing fell out contrary to expectation, or if any tidings
were brought that were grieuous, they of the land knowing to whom the
ſtate was left, might not be troubled.25Againe conſidering, how that the
princes that are borderers, and neighbors vnto my kingdome, waite for
opportunities, and expect what ſhalbe the euent, I haue appointed my
ſonne Antiochus king, whom I often cōmitted, and cōmended vnto
many of you, when I went vp into the high prouinces, to whom I haue
written as followeth.26Therefore I pray, and requeſt you to remember
the benefits that I haue done vnto you generally, and in ſpeciall, and that
euery man will be ſtill faithfull to me, and my ſonne.27For I am
perſwaded that hee vnderſtanding my minde, will fauourably &
graciouſly yeeld to your deſires.28Thus the murtherer, and blaſphemer
hauing ſuffered moſt grieuouſly, as he entreated other men, ſo died he a
miſerable death in a ſtrange countrey in the mountaines.29And Philip
that was brought vp with him, caried away his body, who alſo fearing
the ſon of Antiochus, went into Egypt to Ptolomeus Philometor.
CHAPTER 10 1Now Maccabeus, and his company, the Lord guiding
them, recouered the Temple, and the citie.2But the altars, which the
heathen had built in the open ſtreet, & alſo the Chappels they pulled
downe.3And hauing cleanſed the Temple, they made another Altar, and
ſtriking ſtones, they tooke fire out of them, and offered a ſacrifice after
two yeeres, & ſet forth incenſe, & lights, and Shewbread.4When that was
done, they fell flat downe, and beſought the Lord that they might come
no more into ſuch troubles: but if they ſinned any more againſt him, that
he himſelfe would chaſten them with mercie, and that they might not
bee deliuered vnto the blaſphemous, and barbarous nations.5Now vpon
the ſame day that the ſtrangers prophaned the Temple, on the very ſame
day it was cleanſed againe, euen the fiue and twentieth day of the ſame
moneth, which is Caſleu.6And they kept eight dayes with gladnes as in
the feaſt of the Tabernacles, remembring that not long afore they had
helde the feaſt of the Tabernacles, when as they wandered in the
mountaines, and dennes, like beaſts.7Therefore they bare branches, and
faire boughes and palmes alſo, and ſang Pſalmes vnto him, that had
giuen them good ſucceſse in clenſing his place.8They ordeined alſo by a
common ſtatute, and decree, That euery yeere thoſe dayes ſhould be
kept of the whole nation of the Iewes.9And this was the ende of
Antiochus called Epiphanes.10Now will wee declare the acts of
Antiochus Eupator, who was the ſonne of this wicked man, gathering
briefly the calamities of the warres.11So when he was come to þe crowne,
he ſet one Lyſias ouer the affaires of his Realme, and *appointed him* chiefe
gouernour of Coeloſyria and Phenice.12For Ptolomeus that was called
Macron, choſing rather to doe iuſtice vnto the Iewes, for the wrong that
had bene done vnto them, endeuoured to continue peace with
them.13Whereupon being accuſed of *the kingſ* friends, before Eupator, &
called traitor at euery word, becauſe he had left Cyprus that Philometor
had cōmitted vnto him, & departed to Antiochus Epiphanes; and ſeeing
that hee was in no honorable place, he was ſo diſcouraged, that he
poyſoned himſelfe and died.14But when Gorgias was gouernour of the
holds, hee hired ſouldiers, and nouriſhed warre continually with the
Iewes:15And therewithall the Idumeans hauing gotten into their handes
the moſt commodious holdes, kept the Iewes occupied, and receiuing
thoſe that were baniſhed from Ieruſalem, they went about to nouriſh
warre.16Then they that were wich Maccabeus made ſupplication, &

beſought God, that he would be their helper, and ſo they ranne with violence vpon the ſtrong holds of the Idumeans,17And aſsaulting them ſtrongly, they wanne the holds, and kept off all that fought vpon the wall, and ſlew all that fell into their hands, and killed no fewer then twentie thouſand.18And becauſe certaine (who were no leſſe then nine thouſand) were fled together into two very ſtrong caſtles, hauing all maner of things conuenient to ſuſtaine the ſiege,19Maccabeus left Simon, & Ioſeph, and Zaccheus alſo, and them that were with him, who were enow to beſiege them, and departed himſelfe vnto thoſe places, which more needed his helpe.20Now they that were with Simon, being led with couetouſnes, were perſwaded for money (through certaine of thoſe that were in the caſtle) and tooke ſeuentie thouſand drachmes, and let ſome of them eſcape.21But when it was told Maccabeus what was done, hee called the gouernours of the people together, and accuſed thoſe men, that they had ſold their brethren for money, & let their enemies free to fight againſt them.22So he ſlew thoſe that were found traitors, and immediatly tooke the two caſtles.23And hauing good ſuccesſe with his weapons in all things hee tooke in hand, hee ſlew in the two holdes, more then twentie thouſand.24Now Timotheus whom the Iewes had ouercome before, when he had gathered a great multitude of forraine forces, and horſes out of Aſia not a few, came as though hee would take Iewrie by force of armes.25But when hee drew neere, they that were with Maccabeus, turned themſelues to pray vnto God, and ſprinckled earth vpon their heads, and girded their loynes with ſackcloth,26And fell downe at the foot of the Altar, and beſought him to be mercifull to them, and to be an enemie to their enemies, and an aduerſarie to their aduerſaries, as the Law declareth.27So after the prayer, they tooke their weapons, & went on further from the city: and when they drew neere to their enemies, they kept by themſelues.28Now the Sunne being newly riſen, they ioyned both together; the one part hauing, together with their vertue, their refuge alſo vnto the Lord, for a pledge of their ſuccesſe and victorie: the other ſide making their rage leader of their battell.29But when the battaile waxed ſtrong, there appeared vnto the enemies from heauen, fiue comely men vpon horſes, with bridles of golde, and two of them ledde the Iewes,30And tooke Maccabeus betwixt them, and couered him on euery ſide with their weapons, and kept him ſafe, but ſhot arrowes & lightenings againſt the enemies: ſo that being confounded with blindneſse, and full of trouble, they were killed.31And there were ſlaine *of footemen* twentie thouſand and fiue hundred, and ſixe hundred horſemen.32As for Timotheus himſelfe, hee fled into a very ſtrong holde, called Gazara, where Chereas was gouernour.33But they that were with Maccabeus, laid ſiege againſt the fortreſse couragiouſly foure dayes.34And they þt were within, truſting to the ſtrength of the place, blaſphemed exceedingly, & vttered wicked words.35Neuertheleſſe, vpon the fifth day early, twentie yong men of Maccabeus company, inflamed with anger becauſe of the blaſphemies, aſsaulted the wall manly, and with a fierce courage killed all that they met withall.36Others likewiſe aſcending after them, whiles they were buſied with them that were within, burnt the towres, and kindling fires, burnt the blaſphemers aliue, and others broke open the gates, and hauing receiued in the reſt of the army, tooke the city,37And killed Timotheus that was hidde in a certaine pit, and Chereas his brother, with Apollophanes.38When this was done, they praiſed the Lord with Pſalmes and thankeſgiuing, who had done ſo great things for Iſrael, and giuen them the victory.

CHAPTER 111Not long after this, Lyſias the kings protectour & couſin, who alſo managed the affaires, tooke ſore diſpleaſure for the things that were done.2And when he had gathered about foureſcore thouſand, with all the horſemen, he came againſt the Iewes, thinking to make the citie an habitation of the Gentiles,3And to make a gaine of the Temple, as of the other Chappels of the heathen, and to ſet the high Prieſthood to ſale euery yeere:4Not at all conſidering the power of God, but puffed vp with his ten thouſand footmen, and his thouſand horſemen, and his foureſcore Elephants.5So he came to Iudea, & drew neere to Bethſura, which was a ſtrong town, but diſtant from Ieruſalem about fiue furlongs, and he laid ſore ſiege vnto it.6Now when they that were with Maccabeus heard that he beſieged the holdes, they and all the people with lamentation and teares beſought the Lord, that he would ſend a good Angel to deliuer Iſrael.7Then Maccabeus himſelfe firſt of all tooke weapons, exhorting the other, that they would ieopard themſelues together with him, to helpe their brethren: ſo they went forth together with a willing minde.8And as they were at Ieruſalem, there appeared before them on horſebacke, one in white clothing, ſhaking his armour of gold.9Then they praiſed the mercifull God altogether, and tooke heart, inſomuch that they were ready not onely to fight with men, but with moſt cruell beaſts, & to pierce through wals of yron.10Thus they marched forward in their armour, hauing an helper from heauen: for the Lord was mercifull vnto them.11And giuing a charge vpō their enemies like lions, they ſlew eleuen thouſand footmen, & ſixteene hundred horſemen, and put all the other to flight.12Many of them alſo being wounded, eſcaped naked, and Lyſias himſelfe fled away ſhamefully, and ſo eſcaped.13Who as hee was a man of vnderſtanding, caſting with himſelfe what loſſe he had had, and conſidering that the Hebrewes could not be ouercome, becauſe the Almighty God helped them, he ſent vnto them,14And perſwaded them to agree to all reaſonable conditions, & *promiſed* that hee would perſwade the king, that he muſt needs be a friend vnto them.15Then Maccabeus conſented to all that Lyſias deſired, being carefull of the common good; and whatſoeuer Maccabeus wrote vnto Lyſias concerning the Iewes, the king granted it.16For there were letters written vnto the Iewes from Lyſias, to this effect: Lyſias vnto the people of the Iewes, ſendeth greeting.17Iohn and Abſalon, who were ſent from you, deliuered me the petition ſubſcribed, and made requeſt for the performance of the contents thereof.18Therefore what things ſoeuer were meet to be reported to the king, I haue declared them, and he hath granted as much as might be.19If then you wil keepe your ſelues loyall to the ſtate, hereafter alſo will I endeuour to be a meanes of your good.20But of the particulars I haue giuen order, both to theſe, & the other that came from me, to commune with you.21Fare ye wel. The hundred & eight and fortie yeere, the foure and twentie day of the moneth Dioſcorinthius.22Now the kings letter conteined theſe words, King Antiochus vnto his brother Lyſias ſendeth greeting.23Since our father is tranſlated vnto þe gods, our will is, that they that are in our realme liue quietly, that euery one may attend vpon his own affaires.24Wee vnderſtand alſo that the Iewes would not conſent to our father for to bee brought vnto the cuſtome of the Gentiles, but had rather keepe their owne manner of liuing: for the which cauſe they require of vs that we ſhould ſuffer thē to liue after their own lawes.25Wherefore our mind is, that this nation ſhall be in reſt, and we haue determined to reſtore them their Temple, that they may liue according to the cuſtomes of their forefathers.26Thou ſhalt doe well therefore to ſend vnto them, and grant them peace, that whē they are certified of our mind, they may be of good comfort, & euer goe cheerefully about their owne affaires.27And the letter of þe king vnto the nation of the Iewes was after this maner: king Antiochus ſendeth greeting vnto the counſel, & the reſt of the Iewes28If ye fare well, we haue our deſire, we are alſo in good health.29Menelaus declared vnto vs, that your deſire was to returne home, and to follow your owne buſineſse.30Wherefore they that will depart ſhall haue ſafe conduct, till the thirtieth day of Xanthicus with ſecuritie.31And the Iewes ſhal vſe their owne kind of meats, and lawes, as before, and none of them any maner of wayes ſhal be moleſted for things ignorantly done.32I haue ſent alſo Menelaus, that he may comfort you.33Fare ye wel. In the hundred, forty and eight yeere, and the fifteenth day of the moneth Xanthicus.34The Romanes alſo ſent vnto them a letter containing theſe wordes: Quintus Memmius, & Titus Manlius embaſſadours of þe Romanes, ſend greeting vnto the people of the Iewes.35Whatſoeuer Lyſias the kings couſin hath granted, therewith we alſo are well pleaſed.36But touching ſuch things as hee iudged to be referred to the king: after you haue aduiſed therof, ſend one forthwith, that we may declare as it is conuenient for you: for we are now going to Antioch.37Therefore ſend ſome with ſpeed, that we may know what is your mind.38Farewell, this hundred and eight and fortie yeere, the fifteenth day of the moneth Xanthicus.

CHAPTER 12 1When theſe Couenants were made, Lyſias went vnto the king, and the Iewes were about their huſbandrie.2But of the gouernours of ſeueral places, Timotheus, and Apollonius the ſonne of Genneus, alſo Hieronymus, and Demophon, and beſides them Nicanor þe gouernor of Cyprus would not ſuffer them to be quiet, and liue in peace.3The men of Ioppe alſo did ſuch an vngodly deed: they prayed the Iewes that dwelt among them, to goe with their wiues, and children into

the boats which they had prepared, as though they had meant them no
hurt. 4Who accepted of it according to the common decree of the citie,
as being defirous to liue in peace, and fufpecting nothing: but when they
were gone forth into the deepe, they drowned no leffe then two hundred
of them. 5When Iudas heard of this crueltie done vnto his countrey men,
he commanded thofe that were with him *to make them ready.* 6And calling
vpon God the righteous iudge, he came againft thofe murtherers of his
brethren, & burnt the hauen by night, and fet the boats on fire, and
thofe that fled thither, he flew. 7And when the towne was fhut vp, he
went backward, as if he would returne to root out all them of the citie
of Ioppe. 8But when he heard that þe Iamnites were minded to doe in
like maner vnto the Iewes þt dwelt among them, 9He came vpon the
Iamnites alfo by night, and fet fire on the hauen, & the nauy, fo that the
light of the fire was feene at Ierufalem, two hundred and fortie furlongs
off. 10Now when they were gone from thence nine furlongs in their
iourney toward Timotheus, no fewer then fiue thoufand men on foote,
& fiue hundred horfe men of the Arabians, fet vpon him. 11Whereupon
there was a very fore battell; but Iudas fide by the helpe of God got the
victory, fo that the Nomades of Arabia being ouercome, befought Iudas
for peace, promifing both to giue him cattell, and to pleafure him
otherwife. 12Then Iudas thinking indeede that they would be profitable
in many things, granted them peace, wherupon they fhooke hands, and
fo they departed to their tents. 13Hee went alfo about to make a bridge
to a certaine ftrong citie, which was fenced about with walles, and
inhabited by people of diuers countries, and the name of it was
Cafpis. 14But they that were within it put fuch truft in the ftrength of the
walles, and prouifion of victuals, that they behaued themfelues rudely
towards them that were with Iudas, railing, and blafpheming, and
vttering fuch words, as were not to be fpoken. 15Wherefore Iudas with
his company, calling vpon the great Lord of the world (who without any
rammes, or engines of warre did caft downe Iericho in the time of Iofua)
gaue a fierce afsault againft the walles, 16And tooke the citie by the will
of God, and made vnfpeakable flaughters, infomuch that a lake two
furlongs broad, neere adioining thereunto, being filled ful, was feen
running with blood. 17Then departed they from thence feuen hundred
and fifty furlongs, and came to Characa vnto the Iewes that are called
Tubieni. 18But as for Timotheus they found him not in the places, for
before hee had difpatched any thing, he departed from thence, hauing
left a very ftrong garrifon in a certaine hold: 19Howbeit, Dofitheus, and
Sofipater, who were of Maccabeus captaines, went forth, and flew thofe
that Timotheus had left in the fortrefse, aboue tenne thoufand
men. 20And Maccabeus ranged his armie by bands, & fet them ouer the
bands, and went againft Timotheus, who had about him & hundred and
twentie thoufand men of foote, and two thoufand, and fiue hundred
horfemen. 21Nowe when Timotheus had knowledge of Iudas comming,
he fent the women and children, and the other baggage vnto a fortrefse
called Carnion (for the towne was hard to befiege and vneafie to come
vnto, by reafon of the ftraitnefse of all the places.) 22But when Iudas his
firft band came in fight, the enemies (being fmitten with feare, and
terrour through the appearing of him that feeth all thingf) fled amaine,
one running this way, another that way, fo as that they were often hurt
of their owne men, and wounded with þe points of their owne
fwordf 23Iudas alfo was very earneft in purfuingthem, killing thofe
wicked wretches, of whom he flew about thirtie thoufand
men. 24Moreouer, Timotheus himfelfe fell into the hands of Dofitheus,
& Sofipater, whom he befought with much craft to let him goe with his
life, becaufe hee had many of the Iewes parents, and the brethren of
fome of them, who, if they put him to death, fhould not be
regarded. 25So when hee had afsured them with many words, that hee
would reftore them without hurt according to the agreement, they let
him goe for the fauing of their brethren. 26Then Maccabeus marched
forth to Carnion, & to the Temple of Atargatis, and there he flew fiue
and twenty thoufand perfons. 27And after he had put to flight, and
deftroyed them, Iudas remooued the hofte towards Ephron, a ftrong
citie, wherin Lyfias abode, and a great multitude of diuers nations, and
the ftrong yong men kept the wals, and defended them mightily: wherin
alfo was great prouifion of engines, and darts. 28But when Iudas and his
company had called vpon Almighty God (who with his power breaketh
the ftrength of his enemief) they wanne the citie, and flew twentie and
fiue thoufand of them that were within. 29From thence they departed to
Scythopolis, which lieth fixe hundreth furlongs from Ierufalem. 30But
when the Iewes that dwelt there had teftified that the Scythopolitans
dealt louingly with them, and entreated them kindely in the time of their
aduerfitie: 31They gaue them thankes, defiring them to be friendly ftil
vnto them, and fo they came to Ierufalem, the feaft of the weekes
approching. 32And after the feaft called Pentecoft, they went foorth
againft Gorgias the gouernour of Idumea, 33Who came out *wt* three
thoufand men of foot, & foure hundred horfemen. 34And it happened
that in their fighting together, a few of the Iewes were flaine. 35At which
time Dofitheus one of Bacenors company, who was on horfbacke, and
a ftrong man, was ftill vpon Gorgias, and taking hold of his coate, drew
him by force, and when he would haue taken that curfed man aliue, a
horfeman of Thracia comming vpon him, fmote off his fhoulder, fo that
Gorgias fled vnto Marifa. 36Now when they that were with Gorgias had
fought long & were wearie, Iudas called vpon the Lord that he would
fhew himfelfe to be their helper, and leader of the battell. 37And with
that he beganne in his owne language, & fung Pfalmes with a lowd
voyce, & rufhing vnawares vpon Gorgias men, he put them to
flight. 38So Iudas gathered his hoft, and came into the city of Odollam.
And when the feuenth day came, they purified themfelues (as the
cuftome waf) and kept the Sabbath in the fame place. 39And vpon the
day following as the vfe had bene, Iudas and his company came to take
vp the bodies of them that were flaine, and to bury them with their
kinfmen, in their fathers graues. 40Now vnder the coats of euery one that
was flaine, they found things confecrated to the idoles of the Iamnites,
which is forbidden the Iewes by the Law. Then euery man faw that this
was þe caufe wherefore they were flaine. 41All men therefore praifing the
Lord the righteous Iudge, who had opened the things that were
hid, 42Betooke themfelues vnto praier, and befought him that the finne
committed, might wholy bee put out of remembrance. Befides, that
noble Iudas exhorted the people to keep themfelues from finne,
forfomuch as they faw before their eyes the things that came to paffe,
for the finne of thofe þt were flaine. 43And when he had made a
gathering throughout the company, to the fum of two thoufand
drachmes of filuer, hee fent it to Ierufalem to offer a finne offering,
doing therein very well, and honeftly, in that he was mindfull of the
refurrection. 44(For if he had not hoped that they that were flaine fhould
haue rifen againe, it had bin fuperfluous and vaine, to pray for the
dead.) 45And alfo in that he perceiued that there was great fauour layed
vp for thofe that died godly. (It was an holy, and good thought)
wherupon he made a reconciliation for the dead, that they might be
deliuered from finne.
CHAPTER 13 1In the hundreth forty and ninth yere it was told Iudas
that Antiochus Eupator was cōming with a great power into Iudea; 2And
with him Lyfias his protector, and ruler of his affaires, hauing either of
them a Grecian power of footemen, an hundred and ten thoufand, and
horfmen fiue thoufand, & three hundred, and Elephants two & twenty,
and three hundred charets armed *wt* hooks. 3Menelaus alfo ioyned
himfelf with them, and with great difsimulation encouraged Antiochus,
not for the fafegard of the countrey, but becaufe hee thought to haue
bin made gouernour. 4But the King of kings mooued Antiochus minde
againft this wicked wretch, and Lyfias enformed the king, that this man
was the caufe of all mifchiefe, fo that the king commanded to bring him
vnto Berea, and to put him to death, as the maner is in that place. 5Now
there was in that place a towre of fifty cubites high full of afhes, and it
had a round inftrumēt which on euery fide hanged down into the
afhes. 6And whofoeuer was condemned of facriledge, or had committed
any other grieuous crime, there did all men thruft him vnto death. 7fuch
a death it happened that wicked man to die, not hauing fo much as
buriall in the earth, & that moft iuftly. 8For inafmuch as he had
committed many finnes about the altar whofe fire and afhes were holy,
hee receiued his death in afhes. 9Now þe king came with a barbarous &
hautie mind, to do far worfe to þe Iewes then had beene done in his
fathers time. 10Which things when Iudas perceiued, hee commanded the
multitude to call vpon the Lord night & day, that if euer at any other
time, he would now alfo helpe them, being at the point to be put from
their Law, from their country, and from the holy Temple: 11And that hee
would not fuffer the people, that had euen now been but a little
refrefhed, to be in fubiection to the blafphemous nations. 12So when they
had all done this together, and befought the mercifull Lord with

weeping, and faſting, and lying flat vpon the ground three daies long,
Iudas hauing exhorted them, commanded they ſhould be in a
readineſse. 13And Iudas being apart with the Elders, determined before
the kings hoſt ſhould enter into Iudea and get the city, to goe foorth and
try the matter *in fight* by the helpe of the Lord. 14So when he had
committed *all* to the Creator of the world, & exhorted his ſouldiers to
fight manfully, euen vnto death, for the Lawes, the Temple, the city, the
country, and the common-wealth, he camped by Modin. 15And hauing
giuen the watchword to them that were about him, Uictory is of God;
with the moſt valiant and choice yong men, he went in into the kings
tent by night, & ſlewe in the campe about foure thouſand men, and the
chiefeſt of the Elephants, with all that were vpon him. 16And at laſt they
filled the campe with feare and tumult, and departed with good
ſucceſse. 17This was done in the breake of the day, becauſe the
protection of the Lord did helpe him. 18Now when the king had taken a
taſte of the manlineſse of the Iewes, hee went about to take the holds
by policie, 19And marched towards Bethſura, which was a ſtrōghold of
þͤ Iews, but he was put to flight, failed, & loſt of his men. 20For Iudas
had conueyed vnto them þͭ were in it, ſuch things as were
neceſsary. 21But Rhodocus who was in þͤ Iewes hoſte, diſcloſed the
ſecrets to the enemies, therefore he was ſought out, & when they had
gotten him, they put him in priſon. 22The king treated with them in
Bethſura the ſecond time, gaue his hand, tooke theirs, departed, fought
with Iudas, was ouercome: 23Heard that Philip who was left ouer the
affaires in Antioch was deſperately bent, confounded, intreated the
Iewes, ſubmitted himſelfe, and ſware to all equal conditions, agreed with
them, and offred ſacrifice, honoured the Temple, and dealt kindly with
the place, 24And accepted well of Maccabeus, made him principall
gouernor from Ptolemais vnto the Gerrhenians, 25Came to Ptolemais,
the people there were grieued for the couenants: for they ſtormed
becauſe they would make their couenants voide. 26Lyſias went vp to the
iudgement ſeat, ſaid as much as could be in defence of the cauſe,
perſwaded, pacified, made them well affected, returned to Antioch.
Thus it went touching the kings comming and departing.

CHAPTER 14 1After three yeres was Iudas enformed that Demetrius
the ſonne of Seleucus hauing entred by the hauen of Tripolis with a great
power and nauie, 2Had taken the countrey, and killed Antiochus, and
Lyſias his protectour. 3Now one Alcimus who had beene hie Prieſt, and
had defiled himſelfe wilfully in the times of their mingling (with the
Gentileſ) ſeeing that by no meanes hee could ſaue himſelfe, nor haue
any more acceſse to the holy Altar, 4Came to king Demetrius in the
hundreth and one and fiftieth yeere, preſenting vnto him a crowne of
golde, and a palme, and alſo of the boughes which were vſed ſolemnly
in the Temple: and ſo that day he helde his peace. 5Howbeit hauing
gotten opportunity to further his fooliſh enterpriſe, *and* being called into
counſel by Demetrius, & aſked how the Iewes ſtood affected, and what
they intēdĕd, he anſwered therunto; 6Thoſe of the Iewes that bee called
Aſideans (whoſe captaine is Iudas Maccabeuſ) nouriſh warre, and are
ſeditious; and will not let the realme be in peace. 7Therfore I being
depriued of mine anceſtors honor (I meane the hie Prieſthood) am now
come hither. 8Firſt verily for the vnfained care I haue of things pertaining
to the king, and ſecondly, euen for that I intend the good of mine owne
countrey men: for all our nation is in no ſmall miſery, through the
vnaduiſed dealing of them aforeſaid. 9Wherefore, O king, ſeeing thou
knoweſt all theſe things, bee carefull for the countrey, and our nation,
which is preſſed on euery ſide, according to the clemency that thou
readily ſheweſt vnto all. 10For as long as Iudas liueth, it is not poſsible
that the ſtate ſhould be quiet. 11This was no ſooner ſpoken of him, but
others of the kings friends being malitiouſly ſet againſt Iudas, did more
incenſe Demetrius. 12And foorthwith calling Nicanor, who had bene
maſter of the Elephants, and making him gouernour ouer Iudea, he ſent
him forth, 13Cōmanding him to ſlay Iudas, & to ſcatter them that
were *wt* him, & to make Alcimus high prieſt of the great Temple. 14Then
the heathen that had fled out of Iudea from Iudas, came to Nicanor by
flocks, thinking the harme and calamities of the Iewes, to be their well-
fare. 15Now when the Iewes heard of Nicanors comming, and that the
heathen were vp againſt them, they caſt earth vpon their heads, and
made ſupplication to him that had ſtabliſhed his people for euer, and
who alwayes helpeth his portion with manifeſtation of his preſence. 16So
at the commandement of the captaine, they remooued ſtraightwayes
from thence, and came neere vnto them, at the towne of Deſſaro. 17Now
Simon, Iudas brother, had ioyned battell with Nicanor, but was
ſomewhat diſcomfited, through the ſuddaine ſilence of his
enemies. 18Neuertheleſſe Nicanor hearing of the manlineſse of them that
were with Iudas, and the courageouſnes that they had to fight for their
countrey, durſt not try the matter by the ſword. 19Wherefore he ſent
Poſidonius, and Theodotus, & Mattathias to make peace. 20So when they
had taken long aduiſement thereupon, and the captaine had made
þͤ multitude acquainted therewith, and it appeared that they were all of
one minde, they conſented to the couenants, 21And appointed a day to
meet in together by themſelues, & when the day came, and ſtooles were
ſet for either of them, 22Iudas placed armed men ready in conuenient
places, leſt ſome treachery ſhould bee ſuddenly practiſed by the enemies;
ſo they made a peaceable cōference. 23Now Nicanor abode in Ieruſalem,
and did no hurt, but ſent away the people that came flocking vnto
him. 24And hee would not willingly haue Iudas out of his ſight: for hee
loued the man from his heart. 25He praied him alſo to take a wife, and
to beget children: ſo he maried, was quiet, and tooke part of this
life. 26But Alcimus perceiuing the loue that was betwixt them, and
conſidering the couenants that were made, came to Demetrius, and
tolde him that Nicanor was not well affected towards the ſtate, for that
he had ordained Iudas, a traitor to his realme, to be the kings
ſucceſsour. 27Then the king being in a rage, and prouoked with the
accuſations of the moſt wicked man, wrote to Nicanor, ſignifying that
he was much diſpleaſed with the couenants, and commaunding him that
hee ſhould ſend Maccabeus priſoner in all haſte vnto Antioch. 28When
this came to Nicanors hearing, he was much cōfounded in himſelfe, and
tooke it grieuouſly, that hee ſhould make voyd the articles which were
agreed vpon, the man being in no fault. 29But becauſe there was no
dealing againſt the king, hee watched his time to accompliſh this thing
by pollicie. 30Notwithſtāding when Maccabeus ſaw that Nicanor began
to bee churliſh vnto him, and that he entreated him more roughly then
he was wont, perceiuing þͭ ſuch ſowre behauiour came not of good, hee
gathered together not a few of his men, and withdrew himſelfe frō
Nicanor. 31But the other knowing that he was notably preuented by
Iudas policie, came into the great and holy Temple, and commanded the
Prieſtes that were offering their vſual ſacrifices, to deliuer him
þͤ man. 32And whē they ſware that they could not tel where þͤ man was,
whō he ſought, 33Hee ſtretched out his right hand toward the Temple, &
made an oath in this maner: If you wil not deliuer me Iudas as a priſoner,
I will lay this Temple of God euen with the ground, and I will breake
downe the Altar, and erect a notable temple vnto Bacchus. 34After theſe
words he departed; then the Prieſts lift vp their handes towards heauen,
& beſought him þͭ was euer a defēder of their nation, ſaying in this
maner: 35Thou, O Lord of all things, who haſt neede of nothing, waſt
pleaſed that the Temple of thine habitation ſhould be among
vs. 36Therefore now, O holy Lord of all holineſſe, keepe this houſe euer
vndefiled, which lately was cleanſed, and ſtop euery vnrighteous
mouth. 37Now was there accuſed vnto Nicanor, one Razis, one of the
Elders of Ieruſalem, a louer of his countrey men, and a man of very
good report, who for his kindneſſe was called a father of þͤ Iewes. 38For
in the former times, when they mingled not themſelues with the
Gentiles, he had bin accuſed of Iudaiſme, and did boldly ieopard his
body and life with al vehemency for the religion of þͤ Iewes. 39So
Nicanor willing to declare the hate that he bare vnto the Iewes, ſent
aboue fiue hūdred men of war to take him. 40For he thought by taking
him to do *the Iewes* much hurt. 41Now when the multitude would haue
taken the towre, and violently broken into the vtter doore, and bade that
fire ſhould be brought to burne it, he being ready to be taken on euery
ſide, fell vpon his ſword, 42Chuſing rather to die manfully, then to come
into the hands of the wicked to be abuſed otherwiſe then beſeemed his
noble birth. 43But miſsing his ſtroke through haſte, the multitude alſo
ruſhing within the doores, he ran boldly vp to the wall, and caſt himſelfe
downe manfully among the thickeſt of them. 44But they quickly giuing
backe, and a ſpace being made, he fell downe into the midſt of the void
place. 45Neuertheleſſe while there was yet breath within him, being
inflamed with anger, he roſe vp, and though his blood guſhed out like
ſpouts of water, and his wounds were grieuous, yet hee ranne through
the midſt of the throng, and ſtanding vpon a ſteepe rocke, 46When as his
blood was now quite gone, hee pluckt out his bowels, & taking them in

both his hands, hee caſt them vpon the throng, and calling vpon the Lord of life and ſpirit to reſtore him thoſe againe, he thus died.

CHAPTER 15 1But Nicanor hearing that Iudas and his company were in the ſtrong places about Samaria, reſolued without any danger to ſet vpon them on þͤ ſabbath day.2Neuertheles, the Iewes that were compelled to go with him, ſaid, O deſtroy not ſo cruelly and barbarouſly, but giue honour to that day, which he that ſeeth all things, hath honoured with holineſſe aboue *other dayes.*3Then this moſt vngracious wretch demanded, if there were a mightie one in heauen that had commanded the Sabbath day to be kept.4And when they ſaid, There is in heauen a liuing Lord, and mightie, who commanded the ſeuenth day to be kept,5Then ſaid the other, And I alſo am mightie vpon earth, & I cōmand to take armes, and to do the kings buſines: yet he obteined not to haue his wicked wil done.6So Nicanor in exceeding pride and haughtineſse, determined to ſet vp a publike moument of his victorie ouer Iudas, and them that were with him.7But Maccabeus had euer ſure confidence that the Lord would helpe him.8Wherfore he exhorted his people not to feare the comming of the heathen againſt them, but to remember the helpe which in former times they had receiued from heauen, and now to expect the victory, and aid which ſhould come vnto them from the Almightie.9And ſo comforting them out of the law, and the prophets, and withall putting them in mind of the battels that they won afore, he made them more cheerefull.10And when he had ſtirred vp their minds, he gaue them their charge, ſhewing them therewithall the falſhood of the heathen, and the breach of othes.11Thus he armed euery one of them not ſo much with defence of ſhields and ſpeares, as with comfortable and good words: and beſides that, he tolde them a dreame worthy to be beleeued, as if it had bin ſo indeed, which did not a litle reioyce them.12And this was his viſion: that Onias, who had bin high Prieſt, a vertuous, and a good man, reuerend in conuerſation, gentle in condition, well ſpoken alſo, and exerciſed from a child in all points of vertue, holding vp his hands, prayed for the whole bodie of the Iewes.13This done, in like maner there appeared a man with gray haires, & exceeding glorious, who was of a wonderfull and excellent maieſtie.14Then Onias anſwered, ſaying, This is a louer of the brethren, who prayeth much for the people, and for the holy citie, (to wit) Ieremias þͤ prophet of God.15Whereupon Ieremias, holding forth his right hand, gaue to Iudas a ſword of gold, and in giuing it ſpake thus:16Take this holy ſword a gift from God, with the which thou ſhalt wound the aduerſaries.17Thus being well comforted by the words of Iudas, which were very good, and able to ſtirre them vp to valour, and to encourage the hearts of the yong men, they determined not to pitch campe, but couragiouſly to ſet vpon them, and manfully to trie the matter by conflict, becauſe the citie, and the Sanctuarie, and the Temple were in danger.18For the care that they tooke for their wiues, and their children, their brethren, and kinſfolkes, was in leaſt account with them: but the greateſt, and principall feare, was for the holy Temple.19Alſo they that were in the citie, tooke not the leaſt care, being troubled for the conflict abroad.20And now when as all looked what ſhould bee þͤ triall, & the enemies were already come neere, and the armie was ſet in aray, and the beaſts conueniently placed, and the horſemen ſet in wings:21Maccabeus ſeeing the comming of the multitude, and the diuers preparations of armour, and the fierceneſse of the beaſts, ſtretched out his hands towards heauen, and called vpon the Lord, that worketh wonders, knowing that victorie commeth not by armes, but euen as it ſeemeth good to him, he giueth it to ſuch as are worthy:22Therefore in his prayer he ſaid after this maner: O Lord, thou diddeſt ſend thine Angel in the time of Ezekias king of Iudea, and diddeſt ſlay in the hoſt of Sennacherib, an hundred, foureſcore, and fiue thouſand.23Wherfore now alſo O Lord of heauen, ſend a good Angel before vs, for a feare, and dread vnto them.24And through the might of thine arme, let thoſe bee ſtricken with terror, that come againſt thy holy people to blaſpheme. And he ended thus.25Then Nicanor, and they that were with him came forward with trumpets, and ſongs.26But Iudas, and his company encountred the enemies with inuocation, and prayer.27So that fighting with their hands, and praying vnto God with their hearts, they ſlew no leſſe then thirty and fiue thouſand men: for through the appearance of God, they were greatly cheered.28Now when the battell was done, returning againe with ioy, they knew that Nicanor lay dead in his harneſse.29Then they made a great ſhout, and a noiſe, praiſing the Almighty in their owne language:30And Iudas, who was euer the chiefe defender of the citizens both in body, and minde, and who continued his loue towards his countrymen all his life, commanded to ſtrike off Nicanors head, and his hand, with his ſhoulder, & bring them to Ieruſalem.31So when he was there, and had called them of his nation together, and ſet the prieſts before the altar, he ſent for them that were of the Towre,32And ſhewed them vile Nicanors head, and the hand of that blaſphemer, which with proud brags he had ſtretched out againſt the holy Temple of the Almightie.33And when he had cut out the tongue of that vngodly Nicanor, he commanded that they ſhould giue it by pieces vnto the foules, and hang vp the reward of his madneſse before the Temple.34So euery man praiſed towards the heauen the glorious Lord, ſaying, Bleſſed be hee that hath kept his owne place vndefiled.35He hanged alſo Nicanors head vpon the Towre, an euident, and manifeſt ſigne vnto all, of the helpe of the Lord.36And they ordained all with a common decree, in no caſe to let that day paſſe without ſolemnitie: but to celebrate the thirteenth day of the twelfth moneth, which in the Syrian tongue is called Adar, the day before Mardocheus day.37Thus went it with Nicanor, and from that time forth, the Hebrewes had the citie in their power: and heere will I make an end.38And if I haue done well, and as is fitting the ſtory, it is that which I deſired: but if ſlenderly, and meanly, it is that which I could attaine vnto.39For as it is hurtfull to drinke wine, or water alone; & as wine mingled with water is pleaſant, and delighteth the taſt: euen ſo ſpeech finely framed, delighteth the eares of them that read the ſtorie. And heere ſhall be an end.

THE NEW TESTAMENT

MATTHEW

CHAPTER 1[1]The booke of the generation of Ieſus Chriſt, the ſonne
of Dauid, the ſonne of Abraham.[2]Abraham begate Iſaac, and Iſaac
begate Iacob, and Iacob begate Iudas and his brethren.[3]And Iudas
begate Phares and Zara of Thamar, and Phares begate Eſrom, and
Eſrom begate Aram.[4]And Aram begate Aminadab, and Aminadab
begate Naaſson, and Naaſson begate Salmon.[5]And Salmon begat Boos
of Rachab, and Boos begate Obed of Ruth, and Obed begate Ieſſe.[6]And
Ieſſe begate Dauid the King, & Dauid the King begat Solomon of her
that had bin the wife of Urias.[7]And Solomon begat Roboam, and
Roboam begate Abia, and Abia begate Aſa.[8]And Aſa begate Ioſaphat,
and Ioſaphat begate Ioram, and Ioram begate Ozias.[9]And Ozias begat
Ioatham, and Ioatham begate Achas, and Achas begate Ezekias.[10]And
Ezekias begate Manaſſes, and Manaſſes begate Amon, and Amon begate
Ioſias.[11]And Ioſias begate Iechonias and his brethren, about the time
they were caried away to Babylon.[12]And after they were brought to
Babylon, Iechonias begat Salathiel, and Salathiel begate
Zorobabel.[13]And Zorobabel begat Abiud, and Abiud begat Eliakim, and
Eliakim begate Azor.[14]And Azor begat Sadoc, & Sadoc begat Achim,
and Achim begat Eliud.[15]And Eliud begate Eleazar, and Eleazar begate
Matthan, and Matthan begate Iacob.[16]And Iacob begate Ioſeph the
huſband of Mary, of whom was borne Ieſus, who is called Chriſt.[17]So
all the generations from Abraham to Dauid, are fourteene generations:
and from Dauid vntill the carying away into Babylon, are foureteene
generations: and from the carying away into Babylon vnto Chriſt, are
fourteene generations.[18]Now the birth of Ieſus Chriſt was on this wiſe:
When as his mother Mary was eſpouſed to Ioſeph (before they came
together) ſhee was found with childe of the holy Ghoſt.[19]Then Ioſeph
her huſband being a iuſt man, and not willing to make her a publique
example, was minded to put her away priuily.[20]But while hee thought
on theſe things, behold, the Angel of the Lord appeared vnto him in a
dreame, ſaying, Ioſeph thou ſonne of Dauid, feare not to take vnto thee
Mary thy wife: for that which is conceiued in her, is of the holy
Ghoſt.[21]And ſhe ſhall bring forth a ſonne, and thou ſhalt call his Name
Ieſus: for hee ſhall ſaue his people from their ſinnes.[22](Now all this was
done, that it might be fulfilled which was ſpoken of the Lord by the
Prophet, ſaying,[23]Behold, a Uirgin ſhall be with childe, and ſhall bring
foorth a ſonne, and they ſhall call his name Emmanuel, which being
interpreted, is, God with vs.)[24]Then Ioſeph, being raiſed from ſleepe,
did as the Angel of the Lord had bidden him, & tooke vnto him his
wife:[25]And knewe her not, till ſhee had brought forth her firſt borne
ſonne, and he called his name Ieſus.

CHAPTER 2[1]Now when Ieſus was borne in Bethlehem of Iudea, in
the dayes of Herod the king, behold, there came Wiſe men from the
Eaſt to Hieruſalem,[2]Saying, Where is he that is borne King of the Iewes?
for we haue ſeene his Starre in the Eaſt, and are come to worſhip
him.[3]When Herod the king had heard theſe things, he was troubled, and
all Hieruſalem with him.[4]And when he had gathered all the chiefe Prieſts
and Scribes of the people together, hee demanded of them where Chriſt
ſhould be borne.[5]And they ſaid vnto him, In Bethlehem of Iudea: For
thus it is written by the Prophet;[6]And thou Bethlehem in the land of
Iuda, art not the leaſt among the Princes of Iuda: for out of thee ſhall
come a Gouernour, that ſhall rule my people Iſrael.[7]Then Herod, when
he had priuily called the Wiſe men, enquired of them diligently what
time the Starre appeared:[8]And he ſent them to Bethlehem, and ſaid,
Goe, and ſearch diligently for the yong child, and when ye haue found
him, bring me word againe, that I may come and worſhip him
alſo.[9]When they had heard the King, they departed, and loe, the Starre
which they ſaw in the Eaſt, went before them, till it came and ſtood ouer
where the young childe was.[10]When they ſaw the Starre, they reioyced
with exceeding great ioy.[11]And when they were come into the houſe,
they ſaw the yong child with Mary his mother, and fell downe, and
worſhipped him: and when they had opened their treaſures, they
preſented vnto him gifts, gold, and frankincenſe, and myrrhe.[12]And
being warned of God in a dreame, that they ſhould not returne to
Herode, they departed into their owne countrey another way.[13]And
when they were departed, behold, the Angel of the Lord appeareth to
Ioſeph in a dreame, ſaying, Ariſe and take the young childe, and his
mother, and flee into Egypt, and bee thou there vntill I bring thee word:
for Herode will ſeeke the young childe, to deſtroy him.[14]When he aroſe,
he tooke the yong childe and his mother by night, and departed into
Egypt:[15]And was there vntill the death of Herode, that it might be
fulfilled which was ſpoken of the Lord by the Prophet, ſaying, Out of
Egypt haue I called my ſonne.[16]Then Herode, when hee ſaw that hee
was mocked of the Wiſe men, was exceeding wroth, and ſent foorth,
and ſlewe all the children that were in Bethlehem, and in all the coaſts
thereof, from two yeeres olde and vnder, according to the time, which
he had diligently enquired of the Wiſe men.[17]Then was fulfilled that
which was ſpoken by Ieremie the Prophet, ſaying,[18]In Rama was there
a voice heard, lamentation, and weeping, and great mourning, Rachel
weeping for her children, and would not be comforted, becauſe they are
not.[19]But when Herode was dead, behold, an Angel of the Lord
appeareth in a dreame to Ioſeph in Egypt,[20]Saying, Ariſe, and take the
yong childe and his mother, and goe into the land of Iſrael: for they are
dead which ſought the yong childes life.[21]And he aroſe, and tooke the
yong childe and his mother, and came into the land of Iſrael.[22]But when
he heard that Archelaus did reigne in Iudea in the roome of his father
Herod, hee was afraid to goe thither: notwithſtanding, beeing warned of
God in a dreame, he turned aſide into the parts of Galilee:[23]And hee
came and dwelt in a city called Nazareth, that it might be fulfilled which
was ſpoken by the Prophets, He ſhalbe called a Nazarene.

CHAPTER 3[1]In thoſe daies came Iohn the Baptiſt, preaching in the
wilderneſſe of Iudea,[2]And ſaying, Repent yee: for the kingdome of
heauen is at hand.[3]For this is he that was ſpoken of by the Prophet
Eſaias, ſaying, The voyce of one crying in the wildernes, Prepare ye the
way of the Lord, make his paths ſtraight.[4]And the ſame Iohn had his
raiment of camels haire, and a leatherne girdle about his loynes, and his
meate was locuſts and wilde hony.[5]Then went out to him Hieruſalem,
and all Iudea, and all the region round about Iordane,[6]And were
baptized of him in Iordane, confeſsing their ſinnes.[7]But when he ſaw
many of the PhAriſees and Sadducees come to his Baptiſme, he ſaid
vnto them, O generation of vipers, who hath warned you to flee from
the wrath to come?[8]Bring forth therefore fruits meet for
repentance.[9]And thinke not to ſay within your ſelues, Wee haue
Abraham to our father: For I ſay vnto you, that God is able of theſe
ſtones to raiſe vp children vnto Abraham.[10]And now alſo the axe is layd
vnto the root of the trees: Therefore euery tree which bringeth not
foorth good fruite, is hewen downe, and caſt into the fire.[11]I indeed
baptize you with water vnto repentance: but he that commeth after mee,
is mightier then I, whoſe ſhooes I am not worthy to beare, hee ſhall
baptize you with the holy Ghoſt, and with fire.[12]Whoſe fanne is in his
hand, and he will throughly purge his floore, and gather his wheat into
the garner: but wil burne vp the chaffe with vnquenchable fire.[13]Then
commeth Ieſus from Galilee to Iordane, vnto Iohn, to be baptized of
him:[14]But Iohn forbade him, ſaying, I haue need to bee baptized of thee,
and commeſt thou to me?[15]And Ieſus anſwering, ſaid vnto him, Suffer
it to be ſo now: for thus it becommeth vs to fulfill all righteouſneſſe.
Then he ſuffered him.[16]And Ieſus, when hee was baptized, went vp
ſtraightway out of the water: and loe, the heauens were opened vnto
him, and he ſaw the Spirit of God deſcending like a doue, and lighting
vpon him.[17]And loe, a voice from heauen, ſaying, This is my beloued
Sonne, in whom I am well pleaſed.

CHAPTER 4[1]Then was Ieſus led vp of the Spirit into the wilderneſſe,
to bee tempted of the deuill.[2]And when hee had faſted forty dayes and
forty nights, hee was afterward an hungred.[3]And when the tempter came
to him, hee ſaid, If thou be the ſonne of God, command that theſe
ſtones bee made bread.[4]But he anſwered, and ſaid, It is written, Man
ſhall not liue by bread alone, but by euery word that proceedeth out of
the mouth of God.[5]Then the deuill taketh him vp into the holy Citie,
and ſetteth him on a pinacle of the Temple,[6]And ſaith vnto him, If thou
bee the Sonne of God, caſt thy ſelfe downe: For it is written, He ſhall
giue his Angels charge concerning thee, & in their handes they ſhall
beare thee vp, leſt at any time thou daſh thy foote againſt a ſtone.[7]Ieſus
ſaid vnto him, It is written againe, Thou ſhalt not tempt the Lord thy
God.[8]Againe the Deuill taketh him vp into an exceeding high
mountaine, and ſheweth him all the kingdomes of the world, and the
glory of them:[9]And ſaith vnto him, All theſe things will I giue thee, if

thou wilt fall downe and worſhip me.10Then ſaith Ieſus vnto him, Get thee hence, Satan: for it is written, Thou ſhalt worſhip the Lord thy God, and him onely ſhalt thou ſerue.11Then the deuill leaueth him, and behold, Angels came and miniſtred vnto him.12Now when Ieſus had heard that Iohn was caſt into priſon, he departed into Galilee.13And leauing Nazareth, he came and dwelt in Capernaum, which is vpon the ſea coaſt, in the borders of Zabulon and Nephthali:14That it might be fulfilled which was ſpoken by Eſaias the Prophet, ſaying,15The land of Zabulon, and the land of Nephthali, by the way of the ſea beyond Iordane, Galilee of the Gentiles:16The people which ſate in darkeneſſe, ſaw great light: and to them which ſate in the region and ſhadow of death, light is ſprung vp.17From that time Ieſus began to preach, and to ſay, Repent, for the kingdome of heauen is at hand.18And Ieſus walking by the ſea of Galilee, ſaw two brethren, Simon, called Peter, and Andrew his brother, caſting a net into the ſea (for they were fiſherſ)19And he ſaith vnto them, Follow mee: and I will make you fiſhers of men.20And they ſtraightway left their nets, and followed him.21And going on from thence, hee ſawe other two brethren, Iames the ſonne of Zebedee, and Iohn his brother, in a ſhip with Zebedee their father, mending their nets: and he called them.22And they immediatly left the ſhippe and their father, and followed him.23And Ieſus went about all Galilee, teaching in their Synagogues, and preaching the Goſpel of the kingdome, and healing all maner of ſickeneſse, and all maner of diſeaſe among the people.24And his fame went thorowout all Syria: and they brought vnto him all ſicke people that were taken with diuerſe diſeaſes and torments, and thoſe which were poſſeſſed with deuils, and thoſe which were lunaticke, and thoſe that had the palſie, and he healed them.25And there followed him great great multitudes of people, from Galilee, and from Decapolis, and from Hieruſalem, and from Iudea, and from beyond Iordane.

CHAPTER 51And ſeeing the multitudes, he went vp into a mountaine: and when he was ſet, his diſciples came vnto him.2And he opened his mouth, and taught them, ſaying,3Bleſſed are the poore in ſpirit: for theirs is the kingdome of heauen.4Bleſſed are they that mourne: for they ſhall be comforted.5Bleſſed are the meeke: for they ſhall inherit the earth.6Bleſſed are they which doe hunger and thirſt after righteouſneſſe: for they ſhall be filled.7Bleſſed are the mercifull: for they ſhall obtaine mercie.8Bleſſed are the pure in heart: for they ſhall ſee God.9Bleſſed are the peacemakers: for they ſhall bee called the children of God.10Bleſſed are they which are perſecuted for righteouſneſſe ſake: for theirs is the kingdome of heauen.11Bleſſed are ye, when men ſhall reuile you, and perſecute you, and ſhal ſay all manner of euill againſt you falſly for my ſake.12Reioyce, and be exceeding glad: for great is your reward in heauen: For ſo perſecuted they the Prophets which were before you.13Yee are the ſalt of the earth: But if the ſalt haue loſt his ſauour, wherewith ſhall it bee ſalted? It is thenceforth good for nothing, but to be caſt out, and to be troden vnder foote of men.14Yee are the light of the world. A citie that is ſet on an hill, cannot be hid.15Neither doe men light a candle, and put it vnder a buſhell: but on a candleſticke, and it giueth light vnto all that are in the houſe.16Let your light ſo ſhine before men, that they may ſee your good workes, and glorifie your father which is in heauen.17Thinke not that I am come to deſtroy the lawe or the Prophets. I am not come to deſtroy, but to fulfill.18For verily I ſay vnto you, Till heauen and earth paſſe, one iote or one title, ſhall in no wiſe paſſe from the law, till all be fulfilled.19Whoſoeuer therfore ſhall breake one of theſe leaſt commaundements, and ſhall teach men ſo, he ſhall be called the leaſt in the kingdome of heauen: but whoſoeuer ſhall doe, and teach them, the ſame ſhall be called great in the kingdome of heauen.20For I ſay vnto you, That except your righteouſneſſe ſhall exceede the righteouſneſſe of the Scribes and PhAriſees, yee ſhall in no caſe enter into the kingdome of heauen.21Yee haue heard, that it was ſaide by them of old time, Thou ſhalt not kill: and, Whoſoeuer ſhall kill, ſhalbe in danger of the iudgement.22But I ſay vnto you, that whoſoeuer is angry with his brother without a cauſe, ſhall be in danger of the Iudgement: and whoſoeuer ſhall ſay to his brother, Racha, ſhal be in danger of the counſell: but whoſoeuer ſhall ſay, Thou foole, ſhalbe in danger of hell fire.23Therefore if thou bring thy gift to the altar, and there remembreſt that thy brother hath ought againſt thee:24Leaue there thy gift before the altar, and goe thy way, firſt be reconciled to thy brother, and then come and offer thy gift.25Agree with thine aduerſarie quickly, whiles thou art in the way with him: leaſt at any time the aduerſarie deliuer thee to the iudge, and the iudge deliuer thee to the officer, and thou be caſt into priſon.26Uerily I ſay vnto thee, thou ſhalt by no meanes come out thence, till thou haſt payd the vttermoſt farthing.27Yee haue heard that it was ſaid by them of old time, Thou ſhalt not commit adulterie.28But I ſay vnto you, That whoſoeuer looketh on a woman to luſt after her, hath committed adulterie with her already in his heart.29And if thy right eie offend thee, plucke it out, and caſt it from thee. For it is profitable for thee that one of thy members ſhould periſh, and not that thy whole body ſhould be caſt into hell.30And if thy right hand offend thee, cut it off, and caſt it from thee. For it is profitable for thee that one of thy members ſhould periſh, and not that thy whole body ſhould be caſt into hell.31It hath beene ſaid, Whoſoeuer ſhall put away his wife, let him giue her a writing of diuorcement.32But I ſay vnto you, that whoſoeuer ſhall put away his wife, ſauing for the cauſe of fornication, cauſeth her to commit adultery: and whoſoeuer ſhall marie her that is diuorced, committeth adulterie.33Againe, yee haue heard that it hath beene ſaid by them of old time, Thou ſhalt not forſweare thy ſelfe, but ſhalt performe vnto the Lord thine othes.34But I ſay vnto you, Sweare not at all, neither by heauen, for it is Gods throne:35Nor by the earth, for it is his footſtoole: neither by Hieruſalem, for it is the citie of the great king.36Neither ſhalt thou ſweare by thy head, becauſe thou canſt not make one haire white or blacke.37But let your communication bee Yea, yea: Nay, nay: For whatſoeuer is more then theſe, commeth of euill.38Yee haue heard that it hath beene ſaid, An eie for an eie, and a tooth for a tooth.39But I ſay vnto you, that yee reſiſt not euill: but whoſoeuer ſhall ſmite thee on thy right cheeke, turne to him the other alſo.40And if any man will ſue thee at the law, and take away thy coate, let him haue thy cloake alſo.41And whoſoeuer ſhall compell thee to goe a mile, goe with him twaine.42Giue to him that aſketh thee: and from him that would borrow of thee, turne not thou away.43Yee haue heard, that it hath beene ſaid, Thou ſhalt loue thy neighbour, and hate thine enemie:44But I ſay vnto you, Loue your enemies, bleſſe them that curſe you, doe good to them that hate you, and pray for them which deſpitefully vſe you, and perſecute you:45That yee may be the children of your father which is in heauen: for he maketh his ſunne to riſe on the euill and on the good, and ſendeth raine on the iuſt, and on the vniuſt.46For if yee loue them which loue you, what reward haue yee? Doe not euen the Publicanes the ſame?47And if yee ſalute your brethren only, what do you more then others? Doe not euen the Publicanes ſo?48Be yee therefore perfect, euen as your father, which is in heauen, is perfect.

CHAPTER 61Take heed that yee doe not your almes before men, to bee ſeene of them: otherwiſe yee haue no reward of your father which is in heauen.2Therefore, when thou doeſt thine almes, doe not ſound a trumpet before thee, as the hypocrites doe, in the Synagogues, and in the ſtreetes, that they may haue glory of men. Uerily, I ſay vnto you, they haue their reward.3But when thou doeſt almes, let not thy left hand know, what thy right doeth:4That thine almes may be in ſecret: And thy father which ſeeth in ſecret, himſelfe ſhall reward thee openly.5And when thou prayeſt, thou ſhalt not be as the hypocrites are: for they loue to pray ſtanding in the Synagogues, and in the corners of the ſtreets, that they may be ſeene of men. Uerily I ſay vnto you, they haue their reward.6But thou when thou prayeſt, enter into thy cloſet, and when thou haſt ſhut thy doore, pray to thy father which is in ſecret, and thy father which ſeeth in ſecret, ſhall reward thee openly.7But when yee pray, vſe not vaine repetitions, as the heathen doe. For they thinke that they ſhall be heard for their much ſpeaking.8Be not yee therefore like vnto them: For your father knoweth what things yee haue neede of, before yee aſke him.9After this maner therefore pray yee: Our father which art in heauen, hallowed be thy name.10Thy kingdome come. Thy will be done, in earth, as it is in heauen.11Giue vs this day our daily bread.12And forgiue vs our debts, as we forgiue our debters.13And lead vs not into temptation, but deliuer vs from euill: For thine is the kingdome, and the power, and the glory, for euer, Amen.14For, if yee forgiue men their treſpaſſes, your heauenly father will alſo forgiue you.15But, if yee forgiue not men their treſpaſſes, neither will your father forgiue your treſpaſſes.16Moreouer, when yee faſt, be not as the Hypocrites, of a ſad countenance: for they diſfigure their faces, that they may appeare vnto men to faſt: Uerily I ſay vnto you, they haue their reward.[17]But thou, when thou faſteſt, anoint thine head, and waſh thy face:[18]That thou appeare not vnto men to faſt, but vnto thy father which is in ſecret: and thy father which ſeeth in ſecret, ſhall reward thee openly.[19]Lay not vp for your ſelues treaſures vpon earth, where moth and ruſt doth corrupt, and where theeues breake thorow, and ſteale.[20]But lay vp for your ſelues treaſures in heauen, where neither moth nor ruſt doth corrupt, & where theeues doe not breake thorow, nor ſteale.[21]For where your treaſure is, there will your heart be alſo.[22]The light of the body is the eye: If therefore thine eye be ſingle, thy whole body ſhalbe full of light.[23]But if thine eye be euill, thy whole body ſhall be full of darkneſſe. If therfore the light that is in thee be darkeneſſe, how great is that darkeneſſe?[24]No man can ſerue two maſters: for either he will hate the one and loue the other, or elſe hee will holde to the one, and deſpiſe the other. Ye cannot ſerue God and Mammon.[25]Therfore I ſay vnto you, Take no thought for your life, what yee ſhall eate, or what ye ſhall drinke, nor yet for your body, what yee ſhall put on: Is not the life more then meate? and the body then raiment?[26]Behold the foules of the aire: for they ſow not, neither do they reape, nor gather into barnes, yet your heauenly father feedeth them. Are yee not much better then they?[27]Which of you by taking thought, can adde one cubite vnto his ſtature?[28]And why take ye thought for raiment? Conſider the lillies of the field, how they grow: they toile not, neither doe they ſpinne.[29]And yet I ſay vnto you, that euen Solomon in all his glory, was not arayed like one of theſe.[30]Wherefore, if God ſo clothe the graſſe of the field, which to day is, and to morrow is caſt into the ouen: ſhall he not much more clothe you, O yee of little faith?[31]Therefore take no thought, ſaying, What ſhall we eate? or, what ſhall we drinke? or wherewithall ſhall wee be clothed?[32](For after all theſe things doe the Gentiles ſeeke:) for your heauenly father knoweth that ye haue neede of all theſe things.[33]But ſeeke ye firſt the kingdome of God, and his righteouſneſſe, and all theſe things ſhalbe added vnto you.[34]Take therefore no thought for the morrow: for the morrow ſhall take thought for the things of it ſelfe: ſufficient vnto the day is the euill thereof.

CHAPTER 7[1]Iudge not, that ye be not iudged.[2]For with what iudgment ye iudge, yee ſhall be iudged: and with what meaſure ye mete, it ſhall be meaſured to you againe.[3]And why beholdeſt thou the mote that is in thy brothers eye, but conſidereſt not the beame that is in thine owne eye?[4]Or how wilt thou ſay to thy brother, Let mee pull out the mote out of thine eye, and beholde, a beame is in thine owne eye?[5]Thou hypocrite, firſt caſt out the beame out of thine owne eye: and then ſhalt thou ſee clearely to caſt out the mote out of thy brothers eye.[6]Giue not that which is holy vnto the dogs, neither caſt ye your pearles before ſwine: leſt they trample them vnder their feete, and turne againe and rent you.[7]Aſke, and it ſhalbe giuen you: ſeeke, and ye ſhall finde: knocke, and it ſhalbe opened vnto you.[8]For euery one that aſketh, receiueth: and he that ſeeketh, findeth: and to him that knocketh, it ſhalbe opened.[9]Or what man is there of you, whom if his ſonne aſke bread, will hee giue him a ſtone?[10]Or if he aſke a fiſh, will hee giue him a ſerpent?[11]If ye then being euill, know how to giue good giftes vnto your children, how much more ſhall your Father which is in heauen, giue good things to them that aſke him?[12]Therefore all things whatſoeuer ye would that men ſhould doe to you, doe ye euen ſo to them: for this is the Law and the Prophets.[13]Enter ye in at the ſtrait gate, for wide is the gate, and broad is the way that leadeth to deſtruction, and many there be which goe in thereat:[14]Becauſe ſtrait is the gate, and narrow is the way which leadeth vnto life, and few there be that finde it.[15]Beware of falſe prophets which come to you in ſheepes clothing, but inwardly they are rauening wolues.[16]Yee ſhall knowe them by their fruits: Doe men gather grapes of thornes, or figges of thiſtles?[17]Euen ſo, euery good tree bringeth forth good fruit: but a corrupt tree bringeth forth euill fruit.[18]A good tree cannot bring forth euil fruit, neither can a corrupt tree bring forth good fruit.[19]Euery tree that bringeth not forth good fruit, is hewen downe, and caſt into the fire.[20]Wherefore by their fruits ye ſhall know them.[21]Not euery one that ſaith vnto me, Lord, Lord, ſhall enter into the kingdome of heauen: but he that doth the will of my father which is in heauen.[22]Many will ſay to me in that day, Lord, Lord, haue we not prophecied in thy name? and in thy name haue caſt out deuils? and in thy name done many wonderfull works?[23]And then wil I profeſse vnto them, I neuer knew you: Depart from me, ye that worke iniquity.[24]Therefore, whoſoeuer heareth theſe ſayings of mine, and doeth them, I wil liken him vnto a wiſe man, which built his houſe vpon a rocke:[25]And the raine deſcended, and the floods came, and the windes blew, and beat vpon that houſe: and it fell not, for it was founded vpon a rocke.[26]And euery one that heareth theſe ſayings of mine, and doeth them not, ſhall bee likened vnto a fooliſh man, which built his houſe vpon the ſand:[27]And the raine deſcended, and the floods came, and the windes blew, and beat vpon that houſe, and it fell, and great was the fall of it.[28]And it came to paſſe, when Ieſus had ended theſe ſayings, the people were aſtoniſhed at his doctrine.[29]For he taught them as one hauing authoritie, and not as the Scribes.

CHAPTER 8[1]When he was come downe from the Mountaine, great multitudes folowed him.[2]And behold, there came a leper, and worſhipped him, ſaying, Lord, If thou wilt, thou canſt make me cleane.[3]And Ieſus put forth his hand, and touched him, ſaying, I will, bee thou cleane. And immediately his leproſie was cleanſed.[4]And Ieſus ſaith vnto him, ſee thou tell no man, but go thy way, ſhew thy ſelfe to the prieſt, and offer the gift that Moſes commanded, for a teſtimonie vnto them.[5]And when Ieſus was entred into Capernaum, there came vnto him a Centurion, beſeeching him,[6]And ſaying, Lord, my ſeruant lieth at home ſicke of the palſie, grieuouſly tormented.[7]And Ieſus ſaith vnto him, I will come, and heale him.[8]The Centurion anſwered, and ſaid, Lord, I am not worthy that thou ſhouldeſt come vnder my roofe: but ſpeake the word onely, and my ſeruant ſhalbe healed.[9]For I am a man vnder authority, hauing ſouldiers vnder me: and I ſay to this man, Goe, and he goeth: and to another, Come, and he commeth: and to my ſeruant, Doe this, and he doth it.[10]When Ieſus heard it, he marueiled, and ſaid to them that followed, Uerely, I ſay vnto you, I haue not found ſo great faith, no not in Iſrael.[11]And I ſay vnto you, that many ſhall come from the Eaſt and Weſt, and ſhal ſit downe with Abraham, and Iſaac, & Iacob, in the kingdome of heauen:[12]But the children of the kingdome ſhall be caſt out into outer darkeneſſe: there ſhalbe weeping and gnaſhing of teeth.[13]And Ieſus ſaid vnto the Centurion, Go thy way, and as thou haſt beleeued, ſo be it done vnto thee. And his ſeruant was healed in the ſelf ſame houre.[14]And when Ieſus was come into Peters houſe, hee ſaw his wiues mother laid, and ſicke of a feuer:[15]And he touched her hand, and the feuer left her: and ſhe aroſe, and miniſtred vnto them.[16]When the Euen was come, they brought vnto him many that were poſſeſſed with deuils: and hee caſt out the ſpirits with his worde, and healed all that were ſicke,[17]That it might be fulfilled which which was ſpoken by Eſaias the Prophet, ſaying, Himſelfe tooke our infirmities, and bare our ſickneſses.[18]Now when Ieſus ſaw great multitudes about him, hee gaue commaundement to depart vnto the other ſide.[19]And a certaine Scribe came, and ſaid vnto him, Maſter, I will follow thee whitherſoeuer thou goeſt.[20]And Ieſus ſaith vnto him, The Foxes haue holes, and the birds of the ayre haue neſts: but the ſonne of man hath not where to lay his head.[21]And another of his Diſciples ſaid vnto him, Lord, ſuffer me firſt to goe, and bury my father.[22]But Ieſus ſaid vnto him, Follow me, & let the dead, bury their dead.[23]And when he was entred into a ſhip, his Diſciples followed him.[24]And behold, there aroſe a great tempeſt in the ſea, inſomuch that the ſhip was couered with the waues: but he was aſleepe.[25]And his Diſciples came to him, and awoke, ſaying, Lord, ſaue vs: we periſh.[26]And he ſaith vnto them, Why are yee fearefull, O yee of litle faith? Then hee aroſe, and rebuked the winds and the ſea, and there was a great calme.[27]But the men marueiled, ſaying, What maner of man is this, that euen the winds and the ſea obey him?[28]And when hee was come to the other ſide, into the countrey of the Gergeſenes, there met him two poſſeſſed with deuils, comming out of the tombes, exceeding fierce, ſo that no man might paſſe by that way.[29]And behold, they cryed out, ſaying, What haue we to doe with thee, Ieſus thou ſonne of God? Art thou come hither to torment vs befor þe time?[30]And there was a good way off from them, an heard of many ſwine, feeding.[31]So the deuils beſought him, ſaying, If thou caſt vs out, ſuffer vs to goe away into the herd of ſwine.[32]And he ſaid vnto them, Goe. And when they were come out, they went into the herd of ſwine: and behold, the whole herd of ſwine ranne violently downe a ſteepe place into the ſea, and periſhed in the waters.[33]And they that kept them, fled, and went their waies into the citie, and told euery thing, and what was befallen to the poſſeſſed of the deuils.[34]And behold, the whole citie came out to meete Ieſus: and when they ſaw him, they beſought him that hee would depart out of their coaſts.

CHAPTER 9 1 And hee entred into a ſhip, and paſſed ouer, and came into his owne citie. 2 And behold, they brought to him a man ſicke of the palſie, lying on a bed: and Ieſus ſeeing their faith, ſaid vnto the ſicke of the palſie, Sonne, be of good cheere, thy ſinnes be forgiuen thee. 3 And behold, certaine of the Scribes ſaid within themſelues, This man blaſphemeth. 4 And Ieſus knowing their thoughts, ſaid, Wherefore thinke yee euill in your hearts? 5 For whether is eaſier to ſay, Thy ſinnes be forgiuen thee: or to ſay, Ariſe, and walke? 6 But that yee may know that the ſonne of man hath power on earth to forgiue ſinnes, (Then ſaith hee to the ſicke of the palſie) Ariſe, take vp thy bed, and goe vnto thine houſe. 7 And he aroſe, and departed to his houſe. 8 But when the multitudes ſaw it, they marueiled, & glorified God, which had giuen ſuch power vnto men. 9 And as Ieſus paſſed forth from thence, he ſaw a man named Matthew, ſitting at the receite of cuſtome: and he ſaith vnto him, Follow me. And he aroſe and followed him. 10 And it came to paſſe, as Ieſus ſate at meate in the houſe, behold, many publicanes and ſinners, came and ſate downe with him and his Diſciples. 11 And when the PhAriſees ſaw it, they ſaid vnto his diſciples, Why eateth your maſter with publicanes & ſinners. 12 But when Ieſus heard that, hee ſaid vnto them, They that be whole neede not a Phyſicion, but they that are ſicke. 13 But goe ye and learne what that meaneth, I will haue mercy and not ſacrifice: for I am not come to call the righteous, but ſinners to repentance. 14 Then came to him the diſciples of Iohn, ſaying, Why doe we and the PhAriſees faſt oft, but thy diſciples faſt not? 15 And Ieſus ſaide vnto them, Can the children of the bride-chamber mourne, as long as the bridegrome is with them? But the dayes will come when the bridegrome ſhall bee taken from them, and then ſhall they faſt. 16 No man putteth a piece of new cloth vnto an olde garment: for that which is put in to fill it vp, taketh from the garment, & the rent is made worſe. 17 Neither doe men put new wine into old bottels: elſe the bottels breake, and the wine runneth out, and the bottels periſh: but they put new wine into new bottels, and both are preſerued. 18 While hee ſpake theſe things vnto them, beholde, there came a certaine ruler and worſhipped him, ſaying, My daughter is euen now dead: but come, and lay thy hand vpon her, and ſhe ſhall liue. 19 And Ieſus aroſe, and followed him, and ſo did his diſciples. 20 (And behold, a woman which was diſeaſed with an iſſue of blood twelue yeeres, came behinde him, and touched the hemme of his garment. 21 For ſhe ſaid within her ſelfe, If I may but touch his garment, I ſhall be whole. 22 But Ieſus turned him about, and when he ſaw her, he ſaid, Daughter, bee of good comfort, thy faith hath made thee whole. And the woman was made whole from that houre.) 23 And when Ieſus came into the rulers houſe, and ſaw the minſtrels and the people making a noiſe, 24 He ſaid vnto them, Giue place, for the mayd is not dead, but ſleepeth. And they laughed him to ſcorne. 25 But when the people were put foorth, he went in, and tooke her by the hand: and the mayd aroſe. 26 And the fame hereof went abroad into all that land. 27 And when Ieſus departed thence, two blinde men followed him, crying, and ſaying, Thou ſonne of Dauid, haue mercy on vs. 28 And when he was come into the houſe, the blinde men came to him: and Ieſus ſaith vnto them, Beleeue ye that I am able to doe this? They ſaid vnto him, Yea, Lord. 29 Then touched he their eyes, ſaying, According to your faith, bee it vnto you. 30 And their eyes were opened: and Ieſus ſtraitly charged them, ſaying, ſee that no man know it. 31 But they, when they were departed, ſpread abroad his fame in all that countrey. 32 As they went out, beholde, they brought to him a dumbe man poſſeſſed with a deuill. 33 And when the deuil was caſt out, the dumbe ſpake, and the multitudes marueiled, ſaying, It was neuer ſo ſeene in Iſrael. 34 But the PhAriſees ſaid, He caſteth out the deuils through the prince of the deuils. 35 And Ieſus went about all the cities and villages, teaching in their Synagogues, and preaching the Goſpel of the kingdome, and healing euery ſickeneſse, and euery diſeaſe among the people. 36 But when he ſaw the multitudes, he was moued with compaſſion on them, becauſe they fainted, and were ſcattered abroad, as ſheepe hauing no ſhepheard. 37 Then ſaith he vnto his diſciples, The harueſt truely is plenteous, but the labourers are few. 38 Pray ye therefore the Lord of the harueſt, that hee will ſend foorth labourers into his harueſt.

CHAPTER 10 1 And when hee had called vnto him his twelue diſciples, he gaue them power againſt vncleane ſpirits, to caſt them out, and to heale all maner of ſickeneſse, and all maner of diſeaſe. 2 Now the names of the twelue Apoſtles are theſe: The firſt, Simon, who is called Peter, and Andrew his brother, Iames the ſonne of Zebedee, and Iohn his brother: 3 Philip, and Bartholomew, Thomas, and Matthew the Publicane, Iames the ſonne of Alpheus, and Lebbeus, whoſe ſurname was Thaddeus: 4 Simon the Canaanite, and Iudas Iſcariot, who alſo betrayed him. 5 Theſe twelue Ieſus ſent foorth, and commanded them, ſaying, Goe not into the way of the Gentiles, and into any city of the Samaritans enter ye not: 6 But goe rather to the loſt ſheepe of the houſe of Iſrael. 7 And as yee goe, preach, ſaying, The kingdome of heauen is at hand: 8 Heale the ſicke, cleanſe the lepers, raiſe the dead, caſt out deuils: freely ye haue receiued, freely giue. 9 Prouide neither gold, nor ſiluer, nor braſſe in your purſes: 10 Nor ſcrippe for your iourney, neither two coats, neither ſhooes, nor yet ſtaues: (for the workeman is worthy of his meat.) 11 And into whatſoeuer city or towne ye ſhall enter, inquire who in it is worthy, and there abide till yee goe thence. 12 And when ye come into an houſe, ſalute it. 13 And if the houſe be worthy, let your peace come vpon it: but if it be not worthy, let your peace returne to you. 14 And whoſoeuer ſhall not receiue you, nor heare your words: when yee depart out of that houſe, or city, ſhake off the duſt of your feete. 15 Uerely I ſay vnto you, it ſhall be more tolerable for the land of Sodom and Gomorrha in the day of iudgment, then for that citie. 16 Behold, I ſend you foorth as ſheepe in the middeſt of wolues: be yee therefore wiſe as ſerpents, and harmeleſſe as doues. 17 But beware of men: for they will deliuer you vp to the Councils, and they will ſcourge you in their Synagogues, 18 And yee ſhall be brought before Gouernours and Kings for my ſake, for a teſtimonie againſt them, and the Gentiles. 19 But when they deliuer you vp, take no thought, how or what ye ſhall ſpeake, for it ſhall bee giuen you in that ſame houre what ye ſhall ſpeake. 20 For it is not yee that ſpeake, but the Spirit of your Father, which ſpeaketh in you. 21 And the brother ſhall deliuer vp the brother to death, and the father the childe: and the children ſhall riſe vp againſt their parents, and cauſe them to be put to death. 22 And yee ſhall be hated of all men for my Names ſake: but he that endureth to the end, ſhalbe ſaued. 23 But when they perſecute you in this citie, flee ye into another: for verely I ſay vnto you, ye ſhall not haue gone ouer the cities of Iſrael, till the Sonne of man be come. 24 The diſciple is not aboue his maſter, nor the ſeruant aboue his lord. 25 It is enough for the diſciple that he be as his maſter, and the ſeruant as his Lord: If they haue called the Maſter of the houſe of Beelzebub, how much more ſhall they call them of his houſehold? 26 Feare them not therefore: for there is nothing couered, that ſhall not be reueiled; and hidde, that ſhall not be knowen. 27 What I tell you in darkeneſſe, that ſpeake yee in light: and what yee heare in the eare, that preach yee vpon the houſe tops. 28 And feare not them which kill the body, but are not able to kill the ſoule: but rather feare him which is able to deſtroy both ſoule and body in hell. 29 Are not two Sparrowes ſolde for a farthing? And one of them ſhall not fall on the ground without your Father. 30 But the very haires of your head are all numbred. 31 Feare yee not therefore, ye are of more value then many Sparrowes. 32 Whoſoeuer therefore ſhall confeſse mee before men, him will I confeſse alſo before my Father which is in heauen. 33 But whoſoeuer ſhall deny me before men, him will I alſo deny before my Father which is in heauen. 34 Thinke not that I am come to ſend peace on earth: I came not to ſend peace, but a ſword. 35 For I am come to ſet a man at variance againſt his father, & the daughter againſt her mother, and the daughter in law againſt her mother in law. 36 And a mans foes ſhalbe they of his owne houſhold. 37 He that loueth father or mother more then me, is not worthy of me: and he that loueth ſonne or daughter more then me, is not worthy of me. 38 And he that taketh not his croſſe, and followeth after me, is not worthy of me. 39 He that findeth his life, ſhall loſe it: and he that loſeth his life for my ſake, ſhall find it. 40 He that receiueth you, receiueth me: and he that receiueth mee, receiueth him that ſent me. 41 He that receiueth a Prophet in the name of a Prophet, ſhall receiue a Prophets reward: and he that receiueth a righteous man, in the name of a righteous man, ſhal receiue a righteous mans reward. 42 And whoſoeuer ſhall giue to drinke vnto one of theſe litle ones, a cup of cold water onely, in the name of a diſciple, verily I ſay vnto you, hee ſhall in no wiſe loſe his reward.

CHAPTER 11 1And it came to paſſe, when Ieſus had made an end of commaunding his twelue Diſciples, hee departed thence to teach and to preach in their cities.2Now when Iohn had heard in the priſon the workes of Chriſt, he ſent two of his diſciples,3And ſaid vnto him, Art thou hee that ſhould come? Or doe wee looke for another?4Ieſus anſwered and ſaide vnto them, Go and ſhew Iohn againe thoſe things which we doe heare and ſee:5The blind receiue their ſight, and the lame walke, the lepers are cleanſed, and the deafe heare, the dead are raiſed vp, and the poore haue the Goſpel preached to them.6And bleſſed is he, whoſeouer ſhal not be offended in me.7And as they departed, Ieſus began to ſay vnto the multitudes concerning Iohn, what went ye out into the wilderneſſe to ſee? a reede ſhaken with the winde?8But what went ye out for to ſee? A man clothed in ſoft raiment? Behold, they that weare ſoft cloathing, are in kings houſes.9But what went ye out for to ſee? A Prophet? yea, I ſay vnto you, and more then a Prophet.10For this is he of whom it is written, Behold, I ſend my meſſenger before thy face, which ſhall prepare thy way before thee.11Uerely I ſay vnto you, Among them that are borne of women, there hath not riſen a greater then Iohn the Baptiſt: notwithſtanding, hee that is leaſt in the kingdome of heauen, is greater then he.12And from the dayes of Iohn the Baptiſt, vntill now, the kingdome of heauen ſuffereth violence, and the violent take it by force.13For all the Prophets, and the Law prophecied vntill Iohn.14And if ye wil receiue it, this is Elias which was for to come.15Hee that hath eares to heare, let him heare.16But whereunto ſhall I liken this generation? It is like vnto children, ſitting in the markets, and calling vnto their fellowes,17And ſaying, we haue piped vnto you, and ye haue not danced: wee haue mourned vnto you, and ye haue not lamented.18For Iohn came neither eating nor drinking, and they ſay, he hath a deuill.19The ſonne of man came eating and drinking, and they ſay, Behold a man gluttonous, and a wine bibber, a friend of publicanes and ſinners: but wiſedom is iuſtified of her children.20Then began he to vpbraid the cities wherein moſt of his mighty works were done, becauſe they repented not.21Woe vnto thee Chorazin, woe vnto thee Bethſaida: for if the mightie workes which were done in you, had bene done in Tyre and Sidon, they would haue repented long agoe in ſackcloth and aſhes.22But I ſay vnto you, It ſhall bee more tolerable for Tyre and Sidon at the day of iudgement, then for you.23And thou Capernaum, which art exalted vnto heauen, ſhalt be brought downe to hell: For if the mighty works which haue beene done in thee, had bin done in Sodome, it would haue remained vntil this day.24But I ſay vnto you, that it ſhall be more tolerable for the land of Sodom, in þe day of iudgment, then for thee.25At that time Ieſus anſwered, and ſaid, I thanke thee, O Father, Lord of heauen and earth, becauſe thou haſt hid theſe things frō the wiſe & prudent, & haſt reueiled them vnto babes.26Euen ſo, Father, for ſo it ſeemed good in thy ſight.27All things are deliuered vnto me of my father: and no man knoweth the ſonne but the father: neither knoweth any man the father, ſaue the ſonne, and hee to whomſoeuer the ſonne will reueile him.28Come vnto me all yee that labour, and are heauy laden, and I will giue you reſt.29Take my yoke vpon you, and learne of me, for I am meeke and lowly in heart: and yee ſhall find reſt vnto your ſoules.30For my yoke is eaſie, and my burden is light.

CHAPTER 12 1At that time, Ieſus went on the Sabbath day thorow the corne, & his Diſciples were an hungred, and beganne to pluck the eares of corne, and to eate.2But when the PhAriſes ſaw it, they ſaid vnto him, Behold, thy Diſciples doe that which is not lawfull to doe vpon the Sabbath day.3But he ſaid vnto them, Haue yee not read what Dauid did when hee was an hungred, and they that were with him,4How he entred into the houſe of God, and did eate the ſhew bread, which was not lawfull for him to eate, neither for them which were with him, but, only for the Prieſts?5Or haue yee not read in the law, how that on the Sabbath dayes the Prieſts in the Temple profane the Sabbath, and are blameleſſe?6But I ſaye vnto you, that in this place is one greater then the Temple.7But if yee had knowen what this meaneth, I will haue mercy, and not ſacrifice, yee would not haue condemned the guiltleſſe.8For the ſonne of man is Lord euen of the Sabbath day.9And when hee was departed thence, he went into their Synagogue.10And behold, there was a man which had his hand withered, and they aſked him, ſaying, Is it lawfull to heale on the Sabbath dayes? that they might accuſe him.11And hee ſaid vnto them, What man ſhal there be among you, that ſhall haue one ſheepe: and if it fall into a pit on the Sabbath day, will hee not lay hold on it, and lift it out?12How much then is a man better then a ſhepe? Wherfore it is lawfull to doe well on the Sabbath dayes.13Then ſaith he to the man, Stretch forth thine hand: and hee ſtretched it forth, and it was reſtored whole, like as the other.14Then the PhAriſes went out, and held a counſell againſt him, how they might deſtroy him.15But when Ieſus knew it, hee withdrew himſelfe from thence: and great multitudes followed him, and he healed them all,16And charged them that they ſhould not make him knowen:17That it might be fulfilled which was ſpoken by Eſaias the Prophet, ſaying,18Behold, my ſeruant whom I haue choſen, my beloued in whom my ſoule is well pleaſed: I will put my ſpirit vpon him, and he ſhall ſhew iudgement to the Gentiles.19He ſhall not ſtriue, nor cry, neither ſhall any man heare his voice in the ſtreets.20A bruiſed reed ſhal he not breake, and ſmoking flaxe ſhall he not quench, till he ſend forth iudgment vnto victory.21And in his name ſhall the Gentiles truſt.22Then was brought vnto him one poſſeſſed with a deuill, blinde, and dumbe: and hee healed him, inſomuch that the blinde and dumbe both ſpake and ſaw.23And all the people were amazed, and ſaid, Is this the ſonne of Dauid?24But when the PhAriſees heard it, they ſaid, This fellow doeth not caſt out deuils, but by Beelzebub the prince of the deuils.25And Ieſus knew their thoughts, and ſaid vnto them, Euery kingdome diuided againſt it ſelfe, is brought to deſolation: and euery citie or houſe diuided againſt it ſelfe, ſhall not ſtand.26And if Satan caſt out Satan, he is diuided againſt himſelfe; how ſhall then his kingdome ſtand?27And if I by Beelzebub caſt out deuils, by whom doe your children caſt them out? Therefore they ſhall be your Iudges.28But if I caſt out deuils by the Spirit of God, then the kingdome of God is come vnto you.29Or elſe, how can one enter into a ſtrong mans houſe, & ſpoile his goods, except hee firſt binde the ſtrong man, and then he will ſpoile his houſe.30He that is not with me, is againſt me: and hee that gathereth not with me, ſcattereth abroad.31Wherefore I ſay vnto you, All maner of ſinne and blaſphemie ſhall be forgiuen vnto men: but the blaſphemie againſt the holy Ghoſt, ſhall not bee forgiuen vnto men.32And whoſoeuer ſpeaketh a word againſt the ſonne of man, it ſhall be forgiuen him: but whoſoeuer ſpeaketh againſt the holy Ghoſt, it ſhall not be forgiuen him, neither in this world, neither in the world to come.33Either make the tree good, and his fruit good: Or elſe make the tree corrupt, and his fruit corrupt: For the tree is knowen by his fruit.34O generation of vipers, how can ye, being euil, ſpeake good things? For out of the abundance of the heart the mouth ſpeaketh.35A good man out of the good treaſure of the heart, bringeth foorth good things: and an euill man out of the euill treaſure, bringeth foorth euill things.36But I ſay vnto you, That euery idle word that men ſhall ſpeake, they ſhall giue accompt thereof in the day of Iudgement.37For by thy wordes thou ſhalt bee iuſtified, and by thy words thou ſhalt be condemned.38Then certaine of the Scribes, and of the PhAriſees, anſwered, ſaying, Maſter, we would ſee a ſigne from thee.39But hee anſwered, and ſaid to them, An euill and adulterous generation ſeeketh after a ſigne, and there ſhall no ſigne be giuen to it, but the ſigne of the Prophet Ionas.40For as Ionas was three dayes and three nights in the whales belly: ſo ſhal the ſonne of man be three daies and three nights in the heart of the earth.41The men of Nineue ſhall riſe in iudgement with this generation, and ſhall condemne it, becauſe they repented at the preaching of Ionas, and behold, a greater then Ionas is here.42The Queene of the South ſhall riſe vp in the iudgement with this generation, and ſhall condemne it: for ſhe came from the vttermoſt parts of the earth to heare the wiſedome of Solomon, and behold, a greater then Solomon is here.43When the vncleane ſpirit is gone out of a man, hee walketh thorow dry places, ſeeking reſt, and findeth none.44Then he ſaith, I will returne into my houſe from whence I came out; And when he is come, he findeth it emptie, ſwept, and garniſhed.45Then goeth he, and taketh with himſelfe ſeuen other ſpirits more wicked then himſelfe, and they enter in and dwell there: And the laſt ſtate of that man is worſe then the firſt. Euen ſo ſhal it be alſo vnto this wicked generation.46While he yet talked to the people, behold, his mother and his brethren ſtood without, deſiring to ſpeake with him.47Then one ſaide vnto him, Behold, thy mother and thy brethren ſtand without, deſiring to ſpeake with thee.48But he anſwered, and ſaid

vnto him that told him, Who is my mother? And who are my
brethren?49And hee ſtretched forth his hand toward his diſciples, and
ſaid, Behold, my mother and my brethren.50For whoſoeuer ſhall doe
the will of my Father which is in heauen, the ſame is my brother, and
ſiſter, and mother.

CHAPTER 131The ſame day went Ieſus out of the houſe, and ſate by
the ſea ſide.2And great multitudes were gathered together vnto him, ſo
that hee went into a ſhip, and ſate, and the whole multitude ſtood on
the ſhore.3And hee ſpake many things vnto them in parables, ſaying,
Behold, a ſower went foorth to ſow.4And when he ſowed, ſome ſeedes
fell by the wayes ſide, and the foules came, and deuoured them
vp.5Some fell vpon ſtony places, where they had not much earth: and
foorth with they ſprung vp, becauſe they had no deepeneſse of
earth.6And when the Sunne was vp, they were ſcorched: and becauſe
they had not root, they withered away.7And ſome fell among thorns:
and the thornes ſprung vp, & choked them.8But other fell into good
ground, and brought foorth fruit, ſome an hundred folde, ſome ſixtie
folde, ſome thirty folde.9Who hath eares to heare, let him heare.10And
the diſciples came, and ſayd vnto him, Why ſpeakeſt thou vnto them in
parables?11He anſwered, and ſaid vnto them, Becauſe it is giuen vnto
you to know the myſteries of the kingdome of heauen, but to them it is
not giuen.12For whoſoeuer hath, to him ſhall be giuen, and he ſhall haue
more abundance: but whoſoeuer hath not, from him ſhall be taken away,
euen that hee hath.13Therefore ſpeake I to then in parables: becauſe they
ſeeing, ſee not: and hearing, they heare not, neither doe they
vnderſtand.14And in them is fulfilled the prophecie of Eſaias, which
ſaith, By hearing ye ſhall heare, and ſhall not vnderſtand: and ſeeing yee
ſhall ſee, and ſhall not perceiue.15For this peoples heart is waxed groſse,
and their eares are dull of hearing, and their eyes they haue cloſed, leſt
at any time they ſhould ſee with their eyes, and heare with their eares,
and ſhould vnderſtand with their heart, and ſhould be conuerted, and I
ſhould heale them.16But bleſſed are your eyes, for they ſee: and your
eares, for they heare.17For verely I ſay vnto you, that many Prophets,
and righteous men haue deſired to ſee thoſe things which yee ſee, and
haue not ſeene them: and to heare thoſe things which ye heare, and haue
not heard them.18Heare ye therefore the parable of the ſower.19When
any one heareth the word of the kingdome, and vnderſtandeth it not,
then commeth the wicked one, and catcheth away that which was ſowen
in his heart: this is hee which receiued ſeede by the way ſide.20But he
that receiued the ſeed into ſtony places, the ſame is he that heareth the
word, & anon with ioy receiueth it:21Yet hath hee not root in himſelfe,
but dureth for a while: for when tribulation or perſecution Ariſeth
becauſe of the word, by and by he is offended.22He alſo that receiued
ſeed among the thorns, is he that heareth the word, and the care of this
world, and the deceitfulneſse of riches choke the word, and he
becommeth vnfruitfull.23But he that receiued ſeed into the good ground,
is hee that heareth the word, and vnderſtandeth it, which alſo beareth
fruit, and bringeth foorth, ſome an hundred fold, ſome ſixtie, ſome
thirty.24Another parable put he forth vnto them, ſaying; The kingdome
of heauen is likened vnto a man which ſowed good ſeed in his field:25But
while men ſlept, his enemy came & ſowed tares among the wheat, and
went his way.26But when the blade was ſprung vp, and brought forth
fruit, then appeared the tares alſo.27So the ſeruants of the houſholder
came, and ſaid vnto him, Sir, didſt not thou ſow good ſeede in thy field?
from whence then hath it tares?28He ſaid vnto them, An enemy hath
done this. The ſeruants ſaid vnto him, Wilt thou then that we goe and
gather them vp?29But he ſaid, Nay: leſt while yee gather vp the tares, ye
root vp alſo the wheat with them.30Let both grow together vntil the
harueſt: and in the time of harueſt, I will ſay to the reapers, Gather ye
together firſt the tares, and binde them in bundels to burne them: but
gather the wheat into my barne.31Another parable put he foorth vnto
them, ſaying, The kingdome of heauen is like to a graine of muſtard
ſeed, which a man tooke, and ſowed in his field.32Which indeed is the
leaſt of al ſeeds: but when it is growen, it is the greateſt among herbes,
and becommeth a tree: ſo that the birds of the aire come and lodge in
the branches thereof.33Another parable ſpake he vnto them, The
kingdome of heauen is like vnto leauen, which a woman tooke, and hid
in three meaſures of meale, till the whole was leauened.34All theſe things
ſpake Ieſus vnto the multitude in parables, and without a parable ſpake
hee not vnto them:35That it might bee fulfilled which was ſpoken by the
Prophet, ſaying, I will open my mouth in parables, I wil vtter things
which haue bin kept ſecret from the foundation of the world.36Then
Ieſus ſent the multitude away, and went into the houſe: and his diſciples
came vnto him, ſaying, Declare vnto vs the parable of the tares of the
field.37He anſwered, and ſaid vnto them, Hee that ſoweth the good ſeed,
is the ſonne of man.38The field is the world. The good ſeed, are the
children of the kingdome: but the tares are the children of the wicked
one.39The enemie that ſowed them, is the deuill. The harueſt, is the ende
of the world. And the reapers are the Angels.40As therefore the tares
are gathered and burnt in the fire: ſo ſhall it be in the end of this
world.41The Sonne of man ſhall ſend forth his Angels, and they ſhall
gather out of his kingdome all things that offend, and them which doe
iniquitie:42And ſhall caſt them into a furnace of fire: there ſhall be
wayling and gnaſhing of teeth.43Then ſhall the righteous ſhine foorth as
the Sunne, in the kingdome of their father. Who hath eares to heare, let
him heare.44Againe, the kingdome of heauen is like vnto treaſure hid in
a field: the which when a man hath found, hee hideth, and for ioy
thereof goeth and ſelleth all that hee hath, and buyeth that
field.45Againe, the kingdome of heauen is like vnto a marchant man,
ſeeking goodly pearles:46Who when hee had found one pearle of great
price, he went and ſolde all that he had, and bought it.47Againe, the
kingdome of heauen is like vnto a net that was caſt into the ſea, and
gathered of euery kind,48Which, when it was full, they drew to ſhore,
and ſate downe, and gathered the good into veſſels, but caſt the bad
away.49So ſhall it be at the ende of the world: the Angels ſhal come
forth, and ſeuer the wicked from among the iuſt,50And ſhal caſt them
into the furnace of fire: there ſhall be wailing, and gnaſhing of
teeth.51Ieſus ſaith vnto them, Haue ye vnderſtood all theſe things? They
ſay vnto him, Yea, Lord.52Then ſaid he vnto them, Therefore euery
Scribe which is inſtructed vnto the kingdom of heauen, is like vnto a
man that is an houſholder, which bringeth foorth out of his treaſure
things new and old.53And it came to paſſe, that when Ieſus had finiſhed
theſe parables, hee departed thence.54And when hee was come into his
owne countrey, he taught them in their Synagogue, inſomuch that they
were aſtoniſhed, and ſaid, Whence hath this man this wiſedome, and
theſe mighty works?55Is not this the Carpenters ſonne? Is not his
mother called Marie? and his brethren, Iames, and Ioſes, and Simon, and
Iudas?56And his ſiſters, are they not all with vs? whence then hath this
man all theſe things?57And they were offended in him. But Ieſus ſaid
vnto them, A Prophet is not without honour, ſaue in his owne countrey,
and in his owne houſe.58And hee did not many mighty workes there,
becauſe of their vnbeliefe.

CHAPTER 141At that time Herod the Tetrarch heard of the fame of
Ieſus,2And ſaid vnto his ſeruants, This is Iohn the Baptiſt, hee is riſen
from the dead, and therfore mighty workes doe ſhew foorth themſelues
in him.3For Herode had layd hold on Iohn, and bound him, and put him
in priſon for Herodias ſake, his brother Philips wife.4For Iohn ſaid vnto
him, It is not lawfull for thee to haue her.5And when he would haue put
him to death, hee feared the multitude, becauſe they counted him as a
Prophet.6But when Herods birth day was kept, the daughter of
Herodias daunced before them, and pleaſed Herode.7Whereupon he
promiſed with an oath, to giue her whatſoeuer ſhe would aſke.8And ſhe,
being before inſtructed of her mother, ſaid, Giue me heere Iohn Baptiſts
head in a charger.9And the king was ſorie: neuertheleſſe for the othes
ſake, and them which ſate with him at meate, he commanded it to be
giuen her:10And he ſent, and beheaded Iohn in the priſon.11And his
head was brought in a charger, and giuen to the Damſell: and ſhe
brought it to her mother.12And his Diſciples came, and took vp the
body, and buried it, and went and told Ieſus.13When Ieſus heard of it,
he departed thence by ſhip, into a deſert place apart: and when the
people had heard thereof, they followed him on foote, out of the
cities.14And Ieſus went forth, and ſaw a great multitude, and was
mooued with compaſſion toward them, and he healed their ſicke.15And
when it was euening, his Diſciples came to him, ſaying, This is a deſert
place, and the time is now paſt; ſend the multitude away, that they may
goe into the villages, and buy themſelues victuals.16But Ieſus ſaid vnto
them, They neede not depart; giue yee them to eate.17And they ſay vnto
him, We haue heere but fiue loaues, and two fiſhes.18He ſaid, Bring
them hither to me.19And hee commanded the multitude to ſit downe

on the graſſe, & tooke the fiue loaues, and the two fiſhes, and looking vp to heauen, hee bleſſed, and brake, and gaue the loaues to his Diſciples, and the Diſciples to the multitude.[20]And they did all eat, & were filled: and they tooke vp of the fragments that remained twelue baſkets full.[21]And they that had eaten, were about fiue thouſand men, beſide women and children.[22]And ſtraightway Ieſus conſtrained his Diſciples to get into a ſhip, and to goe before him vnto the other ſide, while he ſent the multitudes away.[23]And when he had ſent the multitudes away, he went vp into a mountaine apart to pray: and when the euening was come, he was there alone:[24]But the ſhip was now in the midſt of the ſea, toſsed with waues: for the wind was contrary.[25]And in the fourth watch of the night, Ieſus went vnto them, walking on the ſea.[26]And when the Diſciples ſaw him walking on the ſea, they were troubled, ſaying, It is a ſpirit: and they cried out for feare.[27]But ſtraightway Ieſus ſpake vnto them, ſaying, Be of good cheere: it is I, be not afraid.[28]And Peter anſwered him, and ſaid, Lord, if it be thou, bid me come vnto thee on the water.[29]And he ſaid, Come. And when Peter was come downe out of the ſhip, he walked on the water, to go to Ieſus.[30]But when he ſaw the wind boyſterous, he was afraid: and beginning to ſinke, he cried, ſaying, Lord ſaue me.[31]And immediately Ieſus ſtretched foorth his hand, and caught him, and ſaid vnto him, O thou of little faith, wherefore didſt thou doubt?[32]And when they were come into the ſhip, the wind ceaſed.[33]Then they that were in the ſhip, came and worſhipped him, ſaying, Of a trueth thou art the ſonne of God.[34]And when they were gone ouer, they came into þͤ land of Geneſaret.[35]And when the men of that place had knowledge of him, they ſent out into all that countrey round about, and brought vnto him al that were diſeaſed,[36]And beſought him, that they might onely touch the hemme of his garment; and as many as touched, were made perfectly whole.

CHAPTER 15[1]Then came to Ieſus Scribes and PhAriſees, which were of Hieruſalem, ſaying,[2]Why do thy diſciples tranſgreſse the tradition of the Elders? for they waſh not their handes when they eat bread.[3]But hee anſwered, and ſaid vnto them, Why doe you alſo tranſgreſse the Commandement of God by your tradition?[4]For God commaunded, ſaying, Honour thy father and mother: And hee that curſeth father or mother, let him die the death.[5]But yee ſay, Whoſoeuer ſhall ſay to his father or his mother, It is a gift by whatſoeuer thou mighteſt bee profited by me,[6]And honour not his father or his mother, hee ſhall be free. Thus haue yee made the Commaundement of God of none effect by your tradition.[7]Yee hypocrites, well did Eſaias prophecie of you, ſaying,[8]This people draweth nigh vnto mee with their mouth, and honoureth mee with their lips: but their heart is farre from me.[9]But in vaine they do worſhip me, teaching for doctrines, the commandements of men.[10]And he called the multitude, and ſaid vnto them, Heare and vnderſtand.[11]Not that which goeth into the mouth defileth a man: but that which commeth out of the mouth, this defileth a man.[12]Then came his diſciples, and ſaid vnto him, Knoweſt thou that the PhAriſees were offended after they heard this ſaying?[13]But he anſwered and ſaid, Euery plant which my heauenly father hath not planted, ſhalbe rooted vp.[14]Let them alone: they be blinde leaders of the blinde. And if the blinde lead the blinde, both ſhall fall into the ditch.[15]Then anſwered Peter, and ſaid vnto him, Declare vnto vs this parable.[16]And Ieſus ſaid, Are yee alſo yet without vnderſtanding?[17]Doe not yee yet vnderſtand, that whatſoeuer entreth in at the mouth, goeth into the belly, and is caſt out into the draught?[18]But thoſe things which proceed out of the mouth, come forth from the heart, and they defile the man.[19]For out of the heart proceed euill thoughts, murders, adulteries, fornications, thefts, falſe witnes, blaſphemies.[20]Theſe are the things which defile a man: But to eate with vnwaſhen hands, defileth not a man.[21]Then Ieſus went thence, and departed into the coaſtes of Tyre and Sidon.[22]And behold, a woman of Canaan came out of the ſame coaſts, & cried vnto him, ſaying, Haue mercy on me, O Lord, thou ſonne of Dauid, my daughter is grieuouſly vexed with a deuill.[23]But he anſwered her not a word. And his diſciples came, and beſought him, ſaying, Send her away, for ſhe cryeth after vs.[24]But he anſwered, and ſaid, I am not ſent, but vnto the loſt ſheepe of the houſe of Iſrael.[25]Then came ſhe, and worſhipped him, ſaying, Lord, helpe me.[26]But he anſwered, and ſaid, It is not meete to take the childrens bread, and to caſt it to dogs.[27]And ſhe ſaid, Trueth Lord: yet the dogs eat of the crummes which fall from their maſters table.[28]Then Ieſus anſwered, and ſaid vnto her, O woman, great is thy faith: be it vnto thee euen as thou wilt. And her daughter was made whole from that very houre.[29]And Ieſus departed frō thence, and came nigh vnto the ſea of Galile, and went vp into a mountaine, and ſate downe there.[30]And great multitudes came vnto him, hauing with them thoſe that were lame, blinde, dumbe, maimed, and many others, and caſt them downe at Ieſus feet, and he healed them:[31]Inſomuch that the multitude wondred, when they ſaw the dumbe to ſpeake, the maimed to be whole, the lame to walke, and the blind to ſee: and they glorified the God of Iſrael.[32]Then Ieſus called his diſciples vnto him, and ſaid, I haue compaſſion on the multitude, becauſe they continue with me now three dayes, and haue nothing to eate: and I will not ſend them away faſting, leſt they faint in the way.[33]And his diſciples ſay vnto him, Whence ſhould we haue ſo much bread in the wilderneſſe, as to fill ſo great a multitude?[34]And Ieſus ſaith vnto them, How many loaues haue yee? And they ſaid, Seuen, and a few little fiſhes.[35]And hee commaunded the multitude to ſit downe on the ground.[36]And he tooke the ſeuen loaues and the fiſhes, and gaue thankes, and brake them, and gaue to his diſciples, and the diſciples to the multitude.[37]And they did all eate, and were filled: and they tooke vp of the broken meate that was left, ſeuen baſkets full.[38]And they that did eat, were foure thouſand men, beſide women and children.[39]And he ſent away the multitude, and tooke ſhip, and came into the coaſts of Magdala.

CHAPTER 16[1]The PhAriſes alſo, with the Sadduces, came, and tempting, deſired him that hee would ſhew them a ſigne from heauen.[2]He anſwered, and ſaid vnto them, When it is euening, yee ſay, It will bee faire weather: for the ſkie is red.[3]And in the morning, It will be foule weather to day: for the ſkie is red and lowring. O ye hypocrites, yee can diſcerne the face of the ſkie, but can ye not diſcerne the ſignes of the times?[4]A wicked and adulterous generation ſeeketh after a ſigne, and there ſhall no ſigne be giuen vnto it, but the ſigne of the Prophet Ionas. And hee left them, and departed.[5]And when his diſciples were come to the other ſide, they had forgotten to take bread.[6]Then Ieſus ſaid vnto them, Take heed and beware of the leauen of the PhAriſes, and of the Sadduces.[7]And they reaſoned among themſelues, ſaying, It is becauſe we haue taken no bread.[8]Which when Ieſus perceiued, he ſaid vnto them, O ye of little faith, why reaſon ye among your ſelues, becauſe ye haue brought no bread?[9]Doe ye not yet vnderſtand, neither remember the fiue loaues of the fiue thouſand, and how many baſkets ye tooke vp?[10]Neither the ſeuen loaues of the foure thouſand, and how many baſkets ye tooke vp?[11]How is it that ye doe not vnderſtand, that I ſpake it not to you concerning bread, that ye ſhould beware of the leauen of the PhAriſes, and of the Sadduces?[12]Then vnderſtood they how that he bade them not beware of the leauen of bread: but of the doctrine of the PhAriſees, and of the Sadduces.[13]When Ieſus came into the coaſts of Ceſarea Philippi, he aſked his diſciples, ſaying, Whom doe men ſay, that I, the ſonne of man, am?[14]And they ſaid, Some ſay that thou art Iohn the Baptiſt, ſome Elias, and others Ieremias, or one of þͤ Prophets.[15]He ſaith vnto them, But whom ſay ye that I am?[16]And Simon Peter anſwered, and ſaid, Thou art Chriſt the ſonne of the liuing God.[17]And Ieſus anſwered, and ſaid vnto him, Bleſſed art thou Simon Bar Iona: for fleſh and blood hath not reueiled it vnto thee, but my Father which is in heauen.[18]And I ſay alſo vnto thee, that thou art Peter, and vpon this rocke I will build my Church: and the gates of hell ſhall not preuaile againſt it.[19]And I will giue vnto thee the keyes of the kingdome of heauen: and whatſoeuer thou ſhalt bind on earth, ſhall be bound in heauen: whatſoeuer thou ſhalt looſe on earth, ſhall be looſed in heauen.[20]Then charged hee his diſciples that they ſhould tel no man that he was Ieſus the Chriſt.[21]From that time foorth began Ieſus to ſhew vnto his diſciples, how that he muſt goe vnto Hieruſalem, and ſuffer many things of the Elders and chiefe Prieſts & Scribes, and be killed, and be raiſed againe the third day.[22]Then Peter tooke him, and began to rebuke him, ſaying, Be it farre from thee Lord: This ſhal not be vnto thee.[23]But he turned, and ſaid vnto Peter, Get thee behind mee, Satan, thou art an offence vnto me: for thou ſauoureſt not the things that be of God, but thoſe that be of men.[24]Then ſaid Ieſus vnto his diſciples, If any man will come after me, let him denie himſelfe, and take vp his croſse, and follow me.[25]For whoſoeuer will ſaue his life, ſhall loſe it: and whoſoeuer will loſe his his life for my ſake, ſhall finde it.[26]For what is a man profited, if hee ſhal gaine the whole world, and loſe his owne ſoule?

Or what ſhall a man giue in exchange for his ſoule?27For the ſonne of man ſhall come in the glory of his father, with his Angels: and then he ſhall reward euery man according to his works.28Uerely I ſay vnto you, There be ſome ſtanding here, which ſhall not taſte of death, till they ſee the Sonne of man comming in his Kingdome.

CHAPTER 171And after ſixe dayes, Ieſus taketh Peter, Iames, and Iohn his brother, and bringeth them vp into an high mountaine apart,2And was tranſfigured before them, and his face did ſhine as the Sunne, and his raiment was white as the light.3And behold, there appeared vnto them Moſes, and Elias, talking with him.4Then anſwered Peter, and ſaide vnto Ieſus, Lord, it is good for vs to be here: If thou wilt, let vs make here three tabernacles: one for thee, and one for Moſes, and one for Elias.5While he yet ſpake, behold, a bright cloud ouerſhadowed them: and behold a voyce out of the cloude, which ſaide, This is my beloued ſonne, in whom I am well pleaſed: heare ye him.6And when the diſciples heard it, they fell on their face, and were ſore afraid.7And Ieſus came and touched them, and ſaid, Ariſe, and be not afraid.8And when they had lift vp their eyes, they ſaw no man, ſaue Ieſus only.9And as they came downe from the mountaine, Ieſus charged them, ſaying, Tell the viſion to no man, vntil the ſonne of man bee riſen againe from the dead.10And his diſciples aſked him, ſaying, Why then ſay the Scribes that Elias muſt firſt come?11And Ieſus anſwered, and ſaid vnto them, Elias truely ſhall firſt come, and reſtore all things:12But I ſay vnto you, that Elias is come already, and they knew him not, but haue done vnto him whatſoeuer they liſted: Likewiſe ſhall alſo the Son of man ſuffer of them.13Then the Diſciples vnderſtood that he ſpake vnto them of Iohn the Baptiſt.14And when they were come to the multitude, there came to him a certaine man, kneeling downe to him, and ſaying,15Lord, haue mercie on my ſonne, for he is lunatike, and ſore vexed: for oft times he falleth into the fire, and oft into the water.16And I brought him to thy diſciples, and they could not cure him.17Then Ieſus anſwered, and ſaid, O faithleſſe and peruerſe generation, how long ſhall I bee with you? howe long ſhal I ſuffer you? bring him hither to me.18And Ieſus rebuked the deuill, and hee departed out of him: and the childe was cured from that very houre.19Then came the Diſciples to Ieſus apart, and ſaid, Why could not we caſt him out?20And Ieſus ſaid vnto them, Becauſe of your vnbeliefe: for verily I ſay vnto you, If yee haue faith as a graine of muſtard ſeed, yee ſhall ſay vnto this mountaine; Remoue hence to yonder place: and it ſhall remoue, and nothing ſhall be vnpoſſible vnto you.21Howbeit, this kind goeth not out, but by prayer and faſting.22And while they abode in Galilee, Ieſus ſaid vnto them, The ſonne of man ſhall be betraied into the hands of men:23And they ſhall kill him, and the third day he ſhall be raiſed againe: And they were exceeding ſorie.24And when they were come to Capernaum, they that receiued tribute money, came to Peter, and ſaid, Doeth not your maſter pay tribute?25Hee ſaith, Yes. And when hee was come into the houſe, Ieſus preuented him, ſaying, What thinkeſt thou, Simon? of whom doe the kings of the earth take cuſtome or tribute? of their owne children, or of ſtrangers?26Peter ſaith vnto him, Of ſtrangers. Ieſus ſaith vnto him, Then are the children free.27Notwithſtanding, leaſt we ſhould offend them, goe thou to the ſea, and caſt an hooke, and take vp the fiſh that firſt commeth vp: and when thou haſt opened his mouth, thou ſhalt find a piece of money: that take, and giue vnto them for me, and thee.

CHAPTER 181At the ſame time came the Diſciples vnto Ieſus, ſaying, Who is the greateſt in the Kingdome of heauen?2And Ieſus called a little child vnto him, and ſet him in the midſt of them,3And ſaid, Uerily I ſay vnto you, Except yee be conuerted, and become as little children, yee ſhall not enter into the kingdome of heauen.4Whoſoeuer therefore ſhall humble himſelfe as this little childe, the ſame is greateſt in the Kingdome of heauen.5And who ſo ſhall receiue one ſuch little child in my name, receiueth me.6But who ſo ſhall offend one of theſe little ones which beleeue in me, it were better for him that a milſtone were hanged about his necke, and that hee were drowned in the depth of the ſea.7Woe vnto the world becauſe of offences: for it muſt needs be that offences come: but wo to that man by whom the offence commeth.8Wherefore if thy hand or thy foote offend thee, cut them off, and caſt them from thee: it is better for thee to enter into life halt or maimed, rather then hauing two hands or two feete, to be caſt into euerlaſting fire.9And if thine eie offend thee, plucke it out, and caſt it from thee: it is better for thee to enter into life with one eie, rather then hauing two eies, to be caſt into hell fire.10Take heed that yee deſpiſe not one of theſe little ones: for I ſay vnto you, that in heauen their Angels do alwaies behold the face of my father which is in heauen.11For the ſonne of man is come to ſaue that which was loſt.12How thinke yee? if a man haue an hundred ſheepe, and one of them be gone aſtray, doth he not leaue the ninetie and nine, and goeth into the mountaines, and ſeeketh that which is gone aſtray?13And if ſo be that he find it, Uerily I ſay vnto you, hee reioyceth more of that ſheepe, then of the ninetie and nine which went not aſtray.14Euen ſo, it is not the will of your father which is in heauen, that one of theſe little ones ſhould periſh.15Moreouer, if thy brother ſhall treſpaſſe againſt thee, goe and tell him his fault betweene thee and him alone: if he ſhall heare thee, thou haſt gained thy brother.16But if he will not heare thee, then take with thee one or two more, that in the mouth of two or three witneſſes, euery word may be eſtabliſhed.17And if hee ſhall neglect to heare them, tell it vnto the Church: But if he neglect to heare the Church, let him be vnto thee as an heathen man, and a Publicane.18Uerily I ſay vnto you, Whatſoeuer ye ſhall binde on earth, ſhall bee bound in heauen: and whatſoeuer yee ſhall looſe on earth, ſhall bee looſed in heauen.19Againe I ſay vnto you, that if two of you ſhall agree on earth as touching any thing that they ſhall aſke, it ſhall bee done for them of my father which is in heauen.20For where two or three are gathered together in my Name, there am I in the midſt of them.21Then came Peter to him, and ſaid, Lord, how oft ſhall my brother ſinne againſt mee, and I forgiue him? till ſeuen times?22Ieſus ſaith vnto him, I ſay not vnto thee, Untill ſeuen times: but, Untill ſeuentie times ſeuen.23Therefore is the kingdome of heauen likened vnto a certaine king, which would take accompt of his ſeruants.24And when hee had begun to reckon, one was brought vnto him which ought him ten thouſand talents.25But foraſmuch as hee had not to pay, his lord commanded him to bee ſold, and his wife, and children, and all that he had, and payment to be made.26The ſeruant therfore fell downe, and worſhipped him, ſaying, Lord, haue patience with mee, and I will pay thee all.27Then the Lord of that ſeruant was moued with compaſſion, and looſed him, and forgaue him the debt.28But the ſame ſeruant went out, and found one of his fellow-ſeruants, which ought him an hundred pence: and hee layd handes on him, and tooke him by the throte, ſaying, Pay mee that thou oweſt.29And his fellow ſeruant fell downe at his feete, and beſought him, ſaying, Haue patience with me, and I will pay thee all.30And he would not: but went and caſt him into priſon, till hee ſhould pay the debt.31So when his fellow-ſeruants ſaw what was done, they were very ſorie, and came, and told vnto their lord all that was done.32Then his lord, after that hee had called him, ſaid vnto him, O thou wicked ſeruant, I forgaue thee all that debt becauſe thou deſiredſt me:33Shouldeſt not thou alſo haue had compaſſion on thy fellow-ſeruant, euen as I had pitie on thee?34And his lord was wroth, and deliuered him to the tormentors, till hee ſhould pay all that was due vnto him.35So likewiſe ſhall my heauenly Father doe alſo vnto you, if yee from your hearts forgiue not euery one his brother their treſpaſſes.

CHAPTER 191And it came to paſſe, that when Ieſus had finiſhed theſe ſayings, he departed from Galilee, and came into the coaſtes of Iudea, beyond Iordane:2And great multitudes followed him, and he healed them there.3The PhAriſees alſo came vnto him, tempting him, and ſaying vnto him, Is it lawfull for a man to put away his wife for euery cauſe?4And hee anſwered, and ſaid vnto them, Haue ye not read, that he which made them at the beginning, made them male and female?5And ſaid, For this cauſe ſhall a man leaue father and mother, and ſhall cleaue to his wife: and they twaine ſhalbe one fleſh.6Wherefore they are no more twaine, but one fleſh. What therefore God hath ioyned together, let not man put aſunder.7They ſay vnto him, Why did Moſes then command to giue a writing of diuorcement, and to put her away?8Hee ſaith vnto them, Moſes, becauſe of the hardneſe of your hearts, ſuffered you to put away your wiues: but from the beginning it was not ſo.9And I ſay vnto you, Whoſoeuer ſhall put away his wife, except it be for fornication, and ſhall marry another, committeth adultery: and whoſo marrieth her which is put away, doth commit adultery.10His diſciples ſay vnto him, If the caſe of the man be ſo with his wife, it is not good to marrie.11But hee ſaid vnto them, All men cannot receiue this ſaying, ſaue they to whom it is giuen.12For there are ſome Eunuches, which were ſo borne from their mothers wombe: and there are ſome Eunuches, which were made Eunuches of men: and

there be Eunuches, which haue made themſelues Eunuches for the
kingdome of heauens ſake. He that is able to receiue it, let him receiue
it.13Then were there brought vnto him little children, that he ſhould put
his hands on them, and pray: and the diſciples rebuked them.14But Ieſus
ſaid, Suffer little children, and forbid them not to come vnto me: for of
ſuch is þe kingdome of heauen.15And he laide his hands on them, and
departed thence.16And behold, one came and ſaid vnto him, Good
maſter, what good thing ſhall I do, that I may haue eternall life?17And
he ſaid vnto him, Why calleſt thou me good? there is none good but
one, that is God: but if thou wilt enter into life, keep the
commandements.18He ſaith vnto him, Which? Ieſus ſaid, Thou ſhalt do
no murder, Thou ſhalt not commit adultery, Thou ſhalt not ſteale, Thou
ſhalt not beare falſe witneſſe,19Honour thy father and thy mother: and,
Thou ſhalt loue thy neighbour as thy ſelfe.20The young man ſaith vnto
him, All theſe things haue I kept from my youth vp: what lacke I
yet?21Ieſus ſaid vnto him, If thou wilt be perfect, goe and ſell that thou
haſt, and giue to the poore, and thou ſhalt haue treaſure in heauen: and
come and follow me.22But when the young man heard that ſaying, he
went away ſorrowfull: for he had great poſſeſſions.23Then ſaid Ieſus
vnto his diſciples, Uerely I ſay vnto you, that a rich man ſhall hardly
enter into the kingdome of heauen.24And againe I ſay vnto you, It is
eaſier for a camel to goe thorow the eye of a needle, then for a rich man
to enter into the kingdome of God.25When his diſciples heard it, they
were exceedingly amazed, ſaying, Who then can be ſaued?26But Ieſus
beheld them, and ſaid vnto them, With men this is vnpoſſible, but with
God al things are poſſible.27Then anſwered Peter, and ſaid vnto him,
Behold, we haue forſaken all, and followed thee, what ſhall we haue
therefore?28And Ieſus ſaid vnto them, Uerily I ſay vnto you, that ye
which haue followed me, in the regeneration when the Sonne of man
ſhal ſit in the throne of his glory, ye alſo ſhal ſit vpon twelue thrones,
iudging the twelue tribes of Iſrael.29And euery one that hath forſaken
houſes, or brethren, or ſiſters, or father, or mother, or wife, or children,
or lands, for my Names ſake, ſhall receiue an hundred fold, and ſhall
inherite euerlaſting life.30But many that are firſt, ſhall be laſt, and the laſt
ſhall be firſt.
CHAPTER 20 1For the kingdome of heauen is like vnto a man that is
an houſholder, which went out early in the morning to hire labourers
into his vineyard.2And when hee had agreed with the labourers for a
peny a day, he ſent them into his vineyard.3And he went out about the
third houre, and ſaw others ſtanding idle in the market place,4And ſaid
vnto them, Go ye alſo into the vineyard, & whatſoeuer is right, I wil giue
you. And they went their way.5Againe he went out about the ſixth and
ninth houre, and did likewiſe.6And about the eleuenth houre, he went
out, and found others ſtanding idle, and ſaith vnto them, Why ſtand ye
here all the day idle?7They ſay vnto him, Becauſe no man hath hired vs.
He ſaith vnto them, Go ye alſo into the vineyard: and whatſoeuer is
right, that ſhall ye receiue.8So when euen was come, the lord of the
vineyard ſaith vnto his Steward, Call the labourers, and giue them their
hire, beginning from the laſt, vnto the firſt.9And when they came that
were hired about the eleuenth houre, they receiued euery man a
penie.10But when the firſt came, they ſuppoſed that they ſhould haue
receiued more, and they likewiſe receiued euery man a penie.11And when
they had receiued it, they murmured againſt the good man of the
houſe,12Saying, Theſe laſt haue wrought but one houre, and thou haſt
made them equall vnto vs, which haue borne the burden, and heat of
the day.13But he anſwered one of them and ſaid, Friend, I do thee no
wrong: didſt not thou agree with me for a penie?14Take that thine is,
and goe thy way, I will giue vnto this laſt, euen as vnto thee.15Is it not
lawfull for mee to doe what I wil with mine owne? Is thine eye euill,
becauſe I am good?16So the laſt ſhall be firſt, and the firſt laſt: for many
bee called, but fewe choſen.17And Ieſus going vp to Hieruſalem, tooke
the twelue diſciples apart in the way, and ſaid vnto them,18Behold, we
goe vp to Hieruſalem, and the Sonne of man ſhall be betraied vnto the
chiefe Prieſts, and vnto the Scribes, and they ſhall condemne him to
death,19And ſhal deliuer him to the Gentiles to mocke, and to ſcourge,
and to crucifie him: and the third day he ſhall riſe againe.20Then came
to him the mother of Zebedees children, with her ſonnes, worſhipping
him, and deſiring a certain thing of him.21And he ſaid vnto her, What
wilt thou? She ſaith vnto him, Grant, that theſe my two ſonnes may ſit,
the one on thy right hand, and the other on the left in thy
kingdome.22But Ieſus anſwered, and ſaid, Ye know not what ye aſke.
Are ye able to drinke of the cup that I ſhall drinke of, and to be baptized
with the baptiſme that I am baptized with? They ſay vnto him, We are
able.23And he ſaith vnto them, Yee ſhall drinke indeed of my cup, and
be baptized with the baptiſme that I am baptized with: but to ſit on my
right hand, and on my left, is not mine to giue, but it ſhall be giuen to
them for whom it is prepared of my father.24And when the ten heard it,
they were moued with indignation againſt the two brethren.25But Ieſus
called them vnto him, and ſaid, Ye know that the princes of the Gentiles
exerciſe dominion ouer them, and they that are great, exerciſe authoritie
vpon them.26But it ſhall not be ſo among you: But whoſoeuer will bee
great among you, let him be your miniſter.27And whoſoeuer will be
chiefe among you, let him be your ſeruant.28Euen as the Sonne of man
came not to be miniſtred vnto, but miniſter, and to giue his life a
ranſome for many.29And as they departed from Hiericho, a great
multitude followed him.30And behold, two blind men ſitting by the way
ſide, when they heard that Ieſus paſſed by, cried out, ſaying, Haue mercie
on vs, O Lord, thou ſonne of Dauid.31And the multitude rebuked them,
becauſe they ſhould holde their peace: but they cried the more, ſaying,
Haue mercie on vs, O Lord, thou ſonne of Dauid.32And Ieſus ſtood ſtill,
and called them, and ſaide, What will yee that I ſhall doe vnto
you?33They ſay vnto him, Lord, that our eyes may be opened.34So Ieſus
had compaſſion on them, and touched their eyes: and immediatly their
eyes receiued ſight, and they followed him.
CHAPTER 21 1And when they drewe nigh vnto Hieruſalem, and were
come to Bethphage, vnto the mount of Oliues, then ſent Ieſus two
Diſciples,2Saying vnto them, Goe into the village ouer againſt you, and
ſtraightway yee ſhall find an Aſſe tied, and a colt with her: looſe them,
and bring them vnto me.3And if any man ſay ought vnto you, yee ſhall
ſay, The Lord hath need of them, and ſtraightway hee will ſend
them.4All this was done, that it might be fulfilled which was ſpoken by
the Prophet, ſaying,5Tell yee the daughter of Sion, Behold, thy king
commeth vnto thee, meeke, and ſitting vpon an Aſſe, and a colt, the
foale of an Aſſe.6And the Diſciples went, and did as Ieſus commanded
them,7And brought the Aſſe, and the colt, and put on them their
clothes, and they ſet him thereon.8And a very great multitude ſpread
their garments in the way, others cut downe branches from the trees,
and ſtrawed them in the way.9And the multitudes that went before, and
that followed, cried, ſaying, Hoſanna to the ſonne of Dauid: Bleſſed is
he that commeth in the Name of the Lord, Hoſanna in the
higheſt.10And when hee was come into Hieruſalem, all the citie was
mooued, ſaying, Who is this?11And the multitude ſaid, This is Ieſus the
Prophet of Nazareth of Galilee.12And Ieſus went into the temple of
God, and caſt out all them that ſold and bought in the Temple, and
ouerthrew the tables of the money changers, and the ſeats of them that
ſolde doues,13And ſaid vnto them, It is written, My houſe ſhall be called
the houſe of prayer, but yee haue made it a denne of theeues.14And the
blind and the lame came to him in the Temple, & he healed them.15And
when the chiefe Prieſts and Scribes ſaw the wonderfull things that he
did, & the children crying in the temple, & ſaying, Hoſanna to the ſonne
of Dauid, they were ſore diſpleaſed,16And ſaid vnto him, Heareſt thou
what theſe ſay? And Ieſus ſaith vnto them, Yea, haue yee neuer read,
Out of the mouth of babes and ſucklings thou haſt perfected
praiſe?17And he left them, and went out of the citie into Bethany, and
he lodged there.18Now in the morning, as hee returned into the citie, he
hungred.19And when he ſaw a figge tree in the way, hee came to it, and
found nothing thereon but leaues only, and ſaid vnto it, Let no fruite
growe on thee hence forward for euer. And preſently the figge tree
withered away.20And when the Diſciples ſaw it, they marueiled, ſaying,
How ſoone is the figge tree withered away?21Ieſus anſwered, and ſaid
vnto them, Uerily I ſay vnto you, if yee haue faith, and doubt not, yee
ſhall not onely doe this which is done to the figge tree, but alſo, if ye
ſhall ſay vnto this mountaine, Be thou remoued, and be thou caſt into
the ſea, it ſhall be done.22And all things whatſoeuer yee ſhall aſke in
prayer, beleeuing, ye ſhall receiue.23And when he was come into the
temple, the chiefe Prieſts and the Elders of the people came vnto him
as he was teaching, and ſaid, By what authoritie doeſt thou theſe things?
and who gaue thee this authoritie?24And Ieſus anſwered, and ſaid vnto
them, I alſo will aſke you one thing, which if ye tell me, I in like wiſe will

tell you by what authoritie I doe theſe things.[25]The baptiſme of Iohn, whence was it? from heauen, or of men? and they reaſoned with themſelues ſaying, If we ſhall ſay, From heauen, hee will ſay vnto vs, Why did ye not then beleeue him?[26]But if we ſhall ſay, Of men, we feare the people, for all hold Iohn as a Prophet.[27]And they anſwered Ieſus, and ſaid, We cannot tell. And he ſaid vnto them, Neither tell I you by what authoritie I doe theſe things.[28]But what thinke you? A certaine man had two ſonnes, and he came to the firſt, and ſaid, Sonne, goe worke to day in my vineyard.[29]He anſwered, & ſaid, I will not: but afterward he repented, and went.[30]And hee came to the ſecond, and ſaid likewiſe: and hee anſwered, and ſaid, I goe ſir, and went not.[31]Whether of them twaine did the will of his father? They ſay vnto him, The firſt. Ieſus ſaith vnto them, Uerely I ſay vnto you, that the Publicanes and the harlots go into the kingdome of God before you.[32]For Iohn came vnto you in the way of righteouſneſſe, and ye beleeued him not: but the Publicanes and the harlots beleeued him. And ye when ye had ſeene it, repented not afterward, that ye might beleeue him.[33]Heare another parable. There was a certaine houſe-holder, which planted a Uineyard, and hedged it round about, and digged a wine-preſse in it, and built a tower, and let it out to huſbandmen, and went into a farre countrey.[34]And when the time of the fruite drew neere, he ſent his ſeruants to the huſbandmen, that they might receiue the fruits of it.[35]And the huſbandmen tooke his ſeruants, and beat one, and killed another, and ſtoned another.[36]Againe hee ſent other ſeruants, moe then the firſt, and they did vnto them likewiſe.[37]But laſt of all, he ſent vnto them his ſonne, ſaying, They will reuerence my ſonne.[38]But when the huſbandmen ſaw the ſonne, they ſaid among themſelues, This is the heire, come, let vs kill him, and let vs ſeaſe on his inheritance.[39]And they caught him, and caſt him out of the Uineyard, and ſlew him.[40]When the Lord therefore of the Uineyard commeth, what will he doe vnto thoſe huſbandmen?[41]They ſay vnto him, He will miſerably deſtroy thoſe wicked men, and will let out his Uineyard vnto other huſbandmen, which ſhall render him the fruits in their ſeaſons.[42]Ieſus ſaith vnto them, Did ye neuer reade in the Scriptures, The ſtone which the builders reiected, the ſame is become the head of the corner? This is the Lords doing, and it is marueilous in our eyes.[43]Therefore ſay I vnto you, the kingdome of God ſhall be taken from you, and giuen to a nation bringing forth the fruits thereof.[44]And whoſoeuer ſhall fall on this ſtone, ſhalbe broken: but on whom ſoeuer it ſhall fall, it will grinde him to powder.[45]And when the chiefe Prieſts and PhAriſees had heard his parables, they perceiued that he ſpake of them.[46]But when they ſought to lay hands on him, they feared the multitude, becauſe they tooke him for a Prophet.

CHAPTER 22[1]And Ieſus anſwered, and ſpake vnto them againe by parables, and ſaid,[2]The Kingdome of heauen is like vnto a certaine King, which made a marriage for his ſonne,[3]And ſent forth his ſeruants to call them that were bidden to the wedding, and they would not come.[4]Againe, hee ſent foorth other ſeruants, ſaying, Tell them which are bidden, Beholde, I haue prepared my dinner; my oxen, and my fatlings are killed, and all things are ready: come vnto the marriage.[5]But they made light of it, and went their wayes, one to his farme, another to his merchandize:[6]And the remnant tooke his ſeruants, and intreated them ſpitefully, and ſlew them.[7]But when the king heard thereof, he was wroth, and hee ſent foorth his armies, and deſtroyed thoſe murderers, and burnt vp their citie.[8]Then ſaith hee to his ſeruants, The wedding is ready, but they which were bidden, were not worthy.[9]Goe yee therefore into the high wayes, and as many as yee ſhall finde, bid to the marriage.[10]So thoſe ſeruants went out into the high wayes, and gathered together all as many as they found, both bad and good, and the wedding was furniſhed with gheſts.[11]And when the King came in to ſee the gueſts, hee ſawe there a man, which had not on a wedding garment,[12]And hee ſayth vnto him, Friend, how cameſt thou in hither, not hauing a wedding garment? And hee was ſpeechleſſe.[13]Then ſaid the king to the ſeruants, Binde him hand and foot, and take him away, and caſt him into outer darkeneſſe, there ſhall be weeping and gnaſhing of teeth.[14]For many are called, but few are choſen.[15]Then went the PhAriſes, and tooke counſell, how they might intangle him in his talke.[16]And they ſent out vnto him their diſciples, with the Herodians, ſaying, Maſter, wee know that thou art true, and teacheſt the way of God in trueth, neither careſt thou for any man; for thou regardeſt not the perſon of men.[17]Tell vs therefore, what thinkeſt thou? Is it lawfull to giue tribute vnto Ceſar, or not?[18]But Ieſus perceiued their wickedneſſe, and ſaid, Why tempt ye me, ye hypocrites?[19]ſhew me the tribute money. And they brought vnto him a peny.[20]And he ſayth vnto them, Whoſe is this image and ſuperſcription?[21]They ſay vnto him, Ceſars. Then ſayth he vnto them, Render therefore vnto Ceſar, the things which are Ceſars: and vnto God, the things that are Gods.[22]When they had heard theſe wordes, they marueiled, and left him, and went their way.[23]The ſame day came to him the Sadduces, which ſay that there is no reſurrection, and aſked him,[24]Saying, Maſter, Moſes ſaid, If a man die, hauing no children, his brother ſhall marrie his wife, and raiſe vp ſeed vnto his brother.[25]Now there were with vs ſeuen brethren, and the firſt when he had maried a wife, deceaſed, and hauing no iſsue, left his wife vnto his brother.[26]Likewiſe the ſecond alſo, and the third, vnto the ſeuenth.[27]And laſt of al the woman died alſo.[28]Therefore, in the reſurrection, whoſe wife ſhall ſhe be of the ſeuen? for they all had her.[29]Ieſus anſwered, and ſaid vnto them, Yee doe erre, not knowing the Scriptures, nor the power of God.[30]For in the reſurrection they neither marry, nor are giuen in marriage, but are as the Angels of God in heauen.[31]But as touching the reſurrection of the dead, haue ye not read that which was ſpoken vnto you by God, ſaying,[32]I am the God of Abraham, and the God of Iſaac, and the God of Iacob? God is not the God of the dead, but of the liuing.[33]And when the multitude heard this, they were aſtoniſhed at his doctrine.[34]But when the PhAriſes had heard that he had put the Sadduces to ſilence, they were gathered together.[35]Then one of them, which was a Lawyer, aſked him a queſtion, tempting him, and ſaying,[36]Maſter, which is the great Commandement in the Law?[37]Ieſus ſayd vnto him, Thou ſhalt loue the Lord thy God with all thy heart, and with all thy ſoule, and with all thy minde.[38]This is the firſt and great Commandement.[39]And the ſecond is like vnto it, Thou ſhalt loue thy neighbour as thy ſelfe.[40]On theſe two Commandements hang all the Law and the Prophets.[41]While the PhAriſes were gathered together, Ieſus aſked them,[42]Saying, What thinke yee of Chriſt? whoſe ſonne is hee? They ſay vnto him, The ſonne of Dauid.[43]He ſaith vnto them, How then doth Dauid in ſpirit call him Lord, ſaying,[44]The Lord ſaid vnto my Lord, Sit thou on my right hand, till I make thine enemies thy footſtoole?[45]If Dauid then call him Lord, how is he his ſonne?[46]And no man was able to anſwere him a word, neither durſt any man (from that day foorth) aſke him any moe queſtions.

CHAPTER 23[1]Then ſpake Ieſus to the multitude, and to his diſciples,[2]Saying, The Scribes and the PhAriſes ſit in Moſes ſeate:[3]All therefore whatſoeuer they bid you obſerue, that obſerue and doe, but doe not ye after their workes: for they ſay, and doe not.[4]For they binde heauie burdens, and grieuous to be borne, and lay them on mens ſhoulders , but they themſelues will not mooue them with one of their fingers.[5]But all their workes they doe, for to be ſeene of men: they make broad their phylacteries, and enlarge the borders of their garments,[6]And loue the vppermoſt roomes at feaſts, and the chiefe ſeats in the Synagogues,[7]And greetings in the markets, and to be called of men, Rabbi, Rabbi.[8]But be not ye called Rabbi: for one is your Maſter, euen Chriſt, and all ye are brethren.[9]And call no man your father vpon the earth: for one is your father which is in heauen.[10]Neither be ye called maſters: for one is your Maſter, euen Chriſt.[11]But hee that is greateſt among you, ſhall be your ſeruant.[12]And whoſoeuer ſhall exalt himſelfe, ſhall be abaſed: and he that ſhall humble himſelfe, ſhall be exalted.[13]But woe vnto you, Scribes and PhAriſees, hypocrites; for yee ſhut vp the kingdom of heauen againſt men: For yee neither goe in your ſelues, neither ſuffer ye them that are entring, to goe in.[14]Woe vnto you Scribes and PhAriſees, hypocrites; for yee deuoure widowes houſes, and for a pretence make long prayer; therefore ye ſhall receiue the greater damnation.[15]Woe vnto you Scribes and PhAriſes, hypocrites; for yee compaſſe ſea and land to make one Proſelyte, and when hee is made, yee make him two fold more the childe of hell then your ſelues.[16]Woe vnto you, yee blind guides, which ſay, Whoſoeuer ſhall ſweare by the Temple, it is nothing: but whoſoeuer ſhal ſweare by the gold of the Temple, he is a debter.[17]Ye fooles and blind: for whether is greater, the gold, or the Temple that ſanctifieth the gold?[18]And whoſoeuer ſhall ſweare by the Altar, it is nothing: but whoſoeuer ſweareth by the gift that is vpon it, he is guiltie.[19]Ye fooles and blind: for whether is greater, the gift, or the Altar that ſanctifieth the gift?[20]Who ſo therefore ſhall ſweare by the Altar, ſweareth by it, and by all things thereon.[21]And who ſo ſhall ſweare by the Temple, ſweareth by it, and by him that dwelleth therein.[22]And he that ſhall ſweare by heauen, ſweareth by the throne of God, and by him that ſitteth thereon.[23]Woe vnto you Scribes and PhAriſees, hypocrites; for yee pay tithe of mint, and anniſe, and cummine, and haue omitted the weightier matters of the Law, iudgement, mercie and faith: theſe ought ye to haue done, and not to leaue the other vndone.[24]Ye blind guides, which ſtraine at a gnat, and ſwallow a camel.[25]Woe vnto you Scribes and PhAriſees, hypocrites; for yee make cleane the outſide of the cup, and of the platter, but within they are full of extortion and exceſse.[26]Thou blind PhAriſee, cleanſe firſt that which is within the cup and platter, that the outſide of them may bee cleane alſo.[27]Woe vnto you Scribes and PhAriſees, hypocrites, for yee are like vnto whited ſepulchres, which indeed appeare beautifull outward, but are within full of dead mens bones, and of all vncleanneſſe.[28]Euen ſo, yee alſo outwardly appeare righteous vnto men, but within ye are full of hypocriſie and iniquitie.[29]Woe vnto you Scribes and PhAriſees, hypocrites, becauſe ye build the tombes of the Prophets, and garniſh the ſepulchres of the righteous,[30]And ſay, If wee had beene in the dayes of our fathers, wee would not haue bene partakers with them in the blood of the Prophets.[31]Wherefore ye bee witneſſes vnto your ſelues, that yee are the children of them which killed the Prophets.[32]Fil ye vp then the meaſure of your fathers.[33]Yee ſerpents, yee generation of vipers, How can yee eſcape the damnation of hell?[34]Wherefore behold, I ſend vnto you Prophets, and wiſemen, and Scribes, and ſome of them yee ſhall kill and crucifie, and ſome of them ſhall yee ſcourge in your ſynagogues, and perſecute them from citie to citie:[35]That vpon you may come all the righteous blood ſhed vpon the earth, from the blood of righteous Abel, vnto the blood of Zacharias, ſonne of Barachias, whom yee ſlew betweene the temple and the altar.[36]Uerily I ſay vnto you, All theſe things ſhal come vpon this generation.[37]O Hieruſalem, Hieruſalem, thou that killeſt the Prophets, and ſtoneſt them which are ſent vnto thee, how often would I haue gathered thy children together, euen as a hen gathereth her chickens vnder her wings, and yee would not?[38]Behold, your houſe is left vnto you deſolate.[39]For I ſay vnto you, yee ſhall not ſee me henceforth, till ye ſhall ſay, Bleſſed is he that commeth in the Name of the Lord.

CHAPTER 24[1]And Ieſus went out, and departed from the temple, and his Diſciples came to him, for to ſhew him the buildings of the temple.[2]And Ieſus ſaid vnto them, ſee yee not all theſe things? Uerily I ſay vnto you, there ſhall not be left heere one ſtone vpon another, that ſhall not be throwen downe.[3]And as he ſate vpon the mount of Oliues, the Diſciples came vnto him priuately, ſaying, Tell vs, when ſhall theſe things be? And what ſhall be the ſigne of thy coming, and of the end of the world?[4]And Ieſus anſwered, and ſaid vnto them, Take heed that no man deceiue you.[5]For many ſhall come in my name, ſaying, I am Chriſt: and ſhall deceiue many.[6]And yee ſhall heare of warres, and rumors of warres: ſee that yee be not troubled: for all theſe things muſt come to paſſe, but the end is not yet.[7]For nation ſhall riſe againſt nation, and kingdome againſt kingdome, and there ſhall be famines, and peſtilences, and earthquakes in diuers places.[8]All theſe are the beginning of ſorrowes.[9]Then ſhall they deliuer you vp to be afflicted, and ſhall kill you: and yee ſhall bee hated of all nations for my names ſake.[10]And then ſhall many be offended, and ſhall betray one another, and ſhall hate one another.[11]And many falſe Prophets ſhall riſe, and ſhall deceiue many.[12]And becauſe iniquitie ſhal abound, the loue of many ſhall waxe cold.[13]But he that ſhall endure vnto the end, the ſame ſhall be ſaued.[14]And this Goſpell of the kingdome ſhall be preached in all the world, for a witneſſe vnto al nations, and then ſhall the end come.[15]When yee therefore ſhall ſee the abomination of deſolation, ſpoken of by Daniel the Prophet, ſtand in the holy place, (who ſo readeth, let him vnderſtand.)[16]Then let them which be in Iudea, flee into the mountaines.[17]Let him which is on the houſe top, not come downe, to take any thing out of his houſe:[18]Neither let him which is in the field, returne backe to take his clothes.[19]And woe vnto them that are with child, and to them that giue ſucke in thoſe dayes.[20]But pray yee that your flight bee not in the winter, neither on the Sabbath day:[21]For then ſhall be great tribulation, ſuch as was not ſince the beginning of the world to this time, no, nor euer ſhall be.[22]And except thoſe dayes ſhould be ſhortned, there ſhould no fleſh be ſaued: but for the elects ſake, thoſe dayes ſhall be ſhortned.[23]Then if any man ſhall ſay vnto you, Loe, heere is Chriſt, or there: beleeue it not.[24]For there ſhall Ariſe falſe Chriſts, and falſe prophets, and ſhal ſhew great ſignes and wonders: inſomuch that (if it were poſsible,) they ſhall deceiue the very elect.[25]Behold, I haue told you before.[26]Wherefore, if they ſhall ſay vnto you, Behold, he is in the deſert, goe not foorth: Behold, he is in the ſecret chambers, beleeue it not.[27]For as the lightening commeth out of the Eaſt, and ſhineth euen vnto the Weſt: ſo ſhall alſo the coming of the Sonne of man be.[28]For whereſoeuer the carkeiſeis, there will the Eagles bee gathered together.[29]Immediately after the tribulation of thoſe dayes, ſhall the Sunne be darkned, and the Moone ſhall not giue her light, and the ſtarres ſhall fall from heauen, and the powers of the heauens ſhall be ſhaken.[30]And then ſhall appeare the ſigne of the Sonne of man in heauen: and then ſhall all the Tribes of the earth mourne, and they ſhall ſee the Sonne of man coming in the clouds of heauen, with power and great glory.[31]And hee ſhall ſend his Angels with a great ſound of a trumpet, and they ſhall gather together his Elect from the foure windes, from one end of heauen to the other.[32]Now learne a parable of the figtree: when his branch is yet tender, and putteth foorth leaues, yee know that Summer is nigh:[33]So likewiſe yee, when ye ſhall ſee all theſe things, know that it is neere, euen at the doores.[34]Uerely I ſay vnto you, this generation ſhall not paſſe, till all theſe things be fulfilled.[35]Heauen and earth ſhall paſſe away, but my wordes ſhall not paſſe away.[36]But of that day and houre knoweth no man, no, not the Angels of heauen, but my Father onely.[37]But as the dayes of Noe were, ſo ſhall alſo the comming of the Sonne of man be.[38]For as in the dayes that were before the Flood, they were eating, and drinking, marrying, and giuing in mariage, vntill the day that Noe entred into the Arke,[39]And knew not vntill the Flood came, and tooke them all away: ſo ſhall alſo the comming of the Sonne of man be.[40]Then ſhall two be in the field, the one ſhalbe taken, and the other left.[41]Two women ſhall be grinding at the mill: the one ſhall be taken, and the other left.[42]Watch therfore, for ye know not what houre your Lord doth come.[43]But know this, that if the good man of the houſe had knowen in what watch the thiefe would come, he would haue watched, and would not haue ſuffered his houſe to be broken vp.[44]Therefore be yee alſo ready: for in ſuch an houre as you thinke not, the ſonne of man commeth.[45]Who then is a faithfull and wiſe ſeruant, whom his Lord hath made ruler ouer his houſhold, to giue them meat in due ſeaſon?[46]Bleſſed is that ſeruant, whome his Lord when he commeth, ſhall finde ſo doing.[47]Uerely I ſay vnto you, that hee ſhal make him ruler ouer all his goods.[48]But and if that euill ſeruant ſhal ſay in his heart, My Lord delayeth his comming,[49]And ſhall begin to ſmite his fellow ſeruants, and to eate and drinke with the drunken:[50]The Lord of that ſeruant ſhall come in a day when hee looketh not for him, and in an houre that hee is not ware of:[51]And ſhall cut him aſunder, and appoint him his portion with the hypocrites: there ſhall be weeping and gnaſhing of teeth.

CHAPTER 25[1]Then ſhall the kingdome of heauen be likened vnto ten Uirgins, which tooke their lamps, & went forth to meet the bridegrome.[2]And fiue of them were wiſe, and fiue were fooliſh.[3]They that were fooliſh tooke their lampes, and tooke no oyle with them:[4]But the wiſe tooke oyle in their veſſels with their lampes.[5]While the bridegrome taried, they all ſlumbred and ſlept.[6]And at midnight there was a cry made, Behold, the bridegrome commeth, goe ye out to meet him.[7]Then all thoſe virgins aroſe, and trimmed their lampes.[8]And the fooliſh ſaid vnto the wiſe, Giue vs of your oyle, for our lampes are gone out.[9]But the wiſe anſwered, ſaying, Not ſo, leſt there be not ynough for vs and you, but goe ye rather to them that ſell, and buy for your ſelues.[10]And while they went to buy, the bridegrome came, and they that were ready, went in with him to the marriage, and the doore was ſhut.[11]Afterward came alſo the other virgines, ſaying, Lord, Lord, open to vs.[12]But he anſwered, and ſaid, Uerely I ſay vnto you, I know you not.[13]Watch therefore, for ye know neither the day, nor the houre, wherein the Sonne of man commeth.[14]For the kingdome of heauen is as a man trauailing into a farre countrey, who called his owne ſeruants,

and deliuered vnto them his goods:15And vnto one he gaue fiue talents,
to another two, and to another one, to euery man according to his
ſeuerall ability, & ſtraightway tooke his iourney.16Then hee that had
receiued the fiue talents, went and traded with the ſame, and made them
other fiue talents.17And likewiſe he that had receiued two, he alſo gained
other two.18But hee that had receiued one, went and digged in the earth,
and hid his lordes money.19After a long time, the lord of thoſe ſeruants
commeth, and reckoneth with them.20And ſo hee that had receiued fiue
talents, came and brought other fiue talents, ſaying, Lord, thou
deliueredſt vnto me fiue talents, behold, I haue gained beſides them, fiue
talents moe.21His lord ſaid vnto him, Well done, thou good and faithfull
ſeruant, thou haſt been faithfull ouer a few things, I wil make thee ruler
ouer many things: enter thou into the ioy of thy lord.22He alſo that had
receiued two talents, came and ſaid, Lord, thou deliueredſt vnto me two
talents: behold, I haue gained two other talents beſides them.23His lord
ſaid vnto him, Well done, good and faithfull ſeruant, thou haſt beene
faithfull ouer a few things, I wil make thee ruler ouer many things: enter
thou into the ioy of thy lord.24Then he which had receiued the one
talent, came & ſaid, Lord, I knew thee that thou art an hard man, reaping
where thou haſt not ſowen, & gathering where thou haſt not
ſtrawed:25And I was afraid, and went and hidde thy talent in the earth:
loe, there thou haſt that is thine.26His lord anſwered, and ſaid vnto him,
Thou wicked and ſlouthfull ſeruant, thou kneweſt that I reape where I
ſowed not, and gather where I haue not ſtrawed:27Thou oughteſt
therefore to haue put my money to the exchangers, and then at my
comming I ſhould haue receiued mine owne with vſurie.28Take
therefore the talent from him, and giue it vnto him which hath ten
talents.29For vnto euery one that hath ſhall be giuen, and he ſhall haue
abundance: but from him that hath not, ſhal be taken away, euen that
which he hath.30And caſt yee the vnprofitable ſeruant into outer
darkeneſſe, there ſhall be weeping and gnaſhing of teeth.31When the
Sonne of man ſhall come in his glory, and all the holy Angels with him,
then ſhall hee ſit vpon the throne of his glory:32And before him ſhall be
gathered all nations, and he ſhall ſeparate them one from another, as a
ſhepheard diuideth his ſheepe from the goats.33And he ſhall ſet the
ſheepe on his right hand, but the goats on the left.34Then ſhall the King
ſay vnto them on his right hand, Come ye bleſſed of my Father, inherit
the kingdome prepared for you from the foundation of the world.35For
I was an hungred, and yee gaue me meate: I was thirſtie, and ye gaue me
drinke: I was a ſtranger, and ye tooke me in:36Naked, and ye clothed me:
I was ſicke, and yee viſited me: I was in priſon, and ye came vnto
me.37Then ſhal the righteous anſwere him, ſaying, Lord, when ſaw we
thee an hungred, and fedde thee? or thirſtie, and gaue thee
drinke?38When ſaw wee thee a ſtranger, and tooke thee in? or naked,
and clothed thee?39Or when ſaw we thee ſicke, or in priſon, and came
vnto thee?40And the King ſhall anſwere, and ſay vnto them, Uerely I ſay
vnto you, in as much as ye haue done it vnto one of the leaſt of theſe
my brethren, ye haue done it vnto me.41Then ſhall he ſay alſo vnto them
on the left hand, Depart from me, ye curſed, into euerlaſting fire,
prepared for the deuill and his angels.42For I was an hungred, and yee
gaue me no meat: I was thirſtie, and ye gaue me no drinke:43I was a
ſtranger, and yee tooke me not in: naked, and ye clothed mee not: ſicke,
and in priſon, and yee viſited me not.44Then ſhall they alſo anſwere him,
ſaying, Lord, when ſaw we thee an hungred, or athirſt, or a ſtranger, or
naked, or ſicke, or in priſon, and did not miniſter vnto thee?45Then ſhall
he anſwere them, ſaying, Uerely, I ſay vnto you, in as much as ye did it
not to one of the leaſt of theſe, ye did it not to me.46And theſe ſhall goe
away into euerlaſting puniſhment: but the righteous into life eternall.
CHAPTER 261And it came to paſſe, when Ieſus had finiſhed al theſe
ſayings, hee ſaid vnto his diſciples,2Ye know that after two dayes is the
feaſt of the Paſſeouer, and the Sonne of man is betrayed to be
crucified.3Then aſſembled together the chiefe Prieſts, and the Scribes,
and the Elders of the people, vnto the palace of the high Prieſt, who
was called Caiaphas,4And conſulted that they might take Ieſus by
ſubtiltie, and kill him.5But they ſaid, Not on the feaſt day, leſt there bee
an vproare among the people.6Now when Ieſus was in Bethanie, in the
houſe of Simon the leper,7There came vnto him a woman, hauing an
alabaſter boxe of very precious ointment, and powred it on his head, as
he ſate at meat.8But when his diſciples ſaw it, they had indignation,
ſaying, To what purpoſe is this waſte?9For this ointment might haue bin
ſold for much, and giuen to the poore.10When Ieſus vnderſtood it, he
ſaid vnto them, Why trouble ye the woman? for ſhe hath wrought a
good worke vpon me.11For ye haue the poore alwayes with you, but me
ye haue not alwayes.12For in that ſhe hath powred this ointment on my
body, ſhee did it for my buriall.13Uerely I ſay vnto you, Whereſoeuer this
Goſpel ſhall be preached in the whole world, there ſhall alſo this, that
this woman hath done, be told for a memoriall of her.14Then one of the
twelue, called Iudas Iſcariot, went vnto the chiefe Prieſts,15And ſaid
vnto them, What will ye giue me, and I will deliuer him vnto you? and
they couenanted with him for thirtie pieces of ſiluer.16And from that
time he ſought opportunitie to betray him.17Now the firſt day of the
feaſt of vnleauened bread, the diſciples came to Ieſus, ſaying vnto him,
Where wilt thou that we prepare for thee to eat the Paſſeouer?18And he
ſaid, Goe into the citie to ſuch a man, and ſay vnto him, The Maſter
ſaith, My time is at hand, I will keepe the Paſſeouer at thy houſe with
my diſciples.19And the diſciples did, as Ieſus had appointed them, and
they made ready the Paſſeouer.20Now when the euen was come, he ſate
downe with the twelue.21And as they did eate, he ſaid, Uerely I ſay vnto
you, that one of you ſhal betray me.22And they were exceeding
ſorowfull, and began euery one of them to ſay vnto him, Lord, Is it
I?23And he anſwered and ſaid, Hee that dippeth his hand with mee in
the diſh, the ſame ſhall betray me.24The ſonne of man goeth as it is
written of him: but woe vnto that man by whom the ſonne of man is
betrayed: It had bin good for that man, if hee had not bene
borne.25Then Iudas, which betrayed him, anſwered, and ſaid, Maſter, Is
it I? He ſaid vnto him, Thou haſt ſaid.26And as they were eating, Ieſus
took bread, and bleſſed it, and brake it, and gaue it to the Diſciples, and
ſaid, Take, eate, this is my body.27And he tooke the cup, and gaue
thankes, and gaue it to them, ſaying, Drinke ye all of it:28For this is my
blood of the new Teſtament, which is ſhed for many for the remiſsion
of ſinnes.29But I ſay vnto you, I will not drinke henceforth of this fruite
of the vine, vntill that day when I drinke it new with you in my fathers
kingdom.30And when they had ſung an hymne, they went out into the
mount of Oliues.31Then ſaith Ieſus vnto them, All ye ſhall be offended
becauſe of me this night, For it is written, I will ſmite the Shepheard,
and the ſheepe of the flocke ſhall be ſcattered abroad.32But after I am
riſen againe, I will goe before you into Galilee.33Peter anſwered, and ſaid
vnto him, Though all men ſhall be offended becauſe of thee, yet will I
neuer be offended.34Ieſus ſaid vnto him, Uerily I ſay vnto thee, that this
night before the cocke crow, thou ſhalt denie me thriſe.35Peter ſaid vnto
him, Though I ſhould die with thee, yet will I not denie thee. Likewiſe
alſo ſaid all the Diſciples.36Then commeth Ieſus with them vnto a place
called Gethſemane, and ſaith vnto the Diſciples, Sit yee heere, while I
goe and pray yonder.37And hee tooke with him Peter, and the two
ſonnes of Zebedee, and beganne to be ſorrowful, and very
heauie.38Then ſaith he vnto them, My ſoule is exceeding ſorrowfull,
euen vnto death: tary ye heere, & watch with me.39And he went a little
further, and fell on his face, and prayed, ſaying, O my father, if it be
poſsible, let this cup paſſe from me: neuertheleſſe, not as I will, but as
thou wilt.40And he commeth vnto the Diſciples, and findeth them
aſleepe, and ſaith vnto Peter, What, could ye not watch with me one
houre?41Watch and pray, that yee enter not into temptation: The ſpirit
indeed is willing, but the fleſh is weake.42He went away again the ſecond
time, and prayed, ſaying, O my father, if this cup may not paſſe away
from me, except I drinke it, thy will be done.43And he came and found
them aſleep againe: For their eies were heauie.44And he left them, and
went away againe, and prayed the third time, ſaying the ſame
words.45Then commeth he to his Diſciples, and ſaith vnto them, Sleepe
on now, and take your reſt, behold, the houre is at hand, and the ſonne
of man is betrayed into the hands of ſinners.46Riſe, let vs be going:
behold, he is at hand that doeth betray me.47And while yet ſpake, loe,
Iudas one of the twelue came, and with him a great multitude with
ſwords and ſtaues from the chiefe Prieſts and Elders of the
people.48Now he that betrayed him, gaue them a ſigne, ſaying,
Whomſoeuer I ſhall kiſſe, that ſame is he, hold him faſt.49And forthwith
hee came to Ieſus, and ſaid, Haile maſter, and kiſſed him.50And Ieſus
ſaid vnto him, Friend, Wherefore art thou come? Then came they, and
laid handes on Ieſus, and tooke him.51And behold, one of them which

were with Ieſus, ſtretched out his hand, and drew his ſword, and ſtroke a ſeruant of the high Prieſts, and ſmote off his eare. 52 Then ſaid Ieſus vnto him, Put vp againe thy ſword into his place: for all they that take the ſword, ſhall periſh with the ſword. 53 Thinkeſt thou that I cannot now pray to my father, and he ſhall preſently giue me more then twelue legions of Angels? 54 But how then ſhall the Scriptures be fulfilled, that thus it muſt be? 55 In that ſame houre ſaid Ieſus to the multitudes, Are ye come out as againſt a thiefe with ſwords and ſtaues for to take mee? I ſate daily with you teaching in the Temple, and ye laide no hold on me. 56 But all this was done, that the Scriptures of the Prophets might be fulfilled. Then all the Diſciples forſooke him, and fled: 57 And they that had laid hold on Ieſus, led him away to Caiaphas the high Prieſt, where the Scribes and the Elders were aſſembled. 58 But Peter followed him afarre off, vnto the high Prieſts palace, and went in, and ſate with the ſeruants to ſee the end. 59 Now the chiefe Prieſts and Elders, and all the councell, ſought falſe witneſſe againſt Ieſus to put him to death, 60 But found none: yea, though many falſe witneſſes came, yet found they none. At the laſt came two falſe witneſſes, 61 And ſaid, This fellow ſaid, I am able to deſtroy the Temple of God, and to build it in three dayes. 62 And the high Prieſt aroſe, and ſaid vnto him, Anſwereſt thou nothing? what is it, which theſe witneſſe againſt thee? 63 But Ieſus held his peace. And the high Prieſt anſwered, and ſaid vnto him, I adiure thee by the liuing God, that thou tell vs, whether thou bee the Chriſt the Sonne of God. 64 Ieſus ſaith vnto him, Thou haſt ſaide: Neuertheleſſe I ſay vnto you, Hereafter ſhall yee ſee the Sonne of man ſitting on the right hand of power, and coming in the clouds of heauen. 65 Then the high Prieſt rent his clothes, ſaying, He hath ſpoken blaſphemie: what further need haue wee of witneſſes? Behold, now ye haue heard his blaſphemie. 66 What thinke ye? They anſwered and ſaid, He is guiltie of death. 67 Then did they ſpit in his face, and buffeted him, and others ſmote him with the palmes of their hands, 68 Saying, Prophecie vnto vs, thou Chriſt, who is he that ſmote thee? 69 Now Peter ſate without in the palace: and a damoſell came vnto him, ſaying, Thou alſo waſt with Ieſus of Galilee. 70 But hee denied before them all, ſaying, I know not what thou ſaieſt. 71 And when he was gone out into the porch, another maide ſaw him, and ſaide vnto them that were there, This fellow was alſo with Ieſus of Nazareth. 72 And againe hee denied with an oath, I doe not know the man. 73 And after a while came vnto him they that ſtood by, and ſaide to Peter, Surely thou alſo art one of them, for thy ſpeech bewrayeth thee. 74 Then beganne hee to curſe and to ſweare, ſaying, I know not the man. And immediatly the cocke crew. 75 And Peter remembred the words of Ieſus, which ſaid vnto him, Before the cocke crow, thou ſhalt denie mee thrice. And hee went out, and wept bitterly.

CHAPTER 27 1 When the morning was come, all the chiefe Prieſts and Elders of the people, tooke counſell againſt Ieſus to put him to death. 2 And when they had bound him, they led him away, and deliuered him to Pontius Pilate the gouernour. 3 Then Iudas, which had betraied him, when he ſaw that hee was condemned, repented himſelfe, and brought againe the thirtie pieces of ſiluer to the chiefe Prieſts and Elders, 4 Saying, I haue ſinned, in that I haue betraied the innocent blood. And they ſaid, What is that to vs? ſee thou to that. 5 And hee caſt downe the pieces of ſiluer in the Temple, and departed, and went and hanged himſelfe. 6 And the chiefe Prieſts tooke the ſiluer pieces, and ſaid, It is not lawfull for to put them into the treaſurie, becauſe it is the price of blood. 7 And they tooke counſell, and bought with them the potters field, to burie ſtrangers in. 8 Wherefore that field was called, The field of blood vnto this day. 9 (Then was fulfilled that which was ſpoken by Ieremie the Prophet, ſaying, And they tooke the thirtie pieces of ſiluer, the price of him that was valued, whom they of the children of Iſrael did value: 10 And gaue them for the potters field, as the Lord appointed me.) 11 And Ieſus ſtood before the gouernour, and the gouernour aſked him, ſaying; Art thou the King of the Iewes? And Ieſus ſayd vnto him, Thou ſayeſt. 12 And when hee was accuſed of the chiefe Prieſts and Elders, he anſwered nothing. 13 Then ſaith Pilate vnto him, Heareſt thou not how many things they witneſſe againſt thee? 14 And he anſwered him to neuer a word: inſomuch that the Gouernour marueiled greatly. 15 Now at that feaſt the Gouernor was woont to releaſe vnto the people a priſoner, whom they would. 16 And they had then a notable priſoner, called Barabbas. 17 Therefore when they were gathered together, Pilate ſaid vnto them, Whom will ye that I releaſe vnto you? Barabbas, or Ieſus, which is called Chriſt? 18 For hee knew that for enuie they had deliuered him. 19 When he was ſet downe on the Iudgement ſeate, his wife ſent vnto him, ſaying, Haue thou nothing to doe with that iuſt man: for I haue ſuffered many things this day in a dreame, becauſe of him. 20 But the chiefe Prieſtes and Elders perſwaded the multitude that they ſhould aſke Barabbas, & deſtroy Ieſus. 21 The Gouernour anſwered, and ſaid vnto them, Whether of the twaine will ye that I releaſe vnto you? They ſaid, Barabbas. 22 Pilate ſaid vnto them, What ſhall I doe then with Ieſus, which is called Chriſt? They all ſayde vnto him, Let him be crucified. 23 And the Gouernour ſaid, Why, what euil hath he done? But they cried out þe more, ſaying, Let him be crucified. 24 When Pilate ſaw that he could preuaile nothing, but that rather a tumult was made, hee tooke water, and waſhed his hands before the multitude, ſaying, I am innocent of the blood of this iuſt perſon: ſee yee to it. 25 Then anſwered all the people, and ſaid, His blood be on vs, and on our children. 26 Then releaſed hee Barabbas vnto them, and when he had ſcourged Ieſus, he deliuered him to be crucified. 27 Then the ſouldiers of the Gouernour tooke Ieſus into the common hall, and gathered vnto him the whole band of ſouldiers. 28 And they ſtripped him, and put on him a ſcarlet robe. 29 And when they had platted a crowne of thornes, they put it vpon his head, and a reed in his right hand: and they bowed the knee before him, and mocked him, ſaying, Haile king of the Iewes. 30 And they ſpit vpon him, and tooke the reed, and ſmote him on the head. 31 And after that they had mocked him, they tooke the robe off from him, and put his owne raiment on him, and led him away to crucifie him. 32 And as they came out, they found a man of Cyrene, Simon by name: him they compelled to beare his Croſse. 33 And when they were come vnto a place called Golgotha, that is to ſay, a place of a ſkull, 34 They gaue him vineger to drinke, mingled with gall: and when hee had taſted thereof, hee would not drinke. 35 And they crucified him, and parted his garments, caſting lots: that it might be fulfilled which was ſpoken by the Prophet, They parted my garments among them, and vpon my veſture did they caſt lots. 36 And ſitting downe, they watched him there: 37 And ſet vp ouer his head, his accuſation written, THIS IS IESVS THE KING OF THE IEWES. 38 Then were there two theeues crucified with him: one on the right hand, and another on the left. 39 And they that paſſed by, reuiled him, wagging their heads, 40 And ſaying, Thou that deſtroyeſt the Temple, & buildeſt it in three dayes, ſaue thy ſelfe: If thou be the Sonne of God, come downe from the Croſse. 41 Likewiſe alſo the chiefe Prieſts mocking him, with the Scribes and Elders, ſaid, 42 He ſaued others, himſelfe he cannot ſaue: If he be the King of Iſrael, let him now come downe from the Croſse, and we will beleeue him. 43 He truſted in God, let him deliuer him now if hee will haue him: for he ſaid, I am the Sonne of God. 44 The thieues alſo which were crucified with him, caſt þe ſame in his teeth. 45 Now from the ſixth houre there was darkeneſſe ouer all the land vnto the ninth houre. 46 And about the ninth houre, Ieſus cried with a loud voyce, ſaying, Eli, Eli, Lamaſabachthani, that is to ſay, My God, my God, why haſt thou forſaken mee? 47 Some of them that ſtood there, when they heard that, ſaid, This man calleth for Elias. 48 And ſtraightway one of them ran, and tooke a ſpunge, and filled it with vineger, and put it on a reede, and gaue him to drinke. 49 The reſt ſaid, Let bee, let vs ſee whether Elias will come to ſaue him. 50 Ieſus, when hee had cried againe with a loud voice, yeelded vp the ghoſt. 51 And behold, the vaile of the Temple was rent in twaine, from the top to the bottome, and the earth did quake, and the rocks rent. 52 And the graues were opened, and many bodies of Saints which ſlept, aroſe, 53 And came out of the graues after his reſurrection, and went into the holy citie, and appeared vnto many. 54 Now when the Centurion, and they that were with him, watching Ieſus, ſaw the earthquake, & thoſe things that were done, they feared greatly, ſaying, Truely this was the Son of God. 55 And many women were there (beholding afarre off) which followed Ieſus from Galilee, miniſtring vnto him. 56 Among which was Mary Magdalene, & Mary the mother of Iames and Ioſes, and the mother of Zebedees children. 57 When the Euen was come, there came a rich man of Arimathea, named Ioſeph, who alſo himſelfe was Ieſus diſciple: 58 He went to Pilate, and begged the body of Ieſus: then Pilate commanded the body to be deliuered. 59 And when Ioſeph had taken the body, hee wrapped it in a cleane linnen cloth, 60 And laide it in his owne newe

tombe, which he had hewen out in the rocke: and he rolled a great ſtone
to the doore of the ſepulchre, and departed.61And there was Mary
Magdalene, and the other Mary, ſitting ouer againſt the ſepulchre.62Now
the next day that followed the day of the preparation, the chiefe Prieſts
and PhAriſees came together vnto Pilate,63Saying, Sir, we remember
that that deceiuer ſaid, while he was yet aliue, After three daies I wil riſe
againe.64Command therfore that the ſepulchre be made ſure, vntill the
third day, leſt his diſciples come by night, & ſteale him away, and ſay
vnto the people, He is riſen from the dead: ſo the laſt errour ſhalbe
worſe then the firſt.65Pilate ſaid vnto them, Yee haue a watch, goe your
way, make it as ſure as you can.66So they went, and made the ſepulchre
ſure, ſealing the ſtone, and ſetting a watch.
CHAPTER 28 1In the ende of the Sabbath, as it began to dawne
towards the firſt day of the weeke, came Mary Magdalene, and the other
Mary, to ſee the ſepulchre.2And behold, there was a great earthquake,
for the Angel of the Lord deſcended from heauen, and came and rolled
backe the ſtone from the doore, and ſate vpon it.3His countenance was
like lightning, and his raiment white as ſnowe.4And for feare of him, the
keepers did ſhake, and became as dead men.5And the Angel anſwered,
and ſaid vnto the women, Feare not ye: for I know that ye ſeeke Ieſus,
which was crucified.6He is not here: for he is riſen, as hee ſaid: Come,
ſee the place where the Lord lay.7And goe quickly, and tell his diſciples
that he is riſen from the dead. And behold, hee goeth before you into
Galilee, there ſhall ye ſee him: loe, I haue told you.8And they departed
quickly from the ſepulchre, with feare and great ioy, and did run to bring
his diſciples word.9And as they went to tell his diſciples, behold, Ieſus
met them, ſaying, All haile. And they came, and held him by the feet,
and worſhipped him.10Then ſaid Ieſus vnto them, Be not afraid: Goe
tell my brethren that they goe into Galilee, and there ſhall they ſee
me.11Now when they were going, behold, ſome of the watch came into
the citie, and ſhewed vnto the chiefe Prieſts all the things that were
done.12And when they were aſſembled with the Elders, and had taken
counſell, they gaue large money vnto the ſouldiers,13Saying, ſay ye, His
diſciples came by night, and ſtole him away while we ſlept.14And if this
come to the gouernours eares, wee will perſwade him, and ſecure
you.15So they tooke the money, and did as they were taught. And this
ſaying is commonly reported among the Iewes vntill this day.16Then the
eleuen diſciples went away into Galilee, into a mountaine where Ieſus
had appointed them.17And when they ſaw him, they worſhipped him:
but ſome doubted.18And Ieſus came, and ſpake vnto them, ſaying, All
power is giuen vnto me in heauen and in earth.19Goe ye therefore, and
teach all nations, baptizing them in the Name of the Father, and of the
Sonne, and of the holy Ghoſt:20Teaching them to obſerue all things,
whatſoeuer I haue commanded you: and loe, I am with you alway, euen
vnto the end of the world. Amen.

MARKE (MARK)

CHAPTER 1 1The beginning of the Goſpel of Ieſus Chriſt, the Sonne
of God,2As it is written in the Prophets, Behold, I ſend my meſſenger
before thy face, which ſhall prepare thy way before thee.3The voice of
one crying in the wilderneſſe, Prepare ye the way of the Lord, make his
paths ſtraight.4Iohn did baptize in the wilderneſſe, and preach the
baptiſme of repentance, for the remiſsion of ſinnes.5And there went out
vnto him all the land of Iudea, and they of Ieruſalem, and were all
baptized of him in the riuer of Iordane, cōfeſsing their ſinnes.6And Iohn
was clothed with camels haire, and with a girdle of a ſkin about his
loines: and he did eat locuſts and wilde honie,7And preached, ſaying,
There commeth one mightier then I after me, the latchet of whoſe
ſhooes I am not worthy to ſtoupe downe, and vnlooſe.8I indeed haue
baptized you with water: but hee ſhall baptize you with the holy
Ghoſt.9And it came to paſſe in thoſe daies, that Ieſus came from
Nazareth of Galilee, and was baptized of Iohn in Iordane.10And
ſtraightway comming vp out of the water, hee ſaw the heauens opened,
and the Spirit like a doue deſcending vpon him.11And there came a voice
from heauen, ſaying, Thou art my beloued Sonne, in whom I am well
pleaſed.12And immediately the Spirit driueth him into the
wilderneſſe.13And he was there in the wilderneſſe fourtie daies tempted
of Satan, and was with the wildbeaſts, and the Angels miniſtred vnto
him.14Now after that Iohn was put in priſon, Ieſus came into Galilee,
preaching the Goſpell of the kingdome of God,15And ſaying, The time
is fulfilled, and the kingdome of God is at hand: repent ye, and beleeue
the Goſpell.16Now as he walked by the ſea of Galilee, he ſaw Simon,
and Andrew his brother, caſting a net into the ſea (for they were
fiſhers.)17And Ieſus ſaid vnto them, Come ye after me; and I will make
you to become fiſhers of men.18And ſtraightway they forſooke their
nets, and followed him.19And when hee had gone a little further thence,
hee ſaw Iames the ſonne of Zebedee, and Iohn his brother, who alſo
were in the ſhip mending their nets.20And ſtraightway he called them:
and they left their father Zebedee in the ſhip with the hired ſeruants,
and went after him.21And they went into Capernaum, and ſtraightway
on the Sabbath day he entred into the Synagogue, and taught.22And they
were aſtoniſhed at his doctrine: for hee taught them as one that had
authority, and not as the Scribes.23And there was in their Synagogue a
man with an vncleane ſpirit, and he cried out,24Saying, Let vs alone, what
haue we to doe with thee, thou Ieſus of Nazareth? Art thou come to
deſtroy vs? I know thee who thou art, the holy One of God.25And Ieſus
rebuked him, ſaying, Hold thy peace, and come out of him.26And when
the vncleane ſpirit had torne him, and cried with a lowd voice, he came
out of him.27And they were all amaſed, inſomuch that they queſtioned
among themſelues, ſaying, What thing is this? What new doctrine is this?
For with authoritie commandeth he euen the vncleane ſpirits, and they
doe obey him.28And immediatly his fame ſpread abroad throughout al
the region round about Galilee.29And forth with, when they were come
out of the Synagogue, they entered into the houſe of Simon, and
Andrew, with Iames and Iohn.30But Simons wiues mother lay ſicke of a
feuer: and anone they tell him of her.31And he came and tooke her by
the hand, and lift her vp, and immediately the feuer left her, and ſhe
miniſtred vnto them.32And at euen, when the Sunne did ſet, they
brought vnto him all that were diſeaſed, and them that were poſſeſſed
with diuels:33And all the citie was gathered together at the doore.34And
he healed many that were ſicke of diuers diſeaſes, and caſt out many
deuils, and ſuffered not the deuils to ſpeake, becauſe they knew
him.35And in the morning, riſing vp a great while before day, hee went
out, and departed into a ſolitarie place, and there prayed.36And Simon,
and they that were with him, followed after him:37And when they had
found him, they ſaid vnto him, All men ſeek for thee.38And he ſaid vnto
them, Let vs goe into ye next townes, that I may preach there alſo: for
therefore came I foorth.39And he preached in their Synagogues
throughout all Galilee, and caſt out deuils.40And there came a leper to
him, beſeeching him, and kneeling downe to him, and ſaying vnto him,
If thou wilt, thou canſt make me cleane.41And Ieſus mooued with
compaſſion, put foorth his hand, and touched him, and ſaith vnto him,
I will, be thou cleane.42And aſsoone as he had ſpoken, immediately the
leproſie departed from him, and he was cleanſed.43And he ſtraitly
charged him, and forth with ſent him away,44And ſaith vnto him, ſee
thou ſay nothing to any man: but goe thy way, ſhew thy ſelfe to the
Prieſt, and offer for thy clenſing thoſe things which Moſes commanded,
for a teſtimony vnto them.45But he went out, and beganne to publiſh it
much, and to blaſe abroad the matter: inſomuch that Ieſus could no
more openly enter into the citie, but was without in deſert places: and
they came to him from euery quarter.
CHAPTER 2 1And againe hee entred into Capernaum after ſome dayes,
and it was noyſed that he was in the houſe.2And ſtraightway many were
gathered together, inſomuch that there was no roome to receiue them,
no not ſo much as about the doore: and he preached the word vnto
them.3And they come vnto him, bringing one ſicke of the palſie, which
was borne of foure.4And when they could not come nigh vnto him for
preaſſe, they vncouered the roofe where he was: and when they had
broken it vp, they let downe the bed wherin the ſick of the palſie
lay.5When Ieſus ſaw their faith, hee ſaid vnto the ſicke of the palſie,
Sonne, thy ſinnes be forgiuen thee.6But there were certaine of the
Scribes ſitting there, and reaſoning in their hearts,7Why doeth this man
thus ſpeake blaſphemies? Who can forgiue ſinnes but God onely?8And
immediatly, when Ieſus perceiued in his Spirit, that they ſo reaſoned
within themſelues, he ſaid vnto them, Why reaſon ye theſe things in your

hearts?9Whether is it eaſier to ſay to the ſicke of the palſie, Thy ſinnes be forgiuen thee: or to ſay, Ariſe, and take vp thy bed and walke?10But that yee may know that the Sonne of man hath power on earth to forgiue ſinnes, (Hee ſaith to the ſicke of the palſie,)11I ſay vnto thee, Ariſe, & take vp thy bed, & goe thy way into thine houſe.12And immediatly he aroſe, tooke vp the bed, and went foorth before them all, inſomuch that they were all amazed, and glorified God, ſaying, Wee neuer ſaw it on this faſhion.13And he went foorth againe by the ſea ſide, and all the multitude reſorted vnto him, and he taught them.14And as he paſſed by, he ſaw Leui the ſon of Alpheus ſitting at the receit of Cuſtome, and ſaid vnto him, Follow me. And he aroſe, and followed him.15And it came to paſſe, that as Ieſus ſate at meate in his houſe, many Publicanes and ſinners ſate alſo together with Ieſus and his diſciples: for there were many, & they followed him.16And when the Scribes and PhAriſees ſaw him eate with Publicanes and ſinners, they ſaid vnto his diſciples, How is it that hee eateth and drinketh with Publicanes and ſinners?17When Ieſus heard it, he ſaith vnto them, They that are whole, haue no need of the Phyſition, but they that are ſicke: I came not to call the righteous, but ſinners to repentance.18And the diſciples of Iohn, and of the PhAriſees vſed to faſt; and they come, and ſay vnto him, Why doe the diſciples of Iohn, and of the PhAriſees faſt, but thy diſciples faſt not?19And Ieſus ſaid vnto them, Can the children of the bride-chamber faſt, while the Bridegrome is with them? As long as they haue the Bridegrome with them, they cannot faſt.20But the dayes will come, when the Bridegrome ſhall bee taken away from them, and then ſhall they faſt in thoſe dayes.21No man alſo ſoweth a piece of new cloth on an old garment: elſe the new piece that filled it vp, taketh away from the old, & the rent is made worſe.22And no man putteth new wine into old bottles, elſe the new wine doeth burſt the bottles, and the wine is ſpilled, and the bottles will bee marred: But new wine muſt bee put into new bottles.23And it came to paſſe, that he went thorow the corne fields on the Sabbath day, & his diſciples began as they went, to plucke the eares of corne.24And the PhAriſees ſaide vnto him, Behold, why do they on the Sabbath day that which is not lawfull?25And he ſaid vnto them, Haue ye neuer read what Dauid did, when hee had need, and was an hungred, he, and they that were with him?26How hee went into the houſe of God in the dayes of Abiathar the high Prieſt, and did eate the Shew-bread, which is not lawfull to eate, but for the Prieſts, and gaue alſo to them which were with him?27And hee ſaid vnto them, The Sabbath was made for man, and not man for the Sabbath:28Therefore the Sonne of man is Lord alſo of the Sabbath.

CHAPTER 31And he entred againe into the Synagogue, and there was a man there which had a withered hand:2And they watched him, whether hee would heale him on the Sabbath day, that they might accuſe him.3And he ſaith vnto the man which had the withered hand, ſtand forth.4And hee ſaith vnto them, Is it lawfull to doe good on the Sabbath dayes, or to doe euill? to ſaue life, or to kill? but they held their peace.5And when he had looked round about on them with anger, being grieued for the hardneſse of their hearts, He ſaith vnto the man, Stretch foorth thine hand. And he ſtretched it out: and his hand was reſtored whole as the other.6And the PhAriſees went forth, and ſtraightway tooke counſel with the Herodians againſt him, how they might deſtroy him.7But Ieſus withdrew himſelfe with his diſciples to the ſea: and a great multitude from Galilee followed him, and from Iudea,8And from Hieruſalem, and from Idumea, and from beyond Iordane, and they about Tyre & Sydon, a great multitude, when they had heard what great things he did, came vnto him.9And he ſpake to his diſciples that a ſmall ſhip ſhould wait on him, becauſe of the multitude, leſt they ſhould throng him.10For he had healed many, inſomuch that they preaſſed vpon him, for to touch him, as many as had plagues.11And vncleane ſpirits, when they ſaw him, fell downe before him, and cried, ſaying, Thou art the Sonne of God.12And he ſtraitly charged them, that they ſhould not make him knowen.13And he goeth vp into a mountaine, and calleth vnto him whom he would: and they came vnto him.14And he ordeined twelue, that they ſhould be with him, and that hee might ſend them foorth to preach:15And to haue power to heale ſickeneſses, and to caſt out deuils.16And Simon he ſurnamed Peter.17And Iames the ſonne of Zebedee, and Iohn the brother of Iames (and he ſurnamed them Boanerges, which is, The ſonnes of thunder.)18And Andrew, and Philip, and Bartholomew, and Matthew, and Thomas, and Iames the ſonne of Alpheus, and Thaddeus, and Simon the Canaanite,19And Iudas Iſcariot, which alſo betrayed him: and they went into an houſe.20And the multitude commeth together againe, ſo that they could not ſo much as eate bread.21And when his friends heard of it, they went out to lay hold on him, for they ſaid, He is beſide himſelfe.22And the Scribes which came downe from Hieruſalem, ſaid, He hath Beelzebub, and by the prince of the deuils, caſteth he out deuils.23And he called them vnto him, and ſaid vnto them in parables, Howe can Satan caſt out Satan?24And if a kingdome be diuided againſt it ſelfe, that kingdome cannot ſtand.25And if a houſe be diuided againſt it ſelfe, that houſe cannot ſtand.26And if Satan riſe vp againſt himſelfe, and be diuided, hee cannot ſtand, but hath an end.27No man can enter into a ſtrong mans houſe, and ſpoile his goods, except he will firſt bind the ſtrong man, and then he will ſpoile his houſe.28Uerely I ſay vnto you, All ſinnes ſhalbe forgiuen vnto the ſonnes of men, and blaſphemies, wherewith ſoeuer they ſhall blaſpheme:29But he that ſhal blaſpheme againſt the holy Ghoſt, hath neuer forgiueneſse, but is in danger of eternall damnation.30Becauſe they ſaid, He hath an vncleane ſpirit.31There came then his brethren, and his mother, and ſtanding without, ſent vnto him, calling him.32And the multitude ſate about him and they ſaid vnto him, Behold, thy mother and thy brethren without ſeeke for thee.33And he anſwered them, ſaying, Who is my mother, or my brethren?34And he looked round about on them which ſate about him, and ſaide, Behold my mother and my brethren.35For whoſoeuer ſhall doe the will of God, the ſame is my brother, and my ſiſter, and mother.

CHAPTER 41And he beganne againe to teach by the ſea ſide: and there was gathered vnto him a great multitude, ſo that he entred into a ſhip, and ſate in the ſea: and the whole multitude was by the ſea on the land.2And he taught them many things by parables, and ſaid vnto them in his doctrine,3Hearken, Behold, there went out a ſower to ſow:4And it came to paſſe as he ſowed, ſome fell by the way ſide, and the foules of the aire came, & deuoured it vp.5And ſome fell on ſtonie ground, where it had not much earth: and immediately it ſprang vp, becauſe it had no depth of earth.6But when the Sunne was vp, it was ſcorched, and becauſe it had no roote, it withered away.7And ſome fell among thornes, and the thornes grew vp, and choked it, and it yeelded no fruite.8And other fell on good ground, and did yeeld fruite that ſprang vp, and increaſed, and brought foorth ſome thirtie, & ſome ſixtie, & ſome an hundred.9And he ſaid vnto them, He that hath eares to heare, let him heare.10And when hee was alone, they that were about him, with the twelue, aſked of him the parable.11And he ſaid vnto them, Unto you it is giuen to know the myſtery of the kingdome of God: but vnto them that are without, all theſe things are done in parables:12That ſeeing they may ſee, and not perceiue, and hearing they may heare, and not vnderſtand, leſt at any time they ſhould be conuerted, and their ſinnes ſhould be forgiuen them.13And he ſaid vnto them, Know ye not this parable? And how then will you know all parables?14The Sower ſoweth the word.15And theſe are they by the way ſide, where the word is ſowen, but when they haue heard, Satan commeth immediately, and taketh away the word that was ſowen in their hearts.16And theſe are they likewiſe which are ſowen on ſtonie ground, who when they haue heard the word, immediately receiue it with gladneſſe:17And haue no roote in themſelues, and ſo endure but for a time: afterward when affliction or perſecution Ariſeth for the words ſake, immediately they are offended.18And theſe are they which are ſowen among thorns: ſuch as heare the word,19And the cares of this world, and the deceitfulneſse of riches, and the luſts of other things entring in, choke the word, and it becommeth vnfruitfull.20And theſe are they which are ſowen on good ground, ſuch as heare the word, and receiue it, & bring foorth fruit, ſome thirty fold, ſome ſixtie, and ſome an hundred.21And he ſaid vnto them, Is a candle brought to be put vnder a buſhell, or vnder a bed? & not to be ſet on a candleſticke?22For there is nothing hid, which ſhall not be manifeſted: neither was any thing kept ſecret, but that it ſhould come abroad.23If any man haue eares to heare, let him heare.24And he ſaid vnto them, Take heed what you heare: With what meaſure ye mete, it ſhalbe meaſured to you: And vnto you that heare, ſhal more be giuen.25For he that hath, to him ſhall be giuen: and he that hath not, from him ſhall be taken, euen that which he hath.26And he ſaid, So is the kingdome of God, as if a man ſhould caſt ſeede into the ground,[27]And ſhould ſleepe, and riſe night and day, and the ſeed ſhould ſpring, and grow vp, he knoweth not how.[28]For the earth bringeth foorth fruite of herſelfe, firſt the blade, then the eare, after that the full corne in the eare.[29]But when the fruite is brought foorth, immediately he putteth in the ſickle, becauſe the harueſt is come.[30]And he ſaid, Wherunto ſhal we liken the kingdome of God? Or with what compariſon ſhall we compare it?[31]It is like a graine of muſtard ſeed: which when it is ſowen in the earth, is leſſe then all the ſeedes that be in the earth.[32]But when it is ſowen, it groweth vp, and becommeth greater then all herbes, & ſhooteth out great branches, ſo that the fowles of the aire may lodge vnder the ſhadow of it.[33]And with many ſuch parables ſpake hee the word vnto them, as they were able to heare it.[34]But without a parable ſpake he not vnto them, and when they were alone, hee expounded all things to his diſciples.[35]And the ſame day, when the Euen was come, he ſaith vnto them, Let vs paſſe ouer vnto the other ſide.[36]And when they had ſent away the multitude, they tooke him, euen as he was in the ſhip, and there were alſo with him other litle ſhips.[37]And there aroſe a great ſtorme of wind, and the waues beat into the ſhip, ſo that it was now full.[38]And he was in the hinder part of the ſhip aſleepe on a pillow: and they awake him, and ſay vnto him, Maſter, careſt thou not, that we periſh?[39]And hee aroſe, and rebuked the winde, and ſaid vnto the ſea, Peace, be ſtill: and the winde ceaſed, and there was a great calme.[40]And he ſaid vnto them, Why are ye ſo fearefull? How is it that you haue no faith?[41]And they feared exceedingly, and ſaide one to another, What maner of man is this, that euen the winde and the ſea obey him?

CHAPTER 5[1]And they came ouer vnto the other ſide of the ſea, into the countrey of the Gadarenes.[2]And when hee was come out of the ſhip, immediatly there met him out of the tombes, a man with an vncleane ſpirit,[3]Who had his dwelling among the tombs, and no man could binde him, no not with chaines:[4]Becauſe that hee had bene often bound with fetters and chaines, and the chaines had bene plucked aſunder by him, and the fetters broken in pieces: neither could any man tame him.[5]And alwayes night and day, hee was in the mountaines, and in the tombes, crying, and cutting himſelfe with ſtones.[6]But when hee ſaw Ieſus afarre off, he came and worſhipped him,[7]And cried with a lowd voice, and ſaid, What haue I to doe with thee, Ieſus, thou Sonne of the moſt high God? I adiure thee by God, that thou torment me not.[8](For he ſaid vnto him, Come out of the man, thou vncleane ſpirit.)[9]And he aſked him, What is thy name? And hee anſwered, ſaying, My name is Legion: for we are many.[10]And hee beſought him much, that he would not ſend them away out of the countrey.[11]Now there was there nigh vnto the mountaines a great herd of ſwine, feeding.[12]And all the deuils beſought him, ſaying, Send vs into the ſwine, that we may enter into them.[13]And forthwith Ieſus gaue them leaue. And the vncleane ſpirits went out, and entred into the ſwine, and the herd ranne violently downe a ſteepe place into the ſea (they were about two thouſand) and were choked in the ſea.[14]And they that fed the ſwine fled, and tolde it in the citie, and in the countrey. And they went out to ſee what it was that was done.[15]And they come to Ieſus, and ſee him that was poſſeſſed with the deuill, and had the Legion, ſitting, and clothed, and in his right minde: and they were afraid.[16]And they that ſaw it, tolde them how it befell to him that was poſſeſſed with the deuill, and alſo concerning the ſwine.[17]And they began to pray him to depart out of their coaſts.[18]And when hee was come into the ſhip, he that had bene poſſeſſed with the deuill prayed him that hee might bee with him.[19]Howbeit Ieſus ſuffered him not, but ſaith vnto him, Goe home to thy friends, and tel them how great things the Lord hath done for thee, and hath had compaſſion on thee.[20]And hee departed, and began to publiſh in Decapolis, how great things Ieſus had done for him: and all men did marueile.[21]And when Ieſus was paſſed ouer againe by ſhip vnto the other ſide, much people gathered vnto him, and he was nigh vnto the ſea.[22]And behold, there commeth one of the Rulers of the Synagogue, Iairus by name, and when he ſaw him, he fell at his feete,[23]And beſought him greatly, ſaying, My litle daughter lieth at the point of death, I pray thee come and lay thy hands on her, that ſhee may be healed, and ſhe ſhall liue.[24]And Ieſus went with him, and much people followed him, and thronged him.[25]And a certaine woman which had an iſſue of blood twelue yeeres,[26]And had ſuffered many things of many Phyſicians, and had ſpent all that ſhe had, and was nothing bettered, but rather grew worſe,[27]When ſhee had heard of Ieſus, came in the preaſe behinde, and touched his garment.[28]For ſhe ſaid, If I may touch but his clothes, I ſhalbe whole.[29]And ſtraightway the fountaine of her blood was dried vp: and ſhe felt in her body that ſhe was healed of that plague.[30]And Ieſus immediatly knowing in himſelfe that vertue had gone out of him, turned him about in the preaſſe, and ſaid, Who touched my clothes?[31]And his diſciples ſaid vnto him, Thou ſeeſt the multitude thronging thee, and ſayeſt thou, Who touched me?[32]And he looked round about to ſee her that had done this thing.[33]But the woman fearing and trembling, knowing what was done in her, came and fell downe before him, and tolde him all the trueth.[34]And he ſaid vnto her, Daughter, thy faith hath made thee whole, goe in peace, and be whole of thy plague.[35]While hee yet ſpake, there came from the Ruler of the Synagogues houſe, certaine which ſaid, Thy daughter is dead, why troubleſt thou the Maſter any further?[36]Aſſoone as Ieſus heard the word that was ſpoken, he ſaith vnto the Ruler of the Synagogue, Be not afraid, onely beleeue.[37]And he ſuffered no man to follow him, ſaue Peter, & Iames, and Iohn the brother of Iames.[38]And hee commeth to the houſe of the Ruler of the Synagogue, and ſeeth the tumult, and them that wept and wailed greatly.[39]And when he was come in, hee ſaith vnto them, Why make yee this adoe, and weepe? the damoſell is not dead, but ſleepeth.[40]And they laughed him to ſcorne: but when he had put them all out, hee taketh the father and the mother of the damoſell, and them that were with him, and entreth in where the damoſell was lying.[41]And he tooke the damoſell by the hand, and ſaid vnto her, Talitha cumi, which is, being interpreted, Damoſell (I ſay vnto thee) Ariſe.[42]And ſtraightway the damoſell aroſe, and walked, for ſhee was of the age of twelue yeeres: and they were aſtoniſhed with a great aſtoniſhment.[43]And hee charged them ſtraitly, that no man ſhould know it: and commanded that ſome thing ſhould be giuen her to eate.

CHAPTER 6[1]And hee went out from thence, and came into his owne countrey, and his diſciples follow him.[2]And when the Sabbath day was come, he began to teach in the Synagogue: and many hearing him, were aſtoniſhed, ſaying, From whence hath this man theſe things? And what wiſedome is this which is giuen vnto him, that euen ſuch mightie workes are wrought by his hands?[3]Is not this the carpenter, the ſonne of Mary, the brother of Iames and Ioſes, and of Iuda, and Simon? And are not his ſiſters heere with vs? And they were offended at him.[4]But Ieſus ſayde vnto them, A Prophet is not without honour, but in his owne countrey, and among his owne kinne, and in his owne houſe.[5]And he could there doe no mightie worke, ſaue that he laid his hands vpon a few ſicke folke, and healed them.[6]And he marueiled becauſe of their vnbeliefe. And he went round about the villages, teaching.[7]And he calleth vnto him the twelue, and began to ſend them foorth, by two and two, and gaue them power ouer vncleane ſpirits,[8]And commanded them that they ſhould take nothing for their iourney, ſaue a ſtaffe onely: no ſcrip, no bread, no money in their purſe:[9]But be ſhod with ſandales: and not put on two coats.[10]And he ſaid vnto them, In what place ſoeuer yee enter into an houſe, there abide til ye depart from that place.[11]And whoſoeuer ſhall not receiue you, nor heare you, when yee depart thence, ſhake off the duſt vnder your feet, for a teſtimonie againſt them: Uerely I ſay vnto you, it ſhalbe more tolerable for Sodom and Gomorrha in the day of iudgement, then for that citie.[12]And they went out, and preached that men ſhould repent.[13]And they caſt out many deuils, and anointed with oyle many, that were ſicke, and healed them.[14]And king Herod heard of him (for his name was ſpread abroad:) and hee ſaid that Iohn the Baptiſt was riſen from the dead, and therefore mightie workes doe ſhew foorth themſelues in him.[15]Others ſaid, That it is Elias. And others ſaid, That it is a Prophet, or as one of the Prophets.[16]But when Herod heard thereof, he ſaid, It is Iohn, whome I beheaded, he is riſen from the dead.[17]For Herod himſelfe had ſent forth and laid hold vpon Iohn, and bound him in priſon for Herodias ſake, his brother Philips wife, for hee had maried her.[18]For Iohn had ſaid vnto Herod, It is not lawfull for thee to haue thy brothers wife.[19]Therfore Herodias had a quarrel againſt him, & would haue killed him, but ſhe could not.[20]For Herod feared Iohn, knowing that he was a iuſt man, and an holy, and obſerued him: and when he heard him, hee did many things, and heard him gladly.[21]And when a conuenient day was come, that Herod on his birth day made a ſupper to his lords, high captaines, and chiefe eſtates of Galilee:[22]And when the daughter of the ſaid Herodias came in, and danced, and pleaſed Herod, and them that ſate with him, the king ſaid vnto the damoſell, Aſke of me whatſoeuer thou wilt, and I will giue it thee.[23]And he ſware vnto her, Whatſoeuer thou ſhalt aſke of me, I will giue it thee, vnto the halfe of my kingdome.[24]And ſhe went forth, and ſaid vnto her mother, What ſhall I aſke? And ſhe ſaid, The head of Iohn þe Baptiſt.[25]And ſhe came in ſtraightway with haſte, vnto the king, and aſked, ſaying, I will that thou giue me by and by in a charger, the head of Iohn the Baptiſt.[26]And the king was exceeding ſory, yet for his othes ſake, and for their ſakes which ſate with him, hee would not reiect her.[27]And immediatly the king ſent an executioner, and commaunded his head to be brought, and he went, and beheaded him in the priſon,[28]And brought his head in a charger, and gaue it to the damoſell, and the damoſell gaue it to her mother.[29]And when his diſciples heard of it, they came and tooke vp his corpſe, and laid it in a tombe.[30]And the Apoſtles gathered themſelues together vnto Ieſus, and tolde him all things, both what they had done, and what they had taught.[31]And he ſaid vnto them, Come yee your ſelues apart into a deſert place, and reſt a while. For there were many comming and going, and they had no leiſure ſo much as to eate.[32]And they departed into a deſert place by ſhip priuately.[33]And the people ſaw them departing, and many knew him, and ranne afoote thither out of all cities, and outwent them, and came together vnto him.[34]And Ieſus when he came out, ſaw much people, and was moued with compaſſion toward them, becauſe they were as ſheepe not hauing a ſhepherd: and hee beganne to teach them many things.[35]And when the day was now far ſpent, his Diſciples came vnto him, and ſaid, This is a deſert place, and now the time is farre paſſed.[36]Send them away, that they may goe into the countrey round about, and into the villages, and buy themſelues bread: for they haue nothing to eate.[37]He anſwered and ſaid vnto them, Giue yee them to eate. And they ſay vnto him, Shall we goe and buy two hundred penniworth of bread, and giue them to eate?[38]He ſaith vnto them, How many loaues haue yee? goe, and ſee. And when they knew, they ſay, Fiue, and two fiſhes.[39]And he commanded them to make all ſit downe by companies vpon the greene graſſe.[40]And they ſate downe in rankes by hundreds, and by fifties.[41]And when he had taken the fiue loaues, and the two fiſhes, he looked vp to heauen, and bleſſed, and brake the loaues, and gaue them to his diſciples to ſet before them; and the two fiſhes diuided he among them all.[42]And they did all eate, and were filled.[43]And they tooke vp twelue baſkets full of the fragments, and of the fiſhes.[44]And they that did eate of the loaues, were about fiue thouſand men.[45]And ſtraightway he conſtrained his diſciples to get into the ſhip, and to goe to the other ſide before vnto Bethſaida, while he ſent away the people.[46]And when hee had ſent them away, he departed into a mountaine to pray.[47]And when Euen was come, the ſhip was in the midſt of the ſea, and he alone on the land.[48]And he ſaw them toiling in rowing (for the wind was contrary vnto them:) and about the fourth watch of the night, he commeth vnto them, walking vpon the ſea, and would haue paſſed by them.[49]But when they ſaw him walking vpon the ſea, they ſuppoſed it had bene a ſpirit, and cried out.[50](For they all ſaw him, and were troubled) and immediately hee talked with them, and ſaith vnto them, Be of good cheere, It is I, be not afraid.[51]And hee went vp vnto them into the ſhip, and the wind ceaſed: and they were ſore amazed in themſelues beyond meaſure, and wondered.[52]For they conſidered not the miracle of the loaues, for their heart was hardened.[53]And when they had paſſed ouer, they came into the land of Geneſareth, and drew to the ſhore.[54]And when they were come out of the ſhip, ſtraightway they knew him,[55]And ran through that whole region round about, and beganne to carrie about in beds, thoſe that were ſicke, where they heard he was.[56]And whitherſouer he entred, into villages, or cities, or countrie, they laide the ſicke in the ſtreetes, & beſought him that they might touch if it were but the border of his garment: and as many as touched him, were made whole.

CHAPTER 7[1]Then came together vnto him the PhAriſes, and certain of the Scribes, which came from Hieruſalem.[2]And when they ſaw ſome of his diſciples eate bread with defiled (that is to ſay, with vnwaſhen) hands, they found fault.[3]For the PhAriſes and all the Iewes, except they waſh their hands oft, eate not, holding the tradition of the elders.[4]And when they come from the market, except they waſh, they eate not. And many other things there be, which they haue receiued to hold, as the waſhing of cups and pots, braſen veſſels, and of tables.[5]Then the PhAriſes and Scribes aſked him, Why walke not thy diſciples according to the tradition of the Elders, but eate bread with vnwaſhen hands?[6]He anſwered and ſaid vnto them, Well hath Eſaias propheſied of you Hypocrites, as it is written, This people honoureth mee with their lips, but their heart is farre from me.[7]Howbeit in vaine doe they worſhip me, teaching for doctrines, the commandements of men.[8]For laying aſide the Commandement of God, yee hold the tradition of men, as the waſhing of pots, and cups: and many other ſuch like things ye doe.[9]And he ſaid vnto them, Full well ye reiect the Commandement of God, that ye may keepe your owne tradition.[10]For Moſes ſaid, Honour thy father & thy mother: and who ſo curſeth father or mother, let him die the death.[11]But ye ſay, If a man ſhall ſay to his father or mother, It is Corban, that is to ſay, a gift, by whatſoeuer thou mighteſt be profited by me: he ſhalbe free.[12]And ye ſuffer him no more to doe ought for his father, or his mother:[13]Making the word of God of none effect through your tradition, which ye haue deliuered: And many ſuch like things doe ye.[14]And when he had called all the people vnto him, hee ſaid vnto them, Hearken vnto me euery one of you, and vnderſtand.[15]There is nothing from without a man that entring into him, can defile him: but the things which come out of of him, thoſe are they that defile the man.[16]If any man haue eares to heare, let him heare.[17]And when hee was entred into the houſe from the people, his diſciples aſked him concerning the parable.[18]And he ſaith vnto them, Are ye ſo without vnderſtanding alſo? Doe yee not perceiue that whatſoeuer thing from without entreth into the man, it cannot defile him,[19]Becauſe it entreth not into his heart, but into the belly, and goeth out into the draught, purging all meats?[20]And he ſaid, That which commeth out of the man, that defileth the man.[21]For from within, out of the heart of men, proceed euill thoughts, adulteries, fornications, murders,[22]Thefts, couetouſneſſe, wickedneſſe, deceit, laſciuiouſneſse, an euill eye, blaſphemie, pride, fooliſhneſse:[23]All theſe euill things come from within, and defile the man.[24]And from thence he aroſe, and went into the borders of Tyre and Sidon, and entred into an houſe, and would haue no man know it, but hee could not be hid.[25]For a certaine woman, whoſe yong daughter had an vncleane ſpirit, heard of him, and came and fell at his feete.[26](The woman was a Greek: a Syrophenician by nation:) and ſhe beſought him that he would caſt forth the deuill out of her daughter.[27]But Ieſus ſaid vnto her, Let the children firſt be filled: for it is not meet to take the childrens bread, and to caſt it vnto the dogges.[28]And ſhe anſwered and ſaid vnto him, Yes Lord, yet the dogges vnder the table eat of the childrens crummes.[29]And hee ſaid vnto her, For this ſaying, goe thy way, the deuill is gone out of thy daughter.[30]And when ſhee was come to her houſe, ſhe found the deuill gone out, and her daughter laied vpon the bed.[31]And againe departing from the coaſtes of Tyre and Sidon, he came vnto the ſea of Galilee, thorow the midſt of the coaſts of Decapolis.[32]And they bring vnto him one that was deafe, and had an impediment in his ſpeech: and they beſeech him to put his hand vpon him.[33]And he tooke him aſide from the multitude, and put his fingers into his eares, and he ſpit, and touched his tongue,[34]And looking vp to heauen, hee ſighed, and ſaith vnto him, Ephphatha, that is, Be opened.[35]And ſtraightway his eares were opened, and the ſtring of his tongue was looſed, and he ſpake plaine.[36]And hee charged them that they ſhould tell no man: but the more hee charged them, ſo much the more a great deale they publiſhed it,[37]And were beyond meaſure aſtoniſhed, ſaying, Hee hath done all things well: hee maketh both the deafe to heare, and the dumbe to ſpeake.

CHAPTER 8[1]In thoſe dayes the multitude being very great, and hauing nothing to eat. Ieſus called his diſciples vnto him, & ſaith vnto them,[2]I haue compaſſion on the multitude, becauſe they haue now bene with me three daies, and haue nothing to eat:[3]And if I ſend them away faſting to their owne houſes, they will faint by the way: for diuers of them came from farre.[4]And his diſciples anſwered him, From whence can a man ſatiſfie theſe men with bread here in the wildernes?[5]And hee aſked them, How many loaues haue ye? And they ſaid, Seuen.[6]And he commanded the people to ſit downe on the ground: and he tooke the ſeuen loaues, and gaue thanks, and brake, and gaue to his diſciples to ſet before them: and they did ſet them before the people.[7]And they had a few ſmall fiſhes: and he bleſſed, and commaunded to ſet them alſo before them.8So they did eate, and were filled: and they tooke vp, of the broken meate that was left, ſeuen baſkets.9And they that had eaten were about foure thouſand, and he ſent them away.10And ſtraightway he entred into a ſhip with his diſciples, and came into the parts of Dalmanutha.11And the PhAriſees came foorth, and began to queſtion with him, ſeeking of him a ſigne from heauen, tempting him.12And he ſighed deepely in his ſpirit, and ſaith, Why doeth this generation ſeeke after a ſigne? Uerely I ſay vnto you, There ſhall no ſigne be giuen vnto this generation.13And he left them, & entring into the ſhip againe, departed to the other ſide.14Now the diſciples had forgotten to take bread, neither had they in the ſhip with them more then one loafe.15And hee charged them, ſaying, Take heed, beware of the leauen of the PhAriſees, and of the leauen of Herode.16And they reaſoned among themſelues, ſaying, It is, becauſe we haue no bread.17And when Ieſus knew it, he ſaith vnto them, Why reaſon ye, becauſe yee haue no bread? Perceiue ye not yet, neither vnderſtand? Haue yee your heart yet hardened?18Hauing eyes, ſee ye not? and hauing eares heare ye not? And doe ye not remember?19When I brake the fiue loaues among fiue thouſand, how many baſkets full of fragments tooke yee vp? They ſay vnto him, Twelue.20And when the ſeuen among foure thouſand: how many baſkets full of fragments tooke ye vp? And they ſaid, Seuen.21And he ſaid vnto them, How is it that ye doe not vnderſtand?22And he commeth to Bethſaida, and they bring a blind man vnto him, and beſought him to touch him:23And he tooke the blind man by the hand, and led him out of the towne, and when he had ſpit on his eyes, & put his hands vpon him, he aſked him, if hee ſaw ought.24And he looked vp, and ſaide, I ſee men as trees, walking.25After that hee put his handes againe vpon his eies, and made him look vp: and he was reſtored, and ſaw euery man clearely.26And hee ſent him away to his houſe, ſaying, Neither goe into the towne, nor tell it to any in the towne.27And Ieſus went out, and his diſciples, into the townes of Ceſarea Philippi: and by the way he aſked his diſciples, ſaying vnto them, Whom doe men ſay that I am?28And they anſwered, Iohn the Baptiſt: but ſome ſay, Elias: & others, one of the Prophets.29And hee ſaith vnto them, But whom ſay yee that I am? And Peter anſwereth and ſaith vnto him, Thou art the Chriſt.30And he charged them that they ſhould tell no man of him.31And hee beganne to teach them, that the Sonne of man muſt ſuffer many things, and be reiected of the Elders, and of the chiefe Prieſts, & Scribes, and be killed, & after three dayes riſe againe.32And he ſpake that ſaying openly. And Peter tooke him, and beganne to rebuke him.33But when he had turned about, and looked on his diſciples, he rebuked Peter, ſaying, Get thee behind me, Satan: for thou ſauoureſt not the things that be of God, but the things that be of men.34And when he had called the people vnto him, with his diſciples alſo, he ſaid vnto them, Whoſoeuer will come after me, let him denie himſelfe, and take vp his croſſe and follow mee.35For whoſoeuer will ſaue his life ſhall loſe it, but whoſoeuer ſhall loſe his life for my ſake and the Goſpels, the ſame ſhall ſaue it.36For what ſhall it profit a man, if he ſhall gaine the whole world, and loſe his owne ſoule?37Or what ſhall a man giue in exchange for his ſoule?38Whoſoeuer therefore ſhall be aſhamed of me, and of my words, in this adulterous and ſinfull generation, of him alſo ſhall the Sonne of man bee aſhamed, when he commeth in the glory of his Father, with the holy Angels.

CHAPTER 91And hee ſaid vnto them, Uerely I ſay vnto you, that there be ſome of them that ſtand here, which ſhal not taſte of death, till they haue ſeene the kingdome of God come with power.2And after ſixe dayes, Ieſus taketh with him Peter, and Iames, and Iohn, and leadeth them vp into an high mountaine apart by themſelues: and he was tranſfigured before them.3And his raiment became ſhining, exceeding white as ſnow: ſo as no Fuller on earth can white them.4And there appeared vnto them Elias with Moſes: and they were talking with Ieſus.5And Peter anſwered, and ſaide to Ieſus, Maſter, it is good for vs to bee here, and let vs make three Tabernacles; one for thee, and one for Moſes, and one for Elias.6For he wiſt not what to ſay, for they were ſore afraid.7And there was a cloud that ouerſhadowed them: and a voyce came out of the cloud, ſaying, This is my beloued Sonne: heare him.8And ſuddenly when they had looked round about, they ſaw no man any more, ſaue Ieſus only with themſelues.9And as they came downe from the mountaine, he charged them that they ſhould tell no man, what things they had ſeene, till the Sonne of man were riſen from the dead.10And they kept that ſaying with themſelues, queſtioning one with another, what the riſing from the dead ſhould meane.11And they aſked him, ſaying, Why ſay the Scribes that Elias muſt firſt come?12And he anſwered, and told them, Elias verely commeth firſt, and reſtoreth al things, and how it is written of the Sonne of man, that he muſt ſuffer many things, and be ſet at nought.13But I ſay vnto you, that Elias is indeed come, and they haue done vnto him whatſoeuer they liſted, as it is written of him.14And when he came to his diſciples, he ſaw a great multitude about them, and the Scribes queſtioning with them.15And ſtraightway all the people, when they beheld him, were greatly amazed, & running to him, ſaluted him.16And he aſked the Scribes, What queſtion ye with them?17And one of the multitude anſwered, and ſaid, Maſter, I haue broughe vnto thee my ſon, which hath a dumbe ſpirit:18And whereſoeuer he taketh him, he teareth him, & he fometh, and gnaſheth with his teeth, and pineth away: and I ſpake to thy diſciples, that they ſhould caſt him out, and they could not.19He anſwereth him, and ſaith, O faithleſſe generation, how long ſhall I be with you, how long ſhall I ſuffer you? Bring him vnto me.20And they brought him vnto him: and when he ſaw him, ſtraightway the ſpirit tare him, and he fel on the ground, and wallowed, foming.21And he aſked his father, Howe long is it agoe ſince this came vnto him? And he ſaid, Of a child.22And oft times it hath caſt him into the fire, and into the waters to deſtroy him: but if thou canſt doe any thing, haue compaſſion on vs, and helpe vs.23Ieſus ſaid vnto him, If thou canſt beleeue, all things are poſsible to him that beleeueth.24And ſtraightway the father of the child cried out and ſaid with teares, Lord, I beleeue, helpe thou mine vnbeliefe.25When Ieſus ſaw that the people came running together, he rebuked the foule ſpirit, ſaying vnto him, Thou dumbe and deafe ſpirit, I charge thee come out of him, and enter no more into him.26And the ſpirit cried, and rent him ſore, and came out of him, and he was as one dead, inſomuch that many ſaid, He is dead.27But Ieſus tooke him by the hand, and lifted him vp, and he aroſe.28And when he was come into the houſe, his diſciples aſked him priuately, Why could not we caſt him out?29And hee ſaid vnto them, This kind can come forth by nothing, but by prayer, and faſting.30And they departed thence, and paſſed through Galilee, and he would not þt any man ſhould know it.31For he taught his diſciples, and ſaid vnto them, The ſonne of man is deliuered into the hands of men, and they ſhall kill him, and after that he is killed, he ſhall riſe the third day.32But they vnderſtood not that ſaying, and were afraid to aſke him.33And he came to Capernaum; and being in the houſe, he aſked them, What was it that yee diſputed among your ſelues by the way?34But they held their peace: For by the way they had diſputed among themſelues, who ſhould be the greateſt.35And he ſate downe, and called the twelue, and ſaith vnto them, If any man deſire to be firſt, the ſame ſhall be laſt of all, and ſeruant of all.36And he tooke a child, and ſet him in the midſt of them: & when he had taken him in his arms, he ſaid vnto them,37Whoſoeuer ſhall receiue one of ſuch children in my Name, receiueth me: and whoſoeuer ſhall receiue me, receiueth not me, but him that ſent me.38And Iohn anſwered him, ſaying, Maſter, we ſaw one caſting out deuils in thy Name, and he followeth not vs, and we forbade him, becauſe he followeth not vs.39But Ieſus ſaid, Forbid him not, for there is no man, which ſhall doe a miracle in my Name, that can lightly ſpeake euill of me.40For he that is not againſt vs, is on our part.41For whoſoeuer ſhall giue you a cup of water to drinke in my Name, becauſe yee belong to Chriſt: Uerily I ſay vnto you, he ſhall not loſe his reward.42And whoſoeuer ſhall offend one of theſe litle ones that beleeue in me, it is better for him, that a milſtone were hanged about his necke, and he were caſt into the ſea.43And if thy hand offend thee, cut it off: It is better for thee to enter into life maimed, then hauing two hands, to goe into hell, into the fire that neuer ſhall be quenched:44Where their worme dieth not, and the fire is not quenched.45And if thy foote offend thee, cut it off: it is better for thee to enter halt into life, then hauing two feete, to be caſt into hell, into the fire that neuer ſhall be quenched:46Where their worme dieth not, and the fire is not quenched.47And if thine eye offend thee, pluck it out: it is better for thee to enter into the kingdom of God with one eye, then hauing two eyes, to be caſt into helfire:48Where their worme dieth not, and the fire is not quenched.49For euery one ſhall be ſalted with fire, and euery ſacrifice ſhall be ſalted with ſalt.50Salt is good: but if the ſalt haue loſt his ſaltneſse, wherewith will you ſeaſon it? Haue ſalt in your ſelues, and haue peace one with another.

CHAPTER 10 1And he roſe from thence, & commeth into the coaſts of Iudea by the farther ſide of Iordan: and the people reſort vnto him againe, and as he was wont, he taught them againe. 2And the PhAriſes came to him, and aſked him, Is it lawfull for a man to put away his wife? tempting him. 3And he anſwered, and ſaide vnto them, What did Moſes command you? 4And they ſaid, Moſes ſuffered to write a bill of diuorcement, and to put her away. 5And Ieſus anſwered, and ſaid vnto them, For the hardneſse of your heart, he wrote you this precept. 6But from the beginning of the creation, God made them male, and female. 7For this cauſe ſhall a man leaue his father and mother, and cleaue to his wife, 8And they twaine ſhalbe one fleſh: ſo then they are no more twaine, but one fleſh. 9What therefore God hath ioyned together, let not man put aſunder. 10And in the houſe his diſciples aſked him againe of the ſame matter. 11And he ſaith vnto them, Whoſoeuer ſhall put away his wife, and marry another, committeth adultery againſt her. 12And if a woman ſhall put away her huſband, and bee married to another, ſhe committeth adulterie. 13And they brought yong children to him, that he ſhould touch them, and his diſciples rebuked thoſe that brought them. 14But when Ieſus ſaw it, hee was much diſpleaſed, and ſaid vnto them, Suffer the little children to come vnto mee, and forbid them not: for of ſuch is the kingdome of God. 15Uerily I ſay vnto you, Whoſoeuer ſhall not receiue the kingdome of God as a little childe, he ſhall not enter therein. 16And hee tooke them vp in his armes, put his handes vpon them, and bleſſed them. 17And when he was gone forth into the way, there came one running, and kneeled to him, and aſked him, Good maſter, what ſhall I doe that I may inherit eternall life? 18And Ieſus ſaid vnto him, Why calleſt thou me good? There is no man good, but one, that is God. 19Thou knoweſt the Commandements, Doe not commit adulterie, Doe not kill, Doe not ſteale, Doe not beare falſe witneſſe, Defraud not, Honour thy father, and mother. 20And hee anſwered, and ſaide vnto him, Maſter, all theſe haue I obſerued from my youth. 21Then Ieſus beholding him, loued him, and ſaid vnto him, One thing thou lackeſt; Goe thy way, ſell whatſoeuer thou haſt, and giue to the poore, and thou ſhalt haue treaſure in heauen, and come, take vp the croſse & folow me. 22And hee was ſad at that ſaying, and went away grieued: for hee had great poſſeſſions. 23And Ieſus looked round about, and ſaith vnto his diſciples, How hardly ſhall they that haue riches enter into the kingdome of God? 24And the diſciples were aſtoniſhed at his words. But Ieſus anſwereth againe, and ſaith vnto them, Children, how hard is it for them that truſt in riches, to enter into the kingdom of God? 25It is eaſier for a camel to goe thorow the eye of a needle, then for a rich man to enter into the kingdom of God. 26And they were aſtoniſhed out of meaſure, ſaying among themſelues, Who then can be ſaued? 27And Ieſus looking vpon them, ſaith, With men it is impoſsible, but not with God: for with God all things are poſsible. 28Then Peter began to ſay vnto him, Loe, we haue left all, and haue followed thee. 29And Ieſus anſwered, and ſaid, Uerily I ſay vnto you, There is no man that hath left houſe, or brethren, or ſiſters, or father, or mother, or wife, or children, or lands, for my ſake, and the Goſpels, 30But hee ſhall receiue an hundred fold now in this time, houſes, and brethren, and ſiſters, and mothers, and children, and lands, with perſecutions; and in the world to come eternall life: 31But many that are firſt, ſhall be laſt: and the laſt, firſt. 32And they were in the way going vp to Hieruſalem: and Ieſus went before them, and they were amazed, and as they followed, they were afraid: and he tooke againe the twelue, and began to tell them what things ſhould happen vnto him, 33Saying, Behold, we go vp to Hieruſalem, and the Sonne of man ſhall be deliuered vnto the chiefe Prieſts, and vnto the Scribes: and they ſhall condemne him to death, and ſhall deliuer him to the Gentiles. 34And they ſhall mocke him, and ſhall ſcourge him, and ſhall ſpit vpon him, and ſhall kill him, and the third day he ſhall riſe againe. 35And Iames, and Iohn the ſonnes of Zebedee come vnto him, ſaying, Maſter, we would þt thou ſhouldeſt do for vs whatſoeuer we ſhall deſire. 36And hee ſaide vnto them, What would ye that I ſhould doe for you? 37They ſaid vnto him, Grant vnto vs that wee may ſit, one on thy right hand, and the other on thy left hand, in thy glory. 38But Ieſus ſaid vnto them, Yee know not what ye aſke: Can ye drinke of the cup that I drinke of? and be baptized with the baptiſme that I am baptized with? 39And they ſaid vnto him, Wee can. And Ieſus ſaid vnto them, Ye ſhall indeed drinke of the cup that I drinke of: and with the baptiſme that I am baptized withall, ſhall ye be baptized: 40But to ſit on my right hand and on my left hand, is not mine to giue, but it ſhall be giuen to them for whom it is prepared. 41And when the ten heard it, they beganne to bee much diſpleaſed with Iames and Iohn. 42But Ieſus called them to him, and ſaith vnto them, Yee know that they which are accompted to rule ouer the Gentiles, exerciſe Lordſhip ouer them: and their great ones exerciſe authoritie vpon them. 43But ſo ſhall it not be among you: but whoſoeuer will bee great among you, ſhall be your miniſter: 44And whoſoeuer of you will bee the chiefeſt, ſhalbe ſeruant of all. 45For euen the Sonne of man came not to bee miniſtred vnto, but to miniſter, and to giue his life a ranſome for many. 46And they came to Iericho: and as he went out of Iericho with his diſciples, and a great number of people; blinde Bartimeus, the ſon of Timeus, ſate by the high wayes ſide, begging. 47And when he heard that it was Ieſus of Nazareth, he began to cry out, and ſay, Ieſus thou Sonne of Dauid, haue mercie on me. 48And many charged him, that he ſhould hold his peace: But he cried the more a great deale, Thou Sonne of Dauid, haue mercy on me. 49And Ieſus ſtood ſtill, and commanded him to bee called: and they call the blinde man, ſaying vnto him, Be of good comfort, riſe, he calleth thee. 50And hee caſting away his garment, roſe, and came to Ieſus. 51And Ieſus anſwered, and ſaid vnto him, What wilt thou that I ſhould doe vnto thee? The blinde man ſaid vnto him, Lord, that I might receiue my ſight. 52And Ieſus ſaide vnto him, Goe thy way, thy faith hath made thee whole: And immediatly hee receiued his ſight, & followed Ieſus in the way.

CHAPTER 11 1And when they came nigh to Hieruſalem, vnto Bethphage, and Bethanie, at the mount of Oliues, hee ſendeth foorth two of his diſciples, 2And ſaith vnto them, Goe your way into the village ouer againſt you, and aſſoone as ye bee entred into it, yee ſhall finde a colt tied, whereon neuer man ſate, looſe him, and bring him. 3And if any man ſay vnto you, Why doe yee this? ſay yee, that the Lord hath need of him: and ſtraightway he will ſend him hither. 4And they went their way, and found the colt tied by the doore without, in a place where two wayes met: and they looſe him. 5And certaine of them that ſtood there, ſaid vnto them, What doe ye looſing the colt? 6And they ſaid vnto them euen as Ieſus had commanded: and they let them goe. 7And they brought the colt to Ieſus, and caſt their garments on him, and he ſate vpon him. 8And many ſpread their garments in the way: and others cut downe branches of the trees, and ſtrawed them in the way. 9And they that went before, and they that followed, cryed, ſaying, Hoſanna, bleſſed is hee that commeth in the Name of the Lord. 10Bleſſed be the kingdome of our father Dauid, that commeth in the Name of the Lord, Hoſanna in the higheſt. 11And Ieſus entred into Hieruſalem, and into the Temple, and when hee had looked round about vpon all things, & now the euentide was come, he went out vnto Bethanie with the twelue. 12And on the morow when they were come from Bethanie, hee was hungry. 13And ſeeing a figtree a farre off, hauing leaues, hee came, if haply hee might find any thing thereon, & when he came to it, hee found nothing but leaues: for the time of figs was not yet. 14And Ieſus anſwered, and ſaid vnto it, No man eate fruite of thee hereafter for euer. And his diſciples heard it. 15And they come to Hieruſalem, and Ieſus went into the Temple, and beganne to caſt out them that ſold and bought in the Temple, and ouerthrew the tables of the money changers, and the ſeats of them that ſold doues, 16And would not ſuffer that any man ſhould carie any veſſell thorow the Temple. 17And he taught, ſaying vnto them, Is it not written, My houſe ſhalbe called of all nations the houſe of prayer? but ye haue made it a den of theeues. 18And the Scribes and chiefe Prieſts heard it, and ſought how they might deſtroy him: for they feared him, becauſe all the people was aſtoniſhed at his doctrine. 19And when Euen was come, Hee went out of the citie. 20And in the morning, as they paſſed by, they ſaw the fig tree dried vp from the roots. 21And Peter calling to remembrance ſaith vnto him, Maſter, behold, the fig tree which thou curſedſt, is withered away. 22And Ieſus anſwering, ſaith vnto them, Haue faith in God. 23For verely I ſay vnto you, that whoſoeuer ſhall ſay vnto this mountaine, Bee thou remoued, and bee thou caſt into the ſea, and ſhall not doubt in his heart, but ſhall beleeue that thoſe things which hee ſaith, ſhall come to paſſe: he ſhal haue whatſoeuer he ſaith.[24]Therfore I ſay vnto you, What things ſoeuer ye deſire when ye pray, beleeue that ye receiue them, and ye ſhall haue them.[25]And when ye ſtand, praying, forgiue, if ye haue ought againſt any: that your Father alſo which is in heauen, may forgiue you your treſpaſſes.[26]But if you doe not forgiue, neither will your Father which is in heauen, forgiue your treſpaſſes.[27]And they come againe to Hieruſalem, and as he was walking in the Temple, there come to him the chiefe Prieſts, and the Scribes, & the Elders,[28]And ſay vnto him, By what authoritie doeſt thou theſe things? and who gaue thee this authority to doe theſe things?[29]And Ieſus anſwered, and ſaide vnto them, I will alſo aſke of you one queſtion, and anſwere me, and I will tell you by what authoritie I doe theſe things.[30]The baptiſme of Iohn, was it from heauen, or of men? Anſwere me.[31]And they reaſoned with themſelues, ſaying, If we ſhall ſay, From heauen, he will ſay, Why then did ye not beleeue him?[32]But if we ſhall ſay, Of men, they feared the people: for all men counted Iohn, that he was a Prophet indeed.[33]And they anſwered and ſaid vnto Ieſus, We cannot tell. And Ieſus anſwering, ſaith vnto them, Neither do I tell you by what authority I doe theſe things.

CHAPTER 12[1]And hee began to ſpeake vnto them by parables. A certaine man planted a vineyard, and ſet an hedge about it, and digged a place for the wine fat, and built a towre, and let it out to huſbandmen, and went into a farre countrey.[2]And at the ſeaſon, he ſent to the huſbandmen a ſeruant, that he might receiue from the huſbandmen of the fruite of the vineyard.[3]And they caught him, and beat him, and ſent him away emptie.[4]And againe, hee ſent vnto them another ſeruant; and at him they caſt ſtones, and wounded him in the head, and ſent him away ſhamefully handled.[5]And againe, he ſent another, and him they killed: and many others, beating ſome, and killing ſome.[6]Hauing yet therefore one ſonne his welbeloued, he ſent him alſo laſt vnto them, ſaying, They will reuerence my ſonne.[7]But thoſe huſbandmen ſaid amongſt themſelues, This is the heire, come, let vs kill him, and the inheritance ſhall be ours.[8]And they tooke him, and killed him, and caſt him out of the vineyard.[9]What ſhall therefore the Lord of the vineyard doe? He will come and deſtroy the huſbandmen, and will giue the vineyard vnto others.[10]And haue ye not read this Scripture? The ſtone which the builders reiected, is become the head of the corner:[11]This was the Lords doing, and it is maruellous in our eies.[12]And they ſought to lay hold on him, but feared the people, for they knew that he had ſpoken the parable againſt them: and they left him, and went their way.[13]And they ſend vnto him certaine of the PhAriſes, and of the Herodians, to catch him in his words.[14]And when they were come, they ſay vnto him, Maſter, we know that thou art true, and careſt for no man: for thou regardeſt not the perſon of men, but teacheſt the way of God in truth. Is it lawfull to giue tribute to Ceſar, or not?[15]Shall we giue, or ſhall we not giue? But he knowing their hypocriſie, ſaid vnto them, Why tempt yee mee? Bring me a penny that I may ſee it.[16]And they brought it: and he ſaith vnto them, Whoſe is this image and ſuperſcription? And they ſaid vnto him, Ceſars.[17]And Ieſus anſwering, ſaid vnto them, Render to Ceſar the things that are Ceſars: and to God the things that are Gods. And they maruailed at him.[18]Then come vnto him the Sadducees, which ſay there is no reſurrection, and they aſked him, ſaying,[19]Maſter, Moſes wrote vnto vs, If a mans brother die, and leaue his wife behind him, and leaue no children, that his brother ſhould take his wife, and raiſe vp ſeed vnto his brother.[20]Now there were ſeuen brethren: and the firſt tooke a wife, and dying left no ſeede.[21]And the ſecond tooke her, and died, neither left he any ſeed, and the third likewiſe.[22]And the ſeuen had her, and left no ſeede: laſt of all the woman died alſo.[23]In the reſurrection therefore, when they ſhall riſe, whoſe wife ſhall ſhe be of them? for the ſeuen had her to wife.[24]And Ieſus anſwering, ſaid vnto them, Doe ye not therefore erre, becauſe yee know not the ſcriptures, neither the power of God?[25]For when they ſhall riſe from the dead, they neither marry, nor are giuen in marriage: but are as the Angels which are in heauen.[26]And as touching the dead, that they riſe: haue ye not read in the booke of Moſes, how in the buſh God ſpake vnto him, ſaying, I am the God of Abraham, and the God of Iſahac, and the God of Iacob?[27]Hee is not the God of the dead, but the God of the liuing: yee therefore doe greatly erre.[28]And one of the Scribes came, and hauing heard them reaſoning together, and perceiuing that he had anſwered them well, aſked him which is the firſt commandement of all.[29]And Ieſus anſwered him, The firſt of al the commandements is, Heare, O Iſrael, the Lord our God is one Lord:[30]And thou ſhalt loue the Lord thy God with all thy heart, and with all thy ſoule, and with all thy minde, and with all thy ſtrength: This is the firſt commandement.[31]And the ſecond is like, namely this, Thou ſhalt loue thy neighbour as thy ſelfe: there is none other commandement greater then theſe.[32]And the Scribe ſaid vnto him, Well maſter, thou haſt ſaid the truth: for there is one God, and there is none other but he.[33]And to loue him with all the heart, and with all the vnderſtanding, and with all the ſoule, and with all the ſtrength, and to loue his neighbour as himſelfe, is more then all whole burnt offerings and ſacrifices.[34]And when Ieſus ſaw that he anſwered diſcreetly, hee ſaide vnto him, Thou art not far from the kingdome of God. And no man after that durſt aſke him any queſtion.[35]And Ieſus anſwered, and ſaid, while hee taught in the Temple, How ſay the Scribes that Chriſt is the ſonne of Dauid?[36]For Dauid himſelfe ſaid by the holy Ghoſt, The Lord ſaid to my Lord, Sit thou on my right hand, til I make thine enemies thy footſtoole.[37]Dauid therefore himſelfe calleth him Lord, and whence is hee then his ſonne? And the common people heard him gladly.[38]And he ſaid vnto them in his doctrine, Beware of the Scribes, which loue to goe in long clothing, and loue ſalutations in the market places,[39]And the chiefe ſeates in the Synagogues, and the vppermoſt roomes at feaſts:[40]Which deuoure widowes houſes, and for a pretence make long prayers: Theſe ſhall receiue greater damnation.[41]And Ieſus ſate ouer againſt the treaſurie, and beheld how the people caſt money into the treaſurie: and many that were rich, caſt in much.[42]And there came a certaine poore widow, and ſhe threw in two mites, which make a farthing.[43]And he called vnto him his diſciples, and ſaith vnto them, Uerily I ſay vnto you, that this poore widow hath caſt more in, then all they which haue caſt into the treaſurie.[44]For all they did caſt in of their aboundance: but ſhe of her want, did caſt in all that ſhe had, euen all her liuing.

CHAPTER 13[1]And as he went out of the Temple, one of his diſciples ſaith vnto him, Maſter, ſee what maner of ſtones, and what buildings are here.[2]And Ieſus anſwering, ſaid vnto him, Seeſt thou theſe great buildings? there ſhall not be left one ſtone vpon an other, that ſhal not be throwen downe.[3]And as he ſate vpon the mount of Oliues, ouer againſt the Temple, Peter, and Iames, and Iohn, and Andrew aſked him priuately,[4]Tell vs, when ſhall theſe things be? And what ſhalbe the ſigne when all theſe things ſhalbe fulfilled?[5]And Ieſus anſwering them, began to ſay, Take heed leſt any man deceiue you.[6]For many ſhal come in my Name, ſaying, I am Chriſt: and ſhall deceiue many.[7]And when yee ſhall heare of warres, and rumors of warres, be yee not troubled: For ſuch things muſt needs be, but the end ſhall not be yet.[8]For nation ſhall riſe againſt nation, and kingdome againſt kingdome: and there ſhalbe earthquakes in diuers places, and there ſhall be famines, and troubles: theſe are the beginnings of ſorrowes.[9]But take heed to your ſelues: for they ſhall deliuer you vp to councels, and in the Synagogues ye ſhall be beaten, and ye ſhalbe brought before rulers and kings for my ſake, for a teſtimony againſt them.[10]And the Goſpel muſt firſt be publiſhed among all nations.[11]But when they ſhall lead you, and deliuer you vp, take no thought before hand what ye ſhall ſpeake, neither doe yee premeditate: but whatſoeuer ſhall bee giuen you in that houre, that ſpeake yee: for it is not yee that ſpeake, but the holy Ghoſt.[12]Now the brother ſhall betray the brother to death, and the father the ſonne: and children ſhall riſe vp againſt their parents, and ſhall cauſe them to be put to death.[13]And ye ſhall bee hated of all men for my Names ſake: but hee that ſhall endure vnto the ende, the ſame ſhall be ſaued.[14]But when ye ſhall ſee the abomination of deſolation ſpoken of by Daniel the Prophet, ſtanding where it ought not (let him that readeth vnderſtand) then let them that be in Iudea, flee to the mountaines:[15]And let him that is on the houſe top, not goe downe into the houſe, neither enter therin, to take any thing out of his houſe.[16]And let him that is in the field, not turne backe againe for to take vp his garment.[17]But woe to them that are with child, and to them that giue ſuck in thoſe dayes.[18]And pray ye that your flight bee not in the winter.[19]For in thoſe dayes ſhall be affliction, ſuch as was not from the beginning of the creation which God created, vnto this time, neither ſhall be.[20]And except that the Lord had ſhortened thoſe dayes, no fleſh ſhould be ſaued: but for the elects ſake whome he hath choſen, he hath ſhortned the daies.[21]And then, if any man ſhall ſay to you, Loe, here is Chriſt, or loe, hee is there: beleeue him not.[22]For falſe Chriſts

and falſe prophets ſhall riſe, and ſhall ſhewe ſignes and wonders, to
ſeduce, if it were poſsible, euen the elect.23But take ye heed: behold, I
haue foretold you all things.24But in thoſe dayes, after that tribulation,
the Sunne ſhalbe darkned, and the Moone ſhall not giue her light.25And
the Starres of heauen ſhall fall, and the powers that are in heauen ſhall
be ſhaken.26And then ſhal they ſee the Sonne of man comming in the
cloudes, with great power and glory.27And then ſhal he ſend his Angels,
and ſhall gather together his elect from the foure winds, from the
vttermoſt part of the earth, to the vttermoſt part of heauen.28Now
learne a parable of the fig tree. When her branch is yet tender, and
putteth forth leaues, ye know that ſummer is neere:29So ye in like maner,
when ye ſhal ſee theſe things come to paſſe, knowe that it is nigh, euen
at the doores.30Uerely I ſay vnto you, that this generation ſhall not paſſe,
till all theſe things be done.31Heauen and earth ſhal paſſe away: but my
words ſhall not paſſe away.32But of that day and that houre knoweth no
man, no not the Angels which are in heauen, neither the Son, but the
Father.33Take ye heed, watch and pray: for ye know not when the time
is.34For the Sonne of man is as a man taking a farre iourney, who left
his houſe, and gaue authority to his ſeruants, and to euery man his
worke, and commanded the porter to watch:35Watch ye therefore (for
ye knowe not when the maſter of the houſe commeth, at Euen, or at
midnight, or at the cocke crowing, or in the morning.)36Leſt comming
ſuddenly, he finde you ſleeping.37And what I ſay vnto you, I ſay vnto
all, Watch.
CHAPTER 141After two dayes was the feaſt of the Paſſeouer, and of
vnleauened bread: and the chiefe Prieſts, and the Scribes ſought how
they might take him by craft, and put him to death.2But they ſaid, Not
on the feaſt day, leſt there be an vprore of the people.3And being in
Bethanie, in the houſe of Simon the leper, as he ſate at meat, there came
a woman, hauing an Alabaſter boxe of oyntment of ſpikenard very
precious, and ſhee brake the boxe, and powred it on his head.4And there
were ſome that had indignation within themſelues, and ſaid, Why was
this waſte of the oyntment made?5For it might haue bene ſolde for more
then three hundred pence, and haue bene giuen to the poore: and they
murmured againſt her.6And Ieſus ſaid, Let her alone, why trouble you
her? Shee hath wrought a good worke on me.7For ye haue the poore
with you alwayes, and whenſoeuer ye will yee may doe them good: but
me ye haue not alwayes.8She hath done what ſhe could: ſhe is come
aforehand to anoint my body to the burying.9Uerely I ſay vnto you,
Whereſoeuer this Goſpel ſhalbe preached thorowout the whole world,
this alſo that ſhe hath done, ſhall be ſpoken of for a memoriall of
her.10And Iudas Iſcariot, one of the twelue, went vnto the chiefe Prieſts,
to betray him vnto them.11And when they heard it, they were glad, and
promiſed to giue him money. And he ſought how he might conueniently
betray him.12And the firſt day of vnleauened bread, when they killed the
Paſſeouer, his diſciples ſaid vnto him, Where wilt thou that we goe, and
prepare, that thou mayeſt eate the Paſſeouer?13And he ſendeth forth two
of his diſciples, and ſaith vnto them, Goe yee into the citie, and there
ſhall meet you a man bearing a pitcher of water: follow him.14And
whereſoeuer he ſhall goe in, ſay yee to the good man of the houſe, The
Maſter ſaith, Where is the gueſt chamber, where I ſhall eate the
Paſſeouer with my diſciples?15And he will ſhew you a large vpper roome
furniſhed, and prepared: there make ready for vs.16And his diſciples
went forth, and came into the citie, and found as hee had ſaid vnto them:
and they made readie the Paſſeouer.17And in the euening hee commeth
with the twelue.18And as they ſate, and did eat, Ieſus ſaid, Uerily I ſay
vnto you, one of you which eateth with me, ſhall betray mee.19And they
began to be ſorowfull, and to ſay vnto him, one by one, Is it I? And
another ſaid, Is it I?20And he anſwered, and ſaide vnto them, It is one
of the twelue, that dippeth with me in the diſh.21The ſonne of man
indeed goeth, as it is written of him: but woe to that man by whom the
Sonne of man is betrayed: Good were it for that man, if he had neuer
bene borne.22And as they did eate, Ieſus tooke bread, and bleſſed, and
brake it, and gaue to them, and ſaid, Take, eate: this is my body.23And
he tooke the cup, and when he had giuen thanks, he gaue it to them: and
they all dranke of it.24And he ſaid vnto them, This is my blood of the
new Teſtament, which is ſhed for many.25Uerely I ſay vnto you, I will
drinke no more of the fruit of the Uine, vntill that day that I drinke it
new in the kingdome of God.26And when they had ſung an hymne, they
went out into the mount of Oliues.27And Ieſus ſaith vnto them, All ye
ſhall be offended becauſe of mee this night: for it is written, I will ſmite
the ſhepheard, and the ſheepe ſhall be ſcattered.28But after that I am
riſen, I will goe before you into Galilee.29But Peter ſaid vnto him,
Although al ſhalbe offended, yet wil not I.30And Ieſus ſaith vnto him,
Uerily I ſay vnto thee, that this day, euen in this night before the cocke
crow twiſe, thou ſhalt denie me thriſe.31But he ſpake the more
vehemently, If I ſhould die with thee, I will not denie thee in any wiſe.
Likewiſe alſo ſaid they all.32And they came to a place which was named
Gethſemani, and hee ſaith to his diſciples, Sit yee here, while I ſhall
pray.33And hee taketh with him Peter, and Iames, and Iohn, and began
to be ſore amazed, and to be very heauy,34And ſaith vnto them, My ſoule
is exceeding ſorowful vnto death: tarie ye here, and watch.35And he went
forward a litle, and fell on the ground, and prayed, that if it were poſsible,
the houre might paſſe from him.36And he ſaid, Abba, father, all things
are poſsible vnto thee, take away this cup from me: Neuertheleſſe, not
that I will, but what thou wilt.37And hee commeth, and findeth them
ſleeping, and ſaith vnto Peter, Simon, ſleepeſt thou? Couldeſt not thou
watch one houre?38Watch ye and pray, leſt yee enter into temptation:
The ſpirit truly is ready, but the fleſh is weake.39And againe he went
away, and prayed, and ſpake the ſame words.40And when he returned,
he found them aſleepe againe, (for their eies were heauie) neither wiſt
they what to anſwere him.41And he commeth the third time, and ſaith
vnto them, Sleepe on now, and take your reſt: it is enough, the houre is
come, behold, the Son of man is betrayed into the hands of
ſinners.42Riſe vp, let vs goe, Loe, he that betrayeth me, is at hand.43And
immediately, while hee yet ſpake, commeth Iudas, one of the twelue,
and with him a great multitude with ſwords, and ſtaues, from the chiefe
Prieſts, and the Scribes, & the Elders.44And he that betrayed him, had
giuen them a token, ſaying, Whomſoeuer I ſhall kiſſe, that ſame is he;
take him, and lead him away ſafely.45And aſsoone as he was come, he
goeth ſtraightway to him, and ſayeth, Maſter, Maſter, and kiſſed
him.46And they layed their hands on him, and tooke him.47And one of
them that ſtood by, drew a ſword, and ſmote a ſeruant of the high Prieſt,
and cut off his eare.48And Ieſus anſwered, & ſaid vnto thē, Are ye come
out as againſt a theefe, with ſwords, & with ſtaues to take me?49I was
daily with you in the Temple, teaching, and yee tooke me not; but the
Scriptures muſt be fulfilled.50And they all forſooke him, & fled.51And
there followed him a certaine yong man, hauing a linnen cloth caſt about
his naked body, and the yong men laid hold on him.52And he left the
linnen cloth, and fled from them naked.53And they led Ieſus away to the
high Prieſt, and with him were aſſembled all the chiefe Prieſts, and the
Elders, and the Scribes.54And Peter followed him a farre off, euen into
the pallace of the high Prieſt: and he ſate with the ſeruants, and warmed
himſelfe at the fire.55And the chiefe Prieſts, and all the counſell ſought
for witneſſe againſt Ieſus, to put him to death, & found none.56For
many bare falſe witneſſe againſt him, but their witneſſe agreed not
together.57And there aroſe certaine, and bare falſe witneſſe againſt him,
ſaying,58We heard him ſay, I will deſtroy this Temple that is made with
hands, and within three dayes I will build another made without
hands.59But neither ſo did their witneſſe agree together.60And the high
Prieſt ſtood vp in the mids, and aſked Ieſus, ſaying, Anſwereſt thou
nothing? What is it which theſe witneſſe againſt thee?61But he held his
peace, and anſwered nothing. Againe, the high Prieſt aſked him, and ſaid
vnto him, Art thou the Chriſt, the ſonne of the Bleſſed?62And Ieſus ſaid,
I am: and yee ſhall ſee the ſonne of man ſitting on the right hand of
power, and comming in the clouds of heauen.63Then the high Prieſt rent
his clothes, and ſaith, What neede we any further witneſſes?64Yee haue
heard the blaſphemy: what thinke yee? And they all condemned him to
be guilty of death.65And ſome beganne to ſpit on him, and to couer his
face, and to buffet him, and to ſay vnto him, Prophecie: And the
ſeruants did ſtricke him with the palmes of their hands.66And as Peter
was beneath in the palace, there commeth one of the maides of the high
Prieſt.67And when ſhe ſaw Peter warning himſelfe, ſhe looked vpon
him, and ſaid, And thou alſo waſt with Ieſus of Nazareth.68But hee
denied, ſaying, I know not, neither vnderſtand I what thou ſayeſt. And
he went out into the porch, and the cocke crew.69And a maide ſaw him
againe, and beganne to ſay to them that ſtood by, This is one of
them.70And he denied it againe. And a little after, they that ſtood by ſaid

againe to Peter, Surely thou art one of them: for thou art a Galilean, and
thy ſpeach agreeth thereto. 71 But he beganne to curſe and to ſweare,
ſaying, I know not this man of whom yee ſpeake. 72 And the ſecond time
the cocke crew: and Peter called to minde the word that Ieſus ſaid vnto
him, Before the cockecrow twiſe, thou ſhalt denie me thriſe. And when
he thought thereon, he wept.
CHAPTER 15 1 And ſtraightway in the morning the chiefe Prieſts helde
a conſultation with the Elders and Scribes, and the whole Councell, and
bound Ieſus, and caried him away, and deliuered him to Pilate. 2 And
Pilate aſked him, Art thou the King of the Iewes? And hee anſwering,
ſaid vnto him, Thou ſayeſt it. 3 And the chiefe Prieſts accuſed him of
many things: but hee anſwered nothing. 4 And Pilate aſked him againe,
ſaying, Anſwereſt thou nothing? behold how many things they witneſſe
againſt thee. 5 But Ieſus yet anſwered nothing, ſo that Pilate
marueiled. 6 Now at that Feaſt he releaſed vnto them one priſoner,
whomſoeuer they deſired. 7 And there was one named Barabbas, which
lay bound with them that had made inſurrection with him, who had
committed murder in the inſurrection. 8 And the multitude crying alowd,
began to deſire him to doe as he had euer done vnto them. 9 But Pilate
anſwered them, ſaying, Will ye that I releaſe vnto you the King of the
Iewes? 10 (For hee knew that the chiefe Prieſts had deliuered him for
enuie.) 11 But the chiefe Prieſts mooued the people, that hee ſhould rather
releaſe Barabbas vnto them. 12 And Pilate anſwered, and ſaid againe vnto
them, What will yee then that I ſhall do vnto him whom ye call the King
of the Iewes? 13 And they cried out againe, Crucifie him. 14 Then Pilate
ſaide vnto them, Why, what euill hath hee done? And they cried out the
more exceedingly, Crucifie him. 15 And ſo Pilate, willing to content the
people, releaſed Barabbas vnto them, and deliuered Ieſus, when he had
ſcourged him, to be crucified. 16 And the ſouldiers led him away into the
hall, called Pretorium, and they call together the whole band. 17 And they
clothed him with purple, and platted a crowne of thornes, and put it
about his head, 18 And beganne to ſalute him, Haile King of the
Iewes. 19 And they ſmote him on the head with a reed, and did ſpit vpon
him, and bowing their knees, worſhipped him. 20 And when they had
mocked him, they tooke off the purple from him, and put his owne
clothes on him, and led him out to crucifie him. 21 And they compell one
Simon a Cyrenian, who paſſed by, comming out of the country, the
father of Alexander and Rufus, to beare his Croſse. 22 And they bring him
vnto the place Golgotha, which is, being interpreted, the place of a
ſkull. 23 And they gaue him to drinke, wine mingled with myrrhe: but he
receiued it not. 24 And when they had crucified him, they parted his
garments, caſting lots vpon them, what euery man ſhould take. 25 And it
was the third houre, and they crucified him. 26 And the ſuperſcription of
his accuſation was written ouer, THE KING OF THE IEWES. 27 And
with him they crucifie two theeues, the one on his right hand, and the
other on his left. 28 And the Scripture was fulfilled, which ſayeth, And
hee was numbred with the tranſgreſsours. 29 And they that paſſed by,
railed on him, wagging their heads, and ſaying, Ah thou that deſtroyeſt
the Temple, and buildeſt it in three dayes, 30 Saue thy ſelfe, and come
downe from the Croſse. 31 Likewiſe alſo the chiefe Prieſts mocking, ſaid
among themſelues with the Scribes, He ſaued others, himſelfe he cannot
ſaue. 32 Let Chriſt the King of Iſrael deſcend now from the Croſse, that
we may ſee and beleeue: And they that were crucified with him, reuiled
him. 33 And when the ſixth houre was come, there was darkeneſſe ouer
the whole land, vntill the ninth houre. 34 And at the ninth houre, Ieſus
cryed with a loude voice, ſaying, Eloi, Eloi, lamaſabachthani? which is,
being interpreted, My God, my God, why haſt thou forſaken me? 35 And
ſome of them that ſtood by, when they heard it, ſaid, Behold, he calleth
Elias. 36 And one ranne, and filled a ſpunge full of vineger, and put it on
a reed, and gaue him to drinke, ſaying, Let alone, let vs ſee whether Elias
will come to take him downe. 37 And Ieſus cryed with a loude voice, and
gaue vp the ghoſt. 38 And the vaile of the Temple was rent in twaine,
from the top to the bottome. 39 And when the Centurion which ſtood
ouer againſt him, ſaw that hee ſo cryed out, and gaue vp the ghoſt, hee
ſaid, Truely this man was the Sonne of God. 40 There were alſo women
looking on afarre off, among whom was Mary Magdalene, and Mary the
mother of Iames the leſſe, and of Ioſes, and Salome: 41 Who alſo when
hee was in Galile, followed him, and miniſtred vnto him, and many other
women which came vp with him vnto Hieruſalem. 42 And now when the
euen was come, (becauſe it was the Preparation, that is, the day before
the Sabbath) 43 Ioſeph of Arimathea, an honourable counſeller, which
alſo waited for the kingdome of God, came, and went in boldly vnto
Pilate, and craued the body of Ieſus. 44 And Pilate marueiled if he were
already dead, and calling vnto him the Centurion, hee aſked him whether
hee had beene any while dead. 45 And when he knew it of the Centurion,
he gaue the body to Ioſeph. 46 And hee bought fine linnen, and tooke
him downe, and wrapped him in the linnen, and laide him in a ſepulchre,
which was hewen out of a rocke, and rolled a ſtone vnto the doore of
the ſepulchre. 47 And Mary Magdalene, and Mary the mother of Ioſes
behelde where he was laide.
CHAPTER 16 1 And when the Sabbath was paſt, Mary Magdalene, and
Mary the mother of Iames, and Salome, had bought ſweete ſpices, that
they might come and anoint him. 2 And very early in the morning, the
firſt day of the week they came vnto the ſepulchre, at the riſing of the
ſunne: 3 And they ſaid among themſelues, who ſhall roll vs away the ſtone
from the doore of the ſepulchre? 4 (And when they looked, they ſaw that
the ſtone was rolled away) for it was very great. 5 And entring into the
ſepulchre, they ſawe a young man ſitting on the right ſide, clothed in a
long white garment, and they were affrighted. 6 And hee ſayth vnto them,
Be not affrighted; ye ſeeke Ieſus of Nazareth, which was crucified: he is
riſen, hee is not here: behold the place where they laide him. 7 But goe
your way, tell his diſciples, and Peter, that hee goeth before you into
Galile, there ſhall ye ſee him, as he ſaid vnto you. 8 And they went out
quickely, and fledde from the ſepulchre, for they trembled, and were
amazed, neither ſayd they any thing to any man, for they were
afraid. 9 Now when Ieſus was riſen early, the firſt day of the weeke, he
appeared firſt to Mary Magdalene, out of whom he had caſt ſeuen
deuils. 10 And ſhe went and told them that had beene with him, as they
mourned and wept. 11 And they, when they had heard that he was aliue,
and had beene ſeene of her, beleeued not. 12 After that, he appeared in
another forme vnto two of them, as they walked, and went into the
countrey. 13 And they went and tolde it vnto the reſidue, neither beleeued
they them. 14 Afterward he appeared vnto the eleuen, as they ſate at meat,
and vpbraided them with their vnbeliefe, and hardneſse of heart,
becauſe they beleeued not them, which had ſeene him after he was
riſen. 15 And he ſaid vnto them, Goe yee into all the world, and preach
the Goſpel to euery creature. 16 He that beleeueth and is baptized, ſhalbe
ſaued, but he that beleeueth not, ſhall be damned. 17 And theſe ſignes ſhal
follow them that beleeue, In my Name ſhall they caſt out deuils, they
ſhall ſpeake with new tongues, 18 They ſhall take vp ſerpents, and if they
drinke any deadly thing, it ſhall not hurt them, they ſhall lay hands on
the ſicke, and they ſhall recouer. 19 So then after the Lord had ſpoken
vnto them, he was receiued vp into heauen, and ſate on the right hand
of God. 20 And they went foorth, and preached euery where, the Lord
working with them, and confirming the worde with ſignes following.
Amen.

LUKE

CHAPTER 1 1 Foraſmuch as many haue taken in hande to ſet foorth in
order a declaration of thoſe things which are moſt ſurely beleeued
among vs, 2 Euen as they deliuered them vnto vs, which from the
beginning were eye-witneſſes, & miniſters of the word: 3 It ſeemed good
to me alſo, hauing had perfect vnderſtanding of things from the very
firſt, to write vnto thee in order, moſt excellent Theophilus, 4 That thou
mighteſt know the certainetie of thoſe things wherein thou haſt bene
inſtructed. 5 There was in the dayes of Herode the king of Iudea, a
certaine Prieſt, named Zacharias, of the courſe of Abia, and his wife was
of the daughters of Aaron, and her name was Elizabeth. 6 And they were
both righteous before God, walking in all the Commandements and
ordinances of the Lord, blameleſſe. 7 And they had no childe, becauſe
that Elizabeth was barren, and they both were now well ſtriken in
yeeres. 8 And it came to paſſe, that while he executed the Prieſts office
before God in the order of his courſe, 9 According to the cuſtome of the
Prieſts office, his lot was to burne incenſe when he went into the Temple
of the Lord. 10 And the whole multitude of the people were praying

without, at the time of incenſe.11And there appeared vnto him an Angel
of the Lord, ſtanding on the right ſide of the Altar of incenſe.12And
when Zacharias ſawe him, hee was troubled, and feare fell vpon
him.13But the Angel ſaid vnto him, Feare not, Zacharias, for thy prayer
is heard, and thy wife Elizabeth ſhall beare thee a ſonne, and thou ſhalt
call his name Iohn.14And thou ſhalt haue ioy and gladneſſe, and many
ſhall reioyce at his birth:15For he ſhall be great in the ſight of the Lord,
and ſhal drinke neither wine, nor ſtrong drinke, and he ſhall bee filled
with the holy Ghoſt, euen from his mothers wombe.16And many of the
children of Iſrael ſhall hee turne to the Lord their God.17And hee ſhall
goe before him in the ſpirit and power of Elias, to turne the hearts of
the fathers to the children, and the diſobedient to the wiſedome of the
iuſt, to make ready a people prepared for the Lord.18And Zacharias ſaid
vnto the Angel, Whereby ſhall I know this? For I am an old man, and
my wife well ſtriken in yeeres.19And the Angel anſwering, ſaid vnto him,
I am Gabriel that ſtand in the preſence of God, and am ſent to ſpeake
vnto thee, and to ſhew thee theſe glad tidings.20And behold, thou ſhalt
be dumbe, and not able to ſpeake, vntill the day that theſe things ſhall
bee performed, becauſe thou beleeueſt not my words, which ſhall bee
fulfilled in their ſeaſon.21And the people waited for Zacharias, and
maruelled that hee taried ſo long in the temple.22And when he came out,
he could not ſpeake vnto them: and they perceiued that he had ſeene a
viſion in the temple: for he beckened vnto them, and remained
ſpeechleſſe.23And it came to paſſe, that as ſoone as the dayes of his
miniſtration were accompliſhed, he departed to his owne houſe.24And
after thoſe dayes his wife Elizabeth conceiued, and hid her ſelfe fiue
moneths, ſaying,25Thus hath the Lord dealt with me in the dayes
wherein he looked on me, to take away my reproch among men.26And
in the ſixt moneth, the Angel Gabriel was ſent from God, vnto a citie of
Galilee, named Nazareth,27To a virgine eſpouſed to a man whoſe name
was Ioſeph, of the houſe of Dauid, and the virgins name was
Marie.28And the Angel came in vnto her, and ſaid, Haile thou that art
highly fauoured, the Lord is with thee: Bleſſed art thou among
women.29And when ſhe ſaw him, ſhe was troubled at his ſaying, and caſt
in her minde what maner of ſalutation this ſhould be.30And the Angel
ſaid vnto her, Feare not, Marie, for thou haſt found fauour with
God.31And behold, thou ſhalt conceiue in thy wombe, and bring forth
a ſonne, and ſhalt call his name Ieſus.32He ſhall be great, and ſhall be
called the ſonne of the Higheſt, and the Lord God ſhall giue vnto him
the throne of his father Dauid.33And hee ſhall reigne ouer the houſe of
Iacob for euer, and of his kingdome there ſhall be no end.34Then ſaid
Marie vnto the Angel, How ſhall this be, ſeeing I know not a man?35And
the Angel anſwered and ſaid vnto her, The holy Ghoſt ſhall come vpon
thee, and the power of the Higheſt ſhall ouerſhadow thee. Therefore
alſo that holy thing which ſhall bee borne of thee, ſhall bee called the
ſonne of God.36And behold, thy couſin Elizabeth, ſhe hath alſo
conceiued a ſonne in her old age, and this is the ſixt moneth with her,
who was called barren.37For with God no thing ſhall be
vnpoſsible.38And Marie ſaid, Behold the handmaide of the Lord, be it
vnto me according to thy word: and the Angel departed from her.39And
Marie aroſe in thoſe dayes, and went into the hill countrey with haſte,
into a citie of Iuda,40And entred into the houſe of Zacharias, and ſaluted
Elizabeth.41And it came to paſſe that when Elizabeth heard the
ſalutation of Marie, the babe leaped in her wombe, and Elizabeth was
filled with the holy Ghoſt.42And ſhe ſpake out with a loud voyce, and
ſaide, Bleſſed art thou among women, and bleſſed is the fruite of thy
wombe.43And whence is this to me, that the mother of my Lord ſhould
come to mee?44For loe, aſsoone as the voice of thy ſalutation ſounded
in mine eares, the babe leaped in my wombe for ioy.45And bleſſed is ſhe
that beleeued, for there ſhalbe a performance of thoſe things, which
were told her from the Lord.46And Marie ſaid, My ſoule doth magnifie
the Lord.47And my ſpirit hath reioyced in God my ſauiour.48For hee
hath regarded the low eſtate of his handmaiden: for behold, from
hencefoorth all generations ſhall call me bleſſed.49For he that is mighty
hath done to mee great things, and holy is his Name.50And his mercy is
on them that feare him, from generation to generation.51Hee hath
ſhewed ſtrength with his arme, he hath ſcattered the proud, in the
imagination of their hearts.52He hath put downe the mighty from their
ſeates, and exalted them of low degree.53Hee hath filled the hungry with
good things, and the rich hee hath ſent emptie away.54Hee hath holpen
his ſeruant Iſrael, in remembrance of his mercy,55As he ſpake to our
fathers, to Abraham, and to his ſeed for euer.56And Mary abode with
her about three moneths, and returned to her owne houſe.57Now
Elizabeths full time came, that ſhee ſhould be deliuered, and ſhee
brought foorth a ſonne.58And her neighbours and her couſins heard
how the Lord had ſhewed great mercy vpon her, and they reioyced with
her.59And it came to paſſe that on the eight day they came to circumciſe
the childe, and they called him Zacharias, after the name of his
father.60And his mother anſwered, and ſaid, Not ſo, but he ſhalbe called
Iohn.61And they ſaid vnto her, There is none of thy kinred that is called
by this name.62And they made ſignes to his father, how he would haue
him called.63And he aſked for a writing table, and wrote, ſaying, His
name is Iohn: and they marueiled all.64And his mouth was opened
immediatly, and his tongue looſed, and hee ſpake, and praiſed
God.65And feare came on all that dwelt round about them, and all theſe
ſayings were noiſed abroad thorowout all the hill countrey of
Iudea.66And all they that had heard them, layde them vp in their hearts,
ſaying, What maner of childe ſhal this be? And the hand of the Lord was
with him.67And his father Zacharias was filled with the holy Ghoſt, and
propheſied, ſaying,68Bleſſed bee the Lord God of Iſrael, for hee hath
viſited and redeemed his people,69And hath raiſed vp an horne of
ſaluation for vs, in the houſe of his ſeruant Dauid,70As he ſpake by the
mouth of his holy Prophets, which haue bene ſince the world
began:71That wee ſhould be ſaued from our enemies, and from the hand
of all that hate vs,72To performe the mercy promiſed to our fathers, and
to remember his holy Couenant,73The oath which he ſware to our father
Abraham,74That hee would grant vnto vs, that wee beeing deliuered out
of the hands of our enemies, might ſerue him without feare,75In
holineſſe and righteouſneſſe before him, all the dayes of our life.76And
thou childe ſhalt bee called the Prophet of the Higheſt: for thou ſhalt
goe before the face of the Lord to prepare his wayes.77To giue
knowledge of ſaluation vnto his people, by the remiſsion of their
ſinnes,78Through the tender mercy of our God, whereby the day-ſpring
from on high hath viſited vs,79To giue light to them that ſit in darknes,
and in the ſhadow of death, to guide our feet into the way of
peace.80And the childe grew, and waxed ſtrong in ſpirit, and was in the
deſerts, till the day of his ſhewing vnto Iſrael.
CHAPTER 2 1And it came to paſſe in thoſe dayes, that there went out
a decree from Ceſar Auguſtus, that all the world ſhould be taxed.2(And
this taxing was firſt made whē Cyrenius was gouernor of Syria)3And all
went to bee taxed, euery one into his owne citie.4And Ioſeph alſo wēt
vp frō Galilee, out of the citie of Nazareth, into Iudea, vnto the citie of
Dauid, which is called Bethlehem, (becauſe he was of the houſe and
linage of Dauid,)5To be taxed with Mary his eſpouſed wife, being great
with child.6And ſo it was, that while they were there, the dayes were
accompliſhed that ſhe ſhould be deliuered.7And ſhe brought foorth her
firſt borne ſonne, and wrapped him in ſwadling clothes, and laid him in
a manger, becauſe there was no roome for them in the Inne.8And there
were in the ſame countrey ſhepheards abiding in þe field, keeping watch
ouer their flocke by night.9And loe, the Angel of the Lord came vpon
them, and the glory of the Lord ſhone round about them, and they were
ſore afraid.10And the Angel ſaid vnto them, Feare not: For behold, I
bring you good tidings of great ioy, which ſhall be to all people.11For
vnto you is borne this day, in the citie of Dauid, a Sauiour, which is
Chriſt the Lord.12And this ſhall be a ſigne vnto you; yee ſhall find the
babe wrapped in ſwadling clothes lying in a manger.13And ſuddenly
there was with the Angel a multitude of the heauenly hoſte praiſing God,
and ſaying,14Glory to God in the higheſt, and on earth peace, good wil
towards men.15And it came to paſſe, as the Angels were gone away from
them into heauen, the ſhepheards ſaid one to another, Let vs now goe
euen vnto Bethlehem, and ſee this thing which is come to paſſe, which
the Lord hath made knowen vnto vs.16And they came with haſte, and
found Mary and Ioſeph, and the babe lying in a manger.17And when
they had ſeene it, they made knowen abroad the ſaying, which was told
them, concerning this child.18And all they that heard it, wondered at
thoſe things, which were tolde them by the ſhepheards.19But Mary kept
all theſe things, and pondered them in her heart.20And the ſhepheards

returned, glorifying & praiſing God for all the things that they had heard and ſeene, as it was told vnto them.21And when eight dayes were accompliſhed for the circumciſing of the childe, his name was called Ieſus, which was ſo named of the Angel before he was conceiued in the wombe.22And when the dayes of her purification according to the law of Moſes, were accompliſhed, they brought him to Hieruſalem, to preſent him to the Lord,23(As it is written in the law of the Lord, Euery male that openeth the wombe, ſhalbe called holy to the Lord)24And to offer a ſacrifice according to that which is ſaid in the Law of the Lord, a paire of turtle doues, or two yong pigeons.25And behold, there was a man in Hieruſalem, whoſe name was Simeon, and the ſame man was iuſt and deuout, waiting for the conſolation of Iſrael: and the holy Ghoſt was vpon him.26And it was reuealed vnto him by the holy Ghoſt, that he ſhould not ſee death, before he had ſeene the Lords Chriſt.27And hee came by the ſpirit into the Temple: and when the parents brought in the child Ieſus, to doe for him after the cuſtome of the Lawe,28Then tooke hee him vp in his armes, and bleſſed God, and ſaid,29Lord now letteſt thou thy ſeruant depart in peace, according to thy word.30For mine eyes haue ſeene thy ſaluation.31Which thou haſt prepared before the face of all people.32A light to lighten the Gentiles, and the glory of thy people Iſrael.33And Ioſeph and his mother marueiled at thoſe things which were ſpoken of him.34And Simeon bleſſed them, and ſaid vnto Marie his mother, Behold, this child is ſet for the fall and riſing againe of many in Iſrael: and for a ſigne which ſhall be ſpoken againſt,35(Yea a ſword ſhall pearce thorow thy owne ſoule alſo) that the thoughts of many hearts may be reuealed.36And there was one Anna a Propheteſse, the daughter of Phanuel, of the tribe of Aſer; ſhe was of a great age, and had liued with an huſband ſeuen yeeres from her virginitie.37And ſhe was a widow of about foureſcore and foure yeeres, which departed not from the Temple, but ſerued God with faſtings and prayers night and day.38And ſhe comming in that inſtant, gaue thankes likewiſe vnto the Lord, and ſpake of him to al them that looked for redemption in Hieruſalem.39And when they had performed all things according to the Lawe of the Lord, they returned into Galilee, to their owne citie Nazareth.40And the child grew, and waxed ſtrong in ſpirit filled with wiſedome, and the grace of God was vpon him.41Now his parents went to Hieruſalem euery yeere, at the feaſt of the Paſſeouer.42And when he was twelue yeeres old, they went vp to Hieruſalem, after the cuſtome of the feaſt.43And when they had fulfilled the dayes, as they returned, the childe Ieſus taried behind in Hieruſalem, and Ioſeph and his mother knew not of it.44But they ſuppoſing him to haue bene in the company, went a daies iourney, and they ſought him among their kinſefolke and acquaintance.45And when they found him not, they turned backe againe to Hieruſalem, ſeeking him.46And it came to paſſe, that after three daies they found him in the Temple, ſitting in the midſt of the Doctours, both hearing them, and aſking them queſtions.47And all that heard him were aſtoniſhed at his vnderſtanding, and anſweres.48And when they ſawe him, they were amazed: and his mother ſaid vnto him, Sonne, why haſt thou thus dealt with vs? Behold, thy father and I haue ſought thee ſorrowing.49And he ſaid vnto them, How is it that ye ſought me? Wiſt yee not that I muſt bee about my fathers buſineſse?50And they vnderſtood not the ſaying which he ſpake vnto them.51And he went downe with them, and came to Nazareth, and was ſubiect vnto them: But his mother kept all theſe ſayings in her heart.52And Ieſus increaſed in wiſedom and ſtature, and in fauour with God and man.

CHAPTER 31Now in the fifteenth yeere of the reigne of Tiberius Ceſar, Pontius Pilate being Gouernour of Iudea, & Herode being Tetrarch of Galilee, and his brother Philip Tetrarch of Iturea, and of the region of Trachonitis, and Lyſanias the Tetrarch of Abilene,2Annas and Caiaphas being the high Prieſts, the word of God came vnto Iohn the ſonne of Zacharias, in the wilderneſſe.3And he came into all the countrey about Iordane, preaching the baptiſme of repentance, for the remiſsiō of ſinnes,4As it is written in the book of the words of Eſaias the Prophet, ſaying, The voyce of one crying in the wilderneſſe, Prepare ye the way of the Lord, make his paths ſtraight.5Euery valley ſhall be filled, and euery mountaine and hill ſhalbe brought low, and the crooked ſhall bee made ſtraight, and the rough wayes ſhall be made ſmooth.6And all fleſh ſhal ſee the ſaluation of God.7Then ſaid hee to the multitude that came forth to bee baptized of him, O generation of vipers, who hath warned you to flee from the wrath to come?8Bring forth therfore fruits worthy of repentance, and begin not to ſay within your ſelues, We haue Abraham to our father: For I ſay vnto you, that God is able of theſe ſtones to raiſe vp children vnto Abraham.9And now alſo the axe is laid vnto the root of the trees: Euery tree therefore which bringeth not foorth good fruit, is hewen downe, and caſt into the fire.10And the people aſked him, ſaying, What ſhall we doe then?11He anſwereth, and ſaith vnto them, He that hath two coats, let him impart to him that hath none, and he that hath meat, let him doe likewiſe.12Then came alſo Publicanes to be baptized, and ſaid vnto him, Maſter, what ſhall we doe?13And he ſaid vnto them, Exact no more then that which is appointed you.14And the ſouldiers likewiſe demanded of him, ſaying, And what ſhall we doe? And he ſaid vnto them, Doe violence to no man, neither accuſe any falſely, & be content with your wages.15And as the people were in expectation, and all men muſed in their hearts of Iohn, whether he were the Chriſt or not:16Iohn anſwered, ſaying vnto them all, I indeede baptize you with water, but one mightier then I commeth, the latchet of whoſe ſhooes I am not worthy to vnlooſe, he ſhall baptize you with the holy Ghoſt, and with fire.17Whoſe fanne is in his hand, and he will thorowly purge his floore, and will gather the wheat into his garner, but the chaffe he will burne with fire vnquencheable.18And many other things in his exhortation preached he vnto the people.19But Herode the Tetrarch being reprooued by him for Herodias his brother Philips wife, and for all the euils which Herode had done,20Added yet this aboue all, that he ſhut vp Iohn in priſon.21Now when all the people were baptized, and it came to paſſe that Ieſus alſo being baptized, and praying, the heauen was opened:22And the holy Ghoſt deſcended in a bodily ſhape like a Doue vpon him, and a voice came from heauen, which ſaid, Thou art my beloued ſonne, in thee I am well pleaſed.23And Ieſus himſelfe began to be about thirty yeeres of age, being (as was ſuppoſed) the ſonne of Ioſeph, which was the ſonne of Heli,24Which was the ſonne of Matthat, which was the ſonne of Leui, which was the ſonne of Melchi, which was the ſonne of Ianna, which was the ſonne of Ioſeph,25Which was the ſonne of Matthathias, which was the ſonne of Amos, which was the ſonne of Naum, which was the ſonne of Eli, which was the ſonne of Nagge,26Which was the ſonne of Maath, which was the ſonne of Matthathias, which was the ſonne of Semei, which was the ſonne of Ioſeph, which was the ſonne of Iuda,27Which was the ſonne of Ioanna, which was the ſonne of Rheſa, which was the ſonne of Zorobabel, which was the ſonne of Salathiel, which was the ſonne of Neri,28Which was the ſonne of Melchi, which was the ſonne of Addi, which was the ſonne of Coſam, which was the ſonne of Elmodam, which was the ſonne of Er,29Which was the ſonne of Ioſe, which was the ſonne of Eliezer, which was the ſonne of Iorim, which was the ſonne of Matthat, which was the ſonne of Leui,30Which was the ſonne of Simeon, which was the ſonne of Iuda, which was the ſonne of Ioſeph, which was the ſonne of Ionan, which was the ſonne of Eliakim,31Which was the ſonne of Melea, which was the ſonne of Menam, which was the ſonne of Mattatha, which was the ſonne of Nathan, which was the ſonne of Dauid,32Which was the ſonne of Ieſſe, which was the ſonne of Obed, which was the ſonne of Booz, which was the ſonne of Salmon, which was the ſonne of Naſson,33Which was the ſonne of Aminadab, which was the ſonne of Aram, which was the ſonne of Efrom, which was the ſonne of Phares, which was the ſonne of Iuda,34Which was the ſonne of Iacob, which was the ſonne of Iſaac, which was the ſonne of Abraham, which was the ſonne of Thara, which was the ſonne of Nachor,35Which was the ſonne of Saruch, which was the ſonne of Ragau, which was the ſonne of Phaleg, which was the ſonne of Heber, which was the ſonne of Sala,36Which was the ſonne of Cainan, which was the ſonne of Arphaxad, which was the ſonne of Sem, which was the ſonne of Noe, which was the ſonne of Lamech,37Which was the ſonne of Mathuſala, which was the ſonne of Enoch, which was the ſonne of Iared, which was the ſonne of Maleleel, which was the ſonne of Cainan,38Which was the ſonne of Enos, which was the ſonne of Seth, which was the ſonne of Adam, which was the ſonne of God.

CHAPTER 41And Ieſus being full of the holy Ghoſt, returned from Iordane, and was led by the ſpirit into the wilderneſſe,2Being fourtie dayes tempted of the deuil, and in thoſe dayes he did eat nothing: and when they were ended, he afterward hungred.3And the deuil ſaide vnto him, If thou be the Sonne of God, command this ſtone that it be made

bread.4And Ieſus anſwered him, ſaying, It is written, that man ſhall not
liue by bread alone, but by euery word of God.5And the deuil taking
him vp into an high mountaine, ſhewed vnto him all the kingdomes of
the world in a moment of time.6And the deuil ſaid vnto him, All this
power will I giue thee, and the glory of them; for that is deliuered vnto
me, & to whomſoeuer I will, I giue it.7If thou therefore wilt worſhip me,
all ſhalbe thine.8And Ieſus anſwered and ſaid vnto him, Get thee
behinde me, Satan: for it is written, Thou ſhalt worſhip the Lord thy
God, and him onely ſhalt thou ſerue.9And hee brought him to
Hieruſalem, and ſet him on a pinacle of the Temple, and ſaid vnto him,
If thou be the Sonne of God, caſt thy ſelfe downe from hence.10For it
is written, He ſhall giue his Angels charge ouer thee, to keepe thee.11And
in their handes they ſhall beare thee vp, leſt at any time thou daſh thy
foot againſt a ſtone.12And Ieſus anſwering, ſaid vnto him, It is ſaid, Thou
ſhalt not tempt the Lord thy God.13And when the deuil had ended all
the temptation, hee departed from him for a ſeaſon.14And Ieſus
returned in the power of the Spirit into Galilee, and there went out a
fame of him through all the region round about.15And hee taught in
their Synagogues, being glorified of all.16And hee came to Nazareth,
where he had bene brought vp, and as his cuſtome was, he went into
the Synagogue on the Sabbath day, and ſtood vp for to reade.17And
there was deliuered vnto him the booke of the Prophet Eſaias, and when
he had opened the Booke, he found the place where it was written,18The
Spirit of the Lord is vpon mee, becauſe hee hath anointed mee, to preach
the Goſpel to the poore, he hath ſent mee to heale the broken hearted,
to preach deliuerance to the captiues, and recouering of ſight to the
blinde, to ſet at libertie them that are bruiſed,19To preach the acceptable
yeere of the Lord.20And he cloſed the booke, and hee gaue it againe to
the miniſter, and ſate downe: and the eyes of all them that were in the
Synagogue were faſtened on him.21And hee began to ſay vnto them,
This day is this Scripture fulfilled in your eares.22And all bare him
witneſſe, and wondered at the gracious wordes, which proceeded out of
his mouth. And they ſaid, Is not this Ioſephs ſonne?23And hee ſaid vnto
them, Yee will ſurely ſay vnto me this prouerbe, Phyſition, heale thy
ſelfe: Whatſoeuer wee haue heard done in Capernaum, doe alſo here in
thy countrey.24And hee ſaid, Verely I ſay vnto you, no Prophet is
accepted in his owne countrey.25But I tell you of a trueth, many widowes
were in Iſrael in the dayes of Elias, when the heauen was ſhut vp three
yeres and ſixe moneths: when great famine was throughout all the
land:26But vnto none of them was Elias ſent, ſaue vnto Sarepta a citie
of Sidon, vnto a woman that was a widow.27And many lepers were in
Iſrael in the time of Elizeus the Prophet: and none of them was cleanſed,
ſauing Naaman the Syrian.28And all they in the Synagogue, when they
heard theſe things, were filled with wrath,29And roſe vp, and thruſt him
out of the citie, & led him vnto the brow of the hill (whereon their city
was built) that they might caſt him downe headlong.30But he paſsing
thorow the mids of them, went his way:31And came downe to
Capernaum, a citie of Galile, and taught them on the Sabbath
dayes.32And they were aſtoniſhed at his doctrine: for his worde was with
power.33And in the Synagogue there was a man which had a ſpirit of an
vncleane deuill, and cryed out with a loud voice,34Saying, Let vs alone,
what haue wee to doe with thee, thou Ieſus of Nazareth? art thou come
to deſtroy vs? I know thee who thou art, the Holy One of God.35And
Ieſus rebuked him, ſaying, Holde thy peace, and come out of him. And
when the deuill had throwen him in the middes, hee came out of him,
and hurt him not.36And they were all amazed, and ſpake among
themſelues, ſaying, What a word is this? for with authoritie and power
hee commaundeth the vncleane ſpirits, and they come out.37And the
fame of him went out into euery place of the countrey round
about.38And he aroſe out of the Synagogue, and entred into Simons
houſe: and Simons wiues mother was taken with a great feuer, and they
beſought him for her.39And he ſtood ouer her, and rebuked the feuer,
& it left her. And immediatly ſhe aroſe, & miniſtred vnto them.40Now
when the Sunne was ſetting, all they that had any ſicke with diuers
diſeaſes, brought them vnto him: and hee laid his handes on euery one
of them, and healed them.41And deuils alſo came out of many, crying
out, and ſaying, Thou art Chriſt the Sonne of God. And hee rebuking
them, ſuffered them not to ſpeake: for they knewe that hee was
Chriſt.42And when it was day, he departed, and went into a deſert place:
and the people ſought him, and came vnto him, and ſtayed him, that he
ſhould not depart from them.43And hee ſaid vnto them, I muſt preach
the kingdome of God to other cities alſo: for therefore am I ſent.44And
hee preached in the Synagogues of Galile.

CHAPTER 51And it came to paſſe, that as the people preaſſed vpon
him to heare the word of God, hee ſtood by the lake of Geneſareth,2And
ſawe two ſhips ſtanding by the lake: but the fiſhermen were gone out of
them, and were waſhing their nets.3And he entred into one of the ſhips,
which was Simons, and prayed him, that he would thruſt out a little from
the land: and he ſate downe, and taught the people out of the ſhip.4Now
when he had left ſpeaking, he ſaid vnto Simon, Lanch out into the deepe,
and let downe your nets for a draught.5And Simon anſwering, ſaid vnto
him, Maſter, wee haue toiled all the night, and haue taken nothing:
neuertheleſſe at thy word I will let downe the net.6And when they had
this done, they incloſed a great multitude of fiſhes, and their net
brake:7And they beckened vnto their partners, which were in the other
ſhip, that they ſhould come and helpe them. And they came, & filled
both the ſhips, ſo that they began to ſinke.8When Simon Peter ſaw it,
he fell downe at Ieſus knees, ſaying, Depart from me, for I am a ſinfull
man, O Lord.9For he was aſtoniſhed, and al that were with him, at the
draught of the fiſhes which they had taken.10And ſo was alſo Iames, and
Iohn the ſonnes of Zebedee, which were partners with Simon. And
Ieſus ſaid vnto Simon, Feare not, from henceforth thou ſhalt catch
men.11And when they had brought their ſhips to land, they forſooke all,
and followed him.12And it came to paſſe, when he was in a certaine citie,
behold a man full of leproſie: who ſeeing Ieſus, fell on his face, &
beſought him, ſaying, Lord, if thou wilt, thou canſt make me
cleane.13And he put forth his hand, and touched him, ſaying, I wil: be
thou cleane. And immediatly the leproſie departed from him.14And hee
charged him to tell no man: but, Goe, and ſhewe thy ſelfe to the Prieſt,
and offer for thy clenſing, according as Moſes commanded, for a
teſtimonie vnto them.15But ſo much the more went there a fame abroad
of him, and great multitudes came together to heare, and to be healed
by him of their infirmities.16And he withdrew himſelfe into the
wilderneſſe, and prayed.17And it came to paſſe on a certaine day, as hee
was teaching, that there were PhAriſees and Doctours of the Law ſitting
by, which were come out of euery towne of Galilee, and Iudea, and
Hieruſalem: and the power of the Lord was preſent to heale them.18And
behold, men brought in a bed a man which was taken with a palſie: and
they ſought meanes to bring him in, and to lay him before him.19And
when they could not find by what way they might bring him in, becauſe
of the multitude, they went vpon the houſe top, & let him downe
through the tiling with his couch, into the midſt before Ieſus.20And
when he ſaw their faith, hee ſaid vnto him, Man, thy ſinnes are forgiuen
thee.21And the Scribes and the PhAriſees began to reaſon, ſaying, Who
is this which ſpeaketh blaſphemies? Who can forgiue ſinnes, but God
alone?22But when Ieſus perceiued their thoughts, he anſwering, ſaide
vnto them, What reaſon ye in your hearts?23Whether is eaſier to ſay, Thy
ſinnes be forgiuen thee: or to ſay, Riſe vp and walke?24But that ye may
know that the Sonne of man hath power vpon earth to forgiue ſinnes
(he ſaid vnto the ſicke of the palſie,) I ſay vnto thee, Ariſe, and take vp
thy couch, and go into thine houſe.25And immediatly he roſe vp before
them, and tooke vp that whereon hee lay, and departed to his owne
houſe, glorifying God.26And they were all amazed, and they glorified
God, and were filled with feare, ſaying, Wee haue ſeene ſtrange things
to day.27And after theſe things hee went foorth, and ſawe a Publicane,
named Leui, ſitting at the receit of cuſtome: and hee ſaid vnto him,
Follow me.28And he left all, roſe vp, and followed him.29And Leui made
him a great feaſt in his owne houſe: and there was a great company of
Publicanes, and of others that ſate downe with them.30But their Scribes
and PhAriſees murmured againſt his diſciples, ſaying, Why doe ye eate
and drinke with Publicanes and ſinners?31And Ieſus anſwering, ſaid vnto
them, They that are whole need not a phyſician: but they that are
ſicke.32I came not to call the righteous, but ſinners to repentance.33And
they ſaid vnto him, Why doe the diſciples of Iohn faſt often, and make
prayers, and likewiſe the diſciples of the PhAriſees: but thine eat and
drinke?34And he ſaid vnto them, Can yee make the children of the
Bride-chamber faſt, while the Bridegrome is with them?35But the dayes
will come, when the Bridegrome ſhall bee taken away from them, and
then ſhall they faſt in thoſe dayes.36And he ſpake alſo a parable vnto

them, No man putteth a piece of a newe garment vpon an olde: if otherwiſe, then both the newe maketh a rent, and the piece that was taken out of the new, agreeth not with the olde.[37]And no man putteth new wine into old bottles: elſe the new wine will burſt the bottles, and be ſpilled, and the bottles ſhall periſh.[38]But newe wine muſt be put into newe bottles, and both are preſerued.[39]No man alſo hauing drunke olde wine, ſtraightway deſireth new: for he ſaith, The old is better.

CHAPTER 6[1]And it came to paſſe on the ſecond Sabbath after the firſt, that he went thorow the corne fields: and his diſciples plucked the eares of corne, and did eate, rubbing them in their hands.[2]And certaine of the PhAriſees ſaid vnto them, Why doe yee that which is not lawfull to doe on the Sabbath dayes?[3]And Ieſus anſwering them, ſaid, Haue yee not read ſo much as this what Dauid did, when himſelfe was an hungred, and they which were with him:[4]How he went into the houſe of God, and did take and eate the ſhew bread, and gaue alſo to them that were with him, which it is not lawful to eate but for the Prieſts alone?[5]And he ſaid vnto them, That the ſonne of man is Lord alſo of the Sabbath.[6]And it came to paſſe alſo on another Sabbath, that he entred into the Synagogue, and taught: and there was a man whoſe right hand was withered.[7]And the Scribes and PhAriſees watched him, whether he would heale on the Sabbath day: that they might find an accuſation againſt him.[8]But he knew their thoughts, and ſaid to the man which had the withered hand, Riſe vp, and ſtand foorth in the mids. And he aroſe, and ſtood foorth.[9]Then ſaid Ieſus vnto them, I will aſke you one thing, Is it lawfull on the Sabbath dayes to doe good, or to doe euill? to ſaue life, or to deſtroy it?[10]And looking round about vpon them all, he ſaid vnto the man, Stretch foorth thy hand. And he did ſo: and his hand was reſtored whole as the other.[11]And they were filled with madneſſe, and communed one with another what they might doe to Ieſus.[12]And it came to paſſe in thoſe dayes, that hee went out into a mountaine to pray, and continued all night in prayer to God.[13]And when it was day, he called vnto him his diſciples: and of them he choſe twelue; whom alſo hee named Apoſtles:[14]Simon, (whom he alſo named Peter,) and Andrew his brother: Iames and Iohn, Philip and Bartholomew,[15]Matthew and Thomas, Iames the ſonne of Alpheus, and Simon, called Zelotes,[16]And Iudas the brother of Iames, and Iudas Iſcariot, which alſo was the traitour.[17]And hee came downe with them, and ſtood in the plaine, and the company of his diſciples, and a great multitude of people, out of all Iudea and Hieruſalem, and from the ſea coaſt of Tyre and Sidon, which came to heare him, and to be healed of their diſeaſes,[18]And they that were vexed with vncleane ſpirits: and they were healed.[19]And the whole multitude ſought to touch him: for there went vertue out of him, and healed them all.[20]And hee lifted vp his eyes on his diſciples, and ſaid, Bleſſed be yee poore: for yours is the kingdome of God.[21]Bleſſed are yee that hunger now: for yee ſhall be filled. Bleſſed are yee that weepe now, for yee ſhall laugh.[22]Bleſſed are yee when men ſhall hate you, and when they ſhall ſeparate you from their company, and ſhal reproach you, and caſt out your name as euill, for the Sonne of mans ſake.[23]Reioice yee in that day, and leape for ioy: for behold, your reward is great in heauen for in the like maner did their fathers vnto the Prophets.[24]But woe vnto you that are rich: for yee haue receiued your conſolation.[25]Woe vnto you that are full: for yee ſhall hunger. Woe vnto you that laugh now: for yee ſhall mourne and weepe.[26]Woe vnto you when all men ſhall ſpeake well of you: for ſo did their fathers to the falſe Prophets.[27]But I ſay vnto you which heare, Loue your enemies, doe good to them which hate you,[28]Bleſſe them that curſe you, & pray for them which deſpitefully vſe you.[29]And vnto him that ſmiteth thee on the one cheeke, offer alſo the other: and him that taketh away thy cloake, forbid not to take thy coat alſo.[30]Giue to euery man that aſketh of thee, and of him that taketh away thy goods, aſke them not againe.[31]And as yee would that men ſhould doe to you, doe yee alſo to them likewiſe.[32]For if yee loue them which loue you, what thanke haue ye? for ſinners alſo loue thoſe that loue them.[33]And if ye doe good to them which doe good to you, What thanke haue ye? for ſinners alſo doe euen the ſame.[34]And if ye lend to them of whom ye hope to receiue, What thanke haue ye? for ſinners alſo lend to ſinners, to receiue as much againe.[35]But loue yee your enemies, and doe good, and lend, hoping for nothing againe: and your reward ſhall bee great, and ye ſhalbe the children of the Higheſt: for hee is kinde vnto the vnthankfull, and to the euill.[36]Be ye therefore mercifull, as your Father alſo is mercifull.[37]Iudge not, and ye ſhall not bee iudged: condemne not, and ye ſhall not be condemned: forgiue, and ye ſhall be forgiuen.[38]Giue, and it ſhall bee giuen vnto you, good meaſure, preaſſed downe, and ſhaken together, and running ouer, ſhall men giue into your boſome: for with the ſame meaſure that ye mete withall, it ſhall bee meaſured to you againe.[39]And hee ſpake a parable vnto them, Can the blinde leade the blinde? Shall they not both fall into the ditch?[40]The diſciple is not aboue his maſter: but euery one that is perfect ſhalbe as his maſter.[41]And why beholdeſt thou the mote that is in thy brothers eye, but perceiueſt not the beame that is in thine owne eye?[42]Either how canſt thou ſay to thy brother, Brother, let mee pull out the mote that is in thine eye: when thou thy ſelfe beholdeſt not the beame that is in thine owne eye? Thou hypocrite, caſt out firſt the beame out of thine owne eye, and then ſhalt thou ſee clearly to pul out the mote that is in thy brothers eye.[43]For a good tree bringeth not foorth corrupt fruit: neither doeth a corrupt tree bring foorth good fruit.[44]For euery tree is knowen by his owne fruit: for of thornes men doe not gather figs, nor of a bramble buſh gather they grapes.[45]A good man out of the good treaſure of his heart, bringeth foorth that which is good: and an euill man out of the euill treaſure of his heart, bringeth foorth that which is euill: For of the abundance of the heart, his mouth ſpeaketh.[46]And why call ye mee Lord, Lord, and doe not the things which I ſay?[47]Whoſoeuer commeth to me, and heareth my ſayings, and doeth them, I will ſhew you to whom he is like.[48]He is like a man which built an houſe, and digged deepe, and layd the foundation on a rocke. And when the flood aroſe, the ſtreame beat vehemently vpon that houſe, and could not ſhake it: for it was founded vpon a rocke.[49]But he that heareth, and doeth not, is like a man that without a foundation built an houſe vpon the earth: againſt which the ſtreame did beate vehemently, and immediatly it fell, and the ruine of that houſe was great.

CHAPTER 7[1]Now when hee had ended all his ſayings in the audience of the people, hee entred into Capernaum.[2]And a certaine Centurions ſeruant, who was deare vnto him, was ſicke and ready to die.[3]And when he heard of Ieſus, he ſent vnto him the Elders of the Iewes, beſeeching him that he would come and heale his ſeruant.[4]And when they came to Ieſus, they beſought him inſtantly, ſaying, that hee was worthy for whome hee ſhould doe this.[5]For he loueth our nation, and hee hath built vs a Synagogue.[6]Then Ieſus went with them. And when he was now not farre from the houſe, the Centurion ſent friends to him, ſaying vnto him, Lord, trouble not thy ſelfe: for I am not worthy that thou ſhouldeſt enter vnder my roofe.[7]Wherefore neither thought I my ſelfe worthy to come vnto thee: but ſay in a worde, and my ſeruant ſhall bee healed.[8]For I alſo am a man ſet vnder authoritie, hauing vnder mee ſouldiers: and I ſay vnto one, Goe, and he goeth: and to another, Come, and hee commeth: and to my ſeruant, Doe this, and he doeth it.[9]When Ieſus heard theſe things, hee marueiled at him, and turned him about, and ſaide vnto the people that followed him, I ſay vnto you, I haue not found ſo great faith, no, not in Iſrael.[10]And they that were ſent, returning to the houſe, found the ſeruant whole that had bene ſicke.[11]And it came to paſſe the day after, that he went into a citie called Naim: and many of his diſciples went with him, and much people.[12]Now when he came nigh to the gate of the citie, behold, there was a dead man caried out, the onely ſonne of his mother, and ſhee was a widow: and much people of the citie was with her.[13]And when the Lord ſaw her, he had compaſſion on her, and ſaide vnto her, Weepe not.[14]And hee came and touched the beere (and they that bare him, ſtood ſtill.) And he ſaid, Yong man, I ſay vnto thee, Ariſe.[15]And he that was dead, ſate vp, and began to ſpeake: and he deliuered him to his mother.[16]And there came a feare on all, and they glorified God, ſaying, that a great Prophet is riſen vp among vs, and that God hath viſited his people.[17]And this rumour of him went foorth throughout all Iudea, and throughout all the region round about.[18]And the diſciples of Iohn ſhewed him of all theſe things.[19]And Iohn calling vnto him two of his diſciples, ſent them to Ieſus, ſaying, Art thou hee that ſhould come, or looke we for another?[20]When the men were come vnto him, they ſaid, Iohn Baptiſt hath ſent vs vnto thee, ſaying, Art thou hee that ſhould come, or looke we for another?[21]And in that ſame houre hee cured many of their infirmities and plagues, and of euill ſpirits, and vnto many that were

blind, he gaue ſight.22Then Ieſus anſwering, ſaid vnto them, Go your
way, and tell Iohn what things ye haue ſeene and heard, how that the
blind ſee, the lame walke, the lepers are clenſed, the deafe heare, the
dead are raiſed, to the poore the Goſpel is preached.23And bleſſed is he
whoſoeuer ſhall not be offended in me.24And when the meſſengers of
Iohn were departed, hee beganne to ſpeake vnto þe people concerning
Iohn: What went ye out into the wilderneſſe for to ſee? A reede ſhaken
with the winde?25But what went ye out for to ſee? A man clothed in ſoft
raiment? Behold, they which are gorgeouſly apparelled, and liue
delicately, are in kings courts.26But what went ye out for to ſee? A
Prophet? Yea, I ſay vnto you, and much more then a Prophet.27This is
he of whome it is written, Behold, I ſend my meſſenger before thy face,
which ſhall prepare thy way before thee.28For I ſay vnto you, among
thoſe that are borne of women, there is not a greater Prophet then Iohn
the Baptiſt: but he that is leaſt in the kingdome of God, is greater then
he.29And all the people that heard him, and the Publicanes, iuſtified
God, being baptized with the baptiſme of Iohn.30But the PhAriſees and
Lawyers reiected the counſell of God againſt themſelues, being not
baptized of him.31And the Lord ſaid, whereunto then ſhall I liken the
men of this generation? and to what are they like?32They are like vnto
children ſitting in the market place, & calling one to another, and ſaying,
We haue piped vnto you, and ye haue not danced: wee haue mourned
to you, and yee haue not wept.33For Iohn the Baptiſt came, neither
eating bread, nor drinking wine, and ye ſay, He hath a deuill.34The ſonne
of man is come, eating, and drinking, and ye ſay, Behold a gluttonous
man, and a wine bibber, a friend of Publicanes and ſinners.35But
wiſedome is iuſtified of all her children.36And one of the PhAriſees
deſired him that he would eat with him. And he went into the PhAriſees
houſe, and ſate downe to meat.37And behold, a woman in the citie which
was a ſinner, when ſhee knew that Ieſus ſate at meat in the PhAriſees
houſe, brought an Alabaſter boxe of ointment,38And ſtood at his feet
behind him, weeping, and began to waſh his feete with teares, and did
wipe them with the haires of her head, and kiſſed his feet, and anointed
them with the oyntment.39Now when the PhAriſee which had bidden
him, ſaw it, he ſpake within himſelfe, ſaying, This man, if he were a
Prophet, would haue knowen who, and what maner of woman this is
that toucheth him: for ſhe is a ſinner.40And Ieſus anſwering, ſaid vnto
him, Simon, I haue ſomewhat to ſay vnto thee. And he ſaith, Maſter, ſay
on.41There was a certaine creditour, which had two debtors: the one
ought fiue hundred pence, and the other fiftie.42And when they had
nothing to pay, he frankly forgaue them both. Tell me therefore, which
of them will loue him moſt?43Simon anſwered, and ſaide, I ſuppoſe, that
hee to whome he forgaue moſt. And he ſaid vnto him, Thou haſt rightly
iudged.44And hee turned to the woman, and ſaid vnto Simon, Seeſt thou
this woman? I entred into thine houſe, thou gaueſt me no water for my
feete: but ſhee hath waſhed my feete with teares, and wiped them with
the haires of her head.45Thou gaueſt me no kiſſe: but this woman, ſince
the time I came in, hath not ceaſed to kiſſe my feet.46Mine head with
oile thou didſt not anoint: but this woman anointed my feet with
oyntment.47Wherefore, I ſay vnto thee, her ſinnes, which are many, are
forgiuen, for ſhe loued much: but to whom litle is forgiuen, the ſame
loueth litle.48And he ſaid vnto her, Thy ſinnes are forgiuen.49And they
that ſate at meat with him, began to ſay within themſelues, Who is this
that forgiueth ſinnes alſo?50And he ſaid to the woman, Thy faith hath
ſaued thee, goe in peace.
CHAPTER 81And it came to paſſe afterward, þt he went throughout
euery citie and village preaching, and ſhewing the glad tidings of the
kingdome of God: and the twelue were with him,2And certaine women
which had bene healed of euill ſpirits and infirmities, Mary called
Magdalene out of whom went ſeuen deuils,3And Ioanna the wife of
Chuza, Herods ſteward, and Suſanna, and many others which miniſtred
vnto him of their ſubſtance.4And when much people were gathered
together, and were come to him out of euery citie, he ſpake by a
parable:5A Sower went out to ſowe his ſeed: and as he ſowed, ſome fell
by the wayes ſide, and it was troden downe, and the foules of the aire
deuoured it.6And ſome fell vpon a rocke, and aſſoone as it was ſprung
vp, it withered away, becauſe it lacked moiſture.7And ſome fell among
thornes, and the thornes ſprang vp with it, and choked it.8And other fell
on good ground, and ſprang vp, and bare fruite an hundred fold. And
when hee ſaide theſe things, he cryed, He that hath eares to heare, let
him heare.9And his diſciples aſked him, ſaying, What might this parable
be?10And he ſaid, Unto you it is giuen to know the myſteries of the
kingdome of God: but to others in parables, that ſeeing, they might not
ſee, and hearing, they might not vnderſtand.11Now the parable is this:
The ſeed is the word of God.12Thoſe by the way ſide, are they that heare:
then commeth the deuil, and taketh away the word out of their hearts,
leaſt they ſhould beleeue, and be ſaued.13They on the rocke, are they
which when they heare, receiue the word with ioy; and theſe haue no
roote, which for a while beleeue, and in time of temptation fall
away.14And that which fell among thornes, are they, which when they
haue heard, goe forth, and are choked with cares and riches, and
pleaſures of this life, and bring no fruite to perfection.15But that on the
good ground, are they, which in an honeſt and good heart hauing heard
the word, keepe it, and bring foorth fruite with patience.16No man when
he hath lighted a candle, couereth it with a veſſell, or putteth it vnder a
bed: but ſetteth it on a candleſticke, that they which enter in, may ſee
the light.17For nothing is ſecret, that ſhall not be made manifeſt: neither
any thing hid, that ſhall not be knowen, and come abroad.18Take heede
therefore how yee heare: for whoſoeuer hath, to him ſhall bee giuen;
and whoſoeuer hath not, from him ſhall be taken, euen that which he
ſeemeth to haue.19Then came to him his mother and his brethren, and
could not come at him for the preaſe.20And it was told him by certaine
which ſaide, Thy mother and thy brethren ſtand without, deſiring to ſee
thee.21And hee anſwered and ſaid vnto them, My mother and my
brethren are theſe which heare the word of God, and doe it.22Now it
came to paſſe on a certaine day, that he went into a ſhip, with his
diſciples: and hee ſaid vnto them, Let vs goe ouer vnto the other ſide of
the lake, and they lanched foorth.23But as they ſailed, he fell aſleepe, and
there came downe a ſtorme of wind on the lake, and they were filled
with water, and were in ieopardie.24And they came to him, and awoke
him, ſaying, Maſter, maſter, we periſh. Then he roſe, and rebuked the
wind, and the raging of the water: and they ceaſed, and there was a
calme.25And he ſaide vnto them, Where is your faith? And they being
afraide wondred, ſaying one to another, What maner of man is this? For
he commandeth euen the winds and water, and they obey him.26And
they arriued at the countrey of the Gadarenes, which is ouer againſt
Galilee.27And when he went forth to land, there met him out of the citie
a certaine man which had deuils long time, and ware no clothes, neither
abode in any houſe, but in the tombes.28When he ſaw Ieſus, he cried
out, and fell downe before him, and with a loud voyce ſaid, What haue
I to doe with thee, Ieſus, thou ſonne of God moſt high? I beſeech thee
torment me not.29(For he had commanded the vncleane ſpirit to come
out of the man: For oftentimes it had caught him, and he was kept
bound with chaines, and in fetters: and he brake the bands, and was
driuen of the deuil into the wilderneſſe.)30And Ieſus aſked him, ſaying,
What is thy name? And he ſaid, Legion: becauſe many deuils were entred
into him.31And they beſought him, that he would not command them
to goe out into the deepe.32And there was there an herd of many ſwine
feeding on the mountaine: and they beſought him that he would ſuffer
them to enter into them: and he ſuffered them.33Then went the deuils
out of the man, and entred into the ſwine: and the herd ran violently
downe a ſteepe place into the lake, and were choked.34When they that
fed them ſaw what was done, they fled, and went, and tolde it in the
citie, and in the countrey.35Then they went out to ſee what was done,
and came to Ieſus, and found the man, out of whom the deuils were
departed, ſitting at the feete of Ieſus, clothed, and in his right minde:
and they were afraid.36They alſo which ſaw it, told them by what meanes
he that was poſſeſſed of the deuils, was healed.37Then the whole
multitude of the countrey of the Gadarenes round about, beſought him
to depart from them, for they were taken with great feare: and he went
vp into the ſhip, and returned back againe.38Now the man, out of whom
the deuils were departed, beſought him that he might be with him: but
Ieſus ſent him away, ſaying,39Returne to thine owne houſe, and ſhew
how great things God hath done vnto thee. And he went his way, and
publiſhed throughout the whole citie how great things Ieſus had done
vnto him.40And it came to paſſe, that when Ieſus was returned, the
people gladly receiued him: for they were all waiting for him.41And
behold, there came a man named Iairus, and hee was a ruler of the
Synagogue, and hee fell downe at Ieſus feete, and beſought him that hee

would come into his houſe:42For hee had one onely daughter about
twelue yeeres of age, and ſhe lay a dying. (But as hee went the people
thronged him.43And a woman hauing an iſſue of blood twelue yeres,
which had ſpent all her liuing vpon Phiſitions, neither could be healed
of any,44Came behinde him, and touched the border of his garment:
and immediatly her iſſue of blood ſtanched.45And Ieſus ſaide, Who
touched mee? When all denied, Peter and they that were with him, ſaid,
Maſter, the multitude throng thee, and preaſſe thee, and ſayeſt thou,
Who touched me?46And Ieſus ſaide, Some body hath touched mee: for
I perceiue that vertue is gone out of me.47And when the woman ſaw
that ſhe was not hid, ſhee came trembling, and falling downe before him,
ſhee declared vnto him before all the people, for what cauſe ſhee had
touched him, and how ſhe was healed immediatly.48And he ſaid vnto
her, Daughter, be of good comfort, thy faith hath made thee whole, goe
in peace.)49While hee yet ſpake, there commeth one from the ruler of
the Synagogues houſe, ſaying to him, Thy daughter is dead, trouble not
the Maſter.50But when Ieſus heard it, he anſwered him, ſaying, Feare
not, beleeue onely, and ſhe ſhalbe made whole.51And when hee came
into the houſe, hee ſuffered no man to goe in, ſaue Peter, and Iames,
and Iohn, and the father and the mother of the mayden.52And all wept,
and bewailed her: but he ſaid, Weepe not, ſhe is not dead, but
ſleepeth.53And they laughed him to ſcorne, knowing that ſhe was
dead.54And hee put them all out, and tooke her by the hand, and called,
ſaying, Mayd, Ariſe.55And her ſpirit came againe, and ſhee aroſe
ſtraightway: and hee commanded to giue her meat.56And her parents
were aſtoniſhed: but hee charged them that they ſhould tell no man what
was done.

CHAPTER 91Then he called his twelue diſciples together, and gaue
them power and authority ouer all deuils, and to cure diſeaſes.2And hee
ſent them to preach the Kingdome of God, and to heale the ſicke.3And
he ſaid vnto them, Take nothing for your iourney, neither ſtaues, nor
ſcrip, neither bread, neither money, neither haue two coates
apeece.4And whatſoeuer houſe yee enter into, there abide, and thence
depart.5And whoſoeuer will not receiue you, when ye goe out of that
city, ſhake off the very duſt from your feete, for a teſtimonie againſt
them.6And they departed, and went through the townes, preaching the
Goſpel, and healing euery where.7Now Herode the Tetrarch heard of
all that was done by him: and hee was perplexed, becauſe that it was ſaid
of ſome, that Iohn was riſen from the dead:8And of ſome, that Elias had
appeared: and of others, that one of the olde Prophets was riſen
againe.9And Herode ſaid, Iohn haue I beheaded: but who is this of
whom I heare ſuch things? And hee deſired to ſee him.10And the
Apoſtles when they were returned, tolde him all that they had done. And
hee tooke them, and went aſide priuately into a deſert place, belonging
to the citie called Bethſaida.11And the people when they knew it,
followed him, and he receiued them, and ſpake vnto them of the
kingdome of God, and healed them that had need of healing.12And
when the day beganne to weare away, then came the twelue, and ſaid
vnto him, Send the multitude away, that they may go into the townes
and countrey round about, and lodge, and get victuals: for we are here
in a deſert place.13But he ſaid vnto them, Giue yee them to eate. And
they ſaid, Wee haue no more but fiue loaues and two fiſhes, except we
ſhould goe and buy meate for all this people.14For they were about fiue
thouſand men. And he ſaid to his diſciples, Make them ſit downe by
fifties in a company.15And they did ſo, and made them all ſit
downe.16Then he tooke the fiue loaues and the two fiſhes, and looking
vp to heauen, hee bleſſed them, and brake, and gaue to the diſciples to
ſet before the multitude.17And they did eate, and were all filled. And
there was taken vp of fragments that remained to them, twelue
baſkets.18And it came to paſſe, as he was alone praying, his diſciples
were with him: and he aſked them, ſaying, Whom ſay the people that I
am?19They anſwering, ſaid, Iohn the Baptiſt: but ſome ſay, Elias: and
others ſay, that one of the old Prophets is riſen againe.20He ſaid vnto
them, But whom ſay yee that I am? Peter anſwering, ſaid, The Chriſt of
God.21And he ſtraitly charged them, and commanded them to tell no
man that thing,22Saying, The Sonne of man muſt ſuffer many things,
and be reiected of the Elders, and chiefe Prieſts, and Scribes, and be
ſlaine, and be raiſed the third day.23And he ſaid to them all, If any man
will come after me, let him denie himſelfe, and take vp his croſſe daily,
and follow me.24For whoſoeuer will ſaue his life, ſhall loſe it: but
whoſoeuer will loſe his life for my ſake, the ſame ſhall ſaue it.25For what
is a man aduantaged, if hee gaine the whole world, and loſe himſelfe, or
be caſt away?26For whoſoeuer ſhall bee aſhamed of me, and of my
wordes, of him ſhall the Sonne of man be aſhamed, when he ſhall come
in his owne glory, and in his Fathers, and of the holy Angels.27But I tell
you of a trueth, there be ſome ſtanding here, which ſhall not taſte of
death, till they ſee the kingdome of God.28And it came to paſſe, about
an eight dayes after theſe ſayings, hee tooke Peter, and Iohn, and Iames,
and went vp into a mountaine to pray:29And as hee prayed, the faſhion
of his countenance was altered, and his raiment was white and
gliſtering.30And behold, there talked with him two men, which were
Moſes and Elias,31Who appeared in glory, and ſpake of his deceaſe,
which he ſhould accompliſh at Hieruſalem.32But Peter, and they that
were with him, were heauie with ſleepe: and when they were awake, they
ſaw his glory, and the two men that ſtood with him.33And it came to
paſſe, as they departed from him, Peter ſaid vnto Ieſus, Maſter, it is good
for vs to be here, and let vs make three tabernacles, one for thee, and
one for Moſes, and one for Elias: not knowing what he ſaid.34While he
thus ſpake, there came a cloud, and ouerſhadowed them, & they feared,
as they entred into the cloude.35And there came a voice out of the cloud,
ſaying, This is my beloued Son, heare him.36And when the voyce was
paſt, Ieſus was found alone, and they kept it cloſe, & told no man in
thoſe dayes any of thoſe things which they had ſeene.37And it came to
paſſe, that on the next day, when they were come downe from the hill,
much people met him.38And behold, a man of the companie cried out,
ſaying, Maſter, I beſeech thee looke vpon my ſonne, for he is mine onely
child.39And loe, a ſpirit taketh him, and hee ſuddenly crieth out, and it
teareth him that he fometh againe, and bruiſing him, hardly departeth
from him.40And I beſought thy diſciples to caſt him out, and they could
not.41And Ieſus anſwering, ſaid, O faithleſſe, and peruerſe generation,
how long ſhal I be with you, and ſuffer you? bring thy ſonne
hither.42And as he was yet a comming, the deuill threw him downe, and
tare him: and Ieſus rebuked the vncleane ſpirit, and healed the child, and
deliuered him againe to his father.43And they were al amazed at the
mightie power of God: But while they wondred euery one at all things
which Ieſus did, he ſaid vnto his diſciples,44Let theſe ſayings ſinke
downe into your eares: for the Sonne of man ſhall bee deliuered into the
handes of men.45But they vnderſtood not this ſaying, and it was hid
from them, that they perceiued it not: and they feared to aſke him of
that ſaying.46Then there aroſe a reaſoning among them, which of them
ſhould be greateſt.47And Ieſus perceiuing þe thought of their heart,
tooke a child, and ſet him by him,48And ſaid vnto them, Whoſoeuer
ſhall receiue this child in my Name, receiueth me: and whoſoeuer ſhal
receiue me, receiueth him that ſent me: For hee that is leaſt among you
all, the ſame ſhalbe great.49And Iohn anſwered, and ſaid, Maſter, we ſaw
one caſting out deuils in thy Name, and we forbade him, becauſe he
followeth not with vs.50And Ieſus ſaid vnto him, Forbid him not: for he
that is not againſt vs, is for vs.51And it came to paſſe, when the time was
come that he ſhould bee receiued vp, he ſtedfaſtly ſet his face to goe to
Hieruſalem,52And ſent meſſengers before his face, and they went and
entred into a village of the Samaritanes to make ready for him.53And
they did not receiue him, becauſe his face was as though he would goe
to Hieruſalem.54And when his diſciples, Iames and Iohn ſawe this, they
ſaid, Lord, wilt thou that wee command fire to come downe from
heauen, and conſume them, euen as Elias did?55But he turned, and
rebuked them, and ſaid, Ye know not what maner ſpirit ye are of.56For
the Sonne of man is not come to deſtroy mens liues, but to ſaue them.
And they went to another village.57And it came to paſſe that as they
went in the way, a certaine man ſaid vnto him, Lord, I wil follow thee
whitherſoeuer thou goeſt.58And Ieſus ſaid vnto him, Foxes haue holes,
and birds of the aire haue neſts, but the Sonne of man hath not where
to lay his head.59And he ſaid vnto another, Follow me: But he ſaid,
Lord, ſuffer mee firſt to goe and bury my father.60Ieſus ſaid vnto him,
Let the dead bury their dead: but go thou and preach the kingdome of
God.61And another alſo ſaid, Lord, I will follow thee: but let me firſt
goe bid them farewel, which are at home at my houſe.62And Ieſus ſaid
vnto him, No man hauing put his hand to the plough, and looking
backe, is fit for the kingdome of God.

CHAPTER 10 1 After theſe things, the Lord appointed other ſeuenty alſo, and ſent them two and two before his face, into euery citie and place, whither hee himſelfe would come. 2 Therefore ſaid hee vnto them, The harueſt truly is great, but the labourers are few; pray ye therefore the Lord of the harueſt, that he would ſend foorth labourers into his harueſt. 3 Go your wayes: Behold, I ſend you forth as lambes among wolues. 4 Cary neither purſe nor ſcrip, nor ſhoes, and ſalute no man by the way. 5 And into whatſoeuer houſe yee enter, firſt ſay, Peace bee to this houſe. 6 And if the ſonne of peace be there, your peace ſhall reſt vpon it: if not, it ſhall turne to you againe. 7 And in the ſame houſe remaine, eating and drinking ſuch things as they giue: For the labourer is worthy of his hire. Goe not from houſe to houſe. 8 And into whatſoeuer citie yee enter, and they receiue you, eate ſuch things as are ſet before you: 9 And heale the ſicke that are therein, and ſay vnto them, The kingdome of God is come nigh vnto you. 10 But into whatſoeuer citie yee enter, and they receiue you not, goe your waies out into the ſtreetes of the ſame, and ſay, 11 Euen the very duſt of your citie which cleaueth on vs, we doe wipe off againſt you: notwithſtanding, be yee ſure of this, that the kingdome of God is come nigh vnto you. 12 But I ſay vnto you, That it ſhall be more tolerable in that day for Sodome, then for that citie. 13 Woe vnto thee Chorazin, wo vnto thee Bethſaida: For if the mighty workes had beene done in Tyre and Sidon, which haue beene done in you, they had a great while agoe repented, ſitting in ſackcloth and aſhes. 14 But it ſhall be more tolerable for Tyre and Sidon at the iudgment, then for you. 15 And thou Capernaum, which art exalted to heauen, ſhalt be thruſt downe to hell. 16 Hee that heareth you, heareth me: and he that deſpiſeth you, deſpiſeth me: and he that deſpiſeth me, deſpiſeth him that ſent me. 17 And the ſeuenty returned againe with ioy, ſaying, Lord, euen the deuils are ſubiect vnto vs through thy name. 18 And he ſaid vnto them, I beheld Satan as lightning fall from heauen. 19 Behold, I giue vnto you power to tread on ſerpents and ſcorpions, and ouer all the power of the enemie: and nothing ſhall by any meanes hurt you. 20 Notwithſtanding in this reioyce not, that the ſpirits are ſubiect vnto you: but rather reioyce, becauſe your names are written in heauen. 21 In that houre Ieſus reioyced in ſpirit, and ſaid, I thanke thee, O father, Lord of heauen and earth, that thou haſt hid theſe things from the wiſe and prudent, and haſt reuealed them vnto babes: euen ſo father, for ſo it ſeemed good in thy ſight. 22 All things are deliuered to me of my father: and no man knoweth who the ſonne is, but the father: and who the father is, but the ſonne, and he to whom the ſonne will reueale him. 23 And he turned him vnto his diſciples, and ſaid priuately, Bleſſed are the eyes which ſee the things that yee ſee. 24 For I tell you, that many Prophets, and kings haue deſired to ſee thoſe things which yee ſee, and haue not ſeene them: & to heare thoſe things which yee heare, and haue not heard them. 25 And behold, a certaine Lawyer ſtood vp, and tempted him, ſaying, Maſter, what ſhall I doe to inherite eternall life? He ſaid vnto him, 26 What is written in the law? how readeſt thou? 27 And he anſwering, ſaid, Thou ſhalt loue the Lord thy God with all thy heart, and with all thy ſoule, and with all thy ſtrength, and with all thy minde, and thy neighbour as thy ſelfe. 28 And he ſaid vnto him, Thou haſt anſwered right: this do, and thou ſhalt liue. 29 But he willing to iuſtifie himſelfe, ſaid vnto Ieſus, And who is my neighbour? 30 And Ieſus anſwering, ſaid, A certaine man went downe from Hieruſalem to Iericho, and fel among theeues, which ſtripped him of his raiment, and wounded him, and departed, leauing him halfe dead. 31 And by chaunce there came downe a certaine Prieſt that way, and when he ſaw him, he paſſed by on the other ſide. 32 And likewiſe a Leuite, when hee was at the place, came and looked on him, and paſſed by on the other ſide. 33 But a certaine Samaritane as he iourneyed, came where he was; and when hee ſaw him, hee had compaſſion on him, 34 And went to him, and bound vp his wounds, powring in oile and wine, and ſet him on his owne beaſt, and brought him to an Inne, and tooke care of him. 35 And on the morrow when he departed, hee tooke out two pence, and gaue them to the hoſte, and ſaide vnto him, Take care of him, and whatſoeuer thou ſpendeſt more, when I come againe I will repay thee. 36 Which now of theſe three, thinkeſt thou, was neighbour vnto him that fell among the theeues? 37 And he ſaid, He that ſhewed mercie on him. Then ſaid Ieſus vnto him, Goe, and doe thou likewiſe. 38 Now it came to paſſe, as they went, that he entred into a certaine village: and a certaine woman named Martha, receiued him into her houſe. 39 And ſhee had a ſiſter called Mary, which alſo ſate at Ieſus feet, and heard his word: 40 But Martha was cumbred about much ſeruing, and came to him, and ſaid, Lord, doeſt thou not care that my ſiſter hath left mee to ſerue alone? Bid her therefore that ſhe helpe me. 41 And Ieſus anſwered, and ſaide vnto her, Martha, Martha, thou art carefull, and troubled about many things: 42 But one thing is needefull, and Mary hath choſen that good part, which ſhall not bee taken away from her.

CHAPTER 11 1 And it came to paſſe, that as he was praying in a certaine place, when hee ceaſed, one of his diſciples ſaid vnto him, Lord, teach vs to pray, as Iohn alſo taught his diſciples. 2 And hee ſaid vnto them, When ye pray, ſay, Our Father which art in heauen, Halowed be thy Name, Thy kingdome come, Thy will be done as in heauen, ſo in earth. 3 Giue vs day by day our dayly bread. 4 And forgiue vs our ſinnes: for we alſo forgiue euery one that is indebted to vs. And lead vs not into temptation, but deliuer vs from euill. 5 And he ſaid vnto them, Which of you ſhall haue a friend, and ſhall goe vnto him at midnight, and ſay vnto him, Friend, lend me three loaues. 6 For a friend of mine in his iourney is come to me, and I haue nothing to ſet before him, 7 And he from within ſhal anſwere and ſay, Trouble mee not, the doore is now ſhut, and my children are with me in bed: I cannot riſe and giue thee. 8 I ſay vnto you, Though he will not riſe, and giue him, becauſe he is his friend: yet becauſe of his importunitie, hee will riſe and giue him as many as he needeth. 9 And I ſay vnto you, Aſke, and it ſhalbe giuen you: ſeeke, and ye ſhal find: knocke, and it ſhalbe opened vnto you. 10 For euery one that aſketh, receiueth: and he that ſeeketh, findeth: and to him that knocketh, it ſhalbe opened. 11 If a ſonne ſhall aſke bread of any of you that is a father, will hee giue him a ſtone? Or if he aſke a fiſh, will he for a fiſh giue him a ſerpent? 12 Or if he ſhall aſke an egge, will he offer him a ſcorpion? 13 If ye then, being euill, know how to giue good gifts vnto your children: how much more ſhall your heauenly Father giue the holy Spirit to them that aſke him? 14 And he was caſting out a deuil, and it was dumbe. And it came to paſſe, when the deuill was gone out, the dumbe ſpake: and the people wondred. 15 But ſome of them ſaid, Hee caſteth out deuils through Beelzebub the chiefe of the deuils. 16 And other tempting him, ſought of him a ſigne from heauen. 17 But he knowing their thoughts, ſaid vnto them, Euery kingdome diuided againſt it ſelfe, is brought to deſolation: and a houſe diuided againſt a houſe, falleth. 18 If Satan alſo be diuided againſt himſelfe, how ſhall his kingdom ſtand? Becauſe yee ſay that I caſt out deuils through Beelzebub. 19 And if I by Beelzebub caſt out deuils, by whom doe your ſonnes caſt them out? therefore ſhall they be your iudges. 20 But if I with the finger of God caſt out deuils, no doubt the kingdome of God is come vpon you. 21 When a ſtrong man armed keepeth his palace, his goods are in peace: 22 But when a ſtronger then he ſhal come vpon him, and ouercome him, hee taketh from him all his armour wherein he truſted, and diuideth his ſpoiles. 23 He that is not with me, is againſt me: and hee that gathereth not with me, ſcattereth. 24 When the vncleane ſpirit is gone out of a man, he walketh through drie places, ſeeking reſt: and finding none, he ſayth, I will returne vnto my houſe whence I came out. 25 And when hee commeth, hee findeth it ſwept and garniſhed. 26 Then goeth he, and taketh to him ſeuen other ſpirits more wicked then himſelfe, and they enter in, and dwell there, and the laſt ſtate of that man is worſe then the firſt. 27 And it came to paſſe as hee ſpake theſe things, a certaine woman of the company lift vp her voice, and ſaid vnto him, Bleſſed is the wombe that bare thee, and the pappes which thou haſt ſucked. 28 But hee ſaid, Yea, rather bleſſed are they that heare the word of God, and keepe it. 29 And when the people were gathered thicke together, hee began to ſay, This is an euill generation, they ſeeke a ſigne, and there ſhall no ſigne be giuen it, but the ſigne of Ionas the Prophet: 30 For as Ionas was a ſigne vnto the Nineuites, ſo ſhall alſo the Sonne of man be to this generation. 31 The Queene of the South ſhall riſe vp in the iudgement with the men of this generation, & condemne them: for ſhee came from the vtmoſt parts of the earth, to heare the wiſedome of Solomon: and behold, a greater then Solomon is here. 32 The men of Nineue ſhall riſe vp in the iudgement with this generation, and ſhall condemne it: for they repented at the preaching of Ionas, and behold, a greater then Ionas is here. 33 No man when he hath lighted a candle, putteth it in a ſecret place, neither vnder a buſhell, but on a candleſticke, that they which come in may ſee the light. 34 The light of the body is the eye: therefore when thine eye is ſingle, thy whole body alſo is full of light: but when thine eye is euill, thy body

alſo is full of darkeneſſe. 35 Take heede therefore, that the light which is
in thee, be not darkneſſe. 36 If thy whole body therefore be full of light,
hauing no part darke, the whole ſhalbe full of light, as when the bright
ſhining of a candle doeth giue thee light. 37 And as he ſpake, a certaine
PhAriſe beſought him to dine with him: and he went in, and ſate downe
to meate. 38 And when the PhAriſe ſaw it, he marueiled that he had not
firſt waſhed before dinner. 39 And the Lord ſaid vnto him, Now doe ye
PhAriſes make cleane the outſide of the cup and the platter: but your
inward part is full of rauening and wickedneſſe. 40 Yee fooles, did not he
that made that which is without, make that which is within alſo? 41 But
rather giue almes of ſuch things as you haue: and behold, all things are
cleane vnto you. 42 But woe vnto you PhAriſes: for ye tythe Mint and
Rue, and all maner of herbes, and paſſe ouer iudgement, and the loue of
God: theſe ought yee to haue done, and not to leaue the other
vndone. 43 Woe vnto you PhAriſees: for ye loue the vppermoſt ſeats in
the Synagogues, and greetings in the markets. 44 Woe vnto you Scribes
and PhAriſees, hypocrites: for ye are as graues which appeare not, and
the men that walk ouer them, are not aware of them. 45 Then anſwered
one of the Lawyers, and ſaid vnto him, Maſter, thus ſaying, thou
reprocheſt vs alſo. 46 And he ſaid, Woe vnto you alſo ye lawyers: for ye
lade men with burdens grieuous to be borne, and ye your ſelues touch
not the burdens with one of your fingers. 47 Woe vnto you: for ye build
the ſepulchres of the Prophets, and your fathers killed them. 48 Truely ye
beare witneſſe that ye allowe the deeds of your fathers: for they indeed
killed them, and yee build their ſepulchres. 49 Therefore alſo ſaid the
wiſedome of God, I wil ſend them Prophets and Apoſtles, and ſome of
them they ſhal ſlay and perſecute: 50 That the blood of all the Prophets,
which was ſhed from the foundation of the world, may be required of
this generation, 51 From the blood of Abel vnto the blood of Zacharias,
which periſhed betweene the Altar and the Temple: Uerely I ſay vnto
you, it ſhall be required of this generation. 52 Woe vnto you Lawyers: for
ye haue taken away the key of knowledge: ye entred not in your ſelues,
and them that were entring in, ye hindred. 53 And as he ſaid theſe things
vnto them, the Scribes and the PhAriſees began to vrge him vehemently,
and to prouoke him to ſpeake of many things: 54 Laying wait for him,
and ſeeking to catch ſomething out of his mouth, that they might accuſe
him.
CHAPTER 12 1 In the meane time, when there were gathered together
an innumerable multitude of people, inſomuch that they trode one vpon
another, he began to ſay vnto his diſciples firſt of all, Beware yee of the
leauen of the PhAriſees, which is hypocriſie. 2 For there is nothing
couered, that ſhall not be reuealed, neither hid, that ſhall not be
knowen. 3 Therefore, whatſoeuer yee haue ſpoken in darkeneſſe, ſhall bee
heard in the light: and that which yee haue ſpoken in the eare, in cloſets,
ſhal be proclaimed vpon the houſe tops. 4 And I ſay vnto you my friends,
Be not afraid of them that kill the body, and after that, haue no more
that they can doe. 5 But I will forewarne you whom you ſhall feare: Feare
him, which after he hath killed, hath power to caſt into hell, yea, I ſay
vnto you, Feare him. 6 Are not fiue ſparrowes ſolde for two farthings,
and not one of them is forgotten before God? 7 But euen the very haires
of your head are all numbred: Feare not therefore, ye are of more value
then many ſparrowes. 8 Alſo I ſay vnto you, Whoſoeuer ſhall confeſse me
before men, him ſhall the Sonne of man alſo confeſse before the Angels
of God. 9 But he that denieth me before men, ſhalbe denied before the
Angels of God. 10 And whoſoeuer ſhall ſpeake a word againſt the Sonne
of man, it ſhall be forgiuen him: but vnto him that blaſphemeth againſt
the holy Ghoſt, it ſhal not be forgiuen. 11 And when they bring you vnto
the Synagogues, and vnto Magiſtrates, & powers, take yee no thought
how or what thing ye ſhall anſwere, or what ye ſhall ſay: 12 For the holy
Ghoſt ſhal teach you in the ſame houre, what ye ought to ſay. 13 And one
of the company ſaide vnto him, Maſter, ſpeake to my brother, that he
diuide the inheritance with me. 14 And he ſaid vnto him, Man, who made
mee a iudge, or a diuider ouer you? 15 And he ſaid vnto them, Take heed
and beware of couetouſnes: for a mans life conſiſteth not in the
abundance of the things which he poſſeſſeth. 16 And he ſpake a parable
vnto them, ſaying, The ground of a certaine rich man brought foorth
plentifully. 17 And he thought within himſelfe, ſaying, What ſhall I doe,
becauſe I haue no roome where to beſtow my fruits? 18 And he ſaid, This
will I doe, I will pull downe my barnes, and build greater, and there will
I beſtow all my fruits, and my goods. 19 And I will ſay to my ſoule, Soule,
thou haſt much goods layd vp for many yeeres, take thine eaſe, eate,
drinke, and be merry. 20 But God ſaid vnto him, Thou foole, this night
thy ſoule ſhal be required of thee: then whoſe ſhal thoſe things be which
thou haſt prouided? 21 So is he that laieth vp treaſure for himſelfe, and is
not rich towards God. 22 And he ſaid vnto his diſciples, Therefore I ſay
vnto you, Take no thought for your life what yee ſhall eate, neither for
the body what yee ſhall put on. 23 The life is more then meate, and the
body is more then raiment. 24 Conſider the rauens, for they neither ſow
nor reape, which neither haue ſtorehouſe nor barne, and God feedeth
them: How much more are yee better then the foules? 25 And which of
you with taking thought can adde to his ſtature one cubite? 26 If yee then
bee not able to doe that thing which is leaſt, why take yee thought for
the reſt? 27 Conſider the Lillies how they growe, they toile not; they
ſpinne not: and yet I ſay vnto you, that Solomon in all his glory, was not
arayed like one of theſe. 28 If then God ſo clothe the graſſe, which is to
day in the field, and to morrow is caſt into the ouen: how much more
will he clothe you, O ye of litle faith? 29 And ſeeke not yee what yee ſhall
eate, or what ye ſhall drinke, neither be ye of doubtfull minde. 30 For all
theſe things doe the nations of the world ſeeke after: and your father
knoweth that yee haue neede of theſe things. 31 But rather ſeeke yee the
kingdome of God, and all theſe things ſhall be added vnto you. 32 Feare
not, litle flocke, for it is your fathers good pleaſure to giue you the
kingdome. 33 Sell that yee haue, and giue almes: prouide your ſelues
bagges which waxe not old, a treaſure in the heauens that faileth not,
where no theefe approcheth, neither moth corrupteth. 34 For where your
treaſure is, there will your heart be alſo. 35 Let your loines be girded about,
and your lights burning, 36 And ye your ſelues like vnto men that waite
for their Lord, when he will returne from the wedding, that when he
commeth and knocketh, they may open vnto him immediately. 37 Bleſſed
are thoſe ſeruants, whom the Lord when he commeth, ſhall find
watching: Uerily, I ſay vnto you, That he ſhall girde himſelfe, and make
them to ſit downe to meate, and will come foorth and ſerue them. 38 And
if he ſhall come in the ſecond watch, or come in the third watch, and
find them ſo, bleſſed are thoſe ſeruants. 39 And this know, that if the good
man of the houſe had knowen what houre the theefe would come, he
would haue watched, and not haue ſuffred his houſe to be broken
thorow. 40 Be yee therefore ready alſo: for the ſonne of man commeth at
an houre when yee thinke not. 41 Then Peter ſaid vnto him, Lord,
ſpeakeſt thou this parable vnto vs, or euen to all? 42 And the Lord ſaid,
Who then is that faithfull and wiſe ſteward, whom his Lord ſhall make
ruler ouer his houſhold, to giue them their portion of meate in due
ſeaſon? 43 Bleſſed is that ſeruant, whom his Lord when he commeth, ſhall
find ſo doing. 44 Of a trueth, I ſay vnto you, that hee will make him ruler
ouer all that he hath. 45 But and if that ſeruant ſay in his heart, My Lord
delayeth his comming and ſhall beginne to beat the men ſeruants, and
maidens, and to eate and drinke, and to be drunken: 46 The Lord of that
ſeruant will come in a day when hee looketh not for him, and at an houre
when hee is not ware, and will cut him in ſunder, and will appoint him
his portion with the vnbeleeuers. 47 And that ſeruant which knew his
Lords will, and prepared not himſelfe, neither did according to his will,
ſhalbe beaten with many ſtripes. 48 But hee that knew not, and did
commit things worthy of ſtripes, ſhall bee beaten with few ſtripes. For
vnto whomſoeuer much is giuen, of him ſhal bee much required: and to
whom men haue committed much, of him they will aſke the more. 49 I
am come to ſend fire on the earth, and what will I, if it be already
kindled? 50 But I haue a baptiſme to be baptized with, and how am I
ſtraitned till it be accompliſhed? 51 Suppoſe yee that I am come to giue
peace on earth? I tell you, Nay, but rather diuiſion. 52 For from
henceforth there ſhalbe fiue in one houſe diuided, three againſt two, and
two againſt three. 53 The father ſhall bee diuided againſt the ſonne, and
the ſonne againſt the father: the mother againſt the daughter, and the
daughter againſt the mother: the mother in lawe againſt her daughter in
lawe, and the daughter in law againſt her mother in lawe. 54 And he ſaid
alſo to the people, When ye ſee a cloud riſe out of the Weſt, ſtraightway
yee ſay, There commeth a ſhowre, and ſo it is. 55 And when ye ſee the
Southwind blow, ye ſay, There will be heat, and it commeth to
paſſe. 56 Ye hypocrites, ye can diſcerne the face of the ſkie, and of the
earth: but how is it that yee doe not diſcerne this time? 57 Yea, and why

euen of your ſelues iudge ye not what is right?58When thou goeſt with
thine aduerſary to the magiſtrate, as thou art in the way, giue diligence
that thou mayeſt be deliuered from him, leſt hee hale thee to the Iudge,
and the Iudge deliuer thee to the officer, and the officer caſt thee into
priſon.59I tell thee, Thou ſhalt not depart thence, till thou haſt payd the
very laſt mite.
CHAPTER 131There were preſent at that ſeaſon, ſome that told him
of the Galileans, whoſe blood Pilate had mingled with their
ſacrifices.2And Ieſus anſwering, ſaid vnto them, Suppoſe ye that theſe
Galileans were ſinners aboue all the Galileans, becauſe they ſuffered
ſuch things?3I tell you, Nay: but except yee repent, ye ſhall all likewiſe
periſh.4Or thoſe eighteene, vpon whom the towre in Siloe fell, and ſlew
them, thinke ye that they were ſinners aboue all men that dwelt in
Hieruſalem?5I tell you, Nay; but except yee repent, ye ſhall all likewiſe
periſh.6Hee ſpake alſo this parable, A certaine man had a figtree planted
in his Uineyard, and he came and ſought fruit thereon, and found
none.7Then ſaid hee vnto the dreſſer of his Uineyard, Beholde, theſe
three yeeres I come ſeeking fruit on this figtree, and finde none: cut it
downe, why cumbreth it the ground?8And he anſwering, ſaid vnto him,
Lord, let it alone this yeere alſo, till I ſhall digge about it, and doung
it:9And if it beare fruit, Well: and if not, then after that, thou ſhalt cut it
downe.10And he was teaching in one of the Synagogues on the
Sabbath.11And beholde, there was a woman which had a ſpirit of
infirmitie eighteene yeeres, and was bowed together, and could in no
wiſe lift vp her ſelfe.12And when Ieſus ſaw her, he called her to him, and
ſaid vnto her, Woman, thou art looſed frō thy infirmitie.13And hee layd
his handes on her, and immediatly ſhe was made ſtraight, and glorified
God.14And the ruler of the Synagogue anſwered with indignation,
becauſe that Ieſus had healed on the Sabbath day, and ſaid vnto the
people, There are ſixe dayes in which men ought to worke: in them
therefore come and be healed, and not on the Sabbath day.15The Lord
then anſwered him, and ſaid, Thou hypocrite, doeth not each one of you
on the Sabbath looſe his oxe or his aſſe from the ſtall, and leade him
away to watering?16And ought not this woman being a daughter of
Abraham, whom Satan hath bound, loe theſe eighteene yeeres, be looſed
from this bond on the Sabbath day?17And when hee had ſaid theſe
things, all his aduerſaries were aſhamed: & all the people reioyced for all
the glorious things that were done by him.18Then ſaid he, Unto what is
the kingdome of God like? and whereunto ſhall I reſemble it?19It is like
a graine of muſtard ſeed, which a man tooke, and caſt into his garden,
and it grew, and waxed a great tree: and the foules of the aire lodged in
the branches of it.20And againe hee ſaid, Whereunto ſhall I liken the
kingdome of God?21It is like leauen, which a woman tooke and hidde in
three meaſures of meale, till the whole was leauened.22And he went
thorow the cities and villages, teaching and iourneying towards
Hieruſalem.23Then ſaid one vnto him, Lord, are there few that be ſaued?
And he ſaid vnto them,24Striue to enter in at the ſtrait gate: for many, I
ſay vnto you, will ſeeke to enter in, and ſhall not be able.25When once
the maſter of the houſe is riſen vp, & hath ſhut to the doore, and ye
begin to ſtand without, & to knocke at the doore, ſaying, Lord, Lord,
open vnto vs, and he ſhal anſwere, & ſay vnto you, I know you not
whence you are:26Then ſhall ye begin to ſay, Wee haue eaten and drunke
in thy preſence, and thou haſt taught in our ſtreets.27But he ſhall ſay, I
tell you, I know you not whence you are; depart from me all ye workers
of iniquitie.28There ſhall be weeping and gnaſhing of teeth, when yee
ſhall ſee Abraham, and Iſaac, and Iacob, and all the Prophets in the
kingdome of God, and you your ſelues thruſt out.29And they ſhall come
from the Eaſt, and from the Weſt, and from the North, and from the
South, and ſhall ſit downe in the kingdome of God.30And behold, there
are laſt, which ſhall be firſt; and there are firſt, which ſhall be laſt.31The
ſame day there came certaine of the PhAriſes, ſaying vnto him, Get thee
out, and depart hence; for Herode will kill thee.32And he ſaid vnto them,
Go ye and tell that Foxe, behold, I caſt out deuils, and I doe cures to
day and to morrow, and the third day I ſhall be
perfected.33Neuertheleſſe, I muſt walke to day and to morrow, and the
day following: for it cannot be that a Prophet periſh out of
Hieruſalem.34O Hieruſalem, Hieruſalem, which killeſt the Prophets, and
ſtoneſt them that are ſent vnto thee; how often would I haue gathered
thy children together, as a henne doeth gather her brood vnder her
wings, & ye would not?35Behold, your houſe is left vnto you deſolate.
And verely I ſay vnto you, ye ſhall not ſee me, vntill the time come when
yee ſhall ſay, Bleſſed is hee that commeth in the Name of the Lord.
CHAPTER 141And it came to paſſe, as he went into the houſe of one
of the chief PhAriſes to eat bread on þe Sabbath day, that they watched
him.2And behold, there was a certaine man before him, which had the
dropſie.3And Ieſus anſwering, ſpake vnto the Lawyers and PhAriſes,
ſaying, Is it lawfull to heale on the Sabbath day?4And they held their
peace. And he tooke him, and healed him, & let him go,5And anſwered
them, ſaying, Which of you ſhall haue an aſſe or an oxe fallen into a pit,
and will not ſtraightway pull him out on the Sabbath day?6And they
could not anſwere him againe to theſe things.7And he put foorth a
parable to thoſe which were bidden, when he marked howe they choſe
out the chiefe roumes, ſaying vnto them,8When thou art bidden of any
man to a wedding, ſit not downe in the higheſt roume: leſt a more
honourable man then thou be bidden of him,9And hee that bade thee
and him, come, and ſay to thee, Giue this man place: and thou begin
with ſhame to take the loweſt roume.10But when thou art bidden, goe
and ſit downe in the loweſt roume, that when he that bade thee
commeth, hee may ſay vnto thee, Friend, goe vp higher: then ſhalt thou
haue worſhip in the preſence of them that ſit at meate with thee.11For
whoſoeuer exalteth himſelfe, ſhalbe abaſed: and hee that humbleth
himſelfe, ſhalbe exalted.12Then ſaid hee alſo to him that bade him, When
thou makeſt a dinner or a ſupper, call not thy friends, nor thy brethren,
neither thy kinſemen, nor thy rich neighbours, leſt they alſo bid thee
againe, and a recompence be made thee.13But when thou makeſt a feaſt,
call the poore, the maimed, the lame, the blinde,14And thou ſhalt be
bleſſed, for they cannot recompenſe thee: for thou ſhalt be recompenſed
at the reſurrection of the iuſt.15And when one of them that ſate at meate
with him, heard theſe things, he ſaid vnto him, Bleſſed is hee that ſhall
eate bread in the kingdom of God.16Then ſaid hee vnto him, A certaine
man made a great ſupper, and bade many:17And ſent his ſeruant at
ſupper time, to ſay to them that were bidden, Come, for all things are
now ready.18And they all with one conſent began to make excuſe: The
firſt ſaid vnto him, I haue bought a piece of ground, and I muſt needs
goe and ſee it: I pray thee haue me excuſed.19And another ſaid, I haue
bought fiue yoke of oxen, and I goe to prooue them: I pray thee haue
me excuſed.20And another ſaid, I haue maried a wife: and therefore I
cannot come.21So that ſeruant came, and ſhewed his lord theſe things.
Then the maſter of the houſe being angry, ſayde to his ſeruant, Goe out
quickely into the ſtreetes and lanes of the city, and bring in hither the
poore, and the maimed, and the halt, and the blinde.22And the ſeruant
ſaid, Lord, it is done as thou haſt commanded, and yet there is
roume.23And the Lord ſaid vnto the ſeruant, Goe out into the high
wayes and hedges, and compell them to come in, that my houſe may be
filled.24For I ſay vnto you, that none of thoſe men which were bidden,
ſhall taſte of my ſupper.25And there went great multitudes with him: and
hee turned, and ſaid vnto them,26If any man come to me, and hate not
his father, and mother, and wife, and children, and brethren, and ſiſters,
yea and his owne life alſo, hee cannot be my diſciple.27And whoſoeuer
doeth not beare his croſſe, and come after me, cannot be my
diſciple.28For which of you intending to build a towre, ſitteth not downe
firſt, and counteth the coſt, whether he haue ſufficient to finiſh it?29Leſt
haply after hee hath laide the foundation, and is not able to finiſh it, all
that behold it, begin to mock him,30Saying, This man beganne to build,
and was not able to finiſh.31Or what king going to make war againſt
another king, ſitteth not downe firſt, and conſulteth whether he be able
with ten thouſand, to meete him that commeth againſt him with twentie
thouſand?32Or elſe, while the other is yet a great way off, hee ſendeth an
ambaſſage, and deſireth conditions of peace.33So likewiſe, whoſoeuer he
be of you, that forſaketh not all that he hath, he cannot be my
diſciple.34Salt is good: but if the ſalt haue loſt his ſauour, wherewith ſhall
it be ſeaſoned?35It is neither fit for the land, nor yet for the dunghill: but
men caſt it out. He that hath eares to heare, let him heare.
CHAPTER 151Then drew neere vnto him all the Publicanes and
ſinners, for to heare him.2And the PhAriſes and Scribes murmured,
murmured, ſaying, This man receiueth ſinners, and eateth with
them.3And he ſpake this parable vnto them, ſaying,4What man of you
hauing an hundred ſheepe, if he looſe one of them, doth not leaue the
ninety and nine in the wilderneſſe, and goe after that which is loſt, vntill
he find it?5And when he hath found it, hee layeth it on his ſhoulders ,

reioycing.6And when he commeth home, he calleth together his friends, and neighbours, ſaying vnto them, Reioyce with me, for I haue found my ſheepe which was loſt.7I ſay vnto you, that likewiſe ioy ſhall be in heauen ouer one ſinner that repenteth, more then ouer ninety and nine iuſt perſons, which need no repentance.8Either what woman hauing ten pieces of ſiluer, if ſhe loſe one piece, doth not light a candle, and ſweepe the houſe, and ſeeke diligently till ſhee find it?9And when ſhe hath found it, ſhe calleth her friends and her neighbours together, ſaying, Reioyce with me, for I haue found þe piece which I had loſt.10Likewiſe I ſay vnto you, there is ioy in the preſence of the Angels of God, ouer one ſinner that repenteth.11And hee ſaid, A certaine man had two ſonnes:12And the yonger of them ſaid to his father, Father, giue me the portion of goods that falleth to me. And he diuided vnto them his liuing.13And not many dayes after, the yonger ſonne gathered al together, and tooke his iourney into a farre countrey, and there waſted his ſubſtance with riotous liuing.14And when he had ſpent all, there aroſe a mighty famine in that land, and he beganne to be in want.15And he went and ioyned himſelfe to a citizen of that countrey, and he ſent him into his fields to feed ſwine.16And he would faine haue filled his belly with the huſkes that the ſwine did eate: & no man gaue vnto him.17And when he came to himſelfe, he ſaid, How many hired ſeruants of my fathers haue bread inough and to ſpare, and I periſh with hunger?18I will Ariſe and goe to my father, and will ſay vnto him, Father, I haue ſinned againſt heauen and before thee.19And am no more worthy to be called thy ſonne: make me as one of thy hired ſeruants.20And he aroſe and came to his father. But when he was yet a great way off, his father ſaw him, and had compaſſion, and ranne, and fell on his necke, and kiſſed him.21And the ſonne ſaid vnto him, Father, I haue ſinned againſt heauen, and in thy ſight, and am no more worthy to be called thy ſonne.22But the father ſaide to his ſeruants, Bring foorth the beſt robe, and put it on him, and put a ring on his hand, and ſhooes on his feete.23And bring hither the fatted calfe, and kill it, and let vs eate and be merrie.24For this my ſonne was dead, and is aliue againe; hee was loſt, & is found. And they began to be merie.25Now his elder ſonne was in the field, and as he came and drew nigh to the houſe, he heard muſicke & dauncing,26And he called one of the ſeruants, and aſked what theſe things meant.27And he ſaid vnto him, Thy brother is come, and thy father hath killed the fatted calfe, becauſe he hath receiued him ſafe and found.28And he was angry, and would not goe in: therefore came his father out, and intreated him.29And he anſwering ſaid to his father, Loe, theſe many yeeres doe I ſerue thee, neither tranſgreſſed I at any time thy commandement, and yet thou neuer gaueſt mee a kid, that I might make merry with my friends:30But as ſoone as this thy ſonne was come, which hath deuoured thy liuing with harlots, thou haſt killed for him the fatted calfe.31And he ſaid vnto him, Sonne, thou art euer with me, and all that I haue is thine.32It was meete that we ſhould make merry, and be glad: for this thy brother was dead, and is aliue againe: and was loſt, and is found.

CHAPTER 161And hee ſaid alſo vnto his diſciples, There was a certaine rich man which had a Steward, and the ſame was accuſed vnto him that he had waſted his goods.2And hee called him, and ſaid vnto him, How is it that I heare this of thee? Giue an accompt of thy ſtewardſhip: for thou mayeſt bee no longer Steward.3Then the Steward ſaid within himſelfe, What ſhall I doe, for my lord taketh away from mee the Stewardſhip? I cannot digge, to begge I am aſhamed.4I am reſolued what to doe, that when I am put out of the ſtewardſhip, they may receiue me into their houſes.5So hee called euery one of his lords detters vnto him, and ſaid vnto the firſt, How much oweſt thou vnto my lord?6And hee ſaid, An hundred meaſures of oyle. And hee ſaide vnto him, Take thy bill, and ſit downe quickly, and write fiftie.7Then ſaid hee to another, And how much oweſt thou? And hee ſaid, An hundred meaſures of wheat. And hee ſaide vnto him, Take thy bill and write foureſcore.8And the lord commended the vniuſt Steward, becauſe he had done wiſely: for the children of this world are in their generation wiſer then the children of light.9And I ſay vnto you, Make to your ſelues friends of the Mammon of vnrighteouſneſſe, that when ye faile, they may receiue you into euerlaſting habitations.10Hee that is faithfull in that which is leaſt, is faithfull alſo in much: and he that is vniuſt in the leaſt, is vniuſt alſo in much.11If therefore yee haue not bene faithfull in the vnrighteous Mammon, who will commit to your truſt the true riches?12And if ye haue not bene faithful in that which is another mans, who ſhall giue you that which is your owne?13No ſeruant can ſerue two maſters, for either he will hate the one, and loue the other: or elſe he will hold to the one, and deſpiſe the other: yee cannot ſerue God and Mammon.14And the PhAriſees alſo who were couetous, heard all theſe things: and they derided him.15And he ſaid vnto them, Ye are they which iuſtifie your ſelues before men, but God knoweth your hearts: for that which is highly eſteemed amongſt men, is abomination in the ſight of God.16The law and the Prophets were vntill Iohn: ſince that time the kingdome of God is preached, and euery man preaſſeth into it.17And it is eaſier for heauen and earth to paſſe, then one title of the law to faile.18Whoſoeuer putteth away his wife, & marrieth another, committeth adultery: and whoſoeuer marrieth her that is put away from her huſband, committeth adultery.19There was a certaine rich man, which was clothed in purple and fine linnen, and fared ſumptuouſly euery day.20And there was a certaine begger named Lazarus, which was layde at his gate full of ſores,21And deſiring to bee fed with the crummes which fel from the rich mans table: moreouer the dogges came and licked his ſores.22And it came to paſſe that the begger died, and was caried by the Angels into Abrahams boſome: the rich man alſo died, and was buried.23And in hell he lift vp his eyes being in torments, and ſeeth Abraham afarre off, and Lazarus in his boſome:24And he cried, and ſaid, Father Abraham, haue mercy on mee, and ſend Lazarus, that he may dip the tip of his finger in water, and coole my tongue, for I am tormented in this flame.25But Abraham ſaide, Sonne, remember that thou in thy life-time receiuedſt thy good things, and likewiſe Lazarus euill things, but now he is comforted, and thou art tormented.26And beſides all this, betweene vs and you there is a great gulfe fixed, ſo that they which would paſſe from hence to you, cannot, neither can they paſſe to vs, that would come from thence.27Then he ſaid, I pray thee therefore father, that thou wouldeſt ſend him to my fathers houſe:28For I haue fiue brethren, that he may teſtifie vnto them, leſt they alſo come into this place of torment.29Abraham ſaith vnto him, They haue Moſes and the Prophets, let them heare them.30And hee ſaid, Nay, father Abraham: but if one went vnto them from the dead, they will repent.31And hee ſaid vnto him, If they heare not Moſes and the Prophets, neither will they be perſwaded, though one roſe from the dead.

CHAPTER 171Then ſaid he vnto the diſciples, It is impoſſible but that offences will come, but wo vnto him through whom they come.2It were better for him that a milſtone were hanged about his necke, and he caſt into the ſea, then that he ſhould offend one of theſe little ones.3Take heed to your ſelues: If thy brother treſpaſſe againſt thee, rebuke him, and if he repent, forgiue him.4And if hee treſpaſſe againſt thee ſeuen times in a day, and ſeuen times in a day turne againe to thee, ſaying, I repent, thou ſhalt forgiue him.5And the Apoſtles ſaid vnto the Lord, Increaſe our faith.6And the Lord ſaid, If yee had faith as a graine of muſtard ſeede, yee might ſay vnto this Sycamine tree, Be thou plucked vp by the root, and be thou planted in the ſea, & it ſhould obey you.7But which of you hauing a ſeruant plowing, or feeding cattell, will ſay vnto him by & by when he is come from the field, Goe and ſit downe to meate?8And will not rather ſay vnto him, Make ready wherewith I may ſuppe, and gird thy ſelfe, and ſerue me, till I haue eaten and drunken: and afterward thou ſhalt eate and drinke.9Doeth he thanke that ſeruant, becauſe hee did the things that were commanded him? I trow not.10So likewiſe ye, when ye ſhal haue done all thoſe things which are commanded you, ſay, Wee are vnprofitable ſeruants: Wee haue done that which was our duety to doe.11And it came to paſſe, as he went to Hieruſalem, that hee paſſed thorow the mids of Samaria and Galile.12And as he entred into a certaine village, there met him tenne men that were lepers, which ſtood afarre off.13And they lifted vp their voices, and ſaid, Ieſus maſter haue mercy on vs.14And when he ſaw them, hee ſaid vnto them, Goe ſhew your ſelues vnto the Prieſts. And it came to paſſe, that as they went, they were cleanſed.15And one of them when hee ſawe that he was healed, turned backe, and with a loud voice glorified God,16And fell downe on his face at his feet, giuing him thanks: and he was a Samaritane.17And Ieſus anſwering, ſaid, Were there not ten cleanſed, but where are the nine?18There are not found that returned to giue glory to God, ſaue this ſtranger.19And he ſaid vnto him, Ariſe, go thy way, thy faith hath made thee whole.20And when hee was demanded of the PhAriſes, when the kingdome of God ſhould come, hee anſwered them, and ſaid, The kingdome of God commeth not with obſeruation.21Neither ſhall they ſay, Loe here, or loe there: for behold, the kingdome of God is within you.22And hee ſaid vnto the diſciples, The dayes will come, when ye ſhall deſire to ſee one of the dayes of the Sonne of man, and ye ſhall not ſee it.23And they ſhall ſay to you, ſee here, or ſee there: Goe not after them, nor follow them.24For as the lightning that lighteneth out of the one part vnder heauen, ſhineth vnto the other part vnder heauen: ſo ſhall alſo the Sonne of man be in his day.25But firſt muſt hee ſuffer many things, & be reiected of this generation.26And as it was in the dayes of Noe: ſo ſhal it be alſo in the dayes of the Sonne of man.27They did eate, they dranke, they married wiues, they were giuen in mariage, vntill the day that Noe entred into the arke: and the flood came, and deſtroyed them all.28Likewiſe alſo as it was in the dayes of Lot, they did eat, they dranke, they bought, they ſold, they planted, they builded:29But the ſame day that Lot went out of Sodome, it rained fire and brimſtone from heauen, & deſtroyed them all:30Euen thus ſhall it bee in the day when the Sonne of man is reuealed.31In that day he which ſhall be vpon the houſe top, and his ſtuffe in the houſe, let him not come downe to take it away: and he that is in the field, let him likewiſe not returne backe.32Remember Lots wife.33Whoſoeuer ſhall ſeeke to ſaue his life, ſhall loſe it, and whoſoeuer ſhall loſe his life, ſhall preſerueit.34I tell you, in that night there ſhall be two men in one bed; the one ſhal be taken, the other ſhall be left.35Two women ſhall bee grinding together; the one ſhall be taken, and the other left.36Two men ſhall be in the field; the one ſhall be taken, and the other left.37And they anſwered, and ſaid vnto him, Where, Lord? And he ſaid vnto them, Whereſoeuer the body is, thither will the Eagles be gathered together.

CHAPTER 181And he ſpake a parable vnto them, to this ende, that men ought alwayes to pray, and not to faint,2Saying, There was in a city a Iudge, which feared not God neither regarded man.3And there was a widowe in that citie, and ſhe came vnto him, ſaying, Auenge me of mine aduerſarie:4And hee would not for a while. But afterward he ſaid within himſelfe, Though I feare not God, nor regard man,5Yet becauſe this widow troubleth me, I will auenge her, leſt by her continuall comming, ſhe wearie me.6And the Lord ſaid, Heare what the vniuſt iudge ſaith.7And ſhall not God auenge his owne elect, which crie day and night vnto him, thogh he beare long with them?8I tell you that he wil auenge them ſpeedily. Neuertheleſſe, when the Son of man commeth, ſhall hee find faith on the earth?9And he ſpake this parable vnto certaine which truſted in themſelues that they were righteous, & deſpiſed other:10Two men went vp into the Temple to pray, the one a PhAriſee, and the other a Publicane.11The PhAriſee ſtood and prayed thus with himſelfe, God, I thank thee, that I am not as other men are, extortioners, vniuſt, adulterers, or euen as this Publicane.12I faſt twiſe in the weeke, I giue tithes of all that I poſſeſſe.13And the Publicane ſtanding afarre off, would not lift vp ſo much as his eyes vnto heauen: but ſmote vpon his breaſt, ſaying, God me mercifull to mee a ſinner.14I tell you, this man went downe to his houſe iuſtified rather then the other: For euery one that exalteth himſelfe, ſhall be abaſed: and hee that humbleth himſelfe, ſhall be exalted.15And they brought vnto him alſo infants, that he would touch them: but when his diſciples ſaw it, they rebuked them.16But Ieſus called them vnto him, and ſaid, Suffer litle children to come vnto me, and forbid them not: for of ſuch is the kingdome of God.17Uerely I ſay vnto you, whoſoeuer ſhall not receiue the kingdome of God as a litle child, ſhal in no wiſe enter therein.18And a certaine ruler aſked him, ſaying, Good maſter, what ſhall I doe to inherit eternall life?19And Ieſus ſaid vnto him, Why calleſt thou mee good? None is good ſaue one, that is God.20Thou knoweſt the commaundements, Doe not commit adulterie, Doe not kill, Doe not ſteale, Doe not beare falſe witneſſe, Honour thy father and thy mother.21And he ſaid, All theſe haue I kept from my youth vp.22Now when Ieſus heard theſe things, hee ſaid vnto him, Yet lackeſt thou one thing: Sell all that thou haſt, and diſtribute vnto the poore, and thou ſhalt haue treaſure in heauen, and come, follow me.23And when he heard this, he was very ſorowfull, for he was very rich.24And when Ieſus ſaw that hee was very ſorrowfull, he ſaid, How hardly ſhal they that haue riches, enter into the kingdome of God?25For it is eaſier for a camel to goe thorow a needles eye, then for a rich man to enter into the kingdom of God.26And they that heard it, ſaid, Who then can be ſaued?27And he ſaid, The things which are vnpoſſible with men, are poſſible with God.28Then Peter ſaid, Loe, we haue left all, and followed thee.29And he ſaid vnto them, Uerily, I ſay vnto you, there is no man that hath left houſe, or parents, or brethren, or wife, or children, for the kingdome of Gods ſake,30Who ſhall not receiue manifold more in this preſent time, and in the world to come life euerlaſting.31Then hee tooke vnto him the twelue, and ſaid vnto them, Behold, we goe vp to Hieruſalem, and al things that are written by the Prophets concerning the ſonne of man, ſhall be accompliſhed.32For he ſhall be deliuered vnto the Gentiles, and ſhall be mocked, and ſpitefully intreated, and ſpitted on:33And they ſhall ſcourge him, and put him to death, and the third day he ſhall riſe againe.34And they vnderſtood none of theſe things: and this ſaying was hid from them, neither knew they the things which were ſpoken.35And it came to paſſe, that as he was come nigh vnto Iericho, a certaine blinde man ſate by the way ſide, begging,36And hearing the multitude paſſe by, he aſked what it meant.37And they tolde him that Ieſus of Nazareth paſſeth by.38And he cried, ſaying, Ieſus thou ſonne of Dauid, haue mercie on me.39And they which went before, rebuked him, that hee ſhould holde his peace: but hee cried ſo much the more, Thou Sonne of Dauid, haue mercie on mee.40And Ieſus ſtood and commanded him to be brought vnto him: and when he was come neere, he aſked him,41Saying, What wilt thou that I ſhall doe vnto thee? And he ſaid, Lord, that I may receiue my ſight.42And Ieſus ſaid vnto him, Receiue thy ſight, thy faith hath ſaued thee.43And immediately he receiued his ſight, and followed him, glorifying God: and all the people when they ſaw it, gaue praiſe vnto God.

CHAPTER 191And Ieſus entred, and paſſed thorow Iericho.2And behold, there was a man named Zacheus, which was the cheefe among the Publicanes, and he was rich.3And he ſought to ſee Ieſus who he was, and could not for the preaſe, becauſe he was litle of ſtature.4And he ranne before, and climed vp into a ſycomore tree to ſee him, for he was to paſſe that way.5And when Ieſus came to the place, he looked vp and ſaw him, and ſaid vnto him, Zacheus, make haſte, & come downe, for to day I muſt abide at thy houſe.6And he made haſte, and came downe, and receiued him ioyfully.7And when they ſaw it, they all murmured, ſaying, That he was gone to be gueſt with a man that is a ſinner.8And Zacheus ſtood, and ſaid vnto the Lord, Behold, Lord, the halfe of my goods I giue to the poore, & if I haue taken any thing from any man by falſe accuſation, I reſtore him foure fold.9And Ieſus ſaid vnto him, This day is ſaluation come to this houſe, forſomuch as he alſo is the ſonne of Abraham.10For the ſonne of man is come to ſeeke, and to ſaue that which was loſt.11And as they heard theſe things, he added, and ſpake a parable, becauſe he was nigh to Hieruſalem, and becauſe they thought that the kingdome of God ſhould immediately appeare.12He ſaid therefore, A certaine noble man went into a farre countrey, to receiue for himſelfe a kingdome, and to returne.13And hee called his ten ſeruants, and deliuered them ten pounds, and ſaid vnto them, Occupy till I come.14But his citizens hated him, and ſent a meſſage after him, ſaying, We wil not haue this man to reigne ouer vs.15And it came to paſſe, that when he was returned, hauing receiued the kingdome, then hee commaunded theſe ſeruants to be called vnto him, to whom he had giuen the money, that hee might know how much euery man had gained by trading.16Then came the firſt, ſaying, Lord, thy pound hath gained ten pounds.17And he ſaid vnto him, Well, thou good ſeruant: becauſe thou haſt bene faithfull in a very little, haue thou authoritie ouer ten cities.18And the ſecond came, ſaying, Lord, thy pound hath gained fiue pounds.19And hee ſaid likewiſe to him, Bee thou alſo ouer fiue cities.20And another came, ſaying, Lord, behold, here is thy pound which I haue kept layd vp in a napkin:21For I feared thee, becauſe thou art an auſtere man: thou takeſt vp that thou layedſt not downe, and reapeſt that thou didſt not ſow.22And hee ſaith vnto him, Out of thine owne mouth will I iudge thee, thou wicked ſeruant: Thou kneweſt that I was an auſtere man, taking vp that I layde not downe, and reaping that I did not ſow.23Wherefore then gaueſt not thou my money into the bancke, that at my comming I might haue required mine owne with vſury?24And he ſaid vnto them that ſtood by, Take from him the pound, and giue it to him that hath ten pounds.25And they ſaid vnto him, Lord, he hath ten pounds.26For I ſay vnto you, That vnto euery one which hath, ſhalbe giuen, and from him that hath not, euen that hee hath ſhalbe

taken away from him.[27]But thoſe mine enemies which would not that I
ſhould reigne ouer them, bring hither, and ſlay them before mee.[28]And
when he had thus ſpoken, he went before, aſcending vp to
Hieruſalem.[29]And it came to paſſe when he was come nigh to
Bethphage and Bethanie, at the mount called the mount of Oliues, he
ſent two of his diſciples,[30]Saying, Goe ye into the village ouer againſt
you, in the which at your entring ye ſhall find a Colt tied, whereon yet
neuer man ſate: looſe him, and bring him hither.[31]And if any man aſke
you, Why do ye looſe him? Thus ſhall ye ſay vnto him, Becauſe the Lord
hath neede of him.[32]And they that were ſent, went their way, and found
euen as hee had ſaid vnto them.[33]And as they were looſing the colt, the
owners thereof ſaid vnto them, Why looſe ye the Colt?[34]And they ſaid,
The Lord hath need of him.[35]And they brought him to Ieſus: and they
caſt their garments vpon the Colt, and they ſet Ieſus thereon.[36]And as
he went, they ſpread their clothes in the way.[37]And when he was come
nigh euen now at the deſcent of the mount of Oliues, the whole
multitude of the diſciples began to reioyce and praiſe God with a loud
voice, for all the mighty workes that they had ſeene,[38]Saying, Bleſſed
bee the King that commeth in the Name of the Lord, peace in heauen,
and glory in the Higheſt.[39]And ſome of the PhAriſees from among the
multitude ſaide vnto him, Maſter, rebuke thy diſciples.[40]And he
anſwered, and ſaid vnto them, I tell you, that if theſe ſhould holde their
peace, the ſtones would immediatly cry out.[41]And when he was come
neere, he beheld the city and wept ouer it,[42]Saying, If thou hadſt
knowen, euen thou, at leaſt in this thy day, the things which belong vnto
thy peace! but now they are hid from thine eyes.[43]For the dayes ſhall
come vpon thee, that thine enemies ſhall caſt a trench about thee, and
compaſſe thee round, and keepe thee in on euery ſide,[44]And ſhall lay
thee euen with the ground, and thy children within thee: and they ſhall
not leaue in thee one ſtone vpon another, becauſe thou kneweſt not the
time of thy viſitation.[45]And he went into the Temple, and began to caſt
out them that ſolde therein, and them that bought,[46]Saying vnto them,
It is written, My houſe is the houſe of prayer: but ye haue made it a
denne of theeues.[47]And he taught daily in the Temple. But the chiefe
Prieſtes and the Scribes, and the chiefe of the people ſought to deſtroy
him,[48]And could not finde what they might doe: for all the people were
very attentiue to heare him.

CHAPTER 20[1]And it came to paſſe, that on one of thoſe dayes, as he
taught the people in the Temple, and preached the Goſpel, the chiefe
Prieſts and the Scribes came vpon him, with the Elders,[2]And ſpake vnto
him, ſaying, Tell vs, by what authoritie doeſt thou theſe things? or who
is hee that gaue thee this authoritie?[3]And hee anſwered, and ſaid vnto
them, I will alſo aſke you one thing, and anſwere me.[4]The Baptiſme of
Iohn, was it from heauen, or of men?[5]And they reaſoned with
themſelues, ſaying, If wee ſhall ſay, From heauen, he will ſay, Why then
beleeued yee him not?[6]But and if we ſay, Of men, all the people will
ſtone vs: for they be perſwaded that Iohn was a Prophet.[7]And they
anſwered, that they could not tell whence it was.[8]And Ieſus ſaid vnto
them, Neither tell I you by what authoritie I doe theſe things.[9]Then
began hee to ſpeake to the people this parable: A certaine man planted
a vineyard, and let it foorth to huſbandmen, and went into a farre
countrey for a long time.[10]And at the ſeaſon, hee ſent a ſeruant to the
huſbandmen, that they ſhould giue him of the fruit of the vineyard, but
the huſbandmen beat him, and ſent him away emptie.[11]And againe hee
ſent another ſeruant, and they beat him alſo, and entreated him
ſhamefully, and ſent him away emptie.[12]And againe he ſent the third,
and they wounded him alſo, & caſt him out.[13]Then ſaid the lord of the
vineyard, What ſhall I doe? I will ſend my beloued ſonne: it may be they
will reuerence him when they ſee him.[14]But when the huſbandmen ſaw
him, they reaſoned among themſelues, ſaying, This is þe heire, come, let
vs kill him, that the inheritance may be ours.[15]So they caſt him out of
the vineyard, and killed him. What therefore ſhall the lord of the
vineyard doe vnto them?[16]Hee ſhall come and deſtroy theſe
huſbandmen, and ſhall giue the vineyard to others. And when they heard
it, they ſaid, God forbid.[17]And hee beheld them, and ſaid, What is this
then that is written, The ſtone which the builders reiected, the ſame is
become the head of the corner?[18]Whoſoeuer ſhall fall vpon that ſtone,
ſhalbe broken: but on whomſoeuer it ſhall fall, it will grinde him to
powder.[19]And the chiefe Prieſts and the Scribes the ſame houre ſought
to lay hands on him, and they feared the people: for they perceiued that
he had ſpoken this parable againſt them.[20]And they watched him, and
ſent foorth ſpies, which ſhould faine themſelues iuſt men, that they
might take holde of his words, that ſo they might deliuer him vnto the
power and authoritie of the gouernour.[21]And they aſked him, ſaying,
Maſter, we know that thou ſayeſt and teacheſt rightly, neither accepteſt
thou the perſon of any, but teacheſt the way of God truely.[22]Is it lawfull
for vs to giue tribute vnto Ceſar, or no?[23]But he perceiued their craftines,
and ſaid vnto them, Why tempt ye me?[24]ſhew me a peny: whoſe image
and ſuperſcription hath it? They anſwered, and ſaid, Ceſars.[25]And he
ſaid vnto them, Render therefore vnto Ceſar the things which be Ceſars,
and vnto God the things which be Gods.[26]And they could not take
holde of his wordes before the people, and they marueiled at his
anſwere, and helde their peace.[27]Then came to him certaine of the
Sadduces (which denie that there is any reſurrection) and they aſked
him,[28]Saying, Maſter, Moſes wrote vnto vs, If any mans brother die,
hauing a wife, and hee die without children, that his brother ſhould take
his wife, and raiſe vp ſeede vnto his brother.[29]There were therefore
ſeuen brethren, and the firſt tooke a wife, and died without
children.[30]And the ſecond tooke her to wife, and he died
childleſſe.[31]And the third tooke her, and in like maner the ſeuen alſo.
And they left no children, and died.[32]Laſt of all the woman died
alſo.[33]Therefore in the reſurrection, whoſe wife of them is ſhe? for ſeuen
had her to wife.[34]And Ieſus anſwering, ſaid vnto them, The children of
this world, marrie, and are giuen in marriage:[35]But they which ſhall be
accompted worthy to obtaine that world, and the reſurrection from the
dead, neither marrie, nor are giuen in marriage.[36]Neither can they die
any more; for they are equall vnto the Angels, and are the children of
God, being the children of the reſurrection.[37]Now that the dead are
raiſed, euen Moſes ſhewed at the buſh, when he calleth the Lord, the
God of Abraham, and the God of Iſahac, and the God of Iacob.[38]For
he is not a God of the dead, but of the liuing for all liue vnto him.[39]Then
certaine of the Scribes anſwering, ſaid, Maſter, Thou haſt well
ſaid.[40]And after that, they durſt not aſke him any queſtion at all.[41]And
he ſaid vnto them, How ſay they that Chriſt is Dauids ſonne?[42]And
Dauid himſelfe ſaith in the booke of Pſalmes, The Lord ſaid to my Lord,
Sit thou on my right hand,[43]Till I make thine enemies thy
footeſtoole.[44]Dauid therefore calleth him, Lord, how is he then his
ſonne?[45]Then in the audience of all the people, he ſaid vnto his
diſciples,[46]Beware of the Scribes, which deſire to walke in long robes,
and loue greetings in the markets, and the higheſt ſeates in the
Synagogues, and the chiefe roumes at feaſts:[47]Which deuoure widowes
houſes and for a ſhew make long prayers: the ſame ſhall receiue greater
damnation.

CHAPTER 21[1]And he looked vp, and ſaw the rich men caſting their
giftes into the treaſurie.[2]And hee ſaw alſo a certaine poore widow,
caſting in thither two mites.[3]And he ſaid, Of a truth, I ſay vnto you, that
this poore widow hath caſt in more then they all.[4]For all theſe haue of
their abundance caſt in vnto the offerings of God, but ſhee of her
penurie hath caſt in all the liuing that ſhe had.[5]And as ſome ſpake of the
Temple, how it was adorned with goodly ſtones, and gifts, he ſaid,[6]As
for theſe things which yee behold, the dayes will come, in the which
there ſhal not be left one ſtone vpon another, that ſhal not be throwen
downe.[7]And they aſked him, ſaying, Maſter, but when ſhall theſe things
be? and what ſigne wil there be, when theſe things ſhall come to
paſſe?[8]And he ſaid, Take heede that yee be not deceiued: for many ſhall
come in my Name, ſaying, I am Chriſt, and the time draweth neere: goe
yee not therefore after them.[9]But when ye ſhall heare of wars, and
commotions, be not terrified: for theſe things muſt firſt come to paſſe,
but the end is not by and by.[10]Then ſaid he vnto them, Nation ſhall riſe
againſt nation, and kingdome againſt kingdome:[11]And great earthquakes
ſhall be in diuers places, and famines, and peſtilences: and fearefull ſights
and great ſignes ſhall there be from heauen.[12]But before all theſe, they
ſhall lay their hands on you, and perſecute you, deliuering you vp to the
Synagogues, and into priſons, being brought before Kings and rulers for
my Names ſake.[13]And it ſhall turne to you for a teſtimony.[14]Settle it
therfore in your hearts, not to meditate before what ye ſhall
anſwere.[15]For I will giue you a mouth and wiſedome, which all your
aduerſaries ſhall not be able to gainſay, nor reſiſt.[16]And yee ſhall be

betrayed both by parents and brethren, and kinſefolkes and friends, and ſome of you ſhall they cauſe to be put to death. 17 And ye ſhalbe hated of all men for my Names ſake. 18 But there ſhall not a haire of your head periſh. 19 In your patience poſſeſſe ye your ſoules. 20 And when yee ſhall ſee Hieruſalem compaſſed with armies, then know that the deſolation thereof is nigh. 21 Then let them which are in Iudea, flee to the mountaines, and let them which are in the midſt of it, depart out, and let not them that are in the countreys, enter thereinto. 22 For theſe be the dayes of vengeance, that all things which are written may be fulfilled. 23 But woe vnto them that are with childe, and to them that giue ſucke in thoſe dayes, for there ſhalbe great diſtreſſe in the land, and wrath vpon this people. 24 And they ſhall fall by the edge of the ſword, and ſhall bee led away captiue into all nations, and Hieruſalem ſhall be troden downe of the Gentiles, vntill the times of the Gentiles bee fulfilled. 25 And there ſhalbe ſignes in the Sunne, and in the Moone, and in the Starres, and vpon the earth diſtreſſe of nations, with perplexity, the ſea and the waues roaring, 26 Mens hearts failing them for feare, and for looking after thoſe things which are comming on the earth; For the powers of heauen ſhall be ſhaken. 27 And then ſhall they ſee the ſonne of man comming in a cloud with power and great glory. 28 And when theſe things begin to come to paſſe, then looke vp, and lift vp your heads, for your redemptiou draweth nigh. 29 And he ſpake to them a parable, Behold the figge tree, and all the trees, 30 When they now ſhoot foorth, yee ſee and know of your owne ſelues, that ſummer is now nigh at hand. 31 So likewiſe yee, when yee ſee theſe things come to paſſe, know ye that the kingdome of God is nigh at hand. 32 Uerily I ſay vnto you, this generation ſhall not paſſe away, till all be fulfilled. 33 Heauen and earth ſhall paſſe away, but my words ſhall not paſſe away. 34 And take heed to your ſelues, leaſt at any time your hearts be ouercharged with ſurfetting, and drunkenneſse, and cares of this life, and ſo that day come vpon you vnawares. 35 For as a ſnare ſhall it come on all them that dwell on the face of the whole earth. 36 Watch ye therefore, and pray alwayes, that ye may be accompted worthy to eſcape all theſe things that ſhall come to paſſe, and to ſtand before the ſonne of man. 37 And in the day time he was teaching in the Temple, and at night hee went out, and abode in the mount that is called the mount of Oliues. 38 And all the people came earely in the morning to him in the Temple, for to heare him.

CHAPTER 22 1 Now þe feaſt of vnleuened bread drew nigh, which is called the Paſſeouer. 2 And the chiefe Prieſts and Scribes ſought how they might kill him; for they feared the people. 3 Then entred Satan into Iudas ſurnamed Iſcariot, being of the number of the twelue. 4 And he went his way, and communed with the chiefe Prieſts and captaines, how he might betray him vnto them. 5 And they were glad, and couenanted to giue him money. 6 And he promiſed, and ſought opportunitie to betray him vnto them in the abſence of the multitude. 7 Then came the day of vnleauened bread, when the Paſſeouer muſt be killed. 8 And he ſent Peter and Iohn, ſaying, Goe and prepare vs the Paſſeouer, that we may eate. 9 And they ſaid vnto him, Where wilt thou that we prepare? 10 And he ſaid vnto them, Behold, when ye are entred into the citie, there ſhall a man meet you, bearing a pitcher of water, follow him into the houſe where he entreth in. 11 And yee ſhall ſay vnto the goodman of the houſe, The Maſter ſaith vnto thee, Where is the gheſt-chamber where I ſhall eate the Paſſeouer with my diſciples? 12 And he ſhall ſhew you a large vpper roume furniſhed, there make ready. 13 And they went, and found as hee had ſaid vnto them, and they made readie the Paſſeouer. 14 And when the houre was come, he ſate downe, and the twelue Apoſtles with him. 15 And he ſaid vnto them, With deſire I haue deſired to eate this Paſſeouer with you before I ſuffer. 16 For I ſay vnto you, I will not any more eate thereof, vntill it be fulfilled in the kingdome of God. 17 And hee tooke the cup, and gaue thanks, and ſaid, Take this, and diuide it among your ſelues. 18 For I ſay vnto you, I will not drinke of the fruit of the Uine, vntill the kingdome of God ſhall come. 19 And hee tooke bread, and gaue thankes, and brake it, and gaue vnto them, ſaying, This is my body which is giuen for you, this doe in remembrance of me. 20 Likewiſe alſo the cup after ſupper, ſaying, This cup is the New Teſtament in my blood, which is ſhed for you. 21 But beholde, the hand of him that betrayeth mee, is with mee on the table. 22 And truly the Sonne of man goeth as it was determined, but woe vnto that man by whom he is betraied. 23 And they began to enquire among themſelues, which of them it was that ſhould doe this thing. 24 And there was alſo a ſtrife among them, which of them ſhould bee accompted the greateſt. 25 And hee ſaide vnto them, The Kings of the Gentiles exerciſe lordſhip ouer them, & they that exerciſe authoritie vpon them, are called benefactors. 26 But ye ſhall not be ſo; but he that is greateſt among you, let him be as the yonger, and he that is chiefe, as he that doeth ſerue. 27 For whether is greater, hee that ſitteth at meat, or hee that ſerueth? Is not he that ſitteth at meat? But I am among you as he that ſerueth. 28 Ye are they which haue continued with me in my temptations. 29 And I appoint vnto you a kingdome, as my Father hath appointed vnto me, 30 That yee may eate and drinke at my table in my kingdome, and ſit on thrones iudging the twelue Tribes of Iſrael. 31 And the Lord ſaid, Simon, Simon, beholde, Satan hath deſired to haue you, that he may ſift you as wheat: 32 But I haue prayed for thee, that thy faith faile not; and when thou art conuerted, ſtrengthen thy brethren. 33 And hee ſaid vnto him, Lord, I am ready to goe with thee both into priſon, and to death. 34 And hee ſaid, I tell thee Peter, the cocke ſhall not crow this day, before that thou ſhalt thriſe denie that thou knoweſt me. 35 And he ſaid vnto them, When I ſent you without purſe, and ſcrip, and ſhooes, lacked ye any thing? And they ſaid, Nothing. 36 Then ſaide hee vnto them, But now he that hath a purſe, let him take it, and likewiſe his ſcrip: and hee that hath no ſword, let him ſel his garment, and buy one. 37 For I ſay vnto you, that this that is written, muſt yet be accompliſhed in me, And he was reckoned among the tranſgreſsors: For the things concerning me haue an end. 38 And they ſaid, Lord, behold, here are two ſwords. And hee ſaide vnto them, It is ynough. 39 And he came out, and went, as hee was wont, to the mount of Oliues, and his diſciples alſo followed him. 40 And when he was at the place, he ſaid vnto them, Pray, that yee enter not into temptation. 41 And he was withdrawen from them about a ſtones caſt, and kneeled downe, and prayed, 42 Saying, Father, if thou be willing, remooue this cup from me: neuertheleſſe, not my will, but thine be done. 43 And there appeared an Angel vnto him from heauen, ſtrengthening him. 44 And being in an agonie, he prayed more earneſtly, and his ſweat was as it were great drops of blood falling downe to the ground. 45 And when he roſe vp from prayer, and was come to his diſciples, hee found them ſleeping for ſorrow, 46 And ſaid vnto them, Why ſleepe yee? Riſe, and pray, leſt yee enter into temptation. 47 And while he yet ſpake, behold, a multitude, and hee that was called Iudas, one of the twelue, went before them, and drewe neere vnto Ieſus, to kiſſe him. 48 But Ieſus ſaid vnto him, Iudas, betrayeſt thou the ſonne of man with a kiſſe? 49 When they which were about him, ſaw what would follow, they ſaid vnto him, Lord, ſhall wee ſmite with the ſword? 50 And one of them ſmote the ſeruant of the high Prieſt, and cut off his right eare. 51 And Ieſus anſwered, and ſaid, Suffer ye thus farre. And he touched his eare, and healed him. 52 Then Ieſus ſaid vnto the chiefe Prieſts, and captaines of the Temple, and the Elders which were come to him, Be ye come out as againſt a thiefe, with ſwords and ſtaues? 53 When I was daily with you in the Temple, yee ſtretched foorth no hands againſt mee: but this is your houre, and the power of darkeneſſe. 54 Then tooke they him, and led him, and brought him into the high Prieſts houſe, and Peter followed afarre off. 55 And when they had kindled a fire in the middes of the hall, and were ſet downe together, Peter ſate downe among them. 56 But a certaine maide beheld him as he ſate by the fire, and earneſtly looked vpon him, and ſaid, This man was alſo with him. 57 And he denied him, ſaying, Woman, I know him not. 58 And after a little while another ſaw him, & ſaid, Thou art alſo of them. And Peter ſaid, Man, I am not. 59 And about the ſpace of one houre after, another confidently affirmed, ſaying, Of a trueth this fellow alſo was with him; for he is a Galilean. 60 And Peter ſaid, Man, I know not what thou ſayeſt. And immediately while he yet ſpake, the cocke crew. 61 And the Lord turned, and looked vpon Peter; and Peter remembred the word of the Lord, how he had ſaid vnto him, Before the cocke crow, thou ſhalt deny me thriſe. 62 And Peter went out, and wept bitterly. 63 And the men that helde Ieſus, mocked him, and ſmote him. 64 And when they had blindfolded him, they ſtroke him on the face, and aſked him, ſaying, Propheſie, who is it that ſmote thee? 65 And many other things blaſphemouſly ſpake they againſt him. 66 And aſſoone as it was day, the Elders of the people, & the chiefe Prieſts and the Scribes came together, and led him into their Councell, ſaying, 67 Art thou the

Chriſt? Tell vs. And hee ſaid vnto them, If I tell you, you will not beleeue.68And if I alſo aſke you, you will not anſwere me, nor let me goe.69Hereafter ſhal the ſonne of man ſit on the right hand of the power of God.70Then ſaid they all, Art thou then the Sonne of God? And hee ſaid vnto them, Ye ſay that I am.71And they ſaid, What need we any further witneſſe? For wee our ſelues haue heard of his owne mouth.

CHAPTER 231And the whole multitude of them aroſe, and led him vnto Pilate.2And they began to accuſe him, ſaying, We found this fellow peruerting the nation, and forbidding to giue tribute to Ceſar, ſaying, that he himſelfe is Chriſt a king.3And Pilate aſked him, ſaying, Art thou the king of the Iewes? And he anſwered him, & ſaid, Thou ſayeſt it.4Then ſaide Pilate to the chiefe Prieſts, and to the people, I finde no fault in this man.5And they were the more fierce, ſaying, He ſtirreth vp the people, teaching thorowout all Iurie, beginning from Galilee to this place.6When Pilate heard of Galilee, he aſked whether the man were a Galilean.7And aſsoone as he knew that hee belonged vnto Herods iuriſdiction, hee ſent him to Herode, who himſelfe alſo was at Hieruſalem at that time.8And when Herode ſaw Ieſus, he was exceeding glad, for hee was deſirous to ſee him of a long ſeaſon, becauſe he had heard many things of him, and hee hoped to haue ſeene ſome miracle done by him.9Then he queſtioned with him in many words, but he anſwered him nothing.10And the chiefe Prieſts and Scribes ſtood, and vehemently accuſed him.11And Herod with his men of warre ſet him at naught, and mocked him, and arayed him in a gorgeous robe, and ſent him againe to Pilate.12And the ſame day Pilate and Herod were made friends together; for before, they were at enmitie betweene themſelues.13And Pilate, when hee had called together the chiefe Prieſts, and the rulers, and the people,14Said vnto them, Ye haue brought this man vnto me, as one that peruerteth the people, and behold, I hauing examined him before you, haue found no fault in this man, touching thoſe things whereof ye accuſe him.15No, nor yet Herod: for I ſent you to him, and loe, nothing worthy of death is done vnto him.16I will therefore chaſtiſe him, and releaſe him.17For of neceſsitie hee muſt releaſe one vnto them at the Feaſt.18And they cried out all at once, ſaying, Away with this man, and releaſe vnto vs Barabbas,19Who for a certaine ſedition made in the citie, and for murder, was caſt in priſon.20Pilate therefore willing to releaſe Ieſus, ſpake againe to them:21But they cried, ſaying, Crucifie him, crucifie him.22And hee ſaid vnto them the third time, Why, what euill hath he done? I haue found no cauſe of death in him, I will therefore chaſtiſe him, & let him goe.23And they were inſtant with loud voyces, requiring that he might be crucified: and the voyces of them, and of the chiefe Prieſts preuailed.24And Pilate gaue ſentence that it ſhould be as they required.25And he releaſed vnto them, him that for ſedition and murder was caſt into priſon, whom they had deſired, but he deliuered Ieſus to their will.26And as they led him away, they laid hold vpon one Simon a Cyrenian, comming out of the countrey, and on him they laid the croſse, that hee might beare it after Ieſus.27And there followed him a great company of people, and of women, which alſo bewailed & lamented him.28But Ieſus turning vnto them, ſaid, Daughters of Hieruſalem, weepe not for me, but weepe for your ſelues, and for your children.29For beholde, the dayes are comming, in the which they ſhall ſay, Bleſſed are the barren, and the wombs that neuer bare, and the paps which neuer gaue ſucke.30Then ſhall they begin to ſay to the mountaines, Fall on vs, and to the hils, Couer vs.31For if they doe theſe things in a green tree, what ſhalbe done in the drie?32And there were alſo two other malefactors led with him, to bee put to death.33And when they were come to the place which is called Caluarie, there they crucified him, and the malefactors, one on the right hand, and the other on the left.34Then ſaid Ieſus, Father, forgiue them, for they know not what they doe: And they parted his raiment, and caſt lots.35And the people ſtood beholding, & the rulers alſo with them derided him, ſaying, Hee ſaued others, let him ſaue himſelfe, if he be Chriſt, þe choſen of God.36And the ſouldiers alſo mocked him, comming to him, and offering him vineger,37And ſaying, If thou be the king of the Iewes, ſaue thy ſelfe.38And a ſuperſcription alſo was written ouer him in letters of Greeke, and Latin, & Hebrew, THIS IS THE KING OF THE IEWES.39And one of þe malefactors, which were hanged, railed on him, ſaying, If thou be Chriſt, ſaue thy ſelfe and vs.40But the other anſwering, rebuked him, ſaying, Doeſt not thou feare God, ſeeing thou art in the ſame condemnation?41And we indeed iuſtly; for we receiue the due reward of our deeds, but this man hath done nothing amiſse.42And he ſaid vnto Ieſus, Lord, remember me when thou commeſt into thy kingdome.43And Ieſus ſaid vnto him, Uerily, I ſay vnto thee, to day ſhalt thou be with me in Paradiſe.44And it was about the ſixt houre, and there was a darkeneſſe ouer all the earth, vntill the ninth houre.45And the Sunne was darkened, and the vaile of the temple was rent in the mids.46And when Ieſus had cried with a loud voice, he ſaid, Father, into thy hands I commend my ſpirit: And hauing ſaid thus, he gaue vp the ghoſt.47Now when the Centurion ſaw what was done, he glorified God, ſaying, Certainly this was a righteous man.48And all the people that came together to that ſight, beholding the things which were done, ſmote their breaſts, and returned.49And all his acquaintance, and the women that followed him from Galilee, ſtood a farre off, beholding theſe things.50And behold, there was a man named Ioſeph, a counſeller, and hee was a good man, and a iuſt.51(The ſame had not conſented to the counſell and deede of them) he was of Arimathea, a city of the Iewes (who alſo himſelfe waited for the kingdome of God.)52This man went vnto Pilate, and begged the body of Ieſus.53And he tooke it downe, and wrapped it in linnen, and layd it in a Sepulchre that was hewen in ſtone, wherein neuer man before was layd.54And that day was the Preparation, and the Sabbath drew on.55And the women alſo which came with him from Galilee, followed after, and beheld the Sepulchre, and how his body was layd.56And they returned, and prepared ſpices and ointments, and reſted the Sabbath day, according to the commandement.

CHAPTER 241Now vpon the firſt day of the weeke, very earely in the morning, they came vnto the Sepulchre, bringing the ſpices which they had prepared, and certaine others with them.2And they found the ſtone rolled away from the Sepulchre.3And they entred in, and found not the body of the Lord Ieſus.4And it came to paſſe, as they were much perplexed thereabout, behold, two men ſtood by them in ſhining garments.5And as they were afraid, and bowed downe their faces to the earth, they ſaid vnto them, Why ſeek ye the liuing among the dead?6He is not heere, but is riſen: Remember how he ſpake vnto you when he was yet in Galilee,7Saying, The Sonne of man muſt be deliuered into the hands of ſinfull men, and be crucified, and the third day riſe againe.8And they remembred his words,9And returned from the Sepulchre, and told all theſe things vnto the eleuen, and to all the reſt.10It was Marie Magdalene, & Ioanna, & Mary the mother of Iames, and other women that were with them, which tolde theſe things vnto the Apoſtles.11And their words ſeemed to them as idle tales, and they beleeued them not.12Then aroſe Peter, and ranne vnto the Sepulchre, and ſtowping downe, hee behelde the linnen clothes layd by themſelues, and departed, wondering in himſelfe at that which was come to paſſe.13And behold, two of them went that ſame day to a village called Emaus, which was from Hieruſalem about threeſcore furlongs.14And they talked together of all theſe things which had happened.15And it came to paſſe, that while they communed together, and reaſoned, Ieſus himſelfe drew neere, and went with them.16But their eyes were holden, that they ſhould not know him.17And he ſaid vnto them, What maner of communications are theſe that yee haue one to another as yee walke, and are ſad?18And the one of them, whoſe name was Cleophas, anſwering, ſaide vnto him, Art thou onely a ſtranger in Hieruſalem, and haſt not knowen the things which are come to paſſe there in theſe dayes?19And hee ſaide vnto them, What things? And they ſaid vnto him, Concerning Ieſus of Nazareth, which was a Prophet, mighty in deede and word before God, and all the people.20And how the chiefe Prieſts and our rulers deliuered him to be condemned to death, and haue crucified him.21But wee truſted that it had bene hee, which ſhould haue redeemed Iſrael: and beſide all this, to day is the third day ſince theſe things were done.22Yea, and certaine women alſo of our company made vs aſtoniſhed, which were early at the Sepulchre:23And when they found not his bodie, they came, ſaying, that they had alſo ſeene a viſion of Angels, which ſaide that he was aliue.24And certaine of them which were with vs, went to the Sepulchre, and found it euen ſo as the women had ſaid, but him they ſaw not.25Then hee ſaide vnto them, O fooles, and ſlow of heart to beleeue all that the Prophets haue ſpoken:26Ought not Chriſt to haue ſuffered theſe things, and to enter into his glorie?27And beginning at Moſes, and all the Prophets, hee expounded vnto them in all the Scriptures, the things concerning himſelfe.[28]And they drew nigh vnto the village, whither they went, and hee made as though hee would haue gone further.[29]But they conſtrained him, ſaying, Abide with vs, for it is towards euening, and the day is farre ſpent: And he went in, to tarrie with them.[30]And it came to paſſe, as hee ſate at meate with them, hee tooke bread, and bleſſed it, and brake, and gaue to them.[31]And their eyes were opened, and they knew him, and he vaniſhed out of their ſight.[32]And they ſaid one vnto another, Did not our heart burne within vs, while hee talked with vs by the way, and while hee opened to vs the Scriptures?[33]And they roſe vp the ſame houre, and returned to Hieruſalem, and found the eleuen gathered together, and them that were with them,[34]Saying, The Lord is riſen indeed, and hath appeared to Simon.[35]And they told what things were done in the way, & how he was knowen of them in breaking of bread.[36]And as they thus ſpake, Ieſus himſelfe ſtood in the midſt of them, and ſayeth vnto them, Peace bee vnto you.[37]But they were terrified, and afrighted, and ſuppoſed that they had ſeene a ſpirit.[38]And he ſaid vnto them, Why are yee troubled, and why doe thoughts Ariſe in your hearts?[39]Beholde my hands and my feete, that it is I my ſelfe: handle me, and ſee, for a ſpirit hath not fleſh and bones, as ye ſee me haue.[40]And when hee had thus ſpoken, hee ſhewed them his handes and his feete.[41]And while they yet beleeued not for ioy, and wondered, hee ſaide vnto them, Haue ye here any meat?[42]And they gaue him a piece of a broyled fiſh, and of an hony combe.[43]And he tooke it, and did eate before them.[44]And hee ſaid vnto them, Theſe are the words which I ſpake vnto you, while I was yet with you, þ[t] all things muſt be fulfilled, which were written in the Law of Moſes, & in the Prophets, and in the Pſalmes concerning me.[45]Then opened he their vnderſtanding, that they might vnderſtand the Scriptures,[46]And ſaid vnto them, Thus it is written, & thus it behoued Chriſt to ſuffer, & to riſe from the dead the third day:[47]And that repentance and remiſsion of ſinnes ſhould be preached in his Name, among all nations, beginning at Hieruſalem.[48]And yee are witneſſes of theſe things.[49]And behold, I ſend the promiſe of my Father vpon you: but tarie ye in the citie of Hieruſalem, vntill ye be indued with power from on high.[50]And he led them out as farre as to Bethanie, and hee lift vp his hands, and bleſſed them.[51]And it came to paſſe, while hee bleſſed them, hee was parted from them, and caried vp into heauen.[52]And they worſhipped him, and returned to Hieruſalem, with great ioy:[53]And were continually in the Temple, praiſing and bleſſing God. Amen.

IOHN (JOHN)

CHAPTER 1[1]In the beginning was the Word, & the Word was with God, and the Word was God.[2]The ſame was in the beginning with God.[3]All things were made by him, and without him was not any thing made that was made.[4]In him was life, and the life was the light of men.[5]And the light ſhineth in darkneſſe, and the darkneſſe comprehended it not.[6]There was a man ſent from God, whoſe name was Iohn.[7]The ſame came for a witneſſe, to beare witneſſe of the light, that all men through him might beleeue.[8]Hee was not that light, but was ſent to beare witneſſe of that light.[9]That was the true light, which lighteth euery man that commeth into the world.[10]Hee was in the world, and the world was made by him, and the world knew him not.[11]Hee came vnto his owne, and his owne receiued him not.[12]But as many as receiued him, to them gaue hee power to become the ſonnes of God, euen to them that beleeue on his Name:[13]Which were borne, not of blood, nor of the will of the fleſh, nor of the will of man, but of God.[14]And the Word was made fleſh, and dwelt among vs (& we beheld his glory, the glory as of the onely begotten of the Father) full of grace and trueth.[15]Iohn bare witneſſe of him, and cried, ſaying, This was he of whom I ſpake, He that commeth after me, is preferred before me, for he was before me.[16]And of his fulneſse haue all wee receiued, and grace for grace.[17]For the Law was giuen by Moſes, but grace and trueth came by Ieſus Chriſt.[18]No man hath ſeene God at any time: the onely begotten Sonne, which is in the boſome of the Father, he hath declared him.[19]And this is the record of Iohn, when the Iewes ſent Prieſts and Leuites from Hieruſalem, to aſke him, Who art thou?[20]And he confeſsed, and denied not: but confeſsed, I am not the Chriſt.[21]And they aſked him, What then? Art thou Elias? And he ſaith, I am not. Art thou that Prophet? And hee anſwered, No.[22]Then ſaid they vnto him, Who art thou, that we may giue an anſwere to them that ſent vs? What ſayeſt thou of thy ſelfe?[23]He ſaid, I am the voice of one crying in the wilderneſſe: Make ſtraight the way of the Lord, as ſaid the Prophet Eſaias.[24]And they which were ſent, were of the PhAriſes.[25]And they aſked him, and ſaid vnto him, Why baptizeſt thou then, if thou be not that Chriſt, nor Elias, neither that Prophet?[26]Iohn anſwered them, ſaying, I baptize with water, but there ſtandeth one among you, whom ye know not,[27]He it is, who comming after me, is preferred before me, whoſe ſhoes latchet I am not worthy to vnlooſe.[28]Theſe things were done in Bethabara beyond Iordane, where Iohn was baptizing.[29]The next day, Iohn ſeeth Ieſus comming vnto him, and ſaith, Behold the Lambe of God, which taketh away the ſinne of the world.[30]This is he of whom I ſaid, After me commeth a man, which is preferred before me: for he was before me.[31]And I knew him not: but that he ſhould be made manifeſt to Iſrael, therfore am I come baptizing with water.[32]And Iohn bare record ſaying, I ſaw the Spirit deſcending from heauen, like a Doue, and it abode vpon him.[33]And I knew him not: but he that ſent me to baptize with water, the ſame ſaid vnto me, Upon whom thou ſhalt ſee the Spirit deſcending, & remaining on him, the ſame is he which baptizeth with the holy Ghoſt.[34]And I ſaw, and bare record, that this is the ſonne of God.[35]Againe the next day after, Iohn ſtood, and two of his diſciples.[36]And looking vpon Ieſus as he walked, he ſaith, Behold the Lambe of God.[37]And the two diſciples heard him ſpeake, and they followed Ieſus.[38]Then Ieſus turned, and ſaw them following, and ſaith vnto them, What ſeeke ye? They ſaid vnto him, Rabbi, (which is to ſay being interpreted, Maſter) where dwelleſt thou?[39]He ſaith vnto them, Come and ſee. They came and ſaw where he dwelt, and abode with him that day: for it was about the tenth houre.[40]One of the two which heard Iohn ſpeake, and followed him, was Andrew, Simon Peters brother.[41]He firſt findeth his owne brother Simon, and ſaith vnto him, We haue found the Meſsias, which is, being interpreted, the Chriſt.[42]And he brought him to Ieſus. And when Ieſus beheld him, he ſaid, Thou art Simon the ſonne of Iona, thou ſhalt be called Cephas, which is by interpretation, a ſtone.[43]The day following, Ieſus would goe foorth into Galilee, & findeth Philip, & ſaith vnto him, Follow me.[44]Now Philip was of Bethſaida, the citie of Andrew and Peter.[45]Philip findeth Nathaneel, and ſaith vnto him, We haue found him of whom Moſes in the Law, and the Prophets did write, Ieſus of Nazareth the ſonne of Ioſeph.[46]And Nathaneel ſaid vnto him, Can there any good thing come out of Nazareth? Philip ſaith vnto him, Come and ſee.[47]Ieſus ſaw Nathaneel comming to him, and ſaith of him, Behold an Iſraelite indeed in whom is no guile.[48]Nathaneel ſayeth vnto him, Whence knoweſt thou me? Ieſus anſwered, and ſaid vnto him, Before that Philip called thee, when thou waſt vnder the figge tree, I ſaw thee.[49]Nathaneel anſwered, and ſaith vnto him, Rabbi, thou art the Sonne of God, thou art the king of Iſrael.[50]Ieſus anſwered, and ſaid vnto him, Becauſe I ſaid vnto thee, I ſaw thee vnder the figge tree, beleeueſt thou? thou ſhalt ſee greater things then theſe.[51]And hee ſaith vnto him, Uerily, verily I ſay vnto you, heereafter yee ſhall ſee heauen open, and the Angels of God aſcending, and deſcending vpon the ſonne of man.

CHAPTER 2[1]And the third day there was a mariage in Cana of Galilee, and the mother of Ieſus was there.[2]And both Ieſus was called, and his diſciples, to the mariage.[3]And when they wanted wine, the mother of Ieſus ſaith vnto him, They haue no wine.[4]Ieſus ſaith vnto her, Woman, what haue I to doe with thee? mine houre is not yet come.[5]His mother ſaith vnto þ[e] ſeruants, Whatſoeuer he ſaith vnto you, doe it.[6]And there were ſet there ſixe water pots of ſtone, after the maner of the purifying of the Iewes, conteining two or three firkins apeece.[7]Ieſus ſaith vnto them, Fill the water pots with water. And they filled them vp to the brimme.[8]And hee ſaith vnto them, Drawe out now, and beare vnto the gouernor of the feaſt. And they bare it.[9]When the ruler of the feaſt had taſted the water that was made wine, and knew not whence it was, (but the ſeruants which drew the water knew) the gouernor of the feaſt called the bridegrome,[10]And ſaith vnto him, Euery man at the beginning doth ſet foorth good wine, and when men haue well drunke, then that which is worſe: but thou haſt kept the good wine vntill now.[11]This beginning of miracles did Ieſus in Cana of Galilee, and manifeſted forth his glory, and his diſciples beleeued on him.[12]After this hee went downe to Capernaum, hee and his mother, and his brethren, and his diſciples, and they continued there not many dayes.[13]And the Iewes Paſſeouer was at hand, & Ieſus went vp to Hieruſalem[14]And found in the Temple thoſe that ſold oxen, and ſheepe, and doues, and the changers of money, ſitting.[15]And when he had made a ſcourge of ſmall cordes, he droue them all out of the Temple, and the ſheepe & the oxen, and powred out the changers money, and ouerthrew the tables,[16]And ſaid vnto them that ſold doues Take theſe things hence, make not my fathers houſe an houſe of merchandize.[17]And his diſciples remembred that it was written, The zeale of thine houſe hath eaten me vp.[18]Then anſwered the Iewes, and ſaid vnto him, What ſigne ſheweſt thou vnto vs, ſeeing that thou doeſt theſe things?[19]Ieſus anſwered, and ſaid vnto them, Deſtroy this temple, and in three dayes I will raiſe it vp.[20]Then ſaid the Iewes, Fourty and ſix yeres was this Temple in building, and wilt thou reare it vp in three dayes?[21]But he ſpake of the temple of his body.[22]When therefore hee was riſen from the dead, his diſciples remembred that hee had ſaid this vnto them: and they beleeued the Scripture, and the word which Ieſus had ſaid.[23]Now when hee was in Hieruſalem at the Paſſeouer, in the feaſt day, many beleeued in his Name, when they ſaw the miracles which he did.[24]But Ieſus did not commit himſelfe vnto them, becauſe he knew al men,[25]And needed not that any ſhould teſtifie of man: for hee knew what was in man.

CHAPTER 3[1]There was a man of the PhAriſees, named Nicodemus, a ruler of þe Iewes:[2]The ſame came to Ieſus by night, and ſaid vnto him, Rabbi, wee know that thou art a teacher come from God: for no man can doe theſe miracles that thou doeſt, except God be with him.[3]Ieſus anſwered, and ſaid vnto him, Uerily, verily I ſay vnto thee, except a man be borne againe, he cannot ſee the kingdome of God.[4]Nicodemus ſaith vnto him, How can a man be borne when he is old? can he enter the ſecond time into his mothers wombe, and be borne?[5]Ieſus anſwered, Uerily, verily I ſay vnto thee, except a man be borne of water and of the ſpirit, he cannot enter into the kingdome of God.[6]That which is borne of the fleſh, is fleſh, and that which is borne of the ſpirit, is ſpirit.[7]Marueile not that I ſaide vnto thee, Ye muſt be borne againe.[8]The winde bloweth where it liſteth, and thou heareſt the ſound thereof, but canſt not tel whence it commeth, and whither it goeth: So is euery one that is borne of the Spirit.[9]Nicodemus anſwered, and ſaid vnto him, How can theſe things be?[10]Ieſus anſwered, and ſaide vnto him, Art thou a maſter of Iſrael, and knoweſt not theſe things?[11]Uerely, verely I ſay vnto thee, We ſpeake that we doe know, and teſtifie that wee haue ſeene; and yee receiue not our witneſſe.[12]If I haue tolde you earthly things, and ye beleeue not: how ſhall ye beleeue if I tell you of heauenly things?[13]And no man hath aſcended vp to heauen, but hee that came downe from heauen, euen the Sonne of man which is in heauen.[14]And as Moſes lifted vp the ſerpent in the wilderneſſe: euen ſo muſt the Sonne of man be lifted vp:[15]That whoſoeuer beleeueth in him, ſhould not periſh, but haue eternall life.[16]For God ſo loued þe world, that he gaue his only begotten Sonne: that whoſoeuer beleeueth in him, ſhould not periſh, but haue euerlaſting life.[17]For God ſent not his Sonne into the world to condemne the world: but that the world through him might be ſaued.[18]He that beleeueth on him, is not condemned: but hee that beleeueth not, is condemned already, becauſe hee hath not beleeued in the Name of the onely begotten Sonne of God.[19]And this is the condemnation, that light is come into the world, and men loued darkneſſe rather then light, becauſe their deedes were euill.[20]For euery one that doeth euill, hateth the light, neither commeth to the light, leſt his deeds ſhould be reproued.[21]But hee that doeth trueth, commeth to the light, that his deeds may be made manifeſt, that they are wrought in God.[22]After theſe things, came Ieſus and his diſciples into the land of Iudea, and there hee taried with them, and baptized.[23]And Iohn alſo was baptizing in Aenon, neere to Salim, becauſe there was much water there: and they came, and were baptized.[24]For Iohn was not yet caſt into priſon.[25]Then there aroſe a queſtion between ſome of Iohns diſciples and the Iewes, about purifying.[26]And they came vnto Iohn, and ſaid vnto him, Rabbi, he that was with thee beyond Iordane, to whom thou bareſt witneſſe, behold, the ſame baptizeth, and all men come to him.[27]Iohn anſwered, and ſaid, A man can receiue nothing, except it be giuen him from heauen.[28]Ye your ſelues beare me witneſſe, that I ſaid, I am not the Chriſt, but that I am ſent before him.[29]He that hath the bride, is the bridegrome: but the friend of the bridegrome, which ſtandeth and heareth him, reioyceth greatly becauſe of the bridegromes voice: This my ioy therefore is fulfilled.[30]Hee muſt increaſe, but I muſt decreaſe.[31]Hee that commeth from aboue, is aboue all: hee that is of the earth, is earthly, and ſpeaketh of the earth: hee that cōmeth from heauen is aboue all:[32]And what hee hath ſeene and heard, that he teſtifieth, and no man receiueth his teſtimony:[33]He that hath receiued his teſtimonie, hath ſet to his ſeale, that God is true.[34]For he whom God hath ſent, ſpeaketh the words of God: For God giueth not the Spirit by meaſure vnto him.[35]The Father loueth the Sonne, and hath giuen al things into his hand.[36]He that beleeueth on the Sonne, hath euerlaſting life: and he that beleeueth not the Sonne, ſhall not ſee life: but the wrath of God abideth on him.

CHAPTER 4[1]When therefore the Lord knew how the PhAriſees had heard that Ieſus made and baptized moe diſciples then Iohn,[2](Though Ieſus himſelfe baptized not, but his diſciples:)[3]He left Iudea, and departed againe into Galile.[4]And hee muſt needs goe thorow Samaria.[5]Then commeth he to a city of Samaria, which is called Sychar, neere to the parcell of ground that Iacob gaue to his ſonne Ioſeph.[6]Now Iacobs Well was there. Ieſus therefore being wearied with his iourney, ſate thus on the Well: and it was about the ſixth houre.[7]There commeth a woman of Samaria to draw water: Ieſus ſayth vnto her, Giue me to drinke.[8]For his diſciples were gone away vnto the city to buy meate.[9]Then ſaith the woman of Samaria vnto him, How is it that thou, being a Iewe, aſkeſt drinke of me, which am a woman of Samaria? For the Iewes haue no dealings with the Samaritanes.[10]Ieſus anſwered, and ſaid vnto her, If thou kneweſt the gift of God, and who it is that ſayth to thee, Giue me to drinke; thou wouldeſt haue aſked of him, and hee would haue giuen thee liuing water.[11]The woman ſaith vnto him, Sir, thou haſt nothing to drawe with, and the Well is deepe: from whence then haſt thou that liuing water?[12]Art thou greater then our father Iacob, which gaue vs the Well, and dranke thereof himſelfe, and his children, and his cattell?[13]Ieſus anſwered, and ſaid vnto her, Whoſoeuer drinketh of this water, ſhall thirſt againe:[14]But whoſoeuer drinketh of the water that I ſhal giue him, ſhall neuer thirſt: but the water that I ſhall giue him, ſhalbe in him a well of water ſpringing vp into euerlaſting life.[15]The woman ſaith vnto him, Sir, giue me this water, that I thirſt not, neither come hither to draw.[16]Ieſus ſaith vnto her, Goe, call thy huſband, and come hither.[17]The woman anſwered, and ſaid, I haue no huſband. Ieſus ſaid vnto her, Thou haſt well ſaid, I haue no huſband:[18]For thou haſt had fiue huſbands, and he whom thou now haſt, is not thy huſband: In that ſaideſt thou truely.[19]The woman ſaith vnto him, Sir, I perceiue that thou art a Prophet.[20]Our fathers worſhipped in this mountaine, and ye ſay, that in Hieruſalem is the place where men ought to worſhip.[21]Ieſus ſaith vnto her, Woman, beleeue me, the houre commeth when ye ſhall neither in this mountaine, nor yet at Hieruſalem, worſhip the Father.[22]Ye worſhip ye know not what: we know what we worſhip: for ſaluation is of the Iewes.[23]But the houre commeth, and now is, when the true worſhippers ſhall worſhip the Father in ſpirit, and in trueth: for the Father ſeeketh ſuch to worſhip him.[24]God is a Spirit, and they that worſhip him, muſt worſhip him in ſpirit, and in trueth.[25]The woman ſaith vnto him, I know that Meſsias commeth, which is called Chriſt: when he is come, hee will tell vs all things.[26]Ieſus ſayth vnto her, I that ſpeake vnto thee, am hee.[27]And vpon this came his diſciples, and marueiled that he talked with the woman: yet no man ſaid, What ſeekeſt thou, or, Why talkeſt thou with her?[28]The woman then left her waterpot, and went her way into the city, and ſayth to the men,[29]Come, ſee a man, which tolde me all things that euer I did: Is not this the Chriſt?[30]Then they went out of the citie, and came vnto him.[31]In the meane while his diſciples prayed him, ſaying, Maſter, eate.[32]But hee ſaid vnto them, I haue meate to eate that ye know not of.[33]Therefore ſaid the diſciples one to another, Hath any man brought him ought to eate?[34]Ieſus ſaith vnto them, My meat is, to doe the will of him that ſent mee, and to finiſh his worke.[35]ſay not ye, There are yet foure moneths, and then commeth harueſt? Behold, I ſay vnto you, Lift vp your eyes, and looke on the fields: for they are white already to harueſt.[36]And hee that reapeth receiueth wages, and gathereth fruite vnto life eternall: that both he that ſoweth, and he that reapeth, may reioyce together.[37]And herein is that ſaying true: One ſoweth, and another reapeth.[38]I ſent you to reape that, whereon ye beſtowed no labour: other men laboured, and yee are entred into their labours.[39]And many of the Samaritanes of that citie beleeued on him, for the ſaying of the woman, which teſtified, Hee told me all that euer I did.[40]So when the Samaritanes were come vnto him, they beſought him that he would tarie with them, and he abode there two dayes.[41]And many moe beleeued, becauſe of his owne word:[42]And ſaid vnto the woman, Now we beleeue, not becauſe of thy ſaying, for we haue heard him our ſelues, and know that this is indeed the Chriſt, the Sauiour of the world.[43]Now after two dayes he departed thence, and went into Galilee:[44]For Ieſus himſelfe teſtified, that a Prophet hath no honour in his owne countrey.[45]Then when hee was come into Galilee, the Galileans receiued him, hauing ſeene all the things that hee did at Hieruſalem at the Feaſt: for they alſo went vnto the Feaſt.[46]So Ieſus came againe into Cana of Galilee, where hee made the water wine. And there was a certaine noble man, whoſe ſonne was ſicke at Capernaum.[47]When he heard that Ieſus was come out of Iudea into Galilee, hee went vnto him, and beſought him that he would come downe, and heale his ſonne: for he was at the point of death.[48]Then ſaid Ieſus vnto him, Except ye ſee ſignes and wonders, yee will not beleeue.[49]The noble man ſaith vnto him, Syr, come downe ere my child die.[50]Ieſus ſaith vnto him, Go thy way, thy ſonne liueth. And the man beleeued the word that Ieſus had ſpoken vnto him, and he went his way.[51]And as he was now going down, his ſeruants met him, and told him, ſaying, Thy ſonne liueth.[52]Then inquired hee of them the houre when he began to amend: and they ſaid vnto him, Yeſterday at the ſeuenth houre the feuer left him.[53]So the father knewe that it was at the ſame houre, in the which Ieſus ſaid vnto him, Thy ſonne liueth, and himſelfe beleeued, and his whole houſe.[54]This is againe the ſecond miracle that Ieſus did, when hee was come out of Iudea into Galilee.

CHAPTER 5[1]After this there was a feaſt of the Iewes, and Ieſus went vp to Hieruſalem.[2]Now there is at Hieruſalem by the ſheepe market, a poole, which is called in the Hebrew tongue Betheſda, hauing fiue porches.[3]In theſe lay a great multitude of impotent folke, of blind, halt, withered, waiting for the mouing of the water.[4]For an Angel went downe at a certaine ſeaſon into the poole, and troubled the water: whoſoeuer then firſt after the troubling of the water ſtepped in, was made whole of whatſoeuer diſeaſe he had.[5]And a certaine man was there, which had an infirmitie thirtie and eight yeeres.[6]When Ieſus ſaw him lie, & knew that hee had beene now a long time in that caſe, he ſayth vnto him, Wilt thou be made whole?[7]The impotent man anſwered him, Sir, I haue no man when the water is troubled, to put mee into the poole: but while I am comming, another ſteppeth downe before me.[8]Ieſus ſayth vnto him, Riſe, take vp thy bed, and walke.[9]And immediatly the man was made whole, and tooke vp his bed, and walked: And on the ſame day was the Sabbath.[10]The Iewes therefore ſaid vnto him that was cured, It is the Sabbath day, it is not lawfull for thee to cary thy bed.[11]He anſwered them, He that made me whole, the ſame ſaid vnto me, Take vp thy bed, and walke.[12]Then aſked they him, What man is that which ſaid vnto thee, Take vp thy bed, and walke?[13]And he that was healed, wiſt not who it was: for Ieſus had conueyed himſelfe away, a multitude being in that place.[14]Afterward Ieſus findeth him in the Temple, & ſaid vnto him, Behold, thou art made whole: ſinne no more, leſt a worſe thing come vnto thee.[15]The man departed, and tolde the Iewes that it was Ieſus which had made him whole.[16]And therefore did the Iewes perſecute Ieſus, and ſought to ſlay him, becauſe he had done theſe things on the Sabbath day.[17]But Ieſus anſwered them, My Father worketh hitherto, & I worke.[18]Therefore the Iewes ſought the more to kill him, not onely becauſe hee had broken the Sabbath, but ſaid alſo, that God was his father, making himſelfe equall with God.[19]Then anſwered Ieſus, and ſaide vnto them, Uerily, verily I ſay vnto you, The ſonne can doe nothing of himſelfe, but what he ſeeth the Father doe: for what things ſoeuer he doeth, theſe alſo doth the ſonne likewiſe.[20]For the father loueth the ſonne, and ſheweth him all things that himſelfe doth: & he will ſhew him greater works then theſe, that ye may marueile.[21]For as the Father raiſeth vp the dead, and quickeneth them: euen ſo the Sonne quickeneth whom he will.[22]For the Father iudgeth no man: but hath committed all iudgement vnto the Sonne:[23]That all men ſhould honour the Son, euen as they honour the Father. He that honoureth not þe Sonne, honoreth not þe Father which hath ſent him.[24]Uerily, verily I ſay vnto you, Hee that heareth my word, & beleeueth on him that ſent mee, hath euerlaſting life, and ſhall not come into condemnation: but is paſſed from death vnto life.[25]Uerily, verily I ſay vnto you, The houre is comming, & now is, when the dead ſhall heare the voice of the Sonne of God: and they that heare, ſhall liue.[26]For as the Father hath life in himſelfe: ſo hath he giuen to the Sonne to haue life in himſelfe:[27]And hath giuen him authority to execute iudgement alſo, becauſe he is the Sonne of man.[28]Marueile not at this: for the houre is comming, in the which all that are in the graues ſhall heare his voice,[29]And ſhall come foorth, they that haue done good, vnto the reſurrection of life, and they that haue done euill, vnto the reſurrection of damnation.[30]I can of mine owne ſelfe doe nothing: as I heare, I iudge: and my iudgement is iuſt, becauſe I ſeeke not mine owne will, but the will of the Father, which hath ſent me.[31]If I beare witneſſe of my ſelfe, my witneſſe is not true.[32]There is another that beareth witneſſe of me, & I know that the witneſſe which he witneſſeth of me, is true.[33]Ye ſent vnto Iohn, and he bare witneſſe vnto the trueth.[34]But I receiue not teſtimonie from man: but theſe things I ſay, that ye might be ſaued.[35]He was a burning and a ſhining light: and ye were willing for a ſeaſon to reioyce in his light.[36]But I haue greater witneſſe then that of Iohn: for the workes which the Father hath giuen me to finiſh, the ſame workes that I doe, beare witneſſe of mee, that the Father hath ſent me.[37]And the Father himſelfe which hath ſent me, hath borne witneſſe of me. Ye haue neither heard his voyce at any time, nor ſeene his ſhape.[38]And ye haue not his word abiding in you: for whom he hath ſent, him ye beleeue not.[39]ſearch the Scriptures, for in them ye thinke ye haue eternall life, and they are they which teſtifie of me.[40]And ye will not come to me, that ye might haue life.[41]I receiue not honour from men.[42]But I know you, that ye haue not the loue of God in you.[43]I am come in my Fathers name, and ye receiue me not: if another ſhall come in his owne Name, him ye will receiue.[44]How can ye beleeue, which receiue honour one of another, & ſeeke not the honour that commeth from God onely?[45]Doe not thinke that I will accuſe you to the Father: there is one that accuſeth you, euen Moſes, in whom ye truſt?[46]For had ye beleeued Moſes, ye would haue beleeued me: for he wrote of me.[47]But if ye beleeue not his writings, how ſhall ye beleeue my words?

CHAPTER 6[1]After theſe things Ieſus went ouer the ſea of Galilee, which is the ſea of Tiberias:[2]And a great multitude followed him, becauſe they ſaw his miracles which hee did on them that were diſeaſed.[3]And Ieſus went vp into a mountaine, and there hee ſate with his diſciples.[4]And the Paſſeouer, a feaſt of the Iewes, was nigh.[5]When Ieſus then lift vp his eyes, and ſaw a great company come vnto him, he ſaith vnto Philip, Whence ſhall we buy bread, that theſe may eate?[6](And this he ſaid to proue him: for he himſelfe knew what he would doe)[7]Philip anſwered him, Two hundred peny-worth of bread is not ſufficient for them, that euery one of them may take a litle.[8]One of his diſciples, Andrew, Simon Peters brother, ſaith vnto him,[9]There is a lad here, which hath fiue barley loaues, and two ſmall fiſhes: but what are they among ſo many?[10]And Ieſus ſaid, Make the men ſit downe. Now there was much graſſe in the place. So the men ſate downe, in number about fiue thouſand.[11]And Ieſus tooke the loaues, and when he had giuen thankes, hee diſtributed to the diſciples, and the diſciples to them that were ſet downe, and likewiſe of the fiſhes, as much as they would.[12]When they were filled, he ſaid vnto his diſciples, Gather vp the fragments that remaine, that nothing be loſt.[13]Therefore they gathered them together, and filled twelue baſkets with the fragments of the fiue barley loaues, which remained ouer and aboue, vnto them that had eaten.[14]Then thoſe men, when they had ſeene the miracle that Ieſus did, ſaid, This is of a trueth that Prophet that ſhould come into the world.[15]When Ieſus therefore perceiued that they would come and take him by force, to make him a King, hee departed againe into a mountaine, himſelfe alone.[16]And when euen was now come, his diſciples went downe vnto the ſea,[17]And entred into a ſhip, and went ouer the ſea towards Capernaum: and it was now darke, and Ieſus was not come to them.[18]And the ſea aroſe, by reaſon of a great winde that blew.[19]So when they had rowed about fiue and twentie, or thirtie furlongs, they

ſee Ieſus walking on the ſea, and drawing nigh vnto the ſhip: and they
were afraid.20But he ſaith vnto them, It is I, be not afraid.21Then they
willingly receiued him into the ſhip, and immediatly the ſhip was at the
land whither they went.22The day following, when the people which
ſtood on the other ſide of the ſea, ſaw that there was none other boat
there, ſaue that one whereinto his diſciples were entred, and that Ieſus
went not with his diſciples into the boat, but that his diſciples were gone
away alone:23Howbeit there came other boats from Tiberias, nigh vnto
the place where they did eate bread, after that the Lord had giuen
thankes:24When the people therefore ſaw that Ieſus was not there,
neither his diſciples, they alſo tooke ſhipping, and came to Capernaum,
ſeeking for Ieſus.25And when they had found him on the other ſide of
the ſea, they ſaide vnto him, Rabbi, when cameſt thou hither?26Ieſus
anſwered them, and ſaid, Uerely, verely I ſay vnto you, Ye ſeeke me, not
becauſe ye ſaw the miracles, but becauſe yee did eate of the loaues, and
were filled.27Labour not for the meat which periſheth, but for that meat
which endureth vnto euerlaſting life, which the Sonne of man ſhall giue
vnto you: for him hath God the Father ſealed.28Then ſaid they vnto him,
What ſhall we doe, that we might worke the workes of God?29Ieſus
anſwered, and ſaid vnto them, This is the worke of God, that ye beleeue
on him whom he hath ſent.30They ſaid therefore vnto him, What ſigne
ſheweſt thou then, that we may ſee, and beleeue thee? What doeſt thou
worke?31Our fathers did eate Manna in the deſert, as it is written, He
gaue them bread from heauen to eate.32Then Ieſus ſaid vnto them,
Uerely, verely I ſay vnto you, Moſes gaue you not that bread from
heauen, but my Father giueth you the true bread from heauen.33For the
bread of God is hee which commeth downe from heauen, and giueth
life vnto the world.34Then ſaid they vnto him, Lord, euermore giue vs
this bread.35And Ieſus ſaid vnto them, I am the bread of life: hee that
commeth to me, ſhall neuer hunger: and he that beleeueth on me, ſhall
neuer thirſt.36But I ſaid vnto you, that ye alſo haue ſeene me, and
beleeue not.37All that the Father giueth mee, ſhall come to mee; and him
that commeth to me, I will in no wiſe caſt out.38For I came downe from
heauen, not to doe mine owne will, but the will of him that ſent
me.39And this is the Fathers wil which hath ſent me, that of all which
he hath giuen mee, I ſhould loſe nothing, but ſhould raiſe it vp againe at
the laſt day.40And this is the will of him that ſent me, that euery one
which ſeeth the Sonne, and beleeueth on him, may haue euerlaſting life:
and I will raiſe him vp at the laſt day.41The Iewes then murmured at
him, becauſe hee ſaid, I am the bread which came downe from
heauen.42And they ſaid, Is not this Ieſus the ſonne of Ioſeph, whoſe
father and mother we know? How is it then that hee ſayth, I came downe
from heauen?43Ieſus therefore anſwered, and ſaid vnto them, Murmure
not among your ſelues.44No man can come to me, except the Father
which hath ſent me, draw him: and I will raiſe him vp at the laſt day.45It
is written in the Prophets, And they ſhall be all taught of God. Euery
man therefore that hath heard, and hath learned of the Father, commeth
vnto me,46Not that any man hath ſeene the Father; ſaue hee which is of
God, hee hath ſeene the Father.47Uerely, verely I ſay vnto you, Hee that
beleeueth on me, hath euerlaſting life.48I am that bread of life.49Your
fathers did eate Manna in the wilderneſſe, and are dead.50This is the
bread which commeth downe from heauen, that a man may eate thereof,
and not die.51I am the liuing bread, which came downe from heauen. If
any man eate of this bread, he ſhall liue for euer: and the bread that I
will giue, is my fleſh, which I will giue for the life of the world.52The
Iewes therefore ſtroue amongſt themſelues, ſaying, How can this man
giue vs his fleſh to eate?53Then Ieſus ſayd vnto them, Uerely, verely I
ſay vnto you, Except yee eate the fleſh of the ſonne of man, and drinke
his blood, yee haue no life in you.54Whoſo eateth my fleſh, and drinketh
my blood, hath eternall life, and I will raiſe him vp at the laſt day.55For
my fleſh is meate indeed, and my blood is drinke indeed.56He that eateth
my fleſh, and drinketh my blood, dwelleth in me, and I in him.57As the
liuing Father hath ſent me, and I liue by the Father: ſo, he that eateth
me, euen he ſhall liue by me.58This is that bread which came downe
from heauen: not as your fathers did eate Manna, and are dead: he that
eateth of this bread, ſhall liue for euer.59Theſe things ſaid hee in the
Synagogue, as he taught in Capernaum.60Many therefore of his diſciples,
when they had heard this, ſaid, This is an hard ſaying, who can heare
it?61When Ieſus knew in himſelfe, that his diſciples murmured at it, hee
ſaid vnto them, Doeth this offend you?62What and if yee ſhall ſee the
ſonne of man aſcend vp where hee was before?63It is the Spirit that
quickeneth, the fleſh profiteth nothing: the wordes that I ſpeake vnto
you, they are Spirit, and they are life.64But there are ſome of you that
beleeue not. For Ieſus knew from the beginning, who they were that
beleeued not, and who ſhould betray him.65And he ſaid, Therefore ſaid
I vnto you, that no man can come vnto me, except it were giuen vnto
him of my Father.66From that time many of his diſciples went backe,
and walked no more with him.67Then ſaid Ieſus vnto the twelue, Will
ye alſo goe away?68Then Simon Peter anſwered him, Lord, to whom
ſhall we goe? Thou haſt the words of eternall life.69And we beleeue and
are ſure that thou art that Chriſt, the Sonne of the liuing God.70Ieſus
anſwered them, Haue not I choſen you twelue, and one of you is a
deuill?71He ſpake of Iudas Iſcariot the ſonne of Simon: for hee it was
that ſhould betray him, being one of the twelue.
CHAPTER 71After theſe things, Ieſus walked in Galilee: for hee would
not walk in Iurie, becauſe the Iewes ſought to kill him.2Now the Iewes
feaſt of Tabernacles was at hand.3His brethren therefore ſaide vnto him,
Depart hence, and go into Iudea, that thy Diſciples alſo may ſee the
works that thou doeſt.4For there is no man that doth any thing in ſecret,
and hee himſelfe ſeeketh to be knowen openly: If thou doe theſe things,
ſhew thy ſelfe to þe world.5For neither did his brethren beleeue in
him.6Then Ieſus ſaid vnto them, My time is not yet come: but your time
is alway ready.7The world cannot hate you, but me it hateth, becauſe I
teſtifie of it, that the workes thereof are euill.8Goe ye vp vnto this feaſt:
I goe not vp yet vnto this feaſt, for my time is not yet full come.9When
he had ſaid theſe words vnto them, he abode ſtill in Galilee.10But when
his brethren were gone vp, then went he alſo vp vnto the feaſt, not
openly, but as it were in ſecret.11Then the Iewes ſought him at the feaſt,
and ſaid, Where is he?12And there was much murmuring among the
people, concerning him: For ſome ſaid, Hee is a good man: Others ſaid,
Nay, but he deceiueth the people.13Howbeit, no man ſpake openly of
him, for feare of the Iewes.14Now about the middeſt of the feaſt, Ieſus
went vp into the Temple, and taught.15And the Iewes marueiled, ſaying,
How knoweth this man letters, hauing neuer learned?16Ieſus anſwered
them, My doctrine is not mine, but his that ſent me.17If any man will
doe his will, he ſhall know of the doctrine, whether it be of God, or
whether I ſpeake of my ſelfe.18He that ſpeaketh of himſelfe, ſeeketh his
owne glory: but he that ſeeketh his glory that ſent him, the ſame is true,
and no vnrighteouſneſſe is in him.19Did not Moſes giue you the Law,
and yet none of you keepeth the Law? Why goe ye about to kill
me?20The people anſwered, and ſayd, Thou haſt a deuill: Who goeth
about to kill thee?21Ieſus anſwered, and ſaide vnto them, I haue done
one worke, and yee all marueile.22Moſes therefore gaue vnto you
Circumciſion (not becauſe it is of Moſes, but of the fatherſ) and yee on
the Sabbath day circumciſe a man.23If a man on the Sabbath day receiue
circumciſion, that the Lawe of Moſes ſhould not be broken; are ye angry
at me, becauſe I haue made a man euery whit whole on the Sabbath
day?24Iudge not according to the appearance, but iudge righteous
iudgement.25Then ſaid ſome of them of Hieruſalem, Is not this hee,
whome they ſeeke to kill?26But loe, he ſpeaketh boldly, and they ſay
nothing vnto him: Doe the rulers know indeede that this is the very
Chriſt?27Howbeit wee know this man whence he is: but when Chriſt
commeth, no man knoweth whence he is.28Then cried Ieſus in the
Temple as he taught, ſaying, Ye both know me, and ye know whence I
am, and I am not come of my ſelfe, but he that ſent me, is true, whom
ye know not.29But I know him, for I am from him, and he hath ſent
me.30Then they ſought to take him: but no man laid hands on him,
becauſe his houre was not yet come.31And many of the people beleeued
on him, & ſaid, When Chriſt commeth, will hee doe moe miracles then
theſe which this man hath done?32The PhAriſees heard that the people
murmured ſuch things concerning him: And the PhAriſees and the
chiefe Prieſts ſent officers to take him.33Then ſaid Ieſus vnto them, Yet
a litle while am I with you, and then I goe vnto him that ſent me.34Ye
ſhall ſeeke me, and ſhall not find me: and where I am, thither yee cannot
come.35Then ſaide the Iewes among themſelues, Whither will hee goe,
that we ſhall not find him? will he goe vnto the diſperſed among the
Gentiles, and teach the Gentiles?36What maner of ſaying is this that he
ſaid, Ye ſhall ſeeke me, and ſhall not find me? and where I am, thither

ye cannot come?37In the laſt day, that great day of the feaſt, Ieſus ſtood, and cried, ſaying, If any man thirſt, let him come vnto me, and drinke.38He that beleeueth on me, as the Scripture hath ſaide, out of his belly ſhall flow riuers of liuing water.39(But this ſpake he of the Spirit which they that beleeue on him, ſhould receiue. For the holy Ghoſt was not yet giuen, becauſe that Ieſus was not yet glorified.)40Many of the people therefore, when they heard this ſaying, ſaide, Of a trueth this is the Prophet.41Others ſaid, This is the Chriſt. But ſome ſaid, Shall Chriſt come out of Galilee?42Hath not the Scripture ſaide, that Chriſt commeth of the ſeede of Dauid, and out of the towne of Bethlehem, where Dauid was?43So there was diuiſion among the people becauſe of him.44And ſome of them would haue taken him, but no man layed hands on him.45Then came the officers to the chiefe Prieſts and PhAriſes, and they ſaid vnto them, Why haue ye not brought him?46The officers anſwered, Neuer man ſpake like this man.47Then anſwered them the PhAriſees, Are ye alſo deceiued?48Haue any of the rulers, or of the PhAriſes beleeued on him?49But this people who knoweth not the Law, are curſed.50Nicodemus ſaith vnto them, (He that came to Ieſus by night, being one of them,)51Doth our Law iudge any man before it heare him, & know what he doth?52They anſwered, and ſaid vnto him, Art thou alſo of Galilee? ſearch, and looke: for out of Galilee Ariſeth no Prophet.53And euery man went vnto his owne houſe.

CHAPTER 81Ieſus went vnto þe Mount of Oliues:2And earely in the morning hee came againe into the Temple, and all the people came vnto him, and he ſate downe, and taught them.3And the Scribes and PhAriſees brought vnto him a woman taken in adultery, and when they had ſet her in the mids,4They ſay vnto him, Maſter, this woman was taken in adultery, in the very act.5Now Moſes in the Law commanded vs, that ſuch ſhould be ſtoned: but what ſayeſt thou?6This they ſaid, tempting him, that they might haue to accuſe him. But Ieſus ſtouped downe, and with his finger wrote on the ground as though he heard them not.7So when they continued aſking him, hee lift vp himſelfe, and ſaide vnto them, Hee that is without ſinne among you, let him firſt caſt a ſtone at her.8And againe, hee ſtouped downe, and wrote on the ground.9And they which heard it, being conuicted by their owne conſcience, went out one by one, beginning at the eldeſt, euen vnto the laſt: and Ieſus was left alone, and the woman ſtanding in the midſt.10When Ieſus had lift vp himſelfe, and ſaw none but the woman, hee ſaid vnto her, Woman, where are thoſe thine accuſers? Hath no man condemned thee?11She ſaide, No man, Lord. And Ieſus ſaide vnto her, Neither doe I condemne thee: Goe, and ſinne no more.12Then ſpake Ieſus againe vnto them, ſaying, I am the light of the world: he that followeth mee, ſhall not walke in darkeneſſe, but ſhall haue the light of life.13The PhAriſees therefore ſaid vnto him, Thou beareſt record of thy ſelfe, thy record is not true.14Ieſus anſwered, and ſaid vnto them, Though I beare record of my ſelfe, yet my record is true: for I know whence I came, and whither I goe: but ye cannot tell whence I come, and whither I goe.15Yee iudge after the fleſh, I iudge no man.16And yet if I iudge, my iudgement is true: for I am not alone, but I and the Father that ſent me.17It is alſo written in your Law, that the teſtimonie of two men is true.18I am one that beare witneſſe of my ſelfe, and the Father that ſent mee, beareth witneſſe of me.19Then ſaid they vnto him, Where is thy Father? Ieſus anſwered, Ye neither know me, nor my Father: if ye had knowen mee, yee ſhould haue knowen my Father alſo.20Theſe words ſpake Ieſus in the treaſury, as hee taught in the Temple: and no man layd hands on him, for his houre was not yet come.21Then ſaide Ieſus againe vnto them, I goe my way, and ye ſhall ſeeke me, & ſhall die in your ſinnes: Whither I goe, ye cannot come.22Then ſaid the Iewes, Will hee kill himſelfe? becauſe he ſaith, Whither I goe, ye cannot come.23And hee ſaid vnto them, Yee are from beneath, I am from aboue: Yee are of this world, I am not of this world.24I ſaid therefore vnto you, that ye ſhall die in your ſinnes. For if yee beleeue not that I am hee, yee ſhall die in your ſinnes.25Then ſaid they vnto him, Who art thou? And Ieſus ſaith vnto them, Euen the ſame that I ſaide vnto you from the beginning.26I haue many things to ſay, and to iudge of you: But hee that ſent mee is true, and I ſpeake to the world, thoſe things which I haue heard of him.27They vnderſtood not that hee ſpake to them of the Father.28Then ſaide Ieſus vnto them, When yee haue lift vp the Sonne of man, then ſhall ye know that I am he, and that I doe nothing of my ſelfe: but as my Father hath taught mee, I ſpeake theſe things.29And he that ſent me, is with me: the Father hath not left mee alone: for I doe alwayes thoſe things that pleaſe him.30As hee ſpake thoſe words, many beleeued on him.31Then ſaid Ieſus to thoſe Iewes which beleeued on him, If ye continue in my word, then are yee my diſciples indeed.32And ye ſhall know the Trueth, and the Trueth ſhall make you free.33They anſwered him, We be Abraham ſeed, and were neuer in bondage to any man: how ſayeſt thou, Yee ſhall be made free?34Ieſus anſwered them, Uerily, verily I ſay vnto you, Whoſoeuer committeth ſinne, is the ſeruant of ſinne.35And the ſeruant abideth not in the houſe for euer: but the Sonne abideth euer.36If the Sonne therfore ſhall make you free, ye ſhall be free indeed.37I know that yee are Abrahams ſeed, but ye ſeeke to kill mee, becauſe my word hath no place in you.38I ſpeake that which I haue ſeene with my Father: and ye do that which ye haue ſeene with your father.39They anſwered, and ſaid vnto him, Abraham is our father. Ieſus ſayth vnto them, If yee were Abrahams children, ye would doe the works of Abraham.40But now yee ſeeke to kill me, a man that hath tolde you the trueth, which I haue heard of God: this did not Abraham.41Ye doe the deeds of your father. Then ſaid they to him, We be not borne of fornication, wee haue one Father, euen God.42Ieſus ſaid vnto them, If God were your Father, yee would loue me, for I proceeded foorth, and came from God: neither came I of my ſelfe, but he ſent me.43Why doe yee not vnderſtand my ſpeech? euen becauſe yee cannot heare my word.44Ye are of your father the deuill, and the luſts of your father ye will doe: hee was a murtherer from the beginning, and abode not in the trueth, becauſe there is no truth in him. When he ſpeaketh a lie, he ſpeaketh of his owne: for he is a liar, and the father of it.45And becauſe I tell you the truth, ye beleeue me not.46Which of you conuinceth mee of ſinne? And if I ſay the trueth, why doe ye not beleeue me?47He that is of God, heareth Gods words: ye therefore heare them not, becauſe ye are not of God.48Then anſwered the Iewes, and ſaid vnto him, ſay wee not well that thou art a Samaritane, & haſt a deuill?49Ieſus anſwered, I haue not a deuill: but I honour my Father, and ye doe diſhonour me.50And I ſeeke not mine owne glory, there is one that ſeeketh & iudgeth.51Uerely, verely I ſay vnto you, If a man keepe my ſaying, hee ſhall neuer ſee death.52Then ſaid the Iewes vnto him, Now we know that thou haſt a deuill. Abraham is dead, and the Prophets: and thou ſayeſt, If a man keepe my ſaying, he ſhall neuer taſte of death.53Art thou greater then our father Abraham, which is dead? and the Prophets are dead: whom makeſt thou thy ſelfe?54Ieſus anſwered, If I honour myſelfe, my honour is nothing: it is my Father that honoureth me, of whom ye ſay, that he is your God:55Yet ye haue not knowen him, but I know him: and if I ſhould ſay, I know him not, I ſhalbe a lyar like vnto you: but I know him, and keepe his ſaying.56Your father Abraham reioyced to ſee my day: and he ſaw it, & was glad.57Then ſaid the Iewes vnto him, Thou art not yet fiftie yeeres olde, and haſt thou ſeene Abraham?58Ieſus ſaid vnto them, Uerely, verely I ſay vnto you, Before Abraham was, I am.59Then tooke they vp ſtones to caſt at him: but Ieſus hidde himſelfe, and went out of the Temple, going thorow the midſt of them, and ſo paſſed by.

CHAPTER 91And as Ieſus paſſed by, he ſaw a man which was blinde from his birth.2And his diſciples aſked him, ſaying, Maſter, who did ſinne, this man, or his parents, that he was borne blinde?3Ieſus anſwered, Neither hath this man ſinned, nor his parents: but that the workes of God ſhould be made manifeſt in him.4I muſt worke the workes of him that ſent me, while it is day: the night commeth when no man can worke.5As long as I am in the world, I am the light of the world.6When he had thus ſpoken, he ſpat on the ground, and made clay of the ſpettle, and he anointed the eyes of the blinde man with the clay,7And ſaid vnto him, Goe waſh in the poole of Siloam (which is by interpretation, Sent.) He went his way therfore, and waſhed, and came ſeeing.8The neighbours therefore, and they which before had ſeene him, that he was blinde, ſaid, Is not this he that ſate and begged?9Some ſaid, This is hee: others ſaid, Hee is like him: but hee ſayd, I am hee.10Therefore ſaid they vnto him, How were thine eyes opened?11He anſwered and ſaid, A man that is called Ieſus, made clay, and anointed mine eyes, and ſaid vnto me, Goe to the poole of Siloam, and waſh: and I went and waſhed, and I receiued ſight.12Then ſaid they vnto him, Where is he? He ſaid, I know not.13They brought to the PhAriſees him that aforetime was blind.14And

it was the Sabbath day when Ieſus made the clay, and opened his
eyes.15Then againe the PhAriſees alſo aſked him how he had receiued
his ſight. He ſaid vnto them, Hee put clay vpon mine eyes, and I waſhed,
and doe ſee.16Therefore ſaid ſome of the PhAriſees, This man is not of
God, becauſe hee keepeth not the Sabbath day. Others ſaid, How can a
man that is a ſinner, doe ſuch miracles? and there was a diuiſion among
them.17They ſay vnto the blind man againe, What ſayeſt thou of him,
that he hath opened thine eyes? He ſaid, Hee is a Prophet.18But the
Iewes did not beleeue concerning him, that hee had bin blind, and
receiued his ſight, vntill they called the parents of him that had receiued
his ſight.19And they aſked them, ſaying, Is this your ſonne, who ye ſay
was borne blind? how then doth he now ſee?20His parents anſwered
them, and ſaid, We know that this is our ſonne, and that he was borne
blind:21But by what meanes he now ſeeth, we know not, or who hath
opened his eyes we know not: hee is of age, aſke him, he ſhall ſpeake for
himſelfe.22Theſe words ſpake his parents, becauſe they feared the Iewes:
for the Iewes had agreed already, that if any man did confeſse that he
was Chriſt, he ſhould be put out of the Synagogue.23Therefore ſaid his
parents, He is of age, aſke him.24Then againe called they the man that
was blind, and ſaid vnto him, Giue God the praiſe, we know that this
man is a ſinner.25He anſwered, and ſaid, Whether he be a ſinner or no,
I know not: One thing I know, that whereas I was blind, now I
ſee.26Then ſaide they to him againe, What did he to thee? How opened
hee thine eyes?27He anſwered them, I haue told you already, and ye did
not heare: wherfore would you heare it againe? Will ye alſo be his
diſciples?28Then they reuiled him, and ſaid, Thou art his diſciple, but we
are Moſes diſciples.29Wee know that God ſpake vnto Moſes: as for this
fellow, we knowe not from whence he is.30The man anſwered, and ſaid
vnto them, Why herein is a marueilous thing, that ye know not from
whence he is, and yet he hath opened mine eyes.31Now we know that
God heareth not ſinners: but if any man bee a worſhipper of God, and
doth his will, him he heareth.32Since the world began was it not heard
that any man opened the eyes of one that was borne blinde:33If this man
were not of God, he could doe nothing.34They anſwered, and ſaide vnto
him, Thou waſt altogether borne in ſinnes, and doeſt thou teach vs? And
they caſt him out.35Ieſus heard that they had caſt him out; and when hee
had found him, he ſaid vnto him, Doeſt thou beleeue on the Sonne of
God?36He anſwered and ſaid, Who is he, Lord, that I might beleeue on
him?37And Ieſus ſaid vnto him, Thou haſt both ſeene him, and it is he
that talketh with thee.38And he ſaid, Lord, I beleeue: and he worſhipped
him.39And Ieſus ſaid, For iudgment I am come into this world, that they
which ſee not, might ſee, and that they which ſee, might be made
blind.40And ſome of the PhAriſees which were with him, heard theſe
words, and ſaide vnto him, Are wee blinde alſo?41Ieſus ſaide vnto them,
If yee were blind, ye ſhould haue no ſinne: but now ye ſay, We ſee,
therfore your ſinne remaineth.

CHAPTER 101Uerily, verily I ſay vnto you, He that entreth not by
þe doore into the ſheepefold, but climeth vp ſome other way, the ſame
is a theefe, and a robber.2But hee that entreth in by the doore, is the
ſhepherd of the ſheepe.3To him the porter openeth, and the ſheepe
heare his voyce, and he calleth his owne ſheepe by name, and leadeth
them out.4And when he putteth foorth his owne ſheepe, he goeth
before them, and the ſheepe follow him: for they know his voyce.5And
a ſtranger will they not follow, but will flee from him, for they know not
the voyce of ſtrangers.6This parable ſpake Ieſus vnto them: but they
vnderſtood not what things they were which he ſpake vnto them.7Then
ſaid Ieſus vnto them againe, Uerily, verily I ſay vnto you, I am the doore
of the ſheepe.8All that euer came before me, are theeues and robbers:
but the ſheepe did not heare them.9I am the doore by me if any man
enter in, he ſhall be ſaued, and ſhall goe in and out, and find
paſture.10The theefe commeth not, but for to ſteale and to kill, and to
deſtroy: I am come that they might haue life, and that they might haue
it more abundantly.11I am the good ſhepheard: the good ſhepheard
giueth his life for the ſheepe.12But hee that is an hireling and not the
ſhepheard, whoſe owne the ſheepe are not, ſeeth the woolfe coming,
and leaueth the ſheep, and fleeth: and the woolfe catcheth them, and
ſcattereth the ſheepe.13The hireling fleeth, becauſe he is an hireling, &
careth not for the ſheepe.14I am the good ſhepheard, and know my
ſheepe, and am knowen of mine.15As the father knoweth me, euen ſo
know I the father: & I lay downe my life for the ſheepe.16And other
ſheepe I haue, which are not of this fold: them alſo I muſt bring, and
they ſhall heare my voyce; and there ſhall be one fold, and one
ſhepheard.17Therefore doth my father loue me, becauſe I lay downe my
life that I might take it againe.18No man taketh it from me, but I lay it
downe of my ſelfe: I haue power to lay it downe, and I haue power to
take it againe. This commandement haue I receiued of my
father.19There was a diuiſion therefore againe among the Iewes for theſe
ſayings.20And many of them ſaid, He hath a deuill, and is mad, why
heare ye him?21Others ſaid, Theſe are not the words of him that hath a
deuill. Can a deuill open the eyes of the blind?22And it was at Hieruſalem
the feaſt of the dedication, & it was winter.23And Ieſus walked in the
temple in Solomons porch.24Then came the Iewes round about him,
and ſaid vnto him, How long doeſt thou make vs to doubt? If thou be
the Chriſt, tell vs plainely.25Ieſus anſwered them, I told you, and ye
beleeued not: the workes that I doe in my Fathers name, they beare
witneſſe of me.26But ye beleeue not, becauſe ye are not of my ſheepe,
as I ſaid vnto you.27My ſheepe heare my voyce, and I know them, and
they follow me.28And I giue vnto them eternall life, and they ſhall neuer
periſh, neither ſhall any man plucke them out of my hand.29My father
which gaue them me, is greater then all: and no man is able to plucke
them out of my fathers hand.30I and my father are one.31Then the Iewes
tooke vp ſtones againe to ſtone him.32Ieſus anſwered them, Many good
workes haue I ſhewed you from my Father; for which of thoſe workes
doe ye ſtone me?33The Iewes anſwered him, ſaying, For a good worke
we ſtone thee not, but for blaſphemy, and becauſe that thou, being a
man, makeſt thy ſelfe God.34Ieſus anſwered them, Is it not written in
your law, I ſaid, ye are gods?35If hee called them gods, vnto whom the
word of God came, and the Scripture cannot be broken:36ſay ye of him,
whom the father hath ſanctified and ſent into the world, Thou
blaſphemeſt; becauſe I ſaid, I am the Sonne of God?37If I doe not the
workes of my Father, beleeue me not.38But if I doe, though yee beleeue
not me, beleeue the works: that ye may know and beleeue that the Father
is in me, and I in him.39Therefore they ſought againe to take him: but
hee eſcaped out of their hand,40And went away againe beyond Iordane,
into the place where Iohn at firſt baptized: and there he abode.41And
many reſorted vnto him, and ſaid, Iohn did no miracle: but all things
that Iohn ſpake of this man, were true.42And many beleeued on him
there.

CHAPTER 111Now a certaine man was ſicke, named Lazarus of
Bethanie, the towne of Mary, and her ſiſter Martha.2(It was that Mary
which anoynted the Lord with oyntment, and wiped his feete with her
haire, whoſe brother Lazarus was ſicke.)3Therefore his ſiſter ſent vnto
him, ſaying, Lord, behold, hee whom thou loueſt, is ſicke.4When Ieſus
heard that, hee ſaid, This ſickneſse is not vnto death, but for the glory
of God, that the Sonne of God might be glorified thereby.5Now Ieſus
loued Martha, and her ſiſter, and Lazarus.6When he had heard therefore
that he was ſicke, he abode two dayes ſtill in the ſame place where he
was.7Then after that, ſaith hee to his diſciples, Let vs go into Iudea
againe.8His diſciples ſay vnto him, Maſter, the Iewes of late ſought to
ſtone thee, and goeſt thou thither againe?9Ieſus anſwered, Are there not
twelue houres in the day? If any man walke in the day, he ſtumbleth not,
becauſe he ſeeth the light of this world.10But if a man walke in the night,
hee ſtumbleth, becauſe there is no light in him.11Theſe things ſaid hee,
and after that, hee ſaith vnto them, Our friend Lazarus ſleepeth, but I
goe, that I may awake him out of ſleepe.12Then ſaid his diſciples, Lord,
if he ſleepe, he ſhall doe well.13Howbeit Ieſus ſpake of his death: but
they thought that hee had ſpoken of taking of reſt in ſleepe.14Then ſaide
Ieſus vnto them plainly, Lazarus is dead:15And I am glad for your ſakes,
that I was not there (to the intent yee may beleeue:) Neuertheleſſe, let
vs goe vnto him.16Then ſaid Thomas, which is called Didymus, vnto his
fellow diſciples, Let vs alſo goe, that we may die with him.17Then when
Ieſus came, hee found that hee had lien in the graue foure dayes
already.18(Now Bethanie was nigh vnto Hieruſalem, about fifteene
furlongs off:)19And many of the Iewes came to Martha, and Mary, to
comfort them concerning their brother.20Then Martha, as ſoone as ſhee
heard that Ieſus was comming, went and met him: but Mary ſate ſtill in
the houſe.21Then ſaide Martha vnto Ieſus, Lord, if thou hadſt bene here,
my brother had not died.22But I know, that euen now, whatſoeuer thou

wilt aſke of God, God will giue it thee.23Ieſus ſaith vnto her, Thy brother
ſhall riſe againe.24Martha ſayeth vnto him, I know that he ſhall riſe
againe in the reſurrection at the laſt day.25Ieſus ſaid vnto her, I am the
reſurrection, and the life: hee that beleeueth in me, though he were dead,
yet ſhall he liue.26And whoſoeuer liueth, and beleeueth in mee, ſhall
neuer die. Beleeueſt thou this?27She ſaith vnto him, Yea Lord, I beleeue
that thou art the Chriſt the Sonne of God, which ſhould come into the
world.28And when ſhee had ſo ſaid, ſhee went her way, and called Mary
her ſiſter ſecretly, ſaying, The Maſter is come, and calleth for
thee.29Aſsoone as ſhe heard that, ſhe aroſe quickely, and came vnto
him.30Now Ieſus was not yet come into the towne, but was in that place
where Martha met him.31The Iewes then which were with her in the
houſe, and comforted her, when they ſaw Mary that ſhe roſe vp haſtily,
and went out, followed her, ſaying, Shee goeth vnto the graue, to weepe
there.32Then when Mary was come where Ieſus was, and ſaw him, ſhee
fell downe at his feete, ſaying vnto him, Lord, if thou hadſt beene here,
my brother had not dyed.33When Ieſus therefore ſawe her weeping, and
the Iewes alſo weeping which came with her, hee groned in the Spirit,
and was troubled,34And ſaid, Where haue ye laid him? They ſay vnto
him, Lord, come, & ſee.35Ieſus wept.36Then ſaid the Iewes, Behold, how
he loued him.37And ſome of them ſaid, Could not this man, which
opened the eyes of the blinde, haue cauſed that euen this man ſhould
not haue died?38Ieſus therefore againe groning in himſelfe, commeth to
the graue. It was a caue, and a ſtone lay vpon it.39Ieſus ſaid, Take yee
away the ſtone. Martha, the ſiſter of him that was dead, ſayth vnto him,
Lord, by this time he ſtinketh: for he hath beene dead foure
dayes.40Ieſus ſaith vnto her, Said I not vnto thee, that if thou wouldſt
beleeue, thou ſhouldeſt ſee the glory of God?41Then they tooke away
the ſtone from the place where the dead was laid. And Ieſus lift vp his
eyes, and ſaid, Father, I thanke thee, that thou haſt heard me.42And I
knewe that thou heareſt me alwayes: but becauſe of the people which
ſtand by, I ſaid it, that they may beleeue that thou haſt ſent me.43And
when hee thus had ſpoken, he cryed with a loude voice, Lazarus, come
foorth.44And he that was dead, came forth, bound hand & foot with
graue-clothes: and his face was bound about with a napkin. Ieſus ſaith
vnto them, Looſe him, and let him goe.45Then many of the Iewes which
came to Mary, and had ſeene the things which Ieſus did, beleeued on
him.46But ſome of them went their wayes to the PhAriſes, and tolde
them what things Ieſus had done.47Then gathered þe chiefe Prieſts and
the PhAriſes a councell, and ſaid, What doe wee? for this man doeth
many miracles.48If we let him thus alone, all men will beleeue on him,
and the Romanes ſhall come, and take away both our place and
nation.49And one of them named Caiaphas, being the high Prieſt that
ſame yeere, ſaid vnto them, Ye know nothing at all,50Nor conſider that
it is expedient for vs, that one man ſhould die for the people, and that
the whole nation periſh not.51And this ſpake he not of himſelfe: but
being high Prieſt that yeere, he prophecied that Ieſus ſhould die for that
nation:52And not for that nation only, but that alſo hee ſhould gather
together in one, the children of God that were ſcattered abroad.53Then
from that day foorth, they tooke counſell together for to put him to
death.54Ieſus therefore walked no more openly among the Iewes: but
went thence vnto a countrey neere to the wilderneſſe, into a city called
Ephraim, and there continued with his diſciples.55And the Iewes
Paſſeouer was nigh at hand, and many went out of the countrey vp to
Hieruſalem before the Paſſeouer to purifie themſelues.56Then ſought
they for Ieſus, and ſpake among themſelues, as they ſtood in the Temple,
What thinke ye, that he will not come to the feaſt?57Now both the chiefe
Prieſts and the PhAriſes had giuen a commandement, that if any man
knew where hee were, he ſhould ſhew it, that they might take him.
CHAPTER 121Then Ieſus, ſixe dayes before the Paſsouer, came to
Bethanie, where Lazarus was, which had bene dead, whom hee raiſed
from the dead.2There they made him a ſupper, and Martha ſerued: but
Lazarus was one of them þt ſate at the table with him.3Then tooke Mary
a pound of ointment, of Spikenard, very coſtly, and anointed the feet of
Ieſus, & wiped his feet with her haire: and the houſe was filled with the
odour of the ointment.4Then ſaith one of his diſciples, Iudas Iſcariot,
Simons ſonne, which ſhould betray him,5Why was not this ointment
ſold for three hundred pence, and giuen to the poore?6This he ſaid, not
that he cared for the poore: but becauſe hee was a thiefe, and had the
bag, and bare what was put therein.7Then ſaid Ieſus, Let her alone,
againſt the day of my burying hath ſhe kept this.8For the poore alwayes
yee haue with you: but me ye haue not alwayes.9Much people of the
Iewes therefore knew that he was there: and they came, not for Ieſus
ſake onely, but that they might ſee Lazarus alſo, whom he had raiſed
from the dead.10But the chiefe Prieſts conſulted, þt they might put
Lazarus alſo to death,11Becauſe that by reaſon of him many of the Iewes
went away and beleeued on Ieſus.12On the next day, much people that
were come to the feaſt, when they heard that Ieſus was comming to
Hieruſalem,13Tooke branches of Palme trees, and went foorth to meet
him, and cried, Hoſanna, bleſſed is the king of Iſrael that cōmeth in the
Name of the Lord.14And Ieſus, when he had found a yong aſſe, ſate
thereon, as it is written,15Feare not, daughter of Sion, behold, thy King
commeth, ſitting on an aſſes colt.16Theſe things vnderſtood not his
diſciples at the firſt: but when Ieſus was glorified, then remēbred they
that theſe things were written of him, and that they had done theſe
things vnto him.17The people therefore that was with him, when he
called Lazarus out of his graue, and raiſed him from the dead, bare
record.18For this cauſe the people alſo met him, for that they heard that
hee had done this miracle.19The PhAriſees therefore ſaide among
themſelues, Perceiue ye how yee preuaile nothing? Behold, the world is
gone after him.20And there were certaine Greeks among them, that
came vp to worſhip at the feaſt:21The ſame came therefore to Philip
which was of Bethſaida of Galilee, and deſired him, ſaying, Sir, we would
ſee Ieſus.22Philip commeth and telleth Andrew: and againe Andrew and
Philip told Ieſus.23And Ieſus anſwered them, ſaying, The houre is come,
that the Sonne of man ſhould be glorified.24Uerely, verely, I ſay vnto
you, Except a corne of wheat fall into the ground, and die, it abideth
alone: but if it die, it bringeth forth much fruit.25He that loueth his life,
ſhall loſe it: and hee that hateth his life in this world, ſhall keepe it vnto
life eternall.26If any man ſerue me, let him follow me, and where I am,
there ſhall alſo my ſeruant be: If any man ſerue me, him will my father
honour.27Now is my ſoule troubled, and what ſhall I ſay? Father, ſaue
me from this houre, but for this cauſe came I vnto this houre.28Father,
glorifie thy Name. Then came there a voice from heauen, ſaying, I haue
both glorified it, and wil glorifie it againe.29The people therefore that
ſtood by, and heard it, ſaid, that it thundered: others ſaid, An Angel
ſpake to him.30Ieſus anſwered, and ſaid, This voice came not becauſe of
mee, but for your ſakes.31Now is the iudgement of this world: now ſhall
the prince of this world be caſt out.32And I, if I be lifted vp from the
earth, will draw all men vnto me.33(This hee ſaid, ſignifying what death
he ſhould die)34The people anſwered him, We haue heard out of the
Law, that Chriſt abideth for euer: and how ſayeſt thou, The Sonne of
man muſt bee lift vp? Who is this Sonne of man?35Then Ieſus ſaid vnto
them, Yet a little while is the light with you: walke while ye haue the
light, leſt darkdeſse come vpon you: For he that walketh in darkeneſſe,
knoweth not whither he goeth.36While ye haue light, beleeue in the light,
that ye may bee the children of light. Theſe things ſpake Ieſus, and
departed, and did hide himſelfe from them.37But though he had done
ſo many miracles before them, yet they beleeued not on him:38That the
ſaying of Eſaias the Prophet might be fulfilled, which hee ſpake, Lord,
who hath beleeued our report? and to whom hath the arme of the Lord
beene reuealed?39Therefore they could not beleeue, becauſe that Eſaias
ſaid againe,40He hath blinded their eyes, and hardned their heart, that
they ſhould not ſee with their eyes, nor vnderſtand with their heart, and
be conuerted, and I ſhould heale them.41Theſe things ſaid Eſaias, when
he ſaw his glory, and ſpake of him.42Neuertheleſſe, among the chiefe
rulers alſo, many beleeued on him; but becauſe of the PhAriſees they
did not confeſse him, leſt they ſhould be put out of the Synagogue.43For
they loued the praiſe of men, more then the praiſe of God.44Ieſus cried,
and ſaid, He that beleeueth on me, beleeueth not on me, but on him
that ſent me.45And he that ſeeth me, ſeeth him that ſent me.46I am come
a light into the world, that whoſoeuer beleeueth on me, ſhould not abide
in darkeneſſe.47And if any man heare my words, and beleeue not, I
iudge him not; For I came not to iudge the world, but to ſaue the
world.48He that reiecteth me, and receiueth not my words, hath one that
iudgeth him: þe word that I haue ſpoken, the ſame ſhall iudge him in the
laſt day.49For I haue not ſpoken of my ſelfe; but the Father which ſent
me, he gaue me a commaundement what I ſhould ſay, and what I ſhould

ſpeake.50And I know that his commandement is life euerlaſting: whatſoeuer I ſpeake therefore, euen as the Father ſaid vnto me, ſo I ſpeake.

CHAPTER 131Now before the feaſt of the Paſſeouer, when Ieſus knew that his houre was come, that he ſhould depart out of this world vnto the Father, hauing loued his owne which were in the world, he loued them vnto the end.2And ſupper being ended (the deuill hauing now put into the heart of Iudas Iſcariot Simons ſonne to betray him.)3Ieſus knowing that the Father had giuen all things into his hands, and that he was come from God, and went to God:4He riſeth from ſupper, and layed aſide his garments, and tooke a towell, and girded himſelfe.5After that, he powreth water into a baſon, and beganne to waſh the diſciples feete, and to wipe them with the towell wherewith he was girded.6Then commeth he to Simon Peter: and Peter ſaith vnto him, Lord, doeſt thou waſh my feete?7Ieſus anſwered, and ſaid vnto him, What I doe, thou knoweſt not now: but thou ſhalt know heereafter.8Peter ſaith vnto him, Thou ſhalt neuer waſh my feete. Ieſus anſwered him, If I waſh thee not, thou haſt no part with me.9Simon Peter ſaith vnto him, Lord, not my feete only, but alſo my hands, and my head.10Ieſus ſaith to him, He that is waſhed, needeth not, ſaue to waſh his feet, but is cleane euery whit: and ye are cleane, but not all.11For he knew who ſhould betray him, therefore ſaid he, Ye are not all cleane.12So after he had waſhed their feet, and had taken his garments, and was ſet downe againe, he ſaid vnto them, Know ye what I haue done to you?13Ye call me Maſter and Lord, and ye ſay well: for ſo I am.14If I then your Lord and Maſter haue waſhed your feete, yee alſo ought to waſh one anothers feete.15For I haue giuen you an example, that yee ſhould doe, as I haue done to you.16Uerily, verily I ſay vnto you, the ſeruant is not greater then his lord, neither he that is ſent, greater then hee that ſent him.17If yee know theſe things, happy are ye if ye doe them.18I ſpeake not of you all, I know whom I haue choſen: but that the Scripture may be fulfilled, He that eateth bread with mee, hath lift vp his heele againſt me.19Now I tell you before it come, that when it is come to paſſe, yee may beleeue that I am he.20Uerily, verily I ſay vnto you, he that receiueth whomſoeuer I ſend, receiueth me: and he that receiueth me, receiueth him that ſent me.21When Ieſus had thus ſayd, hee was troubled in ſpirit, and teſtified, and ſaid, Uerily, verily I ſay vnto you, that one of you ſhall betray me.22Then the diſciples looked one on another, doubting of whom hee ſpake.23Now there was leaning on Ieſus boſome one of his diſciples, whom Ieſus loued.24Simon Peter therefore beckened to him, that he ſhould aſke who it ſhould be of whom he ſpake.25Hee then lying on Ieſus breaſt, ſaith vnto him, Lord, who is it?26Ieſus anſwered, Hee it is to whom I ſhall giue a ſoppe, when I haue dipped it. And when he had dipped the ſop, he gaue it to Iudas Iſcariot the ſonne of Simon.27And after the ſoppe, Satan entred into him, Then ſaid Ieſus vnto him, That thou doeſt, doe quickly.28Now no man at the table knew, for what intent he ſpake this vnto him.29For ſome of them thought, becauſe Iudas had the bagge, that Ieſus had ſayd vnto him, Buy thoſe things that wee haue need of againſt the feaſt: or that he ſhould giue ſome thing to the poore.30He then hauing receiued the ſop, went immediatly out: and it was night.31Therefore when hee was gone out, Ieſus ſayd, Now is the Sonne of man glorified: and God is glorified in him.32If God be glorified in him, God ſhall alſo glorifie him in himſelfe, and ſhall ſtraightway glorifie him.33Litle children, yet a litle while I am with you. Ye ſhall ſeeke mee, and as I ſaid vnto the Iewes, whither I go, ye cannot come: ſo now I ſay to you.34A new commandement I giue vnto you, That yee loue one another, as I haue loued you, that yee alſo loue one another.35By this ſhall all men know that ye are my diſciples, if yee haue loue one to another.36Simon Peter ſayd vnto him, Lord, whither goeſt thou? Ieſus anſwered him, Whither I goe, thou canſt not follow me now: but thou ſhalt follow me afterwards.37Peter ſaid vnto him, Lord, why can not I follow thee now? I will lay downe my life for thy ſake.38Ieſus anſwered him, Wilt thou lay downe thy life for my ſake? Uerily, verily I ſay vnto thee, the Cocke ſhall not crow, til thou haſt denied me thriſe.

CHAPTER 141Let not your heart be troubled: yee beleeue in God, beleeue alſo in me.2In my Fathers houſe are many manſions; if it were not ſo, I would haue told you: I goe to prepare a place for you.3And if I goe and prepare a place for you, I will come againe, and receiue you vnto my ſelfe, that where I am, there ye may be alſo.4And whither I goe yee know, and the way ye know.5Thomas ſaith vnto him, Lord, we know not whither thou goeſt: and how can we know the way?6Ieſus ſaith vnto him, I am the Way, the Trueth, and the Life: no man commeth vnto the Father but by mee.7If ye had knowen me, ye ſhould haue knowen my Father alſo: and from henceforth ye know him, and haue ſeene him.8Philip ſayth vnto him, Lord, ſhew vs the Father, and it ſufficeth vs.9Ieſus ſaith vnto him, Haue I bin ſo long time with you, and yet haſt thou not knowen me, Philip? he that hath ſeene me, hath ſeene the father, and how ſayeſt thou then, ſhew vs the father?10Beleeueſt thou not that I am in the father, and the father in mee? The words that I ſpeake vnto you, I ſpeak not of my ſelfe: but the Father that dwelleth in me, he doth the works.11Beleeue me that I am in the Father, and the Father in mee: or elſe beleeue me for the very workes ſake.12Uerely, verely I ſay vnto you, he that beleeueth on me, the works that I doe, ſhall hee doe alſo, and greater workes then theſe ſhall he doe, becauſe I goe vnto my Father.13And whatſoeuer ye ſhall aſke in my Name, that will I doe, that the Father may be glorified in the Sonne.14If ye ſhall aſke any thing in my Name, I will doe it.15If ye loue me, keepe my commandements.16And I will pray the Father, and hee ſhall giue you another Comforter, that he may abide with you for euer,17Euen the Spirit of trueth, whom the world cannot receiue, becauſe it ſeeth him not, neither knoweth him: but ye know him, for hee dwelleth with you, and ſhall be in you.18I wil not leaue you comfortleſſe, I will come to you.19Yet a litle while, and the world ſeeth me no more: but ye ſee me, becauſe I liue, ye ſhall liue alſo.20At that day ye ſhall know, that I am in my Father, and you in me, and I in you.21He that hath my commandements, and keepeth them, hee it is that loueth me: and he that loueth me ſhall be loued of my Father, and I will loue him, and will manifeſt my ſelfe to him.22Iudas ſaith vnto him, not Iſcariot, Lord, how is it that thou wilt manifeſt thy ſelfe vnto vs, and not vnto the world?23Ieſus anſwered, and ſaide vnto him, If a man loue mee, he will keepe my wordes: and my Father will loue him, and wee will come vnto him, and make our abode with him.24He that loueth mee not, keepeth not my ſayings, and the word which you heare, is not mine, but the Fathers which ſent mee.25Theſe things haue I ſpoken vnto you, being yet preſent with you.26But the Comforter, which is the holy Ghoſt, whom the Father wil ſend in my name, he ſhal teach you al things, & bring al things to your remembrance, whatſoeuer I haue ſaid vnto you.27Peace I leaue with you, my peace I giue vnto you, not as the world giueth, giue I vnto you: let not your heart bee troubled, neither let it bee afraid.28Ye haue heard how I ſaide vnto you, I goe away, and come againe vnto you. If ye loued mee, yee would reioyce, becauſe I ſaid, I go vnto the Father: for my Father is greater then I.29And now I haue told you before it come to paſſe, that when it is come to paſſe, ye might beleeue.30Heereafter I will not talke much with you: for the prince of this world commeth, and hath nothing in me.31But that the world may know that I loue the Father: and as the Father gaue me commandement, euen ſo I doe: Ariſe, let vs goe hence.

CHAPTER 151I am the true vine, and my Father is þe huſbandman.2Euery branch in me that beareth not fruit, hee taketh away: and euery branch that beareth fruit, he purgeth it, that it may bring foorth more fruit.3Now ye are cleane through the word which I haue ſpoken vnto you.4Abide in me, and in you: As the branch cannot beare fruit of itſelfe, except it abide in the vine: no more can ye, except ye abide in me.5I am the vine, ye are the branches: He that abideth in me, and I in him, the ſame bringeth forth much fruit: for without me ye can doe nothing.6If a man abide not in me, he is caſt forth as a branch, and is withered, and men gather them, and caſt them into the fire, and they are burned.7If ye abide in me, and my words abide in you, ye ſhall aſke what ye will, and it ſhall be done vnto you.8Herein is my Father glorified, that ye beare much fruit, ſo ſhall ye bee my Diſciples.9As the Father hath loued me, ſo haue I loued you: continue ye in my loue.10If ye keepe my Commandements, ye ſhal abide in my loue, euen as I haue kept my Fathers Commandements, and abide in his loue.11Theſe things haue I ſpoken vnto you, that my ioy might remaine in you, and that your ioy might be full.12This is my Commaundement, that ye loue one another, as I haue loued you.13Greater loue hath no man then this, that a man lay downe his life for his friends.14Ye are my friends, if ye do whatſoeuer I command you.15Henceforth I call you not ſeruants, for the ſeruant knoweth not what his lord doth, but I haue called you friends: for all things that I haue heard of my Father, I haue made knowen vnto you.16Ye haue not choſen me, but I haue choſen you, and ordeined you, that you ſhould goe and bring foorth fruit, and that your fruite ſhould remaine: that whatſoeuer ye ſhall aſke of the Father in my Name, he may giue it you.17Theſe things I commaund you, that ye loue one another.18If the world hate you, yee know that it hated me before it hated you.19If ye were of the world, the world would loue his owne: But becauſe yee are not of the world, but I haue choſen you out of the world, therfore the world hateth you.20Remember the word that I ſaid vnto you, The ſeruant is not greater then the Lord: if they haue perſecuted me, they will alſo perſecute you: if they haue kept my ſaying, they will keepe yours alſo.21But all theſe things will they doe vnto you for my Names ſake, becauſe they know not him that ſent me.22If I had not come, and ſpoken vnto them, they had not had ſinne: but now they haue no cloke for their ſinne.23He that hateth me, hateth my Father alſo.24If I had not done among thē the works which none other man did, they had not had ſinne: but now haue they both ſeene, & hated both me & my father.25But this commeth to paſſe, that the word might be fulfilled that is written in their law, They hated me without a cauſe.26But when the Comforter is come, whom I wil ſend vnto you from the Father, euen the Spirit of trueth, which proceedeth from the Father, hee ſhall teſtifie of me.27And ye alſo ſhall beare witneſſe, becauſe ye haue bene with me from the beginning.

CHAPTER 161Theſe things haue I ſpoken vnto you, that yee ſhould not be offended.2They ſhall put you out of the Synagogues: yea, the time commeth, that whoſoeuer killeth you, will thinke that hee doeth God ſeruice.3And theſe things will they doe vnto you, becauſe they haue not knowen the Father, nor me.4But theſe things haue I told you, that when the time ſhall come, ye may remember that I told you of them. And theſe things I ſaid not vnto you at the beginning, becauſe I was with you.5But now I goe my way to him that ſent mee, and none of you aſketh me, Whither goeſt thou?6But becauſe I haue ſaide theſe things vnto you, ſorow hath filled your heart.7Neuertheleſſe; I tell you the trueth, it is expedient for you that I goe away: for if I goe not away, the Comforter will not come vnto you: but if I depart, I will ſend him vnto you.8And when he is come, he will reproue the world of ſinne, and of righteouſneſſe, and of iudgement.9Of ſinne, becauſe they beleeue not on me.10Of righteouſneſſe, becauſe I goe to my Father, and ye ſee me no more.11Of iudgement, becauſe the prince of this world is iudged.12I haue yet many things to ſay vnto you, but ye cannot beare them now:13Howbeit, when hee the ſpirit of trueth is come, he wil guide you into all trueth: For he ſhall not ſpeake of himſelfe: but whatſoeuer he ſhall heare, that ſhall he ſpeake, and he will ſhew you things to come.14He ſhall glorifie me, for he ſhall receiue of mine, and ſhall ſhew it vnto you.15All things that the Father hath, are mine: therefore ſaid I that he ſhall take of mine, and ſhal ſhew it vnto you.16A litle while, and ye ſhall not ſee me: and againe a litle while, & ye ſhall ſee me: becauſe I goe to the Father.17Then ſaide ſome of his diſciples among themſelues, What is this that he ſaith vnto vs, A litle while, and ye ſhal not ſee me: and againe, a litle while, and ye ſhall ſee me: and, becauſe I goe to the Father?18They ſaid therefore, What is this that he ſaith, A litle while? we cannot tell what he ſaith.19Now Ieſus knew that they were deſirous to aſke him, & ſaid vnto them, Doe ye enquire among your ſelues of that I ſaide, A litle while, and ye ſhall not ſee mee: and againe; A little while and ye ſhall ſee me?20Uerily, verily I ſay vnto you, that ye ſhall weepe and lament, but the world ſhall reioyce: And ye ſhall be ſorrowfull, but your ſorrow ſhall be turned into ioy.21A woman, when ſhe is in trauaile, hath ſorrow, becauſe her houre is come: but aſſoone as ſhe is deliuered of the child, ſhe remembreth no more the anguiſh, for ioy that a man is borne into the world.22And ye now therefore haue ſorrow: but I will ſee you againe, and your heart ſhall reioyce, and your ioy no man taketh from you.23And in that day ye ſhall aſke me nothing: Uerily, verily I ſay vnto you, Whatſoeuer yee ſhall aſke the Father in my Name, he will giue it you.24Hitherto haue ye aſked nothing in my Name: aſke, and ye ſhall receiue, that your ioy may be full.25Theſe things haue I ſpoken vnto you in prouerbs: the time commeth when I ſhall no more ſpeake vnto you in prouerbes, but I ſhall ſhew you plainly of the Father.26At that day ye ſhall aſke in my Name: and I ſay not vnto you that I will pray the Father for you:27For the Father himſelfe loueth you, becauſe ye haue loued me and haue beleeued that I came out from God.28I came foorth from the Father, and am come into the world: againe, I leaue the world, and goe to the Father.29His diſciples ſaid vnto him, Loe, now ſpeakeſt thou plainly, and ſpeakeſt no prouerbe.30Now are we ſure that thou knoweſt al things, and needeſt not that any man ſhould aſke thee: By this we beleeue that thou cameſt foorth from God.31Ieſus anſwered them, Doe yee now beleeue?32Behold, the houre commeth, yea is now come, that ye ſhall be ſcattered, euery man to his owne, and ſhall leaue me alone: and yet I am not alone, becauſe the Father is with me.33Theſe things I haue ſpoken vnto you, that in me ye might haue peace, in the world ye ſhall haue tribulation: but be of good cheare, I haue ouercome the world.

CHAPTER 171Theſe words ſpake Ieſus, and lift vp his eyes to heauen, and ſaid, Father, the houre is come, glorifie thy Sonne, that thy Sonne alſo may glorifie thee.2As thou haſt giuen him power ouer all fleſh, that he ſhould giue eternall life to as many as thou haſt giuen him.3And this is life eternall, that they might know thee the onely true God, and Ieſus Chriſt whom thou haſt ſent.4I haue glorified thee on the earth: I haue finiſhed the worke which thou gaueſt me to doe.5And now O Father, glorifie thou me, with thine owne ſelfe, with the glory which I had with thee before the world was.6I haue manifeſted thy Name vnto the men which thou gaueſt me out of the world: thine they were; and thou gaueſt them me; and they haue kept thy word.7Now they haue knowen that all things whatſoeuer thou haſt giuen me, are of thee.8For I haue giuen vnto them the words which thou gaueſt me, and they haue receiued them, and haue knowen ſurely that I came out from thee, and they haue beleeued that thou didſt ſend me.9I pray for them, I pray not for the world: but for them which thou haſt giuen me, for they are thine.10And all mine are thine, and thine are mine: and I am glorified in them.11And now I am no more in the world, but theſe are in the world, and I come to thee. Holy Father, keep through thine owne Name, thoſe whom thou haſt giuen mee, that they may bee one, as we are.12While I was with them in the world, I kept them in thy Name: thoſe that thou gaueſt me, I haue kept, and none of them is loſt, but the ſonne of perdition: that the Scripture might be fulfilled.13And now come I to thee, and theſe things I ſpeake in the world, that they might haue my ioy fulfilled in themſelues.14I haue giuen them thy word, and the world hath hated them, becauſe they are not of the world, euen as I am not of the world.15I pray not that thou ſhouldeſt take them out of the world, but that thou ſhouldeſt keepe them from the euill.16They are not of the world, euen as I am not of the world.17ſanctifie them through thy trueth: thy word is trueth.18As thou haſt ſent mee into the world: euen ſo haue I alſo ſent them into the world.19And for their ſakes I ſanctifie my ſelfe, that they alſo might be ſanctified through the trueth.20Neither pray I for theſe alone; but for them alſo which ſhall beleeue on me through their word:21That they all may be one, as thou Father art in mee, and I in thee, that they alſo may bee one in vs: that the world may beleeue that thou haſt ſent mee.22And the glory which thou gaueſt me, I haue giuen them: that they may be one, euen as we are one:23I in them, and thou in mee, that they may bee made perfect in one, and that the world may know that thou haſt ſent me, and haſt loued them, as thou haſt loued me.24Father, I will that they alſo whom thou haſt giuen me, be with me where I am, that they may behold my glory which thou haſt giuen mee: for thou louedſt mee before the foundation of the world.25O righteous Father, the world hath not knowen thee, but I haue knowen thee, and theſe haue knowen that thou haſt ſent me.26And I haue declared vnto them thy Name, and will declare it: that the loue wherewith thou haſt loued mee, may be in them, and I in them.

CHAPTER 181When Ieſus had ſpoken theſe wordes, hee went foorth with his diſciples ouer the Brooke Cedron, where was a garden, into the which hee entred and his diſciples.2And Iudas alſo which betrayed him, knew the place: for Ieſus oft times reſorted thither with his diſciples.3Iudas then hauing receiued a band of men, and officers from the chiefe Prieſts and PhAriſees, commeth thither with lanternes and torches, and weapons.4Ieſus therefore knowing all things that ſhould come vpon him, went foorth, and ſayde vnto them, Whom ſeeke ye?5They anſwered him, Ieſus of Nazareth. Ieſus ſaith vnto them, I am hee. And Iudas alſo which betraied him, ſtood with them.6Aſſoone then as he had ſaid vnto them, I am he, they went backeward, and fell to the ground.7Then aſked hee them againe, Whom ſeeke ye? And they ſaid,

Ieſus of Nazareth.8Ieſus anſwered, I haue tolde you that I am he: If
therefore ye ſeeke me, let theſe goe their way:9That the ſaying might be
fulfilled which he ſpake, Of them which thou gaueſt me, haue I loſt
none.10Then Simon Peter hauing a ſword, drewe it, and ſmote the high
Prieſts ſeruant, & cut off his right eare: The ſeruants name was
Malchus.11Then ſaid Ieſus vnto Peter, Put vp thy ſword into the ſheath:
the cup which my father hath giuen me, ſhall I not drinke it?12Then the
band and the captaine, and officers of the Iewes, tooke Ieſus, and bound
him,13And led him away to Annas firſt, (for he was father in law to
Caiaphaſ) which was the high Prieſt that ſame yeere.14Now Caiaphas
was he which gaue counſell to the Iewes, that it was expedient that one
man ſhould die for the people.15And Simon Peter followed Ieſus, and
ſo did another diſciple: that diſciple was knowen vnto the high Prieſt,
and went in with Ieſus into the palace of the high Prieſt.16But Peter
ſtood at the doore without. Then went out that other diſciple, which
was knowen vnto the high Prieſt, and ſpake vnto her that kept the doore,
and brought in Peter.17Then ſaith the damoſell that kept the doore vnto
Peter, Art not thou alſo one of this mans diſciples? He ſayth, I am
not.18And the ſeruants and officers ſtood there, who had made a fire of
coales, (for it was colde) and they warmed themſelues: and Peter ſtood
with them, and warmed himſelfe.19The high Prieſt then aſked Ieſus of
his diſciples, and of his doctrine.20Ieſus anſwered him, I ſpake openly to
the world, I euer taught in the Synagogue, and in the Temple, whither
the Iewes alwayes reſort, and in ſecret haue I ſaid nothing:21Why aſkeſt
thou me? Aſke them which heard me, what I haue ſaid vnto them:
behold, they know what I ſaid.22And when hee had thus ſpoken, one of
the officers which ſtood by, ſtroke Ieſus with the palme of his hand,
ſaying, Anſwereſt thou the hie prieſt ſo?23Ieſus anſwered him, If I haue
ſpoken euill, beare witneſſe of the euill: but if well, why ſmiteſt thou
me?24Now Annas had ſent him bound vnto Caiaphas the high
Prieſt.25And Simon Peter ſtood and warmed himſelfe: They ſaid
therefore vnto him, Art not thou alſo one of his diſciples? Hee denied
it, and ſaid, I am not.26One of the ſeruants of the high Prieſts (being his
kinſman whoſe eare Peter cut off) ſaith, Did not I ſee thee in the garden
with him?27Peter then denied againe, and immediatly the cocke
crew.28Then led they Ieſus from Caiaphas vnto the hall of Iudgement:
And it was earely, and they themſelues went not into the Iudgement hall,
leſt they ſhould be defiled: but that they might eat the Paſſeouer.29Pilate
then went out vnto them, and ſaid, What accuſation bring you againſt
this man?30They anſwered, & ſaid vnto him, If he were not a malefactor,
we would not haue deliuered him vp vnto thee.31Then ſaide Pilate vnto
them, Take ye him, and iudge him according to your law. The Iewes
therefore ſaid vnto him, It is not lawfull for vs to put any man to
death:32That the ſaying of Ieſus might be fulfilled, which hee ſpake,
ſignifying what death he ſhould die.33Then Pilate entred into the
Iudgement hall againe, and called Ieſus, and ſaide vnto him, Art thou
the King of the Iewes?34Ieſus anſwered him, Sayeſt thou this thing of
thy ſelfe? or did others tell it thee of me?35Pilate anſwered, Am I a Iew?
Thine owne nation, and the chiefe Prieſts haue deliuered thee vnto mee:
What haſt thou done?36Ieſus anſwered, My kingdome is not of this
world: if my kingdome were of this world, then would my ſeruants fight,
that I ſhould not be deliuered to the Iewes: but now is my kingdome not
from hence.37Pilate therefore ſaide vnto him, Art thou a King then?
Ieſus anſwered, Thou ſaieſt that I am a King. To this end was I borne,
and for this cauſe came I into the world, that I ſhould beare witneſſe
vnto the trueth: euery one that is of the trueth heareth my voice.38Pilate
ſaith vnto him, What is trueth? And when hee had ſaid this, he went out
againe vnto the Iewes, and ſaith vnto them, I find in him no fault at
all.39But yee haue a cuſtome that I ſhould releaſe vnto you one at the
Paſſeouer: will ye therefore that I releaſe vnto you the king of the
Iewes?40Then cried they all againe, ſaying, Not this man, but Barabbas.
Now Barabbas was a robber.

CHAPTER 19 1Then Pilate therfore tooke Ieſus, and ſcourged
him.2And the ſouldiers platted a crowne of thornes, and put it on his
head, and they put on him a purple robe,3And ſaid, Haile king of the
Iewes: and they ſmote him with their hands.4Pilate therefore went
foorth againe, and ſaith vnto them, Behold, I bring him foorth to you,
that yee may know that I find no fault in him.5Then came Ieſus forth,
wearing the crowne of thornes, and the purple robe: and Pilate ſaith
vnto them, Behold the man.6When the chiefe Prieſts therefore and
officers ſaw him, they cried out, ſaying, Crucifie him, crucifie him. Pilate
ſaith vnto them, Take ye him, and crucifie him: for I find no fault in
him.7The Iewes anſwered him, We haue a law, and by our law he ought
to die, becauſe hee made himſelfe the Son of God.8When Pilate
therefore heard that ſaying, he was the more afraid,9And went againe
into the iudgement hall, & ſaith vnto Ieſus, Whence art thou? But Ieſus
gaue him no anſwere.10Then ſaith Pilate vnto him, Speakeſt thou not
vnto me? Knoweſt thou not, that I haue power to crucifie thee, and haue
power to releaſe thee?11Ieſus anſwered, Thou couldeſt haue no power
at all againſt me, except it were giuen thee from aboue: therfore he that
deliuered me vnto thee, hath the greater ſinne.12And from thencefore
Pilate ſought to releaſe him: but the Iewes cried out, ſaying, If thou let
this man goe, thou art not Ceſars friend: whoſoeuer maketh himſelfe a
king, ſpeaketh againſt Ceſar.13When Pilate therefore heard that ſaying,
he brought Ieſus foorth, and ſate downe in the iudgement ſeate, in a
place that is called the pauement, but in the Hebrew, Gabbatha.14And
it was the preparation of the Paſſeouer, and about the ſixt houre: and he
ſaith vnto the Iewes, Beholde your King.15But they cried out, Away with
him, away with him, crucifie him. Pilate ſaith vnto them, Shall I crucifie
your King? The chiefe Prieſts anſwered, Wee haue no king but
Ceſar.16Then deliuered he him therfore vnto them to be crucified: and
they took Ieſus, and led him away.17And he bearing his croſse, went
foorth into a place called the place of a ſkull, which is called in the
Hebrewe, Golgotha:18Where they crucified him, and two other with
him, on either ſide one, and Ieſus in the middeſt.19And Pilate wrote a
title, and put it on the croſse. And the writing was, IESVS OF
NAZARETH, THE KING OF THE IEWES.20This title then read
many of the Iewes: for the place where Ieſus was crucified, was nigh to
the citie, and it was written in Hebrewe, and Greeke, and Latine.21Then
ſaid the chiefe Prieſts of the Iewes to Pilate, Write not, The king of the
Iewes: but that he ſaid, I am King of the Iewes.22Pilate anſwered, What
I haue written, I haue written.23Then the ſouldiers, when they had
crucified Ieſus, tooke his garments, (and made foure parts, to euery
ſouldier a part) and alſo his coat: Now the coate was without ſeame,
wouen from the top thorowout.24They ſaid therefore among
themſelues, Let not vs rent it, but caſt lots for it, whoſe it ſhall bee: that
the Scripture might bee fulfilled, which ſaith, They parted my raiment
among them, and for my veſture they did caſt lots. Theſe things
therefore the ſouldiers did.25Now there ſtood by the croſse of Ieſus, his
mother, and his mothers ſiſter, Mary the wife of Cleophas, and Mary
Magdalene.26When Ieſus therefore ſaw his mother, and the diſciple
ſtanding by, whom he loued, he ſaith vnto his mother, Woman, behold
thy ſonne.27Then ſaith he to the diſciple, Behold thy mother. And from
that houre that diſciple tooke her vnto his owne home.28After this, Ieſus
knowing that all things were now accompliſhed, that the Scripture might
be fulfilled, ſaith, I thirſt.29Now there was ſet a veſſell, full of vineger:
And they filled a ſpunge with vineger, and put it vpon hyſsope, and put
it to his mouth.30When Ieſus therefore had receiued the vineger, he ſaid,
It is finiſhed, and he bowed his head, and gaue vp the ghoſt.31The Iewes
therefore, becauſe it was the preparation, that the bodies ſhould not
remaine vpon the Croſse on the Sabbath day (for that Sabbath day was
an high day) beſought Pilate that their legs might be broken, and that
they might be taken away.32Then came the ſouldiers, and brake the legs
of the firſt, and of the other, which was crucified with him.33But when
they came to Ieſus, and ſaw that he was dead already, they brake not his
legs.34But one of the ſouldiers with a ſpeare pierced his ſide, and
forthwith came there out blood and water.35And he that ſaw it, bare
record, and his record is true, and he knoweth that hee ſaith true, that
yee might beleeue.36For theſe things were done, that the Scripture
ſhould be fulfilled, A bone of him ſhall not be broken.37And againe
another Scripture ſaith, They ſhall looke on him whom they
pierſed.38And after this, Ioſeph of Arimathea (being a diſciple of Ieſus,
but ſecretly for feare of the Ieweſ) beſought Pilate that he might take
away the body of Ieſus, and Pilate gaue him leaue: he came therefore,
and tooke the body of Ieſus.39And there came alſo Nicodemus, which
at the firſt came to Ieſus by night, and brought a mixture of myrrhe and
aloes, about an hundred pound weight.40Then tooke they the body of
Ieſus, & wound it in linnen clothes, with the ſpices, as the maner of the

Iewes is to burie:41Now in the place where he was crucified, there was
a garden, and in the garden a new Sepulchre, wherein was neuer man yet
layd.42There laid they Ieſus therefore, becauſe of the Iewes preparation
day, for the Sepulchre was nigh at hand.
CHAPTER 201The firſt day of the weeke, commeth Mary Magdalene
earely when it was yet darke, vnto the Sepulchre, and ſeeth the ſtone
taken away from the Sepulchre.2Then ſhe runneth and commeth to
Simon Peter, and to the other diſciple whom Ieſus loued, and ſaith vnto
them, They haue taken away the Lord out of the Sepulchre, and we
know not where they haue laid him.3Peter therefore went forth, and that
other diſciple, and came to the Sepulchre.4So they ranne both together,
and the other diſciple did outrun Peter, and came firſt to the
Sepulchre.5And he ſtouping downe and looking in, ſaw the linnen
clothes lying, yet went he not in.6Then commeth Simon Peter following
him, and went into the Sepulchre, and ſeeth the linnen clothes lie,7And
the napkin that was about his head, not lying with the linnen clothes,
but wrapped together in a place by it ſelfe.8Then went in alſo that other
diſciple which came firſt to the Sepulchre, and he ſaw, and
beleeued.9For as yet they knew not the Scripture, that hee muſt riſe
againe from the dead.10Then the diſciples went away againe vnto their
owne home.11But Mary ſtood without at the ſepulchre, weeping: & as
ſhee wept, ſhe ſtouped downe, and looked into the Sepulchre,12And
ſeeth two Angels in white, ſitting, the one at the head, and the other at
the feete, where the body of Ieſus had layen:13And they ſay vnto her,
Woman, why weepeſt thou? Shee ſaith vnto them, Becauſe they haue
taken away my Lord, and I know not where they haue laied him.14And
when ſhe had thus ſaid, ſhe turned herſelfe backe, and ſaw Ieſus
ſtanding, and knew not that it was Ieſus.15Ieſus ſaith vnto her, Woman,
why weepeſt thou? whom ſeekeſt thou? She ſuppoſing him to be the
gardiner, ſaith vnto him, Sir, if thou haue borne him hence, tell me where
thou haſt laied him, and I will take him away.16Ieſus ſaith vnto her, Mary.
She turned herſelfe, and ſaith vnto him, Rabboni, which is to ſay,
Maſter.17Ieſus ſaith vnto her, Touch me not: for I am not yet aſcended
to my Father: but goe to my brethren, and ſay vnto them, I aſcend vnto
my Father, and your Father, and to my God, and your God.18Mary
Magdalene came and told the diſciples that ſhee had ſeene the Lord, and
that hee had ſpoken theſe things vnto her.19Then the ſame day at
euening, being the firſt day of the weeke, when the doores were ſhut,
where the diſciples were aſſembled for feare of the Iewes, came Ieſus,
and ſtood in the midſt, and ſaith vnto them, Peace bee vnto you.20And
when hee had ſo ſaide, hee ſhewed vnto them his hands and his ſide.
Then were the diſciples glad, when they ſaw the Lord.21Then ſaid Ieſus
to them againe, Peace be vnto you: As my Father hath ſent me, euen ſo
ſend I you.22And when he had ſaid this, hee breathed on them, and ſaith
vnto them, Receiue ye the holy Ghoſt.23Whoſe ſoeuer ſinnes yee remit,
they are remitted vnto them, and whoſe ſoeuer ſinnes yee retaine, they
are retained.24But Thomas one of the twelue, called Didymus, was not
with them when Ieſus came.25The other diſciples therefore ſaid vnto
him, We haue ſeene the Lord. But he ſaid vnto them, Except I ſhall ſee
in his hands the print of the nailes, and put my finger into the print of
the nailes, and thruſt my hand into his ſide, I will not beleeue.26And
after eight dayes, againe his diſciples were within, and Thomas with
them: Then came Ieſus, the doores being ſhut, and ſtood in the midſt,
and ſaid, Peace be vnto you.27Then ſaith he to Thomas Reach hither thy
finger, and beholde my hands, and reach hither thy hand, and thruſt it
into my ſide, and bee not faithleſſe, but beleeuing.28And Thomas
anſwered, and ſaid vnto him, My Lord, and my God.29Ieſus ſaith vnto
him, Thomas, becauſe thou haſt ſeene mee, thou haſt beleeued: bleſſed
are they that haue not ſeene, and yet haue beleeued.30And many other
ſignes truely did Ieſus in the preſence of his diſciples, which are not
written in this booke:31But theſe are written, that yee might beleeue that
Ieſus is the Chriſt the Sonne of God, and that beleeuing ye might haue
life through his Name.
CHAPTER 211After theſe things Ieſus ſhewed himſelfe againe to the
diſciples at the ſea of Tiberias, and on this wiſe ſhewed he
himſelfe.2There were together Simon Peter, and Thomas called
Didymus, and Nathaneel of Cana in Galilee, and the ſonnes of Zebedee,
and two other of his diſciples.3Simon Peter ſaith vnto them, I goe a
fiſhing. They ſay vnto him, Wee alſo goe with thee. They went foorth
and entred into a ſhip immediatly, and that night they caught
nothing.4But when the morning was now come, Ieſus ſtood on the
ſhore: but the diſciples knewe not that it was Ieſus.5Then Ieſus ſaith
vnto them, Children, haue ye any meat? They anſwered him, No.6And
he ſaid vnto them, Caſt the net on the right ſide of the ſhip, and yee ſhall
finde. They caſt therfore, and now they were not able to draw it, for the
multitude of fiſhes.7Therefore that Diſciple whome Ieſus loued, ſaith
vnto Peter, It is the Lord. Now when Simon Peter heard that it was the
Lord, he girt his fiſhers coate vnto him, (for hee was naked) & did caſt
himſelfe into the ſea.8And the other diſciples came in a litle ſhip (for
they were not farre from land, but as it were two hundred cubiteſ)
dragging the net with fiſhes.9Aſsoone then as they were come to land,
they ſaw a fire of coales there, and fiſh laid thereon, and bread.10Ieſus
ſaith vnto them, Bring of the fiſh, which ye haue now caught.11Simon
Peter went vp, & drewe the net to land full of great fiſhes, an hundred
and fiftie and three: and for all there were ſo many, yet was not the net
broken.12Ieſus ſaith vnto them, Come, and dine. And none of the
diſciples durſt aſke him, Who art thou? knowing that it was the
Lord.13Ieſus then commeth, and taketh bread, and giueth them, and fiſh
likewiſe.14This is nowe the third time that Ieſus ſhewed himſelfe to his
diſciples, after that hee was riſen from the dead.15So when they had
dined, Ieſus ſaith to Simon Peter, Simon, ſonne of Ionas, loueſt thou
mee more then theſe? He ſaith vnto him, Yea, Lord, thou knoweſt that
I loue thee. He ſaith vnto him, Feed my lambes.16He ſaith to him againe
the ſecond time, Simon ſonne of Ionas, loueſt thou me? He ſaith vnto
him, Yea Lord, thou knoweſt that I loue thee. He ſaith vnto him, Feed
my ſheepe.17He ſaid vnto him the third time, Simon ſonne of Ionas,
loueſt thou mee? Peter was grieued, becauſe hee ſaide vnto him the third
time, Loueſt thou me? And he ſaid vnto him, Lord, thou knoweſt all
things, thou knoweſt that I loue thee. Ieſus ſayth vnto him, Feed my
ſheepe.18Uerily, verily I ſay vnto thee, whē thou waſt yong, thou girdedſt
thy ſelfe, and walkedſt whither thou wouldeſt: but when thou ſhalt be
old, thou ſhalt ſtretch forth thy hands, and another ſhall gird thee, and
carie thee whither thou wouldeſt not.19This ſpake hee, ſignifying by
what death he ſhould glorifie God. And when he had ſpoken this, he
ſayth vnto him, Follow me.20Then Peter turning about, ſeeth the
Diſciple whom Ieſus loued, following, which alſo leaned on his breaſt
at ſupper, and ſaid, Lord, which is hee that betraieth thee?21Peter ſeeing
him, ſaith to Ieſus, Lord, and what ſhall this man doe?22Ieſus ſaith vnto
him, If I will that he tary till I come, what is that to thee? Follow thou
me.23Then went this ſaying abroad among the brethren, that that
Diſciple ſhould not die: yet Ieſus ſayd not vnto him, He ſhall not die:
but, If I will that he tary till I come, what is that to thee?24This is the
Diſciple which teſtifieth of theſe things, and wrote theſe things, and we
know that his teſtimonie is true.25And there are alſo many other things
which Ieſus did, the which if they ſhould be written euery one, I ſuppoſe
that euen the world it ſelfe could not conteine the bookes that ſhould
be written, Amen.

THE ACTES (ACTS)

CHAPTER 11The former treatiſe haue I made, O Theophilus, of al that
Ieſus began both to doe and teach,2Untill the day in which hee was taken
vp, after that he through the holy Ghoſt had giuen commaundements
vnto the Apoſtles, whom he had choſen.3To whom alſo he ſhewed
himſelfe aliue after his paſsion, by many infallible proofes, being ſeene
of them fourty dayes, and ſpeaking of the things perteining to the
kingdome of God:4And being aſſembled together with them,
commanded them that they ſhould not depart from Hieruſalem, but
wait for the promiſe of the Father, which, ſaith he, ye haue heard of
me.5For Iohn truely baptized with water, but ye ſhall be baptized with
the holy Ghoſt, not many dayes hence.6When they therefore were come
together, they aſked of him, ſaying, Lord, wilt thou at this time reſtore
againe the kingdome to Iſrael?7And he ſaid vnto them, It is not for you
to knowe the times or the ſeaſons, which the Father hath put in his owne
power.8But ye ſhall receiue power after that the holy Ghoſt is come
vpon you, and ye ſhall be witneſſes vnto me, both in Hieruſalem, and in
all Iudea, and in Samaria, and vnto the vttermoſt part of the earth.9And
when hee had ſpoken theſe things, while they beheld, hee was taken vp,

and a cloud receiued him out of their ſight.[10]And while they looked ſtedfaſtly toward heauen, as he went vp, behold, two men ſtood by them in white apparell,[11]Which alſo ſaid, Yee men of Galililee, why ſtand yee gazing vp into heauen? This ſame Ieſus, which is taken vp from you into heauen, ſhall ſo come, in like maner as yee haue ſeene him goe into heauen.[12]Then returned they vnto Hieruſalem, from the mount called Oliuet, which is from Hieruſalem a Sabbath dayes iourney.[13]And when they were come in, they went vp into an vpper roome, where abode both Peter & Iames, & Iohn, and Andrew, Philip, and Thomas, Bartholomew, and Matthew, Iames the ſonne of Alpheus, and Simon Zelotes, and Iudas the brother of Iames.[14]Theſe all continued with one accord in prayer and ſupplication, with the women, and Mary the mother of Ieſus, and with his brethen.[15]And in thoſe dayes Peter ſtood vp in the mids of the diſciples, and ſaid, (The number of names together were about an hundred and twentie)[16]Men and brethren, This Scripture muſt needs haue beene fulfilled, which the holy Ghoſt by the mouth of Dauid ſpake before concerning Iudas, which was guide to them þ^t took Ieſus.[17]For hee was numbred with vs, and had obtained part of this miniſterie.[18]Now this man purchaſed a field with the reward of iniquity, and falling headlong, he burſt aſunder in the mids, and all his bowels guſhed out.[19]And it was knowen vnto all the dwellers at Hieruſalem, inſomuch as that field is called in their proper tongue, Aceldama, that is to ſay, The field of blood.[20]For it is written in the booke of Pſalmes, Let his habitation be deſolate, and let no man dwell therein: And his Biſhopricke let another take.[21]Wherefore of theſe men which haue companied with vs all the time that the Lord Ieſus went in and out among vs,[22]Beginning from the baptiſme of Iohn, vnto that ſame day that he was taken vp from vs, muſt one be ordained to be a witneſſe with vs of his reſurrection.[23]And they appointed two, Ioſeph called Barſabas, who was ſurnamed Iuſtus, and Matthias.[24]And they prayed, and ſaid, Thou Lord, which knoweſt the hearts of all men, ſhew whether of theſe two thou haſt choſen,[25]That hee may take part of this miniſterie and Apoſtleſhip, from which Iudas by tranſgreſſion fell, that hee might goe to his owne place.[26]And they gaue foorth their lots, and the lot fell vpon Matthias, and hee was numbred with the eleuen Apoſtles.

CHAPTER 2[1]And when the day of Pentecoſt was fully come, they were all with one accord in one place.[2]And ſuddenly there came a ſound from heauen as of a ruſhing mighty wind, and it filled all the houſe where they were ſitting.[3]And there appeared vnto them clouen tongues, like as of fire, and it ſate vpon each of them.[4]And they were all filled with the holy Ghoſt, and began to ſpeake with other tongues, as the ſpirit gaue them vtterance.[5]And there were dwelling at Hieruſalem Iewes, deuout men, out of euery nation vnder heauen.[6]Now when this was noiſed abroad, the multitude came together, and were confounded, becauſe that euery man heard them ſpeake in his owne language.[7]And they were all amazed, and marueiled, ſaying one to another, Behold, are not all theſe which ſpeake, Galileans?[8]And how heare we euery man in our owne tongue, wherein we were borne?[9]Parthians, and Medes, and Elamites, and the dwellers in Meſopotamia, and in Iudea, and Cappadocia, in Pontus, and Aſia,[10]Phrygia, and Pamphylia, in Egypt, and in the parts of Libya, about Cyrene, & ſtrangers of Rome, Iewes and Proſelites,[11]Cretes, and Arabians, we doe heare them ſpeake in our tongues the wonderfull workes of God.[12]And they were all amazed, and were in doubt, ſaying one to another, What meaneth this?[13]Others mocking ſaid, Theſe men are full of new wine.[14]But Peter ſtanding vp with the eleuen, lift vp his voyce, and ſaid vnto them, Ye men of Iudea, & all ye that dwell at Hieruſalem, be this knowen vnto you, and hearken to my words:[15]For theſe are not drunken, as ye ſuppoſe, ſeeing it is but the third houre of the day.[16]But this is that which was ſpoken by the Prophet Ioel,[17]And it ſhall come to paſſe in the laſt dayes (ſaith God) I will powre out of my Spirit vpon all fleſh: and your ſonnes and your daughters ſhall propheſie, and your yong men ſhall ſee viſions, and your old men ſhall dreame dreames:[18]And on my ſeruants, and on my handmaidens, I will powre out in thoſe daies of my Spirit, and they ſhall propheſie:[19]And I wil ſhew wonders in heauen aboue, and ſignes in the earth beneath: blood, and fire, and vapour of ſmoke.[20]The Sunne ſhall be turned into darkeneſſe, and the Moone into blood, before that great and notable day of the Lord come.[21]And it ſhall come to paſſe, that whoſoeuer ſhall call on the Name of the Lord, ſhalbe ſaued.[22]Yee men of Iſrael, heare theſe words, Ieſus of Nazareth, a man approued of God among you, by miracles, wonders, and ſignes, which God did by him in the midſt of you, as yee your ſelues alſo know:[23]Him, being deliuered by the determinate counſell and foreknowledge of God, yee haue taken, and by wicked hands, haue crucified, and ſlaine:[24]Whom God hath raiſed vp, hauing looſed the paines of death: becauſe it was not poſsible that hee ſhould be holden of it.[25]For Dauid ſpeaketh concerning him, I foreſaw the Lord alwayes before my face, for he is on my right hand, that I ſhould not be moued.[26]Therefore did my heart reioyce, and my tongue was glad: Moreouer alſo, my fleſh ſhall reſt in hope,[27]Becauſe thou wilt not leaue my ſoule in hell, neither wilt thou ſuffer thine Holy one to ſee corruption.[28]Thou haſt made knowen to mee the wayes of life, thou ſhalt make mee full of ioy with thy countenance.[29]Men and brethren, let me freely ſpeake vnto you of the Patriarch Dauid, that he is both dead & buried, and his ſepulchre is with vs vnto this day:[30]Therefore being a Prophet, and knowing that God had ſworne with an oath to him, that of the fruit of his loines, according to the fleſh, hee would raiſe vp Chriſt, to ſit on his throne:[31]He ſeeing this before, ſpake of the reſurrection of Chriſt, that his ſoule was not left in hell, neither his fleſh did ſee corruption.[32]This Ieſus hath God raiſed vp, whereof we all are witneſſes.[33]Therefore being by the right hand of God exalted, and hauing receiued of the Father the promiſe of the holy Ghoſt, he hath ſhed forth this, which ye now ſee and heare.[34]For Dauid is not aſcended into the heauens, but he ſaith himſelfe, The Lord ſaid vnto my Lord, Sit thou on my right hand,[35]Untill I make thy foes thy footſtoole.[36]Therefore let all the houſe of Iſrael know aſsuredly, that God hath made that ſame Ieſus, whom ye haue crucified, both Lord and Chriſt.[37]Now when they heard this, they were pricked in their heart, and ſaid vnto Peter, and to the reſt of the Apoſtles, Men and brethren, What ſhall we doe?[38]Then Peter ſaid vnto them, Repent, and be baptized euery one of you in the Name of Ieſus Chriſt, for the remiſsion of ſinnes, and ye ſhal receiue the gift of the holy Ghoſt.[39]For the promiſe is vnto you, and to your children, and to all that are afarre off, euen as many as the Lord our God ſhall call.[40]And with many other words did hee teſtifie and exhort, ſaying, Saue your ſelues from this vntoward generation.[41]Then they that gladly receiued his word, were baptized: and the ſame day there were added vnto them about three thouſand ſoules.[42]And they continued ſtedfaſtly in the Apoſtles doctrine and fellowſhip, and in breaking of bread, and in praiers.[43]And feare came vpon euery ſoule: and many wonders and ſignes were done by the Apoſtles.[44]And all that beleeued were together, and had all things common,[45]And ſolde their poſſeſſions and goods, and parted them to all men, as euery man had need.[46]And they continuing daily with one accord in the Temple, and breaking bread from houſe to houſe, did eat their meat with gladneſſe and ſingleneſse of heart,[47]Praiſing God, and hauing fauour with all the people. And the Lord added to the Church dayly ſuch as ſhould be ſaued.

CHAPTER 3[1]Nowe Peter and Iohn went vp together into the Temple at the houre of prayer, beeing the ninth houre.[2]And a certaine man lame from his mothers womb was caried, whom they laide daily at the gate of the Temple which is called Beautifull, to aſke almes of them that entred into the Temple.[3]Who ſeeing Peter & Iohn about to go into the Temple, aſked an almes.[4]And Peter faſtening his eyes vpon him, with Iohn, ſaid, Looke on vs.[5]And he gaue heede vnto them, expecting to receiue ſomething of them.[6]Then Peter ſaid, ſiluer and gold haue I none, but ſuch as I haue, giue I thee: In the Name of Ieſus Chriſt of Nazareth, riſe vp and walke.[7]And hee tooke him by the right hand, & lift him vp: aud immediatly his feete and ancle bones receiued ſtrength.[8]And hee leaping vp, ſtood, and walked, and entred with them into the Temple, walking, and leaping, and praiſing God.[9]And all the people ſaw him walking, and praiſing God.[10]And they knew that it was hee which ſate for almes at the beautifull gate of the Temple: and they were filled with wonder and amazement at that which had happened vnto him.[11]And as the lame man which was healed, helde Peter and Iohn, all the people ranne together vnto them in the porch, that is called Solomons, greatly wondring.[12]And when Peter ſawe it, hee anſwered vnto the people, Yee men of Iſrael, why marueile ye at this? or why looke yee ſo earneſtly on vs, as though by our owne power or holineſſe we had made this man to walke?[13]The God of Abraham, and of Iſaac, and of Iacob, the God of our fathers hath glorified his ſonne Ieſus, whom ye deliuered vp, and

denied him in the preſence of Pilate, when hee was determined to let
him goe.14But ye denied the Holy one, and the Iuſt, and deſired a
murderer to be granted vnto you,15And killed the Prince of life, whom
God hath raiſed from the dead, whereof we are witneſſes.16And his
Name through faith in his Name hath made this man ſtrong, whom ye
ſee and know: yea, the faith which is by him, hath giuen him this perfect
ſoundneſse in the preſence of you all.17And now brethren, I wote that
through ignorance yee did it, as did alſo your rulers.18But thoſe things
which God before had ſhewed by the mouth of all his Prophets, that
Chriſt ſhould ſuffer, hee hath ſo fulfilled.19Repent yee therefore, and
bee conuerted, that your ſins may be blotted out, when the times of
refreſhing ſhal come from the preſence of the Lord.20And hee ſhall ſend
Ieſus Chriſt, which before was preached vnto you.21Whom the heauen
muſt receiue, vntill the times of reſtitution of all things, which God hath
ſpoken by the mouth of all his holy Prophets ſince the world
began.22For Moſes truely ſaid vnto the fathers, A Prophet ſhall the Lord
your God raiſe vp vnto you of your brethren, like vnto me; him ſhall yee
heare in all things whatſoeuer he ſhal ſay vnto you.23And it ſhall come
to paſſe, that euery ſoule which will not heare that Prophet, ſhalbe
deſtroyed from among the people.24Yea and all the Prophets from
Samuel, and thoſe that follow after, as many as haue ſpoken, haue
likewiſe foretold of theſe dayes.25Yee are the children of the Prophets,
and of the couenant which God made with our fathers, ſaying vnto
Abraham, And in thy ſeed ſhall all the kinreds of the earth be
bleſſed.26Unto you firſt, God hauing raiſed vp his Sonne Ieſus, ſent him
to bleſſe you, in turning away euery one of you from his iniquities.
CHAPTER 41And as they ſpake vnto the people, the Prieſts and the
captaine of the Temple, and the Sadduces came vpon them,2Being
grieued that they taught the people, and preached through Ieſus the
reſurrection from the dead.3And they laid hands on them, and put them
in hold vnto the next day: for it was now euentide.4Howbeit, many of
them which heard the word, beleeued, and the number of the men was
about fiue thouſand.5And it came to paſſe on the morow, that their
rulers, and Elders, and Scribes,6And Annas the high Prieſt, and Caiphas,
and Iohn, and Alexander, and as many as were of the kinred of the high
Prieſt, were gathered together at Hieruſalem.7And when they had ſet
them in the middeſt, they aſked, By what power, or by what name haue
ye done this?8Then Peter filled with the holy Ghoſt, ſaid vnto them, Ye
rulers of the people, and Elders of Iſrael,9If we this day be examined of
the good deed done to the impotent man, by what meanes he is made
whole,10Be it knowen vnto you all, and to all the people of Iſrael, that
by the Name of Ieſus Chriſt of Nazareth, whom ye crucified, whome
God raiſed from the dead, euen by him, doeth this man ſtand here
before you, whole.11This is the ſtone which was ſet at nought of you
builders, which is become the head of the corner.12Neither is there
ſaluation in any other: for there is none other name vnder heauen giuen
among men whereby we muſt be ſaued.13Now when they ſawe the
boldneſse of Peter and Iohn, and perceiued that they were vnlearned
and ignorant men, they marueiled, and they tooke knowledge of them,
that they had bene with Ieſus.14And beholding the man which was
healed, ſtanding with them, they could ſay nothing againſt it.15But when
they had commanded them to go aſide out of the Council, they
conferred among themſelues,16Saying, What ſhall we do to theſe men?
for that indeed a notable miracle hath bene done by them, is manifeſt to
all them that dwell in Hieruſalem, and we cannot denie it.17But that it
ſpread no farther among the people, let vs ſtraitly threaten them, that
they ſpeake henceforth to no man in this Name.18And they called them,
and commanded them, not to ſpeake at all, nor teach in the Name of
Ieſus.19But Peter and Iohn anſwered, and ſaid vnto them, Whether it be
right in the ſight of God, to hearken vnto you more then vnto God,
iudge ye.20For wee cannot but ſpeake the things which we haue ſeene
and heard.21So when they had further threatned them, they let them goe,
finding nothing how they might puniſh them, becauſe of the people: for
all men glorified God for that which was done.22For the man was aboue
fourtie yeeres olde, on whome this miracle of healing was ſhewed.23And
being let goe, they went to their owne company, and reported all that
the chiefe Prieſts and Elders had ſaid vnto them.24And when they heard
that, they lift vp their voyce to God with one accord, & ſaid, Lord, thou
art God which haſt made heauen and earth, and the ſea, and all that in
them is,25Who by the mouth of thy ſeruant Dauid haſt ſaide, Why did
the heathen rage, and the people imagine vaine things?26The Kings of
the earth ſtood vp, and the rulers were gathered together againſt the
Lord, & againſt his Chriſt.27For of a trueth againſt thy holy child Ieſus,
whom thou haſt anointed, both Herod, and Pontius Pilate, with the
Gentiles, and the people of Iſrael were gathered together,28For to doe
whatſoeuer thy hand and thy counſell determined before to be
done.29And now Lord, behold their threatnings, and graunt vnto thy
ſeruants, that with all boldneſse they may ſpeake thy word,30By
ſtretching foorth thine hand to heale: and that ſignes and wonders may
be done by the Name of thy holy child Ieſus.31And when they had
prayed, the place was ſhaken where they were aſſembled together, and
they were all filled with the holy Ghoſt, and they ſpake the word of God
with boldneſse.32And the multitude of them that beleeued, were of one
heart, and of one ſoule: Neither ſaid any of them, that ought of the
things which he poſſeſſed, was his owne, but they had all things
common.33And with great power gaue the Apoſtles witneſſe of the
reſurrection of the Lord Ieſus, and great grace was vpon them
all.34Neither was there any among them that lacked: For as many as were
poſseſsors of lands, or houſes, ſold them, and brought the prices of the
things that were ſolde,35And laide them downe at the Apoſtles feete:
And diſtribution was made vnto euery man according as hee had
neede.36And Ioſes, who by the Apoſtles was ſurnamed Barnabas (which
is, being interpreted, The ſonne of conſolation) a Leuite, and of the
Countrey of Cyprus,37Hauing land, ſold it, and brought the money, &
laid it at the Apoſtles feet.
CHAPTER 51But a certaine man named Ananias, with Sapphira his
wife, ſolde a poſſeſſion,2And kept backe part of the price, his wife alſo
being priuy to it, and brought a certaine part, and layd it at the Apoſtles
feete.3But Peter ſaid, Ananias, Why hath Satan filled thine heart to lie to
the holy Ghoſt, and to keepe backe part of the price of the land?4Whiles
it remained, was it not thine owne? and after it was ſold, was it not in
thine owne power? why haſt thou conceiued this thing in thine heart?
thou haſt not lied vnto men, but vnto God.5And Ananias hearing theſe
words, fell downe, and gaue vp the ghoſt: and great feare came on all
them that heard theſe things.6And the yong men aroſe, wound him vp,
and caried him out, and buried him.7And it was about the ſpace of three
houres after, when his wife, not knowing what was done, came in.8And
Peter anſwered vnto her, Tell me whether ye ſold the land for ſo much.
And ſhe ſaide, Yea, for ſo much.9Then Peter ſaide vnto her, How is it
that ye haue agreed together, to tempt the Spirit of the Lord? behold,
the feete of them which haue buried thy huſband, are at the doore, and
ſhall cary thee out.10Then fell ſhe downe ſtraightway at his feete, and
yeelded vp the ghoſt: And the yong men came in, and found her dead,
and carying her forth, buried her by her huſband.11And great feare came
vpon all the Church, and vpon as many as heard theſe things.12And by
the hands of the Apoſtles, were many ſignes and wonders wrought
among the people. (And they were all with one accord in Solomons
porch.13And of the reſt durſt no man ioyne himſelfe to them: But the
people magnified them.14And beleeuers were the more added to the
Lord, multitudes both of men and women.)15Inſomuch þt they brought
foorth the ſicke into the ſtreetes, and layed them on beds and couches,
that at the leaſt the ſhadow of Peter paſsing by, might ouerſhadow ſome
of them.16There came alſo a multitude out of the cities round about
vnto Hieruſalem, bringing ſicke folkes, and them which were vexed with
vncleane ſpirits: and they were healed euery one.17Then the high Prieſt
roſe vp, and al they that were with him, (which is the ſect of the
Sadduceſ) and were filled with indignation,18And laid their hands on the
Apoſtles, & put them in the common priſon.19But the Angel of the Lord
by night opened the priſon doores, and brought them foorth, and
ſaid,20Goe, ſtand and ſpeake in the Temple to the people all the words
of this life.21And when they heard that, they entred into the Temple early
in the morning, & taught: but the high Prieſt came, and they that were
with him, and called the Councill together, and all the Senate of the
children of Iſrael, and ſent to the priſon to haue them brought.22But
when the officers came, and found them not in the priſon, they returned,
and told,23Saying, The priſon truely found we ſhut with all ſafety, and
the keepers ſtanding without before the doores, but when we had
opened, we found no man within.24Now when the high Prieſt, and the
captaine of the Temple, and the chiefe Prieſts heard theſe things, they
doubted of them wherunto this would grow.25Then came one, and told

them, ſaying, Behold, the men whom ye put in priſon, are ſtanding in
the Temple, and teaching the people.26Then went the captaine with the
officers, and brought them without violence: (For they feared the
people, leſt they ſhould haue bene ſtoned.)27And when they had brought
them, they ſet them before the Councill, and the high Prieſt aſked
them,28Saying, Did not wee ſtraitly command you, that you ſhould not
teach in this Name? And behold, yee haue filled Hieruſalem with your
doctrine, and intend to bring this mans blood vpon vs.29Then Peter, and
the other Apoſtles anſwered, and ſaide, Wee ought to obey God rather
then men.30The God of our fathers raiſed vp Ieſus, whom yee ſlew and
hanged on a tree.31Him hath God exalted with his right hand to bee a
Prince and a Sauiour, for to giue repentance to Iſrael, and forgiueneſse
of ſinnes.32And we are his witneſſes of theſe things, and ſo is alſo the
holy Ghoſt, whom God hath giuen to them that obey him.33When they
heard that, they were cut to the heart, and tooke counſell to ſlay
them.34Then ſtood there vp one in the Councill, a PhAriſee, named
Gamaliel, a doctour of Law, had in reputation among all the people, and
commanded to put the Apoſtles forth a litle ſpace,35And ſaid vnto them,
Yee men of Iſrael, take heed to your ſelues, what ye intend to doe as
touching theſe men.36For before theſe dayes roſe vp Theudas, boaſting
himſelfe to be ſome body, to whom a number of men, about foure
hundred, ioyned themſelues: who was ſlaine, and all, as many as obeied
him, were ſcattered, & brought to nought.37After this man roſe vp Iudas
of Galilee, in the dayes of the taxing, and drew away much people after
him: hee alſo periſhed, and all, euen as many as obeyed him, were
diſperſed.38And now I ſay vnto you, refraine from theſe men, and let
them alone: for if this counſell or this worke be of men, it will come to
nought.39But if it be of God, ye cannot ouerthrow it, leſt haply yee be
found euen to fight againſt God.40And to him they agreed: and when
they had called the Apoſtles, and beaten them, they commanded that
they ſhould not ſpeake in the Name of Ieſus, and let them goe.41And
they departed from the preſence of the Councill, reioycing that they
were counted worthy to ſuffer ſhame for his Name.42And dayly in the
Temple, and in euery houſe, they ceaſed not to teach and preach Ieſus
Chriſt.
CHAPTER 61And in thoſe dayes when the number of the Diſciples
was multiplied, there aroſe a murmuring of the Grecians againſt the
Hebrewes, becauſe their widowes were neglected in the daily
miniſtration.2Then the twelue called the multitude of the diſciples vnto
them, and ſaid, It is not reaſon that we ſhould leaue the word of God,
and ſerue tables.3Wherefore brethren, looke ye out among you ſeuen
men of honeſt report, full of the holy Ghoſt, and wiſedome, whom we
may appoint ouer this buſineſse.4But we will giue our ſelues continually
to prayer, and to the miniſterie of the word.5And the ſaying pleaſed the
whole multitude: and they choſe Steuen, a man full of faith and of the
holy Ghoſt, and Philip, and Prochorus, and Nicanor, and Timon, and
Permenas, and Nicolas a proſelyte of Antioch.6Whom they ſet before
the Apoſtles: and when they had praied, they layd their hands on
them.7And the word of God encreaſed, and the number of the Diſciples
multiplied in Hieruſalem greatly, and a great company of the Prieſts were
obedient to the faith.8And Steuen full of faith and power, did great
wonders and miracles among the people.9Then there aroſe certaine of
the Synagogue, which is called the Synagogue of the Libertines, and
Cyrenians, and Alexandrians, and of them of Cilicia, and of Aſia,
diſputing with Steuen.10And they were not able to reſiſt the wiſedome
and the ſpirit by which he ſpake.11Then they ſuborned men which ſaid,
We haue heard him ſpeake blaſphemous words againſt Moſes, and
againſt God.12And they ſtirred vp the people, and the Elders, and the
Scribes, and came vpon him, and caught him, and brought him to the
Councell,13And ſet vp falſe witneſſes, which ſaid, This man ceaſeth not
to ſpeake blaſphemous words againſt this holy place, and the Law.14For
we haue heard him ſay, that this Ieſus of Nazareth ſhall deſtroy this
place, & ſhall change the Cuſtomes which Moſes deliuered vs.15And all
that ſate in the Councell, looking ſtedfaſtly on him, ſaw his face as it had
bene the face of an Angel.
CHAPTER 71Then ſaid the high Prieſt, Are theſe things ſo?2And hee
ſaid, Men, brethren, and fathers, hearken: The God of glory appeared
vnto our father Abraham, when he was in Meſopotamia, before he dwelt
in Charran,3And ſaid vnto him, Get thee out of thy countrey, and from
thy kinred, and come into the land which I ſhall ſhew thee.4Then came
he out of the land of the Chaldeans, and dwelt in Charran: and from
thence, when his father was dead, he remoued him into this lande
wherein ye now dwell.5And he gaue him none inheritance in it, no not
ſo much as to ſet his foote on: yet he promiſed that he would giue it to
him for a poſſeſſion, and to his ſeed after him, when as yet he had no
child.6And God ſpake on this wiſe, that his ſeede ſhould ſoiourne in a
ſtrange land, and that they ſhould bring them into bondage, and intreate
them euill foure hundreth yeeres.7And the nation to whom they ſhal bee
in bondage, will I iudge, ſaide God: And after that ſhall they come forth,
and ſerue me in this place.8And he gaue him the couenant of
Circumciſion: and ſo Abraham begate Iſaac, and circumciſed him the
eight day: and Iſaac begate Iacob, and Iacob begate the twelue
Patriarchs.9And the Patriarchs moued with enuie, ſold Ioſeph into
Egypt: but God was with him,10And deliuered him out of all his
afflictions, and gaue him fauour and wiſedome in the ſight of Pharao
king of Egypt: and he made him gouernour ouer Egypt and all his
houſe.11Now there came a dearth ouer all the land of Egypt, and
Chanaan, and great affliction, and our fathers found no ſuſtenance.12But
when Iacob heard that there was corne in Egypt, he ſent out our fathers
firſt.13And at the ſecond time Ioſeph was made knowen to his brethren,
and Ioſephs kinred was made knowen vnto Pharao.14Then ſent Ioſeph,
and called his father Iacob to him, and all his kinred, threeſcore and
fifteeene ſoules.15So Iacob went downe into Egypt, and died, he and our
fathers,16And were caried ouer into Sichem, and laid in the ſepulchre
that Abraham bought for a ſumme of money of the ſonnes of Emor the
father of Sichem.17But when the time of the promiſe drew nigh, which
God had ſworne to Abraham, the people grew and multiplied in
Egypt,18Till another king aroſe, which knew not Ioſeph.19The ſame
dealt ſubtilly with our kinred, and euill intreated our fathers, ſo that they
caſt out their yong children, to the end they might not liue.20In which
time Moſes was borne, and was exceeding faire, and nouriſhed vp in his
fathers houſe three moneths:21And when he was caſt out, Pharaohs
daughter tooke him vp, and nouriſhed him for her owne ſonne.22And
Moſes was learned in all the wiſedome of the Egyptians, and was mightie
in words and in deeds.23And when he was full forty yeres old, it came
into his heart to viſit his brethren the children of Iſrael.24And ſeeing one
of them ſuffer wrong, he defended him, and auenged him that was
oppreſſed, and ſmote the Egyptian:25For he ſuppoſed his brethren
would haue vnderſtood, how that God by his hand would deliuer them,
but they vnderſtood not.26And the next day he ſhewed himſelfe vnto
them as they ſtroue, and would haue ſet them at one againe, ſaying, Sirs,
ye are brethren, Why doe yee wrong one to another?27But hee that did
his neighbour wrong, thruſt him away, ſaying, Who made thee a ruler
and a Iudge ouer vs?28Wilt thou kill me, as thou diddeſt the Egyptian
yeſterday?29Then fled Moſes at this ſaying, and was a ſtranger in the land
of Madian, where he begate two ſonnes.30And when fourtie yeeres were
expired, there appeared to him in the wildernes of mount Sina, an Angel
of the Lord in a flame of fire in a buſh.31When Moſes ſaw it, he wondred
at the ſight: and as he drew neere to behold it, the voyce of the Lord
came vnto him,32Saying, I am the God of thy fathers, the God of
Abraham, and the God of Iſaac, and the God of Iacob. Then Moſes
trembled, and durſt not behold.33Then ſaid the Lord to him, Put off thy
ſhooes from thy feet: for the place where thou ſtandeſt, is holy
ground.34I haue ſeene, I haue ſeene the affliction of my people which is
in Egypt, and I haue heard their groning, & am come downe to deliuer
them: And now come, I will ſend thee into Egypt.35This Moſes whom
they refuſed, ſaying, Who made thee a ruler and a Iudge? the ſame did
God ſend to bee a ruler and a deliuerer, by the handes of the Angel
which appeared to him in the buſh.36He brought them out, after that he
had ſhewed wonders and ſignes in the land of Egypt, and in the red ſea,
and in the wilderneſſe fortie yeeres.37This is that Moſes which ſaid vnto
the children of Iſrael, A Prophet ſhall the Lord your God raiſe vp vnto
you of your brethren, like vnto mee: him ſhall ye heare.38This is he that
was in þe Church in the wilderneſſe with the Angel, which ſpake to him
in the mount Sina, and with our fathers: who receiued the liuely oracles,
to giue vnto vs.39To whom our fathers would not obey, but thruſt him
from them, and in their hearts turned backe againe into Egypt,40Saying
vnto Aaron, Make vs gods to goe before vs. For as for this Moſes, which
brought vs out of the land of Egypt, we wote not what is become of

him. 41 And they made a calfe in thoſe dayes, and offered ſacrifice vnto
the idole, and reioyced in the workes of their owne hands. 42 Then God
turned, and gaue them vp to worſhip the hoſte of heauen, as it is written
in the booke of the Prophets, O ye houſe of Iſrael, haue ye offered to
me ſlaine beaſts, and ſacrifices, by the ſpace of fourty yeeres in the
wilderneſſe? 43 Yea, ye tooke vp the Tabernacle of Moloch, and the ſtarre
of your God Remphan, figures which ye made, to worſhip them: and I
will carie you away beyond Babylon. 44 Our fathers had the Tabernacle
of witneſſe in the wilderneſſe, as hee had appointed, ſpeaking vnto
Moſes, that he ſhould make it according to the faſhion that he had
ſeene. 45 Which alſo our fathers that came after, brought in with Ieſus
into the poſſeſſion of the Gentiles, whom God draue out before the
face of our fathers, vnto the dayes of Dauid, 46 Who found fauour before
God, and deſired to find a Tabernacle for the God of Iacob. 47 But
Solomon built him an houſe. 48 Howbeit the moſt high dwelleth not in
temples made with hands, as ſaith the Prophet, 49 Heauen is my throne,
and earth is my footeſtoole: What houſe will ye build me, ſaith the Lord?
Or what is the place of my reſt? 50 Hath not my hand made all theſe
things? 51 Ye ſtifnecked and vncircumciſed in heart, and eares, ye doe
alwayes reſiſt the holy Ghoſt? as your fathers did, ſo doe ye. 52 Which of
the Prophets haue not your fathers perſecuted? And they haue ſlaine
them which ſhewed before of the comming of the Iuſt one, of whom ye
haue bene now the betrayers and murderers: 53 Who haue receiued the
Lawe by the diſpoſition of Angels, and haue not kept it. 54 When they
heard theſe things, they were cut to the heart, and they gnaſhed on him
with their teeth. 55 But hee being full of the holy Ghoſt, looked vp
ſtedfaſtly into heauen, and ſaw the glory of God, and Ieſus ſtanding on
the right hand of God, 56 And ſaid, Behold, I ſee the heauens opened,
and the Sonne of man ſtanding on the right hand of God. 57 Then they
cried out with a loud voice, and ſtopped their eares, and ran vpon him
with one accord, 58 And caſt him out of the citie, and ſtoned him: and
the witneſſes layd downe their clothes at a yong mans feete, whoſe name
was Saul. 59 And they ſtoned Steuen, calling vpon God, and ſaying, Lord
Ieſus receiue my ſpirit. 60 And he kneeled downe, and cried with a loud
voice, Lord lay not this ſinne to their charge. And when he had ſaid this,
he fell aſleepe.
CHAPTER 8 1 And Saul was conſenting vnto his death. And at that time
there was a great perſecution againſt the Church which was at
Hieruſalem, and they were all ſcattered abroad through out the regions
of Iudea, and Samaria, except the Apoſtles. 2 And deuout men carried
Steuen to his buriall, and made great lamentation ouer him. 3 As for Saul,
he made hauocke of the Church, entring into euery houſe, and hailing
men and women, committed them to priſon. 4 Therefore they that were
ſcattered abroad, went euery where preaching the word. 5 Then Philip
went downe to the citie of Samaria, and preached Chriſt vnto
them. 6 And the people with one accord gaue heed vnto thoſe things
which Philip ſpake, hearing and ſeeing the miracles which he did. 7 For
vncleane ſpirits, crying with lowd voyce, came out of many that were
poſſeſſed with them: and many taken with palſies, and that were lame,
were healed. 8 And there was great ioy in that citie. 9 But there was a
certaine man called Simon, which before time in the ſame citie vſed
ſorcery, and bewitched the people of Samaria, giuing out that himſelfe
was ſome great one. 10 To whom they all gaue heed from the leaſt to the
greateſt, ſaying, This man is the great power of God. 11 And to him they
had regard, becauſe that of long time he had bewitched them with
ſorceries. 12 But when they beleeued Philip preaching the things
concerning the kingdome of God, and the Name of Ieſus Chriſt, they
were baptized, both men and women. 13 Then Simon himſelfe beleeued
alſo: and when hee was baptized, hee continued with Philip, and
wondered, beholding the miracles and ſignes which were done. 14 Now
when the Apoſtles which were at Hieruſalem, heard that Samaria had
receiued the word of God, they ſent vnto them Peter and Iohn. 15 Who
when they were come downe, praied for them that they might receiue
the holy Ghoſt. 16 (For as yet hee was fallen vpon none of them: onely
they were baptized in the Name of the Lord Ieſus.) 17 Then layde they
their hands on them, and they receiued the holy Ghoſt. 18 And when
Simon ſaw that through laying on of the Apoſtles hands, the holy Ghoſt
was giuen, hee offered them money, 19 Saying, Giue me alſo this power,
that on whomſoeuer I lay handes, hee may receiue the holy Ghoſt. 20 But
Peter ſaid vnto him, Thy money periſh with thee, becauſe thou haſt
thought that the gift of God may be purchaſed with money. 21 Thou haſt
neither part nor lot in this matter, for thy heart is not right in the ſight
of God. 22 Repent therefore of this thy wickedneſſe, and pray God, if
perhaps the thought of thine heart may be forgiuen thee. 23 For I perceiue
that thou art in the gall of bitterneſse, and in the bond of
iniquitie. 24 Then anſwered Simon, and ſaid, Pray ye to the Lord for mee,
that none of theſe things which ye haue ſpoken, come vpon me. 25 And
they, when they had teſtified and preached the word of the Lord,
returned to Hieruſalem, and preached the Goſpel in many villages of the
Samaritanes. 26 And the Angel of the Lord ſpake vnto Philip, ſaying,
Ariſe, and goe toward the South, vnto the way that goeth downe from
Hieruſalem vnto Gaza, which is deſert. 27 And hee aroſe, and went: and
behold, a man of Ethiopia, an Eunuch of great authority vnder Candace
queene of the Ethiopians, who had the charge of all her treaſure, and
had come to Hieruſalem for to worſhip, 28 Was returning, and ſitting in
his charet, read Eſaias the Prophet. 29 Then the Spirit ſaide vnto Philip,
Goe neere, and ioyne thy ſelfe to this charet. 30 And Philip ran thither to
him, and heard him reade the Prophet Eſaias, and ſaid, Underſtandeſt
thou what thou readeſt? 31 And hee ſaid, How can I, except ſome man
ſhould guide me? And he deſired Philip, that hee would come vp, and
ſit with him. 32 The place of the Scripture, which hee read, was this, Hee
was led as a ſheepe to the ſlaughter, & like a Lambe dumbe before the
ſhearer, ſo opened he not his mouth: 33 In his humiliation, his Iudgement
was taken away: and who ſhall declare his generation? For his life is
taken from the earth. 34 And the Eunuch anſwered Philip, and ſaid, I pray
thee, of whom ſpeaketh the Prophet this? of himſelfe, or of ſome other
man? 35 Then Philip opened his mouth, and began at the ſame Scripture,
and preached vnto him Ieſus. 36 And as they went on their way, they came
vnto a certaine water: and the Eunuch ſaid, See, here is water, what
doeth hinder me to be baptized? 37 And Philip ſaid, If thou beleeueſt with
all thine heart, thou mayeſt. And he anſwered, and ſaid, I beleeue that
Ieſus Chriſt is the Sonne of God. 38 And he commanded the charet to
ſtand ſtill: and they went downe both into the water, both Philip, and
the Eunuch, and he baptized him. 39 And when they were come vp out
of the water, the Spirit of the Lord caught away Philip, that the Eunuch
ſaw him no more: and hee went on his way reioycing. 40 But Philip was
found at Azotus: and paſsing thorow he preached in all the cities, till he
came to Ceſarea.
CHAPTER 9 1 And Saul yet breathing out threatnings & ſlaughter
againſt the diſciples of the Lord, went vnto the high Prieſt, 2 And deſired
of him letters to Damaſcus, to the Synagogues, that if hee found any of
this way, whether they were men or women, hee might bring them
bound vnto Hieruſalem. 3 And as he iourneyed he came neere Damaſcus,
and ſuddenly there ſhined round about him a light from heauen. 4 And
he fel to the earth, and heard a voice ſaying vnto him, Saul, Saul, why
perſecuteſt thou me? 5 And he ſaid, Who art thou Lord? And the Lord
ſaid, I am Ieſus whom thou perſecuteſt: It is hard for thee to kicke
againſt the prickes. 6 And he trembling and aſtoniſhed, ſaid, Lord, what
wilt thou haue mee to doe? And the Lord ſaid vnto him, Ariſe, and goe
into the citie, and it ſhall be told thee what thou muſt doe. 7 And the men
which iourneyed with him, ſtood ſpeechleſſe, hearing a voice, but ſeeing
no man. 8 And Saul aroſe from the earth, and when his eyes were opened,
he ſaw no man: but they led him by the hand, and brought him into
Damaſcus. 9 And he was three dayes without ſight, and neither did eate,
nor drinke. 10 And there was a certaine diſciple at Damaſcus, named
Ananias, and to him ſaid the Lord in a viſion, Ananias. And he ſaid,
Behold, I am here, Lord. 11 And the Lord ſaid vnto him, Ariſe, and goe
into the ſtreet, which is called Straight, and inquire in the houſe of Iudas,
for one called Saul of Tarſus: for behold, he prayeth, 12 And hath ſeene
in a viſion a man named Ananias, comming in, and putting his hand on
him, that he might receiue his ſight. 13 Then Ananias anſwered, Lord, I
haue heard by many of this man, how much euill hee hath done to thy
Saints at Hieruſalem: 14 And here he hath authoritie from the chiefe
Prieſts, to binde all that call on thy Name. 15 But the Lord ſaid vnto him,
Goe thy way: for hee is a choſen veſſell vnto me, to beare my Name
before the Gentiles, and Kings, and the children of Iſrael. 16 For I will
ſhew him how great things hee muſt ſuffer for my Names ſake. 17 And
Ananias went his way, and entred into the houſe, and putting his hands
on him, ſaid, Brother Saul, the Lord (euen Ieſus that appeared vnto thee

in the way as thou cameſt) hath ſent me, that thou mighteſt receiue thy ſight, and be filled with the holy Ghoſt.[18]And immediatly there fell from his eyes as it had bene ſcales, and he receiued ſight forthwith, and aroſe, and was baptized.[19]And when hee had receiued meat, he was ſtrengthened. Then was Saul certaine dayes with the diſciples which were at Damaſcus.[20]And ſtraightway hee preached Chriſt in the Synagogues, that hee is the Sonne of God.[21]But all that heard him, were amazed, and ſaid, Is not this he that deſtroyed them which called on this Name in Hieruſalem, and came hither for that intent that he might bring them bound vnto the chiefe Prieſts?[22]But Saul increaſed the more in ſtrength, and confounded the Iewes which dwelt at Damaſcus, proouing that this is very Chriſt.[23]And after that many dayes were fulfilled, the Iewes tooke counſel to kill him.[24]But their laying awaite was knowen of Saul: and they watched the gates day and night to kill him.[25]Then the diſciples tooke him by night, and let him downe by the wall in a baſket.[26]And when Saul was come to Hieruſalem, he aſsayed to ioyne himſelfe to the diſciples, but they were all afraid of him, and beleeued not that he was a diſciple.[27]But Barnabas tooke him, and brought him to the Apoſtles, and declared vnto them how hee had ſeene the Lord in the way, and that hee had ſpoken to him, and how hee had preached boldly at Damaſcus in the Name of Ieſus.[28]And he was with them comming in, and going out at Hieruſalem.[29]And he ſpake boldly in the Name of the Lord Ieſus, and diſputed againſt the Grecians: but they went about to ſlay him.[30]Which when the brethren knewe, they brought him downe to Ceſarea, and ſent him foorth to Tarſus.[31]Then had the Churches reſt thorowout all Iudea, and Galilee, and Samaria, and were edified, and walking in the feare of the Lord, and in the comfort of the holy Ghoſt, were multiplied.[32]And it came to paſſe, as Peter paſſed thorowout all quarters, he came downe alſo to the Saints, which dwelt at Lydda.[33]And there he found a certaine man named Aeneas, which had kept his bed eight yeeres, and was ſicke of the palſie.[34]And Peter ſaid vnto him, Aeneas, Ieſus Chriſt maketh thee whole: Ariſe, and make thy bed. And he aroſe immediately.[35]And all that dwelt at Lydda, and Saron, ſaw him, and turned to the Lord.[36]Now there was at Ioppa a certain diſciple, named Tabitha, which by interpretation is called Dorcas: This woman was full of good works, and almes deeds, which ſhe did.[37]And it came to paſſe in thoſe dayes that ſhe was ſicke, and died: whome when they had waſhed, they laid her in an vpper chamber.[38]And foraſmuch as Lydda was nigh to Ioppa, and the diſciples had heard that Peter was there, they ſent vnto him two men, deſiring him that he would not delay to come to them.[39]Then Peter aroſe and went with them: when he was come, they brought him into the vpper chamber: And all the widowes ſtood by him weeping, and ſhewing the coats and garments which Dorcas made, while ſhee was with them.[40]But Peter put them all forth, and kneeled downe, and prayed, and turning him to the body, ſaid, Tabitha, Ariſe. And ſhe opened her eyes, and when ſhe ſaw Peter, ſhe ſate vp.[41]And he gaue her his hand, and lift her vp: and when hee had called the Saints & widowes, preſented her aliue.[42]And it was knowen thorowout all Ioppa, and many beleeued in the Lord.[43]And it came to paſſe, that he taried many dayes in Ioppa, with one Simon a Tanner.

CHAPTER 10[1]There was a certaine man in Ceſarea, called Cornelius, a Centurion of þe band called the Italian band,[2]A deuout man, and one that feared God with all his houſe, which gaue much almes to the people, and prayed to God alway.[3]He ſaw in a viſion euidently, about the ninth houre of the day, an Angel of God comming in to him, and ſaying vnto him Cornelius.[4]And when he looked on him, hee was afraid, and ſaid, What is it, Lord? And he ſaid vnto him, Thy praiers and thine almes are come vp for a memorial before God.[5]And now ſend men to Ioppa, and call for one Simon, whoſe ſirname is Peter.[6]Hee lodgeth with one Simon a Tanner, whoſe houſe is by the ſea ſide; he ſhall tell thee what thou oughteſt to doe.[7]And when the Angel which ſpake vnto Cornelius, was departed, he called two of his houſhold ſeruants, and a deuout ſouldier of them that waited on him continually.[8]And when he had declared all theſe things vnto them, he ſent them to Ioppa.[9]On the morrow as they went on their iourney, and drew nigh vnto the citie, Peter went vp vpon the houſe to pray, about the ſixth houre.[10]And he became very hungry, and would haue eaten: But while they made ready, he fell into a traunce,[11]And ſaw heauen opened, and a certaine veſſell deſcending vnto him, as it had beene a great ſheete, knit at the foure corners, and let downe to the earth:[12]Wherein were all maner of foure footed beaſts of the earth, and wilde beaſts, and creeping things, and foules of the ayre.[13]And there came a voyce to him, Riſe, Peter: kill, and eate.[14]But Peter ſaid, Not ſo, Lord; for I haue neuer eaten any thing that is common or vncleane.[15]And the voice ſpake vnto him againe the ſecond time, What God hath cleanſed, that call not thou common.[16]This was done thriſe: & the veſsel was receiued vp againe into heauen.[17]Now while Peter doubted in himſelfe what this viſion which he had ſeene, ſhould meane: behold, the men which were ſent from Cornelius, had made inquirie for Simons houſe, and ſtood before the gate,[18]And called, and aſked whether Simon, which was ſirnamed Peter, were lodged there.[19]While Peter thought on the viſion, the ſpirit ſaid vnto him, Behold, three men ſeeke thee.[20]Ariſe therefore, and get thee downe, and goe with them, doubting nothing: for I haue ſent them.[21]Then Peter went downe to the men, which were ſent vnto him from Cornelius, and ſaid, Behold, I am hee, whom ye ſeeke: what is the cauſe wherefore ye are come?[22]And they ſaide, Cornelius the Centurion, a iuſt man, and one that feareth God, and of good report among all the nation of the Iewes, was warned from God by an holy Angel, to ſend for thee into his houſe, and to heare words of thee.[23]Then called he them in, and lodged them: And on the morrowe Peter went away with them, and certaine brethren from Ioppa accōpanied him.[24]And the morrow after they entred into Ceſarea: and Cornelius waited for them, and had called together his kinſmen and neere friends.[25]And as Peter was comming in, Cornelius met him, and fell downe at his feete, and worſhipped him.[26]But Peter tooke him vp, ſaying, ſtand vp, I my ſelfe alſo am a man.[27]And as he talked with him, hee went in, and found many that were come together.[28]And he ſaid vnto them, Ye know how that it is an vnlawfull thing for a man that is a Iewe, to keepe company or come vnto one of another nation: but God hath ſhewed me, that I ſhould not call any man common or vncleane.[29]Therfore came I vnto you without gaineſaying, as ſoone as I was ſent for. I aſke therefore, for what intent ye haue ſent for me.[30]And Cornelius ſaid, Foure daies agoe I was faſting vntill this houre, and at the ninth houre I prayed in my houſe, and behold, a man ſtood before me in bright clothing,[31]And ſaid, Cornelius, thy prayer is heard, and thine almes are had in remembrance in the ſight of God.[32]Send therfore to Ioppa, and call hither Simon, whoſe ſirname is Peter; he is lodged in the houſe of one Simon a Tanner, by the ſea ſide, who when he cōmeth, ſhall ſpeake vnto thee.[33]Immediately therefore I ſent to thee, and thou haſt well done, that thou art come. Now therefore are we all heere preſent before God, to heare all things that are cōmanded thee of God.[34]Then Peter opened his mouth, and ſaid, Of a trueth I perceiue þt God is no reſpecter of perſons:[35]But in euery nation, he that feareth him, and worketh righteouſneſſe, is accepted with him.[36]The word which God ſent vnto the children of Iſrael, preaching peace by Ieſus Chriſt (he is Lord of all.)[37]That word (I ſay) you knowe which was publiſhed thorowout all Iudea, and began from Galilee, after the baptiſme which Iohn preached:[38]How God anointed Ieſus of Nazareth with the holy Ghoſt, and with power, who went about doing good, and healing all that were oppreſſed of the deuill: for God was with him.[39]And we are witneſſes of all things which hee did both in the land of the Iewes, and in Hieruſalem, whom they ſlew and hanged on a tree,[40]Him God raiſed vp the third day, and ſhewed him openly,[41]Not to all the people, but vnto witneſſes, choſen before of God, euen to vs who did eate and drinke with him after he roſe from the dead.[42]And he commanded vs to preach vnto the people, and to teſtifie that it is he which was ordeined of God to be the Iudge of quicke and dead.[43]To him giue all the Prophets witneſſe, that through his Name whoſoeuer beleeueth in him, ſhall receiue remiſsion of ſinnes.[44]While Peter yet ſpake theſe words, the holy Ghoſt fell on all them which heard the word.[45]And they of the circumciſion which beleeued, were aſtoniſhed, as many as came with Peter, becauſe that on the Gentiles alſo was powred out the gift of the holy Ghoſt.[46]For they heard them ſpeake with tongues, and magnifie God. Then anſwered Peter,[47]Can any man forbid water, that theſe ſhould not bee baptized, which haue receiued the holy Ghoſt, as well as wee?[48]And hee commanded them to be baptized in the Name of the Lord. Then prayed they him to tarie certaine dayes.

CHAPTER 11 1And the Apoſtles, and brethren that were in Iudea, heard that the Gentiles had alſo receiued the word of God.2And when Peter was come vp to Hieruſalem, they that were of the circumciſion contended with him,3Saying, Thou wenteſt in to men vncircumciſed, & didſt eate with them.4But Peter rehearſed the matter from the beginning, and expounded it by order vnto them, ſaying,5I was in the citie of Ioppa praying, and in a trance I ſaw a viſion, a certaine veſſell deſcend, as it had beene a great ſheete, let downe from heauen by foure corners, and it came euen to me.6Upon the which when I had faſtened mine eyes, I conſidered, and ſaw foure footed beaſts of the earth, and wild beaſts, and creeping things, and foules of the aire.7And I heard a voyce, ſaying vnto me, Ariſe Peter, ſlay, and eate.8But I ſaid, Not ſo, Lord: for nothing common or vncleane hath at any time entred into my mouth.9But the voyce anſwered me againe from heauen, What God hath cleanſed, that call not thou common.10And this was done three times: and all were drawen vp againe into heauen.11And behold, immediately there were three men already come vnto the houſe where I was, ſent from Ceſarea vnto me.12And the ſpirit bad me goe with them, nothing doubting: Moreouer, theſe ſixe brethren accompanied me, and we entred into the mans houſe:13And he ſhewed vs how hee had ſeene an Angell in his houſe, which ſtood and ſaid vnto him, Send men to Ioppa, and call for Simon, whoſe ſirname is Peter:14Who ſhall tell thee words, wherby thou, and all thy houſe ſhal be ſaued.15And as I began to ſpeake, the holy Ghoſt fell on them, as on vs at the beginning.16Then remembred I the word of the Lord, how that he ſaid, Iohn indeede baptized with water: but ye ſhall be baptized with the holy Ghoſt.17Foraſmuch then as God gaue them the like gift as hee did vnto vs, who beleeued on the Lord Ieſus Chriſt: what was I that I could withſtand God?18When they heard theſe things, they held their peace, and glorified God, ſaying, Then hath God alſo to the Gentiles granted repentance vnto life.19Now they which were ſcattered abroad vpon the perſecution that aroſe about Steuen, trauailed as farre as Phenice, and Cyprus, and Antioch, preaching the word to none, but vnto the Iewes onely.20And ſome of them were men of Cyprus, and Cyrene, which when they were come to Antioch, ſpake vnto the Grecians, preaching the Lord Ieſus.21And the hand of the Lord was with them: and a great number beleeued, and turned vnto the Lord.22Then tidings of theſe things came vnto the eares of the Church, which was in Hieruſalem: and they ſent foorth Barnabas, that hee ſhould goe as farre as Antioch.23Who when hee came, and had ſeene the grace of God, was glad, and exhorted them all, that with purpoſe of heart they would cleaue vnto the Lord.24For he was a good man, and full of the holy Ghoſt, and of faith: and much people was added vnto the Lord.25Then departed Barnabas to Tarſus, for to ſeeke Saul.26And when he had found him, he brought him vnto Antioch. And it came to paſſe, that a whole yeere they aſſembled themſelues with the Church, and taught much people, and the diſciples were called Chriſtians firſt in Antioch.27And in theſe dayes, came Prophets from Hieruſalem vnto Antioch.28And there ſtood vp one of them, named Agabus, and ſignified by the ſpirit, that there ſhould be great dearth throughout all the world: which came to paſſe in the dayes of Claudius Ceſar.29Then the diſciples, euery man according to his abilitie, determined to ſend reliefe vnto the brethren which dwelt in Iudea.30Which alſo they did, and ſent it to the Elders by the hands of Barnabas and Saul.

CHAPTER 12 1Now about that time, Herode the King ſtretched foorth his hands, to vexe certaine of the Church.2And he killed Iames the brother of Iohn with the ſword.3And becauſe he ſaw it pleaſed the Iewes, hee proceeded further, to take Peter alſo. (Then were the dayes of vnleauened bread.)4And when hee had apprehended him, hee put him in priſon, and deliuered him to foure quaternions of ſouldiers to keepe him, intending after Eaſter to bring him forth to the people.5Peter therefore was kept in priſon, but prayer was made without ceaſing of the Church vnto God for him.6And when Herode would haue brought him foorth, the ſame night Peter was ſleeping betweene two Souldiers, bound with two chaines, and the Keepers before the doore kept the priſon.7And beholde, the Angel of the Lord came vpon him, and a light ſhined in the priſon: and hee ſmote Peter on the ſide, and raiſed him vp, ſaying, Ariſe vp quickely. And his chaines fell off from his hands.8And the Angel ſaid vnto him, Girde thy ſelfe, and binde on thy ſandales: And ſo he did. And he ſayth vnto him, Caſt thy garment about thee, and follow me.9And hee went out, and followed him, and wiſt not that it was true which was done by the Angel: but thought he ſaw a viſion.10When they were paſt the firſt and the ſecond ward, they came vnto the yron gate that leadeth vnto the citie, which opened to them of his owne accord: and they went out and paſſed on thorow one ſtreete, and foorthwith the Angel departed from him.11And when Peter was come to himſelfe, hee ſaid, Now I know of a ſuretie, that the Lord hath ſent his Angel, and hath deliuered mee out of the hand of Herode, and from all the expectation of the people of the Iewes.12And when he had conſidered the thing, he came to the houſe of Mary the mother of Iohn whoſe ſirname was Marke, where many were gathered together praying.13And as Peter knocked at the doore of the gate, a damoſell came to hearken, named Rhoda.14And when ſhe knew Peters voice, ſhe opened not the gate for gladnes, but ran in, and told how Peter ſtood before the gate.15And they ſaid vnto her, Thou art mad. But ſhe conſtantly affirmed that it was euen ſo. Then ſaid they, It it his Angel.16But Peter continued knocking: and when they had opened the doore, and ſaw him, they were aſtoniſhed.17But he beckening vnto them with the hand, to hold their peace, declared vnto them how the Lord had brought him out of the priſon: And he ſaid, Goe ſhew theſe things vnto Iames, and to the brethren. And he departed, and went into another place.18Now aſſoone as it was day, there was no ſmal ſtirre among the ſouldiers, what was become of Peter.19And when Herode had ſought for him, and found him not, hee examined the keepers, and commanded that they ſhould be put to death. And hee went downe from Iudea to Ceſarea, & there abode.20And Herode was highly diſpleaſed with them of Tyre and Sidon: but they came with one accord to him, and hauing made Blaſtus the kings chamberlaine their friend, deſired peace, becauſe their countrey was nouriſhed by the kings countrey.21And vpon a ſet day Herod arayed in royall apparell, ſate vpon his throne, and made an Oration vnto them.22And the people gaue a ſhout, ſaying, It is the voice of a God, and not of a man.23And immediatly the Angel of the Lord ſmote him, becauſe hee gaue not God the glory, and hee was eaten of wormes, and gaue vp the ghoſt.24But the word of God grewe, and multiplied.25And Barnabas and Saul returned from Hieruſalem, when they had fulfilled their miniſterie, and tooke with them Iohn, whoſe ſyrname was Marke.

CHAPTER 13 1Nowe there were in the Church that was at Antioch, certaine Prophets and teachers: as Barnabas, and Simeon that was called Niger, and Lucius of Cyrene, and Manaen, which had bene brought vp with Herod the Tetrarch, and Saul.2As they miniſtred to the Lord, and faſted, the holy Ghoſt ſaid, Separate me Barnabas and Saul, for the worke whereunto I haue called them.3And when they had faſted and prayed, and laid their handes on them, they ſent them away.4So they being ſent forth by the holy Ghoſt, departed vnto Seleucia, and from thence they ſailed to Cyprus.5And when they were at Salamis, they preached the word of God in the Synagogues of the Iewes: and they had alſo Iohn to their Miniſter.6And when they had gone thorow the Ile vnto Paphos, they found a certaine ſorcerer, a falſe prophet, a Iewe, whoſe name was BarIeſus:7Which was with the deputie of the countrey Sergius Paulus, a prudent man: who called for Barnabas and Saul, and deſired to heare the word of God.8But Elymas the ſorcerer (for ſo is his name by interpretation) withſtood them, ſeeking to turne away the deputy from the faith.9Then Saul (who alſo is called Paul) filled with the holy Ghoſt, ſet his eyes on him,10And ſaid, O full of all ſubtilty and all miſchiefe, thou child of the deuil, thou enemie of all righteouſneſſe, wilt thou not ceaſe to peruert the right wayes of the Lord?11And now behold, the hand of the Lord is vpon thee, & thou ſhalt be blind, not ſeeing the Sunne for a ſeaſon. And immediately there fell on him a miſt and a darkenes, and he went about, ſeeking ſome to lead him by the hand.12Then the Deputie when he ſawe what was done, beleeued, being aſtoniſhed at the doctrine of the Lord.13Now when Paul and his company looſed from Paphos, they came to Perga in Pamphylia: and Iohn departing from them, returned to Hieruſalem.14But when they departed from Perga, they came to Antioch in Piſidia, and went into the ſynagogue on the Sabbath day, and ſate downe.15And after the reading of the Law and the Prophets, the rulers of the ſynagogue ſent vnto them, ſaying, Ye men and brethren, if ye haue any word of exhortation for the people, ſay on.16Then Paul ſtood vp, and beckning with his hand, ſaid, Men of Iſrael, and ye that feare God, giue audience.17The God of this

people of Iſrael choſe our fathers, and exalted the people when they
dwelt as ſtrangers in the land of Egypt, and with an high arme brought
he them out of it.18And about the time of fourtie yeeres ſuffered he their
maners in the wilderneſſe.19And when he had deſtroyed ſeuen nations
in the land of Chanaan, he diuided their land to them by lot:20And after
that he gaue vnto them iudges, about the ſpace of foure hundred and
fifty yeeres vntill Samuel the Prophet.21And afterward they deſired a
King, and God gaue vnto them Saul the ſonne of Cis, a man of the tribe
of Beniamin, by the ſpace of fourty yeres.22And when he had remoued
him, hee raiſed vp vnto them Dauid to be their king, to whom alſo he
gaue teſtimonie, and ſaid, I haue found Dauid the ſonne of Ieſſe, a man
after mine own heart, which ſhal fulfill all my wil.23Of this mans ſeed
hath God, according to his promiſe, raiſed vnto Iſrael a Sauiour,
Ieſus:24When Iohn had firſt preached before his coming, the baptiſme
of repentance to all the people of Iſrael.25And as Iohn fulfilled his
courſe, he ſaid, Whom thinke ye that I am? I am not he. But behold,
there commeth one after me, whoſe ſhooes of his feete I am not worthy
to looſe.26Men and brethren, children of the ſtocke of Abraham, and
whoſoeuer among you feareth God, to you is the word of this ſaluation
ſent.27For they that dwell at Hieruſalem, & their rulers, becauſe they
knew him not, nor yet the voices of the Prophets which are read euery
Sabbath day, they haue fulfilled them in condemning him.28And though
they found no cauſe of death in him, yet deſired they Pilate that he
ſhould be ſlaine.29And when they had fulfilled all that was written of
him, they tooke him downe from the tree, and layd him in a
Sepulchre.30But God raiſed him frō the dead:31And he was ſeene many
dayes of them which came vp with him from Galilee to Hieruſalem, who
are his witneſſes vnto the people.32And we declare vnto you glad tidings,
how that the promiſe which was made vnto the fathers,33God hath
fulfilled the ſame vnto vs their children, in that he hath raiſed vp Ieſus
againe, as it is alſo written in the ſecond Pſalme: Thou art my Sonne,
this day haue I begotten thee.34And as concerning that he raiſed him vp
from the dead, now no more to returne to corruption, he ſaid on this
wiſe, I will giue you the ſure mercies of Dauid.35Wherfore he ſaith alſo
in another Pſalme, Thou ſhalt not ſuffer thine holy one to ſee
corruption.36For Dauid after he had ſerued his owne generation by the
will of God, fell on ſleepe, and was laide vnto his fathers, and ſaw
corruption:37But hee whom God raiſed againe, ſaw no corruption.38Be
it knowen vnto you therefore, men and brethren, that through this man
is preached vnto you the forgiueneſse of ſinnes.39And by him all
þt beleeue, are iuſtified from all things, from which ye could not be
iuſtified by the Law of Moſes.40Beware therefore, leaſt that come vpon
you which is ſpoken of in the Prophets,41Behold, yee deſpiſers, and
wonder, and periſh: for I worke a worke in your dayes, a worke which
you ſhall in no wiſe beleeue, though a man declare it vnto you.42And
when the Iewes were gone out of the Synagogue, the Gentiles beſought
that theſe words might be preached to them the next Sabbath.43Now
when the Congregation was broken vp, many of the Iewes, and religious
Proſelytes followed Paul and Barnabas, who ſpeaking to them,
perſwaded them to continue in the grace of God.44And the next
Sabbath day came almoſt the whole citie together to heare the word of
God.45But when the Iewes ſaw the multitudes, they were filled with
enuie, and ſpake againſt thoſe things which were ſpoken by Paul,
contradicting, and blaſpheming.46Then Paul and Barnabas waxed bold,
and ſaid, It was neceſsary that the word of God ſhould firſt haue bene
ſpoken to you: but ſeeing yee put it from you, and iudge your ſelues
vnworthy of euerlaſting life, loe, we turne to the Gentiles.47For ſo hath
the Lord cōmanded vs, ſaying, I haue ſet thee to bee a light of the
Gentiles, that thou ſhouldeſt be for ſaluation vnto the ends of the
earth.48And when the Gentiles heard this, they were glad, and glorified
the word of the Lord: and as many as were ordeined to eternall life,
beleeued.49And the word of the Lord was publiſhed throughout all the
region.50But the Iewes ſtirred vp the deuout and honourable women,
and the chiefe men of the citie, and raiſed perſecution againſt Paul and
Barnabas, and expelled them out of their coaſts.51But they ſhooke off
the duſt of their feete againſt them, and came vnto Iconium.52And the
diſciples were filled with ioy, and with the holy Ghoſt.
CHAPTER 141And it came to paſſe in Iconium, that they went both
together into the ſynagogue of the Iewes, and ſo ſpake, that a great
multitude both of the Iewes, and alſo of the Greekes, beleeued.2But the
vnbeleeuing Iewes ſtirred vp the Gentiles, and made their mindes euill
affected againſt the brethren.3Long time therefore abode they ſpeaking
boldly in the Lord, which gaue teſtimonie vnto the word of his grace,
and granted ſignes and wonders to be done by their hands.4But the
multitude of the city was diuided: and part held with the Iewes, and part
with the Apoſtles.5And when there was an aſsault made both of the
Gentiles, and alſo of the Iewes, with their rulers, to vſe them deſpitefully,
and to ſtone them,6They were ware of it, and fled vnto Lyſtra and
Derbe, cities of Lycaonia, and vnto the region that lyeth round
about.7And there they preached the Goſpell.8And there ſate a certaine
man at Lyſtra, impotent in his feete, being a creeple from his mothers
wombe, who neuer had walked.9The ſame heard Paul ſpeake: who
ſtedfaſtly beholding him, and perceiuing that he had faith to be
healed,10Said with a lowd voice, ſtand vpright on thy feete; And he
leaped and walked.11And when the people ſaw what Paul had done, they
lift vp their voyces, ſaying in the ſpeech of Lycaonia, The gods are come
downe to vs in the likeneſſe of men.12And they called Barnabas Iupiter,
and Paul Mercurius, becauſe hee was the chiefe ſpeaker.13Then the prieſt
of Iupiter, which was before their city, brought oxen, and garlands vnto
the gates, and would haue done ſacrifice with the people.14Which when
the Apoſtles, Barnabas and Paul heard of, they rent their clothes, and
ranne in among the people, crying out,15And ſaying, Sirs, Why doe yee
theſe things? Wee alſo are men of like paſsions with you, and preach
vnto you, that ye ſhould turne from theſe vanities, vnto the liuing God,
which made heauen and earth, and the ſea, and all things that are
therein.16Who in times paſt, ſuffred all nations to walke in their owne
wayes.17Neuertheleſſe, he left not himſelfe without witneſſe, in that he
did good, and gaue vs raine from heauen, and fruitful ſeaſons, filling our
hearts with food and gladneſſe.18And with theſe ſayings ſcarſe reſtrained
they the people, that they had not done ſacrifice vnto them.19And there
came thither certaine Iewes from Antioch and Iconium, who perſwaded
the people, and hauing ſtoned Paul, drew him out of the citie, ſuppoſing
he had beene dead.20Howbeit, as the diſciples ſtood round about him,
he roſe vp, and came into the citie, and the next day he departed with
Barnabas to Derbe.21And when they had preached the Goſpel to that
city, and had taught many, they returned againe to Lyſtra, and to
Iconium, and Antioch,22Confirming the ſoules of the diſciples, and
exhorting them to continue in the faith, aud that we muſt through much
tribulation enter into the kingdome of God.23And when they had
ordeined them Elders in euery Church, and had prayed with faſting, they
commended them to the Lord, on whom they beleeued.24And after they
had paſſed throughout Piſidia, they came to Pamphylia.25And when they
had preached the word in Perga, they went downe into Attalia,26And
thence ſailed to Antioch, from whence they had been recommended to
the grace of God, for the worke which they fulfilled.27And when they
were come, and had gathered the Church together, they rehearſed all
that God had done with them, and how he had opened the doore of
faith vnto the Gentiles.28And there they abode long time with the
diſciples.
CHAPTER 151And certaine men which came downe from Iudea,
taught the brethren, and ſaid, Except ye be circumciſed after the manner
of Moſes, ye cannot be ſaued.2When therefore Paul and Barnabas had
no ſmall diſsention and diſputation with them, they determined that
Paul and Barnabas, and certeine other of them, ſhould goe vp to
Hieruſalem vnto the Apoſtles and Elders about this queſtion.3And being
brought on their way by the Church, they paſſed thorow Phenice and
Samaria, declaring the conuerſion of the Gentiles: and they cauſed great
ioy vnto all the brethren.4And when they were come to Hieruſalem, they
were receiued of the Church, and of the Apoſtles, and Elders, and they
declared all things that God had done with them.5But there roſe vp
certaine of the ſect of the PhAriſees which beleeued, ſaying, that it was
needfull to circumciſe them, and to cōmand them to keepe the Law of
Moſes.6And the Apoſtles & Elders came together for to conſider of this
matter.7And when there had bene much diſputing, Peter roſe vp, and
ſaid vnto them, Men and brethren, ye know how that a good while agoe,
God made choiſe among vs, that the Gentiles by my mouth ſhould heare
the worde of the Goſpel, and beleeue.8And God which knoweth the
hearts, bare them witnes, giuing them the holy Ghoſt, euen as he did
vnto vs,9And put no difference between vs & them, purifying their

hearts by faith.10Now therfore why tempt ye God, to put a yoke vpon
the necke of the diſciples, which neither our fathers nor we were able to
beare?11But we beleeue that through the grace of the Lord Ieſus Chriſt,
we ſhal be ſaued euen as they.12Then all the multitude kept ſilence, and
gaue audience to Barnabas and Paul, declaring what miracles and
wonders God had wrought among the Gentiles by them.13And after
they had helde their peace, Iames anſwered, ſaying, Men and brethren,
hearken vnto me.14Simeon hath declared how God at the firſt did viſite
the Gentiles to take out of them a people for his Name.15And to this
agree the words of the Prophets, as it is written,16After this I will
returne, and wil build againe the Tabernacle of Dauid, which is fallen
downe: and I will build againe the ruines thereof, and I will ſet it
vp:17That the reſidue of men might ſeeke after the Lord, and all the
Gentiles, vpon whom my Name is called, ſayth the Lord, who doeth all
theſe things.18Knowen vnto God are all his workes frō the beginning of
the world.19Wherefore my ſentence is, that we trouble not them, which
from among the Gentiles are turned to God:20But that wee write vnto
them, that they abſtaine from pollutions of Idoles, and from fornication,
and from things ſtrangled, and from blood.21For Moſes of olde time
hath in euery citie them that preach him, being read in the Synagogues
euery Sabbath day.22Then pleaſed it the Apoſtles and Elders with the
whole Church, to ſend choſen men of their owne company to Antioch,
with Paul and Barnabas: namely, Iudas ſurnamed Barſabas, & Silas,
chiefe men among the brethren,23And wrote letters by them after this
maner, The Apoſtles and Elders, and brethren, ſend greeting vnto the
brethren, which are of the Gentiles in Antioch, and Syria, and
Cilicia.24Foraſmuch as we haue heard, that certaine which went out
from vs, haue troubled you with words, ſubuerting your ſoules, ſaying,
Ye muſt be circumciſed, and keepe the Law, to whom we gaue no ſuch
commandement:25It ſeemed good vnto vs, being aſſembled with one
accord, to ſend choſen men vnto you, with our beloued Barnabas and
Paul,26Men that haue hazarded their liues for the Name of our Lord
Ieſus Chriſt.27Wee haue ſent therefore Iudas and Silas, who ſhall alſo tell
you the ſame things by mouth.28For it ſeemed good to the holy Ghoſt,
and to vs, to lay vpon you no greater burden then theſe neceſsarie
things;29That ye abſtaine from meates offered to idoles, and from blood,
& from things ſtrangled, and from fornication: from which if ye keepe
your ſelues, yee ſhall doe well. Fare ye well.30So when they were
diſmiſsed, they came to Antioch: and when they had gathered the
multitude together, they deliuered the Epiſtle.31Which when they had
read, they reioyced for the conſolation.32And Iudas and Silas, being
Prophets alſo themſelues, exhorted the brethren with many words, and
confirmed them:33And after they had taried there a ſpace, they were let
goe in peace from the breehren vnto the Apoſtles.34Notwithſtanding it
pleaſed Silas to abide there ſtill.35Paul alſo and Barnabas continued in
Antioch, teaching and preaching the word of the Lord, with many others
alſo.36And ſome dayes after, Paul ſaid vnto Barnabas, Let vs go againe
and viſit our brethren, in euery city where we haue preached the word
of the Lord, and ſee how they doe.37And Barnabas determined to take
with them Iohn, whoſe ſurname was Marke.38But Paul thought not
good to take him with them; who departed from them from Pamphylia,
and went not with them to the worke.39And the contention was ſo
ſharpe betweene them, that they departed aſunder one from the other:
& ſo Barnabas tooke Marke, & ſailed vnto Cyprus.40And Paul choſe
Silas, and departed, being recommended by the brethren vnto the grace
of God.41And he went thorow Syria and Cilicia, confirming the
Churches.
CHAPTER 161Then came he to Derbe, and Lyſtra: and behold, a
certaine diſciple was there, named Timotheus, the ſon of a certaine
woman which was a Iewefse, and beleeued: but his father was a
Greeke:2Which was well reported of by the brethren that were at Lyſtra
and Iconium.3Him would Paul haue to go forth with him, and tooke,
and circumciſed him, becauſe of the Iewes which were in thoſe quarters:
for they knew all, that his father was a Greeke.4And as they went
through the cities, they deliuered them the decrees for to keepe, that
were ordeined of the Apoſtles and Elders, which were at
Hieruſalem.5And ſo were the Churches eſtabliſhed in the faith, and
increaſed in number dayly.6Now when they had gone thorowout
Phrygia, and the region of Galatia, and were forbidden of the holy Ghoſt
to preach the word in Aſia,7After they were come to Myſia, they aſsayed
to goe into Bithynia: but the Spirit ſuffered them not.8And they paſsing
by Myſia, came downe to Troas.9And a viſion appeared to Paul in the
night: There ſtood a man of Macedonia, and prayed him, ſaying, Come
ouer into Macedonia, and helpe vs.10And after he had ſeene the viſion,
immediatly we endeuoured to goe into Macedonia, aſsuredly gathering,
that the Lord had called vs for to preach the Goſpel vnto
them.11Therfore looſing from Troas, we came with a ſtraight courſe to
Samothracia, and the next day to Neapolis:12And from thence to
Philippi, which is the chiefe citie of that part of Macedonia, and a
Colonie: and we were in that citie abiding certaine dayes.13And on the
Sabboth we went out of the citie by a riuer ſide, where prayer was wont
to be made, & we ſate downe, and ſpake vnto the women which reſorted
thither.14And a certaine woman named Lydia, a ſeller of purple, of the
citie of Thyatira, which worſhipped God, heard vs: whoſe heart the Lord
opened, that ſhe attended vnto the things which were ſpoken of
Paul.15And when ſhe was baptized, and her houſhold, ſhe beſought vs,
ſaying, If ye haue iudged me to bee faithfull to the Lord, come into my
houſe, and abide there. And ſhe conſtrained vs.16And it came to paſſe,
as we went to prayer, a certaine Damoſell poſſeſſed with a ſpirit of
diuination, met vs: which brought her maſters much gaine by
ſoothſaying.17The ſame followed Paul and vs, and cried, ſaying, Theſe
men are the ſeruants of the moſt hie God, which ſhew vnto vs the way
of ſaluation.18And this did ſhe many dayes: but Paul being grieued,
turned and ſaid to the ſpirit, I command thee in the Name of Ieſus
Chriſt, to come out of her. And he came out the ſame houre.19And
when her Maſters ſaw that the hope of their gaines was gone, they
caught Paul and Silas, and drew them into the market place, vnto the
rulers,20And brought them to the Magiſtrates, ſaying, Theſe men being
Iewes, do exceedingly trouble our city,21And teach cuſtomes which are
not lawfull for vs to receiue, neither to obſerue, being Romanes.22And
the multitude roſe vp together againſt them, and the Magiſtrates rent off
their clothes, and commanded to beate them.23And when they had layed
many ſtripes vpon them, they caſt them into priſon, charging the Iaylour
to keepe them ſafely.24Who hauing receiued ſuch a charge, thruſt them
into the inner priſon, & made their feet faſt in the ſtockes.25And at
midnight, Paul and Silas prayed, and ſang praiſes vnto God: and the
priſoners heard them.26And ſuddenly there was a great earthquake, ſo
that the foundations of the priſon were ſhaken: and immediately all the
doores were opened, and euery ones bands were looſed.27And the
keeper of the priſon awaking out of his ſleepe, and ſeeing the priſon
doores open, he drew out his ſword, and would haue killed himſelfe,
ſuppoſing that the priſoners had beene fled.28But Paul cried with a loud
voice, ſaying, Doe thy ſelfe no harme, for we are all heere.29Then hee
called for a light, and ſprang in, and came trembling, and fell downe
before Paul and Silas,30And brought them out, and ſaid, Sirs, what muſt
I doe to be ſaued?31And they ſaide, Beleeue on the Lord Ieſus Chriſt,
and thou ſhalt be ſaued, and thy houſe.32And they ſpake vnto him the
word of the Lord, and to all that were in his houſe.33And hee tooke them
the ſame houre of the night, and waſhed their ſtripes, and was baptized,
hee and all his, ſtraightway.34And when he had brought them into his
houſe, hee ſet meat before them, and reioyced, beleeuing in God with
all his houſe.35And when it was day, the Magiſtrates ſent the Sergeants,
ſaying, Let thoſe men goe.36And the keeper of the priſon told this ſaying
to Paul, The Magiſtrates haue ſent to let you goe: Now therefore depart,
and goe in peace.37But Paul ſaid vnto them, They haue beaten vs openly
vncondemned, being Romanes, and haue caſt vs into priſon, and now
doe they thruſt vs out priuily? Nay verily, but let them come themſelues,
and fetch vs out.38And the Sergeants tolde theſe words vnto the
Magiſtrates: and they feared when they heard that they were
Romanes.39And they came and beſought them, and brought them out,
and deſired them to depart out of the citie.40And they went out of the
priſon, and entred into the houſe of Lydia, and when they had ſeene the
brethren, they comforted them, and departed.
CHAPTER 171Now when they had paſſed thorow Amphipolis, and
Apollonia, they came to Theſsalonica, where was a ſynagogue of the
Iewes.2And Paul, as his maner was, went in vnto them, and three
Sabbath dayes reaſoned with them out of the Scriptures,3Opening and
alleadging, that Chriſt muſt needs haue ſuffered and riſen againe from
the dead: and that this Ieſus whom I preach vnto you, is Chriſt.4And

ſome of them beleeued, and conſorted with Paul and Silas: and of the deuout Greekes a great multitude, and of the chiefe women not a few.5But the Iewes which beleeued not, mooued with enuie, tooke vnto them certaine lewd fellowes of the baſer ſort, and gathered a company, and ſet all the citie on an vprore, and aſsaulted the houſe of Iaſon, and ſought to bring them out to the people.6And when they found them not, they drew Iaſon, and certaine brethren vnto the rulers of the citie, crying, Theſe that haue turned the world vpſide downe, are come hither alſo,7Whom Iaſon hath receiued: and theſe all doe contrary to the decrees of Ceſar, ſaying, that there is another King, one Ieſus.8And they troubled the people, and the rulers of the citie, when they heard theſe things.9And when they had taken ſecuritie of Iaſon, and of the other, they let them goe.10And the brethren immediatly ſent away Paul and Silas by night vnto Berea: who comming thither, went into the Synagogue of the Iewes.11Theſe were more noble then thoſe in Theſsalonica, in that they receiued the word with all readineſse of minde, and ſearched the Scriptures dayly, whether thoſe things were ſo.12Therefore many of them beleeued: alſo of honourable women which were Greekes, and of men not a few.13But when the Iewes of Theſsalonica had knowledge that the word of God was preached of Paul at Berea, they came thither alſo, and ſtirred vp the people.14And then immediatly the brethren ſent away Paul, to goe as it were to the ſea: but Silas and Timotheus abode there ſtill.15And they that conducted Paul, brought him vnto Athens, and receiuing a commaundement vnto Silas and Timotheus, for to come to him with all ſpeed, they departed.16Now while Paul waited for them at Athens, his ſpirit was ſtirred in him, when hee ſaw the city wholy giuen to idolatrie.17Therefore diſputed he in the Synagogue with the Iewes, and with the deuout perſons, and in the market dayly with them that met with him.18Then certaine Philoſophers of the Epicureans, and of the Stoikes, encountred him: and ſome ſaid, What will this babbler ſay? Otherſome, He ſeemeth to be a ſetter foorth of ſtrange gods: becauſe hee preached vnto them Ieſus, and the reſurrection.19And they tooke him, and brought him vnto Areopagus, ſaying, May we know what this new doctrine, whereof thou ſpeakeſt, is?20For thou bringeſt certaine ſtrange things to our eares: we would know therefore what theſe things meane.21(For all the Athenians and ſtrangers which were there, ſpent their time in nothing elſe, but either to tell or to heare ſome new thing.)22Then Paul ſtood in the mids of Marſ-hill, and ſaid, Yee men of Athens, I perceiue that in all things yee are too ſuperſtitious.23For as I paſſed by, and beheld your deuotions, I found an Altar with this inſcription, TO THE VNKNOWEN GOD. Whom therefore yee ignorantly worſhip, him declare I vnto you.24God that made the world, and all things therein, ſeeing that hee is Lord of heauen and earth, dwelleth not in Temples made with hands:25Neither is worſhipped with mens hands as though he needed any thing, ſeeing hee giueth to all, life and breath, and all things,26And hath made of one blood all nations of men, for to dwell on all the face of the earth, and hath determined the times before appointed, and the bounds of their habitation:27That they ſhould ſeeke the Lord, if haply they might feele after him and finde him, though he be not farre from euery one of vs.28For in him we liue, and mooue, and haue our being, as certaine alſo of your owne Poets haue ſaid, For we are alſo his offſpring.29Foraſmuch then as wee are the offſpring of God, wee ought not to thinke that the Godhead is like vnto golde, or ſiluer, or ſtone grauen by arte, and mans deuice.30And the times of this ignorance God winked at, but now commandeth all men euery where to repent:31Becauſe hee hath appointed a day in the which he will iudge the world in righteouſneſſe, by that man whom hee hath ordeined, whereof he hath giuen aſsurance vnto all men, in that he hath raiſed him from the dead.32And when they heard of the reſurrection of the dead, ſome mocked: and others ſaid, Wee will heare thee againe of this matter.33So Paul departed from among them.34Howbeit, certaine men claue vnto him, and beleeued: among the which was Dionyſius the Areopagite, and a woman named Damaris, and others with them.

CHAPTER 181After theſe things, Paul departed from Athens, and came to Corinth,2And found a certaine Iewe named Aquila, borne in Pontus, lately come from Italy, with his wife Priſcilla, (becauſe that Claudius had commanded all Iewes to depart from Rome) and came vnto them.3And becauſe hee was of the ſame craft, he abode with them, and wrought (for by their occupation they were tentmakers.)4And hee reaſoned in the Synagogue euery Sabbath, and perſwaded the Iewes, and the Greekes.5And when Silas and Timotheus were come from Macedonia, Paul was preſſed in ſpirit, and teſtified to the Iewes, that Ieſus was Chriſt.6And when they oppoſed themſelues, and blaſphemed, he ſhooke his raiment, and ſaid vnto them, Your blood be vpon your owne heads, I am cleane: from henceforth I will goe vnto the Gentiles.7And hee departed thence, and entred into a certaine mans houſe, named Iuſtus, one that worſhipped God, whoſe houſe ioyned hard to the Synagogue.8And Criſpus, the chiefe ruler of the Synagogue, beleeued on the Lord, with all his houſe: and many of the Corinthians, hearing, beleeued, and were baptized.9Then ſpake the Lord to Paul in the night by a viſion, Be not afraid, but ſpeake, and holde not thy peace:10For I am with thee, and no man ſhal ſet on thee, to hurt thee: for I haue much people in this city.11And hee continued there a yeere and ſixe monethes, teaching the word of God among them.12And when Gallio was the Deputie of Achaia, the Iewes made inſurrection with one accord againſt Paul, and brought him to the iudgement ſeat,13Saying, This fellow perſwadeth men to worſhip God contrary to the Law.14And when Paul was now about to open his mouth, Gallio ſaid vnto the Iewes, If it were a matter of wrong, or wicked lewdneſse, O yee Iewes, reaſon would that I ſhould beare with you.15But if it be a queſtion of words, and names, and of your law, looke ye to it: for I wil be no iudge of ſuch matters.16And he draue them from the iudgment ſeate.17Then all the Greekes tooke Soſthenes the chiefe ruler of the Synagogue, and beat him before the Iudgement ſeat: and Gallio cared for none of thoſe things.18And Paul after this taried there yet a good while, and then tooke his leaue of the brethren, and ſailed thence into Syria, and with him Priſcilla and Aquila: hauing ſhorne his head in Cenchrea: for he had a vow.19And he came to Epheſus, and left them there: but he himſelfe entred into the Synagogue, and reaſoned with the Iewes.20When they deſired him to tary longer time with them, hee conſented not:21But bade them farewell, ſaying, I muſt by all meanes keepe this feaſt that commeth, in Hieruſalem; but I will returne againe vnto you, if God will: and he ſailed from Epheſus.22And when he had landed at Ceſarea, and gone vp, and ſaluted the Church, he went downe to Antioch.23And after he had ſpent ſome time there, hee departed, and went ouer all the countrey of Galatia and Phrygia in order, ſtrengthening all the diſciples.24And a certaine Iew, named Apollos, borne at Alexandria, an eloquent man, and mightie in the Scriptures, came to Epheſus.25This man was inſtructed in the way of the Lord, and being feruent in the ſpirit, he ſpake and taught diligently the things of the Lord, knowing onely the baptiſme of Iohn.26And he began to ſpeake boldly in the Synagogue: whom when Aquila and Priſcilla had heard, they tooke him vnto them, and expounded vnto him the way of God more perfectly.27And when hee was diſpoſed to paſſe into Achaia, the brethren wrote, exhorting the diſciples to receiue him: who, when he was come, helped them much which had beleeued throgh grace.28For hee mightily conuinced the Iewes, and that publikely, ſhewing by the ſcriptures, that Ieſus was Chriſt.

CHAPTER 191And it came to paſſe, that while Apollos was at Corinth, Paul hauing paſſed thorow the vpper coaſts, came to Epheſus, and finding certaine diſciples,2He ſaid vnto them, Haue ye receiued the holy Ghoſt ſince yee beleeued? And they ſaide vnto him, Wee haue not ſo much as heard whether there be any holy Ghoſt.3And he ſaid vnto them, Unto what then were ye baptized? And they ſaide, Unto Iohns Baptiſme.4Then ſaide Paul, Iohn verely baptized with the baptiſme of repentance, ſaying vnto the people, that they ſhould beleeue on him which ſhould come after him, that is, on Chriſt Ieſus.5When they heard this, they were baptized in the Name of the Lord Ieſus.6And when Paul had laide his hands vpon them, the holy Ghoſt came on them, and they ſpake with tongues, and prophecied.7And all þe men were about twelue.8And hee went into the Synagogue, and ſpake boldly for the ſpace of three moneths, diſputing and perſwading the things concerning the Kingdome of God.9But when diuers were hardened, and beleeued not, but ſpake euill of that way before the multitude, he departed from them, and ſeparated the diſciples, diſputing daily in the ſchoole of one Tyrannus.10And this continued by the ſpace of two yeeres, ſo that all they which dwelt in Aſia, heard the word of the Lord Ieſus, both Iewes and Greeks.11And God wrought ſpeciall miracles by the hands of Paul:12So that from his body were brought vnto the ſicke handkerchiefs or aprons, and the diſeaſes departed from them, and the euill ſpirits went out of them.[13]Then certaine of the vagabond Iewes, exorciſtes, tooke vpon them to call ouer them which had euill ſpirits, the Name of the Lord Ieſus, ſaying, We adiure you by Ieſus whom Paul preacheth.[14]And there were ſeuen ſonnes of one Sceua a Iewe, and chiefe of the Prieſts, which did ſo.[15]And the euill ſpirit anſwered, and ſaid, Ieſus I knowe, and Paul I know, but who are ye?[16]And the man in whom the euill ſpirit was, leapt on them, and ouercame them, and preuailed againſt them, ſo that they fled out of that houſe naked and wounded.[17]And this was knowen to all the Iewes and Greekes alſo dwelling at Epheſus, and feare fell on them all, and the Name of the Lord Ieſus was magnified.[18]And many that beleeued came, and confeſsed, and ſhewed their deedes.[19]Many alſo of them which vſed curious arts, brought their bookes together and burned them before all men: and they counted the price of them, and found it fifty thouſand pieces of ſiluer.[20]So mightily grew the word of God, and preuailed.[21]After theſe things were ended, Paul purpoſed in the ſpirit, when hee had paſſed thorow Macedonia and Athaia, to go to Hieruſalem, ſaying, After I haue bin there, I muſt alſo ſee Rome.[22]So hee ſent into Macedonia two of them that miniſtred vnto him, Timotheus and Eraſtus, but he himſelfe ſtayed in Aſia for a ſeaſon.[23]And the ſame time there aroſe no ſmall ſtirre about that way.[24]For a certaine man named Demetrius, a ſiluer ſmith, which made ſiluer ſhrines for Diana, brought no ſmall gaine vnto the craftſmen:[25]Whom he called together, with the workemen of like occupation, and ſaid, Sirs, ye know that by this craft we haue our wealth.[26]Moreouer, ye ſee & heare, that not alone at Epheſus, but almoſt throughout all Aſia, this Paul hath perſwaded and turned away much people, ſaying, that they bee no gods, which are made with hands.[27]So that not only this our craft is in danger to be ſet at nought: but alſo that the Temple of the great goddeſse Diana ſhould be deſpiſed, and her magnificence ſhould be deſtroyed, whom all Aſia, and the world worſhippeth.[28]And when they heard theſe ſayings, they were ful of wrath, & cried out, ſaying, Great is Diana of þe Epheſians.[29]And the whole citie was filled with confuſion, and hauing caught Gaius and Ariſtarchus men of Macedonia Pauls companions in trauaile, they ruſhed with one accord into the Theatre.[30]And when Paul would haue entred in vnto the people, the diſciples ſuffered him not.[31]And certaine of the chiefe of Aſia, which were his friends, ſent vnto him, deſiring him that he would not aduenture himſelfe into the Theatre.[32]Some therefore cried one thing, and ſome another: for the aſſembly was confuſed, and the more part knew not wherefore they were come together.[33]And they drew Alexander out of the multitude, the Iewes putting him forward. And Alexander beckened with the hand, and would haue made his defence vnto the people.[34]But when they knew that he was a Iewe, all with one voyce about the ſpace of two houres cried out, Great is Diana of the Epheſians.[35]And when the towne clarke had appeaſed the people, he ſaid, Ye men of Epheſus, what man is there þt knoweth not how that the citie of the Epheſians is a worſhipper of the great goddeſse Diana, and of the image which fell downe from Iupiter?[36]Seeing then that theſe things cannot be ſpoken againſt, ye ought to be quiet, and to doe nothing raſhly.[37]For ye haue brought hither theſe men, which are neither robbers of Churches, nor yet blaſphemers of your goddeſse:[38]Wherefore if Demetrius, and the crafteſmen which are with him, haue a matter againſt any man, the law is open, and there are deputies, let them implead one another.[39]But if yee enquire any thing concerning other matters, it ſhalbe determined in a lawfull aſſembly.[40]For we are in danger to be called in queſtion for this dayes vprore, there being no cauſe whereby we may giue an accompt of this concourſe.[41]And when hee had thus ſpoken, he diſmiſsed the aſſembly.

CHAPTER 20[1]And after the vprore was ceaſed, Paul called vnto him the diſciples, and imbraced them, & departed, for to go into Macedonia.[2]And when he had gone ouer thoſe parts, and had giuen them much exhortation, he came into Greece,[3]And there abode three moneths: and when the Iewes layed waite for him, as hee was about to ſaile into Syria, hee purpoſed to returne thorow Macedonia.[4]And there accompanied him into Aſia, Sopater of Berea: and of the Theſsalonians, Ariſtarchus, and Secundus, and Gaius of Derbe, and Timotheus: and of Aſia Tychicus and Trophimus.[5]Theſe going before, taried for vs at Troas:[6]And wee ſailed away from Philippi, after the dayes of vnleauened bread, and came vnto them to Troas in fiue dayes, where we abode ſeuen daies.[7]And vpon the firſt day of the weeke, when the diſciples came together to breake bread, Paul preached vnto them, ready to depart on the morrow, and continued his ſpeach vntill midnight.[8]And there were many lights in the vpper chamber where they were gathered together.[9]And there ſate in a window a certaine yong man named Eutychus, being fallen into a deepe ſleepe, and as Paul was long preaching, hee ſunke downe with ſleepe, and fel downe from the third loft, and was taken vp dead.[10]And Paul went downe, and fell on him, and embracing him, ſaide, Trouble not your ſelues, for his life is in him.[11]When hee therefore was come vp againe, & had broken bread, and eaten, and talked a long while, euen till breake of day, ſo he departed.[12]And they brought the yong man aliue, and were not a little comforted.[13]And wee went before to ſhip, and ſailed vnto Aſsos, there intending to take in Paul: for ſo had hee appointed, minding himſelfe to goe afoote.[14]And when he met with vs at Aſsos, wee tooke him in, and came to Mitylene.[15]And wee ſailed thence, and came the next day ouer againſt Chios, and the next day we arriued at Samos, and taried at Trogyllium: and the next day we came to Miletus.[16]For Paul had determined to ſaile by Epheſus, becauſe he would not ſpend the time in Aſia: for he haſted, if it were poſsible for him, to be at Hieruſalem the day of Pentecoſt.[17]And from Miletus hee ſent to Epheſus, and called the Elders of the Church.[18]And when they were come to him, he ſaid vnto them, Ye know from the firſt day that I came into Aſia, after what maner I haue bene with you at all ſeaſons,[19]Seruing the Lord with all humilitie of minde, and with many teares, and temptations, which befell me by the lying in wait of the Iewes:[20]And how I kept backe nothing that was profitable vnto you, but haue ſhewed you, and haue taught you publikely, and from houſe to houſe,[21]Teſtifying both to the Iewes and alſo to the Greekes, repentance toward God, and faith toward our Lord Ieſus Chriſt.[22]And now behold, I goe bound in the ſpirit vnto Hieruſalem, not knowing the things that ſhal befall me there:[23]Saue that the holy Ghoſt witneſſeth in euery city, ſaying that bonds and afflictions abide me.[24]But none of theſe things mooue me, neither count I my life deare vnto my ſelf, ſo that I might finiſh my courſe with ioy, & the miniſtery which I haue receiued of the Lord Ieſus, to teſtifie the Goſpel of the grace of God.[25]And now behold, I know that ye all, among whom I haue gone preaching the kingdom of God, ſhall ſee my face no more.[26]Wherefore I take you to record this day, that I am pure from the blood of all men.[27]For I haue not ſhunned to declare vnto you all the counſell of God.[28]Take heed therefore vnto your ſelues, & to all the flocke, ouer the which the holy Ghoſt hath made you ouerſeers, to feed the Church of God, which he hath purchaſed with his own blood.[29]For I know this, that after my departing ſhall grieuous wolues enter in among you, not ſparing the flocke.[30]Alſo of your owne ſelues ſhal men Ariſe, ſpeaking peruerſe things, to draw away diſciples after them.[31]Therefore watch, and remember that by the ſpace of three yeeres, I ceaſed not to warne euery one night and day with teares.[32]And now brethren, I commend you to God, and to the word of his grace, which is able to build you vp, and to giue you an inheritance among all them which are ſanctified.[33]I haue coueted no mans ſiluer, or golde, or apparell.[34]Yea, you your ſelues know, that theſe handes haue miniſtred vnto my neceſsities, and to them that were with me.[35]I haue ſhewed you all things, how that ſo labouring, yee ought to ſupport the weake, and to remember the words of the Lord Ieſus, how he ſaid, It is more bleſſed to giue, then to receiue.[36]And when he had thus ſpoken, he kneeled downe, & prayed with them all.[37]And they all wept ſore, and fell on Pauls necke, and kiſſed him,[38]Sorrowing moſt of all for the words which he ſpake, that they ſhould ſee his face no more. And they accompanied him vnto the ſhip.

CHAPTER 21[1]And it came to paſſe, that after wee were gotten frō them, and had lanched, wee came with a ſtraight courſe vnto Choos, and the day following vnto Rhodes, and from thence vnto Patara.[2]And finding a ſhip ſailing ouer vnto Phenicea, wee went abroad, and ſet foorth.[3]Now when wee had diſcouered Cyprus, we left it on the left hand, and ſailed into Syria, and landed at Tyre: for there the ſhippe was to vnlade her burden.[4]And finding diſciples, wee taried there ſeuen dayes: who ſaid to Paul through the Spirit, that hee ſhould not goe vp to Hieruſalem.[5]And when we had accompliſhed thoſe dayes, we departed, and went our way, and they all brought vs on our way, with wiues and children, till wee were out of the citie: and wee kneeled downe

on the ſhore, and prayed.6And when we had taken our leaue one of
another, we tooke ſhip, and they returned home againe.7And when wee
had finiſhed our courſe from Tyre, wee came to Ptolemais, and ſaluted
the brethren, and abode with them one day.8And the next day we that
were of Pauls company, departed, and came vnto Ceſarea, and wee
entred into the houſe of Philip the Euangeliſt (which was one of the
ſeuen) & abode with him.9And þe ſame man had foure daughters,
virgins, which did propheſie.10And as wee taried there many dayes, there
came downe from Iudea a certaine Prophet, named Agabus.11And when
he was come vnto vs, he tooke Pauls girdle, and bound his owne hands
and feete, and ſaid, Thus ſayth the holy Ghoſt, So ſhall the Iewes at
Hieruſalem binde the man that oweth this girdle, and ſhall deliuer him
into the hands of the Gentiles.12And when we heard theſe things, both
we and they of that place, beſought him not to goe vp to
Hieruſalem.13Then Paul anſwered, What meane ye to weepe and to
breake mine heart? for I am ready, not to bee bound onely, but alſo to
die at Hieruſalem for the Name of the Lord Ieſus.14And when he would
not bee perſwaded, we ceaſed, ſaying, The will of the Lord be
done.15And after thoſe dayes we tooke vp our cariages, & went vp to
Hieruſalem.16There went with vs alſo certaine of the diſciples of
Ceſarea, and brought with them one Mnaſon of Cyprus, an old diſciple,
with whō we ſhould lodge.17And when we were come to Hieruſalem,
the brethren receiued vs gladly18And the day following Paul went in with
vs vnto Iames, and all the Elders were preſent.19And when hee had
ſaluted them, hee declared particularly what things God had wrought
among the Gentiles by his miniſterie.20And when they heard it, they
glorified the Lord, & ſaid vnto him, Thou ſeeſt, brother, how many
thouſands of Iewes there are which beleeue, and they are all zealous of
the Law.21And they are informed of thee, that thou teacheſt all the Iewes
which are among the Gentiles, to forſake Moſes, ſaying, that they ought
not to circumciſe their children, neither to walke after the
cuſtomes.22What is it therefore? the multitude muſt needs come
together: for they will heare that thou art come.23Doe therefore this that
we ſay to thee: Wee haue foure men which haue a vow on them,24Then
take, and purifie thy ſelfe with them, & bee at charges with them, that
they may ſhaue their heads: and all may know that thoſe things wherof
they were informed concerning thee, are nothing, but that thou thy ſelfe
alſo walkeſt orderly, and keepeſt the Law.25As touching the Gentiles
which beleeue, wee haue written and concluded, that they obſerue no
ſuch thing, ſaue onely that they keepe themſelues from things offered to
idoles, and from blood, and from ſtrangled, and from
fornication.26Then Paul tooke the men, and the next day purifying
himſelfe with them, entred into the Temple, to ſignifie the
accompliſhment of the dayes of purification, vntill that an offering
ſhould be offered for euery one of them:27And when the ſeuen dayes
were almoſt ended, the Iewes which were of Aſia, when they ſaw him in
the Temple, ſtirred vp all the people, and laide hands on him,28Crying
out, Men of Iſrael, helpe: this is þe man that teacheth al men euery where
againſt the people, and the law, and this place: and farther brought
Greeks alſo into the Temple, and hath polluted this holy place.29(For
they had ſeene before with him in the citie, Trophimus an Epheſian,
whome they ſuppoſed that Paul had brought into the Temple.)30And all
the citie was moued, and the people ran together: and they tooke Paul,
and drew him out of the Temple: and forthwith the doores were
ſhut.31And as they went about to kil him, tidings came vnto the chiefe
captaine of the band, that all Hieruſalem was in an vprore.32Who
immediatly tooke ſouldiers, and Centurions, and ran downe vnto them:
and when they ſaw the chiefe captaine and the ſouldiers, they left beating
of Paul.33Then the chiefe captain came neere, and tooke him, &
commanded him to be bound with two chains, and demanded who he
was, and what hee had done.34And ſome cried one thing, ſome another,
among the multitude: and when he could not know the certaintie for the
tumult, he commanded him to be caried into the caſtle.35And when he
came vpon þe ſtaires, ſo it was that he was borne of the ſouldiers, for
the violence of the people.36For the multitude of the people followed
after, crying, Away with him.37And as Paul was to bee led into the caſtle,
hee ſaide vnto the chiefe captaine, May I ſpeake vnto thee? Who ſaide,
Canſt thou ſpeake Greeke?38Art not thou that Egyptian which before
theſe daies madeſt an vprore, and leddeſt out into the wilderneſſe foure
thouſand men that were murtherers?39But Paul ſaid, I am a man which
am a Iew of Tarſus, a citie in Cilicia, a citizen of no meane citie: & I
beſeech thee ſuffer me to ſpeake vnto the people.40And when he had
giuen him licence, Paul ſtood on the ſtaires, and beckened with the hand
vnto the people: and when there was made a great ſilence, he ſpake vnto
them in the Hebrew tongue, ſaying.
CHAPTER 221Men, brethren, and fathers, heare ye my defence which
I make now vnto you.2(And when they heard that hee ſpake in the
Hebrew tongue to them, they kept the more ſilence: and he ſaith,)3I am
verely a man which am a Iew, borne in Tarſus a citie in Cilicia, yet
brought vp in this citie at the feete of Gamaliel, and taught according to
the perfect maner of the law of the fathers, and was zealous towards
God, as ye all are this day.4And I perſecuted this way vnto the death,
binding and deliuering into priſons both men and women,5As alſo the
high Prieſt doth beare me witneſſe, and all the eſtate of the elders: from
whom alſo I receiued letters vnto the brethren, and went to Damaſcus,
to bring them which were there, bound vnto Hieruſalem, for to be
puniſhed.6And it came to paſſe, that as I made my iourney, & was come
nigh vnto Damaſcus about noone, ſuddenly there ſhone from heauen a
great light round about me.7And I fell vnto the ground, and heard a
voice ſaying vnto mee, Saul, Saul, why perſecuteſt thou me?8And I
anſwered, Who art thou, Lord? And he ſaid vnto me, I am Ieſus of
Nazareth whō thou perſecuteſt.9And they that were with me ſaw
indeede the light, and were afraid; but they heard not the voice of him
that ſpake to me.10And I ſaide, What ſhall I doe, Lord? And the Lord
ſaid vnto me, Ariſe, and goe into Damaſcus, and there it ſhall be told
thee of all things which are appointed for thee to doe.11And when I
could not ſee for the glory of that light, being led by the hand of them
that were with me, I came into Damaſcus.12And one Ananias, a deuout
man according to the law, hauing a good report of al the Iewes which
dwelt there,13Came vnto me, and ſtood, & ſaid vnto me, Brother Saul,
receiue thy ſight. And the ſame houre I looked vp vpon him.14And he
ſaid, The God of our fathers hath choſen thee, þt thou ſhouldeſt know
his will, & ſee that Iuſt one, and ſhouldeſt heare the voice of his
mouth.15For thou ſhalt be his witnes vnto al men, of what thou haſt
ſeene & heard.16And now, why tarieſt thou? Ariſe, and be baptized, and
waſh away thy ſinnes, calling on the name of the Lord.17And it came to
paſſe, that when I was come againe to Hieruſalem, euen while I prayed
in the temple, I was in a trance,18And ſaw him ſaying vnto mee, Make
haſte, and get thee quickly out of Hieruſalem: for they will not receiue
thy teſtimony concerning me.19And I ſaid, Lord, they know that I
impriſoned, and beat in euery ſynagogue them that beleeued on
thee.20And when þe blood of thy martyr Steuen was ſhed, I alſo was
ſtanding by, and conſenting vnto his death, and kept the raiment of them
that ſlew him.21And he ſaid vnto me, Depart: for I will ſend thee farre
hence, vnto the Gentiles.22And they gaue him audience vnto this word,
and then lift vp their voices, and ſaid, Away with ſuch a fellow from the
earth: for it is not fit that he ſhould liue.23And as they cried out, and caſt
off their clothes, & threw duſt into the aire,24The chiefe captaine
commanded him to be brought into the caſtle, and bade that hee ſhould
be examined by ſcourging: that he might know wherfore they cried ſo
againſt him.25And as they bound him with thongs, Paul ſaid vnto the
Centurion that ſtood by, Is it lawfull for you to ſcourge a man that is a
Romane, and vncondemned?26When the Centurion heard that, hee
went and told the chiefe captaine, ſaying, Take heede what thou doeſt,
for this man is a Romane.27Then the chiefe captaine came; and ſaid vnto
him, Tell me, art thou a Romane? He ſaid, Yea.28And the chiefe captaine
anſwered, With a great ſumme obteined I this freedome. And Paul ſaid,
But I was free borne.29Then ſtraightway they departed from him which
ſhould haue examined him: and the chiefe captaine alſo was afraid after
he knew that he was a Romane, & becauſe he had bound him.30On the
morrow, becauſe he would haue knowen the certaintie wherefore he was
accuſed of the Iewes, he looſed him from his bands, and commanded
the chiefe Prieſts and all their Councill to appeare, and brought Paul
downe, and ſet him before them.
CHAPTER 231And Paul earneſtly beholding the council, ſaid, Men and
brethren, I haue liued in all good conſcience before God vntill this
day.2And the high Prieſt Ananias commanded them that ſtood by him,
to ſmite him on the mouth.3Then ſaith Paul vnto him, God ſhall ſmite
thee, thou whited wall: for ſitteſt thou to iudge mee after the Law, and
commandeſt mee to be ſmitten contrary to the Law?4And they that

ſtood by, ſaid, Reuileſt thou Gods high Prieſt?5Then ſaid Paul, I wiſt
not, brethren, that hee was the high Priſt: For it is written, Thou ſhalt
not ſpeake euill of the ruler of thy people.6But when Paul perceiued that
the one part were Sadducees, and the other PhAriſees, hee cryed out in
the Councill, Men and brethren, I am a PhAriſee, the ſonne of a
PhAriſee: of the hope and reſurrection of the dead, I am called in
queſtion.7And when hee had ſo ſaid, there aroſe a diſsenſion betweene
the PhAriſees and the Sadducees: and the multitude was diuided.8For
the Sadducees ſay that there is no reſurrection, neither Angel, nor ſpirit:
but the PhAriſees confeſse both.9And there aroſe a great cry: and the
Scribes that were of the PhAriſees part aroſe, and ſtroue, ſaying, Wee
finde no euill in this man: but if a ſpirit or an Angel hath ſpoken to him,
let vs not fight againſt God.10And when there aroſe a great diſsenſion,
the chiefe captaine fearing leſt Paul ſhould haue bene pulled in pieces of
them, commanded the ſouldiers to goe downe, and to take him by force
from among them, and to bring him into the caſtle.11And the night
folowing, the Lord ſtood by him, and ſaide, Bee of good cheere, Paul:
for as thou haſt teſtified of mee in Hieruſalem, ſo muſt thou beare
witneſſe alſo at Rome.12And when it was day, certaine of the Iewes
banded together, and bound themſelues vnder a curſe, ſaying, that they
would neither eate nor drinke till they had killed Paul.13And they were
more then fourtie which had made this conſpiracie.14And they came to
the chiefe Prieſts and Elders, and ſaid, Wee haue bound our ſelues vnder
a great curſe, that wee will eate nothing vntill wee haue ſlaine
Paul.15Now therefore ye with the Councill, ſignifie to the chiefe captaine
that he bring him downe vnto you to morrow, as though yee would
enquire ſomething more perfectly concerning him: and we, or euer he
come neere, are ready to kill him.16And when Pauls ſiſters ſonne heard
of their laying in wait, hee went and entred into the caſtle, & told
Paul.17Then Paul called one of the Centurions vnto him, and ſaid, Bring
this yong man vnto the chiefe captaine: for he hath a certaine thing to
tell him.18So he took him, and brought him to the chiefe captaine, and
ſaid, Paul the priſoner called me vnto him, and praied mee to bring this
yong man vnto thee, who hath ſomething to ſay vnto thee.19Then the
chiefe captaine tooke him by the hand, and went with him aſide
priuately, and aſked him, What is that thou haſt to tell me?20And he ſaid,
The Iewes haue agreed to deſire thee, that thou wouldeſt bring downe
Paul to morrow into the Council, as though they would enquire
ſomewhat of him more perfectly.21But do not thou yeeld vnto them: for
there lie in wait for him of them moe then fourtie men, which haue
bound themſelues with an othe, that they will neither eate nor drinke,
till they haue killed him: and now are they ready, looking for a promiſe
from thee.22So the chiefe captaine then let the yong man depart, and
charged him, ſee thou tell no man, that thou haſt ſhewed theſe things to
me.23And he called vnto him two Centurions, ſaying, Make ready two
hundred ſouldiers to goe to Ceſarea, and horſemen threeſcore and ten,
and ſpearemen two hundred, at the third houre of the night.24And
prouide them beaſts, that they may ſet Paul on, and bring him ſafe vnto
Felix the gouernour.25And hee wrote a letter after this
manner:26Claudius Lyſias, vnto the moſt excellent Gouernour Felix,
ſendeth greeting.27This man was taken of the Iewes and ſhould haue
beene killed of them: Then came I with an armie, and reſcued him,
hauing vnderſtood that he was a Romane.28And when I would haue
knowen the cauſe wherefore they accuſed him, I brought him foorth
into their Council.29Whom I perceiued to be accuſed of queſtions of
their lawe, but to haue nothing laide to his charge worthy of death or of
bonds.30And when it was tolde me, how that the Iewes laid waite for
the man, I ſent ſtraightway to thee, and gaue commandement to his
accuſers alſo, to ſay before thee what they had againſt him.
Farewell.31Then the ſouldiers, as it was commaunded them, tooke Paul,
and brought him by night to Antipatris.32On the morow, they left the
horſemen to goe with him, and returned to the caſtle.33Who when they
came to Ceſarea, and deliuered the Epiſtle to the gouernour, preſented
Paul alſo before him.34And when the gouernour had read the letter, he
aſked of what prouince he was. And when he vnderſtood that he was of
Cilicia:35I will heare thee, ſaid hee, when thine accuſers are alſo come.
And hee commanded him to be kept in Herods iudgement hall.

CHAPTER 241And after fiue dayes, Ananias the hie Prieſt deſcended
with the Elders, and with a certaine Oratour named Tertullus, who
enformed the gouernour againſt Paul.2And when he was called foorth,
Tertullus began to accuſe him, ſaying, Seeing that by thee we enioy great
quietneſse, and that very worthy deeds are done vnto this natiō by thy
prouidence:3Wee accept it alwayes, and in all places, moſt noble Felix,
with all thankfulneſse.4Notwithſtanding, that I be not farther tedious
vnto thee, I pray thee, that thou wouldeſt heare vs of thy clemencie a
few words.5For we haue found this man a peſtilent fellow, and a moouer
of ſedition among all the Iewes throughout the world, and a ringleader
of the ſect of the Nazarenes.6Who alſo hath gone about to profane the
Temple: whom we tooke, and would haue iudged according to our
lawe.7But the chiefe captaine Lyſias came vpon vs, and with great
violence tooke him away out of our hands:8Commanding his accuſers
to come vnto thee, by examining of whom thy ſelfe mayeſt take
knowledge of all theſe things, whereof we accuſe him.9And the Iewes
alſo aſſented, ſaying that theſe things were ſo.10Then Paul, after that the
gouernour had beckened vnto him to ſpeake, anſwered, Foraſmuch as I
know that thou haſt been of many yeeres a Iudge vnto this nation, I do
the more cheerefully anſwere for my ſelfe:11Becauſe that thou mayeſt
vnderſtand, that there are yet but twelue dayes, ſince I went vp to
Hieruſalem for to worſhip.12And they neither found me in the Temple
diſputing with any man, neither raiſing vp the people, neither in the
Synagogues, nor in the citie:13Neither can they proue the things whereof
they now accuſe me.14But this I confeſse vnto thee, that after the way
which they call hereſie, ſo worſhip I the God of my fathers, beleeuing
all things which are written in the Law and the Prophets,15And haue
hope towards God, which they themſelues alſo allow, that there ſhall be
a reſurrection of the dead, both of the iuſt and vniuſt.16And herein doe
I exerciſe my ſelfe to haue alwayes a conſcience void of offence toward
God, and toward men.17Now after many yeeres, I came to bring almes
to my nation, & offrings:18Wherupon certaine Iewes from Aſia found
me purified in the Temple, neither with multitude, nor with
tumult:19Who ought to haue beene here before thee, and obiect, if they
had ought againſt me.20Or elſe let theſe ſame here ſay, if they haue found
any euill doing in mee, while I ſtood before the Councill,21Except it be
for this one voice, that I cried ſtanding among them, Touching the
reſurrection of the dead I am called in queſtion by you this day.22And
when Felix heard theſe things, hauing more perfect knowledge of that
way, he deferred them and ſaid, When Lyſias the chiefe captaine ſhall
come downe, I will know the vttermoſt of your matter.23And he
commanded a Centurion to keepe Paul, and to let him haue libertie, and
that he ſhould forbid none of his acquaintance to miniſter, or come vnto
him.24And after certaine dayes, when Felix came with his wife Druſilla,
which was a Iew, he ſent for Paul, and heard him cōcerning the faith in
Chriſt.25And as he reaſoned of righteouſneſſe, temperance, and
iudgement to come, Felix trembled and anſwered, Go thy way for this
time, when I haue a conuenient ſeaſon, I will call for thee.26He hoped
alſo that money ſhould haue bene giuen him of Paul, that hee might
looſe him: wherefore hee ſent for him the oftner, and cōmuned with
him.27But after two yeeres, Portius Feſtus came into Felix roome: and
Felix willing to ſhew the Iewes a pleaſure, left Paul bound.

CHAPTER 251Nowe when Feſtus was come into the prouince, after
three dayes he aſcended frō Ceſarea to Hieruſalem.2Then the high Prieſt,
and the chiefe of the Iewes informed him againſt Paul, and beſought
him,3And deſired fauour againſt him, that he would ſend for him to
Hieruſalem, laying wait in the way to kill him.4But Feſtus anſwered, that
Paul ſhould be kept at Ceſarea, and that hee himſelfe would depart
ſhortly thither.5Let them therefore, ſaid he, which among you are able,
go downe with me, and accuſe this man, if there be any wickedneſſe in
him.6And when hee had taried among them more then ten dayes, hee
went downe vnto Ceſarea, and the next day ſitting in the iudgement ſeat,
commanded Paul to be brought.7And when hee was come, the Iewes
which came downe from Hieruſalem, ſtood round about, and laide
many and grieuous complaints againſt Paul, which they could not
proue,8While hee anſwered for himſelfe, Neither againſt the law of the
Iewes, neither againſt the Temple, nor yet againſt Ceſar, haue I offended
any thing at all.9But Feſtus willing to doe the Iewes a pleaſure, anſwered
Paul, and ſaid, Wilt thou goe vp to Hieruſalem, and there be iudged of
theſe things before me?10Then ſaid Paul, I ſtand at Ceſars iudgement
ſeat, where I ought to bee iudged; to the Iewes haue I done no wrong,
as thou very well knoweſt.11For if I be an offender, or haue committed
any thing worthy of death, I refuſe not to die: but if there be none of

theſe things whereof theſe accuſe me, no man may deliuer me vnto
them. I appeale vnto Ceſar.12Then Feſtus when he had conferred with
the Councill, anſwered, Haſt thou appealed vnto Ceſar? vnto Ceſar ſhalt
thou goe.13And after certaine dayes, king Agrippa and Bernice, came
vnto Ceſarea, to ſalute Feſtus.14And when they had beene there many
dayes, Feſtus declared Pauls cauſe vnto the king, ſaying, There is a
certaine man left in bonds by Felix:15About whom when I was at
Hieruſalem, the chiefe Prieſts and the Elders of the Iewes enformed me,
deſiring to haue iudgement againſt him.16To whom I anſwered, It is not
the maner of the Romanes to deliuer any man to die, before that he
which is accuſed, haue the accuſers face to face, and haue licence to
anſwere for himſelfe concerning the crime laid againſt him.17Therefore
when they were come hither, without any delay, on the morrow I ſate
on the iudgement ſeate, and cōmanded the man to be brought
forth.18Againſt whom when the accuſers ſtood vp, they brought none
accuſation of ſuch things as I ſuppoſed:19But had certaine queſtions
againſt him of their owne ſuperſtition, and of one Ieſus, which was dead,
whom Paul affirmed to be aliue.20And becauſe I doubted of ſuch maner
of queſtions, I aſked him whether he would goe to Hieruſalem, and there
be iudged of theſe matters.21But when Paul had appealed to bee
referuedvnto the hearing of Auguſtus, I commanded him to be kept, till
I might ſend him to Ceſar.22Then Agrippa ſaid vnto Feſtus, I would alſo
heare the man my ſelfe. To morrow, ſaid he, thou ſhalt heare him.23And
on the morrow when Agrippa was come and Bernice, with great pompe,
and was entred into the place of hearing, with the chiefe captaines, and
principall men of the citie; at Feſtus commaundement Paul was brought
foorth.24And Feſtus ſaid, King Agrippa, and all men which are heere
preſent with vs, ye ſee this man, about whom all the multitude of the
Iewes haue dealt with me, both at Hieruſalem, and alſo heere, crying that
he ought not to liue any longer.25But when I found that he had
committed nothing worthy of death, and that he himſelfe hath appealed
to Auguſtus, I haue determined to ſend him.26Of whom I haue no
certaine thing to write vnto my Lord: Wherefore I haue brought him
foorth before you, and ſpecially before thee, O king Agrippa, that after
examination had, I might haue ſomewhat to write.27For it ſeemeth to
me vnreaſonable, to ſend a priſoner, and not withall to ſignifie the
crimes laid againſt him.

CHAPTER 261Then Agrippa ſaid vnto Paul, Thou art permitted to
ſpeake for thy ſelfe. Then Paul ſtretched foorth the hand, and anſwered
for himſelfe,2I thinke my ſelfe happy, king Agrippa, becauſe I ſhall
anſwere for my ſelfe this day before thee touching all the things whereof
I am accuſed of the Iewes:3Eſpecially, becauſe I know thee to be expert
in all cuſtomes and queſtions which are among the Iewes: wherefore I
beſeech thee to heare mee patiently.4My maner of life from my youth,
which was at the firſt among mine owne nation at Hieruſalem, know all
the Iewes,5Which knew me from the beginning, (if they would teſtifie)
that after the moſt ſtraiteſt ſect of our religion, I liued a PhAriſee.6And
now I ſtand, and am iudged for the hope of the promiſe made of God
vnto our fathers:7Vnto which promiſe our twelue tribes inſtantly ſeruing
God day and night, hope to come: For which hopes ſake, King Agrippa,
I am accuſed of the Iewes.8Why ſhould it be thought a thing incredible
with you, that God ſhould raiſe the dead?9I verily thought with my ſelfe,
that I ought to doe many things contrary to the name of Ieſus of
Nazareth:10Which thing I alſo did in Hieruſalem, and many of the Saints
did I ſhut vp in priſon, hauing receiued authoritie from the chiefe Prieſts,
and when they were put to death, I gaue my voyce againſt them.11And I
puniſhed them oft in euery Synagogue, and compelled them to
blaſpheme, and being exceedingly mad againſt them, I perſecuted them
euen vnto ſtrange cities.12Whereupon, as I went to Damaſcus, with
authoritie and commiſsion from the chiefe Prieſts:13At midday, O king,
I ſaw in the way a light from heauen, aboue the brightnes of the Sunne,
ſhining round about mee, and them which iourneyed with me.14And
when wee were all fallen to the earth, I heard a voice ſpeaking vnto me,
and ſaying in the Hebrew tongue, Saul, Saul, why perſecuteſt thou me?
It is hard for thee to kicke againſt the prickes.15And I ſaid, Who art thou,
Lord? And hee ſaid, I am Ieſus whom thou perſecuteſt.16But riſe, and
ſtand vpon thy feete, for I haue appeared vnto thee for this purpoſe, to
make thee a miniſter and a witneſſe, both of theſe things which thou
haſt ſeene, & of thoſe things in the which I will appeare vnto
thee,17Deliuering thee from the people, and from the Gentiles, vnto
whom now I ſend thee,18To open their eyes, and to turne them from
darkneſſe to light, and from the power of Satan vnto God, that they may
receiue forgiueneſse of ſinnes, and inheritance among them which are
ſanctified by faith that is in me.19Whereupon, O king Agrippa, I was not
diſobedient vnto the heauenly viſion:20But ſhewed firſt vnto them of
Damaſcus, and at Hieruſalem, and thorowout all the coaſts of Iudea,
and then to the Gentiles, that they ſhould repent and turne to God, and
do works meete for repentance.21For theſe cauſes the Iewes caught mee
in the Temple, and went about to kill me.22Hauing therefore obteined
helpe of God, I continue vnto this day, witneſsing both to ſmall and
great, ſaying none other things then thoſe which the Prophets and
Moſes did ſay ſhould come:23That Chriſt ſhould ſuffer, and that hee
ſhould be the firſt that ſhould riſe from the dead, & ſhould ſhew light
vnto the people, and to the Gentiles.24And as hee thus ſpake for
himſelfe, Feſtus ſaide with a lowd voyce, Paul, thou art beſide thy ſelfe,
much learning doeth make thee mad.25But he ſaid, I am not mad, moſt
noble Feſtus, but ſpeake foorth the words of trueth and
ſoberneſse.26For the King knoweth of theſe things, before whom alſo I
ſpeake freely: for I am perſwaded, that none of theſe things are hidden
from him, for this thing was not done in a corner.27King Agrippa,
beleeueſt thou the Prophets? I know that thou beleeueſt.28Then Agrippa
ſaide vnto Paul, Almoſt thou perſwadeſt mee to bee a Chriſtian.29And
Paul ſaid, I would to God, that not onely thou, but alſo all that heare
mee this day, were both almoſt, and altogether ſuch as I am, except theſe
bonds.30And when hee had thus ſpoken, the king roſe vp, and the
gouernour, and Bernice, & they that ſate with them.31And when they
were gone aſide, they talked betweene themſelues, ſaying, This man
doeth nothing worthy of death, or of bonds.32Then ſaid Agrippa vnto
Feſtus, This man might haue bene ſet at libertie, if he had not appealed
vnto Ceſar.

CHAPTER 271And when it was determined, that wee ſhould ſaile into
Italy, they deliuered Paul, & certaine other priſoners, vnto one named
Iulius, a centurion of Auguſtus band.2And entring into a ſhip of
Adramyttium, wee lanched, meaning to ſaile by the coaſts of Aſia, one
Ariſtarchus a Macedonian, of Theſsalonica, beeing with vs.3And the
next day wee touched at Sidon: And Iulius courteouſly entreated Paul,
and gaue him libertie to goe vnto his friends to refreſh himſelfe.4And
when we had lanched from thence, we ſailed vnder Cyprus, becauſe the
winds were contrary.5And when we had ſailed ouer the ſea of Cilicia and
Pamphylia, wee came to Myra a citie of Lyſia.6And there the Centurion
found a ſhip of Alexandria ſailing into Italy, and he put vs therein.7And
when wee had ſailed ſlowly many dayes, and ſcarſe were come ouer
againſt Gnidus, the wind not ſuffering vs, wee ſailed vnder Creete, ouer
againſt Salmone,8And hardly paſsing it, came vnto a place which is called
the Faire hauens, nigh whereunto was the citie of Laſea.9Now when
much time was ſpent, and when ſailing was now dangerous, becauſe the
Faſt was now alreadie paſt, Paul admoniſhed them,10And ſaid vnto
them, Sirs, I perceiue that this voyage will be with hurt and much
damage, not onely of the lading & ſhip, but alſo of our
liues.11Neuertheleſſe, the Centurion beleeued the maſter and the owner
of the ſhippe, more then thoſe things which were ſpoken by Paul.12And
becauſe the hauen was not commodious to winter in, the more part
aduiſed to depart thence alſo, if by any meanes they might attaine to
Phenice, and there to winter; which is an hauen of Creete, and lieth
toward the Southweſt, and Northweſt.13And when the South wind blew
ſoftly, ſuppoſing that they had obtained their purpoſe, looſing thence,
they ſailed cloſe by Creete.14But not long after, there aroſe againſt it a
tempeſtuous winde, called Euroclydon.15And when the ſhip was caught,
and could not beare vp into the winde, we let her driue.16And running
vnder a certaine yland, which is called Clauda, wee had much worke to
come by the boate:17Which when they had taken vp, they vſed helps,
vnder-girding the ſhip; and fearing leſt they ſhould fall into the quicke-
ſands, ſtrake ſaile, and ſo were driuen.18And being exceedingly toſsed
with a tempeſt the next day, they lightened the ſhip:19And the third day
we caſt out with our owne handes the tackling of the ſhippe.20And when
neither Sunne nor ſtarres in many dayes appeared, and no ſmall tempeſt
lay on vs; all hope that wee ſhould be ſaued, was then taken away.21But
after long abſtinence, Paul ſtood foorth in the middes of them, and ſaid,
Sirs, yee ſhould haue hearkened vnto mee, and not haue looſed from
Creete, and to haue gained this harme and loſse.22And now I exhort you

to be of good cheere: for there ſhall be no loſſe of any mans life among
you, but of the ſhippe.23For there ſtood by me this night the Angel of
God, whoſe I am, and whom I ſerue,24Saying, Feare not Paul, thou muſt
be brought before Ceſar, and loe, God hath giuen thee all them that ſaile
with thee.25Wherefore, ſirs, be of good cheere: for I beleeue God, that
it ſhall be euen as it was tolde me.26Howbeit, we muſt be caſt vpon a
certaine Iland.27But when the fourteenth night was come, as wee were
driuen vp and downe in Adria about midnight, the ſhipmen deemed that
they drew neere to ſome countrey:28And ſounded, and found it twentie
fathoms: and when they had gone a little further, they ſounded againe,
and found it fifteene fathoms.29Then fearing leſt we ſhould haue fallen
vpon rockes, they caſt foure ancres out of the ſterne, and wiſhed for the
day.30And as the ſhipmen were about to flee out of the ſhip, when they
had let downe the boat into the ſea, vnder colour as though they would
haue caſt ancres out of the fore-ſhip,31Paul ſaid to the Centurion, and to
the ſouldiers, Except theſe abide in the ſhip, ye cannot be ſaued.32Then
the ſouldiers cut off the ropes of the boat, and let her fall off.33And
while the day was comming on, Paul beſought them all to take meat,
ſaying, This day is the fourteenth day that ye haue taried, and continued
faſting, hauing taken nothing.34Wherefore, I pray you to take ſome
meat, for this is for your health: for there ſhall not an haire fall from the
head of any of you.35And when hee had thus ſpoken, hee tooke bread,
and gaue thankes to God in preſence of them all, and when he had
broken it, he began to eate.36Then were they all of good cheere, and
they alſo tooke ſome meat.37And we were in all, in the ſhip, two
hundred, threeſcore and ſixteene ſoules.38And when they had eaten
enough, they lightened the ſhip, and caſt out the wheat into the
ſea.39And when it was day, they knew not the land: but they diſcouered
a certaine creek, with a ſhore, into the which they were minded, if it were
poſsible, to thruſt in the ſhip.40And when they had taken vp the ankers,
they committed themſelues vnto the ſea, & looſed the rudder bands, and
hoiſed vp the maine ſaile to the winde, and made toward ſhore.41And
falling into a place where two ſeas met, they ranne the ſhippe a ground,
and the forepart ſtucke faſt, and remained vnmoueable, but the hinder
part was broken with the violence of the waues.42And the ſouldiers
counſel was to kil the priſoners, leſt any of them ſhould ſwimme out,
and eſcape.43But the Centurion, willing to ſaue Paul, kept them from
their purpoſe, and commanded that they which could ſwimme, ſhould
caſt themſelues firſt into the ſea, and get to land:44And the reſt, ſome
on boords, and ſome on broken pieces of the ſhip: and ſo it came to
paſſe that they eſcaped all ſafe to land.
CHAPTER 28 1And when they were eſcaped, then they knew that the
Iland was called Melita.2And the barbarous people ſhewed vs no little
kindneſse: for they kindled a fire, and receiued vs euery one becauſe of
the preſent raine, and becauſe of the cold.3And when Paul had gathered
a bundle of ſtickes, and layde them on the fire, there came a Uiper out
of the heat, and faſtened on his hand.4And when the Barbarians ſaw the
venomous beaſt hang on his hand, they ſaide among themſelues, No
doubt this man is a murtherer, whom though hee hath eſcaped the ſea,
yet Uengeance ſuffereth not to liue.5And hee ſhooke off the beaſt into
the fire, and felt no harme.6Howbeit, they looked when hee ſhould haue
ſwollen, or fallen downe dead ſuddenly: but after they had looked a great
while, and ſaw no harme come to him, they changed their minds, and
ſaid that he was a God.7In the ſame quarters were poſſeſſions of the
chiefe man of the Iland, whoſe name was Publius, who receiued vs, and
lodged vs three dayes courteouſly.8And it came to paſſe that the father
of Publius lay ſicke of a feuer, and of a bloody-flixe, to whom Paul
entred in, and prayed, and layed his hands on him, and healed him.9So
when this was done, others alſo which had diſeaſes in the Iland, came,
and were healed:10Who alſo honoured vs with many honours, and when
wee departed, they laded vs with ſuch things as were neceſsary.11And
after three moneths wee departed in a ſhip of Alexandria, which had
wintered in the Ile, whoſe ſigne was Caſtor and Pollux.12And landing at
Syracuſe wee taried there three dayes.13And from thence wee fet a
compaſſe, and came to Rhegium, and after one day the South winde
blew, and we came the next day to Puteoli:14Where wee found brethren,
and were deſired to tary with them ſeuen dayes: and ſo we went toward
Rome.15And from thence, when the brethren heard of vs, they came to
meet vs as farre as Appii forum, and the three Tauernes: whom when
Paul ſaw, he thanked God, and tooke courage.16And when we came to
Rome, the Centurion deliuered the priſoners to the Captaine of the
guard: but Paul was ſuffered to dwell by himſelfe, with a ſouldier that
kept him.17And it came to paſſe, that after three dayes, Paul called the
chiefe of the Iewes together. And when they were come together, he
ſaid vnto them, Men and brethren, though I haue committed nothing
againſt the people, or cuſtomes of our fathers, yet was I deliuered
priſoner from Hieruſalem into the hands of the Romanes.18Who when
they had examined me, would haue let me goe, becauſe there was no
cauſe of death in me.19But when the Iewes ſpake againſt it, I was
conſtrained to appeale vnto Ceſar, not that I had ought to accuſe my
nation of.20For this cauſe therefore haue I called for you, to ſee you, and
to ſpeake with you: becauſe that for the hope of Iſrael I am bound with
this chaine.21And they ſaide vnto him, Wee neither receiued letters out
of Iudea concerning thee, neither any of the brethren that came, ſhewed
or ſpake any harme of thee.22But we deſire to heare of thee what thou
thinkeſt: for as concerning this ſect, we know that euery where it is
ſpoken againſt.23And when they had appointed him a day, there came
many to him into his lodging, to whom he expounded and teſtified the
kingdome of God, perſwading them concerning Ieſus, both out of the
law of Moſes, and out of the Prophets, from morning till euening.24And
ſome beleeued the things which were ſpoken, and ſome beleeued
not.25And when they agreed not among themſelues, they departed, after
that Paul had ſpoken one word, Well ſpake the holy Ghoſt by Eſaias the
Prophet, vnto our fathers,26Saying, Goe vnto this people, and ſay,
Hearing ye ſhall heare, and ſhall not vnderſtand, and ſeeing ye ſhall ſee,
and not perceiue.27For the heart of this people is waxed groſse, and their
eares are dull of hearing, and their eyes haue they cloſed, leſt they ſhould
with their eyes, and heare with their eares, and vnderſtand with their
heart, and ſhould bee conuerted, and I ſhould heale them.28Be it knowen
therfore vnto you, that the ſaluation of God is ſent vnto the Gentiles,
and that they wil heare it.29And when hee had ſaide theſe words, the
Iewes departed, and had great reaſoning among themſelues.30And Paul
dwelt two whole yeeres in his owne hired houſe, and receiued all that
came in vnto him,31Preaching the kingdome of God, and teaching thoſe
things which concerne the Lord Ieſus Chriſt, with all confidence, no
man forbidding him.

THE EPIſTLE TO THE ROMANES (ROMANS)

CHAPTER 1 1Paul a ſeruant of Ieſus Chriſt, called to bee an Apoſtle,
ſeparated vnto the Goſpel of God,2(Which he had promiſed afore by
his Prophets in the holy Scriptures,)3Concerning his Sonne Ieſus Chriſt
our Lord, which was made of the ſeed of Dauid according to the
fleſh,4And declared to be the Sonne of God, with power, according to
the Spirit of holineſſe, by the reſurrection from the dead.5By whom we
haue receiued grace and Apoſtleſhip for obedience to the faith among
all nations for his Name,6Among whom are ye alſo the called of Ieſus
Chriſt.7To all that be in Rome, beloued of God, called to be Saints:
Grace to you and peace from God our Father, and the Lord Ieſus
Chriſt.8Firſt I thanke my God through Ieſus Chriſt for you all, that your
faith is ſpoken of throughout the whole world.9For God is my witneſſe,
whom I ſerue with my ſpirit in the Goſpel of his Sonne, that without
ceaſing I make mention of you, alwayes in my prayers,10Making requeſt,
(if by any meanes now at length I might haue a proſperous iourney by
the will of God) to come vnto you.11For I long to ſee you, that I may
impart vnto you ſome ſpirituall gift, to the end you may be
eſtabliſhed,12That is, that I may be comforted together with you, by the
mutual faith both of you and me.13Now I would not haue you ignorant,
brethren, that oftentimes I purpoſed to come vnto you, (but was let
hitherto) that I might haue ſome fruit among you alſo, euen as among
other Gentiles.14I am debter both to the Greeks, and to the Barbarians,
both to the wiſe, and to the vnwiſe.15So, as much as in mee is, I am
ready to preach the Goſpel to you that are at Rome alſo.16For I am not
aſhamed of the Gopel of Chriſt: for it is the power of God vnto
ſaluation, to euery one that beleeueth, to the Iew firſt, and alſo to the
Greeke.17For therein is the righteouſneſſe of God reueiled from faith to

faith: as it is written, The iuſt ſhall liue by faith.[18]For the wrath of God is reueiled from heauen againſt all vngodlineſse, and vnrighteouſneſſe of men, who hold the trueth in vnrighteouſneſſe.[19]Becauſe that which may bee knowen of God, is manifeſt in them, for God hath ſhewed it vnto them.[20]For the inuiſible things of him from the Creation of the world, are cleareely ſeene, being vnderſtood by the things that are made, euen his eternall Power and Godhead, ſo that they are without excuſe:[21]Becauſe that when they knew God, they glorified him not as God, neither were thankefull, but became vaine in their imaginations, and their fooliſh heart was darkened:[22]Profeſsing themſelues to be wiſe, they became fooles:[23]And changed the glory of the vncorruptible God, into an image made like to corruptible man, and to birdes, and foure footed beaſts, and creeping things:[24]Wherefore God alſo gaue them vp to vncleanneſſe, through the luſts of their owne hearts, to diſhonour their owne bodies betweene themſelues:[25]Who changed the trueth of God into a lye, and worſhipped and ſerued the creature more then the Creatour, who is bleſſed for euer. Amen.[26]For this cauſe God gaue them vp vnto vile affections: for euen their women did change the naturall vſe into that which is againſt nature:[27]And likewiſe alſo the men, leauing the naturall vſe of the woman, burned in their luſt one towards another, men with men working that which is vnſeemely, and receiuing in themſelues that recompenſe of their errour which was meet.[28]And euen as they did not like to retaine God in their knowledge, God gaue them ouer to a reprobate minde, to doe thoſe things which are not conuenient:[29]Being filled with all vnrighteouſnes, fornication, wickedneſſe, couetouſnes, maliciouſnes, full of enuie, murther, debate, deceit, malignitie, whiſperers,[30]Backbiters, haters of God, deſpitefull, proude, boaſters, inuenters of euill things, diſobedient to parents;[31]Without vnderſtanding, couenant breakers, without naturall affection, implacable, vnmercifull;[32]Who knowing the iudgement of God, (that they which commit ſuch things, are worthy of death) not onely do the ſame, but haue pleaſure in them that doe them.

CHAPTER 2[1]Therefore, thou art inexcuſable, O man, whoſoeuer thou art that iudgeſt: for wherein thou iudgeſt another, thou condemneſt thy ſelfe, for thou that iudgeſt doeſt the ſame things.[2]But wee are ſure that the iudgement of God is according to trueth, againſt them which commit ſuch things.[3]And thinkeſt thou this, O man, that iudgeſt them which doe ſuch things, and doeſt the ſame, that thou ſhalt eſcape the iudgement of God?[4]Or deſpiſeſt thou the riches of his goodneſse, and forbearance, and long ſuffering, not knowing that the goodnes of God leadeth thee to repentance?[5]But after thy hardneſse, and impenitent heart, treaſureſt vp vnto thy ſelfe wrath, againſt the day of wrath, and reuelation of the righteous iudgement of God:[6]Who will render to euery man according to his deedes:[7]To them, who by patient continuance in well doing, ſeeke for glorie, and honour, and immortalitie, eternall life:[8]But vnto them that are contentious, & doe not obey the trueth, but obey vnrighteouſnes, indignation, & wrath,[9]Tribulation, and anguiſh vpon euery ſoule of man that doeth euill, of the Iew firſt, and alſo of the Gentile.[10]But glory, honour, and peace, to euery man that worketh good, to the Iew firſt, and alſo to the Gentile.[11]For there is no reſpect of perſons with God.[12]For as many as haue ſinned without Law, ſhall alſo periſh without Law: and as many as haue ſinned in the Law, ſhalbe iudged by the Law.[13](For not the hearers of the Law are iuſt before God, but the doers of the Law ſhalbe iuſtified;[14]For when the Gentiles which haue not the Law, doe by nature the things contained in the Law: theſe hauing not the Law, are a Law vnto themſelues,[15]Which ſhew the worke of the Law written in their hearts, their conſcience alſo bearing witneſſe, and their thoughts the meane while accuſing, or elſe excuſing one another:[16]In the day when God ſhall iudge the ſecrets of men by Ieſus Chriſt, according to my Goſpel.[17]Behold, thou art called a Iew, and reſteſt in the Law, and makeſt thy boaſt of God:[18]And knoweſt his will, and approueſt the things that are more excellent, being inſtructed out of the Law,[19]And art confident that thou thy ſelfe art a guide of the blinde, a light of them which are in darkeneſſe:[20]An inſtructour of the fooliſh, a teacher of babes: which haſt the forme of knowledge and of the trueth in the Law:[21]Thou therefore which teacheſt another, teacheſt thou not thy ſelfe? thou that preacheſt a man ſhould not ſteale, doeſt thou ſteale?[22]Thou that ſayeſt a man ſhould not commit adulterie, doeſt thou commit adulterie? thou that abhorreſt idols, doeſt thou commit ſacriledge?[23]Thou that makeſt thy boaſt of the Law, through breaking the Law diſhonoureſt thou God?[24]For the Name of God is blaſphemed among the Gentiles, through you, as it is written:[25]For Circumciſion verily profiteth if thou keepe the Law: but if thou be a breaker of the Law, thy Circumciſion is made vncircumciſion.[26]Therefore, if the vncircumciſion keepe the righteouſneſſe of the Law, ſhall not his vncircumciſion be counted for Circumciſion?[27]And ſhall not vncircumciſion which is by nature, if it fulfill the Law, iudge thee, who by the letter, and Circumciſion, doeſt tranſgreſse the Law?[28]For hee is not a Iew, which is one outwardly, neither is that Circumciſion, which is outward in the fleſh:[29]But he is a Iew which is one inwardly, and Circumciſion is, that of the heart, in the ſpirit, and not in the letter, whoſe praiſe is not of men, but of God.

CHAPTER 3[1]What aduantage then hath the Iew? or what profit is there of Circumciſion?[2]Much euery way: chiefly, becauſe that vnto them were committed the Oracles of God.[3]For what if ſome did not beleeue? ſhall their vnbeliefe make the faith of God without effect?[4]God forbid: yea, let God be true, but euery man a lier, as it is written, That thou mighteſt be iuſtified in thy ſayings, and mighteſt ouercome when thou art iudged.[5]But if our vnrighteouſneſſe commend the righteouſneſſe of God, what ſhall we ſay? is God vnrighteous who taketh vengeance? (I ſpeake as a man)[6]God forbid: for then how ſhall God iudge the world?[7]For if the trueth of God hath more abounded through my lye vnto his glory; why yet am I alſo iudged as a ſinner?[8]And not rather as wee be ſlanderouſly reported, and as ſome affirme that we ſay, Let vs doe euill, that good may come: whoſe damnation is iuſt.[9]What then? are wee better then they? No in no wiſe: for we haue before proued both Iewes, and Gentiles, that they are all vnder ſinne,[10]As it is written, There is none righteous, no not one:[11]There is none that vnderſtandeth, there is none that ſeeketh after God.[12]They are all gone out of the way, they are together become vnprofitable, there is none that doeth good, no not one.[13]Their throat is an open ſepulchre, with their tongues they haue vſed deceit, the poyſon of Aſpes is vnder their lippes:[14]Whoſe mouth is full of curſing and bitterneſse:[15]Their feet are ſwift to ſhed blood.[16]Deſtruction & miſery are in their wayes:[17]And the way of peace haue they not knowen.[18]There is no feare of God before their eyes.[19]Now we know that what things ſoeuer the Law ſaith, it ſaith to them who are vnder the Law: that euery mouth may bee ſtopped, and all the world may become guilty before God.[20]Therefore by the deedes of the Law, there ſhall no fleſh be iuſtified in his ſight: for by the Law is the knowledge of ſinne.[21]But nowe the righteouſneſſe of God without the Lawe is manifeſted, being witneſſed by the Lawe and the Prophets.[22]Euen the righteouſneſſe of God, which is by faith of Ieſus Chriſt vnto all, and vpon all them that beleeue: for there is no difference:[23]For all haue ſinned, and come ſhort of the glory of God,[24]Being iuſtified freely by his grace, through the redemption that is in Ieſus Chriſt:[25]Whom God hath ſet forth to bee a propitiation, through faith in his blood, to declare his righteouſneſſe for the remiſsion of ſinnes, that are paſt, through the forbearance of God.[26]To declare, I ſay, at this time his righteouſneſſe: that hee might bee iuſt, and the iuſtifier of him which beleeueth in Ieſus.[27]Where is boaſting then? It is excluded. By what Law? Of works? Nay: but by the Law of faith.[28]Therefore wee conclude, that a man is iuſtified by faith, without the deeds of the Law.[29]Is he the God of the Iewes only? Is he not alſo of the Gentiles? Yes, of the Gentiles alſo:[30]Seeing it is one God which ſhal iuſtifie the circumciſion by faith, and vncircumciſion through faith.[31]Doe we then make void the lawe through faith? God forbid: yea, we eſtabliſh the Law.

CHAPTER 4[1]What ſhall we ſay then, that Abraham our father, as perteining to the fleſh, hath found?[2]For if Abraham were iuſtified by workes, hee hath whereof to glory, but not before God.[3]For what ſaith the Scripture? Abraham beleeued God, and it was counted vnto him for righteouſnes.[4]Now to him that worketh, is the reward not reckoned of grace, but of debt.[5]But to him that worketh not, but beleeueth on him that iuſtifieth the vngodly; his faith is counted for righteouſneſſe.[6]Euen as Dauid alſo deſcribeth the bleſſedneſse of the man, vnto whom God imputeth righteouſneſſe without works:[7]Saying, Bleſſed are they whoſe iniquities are forgiuen, and whoſe ſinnes are couered.[8]Bleſſed is the man to whome the Lord will not impute ſinne.[9]Commeth this bleſſednes then vpon the circumciſion onely, or vpon the vncircumciſion alſo? for

wee ſay that faith was reckoned to Abraham for righteouſneſſe.10How
was it then reckoned? when he was in circumciſion, or in
vncircumciſion? not in circumciſion, but in vncircumciſion.11And hee
receiued the ſigne of circumciſion, a ſeale of the righteouſneſſe of the
faith, which hee had yet being vncircumciſed: that he might be the father
of all them that beleeue, though they be not circumciſed; that
righteouſneſſe might be imputed vnto them alſo:12And the father of
circumciſion, to them who are not of the circumciſion onely, but alſo
walke in the ſteppes of that faith of our father Abraham, which he had
being yet vncircumciſed.13For the promiſe that he ſhould be the heire
of the world, was not to Abraham, or to his ſeed through the Lawe, but
through the righteouſneſſe of faith.14For if they which are of the law be
heires, faith is made voide, and the promiſe made of none
effect.15Becauſe the law worketh wrath: for where no Lawe is, there is
no tranſgreſsion.16Therefore it is of faith, that it might bee by grace; to
the ende the promiſe might be ſure to all the ſeede, not to that onely
which is of the Law, but to that alſo which is of the faith of Abraham,
who is the father of vs all,17(As it is written, I haue made thee a father
of many nationſ) before him whom he beleeued, euen God who
quickeneth the dead, and calleth thoſe things which bee not, as though
they were,18Who againſt hope, beleeued in hope, that hee might become
the father of many nations: according to that which was ſpoken, So ſhall
thy ſeede bee.19And being not weake in faith, hee conſidered not his
owne body now dead, when hee was about an hundred yere old, neither
yet the deadnes of Saraes wombe.20Hee ſtaggered not at the promiſe of
God through vnbeliefe: but was ſtrong in faith, giuing glory to
God:21And being fully perſwaded, that what he had promiſed, he was
able alſo to performe.22And therefore it was imputed to him for
righteouſneſſe.23Now it was not written for his ſake alone, that it was
imputed to him:24But for vs alſo, to whome it ſhall bee imputed, if wee
beleeue on him that raiſed vp Ieſus our Lord from the dead,25Who was
deliuered for our offences, and was raiſed againe for our iuſtification.
CHAPTER 5 1Therefore being iuſtified by faith, wee haue peace with
God, through our Lord Ieſus Chriſt.2By whom alſo wee haue acceſse by
faith, into this grace wherein wee ſtand, and reioyce in hope of the glory
of God.3And not onely ſo, but we glory in tribulations alſo, knowing
that tribulation worketh patience:4And patience, experience: and
experience, hope:5And hope maketh not aſhamed, becauſe the loue of
God is ſhed abroad in our hearts, by the holy Ghoſt, which is giuen vnto
vs.6For when wee were yet without ſtrength, in due time, Chriſt died for
the vngodly.7For ſcarcely for a righteous man will one die: yet
peraduenture for a good man, ſome would euen dare to dye.8But God
commendeth his loue towards vs, in that, while we were yet ſinners,
Chriſt died for vs.9Much more then being now iuſtified by his blood,
we ſhalbe ſaued from wrath through him.10For if when wee were
enemies, we were reconciled to God, by the death of his ſonne: much
more being reconciled, we ſhalbe ſaued by his life.11And not onely ſo,
but wee alſo ioy in God, through our Lorde Ieſus Chriſt, by whom we
haue now receiued the atonement.12Wherefore, as by one man ſinne
entred into the world, and death by ſin: and ſo death paſſed vpon all
men, for that all haue ſinned.13For vntill the Law ſinne was in the world:
but ſin is not imputed when there is no Law.14Neuertheles, death
reigned from Adam to Moſes, euen ouer them that had not ſinned after
the ſimilitude of Adams tranſgreſsion, who is the figure of him that was
to come:15But not as the offence, ſo alſo is the free gift: for if through
the offence of one, many bee dead: much more the grace of God, and
the gift by grace, which is by one man Ieſus Chriſt, hath abounded vnto
many.16And not as it was by one that ſinned, ſo is the gift: for the
iudgement was by one to condemnation: but the free gift is of many
offences vnto iuſtification.17For if by one mans offence, death raigned
by one, much more they which receiue abundance of grace and of the
gift of righteouſnes, ſhall reigne in life by one, Ieſus Chriſt.18Therfore
as by the offence of one, iudgment came vpon all men to condemnation:
euen ſo by the righteouſnes of one, the free gift came vpon all men vnto
iuſtification of life.19For as by one mans diſobedience many were made
ſinners: ſo by the obedience of one, ſhall many bee made
righteous.20Moreouer, the Lawe entred, that the offence might abound:
but where ſinne abounded, grace did much more abound.21That as ſinne
hath reigned vnto death; euen ſo might grace reigne thorow righteouſnes
vnto eternall life, by Ieſus Chriſt our Lord.
CHAPTER 6 1What ſhall we ſay then? ſhall wee continue in ſinne: that
grace may abound?2God forbid: how ſhall wee that are dead to ſinne,
liue any longer therein?3Know ye not, that ſo many of vs as were
baptized into Ieſus Chriſt, were baptized into his death?4Therefore wee
are buryed with him by baptiſme into death, that like as Chriſt was raiſed
vp from the dead by the glorie of the Father: euen ſo wee alſo ſhould
walke in newneſse of life.5For if we haue bene planted together in the
likeneſſe of his death: wee ſhalbe alſo in the likeneſſe of his
reſurrection:6Knowing this, that our old man is crucified with him, that
the bodie of ſinne might bee deſtroyed, that hencefoorth we ſhould not
ſerue ſinne.7For he that is dead, is freed from ſinne.8Now if we be dead
with Chriſt, we beleeue that we ſhal alſo liue with him:9Knowing that
Chriſt being rayſed from the dead, dieth no more, death hath no more
dominion ouer him.10For in that he dyed, he dyed vnto ſinne once: but
in that hee liueth, hee liueth vnto God.11Likewiſe reckon yee alſo your
ſelues to be dead indeed vnto ſinne: but aliue vnto God, through Ieſus
Chriſt our Lord.12Let not ſinne reigne therfore in your mortall body, that
ye ſhould obey it in the luſts thereof.13Neither yeeld yee your members
as inſtruments of vnrighteouſnes vnto ſinne: but yeelde your ſelues vnto
God, as thoſe that are aliue from the dead, and your members as
inſtruments of righteouſneſſe vnto God.14For ſinne ſhall not haue
dominion ouer you, for yee are not vnder the Law, but vnder
Grace.15What then? ſhal we ſinne, becauſe wee are not vnder the Law,
but vnder Grace? God forbid.16Know ye not, that to whom yee yeeld
your ſelues ſeruants to obey, his ſeruants ye are to whom ye obey:
whether of ſinne vnto death, or of obedience vnto righteouſneſſe?17But
God bee thanked, that yee were the ſeruants of ſinne: but ye haue
obeyed from the heart that fourme of doctrine, which was deliuered
you.18Being then made free from ſinne, yee became the ſeruants of
righteouſneſſe.19I ſpeake after the maner of men, becauſe of the
infirmitie of your fleſh: for as yee haue yeelded your members ſeruants
to vncleanneſſe and to iniquitie, vnto iniquitie: euen ſo now yeelde your
members ſeruants to righteouſneſſe, vnto holineſſe.20For when yee were
the ſeruants of ſinne ye were free from righteouſneſſe.21What fruit had
yee then in thoſe things, whereof ye are now aſhamed? for the end of
thoſe things is death.22But now being made free from ſinne, and become
ſeruants to God, yee haue your fruit vnto holineſſe, and the end
euerlaſting life.23For the wages of ſinne is death: but the gift of God is
eternall life, through Ieſus Chriſt our Lord.
CHAPTER 7 1Know ye not, brethren (for I ſpeake to them that knowe
the Lawe) how that the Lawe hath dominion ouer a man, as long as he
liueth?2For the woman which hath an huſbaud, is bound by the law to
her huſband, ſo long as he liueth: but if the huſband be dead, ſhe is
looſed from the law of the huſband.3So then if while her huſband liueth,
ſhee be married to another man, ſhee ſhalbe called an adultereſse: but if
her huſband be dead, ſhee is free from that law, ſo that ſhe is no
adultereſse, though ſhe be married to another man.4Wherefore my
brethren, yee alſo are become dead to the law by the body of Chriſt, that
ye ſhould be married to another, euen to him who is raiſed from the
dead, that wee ſhould bring forth fruit vnto God,5For when wee were
in the fleſh, the motions of ſinnes which were by the law, did worke in
our members, to bring foorth fruit vnto death.6But now wee are
deliuered from the law, that being dead wherein we were held, that we
ſhould ſerue in newneſse of ſpirit, and not in the oldneſse of the
letter.7What ſhall wee ſay then? is the law ſinne? God forbid. Nay, I had
not knowen ſinne, but by the lawe: for I had not knowen luſt, except
the Law had ſaid, Thou ſhalt not couet.8But ſinne taking occaſion by
the commaundement, wrought in me all maner of concupiſcence. For
without the Law ſinne was dead.9For I was aliue without the Law once,
but when the commandement came, ſinne reuiued, and I died.10And the
commandement which was ordained to life, I found to be vnto
death.11For ſinne taking occaſion by the commandement, deceiued me,
and by it ſlew me.12Wherefore the Law is holy, and the Commandement
holy, and iuſt, and good.13Was that then which is good, made death vnto
me? God forbid. But ſinne, that it might appeare ſinne, working death
in mee by that which is good: that ſinne by the Commaundement might
become exceeding ſinfull.14For wee know that the Law is ſpirituall: but
I am carnall, ſold vnder ſinne.15For that which I do, I allow not: for
what I would, that do I not, but what I hate, that doe I.16If then I doe
that which I would not, I conſent vnto the Law, that it is good.17Now

then, it is no more I that doe it: but ſinne that dwelleth in me.[18]For I
know, that in me (that is, in my fleſh) dwelleth no good thing. For to
will is preſent with me: but how to performe that which is good, I find
not.[19]For the good that I would, I do not: but the euill which I would
not, that I doe.[20]Now if I doe that I would not, it is no more I that do
it, but ſinne that dwelleth in me.[21]I find then a Law, that when I would
do good, euil is preſent with me.[22]For I delight in the Lawe of God, after
the inward man.[23]But I ſee another Lawe in my members, warring
againſt the Lawe of my minde, and bringing me into captiuity to the Law
of ſinne, which is in my members.[24]O wretched man that I am: who
ſhall deliuer me from the body of this death?[25]I thanke God through
Ieſus Chriſt our Lord. So then, with the mind I my ſelf ſerue the Law of
God: but with the fleſh, the law of ſinne

CHAPTER 8[1]There is therefore now no condemnation to them which
are in Chriſt Ieſus, who walke not after the fleſh, but after the ſpirit.[2]For
the law of the ſpirit of life, in Chriſt Ieſus, hath made me free from the
law of ſinne and death.[3]For what the law could not doe, in that it was
weake through the fleſh, God ſending his owne Sonne, in the likeneſſe
of ſinnefull fleſh, and for ſinne condemned ſinne in the fleſh:[4]That the
righteouſneſſe of the law might be fulfilled in vs, who walke not after
the fleſh, but after the ſpirit.[5]For they that are after the fleſh, doe minde
the things of the fleſh: but they that are after the ſpirit, the things of the
ſpirit.[6]For to be carnally minded, is death: but to be ſpiritually minded,
is life and peace:[7]Becauſe the carnall minde is enmitie againſt God: for
it is not ſubiect to the law of God, neither indeed can be.[8]So then they
that are in the fleſh, cannot pleaſe God.[9]But ye are not in the fleſh, but
in the ſpirit, if ſo be that the ſpirit of God dwell in you. Now if any man
haue not the ſpirit of Chriſt, he is none of his.[10]And if Chriſt in you, the
body is dead becauſe of ſinne: but the ſpirit is life, becauſe of
righteouſneſſe.[11]But if the ſpirit of him that raiſed vp Ieſus from the
dead, dwell in you: he that raiſed vp Chriſt from the dead, ſhall alſo
quicken your mortall bodies, by his ſpirit that dwelleth in you.[12]Therfore
brethren, we are detters, not to the fleſh, to liue after the fleſh.[13]For if
ye liue after the fleſh, ye ſhall die: but if ye through the ſpirit doe mortifie
the deeds of the body, ye ſhall liue.[14]For as many as are led by the ſpirit
of God, they are the ſonnes of God.[15]For ye haue not receiued the ſpirit
of bondage againe to feare: but ye haue receiued the ſpirit of adoption,
whereby we cry, Abba, father.[16]The ſpirit it ſelfe beareth witnes with
our ſpirit, that we are the children of God.[17]And if children, then heires,
heires of God, and ioynt heires with Chriſt: if ſo be that we ſuffer with
him, that wee may be alſo glorified together.[18]For I reckon, that the
ſufferings of this preſent time, are not worthy to be compared with the
glory which ſhall be reuealed in vs.[19]For the earneſt expectation of the
creature, waiteth for the manifeſtation of the ſonnes of God.[20]For the
creature was made ſubiect to vanitie, not willingly, but by reaſon of him
who hath ſubiected the ſame in hope:[21]Becauſe the creature it ſelfe alſo
ſhall bee deliuered from the bondage of corruption, into the glorious
libertie of the children of God.[22]For wee know that the whole creation
groaneth, and trauaileth in paine together vntill now.[23]And not only
they, but our ſelues alſo which haue the firſt fruites of the ſpirit, euen
we our ſelues groane within our ſelues, waiting for the adoption, to wit,
the redemption of our body.[24]For wee are ſaued by hope: but hope that
is ſeene, is not hope: for what a man ſeeth, why doth he yet hope
for?[25]But if wee hope for that wee ſee not, then doe wee with patience
waite for it.[26]Likewiſe the ſpirit alſo helpeth our infirmities: for we know
not what wee ſhould pray for as wee ought: but the ſpirit it ſelfe maketh
interceſsion for vs with groanings, which cannot bee vttered.[27]And he
that ſearcheth the hearts, knoweth what is the minde of the ſpirit,
becauſe he maketh interceſsion for the Saints, according to the will of
God.[28]And wee know that all things worke together for good, to them
that loue God, to them who are the called according to his
purpoſe.[29]For whom he did foreknow, he alſo did predeſtinate to be
conformed to the image of his ſonne, that hee might bee the firſt borne
amongſt many brethren.[30]Moreouer, whom he did predeſtinate, them
he alſo called: and whom he called, them he alſo iuſtified: and whom he
iuſtified, them he alſo glorified.[31]What ſhall wee then ſay to theſe things?
If God be for vs, who can bee againſt vs?[32]He that ſpared not his owne
ſon, but deliuered him vp for vs all: how ſhall hee not with him alſo
freely giue vs all things?[33]Who ſhall lay any thing to the charge of Gods
elect? It is God that iuſtifieth:[34]Who is he that condemneth? It is Chriſt
that died, yea rather that is riſen againe, who is euen at the right hand of
God, who alſo maketh interceſsion for vs.[35]Who ſhall ſeparate vs from
the loue of Chriſt? ſhall tribulation, or diſtreſſe, or perſecution, or
famine, or nakedneſse, or perill, or ſword?[36](As it is written, for thy ſake
we are killed all the day long, wee are accounted as ſheepe for the
ſlaughter.)[37]Nay in all theſe things wee are more then conquerours,
through him that loued vs.[38]For I am perſwaded, that neither death, nor
life, nor angels, nor principalities, nor powers, nor things preſent, nor
things to come,[39]Nor height, nor depth, nor any other creature, ſhalbe
able to ſeparate vs from the loue of God, which is in Chriſt Ieſus our
Lord.

CHAPTER 9[1]I ſay the trueth in Chriſt, I lie not, my conſcience alſo
bearing mee witneſſe in the holy Ghoſt,[2]That I haue great heauineſse,
and continuall ſorrow in my heart.[3]For I could wiſh that my ſelfe were
accurſed from Chriſt, for my brethren my kinſemen according to the
fleſh:[4]Who are Iſraelites: to whom perteineth the adoption, and the
glory, and the couenants, and the giuing of the Law, and the ſeruice of
God, and the promiſes:[5]Whoſe are the fathers, and of whom as
concerning the fleſh Chriſt came, who is ouer all, God bleſſed for euer,
Amen.[6]Not as though the word of God hath taken none effect. For they
are not all Iſrael which are of Iſrael:[7]Neither becauſe they are the ſeed
of Abraham are they all children: but in Iſaac ſhall thy ſeed be
called.[8]That is, They which are the children of the fleſh, theſe are not
the children of God: but the children of the promiſe are counted for the
ſeed.[9]For this is the word of promiſe, At this time will I come, and Sara
ſhall haue a ſonne.[10]And not onely this, but when Rebecca alſo had
conceiued by one, euen by our father Iſaac,[11](For the children being not
yet borne, neither hauing done any good or euil, that the purpoſe of
God according to election might ſtand, not of workes, but of him that
calleth.)[12]It was ſaid vnto her, The elder ſhall ſerue the yonger.[13]As it is
written, Iacob haue I loued, but Eſau haue I hated.[14]What ſhall we ſay
then? Is there vnrighteouſnes with God? God forbid.[15]For hee ſaith to
Moſes, I will haue mercy on whom I wil haue mercie, and I will haue
compaſſion on whom I will haue compaſſion.[16]So then it is not of him
that willeth, nor of him that runneth, but of God that ſheweth
mercy.[17]For the Scripture ſaith vnto Pharaoh, Euen for this ſame
purpoſe haue I raiſed thee vp, that I might ſhew my power in thee, and
that my Name might bee declared throughout all the earth.[18]Therefore
hath hee mercie on whom hee will haue mercy, and whom he will, he
hardeneth.[19]Thou wilt ſay then vnto mee; Why doeth he yet find fault?
For who hath reſiſted his will?[20]Nay but O man, who art thou that
replieſt againſt God? Shall the thing formed ſay to him that formed it,
Why haſt thou made me thus?[21]Hath not the potter power ouer the clay,
of the ſame lumpe, to make one veſſell vnto honour, and another vnto
diſhonour?[22]What if God, willing to ſhew his wrath, & to make his
power knowen, indured with much long ſuffering the veſſels of wrath
fitted to deſtruction:[23]And that he might make knowen the riches of his
glory on the veſſels of mercy, which hee had afore prepared vnto
glorie?[24]Euen vs whom hee hath called, not of the Iewes onely, but alſo
of the Gentiles.[25]As he ſaith alſo in Oſee, I will call them my people,
which were not my people: and her, beloued, which was not
beloued.[26]And it ſhall come to paſſe, that in the place where it was ſaide
vnto them, Ye are not my people, there ſhall they bee called the children
of the liuing God.[27]Eſaias alſo crieth concerning Iſrael, Though the
number of the children of Iſrael be as the ſand of the ſea, a remnant
ſhalbe ſaued.[28]For he will finiſh the worke, and cut it ſhort in
righteouſneſſe: becauſe a ſhort worke will the Lord make vpon the
earth.[29]And as Eſaias ſaid before, Except the Lord of Sabboth had left
vs a ſeed, we had bene as Sodoma, and bene made like vnto
Gomorrha.[30]What ſhall wee ſay then? That the Gentiles which followed
not after righteouſneſſe, haue attained to righteouſneſſe, euen the
righteouſneſſe which is of faith:[31]But Iſrael which followed after the
Law of righteouſneſſe, hath not attained to the Law of
righteouſnes.[32]Wherefore? becauſe they ſought it, not by faith, but as it
were by the works of the Law: for they ſtumbled at that ſtumbling
ſtone,[33]As it is written, Beholde, I lay in Sion a ſtumbling ſtone, and
rocke of offence: and whoſoeuer beleeueth on him, ſhall not be
aſhamed.

CHAPTER 10 1Brethren, my hearts deſire and prayer to God for Iſrael
is, that they might be ſaued.2For I beare them record, that they haue a
zeale of God, but not according to knowledge.3For they being ignorant
of Gods righteouſneſſe, and going about to eſtabliſh their owne
righteouſneſſe, haue not ſubmitted themſelues vnto the righteouſneſſe
of God.4For Chriſt is the end of the Law for righteouſnes to euery one
that beleeueth.5For Moſes deſcribeth the righteouſneſſe which is of the
Law, that the man which doeth thoſe things ſhall liue by them.6But the
righteouſneſſe which is of faith, ſpeaketh on this wiſe: ſay not in thine
heart, Who ſhall aſcend into heauen? That is to bring Chriſt down from
aboue.7Or, Who ſhall deſcend into the deepe? That is to bring vp Chriſt
againe from the dead.8But what ſaith it? The word is nigh thee, euen in
thy mouth, and in thy heart, that is the word of faith which we
preach,9That if thou ſhalt confeſse with thy mouth the Lord Ieſus, and
ſhalt beleeue in thine heart, that God hath raiſed him from the dead,
thou ſhalt be ſaued.10For with the heart man beleeueth vnto
righteouſneſſe, and with the mouth confeſsion is made vnto
ſaluation.11For the Scripture ſaith, Whoſoeuer beleeueth on him, ſhall
not bee aſhamed.12For there is no difference betweene the Iew and the
Greeke: for the ſame Lord ouer all, is rich vnto all, that call vpon
him.13For whoſoeuer ſhall call vpon the Name of the Lord, ſhall be
ſaued.14How then ſhall they call on him in whom they haue not
beleeued? and how ſhal they beleeue in him, of whom they haue not
heard? and how ſhall they heare without a Preacher?15And how ſhall
they preach, except they be ſent? as it is written: How beautifull are the
feete of them that preach the Goſpel of peace, and bring glad tidings of
good things!16But they haue not all obeyed the Goſpel. For Eſaias ſaith,
Lord, who hath beleeued our report?17So then, faith commeth by
hearing, and hearing by the word of God.18But I ſay, haue they not
heard? yes verely, their ſound went into all the earth, and their words
vnto the ends of the world.19But I ſay, Did not Iſrael know? Firſt Moſes
ſaith, I will prouoke you to iealouſie by them that are no people, & by a
fooliſh nation I will anger you.20But Eſaias is very bold, and ſaith, I was
found of them that ſought me not: I was made manifeſt vnto them, that
aſked not after me.21But to Iſrael he ſayth, All day long I haue ſtretched
foorth my hands vnto a diſobedient and gaineſaying people.
CHAPTER 11 1I ſay then, Hath God caſt away his people? God
forbidde. For I alſo am an Iſraelite of the ſeede of Abraham, of the tribe
of Beniamin.2God hath not caſt away his people which hee foreknew.
Wote yee not what the Scripture ſaieth of Elias? how hee maketh
interceſsion to God againſt Iſrael, ſaying,3Lord, they haue killed thy
Prophets, and digged downe thine Altars, and I am left alone, and they
ſeeke my life.4But what ſaieth the anſwere of God vnto him? I haue
reſeruedto my ſelfe ſeuen thouſand men, who haue not bowed the knee
to the image of Baal.5Euen ſo then at this preſent time alſo there is a
remnant according to the election of grace.6And if by grace, then is it
no more of workes: otherwiſe grace is no more grace. But if it bee of
workes, then is it no more grace, otherwiſe worke is no more
worke.7What then? Iſrael hath not obtained that which he ſeeketh for,
but the election hath obtained it, and the reſt were blinded,8According
as it is written, God hath giuen them the ſpirit of ſlumber: eyes that they
ſhould not ſee, and eares that they ſhould not heare vnto this day.9And
Dauid ſayth, Let their table be made a ſnare, and a trap, and a ſtumbling
blocke, and a recompenſe vnto them.10Let their eyes be darkened, that
they may not ſee, and bow downe their backe alway.11I ſay then; Haue
they ſtumbled that they ſhould fall? God forbid. But rather through their
fall, ſaluation is come vnto the Gentiles, for to prouoke them to
ielouſie.12Now if the fall of them be the riches of the world, and the
diminiſhing of them, the riches of the Gentiles: how much more their
fulneſse?13For I ſpeake to you Gentiles, in as much as I am the Apoſtle
of the Gentiles, I magnifie mine office:14If by any means I may prouoke
to emulation them which are my fleſh, and might ſaue ſome of
them.15For if the caſting away of them be the reconciling of the world:
what ſhal the receiuing of them be, but life from the dead?16For if the
firſt fruite bee holy, the lumpe is alſo holy: and if the root be holy, ſo are
the branches.17And if ſome of the branches bee broken off, and thou
being a wilde oliue tree wert graffed in amongſt them, and with them
partakeſt of the roote and fatneſſe of the Oliue tree:18Boaſt not againſt
the branches: but if thou boaſt, thou beareſt not the root, but the root
thee.19Thou wilt ſay then, The branches were broken off, that I might
bee graffed in.20Well: becauſe of vnbeliefe they were broken off, and
thou ſtandeſt by fayth. Be not high minded, but feare.21For if God
ſpared not the natural branches, take heede leaſt hee alſo ſpare not
thee.22Beholde therefore the goodneſſe and ſeueritie of God: on them
which fell, ſeueritie; but towards thee, goodneſse, if thou continue in his
goodneſse: otherwiſe thou alſo ſhalt be cut off.23And they alſo, if they
bide not ſtill in vnbeliefe, ſhall be graffed in: for God is able to graffe
them in againe.24For if thou wert cut out of the Oliue tree which is wilde
by nature, and wert graffed contrary to nature into a good Oliue tree:
how much more ſhall theſe which be the naturall branches, bee graffed
into their owne Oliue tree?25For I would not, brethren, that ye ſhould
bee ignorant of this myſterie (leaſt yee ſhould bee wiſe in your owne
conceitſ) that blindneſse in part is happened to Iſrael, vntill the fulnes
of the Gentiles be come in.26And ſo all Iſrael ſhall be ſaued, as it is
written, There ſhall come out of Sion the Deliuerer, and ſhall turne away
vngodlineſse from Iacob.27For this is my couenant vnto them, when I
ſhall take away their ſinnes.28As concerning the Goſpel, they are
enemies for your ſake: but as touching the election, they are beloued for
the fathers ſakes.29For the gifts and calling of God are without
repentance.30For as yee in times paſt haue not beleeued God, yet haue
now obtained mercy through their vnbeliefe:31Euen ſo haue theſe alſo
now not beleeued, that through your mercy they alſo may obtaine
mercy.32For God hath concluded them all in vnbeliefe, that he might
haue mercy vpon all.33O the depth of the riches both of the wiſedome
and knowledge of God! how vnſearchable are his iudgements, and his
wayes paſt finding out!34For who hath knowen the mind of the Lord,
or who hath bene his counſeller?35Or who hath firſt giuen to him, and
it ſhall bee recompenſed vnto him againe?36For of him, and through
him, and to him are all things: to whom be glory for euer. Amen.
CHAPTER 12 1I beſeech you therefore brethren, by the mercies of
God, that yee preſent your bodies a liuing ſacrifice, holy, acceptable vnto
God, which is your reaſonable ſeruice.2And bee not conformed to this
world: but be ye tranſformed by the renuing of your minde, that ye may
proue what is that good, that acceptable and perfect will of God.3For I
ſay, through the grace giuen vnto mee, to euery man that is among you,
not to thinke of himſelfe more highly then hee ought to thinke, but to
thinke ſoberly, according as God hath dealt to euery man the meaſure
of faith.4For as we haue many members in one body, and all members
haue not the ſame office:5So we being many are one bodie in Chriſt, and
euery one members one of another.6Hauing then gifts, differing
according to the grace that is giuen to vs, whether prophecie, let vs
prophecie according to the proportion of faith.7Or miniſtery, let vs wait,
on our miniſtring: or hee that teacheth, on teaching:8Or he that
exhorteth, on exhortation: he that giueth, let him doe it with ſimplicitie:
hee that ruleth, with diligence: hee that ſheweth mercy, with
cheerefulneſse.9Let loue bee without diſsimulation: abhorre that which
is euill, cleaue to that which is good.10Bee kindly affectioned one to
another with brotherly loue, in honour preferring one another.11Not
ſlouthfull in buſines: feruent in ſpirit, ſeruing the Lord.12Reioycing in
hope, patient in tribulation, continuing inſtant in prayer.13Diſtributing
to the neceſsitie of Saints; giuen to hoſpitalitie.14Bleſſe them which
perſecute you, bleſſe, and curſe not.15Reioyce with them that doe
reioice, and weepe with them that weepe.16Be of the ſame mind one
towards another. Minde not high things, but condeſcend to men of low
eſtate. Bee not wiſe in your owne conceits.17Recompence to no man
euill for euill. Prouide things honeſt in the ſight of all men.18If it be
poſsible, as much as lyeth in you, liue peaceably with all men.19Dearely
beloued, auenge not your ſelues, but rather giue place vnto wrath: for it
is written, Uengeance is mine, I will repay, ſaith the Lord.20Therefore if
thine enemie hunger, feed him: if he thirſt, giue him drink. For in ſo
doing thou ſhalt heape coales of fire on his head.21Be not ouercome of
euill, but ouercome euill with good.
CHAPTER 13 1Let euery ſoule bee ſubiect vnto the higher powers: For
there is no power but of God. The powers that be, are ordeined of
God.2Whoſoeuer therefore reſiſteth the power, reſiſteth the ordinance
of God: and they that reſiſt, ſhall receiue to themſelues damnation.3For
rulers are not a terrour to good works, but to the euill. Wilt thou then
not bee afraide of the power? doe that which is good, and thou ſhalt

haue praiſe of the ſame.4For hee is the miniſter of God to thee for good:
but if thou do that which is euill, be afraid: for he beareth not the ſword
in vaine: for he is the miniſter of God, a reuenger to execute wrath vpon
him that doeth euill.5Wherfore ye muſt needs be ſubiect, not onely for
wrath, but alſo for conſcience ſake.6For, for this cauſe pay you tribute
alſo: for they are Gods miniſters, attending continually vpon this very
thing.7Render therfore to all their dues, tribute to whom tribute is due,
cuſtome to whome cuſtome, feare to whome feare, honour to whom
honour.8Owe no man any thing, but to loue one another: for hee that
loueth another hath fulfilled the Law.9For this, Thou ſhalt not commit
adulterie, Thou ſhalt not kill, Thou ſhalt not ſteale, Thou ſhalt not beare
falſe witneſſe, Thou ſhalt not couet: and if there be any other
commandement, it is briefly comprehended in this ſaying, namely, Thou
ſhalt loue thy neighbour as thy ſelfe.10Loue worketh no ill to his
neighbour, therefore loue is the fulfilling of the Law.11And that,
knowing the time, that now it is high time to awake out of ſleepe: for
now is our ſaluation neerer then when we beleeued.12The night is farre
ſpent, the day is at hand: let vs therefore caſt off the workes of
darkeneſſe, and let vs put on the armour of light.13Let vs walke honeſtly
as in the day, not in rioting and drunkenneſse, not in chambring and
wantonnes, not in ſtrife and enuying.14But put yee on the Lord Ieſus
Chriſt, and make not prouiſion for the fleſh, to fulfill the luſts thereof.
CHAPTER 141Him that is weake in the faith receiue you, but not to
doubtfull diſputations.2For one beleeueth that he may eat all things:
another who is weake, eateth herbes.3Let not him that eateth, deſpiſe
him that eateth not: and let not him which eateth not, iudge him that
eateth. For God hath receiued him.4Who art thou that iudgeſt an other
mans ſeruant? to his owne maſter he ſtandeth or falleth; Yea he ſhall bee
holden vp: for God is able to make him ſtand.5One man eſteemeth one
day aboue another: another eſteemeth euery day alike. Let euery man
bee fully perſwaded in his owne minde.6He that regardeth a day,
regardeth it vnto the Lord; and hee that regardeth not the day, to the
Lord hee doeth not regard it. He that eateth, eateth to the Lord, for hee
giueth God thankes: and hee that eateth not, to the Lord hee eateth not,
and giueth God thankes.7For none of vs liueth to himſelfe, and no man
dieth to himſelfe.8For whether we liue, we liue vnto the Lord: and
whether wee die, we die vnto the Lord: whether wee liue therefore or
die, we are the Lords.9For to this ende Chriſt both died, and roſe, and
reuiued, that hee might be Lord both of the dead and liuing.10But why
doeſt thou iudge thy brother? or why doſt thou ſet at nought thy
brother? wee ſhall all ſtand before the Iudgement ſeat of Chriſt.11For it
is written, As I liue, ſaith the Lord, euery knee ſhall bow to mee, and
euery tongue ſhall confeſse to God.12So then euery one of vs ſhall giue
accompt of himſelfe to God.13Let vs not therefore iudge one another
any more: but iudge this rather, that no man put a ſtumbling blocke, or
an occaſion to fall in his brothers way.14I know, and am perſwaded by
the Lord Ieſus, that there is nothing vncleane of it ſelfe: but to him that
eſteemeth any thing to bee vncleane, to him it is vncleane.15But if thy
brother be grieued with thy meate: now walkeſt thou not charitably.
Deſtroy not him with thy meat, for whom Chriſt died.16Let not then
your good be euill ſpoken of.17For the kingdome of God is not meat
and drinke; but righteouſnes, and peace, and ioy in the holy Ghoſt.18For
hee that in theſe things ſerueth Chriſt, is acceptable to God, and
approued of men.19Let vs therefore follow after the things which make
for peace, and things wherewith one may edifie an other.20For meat,
deſtroy not the worke of God: all things indeed are pure; but it is euill
for that man who eateth with offence.21It is good neither to eate fleſh,
nor to drinke wine, nor any thing whereby thy brother ſtumbleth, or is
offended, or is made weake.22Haſt thou faith? haue it to thy ſelfe before
God. Happie is he that condemneth not himſelfe in that thing which
hee alloweth.23And hee that doubteth, is damned if hee eate, becauſe
hee eateth not of faith: For whatſoeuer is not of faith, is ſinne.
CHAPTER 151Wee then that are ſtrong, ought to beare the infirmities
of the weake, and not to pleaſe our ſelues.2Let euery one of vs pleaſe his
neighbour for his good to edification.3For euen Chriſt pleaſed not
himſelfe, but as it is written, The reproches of them that reproched thee,
fell on mee.4For whatſoeuer things were written aforetime, were written
for our learning, that we through patience and comfort of the Scriptures
might haue hope.5Now the God of patience and conſolation graunt you
to be like minded one towards another, according to Chriſt Ieſus:6That
ye may with one mind and one mouth glorifie God, euen the Father of
our Lord Ieſus Chriſt.7Wherfore receiue yee one another, as Chriſt alſo
receiued vs, to the glory of God.8Now I ſay, that Ieſus Chriſt was a
Miniſter of the circumciſion for the trueth of God, to confirme the
promiſes made vnto the fathers:9And that the Gentiles might glorifie
God for his mercie, as it is written, For this cauſe I will confeſse to thee
among the Gentiles, and ſing vnto thy Name.10And againe he ſaith,
Reioyce yee Gentiles with his people.11And againe, Praiſe the Lord all
ye Gentiles, and laud him all ye people.12And againe Eſaias ſaith, There
ſhal be a roote of Ieſſe, and he that ſhal riſe to raigne ouer the Gentiles,
in him ſhall the Gentiles truſt.13Nowe the God of hope fill you with all
ioy and peace in beleeuing, that yee may abound in hope through the
power of the holy Ghoſt.14And I my ſelfe alſo am perſwaded of you, my
brethren, that ye alſo are full of goodneſse, filled with all knowledge,
able alſo to admoniſh one another.15Neuertheleſſe, brethren, I haue
written the more boldly vnto you, in ſome ſort, as putting you in mind,
becauſe of the grace that is giuen to mee of God,16That I ſhould be the
miniſter of Ieſus Chriſt to the Gentiles, miniſtring the Goſpel of God,
that the offering vp of the Gentiles might be acceptable, being ſanctified
by the holy Ghoſt.17I haue therfore whereof I may glory through Ieſus
Chriſt, in thoſe things which pertaine to God.18For I will not dare to
ſpeake of any of thoſe things, which Chriſt hath not wrought by me, to
make the Gentiles obedient, by word and deede,19Through mighty
ſignes and wonders, by the power of the Spirit of God, ſo that from
Hieruſalem and round about vnto Illyricum, I haue fully preached the
Goſpel of Chriſt.20Yea, ſo haue I ſtriued to preach the Goſpel, not
where Chriſt was named, leſt I ſhould build vpon another mans
foundation:21But as it is written, To whom hee was not ſpoken of, they
ſhall ſee: and they that haue not heard, ſhall vnderſtand.22For which
cauſe alſo I haue been much hindered from coming to you.23But now
hauing no more place in theſe parts, and hauing a great deſire theſe many
yeeres to come vnto you:24Whenſoeuer I take my iourney into Spaine, I
will come to you: for I truſt to ſee you in my iourney, and to be brought
on my way thitherward by you, if firſt I be ſomewhat filled with your
company.25But now I goe vnto Hieruſalem, to miniſter vnto the
Saints.26For it hath pleaſed them of Macedonia and Achaia, to make a
certaine contribution for the poore Saints which are at Hieruſalem.27It
hath pleaſed them verely, and their detters they are. For if the Gentiles
haue bene made partakers of their ſpirituall things, their duetie is alſo to
miniſter vnto them in carnall things.28When therefore I haue performed
this, and hane ſealed to them this fruit, I will come by you into
Spaine.29And I am ſure that when I come vnto you, I ſhall come in the
fulnes of the bleſſing of þe Goſpel of Chriſt.30Now I beſeech you,
brethren, for the Lord Ieſus Chriſts ſake, and for the loue of the Spirit,
that ye ſtriue together with me, in your praiers to God for me,31That I
may bee deliuered from them that do not beleeue in Iudea, and that my
ſeruice which I haue for Hieruſalem, may bee accepted of the
Saints:32That I may come vnto you with ioy by the will of God, and may
with you be refreſhed.33Now the God of peace bee with you all. Amen.
CHAPTER 161I commend vnto you Phebe our ſiſter, which is a
ſeruant of the Church which is at Cenchrea:2That ye receiue her in the
Lord as becommeth Saints, and that ye aſsiſt her in whatſoeuer buſineſse
ſhe hath need of you: for ſhe hath beene a ſuccourer of many, and of
my ſelfe alſo.3Greete Priſcilla and Aquila, my helpers in Chriſt
Ieſus:4(Who haue for my life laid downe their owne neckes: vnto whome
not onely I giue thankes, but alſo all the Churches of the
Gentiles.)5Likewiſe greet the Church that is in their houſe. Salute my
welbeloued Epenetus, who is the firſt fruits of Achaia vnto
Chriſt.6Greete Marie, who beſtowed much labour on vs.7Salute
Andronicus and Iunia my kinſmen, and my fellow priſoners, who are of
note among the Apoſtles, who alſo were in Chriſt before me.8Greet
Amplias my beloued in the Lord.9Salute Urbane our helper in Chriſt,
and Stachys my beloued.10Salute Appelles approoued in Chriſt. Salute
them which are of Ariſtobulus houſhold.11Salute Herodion my kinſman.
Greet them that be of the houſhold of Narciſsus, which are in the
Lord.12Salute Tryphena and Tryphoſa, who labour in the Lord. Salute
the beloued Perſis, which laboured much in the Lord.13Salute Rufus
choſen in the Lord, and his mother and mine.14Salute Aſyncritus,
Phlegon, Hermas, Patrobas, Hermes, and the brethren which are with
them.15Salute Philologus & Iulia, Nereus, and his ſiſter, and Olympas,

and all the Saints which are with them.16Salute one another with an holy kiſſe. The Churches of Chriſt ſalute you.17Now I beſeech you, brethren, marke them which cauſe diuiſions and offences, contrary to the doctrine which ye haue learned, and auoide them.18For they that are ſuch, ſerue not our Lord Ieſus Chriſt, but their owne belly, and by good wordes and faire ſpeeches deceiue the hearts of the ſimple.19For your obedience is come abroad vnto all men. I am glad therefore on your behalfe: but yet I would haue you wiſe vnto that which is good, and ſimple concerning euill.20And the God of peace ſhal bruiſe Satan vnder your feete ſhortly. The grace of our Lord Ieſus Chriſt be with you. Amen.21Timotheus my worke-fellow, and Lucius, and Iaſon, and Soſipater my kinſemen ſalute you.22I Tertius who wrote this Epiſtle, ſalute you in the Lord.23Gaius mine hoſte, and of the whole Church, ſaluteth you. Eraſtus the Chamberlaine of the citie ſaluteth you, and Quartus a brother.24The grace of our Lord Ieſus Chriſt be with you all. Amen.25Now to him that is of power to ſtabliſh you according to my Goſpel, and the preaching of Ieſus Chriſt, according to the reuelation of the the myſterie, which was kept ſecret ſince the world began:26But now is made manifeſt, and by the Scriptures of the Prophets according to the commandement of the euerlaſting God, made knowen to all nations for the obedience of faith,27To God, onely wiſe, bee glorie through Ieſus Chriſt, for euer. Amen.Written to the Romanes from Corinthus, and ſent by Phebe ſeruant of the Church at Cenchrea.

1 CORINTHIANS

CHAPTER 11Paul called to be an Apoſtle of Ieſus Chriſt, through the will of God, and Soſthenes our brother,2Unto the Church of God which is at Corinth, to them that are ſanctified in Chriſt Ieſus, called to be Saints, with all that in euery place call vpon the Name of Ieſus Chriſt our Lord, both theirs and ours.3Grace be vnto you, and peace from God our Father, and from the Lord Ieſus Chriſt.4I thanke my God alwayes on your behalfe, for the grace of God which is giuen you by Ieſus Chriſt,5That in euery thing yee are enriched by him, in all vtterance, and in all knowledge:6Euen as the Teſtimony of Chriſt was confirmed in you.7So that yee come behinde in no gift; wayting for the comming of our Lord Ieſus Chriſt,8Who ſhall alſo confirme you vnto the end, that yee may be blameleſſe in the day of our Lord Ieſus Chriſt.9God is faithful by whom ye were called vnto the felowſhip of his Sonne Ieſus Chriſt our Lord.10Now I beſeech you brethren by the Name of our Lord Ieſus Chriſt, that yee all ſpeake the ſame thing, and that there be no diuiſions among you: but that ye be perfectly ioyned together in the ſame minde, and in the ſame iudgement.11For it hath bene declared vnto me of you, my brethren, by them which are of the houſe of Cloe, that there are contentions among you.12Now this I ſay, that euery one of you ſaith, I am of Paul, and I of Apollo, and I of Cephas, and I of Chriſt.13Is Chriſt diuided? was Paul crucified for you? or were yee baptized in the name of Paul?14I thanke God that I baptized none of you, but Criſpus and Gaius:15Leſt any ſhould ſay, that I had baptized in mine owne name.16And I baptized alſo the houſehold of Stephanas: beſides, I know not whether I baptized any other.17For Chriſt ſent me not to baptize, but to preach the Goſpel: not with wiſedome of words, leſt the Croſse of Chriſt ſhould be made of none effect.18For the preaching of the Croſse is to them that periſh, fooliſhneſse: but vnto vs which are ſaued, it is the power of God.19For it is written, I will deſtroy the wiſedome of the wiſe, and wil bring to nothing the vnderſtanding of the prudent.20Where is the wiſe? where is the Scribe? where is the diſputer of this world? Hath not God made fooliſh the wiſedome of this world?21For after that, in the wiſedom of God, the world by wiſedome knew not God, it pleaſed God by the fooliſhneſse of preaching, to ſaue them that beleeue.22For the Iewes require a ſigne, and the Greekes ſeeke after wiſedome.23But wee preach Chriſt crucified, vnto the Iewes a ſtumbling block, and vnto the Greekes, fooliſhneſse:24But vnto them which are called, both Iewes and Greekes, Chriſt, the power of God, & the wiſedome of God.25Becauſe the fooliſhneſse of God is wiſer then men: and the weakeneſse of God is ſtronger then men.26For ye ſee your calling, brethren, how that not many wiſe men after the fleſh, not many mighty, not many noble are called.27But God hath choſen the fooliſh things of the world, to confound the wiſe: and God hath choſen the weake things of the world, to confound the things which are mighty:28And baſe things of the world, and things which are deſpiſed, hath God choſen, yea and things which are not, to bring to nought things that are,29That no fleſh ſhould glory in his preſence.30But of him are ye in Chriſt Ieſus, who of God is made vnto vs wiſedome, and righteouſneſſe, and ſanctification, and redemption:31That according as it is written, He that glorieth, let him glory in the Lord.

CHAPTER 21And I, brethren, when I came to you, came not with excellencie of ſpeech, or of wiſedome, declaring vnto you the teſtimony of God.2For I determined not to know any thing amōg you, ſaue Ieſus Chriſt, and him crucified.3And I was with you in weakeneſse, and in feare, and in much trembling.4And my ſpeech, and my preaching was not with entiſing words of mans wiſedome, but in demonſtration of the Spirit, and of power:5That your faith ſhould not ſtand in the wiſdome of men, but in the power of God.6Howbeit wee ſpeake wiſedome among them that are perfect: yet not the wiſedome of this worlde, nor of the Princes of this worlde, that come to nought:7But wee ſpeake the wiſedome of God in a myſterie, euen the hidden wiſedome which God ordeined before the world, vnto our glory.8Which none of the princes of this world knewe: for had they knowen it, they would not haue crucified the Lord of glory.9But as it is written, Eye hath not ſeene, nor eare heard, neither haue entred into the heart of man, the things which God hath prepared for them that loue him.10But God hath reueiled them vnto vs by his Spirit: for the Spirit ſearcheth all things, yea, the deepe things of God.11For what man knoweth the things of a man, ſaue the ſpirit of man which is in him? Euen ſo the things of God knoweth no man, but the Spirit of God.12Now wee haue receiued, not the ſpirit of the world, but the Spirit which is of God, that wee might know the things that are freely giuen to vs of God.13Which things alſo we ſpeake, not in the words which mans wiſedome teacheth, but which the holy Ghoſt teacheth, comparing ſpiritual things with ſpirituall.14But the naturall man receiueth not the things of the Spirit of God, for they are fooliſhneſse vnto him: neither can he know them, becauſe they are ſpiritually diſcerned.15But he that is ſpirituall, iudgeth all things, yet he himſelfe is iudged of no man.16For who hath knowen the mind of the Lord that he may inſtruct him? But we haue the mind of Chriſt.

CHAPTER 31And I, brethren, could not ſpeake vnto you as vnto ſpirituall, but as vnto carnall, euen as vnto babes in Chriſt.2I haue fed you with milke, and not with meate: for hitherto yee were not able to beare it, neither yet now are ye able.3For ye are yet carnall: for whereas there is among you enuying, and ſtrife, and diuiſions, are ye not carnall, and walke as men?4For while one ſaieth, I am of Paul, and another, I am of Apollo, are ye not carnall?5Who then is Paul? and who is Apollo? but miniſters by whom ye beleeued, euen as the Lord gaue to euery man.6I haue planted, Apollo watered: but God gaue the encreaſe.7So then, neither is he that planteth any thing, neither hee that watereth: but God that giueth the increaſe.8Now hee that planteth, and hee that watereth, are one: and euery man ſhal receiue his own reward according to his owne labour.9For wee are labourers together with God, ye are Gods huſbandry, yee are Gods building.10According to the grace of God which is giuen vnto mee, as a wiſe maſter builder I haue laid the foundation, and another buildeth thereon. But let euery man take heede how hee buildeth thereupon.11For other foundation can no man lay, then that is laide, which is Ieſus Chriſt.12Now if any man build vpon this foundation, gold, ſiluer, precіouſſtones, wood, hay, ſtubble:13Euery mans worke ſhall be made manifeſt. For the day ſhall declare it, becauſe it ſhall bee reuealed by fire, and the fire ſhall trie euery mans worke of what ſort it is.14If any mans worke abide which he hath built thereupon, he ſhal receiue a reward.15If any mans worke ſhall bee burnt, he ſhall ſuffer loſse: but he himſelfe ſhall be ſaued: yet ſo, as by fire.16Knowe yee not that yee are the Temple of God, and that the Spirit of God dwelleth in you?17If any man defile the Temple of God, him ſhall God deſtroy: for the Temple of God is holy, which Temple ye are.18Let no man deceiue himſelfe: If any man among you ſeemeth to bee wiſe in this world, let him become a foole, that he may be wiſe.19For the wiſedome of this world is fooliſhneſse with God: for it is written, Hee taketh the wiſe in their owne craftineſse.20And againe, The Lord knoweth the thoughts of the wiſe, that they are vaine.21Therefore let no man glory in men, for all things are yours.22Whether Paul, or Apollo, or Cephas, or the world, or life, or death, or things preſent, or things to come, all are yours.23And yee are Chriſts, and Chriſt is Gods.

CHAPTER 41Let a man ſo account of vs, as of the miniſters of Chriſt, and ſtewards of the myſteries of God.2Moreouer, it is required in ſtewards, that a man be found faithfull.3But with mee it is a very ſmall thing that I ſhould bee iudged of you, or of mans iudgement: yea, I iudge not mine owne ſelfe.4For I know nothing by my ſelfe, yet am I not hereby iuſtified: but hee that iudgeth me is the Lord.5Therefore iudge nothing before the time, vntill the Lord come, who both will bring to light the hidden things of darkeneſſe, and will make manifeſt the counſels of the hearts: and then ſhall euery man haue prayſe of God.6And theſe things, brethren, I haue in a figure tranſferred to my ſelfe, and to Apollo, for your ſakes: that ye might learne in vs not to thinke of men, aboue that which is written, that no one of you bee puffed vp for one againſt another.7For who maketh thee to differ from another? And what haſt thou that thou didſt not receiue? Now if thou didſt receiue it, why doeſt thou glory as if thou hadſt not receiued it?8Now ye are full, now ye are rich, ye haue reigned as kings without vs, and I would to God ye did reigne, that we alſo might reigne with you.9For I thinke that God hath ſet forth vs the Apoſtles laſt, as it were approued to death. For wee are made a ſpectacle vnto the world, and to Angels, and to men.10We are fooles for Chriſts ſake, but ye are wiſe in Chriſt. We are weake, but ye are ſtrong: yee are honourable, but we are deſpiſed.11Euen vnto this preſent houre we both hunger and thirſt, and are naked, and are buffeted, and haue no certaine dwelling place,12And labour, working with our owne hands: being reuiled, wee bleſſe: being perſecuted, we ſuffer it:13Being defamed, we intreate: we are made as the filth of the world, and are the off-ſcouring of all things vnto this day.14I write not theſe things to ſhame you, but as my beloued ſonnes I warne you.15For though you haue ten thouſand inſtructors in Chriſt, yet haue yee not many fathers: For in Chriſt Ieſus I haue begotten you through the Goſpel.16Wherefore I beſeech you, be yee followers of me.17For this cauſe haue I ſent vnto you Timotheus, who is my beloued ſonne, and faithfull in the Lord, who ſhal bring you into remembrance of my wayes which be in Chriſt, as I teach euery where in euery Church.18Nowe ſome are puffed vp as though I would not come to you.19But I wil come to you ſhortly, if the Lord will, and will knowe, not the ſpeach of them which are puffed vp, but the power.20For the kingdome of God is not in word, but in power.21What will ye? Shall I come vnto you with a rod, or in loue, and in the ſpirit of meekeneſse?

CHAPTER 51It is reported commonly, that there is fornication among you, and ſuch fornication, as is not ſo much as named amongſt the Gentiles, that one ſhould haue his fathers wife.2And yee are puffed vp, and haue not rather mourned, that he that hath done this deed, might bee taken away from among you.3For I verily as abſent in body, but preſent in ſpirit, haue iudged alreadie, as though I were preſent, concerning him that hath ſo done this deed,4In the Name of our Lord Ieſus Chriſt, when yee are gathered together, and my ſpirit, with the power of our Lord Ieſus Chriſt,5To deliuer ſuch a one vnto Satan for the deſtruction of the fleſh, that the ſpirit may be ſaued in the day of the Lord Ieſus.6Your glorying is not good: know ye not that a little leauen leaueneth the whole lumpe?7Purge out therefore the olde leauen, that ye may be a new lumpe, as ye are vnleauened. For euen Chriſt our Paſſeouer is ſacrificed for vs.8Therefore let vs keepe the Feaſt, not with old leauen, neither with the leauen of malice and wickedneſſe: but with the vnleauened bread of ſinceritie and trueth.9I wrote vnto you in an Epiſtle, not to company with fornicators.10Yet not altogether with the fornicatours of this world, or with the couetous, or extortioners, or with idolaters; for then muſt yee needs goe out of the world.11But now I haue written vnto you, not to keepe company, if any man that is called a brother bee a fornicator, or couetous, or an idolater, or a railer, or a drunkard, or an extortioner: with ſuch a one, no, not to eate.12For what haue I to doe to iudge them alſo that are without? doe not ye iudge them that are within?13But them that are without, God iudgeth. Therefore put away from among your ſelues that wicked perſon.

CHAPTER 61Dare any of you, hauing a matter againſt another, goe to law before the vniuſt, and not before the Saints?2Do ye not know that the Saints ſhall iudge the world? And if the world ſhalbe iudged by you, are ye vnworthy to iudge the ſmalleſt matters?3Know ye not that we ſhall iudge Angels? How much more things that perteine to this life?4If then yee haue iudgements of things perteining to this life, ſet them to iudge who are leaſt eſteemed in the Church.5I ſpeake to your ſhame. Is it ſo, that there is not a wiſe man amongſt you? no not one that ſhall bee able to iudge betweene his brethren?6But brother goeth to law with brother, & that before the vnbeleeuers?7Now therefore, there is vtterly a fault among you, becauſe yee goe to law one with another: Why doe ye not rather take wrong? Why doe yee not rather ſuffer your ſelues to be defrauded?8Nay, you do wrong and defraud, and that your brethren.9Know yee not that the vnrighteous ſhall not inherite the kingdome of God? Be not deceiued: neither fornicatours, nor idolaters, nor adulterers, nor effeminate, nor abuſers of themſelues with mankinde,10Nor theeues, nor couetous, nor drunkards, nor reuilers, nor extortioners, ſhall inherit the kingdom of God.11And ſuch were ſome of you: but ye are waſhed, but ye are ſanctified, but ye are iuſtified in the Name of the Lord Ieſus, and by the Spirit of our God.12All things are lawfull vnto mee, but all things are not expedient: all things are lawfull for mee, but I will not bee brought vnder the power of any.13Meats for the belly, and the belly for meates: but God ſhall deſtroy both it and them. Now the body is not for fornication, but for the Lord: and the Lord for the body.14And God hath both raiſed vp the Lord, and will alſo raiſe vp vs by his owne power.15Know yee not that your bodies are the members of Chriſt? Shall I then take the members of Chriſt, and make them the members of an harlot? God forbid.16What, know ye not that he which is ioyned to an harlot, is one body? for two (ſaith he) ſhalbe one fleſh.17But hee that is ioyned vnto the Lord, is one ſpirit.18Flee fornication: Euery ſinne that a man doeth, is without the body: but he that committeth fornication, ſinneth againſt his owne body.19What, know ye not that your body is the Temple of the holy Ghoſt which is in you, which yee haue of God, and ye are not your owne?20For yee are bought with a price: therefore glorifie God in your body, and in your ſpirit, which are Gods.

CHAPTER 71Now cōcerning the things wherof ye wrote vnto me, It is good for a man not to touch a woman.2Neuertheleſſe, to auoid fornication, let euery man haue his owne wife, and let euery woman haue her owne huſband.3Let the huſband render vnto the wife due beneuolence: and likewiſe alſo the wife vnto the huſband.4The wife hath not power of her owne body, but the huſband: and likewiſe alſo the huſband hath not power of his owne body, but the wife.5Defraud you not one the other, except it bee with conſent for a time, that yee may giue your ſelues to faſting and prayer, and come together againe, that Satan tempt you not for your incontinencie.6But I ſpeake this by permiſsion, and not of commandement.7For I would that all men were euen as I my ſelfe: but euery man hath his proper gift of God, one after this maner, and another after that.8I ſay therefore to the vnmaried and widowes, It is good for them if they abide euen as I.9But if they cannot conteine, let them marry: for it is better to marrie then to burne.10And vnto the married, I command, yet not I, but the Lord, Let not the wife depart from her huſband:11But and if ſhee depart, let her remaine vnmaried, or be reconciled to her huſband: and let not the huſband put away his wife.12But to the reſt ſpeake I, not the Lord, If any brother hath a wife that beleeueth not, and ſhee bee pleaſed to dwell with him, let him not put her away.13And the woman which hath an huſband that beleeueth not, and if hee be pleaſed to dwell with her, let her not leaue him.14For the vnbeleeuing huſband is ſanctified by the wife, and the vnbeleeuing wife is ſanctified by the huſband; elſe were your children vncleane, but now are they holy.15But if the vnbeleeuing depart, let him depart. A brother or a ſiſter is not vnder bondage in ſuch caſes: but God hath called vs to peace.16For what knoweſt thou, O wife, whether thou ſhalt ſaue thy huſband? or how knoweſt thou, O man, whether thou ſhalt ſaue thy wife?17But as God hath diſtributed to euery man, as the Lord hath called euery one, ſo let him walke, and ſo ordeine I in all Churches.18Is any man called being circumciſed? let him not become vncircumciſed: Is any called in vncircumciſion? let him not be circumciſed.19Circumciſion is nothing, and vncircumciſion is nothing, but the keeping of the Commandements of God.20Let euery man abide in the ſame calling wherein he was called.21Art thou called being a ſeruant? care not for it: but if thou maiſt be made free, vſe it rather.22For he that is called in the Lord, being a ſeruant, is the Lords free man:

likewiſe alſo hee that is called being free, is Chriſts ſeruant.23Ye are
bought with a price, be not ye the ſeruants of men.24Brethren, let euery
man wherin he is called, therein abide with God.25Nowe concerning
virgins, I haue no commaundement of the Lord: yet I giue my
iudgement as one that hath obtained mercy of the Lord to be faithfull.26I
ſuppoſe therefore that this is good for the preſent diſtreſſe, I ſay, that it
is good for a man ſo to be.27Art thou bound vnto a wife? ſeeke not to
bee looſed. Art thou looſed from a wife? ſeeke not a wife.28But and if
thou marry, thou haſt not ſinned, and if a virgin marry, ſhee hath not
ſinned: neuertheleſſe, ſuch ſhall haue trouble in the fleſh: but I ſpare
you.29But this I ſay, brethren, the time is ſhort. It remaineth, that both
they that haue wiues, be as though they had none:30And they that weepe,
as though they wept not: and they that reioyce, as though they reioyced
not: and they that buy, as though they poſſeſſed not:31And they that vſe
this world, as not abuſing it: for the faſhion of this world paſſeth
away.32But I would haue you without carefulneſse. He that is vnmarried,
careth for the things that belõgeth to the Lord, how he may pleaſe the
Lord:33But hee that is maried, careth for the things that are of the world,
how he may pleaſe his wife.34There is difference alſo between a wife and
a virgin: the vnmaried woman careth for the things of the Lord, that
ſhee may be holy, both in body and in ſpirit: but ſhe that is married,
careth for the things of the worlde, how ſhee may pleaſe her
huſband.35And this I ſpeake for your owne profite, not that I may caſt
a ſnare vpon you, but for that which is comely, and that you may attend
vpon the Lord without diſtraction.36But if any man thinke that he
behaueth himſelfe vncomely toward his virgin, if ſhe paſſe the floure of
her age, and neede ſo require, let him doe what hee will, hee ſinneth not:
let them marry.37Neuertheleſſe, hee that ſtandeth ſtedfaſt in his heart,
hauing no neceſsitie, but hath power ouer his owne will, and hath ſo
decreed in his heart that he will keepe his virgin, doeth well.38So then
he that giueth her in mariage, doeth wel: but he that giueth her not in
mariage, doeth better.39The wife is bound by the Lawe as long as her
huſband liueth: but if her huſband bee dead, ſhee is at liberty to bee
maried to whom ſhee will, onely in the Lord.40But ſhee is happier if ſhee
ſobide, after my iudgment: and I thinke alſo that I haue the Spirit of
God.
CHAPTER 81Now as touching things offered vnto idoles, wee know
that wee all haue knowledge. Knowledge puffeth vp: but Charitie
edifieth.2And if any man thinke that hee knoweth any thing, hee
knoweth nothing yet as he ought to know.3But if any man loue God, the
ſame is knowen of him.4As concerning therefore the eating of thoſe
things that are offered in ſacrifice vnto idoles, wee know that an idole is
nothing in the world, and that there is none other God but one.5For
though there bee that are called gods, whether in heauen or in earth (as
there be gods many, and lords many:)6But to vs there is but one God,
the Father, of whom are all things, and we in him, and one Lord Ieſus
Chriſt, by whom are all things, and we by him.7Howbeit there is not in
euerie man that knowledge: for ſome with conſcience of the idole vnto
this houre, eate it as a thing offred vnto an idole, and their conſcience
being weake, is defiled.8But meate commendeth vs not to God: for
neither if we eate, are we the better: neither if wee eate not, are we the
worſe.9But take heed leſt by any meanes, this libertie of yours become a
ſtumbling blocke to them that are weake.10For if any man ſee thee which
haſt knowledge, ſit at meat in the idols temple: ſhall not the conſcience
of him which is weake, be emboldened to eat thoſe things which are
offered to idols?11And through thy knowledge ſhal the weake brother
periſh, for whome Chriſt died?12But when ye ſinne ſo againſt the
brethren, and wound their weake conſcience, ye ſinne againſt
Chriſt.13Wherefore if meate make my brother to offend, I will eat no
fleſh while the world ſtandeth, leſt I make my brother to offend.
CHAPTER 91Am I not an Apoſtle? am I not free? haue I not ſeene
Ieſus Chriſt our Lord? Are not you my worke in the Lord?2If I bee not
an Apoſtle vnto others, yet doubtleſſe I am to you: for the ſeale of mine
Apoſtleſhip are yee in the Lord.3Mine anſwere to them that doe examine
me, is this:4Haue wee not power to eate and to drinke?5Haue we not
power to lead about a ſiſter a wife aſwel as other Apoſtles, and as the
brethren of the Lord, and Cephas?6Or I onely and Barnabas, haue not
we power to forbeare working?7Who goeth a warfare any time at his
owne charges? who planteth a vineyard, and eateth not of the fruite
thereof? or who feedeth a flocke, and eateth not of the milke of the
flocke?8ſay I theſe things as a man? or ſaith not the Law the ſame
alſo?9For it is written in the Law of Moyſes, Thou ſhalt not muzzell the
mouth of the oxe that treadeth out the corne: doth God take care for
oxen?10Or ſaith hee it altogether for our ſakes? for our ſakes, no doubt,
this is written: that hee that ploweth, ſhould plow in hope: and that hee
that threſheth in hope, ſhould bee partaker of his hope.11If we haue
ſowen vnto you ſpirituall things, is it a great thing if wee ſhall reape your
carnall things?12If others bee partakers of this power ouer you, are not
we rather? Neuertheleſſe, we haue not vſed this power: but ſuffer all
things, leſt wee ſhould hinder the Goſpel of Chriſt.13Do ye not know
that they which miniſter about holy things, liue of the things of the
Temple? and they which wait at the altar, are partakers with the
altar?14Euen ſo hath the Lord ordeined, that they which preach the
Goſpel, ſhould liue of the Goſpel.15But I haue vſed none of theſe things.
Neither haue I written theſe things, that it ſhould bee ſo done vnto me:
for it were better for me to die, then that any man ſhould make my
glorying voyd.16For though I preach the Goſpel, I haue nothing to glorie
of: for neceſsitie is laid vpon mee, yea, woe is vnto me, if I preach not
the Goſpel.17For if I doe this thing willingly, I haue a reward: but if
againſt my will, a diſpenſation of the Goſpel is committed vnto
me.18What is my reward then? verily that when I preach the Goſpel, I
may make the Goſpel of Chriſt without charge, that I abuſe not my
power in the Goſpel.19For though I bee free from all men, yet haue I
made my ſelfe ſeruant vnto all, that I might gaine the more.20And vnto
the Iewes, I became as a Iew, that I might gaine the Iewes: to them that
are vnder the Law, as vnder the Law, that I might gaine them that are
vnder the Law:21To them that are without Law, as without Law (being
not without Law to God, but vnder the Law to Chriſt,) that I might
gaine them that are without Law.22To the weake became I as weake, that
I might gaine the weake: I am made all things to all men, that I might by
all meanes ſaue ſome.23And this I doe for the Goſpels ſake, that I might
be partaker thereof with you.24Know yee not that they which runne in
a race, runne all, but one receiueth the price? So runne, that yee may
obtaine.25And euery man that ſtriueth for the maſterie, is temperate in
all things: Now they doe it to obtaine a corruptible crowne, but we an
incorruptible.26I therefore ſo runne, not as vncertainely: ſo fight I, not
as one that beateth the ayre:27But I keepe vnder my body, and bring it
into ſubiection: leſt that by any meanes when I haue preached to others,
I my ſelfe ſhould be a caſtaway.
CHAPTER 101Moreouer brethren, I would not that yee ſhould be
ignorant, how that all our fathers were vnder the cloud, and all paſſed
thorow the ſea:2And were all baptized vnto Moyſes in the cloud, and in
the ſea:3And did all eat the ſame ſpirituall meat:4And did all drinke the
ſame ſpirituall drinke: (for they dranke of that ſpirituall Rocke that
followed them: and that Rocke was Chriſt)5But with many of them God
was not well pleaſed: for they were ouerthrowen in the
wilderneſſe.6Now theſe things were our examples, to the intent wee
ſhould not luſt after euil things, as they alſo luſted.7Neither be ye
idolaters, as were ſome of them, as it is written, The people ſate downe
to eate and drinke, and roſe vp to play.8Neither let vs commit
fornication, as ſome of them committed, and fell in one day three and
twentie thouſand.9Neither let vs tempt Chriſt, as ſome of them alſo
tempted, and were deſtroyed of ſerpents.10Neither murmure ye, as ſome
of them alſo murmured, and were deſtroyed of the deſtroyer.11Now all
theſe things happened vnto them for enſamples: and they are written
for our admonition, vpon whom the ends of the world are
come.12Wherefore, let him that thinketh he ſtandeth, take heed leſt he
fall.13There hath no temptation taken you, but ſuch as is common to
man: but God is faithfull, who wil not ſuffer you to bee tempted aboue
that you are able: but will with the temptation alſo make a way to eſcape,
that ye may bee able to beare it.14Wherefore my dearely beloued, flee
from idolatrie.15I ſpeake as to wiſe men: iudge ye what I ſay.16The cup
of bleſſing which wee bleſſe, is it not the communion of the blood of
Chriſt? The bread which we breake, is it not the communion of the body
of Chriſt?17For we being many are one bread, and one body: for we are
all partakers of that one bread.18Behold Iſrael after the fleſh: are not
they which eat of the ſacrifices, partakers of the Altar?19What ſay I then?
that the idole is any thing? or that which is offered in ſacrifice to idols is
any thing?20But I ſay that the things which the Gentiles ſacrifice, they

ſacrifice to deuils, and not to God: and I would not that yee ſhould haue fellowſhip with deuils.[21]Yee cannot drinke the cup of the Lord, and the cup of deuils: ye cannot be partakers of the Lords Table, and of the table of deuils.[22]Doe we prouoke the Lord to iealouſie? are we ſtronger then he?[23]All things are lawfull for me, but all things are not expedient: All things are lawfull for mee, but all things edifie not.[24]Let no man ſeeke his owne: but euery man anothers wealth.[25]Whatſoeuer is ſolde in the ſhambles, that eate, aſking no queſtion for conſcience ſake.[26]For the earth is the Lords, and the fulneſse thereof.[27]If any of them that beleeue not, bid you to a feaſt, and yee be diſpoſed to goe, whatſoeuer is ſet before you, eate, aſking no queſtion for conſcience ſake.[28]But if any man ſay vnto you, This is offered in ſacrifice vnto idoles, eate not for his ſake that ſhewed it, and for conſcience ſake. The earth is the Lords, and the fulneſse thereof.[29]Conſcience I ſay, not thine owne, but of the others: for why is my libertie iudged of another mans conſcience?[30]For, if I by grace be a partaker, why am I euill ſpoken of, for that for which I giue thankes?[31]Whether therfore ye eat or drinke, or whatſoeuer ye doe, doe all to the glory of God.[32]Giue none offence, neither to the Iewes, nor to the Gentiles, nor to the Church of God:[33]Euen as I pleaſe all men in all things, not ſeeking mine owne profit, but the profit of many, that they may be ſaued.

CHAPTER 11[1]Be yee followers of mee, euen as I alſo am of Chriſt.[2]Now I prayſe you, brethren, that you remember me in all things, and keepe the ordinances, as I deliuered them to you.[3]But I would haue you knowe, that the head of euery man is Chriſt: and the head of the woman is the man, and the head of Chriſt is God.[4]Euery man praying or prophecying, hauing his head couered, diſhonoureth his head.[5]But euery woman that prayeth or propheſieth with her head vncouered, diſhonoureth her head: for that is euen all one as if ſhe were ſhauen.[6]For if the woman be not couered, let her alſo bee ſhorne: but if it bee a ſhame for a woman to be ſhorne or ſhauen, let her be couered.[7]For a man in deede ought not to couer his head, foraſmuch as hee is the image and glory of God: but the woman is the glory of the man.[8]For the man is not of the woman: but the woman of the man.[9]Neither was the man created for the woman: but the woman for the man.[10]For this cauſe ought the woman to haue power on her head, becauſe of the Angels.[11]Neuertheleſſe, neither is the man without the woman, neither the woman without the man in the Lord.[12]For as the woman is of the man: euen ſo is the man alſo by the woman; but all things of God.[13]Iudge in your ſelues, is it comely that a woman pray vnto God vncouered?[14]Doeth not euen nature it ſelfe teach you, that if a man haue long haire, it is a ſhame vnto him?[15]But if a woman haue long haire, it is a glory to her: for her haire is giuen her for a couering.[16]But if any man ſeeme to be contentious, we haue no ſuch cuſtome, neither the Churches of God.[17]Now in this that I declare vnto you, I praiſe you not, that you come together not for the better, but for the worſe.[18]For firſt of all when yee come together in the Church, I heare that there be diuiſions among you, and I partly beleeue it.[19]For there muſt bee alſo hereſies among you, that they which are approued may be made manifeſt among you.[20]When yee come together therefore into one place, this is not to eate the Lords Supper.[21]For in eating, euery one taketh before other, his owne ſupper: and one is hungry, and an other is drunken.[22]What, haue ye not houſes to eate and to drinke in? Or deſpiſe yee the Church of God, and ſhame them that haue not? What ſhall I ſay to you? ſhall I praiſe you in this? I prayſe you not.[23]For I haue receiued of the Lord that which alſo I deliuered vnto you, that the Lord Ieſus, the ſame night in which he was betrayed, tooke bread:[24]And when he had giuen thanks, he brake it, and ſayd, Take, eate, this is my body, which is broken for you: this doe in remembrance of mee.[25]After the ſame manner alſo hee tooke the cup when he had ſupped, ſaying, This cup is the new Teſtament in my blood: this do ye, as oft as ye drinke it, in remembrance of me.[26]For as often as ye eate this bread, and drinke this cup, yee doe ſhew the Lords death till he come.[27]Wherefore, whoſoeuer ſhall eate this bread, and drinke this cup of the Lord vnworthily, ſhall be guilty of the body and blood of the Lord.[28]But let a man examine himſelfe, and ſo let him eate of that bread, and drinke of that cup.[29]For hee that eateth and drinketh vnworthily, eateth and drinketh damnation to himſelfe, not diſcerning the Lords body.[30]For this cauſe many are weake and ſickly among you, and many ſleepe.[31]For if we would iudge our ſelues, we ſhould not be iudged.[32]But when we are iudged, we are chaſtened of the Lord, that wee ſhould not be condemned with the world.[33]Wherefore my brethren, when ye come together to eate, tary one for another.[34]And if any man hunger, let him eate at home, that ye come not together vnto condemnation. And the reſt wil I ſet in order, when I come.

CHAPTER 12[1]Now concerning ſpirituall giftes, brethren, I would not haue you ignorant.[2]Yee know that yee were Gentiles, caryed away vnto theſe dumbe idoles, euen as ye were led.[3]Wherefore I giue you to vnderſtand, that no man ſpeaking by the ſpirit of God, calleth Ieſus accurſed: and that no man can ſay that Ieſus is the Lord, but by the holy Ghoſt.[4]Nowe there are diuerſities of gifts, but the ſame ſpirit.[5]And there are differences of adminiſtrations, but the ſame Lord.[6]And there are diuerſities of operations, but it is the ſame God, which worketh all in all.[7]But the manifeſtation of the ſpirit, is giuen to euery man to profit withall.[8]For to one is giuen by the ſpirit, the word of wiſedome, to another the word of knowledge, by the ſame ſpirit.[9]To another faith, by the ſame ſpirit: to another the gifts of healing, by the ſame ſpirit:[10]To another the working of miracles, to another prophecie, to another diſcerning of ſpirits, to another diuers kindes of tongues, to another the interpretation of tongues.[11]But all theſe worketh that one and the ſelfe ſame ſpirit, diuiding to euery man ſeuerally as he will.[12]For as the body is one, and hath many members, and all the membrs of that one body, being many, are one bodie: ſo alſo is Chriſt.[13]For by one ſpirit are we all baptized into one bodie, whether wee bee Iewes or Gentiles, whether wee bee bond or free: and haue beene all made to drinke into one ſpirit.[14]For the body is not one member, but many.[15]If the foot ſhall ſay, Becauſe I am not the hand, I am not of the body: is it therefore not of the body?[16]And if the eare ſhall ſay, Becauſe I am not the eye, I am not of the body: is it therefore not of the body?[17]If the whole body were an eye, where were the hearing? If the whole were hearing, where were the ſmelling?[18]But now hath God ſet the members, euery one of them in the body, as it hath pleaſed him.[19]And if they were all one member, where were the body?[20]But now are they many members, yet but one body.[21]And the eye cannot ſay vnto the hand, I haue no need of thee: nor againe, the head to the feete, I haue no neede of you.[22]Nay, much more thoſe members of the bodie, which ſeeme to bee more feeble, are neceſsary.[23]And thoſe members of the bodie, which wee thinke to bee leſſe honourable, vpon theſe we beſtow more abundant honour, and our vncomely parts haue more abundant comelineſse.[24]For our comely parts haue no need: but God hath tempered the bodie together, hauing giuen more abundant honour to that part which lacked:[25]That there ſhould be no ſchiſme in the body: but that the members ſhould haue the ſame care one for another.[26]And whether one member ſuffer, all the members ſuffer with it: or one member be honoured, all the members reioyce with it.[27]Now yee are the body of Chriſt, and members in particular.[28]And God hath ſet ſome in the Church, firſt Apoſtles, ſecondarily Prophets, thirdly Teachers, after that miracles, then gifts of healings, helpes in gouernmēts, diuerſities of tongues.[29]Are all Apoſtles? are all Prophets? are all Teachers? are all workers of miracles?[30]Haue all the gifts of healing? doe all ſpeake with tongues? doe all interpret?[31]But couet earneſtly the beſt gifts: And yet ſhew I vnto you a more excellent way.

CHAPTER 13[1]Though I ſpeake with the tongues of men & of Angels, and haue not charity, I am become as ſounding braſſe or a tinkling cymbal.[2]And though I haue the gift of propheſie, and vnderſtand all myſteries and all knowledge: and though I haue all faith, ſo that I could remooue mountaines, and haue no charitie, I am nothing.[3]And though I beſtowe all my goods to feede the poore, and though I giue my body to bee burned, and haue not charitie, it profiteth me nothing.[4]Charitie ſuffereth long, and is kinde: charitie enuieth not: charitie vaunteth not it ſelfe, is not puffed vp,[5]Doeth not behaue it ſelfe vnſeemly, ſeeketh not her owne, is not eaſily prouoked, thinketh no euill,[6]Reioyceth not in iniquitie, but reioyceth in the trueth:[7]Beareth all things, beleeueth all things, hopeth all things, endureth all things.[8]Charitie neuer faileth: but whether there be propheſies, they ſhall faile; whether there bee tongues, they ſhall ceaſe; whether there bee knowledge, it ſhall vaniſh away.[9]For we know in part, and we propheſie in part.[10]But when that which is perfect is come, then that which is in part, ſhalbe done away.[11]When I

was a childe, I ſpake as a childe, I vnderſtood as a childe, I thought as a
childe: but when I became a man, I put away childiſh things.12For now
we ſee through a glaſſe, darkely: but then face to face: now I know in
part, but then ſhall I know euen as alſo I am knowen.13And now abideth
faith, hope, charitie, theſe three, but the greateſt of theſe is charitie.
CHAPTER 141Follow after charitie, and deſire ſpirituall giftes, but
rather that yee may propheſie.2For he that ſpeaketh in an vnknowen
tongue, ſpeaketh not vnto men, but vnto God: for no man
vnderſtandeth him: howbeit in the ſpirit he ſpeaketh myſteries.3But he
that propheſieth, ſpeaketh vnto men to edification, and exhortation, and
comfort.4He that ſpeaketh in an vnknowen tongue, edifieth himſelfe:
but hee that propheſieth, edifieth the Church.5I would that yee all ſpake
with tongues, but rather that ye propheſied: for greater is hee that
propheſieth, then hee that ſpeaketh with tongues, except hee interprete,
that the Church may receiue edifying.6Now brethren, if I come vnto you
ſpeaking with tongues, what ſhall I profit you, except I ſhall ſpeake to
you either by reuelation, or by knowledge, or by propheſying, or by
doctrine?7And euen things without life giuing ſound, whether pipe or
harpe, except they giue a diſtinction in the ſounds, how ſhall it be
knowen what is piped or harped?8For if the trumpet giue an vncertaine
ſound, who ſhall prepare himſelfe to the battell?9So likewiſe you, except
ye vtter by the tongue words eaſie to be vnderſtood, how ſhall it be
knowen what is ſpoken? for ye ſhall ſpeake into the aire.10There are, it
may bee, ſo many kindes of voices in the world, and none of them are
without ſignification.11Therefore if I know not the meaning of the
voyce, I ſhall bee vnto him that ſpeaketh, a Barbarian, and he that
ſpeaketh ſhall be a Barbarian vnto mee.12Euen ſo ye, foraſmuch as yee
are zealous of ſpirituall gifts, ſeeke that yee may excell to the edifying of
the Church.13Wherefore let him that ſpeaketh in an vnknowen tongue,
pray that he may interprete.14For if I pray in an vnknowen tongue, my
ſpirit prayeth, but my vnderſtanding is vnfruitfull.15What is it then? I
will pray with the ſpirit, and wil pray with vnderſtanding alſo: I will ſing
with the ſpirit, and I will ſing with the vnderſtanding alſo.16Elſe, when
thou ſhalt bleſſe with the ſpirit, how ſhall hee that occupieth the roome
of the vnlearned, ſay Amen at thy giuing of thankes, ſeeing he
vnderſtandeth not what thou ſayeſt?17For thou verily giueſt thankes
well: but the other is not edified.18I thanke my God, I ſpeake with
tongues more then you all.19Yet in the Church I had rather ſpeake fiue
words with my vnderſtanding, that by my voyce I might teach others
alſo, then ten thouſand words in an vnknowen tongue.20Brethren, bee
not children in vnderſtanding: how be it, in malice be yee children, but
in vnderſtanding be men.21In the Law it is written, With men of other
tongues, and other lippes will I ſpeake vnto this people: and yet for all
that will they not heare me, ſaith the Lord.22Wherfore tongues are for a
ſigne, not to them that beleeue, but to them that beleeue not: But
propheſying ſerueth not for them that beleeue not, but for them which
beleeue.23If therefore the whole Church be come together into ſome
place, and all ſpeake with tongues, & there come in thoſe that are
vnlearned, or vnbeleeuers, will they not ſay that ye are mad?24But if all
propheſie, and there come in one that beleeueth not, or one vnlearned:
he is conuinced of all, he is iudged of all.25And thus are the ſecrets of
his heart made manifeſt, and ſo falling downe on his face, hee will
worſhip God, and report that God is in you of a trueth.26How is it then
brethren? when ye come together, euery one of you hath a Pſalme, hath
a doctrine, hath a tongue, hath a reuelatiō, hath an interpretatiō: Let all
things be done vnto edifying.27If any man ſpeake in an vnknowen
tongue, let it be by two, or at the moſt by three, and that by courſe, and
let one interprete.28But if there be no interpreter, let him keepe ſilence
in the Church, and let him ſpeake to himſelfe, and to God.29Let the
Prophets ſpeake two or three, and let the other iudge.30If any thing be
reueiled to another that ſitteth by, let the firſt hold his peace.31For yee
may all propheſie one by one, that all may learne, and all may be
comforted.32And the ſpirits of the Prophets are ſubiect to the
Prophets.33For God is not the authour of confuſion, but of peace, as in
all Churches of the Saints.34Let your women keepe ſilence in the
Churches, for it is not permitted vnto them to ſpeake; but they are
commanded to bee vnder obedience: as alſo ſaith the Law.35And if they
will learne any thing, let them aſke their huſbands at home: for it is a
ſhame for women to ſpeake in the Church.36What? came the word of
God out from you? or came it vnto you onely?37If any man thinke
himſelfe to be a Prophet, or ſpiritual, let him acknowledge, that the
things that I write vnto you, are the commandements of the Lord.38But
if any man bee ignorant, let him be ignorant.39Wherefore brethren,
couet to propheſie, and forbid not to ſpeake with tongues.40Let all
things be done decently, and in order.
CHAPTER 151Moreouer brethren, I declare vnto you the Goſpel
which I preached vnto you, which alſo you haue receiued, and wherein
yee ſtand.2By which alſo yee are ſaued, if yee keepe in memorie what I
preached vnto you, vnleſſe yee haue beleeued in vaine.3For I deliuered
vnto you firſt of all, that which I alſo receiued, how that Chriſt died for
our ſinnes according to the Scriptures:4And that he was buried, and that
he roſe againe the third day according to the Scriptures.5And that he
was ſeene of Cephas, then of the twelue.6And that hee was ſeene of
aboue fiue hundred brethren at once: of whom the greater part remaine
vnto this preſent, but ſome are fallen aſleepe.7After that, he was ſeen of
Iames, then of all the Apoſtles.8And laſt of all he was ſeene of me alſo,
as of one borne out of due time.9For I am the leaſt of the Apoſtles, that
am not meet to be called an Apoſtle becauſe I perſecuted þe Church of
God.10But by the grace of God I am what I am: and his grace which
was beſtowed vpō me, was not in vaine: But I laboured more abundantly
then they all, yet not I, but the grace of God which was with
me:11Therefore, whether it were I or they, ſo we preach, aud ſo ye
beleeued.12Now if Chriſt be preached that he roſe from the dead, how
ſay ſome among you, that there is no reſurrection of the dead?13But if
there be no reſurrection of the dead, then is Chriſt not riſen.14And if
Chriſt be not riſen, then is our preaching vaine, and your faith is alſo
vaine:15Yea, and we are found falſe witneſſes of God, becauſe we haue
teſtified of God, that he raiſed vp Chriſt: whom hee raiſed not vp, if ſo
bee that the dead riſe not.16For if the dead riſe not, then is not Chriſt
raiſed.17And if Chriſt be not raiſed, your faith is vaine, ye are yet in your
ſinnes.18Then they alſo which are fallen aſleepe in Chriſt, are
periſhed.19If in this life only we haue hope in Chriſt, wee are of all men
moſt miſerable.20But now is Chriſt riſen from the dead, and become the
firſt fruits of them that ſlept.21For ſince by man came death, by man
came alſo the reſurrection of the dead.22For as in Adam all die, euen ſo
in Chriſt ſhall all be made aliue.23But euery man in his owne order. Chriſt
the firſt fruits, afterward they that are Chriſts, at his comming.24Then
commeth the end, when he ſhall haue deliuered vp the kingdome to
God euen the Father, when he ſhall haue put downe all rule, and all
authority and power.25For he muſt reigne, till hee hath put all enemies
vnder his feete.26The laſt enemie that ſhall be deſtroyed, is death.27For
he hath put all things vnder his feete; but when hee ſaith all things are
put vnder him, it is manifeſt that he is excepted which did put all things
vnder him.28And when all things ſhall bee ſubdued vnto him, then ſhal
the Sonne alſo himſelfe bee ſubiect vnto him that put all things vnder
him, that God may be all in all.29Elſe what ſhal they do, which are
baptized for the dead, if the dead riſe not at all, why are they then
baptized for the dead?30And why ſtand we in ieopardy euery houre?31I
proteſt by your reioycing which I haue in Chriſt Ieſus our Lord, I die
dayly.32If after the maner of men I haue fought with beaſts at Epheſus,
what aduantageth it me, if the dead riſe not? let vs eate and drinke, for
to morrowe wee die.33Bee not deceiued: euill communications corrupt
good manners.34Awake to righteouſneſſe, and ſinne not: for ſome haue
not the knowledge of God, I ſpeake this to your ſhame.35But ſome man
will ſay, How are the dead rayſed vp? and with what body doe they
come?36Thou foole, that which thou ſoweſt, is not quickened except it
die.37And that which thou ſoweſt, thou ſoweſt not that body that ſhall
be, but bare graine, it may chance of wheate, or of ſome other
graine.38But God giueth it a body as it hath pleaſed him, and to euery
ſeed his owne body.39All fleſh is not the ſame fleſh, but there is one kind
of fleſh of men, another fleſh of beaſts, another of fiſhes, and another
of birds.40There are alſo celeſtiall bodies, and bodies terreſtriall: But the
glorie of the celeſtiall is one, and the glorie of the terreſtriall is
another.41There is one glory of the ſunne, another of the moone, and
another glorie of the ſtarres: for one ſtarre differeth from another ſtarre
in glorie.42So alſo is the reſurrection of the dead, it is ſowen in
corruption, it is raiſed in incorruption.43It is ſowen in diſhonour, it is
rayſed in glorie: it is ſowen in weakeneſse, it is rayſed in power:44It is
ſowen a naturall body, it is raiſed a ſpirituall bodie. There is a naturall

bodie, and there is a ſpirituall bodie.45And ſo it is written: The firſt man
Adam was made a liuing ſoule, the laſt Adam was made a quickening
ſpirit.46Howbeit that was not firſt which is ſpirituall: but that which is
naturall, and afterward that which is ſpirituall.47The firſt man is of the
earth, earthy: The ſecond man is the Lord from heauen.48As is the
earthy, ſuch are they that are earthy, and as is the heauenly, ſuch are they
alſo that are heauenly.49And as we haue borne the image of the earthy,
wee ſhall alſo beare the image of the heauenly.50Now this I ſay,
brethren, that fleſh & blood cannot inherite the kingdome of God:
neither doth corruption inherite incorruption.51Behold, I ſhew you a
myſterie: we ſhall not all ſleepe, but wee ſhall all be changed,52In a
moment, in the twinckling of an eye, at the laſt trumpe, (for the trumpet
ſhall ſound, and the dead ſhall be raiſed incorruptible, and we ſhall be
changed.)53For this corruptible muſt put on incorruption, and this
mortall muſt put on immortalitie.54So when this corruptible ſhall haue
put on incorruption, & this mortall ſhall haue put on immortality, then
ſhall be brought to paſſe the ſaying that is written, Death is ſwallowed
vp in victorie.55O death, where is thy ſting? O graue, where is thy
victorie?56The ſting of death is ſinne, and the ſtrength of ſinne is the
law.57But thankes bee to God, which giueth vs the victorie, through our
Lord Ieſus Chriſt.58Therefore my beloued brethren, be yee ſtedfaſt,
vnmoueable, alwayes abounding in the worke of the Lord, foraſmuch as
you know that your labour is not in vaine in the Lord.

CHAPTER 161Now concerning the collection for the Saints, as I haue
giuen order to the Churches of Galatia, euen ſo doe ye.2Upon the firſt
day of the weeke, let euery one of you lay by him in ſtore, as God hath
proſpered him, that there be no gatherings when I come.3And when I
come, whomſoeuer you ſhall approue by your letters, them wil I ſend to
bring your liberality vnto Ieruſalem.4And if it be meet that I goe alſo,
they ſhall goe with me.5Now I wil come vnto you, when I ſhall paſſe
through Macedonia: for I doe paſſe through Macedonia.6And it may bee
that I will abide, yea, and winter with you, that yee may bring me on my
iourny, whitherſoeuer I goe.7For I will not ſee you now by the way, but
I truſt to tarry a while with you, if the Lord permit.8But I will tarry at
Epheſus vntill Pentecoſt.9For a great doore and effectuall is opened
vnto mee, and there are many aduerſaries.10Now if Timotheus come,
ſee that he may be with you without feare: for hee worketh the worke
of the Lord, as I alſo doe.11Let no man therefore deſpiſe him: but
conduct him forth in peace, that hee may come vnto me: for I looke for
him with the brethren.12As touching our brother Apollos, I greatly
deſired him to come vnto you with þe brethren, but his wil was not at
all to come at this time: but he wil come when hee ſhall haue conuenient
time.13Watch yee, ſtand faſt in the faith, quit you like men: be
ſtrong.14Let all your things be done with charitie.15I beſeech you,
brethren, (ye know the houſe of Stephanas, that it is the firſt fruits of
Achaia, and that they haue addicted themſelues to the miniſtery of the
Saints,)16That ye ſubmit your ſelues vnto ſuch, and to euery one that
helpeth with vs and laboureth.17I am glad of the comming of Stephanas,
and Fortunatus, and Achaicus: for that which was lacking on your part,
they haue ſupplied.18For they haue refreſhed my ſpirit and yours:
therefore acknowledge yee them that are ſuch.19The Churches of Aſia
ſalute you: Aquila and Priſcilla ſalute you much in the Lord, with the
Church that is in their houſe.20All the brethren greet you: greet ye one
another with an holy kiſſe.21The ſalutation of me Paul, with mine owne
hand.22If any man loue not the Lord Ieſus Chriſt, let him bee Anathema
Maranatha.23The grace of our Lord Ieſus Chriſt be with you.24My loue
be with you all in Chriſt Ieſus, Amen. The firſt Epiſtle to the Corinthians
was written from Philippi by Stephanas, and Fortunatus, and Achaicus,
and Timotheus..

2 CORINTHIANS

CHAPTER 11Paul an Apoſtle of Ieſus Chriſt by the will of God, and
Timothie our brother, vnto the Church of God, which is at Corinth,
with all the Saints, which are in all Achaia:2Grace bee to you and peace,
from God our Father, and from the Lord Ieſus Chriſt.3Bleſſed be God,
euen the Father of our Lord Ieſus Chriſt, the Father of mercies, and the
God of all comfort,4Who comforteth vs in all our tribulation, that we
may be able to comfort them which are in any trouble, by the comfort,
wherewith we our ſelues are comforted of God.5For as the ſufferings of
Chriſt abound in vs, ſo our conſolation alſo aboundeth by Chriſt.6And
whether we be afflicted, it is for your conſolation and ſaluation, which
is effectuall in the enduring of the ſame ſufferings, which wee alſo ſuffer:
or whether we be comforted, it is for your conſolation, and
ſaluation.7And our hope of you is ſtedfaſt, knowing, that as you are
partakers of the ſufferings, ſo ſhall yee be alſo of the conſolatiou.8For
we would not, brethren, haue you ignorant of our trouble which came
to vs in Aſia, that we were preſſed out of meaſure, aboue ſtrength, in ſo
much that we diſpaired euen of life.9But we had the ſentence of death
in our ſelues, that we ſhould not truſt in our ſelues, but in God which
raiſeth the dead.10Who deliuered vs from ſo great a death, and doeth
deliuer: in whom we truſt that he will yet deliuer vs:11You alſo helping
together by prayer for vs, that for the gift beſtowed vpon vs by the
meanes of many perſons, thankes may bee giuen by many on our
behalfe.12For our reioycing is this, the teſtimony of our conſcience, that
in ſimplicitie and godly ſinceritie, not with fleſhly wiſedome, but by the
grace of God, wee haue had our conuerſation in the world, and more
aboundantly to youwards.13For we write none other things vnto you,
then what you reade or acknowledge, and I truſt you ſhall acknowledge
euen to the end.14As alſo you haue acknowledged vs in part, that we are
your reioycing, euen as ye alſo are ours, in the day of the Lord
Ieſus.15And in this confidence I was minded to come vnto you before,
that you might haue a ſecond benefit:16And to paſſe by you into
Macedonia, and to come againe out of Macedonia vnto you, and of you
to bee brought on my way toward Iudea.17When I therefore was thus
minded, did I vſe lightneſse? or the things that I purpoſe, doe I purpoſe
according to the fleſh, that with mee there ſhould be yea yea, and nay
nay?18But as God is true, our word toward you, was not yea and
nay.19For the Sonne of God Ieſus Chriſt, who was preached among you
by vs, euen by me, and Syluanus and Timotheus, was not Yea, and Nay,
but in him, was yea.20For all the promiſes of God in him are Yea, and
in him Amen, vnto the glory of God by vs.21Now hee which ſtabliſheth
vs with you, in Chriſt, and hath anoynted vs, is God,22Who hath alſo
ſealed vs, and giuen the earneſt of the Spirit in our hearts.23Moreouer, I
call God for a record vpō my ſoule, that to ſpare you I came not as yet
vnto Corinth.24Not for that we haue dominion ouer your faith, but are
helpers of your ioy: for by faith ye ſtand.

CHAPTER 21But I determined this with my ſelfe, that I would not
come againe to you in heauineſse.2For if I make you ſorie, who is hee
then that maketh mee glad, but the ſame which is made ſorie by me.3And
I wrote this ſame vnto you, leaſt when I came, I ſhould haue ſorrow
from them of whome I ought to reioyce, hauing confidence in you all,
that my ioy is the ioy of you all.4For out of much affliction and anguiſh
of heart, I wrote vnto you with many teares, not that you ſhould bee
grieued, but that yee might knowe the loue which I haue more
abundantly vnto you.5But if any haue cauſed griefe, hee hath not grieued
mee, but in part: that I may not ouercharge you all.6Sufficient to ſuch a
man is this puniſhment, which was inflicted of many.7So that
contrarywiſe, yee ought rather to forgiue him, and comfort him, leſt
perhaps, ſuch a one ſhould be ſwallowed vp with ouermuch
ſorrow.8Wherefore I beſeech you, that you would confirme your loue
towards him.9For to this end alſo did I write, that I might know the
proofe of you, whether ye be obedient in all things.10To whom yee
forgiue any thing, I forgiue alſo: for if I forgaue any thing, to whom I
forgaue it, for your ſakes forgaue I it, in the perſon of Chriſt,11Leſt Satan
ſhould get an aduantage of vs: for wee are not ignorant of his
deuices.12Furthermore when I came to Troas, to preach Chriſts Goſpel,
and a doore was opened vnto mee of the Lord,13I had no reſt in my
ſpirit, becauſe I found not Titus my brother, but taking my leaue of
them, I went from thence into Macedonia.14Now thankes bee vnto
God, which alwayes cauſeth vs to triumph in Chriſt, and maketh
manifeſt the ſauour of his knowledge by vs in euery place.15For wee are
vnto God, a ſweet ſauour of Chriſt, in them that are ſaued, and in them
that periſh.16To the one wee are the ſauour of death vnto death; and to
the other, the ſauour of life vnto life: and who is ſufficient for theſe
things?17For wee are not as many which corrupt the word of God: but
as of ſinceritie, but as of God, in the ſight of God ſpeake we in Chriſt.

CHAPTER 3 1Doe wee begin againe to commend our ſelues? or need wee, as ſome others, Epiſtles of commendation to you, or letters of commendation from you? 2Ye are our Epiſtle written in our hearts, knowen and read of all men. 3Foraſmuch as yee are manifeſtly declared to be the Epiſtle of Chriſt miniſtred by vs, written not with inke, but with the ſpirit of the liuing God, not in tables of ſtone, but in fleſhy tables of the heart. 4And ſuch truſt haue wee through Chriſt to Godward: 5Not that wee are ſufficient of our ſelues to thinke any thing as of our ſelues: but our ſufficiencie is of God: 6Who alſo hath made vs able miniſters of the New Teſtament, not of the letter, but of the ſpirit: for the letter killeth, but the ſpirit giueth life. 7But if the miniſtration of death written, and ingrauen in ſtones, was glorious, ſo that the children of Iſrael could not ſtedfaſtly beholde the face of Moſes, for the glory of his countenance, which glorie was to be done away: 8How ſhall not the miniſtration of the ſpirit, be rather glorious? 9For if the miniſtration of condemnation bee glory, much more doth the miniſtration of righteouſneſſe exceed in glorie. 10For euen that which was made glorious, had no glorie in this reſpect by reaſon of the glorie that excelleth. 11For if that which is done away, was glorious, much more that which remaineth is glorious. 12Seeing then that wee haue ſuch hope, we vſe great plainneſse of ſpeech. 13And not as Moſes, which put a vaile ouer his face, that the children of Iſrael could not ſtedfaſtly looke to the end of that which is aboliſhed; 14But their mindes were blinded: for vntill this day remaineth the ſame vaile vntaken away, in the reading of the old teſtament: which vaile is done away in Chriſt. 15But euen vnto this day, when Moſes is read, the vaile is vpon their heart. 16Neuertheleſſe, when it ſhall turne to the Lord, the vaile ſhall be taken away. 17Now the Lord is that ſpirit, and where the Spirit of the Lord is, there is libertie. 18But we all, with open face beholding as in a glaſſe the glory of the Lord, are changed into the ſame image, from glorie to glorie, euen as by the ſpirit of the Lord.

CHAPTER 4 1Therefore, ſeeing we haue this miniſtery, as we haue receiued mercie wee faint not: 2But haue renounced the hidden things of diſhoneſty, not walking in craftines, nor handling the word of God deceitfully, but by manifeſtation of the trueth, commending our ſelues to euery mans conſcience, in the ſight of God. 3But if our Goſpel be hid, it is hid to them that are loſt: 4In whom the God of this world hath blinded the minds of them which beleeue not, leſt the light of the glorious Goſpel of Chriſt, who is the image of God, ſhould ſhine vnto them. 5For we preach not our ſelues, but Chriſt Ieſus the Lord, and our ſelues your ſeruants for Ieſus ſake. 6For God who commaunded the light to ſhine out of darkenes, hath ſhined in our hearts, to giue the light of the knowledge of the glory of God, in the face of Ieſus Chriſt. 7But we haue this treaſure in earthen veſſels, that the excellencie of the power may be of God, and not of vs. 8Wee are troubled on euery ſide, yet not diſtreſſed; we are perplexed, but not in deſpaire, 9Perſecuted, but not forſaken; caſt downe, but not deſtroyed. 10Alwayes bearing about in the body, the dying of the Lord Ieſus, that the life alſo of Ieſus might bee made manifeſt in our body. 11For we which liue, are always deliuered vnto death for Ieſus ſake, that the life alſo of Ieſus might bee made manifeſt in our mortall fleſh. 12So then death worketh in vs, but life in you. 13We hauing the ſame ſpirit of faith, according as it is written, I beleeued, and therefore haue I ſpoken: wee alſo beleeue, and therefore ſpeake. 14Knowing that hee which raiſed vp the Lord Ieſus, ſhall raiſe vp vs alſo by Ieſus, and ſhall preſent vs with you. 15For all things are for your ſakes, that the abundāt grace might, through the thankeſgiuing of many, redound to the glory of God. 16For which cauſe we faint not, but though our outward man periſh, yet the inward man is renewed day by day. 17For our light affliction, which is but for a momēt, worketh for vs a farre more exceeding and eternall waight of glory, 18While we looke not at the things which are ſeene, but at þe things which are not ſeene: for the things which are ſeene, are temporall, but the things which are not ſeene, are eternall.

CHAPTER 5 1For we know, that if our earthly houſe of this Tabernacle were diſſolued, wee haue a building of God, an houſe not made with hand, eternall in the heauens. 2For in this we grone earneſtly, deſiring to be clothed vpō with our houſe, which is from heauen. 3If ſo be that being clothed we ſhal not be found naked. 4For, we that are in this tabernacle, doe grone, being burdened, not for that wee would bee vnclothed, but clothed vpon, that mortalitie might bee ſwallowed vp of life. 5Now he þt hath wrought vs for the ſelfe ſame thing, is God, who alſo hath giuen vnto vs the earneſt of the ſpirit. 6Therefore we are alwayes confident, knowing that whileſt wee are at home in the body, wee are abſent from the Lord. 7(For we walke by faith, not by ſight.) 8We are confident, I ſay, and willing rather to be abſent from the body, and to be preſent with the Lord. 9Wherefore we labour, that whether preſent or abſent, we may be accepted of him. 10For we muſt all appeare before the iudgement ſeat of Chriſt, that euery one may receiue the things done in his body, according to that hee hath done, whether it be good or bad. 11Knowing therefore the terrour of the Lord, we perſwade men; but we are made manifeſt vnto God, & I truſt alſo, are made manifeſt in your conſciences. 12For we commend not our ſelues againe vnto you, but giue you occaſion to glory on our behalfe, that you may haue ſomewhat to anſwere them, which glory in appearance, and not in heart. 13For whether wee bee beſides our ſelues, it is to God: or whether we bee ſober, it is for your cauſe. 14For the loue of Chriſt conſtreineth vs, becauſe wee thus iudge: that if one died for all, then were all dead: 15And that he died for all, that they which liue, ſhould not hencefoorth liue vnto themſelues, but vnto him which died for them, and roſe againe. 16Wherefore hencefoorth know we no man, after the fleſh: yea, though we haue knowen Chriſt after the fleſh, yet now hencefoorth knowe wee him no more. 17Therfore if any man be in Chriſt, hee is a new creature: old things are paſt away, behold, al things are become new. 18And all things are of God, who hath reconciled vs to himſelfe by Ieſus Chriſt, and hath giuen to vs the miniſtery of reconciliation, 19To wit, that God was in Chriſt, reconciling the world vnto himſelfe, not imputing their treſpaſſes vnto them, and hath committed vnto vs the word of reconciliation. 20Now then we are Ambaſsadors for Chriſt, as though God did beſeech you by vs; we pray you in Chriſts ſtead, that be ye reconciled to God. 21For he hath made him to be ſinne for vs, who knewe no ſinne, that wee might bee made the righteouſneſſe of God in him.

CHAPTER 6 1Wee then, as workers together with him, beſeech you alſo, that ye receiue not the grace of God in vaine. 2(For he ſaith, I haue heard thee in a time accepted, and in the day of ſaluation haue I ſuccoured thee: beholde, now is the accepted time, behold, now is the day of ſaluation) 3Giuing no offence in any thing, that the miniſtery be not blamed: 4But in all things approuing our ſelues, as the Miniſters of God, in much patience, in afflictions, in neceſsities, in diſtreſſes, 5In ſtripes, in impriſonments, in tumults, in labours, in watchings, in faſtings, 6By pureneſse, by knowledge, by long ſuffering, by kindneſse, by the holy Ghoſt, by loue vnfained, 7By the worde of trueth, by the power of God, by the armour of righteouſneſſe, on the right hand, and on the left, 8By honour and diſhonour, by euil report and good report, as deceiuers and yet true: 9As vnknowen, & yet wel knowen: as dying, and behold, we liue: as chaſtened, and not killed: 10As ſorrowfull, yet alway reioycing: as poore, yet making many rich: as hauing nothing, and yet poſseſsing all things. 11O yee Corinthians, our mouth is open vnto you, our heart is enlarged. 12Yee are not ſtraitened in vs, but yee are ſtraitned in your owne bowels. 13Nowe for a recompenſe in the ſame, (I ſpeake as vnto my children) be ye alſo inlarged. 14Be ye not vnequally yoked together with vnbeleeuers: for what fellowſhip hath righteouſneſſe with vnrighteouſneſſe? and what communion hath light with darkneſſe? 15And what concord hath Chriſt with Belial? or what part hath he that beleeueth, with an infidel? 16And what agreement hath the Temple of God with idoles? for ye are the Temple of the liuing God, as God hath ſaide, I will dwell in them, and walke in them, and I will be their God, and they ſhall be my people. 17Wherefore come out from among them, and bee yee ſeparate, ſaieth the Lord, and touch not the vncleane thing, and I will receiue you, 18And will bee a Father vnto you, and ye ſhall bee my ſonnes and daughters, ſaith the Lord Almightie.

CHAPTER 7 1Hauing therefore theſe promiſes (dearely beloued) let vs cleanſe our ſelues from all filthines of the fleſh and ſpirit, perfecting holineſſe in the feare of God. 2Receiue vs, we haue wronged no man, wee haue corrupted no man, wee haue defrauded no man. 3I ſpeake not this to condemne you: for I haue ſaid before, that you are in our hearts to die and liue with you. 4Great is my boldneſse of ſpeach toward you, great is my glorying of you, I am filled with comfort, I am exceeding ioyfull in all our tribulation. 5For when wee were come into Macedonia, our fleſh had no reſt, but we were troubled on euery ſide; without were

fightings, within were feares.6Neuertheleſſe, God that comforteth thoſe
that are caſt downe, comforted vs by the comming of Titus.7And not
by his comming onely, but by the conſolation wherewith hee was
comforted in you, when he told vs your earneſt deſire, your mourning,
your feruent minde toward me, ſo that I reioyced the more.8For though
I made you ſory with a letter, I doe not repent, though I did repent: For
I perceiue that the ſame Epiſtle hath made you ſory, thogh it were but
for a ſeaſon.9Now I reioyce, not that ye were made ſorie, but that ye
ſorrowed to repentance: for ye were made ſorie after a godly maner, that
ye might receiue damage by vs in nothing.10For godly ſorrow worketh
repentance to ſaluation not to be repented of, but the ſorrow of the
world worketh death.11For behold this ſelfe ſame thing that yee
ſorrowed after a godly ſort, what carefulneſse it wrought in you, yea,
what clearing of your ſelues, yea, what indignation, yea what feare, yea
what vehement deſire, yea what zeale, yea what reuenge; In all things yee
haue approued your ſelues to be cleare in this matter.12Wherefore
though I wrote vnto you, I did it not for his cauſe that had done the
wrong, nor for his cauſe that ſuffered wrong, but that our care for you
in the ſight of God might appeare vnto you.13Therefore we were
comforted in your comfort, yea and exceedingly the more ioyed wee for
the ioy of Titus, becauſe his ſpirit was refreſhed by you all.14For if I haue
boaſted any thing to him of you, I am not aſhamed; but as we ſpake all
things to you in trueth, euen ſo our boaſting which I made before Titus,
is found a trueth.15And his inward affection is more aboundant toward
you, whileſt he remembreth the obedience of you all, how with feare
and trembling you receiued him.16I reioyce therefore that I haue
confidence in you in all things.

CHAPTER 8 1Moreouer, brethren, wee do you to wit of the grace of
God beſtowed on the Churches of Macedonia,2How that in a great trial
of affliction, the abundance of their ioy, and their deepe pouertie,
abounded vnto the riches of their liberalitie.3For to their power (I beare
record) yea, and beyond their power they were willing of
themſelues:4Praying vs with much entreatie, that we would receiue the
gift, and take vpon vs the fellowſhip of the miniſtring to the Saints.5And
this they did, not as we hoped, but firſt gaue their owne ſelues to the
Lord, and vnto vs, by the will of God.6In ſo much that wee deſired
Titus, that as he had begun, ſo hee would alſo finiſh in you, the ſame
grace alſo.7Therefore (as ye abound in euery thing, in faith, and
vtterance, & knowledge, and in all diligence, and in your loue to vſ) ſee
that yee abound in this grace alſo.8I ſpeake not by commandement, but
by occaſion of the forwardneſse of others, and to prooue the ſinceritie
of your loue.9For yee know the grace of our Lord Ieſus Chriſt, that
though he was rich, yet for your ſakes he became poore, that yee through
his pouertie might be rich.10And herein I giue my aduice, for this is
expedient for you, who haue begun before, not onely to doe, but alſo to
be forward a yeere agoe.11Now therefore performe the doing of it, that
as there was a readineſse to will, ſo there may be a performance alſo out
of that which you haue.12For if there bee firſt a willing minde, it is
accepted according to that a man hath, and not according to that he hath
not.13For I meane not that other men bee eaſed, and you
burthened:14But by an equalitie: that now at this time your abundance
may be a ſupply for their want, that their abundance alſo may be a ſupply
for your want, that there may be equalitie,15As it is written, Hee that had
gathered much, had nothing ouer, and hee that had gathered little, had
no lacke.16But thankes bee to God which put the ſame earneſt care into
the heart of Titus for you.17For indeed he accepted the exhortation, but
being more forward, of his owne accord he went vnto you.18And wee
haue ſent with him the brother, whoſe praiſe is in the Goſpel,
throughout all the Churches.19And not that onely, but who was alſo
choſen of the Churches to trauaile with vs with this grace which is
adminiſtred by vs to the glorie of the ſame Lord, and declaration of your
readie minde.20Auoyding this, that no man ſhould blame vs in this
aboundance which is adminiſtred by vs.21Prouiding for honeſt things,
not onely in the ſight of the Lord, but in the ſight of men.22And we haue
ſent with them our brother, whom wee haue often times proued diligent
in many things, but now much more diligent, vpon the great confidence
which I haue in you.23Whether any doe enquire of Titus; he is my partner
and fellow helper concerning you: or our brethren bee enquired of, they
are the meſſengers of the Churches, and the glorie of
Chriſt.24Wherefore ſhew ye to them, and before the Churches, the
proofe of your loue, & of our boaſting on your behalfe.

CHAPTER 9 1For as touching the miniſtring to the Saints, it is
ſuperfluous for mee to write to you.2For I know the forwardneſse of
your mind, for which I boaſt of you to them of Macedonia, that Achaia
was ready a yeere agoe, and your zeale hath prouoked very many.3Yet
haue I ſent the brethren, leaſt our boaſting of you ſhould bee in vaine in
this behalfe, that as I ſaide, yee may be readie.4Leſt happily if they of
Macedonia come with mee, & find you vnprepared, wee (that wee ſay
not, you) ſhould bee aſhamed in this ſame confident
boaſting.5Therefore I thought it neceſsary to exhort the brethren, that
they would go before vnto you, and make vp before hand your bountie,
whereof yee had notice before, that the ſame might bee readie, as a
matter of bountie, not of couetouſneſſe.6But this I ſay, Hee which
ſoweth ſparingly, ſhall reape ſparingly: and he which ſoweth bountifully,
ſhall reape bountifully.7Euerie man according as he purpoſeth in his
heart, ſo let him giue; not grudgingly, or of neceſsitie: for God loueth a
cheerefull giuer.8And God is able to make all grace abound towards you,
that ye alwayes hauing all ſufficiencie in all things, may abound to euery
good worke,9(As it is written: Hee hath diſperſed abroad: Hee hath
giuen to the poore: his righteouſneſſe remaineth for euer.10Now he that
miniſtreth ſeede to the ſower, both miniſter bread for your foode, and
multiply your ſeede ſowen, and encreaſe the fruites of your
righteouſneſſe)11Being enriched in euery thing to al bountifulnes, which
cauſeth through vs thankeſgiuing to God.12For the adminiſtration of
this ſeruice, not onely ſupplieth the want of the Saints, but is abundant
alſo by many thankſgiuings vnto God,13Whiles by the experiment of this
miniſtration, they glorifie God for your profeſsed ſubiection vnto the
Goſpel of Chriſt, and for your liberall diſtribution vnto them, and vnto
all men:14And by their prayer for you, which long after you for the
exceeding grace of God in you.15Thanks be vnto God for his
vnſpeakeable gift.

CHAPTER 10 1Now I Paul my ſelfe beſeech you, by the meekenes and
gentleneſse of Chriſt, who in preſence am baſe among you, but being
abſent, am bold toward you:2But I beſeech you, that I may not bee bold
when I am preſent, with that confidence wherewith I thinke to be bold
againſt ſome, which thinke of vs as if wee walked according to the
fleſh.3For though we walke in the fleſh, we doe not warre after the
fleſh:4(For the weapons of our warfare are not carnal, but mighty
through God to the pulling downe of ſtrong holds.)5Caſting down
imaginations, and euery high thing that exalteth it ſelfe againſt the
knowledge of God, and bringing into captiuitie euery thought to the
obedience of Chriſt:6And hauing in a readineſse to reuenge all
diſobedience, when your obedience is fulfilled.7Doe ye looke on things
after the outward appearance? if any man truſt to himſelfe, that he is
Chriſts, let him of himſelfe thinke this againe, that as he is Chriſts, euen
ſo are we Chriſts.8For though I ſhould boaſt ſomewhat more of our
authority (which the Lord hath giuen vs for edification, and not for your
deſtruction) I ſhould not be aſhamed:9That I may not ſeeme as if I
would terrifie you by letters.10For his letters (ſay they) are waighty and
powerfull, but his bodily preſence is weake, and his ſpeach
contemptible.11Let ſuch a one thinke this: that ſuch as we are in word
by letters, when we are abſent, ſuch will we be alſo in deede when we
are preſent.12For we dare not make our ſelues of the number, or
compare our ſelues with ſome that commend themſelues: but they
meaſuring themſelues by themſelues, and comparing themſelues
amongſt themſelues, are not wiſe.13But we will not boaſt of things
without our meaſure, but according to the meaſure of the rule, which
God hath diſtributed to vs, a meaſure to reach euen vnto you.14For we
ſtretch not our ſelues beyond our meaſure as though wee reached not
vnto you, for wee are come as farre as to you alſo, in preaching the
Goſpel of Chriſt.15Not boaſting of things without our meaſure, that is,
of other mens labours, but hauing hope, when your faith is increaſed,
that wee ſhall bee enlarged by you, according to our rule
abundantly.16To preach the Goſpel in the regions beyond you, and not
to boaſt in another mans line of things made ready to our hand.17But he
that glorieth, let him glory in the Lord.18For, not he that commendeth
himſelfe is approued, but whom the Lord commendeth.

CHAPTER 11 1Would to God you could beare with mee a little in my
folly, & in deede beare with me.2For I am iealous ouer you with godly

iealouſie, for I haue eſpouſed you to one huſband, that I may preſent
you as a chaſte virgin to Chriſt.3But I feare leſt by any meanes, as the
Serpent beguiled Eue through his ſubtilty, ſo your mindes ſhould bee
corrupted from the ſimplicitie that is in Chriſt.4For if he that commeth
preacheth another Ieſus whome wee haue not preached, or if yee receiue
another ſpirit, which ye haue not receiued, or another Goſpel, which ye
haue not accepted, yee might well beare with him.5For, I ſuppoſe, I was
not a whit behinde the very chiefeſt Apoſtles.6But though I be rude in
ſpeach, yet not in knowledge; but we haue bene throughly made
manifeſt among you in all things.7Haue I committed an offence in
abaſing my ſelfe, that you might be exalted, becauſe I haue preached to
you the Goſpel of God freely?8I robbed other Churches, taking wages
of them to doe you ſeruice.9And when I was preſent with you, and
wanted, I was chargeable to no man: For that which was lacking to mee,
the brethren which came from Macedonia ſupplied, and in all things I
haue kept my ſelfe from being burthenſome to you, and ſo will I keepe
my ſelfe.10As the trueth of Chriſt is in mee, no man ſhall ſtop mee of
this boaſting in the regions of Achaia.11Wherefore? becauſe I loue you
not? God knoweth.12But what I doe, that I wil doe, that I may cut off
occaſion from them which deſire occaſion, that wherein they glory, they
may bee found euen as we.13For ſuch are falſe Apoſtles, deceitfull
workers, tranſforming themſelues into the Apoſtles of Chriſt.14And no
marueile, for Sathan himſelfe is tranſformed into an Angel of
light.15Therefore it is no great thing if his miniſters alſo bee tranſformed
as the miniſters of righteouſneſſe, whoſe end ſhall be according to their
workes.16I ſay againe, Let no man thinke mee a foole; if otherwiſe, yet
as a foole receiue me, that I may boaſt my ſelfe a little.17That which I
ſpeake, I ſpeake it not after the Lord, but as it were fooliſhly in this
confidence of boaſting.18Seeing that many glory after the fleſh, I will
glory alſo.19For ye ſuffer fooles gladly, ſeeing ye your ſelues are
wiſe.20For ye ſuffer if a man bring you into bondage, if a man deuoure
you, if a man take of you, if a man exalt himſelfe, if a man ſmite you on
the face.21I ſpeake as concerning reproch, as though we had bene weake:
howbeit, wherein ſoeuer any is bold, I ſpeake fooliſhly, I am bold
alſo.22Are they Hebrewes? ſo am I: are they Iſraelites? ſo am I: are they
the ſeed of Abraham? ſo am I:23Are they miniſters of Chriſt? I ſpeake as
a foole, I am more: in labors more abundant: in ſtripes aboue meaſure:
in priſons more frequent: in deaths oft.24Of the Iewes fiue times
receiued I forty ſtripes ſaue one.25Thrice was I beaten with rods, once
was I ſtoned: thrice I ſuffered ſhipwracke: a night and a day I haue bene
in the deepe.26In iourneying often, in perils of waters, in perils of
robbers, in perils by my owne countreymen, in perils by the heathen, in
perils in the citie, in perils in the wilderneſſe, in perils in the ſea, in perils
among falſe brethren,27In wearineſse and painfulneſse, in watchings
often, in hunger & thirſt, in faſtings often, in cold and
nakednes.28Beſides thoſe things that are without, that which commeth
vpon me dayly, the care of all the Churches.29Who is weake, and I am
not weake? who is offended, and I burne not?30If I muſt needes glory,
I will glory of the things which concerne mine infirmities.31The God and
Father of our Lord Ieſus Chriſt, which is bleſſed for euermore, knoweth
that I lie not.32In Damaſcus the gouernour vnder Aretas the King, kept
the citie with a gariſon, deſirous to apprehend mee.33And through a
window in a baſket was I let downe, by the wall, and eſcaped his hands.
CHAPTER 12 1It is not expedient for me, doubtleſſe, to glory, I wil
come to viſions and reuelations of the Lord.2I knewe a man in Chriſt
aboue foureteene yeeres agoe, whether in the body, I cannot tell, or
whether out of the body, I cannot tell, God knoweth: ſuch a one, caught
vp to the third heauen.3And I knew ſuch a man (whether in the body,
or out of the body, I cannot tell, God knoweth.)4How that he was
caught vp into Paradiſe, and heard vnſpeakeable wordes, which it is not
lawfull for a man to vtter.5Of ſuch a one will I glory, yet of my ſelfe I
will not glory, but in mine infirmities.6For though I would deſire to
glory, I ſhall not be a foole: for I will ſay the trueth. But now I forbeare,
leſt any man ſhould thinke of me aboue that which hee ſeeth me to bee,
or that hee heareth of me:7And leaſt I ſhould bee exalted aboue meaſure
through the abundance of the reuelations, there was giuen to me a
thorne in the fleſh, the meſſenger of Sathan to buffet me, leſt I ſhould
be exalted aboue meaſure.8For this thing I beſought the Lord thrice,
that it might depart from mee.9And he ſaid vnto me, My grace is
ſufficient for thee: for my ſtrength is made perfect in weaknes. Moſt
gladly therefore will I rather glory in my infirmities, that the power of
Chriſt may reſt vpon me.10Therefore I take pleaſure in infirmities, in
reproches, in neceſsities, in perſecutions, in diſtreſſes for Chriſtes ſake:
for when I am weake, then am I ſtrong.11I am become a foole in
glorying, ye haue compelled me. For I ought to haue beene commended
of you: for in nothing am I behinde the very chiefeſt Apoſtles, though I
be nothing.12Truely the ſignes of an Apoſtle were wrought among you
in all patience, in ſignes and wonders, and mightie deeds.13For what is it
wherein yee were inferior to other Churches, except it bee that I my ſelfe
was not burthenſome to you? forgiue me this wrong.14Behold, the third
time I am readie to come to you, and I will not bee burthenſome to you;
for I ſeeke not yours, but you: for the children ought not to lay vp for
the parents, but the parents for the children.15And I wil very gladly
ſpend and bee ſpent for you, though the more abundantly I loue you,
the leſſe I bee loued.16But be it ſo: I did not burthen you: neuertheleſſe
beeing craftie, I caught you with guile.17Did I make a gaine of you by
any of them, whom I ſent vnto you?18I deſired Titus, and with him I
ſent a brother: did Titus make a gaine of you? Walked wee not in the
ſame ſpirit? walked wee not in the ſame ſteps?19Againe, thinke you that
we excuſe our ſelues vnto you? wee ſpeake before God in Chriſt: but
wee doe all things, dearely beloued, for your edifying.20For I feare leſt
when I come, I ſhall not find you ſuch as I would, and that I ſhall bee
found vnto you ſuch as ye would not, leſt there bee debates, enuyings,
wraths, ſtrifes, backebitings, whiſperings, ſwellings, tumults,21And leaſt
when I come againe, my God will humble mee among you, and that I
ſhall bewaile many which haue ſinned alreadie, and haue not repented
of the vncleanneſſe, and fornication, and laſciuiouſneſse which they
haue committed.
CHAPTER 13 1This is the third time I am comming to you: in the
mouth of two or three witneſſes ſhal euery word be eſtabliſhed.2I told
you before, and foretell you as if I were preſent the ſecond time, and
being abſent, now I write to them which heretofore haue ſinned, and to
all other, that if I come againe I will not ſpare:3Since ye ſeeke a proofe
of Chriſt, ſpeaking in me, which to you-ward is not weake, but is mightie
in you.4For though hee was crucified through weakneſse, yet he liueth
by the power of God: for wee alſo are weake in him, but wee ſhall liue
with him by the power of God toward you.5Examine your ſelues,
whether ye be in the faith: proue your owne ſelues. Know yee not your
owne ſelues, how that Ieſus Chriſt is in you, except ye be
reprobates?6But I truſt that yee ſhall knowe that we are not
reprobates.7Now I pray to God, that ye doe no euill, not that we ſhould
appeare approued, but that ye ſhould doe þt which is honeſt, though we
be as reprobates.8For wee can doe nothing againſt the trueth, but for
the trueth.9For wee are glad when wee are weake, and ye are ſtrong: and
this alſo we wiſh, euen your perfection.10Therefore I write theſe things
being abſent, leſt being preſent I ſhould vſe ſharpneſse, according to the
power which the Lord hath giuen me to edification, and not to
deſtruction.11Finally, brethren, farewell: Bee perfect, bee of good
comfort, bee of one minde, liue in peace, and the God of loue and peace
ſhalbe with you.12Greet one another with an holy kiſſe.13All the Saints
ſalute you.14The grace of the Lord Ieſus Chriſt, and the loue of God,
and the communion of the holy Ghoſt, be with you all. Amen. The
ſecond Epiſtle to the Corinthians, was written from Philippos a citie of
Macedonia, by Titus and Lucas.

GALATIANS

CHAPTER 1 1Paul an Apoſtle, not of men, neither by man, but by Ieſus
Chriſt, and God the Father, who raiſed him frō the dead,2And all the
brethren which are with mee, vnto the Churches of Galatia:3Grace bee
to you and peace, from God the Father, and from our Lord Ieſus
Chriſt,4Who gaue himſelfe for our ſinnes, that he might deliuer vs from
this preſent euill world, according to the will of God, and our Father,5To
whom bee glorie for euer and euer, Amen.6I marueile, that you are ſo
ſoone remoued from him, that called you into the grace of Chriſt, vnto
an other Goſpel:7Which is not another; but there bee ſome that trouble
you, and would peruert the Goſpel of Chriſt.8But though we, or an

Angel from heauen, preach any other Goſpel vnto you, then that which wee haue preached vnto you, let him be accurſed.9As we ſaid before, ſo ſay I now againe, If any man preach any other Goſpel vnto you, then that yee haue receiued, let him be accurſed.10For doe I now perſwade men, or God? or doe I ſeeke to pleaſe men? For if I yet pleaſed men, I ſhould not bee the ſeruant of Chriſt.11But I certifie you, brethren, that the Goſpel which was preached of me, is not after man.12For I neither receiued it of man, neither was I taught it, but by the reuelation of Ieſus Chriſt.13For yee haue heard of my couuerſation in time paſt, in the Iewes Religion, how that beyond meaſure I perſecuted the Church of God, and waſted it:14And profited in the Iewes Religion, aboue many my equals in mine owne nation, being more exceedingly zealous of the traditions of my fathers.15But when it pleaſed God, who ſeparated me from my mothers wombe, and called me by his grace,16To reueale his ſonne in mee, that I might preach him among the heathen, immediatly I conferred not with fleſh and blood:17Neither went I vp to Ieruſalem, to them which were Apoſtles before me, but I went into Arabia, and returned againe vnto Damaſcus.18Then after three yeeres, I went vp to Ieruſalem to ſee Peter, and abode with him fifteene dayes.19But other of the Apoſtles ſaw I none, ſaue Iames the Lords brother.20Now the things which I write vnto you, behold, before God I lye not.21Afterwards I came into the regions of Syria and Cilicia,22And was vnknowen by face vnto the Churches of Iudea, which were in Chriſt.23But they had heard onely, that he which perſecuted vs in times paſt, now preacheth the faith, which once hee deſtroyed.24And they glorified God in me.

CHAPTER 21Then fourteene yeeres after, I went vp againe to Ieruſalem with Barnabas, and tooke Titus with me alſo.2And I went vp by reuelation, and communicated vnto them that Goſpel, which I preach among the Gentiles, but priuately to them which were of reputation, leſt by any meanes I ſhould runne, or had runne in vaine.3But neither Titus, who was with me, being a Greeke, was compelled to be circumciſed:4And that becauſe of falſe brethren vnawares brought in, who came in priuily to ſpie out our libertie, which wee haue in Chriſt Ieſus, that they might bring vs into bondage.5To whom wee gaue place by ſubiection, no not for an houre, that the trueth of the Goſpel might continue with you.6But of theſe, who ſeemed to bee ſomewhat, (whatſoeuer they were, it maketh no matter to mee, God accepteth no mans perſon,) for they who ſeemed to be ſomewhat, in conference added nothing to me.7But contrariwiſe, when they ſaw that the Goſpel of the vncircumciſion was committed vnto me, as the Goſpel of the circumciſion was vnto Peter:8(For he that wrought effectually in Peter to the Apoſtleſhip of the circumciſion, the ſame was mightie in me towards the Gentiles.)9And when Iames, Cephas and Iohn, who ſeemed to bee pillars, perceiued the grace that was giuen vnto me, they gaue to me and Barnabas the right hands of fellowſhip, that wee ſhould goe vnto the heathen, and they vnto the circumciſion.10Onely they would that wee ſhould remember the poore, the ſame which I alſo was forward to doe.11But when Peter was come to Antioch, I withſtood him to the face, becauſe he was to be blamed.12For before that certaine came from Iames, he did eate with the Gentiles: but when they were come, hee withdrew, and ſeparated himſelfe, fearing them which were of the Circumciſiō.13And the other Iewes diſsembled likewiſe with him, inſomuch that Barnabas alſo was caried away with their diſsimulation.14But when I ſaw that they walked not vprightly according to the truth of the Goſpel, I ſaid vnto Peter before them al, If thou, being a Iew, liueſt after the maner of Gentiles, and not as doe the Iewes, why compelleſt thou the Gentiles to liue as do the Iewes?15We who are Iewes by nature, and not ſinners of the Gentiles,16Knowing that a man is not iuſtified by the works of the Law, but by the faith of Ieſus Chriſt, euen we haue beleeued in Ieſus Chriſt, that we might be iuſtified by the faith of Chriſt, and not by the workes of the Law: for by the workes of the Law ſhall no fleſh be iuſtified.17But if while we ſeeke to be iuſtified by Chriſt, wee our ſelues alſo are found ſinners, is therefore Chriſt the miniſter of ſinne? God forbid.18For if I build againe the things which I deſtroyed, I make my ſelfe a tranſgreſsour.19For I through þe Law, am dead to the Law, that I might liue vnto God.20I am crucified with Chriſt. Neuertheles, I liue, yet not I, but Chriſt liueth in me, and the life which I now liue in the fleſh, I liue by the faith of the ſonne of God, who loued mee, and gaue himſelfe for me.21I doe not fruſtrate the grace of God: for if righteouſnes come by the Lawe, then Chriſt is dead in vaine.

CHAPTER 31O fooliſh Galatians, who hath bewitched you, that you ſhould not obey the trueth, before whoſe eyes Ieſus Chriſt hath been euidently ſet forth, crucified among you?2This onely would I learne of you, receiued ye the ſpirit, by the works of the Law, or by the hearing of faith?3Are ye ſo fooliſh? hauing begun in the Spirit, are ye now made perfect by the fleſh?4Haue ye ſuffered ſo many things in vaine? if it be yet in vaine.5He therfore that miniſtreth to you the Spirit, and worketh miracles among you, doeth he it by the workes of the Law, or by the hearing of faith?6Euen as Abraham beleeued God, and it was accounted to him for righteouſneſſe.7Knowe yee therefore, that they which are of faith, the ſame are the children of Abraham.8And the Scripture foreſeeing that God would iuſtifie the heathen through faith, preached before the Goſpel vnto Abraham, ſaying, In thee ſhall all nations be bleſſed.9So then, they which bee of faith, are bleſſed with faithfull Abraham.10For as many as are of the works of the lawe, are vnder the curſe: for it is written, Curſed is euery one that continueth not in all things which are written in the booke of the Law to doe them.11But that no man is iuſtified by the Lawe in the ſight of God, it is euident: for, The iuſt ſhall liue by faith.12And the Law is not of faith: but the man that doeth them, ſhall liue in them.13Chriſt hath redeemed vs from the curſe of the Law, being made a curſe for vs: for it is written, Curſed is euery one that hangeth on tree:14That the bleſſing of Abraham might come on the Gentiles, through Ieſus Chriſt: that wee might receiue the promiſe of the Spirit through faith.15Brethren, I ſpeake after the maner of men: though it be but a mans couenant, yet if it bee confirmed, no man diſanulleth, or addeth thereto.16Now to Abraham and his ſeede were the promiſes made. He ſaith not, And to ſeeds, as of many, but as of one, And to thy ſeed, which is Chriſt.17And this I ſay, that the Couenant that was confirmed before of God in Chriſt, the Lawe which was foure hundred and thirtie yeres after, cannot diſanul, that it ſhould make the promiſe of none effect.18For if the inheritance bee of the Law, it is no more of promiſe: but God gaue it to Abraham by promiſe.19Wherefore then ſerueth the Law? it was added becauſe of tranſgreſſions, till the ſeed ſhould come, to whome the promiſe was made, and it was ordeyned by Angels in the hand of a Mediatour.20Now a mediatour is not a Mediatour of one, but God is one.21Is the Lawe then againſt the promiſes of God? God forbid: for if there had beene a Lawe giuen which could haue giuen life, verily righteouſneſſe ſhould haue bene by the Law.22But the Scripture hath concluded all vnder ſinne, that the promiſe by faith of Ieſus Chriſt might be giuen to them that beleeue.23But before faith came, wee were kept vnder the Law, ſhut vp vnto the faith, which ſhould afterwards bee reuealed.24Wherefore the Law was our Schoolemaſter to bring vs vnto Chriſt, that we might be iuſtified by Faith.25But after that Faith is come, we are no longer vnder a Schoolemaſter.26For ye are all the children of God by faith in Chriſt Ieſus.27For as many of you as haue bene baptized into Chriſt, haue put on Chriſt.28There is neither Iewe, nor Greeke, there is neither bond nor free, there is neither male nor female: for ye are all one in Chriſt Ieſus.29And if yee be Chriſts, then are ye Abrahams ſeed, and heires according to the promiſe.

CHAPTER 41Now I ſay, that the heire, as long as hee is a child, differeth nothing from a ſeruant, though hee bee Lord of all,2But is vnder tutors and gouernours vntill the time appointed of the father.3Euen ſo we, when wee were children, were in bondage vnder the Elements of the world:4But when the fulnes of the time was come, God ſent foorth his Sonne made of a woman, made vnder the Law,5To redeeme them that were vnder the Law, that we might receiue the adoption of ſonnes.6And becauſe yee are ſonnes, God hath ſent foorth the ſpirit of his Sonne into your hearts, crying Abba, Father.7Wherefore thou art no more a ſeruant, but a ſonne; and if a ſonne, then an heire of God through Chriſt.8Howbeit, then when ye knew not God, yee did ſeruice vnto them which by nature are no Gods.9But now after that yee haue knowen God, or rather are knowen of God, how turne ye againe to the weak and beggerly Elements, whereunto ye deſire againe to be in bondage?10Yee obſerue dayes, and moneths, and times, and yeeres.11I am afraide of you, leſt I haue beſtowed vpon you labour in vaine.12Brethren, I beſeech you, be as I am; for I am as ye are, ye haue not iniured me at all.13Ye know how through infirmitie of the fleſh, I preached the Goſpel vnto you at the firſt.14And my temptation which was in my fleſh ye deſpiſed not, nor reiected, but receiued mee as an Angel of God, euen as Chriſt Ieſus.15Where is then the bleſſednes you ſpake of? for I beare you record, that if it had bin poſsible, ye would haue plucked out your own eyes, and haue giuen them to me.16Am I therefore become your enemie, becauſe I tell you the trueth?17They zelouſly affect you, but not well: yea, they would exclude you, that you might affect them.18But it is good to bee zealouſly affected alwayes in a good thing, and not onely when I am preſent with you.19My litle children, of whom I trauaile in birth againe, vntill Chriſt bee formed in you:20I deſire to bee preſent with you now, and to change my voyce, for I ſtand in doubt of you.21Tell me, ye that deſire to be vnder the Law, doe ye not heare the Law?22For it is written, that Abraham had two ſonnes, the one by a bondmaid, the other by a freewoman.23But he who was of the bondwoman, was borne after the fleſh: but hee of the freewoman, was by promiſe.24Which things are an Allegorie; for theſe are the two Couenants; the one from the mount Sinai, which gendereth to bondage, which is Agar.25For this Agar is mount Sinai in Arabia, and anſwereth to Ieruſalem, which now is, and is in bondage with her children.26But Ieruſalem which is aboue is free, which is the mother of vs all.27For it is written, Reioyce thou barren that beareſt not, breake foorth and cry thou that traueileſt not; for the deſolate hath many moe children then ſhe which hath an huſband.28Now wee, brethren, as Iſaac was, are the children of promiſe.29But as then hee that was borne after the fleſh, perſecuted him that was borne after the Spirit, euen ſo it is now.30Neuertheleſſe, what ſaith the Scripture? Caſt out the bondwoman and her ſonne: for the ſon of the bondwoman ſhall not bee heire with the ſon of the freewoman.31So then, brethren, we are not children of the bondwoman, but of the free.

CHAPTER 51ſtand faſt therefore in the libertie wherewith Chriſt hath made vs free, and bee not intangled againe with the yoke of bondage.2Beholde, I Paul ſay vnto you that if ye be circumciſed, Chriſt ſhal profite you nothing.3For I teſtifie againe to euery man that is circumciſed, that he is a debtor to doe the whole Law.4Chriſt is become of no effect vnto you, whoſoeuer of you are iuſtified by the Law: ye are fallen from grace.5For we through the ſpirit waite for the hope of righteouſneſſe by faith.6For in Ieſus Chriſt, neither circumciſion auaileth any thing, nor vncircumciſion, but faith which worketh by loue.7Ye did run well; who did hinder you, that ye ſhould not obey the trueth?8This perſwaſion commeth not of him that calleth you.9A little leauen leaueneth the whole lumpe.10I haue confidence in you through the Lord, that you will be none otherwiſe minded; but he that troubleth you, ſhall beare his iudgement, whoſoeuer hee be.11And I, brethren, if I yet preach circumciſion, why doe I yet ſuffer perſecution? then is the offence of the croſse ceaſed.12I would they were euen cut off which trouble you.13For brethren, ye haue beene called vnto liberty, onely vſe not libertie for an occaſion to the fleſh, but by loue ſerue one another.14For all the Law is fulfilled in one word, euen in this: Thou ſhalt loue thy neighbour as thy ſelfe.15But if yee bite and deuoure one another, take heed ye be not conſumed one of another.16This I ſay then, Walke in the ſpirit, and ye ſhall not fulfill the luſt of the fleſh.17For the fleſh luſteth againſt the Spirit, and the ſpirit againſt the fleſh: and theſe are contrary the one to the other: ſo that yee cannot doe the things that yee would.18But if yee be lead of the ſpirit, yee are not vnder the Law.19Nowe the workes of the fleſh are manifeſt, which are theſe, adulterie, fornication, vncleanneſſe, laſciuiouſneſe,20Idolatrie, witchcraft, hatred, variance, emulations, wrath, ſtrife, ſeditions, hereſies,21Enuyings, murthers, drunkenneſse, reuellings, and ſuch like: of the which I tell you before, as I haue alſo tolde you in time paſt, that they which do ſuch things ſhall not inherite the kingdome of God.22But the fruit of the ſpirit is loue, ioy, peace, long ſuffering, gentleneſse, goodneſse, faith,23Meekeneſse, temperance: againſt ſuch there is no law.24And they that are Chriſts, haue crucified the fleſh with the affections and luſtes.25If we liue in the Spirit, let vs alſo walke in the Spirit.26Let vs not be deſirous of vaine glory, prouoking one another, enuying one another.

CHAPTER 61Brethren, if a man bee ouertaken in a fault: yee which are ſpirituall, reſtore ſuch a one in the ſpirit of meekneſse, conſidering thy ſelfe leaſt thou alſo be tempted.2Beare ye one anothers burthens, and ſo fulfill the Law of Chriſt.3For if a man thinke himſelfe to be ſomething, when he is nothing, hee deceiueth himſelfe.4But let euery man prooue his owne worke, and then ſhall he haue reioycing in him ſelfe alone, and not in an other.5For euery man ſhall beare his owne burthen.6Let him that is taught in the word, communicate vnto him that teacheth, in all good things.7Be not deceiued, God is not mocked: for whatſoeuer a man ſoweth, that ſhall he alſo reape.8For hee that ſoweth to his fleſh, ſhall of the fleſh reape corruption: but he that ſoweth to the ſpirit, ſhall of the ſpirit reape life euerlaſting.9And let vs not bee weary in well doing: for in due ſeaſon we ſhall reape, if we faint not.10As we haue therefore opportunitie, let vs doe good vnto all men, eſpecially vnto them who are of the houſehold of faith.11Ye ſee how large a letter I haue written vnto you with mine owne hand.12As many as deſire to make a faire ſhew in the fleſh, they conſtraine you to be Circumciſed: onely leaſt they ſhould ſuffer perſecution for the Croſse of Chriſt.13For neither they themſelues who are circumciſed, keepe the Law, but deſire to haue you circumciſed, that they may glory in your fleſh.14But God forbid that I ſhould glory, ſaue in the Croſse of our Lord Ieſus Chriſt, by whom the world is crucified vnto me, & I vnto the world.15For in Chriſt Ieſus neither circumciſion auaileth any thing nor vncircumciſion, but a new creature.16And as many as walke according to this rule, peace be on them, and mercie, and vpon the Iſrael of God.17From henceforth let no man trouble mee, for I beare in my body the markes of the Lord Ieſus.18Brethren, the grace of our Lord Ieſus Chriſt be with your ſpirit. Amen. Unto the Galatians, written from Rome.

EPHEſIANS (EPHESIANS)

CHAPTER 11Paul an Apoſtle of Ieſus Chriſt by the will of God, to the Saincts which are at Epheſus, and to the faithfull in Chriſt Ieſus.2Grace be to you, and peace from God our Father, and from the Lord Ieſus Chriſt.3Bleſſed be the God and Father of our Lord Ieſus Chriſt, who hath bleſſed vs with all ſpirituall bleſſings in heauenly places in Chriſt:4According as he hath choſen vs in him, before the foundation of the world, that wee ſhould bee holy, and without blame before him in loue:5Hauing predeſtinated vs vnto the adoption of children by Ieſus Chriſt to himſelfe, according to the good pleaſure of his will:6To the praiſe of the glorie of his grace, wherein he hath made vs accepted in the beloued:7In whom wee haue redemption through his blood, the forgiueneſe of ſinnes, according to the riches of his grace,8Wherein hee hath abounded toward vs in all wiſedome and prudence:9Hauing made knowen vnto vs the myſterie of his will, according to his good pleaſure, which he had purpoſed in himſelfe,10That in the diſpenſation of the fulneſe of times, he might gather together in one all things in Chriſt, both which are in heauen, and which are on earth, euen in him:11In whom alſo we haue obteined an inheritance, being predeſtinated according to the purpoſe of him who worketh all things after the counſell of his owne will:12That we ſhould be to the praiſe of his glorie, who firſt truſted in Chriſt.13In whom ye alſo truſted, after that ye heard the word of trueth, the Goſpel of your ſaluation: in whom alſo after that yee beleeued, yee were ſealed with that holy Spirit of promiſe,14Which is the earneſt of our inheritance, vntill the redemption of the purchaſed poſſeſſion, vnto the praiſe of his glorie.15Wherefore I alſo, after I heard of your faith in the Lord Ieſus, and loue vnto all the Saints,16Ceaſe not to giue thankes for you, making mention of you in my prayers,17That the God of our Lord Ieſus Chriſt the Father of glorie, may giue vnto you the Spirit of wiſedome and reuelation in the knowledge of him:18The eyes of your vnderſtanding being inlightned: that yee may know what is the hope of his calling, and what the riches of the glorie of his inheritance in the Saints:19And what is the exceeding greatneſſe of his power to vſ-ward who beleeue, according to the working of his mightie power:20Which he wrought in Chriſt when he raiſed him from the dead, and ſet him at his owne right hand in the heauenly places,21Farre aboue all principalitie, and power, and might, and dominion, and euery name that is named, not onely in this world, but alſo in that which is to come:22And hath put all things vnder his feete, and gaue him to be the head ouer all things to the Church,23Which is his body, the fulneſe of him that filleth all in all.

CHAPTER 2 1And you hath hee quickned who were dead in treſpaſſes, and ſinnes,2Wherein in time paſt ye walked according to the courſe of this world, according to the prince of the power of the aire, the ſpirit that now worketh in the children of diſobedience,3Among whom alſo we all had our conuerſation in times paſt, in the luſts of our fleſh, fulfilling the deſires of the fleſh, and of the minde, and were by nature the children of wrath, euen as others:4But God who is rich in mercie, for his great loue wherewith hee loued vs,5Euen when wee were dead in ſinnes, hath quickned vs together with Chriſt, (by grace ye are ſaued)6And hath raiſed vs vp together, and made vs ſit together in heauenly places in Chriſt Ieſus:7That in the ages to come, hee might ſhew the exceeding riches of his grace, in his kindeneſse towards vs, through Chriſt Ieſus.8For by grace are ye ſaued, through faith, and that not of your ſelues: it is the gift of God:9Not of workes, leſt any man ſhould boaſt.10For wee are his workemanſhip, created in Chriſt Ieſus vnto good workes, which God hath before ordeined, that we ſhould walke in them.11Wherefore remember that ye being in time paſſed Gentiles in the fleſh, who are called vncircumciſion by that which is called the Circumciſion in the fleſh made by hands,12That at that time yee were without Chriſt, being aliens from the common wealth of Iſrael, and ſtrangers from the couenants of promiſe, hauing no hope, & without God in the world.13But now in Chriſt Ieſus, ye who ſometimes were far off, are made nigh by the blood of Chriſt.14For hee is our peace, who hath made both one, and hath broken downe the middle wall of partition betweene vs:15Hauing aboliſhed in his fleſh the enmitie, euen the Lawe of Commandements conteined in Ordinances, for to make in himſelfe, of twaine, one newe man, ſo making peace.16And that he might reconcile both vnto God in one body by the croſse, hauing ſlaine the enmitie thereby,17And came, and preached peace to you, which were afarre off, and to them that were nigh.18For through him wee both haue an acceſse by one Spirit vnto the Father.19Now therefore yee are no more ſtrangers and forreiners; but fellow citizens with the Saints, and of the houſhold of God,20And are built vpon the foundation of the Apoſtles and Prophets, Ieſus Chriſt himſelfe being the chiefe corner ſtone,21In whom all the building fitly framed together, groweth vnto an holy Temple in the Lord:22In whom you alſo are builded together for an habitation of God thorow the Spirit.

CHAPTER 3 1For this cauſe I Paul, the priſoner of Ieſus Chriſt for you Gentiles,2If ye haue heard of the diſpenſation of the grace of God, which is giuen me to youward:3How that by reuelation hee made knowen vnto me the myſterie, (as I wrote afore in few words,4Whereby when ye reade, ye may vnderſtand my knowledge in the myſterie of Chriſt.)5Which in other ages was not made knowen vnto the ſonnes of men, as it is now reueiled vnto his holy Apoſtles and Prophets by the Spirit,6That the Gentiles ſhould be fellow heires, and of the ſame body, and partakers of his promiſe in Chriſt, by the Goſpel:7Whereof I was made a Miniſter, according to the gift of the grace of God giuen vnto mee, by the effectuall working of his power.8Unto mee, who am leſſe then the leaſt of all Saints, is this grace giuen, that I ſhould preach among the Gentiles the vnſearchable riches of Chriſt,9And to make all men ſee, what is the fellowſhip of the myſterie, which from the beginning of the world, hath bene hid in God, who created all things by Ieſus Chriſt:10To the intent that now vnto the principalities and powers in heauenly places, might be knowen by the church, the manifold wiſedome of God,11According to the eternall purpoſe which he purpoſed in Chriſt Ieſus our Lord:12In whom we haue boldneſse and acceſse, with confidence, by the faith of him.13Wherefore I deſire that yee faint not at my tribulations for you, which is your glory.14For this cauſe I bow my knees vnto the Father of our Lord Ieſus Chriſt,15Of whom the whole family in heauen and earth is named,16That he would grant you according to the riches of his glory, to bee ſtrengthened with might, by his Spirit in the inner man,17That Chriſt may dwell in your hearts by faith, that yee being rooted and grounded in loue,18May be able to comprehend with all Saints, what is the breadth, and length, and depth, and height:19And to know the loue of Chriſt, which paſſeth knowledge, that yee might bee filled with all the fulneſse of God.20Now vnto him that is able to do exceeding abundantly aboue all that wee aſke or thinke, according to the power that worketh in vs,21Unto him be glory in the Church by Chriſt Ieſus, throughout all ages, world without end. Amen.

CHAPTER 4 1I therefore the priſoner of the Lord, beſeech you that yee walke worthy of the vocation wherewith ye are called,2With all lowlineſse and meekeneſse, with long ſuffering, forbearing one another in loue.3Endeuouring to keepe the vnitie of the Spirit in the bond of peace.4There is one body, and one ſpirit, euen as yee are called in one hope of your calling.5One Lord, one Faith, one Baptiſme,6One God and Father of all, who is aboue all, & through all, & in you all.7But vnto euery one of vs is giuen grace, according to the meaſure of the gift of Chriſt.8Wherefore he ſaith: When he aſcended vp on high, he led captiuitie captiue, and gaue gifts vnto men.9(Now that he aſcended, what is it but that hee alſo deſcended firſt into the lower parts of the earth?10He that deſcended, is the ſame alſo that aſcended vp far aboue all heauens, that he might fill all things.)11And he gaue ſome, Apoſtles: and ſome, Prophets: and ſome, Euangeliſts: and ſome, Paſtors, and teachers:12For the perfecting of the Saints, for the worke of the miniſterie, for the edifying of the body of Chriſt:13Till we all come in the vnitie of the faith, and of the knowledge of the Sonne of God, vnto a perfect man, vnto the meaſure of the ſtature of the fulneſse of Chriſt:14That we hencefoorth be no more children, toſsed to and fro, and caried about with euery winde of doctrine, by the ſleight of men, and cunning craftineſse, whereby they lye in waite to deceiue:15But ſpeaking the trueth in loue, may grow vp into him in all things which is the head, euen Chriſt:16From whom the whole body fitly ioyned together, and compacted by that which euery ioynt ſupplyeth, according to the effectuall working in the meaſure of euery part, maketh increaſe of the body, vnto the edifying of it ſelfe in loue.17This I ſay therefore and teſtifie in the Lord, that yee henceforth walke not as other Gentiles walke in the vanitie of their minde,18Hauing the vnderſtanding darkened, being alienated from the life of God, through the ignorance that is in them, becauſe of the blindneſse of their heart:19Who being paſt feeling, haue giuen themſelues ouer vnto laſciuiouſneſse, to worke all vncleanneſſe with greedineſse.20But ye haue not ſo learned Chriſt:21If ſo be that ye haue heard him, and haue bene taught by him, as the trueth is in Ieſus,22That yee put off concerning the former conuerſation, the olde man, which is corrupt according to the deceitfull luſts:23And bee renewed in the ſpirit of your minde:24And that yee put on that new man, which after God is created in righteouſneſſe, and true holineſſe.25Wherefore putting away lying, ſpeake euery man truth with his neighbour: for we are members one of another.26Be ye angry and ſinne not, let not the Sunne go down vpon your wrath:27Neither giue place to the deuill.28Let him that ſtole, ſteale no more: but rather let him labour, working with his handes the thing which is good, that he may haue to giue to him that needeth.29Let no corrupt communication proceede out of your mouth, but that which is good to the vſe of edifying, that it may miniſter grace vnto the hearers.30And grieue not the holy Sririt of God, whereby yee are ſealed vnto the day of redemption.31Let all bitternes, and wrath, and anger, and clamour, and euill ſpeaking, be put away from you, with all malice,32And bee ye kinde one to another. tender hearted, forgiuing one another, euen as God for Chriſts ſake hath forgiuen you.

CHAPTER 5 1Be ye therefore followers of God, as deare children.2And walke in loue, as Chriſt alſo hath loued vs, and hath giuen himſelfe for vs, an offering and a ſacrifice to God for a ſweet ſmelling ſauour;3But fornication and all vncleanneſſe, or couetouſneſſe, let it not be once named amongſt you, as becommeth Saints:4Neither filthineſse, nor fooliſh talking, nor ieſting, which are not conuenient: but rather giuing of thankes.5For this ye know, that no whoremonger, nor vncleane perſon, nor couetous man who is an idolater, hath any inheritance in the kingdome of Chriſt, and of God.6Let no man deceiue you with vaine words: for becauſe of theſe things commeth the wrath of God vpon the children of diſobedience.7Bee not yee therefore partakers with them.8For yee were ſometimes darkeneſſe, but now are yee light in the Lord: walke as children of light,9(For the fruite of the ſpirit is in all goodneſſe and righteouſneſſe & trueth.)10Proouing what is acceptable vnto the Lord:11And haue no fellowſhip with the vnfruitfull workes of darkeneſſe, but rather reproue them.12For it is a ſhame euen to ſpeake of thoſe things which are done of them in ſecret.13But all things that are reproued, are made manifeſt by the light: for whatſoeuer doth make manifeſt, is light.14Wherfore hee ſaith: Awake thou that ſleepeſt, and

Ariſe from the dead, and Chriſt ſhall giue thee light. 15 ſee then that yee walke circumſpectly, not as fooles, but as wiſe, 16 Redeming the time, becauſe the dayes are euill. 17 Wherefore be ye not vnwiſe, but vnderſtanding what the will of the Lord is. 18 And bee not drunke with wine, wherein is exceſse: but bee filled with the Spirit: 19 Speaking to your ſelues, in Pſalmes, and Hymnes, and Spirituall ſongs, ſinging and making melodie in your heart to the Lord, 20 Giuing thankes alwayes for all things vnto God, and the Father, in the Name of our Lord Ieſus Chriſt, 21 Submitting your ſelues one to another in the feare of God. 22 Wiues, ſubmit your ſelues vnto your own huſbands, as vnto the Lord. 23 For the huſband is the head of the wife, euen as Chriſt is the head of the Church: and he is the ſauiour of the body. 24 Therefore as the Church is ſubiect vnto Chriſt, ſo let the wiues bee to their owne huſbands in euery thing. 25 Huſbands, loue your wiues, euen as Chriſt alſo loued the Church, and gaue himſelfe for it: 26 That he might ſanctifie & cleanſe it with the waſhing of water, by the word, 27 That hee might preſent it to himſelfe a glorious Church, not hauing ſpot or wrinckle, or any ſuch thing: but that it ſhould bee holy and without blemiſh. 28 So ought men to loue their wiues, as their owne bodies: hee that loueth his wife, loueth himſelfe. 29 For no man euer yet hated his owne fleſh: but nouriſheth and cheriſheth it, euen as the Lord the Church: 30 For we are members of his body, of his fleſh, and of his bones. 31 For this cauſe ſhall a man leaue his father and mother, and ſhall be ioyned vnto his wife, and they two ſhalbe one fleſh. 32 This is a great myſterie: but I ſpeake concerning Chriſt and the Church. 33 Neuertheleſſe, let euery one of you in particular, ſo loue his wife euen as himſelfe, and the wife ſee that ſhe reuerence her huſband

CHAPTER 6 1 Children, obey your parents in the Lord: for this is right. 2 Honour thy father and mother, (which is the firſt commandement with promiſe,) 3 That it may bee well with thee, and thou maieſt liue long on the earth. 4 And yee fathers, prouoke not your children to wrath: but bring them vp in the nourture and admonition of the Lord. 5 Seruants, bee obedient to them that are your maſters according to the fleſh, with feare and trembling, in ſinglenefse of your heart, as vnto Chriſt: 6 Not with eye ſeruice as men pleaſers, but as the ſeruants of Chriſt, doing the will of God from the heart: 7 With good will doing ſeruice, as to the Lord, and not to men, 8 Knowing that whatſoeuer good thing any man doeth, the ſame ſhall he receiue of the Lord, whether he be bond or free. 9 And ye maſters, do the ſame things vnto them, forbearing threatning: knowing that your maſter alſo is in heauen, neither is there reſpect of perſons with him. 10 Finally, my brethren, be ſtrong in the Lord, & in the power of his might. 11 Put on the whole armour of God, that ye may be able to ſtand againſt the wiles of the deuill. 12 For wee wreſtle not againſt fleſh and blood, but againſt principalities, againſt powers, againſt the rulers of the darknes of this world, againſt ſpirituall wickednes in high places. 13 Wherfore take vnto you the whole armour of God, that yee may be able to withſtand in the euill day, and hauing done all, to ſtand. 14 ſtand therefore, hauing your loynes girt about with trueth, and hauing on the breaſt-plate of righteouſneſſe: 15 And your feete ſhod with the preparation of the Goſpel of peace. 16 Aboue all, taking the ſhielde of Faith, wherewith yee ſhall bee able to quench all the fierie dartes of the wicked. 17 And take the helmet of ſaluation, and the ſword of the Spirit, which is the word of God: 18 Praying alwayes with all prayer and ſupplication in the ſpirit, and watching thereunto with all perſeuerance, and ſupplication for all Saints, 19 And for mee, that vtterance may be giuen vnto me, that I may open my mouth boldly, to make knowen the myſterie of the Goſpel: 20 For which I am an ambaſsador in bonds, that therein I may ſpeake boldly, as I ought to ſpeake. 21 But that yee alſo may know my affaires, and how I doe, Tychicus a beloued brother, and faithfull miniſter in the Lord, ſhall make knowen to you all things. 22 Whom I haue ſent vnto you for the ſame purpoſe, that yee might know our affaires, and that he might comfort your hearts. 23 Peace be to the brethren, and loue, with faith from God the Father, and the Lord Ieſus Chriſt. 24 Grace be with all them that loue our Lord Ieſus Chriſt in ſinceritie. Written from Rome vnto the Epheſians by Tychicus.

PHILIPPIANS

CHAPTER 1 1 Paul and Timotheus the ſeruants of Ieſus Chriſt, to all the Saints in Chriſt Ieſus, which are at Philippi, with the Biſhops and Deacons: 2 Grace be vnto you, and peace, from God our Father, and from the Lord Ieſus Chriſt. 3 I thanke my God vpon euery remembrance of you, 4 Alwayes in euery prayer of mine for you all making requeſt, with ioy 5 For your felowſhip in the Goſpel from the firſt day vntill now; 6 Being confident of this very thing, that he which hath begun a good work in you, will performe it vntil the day of Ieſus Chriſt: 7 Euen as it is meete for mee to thinke this of you all, becauſe I haue you in my heart, in as much as both in my bonds, and in the defence and confirmation of the Goſpel, ye all are partakers of my grace. 8 For God is my record, how greatly I long after you all, in the bowels of Ieſus Chriſt. 9 And this I pray, that your loue may abound yet more & more in knowledge, and in all iudgment. 10 That ye may approue things that are excellent, that ye may be ſincere, and without offence till the day of Chriſt. 11 Being filled with the fruites of righteouſneſſe, which are by Ieſus Chriſt vnto the glory and praiſe of God. 12 But I would yee ſhould vnderſtand brethren, that the things which happened vnto mee, haue fallen out rather vnto the furtherance of the Goſpel. 13 So that my bonds in Chriſt, are manifeſt in all the palace, and in all other places. 14 And many of the brethren in the Lord, waxing confident, by my bonds, are much more bold to ſpeake the word without feare. 15 Some in deed preach Chriſt, euen of enuie and ſtrife, and ſome alſo of good will. 16 The one preach Chriſt of contention, not ſyncerely, ſuppoſing to adde affliction to my bonds: 17 But the other of loue, knowing that I am ſet for the defence of the Goſpel. 18 What then? Notwithſtanding euery way, whether in pretence, or in trueth: Chriſt is preached, and I therein doe reioyce, yea, and will reioyce. 19 For I know that this ſhall turne to my ſaluation through your prayer, and the ſupplie of the ſpirit of Ieſus Chriſt, 20 According to my earneſt expectation, and my hope, that in nothing I ſhalbe aſhamed: but that with all boldnes, as alwayes, ſo now alſo Chriſt ſhal be magnified in my body, whether it be by life or by death. 21 For to me to liue is Chriſt, and to die is gaine. 22 But if I liue in the fleſh, this is the fruit of my labour: yet what I ſhal chuſe, I wote not. 23 For I am in a ſtrait betwixt two, hauing a deſire to depart, & to bee with Chriſt, which is farre better. 24 Neuertheles, to abide in the fleſh, is more needfull for you. 25 And hauing this confidence, I know that I ſhall abide and continue with you all, for your furtherance and ioy of faith, 26 That your reioycing may bee more abundant in Ieſus Chriſt for me, by my comming to you againe. 27 Onely let your conuerſation bee as it becommeth the Goſpel of Chriſt, that whether I come and ſee you, or elſe be abſent, I may heare of your affaires, that yee ſtand faſt in one ſpirit, with one minde, ſtriuing together for the faith of the Goſpel, 28 And in nothing terrified by your aduerſaries, which is to them an euident token of perdition: but to you of ſaluation, and that of God. 29 For vnto you it is giuen in the behalfe of Chriſt, not onely to beleeue on him, but alſo to ſuffer for his ſake, 30 Hauing the ſame conflict which ye ſaw in me, and now heare to be in me.

CHAPTER 2 1 If there bee therefore any conſolation in Chriſt, if any comfort of loue, if any fellowſhip of the Spirit, if any bowels, & mercies; 2 Fulfill ye my ioy, that yee be like minded, hauing the ſame loue, being of one accord, of one minde. 3 Let nothing bee done through ſtrife, or vaine glory, but in lowlineſse of minde let each eſteeme other better then themſelues. 4 Looke not euery man on his owne things, but euery man alſo on the things of others. 5 Let this minde bee in you, which was alſo in Chriſt Ieſus: 6 Who being in the forme of God, thought it not robbery to bee equall with God: 7 But made himſelfe of no reputation, and tooke vpon him the forme of a ſeruant, and was made in the likeneſſe of men. 8 And being found in faſhion as a man, he humbled himſelfe, and became obedient vnto death, euen the death of the Croſse. 9 Wherefore God alſo hath highly exalted him, and giuen him a Name which is aboue euery name: 10 That at the Name of Ieſus euery knee ſhould bow, of things in heauen, and things in earth, and things vnder the earth: 11 And that euery tongue ſhould confeſse, that Ieſus Chriſt is Lord, to the glory of God the Father. 12 Wherefore, my beloued, as yee haue alwayes obeyed, not as in my preſence onely, but now much more in my abſence; worke out your owne ſaluation with feare, and trembling. 13 For it is God which worketh in you, both to will, and to doe, of his good pleaſure.14Doe all things without murmurings, and diſputings:15That yee may bee blameleſſe and harmeleſſe, the ſonnes of God, without rebuke, in the middes of a crooked and peruerſe nation, among whom ye ſhine as lights in the world:16Holding foorth the word of life, that I may reioyce in the day of Chriſt, that I haue not runne in vaine, neither laboured in vaine.17Yea, and if I bee offered vpon the ſacrifice and ſeruice of your faith, I ioy, and reioyce with you all.18For the ſame cauſe alſo doe ye ioy, and reioyce with me.19But I truſt in the Lord Ieſus, to ſend Timotheus ſhortly vnto you, that I alſo may bee of good comfort, when I know your ſtate.20For I haue no man like minded, who will naturally care for your ſtate.21For all ſeeke their owne, not the things which are Ieſus Chriſts.22But ye know the proofe of him, That as a ſonne with the father, hee hath ſerued with me, in the Goſpel.23Him therefore I hope to ſend preſently, ſo ſoone as I ſhall ſee how it wil goe with me.24But I truſt in the Lord, that I alſo my ſelfe ſhall come ſhortly.25Yet I ſuppoſed it necesſary, to ſend to you Epaphroditus my brother and companion in labour, and fellow ſouldiour, but your meſſenger, and hee that miniſtred to my wants.26For hee longed after you all, and was full of heauineſse, becauſe that yee had heard that he had bene ſicke.27For indeed he was ſicke nigh vnto death, but God had mercy on him: and not on him onely, but on mee alſo, leſt I ſhould haue ſorow vpon ſorow.28I ſent him therefore the more carefully, that when ye ſee him againe, ye may reioyce, and that I may bee the leſſe ſorrowfull.29Receiue him therfore in the Lord with all gladneſſe, and hold ſuch in reputation:30Becauſe for the worke of Chriſt he was nigh vnto death, not regarding his life, to ſupply your lacke of ſeruice toward me.

CHAPTER 31Finally, my brethren, reioyce in the Lorde. To write the ſame things to you, to me indeed is not grieuous: but for you it is ſafe.2Beware of dogs, beware of euill workers: beware of the concition.3For we are the circumcition, which worſhip God in the ſpirit, and reioyce in Chriſt Ieſus, and haue no confidence in the fleſh.4Though I might alſo haue confidence in the fleſh. If any other man thinketh that hee hath whereof hee might truſt in the fleſh, I more:5Circumciſed the eight day, of the ſtocke of Iſrael, of the tribe of Beniamin, an Hebrew of the Hebrewes, as touching the Law, a PhAriſe:6Concerning zeale, perſecuting the Church: touching the righteouſneſſe which is in the Law, blameleſſe.7But what things were gaine to me, thoſe I counted loſſe for Chriſt.8Yea doubtleſſe, and I count all things but loſse, for the excellencie of the knowledge of Chriſt Ieſus my Lord: for whom I haue ſuffered the loſſe of all things, and doe count them but doung, that I may win Chriſt,9And be found in him, not hauing mine owne righteouſneſſe, which is of the Law, but that which is through the faith of Chriſt, the righteouſneſſe which is of God by faith:10That I may know him, and the power of his reſurrection, and the fellowſhip of his ſufferings, being made conformable vnto his death,11If by any meanes I might attaine vnto the reſurrection of the dead.12Not as though I had already attained, either were already perfect: but I follow after, if that I may apprehend that for which alſo I am apprehended of Chriſt Ieſus.13Brethren, I count not my ſelfe to haue apprehended: but this one thing I doe, forgetting thoſe things which are behinde, and reaching forth vnto thoſe things which are before,14I preſse toward the marke, for the price of the high calling of God in Chriſt Ieſus.15Let vs therefore, as many as bee perfect, bee thus minded: and if in any thing ye be otherwiſe minded, God ſhal reueale euen this vnto you.16Neuertheleſſe, whereto wee haue alreadie attained, let vs walke by the ſame rule, let vs minde the ſame thing.17Brethren, be followers together of me, and marke them which walke ſo, as ye haue vs for an enſample.18(For many walke, of whome I haue told you often, and now tell you euen weeping, that they are the enemies of the croſse of Chriſt:19Whoſe end is deſtruction, whoſe God is their belly, and whoſe glorie is in their ſhame, who minde earthly things.)20For our conuerſation is in heauen, from whence alſo we looke for the Sauiour, the Lord Ieſus Chriſt:21Who ſhall change our vile bodie, that it may bee faſhioned like vnto his glorious body, according to the working whereby he is able euen to ſubdue all things vnto himſelfe.

CHAPTER 41Therefore, my brethren, dearely beloued and longed for, my ioy and crowne, ſo ſtand faſt in the Lord, my dearely beloued.2I beſeech Euodias, and beſeech Syntiche, that they be of the ſame mind in the Lord.3And I entreat thee alſo, true yokefellow, helpe thoſe women which laboured with me in the Goſpel, with Clement alſo, and with other my fellow labourers, whoſe names are in the booke of life.4Reioyce in the Lord alway: and againe I ſay, Reioyce.5Let your moderation be knowen vnto all men. The Lord is at hand.6Bee carefull for nothing: but in euery thing by prayer and ſupplication with thankeſgiuing, let your requeſt be made knowen vnto God.7And the peace of God which paſſeth all vnderſtanding, ſhall keepe your hearts & minds through Chriſt Ieſus.8Finally, brethren, whatſoeuer things are true, whatſoeuer things are honeſt, whatſoeuer things are iuſt, whatſoeuer things are pure, whatſoeuer things are louely, whatſoeuer things are of good report: if there bee any vertue, and if there bee any praiſe, thinke on theſe things:9Thoſe things which ye haue both learned and receiued, and heard, and ſeene in mee, doe: and the God of peace ſhall be with you.10But I reioyced in the Lorde greatly, that now at the laſt your care of me hath flouriſhed againe, wherein yee were alſo carefull, but ye lacked opportunitie.11Not that I ſpeake in reſpect of want: for I haue learned in whatſoeuer ſtate I am, therewith to bee content.12I know both how to bee abaſed, and I knowe how to abound: euerie where, and in all things I am inſtructed, both to bee full, and to bee hungrie, both to abound, and to ſuffer need.13I can do all things through Chriſt, which ſtrengtheneth me.14Notwithſtanding, yee haue well done, that ye did communicate with my affliction.15Now ye Philippians know alſo, that in the beginning of the Goſpel, when I departed from Macedonia, no Church communicated with mee, as concerning giuing and receiuing, but ye onely.16For euen in Theſsalonica, ye ſent once, and againe vnto my neceſsitie.17Not becauſe I deſire a gift: but I deſire fruit that may abound to your account.18But I haue all, and abound. I am full, hauing receiued of Epaphroditus the things which were ſent from you, an odour of a ſweet ſmell, a ſacrifice acceptable, well pleaſing to God.19But my God ſhall ſupply all your need, according to his riches in glory, by Chriſt Ieſus.20Now vnto God and our Father be glory for euer and euer. Amen.21Salute euery Saint in Chriſt Ieſus: the brethren which are with me, greet you.22All the Saints ſalute you, chiefly they that are of Ceſars houſhold.23The grace of our Lord Ieſus Chriſt be with you all. Amen. It was written to the Philippians from Rome, by Epaphroditus.

COLOſSIANS (COLOSSIANS)

CHAPTER 11Paul an Apoſtle of Ieſus Chriſt, by þe will of God, and Timotheus our brother,2To the ſaints and faithfull brethren in Chriſt, which are at Coloſse, grace be vnto you, and peace from God our Father, and the Lord Ieſus Chriſt.3We giue thanks to God, and the Father of our Lord Ieſus Chriſt, praying alwayes for you,4Since we heard of your faith in Chriſt Ieſus, and of the loue which yee haue to all the Saints,5For the hope which is layd vp for you in heauen, whereof ye heard before in the word of the trueth of the Goſpel,6Which is come vnto you as it is in all the world, and bringeth foorth fruit, as it doth alſo in you, ſince the day yee heard of it, and knew the grace of God in trueth,7As yee alſo learned of Epaphras our deare felow ſeruant, who is for you a faithfull Miniſter of Chriſt:8Who alſo declared vnto vs your loue in the ſpirit.9For this cauſe wee alſo, ſince the day we heard it, doe not ceaſe to pray for you, and to deſire that ye might be filled with the knowledge of his will, in all wiſedome and ſpirituall vnderſtanding:10That ye might walke worthy of the Lord vnto all pleaſing, being fruitfull in euery good worke, & increaſing in the knowledge of God:11Strengthened with all might according to his glorious power, vnto all patience and long ſuffering with ioyfulneſse:12Giuing thanks vnto the Father, which hath made vs meete to be partakers of the inheritance of the Saints in light:13Who hath deliuered vs from the power of darkeneſſe, and hath tranſlated vs into the kingdome of his deare Sonne,14In whom we haue redemption through his blood, euen the forgiueneſse of ſinnes:15Who is the image of the inuiſible God, the firſt borne of euery creature.16For by him were all things created that are in heauen, and that are in earth, viſible and inuiſible, whether they be thrones, or dominions, or principalities, or powers: all things were created by him, and for him.17And he is before all things, and by him all things conſiſt.18And hee is the head of the body, the Church: who is the beginning, the firſt borne from the dead, that in all things he might haue the preeminence:19For it pleaſed the Father that in him ſhould all fulneſse dwell,20And (hauing made peace through the blood of his croſse) by him to reconcile all things vnto himſelf, by him, I ſay, whether they bee things in earth, or things in heauen.21And you that were ſometimes alienated, and enemies in your minde by wicked workes, yet now hath hee reconciled,22In the body of his fleſh through death, to preſent you holy & vnblameable, and vnreprooueable in his ſight,23If ye continue in the faith grounded and ſetled, and be not moued away from the hope of the Goſpel, which yee haue heard, and which was preached to euery creature which is vnder heauen, whereof I Paul am made a Miniſter.24Who now reioyce in my ſufferings for you, and fill vp that which is behind of the afflictions of Chriſt in my fleſh, for his bodies ſake, which is the Church,25Whereof I am made a Miniſter, according to the diſpenſation of God, which is giuen to mee for you, to fulfill the word of God:26Euen the myſtery which hath been hid from ages, and from generations, but now is made manifeſt to his ſaints,27To whom God would make knowen what is the riches of the glory of this myſterie among the Gentiles, which is Chriſt in you, the hope of glory:28Whom we preach, warning euery man, and teaching euery man in all wiſedome, that we may preſent euery man perfect in Chriſt Ieſus.29Whereunto I alſo labour, ſtriuing according to his working, which worketh in me mightily.

CHAPTER 21For I would that ye knew what great conflict I haue for you, and for them at Laodicea, and for as many as haue not ſeene my face in the fleſh:2That their hearts might be comforted, being knit together in loue, and vnto all riches of the full aſsurance of vnderſtanding, to the acknowledgement of the myſterie of God, and of the Father, and of Chriſt,3In whom are hid all the treaſures of wiſedome, and knowledge.4And this I ſay, leſt any man ſhould beguile you with entiſing words.5For though I bee abſent in the fleſh, yet am I with you in the ſpirit, ioying and beholding your order, and the ſtedfaſtneſse of your faith in Chriſt.6As yee haue therefore receiued Chriſt Ieſus the Lord, ſo walke yee in him:7Rooted and built vp in him, and ſtabliſhed in the faith, as yee haue bene taught, abounding therein with thankeſgiuing.8Beware leſt any man ſpoile you through Philoſophie and vaine deceit, after the tradition of men, after the rudiments of the world, and not after Chriſt:9For in him dwelleth all the fulneſse of the Godhead bodily.10And ye are complete in him, which is the head of all principalitie, & power.11In whom alſo ye are circumciſed with the Circumciſion made without handes, in putting off the body of the ſinnes of the fleſh, by the Circumciſion of Chriſt:12Buried with him in Baptiſme, wherein alſo you are riſen with him through the faith of the operation of God, who hath raiſed him from the dead.13And you being dead in your ſinnes, and the vncircumciſion of your fleſh, hath hee quickened together with him, hauing forgiuen you all treſpaſſes,14Blotting out the handwriting of ordinances, that was againſt vs, which was contrary to vs, and tooke it out of the way, nayling it to his Croſse:15And hauing ſpoyled principalities and powers, he made a ſhew of them openly, triumphing ouer them in it.16Let no man therefore iudge you in meat, or in drinke, or in reſpect of an Holy day, or of the New moone, or of the Sabbath dayes:17Which are a ſhadow of things to come, but the body is of Chriſt.18Let no man beguile you of your reward, in a voluntary humilitie, and worſhipping of Angels, intruding into thoſe things which hee hath not ſeene, vainely puft vp by his fleſhly minde:19And not holding the head, from which all the body by ioynts and bands hauing nouriſhment miniſtred, and knit together, increaſeth with the increaſe of God.20Wherefore if yee bee dead with Chriſt frō the rudiments of the world: why, as though liuing in the world, are ye ſubiect to ordinances?21(Touch not, taſte not, handle not:22Which all are to periſh with the vſing) after the commandements and doctrines of men:23Which things haue in deed a ſhew of wiſedome in will-worſhip and humilitie, and neglecting of the body, not in any honour to the ſatiſfying of the fleſh.

CHAPTER 31If yee then bee riſen with Chriſt, ſeeke thoſe things which are aboue, where Chriſt ſitteth on the right hand of God:2Set your affection on things aboue, not on things on the earth.3For yee are dead, and your life is hid with Chriſt in God.4When Chriſt, who is our life, ſhall appeare, then ſhall yee alſo appeare with him in glorie.5Mortifie therefore your members which are vpon the earth: fornication, vncleanneſſe, inordinate affection, euill concupiſcence, and couetouſneſſe, which is idolatrie:6For which things ſake, the wrath of God commeth on the children of diſobedience,7In the which yee alſo walked ſometime, when ye liued in them.8But now you alſo put off all theſe, anger, wrath, malice, blaſphemie, filthy communication out of your mouth.9Lie not one to another, ſeeing that yee haue put off the old man with his deedes:10And haue put on the new man, which is renued in knowledge, after the image of him that created him,11Where there is neither Greeke, nor Iew, circumciſion, nor vncircumciſion, Barbarian, Scythian, bond, nor free: but Chriſt is all, and in all.12Put on therefore (as the elect of God, holy and beloued) bowels of mercies, kindneſse, humbleneſse of minde, meekeneſse, long ſuffering,13Forbearing one another, and forgiuing one another, if any man haue a quarrell againſt any: euen as Chriſt forgaue you, ſo alſo doe yee.14And aboue all theſe things put on charitie, which is the bond of perfectneſse.15And let the peace of God rule in your hearts, to the which alſo yee are called in one body: and be yee thankefull.16Let the word of Chriſt dwell in you richly in all wiſdome, teaching and admoniſhing one another in Pſalmes, and Hymnes, and Spirituall ſongs, ſinging with grace in your hearts to the Lord.17And whatſoeuer yee doe in word or deed, doe all in the Name of the Lord Ieſus, giuing thankes to God and the Father, by him.18Wiues, ſubmit your ſelues vnto your owne huſbands, as it is fit in the Lord.19Huſbands, loue your wiues, and be not bitter againſt them.20Children, obey your parents in all things, for this is well pleaſing vnto the Lord.21Fathers, prouoke not your children to anger, leſt they be diſcouraged.22Seruants, obey in all things your maſters according to the fleſh: not with eye ſeruice as men pleaſers, but in ſingleneſse of heart, fearing God:23And whatſoeuer yee doe, doe it heartily, as to the Lord, and not vnto men:24Knowing, that of the Lord yee ſhall receiue the reward of the inheritance: for ye ſerue the Lord Chriſt.25But he that doeth wrong, ſhall receiue for the wrong which hee hath done: and there is no reſpect of perſons.

CHAPTER 41Maſters, giue vnto your ſeruants that which is iuſt and equall, knowing that yee alſo haue a Maſter in heauen.2Continue in prayer, and watch in the ſame with thankeſgiuing:3Withall, praying alſo for vs, that God would open vnto vs a doore of vtterance, to ſpeake the myſtery of Chriſt, for which I am alſo in bonds:4That I may make it manifeſt, as I ought to ſpeake.5Walke in wiſdome toward them that are without, redeeming the time.6Let your ſpeech bee alway with grace, ſeaſoned with ſalt, that you may know how yee ought to anſwere euery man.7All my ſtate ſhall Tychicus declare vnto you, who is a beloued brother, and a faithfull miniſter, and fellow ſeruant in the Lord:8Whom I haue ſent vnto you for the ſame purpoſe, that hee might know your eſtate, and comfort your hearts.9With Oneſimus a faithfull and beloued brother, who is one of you. They ſhall make knowen vnto you all things which are done here.10Ariſtarchus my fellow priſoner ſaluteth you, and Marcus ſiſters ſonne to Barnabas, (touching whome yee receiued commandements; if he come vnto you, receiue him:)11And Ieſus, which is called Iuſtus, who are of the circumciſion. Theſe onely are my fellow workers vnto the kingdome of God, which haue beene a comfort vnto me.12Epaphras, who is one of you, a ſeruant of Chriſt, ſaluteth you, alwaies labouring feruently for you in praiers, that ye may ſtand perfect, and complete in all the will of God.13For I beare him record, that hee hath a great zeale for you, and them that are in Laodicea, and them in Hierapolis.14Luke the beloued phyſician, and Demas greet you.15Salute the brethren which are in Laodicea, and Nymphas, & the church which is in his houſe.16And when this Epiſtle is read amongſt you, cauſe that it be read alſo in the church of the Laodiceans: and that ye likewiſe reade the Epiſtle from Laodicea,17And ſay to Archippus, Take heede to the miniſterie, which thou haſt receiued in the Lord, that thou fulfill it.18The ſalutation by the hand of me Paul. Remember my bonds. Grace be with you. Amen. Written from Rome to the Coloſsians, by Tychicus and Oneſimus.

1 THEſſALONIANS (1 THESSALONIANS)

CHAPTER 1 1Paul and Siluanus, and Timotheus, vnto the Church of the Theſsalonians, which is in God the Father, and in the Lord Ieſus Chriſt: grace be vnto you, and peace from God our Father, and the Lord Ieſus Chriſt.2We giue thankes to God alwaies for you all, making mention of you in our prayers,3Remembring without ceaſing your worke of faith, and labour of loue, and patience of hope in our Lord Ieſus Chriſt, in the ſight of God and our Father:4Knowing, brethren beloued, your election of God.5For our Goſpel came not vnto you in word onely: but alſo in power, and in the holy Ghoſt, and in much aſsurance, as yee know what maner of men we were among you for your ſake.6And yee became followers of vs, and of the Lord, hauing receiued the word in much affliction, with ioy of the holy Ghoſt:7So that ye were enſamples to all that beleeue in Macedonia and Achaia.8For from you ſounded out the Word of the Lord, not onely in Macedonia & Achaia, but alſo in euery place your faith to Godward is ſpred abroad, ſo that we need not to ſpeak any thing.9For they themſelues ſhew of vs, what maner of entring in we had vnto you, and how yee turned to God from idols, to ſerue the liuing, and true God,10And to waite for his ſonne from heauen whom he raiſed from the dead, euen Ieſus which deliuered vs from the wrath to come.

CHAPTER 2 1For your ſelues, brethren, knowe our entrance in vnto you, that it was not in vaine.2But euen after that wee had ſuffered before, and were ſhamefully entreated, as ye know, at Philippi, wee were bold in our God, to ſpeake vnto you the Goſpel of God with much contention.3For our exhortation was not of deceite, nor of vncleanneſſe, nor in guile:4But as we were allowed of God to bee put in truſt with the Goſpel, euen ſo wee ſpeake, not as pleaſing men, but God, which trieth our hearts.5For neither at any time vſed wee flattering wordes, as yee knowe, nor a cloke of couetouſneſſe, God is witneſſe:6Nor of men ſought we glorie, neither of you, nor yet of others, when we might haue beene burdenſome, as the Apoſtles of Chriſt.7But wee were gentle among you, euen as a nurſe cheriſheth her children:8So being affectionately deſirous of you, we were willing to haue imparted vnto you, not the Goſpel of God only, but alſo our owne ſoules, becauſe ye were deare vnto vs.9For yee remember, brethren, our labour and trauaile: for labourng night and day, becauſe wee would not bee chargeable vnto any of you, wee preached vnto you the Goſpel of God.10Yee are witneſſes, and God alſo, how holily, and iuſtly, and vnblameably wee behaued our ſelues among you that beleeue.11As you know, how wee exhorted and comforted, and charged euery one of you, (as a father doeth his children,)12That ye would walke worthy of God, who hath called you vnto his kingdome and glory.13For this cauſe alſo thanke wee God without ceaſing, becauſe when yee receiued the word of God, which yee heard of vs, yee receiued it not as the word of men, but (as it is in trueth) the word of God, which effectually worketh alſo in you that beleeue.14For yee, brethren, became followers of the Churches of God, which in Iudea are in Chriſt Ieſus: for ye alſo haue ſuffered like things of your owne countreymen, euen as they haue of the Iewes:15Who both killed the Lord Ieſus, and their owne Prophets, and haue perſecuted vs: and they pleaſe not God, and are contrary to all men:16Forbidding vs to ſpeake to the Gentiles, that they might bee ſaued, to fill vp their ſinnes alway: for the wrath is come vpon them to the vttermoſt.17But wee, brethren, beeing taken from you for a ſhort time, in preſence, not in heart, endeuored the more abundantly to ſee your face with great deſire.18Wherefore we would haue come vnto you (euen I Paul) once & againe: but Satan hindered vs.19For what is our hope, or ioy, or crowne of reioycing? Are not euen ye in the preſence of our Lord Ieſus Chriſt at his comming?20For, ye are our glory and ioy.

CHAPTER 3 1Wherefore when wee could no longer forbeare, wee thought it good to bee left at Athens alone:2And ſent Timotheus our brother and miniſter of God, and our fellow labourer in the Goſpel of Chriſt, to eſtabliſh you, and to comfort you concerning your faith:3That no man ſhould be mooued by theſe afflictions: for your ſelues know that we are appointed therunto.4For verily when wee were with you, we told you before, that we ſhould ſuffer tribulation, euen as it came to paſſe and ye know.5For this cauſe when I could no longer forbeare, I ſent to know your faith, leſt by ſome meanes the tempter haue tempted you, and our labor be in vaine.6But now when Timotheus came from you vnto vs, and brought vs good tidings of your faith and charitie, and that ye haue good remembrance of vs alwayes, deſiring greatly to ſee vs, as we alſo to ſee you:7Therefore brethren, wee were comforted ouer you in all our affliction and diſtreſſe, by your faith:8For now we liue, if ye ſtand faſt in the Lord.9For what thankes can we render to God againe for you, for all the ioy wherewith wee ioy for your ſakes before our God,10Night & day praying exceedingly that we might ſee your face, and might perfect that which is lacking in your faith?11Now God himſelfe and our Father, and our Lord Ieſus Chriſt direct our way vnto you.12And the Lorde make you to increaſe, & abound in loue one towards another, and towards all men, euen as we doe towards you:13To the end hee may ſtabliſh your hearts vnblameable in holineſſe before God euen our Father, at the comming of our Lord Ieſus Chriſt with all his Saints.

CHAPTER 4 1Furthermore then we beſeech you, brethren, and exhort you by the Lord Ieſus, that as yee haue receiued of vs, how ye ought to walke, and to pleaſe God, ſo yee would abound more and more.2For yee know what commandements wee gaue you, by the Lord Ieſus.3For this is the will of God, euen your ſanctification, that yee ſhould abſteine from fornication:4That euery one of you ſhould know how to poſſeſſe his veſſell in ſanctification and honour:5Not in the luſt of concupiſcence, euen as the Gentiles which know not God:6That no man goe beyond and defraud his brother in any matter, becauſe that the Lord is the auenger of all ſuch; as we alſo haue forewarned you, and teſtified:7For God hath not called vs vnto vncleanneſſe, but vnto holineſſe.8He therefore that deſpiſeth, deſpiſeth not man, but God, who hath alſo giuen vnto vs his holy Spirit.9But as touching brotherly loue, ye need not that I write vnto you: for yee your ſelues are taught of God to loue one an other.10And in deed ye doe it towards all the brethren, which are in all Macedonia: but we beſeech you, brethren, that ye increaſe more and more:11And that ye ſtudie to be quiet, and to doe your owne buſineſse, and to worke with your owne hands, (as wee commanded you:)12That ye may walke honeſtly toward them that are without, and that ye may haue lacke of nothing.13But I would not haue you to be ignorant, brethren, concerning them which are aſleepe, that ye ſorrow not, euen as others which haue no hope.14For if we beleeue that Ieſus died, and roſe againe: euen ſo them alſo which ſleepe in Ieſus, will God bring with him.15For this we ſay vnto you by the word of the Lord, That we which are aliue and remaine vnto the comming of the Lord, ſhall not preuent them which are aſleepe.16For the Lord himſelfe ſhall deſcend from heauen with a ſhout, with the voyce of the Archangel, and with the trumpe of God: and the dead in Chriſt ſhall riſe firſt.17Then we which are aliue, and remaine, ſhalbe caught vp together with them in the clouds, to meet the Lord in the aire: and ſo ſhall wee euer bee with the Lord.18Wherefore, comfort one an other with theſe words.

CHAPTER 5 1But of the times and the ſeaſons, brethren, yee haue no need that I write vnto you.2For your ſelues knowe perfectly that the day of the Lord ſo commeth as a thiefe in the night.3For when they ſhal ſay, Peace and ſafety: then ſudden deſtructiō commeth vpon them, as trauaile vpon a woman with childe, and they ſhall not eſcape.4But ye, brethren, are not in darkeneſſe, that that day ſhould ouertake you as a thiefe.5Yee are all the children of light, and the children of the day: we are not of the night, nor of darkeneſſe.6Therefore let vs not ſleepe, as doe others: but let vs watch and be ſober.7For they that ſleepe, ſleepe in the night, and they that bee drunken, are drunken in the night.8But let vs who are of the day, bee ſober, putting on the breſtplate of faith and loue, and for an helmet, the hope of ſaluation.9For God hath not appointed vs to wrath: but to obtaine ſaluation by our Lord Ieſus Chriſt,10Who died for vs, that whether we wake or ſleepe, we ſhould liue together with him.11Wherefore, comfort your ſelues together, and edifie one another, euen as alſo ye doe.12And we beſeech you, brethren, to know them which labour among you, and are ouer you in the Lord, and admoniſh you:13And to eſteeme them very highly in loue for their workes ſake, and be at peace among your ſelues.14Now we exhort you, brethren, warne them that are vnruly, comfort the feeble minded, ſupport the weake, be patient toward all men.15ſee that none render euill for euill vnto any man: but euer follow that which is good, both among your ſelues and to all men.16Reioyce euermore:17Pray without ceaſing:18In euery thing giue thankes: for this is the will of God in Chriſt Ieſus concerning you.19Quench not the ſpirit:20Deſpiſe not prophecyings:21Proue all things: hold faſt that which is good.22Abſtaine from all appearance of euill.23And the very God of peace ſanctifie you wholly: and I pray God your whole ſpirit, and ſoule, and body be preſerued blameleſſe vnto the comming of our Lord Ieſus Chriſt.24Faithfull is hee that calleth you, who alſo will doe it.25Brethren, pray for vs.26Greete all the brethren with an holy kiſſe.27I charge you by the Lord, that this Epiſtle bee read vnto all the holy brethren.28The grace of our Lord Ieſus Chriſt be with you, Amen. The firſt Epiſtle vnto the Theſsalonians, was written from Athens.

2 THEſſALONIANS (2 THESSALONIANS)

CHAPTER 11Paul and Siluanus, and Timotheus vnto the Church of the Theſsaloniãs, in God our Father, and the Lord Ieſus Chriſt:2Grace vnto you, and peace from God our Father, and the Lorde Ieſus Chriſt.3Wee are bound to thanke God alwayes for you, brethren, as it is meete, becauſe that your faith groweth exceedingly, and the charitie of euery one of you al towards each other aboundeth:4So that wee our ſelues glorie in you in the Churches of God, for your patience and faith in all your perſecutions and tribulations that yee endure.5Which is a manifeſt token of the righteous iudgement of God, that yee may bee counted worthy of the kingdome of God, for which yee alſo ſuffer;6Seeing it is a righteous thing with God to recompence tribulation to them that trouble you:7And to you who are troubled, reſt with vs, when the Lord Ieſus ſhalbe reuealed from heauen, with his mightie Angels,8In flaming fire, taking vengeance on them that know not God, and that obey not the Goſpel of our Lorde Ieſus Chriſt,9Who ſhalbe puniſhed with euerlaſting deſtruction from the preſence of the Lord, and from the glory of his power:10When hee ſhall come to bee glorified in his Saints, and to bee admired in all them that beleeue (becauſe our teſtimony among you was beleeued) in that day.11Wherefore alſo we pray alwayes for you, that our God would count you worthy of this calling, and fulfill all the good pleaſure of his goodneſse, and the worke of faith with power:12That the Name of our Lord Ieſus Chriſt may bee glorified in you, and ye in him, according to the grace of our God, and the Lord Ieſus Chriſt.

CHAPTER 21Now wee beſeech you, brethren, by the comming of our Lord Ieſus Chriſt, and by our gathering together vnto him,2That yee bee not ſoone ſhaken in minde, or bee troubled, neither by ſpirit, nor by word, nor by letter, as from vs, as that the day of Chriſt is at hand,3Let no man deceiue you by any meanes, for that day ſhall not come, except there come a falling away firſt, and that man of ſinne bee reuealed, the ſonne of perdition,4Who oppoſeth and exalteth himſelfe aboue all that is called God, or that is worſhipped: ſo that he as God, ſitteth in the Temple of God, ſhewing himſelfe that he is God.5Remember yee not, that when I was yet with you, I tolde you theſe things?6And now yee know what withholdeth, that hee might bee reuealed in his time.7For the myſterie of iniquitie doth alreadie worke: onely he who now letteth, will let, vntill he be taken out of the way.8And then ſhall that wicked bee reuealed, whome the Lord ſhall conſume with the ſpirit of his mouth, and ſhall deſtroy with the brightneſse of his comming:9Euen him whoſe comming is after the working of Satan, with all power and ſignes, and lying wonders,10And with all deceiueableneſse of vnrighteouſneſſe, in them that periſh: becauſe they receiued not the loue of the trueth, that they might be ſaued.11And for this cauſe God ſhall ſend them ſtrong deluſion, that they ſhould beleeue a lye:12That they all might bee damned who beleeued not the trueth, but had pleaſure in vnrighteouſnes.13But we are bound to giue thanks alway to God for you, brethren, beloued of the Lord, becauſe God hath from the beginning choſen you to ſaluation, through ſanctification of the ſpirit, and beleefe of the trueth,14Whereunto he called you by our Goſpel, to the obteining of the glorie of the Lord Ieſus Chriſt.15Therefore, brethren, ſtand faſt, and hold the traditions which yee haue beene taught, whether by word or our Epiſtle.16Now our Lorde Ieſus Chriſt himſelfe, and God euen our Father, which hath loued vs, and hath giuen vs euerlaſting conſolation, and good hope through grace,17Comfort your hearts, and ſtabliſh you in euery good word and worke.

CHAPTER 31Finally, brethren, pray for vs, that the word of the Lord may haue free courſe, and be glorified, euen as it is with you:2And that we may bee deliuered from vnreaſonable and wicked men: for all men haue not faith.3But the Lord is faithfull, who ſhall ſtabliſh you, and keepe you from euill.4And wee haue confidence in the Lord touching you, that yee both doe, and will doe the things which we command you.5And the Lord direct your hearts into the loue of God, and into the patient waiting for Chriſt.6Now we command you, brethren, in the Name of our Lord Ieſus Chriſt, that ye withdraw your ſelues from euery brother that walketh diſorderly, and not after the tradition which hee receiued of vs.7For your ſelues know how yee ought to follow vs: for wee behaued not our ſelues diſorderly among you,8Neither did wee eate any mans bread for nought: but wrought with labour and trauaile night and day, that wee might not bee chargeable to any of you.9Not becauſe we haue not power, but to make our ſelues an enſample vnto you to follow vs.10For euen when wee were with you, this wee commanded you, that if any would not worke, neither ſhould he eate.11For we heare that there are ſome which walke among you diſorderly, working not at all, but are buſi-bodies.12Now them that are ſuch, we command, and exhort by our Lord Ieſus Chriſt, that with quietneſse they worke, and eat their owne bread.13But ye, brethren, be not wearie in well doing.14And if any man obey not our word, by this Epiſtle note that man, and haue no company with him, that he may be aſhamed,15Yet count him not as an enemie, but admoniſh him as a brother.16Now the Lord of peace himſelfe, giue you peace alwayes, by all meanes. The Lord be with you all.17The ſalutation of Paul, with mine owne hand, which is the token in euery Epiſtle: ſo I write.18The grace of our Lord Ieſus Chriſt be with you all, Amen. The ſecond Epiſtle to the Theſsalonians was written from Athens.

1 TIMOTHEUS (1 TIMOTHY)

CHAPTER 11Paul an Apoſtle of Ieſus Chriſt by the commaundement of God our Sauiour, & Lord Ieſus Chriſt which is our hope,2Unto Timothie my own ſonne in the Faith: Grace, mercie, and peace from God our Father, and Ieſus Chriſt our Lord.3As I beſought thee to abide ſtill at Epheſus when I went into Macedonia, that thou mighteſt charge ſome that they teach no other doctrine,4Neither giue heed to fables, and endleſſe genealogies, which miniſter queſtions, rather then edifying which is in faith: ſo doe.5Now the end of the commandement is charity, out of a pure heart, and of a good conſcience, and of faith vnfained.6From which ſome hauing ſwarued, haue turned aſide vnto vaine iangling,7Deſiring to bee teachers of the Law, vnderſtãding neither what they ſay, nor whereof they affirme.8But we know that the Law is good, if a man vſe it lawfully.9Knowing this, that the Law is not made for a righteous man, but for the lawleſſe and diſobedient, for the vngodly, and for ſinners, for vnholy, and profane, for murderers of fathers, and murderers of mothers, for manſlayers,10For whoremongers, for them that defile themſelues with mankinde, for men-ſtealers, for liars, for periured perſons, and if there be any other thing that is contrary to ſound doctrine,11According to the glorious Goſpel of the bleſſed God, which was committed to my truſt.12And I thanke Chriſt Ieſus our Lord, who hath enabled mee: for that he counted me faithfull, putting me into the Miniſterie,13Who was before a blaſphemer, and a perſecuter, and iniurious. But I obtained mercie, becauſe I did it ignorantly, in vnbeliefe.14And the grace of our Lord was exceeding abundant, with faith, & loue, which is in Chriſt Ieſus.15This is a faithfull ſaying, and worthy of all acceptation, that Chriſt Ieſus came into the world to ſaue ſinners, of whom I am chiefe.16Howbeit, for this cauſe I obtained mercy, that in me firſt, Ieſus Chriſt might ſhew foorth all long ſuffering, for a paterne to them which ſhould hereafter beleeue on him to life euerlaſting.17Now vnto þe king eternal, immortall, inuiſible, the onely wiſe God, be honour and glory for euer & euer. Amen.18This charge I commit vnto thee, ſonne Timothie, according to the propheſies which went before on thee, that thou by them mighteſt warre a good warfare,19Holding faith, and a good conſcience, which ſome hauing put away, concerning faith, haue made ſhipwracke.20Of whom is Hymeneus and Alexander, whome I haue deliuered vnto Satan, that they may learne not to blaſpheme.

CHAPTER 21I exhort therefore, that firſt of all, ſupplications, prayers, intercesſions, and giuing of thanks be made for all men:2For Kings, and for all that are in authoritie, that we may leade a quiet and peaceable life in all godlineſse and honeſtie.3For this is good and acceptable in the ſight of God our Sauiour,4Who will haue all men to bee ſaued, and to come vnto the knowledge of the trueth.5For there is one God, and one Mediatour betweene God and men, the man Chriſt Ieſus,6Who gaue himſelfe a ranſome for all, to be teſtified in due time.7Whereunto I am ordained a preacher, and an Apoſtle (I ſpeake the trueth in Chriſt, and lie not) a teacher of the Gentiles in faith and veritie.8I will therefore that men pray euery where, lifting vp holy handes without wrath, and doubting.9In like maner alſo, that women adorne themſelues in modeſt apparell, with ſhamefaſtneſse and ſobrietie, not with broided haire, or gold, or pearles, or coſtly aray,10But (which becommeth women profeſsing godlineſ) with good works.11Let the woman learne in ſilence with all ſubiection:12But I ſuffer not a woman to teach, nor to vſurpe authoritie ouer the man, but to be in ſilence.13For Adam was firſt formed, then Eue:14And Adam was not deceiued, but the woman being deceiued was in the tranſgreſsion:15Notwithſtanding ſhe ſhall be ſaued in child-bearing, if they continue in faith and charitie, and holineſſe, with ſobrietie.

CHAPTER 31This is a true ſaying: If a man deſire the office of a Biſhop, he deſireth a good worke.2A Biſhop then muſt be blameleſſe, the huſband of one wife, vigilant, ſober, of good behauiour, giuen to hoſpitalitie, apt to teach;3Not giuen to wine, no ſtriker, not greedy of filthy lucre, but patient, not a brawler, not couetous;4One that ruleth well his owne houſe, hauing his children in ſubiection with all grauitie.5(For if a man know not how to rule his owne houſe, how ſhall he take care of the Church of God?)6Not a nouice, leſt being lifted vp with pride, hee fall into the condemnation of the deuill.7Moreouer, hee muſt haue a good report of them which are without, leſt he fall into reproch, and the ſnare of the deuill.8Likewiſe muſt the Deacons bee graue, not double tongued, not giuen to much wine, not greedy of filthy lucre,9Holding the myſterie of the faith in a pure conſcience.10And let theſe alſo firſt be proued; then let them vſe the office of a Deacon, being found blameleſſe.11Euen ſo muſt their wiues be graue; not ſlanderers, ſober, faithfull in all things.12Let the Deacons be the huſbands of one wife, ruling their children, and their owne houſes well.13For they that haue vſed the office of a Deacon well, purchaſe to themſelues a good degree, and great boldneſse in the faith, which is in Chriſt Ieſus.14Theſe things write I vnto thee, hoping to come vnto thee ſhortly.15But if I tary long, that thou mayeſt know how thou oughteſt to behaue thy ſelfe in the Houſe of God, which is the Church of the liuing God, the pillar and ground of the trueth.16And without controuerſie, great is the myſterie of godlineſse: God was manifeſt in the fleſh, iuſtified in the Spirit, ſeene of Angels, preached vnto the Gentiles, beleeued on in the world, receiued vp into glory.

CHAPTER 41Now the Spirit ſpeaketh expreſly, that in the latter times ſome ſhall depart from the faith, giuing heed to ſeducing ſpirits, and doctrines of deuils:2Speaking lies in hypocriſie, hauing their conſcience ſeared with a hote iron,3Forbidding to marry, and commanding to abſteine from meates, which God hath created to bee receiued with thankeſgiuing of them which beleeue, and know the trueth.4For euery creature of God is good, and nothing to be refuſed, if it be receiued with thankeſgiuing:5For it is ſanctified by the word of God, and prayer.6If thou put the brethren in remembrance of theſe things, thou ſhalt be a good miniſter of Ieſus Chriſt, nouriſhed vp in the wordes of faith, and of good doctrine, whereunto thou haſt attained.7But refuſe prophane and olde wiues fables, and exerciſe thy ſelfe rather vnto godlineſse.8For bodily exerciſe profiteth litle, but godlineſse is profitable vnto all things, hauing promiſe of the life that now is, and of that which is to come.9This is a faithful ſaying, and worthy of all acceptation:10For therfore we both labour, and ſuffer reproch, becauſe we truſt in the liuing God, who is the Sauiour of all men, ſpecially of thoſe that beleeue.11Theſe things command & teach.12Let no man deſpiſe thy youth, but be thou an example of the beleeuers, in word, in conuerſation, in charitie, in ſpirit, in faith, in puritie.13Till I come, giue attendance to reading, to exhortation, to doctrine.14Neglect not the gift that is in thee, which was giuen thee by propheſie, with the laying on of the hands of the Preſbyterie.15Meditate vpon theſe things, giue thy ſelfe wholly to them, that thy profiting may appeare to all.16Take heed vnto thy ſelfe, and vnto the doctrine: continue in them: for in doing this, thou ſhalt both ſaue thy ſelfe, and them that heare thee.

CHAPTER 51Rebuke not an Elder, but intreate him as a father, and the yonger men as brethren:2The elder women as mothers, the yonger as ſiſters with all puritie.3Honour widowes that are widowes indeed.4But if any widow haue children or nephewes, let them learne firſt to ſhew pietie at home, and to requite their parents: for that is good and acceptable before God.5Now ſhe that is a widow in deed, and deſolate, truſteth in God, and continueth in ſupplications and prayers night and day.6But ſhe that liueth in pleaſure, is dead while ſhe liueth.7And theſe things giue in charge, that they may be blameleſſe.8But if any prouide not for his owne, & ſpecially for thoſe of his owne houſe, hee hath denied the faith, and is worſe then an infidel.9Let not a widow bee taken into the number, vnder threeſcore yeeres old, hauing bene the wife of one man,10Well reported of for good works, if ſhee haue brought vp children, if ſhee haue lodged ſtrangers, if ſhe haue waſhed the Saints feet, if ſhee haue releeued the afflicted, if ſhee haue diligently followed euery good worke.11But the yonger widowes refuſe: for when they haue begunne to waxe wanton againſt Chriſt, they will marry,12Hauing damnation, becauſe they haue caſt off their firſt faith.13And withall they learne to bee idle, wandering about from houſe to houſe; and not onely idle, but tatlers alſo, and buſibodies, ſpeaking things which they ought not.14I will therefore that the yonger women marry, beare children, guid the houſe, giue none occaſion to the aduerſary to ſpeake reprochfully.15For ſome are already turned aſide after Satan.16If any man or woman that beleeueth haue widowes, let them relieue them, and let not the Church be charged, that it may relieue them that are widowes indeed.17Let the Elders that rule well, be counted worthy of double honour, eſpecially they who labour in the word and doctrine.18For the Scripture ſaith, Thou ſhalt not mouſell the oxe that treadeth out the corne: and, The labourer is worthy of his reward.19Againſt an Elder receiue not an accuſation, but before two or three witneſſes.20Them that ſinne rebuke before all, that others alſo may feare.21I charge thee before God, and the Lord Ieſus Chriſt, and the elect Angels, that thou obſerue theſe things without preferring one before another, doing nothing by partialitie.22Lay hands ſuddenly on no man, neither bee partaker of other mens ſinnes. Keepe thy ſelfe pure.23Drinke no longer water, but vſe a little wine for thy ſtomackes ſake, and thine often infirmities.24Some mens ſinnes are open before hand, going before to iudgement: and ſome men they follow after.25Likewiſe alſo the good works of ſome are manifeſt before hand, and they that are otherwiſe, cannot be hid.

CHAPTER 61Let as many ſeruants as are vnder the yoke, count their owne maſters worthy of all honour, that the Name of God, and his doctrine be not blaſphemed.2And they that haue beleeuing maſters, let them not deſpiſe them becauſe they are brethren: but rather doe them ſeruice, becauſe they are faithfull and beloued, partakers of the benefite: Theſe things teach and exhort.3If any man teach otherwiſe, and conſent not to wholeſome words, euen the wordes of our Lord Ieſus Chriſt, and to the doctrine which is according to godlineſse:4Hee is proud, knowing nothing, but doting about queſtions, and ſtrifes of wordes, whereof commeth enuie, ſtrife, railings, euill ſurmiſings,5Peruerſe diſputings of men of corrupt mindes, and deſtitute of the trueth, ſuppoſing that gaine is godlineſse: From ſuch withdraw thy ſelfe.6But godlineſse with contentment is great gaine.7For we brought nothing into this world, and it is certaine we can cary nothing out.8And hauing food and raiment let vs be therewith content.9But they that will be rich, fall into temptation and a ſnare, and into many fooliſh & hurtfull luſts, which drowne men in deſtruction and perdition.10For the loue of money is the root of all euill, which while ſome coueted after, they haue erred from the faith, and pierced themſelues through with many ſorrowes.11But thou, O man of God, flie theſe things; and follow after righteouſneſſe, godlineſse, faith, loue, patience, meekeneſse.12Fight the good fight of faith, lay hold on eternall life, whereunto thou art alſo called, and haſt profeſsed a good profeſsion before many witneſſes.13I giue thee charge in the ſight of God, who quickneth all things, and before Chriſt Ieſus, who before Pontius Pilate witneſſed a good Confeſsion,14That thou keepe this commandement without ſpot, vnrebukeable, vntill the appearing of our Lord Ieſus Chriſt.15Which in his times he ſhall ſhew, who is the bleſſed, and onely Potentate, the King of kings, and Lord of lords:16Who onely

hath immortalitie, dwelling in the light, which no man can approch vnto,
whom no man hath ſeene, nor can ſee: to whom be honour and power
euerlaſting. Amen. 17 Charge them that are rich in this world, that they
bee not high minded, nor truſt in vncertaine riches, but in the liuing
God, who giueth vs richly all things to enioy, 18 That they doe good, that
they be rich in good works, ready to diſtribute, willing to
communicate, 19 Laying vp in ſtore for themſelues a good foundation
againſt the time to come, that they may lay holde on eternall life. 20 O
Timothie, keepe that which is committed to thy truſt, auoyding
prophane and vaine bablings, and oppoſitions of ſcience, faſly ſo
called: 21 Which ſome profeſsing, haue erred concerning the faith. Grace
be with thee. Amen. The firſt to Timothie was written from Laodicea,
which is the chiefeſt citie of Phrygia Pacaciana.

2 TIMOTHEUS (2 TIMOTHY)

CHAPTER 1 1 Paul an Apoſtle of Ieſus Chriſt by the will of God,
according to the promiſe of life, which is in Chriſt Ieſus, 2 To Timothie
my dearely beloued ſonne: grace, mercie, and peace from God the
Father, and Chriſt Ieſus our Lord. 3 I thanke God, whom I ſerue from
my forefathers with pure conſcience, that without ceaſing I haue
remembrance of thee in my prayers night and day, 4 Greatly deſiring to
ſee thee, being mindfull of thy teares, that I may bee filled with
ioy, 5 When I call to remembrance the vnfained faith that is in thee, which
dwelt firſt in thy grandmother Lois, and thy mother Eunice: and I am
perſwaded that in thee alſo. 6 Wherefore I put thee in remembrance, that
thou ſtirre vp the gift of God which is in thee, by the putting on of my
hands. 7 For God hath not giuen vs the ſpirit of feare, but of power, of
loue, and of a ſound minde. 8 Bee not thou therefore aſhamed of the
teſtimony of our Lord, nor of me his priſoner, but bee thou partaker of
the afflictions of the Goſpel according to the power of God, 9 Who hath
ſaued vs, and called vs with an holy calling, not according to our workes,
but according to his owne purpoſe and grace, which was giuen vs in
Chriſt Ieſus, before the world began, 10 But is now made manifeſt by the
appearing of our Sauiour Ieſus Chriſt, who hath aboliſhed death, and
hath brought life and immortalitie to light, through the
Goſpel: 11 Whereunto I am appointed a Preacher, and an Apoſtle, and a
teacher of the Gentiles. 12 For the which cauſe I alſo ſuffer theſe things;
neuertheleſſe, I am not aſhamed: for I know whom I haue beleeued, and
I am perſwaded that he is able to keepe that which I haue committed
vnto him againſt that day. 13 Holde faſt the fourme of ſound words, which
thou haſt heard of mee, in faith and loue, which is in Chriſt Ieſus. 14 That
good thing which was committed vnto thee, keepe, by the holy Ghoſt
which dwelleth in vs. 15 This thou knoweſt, that all they which are in Aſia
be turned away from me, of whom are Phygellus and
Hermogenes. 16 The Lord giue mercie vnto the houſe of Oneſiphorus,
for hee oft refreſhed mee, and was not aſhamed of my chaine. 17 But
when he was in Rome, hee ſought mee out very diligently, and found
me. 18 The Lord grant vnto him, that he may finde mercie of the Lord in
that day: And in how many things hee miniſtred vnto mee at Epheſus,
thou knoweſt very well.

CHAPTER 2 1 Thou therefore, my ſonne, be ſtrong in the grace that is
in Chriſt Ieſus. 2 And the things that thou haſt heard of mee among many
witneſſes, the ſame commit thou to faithfull men, who ſhall be able to
teach others alſo. 3 Thou therefore indure hardneſse, as a good ſouldier
of Ieſus Chriſt. 4 No man that warreth, intangleth himſelfe with the
affaires of this life, that hee may pleaſe him who hath choſen him to be
a ſouldier. 5 And if a man alſo ſtriue for maſteries, yet is hee not crowned
except hee ſtriue lawfully. 6 The huſbandman that laboureth, muſt bee
firſt partaker of the fruites. 7 Conſider what I ſay, and the Lord giue thee
vnderſtanding in all things. 8 Remember that Ieſus Chriſt of the ſeede of
Dauid, was raiſed from the dead, according to my Goſpel: 9 Wherein I
ſuffer trouble as an euill doer, euen vnto bonds: but the word of God is
not bound. 10 Therefore I indure all things for the elects ſakes, that they
may alſo obtaine the ſaluation which is in Chriſt Ieſus, with eternall
glory. 11 It is a faithfull ſaying: for if we bee dead with him, wee ſhall alſo
liue with him. 12 If we ſuffer, we ſhall alſo reigne with him: if wee denie
him, hee alſo will denie vs. 13 If we beleeue not, yet he abideth faithfull,
he cannot denie himſelfe. 14 Of theſe things put them in remembrance,
charging them before the Lord, that they ſtriue not about words to no
profite, but to the ſubuerting of the hearers. 15 Studie to ſhewe thy ſelfe
approued vnto God, a workman that needeth not to be aſhamed, rightly
diuiding the word of trueth. 16 But ſhun profane and vaine bablings, for
they will increaſe vnto more vngodlineſse. 17 And their word will eate as
doth a canker: of whom is Hymeneus and Philetus. 18 Who concerning
the trueth haue erred, ſaying that the reſurrection is paſt alreadie, and
ouerthrow the faith of ſome. 19 Neuertheleſſe the foundation of God
ſtandeth ſure, hauing the ſeale, the Lord knoweth them that are his. And,
let euery one that nameth the Name of Chriſt, depart from
iniquitie. 20 But in a great houſe, there are not onely veſſels of gold, and
of ſiluer, but alſo a wood, & of earth: and ſome to honour, and ſome to
diſhonour. 21 If a man therefore purge himſelfe from theſe, he ſhal be a
veſſell vnto honour, ſanctified, and meete for the Maſters vſe, and
prepared vnto euery good worke. 22 Flie alſo youthfull luſts: but follow
righteouſneſſe, faith, charitie, peace with them that call on the Lord out
of a pure heart. 23 But fooliſh and vnlearned queſtions auoid, knowing
that they doe gender ſtrifes. 24 And the ſeruant of the Lord muſt not
ſtriue: but bee gentle vnto all men, apt to teach, patient, 25 In meekeneſse
inſtructing thoſe that oppoſe themſelues, if God peraduenture will giue
them repentance to the acknowledging of the trueth. 26 And that they
may recouer themſelues out of the ſnare of the deuill, who are taken
captiue by him at his will.

CHAPTER 3 1 This know alſo, that in the laſt dayes perillous times ſhall
come. 2 For men ſhall bee louers of their owne ſelues, couetous, boaſters,
proude, blaſphemers, diſobedient to parents, vnthankfull,
vnholy, 3 Without naturall affection, trucebreakers, falſe accuſers,
incontinent, fierce, deſpiſers of thoſe that are good, 4 Traitours, heady,
high minded, louers of pleaſures more then louers of God, 5 Hauing a
forme of godlineſse, but denying the power thereof: from ſuch turne
away. 6 For of this ſort are they which creep into houſes, and leade
captiue ſilly women laden with ſinnes, led away with diuers luſts, 7 Euer
learning, and neuer able to come to the knowledge of the trueth. 8 Now
as Iannes and Iambres withſtood Moſes, ſo do theſe alſo reſiſt the
trueth: men of corrupt mindes, reprobate concerning the faith. 9 But they
ſhal proceede no further: for their folly ſhall be manifeſt vnto all men,
as theirs alſo was. 10 But thou haſt fully knowen my doctrine, maner of
life, purpoſe, faith, long ſuffering, charitie, patience, 11 Perſecutions,
afflictions which came vnto me at Antioch, at Iconium, at Lyſtra, what
perſecutions I indured: but out of them all the Lord deliuered me. 12 Yea,
and all that will liue godly in Chriſt Ieſus, ſhall ſuffer perſecution. 13 But
euill men and ſeducers ſhall waxe worſe and worſe, deceiuing, and being
deceiued. 14 But continue thou in the things which thou haſt learned, and
haſt been aſsured of, knowing of whome thou haſt learned them. 15 And
that from a childe thou haſt knowen the holy Scriptures, which are able
to make thee wiſe vnto ſaluation through faith which is in Chriſt
Ieſus. 16 All Scripture is giuen by inſpiration of God, & is profitable for
doctrine, for reproofe, for correction, for inſtrution in
righteouſneſſe, 17 That the man of God may be perfect, throughly
furniſhed vnto all good workes.

CHAPTER 4 1 I charge thee therefore before God, and the Lord Ieſus
Chriſt, who ſhall iudge the quicke and the dead at his appearing, and his
kingdome: 2 Preach the word, be inſtant in ſeaſon, out of ſeaſon,
reprooue, rebuke, exhort with all long ſuffering & doctrine. 3 For the time
wil come when they will not endure ſound doctrine, but after their owne
luſts ſhall they heape to themſelues teachers, hauing itching eares: 4 And
they ſhall turne away their eares from the trueth, and ſhall be turned
vnto fables. 5 But watch thou in all things, indure afflictions, doe the
worke of an Euangeliſt, make full proofe of thy miniſtery. 6 For I am now
readie to bee offered, and the time of my departure is at hand. 7 I haue
fought a good fight, I haue finiſhed my courſe, I haue kept the
faith. 8 Hencefoorth there is layde vp for me a crowne of righteouſneſſe,
which the Lord the righteous iudge ſhall giue me at that day: and not to
me only, but vnto them alſo that loue his appearing. 9 Doe thy diligence
to come ſhortly vnto me: 10 For Demas hath forſaken me, hauing loued
this preſent world, and is departed vnto Theſsalonica: Creſcens to
Galatia, Titus vnto Dalmatia. 11 Onely Luke is with me. Take Marke and

bring him with thee: for he is profitable to me for the miniſterie.12And Tychicus haue I ſent to Epheſus.13The cloke that I left at Troas with Carpus, when thou commeſt, bring with thee, but eſpecially the parchments.14Alexander the Copperſmith did mee much euill, the Lord reward him according to his works.15Of whom bee thou ware alſo, for he hath greatly withſtood our words.16At my firſt anſwere no man ſtood with mee, but all men forſooke mee: I pray God that it may not bee laid to their charge.17Notwithſtanding the Lord ſtood with me, and ſtrengthened me, that by me the preaching might be fully knowen, and that all the Gentiles might heare: and I was deliuered out of the mouth of the Lyon.18And the Lord ſhall deliuer mee from euery euill worke, and will preſerueme vnto his heauenly kingdome; to whom bee glory for euer, and euer. Amen.19Salute Priſca and Aquila, and the houſhold of Oneſiphorus.20Eraſtus abode at Corinth: but Trophimus haue I left at Miletum ſicke.21Doe thy diligence to come before winter. Eubulus greeteth thee, and Pudens, and Linus, and Claudia, and all the brethren.22The Lord Ieſus Chriſt bee with thy ſpirit. Grace be with you. Amen. *The ſecond Epiſtle vnto Timotheus, ordeined the firſt Biſhop of the Church of the Epheſians, was written from Rome, when Paul was brought before Nero the ſecond time.*

TITUS

CHAPTER 11Paul a ſeruant of God, and an Apoſtle of Ieſus Chriſt, according to the Faith of Gods Elect, and the acknowledging of the trueth which is after godlineſse,2In hope of eternall life, which God that cannot lie, promiſed before the world began:3But hath in due times manifeſted his word through preaching, which is committed vnto mee according to the commandement of God our Sauiour:4To Titus mine owne Sonne after the common faith, Grace, mercie, and peace from God the Father, and the Lord Ieſus Chriſt our Sauiour.5For this cauſe left I thee in Crete, that thou ſhouldeſt ſet in order the things that are wanting, and ordaine Elders in euery citie, as I had appointed thee.6If any be blameleſſe, the huſband of one wife, hauing faithfull children, not accuſed of riot, or vnruly.7For a Biſhop muſt be blameles, as the ſteward of God: not ſelfewilled, not ſoone angry, not giuen to wine, no ſtriker, not giuen to filthie lucre,8But a louer of hoſpitality, a louer of good men, ſober, iuſt, holy, temperate,9Holding faſt the faithfull word, as hee hath beene taught, that he may bee able by ſound doctrine, both to exhort and to conuince the gainſayers.10For there are many vnruly and vaine talkers and deceiuers, ſpecially they of the circumciſion:11Whoſe mouthes muſt be ſtopped, who ſubuert whole houſes, teaching things which they ought not, for filthie lucres ſake.12One of themſelues, euen a Prophet of their owne, ſaid: The Cretians are alway lyers, euill beaſts, ſlow bellies.13This witneſſe is true: wherefore rebuke them ſharpely that they may be ſound in the faith;14Not giuing heede to Iewiſh fables, and commandements of men that turne from the trueth.15Unto the pure all things are pure, but vnto them that are defiled, and vnbeleeuing, is nothing pure: but euen their mind and conſcience is defiled.16They profeſse that they know God; but in workes they deny him, being abominable, and diſobedient, and vnto euery good worke reprobate.

CHAPTER 21But ſpeake thou the things which become ſound doctrine:2That the aged men be ſober, graue, temperate, ſound in faith, in charitie, in patience.3The aged women likewiſe that they be in behauiour as becommeth holineſſe, not falſe accuſers, not giuen to much wine, teachers of good things,4That they may teach the young women to bee ſober, to loue their huſbands, to loue their children,5To be diſcreet, chaſte, keepers at home, good, obedient to their own huſbands, that the word of God bee not blaſphemed.6Yong men likewiſe exhort, to bee ſober minded.7In all things ſhewing thy ſelfe a patterne of good workes: in doctrine ſhewing vncorruptneſse, grauity, ſinceritie,8Sound ſpeech that cannot be condemned, that hee that is of the contrarie part, may bee aſhamed, hauing no euill thing to ſay of you.9Exhort ſeruants to be obedient vnto their own maſters, and to pleaſe them well in all things, not anſwering againe:10Not purloyning, but ſhewing all good fidelitie, that they may adorne the doctrine of God our Sauiour in all things.11For the grace of God that bringeth ſaluatiō, hath appeared to all men,12Teaching vs that denying vngodlineſse and worldly luſts we ſhould liue ſoberly, righteouſly and godly in this preſent world,13Looking for that bleſſed hope, and the glorious appearing of the great God, and our Sauiour Ieſus Chriſt,14Who gaue himſelfe for vs, that he might redeeme vs from all iniquitie, and purifie vnto himſelfe a peculiar people, zealous of good workes.15Theſe things ſpeake and exhort, and rebuke with all authoritie. Let no man deſpiſe thee.

CHAPTER 31Put them in minde to bee ſubiect to Principalities & Powers, to obey magiſtrates, to be ready to euery good worke,2To ſpeake euill of no man, to bee no brawlers, but gentle, ſhewing all meekeneſse vnto all men.3For we our ſelues alſo were ſometimes fooliſh, diſobedient, deceiued, ſeruing diuers luſts and pleaſures, liuing in malice and enuy, hatefull, and hating one another.4But after that the kindneſſe and loue of God our Sauiour toward man appeared,5Not by workes of righteouſneſſe which wee haue done, but according to his mercy he ſaued vs, by the waſhing of regeneration, and renewing of the holy Ghoſt,6Which hee ſhed on vs abundantly, through Ieſus Chriſt our Sauiour:7That being iuſtified by his grace, we ſhould bee made heires according to the hope of eternall life.8This is a faithfull ſaying, and theſe things I will that thou affirme conſtantly, that they which haue beleeued in God, might be carefull to maintaine good works: theſe things are good and profitable vnto men.9But auoyd fooliſh queſtions, and genealogies, and contentions, and ſtriuings about the lawe; for they are vnprofitable and vaine.10A man that is an heretike, after the firſt and ſecond admonition, reiect:11Knowing that hee that is ſuch, is ſubuerted, and ſinneth, being condemned of himſelfe.12When I ſhall ſend Artemas vnto thee, or Tychicus, be diligent to come vnto mee to Nicopolis: for I haue determined there to winter.13Bring Zenas the Lawyer, and Apollos, on their iourney diligently, that nothing be wanting vnto them.14And let ours alſo learne to maintaine good workes for neceſsarie vſes, that they be not vnfruitfull.15All that are with mee ſalute thee. Greete them that loue vs in the faith. Grace be with you all. Amen. *It was written to Titus ordeined the firſt Biſhop of the Church of the Cretians, from Nicopolis of Macedonia*

PHILEMON

CHAPTER 11Paul a priſoner of Ieſus Chriſt, & Timothie our brother vnto Philemon our dearely beloued, and fellow labourer,2And to our beloued Apphia, and Archippus our fellow Souldier, and to the Church in thy houſe.3Grace to you, and peace from God our Father, and the Lord Ieſus Chriſt.4I thanke my God, making mention of thee alwayes in my prayers,5Hearing of thy loue, and faith, which thou haſt toward the Lord Ieſus, and toward all Saints:6That the communication of thy faith may become effectuall by the acknowledging of euery good thing, which is in you in Chriſt Ieſus.7For wee haue great ioy and conſolation in thy loue, becauſe the bowels of the Saints are refreſhed by thee, brother.8Wherefore, though I might bee much bolde in Chriſt to enioyne thee that which is conuenient;9Yet for loues ſake I rather beſeech thee, being ſuch a one as Paul the aged, and now alſo a priſoner of Ieſus Chriſt.10I beſeech thee for my ſonne Oneſimus, whome I haue begotten in my bonds,11Which in time paſt was to thee vnprofitable: but now profitable to thee and to me:12Whom I haue ſent againe: thou therfore receiue him, that is mine owne bowels.13Whome I would haue reteined with mee, that in thy ſtead hee might haue miniſtred vnto me in the bonds of the Goſpel.14But without thy minde would I doe nothing, that thy benefite ſhould not bee as it were of neceſsitie, but willingly.15For perhaps hee therefore departed for a ſeaſon, that thou ſhouldeſt receiue him for euer:16Not now as a ſeruant, but aboue a ſeruant, a brother beloued, ſpecially to mee, but how much more vnto thee, both in the fleſh, and in the Lord?17If thou count mee therefore a partner, receiue him as my ſelfe.18If hee hath wronged thee, or oweth thee ought, put that on mine account.19I Paul haue written it with mine own hand, I will repay it: albeit I doe not ſay to thee how thou oweſt vnto me, euen thine owne ſelfe beſides:20Yea, brother, let mee haue ioy of thee in the Lord: refreſh my bowles in the Lord.21Hauing confidence in thy obedience, I wrote vnto thee, knowing that thou wilt alſo doe more then I ſay.22But withall prepare mee alſo a lodging: for I truſt that through your prayers I ſhall be giuen vnto you.23There ſalute thee Epaphras, my fellow priſoner in Chriſt Ieſus:24Marcus, Ariſtarchus, Demas, Lucas, my fellow labourers.25The grace of our Lord Ieſus Chriſt be with your ſpirit. Amen.Written from Rome to Philemon, by Oneſimus a ſeruant.

HEBREWS

CHAPTER 11God who at ſundry times, and in diuers manners, ſpake in time paſt vnto the Fathers by the Prophets,2Hath in theſe laſt dayes ſpoken vnto vs by his Sonne, whom he hath appointed heire of all things, by whom alſo he made the worlds,3Who being the brightneſſe of his glory, and the expreſſe image of his perſon, and vpholding all things by the word of his power, when hee had by himſelfe purged our ſinnes, ſate down on þe right hand of the Maieſtie on high,4Being made ſo much better then the Angels, as hee hath by inheritance obtained a more excellent Name then they.5For vnto which of the Angels ſaid he at any time, Thou art my ſonne, this day haue I begotten thee? And again, I will be to him a Father, and he ſhall be to me a Sonne.6And againe, when he bringeth in the firſt begotten into the world, hee ſaith, And let all the Angels of God worſhip him.7And of the Angels he ſaith: Who maketh his Angels ſpirits, and his miniſters a flame of fire.8But vnto the Sonne, he ſaith, Thy throne, O God, is for euer and euer: a ſcepter of righteouſneſſe is the ſcepter of thy kingdome.9Thou haſt loued righteouſneſſe, and hated iniquitie, therefore God, euen thy God hath anointed thee with the oyle of gladneſſe aboue thy fellowes.10And, thou Lord in the beginning haſt layed the foundation of the earth: and the heauens are the works of thine hands.11They ſhall periſh, but thou remaineſt: and they all ſhal waxe old as doth a garment.12And as a veſture ſhalt thou fold them vp, and they ſhall be changed, but thou art the ſame, and thy yeeres ſhall not faile?13But to which of the Angels ſaid hee at any time, Sit on my right hand, vntill I make thine enemies thy footſtoole?14Are they not all miniſtring ſpirits, ſent foorth to miniſter for them, who ſhall be heires of ſaluation?

CHAPTER 21Therefore we ought to giue the more earneſt heede to the things which we haue heard, leſt at any time we ſhould let them ſlip.2For if the word ſpoken by Angels was ſtedfaſt, and euery tranſgreſſion and diſobedience receiued a iuſt recompenſe of reward:3How ſhall we eſcape, if we neglect ſo great ſaluation, which at the firſt began to be ſpoken by the Lord, and was confirmed vnto vs by them that heard him,4God alſo bearing them witneſſe, both with ſignes & wonders, and with diuers miracles, and gifts of the holy Ghoſt, according to his owne will?5For vnto the Angels hath he not put in ſubiection the world to come, whereof we ſpeake.6But one in a certaine place teſtified, ſaying: What is man, that thou art mindfull of him: or the Sonne of man that thou viſiteſt him?7Thou madeſt him a little lower then the Angels, thou crownedſt him with glory and honor, and didſt ſet him ouer the workes of thy hands.8Thou haſt put all things in ſubiection vnder his feete. For in that he put all in ſubiection vnder him, hee left nothing that is not put vnder him. But now wee ſee not yet all things put vnder him.9But wee ſee Ieſus, who was made a little lower then the Angels, for the ſuffering of death, crowned with glory and honour, that hee by the grace of God ſhould taſte death for euery man.10For it became him, for whom are all things, and by whom are all things, in bringing many ſonnes vnto glory, to make the Captaine of their ſaluation perfect through ſufferings.11For both hee that ſanctifieth, and they who are ſanctified, are all of one: for which cauſe he is not aſhamed to cal them brethren,12Saying, I will declare thy Name vnto my brethren, in the midſt of the Church will I ſing praiſe vnto thee.13And againe, I will put my truſt in him: and againe, Behold, I, and the children which God hath giuen me.14Foraſmuch then as the children are partakers of fleſh and blood, he alſo himſelfe likewiſe took part of the ſame, that through death hee might deſtroy him that had the power of death, that is, the deuill:15And deliuer them, who through feare of death were all their life time ſubiect to bondage.16For verely he tooke not on him the nature of Angels: but he tooke on him the ſeed of Abraham.17Wherfore in all things it behooued him to bee made like vnto his brethren, that he might be a mercifull and faithfull high Prieſt, in things pertaining to God, to make reconciliation for the ſinnes of the people.18For in that he himſelfe hath ſuffered, being tempted, he is able to ſuccour them that are tempted.

CHAPTER 31Wherfore holy brethrē, partakers of the heauenly calling, conſider the Apoſtle and high Prieſt of our profeſsion Chriſt Ieſus,2Who was faithful to him that appointed him, as alſo Moſes was faithfull in all his houſe.3For this man was counted worthy of more glory then Moſes, in as much as he who hath builded the houſe, hath more honour then the houſe.4For euery houſe is builded by ſome man, but hee that built all things is God.5And Moſes verely was faithfull in all his houſe as a ſeruant, for a teſtimonie of thoſe things which were to be ſpoken after.6But Chriſt as a Sonne ouer his owne houſe, whoſe houſe are wee, if we hold faſt the confidence, and the reioycing of the hope firme vnto the end.7Wherfore as the holy Ghoſt ſaith, To day if ye will heare his voyce,8Harden not your hearts, as in the prouocation, in the day of temptation in the wilderneſſe:9When your fathers tempted me, prooued me, and ſaw my works fourty yeeres.10Wherefore I was grieued with that generation, and ſayd, They doe alway erre in their hearts, and they haue not knowen my wayes.11So I ſware in my wrath: they ſhall not enter into my reſt.12Take heed, brethren, leſt there be in any of you an euill heart of vnbeleefe, in departing from the liuing God.13But exhort one another dayly, while it is called To day, leaſt any of you be hardned through the deceitfulneſſe of ſinne.14For wee are made partakers of Chriſt, if we hold the beginning of our confidence ſtedfaſt vnto the end.15Whileſt it is ſayd, To day if yee will heare his voice, harden not your hearts, as in the prouocation.16For ſome when they had heard, did prouoke: howbeit not all that came out of Egypt by Moſes.17But with whom was he grieued fourty yeeres? was it not with them that had ſinned, whoſe carcaſes fell in the wilderneſſe?18And to whom ſware he that they ſhould not enter into his reſt, but to them that beleeued not?19So we ſee that they could not enter in, becauſe of vnbeleefe.

CHAPTER 41Let vs therefore feare, leſt a promiſe being left vs, of entring into his reſt, any of you ſhould ſeeme to come ſhort of it.2For vnto vs was the Goſpel preached, as well as vnto thē: but the word preached did not profit them, not being mixed with faith in them that heard it.3For we which haue beleeued do enter into reſt, as hee ſaid, As I haue ſworne in my wrath, if they ſhall enter into my reſt, although the works were finiſhed from the foundation of the world.4For he ſpake in a certaine place of the ſeuenth day on this wiſe: And God did reſt the ſeuenth day from all his works.5And in this place againe: If they ſhall enter into my reſt.6Seeing therfore it remaineth that ſome muſt enter therein, and they to whom it was firſt preached, entred not in becauſe of vnbeleefe:7Againe, hee limiteth a certaine day, ſaying in Dauid, To day, after ſo long a time; as it is ſaide, To day if ye will heare his voyce, harden not your hearts.8For if Ieſus had giuen them reſt, then would he not afterward haue ſpoken of another day.9There remaineth therefore a reſt to the people of God.10For he that is entred into his reſt, hee alſo hath ceaſed from his owne works, as God did from his.11Let vs labour therefore to enter into that reſt, leſt any man fall after the ſame example of vnbeleefe.12For the word of God is quicke and powerfull, and ſharper then any two edged ſword, pearcing euen to the diuiding aſunder of ſoule and ſpirit, and of the ioynts and marrowe, and is a diſcerner of the thoughts and intents of the heart.13Neither is there any creature that is not manifeſt in his ſight: but all things are naked, and opened vnto the eyes of him with whome wee haue to doe.14Seeing then that wee haue a great high Prieſt, that is paſſed into the heauens, Ieſus the Sonne of God, let vs hold faſt our profeſsion.15For wee haue not an high Prieſt which cannot bee touched with the feeling of our infirmities: but was in all points tempted like as we are, yet without ſinne.16Let vs therefore come boldly vnto the throne of grace, that wee may obtaine mercy, and finde grace to helpe in time of need.

CHAPTER 51For euery high Prieſt taken from among men, is ordeined for men in things pertaining to God, that hee may offer both giftes & ſacrifices for ſins.2Who can haue compaſſion on the ignorant, and on them that are out of the way, for that he himſelfe alſo is compaſſed with infirmitie.3And by reaſon heereof hee ought as for the people, ſo alſo for himſelfe, to offer for ſinnes.4And no man taketh this honour vnto

himſelfe, but hee that is called of God, as was Aaron. 5 So alſo, Chriſt
glorified not himſelfe, to bee made an High Prieſt: but hee that ſaide
vnto him, Thou art my Sonne, to day haue I begotten thee. 6 As he ſaith
alſo in another place, Thou art a Prieſt for euer after the order of
Melchiſedec. 7 Who in the dayes of his fleſh, when hee had offered vp
prayers and ſupplications, with ſtrong crying and teares, vnto him that
was able to ſaue him from death, and was heard, in that he
feared. 8 Though hee were a Sonne, yet learned hee obedience, by the
things which he ſuffered: 9 And being made perfect, he became the
authour of eternall ſaluation vnto all them that obey him, 10 Called of
God an high Prieſt after the order of Melchiſedec: 11 Of whom we haue
many things to ſay, and hard to be vttered, ſeeing ye are dull of
hearing. 12 For when for the time yee ought to bee teachers, yee haue
neede that one teach you againe which be the firſt principles of the
Oracles of God, and are become ſuch as haue need of milke, and not of
ſtrong meat. 13 For euery one that vſeth milke, is vnſkilful in the word of
righteouſnes: for he is a babe. 14 But ſtrong meate belongeth to them that
are of full age, euen thoſe who by reaſon of vſe haue their ſenſes
exerciſed to diſcerne both good and euil.

CHAPTER 6 1 Therefore leauing the principles of the doctrine of
Chriſt, let vs goe on vnto perfection, not laying againe the foundation
of repentance from dead workes, and of faith towards God, 2 Of the
doctrine of Baptiſmes, and of laying on of hands, and of reſurrection of
the dead, and of eternall iudgement. 3 And this will we doe, if God
permit. 4 For it is impoſsible for thoſe who were once inlightned, and
haue taſted of the heauenly gift, and were made partakers of the holy
Ghoſt, 5 And haue taſted the good word of God, and the powers of the
world to come; 6 If they ſhall fall away, to renue them againe vnto
repentance: ſeeing they crucifie to themſelues the Sonne of God afreſh,
and put him to an open ſhame. 7 For the earth which drinketh in the raine
that commeth oft vpon it, and bringeth forth herbes meet for them by
whome it is dreſſed, receiueth bleſſing from God. 8 But that which
beareth thornes and briers, is reiected, and is nigh vnto curſing, whoſe
end is to be burned. 9 But beloued, wee are perſwaded better things of
you, and things that accompany ſaluation, though we thus ſpeake. 10 For
God is not vnrighteous, to forget your worke and labour of loue, which
yee haue ſhewed toward his Name, in that yee haue miniſtred to the
Saints, and doe miniſter. 11 And wee deſire, that euery one of you doe
ſhewe the ſame diligence, to the full aſsurance of hope vnto the
ende: 12 That yee be not ſlothfull, but followers of them, who through
faith and patience inherite the promiſes. 13 For when God made promiſe
to Abraham, becauſe hee could ſweare by no greater, he ſware by
himſelfe, 14 Saying, Surely, bleſſing I will bleſſe thee, and multiplying I wil
multiply thee. 15 And ſo after he had patiently indured, he obtained the
promiſe. 16 For men verily ſweare by the greater, and an oath for
confirmation is to them an end of all ſtrife. 17 Wherein God willing more
abundantly to ſhewe vnto the heyres of promiſe the immutabilitie of his
counſell, confirmed it by an oath: 18 That by two immutable things, in
which it was impoſsible for God to lye, wee might haue a ſtrong
conſolation, who haue fled for refuge to lay hold vpon the hope ſet
before vs. 19 Which hope we haue as an anker of the ſoule both ſure and
ſtedfaſt, and which entreth into that within the vaile, 20 Whither the
forerunner is for vs entrrd; euen Ieſus, made an high Prieſt for euer after
the order of Melchiſedec.

CHAPTER 7 1 For this Melchiſedec king of Salem, Prieſt of the moſt
high God, who met Abraham returning from the ſlaughter of the Kings,
and bleſſed him: 2 To whom alſo Abraham gaue a tenth part of all: firſt
being by interpretation king of righteouſneſſe, and after that alſo king
of Salem, which is, king of peace. 3 Without father, without mother,
without deſcent, hauing neither beginning of dayes nor end of life: but
made like vnto the Sonne of God, abideth a Prieſt continually. 4 Now
conſider how great this man was, vnto whō euen the patriarch Abraham
gaue the tenth of the ſpoiles. 5 And verily they that are of the ſonnes of
Leui, who receiue the office of the Prieſthood, haue a commandement
to take Tithes of the people according to the Law, that is of their
brethren, though they come out of the loines of Abraham: 6 But he
whoſe deſcent is not counted from them, receiued tithes of Abraham,
and bleſſed him that had the promiſes. 7 And without all contradiction,
the leſſe is bleſſed of the better. 8 And here men that die receiue tithes:
but there hee receiueth them, of whom it is witneſſed that he
liueth. 9 And as I may ſo ſay, Leui alſo who receiueth tithes, payed tithes
in Abraham. 10 For hee was yet in the loynes of his Father when
Melchiſedec met him. 11 If therefore perfection were by the Leuiticall
Prieſthood (for vnder it the people receiued the Law) what further neede
was there, that another Prieſt ſhould riſe after the order of Melchiſedec,
and not bee called after the order of Aaron? 12 For the Prieſthood being
chaunged, there is made of neceſsitie a change alſo of the Law. 13 For hee
of whom theſe things are ſpoken, pertaineth to another tribe, of which
no man gaue attendance at the Altar. 14 For it is euident that our Lorde
ſprang out of Iuda, of which tribe Moſes ſpake nothing cōcerning
Prieſthood. 15 And it is yet farre more euident: for that after the ſimilitude
of Melchiſedec there Ariſeth another Prieſt, 16 Who is made not after the
Law of a carnall commandement, but after the power of an endles
life. 17 For hee teſtifieth; Thou art a Prieſt for euer, after the order of
Melchiſedec. 18 For there is verily a diſanulling of the commandement
going before, for the weakeneſse and vnprofitableneſse thereof. 19 For
the Law made nothing perfect, but the bringing in of a better hope did:
by the which wee draw nigh vnto God. 20 And in as much as not without
an othe he was made Prieſt, 21 (For thoſe Prieſts were made without an
oath: but this with an oath, by him þt ſaid vnto him, The Lord ſware and
wil not repent, thou art a Prieſt for euer after the order of
Melchiſedec) 22 By ſo much was Ieſus made a ſuertie of a better
Teſtament. 23 And they truely were many Prieſts, becauſe they were not
ſuffered to continue by reaſon of death. 24 But this man becauſe hee
continueth euer, hath an vnchangeable Prieſthood. 25 Wherefore he is
able alſo to ſaue them to the vttermoſt, that come vnto God by him,
ſeeing hee euer liueth to make interceſsion for them. 26 For ſuch an high
Prieſt became vs, who is holy, harmeleſſe, vndefiled, ſeparate from
ſinners, and made higher then the heauens. 27 Who needeth not daily, as
thoſe high Prieſts, to offer vp ſacrifice, firſt for his owne ſins and then
for the peoples: for this he did once, when he offered vp himſelfe. 28 For
the Law maketh men high Prieſts which haue infirmitie, but the word
of the othe which was ſince the Law, maketh the Sonne, who is
conſecrated for euermore.

CHAPTER 8 1 Now of the things which we haue ſpoken, this is the
ſumme: wee haue ſuch an high Prieſt, who is ſet on the right hand of
the throne of the Maieſtie in the heauens: 2 A miniſter of the Sanctuary,
and of the true Tabernacle, which the Lord pitched, and not man. 3 For
euery high Prieſt is ordeined to offer gifts and ſacrifices: wherefore it is
of neceſsitie that this man haue ſomewhat alſo to offer. 4 For if he were
on earth, he ſhould not bee a Prieſt, ſeeing that there are Prieſts that
offer gifts according to the Law: 5 Who ſerue vnto the example and
ſhadow of heauenly things, as Moſes was admoniſhed of God when he
was about to make the Tabernacle. For ſee (ſaith he) that thou make all
things according to the paterne ſhewed to thee in the mount. 6 But now
hath he obtained a more excellent miniſterie, by how much alſo he is
the Mediatour of a better Couenant, which was eſtabliſhed vpon better
promiſes. 7 For if that firſt Couenant had bene faultles, then ſhould no
place haue bene ſought for the ſecond. 8 For finding fault with them, hee
ſaith, Behold, the dayes come (ſaith the Lord) when I will make a new
couenant with the houſe of Iſrael, and the houſe of Iudah. 9 Not
according to the Couenant that I made with their fathers, in the day
when I tooke them by the hand to lead them out of the land of Egypt,
becauſe they continued not in my Couenant, and I regarded them not,
ſaith the Lord. 10 For this is the Couenant that I will make with the houſe
of Iſrael after thoſe dayes, ſaith the Lord: I wil put my Lawes into their
minde, and write them in their hearts: and I will be to them a God, and
they ſhalbe to me a people. 11 And they ſhall not teach euery man his
neighbour, and euery man his brother, ſaying, Know the Lord: For all
ſhall know me, from the leaſt to the greateſt. 12 For I will be mercifull to
their vnrighteouſnes, and their ſins & their iniquities will I remember no
more. 13 In that he ſaith, A new Couenant, he hath made the firſt olde.
Now that which decayeth and waxeth old, is readie to vaniſh away.

CHAPTER 9 1 Then verily the firſt Couenant had alſo ordinances of
diuine Seruice, and a worldly Sanctuary. 2 For there was a Tabernacle
made, the firſt, wherein was the Candleſticke, and the Table, and the
Shewbread, which is called the Sanctuarie. 3 And after the ſecond vaile,
the Tabernacle which is called þe Holieſt of all: 4 Which had the golden
Cenſor, and the Arke of the Couenant ouerlayed round about with gold,
wherein was the Golden pot that had Manna, and Aarons rod that

budded, and the Tables of the Couenant. 5 And ouer it the Cherubims of
glory ſhadowing the Mercyſeat; of which we cannot now ſpeake
particularly. 6 Now when theſe things were thus ordained, the Prieſtes
went alwayes into the firſt Tabernacle, accompliſhing the ſeruice of
God. 7 But into the ſecond went the high Prieſt alone once euery yeere,
not without blood, which he offered for himſelfe, and for the errors of
the people. 8 The holy Ghoſt this ſignifying, that the way into the Holieſt
of all, was not yet made manifeſt, while as the firſt Tabernacle was yet
ſtanding: 9 Which was a figure for the time then preſent, in which were
offred both gifts and ſacrifices, that could not make him that did the
ſeruice perfect, as pertayning to the conſcience, 10 Which ſtood onely in
meates and drinkes, and diuers waſhings, and carnall ordinances
impoſed on them vntill the time of reformation. 11 But Chriſt being come
an high Prieſt of good things to come, by a greater and more perfect
Tabernacle, not made with hands, that is to ſay, not of this
building: 12 Neither by the blood of Goats and Calues: but by his owne
blood hee entred in once into the Holy place, hauing obtained eternall
redemption for vs. 13 For if the blood of Bulls, and of goats, and the aſhes
of an heifer ſprinkling the vncleane, ſanctifieth to the purifying of the
fleſh: 14 How much more ſhall the blood of Chriſt, who through the
eternal Spirit, offered himſelfe without ſpot to God, purge your
conſcience from dead workes, to ſerue the liuing God? 15 And for this
cauſe hee is the Mediatour of the New Teſtament, that by meanes of
death, for the redemption of the tranſgreſſions that were vnder the firſt
Teſtament, they which are called, might receiue the promiſe of eternall
inheritance. 16 For where a Teſtament is, there muſt alſo of neceſsitie bee
the death of the Teſtatour. 17 For a Teſtament is of force after men are
dead: otherwiſe it is of no ſtrength at all whileſt the Teſtatour
liueth. 18 Whereupon, neither the firſt Teſtament was dedicated without
blood. 19 For when Moſes had ſpoken euery precept to all the people
according to the Law, he tooke the blood of Calues and of Goates, with
water and ſcarlet wooll, and hyſope, and ſprinckled both the booke and
all the people, 20 Saying, This is the blood of the Teſtament which God
hath enioyned vnto you. 21 Moreouer, hee ſprinkled with blood both the
Tabernacle, and all the veſſels of the Miniſtery. 22 And almoſt all things
are by the Law purged with blood: and without ſhedding of blood is no
remiſsion. 23 It was therefore neceſsary that the patterns of things in the
heauens ſhould bee purified with theſe, but the heauenly things
themſelues with better ſacrifices then theſe. 24 For Chriſt is not entred
into the Holy places made with handes, which are the figures of the true,
but into heauen it ſelfe, now to appeare in the preſence of God for
vs. 25 Nor yet that he ſhould offer himſelfe often, as the high Prieſt
entreth into the Holy place, euery yeere with blood of others: 26 For then
muſt hee often haue ſuffered ſince the foundation of the world: but now
once in the end of the world, hath he appeared to put away ſinne by the
ſacrifice of himſelfe. 27 And as it is appointed vnto men once to die, but
after this the Iudgement: 28 So Chriſt was once offered to beare the ſinnes
of many, & vnto them that looke for him ſhall hee appeare the ſecond
time without ſinne, vnto ſaluation.

CHAPTER 10 1 For the Law hauing a ſhadow of good things to come,
and not the very Image of the things, can neuer with thoſe ſacrifices
which they offered yeere by yeere continually, make the commers
thereunto perfect: 2 For then would they not haue ceaſed to be offered,
becauſe that the worſhippers once purged, ſhould haue had no more
conſcience of ſinnes? 3 But in thoſe ſacrifices there is a remembrance
againe made of ſinnes euery yeere. 4 For it is not poſsible that the blood
of Bulles and of Goats, ſhould take away ſinnes. 5 Wherefore when hee
commeth into the world, he ſaith, Sacrifice and offering thou wouldeſt
not, but a body haſt thou prepared mee: 6 In burnt offerings, and
ſacrifices for ſinne thou haſt had no pleaſure: 7 Then ſaid I, Loe, I come.
(In the volume of the booke it is written of me) to doe thy will, O
God. 8 Aboue when hee ſaid, Sacrifice, and offering, and burnt offerings,
and offering for ſinne thou wouldeſt not, neither hadſt pleaſure therein,
which are offered by the Law: 9 Then ſaid he, Loe, I come to doe thy will
(O God:) He taketh away the firſt, that he may eſtabliſh the ſecond. 10 By
the which will wee are ſanctified, through the offering of the body of
Ieſus Chriſt once for all. 11 And euery Prieſt ſtandeth dayly miniſtring and
offering oftentimes the ſame ſacrifices which can neuer take away
ſinnes. 12 But this man after he had offered one ſacrifice for ſinnes for
euer, ſate downe on the right hand of God, 13 From henceforth expecting
till his enemies be made his footſtoole. 14 For by one offering hee hath
perfected for euer them that are ſanctified. 15 Whereof the holy Ghoſt
alſo is a witneſſe to vs: for after that he had ſaid before, 16 This is the
Couenant that I wil make with them after thoſe dayes, ſaith the Lord: I
will put my Lawes into their hearts, and in their mindes will I write
them: 17 And their ſinnes and iniquities will I remember no more. 18 Now,
where remiſsion of theſe is, there is no more offering for ſinne. 19 Hauing
therefore, brethren, boldneſse to enter into the Holieſt by the blood of
Ieſus, 20 By a new and liuing way which hee hath conſecrated for vs,
through the vaile, that is to ſay, His fleſh: 21 And hauing an high Prieſt
ouer the houſe of God: 22 Let vs drawe neere with a true heart in full
aſsurance of faith, hauing our hearts ſprinkled from an euill conſcience,
and our bodies waſhed with pure water. 23 Let vs hold faſt the profeſsion
of our faith without wauering (for he is faithfull that promiſed) 24 And let
vs conſider one another to prouoke vnto loue, and to good
workes: 25 Not forſaking the aſſembling of our ſelues together, as the
manner of ſome is: but exhorting one another, and ſo much the more,
as ye ſee the day approching. 26 For if we ſinne wilfully after that we haue
receiued the knowledge of the trueth, there remaineth no more ſacrifice
for ſinnes, 27 But a certaine fearefull looking for of iudgement, and fiery
indignation, which ſhall deuoure the aduerſaries. 28 Hee that deſpiſed
Moſes Lawe, died without mercy, vnder two or three witneſſes. 29 Of
how much ſorer puniſhment ſuppoſe ye, ſhall hee be thought worthy,
who hath troden vnder foote þe Sonne of God, and hath counted the
blood of the couenant wherwith he was ſanctified, an vnholy thing, and
hath done deſpite vnto the ſpirit of grace? 30 For we know him that hath
ſaid, Uengeance belongeth vnto me, I wil recompence, ſaith the Lord:
and again, The Lord ſhall iudge his people. 31 It is a fearefull thing to fall
into the hands of the liuing God. 32 But call to remembrance the former
dayes, in which after yee were illuminated, ye indured a great fight of
afflictions: 33 Partly whileſt ye were made a gazing ſtocke both by
reproches & afflictions, and partly whileſt ye became companions of
them that were ſo vſed. 34 For yee had compaſſion of me in my bonds,
and tooke ioyfully the ſpoyling of your goods, knowing in your ſelues
that yee haue in heauen a better and an induring ſubſtance. 35 Caſt not
away therfore your confidence which hath great recompenſe of
reward. 36 For ye haue need of patience, that ſhall after ye haue done the
will of God ye might receiue the promiſe. 37 For yet a litle while, and he
that ſhall come will come, and will not tary. 38 Now the iuſt ſhall liue by
faith: but if any man drawe backe, my ſoule ſhall haue no pleaſure in
him. 39 But wee are not of them who draw backe vnto perdition: but of
them that beleeue, to the ſauing of the ſoule.

CHAPTER 11 1 Now faith is the ſubſtance of things hoped for, the
euidence of things not ſeen. 2 For by it the Elders obtained a good
report. 3 Through faith we vnderſtand that the worlds were framed by the
word of God, ſo that things which are ſeene were not made of things
which doe appeare. 4 By faith Abel offered vnto God a more excellent
ſacrifice then Kain, by which he obtained witnes that he was righteous,
God teſtifying of his gifts: and by it he being dead, yet ſpeaketh. 5 By faith
Enoch was tranſlated, that he ſhould not ſee death, and was not found,
becauſe God had tranſlated him: For before his tranſlation he had this
teſtimonie, that he pleaſed God. 6 But without faith it is impoſsible to
pleaſe him: for hee that commeth to God, muſt beleeue that he is, and
that he is a rewarder of them that diligently ſeeke him. 7 By faith Noah
being warned of God of things not ſeene as yet, moued with feare,
prepared an Arke to the ſauing of his houſe, by the which he condemned
the world, and became heire of the righteouſneſſe which is by faith. 8 By
faith Abraham when he was called to goe out into a place which hee
ſhould after receiue for an inheritance, obeyed, and he went out, not
knowing whither he went. 9 By faith hee ſoiourned in the land of promiſe,
as in a ſtrange countrey, dwelling in tabernacles with Iſaac and Iacob,
the heires with him of the ſame promiſe. 10 For hee looked for a citie
which hath foundations, whoſe builder and maker is God. 11 Through
faith alſo Sara her ſelfe receiued ſtrength to conceiue ſeede, and was
deliuered of a child when ſhe was paſt age, becauſe ſhe iudged him
faithful who had promiſed. 12 Therfore ſprang there euen of one, and him
as good as dead, ſo many as the ſtarres of the ſkie in multitude, and as
the ſand which is by the ſea ſhore innumerable. 13 Theſe all died in faith,
not hauing receiued the promiſes, but hauing ſeene them a farre off, and
were perſwaded of them, and embraced them, and confeſsed that they

were ſtrangers and pilgrims on the earth.14For they that ſay ſuch things,
declare plainly that they ſeeke a countrey.15And truly if they had been
mindfull of that countrey, from whence they came out, they might haue
had opportunitie to haue returned:16But now they deſire a better
countrey, that is, an heauenly: wherefore God is not aſhamed to bee
called their God: for he hath prepared for thē a city.17By faith Abraham
when he was tried, offered vp Iſaac: and he that had receiued the
promiſes, offered vp his onely begotten ſonne,18Of whom it was ſaid,
That, in Iſaac ſhall thy ſeed be called:19Accounting that God was able to
raiſe him vp, euen from the dead: from whence alſo he receiued him in
a figure.20By faith Iſaac bleſſed Iacob and Eſau concerning things to
come.21By faith Iacob when hee was a dying, bleſſed both the ſonnes of
Ioſeph, and worſhipped leaning vpon the top of his ſtaffe.22By faith,
Ioſeph when hee died, made mention of the departing of the children
of Iſrael: and gaue commandement concerning his bones.23By faith;
Moſes when hee was borne was hid three moneths of his parents,
becauſe they ſaw he was a proper childe, and they not afraid of the Kings
commandement.24By faith Moſes when hee was come to yeeres, refuſed
to bee called the ſonne of Pharaohs daughter,25Chuſing rather to ſuffer
affliction with the people of God, then to enioy the pleaſures of ſinne
for a ſeaſon:26Eſteeming the reproch of Chriſt greater riches then the
treaſures in Egypt: for he had reſpect vnto the recompenſe of the
reward.27By faith hee forſooke Egypt, not fearing the wrath of the king:
for he indured, as ſeeing him who is inuiſible.28Through faith he kept
the Paſſeouer, and the ſprinkling of blood, leſt he that deſtroyed the firſt
borne, ſhould touch them.29By faith they paſſed through the red ſea, as
by drie land: which the Egyptians aſſaying to do, were drowned.30By
faith the walles of Iericho fell downe, after they were compaſſed about
ſeuen dayes.31By faith the harlot Rahab periſhed not with them that
beleeued not, when ſhee had receiued the ſpies with peace.32And what
ſhall I more ſay? for the time would faile mee to tell of Gideon, and of
Barak, and of Sampſon, and of Iephthah, of Dauid alſo and Samuel, and
of the Prophets:33Who through faith ſubdued kingdomes, wrought
righteouſneſſe, obteined promiſes, ſtopped the mouthes of
Lions,34Quenched the violence of fire, eſcaped the edge of the ſword,
out of weakeneſse were made ſtrong, waxed valiant in fight, turned to
flight the armies of the aliens.35Women receiued their dead raiſed to life
againe: and others were tortured, not accepting deliuerance, that they
might obtaine a better reſurrection.36And others had triall of cruell
mockings and ſcourgings, yea moreouer, of bonds and
impriſonment.37They were ſtoned, they were ſawen aſunder, were
tempted, were ſlaine with the ſword: they wandered about in
ſheepſkinnes, and goat ſkins, being deſtitute, afflicted, tormented.38Of
whome the world was not worthy: they wandered in deſerts, and in
mountains, and in dennes and caues of the earth.39And theſe all hauing
obtained a good report through faith, receiued not the promiſe:40God
hauing prouided ſome better thing for vs, that they without vs, ſhould
not be made perfect.

CHAPTER 121Wherefore, ſeeing wee alſo are compaſſed about with
ſo great a cloude of witneſſes, let vs lay aſide euery weight, & the ſinne
which doth ſo eaſily beſet vs, and let vs runne with patience vnto the
race that is ſet before vs,2Looking vnto Ieſus the Authour and finiſher
of our faith, who for the ioy that was ſet before him, endured the croſse,
deſpiſing the ſhame, and is ſet down at the right hand of the throne of
God.3For conſider him that indured ſuch contradiction of ſinners
againſt himſelfe, leſt ye be wearied and faint in your mindes.4Yee haue
not yet reſiſted vnto blood, ſtriuing againſt ſinne.5And ye haue forgotten
the exhortation which ſpeaketh vnto you as vnto children, My ſonne,
deſpiſe not thou the chaſtening of the Lord, nor faint when thou art
rebuked of him.6For whome the Lord loueth hee chaſteneth, and
ſcourgeth euery ſonne whom he receiueth.7If yee endure chaſtening,
God dealeth with you as with ſonnes: for what ſonne is he whom the
father chaſteneth not?8But if ye be without chaſtiſement, whereof all are
partakers, then are ye baſtards, and not ſonnes.9Furthermore, wee haue
had fathers of our fleſh, which corrected vs, and we gaue them
reuerence: ſhall we not much rather bee in ſubiection vnto the Father of
Spirits, and liue?10For they verily for a fewe dayes chaſtened vs after
their owne pleaſure, but hee for our profit, that we might bee partakers
of his holineſſe.11Now no chaſtening for the preſent ſeemeth to be
ioyous, but grieuous: neuertheleſſe, afterward it yeeldeth the peaceable
fruite of righteouſneſſe, vnto them which are exerciſed
thereby.12Wherefore lift vp the handes which hang downe, and the
feeble knees.13And make ſtraight paths for your feete, leſt that which is
lame bee turned out of the way, but let it rather bee healed.14Followe
peace with all men, and holineſſe, without which no man ſhall ſee the
Lord:15Looking diligently, leſt any man faile of the grace of God, leſt
any roote of bitterneſse ſpringing vp, trouble you, and thereby many be
defiled:16Leſt there bee any fornicatour, or profane perſon, as Eſau, who
for one morſell of meat ſold his birthright.17For yee know how that
afterward when hee would haue inherited the bleſſing, hee was reiected:
for hee found no place of repentance, though he ſought it carefully with
teares.18For yee are not come vnto the mount that might be touched,
and that burned with fire, nor vnto blackneſse, and darknes, and
tempeſt,19And the ſound of a trumpet, and the voyce of wordes, which
voyce they that heard, entreated that the word ſhould not bee ſpoken to
them any more.20For they could not indure that which was
commaunded: And if ſo much as a beaſt touch the Mountaine, it ſhall
be ſtoned, or thruſt thorow with a dart.21And ſo terrible was the ſight,
that Moſes ſayde, I exceedingly feare, and quake.22But ye are come vnto
mount Sion, and vnto the citie of the liuing God the heauenly Ieruſalem,
and to an innumerable company of Angels:23To the generall aſſembly,
and Church of the firſt borne which are written in heauen, and to God
the Iudge of all, and to the ſpirits of iuſt men made perfect:24And to
Ieſus the mediatour of the new Couenant, and to the blood of
ſprinckling, that ſpeaketh better things then that of Abel.25ſee that yee
refuſe not him that ſpeaketh: for if they eſcaped not who refuſed him
that ſpake on earth, much more ſhall not we eſcape if wee turne away
from him that ſpeaketh from heauen.26Whoſe voice then ſhooke the
earth, but now he hath promiſed, ſaying, Yet once more I ſhake not the
earth onely, but alſo heauen.27And this word Yet once more, ſignifieth
the remouing of thoſe things that are ſhaken, as of things that are made,
that thoſe things which cannot be ſhaken may remaine.28Wherefore wee
receiuing a kingdome which cannot bee moued, let vs haue grace,
whereby wee may ſerue God acceptably, with reuerence and godly
feare.29For our God is a conſuming fire.

CHAPTER 131Let brotherly loue continue.2Bee not forgetfull to
entertaine ſtrangers, for thereby ſome haue entertayned Angels
vnawares.3Remember them that are in bonds, as bound with them; and
them which ſuffer aduerſitie, as being your ſelues alſo in the
body.4Mariage is honorable in all, and the bed vndefiled: but
whoremongers, and adulterers God will iudge.5Let your conuerſation
bee without couetouſneſſe: and be content with ſuch things as yee haue.
For hee hath ſaid, I will neuer leaue thee, nor forſake thee.6So that wee
may boldly ſay, The Lord is my helper, and I will not feare what man
ſhall doe vnto me.7Remember them which haue the rule ouer you, who
haue ſpoken vnto you the word of God, whoſe faith follow, conſidering
the end of their conuerſation.8Ieſus Chriſt the ſame yeſterday, and to
day, and for euer.9Be not caried about with diuers and ſtrange doctrines:
for it is a good thing that the heart be eſtabliſhed with grace, not with
meates, which haue not profited them that haue beene occupied
therein.10Wee haue an altar whereof they haue no right to eate, which
ſerue the Tabernacle.11For the bodies of thoſe beaſts, whoſe blood is
brought into the Sanctuary by the high Prieſt for ſinne, are burnt without
the campe.12Wherefore Ieſus alſo, that hee might ſanctifie the people
with his own blood, ſuffered without the gate.13Let vs goe foorth
therefore vnto him without the campe, bearing his reproch.14For here
haue we no continuing citie, but we ſeeke one to come.15By him
therefore let vs offer the ſacrifice of praiſe to God continually, that is,
the fruit of our lippes, giuing thankes to his Name.16But to doe good,
and to communicate forget not, for with ſuch ſacrifices God is well
pleaſed.17Obey them that haue the rule ouer you, and ſubmit your
ſelues: for they watch for your ſoules, as they that muſt giue account,
that they may doe it with ioy, and not with griefe: for that is vnprofitable
for you.18Pray for vs: for we truſt wee haue a good conſcience in all
things, willing to liue honeſtly.19But I beſeech you the rather to doe this,
that I may be reſtored to you the ſooner.20Now the God of peace, that
brought againe from the dead our Lord Ieſus, that great ſhepheard of
the ſheepe, through the blood of the euerlaſting Couenant,21Make you

perfect in euery good worke to doe his will, working in you that which is well pleaſing in his ſight, through Ieſus Chriſt, to whom be glorie for euer and euer. Amen.22And I beſeech you brethren, ſuffer the word of exhortation, for I haue written a letter vnto you in few words.23Know yee, that our brother Timothie is ſet at libertie, with whom if he come ſhortly, I will ſee you.24Salute all them that haue the rule ouer you, and al the Saints. They of Italy ſalute you.25Grace be with you all. Amen. *Written to the Hebrewes, from Italy, by Timothie.*

THE EPIſTLE OF IAMES (JAMES)

CHAPTER 11Iames a ſeruant of God, and of the Lord Ieſus Chriſt, to the twelue Tribes which are ſcattered abroad, greeting.2My brethren, count it all ioy when ye fall into diuers temptations,3Knowing this, that the trying of your faith worketh patience,4But let patience haue her perfect worke, that ye may be perfect, and entier, wanting nothing.5If any of you lacke wiſedome, let him aſke of God, that giueth to all men liberally, and vpbraideth not: and it ſhalbe giuen him.6But let him aſke in faith, nothing wauering: for he that wauereth is like a waue of the ſea, driuen with the wind, and toſsed.7For let not that man thinke that he ſhall receiue any thing of the Lord.8A double minded man is vnſtable in all his wayes.9Let the brother of low degree, reioyce in that he is exalted:10But the rich, in that hee is made low: becauſe as the floure of the graſſe he ſhall paſſe away.11For the Sunne is no ſooner riſen with a burning heate, but it withereth the graſſe; and the flowre thereof falleth, and the grace of the faſhion of it periſheth: ſo alſo ſhall the rich man fade away in his wayes.12Bleſſed is the man that endureth temptation: for when hee is tried, hee ſhall receiue the crowne of life, which the Lord hath promiſed to them that loue him.13Let no man ſay when he is tempted, I am tempted of God: for God cannot be tempted with euill, neither tempteth he any man.14But euery man is tempted, when hee is drawen away of his owne luſt, and entiſed.15Then when luſt hath conceiued, it bringeth forth ſinne: and ſinne, when it is finiſhed, bringeth forth death.16Doe not erre, my beloued brethren.17Euery good gift, and euery perfect gift is from aboue, & commeth downe from the Father of lights, with whom is no variableneſse, neither ſhadow of turning.18Of his owne will begate hee vs, with the word of Trueth, that wee ſhould bee a kinde of firſt fruites of his creatures.19Wherefore my beloued brethren, let euery man bee ſwift to heare, ſlow to ſpeake, ſlow to wrath.20For the wrath of man worketh not the righteouſneſſe of God.21Wherefore lay apart all filthineſse, and ſuperfluitie of naughtineſse, & receiue with meekneſse the engrafted word, which is able to ſaue your ſoules.22But be ye doers of the word, and not hearers onely, receiuing your owne ſelues.23For if any be a hearer of the word and not a doer, he is like vnto a man beholding his naturall face in a glaſſe:24For hee beholdeth himſelfe, and goeth his way, and ſtraightway forgetteth what maner of man he was.25But who ſo looketh into the perfect Law of libertie, and continueth therein, he being not a forgetfull hearer, but a doer of the worke, this man ſhall be bleſſed in his deed.26If any man among you ſeeme to be religious, & bridleth not his tongue, but deceiueth his owne heart, this mans religion is vaine.27Pure religion and vndefiled before God and the Facher, is this, to viſit the fatherleſſe and widowes in their affliction, and to keepe himſelfe vnſpotted from the world.

CHAPTER 21My brethren, haue not the faith of our Lord Ieſus Chriſt the Lord of glorie, with reſpect of perſons.2For if there come vnto your aſſembly a man with a gold ring, in goodly apparel, and there come in alſo a poore man, in vile raiment:3And yee haue reſpect to him that weareth the gay clothing, and ſay vnto him, Sit thou here in a good place: and ſay to the poore, ſtand thou there, or ſit here vnder my footſtoole:4Are yee not then partiall in your ſelues, and are become iudges of euill thoughts?5Hearken, my beloued brethren, Hath not God choſen the poore of this world, rich in faith, and heires of the kingdome, which hee hath promiſed to them that loue him?6But yee haue deſpiſed the poore. Doe not rich men oppreſſe you, and draw you before the Iudgement ſeats?7Doe not they blaſpheme that worthy Name, by the which ye are called?8If ye fulfil the royall Law, according to the Scripture, Thou ſhalt loue thy neighbour as thy ſelfe, ye doe well.9But if ye haue reſpect to perſons, ye commit ſinne, and are conuinced of the Law, as tranſgreſsours.10For whoſoeuer ſhall keepe the whole Law, & yet offend in one point, he is guilty of all.11For he that ſaid, Doe not commit adultery; ſayd alſo, Do not kill. Now if thou commit no adultery, yet if thou kill, thou art become a tranſgreſsour of the Law.12So ſpeake ye, and ſo doe, as they that ſhall bee iudged by the Law of libertie.13For he ſhall haue iudgement without mercie, that hath ſhewed no mercy, & mercie reioyceth againſt iudgement.14What doth it profit, my brethren, though a man ſay hee hath faith, and haue not workes? can faith ſaue him?15If a brother or ſiſter be naked, and deſtitute of dayly foode,16And one of you ſay vnto them, Depart in peace, be you warmed & filled: notwithſtanding ye giue them not thoſe things which are needfull to the body: what doth it profit?17Euen ſo faith, if it hath not works, is dead being alone.18Yea, a man may ſay, Thou haſt faith, and I haue workes: ſhew mee thy faith without thy workes, and I will ſhew thee my faith by my workes.19Thou beleeueſt that there is one God, thou doeſt well: the deuils alſo beleeue, and tremble.20But wilt thou knowe, O vaine man, that faith without workes is dead?21Was not Abraham our father iuſtified by works, when hee had offered Iſaac his ſonne vpon the altar?22Seeſt thou how faith wrought with his works, and by works was faith made perfect?23And the Scripture was fullfiled which ſaith, Abraham beleeued God, and it was imputed vnto him for righteouſnes: and he was called the friend of God.24Ye ſee then, how that by workes a man is iuſtified, and not by faith only.25Likewiſe alſo, was not Rahab the harlot iuſtified by works, when ſhe had receiued the meſſengers, and had ſent them out another way?26For as the body without the ſpirit is dead, ſo faith without workes is dead alſo.

CHAPTER 31My brethren, bee not many maſters, knowing that we ſhall receiue the greater condemnation.2For in many things we offend all. If any man offend not in word, the ſame is a perfect man, and able alſo to bridle the whole body.3Behold, we put bittes in the horſes mouthes, that they may obey vs, and we turne about their whole body.4Behold alſo the ſhips, which though they be ſo great, and are driuen of fierce windes, yet are they turned about with a very ſmall helme, whitherſoeuer the gouernour liſteth.5Euen ſo the tongue is a little member, and boaſteth great things: behold, how great a matter a litle fire kindleth.6And the tongue is a fire, a world of iniquitie: ſo is the tongue amongſt our members, that it defileth the whole body, and ſetteth on fire the courſe of nature, and it is ſet on fire of hell.7For euery kind of beaſts, and of birds, and of ſerpents, and things in the ſea, is tamed, and hath been tamed of mankind.8But the tongue can no man tame, it is an vnruly euill, ful of deadly poyſon.9Therewith bleſſe wee God, euen the Father: and therewith curſe wee men, which are made after the ſimilitude of God.10Out of the ſame mouth proceedeth bleſſing and curſing: my brethren, theſe things ought not ſo to be.11Doeth a fountaine ſend foorth at the ſame place ſweet water and bitter?12Can þe figtree, my brethren, beare oliue berries? either a vine, figs? ſo can no fountaine both yeeld ſalt water & freſh.13Who is a wiſe man and indued with knowledge amongſt you? let him ſhew out of a good conuerſation his workes with meekenes of wiſedome.14But if ye haue bitter enuying and ſtrife in your hearts glory not, and lie not againſt the trueth.15This wiſedome deſcendeth not from aboue, but is earthly, ſenſuall, deuiliſh.16For where enuying and ſtrife is, there is confuſion, and euery euill worke.17But the wiſedome that is from aboue, is firſt pure, then peaceable, gentle, and eaſie to be intreated, full of mercy, and good fruits, without partialitie, and without hypocriſie.18And the fruit of righteouſneſſe is ſowen in peace, of them that make peace.

CHAPTER 41From whence come warres and fightings among you? come they not hence, euen of your luſts, that warre in your members?2Ye luſt, and haue not: yee kill, and deſire to haue, and cannot obtaine: yee fight and warre, yet yee haue not, becauſe ye aſke not.3Ye aſke and receiue not, becauſe ye aſke amiſse, that yee may conſume it vpon your luſts.4Ye adulterers, and adultereſses, know yee not that the friendſhip of the world is enmity with God? whoſoeuer therefore will be a friend of the world, is the enemy of God.5Doe ye thinke that the Scripture ſaith in vaine, the ſpirit that dwelleth in vs luſteth to enuy?6But he giueth more grace, wherefore he ſaith, God reſiſteth the proude, but giueth grace vnto the humble.7Submit your ſelues therefore to God:

reſiſt the deuill, and hee will flee from you.8Draw nigh to God, and hee
will draw nigh to you: cleanſe your hands ye ſinners, and purifie your
hearts yee double minded.9Bee afflicted, and mourne, and weepe: let
your laughter be turned to mourning, and your ioy to
heauineſse.10Humble your ſelues in the ſight of the Lord, and he ſhall
lift you vp.11Speake not euill one of another (brethren:) he that ſpeaketh
euill of his brother, and iudgeth his brother, ſpeaketh euill of the Law,
and iudgeth the Law: but if thou iudge the Law, thou art not a doer of
the Law, but a iudge.12There is one Lawgiuer, who is able to ſaue, and
to deſtroy: who art thou that iudgeſt another?13Goe to now ye that ſay,
To day or to morrow wee will goe into ſuch a city and continue there a
yere, and buy, and ſell, and get gaine:14Whereas yee know not what
ſhalbe on the morow: for what is your life? It is euen a vapour that
appeareth for a litle time, and then vaniſheth away.15For that yee ought
to ſay, if the Lord will, we ſhall liue, and doe this, or that.16But now yee
reioyce in your boaſtings: all ſuch reioycing is euill.17Therefore to him
that knoweth to doe good, and doth it not, to him it is ſinne.
CHAPTER 5 1Goe to now, yee rich men, weepe and howle for your
miſeries that ſhall come vpon you.2Your riches are corrupted, and your
garments motheaten:3Your gold and ſiluer is cankered, and the ruſt of
them ſhall bee a witneſſe againſt you, and ſhall eate your fleſh as it were
fire: ye haue heaped treaſure together for the laſt dayes.4Beholde, the
hire of the labourers which haue reaped downe your fieldes, which is of
you kept backe by fraud, cryeth: and the cryes of them which haue
reaped, are entred into the eares of the Lord of Sabaoth.5Yee haue liued
in pleaſure on the earth, and bene wanton: ye haue nouriſhed your
hearts, as in a day of ſlaughter:6Yee haue condemned, and killed the iuſt,
and he doth not reſiſt you.7Be patient therefore, brethren, vnto the
comming of the Lord: behold, the huſbandman waiteth for the precious
fruit of the earth, and hath long patience for it, vntill hee receiue the
early and latter raine.8Be yee alſo patient; ſtabliſh your hearts: for the
comming of the Lorde draweth nigh.9Grudge not one againſt another,
brethren, leſt ye be condemned: behold, the Iudge ſtandeth before the
doore.10Take, my brethren, the Prophets, who haue ſpoken in the Name
of the Lord, for an example of ſuffering affliction, and of
patience.11Beholde, wee count them happie which endure. Ye haue
heard of the patience of Iob, and haue ſeene the end of the Lord: that
the Lord is very pitifull and of tender mercie.12But aboue all things, my
brethren, ſweare not, neither by heauen, neither by the earth, neither by
any other othe: but let your yea, be yea, and your nay, nay: leſt yee fall
into condemnation.13Is any among you afflicted? let him pray. Is any
merry? let him ſing Pſalmes.14Is any ſicke among you? let him call for
the Elders of the Church, and let them pray ouer him, anointing him
with oyle in the Name of the Lord:15And the prayer of Faith ſhall ſaue
the ſicke, and the Lord ſhall raiſe him vp: and if hee haue committed
ſinnes, they ſhall be forgiuen him.16Confeſse your faults one to another,
and pray one for another, that yee may bee healed: the effectuall feruent
prayer of a righteous man auaileth much.17Elias was a man ſubiect to
like paſsions as we are, and he prayed earneſtly that it might not raine:
and it rained not on the earth by the ſpace of three yeeres and ſixe
monethes.18And hee prayed againe, and the heauen gaue raine, and the
earth brought foorth her fruit.19Brethren, if any of you doe erre from
the trueth, and one conuert him,20Let him know, that hee which
conuerteth the ſinner from the errour of his way, ſhall ſaue a ſoule from
death, and ſhall hide a multitude of ſinnes.

1 PETER

CHAPTER 1 1Peter an Apoſtle of Ieſus Chriſt, to the ſtrangers ſcattred
thorowout Pontus, Galatia, Cappadocia, Aſia, and Bithynia,2Elect,
according to the foreknowledge of God the Father, through
ſanctification of the Spirit vnto obedience, and ſprinkling of the blood
of Ieſus Chriſt: Grace vnto you and peace be multiplied.3Bleſſed be the
God and Father of our Lord Ieſus Chriſt, which according to his
abundant mercy, hath begotten vs againe vnto a liuely hope, by the
reſurrection of Ieſus Chriſt from the dead,4To an inheritance
incorruptible, and vndefiled, and that fadeth not away, reſeruedin
heauen for you,5Who are kept by the power of God through faith vnto
ſaluation, ready to be reuealed in the laſt time.6Wherin ye greatly reioyce,
though now for a ſeaſon (if neede bee) yee are in heauineſse through
manifolde temptations:7That the triall of your faith, being much more
precious then of golde that periſheth, though it bee tryed with fire, might
be found vnto praiſe, and honor, and glory, at the appearing of Ieſus
Chriſt:8Whom hauing not ſeene, yee loue, in whom though now ye ſee
him not, yet beleeuing, ye reioyce with ioy vnſpeakeable, and full of
glory,9Receiuing the ende of your faith, euen the ſaluation of your
ſoules:10Of which ſaluation the Prophets haue inquired, and ſearched
diligently, who propheſied of the grace that ſhould come vnto
you,11ſearching what, or what maner of time the Spirit of Chriſt which
was in them did ſignifie, when it teſtified beforehand the ſuffrings of
Chriſt, and the glory that ſhould follow.12Unto whome it was reuealed,
that not vnto themſelues, but vnto vs, they did miniſter the things which
are now reported vnto you, by them that haue preached the Goſpel vnto
you, with the holy Ghoſt ſent downe from heauen, which things the
Angels deſire to looke into.13Wherefore gird vp the loynes of your
minde, bee ſober, and hope to the end, for the grace that is to bee
brought vnto you at the reuelation of Ieſus Chriſt:14As obedient
children, not faſhioning your ſelues according to the former luſts, in
your ignorance:15But as hee which hath called you is holy, ſo be ye holy
in all maner of conuerſation;16Becauſe it is written, Be ye holy, for I am
holy.17And if ye call on the Father, who without reſpect of perſons
iudgeth according to euery mans worke, paſſe the time of your
ſoiourning here in feare:18For as much as ye know that yee were not
redeemed with corruptible things, as ſiluer and golde, from your vaine
conuerſation receiued by tradition from your fathers;19But with the
precious blood of Chriſt, as of a Lambe without blemiſh and without
ſpot,20Who verily was foreordeined before the foundation of the world,
but was manifeſt in theſe laſt times for you.21Who by him do beleeue in
God that raiſed him vp from the dead, and gaue him glorie, that your
faith and hope might be in God.22Seeing yee haue purified your ſoules
in obeying the truth through the Spirit, vnto vnfained loue of the
brethren: ſee that ye loue one another with a pure heart feruently,23Being
borne againe, not of corruptible ſeed, but of incorruptible, by the word
of God which liueth and abideth for euer.24For all fleſh is as graſſe, and
all the glory of man as the flowre of graſſe: the graſſe withereth, and the
flowre thereof falleth away.25But the word of the Lord endureth for
euer: & this is the word which by the Goſpel is preached vnto you.
CHAPTER 2 1Wherefore laying aſide all malice, and all guile, and
hypocriſies, and enuies, and euill ſpeakings,2As new borne babes deſire
the ſincere milke of the word, that ye may grow thereby,3If ſo bee yee
haue taſted that the Lord is gracious.4To whom comming as vnto a
liuing ſtone, diſallowed in deed of men, but choſen of God, and
precious,5Ye alſo as liuely ſtones, are built vp a ſpirituall houſe, an holy
Prieſthood to offer vp ſpirituall ſacrifice, acceptable to God by Ieſus
Chriſt.6Wherefore it is conteined in the Scripture, Beholde, I lay in Sion
a chiefe corner ſtone, elect, precious, and he that beleeueth on him, ſhall
not be confounded.7Unto you therfore which beleeue hee is precious;
but vnto them which be diſobedient, the ſtone which the builders
diſallowed, the ſame is made the head of the corner,8And a ſtone of
ſtumbling, and a Rocke of offence, euen to them which ſtumble at the
word, being diſobedient, whereunto alſo they were appointed.9But yee
are a choſen generation, a royall Prieſthood, an holy nation, a peculiar
people, that yee ſhould ſhewe forth the praiſes of him, who hath called
you out of darknes into his marueilous light:10Which in time paſt were
not a people, but are now the people of God: which had not obteined
mercie, but now haue obteined mercy.11Dearely beloued, I beſeech you
as ſtrangers and pilgrimes, abſtaine from fleſhly luſts, which warre
againſt the ſoule,12Hauing your conuerſation honeſt among the Gentiles,
that whereas they ſpeake againſt you as euill doers, they may by your
good works which they ſhall behold, glorifie God in the day of
viſitation.13Submit your ſelues to euery ordinance of man for the Lordes
ſake, whether it be to the King, as ſupreme,14Or vnto gouernours, as
vnto them that are ſent by him, for the puniſhment of euil doers, and
for the praiſe of them that doe well.15For ſo is the will of God, that with
well doing yee may put to ſilence the ignorance of fooliſh men.16As free,
and not vſing your libertie for a cloake of malicioufneſse, but as the
ſeruants of God.17Honour all men. Loue the brotherhood. Feare God.

Honour the King.[18]Seruants, be ſubiect to your maſters with al feare,
not only to the good and gentle, but alſo to the froward.[19]For this is
thanke-worthie, if a man for conſcience toward God endure griefe,
ſuffering wrongfully.[20]For what glory is it, if when yee be buffeted for
your faults, ye ſhall take it patiently: but if when yee doe well, and ſuffer
for it, ye take it patiently, this is acceptable with God.[21]For euen
hereunto were ye called: becauſe Chriſt alſo ſuffered for vs, leauing vs
an example, that yee ſhould follow his ſteps.[22]Who did no ſinne, neither
was guile found in his mouth.[23]Who when hee was reuiled, reuiled not
againe; when hee ſuffered, hee threatned not, but committed himſelfe
to him that iudgeth righteouſly.[24]Who his owne ſelfe bare our ſinnes in
his owne body on the tree, that wee being dead to ſinnes, ſhould liue
vnto righteouſneſſe, by whoſe ſtripes ye were healed.[25]For yee were as
ſheepe going aſtray, but are now returned vnto the ſhepheard and
Biſhop of your ſoules.
CHAPTER 3[1]Likewiſe, ye wiues, be in ſubiection to your owne
huſbands, that if any obey not the word, they alſo may without the word
be wonne by the conuerſation of the wiues:[2]While they beholde your
chaſte conuerſation coupled with feare:[3]Whoſe adorning, let it not bee
that outward adorning, of plaiting the haire, and of wearing of gold, or
of putting on of apparell.[4]But let it bee the hidden man of the heart, in
that which is not corruptible, euen the ornament of a meeke and quiet
ſpirit, which is in the ſight of God of great price.[5]For after this manner
in the olde time, the holy women alſo who truſted in God adorned
themſelues, beeing in ſubiection vnto their owne huſbands.[6]Euen as
Sara obeyed Abraham, calling him Lord, whoſe daughters ye are as long
as ye doe well, and are not afraid with any amazement.[7]Likewiſe ye
huſbands, dwel with them according to knowledge, giuing honour vnto
the wife as vnto the weaker veſsel, and as being heires together of the
grace of life, that your prayers be not hindered.[8]Finally be ye all of one
minde, hauing compaſſion one of another, loue as brethren, be pitifull,
be courteous,[9]Not rendring euill for euill, or railing for railing: but
contrarywiſe bleſſing, knowing that yee are thereunto called, that ye
ſhould inherite a bleſſing.[10]For hee that will loue life, and ſee good
dayes, let him refraine his tongue from euil, and his lips that they ſpeake
no guile:[11]Let him eſchew euil and do good, let him ſeeke peace and
enſue it.[12]For the eyes of the Lord are ouer the righteous, and his eares
are open vnto their prayers: but the face of the Lord is againſt them that
doe euill.[13]And who is hee that will harme you, if ye bee followers of
that which is good?[14]But and if ye ſuffer for righteouſnes ſake, happy
are ye, and be not afraid of their terrour, neither be troubled:[15]But
ſanctifie the Lord God in your hearts, & be ready alwayes to giue an
anſwere to euery man that aſketh you a reaſon of the hope that is in you,
with meekeneſse and feare:[16]Hauing a good conſcience, that whereas
they ſpeake euill of you, as of euill doers, they may bee aſhamed that
falſly accuſe your good conuerſation in Chriſt.[17]For it is better, if the
will of God be ſo, that yee ſuffer for well doing, then for euill
doing.[18]For Chriſt alſo hath once ſuffered for ſinnes, the iuſt for the
vniuſt, that he might bring vs to God, being put to death in the fleſh,
but quickened by the Spirit.[19]By which alſo he went and preached vnto
the ſpirits in priſon,[20]Which ſometime were diſobedient, when once the
long-ſuffering of God waited in the dayes of Noah, while the Arke was
a preparing: wherein few, that is, eight ſoules were ſaued by water.[21]The
like figure whereunto, euen Baptiſme, doth alſo now ſaue vs, (not the
putting away of the filth of the fleſh, but the anſwere of a good
conſcience toward God,) by the reſurrection of Ieſus Chriſt.[22]Who is
gone into heauen, and is on the right hand of God, Angels, and
authorities, and powers being made ſubiect vnto him.
CHAPTER 4[1]For aſmuch then as Chriſt hath ſuffered for vs in the
fleſh, arme your ſelues likewiſe with the ſame minde: for hee that hath
ſuffered in the fleſh, hath ceaſſed from ſinne:[2]That he no longer ſhould
liue the reſt of his time in the fleſh, to the luſts of men, but to the will
of God.[3]For the time paſt of our life may ſuffice vs to haue wrought the
will of the Gentiles, when we walked in laſciuiouſnes, luſts, exceſse of
wine, reuellings, banquetings, and abhominable idolatries.[4]Wherein they
thinke it ſtrange, that you runne not with them to the ſame exceſse of
riot, ſpeaking euil of you:[5]Who ſhal giue accompt to him that is ready
to iudge the quicke & the dead.[6]For, for this cauſe was the Goſpel
preached alſo to them that are dead, that they might bee iudged
according to men in the fleſh, but liue according to God in the
ſpirit.[7]But the ende of all things is at hand: be ye therefore ſober and
watch vnto prayer.[8]And aboue all things haue feruent charitie among
your ſelues: for charity ſhall couer the multitude of ſinnes.[9]Uſe
hoſpitalitie one to another without grudging.[10]As euery man hath
receiued the gift, euen ſo miniſter the ſame one to another, as good
ſtewards of the manifold grace of God.[11]If any man ſpeake, let him
ſpeake as the oracles of God: if any man miniſter, let him doe it as of
the ability which God giueth, that God in all things may bee glorified
through Ieſus Chriſt, to whom be praiſe and dominion for euer and euer.
Amen.[12]Beloued, thinke it not ſtrange concerning the fiery triall, which
is to try you, as though ſome ſtrange thing happened vnto you.[13]But
reioyce in as much as yee are partakers of Chriſtes ſufferings; that when
his glory ſhalbe reueiled, ye may be glad alſo with exceeding ioy.[14]If ye
be reproched for the Name of Chriſt, happie are ye, for the ſpirit of
glory, and of God reſteth vpon you: on their part hee is euill ſpoken of,
but on your part he is glorified.[15]But let none of you ſuffer as a
murtherer, or as a theefe, or as an euill doer, or as a buſibody in other
mens matters.[16]Yet if any man ſuffer as a Chriſtian, let him not be
aſhamed, but let him glorifie God on this behalfe.[17]For the time is come
that iudgement muſt begin at the houſe of God: and if it firſt begin at
vs, what ſhall the ende bee of them that obey not the Goſpel of
God?[18]And if the righteous ſcarcely be ſaued, where ſhall the vngodly
and the ſinner appeare?[19]Wherfore, let them that ſuffer according to the
will of God, commit the keeping of their ſoules to him in well doing, as
vnto a faithfull Creator.
CHAPTER 5[1]The Elders which are among you I exhort, who am alſo
an Elder, and a witneſſe of the ſufferings of Chriſt, and alſo a partaker
of the glory that ſhall be reuealed.[2]Feede the flocke of God which is
among you, taking the ouerſight thereof, not by conſtraint, but willingly:
not for filthy lucre, but of a ready minde:[3]Neither as being lords ouer
Gods heritage: but being enſamples to the flocke.[4]And when the chiefe
ſhepheard ſhall appeare, ye ſhall receiue a crowne of glory that fadeth
not away.[5]Likewiſe ye yonger, ſubmit your ſelues vnto the elder: yea, all
of you bee ſubiect one to another, and bee clothed with humilitie: for
God reſiſteth the proud, and giueth grace to the humble.[6]Humble
yourſelues therefore vnder the mighty hand of God, that hee may exalt
you in due time,[7]Caſting all your care vpon him, for he careth for
you.[8]Be ſober, be vigilant: becauſe your aduerſary the deuill, as a roaring
Lion walketh about, ſeeking whom he may deuoure.[9]Whom reſiſt
ſtedfaſt in the faith, knowing that the ſame afflictions are accompliſhed
in your brethren that are in the world.[10]But the God of all grace who
hath called vs into his eternall glory by Chriſt Ieſus, after that ye haue
ſuffered a while, make you perfect, ſtabliſh, ſtrengthen, ſettle you.[11]To
him bee glory and dominion for euer and euer. Amen.[12]By Syluanus a
faithfull brother vnto you, (as I ſuppoſe) I haue written briefly,
exhorting, & teſtifying, that this is the true grace of God wherein ye
ſtand.[13]The Church that is at Babylon elected, together with you,
ſaluteth you, and ſo doth Marcus my ſonne.[14]Greete yee one another
with a kiſſe of charity: Peace bee with you all that are in Chriſt Ieſus.
Amen.

2 PETER

CHAPTER 1[1]Simon Peter, a ſeruant & an Apoſtle of Ieſus Chriſt, to
them that haue obtained like precious Faith with vs, through the
righteouſnes of God, and our Sauiour Ieſus Chriſt.[2]Grace and peace be
multiplied vnto you through the knowledge of God, and of Ieſus our
Lord,[3]According as his diuine power hath giuen vnto vs all things that
pertain vnto life and godlines, through the knowledge of him that hath
called vs to glory and vertue.[4]Whereby are giuen vnto vs exceeding great
and precious promiſes, that by theſe you might bee partakers of the
diuine nature, hauing eſcaped the corruption that is in the world through
luſt.[5]And beſides this, giuing all diligence, adde to your faith, vertue; and
to vertue knowledge;[6]And to knowledge, temperance; and to
temperance, patience; and to patience, godlineſe;[7]And to godlineſse,
brotherly kindneſse; and to brotherly kindneſse, charitie.[8]For if theſe
things be in you, and abound, they make you that yee ſhall neither be

barren, nor vnfruitfull in the knowledge of our Lord Ieſus Chriſt.9But hee that lacketh theſe things, is blind, and cannot ſee farre off, and hath forgotten that hee was purged from his old ſinnes.10Wherefore, the rather, brethren, giue diligence to make your calling and election ſure: for if ye doe theſe things, ye ſhall neuer fall.11For ſo an entrance ſhall be miniſtred vnto you abundantly, into the euerlaſting kingdome of our Lord and Sauiour Ieſus Chriſt.12Wherefore I wil not be negligent to put you alwayes in remembrance of theſe things, though yee know them, and be ſtabliſhed in the preſent trueth.13Yea, I thinke it meete, as long as I am in this tabernacle, to ſtirre you vp, by putting you in remembrance:14Knowing that ſhortly I muſt put off this my Tabernacle, euen as our Lord Ieſus Chriſt hath ſhewed mee.15Moreouer, I will endeuour, that you may bee able after my deceaſe, to haue theſe things alwayes in remembrance.16For wee haue not followed cunningly deuiſed fables, when wee made knowen vnto you the power and comming of our Lord Ieſus Chriſt, but were eye witneſſes of his Maieſtie.17For hee receiued from God the Father, honour and glory, when there came ſuch a voice to him from the excellent glory, This is my beloued Sonne in whom I am well pleaſed.18And this voice which came from heauen wee heard, when we were with him in the holy mount.19We haue alſo a more ſure word of prophecie, whereunto yee doe well that ye take heede, as vnto a light that ſhineth in a darke place, vntill the day dawne, and the day ſtarre Ariſe in your hearts:20Knowing this firſt, that no prophecy of the Scripture is of any priuate Interpretation:21For the prophecie came not in olde time by the will of man: but holy men of God ſpake as they were moued by the holy Ghoſt.

CHAPTER 21But there were falſe prophets alſo among the people, euen as there ſhall bee falſe teachers among you, who priuily ſhall bring in damnable hereſies, euen denying the Lord that bought them, and bring vpon themſelues ſwift deſtruction.2And many ſhall follow their pernicious wayes, by reaſon of whom the way of trueth ſhall be euill ſpoken of:3And through couetouſneſſe ſhall they with fained words, make marchandiſe of you, whoſe iudgement now of a long time lingereth not, and their damnation ſlumbreth not.4For if God ſpared not the Angels that ſinned, but caſt them downe to hell, and deliuered them into chaines of darkeneſſe, to be reſeruedvnto iudgment:5And ſpared not the old world, but ſaued Noah the eight perſon a preacher of righteouſneſſe, bringing in the flood vpon the world of the vngodly:6And turning the cities of Sodom and Gomorrha into aſhes, condemned them with an ouerthrowe, making them an enſample vnto thoſe that after ſhould liue vngodly:7And deliuered iuſt Lot, vexed with the filthy conuerſation of the wicked:8(For that righteous man dwelling among them, in ſeeing & hearing, vexed his righteous ſoule from day to day, with their vnlawfull deeds.)9The Lord knoweth how to deliuer the godly out of temptations, and to reſerue the vniuſt vnto the day of iudgement to be puniſhed:10But chiefly them that walke after the fleſh in the luſt of vncleanneſſe, and deſpiſe gouernment. Preſumptuous are they; ſelfe willed: they are not afraid to ſpeake euill of dignities:11Whereas Angels which are greater in power and might, bring not railing accuſation againſt them before the Lord.12But theſe, as natural bruit beaſts made to bee taken and deſtroyed ſpeake euill of the things that they vnderſtand not, and ſhall vtterly periſh in their owne corruption,13And ſhall receiue the reward of vnrighteouſneſſe, as they that count it pleaſure to riot in the day time: Spots they are and blemiſhes, ſporting themſelues with their owne deceiuings, while they feaſt with you:14Hauing eyes ful of adulterie and that cannot ceaſe from ſinne, beguiling vnſtable ſoules: an heart they haue exerciſed with couetous practiſes: curſed children:15Which haue forſaken the right way, and are gone aſtray, following the way of Balaam the ſonne of Boſor, who loued the wages of vnrighteouſneſſe,16But was rebuked for his iniquity: the dumbe aſſe ſpeaking with mais voice, forbade the madneſse of the Prophet.17Theſe are welles without water, cloudes that are caried with a tempeſt, to whom the miſt of darkeneſſe is reſeruedfor euer.18For when they ſpeake great ſvelling words of vanitie, they alure through the luſts of the fleſh, through much wantonneſse, thoſe that were cleane eſcaped from them who liue in errour.19While they promiſe them libertie, they themſelues are the ſeruants of corruption: for of whom a man is ouercome, of the ſame is he brought in bondage.20For if after they haue eſcaped the pollutions of the world through the knowledge of the Lord and Sauiour Ieſus Chriſt, they are againe intangled therein, and ouercome, the latter end is worſe with them then the beginning.21For it had bin better for them not to haue knowen the way of righteouſneſſe, then after they haue knowen it, to turne from the holy commandement deliuered vnto them.22But it is happened vnto them according to the true prouerbe: The dog is turned to his own vomit againe, and the ſowe that was waſhed, to her wallowing in the mire.

CHAPTER 31This ſecond Epiſtle (beloued) I now write vnto you, in both which I ſtir vp your pure mindes by way of remembrance:2That yee may be mindfull of the wordes which were ſpoken before by the holy Prophets, and of the Commandement of vs the Apoſtles of the Lord and Sauiour:3Knowing this firſt, that there ſhall come in the laſt dayes ſcoffers, walking after their owne luſts,4And ſaying, Where is the promiſe of his comming? For ſince the fathers fell aſleepe, all things continue as they were frō the beginning of the creation.5For this they willingly are ignorant of, that by the word of God the heauens were of olde, and the earth ſtanding out of the water, and in the water,6Whereby the world that then was, being ouerflowed with water, periſhed.7But the heauens and the earth which are now, by the ſame word are kept in ſtore, reſeruedvnto fire againſt the day of Iudgement, and perdition of vngodly men.8But (beloued) bee not ignorant of this one thing, that one day is with the Lord as a thouſand yeeres, and a thouſand yeeres as one day.9The Lord is not ſlacke cōcerning his promiſe (as ſome men count ſlackneſse) but is long-ſuffring to vſ-ward, not willing that any ſhould periſh, but that all ſhould come to repentance.10But the day of the Lord wil come as a thiefe in the night, in the which the heauens ſhall paſſe away with a great noiſe, and the Elements ſhall melt with feruent heate, the earth alſo and the works that are therin ſhalbe burnt vp.11Seeing then that all theſe things ſhall be diſſolued, What maner of perſons ought ye to be in all holy conuerſation, and godlineſse,12Looking for and haſting vnto the comming of the day of God, wherein the heauens being on fire ſhalbe diſſolued, and the Elements ſhall melt with feruent heat.13Neuertheleſſe wee, according to his promiſe, looke for new heauens, and a new earth, wherein dwelleth righteouſneſſe.14Wherefore (beloued) ſeeing that ye looke for ſuch things, be diligent that ye may be found of him in peace, without ſpot, and blameleſſe.15And account that the long ſuffering of the Lord is ſaluation, euen as our beloued brother Paul alſo, according to the wiſedome giuen vnto him, hath written vnto you.16As alſo in all his Epiſtles, ſpeaking in them of theſe things, in which are ſome things hard to be vnderſtood, which they that are vnlearned and vnſtable wreſt, as they doe alſo the other Scriptures, vnto their owne deſtruction.17Ye therefore, beloued, ſeeing yee know theſe things before, beware leſt yee alſo being led away with the errour of the wicked, fall from your owne ſtedfaſtneſse.18But growe in grace, and in the knowledge of our Lord and Sauiour Ieſus Chriſt: to him be glory both now and for euer. Amen.

1 IOHN (1 JOHN)

CHAPTER 11That which was from þe beginning, which wee haue heard, which wee haue ſeene with our eyes, which wee haue looked vpon, and our hands haue handled of the word of life.2(For the life was manifeſted, and we haue ſeene it, and beare witnes, and ſhew vnto you that eternall life which was with the Father, and was manifeſted vnto vs.)3That which wee haue ſeene and heard, declare we vnto you, that ye alſo may haue felowſhip with vs; and truely our fellowſhip is with the Father, and with his Sonne Ieſus Chriſt.4And theſe things write we vnto you, that your ioy may be full.5This then is the meſsage which we haue heard of him, and declare vnto you, that God is light, and in him is no darkeneſſe at all.6If we ſay that we haue felowſhip with him, and walke in darkeneſſe, we lie, and doe not the trueth.7But if wee walke in the light, as he is in the light, wee haue fellowſhip one with another, and the blood of Ieſus Chriſt his Sonne clenſeth vs from all ſinne.8If we ſay that we haue no ſinne, we deceiue our ſelues, and the trueth is not in vs.9If we confeſse our ſinnes, hee is faithfull, & iuſt to forgiue vs our ſinnes, and to cleanſe vs from all vnrighteouſneſſe.10If we ſay that we haue not ſinned, wee make him a liar, and his word is not in vs.

CHAPTER 21My little children, theſe things write I vnto you, that ye ſinne not. And if any man ſinne, we haue an Aduocate with the Father,

Ieſus Chriſt the righteous:2And he is the propitiation for our ſinnes: and
not for ours onely, but alſo for the ſinnes of the whole world.3And
hereby wee doe knowe that we know him, if we keepe his
commandements.4He that ſaith, I knowe him, and keepeth not his
commandements, is a lyer, and the trueth is not in him.5But who ſo
keepeth his word, in him verely is the loue of God perfected: hereby
know we that we are in him.6He that ſayeth he abideth in him, ought
himſelfe alſo ſo to walke, euen as he walked.7Brethren, I write no new
commandement vnto you, but an olde commandement which ye had
from the beginning: the old commandement is the word which ye haue
heard from the beginning.8Againe, a new commandement I write vnto
you, which thing is true in him and in you: becauſe the darkeneſſe is
paſt, and the true light now ſhineth.9He that ſaith he is in the light, and
hateth his brother, is in darkeneſſe euen vntill now.10Hee that loueth his
brother, abideth in the light, and there is none occaſion of ſtumbling in
him.11But he that hateth his brother, is in darkneſſe, and walketh in
darkneſſe, and knoweth not whither hee goeth, becauſe that darkneſſe
hath blinded his eyes.12I write vnto you, little children, becauſe your
ſinnes are forgiuen you for his Names ſake.13I write vnto you, fathers,
becauſe yee haue knowen him that is from the beginning. I write vnto
you, young men, becauſe you haue ouercome the wicked one. I write
vnto you, little children, becauſe yee haue knowen the Father.14I haue
written vnto you, fathers, becauſe ye haue knowen him that is from the
beginning. I haue written vnto you, young men, becauſe yee are ſtrong,
and the word of God abideth in you, and yee haue ouercome the wicked
one.15Loue not the world, neither the things that are in the world. If any
man loue the world, the loue of the Father is not in him.16For all that is
in the world, the luſt of the fleſh, the luſt of the eyes, and the pride of
life, is not of the Father, but is of the world.17And the world paſſeth
away, and the luſt thereof, but hee that doeth the will of God, abideth
for euer.18Little children, it is the laſt time: and as yee haue heard that
Antichriſt ſhall come, euen now are there many Antichriſts, whereby
wee know that it is the laſt time.19They went out from vs, but they were
not of vs: for if they had beene of vs, they would no doubt haue
continued with vs: but they went out that they might be made manifeſt,
that they were not all of vs.20But ye haue an vnction from the holy One,
and ye know all things.21I haue not written vnto you, becauſe yee know
not the trueth: but becauſe ye know it, and that no lie is of the
trueth.22Who is a lier, but hee that denieth that Ieſus is the Chriſt? hee
is Antichriſt, that denyeth the Father, and the Sonne.23Whoſoeuer
denieth the Sonne, the ſame hath not the Father: but he that
acknowledgeth the Sonne, hath the Father alſo.24Let that therefore
abide in you which yee haue heard from the beginning: if that which ye
haue heard from the beginning ſhall remaine in you, yee alſo ſhall
continue in the Sonne, and in the Father.25And this is the promiſe that
hee hath promiſed vs, euen eternall life.26Theſe things haue I written
vnto you, concerning them that ſeduce you.27But the anointing which
ye haue receiued of him, abideth in you: and yee need not that any man
teach you: But, as the ſame anointing teacheth you of all things, and is
trueth, and is no lye: and euen as it hath taught you, ye ſhall abide in
him.28And now, little children, abide in him, that when hee ſhall
appeare, wee may haue confidence, and not bee aſhamed before him at
his comming.29If ye know that he is righteous, ye know that euery one
which doeth righteouſneſſe, is borne of him.
CHAPTER 3 1Beholde, what manner of loue the Father hath beſtowed
vpon vs, that wee ſhould be called the ſonnes of God: therfore the world
knoweth vs not, becauſe it knewe him not.2Beloued, now are we the
ſonnes of God, and it doeth not yet appeare, what wee ſhall be: but wee
know, that when he ſhall appeare, we ſhall bee like him: for we ſhall ſee
him as he is.3And euery man that hath this hope in him, purifieth
himſelfe, euen as he is pure.4Whoſoeuer committeth ſinne, tranſgreſseth
alſo the lawe: for ſinne is the tranſgreſſion of the law.5And ye know that
hee was manifeſted to take away our ſinnes, and in him is no
ſinne.6Whoſoeuer abideth in him, ſinneth not: whoſoeuer ſinneth, hath
not ſeene him, neither knowen him.7Little children, let no man deceiue
you: he that doth righteouſnes, is righteous, euen as he is righteous.8He
that committeth ſinne, is of the deuill, for the deuill ſinneth from the
beginning: for this purpoſe the Sonne of God was manifeſted, that he
might deſtroy the works of the deuill.9Whoſoeuer is borne of God, doth
not commit ſinne: for his ſeede remaineth in him, and he cannot ſinne,
becauſe he is borne of God.10In this the children of God are manifeſt,
and the children of the deuill: whoſoeuer doeth not righteouſneſſe, is
not of God, neither hee that loueth not his brother.11For this is the
meſsage that yee heard from the beginning, that wee ſhould loue one
another.12Not as Cain, who was of that wicked one, and ſlewe his
brother: and wherefore ſlewe hee him? becauſe his owne workes were
euill, and his brothers righteous.13Marueile not, my brethren, if the
world hate you.14Wee know that wee haue paſſed from death vnto life,
becauſe wee loue the brethren: he that loueth not his brother, abideth
in death.15Whoſoeuer hateth his brother, is a murtherer, and yee knowe
that no murtherer hath eternall life abiding in him.16Hereby perceiue
wee the loue of God, becauſe he layd downe his life for vs, and wee
ought to lay downe our liues for the brethren.17But who ſo hath this
worlds good, and ſeeth his brother hath need, and ſhutteth vp his bowels
of compaſſion from him; how dwelleth the loue of God in him?18My
little children, let vs not loue in word, neither in tongue, but indeede and
in trueth.19And hereby wee know that wee are of the trueth, and ſhall
aſsure our hearts before him.20For if our heart condemne vs, God is
greater then our heart, and knoweth all things.21Beloued, if our heart
condemne vs not, then haue wee confidence towards God.22And
whatſoeuer we aſke, wee receiue of him, becauſe we keepe his
commandement, and doe thoſe things that are pleaſing in his ſight.23And
this is his commandement, that we ſhould beleeue on the Name of his
Sonne Ieſus Chriſt, and loue one another, as hee gaue vs
commandement.24And hee that keepeth his commandements dwelleth
in him, and hee in him: and hereby wee know that hee abideth in vs, by
the ſpirit which hee hath giuen vs.
CHAPTER 4 1Beloued, beleeue not euery ſpirit, but trie the ſpirits,
whether they are of God: becauſe many falſe prophets are gone out into
the world.2Hereby know ye the ſpirit of God: euery ſpirit that confeſseth
that Ieſus Chriſt is come in the fleſh, is of God.3And euery Spirit that
confeſseth not that Ieſus Chriſt is come in the fleſh, is not of God: and
this is that ſpirit of Antichriſt, whereof you haue heard, that it ſhould
come, and euen now already is it in the world.4Ye are of God, little
children, and haue ouercome them: becauſe greater is he that is in you,
then he that is in the world.5They are of the world: therefore ſpeake they
of the world, and the world heareth them.6We are of God: hee that
knoweth God, heareth vs: he that is not of God heareth not vs, hereby
know wee the ſpirit of trueth, and the ſpirit of errour.7Beloued, let vs
loue one another; for loue is of God: and euery one that loueth, is borne
of God and knoweth God.8Hee that loueth not, knoweth not God: for
God is loue.9In this was manifeſted the loue of God towards vs, becauſe
that God ſent his only begotten Sonne into the world, that we might liue
through him.10Herein is loue, not that wee loued God, but that he loued
vs, and ſent his Sonne to be þe propitiation for our ſins.11Beloued, if
God ſo loued vs, wee ought alſo to loue one another.12No man hath
ſeene God at any time. If wee loue one another, God dwelleth in vs, and
his loue is perfected in vs.13Hereby know wee that we dwell in him and
he in vs, becauſe hee hath giuen vs of his Spirit.14And we haue ſeene,
and doe teſtifie, that the Father ſent the Sonne to be the Sauiour of the
world.15Whoſoeuer ſhall confeſse that Ieſus is the Sonne of God, God
dwelleth in him, and he in God.16And we haue knowen and beleeued
the loue that God hath to vs. God is loue, and hee that dwelleth in loue,
dwelleth in God, and God in him.17Herein is our loue made perfect,
that wee may haue boldneſse in the day of Iudgement, becauſe as hee is,
ſo are we in this world.18There is no feare in loue, but perfect loue
caſteth out feare: becauſe feare hath torment: hee that feareth, is not
made perfect in loue.19We loue him: becauſe hee firſt loued vs.20If a
man ſay, I loue God, and hateth his brother, he is a lyar. For hee that
loueth not his brother whom hee hath ſeene, how can he loue God
whom he hath not ſeene?21And this commandement haue we from him,
that he who loueth God, loue his brother alſo.
CHAPTER 5 1Whoſoeuer beleeueth that Ieſus is the Chriſt, is borne of
God: and euery one that loueth him that begate, loueth him alſo that is
begotten of him.2By this wee know that wee loue the children of God,
when we loue God and keepe his commandements.3For this is the loue
of God, that we keepe his commandements, and his commandements
are not grieuous.4For whatſoeuer is borne of God, ouercommeth the
world, and this is the victorie that ouercommeth the world, euen our
faith.5Who is he that ouercommeth the world, but he that beleeueth that

Ieſus is the Sonne of God?6This is hee that came by water and blood,
euen Ieſus Chriſt, not by water onely, but by water and blood: and it is
the Spirit that beareth witneſſe, becauſe the Spirit is trueth.7For there
are three that beare record in heauen, the Father, the Word, and the holy
Ghoſt: and theſe three are one.8And there are three that beare witneſſe
in earth, the Spirit, and the Water, and the Blood, and theſe three agree
in one.9If we receiue the witneſſe of men, the witneſſe of God is greater:
for this is the witneſſe of God, which hee hath teſtified of his
Sonne.10Hee that beleeueth on the Sonne of God, hath the witneſſe in
himſelfe: he that beleeueth not God, hath made him a liar, becauſe he
beleeueth not the record that God gaue of his Sonne.11And this is the
record, that God hath giuen to vs eternall life, and this life is in his
Sonne.12Hee that hath the Sonne, hath life; and hee that hath not the
Sonne, hath not life.13Theſe things haue I written vnto you that beleeue
on the Name of the Sonne of God, that ye may know, that ye haue
eternall life, and that yee may beleeue on the Name of the Sonne of
God.14And this is the confidence that we haue in him, that if wee aſke
any thing according to his will, hee heareth vs.15And if we know that he
heare vs, whatſoeuer wee aſke, wee know that we haue the petitions that
wee deſired of him.16If any man ſee his brother ſinne a ſinne which is
not vnto death, hee ſhall aſke, and he ſhall giue him life for them that
ſinne not vnto death. There is a ſinne vnto death: I doe not ſay that he
ſhall pray for it.17All vnrighteouſnes is ſinne, and there is a ſinne not
vnto death.18We know that whoſoeuer is borne of God, ſinneth not: but
hee that is begotten of God, keepeth himſelfe, and that wicked one
toucheth him not.19And we know that we are of God, and the whole
world lieth in wickedneſſe.20And we know that the Sonne of God is
come, and hath giuen vs an vnderſtanding that wee may know him that
is true: and wee are in him that is true, euen in his Sonne Ieſus Chriſt.
This is the true God, and eternall life.21Little children, keepe your ſelues
from Idoles. Amen.

2 IOHN (2 JOHN)

CHAPTER 11The Elder vnto the elect Lady, and her children, whome
I loue in the trueth: and not I onely, but alſo all they that haue knowen
þe trueth:2For the trueths ſake which dwelleth in vs, and ſhalbe with vs
for euer:3Grace bee with you, mercie, and peace from God the Father,
and from the Lord Ieſus Chriſt, the Sonne of the Father in trueth and
loue.4I reioyced greatly, that I found of thy children walking in trueth,
as wee haue receiued a commaundement from the Father.5And now, I
beſeech thee Lady, not as though I wrote a new commandement vnto
thee: but that which wee had from the beginning, that wee loue one
another.6And this is loue, that wee walke after his Commandements.
This is the Commandement, that as yee haue heard from the beginning,
yee ſhould walke in it.7For many deceiuers are entred into the world,
who confeſse not that Ieſus Chriſt is come in the fleſh. This is a deceiuer,
and an Antichriſt.8Looke to your ſelues, that wee loſe not thoſe things
which wee haue wrought, but that we receiue a full reward.9Whoſoeuer
tranſgreſseth and abideth not in the doctrine of Chriſt, hath not God:
hee that abideth in the doctrine of Chriſt, he hath both the Father and
the Sonne.10If there come any vnto you, and bring not this doctrine,
receiue him not into your houſe, neither bid him, God ſpeed.11For hee
that biddeth him God ſpeed, is partaker of his euill deeds.12Hauing many
things to write vnto you, I would not write with paper and inke, but I
truſt to come vnto you, and ſpeake face to face, that our ioy may be
full.13The children of thy elect ſiſter greet thee. Amen.

3 IOHN (3 JOHN)

CHAPTER 11The Elder vnto the welbeloued Gaius, whom I loue in
the trueth:2Beloued, I wiſh aboue all things that thou mayeſt proſper
and be in health, euen as thy ſoule proſpereth.3For I reioyced greatly
when the brethren came and teſtified of the truth that is in thee, euen as
thou walkeſt in the trueth.4I haue no greater ioy, then to heare that my
children walke in truth.5Beloued, thou doeſt faithfully whatſoeuer thou
doeſt to the Brethren, and to ſtrangers:6Which haue borne witneſſe of
thy charitie before the Church: whome if thou bring forward on their
iourney after a godly ſort, thou ſhalt doe well:7Becauſe that for his
Names ſake they went foorth, taking nothing of the Gentiles.8We
therefore ought to receiue ſuch, that we might be fellow helpers to the
trueth.9I wrote vnto the Church, but Diotrephes, who loueth to haue
the preeminence among them, receiueth vs not.10Wherefore if I come,
I will remember his deeds which he doeth, prating againſt vs with
malicious words: and not content therewith, neither doth hee himſelfe
receiue the brethren, and forbiddeth them that would, and caſteth them
out of the Church.11Beloued, follow not that which is euill, but that
which is good. He that doth good, is of God: but hee that doth euill,
hath not ſeene God.12Demetrius hath good report of all men, and of the
trueth it ſelfe: yea, and we alſo beare record, and ye know that our record
is true.13I had many things to write, but I will not with inke and pen
write vnto thee.14But I truſt I ſhall ſhortly ſee thee, and wee ſhall ſpeake
face to face. Peace bee to thee. Our friends ſalute thee. Greet the friends
by name.

IUDE (JUDE)

CHAPTER 11Iude the ſeruant of Ieſus Chriſt, and brother of Iames,
to them that are ſanctified by God the Father, and preſerued in Ieſus
Chriſt, & called:2Mercie vnto you, and peace, and loue be
multiplied.3Beloued, when I gaue all diligence to write vnto you of the
common ſaluation: it was needfull for mee to write vnto you, and exhort
you that ye ſhould earneſtly contend for the faith which was once
deliuered vnto the Saints.4For there are certaine men crept in vnawares,
who were before of olde ordained to this condemnation, vngodly men,
turning the grace of our God into laſciuiouſneſse, and denying the onely
Lord God, & our Lord Ieſus Chriſt.5I will therefore put you in
remembrance, though ye once knew this, how that the Lord hauing
ſaued the people out of the land of Egypt afterward deſtroied them that
beleeued not.6And the Angels which kept not their firſt eſtate, but left
their own habitation, he hath reſeruedin euerlaſting chaines vnder
darkeneſſe, vnto the iudgement of the great day.7Euen as Sodom and
Gomorrha, and the cities about them, in like maner giuing themſelues
ouer to fornication, and going after ſtrange fleſh, are ſet forth for an
example, ſuffring the vengeance of eternall fire.8Likewiſe alſo theſe
filthy dreamers defile the fleſh, deſpiſe dominion, and ſpeake euill of
dignities.9Yet Michael the Archangel, when contending with the deuill,
he diſputed about the body of Moſes, durſt not bring againſt him a
railing accuſation, but ſaid, The Lord rebuke thee.10But theſe ſpeake
euill of thoſe things, which they know not: but what they knowe
naturally, as brute beaſtes, in thoſe things they corrupt themſelues.11Wo
vnto them, for they haue gone in the way of Kain, and ranne greedily
after the errour of Balaam, for reward, and periſhed in the gainſaying of
Core.12Theſe are ſpottes in your feaſts of charitie, when they feaſt with
you, feeding themſelues without feare: cloudes they are without water,
caried about of winds, trees whoſe fruit withereth, without fruit, twiſe
dead, plucked vp by the rootes.13Raging waues of the ſea, foming out
their owne ſhame, wandring ſtars, to whom is reſeruedthe blackneſse of
darkeneſſe for euer.14And Enoch alſo, the ſeuenth from Adam,
propheſied of theſe, ſaying, Behold, the Lord commeth with ten
thouſands of his Saints,15To execute iudgement vpon all, and to
conuince all that are vngodly among them, of all their vngodly deeds
which they haue vngodly committed, and of all their heard ſpeaches,
which vngodly ſinners haue ſpoken againſt him.16Theſe are murmurers
complainers, walking after their owne luſtes, and their mouth ſpeaketh
great ſwelling wordes, hauing mens perſons in admiration becauſe of
aduantage.17But beloued, remember yee the words, which were ſpoken
before of the Apoſtles of our Lord Ieſus Chriſt:18How that they tolde
you there ſhould be mockers in the laſt time, who ſhould walke after
their own vngodly luſtes.19Theſe be they who ſeparate themſelues,
ſenſual, hauing not the ſpirit.20But yee beloued, building vp your ſelues
on your moſt holy faith, praying in the holy Ghoſt,21Keepe your ſelues
in the loue of God, looking for the mercy of our Lord Ieſus Chriſt vnto
eternall life.22And of ſome haue compaſſion, making a difference:23And
others ſaue with feare, pulling them out of the fire: hating euen the

garment ſpotted by the fleſh.24Now vnto him that is able to keepe you from falling, and to preſent you faultleſſe before the preſence of his glory with exceeding ioy,25To the onely wiſe God our Sauiour, be glory and maieſtie, dominion and power, now and euer. Amen.

REUELATION (REVELATION)

CHAPTER 11The Reuelation of Ieſus Chriſt, which God gaue vnto him, to ſhewe vnto his ſeruants things which muſt ſhortly come to paſſe; and he ſent and ſignified it by his Angel vnto his ſeruant Iohn,2Who bare record of the word of God, and of the teſtimonie of Ieſus Chriſt, and of all things that he ſaw.3Bleſſed is hee that readeth, and they that heare the words of this propheſie, and keepe thoſe things which are written therein: for the time is at hand.4Iohn to the ſeuen Churches in Aſia, Grace be vnto you, & peace, from him which is, and which was, and which is to come, and from the ſeuen ſpirits which are before his throne:5And from Ieſus Chriſt, who is the faithful witneſſe, and the firſt begotten of the dead, and the Prince of the kings of the earth: vnto him that loued vs, and waſhed vs from our ſinnes in his owne blood,6And hath made vs Kings and Prieſts vnto God and his Father: to him be glory and dominion for euer and euer, Amen.7Behold he commeth with clouds, and euery eye ſhal ſee him, and they alſo which pearced him: and all kinreds of the earth ſhall waile becauſe of him: euen ſo. Amen.8I am Alpha and Omega, the beginning and the ending, ſaith the Lord, which is, and which was, and which is to come, the Almighty.9I Iohn, who alſo am your brother, and companion in tribulation, and in the kingdome and patience of Ieſus Chriſt, was in the Iſle that is called Patmos, for the word of God, and for the teſtimonie of Ieſus Chriſt.10I was in the ſpirit on the Lords day, and heard behind me a great voice, as of a trumpet,11Saying, I am Alpha and Omega, the firſt and the laſt: and what thou ſeeſt, write in a booke, and ſend it vnto the ſeuen Churches which are in Aſia, vnto Epheſus, and vnto Smyrna, and vnto Pergamos, and vnto Thyatira, and vnto Sardis, and Philadelphia, and vnto Laodicea.12And I turned to ſee the voice that ſpake with mee. And being turned, I ſaw ſeuen golden Candleſticks,13And in the midſt of the ſeuen candleſtickes, one like vnto the Sonne of man, clothed with a garment downe to the foot, and girt about the paps with a golden girdle.14His head, and his haires were white like wooll as white as ſnow, and his eyes were as a flame of fire,15And his feet like vnto fine braſſe, as if they burned in a furnace: and his voice as the ſound of many waters.16And hee had in his right hand ſeuen ſtarres: and out of his mouth went a ſharpe two edged ſword: and his countenance was as the Sunne ſhineth in his ſtrength.17And when I ſawe him, I fell at his feete as dead: and hee laid his right hand vpon me, ſaying vnto mee, Feare not, I am the firſt, and the laſt.18I am hee that liueth, and was dead: and behold, I am aliue for euermore, Amen, and haue the keyes of hell and of death.19Write the things which thou haſt ſeene, and the things which are, and the things which ſhall be hereafter,20The myſterie of the ſeuen ſtarres which thou ſaweſt in my right hand, and the ſeuen golden Candleſtickes. The ſeuen Starres are the Angels of the ſeuen Churches: and the ſeuen candleſtickes which thou ſaweſt, are the ſeuen Churches.

CHAPTER 21Vnto the Angel of the church of Epheſus, write, Theſe things ſaith he that holdeth the ſeuen ſtarres in his right hand, who walketh in the midſt of the ſeuen golden Candleſticks:2I know thy workes, and thy labour, and thy patience, and how thou canſt not beare them which are euil, and thou haſt tried them which ſay they are Apoſtles, and are not, and haſt found them lyers:3And haſt borne, and haſt patience, and for my Names ſake haſt laboured, and haſt not fainted.4Neuertheleſſe, I haue ſomewhat againſt thee, becauſe thou haſt left thy firſt loue.5Remember therfore from whence thou art fallen, and repent, and doe the firſt workes, or elſe I will come vnto thee quickly, and will remoue thy Candleſticke out of his place, except thou repent.6But this thou haſt, that thou hateſt the deeds of the Nicolaitans, which I alſo hate.7Hee that hath an eare, let him heare what the Spirit ſaith vnto the Churches: To him that ouercommeth will I giue to eate of the tree of life, which is in the middeſt of the Paradiſe of God.8And vnto the Angel of the Church in Smyrna, write, Theſe things ſaith the firſt and the laſt, which was dead, and is aliue,9I know thy works, and tribulation, and pouertie, but thou art rich, and I know the blaſphemie of them which ſay they are Iewes and are not, but are the Synagogue of Satan.10Feare none of thoſe things which thou ſhalt ſuffer: behold, the deuill ſhal caſt ſome of you into priſon, that ye may be tried, and yee ſhall haue tribulation tenne dayes: bee thou faithfull vnto death, and I will giue thee a crowne of life.11He that hath an eare, let him heare what the ſpirit ſaith vnto the churches. He that ouercommeth, ſhall not be hurt of the ſecond death.12And to the Angel of the Church in Pergamos, write, Theſe things ſaith hee, which hath the ſharpe ſword with two edges:13I know thy workes, and where thou dwelleſt, euen where Satans ſeat is, and thou holdeſt faſt my Name, and haſt not denied my faith, euen in thoſe daies, wherein Antipas was my faithful Martyr, who was ſlaine among you, where Satan dwelleth.14But I haue a fewe things againſt thee, becauſe thou haſt there them that holde the doctrine of Balaam, who taught Balac to caſt a ſtumbling blocke before the children of Iſrael, to eate things ſacrificed vnto idoles, and to commit fornication.15So haſt thou alſo them that hold the doctrine of the Nicolaitans, which thing I hate.16Repent, or elſe I will come vnto thee quickly, and wil fight againſt them with the ſword of my mouth.17Hee that hath an eare, let him heare what the Spirit ſaith vnto the Churches. To him that ouercommeth will I giue to eate of the hidden Manna, and will giue him a white ſtone, and in the ſtone a new name written, which no man knoweth, ſauing hee that receiueth it.18And vnto the Angel of the church in Thyatira, write, Theſe things ſaith the Sonne of God, who hath his eyes like vnto a flame of fire, and his feete are like fine braſſe:19I know thy works, and charitie, and ſeruice, and faith, and thy patience, and thy workes, and the laſt to bee more then the firſt.20Notwithſtanding, I haue a few things againſt thee, becauſe thou ſuffereſt that woman Iezebel, which calleth herſelfe a Propheteſse, to teach and to ſeduce my ſeruants to commit fornication, and to eat things ſacrificed vnto idoles.21And I gaue her ſpace to repent of her fornication, and ſhe repented not.22Behold, I will caſt her into a bed, and them that commit adultery with her, into great tribulation, except they repent of their deeds.23And I will kill her children with death, and all the Churches ſhall know that I am hee which ſearcheth the reines and hearts: and I will giue vnto euery one of you according to your workes.24But vnto you I ſay, and vnto the reſt in Thyatira, as many as haue not this doctrine, and which haue not knowen the depthes of Satan, as they ſpeake, I will put vpon you none other burden:25But that which ye haue already, hold faſt till I come.26And hee that ouercommeth, and keepeth my workes vnto the ende, to him will I giue power ouer the nations:27(And he ſhall rule them with a rod of yron: as the veſſels of a potter ſhall they be broken to ſhiuers:) euen as I receiued of my Father.28And I will giue him the morning ſtarre.29He that hath an eare, let him heare what the Spirit ſaith vnto the Churches.

CHAPTER 31And vnto the Angel of the Church in Sardis write, Theſe things ſaith he that hath the ſeuen Spirits of God, & the ſeuen ſtarres; I know thy workes, that thou haſt a name that thou liueſt, and art dead.2Be watchfull, and ſtrengthen the things which remaine, that are ready to die: for I haue not found thy works perfect before God.3Remember therefore, how thou haſt receiued and heard, and hold faſt, and repent. If therefore thou ſhalt not watch, I will come on thee as a thiefe, and thou ſhalt not know what houre I will come vpon thee.4Thou haſt a few names euen in Sardis, which haue not defiled their garments, and they ſhall walke with me in white: for they are worthy.5Hee that ouercommeth, the ſame ſhalbe clothed in white raiment, and I will not blot out his name out of the booke of life, but I will confeſse his name before my Father, and before his Angels.6Hee that hath an eare, let him heare what the Spirit ſaith vnto the Churches.7And to the Angel of the Church in Philadelphia write, Theſe things ſaith he that is Holy, he that is true, he that hath the key of Dauid, he that openeth, and no man ſhutteth, and ſhutteth, and no man openeth;8I know thy workes: behold, I haue ſet before thee an open doore, and no man can ſhut it: for thou haſt a little ſtrength, and haſt kept my word, and haſt not denied my Name.9Behold, I will make them of the ſynagogue of Satan, which ſay they are Iewes, and are not, but doe lie: behold, I will make them to come and worſhip before thy feete, and to know that I haue loued thee.10Becauſe thou haſt kept the word of my patience, I alſo will keepe thee from the houre of temptation, which ſhall come vpon all the world, to try them that dwell vpon the earth.11Beholde, I come quickly, hold that faſt which thou haſt, that no man take thy crowne.12Him that ouercommeth, will I make a pillar in the Temple of my God, and he ſhall goe no more out: and I wil write vpon him the Name of my God, and the name of the Citie of my God, which is new Hieruſalem, which commeth downe out of heauen from my God: And I will write vpon him my New name.13Hee that hath an eare, let him heare what the Spirit ſaith vnto the Churches.14And vnto the Angel of the Church of the Laodiceans, write, Theſe things ſaith the Amen, the faithfull and true witneſſe, the beginning of the creation of God:15I know thy workes, that thou art neither cold nor hot, I would thou wert cold or hot.16So then becauſe thou art lukewarme, and neither cold nor hot, I wil ſpew thee out of my mouth:17Becauſe thou ſayeſt, I am rich, and increaſed with goods, and haue need of nothing: and knoweſt not that thou art wretched, and miſerable, and poore, and blinde, and naked.18I counſell thee to buy of me gold tried in the fire, that thou mayeſt bee rich, and white raiment, that thou mayeſt be clothed, and that the ſhame of thy nakedneſſe doe not appeare, and anoint thine eyes with eye ſalue, that thou mayeſt ſee.19As many as I loue, I rebuke and chaſten, be zealous therefore, and repent.20Behold, I ſtand at the doore, and knocke: if any man heare my voyce, and open the doore, I will come in to him, and will ſup with him, and he with me.21To him that ouercommeth, will I graunt to ſit with mee in my throne, euen as I alſo ouercame, and am ſet downe with my Father in his throne.22Hee that hath an eare, let him heare what the Spirit ſaith vnto the Churches.

CHAPTER 4 1After this I looked, and beholde, a doore was opened in heauen: and the firſt voice which I heard, was as it were of a trumpet, talking with me, which ſaid, Come vp hither, and I will ſhew thee things which muſt be hereafter.2And immediatly I was in the ſpirit: and beholde, a Throne was ſet in heauen, and one ſate on the Throne.3And he that ſate was to looke vpon like a Iaſper, and a Sardine ſtone: and there was a rainebow round about the Throne, in ſight like vnto an Emeralde.4And round about the Throne were foure and twentie ſeates, and vpon the ſeates I ſaw foure and twentie Elders ſitting, clothed in white rayment, and they had on their heades crownes of golde.5And out of the Throne proceeded lightnings, and thundrings, and voyces: and there were ſeuen lampes of fire burning before the Throne, which are the ſeuen Spirits of God.6And before the Throne there was a ſea of glaſſe like vnto Chryſtall: and in the middeſt of the throne, and round about the Throne, were foure beaſtes full of eyes before and behinde.7And the firſt beaſt was like a Lion, and the ſecond beaſt like a Calfe, and the third beaſt had a face as a man, and the fourth beaſt was like a flying Egle.8And the foure beaſts had each of them ſixe wings about him, and they were full of eyes within, and they reſt not day and night, ſaying, Holy, holy, holy, Lord God Almighty, which was, and is, and is to come.9And when thoſe beaſts giue glory, and honour, and thankes to him that ſate on the Throne, who liueth for euer and euer,10The foure and twentie Elders fall downe before him that ſate on the Throne, and worſhip him that liueth for euer and euer, and caſt their crownes before the Throne, ſaying,11Thou art worthy, O Lord, to receiue glorie, and honour, and power: for thou haſt created all things, and for thy pleaſure they are, and were created.

CHAPTER 5 1And I ſaw in þe right hand of him that ſate on the Throne, a booke written within, & on the backeſide, ſealed with ſeuen ſeales.2And I ſaw a ſtrong Angel proclaiming with a loude voice; Who is worthy to open the booke, and to looſe the ſeales thereof?3And no man in heauen, nor in earth, neither vnder the earth, was able to open the booke, neither to looke thereon.4And I wept much, becauſe no man was found worthy to open, and to reade the booke, neither to looke thereon.5And one of the Elders ſaith vnto me, Weepe not: beholde, the Lion of the tribe of Iuda, the roote of Dauid, hath preuailed to open the booke, and to looſe the ſeuen ſeales thereof.6And I beheld, and loe, in the middeſt of the Throne, and of the foure beaſtes, and in the midſt of the Elders ſtood a Lambe as it had beene ſlaine, hauing ſeuen hornes and ſeuen eyes, which are the ſeuen Spirits of God, ſent foorth into all the earth.7And he came, and tooke the booke out of the right hand of him that ſate vpon the Throne.8And when he had taken the booke, the foure Beaſts, and foure and twenty Elders fel down before the Lambe, hauing euery one of them harps, and golden vials full of odours, which are the prayers of Saints.9And they ſung a new ſong, ſaying, Thou art worthy to take the Booke, and to open the ſeales thereof: for thou waſt ſlaine, and haſt redeemed vs to God by thy blood, out of euery kinred, and tongue, and people, and nation:10And haſt made vs vnto our God Kings and Prieſts, and we ſhall reigne on the earth.11And I beheld, and I heard the voyce of many Angels, round about the Throne, and the beaſts and the Elders, and the number of them was ten thouſand times tenne thouſand, and thouſands of thouſands,12Saying with a lowd voice, Worthy is the Lambe that was ſlaine, to receiue power, and riches, and wiſedome, and ſtrength, and honour, and glory, and bleſſing.13And euery creature which is in heauen, and on the earth, and vnder the earth, and ſuch as are in the ſea, and all that are in them, heard I, ſaying, Bleſſing, honour, glory, and power bee vnto him that ſitteth vpon the Throne, and vnto the Lambe for euer and euer.14And the foure beaſts ſaid, Amen. And the foure and twenty Elders fell downe and worſhipped him that liueth for euer and euer.

CHAPTER 6 1And I ſawe when the Lambe opened one of the ſeales, and I heard as it were the noiſe of thunder, one of the foure beaſtes, ſaying, Come and ſee.2And I ſaw, and behold, a white horſe, and hee that ſate on him had a bowe, and a crowne was giuen vnto him, and hee went foorth conquering, and to conquere.3And when hee had opened the ſecond ſeale, I heard the ſecond beaſt ſay, Come and ſee.4And there went out another horſe that was red: and power was giuen to him that ſate thereon to take peace from the earth, and that they ſhould kill one another: and there was giuen vnto him a great ſword.5And when hee had opened the third ſeale, I heard the third beaſt ſay, Come and ſee. And I beheld, and loe, a blacke horſe: and hee that ſate on him had a paire of balances in his hand.6And I heard a voice in the midſt of the foure beaſtes ſay, A meaſure of wheate for a penie, and three meaſures of barley for a penie, and ſee thou hurt not the oyle and the wine.7And when hee had opened the fourth ſeale, I heard the voice of the fourth beaſt ſay, Come and ſee.8And I looked, and behold, a pale horſe, & his name that ſate on him was Death, and hell followed with him: and power was giuen vnto them, ouer the fourth part of the earth to kill with ſword, & with hunger, and with death, and with the beaſtes of the earth.9And when hee had opened the fift ſeale, I ſaw vnder the altar, the ſoules of them that were ſlaine for the word of God, and for the teſtimony which they held.10And they cried with a lowd voice, ſaying, How long, O Lord, holy and true, doeſt thou not iudge and auenge our blood on them that dwell on the earth?11And white robes were giuen vnto euery one of them, and it was ſayd vnto them, that they ſhould reſt yet for a little ſeaſon, vntill their fellow ſeruants alſo, and their brethren that ſhould be killed as they were, ſhould be fulfilled.12And I beheld when he had opened the ſixt ſeale, and loe, there was a great earthquake, and the Sunne became blacke as ſackecloth of haire, and the Moone became as blood.13And the ſtarres of heauen fell vnto the earth, euen as a figge tree caſteth her vntimely figs when ſhe is ſhaken of a mighty winde.14And the heauen departed as a ſcrowle when it is rolled together, and euery mountaine and Iſland were moued out of their places.15And the kings of the earth, and the great men, and the rich men, and the chiefe captaines, and the mighty men, and euery bondman, and euery free man, hid themſelues in the dennes, and in the rockes of the mountaines,16And ſaid to the mountaines and rockes, Fall on vs, and hide vs from the face of him that ſitteth on the throne, and from the wrath of the Lambe:17For the great day of his wrath is come, and who ſhall be able to ſtand?

CHAPTER 7 1And after theſe things, I ſaw foure Angels ſtanding on the foure corners of the Earth, holding the foure windes of the earth, that the winde ſhould not blow on the earth, nor on the ſea, nor on any tree.2And I ſaw another Angel aſcending from the Eaſt, hauing the ſeale of the liuing God: and he cried with a loud voice to the foure Angels to whom it was giuen to hurt the earth and the ſea,3Saying, Hurt not the earth, neither the ſea, nor the trees, till wee haue ſealed the ſeruants of our God in their foreheads.4And I heard the number of them which were ſealed: and there were ſealed an hundreth and fourty and foure thouſand, of all the tribes of the children of Iſrael.5Of the tribe of Iuda were ſealed twelue thouſand. Of the tribe of Ruben were ſealed twelue thouſand. Of the tribe of Gad were ſealed twelue thouſand.6Of the tribe of Aſer were ſealed twelue thouſand. Of the tribe of Nepthali were ſealed twelue thouſand. Of the tribe of Manaſſes were ſealed twelue thouſand.7Of the tribe of Simeon were ſealed twelue thouſand. Of the tribe of Leui were ſealed twelue thouſand. Of the tribe of Iſachar were ſealed twelue thouſand.8Of the tribe of Zabulon were ſealed twelue thouſand. Of the tribe of Ioſeph were ſealed twelue thouſand. Of the tribe of Beniamin were ſealed twelue thouſand.9After this I beheld, and lo, a great multitude, which no man could nũber, of all nations, and kindreds, and people, & tongues, ſtood before the throne, & before the Lamb, clothed with white robes, and palmes in their hands:10And cryed with a loude voice, ſaying, Saluation to our God, which ſitteth vpon the Throne, and vnto the Lambe.11And all the Angels ſtood round about the Throne, and about the Elders, and the foure beaſts, and fell before the throne on their faces, and worſhipped God,12Saying, Amen: Bleſſing, and glorie, and wiſedome, and thankeſgiuing, and honour, & power, and might be vnto our God for euer & euer, Amen.13And one of the Elders anſwered, ſaying vnto mee, What are theſe which are arayed in white robes? and whence came they?14And I ſaid vnto him, Sir, thou knoweſt. And he ſaid to me, Theſe are they which came out of great tribulation, and haue waſhed their robes, and made them white in the blood of the Lambe.15Therefore are they before the throne of God, and ſerue him day and night in his Temple: and hee that ſitteth on the Throne ſhal dwell among them.16They ſhall hunger no more, neither thirſt any more, neither ſhall the Sunne light on them, nor any heate.17For the Lambe, which is in the middeſt of the throne, ſhall feede them, and ſhall leade them vnto liuing fountaines of waters: and God ſhal wipe away all teares from their eyes.

CHAPTER 81And when hee had opened the ſeuenth ſeale, there was ſilence in heauen about the ſpace of halfe an houre.2And I ſawe the ſeuen Angels which ſtood before God, and to them were giuen ſeuen trumpets.3And another Angel came & ſtood at the altar, hauing a golden cenſer, and there was giuen vnto him much incenſe, that hee ſhould offer it with the prayers of all Saints vpon the golden altar which was before the throne.4And the ſmoke of the incenſe which came with the prayers of the Saints, aſcended vp before God, out of the Angels hand.5And the Angel tooke the cenſer, and filled it with fire of the altar, and caſt it into the earth: and there were voyces, and thunderings, and lightnings, and an earthquake:6And the ſeuen Angels which had the ſeuen trumpets, prepared themſelues to ſound.7The firſt Angel ſounded, and there followed haile, and fire mingled with blood, and they were caſt vpon the earth, and the third part of trees was burnt vp, and all greene graſſe was burnt vp.8And the ſecond Angel ſounded, and as it were a great mountaine burning with fire was caſt into the ſea, and the third part of the ſea became blood.9And the thirde part of the creatures which were in the ſea, and had life, died, and the third part of the ſhips were deſtroyed.10And the third Angel ſounded, and there fell a great ſtarre from heauen, burning as it were a lampe, and it fell vpon the third part of the riuers, and vpon the fountaines of waters:11And the name of the ſtarre is called Wormewood, and the third part of the waters became wormewood, and many men dyed of the waters, becauſe they were made bitter.12And the fourth Angel ſounded, and the thirde part of the Sunne was ſmitten, & the third part of the Moone, and the third part of the ſtarres, ſo as the third part of them was darkened: and the day ſhone not for a third part of it, and the night likewiſe.13And I beheld, and heard an Angel flying through the midſt of heauen, ſaying with a loude voice, Woe, woe, woe, to the inhabiters of the earth, by reaſon of the other voyces of the trumpet of the three Angels which are yet to ſound.

CHAPTER 91And the fift Angel ſounded, and I ſaw a ſtarre fall from heauen vnto the earth: and to him was giuen the key of the bottomleſſe pitte.2And hee opened the bottomeleſſe pit, and there aroſe a ſmoke out of the pit, as the ſmoke of a great fornace, and the ſunne and the ayre were darkened, by reaſon of the ſmoke of the pit.3And there came out of the ſmoke locuſts vpon the earth, and vnto them was giuen power, as the Scorpions of the earth haue power.4And it was commaunded them that they ſhould not hurt the graſſe of the earth, neither any greene thing, neither any tree: but only thoſe men which haue not the ſeale of God in their foreheads.5And to them it was giuen that they ſhould not kill them, but that they ſhould be tormented fiue moneths, and their torment was as the torment of a Scorpion, when he ſtriketh a man.6And in thoſe daies ſhal men ſeeke death, and ſhall not finde it, and ſhall deſire to die, and death ſhall flee from them.7And the ſhapes of the Locuſts were like vnto horſes prepared vnto battell, and on their heades were as it were crownes like golde, and their faces were as the faces of men.8And they had haire as the haire of women, and their teeth were as the teeth of Lions.9And they had breſtplates, as it were breſtplates of iron, and the ſound of their wings was as the ſound of charets of many horſes running to battell.10And they had tayles like vnto Scorpions, and there were ſtings in their tayles: and their power was to hurt men fiue moneths.11And they had a king ouer them, which is the Angel of the bottomleſſe pit, whoſe name in the Hebrew tongue is Abaddon, but in the Greeke tongue hath his name Apollyon.12One woe is paſt, and behold there come two woes more hereafter.13And the ſixt Angel ſounded, and I heard a voyce from the foure hornes of þe golden altar, which is before God,14Saying to the ſixt Angel which had the trumpet, Looſe the foure Angels which are bound in the great riuer Euphrates.15And the foure Angels were looſed, which were prepared for an houre, and a day, and a moneth, and a yeere, for to ſlay the third part of men.16And the number of the armie of the horſemen were two hundred thouſand thouſand: and I heard the number of them.17And thus I ſawe the horſes in the viſion, and them that ſate on them, hauing breſt-plates of fire and of Iacinct, and brimſtone, & the heades of the horſes were as the heads of Lions, and out of their mouthes iſſued fire, and ſmoke, and brimſtone.18By theſe three was the third part of men killed, by the fire, and by the ſmoke, and by the brimſtone which iſſued out of their mouthes.19For their power is in their mouth, and in their tailes: for their tailes were like vnto ſerpents, and had heads, and with them they doe hurt.20And the reſt of the men which were not killed by theſe plagues, yet repented not of the works of their hands, that they ſhould not worſhip deuils, and idoles of golde, and ſiluer, and braſſe, and ſtone, and of wood, which neither can ſee, nor heare, nor walke:21Neither repented they of their murders, nor of their ſorceries, nor of their fornication, nor of their thefts.

CHAPTER 101And I ſaw another mighty Angel come down from heauen, clothed with a cloud, and a rainebow was vpon his head, and his face was as it were the Sunne, and his feet as pillars of fire.2And hee had in his hand a little booke open: and hee ſet his right foote vpon the ſea, and his left foote on the earth,3And cryed with a loude voice, as when a Lion roareth: and when hee had cried, ſeuen thunders vttered their voices.4And when the ſeuen thunders had vttered their voices, I was about to write: and I heard a voice from heauen, ſaying vnto mee, ſeale vp thoſe things which the ſeuen thunders vttered, and write them not.5And the Angel which I ſaw ſtand vpon the ſea, and vpon the earth, lifted vp his hand to heauen,6And ſware by him that liueth for euer and euer, who created heauen, and the things that therein are, and the earth, and the things that therein are, and the ſea, and the things which are therein, that there ſhould bee time no longer.7But in the dayes of the voice of the ſeuenth Angel, when he ſhall begin to ſound, the myſterie of God ſhould be finiſhed, as hee hath declared to his ſeruants the Prophets.8And the voice which I heard from heauen ſpake vnto me againe, and ſaid, Go, and take the litle booke which is open in the hand of the Angel which ſtandeth vpon the ſea, and vpon the earth.9And I went vnto the Angel, and ſaid vnto him, Giue me the little booke. And he ſayd vnto me, Take it, and eat it vp, and it ſhall make thy belly bitter, but it ſhall bee in thy mouth ſweete as hony.10And I tooke the little booke out of the Angels hand, and ate it vp, and it was in my mouth ſweet as honie: and as ſoone as I had eaten it, my belly was bitter.11And he ſayd vnto me, Thou muſt propheſie againe before many peoples, and nations, and tongues, and kings.

CHAPTER 111And there was giuen me a reede like vnto a rod, and the Angel ſtood, ſaying, Riſe, and meaſure the Temple of God, and the Altar, and them that worſhip therein.2But the Court which is without the Temple leaue out, and meaſure it not: for it is giuen vnto the Gentiles, and the holy citie ſhall they tread vnder foote fourty and two moneths.3And I will giue power vnto my two witneſſes, and they ſhall propheſie a thouſand two hundred and threeſcore dayes clothed in ſackcloth.4Theſe are the two oliue trees, and the two candleſtickes, ſtanding before the God of the earth.5And if any man will hurt them, fire proceedeth out of their mouth, and deuoureth their enemies: and if any man will hurt them, hee muſt in this maner be killed.6Theſe haue power to ſhut heauen, that it raine not in the dayes of their propheſie: and haue power ouer waters to turne them to blood, and to ſmite the earth with all plagues, as often as they will.7And when they ſhall haue finiſhed their teſtimonie, the beaſt that aſcendeth out of the bottomleſſe pit, ſhall make warre againſt them, and ſhall ouercome them, and kill them.8And their dead bodies ſhall lie in the ſtreet of the great citie, which ſpiritually is called Sodome and Egypt, where alſo our Lord was crucified.[9]And they of the people, and kinreds, and tongues, and nations, ſhal ſee their dead bodies three dayes and an halfe, and ſhall not ſuffer their dead bodies to be put in graues.[10]And they that dwell vpon the earth ſhall reioyce ouer them, and make merry, and ſhall ſend gifts one to another, becauſe theſe two Prophets tormented them that dwelt on the earth.[11]And after three dayes and an halfe the Spirit of life from God, entred into them: and they ſtood vpon their feete, and great feare fell vpon them which ſaw them.[12]And they heard a great voyce from heauen, ſaying vnto them, Come vp hither. And they aſcended vp to heauen in a cloud, and their enemies beheld them.[13]And the ſame houre was there a great earthquake, and the tenth part of the city fell, and in the earthquake were ſlaine of men ſeuen thouſand: and the remnant were affrighted, and gaue glory to the God of heauen.[14]The ſecond woe is paſt, and behold, the third woe commeth quickly.[15]And the ſeuenth Angel ſounded, and there were great voyces in heauen, ſaying, The kingdomes of this world are become the kingdomes of our Lord, and of his Chriſt, and he ſhall reigne for euer and euer.[16]And the foure and twentie Elders which ſate before God on their ſeates, fell vpon their faces, and worſhipped God,[17]Saying, Wee giue thee thankes, O Lord God Almightie, which art, and waſt, and art to come; becauſe thou haſt taken to thee thy great power, and haſt reigned.[18]And the nations were angry, and thy wrath is come, and the time of the dead that they ſhould bee iudged, and that thou ſhouldeſt giue reward vnto thy ſeruants the Prophets, and to the Saints, & them that feare thy Name, ſmall and great, and ſhouldeſt deſtroy them which deſtroy the earth.[19]And the Temple of God was opened in heauen, and there was ſeene in his Temple the Arke of his Teſtament, and there were lightnings, and voyces, and thundrings, and an earthquake, and great haile.

CHAPTER 12[1]And there appeared a great wonder in heauen, a woman clothed with the Sunne, & the Moone vnder her feete, and vpon her head a Crowne of twelue ſtarres:[2]And ſhee being with childe, cried, trauailing in birth, and pained to be deliuered.[3]And there appeared another wonder in heauen, and behold a great red dragon, hauing ſeuen heads, and ten hornes, and ſeuen crownes vpon his heads.[4]And his taile drew the third part of the ſtarres of heauen, and did caſt them to the earth: And the dragon ſtood before the woman which was ready to be deliuered, for to deuoure her childe as ſoone as it was borne.[5]And ſhee brought foorth a man child, who was to rule all nations with a rod of yron: and her child was caught vp vnto God, and to his Throne.[6]And the woman fled into the wilderneſſe, where ſhee hath a place prepared of God, that they ſhould feed her there a thouſand, two hundred, and threeſcore dayes.[7]And there was warre in heauen, Michael and his Angels fought againſt the dragon, & the dragon fought and his angels,[8]And preuailed not, neither was their place found any more in heauen.[9]And the great dragon was caſt out, that old ſerpent, called the deuill and Satan, which deceiueth the whole world: hee was caſt out into the earth, and his angels were caſt out with him.[10]And I heard a lowd voyce ſaying in heauen, Now is come ſaluation, and ſtrength, and the kingdome of our God, and the power of his Chriſt: for the accuſer of our brethren is caſt down, which accuſed them before our God day and night.[11]And they ouercame him by the blood of the Lambe, and by the word of their Teſtimony, and they loued not their liues vnto the death.[12]Therefore reioyce, yee heauens, and yee that dwell in them; Woe to the inhabiters of the earth, and of the ſea: for the deuill is come downe vnto you, hauing great wrath, becauſe he knoweth that he hath but a ſhort time.[13]And when the dragon ſaw that he was caſt vnto the earth, hee perſecuted the woman which brought foorth the man childe.[14]And to the woman were giuen two wings of a great Eagle, that ſhee might flee into the wilderneſſe into her place, where ſhe is nouriſhed for a time, and times, and halfe a time, from the face of the ſerpent.[15]And the ſerpent caſt out of his mouth water as a flood, after the woman: that he might cauſe her to bee caried away of the flood.[16]And the earth helped the woman, and the earth opened her mouth, and ſwallowed vp the flood which the dragon caſt out of his mouth.[17]And the dragon was wroth with the woman, and went to make warre with the remnant of her ſeed, which keepe the Commaundements of God, and haue the teſtimony of Ieſus Chriſt.

CHAPTER 13[1]And I ſtoode vpon the ſand of the ſea: and ſaw a beaſt riſe vp out of the ſea, hauing ſeuen heads, and tenne hornes, and vpon his hornes tenne crownes, and vpon his heads, the name of blaſphemie.[2]And the beaſt which I ſaw, was like vnto a Leopard, and his feet were as the feet of a Beare, and his mouth as the mouth of a Lion: and the dragon gaue him his power, and his ſeat, and great authoritie.[3]And I ſaw one of his heads as it were wounded to death, and his deadly wound was healed: and al the world wondered after the beaſt.[4]And they worſhipped the dragon which gaue power vnto the beaſt, and they worſhipped the beaſt, ſaying, Who is like vnto the beaſt? Who is able to make warre with him?[5]And there was giuen vnto him a mouth, ſpeaking great things, and blaſphemies, and power was giuen vnto him to continue fortie and two moneths.[6]And he opened his mouth in blaſphemie againſt God, to blaſpheme his Name, and his Tabernacle, and them that dwelt in heauen.[7]And it was giuen vnto him to make warre with the Saints, and to ouercome them: And power was giuen him ouer all kinreds, and tongues, and nations.[8]And all that dwel vpon the earth, ſhall worſhip him, whoſe names are not written in the booke of life of the Lambe, ſlaine from the foundation of the world.[9]If any man haue an eare, let him heare:[10]Hee that leadeth into captiuitie, ſhall goe into captiuitie: Hee that killeth with the ſword, muſt be killed with the ſword. Here is the patience and the faith of the Saints.[11]And I beheld another beaſt comming vp out of the earth, and hee had two hornes like a lambe, and hee ſpake as a dragon.[12]And he exerciſeth all the power of the firſt beaſt before him, and cauſeth the earth and them which dwell therein, to worſhip the firſt beaſt, whoſe deadly wound was healed.[13]And hee doeth great wonders, ſo that hee maketh fire come downe from heauen on the earth in the ſight of men,[14]And deceiueth them that dwel on the earth, by the meanes of thoſe miracles which he had power to do in the ſight of the beaſt, ſaying to them that dwell on the earth, that they ſhould make an Image to the beaſt which had the wound by a ſword, and did liue.[15]And he had power to giue life vnto the Image of the beaſt, that the Image of the beaſt ſhould both ſpeake, and cauſe that as many as would not worſhip the Image of the beaſt, ſhould be killed.[16]And he cauſeth all, both ſmal and great rich and poore, free and bond, to receiue a marke in their right hand, or in their foreheads:[17]And that no man might buy or ſell, ſaue he that had the marke, or the name of the beaſt, or the number of his name.[18]Here is wiſedome. Let him that hath vnderſtanding, count the number of the beaſt: for it is the number of a man, and his number is, ſixe hundred threeſcore and ſixe.

CHAPTER 14[1]And I looked, and loe, a Lambe ſtood on the mount Sion, and with him an hundreth fourty and foure thouſand, hauing his Fathers Name written in their foreheads.[2]And I heard a voice from heauen, as the voice of many waters, and as the voyce of a great thunder: and I heard the voyce of harpers, harping with their harpes.[3]And they ſung as it were a new ſong before the throne, and before the foure beaſts, and the Elders, and no man could learne that ſong, but the hundreth and fourtie and foure thouſand, which were redeemed from the earth.[4]Theſe are they which were not defiled with women: for they are virgines: Theſe are they which follow the Lambe whitherſoeuer hee goeth: Theſe were redeemed from among men, being the firſt fruits vnto God, and to the Lambe.[5]And in their mouth was found no guile: for they are without fault before the throne of God.[6]And I ſaw another Angel flie in the midſt of heauen, hauing the euerlaſting Goſpel, to preach vnto them that dwel on the earth, and to euery nation, and kinred, and tongue, and people,[7]Saying with a loud voice, Feare God, and giue glory to him, for the houre of his iudgement is come: and worſhippe him that made heauen and earth, and the ſea, and the fountains of waters.[8]And there followed another Angel, ſaying, Babylon is fallen, is fallen, that great citie, becauſe ſhe made all nations drinke of the wine of the wrath of her fornication.[9]And the third Angel followed them, ſaying with a lowd voice, If any man worſhip the beaſt and his image, and receiue his marke in his forehead, or in his hand,[10]The ſame ſhall drinke of the wine of the wrath of God, which is powred out without mixture into the cup of his indignation, and hee ſhall be tormented with fire and brimſtone, in the preſence of the holy Angels, and in the preſence of the Lambe:[11]And the ſmoke of their torment aſcendeth vp for euer and euer. And they haue no reſt day nor night, who worſhip the beaſt and his image, and whoſoeuer receyueth the marke of his name.[12]Here is the patience of the Saints: Here are they that keepe the Commandements of God, and the faith of Ieſus.[13]And I heard a voyce from heauen, ſaying vnto me, Write, Bleſſed are the dead

which die in the Lord, from hencefoorth, yea, ſaith the Spirit, that they
may reſt from their labours, and their workes doe follow them.14And I
looked, and beholde, a white cloud, and vpon the cloude one ſate like
vnto the ſonne of man, hauing on his head a golden crowne, and in his
hand a ſharpe ſickle.15And another Angel came out of the Temple crying
with a loude voice to him that ſate on the cloud: Thruſt in thy ſickle and
reape, for the time is come for thee to reape, for the harueſt of the earth
is ripe.16And hee that ſate on the cloude thruſt in his ſickle on the earth,
and the earth was reaped.17And another Angel came out of the Temple
which is in heauen, he alſo hauing a ſharpe ſickle.18And another Angel
came out from the Altar, which had power ouer fire, and cryed with a
loud cry to him, that had the ſharpe ſickle, ſaying, Thruſt in thy ſharpe
ſickle, and gather the cluſters of the vine of the earth, for her grapes are
fully ripe.19And the Angel thruſt in his ſickle into the earth, and gathered
the vine of the earth, & caſt it into the great winepreſſe of the wrath of
God.20And the winepreſſe was troden without the citie, and blood came
out of the winepree, euen vnto the horſe bridles, by the ſpace of a
thouſand and ſixe hundred furlongs.
CHAPTER 151And I ſaw another ſigne in heauen great and
marueilous, ſeuen Angels hauing the ſeuen laſt plagues, for in them is
filled vp the wrath of God.2And I ſaw as it were a ſea of glaſſe, mingled
with fire, and them that had gotten the victorie ouer the beaſt, and ouer
his image, and ouer his marke, and ouer the number of his name, ſtand
on the ſea of glaſſe, hauing the harpes of God.3And they ſing the ſong
of Moſes the ſeruant of God, and the ſong of the Lambe, ſaying, Great
and marueilous are thy workes, Lord God Almightie, iuſt and true are
thy wayes, thou king of ſaints.4Who ſhall not feare thee, O Lord, and
glorifie thy Name? for thou onely art holy: for all nations ſhall come and
worſhip before thee, for thy iudgements are made manifeſt.5And after
that I looked, and behold, the Temple of the tabernacle of the teſtimony
in heauen was opened:6And the ſeuen Angels came out of the Temple,
hauing the ſeuen plagues, clothed in pure and white linnen, and hauing
their breaſts girded with golden girdles.7And one of the foure beaſts
gaue vnto the ſeuen Angels, ſeuen golden vials, full of the wrath of God,
who liueth for euer and euer.8And the Temple was filled with ſmoke
from the glory of God, and from his power, and no man was able to
enter into the Temple, till the ſeuen plagues of the ſeuen Angels were
fulfilled.
CHAPTER 161And I heard a great voyce out of the Temple, ſaying to
the ſeuen Angels, Goe your wayes, and powre out the vials of the wrath
of God vpō the earth.2And the firſt went, and powred out his viall vpon
the earth, and there fell a noyſome and grieuous ſore vpon the men
which had the marke of the beaſt, and vpon them which worſhipped his
image.3And the ſecond Angel powred out his viall vpon the ſea, and it
became as the blood of a dead man: and euery liuing ſoule died in the
ſea.4And the third Angel powred out his viall vpon the riuers and
fountaines of waters, & they became blood.5And I heard the Angel of
the waters ſay, Thou art righteous, O Lord, which art, and waſt, and
ſhalt be, becauſe thou haſt iudged thus:6For they haue ſhedde the blood
of Saints and Prophets, and thou haſt giuen them blood to drinke: for
they are worthy.7And I heard another out of the altar ſay, Euen ſo, Lord
God Almightie, true and righteous are thy iudgements.8And the fourth
Angel powred out his viall vpon the Sunne, and power was giuen vnto
him to ſcorch men with fire.9And men were ſcorched with great heat,
and blaſphemed the Name of God, which hath power ouer theſe
plagues: and they repented not, to giue him glory.10And the fift Angel
powred out his viall vpon the ſeat of the beaſt, and his kingdome was
full of darkeneſſe, and they gnawed their tongues for paine,11And
blaſphemed the God of heauen, becauſe of their paines, and their ſores,
and repented not of their deeds.12And the ſixt Angel powred out his viall
vpon the great riuer Euphrates, and the water thereof was dried vp, that
the way of the Kings of the Eaſt might be prepared.13And I ſaw three
vncleane ſpirits like frogs come out of the mouth of the dragon, & out
of the mouth of the beaſt, & out of the mouth of the falſe prophet.14For
they are the ſpirits of deuils working miracles, which goe forth vnto the
Kings of the earth, and of the whole world, to gather them to the battell
of that great day of God Almighty.15Behold, I come as a thiefe. Bleſſed
is he that watcheth, and keepeth his garments, leaſt hee walke naked,
and they ſee his ſhame.16And hee gathered them together into a place,
called in the Hebrewe tongue, Armageddon.17And the ſeuenth Angel
powred out his viall into the ayre, and there came a great voyce out of
the Temple of heauen, from the throne, ſaying, It is done.18And there
were voices and thunders, and lightnings: and there was a great
earthquake, ſuch as was not ſince men were vpon the earth, ſo mighty
an earthquake, and ſo great.19And the great Citie was diuided into three
parts, and the Cities of the nations fell: and great Babylon came in
remembrance before God, to giue vnto her the cup of the wine of the
fierceneſse of his wrath.20And euery yland fled away, and the
mountaines were not found.21And there fell vpon men a great haile out
of heauen, euery ſtone about the weight of a talent, and men blaſphemed
God, becauſe of the plague of the hayle: for the plague thereof was
exceeding great.
CHAPTER 171And there came one of the ſeuen Angels, which had the
ſeuen vials, and talked with me, ſaying vnto mee, Come hither, I will
ſhew vnto thee the iudgement of the great Whore, that ſitteth vpon
many waters:2With whom the kings of the earth haue committed
fornication, and the inhabiters of the earth haue beene made drunk with
the wine of her fornication.3So he caried me away in the Spirit into the
wilderneſſe: and I ſaw a woman ſit vpō a ſcarlet coloured beaſt, full of
names of blaſphemy, hauing ſeuen heads, and ten hornes.4And the
woman was arayed in purple and ſcarlet colour, and decked with gold,
and precious ſtone & pearles, hauing a golden cup in her hand, full of
abominations and filthineſse of her fornication.5And vpon her forehead
was a name written, Myſtery, Babylon The Great, The Mother Of
Harlots, And Abominations Of The Earth.6And I ſaw the woman
drunken with the blood of the Saints, and with the blood of the Martyrs
of Ieſus: and when I ſaw her, I wondred with great admiration.7And the
Angel ſaide vnto mee, Wherefore didſt thou marueile? I will tell thee the
myſtery of the woman, and of the beaſt that carieth her, which hath the
ſeuen heads, and ten hornes.8The beaſt that thou ſaweſt, was, and is not,
and ſhall aſcend out of the bottomleſſe pit, and goe into perdition, and
they that dwell on the earth ſhall wonder, (whoſe names were not
written in the booke of life from the foundation of the world) when they
behold the beaſt that was, and is not, and yet is.9And here is the mind
which hath wiſedome. The ſeuen heads are ſeuen mountaines, on which
the woman ſitteth.10And there are ſeuen Kings, fiue are fallen, and one
is, and the other is not yet come: and when he commeth, he muſt
continue a ſhort ſpace.11And the beaſt that was, and is not, euen he is
the eighth, & is of the ſeuen, and goeth into perdition.12And the tenne
hornes which thou ſaweſt, are ten kings, which haue receiued no
kingdom as yet: but receiue power as kings one houre with the
beaſt.13Theſe haue one minde, and ſhall giue their power and ſtrength
vnto the beaſt.14Theſe ſhal make warre with the Lambe, and the Lambe
ſhal ouercome them: For he is Lord of Lords, and King of kings, and
they that are with him, are called, & choſen, and faithfull.15And he ſaith
vnto me, The waters which thou ſaweſt, where the whore ſitteth, are
peoples, and multitudes, and nations, and tongues.16And the ten hornes
which thou ſaweſt vpon the beaſt, theſe ſhall hate the whore, and ſhall
make her deſolate, and naked, and ſhall eate her fleſh, and burne her
with fire.17For God hath put in their hearts to fulfill his will, and to
agree, and giue their kingdome vnto the beaſt, vntil the words of God
ſhall be fulfilled.18And the woman which thou ſaweſt, is that great Citie
which reigneth ouer the kings of the earth.
CHAPTER 181And after theſe things, I ſaw another Angel come
downe from heauen, hauing great power, and the earth was lightened
with his glory.2And he cryed mightily with a ſtrōg voyce, ſaying, Babylon
the great is fallen, is fallen, and is become the habitation of deuils, and
the hold of euery foule ſpirit, and a cage of euery vncleane and hatefull
bird:3For all nations haue drunke of the wine of the wrath of her
fornication, and the Kings of the earth haue committed fornication with
her, & the Merchants of the earth are waxed rich thorow the abundance
of her delicacies.4And I heard another voice from heauen, ſaying, Come
out of her, my people, that yee be not partakers of her ſinnes, and that
yee receiue not of her plagues:5For her ſinnes haue reached vnto heauen,
and God hath remembred her iniquities.6Reward her euen as ſhe
rewarded you, and double vnto her double according to her works: in
the cup which ſhe hath filled, fill to her double.7How much ſhe hath
glorified her ſelfe, and liued deliciouſly, ſo much torment and ſorrow
giue her: for ſhe ſaith in her heart, I ſit a Queene, and am no widow, and
ſhall ſee no ſorrow.8Therefore ſhall her plagues come in one day, death,

and mourning, and famine, and ſhe ſhall bee vtterly burnt with fire, for ſtrong is the Lord God, who iudgeth her.[9]And the Kings of the earth, who haue committed fornication, and liued deliciouſly with her, ſhall bewaile her and lament for her, when they ſhall ſee the ſmoke of her burning:[10]Standing afarre off for the feare of her torment, ſaying, Alas, alas, that great citie Babylon, that mighty citie: for in one houre is thy iudgement come.[11]And the Merchants of the earth ſhall weepe and mourne ouer her, for no man buyeth their merchandiſe any more.[12]The merchandiſe of gold, and ſiluer, and pretious ſtones, and of pearles, and fine linnen, and purple, and ſilke, and ſcarlet, and all Thine wood, and all maner veſſels of Yuorie, and all maner veſſels of moſt precious wood, and of braſſe, and iron, and marble,[13]And Cynamome, and odours, and ointments, and frankincenſe, & wine, and oile, and fine floure, and wheat, and beaſts, and ſheepe, and horſes, and chariots, and ſlaues, and ſoules of men.[14]And the fruits that thy ſoule luſted after, are departed from thee, and all things which were daintie, and goodly, are departed from thee, and thou ſhalt finde them no more at all.[15]The Merchants of theſe things which were made riche by her, ſhall ſtand afarre off for the feare of her torment, weeping and wailing.[16]And ſaying, Alas, alas, that great city, that was clothed in fine linnen, and purple and ſcarlet, and decked with gold, and pretious ſtones, and pearles:[17]For in one houre ſo great riches is come to nought. And euery ſhipmaſter, and all the company in ſhips, and ſailers, and as many as trade by ſea, ſtood a farre off,[18]And cryed when they ſaw the ſmoke of her burning, ſaying, What city is like vnto this great citie?[19]And they caſt duſt on their heads, and cried, weeping, and wailing, ſaying, Alas, alas, that great citie, wherein were made rich all that had ſhips in the ſea, by reaſon of her coſtlineſse, for in one houre is ſhe made deſolate.[20]Reioyce ouer her thou heauen, and ye holy Apoſtles and Prophets, for God hath auenged you on her.[21]And a mightie Angel tooke vp a ſtone like a great milſtone, and caſt it into the ſea, ſaying, Thus with violence ſhall that great citie Babylon bee throwen downe, and ſhall bee found no more at all.[22]And the voyce of harpers and muſitions, and of pipers, and trumpetters, ſhall bee heard no more at all in thee: and no craftſman, of whatſoeuer craft hee be, ſhall be found any more in thee: and the ſound of a milſtone ſhalbe heard no more at all in thee:[23]And the light of a candle ſhall ſhine no more at all in thee: and the voice of the bridegrome and of the bride ſhalbe heard no more at all in thee: for thy Merchants were the great men of the earth: for by thy ſorceries were all nations deceiued.[24]And in her was found the blood of Prophets, and of Saints, and of all that were ſlaine vpon the earth.

CHAPTER 19[1]And after theſe things I heard a great voyce of much people in heauen, ſaying, Alleluia: ſaluation, and glorie, and honour, and power vnto the Lord our God:[2]For true and righteous are his iudgements, for hee hath iudged the great whore which did corrupt the earth with her fornication, and hath auenged the blood of his ſeruants at her hand.[3]And againe they ſayd, Alleluia: and her ſmoke roſe vp for euer & euer.[4]And the foure and twentie Elders, and the foure beaſts fell downe, and worſhipped God that ſate on the throne, ſaying, Amen, Alleluia.[5]And a voice came out of the throne, ſaying, Praiſe our God all yee his ſeruants, and ye that feare him, both ſmall and great.[6]And I heard as it were the voice of a great multitude, and as the voice of many waters, and as the voice of mightie thundrings, ſaying, Alleluia: for the Lord God omnipotent reigneth.[7]Let vs bee glad and reioyce, and giue honour to him: for the mariage of the Lambe is come, and his wife hath made herſelfe readie.[8]And to her was granted, that ſhe ſhould bee arayed in fine linnen, cleane and white: for the fine linnen is the righteouſneſſe of Saints.[9]And hee ſaith vnto mee, Write, Bleſſed are they which are called vnto the marriage ſupper of the Lambe. And he ſaith vnto mee, Theſe are the true ſayings of God.[10]And I fell at his feete to worſhip him: And he ſaid vnto me, ſee thou doe it not: I am thy fellow ſeruant, and of thy brethren, that haue the teſtimonie of Ieſus, Worſhip God: for the teſtimony of Ieſus, is the ſpirit of prophecie.[11]And I ſawe heauen opened, and behold a white horſe, and hee that ſate vpon him was called faithful and true, and in righteouſnes hee doth iudge and make warre.[12]His eyes were as a flame of fire, and on his head were many crownes, and hee had a name written, that no man knew but he himſelfe.[13]And hee was clothed with a veſture dipt in blood, and his name is called, The word of God.[14]And the armies which were in heauen followed him vpon white horſes, clothed in fine linnen, white and cleane.[15]And out of his mouth goeth a ſharpe ſword, that with it hee ſhould ſmite the nations: and he ſhal rule them with a rod of yron: and he treadeth the winepreſſe of the fierceneſse and wrath of Almighty God.[16]And he hath on his veſture, and on his thigh a name written, King Of Kings, And Lord Of Lords.[17]And I ſaw an Angel ſtanding in the Sunne, and hee cried with a lowd voyce, ſaying to all the foules that flie in the midſt of heauen, Come and gather your ſelues together vnto the ſupper of the great God:[18]That yee may eate the fleſh of Kings, and the fleſh of Captaines, and the fleſh of mighty men, and the fleſh of horſes, and of them that ſit on them, and the fleſh of all men both free and bond, both ſmall and great.[19]And I ſaw the beaſt, & the Kings of the earth, and their armies gathered together to make warre againſt him that ſate on the horſe, and againſt his armie.[20]And the beaſt was taken, & with him the falſe prophet, that wrought miracles before him, with which he deceiued them that had receiued the marke of the beaſt, and them that worſhipped his image. Theſe both were caſt aliue into a lake of fire burning with brimſtone.[21]And the remnant were ſlain with the ſword of him that ſate vpon the horſe, which ſword proceeded out of his mouth: and all the foules were filled with their fleſh.

CHAPTER 20[1]And I ſaw an Angel come down from heauen, hauing the key of the bottomles pit, & a great chaine in his hand.[2]And hee laid hold on the dragon that old ſerpent, which is the deuill and Satan, and bound him a thouſand yeres,[3]And caſt him into the bottomleſſe pit, and ſhut him vp, and ſet a ſeale vpon him, that he ſhould deceiue the nations no more, till the thouſand yeeres ſhould bee fulfilled: and after that hee muſt be looſed a little ſeaſon.[4]And I ſaw thrones, and they ſate vpon them, and iudgement was giuen vnto them: & I ſaw the ſoules of them that were beheaded for the witneſſe of Ieſus, and for the word of God, and which had not worſhipped the beaſt, neither his image, neither had receiued his marke vpon their foreheads, or in their hands; and they liued and reigned with Chriſt a thouſand yeeres.[5]But the reſt of the dead liued not againe vntill the thouſand yeeres were finiſhed. This is the firſt reſurrection.[6]Bleſſed & holy is he that hath part in þe firſt reſurrection: on ſuch the ſecond death hath no power, but they ſhall be Prieſts of God, and of Chriſt, and ſhall reigne with him a thouſand yeeres.[7]And when the thouſand yeeres are expired, Satan ſhall be looſed out of his priſon,[8]And ſhall goe out to deceiue the nations which are in the foure quarters of the earth, Gog & Magog, to gather them together to battell: the number of whom is as the ſand of the ſea.[9]And they went vp on the breadth of the earth, and compaſſed the campe of the Saints about, and the beloued citie: and fire came downe from God out of heauen, and deuoured them.[10]And the deuil that deceiued them, was caſt into the lake of fire and brimſtone, where the beaſt and the falſe prophet are, and ſhall be tormented day and night, for euer and euer.[11]And I ſaw a great white throne, and him that ſate on it, from whoſe face the earth and the heauen fled away, and there was found no place for them.[12]And I ſawe the dead, ſmall and great, ſtand before God: and the books were opened: & another booke was opened, which is the booke of life: and the dead were iudged out of thoſe things which were written in the books, according to their works.[13]And the ſea gaue vp the dead which were in it: and death and hell deliuered vp the dead which were in them: and they were iudged euery man according to their works.[14]And death and hell were caſt into the lake of fire: this is the ſecond death.[15]And whoſoeuer was not found written in the booke of life, was caſt into the lake of fire.

CHAPTER 21[1]And I ſaw a new heauen, and a new earth: for the firſt heauen, and the firſt earth were paſſed away, and there was no more ſea.[2]And I Iohn ſaw the holy City, new Hieruſalem comming down from God out of heauen, prepared as a bride adorned for her huſband.[3]And I heard a great voice out of heauen, ſaying, Behold, the Tabernacle of God is with men, and he wil dwell with them, and they ſhall be his people, and God himſelfe ſhalbe with them, and be their God.[4]And God ſhall wipe away all teares from their eyes: and there ſhall bee no more death, neither ſorrow, nor crying, neither ſhall there bee any more paine: for the former things are paſſed away.[5]And he that ſate vpon the throne, ſaid, Behold, I make all things new. And hee ſaid vnto me, Write: for theſe words are true and faithfull.[6]And he ſaid vnto mee, It is done: I am Alpha and Omega, the beginning and the end. I will giue vnto him that is athirſt, of the fountaine of the water of life, freely.[7]He that ouercommeth, ſhall inherite all things, and I will bee his God, and he ſhall be my ſonne.8But the fearefull, and vnbeleeuing, and the abominable, and murderers, and whore mongers, and ſorcerers, and idolaters, and all lyars, ſhall haue their part in the lake which burneth with fire and brimſtone: which is the ſecond death.9And there came vnto me one of the ſeuen Angels, which had the ſeuen vials full of the ſeuen laſt plagues, and talked with me, ſaying, Come hither, I will ſhew thee the Bride, the Lambes wife.10And he caried me away in the ſpirit to a great and high mountaine, and ſhewed me that great citie, the holy Hieruſalem, deſcending out of heauen from God,11Hauing the glory of God: and her light was like vnto a ſtone moſt precious; euen like a iaſper ſtone, cleare as chriſtal,12And had a wall great and high, and had twelue gates, and at the gates twelue Angels, & names written thereon, which are the names of the twelue tribes of the children of Iſrael.13On the Eaſt three gates, on the North three gates, on the South three gates, and on the Weſt three gates.14And the wall of the citie had twelue foundations, and in them the names of the twelue Apoſtles of the Lambe.15And hee that talked with mee, had a golden reede to meaſure the citie, and the gates thereof, and the wall thereof.16And the city lieth foure ſquare, and the length is as large as the breadth: and he meaſured the city with the reed, twelue thouſand furlongs: the length, and the breadth, and the height of it are equall.17And he meaſured the wall thereof, an hundred, and fourtie, and foure cubites, according to the meaſure of a man, that is, of the Angel.18And the building of the wall of it was of Iaſper, and the city was pure gold, like vnto cleare glaſſe.19And the foundations of the wall of the city were garniſhed with all maner of precious ſtones. The firſt foundation was Iaſper, the ſecond Saphir, the third a Chalcedony, the fourth an Emerald,20The fift Sardonix, the ſixt Sardius, the ſeuenth Chryſolite, the eight Beryl, the ninth a Topas, the tenth a Chryſopraſus, the eleuenth a Iacinct, the twelfth an Amethyſt.21And the twelue gates were twelue pearles, euery ſeuerall gate was of one pearle, and the ſtreete of the city was pure golde, as it were tranſparent glaſſe.22And I ſaw no Temple therein: For the Lord God Almightie, and the Lambe, are the Temple of it.23And the citie had no need of the Sunne, neither of the Moone to ſhine in it: for the glory of God did lighten it, and the Lambe is the light thereof.24And the nations of them which are ſaued, ſhall walke in the light of it: and the kings of the earth doe bring their glory and honour into it.25And the gates of it ſhall not bee ſhut at all by day: for there ſhall bee no night there.26And they ſhall bring the glorie and honour of the nations into it.27And there ſhall in no wiſe enter into it any thing that defileth, neither whatſoeuer worketh abomination, or maketh a lie: but they which are written in the Lambes booke of life.

CHAPTER 221And he ſhewed mee a pure riuer of water of life, cleere as Chryſtall, proceeding out of the throne of God, and of the Lambe.2In the middeſt of the ſtreet of it, and of either ſide of the riuer, was there the tree of life, which bare twelue manner of fruits, and yeelded her fruit euery moneth: and the leaues of the tree were for the healing of the nations.3And there ſhall be no more curſe, but the throne of God, & of the Lambe ſhall bee in it, and his ſeruants ſhall ſerue him.4And they ſhall ſee his face, and his Name ſhall be in their foreheads.5And there ſhalbe no night there, and they need no candle, neither light of the Sunne, for the Lord God giueth them light, and they ſhall reigne for euer and euer.6And hee ſaid vnto mee, Theſe ſayings are faithfull and true. And the Lord God of the holy Prophets ſent his Angel to ſhew vnto his ſeruants the things which muſt ſhortly be done.7Beholde, I come quickly: Bleſſed is he that keepeth the ſayings of the prophecie of this booke.8And I Iohn ſaw theſe things, and heard them. And when I had heard and ſeene, I fell downe, to worſhip before the feete of the Angel, which ſhewed me theſe things.9Then ſaith he vnto me, ſee thou doe it not: for I am thy fellow ſeruant, and of thy brethren the Prophets, and of them which keepe the ſayings of this booke: worſhip God.10And hee ſaith vnto mee, ſeale not the ſayings of the propheſie of this booke: for the time is at hand.11He that is vniuſt, let him be vniuſt ſtill: and he which is filthy, let him be filthy ſtill: and hee that is righteous, let him bee righteous ſtill: and hee that is holy, let him be holy ſtill.12And behold, I come quickly, and my reward is with mee, to giue euery man according as his worke ſhall be.13I am Alpha and Omega, the beginning and the end, the firſt & the laſt.14Bleſſed are they that do his commandements, that they may haue right to the tree of life, and may enter in thorow the gates into the citie.15For without are dogs, and ſorcerers, and whoremongers, and murderers, and idolaters, and whoſoeuer loueth and maketh a lie.16I Ieſus haue ſent mine Angel, to teſtifie vnto you theſe things in the Churches. I am the roote and the offſpring of Dauid, and the bright and morning ſtarre.17And the Spirit and the Bride ſay, Come. And let him that heareth, ſay, Come. And let him that is a thirſt, come. And whoſoeuer will, let him take the water of life freely.18For I teſtifie vnto euery man that heareth the wordes of the propheſie of this booke, If any man ſhal adde vnto theſe things, God ſhall adde vnto him the plagues, that are written in this booke.19And if any man ſhall take away from the wordes of the booke of this propheſie, God ſhal take away his part out of the booke of life, and out of the holy citie, and from the things which are written in this booke.20Hee which teſtifieth theſe things, ſaith, Surely, I come quickly. Amen. Euen ſo, Come Lord Ieſus.21The grace of our Lord Ieſus Chriſt be with you all. Amen.

Made in United States
Orlando, FL
09 December 2024

55238731R00293